UNDERSTANDING THE VOLATILE AND DANGEROUS MIDDLE EAST

A comprehensive analysis

Also by Steven Carol

Encyclopedia of Days: Start the Day with History

From Jerusalem to the Lion of Judah and Beyond

UNDERSTANDING THE VOLATILE AND DANGEROUS MIDDLE EAST

A comprehensive analysis

Steven Carol

iUniverse

**UNDERSTANDING THE VOLATILE AND DANGEROUS MIDDLE EAST
A COMPREHENSIVE ANALYSIS**

iUniverse books may be ordered through booksellers or by contacting:

iUniverse
1663 Liberty Drive
Bloomington, IN 47403
www.iuniverse.com
1-800-Authors (1-800-288-4677)

Because of the dynamic nature of the Internet, any web addresses or links contained in this book may have changed since publication and may no longer be valid. The views expressed in this work are solely those of the author and do not necessarily reflect the views of the publisher, and the publisher hereby disclaims any responsibility for them.

ISBN: 978-1-4917-6657-6 (sc)
ISBN: 978-1-4917-6658-3 (e)

Print information available on the last page.

iUniverse rev. date: 08/24/2015

To Hadara, for her encouragement, support, and love.
To Shelli and David, with love for them and their posterity.

TABLE OF CONTENTS

LIST OF MAPS

Please note that the maps in this book are placed in context with the accompanying applicable text, rather than in chronological order.

LIST OF MAPS

The following is a chronological listing of the maps that appear in this book.

LIST OF TABLES

LIST OF BASIC PRINCIPLES

Critical Geographic Features

1. Throughout history, the Middle East has held a place of importance greater than that of any other region of the world.

2. Many strategic and vital waterways are concentrated in the Middle East.

3. Contrary to Arab/Muslim propaganda, the depictions of Israel as an immense expansionist country are false. In reality, Israel is a tiny Jewish "island" in a vast Arab/Muslim sea.

4. The terms "Middle East" and "Near East" continue to be used interchangeably.

5. Middle East countries have been "created" but Israel is not one of them.

6. Distance in the Middle East *is* important.

7. Geographic denial, omissions and substitutions are prevalent on Arab/Muslim maps of the region.

Demographics of the Region

8. The Middle East is not an exclusively Arab region.

9. The so-called "Arab Middle East" is not exclusively Muslim.

10. The "refugee problem" connected with the Arab–Israeli conflict, is not one of "Palestinian Arab" refugees alone.

11. The Arab/Muslim claim that Israeli towns and villages in the "occupied areas," must be removed is but a first step to eradicating all of Israel.

Traditions and the Historic Record

12. Tradition is a powerful force in the Arab/Muslim world.

13. Israel is one of the oldest nations in the world with a common religion and language.

14. Jerusalem is the eternal capital of the Jewish nation as Jews have lived there for three millennia.

15. Since biblical times and throughout history, the name for the mountainous highlands in the center of the Land of Israel has been Judea and Samaria.

16. The League of Nations established the international legal basis for reestablishing Jewish sovereignty in the British Mandate of Palestine.

17. Throughout the entire Middle East, only one country bears an uncanny political, demographic, and historic similarity to the United States—that country is Israel.

18. The Kurds, the fourth most numerous people in the region, have never achieved national sovereignty, but have played a leading role in the history of the Middle East.

19. In the Arab/Muslim culture, pride, dignity, and honor outrank truth on any scale of political values.

20. Throughout history, there has been East-West confrontation in the Middle East. At the nexus of three continents, the region has been both an invasion route and the main east-west conduit of commerce.

21. The Arab/Muslim world views their history as starting in 622 C.E. anything that happened before that is an irrelevant myth.

22. Arab/Muslim conquerors have a penchant for destroying other people's religious shrines and many times building their own on the ruins as a mark of supremacy. It was, and remains, Islam's way of saying, "We have defeated you, we rule you, and our god—Allah—is greater than your god."

23. For over one hundred years, the Arab/Muslim world has claimed to be "victims" entitled to compensation and acquiescence to their maximal demands.

24. Since 1921, a Palestinian Arab state has existed in the Middle East, created by the British and then named the Hashemite Emirate of Transjordan.

25. To fully understand the Arab/Muslim war against Jewish sovereignty in the Land of Israel, one must comprehend that there has been a continual and massive Arab/Muslim policy of role reversal and grotesque transformation of historical facts.

26. Due in large part to its geographic proximity to the Middle East, Russia has been a major power player in the region. This has been especially true since the late-seventeenth century with a few relatively short exceptions.

Influence of Islam on the Region

27. The ideology of Islam is based on the Qur'an, which is believed by most Muslims to be the literal word of Allah—perfect, complete, immutable and valid for all of eternity.

28. All Muslim religious scholars and authorities consider Islam to be a "complete way of life."

29. Muslim women and children are dispensable. Infidel women and children are prime targets for rape, slavery and genocide.

30. Suicide is a sin in Islam except when done to kill infidels. It then becomes a virtue rewarded in Paradise, with seventy-two virgins.

31. Throughout history, Islam sought to conquer the West and destroy its civilization.

32. The concept of *dhimmitude* has been part of Qur'anic Muslim tradition.

Political Processes

33. In the Middle East, disputed areas are known by different names strictly for political motives.

34. While Israel is often described as a "thriving democracy" and the "only democracy in the Middle East," it does not follow exactly the democratic model of the United States.

35. Elections do not make a true democracy in the Middle East.

36. Assassination, an accepted means of political activity in most Arab/Muslim countries, is often used to replace key political leaders in the Middle East.

37. Since before World War II, "revolutions" and military takeovers—coups d'état—have been the most prevalent means of seizing political power throughout the Arab/Muslim world.

38. The power that dominates the Nile Valley has been and continues to be the rival of the power that controls the Tigris–Euphrates Valley.

39. The goal of pan-Arab unity has been largely illusory, akin to a mirage in the desert.

Ever Shifting Alliances

40. For most of its modern history, Israel has been one of the most steadfast allies of the United States, though no formal alliance exists between the two nations.

41. The maxim "the enemy of my enemy is my friend" applies in many cases to Middle Eastern history and politics.

42. Turkey usually allies itself with whichever power opposes Russia. Additionally, Turkey has always been a regional rival of Persia/Iran.

43. In the Middle East, weakness guarantees aggression.

44. The constant reference to the "Israeli-Palestinian conflict" is based on a false premise that historically the conflict was only between Israel and the Palestinian Arabs.

45. The Arab/Muslim exaggerated emphasis on the "Palestinian-Israeli conflict" has by and large, obscured the far worse conflicts, ethnic and sectarian cleansings, murders, assassinations and destruction perpetrated within the Islamic world as well as jihadist attacks worldwide against the West.

46. The Arab proverb, "I against my brother, I and my brothers against my cousins, I and my brothers and my cousins against the world," is taken and practiced literally through much of the Muslim world.

47. Arab/Muslim states can always set aside their rivalries and differences for common action against Israel.

48. In addition to its continued military, diplomatic, and propaganda war against Israel, the Arab League for over a half-century has waged economic warfare against the Jewish state.

49. The Arabs have practiced limited liability war against the Jews in the Land of Israel for some eighty years.

50. Throughout the ongoing Arab/Muslim conflict against Israel, the Jewish state has been forced by foreign and domestic pressures to return territory acquired in defensive wars.

51. Arab/Muslim forces have historically relied on terrorist and unconventional warfare, primarily against civilians, especially when confronting a militarily superior foe.

52. Throughout the greater Middle East and beyond, Middle Eastern-related airplane, bus, train, and ship hijackings—sometimes coupled with the destruction of aircraft—have been a method of waging war against the West. Holding passengers and crews hostage, and seizing cargoes, all to be held for ransom, have been historic practices of some countries and various terrorist groups.

53. The use of human shields is a favored tactic of the Arab/Muslim side in their conflicts with the West.

54. Since 1973, every Arab state or terrorist organization that has gone to war against Israel has benefited from its aggression.

55. Since the early 1960s, several Arab/Muslim states have engaged in development of, threats to use, and actual usage of biological, chemical and nuclear weapons–weapons of mass destruction—WMDs.

56. The principle in international law of *ex injuria jus non oritur*— "right cannot originate from wrong"—i.e. the aggressor must be punished and penalized, applies globally, but has been unjustly denied to Israel.

57. Throughout the conflict between Arab/Muslim forces and the Jewish people in Israel, the Arab/Muslim side voiced its opposition to Zionism, tried to equate Zionism with racism, and brand it a colonizing imperialistic ideology.

58. Throughout its modern history, the State of Israel, time and again at the last possible second before the stroke of disaster, has relied on a policy of *ayn breira*—"no alternative"—in dealing with threats to its existence.

59. Israel has long been known to have nuclear warfare capacity. However, though under constant attack and threat of annihilation, it has never threatened any nation with its nuclear arsenal.

Perpetual Negotiations

60. Israeli control of recovered territory is legal, and pales by comparison to occupation of territories by other nations.

61. The historic experience of Arab (Jordanian) occupation of Jerusalem, from 1948 to 1967, and its demonstrated blatant disregard for Jewish and Christian religious sentiments by Muslims, is likely to be repeated if Jerusalem is ever divided again.

62. The Jews/Israelis have consistently attempted to reach a compromise with their hostile Arab/Muslim neighbors only to be rejected time and time again.

63. The most often quoted and misunderstood United Nations Security Council resolution dealing with the Middle East is United Nations Security Council Resolution 242.

64. Arab/Muslim countries practice bazaar diplomacy.

65. What the parties negotiated and promised in concluded agreements in English, French, German and other Western languages is inconsequential. What is stated publicly in Arabic or Farsi is what counts.

66. There is an Arab proverb that states, "There is no tax on words." It succinctly expresses the negotiating style of the Arab/Muslim Middle East.

67. There is also *taqiyya* or *kitman* ("deception") applied to Arab/Muslim deeds. One of Muhammad's companions, Abu Jabir Abdullah related, "Muhammad said, 'War is deceit.'"

68. In the Islamic Middle East, the rational desire for peace is often perceived as weakness—a despised trait in that culture.

Attempts at Security

69. The United Nations has failed to maintain peace and security in the Middle East. Additionally, in a short period the UN became biased and often hostile to Israel, far from the popular image of being an impartial mediator. Furthermore, UN "peacekeeping" efforts in the greater Middle East have been far from effective.

70. International guarantees, especially when applied to the Middle East, are often broken and do not provide security.

71. Security barriers are not obstacles to peace.

Role of the Media

72. There is no such thing as a free press in the Arab/Muslim Middle East.

73. Arab/Muslim indoctrination is a highly successful industry. It is well organized and is without opposition. It makes use of exaggeration, disinformation, manipulation, selective omissions, distortion of key facts, lack of context, oversimplification of complex issues and historical inaccuracy.

74. The use of specific vocabulary can change reality to fiction over time. It can also obliterate history and create new truths from the fabric of the big lie technique. If someone tells a lie big enough and keeps repeating it, people will eventually come to believe it. As British, Prime Minister Winston Churchill once cautioned, "A lie gets halfway around the world before the truth has a chance to get its pants on."

75. Transliterating Arabic words and phrases into their precise English phonetic equivalents is an exercise of great complexity.

ABOUT THE AUTHOR

A true teacher is one who, keeping the past alive is also able to understand the present.
Confucius

Dr. Steven Carol received his M.A. in History from Queens College and his Ph.D. in History from St. John's University, New York. His specialties are the Modern Middle East, United States history and government, the World Wars of the twentieth century and the Cold War.

Now retired, he taught for nearly four decades, both on the East Coast (including Adelphi University and Long Island University) and in Arizona on the high school, college (at Mesa Community College, and Scottsdale Community College) and graduate levels.

Dr. Carol is the author of six books as well as articles, songs, visual aids, and educational games. He has written numerous articles about the Middle East, which has appeared in newspapers in the United States and Canada. They have also appeared on the worldwide web at Israel National News, UnityCoalitionforIsrael.org, Israpundit, Think-Israel.org, One Jerusalem.org, and the Israel Insider.

Dr. Carol has spoken to civic and political groups throughout the United States at churches, synagogues, universities, schools, and service organizations on topics related to the history of the Arab–Israeli conflict, terrorism and about a forgotten rescuer of the Holocaust period, Portuguese diplomat, Dr. Aristides de Sousa Mendes.

Since 2003, Dr. Carol, has been the official historian of "The Middle East Radio Forum" (MERF) and Middle East Consultant to the Salem Radio Network. He is the most frequent guest (over 250 appearances) on the show, providing detailed historical overviews, perspectives and analysis, frequently relating these to current developments. Additionally, he has been a featured guest on various radio shows across the United States and in Israel.

He has been affiliated with the Arizona Humanities Council as part of the "9/11 Conversations" programs and has spoken about the war against radical Islam as well as the origins of the Arab-Israeli Conflict, among other subjects.

Dr. Carol also was a consultant for the New York State and Arizona Departments of Education. In 1987, New York State named him "Outstanding Teacher." He currently continues to write, speak to groups and appear on radio.

ACKNOWLEDGEMENTS

Special thanks go to Tzvi and Yosefa for their generous assistance in helping make this book possible. So, too, my thanks to my son David, for his critical evaluation and editing, to William Wolf for his foreword to this volume, to Dr. Carl Goldberg and Harry J. Sweeney for their suggestions regarding Islam. Words are not enough to express my thanks to my wife, Hadara, for her tireless efforts in editing and the numerous suggestions she's made, as well as her assistance, encouragement, and patience. Without her most thorough proof reading of the manuscript, additional help, support, and love, this study could not have been completed. While the original map work for this book was researched, drawn, produced, and copyrighted by the author, extra special thanks must go to Kurt Sweeney, for his exceptional computer skills in adapting the maps into black-and-white format.

NOTE ON CALENDARS

All dates in the chronologies and the body of the book are given in the calendar traditionally referring to events before the birth of Jesus (B.C.) and continuing after his birth (A.D.), and now universally adopted and known to scholars as Before the Common Era (B.C.E.) and the Common Era (C.E.).

FOREWORD

It is my privilege to recommend to you Dr. Steven Carol's book, *Understanding the Volatile and Dangerous Middle East: A comprehensive analysis.* This unique book is designed for the public and is a prime resource for any scholar or researcher who wishes to assess or write about any aspect of Middle Eastern affairs.

As a student of the Middle East for decades, traveling there thirteen times, and hosting a radio show about the region—*Middle East Radio Forum*—I have done my best to keep informed. However, I became frustrated with the bewildering volume of material, some of very questionable accuracy and objectivity. Political correctness and a specific agenda often dominate the reporting, making the truth difficult to decipher, if even present in the first place. It was not until I had the pleasure to meet historian Dr. Steve Carol that I was able to really grasp the significance and importance of the greater Middle East.

The author's intent is to give the reader a set of facts, in-depth analyses and clarity, about the greater Middle East region in general and Israel in particular. This will help avoid the all too common traps of Arab/Muslim propaganda and expose anti-American and anti-Israel media bias. In this, I believe Dr. Carol has superbly succeeded.

Dr. Carol's book is the culmination of his years of research and study—including his own thirteen trips to the region—and is presented to anyone who desires to understand the morass and enigma that unfortunately largely dominates what we know as the greater Middle East. The book establishes a solid foundational roadmap written in a concise, logical and clear manner. His scholarship and expertise are evident from his over 250 appearances as the most frequent guest on my radio show. Therefore, I named him "official historian" of the show.

The breadth and depth of Dr. Carol's knowledge of the Middle East are evident in his sharp analyses and commentary about historical events and how these issues relate to the current situation. As a long-time listener, Stuart Citron astutely observed, "If ever there was a man who not only has the intellectual capacity, but also has the heart and passion for his subject, it is Dr. Steve Carol. He has the ability to explain a subject in a clear, comprehensive and understandable manner. His contribution to our knowledge is immeasurable. Just listen to the radio show where he is the most frequent contributor for some twelve years and counting. Dr. Carol has a style that differs from others. He connects the dots that pull together the historic, political, economic, diplomatic, military, cultural, and religious pieces of the complex Middle East puzzle, in a way that is relevant for today and tomorrow. His tag line is "Dr. History." He could also be called "Dr. Insightful."

This book will be your go-to guide when examining information that appears in the media or in other books on the subject. His book will assist readers to become informed and finally be able to understand the amount of inaccurate information, or even disinformation, one encounters in the news, editorials or popular literature about this highly controversial field.

The author's perceptive comprehension of the subject is backed by well-documented facts, which are copiously footnoted. It truly deserves to be read and re-read. This gem of knowledge should be shared with all who want to avail themselves of the fruit of Dr Carol's scholarship. Its importance cannot be overstated. Moreover, unlike many other books in this field, it will not be readily dated because the facts compiled here will remain valid and immutable. I heartily recommend *Understanding the Volatile and Dangerous Middle East: A comprehensive analysis* to everyone. For anyone who seeks the truth based on facts, this definitely is one book to keep handy on your library shelf.

William J. Wolf, Esq.
Founder and host of
Middle East Radio Forum
www.middleeastradioforum.org

INTRODUCTION

For Zion's sake, I will not keep silent, and for Jerusalem's sake, I will not be quiet, until
her righteousness goes forth as brightness, and her salvation as a burning torch.
Isaiah 62:1

The Middle East is not a region of amity or tranquility. Historically, it is and has been a volatile, dangerous and bewildering place for the West in general and American interests in particular. In the context of this book, the term "Middle East" refers to the region that ranges, at its greatest extent, from Mauritania, Western Sahara and Morocco on the west, through Iran in the east, and from Turkey* and Cyprus† in the north, to Sudan, the Arabian Peninsula, and the Horn of Africa in the south. This broad definition of the "Middle East" is based on the historical, political, military, religious, cultural, linguistic, and economic links among the various countries, which make up the region.

Throughout this book, I use the term "misojudaism." Misojudaism is a more accurate descriptor of the widespread hatred of Jews (*sin'at Yehudim* in Hebrew) than the commonly used "anti-Semitism." Like "misogyny," the hatred of women; "misogamy," the hatred of marriage; "misoneism," the hatred of innovation; or "misanthropy," the hatred of humankind; "misojudaism" is a more precise term. Islamic misojudaism did not begin as an Arab/Muslim reaction to the reestablishment of Jewish sovereignty in the Land of Israel or with the earlier nineteenth century Jewish immigration to that section of the Ottoman Empire. Islamic misojudaism is rooted in mainstream, orthodox Islamic teachings that dates back 1,400 years and are embedded in the Qur'an. In May 627 c.e., after driving out various Jewish tribes from Arabia, Muhammad decided to destroy the last Jewish tribe—the Banu Qurayzah. After forcing them to surrender, an estimated 800 to 900 men and one woman of the tribe were beheaded all in one day, while Muhammad watched. This became the standard of how to deal with the Jews.

Many of Israel's Arab/Muslim enemies have claimed, with anthropological accuracy, that they cannot be "anti-Semites," because they also are Semites. Therefore, "anti-Semitism" is a misnomer and a racist term. Instead, these enemies use the term "anti-Zionist" to camouflage their vehement misojudaic hostility. PLO Chairman Yasser Arafat was always misojudaic. Up to the eve of the Oslo Accords, he constantly vilified the Jews using strong religious imagery. In his book, *Revolution until Victory?: The Politics and History of the PLO*, Barry Rubin, Middle Eastern affairs and terrorism expert, explains that others in the PLO held the same attitudes, such as Salah Khalaf (also known as "Abu Iyad," the organization's leading ideologue as well as its intelligence chief), who stated "Damn their [the Jews] fathers. The dogs. Filth and dirt. Treachery flows in their blood, as the Qur'an testifies."[1] After the signing of the September 13, 1993 Oslo Accords, Arafat emphasized that he was not misojudaic, i.e. anti-Semite, by claiming with a straight face, he was merely "anti-Zionist."

---

* Though a tiny part of modern Turkey lies geographically within Europe, Turkey is overwhelmingly part of the Middle East based on its history, politics, religion, culture, and commerce.

† Situated in the eastern Mediterranean Sea, where Europe meets Asia, the island of Cyprus sits astride a major ethno-religious strategic fault line between East and West and between Christianity and Islam. As such, historically it has been fought over by the ancient Greeks and Persians, the Venetians and the Ottoman Turks (from the fifteenth to the eighteenth centuries), and in modern times, between Greeks and Turks.

Since shortly after attaining political independence from Great Britain, the United States has been engaged with the Middle East. In fact, two of America's earliest foreign wars were those with Algiers and Tripoli. Those wars were in response to acts of aggression against the United States including attacks on its fledgling maritime trade, the seizure of hostages, and the demands for ransom and "protection" payments by the Arab/Muslim city-states of North Africa. Prior to World War II, United States activities in the region were primarily private and generally commercial, cultural, educational, medical, philanthropic and religious in nature. Official actions were severely limited.

American involvement in the greater Middle East region increased dramatically after World War II. This was largely in reaction to the growing challenges posed by the ambitions of the Soviet Union. US ambitions were primarily to extend its policy of containment as well as prevent the Soviet Union from controlling the oil fields and the strategic landmass and waterways. This enlarged American involvement coincided with dramatic changes taking place in the region, including the diminishment of the roles and presence of the United Kingdom and France, the reestablishment of Jewish sovereignty, after 1,875 years of exile and dispersion, in the Land of Israel, and the rise of anti-Western Arab nationalism. Despite the increased engagement for most Americans, the Middle East was and is a part of the world about which they know little and understand less.

Based on my personal experiences in both high schools and colleges in New York and Arizona, for the last half of the twentieth century, the region's history, politics, diplomacy, culture and religious beliefs were barely mentioned in American high schools or colleges, unless one chose to take specialty courses, often not available. The 1973–74 Arab oil embargo, the 1979 Islamic Iranian Revolution, and the September 11, 2001, Islamic supremacist attacks on New York and Washington, DC, all triggered more interest in the region. However, by the dawn of the twenty-first century, a noticeable shift had occurred in media coverage of the region, from fact-based to agenda-driven news coverage. Furthermore, news, editorials, and popular literature on this highly controversial subject are often plagued by errors of commission and omission.

Many changes have occurred in the past few years in the Middle East. The United States, under the Obama administration adopted an Islamist-centric Middle East policy. Additionally, it decided to dramatically scale back its engagement in the region, with withdrawals from Iraq and Afghanistan, as well as inducing strains with long-term allies—Egypt, Israel, and Saudi Arabia, to name the most prominent. Russia, on the other hand, reemerged as an active great power player both diplomatically and militarily. Turkey, a NATO ally of the United States, shifted its political orientation and moved toward the Islamist camp. Israel fought four short, intentionally non-conclusive, wars against Hezbollah in Lebanon and the Islamic Resistance Movement, better known by its Arabic acronym Hamas, in the Gaza Strip—both terrorist organizations. Overall, the Arab/Muslim coalition aligned against Israel rearmed and increased the number of rockets aimed at the Jewish state for the next war. Long-entrenched regimes in Tunisia, Egypt, Yemen, and Libya were overthrown as demonstrations, violence, and in the case of the latter, civil war and foreign intervention ended those governments.

A revival of Islamist fundamentalism swept the region and brought to power in Egypt briefly, an Islamist government dominated by the Muslim Brotherhood. Syria was plunged into a multi-faceted civil war as the Assad regime ruthlessly suppressed its own people with military force, including the use of poison gas. Egypt's military ousted the Muslim Brotherhood after a year in power. Far from being defeated and eliminated as threats to the United States and the West, the Taliban and Al Qaeda, have bounced back from the brink of oblivion. The latter like a hydra, spread far afield across the Middle East and beyond. Al-Qaeda franchises like the Egyptian Islamic Jihad, Al-Qaeda in Mesopotamia, which became Al-Qaeda in Iraq, and then morphed into the Islamic State of Iraq and the Levant (ISIL),* Al-Qaeda in the Arabian Peninsula, Al-Qaeda in the Islamic Maghreb, Qaedat al-Jihad in the Indian Subcontinent, Al-Shabaab in Somalia, and Boko Haram in Nigeria, to name the most infamous—all spewed murder, mayhem and terror in their wake. All the while, Iran furiously pressed ahead to complete its nuclear weapons program and long-range missile development, despite United Nations sanctions

This book endeavors to clarify the confusing nature of Middle East affairs and combat the mistaken beliefs, misrepresentations, and outright fabrications that have been perpetrated to the present. In an effort to reclaim the historic truth, I have postulated a series of basic principles in respect to ten relevant subjects concerning the Middle East. Each basic principle has factual supporting evidence to prove its validity, all in a clear understandable manner. The volume is reader-friendly, with maps, tables, a glossary, annotated appendices, a large suggested reading list and an index. It is my hope that the reader will gain understanding by applying these guidelines when faced with any source of information pertaining to the Middle East. The book is designed to be a valuable educational tool for all those interested in the region. Although the region faces constant uncertainty, the principles outlined in this book are valid and timeless.

---

* The Levant is a geographic and cultural region consisting of the eastern Mediterranean littoral (shoreline and hinterlands) between Anatolia (the bulk of Turkey) and the Sinai Peninsula. The Levant today consists of the island of Cyprus, part of southeastern Turkey, Syria, Lebanon, Israel, and Jordan.

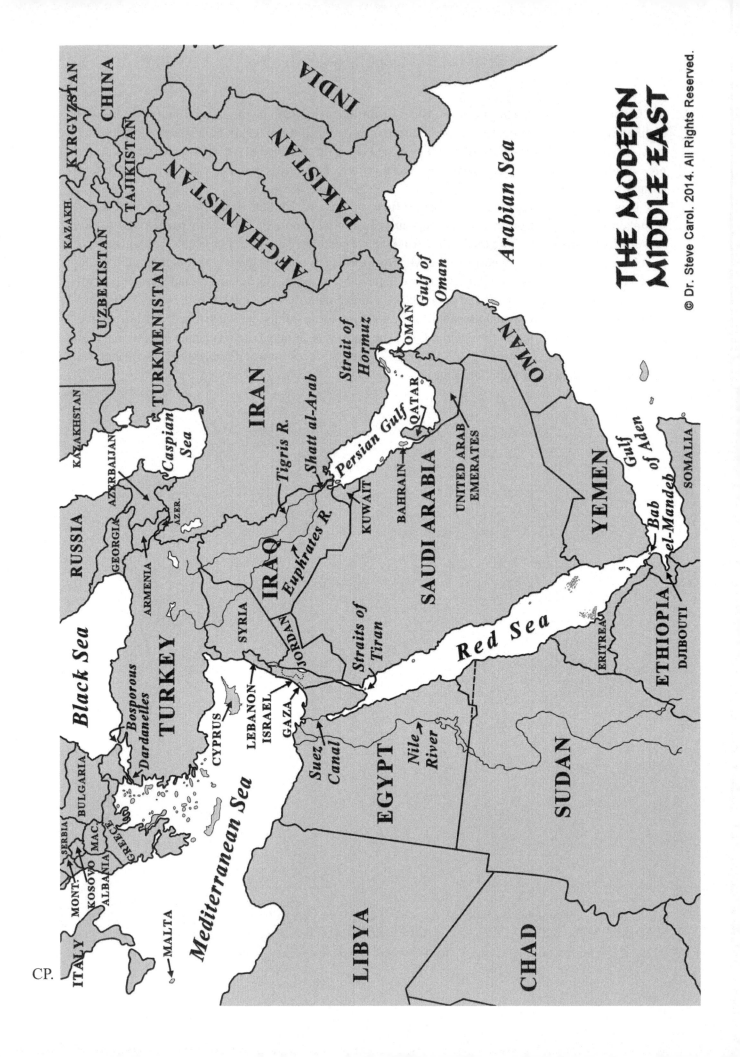

THE MODERN MIDDLE EAST

CRITICAL GEOGRAPHIC FEATURES

A society without knowledge of geography is like a sailor without a compass and a sextant.
Anonymous

The Middle East, isn't that somewhere near the Midwest?
Anonymous

The region known as the greater Middle East encompasses a strategic section of the world. There is daily news coverage of events in the region, yet, its geographic importance and dimensions are not well known. Even the geographic extent of the area has been debated. Additionally, geographic controversies and disputes affect many of the states in the region.

1. Throughout history, the Middle East has held a place of importance greater than that of any other region of the world.

The Middle East is the cradle of Western civilization. Some of the earliest recorded societies began and grew in the Nile River Valley and in the Tigris–Euphrates River Valley. Many ancient civilizations, including the Akkadians, Sumerians, Phoenicians, Hebrews, Babylonians, and Egyptians had their origins there, and the region is the birthplace of three monotheistic faiths: Judaism, Christianity and Islam. However, as noted Catholic theologian, George P. Weigel, accurately reflected, "To speak of Judaism, Christianity, and Islam as the 'three Abrahamic faiths,' the 'three religions of the Book,' or the three monotheisms, obscures rather than illuminates. These familiar tropes ought to be retired."[1]

The Middle East has the immense geographic importance of being the land bridge between three continents—Europe, Asia and Africa. Throughout history, invasion routes have passed through this region. It also contains water routes of enormous geographic, economic, historic, and political importance. Of economic consequence are the vast reserves of petroleum located in the region (*see* "Major Oilfields of the Persian Gulf" map). The Middle East became a major source of oil beginning with commercial production by Iran (1908). This was followed by Iraq (1930), Saudi Arabia and Kuwait (1938), Bahrain (1940), Algeria (1956), Abu Dhabi (1962), Libya (1962), Oman (1967), Dubai (1969), Sharjah (1972), and Sudan (1999).

MAJOR OILFIELDS

SECESSIONIST AREAS 1945-1946

Azerbaijan People's Government
Dec. 12, 1945-Dec. 11, 1946

Kurdish Republic of Mahabad
Jan. 22,-Dec. 15, 1946

2. Many strategic and vital waterways are concentrated in the Middle East.

The Nile River, the Tigris River and Euphrates River, as well as the Shatt al-Arab, the confluence of the Tigris and the Euphrates that flows into the Persian Gulf, are all in the region. Five of the most important straits in the world are situated in the Middle East including the Dardanelles, Bosporus, Tiran, Bab el-Mandeb and Hormuz. Also located in the area is one of the great maritime highways, the Suez Canal. For a better understanding of the importance of these waterways, a closer examination is needed.

THE TURKISH STRAITS

The Turkish Straits refer to two narrow straits that link the Black Sea to the Aegean Sea and the Mediterranean beyond. The Bosporus measures 16 miles long, 1 mile wide, and in some places less than 700 yards wide. The Sea of Marmara is 130 miles long and 40 miles wide. Within that sea, Turkey maintains the prison island of Imrali. The Dardanelles (the Hellespont of antiquity) is 25 miles long, 4.5 miles wide in the south and 2.5 miles wide in the north. The Persians invaded ancient Greece by crossing the Straits. During World War I, the famous Gallipoli campaign occurred on its shores in 1915 (*see* the Turkish Straits map). The treaty that governs the use of the Straits is:

THE MONTREUX CONVENTION[2]
July 20, 1936

- The treaty restored Turkish sovereignty over the Straits, the Bosporus and Dardanelles, allowing Turkey to remilitarize the zone along the Straits.
- It provided for the free navigation of the Straits by all nations' commercial vessels in peacetime.
- It permitted Turkey to close the Straits to all enemy ships in wartime.
- The pact specified that Turkey be notified eight days in advance (or fifteen days for ships of non-Black Sea nations) of any ship passing through the Straits.
- It required that ships pass through the Straits singly, unsubmerged, and only in the daytime.
- Warships from non-Black Sea nations can only stay in the basin for up to 21 days consecutively.

THE STRAITS

Black Sea

Bosporus

Istanbul

Sea of Marmara

Edirne

TURKEY

TURKEY

BULGARIA

GREECE

Alexandroupolis

Gallipoli

Dardanelles

Aegean
Sea

THE SUEZ CANAL

The Suez Canal, a sea-level canal, is one of the world's great man-made waterways. It connects the Mediterranean Sea and the Red Sea measuring 101 miles in length. Its northern outlet is at the city of Port Sa'id. Its southern exit is at the city of Suez. Use of the canal shortens shipping times as reflected in the chart below.

SAILING DISTANCES WITH AND WITHOUT THE USE OF THE SUEZ CANAL		
From/To	No Suez Canal	Via The Suez Canal
London, United Kingdom to the Persian Gulf	11,310 miles	6,537 miles
Naples, Italy to Massawa, Eritrea	10,850 miles	2,178 miles
Rotterdam, the Netherlands to Tokyo, Japan	15,045 miles	11,302

The most pivotal event in the history of the Suez Canal occurred when Egyptian President Gamal Abdel Nasser nationalized the *Compagnie Universelle du Canal de Suez* (Suez Canal Company) on July 26, 1956. It is important to explain who Nasser was, what his goals were, and how that impacted the Suez Canal and the entire Middle East.

On July 23, 1952, the Free Officers Movement within the Egyptian army staged a bloodless coup that toppled the Egyptian monarchy of King Farouk. The leaders of the coup were Muhammad Naguib and Gamal Abdel Nasser. A year later on June 18, 1953, the monarchy was officially abolished and a republic proclaimed. By April 17, 1954, Naguib had been pushed aside and Nasser became Premier of Egypt. His goals were outlined in his book *Philosophy of the Revolution*. He wanted to promote Arab socialism, i.e. public ownership of industry, and Pan-Arabism, the concept of unifying the Arab world, from the Atlantic to the Arabian Sea, into one nation-state with himself at its head.

Nasser detested the "temporary" British occupation of Egypt that lasted from 1888 to 1954 as well as British colonial rule and influence elsewhere in the Arab world—namely in Sudan, Eritrea, Jordan, Iraq, the Trucial States, Kuwait, Bahrain, Qatar, Oman and Aden. He vowed to eliminate British influence, build up Egypt as the leader of the Arab world and eliminate Israel, which had militarily defeated Egypt in the 1948–49 war. His foreign policy was based purely on what was good for Egypt and what could further his goals. Nasser saw his influence over the principle sources of foreign aid—the United States and the Soviet Union as follows: speaking as the leader of Egypt he could get "x" results; speaking as the leader of the Arab world he could get "x^2" results; speaking as the head of the Islamic world he could get "x^3" results, and speaking as leader of the Non-Aligned world he could get "x^4" results. Using this strategy, Nasser would free Egypt from British colonialism and influence, nationalize the Suez Canal, gain military power, confront Israel, and put the Non-Aligned countries on the diplomatic world stage.

Nasser from 1954 onwards played off the United States against the Soviet Union for both military equipment requests and for economic assistance, primarily for his major project, the construction of the Aswan High Dan across the Nile River. He began simultaneous negotiations with the two superpowers, openly with the United States and the West and covertly with the Soviet Union. By

January 1955, Nasser had made a deal of "cotton for arms" with Czechoslovakia standing in as a surrogate for the Soviet Union. The first arm shipment was in Egypt by July 1955 in time of the July 26 Revolution anniversary parade. Nasser saw the arms deal in political (not military as he later claimed) terms. He needed the arms to survive domestic opposition (mainly from the Muslim Brotherhood, which attempted to assassinate him. The arms deal with the Soviets would break the Western arms monopoly (*see* Appendix 6) and reduce the Western sphere of influence. Furthermore, it would unfreeze the territorial and political status quo including his desire to push Pan-Arabism, his ongoing rivalry with pro-British Iraq, and his hoped for ultimate confrontation with Israel.

Openly Nasser negotiated with the United States, the United Kingdom and the World Bank for a loan to help finance the construction of the Aswan High Dam. To allay any Western doubts, on September 2, 1954, Nasser publicly proclaimed his support for the West in the Cold War. Thus, on October 19, 1954, the United Kingdom and Egypt concluded a treaty by which the British would remove its armed forces from the Suez Canal Zone within the next twenty months. An additional provision allowed the British to militarily reoccupy the Zone for the next seven years if Turkey or any Arab country were attacked. Egypt could now use the Suez Canal as a bargaining chip to obtain foreign aid for the construction of the Aswan High Dam. With this knowledge in mind, Egyptian leader Gamal Abdel Nasser prepared plans for the nationalization of the canal. The last British troops evacuated the Suez Canal Zone on June 12, 1956. There was now no roadblock to an Egyptian nationalization of the canal at any time of Nasser's choosing.

The West however wanted Egypt to be the focal point of a new Western (anti-Soviet) alliance in the Middle East to link the North Atlantic Treaty Organization (NATO) with the Southeast Asia Treaty Organization (SEATO). Nasser, despite the offers of Western aid, refused. The United States and the United Kingdom began to have second thoughts about Nasser's policies and withdrew their aid offer to finance the construction of the Aswan High Dam, on July 19, 1956. That move provided Nasser with the pretext needed to proceed with the nationalization of the canal. As the fates would have it, Egypt's seizure of the canal was obscured by a major maritime crisis, as a collision at sea between the SS *Andrea Doria* and the MS *Stockholm*, riveted the attention of much of the world, but did not deter Nasser from moving swiftly to seize the canal (*see* "Causes of the Sinai-Suez War map).

In a speech on July 26, 1956, delivered at Mansheyya Square, in Alexandria, Nasser listed the humiliations Egypt suffered over 200 years at the hands of the Western powers, primarily the United Kingdom, France and the United States.

The speech was the vehicle for delivering the signal for the canal's takeover. Nasser criticized the political conditions attached to Western aid, declaring Egypt could not be bought with aid. Turning to the matter of Egypt's quest for military equipment, he stated emphatically "I do not know whether they are 'communist arms', or 'non-communist arms.' In Egypt these arms are Egyptian arms."[3] Nasser thus admitted that he had received Soviet-supplied arms. Characterizing the High Dam negotiations as long and bitter, Nasser said the West's terms constituted "imperialism without soldiers. They are punishing Egypt because she refused to side with military blocs."[4] Nasser related that during the negotiations, Mr. Black (head of the World Bank), made him feel as if he was sitting "in front of Ferdinand de Lesseps"[5] the chief engineer in the construction of the canal. The name "Ferdinand de Lesseps" was the secret signal for Egyptian forces to seize the canal. It was repeated fourteen times in the space of 10 minutes! With that signal Egyptian personnel seized the company headquarters at Ismailia on the canal as well as the two other control points of the canal, Port Sa'id at the northern end of the waterway, and Port Tewfik (now Suez Port) at the southern end. Nasser declared that Egypt "shall build the High Dam"[6] with the revenues from the Suez Canal. Egypt also seized the account of the Suez Canal Company in the Ottoman Bank in Cairo, amounting to E£ 5 million. The British government held 44 percent of the shares in the company as did France.

The nationalization of the Suez Canal symbolized the modern Arab world's declaration of independence. Nasser correctly calculated that the British had to intervene immediately, if at all, remarking, "It must appear as a direct reaction. If [British Prime Minister Anthony] Eden delays, the pressure against him will increase." Nasser considered that the peak period of danger for Egypt would be 80 percent at the beginning of August 1956, one week after the nationalization, "decreasing each week through political activities." By the end of September, the danger of British military intervention would be reduced to 20 percent. Since Nasser estimated that the British could not intervene for at least two months, the chance for Egyptian success in keeping the canal was, to say the least, encouraging.

The British and French did intervene militarily, but their intervention only began on October 31, and was stopped before they could achieve their objectives (*see* "Sinai-Suez War "map). This case was a classic example of an opponent, (the British and French) which possessed the potential to retaliate against a *fait accompli* (Nasser's seizure of the canal) being unable to do so, since they required an excessive length of time for their military preparations in order to go back to status quo ante. Similar circumstances befell the United States, at the time of the November 1979 seizure of US diplomatic hostages and its embassy in Tehran, Iran.

From 1948, Egypt, illegally barred Israeli ships and cargoes bound to or from Israel on third party vessels. This was in violation of the Constantinople Convention (*see* Appendix 1). On October 31, 1952, a cargo of meat from Incode, on the Norwegian vessel MV *Rimfrost,* proceeding from Massawa to Haifa through the Suez Canal, was confiscated. Under international pressure, the cargo was returned in useless condition three months later.

On two occasions, Egypt's closure of the Suez Canal to Israeli ships and cargo to and from Israel on third party vessels was raised in the United Nations Security Council. On September 1, 1951, there was a lengthy debate in the Security Council on this subject. In the resolution that followed (S/2322), Egyptian interference with navigation to Israel and the maintenance of the blockade were denounced as being "inconsistent with the objective of a peaceful settlement between the parties and the establishment of permanent peace in Palestine set forth in the armistice agreement* between Egypt and Israel."[7] Furthermore, the Security Council:

> called upon Egypt to terminate the restrictions on the passage of international
> commercial shipping and goods through the Suez Canal wherever bound and to cease
> all interference with such shipping beyond that essential to the safety of shipping in
> the Canal itself and to the observance of the international conventions in force.[8]

The resolution was adopted by a vote of eight in favor, none against, and three abstentions (China, India, and the Soviet Union). Nevertheless, there was no Security Council enforcement of the resolution and Egypt continued its blockade of both the Suez Canal and the Straits of Tiran (for the latter, *see* below). The Security Council discussed the matter again in February and March 1954, with special reference to Egyptian interference with shipping proceeding to Eilat. On that occasion the representative of New Zealand, introduced a draft resolution (which was supported also by the United

---

* It should be understood that under binding international law, an armistice agreement is not a war-terminating arrangement. Always, it is merely a pledge temporarily to cease hostilities, within a protracted or extended conflict.

States, the United Kingdom, France, Brazil, Colombia, Turkey and Denmark) which noted "with grave concern" Egyptian noncompliance and called for the implementation of the 1951 resolution adding:

> The final paragraph of the draft resolution, Para. 6, refers only to the complaint of interference with shipping in the Gulf of Aqaba. In the view of my delegation, the arguments advanced by the representative of Egypt in justification of that interference cannot be sustained and, in fact, have already been rejected by the Council.

> Any impartial survey of events since the resolution of September 1, 1951, must record that the Egyptian Government has, with every appearance of deliberation, ignored the injunctions of this Council. This course of conduct, persisted in for over two years, has resulted in many ships, which would otherwise have gone on their lawful occasions through the Suez Canal or the Gulf of Aqaba, being deterred from trading with Israel, or diverted at great cost over other routes to their destination. No government interested in the preservation of the rule of law in international affairs and least of all any government depending for the livelihood of its people on maritime trade, can contemplate this unhappy state of affairs without an earnest desire to bring it to an end.[9]

The draft resolution was killed by a Soviet veto.

Israel attempted to compel the United Nations Security Council to enforce its rulings with regard to passage through the Suez Canal. On September 28, 1954, an Israeli freighter *SS Bat Galim,* bound from Eritrea to Haifa, Israel, with ninety-three tons of meat, forty-two tons of plywood and three tons of hides, attempted to enter the southern end of the Suez Canal. The ship was immediately detained. Its cargo was confiscated and its crew was thrown in jail under a charge of having opened fire on Egyptian fishermen at the entrance to the Canal. False names for the alleged fishermen were fabricated. The Egyptian-Israeli Mixed Armistice Commission dismissed the Egyptian story as a total fiction. Under United Nations pressure, Egypt released the crew from prison on January 1, 1955. The Egyptian delegate at the United Nations had pledged that the ship and cargo would also be returned. They were not. The cargo was appropriated and the confiscated ship was commissioned into the Egyptian Navy. Any United Nations Security Council action was blocked by a veto from the Soviet Union, which already began to support the Arab position openly in the Arab-Israeli conflict. It was these actions incidentally, both at the Suez Canal and at the Straits of Tiran, which led Israel to take military action in the Sinai Campaign*—Operation *Kadesh*—of 1956, to insure the freedom of navigation through the Straits of Tiran.

For a short period after the 1956 Sinai-Suez War, the Egyptian government allowed Israeli cargo to go through the Suez Canal in ships flying the flags of other nations. This was part of a verbal arrangement between Egyptian President Gamal Abdel Nasser and UN Secretary-General Dag Hammarskjold. But soon thereafter, cargos consigned to Israel on foreign flag vessels were refused transit if they appeared on an arbitrary "contraband list." Foreign vessels carrying cargo to Israel were blacklisted. In 1959, Egypt extended these restrictions to cargo from Israel proceeding southward to ports in Africa and Asia. On several occasions, Egypt (then the United Arab Republic) unlawfully interfered with the freedom of passage through the Suez Canal. On February 26, 1959, the SS *Capetan*

---

* The Sinai Campaign was the Israeli portion of the larger Sinai-Suez War of 1956.

Manolis, flying the Liberian flag, was detained and its cargo impounded.[10] On March 17, 1959, the Federal Republic of (West) German ship SS *Laglott* was detained and its cargo was unloaded and seized.[11]

In a celebrated case, on May 21, 1959, the Danish ship, SS *Inge Toft* arrived at Port Sa'id from Haifa, bound for Hong Kong. It carried a cargo of potash, marble and scrap brass. The captain refused to offload the cargo and Egyptian authorities detained the ship for nine months. On February 17, 1960, the *Inge Toft* was allowed to return to Haifa, but its cargo was confiscated. During those nine months, many protests were made in direct communications to the Egyptian government and in debates in the United Nations General Assembly against Cairo's flagrant violation of international rights and decisions. None had any effect. While the *Inge Toft* was still being detained, on December 17, 1959, the Greek vessel, SS *Astypalea,* arrived at Port Sa'id with a cargo of cement. It was bound from Haifa to Djibouti and was detained. After four months of international protests, her owners submitted to Egyptian demands and allowed the cargo to be confiscated. The result of all these cases was that the United Nations did nothing and Egypt continued its illegal closure of the Suez Canal to Israeli ships and cargoes bound to or from Israel.

In part, because of these and other issues, four wars have been fought over and along the canal: Sinai-Suez War of 1956; the Six-Day War of 1967; the 1,000-Day War of Attrition, which lasted from 1967 to 1970; and the Yom Kippur War of 1973. The Egypt–Israel Peace Treaty of March 26, 1979, stated (Article V, Sec. 1):

> Ships of Israel, and cargoes destined for or coming from Israel, shall enjoy the right of free passage through the Suez Canal and its approaches through the Gulf of Suez and the Mediterranean Sea on the basis of the Constantinople Convention of 1888, applying to all nations, Israeli nationals, vessels and cargoes, as well as persons, vessels and cargoes destined for or coming from Israel, shall be accorded non-discriminatory treatment in all matters connected with usage of the canal.

THE SUEZ CANAL HISTORIC TIMELINE	
Date	**Event**
1,800–1,200 B.C.E.	Ancient Egyptians built the first version of the Suez Canal.
641 C.E.	The ancient canal was re-dug by Caliph Umar.
1798	Napoleon Bonaparte had the area surveyed as a site for a new canal.
1832	Ferdinand de Lesseps, French consul in Egypt, studied the feasibility of constructing a new canal.
November 30, 1854	De Lesseps obtained a license for construction and subsequent operation of a canal from the Viceroy of Egypt, Sa'id Pasha. He obtained a second more detailed lease on January 6, 1856, which ran for ninety-nine years.
December 15, 1858	De Lesseps formed the *Compagnie Universelle du Canal de Suez* (Suez Canal Company). Sa'id Pasha controlled 22 percent of the company, the remainder was held by private French interests.
April 25, 1859	Construction of the canal began.
November 17, 1869	The official opening of the Suez Canal took place.
November 25, 1875	The United Kingdom gained 44 percent interest in the Suez Canal. French syndicates controlled the remaining shares.

August 25, 1882	The United Kingdom took control of the canal.
March 2, 1888	The Constantinople Convention guaranteed right of passage of all ships through the Suez Canal during war and peace (*see* Appendix 1).
January 14, 1915	During World War I: Some 25,000 Turkish troops, commanded by Djemal Pasha launched an offensive westward across the Sinai Peninsula to attack the Suez Canal.
February 3, 1915	Turkish troops attempted to cross the Suez Canal but their attack failed and British-officered Indian troops as well as the guns of British and French ships guarding the canal forced them to retreat.
July 19, 1916	Some 18,000 Turkish troops, commanded by German General Friedrich Freiherr Kress Kressenstein, launched their second attack on the Suez Canal. They advanced to within 10 miles of Romani, a rail junction some 23 miles to the east of the canal.
August 3–5, 1916	Turkish forces launched an attack on Romani in a bid to reach the canal but were pushed back by New Zealand and other British Empire forces. The Turks suffered some 9,000 casualties.
November 14, 1936	The British established a Suez Canal Zone under their military control.
January 1941–July 1942	During World War II: The German *Luftwaffe* operating from the island of Rhodes, closed the Suez Canal with mines for 21 days in February 15 days in March and 17 days in May. Between January 1941 and July 1942, the canal experienced sixty-four air raids, sinking sixteen ships in transit and eleven other vessels.
1948–April 30, 1979	Egypt in defiance of international treaty, international law and a United Nations Security Council resolution illegally closed the Suez Canal to Israeli ships and cargoes bound to or from Israel in third party vessels.
June 13, 1956	The last British military forces evacuated the canal zone and it reverted to Egyptian control.
July 26, 1956	Egyptian President Gamal Abdel Nasser nationalized the canal.
November 5, 1956–April 8, 1957	During the Sinai-Suez War, Egyptian President Nasser blocked the canal to international shipping with forty-seven ships filled with concrete, and the canal was closed.
June 5, 1967–April 10, 1975	During the Six-Day War, Egypt again blocked the canal, which remained closed for almost eight years. Fourteen ocean-going ships remained trapped in the Great Bitter Lake within the canal for that period.
June 10, 1975	The Suez Canal officially reopened to international shipping.
April 30, 1979	Because of the Egypt–Israel Peace Treaty, the first Israeli ship—the cargo vessel *Ashdod*—passed through the Suez Canal.

With the future of the Egypt–Israel Peace Treaty in doubt, after the Egyptian political upheaval of 2011–12, as well as the subsequent Egyptian military coup of July 3, 2013, the Suez Canal once again may be blocked illegally, to Israeli shipping and cargoes going to or from Israel.

THE STRAITS OF TIRAN

As has been mentioned above, the Suez Canal is a vital maritime link between the Mediterranean Sea, via the Gulf of Suez, and Red Sea. There is however, a nearby alternate route. Israel, apart from Egypt, is the only country in the world, which has a coastline both on the Mediterranean and on the Red Sea. Cargo can travel from Israel's port of Ashdod on the Mediterranean coast, overland to the Israeli southern port of Eilat, and from there by sea, southward through the Gulf of Aqaba (Eilat) through the Straits of Tiran into the Red Sea. Ashdod is the largest port in Israel, handling about 60 percent of Israel's port cargo. Similarly, in a reverse flow, goods can travel via the Gulf of Aqaba across Israel to Ashdod. In 1968, Israel constructed the 158-mile long, 42-inch diameter Trans-Israel oil pipeline* that connects Israel's Mediterranean port of Ashkelon with Eilat. The Trans-Israel pipeline can transport crude oil cargoes in either direction.

As a major step to increase Israel's economic and strategic position in the Middle East, on July 3, 2012, Israeli Transport Minister Yisrael Katz and China's Minister of Transport Li Shenglin signed a memorandum of understanding in Beijing, whereby China will construct a high speed double-track (one for passenger traffic, the other for cargo) electrified rail line between the Israeli port of Ashdod and Eilat.[12] There are plans also to possibly extend the line to Jordan's sole port of Aqaba. The $2 billion, 187-mile projected railway, dubbed the "Red-Med line," is to have an estimated maximum speed of 140 to 190 mph. It is expected to begin operation five years from the start of construction as early as 2019. It also enhances world trade patterns. As Israeli Prime Minister Benjamin Netanyahu observed, "It's the first time we'd be able to assist the countries in Europe and Asia to make sure they always have an open connection between Europe and Asia and between Asia and Europe."[13] Thus, free passage through the Gulf of Aqaba is vital to Israel's economy as well as the economic health of both Europe and Asia. Given the volatile nature of the region, this is especially true if Suez Canal traffic is curtailed or stopped for political or military reasons.

The Gulf of Aqaba is 100 miles long and has a total coastline of 230 miles, which is shared by four countries—Egypt, Israel, Jordan, and Saudi Arabia. At the northern end of the Gulf, the width of which varies from 12 to 17 miles, there are two ports: Eilat, Israel, and Aqaba, Jordan. For Jordan, Aqaba is its sole port.

Two islands are situated at the southern end of the Gulf of Aqaba, Tiran and Sanafir. Interestingly, both islands were Jewish trading posts in the third century C.E.[14] The only navigable channel leading from the Red Sea to the Gulf of Aqaba passes between Tiran Island and the coast of the Sinai Peninsula. It is the narrow Enterprise Passage, a shipping channel only 1,300 yards wide and running parallel to the shore. The point on the Sinai coast directly facing the island of Tiran is known as Ras Nasrani, to the south of which, at the southern tip of the Sinai Peninsula, lays Sharm el-Sheikh (*see* "Straits of Tiran" map).

---

* Earlier in late 1957, Israel built an 8-inch diameter oil pipeline from Eilat to Beersheba. From there, the oil was transported by railway tanker cars to the main oil refinery in Haifa. In 1960 a new line was laid (16-inch diameter) from Eilat directly to the Haifa Oil Refinery

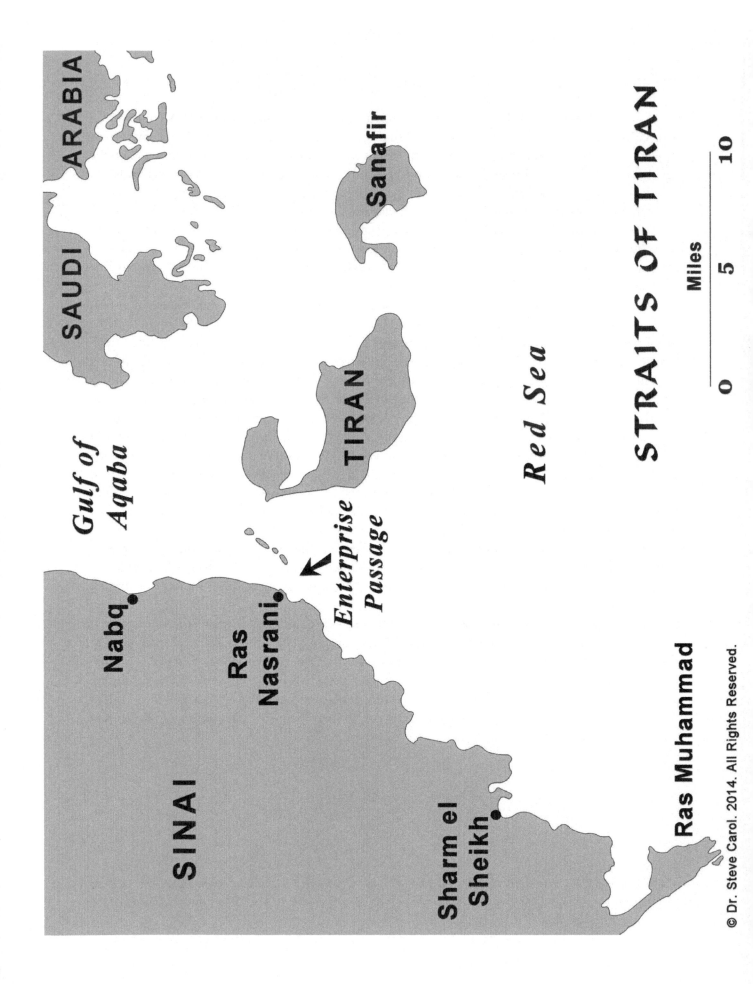

STRAITS OF TIRAN

Miles

0   5   10

Historically, Israel has always regarded the Gulf of Aqaba as its gateway to the Red Sea, Africa, Asia, and beyond. King Solomon of Israel had a port on the Red Sea as is described in I Kings 9:26–28:

> And King Solomon made a navy of ships in Ezion-geber, which is beside Eloth [Eilat], on the shore of the Red Sea, in the land of Edom. And Hiram sent in the navy his servants, shipmen that had knowledge of the sea, with the servants of Solomon. And they came to Ophir and fetched from there gold, four hundred and twenty talents and brought it to King Solomon.

After the First World War, the northern and eastern shores of the Gulf of Aqaba came to be divided between the British mandated territory of Palestine (which included the Emirate of Transjordan) and the Kingdom of Saudi Arabia. After the termination of the British Mandate in 1948, the areas on the northern shore of the gulf, which had previously been under British Mandate, became part of Israel and Transjordan respectively.

In December 1949, Egypt erected military installations on the uninhabited islands of Tiran and Sanafir and on the Sinai coast opposite the islands. In reply to an inquiry on the subject addressed to it by the American Embassy in Cairo, the Egyptian Government on January 28, 1950, stated it had no intention of interfering in any way with peaceful shipping. It added that "it goes without saying that this passage [through the Straits of Tiran] will remain free [i.e. from visit, search, and seizure] as in the past in conformity with international practice and with the recognized principle of international law."[15]

In mid-1951, despite the Egyptian promise to the United States and of its acknowledgment that the Gulf of Aqaba was an international waterway, Egypt began to enforce a blockade of the Straits of Tiran, the entrance to the Gulf of Aqaba. This was done as part of the continued Arab League economic war against the Jewish state. The blockade and economic war continued even after armistice agreements had been signed between Israel and several of its Arab neighbors—with Egypt on February 25, 1949, with Lebanon on March 23, 1949, with Transjordan on April 3, 1949, and with Syria on July 20, 1949. All these agreements expressly prohibited all warlike or hostile actions between the parties.

Egypt set up six gun emplacements—two were six-inch guns and four were three-inch guns—at Ras Nasrani, for the sole purpose of preventing ships from entering the gulf to call at the Israeli port of Eilat. As an added benefit, Egypt used the blockade to restrict ships to the Jordanian port of Aqaba. Throughout the 1950s, Egypt on numerous occasions, sought to apply political and economic pressure on Jordan, in various attempts to topple the government of Jordanian King Hussein. As events would show, the blockade remained in effect from July 1, 1951, to November 3, 1956, when the Israel Defense Forces (IDF) captured Ras Nasrani and much of the Sinai Peninsula, during the Sinai-Suez War.

Under Egyptian regulations and decrees, ships about to pass through the Straits of Tiran were required to give seventy-two hours notice in advance to the Egyptian authorities with full particulars of their cargo, passengers and destination. Most of these regulations were actually enacted after the United Nations Security Council had denounced the Egyptian blockade. By a decree issued in November 1953, even foodstuffs were included in the list of "contraband goods" prohibited from being shipped through the Straits of Tiran to Eilat. In an explanatory memorandum accompanying this decree the purpose, underlying it was frankly stated, "Israel was showing increasing economic activity and was establishing a merchant fleet to handle its imports from South and East Africa."[16] The regulations were enforced with ever-increasing severity, despite the strong diplomatic representations of the maritime powers using the gulf.

In the period, from 1951 to 1955, a number of serious incidents occurred in the gulf. The first occurred on July 1, 1951, when the British SS *Empire Roach*, carrying a cargo of arms to the Jordanian port of Aqaba, was fired upon and denied access to the gulf. A second incident took place on December 3, 1952, when the American vessel SS *Albion,* carrying a cargo of US aid—wheat for the relief of famine in Jordan—bound for Aqaba, was fired upon by the Egyptian shore batteries. In apologizing for the incident, the Egyptian authorities explained that they had mistaken the ship's destination as being Eilat.

A third episode transpired on September 2, 1953, when the Greek freighter, *Parnon*, en route from Mombasa, Kenya, to Eilat was detained by Egyptian authorities for eleven days and its cargo was seized. Four months later, on January 1, 1954, Egyptian gunfire was directed against the Italian ship *Maria Antonia* en route from Massawa, Ethiopia to Eilat. The vessel was forced to return to its port of origin. Yet another incident occurred on April 10, 1955, when the British SS *Argobec* was stopped by shots fired across its bow, and this led to a formal protest by the United Kingdom. The final interference with the right of free navigation in the gulf before the Sinai-Suez War took place on July 3, 1955, when the British ship SS *Anshun*, engaged in carrying pilgrims to Mecca, was fired upon and actually hit.

These incidents clearly showed that Egypt acted in utter disregard of international law governing navigation through straits, which connect two parts of the high seas. Such straits, even when technically forming part of territorial waters, constitute international waterways. The law of international waterways provides for the full freedom of innocent passage. These principles were reaffirmed in 1949, by the International Court of Justice in a judgment of general application—the Corfu Channel Case. The court ruled that when straits are geographically part of a highway used in fact for international navigation, then the vessels of all nations enjoy the rights of free navigation therein, whether or not the straits are entirely or partly within the territorial waters of one or more states.[17] The judgment continued:

> It is in the opinion of the Court generally recognized and in accordance with international custom that States in time of peace have a right to send their warships through straits used for international navigation between two parts of the high seas without the previous authorization of a coastal state, provided that the passage is innocent. Unless otherwise prescribed in an international convention, there is no right for a coastal state to prohibit such passage through straits in time of peace." The narrow passage at Tiran is clearly a strait within this general rule.[18]

In May 1967, Egypt's Nasser again ordered a blockade of the Straits of Tiran, an act of war, which precipitated the Six-Day War.* The blockade lasted from May 22, 1967, until June 7, 1967, when Sharm el-Sheikh and Ras Nasrani fell to the IDF (*see* the "Six-Day War, June 5–10, 1967, Israeli Attack" map).

The Egypt–Israel Peace Treaty of March 26, 1979, stated (Article V, Sec. 2):

> The Parties consider the Straits of Tiran and the Gulf of Aqaba to be international waterways open to all nations for unimpeded and non-suspendable freedom of navigation and overflights. The parties will respect each other's right to navigation

---

* Many contemporary historians and journalists ignore or conveniently forget that Egypt's blockade is what started the Six-Day War. Such authors, out of ignorance or with a political agenda, prefer to claim Israel started the war with its pre-emptive air strikes of June 5, 1967.

and overflights for access to either country through the Straits of Tiran and the Gulf of Aqaba.

Of related interest, in 1988, Egypt and Saudi Arabia began discussions for the construction of a 20-mile-long road and rail bridge across the Straits of Tiran from Ras Nasrani, in the Sinai Peninsula, near Sharm el-Sheikh, to Ras Hamid in northwestern Saudi Arabia. Part of the project was to be a suspension bridge. In 2006, then Egyptian President Hosni Mubarak abruptly shelved the mammoth project shortly before construction began after Israel expressed security concerns, because of escalating terrorist attacks in the region.

With the ouster of the Mubarak regime in February 2011, the bridge project was put back on track. In July 2011, Egypt's interim Prime Minister Essam Sharaf put General Abdul Aziz, chairperson of the Arab Road Association, in charge of overseeing the project. Officials believe that tolls paid by millions of Muslim pilgrims on their way to holy sites in Saudi Arabia could pay for the roughly $5 billion the bridge is expected to cost. They also believe the bridge will significantly increase the number of pilgrims.[19] With the ouster of the Morsi regime in July 2013, the future status of the bridge project is again in a state of limbo.

BAB EL-MANDEB

At its southern end, the Red Sea gradually narrows to a point where the tip of the Arabian Peninsula and the coast of Africa are separated by a distance of only 22 miles. The Strait of Bab el-Mandeb ("The Gate of Tears") connecting the Red Sea with the Gulf of Aden and the Indian Ocean beyond, is bisected by Perim Island, controlled since the end of 1967 by the People's Democratic Republic of Yemen (PDRY)—today part of Yemen. Facing Perim on the African coast is the Republic of Djibouti—and the southern part of the Eritrean coast. Since the narrow passage between the mainland of Yemen and Perim, measuring 1.75 miles wide, is dangerous for navigation, the main passage into the Red Sea has been the 16.5-mile-wide channel between Perim and the African coast, which is relatively deep and free of obstructions. An estimated 3.8 million bbl/d of crude oil and refined petroleum products flowed through this waterway in 2013.[20]

The British withdrew from the Federation of South Arabia (their former Aden colony and protectorate) on November 30, 1967, and the independence of the PDRY was proclaimed. The British had a tentative plan to internationalize Perim under the supervision of the United Nations,[21] but this was not implemented and the island came under PDRY administration. The PDRY announced that it would use Perim to block the passage of Israeli ships through the Strait of Bab el-Mandeb. The PDRY was ideologically related to the Marxist-oriented Palestinian cause and opposed the existence of Israel. At that time, there were worldwide discussions being held on the Law of the Sea. The extension of territorial limits at sea, to 12 miles in this case, could have the most explosive potential effects.

In fact, the right of innocent passage through the Bab el-Mandeb was challenged on June 11, 1971, when an Israeli-chartered Liberian flag tanker, SS *Coral Sea* was attacked in that waterway by a Palestinian guerrilla unit based on Perim, with the collusion of some of the PDRY leaders. Two years later, the Arabs imposed a blockade on this international waterway during the 1973 Yom Kippur War (*see* "Bab el-Mandeb" map).

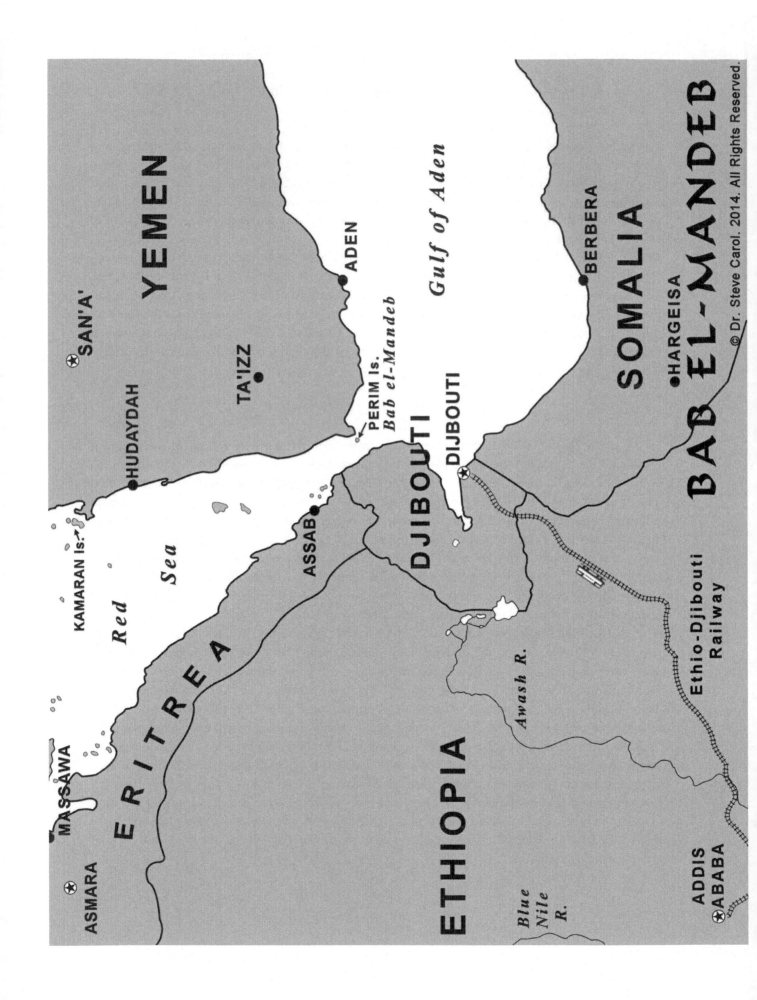

SHATT AL-ARAB

The Shatt al-Arab (known as Arvand Rud in Iran) is the name given to the confluence of the Tigris River and the Euphrates River, at Qurna, as it flows about 120 miles southeast into the Persian Gulf. The southern end of the Shatt al-Arab constitutes the border between Iraq and Iran. Iraq is nearly land-locked with a Persian Gulf coastline of only 25 miles. Iraq's chief port Basra, and two of Iran's key ports, Khorramshahr and Abadan, are located on the Arvand Rud/Shatt al-Arab. It also provides the outlet for the southern Iraqi oil fields, and the Iranian refineries at Abadan (*see* "Shatt al-Arab" map).

Historically, the Shatt al-Arab, which literally means "the Arab shore," has long marked the boundary between the Ottoman Empire (then including present-day Iraq) and Persia (modern Iran). It marked the eastern border of the Arab world. The boundary was disputed by one party or the other since the May 17, 1639 Treaty of Zuhab. At least eighteen treaties have dealt with that frontier and various attempts were made at demarcation. The issue of the Shatt al-Arab waterway did not arise until the Treaty of Erzurum signed on May 31, 1847. At that time, the waterway's boundary was set at the eastern bank, so that the entire waterway remained under Ottoman control. A more precise delineation of the border, including the waterway, was agreed upon in the Constantinople Protocol of November 17, 1913. The signatories were the Ottoman Empire, Persia, Russia and the United Kingdom.

The protocol gave sovereignty over the entire Shatt al-Arab and both banks of the river to Turkey, with the exception in the area surrounding the Persian town of Khorramshahr, where the boundary was to follow the thalweg. The thalweg line is the rule of international law, which determines the exact location of the boundary of two states separated by a navigable river. The thalweg or "downway" is the middle of the main, deepest channel or downstream current. The law is also applicable to estuaries and bays.

With the collapse of the Ottoman Empire in 1918, and the emergence of new nations, the Shatt al-Arab marked the boundary between Iraq and soon to be renamed Persia, i.e. Iran. Under Shah Reza Khan, Iran challenged the Constantinople Protocol in 1934. Presentations were made to the League of Nations without any resolution of the dispute. In part this was due to the fact that the United Kingdom dominated the League with six votes (itself and other British Empire members—Australia, Canada, India, New Zealand and South Africa). Therefore, there were new negotiations resulting in the Iran–Iraq Frontier Treaty of July 8, 1937, signed in Tehran. The United Kingdom, ever mindful of its own strategic interests, negotiated for Iraq, and thus imposed pressure on Iran to accept the Constantinople Protocol with an additional exception. The boundary around the area in the immediate vicinity of the Iranian town of Abadan, would also follow the thalweg line. However, this did not settle the issue of freedom of navigation along the entire length of the Shatt al-Arab.

On April 19, 1969, Iran, under Shah Mohammad Reza Pahlavi, abrogated the Iran-Iraq Frontier Treaty of 1937. Iran claimed that the Shatt al-Arab was a border river between the two states and that it should be divided according to the thalweg line. Thus, the boundary dispute erupted again. The Shatt al-Arab boundary was a contentious issue between Iraq and Iran from 1932 to 1975. The Algiers Agreement of March 6, 1975, settled the dispute for a while, but it was revived by the abrogation of the Algiers Agreement by the Iraqi regime of Saddam Hussein on September 17, 1980. The Iraqi move came just days before the Iraqi attack on Iran starting the Iran–Iraq War (1980–88). In August 1990, Iraq declared its acceptance of the Algiers Agreement, which divided the Shatt al-Arab between the two nations, along the thalweg line.

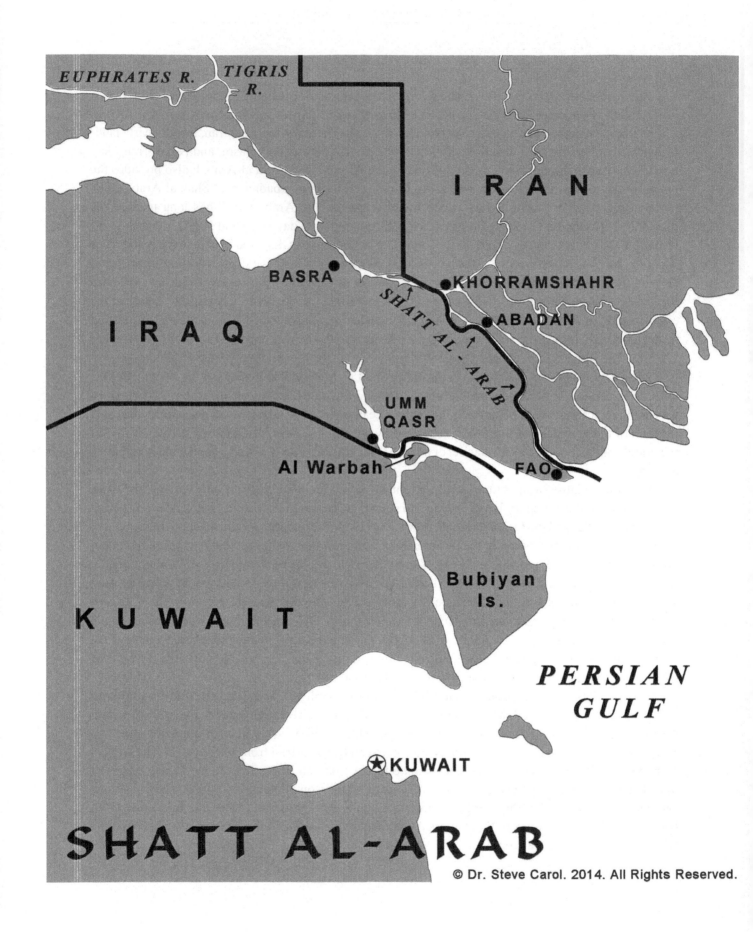

SHATT AL-ARAB

STRAIT OF HORMUZ

The Strait of Hormuz is the body of water that connects the Persian Gulf to the Gulf of Oman, the Arabian Sea and the Indian Ocean beyond. It is 33.5 miles wide (18.6 miles at its narrowest) and 170 miles long. Territorially, it is flanked by Iran to the north and Oman's 51 mile-long enclave, Ruus al Jibal, on the Ras Mussandam Peninsula to the south (*see* "Strait of Hormuz and the UAE" map). Both Iran and Oman claim twelve mile-wide limits thus, leaving a four mile-wide slot of international waters. Within that four mile-wide area are two shipping lanes, each one-mile wide—the more northerly inbound channel and to its south, the outbound channel. A two-mile buffer in the midst of which are the disputed islands of Greater and Lesser Tunb separate them. Iran has occupied the islands since 1971 and has military forces as well as anti-ship missiles stationed on the islands.

According to the US Energy Information Administration, on average, 15 crude oil tankers, carrying 17 million barrels of oil passed through the Strait of Hormuz daily (2014 figures). In addition, there are tankers carrying other petroleum products and liquefied natural gas. This represents 30 percent of the world's seaborne oil shipments, and 20 percent of all world shipments. This volume varies according to weather conditions, currents, and whether it is day or night. The traffic during the navigable hours tends to be heavy, no more than 6 minutes between each vessel. It is on this vital waterway that the United States receives 12 percent of its oil and Western Europe and Japan get 25 to 66 percent of their oil respectively. Thus, the Strait of Hormuz is one of the world's most strategically important oil choke points.[22]

In June 2012, Abu Dhabi, part of the United Arab Emirates (UAE), announced the completion of the 224-mile-long Habshan–Fujairah oil pipeline, which connects Abu Dhabi on the Persian Gulf with the Emirate of Fujairah on the Gulf of Oman. The 48-inch pipeline has a capacity of 1.5 million barrels per day and bypasses the Strait of Hormuz, thus providing an alternate route in case the strait is blockaded or mined.

A territorial dispute existed between the UAE and Iran over ownership of three islands—Abu Musa, Greater Tunb Island, and Lesser Tunb Island—all strategically located at the mouth of the Strait of Hormuz (*see* "The Strait of Hormuz and the UAE" map). Iran claimed the islands as part of the Persian Empire, dating back to the twelfth century and lasting until the early twentieth century. The United Kingdom controlled the islands from the early years of the twentieth century, as well as exercised a protectorate over the Trucial states. Greater and Lesser Tunb islands belonged to the emirate of Ras al Khaimah. On November 29, 1971, Iran (under the Shah) and the emirate of Sharjah signed an agreement for joint administration of Abu Musa island. The next day, November 30, Iran forcibly occupied the Greater Tunb and Lesser Tunb islands, which belonged to the emirate of Ras al Khaimah. Less than 48 hours later, the Trucial states under a new name—the United Arab Emirates— became an independent country. In March 1992, Iran expelled all foreigners from the islands. In September, Iran declared full sovereignty over the islands.

In 1995, the Iranian Foreign Ministry claimed that the islands were "an inseparable part of Iran" and deployed 4,000 troops, artillery, surface-to-air missiles and anti-ship missiles to Abu Musa. In March 1996, an airfield was built on Abu Musa and a squadron of Su-25 jet fighters was deployed there. Iran rejected a 1996 proposal by the Gulf Cooperation Council[*] (GCC) for the dispute to be resolved by the International Court of Justice, an option supported by the UAE.

On December 31, 2001, the GCC issued a statement reiterating its support for the UAE's sovereignty over Abu Musa and the Tunb Islands, declared Iran's claims on the islands as "null and void," and

---

[*] The GCC is comprised of Bahrain, Kuwait, Oman, Qatar, Saudi Arabia, and the United Arab Emirates.

backed "all measures … by the UAE to regain sovereignty on its three islands peacefully." The UAE and Oman were supported by the United States, which guaranteed their security (United States–Oman Defense agreement of 1980) by keeping a naval carrier task force in the Persian Gulf area. Tensions between Iran and the United States grew over the former's quest for nuclear weapons. In 2013, the Iranian Revolutionary Guard Command inaugurated a naval base on Abu Musa.

However, during the latter portion of 2013, the UAE and Iran engaged in secretive talks with the help of the Omani government about resolving the dispute. In January 2014, an agreement was reached between Iran and the UAE. The Greater and Lesser Tunbs, were to be returned to the UAE while the status of Abu Musa was finalized. According to the accord:

> Iran will retain the seabed rights around the three islands while the UAE will hold sovereignty over the land. [At the same time an agreement was reached with Oman whereby] Oman will grant Iran a strategic location on Ras Musandam mountain, which is a very strategic point overlooking the whole gulf region. In return for Ras Musandam, Oman will receive free gas and oil from Iran once a pipeline is constructed within the coming two years.[23]

It remains to be seen if the Iran–UAE, and Iran–Oman set of agreements will hold. If the Geneva interim agreement on the Iranian nuclear program of November 2013, does not result in a satisfactory final accord, tensions in the Persian Gulf region will quickly escalate. Iran has the military capability to reoccupy the strategic islands quickly.

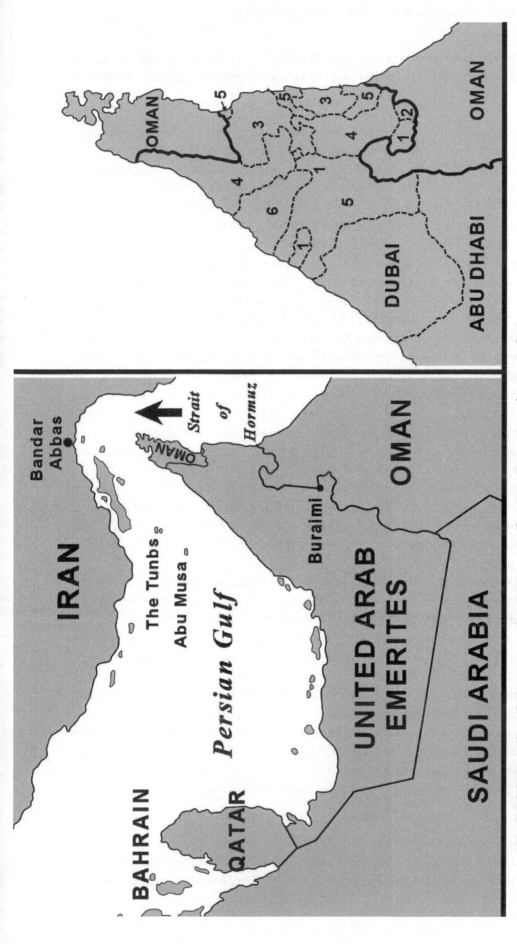

STRAIT OF HORMUZ

1 'AJMAN
2 DUBAI
3 FUJAIRA
4 RAS AL-KHAIMA
5 SHARJAH
6 UMM AL-QAIWAIN

IRAN

Bandar Abbas

The Tunbs
Abu Musa

Persian Gulf

Strait of Hormuz

OMAN

BAHRAIN

QATAR

UNITED ARAB EMERITES

Buraimi

OMAN

SAUDI ARABIA

OMAN

OMAN

DUBAI

ABU DHABI

3. Contrary to Arab/Muslim propaganda, the depictions of Israel as an immense expansionist country are false. In reality, Israel is a tiny Jewish "island" in a vast Arab/Muslim sea.

Throughout history, the Land of Israel was the geo-strategic pivotal point squeezed in between larger competing empires and more frequently than not, surrounded by enemies. It was not necessarily an asset to be located at the crossroads of three continents on historic invasion routes. Strong enemies have challenged the religious and cultural integrity as well as the physical survival of the Jewish nation. The Land of Israel—*Eretz Yisrael*—was invaded both from the southwest and from the northeast numerous times. To survive in that geopolitical hot spot, a nation needs a strong military, which explains modern Israel's emphasis on defense and security.

Modern Israel's area is 8,019/8,522[24] square miles, smaller than the State of New Jersey (8,721 square miles). One can drive across Israel near its widest extent—from the shore of the Dead Sea to the Mediterranean on the other side—in just over ninety minutes. From north to south, i.e. from Kiryat Shmona to Eilat, Israel is but a short 263 miles. A modern fighter jet can cover the space between Israel's two most distant points in less than 10 minutes. Israel comprises less 0.5 percent of the Middle East's territory. The twenty-one Arab states have a total area of 5,208,801square miles, which is slightly less than one and one-half times the size of the fifty United States (3,794,085 square miles). The ratio of Arab to Jewish land is over 640:1. Syria alone (71,498 square miles) is seven times the size of Israel.

There is one Jewish state. Israel, with 8,522 square miles as noted above, including the recovered territories—Judea, Samaria and the Gaza Strip (what is erroneously called "occupied" territories. Neither, for that matter, are these territories, "disputed territories," because the Arab claim to them is not of equal juridical weight to the Jewish legal right to them). There are fifty-six Muslim states with 12,277,290 square miles.[25] Why one tiny country is sufficient for Jews, but fifty-six countries are not enough for Muslims? Why are over 12 million square miles so insufficient for the Muslim world, that they must go to war over another 2,402 square miles, from Israel's heartland, to expand Muslim lands by an infinitesimal 0.02 percent?

Forty-five American states are larger than Israel. Texas is 267,339 square miles. Israel can fit into Texas over thirty-three times (33.33). Arizona is 113,642 square miles. Israel can fit into Arizona over fourteen times (14.17). Lake Erie is larger than Israel and Lake Michigan more than twice as large. If Israel were dropped into Lake Michigan, it would disappear from view without a trace. Israel is less than the size of Maricopa County, Arizona (9,224 square miles). It is less than one-half the size of San Bernardino County, California. The distance from Israel's capital in Jerusalem to Bethlehem in the Palestinian Arab territory is only a fraction of the distance from Washington, DC, to Baltimore, Maryland. Israel, including Judea and Samaria, Gaza, and the Golan Heights, is 10,846 square miles. The Gaza Strip is 139 square miles. It shares a 32-mile frontier with Israel, a 7-mile border with Egypt and has 25 miles of Mediterranean coastline. The territory of Judea and Samaria is 2,263 square miles in area. The Golan Heights is 451 square miles. It measures (from north to south) just 40 miles. At its widest point (east to west), the Golan Heights is 15.5 miles and at its narrowest, 7.5 miles.

For Israel, the territory of Judea and Samaria has great strategic importance. The area is a territorial barrier protecting the vulnerable Gush Dan coastal plain from armed attack from the east. The Gush Dan plain contains more than 70 percent of Israel's population and 80 percent of its industrial capacity.

The mountain ridge of Judea and Samaria reaches only 3,346 feet at its highest point, Mount Hebron. However, to the east lies the Jordan Valley-Dead Sea Rift, the lowest point on Earth, dropping down to 1,371 feet below sea level. This means that the eastern slope of the Judea and Samaria mountain ridge forms a 4,717-foot barrier that is relatively steep for an attacking ground force to scale.

Radar arrays and electronic signals intelligence (ELINT) sites atop this mountain ridge give Israel an early warning system against enemy aircraft from the east. An enemy fighter-bomber needs less than 45 seconds to cross the 42 miles from the Jordan River over Judea and Samaria and Israel to the Mediterranean. The distance from the Jordan River to the apex of the mountain ridge is roughly 8 to 12 miles, and the entire Judea and Samaria region is about 33 miles wide. Israeli control of the eastern slopes of the mountain ridge as well as the Jordan River Valley gives it a defensive line, which would buy time and enable the IDF to mobilize to face advancing aggressor ground forces from the east. Additionally, Israel's military control of the Jordan Valley allows it to prevent the smuggling of advanced weapons to various terrorist groups. Israel has only to patrol a border that is 62 miles long as opposed to the 1949 armistice line—the "Green Line"*—that is 223 miles in length.

The Golan Heights is a rocky plateau that rises from 1,968 feet to 2,952 feet above sea level. For nineteen years, Syrian artillery (well hidden and not visible by the Israelis) was trained on the Hula Valley, the northern Galilee and the Sea of Galilee (alternatively known as Lake Kinneret or Lake Tiberias) below. These guns disrupted and threatened the lives of Israelis working the farms on both shores of the sea and beyond, as well as the fishermen on the sea itself. By 1963, so many Israeli farmers and fishermen had lost their lives to Syrian gunfire that armored-plated tractors and fishing vessels became standard equipment.[26] Additionally, the Syrians were at the forefront of the Arab plan to divert the headwaters of the Jordan River—that channel 40 percent of Israel's water supply† into the Sea of Galilee—and actually began such diversion (for details *see* "Basic Principle 44" and "Basic Principle 69").

The cliffs of the Palisades on the west side of the lower Hudson River, located in northeastern New Jersey, are very similar in topography to the Golan Heights, only much lower, rising 300 feet on average above sea level. Imagine hostile forces atop the Palisades firing their guns, and wreaking havoc on excursion boats in the Hudson River, on gardeners tilling the soil on the narrow shoreline below, or on Manhattan Island across the river. That would replicate the situation Israel faced from the Golan Heights during the period 1949–67.

MIDDLE EAST TERRITORIAL COMPARISON	
Country	Territory (in square miles)
Mauritania*	419,229
Morocco*	275,410 [27]
Algeria*	919,595
Tunisia*	63,378
Libya*	679,358

* The armistice lines were colored green on the original maps drawn up at the negotiations on the island of Rhodes in 1949, hence the name "Green Line."

† An additional 40 percent of Israel's water supply comes from the aquifer under Judea and Samaria.

Egypt*	386,874
Sudan*	728,215
Djibouti*	8,880
Somalia*	246,261
Comoros*	863
Saudi Arabia*	829,995
Yemen*	203,850
Oman*	119,500
United Arab Emirates*	32,278
Qatar*	4,473
Bahrain*	290
Kuwait*	6,880
Turkey	302,535
Cyprus	3,572
Syria*	71,498
Lebanon*	4,036
Jordan*	35,468
Iraq*	172,476
Iran	636,293
Total Arab world	5,208,801
Total Arab world plus Iran	**5,845,094**
Israel	8,522 [28]

* Member of the Arab League

One additional territorial factor must be considered. A disproportionate territorial exchange took place between the Arab states and Israel. Over 881,000 Jews were forced to flee Arab countries since 1948. They abandoned their homes and forfeited their property. The Arabs gained between 38,625[29] and 100,000 square miles[30] from their Jewish residents without compensation. The Arabs gained a land mass that is between nearly five times to over twelve times the size of Israel (8, 019 square miles), or between three and one-half to over nine times the size all of the recovered territories and Israel combined (10,872 square miles), depending on which land mass area is selected.

Since 1948, Israel, in legitimate wars of self-defense, gained just 2,853 square miles of territory (Judea, Samaria, the Gaza Strip and the Golan Heights—about 3 percent of the territory confiscated from Jews in Arab lands). Israel should fully extend Israeli sovereignty to those 2,853 square miles of disputed lands, as the Arabs did with land they acquired from the Jews. In exchange the Arab states should turn those confiscated Jewish properties over to the Palestinian Arabs, who's cause they so fervently espouse.

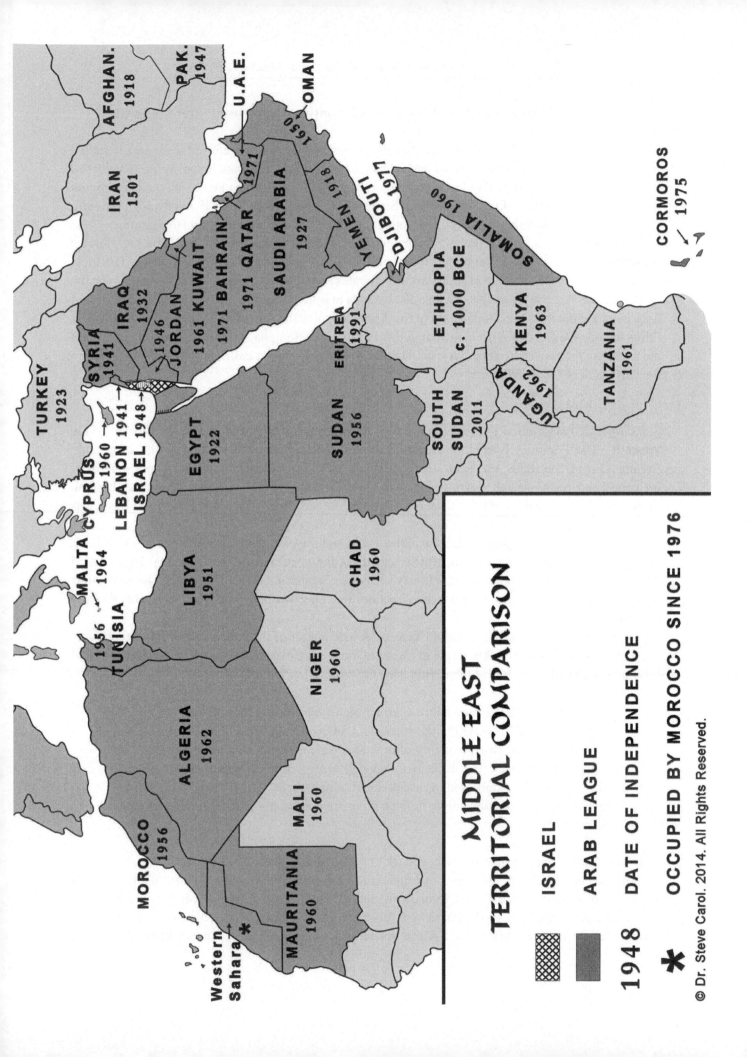

MIDDLE EAST
TERRITORIAL COMPARISON

ISRAEL

ARAB LEAGUE

1948 DATE OF INDEPENDENCE

✳ OCCUPIED BY MOROCCO SINCE 1976

© Dr. Steve Carol. 2014. All Rights Reserved.

4. The terms "Middle East" and "Near East" continue to be used interchangeably.

Prior to 1954, the term "Near East" was used extensively and generally referred to an area bounded by Egypt to the west, Iraq to the east and included Israel, Jordan, Lebanon and Syria. It stretched from Turkey in the north, and extended to the southern tip of the Arabian Peninsula including Saudi Arabia, Kuwait, Bahrain, Qatar, the Trucial States, Aden and Yemen. From 1954 onwards, the term "Middle East" became the prevalent description, though it has not been the exclusive name.

Since the second half of the twentieth century, the geographic parameters of the region have broadened. This was due in large part to the political independence of several countries. The most far-reaching description of the Middle East incorporates Mauritania, Western Sahara, Morocco on the west, includes Algeria, Tunisia and Libya and extends to Iran in the east. It stretches from Turkey and Cyprus in the north to the southern tip of the Arabian Peninsula, including Sudan. Its southernmost limits include the Horn of Africa, including Eritrea, Djibouti, Somalia and the Comoros Islands. With the advent of the twenty-first century, at times even Afghanistan and Pakistan have been included in the definition of the Middle East.

Some historic background is instructive. The Roman Empire started the East-West division of the Western world. For many years, "the Eastern Question" related to Western dealings with the Ottoman Empire. During the 1890s, the Sino-Japanese War of 1894–95, the division of China into spheres of influence, and the massacres of Armenians, Assyrians, Greeks, and other troubles within the Ottoman Empire forced the creation of two "Eastern Questions"—"Far" and "Near." By 1896, "Near East" was widely used to describe the Middle East.

In 1902, Dr. D.G. Hogarth, a British archeologist and traveler, published *The Near East,* a book about the geography of the region, which helped fix the term and define its limits. He included Albania, Montenegro, southern Serbia (today's Kosovo), Bulgaria, Greece, Egypt, the Ottoman lands of Asia, the Arabian Peninsula, and most of modern Iran up to the area between the Caspian Sea and the Indian Ocean.

In September 1902, Captain Alfred Thayer Mahan, author of the authoritative *The Influence of Sea Power upon History* (1890), wrote in *National Review* an article entitled, "The Persian Gulf and International Relations." In it, Mahan first used the term "Middle East." He wrote:

> The Middle East, if I may adopt a term which I have not seen, will someday need its Malta, as well as its Gibraltar; it does not follow that either will be in the Persian Gulf. Naval force has the quality of mobility, which carries with it the privilege of temporary absences; but it needs to find on every scene of operation-established bases of refit, of supply, and in case of disaster, of security. The British Navy should have the facility to concentrate in force if occasion arise, about Aden, India, and the Persian Gulf.[31]

However, Mahan did not specify the boundaries of the "Middle East."

On October 12, 1902, the *Times* of London, ran an article by Valentine Chirol using Mahan's term and helped popularize it, but Chirol distinguished Middle East from the Near East and Far East. In Chirol's view, the Near East centered on Turkey, the Middle East centered on India, and the Far East centered on China. After World War I, the definition of Middle East expanded to include areas previously defined as being in the Near East. Winston Churchill, then Secretary of State for Colonies, established the Colonial Office Middle Eastern Department, to supervise Palestine, Transjordan and Iraq. He was supported by the Royal Geographic Society, which declared that the Middle East extended from the Bosporus to the eastern frontiers of India and the "Near East" denoted the Balkans.

During World War II, the British Army had a Middle East Command centered in Cairo, which included Ethiopia, the Somalilands, Eritrea, Libya, Greece, Crete, Iraq, and Iran but still was vague. During the war, Prime Minister Churchill sometimes referred to the Arab areas as the Near East.

After World War II, Churchill wrote, "I had always felt that the name 'Middle East' for Egypt, the Levant, Syria and Turkey, was ill-chosen. This was the Near East. Persia and Iraq were the Middle East, India, Burma and Malaya—the East; and China and Japan the Far East." This was confusing as the Levant had always included Syria, but Churchill listed them separately.

Clement Attlee, who succeeded Churchillas Prime Minister, took a slightly different approach declaring in April 1946, "It has become the accepted practice to use the term 'Middle East' to cover the Arab world and certain neighboring countries. The practice seems to me convenient and I see no reason to change it."[32] In the March-April 1946 issue of *Geographical Journal,* Attlee was asked about his definition of the term. He remained determined to use "Middle East," but gave a different definition, "at least the area of Egypt, Palestine, Cyrenaica, Syria and Lebanon, Transjordan, Iraq and the Arabian Peninsula, as well as, in most cases, Persia and Turkey."

In 1945, the newly created United Nations assuming that the term "Near East" was dead listed as its member states in the Middle East: Afghanistan, Iran, Iraq, Syria, Lebanon, Turkey, Saudi Arabia, Yemen, Egypt, Ethiopia, and Greece.

On November 1, 1956, in the midst of the Sinai-Suez War, *The New York Times* stated, "The Middle East is now used in preference to Near East to conform to the change in general usage." In 1957, US Secretary of State John Foster Dulles weighed in with his definition: The Middle East is "the area lying between and including Libya on the west, Pakistan on the east, and Turkey on the north, and the Arabian Peninsula to the south." "I think it should also include Ethiopia and the Sudan, which lie in Africa, but of which considerable parts lie north of the southern portion of the Arabian Peninsula."[33] In Dulles' view, "Middle East" and "Near East" were identical. The 1957 Eisenhower Doctrine passed both Houses of Congress with this definition (*see* Appendix 7).

On August 14, 1958, after US forces landed in Lebanon to support its government against United Arab Republic (Egypt and Syria) subversion, *The New York Times* quoted President Dwight D. Eisenhower using the term "Near East." The State Department quickly clarified the "Middle East" and "Near East" as interchangeable for Egypt, Syria, Israel, Jordan, Lebanon, Iraq, Saudi Arabia, and the Persian Gulf sheikhdoms.

In late 1958, the State Department set up its "Aegean and Middle East Division" to cover Greece, Turkey, Cyprus, Iran, Afghanistan, and Pakistan. But if Greece and Turkey are "Aegean" then the rest is the Middle East. All Arab states and Israel were omitted from this division, probably to leave the Soviet Union wondering what was and what was not, covered by the Eisenhower Doctrine.

Currently the US State Department has a Bureau of Near East Affairs dealing with Algeria, Bahrain, Egypt, Iran, Iraq, Israel, Jordan, Kuwait, Lebanon, Libya, Morocco, Oman, Qatar, Saudi Arabia, Syria, Tunisia, United Arab Emirates, and Yemen. Similarly, the American Israel Public Affairs Committee has published a bi-weekly newsletter called the "Near East Report" (for over half a century) and since 1985, there has been a think tank named the Washington Institute for Near East Policy.

Furthermore, the Middle East Institute in Washington, DC defines the Middle East as southwestern Asia and northeastern Africa, from Mauritania and Morocco to Pakistan, including the Caucasus and Central Asian republics of Georgia, Armenia, Azerbaijan, Kazakhstan, Kyrgyzstan, Tajikistan, Turkmenistan, and Uzbekistan.

5. Middle East countries have been "created" but Israel is not one of them.

For a four hundred-year period (ca. 1517–1918), much of the greater Middle East was ruled by the Ottoman Empire. With the collapse of the Ottoman Empire because of its defeat in World War I, borders were created to satisfy European needs, based on interests, geography, and natural resources. Those boundary lines largely ignored the realities of historic ethnic, tribal and sectarian divisions. For the Europeans it made it easier to implement Johann Wolfgang Von Goethe's maxim, "Divide and rule."

It should be understood, however, that by and large, the concept of loyalty to a nation-state is a weak one in the Middle East. Religious and tribal identity far outranks national identity, in part because many of these states were artificially created. Furthermore, that demographic truth is spreading globally with the mass migrations (legal and illegal) being witnessed into Europe, North America and Australia. In the Middle East loyalty is given first to the family, the *hamula* (clan), the tribe and the ethnic group, in that order. Illustrative of this fact are Saddam Hussein, Hafez and Bashir al-Assad and Muammar Qadhafi. Each leader held power for decades due to their closest aides and advisers being from their tribe and hometown. Hussein relied on his Al-bu Nasir tribe from the town of Tikrit, Iraq, the al-Assads, were from the Numailatiyyah faction of the al Matawirah tribe (one of four main Alawite tribes) from their ancestral village of Qardaha in Syria, and Qadhafi, in a similar fashion, depended on members of his Qadhadhfa tribe from around the town of Sirte, Libya.

Several political entities in the Middle East are actually composed of individual clan-families, each of which has (one very large and the others, mini-states) formed a country.

FAMILY-CLAN ENTITIES	
Family-Clan	**Country**
Al Saud	Saudi Arabia
Al Sabah	Kuwait
Al Khalifa	Bahrain
Al Thani	Qatar
Al Nahyan	Abu Dhabi
Al Maktoum	Dubai
Al Nuaim	Ajman
Al Sharqi	Fujairah
Al Qasimi	Ras al Khaimah
Al Qasimi	Sharjah
Al Mu'alla	Umm al Qaiwain

In only three countries of the Middle East, for the most part, does the concept of loyalty to a nation-state come first—Israel, Turkey and Egypt.

Turning to the issue of "creation" of countries in the greater Middle East, the United Kingdom created Sudan, Jordan Iraq, the United Arab Emirates, and Somaliland. It was instrumental in drawing the borders of Iran, Iraq, Jordan, Egypt, Sudan, Somaliland, Yemen, Oman, the United Arab Emirates, Qatar, Kuwait, and Bahrain. A bit further afield, the British did the same for Pakistan and Afghanistan. France created Syria, Lebanon and Djibouti. It was involved in determining the borders of Morocco, Algeria, Tunisia, Lebanon, Syria and Djibouti. Italy was responsible for creating and drawing the borders of Libya, Eritrea and Somalia. Saudi Arabia was "created" by force, by one man, King Abd al-'Aziz ibn Abdur Rahman Al-Feisal Al Sa'ud (commonly known as Ibn Saud) in 1927 (as the Kingdom of Hejaz and Nejd, renamed "Saudi Arabia" in 1932). Included within these borders of all these countries were ethnic, religious, denominational and tribal groups who, throughout history, were often unable to live together in peace.

In contrast, Jewish sovereignty was reestablished as an independent nation in the very land—the Land of Israel—where two previous Jewish sovereign polities had existed before they were conquered by outside aggressors (*see* "Israel's Ancient Monarchies—Kingdom of David and the Kingdom of Solomon" maps). Modern Israel's boundaries are within the boundaries of the Kingdom of Israel, whereas the created Arab countries were established where no such Arab state had previously existed.

JEWISH NATIONAL SOVEREIGNTY IN THE LAND OF ISRAEL	
Time Period	**Number of Years in Existence**
ca. 1400–586 B.C.E.	814 years
539 B.C.E.–73 C.E.	612 years
132–135 C.E.	3 years
Reestablishment of Jewish national sovereignty—the State of Israel—since 1948	67 years and counting
Total	**1,496 years and counting**

Time Period	**Number of Years of Arab Rule**
Arab rule over the Land of Israel 636–969 C.E.	333 years

6. Distance in the Middle East *is* important.

It is often claimed that in an age of missiles, distance is of little importance and need not be emphasized in any negotiations. This is a false premise. In war, while missiles and bombs can inflict great damage, a country can only be conquered by physical occupation of its territory by boots on the ground. In fact, the defensive importance of territorial depth has only been amplified with the increased mobility of armed forces. Military technology is not enough to win in war. Topography is still of major significance. Thus, every mile/kilometer that provides strategic depth and topographical advantage is most important.

For example, the Old City of Jerusalem is less than six-tenths of a mile (a kilometer) across. For tiny countries such as Bahrain, Qatar, Kuwait, Cyprus, Lebanon, and Israel, distance is critical to survival. Every mile or kilometer can be argued over and in many cases fought over. A tiny country can be invaded and occupied quickly. Two modern examples are Turkey's three-day invasion of over one-third of Cyprus in August 1974, and Iraq's 1990 conquest of Kuwait, during which the bulk of Kuwait was overrun in six hours, the complete conquest and occupation of that entire tiny state being accomplished in less than two days. When larger countries claim, in a cavalier-like fashion, that another mile or kilometer here or there does not count, in this age of missile technology, they are being less than honest with someone else's territory. Such cessions of land may prove fatal for a small country. This is especially critical for Israel, surrounded by hostile Arab/Muslim states.

In the latter's case, US General (retired) Alfred M. Gray, Jr., former Commandant, US Marine Corps, expressed the problem succinctly, "Missiles fly over any terrain feature, but they don't negate the strategic significance of territorial depth. The key threat to Israel will remain the invasion and occupation by armored forces. Military success requires more than a few hundred missiles. To defeat Israel would require the Arabs to deploy armor, infantry and artillery into Israel and destroy the IDF on the ground. That was true in 1948, 1967 and 1973, and it remains true in the era of modern missiles."[34]

During the 1949 to 1967 period, Israel's geographic vulnerability was dramatically evident. Indefensible borders, e.g. the 1949 Armistice lines, would create a standing invitation to hostile neighbors to launch an attack at a moment of their choosing and would be a constant cause of friction and instability in the region. As the map illustrates, Israel's narrow geographic waist, as per the 1949 Armistice lines, was 9 miles wide. For the sake of comparison, that is about two-thirds the length of Manhattan Island, or the distance between Battery Park and Columbia University. The distance from LaGuardia Airport to John F. Kennedy Airport in New York City is 10.67 miles.[35] The San Francisco-Oakland Bay Bridge (including approaches, the toll plaza et cetera, is 8.4 miles.[36] In November 1998, then Texas Governor George W. Bush, during a visit to Israel, viewed the narrow waist region from the vantage point of a helicopter ride with then-Israeli Foreign Minister Ariel Sharon. Bush quickly understood the existential peril Israel would be placed in, if forced back to the insecure 1949 Armistice lines. Bush famously remarked, "We've got driveways longer than that in Texas."[37] Pointedly, Israeli Prime Minister Benjamin Netanyahu reminded President Barak Obama in May 2011, "before 1967, Israel was all of nine miles wide. It was half the width of the Washington Beltway."[38] Additionally under the 1949 Armistice lines, Jerusalem was connected to the Israeli coastal plain by a narrow corridor that was just 2 to 4 miles wide.

US Army Lieutenant General (retired) Thomas W. Kelly, director of operations for the Joint Chiefs of Staff in the 1991 Persian Gulf War emphasized the geographic dangers for Israel if it did not retain the mountainous highlands of Judea and Samaria, "I cannot defend this land [Israel] without that terrain...The West Bank [Judea and Samaria] mountains and especially their five approaches, are the critical terrain. If an enemy secures those [east–west] passes, Jerusalem and Israel become uncovered. Without the West Bank [Judea and Samaria], Israel is only 8 (sic) miles wide at its narrowest point. That makes it indefensible."[39]

General Kelly was not the only senior military official to understand the geographical and security implications of the territories Israel acquired in its defensive war of 1967. US Navy Rear Admiral and former White House national security affairs adviser James W. "Bud" Nance expressed his assessment of Israel's security needs in general and of the unique role played by the cliffs and mountains of the Golan Heights and the mountain ridges of Judea and Samaria, "I believe if Israel were to move out of the Golan Heights and the West Bank [Judea and Samaria], it would increase instability and the possibility of war, increase the necessity to preempt in war, and the possibility that nuclear weapons would be used to prevent an Israeli loss, and increase the possibility that the United States would have to become involved in a war"[40] (see "Israel–Insecure Borders–Distances" map).

INSECURE BORDERS

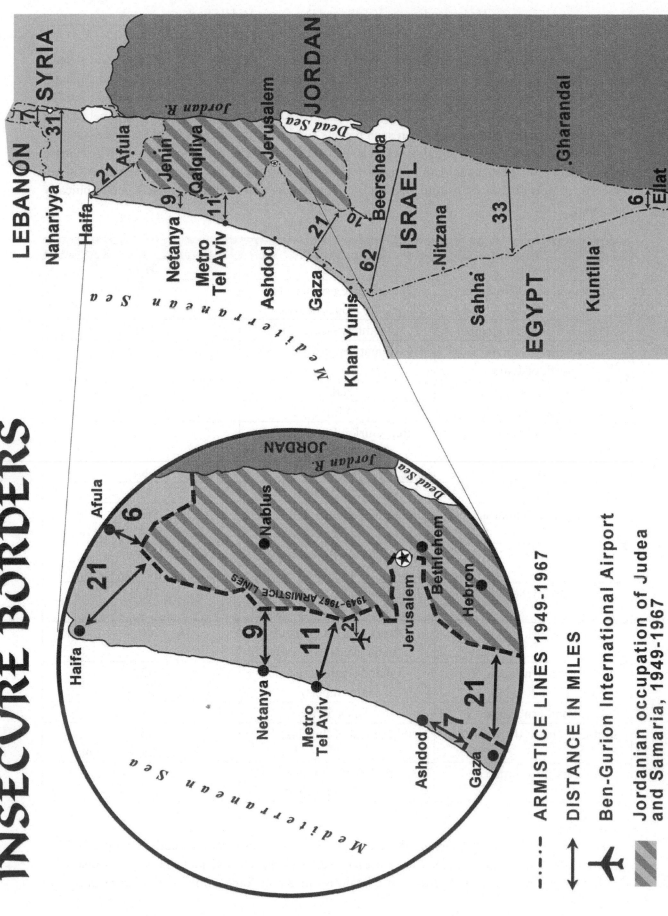

— · — · ARMISTICE LINES 1949-1967

◄───► DISTANCE IN MILES

✈ Ben-Gurion International Airport

▨ Jordanian occupation of Judea and Samaria, 1949-1967

Since 2005, when Israel unilaterally withdrew from the Gaza Strip, its citizens and towns have been subject to constant rocket and mortar attack from that Palestinian Hamas-controlled territory. The rockets employed have grown in sophistication and range. The Gaza Strip has reverted to its old status (one it held from 1949–67) as a dagger pointed at Tel Aviv, Israel's largest city. If Israel were to withdraw from Judea and Samaria then such rockets fired from those areas would have devastating effect as 70 percent of Israel's population and 80 percent of Israel's industrial capacity lie within these rockets' range. In short, Israel cannot make territorial concessions in Judea and Samaria without critically compromising its minimum-security requirements and rendering itself geographically untenable.

DISTANCES INTO ISRAEL FROM THE 1949 ARMISTICE LINES		
From	**To**	**Miles**
Lebanon across to Syria	The extreme northern part of the Upper Galilee	7
Foot of the Golan Heights	Mediterranean Sea	31
Northern Samaria north of Jenin	Ramat David airbase	10.9
Northern Samaria	Haifa	21
Northern Samaria	Afula	6
Western Samaria	Ben-Gurion International Airport	5.9
Tulkarem	Netanya	8.7
Qalqiliya	Kfar Saba	0.43
Western Samaria	Metropolitan Tel Aviv and Sde Dov Airport	12.4
Judea	Ben-Gurion International Airport	4
Bethlehem	Jerusalem; also within range: Tel Nof and Hazor airbases	0.25
Southern Judea	Beersheba (largest city in the Negev Desert)	10.5
Southern Judea	Ashdod (Israel's second largest port)	22
Southern Judea	Gaza Strip	21
Southern end of the Dead Sea	Southern end of the Gaza Strip	62 (Israel's widest point)
Egypt to Jordan	At Israel's southern tip including Eilat	6

For Israel, defensible borders are those that provide sufficient strategic depth and topographical conditions including mountainous terrain that overlooks the coastal plain. This is to insure its small standing army can withstand and contain an invading force until its civilian reserves are mobilized. Therefore, the retention of territory, which has been repeatedly used as a launching platform for additional aggression, is vital as a security buffer against future attacks. Such territorial buffers for small nations become existentially essential in an era, which has witnessed an abundance and proliferation of man-portable air defense systems (MANPADS). Such MANPADS include the Russian-made SA-7 Strela, and the SA-18 Igla, the US-made FIM-82 Stinger, the Chinese-made FN-6, and the Iranian-made Misagh 2, to name the most prominent. Not only are such MANPADS a threat to military aviation, but to civilian air traffic as well.

A territorial buffer buys time for a nation under attack, to mobilize and respond. By trading space for time, a small nation such as Israel, can call up its army, deploy forces, and attack the invaders before the vital heartland is breached. This historically was the case with Russia in dealing with the French invasion (1812) as well as German aggression (1941–44), China during the Sino-Japanese War (1937–45), Israel (then in possession of the Sinai Peninsula) in responding to Egyptian and Syrian attack (1973), and Iran in countering an Iraqi invasion (1980–82).

If geographically large countries like Russia, China, and Iran need territory to provide defense in depth, certainly tiny Israel surrounded by hostile neighbors demonstrating continued enmity and unending religious hatred, merits such territory. Former Israeli Minister of Defense and Foreign Affairs as well as Ambassador to the United States, Moshe Arens concisely explained why Israel could not return to the 1949 Armistice lines reducing it to a small defenseless state:

> Small is precarious. Small is dangerous. Small creates the impression of weakness. Small can be bombed, invaded, and destroyed. Donald Rumsfeld, the former US Secretary of Defense once said, "If we know anything it is that weakness is a provocation." A small-truncated Israel will project weakness and provoke aggression – by terrorists, by armed forces, and by those in possession of nuclear weapons. No security arrangements or demilitarization is going to be of any use in the long run. Reducing the size of Israel will endanger Israel's future.[41]

7. Geographic denial, omissions and substitutions are prevalent on Arab/Muslim maps of the region.

One will not find "Israel" indicated on maps across the Arab/Muslim world. There is a deliberate policy of ongoing educational indoctrination of successive generations, to deny Israel's existence. In a like fashion, the Jewish Quarter of the Old City of Jerusalem does not appear on Arab maps of the city. Israeli cities and towns have Arab names. Moreover, Jewish religious sites such as the Temple Mount, Western Wall, Cave of the Patriarchs, and the Tomb of Rachel are renamed Muslim holy sites.

What will be found where the modern State of Israel has been located for over 67 years (and where earlier Jewish sovereignty existed for 1,279 years), is a non-existent country called "Palestine" for the entire area, from the Jordan River to the Mediterranean Sea, labeled "Occupied Territory of Palestine." Never, in recorded history, has there been an independent sovereign Arab state called "Palestine."

In a similar vein, Syrian maps do not show a separate independent nation of Lebanon. This was re-emphasized by Syrian President Hafez al-Assad on August 26, 1973, when he said, "Syria and Lebanon are one country and one nation, but they have two governments." On July 20, 1976, he declared, "Historically, Syria and Lebanon are one country and one people."[42] Yet again, this was stressed on August 26, 1983, when Assad declared that "Syria and Lebanon are one country, and that both Lebanese and Syrians are one people."[43]

Syrian maps also do not show the province of Hatay (which includes the ancient city of Antioch (now called Antakya) as well as the city and district of Iskenderun) as part of Turkey, but rather as Syrian territory. The area prior to 1939 was known as Alexandretta. In a like manner, the Iranian province of Khuzistan does not exist, only Arabistan is inscribed on Arab maps,[44] and the Persian Gulf is not found, but it is named the "Arabian Gulf."[45] Since the late 1960s to the present, pan-Arabist thought and rhetoric insisted on the creation of a vast unified empire "from the Atlantic Ocean to the Arab Gulf." This continued Arab denial of the water body's historic name, provoked sharp confrontations with Iran and has been rejected by most geographers.

An example of the seriousness of such nomenclature conflicts occurred in 2010. The Second Islamic Solidarity Games, a multinational, multi-sport event among the fifty-seven members of the Organization of Islamic Cooperation (known prior to June 28, 2011, as the Organization of the Islamic Conference), were originally scheduled to take place in October 2009, in Iran. The games were re-scheduled for April 2010, and then cancelled. The cancellation came after a dispute arose between Iran and the Arab world because Tehran inscribed "Persian Gulf" on the tournament's official logo and medals.

DEMOGRAPHICS OF THE REGION

There is very little difference between people, but the little difference there is, makes all the difference in the world.
Anonymous

The Middle East is neither ethnically nor religiously homogeneous. Syria, for example, is comprised of a radically diverse group of ethnic and religious communities—all fearful of the Sunni Arab majority. As a result, there have been conflicts among the different ethnic groups and among different religious denominations. The interaction among the region's peoples have produced several major refugee problems, some of which, deliberately so, linger to this day.

8.   The Middle East is not an exclusively Arab region.

The Middle East is inhabited by other peoples, most of who pre-date the Arabs, who emerged from the Arabian Peninsula in the seventh century C.E. While the Arabs want an exclusively Arab Middle East, the reality is that the region is a pluralistic region, a diverse region made up of the Imazighen (the Berbers), Turks, Tuareg, Toubou, Kurds, Jews, Aramaeans, Greeks, Assyrians, Persians, Armenians, Azeris, Lurs, Turkmen, Gilakis, Mazandaranis, Balochis, Circassians, Nubians, Afars, Somalis, Bannu, Kunama, and Tigrayans, among many other groups, as well as the Arabs.

An illustration of the diversity of population is Iran. Persians make up 61 percent of the population, but there are substantial other groups within the country including Azeri, 16 percent; Kurd, 10 percent; Lur, 6 percent; Baloch, 2 percent; Arab, 2 percent; Turkmen and Turkic tribes, 2 percent; other (including the Gilaki and Mazandarani), 1 percent.[1] (*see* "Major Ethnic Minorities in Iran" map).

ETHNIC MINORITIES

Arabs		Kurds	
Armenians		Lurs	
Azeris		Mazandaranis	
Balochis		Turkmens	
Gilakis			

Every one of the Arab states is an assortment of ethnic, religious and/or tribal groups. The following are examples: Inhabiting Iraq are Arabs, Kurds, Turkmen and Persians who practice at least seven faiths. The Muslims consist of both Sunnis and Shi'ites, and most of the population is splintered along tribal lines. Saddam Hussein imposed his Dulaim tribe on Iraq. During his regime, the Dulaimis formed 10 percent to 20 percent of the Iraqi Republican Guard. Muammar Qadhafi's tribe, the Qadhadhfa, was instrumental in the 1969 military coup that brought him to power in Libya. Many tribal members had influential positions in his government until his downfall in October 2011.

In Syria, the population consists of Arabs, Kurds and Turkmen who are Muslims, Christians, Druze or Alawis. The Muslims are both Sunnis and Shi'ites, and the tribal element is dominant in some areas as well. The Alawis became the ruling force in Syria because of the November 13, 1970 military coup led by Hafez al-Assad. However, as noted Middle East expert Daniel Pipes wrote, "An Alawi ruling Syria is like an untouchable becoming maharajah in India or a Jew becoming tsar in Russia—an unprecedented development shocking to the majority population which had monopolized power for so many centuries."[2]

The population in Jordan is Arab and Circassian. An Arab minority, the Bedouin, are the privileged class over the majority of the population, which is Palestinian. Ruling them is a foreign royal family— the Hashemites—brought in by the British, from Hejaz, the western region of the Arabian Peninsula. There are three demographic divisions in Yemen. Regionally the country has a long history of north versus south. There is a major sectarian division between Zaydis, who are Shi'ite and Shafi'is, who are Sunni. Yemen is also a largely tribal society. The Zaydis are the second-largest sect in Shi'ite Islam. In the north alone for example, there are some 400 Zaydi tribes.[3]

Similar to the comparison of territorial size, Israel's population is but a minute fraction of the Arab states. It is tinier still when compared to the Arab/Muslim population of the Middle East.

MIDDLE EAST POPULATION COMPARISON	
Country	**Population**[4]
Mauritania*	3,200,000
Morocco*	32,400,000 [5]
Algeria*	34,990,000
Tunisia*	10,600,000
Libya*	6,500,000
Egypt*	82,000,000
Sudan*	36,800,000
Djibouti*	750,000
Somalia*	9,900,000
Comoros*	790,000
Saudi Arabia*	26,100,000
Yemen*	24,100,000
Oman*	3,000,000
United Arab Emirates*	5,100,000
Qatar*	840,000
Bahrain*	1,200,000
Kuwait*	2,500,000

Turkey	78,700,000
Cyprus	1,100,000
Syria*	22,500,000
Lebanon*	4,100,000
Jordan*	6,500,000
Iraq*	30,300,000
Iran	77,890,000
Total Arab states	344,170,000
Total Arab states plus Iran	**422,060,000**
Israel	8,345,000[6] (of that number 6,251,000 are Jewish—a full 74.9 percent.* "Israeli Arabs" number 1,730,000, or 20.7 percent of the total population. However, that statistic lumps together Israeli Arab Muslims, Israeli Christians, the Druze, the Bedouin, and the Circassians among others. Additionally, some 364,000 people— some 4.4 percent—are non-Arab Christians or people of other religions, as well as those with no religious affiliation.

* Member of the Arab League

Israel's population of 8.345 million is smaller than that of New Jersey, Virginia or New York City. Over 50 percent of Jewish Israelis are refugees and their descendents from Arab and Muslim lands. The 6,251,000 Jews in Israel represents a miniscule portion of the overall Arab population of the Middle East, which stands at some 344,700,000 people. It should be noted that historically the Jews/Israelis had an aversion to ruling over others, while for Arab/Muslims, a ruler-ruled relationship was normal.

Demographically, the position of the Jewish nation is unique. In this context "nation" is synonymous with "people," whereas a "country" is equivalent to a "sovereign state." Judaism is a combination of nationality, religion, philosophy, tradition, and culture. The Jewish nation was reestablished in its ancestral homeland. These attributes are all inter-twined. No other nationality, religion, or country has such a grouping. Many Jews in the Diaspora deny that Judaism is a nationality, due to over 1,800 years of exile and dispersion. Yet, the term "Jew" originated from the name of the nation of Judea, which existed prior to 135 c.e. For example, the modern State of Israel and the former Soviet Union, both used the term "Jew" to indicate nationality on their identity papers. Some Israeli politicians on the left, like Shimon Peres, Yair Lapid, Tzipi Livni, and Yosef Beilin (the architect of the Oslo Accords), as well as their American Jewish allies on the left, want to reduce Judaism to secular humanism. This is a denial that Judaism is a distinct nationality, and it has been a leftist refrain since Israeli independence in 1948. It is one of the prime factors in explaining the rift between the Jewish political right and the political left both in Israel and in the United States.

---

* Actually, Israel's Jewish population is higher. There are 6.4 million Jews (including some 300,000 Soviet immigrants who are not yet recognized as Jews by the rabbinate)—a full 66 percent of the population in the area from the Jordan River to the Mediterranean Sea—next to 1.69 million Israeli Arabs and 1.65 million Arabs in Judea and Samaria.

While Israel is a Jewish state, it is a common misconception that it is an overwhelmingly religiously Orthodox one (in the American sense, which tends to equate "Orthodox" with *haredi*). Another stereotypical falsehood, which is held by foreigners, is that all religious Jews in Israel are dressed in black. Another fallacy (almost a reverse of the first) is that Israel is overwhelmingly secular (some 80 percent) and only a minority are religious (20 percent).

A survey of Israeli Jews taken in 2009 by the Israel Central Bureau of Statistics, revealed a far different society. Israel's Jews are not divided into two groups but into five: ultra-Orthodox Jews—*haredim*—(8 percent), Orthodox Jews—*dati'im*—(9.8 percent), traditional Jews (includes "traditional-religious" and "traditional-not so religious" Jews)—*masorti'im*—(40.2 percent), and not religious, secular Jews—*hiloni'im*—(41.7 percent).[7]

To clarify, Orthodox Jews are similar to the modern or centrist Orthodox Jews in the Diaspora. They partake in most or all aspects of modern civilization except that they maintain Orthodox observance of Jewish religious law and tradition. The term traditionalism, as used in Israel, refers to a life lived, at least in part, in accordance with tradition, e.g. conduct learned from their parents, the immediate environment, and the extended family. It is religious because so much of it refers to matters of religious concern. Among traditionalists, religious life is governed by habit and by what "seems" right.[8] It flourishes when religion and culture are integrated. Another important aspect is the commitment to the State of Israel, the Jewish people, Jewish religion, Jewish history, their parents and families, or to some combination of these factors.

The traditional-religious Jews are those who came from many backgrounds but most were Sephardim from the Mediterranean or Islamic worlds. They are people who value traditional Jewish life but are prepared to modify *Halacha*.* This group believes that some Jewish practices should be adapted to fit modern times. They cover the whole range of belief and observance, from people of fundamentalist conviction and looser practice to people who have interpreted Judaism in the most modern manner, but retain many of its customs and ceremonies. Many of these traditional-religious Jews differ from the Orthodox ones only in that they drive their cars on the Sabbath, use electricity, watch television, and go to sporting events or to the beach, at times after attending religious services in the morning and the evening beforehand. The traditional-not so religious Jews claim to maintain those practices for family and national reasons rather than for religious ones. The fact that Jewish religious observance has such a strong national component makes it a major element of most Jews' national identity even if they no longer see themselves as believers in the Jewish religion. The largest group of the four is the secular Jews who are not religious, yet from a cultural and historical perspective they, for example, would circumcise their male children and attend a Passover Seder. What emerges from this survey is that 58 percent of Israelis practice a form of Judaism that for the most part Americans would call "Orthodox," in that it recognizes normative Judaism in the rabbinic tradition. This Israeli Jewish majority is growing in number between the Jordan River and the Mediterranean Sea, supporting demographically the statement heard for over 100 years that the State of Israel is a Jewish state. Aside from the five categories mentioned, there are other variations within Judaism as a religion, as well as a wide body of texts, practices, theological positions (many different sects), and forms of organization.

An additional demographic subject needs to be addressed. It is the often cited claim that Israel must give up territory in order to maintain its Jewish identity. Demography is an important component of the Arab/Muslim war on Israel, and plays a role in relation to Israel's long-term security. Since 1948, when Israel's population stood at only 650,000 there were predictions of Israel's Jews being swamped by the larger number of Arabs within the territory it controlled. Since the end of the Six-Day

---

* *Halacha* is the collective body of Jewish religious laws, based on the Written and Oral Torah.

War, the worldwide left, including Americans and Israelis, claimed that Israeli Jews were doomed to become a minority west of the Jordan River, and that the Jewish state should concede territory, to secure Jewish demography. This flawed suggestion produced calls for the futile and suicidal "land for peace" process and Israeli withdrawals from Judea and Samaria as well as the Gaza Strip. They have been either dramatically mistaken or outrageously misleading.[9] "Land for peace" produced nothing but land for terror, and land for rocket launching facilities for the bombardment of what is left of Israel.

DEMOGRAPHIC PREDICTIONS VERSUS REALITY		
Source	Date of prediction and projected number of Jews between the Jordan River and the Mediterranean Sea	The real numbers by the date of the prediction[10]
Shimon Dubnov, the leading Jewish historian/demographer of the period.	In 1898, he declared that by 2000, only 500,000 Jews would reside there.	5,000,000 Jews
Roberto Bacchi, professor of Statistics at the Hebrew University and the founder of the Israel Central Bureau of Statistics.	He stated in 1948, that by 2001, 2,300,000 Jews would reside there, representing a 34 percent minority of the inhabitants.	5,000,000 Jews constituted a 60 percent majority and 67 percent if the Gaza Strip was not included.
Prime Minister Levy Eshkol	He was advised in 1967 that by 1987, there would be an Arab majority.	Jews constituted a 60 percent majority, 67 percent if the Gaza Strip was not included.
Professor of Geography Arnon Sofer of Haifa University, who specialized in demographics.	He projected and predicted on July 6, 1987, that by 2000 there would be an Arab majority.	In 2000, there was a clear Jewish majority, with 5 million Jews and 3.5 million Arabs.
Sofer subsequently revised his estimate.	On August 3, 1988, he stated there would be an Arab majority by 2008. Note, that in 2000, Professor Sofer added 1 million Arabs to his estimate of the population in Judea and Samaria.	By 2013, there were 6.3 million Jews (including some 300,000 Soviet immigrants who are not yet recognized as Jews by the rabbinate)—a full 66 percent of the population—next to 1.67 million Israeli Arabs and 1.65 million Arabs in Judea and Samaria.
Sergio DellaPergola, a professor of Population Studies at the Hebrew University in Jerusalem, specializing in demography and statistics related to the Jewish population all over the world.	On October 23, 1987, he dismissed any prospect of Jewish immigration from the Soviet Union.	Since the 1970s and with the implosion of the Soviet Union in 1991, over one million Jews immigrated to Israel.

In defiance of those fatalistic projections, in 2010 there was a 66 percent Jewish majority in 98.5 percent of the area between the Jordan River and the Mediterranean excluding Gaza, and a 58 percent Jewish majority with Gaza.[11] What attributed to the misreading of the demographic trend? Despite predictions, large numbers of Jews made *aliyah** from the Arab states, Eastern and Western Europe, the former Soviet Union, Ethiopia and even the United States. Unfortunately, it should be noted that since the Oslo Accords of 1993, Israeli governments have downplayed the importance of *aliyah*. That trend needs to be reversed, as *aliyah* is an important growth engine for Israel's demography as the influx of immigrants from the above-mentioned areas attest. For the future, the current 66 percent Jewish majority in the combined area of the pre-1967 Israel, Judea and Samaria would mushroom to "an 80 percent majority in 2035, if Israel pro-actively realized the *aliyah* window of opportunity of 500,000 Jews, in the next ten years,"[12] from Argentina, France, the United Kingdom, Belgium, Germany, the former Soviet Union, and the United States.

Contributing to the false demographic picture were the practices of the Palestinians. In 1997, the Palestinian census exaggerated the Arab population in Judea, Samaria, Gaza and Jerusalem by nearly 50 percent. Indeed, in an interview with the *New York Times*, Hassan Abu Libdeh, the head of the Palestinian Central Bureau of Statistics, boasted that the Palestinian-conducted survey (inflated as it turned out to be) was, in effect, "a civil intifada."[13] The Palestinian Authority (PA) claims were disputed by several Israeli demographers.[14] Rather than 3.8 million Palestinian Arabs (2.4 million in Judea and Samaria, and another 1.5 million in Gaza), it was no more than 2.4 million. A subsequent 2009 audit exposed a 66 percent distortion in the number of Arabs living in Judea and Samaria, 1.55 million and not 2.5 million, as claimed by the PA.[15] The Palestinian Authority Central Bureau of Statistics (PCBS) exaggerated the number of Arabs in its territory in a number of ways. The latest census included some 400,000 overseas residents, double-counted 200,000 Jerusalem Arabs who were also counted as Israeli-Arabs[†] and counted Israeli Arabs in pre-1967 Israel as "Palestinians."[16]

Totally ignored was net emigration from the Palestinian Authority accounting for 321,239 persons during the period 1994–2007, averaging about 23,000 annually. Mustafa Khawaja of the Palestinian Central Bureau of Statistics reported net emigration in 2007, of about 60,000. Jordan, (which monitors the international Jordan River crossings into its territory) recorded 63,000 and 44,000 net emigration from the PA areas, during the first eight months in 2008 and 2009 respectively.[17] There are also cases when deaths are not reported. The World Bank documented a 32 percent gap between the number of Arab births given by the PCBS and that provided by the PA's Ministry of Health and confirmed by its Ministry of Education.[18] Furthermore, the Arab birthrate dropped. PA officials reported that the birthrate in Judea, Samaria and the Gaza Strip stood at 6.0 in 1997, but dropped to 4.6 by 2009.

The trend above has been further confirmed by a new study, authored by Dr. Yaakov Feitelson and published by the Institute for Zionist Strategies, which showed the Arab population in the territories continued to shrink. The study published in late 2013, confirmed the earlier findings that Arab

---

* Literally "the act of going up" as ascending to Jerusalem. The in-gathering of Jewish exiles back to the Land of Israel; Jewish immigration to Israel.

† The PLO/PA refers to all of the Arabs who live in what they term "Palestine" (i.e. from the Jordan River to the Mediterranean Sea)—including "Israeli Arabs"—as Palestinians. There is no distinction in the PA's approach between "Palestinians" and "Arabs." Similarly, when PLO/PA Chairman Mahmoud Abbas speaks of "Israelis," he in fact means "Jews." No distinction is made between "Jews" and "Israelis," when speaking of residents of the territory of the Land of Israel. Even now, Israelis/Jews are not permitted to live inside the PA-controlled territories—Areas A and B—and the sale of land to Jews is punishable by death. Various Christians have testified that it is also enforced if land is sold to Christians.

numbers were inflated and revealed that he Arab population of Judea, Samaria, and Gaza (note this survey included the Gaza Strip) encompassed 2,762,000 Muslims, and roughly 52,000 Christians. This is approximately 1,331,000 people fewer than the number estimated by the PA. Additionally, while the natural increase rate, calculated by looking at birth and mortality rates, for Israeli Jews rose by 41.6 percent from 1995 to 2012, the Arab natural increase rate declined during the same time by 30.6 percent, with the rate now at its lowest level since 1955. Furthermore, a survey of the political and social attitudes of Arab youth, conducted by the Baladna Association for Arab Youth, revealed that roughly 25 percent of Arab youths are considering emigration.[19]

A recent demographic development concerns Israeli Christians. Previously, Israeli Christians were registered as "Arab Christians." On September 16, 2014, Israeli Interior Minister Gideon Sa'ar approved having "Aramaean" as an official nationality on Israeli identification cards, a move warmly received by Israel's Christian-Aramaean community. Earlier, the Israeli Supreme Court found that the Aramaean nationality clearly exists, and has the conditions required to prove its existence, including historical heritage, religion, culture, origin and common language. The Israeli Christians amount to some 2.1 percent of the total population. By and large, these Israeli Christians do not regard themselves as either Arabs or Palestinians. The about 165,000 Christians who live in Israel and belong to one of the Eastern Orthodox churches (Maronite-Syriac, Orthodox Aramaic, Greek Orthodox, Greek Catholic and Syriac Catholic) can now be listed as an Aramaean at their request. It is to be recalled that Aramaic was the spoken language in Judea 2000 years ago at the time of Jesus. The Aramaeans predate the Muslims in the region by some 700 years. This demographic step is proof that Israel protects its citizens, especially the identity of its minorities, unlike what all the Arab/Muslim nations around Israel are doing to their minorities.[20]

9. The so-called "Arab Middle East" is not exclusively Muslim.

Other religions have existed in the Middle East, most of them pre-dating the advent of Islam. Furthermore, within these faiths are denominational subdivisions. These include: Greek Orthodox, Nestorians (Assyrians), Coptic Orthodox, Jacobite (Syrian) Orthodox, Armenian Orthodox, Roman Catholics, Armenian Catholics, Greek Catholics, Syriac Catholics, Chaldean Catholics, Coptic Catholics, Maronite Catholics*, numerous Protestant denominations, Druze, Rabbinical Jews and members of other Jewish sects, including the Karaites and the Samaritans. Other religious groups include the Sabians, Yazidis, Mandaneans, Shabaka, Bahá'ís, Zoroastrians, and animists or practitioners of native religions (*see* "Major Religions in the Middle East" map).

---

* Additionally to not being Muslim, a number of Maronite historians claim that the Maronite Catholics of Lebanon were the descendants of the Phoenicians, and as such do not consider themselves Arabs. Thus, they considered the Muslim Arabs to be invaders of their country. The Maronites were in fact, philo-Judaic. The Maronite Catholic Patriarch, Anthony Peter Arida actually gave an official welcome to the Jews to the Mideast in 1946 and was favorable to the creation of a Zionist state in the Land of Israel as well as a Christian state in Lebanon.

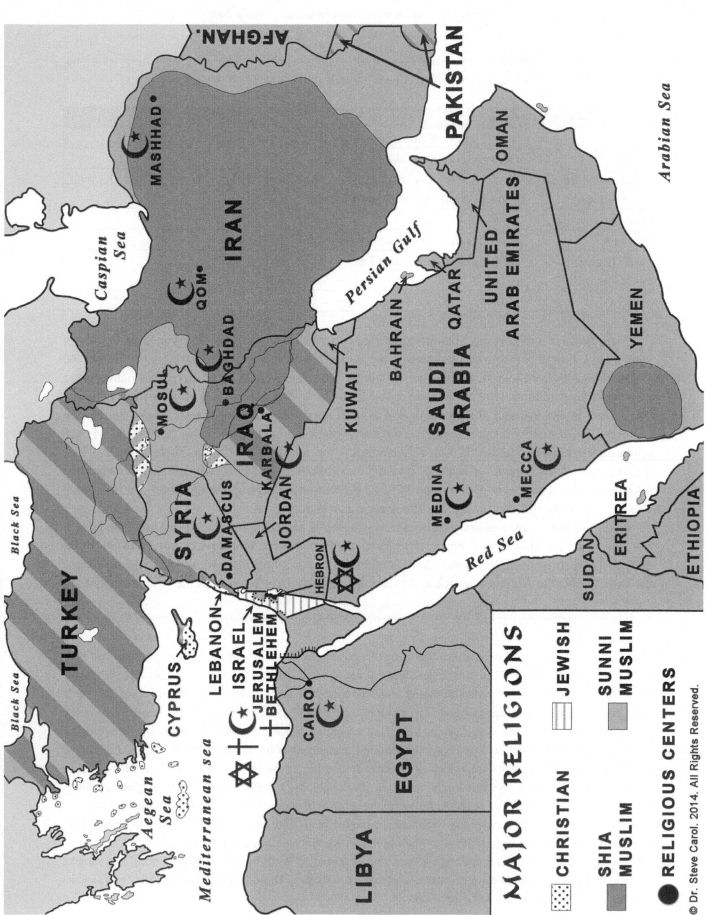

MAJOR RELIGIONS

	CHRISTIAN		JEWISH
	SHIA MUSLIM		SUNNI MUSLIM

● RELIGIOUS CENTERS

Additionally, it must be stressed that Islam itself, is not monolithic. There are, as in most religions, major sects. These include Sunni, Shi'a, Alawi, Isma'ili, Sufi, and Alevi among others.

MUSLIM SECTS IN THE MIDDLE EAST	
Sect	**Countries where they are prominently located**
Sunni	Throughout the Middle East and Pakistan
Shi'a—also known as the Twelvers.*	Iran, Azerbaijan, Iraq, Yemen, Lebanon, Turkey, Saudi Arabia, Kuwait, United Arab Emirates and Bahrain.
Alawi	Syria
Isma'ili	Syria, Iran, Yemen and Afghanistan
Sufi (Islamic mysticism)	Throughout the Middle East
Alevi	Turkey

The Alawi is a dissenting Muslim group related to an offshoot of the Twelver Shi'a branch of Islam. They follow certain rituals derived from both Christianity and Zoroastrianism. Prior to the 1920s, Alawites were known to outsiders by the term "Nusairyoon" (or "Nusayris")—named after Abu Shu'ayb Muhammad ibn Nusayr, the reputed founder of the sect in ninth century Mesopotamia. The term Alawite evolved during the period of the French Mandate over Syria. Under the French Mandate, the Alawites had an autonomous territory, which was created on September 29, 1923. It was renamed the Alawite State—"L' État de Alaouites"—on January 1, 1925. On September 22, 1930, it was renamed the Sanjak† of Latakia. It lasted until February 28, 1937, when it was incorporated into Syria. The Alawites make up some 10 to 12 percent of Syria's population. There are also some Alawites in northern Lebanon and the Hatay region of Turkey.

Many Alawites saw a military career as a way to social and economic mobility. Under the French Mandate, they enlisted in the *Troupes Spéciales,* the French local forces used in the Levant. From 1921 to 1945, three of eight infantry battalions in the *Troupes Spéciales* were Alawite units. Since the early 1960s, the Alawites constituted a disproportionally large number of the Syrian Army high

---

* The Sunni-Shi'a split revolved around the issue of who should lead the *Ummah* (Muslim community) after the death of Muhammad. The Shi'a believe that Muhammad's closest male relative should lead, while the Sunni think the best qualified Muslim should lead. The term "Twelvers" comes from the belief in and efforts to prepare for the Mahdi. The Mahdi is, according to the *Encyclopaedia of Islam and the Muslim World*, the long-prophesied Islamic messiah destined to be "the restorer of religion and justice who will rule before the end of the world." He will be the savior of humankind. A member of the family of the Prophet, Muhammad ibn Hasan al-Mahdī is otherwise known as the Twelfth and last of the Imams, or the Hidden Imam. Shi'ite tradition claims that this mystical figure, was born ca. July 29, 869 C.E. (Sha'aban 15, 255 A.H.) and assumed the Imamate when he was five years old following the death of his father Hasan al-Askari. In the year 941 C.E., at age seventy-one, he disappeared or "occulted" to another plane of existence, but is destined to return at the end of time, reign for seven years before bringing final judgment and the end of the world.

† The 400-year old Ottoman empire was subdivided into vilayets (akin somewhat to provinces) and sanjaks (similar to districts or counties). For example, there were vilayets of Beirut, Damascus and Hejaz and sanjaks of Acre, Alexandretta, Gaza, and Jerusalem.

command and officer corps. Many of these Alawite officers had already joined the Ba'athist Party.* Since the Ba'athist coup of March 8, 1963 (glorified as the "8 March Revolution"), many Alawites have been prevalent in Syria's political leadership, including Salah Jadid, and the al-Assads—Hafez, Rifaat and Bashar, though the latter did not serve in the military.

The Isma'ili is the second largest branch of Shi'a Islam. Also known as, the "Seveners," the Isma'ili were the result of a split in Shi'a Islam ca. 765 C.E., over the issue of who was the true seventh Imam. The Isma'ilis followed Isma'il, the son of the sixth Imam, Ja'far al-Sadeq, who died before his father in 762 C.E. The mainstream Shi'a followed Musa al-Kazim, Isma'il's brother. An Isma'ili group, led by Ubayd Allah al-Mahdi Billah, established the Fatimid Caliphate† in Tunis in 909 C.E., and conquered Egypt in 969 C.E. From Cairo, the Fatimid Caliphate ruled over an empire that stretched from North Africa, Sicily, to the Land of Israel, Syria, the Red Sea coast of Africa, and the western section of the Arabian Peninsula—Hejaz and Yemen—until 1171.

The Sufi sect believes in the inner mystical dimension of Islam, whereby direct knowledge of Allah is attainable through intuition or insight, based on the doctrine and methods derived from the Qur'an. A practitioner of this tradition is generally known as a Sufi. Hasan al Basri (d. 728 C.E.) was one of the founding Sufi personalities and was a proponent of early Muslim asceticism.

Further complicating matters is the pattern of one denominational sect ruling over another, sometimes with a minority sect ruling a majority population of another sect. To make matters worse often the ruling minority discriminated against and persecuted the majority. Some examples are:

MUSLIM MINORITIES RULING MAJORITY SECTS[21]		
Country	**Ruling Group (Minority Sect)**	**Majority of the Population**
Bahrain	Sunni (12 percent)	Shi'a (75 percent)
Iraq (until 2003)‡	Sunni (32–37 percent)	Shi'a (60–65 percent)
Syria	Alawi (10–12 percent)	Sunni (65 percent)
Yemen (until 1962)§	Zaydi Shi'a (35 percent)	Sunni (65 percent)

---

* The Ba'athist (Renaissance) Party was founded on November 29, 1940 by Zaki al-Arsuzi in Syria. Other influential leaders were Michel Aflaq and Salah al-Din al-Bitar. It was influenced by and modeled on the fascist/Nazi program. Branches were created all over the Arab Middle East. The Ba'athist doctrine was Pan Arab (creating a unified Arab state), racist, misojudaic, socialist as well as being vehemently anti-Israel, after 1948. After World War II, the Syrian Ba'athist party would rule that country for over a half century, while its Iraqi branch, ruled the latter for some 35 years from 1968 to 2003.

† An Islamic state led by a supreme religious as well as political leader known as a caliph (meaning literally a successor, i.e. a successor to Islamic prophet Muhammad. It is an Islamic theocracy where there is no separation of "church" (mosque) and state.

‡ Since 2003, the ongoing violence in Iraq is in large part due to the Sunni minority refusal to cooperate in a government of national unity and their ambition to regain the ruling status they had before.

§ Since 2004, the ongoing violence in Yemen is in large part due to the Shi'a-Zaydi-Houthi minority refusal to cooperate in a government of national unity and their ambition to regain the ruling status they had before 1962. called *Al-Shabab al-Mu'minin* ("The Young Believers"). Its flag features the slogan "Death to America, death to Israel, curse on the Jews, victory to Islam."

The Druze is a monotheistic religious community, where nationality and religion are intertwined. Many Druze believe they descended from Jethro, the father in law of Moses, who was loyal to the Jews and aided them, while remaining a non-Jew. Like the Kurds, the Druze find themselves divided among four states. This minority group primarily resides in Syria, Lebanon, Israel and Jordan, but is frequently mentioned in discussions about the Middle East.

THE DRUZE IN THE MIDDLE EAST	
Country	Population
Syria	540,000[22]
Lebanon	324,800[23]
Israel, including the Golan Heights	133,400[24]
Jordan	20,000[25]

The Druze is a closed and non-proselytizing religious group whose tenets are fully known only to the initiated. They have a long tradition of concealing the tenets of their faith from outsiders. The Druze canon includes the Torah, the New Testament, the Qur'an, the works of Socrates, Plato and eastern religions. The Druze stress moral and social principles rather than ritual, and believe in reincarnation. Liberal and pluralistic in their attitudes towards others, as a community they just want to be left alone.

The Druze are not Arab ethnically, but are an Arabic-speaking people. They have abandoned all orthodox Islamic practices and are considered heretical by many other Muslims. For example, a man is permitted only one wife and wives are equal in status to their husbands. Druze women go unveiled and have more rights than their Muslim counterparts. The Druze do not observe the Ramadan fast, or make *hajj*—pilgrimage—to Mecca. Additionally, it is impermissible to convert into or out of the Druze faith. Furthermore, jihad against Muslims could be conducted if there is a military necessity to protect the Druze community.[26] Thus, the Druze are as anti-Muslim as the Muslims are anti-Druze.

The name Druze is derived from the name of Muhammad bin Ismail Nashtakin ad-Darazī who was an early preacher. Although the Druze considers ad-Darazī a heretic, the name "Druze" is still used for identification and for historical reasons. In 1018 ad-Darazi was assassinated for his teachings at the time the sixth Fatimid Caliph Al-Hakim bi-Amr Allah was proclaimed the incarnation of God.

In the modern period, the Druze had an autonomous state—Jabal al-Druze—within the French Mandate of Syria. Home to about 50,000 Druze it was proclaimed on May 1, 1921 with its capital at Sweida. Subsequently, the Druze resisted colonial rule in the Great Druze Revolt against the French that took place from July 21, 1925 to June 1927. The revolt spread to other communities in Syria, but there was little coordination and was crushed by French military force. As a result of the Franco-Syrian Treaty of 1936, Jabal al-Druze ceased to exist as an autonomous entity and was incorporated into Syria.

The Druze have a strong sense of community and this communal solidarity has at times linked them beyond the existence of national frontiers. In 1954, the Lebanese Druze assisted the Syrian Druze against the Shishakli regime in Syria. In May–July 1958, the Syrian Druze aided their coreligionists in Lebanon during the First Lebanese Civil War. In the summer of 1983, Israeli Druze wanted to help the Lebanese Druze fighting in the Shouf Mountains of Lebanon.[27]

The Druze in Israel served and fought in the IDF since 1948. Since 1957, they have been recognized as a distinct separate religious community within Israel. As such they are not subject to Muslim courts and shari'a—Islamic law. A Druze community religious council was set up in 1961 and Druze courts were established in 1962. Noticeably, the Druze refuse to participate in the annual March 30 "Land Day" protests of Israeli Arabs against the policies of the Jewish state, since "Land Day" was initiated in 1976. Druze have been elected as members of the Knesset and served in the Israeli diplomatic corps.[28]

10. The "refugee problem" connected with the Arab–Israeli conflict, is not one of "Palestinian Arab" refugees alone.

The refugee problem as it relates to the Arab-Israel conflict is a twin refugee problem—dealing with both Arab refugees from what became Israel, and Jewish refugees from Arab countries. Both refugee problems need to be addressed and solved by both parties to the conflict. As a result of the 1948–49 Arab invasion of Israel, between 583,000 and 609,000 Arabs fled Israel,[29] while 160,000 remained in the Jewish state. A UN mediator put the figure for Arab refugees even lower, at 472,000.[30] In the 1950's, John Measham Berncastle, under the aegis of the United Nations Conciliation Commission for Palestine, estimated that total assets lost by Palestinian Arab refugees from 1948—including land, buildings, movable property, and frozen bank accounts—amounted to roughly $350 million ($650 per refugee). Adding in an additional $100 million for assets lost by Palestinian Arab refugees because of the Six-Day War, an approximate total is $450 million ($4.4 billion in 2012 prices).[31]

In contrast, at the same time Jews living in Arab countries were subjected to misojudaic discrimination and persecution. They were attacked, dispossessed, displaced, forced to flee or were expelled. The Jews had far more property and assets seized and expropriated in Arab lands than Arabs in what became Israel. The value of assets lost by the Jewish refugees from Arab countries—compiled by a similar methodology—is estimated at $700 million (roughly $6.7 billion today).[32] The World Organization of Jews from Arab Countries estimated in 2003, that the total value of Jewish property and assets was "well over $100 billion."[33] Other estimates range from $16 billion to $300 billion.[34] In any event, the value of Arab assets is far lower than those lost by the Jewish refugees from Arab countries. Between 1948 and 1976 over 880,000 Jews were driven out of ten Arab countries. Israel never referred to them as refugees. They were welcomed as an "ingathering of the exiles," given citizenship on the spot and as quickly as possible, integrated and absorbed into Israeli society. These Jews had lived in the countries from which they were forced to flee far longer than the vast majority of Arabs, who left the small territory that became Israel. In Iraq, for example, the Jewish community dated back to the Babylonian exile, 586–539 B.C.E. In contrast, most of the Arabs who left Israel in 1948 were recent arrivals. They were attracted to what had been an empty and desolate territory by the economic opportunities opened up by Zionist enterprise in the British Mandate of Palestine in the twentieth century. What had occurred, in effect, was a population exchange or population transfer.

There has been a long historic record of population transfers. Transfers and population exchanges have been a solution for many intractable problems in twentieth century history. After World War I and II, transferring populations was considered legal and moral, and the most favored response to inter-ethnic strife. The first population-exchanges involved Bulgaria, Greece, and Turkey. The Treaty of Neuilly of November 27, 1919, provided for 46,000 Greeks from Bulgaria and 96,000 Bulgarians from Greece to switch countries.

After the defeat of the Greek army in the Greek-Turkish War of 1921–22, and the Turkish assault against Greek communities in Turkey, Greek refugees began fleeing their homes in Turkey. Greece and Turkey voluntarily exchanged populations with about 1.3 million Greeks, who were Turkish citizens leaving Anatolia and about 400,000 Turks, who were Greek citizens departing Thrace.[35] Both, the repatriated Greeks and Turks, were absorbed by their respective nations.

In 1937, the Peel Commission in the British Mandate of Palestine concluded in its report:

> An irrepressible conflict has arisen between two national communities within the narrow bounds of one small country. There is no common ground between them. Their national aspirations are incompatible. The Arabs desire to revive the traditions of the Arab golden age. The Jews desire to show what they can achieve when restored to the land in which the Jewish nation was born. Neither of the two national ideals permits of combination in the service of a single State.[36]

The Peel Commission Report recommended for the first time, that Western Palestine be partitioned into Jewish and Arab states. The plan offered 18.4 percent of Western Palestine to the Jews and 81.6 percent to the Arabs. Nevertheless, the Arabs rejected the plan (*see* "The Peel Commission Partition Plan, July 7, 1937" map). If partition was to succeed, the Commission report added, drawing new boundaries and establishing two separate states would not be sufficient. "Sooner or later there should be a transfer of land, and as far as possible, an exchange of population."[37] A number of leading Zionist leaders favored such ideas, as did Presidents Herbert Hoover and Franklin Roosevelt, Czechoslovakian President Edvard Beneš, and three Nobel Peace Prize winners: Sir Norman Angell, Christian Lange, and Philip Noel-Baker.

Of interest too, then as now there were those who felt that Arab economic progress and benefit was the means by which Arab acceptance of a Jewish state could be achieved. They were wrong then, and are wrong today. The Peel Commission noted this early on:

> We have found that, though the Arabs have benefited by the development of the country owing to Jewish immigration, this has had no conciliatory effect. On the contrary … with almost mathematical precision the betterment of the economic situation in Palestine meant the deterioration of the political situation.[38]

However, nothing was achieved due to the outright Arab rejection of the Peel Commission report, the continuing Arab Revolt of 1936–39, and the rapid approach of World War II.

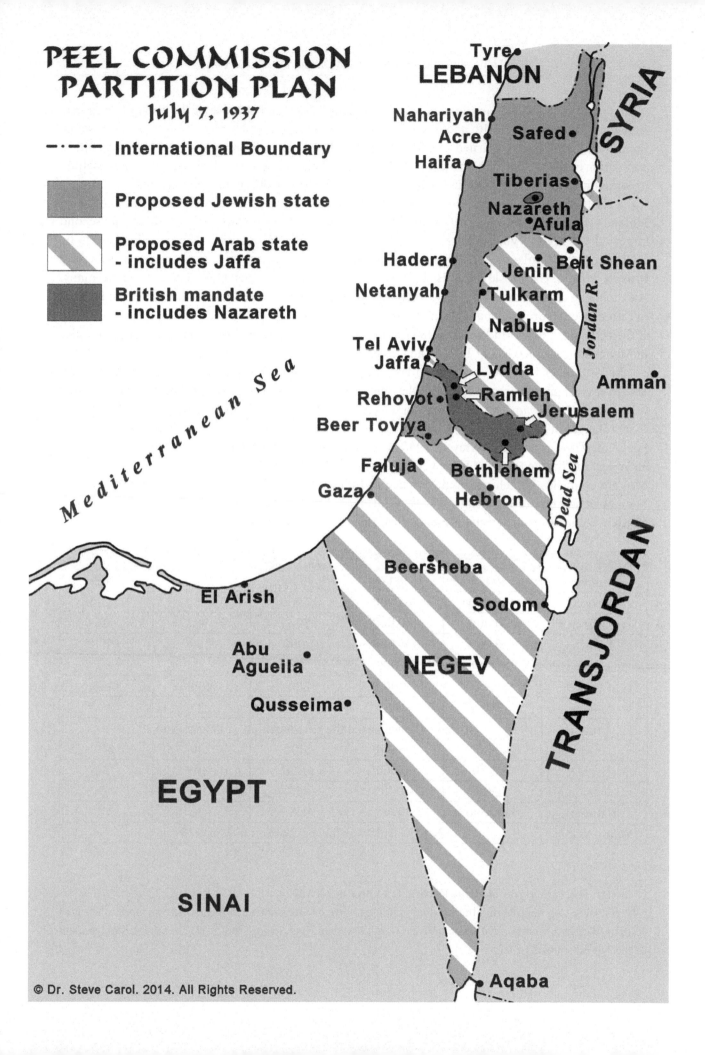

PEEL COMMISSION PARTITION PLAN
July 7, 1937

— - — - — International Boundary

Proposed Jewish state

Proposed Arab state
- includes Jaffa

British mandate
- includes Nazareth

LEBANON

SYRIA

Tyre

Nahariyah
Acre · Safed
Haifa
Tiberias
Nazareth
Afula

Hadera · Beit Shean
Jenin
Netanyah · Tulkarm
Nablus
Jordan R.
Tel Aviv
Jaffa · Lydda
Rehovot · Ramleh
Beer Toviya · Jerusalem
Amman

Faluja · Bethlehem
Gaza · Hebron

Mediterranean Sea

Dead Sea

TRANSJORDAN

El Arish

Beersheba
Sodom

Abu
Agueila
NEGEV

Qusseima

EGYPT

SINAI

Aqaba

Another prominent example of population exchange occurred because of the Treaty of Craiova, signed on September 7, 1940, and recognized by the major European powers. Under its provisions, Southern Dobruja was returned to Bulgaria. It had been under Romanian control. As a result, a population exchange occurred, whereby 80,000 Romanians left Southern Dobruja and were resettled in Romania, and 65,000 Bulgarians from Romanian Northern Dobruja moved to Bulgaria.

Sometimes such transfer/exchange is the result of conflict. As an outcome of the Soviet attack on Finland—the Winter War—of 1939–40, Finland, not only lost its territory of Karelia and its second largest city, Viipuri/Vyborg, but some 400,000 Karelians, virtually the whole population, had to be relocated within Finland. After World War II, fifteen million Germans were transferred from East Prussia, Poland, Czechoslovakia, Hungary, the Soviet Union, and East Germany to West Germany. An exchange of minorities between Czechoslovakia and Hungary also took place. After the borders in Europe were redrawn, smaller transfers were made in parts of Central and Eastern Europe. In Asia, at the conclusion of World War II, 6.289 million Japanese were transferred from their former empire in Manchuria, Korea, China, Taiwan, and Southeast Asia.

In 1948, over 800,000 Jews had to flee Iraq, Yemen, Egypt, Syria and other Arab states after Jewish sovereignty was reestablished in the State of Israel. The urgency of their situation was reflected by the *New York Times* two days after Israel declared independence. In an article entitled, "Jews in Grave Danger in all Moslem Lands: Nine Hundred Thousand in Africa and Asia Face Wrath of Their Foes," the *Times* reported on May 16, 1948, that for nearly four months, the United Nations considered an appeal for "immediate and urgent consideration of the case of the Jewish populations in Arab and Moslem countries stretching from Morocco to India."[39] The article quoted the UN Economic and Social Council report as saying, "The very survival of the Jewish communities in certain Arab and Moslem countries is in serious danger, unless preventive action is taken without delay."[40]

JEWISH POPULATION IN ARAB COUNTRIES, IRAN[41] AND TURKEY					
Country	1945	1948	1976	2001	2015
Morocco	300,000	265,000	17,000	5,230	<2,500
Algeria	150,000	140,000	500	0	0
Tunisia	120,000	105,000	2,000	<1,000	<900
Libya	40,000	38,000	20	1*	0
Egypt	90,000	75,000	200	100	<100
Sudan	350	<350	0	0	0
Jordan	No Jews allowed since the first partition of Palestine in 1921.				
Iraq	140,000	135,000	<400	200	8[42]
Syria	35,000	30,000	4,350	<100	<30
Lebanon	5,200	9,000†	150	<100	40
Bahrain	550–600	N.A.	N.A.	<50	37
Saudi Arabia	No Jews allowed since expulsion in May 628 C.E.				

---

* The last Jew, eighty-year old Rina Debach, left Libya in 2003.

† Lebanon, with a population almost equally divided between Christians and Muslims, was more tolerant of Jews in 1948. Its Jewish population actually grew as it absorbed Jews fleeing from Syria after the reestablishment of the Jewish state of Israel.

Ras al Khaimah (now part of the United Arab Emirates)	No Jews since the third quarter of the twelfth century.				
Oman	No Jews since the end of the nineteenth century.				
Yemen	55,000	55,000	1,200	<400	<190[43]
Aden (later the People's Democratic Republic of [South] Yemen)	8,000	8,000	0	0	0
TOTAL	943,600	860,000	25,620	<6,866	<9,000

	1948	1979	2004	2015
Iran	120,000	70,000	<25,000	8,800[44]
Turkey[45]	80,000	ca. 49,000 (1951)	20,000	<17,300

In Iran, since the Islamic Revolution of 1979, the plight of Jews has steadily deteriorated. The execution of Iranian-Jewish businessman, Habib Elghanian on May 9, 1979, sent shock waves through the 80,000-strong Iranian Jewish community, triggering the beginnings of a mass exodus of Jews that continues to this day. Elghanian, who was the president of the Tehran Jewish Society and acted as the symbolic head of the Iranian Jewish community, was accused of spying for Israel, and economic imperialism. He was tried and executed by firing squad.

Currently, the Iranian Jewish community is under constant surveillance. The teaching of Hebrew is prohibited. Jewish women are forced to follow the same modesty laws imposed on Muslim women. Additionally, Jews are barred from certain jobs and some imprisoned or hanged on trumped up charges of contact with "Zionists" or dealing with the "imperialist" Americans. The latter two charges are punishable by death. Jews who apply for a passport to travel abroad must do so in a special bureau and are immediately put under surveillance.

Additional illustrations of transferred peoples took place in Asia. Some 3 million North Koreans fled to South Korea because of the Korean War (1950–53). At the end of the First Indochina War in 1955, some 800,000 Vietnamese fled from northern to southern Vietnam while 52,000 went from south to north. After the conclusion of the Second Indochina war in 1975, some 1.6 million Cambodians, Laotians, and Vietnamese fled to freedom and were resettled in many nations around the world.

Population transfer was also used to settle the inter-religious enmity between Hindus and Muslims in British India in 1947. Once it became clear the communities could not live together, the subcontinent was partitioned into two states—India and Pakistan. This required the resettlement of some fifteen million people. 7.5 million Muslims left India in 1947–that is ten times the number of Arabs who left Israel in 1947–49. Similarly, 7.5 million Hindus and Sikhs were forced out of Pakistan.

An often overlooked and relatively recent example of population transfer occurred on the island of Cyprus. Historically, Cyprus lies along the East–West dividing line. As such, it was a factor in the struggle between the ancient Persian Empire and the Greek city-states, from 525 B.C.E. to 331 B.C.E. During the Middle Ages, the island was the bone of contention between Arab/Muslim forces and the

Byzantine Empire. During the Renaissance, the fight for control of Cyprus was waged between the Muslim Ottoman Turkish Empire and the Venetian Republic, with the former gaining total control in 1570. Turkey and Greece have struggled over the island since the early nineteenth century, which culminated in the Turkish invasion and occupation of the northern-third of the island, in 1974.

After Turkey invaded and occupied the northern third of Cyprus (36.2 percent of the island) in July 1974 (*see* "Cyprus-Crisis of 1974, Turkish Invasion and Occupation" map), Turkey engaged in ethnic cleansing, forcibly driving out some 200,000 Greek Cypriots who were relocated across the Attila Line—also known as the "Green Line"—the 112-mile long barrier that divides the island. Turkey imported thousands of settlers* from Anatolia to move into the northern part of the country to change permanently the demographic makeup of the island. With a public relations ineptness of major proportions, the Turks decided to call the new demarcation boundary between the Turkish and Greek sections of Cyprus, the "Attila Line." Though Attila is a national hero in Turkey, his name is synonymous with barbarism in the rest of the world. Some 35,000 Turkish Cypriots (the Turks claim 65,000) went north, where they moved into homes abandoned by Greek-Cypriots. The Greek Cypriot refugees resettled in the southern part of the island, a number of them on property owned by Turkish-Cypriots. This transfer of populations was completed by September 7, 1975.

---

* The term "settlers" is a term of the highest international opprobrium when applied to Israel, but rarely mentioned in the case of northern Cyprus.

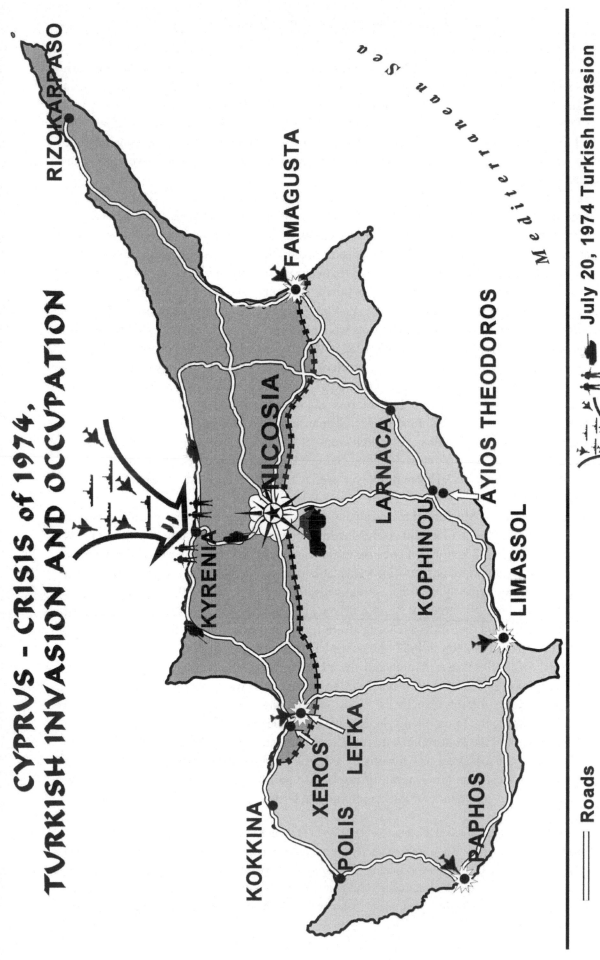

CYPRUS – CRISIS of 1974, TURKISH INVASION AND OCCUPATION

RIZOKARPASO

FAMAGUSTA

NICOSIA

KYRENIA

LARNACA

AYIOS THEODOROS

KOPHINOU

LIMASSOL

XEROS

LEFKA

KOKKINA

POLIS

PAPHOS

Mediterranean Sea

Roads

July 15, 1974
Cyprus National Guard coup
ousted Archbishop Makarios

July 20, 1974 Turkish Invasion

Occupied by Turkey 1974 to date

Attila Line

Additionally, Turkey brought over 120,000 Turks from the mainland to settle in the northern portion of the island from which the Greeks were evicted. This is a violation of Article 49 of the Geneva Convention and is a war crime. Furthermore, while the Turkish population of Cyprus consistently was 18 percent of the total, Turkey forcibly occupied a disproportionate part of the territory, 36.2 percent. This affected the *de facto* partition of Cyprus. Thus, invasion, occupation, ethnic cleansing, forcible relocation, importation of new settlers, all have occurred on the territory of another sovereign state, without repeated international condemnation.

In a case relating to the Greek-Turkish dispute over Cyprus, but with great implications for the Arab–Israel conflict, on March 1, 2010, the European Court of Human Rights rejected the claim of Greek Cypriots for the return of their homes.[46] These Greek Cypriots fled or were driven out of the northern part of the island in 1974. The Court decision noted, "It is not enough for an applicant to claim that a particular place or property is a 'home.' He or she must show that they enjoy concrete and persisting links with the property concerned. Some thirty-five years have elapsed since the applicants lost possession of their property in northern Cyprus in 1974. Generations have passed. The local population has not remained static. Turkish Cypriots who inhabited the north have migrated elsewhere. Turkish Cypriot refugees from the south have settled in the north; Turkish settlers from Turkey have arrived in large numbers and established homes. Much of the Greek Cypriot property changed hands at least once, whether by sale, donation or inheritance."[47] Thus, the passage of time is an important factor, not in term of property ownership, but in terms of a right of return versus compensation.

The ruling by one of the world's most respected international legal institutions on the matter of human rights has great implications for other areas of the world, including the Middle East. According to it, there is no "right of return" as long claimed by the Arab refugees, their descendants and worldwide Muslim supporters.* This may apply as well to the contested Western Sahara, occupied by Morocco since 1976.

Another case in point of Muslim ethnic cleansing and expulsion of a resident people occurred in Kuwait in 1991. Thanks to the incessant Arab/Muslim propaganda machine, one constantly hears of the Palestinians "expelled" from Israel because of the 1948–49 war launched by the Arab states. However, there was little mention, or repetition today, about the expulsion of Palestinian Arabs from that Persian Gulf emirate. Some 443,000 Palestinians resided in Kuwait in 1990.[48] In general, Arab leaders are concerned about potential Palestinian-driven subversion, which caused the expulsion of Arafat, Mahmoud Abbas and their PLO associates from Egypt in the late 1950s, from Syria in 1966, from Jordan in 1970, from Lebanon in 1982–83, as well as from Kuwait in 1991.

In the summer of 1990, Yasser Arafat and the PLO supported Saddam Hussein's invasion, conquest and occupation of Kuwait. As a result, after that emirate was liberated, some 443,000–450,000 Palestinians were forcibly expelled from Kuwait during one week in March 1991.[49] Top Kuwaiti officials, including the Emir of Kuwait, used the word "cleansing"[50] (as in "ethnic cleansing") to describe the expulsion of the Palestinians. It is of noteworthy interest that there was little terrorism or political activism against Kuwait or Kuwaitis by the PLO or any other Palestinian terror group in particular, and the Palestinians in general, in reaction to their expulsion. Yet, this is one of the perverted excuses given by apologists for the heinous acts of terrorism perpetrated against Israelis by

---

* Israel's Arab/Muslim enemies, cite the Universal Declaration of Human Rights (1948) as guarantor of the right to leave and return to one's country. They use it to justify the "Palestinian right of return." However, there is no such "right." The non-binding UN General Assembly Resolution 194 (1948) refers to *all refugees*, [emphasis added] Jewish as well as Arab, and does not confer automatic rights to return. Repatriation (or return) *was suggested as one option,* [emphasis added] but this is based on conditions that the Arabs have never fulfilled.

Palestinians for over six decades. A further example took place after the disintegration of the Soviet Union in 1991. There was a population exchange of thousands of people among the Caucasus areas of Armenia, Nagorno-Karabakh, Azerbaijan, Abkhazia, Chechnya, South Ossetia, and Georgia.

Sudden expulsion of various groups from areas of the Middle East is hardly a thing of the past. As a result of the Gulf Cooperation Council Foreign Ministers meeting in Jeddah, Saudi Arabia, June 10, 2013, tens of thousands of Lebanese Shi'ites working or operating businesses in the Gulf were facing indiscriminate mass expulsions from the six Gulf states. The move was to punish the Hezbollah terrorist group for its "flagrant military intervention in Syria and its participation in shedding the blood of Syrian people." There are an estimated 500,000 Lebanese expatriates in the Gulf Cooperation Council (GCC) states. Some 18 percent are believed to be Shi'ite.[51] According to the Lebanese daily *An Nahar,* the Lebanese expatriates transfer some $4 billion back to Lebanon annually.[52]

The Lebanese expatriates are most susceptible to expulsion when they apply to renew their residency permits, and conduct financial as well as commercial transactions. It is feared that Shi'ites who are not Hezbollah supporters, and other non-Shi'ite groups, as well as Christians could be targeted. Following the GCC decision, eighteen Lebanese were expelled from Qatar and at least ten from Saudi Arabia by June 20, 2013.[53] The Kuwaiti Interior Ministry already had plans to revoke the residency permits of at least 2,000 Lebanese citizens.[54] Saudi ambassador to Beirut Ali Awad Assiri said on June 20, 2013, that Lebanese citizens who support Hezbollah would be deported over the group's role in the Syrian Civil War, including "those who financially support this party."[55] This forced repatriation of masses of Shi'ites will not only be a destabilizing factor in Lebanon, but is bound to raise military tensions between Shi'ite Iran and the Sunni Gulf states.

In none of these cases were the people concerned asked whether they wanted to be resettled, and adequate humanitarian safeguards for an orderly transfer were sorely missing. In any case, few people remember these events today. Furthermore, within the international community, there has also been established the precedent of creating new states based on ethnic, national and even religious boundaries and is becoming the trend. The recent historic tendency has been to move away from attempts to accommodate competing national aspirations in a single state. The former Soviet Union was broken up into fifteen separate states, and may fragment further, witness the separatist movements in the Caucasus. Yugoslavia ruptured into seven countries. Czechoslovakia was split into two, and Cyprus was divided by the Turkish invasion of 1974, into two states, with forced ethnic relocation taking place. Even in Iraq there are those voices which wish to see the creation of three states—Shi'ite, Sunni and Kurdish. Why did the transfer of people described above, as well as the recent disintegration of long established states take place? One main reason is because the two groups involved could not live in peace with one another. That has been the case between Israel and its Arab/Muslim neighbors all along.

It is to be recalled that since the reestablishment of Jewish sovereignty in the modern State of Israel, Arab leaders admitted they were in large part responsible for the Arab refugees existing in the first place. The Arabs were blunt in taking responsibility for starting the war, which began on November 30, 1947, the day after the adoption of the UN Partition plan for Palestine. A frank admission came from Ismayil Safwat, Commander in Chief of the Arab Liberation Army, who declared on March 23, 1948, "The Jews have not attacked any Arab village, unless attacked first."[56] Jamal Husseini, Acting head of the Palestine Arab Higher Committee, told the UN Security Council on April 16, 1948:

> The representative of the Jewish Agency told us yesterday that they were not the attackers, that the Arabs had begun the fighting. We did not deny this. We told the whole world that we were going to fight.[57]

Earlier in April, the 6,000-strong Arab community of Tiberias was similarly forced out by its own leaders, against local Jewish wishes. Several weeks later, Sir Alan Cunningham, the last British High Commissioner of Palestine, reported that the Tiberias Jews "would welcome [the] Arabs back."[58] *Time* magazine reported, in early May, 1948, "The mass evacuation [April 20–21], prompted partly by fear, partly by order of Arab leaders, left the Arab quarter of Haifa a ghost city. By withdrawing Arab workers, their leaders hoped to paralyze Haifa."[59] In 1948, 65 percent of Arabs fled Palestine without ever seeing an Israeli soldier.

General John Bagot Glubb (also known as Glubb Pasha) was the British officer who commanded the Transjordanian Arab Legion, considered by many as the best Arab fighting force in the Middle East. Hardly sympathetic to the Israeli cause, Glubb laid much of the blame on the (Palestinian) Liberation Army. He admitted:

> Early in January [1948], the first detachments of the Arab Liberation Army began to infiltrate into Palestine from Syria. Some came through Jordan and even through Amman . . . They were in reality to strike the first blow in the ruin of the Arabs of Palestine.[60]

In May 1948, Glubb led the Arab Legion as it invaded Judea and Samaria to seize those areas for King Abdullah I of Transjordan. Certainly not sympathetic to the Israeli cause, he nevertheless wrote in the British press that, "The Arab civilians panicked and fled ignominiously. Villages were frequently abandoned before they were threatened by the progress of war."[61]

The leading Christian Arab bishop in the British Mandate of Palestine, George Hakim (and no friend of the Jews) told a Beirut newspaper that, "The refugees were confident they would return within a week or two. Their leaders had promised them that the Arab armies would crush the 'Zionist gangs' very quickly and there was no need for panic or fear of a long exile."[62] Emil Ghoury, Secretary of the Palestine Arab Higher Committee, was quoted in a Beirut newspaper:

> The Arab states which had encouraged the Palestine Arabs to leave their homes temporarily in order to be out of the way of the Arab invasion armies, have failed to keep their promise to help these refugees.[63]

The London *Economist,* a frequent critic of the Zionists and Israelis, reported:

> Of the 62,000 Arabs who formerly lived in Haifa not more than 5,000 or 6,000 remained. Various factors influenced their decision to seek safety in flight. There is but little doubt that the most potent of the factors were the announcements made over the air by the Higher Arab Executive, urging the Arabs to quit.... It was clearly intimated that those Arabs who remained in Haifa and accepted Jewish protection would be regarded as renegades.[64]

The Jordanian newspaper *Falastin* declared in mid-February 1949, "The Arab states encouraged the Palestine Arabs to leave their homes temporarily in order to be out of the way of the Arab invasion armies, have failed to keep their promise to help these refugees."[65] In June 1949, John Troutbeck, the head of the British Middle East Office in Cairo, Egypt, affirmed:

> The refugees speak with utmost bitterness of the Egyptians and other Arab states. They know who their enemies are, and they are referring to their Arab brothers who—they declare—persuaded them unnecessarily to leave their homes.[66]

Most expressive was the recollection by one of the Arabs who had fled, testifying in the Jordanian daily, *Ad-Difaa*, "The Arab governments told us: Get out so that we can get in. So we got out, but they did not get in."[67] Khaled al-Azm, the prime minister of Syria, during the 1948–49 Arab invasion of Israel, analyzed the reasons for the Arab failure (to defeat Israel) in 1948. These were published in his mémoires, released in Beirut in 1973. Al-Azm explained the reasons for the Arab defeat, laying the blame squarely on

> the Arab governments [who appealed] to the inhabitants of Palestine to evacuate it and leave for the bordering Arab countries. Since 1948, we have been demanding the return of the refugees to their homes; but we ourselves are the ones who encouraged them to leave. Only a few months separated our call to them to leave and our appeal to the UN to resolve on their return.... We brought destruction upon a million Arab refugees, by calling upon them and pleading with them to leave their land, their homes, their work and their business.... [Additionally,] we exploited them in executing crimes of murder, arson, and throwing stones upon men, women and children ... all this in the service of political purposes.[68]

Even Mahmoud Abbas, also known as Abu Mazen, the head of both the Palestinian Liberation Organization (PLO) and the Palestinian Authority (PA) admitted the role of the Arab leaders. In an article he wrote for *Falastin al-Thawra,* the official journal of the PLO in Beirut, in March 1976, entitled "What We Have Learned and What We Should Do," Abbas declared:

> The Arab armies entered Palestine to protect the Palestinians from the Zionist tyranny, but instead they abandoned them, *forced them to emigrate* [emphasis added] and to leave their homeland, imposed upon them a political and ideological blockade and threw them into prisons similar to the ghettos in which the Jews used to live in Eastern Europe.[69]

From these testimonies, there should be no doubt as to where a large part of the blame for the Arab refugee problem lies. Now all these facts are swept under the rug as calls go out for the creation of another "Palestinian Arab state."

The Palestinian Arabs, however, already have a state called Jordan, where they make up some 80 percent of the population on 77.5 percent of the original British Mandate of Palestine's territory. Overwhelmingly, those who live in Judea and Samaria as well as the Gaza Strip do not want to have

Jews in their midst, favor the continued use of terror and violence to kill Jews, and wish to destroy Israel. No number of negotiations, or agreements, including the so-called Oslo "peace process," changes these facts.

While Jewish refugees from the Arab/Muslim lands have been integrated into Israeli society, Arab refugees have been made pariahs within Arab states. Whereas the United Nations has one agency, the United Nations High Commissioner for Refugees, (UNHCR), to deal with refugee crises the world over (including most recently the one in Syria), only the Palestinian Arabs have an entire United Nations agency—United Nations Relief and Works Agency for Palestine Refugees in the Near East (UNRWA)—devoted to them. It should be pointed out that the UN did *not* (emphasis added) create any separate special agency, like UNRWA, to assist the larger number of Jewish refugees from Arab countries. UNRWA started out with the intention of resettling the Arab refugees but was thwarted by the Arab countries. It evolved very quickly into an agency for their perpetuation and maintenance as refugees. Sir Alexander Galloway, the former UNRWA director in Jordan, forthrightly stated in April 1952:

> It is perfectly clear, that the Arab nations do not want to solve the refugee problem. They want to keep it as an open sore, as an affront to the United Nations and as a weapon against Israel. Arab leaders don't give a damn whether the refugees live or die.[70]

Initially, UNRWA defined Palestinian Arab refugees as persons whose normal place of residence was the British Mandate of Palestine between June 1946 and May 1948, who lost both their homes and means of livelihood as a result of the 1948 Arab attack against the *Yishuv* (the Jewish community) in the Land of Israel, with the goal of annihilating the fledgling Jewish state.

The majority of Palestinian Arabs have been maintained in fifty-nine UNRWA-run camps in Judea and Samaria (what the Arabs would call the West Bank)—then under Jordanian occupation, the Gaza Strip, then under Egyptian military administration, Jordan, Syria, and Lebanon. The camps, first opened in 1950, do not seek to settle the Arabs elsewhere.

Certainly, no one, including UNWRA and its donors, imagined that refugee status would become a heritable trust* to be bestowed on the refugees' relatives, their children, grandchildren, great grandchildren, ad infinitum. Given that, by 2014, there are so few remaining original Arab refugees being alive, a more accurate term for "Palestinian refugees" would be "Palestinian descendants," which is not the same as "refugees." Furthermore, UNRWA violates international law—specifically, the 1951 Convention Relating to the Status of Refugees (Article 1C, the "Cessation" Clause)—a person stops being a "refugee" once he "has acquired a new nationality, and enjoys the protection of the country of his new nationality."[71] UNRWA illegally insisted that nearly two million people who have been given citizenship in Jordan, Syria, and Lebanon (and who constitute 40 percent of UNRWA's beneficiaries) are still refugees.

John Blandford Jr., the Director of UNRWA, wrote in his report on November 29, 1951, that he expected the Arab governments to assume responsibility for relief by July 1952. Moreover, Blandford stressed the need to end relief operations, "Sustained relief operations inevitably contain the germ of human deterioration."[72] Blandford was wrong. The Arab refugee problem is still with us. In reality, only about 30,000 of the original Arab refugees are still alive.

---

* UNRWA made a little-noticed decision in 1965 that extended the definition of "Palestine refugee" to the descendants of those refugees who are male. We are now up to the fourth and fifth generation of such people.

Now the world (including the US State Department*, as well as many of the world's Jews) accept without protest UNRWA's assertion (as of December 30, 2010) that it provides education, healthcare, social services and emergency aid to over 4.9 million Palestinian refugees,[73] including Arabs living full-time in Jordan, as well as Arabs who long ago emigrated throughout the Middle East and to the West.

Whereas UNHCR has a staff of 7,600 spread across 126 countries,[74] UNWRA has a bloated bureaucracy of over 29,000 persons (in Judea and Samaria, also known as the West Bank, Gaza, Jordan, Lebanon and Syria) and its United Nations General Assembly-approved budget for 2008 was $541 million.[75] UNRWA's biennium regular budget for 2010 and 2011 was USD 1.23 billion.[76] In comparison, UNHCR's budget for only one year—2012—was $2.1 billion,[77] for the entire world excluding the Palestinian Arabs. While UNHCR is about helping refugees worldwide to get out of their refugee status, UNRWA is keeping Palestinians refugees and acting (for some sixty-seven years) as their internationally funded health, education and welfare ministry. An analysis by the academic journal *Refugee Survey Quarterly* projected that if that definition remains intact, there will be 11 million Palestinian refugees by 2040 and 20 million by 2060[78]—even though not one of those who actually left Israel in 1948–49 is likely still to be alive.

Arab countries implemented special laws designed to make it impossible to integrate the refugees. Even descendants of Palestinian refugees who were born in another Arab country, live there their entire lives, can never gain that country's passport. Even if they marry a citizen of an Arab country, they cannot become citizens of their spouse's country. They have been held in perpetual refugee status, passed on from generation to generation, to act as in the words of Egyptian President Gamal Abdel Nasser, "a demographic bomb" against the Jewish state. It was obvious many years ago, that the Arab regimes really cared little for the Arab refugees. Interviewed in Cairo, in April 1956, Nasser revealed this fact candidly to John Laffin, a Western reporter, "The Palestinians are useful to the Arab states as they are. We will always see that they do not become too powerful. Can you imagine yet another nation on the shores of the eastern Mediterranean!"[79] As Ralph Garraway, another former UNRWA director, explained in August 1958, "The Arab states do not want to solve the refugee problem. They want to keep it as an open sore, as an affront to the United Nations and as a weapon against Israel. Arab leaders don't give a damn whether the refugees live or die."[80]

Furthermore, the Palestinian refugees were told by their own leaders that they would be denied Palestinian citizenship even in a future Palestinian state. "They are Palestinians, that's their identity," Abdullah Abdullah, the Palestinian ambassador to Lebanon, stated in 2011. "But … they are not automatically citizens. Even Palestinian refugees who are living in [refugee camps] inside the [Palestinian] state, they are still refugees. They will not be considered citizens." Ambassador Abdullah added, "When we have a state accepted as a member of the United Nations, this is not the end of the conflict. This is not a solution to the conflict. This is only a new framework [i.e. another step in the strategy of stages] that will change the rules of the game."[81] Thus, they must only return to whatever remains of the Jewish state of Israel in order to undermine it demographically.

---

* The US State Department position appears to conflict with the United States Law on Derivative Refugee Status, which allows spouses and children of refugees to apply for derivative status as refugees, but specifically declares that grandchildren are ineligible for derivative refugee status. In other words, US law doesn't permit descendants of refugees to get refugee status inside the United States.

Nevertheless, UNRWA encourages high birth rates by monetarily rewarding families with many children. PLO Chairman Yasser Arafat (also known as Abu Ammar[*]) said the Palestinian woman's womb was his best weapon. All of these actions were designed by the Arab world to perpetuate and exacerbate the Palestinian Arab refugee crisis. As former Israeli Minister of Tourism and Knesset member Benny Elon, currently the head of the Israeli Initiative[82] stated:

> [UNRWA] is an agency that has yet to rehabilitate a single refugee, and will never do so. UNRWA was not created to serve the Palestinian population, but rather, to serve the Palestinian national narrative. As such, it perpetuates the conflict and offers the refugees conflict and blood instead of wellbeing and life.[83]

The Palestinian Arab refugees have become the recipients of constant funding by the outside world, mainly by United States taxpayers (directly or through the United Nations) and the members of the European Union. Until 1973, Israel donated more to UNRWA, than any Arab state. Even by the mid-1990s, Israel's contribution was larger than any Arab state except for Saudi Arabia, Kuwait, and Morocco.

PLEDGES AND CONTRIBUTIONS TO UNRWA[† 84] (Cash and in kind, in US Dollars)	
Donor	**Amount**
United States	$ 239,440,945
European Commission	$ 175,450,364
Saudi Arabia	76,783,911
United Kingdom	76,299,681
Sweden	56,649,690
Norway	31,588,102
Netherlands	26,839,866
Switzerland	24,841,167
Germany	23,469,432
Australia	16,928,891
Japan	15,523,777
Spain	15,112,940
Canada	15,088,854
Denmark	13,908,370
Belgium	13,147,845
France	11,109,564
The Gulf States: Bahrain, Kuwait, Oman, Qatar and the United Arab Emirates	4,594,000
All other Arab countries	3,453,514

---

[*] The term *abu* (e.g. "Abu Ammar, Abu Iyad, Abu Jihad, and Abu Mazen") is a *kunya* or nickname (*umm* is used for women). It is an honorific in placwe of or alongside given names in the Arab/Muslim world.

[†] Pledges for 2011.

As the table above indicates, and the trend has continued, the Agency's largest contributors were from the United States, and other Western countries.[85] The Arab states, which bear a much greater responsibility for launching war against Israel in 1948 and 1967, causing the Arab refugee problem in the first place, have made negligible contributions, little in hard cash but millions in lip service. Much of the UNRWA funding has not gone to the Palestinian Arab people, but rather to their leadership, and ends up in Swiss and offshore bank accounts. That funding is used to purchase weapons for use against Israel.

Since 1950, US contributions to UNRWA amounted to over $3.7 billion. Furthermore, since 2007, US foreign aid to the PLO/PA and to PA-controlled NGOs totaled nearly $2 billion. The question therefore must be asked: Has American foreign aid to the PLO/PA advanced moderation, the peace process and US national security interests? The answer is obvious they have not.

11. The Arab/Muslim claim that Israeli towns and villages in the "occupied areas," must be removed is but a first step to eradicating all of Israel.

As noted in the introduction, the Arab/Muslim world's war against the Jewish people predates the *Yishuv* and the reestablishment of Jewish sovereignty, as the State of Israel in 1948. The first name on the official Israeli governmental list of the fallen—those who died in defense of the Jewish state and pre-state *Yishuv**—is Aharon Hershler. Hershler, a 23-year-old Yeshiva student was killed January 1, 1873, s a result of gunfire of an Arab terrorist cell that penetrated his neighborhood— Mishkenot Shananim—the first Jewish neighborhood outside Jerusalem's Old City's walls.[86] He is buried in the Jewish cemetery on the Mount of Olives in Jerusalem. As of Israel's Memorial Day—*Yom HaZikaron*—23,320 Israelis† through war and terrorism, gave their lives to help secure the Jewish state since 1860, when Jerusalem's Jews first settled outside the Old City of Jerusalem.[87]

Some background is instructive. Terrorism is defined as the deliberate and systematic, violent or destructive acts committed by groups in order to inspire fear and intimidate a population or government into granting their demands. These acts include the murdering, maiming, and menacing of innocent civilians—men, women and children—systematically and deliberately by various means. The hackneyed cliché that "one man's terrorist is another man's freedom fighter" is both false and a gross insult to real historical freedom fighters such as Judah Maccabee, Shimon Bar Kokhba, George Washington, Francis "Swamp Fox" Marion, Daniel Morgan, Simon Bolivar, Bernardo O'Higgins, Mahatma Gandhi, and Martin Luther King, Jr. Yasser Arafat was no George Washington. There are obvious differences between, on the one hand, the American, Algerian, Kenyan and Indonesian revolutionary guerrilla groups and, on the other, the Palestinian guerrilla groups. The resistance movements, which liberated the United States from the United Kingdom (then Great Britain), Algeria from France, Kenya from the United Kingdom, and Indonesia from the Netherlands, did not seek the elimination of the United Kingdom, France or the Netherlands from the historical map of the world or the denial of their national personality. There were no systematic and deliberate attacks on civilians and their places of worship. On the other hand, the PLO, Hamas et al seeks the total destruction of

---

* In 1980, an amendment was made to the General Memorial Day for the Fallen of Israel's Wars Law to include those who were part of the underground movements prior to the State's formation as well *Shin Bet* and Mossad agents.

† As of May 2015.

Israel. Their schools and textbooks continue to teach blind hatred of all things Jewish and Israeli. Their mosques instruct them that Allah seeks the destruction or subjugation of all the Jews.

Additionally, unlike the true revolutionary movements mentioned above, the officers of these Palestinian groups did not go out on raids but rather sent peasants and recruited mercenaries from such countries as Germany, Japan, Turkey and Nicaragua. Furthermore, most of the terrorist attacks perpetrated by the PLO et al were on those targets that had, up to now, under civilized norms been immune to attack including children, passengers on civilian aircraft, ships, busses, trains, parties not involved in the conflict, delegates at international assemblies, and diplomats.

Lastly, the question has been raised over the years, "Isn't the PLO's underground fight for the independence of a Palestinian state similar to the underground fight for the reestablishment of Jewish sovereignty in the Land of Israel? The answer to this question is "No." The Israelis fought for the salvation of a people—the Jews. The PLO fights for the destruction of a people—the Israelis. The Israelis fought against armed men (the British army) and sought to avoid civilian casualties. The PLO fights against innocent civilians and uses their own civilians as shields and human bombs. Finally, the Arab right to self-determination has been more than fulfilled in twenty-one states. The Israeli right to Jewish self-determination depends on Israel alone. The fact remains that Israel has a moral, legal, historical and Biblical right to settle every hill and populate every valley of this ancient land.

The Arabs claim that Israel's settlements are "illegal" and assert that Israel has contravened the Fourth Geneva Convention of 1949 "Relative to the Protection of Civilian Persons in Time of War." This argument is specious and omits the details of history. The primary fact about this convention is that it is not relevant to Jewish settlements in Judea, Samaria and Gaza (or as it is known by its Hebrew acronym, *Yesha*: meaning *Yehuda, Shomron* and *Azza*), or to the Israeli presence there. The convention's applicability is defined precisely in Article 2, which states, "The present convention, shall apply to cases of partial or total occupation of the territory of a High Contracting Party."[88]

Israel does not occupy the territory of a "High Contracting Party." It is true that Israel wrested the territories from Jordan and Egypt during the Six-Day War of 1967, but these territories did not belong to them. Egypt and (then) Transjordan, acquired them in an act of naked aggression in their invasion of Western Palestine in 1948 in the Arab effort to annihilate the fledgling Jewish state. After Israel recovered Judea, Samaria and Gaza in 1967, it set about to reverse the ethnic cleansing of Jews carried out by the Arabs in 1948, in those areas. Thus, Israel rebuilt destroyed towns and villages, and established new ones.

Furthermore, the Arab/Muslim side views *all* (emphasis added) Jewish cities, towns and villages as settlements on "occupied" land. Contrary to what some believe, this practice did not begin after the Six-Day War of 1967 when Israel, in a defensive war, regained control of Judea, Samaria, the Golan Heights and the Gaza Strip. Moreover, the Palestine Liberation Organization (PLO) Charter of 1964 declared that all of Israeli territory is illegal and "occupied" Arab land (*see* Appendix 8). Other evidence of this type of selective disinformation appears on pre-1967 Jordanian maps, especially those of Jerusalem, which labels the land west of the Old City of Jerusalem (then under Jordanian occupation) as the "Occupied Territory of Palestine." The Hamas* Charter, similarly declares that all of Israel, not just Judea, Samaria or Gaza, are "occupied."

---

* Arabic acronym for *Harakat al-Muqawama al-Islamiya* ("Islamic Resistance Movement"). An Islamist Sunni Arab terror group, it is the Palestinian wing of the Muslim Brotherhood in Egypt.

The Arabs and other Muslims claim that the core of the Arab-Israel conflict is "occupation" and "illegitimate settlements." There can be no division of Israel's legitimacy as a Jewish state. If Israel's assertion of its sovereignty is legitimate for example, in Tel Aviv, Rehovot, Nahariya, Safed and Kiryat Shmona, then it is legitimate in Ma'ale Adumim, Kiryat Arba in Hebron, Ariel and other cities and towns in Judea and Samaria. One group of cities and towns does not have a different status from the other group. As Naftali Bennett, leader of the *HaBayit HaYehudi* ("The Jewish Home") party put it accurately, "there is no occupation within one's own land."[89]

Additionally, Israel's enemies worldwide now have morphed the term "settlement" into a misojudaic term. "Settlement" no longer means a new town or village in an unsettled area or region; it now simply means a place where Jews live. Arab terminology considers all of Israel as occupied and illegitimate. PA-controlled TV and cultural events continue to reinforce the message of nonrecognition of Israel, by their ongoing depiction of all of Israel as "Palestine." In April 2011, for example, a Palestinian TV program for teenagers included a short video clip which opened with the words across the screen, "Palestine: We will return one day to our home," and then followed with a series of pictures of cities and regions in Israel, with the names on the screen, including: Tel Aviv, Haifa, Galilee, Negev, Caesarea, Acre, and Jerusalem. PA TV also showed a picture of Masada but incorrectly labeled it "Jericho mountains." The picture of the Galilee, though not labeled, was of the ancient Synagogue in Capernaum. The Christian Bible (i.e. Old and New Testaments) cites the Capernaum Synagogue as a place where Jesus taught on the Sabbath. (Luke 4:31–37).[90] Recent depictions of all of Israel as "Palestine" include songs for children to sing. In addition to the cities named above were also included the cities of Safed, Tiberias, Acre, Nazareth, Beit She'an, Jaffa, and Ramle.[91] It is not occupation but rather the Arab/Muslim preoccupation with destroying the Jewish state that is the core of the conflict. This issue has never been one of "occupation" but rather, whether a sovereign Jewish state has the right to exist in the Middle East.

Either all of Israel is legitimate or none of it is. The end game of Israel's enemies, both foreign and domestic, has always been to achieve the latter. Once achieved, Israel as an "outlaw illegitimate state" can be dismantled and destroyed, in stages or directly. Israel's friends and supporters of all faiths and nationalities must prevent that from happening, lest the world sink into a new morally bankrupt Dark Age.

Of significance, in several instances, the Qur'an cites the Jewish people as belonging in the Middle East with their own nation. The Qur'an (5:20–21) powerfully affirms Jewish sovereignty to the land of Israel, "Remember Moses said to his people: 'O my people! Recall in remembrance the favor of Allah unto you, when He produced prophets among you, made you kings, and gave you what He had not given to any other among the peoples in the world. O my people! Enter the holy land which Allah hath assigned unto you, and turn not back ignominiously, for then will ye be overthrown, to your own ruin.'" *Sura* 7:137 affirms, "We gave as their heritage the eastern and western parts of the land [of Israel] that we had blessed." In *Sura* 17:104 the pledge is repeated, "And after that We said unto the children of Israel: Dwell now securely in the land." However, these citations have been ignored and forgotten.

TRADITIONS AND THE HISTORIC RECORD

A society without a sense of history is like an individual without memory.
Anonymous

History is philosophy with examples.
Henry St John, 1st Viscount Bolingbroke (1678-1751)

Those who cannot remember the past are condemned to repeat it.
George Santayana

*Why is it that nobody listens when history repeats itself? The reason
is that most people were not listening the first time.*
Anonymous

People have a historical memory that goes back to breakfast.
Benjamin Netanyahu

It seems that every time history repeats itself, the price doubles.
Anonymous

The Middle East was home to numerous ancient civilizations and empires. The region is steeped in tradition and history. Among the key historic and modern players in the Middle East are the Jews, the Arabs, the Kurds, the Persians and the Turks. Islamic conquests have been a dominant and continual driving force in the area, marked by many symbols of those conquests. Historically, there has been the drive to force all others to accept the hegemony of the Arab/Muslim world, accompanied by the rejection of all claims for political and religious independence by all non-Arab and non-Muslim peoples. Despite this, the Jewish people, in 1948, became the first people in the region, to defy successfully both Arab and Muslim subjugation and achieved sovereignty and independence.[*] Furthermore, the region has been a cockpit of historic East–West rivalry and for over three centuries, Russia has been a major outside power involved in the region.

12. Tradition is a powerful force in the Arab/Muslim world.

Traditionalism permeates Arab/Muslim life. Religion, the family-clan, personal relationships, sexual behavior, gender apartheid, and to a lesser extent, the traditional arts and crafts, especially the verbal arts, are main concerns of Arab/Muslim culture. All these concerns are held in esteem not merely, because they represent old traditions in Arab/Muslim life, but also because they are hallowed by Islam. Revealed religion is a strong factor in Arab/Muslim traditionalism. The vast majority of Muslim society believes its religion was revealed by Allah at a certain time in the past, to its most beloved

---

[*] Thus far, only two other peoples have similarly achieved sovereignty and independence successfully defying Arab/Muslim rule. They are East Timor, in 2002, (against Indonesian/Muslim rule in southeast Asia) and South Sudan, in 2011, (against Arab/Muslim rule in the greater Middle East).

religious leader, Muhammad. This helps develop a mentality, which considers adherence to religious tradition as a supreme value, and by extension, must come to regard all tradition in the same light.

Primary loyalty to the family-clan[1] with the dominance of a patriarchal environment—a father and male elders—and their veneration brings with it a preference for the staid way of the older generation and their unquestioning adoption and continuation by the younger. It emphasizes the centrality of the family-clan in social organization. This loyalty to the family-clan subordinates the individual and the state to this traditional system. Muhammad could not break the power of Bedouin traditions or their social structure. The family remains the first priority and then that of the clan and tribe. There are no "neighbors" who are not related, the Arabs/Muslims have no responsibilities to any others beyond that. They do not hold their earthly lives in great value; neither do they value anyone else's.[2] Someone may reach for a gun if you insult his or her tradition. This is tied to their concept of honor. View this as a cautionary warning–especially to first time visitors to the region.

13. Israel is one of the oldest nations in the world with a common religion and language.

The Jews are the only nation* that can claim an uninterrupted presence in the Land of Israel—*Eretz Yisrael*—from biblical times to date, and for a significant amount of the time as its rulers (*see* "Jewish National Sovereignty in the Land of Israel" table [above]). The Land of Israel was and is the focal point of spiritual fulfillment, political freedom and national sovereignty for the Jewish people. The land was promised to Abraham and his descendants and it was the territorial goal of Moses and the Israelites in their liberation from slavery in Egypt. It was the target of conquest by Joshua and became the scene of military struggles under judges and kings. The personage of King David and the centrality of the Jewish Holy Temple—*Bet HaMikdash*—in Jerusalem are primary elements of identity, pride and remembrance never to be suspended or forgotten. For countless generations a popular Jewish musical exhortation is "David is the king of Israel / Lives, lives and exists" (transliterated from the Hebrew: *David Melech Yisrael; Chai, Chai, Vekayam*). Furthermore, there is a 2,000-year-old belief that the Third Jewish Temple will be built in Jerusalem. Perhaps Lord Arthur Balfour expressed this fact best when he wrote in 1919, two years after issuing the historic declaration that bears his name, "The position of the Jews is unique. For them race [nationality], religion and country are inter-related, as they are inter-related in the case of no other race, no other religion, and no other country on earth."[3] As has been stated, Israel was not "created" in 1947. In fact, it has a history that spans over 3,250 years.

HISTORY OF ISRAEL	
Date	**Event**
ca. 1400 B.C.E.	The nation of Israel—*am Yisrael*—started to crystallize in the Land of Israel—*Eretz Yisrael*.
ca. 1400 B.C.E.	A hieroglyphic inscription with images, from the reign of Amenhotep III, mentions "Israel" as a known nation.[4]
March 8, 1313 B.C.E.	Joshua led the Israelite tribes across the Jordan River into the Land of Canaan.
ca.1250–1010 B.C.E.	Period of the Judges.

---

* In this context "nation" is synonymous with "people," whereas a "country" is equivalent to a "sovereign state."

ca. 1207 B.C.E.	Israel was a known nation according to the Egyptian Merneptah Stele (a block of granite engraved by Merneptah IV, successor to Ramses II), also referred to by scholars as the "Israel Stele."
ca. 1190 B.C.E.	The Philistines invaded and took over the southern coast of Canaan.
ca. 1050 B.C.E.	The Philistines captured the Ark of the Covenant. After seven months during which time the Philistines suffered several severe afflictions, they sent the Ark back to the Israelites.
ca. 1025 B.C.E.	Saul was anointed first king of Israel. He fought the Philistines and regained some territory.
ca. 1010–968 B.C.E.	The reign of King David, who expelled the Philistines and consolidated as well as expanded the Kingdom of Israel. From Hebron, King David ruled for seven and a half years before he captured and established Jerusalem as Israel's capital, and brought to it the Ark of the Covenant. David purchased Aravna's threshing-floor that was located at the great rock[5] at the center of the current Temple Mount. The rock is called in Hebrew *Even Hashtiyah* ("Rock of Foundation") and in Arabic *El Tzachra* ("the Rock") (*see* "Israel's Ancient Monarchy–Kingdom of David," map).
968–928 B.C.E.	During the reign of King Solomon, the First Jewish Temple was erected. The period was ancient Israel's most prosperous and powerful era (*see* "Israel's Ancient Monarchy–Kingdom of Solomon" map).
928 B.C.E.	King Solomon died and the kingdom was split into two parts. In the north was the Kingdom of Israel, with its capital in Shechem, and in the south, the Kingdom of Judah, with its capital in Jerusalem (*see* the "Divided Monarchy c. 900 B.C.E." map).

ISRAEL'S ANCIENT MONARCHY KINGDOM OF DAVID

CHITTIM (Cyprus)

Orontes R.

Euphrates R.

Tipsah

Hamath

Arvad

ARAM

Tadmor

The Great Sea (Mediterranean)

Gebal

ZABAH

Sidon

Damascus

Tyre

Hazor

Megiddo

Jordan R.

Ramoth-gilead

ISRAEL

Joppa

Rabbath-ammon

Ashdod
Ashkelon
Gaza

Jerusalem

AMMON

Hebron

MOAB

River of Egypt (Wadi El Arish)

JUDAH

EDOM

Ezion-geber

Phoenicia

Philistia

Kingdom of David
ca. 1010-968 B.C.E.

— Reestablishment of Jewish sovereignty in the Land of Israel 1948-1967 Armistice lines

ISRAEL'S ANCIENT MONARCHY KINGDOM OF SOLOMON

CHITTIM (Cyprus)

Orontes R.

Euphrates R.

Tipsah

Hamath

Arvad

ARAM

Tadmor

ZABAH

The Great Sea (Mediterranean)

Gebal

Sidon

Damascus

Tyre

Hazor

Megiddo

Jordan R.

Ramoth-gilead

I S R A E L

Joppa

Rabbath-ammon

Ashdod
Ashkelon
Gaza

Jerusalem

AMMON

Hebron

MOAB

JUDAH

EDOM

River of Egypt (Wadi El Arish)

Ezion-geber

Phoenicia

Philistia

Kingdom of Solomon ca. 968-928 B.C.E.

— **Reestablishment of Jewish sovereignty in the Land of Israel 1948-1967 Armistice lines**

GREAT
(Mediterranean)
SEA

Damascus

Tyre

Dan

Sea of
Galilee

Dor

ISRAEL

Samaria

Shechem

Jordan R.

Bethel

THE DIVIDED
MONARCHY
ca. 900 B.C.E.

Jerusalem

Dead Sea

Gaza

Hebron

JUDAH

Philistia

Phoenicia

Aram

Moab

Contested by
Israel and Moab

Date	Event
878 B.C.E.	King Omri of Israel founded a new capital at Samaria.
ca. 850 B.C.E.	The Tel Dan Stele recorded an Aramaean victory over the "House of David."
ca. 850 B.C.E.	The Mesha Stele recorded the Moabite King Mesha's victory over a coalition of Israel and the "House of David." It bears the earliest known reference to the sacred Hebrew name of God.
842 B.C.E.	Queen Jezebel of Israel imposed the cult of Baal and the people revolted. Weakened by internal turmoil, Israel lost land to the Aramaeans.
ca. 750 B.C.E.	Prophets Amos and Hosea decried exploitation of the poor by the wealthy of Israel.
ca. 740–687 B.C.E.	The Prophet Isaiah admonished the Jewish people to keep the faith of their ancestors and forsake idolatry and pagan practices. He ministered to the people during the reigns of Kings Uzziah, Jotham, Ahaz, Hezekiah and possibly the early years of Manasseh.
738 B.C.E.	The Assyrian Empire exacted heavy tribute from Israel (*see* the "Assyrian Empire, 824–671 B.C.E." map).

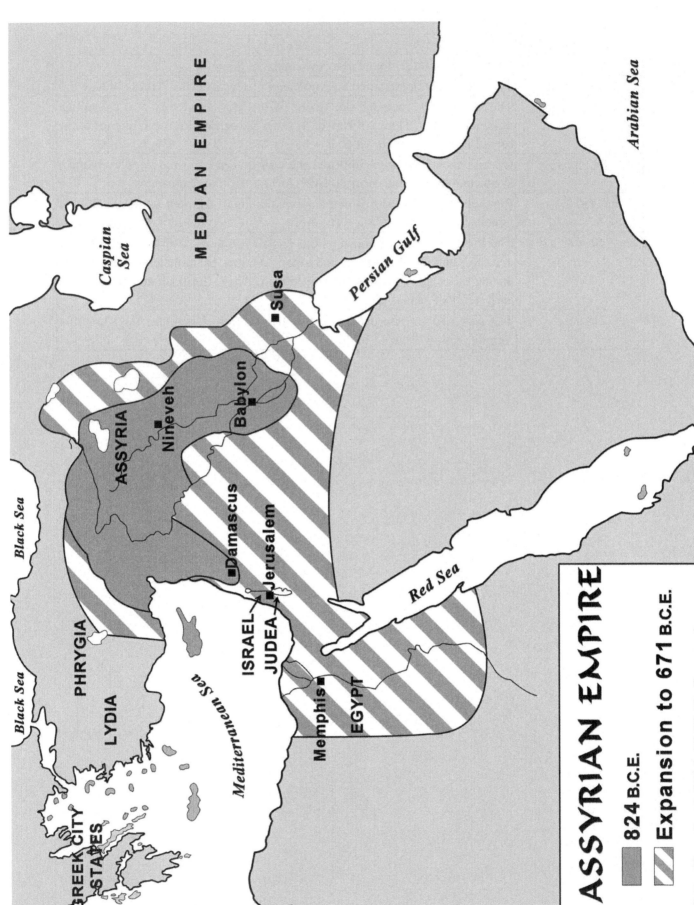

ASSYRIAN EMPIRE

Black Sea

Caspian Sea

MEDIAN EMPIRE

Arabian Sea

Persian Gulf

Susa ■

ASSYRIA

Nineveh ■

Babylon ■

GREEK CITY STATES

PHRYGIA

LYDIA

Mediterranean Sea

Damascus ■

Jerusalem ■
ISRAEL
JUDEA →

Red Sea

Memphis ■

EGYPT

824 B.C.E.

Expansion to 671 B.C.E.

Date	Event
722 B.C.E.	The Assyrian Empire invaded the Kingdom of Israel. Samaria was destroyed and its nobility was exiled. Judah became a vassal state under the Assyrians and forced to pay tribute.
716–687 B.C.E.	King Hezekiah of Judah purified the Jewish religion of Assyrian influences. He built a 600-yard tunnel under Jerusalem, to the Gihon Spring, to ensure a supply of fresh water for the city, which was discharged into a reservoir called the Pool of Siloam (Shiloah).
701 B.C.E.	The Assyrian army led by King Sennacherib, invaded Judah. Some forty-six fortified Jewish towns were destroyed and their populations were deported.
701 B.C.E.	The Assyrians besieged Jerusalem but suddenly called off the siege due to a threat by the Egyptian army. According to Biblical texts, the siege was suddenly lifted after the death of some 185,000 troops, by plague. The Assyrian army withdrew, never to return.
687–642 B.C.E.	After a ten-year period of being co-regent with his father, King Hezekiah, King Manasseh became the sole ruler of Judah in 687 B.C.E. ruling for some 45 years.
639–609 B.C.E.	King Josiah of Judah regained some territory from the Assyrian Empire, whose power was declining. Josiah repaired the First Jewish Temple.
598 B.C.E.	The Chaldeans (New Babylonians) invaded Judah.
March 16, 597 B.C.E.	The Chaldeans captured Jerusalem and deported King Jehoiachin.
597–586 B.C.E.	The reign of King Zedekiah.
588 B.C.E.	The second Chaldean invasion of Judah began.
July 11, 586 B.C.E. (Ninth of Av, 3338,[*] in the Hebrew/Jewish calendar)	Jerusalem fell to the Chaldean forces of King Nebuchadnezzar II. The city and the First Jewish Temple were destroyed. Some 100,000 Jews were slaughtered and millions were exiled. This marked the end of the Davidic Kingdom of Judah (*see* the "Middle East in 586 B.C.E." map).
October 17, 539 B.C.E.	King Cyrus the Great (*Koresh* in Hebrew) of the Persian Empire, began his rule over the Land of Israel. Cyrus allowed 42,360 Jews[6] (including Zerubavel) to return to the Land of Israel, then known as Judea (*see* the "Persian Empire 500 B.C.E." map).
520 B.C.E.	The construction of the Second Jewish Temple was begun by Ezra, in the second year of Darius I (*Daryavesh* in Hebrew).
515 B.C.E.	The Second Jewish Temple was completed.

[*] A discrepancy of about between 154 and 169 years exists between the conventional chronology and the traditional Jewish rabbinic chronology. The discrepancy is due to two factors: conflicting opinions as to the identity of the Persian kings that reigned over the Land of Israel and the number of Persian kings that reigned after the building of the Second Jewish Temple. For a much more detailed discussion of this topic see: Michael First, *Jewish History in Conflict: A Study of the Major Discrepancy between Rabbinic and Conventional Chronology*, Washington, DC: Jason Aronson, Inc., 1997, xvii, 3–7.

486–465 B.C.E.	Reign of King Ahasuerus (prominent in the biblical Book of Esther) over the Land of Israel. The majority of historians agree that Ahasuerus was the Greek-named Xerxes I.*
ca. 445 B.C.E.	The Jewish people living in the Land of Israel are re-energized spiritually thanks to the leadership of Ezra and the Men of the Great Assembly. Ezra read the Torah to the Jews in Jerusalem.
332 B.C.E.	End of the reign of Darius III over the Land of Israel and beginning of Greek rule. Alexander the Great overran Judea on his way east. He had already decisively defeated the Persians in two great battles, the Battle of Granicus (May 3, 334 B.C.E.), and the Battle of Issus (November 5, 333 B.C.E.), seeking primacy in the greater Middle East and Central Asia. His third great victory at the Battle of Gaugamela (October 1, 331 B.C.E.) crushed the Persian Achaemenid Empire and signaled its disintegration (*see* "Empire of Alexander the Great, 323 B.C.E." map). Alexander endorsed the Jewish privileges granted by the Persians earlier.

---

* The conventional chronology places the rule of Ahasuerus/Xerxes I after the building of the Second Jewish Temple, while the traditional Jewish rabbinic chronology places his reign before the building of the Second Jewish Temple.

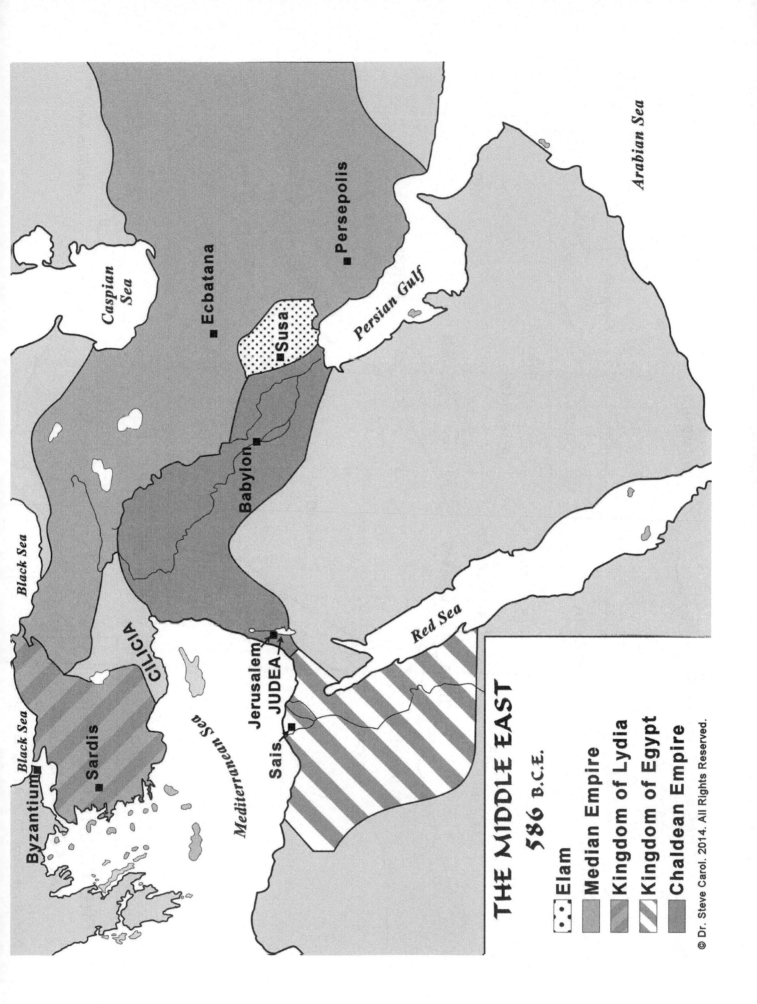

THE MIDDLE EAST
586 B.C.E.

Elam

Median Empire

Kingdom of Lydia

Kingdom of Egypt

Chaldean Empire

Arabian Sea

Persian Gulf

Persepolis

Ecbatana

Susa

Caspian Sea

Black Sea

Black Sea

Byzantium

Sardis

CILICIA

Mediterranean Sea

Babylon

Jerusalem

JUDEA

Sais

Red Sea

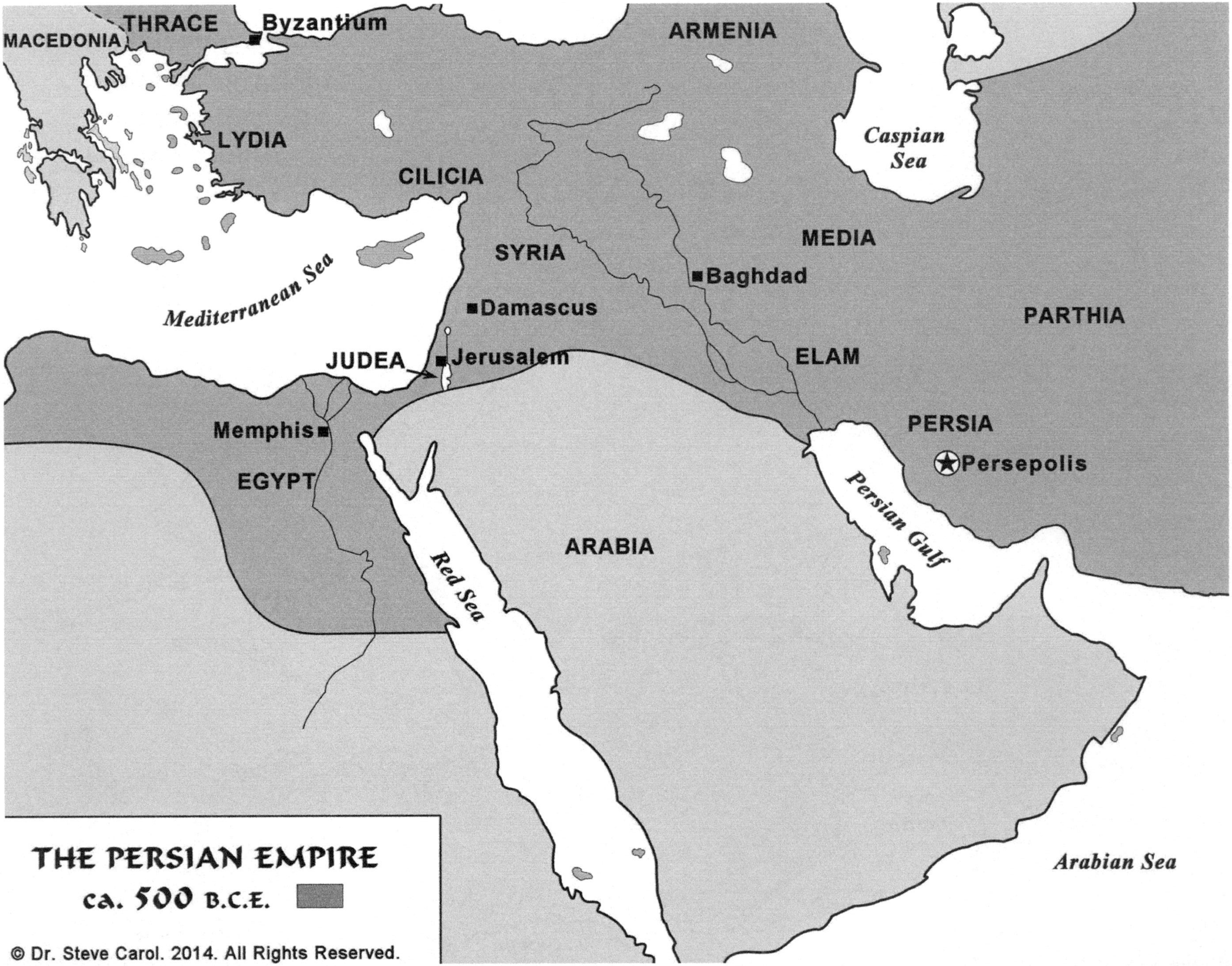

THE PERSIAN EMPIRE
ca. 500 B.C.E.

Labels on map:

Arabian Sea

PARTHIA

Persepolis

PERSIA

Persian Gulf

Caspian Sea

MEDIA

ELAM

Baghdad

ARMENIA

ARABIA

SYRIA

Damascus

Jerusalem

Red Sea

CILICIA

JUDEA

Mediterranean Sea

Byzantium

THRACE

MACEDONIA

LYDIA

Memphis

EGYPT

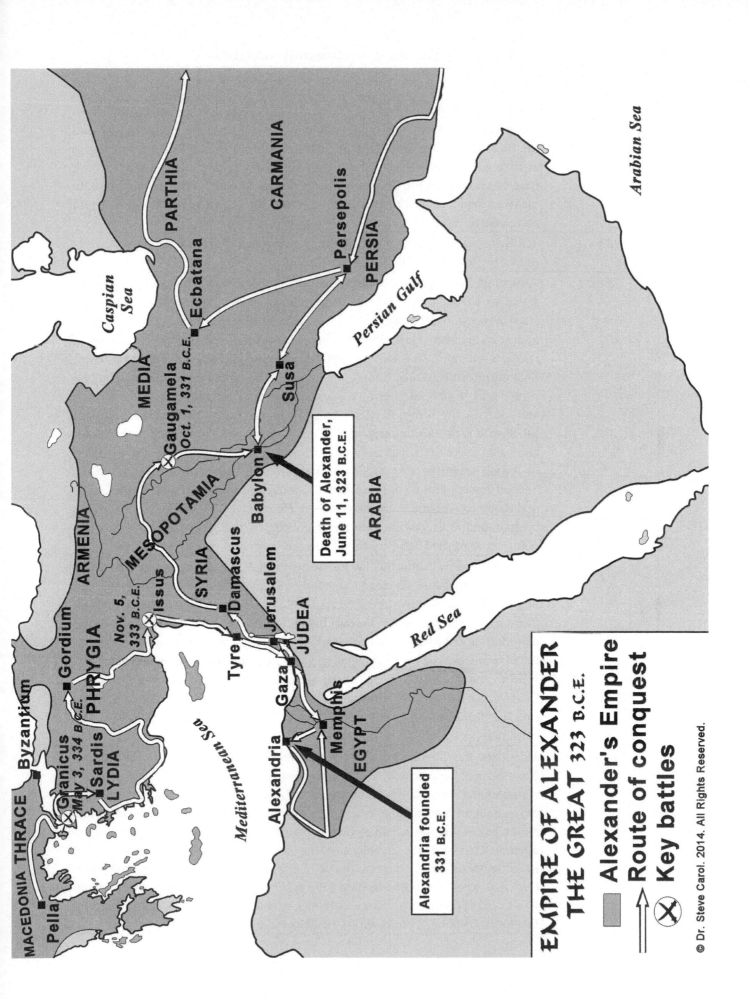

EMPIRE OF ALEXANDER THE GREAT 323 B.C.E.

- Alexander's Empire
- → Route of conquest
- ⊗ Key battles

© Dr. Steve Carol. 2014. All Rights Reserved.

Arabian Sea

Caspian Sea

PARTHIA

CARMANIA

Persepolis

PERSIA

Persian Gulf

Ecbatana

MEDIA

Gaugamela
Oct. 1, 331 B.C.E.

Susa

Babylon

Death of Alexander, June 11, 323 B.C.E.

MESOPOTAMIA

ARMENIA

ARABIA

Issus
Nov. 5, 333 B.C.E.

SYRIA

Damascus

Jerusalem

JUDEA

Tyre

Gaza

Red Sea

Memphis

EGYPT

Alexandria

Alexandria founded 331 B.C.E.

Mediterranean Sea

Byzantium

THRACE

MACEDONIA

Pella

Granicus
May 3, 334 B.C.E.

Gordium

Sardis

LYDIA

PHRYGIA

Date	Event
301 B.C.E.	After the death of Alexander the Great, his empire was divided into three parts—Macedonia, the Seleucid Kingdom (largely Syria, Iraq and parts of Turkey) and the Ptolemaic Kingdom of Egypt. Judea was ruled by the Ptolemys of Egypt at first. The Ptolemys granted the Jews autonomy in domestic matters. Jewish religious and social life flourished. Nevertheless, situated on the border between the two kingdoms, the Land of Israel was militarily contested by Ptolemaic Egypt and Seleucid Syria.
198 B.C.E.	The Seleucid Syrians conquered Judea from Egypt and granted the Jews the right to live by "the laws of their fathers."
175 B.C.E.	Antiochus IV Epiphanes became ruler of the Seleucid Empire. He viewed the Judaeans as being pro-Egyptian, held Judaism in contempt and took deliberate steps between 169 B.C.E. and 167 B.C.E. to Hellenize the Jews of Israel by attempting to destroy Judaism. He banned the observance of the Sabbath, the observance of the New Moon (*Rosh Chodesh*), and the observance of the holidays—Passover, Shavuot, Rosh Hashana, Yom Kippur, and Sukkot. Furthermore, Antiochus IV suppressed Jewish religious practices including circumcision, keeping kosher, and studying the Torah. Women who allowed their sons to be circumcised were killed with their sons tied around their necks. Torah scrolls were publicly burned, and swine were sacrificed over sacred Jewish books to defile them. Possession of Jewish scriptures was made a capital offense. Antiochus IV desecrated the Second Jewish Temple in Jerusalem and converted it into a temple to the Greek god Zeus. Its treasures were confiscated. He removed the High Priest from his position and replaced him with a Hellenized Jew that he controlled. From this point, forward the High Priesthood became, largely, a corrupt institution.
167–142 B.C.E.	These actions by Antiochus IV Epiphanes triggered a revolt and guerrilla war by the Hasmoneans. The revolt was led by Mattathias, a priest from the town of Modi'in, and his five sons, Yehuda (Judah), Yonathan (Jonathan), Shimon (Simon), Yochanan, and Eleazar. Judah was nicknamed *HaMakevet*—"the hammer," and the name came to be applied to the entire Jewish fighting force—the Maccabees. The uprising began as a war for religious freedom and became a war of national liberation against the Seleucid rulers, their Hellenized subjects, in effect a civil war between the Hasmonean forces, and the Hellenized Jews (see the "Middle East at the time of the Hasmonean [Maccabee] Revolt, 165 B.C.E. map.
164 B.C.E.	Jerusalem was liberated by the Hasmoneans. The Second Jewish Temple was cleansed and rededicated. The Jewish festival of Hanukkah is celebrated in commemoration of the Hasmonean revolt, liberation of Jerusalem, rededication of the Second Jewish Temple, and restoration of Judaism to the Land of Israel. Nevertheless, the war would go on for some 25 years as different Seleucid rulers attempted to reconquer Jerusalem and the Land of Israel. In 162 B.C.E. Eleazar fell in battle, thrusting a spear into the belly of a war elephant on which he thought the king was riding, the elephant fell on him crushing him to death. Yehuda was killed at the battle of Elasa in 160 B.C.E. and Yonathan was assassinated by Diodotus Tryphon, a pretender to the Seleucid throne, in 142 B.C.E.

142 B.C.E.	The Greek-Hasmonean War ended, as Seleucid ruler, Demetrius II Nicator, agreed to sign a peace treaty with Shimon, the last survivor of the five sons of Mattathias.
142–37 B.C.E.	The Hasmonean dynasty ruled an independent religious Jewish state in the Land of Israel for some 103 years.

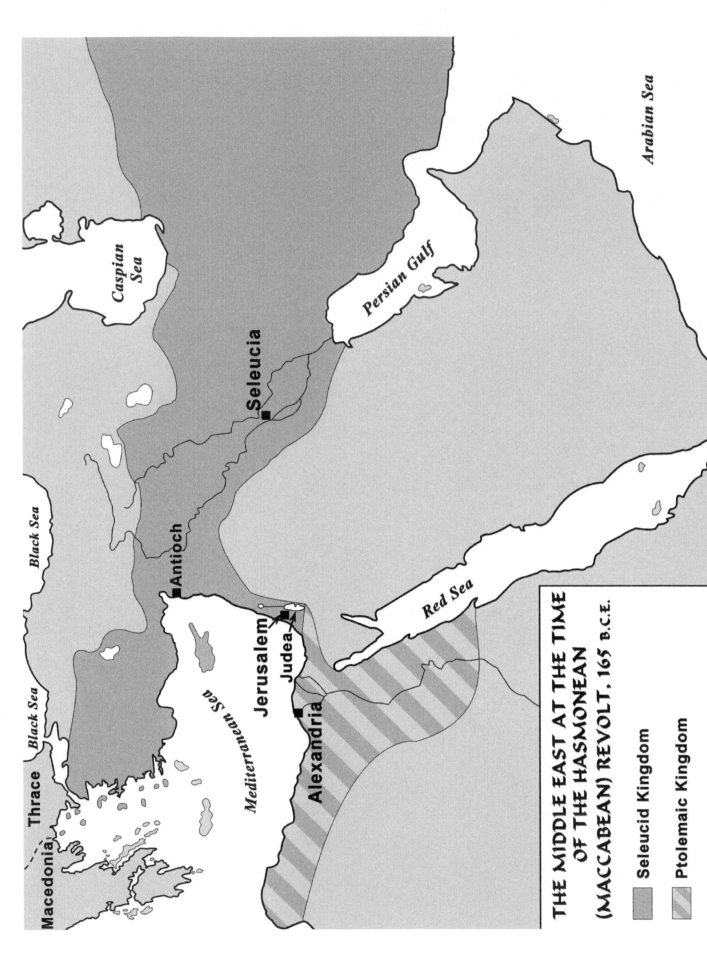

THE MIDDLE EAST AT THE TIME
OF THE HASMONEAN
(MACCABEAN) REVOLT, 165 B.C.E.

Seleucid Kingdom

Ptolemaic Kingdom

Arabian Sea

Caspian
Sea

Persian Gulf

Seleucia

Black Sea

Antioch

Red Sea

Black Sea

Thrace

Mediterranean Sea

Jerusalem

Judea

Macedonia

Alexandria

Date	Event
63 B.C.E.	Roman General Pompey conquered the region, which the Romans named "Judaea." Some 12,000 Jews were slaughtered in Jerusalem alone. From 63 B.C.E. to 44 C.E., Judaea had nominal autonomy within the Roman Empire.
37–4 B.C.E.	King Herod ruled over Judaea as a puppet of the Roman authorities. During his reign, he renovated and expanded the Second Jewish Temple in Jerusalem. He also built the magnificent edifice that is still intact two thousand years later—the Tomb of the Patriarchs atop the Cave of Machpelah in Hebron. It is the burial sites of the Biblical Patriarchs—Abraham, Isaac and Jacob—and Matriarchs—Sarah, Rebecca, and Leah. The Cave of Machpelah also contains the tomb of the first Israelite judge Othniel Ben Kenaz, the tombs of generals and confidants to Kings Saul and David and the tombs of Ruth and Jesse, King David's great-grandmother and his father, respectively. Nevertheless, under Herod, Judaea became a Roman client state.
ca. 20 C.E.	The city of Tiberias was founded on the ruins of a Jewish village. It remained a center of Jewish life for over 1,300 years.
30 C.E.	Jesus was crucified in Jerusalem.
44–46 C.E.	Direct Roman rule was reimposed over Judaea causing unrest among the Jews.
66–73 C.E.	In mid-May 66 C.E., misojudaic riots erupted in Caesarea. Roman troops entered Jerusalem in force. These events triggered the First Jewish Revolt by the Zealots. After driving Roman forces from the city, the Zealots held Jerusalem for four years.
August 2, 70 C.E. (Ninth of Av, 3828, in the Hebrew/ Jewish calendar)	Jerusalem fell to the Roman legions of Emperor Vespasian, led by his son Titus. The Second Jewish Temple was destroyed. Vespasian, gloating over his triumph, ordered the issuance of a series of commemorative coins to celebrate the capture of Judaea and the destruction of the Temple by Titus. The coins bear the legend: *Judaea Capta* ("Judea conquered"). The historian Josephus Flavius in Book 6, Chapter 9 of *The Jewish War,* asserted that some 1.1 million Jews died at the hands of the Romans during the siege and destruction of Jerusalem and another 97,000 were taken captive. Many were either sold into slavery or fed to the lions in the gladiatorial arenas. This was the beginning of the Jewish Diaspora. There was direct Roman rule until 395 C.E. Any remaining Jews were reduced to tenants in their own country. The Temple was not to be rebuilt. Rome levied a tax on all Jews—men, women, children, and the elderly. The tax called *Fiscus Iudaicus* went straight into the Roman Treasury. Only those Jews who abandoned their religion were exempt from paying it.
70–73 C.E.	A band of Jewish Zealots led by Eleazar ben Yair, defied Rome and resisted for another three years atop Masada, an isolated fortified rock plateau overlooking the Dead Sea. Masada fell to the Romans on April 16, 73 C.E., after its defenders committed mass suicide, preferring to die as free men and women rather than live as slaves of Rome. The Diaspora, dating from this time, began a 1,875-year quest to regain Jewish sovereignty and independence.
115–117 C.E.	A second Jewish revolt called the Kitros War or the rebellion of the Diaspora broke out against Rome. It erupted in Cyrene (Cyrenaica) and spread to Egypt, Cyprus, Syria, Mesopotamia, and Judea. The revolt was ruthlessly crushed by Roman legions under the command of general Lusius Quietus, as per the orders of Emperor Trajan. It was a corruption of the general's name that later provided the conflict's name—"Kitos."

132–35 C.E.	In 132 C.E., the third Jewish revolt erupted against the Roman Empire. The revolt was triggered when the Roman Emperor Hadrian forbade the practice of circumcision. It was an attempt by the Jewish sage Rabbi Akiva Ben Joseph and his general Shimon Ben-Kotzivah—better known as Shimon Bar Kokhba—to reestablish Jewish sovereignty over the Land of Israel and rebuild the Holy Temple. The rebellion was triggered in part, by Roman Emperor Hadrian's determination to prevent Jews from living in Jerusalem. At the start of the rebellion a complete Roman legion—the IX Hispania Legion—with auxiliaries was annihilated. The fighting was so intense, that Hadrian had to recall one of his best generals, Sextus Julius Severus from Britain, to quell the uprising. Rome committed no fewer than twelve legions, (at the time there were only twenty-eight legions in the entire Roman Empire), to quell the Jewish determination for independence and reconquer Judaea. Bar Kokhba made his last stand at Betar, southwest of Jerusalem. Betar fell to Roman forces in November or December 135 C.E., and Bar Kokhba was killed (*see* the "Middle East at the time of the Bar Kokhba Rebellion, 132 C.E." map).
135 C.E.	The failure of the Bar Kokhba Rebellion marked the end of autonomous independent Jewish government. Enraged and vindictive, Roman Emperor Hadrian made a determined effort to stamp out Jewish nationhood and statehood. Accordingly, he ordered destroyed 50 Jewish fortresses and 985 villages, as well as slaughtered over 580,000 Jewish fighters in quelling the revolt.[7] The numbers of non-combatant civilians killed is unknown including Jewish children wrapped in Torah scrolls, which were then set ablaze by the Romans.[8] A largely unsuccessful attempt was made to prevent Jews from living in the Land of Israel. Large numbers of Jewish prisoners of war were sold as slaves throughout the empire. Many Jews left or were transported out of the country altogether for the Diaspora communities. Judaean settlements were not rebuilt. The name of the province was changed from Judaea to Syria Palaestina. Jerusalem was turned into a pagan city called Aelia Capitolina and Jews were forbidden to live there. They were permitted to enter the city only once a year on the Ninth of Av to mourn the loss of their Temple and independence. A temple to the Roman god Jupiter was built on the site of the Jewish Temple. Hadrian issued many misojudaic (hatred of Jews) decrees forbidding prayer on the Temple Mount, Torah study, Sabbath observance, circumcision, Jewish courts, meeting in synagogues and other ritual practices.
135–400 C.E.	Nevertheless, Jewish life thrived in the Galilee and Tiberias. *Ha Talmud shel Eretz Yisrael* ("The Talmud of the Land of Israel")—more commonly known as the Jerusalem Talmud)—an ancient work of Jewish instruction and law, was completed in Tiberias, ca. 390 C.E.
ca. 210 C.E.	The Mishnah (Oral Law) was also edited and completed in Tiberias.
313–636 C.E.	The Christian Byzantine Empire ruled over the Land of Israel (*see* the "Middle East, 400 C.E." map).

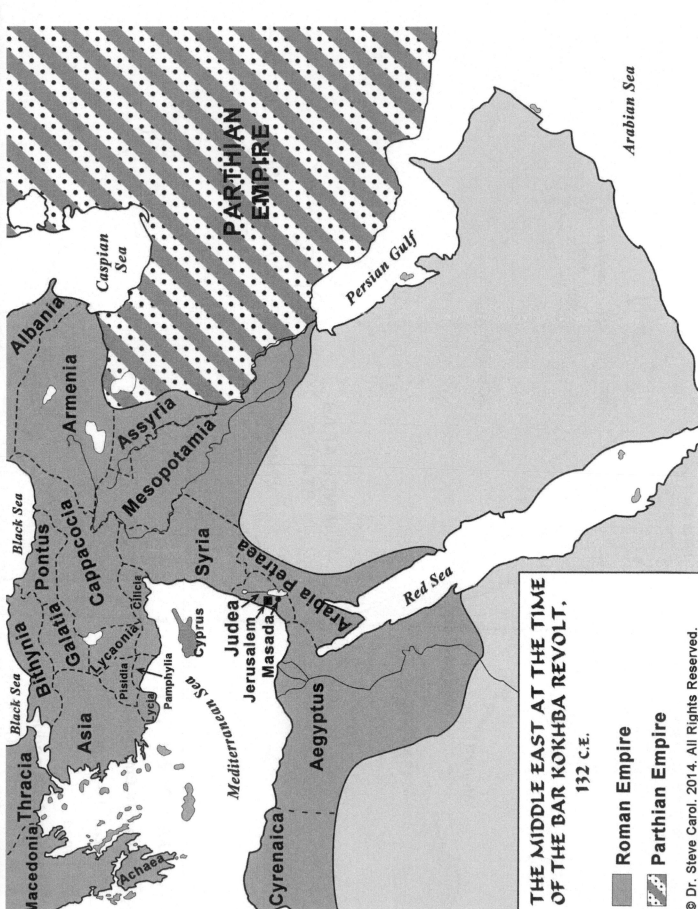

THE MIDDLE EAST AT THE TIME
OF THE BAR KOKHBA REVOLT,
132 C.E.

■ Roman Empire

▨ Parthian Empire

© Dr. Steve Carol. 2014. All Rights Reserved.

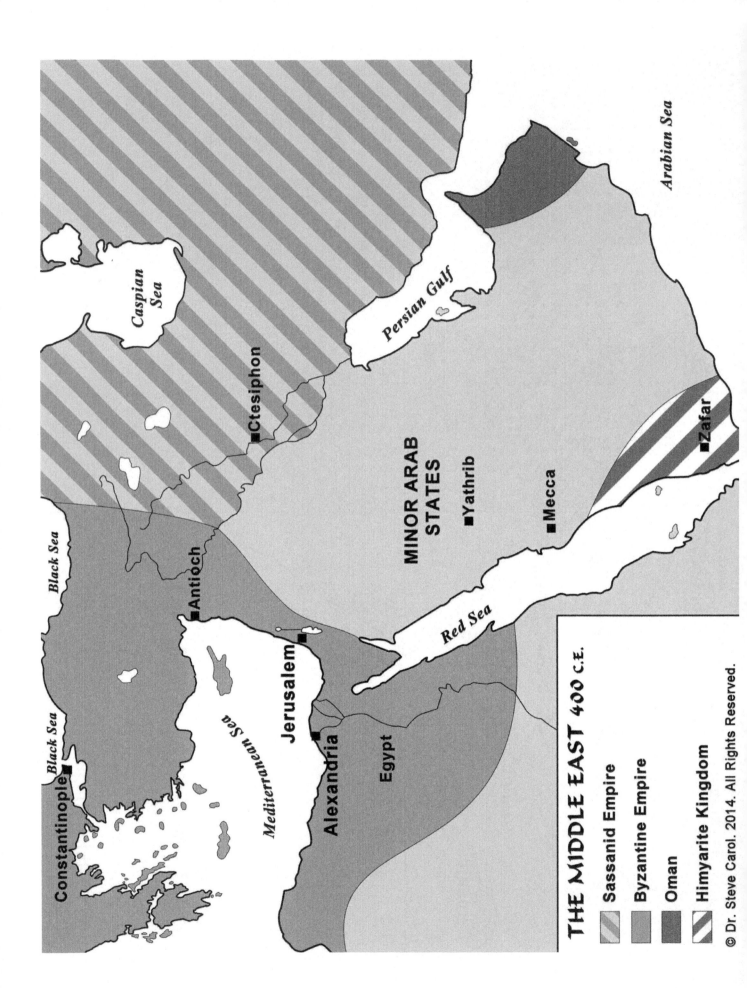

THE MIDDLE EAST 400 C.E.

Sassanid Empire

Byzantine Empire

Oman

Himyarite Kingdom

© Dr. Steve Carol. 2014. All Rights Reserved.

MINOR ARAB
STATES

■Yathrib

■Mecca

■Zafar

■Ctesiphon

■Antioch

Jerusalem

Alexandria

Egypt

Constantinople

Black Sea

Black Sea

Caspian
Sea

Persian Gulf

Arabian Sea

Red Sea

Mediterranean Sea

Date	Event
351–352 C.E.	Due to misojudaic persecution, encouraged by Byzantine Emperor Constantius II and his Caesar of the East Galius, another Jewish revolt occurred in Sepphoris (present day Tzippori) in the Galilee and spread to Lydda before being suppressed.
February 4, 362 C.E.	Roman Emperor Julian II promulgated an edict to guarantee freedom of religion, which applied to Jews as well. This edict proclaimed that all the religions were equal before the law. He allowed Jews to live in Jerusalem again. In 363 C.E., he ordered the Jewish Temple rebuilt and funds were appropriated for that task. However, growing Christian Jerusalemite hostility to the project, coupled with the Galilee earthquake of May 18–19, 363 C.E., as well as Julian's sudden death in battle with the Persians, June 26, 363 C.E. caused the project to be cancelled. The next emperor Jovian restored Christianity as the state religion and abrogated Julian's edicts.
484 C.E.	Persecuted by Byzantine Emperor Zeno, the Samaritans, a Jewish sect, began a revolt in Shechem (Neapolis) in Samaria, which was suppressed. The Samaritans were banned from their sacred Mount Gerizim.
495 C.E.	A second Samaritan revolt erupted against Byzantine Emperor Anastasius I. The Samaritans regained Mount Gerizim but were crushed subsequently by Byzantine forces.
ca. 499 C.E.	The *Gemara* (the section of the Talmud comprising rabbinical analysis of and commentary on the *Mishnah*) was edited and finished and thus completed the "Babylonian" Talmud.
529–31 C.E.	The Samaritans, seeking independence from Byzantine rule, revolted for a third time. They were led by Julianus ben Sabar, who proclaimed himself "King of Israel." Emperor Justinian I ruthlessly crushed the revolt killing and enslaving tens of thousands. He banned the Samaritan faith.
ca. July 555	The fourth Samaritan revolt against Byzantine rule began in the city of Caesarea. Jews and Samaritans were allied in this revolt, which spread as far as Bethlehem. Nevertheless, it was crushed by the Byzantines.
May 613–14	During the Byzantine–Sassanid Persian War (602–28), some 30,000 Jews, led by Nehemiah ben Hushiel and allied with Persian King Khosrau II, revolted against Byzantine Emperor Heraclius. The rebellion originated in Tiberias and the Jews captured Jerusalem. Plans were made to rebuild the Jewish Temple.
614–28	Persian invasion and rule over the Land of Israel. Jewish autonomy was established which lasted only until 617, when the Persians abandoned the Jews after making peace with the Byzantines.
629	The Byzantines, under Emperor Heraclius, reconquered Jerusalem and again expelled its Jewish inhabitants. The Persians were finally defeated but for the Byzantines it was a pyrrhic victory. Having been so weakened by decades of war, the region was easy prey for the rising Islamic empire.
636	The Muslim Rashidun army from the Arabian Peninsula invaded the Land of Israel. Jerusalem was besieged from November 636 to April 637 before it surrendered to Caliph Umar ibn Al-Khattab. The Arabs seized Jewish property and drove the Jewish inhabitants off their land. Furthermore, the Muslim conquerors brought in additional Arabs to colonize, Arabize and Islamize the region.

661–750	The Land of Israel was conquered and ruled by the Umayyad Caliphate.
750–969	The Land of Israel was conquered and ruled by the Abbasid Caliphate.
969–1071	Fatimid conquest and rule over the Land of Israel.
1071–99	The Seljuk Turks conquered and ruled the Land of Israel.
1099–1187	The Crusaders captured Jerusalem on July 15, 1099, and established the Crusader Kingdom of Jerusalem. After making a truce with Saladin, the Crusaders maintained a presence in the Land of Israel via a series of fortified castles.
1187–1250	The Ayyubid dynasty, founded by Saladin, conquered and ruled the Land of Israel. Jerusalem fell to Saladin's forces on October 2, 1187.
1211	A wave of Jews returned to the Land of Israel, led by 300 prominent rabbis from Europe.
1244	Jerusalem was sacked by the Khwarezmian Tartars, who decimated the city's Christian population and drove out the Jews.
1250–1517	The Mamelukes invaded from the south and ruled the Land of Israel.
September 3, 1260	The Mongol invasion of the Land of Israel was stopped at the Battle of Ain Jalut by Mameluke forces in the Jezreel Valley of the Galilee. It marked the high-water mark of Mongol conquests and was the first time a Mongol advance was permanently beaten back in direct combat.
May 19, 1291	The Mameluke Sultan of Egypt al-Ashraf Khalil captured Acre, the last Christian outpost in the Land of Israel, and the era of the Crusades was over.
ca. 1500	The city of Safed became a thriving center of Jewish life and the center of Jewish mysticism.
1517–1917	The Ottoman Turks from the north invaded, conquered and ruled the Land of Israel.
1520–1625	Jews continued to return to the Land of Israel in large numbers despite increasingly harsh treatment by the Ottoman authorities.
1558	Jews began the reconstruction of Tiberius as a center of Jewish life, with the approval of the Turkish sultan.
1860	Jews built the first neighborhood outside the walls of the Old City of Jerusalem.
1864	Jews were the majority once again, in their ancient capital, Jerusalem.
1870	Mikveh Yisrael began as the first modern agricultural settlement in the Land of Israel.
1882–1903	The First *Aliyah*—the ingathering of exiles—took place. Some Jewish pioneers began to farm land they purchased in the Horan region of the Golan Heights (1898) until the Turks evicted them. Their land was then seized illegally.

1890	The Hebrew Language Committee (*Va'ad ha-lashon ha-'Ivrit*) was established in Jerusalem. At that time, the Hebrew language had been used only as a religious language for some 2,500 years of the Jewish Diaspora. There were virtually no native speakers during that period. It was revived in the late nineteenth century in the Land of Israel, largely through the tireless efforts of Eliezer Ben-Yehuda to its status as an active living language with 6.5 million speakers worldwide. Ben-Yehuda correctly assessed that the revival of the Hebrew language in the Land of Israel could unite all Jews worldwide and that Hebrew and Zionism were symbiotic. In 1910, Ben-Yehuda began publishing the *Dictionary of Ancient and Modern Hebrew*. The 17-volume dictionary was completed by his son in 1959. The Hebrew language was fully modernized and used as the daily vernacular in Israel for all purposes. To date, no other ancient language in the world was similarly revived.
1891	Baron Rothschild purchased around 18,000 acres in what is present-day Ramat Magshimim, a town on the Golan Heights. Earlier in the nineteenth century members of the Bnei Yehuda society from Safed purchased land on the Golan, while it was under Turkish control.
1896	Theodor Herzl published his book, *Der Judenstaat* ("The State of the Jews") in which he called for the establishment of an independent sovereign state for the Jewish people.
August 29–31, 1897	Herzl organized the First Zionist Congress in Basel, Switzerland. There he expounded his vision of a Jewish state, inaugurating the modern political movement for the re-attainment of Jewish sovereignty in the Land of Israel. As a result, the Zionist Organization was founded.
December 29, 1901	At the Fifth Zionist Congress in Basel, Switzerland, *Keren Kayemet LeYisrael*—the Jewish National Fund (JNF)—was formed. Its purpose was to purchase land for Jewish settlement in the Land of Israel, then under Ottoman rule. The JNF restored forests, drained swamps, and irrigated dry land.
1904–1914	The Second *Aliyah*—ingathering of exiles—took place.
April 11, 1909	The city of Tel Aviv was founded on the outskirts of the ancient port city of Jaffa.
October 29, 1910	The first rural *kibbutz*, Degania, was established along the southern shore of the Sea of Galilee.
April 11, 1912	The cornerstone was laid in Haifa, for the first university in the Land of Israel, the Technion—the Israel Institute of Technology.
November 2, 1917	The United Kingdom issued the Balfour Declaration calling for the establishment of a Jewish National Home in their ancient homeland—the Land of Israel (*see* Appendix 2).
1917	As a result of Arab riots, Jewish self-defense was organized in Jerusalem.
1917–20	During World War I in the Middle East, the British Empire invaded and conquered the area. British forces, led by General Edmund Allenby, took Beersheba on October 31, 1917, Gaza on November 7, Jaffa on November 16, and Jerusalem on December 10. Palestine was under British military occupation for the next three years until 1920.
February 1919	At the Paris Peace Conference, the Zionist World Organization submitted its first territorial plan for the establishment of a Jewish homeland (*see* "Zionist Plan for Palestine" map). The plan was rejected.

ZIONIST PLAN FOR THE JEWISH STATE, FEBRUARY 1919

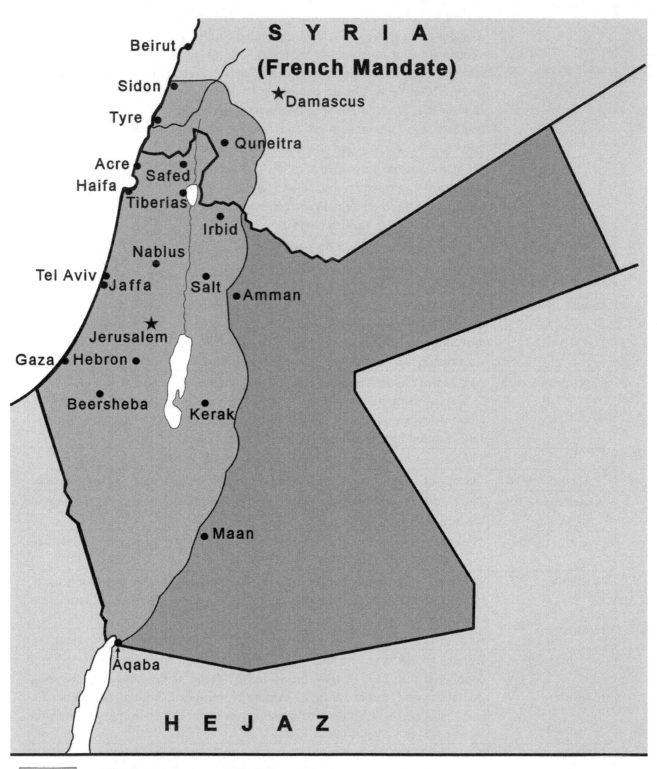

S Y R I A
(French Mandate)

★ Damascus

Beirut

Sidon

Tyre

Quneitra

Acre

Safed

Haifa

Tiberias

Irbid

Nablus

Tel Aviv

Jaffa

Salt

Amman

★ Jerusalem

Gaza ● Hebron ●

Beersheba

Kerak

Maan

Aqaba

H E J A Z

February 1919
Zionist plan for the Jewish State

Date	Event
1919–23	The Third *Aliyah* took place.
March 1–April 25, 1920	The Arabs launched misojudaic attacks against the Jewish Quarter of the Old City of Jerusalem and eight Jewish towns including Tel Hai, Kfar Giladi, Degania and Rosh Pina. This included the Nebi Musa riots in Jerusalem of April 4–7, in which five Jews were killed and 216 were wounded. Four other communities, including Bnei Yehuda and Hamara, had to be abandoned. These attacks spurred Jewish determination to become self-reliant, establish an autonomous infrastructure and a defense organization.
April 24–25, 1920	The San Remo Conference assigned the United Kingdom a mandate over Palestine, which extended from the desert of Mesopotamia (modern Iraq) in the east to the Mediterranean Sea in the west. The primary purpose of the mandate was to facilitate the establishment of a Jewish National Home in their ancient homeland. Modern Israel's international legal basis originated at the San Remo Conference and the Resolution passed on April 25, 1920. The resolution had the force of law upon its being incorporated first, in the Treaty of Sèvres of August 10, 1920 and then confirmed by the Council of the League of Nations on July 24, 1922, in the Mandate for Palestine which charged the British government with administering the area (from the Jordan River to the Mediterranean Sea) earmarked as the future independent Jewish state. Though the League of Nations Mandate for Palestine has expired, the rights derived from it remain in full force and effect under both international law and Israeli law.

As the author of *The Legal Foundation and Borders of Israel under International Law,* Howard Grief, concluded:

> Once international law in the form of the San Remo Resolution recognized that *de jure* sovereignty over all regions of historical Palestine and the Land of Israel had been vested in the Jewish People, neither the Supreme Council of the Principal Allied Powers nor the Council of the League of Nations nor its successor, the United Nations, could thereafter revoke or alter Jewish sovereignty by a new decision.[9]

Thus, by the action of the San Remo Conference, legal ownership or title to the Land of Israel was transferred to the Jewish people in perpetuity. This means no international organizations possess the legal right to deprive the Jewish people from this land, for if they did, the sovereignty of every state in the world to its territory would be jeopardized by such supranational bodies.

Date	Event
June 12, 1920	Due to Arab riots and attacks, the *Yishuv*—the Jewish community in the British Mandate of Palestine—formed an underground militia called the *Haganah,* literally, "defense," for protection. The *Haganah* pursued a policy of *havlaga* (restraint). It prescribed non-retaliation except under direct attack. As a result of this policy, the Arabs were always sure of the initiative and never suffered any counter-attack.

December 1920	The *Histadrut*—the General Federation of Workers in the Land of Israel—labor organization came into being.
March 12–23, 1921	The United Kingdom hosted the Cairo Conference on the Middle East. As a result of a decision reached, later that year the United Kingdom unilaterally detached and then created Transjordan on 77.5 percent (35,468 square miles) of the original mandate land (which had totaled 46,339 square miles). This was the First Partition of Palestine.
May 1–November 7, 1921	Arab misojudaic attacks began in Jaffa and spread to six main Jewish towns including Rehovot, Kfar Saba, Petah Tikva, and Hadera. The riots resulted in the deaths of 47 Jews and 48 Arabs. 146 Jews and 73 Arabs were wounded. In November, Arab attacks occurred against the Jewish Quarter of Jerusalem. In a foolhardy attempt to appease the Arabs, the British High Commissioner, Sir Herbert Samuel, appointed Islamic supremacist Hajj Amin al-Husseini, as Grand Mufti of Jerusalem (May 10). As a further sop to the Arabs, the British suspended temporarily Jewish immigration into the British Mandate of Palestine.
September 11, 1921	The first *moshav,* Nahalal, was established in the Jezreel Valley.
December 1921	A Supreme Muslim Council was formed and charged with supervising the *Waqf** (Muslim religious trust) and shari'a law. Hajj Amin al-Husseini was granted the post of president of this council. From his two positions of leadership, Husseini was able to foment and incite opposition as well as violence against the *Yishuv.*

As the result of the 1920–21 riots, the Arabs learned an important lesson. Maintaining uncompromising political positions and coupling them with violence, brought them unexpected, agreeable and beneficial results in a comparatively short period. In later years, the violence escalated into terrorism. These tactics would be repeated with a good deal of success to the present day.

Date	Event
September 21, 1922	President Warren G. Harding signed into law a unanimously passed Joint Resolution of the Sixty-Seventh Congress Second session, recognizing a future Jewish state in "the whole of Palestine."
September 29, 1922	The League of Nations officially accepted the British Mandate over Palestine.
March 7, 1923	The United Kingdom approved the transfer of the Golan Heights from the British Mandate of Palestine to the French Mandate of Syria under a Franco-British agreement delineating the boundary between the two mandates.
1924–28	The Fourth *Aliyah* took place.
April 1, 1925	Founded in 1918, the Hebrew University campus was opened on Mount Scopus in Jerusalem.

---

* A religious endowment or trust in Islam, typically denoting a building, piece of property, for example the Temple Mount in Jerusalem, or even cash for Muslim religious or charitable purposes.

April 25, 1925	Vladimir (Ze'ev) Jabotinsky founded the Union of Revisionist Zionists (*Hatzohar*), commonly known as the Revisionist Movement. Jabotinsky advocated the "revision" of Labor Zionist guidelines to include the use of force if necessary, to secure a Jewish state within the boundaries of the original British Mandate of Palestine.
August 23–30, 1929	The Grand Mufti of Jerusalem, Hajj Amin al-Husseini, instigated a new wave of Arab misojudaic violence across Palestine, spreading rumors and propaganda, such as the rumor the Jews planned to destroy the Dome of the Rock and the Al-Aqsa Mosque. With cries of *Itbah al-Yahudi* ("Slaughter the Jews"), Arabs attacked and massacred Jews throughout the British Mandate territory. The Jewish community in the biblical town of Hebron was nearly annihilated, 67 being killed, 58 injured and survivors driven out. Upon visiting Hebron after the massacre, the British High Commissioner for Palestine, John Chancellor, wrote to his son, "I do not think that history records many worse horrors in the last few hundred years. I am so tired and disgusted with this country and everything concerned with it that I only want to leave it as soon as I can."[10] For the next thirty-eight years (until Israel's victory in the Six-Day War), no Jews were allowed to live or pray in Hebron. Attacks on other Jewish communities in Jerusalem, Safed, Tel Aviv, Hulda, Beer Ruvia, Bet Alfa and elsewhere, resulted in a total of 133 dead and 339 wounded by Arab mobs.[11] Seven Jewish communities were abandoned, including Shiloah, which in modern times was inhabited by Jews since 1882. The British Mandatory authorities suppressed the violence, killing 110 Arabs. The British Shaw Commission ignored evidence of the Mufti's orchestration of the carnage and recommended reducing Jewish immigration, thus blaming the victims—the Jews—for the murderous Arab pogrom unleashed against them. This pattern of blaming the Jewish victims would continue to the present.
1929–39	The Fifth *Aliyah* took place.
1930–35	Due to the deteriorating economic and political situation in Europe, Jewish immigration to British Mandatory Palestine increased. Between 1930 and 1934, 91,258 immigrants arrived. In 1935 alone, a record influx of 61,854 Jews entered.[12]
April 10, 1931	The National Military Organization in the Land of Israel—*Ha'Irgun H'Tzva'i HaLe'umi BeEretz Yisrael,* abbreviated as *Irgun* and commonly referred to as *Etzel,* (an acronym of the Hebrew initials)—was formed. It was largely in negation to the *Haganah's* policy of *havlaga* ("restraint") that the *Irgun* was established. From 1931 to 1948, the *Irgun* was a pro-active Jewish underground paramilitary group that fought the British across Mandatory Palestine as well as protected the *Yishuv* from Arab attacks.

May 19, 1931	Bowing to Arab pressure, the British Mandatory government issued a King's Order in Council, which banned Jews from blowing the shofar at the Western Wall, despite the fact that this ceremony is an integral part of the Rosh Hashana (Jewish New Year), and Yom Kippur (Day of Atonement) prayer services. The ban deeply offended Jews, and the *Irgun* decided to act. After the imposition of the ban, *Irgun* and Betar (the Revisionist Zionist youth movement) members "smuggled" a shofar into the Western Wall area every Yom Kippur. There a volunteer was waiting to blow the *Tekiah Gedola*, the long blast that marks the end of the fast. This was not easily done, since large numbers of British police officers were stationed along the routes to the Wall and conducted careful searches of the belongings of the Jews visiting the Wall. The shofar blower was usually arrested and jailed.
1934–48	*Aliyah Bet* was an effort to rescue and bring to Mandatory Palestine, European Jews who escaped the persecution of many fascist regimes, and then fled from the ravages of World War II as well as the Holocaust. At the conclusion of the war, the effort concentrated on seeking to circumvent British restrictions and naval patrols to transport the remnants of European Jewry to Mandatory Palestine. Both the *Irgun* and the *Haganah* (the latter only after 1938) were engaged in this clandestine immigration. While some refugees entered Mandatory Palestine by land, the majority attempted to reach their destination by sea. There were 142 voyages by 120 ships, many of which the Royal Navy intercepted and the passengers interned in camps in Cyprus and Mauritius. Some vessels were sunk with large loss of life; most notably the SS *Patria* and the MV *Struma* (*see* below for SS *Patria* and *see* "Basic Principle 36" assassination of Lord Moyne, for details about the MV *Struma*). Both of those sinkings served as rallying points for the *Irgun* and *Lohamei Herut Yisrael* ("Fighters for the Freedom of Israel"—better known by its Hebrew acronym *LEHI*), encouraging their active revolt against the British presence in Mandatory Palestine. *Aliyah Bet* was a powerful unifying and moral weapon used to focus the need for a Jewish state.
September 7–12, 1935	The Revisionist Movement, headed by Vladimir (Ze'ev) Jabotinsky, seceded from the World Zionist Organization and established the New Zionist Organization.
April 15, 1936– November 1936	Opposing Jewish immigration into Mandatory Palestine and sensing British weakness in response to the Italian conquest of Ethiopia, reaction to the Spanish Civil War, and the aggressive acts of Nazi Germany in the Rhineland, the Grand Mufti of Jerusalem, Hajj Amin al-Husseini, launched what was termed the "Arab revolt." Al-Husseini (who had a pathological hatred of Jews), formed and led the Arab Higher Committee. The rebellion began with the murder of Jews traversing the Nablus–Tulkarem road (April 15, 1936), and was followed by incitement as well as calls for violence. Riots broke out in Jaffa (April 19–20) and was followed by a general strike by the Arabs, which lasted until October 12, 1936, when it was suppressed by the British. The rioting and destruction by organized Arab gangs swept across the British Mandate territory. There were acts of sabotage and attacks against British officials as well as military forces. Additionally, civilian Jews were murdered, property destroyed, and orchards burned. In this first phase of the rebellion, there were 985 Arab casualties, including 187 dead. The Jews suffered 388 casualties including 21 dead.[13]

July 7, 1937	In reaction to the first phase of the Arab revolt, the Peel Commission Report recommended for the first time, that Western Palestine be partitioned into Jewish and Arab states. The plan offered 18.4 percent of Western Palestine to the Jews and 81.6 percent to the Arabs. Nevertheless, the Arabs totally rejected the plan (*see* "The Peel Commission Partition Plan, July 7, 1937" map). The Arab revolt continued. During 1938, there were 3,717 casualties, including 69 British, 92 Jewish, and 486 Arab dead, all killed by Arab terrorism. The Arab terrorists killed in response numbered 1,138.[14]
August 1937– September 1, 1939	A second more violent phase of the Arab revolt began in August 1937 and lasted until the outbreak of World War II. Between August 29 and November 11, 1937, there was a surge of Arab attacks on Jews included shootings, stabbings and bombings. Additionally, on September 26, 1937, the British district commissioner for the Galilee, Lewis Yelland Andrews, was shot to death by Arabs associated with Grand Mufti Hajj Amin al-Husseini and the Arab Higher Committee. Both arms and funding for the Arabs flowed into Mandatory Palestine from Nazi Germany. Arab attacks continued and forced the evacuation of Jewish communities in Silwan, Jerusalem, Beisan, and Acre. At the same time, followers of Hajj Amin al-Husseini liquidated most of the Palestinian political opposition, especially the Nashashibi and Nusseibeh clans. In light of the on-going Arab violence and terror against the *Yishuv*, it became obvious that the policy of *havlaga* ("passive defense") was not a deterrent. For the *Yishuv,* passive defense could only end in defeat and destruction.* Therefore, by November 1937, the *Irgun* adopted a policy of *teguva* ("active defense") based on the old adage, "the best defense is a good offense," as well as the biblical admonition of "an eye for an eye"—*ayin tachat ayin.*[15] The United Kingdom bolstered its forces in Mandatory Palestine and it took some 50,000 British troops to suppress the Arab revolt. The cost was high. British security services suffered 262 killed, and some 55 wounded. The Jews sustained some 300 killed and 4 were executed by British authorities. The Arabs lost about 5,000 killed, 15,000 wounded (many in intra-Arab fighting) and 108 were executed by British authorities. Additionally, 12,622 were imprisoned.
October 1, 1937	Five Arab leaders were arrested and deported to the Seychelles islands, and the Arab Higher Committee was outlawed. The Grand Mufti Hajj Amin al-Husseini was deposed from the presidency of the Muslim Supreme Council and fearing arrest, fled to Beirut, Lebanon.

---

* As mentioned above, Arab violence and attacks met by passive defense stimulated appeasement and yielded valuable political rewards for them. The 1920–21 attacks resulted in the First Partition of the Mandate of Palestine in 1921, excluding Jewish immigration and settlement from some 77 percent of the original mandate. The 1936–39 Arab revolt resulted in the MacDonald White Paper of May 1939, which curbed and then ended Jewish immigration as well as limited the sale of land to Jews in the remainder of Mandatory Palestine.

May 17, 1939	With war clouds looming in Europe and mindful of its need for Middle East oil as well as the usage of the Suez Canal, the British government sought to appease the Arab states and the Arab population of Palestine, hoping to retain their loyalty towards the United Kingdom. Thus, the British government approved the MacDonald White Paper (named after British Colonial Secretary, Malcolm MacDonald), which severely restricted Jewish immigration into Palestine to no more than 15,000 per year for the next five years. After that, Jewish immigration would occur only with Arab consent. The purchase of land by Jews was prohibited in some areas and restricted in others. By these moves, the British in effect, cancelled the Balfour Declaration and unilaterally contravened the League of Nations Mandate pledging a Jewish national homeland. Though according to its terms the Arabs would be in total control of Palestine after ten years, the Arabs nevertheless, totally rejected the MacDonald White Paper insisting they be given control immediately.
September 1, 1939	Formal hostilities in World War II began with the Nazi German invasion of Poland, and the subsequent British and French declarations of war against Germany (September 3). The Jewish Agency in Palestine, through their leader David Ben-Gurion declared, "We shall fight in the war against Hitler, as if there were no White Paper, and we shall fight the White Paper as if there were no war."[16] Palestinian Jews declared wholehearted support for the United Kingdom's war against Nazi Germany as subsequently some 119,000 registered to serve in the British armed forces, in any capacity.
1939–47	Jewish underground militias struggled and fought in opposition to British restrictions against Jewish immigration and overall rule.
July 17, 1940	*Lohamei Herut Yisrael* ("Fighters for the Freedom of Israel") was founded and led by Avraham ("Yair") Stern. Known by its Hebrew acronym *LEHI*, it was a small radical group that broke away (for tactical reasons) from the *Irgun,* to pursue the struggle for national liberation from the British in Palestine. The British derogatorily labeled it as the "Stern Gang." The primary difference between the *Irgun* and *LEHI* was its intention to fight the British in Palestine, regardless of their war against Germany. *LEHI* was opposed to all negotiations with the British. Later, additional operational and ideological differences developed that contradicted some of the *Irgun's* guiding principles.
September 9, 1940	Germany's Axis partner Italy bombed Tel Aviv killing 112.
November 25, 1940	In early November 1940, the Royal Navy intercepted three clandestine immigrant ships, SS *Pacific*, SS *Milos* and SS *Atlantic*, which carried Jewish refugees from Nazi-occupied Europe and forced them into Haifa harbor. There, the refugees were forcibly transferred to SS *Patria,* which the British authorities planned to use to deport them from Mandatory Palestine to Mauritius because they lacked entry permits. In an attempt to prevent the British action, the *Haganah,* planted a bomb inside the ship, hoping to blow a small hole in it to allow for the evacuation of the refugees. The blast was more powerful than anticipated and the ship sank in 16 minutes. Of 1,770 refugees aboard, 217 refugees, as well as 50 crew and British soldiers were killed and 172 were wounded.

1941	The Grand Mufti of Jerusalem, Hajj Amin al-Husseini, continued to solicit German aid and intervention on behalf of the Arabs. He lavished praise on Adolf Hitler. In his letter to Hitler on January 20, 1941, the Mufti described the German Führer as a descendent of Muhammad and the savior of Islam. In response to repeated requests by the Mufti, the Germans promised assistance to him and the Arabs. In a cable sent (February 17, 1941) from the office of the *Führer* and *Reichskanzler* Adolf Hitler, the Germans declared, "Germany's fundamental attitude to your questions is quite clear. The merciless fight (without compromise) against world Jewry and (the struggle for) the ultimate destruction of the Jewish national home in Palestine is plainly written on the banner of the Third Reich. The German aim is basically the final destruction of all the Jews living within Arab territories. Germany will provide positive and practical aid to the Arabs who are engaged in the same battle aimed at the total extermination of the entire Jewish people.–Adolf Hitler." The Mufti believed the Axis would win the war. In subsequent correspondence as well as his personal meeting with Hitler on November 28, 1941, he secured a commitment from both Germany and Italy to the formation of a region-wide Arab state. He also asked permission to solve the Jewish problem by the "same method that will be applied for the solution of the Jewish problem in the Axis states" i.e. extermination.[17]
May 9, 1941	The Grand Mufti fled arrest in Mandatory Palestine and arrived in Iraq to assist in a pro-Axis coup there. From Baghdad, he called for a jihad against the British. When the British intervened to secure Iraq, the Mufti fled to Berlin where he continued his collaboration with the Nazis for the entire war. He raised thousands of Muslim troops in Africa, Asia and Europe to fight with the Axis and carry out their genocidal program against Jews and Slavs, especially in the Balkans.
June 7–8, 1941	The Free French with British support invaded Syria and Lebanon from Mandatory Palestine, in an effort to break Vichy power in a key region of the Middle East. Palestinian Jewish Palmach units took part in the invasion, during which Moshe Dayan lost his left eye. Some 30,000 Palestinian Jews fought against Nazi Germany during the war.
October 1942	As the German *Afrikakorps* led by General Erwin Rommel neared the Suez Canal in Egypt, the Nazi high command established "Einsatzgruppe Egypt," based in Athens and headed by SS Colonel Walther Rauff. Rauff had perfected the use of mobile gas chambers in the Nazi conquest of Eastern Europe. As part of Rommel's advancing army in North Africa, Rauff was empowered to carry out "executive measures on the civilian population," the Nazi euphemism for mass murder and enslavement. Plans were laid for the extermination of the entire *Yishuv* in British Mandatory Palestine as well as Jews elsewhere in the Middle East. Extermination camps were planned near Tunis, Baghdad and Jericho.[18] The Grand Mufti Hajj Amin al-Husseini planned to install a gas chamber and crematorium complex in the Dothan Valley near Nablus/Shechem in Samaria, once it was conquered by Axis forces. However, the Nazi plans were thwarted following the Axis' defeat in the Second Battle of El Alamein, by November 11, 1942.

May 1943–March 30, 1944	The Mufti Hajj Amin al-Husseini in Berlin made repeated requests that the German *Luftwaffe* bomb Jerusalem and Tel Aviv, as being the two most heavily Jewish populated cities in Mandatory Palestine.[19] He specified that the Jewish Agency headquarters in Jerusalem be bombed as it served as a provisional government of the *Yishuv*. He even suggesting a date—November 2, 1943, the anniversary of the Balfour Declaration. The Germans only refused because they had more pressing military issues.
February 1, 1944	The *Irgun,* at that time led by Menachem Begin, proclaimed a revolt against the British mandatory government in Palestine. Posters were put up all around the country, stating that all of the Zionist movements would continue to support the Allied Forces (fighting in World War II) and over 25,000 Jews had enlisted in the British military up to that time. The hope to establish a Jewish army had died, while throughout the war the Arabs of the Middle East favored and supported the Axis side. European Jewry was trapped and was being destroyed in the Holocaust. Yet the United Kingdom, for its part, did not allow any rescue missions or admission of Jews to Palestine, as per the White Paper. When the revolt began, the *Irgun* stipulated two restricting conditions: avoidance of individual terror as a method and postponement of attacks on military targets until the war ended. The first attacks by the *Irgun* were against symbols of British power and repression. They successfully bombed the empty buildings, in Jerusalem, Tel Aviv, and Haifa, that housed the British Mandatory government immigration offices (February 12); the income tax offices (February 27); and the British Intelligence and police offices (March 23). In all cases, warnings were posted before the attacks.
September 27, 1944	Prior to Yom Kippur (5705/1944), the *Irgun* posted no less than nine warnings that any British officer who interfered with the blowing of the shofar at the Western Wall at the end of Yom Kippur prayers—an act of rebellious significance carried out by young men of the Betar movement since it was banned in 1931—would be "regarded as a criminal and … be punished accordingly." On September 27, when Yom Kippur prayers ended at the Western Wall, British security forces did not burst forth as they had the year prior. The shofar was blown and no one interfered. It was the "trumpet of revolt," Menachem Begin later wrote. That night, the *Irgun* assaulted police "Tegart" forts in Haifa, Qalqilya, Gedera-Tel Qatra and Beit Dagan. This demonstration of the *Irgun*'s political sophistication and strength helped undermine British morale.
October 6, 1944	Again at the Mufti's urging, the German military high command, agreed to a plan to poison the water system of Tel Aviv. On October 6, 1944, a five-man German and Arab commando team parachuted into Mandatory Palestine and was to poison the Tel Aviv water system. They carried ten containers of toxin. They were apprehended by the British near Jericho, and the plot failed. A subsequent police report stated that the toxin was sufficient to kill some 250,000 people.[20]

November 1944–March 1945	The Jewish Agency, controlled by left wing Labor Zionists, collaborated with the British military and police to destroy their political opposition, the right-wing *Irgun*. In what came to be known as "the *Saison*" ("the Hunting Season"), *Irgun* members were hunted, arrested, tortured and deported. In effect, it was a one-sided civil war. Menachem Begin however, directed his organization not to fight fellow Jews and his followers obeyed him. It was one of the blackest periods of the *Yishuv's* struggle for national independence.
June 29, 1946	Upwards of 25,000 British military and security troops launched a massive series of raids—Operation *Agatha*—against the *Yishuv*. The undertaking came to be known as "Black Saturday" as it was carried out on the Jewish Sabbath. The operation lasted some two weeks across all of the British Mandate of Palestine, striking at Tel Aviv, Jerusalem, Haifa and other Jewish localities. The authorities seized arms caches and arrested some 2,700 Jewish officials, many from the Jewish Agency and *Haganah*. However, the British could not find other Jewish underground leaders. Nevertheless, the British action dealt Jewish morale a severe blow.
July 22, 1946	In retaliation for the "Black Sabbath" raids, the *Irgun*, guided by their motto, *rak kach* ("only this way"), retaliated. They struck—via Operation *Chick*—at the King David Hotel in Jerusalem. The hotel served as both British military headquarters, and the Secretariat of the civil government. The building had been deemed impregnable by the British. By three separate routes the *Irgun* sent telephone warnings beforehand, to evacuate the building. These warnings were ignored, thus resulting in 91 killed and 46 injured in the bomb blast and subsequent collapse of the entire southern wing of the hotel. The proverbial straw broke the British back. After this attack, the British realized that their position in Mandatory Palestine was unsustainable.
February 25, 1947	The United Kingdom turned the Palestine issue over to the United Nations. The British expected that Cold War rivalry between the United States and the Soviet Union, would lead to a deadlock, leaving the British free to use maximum force to deal with the Jews. However, in a rare instance of agreement, both the United States and the Soviet Union (each for their own reasons), favored the Partition Plan.
May 4, 1947	In retaliation for the hanging of four of their members at Acre prison on April 19, 1947, the *Irgun* staged a spectacular prison break from the Acre Fortress Citadel. The Citadel had been turned into an "escape-proof" prison by British authorities. The escapees included thirty *Irgun* and eleven *LEHI* detainees, as well as upward of 185 Arabs.
November 29, 1947	United Nations General Assembly Resolution 181 was adopted. It called for the partition of Palestine. It was a non-legally binding General Assembly resolution. The partition plan merely expressed the willingness of two-thirds of the United Nations General Assembly to accept the establishment of a Jewish state and an Arab state in Palestine. Note, the resolution specifically called for the establishment of a "Jewish state." It did not ensure the establishment of either (*see* "UN Partition Plan, November 29, 1947" map). It should be stressed that the UN did not create Israel, despite the persistent myth that it did. Israel's legal basis in international law had already been established twenty-seven years earlier with the San Remo Resolution.

November 30, 1947–July 20, 1949	What came to be known as the Israeli War of Independence—the first Arab war against Israel—was fought. Starting the day after the UN Partition Plan vote, November 30, 1947, the *Yishuv*—the Jewish community in Palestine—had to fight against three distinct, if interconnected enemies. The first was the Arabs of the Mandate, led by the Arab Higher Committee, headed by Hajj Amin al-Husseini. The second was a pan-Arab volunteer force—the Arab Liberation Army—led by Fawzi al-Qawuqji, a Lebanese, (who competed with the mufti to lead the Arab struggle against the British and the Jews). The third enemy (after May 15) was the regular forces of the five invading Arab armies—Egyptian, Transjordanian, Iraqi, Syrian and Lebanese.
December 8–17, 1947	At an Arab League summit meeting in Cairo, Egypt, agreement was reached to contribute £E1 million, 10,000 rifles and 5 million rounds of ammunition to the Arabs fighting in Palestine. The Arab states pledged to recruit 3,000 volunteers for the Arab Liberation Army.
March 19, 1948	Warren Austin, US ambassador to the United Nations declared that the fighting proved the UN Partition Plan was no longer possible and therefore Palestine should be placed under a UN trusteeship.
April 13, 1948	A medical convoy of Jewish doctors and nurses, going to Hadassah Hospital on Mount Scopus in Jerusalem, was ambushed by Arab forces. Eighty doctors and nurses were killed and some twenty others were wounded.
May 13, 1948	The seven-member Arab League proclaimed a state of war between the League and the Jews of Palestine. On the same day, Kfar Etzion a *kibbutz* situated between Jerusalem and Hebron fell to the forces of the Transjordanian Arab Legion. Those who surrendered were slaughtered. Only three men and a girl survived. The next day, the remaining three *kibbutzim* of the Etzion Bloc were forced to surrender. All the surviving inhabitants were taken prisoner and the four villages were razed by the Arabs. In September 1967, after the Six-Day War, the Etzion Bloc was rebuilt and inhabited by the children of the original inhabitants.
May 14, 1948 (Fifth of Iyar, 5708, in the Jewish calendar)	The reestablishment of Jewish sovereignty over the ancient historic, sacred, and legal Jewish homeland was achieved as the State of Israel was proclaimed. US President Harry Truman extended *de facto* recognition eleven minutes later. The Soviet Union extended full *de jure* recognition on May 17, 1948.
May 15, 1948	Troops from five Arab armies invaded Israel, as the Egyptian Air Force bombed Tel Aviv. This invasion rendered UN General Assembly Resolution 181 null and void. Since then, the entire Arab League has been in a formal and uninterrupted condition of belligerency with the Jewish state.
May 15, 1948– June 7, 1967	The Transjordanian Arab Legion invaded and occupied Judea and Samaria including the Old City of Jerusalem.
May 17, 1948	Egyptian forces occupied Beersheba, and advanced north towards the outskirts of Jerusalem.
May 25, 1948	An Iraqi attack toward Netanya was repulsed.
May 26, 1948	The Israel Defense Forces (IDF) was established.

May 28, 1948	The Jewish Quarter of the Old City of Jerusalem fell to the invading British-officered Transjordanian Arab Legion.
June 6–7, 1948	Egyptian forces captured and occupied Nitzanim, some eighteen miles south of Tel Aviv.
June 11–July 8, 1948	Exhausted and in need of time to reorganize as well as resupply, both Arabs and Israelis accepted a UN thirty-day ceasefire.
June 20–21, 1948	An armed confrontation that came to be known as the *Altalena* Affair, took place between the IDF and the *Irgun* at Kfar Vitkin and later on the beach in north Tel Aviv, regarding the cargo ship, *Altalena.* In anticipation of Israel's fight for independence against attacking Arab armies, the *Irgun* had purchased the ship, which carried some 940 volunteer fighters as well as munitions including 5,000 rifles, 250 Bren guns, and 1,000 grenades, 5 million rounds of ammunition, 50 bazookas, and 10 Bren carriers. The weapons valued at 153 million francs were donated by the French government. Right-wing *Irgun* leader, Menachem Begin had informed the new Israeli government of these moves and assumed there would be no trouble. Begin wanted the weapons to strengthen his forces in their desperate attempt to defend the Old City of Jerusalem, then being attacked by the Transjordanian Arab Legion.[21] Leftist Prime Minister David Ben-Gurion was determined to resist any challenge to his authority, real or imagined. Ben-Gurion was fearful of his political rival and a rival military force, though Begin had only a few thousand fighters at most in comparison to Ben-Gurion's 100,000-strong IDF. Thus, Ben-Gurion saw the opportunity to crush his right-wing political rival, Begin. Ben-Gurion concocted the myth of an "armed revolt," claiming the *Irgun* intended to seize control of the Israeli government in a coup. Hence, he ordered the IDF to fire on the *Altalena* with artillery and machine gun fire. The ship caught fire, burned, sunk and most of its precious cargo lost. *Irgun* fighters were shot as they struggled in the water while evacuating the ship. Begin refused to order his men to return fire, not wanting to start a civil war and have Jews fire upon Jews. Sixteen *Irgun* fighters and three IDF soldiers were killed in the confrontation. Ben-Gurion's government never produced a shred of evidence that Begin and the *Irgun* sought to overthrow the government. While one cannot say with certainty, were it not for Ben-Gurion's politically motivated interference, it is likely that the Old City of Jerusalem would not have been lost in 1948, and then occupied by the Arab attackers.[22] [23]
July 18, 1948	The Arabs agreed to a second UN ceasefire and violated it almost immediately, resorting to guerrilla warfare. The second truce officially ended October 15, 1948.
1948–53	Some 10,000 Egyptian Jews fled or were expelled and were transported to Israel, in Operation *Goshen.*
January 25, 1949	Elections were held for the first Knesset—the Israeli parliament. The first session began on February 14, in Jerusalem.
February 16, 1949	Chaim Weizmann was elected first president of Israel.

February 25–July 20, 1949	Victorious in its War of Independence, Israel concluded armistice agreements with several of its Arab neighbors—with Egypt on February 25, 1949, Lebanon on March 23, Transjordan on April 3, and Syria on July 20. Iraq however, never signed an armistice agreement with Israel (*see* "Armistice lines, 1949" map).

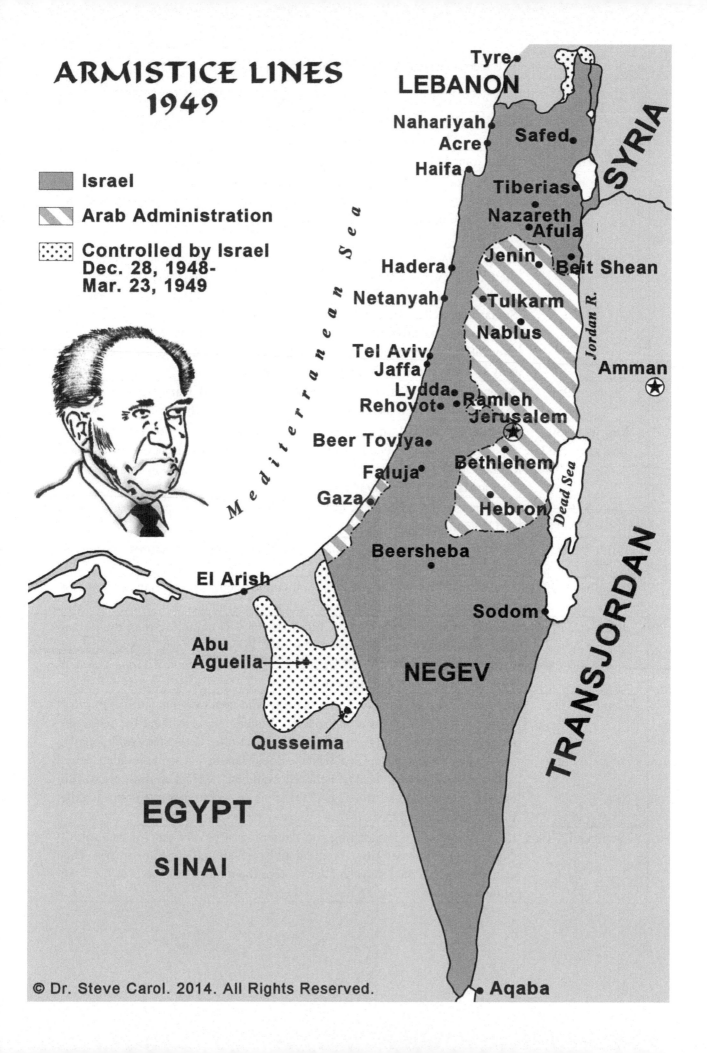

ARMISTICE LINES 1949

Legend:
- Israel
- Arab Administration
- Controlled by Israel Dec. 28, 1948 - Mar. 23, 1949

Tyre

LEBANON

Nahariyah
Acre
Safed
Haifa

SYRIA

Tiberias

Nazareth
Afula

Mediterranean Sea

Hadera
Jenin
Beit Shean

Netanyah
Tulkarm

Nablus

Jordan R.

Tel Aviv
Jaffa
Lydda
Rehovot
Ramleh
Jerusalem

Amman

Beer Toviya
Bethlehem

Faluja
Dead Sea
Gaza
Hebron

Beersheba

El Arish
Sodom

Abu
Aguella

NEGEV

TRANSJORDAN

Qusseima

EGYPT

SINAI

Aqaba

Date	Event
April 1949– December 1951	Via an Israeli sealift, 31,343[24] Libyan Jews were transported to Israel.
May 11, 1949	Israel joined the United Nations as its fifty-ninth member.
June 1949– September 24, 1950	An airlift of some 49,000 Jews from Yemen and Aden to Israel was successfully undertaken. Operation *On Wings of Eagles*,[25] also known as Operation *Magic Carpet*, brought most of a 2,000-year-old Jewish community back to the Land of Israel.
December 1949	Egypt occupied the islands of Tiran and Sanafir at the southern entrance to the Gulf of Aqaba (also known as the Gulf of Eilat), blocking passage to the southern Israeli port of Eilat. Transjordan unilaterally annexed Judea and Samaria as well as the Old City of Jerusalem, conquered by the Arab Legion. The Jordanian Parliament ratified this move on April 4, 1950. The illegal annexation was rejected by the international community and was recognized only by two countries, the United Kingdom and Pakistan.
March 1950	A secret draft peace treaty was initialed by Israel and Transjordan. It did not reach fruition due to the assassination of King Abdullah I on July 20, 1951.
May 18, 1950– February 1952	A large-scale Jewish immigration from Iraq via an airlift was begun. Called Operation *Ezra and Nehemiah* (also known as Operation *Ali Baba*) the transfer of Iraqi Jews was largely completed in July 1951. Some 130,000 Iraqi Jews left Iraq for Israel between 1950 and 1952.
July 5, 1950	The Knesset passed the Law of Return whereby any Jew may return to Israel and become a citizen.
March 1951	Israel began a project to drain the Hula Valley swamps, a breeding ground for malaria-carrying mosquitoes.
September 1, 1951	The United Nations Security Council condemned the Egyptian blockade of Israeli cargo and ships from transiting the Suez Canal.
January 1, 1954	The Egyptian blockade of the Gulf of Aqaba was enforced when the Italian ship *Maria Antonia*, en route from Massawa, Ethiopia to Eilat, Israel, was fired upon by gun batteries at Ras Nasrani, overlooking the Straits of Tiran. The ship was forced to return to Massawa.
January 1955	Egyptian President Gamal Abdel Nasser, who never reconciled to Egyptian defeat in the 1948–49 war with Israel, dramatically escalated the *fedayeen* terrorist attacks on Israel from the Egyptian-controlled Gaza Strip. Additionally, he concluded a major arms deal with the Soviet Union that soon provided Egypt with the weaponry for what he believed would be the final confrontation with Israel (for greater details *see* "Basic Principle 26 – "Russia's role in the Middle East"—entries for 1955).
September 12, 1955	Egypt announced a broadening and tightening of its blockade of the Gulf of Aqaba at the Straits of Tiran, banning all Israeli air and maritime traffic. This event, as well as the *fedayeen* attacks were the major *casus belli* of the 1956 Sinai Campaign.

October 22, 1956	Egypt, Syria, and Jordan signed a military alliance placing all their military forces under the unified command of Egyptian General Abdel Hakim Amer. For Israel, this constituted another automatic *casus belli*.
October 29–November 5, 1956	Israel launched Operation *Kadesh* to destroy the *fedayeen* bases in the Gaza Strip, the growing Soviet-supplied Egyptian military machine in the Sinai Peninsula and reopen the Straits of Tiran. Within the first one hundred hours, Israeli forces reached the Suez Canal (November 2) and then pulled back fifteen kilometers (some nine miles) as it was expected that British and French forces would occupy the Canal Zone, as part of the overall Sinai-Suez War. By November 5, the IDF reached Ras Nasrani and Sharm el-Sheikh reopening the Straits of Tiran and achieving all the goals of Operation *Kadesh* (*see* the "Sinai-Suez War" map). British and French military activity ceased on November 7, 1956.
November 1956	As a result of the Sinai Suez War, some 82,000 Egyptian Jews were stripped of their citizenship, nationality, had their property, and assets confiscated. Furthermore, they were expelled from Egypt. Many left with only one suitcase and £E10 per person. Some 35,000 went to Israel.[26]

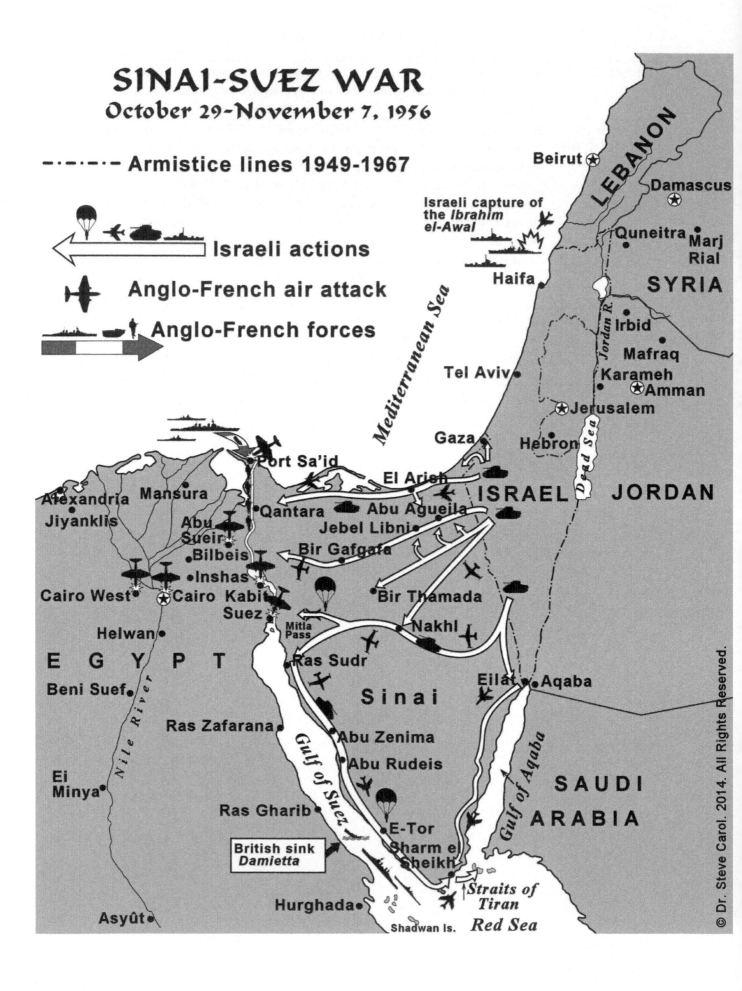

SINAI-SUEZ WAR
October 29-November 7, 1956

— ·· — ·· — Armistice lines 1949-1967

Israeli actions

Anglo-French air attack

Anglo-French forces

Date	Event
April 26, 1960– June 1964	Israel's National Water Carrier was constructed. It carries water eighty-two miles from the Sea of Galilee to Israel's population centers and further south to the Negev Desert.
May 23, 1960	In the Knesset, Prime Minister David Ben-Gurion announced the capture of Nazi war criminal Adolf Eichmann. He was apprehended on May 11, 1960, in a suburb of Buenos Aires, Argentina, to where he had fled after the end of World War II. He was caught by an eight-man Mossad* team headed by Mossad chief Isser Harel. Eichmann was an *SS-Obersturmbannführer* (lieutenant colonel) and one of the major organizers of the Holocaust. Eichmann was put on trial on fifteen criminal charges including war crimes, crimes against humanity, and crimes against the Jewish people. Found guilty on many of these charges, he was sentenced to death by hanging and executed on May 31, 1962. Eichmann's body was cremated and the ashes were scattered by the Israeli Navy in international waters.
1962–64	Some 100,000[†] Moroccan Jews were transported to Israel via Operation *Yakhin*.[27]
May 28, 1964	The Palestine Liberation Organization (PLO) was created[28] as sanctioned by the Arab League at their First Arab Summit Conference in Cairo (January 13–17, 1964). The PLO was created with one objective in mind—the destruction of the Jewish state of Israel. That has been, and remains, the PLO's overarching goal and their *raison d'être*. This elimination of Israel is to be accomplished by "armed struggle" i.e. terrorism, the Phased Plan, the demand for "self-determination" (among the Arabs within Israel) and a *Haq al-Auda* ("right of return") for all Arabs claiming to be "refugees" as well as their descendents. All of the Jewish state of Israel is to be replaced by a greater Palestinian Arab state, incorporating all of present day Israel, the Gaza Strip, Judea and Samaria as well as all of Jordan.
May 18, 1965	Israeli Mossad agent Eli Cohen was exposed and executed in Damascus. From 1961 to 1965 operating under the alias of Kamal Amin Ta'abet, he worked his way up the Syrian Ba'athist Party and government hierarchy including the inner circle of Syrian President Amin al-Hafiz. Cohen even was considered to be named the Syrian Deputy Minister of Defense. During his time in Syria, he passed information to Israel about the Arab water diversion plans (*see* "Arab attempts at Diversion of Water Resources and Israeli Response" map) as well as their fortifications on the Golan Heights. This information helped Israel capture the Golan Heights in only two days during the Six-Day War of 1967.
May 14, 1967	Egypt and other Arab states began mobilizing their armed forces to wage what they termed the final battle with Israel, moving them to the 1949 armistice lines with Israel.
May 19, 1967	Egypt evicted the United Nations Emergency Force (UNEF) from its territory.

---

* The Hebrew acronym for *HaMossad LeBiyyun U'Letafkidim Meyuhadim.* ("Institute for Intelligence and Special Operations"). It is the national foreign intelligence agency of Israel, equivalent to the US CIA.

† The Moroccan Jews were given permission to leave at the cost of $100 per person.

May 23, 1967	Egypt announced the mining of the Straits of Tiran and the re-imposition of a total blockade of all air and maritime traffic, bound for Eilat, Israel's southern port. It was a major move to turn the clock backwards to the situation prior to the Sinai Campaign of 1956. This was the major *casus belli* of the war that was soon to erupt.
June 5–10, 1967	The Six-Day War–the third Arab war against Israel, was fought. While Israel had to deal primarily with the armed forces of Egypt, Jordan and Syria, military forces from five other Arab states participated. Israel emerged militarily victorious (*see* the "Six-Day War June 5–10, 1967–Israeli Attack" map).
June 7, 1967 (28 Iyar 5727, in the Jewish calendar)	Israel Defense Forces (IDF) entered Jerusalem's Old City via the Lions' Gate (at the time known as St. Stephen's Gate). It was only the second time in recorded history that the city was captured from the east, the first being King David's conquest in ca. 1002 B.C.E. In 1967, the IDF promptly made their way to the Temple Mount. Colonel Mordechai Gur, commander of the Paratroopers Brigade, soon broadcast a momentous message to the Israeli nation, "The Temple Mount is [again] in our hands." The city was reunited under Israeli/Jewish sovereignty after 1,897 years (*see* "United Jerusalem" map).

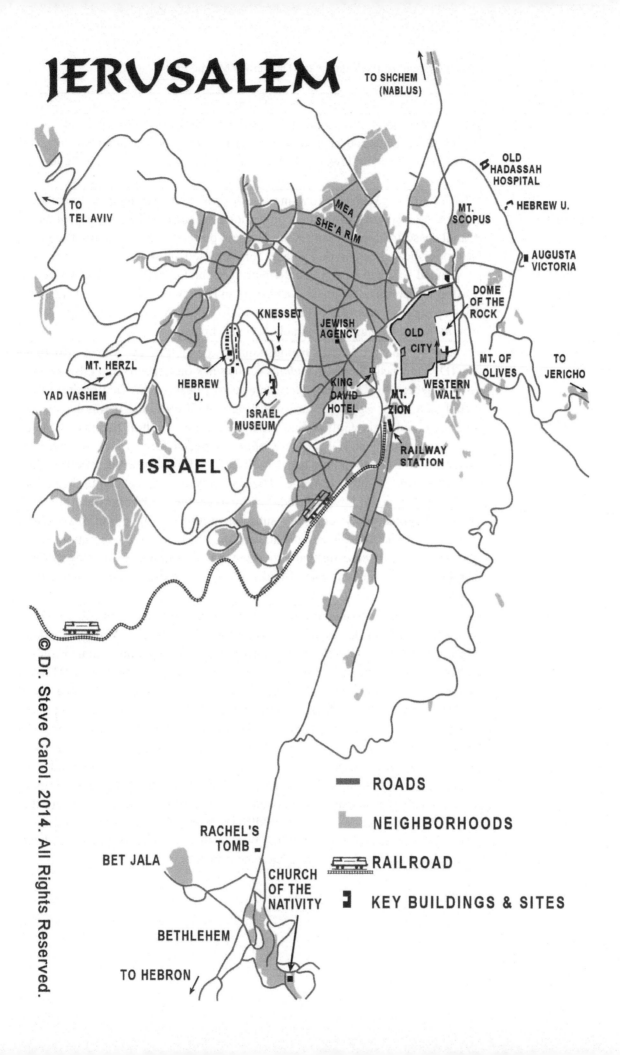

JERUSALEM

TO SHCHEM
(NABLUS)

OLD
HADASSAH
HOSPITAL

HEBREW U.

TO
TEL AVIV

MEA
SHE'A RIM

MT.
SCOPUS

AUGUSTA
VICTORIA

DOME
OF THE
ROCK

KNESSET

JEWISH
AGENCY

OLD
CITY

MT. HERZL

HEBREW
U.

MT. OF
OLIVES

TO
JERICHO

YAD VASHEM

KING
DAVID
HOTEL

WESTERN
WALL

ISRAEL
MUSEUM

MT.
ZION

ISRAEL

RAILWAY
STATION

═══ ROADS

NEIGHBORHOODS

RACHEL'S
TOMB

RAILROAD

BET JALA

CHURCH
OF THE
NATIVITY

KEY BUILDINGS & SITES

BETHLEHEM

TO HEBRON

Date	Event
June 10, 1967	The Soviet Union severed diplomatic relations with Israel, as did Czechoslovakia. Bulgaria, Hungary and Yugoslavia followed suit on June 11, and Poland severed relations on June 12. However, Romania did not break relations with the Jewish state.
July 1, 1967– August 7, 1970	The 1,000-Day War of Attrition—the fourth Arab war against Israel was fought. As Egypt began another conventional war against Israel along the Suez Canal ceasefire line, Jordan's King Hussein provided its archenemy the PLO, with logistical and operational bases for increased anti-Israel terrorism. Israel responded with daring and unanticipated (by the Egyptians) actions based on the biblical precept, "By ruses (*tachboulot* in Hebrew) shall thou wage war, and victory comes with much planning by advisors"[29] (*see* the "1,000-Day War of Attrition–Arab Attacks and Israeli Actions" maps).
July 19, 1969	In an event that marked a turning point in the 1,000-Day War of Attrition, the IDF launched Operation *Bulmus 6*, an attack on Green Island (also known as Al Jazeera Al Khadraa). The island was a heavily fortified position that acted as a major Egyptian early warning and ELINT site. It was located at the north end of the Gulf of Suez, some 2.5 miles south of the city of Suez. In a joint operation, IDF *Sayeret Matkal* (special forces) and *Shayetet 13* (naval commandos) captured and demolished the Egyptian fortifications on the island (*see* the "1,000-Day War of Attrition–Israeli Actions" map). The action opened a gap in the Egyptian radar array to enable the IAF to penetrate and exploit Egyptian air defenses for subsequent air (e.g. Operation *Boxer*–July 20-28, 1969, and some 300 dogfights) and over 80 commando operations until the August 1970 ceasefire that ended the war. It sent a clear message to the Egyptian regime that no part of their military structure was immune to IDF attack.
September 9, 1969	In a move designed to undermine Egyptian morale and expose its vulnerability, Israel launched its sole ground offensive during the 1,000-Day War of Attrition. Operation *Raviv* ("Drizzle") was a 10-hour "armored raid" along Egypt's western Red Sea coast, using captured Arab armor (T-55 tanks and BTR-50 personnel carriers). The IDF strike-force was transported across the Gulf of Suez and landed at A-Dir, south of Ras Sadat. Catching the Egyptians completely by surprise the force raced southward along the coastal road for some 30 miles, destroying a dozen Egyptian military positions, radar sites and a main encampment at Ras Abu-Daraj. The IDF strike-force then embarked near Ras Zafarana, suffering only one slightly wounded soldier before returning to Sinai. The Egyptians suffered between 100 and 200 casualties including the death of a Soviet general (*see* the "1,000-Day War of Attrition–Israeli Actions" map). Nasser was so shocked by the raid he suffered a heart attack and later fired both his Chief of Staff and Navy commander.

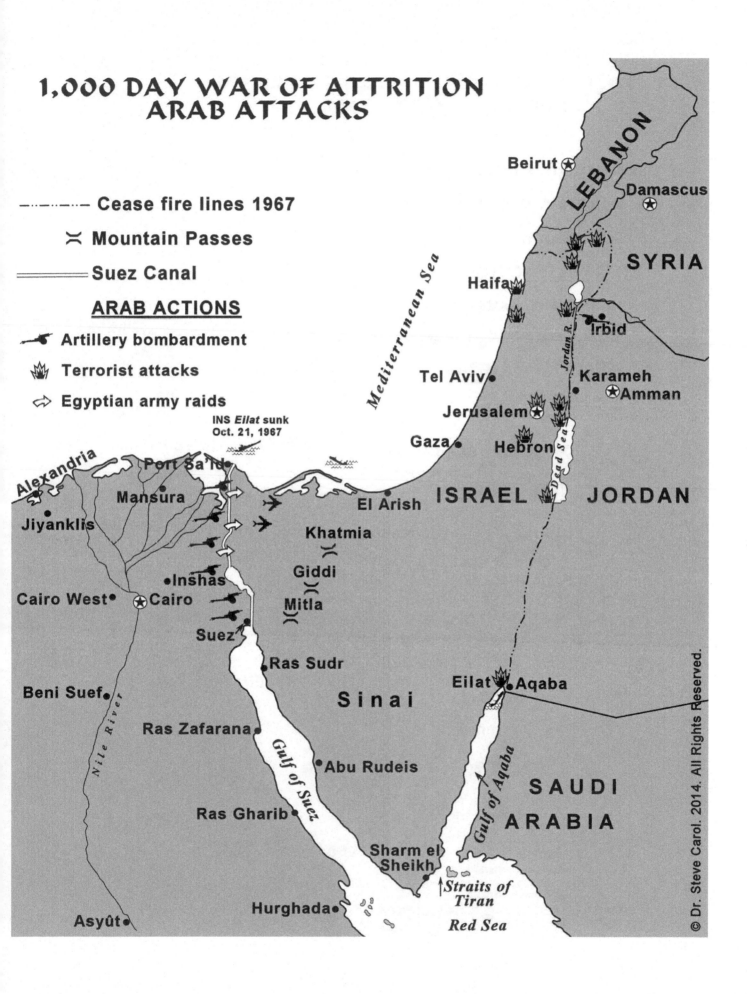

1,000 DAY WAR OF ATTRITION ARAB ATTACKS

- –·–··–··– Cease fire lines 1967
- ⊁ Mountain Passes
- ══════ Suez Canal

ARAB ACTIONS
- Artillery bombardment
- Terrorist attacks
- Egyptian army raids

INS *Eilat* sunk
Oct. 21, 1967

LEBANON

SYRIA

Beirut

Damascus

Haifa

Irbid

Mediterranean Sea

Tel Aviv

Jordan R.

Karameh
Amman

Jerusalem

Gaza

Hebron

Dead Sea

ISRAEL

JORDAN

El Arish

Khatmia

Giddi

Mitla

Alexandria

Port Sa'Id

Mansura

Jiyanklis

Inshas

Cairo West

Cairo

Suez

Ras Sudr

Sinai

Beni Suef

Nile River

Ras Zafarana

Abu Rudeis

Eilat

Aqaba

Gulf of Aqaba

SAUDI

ARABIA

Ras Gharib

Gulf of Suez

Sharm el
Sheikh

Straits of
Tiran

Red Sea

Asyût

Hurghada

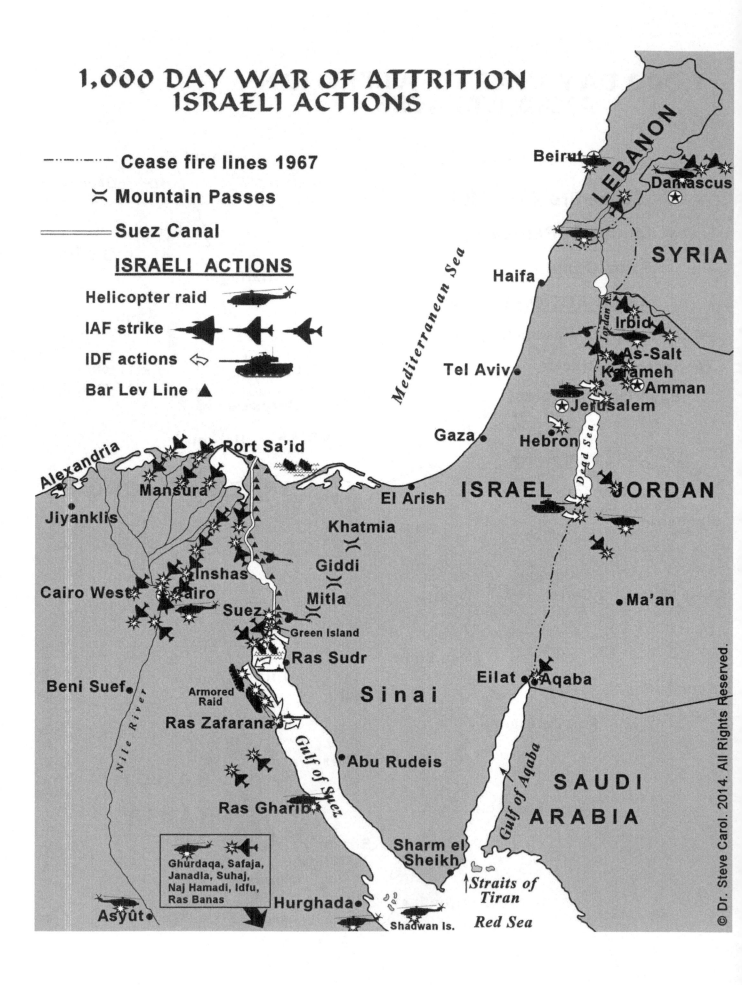

1,000 DAY WAR OF ATTRITION ISRAELI ACTIONS

Legend:
- — · — · — Cease fire lines 1967
-)(Mountain Passes
- ═══ Suez Canal

ISRAELI ACTIONS
- Helicopter raid
- IAF strike
- IDF actions
- Bar Lev Line ▲

Labels:
LEBANON, SYRIA, ISRAEL, JORDAN, SAUDI ARABIA, Sinai

Beirut, Damascus, Haifa, Irbid, As-Salt, Karameh, Amman, Jerusalem, Tel Aviv, Gaza, Hebron, Ma'an

Mediterranean Sea, Dead Sea, Jordan R., Red Sea

Alexandria, Port Sa'id, Mansura, Jiyanklis, El Arish, Khatmia, Giddi, Mitla, Cairo West, Inshas, Cairo, Suez, Green Island, Ras Sudr, Beni Suef, Armored Raid, Ras Zafarana, Nile River, Gulf of Suez, Abu Rudeis, Ras Gharib, Eilat, Aqaba, Gulf of Aqaba, Sharm el Sheikh, Straits of Tiran, Hurghada, Asyût, Shadwan Is.

Ghurdaqa, Safaja, Janadla, Suhaj, Naj Hamadi, Idfu, Ras Banas

Date	Event
1969 to date	Over 1 million Russians of Jewish origin immigrated to Israel.
October 6–26, 1973	In a surprise attack, Egypt and Syria launched the Yom Kippur War—the fifth Arab war against Israel. A total of eleven Arab states contributed troops and material against Israel (*see* the "Yom Kippur War, October 6–24, 1973—Arab Attack and Israeli Counterattack" maps). While suffering heavy losses at the start of the conflict, Israel prevailed militarily by the time of the UN ceasefire.
March–May 1974	Syria waged a war of attrition against the Israeli Golan. There were artillery exchanges, skirmishes, as well as repeated Syrian attempts to capture Mount Hermon, the highest peak in the Golan Heights. The Soviet Union provided Syria with a guarantee against any major Israeli counter-attack by deploying two Cuban armored brigades—airlifted from Angola—into Syria.
April 10, 1975	The Israeli government acknowledged the right of Ethiopian Jews—the *Beta Israel*—to immigrate to Israel under the Law of Return.
July 3–4, 1976	Israeli *Sayeret Matkal* Special Forces freed Israeli and Jewish hostages as well as the Air France crew, held by Palestinian and German terrorists at the airport in Entebbe, Uganda, in Operation *Thunderbolt*, later renamed Operation *Yonatan*.
May 12, 1977	The opposition Likud Party won the national elections. Menachem Begin became prime minister.
March 14–21, 1978	In response to constant PLO and Popular Front for the Liberation of Palestine (PFLP) attacks from Lebanon on civilian targets in northern Israel, culminating in the Coastal Road Massacre of March 11, 1978 (*see* "Basic Principle 52"), Israel launched Operation *Litani*. The IDF invaded southern Lebanon defeating and expelling Palestinian terrorist forces from the region. Israel established a security zone and offered protection to Lebanese Christians. A United Nations Interim Force in Lebanon (UNIFIL) buffer zone was established to keep the peace. However, the UN "peacekeepers" proved totally ineffective (*see* "Basic Principle 69").
March 26, 1979	Egyptian President Anwar el-Sadat and Israeli Prime Minister Menachem Begin signed the Egypt–Israel Peace Treaty in Washington, DC.
April 30, 1979	According to the terms of the Egypt–Israel Peace Treaty the first Israeli ship—the cargo vessel *Ashdod*—passed through the Suez Canal.
June 7, 1981	An Israeli air strike destroyed the Iraqi nuclear facility at Osirak, near Baghdad.
December 14, 1981	Israel extended its "laws, jurisdiction and administration" to the Golan Heights.[30]
April 25, 1982	Israel completed its withdrawal of the Sinai Peninsula returning it to Egypt.

June 6, 1982– September 1982	In a move designed to halt the incessant PLO terrorist attacks against Israel, which emanated from Lebanon since 1972, as well as to destroy PLO bases there once and for all, Israel launched Operation *Peace for Galilee*. Additionally, Israel entered Lebanon, in part to liberate the Lebanese Christians from the brutal, ruthless and murderous occupying PLO terrorist organization. Contrary to media and UN accusations, it was not an act of aggression. Only armistice agreements exist between Israel and Lebanon, and Israel and Syria. Signed on March 23, 1949 with Lebanon, and July 20, 1949 with Syria, these agreements were by definition, not a war-terminating agreement, but merely pledges, still not honored by the Lebanese or Syrians, to cease active hostilities on a temporary basis. Thus, it is not legally possible for Israel to commit "aggression" against Lebanon or Syria. These two Arab states, consider themselves in a formal and uninterrupted condition of belligerency with the Jewish state. A state cannot commit aggression against another state with which it is already at war. This conflict was the sixth Arab war against Israel, and involved the PLO as well as Syria. The Israel–PLO War in Lebanon, also known as the First Lebanon War, lasted until September (*see* "Israel–PLO War in Lebanon" map).

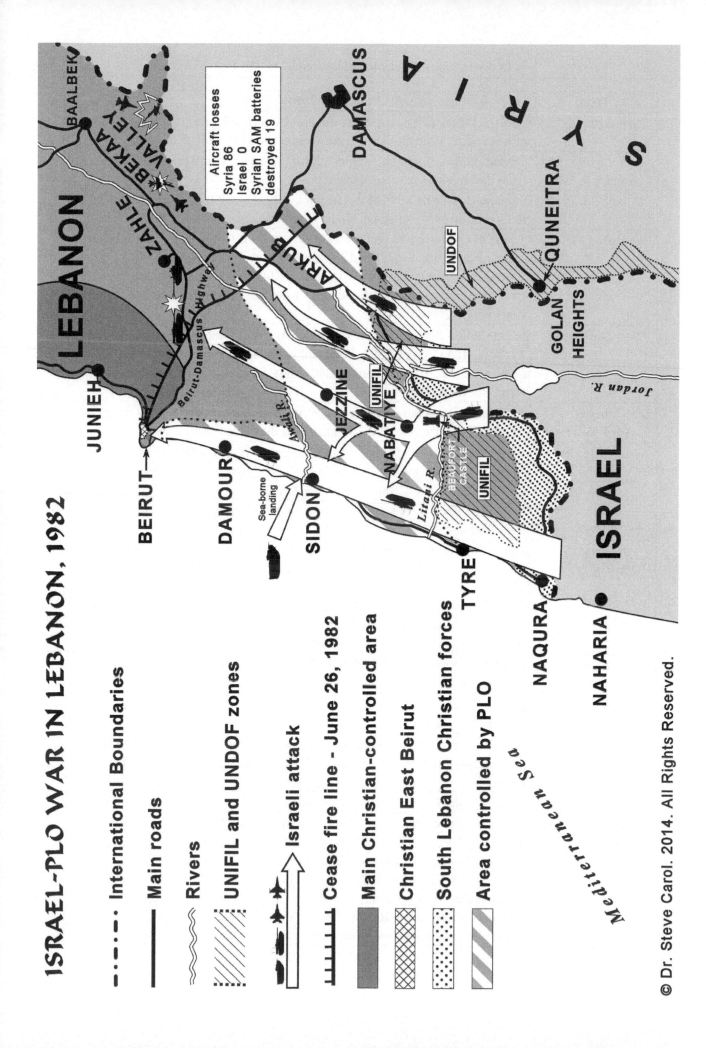

ISRAEL–PLO WAR IN LEBANON, 1982

Legend:
- ▪·▪·▪ International Boundaries
- ▬▬ Main roads
- ～～ Rivers
- ▨ UNIFIL and UNDOF zones
- ✈ / ⬆ Israeli attack
- ⊥⊥⊥ Cease fire line – June 26, 1982
- Main Christian-controlled area
- Christian East Beirut
- South Lebanon Christian forces
- Area controlled by PLO

Aircraft losses
Syria 86
Israel 0
Syrian SAM batteries destroyed 19

Labels: BAALBEK, BEKAA VALLEY, ZAHLE, LEBANON, DAMASCUS, SYRIA, JUNIEH, BEIRUT, Beirut-Damascus Highway, DAMOUR, SIDON, Sea-borne landing, Awali R., JEZZINE, NABATIYE, UNIFIL, Litani R., BEAUFORT CASTLE, TYRE, NAQURA, NAHARIA, ISRAEL, Jordan R., GOLAN HEIGHTS, QUNEITRA, UNDOF, Mediterranean Sea

Date	Event
September 1982	An Israel–Lebanon peace treaty did not reach fruition due to the assassination of Lebanese President-elect Bashir Gemayel on September 14, 1982.
November 21, 1984– January 5, 1985	Operation *Moses* airlifted some 7,900 *Beta Israel* (Ethiopian Jews) to Israel from Sudan via Brussels, Belgium.
March 28, 1985	In a one-day airlift, 494 Ethiopian Jews were rescued from Ethiopia via Sudan in Operation *Sheba* (also known as Operation *Joshua*).
July 1985	The IDF completed its withdrawal from most of Lebanon. A 12.5 mile-deep security zone was established in southern Lebanon on the Israeli–Lebanese frontier, manned by the mostly Lebanese Christian South Lebanon Army. For Israel, the maintenance of the security zone had a deterrent effect for some 15 years (1985–2000).
October 1, 1985	In retaliation for the murder of Israelis off the coast of Cyprus, the Israeli Air Force (IAF) successfully bombed PLO headquarters—Operation *Wooden Leg*—in Tunis, Tunisia, some 1,280 miles from Israel. Fifty-six Palestinian terrorists were killed.
December 6, 1987– April 16, 1993	A Palestinian Arab *intifada* ("shaking off") accompanied by increased terrorism occurred in Judea, Samaria and the Gaza Strip.
March 15, 1989	Israel returned the disputed Taba region to Egypt, after an international commission awarded the enclave to Egypt on September 29, 1988.
1989–91	Some 380,000 Jews from the Soviet Union were transported to Israel via Operation *Exodus*. Since the 1970s, over 1 million Russians of Jewish origin immigrated to Israel.
January 18– February 25, 1991	Israel was hit by thirty-nine Iraqi Scud missiles during the Persian Gulf War. They were aimed at Haifa, Tel Aviv, and the Negev Desert around Dimona where Israel had a nuclear facility.[31] Heavy damage was inflicted to property. Thirteen died and some 230 were injured. The US Patriot missile batteries stationed in Israel were found to be ineffective against and did not succeed in intercepting incoming Scud missiles.
May 24–25, 1991	Operation *Solomon* airlifted 14,325 *Beta Israel* from Ethiopia to Israel in thirty-six hours.
October 18, 1991	After a break of twenty-four years, Israel and the Soviet Union restored diplomatic relations.
December 16, 1991	After a sixteen-year battle, the infamous and abhorrent United Nations General Assembly Resolution 3379, which declared "Zionism as a form of racism," was revoked.
January 24, 1992	Israel and the People's Republic of China established diplomatic relations.
January 29, 1992	Full diplomatic relations were announced between India and Israel.
September 13, 1993	The Israeli–PLO Declaration of Principles, also known as the Oslo Accords, was signed on the White House lawn in Washington, DC, between Israeli Prime Minister Yitzhak Rabin and PLO chief Yasser Arafat. The Palestinians agreed to recognize Israel, renounce terrorism, outlaw terrorist groups, confiscate illegal weaponry and end incitement against Israel and Jews. However, the PLO did not comply with these pledges but continued their quest to destroy Israel.

May 4, 1994	The Gaza–Jericho Agreement was signed between Israel and the PLO, under which Israel agreed to withdraw its forces and administration from Jericho and most of the Gaza Strip. The Palestinians in turn, pledged to recognize Israel and renounce the use of terrorism against it. Israel allowed the creation of the Palestinian National Authority (PA). However once again, the Palestinians refused to accept Israel or stop terrorism. The IDF withdrew on May 13, 1994 from Jericho, transferring authority to the PLO/PA.
June 16, 1994	Israel and Vatican City established full diplomatic relations.
October 26, 1994	The Israel–Jordan Peace Treaty was signed.
September 28, 1995	The Israel–Palestinian Oslo II Agreement (Interim Agreement) was signed in Washington, DC. Israel dissolved its military government in Palestinian areas and handed over the main cities of Jenin, Nablus, Tulkarem, Qalqilya, Ramallah, and Bethlehem. This relinquishment of more than 30 percent of Judea and Samaria occurred despite the fact that the PLO/PA failed to live up to its original Oslo Accords obligations. The PLO/PA continued terrorism, incitement, and on-going misojudaic radicalization of the Palestinian people.
November 4, 1995	Israeli Prime Minister Yitzhak Rabin was assassinated in Tel Aviv.
December 11–27, 1995	The IDF completed its withdrawal from six cities in Judea and Samaria— Bethlehem, Jenin, Nablus, Qalqilya, Ramallah, and Tulkarem.
January 15–17, 1997	The Israeli–Palestinian Hebron Protocol was signed. It called for the redeployment of the IDF from 80 percent of Hebron. Coupled with the earlier 1995 IDF withdrawal from the other main Palestinian cities, virtually all 1.4 million Palestinians living in Judea and Samaria were placed under Palestinian jurisdiction. For its part, the PLO/PA pledged to arrest terrorists, fight terrorism and educate the Palestinian public for peace. While Israel complied with the terms of the agreement, the PLO/PA did not.
October 23, 1998	The Israel–Palestinian Wye River Memorandum agreement was concluded, whereby Israel agreed to withdraw from further territory in two phases. For their part, the PLO/PA promised, yet again, to take all necessary measures to fight terrorism, to confiscate illegal weaponry and to end incitement to hatred and murder against Israel. Israel fulfilled its commitment by withdrawing from 13 percent of Judea and Samaria in the first phase but refused to go further when the PLO/PA did not carry out its commitments.
September 4, 1999	Israel and the PLO/PA signed the Sharm el-Sheikh Memorandum, under which Israel agreed to a further withdrawal from 11 percent of Judea and Samaria in fulfillment of its remaining territorial pledge under the Wye River Memorandum. Additionally, Israel freed 350 Palestinian prisoners. This put 98 percent of the Palestinian population of the territories under PLO/PA control, along with about 45 percent of the land and some important mountain aquifer resources. The PLO/PA again promised to act swiftly and decisively against terrorists. While Israel fulfilled its commitments, the PLO/PA yet again, did not fulfill its pledges.

May 24, 2000	Israel unilaterally completed its withdrawal from its 12.5-mile security zone in southern Lebanon. The hurried withdrawal took place in the dead of night. Israel's ally, the South Lebanon Army (SLA) made up largely of Lebanese Christians, was quick to collapse without Israeli support. SLA soldiers and their families streamed to the Israeli border and had to be hastily taken into Israel, or face slaughter at the hands of Hezbollah. The withdrawal projected Israeli weakness and no doubt encouraged PLO chief Yasser Arafat to launch the Al-Aqsa (Second) *Intifada* four months later. That terror war lasted years and cost the lives of about 1,500 Israelis, most of them civilians. In light of the 2000 Al-Aqsa *Intifada*, the 2006 Hezbollah-launched missile war and the ongoing military buildup by Hezbollah, the Israeli withdrawal proved to be a major strategic mistake.
July 11–25, 2000	The Camp David II Summit convened to reach a final status settlement between Israel and the PLO/PA. The summit collapsed due to Yasser Arafat's demand that Israel withdraw from all the territories captured in the Six-Day War, including the Old City of Jerusalem. Arafat even denied there had ever been a Jewish Temple in Jerusalem.[32] The Arab response to the summit's failure was to launch another violent uprising.
September 28, 2000–February 8, 2005	The Palestinian Arab Al-Aqsa (Second) *Intifada* uprising began and continued for some five years. Increased terrorist acts including suicide bombings were launched against Israel.
March 29–May 3, 2002	Israel launched Operation *Defensive Shield*. The IDF was redeployed into Judea and Samaria into Shechem (Nablus), Jenin and other cities. Its goal was to wipe out terrorist bases. Operation *Determined Path* was launched June 22, 2002, to complete the major objectives of Operation *Defensive Shield* and lasted until the end of July.
August 15–23, 2005	Israel implemented and completed its unilateral disengagement plan from the Gaza Strip and northern Samaria. As a result, twenty-one communities in the Gaza Strip and four in Samaria were demolished and over 9,000 Israelis were uprooted and expelled. The Palestinians rapidly turned the Gaza Strip into a forward launching platform for both rocket and terrorist attacks on Israel. As events subsequently proved, this Israeli withdrawal was a colossal strategic blunder.
July 12–August 14, 2006	The Second Lebanon War, the Hezbollah War—the seventh Arab/Muslim war against Israel—was fought. During this conflict, over 4,000 missiles were fired at Israel causing extensive damage and killing forty-four civilians.[33]
September 6, 2007	An Israeli air strike hit and destroyed a Syrian nuclear weapons facility at Deir Ez-Zour.
December 27, 2008–January 18, 2009	The First Gaza War—Operation *Cast Lead*—was fought. It was the eighth Arab/Muslim war against Israel. The results of the war for Israel were inconclusive. Hamas rearmed and resumed a missile and mortar war against Israel's cities, towns and villages. The quality and quantity of these missiles steadily increased. In 2010, Palestinian terrorists fired 158 missiles. That number increased to 680 in 2011 and to more than 900 rockets and mortars at Israel through November 2012.

November 10–21, 2012	Hamas terrorists fired an anti-tank missile at an IDF patrol in their jeep. Four were injured, two seriously. Israel's return of fire was met by an increased and escalating rocket barrage, initiating the Second Gaza War. Hamas used Fajr-5 missiles supplied by Iran, to hit deep into central Israel striking Tel Aviv and Jerusalem. On November 14, Israel launched a counter-offensive—Operation *Pillar of Cloud* (*Amúd Anán*)[34]. It was also called Operation *Pillar of Defense* because in the commentaries of Rashi *Amúd* Anán also physically blocked the arrows and catapults of the Egyptians, thus it was also a pillar of defense. Due to Israel's successful use of the Iron Dome short-range anti-missile system, it was thought that using the attribute of physically protecting the people of Israel, the second name was better. The second name exists only in English, since in Hebrew it carries both meanings. On November 21, an Egyptian-brokered ceasefire ended the Second Gaza War. Once again, it was inconclusive. It was the ninth Arab/Muslim war against Israel.
June 11, 2014– August 26, 2014	The Third Gaza War (the tenth Arab/Muslim war against Israel) began when Hamas and Islamic Jihad launched a high intensity rocket and missile bombardment of Israel. This escalated the next day with the kidnapping and murder of three Israeli teenagers. The missile bombardment reached a crescendo of some 100 missiles on July 8, 2014. Using long-range missiles, like the Syrian-made M-302 Khaibar missile as well as longer-ranged R-160s, hits were made on Ashdod, Caesarea, Beersheba, Dimona, Tel Aviv, Jerusalem, Hadera, Zikhron Ya'akov, Haifa and Nahariya (some 107 miles from the Gaza Strip). Virtually all of Israel came under Hamas missile fire. In response Israel launched Operation *Protective Edge* (July 8) increased IAF strikes on high value Hamas targets and called up some 86,000 reservists. A limited IDF ground invasion of the Gaza Strip began on July 17, 2014. During the war, Hamas fired some 4,500 rockets and mortars on Israel from within densely populated civilian areas. Eighteen percent of the rockets fired by Hamas (by IDF calculations)—which is to say, about 600 rockets—were fired from schools (including the UNRWA schools), playgrounds, hospitals, mosques, and cemeteries.[35] All such firings from civilian areas are in violation of international law. Thirty-two Hamas terrorist attack tunnels under the Israeli border were discovered and destroyed. Sixty-seven IDF soldiers died in the war and the overall death toll was seventy-two Israelis (five were civilians). Over 900 Hamas terrorists mostly dressed as civilians were killed during the conflict. As in the two previous Gaza wars, the Third Gaza War ended inconclusively with Hamas still standing.

14. Jerusalem is the eternal capital of the Jewish nation as Jews have lived there for three millennia.

No place on earth touches the soul of the Jewish people as deeply as Jerusalem. As the Book of Genesis, 28:17 relates, "How awesome is this place! This is none other than the abode of God, and this is the gate of heaven." No wonder this is a spot that every major conqueror in all of human history has wanted to own. The role Jerusalem occupies in Jewish consciousness is unique in the pages of history.

Until the 1860s, the walled Old City of Jerusalem, measuring less than one-third of a square mile in area, contained the entire city. Within its walls, lie religious sites sacred to Judaism, Christianity, and Islam. The current walls were constructed in 1538 by the Ottoman Turkish Sultan Suleiman the Magnificent. There are eleven gates in the walls, of which seven are currently open (*see* the "Old City of Jerusalem" map).

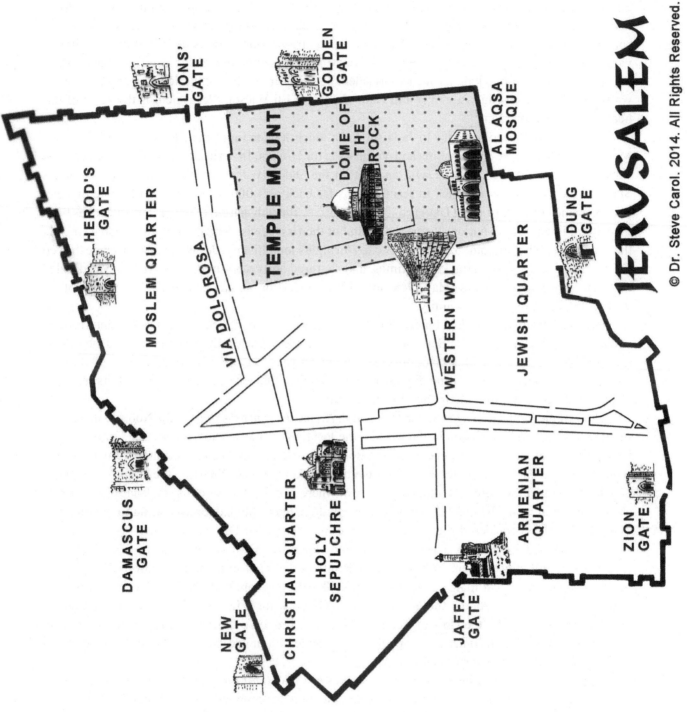

JERUSALEM

On Mount Zion in Jerusalem, one may find today, the Tomb of King David, the Cenacle—the room of the Last Supper, and Dormition Abbey where tradition states the Virgin Mary fell into an eternal sleep. The city was conquered by King David 3,000 years ago, was proclaimed Israel's capital and was the site of the two holy Jewish Temples. As such, it continues to serve as the emotional and spiritual home for the Jewish people. As David Ben-Gurion, soon to be Israel's first prime minister would declare in 1947, "No city in the world, not even Athens or Rome, ever played as great a role in the life of a nation for so long a time as Jerusalem has done in the life of the Jewish people."[36] In the words of Jewish Holocaust survivor and Nobel Laureate Eli Wiesel, "Jerusalem is the heart of our heart, the soul of our soul."[37]

Jerusalem is the holiest city to Judaism for a much longer time, than Rome is for Catholics, Mecca and Medina are for Muslims and Varanasi is for Hindus. In Jerusalem, artifacts found inside excavations around the City of David and within the Old City, the Temple Mount and Solomon's Stables date the Jewish presence in Jerusalem as far back as 1,000 B.C.E., during the time of King David.[38] Since the rule of King David ca. 1010–968 B.C.E., the only nation of which Jerusalem has been the capital is the Jewish nation. It was the capital of the first Jewish kingdom ca.1010–586 B.C.E. and the second Jewish kingdom, 520 B.C.E.–73 C.E. During its long history, Jerusalem has been destroyed twice, besieged 23 times, attacked 52 times, and captured and recaptured 44 times.[39] It was divided only once, for nineteen years (May 1948–June 1967), under Jordanian occupation, in defiance of the will of the international community.

Jews have lived in Jerusalem for over 3,000 years with only two interruptions. The first interruption occurred after the failure of the Bar Kokhba Rebellion in 135 C.E. when the Romans banned them from the city. The second pause took place during the nineteen-year Jordanian occupation (May 1948–June 1967) of the eastern portion of the city including the walled Old City of Jerusalem, with its religious sites including the Temple Mount and Western Wall.

The Temple Mount (in Hebrew *Har Habayit*; in Arabic, *Haram esh-Sharif*, "the Noble Sanctuary"), includes the holiest Jewish site in the world—the location of the two ancient Jewish Temples. Jews have prayed there for centuries even after the Roman destruction in 70 C.E. It sits atop Mount Moriah, which was already sanctified for Jews from the time of Abraham as "Shalem" the "Land of Moriah", and the "Mount of the Lord."[40] It marked the site of where Abraham offered his son Isaac as a sacrifice (Muslims claim it was Ishmael)[41], and where Jacob dreamed of the ladder ascending to heaven. The Temple Mount is considered the place where the *Shechina*—the Divine Presence—rested and, as such, is sanctified for eternity. The original Temple Mount was a 500 square cubit compound (a cubit is an ancient unit of measurement based on the length of the forearm from the elbow to the tip of the middle finger, usually estimated as approximately 18 inches), where both the First Jewish Temple and Second Jewish Temple stood—the *Bet HaMikdash* (Hebrew for "Holy Temple"). Of that area only a smaller section thereof—the Holy of Holies—was too sacred to be entered by those ritually unclean. The current area 37-acre compound known as the Temple Mount was considerably enlarged by King Herod, especially on the north-south axis.

Contrary to widespread misconception, the Western Wall (*HaKotel HaMa'aravi*) is not Judaism's holiest site. It is the outer retaining wall of the Temple Mount compound on which stood both the First Jewish Temple and the Second Jewish Temple. It is the only remaining structure from the compound above it. The 37-acre Temple Mount compound has been a symbol of the deepest connection between the Jewish people—both religious and secular—and Judaism for two thousand years following the destruction of the Second Jewish Temple on *Tisha B'Av*—the ninth day of the Hebrew month of Av—in

70 C.E. The Cave of the Patriarchs in Hebron is the second holiest site, and Rachel's Tomb, on the road between Jerusalem and Bethlehem, is the third holiest site.

From the time of the Ottoman Turkish conquest in 1517 and for the next four hundred years, the Western Wall became the symbol of pilgrimage for Jews since they were denied access to the Temple Mount by the Muslims. After the British conquest of Jerusalem from the Turks in 1917, the term "Wailing Wall," was introduced by non-Jews, due to the heartfelt prayers observed and offered at the Western Wall. However, this name never won a wide following among traditional Jews and the term "Wailing Wall" is not used in Hebrew.

Under the British Mandate from 1921 to 1948, limits on worship at the Western Wall were imposed on Jews under pressure from the Arabs led by the Grand Mufti of Jerusalem, Hajj Amin al-Husseini. British restrictions denied the Jews the right to sit at the wall, separate the sexes by a screen, as well as forbade and declared illegal (from 1931), the blowing of the shofar (a ram's horn trumpet). During the 1930s, at the conclusion of Yom Kippur, young Jews persistently flouted the shofar ban each year and blew the shofar. The consequences of their action were arrest and prosecution, usually resulting in a fine or imprisonment for three to six months. After the Jordanian conquest of the Old City of Jerusalem in 1948 and under Jordanian occupation from May 1948–June 1967, the Jews enjoyed no access to the Western Wall. Jordan reneged on its 1949 Armistice agreement with Israel. Specifically they failed to honor the clause— Article VIII—that guaranteed Jewish access to the Western Wall and other holy sites. Instead, it was turned into an outdoor urinal. With the liberation of Jerusalem from Jordanian occupation on June 7, 1967, Jewish sovereignty was restored to the Western Wall.

As emphasized above, the Jewish presence in Jerusalem is described in the Bible, reinforced by archaeological evidence, and numerous ancient documents. Additionally, a large number of ancient, non-Jewish sources, document the presence of Jews in Jerusalem. These include Assyrian, Babylonian, Persian, Greek and Roman sources. The Taylor Prism is a clay prism inscribed with the annals of the Assyrian king Sennacherib. It was found in the ruins of Nineveh, Iraq, in 1830. Another prism, the Sennacherib Prism, was purchased by James Henry Breasted from a Baghdad antiques dealer in 1919 for the Oriental Institute in Chicago, where it now resides. Both prisms are notable for describing Sennacherib's assault against "Hezekiah, the king of the Jews and his capital city, Jerusalem" in 701 B.C.E. The Babylonian Chronicles, a collection of ancient tablets recording major events in Babylonian history, also tell of the Jews and Jerusalem. The Chronicles are presently found in the British Museum in London. One of the Elephantine Papyri, ca. fifth century B.C.E., composed in the seventeenth year of Persian King Darius, talks about the Jewish Temple in Jerusalem and its priests.

Long before Islam was founded by Muhammad, and aggressively roared out of the Arabian Peninsula on the road of conquest, many Greek and Roman historians were documenting that Jerusalem was a Jewish city. Some of the most notable are listed in the table below.

GREEK AND ROMAN HISTORIANS WHO RECORDED A JEWISH JERUSALEM		
Historian	**Time Period**	**Origin**
Hecataeus of Abdera	Fourth century B.C.E.	Greek
Lysimachus	360–28 B.C.E.	Greco-Macedonian
Manetho	Third century B.C.E.	Greco-Egyptian
Agatharchides	Second century B.C.E.	Greco-Egyptian
Diodorus Siculus	First century B.C.E.	Greek

Cicero	January 3, 106–December 7, 43 B.C.E.	Roman
Livy	59 B.C.E.–17 C.E.	Roman
Apion	ca. 20 B.C.E.–ca. 45/48 C.E.	Roman
Josephus Flavius*	37/38–ca.100 C.E.	Judeo-Roman citizen
Plutarch	ca. 46–120 C.E.	Greco-Roman citizen
Tacitus	ca. 56–ca. 117 C.E.	Roman
Suetonius	ca. 69/75–after 130 C.E.	Roman
Juvenal	Late first–early second century C.E.	Roman
Cassius Dio	ca. 155 or 163/164 C.E. until after 229 C.E.	Roman

Despite the fact that several of these historians were misojudaic, they wrote histories that clearly linked the Jewish people to Jerusalem, and Judaea. They made no mention of this land being "Arab" of being called "Palestine," or its people "Palestinians." On the contrary, they detailed the difference between the native Jews, which Rome was trying to subdue, and the Arabs from the surrounding lands, who decided to join the Romans in the conquest of Judaea.

Jerusalem became the united capital of the modern State of Israel by two wars of liberation. Both wars, in 1947–49 and again in 1967, were launched by the aggressive intent of the Arabs to wipe Israel off the map. Israel merely defended itself. In the first, Israel regained control of the western section of the city. It would have gained total control but Transjordan's King Abdullah I, listening to his British advisers, agreed to an armistice before he lost it all. For nineteen years thereafter, eastern Jerusalem was under Jordanian occupation and illegally annexed (*see* "Divided Jerusalem, 1948–67" map). Jordan violated (while the world stood silent) those same 1949 Armistice Agreements, which provided for free access to all the Jewish religious sites in the Old City of Jerusalem, including the Western Wall, and beyond, including the Mount of Olives Cemetery. Additionally, the Jewish Quarter of the Old City was totally desecrated and destroyed. The famous Hurva Synagogue was dynamited, the second time it was destroyed by Arabs, the first being in 1721, when Arab creditors burned the unfinished structure together with the forty Torah scrolls it contained. All fifty-eight of the Jewish Quarter's synagogues were desecrated or destroyed. Abdullah el-Tell, commander of the Sixth Battalion of the Arab Legion, reported to headquarters, "For the first time in 1,000 years not a single Jew remains in the Jewish Quarter. Not a single building remains intact. This makes the Jews' return here impossible"[42] (*see* the "Old City of Jerusalem under Jordanian occupation, 1948–67" map).

---

* Yosef Ben Matityahu, better known as the historian Josephus Flavius wrote *The Jewish War* (c. 75 C.E.) and *Antiquities and Wars of the Jews,* (c. 94 C.E.), in which he devoted hundreds of pages to the plight of the Jewish people in the Land of Israel and especially Jerusalem and the eventual destruction of their Temple.

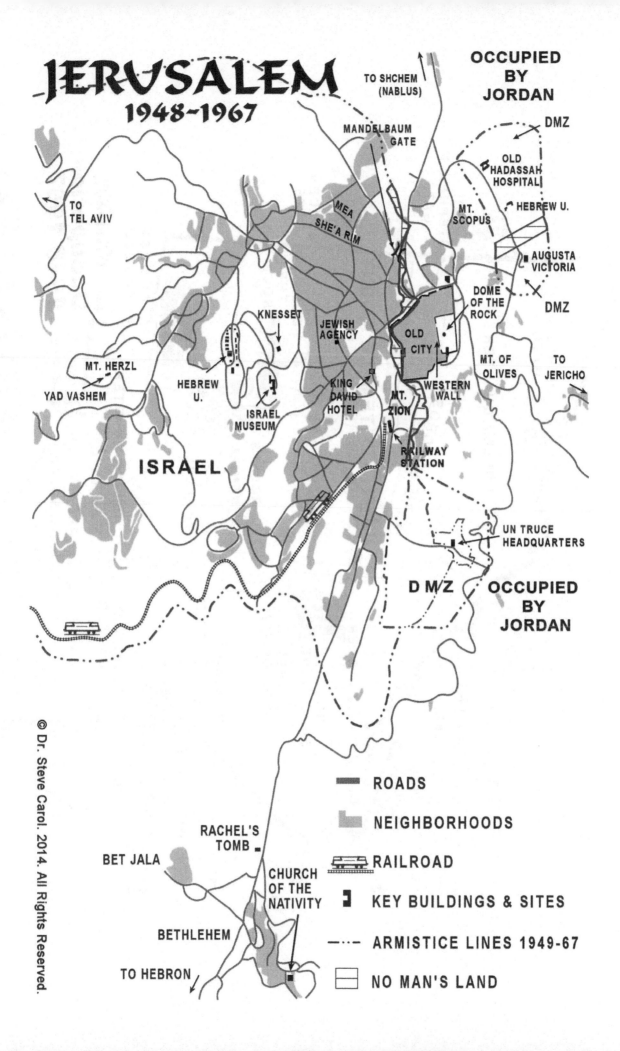

JERUSALEM
1948~1967

TO SHCHEM (NABLUS)

OCCUPIED BY JORDAN

MANDELBAUM GATE

DMZ

OLD HADASSAH HOSPITAL

MT. SCOPUS

HEBREW U.

TO TEL AVIV

MEA SHE'A RIM

AUGUSTA VICTORIA

DOME OF THE ROCK

DMZ

KNESSET

JEWISH AGENCY

OLD CITY

MT. OF OLIVES

TO JERICHO

MT. HERZL

HEBREW U.

KING DAVID HOTEL

WESTERN WALL

YAD VASHEM

ISRAEL MUSEUM

MT. ZION

ISRAEL

RAILWAY STATION

UN TRUCE HEADQUARTERS

D MZ   OCCUPIED BY JORDAN

ROADS

NEIGHBORHOODS

RACHEL'S TOMB

RAILROAD

BET JALA

CHURCH OF THE NATIVITY

KEY BUILDINGS & SITES

BETHLEHEM

ARMISTICE LINES 1949-67

TO HEBRON

NO MAN'S LAND

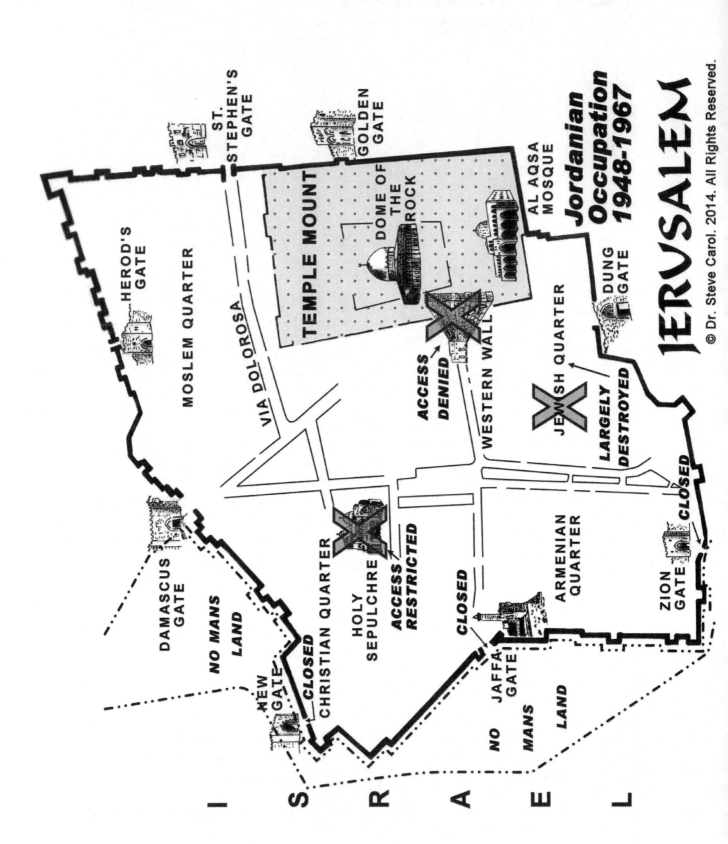

JERUSALEM

Jordanian Occupation 1948-1967

- ST. STEPHEN'S GATE
- GOLDEN GATE
- HEROD'S GATE
- MOSLEM QUARTER
- VIA DOLOROSA
- TEMPLE MOUNT
- DOME OF THE ROCK
- AL AQSA MOSQUE
- *ACCESS DENIED*
- WESTERN WALL
- JEWISH QUARTER
- *LARGELY DESTROYED*
- DUNG GATE
- DAMASCUS GATE
- *NO MANS LAND*
- NEW GATE
- *CLOSED*
- CHRISTIAN QUARTER
- HOLY SEPULCHRE
- *ACCESS RESTRICTED*
- JAFFA GATE *CLOSED*
- *NO MANS LAND*
- ARMENIAN QUARTER
- ZION GATE *CLOSED*

I S R A E L

On June 5, 1967, despite Israeli appeals via three different message-routes, not to enter the war, the Jordanians attacked Jerusalem. Two days later, on June 7, 1967, the second day of the Six-Day War, Israeli paratroopers entered Jerusalem's Old City and liberated it from nineteen years of illegal Jordanian occupation. For the first time in 1,897 years, the Temple Mount was under the control of a sovereign Jewish people. IDF Colonel Mordechai Gur, commander of the Paratroopers Brigade ordered three paratroopers to climb to the top of the Dome of the Rock and unfurl an Israeli flag over it. Four hours later leftwing Israeli Defense Minister Moshe Dayan ordered the flag taken down.[43] Rabbi Shlomo Goren was the chief rabbi of the IDF at the time of the Six-Day War. On that same day, June 7, 1967, he blew a shofar in front of the just liberated Western Wall. The event was famously depicted in a photograph.[44] Goren established his office on the Temple Mount and held a daylong seminar there for reservists from the military rabbinate, which was followed by a tour of the Mount. Goren wanted a Jewish presence as well as the right to pray on the Mount, but that was not to be. With the guns not yet silent, Dayan began to snatch defeat from the jaws of victory as far as the Temple Mount was concerned.

In a second move, Dayan ordered the IDF paratroop company that was supposed to remain permanently stationed in the northern part of the mount to withdraw. General Uzi Narkiss, head of Central Command pleaded with Dayan that the troops should stay, reminding the latter of Jordan's earlier stationing of military forces on the Temple Mount during its occupation of the Old City from 1948 to 1967, and the even earlier stationing of Roman forces in the Antonia Fortress built by Herod (adjacent to the Temple Mount) to maintain order. Dayan, however, was not persuaded. He told Narkiss that it seemed to him the place would have to be left in the hands of the Muslim guards.[45] Dayan added insult to injury, when ten days later on June 17, Dayan met with the Muslim *Waqf* (religious authority) that ran the Temple Mount. At their meeting, Dayan stated:

> This compound was our Temple Mount. Here stood our Temple during ancient time, and it would be inconceivable for Jews not to be able freely to visit this holy place now that Jerusalem is under our rule.[46]

Note that Dayan spoke of the Jews having visiting rights without restriction, (i.e. "freely") at the Temple Mount, but no mention was made of being able to pray there! Dayan thought, and years later even committed the thought to writing, that since for Muslims the mount is a "Muslim prayer mosque" while for Jews it is no more than "a historical site of commemoration of the past...one should not hinder the Arabs from behaving there as they now do."[47]

The Israeli defense minister believed that Islam must be allowed to express its religious sovereignty—as opposed to national sovereignty—over the mount; that the Arab-Israeli conflict must be kept on the territorial-national level; and that the potential for a conflict between the Jewish religion and the Muslim religion must be removed. In granting Jews the right to visit the mount, Dayan sought to placate the Jewish demands for worship and sovereignty there. In giving religious sovereignty over the mount to the Muslims, he believed he was defusing the site as a center of Palestinian nationalism.[48]

Seemingly, Dayan did this due to his misguided assumption that the grateful Muslims would appreciate Jewish magnanimity and reciprocate allowing Jews and Muslims to worship in peaceful harmony on the Mount. The Muslims have not and will not as the Qur'an dictates treatment of Jews as *dhimmis* or worse. Thus, Dayan* committed a disastrous mistake, effectively handing over the keys of the Temple Mount to the *Waqf*, which retained total control and jurisdiction over this extensive area and over the past nearly half-century have increasingly violated Jewish access to the mount, conducted unauthorized digs, construction and other changes to try to permanently de-Judaize and instead Islamize the sacred plateau..

Following the destruction of Jerusalem by the Romans in the year 70 C.E., the area of the Temple was deliberately left in ruins (first by the Romans, then by the Byzantines). These ruins were not removed until the Muslim conquest of the city by the Caliph Umar ibn al-Khattab in 638 C.E. The Muslims recognized the area of the Dome of the Rock on the Temple Mount as holy because of Solomon's Temple, as borne by the Arabic name for Jerusalem, *Al-Quds*; adapted from the original Arabic name for the Temple Mount: *Bayt al-Maqdis*. Umar ordered the clearing of the rubble and debris around the *Ṣakhra* ("rock")—i.e. Mount Moriah and the Temple Mount. After three showers of heavy rain had cleansed the Rock, Umar instituted prayers there. To this day, the place is known as *ḳubbat es ṣakhra*, the "Dome of the Rock."

The Dome of the Rock covers Mount Moriah. It was built not as a mosque, but rather as a shrine. "At the request of the Jews, [Caliph] Umar built the Dome of the Rock sanctuary to serve as a house of prayer for the Jews. This was after the Jews showed him the site where the Holy Temple had stood— and it does not point to Mecca."[49] However, due to recent encroachments by the *Waqf*, the Dome of the Rock has become a *de facto* place of worship. Also on the Temple Mount today is the Al-Aqsa Mosque, which was built as a Muslim house of prayer. It was constructed "outside the boundaries of the original Temple Mount,"[50] which was part of King Herod's extension of the plateau at the southern end of the Temple Mount plaza opposite the Dome of the Rock, and therefore it points southward towards Mecca. According to Muslim tradition, the current Al-Aqsa is identified as the place of the "farthest mosque" (in Arabic, *masjid al-aqsa*) from which the Prophet Mohammed, accompanied by the Angel Gabriel, made the Night Journey (*Shab-e-Me`raj*) to the "farthest mosque" (*see* Qur'an 17:1). However, the "furthest mosque" at that time was nowhere near the City of Jerusalem. In fact the Muslim historians Abu `Abdullah Muhammad Ibn 'Omar Ibn Waqid al-Aslami—commonly referred to as al-Waqidi ca. 748–822 C.E., and the ninth century historian al-Azraqi state that the "farthest mosque" was in Jiranah, a place ten miles from Mecca.[51] An Egyptian scholar, Ahmed Mahmad Oufa, reminded the public of this fact in an article he wrote on August 28, 2003 that Muhammad's Night Journey had nothing to do with Jerusalem.[52]

Jerusalem became the third-holiest city in Islam quite by historical happenstance. In 692 C.E., 'Abd-Allah ibn al-Zubayr, the nephew of Aisha, third wife of Muhammad led a rebellion against the Umayyad Caliphate and conquered Mecca. Pilgrims were prevented from reaching Mecca for the

---

* Rabbi Eliezer Melamed in his recent article, "Judaism: Rabbi Goren and the Temple Mount," Arutz-7, November 16, 2014, (at http://www.israelnationalnews.com/Articles/Article.aspx/15980#.VHJ3v2M0Rx1) explained the nature of Moshe Dayan. The quotes are from that article. Moshe Dayan was a very controversial personality in modern Israeli history. "For years, it was known in Israel that Moshe Dayan had both a dark and a light side jumbled together." On the one hand, Dayan was a true Israeli war hero, in the Sinai Campaign of 1956 and in achieving the miraculous victory in the Six-Day War of 1967. However, on the other hand he was largely to blame for the *Mechdal* ("the Failure") for much of what happened, especially in the opening week of the Yom Kippur War. Furthermore, he was "an adulterer and a thief" of archaeological artifacts. "Apparently, his adultery and thievery tipped the scales against him. That is when he began to lose his public status."

Hajj. This in turn, deprived the fifth Umayyad Caliph Abd al-Malik ibn Marwan of the revenue of the lucrative hajj trade. Not knowing how long the rebellion would last (Ibn al-Zubayr held Mecca for six months before being defeated and killed), Umar searched for a city under his control of equal religiosity to serve as an alternative site for the pilgrimage. He settled on Jerusalem, already the most sacred city for the Jews and of great religious importance to Christians as well. Conveniently, Qur'an 17:1) which dealt with Muhammad's Night Journey to the "farthest mosque" was a perfect fit since "the farthest mosque" was not named. Thus, Jerusalem—though never specifically named—was assigned that role. Despite the fact that at the time, the journey between Mecca and Jerusalem took three days by camel, the Muslims have claimed that Jerusalem was the "farthest mosque" and both the Temple Mount as well as the Western Wall were sacred to Islam. Accordingly, Muhammad tethered his magical steed, *Al-Buraq,* to the Western Wall of the Temple Mount and from there ascended to the seventh heaven. Subsequently, to deny the Jewish historical and religious connection to the Western Wall, the Muslims renamed it the *Al-Buraq* Wall.

Al-Aqsa Mosque was built, expanded and completed in 705 c.e., some 73 years after the death of Muhammad. More rebuilding was necessitated by two earthquakes in 746 and 1033. The present Al-Aqsa Mosque dates from 1035. During the British Mandate period, the Temple Mount was administered by the Supreme Muslim Council headed by the Grand Mufti of Jerusalem, Hajj Amin al-Husseini. This was a tradition originating from the creation of the Islamic *Waqf* in 1432. After the Jordanian conquest of the Old City of Jerusalem including the Temple Mount in 1948, King Abdullah I created a new post in 1951, that of Guardian of the Haram E-Sharif and Supreme Custodian of the Holy Places of All Other Religions.[53] Despite the lofty title, Jewish sites under Jordanian control were obliterated, and Christian sites severely restricted. PLO Chairman Yasser Arafat also referred to an "assertion by the British mandatory government in 1929 that the Western Wall is the Wall of Al-Buraq, and that it is regarded as an Islamic *Waqf* and an historic Islamic right."[54]

On August 16, 1967 (which coincided with the Jewish *Tisha B'Av*—the ninth day of the Hebrew month of Av, the fast day which commemorates the destruction of the First and Second Temples) Rabbi Goren led a group of fifty Jews to pray on the Mount. They carried with them a Torah scroll, an Ark for the scroll and some benches.[55] After the service, Goren announced that he would hold prayer services there on Yom Kippur. However, because of Defense Minister Dayan's insistence (seconded by Chief of Staff Yitzhak Rabin) the Israeli government prohibited any further activities by Goren on the Mount. Dayan was already restricting the rights of Jews vis-à-vis the Temple Mount. So much for unrestricted Jewish access to the holiest site in Judaism. A year later, then-Minister of Justice Yaakov Shimshon Shapira, said at a committee meeting in June 1968, "We [the government] never announced that the entirety of the Temple Mount belongs to the Arabs. We never announced that it is forbidden for Jews to pray there. We never announced that it is forbidden for Jews to establish a synagogue there."[56] Despite Shapira's statement, the leftist Israeli government made no move to counteract Dayan's move. Dayan's action proved to be a colossal blunder—the ramifications of which are felt to the present day. The Jerusalem *Waqf* violated the trust with which it was authorized to respect and protect the holiness of the Temple Mount for *both* (emphasis added) Muslims and Jews. The *Waqf* removed every sign of ancient Jewish presence at the Jewish holy site and consistently destroyed Jewish antiquities on the Temple Mount in a direct violation of a ruling by the Israeli Supreme Court.

After the Six-Day War, Jerusalem was then proclaimed, on two occasions, the united capital of Israel. While it served as a capital of the Crusader "Kingdom of Jerusalem" for eighty-eight years, the Crusaders were not a nation. It has never served as an Arab capital for the simple reason that there has never been an independent Arab state in that area.

The Jews are the only people who have inhabited Jerusalem continuously–with relatively short interruptions imposed by bans of conquerors—for 3,000 years. From the early nineteenth century, Jews constituted the largest ethnic group in the city,[57] and by the end of the nineteenth century, they had become an absolute majority—a position they have kept for over 150 years.

THE POPULATION OF JERUSALEM				
Year	Jewish	Muslim	Christian	Total[58]
1844[59]	7,120	5,760	3,390	16,270
1854[60]	8,000	4,000	3,500	15,500
1876[61]	12,000	7,560	5,470	25,030
1896	28,112	8,560	8,748	45,420
1922[62]	33,971	13,413	14,699	62,578[63]
1931	51,222	19,894	19,335	90,503[64]
1944	92,143	32,039	27,849	152,031
1948[65]	99,320	36,680	31,300	165,000
1961[66][67]	187,700	2,400	1,600	191,700
1967	195,700	54,963	12,646	263,307
1972	261,100	74,400	11,800	347,300
1983	346,700	112,100	13,900	472,700
1988	352,800	125,200	14,400	493,500
1990	378,200	131,800	14,400	524,500

YEAR	JEWISH	MUSLIM	CHRISTIAN	NCBR*	TOTAL
1995[68]	420,900	165,800	13,500	2,400	602,700
2000[69]	439,600	196,900	14,200	6,700	657,500
2005	464,300	232,300	14,900	8,300	719,900
2007[70]	509,600	295,500	15,000	8,500	747,600
2008[71]	479,800	256,700	14,300	9,500	760,400
2009	484,700	264,300	14,500	9,400	773,800
2010	488,200	268,300	11,500/15,400[72]	9,400	777,400
2013[73]	499,400	281,100	14,700	9,000	804,400†

There is no equivalent in any monotheistic religion for Jewish prayers, because some of them go all the way back to biblical times. Psalm 137 admonishes the Jewish people, "If I forget thee, O Jerusalem, let my right hand forget her cunning. If I do not remember thee, let my tongue cleave to the roof of my mouth; if I prefer not Jerusalem above my highest joy." The city is mentioned 658 times by name and 158 times as Zion, in the *Tanakh* (Hebrew/Jewish Bible). In the New Testament, it

---

* Not classified by religion.

† Includes 200 Druze.

is mentioned 154 times (and as Zion, seven times). The Qur'an never mentions Jerusalem—not even once—nor for that manner, does it mention "Palestine."

No matter where Jews lived throughout the world, as the Diaspora for 1,875 years, their thoughts and prayers were directed toward Jerusalem. Despite centuries of exile, the Jews maintained a continuous presence in Jerusalem. Even today, whether in Israel, the United States or anywhere else, Jewish ritual practice, holiday celebration, and lifecycle events include recognition of Jerusalem as a core element of the Jewish experience. Consider that:

- Jews in prayer always turn toward Jerusalem.
- Jerusalem is mentioned twenty-one times in a Jews' daily prayers.
- Arks (the repository traditionally in or against the wall of a synagogue) that hold Torah scrolls in synagogues throughout the world are placed on the wall nearest Jerusalem.
- Jews end the Passover Seders each year with the words, "Next year in Jerusalem." The same words are pronounced at the end of Yom Kippur, the most solemn day of the Jewish year.
- A three-week moratorium on weddings in the summer recalls the breaching of the walls of Jerusalem by the Chaldean (New Babylonian) army in 586 B.C.E. That period culminates in a special day of mourning—*Tisha B'Av* (the ninth day of the Hebrew month of Av)—commemorating the destruction of both the First and Second Jewish Temples.
- Jewish wedding ceremonies—joyous occasions, are marked by sorrow over the loss of Jerusalem. The groom recites a biblical verse from the Babylonian Exile, "If I forget thee, O Jerusalem, let my right hand forget her cunning," and breaks a glass in commemoration of the destruction of the Holy Temples.

Even body language, often said to tell volumes about a person, reflects the importance of Jerusalem to Jews as a people and, arguably, the lower priority the city holds for Muslims:

- As has been mentioned, when Jews pray they face Jerusalem; in Jerusalem Israelis pray facing the Temple Mount, the single holiest place in Judaism. It is not only where the two Jewish Temples stood, it is considered by tradition to be Mount Moriah, the site of the *Akedah Yitzhak*—the place where Isaac was supposed to be sacrificed. (The original Moriah was extended with retaining walls by King Herod, around 19 B.C.E., with his expansion of the Second Temple.
- When Muslims pray, they face Mecca. In Jerusalem, Muslims point their behinds towards the Temple Mount—the Jewish Holy of Holies—and pray with their backs to the city.
- Even at burial, a Muslim face is turned toward Mecca.

Ben-Gurion, reminded the Israeli Parliament, the Knesset, in 1949, "Our ties today with Jerusalem are no less deep than those which existed in the days of Nebuchadnezzar and Titus Flavius ... our fighting youth knew how to sacrifice itself for our holy capital no less than did our forefathers in the days of the First and Second Jewish Temples." In 1950, Abba Eban, Israel's Foreign Minister, would emphasize this theme at the UN Trusteeship Council, "A devotion to the Holy City has been a constant theme of our people for three thousand years."

At the 1991 Madrid Peace Conference, Prime Minister Yitzhak Shamir told the opening session attended by nearly all the region's Arab leaders, "We are the only people who have lived in the Land of Israel without interruption for nearly 4,000 years; we are the only people, except for a short

Crusader kingdom, who have had an independent sovereignty in this land; we are the only people for whom Jerusalem has been a capital; we are the only people whose sacred places are only in the Land of Israel."

It must be further noted that Jerusalem has never been the capital of any Arab or Muslim political entity. Muslim caliphates all regarded other cities far more important than Jerusalem, whether they actually controlled Jerusalem or not.

MUSLIM CALIPHATES		
Muslim Caliphate[*]	Years in Existence	Capital City
Rashidun	632–661	Medina (632–56) Kufa (656–61)
Umayyad	661–750	Damascus
Al-Andalus	756–1031	Córdoba
Abbasid	750–1258	Baghdad
Fatimid	909–1171	Mahdia (909–69) Cairo (969–1171)
Ottoman	1517–1924[†]	Constantinople
Sokoto	1804–March 13, 1903	Gudu (1804) Sokoto (1804-1850), (1851-1902) Birnin Konni (1850)

While Jerusalem is accorded special status in Islamic history, the Qur'an (34:13), nonetheless, confirms that Jerusalem was ruled by the Jewish King Solomon and mentioned his construction there, "they made for him whatever he wished of sanctuaries, and statues, and basins as [large as] great watering-troughs and cauldrons firmly anchored [because of their huge size]."[74] The "sanctuaries" were apparently the great halls of the new Temple.[75] Furthermore, the Qur'an records the destruction of the First and Second Jewish Temples (17:7), "[We raised new enemies against you and allowed them] to disgrace you utterly, and to enter the Holy Temple, as [their forerunners] had entered it once before, and to destroy with utter destruction all that they had conquered."[76]

As late as the fourteenth century, Islamic scholar and theologian Taqi ad-Din Ibn Taymiyya (1263–1328), who was regarded as a superior authority on Islamic knowledge and whose writings influenced the Wahhabist movement in Arabia, ruled that sacred Islamic sites are to be found only in the Arabian Peninsula. Of importance was Ibn Taymiyya's declaration that "in Jerusalem, there is not a place one calls sacred [to Islam], and the same holds true for the tombs of [the Biblical Patriarchs and Matriarchs in] Hebron."[77]

---

[*] The title adopted by Abu Bakr, the first caliph, as the head of the universal Islamic community. The word itself was taken from the phrase *Khalifat Rasul Allah* ("Successor to the Messenger [Muhammad] of Allah"). The institution was known as the caliphate.

[†] On March 3, 1924, the first President of the Turkish Republic, Mustafa Kemal Atatürk, as part of his reforms, constitutionally abolished the institution of the Caliphate.

During the 1930s, the infamous Grand Mufti of Jerusalem, Hajj Amin al-Husseini, began promoting the idea that Jerusalem was the third most important holy city of Islam. He renovated the mosques that had fallen into complete disrepair on the Temple Mount. The Arab/Muslim claim to the city as being a Muslim, not Jewish, city was accelerated after the Six-Day War, when Israel recovered the eastern portion of the city from Jordanian occupation in a war of self-defense.

Recent statements by Arab Muslim leaders that there was never a Jewish presence in Jerusalem are utter nonsense and a crude attempt at re-writing history. The PLO/PA Mufti, Ikrima Sabri, (who was appointed by Yasser Arafat) was interviewed by the German *Die Welt* on the issues of Jerusalem, the Jews and the Arab-Israeli conflict on January 17, 2001. Sabri declared:

> There is not [even] the smallest indication of the existence of a Jewish temple on this place in the past. In the whole city, there is not even a single stone indicating Jewish History. Our right, on the other hand, is very clear. This place belongs to us for 1,500 years. Even when it was conquered by the Crusaders, it remained Al-Aqsa, and we got it back soon afterwards. The Jews do not even know exactly where their temple stood. Therefore, we do not accept that they have any rights, underneath the surface or above it.[78]

The *Die Welt* reporter challenged Sabri as to why he could not respect the Jewish connection to the Western Wall, in light of the fact that it was agreed among archeologists that the Western Wall was part of the foundation of Herod's temple and that the Bible and other ancient sources reported about that site in detail. Sabri with misojudaic invective persisted:

> It is the art of the Jews to deceive the world. But they can't do it to us. There is not a single stone in the Wailing Wall (which he referred to as the "Al Burak Wall") relating to Jewish History. The Jews cannot legitimately claim this wall, neither religiously or historically. The Committee of the League of Nations recommended in 1930, to allow the Jews to pray there, in order to keep them quiet. But by no means did it acknowledge that the wall belongs to them.[79]

The *Die Welt* interviewer asked, "Why don't you allow Israeli scientists to dig there to look for possible remnants and proofs for or against the existence of the Jewish temple?" To which Sabri responded:

> We categorically reject all excavations under the Al-Aqsa Mosque, because they would endanger the historical buildings on the site. Besides, they have already dug everywhere. All they could find were remnants of buildings from the Umayyad period. Everything they excavated was related to Arabs and Muslims.[80]

To the contrary, for decades the Jerusalem *Waqf*—the Muslim religious trust—has been destroying unique Jewish antiquities on the Temple Mount under different pretexts. A case in point occurred with the July 2007 digging of a 400-meter-long, 1.5-meter-deep trench from the northern side of the

Temple Mount compound to the Dome of the Rock,[*] allegedly in order to replace 40-year-old electric cables in the area.[81] In the process of these excavations, between 1999 and 2001, the *Waqf* unearthed, removed and dumped enormous quantities (more than 13,000 tons) of priceless archeological artifacts, from the First and Second Holy Temple periods—what the *Waqf* termed rubble—from the Temple Mount and its substructure. The most striking find, thus far, from this "rubble" is a First Temple period bulla, or seal impression, containing ancient Hebrew writing, which may have belonged to a well-known family of *Kohanim* ("priests") mentioned in the Book of Jeremiah.[82] Two reasons were put forth as to why this removal and dumping was allowed to happen: There was insufficient Israeli government attention paid to what the Muslims were doing; or alternatively, the Israeli government may have known and chose to turn a blind eye so as to avoid a fight with the Muslims.

Running on a parallel track, in another bid to further their ongoing attempts at delegitimizing Israel and denying the Jewish connection to Jerusalem and the Land of Israel, the Arab/Muslim world has created the fiction of two Jerusalems, one Arab and the other Jewish, and that the Arab one was taken from them and needs to be restored. Nothing is further from the historic truth. The division of Jerusalem into two cities is no more valid than the Soviet division of the German capital, Berlin[†] by force, in the early days of the Cold War or the Turkish division by force, of the Cypriot capital, Nicosia[‡] in August 1974.

Israel's Arab/Muslim enemies know very well the Israeli and Jewish connection to Jerusalem and it is precisely that connection they target and now demand, as a minimum the "return" of the northern, eastern and southern parts of Jerusalem, as well as the re-Islamization of the holy city. Israel's Arab/Muslim enemies have openly declared, "Jerusalem is the cornerstone of the spiritual edifice and the Zionist Jewish entity. Were it to be dislodged the whole edifice and the Zionist entity itself would crumble like a deck of cards."[83]

The theme of no Jewish presence on the Temple Mount or in Jerusalem has constantly been repeated by other Arab/Muslim leaders. Yasser Arafat falsely proclaimed, without corroborating historic proof, that the Palestinians' "forefathers, [were] the Canaanites and the Jebusites" in a effort to pre-date the Jewish King David.[84] There is no archeological evidence to support such Palestinian claims. Of note is the fact that the Canaanites spoke a language akin to Hebrew and thus could not have been "Arabs." Archeologists and historians have generally concluded that most, if not all, modern day Palestinian Arabs are "more closely related to the Arabs of Saudi Arabia, Yemen, Jordan and other countries than they are to the ancient Jebusites, Canaanites, or Philistines."[85] Raed Salah Abu Shakra, the leader of the northern branch of the Islamic Movement (Hamas) stated in 2006, "We remind, for the 1,000[th] time, that the entire Al-Aqsa Mosque [on the Temple Mount], including all of its area and alleys above the ground and under it, is exclusive and absolute Muslim property, and no one else has any rights to even one grain of earth in it."[86] In August 2009, Sheik Tayseer Rajab

---

[*] The Dome of the Rock is a shrine and not a mosque, located atop and in the center of the Jewish Temple Mount in the Old City of Jerusalem. First completed in 691 C.E., it was built at the order of Umayyad Caliph Abd al-Malik as a symbol of Muslim supremacy, after the Muslim Arab conquest of the Land of Israel.

[†] In the interest of historical accuracy, it should be noted that the Soviet presence in Berlin, division notwithstanding, was valid as they had been fighting a defensive war against German aggression. This was decidedly unlike the Transjordanian Arab Legion assault and occupation of predominantly Jewish Jerusalem which was part of the overall Arab aggression against the Jewish state in 1948.

[‡] In their invasion and occupation of Nicosia, Turkish forces uprooted and drove out thousands of Greek Cypriots, who have never been allowed to return. Turks have been moved into the northern section, a violation of the Fourth Geneva Convention. Nicosia is currently the last divided capital in the world.

Tamimi, chief Islamic judge of the PLO/PA declared, "[Jerusalem is solely] an Arab and Islamic city and it has always been so."[87] These are but a few examples of the ongoing campaign by the PLO/PA and Islamist groups to erase the Jewish connection to Jerusalem entirely.

Since 1998, the PLO/PA has been conducting a longstanding, systematic campaign to deny Israel's right to exist, first by claiming there was no Jewish history in the Land of Israel and then by fabricating a "Palestinian" narrative for Jewish sites, artifacts and archeological finds. PA academics and religious leaders have claimed that Palestinians, Arabs and Muslims all populated the land of Israel in biblical times and even earlier. In March 2009, the Supreme Islamic Council of the PLO/PA declared that Arabs have been living in the land of "Palestine" since 7,500 B.C.E.[88] This Palestinian Arab narrative is fabricated. It is a brazen attempt to steal Jewish heritage, history, and values, as well as deny its legitimacy as a people and a state.

These purveyors of falsehood need only look at the writings in the Qur'an, as cited above. This fabricated historic revisionism is repeated often in the big lie technique. The big lie technique was put forth by Adolf Hitler, in *Mein Kampf.* "The size of the lie is a definite factor in causing it to be believed, for the vast masses of a nation are in the depths of their hearts more easily deceived than they are consciously and intentionally bad. The primitive simplicity of their minds renders them a more easy prey to a big lie than a small one, for they themselves often tell little lies, but would be ashamed to tell big lies."[89] The Nazi regime perfected the technique and had as its chief purveyor, Reich Minister of Public Enlightenment and Propaganda, Joseph Goebbels.

Aside from the references in the Qur'an, there is a more recent official Muslim acknowledgment of Jerusalem's Jewish history. In 1924, a publicity booklet was published by the Supreme Muslim Council of Jerusalem—the *Waqf*—called *A Brief Guide to al-Haram al-Sharif. Al-haram al-sharif,* the Arabic name for the Temple Mount, is currently the site of the Dome of the Rock, a shrine, and Al-Aqsa Mosque. It is, according to Islamic tradition, where Muhammad ascended to heaven.[90]

Yet it is also, according to the council's booklet, on page four, a site of uncontested importance for the Jews. "The site is one of the oldest in the world. Its sanctity dates from the earliest (perhaps from pre-historic) times. Its identity with the site of Solomon's Temple is beyond dispute." And the booklet quotes the book of 2 Samuel 24:25, "This, too, is the spot, according to the universal belief, on which 'David built there an altar unto the Lord, and offered burnt offering and peace offerings.'"[91] Later on page sixteen, the booklet says the underground structure known as King Solomon's Stables probably dates "as far back as the construction of Solomon's Temple." Citing the historian Josephus Flavius, it claims the stables were likely used as a "place of refuge by the Jews at the time of the conquest of Jerusalem by Titus in the year 70 A.D. [C.E.]."[92] However, those references were expunged in 1954 in favor of a new falsified, historical narrative.

A word about the US position regarding Jerusalem. On April 24, 1990, the US House of Representatives, with the Senate concurring, passed (H. Con. Res. 290) a resolution acknowledging, "Jerusalem is and should remain the capital of the State of Israel" and expressing the belief that "Jerusalem must remain an undivided city in which the rights of every ethnic and religious group are protected." It did so recognizing that "since 1967 Jerusalem had been an united city administered by Israel" and because of "ambiguous statements by the Government of the United States concerning the right of Jews to live in all parts of Jerusalem raise concerns in Israel that Jerusalem might one day be redivided." The resolution passed by a vote of 378 to 34.

The Jerusalem Embassy Act was passed, on October 23, 1995, with overwhelming majorities of both houses of the 104th Congress. The vote was 93 to 5 in the Senate and 374 to 37 in the House. The law went into effect, November 8, 1995. It provided that "Jerusalem should be recognized as the undivided, eternal capital of the State of Israel; and the United States Embassy in Israel should be established in Jerusalem no later than May 31, 1999." It went so far as to cut appropriations to the Executive by 50 percent until the Embassy was opened. The law contains a waiver allowing the President to delay implementation of the act on the grounds of national security interests. To date, every President since Bill Clinton has exercised the waiver and the act has not been implemented. The US Embassy has not been moved to Jerusalem and remains in Tel Aviv.

Finally, it cannot be stressed enough that Israel is the only country in the Middle East that allows genuine freedom of conscience and protects sacred sites of all faiths. Since June 1967, Israel has a proven track record of ensuring full access to Jerusalem's holy sites. It allowed all peoples, including citizens of enemy states, e.g. Kuwaiti Muslims, to visit those holy sites.

15. Since biblical times and throughout history, the name for the mountainous highlands in the center of the Land of Israel has been Judea and Samaria.

Judea and Samaria—*Yehuda VeShomron* (in Hebrew)—are the historical biblical names for the mountainous, highland regions of the Land of Israel, with Samaria in the north and Judea in the south. The geographic and strategic importance of Judea and Samaria has been discussed in a previous chapter. Judea and Samaria is the cradle of the Jewish nation its history, religion, culture, language, and holidays. Both are referred to by name in the Bible. The name "Judea" is a Greek and Roman adaptation of the name "Judah," (the fourth son of Jacob and Leah, as well as the tribe named after him) which originally encompassed the territory of the Israelite tribe of that name and later the ancient Kingdom of Judah. The area was the southern part of the Hasmonean Kingdom and the later Kingdom of Judah, a sub-province in the Roman Empire.

Among many references, Judea is mentioned in Deuteronomy 34:2, "And all Naphtali, and the land of Ephraim, and Manasseh, and all the land of Judah, to the utmost sea;" in I Samuel 22:5, "depart, and get thee into the land of Judah;" as well as in the Book of Ezra 5:1, "When the prophets … prophesized unto the Jews that were in Judea;" and in 5:8, "Be it known unto the king, that we went into the province of Judea." Additionally, the region was mentioned again in the Book of Nehemiah I 11:3, "the cities of Judea" and in 11:20, "were in all the cities of Judea." The Persians named the province around Jerusalem *Yehud* and Nehemiah was governor of *Yehud*—Judea.

Samaria is mentioned in Book I Kings 16:24 "And he [King Omri] bought the mountain Samaria of Shemer for two talents of silver and built on the mountain and called the name of the city which he built, after the name of Shemer, owner of the mountain Samaria." That city was the capital of the Kingdom of Israel. Shomron means "guard" and the mountains of Samaria geographically guarded northwestern Israel, as well as the Jordan rift valley to the east. Judea and Samaria form the geographic heartland of the Land of Israel.

Judea and Samaria are the definitive and proper political and geographic names for the region and have been in general use since Clearchus, a disciple of Aristotle. These two areas have no other names. No one would dream of referring to Sinai as anything but Sinai, or to Sussex (in the United Kingdom), Normandy (in France) or Manhattan (in the US) as anything but Sussex, Normandy or Manhattan. Similarly, with a longer historic pedigree than those areas, Judea is Judea and Samaria is Samaria.

The author has copies of maps in his possession—"Holy Land," by Abraham Ortelius, 1584; "A Map of the Land of Canaan," by O. Lindeman, 1757; and "The Ten Tribes of Israel," by St. D'Anville, 1783—which all feature prominently, the names "Judea" and "Samaria." Furthermore, *The Jefferson Bible,*[93] compiled by the third President of the United States, contains two maps, the first entitled "*Loca Terrae Sanctae,*" and the second labeled "Tabula Geographica." Both prominently display "Judaea" and "Samaria." The term "Palestine" is nowhere to be seen. Noted historians, archeologists and travelers to the region throughout the nineteenth century recorded the area as "Judea and Samaria." These included:

- E. Robinson and E. Smith (*Biblical Researches in Palestine, Mount Sinai and Arabia Petraea: A Journal of Travels in the Year 1838,* 1841)
- C.W. Van de Velde (*Peise durch Syrien und Paletsinea,* 1861)
- Felix Bovet (*Voyage en Terre Sainte,* 1861)
- H. B. Tristram (*The Land of Israel: A Journal of Travels in Palestine,* 1865)
- Mark Twain (*The Innocents Abroad,* 1869)
- R.A. Stewart MacAlister and E.W.G. Masterman (*Palestine Exploration Fund Quarterly,* 1869)
- A.P. Stanley (*Sinai and Palestine in Connection with Their History,* 1877)

The names "Judea and Samaria" were used during the League of Nations Mandate period. They appeared in British government documents,[94] and United Nations documents including the UN Partition Plan of 1947[95]. They appeared in US State Department documents, including a July 18, 1948 map.[96] Even as late as 1961, the *Encyclopaedia Britannica* refers to "Judaea" and "Samaria" in an article on "Palestine."[97]

As was related, Transjordan illegally invaded Judea and Samaria in May 1948 and because of its aggression occupied that region. It needs to be emphasized that overall, the pan-Arab invasion of the nascent State of Israel was more a scramble for territory of the former British Mandate of Palestine than a fight for the national rights of the Arab inhabitants residing there. In any event, that Arab invasion and occupation nullified the UN Partition Plan of 1947.

As the first Secretary General of the Arab League, Abdel Rahman Azzam, once admitted to a British reporter, the goal of King Abdullah I of Transjordan "was to swallow up the central hill regions of Palestine, with access to the Mediterranean at Gaza. The Egyptians would get the Negev. Galilee would go to Syria, except that the coastal part as far as Acre would be added to the Lebanon."[98] Thus in 1948, the invading Arab states were not trying to establish a Palestinian Arab state, but rather were after territorial self-aggrandizement. In December 1949, Transjordan unilaterally annexed Judea and Samaria as well as the Old City of Jerusalem, conquered by the Arab Legion, during the Israeli War of Independence. The Jordanian Parliament ratified the move on April 4, 1950. The illegal annexation, rejected by the international community, was recognized only by two nations, the United Kingdom and Pakistan.

The Arab League, their Muslim supporters, anti-Israel elements and misojudaic peoples, deliberately sought to rob the region of its correct geographic, political and historic name. They had to fabricate a brand new name for they could find no other name for the territory, after forcibly occupying Judea and Samaria. Removing the prefix "Trans" from "Transjordan" was a way to hide the fact that the artificially created kingdom was situated east of the east bank of the Jordan River, but not on both banks. The "West Bank" was the name concocted by King Abdullah I of Transjordan and his British advisors, allowing the king to lay claim to and annex land outside of his kingdom. Deliberately relabeling was the technique used to delegitimize and erase the centuries-old name for the region—Judea and Samaria. Abdullah then changed the name of his kingdom twice, first to "The Hashemite Kingdom of the Jordan," on June 2, 1949, (to reflect his conquests west of the river) but that was quickly rejected since it gave the appearance of a kingdom only along the banks of the Jordan River. The name then was changed again to "The Hashemite Kingdom of Jordan." The term "West Bank" eradicates all historic and on-going Jewish connection to the area, much the same way as Roman Emperor Hadrian did in 135 C.E. by changing "Judaea" to "Syria Palaestina." The use of the term "West Bank," is a political, not a geographic statement in support of the Arab propaganda narrative. It is a sad commentary that many in the West, including the political left, many of Israel's supporters, some Israelis themselves, as well as the naïve and self-delusional who think the name does not matter, have acquiesced to this unilateral change of names and use it in common parlance. But the name does matter. Similarly, the Arabs insist on calling the Persian Gulf, the "Arabian Gulf" and Iran's Khuzistan province, as "Arabistan." Why then does not much of the world call the Persian Gulf, the "Arabian Gulf?" Is there a double standard at work here?

The Arab claim to Judea and Samaria is completely fabricated and artificial with no grounding in international law. The San Remo Resolution and the Mandate for Palestine, both envisaged that Judea and Samaria would be integral parts of the Jewish National Home and not a part of an Arab state. Their classification as "disputed territories" is therefore, an unfortunate distortion of their legal status under both international law and Israeli constitutional law.

Besides the political origins of the phrase "West Bank," one must wonder from a geographical perspective how wide can a riverbank be. A riverbank may be a few feet or so, but not some 30 miles deep from the river! Just because a new name is invented, does not mean the world should adopt it in common usage. Does an aggressor get rewarded with the additional bonus of a geographic name change designed to eradicate the historic name of a region? In March 1939, Germany renamed the present-day Czech Republic, *Böhmen und Mähren,* after seizing that land by aggressive act. During World War II, Germany invaded, occupied and annexed part of Russia calling it *Ostland.* Do we use those terms today? Do we call Texas the "North Bank" because it borders on the Rio Grande? Should we rename Serbia, the "West Bank" (of Europe) because it lies to the west of the Danube River and re-designate Poland the "East Bank" due to its location east of the Oder-Neisse Rivers? Long before most of the media capitulated to protests over Danish cartoons[*] and statements by Pope Benedict XVI,[†] the media and many in the world, out of fear. cowardice, and intellectual laziness, agreed to obfuscate the truth by surrendering the use of the names Judea and Samaria, adopting the term "West Bank."

At this juncture, a brief historic review is in order. The tiny corner of the vast Roman Empire that was the Land of Israel, Judea at the time was a region of defiance, discontent and rebellion. During

---

[*] The twelve cartoons appeared in an editorial—*Muhammeds ansigt* ("The face of Muhammad")—in the Danish newspaper *Jyllands-Posten* on September 30, 2005. The cartoons depicted the prophet Muhammad and included one showing him wearing a bomb as a turban with a lit fuse.

[†] In his speech on September 12, 2006 at Regensburg University in Germany, the Pope quoted an unfavorable remark about Islam written in 1391 by Manuel II Palaiologos, the Byzantine emperor. The passage, in the English translation published by the Vatican, was, "Show me just what Muhammad brought that was new and there you will find things only evil and inhuman, such as his command to spread by the sword the faith he preached."

Emperor Nero's reign, Gessius Florus was the Roman procurator of Judaea. His misojudaic actions helped trigger, the First Jewish Revolt in 66 C.E. The uprising infuriated Vespasian in "that the Jews alone had not submitted [to Roman rule]." He was appointed to suppress the revolt in that year.[99] The Roman historian Tacitus related what followed and left a record, not only of the Jews, but also of the role of the Arabs.

> Early in this year [70 C.E.] Titus … [was] selected by his father [by then, Emperor Vespasian] to complete the subjugation of Judaea. He found in Judaea three legions, the Fifth, the Tenth, and the Fifteenth, all old troops of Vespasian's. To these he added the Twelfth from Syria, and some men belonging to the Eighteenth and Third, whom he had withdrawn from Alexandria. This force was accompanied … by a strong contingent of Arabs, who hated the Jews with the usual hatred of neighbors.[100]

Notice that the Romans had no trouble distinguishing between Judaeans, i.e. Jews and Arabs. The Arabs were foreigners to the land of Judea, acting virtually as scavengers, looking to grab a share of the main Roman spoils. They certainly were not "native Palestinians." Recall, that Islam did not yet exist.

The First Jewish Revolt of 66–73 C.E. was followed by two others in 115–17 C.E., and 132–35 C.E. All had to be suppressed at a great cost to Rome. Furthermore, a Jewish sect had started early Christianity, which was slowly undermining the empire itself. Therefore, after suppressing the Jewish revolt led by Shimon Bar Kokhba, and as an imperial act of supreme punishment, the Roman Emperor Hadrian in 135 C.E., attempted to eradicate Jewish nationhood, statehood, and identity as well as any connection to the Land of Israel. He joined the province of Judaea (comprising Samaria, Judea proper, and Idumea) with Galilee to form a new province of "Syria Palaestina—or simply "Palaestina"—after the Philistines, the ancient non-Semitic, sea people from the eastern Mediterranean or Aegean area, who had been the historic enemies of the Jews/Israelites.

ROMAN ATTEMPT TO REMOVE JEWISH PLACE NAMES FROM THE LAND OF ISRAEL	
Historic Judaean/Jewish name	**Roman imposed name**
Judaea	"Syria Palaestina"
Jerusalem	"Aelia Capitolina"
Shechem	"Flavia Neapolis" ("new city of [the emperor] Flavius")
Rakkat	Tiberias

Seeking to erase the Jewish connection to Jerusalem, the Romans razed the city and named the city built atop the rubble, Aelia Capitolina. Nevertheless, as late as the fourth century, the Christian author, Epiphanius, referred to "Palaestina", that is Judea." Despite this "Palaestina" is still Israel, Aelia Capitolina is still Jerusalem and the "West Bank" is still Judea and Samaria.

In the Arabic language, there is no "p" sound. Thus, after the Arab conquest of the Land of Israel in 637 C.E., Palaestina became *Filastin*. Indeed, every name of every so-called "Arab town" in Israel is nothing more than an Arabic distortion of the original Hebrew, Greek or Latin names for a city. Two examples would be *Habrun*—from the Hebrew *Hevron* (Hebron), and Nablus—from *Nea Polis,* ("New

City") built on the ruins of biblical Shechem. The Arabs also decided to call Jerusalem *Al Quds* and the Temple Mount, *Beit al Muqdas.* These are nothing but Arabized terms from the original Hebrew: *Ha-Kodesh* and *Beit ha-Miqdash*, which respectively mean "the Holy (City)" and "the Holy House" (i.e., "Holy Temple"). Even Israeli cities that were Jewish from their inception have had their name "Arabized," with Beersheba labeled "Bir Assaba" and Tel Aviv also referred to as "Tell Ar-Rabee."

Under the Ottoman Turks for example, the entire area known as "Palestine" was divided between the Vilayet* of Beirut and the Sanjak of Jerusalem, which included Sinai. There never was an Arab, Seljuk, Mameluke, or Ottoman Turkish province of "Palestine." The name "Palestine" remained alive only in Europe. Through the millennia, "Palestine" has never been the name of an independent nation-state. This designation indicated a vague broad, geographical region much like "the Southwest" in the United States, Patagonia in Argentina, Siberia in Russia, or Tibet in China. In the mid-twentieth century, the Arab/Muslim opponents of the reestablishment of Jewish sovereignty in the Land of Israel appropriated the term "Palestine" as an appellation in their war against the Jews. Up until the end of World War I "Palestine" did not exist, even as a unified geopolitical entity. The British re-imported the term for their Mandate after World War I. Even as a non-state legal entity, "Palestine" ceased to exist in 1948, when the United Kingdom relinquished its League of Nations mandate.

The ultimate status of Judea and Samaria remains to be determined. However, with the status of these areas in dispute, the stronger legal claim to that territory as well as the obvious need for security against surrounding enemies makes it highly desirable for Israel to extend Jewish sovereignty and Israeli law to all of Judea and Samaria. If Israel declares its sovereignty over Judea and Samaria, the Jews would still represent a two-thirds majority of residents. Citizenship would be subject to preconditions of no prior membership in terrorist groups such as Hamas or the PLO (which have vowed to destroy the State of Israel) and pledge allegiance to the Jewish state. So annexation threatens neither Israel's democracy nor Jewishness. The final resolution of the status of Judea and Samaria will be that between the Jordan River and the Mediterranean Sea there can only be one sovereignty—either total Jewish sovereignty or total Muslim sovereignty—and the outcome will be that either one or the other will prevail.

16. The League of Nations established the international legal basis for reestablishing Jewish sovereignty in the British Mandate of Palestine.

The legally binding document the "Mandate for Palestine" was conferred on April 24, 1920 at the San Remo Conference, and its terms outlined in the Treaty of Sèvres on August 10, 1920. The Mandate's terms were finalized and unanimously approved on July 24, 1922, by the Council of the League of Nations, which was comprised at that time of fifty-one countries, and became operational on September 29, 1923. It was approved by the United States on December 3, 1924. The United Kingdom's mandate in Palestine encompassed what are now Jordan, Israel, the Golan Heights, Judea and Samaria (what the Arabs call the "West Bank"), and the Gaza Strip (*see* "Original British Mandate of Palestine" map). The conference also affirmed the United Kingdom's 1917 Balfour Declaration, favoring a "national home" in Palestine for the Jewish people (*see* Appendix 2). It incorporated Article

---

* The 400-year old Ottoman empire was subdivided into vilayets (akin somewhat to provinces) and sanjaks (similar to districts or counties). For example, there were vilayets of Beirut, Damascus and Hejaz and sanjaks of Acre, Alexandretta, Gaza, and Jerusalem.

22 of the Covenant of the League of Nations and was the basic document upon which the Mandate for Palestine was constructed. As an aside, it should be noted that when Jordan and Egypt signed peace treaties with Israel in 1979 and 1994 respectively, both nations expressly referred to the League of Nations Mandate for Palestine boundary as the current international border of Israel, demonstrating its continued relevance.

ORIGINAL PALESTINE MANDATE

S Y R I A
(French Mandate)

⊛ Damascus

Beirut
Sidon
Tyre
• Quneitra
Acre
Haifa Safed
Tiberias
Irbid
Nablus
Tel Aviv
Jaffa Salt • Amman
⊛
Jerusalem
Gaza • Hebron •
Beersheba Kerak

**BRITISH MANDATE OF
PALESTINE, 1920**

• Maan

• Aqaba

H E J A Z

While the decision made at San Remo created the Palestine Mandate *de facto*, the mandate document signed by the United Kingdom as the Mandatory and the League of Nations made it *de jure*. Thus, it became a binding treaty—*res judicata*—in international law. The fifty-one member countries—the entire League of Nations—unanimously declared on July 24, 1922:

> Whereas recognition has thereby been given to the historical connection of the Jewish people with Palestine and to the grounds for *reconstituting* [emphasis added] their national home in that country.

This move was unique in history. No such recognition had ever been accorded to anyone, ever. Palestine was to be held for the Jewish people wherever they lived. Thus, the international community recognized not only the Jewish right to the Land of Israel, but recognized the historical pre-existing right of the Jews to that particular territory. It was not the creation of a new right. The Jewish people were chosen to be the political beneficiaries of the British Mandate of Palestine. Similarly, it was the Arab inhabitants were chosen to be the political beneficiaries of the Mandate of Syria (later divided into Syria and Lebanon) and the Mandate of Mesopotamia (later renamed Iraq).

> ARTICLE 2. The Mandatory shall be responsible for placing the country under such political, administrative and economic conditions as will secure the establishment of the Jewish national home, as laid down in the preamble, and the development of self-governing institutions, and for safeguarding the civil and religious rights of all the inhabitants of Palestine, irrespective of race and religion.

Thus, the operative clause specifically referred to the preamble and reiterated that there were no political rights for other inhabitants.

> ARTICLE 5. The Mandatory shall be responsible for seeing that no Palestine territory shall be ceded or leased to, or in any way placed under the control of the Government of any foreign Power.

> ARTICLE 6. The Administration of Palestine, while ensuring that the rights and position of other sections of the population are not prejudiced, shall facilitate Jewish immigration under suitable conditions and shall encourage, in co-operation with the Jewish agency referred to in Article 4, close settlement* by Jews on the land, including State lands and waste lands not required for public purposes.

> ARTICLE 7. The Administration of Palestine shall be responsible for enacting a nationality law. There shall be included in this law provisions framed so as to facilitate the acquisition of Palestinian citizenship by Jews who take up their permanent residence in Palestine.

---

* Thus, the 122 settlements established (as of 2013) west of the Jordan River, in Judea and Samaria since the Six-Day War of 1967, are legal under international law as per the terms of the San Remo Agreement of April 25, 1920 and confirmed by the Council of the League of Nations on July 24, 1922.

De facto, the First Partition of Palestine occurred during March 12–23, 1921 at a Middle East Conference hosted by the United Kingdom in Cairo, Egypt. As a result, later that year the United Kingdom bowing to Arab pressure closed the area east of the Jordan River to Jewish immigration and settlement—but not the area west of it to accelerating Arab migration. The United Kingdom—its mandate now confirmed by the League of Nations—arbitrarily and unilaterally detached and then created Transjordan on 77.5 percent (35,468 square miles) of the original mandate land (which had totaled 46,339 square miles). Winston Churchill, who presided over the Cairo Conference, would later reflect, "I created Transjordan with the stroke of a pen on a Sunday afternoon in Cairo." Yet, under Article 5 of the Mandate, the eastern portion of the British Mandate of Palestine was detached and ceded to the control of a foreign monarch, the Hashemite Abdullah I from Hejaz (in western present-day Saudi Arabia). Thus, the creation of Transjordan was illegal (*see* "First Partition of Palestine" map).

THE FIRST PARTITION OF PALESTINE, 1921

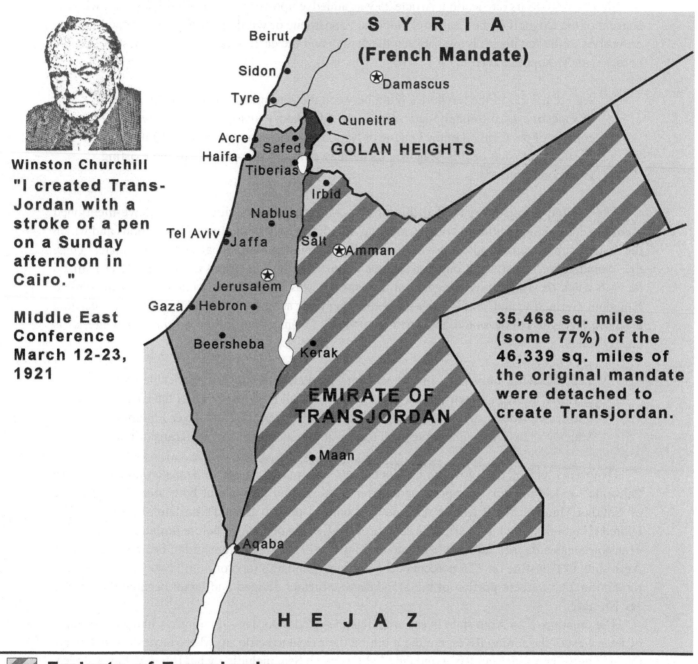

Winston Churchill

"I created Trans-Jordan with a stroke of a pen on a Sunday afternoon in Cairo."

Middle East Conference March 12-23, 1921

S Y R I A
(French Mandate)

Beirut

Sidon

Tyre

Damascus

Quneitra

Acre

Safed

GOLAN HEIGHTS

Haifa

Tiberias

Irbid

Nablus

Tel Aviv

Jaffa

Salt

Amman

Jerusalem

Gaza • Hebron

Beersheba

Kerak

EMIRATE OF TRANSJORDAN

35,468 sq. miles (some 77%) of the 46,339 sq. miles of the original mandate were detached to create Transjordan.

Maan

Aqaba

H E J A Z

Emirate of Transjordan

Area ceded by Great Britain to the French Mandate of Syria 1923

On September 16, 1922, the League of Nations approved the Mandatory Power—the United Kingdom—to partition historic Palestine. All the League of Nations—that was dominated by the British Empire and France (seven votes out of the forty-two original members)—did was rubber stamp Churchill's actions. The Emirate of Transjordan, under Abdullah I, was already established by the time the League took its "official action."

Shortly prior to its ratification, Article 25 was added, empowering the United Kingdom, with the consent of the Council of the League of Nations, to postpone or withhold application of the Mandate provisions to the territories lying between the Jordan and the eastern boundary of Palestine, i.e. the border with Mesopotamia (Iraq).

> ARTICLE 25. In the territories lying between the Jordan and the eastern boundary of Palestine as ultimately determined, the Mandatory shall be entitled, with the consent of the Council of the League of Nations, to postpone or withhold application of such provision of this Mandate, as he may consider inapplicable to the existing local conditions.[101]

The United Kingdom activated this option, to partition Palestine, in the above-mentioned memorandum of September 16, 1922, which the Mandatory sent to the League of Nations and which the League subsequently approved—making it a legally binding integral part of the "Mandate." Thus, the "Mandate for Palestine" brought to fruition a fourth Arab state east of the Jordan River realized in 1946 when the Hashemite Kingdom of Transjordan was granted independence from the United Kingdom. Syria, Iraq and Saudi Arabia being the other three at the time. Not all the clauses concerning a Jewish National Home would apply to this territory (Transjordan) of the original Mandate, as is clearly stated:

> The following provisions of the Mandate for Palestine are not applicable to the territory known as Transjordan, which comprises all territory lying to the east of a line drawn from … up the centre of the Wady Araba, Dead Sea and River Jordan. His Majesty's Government accept[s] full responsibility as Mandatory for Transjordan.[102]

Historians and official government documents continued to refer to Transjordan as "Eastern Palestine" and Mandatory passports and currency were used throughout both areas. The League of Nations Mandate for Palestine remained unchanged despite Britain's unilateral partition. The United Kingdom waited until after the demise of the League of Nations before unilaterally declaring Transjordan as a *de jure* independent state on May 25, 1946. Thus, Transjordan became the *de jure* Arab state in Palestine on 77.5 percent of the original Mandate's territory only two years before the remaining 22.5 percent portion of the Mandate was further divided and Israel became the *de jure* Jewish state.

The creation of an Arab state in eastern Palestine—today Jordan—in no way changed the status of Jews west of the Jordan River, nor did it inhibit their right to settle anywhere in western Palestine, the area between the Jordan River and the Mediterranean Sea, including what is today, Israel, Judea, Samaria, Gaza, and the Golan Heights. Most Israeli settlements today, in Judea and Samaria have been built on land that was state land under the Ottomans, British, and Jordanians and, after the 1967 Six-Day War, under the Israelis, or on property that has been privately purchased.

The United States became a party to the Mandate of Palestine by the Anglo-American Convention, a treaty signed by the United States and the United Kingdom on December 3, 1924. The Convention contained the entire text of the "Mandate for Palestine" including the preamble and stipulated that the United States fully accepted upon itself (it became a contracting party to) the Mandate for Palestine, as a homeland for the Jewish people, which declared all of Judea and Samaria within its borders. The treaty approved by the US Senate on February 20, 1925, signed by President Calvin Coolidge on March 2, 1925, went into force on December 5, 1925. The treaty was never abrogated. Treaties themselves have no statute of limitations, so their rights go on ad infinitum. As has previously been discussed, Israel's presence in Judea and Samaria does not qualify as an "occupation" under international law. Additionally, this is true because of the Anglo-American Convention, the Hague Convention and the Geneva Convention.

The documents mentioned above were the last legally binding documents regarding the status of Judea, Samaria and the Gaza Strip. The September 16, 1922 memorandum was also the last modification of the official terms of the Mandate on record by the League of Nations or by its legal successor, the United Nations, in accordance with Article 27 of the Mandate that stated unequivocally that "the consent of the Council of the League of Nations is required for any modification of the terms of this mandate." The United Nations Charter recognized the UN's obligation to uphold the commitments of its predecessor, the League of Nations. Article 80 of the United Nations Charter, specifically states

> nothing in this Chapter [concerning former League of Nations Mandates and UN trusteeship areas] shall be construed in and of itself to alter in any manner the rights whatsoever of any States or any peoples or the terms of existing international instruments to which Members of the United Nations may respectively be parties.[103]

Thus, the British Mandate of Palestine continued without change. In reaction to Arab violence in Palestine in 1920 and 1921, the British took steps to prevent the Jews from establishing a state on the remainder (22.5 percent) of the land. They blocked Jewish immigration and limited the right of Jews to purchase and settle the land to a tiny portion of the territory.

An important clarification about Jewish immigration to the Land of Israel needs to be addressed at this juncture. There has always been a Jewish presence in the Land of Israel for more than 3,000 years. Even at times of forcible exile, by the Assyrians, Babylonians, Romans, and Muslims (be they Arabs, Seljuks, Mamelukes, or Ottomans), pockets of Jewish population existed and survived. It has never been *judenrein* (ethnically and religiously "cleansed of Jews"), though its enemies persist in trying to make that a fact. In 1695, for example, long before the birth of modern Zionism and the waves of Jewish immigration into the Land of Israel, the Jews constituted a majority of inhabitants there.[104]

Just as Córdoba (711–1236) and Seville (712–1248) returned to Spanish sovereignty after 525 and 536 years of Arab/Muslim occupation respectively, and Granada (711–1492) after 781 years of Arab/Muslim occupation, so too did the Land of Israel return to Jewish sovereignty after 1,093 years of Arab/Muslim occupation. Israel was the Jewish state and is again the Jewish state. If Jews have to return home—to go "back where they came from" as some of Israel's detractors advocate—some 6 million of them have done so, gone back to Israel. Thus, much as their propagandists like to claim, the Arabs were not the only and "original" peoples of the British Mandate of Palestine.

Author Mark Twain visited the Holy Land in 1867 and reflected on his travels in his book, *The Innocents Abroad* (1869), that Ottoman Palestine was

> [A] desolate country whose soil is rich enough, but is given over wholly to weeds-a
> silent mournful expanse....A desolation is here that not even imagination can grace
> with the pomp of life and action....We never saw a human being on the whole route....
> There was hardly a tree or a shrub anywhere. Even the olive and the cactus, those
> fast friends of the worthless soil, had almost deserted the country.[105]

The Muslim Ottoman rulers (as many Muslim rulers before them) imposed the *jizya* on the indigenous Jews living in the Land of Israel. Deprived of funds, the number of Jews was kept low through these discriminatory taxes, which compelled them to emigrate. For example, in 1849, the Jews of Tiberius envisaged emigration[106] because of the brutality, financial burdens forced upon them, and injustice of the Ottoman authorities. Furthermore, Muslim Ottoman rulers increased the Muslim population by providing incentives for Muslim colonists from other parts of their empire, e.g. North Africa and the Balkans, to settle in Ottoman-controlled Palestine. Incentives included free land, twelve years exemption from taxes and exemption from military service.[107] The Ottoman Turkish sultan, Abdul Hamid II was aware of the dearth of loyal Muslim population in Ottoman-controlled Palestine, and in 1878 launched a resettlement scheme to bring Algerians and Circassians to the region. This was just four years before the First *Aliyah*, but very few worldwide paid attention to this influx of outsiders.

From the time of the First *Aliyah*, begun in 1882, much awareness was focused on Jews arriving from Europe, mainly by sea. Scant attention was paid to other arrivals, mainly overland. Arab immigration into Ottoman-controlled and then the British Mandate of Palestine continued unhindered as they crossed poorly monitored land frontiers. These mostly itinerant Arab laborers flocked from the entire Arab-speaking world, from the Maghreb (the "Arab West," which includes the modern countries of Mauritania, Morocco—plus Western Sahara, Algeria, Tunisia, and Libya), as well as from the Mashreq (the "Arab East," consisting of Arabia, Syria, Lebanon, Transjordan, Egypt and Sudan. No less a personality than President Franklin D. Roosevelt observed in 1939, that, "Arab immigration into Palestine since 1921 has vastly exceeded the total Jewish immigration during this whole period."[108]

The Arabs immigrated to the British Mandate of Palestine for one main reason—economics. The indigenous Jews grew in number and turned a backwater of the Ottoman Empire into a thriving area, providing jobs, increased standard of living and benefits, health, education and more. The Arabs came to share in what the Jews created within the British Mandate of Palestine. In this manner, Arab migrants were regarded as natives, whereas the British counted the Jewish immigrants as "foreign" arrivals. Journalist Robert F. Kennedy, working for the *Boston Post* observed in March 1948:

> The Jews point with pride to the fact that over 500,000 Arabs in the 12 years between
> 1932 and 1944, came into Palestine to take advantage of living conditions existing in
> no other Arab state. This is the only country in the Near and Middle East where an
> Arab middle class is in existence.[109]

Even into the twenty-first century, Arab "Palestinian" leaders admit the real origins of their people. On March 23, 2012, Hamas's director of the Al-Aqsa television station and the terror group's "minister" of the interior and national security, Fathi Hamad, was interviewed by Egypt's Al Hekma television station. The interview was translated by the Middle East Media Research Institute (MEMRI).

> We all have Arab roots, and every Palestinian, in Gaza and throughout Palestine,
> can prove his Arab roots—whether from Saudi Arabia, from Yemen, or anywhere.

Personally, half my family is Egyptian. We are all like that. More than 30 families in the Gaza Strip are called Al-Masri ["Egyptian"]. Brothers, half of the Palestinians are Egyptians and the other half are Saudis. Who are the Palestinians? We have many families called Al-Masri, whose roots are Egyptian. Egyptian! They may be from Alexandria, from Cairo, from Dumietta, from the North, from Aswan, from Upper Egypt. We are Egyptians. We are Arabs. We are Muslims.[110]

By no means is al-Masri (Egyptian) the only family name among the "Palestinians" that delineates their places of origin. Other family names include Hejazi (Hejaz in what today is Saudi Arabia), Mugrabi (Moroccan), Ajami (Persian), Haurani (Syrian), Halabi (Aleppan), Kurdi (Kurdish), Hindi (Indian), and many more. Some of these migrant groups, like the Circassian Muslims and Armenian Christians, did not even attempt to assimilate into local "Palestinian" society. As thus defined, the "new Palestinians (i.e. Arab Palestinians—as opposed to the older Palestinian Jews)" are of diverse character. This manifests itself in family, tribal, and sectarian rivalry.

Historically, from the 1920s to the 1940s, while Arab immigrants poured into the British Mandate of Palestine, the British steadily restricted Jewish immigration. This culminated with the release of the infamous MacDonald White Paper of May 17, 1939. According to its provisions, Jewish immigration would be restricted to 10,000 per year for the next five years. During that same period, 25,000 Jewish refugees would be allowed into the British Mandate of Palestine, resulting in a grand total of 75,000 Jews. All subsequent Jewish immigration would be completely halted by 1944. Land sales were immediately restricted to only 5 percent of the country. After ten years, the British promised the Arabs an independent state, though by that time they already had seven independent states. Thus, the British sacrificed Jewish rights to Arab intransigence. In effect, the British had cancelled the Balfour Declaration of 1917. In the short span of twenty-two years, the United Kingdom went from being the primary advocate, promoter and guarantor of the restoration of Jewish sovereignty in the Land of Israel, to being the principal opponent of that reestablishment. This significant shift took place during the most critical time in Jewish history, as millions of Jews perished in the Holocaust, many for lack of a safe refuge. Even as the Holocaust became common knowledge, the British continued to refuse to change their policy, or to admit Jews into the British Mandate of Palestine, from Nazi-controlled Europe.

As World War II ended, the British kept a naval blockade on the Palestinian coast. They were determined to deny thousands of Jewish Holocaust survivors entry to the British Mandate of Palestine. Yet, no one was watching the lengthy land frontiers with Lebanon, Syria, Transjordan, and Egypt and the Arab population increased accordingly.

In late 1946, the British Labor government of Clement Attlee was so determined to appease the Arabs, preserve their preeminent position in the Middle East and safeguard their access to oil, that it asked the British Secret Intelligence Service (MI6) for "proposals for action to deter ships masters and crews from engaging in illegal Jewish immigration and traffic," adding, "action of the nature contemplated is, in fact, a form of intimidation and intimidation is only likely to be effective if some members of the group of people to be intimidated actually suffer unpleasant consequences." The result, according to newly declassified documents from MI6, was Operation *Embarrass* launched in early 1947. Under Operation *Embarrass,* the British government ordered MI6 to prevent ships of Jews sailing to Palestine, even to the point of blowing them up with passengers aboard. This has been detailed in the book by Keith Jeffery, titled *MI6: The History of the Secret Intelligence Service 1909–49.* The British government has independently verified Jeffery's revelations.[111]

Returning to the subject of the British Mandate of Palestine, on March 7, 1923, the United Kingdom approved, unilaterally, the transfer of the Golan Heights to the French mandate of Syria (this will be discussed in more detail, later). This being the case, Israel in 1949 ended up with 17.5 percent of mandate Palestine. Judea and Samaria as well as the Gaza Strip are the remaining unallocated, disputed 5 percent.

It must be re-emphasized that the British Mandate of Palestine has already been partitioned into two states, one Arab and one Jewish, Jordan and Israel, respectively. Now there is the call for a second Arab Palestinian state. Whatever the apportionment of the final 5 percent of the original British Mandate of Palestine, Israel does not and will not have a majority of the land.

17. Throughout the entire Middle East, only one country bears an uncanny political, demographic, and historic similarity to the United States—that country is Israel.

The ancient Jewish nation was the inspiration for the Founding Fathers of the United States of America.

BIBLICAL ISRAEL'S INFLUENCE ON THE UNITED STATES		
	Biblical Israel	**Foundation Stones of the United States of America**
THE BASIS OF THE GOVERNING SYSTEM	The Covenant with God. Religion based on ethical monotheism rooted in the *Tanakh*, i.e. the Hebrew/Jewish Bible.	Religion based on ethical monotheism rooted in the Hebrew Bible. Judeo-Christian values and a federal system of government. The word "federalism" is a derivative of the Latin word for "Covenant"–*foedus*.
EXECUTIVE LEADER	Moses	The President
DEPUTY EXECUTIVE	Aaron	The Vice President
LEGISLATIVE BRANCH	The tribal governors and the legislature of seventy elders.	The US Congress
BASIS FOR LAW	The Ten Commandments	These commandments are in past or present laws of the United States: Commandment VI–"Thou Shalt Not Murder"; Commandment VII–"Thou Shalt Not Commit Adultery"; Commandment VIII–"Thou Shalt Not Steal"; Commandment IX–"Thou Shalt Not Bear False Witness Against Thy Neighbor."
POLITICAL SUBDIVISIONS	Twelve Jewish tribes	The States–originally thirteen, now fifty.

There is a unique bond between Israel and the United States, which includes Judeo-Christian values based on the Ten Commandments. These values impacted the view of the Pilgrims, the Puritans and the Founding Fathers. They are reflected in the US Constitution, the Bill of Rights, the concept of separation of powers, as well as the system of Checks and Balances within American government.

The United States and Israel share a common ancient source that was influential in their foundation—a moral code, rooted deeply in Mosaic Law. They also share a common culture and civilization. Both have a Western democratic ideology with an open and tolerant society, a functioning legislature, rule of law, free multiparty elections, free market economic systems, respect for minorities and individual rights including freedom of expression, and freedom of religion. Both countries were nurtured by immigrants and exiles—an ingathering of peoples from over 100 other countries producing culturally diverse societies. As such, both nations share a common destiny. The unique relationship between the United States and the Jewish state of Israel has evolved around shared values of liberty, democracy and human rights, as well as joint vital interests and mutual threats. Lastly, both countries have had many parallel episodes in their respective histories as outlined in the table below.

PARALLELS IN UNITED STATES AND ISRAELI HISTORY		
	United States	**Israel**
ESTABLISHMENT	The country was established by people seeking to escape tyranny, and religious persecution, as well as to promote liberty. Its inhabitants had a pioneering spirit.	The country was established by people seeking to escape tyranny, and religious persecution, as well as to promote liberty. Its inhabitants had a pioneering spirit.
POPULATION	A nation of immigrants and exiles from over 100 countries.	The 3,000+ year old Jewish nation, in modern times ingathered immigrants and exiles from over 100 countries, fulfilling the words of Ezekiel 36:24, "For I will take you from among the nations and gather you out of all countries, and will bring you [back] into your own land."
SETTLEMENT	There was a need for its citizens to move into the territories to secure those territories for the nation including the establishment of stockaded frontier settlements to help guard against outside attack.	There was a need for its citizens to move into the territories to secure those territories for the nation including the establishment of stockaded frontier settlements to help guard against outside attack.
KEY PUBLICATION THAT ADVOCATED INDEPENDENCE AND SOVEREIGNTY	*Common Sense* by Thomas Paine (1776)	*Der Judenstaat* by Theodor Herzl (1896)

INDEPENDENCE ATTAINED FROM	Great Britain	The United Kingdom (Great Britain)
HOW INDEPENDENCE WAS ATTAINED	Farmers and shopkeepers fought against overwhelming odds, a militarily superior enemy in the Revolutionary War of Independence, 1775–83.	Farmers and shopkeepers fought against overwhelming odds, a militarily superior enemy in the Israeli War of Independence (the Arab–Israeli War of 1947–49).
IN ITS EARLY YEARS, OUTSIDE POWERS HARASSED AND OTHERWISE RESTRICTED THE NEW NATION. THIS INCLUDED SUPPORTING INTERNAL GROUPS WHO ATTACKED THE NEW NATION	Great Britain incited the Native Americans of the Old Northwest, 1776–1815 to attack the new nation. Spain incited the Native Americans of the Old Southwest and Florida, 1776–1819 to attack the new nation. Morocco, Algiers, Tunis, and Tripoli, attacked and seized US ships and held Americans hostage for ransom.	Since 1920, the Arab states (joined since 1979, by Iran), supported Arab terrorist groups in their attacks on Israel and Israeli targets—land, sea, and air—worldwide.
HOW THE NATION DEALT WITH THESE GROUPS	United States–Native American (Indian) Wars, 1794–1890. United States–Tripolitan War, 1801–04. United States–Algerine War, 1815. A US naval presence in the Mediterranean Sea. The Pershing Expedition against Pancho Villa in northern Mexico, 1916–17.	Israeli incursions in Lebanon in 1978, 1982, the late 1980s, and the Iran proxy wars against Israel by Hezbollah from Lebanon in 2006 and by Hamas from Gaza 2007 to date.
THE NEED TO EXERCISE SECURITY CONTROL OVER A MAJOR RIVER VALLEY	The Mississippi River was needed for economic survival: It was the main conduit for Midwest and Southern trade and commerce to the outside world. This included the "right of deposit," at the main port of New Orleans, controlled by foreign powers— Spain and France, 1783–1803. The Mississippi River Valley was needed to maintain security and military control. The United States repelled the British attempt to seize New Orleans, in January 1815. The United States defeated Confederate attempts to control the river valley, 1861–63.	The Jordan River was needed for economic survival: It is Israel's main source of water. Israel resisted Arab attempts to divert the headwaters of the Jordan, 1964–65. The Jordan River Valley is needed to maintain security and military control, in order to prevent hostile forces from crossing the river from the east, entering Judea and Samaria and attacking the Israeli heartland—1948 to date. Militarily, Israel ended terrorist attacks from east-bank Jordan Valley bases between 1967 and 1970.

HOW THE NATION RESPONDED TO A THREAT TO ITS "FREEDOM OF THE SEAS"	The United States fought the War of 1812 (1812–15) and World War I, 1917–18.	Israel fought the Sinai-Suez War, 1956, and the Six-Day War, 1967.
INVOLVEMENT IN A WAR TO EFFECT GEOPOLITICAL CHANGE	Iraq, 2003–11; Afghanistan, 2001–14.	The First Lebanon War (the Israel–PLO War in Lebanon), 1982–85.
COMBATING THE ISLAMIC SUPREMACIST WAR AGAINST THE WEST	War against Al-Qaeda, the Taliban, the Islamic State, and other Islamic supremacist terrorists globally, 2001 to date.	War against Hezbollah, Hamas, Islamic Jihad, Al-Aqsa Martyrs Brigades, Tanzim, the Popular Front, Al-Qaeda and other such groups, 2000 to date.

The United States–Israel bond is the most unique "special relationship" in the world. In many areas—including history, foreign policy, strategic cooperation,[112] economic ties, and intellectual connections—there is an important linkage and partnership.

18. The Kurds, the fourth most numerous people in the region, have never achieved national sovereignty, but have played a leading role in the history of the Middle East.

The Kurds are the fourth most numerous people in the Middle East, between 27 and 38 million (after the Arabs: 286 million; the Turks: 69 million; and the Iranians: 68 million). They speak their own distinctive Indo-European language distantly related to Farsi. They are, for the most part, a moderate, secularly minded predominately Sunni Muslim people, with their own unique culture. The Kurds have historic ties to the Jewish state and the Jewish people. Israel was the first country to support Kurdish independence in Iraq and has a long history of giving the Kurds military assistance and training in that country. The Kurds have had a sense of themselves as a distinct people for many centuries. The Kurds have been betrayed repeatedly in the past 100 years by the international community and its promises. Thus, the Kurds are the world's largest ethnic group without a state.

Kurdistan's geographic area has been neither defined precisely nor been formed as a political unit. It is estimated in size to be between 135,000 and 193,000 square miles.[113] [114] The Kurdish people today, live primarily within the boundaries of six countries—Turkey, Iran, Iraq, Syria, Armenia, and Azerbaijan.

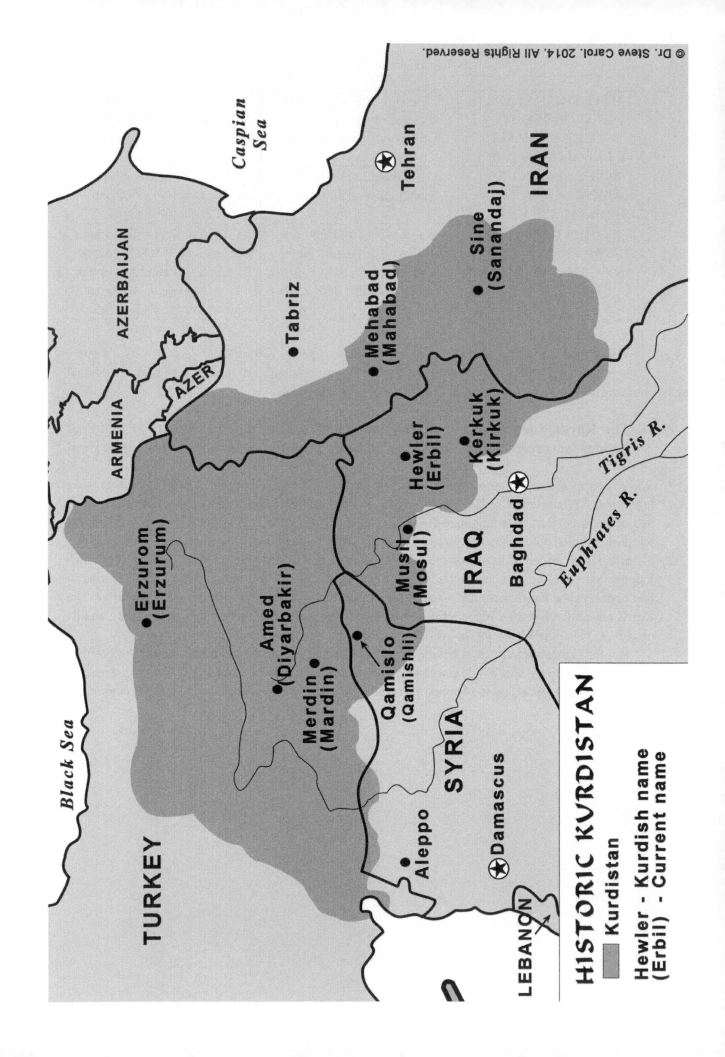

HISTORIC KURDISTAN

Kurdistan

Hewler - Kurdish name
(Erbil) - Current name

TOTAL KURDISH POPULATION: 27–38 MILLION [115] [116]		
Location	**Population**	**Comments**
Turkey	15–21 million[117] [118] [119]	The Kurds were first referred to as "Mountain Turks," and after 1980, as "Eastern Turks." Their language is forbidden.
Iran	4.8–7 million[120]	They live in the northwestern region of Iran.
Iraq	4–6.5 million[121]	They live in the region northeast of the Tigris River in an oil-producing area.
Syria	1.6–2.8 million[122]	They live in the northeastern region of Syria.
Outside "Kurdistan," primarily in Armenia and Azerbaijan.	1.1 million	They live in southern Armenia (150,000)[123] and in the Nakhichevan enclave of Azerbaijan.

The Kurds claim descent from the ancient Aryans. The ancient Sumerians referred to Kurdistan as Kur-a, Gutium (twenty-fourth century B.C.E.), or Land of Karda. Other ancient peoples referred to the Kurds by other names: by the Elamites as Kurdasu, by the Akkadians as Kurtei, by the Assyrians as Kurti, by the Babylonians as Qardu, by the Persians as Medes, by the Greeks as Carduchoi and by the Romans as Corduene.

The famous twelfth century Muslim warrior leader, Salah al-Dīn Yusuf ibn Ayyub—better known as Saladin (ca. 1138–March 4, 1193)—was a Kurd. Interestingly, he was born in Tikrit, in modern day Iraq, which centuries later became the home and powerbase of Saddam Hussein. Saladin battled the Crusaders (during the Second Crusade) and most notably decisively defeated them on July 4, 1187, at the Battle of Hattin, near Tiberius in present day Israel. He recaptured Jerusalem on October 2, 1187, after eighty-eight years of Crusader rule. In January 1189, Saladin would vow, "Then I shall cross this sea to their islands [the islands of the Franks] to pursue them until there remains no one on the face of the earth who does not acknowledge Allah. Or until I die."[124]

The defeat at Hattin and the fall of Jerusalem prompted the Third Crusade, financed in England by a special "Saladin tithe." This Crusade took back Acre, and Saladin's army met King Richard I of England at the Battle of Arsuf on September 7, 1191, at which Saladin was defeated. Richard and Saladin came to an agreement over Jerusalem in the Treaty of Ramla—a five-year armed truce—on September 2, 1192. Under its terms, Jerusalem would remain in Muslim hands but would be open to unarmed Christian pilgrims and the Crusader Latin Kingdom was reduced to a strip along the coast from Tyre to Jaffa, giving access to Muslim traders. Saladin overthrew the Shi'a Fatimid dynasty in Egypt and founded the Ayyubid dynasty, which ruled (1169–1250) Egypt, Syria, Iraq, Hejaz including Mecca and parts of Yemen.

KEY EVENTS IN MODERN KURDISH HISTORY	
Date	**Event**
August 23, 1514	Ottoman Turkey, under Sultan Selim I, won a decisive victory over the Persian Safavid Empire, led by Shah Ismail I, at the Battle of Chaldiran. Turkey annexed Armenia and Kurdistan. As a result, the Turkish Sultan promised to recognize the Kurdish principalities and not to interfere in their internal affairs.
1639	After a series of long wars, Ottoman Turkey and the Safavid rulers of Persia (Iran) demarcated their frontier, cutting through the center of Kurdistan.

1806, 1818, 1832, 1843–46, 1853–55, 1877	Contrary to earlier pledges, the Ottoman Sultan began to interfere in Kurdish affairs. This action triggered a series of disconnected Kurdish revolts by various Kurdish emirates and principalities. All were suppressed and apart from a few provinces annexed by Persia (Iran) all the Kurdish territories fell under Ottoman domination.
1880	A Kurdish landowner and head of the powerful Shemdinan family, Sheikh Ubeydullah launched the first modern Kurdish national uprising. He attempted to unite Turkish and Persian Kurds in a war of independence. He was thwarted by the joint efforts of the Turkish and Persian regimes. Ubeydullah along with other notables was exiled to Constantinople.
1907	Turkish Kurds raided Persian Azerbaijan and spurred anti-Kurdish sentiment. This was demonstrated by rioting against the Sunni Muslim Kurds.
1908	Kurdish political clubs were established in Istanbul, Mosul, Diyarbakir, and Baghdad in an attempt to organize a national movement.
1914–18	Before World War I, most Kurds lived within the boundaries of the Ottoman Empire in the province of Kurdistan. During the war, Persian Kurds cooperated with the Turks and the Germans. They raided Armenian and Assyrian villages.
November 17, 1918	As World War I ended with the defeat of Ottoman Turkey and its Central Power allies, a joint Anglo-French declaration was issued which called for complete and final "liberation of the peoples oppressed" by the Turks. Kurdish chiefs joined other non-Turkish peoples—the Arabs, the Jews, the Druze among others—in demanding their national rights. At first, the Allied Powers envisaged an autonomous region of Kurdistan in eastern Anatolia and the Mosul province of Mesopotamia with an option for later independence.
May 1919	The Kurds in Mesopotamia (Iraq) rebelled against the British occupation forces and established a government at Sulaymaniyah. They were crushed a few weeks later.
1919	A revolt was attempted by Kurdish leader, Ismail Aga, against the Qajar rulers of Persia. It was unsuccessful.
August 10, 1920	The Treaty of Sèvres was signed between the victorious Allied Powers and defeated Turkey. Section III, Article 62 of the treaty provided for "local autonomy for the predominantly Kurdish areas lying east of the Euphrates, south of the southern boundary of Armenia" and the Kurds (Article 64) could request from the Council of the League of Nations "independence" in one year.[125] However, the rise of Mustafa Kemal Atatürk prevented this as his new Republic of Turkey army reconquered areas in Smyrna, Kurdistan and Armenia. Thus, the Treaty of Sèvres was aborted and the promise to the Kurds was broken.
October 20, 1921	France and Turkey signed the Accord of Ankara. By its terms, France took the Kurdish provinces of Jazira and Kurd-Dagh, which were annexed, to the French Mandate of Syria.
July 7, 1923– April 8, 1929	Two Kurdish areas in Soviet-controlled Azerbaijan were unified into an administrative unit called Kurdistan Uyezd or "Red Kurdistan." It was dissolved by Soviet authorities after a brief six-year existence.

July 24, 1923	Due to Turkish militancy, the Treaty of Sèvres proved a dead letter. The Allies accepted the renegotiated Treaty of Lausanne in its place, accepting the border of the modern Republic of Turkey and leaving the Kurds without an autonomous region. Other Kurdish areas were assigned to the new British and French mandated states of Iraq and Syria.

Great power machinations, historic Turkish-Persian enmity, along with constant rivalries between tribes, clans, families, and villages all contributed to the partition of Kurdistan by the opening decades of the twentieth century. After World War I the Kurdish claim to self-determination was ignored, and then repressed. Kurdistan was divided primarily among four states—Turkey, Iran, Iraq, and Syria. The fragmentation of Kurdistan and the very different circumstances prevailing in these four states caused a parallel fragmentation in the Kurdish national movement and its organizations. At times, two or more of these states cooperated against the Kurds, and at other times, these states individually backed various factions of Kurds, both within their borders and across the frontiers of neighboring states, often against other Kurdish factions.

The first and main organization akin to a modern political party was *Khoibun* ("Independence"), founded in Beirut, Lebanon, in 1927. It was an organization of exiles, mostly in Europe. It was pro-Western and non-Socialist. It began to lose influence with the emergence of Kurdish organizations in Kurdistan itself. These included:

- *Heva* ("Hope"), a right-wing party that claimed to have started in 1910 before World War I.
- *Ruzkhari* ("Salvation"), a Marxist party.
- *Komala i-Zhian i-Kurdistan* ("Committee for Kurdish Resurrection") or *Komala* for short, was a left-wing party established in Iran.

The *Komala* society reconstituted itself, in August 1946, as the Kurdish Democratic Party (KDP). It became the focus of Kurdish nationalism, both organizationally and ideologically. It was active in both Iran and Iraq. Mulla Mustafa Barzani became its main leader.

To facilitate the historic timeline of events, it is necessary to look at the relationship of the Kurds with each of the four states in which they resided.

THE KURDS AND TURKEY

Under the Turkish Republic, the very idea of a separate Kurdish people was suppressed. During the 1930s and 1940s, the Turkish government disguised the presence of the Kurds statistically by categorizing them as "Mountain Turks." This was changed to the new euphemism of "Eastern Turks" in 1980. Furthermore, the Kurds had largely been forbidden to wear their traditional costume, or speak, read or possess any material in their language. A Kurdish mother cannot give her baby a Kurdish name. The words "Kurd" and "Kurdistan" have been erased from literature and maps. There was a general forced assimilation of Kurds into Turkish life. Kurdish nationalist organizations remained underground and ruthlessly suppressed.

Date	Event
March 3, 1924	A Turkish decree banned all Kurdish schools, organizations, and publications, along with religious fraternities and *madrasas* (schools attached to a mosque where young men study theology).
March 1925	Sheikh Mehmet Said of Palu attempted a Kurdish insurrection in southern Turkey. It was crushed by the Turkish military employing over 50,000 troops and aerial bombardment against a 15,000-man Kurdish guerilla army.[126] Said was captured and hanged in Diyarbakır, in southeastern Turkey on June 29, 1925.
October 28, 1927	There was a Kurdish uprising in eastern Anatolia, Turkey, around Mount Ararat. The (Kurdish) Republic of Ararat was declared independent. However, it was not recognized by other states and lacked foreign support. The Ararat rebellion was defeated and the Republic of Ararat ceased to exist on September 17, 1930. Turkey resumed control over the disputed area. As a result, the Turkish government announced it had no Kurds, only "Mountain Turks" who had forgotten their native tongue.
1930	General Ihsan Nuri Pasha led another Kurdish rebellion, the Agrı rebellion, against the Turks, which became a part of the ongoing Ararat rebellion. Turkey again used air power to suppress destructively the uprising.
May 1932	Turkey promulgated a law for the deportation and dispersion of the Kurds. Thousands were deported to Central and Western Anatolia.
1934	Turkey adopted new anti-Kurdish legislation whereby the Kurds were to be dispersed across the country and forced their resettlement. The goal was that Kurds would never constitute more than 5 percent of the population in any place they inhabited.
1937	A Kurdish revolt erupted in the Dersim area of eastern Turkey led by Seyid Riza and termed the Dersim Rebellion. As in the case of the earlier tribal rural rebellions—1925, 1927, and 1930—this uprising was ruthlessly suppressed. Aerial bombardment, poison gas and artillery shelling were systematically directed against Kurdish strongholds. Some 40,000 were killed.[127] Riza was captured on September 5, and was hanged.
July 1943	Another Kurdish revolt began in Turkey, led by Sheikh Said Biroki. The rebellion was suppressed.
1945	The Kurds submitted a petition to the newly formed United Nations demanding national rights.
Summer 1960	After the May 27, 1960, military coup in Turkey, the State Planning Organization (DPT) was established to solve the problem of Kurdish separatism and underdevelopment. During this same period, there was a series of small unsuccessful revolts by Kurds in Turkey.
1961	The Turkish DPT prepared a report entitled "The Principles of the State's Development Plan for the East and Southeast," shortened to "Eastern Report." It proposed to defuse Kurdish separatism by encouraging ethnic mixing through migration (to and from the southeast). The Labor Minister at the time, Bülent Ecevit, was of Kurdish ancestry and criticized the report.

November 27, 1978	The Kurdistan Workers' Party–*Partiya Karkaren Kurdistan*–(PKK), a Marxist-Leninist group, was founded with Abdullah Öcalan as its leader. Its goal was to create an independent, socialist Kurdish state in Kurdistan. It employed terrorism as a tactic against Turkey.
1984	The PKK initiated a campaign of violent insurgency comprising of militant attacks against Turkish government forces and civilians in Iraq, Iran, and Turkey in order to create an independent Kurdish state. Approximately 37,000 people were killed by the PKK because of these attacks between 1984 and 2007.[128] The PKK was labeled a terrorist organization by several countries and international organizations including Turkey, the United States, Canada, Australia, and the European Union.
1984–99	The Turkish military engaged in a guerrilla war with the PKK. During the conflict, much of the countryside in southeastern Turkey was depopulated. An estimated 300 Kurdish villages in Turkey were virtually wiped off the map, displacing over 378,000 people.
March 4, 1987	100 Turkish warplanes bombed PKK bases in northern Iraq, killing an estimated 100 persons. The raid was in retaliation for a PKK attack, on February 22, in eastern Turkey.
August 30, 1988	Turkey officially opened its border to Iraqi Kurds fleeing their government's offensive, launched at the end of the Iran–Iraq War. Over 100,000 Kurds entered Turkey since the start of the offensive on July 30. Many refugees claimed to have witnessed poison gas attacks on the Kurds.

The PKK's main sanctuary was Syria, which gave the PKK arms, money and political cover. Saddam Hussein's Iraq also assisted Öcalan's forces by providing bases along the Iraqi-Turkish border. Neither Syria nor Iraq was supporting the Kurds out of any love for the Kurds. Within their respective nations, they treated the Kurds harshly, and fiercely repressed their own Kurdish populations. The main reason for their support was the desire for water. The headwaters of both the Tigris River and the Euphrates River spring forth from Turkey. Both Iraq and Syria want more water and use the Turkish Kurds to apply pressure on Ankara. Turkey controls the flow of both rivers and can turn the water spigot on and off by a series of dams on both rivers. That is the main reason why Turkey refuses to grant any autonomy to the Kurdish regions in the southeast. Turkey has been opposed to giving its section of Kurdistan (about the size of Austria) any autonomy for fear of undercutting the authority of the central government and a possible loss of the water resources.

Date	Event
October 1992	Turkey and the Iraqi Kurds, operating in their safe haven in northern Iraq, launched a joint operation to eliminate PKK camps in northern Iraq.
March 20, 1995	35,000 Turkish troops crossed the border into Iraq in a search and destroy operation against PKK guerrillas. They withdrew from northern Iraq on July 11.

October 20, 1998	PKK leader, Öcalan sought sanctuary in Syria. As the situation deteriorated in Turkey, the Turkish government openly threatened Syria with war over its support for the PKK. As a result of the Turkish threat, the Syrian regime concluded the Adana Agreement with Turkey and forced Öcalan to leave the country, but did not hand him over to Turkish authorities. Öcalan went to Russia first and from there he moved to various countries, including Italy and Greece.
February 15, 1999	Öcalan was captured in Nairobi, Kenya, while being transferred from the Greek embassy to the Nairobi international airport, in an operation by the Turkish National Intelligence Agency (MIT). He was then flown back to Turkey for trial. His capture led thousands of protesting Kurds to seize Greek embassies around the world.
February 17, 1999	Incited by rumors that the Israeli Mossad provided information that led to Öcalan's arrest in Kenya by the MIT, Kurdish protesters in Berlin attacked the Israeli consulate. Israeli security forces fired at the crowd resulting in three protesters killed and another fifteen injured.[129] Efraim Halevy, then head of the Mossad, took the unprecedented step of publicly disassociating Israel from Öcalan's capture. The Mossad does not usually comment publicly on intelligence matters.[130]
2002	Turkey lifted a fifteen-year state of emergency over its southeastern region, which it imposed due to the Kurdish uprising.

From 1999 to 2009, Öcalan was held in solitary confinement as the sole prisoner on İmralı Island in the Sea of Marmara. Despite the fact that all other prisoners formerly at İmralı were transferred to other prisons, there are still over 1,000 Turkish military personnel stationed there guarding him. He was sentenced to death, but this sentence was commuted to life-long aggravated imprisonment when the death penalty was abolished in Turkey in August 2002. In August 2003, the Turkish government passed an amnesty law, providing the group's members a chance to leave the PKK.[131] The PKK ended a self-imposed ceasefire in 2004 and killed 600 in 2006 alone.

Date	Event
March 2005	Öcalan released the Declaration of Democratic Confederalism in Kurdistan in which he asked for a border free confederation between the Kurdish regions of Turkey (called "Northwest Kurdistan" by the PKK), Syria ("Small part of South Kurdistan"), Iraq ("South Kurdistan"), and Iran ("East Kurdistan"). In this zone, three bodies of law would be implemented: EU law, Turkish/Syrian/Iraqi/Iranian law and Kurdish law.
September 28, 2006	Öcalan released a statement calling on the PKK to declare a ceasefire and seek peace with Turkey. Öcalan's statement declared, "The PKK should not use weapons unless it is attacked with the aim of annihilation," and that it is "very important to build a democratic union between Turks and Kurds. With this process, the way to democratic dialogue will be also opened."[132]
February 27, 2007	During a US Senate Armed Services Committee hearing whether Turkey would "stand on the sidelines and watch an independent Kurdistan be formed in the north [of Iraq] without going to war," Director of National Intelligence Vice Admiral J. Michael McConnell said, flatly, "no".

April 8, 2007	As PKK anti-Turkish attacks continued, Turkey accused Iraqi Kurdistan of harboring the PKK terrorists, allowing them to stage cross-border raids into Turkey and return into Iraqi Kurdistan for sanctuary.

The Barzani administration in Iraq provided safe haven and supplies to the PKK. Few restrictions were placed on PKK travel within northern Iraq. The PKK continued to smuggle explosives and carry out attacks in Turkey. Barzani refused to stop weapons trafficking across the border with his own *Peshmerga* militia, and refused the Iraqi army permission to do so. To add to Turkey's anger, Iraqi Kurdish television and newspapers were rampant with incitements to unrest, often referring to Iraqi Kurdistan as "South Kurdistan," thereby implying that large chunks of Turkey must be "North Kurdistan."

Date	Event
April 9, 2007	Turkey challenged Iraqi Kurdish leader Massoud Barzani's claim to oil-rich Kirkuk in northern Iraq. Officials in the Turkish capital said his persistence would lead to the loss of the last trace of stability in Iraq. Barzani in an interview told *Al Arabiya* television, "Turkey is not allowed to intervene in the Kirkuk issue; if it does, we will interfere over Diyarbakir [the largest predominantly Kurdish city] and other cities in Turkey." Ankara replied, "Turkey will not hesitate to take necessary precautions so that Barzani can't even spell the "D" of Diyarkabir. Barzani should know his place."
April 12, 2007	Turkish forces crossed the Iraqi frontier into Iraqi Kurdistan, 12.5 miles deep to target PKK camps east of Zaho and 19 to 25 miles up to the rural areas of Haftanin, Sinaht and Pirbela provinces.
June 6, 2007	As PKK activity continued through May–June, several hundred Turkish troops, backed by armored vehicles and combat aircraft, invaded Iraqi Kurdistan again, in an effort to destroy PKK bases.
February 21, 2008	Turkey yet again sent its military forces into Iraqi Kurdistan to attack PKK bases. The ground incursion was preceded by Turkish Air Force aerial bombardment on PKK facilities, which began on December 16, 2007. Turkish forces withdrew on February 29, 2008, declaring it had achieved its objectives. Turkish military operations against the PKK were ongoing well into 2008.
ca. September 2009	It is highly probable that the Turkish Army used chemical weapons against members of the PKK.[133]
November 2009	As a result of pressure from the Council of Europe's Committee for the Prevention of Torture, Turkish authorities announced that Öcalan would be relocated to a new prison on İmralı, and that they were ending his solitary confinement. Furthermore, they transferred several other PKK prisoners to the island allowing Öcalan to see them for ten hours a week.
December 11, 2009	The Constitutional Court of Turkey banned the Kurdish Democratic Society Party (DTP). It ruled that the party had become the "focal point of activities against the indivisible unity of the state, the country and the nation" and was linked to the Kurdistan Workers' Party (PKK). This triggered demonstrations on December 15, resulting in two killed and at least six wounded.

May 2010	The Turkish Islamist government of Prime Minister Recep Tayyip Erdoğan failed to achieve any agreement with the PKK and its leader Abdullah Öcalan, who abandoned efforts for dialogue. On May 20, 2010, Turkish planes bombed dozens of Kurdish rebel targets in northern Iraq, and on May 31, the PKK retaliated with a rocket attack against a naval base, which left seven soldiers dead. Thus, the Turkish-PKK conflict resumed. The PKK demanded autonomy, freedom for imprisoned Kurdish rebel leader Abdullah Öcalan, an unconditional amnesty for rebel commanders and permission for Kurdish-language education in schools.
August 17, 2011	Turkey launched a large offensive against PKK strongholds in northern Iraq. The main battlefields were the Qandil Mountains region, Sinath-Haftanin, Hakurk and Gara. The US, Turkey, Iran and the Kurdish Regional Government of northern Iraq formed an improbable coalition to cooperate in extinguishing the Kurdish rebellions staged by the PKK against Turkey and the Kurdistan Free Life Party—*Partiya Jiyana Azada Kurdistanê*—(PJAK) against Iran.
January 2012	The Democratic Society Congress (DTK), an umbrella organization of Kurdish groups in Turkey, submitted a proposal to the Turkish Parliament for the new constitution demanding Kurdish regional autonomy. The DTK further proposed that the emphasis on "Turkishness" should be completely removed from the new constitution. Additionally, the DTK demanded education and public services in native languages as well as in scientific, religious and artistic activities.[134]
March 21, 2013	Jailed Kurdish rebel leader Abdullah Öcalan called for an immediate ceasefire and for thousands of his Kurdistan Workers' Party (PKK) fighters to withdraw from Turkish territory.
May 8, 2013	As the result of negotiations between Turkish intelligence—the MIT—and PKK leader Abdullah Öcalan that started in the fall of 2012, some of the estimated 2,000 armed Kurdish PKK rebels began withdrawing from Turkey to their stronghold in the Qandil Mountains in northern Iraq.[135]
September 30, 2013	Turkish Prime Minister Recep Tayyip Erdoğan announced a series of reforms some of which lessened some restrictions on the Kurds of Turkey. Among these were, teaching in Kurdish would be allowed in private schools, though it is still restricted in state schools. Towns would be allowed officially to take their native-language names. Thus, the Turkish-named city of Tunceli would revert to its Kurdish name, Dersim. Additionally, the Prime Minister promised to remove the daily oath of allegiance to the Turkish nation that schoolchildren swear. Furthermore, Erdoğan undertook to review the law under which only parties, which won ten percent of the national vote, would gain seats in parliament. That law could be replaced by a five percent threshold, or even abolished altogether, Erdoğan stated. In the past, the law prevented the main Kurdish party in Turkey—the Peace and Democracy Party (BDP)—from campaigning for parliament.[136]

March 21, 2015	Imprisoned PKK leader Abdullah Öcalan urged his followers to lay down their arms reflecting, "I think it is necessary and historic for the PKK to end the 40 year-long armed struggle against the Republic of Turkey and hold a congress to conform to the new era's spirit."[137]

Turkey cannot solve its Kurdish problem because the Kurds know that time is on their side. The situation of the Kurds in Turkey and the future of Kurdish sovereignty as an independent nation-state will come about because of demography. Ethnic Turks have a fertility rate close to 1.5 children per family, while the Kurdish minority is having 4 children per family. Demographically, Turkish Kurds will comprise half the country's military-age population a generation from now.[138] That is why the PKK Kurdish separatists are confident that their guerilla campaign against Turkish security forces ultimately will triumph.

THE KURDS AND SYRIA

The Kurds consider themselves ethnically different from the Arabs, being non-Semitic and speaking an Indo-European language. The Kurds have little in common with the Arabs of Syria or Iraq apart from their Sunni Muslim faith. Most of the Kurds in Syria live in the Jazira region (the traditional Arabic name for modern-day regions of northwestern Iraq and northeastern Syria. Their "capital" is the city of Al Qamishlo. Many arrived after the Turks crushed their revolt in 1925. There is a small community of Kurds in Damascus dating from the time of Saladin.

The Syrian Arab regimes up until the Syrian Civil War continually practiced racism and apartheid, especially against the Kurdish minority. Kurds in Syria, cannot own property, vote, be publicly employed, travel freely within the country, obtain passports or even practice certain professions (such as medicine or teaching). Couples were deemed "single" and could not share a hotel room or register their children. These 100,000 children of unrecognized marriages were denied access to education, food subsidies and health care. Thus, Kurds are forced to work, aspiring to menial careers of cotton-picking, cigarette selling and shoe shining. Having been denied the right to Syrian nationality, around 300,000 Kurds have been deprived of any social rights, in violation of international law. Furthermore, nearly one quarter million Kurdish farmers have been forced to abandon their farms and move to urban centers, due to the unavailability of water. As has been mentioned above, Turkey has limited the flow of Euphrates River water through Syria and Iraq. According to the findings of a special study by the United Nations, the Euphrates is expected to become completely dry outside Turkey's boundaries.[139]

Date	Event
1957	Kurdish activists Osman Sabri and Daham Miro, along with others, established the Kurdish Democratic Party of Syria (KDPS), demanding that they be recognized as an ethnic group and allowed to practice their own culture.
1958	With the creation of the United Arab Republic (UAR), linking Egypt and Syria, the KDPS was repressed as Nasser sought to eliminate any political rivals to his regime. The UAR government was determined to inflict maximum damage on the Kurds because they were viewed as agents of Israel. In 1960, the Syrian government issued a decree that denied the Kurds the right of grazing livestock on their own land. As a result, millions of livestock perished of starvation, causing the Kurds severe economic hardship. This repressive policy continued even after Syria seceded from the UAR in September 1961.
1962	The Syrian government began a resettlement policy, whereby the government began to seize Kurdish properties and transfer them to Arab ownership.
August 23, 1962	The new Syrian Arab Republic sought to disenfranchise the Kurds by conducting a special census held only in Al-Hasakah Governate, in the northeastern corner of the country, which stripped Kurds of their citizenship rights. Even if Kurds proved Syrian-residency dating from Ottoman Empire or the French mandate periods, or if they had served in the military, they still lost their nationality. Thus, 400,000 Kurds[140] were deprived of Syrian nationality and were classified as aliens. Since then, even if they met requirements for regaining citizenship, they were unable to acquire recognition.
March 8, 1963	After the Ba'athist Party coup, the new Syrian leadership expelled many of the Kurds along the border with Turkey and continued the policy of depriving thousands more of their Syrian nationality. As soon as the Ba'athists came to power, they announced a program of Agrarian Reform, which ostensibly meant the confiscation of Kurdish land. The land would be used to build the "Arab Belt," a euphemism for ethnic cleansing, and serve as a buffer zone between Syrian Kurds and their brethren in Turkey and Iraq. This "Arabization policy" resulted in rendering Syria's 300,000 Kurds "stateless foreigners" and subject to oppression. Syria's Constitution afforded no protection for Kurds, or indeed, for any other minorities. They were rendered "non-citizens" and thereby deprived of basic rights to obtain basic social services. The Syrian Ba'athist government adopted the Iraqi policy of resettling Arabs in the Jazira region while scattering Kurds into the interior of the country.
June 10, 1963	Syria took part in the Iraqi military campaign against the Kurds by providing aircraft, armored vehicles and a force of some 6,000 soldiers.[141]
1965	The Syrian government adopted a plan to deal with the "Kurdish problem"—by destroying the cohesion of the Kurdish community in Syria. Part of the plan was the creation of an Arab *cordon sanitaire* along the Syrian-Turkish border.
1966–71	The Ba'athists began a policy of seizing Kurdish lands. In the 1970s, under Hafez al-Assad, the Arabization policy in Kurdish territory continued as the Syrian regime created forty-five settlements and brought 30,000 Arab families into the al-Hasakah region in the northeastern (Kurdish) portion of the country. By early 1971, some 30,000 Kurds had been moved out of the region. Land confiscations continued into the 1970s and 1980s.

1973	The regime of Hafez al-Assad implemented the 1965 plan to create an "Arab belt"—*al hizam al'-arabi*—a Kurdish-free zone, along the Syrian-Turkish frontier. Originally it was to be 6 to 9 miles wide (though in some areas it was nearly 22 miles deep), 233 miles in length, running from six miles west of Ras al'Ain along the Turkish border as far as Iraq, and then southwards around the Syrian panhandle along the Iraqi border to Tal Kuchik.[142] Kurds were to be ethnically cleansed from this entire swath of territory.
1976	The Syrian government abandoned the resettlement of more Arabs in the Kurdish areas. However, it did not remove those Arabs already settled in forty-one new villages in the *al hizam al'-arabi*, nor did it lead to the reinstatement of the Kurds on their previous land holdings.[143]
March 21, 1986	A few thousand Kurds wearing Kurdish costumes gathered in the Kurdish part of Damascus to celebrate the spring festival of Nowruz. Police warned them that Kurdish dress was prohibited, as was the flying of the Kurdish flag, and it fired on the crowd leaving one person dead.[144]
2000	Bashar al-Assad, (who became president of Syria, July 17, 2000) continued his father's policy by creating a buffer zone along the Iraqi border, to separate Syrian from Iraqi Kurds.[145] Bedouin Arabs from the Euphrates Valley (displaced by the construction of the Tabqa Dam and the creation of Lake Assad) were brought in and resettled in Kurdish areas, while village names were Arabized. The Syrian security agencies in the Kurdish area were given extraordinary powers. They could confiscate, detain, torture, and kill with impunity. The Syrian government did not officially recognize the Kurds as being Kurds. Kurds see themselves as "second class Arabs." Harsh conditions in the Kurdish areas of northeast Syria, in addition to the lack of infrastructure or employment opportunities, forced many Kurds to flee Syria and settle in Germany and Scandinavia.[146]
2003	The Kurdish Democratic Union Party (PYD) was founded. It is affiliated with the PKK and is trained by the latter. There are those who believe that the PYD is an off-shoot of the PKK and as such, like its mentor, is leftist, secular, quasi-Marxist but nevertheless a Kurdish nationalist party seeking Kurdish autonomy in Syria
March 12, 2004	Syrian regime-sponsored Sunni thugs attacked Kurdish soccer fans in Qamishli, a Kurdish city in northeastern Syria. The attack led to three days of Kurdish anti-regime riots. Rioters destroyed regime monuments, including a statue of Hafez al-Assad, and burned government offices.[147] The riots were brutally quelled by security forces, tanks and helicopters. As a result, eighty-five Kurds were dead, hundreds injured and thousands imprisoned. The discovery of oil in the Hasakah region served as further motivation for the Syrian regime to engage in their ethnic cleansing of Kurdish areas.[148]
January 2007	A decree issued by Dr. Adel Safar, Syrian Minister of Agriculture and Agrarian Reform, approved the resettlement of 150 Arab families to the Kurdish region. The decree brought Arabs from the South Abdulaziz Mountains to the Kurdish town of Derrick. Additionally, the Ba'athist regime redrew the boundaries of the Kurdish region, dividing it into four provinces, in order to undermine the Kurdish majority. Moreover, the Syrian regime gerrymandered portions of the Kurdish region to neighboring Arab provinces.[149]

March 21, 2010	Syrian security forces opened fire on a crowd of 5,000 in the northern Syrian town of al-Raqqah. The crowd had gathered to celebrate the Kurdish festival of Nowruz. Three people, including a 15-year-old girl, were killed and over fifty were injured. This episode marked the start of a new wave of Syrian repression of its Kurdish minority.
June–July 2010	The Syrian Army began a military campaign against the Kurds in Syria. This was done with the active cooperation of Turkish generals based at Syrian staff headquarters in Damascus.* Attacks were launched on the large Kurdish town of Qamishli, the mixed Kurdish-Assyrian town of Al Asakah and two others, Qaratshuk and Diwar. Furthermore, Syria sealed the Syrian-Iraqi and Syrian-Lebanese borders to prevent the Kurds from fleeing and in the case of the former, to prevent PKK reinforcements from reaching the fighting. While some Kurds were members of the PKK, the majority were civilians. An estimated 300 were killed and over 1,000 injured. Prisoners captured were turned over to the Turkish military. Additionally, Syrian security forces arrested some 400 Kurds (Kurdish sources claimed 630) allegedly for having links to the PKK.[150]
March 2011	The Syrian government promised to tackle the issue of Kurdish statelessness and grant Syrian citizenship to the 300,000 Kurds.
April 7, 2011	President Bashar al-Assad signed Decree 49, which granted "Syrian Arab nationality" to people registered as "foreigners" in Al-Hasakah,[151] where many Kurds reside. However, a recent report indicated that the actual number of stateless Kurds who have obtained national ID cards since the decree was only 9,381,[152] leaving the rest in limbo.

During the 2011–15 uprising against the regime of Bashar Assad and subsequent Syrian Civil War, at first the Kurds sat on the sidelines. The leaders of the Syrian Kurdish Democratic Union Party (PYD), which is affiliated with the PKK of Kurds in Turkey, wanted to remain uninvolved in the conflict and keep it out of the Kurdistan region in Syria's northeast. The PYD stands separate from the Kurdish National Council (KNC), a coalition of eleven Kurdish parties in Syria that has ties to the autonomous Kurdistan Regional Government in Iraq. The Kurdish groups are far from united

---

* The Turkish government of Prime Minister Tayyip Recep Erdoğan supported the anti-Kurdish Syrian military campaign by using Israeli-supplied *Heron* spy drones which the Jewish state had previously sold to Turkey. The drones were used to track Kurds in flight across Syria's borders, mainly into Lebanon, where Hezbollah helped Syria hunt the refugees down. This action was in violation and despite restrictions in the original Israel-Turkish arms sales contracts which barred the drones use in the service of hostile states or entities. However, one must recall an earlier period, 1955–56, which illustrated this predicament. At that time, Egyptian President Gamal Abdel Nasser purchased arms from the Soviet Union via Czechoslovakia. When the deal was exposed, Nasser declared, "I do not know whether they are 'Communist arms', or 'non-Communist arms.' In Egypt these arms are Egyptian arms." Similarly, Israel and the West long ago had to realize that once weapons are sold to another nation, they can be compromised and fall into the hands of hostile powers. This is what has happened with the Israeli drones sold to Turkey. Thus, the Syrian Army, Hezbollah and Iran have gained the opportunity to study the Israeli drone's sophisticated features in real combat conditions and develop counter-measures to foil the *Heron's* capabilities. Turkey therefore became the first NATO member to make advanced Western military technology available to the Islamic fundamentalist axis of Iran-Syria-and Hezbollah-controlled Lebanon and terrorist groups supported by this axis.

on most issues. The KNC has in the past clashed with the PYD, but since Syria's unrest began in January 2011, the two factions have "signed an agreement sponsored by the Iraqi Kurdish leadership to prevent intra-Kurdish tensions."[153] As the Syrian Civil War continued, Syrian Kurdish leaders began contemplating a Kurdish autonomous zone in Syria, similar to the one in Iraq.

As Turkey openly called for the ouster of the Assad regime, increased border clashes occurred between the two nations. As a result, Assad allowed some 2,000 PKK fighters to move from Iraqi Kurdistan, into northern Syria to conduct operations against Turkey. Since the summer of 2011, over 700 Turks have been killed.

Date	Event
July 16, 2013	During the Syrian Civil War, the People's Protection Units—*Yekîneyên Parastina Gel* (YPG)—of the Kurdish Democratic Union Party (PYD) captured the city of Ra's al-'Ayn (in the al-Hasakah Governorate) on the northern border with Turkey and created an exclusively autonomous Kurdish region. Additionally, the Kurds planned to form a provisional Kurdish government due to the absence of any central authority.
October 26, 2013	Kurdish fighters of the People's Protection Units (YPG) defeated Al-Qaeda affiliates, the Nusra Front (*Ansar Jabhat al-Nusra li-Ahl al-Sha'm*), and the Islamic State in Iraq and the Levant (*ad-Dawla al-Islamiyya fi al-'Irāq wa-sh-Sham*), abbreviated as ISIL (also known as ISIS, but more accurately transliterated ISIL). They captured the Yaribiyah border crossing (known to the Kurds as Tel Kocher) in Hasakah province, between Syria and Iraq. The YPG offensive concluded in early November with the capture of the Ras al-Ayn (Serêkaniyê) area, on the border with Turkey. The YPG forces consolidated their autonomous enclave in northeastern Syria bordering Iraq. The Kurds call this area "Rojavayê," or western Kurdistan.
November 12, 2013	Syrian Kurds announced the formation of a transitional autonomous government for Rojavayê, i.e. western Kurdistan. The region was divided into three areas, each with its own local assembly, as well as representatives to a regional executive body.
January 21, 2014	Syrian Kurds declared an autonomous provincial government—the Cizîre Canton of Western Kurdistan. The autonomous government will have its own president and twenty-two ministries, including foreign affairs, defense, justice and education. Kurdish, Arab, and Assyrian representatives will be appointed to each ministry. Kurdish, Arabic, and Syriac have been designated as the canton's official languages. Ekrem Heso was elected the President of the Cizîre canton. Syriac Elizabet Gewriyê and Arab Husen Ezem were named as vice presidents.

In Syria, much depends on the outcome of the Syrian Civil War. If the Assad regime prevails, again there may be ruthless suppression of the Kurds. If the myriad of rebel groups achieve victory, Syria may become a decentralized federal state with autonomous regions, or fall apart altogether into Alawite, Druze, Kurdish, and Arab/Sunni components. It also remains to be seen if the Kurdish autonomous region in northeastern Syria will join with that in Iraq. Turkey, seeking a buffer between itself and Shi'ite Iran may well reach an accommodation with the Kurds within its own territory as well as the two autonomous regions, providing the Kurds overall, with their best chance to cautiously move forward towards sovereignty and their own nation-state.

THE KURDS AND IRAN	
Date	**Event**
1918–30	Ismail Agha Shikak also known as Simko Shikak revolted in Persia (Iran) during a period of weakness in the Persian government following World War I. Reza Khan took military action to crush the Kurdish rebels. Shikak was forced to abandon his region in the autumn of 1922, and spent eight years in hiding. When the Iranian government persuaded him to come in and negotiate, he was ambushed and killed at Oshnaviyeh (Ushno) on June 30, 1930. After this, Shah Reza Khan pursued a crude but effective policy against the Kurds. Hundreds of Kurdish chiefs were deported and forced into exile. Additionally, their lands were confiscated by the government.[154]
Autumn 1931	Another insurrection by Kurds erupted in Persia, led by Sheikh Jafar. The Persian government incredulously declared it had no Kurdish problem.

From 1931 until World War II, there was a period of relative quiet between the central government of Shah Reza Khan and the Kurds. Relations were better than in Turkey. The Shah's government left traditional society and its tribal patterns of governance undisturbed and did not interfere with the social-cultural activities of the Kurdish people as long as they remained politically loyal to the regime.

Date	**Event**
August 25–September 17, 1941	As Allied troops (British and Soviet, later joined by American forces) entered Iran, Shah Reza Khan was deposed (September 16) for his pro-Axis sympathies. The Iranian Army was quickly dissolved and their ammunition was captured by the Kurds. The sons of Kurdish chiefs seized the opportunity and escaped from their exile in Tehran. A Kurdish chief from Baneh, named Hama Rashid took control of Sardasht, Baneh and Mariwan in western Iran. He was finally driven out of the region by the Iranian Army in the fall of 1944.[155]
September 16, 1942	The *Komala*, a secret Kurdish Marxist, and nationalist society, was founded in Mahabad, Iran. It served as the Kurdish Communist Party.
September 1945	Qazi Muhammad and his two brothers, Kurdish leftists from Mahabad, visited the Soviet Union. They learned that the Soviets were planning to establish a communist state in Iranian Azerbaijan, and that they should do the same in their region in West Azerbaijan. The Soviets persuaded Qazi to take command of the *Komala* society. Qazi included social and land reform demands in the *Komala* platform and pledged a close working relationship with the Soviet Azerbaijan republic.
November 1945	*Komala* came out into the open at Mahabad.
December 15, 1945	The Kurdish Republic of Mahabad (*see* "Major Oilfields and Secessionist Areas" map) proclaimed its independence. The Qazi brothers and a group of urban intellectuals and merchants provided the leadership, while its main armed force was Barzani tribesmen, led by Mulla Mustafa Barzani. In February 1946, Soviet arms were sent to the Kurdish Republic of Mahabad.

May 9, 1946	After several delays and under United States and UN pressure, as well as Iranian duplicity, Soviet troops were withdrawn from northwestern Iran. The withdrawal of Soviet Red Army forces facilitated the collapse of both the "Azerbaijan People's Government" and the Kurdish Republic of Mahabad on December 11, 1946 and December 15, 1946, respectively.
December 15, 1946	Iranian forces entered and secured Mahabad, crushing the short-lived independent Kurdish Republic of Mahabad. Once there, they closed down the Kurdish printing press, banned the teaching of Kurdish, and burned any books that were written in Kurdish that they could find.
March 1947	The Qazis surrendered without a fight. The US ambassador George Allen sought an immediate audience with the Shah. As Allen began his appeal the Shah broke in, "Are you afraid I'm going to have them shot? If so, you can set your mind at rest. I am not." He kept his word with regal duplicity: Twenty Kurdish leaders, including Qazi Muhammad and his brothers were charged with treason and hanged the following dawn, March 31. The public hanging took place in Chuwarchira Square in the center of Mahabad, at the express orders of the Shah! Mulla Mustafa al-Barzani retreated into the Naqadeh area of Iran near the Iraqi border.

Archibald Bulloch Roosevelt, Jr., grandson of former US President Theodore Roosevelt, wrote in *The Kurdish Republic of Mahabad* that a main problem of that regime was that the Kurds needed the assistance of the USSR; only with the Red Army did they have a chance. But this close relationship to Stalin and the USSR caused most of the Western powers to side with Iran. Qazi Muhammad, though not denying the fact that they were funded and supplied by the Soviets, denied that the KDP was a communist party, stating this was a lie fabricated by Iranian military authorities, and adding that his ideals were too different from the Soviets.[156]

During the 1960s, relations between the Shah's government and the Kurds improved as the Shah allowed the Kurdish rebels in Iraq to establish their main base and staging area in the Kurdish region of Iran, aiding them with supplies, arms and ammunition. This assistance continued into the mid-1970s. Relations soured because of the 1975 Algiers Agreement between Iran and Iraq. In return for Iraqi recognition of the *thalweg* line as the delineation of the Shatt al-Arab waterway, known as Arvand Rud in Iran, the Shah of Iran agreed to close Iran's border and stop the flow of aid to the Kurds in rebellion against the Baghdad government. Thus, the Shah denied the Kurds the facilities upon which they depended and their rebellion against Iraq collapsed.

Date	Event
February 10–11, 1979	The Iranian monarchy was overthrown and an Islamist regime, headed by Ayatollah Ruhollah Khomeini, came to power. The *de facto* semi-autonomous status of the Iranian Kurds ended.
February 22, 1979	Over 100 were killed on the Iraq–Iran border in clashes between the Kurds and supporters of the new Iranian Islamic Republic.
March 3, 1979	In Mahabad, after thirty-three years underground, the Kurdish Democratic Party of Iran announced its own legalization to a crowd of 200,000 people gathered in the very same square—Chuwarchira Square—where the leaders of the Kurdish Republic of Mahabad had been hanged in March 1947.

March 18–19, 1979	In Sanandaj, in Iranian Kurdistan, Kurdish *Peshmerga* forces violently clashed with Ayatollah Khomeini's forces. A special envoy, Ayatollah Taleghani, concluded a ceasefire agreement and promised publicly that the Islamic regime would grant autonomous status to Iran's ethnic minorities.
April 1, 1979	The Kurds abstained from voting in a referendum to endorse the creation of an Islamic republic. They were seen by the Islamic authorities as vulnerable to exploitation by foreign powers who wished to destabilize the young republic. (The Kurds are Sunni, unlike the overwhelming majority of their compatriots who are Shi'ite). That referendum institutionalized Shi'a primacy and made no provision for regional autonomy. In August 1979, armed conflict broke out between armed Kurdish factions and the Iranian government's security forces. The Kurdish forces primarily included the Democratic Party of Iranian Kurdistan (KDPI) and the leftist *Komala* (Revolutionary Organization of Kurdish Toilers). In a speech, Ayatollah Khomeini called the concept of ethnic minorities contrary to Islamic doctrines. He also accused those who did not wish Muslim countries to be united in creating the issue of nationalism among minorities. His views were shared by many in the clerical leadership.
April 20–22, 1979	Violent incidents erupted in Naghadeh, which were followed by clashes continuing into August.

The crisis deepened after Kurds were denied seats in the assembly of experts gathering in 1979, who were responsible for writing the new constitution. Therefore, Kurds were deprived of their political rights under the new Iranian constitution, since the majority of them belonged to the Sunni branch of Islam.

Date	Event
August 17, 1979– into Spring 1980	Iranian Supreme Leader, Ayatollah Khomeini issued a *fatwa* (an authoritative Islamic religious decree issued by a Muslim scholar) and declared holy war against the Kurdish organizations fighting with the central government.[157] The Iranian Army, under the command of President Abolhassan Banisadr, launched a general offensive against the *Peshmerga* forces using 110,000 troops complete with tanks, heavy artillery, fighter-bombers and armed helicopters. Khomeini consistently referred to the Kurds as *khofar* ("infidels"). Entire villages and towns were destroyed to force Kurds into submission, including Mahabad, Sinne, Pawe, and Marivan. By September 5, 1979, the main towns of Kurdistan had been occupied by the Iranian military. In early March 1980, there was a temporary ceasefire. However, by the end of March 1980, fighting erupted in Sanandaj, the main market town in Iranian Kurdistan and continued. The Islamic tribunals headed by Chief Justice, Ayatollah Sadegh Khalkhali—dubbed by the press, "the hanging judge"[158]—sentenced thousands of men to execution[159] after summary trials without regard for the rights of the accused. The Iranian Revolutionary Guards Corps—*Pasdaran*—fought to reestablish government control in the Kurdish regions. As a result, more than 10,000 Kurds were killed.[160]

These developments also caused a split in the Kurdish national movement. The KDP had never been fully united and its Iraqi and Iranian branches sometimes followed divergent policies. This was best illustrated during the Iran–Iraq War of 1980–88, when Kurdish rebels in Iran—a KDP faction led by Secretary-General Abdul Rahman Ghassemlou—sometimes collaborated with Iraq and its secret services, while Barzani's KDP in Iraq collaborated to some extent with Iran. The two branches of the KDP thus found themselves on opposite sides in the war but managed to avoid direct clashes with one another.

Date	Event
June 1987	Iraq launched chemical weapons attacks on Iranian Kurdish villages. Some twenty were killed and 2,000 injured.[161]
Autumn 1989	After the Iran–Iraq War, Jalal Talabani tried to broker a meeting between Ghassemlou and Iranian officials. Ghassemlou was assassinated at the meeting in Vienna, Austria, by Iranian agents of the Islamic republic.
September 17, 1992	Ghassemlou's successor to the post of Secretary-General of the KDP, Sadegh Sharafkandi, was likewise assassinated with three others, by Iranian agents, in the Mykonos restaurant in Berlin, Germany.
May 23, 1997	Sunni Kurds took part in the Iranian presidential election. The winner was the reformist candidate, Mohammad Khatami, who praised the glory of Kurdish culture and history. The Kurds demanded fewer restrictions on the use of the Kurdish language and the appointment of top-level officials. In his first term, Khatami appointed Abdollah Ramezanzadeh to be the first Kurdish governor of the Iranian province of Kurdistan. He also appointed several Sunni and Shi'a Kurds as his own advisers or cabinet ministers. In his second term Khatami had two Kurdish cabinet members, both of them Shi'a.
February 1999	Kurdish nationalists took to the streets in several cities such as Mahabad, Sanandaj, and Urmia, staging mass protests against the government as well as in support of Abdullah Öcalan, the Kurdish leader of the PKK. This was viewed as transnationalization of the Kurdish movement.[162] These protests were violently suppressed by government forces. According to human rights groups, at least twenty people were killed.[163]
2004	The Kurdistan Free Life Party—*Partiya Jiyana Azada Kurdistanê* (PJAK)—was founded and was said to be linked to the PKK. The Iranian government began to battle the PJAK, in a bid to win Turkey's favor at the expense of the United States.
July 9–August 2005	As a result of the July 9, 2005 murder of Shivan Qaderi and two other Kurdish leaders by Iranian security men, riots and protests erupted in Kurdish towns and villages throughout eastern Kurdistan. The violence flared in Mahabad, Sinne (Sanandaj), Sardasht, Piranshahr (Xanê), Oshnavieh (Şino), Baneh, Bokan, and Saqiz (and inspired protests in southwestern Iran and in Baluchistan in eastern Iran). Scores were killed and injured, and an untold number arrested without charge. The authorities also shut down several major Kurdish newspapers, arresting reporters and editors. Partly in retaliation, four members of the Iranian police force were taken hostage by the PJAK armed group in West Azerbaijan Province. The PJAK continuously launched militant operations against Iranian army forces so that in less than six months they killed 120 Iranian police and injured many.[164]

2009–10	In a blatant attempt to intimidate the Kurdish minority, the Iranian government jailed (without fair trial), tortured, and executed Kurdish activists, including Ehsan Fattahian (November 2009), Fasih Yasamani (January 2010) as well as Ali Heydarian, Farhad Vakili, Mehdi Eslamian, Shirin Alam Hooli, and Farzad Kamangar (May 2010). These men were charged with unproven offenses and executed for "enmity against God" and belonging to the PJAK. As of May 2010, there were at least sixteen other Kurdish political prisoners on death row. Not one case has been reported as receiving a fair trial.
July 16–17, 2011	Iranian Revolutionary Guard Corps (IRGC) forces crossed the border into Iraqi Kurdistan to attack PJAK guerrillas, as tensions mounted along the border.

THE KURDS AND IRAQ

As has been previously mentioned, the Kurds consider themselves ethnically different from the Arabs, being non-Semitic and speaking an Indo-European language. The Kurds have little in common with the Arabs of Iraq or Syria apart from their Sunni Muslim faith. There was near-constant Kurdish unrest from the liquidation of Ottoman rule in 1918, to the beginnings of British administration over Mesopotamia and the formation of the Kingdom of Iraq on August 23, 1921. At first, this unrest was linked to Turkish efforts to keep the province of Mosul within the new Turkey, but the unrest remained endemic when the province was awarded to the newly created Iraq and when Turkish manipulations gradually ceased.

The British in the early years of control over Iraq also tried to manipulate the various Kurdish sheikhs, sometimes encouraging a degree of *de facto* semi-autonomy, sometimes suppressing the sheikhs' semi-rebellion. It was the classic pattern of divide and rule. During the 1920s and 1930s several Kurdish uprisings occurred.

Date	Event
December 1, 1918	During a meeting in Sulaymaniyah with Colonel Arnold Wilson, the Acting Civil Commissioner for Mesopotamia, Kurdish leaders called for British support for a united and independent Kurdistan under British protection. Between 1919 and 1922, Sheikh Mahmud Barzanji, an influential Kurdish leader based in Sulaymaniyah, formed a Kurdish government.
May 22, 1919	Sheikh Mahmud Barzanji began his first revolt against British rule. The revolt started with the arrest of British officials in Sulaymaniyah and it quickly spread to Mosul and Erbil. Barzanji's goal was to create a free and united Kurdistan.
July 1920	Sixty-two tribal leaders of the region, called for independence of Kurdistan under a British mandate. The objection of the British to Kurdish self-rule was driven by the fear that the success of the Kurdish area would tempt the two Arab areas of Baghdad and Basra to follow suit, hence endangering direct British control over all Mesopotamia.
1922	The United Kingdom restored Sheikh Mahmoud Barzanji to power, hoping that he would organize the Kurds to act as a buffer against the Turks, who had territorial claims over Mosul.

June 18, 1922	Sheikh Mahmoud Barzanji began a second insurrection and declared a Kurdish Kingdom, which lasted from September 1922 to July 1924, with himself as king. He established contact with Ismail Agha Shikak, a Kurdish leader in Persia (Iran). Barzanji sought independence or autonomy for his people. The rebellion was suppressed by the British Army by July 1924, and the Sheikh was exiled to India.
December 16, 1925	The League of Nations Council assigned most of the disputed territory in the oil-rich Mosul region to Iraq, despite strong Turkish protests. For its part, the Iraqi government pledged to recognize Kurdish national "distinctiveness and consciousness." This pledge was ignored by successive Iraqi governments.
1927	By the late 1920s, the Barzani clan, the largest and most prominent Kurdish tribe in Kurdistan, had become vocal supporters of Kurdish rights in Iraq. A Kurdish insurrection erupted in Iraq led by Sheikh Mahmoud Barzani, but it was beset by inter-tribal rivalries.
September 11, 1930	A third Kurdish insurrection erupted in Iraq, again led by Sheikh Barzanji, who had returned from India. In 1929, Barzanji had demanded the formation of a Kurdish province in northern Iraq. Emboldened by these demands, in 1931 Kurdish notables petitioned the League of Nations to set up an independent Kurdish government. The revolt was suppressed by British air and ground forces and the Sheikh surrendered in April 1931. Barzanji was captured by the British and placed under house arrest in Baghdad.
1931–35	Almost immediately, another Kurdish insurrection began in Iraq, led by Sheikh Ahmed Barzani and his brother Mulla Mustafa Barzani. (Mulla was his first name, not a religious title).
August 1931	The Jewish *Yishuv* established contact with the Kurds. A relationship would continue to the present. Reuven Shiloah, who later became founder of the Israeli intelligence community, quickly realized the need for clandestine alliances with all the non-Arab minorities in the Middle East.[165] The Kurds would assist in helping smuggle Iraqi Jews out of Iraq for over two decades.
January–October 1932	As the League of Nations deliberated to terminate the British Mandate of Iraq, granting it independence and admitting it to League membership, a requirement was made on Iraq (Article 9) guaranteeing Kurdish as an official language in the Kurdish regions of Iraq. "The stipulations … are recognized as fundamental laws of Iraq and no law, regulation or official action shall conflict or interfere with these stipulations, nor shall any law, regulation or official action now or in the future prevail over them."[166] Nevertheless, Iraq did not fulfill that commitment.

The Kurdish struggle, at first tribal, became increasingly a national struggle as detribalized urban intelligentsia became more deeply involved. This synthesis of traditional tribal and modern nationalist elements found expression in Mulla Mustafa Barzani's assumption of the Presidency of the KDP in the 1940s.

Date	Event
June 1943	Mulla Mustafa Barzani escaped from house arrest in Iraq.
July–October 1943	Barzani began a Kurdish revolt in the mountainous region of northeast Iraq. The Kurds demanded *sarbasti* ("freedom").
February 12, 1945	Mulla Mustafa Barzani formed the Freedom Party.
August 10, 1945	Barzani began yet another revolt in Iraq.
September–October 1945	Barzani's forces broke through an Iraqi military cordon and reached Iran.
April 25, 1947	Barzani re-crossed the border into Iraq.
May 27–June 15, 1947	Barzani conducted a fighting retreat of some 220 miles into the Soviet Union. Barzani's exile in the Soviet Union earned for him a modicum of notoriety in the Western press, where he was called the "Red Mullah," even though Mulla was his name and not a religious title. The Soviets made him an honorary general in the Red Army.
1954	The Kurdish Democratic Party became the United Democratic Party of Kurdistan (UDPK).
July 17, 1958	After the violent July 14 coup that overthrew the pro-Western monarchy in Iraq, the United Democratic Party of Kurdistan (UDPK) asked the new Iraqi strongman, Abdel Karim Qassem for a degree of Kurdish autonomy.
October 6, 1958	Mulla Mustafa Barzani was permitted to return to Iraq from the Soviet Union. He became Chairman of the United Democratic Party of Kurdistan. The party was reorganized. Barzani was given a cash allowance and a government car. Qassem needed Kurdish support against both the Nasserists and the communists.
April 1959	Kurdish forces clashed with the Iraqi Popular Resistance Force militia.
July 14, 1959	The Iraqi regime perpetrated a massacre of Kurds in Kirkuk.
January 6, 1960	Qassem permitted certain political parties to operate openly. That included the UDPK, which had changed its name back to the Kurdistan Democratic Party (KDP).
February 1961	Qassem clamped down on the Kurds. He tried to incite the Baradost and Zebari tribes against Barzani. The Kurdish Arkou tribe revolted in Iraq.
March 1961	Mulla Mustafa Barzani moved back into the mountains.
June 1961	Barzani and the KDP petitioned Qassem for Kurdish national rights. They wanted autonomy, including cultural and economic rights. The demand for the latter included a 15 percent share of the Iraqi national budget, claiming that the Kirkuk oil fields supplied about 65 percent of the 2.1 million barrels of oil then being produced in Iraq daily.

July 29, 1961	KGB Chairman Alexander Shelepin suggested to Nikita Khrushchev, the Secretary-General of the Soviet Communist Party, that the KGB have Kurdish leader Mulla Mustafa Barzani (code-named *Ra'is,* Arabic for president) "activate the movement of the Kurdish population of Iraq, Iran, and Turkey for creation of an independent Kurdistan." If successful, the rebellion could disadvantage not only the United States and the United Kingdom but also US allies Turkey and Iran.[167] It would also distract the West from the crisis then escalating over West Berlin. The Soviets were always opportunists and they saw the Kurdish uprising as a situation to be exploited for their own ends.
September 16, 1961	The Iraqi government's response to the Kurdish demands was to launch a military offensive against the Kurds. It was the beginning of an 8½ year-long guerrilla war. The Kurds resisted, fielding a fighting force of over 20,000 men—the *Peshmerga*—which literally means, "facing death." Qassem accused the United States, the United Kingdom and foreign oil companies of instigating the Kurdish revolt. The Soviet Union also took an interest in these events in Iraq, as the latter was a client state of the USSR.
1962	Mulla Mustafa Barzani offered to become an ally of the United States. In an interview with Dana Adams Schmidt of the *New York Times,* Barzani said, "Let the Americans give us military aid, openly or secretly, so that we can become truly autonomous, and we will become your loyal partners in the Middle East."[168]

Qassem's government was not able to subdue the Kurdish insurrection. This stalemate irritated powerful factions within the Iraqi military and is said to be one of the main reasons behind the Ba'athist coup against Qassem. On February 8–9, 1963, a combination of civilian Ba'athist party members and nationalist anti-communist military men overthrew the Iraqi government of Abdel Karim Qassem, in a coup—the "14 Ramadan Revolution." Qassem was executed. Abdul Rahman Aref became the new Iraqi strongman.

Date	Event
May 1963	The Mongolian People's Republic requested the United Nations to place the Kurdish question before the United Nations General Assembly. This was a move by the Soviet Union to apply pressure on the new Iraqi regime, which was more opposed to the Iraqi communists than the previous Qassem regime. The request was withdrawn in September.
June 10, 1963	Ba'athist Syria dispatched an army brigade to Iraq to assist the new Ba'athist government in fighting the Kurds. The Iraqi government was unable to end the rebellion partly because of the help the Kurds received from Iran.
June 1963	The short-lived Ba'athist regime dominated by Ali Saleh al-Sa'adi, Secretary General of the party, sought to Arabize Kurdistan. It destroyed thirteen Kurdish villages around Kirkuk and expelled the population of another thirty-four Kurdish villages in the Dubz district near Kirkuk, replacing them with Arabs from central and southern Iraq.[169] This was the beginning of an Iraqi Arab ethnic cleansing of Iraqi Kurdistan. After the Ba'ath party consolidated power nationally, in 1963, the National Guard—*al-Haras al-Qawmi*—recruited Arab Ba'athists and Turkmen who systematically attacked ethnic Kurds.[170]

June 18, 1963	The Soviet Union officially declared its support for the Kurdish movement. In July, the Soviet Union charged Iraq with seeking the "physical elimination of the Kurdish minority."[171]
July 9, 1963	Soviet Foreign Minister Andrei Gromyko sent a note to the ambassadors of Iran, Iraq, Syria, and Turkey warning their governments not to launch a joint military intervention in Iraqi Kurdistan. As a result, Turkey and Iran gave up Operation *Tiger,* the planned link-up with the Iraqi and Syrian troops engaged in Kurdistan.[172]
1963	For their part, the Kurds requested Israeli assistance at the Israeli Embassy in Paris. As has been mentioned, the Kurds had contact with the Jews even before the reestablishment of Jewish sovereignty in the Land of Israel. The Kurds were also of great assistance in getting Iraqi Jews out of Iraq, via Iran, to Israel.[173] Beginning in 1965 and continuing until March 1975, Israel supplied the Kurds with arms and ammunition (of Soviet manufacture), training, a field hospital, medical supplies and eight doctors.[174] It was a classic case of "the enemy of my enemy is my friend." By assisting the Kurds, Israel reduced the threat posed by Iraq, an Arab state that had never signed an armistice with Israel in 1949. The United States knew of this Israeli aid and was favorably disposed to it as it sought to undermine the pro-Soviet Iraqi regime and counter Iraqi designs on the Shah's Iran.
February 1964	Iraqi strongman, Abdul Salam Aref, declared a ceasefire in the war against the Kurds, which provoked a split among Kurdish urban radicals on one hand and traditional forces led by Barzani on the other. Barzani agreed to the ceasefire and fired the radicals from the party. Despite this, the Baghdad government tried once more to defeat Barzani's movement by the use of force. However, this campaign failed in May 1966, when Barzani's forces defeated the Iraqi Army at the Battle of Mount Handrin, near Rawanduz.
May 13, 1966	Negotiations between the Kurds and the Iraqi government of Abdul Rahman Aref (who succeeded his brother a month earlier) were broken off and military operations against the Kurds resumed. During the fighting that same month, Israeli officers apparently assisted the Kurds in Barzani's major victory over the Iraqi army at Mount Handrin.[175]

On June 29, 1966, a twelve point "peace plan" was announced to settle the Kurdish question. It included:

- Partial *de facto* autonomy for the Kurdish provinces to be based on a general decentralization of Iraqi administration.
- Recognition and use of the Kurdish language in local administration and education.
- A fair, proportional share for the Kurds in government, army and civil service
- Freedom of Kurdish political organizations—with a secret clause reportedly permitting the *Peshmerga* to remain intact as a militia.

The Kurds agreed to the peace plan but it was never implemented by the Iraqi government. The ceasefire it entailed was never complete. The Iraqi government of Abdul Rahman Aref was in turn, ousted by the Iraqi Ba'athists on July 17, 1968.

Date	Event
August 16, 1966	Iraqi Captain Munir Redfa flew his MiG-21F-13 to Israel as part of the Mossad's Operation *Diamond*. Redfa, an Iraqi Assyrian Christian, was both discouraged because his rise in the Iraqi Air force had been blocked because of his religious affiliation and distressed by Iraq's genocidal campaign against the Iraqi Kurds, another minority. It was the first time such a sophisticated Soviet-built aircraft had fallen into Western hands. His entire extended family was smuggled safely out of Iraq to Israel with Kurdish assistance.[176]
September 1967	Barzani visited Israel and met with Israeli Defense Minister, Moshe Dayan, presenting the latter with a curved Kurdish dagger. Barzani found Israeli mortars superior to those he had been using and asked for more. Many believed that a particularly successful Kurdish mortar attack on the oil refineries in Kirkuk in March 1969 was the work of the Israelis. Israeli officers working with the Kurds remained in constant radio contact with Israel.[177] Barzani visited Israel on two other occasions, in 1968 and again in 1973. On both occasions, he requested additional weapons.[178]
1968	The Iraqi Ba'athist regime, now under the control of Saddam Hussein, started a campaign to end the Kurdish insurrection. However, the campaign stalled in 1969. This was partly attributed to the internal power struggle in Baghdad as well as growing tensions with Iran. Moreover, the Soviets pressured the Iraqis to come to terms with Barzani and the Kurds.
January 1970	Negotiations began again between the Iraqi government (of President Ahmad Hassan al-Bakr but dominated by Saddam Hussein) and the Kurds.

On March 11, 1970, a ceasefire agreement was signed by the Iraqi government and the Kurdish rebels. Until then over 100 Kurdish villages had been destroyed and 9,000 Iraqi troops had been killed. The new agreement went even further than that of 1966.

- It formally accepted the Kurdish nation as one of two nations forming Iraq.
- The local autonomy granted and the use of the Kurdish language was wider in scope than in the 1966 agreement.
- A Kurdish region was to be formed in the mainly Kurdish provinces of Sulaymaniyah, Erbil, and Dohuk (the last newly created in 1969–70, out of the Kurdish northern parts of Mosul province).
- A "High Committee" was to supervise the implementation of these measures.
- The leading officials in the Kurdish areas were to be Kurdish.
- A Kurd would be named vice-president of Iraq and Kurds were to be appointed to the Revolutionary Command Council.
- Kurds were to be represented proportionally in the parliament, government, and reportedly informally in the army as well as the civil service.

- Kurdish military forces were to be dissolved but a secret clause reportedly permitted a 10–12,000 *Peshmerga* force as border guards and militia.
- The agreement was to be fully implemented within four years.

While a few token steps were taken by the Iraqi government, there was non-implementation of many provisions and several major disagreements. The Iraqis wanted Erbil, not Kirkuk, as the capital of Kurdistan. The Kurds wanted Kirkuk as their capital and a 20 to 25 percent share of the oil revenues. The Kurds also wanted veto power in Baghdad pertaining to the autonomous region of Kurdistan. The Iraqi government meanwhile was encouraging anti-Barzani Kurdish factions to re-emerge. There was persistent disagreement on the delimitation of the Kurdish region, especially concerning the western and southern regions of Mosul and Kirkuk. These areas were of vital importance ever since a British-dominated company struck oil near Kirkuk in 1927.

Date	Event
October 16, 1970	A plebiscite to determine the future of Kirkuk was postponed by the Iraqi government indefinitely. The Iraqi government embarked on an Arabization program in the oil rich regions of Kirkuk and Khanaqin. The Iraqis then moved 50,000 Kurds out of Kirkuk and replaced them with Arabs. This was the beginning of an ongoing ethnic cleansing campaign implemented by Saddam Hussein's Ba'athist regime. Thus, the agreement was again unfulfilled and fighting resumed. The Shah of Iran, Mohammad Reza Pahlavi, supported the Kurds, in part to offset the growing influence of the pro-Soviet Iraqi regime in the region.
May 1972	US President Richard Nixon visited Tehran, Iran. The Shah asked Nixon for the United States to arm the Kurds against Iraq, as the Kurds did not trust the Shah. The CIA, the Defense Department and Presidential Special Advisor Henry Kissinger all advised against such action. Nevertheless, Nixon ordered the operation undertaken and bypassed having it approved by the Forty Committee.[179] As Henry Kissinger later noted in his memoirs, "The benefit of Nixon's Kurdish decision was apparent in just over a year: Only one Iraqi division was available to participate in the October 1973 Yom Kippur War.[180]

In a report from the Pike Committee chaired by Congressman Otis Pike (D-NY), the CIA sent millions of rounds of ammunition and Soviet and Chinese weapons to the Kurds. The US had acquired those in 1970, and they were valued at over $5 million. Thus, "the United States acted in effect as a guarantor that the insurgent group would not be summarily dropped by the foreign head of state [i.e. the Shah]."[181] Covert Israeli aid also continued. According to American reporter Jack Anderson, citing a CIA source, during the years of US assistance, "every month … a secret Israeli envoy slips into the mountains in northern Iraq to deliver $50,000 to Mulla Mustafa Barzani. The subsidy insures Kurdish hostility against Iraq, whose government is militantly anti-Israel."[182]

Date	Event
October 6, 1973	The Yom Kippur War erupted as Egypt and Syria, in a coordinated move, attacked Israel. Iraqi forces joined the Syrians in the fighting on the Golan Heights. The Kurds wanted to launch an offensive against the Iraqis at this time. As the Israelis slowly regained the initiative, US Secretary of State Henry Kissinger did not want to weaken further the Arab cause and opposed the Kurdish suggestion. Furthermore, as the Pike Committee would note, "it is particularly ironic that … the United States … restrained the insurgents [the Kurds] from an all-out offensive on one occasion when such an attack might have been successful because other events were occupying the neighboring country [Iraq]."[183]
October 16, 1973	Kissinger ordered CIA Chief William Colby to send a message to the Kurds, "We do not, repeat not, consider it for you to undertake the offensive military action that another government [the Pike Report states that this refers to Israel] has suggested to you." However, according to Kissinger "the decision to discourage the Kurds from launching a diversionary offensive during the October 1973 war was based on the unanimous view of our intelligence officials and the Shah, that the Kurds would be defeated in such an offensive; this judgment was concurred in by the Israeli government."[184] Clearly, there is a contradiction here. The Israeli government could not at the same time, have urged a Kurdish offensive and agreed with the Americans that it should not take place. In any event, the Kurds honored the US request. After all, the United States was the ally they trusted. It turned out to be the greatest mistake of Barzani's life. For Nixon and Kissinger, their highest priority was dealing with an Arab attack on Israel, an Arab oil embargo—launched October 17—and a super-power confrontation with the Soviet Union—October 24. These events took precedence over what fate might befall the Kurds, as they were abandoned.
March 12, 1974	The Iraqi government issued a fifteen-day deadline for the Kurds to accept an Iraqi formulated "compromise." This "compromise" was designed without the approval of the KDP or its cooperation with no agreement on any of the points in dispute and without including any parts of the provinces of Mosul and Kirkuk. The Kurdish response was, "We will make Kurdistan a pool of blood to drown the enemy." Barzani launched a new insurrection on March 14, officially ending the four-year ceasefire.

General Barzani offered inducements to the United States remarking, "If the United States will help us, openly or secretly, we will meet an ally's obligations. Why shouldn't American companies have concessions to help us develop the oil and mineral resources under the ground here in Kurdistan?"[185]

Date	Event
March 22, 1974	A CIA memorandum read, "Iran, like ourselves, has seen benefit in a stalemate situation … in which Iraq is intrinsically weakened by the Kurds' refusal to relinquish its semi-autonomy. Neither Iran nor ourselves wish to see the matter resolved one way or the other."[186]
March 23, 1974	Soviet Defense Minister Andrei Grechko went to Baghdad to attempt to arrange a compromise between the Iraqi government and the Kurds. The Kurds refused the offer on the advice of the United States.
April 1974	With no progress on implementation of the 1970 agreement, warfare between the Iraqis and Kurds erupted again. Kurdish leader Barzani was so moved by American support that he sent Henry Kissinger three rugs and later a gold and pearl necklace for his new bride.[187] Barzani also sent word to Kissinger that the Kurds were "ready to become the fifty-first state"[188] after liberation. He also declared that he would "turn over the [Iraqi] oilfields to the United States" and that "the United States could look to a friend in OPEC once oil-rich Kurdistan achieved independence."[189]
Late 1974	As warfare continued between the Iraqis and the Kurds, the Soviets flew combat missions against the Kurds on behalf of Saddam Hussein's government.
Early 1975	As the fighting raged on, four-fifths of Iraq's 100,000 troops and nearly half of its 1,390 tanks were pinned down by the 45,000-man Kurdish *Peshmerga* guerrillas.
March 5, 1975	The Algiers Agreement was signed in Algeria, between Iran and Iraq. In return for Iraqi recognition of the *thalweg* line as the delineation of the Shatt al-Arab waterway, the Shah of Iran agreed to close Iran's border to stop the flow of aid ($16 million) to the Kurds in rebellion against the Iraqi government. The Pike Committee report related, "The extent of our ally's [Iran's] leverage over US policy was such that he apparently made no effort to notify his junior American partners that the program's end was near. The United States "had no choice but to acquiesce."[190] "The cut-off of aid … came as a severe shock to its [the Kurds'] leadership," and made it impossible for the Kurdish rebellion to continue.[191] Their adversaries [Iraq], knowing of the impending aid cut-off, launched an all-out search-and-destroy campaign the day after the agreement was signed. The autonomy movement was over."[192]
March 8, 1975	The Iraqi government immediately began an offensive against the Kurds.

March 10, 1975	Barzani sent a message to the CIA, "There is confusion and dismay among our people and forces. Our people's fate [is] in unprecedented danger. Complete destruction [is] hanging over our head. No explanation for all this. We appeal to you and the US government [to] intervene according to your promises."[193] Later that same day, the local CIA station chief cabled CIA Director William Colby, "Is headquarters in touch with Kissinger's office on this; if USG does not handle this situation deftly in a way which will avoid giving the Kurds the impression that we are abandoning them they are likely to go public. Iran's action has not only shattered their political hopes; it endangers lives of thousands."[194] Additionally, General Barzani sent a letter to US Secretary of State Henry Kissinger which in part read, "Our hearts bleed to see that an immediate byproduct of their agreement [between Iran and Iraq] is the destruction of our defenseless people in an unprecedented manner as Iran closed its border and stopped help to us completely and while Iraq began the biggest offensive they have ever launched. We feel, Your Excellency, that the United States has a moral and political responsibility towards our people who have committed themselves to your country's policy. Mr. Secretary, we are anxiously awaiting your quick response."[195]
March 22, 1975	The local CIA station chief again cabled CIA Director Colby, "No reply has been received from Secretary of State Henry Kissinger to the message from Barzani. If the USG intends to take steps to avert a massacre it must intercede with Iran promptly."[196] Nothing was done. In short, an American guarantee was dishonored. The Kurds' first encounter with US foreign policy ended in disaster.

Barzani was told to "get your people out" before the border was sealed off. The conflict resulted in 60,000 civilian and military casualties, the destruction of 40,000 homes in some 700 villages, and 300,000 refugees. 227 leaders of the Kurdish revolt were executed.[197] Some 5,000 Kurds died fleeing the Iraqi attack. Some 200,000 Kurds fled to Iran. Iran then forcibly returned some 40,000 back to Iraq! Thousands of Kurds were killed in the Iraqi offensive and some 30,000 were placed in Iraqi concentration camps. Barzani went into exile in Karaj near Tehran, Iran. He died on March 1, 1979, in exile at Georgetown Hospital in the United States, (where he had gone for treatment for lung cancer). Shortly before Barzani's death, Assistant Secretary of State Harold Saunders denied the dying man access to the Carter White House to press his plea for his people.

Date	Event
1975–76	Iraqi persecution of the Kurds continued unabated. The Iraqi government passed laws fixing the prices of agricultural products at an extremely low level. These laws were only enforced in the Kurdish "autonomous zone"—a misleading term since while it implies self-rule, it was in effect so designated for the purpose of discriminatory legislation. As a result, the government took away nearly 80 percent of the agricultural output at a price close to outright confiscation. The food was then resold in the Arab region at market prices. Nearly all doctors and medical personnel were transferred out of the Kurdish region. Travel by Kurds between Kurdish villages was forbidden except in cases where the government saw its own purposes served. Iraqi law required all owners of cameras and typewriters to register them with the police or face seven years imprisonment. Egyptian families were brought in to settle in the "autonomous zone." In April 1976, the Iraqi Ministry of Tourism ran an ad in Egypt's *Al Ahram* newspaper disclosing its government's intent to build three towns at a cost of $90 million each, and inviting Egyptians to settle in them. The settlement of 2 million Egyptians in Iraqi Kurdistan was the target agreed upon by Iraq and Egypt. This was part of an ongoing "Arabization" process, which included moving some 300,000 Kurds out of their homes to the Arab south and the Iraqi government's monetary incentive bonuses, being offered to Iraqis to marry and assimilate Kurds.
Late 1970s	Mulla Mustafa's sons, Massoud and Idris Barzani tried to rekindle the rebellion, and rebuild the *Peshmerga,* but the Kurdish movement was beset by factionalism. The KDP split, and another Barzani brother, Ubaid-ullah, collaborated with the Iraqi government.
June 1, 1975	Jalal Talabani, a former lieutenant of Mulla Mustafa's, set up a rival political organization, the Patriotic Union of Kurdistan (PUK) in Damascus, Syria. Ba'athist Syria at this time was in dispute with rival Ba'athist Iraq and supported the Talabani faction. Recall that Syria also supported Kurdish guerrillas in Turkey. The PUK advocated Marxist principles and denounced the Barzanis as "reactionary." By 1976, the PUK became the first Kurdish party to return *Peshmerga* forces to Iraq.
1978–79	Six hundred Kurdish villages were burned down in Iraq. Ethnic cleansing continued as around 200,000 Kurds were deported to other parts of the country.[198]
September 22, 1980– August 20, 1988	During the Iran–Iraq War, Kurdish rebels in Iran—a KDP faction led by Abdul Rahman Ghassemlou—sometimes collaborated with Iraq and its secret services, while Barzani's KDP in Iraq collaborated to some extent with Iran. The two branches of the KDP thus found themselves on opposite sides in the war but managed to avoid direct clashes with one another. This was all further complicated by the Iraqi government's attempts to win Jalal Talabani and his PUK supporters as collaborators and partners, but talks broke down in 1984. From early 1985, Talabani and his group rejoined the rebellion against Iraq, though not in cooperation with Barzani's KDP. The PUK began to cultivate ties to Iran, which began to arm PUK activists. To add to the complexity of the situation, there was Turkish-Iraqi cooperation and joint action against both the Turkish and Iraqi Kurds.[199]

October 1980	Israeli Prime Minister Menachem Begin disclosed Israel's long-secret military support for the Kurdish rebellion in Iraq. Begin confirmed that from 1965 to 1975 Israel provided the Kurdish guerrillas with "money, arms, and instructors."[200]
June 1985	Western intelligence sources reported that Libyan leader Muammar Qadhafi was supplying light arms and ammunition to the Kurds fighting in both northern Iraq and southeastern Turkey. The shipment of these arms was facilitated by both Iran and Syria.
January 31, 1987	With the death of Idris Barzani, the leadership of the KDP was solely in the hands of Massoud Barzani. During the war between Iran and Iraq, the KDP was able to set up liberated zones totaling 4,000 square miles along the Iraqi border with Iran. Iran helped arrange in May 1987, a reconciliation of the PUK and the KDP.
March 29, 1987– April 23, 1989	Iraq launched the *Al-Anfal* Campaign designed to eliminate the Kurdish people in Iraq. The Iraqi army, under the command of Ali Hassan al-Majid (a first cousin of Saddam Hussein), carried out a genocidal campaign against Kurds, characterized by the following human rights violations: The widespread use of chemical weapons—on some 250 towns and villages; the wholesale destruction of some 3,800 villages (out of 4,655);[201] and the slaughter of 50,000–100,000 non-combatant civilians including women and children, by the most conservative estimates.[202] Al-Majid had an affinity for using chemical weapons, and was dubbed "Chemical Ali" (for his role in perpetrating these chemical attacks against the Kurds. For his crimes, Al-Majid was hanged in Baghdad, on January 25, 2010.)[203] The large Kurdish town of Qala Dizeh (population 70,000) was destroyed by the Iraqi army. The campaign also included Arabization of Kirkuk, a program to drive Kurds out of the oil-rich city and replace them with Arab settlers from central and southern Iraq.[204] Kurdish sources report the number of dead to be greater than 182,000.[205] As Iraqi forces reclaimed the area, KDP leaders escaped to Iran or Syria.
March 16–17, 1988	A two-day poison gas and nerve agent attack by Iraqi aircraft was launched against the Kurdish city of Halabja, population 80,000. Halabja is located about 150 miles northeast of Baghdad and 8 to 10 miles from the Iranian border. The city was then held by Iranian troops and Iraqi Kurdish *Peshmerga* guerrillas allied with Tehran. The attack on Halabja was the largest-scale chemical weapons attack against a civilian population in modern times. Unequivocally, it was a prime example of the regime's willingness to use WMDs. It began early in the evening of March 16, when a group of eight aircraft began dropping chemical bombs, and the chemical bombardment continued all night. It was known that Iraq had used such gas against Iran in its eight-year war against that nation, including mustard gas, (which burns, blisters and blackens the skin, and can be lethal if inhaled). Iraq also used the nerve agents sarin, tabun (which prompts convulsions, and foaming and bleeding at the mouth before death), and VX. Some sources have also pointed to the blood agent hydrogen cyanide. There were an estimated 5,600[206] fatalities. The injured numbered 7,000 to 10,000.[207]

Between 1963 and 1988, the Ba'athist Iraqi regime destroyed 779 Kurdish villages in the Kirkuk region alone—razing 493 primary schools, 598 mosques, and 40 medical clinics.[208] In order to prevent the return of the Kurds, they burned farms and orchards, confiscated cattle, blew up wells, and obliterated cemeteries. In all, this ethnic cleansing campaign forced 37,726 Kurdish families out of their villages. Given the average rural Kurdish family size of between five and seven people, this policy forced over 200,000 Kurds to flee the region. The Kurds were not the regime's only victims. During the Iran–Iraq War, the central government also destroyed about ten Shi'ite Turkmen villages south of Kirkuk.

The Iraqi government also compelled urban Kurds to leave Kirkuk. It transferred oil company employees, civil servants, and teachers to southern and central Iraq. The Ba'athist government renamed streets and schools in Arabic and forced businesses to adopt Arab names. Kurds could only sell real estate to Arabs; non-Arabs could not purchase property in the city. The government allocated thousands of new residential units for Arabs only.[209]

Date	Event
May 1988	The KDP, the PUK, and six other smaller Kurdish groups came together to form the Iraqi Kurdistan Front (IKF) with Massoud Barzani and Jalal Talabani serving as co-presidents.
September 1988	As the Iran–Iraq War ended, the PUK and IKF members fled across the border to Iran or Syria. According to secret Iraqi documents seized by the Kurds during their March 1991 uprising, at least 100,000 non-combatant Kurds were slaughtered between February and September 1988.[210]
August 1990	When Iraq invaded and occupied Kuwait, the leadership of the KDP was able to return to Iraqi Kurdistan, as the regime of Saddam Hussein was confronted by an international coalition demanding his retreat from Kuwait.
March 3–5, 1991	After the second Gulf War ended, US President George H.W. Bush urged the Kurds of northern Iraq and the Shi'ites of southern Iraq to rise up and depose the regime of Saddam Hussein. Massoud Barzani then began a Kurdish rebellion, by persuading the 100,000-strong local Iraqi army auxiliary force, made up of Kurds to change sides. Within a week, the rebels controlled the Kurdish Autonomous region and large parts of the oil-rich province of Tamim, including its capital Kirkuk. Barzani declared, "I feel that the result of 70 years of struggle … is at hand now. It is the greatest honor for me. It is what I wanted all my life."[211]
March 13, 1991	An Iraqi government counter-offensive, using helicopter gun-ships and its Republican Guards ruthlessly crushed the short-lived uprising. The Iraqi Ba'athist regime in the predominantly Kurdish city of Kirkuk even began to rewrite Kurdish tombstone inscriptions in the Kurdish cemetery with Arabic, in order to alter retroactively the demography of that city. The US-led coalition did not oppose this slaughter and the ethnic cleansing that followed. The failed rebellion caused a massive exodus of 1.5 million Kurds into Turkey and Iran. Both nations closed their border, April 3 and April 7, respectively.

A month after the Gulf War ceasefire, the United States admitted that "the number of Iraqi tanks and armored vehicles that survived the American-led land attack that ended the Persian Gulf War is much greater than American military authorities initially reported ... [and] many of the weapons have been used by the government of President Saddam Hussein to quell resistance by Iraqi insurgents [including the Kurds]." The "new estimates raise questions about the wisdom of the Bush Administration's decision to halt the ground war after 100 hours of fighting"[212] General Norman Schwarzkopf, coalition forces commander, later admitted as much, "[US-led coalition forces] had them in a rout" and could have continued to rain great destruction on them. But the President's decision to halt the war "did leave some escape routes open for them to get back out."[213] It is obvious from later events, that had the United States persisted for one or two more days against Iraqi forces, Saddam Hussein's military machine would have been totally smashed, and quite possibly his regime overthrown, eliminating the need for the US-led coalition campaign in March 2003—Operation *Iraqi Freedom*.

As Saddam Hussein's forces began to crush ruthlessly the Kurdish uprising, Barzani and Talabani, as co-presidents of the Iraqi Kurdish Front, appealed to US President George H.W. Bush for help by reminding him, "You personally called upon the Iraqi people to rise up against Saddam Hussein's brutal dictatorship."[214] Bush did nothing on the ground.

Date	Event
March 20, 1991	The United States began shooting down Iraqi warplanes breaking the Gulf War truce. This led to the creation of a "no-fly" zone—north of latitude 36°—over Iraqi Kurdistan to prevent a repetition of the massacres perpetrated by Saddam Hussein's Iraqi regime. The "no-fly" zone was patrolled by American, British and (until 1998) French aircraft. The Western Allies warned Iraq not to use either fixed-wing aircraft or helicopters in the "no-fly" zone.
April 5, 1991	The United Nations adopted United Nations Security Council Resolution 688, which condemned "the repression of the Iraqi civilian population in many parts of Iraq, including ... in Kurdish populated areas the consequences of which threaten international peace and security in the region" and demanded that "Iraq ... immediately end this repression."[215] UN Security Council Resolution 688 also called on Iraq to allow immediate access to the Kurdish areas by international humanitarian organizations. This was the first international document to mention the Kurds by name since the League of Nations' arbitration of Mosul in 1925.
April 6, 1991	Due in large part to the Iraqi slaughter of the Kurds, the Allies—the United States, the United Kingdom and France—instituted a safe haven in northern Iraq—some 3,600 square miles and launched Operation *Provide Comfort* to bring humanitarian assistance to the Kurds. Iraqi troops were forced to withdraw from the region. In retaliation, Iraq imposed an economic blockade over the region, reducing its oil and food supplies. Faced with this, Iraqi Kurdistan began to function as a semi-independent *de facto* autonomous entity, being ruled by the two principal Kurdish parties—the KDP and the PUK.

May 1992	Legislative Council elections were held in the Kurdish autonomous region and the KDP and PUK shared power almost equally. During this period, the Kurds were subjected to a double embargo: one imposed by the United Nations on Iraq and one imposed by Saddam Hussein on their region. The severe economic hardships caused by these embargoes, fueled tensions between the KDP and the PUK over control of trade routes and resources.[216]
September 15, 1992	The KDP and the PUK agreed to merge but the merger failed. Rivalry and clashes between the two groups continued.
May 1994–1997	Fighting erupted between the KDP and PUK once again.
July–August 1996	As the fighting intensified between the KDP and PUK, each side sought money and arms from outside patrons. The PUK turned to Iran, which intervened with its Iranian Revolutionary Guard Corps (in July) and the KDP turned to the Iraqi regime of Saddam Hussein. The clashes left more than 1,000 fighters and civilians dead and would continue intermittently into 1997.
August 31, 1996	Thirty thousand Iraqi troops intervened in the Kurdish area and assisted the KDP capture the town of Erbil. The United States fearful that Iraq would seek to reoccupy the entire northern Kurdish region responded with Operation *Desert Strike*, on September 3–4, 1996, with cruise missile strikes against Iraqi military targets. Meanwhile, the Iraqi Ba'athist regime passed an "identity law" to force Kurds and other non-Arabs to register as Arab. The government expelled from the region anyone who refused. The bulk of the Iraqi forces withdrew after a week, and the KDP pursued the demoralized PUK and captured its stronghold of Sulaymaniyah on September 9. The PUK retreated to the Iranian border.
October 1996	The PUK launched a counter-offensive and recaptured Sulaymaniyah and other districts. The United States brokered a ceasefire between the KDP and PUK at the end of the month.
December 31, 1996	Operation *Provide Comfort* officially ended. It was immediately replaced by another US-led humanitarian effort.
January 1, 1997	Operation *Northern Watch* was launched by the United States, assisted by the United Kingdom and Turkey, to continue the flow of humanitarian assistance to the northern Kurdish autonomous region. After 1996, thirteen percent of the Iraqi oil sales were allocated for Iraqi Kurdistan and this led to relative prosperity in the region.[217] This assistance continued until after the success of Operation *Iraqi Freedom* in March 2003, and officially ended on May 1, 2003.
1997	The Iraqi government demolished Kirkuk's historic citadel with its mosques and ancient church. Human Rights Watch estimated that between 1991 and 2003, the Iraqi government expelled between 120,000 and 200,000 non-Arabs from Kirkuk and its environs.[218]
September 17, 1998	Direct US mediation led to the Washington Agreement whereby the KDP and PUK agreed to a formal ceasefire, and a more equitable division of the resources of the region.
September 1999	The US State Department reported that the Iraqi government had displaced approximately 900,000 citizens throughout Iraq. The report continued to describe how "[l]ocal officials in the south have ordered the arrest of any official or citizen who provides employment, food, or shelter to newly arriving Kurds."[219]

October 2002	The Erbil-based, Iraqi Kurdistan National Assembly held its first meeting since 1994.
March 2003	Kurdish parties joined forces against the Iraqi government in Operation *Iraqi Freedom*. The Kurdish military forces—the *Peshmerga*—played a key role in the overthrow of the former Iraqi regime.
April 10–11, 2003	During Operation *Iraqi Freedom*, coalition and Kurdish forces occupied the city of Kirkuk.
July 2003	The Israeli government reversed its embargo on Iraq, allowing trade between the two peoples including the export of Israeli military products to the Kurds.[220]
January 30, 2005	In the Iraqi Legislative elections, the KDP and PUK united to form an alliance with several smaller parties—the Democratic Patriotic Alliance of Kurdistan. They received 25.7 percent of the vote and 75 seats in the 275-seat legislature. PUK leader Jalal Talabani was elected President of the new Iraqi administration, while KDP leader Massoud Barzani became President of the Kurdistan Regional Government (KRG).
June 7, 2005	The president of Iraqi Kurdistan Massoud Barzani declared he had no objection to establishing diplomatic relations with Israel. "Establishing relations between the Kurds and Israel is not a crime since many Arab countries have ties with the Jewish state," Barzani said in an interview with the Saudi daily *al-Hayat*. He said when the time comes and an Israeli Embassy is opened in Baghdad he will ask that an Israeli consulate be also established in Erbil, the capital of Iraq's Kurdistan.[221]
October 15, 2005	The authority of the KRG and legality of its laws and regulations were recognized in Articles 113 and 137 of the new Iraqi constitution[222] adopted in a referendum of the people.
March 2007	Indicative of Kurdish-US friction, was PUK leader, Talabani's interview with the Iraqi newspaper *al-Rai*. Talabani challenged US policy as he discussed the potential for Kurdish-Iranian military cooperation to drive Iraq's Sunnis out of Mosul and other disputed areas in northern Iraq.[223] Talabani asserted that Kurdish and Iranian forces could take under their control virtually all of Iraq. Such provocative Talabani comments stirred up ethnic animosity in Iraq and put US forces at greater risk.[224]
August 14, 2007	Al-Qaeda in Iraq suicide bombers drove, and then detonated, three oil-tanker explosives-laden trucks into Qataniya and Adnaniya, two Yazidi Kurdish towns near Mosul. At least 500 were murdered with over 1,000 injured. Within minutes, an ancient indigenous Iraqi sect was turned into a humanitarian problem. Al-Qaeda in Iraq had selected a tiny, isolated, unprotected community of some 150,000 Yazidi Kurds, persecuted by Sunni and Shi'ite Muslims alike, as the victims of its barbarity. The Yazidis live in communities of 5,000 to 20,000, which are clearly defined by religion and ethnic, tribal, and clan kinship. They were isolated and not protected by Allied forces, Iraqi security or local militias. Thus, they were an easy "soft" target.

June 24, 2009	The Kurds in the autonomous region of northern Iraq drew up a new constitution, which enshrined Kurdish claims to territories and the oil and gas beneath them. The constitution defined the Kurdistan region as comprising of their three provinces but also added all of hotly contested and oil-rich Kirkuk Province, as well as other disputed areas in Nineveh and Diyala Provinces.
July 25, 2009	KRG president Massoud Barzani won re-election in regional elections.
Early 2010	Media reports began to appear indicating that Israeli military and intelligence agents were operating in Iraqi Kurdistan once again. Their primary role was to train elite Kurdish commandos in guerrilla warfare and anti-terror tactics. Kurdish commandos also reportedly accompanied Israeli operatives across the Iraq–Iran border in recent years to install sensory devices meant to monitor suspected Iranian nuclear facilities.[225]

In 2013, the KRG completed a pipeline from the Taq Taq and Tawke oil fields, in central Kurdistan, through Khurmala and Dahuk to Faysh Khabur on the Turkey–Iraq border, where it is connected to the Kirkuk-Ceyhan pipeline. The 36-inch diameter pipeline has a capacity of 150,000 barrels per day. Ceyhan, Turkey is a major port in southeastern Turkey on the Mediterranean coast.

May 23. 2014	The KRG announced the first sales of crude oil as well as the departure of "a tanker loaded with over one million barrels of crude oil … from Ceyhan towards Europe."[226] The first tanker—*SCF Altai*—arrived in Ashkelon, Israel, on June 20, 2014.[227] However, it did not arrive directly from Ceyhan. The tanker delivered its cargo to Ashkelon for an unknown buyer. The KRG denied selling oil to Israel directly or indirectly.[228] Yet, Kurdistan has already sent 2 million barrels of oil to Israel via Ceyhan.[229] Oil industry insiders believe that the KRG pays Turkey and Israel a dollar each for every barrel that passes through their territory.[230] From Ashkelon, the oil can be transported westward to European or Western hemisphere purchasers or to Asia via the 158-mile long Trans-Israel oil pipeline to its southern port of Eilat.
July 2, 2014	It is believed that during the Islamic State offensive to capture the Kurdish-held town of Kobanê, Syria, evidence emerged which appeared to point to the use of some kind of chemical agent (probably mustard blister agent), against the fighters of the Kurdish Peoples' Protection Units.[231] These weapons came from the Iraqi chemical stockpiles seized by ISIL in June 2014.
July 3, 2014	KRG President Massoud Barzani called on parliament to form an independent electoral commission that would organize a referendum on independence for the autonomous region.
August 11, 2014	The United States began airlifting large quantities of military equipment to the Kurds in northern Iraq to help the *Peshmerga* forces repel attacks by Islamic State forces. The arms were drawn from US supply depots in both Jordan and Israel. France also began airlifting military equipment to the Kurds on August 13.

The Kurds are truly a people—a nation—in the traditional sense but no one has permitted their liberation and attainment of national sovereignty. Historically, no one has allowed them to create their own country. As the record proves, throughout the history of the modern Middle East, the Kurdish people have been forgotten, neglected, manipulated and betrayed by numerous organizations and countries including but not limited to, the League of Nations, the United Kingdom, Turkey, Iran, Iraq, Syria, the United Nations and the United States (several of these on more than one occasion). The Kurds were used by one or more of the above for their own ends, only to be dropped when it no longer served their purpose. There is great truth to the Kurdish adage: *Kurdan ji çiyayan pêve dostên xwe nînin!* ("Kurds have no friends but the mountains!"). On the plus side, it was an international coalition that twice changed the situation on the ground in Iraqi Kurdistan, albeit not without cost, so that the Kurds today have achieved a remarkable degree of self-rule. The creation of a safe haven after the Gulf War of 1991, and the deposing of the Ba'athist Saddam Hussein dictatorship in 2003, Operation *Iraqi Freedom*, has brought the Kurds to the brink of statehood.

What might the immediate future hold in store for the Kurds? As has been the historic case, Kurdish unity is more theoretical than actual. If a federal democratic Iraq can be firmly established with guaranteed rights for all its citizens regardless of their religious and ethnic background, coupled with a equal sharing of revenues from the nation's oil resources (on the model of Alaska or Kuwait) that would benefit all inhabitants, that could be a solution acceptable to the Kurds.

A second option is to form a confederation—of two or three separate autonomous units, with the central government primarily in charge of defense and foreign policy. In fact, on September 26, 2007, the US Senate passed a non-binding resolution to split Iraq into a loose federation of sectarian-based regions–Kurdish, Sunni and Shi'ite. The resolution was passed by a bipartisan vote of 75 to 23.

The third option, which seems likely, as American forces and power are withdrawn from Iraq, is an independent Kurdistan. This is especially likely if the aforementioned options prove unworkable and Iraq reverts to a military dictatorship as, so often, was the historic case for that country. Such an independent Kurdistan would have to undertake a pledge to Turkey that the existing international border would remain intact. Perhaps there would be a transfer of population with compensation between the two nations. A US supported Kurdistan would be a valuable ally and assist in placing pressure on both Syria and Iran, the rogue terrorist-supporting regimes in the region.

An independent Kurdistan would mean the dissolution of Iraq. The Soviet Union and Yugoslavia were two twentieth century examples of countries welded together and kept that way by force. Yet, the various ethnic components and religious groups eventually caused these countries to fragment into parts, each a separate country. If Muslim Syria could break away from the Muslim United Arab Republic in 1961, if Buddhist-Christian Singapore could break away from Muslim Malaysia in 1965, if Muslim Bangladesh could break away from Muslim Pakistan in 1971, and if Muslim Eritrea could break away from Christian Ethiopia in 1991, (after a 30-year war), and they are acceptable to the international community, why shouldn't Iraq, an artificially created state, undergo similar disintegration, especially if it ends ethnic and religious conflict (though that is far from assured)?

The Kurds have already established a *de facto* state in northern Iraq. After many promises, almost all broken, by the international community, independence can be achieved. With its oil revenues, it would be a viable state and a state friendly to the West, particularly the United States. As to the remainder of Iraq, there would be a Shi'ite state in the south with oil revenues. The remainder, a Sunni state in the center-west in the area called Jazirah (the so-called Sunni triangle) might seek its own statehood or merge with Sunni areas in Syria and/or Saudi Arabia.

If the existing nation of Iraq cannot implement true democratic reforms based on basic human and political rights and equality, including that of faith, opportunity and equal status for women, and if they continue to oppress significant portions of their population, then perhaps the time has come for disintegration and a redrawing of the map. This would be a major step towards acknowledging tolerance, especially of minority groups. It would remove a major stumbling block in setting some of the region's most intractable conflicts: the Arab/Muslim war against Israel, the precarious position of the Christians of Lebanon, and the non-acceptance of the Kurdish people.

A key question is how such dissolution is to take place. One method is by conflict, with its attendant destruction, loss of life, creation of refugee populations, and other problems listed above. This was the method used by Bangladesh, Eritrea and most of the former Yugoslavia. On the other hand, there is ample precedent for peaceful dissolution: Syria from the United Arab Republic, Singapore from Malaysia, Slovakia from the former Czechoslovakia and the relatively peaceful dissolution of the former Soviet Union. An international organization could be involved, as was the case when the European Union took the lead in acknowledging the dissolution of Yugoslavia by according full diplomatic recognition to the newly proclaimed Republics of Croatia and Slovenia on January 15, 1992.

In a similar vein, the Kurds in Syria could achieve a degree of autonomy if Syria were to become a decentralized federal state. There are five main groups in Syria—the Kurds, the Druze, the Alawis (a Shi'ite offshoot), the Sunnis and the Christians. Almost 50 percent of the Syrian population is comprised of Kurds, Druze, Alawi, and Christians. A decentralized federal Syria would boost the power of and protect ethnic and religious minorities. Sherkoh Abbas, President of the Kurdistan National Assembly of Syria (KNAS), echoed these same sentiments in an interview on June 20, 2013, with reporter Joseph Puder. In view of the fratricidal savagery of the Syrian Civil War, Abbas stated that it is vital for the US administration to support a federalized Syria, "by establishing a Kurdish Federal region in the North, a Druze region in the Southwest, an Alawite region in western Syria, in addition to a Sunni region in the rest of Syria."[232] Yet by mid-2015, the savagery, loss of life and destruction of the Syrian Civil War seemed to preclude any thought of a federalized Syrian state. The Alawite regime of Bashar Assad, supported by the Shi'ite bloc of Iran, the Maliki government of Iraq, and Hezbollah in Lebanon, seemed determined to survive and defeat their Sunni opponents, an amalgam of groups including Al-Qaeda, supported by Saudi Arabia, the Gulf States and Turkey. Thus far, the sectarian warfare has excluded the Kurds. The question for the future is, once the Syrian conflict ends (and that might not be for years) will the victors turn on the Kurds once again, as so often has been the historic case?

For Kurds, religion is not as important or emphasized as ethnicity. The Kurds geographic location and acculturation makes them a barrier to the spread of radical Islam—whether Shi'a or Sunni. The Kurds also aspire to become a democratic society modeled after Israel.[233] The Kurds still need to overcome many challenges, among them the need to develop a standardized Kurdish language. Yet, Kurdistan stands at a historic crossroads, perhaps closer to full independence and sovereignty than at any other time in its history.

19. In the Arab/Muslim culture, pride, dignity, and honor outrank truth on any scale of political values.

An Arab/Muslim man's *sharaf*—his sense of honor, pride, and self-respect—is of overriding importance. It is common in Arab/Muslim culture to be exceedingly aware of one's status in the group, other peoples' view of oneself and any signs of any kind of criticism. In that world, a man's honor consists of two primary components: his reputation, as determined by his own actions in the community, and the chastity or virtue of the female members of his family. *Sharaf* is something flexible: depending on a man's behavior, way of talking and acting, his *sharaf* can be acquired, augmented, diminished, lost, and regained, and so on. The specific kind of honor that is connected with women and depends on their proper conduct is called *'ird*. In contrast to a man's *sharaf*, *'ird* is a rigid concept: every woman has her ascribed *'ird*; she is born with it and grows up with it; she cannot augment it because it is something absolute; but it is her duty to preserve it. A sexual offense on her part, however slight, causes her *'ird* to be lost and it can never be regained.[234] Thus, in this culture, a man or his family will be threatened or disgraced, because of the perceived sexual misconduct of a female member of the family. A female holds the family honor within her, unlike her brother, who is only responsible for his own honor. If a female does something herself, or something is done to her against her will to lose that honor, it can never be restored and the family then will be without honor until they kill her, erase her from all records and memory. Only in that way can the family's honor be regained. This is the basis for what is called, honor killing.

Honor killing occurs frequently and has been committed in the Islamic world for over 1,400 years, even pre-dating Islam, as a vestige of traditional patriarchal society. Nevertheless, under Islamic law someone who kills his/her child incurs no legal penalty. i.e. they are "not subject to retaliation." This includes "a father or mother (or their fathers or mothers) for killing their offspring, or offspring's offspring."[235] It remains part of the fundamentalist culture. The decision to kill is often sanctioned by a group of male family members. The deed is usually performed by a relative—a husband, brother, uncle, father or son of the woman who allegedly sullied the family's honor and brought shame upon the family or community. The aggressive response to anything that tarnished the family's honor is seen as an expression of honorable behavior. Violence in defense of a man's *sharaf* is authentic Islam.[236] Men can also be the victims of honor killings by members of the family of a woman with whom they are perceived to have an inappropriate relationship.

The usual method is death by stoning. Stoning is a popular form of punishment in Afghanistan, Iran, Somalia and Sudan. Often the victim is raped first so that the rape victim would not be able to enter paradise. There is now another alternative. In some cases, the daughter can restore her honor and her family's honor by a cash settlement, marriage settlement, non-lethal whipping or volunteering as a suicide bomber.[237] With this in mind, the family therefore may want to put the daughter through the torture and pain of female genital mutilation to avoid the possibility of losing honor later on. Some fathers murder their daughters at birth, or murder a younger sister, to avoid the possibility of future honor problems.

The Middle East practice of honor killing has now spread to both Europe and the Americas by Muslim immigrants. In the book *Guarding the Secrets: Palestinian Terrorism and a Father's Murder of His Too-American Daughter,* by Ellen Harris, (New York: Scribner's, 1995) the author relates an episode from November 1989, in St. Louis, Missouri. The FBI inadvertently taped the murder of a teenage girl being killed by her Palestinian father and Brazilian mother. The FBI agents were looking for evidence of terrorism, which they also found. In a ghastly eight-minute sequence on the tape, the girl was stabbed thirteen times with a butcher's knife while being held down by her mother, who was heard screaming, "Die! Die quickly! Quiet, little one! Die, my daughter, die!" On November 1, 2006, Pakistani immigrant Mohammed Riaz burned to death his wife and four daughters (aged three to sixteen) because they had become too Westernized. Before the murders, he had destroyed Western clothes belonging to the girls.

In a different case, on December 9, 2007, another well-publicized honor killing took place when a Canadian Muslim teenager, Aqsa Parvez was strangled, in Missauga, Canada, and died the next day. Her father was arrested and charged with her murder. Aqsa's offense was trying to establish her own identity by moving out of her family home and for defying her father's command to cover her head with a *hijab*.[238] On December 31, 2007, two sisters, seventeen-year-old Sarah and eighteen-year-old Amina Said, were found dead in a taxicab in Irving, Texas. The vehicle belonged to their father, Yaser Abdel Said, an Egyptian-born cabdriver who reportedly was upset by his daughters' Westernized habits.

In the United States, a contemporary honor killing shocked many. Noor Almaleki was a victim of an honor killing, on October 20, 2009, when her father, Faleh Hassan Almaleki ran her down with his Jeep Cherokee, in Glendale, Arizona. Noor, 20, died from her injuries on November 2, 2009. Her father deliberately targeted and attacked her for becoming too "Westernized." Noor was an aspiring model and actor, worked at the local Applebee's and went to school. All of which, infuriated the father, in that his daughter failed to live by traditional Muslim values. Thereupon, he took her to Iraq and married her off. She had to find her own way back to Arizona and her fiancé, who she loved, only to be killed by her father.[239]

Another contemporary horrific honor killing occurred in December 2009, in the town of Kahta, in southeastern Turkey. A 16-year-old girl was buried alive in a sitting position with her hands tied, in a 2-meter-deep hole dug under a chicken pen outside her house. She was murdered by relatives because she reportedly befriended boys. Two months before her body was discovered, the girl had made a complaint to the police about her grandfather, saying that he beat her because she had made and talked to male friends.[240]

In late June 2014, a young couple, Sajjad Ahmed and his bride, Muafia Bibi were murdered in Satrah, Punjab, Pakistan barely a week after they had married for love. Their throats were slit by the wife's father in an honor killing as a warning to other girls not to marry without the permission of their parents. The town's children were forced to watch as the couple bled to death, as a lesson of what would happen to them if they married someone of their own choice.[241]

A United Nations study reported that at least 5,000 women worldwide were murdered each year in honor killings for alleged infidelity. The true number of honor killings occurring worldwide remains unclear, largely because they are often treated as private family affairs. It is unknown how many women are maimed or disfigured for life in attacks that fall short of murder. Punishment for such crimes is rare. What is of great concern is that most Islamic authorities refuse to denounce explicitly the practice—as opposed to merely denying that Islam sanctions it. This only encourages more of the same. In Western eyes, honor killing is a gross misnomer. There is no honor involved in what is usually a brutal murder.

20. Throughout history, there has been East–West confrontation in the Middle East. At the nexus of three continents, the region has been both an invasion route and the main east-west conduit of commerce.

HISTORIC EAST–WEST RIVALRY AND CONFRONTATION IN THE MIDDLE EAST		
Time Period	**East**	**West**
Fifth century B.C.E.	Persian Empire	Greek states
First century B.C.E.–early third century C.E.	Parthian Empire	Roman Republic and Empire
Third century–fifth century C.E.	Sassanid Empire	Roman Empire
Sixth century–early seventh century C.E.	Sassanid Empire	Byzantine Empire
Seventh century–eleventh century	Arab/Muslim Empire	Byzantine Empire
Eleventh century–twelfth century	Seljuk Turks	Byzantine Empire
Late eleventh century–late thirteenth century	Seljuk Turks and Ayyubid Empire	European Christian states
Mid-sixteenth century–early twentieth century	Ottoman Turkey	Russia
Early nineteenth century and early twentieth century	Ottoman Turkey	The United Kingdom and France
Mid-nineteenth century–early twentieth century	Russia	The United Kingdom and France
Last half of the twentieth century	Soviet Union	United States
First decade of the twenty-first century	Iran	United States

The Gaza Strip was historically the invasion route of the Egyptians. It was the first major campaign on record against the Jewish state at the end of King Solomon's reign in 928 B.C.E. Later, the Gaza route was utilized by the Arabs and in the twentieth century by the British and Arabs again, all from the southwest.

The Jordan Valley was the northeastern invasion route used by the Assyrians, who invaded in 725 B.C.E. That invasion resulted in the fall of Samaria in 722 B.C.E. and the destruction of the Northern Kingdom of Israel. The Chaldean (New Babylonian) invasions, via the same route, in 598 and 588 B.C.E. resulted in the destruction of Jerusalem and of the First Jewish Temple in 586 B.C.E. Later invasions included those by the Persians, Greeks, Romans, Tartars, and Turks. The geopolitics of this area has not changed much over the last 3,000 years.

One of modern Israel's basic strategic vulnerabilities is Israel's tiny geographic size, which attracts invaders. Additionally, Israel does not have the massive population base of its Arab/Muslim enemies. During its War of Independence, it lost 6,373 persons killed, some 1 percent of its population,* which in comparison to the United States would mean the loss of 3.12 million people during a twenty-month period. That is more than all the deaths in all the wars in US history. Furthermore, Israel is beset by

---

* During Israel's War of Independence, some 3,000 volunteers from forty countries—men, women, Jews and non-Jews—participated in the conflict. Of these, 119 were killed including four women and eight non-Jews.

another basic strategic vulnerability—its political weakness both at home and abroad—which make it impossible to fight long wars.

Thus, Israel's first Prime Minister, David Ben-Gurion, asserted that Israel's military doctrine had to be to fight wars on its enemies' territory and to end them as swiftly and as decisively as possible. This was done in the Sinai Campaign of 1956, the Six-Day War of 1967, the 1,000-Day War of Attrition of 1967–70, the Yom Kippur War of 1973, the First Lebanon War, also known as the Israel–PLO War in Lebanon of 1982, the Second Lebanon War (against Hezbollah) of 2006, and the First, Second and Third Gaza Wars (against Hamas) of 2008–09, 2012 and 2014, respectively. This doctrine remains for Israel, the only realistic option today.

21. The Arab/Muslim world views their history as starting in 622 C.E. Anything that happened before that is an irrelevant myth.

Most Muslims do not recognize world history before 622 C.E. The period prior to 622 C.E. is referred to as *jahiliyyah* (the "age of ignorance"). This included the history of the Jewish nation, which continued for some 2,000 years before 622 C.E., and the advent of Islam. Thus, the Arab/Muslim claim that the country they call "Palestine" was theirs and was taken away from them by the Jews is false and lacks any historical and archaeological basis. To date, there never was an independent sovereign Arab Palestine west of the Jordan River. As has been discussed elsewhere in this book, the eastern portion of the British Mandate of Palestine was detached from the original mandate. An Arab Palestinian state named Jordan was created in 1921, and is demographically today, some 80 percent Palestinian Arab.

Israel became a nation in ca. 1300 B.C.E., 2,000 years before the rise of Islam, and long before there was any Arab nation. Israel has been the homeland of the Jewish people since biblical times. In fact, in what must be viewed as more than a coincidence, Deuteronomy 30:5 says, "The Lord your God will bring you back into the land your ancestors possessed, and you will possess it; he will make you prosper there, and you will become even more numerous than your ancestors." This is verse 5708 in the Bible. Israel's rebirth took place on May 14, 1948 on the secular calendar, which on the Hebrew (biblical) calendar was 5 Iyar, 5708!

Israel was subsequently "occupied" more than fifteen times. Among its occupiers were the Egyptians, the Assyrians, the Chaldeans (New Babylonians), the Persians, the Greeks, the Romans, the Byzantines, the Arabs, the Seljuk Turks, the Christian Crusaders, the Ayyubids, the Mamelukes, and the Ottoman Turks. The longest occupiers of the Land of Israel were the Ottoman Turks, who ruled for 400 years between 1517 and 1917. They were followed by the British who ruled under a Mandate of the League of Nations. The Jews had sovereignty over the Land of Israel for over 1,400 years before eventually losing it to the conquering Romans. However, Jews have had a continuous presence in this land for over 3,300 years. Archeological evidence substantiates their presence there.

A recent excavation conducted by archeologist Eilat Mazar in the Ophel area in Jerusalem, revealed a section of an ancient city wall. Mazar uncovered the wall as well as an inner gatehouse for entry into the royal quarter of the ancient city, and an additional royal structure adjacent to the gatehouse, as well as a corner tower. These structures were dated to the tenth century B.C.E.—the time of King Solomon, credited by the Bible for the construction of the ancient First Jewish Temple in Jerusalem. Pottery found at the lowest levels of the dig was dated to this era. Additionally, bullae (seal impressions) with Hebrew names were found, as well as seal impressions on jar handles inscribed with the words "to the king," which means they were employed by the Israelite state in that time. Inscriptions on the jars, which Mazar said were the largest ever found in Jerusalem, showed them to be the property of a royal official. The significance of this extraordinary find is that it provides new proof of the existence and power of the Davidic monarchy, the Israelite state that it led, and the more than 3,000-year-old Jewish presence in Jerusalem.[242] The more the history of the city is uncovered, the less credible becomes the charges that Jews are alien colonists in what the media sometimes wrongly refer to as "traditionally Palestinian" or "Arab" Jerusalem. Any other distinct people, like the Canaanites, who preceded the Jewish presence, no longer exist.

One may recall the prophecy of the Prophet Joel:

> For behold, in those days and in that time, when I shall bring again the captivity of Judah and Jerusalem, I will also gather all nations and will bring them down to the valley of Jehoshaphat, and will plead with them there for My people and for My heritage, Israel, whom they have scattered among the nations, and parted my land (Joel 4:1–2 in the Sinai Edition of the *Tanakh*).[243]

The *Tanakh* is the canon of the Hebrew/Jewish Bible. The word *"Tanakh"* is a Hebrew acronym, which stands for Torah, Prophets, and Writings. It contains the Torah ("Teaching," also known as the Five Books of Moses), the Prophets (*Nevi'im*), which includes several of the historical books (Joshua, Judges, I Samuel, II Samuel, I Kings, II Kings), the three Major Prophets (Isaiah, Jeremiah, Ezekiel), and the twelve Minor Prophets (Hosea, Joel, Amos, Obadiah, Jonah, Micah, Nahum, Habakkuk, Zephaniah, Haggai, Zechariah, Malachi); and the Writings (*Ketuvim*), comprising Psalms, Proverbs, Job, the Song of Songs, Ruth, Lamentations, Ecclesiastes, Esther, Daniel, Ezra, Nehemiah, I Chronicles, II Chronicles. (This order differs significantly from the sequence in the Christian Bible).

22. Arab/Muslim conquerors have a penchant for destroying other people's religious shrines and many times building their own on the ruins as a mark of supremacy. It was, and remains, Islam's way of saying, "We have defeated you, we rule you, and our god—Allah—is greater than your god."

Historically, Muslim rulers have long had the practice known as "erasing the signs," i.e. eliminating the remnants of any civilization that preceded Islam. This has the effect of depriving other cultures of their spiritual base to establish the superiority of Islam and achieve total physical domination over those pre-Islamic sites. Some prominent examples of this practice are discussed below.

Islam's holiest shrine—the Kaaba, a cube-like building in Mecca—is an older pre-Islamic pagan Arab idolatrous shrine. According to Islamic tradition, the first building was constructed by Adam and rebuilt by Abraham (Ibrahim). The Black Stone, possibly a meteorite fragment, is a significant feature of the Kaaba. The Masjid al-Haram mosque was built around the Kaaba.

The Rashidun Caliphate established rule over Hebron in 638 c.e. and converted the Byzantine church there into the Ibrahimi Mosque. The church itself had been built over the second-most venerated Jewish holy site, the Cave of Machpelah—the Tomb of the Patriarchs, Abraham, Isaac, and Jacob. Minarets were built onto the Tomb of the Patriarchs as a symbol of Islamic supremacy. Furthermore, in 1266 while on pilgrimage to Hebron, Mameluke Sultan Baibars, al-Bunduqdari promulgated an edict forbidding Christians and Jews from entering the Tomb of the Patriarchs.[244] The situation at the Tomb became less tolerant of Christians and Jews than it had been under the prior Ayyubid rule. Under the edict, Christian and Jews were only allowed to climb no higher than the fifth step of the staircase at the southeast corner of the structure, but after some time this was increased to the seventh step. On June 7, 1967, Hebron was restored to Jewish control for the first time in 2,000 years. The 701-year-long restriction limiting non-Muslims to the seventh step was lifted.

In 637 C.E. (other sources say 641 C.E.), during the reign of the Caliph Umar ibn al-Khattab, the region around Nineveh (present-day Mosul, Iraq) was conquered by Islamic forces and annexed to the Rashidun Caliphate. Near the ancient remnants of Nineveh was the Tomb of the Biblical prophet Jonah. During the early Byzantine period, a Nestorian-Assyrian Church was built there. With the Muslim conquest, the Nestorian-Assyrian church was razed and the Mosque of the Prophet Yunus (Jonah) was built on the site. Ironically, in a case of an Islamic conqueror destroying an Islamic site, on July 24, 2014, Jonah's tomb, as well as the Mosque of the Prophet Yunus was totally destroyed by the Sunni Islamic State of Iraq and the Levant (ISIL) terrorist group, claiming, "The mosque had become a place for apostasy, not prayer."[245] To add insult to injury, in June 2015, ISIL announced plans to construct a park and "fun city" over the site of Jonah's Tomb and began leveling the area for that purpose.[246] At the time of their conquest of Mosul, Iraq (also in July 2014), ISIL blew up a tomb attributed to the Biblical Prophet Daniel. The destruction of the Tombs of the Jewish prophets Jonah and Daniel was in keeping with Islamic conquerers' policy of rewriting history by obliterating symbols and sites of other religions and cultures.

The Dome of the Rock was built on the ruins of Judaism's holiest site, the Temple Mount, in Jerusalem. The Temple Mount is a broad plateau, currently some 37 acres, where the two Jewish Holy Temples once stood. The Dome of the Rock was erected by the Umayyad Caliph Abd al-Malik and completed in 691 C.E. According to some sources, it was also built to protect the Foundation Stone, which is actually the top of Mount Moriah. Mount Moriah is considered by tradition to be the site of the *Akedah Yitzhak*—the place where Isaac was supposed to be sacrificed. Muslim scholars have endorsed the belief it was Ishmael (not Isaac), Abraham's first son, who was to be sacrificed there. To the present, the entire plateau is also known as *Bayt al-Muqaddas* (alternatively transliterated as *Beit al-Maqdis* or *Bait-ul-Muqaddas*), an Arabic version of *Bet HaMikdash*, and the classical Hebrew term for the Jewish Temple and its immediate surroundings.

Al-Walid, son of al-Malik, erected the Al-Aqsa Mosque at the southern end of the Temple Mount and over the ruins of the Basilica of St. Mary of Justinian, originally built in 560 C.E. Al-Aqsa was built as a reconstruction of the church in 712 C.E., and a dome was added to convert it into a mosque. Recently British archeological records and photos dating from the 1930s revealed the discovery made then (following the 1927 earthquake that affected Jerusalem) of a Byzantine mosaic floor under the Al-Aqsa Mosque. The mosaic dates from between the fifth to seventh century C.E.[247] The main reason for the construction of the Dome of the Rock and Al-Aqsa Mosque was to show the supremacy of Islam over Judaism, as well as Christianity and to be in competition with the Christian Church of the Holy Sepulcher, built nearby centuries earlier. The church is venerated by most Christians as Golgotha, the Hill of Calvary, where tradition says that Jesus was crucified and buried.

After the Muslim conquest of Syria, the Umayyad Grand Mosque of Damascus was erected on the site of the Cathedral of St. John the Baptist in 715 C.E. Within the mosque is a shrine, which contains the head of John the Baptist.

The Grand Mosque of Córdoba in Muslim-occupied Spain (what the Muslims called Al-Andalus, was built on the site of the great Visigoth Church of St. Vincent in that city. Construction and expansion of the mosque lasted from 784 C.E. until 987 C.E. (As part of the Christian *Reconquista*, Córdoba was recaptured from the Muslims by King Ferdinand III of Castile, on June 29, 1236, and the mosque was restored to being a Roman Catholic cathedral).

On October 18, 1009, the Muslim Fatimid Caliph Abu 'Ali Mansur Tariqu'l-Hakim destroyed, down to the bedrock, the Church of the Holy Sepulcher in Jerusalem. Gravestones were also destroyed. Muslim forces tried o dig up all the graves and wipe out all traces of their existence. The site is now within the walled, Old City of Jerusalem. After the capture of Jerusalem on October 2, 1187, the first Ayyubid Sultan, Saladin constructed two mosques, Al Khanqa and Abdul Malek, contiguous to and taller than the Church of the Holy Sepulcher.[248] In 1192, a year after his conquest of Jerusalem, Saladin converted the Church of St. Anne, which stood near Lions' Gate on the Via Dolorosa, into an Islamic seminary, noted by the Arabic inscription *Salahiya* (of Saladin) above the entrance.

In 1193, the Nalanda University complex in Bihar, India was destroyed by Muslim forces led by Bakhtiyar Khalji. It was the greatest repository of Buddhist knowledge in the world at the time, with learning centers, ten temples and monasteries, along with a huge library. The Muslim forces destroyed everything and the library burned for several months.[249] Similarly, a second great Buddhist learning center at Vikramshila, was destroyed a short while later.

At the end of the twelfth century, Al-Aziz Uthman, the second son of Saladin, and second Ayyubid Sultan of Egypt, attempted to destroy the pyramids at Giza, outside of Cairo, Egypt. These were regarded by the Muslims as infidel monuments. Uthman began with the smallest of the three pyramids—the Pyramid of Menkaure. After eight months of extensive labor all that was accomplished was superficial damage and the attempt stopped. It should be noted that there are currently calls from Islamist groups in Egypt, to finish the demolition of the Pyramids and other pharaonic symbols. Abd Al-Munim A-Shahhat, a representative for the Salafi group *Dawa,* has said that Egypt's world-renowned pharaonic archeology—its pyramids, Sphinx and other monuments covered with un-Islamic imagery—should also be hidden from the public eye. "The pharaonic culture is a rotten culture," A-Shahhat told the London-based Arabic daily *A-Sharq Al-Awsat* on August 28, 2011, saying the faces of ancient statues "should be covered with wax, since they are religiously forbidden." He likened the Egyptian relics to the idols, which circled the walls of Mecca in pre-Islamic times.[250] In November 2012, Sheikh Murjan Salem al-Jawhari, a Salafi leader, issued a *fatwa* in which he called for the destruction of all idols, relics, and statues in Egypt, specifically mentioning the Sphinx and the Great Pyramids.

When the Mameluke Sultan Baibars al-Bunduqdari captured the Crusader Krak des Chevaliers fortress in Syria, on April 8, 1271, he converted the Knights Hospitaller chapel to a mosque.

In India, the Hindu Vikramasli Temple was razed to the ground in the thirteenth century, and its foundation stones thrown into the Ganges. Hundreds of Hindu temples were destroyed and converted into mosques. In Iran, there are no ancient Zoroastrians or Manichean shrines left. All were destroyed.

When Constantinople was conquered in 1453 by the Ottoman Turks, the Pantokrator Monastery was looted and converted into the Zeyrek Djami Mosque. After the Muslim conquest of Cyprus (1570–71) by the Ottoman Turks, St. Sophia Cathedral in Nicosia was converted into the Selimiye Mosque. In a like manner, St. Nicholas Cathedral in Famagusta was converted into the Lala Mustafa Pasha Mosque, named after Vizier Lala Mustafa Pasha, the conqueror of Cyprus.

The largest Byzantine cathedral in the world for nearly one thousand years was Hagia Sophia (The Church of the Holy Wisdom) in Constantinople (now Istanbul, Turkey). It had been built between 532 and 537 C.E. by the Byzantine Emperor Justinian. In 1453, Constantinople was conquered by the Muslim Ottoman Turks. Sultan Mehmed II ordered the building be converted into the Aya Sofya Mosque. The bells, altar, religious icon-laden screens, and sacrificial vessels were removed and many of the mosaics defaced and plastered over. Islamic features, such as the *mihrab* and *minbar* were added. A *mihrab* is a crescent-shaped niche in the wall of a mosque that indicates the *qibla,* i.e. the direction of the Kaaba in Mecca and the direction that Muslims should face when praying. A *minbar* is a raised pulpit in the mosque where the imam (prayer leader) stands to deliver sermons. Additionally, four minarets, the sign of Islamic supremacy, were built at each corner of the church's property. In his last will and testament, Mehmed II decreed that Hagia Sophia remain a mosque until "Judgment Day."[251]

With the advent of the more secular Republic of Turkey, Hagia Sophia was closed to the public in 1931, for four years. In 1935, it was reopened having been converted into a "neutral" museum. With the Erdoğan government of Turkey moving steadily towards establishing an Islamic republic, Hagia Sophia may yet again be restored as a mosque. The trend certainly seems to be in that direction. On May 23, 2012, thousands of devout Muslims prayed outside Hagia Sophia protesting a 1934 law that bars formal worship within the sixth century monument. Worshippers shouted, "Break the chains, let Hagia Sophia Mosque open," and *"Allahu akbar."*[252] It should be noted that *"Allahu akbar"* means "Allah is greater"—not, as it is often translated, "Allah is great." Nor does it mean "Thank, God." The significance of this is enormous, as it is essentially a proclamation of Islamic superiority and supremacism. Allah is greater—than any of the gods of the infidels (Judaism, Christianity, Hinduism, and Buddhism among others) and Islam is superior to all other religions. Most recently on May 3, 2014, Hami Yildirim, a deputy in the Grand National Assembly of Turkey submitted a draft law calling for the conversion of Hagia Sophia Museum back to a mosque.[253]

The first Mughal emperor of India, Babur, ordered the construction of the Babri Mosque in Ayodhya, in 1527. Babur's commander-in-chief, Mir Baki, destroyed the existing Hindu temple commemorating the birthplace of Rama—an incarnation of Vishnu—and ruler of Ayodhya, India. In a rare instance of a population trying to return the holy site to its original religious importance, a crowd of over 150,000 attacked and destroyed the Babri Mosque on December 6, 1992. During the period of Mughal rule, 1526–1858, practically no Hindu temples survived Muslim occupation, with an estimated 10,000 destroyed during this Muslim period. Thousands of mosques were built on the foundations of Hindu temples.

From 1609 to 1616, Ottoman Sultan Ahmed I built the Sultan Ahmed Mosque—popularly known as the Blue Mosque—in Constantinople, on the site of the Great Palace of the Byzantine Christian emperors.

The Jewish Quarter in the Old City of Jerusalem was destroyed in 1948–49. Numerous synagogues and religious schools of learning, including the famous Ramban Synagogue constructed in 1267, and the Hurva Synagogue were obliterated.

In Libya, on November 26, 1970, the Catholic Cathedral of the Sacred Heart in Tripoli was converted into the Gamal Abdel Nasser Mosque.

During the Second Lebanese Civil War, PLO terrorists and Lebanese Muslim forces attacked Damour, a Christian Lebanese town on January 20, 1976 (*see* the "Lebanese Civil War, 1976" map). The attackers destroyed the town's buildings. In vile desecration, the Christian cemetery was destroyed, coffins dug up, the dead robbed, vaults opened, and bodies and skeletons thrown across the graveyard. The Church of St. Elias was gutted by grenades and burnt. While, thus far a mosque has not been built on the site, the rubble of the church was turned into a combination repair garage for PLO vehicles,[254] and shooting range. Targets were painted on the eastern wall of the nave. An outside wall was covered with a mural of Fatah* terrorists holding AK-47 rifles and a portrait of Yasser Arafat was placed at one end. Christian civilians were lined up against a wall and sprayed with machine-gun fire. An estimate of the civilian dead was 584.[255] The PLO terrorized the rest of the 25,000 residents into fleeing Damour. Father Mansour Labaky of the Church of St. Elias gave this description of the massacre:

> The PLO came and bombed the church without entering it. They kicked open the door and threw in the grenades. An entire family had been killed, the Can'an family, four children all dead, and the mother, the father, and the grandfather. The mother was still hugging one of the children. And she was pregnant. The eyes of the children were gone and their limbs were cut off. No legs and no arms. It was awful.[256]

---

* Arabic reverse acronym derived from *Harakat al-Tahrir [al-watani] al-Filastiniya* ("Palestine National Liberation Movement"). The actual acronym is "*Hataf*" meaning "sudden death." By reversing the acronym, "Fatah" becomes "conquest" or "victorious conquest" through holy struggle (i.e. jihad). It also refers to the rapid and violent spread of Islam during the first centuries of Islamic history, as well as being the title of Sura 48 in the Qur'an that details the story of the Treaty of Hudaybiyyah.

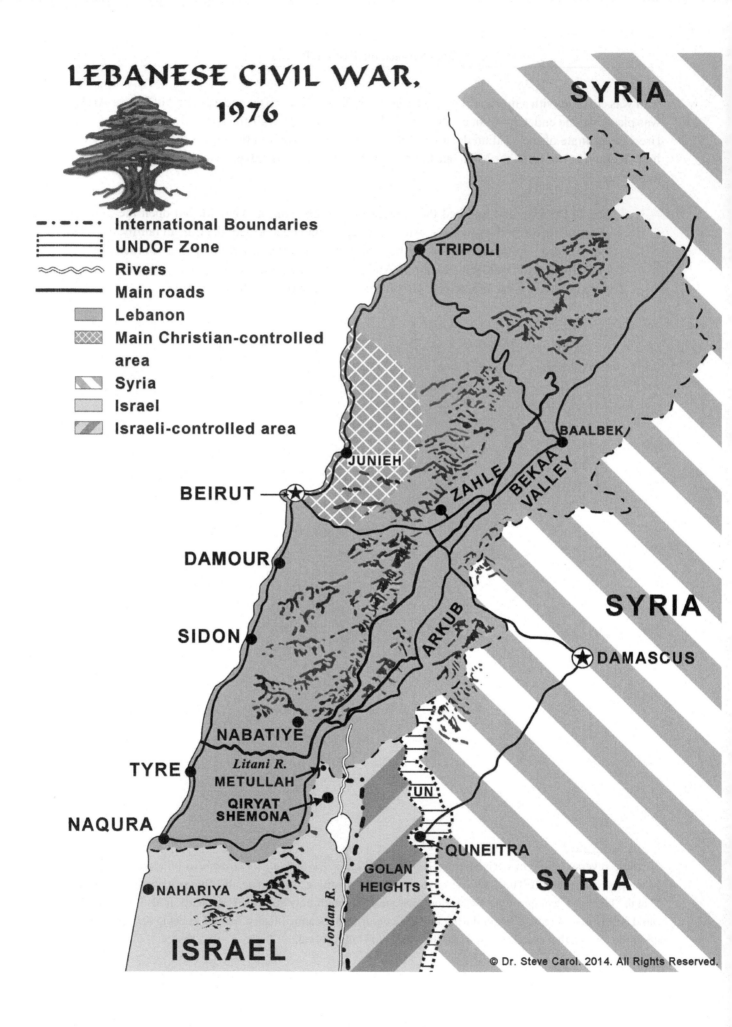

LEBANESE CIVIL WAR, 1976

SYRIA

Legend:
- ─·─·─ International Boundaries
- UNDOF Zone
- ∿∿∿ Rivers
- ─── Main roads
- Lebanon
- Main Christian-controlled area
- Syria
- Israel
- Israeli-controlled area

TRIPOLI

BAALBEK

JUNIEH

ZAHLE

BEKAA VALLEY

BEIRUT

DAMOUR

SYRIA

SIDON

ARKUB

DAMASCUS

NABATIYE

Litani R.
METULLAH

TYRE

QIRYAT SHEMONA

UN

NAQURA

QUNEITRA

SYRIA

GOLAN HEIGHTS

NAHARIYA

Jordan R.

ISRAEL

Despite solemn pledges and signed documents, i.e. the Oslo II Agreement (Interim Agreement) of September 28, 1995, between Israel and the PLO, Jews were denied free, unimpeded and secure access to worship and practice their faith at two holy sites in PA-controlled territory—the first being the Tomb of the Biblical Patriarch Joseph and the second being the 1,500 year-old Shalom Al Yisrael synagogue in Jericho.

The Oslo II Agreement provided specifically for "free, unimpeded and secure access to the relevant Jewish holy site; and … to ensure the peaceful use of such site, to prevent any potential instances of disorder and to respond to any incident," (Art. V and Appendix 4 of Annex I–Protocol Concerning Redeployment and Security Arrangements–and Art. 32(3) of Appendix 1–Powers and Responsibilities for Civil Affairs–to Annex III–Protocol Concerning Civil Affairs).

Despite these solemn written pledges, in September 1996, Palestinian Arabs desecrated and destroyed the Biblical Patriarch Joseph's Tomb, in Shechem (Joshua 24:32), the Biblical town the Arabs call Nablus, including a synagogue. Joseph's Tomb is one of the holiest sites in Judaism as many Jews believe the site to be the final resting place of the biblical patriarch Joseph and his two sons, Ephraim and Manasseh.

On September 28, 2000, when Arafat's PLO/PA began the Al-Aqsa (Second) *Intifada*—the Oslo War—Arab vandals torched and burnt down a large part of the Shalom Al Yisrael synagogue in Jericho. Local Arabs prevented Israeli fire trucks from putting out the fire. Since then it has constantly been defiled by Arab residents.

Shortly thereafter, on October 1, 2000, Arab mobs attacked Joseph's Tomb with gunfire, firebombs, and stones. The IDF defenders in the compound withstood the attacks and stopped several attempts by armed Palestinians to break in. An IDF border police officer, Madhat Yousuf was shot in the neck was not rescued in time and bled to death. Incredulously, Israeli Prime Minister Ehud Barak authorized the evacuation of the site, based on the promises of the PA to respect the Oslo Accords, to safeguard and protect holy sites, Jewish and Christian, and ensure access by all. The PA also pledged to prevent any vandalism and to return Joseph's Tomb to its original condition after the violence settled down.

Then on October 7, 2000, within two hours of the IDF withdrawal from the Tomb compound, Joseph's Tomb, the reconstructed synagogue and yeshiva—*Od Yosef Chai*—which had stood at the site for 25 years, was systematically sacked and burned by Arab mobs. Rabbi Hillel Lieberman, who went there hoping to save Torah scrolls and other holy objects, was murdered. The next day his bullet-ridden body was found in a cave. The Palestinian police stood by, failing to prevent any of these violent activities, despite their commitment to guard the Tomb. Within hours, Joseph's Tomb was reduced to a smoldering heap of rubble.

Within two days, as an Associated Press dispatch reported, "the dome of the tomb was painted green the color of Islam,[257] and bulldozers were seen clearing the surrounding area," as the Palestinian Arabs sought to transform the biblical Joseph's resting place into a Muslim holy site. Under intense United States and international pressure, the dome was repainted white.[258]

On April 22, 2009, Joseph's burial site was desecrated yet again. It was found covered in misojudaic graffiti, swastikas, and boot prints in the concrete, as well as scorch marks and damage to the headstone.[259] Undeterred, Israel restored the tomb and during the night of September 25–26, 2010, brought and lowered a five-ton stone slab into the ancient tomb structure in the exact location where the original stone lay, before it was smashed and burned by the Arab despoilers in October 2000.

Furthermore, on April 24, 2011, PA "security" police opened fire on Jewish worshippers at Joseph's Tomb, killing one and wounding four others. Arab mobs then set fire to the Tomb complex again. On October 5, 2011, Joseph's Tomb was desecrated once again. Incredulously, it was Israel that first armed the PA with rifles as part of the misnamed Oslo "peace" Accords. As has been stated, several agreements between Israel and the PA guaranteed Israel control and the freedom of worship to Jews at Joseph's Tomb. So much for such agreements.[260] Nevertheless, Joseph's Tomb was desecrated yet again in December 2014. Israel should once and for all, extend Israeli sovereignty to Joseph's Tomb, forever restoring it to Jewish exclusive control. The historic record of Arab (Jordanian) occupation of the holy sites in Judea, Samaria and particularly Jerusalem, and the recent record of attacks, desecrations and demolition of such sites by the PLO/PA cast serious doubts as to whether any Palestinian Arab authority can be a trusted custodian of sacred sites.

The desecration of religious holy sites by Muslim fundamentalists is not restricted to the Middle East. In Kosovo in 1999, more than one hundred ancient Orthodox Christian holy places were destroyed, some dating back to the thirteenth through fifteenth century.

Yet another modern example of deliberate Islamic destruction of the symbols and sacred places of other faiths occurred with the destruction of the Buddhas of Bamiyan. These were two giant statues of Buddha—Vairocana (built in 554 C.E.) and Sakyamuni (built in 507 C.E.), measuring 180 and 121 feet high respectively. They were carved into the side of a cliff in the Bamyan Valley in the Hazarajat region of central Afghanistan. The 1,500 year-old statues were deliberately blown up and methodically destroyed over a period of weeks in March 2001. This came after a *fatwa* ordered by the Taliban government, headed by Mullah Mohammed Omar, directed all Afghan "idols" be destroyed as being anti-Muslim and forbidden under shari'a. On a similar note, in the republics of Central Asia— Kazakhstan, Kyrgyzstan, Tajikistan, Turkmenistan, and Uzbekistan—no Buddhist temples remain.

In mid-February 2012, an Islamist mob attacked the national museum of the Maldive Islands. The rampage destroyed 99 percent of the Hindu and Buddhist artifacts associated with the pre-Islamic period of Maldivian history. The Maldives converted to Islam at the end of the twelfth century. About 35 exhibits—mostly images of Buddha and Hindu gods—were destroyed in the attack. Some of the artifacts dated back to the sixth century C.E.[261]

Arab Muslims have attempted to appropriate the tomb of Rabbi Ashi, near *Kibbutz* Menara, in northern Israel on the border with Lebanon. Rabbi Ashi, who died in 427 C.E., was a celebrated Jewish religious scholar, and the first editor of the Babylonian Talmud. The Shi'ite Muslims claim the tomb is not that of Rabbi Ashi, but rather of a Shi'ite leader in Lebanon who died in the seventeenth century. As a result of the Israeli withdrawal from southern Lebanon, completed on May 24, 2000, and a United Nations imposed international boundary line, the border fence runs through the tomb!

In 1996, the Islamic *Waqf* converted an ancient underground Second Temple period structure into a massive new mosque, which was named the Al-Marwani Mosque, located at the southeast corner of the Temple Mount in the area in the structures known since Crusader times as Solomon's Stables near the Eastern Hulda Gate. The new mosque has a large, 7,000 person-capacity. In 1997, the Western Hulda Gate passageway was converted into another mosque named the Al-Aqsa Hakadum. The Hulda Gates are the two sets of now-blocked gates in the Southern Wall of the Temple Mount. The western set is a double arched gate and the eastern is a triple arched gate. Solomon's Stables and both the Eastern and Western Hulda Gate passageways have enormous historical value as pivotal parts of the Jewish Temple during the Herodian era. Neither of these new Islamic prayer sites were ever mosques in the past. In November 1999, a buried Crusader-era door was reopened as an "emergency exit" for the mosque located within the Solomon's Stables area, opening an excavation 18,000 square feet in size and up to 36 feet deep.

In early 2001, Arab bulldozers destroyed an ancient arched structure located adjacent to the eastern wall of the Temple Mount in Jerusalem. Some 6,000 square meters of the Temple Mount were dug up, paved, and declared open-air mosques. Some of the earth and rubble removed was dumped in the El-Azaria and in the Kidron Valleys. Furthermore, there was virtually no archaeological supervision over this digging and countless artifacts were undoubtedly destroyed.

The Islamization of the entire Temple Mount continued, without any real protest and action by the world in general and the Israeli government in particular. As has been mentioned previously, in July 2007, the *Waqf* began digging a ditch from the northern side of the Temple Mount compound to the Dome of the Rock as a prelude to what was termed as "infrastructure work." The vandalism, desecration, and destruction of Jewish antiquities on the Temple Mount continued.

In late May 2014, it was revealed that the *Waqf* planned to lay the groundwork for a fifth mosque in the eastern part of the Temple Mount complex in the underground space beneath the Golden Gate. It is said that the Ottoman Sultan Suleiman the Magnificent sealed off the Golden Gate in 1541, to prevent the entrance of the Jewish Messiah. The Golden Gate remains sealed to this day. According to Dr. Eilat Mazar, an Israeli archaeologist at the Hebrew University of Jerusalem and a member of the Public Committee against the Destruction of Antiquities on the Temple Mount, in the large space underneath the Golden Gate there continues to be "significant, new activity that arouses great concern."[262] All of the construction in 1996, 1997, 1999, 2001, 2007, and 2014, was a deliberate calculated attempt to destroy the physical evidence of the Jewish presence on and claim to the Temple Mount, which is precisely the goal of Israel's Arab/Muslim enemies.

The Mughrabi Gate is the only point of entry for Jews and other non-Muslims to the Temple Mount. In 2005, a landslide made the earthen ramp leading to the Mughrabi Gate unsafe and in danger of collapse. Israel, in 2007, built a temporary wooden pedestrian bridge, called the Mughrabi Bridge, to the Mughrabi Gate and planned to build a permanent access to the gate. Arab/Muslim violence and threats delayed the construction of the permanent structure. There are sections of the temporary span, which are unsupported and could endanger visitors to not only the Temple Mount, but to the Western Wall plaza below, particularly the women's section. The Muslims apparently prefer that a permanent bridge to the Temple Mount not be built so that it is open to Muslims only.

Currently, there is an Arab/Muslim attempt to deny the Jewish connection to both the Cave of Machpelah—the Tomb of the Patriarchs—in Hebron and the Biblical matriarch Rachel's Tomb, located just south of Jerusalem on the northern approaches to Bethlehem. The Arabs claim that the Tomb of the Patriarchs (Cave of Machpelah) is exclusively Muslim. They also claim that Rachel's Tomb is a 1,000-year-old mosque, Bilal Bin Rabbah. There have been numerous Muslim attempted attacks on Rachel's Tomb. The Arab claim is false and was only put forth in 1996 and popularized after 2000.[263] Interestingly enough, as late at April 24, 1994, the Arab League, in testimony to the UN Human Rights Council referred to the site only as Rachel's Tomb.[264] The only Arabic name for the site historically has been *Qubbat Rukhail,* or "The Dome of Rachel."[265]

The Israeli government built security barriers on three sides of the site, to protect tourists and pilgrims from Arab attacks. This in turn, has restricted access to pilgrims and tourists, approaching the site from Israel. On February 22, 2010, the Israeli government announced that it would include the Tomb of the Patriarchs and Rachel's Tomb as part of a comprehensive plan to preserve Israel's national heritage and religious sites and renovate them. The announcement triggered Arab riots. The PA was able, in March 2010, to persuade the United Nations Educational, Scientific, and Cultural Organization's Executive Board, to refer to the Bilal Bin Rabah mosque as "historic."[266] That was followed in October, by an Executive Board vote of 44 to 1 (with 12 abstentions) which declared the "the Palestinian sites of al-Haram al-Ibrahimi/Tomb of the Patriarchs in al-Khalil/Hebron and the Bilal bin Rabah Mosque/Rachel's Tomb in Bethlehem … [were] an integral part of the occupied

Palestinian Territories."[267] These are further examples of the on-going attempts by the Arab/Muslim world to eradicate Jewish history and culture from the Middle East in general, and the Land of Israel in particular.

There should be no doubt; the Jewish connection to both the Cave of Machpelah and Rachel's Tomb precedes the advent of Islam by over 2,000 years. The Book of Genesis 23:16 relates Abraham's purchase of the Cave as a burial site for his wife Sarah and their descendants. Genesis 35:19 relates "and Rachel died and was buried on the way to Ephrath, which is Bethlehem."

By no means is the Arab/Muslim attempt to eradicate any trace of a historic Jewish presence limited to the Palestinian-controlled areas of the Land of Israel. In early January 2010, reports reached the West that the Iraqi government planned to turn the tomb of the Prophet Ezekiel into a mosque and erase all Jewish markings. The tomb is located in Al-Kifl, a small town south of Baghdad. Shlomo Alfassa, Director of Justice for Jews from Arab Countries, reported that Islamic political parties have pressured the Iraqi government to remove the Jewish inscriptions. He quoted the Iraqi news agency *Ur News* as reporting that the writing and ornamentations "are being (or have been) removed ... under the pretext of restoring the site." Alfassa quotes sources to the effect that Iraq's Antiquities and Heritage Authority "has been pressured by Islamists to historically cleanse all evidence of a Jewish connection to Iraq—a land where Jews had lived for over a thousand years before the advent of Islam." The reports were confirmed by Professor Shmuel Moreh, Israel Prize Laureate in Arabic Literature and Professor Emeritus at Hebrew University of Jerusalem. He had received worrisome phone calls from non-Jewish friends in Baghdad about the issue. Professor Moreh, who serves as the Chairman of the Association of Jewish Academics from Iraq, said that the plans were to turn the holy site into a mosque, and "some told me that they are taking off the Hebrew inscriptions."[268]

Attacks on Jewish holy sites in the Middle East were not restricted to the Arab states alone. In December 2010, Iranian Basij militia threatened to tear down and destroy the Tomb of Esther and Mordechai, the Jewish leaders connected to the Jewish festival of Purim. Purim celebrates the deliverance of the Jews of the Persian Empire from a planned extermination plot by Haman, the advisor to the King Ahasuerus (generally identified with Xerxes I) and is related in the biblical Book of Esther. In early January 2011, Iranian authorities downgraded the status of the site. They removed an official sign at the mausoleum, in the city of Hamadan in central Iran that declared it an official pilgrimage site. There was an implicit threat made, by the state-run Iranian news agency Fars, (which is owned by the Iranian Revolutionary Guard Corps) hinting that the fate of the site could be much worse. It said Iran has chosen to ignore, for the time being, "the responsibility of Esther and Mordechai for "the real holocaust,"—the massacre of 75,000 Iranians, which the Jews celebrate at Purim."[269] This bogus charge blatantly falsifies the reason for the celebration of that Jewish holiday.

Furthermore, a new twist was offered on the blood libel devised so often in the past to justify the persecution of and attacks on, Jewish communities. The Fars agency carried a report noting that Jews were used to adding the blood of Muslim children to the "Ears of Haman,"[270] (*hamantashen*) a triangular pastry cake traditionally baked on the Purim festival. Historically, such vile calumnies unleashed wholesale misojudaic rampages. This may well happen now against the less than 9,000 Jews who are the last survivors of the 3,000-year old Iranian Jewish community.

At this point, it is important to explain briefly the "matzo blood libel." It is the false accusations against Jews for allegedly using the blood of non-Jews to make matzo—the unleavened bread eaten during the Passover holiday. It originated among Christians starting in 1144 with the fabricated story of the murder of William of Norwich, England. The accusation of ritual murder associated with the preparation of matzo was common in Europe in the Middle Ages. Today these accusations are widespread and deep rooted in the Muslim world, not the Christian world. The accusation that Jews use the blood of Christian or Muslim blood is quite common in Islamic literature.[271] Scores of books, pamphlets, propaganda tracts, news articles, and TV programs[272] have repeated the noxious lies. A few examples are listed below.

In 1983, Syrian Defense minister (from 1972 to 2004), Mustafa Tlass wrote and published *The Matzah of Zion*, which revived this most vicious misojudaic canard. In his book, Tlass claims that Jews living in Damascus in 1840 killed two Christians and used their blood in preparing matzo.[273] On April 6, 2003, a cartoon was posted on the official website of the Palestinian Authority State Information Center (which regularly posts ugly anti-Israel and anti-American cartoons), depicted then Israeli Prime Minister Ariel Sharon holding a blood-stained cleaver hovering over a "slaughtered blood-soaked child" having a "sale" of "Palestinian blood" with dead children hanging from hooks. Captioned in English (the cartoon was intended for foreign audiences) it reiterated the misojudaic blood libel that Jews kill non-Jewish children.[274] A particularly venomous Syrian-produced TV series—*Al-Shatat*—replete with villainous stereotypes of scheming Jews plotting to murder a Christian child for his blood, was shown on Al-Mamnou' TV (Jordan), October 20, 2005, as well as elsewhere across the Arab Middle East.[275] In July 2014, a top Hamas representative in Lebanon, Osama Hamdan claimed in a television interview that Israelis kill children and linked this to the blood libel.[276] Most recently, a former Jordanian Member of Parliament, Sheik Abd Al-Mun'im Abu Zant, made the comments in an interview, which aired on Hamas's Al-Aqsa TV on September 7, 2014, in which he accused Jews of "cannibalism."[277] The irony of the untruthful blood libel accusation is that the Torah expressly forbids Jews to consume blood in any form (which is part of the process of koshering meat), whereas pagan religions did so as part of their rituals.

Across the Arab/Muslim world, attacks on Christian institutions also continued unabated. During the mass demonstrations, ostensibly for "democratic" change that brought down the Mubarak regime in Egypt, Muslims, on March 5, 2011, assaulted, plundered, and set ablaze an ancient Coptic church in Sool, Egypt, near Cairo. Adding insult to injury, the attackers played "soccer" with the relic-remains of the church's saints and martyrs additionally transforming the desecrated church into a mosque.[278] Afterwards, the Muslim mobs gathered around the scorched building and pounded its walls down with sledgehammers—to cries of *"Allahu akbar."*

While not a religious site, the Twin Towers of the World Trade Center in lower Manhattan, New York City stood as a symbol of Western commerce, industry and civilization. Additionally, the World Trade Center represented New York City, perhaps more than any other landmark aside from the Statue of Liberty. Furthermore, the city itself is both the symbolic and actual home of many American Jews—from the historic Lower East Side to contemporary Crown Heights. On September 11, 2001, the world witnessed the horrors of the attack on, followed by the calamitous collapse of, those Twin Towers. It was an attack motivated by what the Twin Towers represented including an attack directed against New York City's Jews, whom in Muslim eyes are no more than a *dhimmi* people. While not a religious site, no doubt many prayers were said there both during and after the Twin Towers' destruction.

In May 2010, it was announced that two blocks from the ruins of the World Trade Center, reduced to rubble in the name of Islam, an Islamic mosque would rise. This fits the historic pattern of Muslim construction near or atop the ruins of their enemies' symbolic buildings as a mark of Islamic supremacy. The planned mosque was at first named "Córdoba House," a name with much Islamic historic significance. After the Muslim conquest and occupation of the Iberian Peninsula beginning in 711 c.e. and continuing for over 770 years, the region was renamed *Al-Andalus*. During Muslim rule and occupation, Córdoba was the capital of a succession of Islamic states, including an Islamic Caliphate of Córdoba (from 756 to 1031).

Former Speaker of the House of Representatives and historian, Newt Gingrich pointedly stressed the history, meaning and symbolism of a mosque near Ground Zero. He also aptly explained the meaning and significance of the name "Córdoba House:"

> The proposed 'Córdoba House' overlooking the World Trade Center site–where a group of jihadists killed over 3,000 Americans and destroyed one of our most famous landmarks, is a test of the timidity, passivity and historic ignorance of American elites. For example, most of them do not understand that 'Córdoba House' is a deliberately insulting term. It refers to Córdoba, Spain—the capital of Muslim conquerors who symbolized their victory over the Christian Spaniards by transforming a church there into the world's third-largest mosque complex.... In fact, every Islamist in the world recognizes Córdoba as a symbol of Islamic conquest. It is a sign of their contempt for Americans and their confidence in our historic ignorance that they would deliberately insult us this way.... America is experiencing an Islamist cultural-political offensive designed to undermine and destroy our civilization. Sadly, too many of our elites are the willing apologists for those who would destroy them if they could. No mosque. No self-deception. No surrender.[279]

Due to the controversy, publicity and opposition to the planned mosque, the site was renamed "Park51" and designated as a Muslim community center. Even the change of name left doubts. The Imam leading the project referred to the project as "Córdoba House."[280] The Park51 website then clarified that Park51 is the community center, while "Córdoba House "is the "interfaith and religious component of the center."[281] Despite plans for other facilities, the main purpose of the building will be as a mosque. Once built, 1,000 to 2,000 Muslims are expected to pray at the mosque every Friday.[282] A question arises as to whether there is such a large Muslim community living within this area of lower Manhattan? The land for the community center/mosque was bought for $4.85 million in unaccounted for cash. The estimated cost of the new 13-story building that will house the mosque is $100 million. It is to be funded by donations. Just who specifically would be making these donations is another unanswered question?

Moreover, a second group seeks to build an additional mosque near ground zero. The Manhattan Mosque has raised $8.5 million and is seeking an additional $2.5 million to begin construction. While it apparently has not settled on a final location, it has told donors it plans to build very close to where the World Trade Center once stood.[283] In fact, the Manhattan Mosque website states, *"Insha'Allah we will raise the flag of La-Illaha-Illa-Allah* in downtown Manhattan very soon!"[284] The website, updated November 2, 2012, announced that property had been purchased and "is situated in one of the best locations in downtown Manhattan. It is near Wall Street, in Manhattan's downtown Financial Center, close to City Hall, Manhattan South Street Seaport and to major public transportation (Fulton St/Broadway-Nassau station, the City Hall and Brooklyn Bridge stations and the under-construction Fulton St. /*World Trade Center* (emphasis added) Subway Hub)."[285]

The World Trade Center was destroyed in the name of Islam. The Islamic supremacist perpetrators stated that the people who were murdered were not innocent, which is blatantly false. Constructing the Córdoba House Mosque at Ground Zero is like building a tribute to the Japanese military at Pearl Harbor. The planned mosque will be just 600 feet from Ground Zero, at the site of the greatest Islamic supremacist achievement over infidels in hundreds of years.

Furthermore, as if to rub salt in the wound of the September 11, 2001 attacks, another mosque was planned for Shanksville, Pennsylvania at the United Airlines Flight 93 crash site. The site itself marks the culmination point of the efforts by the valiant and patriotic Americans—the forty passengers and crew—who sacrificed themselves in order to protect their nation.

The original plan called for the construction of what was called the "Crescent of Embrace," and was publicized by some as the world's largest open-air mosque disguised as a memorial on 2,200 acres of land. The memorial included a giant half-mile wide Islamic-shaped crescent of maple trees. In the autumn the leaves of these trees turn a brilliant flaming red. Viewed from the sky (either from aircraft flying overhead or via Google Earth photos) the memorial would have shown the Islamic crescent moon—*hilal*—dominating the site.[286] Also incorporated into the original design, whether coincidentally or not, was its orientation toward Mecca for prayer. That would have made the memorial a *mihrab*. A *mihrab* is the semicircular niche in the wall of a mosque that indicates the *qibla;* that is, the direction of the Kaaba in Mecca and hence the direction that Muslims should face when praying. The wall in which a *mihrab* appears is thus the "*qibla* wall." Note that while some *mihrabs* are pointed-arch shaped, the classic *mihrab* is crescent shaped.

According to the original design the center of the crescent at the Flight 93 memorial, pointed less than 2 degrees towards Mecca. If you visualize the crescent as a bow with the bowstring between the two end tips and the arrow lying across the curve of the crescent (f∫) then the arrow points towards Mecca. That makes the Flight 93 Memorial a mosque.[287] Due to a firestorm of protests, the construction drawings were revised. The lower tip of the half-mile wide crescent (about 300 feet), was moved to change the orientation of the crescent by about 4.5 degrees. Thus, instead of pointing less than 2 degrees north of Mecca, the giant Islamic-shaped crescent would point less than 3 degrees south of Mecca. This did not pacify those who viewed this plan as being for an open-air mosque.[288]

It should be noted in fact that a *mihrab* does not have to point exactly at Mecca, for the simple reason that, throughout most of Islamic history, Muslims in far-flung parts of the world had no accurate way to determine the direction to Mecca. As a result, it was established as a matter of religious principle that what matters is intent to face Mecca. This was recently affirmed by Saudi religious authorities, after Meccans realized that some 200 of their local mosques do not face directly towards the Kaaba. "It does not affect the prayers" assured the Saudi Islamic Affairs Ministry.[289]

Another feature of the memorial was the enormous 93-foot minaret-like Tower of Voices, which can easily double as an Islamic prayer-time sundial.[290] Recall the minaret has always been used as a symbolism of supremacy. The tower is shaped like a crescent with a crescent-shaped top. As Mike Rosen of the *Rocky Mountain News* wrote, "On the anniversaries of 9/11, it's not hard to visualize Al-Qaeda celebrating the crescent of maple trees, turning red in the fall, 'embracing' the Flight 93 crash site. To them, it would be a memorial to their fallen martyrs. Why invite that? Just come up with a different design that eliminates the double meaning and the dispute."[291]

Due to the on-going protests and controversy, a modified design—a broken circle rather than a crescent—was adopted. An extra arc of trees was added to create a broken circle. The memorial was renamed the "Circle of Embrace." The two breaks are at the two ends of the extra arc of trees. However, remove the symbolically broken-off parts of the circle and what symbolically remains standing in the wake of 9/11 is still a giant Islamic shaped crescent—the original Crescent of Embrace design—pointing towards Mecca. The first phase of the permanent memorial was completed, opened and dedicated on September 10, 2011. It was autumn and the leaves were turning a bright flaming red.

In summary, three questions should be raised. Are these mosques, at Ground Zero and in Shanksville, to honor the perpetrators of 9/11 rather than its victims? Do these mosques and the Shanksville memorial indicate Islam's triumph and supremacy on that infamous day? Finally, how will the establishment of these mosques and the memorial at Shanksville be viewed in the Arab/Muslim world far into the future?

23. For over one hundred years, the Arab/Muslim world has claimed to be "victims" entitled to compensation and acquiescence to their maximal demands.

Pre-dating the modern Arab/Muslim war against the State of Israel has been a deeply rooted religious element (discussed in more detail in the chapter on "Islam"). It calls for jihad—holy war—against the unbelievers, which includes the Christians, Jews, Hindus, Sikhs, Buddhists, Zoroastrians, Bahá'ís, animists and others. These infidels are blamed by the Muslims for resisting Islam as well as being responsible for the violence perpetrated against them and the absence of peace. The Muslim world is forced to take measures to protect the truth of Islam, by jihad if necessary.[292] Jihad is a communal and religious duty of Muslims against the *harbi*—the unbelievers or infidels. According to Muslims, submission to Islam is the only path to world peace. Muslims will violently react to any perceived slight directed against Muhammad and Islam. Examples include the controversy over the Danish cartoons in 2005, the naming of a teddy bear "Muhammad," by British school teacher Gillian Gibbons in Sudan in 2007, and recently the firebombing of the headquarters of the French satirical newspaper, *Charlie Hebdo,* on November 2, 2011, which ran a special issue with Muhammad as "guest editor-in-chief" and his cartoon depiction on the front page.

Yet at the same time, the Arab/Muslim world claims they were the victims of Ottoman Turkish domination, British and French colonization, US imperialism, Israeli occupation, as well as repression by autocratic and dictatorial Arab/Muslim regimes. For good measure, they now add the charges of being victimized by racism and "Islamophobia." These claims have developed into the veritable cottage industry of perpetual victimhood. There is an expression in Arabic that summarizes this dichotomy, "I hit him and I cried." The Arabs use this sense of victimhood to justify murder, mayhem perpetrated against the West in general, and Israel in particular.

Many in the Arab/Muslim world see their own lives mainly guided by outer factors: a fearsome Allah, an authoritarian father, influential imams, and ancient but strong cultural traditions. Thus, they very easily develop a victim mentality. Accordingly, these 'victims' blame the infidels for their 'plight' and see conspiracies everywhere. This victimization is central in Muslim leaders' rhetoric and politics. It is also found in the extravagant demands of street protestors and agitators for not only economic support, but also for the acceptance of shari'a, and deference to Islamic traditions over that of European laws and customs.

24. Since 1921, a Palestinian Arab state has existed in the Middle East, created by the British and then named the Hashemite Emirate of Transjordan.

Since the first partition of the Palestine Mandate in 1921, into western Palestine, i.e. the British Mandate of Palestine, and eastern Palestine, i.e. the Emirate of Transjordan, there have been numerous attempts to create a second Arab state in the territory west of the Jordan River. Proposals were made in 1937—the Peel Commission partition plan, and 1947—the United Nations Partition Plan, as well as over a dozen proposals since that time. Constant and repeated Arab rejection of all these proposals only accentuates the need to ask the question: Is there a need for a second Palestinian Arab state?

Must all national and ethnic groups that want their own states and have struggled for such a state get one, in the name of self-determination? If so, why have not all of the following areas been granted statehood? Starting with the greater Middle East, why have not the *Imazighen* (Berbers), who predate their Arab conquerors by millennia and who have their own language as well as culture, gained their own state. Why have the Sahrawi people, who are occupied by Morocco, not been granted their own state? Why is there no Riffian state of Arrif to be created from Morocco, a Kabyle state for the Kabyle people to be carved out of Algeria, a Darfur state established for the Fur, Masalit, and Zaghawe peoples of Sudan, as well as a Nuba state of Nubia cut from Sudan? Let us not overlook the need for a Coptic state made from Egypt, a Maronite state fashioned from Lebanon, an Alawite state as well as Jabal al-Druze—a Druze state, both made from Syria, and a Balochistan, and Kurdistan for the Baloch and Kurds respectively to be carved out of Iran.

Turning to Europe, why is there no independent Euskadi state for the Basques of Spain and France? Where are the insular states of the Faroe Islands, Åland Islands, Isle of Man, Canary Islands, Corsica, and a Republic of Sardinia? Why is there no state of Savoy, state of Bavaria, state of South Tyrol, and a Venetian republic? Where is the full statehood for the Republika Srpska, Abkhazia, South Ossetia, and Transnistria? Why deprive the peoples of Andalusia, Aragon, Asturias, Cantabria, Castile, and Galicia from achieving respective states from Spain? In a like fashion, where are the states for the Chechens, Circassians, Gagauz, Ingush, and the Tatars of Russia? Why is there no state for the Welsh of Wales, the Bretons of Brittany, the Flemings of Flanders, the Walloons of Wallonia, the Catalans of Catalonia, the Frisans in the Netherlands, and the Sami people in northern Norway, Sweden, Finland and on the Kola Peninsula of Russia? The preceding seven peoples all have their own distinct languages, cultures and long histories.

Looking at Asia, why is there no state of Tibet and a Uyghur state, both to be separated from China, as well as a Tamil state of Tamil-Eelam in northeastern Sri Lanka? Why is there no state of Badakhshan for the Pamiri people of Afghanistan, and Sindhudesh for the Sindhi people of Pakistan? Why are there no states for the Mizos and Nagas of northeast India, the Karens of Myanmar, the Acehans as well as the West Papuans of Indonesia?

Just briefly reflecting on sub-Saharan Africa (which has hundreds of ethnic groups), why is there no Tuareg state of Azawad, stretching across the Sahara from Mali to Niger, Ibo state of Biafra, Diola state of Casamance (southern Senegal), Lunda state of Katanga, Luba state of South Kasai, Lozi state of Caprivi, Baganda state of Buganda, or a state of Cabinda?

The reader should understand that the above list is but a small part of the various global ethnic and sectarian groups that seek a state, be it independent or autonomous. One important benchmark of nationhood must be the degree of difference from its neighbors, and the need for a state to protect that uniqueness. The Tibetans, for example, have their own special culture, language, and religion, which they will lose if they continue to be ruled by the Chinese. The Kurds have a culture and language unlike that of the Arabs or the Turks, and the Karens, have a language and religion different from that of the Burmese to cite but a few examples—however, the Palestinian Arabs do not. Why must they be given a second Palestinian Arab state? They already make up some 80 percent of the population of Jordan, a nation created by the British in 1921 from 77.5 percent of the original British Mandate of Palestine, which was to be the Jewish National homeland.

During the closing months of 2014, several Western European parliaments (those of Ireland, Sweden, the United Kingdom, France, Spain and Portugal) voted to "recognize" symbolically the non-existent "state of Palestine," perhaps it is time for the international community to extend such recognition to the areas mentioned above.

Hypocritically, cynically and employing a double standard the international community expects all the aforementioned peoples to get along with the nations of which they are a part—the Imazighen with the Arab states of North Africa, the Chechens with Russia, the Basques with Spain, the Tibetans with China, the Sahrawi with Morocco, as well as the others. Why not the Palestinian Arabs? Why give them a second state now? The answer is simple: Arab/Muslim pressure and global appeasement and capitulation to the oil-rich countries of the Middle East. We would do well to heed the words of British Prime Minister Winston Churchill, "An appeaser is one who feeds a crocodile, hoping it will eat him last." The Arab people already have self-determination as expressed in twenty-one sovereign countries. Is there a need for a twenty-second Arab state—a second Palestinian Arab state?

Should the Palestinian Arabs alone be acknowledged by many of deserving not one, but two states? Thus far, the historic record has shown a lack of Palestinian Arab ability to govern and police themselves. Recall that the PLO/PA governed Gaza since 1994, save for the twenty-one Jewish communities located there and subsequently evicted by the Israeli government in 2005. In a bloody coup d'état, that lasted from June 7 to 15, 2007, Hamas ousted PLO/PA Fatah officials and has exercised control of the Gaza Strip ever since. Thus, Hamas became an unelected dictatorship with no legal basis, since it never accepted the Oslo Accords agreements. Hamas turned the territory into a terrorist base as well as a rocket-launching platform from which to bombard Israel.

There never was a separate Palestinian Arab people, distinct from other Arabs during the 1,192 years of Muslim hegemony in Palestine under Arab, Umayyad, Abbasid, Fatimid, Seljuk, Ayyubid, Mameluke, and Ottoman rule. All through the period of the British military occupation and the subsequent British Mandate of Palestine, countless official British Mandate documents speak of the Jews and the Arabs of Palestine—not Jews and Palestinians. The Arab riots, violence, murder and mayhem of 1920, 1921, 1929, and 1936–39, was directed against British mandatory rule, and were misojudaic and anti-Zionist. They were not for the establishment of an Arab Palestinian state. The Arab battle cry was simply *Idbah al-Yahud!* ("slaughter the Jews").

At the start of the Arab Revolt of 1936–39 in the British Mandate of Palestine, the Arab Higher Committee was formed on April 25, 1936. A creation of the Grand Mufti of Jerusalem, Hajj Amin al-Husseini, it became the main political body of the Arab community. Pointedly, it was not called the "Palestinian Arab Higher Committee," or the "Palestinian Higher Committee" for the term "Palestinian" was associated with the Jews as explained below.

In 1937, a local Arab leader Auni Bey Abdul-Hadi, told the Peel Commission, "There is no such country [as Palestine]! 'Palestine' is a term the Zionists invented! There is no Palestine in the Bible. Our country was for centuries, part of Syria."[293] The eminent Arab-American historian Professor Emeritus Philip Hitti, testifying in 1946 before the Anglo-American Committee of Inquiry (also known as the Grady-Morrison Committee), made it clear to the commission that even Middle Eastern Arabs never thought of a separate Arab country in Palestine, "There is no such thing as Palestine in history, absolutely not."[294]

In fact, from 1920 to 1948, the term "Palestinians" and "Palestine" applied almost exclusively to Palestinian Jews and their institutions. The well-known Israeli bank—Bank Leumi, was incorporated on February 27, 1902, as the "Anglo-Palestine Company." Even after Israel's independence in 1948, this Jewish bank issued banknotes (until 1952 when it adopted its current name), inscribed

"Anglo-Palestine Bank, Limited." *Keren Hayesod*, United Israel Appeal, the official fundraising organization for Israel all around the world began as the "Palestine Foundation Fund" in July 1920. The Jewish Agency, a quasi-governmental organization that served the administrative needs of the Jewish community in the British Mandate of Palestine officially recognized in 1922, was initially called the "Jewish Agency for Palestine." *The Jerusalem Post*, an English-language daily newspaper founded on December 1, 1932, was called the *"Palestine Post"* until 1950. Even the Israel Philharmonic Orchestra, the leading symphony orchestra in Israel, was originally called the "Palestine Symphony Orchestra" when it was founded in 1936. Furthermore, a picture of the flag of Palestine in 1939 clearly shows the Jewish connection to the British Mandate. It appears under the listing "Pavillons" in the 1939 French Larousse dictionary. The blue and white vertically bi-colored flag contains, in the center, a gold Star of David, a universally recognized Jewish symbol that is also engraved in the State of Israel's blue-and-white flag.[295] During World War II, some 30,000 Palestinian Jews served in the British Army in two distinct Palestinian groups. The Palestine Regiment formed August 6, 1942, was 75 percent Jewish. The Jewish Brigade formed July 3, 1944, was comprised of almost exclusively Palestinian Jews.

The Palestinian Arabs of today, that reside in Judea, Samaria (what the Arabs call the "West Bank") and Gaza, speak the same dialect of Arabic, share the same Islamic faith, have the same family structure, customs, dress, food, music and social values as is found in Jordan and Syria. Indeed, many have strong family ties to Palestinian Arabs in Jordan and share a common border with the Arabs of Jordan. Furthermore, they live in an environment whose physical landscape, flora, fauna, and climate are indistinguishable from much of Jordan and Syria. These "Palestinians" possess no distinctive history, language or culture, and are not essentially different in the ethnological sense from the Arabs living in the neighboring countries of Syria, Jordan, Lebanon and Iraq.

The use of the name "Palestinians" for Arabs did not take general hold until December 10, 1969, when the UN General Assembly first accorded international recognition to a "Palestinian people" in UNGA 2535, and began passing resolutions thereafter affirming its legitimate and inalienable rights to "Palestine." Perhaps this appellation was adopted in part due to Prime Minister Golda Meir who told the London *Sunday Times* on June 15, 1969, that "there is no such thing as a Palestinian people." Despite the scorn and derision that was heaped on her then, the truth was still the truth and would be proven by the words of the PLO itself (*see* below). Two decades later, Meir's statement was no less true when the former US Ambassador to the United Nations, Jeanne Kirkpatrick observing the PLO's diplomatic successes in the UN General Assembly declared:

> The long march through the UN has produced many benefits for the PLO. It has created a people where there was none, an issue where there was none, a claim where there was none. Now the PLO is seeking to create a state where there already is one.[296]

Twenty-three years afterward, that truth still had not changed. However, it takes courage to state the truth as former Speaker of the US House of Representatives, and 2012 US Presidential candidate, Newt Gingrich, did on December 9, 2011, "I think we've had an invented Palestinian people who are in fact Arabs, and who were historically part of the Arab community."[297] The Palestinian Arabs are an invented people and their professed national identity is bogus not because Golda Meir, Jeanne Kirkpatrick and Newt Gingrich designated them as 'created" or "invented." They are a contrived people and their professed national identity is bogus because they, and their Arab patrons, openly say so.

Various Arab representatives of notable rank and importance have repeatedly admitted that there is a Palestinian state and it is called Jordan. Thus, the concept of a second Palestinian state is a sham designed to weaken Israel by demanding further territorial concessions. King Abdullah I of Transjordan at a meeting of the Arab League in Cairo, on April 12, 1948, told the representatives of the Arab states in attendance, "Palestine and Transjordan are one, for Palestine is the coastline and Transjordan the hinterland of the same country." On August 23, 1959, Hazza al-Majali, the Prime Minister of Jordan declared, "We are the Government of Palestine, the army of Palestine and the refugees of Palestine." Jordanian King Hussein's brother, Crown Prince Hassan, in an address to the Jordanian National Assembly on February 2, 1970, said, "Palestine is Jordan and Jordan is Palestine; there is one people and one land, with one history and one and the same fate." In 1970, PLO chief Yasser Arafat told correspondent Oriana Fallaci, "What you call Jordan is actually Palestine."

Jordan's King Hussein, in August 1972, again reaffirmed that the Jordanian and Palestinian peoples were one people, "We consider it necessary to clarify to one and all, in the Arab world and outside, that the Palestinian people with its nobility and conscience is to be found here on the East Bank [of the Jordan River], the West Bank, and the Gaza Strip. Its overwhelming majority is here [on the East Bank] and nowhere else."[298] Yet again, in February 1973, King Hussein announced, "The Palestinians here constitute not less than one half of the members of the armed forces. They and their brothers, the sons of Transjordan, constitute the members of one family who are equal in everything, in rights and duties."[299]

At the United Nations Security Council on June 11, 1973, Jordan's representative Sharif Al-Hamid Sharaf voiced his nation's prevalent opinion, "The new Jordan, which emerged in 1949, was the creation of the Palestinians of the West Bank and their brothers in the East. While Israel was the negation of the Palestinian right of self-determination, unified Jordan was the expression of it."

President Habib Bourguiba of Tunisia, in July 1973, not only stressed that Transjordan was Palestine, but warned King Hussein of the fate that could await him if he ignored his Palestinian population's aspirations. "With all respect to King Hussein, I suggest that the Emirate of Transjordan was created from whole cloth by the United Kingdom, which for this purpose cut up ancient Palestine. To this desert territory to the east of the Jordan [River], it gave the name Transjordan. But there is nothing in history, which carries this name. While since our earliest time, there was Palestine and Palestinians. I maintain that the matter of Transjordan is an artificial one, and that Palestine is the basic problem. King Hussein should submit to the wishes of the people, in accordance with the principles of democracy and self-determination, so as-to avoid the fate of his grandfather, Abdullah, or of his cousin, Feisal II, both of whom were assassinated."[300]

On March 14, 1977, in an interview with *Newsweek*, Farouk Kaddoumi, then head of the PLO Political Department stated, "There should be a kind of linkage because Jordanians and Palestinians are considered by the PLO as one people." In an interview given to the Dutch newspaper *Trouw*, on March 31, 1977, Zuheir Mohsen, Palestinian leader of the Syrian-controlled As-Sa'iqa terrorist group (between 1971 and 1979), revealed the change in territorial aspirations to include not only Israel but Judea and Samaria as well as the Gaza Strip. In doing so, the PLO admitted that the Palestinian people were in fact a PLO invention:

> The Palestinian people does not exist. The creation of a Palestinian state is only a means for continuing our...[fight against Israel]. In reality, there is no difference between Jordanians, Palestinians, Syrians and Lebanese. Only for political and tactical reasons do we speak today about the existence of a Palestinian people, since

Arab national interests demand that we posit the existence of a distinct 'Palestinian people' to oppose Zionism.

For tactical reasons, Jordan, which is a sovereign state with defined borders, cannot raise claims to Haifa and Jaffa, while as a Palestinian, I can undoubtedly demand Haifa, Jaffa, Beer-Sheva and Jerusalem. However, the moment we reclaim our right to all of Palestine, we will not wait even a minute to unite Palestine and Jordan.[301][302]

While his statement contravened the PLO charter, which affirms the existence of a separate "Palestinian" people with national rights, it was in line with As-Sa'iqa's Syrian-Ba'athist ideology.

Marwan al Hamoud, member of the Jordanian National Consultative Council and former Minister of Agriculture, stated in 1980, "Jordan is not just another Arab state with regard to Palestine but, rather, Jordan is Palestine and Palestine is Jordan in terms of territory, national identity, sufferings, hopes and aspirations, both day and night. Though we are all Arabs and our point of departure is that we are all members of the same people, the Palestinian-Jordanian nation is one and unique, and different from those of the other Arab states."[303] In a like vein, in 1980 Jordan's Prime Minister Abdul Hamid Sharif declared, "The Palestinians and Jordanians do not belong to different nationalities. They hold the same Jordanian passports, are Arabs and have the same Jordanian culture." Furthermore, in an interview with the Paris-based *An-Nahar Al Arabi W'al-Daouli* on December 26, 1981, King Hussein stated, "The truth is that Jordan is Palestine and Palestine is Jordan."

In April 1989, PLO "foreign minister" Farouk Kaddoumi stated unequivocally, "The recovery of but part of our soil will not cause us to forsake our Palestinian land... We will build our tent in those places, which our bullets can reach... This tent will then form the base from which we will later pursue the next phase."[304]

In a 1994 television interview for Israel Channel 2, Israeli Arab professor, Dr. Azmi Bishara explained:

I don't think there's a Palestinian nation. There's an Arab nation. I don't think there's a Palestinian nation. That's a colonial invention. Since when were there Palestinians? I think there's only an Arab nation. Until the end of the nineteenth century, Palestine was the southern part of 'Greater Syria.'[305]

This was two years before Bishara was elected to the Israeli Parliament—the Knesset. He was a leader of the Balad Party made up of Israeli Arab citizens who openly identified with Israel's enemies. In April 2007, Bishara walked into the Israeli embassy in Cairo and resigned from the Knesset after he got word that he was about to be indicted for treason for helping Hezbollah aim rockets against Israel during the 2006 Second Lebanon War. All of the above statements confirm that even officials in the Arab world realize that there already exists a "Palestinian" state and it is currently called Jordan.

Moreover, having tried to overthrow the Hashemite monarchy in Jordan in September 1970 and failed, the PLO nevertheless has on several occasions, made it clear that once Israel is eliminated, they intend to absorb Jordan into their "Palestinian" state. In a letter to the Jordanian Student Council in Baghdad, PLO Chairman Yasser Arafat wrote, "Jordan is ours, Palestine is ours, and we shall build our national entity on the whole of this land after having freed it of both the Zionist presence and the reactionary traitor's [i.e. King Hussein's] presence."[306]

Salah Khalaf, also known as Abu Iyad, the leading ideologue of the PLO and Arafat's deputy, in moments of candor made two admissions. In an interview with the BBC in1985, he admitted, "When we say occupied Palestine … we consider all Palestine occupied. Our resistance will be everywhere inside the territory and that is not defined in terms of the West Bank [Judea and Samaria] and Gaza alone."[307] In 1989, he revealed, that Palestinian territorial aspirations extended to both sides of the Jordan River, "I say that as soon as the Palestinian state is proclaimed on the very next day that state will unite with Jordan. That is because we are one people with one history. You cannot differentiate between a Jordanian and a Palestinian."[308] Thus, the bottom line remains that the idea of a "Palestinian Arab" national identity was created with one goal in mind, to oppose any Jewish sovereignty anywhere in the Land of Israel.

25. To fully understand the Arab/Muslim war against Jewish sovereignty in the Land of Israel, one must comprehend that there has been a continual and massive Arab/Muslim policy of role reversal and grotesque transformation of historical facts.

There is an ongoing Arab/Muslim policy of denying Israel's history and legitimacy, including Jerusalem's Jewish heritage as well as invalidating the Jewish people's experience in the Land of Israel. Furthermore, the Arab/Muslim states maintain that the Jews do not constitute a nation but are only a religion—a minority one at that—and therefore are not entitled to statehood. Hence, they declare Israel should not exist and the Jews should be a *dhimmi* people at best. Jewish history, heritage, and values were stolen, distorted and adapted to the Palestinian Arab propaganda narrative to fit their needs. Jewish vocabulary is appropriated for use by the Arabs. No matter how ludicrous such denials prove to be, they continue to be made by the Arabs as a means of denying Israel's right to exist as a sovereign nation. Endless repetition of these falsehoods becomes accepted "truths" over time. These big lies succeed in part, because many people do not know the history of the Land of Israel in general, and that of Jerusalem in particular.

The Palestinian Authority on numerous occasions denies a Jewish temple ever existed in Jerusalem, calling it "the alleged Temple." Recently, PA TV (Fatah) on June 2, 2011, declared that Psalm 137:5–6, which states, "If I forget thee, O Jerusalem, let my right hand forget her cunning. If I do not remember thee, let my tongue cleave to the roof of my mouth; if I prefer not Jerusalem above my chief joy" was first said by "the Frankish [Christian] Crusader ruler of Acre before he left [the Holy Land and] was borrowed by the Zionist movement, which falsified it in the name of Zionism."[309] For the record, Psalm 137, which mourns the destruction of Jerusalem by the Babylonian army in 586 B.C.E., is part of Jewish tradition and liturgy since then and has appeared in Jewish sources for thousands of years. The oldest surviving manuscript of the *Ketuvim,* or "Writings," which includes the Hebrew Psalms, is dated between 175 and 164 B.C.E. It contains Psalm 137.

Among the Arab/Muslim myths being foisted on a largely uninformed, naive and gullible world are:

- That "the nation of Palestine … [in] the Land of Canaan had a 7,000-year history B.C.E."[310]
- That Biblical patriarch "Abraham [referred to as "Ibrahim bin Azar"] was not a Jew, nor yet a Christian, but a righteous man, who had surrendered [to Allah and thus was a Muslim], and not an idol worshipper."[311] He bound and was prepared to sacrifice Ishmael, his son by his servant Hagar, rather than Isaac, his son by Sarah.
- That the "Palestinians" were the biblical Canaanites, Edomites, Amorites, Midianites, and Amalekites[312] mentioned in the Bible, though there is no archeological, scientific, or secular historiographical proof of such a connection.

- That the "Palestinians" were descended from the biblical Jebusites.[313]
- Denial of the Biblical accounts of the First and Second Jewish Temples.[314]
- That the Western Wall of the Temple Mount was never a Jewish holy site.
- That Jesus, referred to as "Isa," was a Muslim prophet[315] not a Jewish sage or the Christian Savior. He was sent to proclaim the coming of Muhammad.[316]
- That Jesus was a "Palestinian," not a Judaean.
- That Jesus was a *shahid*, a holy martyr of Islam, the only Palestinian prophet, and the first Palestinian *shahid* who was tortured in "Palestine."[317]*
- That at Arab/Muslim insistence, the noted twelfth century Jewish physician and theologian Rabbi Moshe ben Maimon, better known as Moses Maimonides (or by his Hebrew acronym—the Rambam) was classified as a Muslim named "Moussa ben Maimoun" by the United Nations Educational, Scientific and Cultural Organization (UNESCO). Thus, because he had been forcibly converted to Islam (later, in Egypt, he reverted to Judaism) he is categorized as "Muslim" by the UN's revisionist historians.[318]
- That the population of the Palestinian Arabs is always greater than the population of Israel.[319]
- That Israel took over "Palestine," displacing its original inhabitants, except no such independent Arab Palestinian entity ever existed in history.
- That the Arabs were driven into the desert whereas in reality, Arab leaders have vowed to drive the Jews into the sea. This vow reached a crescendo in May–June 1967.
- That the Palestinian Arab "covenant" (charter) replaces the Biblical covenant between the Judeo-Christian God and the Jewish people.
- That the Palestinian Arabs claim a *Haq al-Auda* (right of return) to replace the Israeli Law of Return whereby any Jew may return to Israel and become a citizen.
- That the Israelis are doing to the Arabs what the Nazis did to the Jews (presumably killing them by the millions in gas chambers).
- That the Palestinian Arabs speak of their tragedy as a "holocaust," denying the real Holocaust (*see* below) perpetrated on the Jews from 1939 to 1945.

All this is historical revisionism, or "counter-narrative." No matter what it is called it is a false invented history designed to supplant and replace the authentic history based on archeological evidence of a Jewish state—Israel.

A point of factual historical record needs to be inserted at this juncture. The Holocaust was the systematic, bureaucratic plan by the Nazis, to exterminate the entire Jewish population of the world. They succeeded in murdering six million Jews, though recent discoveries of heretofore unknown graves in Eastern Europe and Ukraine has pushed the figure to an estimated 7 to 7.5 million.[320] The Holocaust was the most profound example of man's inhumanity to man in history. The Holocaust was universal in scale. There were no reprieves and no allowances for children—they were murdered too. The technology used in the destruction of the Jews was of such magnitude that it was unprecedented in the history of humankind.

---

* It is believed that Jesus died between 30 and 33 C.E. The falsification of history according to this bogus "Palestinian" narrative is exposed by the fact that Jesus was supposedly a "Palestinian" some 102 years before the term "Palestine" was even coined by Emperor Hadrian in 135 C.E. Similarly, Jesus was claimed a Muslim some 577 years before Muhammad established Islam 610 C.E.

As the shadow of horrific death descended across Europe, millions of other peoples were swept into this net of cruelty and barbarism. While not all victims were Jews, all Jews were targeted to be victims. The universality of the Holocaust lies in its uniqueness. The event is essentially Jewish, yet its interpretation is universal. By the conclusion of the war, 33 to 40 percent of the world's Jewry was annihilated. The Holocaust was genocide, but not every genocide is a holocaust.

However, it must be emphasized in light of an oft-repeated canard, far too many believe that without the Holocaust there would have been no Israel. President Obama seemingly gave his imprimatur to this misleading linkage in his June 4, 2009 Cairo University speech, when he spoke of "the recognition that the aspiration for a Jewish homeland is rooted in a tragic history that cannot be denied."[321] Worse still, Obama's words reinforced the canard that prevails across the Arab/Muslim world that the Europeans decided to dump the surviving Jews from the Holocaust on unsuspecting Arabs who were living in an area that colonial Europe controlled. This narrative denies the factual historic record.

26. Due in large part to its geographic proximity to the Middle East, Russia has been a major power player in the region. This has been especially true since the late-seventeenth century with a few relatively short exceptions.

RUSSIAN INVOLVEMENT IN THE MIDDLE EAST	
TSARIST RUSSIA	
Seventeenth Century	
Date	**Event**
January 30, 1667	Under the Treaty of Andrusovo, Russia annexed Ukraine. This was confirmed by the Eternal Peace Treaty of May 6, 1686. The annexation brought Russia closer toward the Middle East and established more direct contact with the Ottoman Empire, the major Middle Eastern power, as well as its Crimean vassal—the Khanate of Crimea.
1695–1700	Peter the Great's Russian army captured the area around the Sea of Azov from Ottoman forces. This gave Russia access to the Black Sea, a gateway to the Middle East. From this time forward, Russia and later the Soviet Union, had a perennial desire to establish free access to the Mediterranean Sea and would regularly challenge Turkish hegemony over the Straits (*see* the "Turkish Straits" map).
Eighteenth Century	
Date	**Event**
July 21, 1711	As a result of the Russian defeat in the Russo-Turkish War, 1710–11, under the Treaty of Pruth, Russia returned Azov to Ottoman Turkey.
September 12, 1723	By the terms of the Treaty of St. Petersburg, signed at the conclusion of the Russo-Persian War, 1722–23, Russia annexed the southern and western shores of the Caspian Sea including Baku. However, the territory was returned to Persia by 1735.
June 12, 1724	Due to Turkish intervention in the Russo-Persian War, 1722–23, both Russia and Turkey sought to gain territory at Persia's expense. By the Treaty of Constantinople, Turkey gained territory in western Persia, including Tabriz and Russia gained territory in northern Persia.

October 3, 1739	Due to the Russo-Turkish War, 1736–39, and the terms of the Treaty of Nissa, Russia was forced to give up its claims to the Crimea, but retained control of Azov.
July 21, 1774	Due to the Russo-Turkish War, 1768–74, the Crimea fell under Russian influence again, as per the terms of the Treaty of Kuchuk Kainarji. Russia also received the ambiguous right to protect Christian Orthodox rights in Ottoman Turkish-controlled territory.
April 8, 1783	Under Catherine II (the Great), Russia annexed the entire Crimean Peninsula.
1783	Eastern Georgia voluntarily accepted Russian protection. In 1801, fearing Persian invasion, it was formally incorporated into the Russian Empire.
January 9, 1792	After Turkey's defeat in the Russo-Turkish War, 1787–92, the Treaty of Jassy granted Russia possession of the northwestern coast of the Black Sea.
Nineteenth Century	
Date	**Event**
1801–10	Russian expansion to the south continued, as it acquired territory in the Caucasus—the land bridge to the Middle East—including Abkhazia, Imeritia, Ossetia, and Chechnya.
October 24, 1813	Due to the Russo-Persian War, 1804–13, and the Treaty of Gulistan, Russia gained all of Georgia, Dagestan, Karanakh, and northern Azerbaijan, in the Caucasus region. The subjugation of Dagestan was finally completed in 1859.
1813–1907	From 1813 until the Anglo-Russian Convention of 1907, the British Empire and the Russian Empire engaged in what became known as "the Great Game".[322] "The Great Game" was the strategic rivalry and conflict between the two empires for supremacy in Central Asia.
February 21, 1828	The Treaty of Turkmenchai, concluded at the end of the second Russo-Persian War, 1825–28, expanded Russian territorial holdings—including parts of present-day Armenia and Azerbaijan—up to the Aras River. Persia lost all its territory west of the Caspian Sea. Only Russian warships were henceforth allowed in the Caspian Sea.
February 12, 1829 (January 29 O.S.)	A Persian mob of some 500, egged on by a hysterical nationalistic mullah who had declared a jihad against Russia, marched against the Russian Embassy in Tehran. Russian historians claim that the British Embassy had a hand in instigating the plot. By the time the mob reached the Russian Embassy it numbered over 10,000. The mob stormed the embassy, overpowered the Cossack guards and killed all embassy personnel except for one clerk, who managed to jump over a wall and escape. Russian ambassador Alexander Griboyedov was first decapitated and then torn apart limb by limb. His head was paraded for three days before a jeering populace on the streets of Tehran. The Russian government demanded severe punishments of those persons responsible and threatened war. In fear, the Shah's court apologized and sent the Shah's son, Hosrov-Mirza, to St. Petersburg on a reconciliation mission. There the prince gave the Nadir Shah diamond, weighing 90 carats, to the Russian Tsar Nicholas I, as a present. The diamond had once belonged to India before being stolen during the Mughal invasion and is now on permanent exhibit in the Kremlin Armory. Note the similarity to the Iranian seizure of the US Embassy in 1979, but the difference in outcome!

September 14, 1829	The Treaty of Adrianople concluded the Russo-Turkish War, 1828–29. Aside from considerable European territories, it gave Russia the province of Akhaltsikh (in present-day Georgia) located in the Caucasus region of eastern Ottoman Turkey.
1852	A question of jurisdiction of the Christian Holy Places in Turkish-controlled Jerusalem set Russia on one hand, against the United Kingdom and France on the other. The United Kingdom and France were fearful of Russian expansionist moves into the Middle East, while Russia sought unrestricted egress from the Black Sea into the Mediterranean Sea at the expense of Ottoman Turkey. In July 1853, Russian forces moved into the Danubian principalities to pressure the Ottoman Turks not to change the status regarding the Holy Places. As a result, on October 23, 1853, Turkey declared war on Russia.
November 30, 1853	Russian battleships led by Pavel Nakhimov destroyed an Ottoman fleet at the Battle of Sinop, precipitating hostilities in the Crimean War, 1853–56. When the Russians refused to withdraw, France declared war on Russia, March 27, 1854, followed by the United Kingdom on March 28. Both Western nations supported Turkey.
By 1864	Russia expanded southward towards the Persian Gulf and the Indian Ocean annexing most of present-day Kazakhstan.
March 3, 1878	The Treaty of San Stefano ended the Russo-Turkish War, 1877–78. Defeated, Turkey ceded Batumi, Kars, Ardahan and other territories in the Caucasus, to Russia.
By 1884	Persia was forced to accept the Atrak River as the boundary between Persia and the Russian Empire.
By 1894	Russian expansion moved closer to the Persian Gulf and Indian Ocean reaching the present-day borders with Iran and Afghanistan, and adding the territories of present day Uzbekistan, Turkmenistan, Kyrgyzstan, and Tajikistan to the Russian Empire.
Twentieth Century	
Date	**Event**
By 1903	Azerbaijan was divided between Russia and Persia.
August 31, 1907	The United Kingdom and Russia signed the Anglo-Russian Convention. By its terms, Persia was divided into spheres of influence, with the Russians in the north controlling most large cities, and the British in the south adjacent to British Baluchistan to defend the approaches to India. The remainder of the country, in the southwest was designated neutral (*see* the "Great Game and the Middle East in 1914" map).
November 29, 1911	Russia opposed the financial reform mission to Persia, of American Morgan Schuster, who had been named Treasurer-General by the Persian *Majlis* (parliament). Russia issued three ultimatums and landed additional troops in Persia.
December 24, 1911	The *Majlis* rejected the Russian ultimatums, but the vice-Regent expelled Schuster and his reform efforts came to naught.

1914–18	During the Caucasus Campaign of World War I, Russian forces occupied areas of eastern Anatolia and the northern provinces of Persia (Iran). All Russian-controlled Ottoman territory was relinquished because of the Treaty of Brest-Litovsk, March 3, 1918. The treaty, signed by the new Bolshevik (communist) government of Russia and Germany as well as the other Central Powers effectively ended Russian participation in World War I.
May 16, 1916	The secret Sykes-Picot Agreement was concluded between the United Kingdom and France. Russia became a party to the agreement thanks to the effort of Foreign Minister Sergey Sazonov. Russia was to receive Constantinople, the Turkish Straits and the Ottoman Armenian vilayets of Van, Bitlis, Trabzon, and Erzurum, as well as part of northern Persia (*see* "Sykes-Picot Agreement, 1916" map). When the Bolsheviks seized power in Russia in November 1917, they denounced the secret agreements and renounced the policy of territorial aggrandizement. The Russian push towards the Middle East temporarily halted.

The Sykes-Picot Agreement defined proposed spheres of influence and control for the United Kingdom and France in the Middle East should the Allies succeed in defeating the Ottoman Empire during World War I. Both Russia in 1916, and Italy in 1917, became parties to the agreement. Russia insisted that the area around Jerusalem containing the Holy Sites be made an international area (*see* "Sykes-Picot Agreement" map below). Once the secret deal was exposed by the Bolshevik government of Russia, the British and French disavowed the agreement, yet the San Remo Conference of April 19–26 1920 confirmed and the League of Nations Mandate system established new states in the Middle East that bore uncanny resemblance to the areas both the United Kingdom and France coveted (*see* "Middle East 1920" map). By mid-1921 the states of Lebanon and Transjordan were created from the Mandates of Syria and Palestine respectively (*see* "Middle East mid-1921" map). The Islamic State claims one of the goals of its insurgency is to reverse the effects of the Sykes–Picot Agreement.

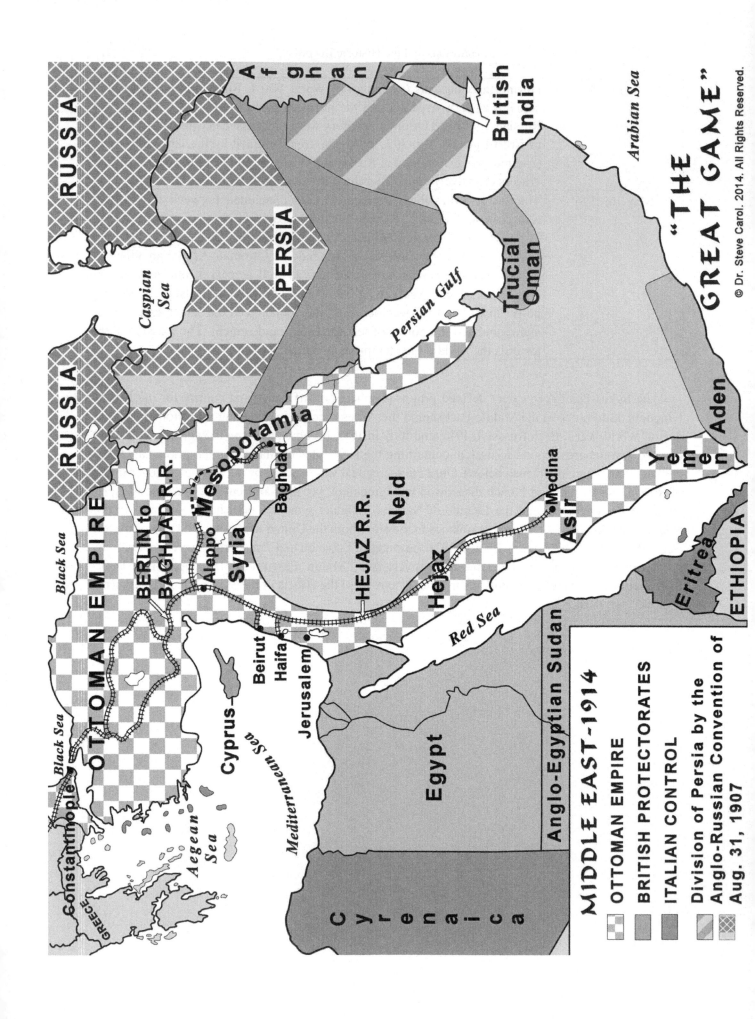

MIDDLE EAST~1914

"THE GREAT GAME"

© Dr. Steve Carol. 2014. All Rights Reserved.

Legend:
- OTTOMAN EMPIRE
- BRITISH PROTECTORATES
- ITALIAN CONTROL
- Division of Persia by the Anglo-Russian Convention of Aug. 31, 1907

Labels on map:

RUSSIA

RUSSIA

PERSIA

Afghan

British India

Arabian Sea

Caspian Sea

Black Sea

Black Sea

OTTOMAN EMPIRE

BERLIN to BAGHDAD R.R.

Mesopotamia

Baghdad

Aleppo

Syria

HEJAZ R.R.

Nejd

Medina

Asir

Yemen

Aden

Hejaz

Trucial Oman

Persian Gulf

Beirut

Haifa

Jerusalem

Cyprus

Mediterranean Sea

Aegean Sea

GREECE

Constantinople

Red Sea

Eritrea

ETHIOPIA

Egypt

Cyrenaica

Anglo-Egyptian Sudan

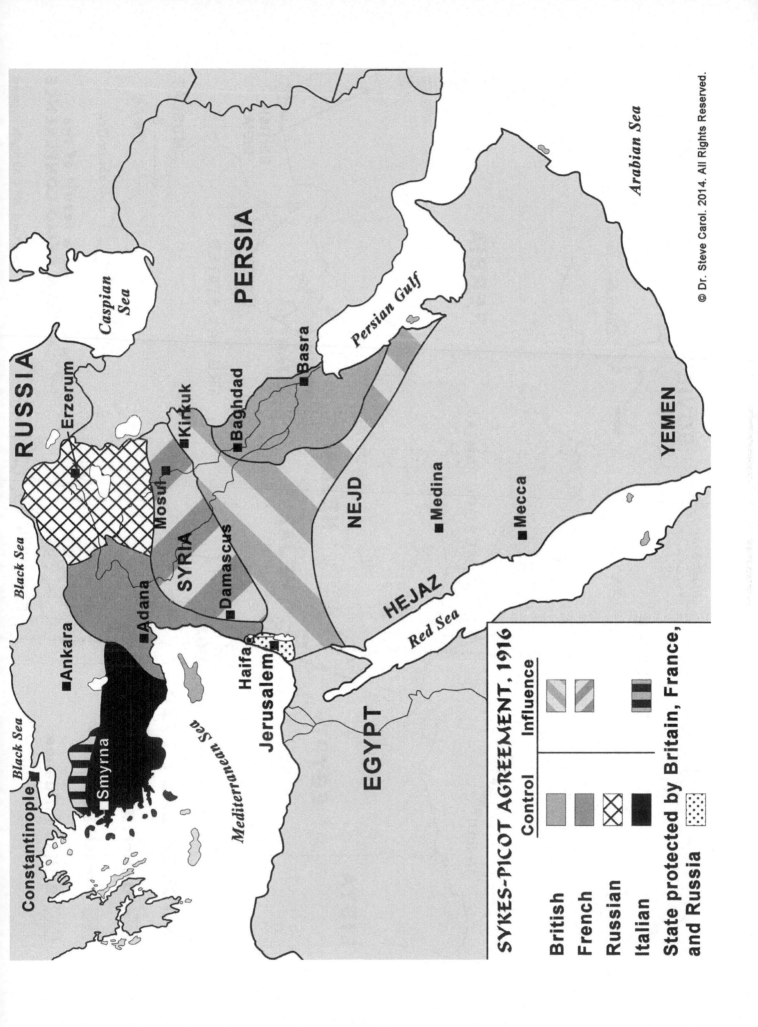

SYKES–PICOT AGREEMENT, 1916

Control   Influence

British

French

Russian

Italian

State protected by Britain, France, and Russia

© Dr. Steve Carol. 2014. All Rights Reserved.

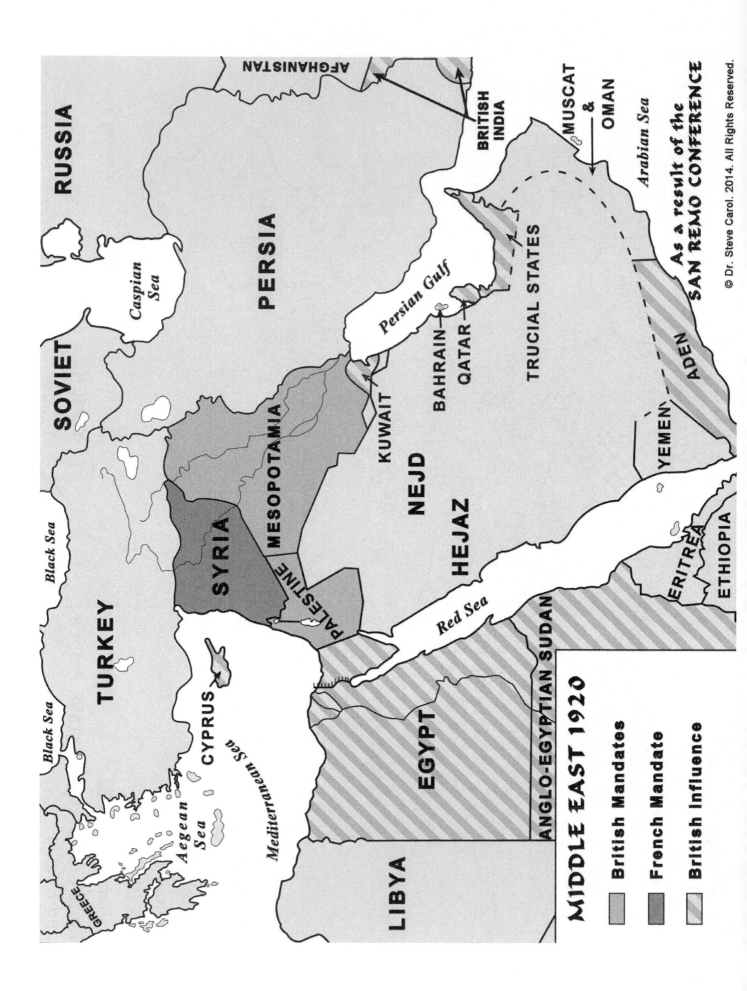

MIDDLE EAST 1920

British Mandates

French Mandate

British Influence

As a result of the SAN REMO CONFERENCE

© Dr. Steve Carol. 2014. All Rights Reserved.

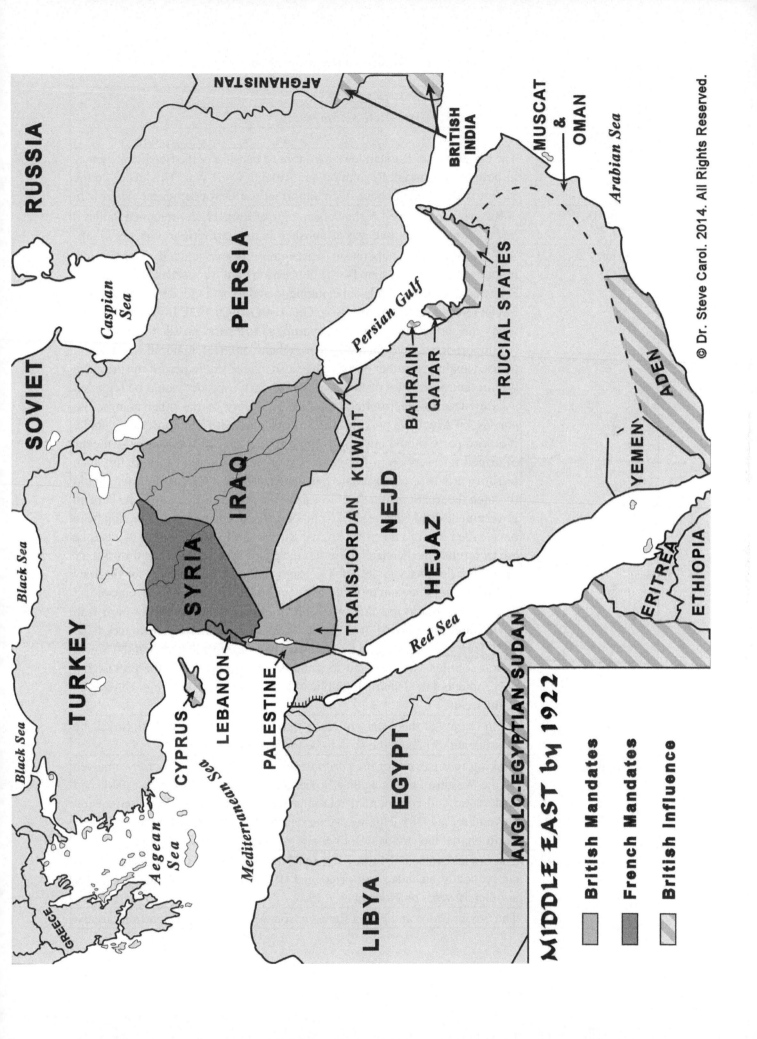

MIDDLE EAST by 1922

- British Mandates
- French Mandates
- British Influence

RUSSIA

SOVIET

TURKEY

Black Sea

Black Sea

GREECE

Aegean Sea

CYPRUS

Mediterranean Sea

LEBANON

PALESTINE

SYRIA

IRAQ

PERSIA

Caspian Sea

AFGHANISTAN

BRITISH INDIA

Persian Gulf

TRANSJORDAN KUWAIT

BAHRAIN

QATAR

NEJD

TRUCIAL STATES

MUSCAT & OMAN

Arabian Sea

HEJAZ

YEMEN

ADEN

Red Sea

EGYPT

LIBYA

ANGLO-EGYPTIAN SUDAN

ERITREA

ETHIOPIA

SOVIET RUSSIA	
Twentieth Century	
Date	**Event**
Post 1917	The emigration of Russian Jews was stopped because of the Bolshevik victory in both the Bolshevik Revolution and Russian Civil War. This deprived the *Yishuv* in the Land of Israel, of an important source for demographic growth.
May 18, 1920	A Russian force landed in the Persian port of Enzeli (later renamed Pahlavi) and a communist regime was established in the northern province of Gilan.
February 26, 1921	A Soviet-Persian Cooperation Agreement was concluded. The Soviets renounced all old Russian Tsarist concessions and properties. The Caspian Sea was recognized as a lake belonging to and to be divided by both nations. Soviet forces were withdrawn from Gilan by October 1921. In Article V of the treaty the parties undertook not to permit a third party hostile to one of them "to import or to convey in transit across their countries, material which could be used against the other party." They also agreed not to permit the presence within their territories of forces of a third party, which "would be regarded as a menace to the frontiers, interests or safety of the other contracting parties."[323] Article VI provided the Soviet Union with an important loophole: if a third party should attempt to carry out a policy of usurpation by means of armed intervention in Persia, or if such power should desire to use such territory as a base of operations against Russia, or if a foreign power should threaten the frontiers of federal Russia or those of its allies, and if the Persian government should not be able to put a stop to such menace after having been once called upon to do so by Russia, Russia shall have the right to advance her troops into the Persian interior for the purpose of carrying out the military operations necessary for its defense. Russia undertakes, however, to withdraw her troops from Persian territory as soon as the danger has been removed.[324] The Soviets would use this provision to occupy sections of northern Iran during and after World War II. In 1959, Iran unilaterally denounced the 1921 Treaty as unequal and inconsistent with the UN Charter, but the Soviet Union continued to insist on its validity. In October 1979, the provisional government of the Islamic Republic of Iran announced its formal abrogation of the treaty.
October 23, 1921	By the terms of the Treaty of Kars, that region was returned to Turkey by Russian authorities in the soon to be formed Soviet Union.
August 1924	Seeking to break out of the *cordon sanitaire* (a protective barrier) imposed by the Western Powers against Soviet Russia, the Soviet Union established diplomatic and commercial relations with Saudi Arabia and Yemen (on November 1, 1928). This was done despite the reactionary nature of these traditionalist monarchies. Both missions were withdrawn in 1938.
December 17, 1925	The Soviet Union and Turkey signed a Non-Aggression treaty. The pact was subsequently amended and prolonged (1929) and was prolonged again for another 10 years on November 7, 1935.
October 1, 1927	The Soviet Union and Persia signed a Non-Aggression and Neutrality treaty.

July 20, 1936	Under the terms of the Montreux Convention, Soviet warships were allowed peacetime passage through the Turkish Straits.
November 25, 1940	The Soviet government accepted the proposal of Nazi Germany that defined "the center" of Russia's "territorial aspirations" as "the area south of Baku and Batum in the general direction of the Persian Gulf." Immediately after World War II, the USSR attempted to implement this delineation.
June and August 1941	During World War II, the United Kingdom and the Soviet Union twice asked the Iranian government to expel the German nationals residing in Iran, and allow the Allies the use of the Trans-Iranian Railway. This led to increased tensions and pro-German rallies in the capital of Tehran. Shah Reza Khan refused the Allied requests.
August 25, 1941	British and Soviet forces cooperated in the land, air and naval invasion of Iran, code-named Operation *Countenance*. British Prime Minister Winston Churchill and Soviet leader Joseph Stalin had agreed that Nazi intrigues in Teheran had to be stopped. Both wanted supply lines through Iran to be kept open. Shah Reza Khan resisted for two days and then capitulated. He was deposed on September 16. By September 17, 1941, British and Soviet forces completed their occupation of Tehran.
January 29, 1942	The Tripartite Treaty was signed by Iran, the United Kingdom and the Soviet Union. Although it reaffirmed Iran's territorial integrity, sovereignty and political independence, the Soviets kept their zone of occupation under firm control, denying Iranian authorities freedom of movement. The Soviets helped found the Tudeh Party ("Masses" Party), a communist group and intrigued with Armenians and Kurds within Iran. Furthermore, the Soviets advocated the separation of Iranian Azerbaijan. Article 5 of the agreement committed the Allies (the United Kingdom, the Soviet Union and later, the United States) to leave Iran "not more than six months after the cessation of hostilities" between the Allies and the Axis.
1943–44	The Soviet Union established diplomatic missions in Egypt, Lebanon and Iraq. They maintained contact with a great variety of political and social groups including the Muslim Brotherhood and the Grand Mufti of Jerusalem, Hajj Amin al-Husseini (who was in Egypt from June 20, 1946). The Soviets also focused on national and religious minorities in the region, for example, the Armenians, Azeris, Kurds, and some Arab Orthodox Christians, who called on the Arabs to look to the Soviet Union for assistance. One noted example of the latter was Issa Daoud El-Issa, founder of the newspaper, *Filastin*.[325]
September 1944	The Soviet Union and Iraq established diplomatic relations.[326]
February 4–11, 1945	At the Yalta Conference in the Crimea, Stalin, Roosevelt, and Churchill agreed to the consolidation of the Jewish National Home in the British Mandate of Palestine, as well as to the opening of that area's doors to Jewish immigration in the immediate post-World War II future.[327]

February 1945	In London, the Soviet delegation at the founding conference of the World Federation of Trade Unions supported a resolution to enable the Jewish people to continue the building up of the British Mandate of Palestine as their national home.[328]
March 20, 1945	The Soviet Union denounced and unilaterally withdrew from the long-standing Soviet-Turkish Treaty of Non-Aggression (signed in 1925, and renewed in 1929, as well as in 1935).
Early Summer 1945–Spring 1947	The Soviets aided and abetted Jewish emigration from Eastern Europe, notably Poland, to the Western occupation zones of Austria and Germany, with the knowledge that the emigrants intended to make their homes in the British Mandate of Palestine. The significance of this assistance to the Jews was in no way mitigated by the fact that it was motivated by Soviet interests in the realm of great power politics, the growing Soviet interest in the Middle East, and not by any desire to help the Jews or the Jewish community in Palestine—the *Yishuv.* The Soviet's primary intention was to create a situation in which the occupation authorities and their respective governments would be faced with a situation in which the displaced persons (DP) camps would be a source of permanent unrest in Austria and Germany. It might create pressure and trouble at home, especially in the United States, and thus give the two Western allies a direct interest in changing the *status quo* in the British Mandate of Palestine in contradiction to declared British policy. In fact, that is what happened.
June 7, 1945	Soviet Foreign Minister Vyacheslav Molotov put forth the following demands on Turkey: that Turkey grant the Soviet Union military bases in the Straits (the Bosporus and the Dardanelles) area (*see* the "Turkish Straits" map); there be a revision of the Montreux Convention of July 20, 1936, to allow passage of warships even in wartime; that Turkey, annul the Treaty of Kars and retrocede the provinces of Kars, Ardahan and Artvin in eastern Turkey, to the Soviet Union (Russia had controlled these areas from 1878 to 1921). Demanded also, was a revision of the Turkish Thracian boundary in favor of Bulgaria, the Soviet proxy in southeastern Europe. These claims were rejected by Turkey, which was supported by the United States and the United Kingdom.
July 1945	The Soviets offered to drop their claim to Artvin, Turkey, in return for a military base at Alexandroupolis, in Thrace (northeastern Greece), near the Turkish border (*see* the "Turkish Straits" map). Again, this offer was rejected by Turkey and the Western Powers.
July 17–August 2, 1945	The Soviet Union made its additional interests in the Middle East clear, when it demanded the following at the Potsdam Conference: control of the Turkish Straits; a UN Trusteeship over Tripolitania (in present-day Libya) because the USSR needed "Mediterranean bases for her merchant fleet;" a voice in control of Syria and Lebanon; and a voice in the control of Tangier, at the western entrance to the Mediterranean Sea. All these claims were rejected by the Western Powers.

December 1945–March 1946	While US and British forces withdrew from Iran, Soviet troops stationed in northwestern Iran not only refused to withdraw but backed revolts that established short-lived, pro-Soviet separatist regimes in the northern provinces of Iran. In doing so, the Soviets violated Article 5 of the Tripartite Treaty.
December 12, 1945	The Tudeh Party set up the communist autonomous "Azerbaijan People's Government" with its capital at Tabriz (*see* "Major Oilfields and Secessionist Areas" map). It was headed by chair Sayyed Ja'far Pishevari and was backed by the Soviet Red Army under the direct orders of Joseph Stalin.[329]
December 15, 1945	With Soviet support, in a similar fashion the Kurdish Republic of Mahabad proclaimed its independence (*see* "Major Oilfields and Secessionist Areas" map).
May 9, 1946	After several delays and due in part to a combination of United States and UN pressure as well as Iranian duplicity, Soviet forces withdrew from Iran. The withdrawal of Soviet Red Army forces facilitated the collapse of both the "Azerbaijan People's Government" and the Kurdish Republic of Mahabad on December 11, 1946 and December 15, 1946, respectively.
May 14, 1947	At the First Special Session of the United Nations General Assembly, Soviet Deputy Foreign Minister Andrei Gromyko outlined the Soviet position on the Palestine question. The USSR would support neither an all-Arab nor all-Jewish Palestine, since it recognized the past and present rights of both peoples in Palestine. The Soviet government therefore, favored a federal Arab-Jewish state. Should that prove unworkable, the Soviet Union would support the establishment in Palestine of two independent states, one Arab and one Jewish.[330]
October 13, 1947	Soviet delegate Semen Tsarapkin, announced to the Ad Hoc Committee of the Second Regular Session of the United Nations General Assembly, that the USSR would support the partition plan recommended by the United Nations Special Committee on Palestine (UNSCOP).[331]
November 29, 1947	The Soviet Union voted in favor of United Nations General Assembly Resolution 181, which called for the partition of the British Mandate of Palestine into an independent Arab state and an independent Jewish state. They did so, not out of any historic love for Jews or Zionism, but for the realization of a Soviet geopolitical goal: the first step in the removal of the most powerful Western force in the region at that time—the British.

Arab attacks on the *Yishuv* escalated sharply after the United Nations General Assembly vote. It was obvious to all that the Jewish state would have to fight to achieve its independence. On May 8, 1947, Soviet Deputy Foreign Minister Gromyko told the First Committee of the United Nations General Assembly that Soviet Jews were not interested in immigrating to the Jewish state.[332] However, contrary to Gromyko's claim, several thousand young Soviet Jewish men viewed the increased fighting and the Israeli War of Independence as a just war of national liberation. It was compared to the Spanish Civil War (1936–39) during which Soviet volunteers went to Spain to fight against fascism.[333] Such sentiments were the last thing Soviet authorities wanted to hear.

Date	Event
Late March– May 1948	The Soviets, eager to get the British out of the Palestine Mandate, allowed Czechoslovakia—by then a Soviet satellite—to sell rifles, machine guns, bombs, ammunition, and Messerschmitt Bf 109F aircraft to the *Yishuv*, which was in urgent need to arm itself against the increasing attacks from the Arabs and neighboring Arab states. The British were actively collaborating with Transjordan's King Abdullah I to reduce the size of the Jewish state by war. At this time, the United States proclaimed an arms embargo and the United Kingdom continued to provide military equipment to Egypt, Transjordan, and Iraq.
May 17, 1948	Three days after the declaration of independence by the State of Israel, the Soviet Union was the first nation to fully recognized Israel *de jure*. Within the next five days, Soviet-dominated nations—Byelorussia, Ukraine, Poland, Czechoslovakia, and Yugoslavia—followed suit. For the Soviets it was a major strategic achievement, as the British gave up their naval base in Haifa, their airfields, including Lydda (Lod), and the Negev Desert, which had provided a land bridge between British forces and bases in Egypt and those in Transjordan and Iraq.
May 20, 1948	In stark contrast to its later pro-Arab policy, the Soviet Union openly supported the Jews and their Zionist quest for statehood. In the United Nations Soviet Foreign Minister Andrei Gromyko declared, "Zionism is the embodiment of the millennial longing of a people driven out of its country by the Roman conquest and dreaming of a Return to Zion—an authentic 'Movement of National Liberation.'"[334] The next day, May 21, Gromyko condemned the Arab states for "sending troops into Palestine and carrying out military operations aimed at the suppression of the [Jewish] National Liberation Movement in Palestine."[335]
March 4, 1949	The Soviet Union voted in favor of United Nations Security Council Resolution 69, which called for Israel's admission to the United Nations. Israel was admitted by the General Assembly, as its fifty-ninth member, on May 11, 1949.

The reestablishment of a sovereign Jewish nation in the Land of Israel after 1,875 years led to the awakening of Jewish consciousness among Soviet Jews. This led to a spontaneous outpouring of support and sympathy for the Jewish state. This was perhaps best exemplified by the arrival of the first Israeli ambassador to the USSR, Mrs. Golda Meyerson (Meir), on September 10, 1948, when she presented her credentials to Soviet authorities. Her appearance at the Moscow Great Synagogue for Rosh Hashana (Jewish New Year) services on October 4, 1948 was electrifying. Thousands of Soviet Jews (some estimates claim 50,000) crowded the synagogue and surrounding streets chanting her name.

This reaction of Soviet Jewry was unexpected by the Soviet government, which had for decades been trying to create the "Soviet man" free of ethnic and national roots. The anti-Jewish campaign already underway coupled with Soviet Jewish sympathy for Israel, convinced Soviet authorities that there should be no contact between Soviet Jews and Israeli officials. Soviet Deputy Foreign Minister

Valerian Zorin informed Israeli ambassador Meyerson that the Soviet government would not tolerate such contacts.[336]

Soviet support for the fledgling Israeli state began to wane within a year. This was due to several factors, which were not directly related to developments in Israel. Starting in the summer of 1946, a misojudaic campaign began in the Soviet Union and its Eastern European satellite states. The campaign escalated in the winter of 1947–48. From December 1948 to April 1949, Soviet authorities conducted an "anti-cosmopolitan" campaign, which quickly became anti-Jewish and anti-Zionist. Anti-Jewish discrimination permeated the government, professions, universities, intellectuals, and students. Jews were publicly accused of disloyalty to their Soviet motherland and connections to the "imperialist camp." This campaign continued until the death of Soviet leader Joseph Stalin in March 1953. Notorious examples of this misojudaic purge included the following evens.

The July 4, 1946, KBG-triggered Polish pogrom in Kielce, which continued for months, resulting in some 2,000 to 3,000 killed. Most of the remaining 300,000 Jews of Poland emigrated shortly thereafter. In Czechoslovakia, Rudolf Slansky, General Secretary of the Czech Communist party, Vladimir Clementis and twelve others were arrested on charges of being "Titoists." The November 20, 1952 show trials that followed were blatantly misojudaic, as it was quickly pointed out that Slansky and ten of the thirteen others were Jews. The defendants were charged with being connected with Israel and world Jewry in a conspiracy against the Soviet Union and the Soviet-controlled states of Eastern Europe.[337] All were found guilty of "Trotskyite-Titoist-Zionist activities in the service of American imperialism" and hanged December 3, 1952. (Posthumously, they were all cleared in April 1963 and fully rehabilitated in May 1968).

On August 12, 1952, twenty-four leading Jewish poets and writers were executed in Lubyanka prison in Moscow, as part of a brutal campaign to eradicate Jewish culture in the USSR. This was followed in August, by the arrest of doctors who treated Stalin and other Soviet leaders. This "Doctor's Plot" was revealed to the public in the pages of *Pravda* on January 13, 1953 under the headline "Chronicles." Nine doctors, six of whom were Jewish, had been arrested, and said to have "Zionist-British-American" intelligence links. They had "confessed" to plotting to kill Soviet leaders. Two Politburo members including Andrei Zhdanov (who organized the Cominform) it was charged, were "murdered" by the "terrorist" doctors. The Jewish character of most of the accused was explicitly indicated. These charges unleashed a wave of misojudaic hostility in the USSR. It is widely believed that Stalin intended to unleash a nationwide misojudaic pogrom and conduct a last great purge of his loyal subordinates. His death in March 1953 precluded that. In April 1953, after Stalin's death, Soviet officials conceded that the charges had been falsified and that the confessions obtained through torture.

The result of the Doctor's Plot trials led to a severance of diplomatic relations with Israel in February 1953. Relations were restored in July 1953 after the death of Stalin.[338] The changes in the Soviet-Israel relationship occurred for the reasons outlined above. But moreover, they occurred due to events that had transpired. Israel had fought its war of independence and survived an Arab onslaught. It had concluded armistice agreements with four of its immediate neighbors. The need for Soviet weaponry was lessened. Israel, as mentioned, was admitted to the United Nations, which gave it international recognition. For their part, the Soviets, having helped Israel come into being had achieved a strategic goal, i.e. the withdrawal of British military forces from the British Mandate of Palestine.

From 1949, Israel was linked increasingly to the United States and what the Soviets termed American "imperialism." Furthermore, the Soviets resented the May 25 1950, US-British-French

Tripartite Declaration, which pledged to control the qualitative and quantitative flow of armaments to the Middle East—to prevent any future imbalance in that region, and to guarantee the territorial status quo as, set forth in the 1949 Armistice Agreements. The Declaration excluded the USSR from the Middle East, a region they were just beginning to penetrate. The Western attempt to maintain an arms balance was an issue that the Soviets would exploit to great advantage as the 1950s progressed.

As the 1950s commenced, the Soviets viewed the increased unrest and anti-British and anti-French activity in the Arab world as a useful tool in the Cold War. The upsurge of nationalism in Africa, Asia, and the Middle East could be used to Soviet advantage. Thus, the Soviets shifted their policy to one of backing the Arab world. Gromyko predicted with accuracy, that the day would come when the Arab states would look to the Soviet Union for assistance.[339]

An early sign of this Soviet shift to a pro-Arab policy occurred in October 1951, when Egypt prevented the formation of the Middle East Command, of which it was to have been a founding member. Egypt rejected the invitation to join, extended to it by the United States, the United Kingdom, France, and Turkey. The Soviet Union, fearful of Western alliance building and encirclement, was most appreciative giving a note to that effect to the Egyptian ambassador to Moscow on November 21, 1951.[340] The Soviets then began to take an active interest in the Egyptian struggle against the British presence in that nation.

Throughout the Cold War era (1945–91), strategic considerations and not ideological preferences shaped Soviet diplomacy in the Middle East. In all instances, local communists were expendable. The hallmark of Soviet policy in the Middle East was persistence rather than success. A primary goal was eroding Western positions and influence in the region. The Soviets supported anti-Western regimes and sought, with notable success, the removal of Western—American, British, and French—bases from the Middle East.

Date	Event
January 16–March 6, 1954	An Egyptian "economic delegation" headed by Deputy Minister of War Hasan Rajab arrived in the Soviet Union for a visit of nearly two months. The delegation visited several Soviet satellite states in Eastern Europe on the way to and from the USSR. The foundation for the later-announced Czechoslovakia–Egypt arms deal (as a "commercial exchange") was laid during this visit.
January 22, 1954 and March 29, 1954	The Soviet Union began its support of the Arab position in the Arab-Israeli conflict, signaling the shift of policy, with the use of a Soviet veto in the United Nations Security Council. The first veto in January was against the B'not Yaacov water project in the Israeli-Syrian demilitarized zone.[341] In March, the Soviets vetoed a New Zealand draft resolution calling on Egypt to comply with a 1951 Security Council resolution, regarding the right of free unhindered Israeli passage through the Suez Canal and the Straits of Tiran.[342] Henceforth, the Soviets would provide diplomatic cover for "progressive" and "friendly" Arab regimes at the United Nations and other international forums.
November 6, 1954	Iraq severed diplomatic relations with the USSR. The Soviets had opposed the proposed creation of a Middle East Defense Organization (MEDO), which would include Iraq. MEDO evolved into the Baghdad Pact formed on February 24, 1955.

End of January 1955	Soviet Foreign Minister Dmitri Shepilov concluded a $250 million arms-for-barter trade agreement with Egypt. In fact, Soviet sources described the transaction as an ordinary commercial exchange.[343] To camouflage this new direct Soviet involvement in the Middle East, the arms deal would be publicized at the appropriate time as a "Czechoslovakia–Egypt arms deal" and shipments made indirectly via Yugoslavia. The Soviets would establish the circuitous route—Soviet Union to Czechoslovakia, via Yugoslavia to Egypt (and later Syria)—with the signing of the Belgrade Declaration between the USSR and Yugoslavia on June 2, 1955. The Soviet–Egypt deal included 200 T-34 tanks, 150 artillery pieces, 120 MiG-15 jet fighters, 50 IL-28 jet bombers, twenty IL-14 jet transport planes, fifteen helicopters, and hundreds of vehicles and thousands of modern rifles and machine guns. Later, through another satellite state, Bulgaria, the Soviets would sell Egypt four destroyers, two submarines, and one frigate for the Egyptian Navy. The Soviet shipments to Egypt exceeded in volume the cumulative total of arms transfers to all the Middle Eastern countries (except Iraq) by all other arms suppliers during the previous five years.

In February 1955, a power struggle in the Kremlin concluded with the faction headed by Nikita Khrushchev emerging in control. Khrushchev favored Soviet involvement in the Middle East. The new Soviet leadership saw opportunities to gain influence in the region at comparatively little cost. It enabled the Soviet Union to leapfrog over the Western containment alliance system, then represented by the Baghdad Pact (*see* the "Baghdad Pact and the Soviets leapfrog into the Middle East" map). It also provided the chance to influence and perhaps control the flow of oil from the region. Additionally, it was an opportunity to begin to win friends and potential allies in the non-committed Arab-Afro-Asian world.

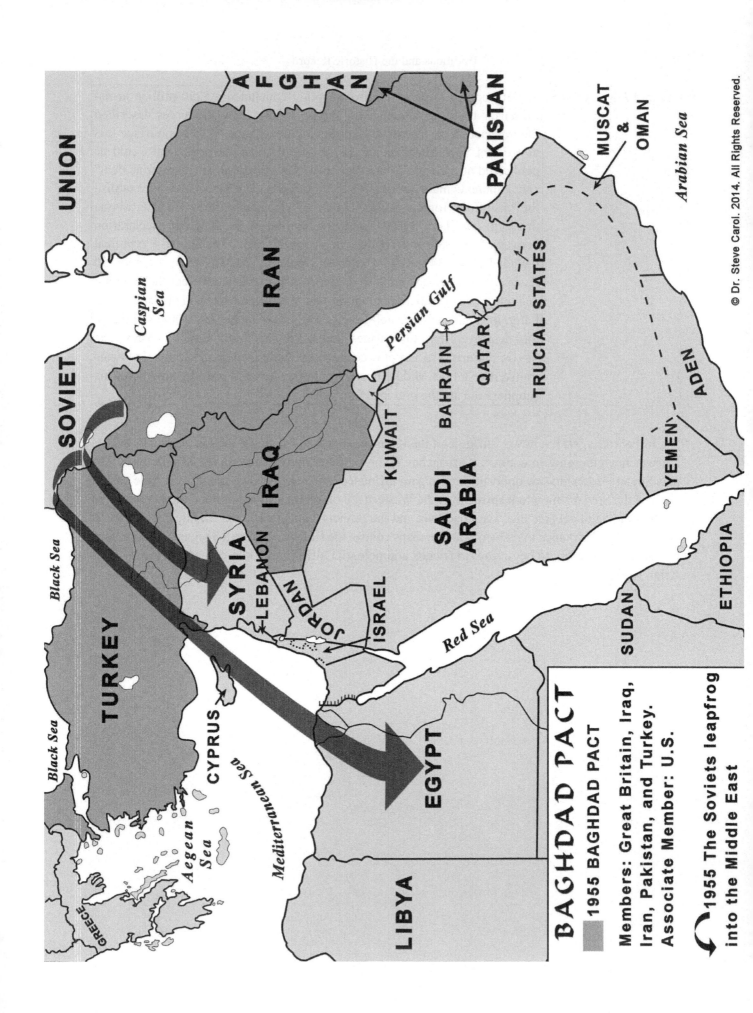

BAGHDAD PACT

■ 1955 BAGHDAD PACT

Members: Great Britain, Iraq, Iran, Pakistan, and Turkey. Associate Member: U.S.

⤺ 1955 The Soviets leapfrog into the Middle East

An important means for spreading Soviet influence was the conclusion of arms deals with various Arab regimes. This would break the Western arms monopolies in the region, and tie the Arab states to the USSR for spare parts and upgrades in weaponry. With the arms, would come instructors, technicians, and advisers as well as the necessity of adopting Soviet military doctrine, hence the need to send officers for courses in the USSR (most notably to Frunze, the Soviet military academy) where they would absorb more than strictly professional skill. Eventually, with the latest and most sophisticated weapons came Soviet crews to operate them. The Soviets implemented a process whereby the Arab states would become dependent on the USSR for military, economic, political, and diplomatic support. Additionally, it enabled the USSR to encourage and support nationalist movements against the West, including Western colonies, bases, and economic concessions. By supplying Egypt with Soviet weapons for example, Egyptian President Gamal Abdel Nasser was able to transfer older equipment to the Algerian Arabs fighting the French in Algeria. Later, Soviet arms via Egypt would flow to Algeria. The Soviets favored this arms transfer policy as it kept the French Army, the largest European component of NATO at the time, pre-occupied and pinned down in Algeria and not facing Soviet bloc forces along the Iron Curtain. It was in the USSR's interest to continue that state of affairs as long as possible.

The Soviets also engaged in economic assistance to various Arab states, specializing in spectacular projects likely to have prestige value. The Aswan High Dam and Helwan Steel complex in Egypt, the Homs oil refinery and Tabqa Dam in Syria, and the deep-water port of Hodeida in Yemen, were notable examples. The foreign trade of those nations, which received Soviet economic aid, was dependent on exports to, and imports from the Soviet Union and the Soviet bloc countries through the Council of Mutual Economic Assistance (COMECON). With all this in mind, arms deals were concluded with Egypt (late January 1955), Syria (October 1955), Yemen (March 1956), Iraq (1958), Algeria (1962), Sudan and PDRY (1967), Iran (1967), Libya (1970), and Lebanon (1971).

Furthermore, the Soviets made use of lease-deal arrangements. Under such an arrangement, the client state kept the Soviet armaments on its own territory but ownership remained with the Soviets until they had been paid for in full. These armaments could be sold and delivered to third parties at Moscow's discretion. Thus, in 1971, Egypt rushed Soviet equipment to India for use in the Indo-Pakistani War and in 1975 Syria sent Soviet armaments to the People's Movement for the Liberation of Angola (MPLA) in Angola for use in that nation's civil war. The lease-deal provided the Soviet Union with additional inventory space and weapons could be brought into use quickly in support of the Kremlin's political and military aims.

Using a growing number of proxies, the Soviets assisted the Arabs of Egypt against the British, the Arabs of Algeria against the French, and the Arabs of then Aden against the British. Additionally, in the coming decades the Soviets would support "progressive" revolutionary states and various terrorist groups against the "conservative" pro-Western regimes in the region. During the 1970s for example, the USSR would support Iraq and the People's Democratic Republic of Yemen (PDRY commonly known as South Yemen), against Saudi Arabia, the PDRY against Oman, Syria and the PLO against Israel as well as Jordan; and Libya against Egypt, Sudan, and Morocco.

Date	Event
March 1955	In the first display of Soviet public support for Syria, Soviet Foreign Minister Vyacheslav Molotov declared "the USSR supports Syria's attitude [against the then-forming Baghdad Pact and against Israel] and is willing to extend to it aid in any form whatsoever."

One of the great fictions in the historiography of the Arab/Muslim war against Israel was the claim that Egypt was forced to purchase weapons from the Soviet Union in September 1955. According to the Egyptian propaganda narrative, Egypt was forced to do this after an Israeli retaliatory raid, February 28–March 1, 1955 (Operation *Black Arrow*), against the city of Gaza. Israel's motive for the raid was to stop the increased Egyptian-sponsored *fedayeen* raids emanating from the Gaza Strip against the Jewish state.

However, the correct time-line of that first Soviet-Arab (i.e. Egyptian) arms deal is most crucial for a factual understanding of the events of 1955–56, culminating in the Sinai Campaign of October–November 1956. As has been noted above, the Soviet Union and Egypt concluded an arms-for-barter arrangement in late January 1955. On February 13, 1955, Cairo's Voice of the Arabs, in a domestic broadcast, announced that a Czech delegation had arrived "recently" to conclude an agreement for the trade of Egyptian cotton for "heavy machinery." The next day, *Agence France Press* declared, "it is learned from a well-informed source that Czechoslovakia is ready to exchange heavy arms for Egyptian cotton."[344] The fact that the Czechoslovakia–Egypt arms deal was concluded in mid-February was even confirmed by the Soviets, but only ten years later, when it declared "Nasser's government concluded in February 1955 a commercial agreement with Czechoslovakia for the delivery of arms."[345]

Date	Event
By the third week of July 1955	The first shipment of heavy weapons arrived in Egypt from the Soviet Union, via Czechoslovakia and Yugoslavia. This included MiG-15 jet fighters, and T-34 tanks. During the July 26, 1955 Egyptian Revolution Day parade in Cairo, fifty of the eighty jets in the fly over were MiGs and over 120 T-34 tanks participated in the parade.
September 27, 1955	The Soviet—i.e. "Czechoslovakia–Egypt arms deal" was publicly announced, but the arms were already in Egypt, since the deal in reality, was concluded earlier at the end of January 1955.
October 1955	The USSR concluded an arms deal with Syria via Czechoslovakia. It would provide 100 T-34 tanks, 100 MiG-15 jet fighters as well as machine guns, rifles and other equipment. The Bulgarians would sell Syria two submarines and a missile boat. As was with the earlier case of Egypt, Syria would deny the deal until officially announcing it on December 10, 1956.
October 1955	The Soviets began discussions with Egypt regarding the construction of the Aswan High Dam. By June 1956, the Soviets had offered Egypt a loan of $1,120,000,000 at 2 percent interest for the construction of the dam.
July–October 1956	The USSR gave full political and diplomatic support to Egypt during the Suez crisis.
October 31, 1956	The Soviet Union reestablished diplomatic relations with Yemen, signing a Treaty of Friendship.

November 5, 1956	During the Sinai-Suez War (October 29–November 7, 1956), the Soviet Union skillfully shifted world attention from its brutal military repression of Hungary (then revolting for freedom from Soviet domination) to the Anglo-Franco-Israeli attack on Egypt. Ominously, Soviet Premier Nikolai Bulganin sent three threatening letters to British Prime Minister Anthony Eden, French Premier Guy Mollet and Israeli Prime Minister David Ben-Gurion. To Eden, Bulganin wrote "in what position would Britain have found herself if she herself had been attacked by more powerful states possessing every kind of modern destructive weapon? And there are countries now, which need not have sent a navy or air force to the coasts of Britain, but could have used other measures, such as a rocket technique. We are filled with determination to use force to crush the aggressors, and to restore peace in the East. We hope you will show the necessary prudence and will draw from this the appropriate conclusions."[346] Bulganin's letter to Ben-Gurion threatened that Israel's "very existence … as a state [would be] in jeopardy."[347] In reality, other than prototypes, the Soviets had no missiles with a range of over 622 miles ready for use. President Eisenhower response to the Soviet missile threat was to have General Alfred Gruenther, Supreme Allied Commander Europe, hold a news conference, at which he declared that if Khrushchev carried out his threat to use rockets against the British Isles, Moscow would be destroyed "as surely as day follows night."[348] As a result, Khrushchev dialed back his bellicose rhetoric. The Soviets then proposed "joint and immediate use" of US and Soviet forces to stop the war; then the Soviets threatened to send "volunteers" to assist Egypt. The warning, coming only a few years after China sent one million "volunteers" to intervene in the Korean War, was taken seriously in the West, though the Soviets had neither the sealift nor airlift capability to send and sustain such an intervention. Arab public opinion credited the Soviet Union as the outside power most instrumental in rescuing Egypt, despite the fact that the Kremlin played only a secondary role, as compared to the United States, in forcing the withdrawal of British, French, and Israeli forces from Egyptian territory.[349] In the aftermath of the war, the Soviet Union emerged as a recognized Middle Eastern power. It played the role of "savior" and protector of Arab nationalism,[350] increased its influence in the Arab world, militarily re-supplied Egypt, and witnessed the continued erosion of Western influence in the region.
March 1957	Czechoslovakia and Syria signed an agreement for "Czech" (i.e. Soviet) construction of Syria's first oil refinery at Homs.
August 27–October 1957	Due to escalating rivalry and violence between Syrian Ba'athists and Syrian Communists and the fear of spillover throughout the region, the Western Powers began to apply pressure on Syria, including Turkish forces conducting military maneuvers along the Turco-Syrian frontier. The Soviets provided political and diplomatic support to Syria and threatened military intervention. To emphasize Soviet strength, Soviet warships visited Latakia, Syria, in September–October 1957. This was the first publicly recorded visit of Soviet warships to a Middle Eastern nation. To underscore the Soviet military threat, on October 7, 1957, (only three days after the Soviet Union launched the first artificial satellite—*Sputnik I*—into orbit) Soviet Premier Khrushchev would threaten, "if the rifles fire [from Turkey], the rockets will start flying." Turkey would "not last one day."

The Lebanon Crisis of 1958 with its accompanying landing of US Marines in that nation, and the US naval quarantine during the 1962 Cuba Missile Crisis, convinced the Soviet leadership of the inadequacy of their naval power. Accordingly, the USSR began to build a "white-water" fleet. Between 1962 and 1972, the Soviets constructed 911 ships, while the United States built only 263. In 1964, Soviet warships began regular patrols in the Mediterranean. From 1965 to the end of the Cold War, there was a constant presence of the Soviet Fifth *Eskadra* ("naval squadron") in the Mediterranean Sea.

Date	Event
July 18, 1958	In the immediate aftermath of the Iraqi Revolution of July 14, 1958, Iraq reestablished diplomatic relations with the Soviet Union.[351] Soviet military, economic, and technical aid followed. Iraq, in contrast to Egypt and Syria, paid for its purchases in hard currency or crude oil.[352] The Soviets were pleased to see Iraq leave the Western-sponsored Baghdad Pact, which collapsed, weakening the Western wall of containment around the USSR. However, in short order, the West reconstituted its alliance system, albeit smaller, as the Central Treaty Organization (CENTO)—formed on August 21, 1959 (*see* "Central Treaty Organization" map).
October 23, 1958	Soviet Premier Nikita Khrushchev announced the start of the construction of the Aswan High Dam across the Nile River in Egypt.
January–March 1960	In January 1960, Syria, then part of the United Arab Republic, heated up the Syrian-Israeli border with a series of shooting incidents. The Soviets began to claim Israel was preparing to attack Syria. The Soviet assessment alarmed Syria and brought UAR leader Gamal Abdel Nasser on an urgent visit to Damascus on January 14, 1960, to evaluate the situation. A day later, the Soviet embassy in Cairo delivered an intelligence report warning of Israeli plans to attack Syria. The Soviets had fed Egypt false information. On January 19, 1960, Egyptian armor (600 tanks) and three infantry brigades began crossing the Suez Canal and massing in the Sinai Desert. On February 1, 1960, in response to the Syrian attacks, Israel launched a retaliatory raid against Tawafiq, Syria, code-named Operation *Grasshopper*. This seemingly gave credibility to the Soviet charges. The Soviets continued to spread the disinformation that Israel was about to attack Syria. According to the Soviet media, this was part of a coordinated "Zionist-imperialist" plot to undermine the "progressive" revolutionary regimes in the Middle East. The Israelis were unaware of the Egyptian military movements for six days. At the time, Israel had only 30 tanks across the Egyptian-Israeli 1949 Armistice line. It was a major Israeli intelligence failure. This forced an Israeli counter-mobilization—Operation *Rotem*—which lasted from February 18 to March 1, 1960. At the end of March, the Egyptian forces returned to their bases west of the Suez Canal. The Arabs claimed a victory and the Soviet Union's image and value as an Arab patron was enhanced.[353] The Soviets would duplicate the disinformation scenario, i.e. Israel was preparing to attack Syria, in May 1967 with more devastating effects. At that time, the Soviets lost control of the situation and war ensued on June 5, 1967.

April 1961	Soviet aid and some 500 experts, helped build the Yemeni deep-water port of Hodeida, which would serve as a Soviet naval facility in the 1970s and 1980s.
July 29, 1961	KGB Chairman Alexander Shelepin suggested to Nikita Khrushchev, the Secretary-General of the Soviet Communist Party, that the KGB have Kurdish leader Mulla Mustafa Barzani (code-named *Ra'is,* Arabic for president) "activate the movement of the Kurdish population of Iraq, Iran, and Turkey for creation of an independent Kurdistan." If successful, the rebellion could disadvantage not only the United States and the United Kingdom, but also US allies Turkey and Iran.[354] It would also distract the West from the crisis then escalating over West Berlin.
September 1962	The Shah of Iran, Mohammad Reza Pahlavi, pledged to the Soviets that he would never allow American missiles to be based in Iran.[355] Ironically, this pledge was made a month before the Cuban Missile Crisis, whereby the USSR sought to base missiles in Cuba directed at the United States.
March 1963	The USSR established diplomatic relations with Kuwait.
June 18, 1963	The Soviet Union officially declared its support for the Kurdish movement. This was a tactical move designed to apply pressure on the new Ba'athist regime in Iraq, which was hostile to the local communists.
July 9, 1963	Soviet Foreign Minister Andrei Gromyko sent a note to the ambassadors of Iran, Iraq, Syria, and Turkey warning their governments not to launch a joint military intervention in Iraqi Kurdistan. Turkey and Iran gave up Operation *Tiger,* the planned link-up with the Iraqi and Syrian troops engaged in Kurdistan.[356]

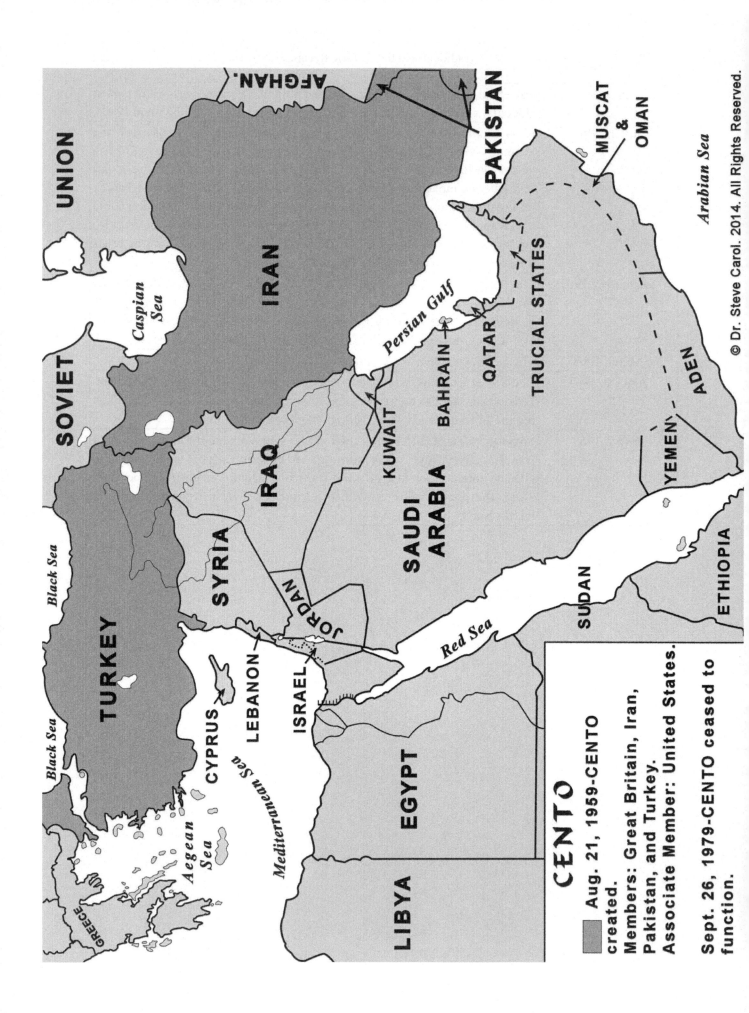

CENTO

Aug. 21, 1959-CENTO created.
Members: Great Britain, Iran, Pakistan, and Turkey.
Associate Member: United States.

Sept. 26, 1979-CENTO ceased to function.

To deepen the dependence on continued military supplies the USSR pursued a deliberate policy of exacerbating the Arab-Israel conflict in 1956, 1967, and 1973. Throughout the period, the USSR pursued a deliberate policy of preventing a settlement, both by further massive arms supplies and by unqualified backing of Arab policies. Thus, even though the Arab states were militarily defeated in 1956, 1967, 1973, and 1982, massive Soviet military resupply provided the war option to the Arab states almost immediately thereafter.

Date	Event
May 1966	Soviet Premier Aleksei Kosygin visited Cairo, Egypt, where he urged "progressive" Arab states (e.g. Egypt, Syria, Iraq, Algeria, and Yemen) to unite into a single anti-imperialist front. Syrian media constantly spoke of "an open and decisive confrontation with Israel,"[357] as the Soviets began an increased propaganda campaign accusing Israel of preparing an "attack on Syria." On May 24, 1966, the Syrian Minister of Defense General Hafez al-Assad declared, "We say, we shall never call for, nor accept peace. We have resolved to drench this land with our blood, to oust you [Israel]…and throw you into the sea for good." It must be remembered that this propaganda onslaught came during a period of relative stability along the Syrian-Israeli 1949 Armistice line.
November 24, 1966	Egyptian Field Marshal Hakim Amer visited Moscow and held discussions with Soviet Field Marshal Andrei Grechko (soon to be named Soviet Minister of Defense). It was during these discussions that the Soviets suggested and encouraged the Egyptians to expel the United Nations Emergency Force (UNEF) that had patrolled the Egyptian-Israeli armistice lines since late in 1956.

Soviet policies, exploitation, and encouragement were among the chief factors determining the course of events that led to the outbreak of war in June 1967. Perhaps the Soviet leaders believed the United States was pre-occupied with its growing involvement in Indochina. The Soviets had witnessed the ouster of pro-Soviet "progressive" leaders such as Ahmed Ben Bella in Algeria (June 30, 1964), Ahmed Sukarno in Indonesia (October 1–2, 1965), and Kwame Nkrumah in Ghana (February 24, 1966), as well as Western military intervention in the Congo (Kinshasa), the Dominican Republic and South Vietnam, in addition to the army coup against the leftist government of Greece in April 1967. Egypt's Gamal Abdel Nasser seemed a likely Western target for ouster. Thus, the Soviets sought to bolster Nasser and their position in the Middle East. The obvious means was to propel him to the leadership of the Arab "final battle" with the Israelis. Towards that end, Egypt and Syria had already concluded a mutual defense pact on November 4, 1966. From December 1966 to January 1967, Field Marshal Amer formulated the idea into an operational plan for removing the UNEF and reoccupying Sharm el-Sheikh overlooking the Straits of Tiran. The plan was passed on to President Nasser (*see* "Causes of the Six-Day War, 1967" map).

Date	Event
March 29, 1967	Soviet Foreign Minister Andrei Gromyko made an unannounced visit to Cairo, which was clouded in secrecy. Yugoslavia's news agency claimed the purpose of the visit was to discuss the future of the UNEF and coordinate Soviet-Egyptian moves.[358]
April 6, 1967	A high-level Syrian delegation sent to Moscow for the funeral of Soviet Defense Minister Rodion Malinovsky (who had died March 31, 1967) was escorted, as they departed, to the airport by Soviet Air Force General Batuv. Just why such a high-ranking Soviet Air Force general accompanied the Syrians was revealed the very next day.
April 7, 1967	The Syrians opened fire on Israeli tractors along the shore of the Sea of Galilee. The Syrians escalated the tempo and this became a furious one-day battle, involving artillery fire and an air battle. The air clash—the first in many years between Syria and Israel—resulted in the loss of six Syrian MiG-21s, (a quarter of their top-of-the-line MiG-21 fleet). It may be sheer coincidence, but Soviet General Batuv's farewell to the Syrian delegation in Moscow, could very well have been the final coordination as to what was to transpire the next day. Moscow would immediately replace the downed MiGs and Syria now had a pretext to invoke its mutual defense pact with Egypt's Nasser. The collusion between the Soviet Union, Syria and Egypt set the stage for the May "crisis" and subsequent Six-Day War.
Early May 1967	The Soviet Union officially "informed" the Egyptians that Israel was massing troops on the Syrian frontier, accusing Israeli actions as being part of an Anglo-American scheme against "progressive" Syria, plotted and financed by the CIA. The Soviets were specific in their charges, claiming that Israel would attack at 0400 on May 17, 1967, with thirteen brigades of troops. The Syrians began echoing the Soviet charge. However, the Soviets were feeding Egypt false information, using components of a ten-year-old Israeli plan—the Neeman Brief—stolen by Soviet agents. The Soviets fed Nasser the substance of the plan without indicating to him that it was a ten-year-old contingency plan. The Israelis for their part offered to take the Soviet ambassador to Israel Dmitri Chuvbakin, to the Sea of Galilee frontier to witness that there was no Israeli military buildup. He refused.[359] This was seconded by an aide mémoire sent by UN Secretary-General U Thant to Egypt on May 18, 1967, which stated, "On the basis of the fully reliable reports received from the Chief of Staff of UNTSO* in Palestine, there have been no recent indications of troop movements or concentrations along any of the lines which should give rise to undue concern."[360]
June 2, 1967	The USSR announced that Egypt was justified in re-imposing an air and naval blockade against Israel at the Straits of Tiran. The Soviets claimed the blockade was necessary and that "the United Arab Republic [Egypt] emphasizes that it is merely reestablishing the position existing prior to 1956, that is, before the Anglo-Franco-Israeli aggression against Egypt."[361]

---

* United Nations Truce Supervisory Organization.

Nasser knew the Soviet charges were false—and he knew that the Soviets knew he knew! Nasser saw these events as a Soviet invitation to escalate a confrontation with Israel. Nasser pretended to believe the Soviet charges. He was concerned of an Israeli reprisal raid against Syria, which would mark the beginning of a US-led campaign against the Egyptian regime. Both in Cairo and Moscow there was fear of a global "counter-revolution" the examples of which had already taken place. On May 14, 1967, the Egyptian Chief of Staff, General Muhammad Fawzi, was sent to Syria and reported there was no Israeli military build-up. This was confirmed at the 1968 trial of the Egyptian War Minister Shams Badran who testified that General Fawzi had reported the Soviets "must have been having hallucinations."[362]

Within the Kremlin, after the fall of Nikita Khrushchev, there was an argument between those (led by Leonid Brezhnev) who favored continuation of aid to "progressive" Third World countries and the faction that was opposed (which included Aleksei Kosygin). The Brezhnev faction prevailed citing the need for a Soviet "victory" to justify the continuation of Soviet policy, as well as stop the US "global counter-revolution." The Soviets wanted to protect "progressive" Syria and deter any Israeli military move. The Soviet leadership had a low opinion of the IDF, and underestimated Israel's ability and willingness to defend its rights. At a May 1967 meeting between Moshe Sneh, Israeli Communist Party leader, and Soviet Ambassador Chubakhin, Sneh told the Ambassador, "Israel will win the war." To which the Soviet diplomat sneering replied, "Who will fight? The espresso boys and the pimps of Dizengoff Street [the main shopping thoroughfare of Tel Aviv]?"[363] The Soviets regarded Egyptian military concentrations in the Sinai as sufficient to deter Israel from striking at Syria. Additionally, these moves would further polarize the Middle East between the "progressive" forces backed by the USSR, and the "reactionaries" and Israel supported by the United States. If Egypt's Nasser achieved any Israeli concessions, or proved victorious on the battlefield as Nasser estimated, that would provide justification for the Soviet policy. A Soviet-sponsored Arab "progressive" victory might even force US concessions over Vietnam. For the Soviets, it seemed like a low risk, win-win situation. The events of the Six-Day War, June 5–10, 1967, proved all these calculations wrong, as Israel won a smashing victory over Egypt, Syria, and Jordan.

Date	Event
June 9, 1967	The Soviet Union broke diplomatic relations with Israel. On June 13, the entire Soviet bloc, with the exception of Romania, but including Yugoslavia, followed suit. The Romanians were appalled by Brezhnev's argument that Israel was "a tool of Western imperialism." When the Romanians asked Brezhnev why he did not cut off with other "imperialists" as well, he lost his temper.

June 10, 1967	As Israeli forces battled their way up the Golan Heights, the Soviet Union threatened to intervene in the Six-Day War, fearing the capture of Damascus and the toppling of the Syrian regime. At 9:05 A.M., Soviet Premier Kosygin used the "hot line" to send an urgent message to US President Lyndon B. Johnson. Kosygin declared a "very crucial moment" had arrived. He went on to speak of the possibility of an "independent decision" by the USSR. He foresaw the risk of a "grave catastrophe" and stated that unless Israel unconditionally halted operations within the next few hours, the Soviet Union would take "necessary actions, including military." Johnson met with US Secretary of Defense, Robert McNamara and asked, "Where is the Sixth Fleet now?" McNamara replied, "It is approximately 300 miles west of the Syrian coast." Johnson then queried, "How fast do these carriers normally travel?" To which McNamara responded, "About 25 knots. Travelling normally they are some ten to twelve hours away from the Syrian coast." Johnson then ordered the fleet to move at top speed to 50 miles from the Syrian coast. As the US ships moved swiftly towards Syria, Soviet intelligence trawlers (tailing the US ships) signaled Moscow of the American move. The Soviet threats ceased, and a ceasefire took effect at 6:30 P.M. that evening.

The Six-Day War, in which a victorious Jewish nation defeated Soviet-armed Arab armies, impacted the Soviet Union also at home. The victory stirred up Zionist feelings and ethnic pride among many Soviet Jews, as well as demands for more freedom to emigrate to the Jewish state. A massive emigration of Soviet citizens from the communist "utopia" was politically undesirable, so at first the Soviets attempted to curb Jewish demands with various new rules and regulations. These included a regulation stating that persons who had been given access at some point in their careers to information vital to Soviet national security were not allowed to leave the country. Another directive invoked a so-called "diploma tax" of up to twenty years salary as a fee on would-be emigrants who received higher education in the Soviet Union. Additionally, the Soviet authorities targeted "Zionists" with a vehement propaganda campaign in the state-controlled mass media and outlawed Hebrew as a political language. Nevertheless, international pressure grew on the USSR to allow more of its citizens to emigrate and the door slowly opened. Since 1969, over 1 million Russians of Jewish origin immigrated to Israel.

The Six-Day War brought Western, notably US, recognition of the Soviet Union as a Middle Eastern power. US–Soviet discussions about the Middle East, especially the Arab-Israeli conflict would continue thereafter both on a bilateral basis, e.g. the Glassboro Summit (June 23–25, 1967) and the multinational deliberations at the United Nations that led to the passage of United Nations Security Council Resolution 242 on November 22, 1967. Before United Nations Security Council Resolution 242 was passed, the Soviet Union attempted a replay of the 1957 scenario turning an Arab defeat into a diplomatic victory. The Soviets demanded an unconditional Israeli withdrawal to the June 4, 1967 (i.e. 1949) armistice lines. They demanded later that Israel pay war reparations to the Arabs, who had been the aggressors! On June 14, the Security Council refused to adopt the Soviet draft resolution.

The Soviet Union quickly replaced all military equipment lost by Egypt, Syria, and Iraq, during the Six-Day War, augmenting it, both quantitatively and qualitatively. By September 1967, the Egyptian Army was completely reorganized and reequipped by the Soviets and stronger than before the Six-Day War of the previous June. Egyptian President Nasser even proposed to the Soviets that a

Soviet Air Force general assume command of Egypt's air defenses. In short, the USSR gave the Arab states the war option once again and denied Israel the political fruits of its military victory. Thanks to this Soviet resupply, Egypt was able to initiate (only twenty days after the conclusion of the Six-Day War) the 1,000-Day War of Attrition against Israel on July 1, 1967 (*see* the "1,000-Day War of Attrition–Arab Attacks" map).

Date	Event
October 21, 1967	Under Soviet guidance, INS *Eilat,* the flagship of the Israeli navy, was sunk 13½ miles off the north Sinai coast by Soviet-supplied Egyptian Styx sea-to-sea missiles, fired from a Soviet-supplied Komar-class Egyptian missile boat anchored inside Port Sa'id harbor. It was a premeditated planned attack. Of its crew of 199, 47 were killed or missing and 152 were saved (of which 91 were injured). It was the first occasion in history in which a warship had been sunk by missile fire (*see* 1,000-Day War of Attrition–Arab Attacks map).

After the Six-Day War the Soviet Union began to assist the PLO, the umbrella organization for a myriad of terrorist groups, including though not limited to, Al Fatah, the Democratic Front for the Liberation of Palestine (DFLP), the Popular Front for the Liberation of Palestine (PFLP), the Popular Front for the Liberation of Palestine-General Command (PFLP-GC), Popular Democratic Front for the Liberation of Palestine (PDFLP), the Arab Liberation Front, and as-Sa'iqa. The assistance included arms, training, finance, intelligence sharing, logistics, and diplomatic support. It was provided by not only the USSR but also Soviet bloc states including Cuba and the Democratic People's Republic of Korea (DPRK) also known as North Korea. This assistance continued to date, despite the collapse of the USSR. Soviet assistance was also extended to the Dhofar Liberation Front (June 1965–September 1968), which changed its name to PFLOAG—the Popular Front for the Liberation of Oman and the Arab Gulf (September 1968–August 9, 1974) and which changed its name yet again to the Popular Front for the Liberation of Oman (August 9, 1974–76).[364] The Soviets used their proxies in the PDRY, as well as Cuban and East German personnel to facilitate assisting the PFLOAG indirectly.

It should be stressed that from its inception in 1964, the PLO had and continues to have as its goal, the destruction of the Jewish state of Israel. The Soviet Union advised Yasser Arafat to reclassify, especially for Western consumption, the PLO from being a terrorist organization to being an organization fighting for "rights" and against Israeli "occupation." After the Oslo Accords of 1993, the PLO established the Palestinian Authority, to administer territory placed under its jurisdiction. Nevertheless, the PLO retains its original goal as outlined in its charter (*see* Appendix 8).

Date	Event
November 30, 1967	South Arabia was proclaimed an independent state as the People's Republic of Southern Yemen (PRSY). The Soviet Union accorded the PRSY immediate recognition.[365] On November 30, 1970, the name of the country was changed to the People's Democratic Republic of Yemen (PDRY). The PDRY provided informal base rights to the USSR, at the Khormaksar and other airfields, as well as the ports of Aden, Mukallah, and later Socotra Island. At these facilities, Soviet aircraft and vessels could find Soviet technicians, equipment, and spare parts as well as enjoy the usual services of a base without the political disadvantages of officially calling it such. By mid-1972, the Soviets delivered two squadrons of MiG-17s to the PDRY and trained sixty PDRY pilots in their use.[366] The Soviets also provided economic and technical aid. The PDRY served as a local actor to serve Soviet interests. Covert Soviet assistance to various "revolutionary," opposition and terrorist groups could be funneled through the PDRY, which became a main base for such groups as the Popular Front for the Liberation of Oman (PFLO), the PFLP, the Popular Democratic Front for the Liberation of Palestine (PDFLP) and the Eritrean Liberation Front (ELF).
December 1, 1967–February 8, 1968	As a result of its defeat in the Six-Day War, the UAR (i.e. Egypt) was forced to withdraw its troops from Yemen, where they had been militarily engaged supporting the Republican regime in the Yemen Civil War. As the last UAR troops left October 16, 1967, the opposing Royalist forces began an offensive against the last main Republican stronghold, the capital city of Sana'a on November 17, 1967. On December 1, 1967, the Royalists began a siege of the city. The Soviet Union launched an emergency airlift of arms, equipment, supplies and technicians to the beleaguered city. Soviet-piloted fighter aircraft flew combat missions in support of the Republicans.[367] This Soviet military intervention prevented the fall of Sana'a and with it the Republican regime. It was an example of early Soviet military intervention outside of Eastern Europe. The Soviet intervention forced the lifting of the siege on February 8, 1968. When Royalist forces again neared Sana'a in late October 1968, Soviet aircraft intervened, attacking Royalist positions. One of their planes was shot down and it was reported that the pilot was a Russian.[368] The Soviet intervention insured that the military stalemate between Royalist and Republican Yemeni forces would continue, until a ceasefire compromise was reached on May 23, 1970 (*see* "The Yemen Civil War–Stalemate and Conclusion" map).
1968	The Soviet Union began construction of the Tabqa Dam on the Euphrates River in Syria.
Between March and June, 1969	Twenty-thousand Soviet military advisors arrived in Egypt.

| 1969–78 | The Soviet Union and Saudi Arabia were at odds over the two Yemens' unification. They did not oppose unification per se, but tried to influence what system would govern such a unified state. Whereas the Soviets favored a "progressive," socialist, radical Marxist model allied with the Soviet bloc, the Saudis preferred a conservative and capitalist system, linked more towards the West. The internal power struggle between "moderates" and "radicals" within the PDRY, as well as intra-Arab rivalries, East–West competition and Soviet-Chinese rivalry over which nation should have predominant influence in the PDRY—made the situation more complex. By 1979, the Soviet Union stopped trying to achieve their form of unification for Yemen, and instead concentrated on building up the PDRY as a Marxist-socialist state allied to the Soviet bloc. |

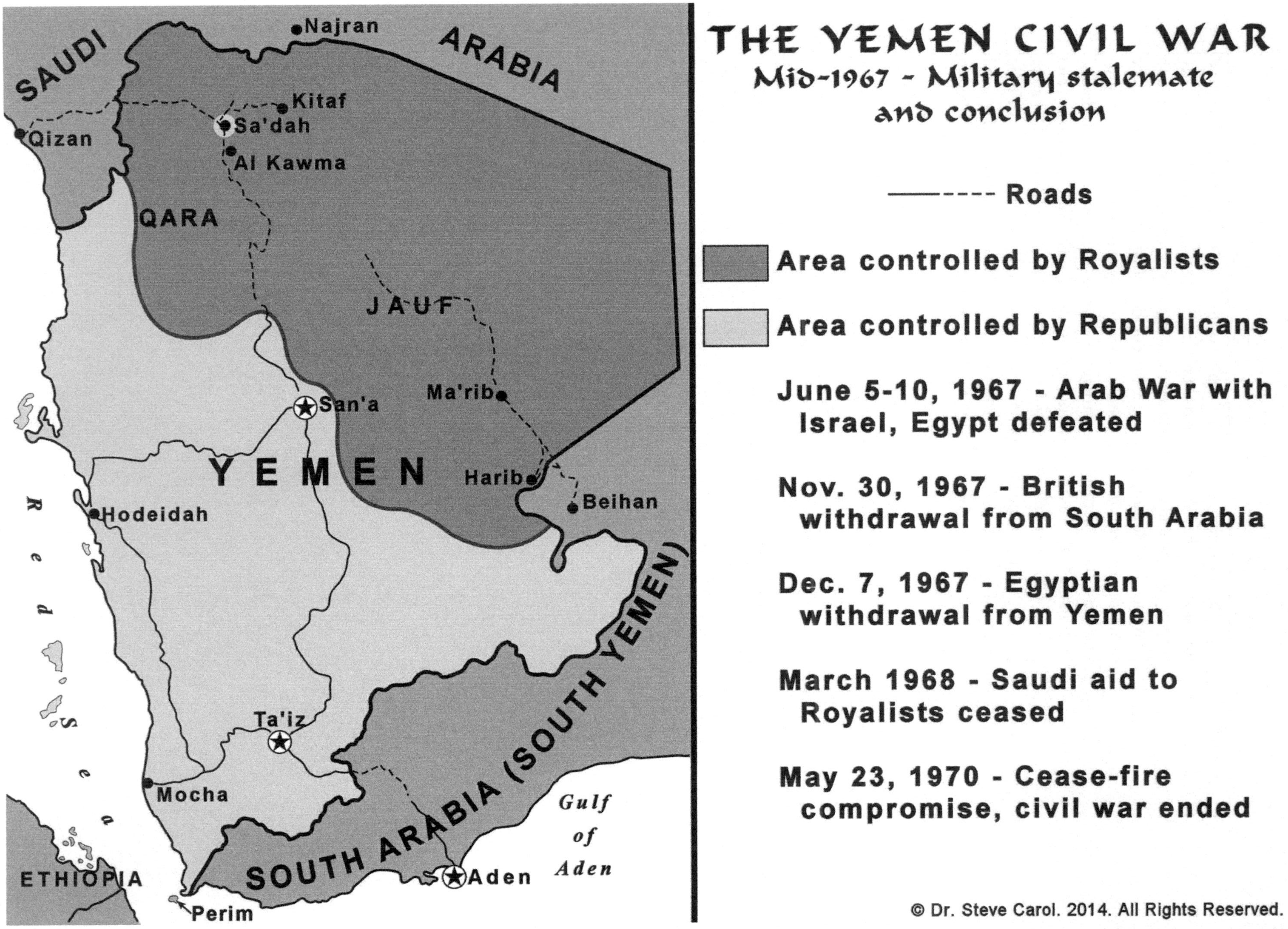

THE YEMEN CIVIL WAR

Mid-1967 – Military stalemate and conclusion

----- Roads

Area controlled by Royalists

Area controlled by Republicans

June 5-10, 1967 - Arab War with Israel, Egypt defeated

Nov. 30, 1967 - British withdrawal from South Arabia

Dec. 7, 1967 - Egyptian withdrawal from Yemen

March 1968 - Saudi aid to Royalists ceased

May 23, 1970 - Cease-fire compromise, civil war ended

SAUDI ARABIA

Najran

Qizan

Kitaf

Sa'dah

Al Kawma

QARA

JAUF

San'a

Ma'rib

Harib

Beihan

Hodeidah

YEMEN

Ta'iz

Mocha

Perim

SOUTH ARABIA (SOUTH YEMEN)

Aden

Gulf of Aden

ETHIOPIA

Red Sea

By 1970, the Soviet Union was openly proclaiming that Soviet ships were "now found where they are demanded by the security and interests of the Soviet Union. The tense atmosphere in the Middle East, created and artificially supported by imperialists in the interests of powerful monopolies, represent a real threat to the security of all Mediterranean states, including the Soviet Union."[369] It was not explained why the Soviet Union was described as a "Mediterranean state" when it had no frontier on that body of water.

Date	Event
February 19, 1970	An entire Soviet Air Defense Division was sent to Egypt, including combat personnel, as part of Operation *Kaykaz*. Soviet advisers in Egypt and Syria were assigned to various military formations down to battalion level. This included Soviet-manned anti-aircraft artillery, radar stations, command and control facilities, the latest versions of SA-2 (NATO code-named Guideline) and SA-3 (NATO code-named Goa)—the latter never before operated in the Middle East. Over 100 SAM sites were constructed in Egypt alone. A MiG-21J interception air brigade was dispatched to Egypt. 150 Soviet aircraft would operate from six bases controlled exclusively by the USSR. Soviet and DPRK pilots began to fly operational combat missions (*see* "The Soviet Presence in Egypt, 1970–73" map).
March 15, 1970	The first Soviet SAM batteries went operational in Egypt.
April 13, 1970	Soviet pilots in Egypt began defensive air patrols along the Nile Valley.
April 18, 1970	Soviet pilots began to fly defensive air cover over Cairo, the Egyptian capital. Soviet Air Defenses began an aggressive campaign to push the Israeli Air Force (IAF) east, back across the Suez Canal and further east back into Sinai. Soviet SA-3s began taking a toll of Israeli aircraft. The United States responded by sending electronic counter measures (ECM) pods to Israel.
July 21, 1970	The Aswan High Dam on the Nile River in Egypt was completed after over eleven years of construction with Soviet assistance, at a cost of $1 to 1.5 billion.
July 25, 1970	Several Soviet piloted MiG-21s attacked two Israeli A-4 Skyhawks along the Suez Canal. One Skyhawk was hit but managed to return to base, as did the other plane.
July 30, 1970	In the first instance of Soviet aerial combat since World War II, a Soviet aerial ambush over the Suez Canal resulted in a clash between twenty Soviet-piloted MiG-21 jets and an Israeli force made up of four F-4 Phantoms and eight Mirages. The Soviets lost five MiGs. Four Soviet pilots were killed.

August 7, 1970	The Soviet Union acted as co-guarantor (with the United States) of a ceasefire that ended the 1,000-Day War of Attrition between Egypt and Israel. Item "C" of the ceasefire terms read, "Both sides will refrain from changing the military status quo within zones extending 32 miles to the east and the west of the ceasefire line [i.e. the Suez Canal]"[370] Nevertheless, on the night of the ceasefire, Egypt and the Soviet Union violated the agreement by installing new SA-2 and SA-3 missiles in the thirty-two mile zone on the Egyptian side of the Canal. Within two weeks, Egypt had constructed between 20 and 30 new sites and moved up more than 500 missiles. The Soviets and Egyptians gambled that Israel would not respond so soon after the ceasefire went into effect—and they were right. Israel did nothing. This would have telling effect three years later, when Egyptian surface-to-air missile (SAM) anti-aircraft batteries along the Suez Canal, effectively battered the IAF in the first days of the October 1973 Yom Kippur War.
September 18, 1970	During the Jordanian Civil War (Black September) between forces of the Hashemite monarchy and the PLO, the Soviets urged Syria to intervene. Syria sent two divisions and 300 tanks into Jordan, on behalf of the PLO. It should be noted that while Syria's *de facto* leader Salah Jadid (1966–70) sent Syrian ground forces, including tanks, to help the PLO, Syrian Minister of Defense, Hafez al-Assad refused to send air cover. The two men were long-time rivals struggling for ultimate total power. At this time there was Soviet control of the Syrian army down to the battalion level (*see* the "Jordanian Civil War, 1970–71" map). It was the Soviet-Syrian-PLO hope to replace King Hussein's government with a pro-Soviet regime dedicated to the destruction of Israel. It would be a badly needed Soviet "win" in the region. There was additional concern that the 17,000 Iraqi troops already in Jordan would also move against the Jordanian monarch. At the same time, the Fifth *Eskadra* of the Soviet Navy was increased to some twenty surface warships and six submarines. By mutual agreement, Soviet amphibious forces were ordered to respond to any landing of US forces. The Syrian forces reached Irbid, Jordan by later that day. The Soviets had sent the United States an urgent note assuring the United States that the Soviet Union would not intervene and that it was doing its best to keep other countries from doing so. Clearly, Syria's actions belied the Soviet's words. The United States responded with placing 20,000 troops, including the Eighty-Second Airborne Division, on alert, secretly convincing the Greek government to provide staging areas, and increasing the US Sixth Fleet to four aircraft carrier battle groups, four additional destroyers, and two attack submarines. The Sixth Fleet moved closer to the Syrian coast on September 19–20, 1970. Furthermore, on September 21, 1970, the United States and Israel agreed to intervene if Syrian forces crossed a line between Irbid and Amman (which would signal the King Hussein's army had been defeated), with the Israelis poised to strike at the Syrian tanks. To convey the seriousness of their purpose, four IAF F-4 Phantoms overflew the tanks in a mock-air strike. The United States would oppose any Soviet-inspired counter-move along the Suez Canal or elsewhere, by use of the Sixth Fleet.

September 22, 1970	US National Security advisor, Henry Kissinger, spoke to the Soviet Minister Counselor Yuly M. Vorontsev, at a dinner party at the Egyptian Embassy in Washington, DC. Kissinger remarked, "The last time you [the Soviet Union] told me that the Syrians would send in no more troops." Vorontsov replied, "We didn't know the Syrians would cross the border, our own military advisers, stopped at the border and went no further." His words indicated that the Soviets were complicit in the Syrian intervention. Kissinger retorted, "Your client started it, you have to end it." King Hussein, with the assurance that both Israel and the United States were behind him, committed his small air force to attacking the Syrian tanks around Irbid. Some 130 T-54 tanks, about one-half of the invading force, were destroyed. The Syrians withdrew on September 23, as the Jordanian army proceeded to crush the PLO. The defeat of Syrian armor precipitated Hafez al-Assad's bloodless coup d'état in Syria, two months later on November 13, 1970.
May 27, 1971	A fifteen-year Soviet-Egyptian Treaty of Friendship and Cooperation was concluded. It was a *de facto* alliance of strategic cooperation. The Soviets gained the use of port facilities at Mersa Matruh, Alexandria, Port Sa'id, and Ras Banas. Additionally, six airfields were placed under exclusive Soviet control—Mansura, Janaklis, Cairo West, Beni Suef, Anshas, and Aswan (*see* the "Soviet Presence in Egypt, 1970–73" map).
October 10, 1971, November 6, 1971, March 10, 1972, and May 16, 1972	Soviet-piloted MiG-25s (NATO code-named Foxbat) flew reconnaissance missions over Israeli-controlled Sinai gathering information for the war that would erupt on October 6, 1973 (*see* the "Soviet Presence in Egypt, 1970–73" map).

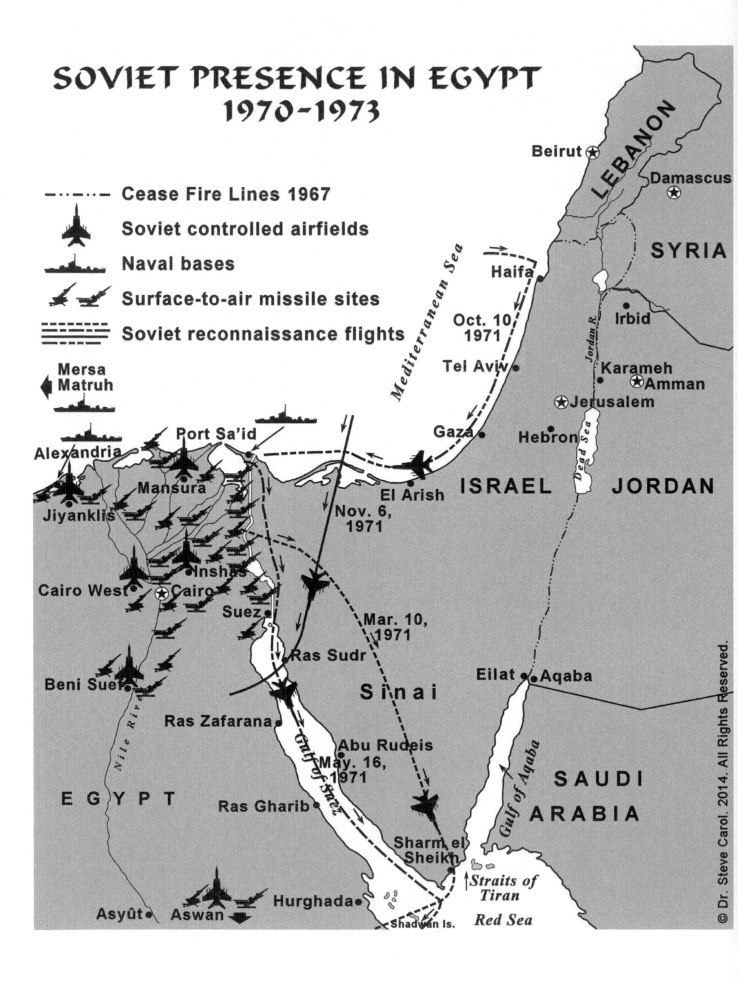

SOVIET PRESENCE IN EGYPT 1970~1973

Cease Fire Lines 1967
Soviet controlled airfields
Naval bases
Surface-to-air missile sites
Soviet reconnaissance flights

Mersa Matruh

Alexandria
Port Sa'id
Mansura
Jiyanklis
Cairo West
Inshas
Cairo
Suez
Beni Suef
Ras Sudr
Ras Zafarana
Abu Rudeis
Ras Gharib
Sharm el Sheikh
Shadwan Is.
Asyût
Aswan
Hurghada

Nile River

Gulf of Suez

E G Y P T

S i n a i

Mediterranean Sea

El Arish
Gaza
Tel Aviv
Haifa
Hebron
Jerusalem
Beirut
Damascus

LEBANON
SYRIA
Irbid
Karameh
Amman
Jordan R.
Dead Sea
ISRAEL
JORDAN

Eilat
Aqaba

Gulf of Aqaba

SAUDI ARABIA

Straits of Tiran
Red Sea

Oct. 10, 1971
Nov. 6, 1971
Mar. 10, 1971
May. 16, 1971

The Soviet-Egyptian Treaty of Friendship and Cooperation served as the model for others that followed across the Middle East and beyond (e.g. the Soviet-Indian Treaty of Friendship and Cooperation of August 9, 1971, the Soviet-Ethiopian Treaty of Friendship and Cooperation of May 4, 1977, and the Soviet-Afghan Treaty of Friendship and Cooperation of December 5, 1978). These treaties all had certain basic components. They perpetuated the dependence of these countries on the Soviet Union, and ran for fifteen years, (the Soviet-PDRY treaty ran for twenty years) unless expressly terminated by one party. They stressed that "indestructible friendship will always exist between the two countries and their peoples."

Dealing specifically with the Arab states, each treaty bound the Arab country in the spheres of defense, economy, foreign policy and domestic policy. In the realm of defense (Article 9 in the Soviet-Iraqi treaty and Article 5 in the Soviet-PDRY treaty), the parties "will continue to develop cooperation in the military field." Training and the supply of military equipment were specifically mentioned. "In the event of a situation developing which, in the opinion of the two parties, constitutes a threat to the peace or a breach of the peace, the parties shall immediately contact each other for the purpose of coordinating their positions in the interests of removing the said threat or of restoring peace." Furthermore, (in the case of the Soviet-Egyptian agreement) their joint communiqué of May 28, 1971, spoke of Soviet "all around aid and support" in the just "struggle against Israeli aggression."[371]

These treaties also contained an article (Article 2 in the Soviet-Egyptian agreement, Article 7 in the Soviet-Syrian agreement and Article 2 in the Soviet-PDRY treaty) which pledged close cooperation for the "maintenance and further development of the social and economic achievements of their peoples."[372] Thus, the Soviets committed themselves to preserve the regimes in the event of a "reactionary rebellion" by some rightist faction or Islamist fundamentalist group (e.g. the Muslim Brotherhood).

The treaties gave the Soviet Union the right of proxy, or direct intervention in order to protect its interests. It also provided for Soviet use of air and sea bases. Securing such bases from which to project Soviet power was the linchpin of Soviet foreign policy. There was also an obligation (Article 10 of the Soviet-Iraqi treaty and Article 12 of the Soviet-PDRY treaty) not to enter into a pact for action against the other party, nor to allow use of the territory of either country for activities (military or otherwise) potentially harmful to the other.[373] [374]

The Soviets were skillful in maintaining good relations with both sides in several Middle East quarrels: Syria and Iraq; Egypt and Libya; Iraq and Iran; the Yemen Arab Republic and the PDRY; and Kuwait and Iraq. In a like-manner, the Soviets shielded prime clients from defeat at the hands of their pro-American opponents: in the Six-Day War (1967), the 1,000-Day War of Attrition, (1967–70), the Yom Kippur War (1973); and Syria's intervention in Lebanon (1976 and again in 1982). Throughout the period of Soviet involvement in the Middle East and even beyond the demise of the Soviet Union, its policy was one of persistence rather than success.

Date	Event
February 14, 1972	The USSR attempted to establish diplomatic relations with the United Arab Emirates. A preliminary announcement to that effect was made.[375] Combined pressure by Saudi Arabia, Qatar, Oman, and Iran succeeded in preventing the establishment of diplomatic ties.[376]

April 9, 1972	A fifteen-year Soviet-Iraqi Treaty of Friendship and Cooperation was concluded. It drew Iraq closer to the Soviet Union, which provided increased military aid to the regime of Saddam Hussein. The Soviets obtained naval facilities at Umm Qasr at the head of the Persian Gulf.
July 18, 1972	Egyptian President Anwar el-Sadat "expelled" Soviet advisers from Egypt. Some claimed at the time, that 21,000 Soviets had been ousted. The US government claimed in February 1975, that it was only 6,000. The International Institute for Strategic Studies stated eventually that only 3,000 had left. The "expulsion" was "completed" by August 6. Some left and returned a short while later. Others were "transferred to Syria" as part of a triangular arrangement among Moscow, Cairo, and Damascus. As President Sadat's close confidant Ihsan Abdel Quddus would relate, "Egypt approved this Syrian stand, in fact supported it, because the national interests required the continued existence of Soviet experts in the region."[377] This was part of Sadat's grand *taqiyya**("deception") in preparation for war with Israel, planned for the next year. In reality, while some Soviet personnel left Egypt because their training mission was complete, others left while new advisors took their place. It was more a military rotation of duty than an expulsion. The fifteen-year Soviet-Egyptian Treaty of Friendship and Cooperation remained intact.
August 1972– February 1973	Officially during this period, Soviet-Egyptian relations were "frozen." Despite that, the USSR promised and delivered to Egypt (and Syria) military material that would change the Arab-Israel military balance in the war that was to break out later that year. The Soviet leadership was determined that Soviet equipment was not to be shown up again as inferior to Western weaponry, as in 1967. Coordinated Soviet-Egyptian diplomatic moves continued as before. Additionally, Sadat renewed the agreement, which allowed the continued Soviet naval use of Egyptian ports.

By the spring of 1973, the Soviet Union had heavily invested in the Arab world for eighteen years and that involvement continued and now moved to new heights as the USSR actively assisted Egypt and Syria to prepare for another war against Israel. The Soviets moved in this direction based on several factors. First, the Soviets had obtained naval bases, and port facilities for support of the Soviet Mediterranean fleet, as well as air bases for strategic reasons. Second, Soviet airlift and sealift capabilities were much improved over 1967. Third, the Suez Canal blocked by the Egyptians at the start of the Six-Day War in June 1967, had remained closed for six and one-half years. The Israeli presence on the eastern bank of the Suez Canal had an effect on the Soviet ability to project its power easily into the Red Sea, Indian Ocean and Persian Gulf. Economically, the closure hampered Soviet ability to provide a means for the winter transportation of goods to the Soviet Far East. Additionally, the Soviets disliked Israel and the Jews, especially because of the international attention they had caused over the plight of Soviet Jews seeking emigration from the USSR. Finally, the Soviets realized the limits of détente at that time. A status quo had been achieved in Europe, the SALT I agreement

---

* *Taqiyya,* deception or lying to "infidels" is permissible in pursuit of Islamic goals andia sanctioned in the Qur'an. For a more complete explanation *see* "Basic Principle 27."

had been concluded with the United States, and the United States was pre-occupied with a serious domestic political scandal—Watergate.

For the Soviet Union, the risk of another Middle East conflict seemed relatively low. The benefits were great. The United States would be isolated in support of Israel, the Arab world would be united against the United States, and there would be serious dissention within NATO. The hardliners in the Kremlin could hope that the United States would become enmeshed in a war with the Muslim world—a war far worse than its recently concluded involvement in Indochina, plus the horrifying moral and political dilemma of the United States standing by while Israel was destroyed. If the Arabs were defeated, it could not be total (the Soviets would prevent that), and it could trigger a process of radicalization throughout the Arab world from which the Soviet Union could only gain. One limiting factor to Soviet behavior would be the possibility of a direct Soviet-American military confrontation. Yet, at a crucial juncture, the two superpowers could step in to bring about a ceasefire. As the history of the Yom Kippur War would reveal, this is precisely what happened.

Date	Event
February 1973	In preparation for the coming war against Israel, the Soviet Union modernized and enlarged Egypt's armored units by supplying almost 600 additional tanks including improved versions of the T-62, sent amphibious PT-76, over 250 armored personnel carriers, approximately 100 additional Soviet aircraft including all-weather and night-flying versions of the MiG-21, more helicopters, and some twenty new naval units. The USSR shipped forty to fifty SAM anti-aircraft batteries and additional T-62 main battle tanks to Syria.[378] The largest and most significant influx of weaponry was in the missile category. At about the same time, the Soviets began to sealift Moroccan troops to Syria to facilitate their participation in the coming war. During the first half of 1973, the Soviet Union supplied Syria with $185 million worth of arms–$35 million more than in the whole of 1972.
March 1973	The Soviets began to ship two brigades of Scud-B surface-to-surface missiles—with a 186 miles range—to Alexandria, Egypt as a deterrent to expected IAF retaliatory deep penetration raids once the war commenced. The Soviet flow of weapons, munitions, and spare parts was re-instituted to the pre-"expulsion" levels.
July–August 1973	The Soviets began to ship advanced weaponry to both Egypt and Syria. This included SA-6 (NATO code-named Gainful) mobile anti-aircraft batteries to defeat the qualitative Israeli air superiority; AT-3 (NATO code-named Sagger) anti-tank missile to overcome Israeli superior use of armor; and advanced Soviet bridging equipment to facilitate an Egyptian crossing of the Suez Canal.
July 1973	A second Moroccan military contingent arrived in Syria, sealifted by the USSR.

The Soviet willingness to commit technologically advanced weapons (some had never before been exposed to combat and possible capture) was a clear indication of the high degree of the Soviet involvement in the Arab-Israeli arms race. What makes the massive buildup of Soviet military hardware even more impressive was that delivery was concentrated into a period of about five months or so, leading up to the war. The Soviets trained both the Egyptians and Syrians in offensive tactics and in the crossing of water obstacles. The Soviets were no longer actively opposed to the Arab plan to go to war. They encouraged the Yom Kippur War by acquiescing to it. They could have discouraged the war by refusing to acquiesce.

Furthermore, the Soviet Union goaded the Arabs to put pressure on the United States. On July 2, 1973, the Soviets broadcast in Arabic, "The political awareness of the Arab countries and other oil-rich countries has grown to a great extent and their solidarity has been consolidated. This has not only enabled them to limit the use of oil by the imperialists, but it also has enabled them to rely more firmly on their oil in the liberation struggle. The Soviet Union and other socialist countries are rendering primary, essential assistance to those countries which have decided to nationalize their natural resources." This pronouncement presaged the use of the Arab oil weapon.

Date	Event
September 24, 1973	The Soviets launched a reconnaissance satellite over the Middle East.[379] This would enable them to have real time information from the battlefronts. During this same period, the Soviets sent supersonic Tu-22 (NATO code-named Blinder) long-range bombers to Iraq.
September 28–29, 1973	The Soviets and their Czech counterparts were complicit in the train hijacking of Jewish emigrants to Austria. The crisis (*see* "Basic Principle 52") was part of the diversionary tactics used to distract Israel from the Egyptian-Syrian buildup for war.
October 2, 1973	The Soviets began to evacuate personnel from Syria. This was a Soviet ploy to create the impression it was disassociating itself from the war. In reality, Soviet advisors remained and only their family members left. At the beginning of October 1973, there were some 1,000 advisors in Egypt, 3,000 in Syria, and 1,500 in Iraq.
October 4, 1973	Units of the Soviet navy began leaving Alexandria and Port Sa'id, Egypt.
October 5, 1973	Although the war would not erupt until the next day, Soviet transport planes began arriving in Cairo and Damascus carrying heavy weapons. The Soviet resupply effort began—*before the war* (emphasis added)! It was the first test of Soviet airlift supply facilities since the expansion of the Soviet air transport force (*see* the "Yom Kippur War, 1973–Soviet Supply to Egypt and Syria" map).
October 6, 1973	Egypt and Syria launched a surprise attack—Operation *Badr* (1973)—against Israel on Yom Kippur, the holiest day of the Hebrew or Jewish calendar at 1:55 P.M. local time (*see* the "Yom Kippur War, October 6–24, 1973—Arab Attack" map).
October 9, 1973	In a letter to Algerian President Houari Boumédiènne, the Soviet Union urged Algeria and the other Arab states to get into the conflict "against a treacherous enemy."[380] It admonished them that the advanced Soviet equipment had been given to them for that very purpose. It praised Iraq for nationalizing the American-owned Basra Petroleum Company and urged other Arab oil producers to do likewise.

October 10, 1973	Twenty Soviet An-22 heavy transport aircraft began an emergency resupplying effort to Syria. The planes flew via Hungary and Yugoslavia through Aleppo. Turkey, though a NATO member, also allowed Soviet overflights to Egypt and Syria. The airlift was of such magnitude that it had to be organized for several days, i.e. *before* the outbreak of the war. From October 9 to 24, the Soviets conducted 934 sorties carrying 15,000 tons of war materials to the Arab states.[381] To offset the Soviet effort the United States mounted Operation *Nickel Grass* with 566 sorties carrying 22,395 tons of materials to Israel, between October 13 and 24. President Nixon, from a national security perspective, could not afford to let Soviet proxies defeat an American ally (*see* the Yom Kippur War, 1973–US Resupply to Israel map).[382] Soviet experts actually participated in one form or another on the Golan front.[383] For example, Soviet personnel drove tanks from Syrian ports to Damascus to make up for Syrian losses and they transported the Moroccan contingents to the Syrian battlefront.
October 11, 1973	The Soviets began a resupply effort to Iraq and placed three airborne divisions on alert.
October 13, 1973	The Soviets dispatched nuclear warheads from the Nikolayev naval base at Odessa, USSR, to Alexandria, Egypt to be fitted to the brigades of Scud-B missiles already based there. Both missile brigades were Soviet-manned and remained so during the Yom Kippur War.[384]
October 24, 1973 (21:35 hours) (04:35 October 25, Moscow time)	The Soviet Union, in an urgent letter—a virtual ultimatum—to US President Richard Nixon, demanded joint Soviet and US military intervention into Egypt. This was in response to the IDF's entrapment of the Egyptian Third Army on the east bank of the Suez Canal. The Soviets sought to impose a ceasefire and a peace settlement on the combatants. Soviet General Secretary Leonid Brezhnev further threatened that if the United States would not act jointly with the Soviet Union, it would act unilaterally. He demanded of Nixon an "immediate and clear reply." At the same time the Soviets began increased military preparations including: a Soviet command post was established in the southern portion of the USSR; 150,000 airborne troops (seven divisions) and two mechanized divisions were put on "comprehensive alert;" East German troops were put on alert; the Soviets began moving airborne troops from Hungary; twelve An-22 transports, each carrying 200 troops, were detected en route to Cairo—the Soviets had the capability of airlifting 5,000 soldiers a day into Egypt; and the Soviet Mediterranean fleet was increased from 60 to 85 ships and later exceeded 100, including nuclear missile submarines. A flotilla of twelve ships including two amphibious vessels headed for Alexandria. Admiral Sergei Gorshkov, commander-in-chief of the Soviet Navy, gave orders for an amphibious troop landing on the east bank of the Suez Canal, in support of the trapped Egyptians. On that same morning, the Soviet vessel bearing the nuclear warheads arrived in Alexandria. The ship remained in port until November 1973 and never unloaded its cargo. In response, in the early hours of October 25, the United States ordered a worldwide DEFCON 3 alert for its military forces. With that American move, the Soviets immediately scaled back on their escalation.

YOM KIPPUR – WAR SOVIET SUPPLY TO EGYPT AND SYRIA

Legend:
- Soviet sealift
- --- Soviet airlift
- Soviet fleet

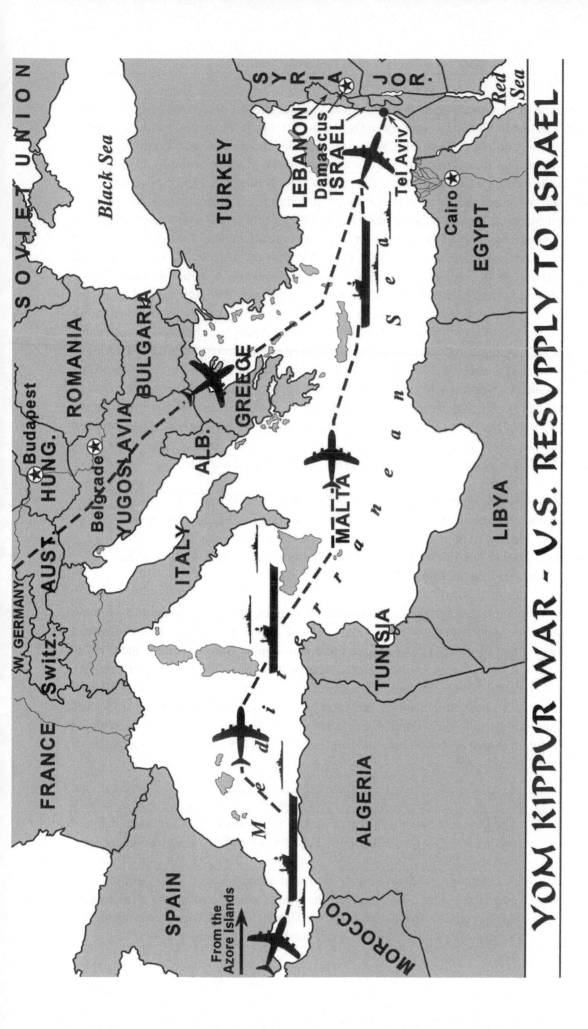

YOM KIPPUR WAR – U.S. RESUPPLY TO ISRAEL

----- U.S. airlift

━━━ U.S. Sixth Fleet.

At the conclusion of the Yom Kippur War, the Soviets immediately replaced the equipment both Egypt and Syria had lost in battle. More importantly, the quality of the weaponry was considerably superior, including Su-20 and MiG-23 aircraft. Sadat later revealed that Egypt had secretly "expanded the period of the naval facilities granted to the Soviet navy in the Mediterranean to 1978."[385] The Soviet position in the Middle East was stronger than at any time previously. The USSR deliberately used aggressive war as an instrument of national policy. It undermined détente, and weakened and isolated the United States. It broke up the solidarity of NATO in this crisis. The Soviets displayed increased military power and capability of intervention. It was the champion of the Arab world and hoped to perpetuate Arab dependence on the USSR. Radio Moscow on February 16, 1974, trumpeted the Soviet role, "The strong Soviet intervention, the stern Soviet warning to Israel, and the alerting of the Soviet forces to go to the Middle East to establish peace and stop the aggression changed the situation completely." The Soviets were content to allow the Americans to get for Egypt through negotiations (i.e. the return of all of the Sinai Peninsula) what the Arabs and the USSR were unable to achieve through military confrontation. An immediate benefit of this strategy was the reopening of the Suez Canal, officially on June 10, 1975. The canal at the time was large enough to accommodate the Soviet Mediterranean squadron's two helicopter carriers, but too small for the assault carriers of the US Sixth Fleet. The Soviets increased their support of the PLO in order to gain a strong foothold in any future Palestinian state, preempting Chinese influence, and as a hedge against peace between Egypt and Israel in the future. That the USSR would continue to support Arab moves against Israel was made clear by a Radio Moscow broadcast on April 4, 1974, which declared:

> The Soviet Union has taken part in all stages of the Arab people's struggle against aggression and expansionism in the Middle East. In the last few years, it has helped in every possible way to tip the balance of power in favor of the Arabs. Without this, it would have been impossible for Egypt and Syria to score these successes in the last war of October 1973, in the Middle East.

The Soviet presence remained in the greater Middle East region. The Soviets showed a greater ability and readiness to project military power into areas of opportunity. This included Soviet involvement in the Angolan Civil War (1977–88), the Ethiopian-Somali War over the Ogaden (1977–78), and intervention in Afghanistan (1979–89). The Soviets used proxies—Cubans, South Yemenis, and North Koreans from the DPRK, the latter in a combat pilot role. The use of proxies allowed the Soviets to have a less perceptible military presence but not a less effective one. The Soviets demonstrated during this period, 1973–89, that they were willing to run higher risks, for regional gain, accepting the international costs and consequences and doing so irrespective of the effect on its relationship with the United States.

Date	Event
December 6, 1973	The IAF shot down a DPRK piloted MiG-21 over the Gulf of Suez, while a second was shot down in error by Egyptian air defense forces along the Suez ceasefire lines.
July 11, 1974	A fifteen-year Soviet-Somali Treaty of Friendship and Cooperation was concluded. The Soviets gained the use of naval facilities at Berbera and Kismayu, as well as air bases such as Uanle Uen from which long-range TU-95 aircraft patrolled the northwest quadrant of the Indian Ocean.[386]

Late 1974	During the Iraqi attempt to crush the ongoing eight and one-half year Kurdish rebellion, the Soviets flew combat missions against the Kurds on behalf of the Iraqi government.
February 1975	The USSR supplied Scud surface-to-surface missiles to Iraq.
March 15, 1976	Egypt formally abrogated the Soviet-Egyptian Treaty of Friendship and Cooperation.
October 1976	The Soviets tried to make inroads into pro-Western Iran (of the Shah) as evidenced by the signing of a $550 million deal with that nation for the sale of SA-7 (NATO code-named Strela) missiles, half-tracks and tank carriers.
March 1977	Through its proxy, President Fidel Castro of Cuba (then visiting Aden, PDRY), the Soviet Union attempted to sponsor and encourage a socialist confederation consisting of Ethiopia, Somalia, Djibouti, and the PDRY, which would also provide for Eritrean autonomy.[387]
July 13, 1977–March 15, 1978	On July 13, 1977, Soviet ally and Arab League member, Somalia, taking advantage of the chaos in Ethiopia, invaded the Ogaden region, in an attempt to wrest it away from Ethiopia. In a dramatic shift of Cold War alliances, the Soviet Union switched from supplying aid to Somalia to supporting Ethiopia, which had previously been backed by the United States, prompting the United States to start supporting Somalia. The Soviets concluded a Treaty of Friendship and Cooperation with Ethiopia on May 4, 1977.[388] Ethiopia received military and logistic support from the Soviet Union, Cuba, and the PDRY. A $220 million arms deal was concluded by the Soviets, with Ethiopia, which included four squadrons of MiG-21 fighters, nearly 200 T-54 tanks, SAM-3 and SAM-7 antiaircraft missiles, as well as wire-guided antitank missiles. Forty Ethiopian pilots were already in the USSR learning to fly the MiG-21s.[389] In retaliation, on November 13, 1977, Somalia ordered all Soviet advisors to leave the country within seven days; ended Soviet use of strategic naval and air bases; abrogated the Soviet-Somali Treaty of Friendship and Cooperation; and broke diplomatic relations with Cuba, ordering all Cuban personnel out of the country within forty-eight hours. The Soviet reaction was not long in coming. On the evening of November 25, 1977, the Soviets launched a massive airlift into Ethiopia, which exceeded any previous airlift to that date (including those of the United States and the USSR during the Yom Kippur War of 1973), using some 250 Soviet transport planes. The airlift brought some 61,000 tons of military hardware as well as food, medical supplies and petroleum. Some 18,000 Cuban[390] (most from garrisons in Angola), 2,000 South Yemeni (from the PDRY), and some 1,500 Soviet personnel and armed forces were involved in military planning and fighting against Somalia. With Soviet assistance, Ethiopia was able to repel the Somalis, regain the Ogaden region, and the war ended. By their actions in Ethiopia (and earlier in Angola), the Soviets were able to demonstrate to other regimes in the Third World, that when faced with a military challenge to perceived vital interests, only one superpower could be relied upon to act—the Soviet Union.

November 18, 1978	As Iran descended into the turmoil of the Iranian Islamic Revolution, Soviet President Leonid Brezhnev warned the United States against intervention stating, "It must be made clear that any interference, let alone military intervention in the affairs of Iran—a state which has a common frontier with the Soviet Union—would be regarded by the USSR as a matter affecting its security interests."[391]
December 5, 1978	A fifteen-year Soviet-Afghan Treaty of Friendship and Cooperation was concluded.
December 1978	The Soviet-built Tabqa Dam in Syria was inaugurated.
October 25, 1979	A twenty-year Soviet-PDRY Treaty of Friendship and Cooperation was concluded. The Soviets gained naval facilities at Aden and on Socotra Island, as well as an air base at Mukallah.[392] The Soviets also provided economic and technical assistance. The PDRY was the only Arab state with a single party of avowedly Marxist orientation—the Yemeni Socialist Party.
November 1979	After the Islamic Revolution in Iran, the Soviet Union began to supply weaponry to the regime via Syria and Libya. Yet, this military aid was short-lived. Despite the Soviet support in the United Nations Security Council blocking sanctions against Iran (e.g. January 31, 1981), Iran began to refer to the USSR as "the big satanic power."[393]
December 24, 1979	The Soviet Union massively invaded Afghanistan to support the country's Marxist government. The Soviets became enmeshed in a ten-year struggle against Afghan *mujahadeen*—Islamic jihadist—forces and withdrew in February 1989.

When Iraq invaded Iran at the start of the Iran–Iraq War in September 1980, the Soviet Union, a large supplier of arms to Iraq, proclaimed its neutrality and instituted an arms embargo against Iraq. By mid-1981 when the war shifted in Iran's favor, the Soviets resumed their arms shipments to Iraq. Some 200 T-55 and T-72 tanks, as well as SA-6 missiles were sent. Economic assistance was also offered.[394] In return, Iraqi strongman, Saddam Hussein proclaimed a general amnesty for Iraqi communists and released many from prison.[395] Soviet arms supplies continued until the end of the conflict.

Date	Event
October 8, 1980	A fifteen-year Soviet-Syrian Treaty of Friendship and Cooperation was concluded. It expanded the Soviet naval use of Tartus and Latakia. Both facilities would be expanded over the years making them Soviet naval bases, which obviated the need for the Soviet fleet of frequent naval transits to homeports in the Black Sea.[396]
January 1983	The USSR and Iraq concluded a $2 billion arms deal, which included T-62 and T-72 tanks. By 1987, Iraq had received 800 T-72 tanks, MiG-23, MiG-25 (and later MiG-29) jet fighters, as well as Scud-B and SS-21 surface-to-surface missiles.[397]
October 9, 1984	A twenty-year Soviet-Yemeni Arab Republic Treaty of Friendship and Cooperation was concluded.

November 15, 1985	The Soviet Union established diplomatic relations with the United Arab Emirates.
1986–87	During the Iran–Iraq War, the Soviet Union sent two frigates and three minesweepers to the Persian Gulf, joining other nations' efforts to keep the Gulf open to shipping. On April 9, 1987, the Soviets announced it would lease three tankers to Kuwait to transport oil.
January 1990	The Soviet Union began to allow large-scale Jewish immigration to Israel.
October 18, 1991	The Soviet Union restored diplomatic relations with Israel after a 24-year break.
December 26, 1991	The Supreme Soviet officially dissolved itself and the Union of Soviet Socialist Republics (USSR).
January 8, 1995	Russia and Iran signed a deal to complete the construction of a 1,300-megawatt nuclear power plant at Bushehr in southern Iran. Construction of the Bushehr plant had started in 1975.

In retrospect, the huge Soviet investment and efforts in the Arab world had brought the USSR relatively few gains. Bolshevik leader, Vladimir Lenin often asked: *kto kogo?*—"Who (does it to) whom?"—or "Who used whom?" In general, the Arabs succeeded in using the Soviet Union more than the Soviets had used the Arabs.

Despite the collapse of the Soviet Union in 1991, Russia continued its historic role as a major power in the Middle East. It continued to supply arms to Iran, Syria, and even Lebanon. In a June 2000 foreign policy concept paper approved by the then Russian Federation President Vladimir Putin, Russia's priorities in the Middle East were defined as seeking "to restore and strengthen its position [in the region], particularly economic ones."[398] Since 2006, Russia moved back into the greater Middle East region resuming its traditional interest and involvement in the area. This included arms supplies, and construction of prestige projects.

RUSSIAN FEDERATION	
Twenty-first Century	
Date	**Event**
2006	The Russians signed an agreement with Syria providing for the sale to the Syrian Air Force of an unspecified number of advanced MiG-29M/M2 fighter-bombers and eight MiG--31E. Iran was to pay for the $1 billion deal. On March 30, 2009, Russian military sources announced that five of the eight MiG-31E's had been delivered. In September 2009, the Russian daily newspaper *Kommersant*,[399] confirmed that a new sale of MiG-31s to Syria had been concluded.
Late January 2007	Russia completed the delivery of twenty-nine TOR-M1 anti-aircraft missile systems to Iran under a $700 million contract signed at the end of 2005. The short-range anti-aircraft missile systems were to protect Iran's nuclear facilities.
December 2007	Russia signed a contract with Iran to sell the S-300 anti-aircraft missile system (NATO code-named SA-20 Gargoyle). Russia was to supply five divisions' worth of S-300PMU-1s for $800 million.

August 9–28, 2008	After separatist Abkhazian forces fired on Georgian forces, a full-scale war between the Russian Federation and the Republic of Georgia erupted. The next day, August 10, 2008, some 9,000 Russian troops entered Abkhazia and remained there. Russia recognized the independence of Abkhazia on August 26, 2008. On August 28, 2008, the Parliament of Georgia passed a resolution declaring Abkhazia a Russian-occupied territory. Nevertheless, Russia established a Black Sea naval base in Abkhazia, thus enabling it to project power into the greater Middle East.
February 3, 2009	Russia bribed and pressured Kyrgyzstan to shut down the US air base at Manas airport, in Bishkek. The air base was a crucial NATO conduit into Afghanistan. Russia promised to provide $150 million in free aid to Kyrgyzstan, a soft loan of $300 million, and another loan of $1.7 billion for the construction of one of the largest hydroelectric power plants in the region, the Kambarata HPP-1 plant.[400] One of the informal conditions of the loan was the closing of the US base in Manas. On December 24, 2012, the President of Kyrgyzstan, Almazbek Atambayev, stated the base would be closed down in 2014.
February 4, 2009	Russia announced the formation of a "rapid reaction force" with six former Soviet republics—Armenia, Belarus and four Central Asian nations, Kazakhstan, Kyrgyzstan, Tajikistan and Uzbekistan.[401] This regional Russian-led strike force is meant to reassert Russian hegemony in the Central Asian Muslim belt north of Afghanistan and is part of a continuing effort to curb US influence in energy-rich Central Asia.
2009	Russia sold ten advanced MiG-29 fighter-bombers to Lebanon. In effect, with Hezbollah dominating the Lebanese political situation, Russia sold the jets to the Shi'ite terrorist group. For the first time, a terrorist organization had its own air force.
May 2009	Russia gained its first maritime foothold in the Persian Gulf by having fleet units obtain provisions and fuel at the ports of Bahrain, and Salalah, Oman.
2009	Employing an old tactic from the days of the Soviet Union, Russia used a proxy to sell its advanced Iskander-M cruise missiles and its advanced S-300 anti-aircraft missile multi-targeting shield systems to Iran and Syria. Belarus was the conduit by which Iran took delivery of all the missiles and diverted part of the shipment to Syria. In August 2010, Iran claimed it had received two S-300 systems from Belarus and two from another nation, despite Russia's declaration in June 2010, that it could not complete the deal due to new UN sanctions.
April 12–July 2009	The Lebanese government announced the arrest and breakup of the Al-Alam spy ring, which allegedly spied for Israel. A second ring was broken up in June 2009. It was revealed that for the first time since the collapse of the Soviet Union, a special unit of the Russian Federal Security Service (FSB), commissioned by Hezbollah's special security apparatus, was responsible for the massive discovery of the spy rings with the help of super-efficient detection systems. This was the first time that the FSB was engaged in anti-Israel activity in the service of an Arab terrorist organization.

July 2009	Russia announced that the Soviet-era naval maintenance base near Tartus, Syria, was to be expanded and modernized to become "fully operational." Such a permanent base for Russia would enable it to project power into the Mediterranean, the Atlantic, the Red Sea, and the Indian Ocean in a matter of days.
July 2009	Russia and the Islamic Republic of Iran agreed to hold joint naval maneuvers in the Caspian Sea for the first time ever.
August 2009	Russia and Saudi Arabia negotiated a $2 billion arms package reported to include up to 150 helicopters (30 Mi-35 attack helicopters and up to 120 Mi-17 transport helicopters), more than 150 T-90S tanks, 250 BMP-3 infantry fighting vehicles and "several dozen" S-400 air defense systems. The S-400 system is the newest version of the S-300 long-range surface to air missile system that Moscow has reportedly been in discussion for several years to sell to Iran. The deal marked a major diversification of arms suppliers for Saudi Arabia, which to this date relied on US, British and French weapons.[402]
May 2010	Russia announced the sale of 25 advanced MiG-29 fighters, 50 truck-mounted Pantsyr S-1 short-range surface-to-air interceptor missile batteries, anti-aircraft artillery systems and armored vehicles to Syria. According to a report released by the Stockholm International Peace Research Institute, Syria imported nearly six times more weapons in 2007–11 than in the previous five-year period, with Russia accounting for 72 percent of the arms supplied, which in addition to the arms described, included air defense systems and anti-ship missiles. In late 2011, Russia signed a $550 million deal for 36 Yak-130 light combat aircraft.
August 22, 2010	There was heavy Russian participation in the Iranian nuclear program, especially the construction of the Bushehr nuclear power plant, which with Russian-supplied fuel rods, started operation on August 22, 2010, and joined the Iranian national power grid on September 3, 2011.
November 2010	The Lebanese Prime Minister Saad Hariri confirmed November 16, 2010, that Russia agreed to supply the Lebanese army with advanced weapons. The new weaponry included thirty-one tanks, 130 mm caliber cannon shells, six attack helicopters and various munitions. The new helicopters are expected to boost significantly Lebanon's air force, which currently has around thirty helicopters, all unarmed, and several jets.[403] It was further revealed that Russian firms plan to bid on Lebanese contracts, including electric, transport, telecommunications and weapons offers.

February 2012	Russia continued its support of the Assad regime, both diplomatically and militarily, during the Syrian Civil War, opposing both the Muslim Brotherhood and al-Qaeda. Russia upgraded its Jabal Al Harrah electronic and surveillance station south of Damascus opposite Israel's Sea of Galilee. This listening post can provide both Syria, but especially Iran, with early warning of an oncoming US or Israeli attack. Before it was boosted by extra advanced technology and manpower, the station covered civilian and military movements in northern Israel as far south as Tel Aviv, northern Jordan and western Iraq. Its current range extends to all parts of Israel and Jordan, the Gulf of Aqaba and northern Saudi Arabia.[404] Additionally, Russia upgraded the Syrian radar stationed on Lebanon's Mount Sannine and connected it to the Jabal Al Harrah facility in Syria. Thus, Russia was able to track US and Israeli naval and aerial movements in the Eastern Mediterranean as far north as Cyprus and Greece.
March 13, 2012	Russian Deputy Defense Minister Alexei Antonov admitted that Russian military technical experts were in Syria, assisting the Assad regime during the Syrian Civil War. Since mid-January of that year, Russian military crews have taken over the operation of the Pantsyr batteries from Syrian personnel.[405]
May 7, 2013	Russia announced it would ship six S-300 anti-aircraft missile batteries carrying 144 missiles to Syria along with Russian missile and air defense specialists, termed "instructors." The missiles had been ordered and paid for by Syria a few years earlier.
May 12, 2013	Russian Navy Commander Admiral Viktor Chirkov announced that Russia was restoring its permanent naval presence in the Mediterranean Sea. Previously, the Soviet Fifth *Eskadra* was stationed in the Mediterranean from 1967 until 1992. It was formed to counter the US Navy Sixth Fleet during the Cold War, and consisted of 30 to 50 warships and auxiliary vessels at different times. The new Russian squadron would comprise of five to six warships and their service vessels as well as nuclear submarines armed with nuclear ballistic missiles.[406]
July 2013,	As the military took over in Egypt, Russia came out in support of the El-Sisi regime, in opposition to the Muslim Brotherhood. It offered to supply advanced fighter-bomber aircraft to Egypt, to replace the F-16 planes, whose delivery the Obama administration suspended on July 24, 2013. The new Egyptian government rapidly soured on its four-decade relationship with the United States (first established by Anwar Sadat and Henry Kissinger), especially in light of the Obama administration's support of the ousted Morsi-Muslim Brotherhood government. For Russia, it was an opportunity to reestablish the old Russian-Egyptian relationship.
September 9, 2013	A Russian diplomatic initiative stopped a planned US military strike against the Assad regime in Syria, over the latter's alleged use of chemical weapons on August 21, 2013.

December 12, 2013	Russia signed a $2 billion arms deal with the new el-Sisi regime in Egypt, including MiG-29 M/M2 fighter jets, MI-35 attack helicopters, air defense missile complexes, anti-ship complexes, short-range Kornet anti-tank missiles, light arms, and ammunition. The sale was to be funded by Saudi Arabia and the United Arab Emirates. In return for these arms, Egypt has agreed to provide the Russian navy with port services in Alexandria and to strengthen the two navies' cooperation in the Mediterranean Sea.[407] The deal signaled a return of Russia as a major power player in the Middle East, as well as a restoration of the primacy of Russian influence in Egypt. This followed a disintegration of US-Egyptian ties following the Obama administrations whole-hearted support of the Muslim Brotherhood Mohamed Morsi regime, which was ousted by massive civilian (upwards of 30 million people) demonstrations in July 2013.
January 26, 2014	For at least the third time it was claimed by Syrian opposition groups that the Israeli Air force had bombed Russian-supplied S-300 missile launchers and components in and around Latakia, Syria. Israel previously warned several times that it would not permit the transfer of these missiles to the Hezbollah terrorists in Lebanon. An earlier alleged Israeli strike took place on July 4, 2013.[408] This was later followed by a series of explosions in September, which were also attributed to the IAF.[409]
February 26, 2014– March 18, 2014	In the aftermath of a political crisis in neighboring Ukraine, Russia used the ouster of Ukrainian President Viktor Yanukovych as the pretext to occupy militarily the Crimean Peninsula (starting February 26, 2014). In short order, a referendum was staged (March 16), and the Crimea was annexed into the Russian Federation (March 18). A strategic factor in this Russian move was to retain absolute Russian control of Sevastopol and Feodosia, the key Crimean naval bases on the Black Sea, from which Russia projected its naval power into the Middle East region.

There has been a historic and ongoing Russian concern that the border regions on Russia's frontiers—what the Russians call "the near abroad"—should be friendly, i.e. non-hostile, and not used by other powers as a springboard against Russia or its interests. This is especially the case with the greater Middle East where Russia continues to have a deep interest because of the region's strategic location, its huge oil resources and its proximity to Russia.

Thus, the Russians have long opposed Western moves in the region. As mentioned earlier, in the mid-twentieth century as the West sought to create the Baghdad Pact, the Russians leapfrogged over that alliance into the Middle East. Later, as the United States caused discomfort for the Russians, by expanding NATO eastward to include the Baltic States—Estonia, Latvia, and Lithuania (former republics of the USSR)—Russia reacted causing worry for the United States by applying counter-pressure in the Middle East, supporting both Iran and Syria. Similarly, Russia supports Venezuela in South America. Historically, Russia fears popular revolution and automatically backs authoritarian rulers. It supports secular governments and seeks stability, even where it was enforced by a dictatorship, because the alternatives tend to be worse from the Russian perspective. This is why Russia assisted Syria for over a half century, continuing today to back the Bashar al-Assad regime, with political and diplomatic support as well as shipments of weaponry.

Given Russian support for Iran and Venezuela, there is a possibility of a new global petro-axis forming that may well dwarf the impact of the OAPEC cartel of the 1970s. The Persian Gulf's littoral states hold over 60 percent of the world's proven petroleum reserves and 40 percent of the natural gas. Russia has 10 percent of the oil reserves and 35 percent of the world's natural gas. Venezuela has over 6 percent of the world's oil reserves. Iran and its neighbors, along with Russia and Venezuela, own 75 percent of the world's oil reserves and 75 percent of the natural gas. An emerging Russian-Iranian-Venezuelan petro-axis would have the world, over a barrel.

Bear in mind that the former Soviet Union dealt with the threat of militant Islamists since its disastrous 1980s war in Afghanistan, and watched as it showed up in parts of Russia's heartland. Russian territory is on the front line of the war against Islamic supremacism. The northern Caucasus, Central Asia, and even the central Volga region are threatened. Its wars in Chechnya were testimony to the Islamic fundamentalist threat. Russia views militant Islamic fundamentalism as an ongoing menace continuing to spread violence across North Africa and West Asia. The Russians condemned recent Western moves that destroyed stable regimes in the greater Middle East, and willfully opened the gates to the Islamic supremacists. The toppling of Mubarak in Egypt, Qadhafi in Libya, and the on-going attempt against Assad in Syria, are cases in point. Such moves open the door to Islamist forces to take power, or expand their base of operations, recent examples being Mali and Algeria in January 2013. Russia's opposition to the events in Libya in 2011 and Syria 2011–15 are further proof of its questioning Western motives, which seem to go against the wisdom of making common cause against the growing Islamist menace. Given the turn of events as one observes the almost unimpeded rise and spread globally of Islamic supremacism, we may witness a reappearance of the "Grand Alliance" of World War II, as Russia and the West come together in common cause, to cooperate, resist and repel the Islamic supremacist threat.

INFLVENCE OF ISLAM ON THE REGION

Islam is not a normal religion like the other religions in the world and Muslim nations are not like normal nations. Muslim nations are very special because they have a command from Allah to rule the entire world and to be over every nation in the world.
Sayeed Abdul A'la Maududi

Allah is our objective; the Quran is our law, the Prophet is our leader; Jihad is our way; and dying in the way of Allah is the highest of our aspirations.
Credo of the Muslim Brotherhood

The mosques are our barracks, the domes our helmets, the minarets our bayonets and the faithful our soldiers.
Recep Tayyip Erdoğan, Mayor of Istanbul, December 1997

Islam is the world's second largest religion. It is the fastest growing religion in the world today, due in part to polygamy and prohibition of abortion (*see* the "Spread of Islam" map). According to a 2010 study and released January 2011, Islam has 1.57 billion adherents,[1] making up over 23 percent of the world population. It is expected to rise to 2.2 billion by 2030.[2] If current trends continue, 79 countries will have a million or more Muslim inhabitants in 2030.[3] Islam is the dominant religion in the Middle East, North Africa, the Horn of Africa, and the Sahel (the semi-arid grasslands from the southern edge of the Sahara Desert extending southward, from the Atlantic Ocean in the west to the Red Sea in the east). However, not to be overlooked is the fact that there are roughly as many Muslims in South Asia (Indian subcontinent—India, Pakistan, and Bangladesh) as there are in the Arab world. There are more Muslims outside the Middle East (in southeastern Europe, the Caucasus, Central Asia, South Asia, western China, and Southeast Asia) than inside it.

A lot more of the world lives under shari'a—Islamic law—than was the case some thirty years ago. Shari'a has official status or a high degree of influence on the legal system in close to a score of countries and regions. It covers family law, criminal law, and in some places, personal beliefs, including penalties for apostasy, blasphemy, and not praying. These countries include Mauritania, northern Nigeria, Sudan, Saudi Arabia, Qatar, certain areas of the United Arab Emirates, Yemen, Iraq, Iran, Pakistan, Afghanistan, Brunei, the Maldive Islands, southern Thailand, certain regions in Indonesia, and Malaysia, especially in the state of Kelantan.[4] More specifically, Pakistan adopted shari'a in 1977, as did Iran in 1979, Sudan in 1984, and Brunei on May 1, 2014.[5] More than fifty years ago, Nigeria lived under English common law. Now, half of that country is under Islamic law. Recently, it was announced that sixteen of Indonesia's thirty-two provinces have passed laws influenced by shari'a. These laws vary widely in form. The laws discriminate against religious minorities and violate Indonesia's policy of *Pancasila,* or "unity in diversity." In Padang, Indonesia, both Muslim and non-Muslim women are required to wear headscarves, while a law in the Indonesian city of Tangerang allows women found "loitering" alone on the street after 10 P.M. to be arrested and charged with prostitution. Other laws stipulate Qur'an literacy among schoolchildren and severe punishment for adultery, alcoholism and gambling.[6] Islam continues to spread. Since the end of 2004, for example, some 10 percent of southern Thailand's Buddhist population has abandoned their homes due to Islamic supremacist pressure, a fact that has largely gone unreported in the Western press.

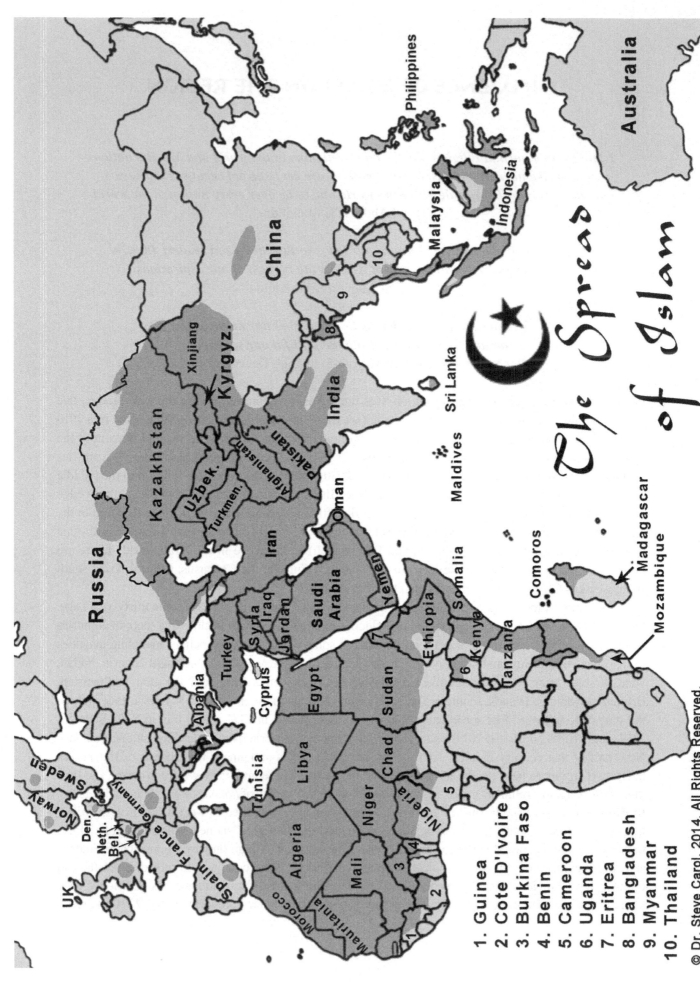

The Spread of Islam

1. Guinea
2. Cote D'Ivoire
3. Burkina Faso
4. Benin
5. Cameroon
6. Uganda
7. Eritrea
8. Bangladesh
9. Myanmar
10. Thailand

Prior to September 11, 2001, many in the Western world (aside from Middle East and Islamic academics, scholars and diplomatic specialists) knew little about Islam. In fact, the public had only been briefly exposed to it in their one-year World History course in high school. Such classes summed up Islam by stating it was one of three great monotheistic faiths with but different names for God (Allah), its place of worship (a *masjid* i.e. mosque), its holy book (the Qur'an), its founder (Muhammad), and its day of rest and worship (Friday). However, contrary to what some people believe, Islam is not just one of three monotheistic religions, with but minor differences. Such explanations are far from accurate, are simplistic and superficial, exposing a great lack of depth of knowledge about Islam.

The events of September 11, 2001, brought Islam into sharp focus with more of the public (albeit not enough) seeking to understand Islam more thoroughly than in the past, not just in theological terms but also in ideological and practical terms. Islam has always been political, and the union of religion and the state has always been essential to its ideology. Simply put, there is no separation of church (in this case, mosque,) and state. With good reason, many would ask the question candidly asked years later by Daniel Greenfield, "If Islam is no different than every other religion and their deity is no different than every other deity, why are so many members of those religions and worshipers of those deities being murdered by the followers of a single religion—not once or twice, but constantly? Year after year."[7] In fact, Islam sees itself as the only religion that is *din al-Haq* ("the true religion") while all of the other religions are *din al-Batel* ("false religion"). Since its founding, Islam is intended to be the world religion.

For a deeper understanding of Islam, it is necessary to understand some critical precepts of Islam. The term "Islam" means "submission" and applies both to the individual's submission to Allah and to a people's acquiescence to conquest and subjugation by Muslim armies. A "Muslim" is one who submits. According to Islam, the world is divided into two parts: *Dar al-Islam,* (the House of Submission) and *Dar al-Harb,* (the House of War). As such, there are no nation states with geographical borders as is understood in the West. *Dar al-Islam* refers to those lands under Islamic rule, while *Dar al-Harb* refers to those lands outside Muslim rule controlled by non-Muslim governments.

The world's people are similarly divided between the believers, i.e. the Muslims and the *kuffar,* who do not believe in Muhammad and the Qur'an. This latter group is known as the *harbi* ("the inhabitants of the *Dar al-Harb*"). They include Christians, Jews, Hindus, Buddhists, Sikhs, Zoroastrians, Bahá'ís, animists, agnostics, polytheists, pagans, and atheists among others. Muhammad established dualistic legal and ethical systems, one set for Muslims, and another for *kuffar.*

Kafir (the original Arabic word as it appears in the Qur'an) is an abusive, derogatory, hateful, and prejudiced pejorative used to describe non-Muslims throughout the Qur'an, Sira, and Hadith. These sacred Islamic texts prescribe the political treatment of all peoples who do not believe in Islam. *Kafir,* and its plural *kuffar,* is directly used 134 times in the Qur'an, its verbal noun "*kufr*" is used 37 times, and the verbal cognates of *kafir* are used about 250 times.[8] In Western languages it came to be translated as "unbeliever," "nonbeliever," "disbeliever," "non-Muslim," and "infidel," though the first four of these terms have a neutral connotation and appear in some translations of the Qur'an. Western translators may have interpreted it that way so as not to offend the sensibilities (political correctness at work here) of Muslims.

Allah classified the *kuffar* in the Qur'an as the "vilest of creatures," or "the worst of beasts,"[9] and they "will abide in the fire of Hell. They are the worst of created beings."[10] The treatment of unbelievers is an integral part of the ideology of Islam. In the Qur'an, the Sira and the Hadith, *kuffar*—unbelievers—are unclean,[11] ignorant,[12] liars,[13] evil[14] and the allies of Satan.[15] They are not to be taken as friends.[16] They can be confused,[17] deceived,[18] cursed,[19] hated[20] mocked,[21] humiliated,[22] disgraced,[23] plotted against,[24] terrorized,[25] robbed,[26] raped,[27] enslaved,[28] killed,[29] murdered,[30] crucified,[31] beheaded,[32] made war on,[33] and annihilated.[34]

Islam divides the world in two ways. The first is Muslims against non-Muslims (i.e. unbelievers) where Muslims are superior to unbelievers both morally and legally. The Qur'an itself, e.g., *Sura* 2:221, confirms this idea that even the lowliest Muslim (a Muslim slave) is superior to any unbeliever. The second division is men versus women, whereby men are superior to women both morally and legally. The status of women will be covered in greater depth in "Basic Principle 29."

For Muslims, the definition of Islam and acceptance of the *Ummah* (the Muslim worldwide nation* or community) rests on the Five Pillars of Islam—*arkan al-Islam*—i.e. five basic obligatory acts for all Muslims. They are a sign of commitment to the faith. The Five Pillars of Islam are: 1) the creed or declaration of the faith—*shahada*, 2) daily prayer—*salat*, 3) voluntary charity or alms giving—*zakat*, 4) fasting—*sawm*—primarily fasting during the month of Ramadan, and 5) pilgrimage—*hajj*—to the holy city of Mecca at least once in a lifetime.

The *Shahada* or declaration of the faith marks the difference between Muslim and nonbeliever. It consists of two clear unambiguous sentences, "I testify there is no God but Allah. I testify that Muhammad is the Prophet of Allah." The first is an affirmation of monotheism and a rejection of polytheism, idolatry, atheism, agnosticism, and the God of the Jews and Christians. The second affirms Muhammad's mission as Allah's final prophet to humankind, after whom there will be no other.

Salat or daily prayer comes in a set formula and must be recited five proscribed times a day—dawn, midday, early afternoon, sunset, and evening. Muslims declare their allegiance and submission to Allah by reciting the opening verses of the Qur'an. The worshipper must face in the direction of the Kaaba, in Mecca, no matter where he/she is in the world.

A recent event of major consequence, Iraq's Shi'ite Prime Minister, Nouri al-Maliki, in December 2013, ordered Muslim prayers to be directed towards the Shi'ite holy city of Karbala, instead of Mecca. This move can only exasperate the growing divide between the Sunni and Shi'a factions of Islam. Karbala is where, in 680 C.E., Imam Husayn ibn Ali, a grandson of Muhammad, was killed for refusing to surrender the Islamic caliphate to Sunni leaders. Regarded as a Shi'ite martyr, his mausoleum is in Karbala. This development comes amidst the rising tensions, violence and threats of all-out sectarian warfare between the Shi'ite bloc (led by Iran) and the Sunni bloc (led by Saudi Arabia), on the battlefields of Iraq, Syria, Lebanon and Yemen, with the backdrop of an emergent nuclear Iran.

Friday, rather than a day of rest, is the day of communal and public prayer as well as public sermon. This day was chosen to be different from the Jewish Sabbath, Saturday, and the Christian Sabbath, Sunday. In some Muslim countries (e.g. Indonesia) it is not considered a day of rest. In

---

* "Nation" in this sense should not be confused with the concept of a Western nation-state—such as Canada, Belgium or Portugal, with fixed geographic borders, which is a secondary definition of the word. In Islam, "nation" is used in its primary definition, meaning "a large body of people." More precisely, a large body of people who feel themselves bound to one another by certain traits: maybe geographical borders, and perhaps ethnicity and language. In the case of Islam, they are bound to one another by the common beliefs as defined in the Koran and the Sunnah. There are other such "nations" without fixed political borders—the Kurds, the Basques, the Jews (in the Diaspora for some 1,875 years), the Lakota, and the Diné (Navajo)—to name but a few. For the Muslim *Ummah* the entire world is their geographic border. In the past there was a Muslim political-religious entity—the caliphate. It is the caliphate that they seek to restore today.

others, (e.g. Pakistan) it is a half a day of rest, and in still others (e.g. the United Arab Emirates) it is a full day of rest.

Zakat, voluntary charity or alms giving, is every Muslim's obligation to contribute to the strengthening of the *Ummah,* the global Islamic community. It is a religious tithe and not charity in the Western sense. Definitively, it includes the funding of violent jihad against non-Muslims.[35] The Sunni Gulf States (Saudi Arabia, Qatar, and the United Arab Emirates) have funded various Islamic supremacist jihadist terrorist groups with petrodollars. Other ideologically similar groups are funded by Shi'ite Iranian petrorials. Muslims are taught that charity means Muslims aiding Muslims, for the purpose of fortifying and extending the *Ummah* until all the world is Islam's domain. "Take alms from their wealth [properties]," instructs Allah in the Qur'an, "for this will cleanse and purify them."[36] Thus, *zakat* may be given only to Muslims. In *Reliance of the Traveller: The Classic Manual of Islamic Sacred Law* (in Arabic, *'Umdat al-Salik*),* a Shafi'i manual of Islamic law, it specifies, "It is not permissible to give *zakat* to a non-Muslim."[37]

In the Qur'an (*Sura* 9:60), the verse most often associated with *zakat,* directs that "alms are for the poor and the needy, and those employed to administer the funds; for those whose hearts have recently reconciled to Truth [i.e., to Islam]; for those in bondage [like those imprisoned terrorists] and in debt; in the cause of Allah; and for the wayfarer. Thus, it is ordained by Allah." Echoing *Reliance,* the official Saudi version of the Qur'an annotates this verse with the clarification that "those who have devoted themselves entirely to the cause of faith [Allah]—be it by spreading, elucidating, or defending it physically or intellectually—or to any selfless pursuits extolled in Allah's message, such as search for knowledge, work for the betterment of man's lot, and so forth; and finally, those who, having suffered personal or material hurt in such pursuits, are henceforth unable to fend for themselves."[38]

In comparison for example, while Americans may give charity to the poor of all faiths via the Salvation Army (whose "ministry extends to all, regardless of age, sex, color, or creed"[39]) and to Japanese, Sri Lankan, Indian tsunami victims, as well as earthquake victims in Haiti, Chile, and Nepal, Muslims will not give charity to those disasters since they are unbelievers, i.e. infidels. *Zakat* would however, be given to Palestinian suicide bombers' families, and *mujahadeen* fighters in Afghanistan, Iraq as well as Syria, because they are Muslims.

Sawm or fasting refers primarily to the fasting during the month of Ramadan. For the duration of Ramadan, believers are required to fast from dawn to dusk for the entire month. The Qur'an (*Suras* 2:179–181, 183) lays down the rules for the fast. Traditions and Muslim jurists amplify the rules. Muslims must abstain from all food, drink, tobacco, sexual relations, and even perfume. Since the Muslim calendar is lunar, the fasting month of Ramadan rotates throughout the entire solar calendar.

The *hajj* or pilgrimage is one of the five basic pillars of Islam. The formal pilgrimage takes place at a fixed time in the first half of the last month of the Muslim year, known as *Dhu'l Hijja.* The same word, *hajj,* is used as a title for those who have performed the pilgrimage. They may indicate this by wearing a green band around their headgear.

Aside from the Five Pillars of Islam, it is also necessary to understand the role of the mosque. A mosque is not just a house of prayer. From the beginning of the Islamic era, the mosque was a propagation center for Islamic supremacist ideology. It is a base for all Islamist activities political as well as non-political. In recent times mosques have been used "to preach hatred; to spread exhortations to terrorist activity; to house a bomb factory; to store weapons; to disseminate messages from bin Laden; to demand (in the US) that non-Muslims conform to Islamic dietary restrictions; to fire on

---

* *Reliance of the Traveller* is endorsed by Al-Azhar University in Cairo, the most prestigious institution in Sunni Islam, as "conforming to the practice and faith of the orthodox Sunni community."

American troops; and to fire upon Indian troops; as well as to train jihadists."[40] This political use of a mosque is validated by Yusuf al-Qaradawi, an Egyptian Islamic theologian and is best known for his program, *al-Sharī'a wa al-Ḥayāh* ("Shari'a and Life"), broadcast on Al Jazeera, which has an estimated audience of 60 million worldwide. Additionally, he is a trustee of the Oxford University Centre for Islamic Studies. Al-Qaradawi is considered one of the most influential Islamic scholars living today. In 2006, al-Qaradawi produced a *fatwa* to answer the question, "Is it permissible to use a mosque for political purposes?" His reply was "Yes it is," and included the following remarks:

> The mosque at the time of the prophet [Muhammad] was his propagation center and the headquarters of the state. This was also the case for his successors, the rightly guided Caliphs: the mosque was their base for all activities political as well as non-political....Politics in itself is neither vice, nor evil, according to Islam.... For Muslims it is part of our religion: doctrine and worship constitute a system for the whole of life.... It must be the role of the mosque to guide the public policy of a nation, raise awareness of critical issues, and reveal its enemies.[41]

Shari'a is Islamic law. The word "shari'a" simply means "the path" or "the way," that is, the Islamic way of conducting affairs. It governs every aspect of the believer's life. Islamic scholars claim that shari'a is perfect, complete, universal and eternal.[42] Shari'a is based on principles found in the Islamic religious and ideological texts. The first is the Qur'an—the literal words of Allah as related to Muhammad. The Qur'an is only a small part of the textual doctrine of Islam. The second compilation of texts is the Sira—the chronological biographies of Muhammad. Two of the most authoritative and important recorders were Ishaq and Al Tabari. The third compilation of sacred texts is the Hadith ("Traditions") which is a verified collection of brief stories with reference to the practices and actions as well as the sayings about and by Muhammad. Hadith with a capital "H" is an entire collection by one recorder. Individual stories are "hadith," the plural of which is "ahadith." Hadith are regarded by traditional Islamic schools of jurisprudence as important tools for understanding the Qur'an and in matters of shari'a—Islamic law. They were written down and assembled into approved collections. The most authoritative Hadith collections are those by Bukhari and Abu Muslim.

Shari'a repudiates the fundamental principle of justice, that is, equality in the eye of the law. In shari'a, Muslims and non-Muslims are not equal. This inequality extends even to the treatment of Muslim women (which will be discussed in detail in "Basic Principle 29"). The inequality of Muslims and non-Muslims is based on the Islamic definition of human rights and is rooted in the Qur'an and shari'a. It is an accepted principle in Islam that the life of a non-Muslim is worth less than that of a Muslim. *Reliance of the Traveller* declares, "The indemnity for the death or injury of a woman is one-half the indemnity paid for a man. The indemnity paid for a Jew or Christian is one-third the indemnity paid for a Muslim. The indemnity paid for a Zoroastrian is one-fifteenth that of a Muslim."[43] A second example is seen in the Saudi law dealing with the concept of blood money. Under this concept, if a person was killed or caused to die by another, the latter has to pay blood money or compensation as follows:

100,000 riyals if the victim is a Muslim man
50,000 riyals if the victim is a Muslim woman
50,000 riyals if the victim is a Christian man
25,000 riyals if the victim is a Christian woman
6,666 riyals if the victim is a Hindu man

3,333 riyals if the victim is a Hindu woman

Thus, a Muslim man's life is worth 33 times that of a Hindu woman.[44]

As such, shari'a is authoritarian, anti-liberty, anti-equality, and intolerant of minority rights. There is no freedom of speech, religion, expression as well as freedom of the press. The liberty to analyze and criticize shari'a itself is curtailed. It also administers cruel and unusual punishments against women, homosexuals and non-Muslims. There is no equal protection under the law for those groups. As such shari'a, is incompatible with the US Constitution, is opposed to Article VI, Section 2, of the US Constitution (which states, "The Constitution is the supreme law of the land") and seeks to eliminate and supersede it.

Shari'a is in stark conflict with the United Nations Universal Declaration of Human Rights (1948) on a large number of issues. The fact remains that wherever shari'a is implemented, people suffer and human rights are violated. It is believed that Islamic domination of the world is foreordained by Allah, "He who obeys Allah and His Messenger, and fear Allah and keep duty (unto Him) [spreading Islam]: such indeed are those who are triumphant."[45] Thus, it is the duty of all Muslims to strive until all governments are ruled by shari'a.

Islam is a comprehensive political, economic, and religious ideology that is theologically driven, totalitarian-collectivist, militaristic, xenophobic, irredentist, and imperialistic. It has been doing the same thing since 622 c.e. and has had the same goals for 1,400 years. This ideology seeks to impose shari'a law upon all aspects of global society. Islam supersedes everything else, demanding a loyalty above national allegiances and even family ties. It has an undiminishable hatred of Western civilization, as exemplified today, by the United States and Israel—dubbed the "Great Satan" and the "Little Satan" respectively, by the Islamic Republic of Iran." It is the centrality of Islamic ideology that motivates, inspires, instigates, arouses, and stirs its adherents toward the unrelenting goal of a global caliphate. Islam has its own system of totalitarian control, which extends far beyond the twentieth century secular totalitarian systems of fascism, Nazism, and communism. It dictates politics, law, transactions, contracts, philosophy, logic, ritual worship, beliefs, punishments, attire, art, culture, morals, manners, including for example, that people should not gamble, the types of music permitted, and even the proper manner to perform bodily functions.

Lest anyone think that these are theoretical guidelines, one should merely examine the new laws and restrictions implemented by the recently proclaimed Islamic State.

> It is absolutely forbidden [in government public schools] to teach art, music, civics education, sociology, history, sports, philosophy, psychology, and religious education, be it Muslim or Christian. (Religious studies are conducted exclusively in the madrasa–religious schools). There should be no mention of the nation-state, Syria, or use of the word 'homeland.' The national anthem is also forbidden. Instead, the students/pupils should learn to say Islamic State or Country of Islam or the Province of Sham (the Levant). In mathematics, no example should be given that would point at calculating interest, or mentioning democracy or elections. In natural science, there will be no mention of Darwin or Darwinism.[46]

In a discussion of Islam, it is essential to distinguish between Islam as a religious ideology and how people who identify themselves as Muslims behave. If we take the term "Islam" to be the body of beliefs and doctrines of Islam, there are no strict or moderate forms. Islam itself does not vary, but what varies is how strictly Muslims adhere to its doctrine. This is an important distinction. The doctrines of Islam exist no matter how strict or lax Muslims may be in following them. Secular Muslims deviate in practice from some of the basic doctrines of Islam. There are those secularists who consider themselves "devout Muslims," even though they reject fundamental Islamic doctrines such as the perpetual jihad against non-Muslims, the total loyalty to the *Ummah,* and the mandatory nature of shari'a law. They fail to practice Islam as defined by Islamic religious authorities.

It is important to distinguish between those Muslims who support the doctrines of Islam and those who do not. Those Muslims who do not support all the doctrines of Islam, will never stand up en masse and say so, largely out of fear for their lives. It is more appropriate and accurate to speak of practitioners of Islam as prescribed by the Islamic holy texts on one hand, and secular Muslims on the other, rather than the mistaken Western-derived categorization of Islam into basically two groups—"radicals" and "moderates." The "moderates" are people who identify themselves as being Muslims who are secular. These secularist Muslims are a tiny minority worldwide and their influence is minimal. In the mainstream of the *Ummah,* they are viewed as hypocrites, heretics or apostates.[47] While there are secular Muslims, there is no such thing as "moderate" Islam. The Turkish Prime Minister Recep Tayyip Erdoğan pointedly demonstrated this fact when speaking on the Kanal D TV's *Arena* program. Erdoğan, himself an Islamist, commented on the term "moderate Islam" often used by the West to describe his AKP party. He said, "these descriptions are very ugly. It is offensive and an insult to our religion. There is no moderate or immoderate Islam. Islam is Islam and that's it."[48] In the Muslim world, and in the established Muslim areas in the West, the true meaning of Islam exists in practice. There is only one form of Islam and not what Western apologists seek to dismiss as only a abnormal form of it to explain away the more violent and sanguinary practices. Islam means censorship, homophobia, pedophilia, misojudaism, misogyny, child marriages (no minimum age limit for girls to be married), wife-beatings, honor killings, beheadings, and murdering infidels, among other practices.

The overwhelming majority of Muslims do not adhere to violent jihad (for more information about jihad, *see* "Basic Principle 31"), but that does not mean that there is not a basis for it in Islamic doctrine. To assign Islamic supremacist beliefs to every single Muslim of the 1.5 billion Muslims on the planet is wrong. Not all Muslims are supremacist. Such groups as the Ahmadis or Ahmadi Muslims, Isma'ilis, modern Sufis, and the Kurdish Muslims of Iraqi and Syrian Kurdistan, are not supremacists. To deny the basis in Islamic doctrine for this entire violent jihad is wrong and it is preventing the West from facing the global war thrust upon us. The practitioners of Islam, who follow the Islamic holy texts—the Qur'an, the Sunnah, and the Hadith, are known by various names—fundamentalists, jihadists, Islamic supremacists, and Islamofascists.* These practitioners number in the hundreds of millions and may

---

* Islamofascism as a term was introduced by French writer Maxine Rodinson (1945–2004) to describe the Iranian Revolution of 1979. The term is used to describe those Islamic supremacists who have been waging war against the West in the latter half of the twentieth century and into the twenty-first century. The twentieth century totalitarian ideology of fascism bears an uncanny resemblance to the ideology of Islam which predates it by some 1,300 years. Islam and fascism have some common elements. The goals of both are more important than the rights of individuals. Both have an anti-humanist character. Both seek to re-create a mystical past. Both seek by force, world conquest and domination as well as the imposition of violent customs and rules on the rest of the world. Both are triumphalist, supremacist, anti-democratic, anti-liberal, populist, intolerant, misogynistic, expansive, imperialistic, aggressive, oppose personal liberty, and glorify war. Additionally, both utilize violence, intimidation, belligerence, superiority over unbelievers (i.e. racism), misojudaism (hatred of Jews), and anti-liberalism.

very well be a majority of the *Dar al-Islam*—the Islamic world. They are engaged in a civilizational war against the West—legalistically, educationally, economically, militarily, and demographically.

One must also note the distinctions between active support, passive support and direct opposition to Islamic terrorism. As Daniel Greenfield points out:

> Those Muslims who support both the ends and the means of Muslim terrorism are active supporters. Those who support the ends of Islamic theocracy, but not the means of Islamic terrorism, can be labeled passive supporters. And the tiny minority of secular extremists who oppose both the ends and the means are the direct opposition.[49]

Every political, economic, diplomatic and military victory brings more adherents to the Islamic supremacist cause. The fact remains that there are violent Islamic supremacists around the world who commit acts of war or terror. While not all Muslims support every act of terror, nearly all Muslims support some acts of terror. They define acts that they disapprove of as terrorism and acts that they approve of as resistance or armed struggle, which makes the formal condemnations of terrorism by Muslim groups completely meaningless. They justify these acts based on Islamic scripture and carry them out to promote Islam. They are following to the letter the Islamic doctrine of violent armed jihad. To the Islamic supremacists we are the enemy, not because of this or that policy or our presence in this or that country. We are the enemy because we are who we are. This truth was enunciated on November 30, 2005, by former US Secretary of State Henry Kissinger when he stated simply that what angers the Islamic supremacists, "What provokes the Islamofascists is our existence—not our policies." Their hatred of America stems from a hatred of the modern Western lifestyle. Let us make no mistake; this is a war of civilizations. To date, the Western powers have persistently played down the Sunni and Shi'ite jihadist political and military potential, and gloss over three essential facts:

Western ideals and values are not universally shared. In fact, Western and Islamic societal values are very different on many subjects including (but not limited to) the sanctity of life, protection of women and children, as well as concepts of peace. Arab/Muslim society has different political, social and cultural values. Fundamentalist Islam has declared a perpetual war on Western law, culture and tradition. This is not rooted in political or social differences, such as the gap between the have-not Muslim and the affluent Westerner, or even in various world disputes like the Arab/Muslim war against Israel, the Kashmir dispute and the wars in Iraq and Afghanistan, which are often held up as expressions of imperialistic injustice. The Islamic supremacists are committed to unending war with the West—be it full scale, low key, or subversive warfare—focused first on the United States and Israel, and then on other western societies. They loathe everything the West stands for, not just because it is infidel but also because it represents modernity with its freedom, individual liberty, religious choice, toleration (religious, sexual, philosophical), social equality (especially for women) and moral attitudes. These fundamentalists are willing to lay down their lives, and the lives of their children, to extinguish all of these.

To challenge and defeat an ideological movement, you have to understand and confront their vision of the world. To his credit, President George W. Bush was not afraid to name the enemy confronting the United States. On October 28, 2005, Bush denounced Islamofascist movements that call for a "violent and political vision: the establishment, by terrorism, subversion and insurgency, of a totalitarian empire that denies all political and religious freedom."[50] Later, President Bush characterized the revelation, in London, of a major terror plot to blow up several trans-Atlantic jetliners, as proof "that this nation is at war with Islamic fascists."[51] The West can only defeat this threat by weakening

Islam, legalistically, educationally, economically, militarily and demographically. If we in the West want to maintain our Judeo-Christian values, we must resist the basic teachings of the Islamic holy texts. One cannot make a violent religion like Islam non-violent by discussion or argument. Islamic supremacism can only be defeated by greater retaliatory force primarily against state sponsors of jihadist terrorism, and drying up the money supply that funds such terrorism, provided by the oil of the Middle East. They must be defeated thoroughly, for if the West does not win, it will lose. There is no middle ground compromise.

27. The ideology of Islam is based on the Qur'an, which is believed by most Muslims to be the literal word[52] of Allah—perfect, complete, immutable and valid for all of eternity.

Islam is not merely a religion in the Judeo-Christian or even East Asian sense. Rather it is a religious ideology and it includes a mandatory and highly specific legal and political plan for all of society. It is this fundamental principle of Islam that has prevented religious Muslims from offering alternative interpretations or deciding that various verses of the Qur'an no longer are valid. Muslims cannot alter or ignore any part of the Qur'an. Hence, all Muslim scholars know that they cannot condemn, on the basis of the Qur'an, the use of violence to expand their religion. This has been followed and practiced for 1,400 years. Historically, Islam is a religion built on war and conquest. The peoples of the world are distinguished from Muslims as *dhimma* (the protected—though second-class—"Peoples of the Book"—Christians and Jews) who are to be tolerated and defended by Islam as long as they submitted to the superior Islamic sovereignty, and the infidels who were to be fought into submission. However, the Arabian Peninsula was to be cleansed of Christians and Jews as per the wishes of Muhammad. "It has been narrated by 'Umar ibn al-Khattib, that he heard the Messenger of Allah [Muhammad] (may peace be upon him) say: I will expel the Jews and Christians from the Arabian Peninsula and will not leave any but Muslim."[53]

Islam is a global totalitarian, supremacist and imperialistic ideology. It is a theocratic and political ideology. Since its inception, it has maintained that it replaces and is a successor to both Judaism and Christianity. It never intended to live side by side with Judaism and Christianity. In the historic past, all religions killed. However, the question must be asked: Which religion has not stopped killing? It should be noted that the political violence of the Qur'an is eternal and universal. The political violence of the Bible was for that particular historical time and place. This is the vast difference between Islam and other ideologies. The violence remains a constant threat to all non-Islamic cultures, now and into the future. Islam is not analogous to Christianity and Judaism in any practical way. Beyond the one-god doctrine, Islam is unique unto itself.[54] Islam served notice and continued to warn unbelievers that it will continue its jihad until all the world is within the *Dar al-Islam*. Islamic theology is supremacist and materialist. It combines an honor-shame code of an old-fashioned tribal culture and driven compulsively by private beliefs inexorably toward confrontations with other societies with destruction and conquest as goals and with deceit, assassination, and war as an acceptable means to an end.

According to Islamic doctrine, everyone born into the world is a Muslim but his parents convert him to Judaism or to Christianity or to Zoroastrianism or to something else.[55] Hence, everyone who is an unbeliever must be given three choices, convert to Islam, submit to a subordinate status (*dhimmitude*) and pay *jizya*—per capita tax tribute—or face war and death. This is not some ancient historic custom, but rather an on-going tradition practiced for over 1,400 years. A recent example occurred in the southern Ethiopian city of Besheno, in Alaba Province. The province, according to the 2007 census, is 93.84 percent Muslim and only 5.82 percent Christian. Ethiopia is a predominantly

Christian nation. On November 9, 2010, the Christian inhabitants of Besheno woke up to find notes tacked to their doors warning them to convert to Islam, leave the city or face death.[56] Thousands of Christians have been forced to flee their homes in western Ethiopia after Muslim extremists set fire to roughly fifty churches and dozens of Christian homes. At least one Christian was killed; many more were injured and anywhere from 3,000 to 10,000 were displaced in the attacks that began March 2, 2011, after a Christian in the community of Asendabo was accused of desecrating the Qur'an.[57] During 2013–14, the Islamic State has forcibly converted or killed thousands across the map of what was then Syria and Iraq,

Muslims must maintain absolute loyalty to Islam and one another, while disavowing, even hating[58] all things un-Islamic—including infidels. This precept is known as *Wala' wa Bara'* ("loyalty and enmity") and is exemplified by Qur'an 5:51. To uphold loyalty and enmity, it is totally acceptable to use deception—*taqiyya* or *kitman*—against the infidel, to advance the goal of spreading Islam. Whereas *taqiyya* is saying something that is not true, *kitman* is lying by omission. As Raymond Ibrahim, Arab history researcher and author, pointed out:

> According to the authoritative Arabic text, *Al-Taqiyya Fi Al-Islam*, '*Taqiyya* [deception] is of fundamental importance in Islam. Practically every Islamic sect agrees to it and practices it. We can go so far as to say that the practice of *taqiyya* is mainstream in Islam, and that those few sects not practicing it diverge from the mainstream...*Taqiyya* is very prevalent in Islamic politics, especially in the modern era.'[59]

The use of *taqiyya* is important especially wherever and whenever Muslim minorities live among non-Muslim majorities. In fact, the Qur'an's primary justification for deception is in the context of loyalty. Using *taqiyya* when necessary, Muslims are permitted to feign friendship and loyalty to non-Muslims. Furthermore, shari'a says that Muslims can lie to avoid a charge in court, even if it is only a damage claim, "If the consequences of telling the truth are more damaging, one is entitled to lie."[60] Abu Muslim, in *Reliance of the Traveller,* recorded that Umm Kulthum discussing *taqiyya* added, "I did not hear him [the Prophet] permit untruth in anything people say, except for three things: war [jihad], settling disagreements, and a man talking with his wife or she with him."[61]

According to Nonie Darwish, an Egyptian-American human rights activist, President of Former Muslims United and founder of Arabs For Israel, "In Arab culture, being truthful is not only considered to be naïve and stupid, but is also considered—believe it or not—rude."[62] Darwish continued, this of course, "was very different from American culture, where people talk freely about their shortcomings and pain without shame."[63] Moreover, she added, "Western-style soul searching or examination of beliefs is almost unheard of in Arab culture. And no subject is more sacred and protected from analysis or criticism than the Qur'an or Islam. Muslims can get violently angry if that is done. To a lesser extent, if a family member, tribe, nation, or culture is perceived to be under attack, then excuses … misrepresentations, and outright lies are the only honorable thing to do. Remember, this is a culture based on pride and shame."[64] (For more on *taqiyya* as a negotiating strategy, *see* "Basic Principle 66").

The supremacist ideology of Islam is based on the "immutable" words of Allah as recorded in the Qur'an. The Qur'an is one book written by one man, Muhammad, during his lifetime. It is to be taken literally, and consists mainly of direct commands. The Qur'an is unlike the Jewish *Tanakh,* which is a collection of books that lays out the foundational historic narrative of the Jewish people including their formation into a nation by God, their trials and tribulations, and their covenant with God, which involves following a way of life bound by a set of religious obligations and civil laws.

Various authors wrote it over a period of hundreds of years. Also, the Qur'an is unlike the Christian Bible, which similar to the *Tanakh* is a collection of writings from various authors, written sometimes hundreds of years apart. It is an anthology of the life, the teachings, the death and the resurrection of Jesus, and includes advice, analogies, dreams, parables, and symbolisms all collected in one book.

The Qur'an contains 114 *suras* (chapters), each containing many *ayahs* (verses). There are over 6,000 *ayahs* in the Qur'an. However, unlike the Jewish Torah or the Christian New Testament, the *suras* of the Qur'an are not arranged in chronological order in regard to the timing in which they were written. The *suras* (except for the first one) are written according to length, longest to shortest. The first eighty-seven *suras* are known as the "Meccan" *suras*—the revelation purportedly received by Muhammad via the messenger/angel Gabriel. These *suras* are widely regarded by experts on Islamic scripture as being the more benign revelations that Muhammad received. These are the passages most favored by Islamists who wish to deceive, especially unbelievers, into thinking Islam is nothing but a religion of peace, harmony, tolerance and love. As Dr. Michael Widlanski of Bar Ilan University explained, there is much theological and linguistic distortion involved in describing Islam as "the religion of peace." While it is true that the word "Islam" in Arabic is related to the word *salaam*, both words from the root S-L-M, like the Hebrew word *shalom*, which comes from the root SH-L-M, in Arabic grammar, Islam is actually the fourth verbal form that means to "give oneself" or "to submit" to God's will.[65]

The following twenty-seven *suras* were "revealed" to Muhammad following his migration, on July 16, 622 C.E., to Yathrib (Medina). These Medinan *suras* and verses are widely regarded by experts on Islamic scripture as being much more belligerent, violent and supremacist than the "Meccan" *suras*. It was in Medina, that Muhammad became a warlord. Once Muhammad was in Medina he nullified, abrogated, and rendered void the earlier more passive and peaceful *ayahs*.

More importantly, the latter "Medinan" *suras* which were revealed to Muhammad* are regarded and upheld as being more *authoritative* (emphasis added) than the former *suras*. Additionally, the later *ayahs* supersede the earlier ones and incite killing, decapitations, maiming, terrorism and religious intolerance. To the present, circumstance dictates which *suras* are to be implemented. When Muslims are weak, they should preach and behave according to the Meccan *suras*; when strong, they should go on the offensive, according to the Medinan *suras*.

The doctrine of abrogation comes into play throughout the Qur'an. Abrogation is the abolition, nullification or cancellation of previously cited *ayahs*, by these later *ayahs*. Some 225 *ayahs* of the Qur'an are abrogated by later ones. Abrogation is based on and justified by two *ayahs* that Allah instructed Muhammad to put into the Qur'an.

> None of Our revelations do We abrogate or cause to be forgotten, but We substitute something better or similar: Knowest thou not that Allah is able to do all things? (*Sura* 2:106)

> When We substitute one revelation for another, and Allah knows best what he reveals (in stages), they say, 'Thou art but inventing': but most of them understand not. (*Sura* 16:101)

---

* The Qur'an was revealed to Muhammad by the Archangel Gabriel over a period of twenty-three years—ten years in Mecca and thirteen years in Medina.

In short, *ayahs* 2:106 and 16:101 explained that Allah could do whatever he wanted and anyone finding fault with that was not a believer and was asking for punishment. An example of abrogation is *Sura* 9:5 which nullifies 124 *ayahs* that call for tolerance and patience. *Sura* 9:5 is called the "verse of the sword" and states, "Then when the sacred months have past [passed], slay the idolaters wherever ye find them, and taken them [captive], and besiege them, and prepare for them each ambush." Another example is *Sura* 9:29 which abrogates *Sura* 5:77 and calls for harsher treatment of the "People of the Book," i.e. Christians and Jews.

It should be noted that one of Islam's classical reference books (in the Arabic language) is entitled *al-Nasikh wal-Mansoukh* ("The Abrogator and the Abrogated"), authored by the revered Muslim scholar Abil-Kasim Hibat-Allah Ibn-Salama Abi-Nasr who set forth which *suras* and *ayahs* were abrogated. The book goes through every *sura* in the Qur'an and cites in detail every *ayat* that was abrogated, i.e. cancelled-out or overridden, by particular *ayahs* that were written later. The author noted that out of 114 *suras* of the Qur'an, there are only 43 *suras* that were not affected by this doctrine.[66] Scholars through the ages have wondered about the need for abrogation. Why was there a need for changes in the Qur'an, if it really contained Allah's words? If Allah were indeed all-powerful and all knowing, why would He need to revise and correct Himself so often?

The Qur'an contains at least 109 *ayahs* that call Muslims to war with unbelievers. Some are quite graphic, with commands to chop off heads and fingers and kill infidels wherever they may be hiding. Muslims who do not join the fight are called "hypocrites" and warned that Allah will send them to Hell if they do not join the slaughter.

Unlike nearly all of the *Tanakh* (Hebrew/Jewish Bible) verses of violence, most of the verses of violence in the Qur'an are open-ended, meaning that the historical context is not embedded within the surrounding text. They are part of the eternal, unchanging word of Allah, and today are just as relevant or subjective as anything else in the Qur'an is. Unfortunately, there are very few verses of tolerance and peace to abrogate or even balance out the many that call for unbelievers to be fought and subdued until they accept humiliation, convert to Islam, or are killed. This proclivity toward violence and Muhammad's own martial legacy, has left a trail of blood and tears across world history.

The following are a broad sampling of the more belligerent, violent and supremacist verses[67][68] in the Qur'an:

- "Lo! Allah is the enemy of the disbelievers" (2:98).
- "[Muslims] Fight against them [the unbelievers] until idolatry is no more and Allah's religion reigns supreme" (2:193).
- "The [only] religion [acceptable] before Allah is Islam" (3:19).
- "If anyone desires a religion other than Islam, never will it be accepted of him" (3:85).
- "You are the noblest community ever raised up for mankind" (3:110).
- "We will put terror into the hearts of the unbelievers" (3:150).
- "Allah has made men superior to women because men spend their wealth to support them. Therefore, virtuous women are obedient, and they are to guard their unseen parts as Allah has guarded them. As for women whom you fear will rebel, admonish them first, and then send them to a separate bed, and then beat them. But if they are obedient after that, then do nothing further; surely Allah is exalted and great!" (4:34).[69]
- "Those who reject our Signs, We shall soon cast into the Fire: as often as their skins are roasted through, We shall change them for fresh skins, that they may taste the penalty: for Allah is Exalted in Power, Wise" (4:56).

- "Hence, let them fight in Allah's cause—all who are willing to barter the life of this world for the life to come; for unto him who fights in Allah's cause, whether he be slain or be victorious, We shall in time grant a mighty reward" (4:74).
- "The true believers fight for the cause of Allah, but the infidels fight for the devil. Fight then against the friends of Satan" (4:76).
- "The unbelievers are your inveterate enemy" (4:101).
- "And never will Allah grant to the unbelievers any way of success over the believers" (4:141).
- "Indeed, the truth denies they who say, 'Behold, Allah is the Christ, son of Mary.' Say 'And who could have prevailed with Allah in any way had it been His will to destroy the Christ, son of Mary, and his mother, and everyone who is on earth—all of them? For Allah is the dominion over the heavens and the earth and all that is between them; He creates what He wills: and Allah has the power to will anything!'" (5:17).
- "The only reward of those who wage war against Allah and His messenger and endeavor to spread corruption on earth, will be that they should be murdered or crucified in great numbers or their hands and their feet should be cut off on opposite sides or they should be expelled out of the land; this shall be as a disgrace for them in this world, and in the Hereafter theirs will be an awful doom" (5:33).
- "O ye who believe! Take neither the Jews nor the Christians for friends. They are friends one to another. He among you who taketh them for friends is (one) of them; behold Allah does not guide such evildoers" (5:51). Twelve *ayahs* in the Qur'an repeat this admonition.
- "Indeed, the truth deny they who say, 'Behold, Allah is the Christ, son of Mary'—seeing that the Christ (himself) said, 'O children of Israel! Worship Allah, who is my Sustainer as well as your Sustainer.' Behold, whoever ascribes divinity to any being beside Allah, unto him will Allah deny paradise, and his goal shall be the fire; and such evildoers will have none to succor them!" (5:72).

Muslims are taught in the Qur'an that Christians are the most monstrous of blasphemers and the most wicked of people because they believe that Jesus is the son of God. This is the greatest sin in Islam, the only sin that Allah will never pardon. Specifically, in *Suras* 5:17 and 9:30 the Qur'an talks about people who believe that Jesus of Nazareth is the son of God. The fact remains that hundreds of millions of Christians have believed that Jesus is the son of God for over 2,000 years. If, however, the Qur'an were to be the law of the land, there would be a problem for these Christians, because the Qur'an explicitly curses and damns these people (9:30), and the Qur'an even expresses the wish that people who believe that Christ is the son of God shall be killed in battle.

- "I shall cast terror into the hearts of the infidels. Strike off their heads; strike off the very tips of their fingers" (8:12). The translation is also rendered as "I will instill terror into the hearts of the Unbelievers: smite ye above their necks and smite all their finger-tips off them."

The above verse, as well as *Sura* 47:4, bring to mind the slaughter by beheadings of Daniel Pearl, reporter for the *Wall Street Journal* on February 1, 2002, American businessman Nicholas Berg on May 7, 2004, Owen Eugene Armstrong, a American contractor on September 20, 2004, American Jack Hensley beheaded the next day, and most recently James Foley (August 20, 2014) and Steven Sotloff (September 1, 2014), American freelance journalists for *GlobalPost* and *TIME* Magazine respectively, in Syria. Pearl and Berg were also killed because they were both Americans and Jews. Increasingly, the practice of beheadings (or attempted beheadings) has appeared in the West more frequently in recent years. These include: Ariel Sellouk, a Jew beheaded by his Saudi "friend," in Houston, Texas, on August 6, 2003; Sébastien Selam, a Jew in Paris, France, on November 20, 2003; Amgad A. Konds and Hany F. Tawadros, both Coptic Christians in Jersey City, New Jersey, around February 7, 2013; and Lee Rigby, a British soldier from Woolwich barracks near London, in the United Kingdom, on May 22, 2013. Not to be forgotten was the assassination of Dutch filmmaker, columnist, author and actor, Theodoor "Theo" van Gogh. On the morning of November 2, 2004, van Gogh, a critic of Islam and great great nephew of post-Impressionist painter Vincent van Gogh, was stabbed and shot to death on the streets of Amsterdam in the Netherlands. He had received death threats over a movie he had made criticizing the treatment of women under Islam. Van Gogh was ritualistically murdered, his head nearly severed from his body, by Dutch-Moroccan dual-national Mohammed Bouyeri. Bouyeri was linked to the jihadist Hofstad group. Terrorist savagery was not limited to civilians. On January 19, 2008, Hezbollah leader Sheikh Hassan Nasrallah stated that his armed group had body parts of Israeli soldiers killed in Lebanon during the 2006 conflict. He said they had the "heads, the hands, the feet and even a nearly intact cadaver from the head down to the pelvis." The public was horrified in each case, when videotapes or photos of these executions were broadcast globally. This is precisely the reaction wanted by the Islamic supremacists—to instill fear and terrorize others into submission (*see* also *Sura* 3:151).

- "Fight them until all opposition ends and all submit to Allah. So fight them until there is no more Fitnah (disbelief [by non-Muslims]) and all submit to the religion of Allah alone (in the whole world)" (8:39).
- "Make war on them [non-Muslims] until idolatry shall cease and Allah's religion shall reign supreme" (8:40).
- "Surely the vilest of animals in Allah's sight are those who disbelieve, then they would not believe" (8:55).
- "Fight and kill the disbelievers wherever you find them, take them captive, harass them, lie in wait and ambush them using every stratagem of war" (9:5).
- "Fight from among the people who have been given the Scripture [the Jews] those who do not believe in Allah and the Last Day and who do not forbid that which Allah and His messenger have forbidden and who do not follow the religion of truth, until they pay the tribute [*jizya*] readily, having been humbled" (9:29).

These verses (9:5 and 9:29) not only command war against people (no matter how innocent) who simply believe in another religion other than Islam, but also denote the superiority of believers over unbelievers (the latter having been humbled).

- "Prophet, make war on the unbelievers and the hypocrites and deal rigorously with them" (9:73 and 66:9).
- "Allah has purchased from the faithful their lives and worldly goods, and in return has promised them Paradise. They will fight for the cause of Allah; they will kill and be killed" (9:111).
- "O ye who believe! Fight; fight those of the unbelievers, who dwell around you. Deal harshly with them" (9:123).

- "But as for those who disbelieve, garments of fire will be cut out for them; boiling fluid will be poured down on their heads, Whereby that which is in their bellies and their skins too, will be melted; And for them are hooked rods of iron. Whenever, in their anguish, they would go forth from thence they are driven back therein and (it is said unto them): Taste the doom of burning" (22:19–22).
- "When you meet the unbelievers in the battlefield, strike off their heads" (47:4).
- "Muhammad is the messenger of Allah. And those with him are hard against the disbelievers and merciful among themselves" (48:29).
- "He it is who has sent his Messenger with guidance and the religion of truth [Islam] to make it conqueror over all religions even though the infidels may be averse" (61:9).
- "The unbelievers among the People of the Book [Jews and Christians] and the idolaters shall burn forever in the fire of Hell. They are the worst of created beings" (98:6).

While on the subject of violence, it has been claimed that the *Tanakh*, (Hebrew/Jewish Bible) and the Christian Bible, (i.e. Old and New Testaments) are equivalent in their call to violence compared to the Qur'an. This attempt at politically correct moral equivalency and relativism is false. The key issue of Biblical violence and cruelty versus Qur'anic violence and cruelty can be summed up as "descriptive" and "prescriptive." Violence (and even brutality) in the Old and New Testaments is descriptive. It relates to particular events of what happened in the past. At no time did God give an open-ended command for the Hebrews and by extension their Jewish descendants, to fight and kill all "unbelievers." In contrast, the violence in the Qur'an is prescriptive. It is an instruction manual for Muslims, which uses generic, open-ended language to command them to bring the entire world into the *Dar al-Islam,* and what they must do now and in the future, including the use of violence and brutality. Most Muslims believe that changing even one word of the Qur'an is blasphemy and a corruption. That is why Islam is hostile to the Western way of life.

Even modern day fundamentalist Jews and Christians do not follow such cruel behavior in the name of religion. Jews do not go around committing atrocities quoting passages from the *Tanakh*. The violence of the Bible is not commanded for all history throughout time as in the Qur'an. The Bible's descriptive verses "nowhere command believers to imitate this behavior, or to believe under any circumstances that God wishes them to act as His instruments of judgment in any situations today."[70] In stark contrast, the Qur'an is always phrased in general terms against unbelievers, Jews, or Christians. It is the general, open-ended nature of the phrasing that prevents it from being limited to a particular historical context. Thus, the Qur'an commands believers to continue, for all time, to use violence until the entire world of all unbelievers (i.e. the *Dar al-Harb)*, agree to convert to Islam, or submit by accepting *dhimmi* status and paying the *jizya,* or else face death.

The noted nineteenth century French historian and political thinker, Alexis de Tocqueville, commented on the difference between Islam and the Gospel. He stated that:

> Mohammed professed to derive from Heaven, and he has inserted in the Koran, not only a body of religious doctrines, but political maxims, civil and criminal laws, and theories of science. The Gospel, on the contrary, only speaks of the general relations of men to God and to each other—beyond which it inculcates and imposes no point of faith.[71]

Religion, even more than nationalism, played a dominant role in the Arab/Muslim war against the Jews in the Land of Israel. It dates from the seventh century (*see* "Basic Principle 31"). With the advent of modern Arab nationalism and Zionism (the Jewish national liberation movement), the religious component was at times obscured (and downplayed by the West) but it is always present. From the 1920s Arab leaders, both religious (e.g. the Grand Mufti of Jerusalem, Hajj Amin al-Husseini, Grand Mufti of Egypt, Sheikh Hasan Ma'moun, and Hamas leader Sheikh Ahmed Ismail Hassan Yassin) and secular (e.g. King Farouk of Egypt, King Abdullah I of Transjordan, Egypt's President Gamal Abdel Nasser, Iraq's strongman Saddam Hussein, and Yasser Arafat) called for jihad against the Jews. It was not a purely nationalist struggle then, nor is it today. Little has changed since the 1920s. The religious component has, if anything, grown with the explosion of radical Islamic fundamentalism starting in the 1970s. It is as Muslims, more than, as Arabs or Iranians, that today's leading enemies of Israel view the Arab/Muslim conflict against the Jewish state.

Historic misojudaism has been camouflaged using a new term—"anti-Zionism." In recent decades, many of Israel's Arab/Muslim enemies, as well as many misojudaic individuals and groups worldwide have latched on to this odious code phrase to pursue their vehement hatred. While legitimate criticism of Israel's government, policies, and actions is to be expected in the free world, much of the criticism of Israel and Jews is not legitimate and is nothing more than disguised misojudaism often behind the mask of "anti-Zionism."

Natan Sharansky, Israel's Minister for Diaspora Affairs and Jerusalem, developed a simple "'3-D' test"[72] for differentiating legitimate criticism of Israel from misojudaism. This "'3-D' test" applies the same criteria to new misojudaism when compared to classical misojudaism. The first "D" of the test stands for demonization. This applies to comparing Israel's actions to the worst evils in history. For example, one such comparison is that of Israelis to Nazis, and another is of the Palestinian refugee camps to the Auschwitz death camp. Such equivocations are clearly misojudaic. Those who draw such analogies either are deliberately ignorant regarding Nazi Germany or are deliberately depicting modern-day Israel as the embodiment of evil. The second "D" of the test stands for double standards. Here, Israel is singled out for criticism while ignoring comparable or worse actions perpetrated by other countries. For example, Israel is singled out for condemnation by the United Nations for perceived human rights abuses even though proven violators of human rights on a massive scale—like Iran, Cuba, the DPRK, China, Saudi Arabia, and Sudan, to name just a few of the biggest violators—are not even mentioned, let alone condemned. The third "D" of the test stands for delegitimization. This is the outright attempt to deny Israel's fundamental right to exist as a nation-state of the Jewish people, by presenting it as, among other things, the prime remnant of imperialist colonialism. While criticism of an Israeli policy may not be misojudaic, the denial of Israel's right to exist is always misojudaic. If other peoples, including twenty-one Arab Muslim states, not to mention the scores of states created in the postcolonial period following World War II, have the right to live securely in their homelands, then the Jewish people have that right as well. Questioning that legitimacy is an example of pure misojudaism.

A demonstrative illustration of the ongoing Arab/Muslim hatred of Jews and Israel can be seen in a *fatwa* issued in 1956. The most authoritative religious educational institution within Sunni Islam is Al-Azhar University,* in Cairo, Egypt. On January 5, 1956, a *fatwa* was written by then Grand Mufti

---

* Al-Azhar is the chief center of Islamic learning, thought and jurisprudence for all of Sunni Islam. Its mission includes the propagation of Islamic religion and culture. To this end, its Islamic scholars (*ulamas*) render edicts (*fatwas*) on disputes submitted to them from all over the Sunni Islamic world regarding proper conduct for Muslim individuals and societies. The grand imam of Al-Azhar, is the nearest equivalent to a pope in Islam.

of Egypt, Sheikh Hasan Ma'moun, and signed by the leading members of the Fatwa Committee of Al-Azhar, and the major representatives of all four Sunni Islamic schools of jurisprudence. [English translation from State Department Telegram 1763/ Embassy (Cairo) Telegram 1256 D441214] This ruling elaborated the following key initial point: that all of historical Palestine having been conquered by jihad, was a permanent possession of the global Muslim *Ummah* (community), "*fay* territory" (booty/spoils), to be governed by Islamic law.

> The question put to us reveals that the land of Palestine has been conquered by the Muslims [i.e., by Jihad in the seventh century] who have lived there for a long time, and has become part of the Muslim territory where minorities of other religions dwell. Accordingly, Palestine has become a territory under the jurisdiction of Islam and governed by Islamic laws. The question further reveals that Jews have taken a part of Palestine and there established their non-Islamic government and have evacuated from that part most of its Muslim inhabitants.
>
> In this case, the Jihad is the duty of all Muslims, not just those who can undertake it. And since all Islamic countries constitute the abode of every Muslim, the Jihad is imperative for both the Muslims inhabiting the territory attacked and Muslims everywhere else because even though some sections have not been attacked directly, the attack nevertheless took place on a part of the Muslim territory, which is a legitimate residence for any Muslim.
>
> Muslims cannot conclude peace with those Jews who have usurped the territory of Palestine and attacked its people and their property in any manner, which allows the Jews to continue as a state in that sacred Muslim territory. Muslims should cooperate regardless of differences in language, color, or race to restore the country to its people … Everyone knows that from the early days of Islam to the present day the Jews have been plotting against Islam and Muslims and the Islamic homeland. They do not propose to be content with the attack they made on Palestine and Al-Aqsa Mosque, but they plan for the possession of all Islamic territories from the Nile to the Euphrates.[73]

It needs to be emphasized that the January 1956 Al-Azhar *fatwa* was issued only eight years after Israel miraculously overcame Arab aggression bent on its destruction within the *1947 UN Partition Plan lines* (emphasis added). It was issued some nine months *before* (emphasis added) the outbreak of the Sinai Campaign (Operation *Kadesh*), which was launched to destroy Nasser's growing Soviet-supplied military machine, that was to be used for the final assault on Israel. The *fatwa* was issued eleven long years *before* (emphasis added) the Six-Day War of June 1967, and the issues of "occupied territories" and "Jerusalem" became standards at the United Nations. In short, the Arab/Muslim war against Jewish sovereignty in the Land of Israel dates back to the early years of Islam itself and its Qur'anic dictates.

The Muslim hatred of the Jews continues to the present. Illustrations of this misojudaism are found continually 24/7, in the Arab and non-Arab Muslim press, radio, television, social media and on the Internet. In fact, Arab/Islamic misojudaism is the most biased, misleading and underreported story of the entire conflict between Arabs/Muslims and the Jews. For example, in May and June 2011, the official PA daily newspaper, *Al-Hayat Al-Jadida,* ran a series of articles in their section on religion, which reemphasized the following points:

- Judaism is a "distorted, corrupted, falsified religion."
- The Jews are inherently evil and inherited this nature from Cain who murdered his brother, Abel.
- Zionism is a religious Jewish plan to rule over the non- Jewish world, and "Goyim [non-Jews] must submit to their will."
- Since Islam's creation, its "enemies" have agreed on "cultivating evil against Islam and uprooting Muslims."
- The creation of Israel is a "malignant cancerous growth."
- "And the conflict between us and the Jews is not a conflict about land and borders, but rather a conflict about faith and existence."[74]

It is this last point that hits the nail on the head. The Arab/Muslim war on the Jewish people in the Land of Israel, ongoing for 140 years, is not about borders, refugees, Jerusalem, water rights, "settlements," and "occupation." These are all tactical issues used to weaken Israel's resolve and divert world attention from the core issue. The war is fundamentally based on religious premises, waged against Jews worldwide, and has continued for 1,400 years. The harsh reality is that all of the misojudaic slaughters perpetrated by Arabs and other Muslims have been motivated to greater or lesser degrees by Islamic misojudaism enshrined in the Islamic sacred texts and incessantly preached, taught and inculcated into the Arab/Muslim population. In a mid-2013 interview, Ayaan Hirsi Ali, Somali-Dutch-American women's rights activist, opponent of Islamist supremacism, and politician put it this way:

> Israel is not the problem nor is it the solution. Even if you give up all the land, it will not solve any of the problems in the Middle East. It will not obliterate despotism, it will not liberate women, and it will not help religious minorities. It will not bring peace to anyone. Even if Israel does not give up an inch of land -- the result will be the same. If you want real, lasting peace, then things have to change first within the Arab Muslim individual, family, school, streets, education, and politics. It is not an Israeli problem.[75]

In sum, there is an overriding realistic understanding about the Arab/Muslim war against the sovereign Jewish state of Israel. This 140-year conflict is irreconcilable due to the fact of its religious, non-secular nature. Islam, by foundational decree and its uncompromising, politico-religious ideology, cannot surrender land it considers *dar al-Islam*—land belonging to, or once belonging to—Islam.

Even today, the language and arguments of the 1956 *fatwa* are indistinguishable from those within the Hamas Charter (*see* Appendix 8), which reveals the same connected motivations of jihad, and conspiratorial Islamic misojudaism. Their charter is unequivocal, "Article 13 … There is no solution to the Palestinian problem except by jihad, for initiatives, proposals and international conferences are nothing but a waste of time and absurd nonsense."

There is a common Arabic exhortation chanted in the Middle East: *Khaybar, Khaybar ya Yahud, jaish-Muhammad saya'ud* ("Khaybar, Khaybar oh Jews, the army of Muhammad will return"). This dates back to the Muslim victory over some of the last Jewish tribes in Arabia in May 628 C.E. Even more commonly prevalent are the cries of *Al-Yahud qalab'na* ("The Jews are our dogs"), and the hair-raising scream of *Idbah al-Yahud!* ("slaughter the Jews!") which have echoed across the Arab/Muslim world for some 1,400 years. The *takbir*—the phrase—*Allahu akbar,* is applicable to all unbelievers and, in part, is designed to inspire fear. This war cry is always shouted out when Islamic supremacists score a victory. Recall that is what was shouted as civilian aircraft plowed into the World Trade Center, the Pentagon and a field near Shanksville, Pennsylvania, on September 11, 2001.

Virulent misojudaism, prevalent and emanating from the Arab/Muslim world, is sanctified by the Qur'an and the Hadith. The Qur'an declares Jews as "the worst of creatures,"[76] "transformed by Allah into apes and pigs,"[77] and even rats.[78] They are cursed forever[79] and the disciples of Satan.[80] The Qur'an and other Islamic writings hold Jews in derision. The vast majority of Muslims are raised with a scripture that regards another people and religion—the Jews—as immoral and sub-human. Thus, it is obvious why there is such hatred and contempt on the part of Muslims for Jews and Israel. One needs only to refer to the Qur'an to find evidence of these sentiments:

- "And humiliation and wretchedness were stamped upon them [the Jews] and they were visited with wrath from Allah. That was because they disbelieved in Allah's revelations and slew the prophets wrongfully. That was for their disobedience and transgression." (2:61)
- "Say: Why, then, did you [the Jews] slay Allah's prophets aforetime, if you were Allah aforetime [the prophets before Muhammad, e.g. Jesus] if you were [truly] believers?" (2:91)
- "But Allah hath cursed them [the Jews] for their disbelief, so they believe not, save a few." (4:46)
- "Worse whom Allah has cursed, them [the Jews] on whom His wrath had fallen! Worse is he of whose sort Allah has turned some to apes and pigs." (5:60)
- "Thou will surely find the most vehement of mankind in hostility to those who believe [the Muslims] (to be) the Jews and the idolaters." (5:82)

Additionally, as has previously been mentioned, are the Qur'anic verses 2:193; 3:85; 3:150; 4:76; 4:101; 5:51; 8:12; 8:55; 9:5; 9:29; 9:123; and 98.6, all of which apply not only to the Jews, but to Christians, Hindus, Sikhs, Buddhists, Zoroastrians, Bahá'ís, animists and others. There is also, the genocidal hadith, which states, "The Day of Judgment will not have come until you fight with the Jews, and the stones and the trees behind which a Jew will be hiding will say: 'O Muslim! There is a Jew hiding behind me, come and kill him!"[81] Witness Ibn Umar reported, "Allah's Messenger peace be upon him as saying: 'You will fight against the Jews and you will kill them until even a stone would say: Come here, Muslim, there is a Jew [hiding himself] behind me; kill him.'"[82] Thus, the Arab Muslims already had their own "final solution" in store for the Jews in the seventh century.

This call to genocide is enshrined in Article 7 of the Hamas Charter, "Allah bless him and grant him salvation, has said: The Day of Judgment will not come about until Muslims fight the Jews [killing the Jews], when the Jew will hide behind stones and trees. The stones and trees will say O Muslims, O Abdullah, there is a Jew behind me, come and kill him. Only the Gharkad tree, [evidently a certain kind of tree] would not do that because it is one of the trees of the Jews." It must be stressed that Hamas makes "no distinctions between Jews, Zionists, and Israelis."[83] Hence, their war is a widespread genocide against all the Jews of planet Earth. Islamic calls for the extermination of the Jews and destruction of Israel, dominate the mosques, seminaries, universities and media outlets throughout the Arab and Muslim worlds. Thus, it is extremely doubtful there can ever be dispute resolution, real peace and reconciliation—*sulha*—between Muslims and Jews, let alone between Arab Muslims and the Jewish state of Israel. Islam, as currently interpreted and practiced, cannot and will not accept a sovereign Jewish state of any size in what is regarded as *Dar al-Islam* (the Muslim domain). A major factor of this misojudaic hatred is the religious and historic Muslim enmity towards any *dhimmi* people having sovereignty over lands Muslims once possessed and which they deemed part of *Dar al-Islam* to be reconquered.

With all of the above in mind, the ingathering of the Jews into modern Israel is an unbearable challenge to the authority of Islam for several reasons. Israel gave shelter to the Jews, whom the Qur'an termed as "wretched people" (2:61, and 5:64). Muslims believe that Jews are not a nation,[84] only a tolerated faith under Islamic rule, and therefore their claim to a separate political existence constituted a violation of the holy tradition of Islam. The fact that Jews sought refuge in Israel defied and exposed to criticism the traditional Muslim allegation that the *dhimmi* people enjoy equality, protection and benevolence under Islamic rulers. Rather than "toleration," Jews, Christians and Zoroastrians have been subjected to general abuse, debasement and suppression. The massive exodus of the Jews from Arab lands belied Muslim contentions of the fair treatment they supposedly received. Those same Jews, condemned to "humiliation and misery" in the Qur'an (2:61, 3:112, 9:29), dared and succeeded (though vastly outnumbered) in defeating on several occasions, the Muslims. Arabs and Muslims in general, despite their assurances to the contrary, regard modern Israelis as descendants of the Qur'anic Jews. To the Arab/Muslim world, as a sovereign people in a sovereign Jewish state, the Israelis can only be regarded as infidels. Only by submitting to Islam and becoming *dhimmis* again, will the Jews be a "protected" though subordinated people.

Palestine had been part of the *Dar al-Islam* since the early seventh century until it was taken over by the British and then by the Jews in the twentieth century. This sovereignty was interrupted only by the rule of the Crusaders, who were eventually defeated by Saladin who restored the land to Islam. Current Islamic thought treats the Jewish usurpation of Palestine as a short-lived Crusader-like colonialist experiment that is doomed to failure because it contradicted the logic of Islamic history. Thus, jihad remains, as it has always been, the legitimate tool of the Muslims to retrieve their lost lands.

Over a century ago, Edwin Sherman Wallace, former US Consul to Ottoman-controlled Palestine (1893–98), provided this seemingly timeless insight regarding Muslims, written in 1908, almost a decade prior to the Balfour Declaration:

> Their religion [Islam] is intolerant. It has little sympathy for the adherents of other
> faiths. It once advocated an extermination of the infidels. Perhaps it would continue
> in that advocacy did its leaders dare.[85]

Since 1979, Iran's theocratic regime strictly forbids the proselytizing of Muslims and targets any citizens believed to have abandoned Islam, human rights watchers say. Under Iran's strict interpretation of Islamic law, anyone leaving Islam for another religion is committing a capital offense, the penalty for which is death. In early 2009, the Iranian Parliament passed a bill calling for execution of Christians on the basis of apostasy.[86] Abe Ghaffari of Iranian Christians International said the death penalty had only been one of several options for punishment, but the new proposed legislation would change that. "The death penalty will become an automatic and mandatory thing for the apostates," he explained. "Anyone who abandons Islam will be executed." The Islamic prophet Muhammad said, "Whoever changes his Islamic religion, then kill him."[87]

In preparation for the official full implementation of shari'a, which occurred on May 1, 2014, Brunei legal experts from the Ministry of Religious Affairs and the Prime Minister's Office told 300 representatives of private education institutions it was an offence to propagate religions other than Islam to a Muslim or atheist. The offence is punishable by a fine of up to $20,000, imprisonment for up to five years or both under Section 209. Exposing beliefs and practices other than Islam to a Muslim child, or a child whose parents are atheist, carries the same punishment. Under Section 212, it is an offence to "persuade, tell, cause, offer payment to, influence, incite, encourage or let" the child accept such teachings. Additionally, it is a crime to expose the child to any ceremony, act of worship or religious activity of any religion beside Islam, or to participate in any activity held for the benefit of other religions. On May 1, 2014, Brunei began enforcing the first phase of the new law, which covered *Ta'zir* or general offences that are punishable by fines, imprisonment or both. These offenses include pregnancy outside marriage and failure to perform Friday prayers.[88] Harsher punishments for serious crimes, such as whipping, amputation of limbs for stealing, will come into force for offences including theft and drinking alcohol. These will be introduced in the second phase, while the death penalty will only come into force in the third phase, pending the finalization of the Syariah (Shari'a) Courts Criminal Procedure Code Order.[89]

Currently, it is politically correct to say that Islam is a "religion of peace," and that the vast majority of Muslims want to live in peace. This may be true, but in light of worldwide Muslim terrorist acts in New York, Washington DC, Boston, Fort Hood, Texas, London, Madrid, Moscow, Bali, Mumbai and elsewhere, the reference to the religion of peace becomes questionable. Using such terms obfuscates the issue by causing a false optimism while diminishing the specter of the fanatics who rampage the globe in the name of Islam. The peaceful majority in Muslim lands is cowed into a non-existent or at least irrelevant force. Unfortunately, at this moment in history, fanatics set the tone in Islamic countries. Peace-loving Muslims have been made immaterial by their silence. It is the fundamentalists like the Iranian mullahs and former Iranian President Mahmoud Ahmadinejad, the Wahhabist movement in Saudi Arabia, or the Muslim Brotherhood across the region, who dictate policies, set the agenda, and cause the majority to remain silent and to progressively even lose their naturally endowed rights to human freedom and dignity.[90]

Many times in history, a small event can become magnified into the spark for a greater conflagration. On December 17, 2010, a street vendor, Mohamed Bouazizi, in protest of the harassment, humiliation and the confiscation of his fruit, by a municipal official and her aides, self-immolated in Sidi Bouzid, Tunisia. His act became the catalyst triggering the deep-rooted long-standing grievances, which gripped much of the Arab world. These grievances included entrenched corrupt dictatorships, bribery-riddled bureaucracies, economic stagnation and lack of opportunity, growing religious sectarian rivalries, tensions and conflicts, as well as an Islamist revivalism—all contributed to the revolutions that followed. Seeing an opportunity with the death of Bouazizi, Al-Jazeera TV's Arabic channel, which is linked to the Muslim Brotherhood and based in Qatar, began a 24/7 news cycle that whipped the masses to revolution in Tunisia and later in other Arab states including Egypt, Yemen, Libya, and Syria. These massive demonstrations, riots, violence and government crack-downs, which swept the Arab world (including far beyond the named countries) from December 2010 to date, were quickly dubbed the "Arab Spring" by main stream mass media, ever quick to label events, with little thought, research and analysis. Perhaps some recalled the "Prague Spring" in Czechoslovakia, of early 1968, when nationalistic communists led by Alexander Dubček, sought to "democratize," "liberalize" and "reform" the harsh system of Soviet-style communism, centralized authority and the domination of Stalinist communists within that country's government. The "Prague Spring" lasted but seven months, from January 8 to August 21, 1968, and was crushed by a massive invasion of 200,000 Soviet and Warsaw Pact troops backed by 5,000 tanks, which promptly ended the "liberalization" of Dubček's regime.

Furthermore, many in the West erroneously viewed the "Arab Spring" of 2010–14, as being one between two opposite sides, pitting the forces of Western-style democracy against the oppressive dictatorial regime. Simplistically, they projected the image of Hungarian "Freedom Fighters" battling the Soviet-imposed dictatorship in 1956, or the more recent people's "revolts" in Eastern Europe after the implosion of the Soviet Union, toppling the last vestiges of communism in Eastern Europe. Nothing could be further from reality. Competition, rivalry and enmity exist between the Islamic fundamentalists on one hand, and the military regimes and/or monarchies on the other. Rather than being on opposite sides, these conflicting forces are at opposite poles of the *same side* (emphasis added), i.e. Islam. These basically, were two competing forms of tyranny. This stark reality has been confirmed repeatedly in the past three years in Libya, Syria, Yemen, and Egypt.

The term "Arab Spring" is a misnomer. No matter how dressed up in the trappings of a Western-style mass movement, with calls for "freedom," "progress," "democracy" and "reform" it was nothing more than a repeat of the cycle prevalent in the Arab/Muslim world for centuries, albeit this time, with more technological devices. The masses rising up against a long-entrenched ruling élite (in the last two centuries the list of targets broadened to include Western-supported rulers), the struggle between the more secularist and more fundamentalist groups within Islam, and the various conflicts between and among the sub-divisions of the Arab/Muslim world—religious, ethnic and tribal—all have occurred numerous times in the past, and would be repeated again and again. Shi'ites, Alawites, Senussis, Maronites, Kurds, to name but a few, have all struggled against forces that are more dominant. The greater Middle East is facing an "Islamic Reawakening," and the movement toward pan-Islamism, which are all legitimized by elections. For the West, it portends to be the fiery eve of an "Islamic Winter," rather than the much hyped and erroneously named "Arab Spring" of Western-style democracy and reforms. To make matters worse, the Obama administration intentionally facilitated the coming to power of the transnational Muslim Brotherhood—which espouses jihad and compliance to shari'a—in Tunisia, Egypt and Libya and favored that faction in the Syrian Civil War. Thus, the upheavals witnessed the ousting of pro-American dictatorial regimes and their replacement with anti-American dictatorial Islamist ones.

To date, the Arab/Muslim world's denunciations are partisan and are directed externally. Family blames tribe, tribe blames party, party blames the regime, and the regime blames the Turks, the British, the French, the Americans, the Zionists—the Western "imperialists" in general, all convenient foreign scapegoats. The reality is that progress comes from internal self-doubt and self-criticism that leads to reform. Only this internal introspection can stimulate reform and change within Islam. Reform comes from denouncing one's self or the system, much the same as Martin Luther denounced the Catholic Church on October 31, 1517, by posting his *Ninety-Five Theses,* on the door of the Castle Church of Wittenberg, Germany. Until and unless such internal reform can come about in the greater Muslim world, the irascible Arab/Muslim world will remain unchanged and a terrible thorn in the side of the West. An expert, Harry J. Sweeney succinctly summarized:

> According to many studies of Islam, including studies by Muslims themselves, one cannot be a *moderate* Muslim in our sense of the word, because the terms are

mutually conflicting. If one is <u>not</u> a *fundamentalist* Muslim, in our sense of the word, then one is not Muslim as far as *non-moderate* Muslims are concerned. Some Muslims have indicated that the *non-fundamentalist* Muslim can be considered as apostate; and as such, he can be killed by anyone who knows his status. As long as the Qur'an retains its present status among Muslims, a celestial, holy text with no author and no beginning, uncreated and eternal, containing Allah's Words exactly; then no significant reforms can be made to the religion or ideology. When people who know use the term Muslim, unsaid but included in that term is *fundamentalist* at least.[91]

Most recently, Egyptian Head of State General Abdel Fattah el-Sisi, called for a reformation in Islam in mid-January 2014, which may be what future history may call the initial catalyst equivalent to Martin Luther's actions in 1517. El-Sisi, who was also First Deputy Prime Minister and Minister of Defense, declared during a speech at the Armed Forces' Department of Moral Affairs that "religious discourse is the greatest battle and challenge facing the Egyptian people, pointing to the need for a new vision and a modern, comprehensive understanding of the religion of Islam—rather than relying on a discourse that has not changed for 800 years." The "800 years" refers to when the most qualified Islamic scholars of that time ruled that all questions about interpretation of Islam had been settled. The "gates" of *ijtihad*—independent reasoning and interpretation of Islam—ended by the year 1258. El-Sisi wanted the "gates" reopened, which would allow for the critical examination that an Islamic reformation needed. Additionally, he stated, "all who follow the true Islam [should] … improve the image of this religion in front of the world, after Islam has been for decades convicted of violence and destruction around the world, due to the crimes falsely committed in the name of Islam." It remains to be seen if President El-Sisi (who took office, June 8, 2014) will follow through on this called for reform.

Earlier, in January 2011, former Egyptian Islamist Tawfik Hamid reported that 25 Islamic scholars, including teachers from Al-Azhar, said that *ijtihad* needed to be resumed. The ten points they listed for renewed examination included the separation of mosque and state, women's rights, relations with non-Muslims and jihad. As Ryan Mauro, National Security Analyst of the Clarion Project stressed, the "ideological underpinning [of Islamist supremacism] must be debated and defeated. The determinations of scholars from 800 years [ago] can no longer be treated as eternal truth, but for what they really are—opinions influenced by the times in which they were made."[92] It remains to be seen if El-Sisi's call will generate popular demand and overcome the long-standing traditional views that Islam cannot be reformed, which is advocated by such groups as the transnational Muslim Brotherhood.

Any call for reform or moderation of radical Islamic ideology must overcome 1,400 years of Islamic tradition and religious scholarship—a religious scholarship which considers any attempt to reinterpret the Qur'an as heresy punishable by death. Simply put, every word of the Qur'an is the word of Allah and is not subject to human modification, ever. As Evelyn Baring, 1st Earl of Cromer, the British Controller-General and later Consul-General of Egypt, would state concisely, and Wafa Sultan, Syrian critic of Islam, would later repeat, "Islam reformed, is Islam no longer."[93]

However, it must be noted that what the world has been experiencing since the 1970s has been in effect an Islamic reformation, if one recalls the basic definition of the word "reform." Reform is the improvement or amendment of what is wrong, corrupt, and unsatisfactory. To the Islamic supremacists, Islam strayed from the path of pure Islam as preached and practiced by Muhammad due to corrupting outside Western and modernizing influences. Thus, the change is to return to original Islam, uncorrupted and unspoiled.

28. All Muslim religious scholars and authorities consider Islam to be a "complete way of life."

As has been noted, Islam is an ideology and a social system, a religion of laws—a religion with a political orientation and with political ambitions. The respected historian and one of the greatest authorities of our time on the Islamic world, Bernard Lewis, has noted that since its birth (in 622 C.E.), Islam has sought to merge religion and state authority, and to expand its influence. Several Islamic sources cite the same explanation for Islam being a complete way of life.

> Islam is not a religion in the common, distorted meaning of the word, confining its scope only to the private life of man. By saying that it is a complete way of life, we mean that it caters for all the fields of human existence. In fact, Islam provides guidance for all walks of life—individual and social, material and moral, economic and political, legal and cultural, national and international. The Qur'an enjoins man to enter the fold of Islam without any reservation and to follow God's [Allah's] guidance in all fields of life.[94]

According to shari'a (i.e., "Islam's way of life," more commonly translated as "Islamic law") every conceivable human act is classified according to five categories (*ahkam*): the obligatory (*wajib*), the recommended (*mustahib*), the permissible (*mubah*), not recommended (*makruh*), and the forbidden (*haram*). Common sense or universal opinion has little to do with Islam's notions of right and wrong. All that matters is what Allah (via the Qur'an) and his prophet Muhammad (through the Hadith) have to say about any given subject, and how Islam's greatest theologians and jurists—collectively known as the *ulama,* (literally, the "ones who know")—have articulated it.

One can find the phrase—"a complete way of life"—on all Muslim websites including the Council of American-Islamic Relations (CAIR). Most non-Muslims have no idea what this really means. Yet, this characteristic of Islam is extremely important because it affects the unwillingness of Muslim immigrants to assimilate in our own, as well as in many other non-Islamic countries. Muslims, according to Islamic law, are required to strive to impose this complete way of life on everybody in the world. Shari'a is a complete code of law that covers, for example, family law, contractual law, criminal law, banking, insurance, and even foreign policy. Additionally, shari'a tells people how to dress, what kind of pictures they can have in their homes, how to use the toilet, what they can eat and when, who can marry whom, who they are allowed to befriend, and who they must fight and subdue. Traditional shari'a has been supported by all the Islamic scholars and religious authorities for 1,400 years.

In the last forty years, Western Europe has not withstood the onslaught of Islam. The list of steady Islamic gains has grown with no end in sight. In general, Muslim residents of these European countries do not assimilate into society. They have established Muslim enclaves demanding that the countries in which they reside bend to Islamic will. These groups issue frenzied calls for shari'a-imposed judicial decisions and established shari'a-controlled semi-autonomous sectors[95] within cities that even police, firefighters and mailmen are afraid to enter for fear of being attacked. Even doctors and ambulances do not enter except if they have no other choice. Some have termed these areas "no-go" zones, France has "some 751"[96] semi-autonomous sectors, Sweden has at least "55"[97] semi-autonomous sectors and the Netherlands at least 40[98], and the United Kingdom at least 12[99] semi-autonomous sectors. These zones exist also in Belgium, Germany and Italy. Women are relegated to second-class status and misojudaic violence has increased. There are parts of Europe where large numbers of Muslims violate laws and the police just stand by and do nothing. For example, in London, Paris and other Western European cities, sometimes-large gatherings of Muslims will get together and pray in huge numbers in streets blocking traffic in violation of zoning laws. They have succeeded thus far, in intimidating and threatening their host governments with violence.

29. Muslim women and children are dispensable. Infidel women and children are prime targets for rape, slavery and genocide.

Religious and sexual apartheid are practiced extensively in Arab/Muslim countries. It is noted in one of the Islamic world's most authoritative commentaries on the teachings of the Qur'an—*Tafsir al-Qurtubi*—that, "Women are like cows, horses, and camels, for all are ridden."[100] Comparing women to animals is common in Islam. Muhammad is recorded saying, "Women, dogs, and donkeys annul a man's prayer."[101] In yet another hadith, women are equated with slaves and camels.[102] The status of women[103] under shari'a, within several categories, can be summarized as follows:

STATUS OF WOMEN IN ISLAM
SOCIETY

In the West, the rights of the individual reign supreme. In the Islamic world, the rights of the dominant religion and culture are paramount. Muslim society is a patriarchal society based on gender apartheid with women reduced to a second-class and lowly state of fear. This gender apartheid, in part, is justified by the Qur'an that men rule women, "men are a degree above them [women],"[104] and "Allah has made men superior to women."[105] Additionally, Muhammad stated that he, "was shown the Hell-fire and that the majority of its dwellers are women."[106] There is no opportunity for women, to have individual freedom and equality. "In accordance with justice, the rights of the wives [with regard to their husbands] are equal to the [husbands'] rights with regard to them although men have precedence over them."[107] For example, in Saudi Arabia woman are required to get a male relative's permission to get married, work, travel, undergo some surgical operations, undertake paid employment or get higher education. Additionally, they are prevented from accessing government agencies that have not established female sections unless they have a male representative.[108]

DRESS

The Qur'an stipulates, "O prophet, tell your wives and daughters and women-folk of the believers to draw their robes close to them; that is more appropriate as a way for them to be recognized and not be vexed. Allah is forgiving and compassionate."[109] On the basis of this verse, many Muslim women are forced to wear certain garments. These include the *hijab*, which is a veil that covers the hair, head, neck, and chest—but reveals the face of the woman. It is particularly worn by a Muslim female beyond the age of puberty in the presence of adult males; a *jilbab*, which is an indoor ankle-length, long-sleeved garment An indoor ankle-length, long-sleeved garment that leaves only the face and hands exposed. It is similar to a caftan; an *abaya,* a garment—traditionally in black—that covers the whole body except the face, feet, and hands. It can be worn with the *niqab,* a face veil covering all but the eyes, more common in Saudi Arabia and the Gulf states; the *chador* (a combined head covering veil and shawl), most prevalent in Iran; or the *burqa,* which is an outer garment that covers the head and body completely and is worn in public.[110] It is prevalent in Afghanistan, Pakistan and Saudi Arabia. While some women wear the *niqab* and *burqa* they are required by neither the Qur'an nor shari'a, in fact are outlawed in some Muslim countries.

With the establishment of the Islamic Republic of Iran in 1979, Ayatollah Khomeini reimposed the veil on the formerly modern and educated women of Iran. Wearing a *hijab* is obligatory in Iran. Elsewhere, Sudanese Muslim officials arrest tens of thousands of women a year for wearing "indecent clothing," including trousers, and many have been fined and subjected to forty whiplashes. According to Sudanese law, "indecent clothing" is clothing that offends public sentiment. In practice, the law is defined according to the police officer's mood. In Khartoum, Sudan's capital, 43,000 women were arrested because of their clothing according to the police general commissioner.[111] In late November 2010, five Islamist members of Parliament in Kuwait proposed that women who wear swimsuits at the beach should be jailed for a year and fined 1,000 Kuwaiti dinars ($3,568). In a proposal to amend Kuwait's penal code, they said the same penalty should apply to women who reveal their upper chest or take part in "indecent behavior."[112]

SEXUALITY

The Qur'an (24:31) commands:

> And tell the believing women to lower their gaze and to be mindful of their chastity, and not to display their charms in public beyond what may decently be apparent thereof; hence let them draw their head-coverings over their bosoms [note: at that time, not all bosoms were covered]. And let them not display more of their charms to any but their husbands, or their fathers, or their husbands' fathers.

The *Reliance of the Traveller,* dictates, "It is offensive for an attractive or young woman to come to the mosque to pray (O: or for her husband to permit her), though not offensive for women who are not young or attractive when this is unlikely to cause temptation."[113] Under no circumstances should a Muslim woman ever have sex, including marriage, with an unbeliever.

Men should have absolute control of a woman's sexuality. Hence, in Saudi Arabia legislation is being considered to stop women from revealing "tempting eyes" in public, despite the fact they are already covered from head to feet in an *abaya* and a *niqab.*[114] This aversion to a woman's display of her physical features even extends to dolls. The Committee for the Propagation of Virtue and Prevention of Vice, as the Saudi religious police are officially known (they are informally known as the *mutaween,)*, totally banned Mattle's Barbie doll in 2003, because the shapely toy was "offensive to Islam." Injecting misojudaic invective, the Saudi religious police declared that the "Jewish Barbie dolls, with their revealing clothes and shameful postures, accessories and tools are a symbol of decadence to the perverted West. Let us beware of her dangers and be careful," said a poster issued by the religious police on their website.[115] In neighboring Iran, clerics since 1996, have complained about Barbie's "destructive cultural and social consequences." In 2012, Iran banned Barbie dolls and replaced them with Sara, while the American Ken, was replaced with Dara, Sara's moral traditional brother.[116]

Love and affection are not qualities that current Islamic fundamentalists want to see between a man and a woman, even in marriage. Valentine's Day, for example, is anathema to fundamentalist Muslims. Each year the Saudi religious police, mobilize ahead of February 14, and institute a nationwide crackdown on stores selling items (which are confiscated), that are red or in any other way allude to the banned celebrations of Valentine's Day. This includes red roses, heart-shaped products or gifts wrapped in red.[117] Similarly, Iran institutes such a ban, sending their police forces around with strict orders to disrupt any Valentine's Day celebrations and arrest the people involved. On February 12, 2013, supporters of Pakistan's main religious party—Jamaat-e-Islami—staged a noisy protest in the city of Peshawar, in anticipation of and against Valentine's Day. They denounced it as being un-Islamic and "spread[ing] immodesty in the world." They condemned the Valentine's Day tradition for encouraging unmarried men and women to live together in sin. Instead, the protestors called for a "day of modesty."[118]

There is a stereotypical view of women as sexual objects and as creatures that cannot resist sexual temptation. Therefore, women may not be alone with any unmarried men, except for close family male members—father, brothers, or sons. This proscription leads to segregation in such areas as schools, universities, sports, careers and friendships.[119] In fact, the restrictions on male–female interaction were further curtailed in early 2014, in the Islamic Republic of Iran. As reported by the Egyptian daily *Al Ahram*, Supreme Leader Ayatollah Ali Khamenei issued a *fatwa* that decreed chatting between the sexes on social networks was immoral. Iran has placed severe restrictions on use of the Internet and social networks, and blocked a WeChat message that is used on smartphones.[120]

Circumcision is mandatory under shari'a law for both men and women, though some Islamic scholars regard female circumcision as not mandatory but a courtesy to the husband.[121] The most frequently stated purpose for female circumcision is to "calm down" the women to diminish their libido.[122] However, in the original Arabic, female circumcision entails the cutting out of the clitoris, which is called *Hufaad*.[123] Thus, the practice of female circumcision is now considered female genital mutilation (FGM). While the practice of FGM has been proven to be aligned with tribal cultures, not religions, its prevalence is higher among Muslim communities in the Middle East and Africa. This practice is widespread in the Levant, the Fertile Crescent including Iraqi Kurdistan, the Arabian Peninsula, and both North Africa and Muslim sub-Saharan Africa.

More than 125 million girls and women alive today have been subjected to FGM in the 29 countries in Africa and the Middle East in which it is concentrated, and 30 million girls are at risk of being cut within the next decade according to a recent (2013) UNICEF report. In Somalia, an Arab League member, it is the rule and 98 percent of women and girls are subjected to FGM. In Egypt, the largest Arab country, it is 91 percent, in Sudan 88 percent and in Mauritania, it is 69 percent, the report revealed.[124] The practice is pervasive among many immigrant groups from all these countries, who go to the West. Many Muslim girls are victims of FGM to deny them any vestige of sexual pleasure. However, contrary to the *fatwas* of many clerics in Islam, the Qur'an contains no requirement for the practice of female genital mutilation. Nobody in Islam has the authority to command that female genital mutilation be practiced—it defies Islamic law in that it harms people and kills many. This is one area, which could be reformed because, except for one weak (*da'if*) hadith,[125] the holy texts are silent.

While the practice pre-dates Islam, local tradition has perpetuated the practice of FGM. A Palestinian-Swiss specialist in Islamic law, Sami A. Aldeeb Abu Sahlieh, cited Muhammad as saying,

"Circumcision is a *sunna* (tradition) for the men and *makruma* (honorable deed) for the women."[126] None of the major Islamic schools of jurisprudence forbids the practice. Some call it obligatory; some call it merely a preference.

In Egypt, the government banned FGM in 1996, but an Egyptian court overturned the ban in July 1997, because of the ferocious uprising of the prominent Shafi'i school of Islamic jurisprudence, which is comprised of Salafists.* The Salafists affirmed that the practice was mandatory in accordance with Muslim tradition,[127] and re-implemented the practice. They are against banning any inherited tradition no matter what it is. In their minds, they believe that reform means they will eventually lose their dominance over women. They will do anything to keep that dominance.

However, the present Grand Mufti of Egypt, Sheikh Ali Gomaa, issued a new *fatwa*[128] indicating that the inheritance of the unfortunate tradition was not reason enough to continue the procedure. The Grand Mufti, not only wants the practice forbidden, but also wants it criminalized. In fact, the consensus of scholars in general, but particularly those at Al-Azhar University, as well as medical authorities in Islam, was that the procedure had no value and in reality, was harmful. It should be noted that the Grand Mufti wrote that all ahadith, including Dawud 41:5251, touching upon FGM were weak, flawed, and without the force of law. There are no religious or other reasons to continue this horrid practice. Nonetheless, the practice may be continued from ignorance or from dedication to traditions despite the egregious consequences—often ending in terrible mutilation and even death.

In addition to the topics mentioned above, female sexual and domestic slavery still exists. Slaves are sexual property of their male owners, "and all married women [are forbidden unto you save] those [captives, i.e. prisoners of war] whom your right hands possess."[129] Furthermore, in Saudi Arabia, Iran, Hamas-controlled Gaza, and many other Arab/Muslim countries, there is sexual orientation discrimination. Gay and lesbian citizens have been imprisoned and executed.

MARRIAGE

There is a preference for close in-family marriages. Men will be reluctant to fight against a neighboring group of which their wives' fathers and brothers are members or into which their daughters or sisters have married. There is no prohibition on marrying one's first cousin under Islam.[130] Basic love and being in love is forbidden. "Marriage is commanded by the prophet even if there be no desire; and if there be desire, then marriage is an indispensable duty. It should be performed in the presence of two free men; or of one free man and two free women."[131] Women do not sign their own marriage certificate. A recent example of forbidden love occurred on April 13, 2009, when a Taliban firing squad killed Gul Pecha and Abdul Aziz for trying to elope. They had been accused of immoral

---

* The *Salafists* are ultraconservative Muslims, who believe themselves to be the direct followers of the teachings of Muhammad. They believe in personal purification and religious observance. They expect everyone else to emulate the piety of the *Salaf* ("the venerable predecessors" or "ancestors"), the earliest Muslims. The term, *Salafist,* has been in use since the Middle Ages, but today it refers especially to a follower of a modern Sunni Islamic movement known as the *Salafiyyah,* which is related to or includes Wahhabism, so that the two terms are sometimes erroneously viewed as synonymous. In modern times, both groups seek to emulate the orthodoxy and austerity of Islam's early years—the first three Muslim generations—from the time of Muhammad. The *salafis* view other Muslim sects as almost bordering on apostasy and more secular Muslim rulers, not sufficiently Muslim according to their interpretation, as targets to be killed, Egypt's Anwar el-Sadat being a case in point.

acts, and a council of conservative clerics ordered their death in Nimruz province in southwestern Afghanistan.

Women must have sex with their husbands whenever he wants it, in effect, sex on demand. A man has all rights to his wife's body. The Qur'an likens a woman's vagina to a plowed field (*tilth*), to be used by a man as he wills, "Your women are a *tilth* for you [to cultivate] so go to your *tilth* as ye will."[132] It is related that Muhammad said, "The marriage vow most rightly expected to be obeyed is the husband's right to enjoy the wife's vagina."[133] This in effect codifies rape. Muhammad made it legal for Muslim men to capture and rape married women unbelievers.[134] Polygamy is the rule rather than the exception. Men are allowed to marry up to four wives, and have sex with slave women. In fact, female concubines in Islam are not deemed human, as the Arabic relative pronoun used in the Qur'an to indicate captive sex-slaves is "it"—as in an animal—not "she" (e.g., Qur'an 4:3).[135] In Shi'ite Islam men are permitted to have "temporary wives" so they can have sex outside of their marriage. "If ye fear that ye shall not be able to deal justly with the orphans, marry women of your choice, two or three or four; but if ye fear that ye shall not be able to deal justly [with them], then only one, or [a captive] that your right hands possess, that will be more suitable, to prevent you from doing injustice."[136] A traditional interpretation of this *ayat* does not mean treating them equally. Rather, as Ismail Ibn Kathir* explained, doing so is only "recommended," and even without equal treatment, "there is no harm on him [i.e. the husband]."[137]

In Saudi Arabia, women are forbidden to date. A fifty-page 2008 report from New York-based Human Rights Watch, entitled "Perpetual Minors: Human Rights Abuses Stemming from Male Guardianship and Sex Segregation in Saudi Arabia," said Saudi court rulings have allowed male family members to prevent, end or force the marriages of adult women and seize custody of their children. Under Saudi law, women must get permission from a father, brother or even a son to marry.[138]

In Iran, enclaves in Iraq and Hezbollah-controlled sections of Lebanon, high school girls are forbidden to hold hands with boyfriends. The Associated Press reported on January 4, 2010, that fifty-two unmarried Muslim couples faced charges of sexual misconduct and possible jail terms after being caught alone in hotel rooms by Malaysia's Islamic morality police during a New Year's Day crackdown. The couples were expected to be charged with *khalwat,* or "close proximity," which under Malaysia's shari'a law is described as couples not married to each other, being alone together in a private place.[139]

Marriage to prepubescent girls is sanctioned in the Qur'an.[140] In some countries, including Yemen and Iran, marriage is allowed to girls as young as nine.[141] Article 1041 of the Civil Code of the Islamic Republic of Iran states that girls can be engaged before the age of nine, and married at nine, "Marriage before puberty (nine full lunar years for girls) is prohibited. Marriage contracted before reaching puberty with the permission of the guardian is valid provided that the interests of the ward are duly observed."[142] An Iranian NGO, the Society For Protecting the Rights of the Child, said 43,459 girls aged under fifteen had married in 2009, compared with 33,383 three years previously. In 2010, 716 girls younger than ten had wed, up from 449 the previous year, according to the organization.[143] Even in Turkey, viewed as a largely secular Muslim country there were more than 181,000 child brides in 2012.[144]

Marriage to prepubescent girls is based on Muhammad's example. Muhammad, at the age of forty-nine married a six-year-old girl, 'Aisha, consummating the marriage with her when she was nine and he was fifty-two, "and she remained with him for nine years [i.e. until his death]."[145] Muhammad

---

* Ismail ibn Kathir (1301–1373) was a Muslim *muhaddith* (hadith specialist), *faqīh* (expert on Islamic jurisprudence), *mufassir* (explainer of the Qur'an), and historian.

is regarded in the Qur'an, as *uswa hasana*—an "excellent model of conduct" (33:21) and *al-insan al-kamil*—the universal man, the prototype of all of creation, and the norm of all perfection—i.e. the "perfect man." Thus, Muhammad's life is considered exemplary and compulsory for Muslims to emulate. As such, ninety-one ayahs command all Muslims to imitate Muhammad. The concept of *sunna*—which is what Sunni Muslims are named after—essentially asserts that anything performed or approved by Muhammad, humanity's most perfect example, is applicable for Muslims today no less than in the past.

Marriage always includes a dowry—*mahr*—paid to the bride's nearest male relative, usually the father. If there is a divorce, it does not have to be returned. Arranged marriages are often to men much, much older. Accordingly, even in modern times we find numerous examples of such marriages. Iran's Ayatollah Ruhollah Khomeini, at the age of twenty-eight, married a ten-year-old. Khomeini called marriage to a prepubescent girl "a divine blessing," and advised the faithful, "Do your best to ensure that your daughters do not see their first blood in your house."[146]

In Saudi Arabia, girls can be married as early as the age of ten. For example, in January 2010, *Al Arabiya* reported the arranged marriage of a Saudi octogenarian marrying an eleven-year-old girl in her hometown of Buraidah, near Riyadh, the Saudi capital. The father of the bride, who took 85,000 riyals ($23,350) in dowry, defended his decision to marry off his eleven-year-old daughter even though his wife vehemently objected. "I don't care about her age," he told the paper. "Her health and her body build make her fit for marriage. I also do not care what her mother thinks. This is a very old custom [in Saudi society] and there is nothing wrong with it whether religiously or socially."[147] In a rare occurrence, this child bride challenged the arrangement. With the assistance of legal counsel, the girl, then twelve at that time, took her case to court in Buraidah. She reached an agreement with her family, and she was granted a divorce. A settlement was handled privately rather than in the courts. But this is more the exception than the rule. In November 2010, another case of an over eighty -year-old man marrying a fourteen-year-old girl made international news. He refused to divorce her unless she paid him back his 17,000 Saudi riyals dowry. The bride's father, Showan Ateen, said his daughter had been forced to marry the octogenarian, though he did not state who forced her. The husband threatened to consummate the marriage by force, unless he was repaid.[148] Saudi Arabia still has no minimum legal age for marriage.[149]

On July 13, 2011, Dr. Salih bin Fawzan, a prominent cleric and member of Saudi Arabia's highest religious council, issued a *fatwa* asserting that there is no minimum age for marriage, and that girls can be married "even if they are in the cradle." He insisted that nowhere does shari'a set an age limit for marrying prepubescent girls.[150] Subsequently, in April 2012, Saudi Arabia's Grand Mufti Abdul Aziz al ash-Shaikh okayed marriage for girls starting at age ten and criticized those who want to raise the legal marriageable age to twenty-five. The Grand Mufti declared, "Our mothers and grandmothers got married when they were barely twelve. Good upbringing makes a girl ready to perform all marital duties at that age."[151]

Child marriages are widespread in Yemen. More than a quarter of the country's females marry before age fifteen.[152] Such early marriages are often dangerous for the women. Women who give birth before they are eighteen are almost eight times more likely to die in labor than those who give birth in their twenties. In some parts of Yemen, women are about sixty times more likely to die in childbirth than in the United States.

The situations of Nujood Ali and Reem al Numeri exemplified the dire straits of prepubescent Muslim girls being forced to marry. In February 2008, ten-year-old Nujood Ali was forcibly married to a man in his thirties. The husband repeatedly beat and raped her. After this abuse, she took herself to court in Sana'a, the Yemeni capital and asked a judge for a divorce. Nujood's father and husband were arrested until the divorce hearing. After a well-publicized trial, she was granted a divorce on April 15, 2008. But based on the principles of shari'a law, her husband was compensated, not prosecuted. Nujood was ordered to pay him more than $200, a huge amount in a country where the United Nations Development Program says 15.7 percent of the population lives on less than $1 a day.[153]

In the case of Reem al Numeri, the girl was eleven when her father forced her to marry a thirty-two-year-old cousin. The father threatened to cut her in half with his dagger if she did not agree to the marriage. Divorced at fourteen, Reem now lives the life of an outcast. Without a husband or father to support her, she cannot attend school. In Yemen, more than half of all young girls are married before age eighteen, mostly to older men.[154] A study carried out in 2008 by the Gender Development Research and Studies Centre at Sana'a University found that 52 percent of Yemeni girls are married before turning eighteen, while a 2007 study by the International Centre for Research on Women put the figure at 48 percent. The latter study ranked Yemen thirteenth in the world for child marriage[155]

In February 2009, Yemen's Parliament passed legislation, which proposed raising the minimum age of marriage to eighteen. But conservative parliamentarians argued that the bill violated shari'a, which does not stipulate a minimum age of marriage. Shari'a supersedes all civil law. More than 100 leading religious clerics called the attempt to restrict the age of marriage "un-Islamic." Thus, the committee of Islamic Legislations and shari'a in the Yemeni Parliament rejected the proposed law to increase the legal age of marriage to eighteen.[156]

Since the establishment of the Islamic Republic of Iran in 1979, extramarital sex is a crime punishable by law. The punishment for a single man or woman guilty of sex outside marriage is 100 lashes. Under Article 86, the punishment for a married person is death by stoning. However, since Iranian law permits polygamy, men have an escape clause. Because Iranian law recognizes "marriages" of even a few hours between men and single women, men can claim that their adulterous relationships are in fact temporary marriages. Thus, men are rarely sentenced to stoning. Married women accused of adultery have access to no such pardon and as such are stoned to death as prescribed in the Hadith.[157]

ASSAULT

The Qur'an tells husbands to beat their disobedient wives. Women and daughters are routinely beaten for even minor offenses.

> Allah has made men superior to women because men spend their wealth to support them. Therefore, virtuous women are obedient, and they are to guard their unseen parts as Allah has guarded them. As for women whom you fear will rebel, admonish them first, and then send them to a separate bed, and then beat them. But if they are obedient after that, then do nothing further; surely Allah is exalted and great![158]

According to a hadith, Muhammad said, "A man will not be asked as to why he beat his wife."[159] Thus, the practice is widespread. Over 90 percent of Pakistani women have been beaten.

In Islam, the victim of rape is to blame, for she has sullied the family's honor by engaging in sexual immorality. The fact that it was forced upon her makes no difference at all. Women who are raped most often are punished, while the rapist is not. The testimony of four male Muslim witnesses, who saw the act, is the standard for establishing guilt in sexual offenses under shari'a law.[160] The testimony of the woman involved is inadmissible. Therefore, if those four male witnesses do not come forward and the victim becomes pregnant, her pregnancy becomes evidence that she has committed adultery. In February 2009, Saudi judges ordered a woman jailed for a year and receive 100 lashes after she was gang-raped. Some 75 percent of women in Pakistani prisons have been jailed for the crime of having been raped. In March 2009, Afghan President Hamid Karzai signed a shari'a-influenced law that legalized Shi'ite marital rape. "It is essential for the woman to submit to the man's sexual desire."[161] The law also declared that women could only seek work, education or doctor's appointments with their husband's permission. The law was signed to curry favor with Shi'ite clerics. Furthermore, "the indemnity for the death or injury of a woman is one-half the indemnity paid for a man. The indemnity paid for a Jew or Christian is one-third of the indemnity paid for a Muslim. The indemnity paid for a Zoroastrian is one-fifteenth of that a Muslim."[162]

From January 2011, sexual assaults including gang rapes plagued Tahrir Square in Cairo, Egypt, the epicenter of the "revolution" that toppled the Mubarak regime and brought the Muslim Brotherhood to power, under the leadership of Mohamed Morsi. These assaults escalated during the numerous protests held in the square, occurred simultaneously in several parts of the square and seemed organized. Groups seeking to assist the assaulted women were themselves attacked, the situations being described as "like war." When women try to file sexual assault cases with police, the reaction is often dismissive or even victim blaming. At times, e.g. in March 2011, the Egyptian police participated in sexual assaults of their own by forcing "virginity tests" on women protesters at Tahrir. All this is part of the chronic problem of sexual harassment in Egypt.[163] It remains to be seen if the status of women will improve given the ouster of the Morsi regime by the Egyptian military on July 3, 2013 and the subsequent inauguration of President Abdel Fattah el-Sisi on June 8, 2014.

Foreign women traveling in the Arab/Muslim Middle East are frequently targeted for rape. A noted case was that of Norwegian interior designer, Marte Deborah Dalelv, who was raped by a co-worker on March 6, 2013, in Dubai, UAE, while on a business trip to the emirate. After reporting the attack to police, her passport was confiscated and she was detained for four days after being accused of having extramarital sex, drinking alcohol, and perjury. She was held in prison until convicted and sentenced, on July 17, to 16 months in jail in Dubai for having sex outside marriage. Her alleged attacker received a 13-month-sentence for out-of-wedlock sex and alcohol consumption. Due to international outcry by rights groups and the Norwegian government, she was pardoned by Dubai's ruler, her passport returned and she was free to leave the country on July 22, 2013. Recall that under shari'a a rape conviction can only be secured after a confession by the rapist or as the result of testimony from four adult male witnesses to the crime.

DIVORCE

Divorce is determined by the husband. For Muslim men, divorce is relatively easy. The husband may invoke *talaq,* saying "I divorce you" three times to be divorced. Islamic divorce procedures "shall apply to those [women] who have not yet menstruated."[164] A husband may get rid of one of his undesirable wives.[165] On the other hand, divorce is forbidden to women. Women thus divorced receive no support and usually lose custody of their children.

A divorced woman is required to wait a period—*iddah*—usually three months or three menstrual cycles, before she can remarry.[166] A wife may remarry her ex-husband if and only if she marries another man, they have sex, and then this second man divorces her.[167] If her husband dies, a woman must wait 4 months and 10 days before remarrying.

FAMILY

Muslims are to have more children to increase the *Ummah*—the community of Muslims. A son's inheritance should be twice the size of that of a daughter. "Allah [thus] directs you as regards your children's [inheritance]: to the male, a portion equal to that of two females."[168]

Some Saudi hospitals require a guardian's permission before a woman or her children can get certain medical treatments. Saudi women are denied the legal right to make even trivial decisions for their children. Women cannot open bank accounts for children, enroll them in school, obtain school files, or travel with their children without written permission from the child's father.[169] Additionally, Saudi judges have repeatedly granted fathers the right to interfere arbitrarily in their adult children's private lives, in serious violation of their right to privacy and to establish families freely. Fathers have imprisoned their adult daughters for "disobedience" and prevented their marriage, and have been granted custody over a grandchild without valid reason, all with the support of the courts. The Saudi government recognizes filial "disobedience" as a crime and denies an adult woman the right to live on her own and to marry of her free will.[170]

EDUCATION AND ECONOMIC INDEPENDENCE

Schooling for women, if it exists, is segregated. Various subjects are deemed appropriate for women whereas other subjects are restricted or forbidden. This is justified by Muhammad's statement to women, "I have not seen any one more deficient in intelligence and religion than you."[171] In Afghanistan, in 2007, 236 schools teaching girls were burned down by the Taliban. In 2008, there were attacks on 256 schools that left 58 dead. In mid-August 2012, thirty-six Iranian government universities announced that 77 BA and BS courses in the coming academic year would be "single gender" and effectively exclusive to men. Under the new policy, women undergraduates would be excluded from a broad range of studies in some of the country's leading institutions, including English literature, English translation, hotel management, archaeology, nuclear physics, computer science, electrical engineering, industrial engineering and business management. It follows years in which Iranian women students outperformed men, a trend at odds with the traditional male-dominated outlook of the country's religious leaders. Women outnumbered men by three to two in passing the 2012 university entrance exam. With the announced withdrawal of American forces from Afghanistan by the end of 2016, it is expected that the Taliban will return to power. Given their previous record, education for females will end.

In Iran, the fields of medicine and health are most sought after by women students, because they provide the greatest job security and independence. For this reason, in the last decade, women's medicine entrance test scores have been consistently higher on average than men's have. For that reason, the government placed quotas on women university entrants, particularly in specific fields, such as medicine and engineering.[172] Turning to the issue of economic independence, in many Islamic societies, women cannot go out of the house to work forcing economic and social dependence on men.

POLITICAL RIGHTS

The Qur'an declares that a woman's testimony is worth half that of a man. "Get two witnesses, out of your own men, and if there are not two men, then a man and two women, such as ye choose, for witnesses, so that if one of them errs, the other can remind her."[173] It is further related that Muhammad asked some women, "Isn't the witness of a woman equal to half that of a man?" The women replied,

"Yes," He said, "This is because of the deficiency of the woman's mind."[174] Another hadith broadened the scope of women's deficiency. Speaking to a group of women, Muhammad commented, "I have witnessed that most of the people in Hell are women. [When asked why, he replied] You swear too much and you show no gratitude to your husbands. I have never come across anyone more lacking in intelligence, or ignorant of their religion than women."[175] Along this line of thinking women were not to lead politically, lest it result in failure.[176] The election and tenure of Benazir Bhutto as Prime Minister of Pakistan (1988–90 and 1993–96), as well as her long tenure in politics (from 1988 until her assassination on December 27, 2007), was one of the few exceptions to this prohibition.

In many Muslim nations, women are not allowed to vote. Saudi law bars women from voting, except for chamber of commerce elections in two cities in recent years, and no woman can sit in the kingdom's Cabinet. In a gesture towards granting some political rights to women, Saudi King Abdullah by royal decree on January 11, 2013, appointed 30 women to the previously all-male 150 member legislative advisory council—the Shura Council. The decree stated that special seating would be allocated for women inside the Shura Council building, and that a special entrance and exit would be built to ensure the segregation of male and female members. Earlier in 2011, King Abdullah announced that women would be allowed to vote and run as candidates in the 2015 municipal elections.

TRAVEL

Women are not allowed to leave the house without a male relative. Saudi Arabia is the only country in the world that bans women from driving. It is enforced by Saudi police through fines and arrests. Only men are permitted to acquire driving licenses. The prohibition forces families to hire live-in drivers and those who cannot afford the $300 to $400 a month for a driver must rely on male relatives to drive them to work, school, shopping, or the doctor.[177] Furthermore, under Saudi law, women must get permission from a father, husband, brother or even a son to travel.

In the Taliban-controlled parts of Afghanistan, in addition to the above-mentioned restrictions, chatting with the other gender is a crime; movies, mixed schools, radios, dish antennas, music (including CDs and CD players) and poetry are banned. Other Salafist groups from Mali, in western Africa, to the al-Qaeda offshoot, Islamic State of Iraq and the Levant (ISIL), have also instituted similar bans. If the Islamic supremacists win the global conflict and reestablish the caliphate that will be the society they would establish. According to a report via Reuters, in Pakistan's North West Frontier Province, Islamist parties banned music on public transport and tore down movie posters featuring women.[178] This is in keeping with Hadith Qudsi 19:5, "The Prophet said that Allah commanded him to destroy all the musical instruments, idols, crosses and all the trappings of ignorance." A recent example occurred in Pakistan, when the traffic police in Karachi, launched a ban on the playing of music on all public methods of transport in mid-February 2014. Drivers caught playing music were fined and music players were confiscated under the crackdown.[179]

In 2009, the Hamas government moved ahead with its goal of enacting shari'a throughout the Gaza Strip, with the establishment of Morality Units to supervise proper public behavior. These units run jointly by the Ministry of the Interior and the Ministry of Religious Affairs enforced the wearing of the *hijab* and *jalabiya* (long gown worn as an outer garment) on female lawyers and students. Additionally, the Morality Units acted to separate the sexes in government departments by imposing a separation between the sexes in offices and waiting rooms. What's more, the units prohibited mixed folk dancing. Moreover, the units asked couples who walked on the beach to present a marriage contract, and asked any woman walking alone on the beach to have an escort i.e. a male relative. The

Morality Units prohibited laughing and talking for women in public, and issued a *fatwa* prohibiting men from swimming in shorts, with the rest of their bodies naked.[180] A 2010 study conducted by the Gaza-based Palestinian Women's Information and Media Center found that Gaza women have increasingly been victims of violence since the Hamas regime seized power in the Gaza Strip in June 2007. A report issued by the Israeli Security Agency (*Shin Bet*) in November 2009, substantiated these restrictions. In addition to the above-mentioned limitations, there is a dress code for women in public, female mannequins may not be exhibited in store windows, and men may not teach in girls' schools. Men are not allowed to go shirtless, even while swimming in the ocean. The death penalty was restored for crimes such as adultery, drug use, murder, and cooperation with Israel.

In July 2010, a wave of new regulations aimed at women, were implemented in the Gaza Strip. On July 17, 2010, the Hamas Interior Ministry announced that women and teenagers would no longer be allowed to smoke *nargilhas* (water pipes) in public. Restaurant and hotel owners reported that they were forced to sign papers stating that they would enforce the new law. Additionally on July 28, 2010, new restraints were placed on women's lingerie and dress stores throughout the Gaza Strip. Banned were displays of lingerie or pajamas in store windows, having fitting rooms or cubicles inside shops, and using tinted glass for store windows. Security cameras inside women's stores were also prohibited. Other bans included a prohibition on women from riding motorcycles and attending wedding parties extending past midnight.[181] While these restrictions and discriminatory practices against women, which constitute gender apartheid, have gone on for centuries, it shows no sign of any modification or abatement. Thus, Muslim women may easily be classified as second-class citizens, because women are considered inferior to men as human beings. However, it should not be forgotten that unbelievers, i.e. non-Muslims—men and women—are considered to be less than human and as such have a third-class political status. Nevertheless, it cannot be overstated that the treatment of women in Muslim-majority countries is the biggest human-rights crisis of our generation. Incredulously, there is nothing but overwhelming and deafening silence from Western feminists, human rights advocates, and liberals.

30. Suicide is a sin in Islam except when done to kill infidels. It then becomes a virtue rewarded in Paradise, with seventy-two virgins.[182]

The Qur'an mentions martyrs going to heaven will get *houris* and the word was taken by early commentators to mean "virgins" (*see* Qur'an 9:111, 44:54, 52:20, 55:54–59, 55:72, 56:12–40, and 76:12–22). In the Hadith Book of Sunanm Vol. IV, Muhammad used the promise of virgins in exhortation to his warriors before the Battle of Badr, March 17, 624 C.E. This is exemplified by *Sura* 9:111 in the Qur'an, which states (several translations follow):

> YUSUF ALI, "Allah hath purchased of the believers their persons and their goods; for theirs (in return) is the garden (of Paradise): they fight in His cause, and slay and are slain: a promise binding on Him in truth, through the Law, the Gospel, and the Qur'an: and who is more faithful to his covenant than Allah? Then rejoice in the bargain which ye have concluded: that is the achievement supreme."

> PICKTHAL, "Lo! Allah hath bought from the believers their lives and their wealth because the Garden will be theirs: they shall fight in the way of Allah and shall slay and be slain. It is a promise, which is binding on Him in the Torah and the Gospel

and the Qur'an. Who fulfilleth His covenant better than Allah? Rejoice then in your bargain that ye have made, for that is the supreme triumph."

SHAKIR, "Surely Allah has bought of the believers their persons and their property for this, that they shall have the garden; they fight in Allah's way, so they slay and are slain; a promise which is binding on Him in the Taurat and the Injeel and the Qur'an; and who is more faithful to his covenant than Allah? Rejoice therefore in the pledge which you have made; and that is the mighty achievement."

This martyrdom verse is taken to mean that the slain martyr need not wait until Judgment Day in order to get his virgins in Paradise. There are scholars who believe that the date of the attacks on the United States by Osama Bin Laden's Al-Qaeda on September 11, 2001—i.e. 9/11 was inspired by this verse. It should not be forgotten that the ringleader of the nineteen Al-Qaeda terrorists, Mohammed Atta, wrote reassuringly to his fellow hijackers shortly before the attacks on the World Trade Center and the Pentagon, "The virgins are calling you."[183]

31. Throughout history, Islam sought to conquer the West and destroy its civilization.

The internationally renowned Muslim historian and philosopher Abu Zayd 'Abdu r-Raḥman bin Muhammad bin Khaldūn Al-Hadrami, more commonly known as Ibn Khaldun (May 27, 1332–March 19, 1406) explained why Islam is the superior religion in his highly influential book, *Muqaddimah of Ibn Khaldun* ("Ibn Khaldun's Introduction [to History]"), written in 1377. He put into words the division of the world into two parts, as mentioned previously, *Dar al-Islam,* (the House of Submission) and *Dar al-Harb,* (the House of War), in this manner:

> In the Muslim community, holy war [jihad] is a religious duty, because of the universalism of the Muslim mission and the obligation to convert everybody to Islam either by persuasion or by force. The other religious groups [specifically Christians and Jews] did not have a universal mission, and the holy war was not a religious duty for them, save only for purposes of defense. But Islam is under obligation to gain power over other nations.[184]

In short, no other religion commands' converting the world through force, but Islam does. Thus, the normal and only justified relationship between the *Dar al-Islam* and the *Dar al-Harb* is a state of perpetual, though not necessarily continuous, war. There can be no peace with non-Muslims, i.e. infidels, only temporary truces—*hudnas*.[185] A *hudna* does not imply the abandonment of jihad, but rather is a suspension of hostilities. It is a temporary or limited truce, armistice, or ceasefire, which can be broken, and hostilities resumed any time a Muslim leader deems it is advantageous.

Shari'a law unequivocally portrays jihad* as a military endeavor to empower Islam. Imposing shari'a law worldwide is a religious duty. The institution of jihad, according to every authoritative Muslim book on Islamic jurisprudence, is nothing less than offensive warfare to spread shari'a, a cause

---

* "Jihad" is mentioned in the Qur'an forty times. In thirty-six of those references the word is used in context of holy war, to subjugate or kill unbelievers—not in the currently PC-vogue definition of "inner struggle." Islamic supremacist groups, including Al-Qaeda, state jihad is used to fight oppression, invasion and injustices, as defined by the Islamic supremacists themselves.

seen as both "holy" and "legitimate" in Islam. Making Islam supreme through jihad is the greatest priority. As such, the impermissible becomes permissible. Thus, anything and everything that is otherwise banned becomes allowable. All that matters is one's intention, or *niyya*.

One hundred and eleven *ayah* in the Qur'an are devoted to jihad. Literally, jihad means to "struggle" or "strive." "Jihad means to war against non-Muslims."[186] "It is a communal obligation. When enough people perform it to successfully accomplish it, it is no longer obligatory upon others; He who provides the equipment for a soldier in jihad has himself performed jihad."[187] However, jihad can take on any form, though its most native and praiseworthy expression revolves around fighting and killing the infidel enemy, even if it costs the Muslim fighter—the *mujahid*—his life (*see* Qur'an 4:74 and 9:11 below). Jihad has been a fundamental feature of Islam since the seventh century. Any act of war or violence against the *Dar al-Harb* is morally justified. Hence, Arab/Muslim states do not denounce or recognize as terrorism any acts perpetrated against Jewish Israel, Hindu India, Orthodox Serbia or Russia, Catholic Philippines, and Buddhist Thailand to cite but a few examples.

Islamic doctrine holds that jihad becomes obligatory upon all Muslims whenever a Muslim land is attacked. (Provocations by Muslims from that Muslim land do not factor into this equation—if the non-Muslim enemy strikes back, that constitutes an invasion of Muslim land). All the schools of Islamic jurisprudence agree that when a non-Muslim force enters a Muslim land, jihad becomes the individual obligation—*fard 'ayn*—of every Muslim. Offensive jihad or *jihad al-talab* ("jihad of conquering") is a compulsory command and is the permanent state of war or hostility between the *Dar al-Islam* and the *Dar al-Harb,* until the infidels conclusive submission to the absolute world supremacy of Islam. Thus, jihad is a mandatory, global and eternal militaristic doctrine.

Any territory conquered during jihad by Muslims is a *Waqf*—a sacred Muslim trust—never to be returned. Islamic doctrine dictates that it is the duty of every Muslim to ensure that land that is under Islamic dominion remains under Islamic dominion and that land once under such dominion, but lost to infidels is considered occupied and must be returned to Islamic dominion by force. Such lands Islamists (*see* Islamic supremacism below) claim, belong exclusively to them (for example *see* Appendix 8, Hamas Charter Article 11). The Arab/Muslim world's historic record reveals that Islamists are never willing to agree to any *permanent* (emphasis added) loss of territory. Thus, places like Spain (called Al-Andalus by its Muslim conquerors), Portugal, southern France, the Italian coast, the islands of the Mediterranean such as Sicily, Cyprus and Rhodes (among others), much of the Balkan Peninsula, Greece, Israel, the Christian portions of Lebanon, East Timor, and South Sudan to name several prominent areas, must be reconquered, or in the words of Hassan al-Banna, the founder of the Muslim Brotherhood, "Must return to the embrace of Islam"[188]—sooner or later. The Hanafi, Maliki, Shafi'i, and Hanbali schools of Sunni jurisprudence further declare that jihad, once it is *fard 'ayn* is no different from prayer and fasting. In other words, to engage in warfare with non-Muslims in that case, is a religious devotion that cannot lawfully be evaded.[189]

The current jihad being waged by Islamic supremacists against the West is being waged simultaneously on five parallel tracks:

- Politically–to soften the public of the target country to be more accommodating to the precepts of Islam and shari'a, as well as to penetrate and influence its government. Additionally, attempts are made to radicalize the existing and growing Muslim population in the target country.
- Subversively–to infiltrate the target country and use its laws to undermine its legal system. This infiltration is being aided by *al-hijra,* or the Islamic doctrine of emigrating from Islamic

lands to other areas of the *Dar al-Harb*. Given the multiple upheavals currently raging across the greater Middle East from Afghanistan to Libya, from Syria to Yemen and Somalia there are tens of thousands of mainly Muslim refugees moving and being resettled in predominantly Western nations and particularly in the United States.[190]

- Economically–to use oil and trade as a weapon.
- Ideologically–to penetrate and influence the educational system of the target country and its mass media.
- Diplomatically–to influence and control the target country's foreign policy.

Jihad manifests itself in three stages. These stages change when circumstances dictate. The first stage is stealth jihad—infiltration. When Muslims are too weak to fight, they promote peace and tolerance outwardly, but never inwardly. This includes offers of interfaith dialogue to indoctrinate non-Muslims. Increased Muslim immigration and birth rates in host countries, takes place. The practice of *taqiyya* is used. *Taqiyya* is the religiously sanctioned Muslim doctrine that allows lying and deception to conceal one's true intentions and beliefs. There are several different styles of deception used by Muslims (for example, *kitman* which is lying by omission) when discussing Islam or their activities as Muslims, but for the purpose of this book, only the overall term "taqiyya" will be used. These are all deception techniques inherent in Arab/Muslim statecraft. Additionally, in this first stage, there are claims of Islamophobia, victimization and charges of racism (even though Islam is not a "race"). All this is accompanied by "creeping shari'a"—the slow, deliberate, methodical advance of Islamic law in non-Muslim countries. Special privileges for Muslims and Islam are sought. Preparations for jihad behind the scenes continue. As explained by the eminent authority on *dhimmitude**, Bat Ye'or:

> Stealth jihad exists in every sector of Western society, in law, culture, schools, universities, policies, banking, economics, and the media. The aim is to destroy Judeo-Christian values and to Islamize Western societies, following the thousand years of Islamic conquest of Christian lands. They are helped in the West by the promoters of multiculturalism and the political Left.[191]

As Newt Gingrich explained, these tools—"political, cultural, societal, religious and intellectual"—designed to speed the implementation of shari'a pose "a mortal threat to the survival of freedom in the United States and in the world, as we know it."[192]

The second stage is defensive jihad. When Muslims are strong enough to fight, but not strong enough to subjugate the unbelievers, they claim persecution in order to justify physical violence and terrorism against their enemies, assassinate critics and look for excuses to attack other groups. There is rejection of the host society's secular laws and culture, as well as demands for the implementation of shari'a.

The last stage is offensive jihad. When Muslims achieve a majority in an area, then Muslims violently subjugate all unbelievers, because they are not Muslims. Shari'a becomes the only law of the land. Western freedoms—such as gender equality, fair treatment for minorities, equal opportunity and social mobility, as well as freedom of speech, the press, association, and religion—are curtailed or eliminated. Additionally, Muslims strive to expand their political dominion conquering non-Muslim

---

* The legal concept, in an Islamic state, of non-Muslims under shari'a who have paid a special tax—the *jizya*—and agree to a long list of strict conditions by which they are subordinated. The *dhimmi* includes Christians, Jews, and Zoroastrians.

lands. Then they rid important Muslim lands of all non-Muslims—by use of ethnic cleansing, ending diversity and tolerance. Historic evidence and symbols of other faiths, and cultures are denied or destroyed. Currently, the United States, Canada, and Australia are in the first stage. Many countries in Europe and some countries of sub-Saharan Africa and Asia are in the second stage. The Arab/ Muslim states of Africa, Asia, and southeastern Europe, are in the last stage.

There have been three historic attempts of Islamic conquest against the West, which has come close on several occasions to extinguishing Western civilization, as we know it. The first concerted effort was made by the Arabs between 634 and 800 C.E. After sweeping out of the Arabian Peninsula, Arab Muslim forces conquered North Africa, and crossed the water strait at the western end of the Mediterranean Sea, dominated by the mountain that still bears the name of the Arab commander, Tariq ibn Ziyad, the mountain of Tariq (*Jabal Tariq* i.e. Gibraltar). Then, Muslim armies overran the entire Iberian Peninsula (present-day Spain and Portugal). The Muslim hordes were stopped by Charles Martel and the Franks at the Battle of Tours (also known as the Battle of Poitiers), France, October 10, 732 C.E. only 183 miles from Paris. During this same period, Arab armies also swept into Persia, Central Asia and the Indian subcontinent.

The second historic period of conquest came between ca. 1021 and 1689 as the Muslim Turkish forces repelled Christian attempts to regain lost Christian territories, which was followed by Muslim attempts to conquer Europe, this time from the east. At first, the Muslim armies were quite successful. When the Byzantine Christian forces fought to protect their besieged capital at Constantinople against attacking Muslim forces, from April 6, 1453 to May 29, 1453, they lost and witnessed the end of their Byzantine Empire, which had lasted for over 1,000 years. Don John of Austria led a multinational fleet to fight and defeat a Muslim fleet at the Battle of Lepanto, October 7, 1571. Likewise, the King of Poland, Jan III Sobieski led a combined Polish-Austrian-German army to demolish the Islamic army of Turks and Tartars[*] outside the gates of Vienna, Austria. The Battle of Vienna marked the high water mark of militant Islam's efforts to subjugate Europe for a second time.

Additionally during this same time, Muslim armies attempted to snuff out the last vestiges of Christianity in northeastern Africa. They were stopped by Ethiopian Emperor Galawdewos who fought and defeated the Muslim armies at the Battle of Wayna Dega, February 21, 1543. It should be noted that isolated Christian Ethiopia resisted repeated Muslim attempts at conquest well into the late nineteenth century. Ethiopian Emperor Yohannes IV fought and defeated invading Egyptian Muslim armies at the Battle of Gundat, November 16, 1875, and at the Battle of Gura, from March 7 through 9, 1876. What is more, he decisively defeated the Muslim Mahdist Sudanese army at the Battle of Gallabat/Metemma, from March 9 to 10, 1889, at the cost of his own life to preserve Ethiopian Christianity and independence.

The third attempt to conquer the West began in the 1970s, with the spread of militant Sunni Wahhabist movement from Saudi Arabia, and after 1979, the spread of similar militant Shi'ite Islam, from Iran. This time the goal is not merely the subjugation of Europe, but of the entire world. This third Islamic thrust is still ongoing globally in the Philippines, Thailand, India, Afghanistan, Iraq, Syria, Chechnya, Dagestan, Somalia, Israel, Kosovo, Algeria, Libya, Egypt, Yemen and in cities scattered across Europe and the United States.

At this juncture, it is important to review the concept of Islamic fundamentalism or as it is sometimes called Islamic revivalism or Islamism. These revivalist fundamentalist groups believe that all the

---

[*] The historic name of this Turkic Muslim people is the Tartars. In modern times they are referred to as Tatars.

problems of the Muslim world were caused through lack of genuine Islamic observance. The status of the Muslim world was due to their not being faithful to the precepts of Islam and following Allah's laws. Thus, they became impoverished, ignorant, corrupt, and weak. This state of affairs could be corrected by strict adherence to the ideology of Islam, and more shari'a compliance. What is implied is that when Islam is truly implemented all the problems human beings face will be solved. Islamic fundamentalism is found today, in varying degrees of strength and popular support, in every Muslim majority country and in many countries with large Muslim minorities.

Islamic fundamentalism is not new. In modern times, it has been around since the mid-eighteenth century. Such revivalist fundamentalist movements seek to reestablish the greatness of Islam and make it supreme again. They reject many aspects of modern and secular societies. These movements seek by force, both overtly and covertly, world conquest and domination as well as the imposition of violent customs and rules on the rest of the world. Among the most prominent of these movements are the Wahhabist movement, the Deobandi movement, the Muslim Brotherhood and the Jamaat-e-Islami.

Since 1740, the Wahhabist movement is a revivalist ultra-conservative faction of Sunni Islam that has as its objective the restoration of the pristine fundamentalist Islam of the Qur'an and Hadith. It was initiated by an eighteenth century theologian, Muhammad ibn Abd al-Wahhab (1703–92) from Nejd, (what today is the central region of Saudi Arabia). Wahhabism is the creed upon which the kingdom of Saudi Arabia was founded and its tremendous oil wealth has made possible the dissemination of Wahhabist ideology and influence throughout the world, through religious propaganda and financial assistance to mosques and madrasas.

A second fundamentalist movement is Deobandi movement, a Sunni Islamic group found primarily in India, Pakistan, Afghanistan and Bangladesh. The Deobandi movement started at the Darul Uloom Deoband, an Islamic seminary in India. The school dates from May 30, 1866, when the foundation of the building was laid. The movement was inspired by Islamic scholar Qutb-ud-Din Ahmad ibn 'Abdul Rahim, better known as Shah Waliullah (1703–62). He attempted to reassess Islamic theology in the light of modern changes.

Contemporary Islamic fundamentalist groups trace their origins to two organizations, the transnational Muslim Brotherhood in the Arab world and Jamaat-e-Islami in the Indian subcontinent. Both groups surfaced as responses to the problems confronting Muslims under British colonial rule or influence, and in reaction to the perceived conformism by secular or modernist Muslim elites to Western ideas and institutions. Turning first to the transnational Muslim Brotherhood—*al-Ikhwan al-Muslimun* (*Ikhwan* for short)—which is the world's largest and one of the oldest Sunni Islamist fundamentalist organizations.

The Muslim Brotherhood's goals are to return to the Islam of Muhammad, the conversion of Muslim countries into states ruled by shari'a law, the reestablishment of the caliphate and ultimately, via civilizational jihad, world dominion. There will be no separation of mosque and state in the caliphate they envision. The Muslim Brotherhood's ideology, which insists that Islam is a superior prescription for governance as well as religion, is the prototypical example of Islamism. Their credo is self-explanatory, "Allah is our objective; the Quran is our law, the Prophet is our leader; Jihad is our way; and dying in the way of Allah is the highest of our aspirations." The Brotherhood is not a fanatical sect of Islam. In reality, it is a resurgence of pure Islam.

With only six members, the Muslim Brotherhood was founded formally in March 1928, by Hassan al-Banna, but it may have existed before in a less formal framework. After ten years, the *Ikhwan* had only 800 members, but the Muslim Brotherhood became a regional force after receiving massive aid from Nazi Germany. It formed a tactical and ideological alliance with the Nazis as well as with Hajj Amin al-Husseini, the Grand Mufti of Jerusalem. It must be stressed that both the Islamists, (whether the Muslim Brotherhood, or the Islamic Arab nationalists led by Hajj Amin al-Husseini) and the Nazis shared parallel and symbiotic ideologies. Both groups developed these doctrines based on their own societies' histories, political traditions, religion and fervently believed in these ideologies. The Islamists continue to believe in and follow these doctrines to this day.

The Brotherhood endorsed Adolf Hitler's goal of eradicating the Jews. Nazi Germany provided significant financial aid to the Brotherhood, specifically to al-Banna. In 1939, they transferred to al-Banna some E£1,000 per month, a substantial sum at the time. In comparison, the Muslim Brotherhood fund-raising for the cause of Palestine yielded only E£500 for that entire year. This Nazi funding enabled the Muslim Brotherhood to expand internationally. By the end of World War II, it had a million members.

The Brotherhood's influence spread across the Middle East and into Africa. For example, Hamas in the Gaza Strip is an offshoot of the Muslim Brotherhood. On June 7, 2011, the Muslim Brotherhood was legalized in Egypt, in the wake of the overthrow of the Mubarak regime. As the result of the Egyptian elections of June 16–17, 2012, the Muslim Brotherhood candidate, Mohamed Morsi was elected president of Egypt. However, as Morsi assumed dictatorial powers and the Muslim Brotherhood regime quickly implemented moves designed to turn Egypt into a more Islamist shari'a-compliant state, opposition grew from several sectors. After four days of massive civilian protest and demonstrations upwards of 30 million people, the Morsi regime was ousted by the Egyptian military led by General Abdel Fattah el-Sisi, who removed Morsi from power on July 3, 2013. Morsi was arrested and detained. On August 19, 2013, the Brotherhood's Supreme Guide, Mohammed Badie, was arrested along with most of the top Muslim Brotherhood leadership. The Muslim Brotherhood was subsequently declared a terrorist group and a threat to Egypt's security, on December 24, 2013, and banned. In a like manner, an Egyptian court outlawed the Muslim Brotherhood's Palestinian offshoot, Hamas, and banned its activities in Egypt. The March 4, 2014 ruling stemmed from Hamas's anti-Egyptian terrorist activities, particularly in the Sinai Peninsula, alongside another terror group Al Qaeda in the Sinai Peninsula.

As the result of the election of May 26–28, 2014, Abdel Fattah el-Sisi became the new Egyptian president backed by massive public support. This was followed by the trials of Muslim Brotherhood officials including Morsi. Moreover, the Egyptian administrative court order of August 9, 2014, dissolved the Freedom and Justice Party, the political wing of the already banned Brotherhood. This ruling is irrevocable and officially prevents the Brotherhood from formally participating in parliamentary elections.[193] It now remains to be seen what the future holds in store for the Brotherhood. A word of caution however, this nearly ninety-year-old organization has survived being forced underground, outlawed, imprisoned and yet it survived to rise to political control of Egypt. It may currently be down, but is it really out?

A second contemporary organization is the Jamaat-e-Islami, a conservative Sunni Islamic fundamentalist movement founded in what was then British India, on August 26, 1941, by Abul Ala Maududi. Upon the partition of the Indian subcontinent and the attainment of independence for India and Pakistan, the movement split into two parts, one in each country—Jamaat-e-Islami Hind and Jamaat-e-Islami Pakistan, respectively. From those two organizations, separate branches developed in Kashmir, Bangladesh and Afghanistan, the latter in 1968. The Jamaat's objective is the establishment of an Islamic state, governed by shari'a law.

It should be noted that even the Organization of Islamic Cooperation is a revivalist organization. This is reflected in its Charter which states that it exists "to work for revitalizing Islam's pioneering role in the world," a euphemism for reestablishing Islam's dominant place in world affairs.[194]

Whatever one's opinion of the various local conflicts around the world—Muslims versus Buddhists in Thailand, Muslims versus Catholics in the Philippines, Muslims versus Hindus in Kashmir, Muslims versus Jews in the Land of Israel, Muslims versus Russian Orthodox in Chechnya, Muslims versus Zoroastrians in Iran, and Muslims versus Christians, in Lebanon, Syria, Iraq, Egypt and across Africa—the fact is that violent armed jihad has held out a long time against very tough enemies. If the Islamic supremacists were not afraid of taking on the Israelis and Russians, why would they fear the Danes, the Swedes, the Dutch, the Belgians, the French, the Spaniards, the Italians, the British or even the Americans? Islam's war against the West has been prosecuted for fourteen centuries in various forms and frequencies. It will not end with the elimination of this or that individual terrorist leader, group or organization. A more detailed historic listing of Islamic conquests, as well as setbacks follows.

TIMELINE OF ISLAM, MUSLIM CONQUESTS AND SETBACKS (Islamic setbacks are italicized)	
Date	**Event**
April 20, 570 C.E.	The Islamic prophet Muhammad (Abu al-Qasim Muhammad Ibn Abd Allah Ibn Abd al-Muttalib Ibn Hashim), founder of Islam, was born in Mecca.
610	Muhammad believed he had a vision and was chosen to serve as the prophet of a new faith—Islam. He began his teachings in Mecca.
July 16, 622	*Warned of a plot to assassinate him, Muhammad and his followers began a 210-mile Hegira (emigration) from Mecca to Yathrib (later renamed Medina).*
September 24, 622	Muhammad completed his Hegira. This marked the beginning of the Islamic era, Year 1 A.H. (after Hegira) in the Islamic calendar.
March 17, 624	Muhammad won a key victory over his enemies, the Quraysh of Mecca, in the Battle of Badr. His victory marked the beginning of the Islamic wars of expansion (*see* "Islamic Expansion" map). The Jews of Medina were massacred within a year.
624	Two Jewish tribes of Medina, the Banu Qaynuqa and the Banu Nadhir who had rejected Muhammad's claim of being the last prophet, were expelled. The Banu Qaynuqa left Arabia, while the Banu Nadhir refugees went to the village of Khaybar.
March 19, 625	*Meccan forces defeated Muhammad's Muslim forces from Medina in the Battle of Uhud near the mountain of the same name, in northwestern Arabia. This was due to Muslim archers deserting their posts in order to quarrel over expected booty.*
March 31–April 26, 627	Meccan forces attacked Muhammad in Yathrib (Medina), in what came to be known as the Battle of the Trench. Adopting defensive positions, and by use of *taqiyya* ("deception") Muhammad's forces prevailed. The larger Meccan attacking force gave up the siege and their attempt to snuff out Islam. It was the crowning victory of Islam over superior forces, which ultimately led to the conquest of Mecca, followed by all of Arabia.

May 627	The last Jewish tribe in Medina, the Banu Qurayzahh had been allied with the Meccan forces. After the Battle of the Trench, Muhammad decided to destroy them. His forces besieged their fortifications for 25 days. After forcing them to surrender, an estimated 800 to 900 men of the Banu Qurayzah tribe were led to the market of Medina to be slaughtered. Trenches were dug and all the men and one woman were beheaded, all in one day. Their decapitated corpses were buried in the trenches while Muhammad watched in attendance. The other women and all children were sold into slavery, a number of them being distributed as gifts among Muhammad's companions, and Muhammad chose one of the Qurayzah women (Rayhana) for himself to serve as a concubine. The Qurayzah's property and other possessions (including weapons) were also divided up as additional booty among the Muslims, to support further jihad campaigns. It was while in Medina that Muhammad changed the direction that Muslims should face when praying, known as the *qibla*, turning their backs on Jerusalem to face in the direction of the Kaaba in Mecca.
March 628	*Muhammad, whose forces already controlled Medina, agreed to a 10-year truce with the pagan Quraysh tribe of Mecca. Muhammad agreed to this arrangement because he realized that his forces were not strong enough to conquer Mecca at the time. Islamic doctrine in fact, forbids Muslims from entering into a jihad or battle without the reasonable certainty of being able to prevail. In such cases, as with Muhammad, Muslims are permitted to enter into a temporary ceasefire or truce (a* hudna*). Thus, Muhammad agreed to the 10-year Treaty of Hudaybiyyah. Muhammad needed time to build his forces for an assault on Mecca. Signing a treaty was the means to that end.*
May 628[195]	Muslim forces defeated the remaining Jews of the Banu Nadhir, at the Battle of Khaybar. Under Muhammad's direct orders, many Jews were killed. The battle marked the end of Jewish presence in Arabia. The imposition of tribute upon the conquered Jews, in the Pact of Khaybar, served as a precedent for provisions in Islamic law requiring the exaction of *jizya*—tribute—from the *dhimma*, i.e. the non-Muslims under Islamic law, and confiscation of land belonging to non-Muslims into the collective property of the *Ummah*—the Islamic worldwide nation or community.
January 630	Contrary to the 10-year truce provision of the Treaty of Hudaybiyyah, less than two years later, seizing on the pretext of the murder of a Muslim by an ally of the Quraysh and having in the interim gained superior strength with some 10,000 fighters, Muhammad broke the treaty. His forces assaulted and conquered Mecca, without resistance and seized all the territory of the Quraysh. The Treaty of Hudaybiyyah became the role model for all subsequent Arab/Muslim negotiations with their opponents.
February 630	Muhammad and his followers were ambushed and nearly routed on the road from Mecca to al-Ta'if. Nevertheless, the Muslims gained a great victory and defeated the Bedouin Hawazin tribe in the Battle of Hunayn. This was followed by the conquest of al-Ta'if. In doing so, the Muslim army captured huge spoils, consisting of 6,000 women and children and 24,000 camels. Muhammad was now the ruler of Arabia. The Battle of Hunayn is one of only two battles mentioned in the Qur'an by name (*Sura 9:25*).
March 632	In Muhammad's farewell address, he said, "I was ordered to fight all men until they say 'There is no god but Allah.'"

June 8, 632	Muhammad died at age 59, in Medina. Islam controlled Hejaz (the western area of the Arabian Peninsula).
June 8, 632–August 23, 634	Abu Bakr, Muhammad's father-in-law, became the first caliph—*khalifa*—("successor"), the absolute religious and political ruler, in effect, a religious emperor. During his reign, he waged the first Ridda War—"apostasy war"—against those followers of Muhammad that left the faith after the latter's death, or refused to follow the new caliph. Abu Bakr was the first of four Rashidun ("Rightly Guided") caliphs, as they had been *as-sahabah* ("the Companions") of Muhammad. Their reigns are considered an extension of Muhammad's rule and collectively form the Rashidun Caliphate.
633–37	The Muslim Arab conquest of Syria took place. Damascus was captured in 635 C.E. The surrounding lands, all Christian at the time, including present-day Israel, as well as Mesopotamia (present-day Iraq) were also taken over. It marked the beginnings of a great wave of Muslim conquests and the rapid advance of Islam outside the Arabian Peninsula (*see* "Islamic Expansion, 622–705 C.E." map).
August 23, 634	Abu Bakr, the first caliph died. He designated Umar bin al-Khattab to become his successor.
August 23, 634–November 7, 644	Umar bin al-Khattab ruled as the second Rashidun caliph. He established a standing jihadi army and conquered the Sassanid Empire of Persia and two-thirds of the Christian Byzantine Empire.
August 15–20, 636	The Battle of Yarmuk took place in southern Syria. The Muslim Arabs, led by Khalid bin Walid, defeated the Christians of the Byzantine Empire under Emperor Heraclius. The Muslim victory ended Byzantine rule south of Anatolia. This opened Syria and the surrounding lands, all Christian—including the Land of Israel and Mesopotamia (Iraq)—to the Caliph Umar.
November 16–19, 636	The Battle of Qadisiyya, a decisive Muslim victory over the Sassanid Persian army insured the dominance of Arab and Islamic rule in Persia. The battle paved the way for the Muslim control of Mesopotamia (modern Iraq).
636–42	Persia was subdued by the Muslims. The Sassanid capital, Ctesiphon, fell to Muslim forces (637). The conquest culminated in the Battle of Nahavand (642) which marked the decisive Arab/Muslim destruction of the Sassanid army and the effective dissolution of the Sassanid Empire.
637–1071	The Arab Muslim conquest and occupation of Jerusalem and the Land of Israel occurred.
639	Armenia and Khuzistan (southwestern Persia) were conquered by Muslim forces.
639–42	Islamic forces, under General Amr ibn al-As, invaded the Nile Valley of Egypt.
640	The second caliph, Umar bin al-Khattab, expelled the Jews and Christians from Hejaz, claiming "the land belongs to Allah and his Messenger, the Messenger of Allah can annul his pact if he so wishes." Umar referred to Muhammad's wish that the "Two religions shall not remain together in the peninsula of the Arabs."[196] The pre-eminence of Islam over all other religions was emphasized in the Qur'an (9:33) and that Islam would reign supreme over all mankind (34:28).

July 6, 640	The Battle of Heliopolis, between Muslim forces and the Byzantine army, resulted in a decisive victory for the Muslims. Babylon on the Nile surrendered on April 9, 641. Alexandria capitulated on November 8, 641. By 642, all of Egypt was conquered for Islam.
643	Libya and Azerbaijan were conquered.
November 7, 644	On November 3, the second caliph, Umar was stabbed multiple times by a Persian slave, Pirouz Nahavandi, as part of an assassination plot in revenge for the Muslim conquest of Persia. Umar died of his wounds (November 7). Umar, on his deathbed formed a committee of six people to choose the next caliph from amongst themselves. Uthman ibn Affan was selected as the third caliph on November 11.
November 11, 644–June 17, 656	Uthman ibn Affan ruled as the third Rashidun caliph. His caliphate expanded into present-day Iran, Afghanistan, Pakistan, Azerbaijan, Armenia, Dagestan, and Turkmenistan. His armies captured much of North Africa (652–65), invaded Nubia (present-day Sudan) and invaded the Iberian Peninsula (652–53).
647	The island of Cyprus was conquered, along with Crete and Rhodes. The invasion of North Africa was begun.
651	With the assassination of Yazdegerd III, the last Sassanid king, the conquest of Zoroastrian Persia was completed (*see* "Islamic Expansion" map).
June 17, 656[197]	The third Caliph, Uthman ibn Affan, was assassinated by political opponents, concerned by issues including the nepotism in his regime. Uthman had appointed family members to governorships of the various provinces of the caliphate and they all gained great wealth.
656–61	*Due to Uthman ibn Affan's murder, an Islamic civil war—the First Fitna—erupted between rival Muslim forces. The Caliph Ali ibn Abi Talib, Muhammad's cousin and son-in-law was opposed by forces, which included Muawiyah bin Abi-Sufyan allied to Aisha, Muhammad's widow. The Battle of Basra ensued, the first between rival Muslim forces and resulted in some 10,000 killed and a victory for the Caliph.*
January 27, 661	The fourth Caliph, Ali ibn Abi Talib was assassinated in Kufa, south of Baghdad. His son, Hasan ibn Ali, briefly succeeded him as the righteous Caliph. Hassan was married to Fatima, Muhammad's daughter. Hasan, not wishing an open break with the ranks of Islam, entered into a treaty with the first Umayyad caliph, Muawiyah ibn Abi Sufyan, who assumed the Caliphate. The treaty stipulated that upon Muawiyah's death, the caliphate should be restored to Hasan. However, Muawiyah sought to keep power in his family and nominated his son, Yazid, as caliph after him.
662–709	Transoxiana (in the present-day Afghanistan region) was conquered. Kabul was captured in 670 while Bukhara became a vassal state in 674.
664–712	Sindh (modern day Pakistan and Kashmir) fell to invading Muslim armies.
March 9 or 30, 670	*Hasan, the eldest son of the murdered Ali, (and successor, as far as the Shi'ites are concerned), was poisoned to death, in Medina, on the orders of the Sunni Umayyad caliph Muawiya I. Sunnis consider Ali the fourth and final of the* Rashidun *(rightly guided Caliphs), while the* Shiat Ali *(Party of Ali)—Shi'as—regard Ali as the first Imam and consider him and his descendants the rightful successors to Muhammad, all of whom are members of the* Ahl al-Bayt, *the household of Muhammad. This disagreement split the Ummah into the Sunni and Shi'a branches.*

672	Muslim forces captured the island of Rhodes.
674–78	First Muslim siege of Constantinople took place but failed in large part due to the Christian use of Greek fire, an incendiary weapon, against the Muslim fleets.
ca. 680–92	*The period of the Second Islamic Civil War—the Second Fitna. It involved challenges to the Umayyad Caliphate after the death of the first Umayyad caliph Muawiya I and his son's (Yazid I) succession. The first challenge involved Husayn ibn Ali and his followers. Husayn ibn Ali was murdered at the Battle of Karbala (see below). The second challenge was by Abd Allah ibn al-Zubayr and his supporters. Al-Zubayr was killed in 692. The Umayyad Caliphate thus prevailed.*
October 10, 680	*(10 Muharram 61 A.H.) Shi'a Imam Husayn ibn Ali, (Ali's younger son) the grandson of Muhammad, and his family, some ninety relatives, including women, children and friends, were murdered, the men being beheaded, by forces under Umayyad Caliph Yazid I of the Sunnis, at the Battle of Karbala, in present-day Iraq. The martyrdom of Husayn ibn Ali is a central theme of Shi'a Islam. It is commemorated by Shi'a Muslims as the Day of Ashura (festival). The split between Shi'a and Sunnis deepened and became definitive. The Shi'a consider Ali as their first Imam, and Husayn as the third Imam.*
681	Muslim forces under General Uqba ibn Nafi (serving the Umayyad caliphate) reached the Atlantic Ocean after crossing and conquering North Africa. Uqba rode his horse into the waves, drew his sword and exclaimed "God of Muhammad! If I heard there was a country beyond these waters, I would go there and carry the glory of your name there as well!"
687–91	The Umayyad (tenth) caliph, Abd al-Malik, began building the Dome of the Rock atop the Jewish Temple Mount in Jerusalem. It was completed in 691 C.E.
698	Roman Carthage (in present day Tunisia) was conquered by Muslim forces commanded by Amir (general) Hasan ibn an-Nu'uman al-Ghasani, who defeated Roman Emperor Tiberios III at the Battle of Carthage. The Roman Exarchate of Africa (administrative region) was thus destroyed.
700	Muslim forces waged military campaigns against the Imazighen (the Berbers), Tuareg, and Toubou peoples in North Africa.
700	*Muslim forces in North Africa, turned southward across the Sahara and attacked the Kingdom of Ghana. They were repulsed.*
700–1606	Nubia (northern Sudan) was subdued and taken by Muslim forces.
701–05	Muslim armies invaded and defeated Armenia (*see* "Islamic Expansion, 622–705 C.E." map).

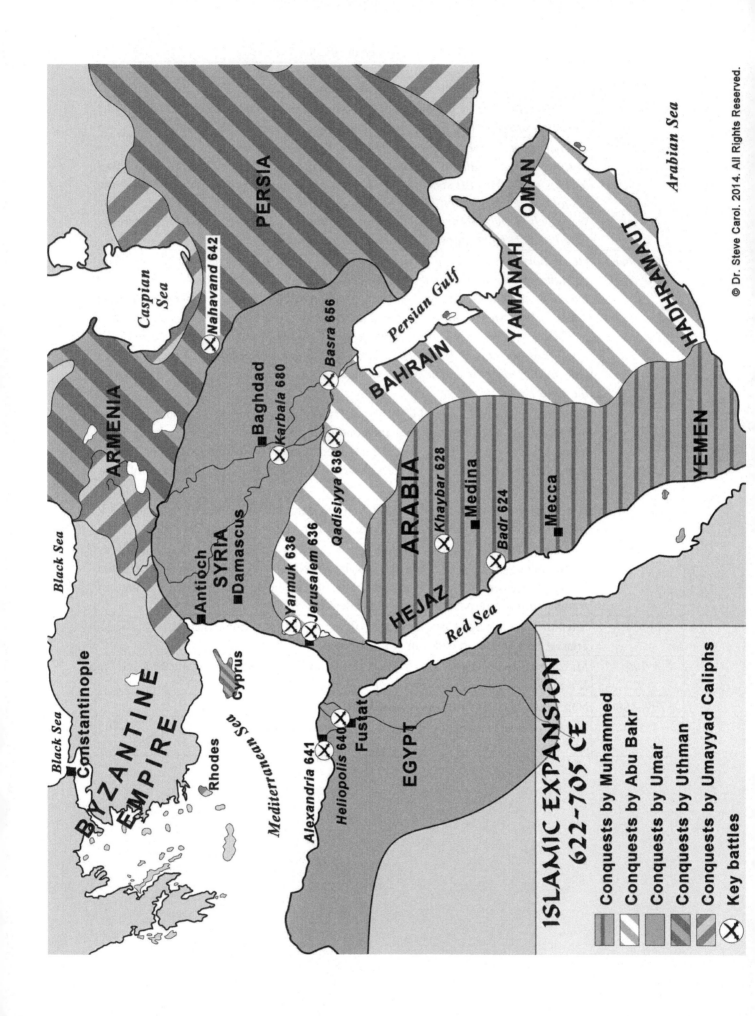

ISLAMIC EXPANSION
622-705 CE

Conquests by Muhammed
Conquests by Abu Bakr
Conquests by Umar
Conquests by Uthman
Conquests by Umayyad Caliphs
⊗ Key battles

Date	Event
705–827 c.e.	Muslim forces launched numerous attacks on Crete. The island was finally conquered in 827.
April 29, 711	Muslim forces began to expand into Europe from the west as Umayyad troops led by Tariq ibn Ziyad (after whom Gibraltar was named—*Jabal Tariq* [the Rock of Tariq]) invaded the Iberian peninsula (present day Spain and Portugal).
July 19, 711	Roderic and the Visigoths in Iberia were defeated in the Battle of Guadalete by Muslim Umayyad Arab invaders led by Tariq ibn Ziyad. Iberia was conquered (711-16) and renamed *Al-Andalus* by the Muslims. Beginning in 718, under Pelagius of Asturias, and continuing some 774 years, Iberia was reconquered—the *Reconquista*—for Christendom. These Christian crusades, unlike the Muslim jihad, were concerned primarily with the defense or reconquest of threatened or lost Christian territory. It was limited to the successful wars for the recovery of Iberia. The last Muslims were expelled in 1492, by King Ferdinand II of Aragon and Queen Isabella I of Castile.
711–750	Muslim armies conquered the Caucasus region.
716–718	The Caliph Sulayman ibn Abd al-Malik dispatched his brother Maslama, with a vast Umayyad Arab/Muslim army to attack and besiege Constantinople, in a second attempt to capture the capital of the Christian Byzantine Empire. Muslim forces numbered a land army of some 120,000 men, as well as a naval force of 2,500 vessels (in two separate fleets) containing an additional 80,000 troops to cut off the Bosporus and starve the city into submission.
August 15, 718	*The second siege of Constantinople was lifted due to several factors: The leadership of Byzantine Emperor Leo III; the use of Greek fire; a harsh winter with Muslim forces starving to death and resorting to cannibalism; being decimated by disease; the intervention of Bulgarian forces on the side of the Byzantines; as well as the defection of Egyptian Copt* dhimmis *from the second Arab fleet. The defeat of the Arab forces stopped the Muslim expansion into southeastern Europe.*
718	Aquitaine, in southwestern France, was invaded by Arab Muslim forces and they attacked Tarragona, Spain, as well.
718	The Islamic conquest of the Iberian Peninsula was completed. The region was renamed *Al-Andalus.*
720	Muslim forces attacked Narbonne, France.
725	Muslim forces attacked Carcassonne, France and occupied Nimes, France.
730	Muslim forces attacked Cerdegna, Italy.
October 10, 732	*Muslim forces attacking Western Europe were finally stopped at the Battle of Tours (also known as the Battle of Poitiers), France. This was regarded as one of the great turning points in world history. The Franks, under Charles Martel (the mayor of the palace of the last Merovingian Kings of France, and grandfather of Charlemagne), defeated a large Andalusian Muslim army led by Abdul Rahman Al Ghafiqi. This victory stopped the northward advance of Islam from the Iberian Peninsula. By 759, the Muslims had been expelled from France. The battle determined that Christianity, rather than Islam, would dominate Europe.*
735	Muslim forces attacked Arles, France.
736	Islamic armies conquered Tbilisi, Georgia.

750	*In the Middle East, the Umayyad Caliphate was destroyed as the Abbasids established their power and established the Abbasid Caliphate.*
751	Arab Muslim forces defeated the Chinese in the Talas River region in present-day Kazakhstan.
756	By this date, the Umayyads controlled most of Spain and Portugal.
805	The Muslims campaigned against the Byzantines; Captured the islands of Rhodes and Cyprus (*see* 'Abbasid Caliphate, 805 C.E." map).

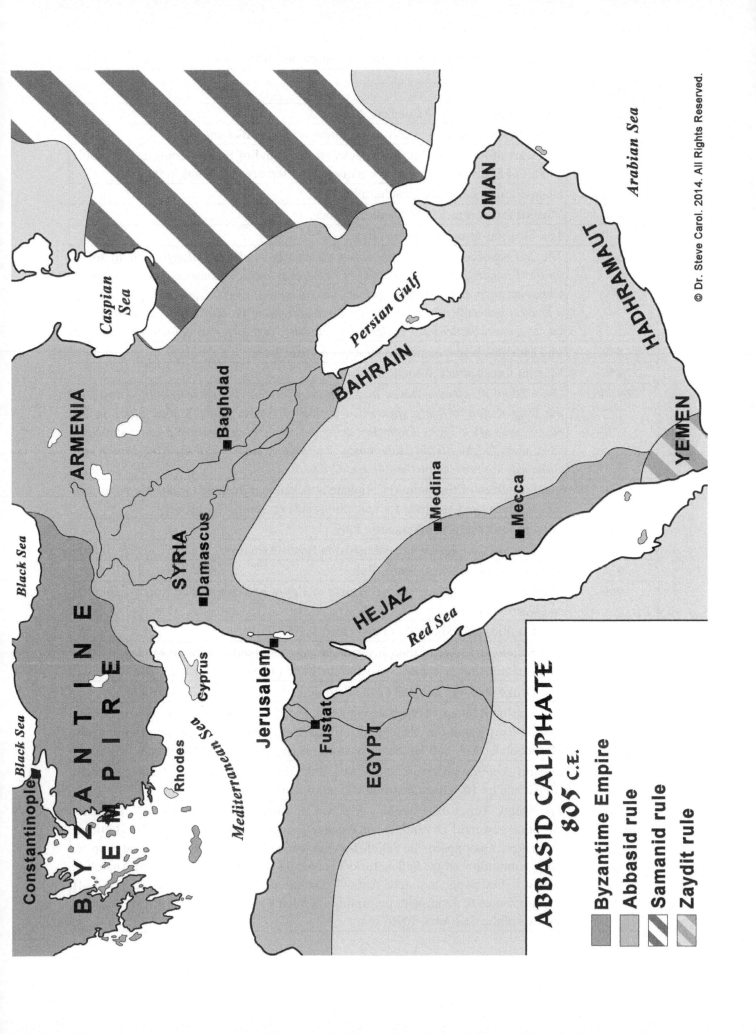

ABBASID CALIPHATE
805 c.e.

- Byzantime Empire
- Abbasid rule
- Samanid rule
- Zaydit rule

BYZANTINE EMPIRE

Constantinople

Black Sea

Black Sea

Caspian Sea

ARMENIA

Baghdad

SYRIA

Damascus

Jerusalem

Fustat

EGYPT

Cyprus

Rhodes

Mediterranean Sea

Red Sea

HEJAZ

Medina

Mecca

BAHRAIN

Persian Gulf

OMAN

HADHRAMAUT

YEMEN

Arabian Sea

Date	Event
813 c.e.	Muslim forces attacked Calabria, Italy.
827	Crete was conquered by the Muslim forces of Abu Hafs Omar.
827–965	The start of numerous Muslim attacks on the island of Sicily. Taomina fell in 902, and all of Sicily was eventually conquered by Berbers and Arabs in 965.
827–902	Islamic forces conquered southern Italy.
838	Muslim forces attacked Marseilles, France.
840	The Muslims attacked Tarento, Italy.
846	*The first papal call for a crusade occurred, when an Arab expedition from Sicily sailed up the Tiber and sacked St. Peter's in Rome. A synod in France issued an appeal to Christian sovereigns to rally against "the enemies of Christ," and the Pope, Leo IV, offered a heavenly reward to those who died fighting the Muslims. A century and a half and many battles later, in 1096, the Crusaders actually arrived in the Middle East.*
849	The Muslims began numerous attacks on Ostia, Italy.
856	Muslim forces attacked Naples, Italy.
869–883	*Over 500,000 African slaves and free men launched a slave revolt—known as the Zanj Rebellion—that spanned a period of fifteen years. It took place in the marshlands of the Tigris-Euphrates delta, near the city of Basra, in present-day Iraq. They were led by Ali bin Muhammad. The vicious and brutal uprising finally was ruthlessly suppressed by the Abbasid Caliphate.*
870	Muslim forces of the Fatimid Caliphate attacked and occupied Malta for some 220 years. It was used as a base for launching raids on southern Europe.
878	Muslim forces attacked Syracuse, Italy.
909	The Fatimid Caliphate was established in North Africa.
934	Muslim forces attacked Genoa, Italy.
969	The Fatimids completed their conquest of Egypt and established a new capital at *al-Qāhirat* (Cairo).
969–1076	The Fatimids gained control of and ruled Syria.
ca. 970	The Seljuk Turks began their invasion of caliphate lands, taking Baghdad in 1055. Additionally, they occupied Syria and the Land of Israel (1070–80).
ca. 1021	The Druze sect was founded by the Fatimid Caliph, al-Hakim bi-Amr Allah.
1053	The Muslim Almoravids began conquering kingdoms south of the Sahara, including Takrur (in present-day Senegal), Sanhaja and Sijilmasa (in present-day eastern Morocco) in 1054, and Aoudaghost (in southern present-day Mauritania) in 1055.
1062	Muslim Almoravid forces, under Abu Bakr ibn Umar, attacked the Kingdom of Ghana and by 1076, the Ghanaian capital of Kumbi was captured.
August 26, 1071	The Seljuk Turks under Sultan Alp Arslan gained a decisive victory defeating the once-powerful Byzantine army under Emperor Romanus IV at the Battle of Manzikert. Unopposed, the Seljuk Turks extended Islam into the Byzantine Empire. The victory allowed the Seljuk Turks to consolidate control of the central Anatolian plateau. They swept on to take Antioch, Damascus and Jerusalem as well as cut off pilgrim routes to Jerusalem, prompting the First Crusade (*see* the "Middle East on the Eve of the Crusades, 1090" map).

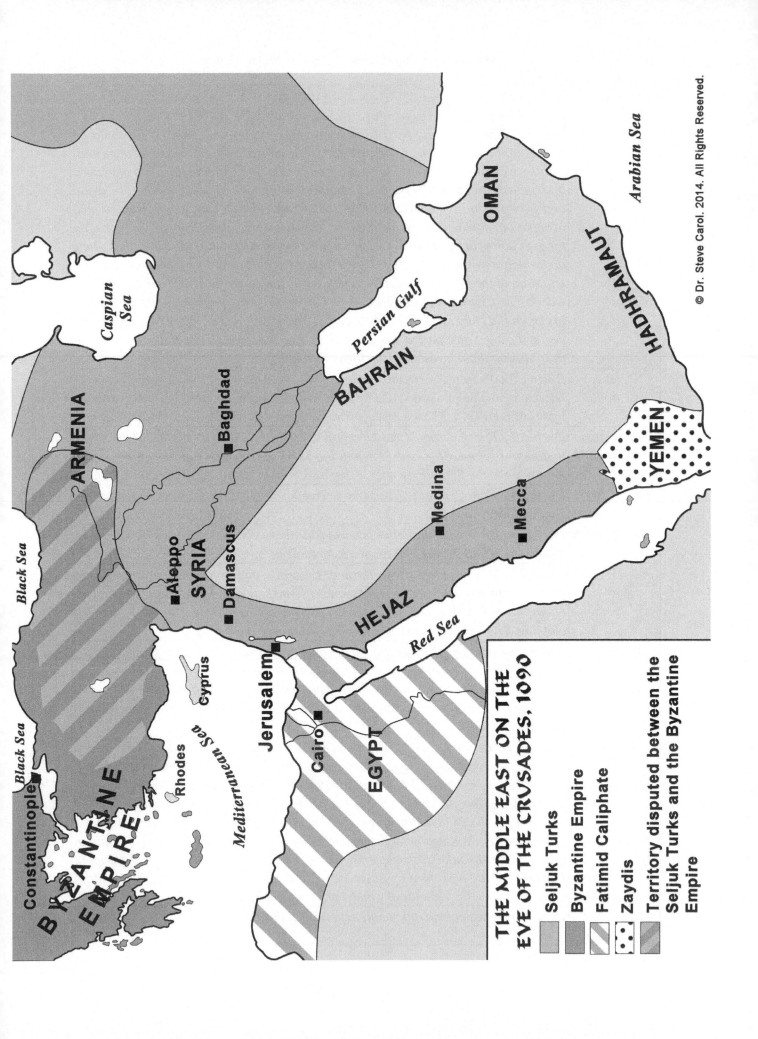

THE MIDDLE EAST ON THE
EVE OF THE CRUSADES, 1090

- Seljuk Turks
- Byzantine Empire
- Fatimid Caliphate
- Zaydis
- Territory disputed between the Seljuk Turks and the Byzantine Empire

Date	Event
November 27, 1095	*At the Council of Clermont, Pope Urban II called for the First Crusade to free the Christian Holy Land from Islamic invasion, seizure and control. It should be understood that the European Crusades that lasted from the tenth to thirteenth century were not "invasions" by outside powers into the Middle East, but a delayed and limited western Christian counterattack against Muslim assault, invasion and occupation. The Crusades were the attempt to free Christians from Islamic occupation, dominance and humiliation. This Islamic aggression had been going on for over 450 years continually, from the founding of Islam until the eleventh century and which continued thereafter. The Crusades were a late, limited, and unsuccessful imitation of the jihad—an attempt to recover by holy war what had been lost by holy war.[198] The Crusades failed. They were not followed by another Christian attempt to regain the Holy Land. Nevertheless, the Crusades bought Europe time, some 200 years, during which period it organized and gained strength to be able to resist the next Muslim jihad invasion in the fifteenth century.*
October 21, 1096	During the Peasants' Crusade, some 20,000 peasants were killed in the Battle of Nicaea, by the Seljuk Turks. Led by Kilij Arslan, the Seljuk Turks suffered very few losses of their own. Those peasants who were not massacred were sold into slavery.
May 14–June 19, 1097	*During the First Crusade, Crusader forces besieged Nicaea, the capital of the Seljuk Sultanate of Rûm. After over a month the Turks surrendered, not to the Crusader forces, but to the Byzantine emperor Alexius I, robbing the Crusaders of their victory.*
July 1, 1097	*During the First Crusade, Crusaders defeated a Seljuk army for the first time at the Battle of Dorylaeum.*
June 28, 1098	*The Crusaders routed the Seljuk army outside the walls of Antioch, Syria. They then moved south and made plans to attack Jerusalem.*
July 15, 1099	*Some 20,000 Crusaders broke through the walls and entered Jerusalem. There they perpetrated a massacre of thousands of Muslims and Jews—men, women and children. Included in those killed were Christians who were dressed in eastern clothing. The Crusaders extended their control over the region.*
August 12, 1099	*Crusader forces under the command of Godfrey of Bouillon defeated Fatimid forces under Al-Afdal Shahanshah, in the Battle of Ashkelon. It was a partial victory as the Crusaders were unable to take the city, which remained in Muslim hands until 1153. Nevertheless, the Fatimids retreated to Egypt. It was the last major engagement of the First Crusade.*
1104	*Leading Crusader forces, Baldwin of Lorraine conquered the city of Acre, which became the main port for the Crusaders in the Holy Land. After four years of fighting, the Crusaders established four states within the over 500-mile-long strip of coastal land they conquered: The County of Edessa, founded in 1098, and ruled by Baldwin of Lorraine; the Principality of Antioch, founded in 1098 and headed by Bohemond of Italy; the Latin Kingdom of Jerusalem, founded in 1099, with Godfrey of Bouillon ruling under the title "Defender of the Holy Sepulcher;" and the County of Tripoli, founded in 1104 and ruled by Raymond of Toulouse. Fortified castles were built in all these states, the remains of which can be seen today in Acre, Sidon, and Tripoli.*
December 4, 1110	*Crusader forces conquered Sidon, in present-day Lebanon.*

1144	Led by Zengi, Emir of Mosul, the Seljuk Turks captured Edessa. This caused Pope Eugenius III to order Bernard of Clairvaux to call a Second Crusade, hoping to regain Edessa.
1147	*Under King Afonso I, the city of Lisbon, Portugal, was liberated from Muslim rule as part of the* Reconquista.
October 25, 1147	During the Second Crusade at the second Battle of Dorylaeum, the Seljuk Turks won a smashing victory over German Crusader forces led by Conrad III, annihilating some 20,000 Christian troops.
July 23–28, 1148	The Crusaders were unsuccessful in their siege of Damascus, Syria, and were forced to retreat. The Second Crusade thus failed in its original goal and Edessa remained in Muslim hands.
1171	Saladin formally ended Fatimid control in Egypt, starting the Ayyubid dynasty and became Sultan of Egypt. He conquered Syria, (Tripoli in 1172, Damascus on November 27, 1174, Aleppo in May 1182), part of Nubia (1172), Hejaz (1173), Yemen (1174), and Mosul in Mesopotamia (1186), thus creating a formidable Ayyubid Empire. By these conquests, Saladin surrounded the Crusader states on three sides (*see* "Ayyubid Empire of Saladin, 1171–89" map).
1185	Saladin declared his intention to lead a jihad to reclaim Jerusalem from the Christians.
July 4, 1187	Saladin surrounded and virtually annihilated the main Crusader army led by Guy of Lusignan, King of Jerusalem, at the Battle of Hattin near Tiberias. Muslim forces proceeded to conquer Tiberias (July 5) Acre (July 10) and later that month, Nablus, Jaffa, Ashkelon, Caesarea, Haifa, Sidon, and Beirut (the latter on August 6).
September 20, 1187	Saladin besieged Jerusalem, which he captured on October 2, 1187, after eighty-eight years of Crusader rule. It was the anniversary of Muhammad's ascension to heaven. Soon afterwards, his forces captured Antioch and Tripoli. Only Tyre remained in the hands of the Crusaders. It was the only remaining city of the Kingdom of Jerusalem. The loss of Jerusalem triggered the Third Crusade.
January 1189	Saladin declared his goals vis-à-vis the Crusaders, "I shall cross this sea to their islands to pursue them until there remain no one on the face of the earth who does not acknowledge Allah.
August 1189	*During the Third Crusade, King Richard I—"the Lionheart"—of England, began a siege of Acre.*
October 4, 1189	Muslim forces won an incomplete victory at the Battle of Acre, east of the city (*see* "Ayyubid Empire of Saladin, 1171-1189" map).

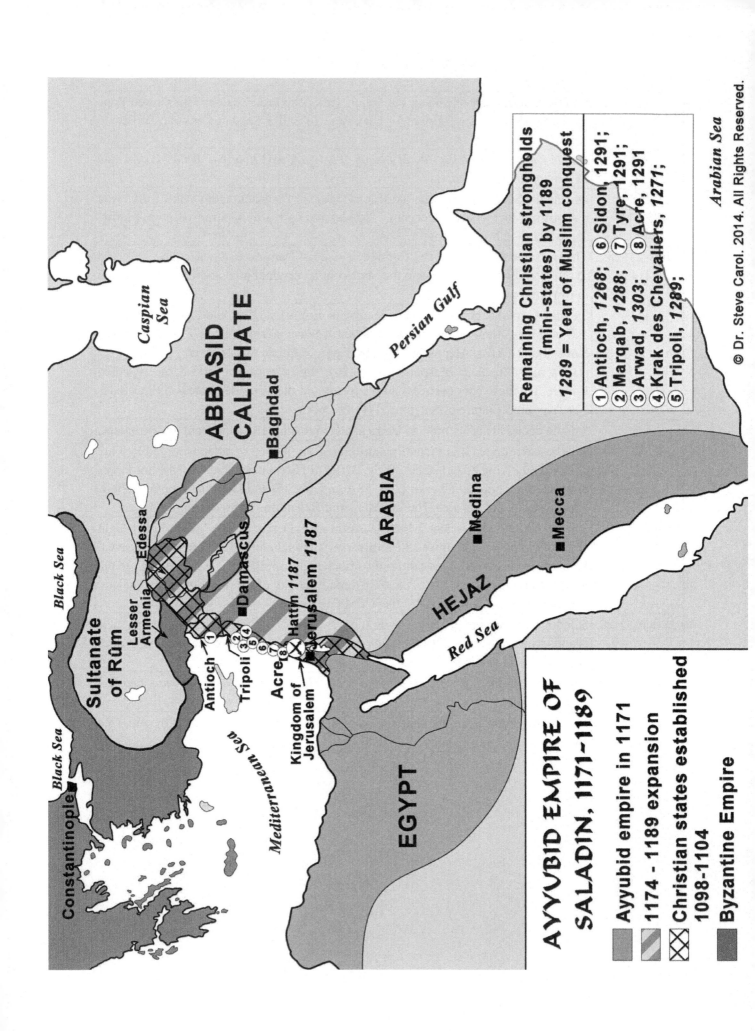

AYYUBID EMPIRE OF SALADIN, 1171-1189

Remaining Christian strongholds (mini-states) by 1189
1289 = Year of Muslim conquest

1. Antioch, 1268;
2. Marqab, 1288;
3. Arwad, 1303;
4. Krak des Chevaliers, 1271;
5. Tripoli, 1289;
6. Sidon, 1291;
7. Tyre, 1291;
8. Acre, 1291

Ayyubid empire in 1171

1174 - 1189 expansion

Christian states established 1098-1104

Byzantine Empire

ABBASID CALIPHATE

Baghdad

Caspian Sea

Black Sea

Sultanate of Rûm

Constantinople

Lesser Armenia

Edessa

Damascus

Hattin 1187

Jerusalem 1187

Antioch

Tripoli

Acre

Kingdom of Jerusalem

Mediterranean Sea

ARABIA

HEJAZ

Medina

Mecca

Red Sea

Persian Gulf

Arabian Sea

EGYPT

Date	Event
July 12, 1191	*Acre was finally captured by the Crusaders.*
September 7, 1191	*Muslim forces under Saladin were defeated in the Battle of Arsuf by the Crusader army of King Richard I. Richard went on to capture Jaffa on September 10, 1191, but was unable to recapture Jerusalem, even though the Crusaders had twice fought to within 12 miles of the city.*
1204	*Venetian forces conquered Crete from its Muslim occupiers.*
1216	The Fifth Crusade adopted the strategy of invading Egypt, the richest and strongest Muslim state and then trying to regain Jerusalem from Egypt.
June 1218	*The Crusaders attacked and besieged Damietta, Egypt, at the mouth of the Nile River. The new Egyptian Sultan Malik al-Kamil tried to negotiate peace with the Crusaders. He offered to trade Damietta for Jerusalem, but Cardinal Pelagius, one of the main leaders, rejected the offer.*
November 1219	*Crusader forces captured Damietta. However, there was disunity and rivalry in the Christian ranks.*
July 1221	As the Crusaders marched on Cairo, they were caught between a Muslim army and the Nile floods. This resulted in military disaster, the abandonment of Damietta, in return for an eight-year truce with al-Kamil and a forced return to Europe in September 1221.
1229	*During the Sixth Crusade, Emperor Frederick II negotiated a ten-year truce, with Ayyubid Sultan Malik al-Kamil, to win possession of Jerusalem and privileges for Christian pilgrims in Jerusalem, Bethlehem, and Nazareth. The truce expired in 1239 and was not renewed by the Muslims.*
1244	The Ayyubids invited the Khwarezmian Turks (Khorezman Tartars) displaced by the Mongols, to reconquer Jerusalem. In the resulting siege and conquest, the Khwarezmians completely razed Jerusalem, killing large numbers of Christians and burning many churches, including the Church of the Holy Sepulcher. The city was left in ruins and useless to both Christians and Muslims.
1248	*King Louis IX of France undertook the leadership of the Seventh Crusade against the Ayyubids of Egypt seeking to be more successful than the Fifth Crusade. He captured Damietta, Egypt in June 1249. In early 1250, the Crusader forces moved towards Cairo.*
1249	*Under King Afonso III, Portugal became the first Iberian nation totally liberated from Muslim rule as part of the* Reconquista.
February 8–11, 1250	At the Battle of Al-Mansurah, Muslim Mameluke forces defeated the Crusader army. In March 1250, King Louis IX finally tried to return to Damietta as disease and famine ravaged his army.
April 6, 1250	At the Battle of Fariskur, the Crusader army was annihilated. King Louis IX was taken captive and forced to pay a ransom of 400,000 dinars for his release. He promised to withdraw from Damietta, and leave Egypt, never to return. He left, May 8, 1250, for Acre. Later, he returned home to France. Meanwhile in Egypt, the Ayyubid Sultan Turanshah was assassinated and the Mamelukes seized power.
1250–60	The Mameluke Sultanate emerged in Egypt and Syria with the decay of the Ayyubid Empire.

December 15, 1256	*The Hashshashin—the Assassins—stronghold at Alamut in present-day Iran was captured and destroyed by Hulagu Khan and the Mongols.*
1258	*Led by Hulagu Khan, the Mongols stormed Baghdad ending the Abbasid Caliphate as the Muslim empire collapsed.*
1268	Antioch fell to Muslim forces.
1289	Tripoli fell to Muslim forces and its harbor was destroyed.
ca. 1290–1320	Ottoman Turkish states emerged in western Anatolia.
May 19, 1291	The Mameluke Sultan of Egypt, al-Ashraf Khalil, captured Acre, the last Christian outpost in the Holy Land, and after 196 years, the era of the Crusades ended.
1299–1453	A series of Byzantine Christian-Muslim Ottoman Turkish Wars were fought.
1308	Muslim forces attacked Thrace, in the Balkans.
1326–66	Muslim Ottoman Turks conquered western Anatolia, Bursa (1326), Nicaea (1331), Gallipoli (1354), and Adrianople (1366). Attacks continued on Thrace, Greece, and Macedonia.
September 26, 1371	A decisive Muslim Ottoman Turkish victory at the Battle of Cirmen enabled further Muslim conquests in the Balkans, including Macedonia and parts of Bulgaria.
1371–75	Muslim Ottoman forces invaded Serbia.
1388	Northeastern Bulgaria fell to the Muslim Turks.
June 15, 1389	Muslim Turkish forces inflicted a decisive defeat on the Serbs and Bosnians at the Field of the Blackbirds, in the First Battle of Kosovo. Christian Serbia became a vassal state under the Ottomans and placed in *dhimmitude* status.
September 25, 1396	Muslim Ottoman Turkish Emperor Bayezid I defeated a coalition of Christian forces—Hungary, the Holy Roman Empire, France, England, the Kingdom of Scotland, the Old Swiss Confederacy, Poland, Wallachia, the Republic of Venice, the Republic of Genoa, and the Knights of St. John—in the Battle of Nicopolis, near the Danubian fortress of the same name (present-day Nikopol), in Bulgaria.
1421	Renewed attacks were made on the Peloponnese Peninsula, Albania, Serbia, and Hungary by the Ottoman Turks.
November 28, 1443	*Gjergj Kastrioti (remembered as Skanderbeg), and his forces liberated Kruja, in central Albania from Muslim Ottoman Turkish rule. There they raised the banner that became Albania's national flag—a black double-headed eagle on a red field.*
November 10, 1444	The Muslim Ottoman Turkish forces of Sultan Murad II defeated the Polish and Hungarian armies under Władysław III of Poland and János Hunyadi, at the Battle of Varna. By this victory, the Turks consolidated their hold on Bulgaria and helped set the stage for the fall of Constantinople.
October 17, 1448	Led by Sultan Murad II, Muslim Ottoman Turkish forces decisively defeated a Hungarian-led Catholic coalition, under János Hunyadi, in the Second Battle of Kosovo. The Christian Balkan states were unable to resist the Muslims after this defeat, eventually falling under control of the Ottoman Empire. This defeat placed the Byzantine capital, Constantinople, in imminent danger.
May 29, 1453	Constantinople fell to Ottoman Turkish forces led by Sultan Mehmed II after a siege. During the battle, the Byzantine Emperor Constantine XI was killed, thus ending the Byzantine Empire, which had lasted for over 1,000 years. The Ottomans made the city the capital of their caliphate and empire. Muslim forces then began expansion into Europe from the east.

1456	Ottoman Turkish forces conquered Athens, Greece.
July 22, 1456	*The siege of Belgrade by Muslim Ottoman Turkish forces led by Mehmed II was broken. The Turks were defeated by Hungarian and Wallachian forces commanded by János Hunyadi, the Regent of the Kingdom of Hungary. These later Christian campaigns, unlike the Muslim Ottoman jihad, were concerned primarily with the defense or reconquest of threatened or lost Christian territories. It was, with few exceptions, limited to the unsuccessful wars to halt the Ottoman advance in the Balkans.*
1463	Bosnia was defeated and annexed by the Ottoman Turkish Empire.
1478	Serbia and the Crimea came under Muslim Turkish control.
1480	Otranto in Italy was captured by the Muslims, prompting the evacuation of Rome. Although Muslim forces held the city for only ten months, it was time enough to behead over 800 Christians who refused to convert to Islam.
1483	Herzegovina was defeated and conquered by the Ottoman Turks.
January 2, 1492	*The Muslim forces of Abu 'Abdallah Muhammad XII, the last Nasrid Arab Muslim ruler in Granada surrendered to their Catholic Highnesses, Ferdinand and Isabella of Spain. After 774 years, the* Reconquista *was over. Spain was restored to Christendom, as Muslim control ended.*
August 3, 1492	Christopher Columbus departed Palos de la Frontera, Spain, with three ships—*Niña, Pinta,* and the *Santa Maria*—to seek a westward all-water route to Asia. One of the prime reasons for Columbus' quest was the control of the direct eastward overland route from Europe by the Muslim Ottoman Turks. The latter, controlling the Middle East, made trade much more difficult and dangerous.
1512	Ottoman Turkish forces attacked and conquered Moldavia.
1516–17	The Ottoman Turks conquered Syria and Egypt destroying the Mameluke Sultanate.
August 1521	Muslim forces captured Belgrade, Serbia.
1522	The Ottoman Turks conquered the island of Rhodes.
1526–1857	Muslim forces conquered and ruled much of the Indian subcontinent.
August 29–30, 1526	Suleiman the Magnificent of the Ottoman Empire defeated and killed the last Jagiellonian king of Hungary and Bohemia at the Battle of Mohács. The Muslim victory broke Hungary's hold on central Europe and threatened Austrian lands.
1527–43	The Muslim Sultanate of Adal invaded Christian Ethiopia. Muslim forces were led by Ahmed ibn Ibrahim al-Ghazi, the *Gragn*. Three-quarters of Ethiopia was brought under Muslim control as they sacked churches and monasteries, destroying centuries of literature and art.
1529	The first, though unsuccessful, siege of Vienna by the Muslim Ottoman Turks took place.
1529–33	Continued attacks in the Danube valley, ended in the Treaty of 1533, when a large portion of eastern Hungary was ceded to the Ottoman Turkish Empire.

September 28, 1538	In 1537, Muslim Ottoman Turkish forces, spearheaded by a large fleet commanded by Hayreddin Barbarossa captured a number of Aegean and Ionian islands belonging to Venice, namely Syros, Aegina, Ios, Paros, Tinos, Karpathos, Kasos and Naxos, thus annexing the Duchy of Naxos to the Ottoman Empire. He then besieged the Venetian stronghold of Corfu and ravaged the Spanish-held Calabrian coast in southern Italy. In response to this threat, Pope Paul III formed the Holy League, in February 1538, to stop the Muslim invasion. The Holy League was comprised of the Republics of Genoa and Venice, the Papal States, Spain and the Knights of Malta. On September 28, 1538, opposing fleets met in the Battle of Preveza, in the Ionian Sea off the coast of Epirus, Greece. The numerically smaller Ottoman Turkish fleet, commanded by Hayreddin Barbarossa, won a decisive victory over the larger "Holy League" fleet commanded by Genovese Captain Andrea Doria. The Ottoman victory paved the way for Muslim dominance over the Aegean, Ionian and eastern Mediterranean Seas.
February 11, 1543	*A combined Ethiopian and Portuguese army defeated an invading Muslim army at the Battle of Wayna Daga, Ethiopia.*
November 5, 1556	The Mughal (Muslim) army of Emperor Akbar the Great defeated the numerically superior Hindu forces of General Hemu at the Second Battle of Panipat, 50 miles north of Delhi, India.
September 11, 1565	*Christian forces led by the Knights Hospitaller (also known as the Order of Saint John of Jerusalem) assisted by troops from the Kingdom of Spain and the Kingdom of Sicily, defeated a vastly superior invading Ottoman Turkish force, lifting the Great Siege of Malta.*
July 1, 1570–August 3, 1571	The Muslim Ottoman Turkish invasion and conquest of Cyprus took place. The Ottoman occupation of Cyprus would last 307 years. From the outset, the Turkish rulers demonstrated a ferocity that the inhabitants of Cyprus never forgot. For example, after the capture of Famagusta on August 3, 1571, the commander of the defending garrison was publicly flogged to death, and then his skin was stuffed with straw and publicly paraded around the island.
April 9, 1571	The Ottoman Turkish government decreed the inhabitants of Caraman in south central Anatolia, be encouraged to settle in Cyprus. This was followed by a second order, September 22, 1572, stipulating that one out of every ten families in Caraman and surrounding provinces be "exiled" to Cyprus. Some 5,720 families (approximately 30,000 inhabitants) were thus moved. Many of the Turks, which populate contemporary Cyprus, are descendants of these original Caramanlis.
October 7, 1571	*The Muslim Ottoman Empire, attempting to expand further into Europe and attack Rome, was decisively defeated by an expanded Holy League multinational fleet led by Don John of Austria. The Holy League was comprised of the Papal States, the Habsburg states of Spain, Naples and Sicily, the Republic of Venice, the Republic of Genoa, the Grand Duchy of Tuscany, the Duchies of Savoy, Parma and Urbino and the Knights of Malta. The Muslim Ottoman fleet was crushed near the Gulf of Corinth in the Battle of Lepanto. It was the greatest naval battle since the Battle of Actium (September 2, 31 B.C.E.), and the last naval battle fought by oar-driven ships.*
1669	Ottoman Turkish forces captured the island of Crete.

September 11–12, 1683	*A combined Polish-Austrian-German force led by Jan III Sobieski, the King of Poland, demolished the invading Muslim army of Turks and Tartars at the Battle of Vienna, Austria. The battle was the high-water-mark and turning point in the 300-year struggle between the forces of the Christian Central European kingdoms, and the Muslim Ottoman Turkish armies attempting to conquer Europe from the east.*
1696	*Catherine the Great's Russian forces captured Azov from the Muslim Ottoman Turks, giving Russia access to the Black Sea.*
1696	Muslim Omani forces conquered Mombasa (in present-day Kenya), Pemba, Kilwa, and Zanzibar (all in present-day Tanzania).
September 11, 1697	*Prince Eugene of Savoy leading a Christian Holy League army of some 50,000, caught and annihilated the larger (100,000 men) Ottoman Muslim army, which was in the process of crossing the Tisa river, at the Battle of Zenta in what today is Senta, Vojvodina, Serbia. As a result of this decisive Habsburg victory, the Ottoman Empire lost the Banat region of Central Europe.*
August 5, 1716	*Prince Eugene of Savoy defeated the Muslim Turks at Peterwardein after their conquests of Crete and Greece. The resulting Treaty of Passorowitz (1718) caused the Turks to quit Hungary, cede Belgrade and parts of Walachia to Austria, and surrender portions of Albania and Dalmatia to Venice.*
July 21, 1774	*A Russian-Turkish War (which began in 1768) ended as Catherine the Great's Russian armies defeated the Turks. This ended a series of attacks on southern Poland and Russia by Muslim forces, and culminated in the Treaty of Kuchuk Kainarji, signed July 21.*
1783	*Russian forces captured and annexed the Crimean Peninsula from the Muslim Tartar Crimean Khanate.*
1787	*Muslim Turkish forces were defeated once again resulting in the end of their influence in southern Poland and nearby Russia.*
1804	Muslim Fulani forces began a jihad that conquered Hausaland (much of present-day northern Nigeria and northern Cameroon).
1817–37	Muslim Fulani forces began attacking the Oyo Empire (in present-day western Nigeria) and by 1837, the capital Old Oyo, was conquered and burned.
July 1860	In Damascus, armed Arab Muslim groups organized pogroms against Christians. In this, they were aided by Ottoman Turkish troops with the connivance of the military authorities. This was accomplished by either direct support or by disarming Christian forces. Churches and missionary schools were set afire. The violence lasted for three days (from July 9 to July 11, 1860). As a result, some 25,000 Christians were killed, including the American and Dutch consuls. Some 380 Christian villages, 560 churches and 40 monasteries were destroyed.[199] Only after Ottoman soldiers quelled the disturbances did French troops intervene. A French expeditionary corps of 6,000 soldiers landed in Beirut on August 16, 1860, under the command of General Beaufort d'Hautpoul.

1875–77	*The Ethiopian–Egyptian War was fought as Ismail Pasha, the Khedive (viceroy) of Egypt, sought to expand along the Red Sea coast at Ethiopia's expense. Emperor Yohannes IV decisively defeated the Egyptian Muslim forces at the Battle of Gundat (November 16, 1875), and the Battle of Gura, southwest of Massawa (March 7–9, 1876).*
June 4, 1878	*The United Kingdom took Cyprus in "trust" from the Ottoman Empire and subsequently annexed the island on November 5, 1914, during World War I. Communal tension and conflict began between the resident Greeks and Turks.*
1887–89	Muslim Mahdist forces invaded Ethiopia from Sudan.
March 9–10, 1889	*Ethiopian forces commanded by Emperor Yohannes IV decisively defeated the Muslim Mahdist Sudanese army at the Battle of Gallabat/Metemma, though Yohannes himself, was killed by a sniper's bullet.*
1894–96	The Muslim Turks massacred Christian Armenians in Central Anatolia and Mesopotamia.

RECENT EXAMPLES OF CONTINUED MUSLIM EXPANSION	
Date	Event
September 1903	Sectarian fighting between Muslims and Christians took place in Beirut, Lebanon. An estimated 20,000 Christians, mainly Maronites, took refuge in the Mount Lebanon range east of the city.
April 1909	The Muslim Turks massacred Christian Armenians in the Vilayet of Adana, in southern Turkey. An estimated 25,000 were killed during the series of pogroms.[200]
November 4, 1914	Shortly after Ottoman Turkey entered World War I on October 29, 1914, Sultan Mehmed V Reshad in his role as caliph proclaimed a jihad against the British, French and Russian Empires. Via a *fatwa*, Turkey urged all faithful Muslims in those realms to rise up in revolt and destroy their Christian masters. Non-Turkish Muslims also had to participate. This included Arabs, Persians, and the Muslims of the Indian subcontinent, French North Africa, and the Russian Caucasus.
April 24, 1915–23	Muslim Turkish officials arrested some 250 Christian Armenian leaders in Constantinople and began the brutal mass deportations and massacres of Armenians. Hundreds of thousands of men, women and children were forced into death marches from their mountain homeland through the desert to Deir ez-Zor in present-day northeast Syria. All told, some 1.5 million perished in what came to be known as the Armenian Genocide. Additionally, some 750,000 Assyrians, Chaldeans, and Syrian Orthodox Christians, and 400,000 Greeks were deported and replaced with Turks in the west.
1918	*The defeat of Ottoman Turkey in World War I ended Ottoman Turkish rule in Arab areas, and in the Land of Israel.*
1921–22	In one of the first cases of massive ethnic cleansing in the twentieth century, Muslim Turkey expelled approximately 1,200,000 Greeks from its territory and replaced them with Turks.
1947–76	The Muslims expelled approximately 880,000 Jews from their Arab homelands, from Morocco to Iraq and from Syria to Yemen.
1947 to date	Since 1947, the Arab League, now numbering 21 countries, fought a continual war—militarily, politically, economically, demographically, and diplomatically—in an attempt to destroy the Jewish state of Israel. Their goal is to occupy *all* (emphasis added) of Israel's territory, and make the Middle East exclusively Muslim and *judenrein* (ethnically and religiously "cleansed of Jews"). To this day, fifty-five of the fifty-seven Islamic members (fifty-six countries plus the non-existent "country" of "Palestine") in the Organization of Islamic Cooperation publicly approve of these actions and the ultimate goal.
1947 to date	There were repeated Muslim attempts, by war and terrorism, to gain control of Kashmir. The Hindus of Pakistan steadily declined from 15 percent (in 1947) to 1.5 percent of the population today.
1947 to date	The Hindus and other non-Muslims fled from Bangladesh (prior to 1971, East Pakistan). Whereas non-Muslims made up 35 percent (in 1947), today they constitute a mere 8 percent of the population in that country.

1948–67	During the Jordanian occupation of Judea and Samaria (what the Arabs call the "West Bank"), having driven out all the Jews from the area, the Muslim Arabs undertook an unsuccessful attempt to make Jerusalem an exclusively Muslim city by forcing out approximately 14,000 Christian inhabitants.
September 6–7, 1955	As part of a policy of forcible Turkification, the Turkish government ethnically cleansed the city of Istanbul of its remaining Christians and Jews, including the 100,000 Greeks, whose right to live in the city was guaranteed by the Treaty of Lausanne (1923). Houses and businesses owned by Armenians, Greeks, and Jews were identified, wire cutters, sledgehammers, welding machines, and other tools distributed, and on the assigned date, 100,000 rioters broke into non-Muslim homes and businesses destroying industrial equipment, personal property, and commercial goods while Christian and Jewish families huddled in terror. Many women were raped, and a dozen Christians were killed. The non-Muslim past was erased by rioters who smashed holy images, crosses, icons and other sacred possessions inside the churches. These artifacts were either destroyed or burnt, or the whole church was set on fire. Greek-Orthodox cemeteries in Şişli and Balıklı were particularly damaged. The assailants not only tore down the epitaphs, but also took out the skeletons, which were either burnt or broken.[201]
1955–72, 1983–2005	The Muslim Arabs of northern Sudan conquered much of southern Sudan, waging genocidal war to convert its Christian and animist population.
1961 to date	Muslim Indonesian genocide against West Papuans resulted in an estimated 100,000 to 400,000 killed.
1963	Muslim Indonesia occupied all of non-Islamic western New Guinea and incorporated it into Indonesia.
1963 to date	Muslim Malays blocked the economic and social development of the predominantly Chinese island of Singapore. There were race riots in 1964. The Malaysian parliament expelled Singapore from the Federation of Malaysia, and Singapore became a separate independent state on August 9, 1965. The remaining non-Muslims—Chinese and Hindus—of Malaysia, saw their relative numbers steadily decline. The non-Muslim peoples came under fierce pressure to convert to Islam (not least the indigenous tribes in Sarawak and Sabah) which only increased as the new Muslim majority felt the need to exercise its power.
Late 1960s to 2014	There was a Muslim insurgency spanning some fifty years in the southern Philippines by the Moro Liberation Front, the Moro Islamic Liberation Front and the Abu Sayyaf movement. Their goal was the establishment of a separate Muslim state, which they name Bangsamoro, or Moro nation. Over 150,000 Filipinos were killed and 1 million displaced in the conflict.
1970 to date	Muslims in northern Nigeria launched religious violence against the largely Christian south.
1974 to date	Muslim Turkey invaded and occupied northern Cyprus, displacing over 200,000 Greek-Cypriots living there (see "Cyprus-Crisis of 1974, Turkish Invasion and Occupation" map).

December 7, 1975– September 20, 1999	Muslim Indonesia invaded and occupied Christian Timor Este (East Timor). The Indonesian occupation was marked by extreme violence and brutality against Christians. Over 200,000 were killed.[202]
February 11, 1979	With the establishment of the Islamic Republic of Iran, its Supreme Leader Ayatollah Ruhollah Khomeini declared, "We shall export our revolution throughout the world … until the calls 'there is no god but Allah and Muhammad is the messenger of Allah' are echoed all over the world."
February 15, 1988	After a ten-year conflict, the Soviet Union left Afghanistan, defeated by the Muslim *mujahadeen*—Islamic jihadist fighters. It was a major victory for Islamic supremacists having defeated the number two superpower.
1989 to date	Muslim militants launched an insurgency in Kashmir. By July 2009, over 47,000 were killed, including 7,000 Indian police and some 20,000 insurgents. Estimates of civilians killed range from 65,000 to 100,000.[203]
1990s to date	Muslim Albania is attempting to enlarge its borders at Christian Macedonia's expense.
1992–2002	The Arab/Muslim government of Sudan waged jihad against the Nuba people, who reside in the Nuba Mountains region in the central portion of the South Kordofan state of Sudan.
1994–96, 1999–2009	Muslims attempted to create an independent Chechnya from Russian territory. This led to two wars and continued terrorist activity. Over 200,000 civilians died in both conflicts.[204]
1997 to date	The East Turkestan Islamic Movement has waged a Uighur insurgency against the Han Chinese residents of the Xinjiang region of China. On July 5, 2009, there were severe riots in Urumqi, the capital of Xinjiang that left some 200 killed. The Muslim Uyghurs seek to detach Xinjiang from China and create an independent "East Turkestan."

February 23, 1998	In what was tantamount to a declaration of war against the West in general, and the United States in particular, a *fatwa* was issued by Sheikh Osama bin Laden, Ayman al-Zawahiri (Emir of the Jihad Group in Egypt), Abu-Yasir Rifa'I Ahmad Taha (Egyptian Islamic Group), Sheikh Mir Hamzah (Secretary of the *Jamiat-ul-Ulama-e-Pakistan*), and Fazlur Rahman (Emir of the Jihad Movement in Bangladesh). Its main provisions were in compliance with Allah's order, we issue the following *fatwa* to all Muslims: The ruling to kill the Americans and their allies—civilians and military—is an individual duty for every Muslim who can do it in any country in which it is possible to do it, in order to liberate the Al-Aqsa Mosque and the holy mosque [Mecca] from their grip, and in order for their armies to move out of all the lands of Islam, defeated and unable to threaten any Muslim. This is in accordance with the words of Almighty Allah, 'and fight the pagans all together as they fight you all together,' and 'fight them until there is no more tumult or oppression, and there prevail justice and faith in Allah.' We—with Allah's help—call on every Muslim who believes in Allah and wishes to be rewarded to comply with Allah's order to kill the Americans and plunder their money wherever and whenever they find it. We also call on Muslim *ulama* (the body of Muslim scholars), leaders, youths, and soldiers to launch the raid on Satan's US troops and the devil's supporters allying with them, and to displace those who are behind them so that they may learn a lesson.[205]
1998 to date	Muslim Indonesia continued its attempt to destroy Christianity in Sulawesi (formerly the Celebes) and elsewhere in the country. There is ongoing discrimination against Christians accompanied by physical attacks, forced circumcisions, forced conversions, beheadings, and the burning of churches. The estimated death toll is over 10,000.
May 3–July 26, 1999	Pakistan and India fought a three-month war in the Kargil district, and elsewhere along the Line of Control (LOC) in Kashmir, India. The fighting, initiated by Islamic Kashmiri militants supported by the Pakistani army, led to the temporary occupation of Indian territory. The fighting was the most serious since the 1971 war between the two now nuclear-armed nations. There was fear that the limited conflict could lead to the use of nuclear or chemical weapons. As a result of Operation *Vijay* ("Victory") the Indian army recaptured their territory, forcing the Pakistanis back across the LOC.
1999 to date	Muslim Kosovo ethnically cleansed its territory of Christian Serbs. Some 200,000 to 250,000 fled to date.

September 11, 2001	Al-Qaeda attacked the United States, destroying the World Trade Center Twin Towers in New York and damaging the Pentagon, in Arlington, Virginia. 2,973 were killed.
Mid-November 2001	Al-Qaeda leader, Osama bin Laden in a videotaped interview declared, "I was ordered to fight people until they say there is no god but Allah, and his Prophet Muhammad."
2002 to date	Boko Haram, an Islamic supremacist terrorist group in northeastern Nigeria, began its jihadist attacks and conquests directed against non-Muslims, especially Christians across all of northern Nigeria. It is affiliated to Al-Qaeda in the Islamic Maghreb and its goal is the establishment of an Islamic state governed by shari'a law throughout Nigeria, though half the country's population of 170 million is Christian. By mid-2014, more than 7,000 people were estimated killed[206] in Boko Haram-related violence, many in brutal ways, such as being hacked to death and being burned alive in their churches. More than 300,000 people have been displaced from their homes.[207]
November 7, 2004 to date	A Muslim rebellion in the southern Thailand provinces of Songkhla, Pattani, Yala and Narathiwat, bordering Muslim Malaysia, seeks to establish a separate Muslim state. More than 4,000 people have been killed and thousands more injured, thus far.[208]
July 12–August 14, 2006	The Islamic terrorist group, Hezbollah, attacked Israel (Second Lebanon War), which officially lasted thirty-four days and ended with the terrorist group still in possession of territory and its weaponry.
December 27, 2008–January 18, 2009	The Hamas terrorist group charter calls for the destruction of Israel and the death of all Jews. Despite a six-month truce brokered by Egypt, Hamas repeatedly violated the truce with continued rocket and mortar fire into the Jewish state, as well as never ceasing the smuggling of more weapons into the Gaza Strip. These events triggered the First Gaza War as Israel sought to stop both the rocket fire and the smuggling. While pounding Hamas, Israel was not successful in achieving either of its main objectives, thus insuring another round.
November 10–21, 2012	Hamas rearmed and resumed a missile and mortar war against Israel's cities, towns and villages. The quality and quantity of these missiles steadily increased. Israel's return of fire was met by an increased and escalating rocket barrage, initiating the Second Gaza War. Again, the war was inconclusive.

2013–to date	A Sunni Islamic supremacist group, (originally an offshoot of Al-Qaeda) calling itself the Islamic State of Iraq and the Levant (ISIL)—*Dawla al-Islāmiyya fi al-'Irāq wa-sh-Shām*—began a rapid military conquest of large areas of both Syria and Iraq, eradicating the border between the two countries in the process. Beginning in early March 2013 with the capture of the northern Syrian town of Raqqa, ISIL issued a directive to all Christians within its control to convert to Islam, accept *dhimmi* status and pay the *jizya*, or face death. This triggered a Christian exodus from Syria and later Iraq as ISIL started attacking and burning churches. Moving into Iraq, ISIL forces overran the unresisting western Iraqi province of Anbar and a row of important towns, including Fallujah in January 2014. By June 10, 2014, ISIL seized control of Mosul, Iraq's second largest city, and then moved south and captured Tikrit, the hometown of former dictator Saddam Hussein, and other cities. In the territory it controls ISIL immediately imposed strict shari'a law. On June 29, 2014, which coincided with the first day of Ramadan (1435 A.H.) ISIL changed its name to the Islamic State and proclaimed its leader, Abu Bakr al-Baghdadi as imam and *khalifa* (caliph). He took the name of Caliph Ibrahim. As the power of the Islamic State grew (thanks to captured American arms given to the government of Iraq), it began waging a barbaric genocide against religious communities such as the Shi'ites, Christians, Yazidis, and other ethnic minorities, using beheadings, including beheading children, stonings, live burials, hangings, crucifixions, rape and murder. As of this writing, little has been done by Iraq, Syria, the United States, or other powers to reverse the conquests of the Islamic State.
June 11, 2014– Augsut 26, 2014	The Third Gaza War was fought, as Hamas and Islamic Jihad began a high intensity rocket and mortar bombardment of Israel. The missile bombardment was more intense and farther reaching than in the previous two Gaza wars. Some 4,500 were fired at Israel during the conflict. Additionally, Hamas planned a massive tunnel offensive against Israeli border towns for the Jewish New Year falling on September 24, 2014, with the purpose of killing and kidnapping large numbers of Israeli civilian residents—including men, women, and children (with kindergarteners being especially targeted). The terrorists' goal was to perpetrate a September 11, 2001-type mega-disaster for Israel. During the conflict, Israel discovered and destroyed some 32-attack tunnels foiling the plot.

As the tables indicate, from its inception to the present, Islam spread whenever it could, through conquest. The majority of what is now known as the Islamic world, or *Dar al-Islam*, was conquered by the sword of Islam. Since the earliest years of jihad over fourteen centuries ago, strategic thinking went into the planning and execution of jihad. This was set forth in a hadith that has been used as a template for that purpose. The circumstances for this hadith occurred prior to the invasion of Persia in 637 C.E. by Muslim forces of the second caliph, Umar ibn Al-Khattab (634–644 C.E.). Umar asked for advice about strategy and was counseled by Al-Hurmuzan. Using a bird as an example Umar was advised "if we were to destroy its head [as opposed to its wings or legs], then the rest of the bird is helpless."[209] In a like fashion, if the United States today were to be severely crippled or destroyed the rest of the Free World—including our NATO allies, our OAS allies, Israel, Japan, the Republic of Korea, Taiwan, the Philippines, and Australia (to name the most prominent)—would soon be helpless. That was the thinking behind the infamous September 11, 2001 attacks on the United States. It remains the Islamic supremacists plan for the present and the future.

Currently, the United States is in a war that was declared and thrust upon us, by Shi'ite Iranian Islamic supremacists since 1979, and by Sunni Islamic supremacists starting in the early 1980s. Since 1979, Iran has been a militant theocratic regime driven by messianic zeal and committed to the worldwide export of its Islamic supremacist ideology. The Islamic Republic of Iran declared war on the United States by its attack on sovereign US territory on November 4, 1979, when it seized the US Embassy in Tehran and held fifty-two Americans hostage for 444 days. Since then the Islamic Republic of Iran has relentlessly waged war against the United States and its allies. From Gaza to Khandahar, Afghanistan, from Beirut, Lebanon to Buenos Aires, Argentina, from Baghdad, Iraq, to Caracas, Venezuela, and from Cairo, Egypt to Central America, Iranian agents have done their best to disrupt and kill. Additionally, Iran granted hospitality and support to numerous terrorist groups.

On August 11, 1988, a Sunni Islamic supremacist multinational organization—Al-Qaeda ("the Base")—was formed, advocating worldwide jihad with the aim of establishing a global Islamic caliphate. It quickly gained notoriety for its indiscriminate actions. This included the February 26, 1993 attempt to topple the World Trade Center in New York City, using a massive bomb in a van parked in the underground garage of the Twin Towers. The plot included the release of cyanide poison (which failed). Six were killed and over 1,000 were injured in the first attack on the United States mainland by Islamic terrorists. They would strike the same target again, with horrific success on September 11, 2001 (*see* "Hijackings" section of "Basic Principle 52" for specific details). In 1996, Osama bin Laden, the head of Al-Qaeda, issued a *fatwa,* officially declaring war on the United States. In a "Declaration of War against the Americans Occupying the Land of the Two Holy Places" bin Laden demanded the United States first leave Saudi Arabia and then the entire Middle East. On August 7, 1998, the eighth anniversary of the arrival of US military forces in Saudi Arabia, Al-Qaeda attacked the US Embassy buildings in Nairobi, Kenya and in Dar es-Salaam, in neighboring Tanzania, both hit simultaneously by truck bomb attacks. As a result, in Kenya at least 213 people died and an estimated 4,000 were wounded, while in Tanzania, the attack killed at least eleven and wounded eighty-five. After failing in a similarly planned attack against the USS *The Sullivans,* (January 3, 2000) in the harbor of Aden, Yemen, Al-Qaeda succeeded with a suicide boat bomb attack on the USS *Cole,* anchored there on October 12, 2000. Seventeen US sailors were killed and thirty-nine were injured.

Furthermore, it was revealed in early June 2010, that Osama bin Laden and several close associates, including Ayman Al-Zawahiri, were granted sanctuary and lived in Iran starting in 2005. The Al-Qaeda leadership resided in the mountainous town of Savzevar in the northeastern Iranian province of Khorasan, about 137 miles west of Mashhad.[210] Subsequently Osama bin Laden moved to Abbottabad, Pakistan. It was at a mansion there, that bin Laden was located and killed by a US Navy SEALs unit on May 2, 2011. Despite the death of bin Laden and several other top leaders, Al-Qaeda has not been decimated, nor has its activities ceased. Al-Qaeda today is like a franchise and has affiliates such as Al-Qaeda in the Arabian Peninsula, the Al-Qaeda offshoot, the Islamic State of Syria and the Levant, Al-Qaeda in the Islamic Maghreb (North Africa) and the newly established Qaedat al-Jihad in the Indian Subcontinent.

William Gawthrop, FBI Counterterrorism analyst, succinctly explained why the West could not afford to focus on one terrorist group or a particular leader, during his lecture to the New York Metro Infragard at the World Financial Center in downtown Manhattan on June 8, 2011. Gawthrop told his audience that the fight against al-Qaida is a "waste," compared to the threat presented by the ideology of Islam itself.

> At the operational level, you have groups such as Hamas, Hezbollah, al-Qaida. Like teeth in a shark, it is irrelevant if you take one group out. We waste a lot of analytic effort talking about the type of weapon, the timing, the tactics. All of that is irrelevant … if you have an Islamic motivation for actions," [Gawthrop said. Even taking down hostile states like Iran is futile, since] "there are still internal forces that will seek to exert Islamic rule again.[211]

It should be stressed that there is a myriad of Islamic supremacist terrorist groups worldwide. These groups may change their name, cease activities (especially if associated with particularly heinous actions) and reestablish themselves under a new appellation. Nevertheless, while their names have changed their goal is the same. For example, in 2008, a new Palestinian Islamist group in the Gaza Strip, modeled on the ideology of Osama bin Laden's Al-Qaeda, was formed. It was associated with Hamas and called *Jaysh al-Ummah*—"Islam's army"—it stated its goals clearly "Muslims all over the world are obliged to fight the Israelis and the infidels [unbelievers] until only Islam rules the earth." Thus, it is not a particular group or groups that the West must combat but rather the ideology of Islamic supremacism itself.

In short, Islamic supremacists of both Sunni and Shi'ite denominations have committed multiple acts of war, attacking our civilians, our embassies, our military personnel, and our military units. The culmination of such attacks occurred on September 11, 2001, against the US mainland. There should be no doubt, we are the victims, and are the aggrieved party. The West is engaged in a war against a totalitarian political ideology—Islamic supremacism. It is a war thrust upon the West. It is conducted by Islamic supremacist religious armies whose war is inspired by their reading of the Qur'an and other Islamic holy texts. The Islamic supremacists are aided and abetted by many Islamic governments, many flush with oil revenues. It is a war against free societies, Western Judeo-Christian religions and values, as well as all unbelievers of other faiths.

As in World War II (against fascism and Nazism) and the Cold War (against communism), the West must defeat Islamic supremacism worldwide in piecemeal fashion rather than in a single decisive battle. The war, termed a "clash of civilizations"* by both Samuel P. Huntington and Bernard Lewis before him, will be long and can end in the defeat of this ideology, but only if we recognize the threat and summon the will to see and understand the scope of the challenge. Former Arkansas Governor and Presidential contender (in both 2008 and 2016) Mike Huckabee summarized what is at stake in the war against Islamic supremacism:

> It is right for us to be on the offense against Islamofascism, and not wait until they attack us on our soil. Unlike any war we have ever fought in this nation, this is not a war for soil. It is a war for our soul. Either we will win it or we will lose it. This nation must rally to the point where we recognize there is no compromise. There is no alternative. We must win; they must lose. Islamofascism must disappear from the face of the earth, or we will.[212]

---

* Whereas Western civilization has a unitary ethical ideal which leads us to equality and freedom, the Islamic supremacist civilization is one of dualism and submission. One or the other must prevail.

Moreover, in this conflict we must not limit our vocabulary or speech, as some have advocated and practiced, failing to use terms like "fundamentalists," "jihadists," "Islamic supremacists," and "Islamofascists." To substitute the name "war on terror" or "war on Al-Qaeda" as the name for the current conflict merely obfuscates who the enemy is and what they stand for. This is a war against Islamic supremacism. The Islamic supremacists have launched a global conflict against Western civilization. One of the tactics they use is terrorism. This conflict is not a war against a particular terrorist group, like Al-Qaeda. This war against Islamic supremacism is no more a war on terror, than World War II was a "war on blitzkrieg and kamikaze," or a "war on the *Schutzstaffel* (SS) and the Gestapo." Additionally, rebranding the "global war of terror" as "overseas contingency operations" as has been done by the Obama administration, moves the public further away from understanding who and what the threat is to the United States and Western civilization. This exercise in doublespeak will not change the identity or motives of the enemy arrayed against the West. As Sun Tzu, the Chinese military general, strategist, philosopher, and author of *The Art of War* would direct "If you know the enemy and know yourself you need not fear the results of a hundred battles." However, as US Army Lt. Col. Matthew Dooley would stress, "Political correctness is killing us. How can we properly identify the enemy, analyze his weaknesses, and defeat him, if we are NEVER [emphasis in the original] permitted to examine him from the most basic doctrinal level?"[213] The reader should not forget that the opposite of political correctness is morality, where there is a distinction between good and evil. We must recall the words of Isaiah 5:20, "Woe to them that call evil, good and good, evil. Who present darkness as light and light as darkness. Who call bitter, sweet and sweet, bitter." We must turn back the evil. We must turn back the darkness. We must turn back the bitter. Therefore, it is both essential and urgent that we recognize this clear and present danger that threatens not only the United States but also the values of Western civilization.

Army Lt. Col. Matthew Dooley was a decorated and highly rated officer who taught a course on radical Islam at the Joint Forces Staff College within the National Defense University. Dooley's course categorized Islam as an ideology, and not just a religion. Bowing to the protestations of Islamic organizations and the prevailing climate of political correctness, General Martin E. Dempsey, Chairman of the Joint Chiefs of Staff, publicly excoriated Dooley, then removed him as instructor, ordered Dooley's career-ending Negative Officer Evaluation Report, and then reassigned him to a remote post. The lesson was meant to serve as a stark warning to anyone else in the Department of Defense who might be tempted to become accurately educated about Islam.[214]

Overall, since coming to office in January 2009, the Obama administration adopted a policy of global withdrawal, engaging rather than confronting rogue states, and appeasing Islamic supremacism. Matters were made more difficult when the Obama administration ordered the removal of all references to Islam in connection with any examination of Islamic jihad terror activity. It has placed off-limits any investigation of the beliefs, motives and goals of jihad terrorists. Some vocabulary was banned, such as the terms "jihad," "jihadist," and "*mujahadeen*." Euphemisms were introduced like, "domestic violence" used to describe, "honor killings." The massacre of US servicemen (13 killed and 31 wounded) at Fort Hood, Texas in November 2009, by an avowed Muslim fundamentalist was redesignated as "workplace violence" by a "lone gunman." The interception of an Islamist terrorist, nicknamed the "underwear bomber," aboard Northwest Airlines Flight 253, en route from Amsterdam to Detroit, Michigan, on December 25, 2009, was described in the media as the avoidance of a "man-made disaster." Added to this deliberate denial of actions by Islamic supremacists were euphemisms such as "criminal acts" and "violent extremism." On April 2, 2015, Islamic supremacists from the Somali-based al-Shabaab terrorist organization perpetrated a massacre of nearly 150 Kenyan students at Garissa University College in northeastern Kenya because of their Christian faith. President Obama engaged in verbal gymnastics to avoid stating exactly who the perpetrators or victims were of this religiously motivated atrocity. He merely identified the victims as "innocent men and women" who "were brazenly and brutally massacred."[215] Thus, in more than one instance, factually inaccurate metaphors were deliberately used by the Obama administration to obfuscate the true nature and origins of the Islamist supremacist terrorist threat against the United States and Western civilization. Furthermore, the US National Security Strategy document that previously outlined the Bush Doctrine of preventative war was scrubbed of its key point that, "the struggle against militant Islamic radicalism is the greatest ideological conflict of the early years of the 21st century."[216] If there is a phobia, from which many Western governments, elites, the main stream media, portions of academia and others suffer, it is veritophobia—fear of the truth. As Dietrich Bonhoeffer, Christian theologian, who was hanged by the Nazis for his views, stated "Failure of people to speak small truths results in the victory of the Big Lie." To defeat an enemy, you must identify him properly and understand what motivates him.

32. The concept of *dhimmitude* has been part of Qur'anic Muslim tradition.

A *dhimmi* is a non-Muslim living under Islamic law, subject to a special tax and long list of strict conditions. The imposed conditions were those under which the *ahl al-kitab* ("People of the Book")—Christians, Jews, Samaritans, as well as Zoroastrians*—living on the lands newly conquered and colonized by Muslims, could hold onto their religion. Commonly, these regulations are known as the Pact of Umar. The Pact of Umar is a foundational medieval Muslim text that set forth Islamic supremacism over other non-Muslim peoples. It formed the pattern of later interaction between the Muslims and the *ahl al-kitab*—to the present.

The Pact of Umar, more accurately *al-shurut al-'umariyya*—"the conditions of Umar," was the set of rules that governed how the *dhimma* live under Islam. However, there were two caliphs named Umar. Historians are not unanimous as to which monarch this pact was actually attributed. The first, Umar bin al-Khattab—Umar the Great—who ruled as caliph from August 23, 634 to November 7, 644—concluded a peace treaty in ca. 637 with the Christians of Syria and what is now present day Israel.

The second was the Umayyad Caliph Umar II, Umar ibn Abd al-Aziz, who ruled from 717 to 720, and concluded the Umari Treaty, ca. 717, which has also been called the Pact of Umar. By a process of a gradual growth and enlargement from established practices and precedents, the Pact was extended. Yet, despite these additions, the whole Pact was ascribed to Umar. There are many variants of the text, and scholars deny that the text as it now stands could have come from the pen of Umar the Great. It is generally assumed that its present form dates from about the ninth century. The Pact increased in stringency over the centuries. In the final analysis, no matter under which Umar these conditions began, the conquering Muslims have implemented them and have been doing so for the past 1,400 years. The Pact of Umar was not some medieval proclamation directed against Christians and Jews, but rather an on-going edict that continues to be implemented in the twenty-first century in many Islamic states. When the jihadist group, Islamic State of Iraq and the Levant (ISIL) occupied the

---

* Muhammad made an exception for the Zoroastrians because they also believe in one god, Ahura Mazda, said to be the one uncreated Creator to whom all worship is ultimately directed.

northern Syrian town of Raqqa, March 3–6, 2013, they issued a directive, which encapsulated the Pact of Umar. Citing the Islamic concept of *dhimma*, the edict required Christians in the city to pay a tax of around half an ounce, 14g, of pure gold in exchange for their safety. The order stated Christians must not make renovations to churches, display crosses or other religious symbols outside churches, ring church bells or pray in public. Christians must not carry arms, and must follow other rules imposed by ISIL on their daily lives. The statement said the group had met Christian representatives and offered them three choices—they could convert to Islam, accept ISIL's conditions, or reject their control and risk being killed. "If they reject, they are subject to being legitimate targets, and nothing will remain between them and ISIL other than the sword," the directive added.[217] Many Christians fled Raqqa after ISIL started attacking and burning churches.

It is important for the reader to understand that the aggressor Arab/Muslim forces imposed degrading and discriminatory rules on the conquered peoples in their own homelands. The Muslims claimed that they were "protecting" these conquered native peoples, but the question immediately arises, protecting the *dhimma* from whom? Furthermore, every condition represents utter contempt for religious beliefs and feelings of the subjugated peoples, their culture, heritage, and dignity. Application of *dhimmi* status was exceptionally harsh on the Jews living within any Muslim political entity. Not supported by any nation-state of their own, the Jews suffered greatly, whereas Christian states would periodically intervene to lessen the pressure and persecution of Christian *dhimmis*.

At this juncture it is important to mention the so-called "Golden Age" of Muslim-Jewish cooperation and toleration that thrived mainly during the Middle Ages. This "golden age" of equal rights was a myth, and belief in it was a result, more than a cause, of Jewish sympathy for Islam. The myth was invented by Jews in nineteenth century Europe as a reprimand to Christians and taken up by Muslims in the twentieth century as an admonishment to Jews (for not consenting to be *dhimmis* to "enjoy the benefits" (sic) of a non-existent "golden age"). This is a narrative favored by those who could generally be categorized as "under-informed"—they think they know the subject but they do not know it enough. This would also include those who omit the historic details of this era of Muslim-Jewish relations. This "golden age" was painted as one of harmony and equality between these two religious groups. It is usually contrasted with the hostility and savagery of the 196-year struggle (1095–1291) by the Christian Crusades to regain control of the Holy Land from Muslim invaders of earlier centuries, as well as the Spanish and Portuguese Inquisitions which triggered some 250 years of peak barbaric and torturing activity (1478–early eighteenth century). In the "golden age" narrative, great emphasis (perhaps too great an emphasis) was and continues to be placed on Christian actions vis-à-vis the Muslims and Jews, while scant mention is made of the continued and on-going 1,400-year series of persecutions, humiliations, physical destruction, forcible conversions, or death, that were perpetrated against permanently categorized (Jewish and Christian) *dhimmi* subjects.

It is true that several hundred individuals, though they represented but a scant few out of the hundreds of thousands of *dhimma,* achieved positions of influence, wealth, and some power, but their number was infinitesimal compared to the multitudes of their co-religionists suffering under *dhimmitude*. Frequently mentioned as a stellar example of Muslim-Jewish amity—a "golden age" success story—was the twelfth century medieval Jewish philosopher, physician, and scholar Moshe ben Maimon, better known as Moses Maimonides—the Rambam. He was forcibly converted to Islam in Morocco (but later in Egypt he resumed his practice of Judaism) and rose in prominence achieving the status of court physician to Saladin. Yet, even from such a beneficiary of the so-called "golden age" as Maimonides, the truth emerged about the treatment and desperate situation of the Jewish *dhimma* under Islam. He had witnessed firsthand, what befell them in Muslim Spain, Morocco and Egypt. He lamented in his *Iggeret Teman* ("Epistle to Yemen") ca, 1172:

> No nation [the the Arab/Muslims] has ever done more harm to Israel. None has matched it in molesting, degrading, debasing and hating us [the Jews]. None has been able to reduce us as they have.[218]

For Maimonides, who knew of the Crusader attacks on Jews across Europe and on their way to the Holy Land, as well as his own family's experiences in Muslim Spain, Morocco and Egypt, this was a damning historic indictment of the "golden age." There were volumes of similar testimony over the centuries from others. Subsequent history repeatedly revealed Muslim discrimination and persecution of *dhimma*. Through the centuries of Muslim domination, any manifestations of a so-called "golden age" were merely pauses in the periods of persecution. Collectively, this historic record should lay to rest the highly and vastly overrated "golden age."

Although for periods, the *dhimma* were unmolested, it did not prevent Muslim rulers from initiating violence and massacres whenever they needed to distract the Muslim masses in times of stress. These bloodbaths included violence, rape, murder, arrests, the sacking of property, including churches, synagogues, and temples as well as forced conversions for example, the massive forced conversion of Jews in Yemen in 1165 and 1678. All these acts of despoliation occurred while the Muslim authorities, be they Arab, Persian, Ottoman, or Arab state police looked on passively or actively assisted the misojudaic and anti-Christian mobs. Even during the European colonial period, the authorities belatedly intervened to stop the carnage. Some of the most infamous episodes are listed below.

MAJOR MISOJUDAIC MASSACRES AND VIOLENCE IN THE ARAB/MUSLIM WORLD TO 1942 [219] (for the sake of clarity, modern day country names are used)	
Date	**Place**
625 C.E.	Medina, Arabia
629	Khaybar, Arabia Jews were expelled from all but the eastern and southern fringes of the Arabian Peninsula, during the reign of Caliph Umar, 634–644.
1010–13	Across Muslim-controlled Spain; Córdoba, Spain (1011)
1012	Cairo, Egypt
1032	Fez and Marrakesh, Morocco
December 30, 1066	Granada, Muslim-controlled Spain In one day, 4–5,000 Jews were put to the sword in a pogrom and their property seized.
1140–42	Dajayya, al-Mahdiya, Subrat and Tura, Libya
1146	Dar'a, Fez, Sijilmassa, and Marrakesh, Morocco

1291	Upon the death of Arghun Khan, Mongol ruler, (rumored to have been poisoned by his Jewish physician and Vizier, Sa'd ad-Daula) a widespread series of Muslim misojudaic attacks swept Iran and Iraq, then part of the Mongol Empire.
1333	Baghdad, Iraq
1465	Fez and other cities in Morocco
1640	The *al-Khada* in Fez, Morocco
1660	Safed in Ottoman-controlled Israel
1679–80	Yemeni Jews were expelled from all parts of the country to the desert region of Mawza, where some two-thirds of the expellees died of starvation and disease.
1720	Jerusalem in Ottoman-controlled Israel
1734–35	Safed and Hebron in Ottoman-controlled Israel
1776	Basra, Iraq
1790	Fez and Tetuan, Morocco
1792	Tetuan, Morocco and Yemen
1801	Algiers, Algeria
1817–31	Baghdad, Iraq
1818	Acre, Safed, Tiberias, Ottoman-controlled Israel
1820	Fez, Morocco
1838	Safed, in Ottoman-controlled Israel
1824	Beirut, Lebanon
1828	Baghdad, Iraq
1834	Tripoli, Lebanon
1838–39	Meshad, Iran
1840	Damascus, Syria
1844	Cairo, Egypt
1847	Dir el-Qamar, Lebanon
1862	Elkaer Kebir, Morocco
1864	Djerba, Tunisia
1864–80	Fez and Marrakesh, Morocco
1866, 1875, the winter of 1892–93, 1897	Hamadan, Iran
1869	Alexandria, Egypt
1869	Tunis, Tunisia
1870–92	Six separate pogroms in Egypt
1875	Debdou, Morocco
1877–1900	A series of pogroms in Tehran, Iran
1880	Nabel, Tunisia
1880s–1908	Port Sa'id, Egypt

1881	Tlemcen, Algeria
1882, 1897 and 1898	Algiers, Algeria
1883	Oran, Algeria
1889	Isfahan, Iran
1892	Hamadan, Iran
1903	Settat and Taza, Morocco
1907	Settat and Casablanca, Morocco
March 16, 1908	Jaffa, in Ottoman-controlled Israel
1909	Durab, Iran
May 21, 1910	Shiraz, Iran
October 30, 1910	Shiraz, Iran
April 18, 1912	Fez, Morocco[*]
August 1917	Tunis, Bizerte, Susa, Mehdia, and Sfax, Tunisia
1929–30	Constantine, Algeria
1931	Yemen
July 1932	Sfax, Tunisia
1933	Aden, Yemen
June–July 1934	Edirne, Turkish Thrace
August 5, 1934	Constantine, Algeria
1936	Damascus, Syria
July 1937	Baghdad, Iraq
May 1938	Oujda and Jerada, Morocco
1938	Mosul, Iraq
1938	Damascus, Syria
1938–39	Alexandria, Tanta, Mansura, Mohala, Cairo, Port Sa'id, Ismailia, and Assuit, Egypt
August 1940	Ebba-Ksour, Keff, Moktar, and Siliana, Tunisia
November 1940	Degache, Tunisia
May 1941	Gabes, Tunisia
June 1–2, 1941[220]	The infamous *Farhud* ("violent dispossession") took place in Baghdad, Iraq.
1941–42	Benghazi and Tripoli, Libya

Such massacres escalated in frequency across the Arab world with the attainment of Arab political independence after World War II, passage of the UN Partition Plan for Palestine of 1947, and the reestablishment of Jewish sovereignty in the Land of Israel in 1948. Thus, riots, mayhem, rape, and murder continued to be directed at resident Jews of the greater Middle East.

---

[*] More Jews were killed, wounded, assaulted and made homeless by the Fez pogrom than in the infamous, but more widely reported 1903 Kishinev, Russia, pogrom.

MAJOR MISOJUDAIC MASSACRES AND VIOLENCE IN THE ARAB/MUSLIM WORLD, 1944–2002 [221] [222] [223]	
Date	**Place**
1944, 1945 and 1949	Damascus, Syria
January 1945	Tripoli, Libya
1945	Tripoli, Lebanon
November 2–3, 1945	Cairo and Alexandria, Egypt
November 4–7,1945; 1947	Tripoli and several smaller towns Zawia, Zanzur, Amrus, Kussabat, and Tawarga, Libya
November 18, 1945, November–December 2, 1947, April 1948	Aleppo, Syria
July 1946, 1948	Baghdad, Iraq
May 1947	Fallujah, Iraq
December 2–4, 1947	Aden
December 5, 1947	Cairo, Egypt
December 5, 1947	Bahrain
1947–48	Yemen
June 7–8, 1948	Oujda and Jerada, Morocco
June 12, 1948	Tripoli, Libya
1948	Tripoli, Benghazi and Hara, Libya
1948	Baghdad, Iraq
May–September 22, 1948	Cairo and other cities in Egypt
September–October 1948	Basra, Iraq
November 2, 1948	Cairo, Egypt
August 5, 1949	Damascus, Syria
December 1949	Baghdad, Iraq
June 1950	Iraqi Kurdistan and Baghdad, Iraq
January 26, 1952	"Black Saturday" in Cairo, Egypt
January 1952	Tunis, Tunisia
March 15, 1952	Tangier*
August 3, 1954	Sidi Kassem-Petitjean, Morocco
1955	Mazagan, Safi, and Oued Zem, Morocco
October 1956	Cairo and Alexandria, Egypt
1957, 1959, 1960, 1961	Tunis, Tunisia
1957	Oran and Medea, Algeria
March 1958	Boghari, Algeria
October 11, 1959	Bou Saada, Algeria
December 12, 1960	Algiers, Algeria
January 1961, 1961–62	Morocco

---

* While directed mainly against European interests, many Jewish-owned businesses were looted and burned.

1961	Oran, Constantine, Algeria
July 5, 1962	Oran, Algeria
1963, June 5, 1967, 1969, 1970, 1978	Tripoli, Libya
June 6, 1967	Tunis, Tunisia
June 1967	Qamishli, Syria
1967, 1971	Lebanon
1968, 1979–80	Iran
September 1973	Damascus, Syria
1982	Djerba, Tunisia
April 11, 2002	Djerba, Tunisia

Over 1,000 Jews were killed during these pogroms, thousands more injured and millions of dollars of damage done to homes and property. In Libya, cities were urged to dig up Jewish cemeteries and throw the bodies of the dead into the sea.[224] This in turn triggered a massive Jewish exodus from Arab lands (*see* "Jewish Population in Arab Countries, Iran and Turkey" table) to Israel. Today, while the Muslims in the majority of their countries continue to implement many of these conditions against all unbelievers, they with a great degree of hypocrisy, demand all human rights in the Western democracies in which they reside, and at the same time seek to bring down those democratic institutions in those countries to their level of intolerance.

The Pact of Umar, from its inception to date, exposes the lies and disinformation that Islam is egalitarian and tolerant. The historic record proves otherwise. There are numerous examples of *dhimmitude*. To cite several:

Christians and Jews had to pay a special head tax—*jizya*—mandated in the Qur'an (9:29) "readily," while "being brought low," with a humiliating ceremony as a token of acceptance of the supremacy of Islam. Both Christians and Jews had to bow to their Muslim masters when they paid the *jizya*). This tax had to be paid in person by each subject, and it had to be paid in a public and humiliating manner. The tax collector had to strike a blow on the neck of the non-Muslim, which was meant as a symbolic beheading. Christians and Jews also had to pay an *avania* or "protection" payment for their safety and well-being as well as the *kharaj*—a tenant tax that acknowledged the land belonged to their Muslim masters. In Muslim Spain, *Al-Andalus*, the Christian peasantry, subjected to heavy taxes, formed a servile class attached to the Arab domains. Many Christians abandoned their land and fled to the towns.[225]

Christians and Jews were excluded from holding public office and kept from professions that might make them superior in any way over Muslims. They also could not give testimony in courts in cases involving Muslims, even if wronged by Muslims. Often Christians and Jews had to hire Muslim "witnesses" to give testimony on their behalf.

Christians and Jews were not allowed to enter certain streets in Muslim towns and cities. They were often confined to special quarters (e.g. the Christian Quarter and the Jewish Quarter in the Old City of Jerusalem)—in effect ghettos (*see* "Old City of Jerusalem" map). In Morocco, these walled ghettos were called *mellahs*. The *mellahs* were usually closed after dark and the Jews were locked in for the night.

Christians and Jews had to get permission to construct buildings. In all cases, the houses of Christians and Jews could never be taller or more elaborate than the houses of their Muslim neighbors. In this context, one should understand the purpose of the minarets that are part of any mosque.

Historically, the minaret has served as a symbol of Islamic political power and aspiration. It is designed to help impose Islam on the surrounding society. As a powerful symbol of Islamic dominance, it is often constructed to be higher than other religious buildings specifically to send the message to both Muslims and those of other faiths that Islam is supreme. It was largely for this reason that Switzerland, by national referendum on November 29, 2009, banned the construction of minarets.[226]

While on the subject of minarets, it is of interest to note, that in 1997, the Mayor of Istanbul, Turkey, Recep Tayyip Erdoğan, publicly read a famous Turkish poem "The Soldier's Prayer," written (in 1912) by Turkish nationalist poet Ziya Gokalp, which included the lines, "The minarets are our bayonets, the domes our helmets, the mosques our barracks and the faithful our army."[227] Erdoğan's pro-Islamist sympathies earned him a conviction for inciting religious hatred in April 1998. He was sentenced to 10 months in jail,[228] but was freed after four. However, because of his criminal record, he was barred from standing in elections or holding political office. The Turkish Parliament in 2001 changed the constitution to allow Erdoğan to stand for a parliamentary seat. He later founded the Justice and Development Party (*Adalet ve Kalkinma Partisi,* or AKP) and was swept to power in 2002, becoming Turkey's Prime Minister. On August 28, 2014, Erdogan assumed the presidency of Turkey steadfastly continuing his Islamization policies in the country.

Christians and Jews were only allowed to restore any place of worship that needed repair. The construction of new churches and synagogues was forbidden. An exception to this prohibition was the construction of "Our Lady of the Rosary," Qatar's first-ever church, which opened in 2008. But it was built minus the cross, bell, dome, steeple, or signboard. Rosary's priest, Father Tom Veneracion, explained their absence, "The idea is to be discreet because we don't want to inflame any sensitivities."[229]

Christian and Jewish places of worship were often ransacked, burned or demolished at the whim of the Muslims. This practice has continued to the present. On April 2, 2002, as the IDF swept into Bethlehem—part of Operation *Defensive Shield*—to root out the terrorists who had taken control of the city, between 150 and 180 Fatah terrorists under Yasser Arafat's command shot their way into the Church of the Nativity in Bethlehem. The church is the oldest continuously operated church in the world. For the next thirty-nine days, they held the sacred site and some 150 clergymen hostage. Three weeks into the siege, three Armenian monks escaped from the church through a side entrance and revealed what was happening inside. Friar Narkiss Koraskian told reporters, "They stole everything. They stole our prayer books and four crosses. They didn't leave anything." When the siege ended, the released hostages told of frequent beatings of clergymen. The terrorists, they told the *Washington Times,* "ate like greedy monsters," gorging themselves on food and slurping down beer, wine and Johnny Walker scotch they stole from the rectory as their hostages went hungry. Catholic priests said that the terrorists used their bibles as toilet paper. Franciscan priest Nicholas Marques from Mexico reported, "Palestinians took candelabras, icons and anything that looked like gold."[230] The siege ended in early May.

A second such atrocity in Bethlehem was revealed via a 2009 interview with Pastor Steven Khoury, of Bethlehem's First Baptist Church. Pastor Khoury reported that his church had been fire bombed fourteen times and two young women were shot to death for inviting non-Christian children to Vacation Bible School. "Persecution has made our church stronger," Pastor Khoury added. "I've been beaten up and shoved in trash cans just for one simple reason: for disciplining other young men who are from another faith." Khoury added, "My father's (Pastor Naem Khoury) been shot at three single separate times for one simple reason, carrying a cross and walking everyday and professing Jesus Christ and Him alone. Our church family gets persecuted every day."[231] In another interview in May 2013, Pastor Khoury declared that the continuous harassment of Christians had not abated. Due to this, many of them refrain from bearing crosses in public and carrying Bibles. He added that they are often told by Muslims to "Convert to Islam. It's the true and right religion."[232]

There has also been outbreaks of violence and destruction directed against Christians in Egypt. According to the Egyptian Initiative for Personal Rights (EIPR), on August 17, 2008, a policeman assigned to guard the Archangel Michael Church in Deshasha in Beni Soueif province south of Cairo, Egypt, hit three women while they were taking sand into the church to fix the floor, which was cracked as result of water collection underneath. On November 26, 2008, the Coptic Orthodox Church of the Virgin Mary in West Ain Shams, Cairo, Egypt, was inaugurated. The Church building was originally a condemned factory that was adapted into a church, which took over five years to complete. The Christian leaders obtained the necessary permits from the authorities to have a Church established there. Some 1,000 Coptic Christians had gathered for prayer inside the church. The building was attacked by a mob of over 20,000 Muslims with stones and butane gas cylinders. The Muslim mob blocked both sides of the street and encircled the church building, broke its doors and demolished its entire first floor. The mob chanted jihad verses as well as slogans saying, "We will demolish the church" and "we sacrifice our blood and souls, we sacrifice ourselves for you, Islam," while the entrapped Christians chanted "Lord have mercy." On April 26, 2009, Egyptian State Security forces attacked and demolished the services building belonging to the Coptic Orthodox Diocese of Masrah Matrouh, assaulting the Coptic priest, Father Matta Zakaria, and Coptic women and men.[233]

Another example of this continuing pattern of attacks occurred after prayers on Friday, September 30, 2011, when Muslim mobs exceeding 3,000 in number, attacked Coptic Christians in the village of Marinab, Egypt, according to a report published in the daily *Al Masry Al Youm*. The village is situated close to the town of Edfu in the Aswan Governorate, located some 500 miles south of Cairo. The attackers set fire to St. George Coptic Church, and demolished its dome.[234] Church attacks in Egypt always occur on Friday, Islam's day of public prayer, and are always accompanied by religious cries of *Allahu akbar*. Nearby Coptic homes were also set afire, and were further ransacked by rioting Muslims, during what in effect was an Islamic pogrom. The church, built nearly 100 years ago, was in a dilapidated state, badly in need of repairs. Approval of the design was sought and given by the local Marinab council and the Aswan Governorate. The church had been restored earlier in September. Nevertheless, local Muslims began complaining, making various demands, including that the church be devoid of crosses and bells—even though the building permit approved them. These demands were followed by a demand that the dome of the church be removed and that the church itself be referred to as a "guest home."[235] Note this attack occurred after the 2011 upheaval that toppled the Mubarak regime, during which promises were made that the "new order" would bring peace and equality between the country's majority and minority populations. Once the protests died down it was back to Muslim discrimination against Copts in Egypt.* With the advent of the Muslim Brotherhood-dominated government of Mohamed Morsi, violence and persecution of Copts in Egypt increased and seemingly knew no bounds.

On April 7, 2013, the St. Mark Coptic Orthodox Cathedral in Cairo, Egypt, was attacked by both Islamist mobs and Egyptian Internal Ministry security forces. Rocks and Molotov cocktails were thrown and gunfire was utilized. Two Christians were killed and dozens wounded. Incredibly, the only people to be arrested were Christians themselves—for daring to protect their holiest site against an Islamic attack. St. Mark's Cathedral is named after the author of the Gospel of the same name, who brought Christianity to Egypt some 600 years before Amr bin al-As brought Islam to that country by the sword. It is the seat of the Coptic Orthodox Pope and is considered the most sacred building for millions of Christians around the world—above and beyond the many millions of Copts in and out of Egypt. Additionally, it is the only apostolic see in the entire continent of Africa. As an apostolic see—the actual seat of an apostle of Christ—the cathedral further possesses historical significance for Christianity in general. With much of the world silent, such attacks are likely to continue and with them a corresponding Coptic emigration out of Egypt. It remains to be seen as to what will befall the Copts of Egypt under the new regime of President Abdel Fattah el-Sisi.

In a like vein, there were attacks against the sacred sites associated with Jewish biblical figures. There was repeated destruction of the traditional Joseph's Tomb in Shechem (Nablus) in 1996, 2000, 2003, and 2009, as well as the desecration of the traditional tomb of the Biblical leader Joshua at Timnat Haress, near Ariel in Samaria on December 18, 2007, and again on December 16, 2010.

Returning to the listing of Islamic prohibitions against *dhimmis,* Christians and Jews had to bury their dead without loud lamentations and prayers. Christian and Jewish graves had to be specially marked to prevent a Muslim from accidentally praying over the grave of an infidel. The cemeteries of Christians and Jews were not respected since they were considered as being from the realm of hell. Commonly they were desecrated or even destroyed, as was the case with the oldest Jewish cemetery (dating back some 3,000 years) on the Mount of Olives in Jerusalem, during the Jordanian occupation, May 1948–June 1967.

Christians and Jews were prohibited from visibly displaying religious symbols (e.g. crucifixes, icons, or Stars of David). It was for this reason that the Church of the Holy Sepulcher in Jerusalem has no cross and no belfry. For the many centuries of being subject to Islamic law and traditions under a succession of Islamic conquerors, including the Ottoman Empire (1517–1917) and the Jordanian occupation of Jerusalem (May 1948–June 1967), the church was stripped of its Christian symbols. This is clearly seen in an engraving by C. Maurand, from a drawing by E. T. Thérond, after a photograph by A. Salzmann, taken in 1856.[236]

Christians and Jews could not pray loudly, ring bells, trumpet shofars (ram's horns used in Jewish ceremonies), or other religious noises within the hearing of any Muslim. Christians and Jews were generally prohibited from publishing or selling non-Muslim religious literature and banned from teaching the Qur'an. Christians could not proselytize on pain of death.

---

* As Samuel Tadros reported in "The Christian Exodus From Egypt," *Wall Street Journal,* October 11, 2012, at http://online.wsj.com/article/SB10000872396390444358804578014733288327450.html?KEYWORDS= SAMUEL+TADROS, "Egyptian Copts were excluded from high government positions. There were no Coptic governors, intelligence officers, deans of schools, or CEOs of government companies. Until 2005, Copts needed presidential approval to build a new church or even build a bathroom in an existing one. Even with approval, state security often blocked construction, citing security concerns."

The prohibition of the ringing of church bells also extended to school bells. In April 2010, Al-Shabaab, Somalia's most powerful Islamist insurgent group, outlawed school bells in Jowhar, a town some 55 miles north of Mogadishu, Somalia's capital. At the same time, more than a dozen radio stations in Mogadishu stopped playing any form of music—even to introduce daily programs like news broadcasts—after another Islamist insurgent group, Hizbul Islam, warned radio stations to cease playing songs or face "serious consequences."[237]

A most shocking example of enforcement of these prohibitions occurred on November 21, 2002, when American Christian missionary Bonnie Penner was murdered—shot in the face three times—at the prenatal clinic at which she worked in Sidon, Lebanon. She was executed for her Christian faith. In Saudi Arabia, the Saudis will not allow the construction of a single church or synagogue on their land. Bibles are banned and burned. Christians engaged in any kind of missionary activity are arrested, tortured, and sometimes killed. Muslim converts to Christianity are put to death.

Christians and Jews were prohibited from critique of Muslim holy texts, denial of Muhammad's status as prophet, and disrespectful references to Islam. Recall the controversy over the Danish cartoons in 2005, the naming of a teddy bear "Muhammad," by British school teacher Gillian Gibbons in Sudan in 2007, and the firebombing of the headquarters of the French satirical newspaper, *Charlie Hebdo,* on November 2, 2011, when they ran a special issue with Muhammad as "guest editor-in-chief" and his cartoon depiction appeared on the front page. The newspaper, which suffered major damage, had "invited" the Islamic prophet Muhammad as a guest editor for its weekly issue. The paper was subtitled "Shari'a Hebdo," in reference to Islamic law. Its front-page of the weekly showed a cartoon-like man with a turban, white robe and beard smiling broadly and saying, in an accompanying bubble, "100 lashes if you don't die laughing." Page two, called "Shari'a Madame," was made up of a series of cartoons featuring women in burqas. The paper's tongue-in-cheek editorial, signed "Muhammad," followed on page three, centered on the victory of Tunisia's Islamist Ennahda Movement in the nation's first free election, and saying that the party's real intention was to impose Islam, not democracy. Each page contained "a word from Muhammad" in the corner and spoofed the news by twisting it into the weekly's current theme.[238]

Christian and Jewish communities were religiously harassed and sometimes forced to convert. A notable example was the serious riots that broke out in Istanbul on September 6–7, 1955. An emotional crowd of thousands of Turkish Muslim militants attacked Greek and Armenian Christian neighborhoods. More than 5,300 properties were destroyed, including homes, businesses, factories, hotels, pharmacies, churches, monasteries, a synagogue, and schools. Nearly a score of individuals were murdered, and over thirty were severely wounded. In addition, dozens of ethnic Greek women were raped and a number of men, mainly priests, were forcibly circumcised by the mob. The pogrom greatly accelerated emigration of ethnic Greeks from Turkey in general and the Istanbul region in particular.

Illustrative of the oppressive *dhimmitude* status imposed by an Arab state on its entire Jewish population was the series of twelve misojudaic laws enacted by Syria after 1967.

1. The Jewish right to emigrate was completely forbidden. This even applied to Jews holding foreign passports.
2. Jews were forbidden to move more than three kilometers (less than 1.9 miles) from their place of residence. A special permit was required to travel further.
3. A special identity card for Jews was stamped in red with the word *Mussawi* (follower of Moses).
4. Jews were subject to a 10 P.M. curfew.

5. Jews were allowed only six years of elementary schooling.
6. Jewish houses in the town of Qamishli were to be marked in red.
7. Jews were barred from jobs in the public service, public institutions and banks.
8. Government officials and military personnel were forbidden to purchase in Jewish shops.
9. Foreigners could not visit the Jewish quarters of various towns, without being escorted by a government official.
10. Jews were forbidden to own telephones, radios or to maintain postal contact with the outside world.
11. No telephones were to be installed in Jewish homes.
12. The property and possessions of deceased Jews were confiscated by the government. Their heirs then had to pay for its use. If they could not, it was to be handed over to the Palestinian Arabs.[239]

A further example of Muslim religious discrimination and persecution of Jews within an Arab country, occurred in Yemen, where it was required that every Jewish orphan child be converted to Islam. In December 2008, Rabbi Moshe Yaish al-Nahari was murdered in the Ridah-Amran district of northern Yemen, for refusing to convert to Islam. His death and continued persecution of his congregants triggered an exodus of some of the last Jews in Yemen.[240]

Christians and Jews could not bear arms. In fact, Christians and Jews were not allowed to raise a hand against their Muslim master, even if in self-defense. Such an act often resulted in the death penalty. If one *dhimmi* harmed a Muslim, the whole community would lose its status of protection, leaving it open to pillage, enslavement and arbitrary killing.

In *Al-Andalus* (modern Spain), the humiliating status imposed on the *dhimma* and the confiscation of their land provoked many revolts, punished by massacres, as in Toledo (761, 784–86, and 797). After another Toledan revolt (806), seven hundred inhabitants were executed. Insurrections erupted in Saragossa (from 781 to 881), Cordova (805), Merida (805–813, 828, 829, and later in 868). When Christians rose up in revolt, yet again in Toledo (811–19), the insurgents were crucified, as prescribed in Qur'an 5:33.[241] The revolt in Cordova of 818 was crushed by three days of massacres and pillage, with 300 notables crucified and 20,000 families expelled.[242]

By no means was the use of crucifixion limited to ancient or medieval times, or restricted to Christians and other non-believers. A recent example was the eight Muslim rebel fighters, who were crucified, on June 28, 2014, in the town square of Deir Hafer in eastern Aleppo province, Syria. They were left there for three days to die. They were crucified by ISIL because they were considered too moderate, belonging to other rebel forces fighting against the Assad regime in the Syrian Civil War.[243]

Christians and Jews could not own or ride horses or camels. While they were allowed to ride donkeys (but only sidesaddle as a woman would do), they were required to dismount upon meeting a Muslim and pass him on foot to show their inferior status. Christians and Jews had to greet a Muslim first when traveling on a road, and walk in the narrowest part of it. In many countries, the Jews were even required to go barefoot. They were also required to walk to the left of the Muslims, discouraging a hostile engagement.

Christians and Jews could not enter into sexual relations or marriage with Muslim women, upon pain of death. In fact, it is a violation of shari'a law for any non-Muslim man to marry a Muslim woman. It is even more of a violation to have illicit sexual relations between a non-Muslim man and a Muslim woman. Muslim men, on the other hand, were permitted to marry Christian and Jewish women because the enslavement of non-Muslims by Muslims was allowed. The children resulting from such unions were automatically deemed Muslim.

Christians and Jews were required to wear distinctive clothing (e.g. *zunar*—wide belts and distinctive conical hats) and patches of distinct colors (e.g. yellow badges for Jews, blue for Christians, and red for Zoroastrians) on their outer garments. These requirements were intended to humiliate as well as to allow their recognition as inferior beings. The yellow badge was first introduced by a caliph in Baghdad in the ninth century, and spread to the West in medieval times, where various Christian countries utilized it. The Nazi regime in Germany copied this practice for Jews living in Germany and German-occupied Europe.

The concept of *dhimmitude* even was extended to diplomatic talks. At every opportunity, Muslim leaders have attempted to impose *dhimmi* status on Israelis, even in negotiations. Since the reestablishment of Jewish sovereignty in the Land of Israel, during negotiations between Arabs and Israelis, the Arabs refused to sit in the same room with Israelis to negotiate. For example, in 1948–49 American mediator, Ralph Bunche, had to shuttle between rooms at the same hotel. Henry Kissinger, in 1973–75, had to shuttle between Jerusalem and Cairo, and Jerusalem and Damascus. The only exceptions were at international forums such as the United Nations General Assembly, the Madrid Middle East Conference of 1991, and the Annapolis Conference of 2007. However, it should be emphasized that at the latter event, the Arabs demanded, and the United States acquiesced, to having the Israelis enter via a service entrance, thus endorsing the concept of *dhimmitude*.

In the period immediately preceding the Six-Day War of June 1967, an ominous phrase was heard in Muslim circles, "First the Saturday people [the Jews], then the Sunday people [the Christians]."[244] With the upsurge of fundamentalist, jihadist Islam, that theme has been repeated. Are the jihadists prepared to tolerate non-Islamic enclaves, whether Jewish in Israel, or Christian in Lebanon, in the heart of the Islamic world? The answer based on the history of over 100 years is "No."

The plight and suffering of the Christians in the Middle East must be discussed further. It bears closer examination. Islam believes that Christianity is a corrupted and distorted religion based on myths and legends. In Islam, Jesus is a Muslim prophet, Christ's divinity is a blasphemy and thus the foundations of Christianity are false.[245] At the time of the Arab/Muslim conquests of the seventh century, most of Anatolia, the Fertile Crescent, the Land of Israel and Egypt were Christian, part of the Byzantine Empire. In the centuries that followed, most of the people in the broader Middle East embraced Islam. They became culturally and linguistically Arabized. The remaining Christians became a minority.

Beginning, on August 26, 1072, with the defeat of Emperor Romanus IV by the Seljuk Turks led by Sultan Alp Arslan at the Battle of Manzikert, the Christian Byzantine Empire was weakened. Islamic power was extended into the empire consolidating Muslim control over the central Anatolian plateau. Christian pilgrimage routes to Jerusalem were cut off, which in turn would prompt the First Crusade. It is to be recalled that the 196-year Crusader period (1095–1291) was not an "invasion" by outsiders of sacred Muslim lands, but rather (in the end) a feeble Christian counter-attack to try to regain the Holy Land conquered by invading Muslim forces. Once the Crusades stopped, the local remaining Christians were accused of collusion with the Crusaders and Muslim forces sought retribution on these Christians. For example in 1320 and again in 1354, the Egyptian Mamelukes attacked Coptic churches throughout Egypt whereby the structures were destroyed on the heads of thousands of worshippers and asylum seekers.[246] The final collapse of the Christian Byzantine Empire was marked by the fall of Constantinople to the Ottoman Turkish forces of Sultan Mehmet II, on May 29, 1453. The Muslims made the city the capital of their caliphate and empire. The Christian position in the Middle East deteriorated from that time.

Overall, through the centuries, under Islamic rule, Christians were subject to discrimination, intimidation, persecution, forced conversion, deportation, attack, rape, and murder. This occurred despite being a "protected people" under Islam and under the humiliation of *dhimmitude*. Under such conditions, increased numbers of Christians were forced to flee seeking refuge and ultimately, exile from their homeland. Whether they were the Christian Maronites in the mountains of Lebanon, who suffered a massacre of thousands in 1860, the Christian Armenians, who were victims of the first great genocide of the twentieth century—the Armenian Genocide—or the Christian Copts of Egypt in the twenty-first century—the pattern described above was the same.

By no means were the Maronites and Armenians the only Christians who suffered. Some of the other groups included the Egyptian Copts, the Assyrian Catholics of Syria, and Chaldean Catholics of Iraq, as well as the Christian Southern Sudanese, who suffered huge losses in two wars directed against them, from 1955 to 1972 and from 1983 to 2005. Some 500,000 perished in the first war. More than two million died of starvation as well as being systematically murdered, raped, brutalized, sold into slavery and banished from their homes in the second conflict.[247]

At the turn of the twentieth century, Christians made up 26 percent of the Middle East's population.[248] Today the Christians in the Middle East number 10.8 million, comprising 3.8 percent of the population of the region.[249] With the advent of Arab nationalism, and more importantly that of Islamic fundamentalism, the status of Christians in the region has sadly declined even more rapidly. In fact, many Christian clergymen in Arab/Muslim countries are so terrified of Islamic aggression that they systematically hide the truth of their oppression and often distort their own theology to win the tolerance of supremacist Islamic authorities. The cases of Lebanon and the city of Bethlehem both dramatically illustrate the decline of Christian populations in the Middle East.

In 1932, Christians made up 55 percent of the population of Lebanon according to the census held that year, the last to date in Lebanon's history. A political power sharing arrangement, the National Pact of 1943 (*see* Appendix 4), was based on the 1932 census. A government estimate in 1956 placed Christians at 54 percent of the population. The Muslim population disputed these statistics and increased the friction between the two main religious groups, each of which was subdivided by numerous religious denominations. The census became a highly charged political issue in Lebanon, because it constituted the ostensible basis for communal representation. By 1958, the estimated Christian population was lowered to some 50 percent.

The growth of the Muslim population of Lebanon to majority status was one of the main causes of the First Lebanon Civil War in 1958. It was the disproportioned apportionment of power sharing in the government that triggered the conflict. The other major factor was Egyptian President Gamal Abdel Nasser's ambition for a larger UAR is mentioned elsewhere in the text. The Christians did not want to readjust the balance, and that was the main cause of the two Lebanese civil wars. Similarly, the continued growth of the Muslim majority as well as the presence of the PLO in Lebanon, led to the bloodier and longer Second Lebanese Civil War from 1975 to 1990. As previously stated but needs to be reemphasized, the underlying factor in both civil wars was the historic Muslim enmity towards any *dhimmi* people having sovereignty over lands Muslims once possessed, which they deemed part of *Dar al-Islam* to be reconquered.

With the unexpected (by the Arab/Muslim world) Israeli military victories in both the Six-Day and Yom Kippur Wars, the priorities of the ominous phrase—"First the Saturday people [the Jews], then the Sunday people [the Christians]"—had to be reversed. Attention was to be paid to "First the

Sunday people [the Christians] and then the Saturday people [the Jews]." This was to be implemented in Lebanon, beginning in 1975.

The Christians were the principal victims in both Lebanese civil wars, subjected to attacks by the Lebanese Muslims as well as UAR elements in the first civil war, and Lebanese Muslims, the PLO and Syria in the second. By 2010, the Christian population was estimated at 39 percent[250] and declining. With growing Hezbollah influence, Syria dominance returning and Iranian meddling, the future for the Christians of Lebanon looks bleak indeed.

The rejection of the concept of a Christian-free Middle East, (with emphasis on Lebanon) or Christians being relegated to *dhimmi* status was forcefully voiced by then President-elect Bashir Gemayel of Lebanon, who delivered a speech at Dayr-Salib, on September 4, 1982, which summed up the precarious position of Christians not only in Lebanon, but throughout the Muslim Middle East.

> In the name of all the Christians of the Middle East, and as Lebanese Christians, let us proclaim that if Lebanon is not to be a Christian national homeland, it will nonetheless remain a homeland for Christians ... a homeland to be protected and preserved, in which our churches may be rebuilt at the time and in the manner we desire.

> Our desire is to remain in the Middle East so that our church bells may ring out our joys and sorrow whenever we wish! We want to continue to christen, to celebrate our rites and traditions, our faith and our creed whenever we wish! We want to be able to assume and testify to our Christianity in the Middle East! And whatever may be the difficulty in offering this testimony, we will never renounce it. We will testify to our Christianity in Lebanon!

> We will testify to our Christianity in the Middle East! As a Christian part of the Middle East, we want to be different from others and possess a land which, without being—let it be repeated—a Christian national homeland, shall be a country for Christians, where we may live in dignity, without being forced by anyone to deny our faith, as we were in the time of the Turks when we were ordered to walk on the[ir] left because we were Christians. We do not want to be forced to wear any sort of discriminatory badge on our body or on our clothes—so that one might know that we were Christians—and we do not want to be transformed into citizens existing in the *dhimmitude* of others! Henceforth, we refuse to live in any *dhimmitude*![251]

For his bold oratory and the expression of these sentiments, President Gemayel paid the ultimate price. He was assassinated in East-Beirut the very afternoon he gave this speech.

A second notable example of the decline of the Christian populations in the Middle East is the city of Bethlehem, the site sacred to Christians as the birthplace of Jesus. Under Israeli administration, from 1967 to 1995, Bethlehem thrived and grew. With the 1967 Israeli liberation of Judea and Samaria, 550 Bethlehem leaders asked Israel to incorporate Bethlehem within Israel's borders, partly because Bethlehem's economy depended on Jerusalem, partly to maintain ready access for Christians to pray at two of Christendom's holiest shrines, Bethlehem's Church of the Nativity, and Jerusalem's Church of the Holy Sepulcher, where Jesus was buried. But the leftist government of Israel declined, fearing the international condemnation that would follow an extension of Israeli sovereignty as well as the prospect of ruling over Bethlehem's substantial Muslim population.[252]

Between the 1993 signing of the Oslo Accords and the 1995 transfer of Bethlehem to the PA, Palestinian Christians lobbied both the United States and Israel against the transfer of the area to the PA. Their request was denied, in order to advance the Oslo "peace process." Those who objected included the heads of Bethlehem and Beit Jala monasteries and the late Christian mayor of Bethlehem, Elias Freij, who pleaded in 1993, not to transfer the area to PLO control. "Bethlehem will become a town of churches devoid of Christians, if you transfer the area to the Palestinian Authority," he said. Freij unsuccessfully lobbied Israel to include Bethlehem in the boundaries of Greater Jerusalem, as was the Jordanian practice until 1967.[253] Then, Israeli Prime Minister Yitzhak Rabin agreed, but only on condition that the heads of the Christian church officially and publicly request that Bethlehem remain under Israeli rule. The church leaders declined, unable to embrace unambiguously Israel for fear of Muslim retaliation against Christians in the Holy Land and elsewhere in the Middle East. Sadly, Freij's prediction became reality.

Bethlehem's Christian population started to drastically decline in 1995, the very year Yasser Arafat's PA took over the holy Christian city in line with the US-backed Oslo Accords. As soon as he took over Bethlehem, Arafat defied tradition by appointing a Muslim, Muhammed Rashad A-Jabar, as governor.[254] Additionally, Arafat unilaterally deposed Bethlehem's city council, which had nine Christians and two Muslims, reducing the number of Christians councilors to a 50-50 split. Arafat then converted a Greek Orthodox monastery next to the Church of Nativity into his official Bethlehem residence.[255]

The PLO/PA then redrew the city's boundaries adding the satellite towns of Beit Sahour and Beit Jala, thus adding some 30,000 Muslims to Bethlehem's population. A PLO/PA rule was instituted forbidding a Christian from selling his property, whether a shop or a house, to another Christian if he decides to move abroad. The sale must be made only to Muslims. This all but guaranteed a Muslim majority in any future Bethlehem municipal elections.[256] Christian businessmen were forced to shut down their businesses because they could no longer afford to pay "protection" money to local Muslim gangs.[257] The dramatic Christian exodus from the city of Jesus' birth began shortly thereafter.

The Christian population of Bethlehem dropped dramatically from 85 percent in 1948 to 12 percent in 2007[258] and to less than 10 percent in 2014.[259] Justus Reid Weiner, an international human rights lawyer and scholar, said, "The systematic persecution of Christian Arabs living in Palestinian areas is being met with nearly total silence by the international community, human rights activists, the media and NGOs." He predicted the complete dissipation of Christian communities in the Palestinian-controlled territories within the next fifteen years (i.e. by 2022).[260]

In the last decade and a half, Christian individuals, churches, and even cemeteries, were frequently attacked, and the latter two defaced. Monasteries had their telephone lines cut, and there have been break-ins at convents.[261] Examples of this pattern of Christian discrimination, persecution and attack occurred in Iraq, Syria, and Egypt. In Iraq on October 31, 2010, Islamic supremacist terrorists attacked the Our Lady of Salvation Assyrian Catholic church, the largest in Baghdad. As some one hundred worshipers celebrated Sunday evening mass, members of Al-Qaeda in Mesopotamia terror group stormed the church. The terrorists walked straight up to the priest, Father Wassim Sabih, who was administering the mass, pushed him to the ground as he grasped a crucifix and pleaded with the gunmen to spare the worshipers, murdered him, riddling his body with bullets.[262] The Muslim terrorists then took the Christian worshipers hostage. As Iraqi security forces stormed the church under US military supervision, the Islamic terrorists threw grenades at the worshipers and four suicide bombers detonated their bomb belts. The death toll reached 58, while 67 were wounded. Iraqi Human Rights Minister Wijdan Michael, a Christian, said at the scene of the Baghdad attack, "What happened was more than a catastrophic and tragic event. In my opinion, it is an attempt to force Iraqi

Christians to leave Iraq and to empty Iraq of Christians."[263] Since the collapse of Saddam Hussein's regime in 2003, more than half of Iraq's Christian population has been forced by targeted violence to seek refuge abroad or to live away from their homes as internally displaced people.

A similar pattern is being repeated among the Christian population of Syria, especially since the advent of the Islamic State of Iraq and the Levant (ISIL) in April 2013. Reminiscent of what the Nazis did marking Jewish businesses and homes with a "J" for "*Jude*," Christians throughout the region controlled by ISIL have had their homes marked with "N" for *Nasrani* ("Nazarenes," i.e. Christians).

Even though Egyptian Copts took part in the 2011 popular revolution that overthrew the Mubarak regime, discrimination against them increased, especially with the advent of the Muslim Brotherhood-dominated Mohamed Morsi government. There was discrimination in housing and education. Many colleges in Egypt limited the enrollment of Copts to a quota of 2 percent, although Christians make up about 10 percent of the population. Christians are excluded from political activities, police departments, security agencies, and academia.[264] Despite the 2013 overthrow of the Morsi Muslim Brotherhood government by the Egyptian public and the military, attacks on the Copts have increased.

The violent oppression of Christian minorities became the pattern in Muslim-majority nations stretching from West Africa and the Middle East to South and Southeast Asia. The Muslim enmity towards Christians goes beyond ethnicities, regions and cultures. While precise figures are hard to come by, the chart below gives an approximation of the decline of Christian populations in selected areas across the greater Middle East.

DECLINING CHRISTIAN POPULATION IN THE ARAB/MUSLIM WORLD		
Entity or Country	**Then**	**Today**
Palestinian Authority Bethlehem	35 percent (1995)	< 10 percent[265]
Palestinian Authority (Judea-Samaria also known as the "West Bank")	15 percent (1994)	< 2 percent
Hamas-controlled Gaza Strip	< 5,000 (2006)[266]	< 1,700 (2011)[267]
Lebanon	54 percent (1932)[268]	< 30 percent
Turkey	2,000,000 (1918)	< 100,000
Syria	< 50 percent (1946)	< 4 percent (was 10 percent in 2010, i.e. 2.3 million)
Jordan	18 percent (1950)	2 percent
Egypt	20 percent (early 1950s)[269]	< 10 percent i.e. < 7,800,000
Turkish Republic of Northern Cyprus	83 percent (1975)	0
Mosul, Iraq	70 percent (1932)	47 percent (1957); 51,815 (2010)[270]
Iraq	1,400,000 (before 2003)	< 300,000[271]
Pakistan	3 percent (1947)[272]	1.6 percent[273] (< 2.8 million)

In contrast, as documented in the Central Bureau of Statistics' Statistical Abstract of Israel 2008 (Chart 2.2), from 1948 to 2007, the Christian population in Israel has grown by more than 400 percent.

THE GROWTH OF CHRISTIAN POPULATION IN ISRAEL[274]	
Year	**Population**
1948	34,000
1968	72,200
1974	78,700
1986	100,900
1995	120,600
2007	151,600

During the twelve-year period (1995–2007), Israel's Christian population grew from 120,600 in 1995 to 151,600 in 2007, representing a growth rate of 25 percent. In fact, the Christian growth rate outpaced the Jewish growth in Israel in that time. In 1995, there were 4,522,300 Jews in Israel and in 2007 there were 5,478,200, representing a growth rate of 21 percent—4 percent less than the Christian population grew during the same period.[275] Today, Israel is the only country in the Middle East where the Christian population is growing.

In fact, Israel is the only safe haven for Christian minorities in the Middle East today. Testimony to that effect was given on September 23, 2014, by Father Gabriel Nadaf, a Greek Orthodox priest from Nazareth and a loyal citizen of the State of Israel, to the United Nations Human Rights Council in Geneva, Switzerland. "Across the Middle East, in the last 10 years, 100,000 Christians have been murdered each year. That means that every five minutes a Christian is killed because of his faith," Nadaf asserted. "In the Middle East today, there is one country where Christianity is not only not persecuted, but affectionately granted freedom of expression, freedom of worship and security," Nadaf declared. "It is Israel, the Jewish State. Israel is the only place where Christians in the Middle East are safe."[276]

As the information above reveals, Arab/Muslim hostility to Christians and Jews is long-standing. The reader should not be distracted from this factual historic record by revisionist propaganda that Arab/Muslim hostility is merely a phenomenon that began with the advent of modern Zionism at the end of the nineteenth century, or with the reestablishment of Jewish sovereignty in the Land of Israel in 1948, or with elements of US foreign policy. It began with the advent of Islam in the seventh century.

POLITICAL PROCESSES

All power tends to corrupt and absolute power corrupts absolutely.
John Dalberg-Acton, 1st Baron Acton

Assassination is the extreme form of censorship.
George Bernard Shaw, 1916.

*Politics is the art of looking for trouble, finding it whether it exists or
not, diagnosing it incorrectly, and applying the wrong remedy.*
Sir Ernest John Pickstone Benn, 2nd Baronet, political publicist.

*If you lie to people to get their money, that is fraud. If you
lie to them to get their votes, that is politics.*
Anonymous

Historically, violence is ever present in the Arab/Muslim Middle East. It has been the primary method of dealing with opponents, both foreign and domestic, as well as both Arab and non-Arab. The contentious political forces in the Middle East have produced numerous disputes and conflicts. There is but a sole Western-style democracy in the region, Israel. For the rest of the Middle East, there are constant unexpected political changes. Often, these changes have manifested themselves by assassination, coups d'état, and "revolutions." Politically, over the centuries there has been rivalry between the power that dominates the Nile Valley and the power that dominates the Tigris–Euphrates Valley. Furthermore, in modern times the quest for pan-Arab unity has been elusive.

Modern Arab political history can be divided into three periods. The first period which ran through the first three-quarters of the twentieth century, was that of semi-colonial monarchic rule dominated by the United Kingdom, France, and Italy. It was exemplified in Morocco, Tunisia, Libya, Egypt, Anglo-Egyptian Sudan, Transjordan, Iraq, the Aden Protectorate and the Gulf emirates.

The second period was a nationalist one, which was largely more anti-colonial, secular, anti-clerical, socialist, and pan-Arab. The era began with the 1952 Free Officers Movement coup that overthrew the Egyptian monarchy of King Farouk. Military strongmen such as Muammar Qadhafi, Gamal Abdel Nasser, Anwar Sadat, Hosni Mubarak, Hafez and Bashar Assad, as well as Saddam Hussein harshly opposed and repressed Islamic fundamentalist elements, jailing and executing them. The most infamous episode of this repression being Hafez al-Assad's destruction of the Muslim Brotherhood's bastion in Hama from February 2 to 28, 1982, during which the Syrian city was subjected to tank and artillery fire, poison gas attack as well as being largely leveled. An estimated 7,000 to 38,000 were killed.

The third period began in 2011, with Islamist revolutions sweeping the Arab world from Tunisia, to Egypt, to Libya, to Yemen, to Syria. However, within a year there was a popular backlash against the Islamic fundamentalist government of Egypt. This in turn triggered the military coup of July 3, 2013, that ousted the Muslim Brotherhood regime of Mohamed Morsi. Similarly, such a reaction had occurred earlier on January 11, 1992, in Algeria, when the military blocked the Islamic Salvation Front from assuming power. Thus, this third period may only be a transitional phase. Whether this will be repeated elsewhere—in Tunisia, Libya, Yemen or Turkey—remains to be seen.

33. In the Middle East, disputed areas are known by different names strictly for political motives.

Examples of the validity of this principle include:

- Hatay = *Livaa aliskenderna*
- Kobanê = Ayn al-Arab (Kurdish town on Syrian-Turkish border)
- Eilat = Umm Rashrash
- Gulf of Eilat = Gulf of Aqaba
- Khuzistan = Arabistan
- Shatt al-Arab = Arvand Rud
- Persian Gulf = Arabian Gulf
- Mount Dov = Shebaa Farms
- Western Sahara = southern Morocco
- Judea and Samaria = the "West Bank"
- The Temple Mount = *Haram esh-Sharif,* or Noble Sanctuary

On a larger scale, the Arab world has sought to deny the Jewish people's historic connection to the Land of Israel, and the fact that a sovereign Jewish political entity existed on that territory for 1,279 years before the Arab conquest and occupation of that area (636–969 C.E.) for a total of 333 years. Hundreds of Jewish town and village place names were Arabized, from the original Hebrew, by adjusting their names to Arabic phonetic patterns. These Hebrew names were evidence of Jewish habitation dating from biblical times. Some of these changes were minor making the older Jewish names recognizable, while others were more obscure. The following are illustrations.

ARAB ATTEMPTS TO REMOVE JEWISH PLACE NAMES FROM THE LAND OF ISRAEL	
Historic Jewish name	**Arab name**
Israel	*Filastin* (Palestine)
Jerusalem	*Al Quds*
Shechem	Nablus
Hebron (site of the Tomb of the Patriarchs, as well as King David's seat of power for seven years before he moved his capital to Jerusalem)	*Al Khalil*
Akko	Akka
Tel Aviv	Sheikh Munis
Ashkelon	Majdal
Eilat	Umm Rashrash

Nahalat Shimon and Shimon HaTzadiq (The latter commemorated Simon the Just, a Jewish high priest from the fourth century C.E. It was purchased by Jews in 1876. Nahalat Shimon was built by Sephardic and Yemenite Jews in 1891.)	Sheikh Jarrah (It was primarily a Jewish neighborhood in the late nineteenth century and remained so up until 1948. At that time, all the Jews were expelled by the invading Transjordanian army.)
Shiloach (site of the Gihon Spring [Isaiah 8:6] and the Pool of Siloam [Nehemiah 3:15] that supplied water to the City of David, the original site of King David's capital at Jerusalem. In modern times it was settled by Yemenite Jews in 1882)	Silwan (All Jews expelled in 1948)
Anathoth (Anatot), some 3 miles north of Jerusalem (the birthplace of the prophet Jeremiah–Book of Jeremiah 1.1)	Anata
Betar, southwest of Jerusalem (was the seat of the Bar Kokhba Rebellion against Rome from 132 to 135 C.E.)	Battir
Beit Horon, northwest of Jerusalem (was where the Maccabees defeated the Seleucid Greeks under the command of Seron, in 166 B.C.E.)	Beit-Hur
Beit She'an, south of Tiberias in the Jordan Valley	Beisan
Beth El, mountain-top town north of Jerusalem (archaeological evidence revealed that for more than 2,000 years this mountain was considered the site of Jacob's dream in which angels ascended and descended the famous ladder–Genesis 28)	Beitin
Ein Gannim	Jenin
Giv'on (where Joshua defeated the Amorite kings–Joshua 10:12)	Jib
Modi'in (where the Hasmonean also known as Maccabeean Revolt broke out in 167–142 B.C.E.)	Midia
Tekoa, south of Jerusalem (birthplace of the prophet Amos– Book of Amos 1:1)	Tequa

34. While Israel is often described as a "thriving democracy" and the "only democracy in the Middle East," it does not follow exactly the democratic model of the United States.

Ideologically, Israel is a democracy like the United States. Freedom House proclaimed in 2013, "Israel remains the region's [i.e. the Middle East] only Free country."[1] However, Israel, unlike France or the United States, has no constitution. Instead, Israel has a variety of "Basic Laws" passed at different times by different governments led by different political parties. Israel's first Basic Law: The Knesset was initiated by the Knesset Law Committee in 1958, ten years after the founding of the State. Other Basic Laws are: Basic Law: Israel Lands (1960); Basic Law: The President of the State (1964); Basic Law: The State Economy (1975); Basic Law: The Military (1979); Basic Law: Jerusalem, Capital of Israel (1980); Basic Law: The Judiciary (1984); Basic Law: The State Comptroller (1988); Basic Law: Human Dignity and Liberty (1992); Basic Law: Freedom of Occupation (1994); Basic Law: The Government (2001); and Basic Law: The Referendum Law (2014).[2] Frequently, any coalition agreement states that any change in the Basic Law must have the agreement of all partners in the government, thus making any changes very difficult.

Under Israel's parliamentary electoral laws, the entire country constitutes a single electoral district for electing Israel's 120-member Knesset. This fact necessitates a Knesset based on proportional representation. This proportional representation is inherited from the political structure of the World Zionist Organization since the late nineteenth century. In this system, voters cast their ballots for nationwide fixed, party-ranked lists of candidates, most of whose names are unknown to the average voter. Each party is then apportioned Knesset seats on the basis of the percentage of votes it obtains. In Israel any party winning 3.2 percent (raised from 2 percent in March 2014[3]) of the popular votes cast in a national election, can win two and possibly three Knesset seats. This permissive electoral threshold further multiplies the number of political parties, whose special interests hinder national unity. (If party X wins 5 percent of the vote, for instance, it gets 120 x .05 or six seats, which go to the top six candidates on its party list). While not without its virtues, chief among which is the parliamentary voice it gives to minorities, proportional representation also has its grave defects. That is why it is practiced in Israel and the Netherlands alone and in hybrid versions in only a few other countries like Finland, and Ireland. A much greater improvement would result by raising the threshold to 5 percent, as is the case in Germany and New Zealand. Such a higher threshold would produce fewer rival parties in the Knesset as well as in the Cabinet. This in turn will enable the Government to pursue a more coherent and decisive national policy.

One of these shortcomings is that, in a country that is religiously, ethnically, or ideologically fractured, proportional representation can produce parliaments with many small parties and no dominating large ones, leading to complex and unstable governing coalitions that are difficult to maintain. In its first sixty-seven years as a modern state, Israel has had thirty-two governments.

An even more severe deficiency is the detachment of voters from the candidates elected by them. Whereas, for example, all Americans have a US Congressman from their district and two US Senators from their state who must take into account their needs, desires, and opinions, Israeli politics has no corresponding representatives. Party X's Knesset members are not personally answerable to the public that elected them. Nor, having been chosen by their parties, can they be rewarded or punished on an individual basis. There is no way to return one member of party X to the Knesset for having done a good job while retiring another member of the same party for having done a bad one. Thus, an incumbent Knesset member does not even have to defend his voting record against a rival candidate in a local election.

Such a system clearly, is capable of producing a fundamental estrangement from politics by the public. As long as Israelis, despite their differences, shared a strong sense of common national purpose, this was balanced by other forces. Once Israeli society began to fragment, however, it became relevant. And as it did, the effective response to it became identity politics—with ethnic, religious, or ideological constituency taking the place of distinct geographical districts. Thus, Israeli politicians campaign for and respond primarily to those groups. A US Republican Congressman/Congresswoman understands that he/she represents his/her entire district. He/She must be attentive to Democrats too, if only because he/she wants as many of their votes as he/she can get in the future. But a Knesset member from single-constituency party X feels no such obligation to voters for parties Y and Z. He/She may never have had the slightest contact with them, having gotten to be a Knesset member in the first place not by winning local elections and working his/her way up the political ladder but by being active in the population group that party X represents and cultivating its leaders (Israel's only local elections are for mayors and few mayors make the jump to the Knesset. However, certain larger parties have seats pre-allocated to geographic regions of voters). Little wonder, then, that many Israelis, especially younger ones, have grown cynical about their politicians.

On the plus side of the Israeli system, every law is read in full and passes first, in committee, and then by three consecutive votes in the Knesset. If the second vote has passed by an overwhelming majority, the final vote might become a sheer formality. In comparison, the recent passage of voluminous bills in the US Congress unread leaves much to be desired.

In Israel, no quorum is required to pass legislation. In fact, Israel's most important Basic Law: Human Dignity and Freedom (1992), was enacted with only a minority of the Knesset present and voting. Additionally, treaties are not ratified by the Knesset; they are merely announced by the Government and published within twenty days thereafter. The Knesset may pass a resolution in favor of a treaty, but this has no legal standing.

Israel has a parliamentary multi-party system. It is typical for more than twenty-five parties to compete in an election, with about twelve to fourteen gaining Knesset seats. Thus, forming a coalition government is necessary and leads to multi-party cabinet government. For example, in the January 22, 2013, elections, thirty-four parties competed for seats in the Knesset. Twelve parties gained over the then minimum 2 percent and three of the twelve had the minimum three seats allowed. Despite this, Israeli election law overall discourages many more splinter parties. Unfortunately, a government can become dependent on the whims of small parties motivated exclusively by their own narrow interests. In fact, Israeli politics seems to be motivated, more by personal aggrandizement and power, than by the national interest. If the coalition cannot stay together, the government in effect, stops functioning. At that point, the leading coalition party seeks to hobble together a new coalition, or failing that, is forced to call new elections where the process starts all over again. Italy, by the way, is a much worse example of this coalition phenomenon than Israel. Since the end of World War II, Italy has had sixty-four governments (as of February 2014).

With so many parties, no one party in Israeli history has come even close to winning a majority of seats (sixty-one) in the 120-member Knesset, which forces the bargain-making process. This means that the cabinet will consist of the leaders of five or more rival parties, each anxious to increase the influence of his or her own party program among the voters before the next election. The party leader able to assemble a Knesset majority coalition becomes prime minister. Since 1990, an absolute majority (61 out of 120) of Knesset members are needed for a no-confidence vote to oust the prime minister. It should be noted that the executive power of the Israeli Prime Minister is far less than that of the US President. The large number of rival parties in the cabinet, each having its own agenda or priorities, not only precludes coherent and resolute national policies, it also produces governments whose average duration in recent times is about two and one-half years.

The American system of checks and balances does not exist in Israel and therefore the country is at the mercy of the political elites. The President of Israel is not elected by the people, but rather appointed by the ruling party in the Knesset. The Israeli presidency is a ceremonial, symbolic, and figurehead position. One of the president's few prerogatives is the right to pick the most suitable candidate for heading a new government after a general election. However, the Israeli presidency under Shimon Peres (2007-14) became a political post, with the president trying to influence and even make policy, undermining the sitting Prime Minister and the executive branch of the Israeli government.

Judges in Israel, including Supreme Court judges, are chosen by a non-elected panel dominated by other judges, and there are no possibilities for impeachment of judges by the Knesset or by ballot initiative. Appointments of judges are not subject to approval by the Knesset. The Israeli Supreme Court is dominated by Ashkenazi, secular, liberal Jews and is hardly representative of the Israeli political, ethnic, and religious spectrum of the Jewish state. Israel's Supreme Court has been controlled by the anti-democratic doctrine of "judicial imperialism" for a generation. "Judicial imperialism" is when judges simply make up imaginary "laws" as they go along, without the need for the legislature— the Knesset—to bother passing them as laws. The unelected justices of the Israeli Supreme Court claim the right, invented by them out of thin air, to be able to overturn laws passed by the elected representatives of the people. There is no constitutional basis in Israel for their claiming such a right. In the United States this process is called "legislating from the bench," though is far worse in Israel. Supreme Court president Aharon Barak (president from 1995 to 2006) construed Basic Law: Human Dignity and Freedom (1992) as endowing the Court with the power of judicial review. This interpretation of Basic Law: Human Dignity and Freedom prompted Barak to decree, "everything is justiciable." Barak made the Court a super-legislature. Such is the Court's unprecedented power– unequaled in any democratic country—that Barak, a leftwing cultural relativist, went so far as to rule in 2005, that Basic Law: Human Dignity and Freedom did not apply to the Government's expulsion of 9,000 Jews from their homes in Gaza and northern Samaria. What is needed in Israel is a judicial system, whereby the President nominates Supreme Court judges subject to confirmation by the Knesset in open public hearings, similar to the US system.

In the words of Robert Bork, one of America's prominent critics of judicial activism, "the pride of place in the international judicial deformation of democratic government goes not to the United States, nor to Canada, but to the State of Israel." In his book *Coercing Values: The Worldwide Rule of Judges,* Bork argued that, "Israel has set a standard for judicial imperialism that can probably never be surpassed and one devoutly hopes will never be equaled elsewhere."[4] Recall, it was American James Madison who said (in a speech at the Virginia Convention to ratify the Federal Constitution, June 6, 1788), "I believe there are more instances of the abridgment of freedoms of the people by gradual and silent encroachment of those in power than by violent and sudden usurpations."[5]

After over sixty-seven years, Israel needs a written constitution. In it, should be enshrined the concept that Israel is a Jewish state and that a super majority would be needed to amend the constitution. Nevertheless, despite its structural and organizational differences, Israel is the Middle East's only democracy and the only country in the region that respects human rights! The remaining countries in the region are governed by a group of tyrants, despots, dictators, autocrats and theocrats.

35. Elections do not make a true democracy in the Middle East.

Middle Eastern elections in and of themselves do not constitute democracy. As Thomas Sowell would insightfully observe, "To hold elections for the sake of holding elections is to abdicate responsibility for the sake of appearances."[6] To the uninformed, the word "democracy" equals liberty and freedom, equality and tolerance. It does not. Democracy is a tool, it is a means to an end. Like most tools, democracy is only as good as those who use it. As Turkish Prime Minister Recep Tayyip Erdoğan once explained, "Democracy is like a streetcar. When you come to your stop, you get off."[7] Democracy is more than the right to vote. Furthermore, democracy as we think of it, and democracy as it is often played out in the Middle East are two different things. Many Arab/Muslim countries are ruled by a dominant party or have no political parties at all. Elections are mainly plebiscites to approve the program of the leader or party in power and are followed by the imposition of authoritarian rule. In those few Arab/Muslim countries that have multiple parties, elections are only mechanisms for regulating the balance among competing ethnic, tribal and religious groups intent on political domination, economic exploitation and social coercion. Such elections can be suspended at the first opportune moment. No Arab nationalist regime or monarchy in the Middle East has ever let itself be voted out of office. The Islamic Iranian government has not abolished itself to date. The new Islamist governments appearing across the Middle East are not likely to do so either. Using a democratic function, i.e. an election, does not mean democratic values will magically appear after that election. As Thomas Sowell understatedly commented, "You cannot create instant democracy like you are making instant coffee."[8]

Adolf Hitler and his Nazi Party gained a plurality in the last two free and fair all-German elections held on July 31, 1932 and November 6, 1932 (only after the military destruction of the Nazi regime were free elections restored in 1949). The Nazis subsequent rise to power in Germany did not bring democracy to that nation. Hitler's victory in those elections is an example of the proponents of tyranny and despotism using one element of the democratic system to gain power and then to destroy that very system. There are numerous such examples in the twentieth century and into the twenty-first century, including Joseph Stalin, Mao Zedong, Gamal Abdel Nasser, Hafez al-Assad and his son, Bashar, Saddam Hussein, Muammar Qadhafi, and Mahmoud Ahmadinejad to name the most notorious of many despots. In Iran in 1979, the act of removing the Shah and replacing him by a tyrannical and cruel Islamic regime run by an Ayatollah, allegedly selected by God, not elected by people—was not democracy in the true meaning of the word.

Today, opponents of tyranny assume that deposing a tyrant will improve the lives of his victims and lead to individual liberty, a free pluralistic and secular society, human rights guarantees, equal rights for women as well as ethnic and religious minorities. Perhaps these opponents are influenced by the Robin Hood legend, whereby the good Robin Hood and his Merry Men toppled the evil tyrant, Prince John and his henchmen, including the Sheriff of Nottingham. Deposing the tyrant can certainly do so, however, there is no assurance that it will. Thus, this belief is sometimes true, but only occasionally. More often, the overthrow of a despot leads to a worse tyranny as the following examples illustrate. In 1917, the Russian people overthrew Tsar Nicholas II, and this resulted in the rule of the Bolsheviks (communists)—Lenin (some 6 to 8 million died during his regime) and Stalin (upwards of 10 million died). The Chinese people overthrew the autocratic rule of Jiang Jieshi (Chiang Kai-shek), which was replaced by Mao Zedong's unprecedented barbarity, which became responsible for the deaths of 76 million Chinese. The Cuban people overthrew Fulgencio Batista in 1959—they got Fidel Castro and a communist regime that continues to rule after more than half a century. The Iranian people overthrew the Shah's reign, which resulted in the Ayatollah Khomeini and the theocratic regime of the mullahs. In all these examples, the regimes established were far more repressive than their authoritarian predecessors were. On the other hand, after the Portuguese overthrew the authoritarian regime of Antonio Salazar and his successor, Marcelo Caetano in 1974, as well as when the various peoples of Eastern Europe toppled the communist regimes during the period 1990 to 1991, they achieved liberty and democracy.

Radical Islamic fundamentalists who are elected to office only use the mantle of democracy in order to prevent and/or destroy the values that support true legitimate democracy, and make it possible. It is peoples and their values that make a nation, not a "democratic" election. Those values include, but are not limited to, liberty, freedom of expression, freedom of religion, respect for individual rights and private property, equal justice, the safeguarding and toleration of both ethnic and religious minority rights, gender equality, use of secret ballots, an independent press, willingness to compromise, and constitutional checks and restraints on government power. Such values must be instilled in a society and learned. Instead of respecting those true democratic ideals and building institutions to sustain them, Islamic supremacists are winning elections with the goal of doing away with them. Islamic supremacists use such elections to advance their radical agenda. As political commentator, Diana West suitably phrased it, "The West enshrines the liberty of the individual, while Islam, like other totalitarian systems, enforces a collective will."[9]

Egyptian Premier Gamal Abdel Nasser staged a plebiscite on January 24, 1954 to ratify a new Egyptian constitution. The population of Egypt at the time was some 22,000,000. Of that number 5,697,467 registered to vote and 5,488,225 or 99.8 percent voted in favor, while 10,045 voted "no." At the same time, Premier Nasser was elected president of Egypt by a greater majority, 5,496,965 or 99.9 percent, of the vote. Despite the large numbers of voters, only 150,000 women participated. Did this election make Egypt a democracy? The answer, which still applies today, is definitely not.

During March 29–30, 1979, the Iranian people were offered a simple yes-or-no vote referendum on creating an Islamic Republic. The result was 98.2 percent voted yes, while only 1.8 percent voted no. The Islamic Republic was established and democracy perished shortly thereafter as opposition parties were crushed, newspapers closed, and enemies of the regime were executed by firing squads and on the gallows.

On December 26, 1991, Algeria's first multi-party parliamentary elections were held for the 430-seat Algerian National Assembly. In the first round of voting, the Islamic Salvation Front (FIS) won 231 seats with more than 50 percent of the votes. Such a result would have led to a FIS victory, which was almost certain to win more than the two-thirds majority of seats required to change the Algerian Constitution. That in turn, would have enabled the FIS to impose an Islamic fundamentalist state, based on shari'a, and end the vestiges of democracy in largely secular Algeria. This was unacceptable to the military, which then intervened. On January 11, 1992, the army declared a state of emergency that limited freedom of speech and assembly as well as canceled the second round of voting. The military intervention, suspended election and subsequent political turmoil resulted in the Algerian Civil War, which was waged from December 26, 1991 to 2006.[10] The war left 200,000 Algerians dead and approximately 15,000 missing.[11] The military forced then-President Chadli Bendjedid to resign and banned all political parties based on religion, including the FIS.

The victories of Islamic parties, not democratic forces in the Western sense, is what occurred across the Middle East during the first two decades of the twenty-first century. This occurred with the election of the Justice and Development Party (AKP) in Turkey in 2002. It also took place with the victory of the Islamic fundamentalist Hamas in the Palestinian Legislative elections of January 25,

2006, in the Gaza Strip. That election was cited by its supporters, both in the Middle East and abroad, as proof that the people have spoken through the democratic process. As a result of this election, the world should now sit down and negotiate with this gang of religiously motivated killers. Although Hamas gained 44.45 percent of the popular vote, it was given 74 seats in the 132-seat legislature, 56 percent of the seats. Fatah, which placed second with 41.43 percent of the popular vote was given 45 seats, which amounted to only 34 percent!

On June 12, 2009, Iran held a presidential election. The twelve-member Council of Guardians, headed by Supreme Leader Ayatollah Ali Khamenei, set out the election rules. Candidates for president had to be approved by the Council. As reported by the BBC, more than 450 Iranians registered as prospective candidates, but only four contenders were accepted. All forty-two women who attempted to run were rejected. The contest was really between Mahmoud Ahmadinejad and his main rival Hossein Mousavi. Eighty-five percent of Iran's 46.2 million eligible voters turned out for the election. The entire process was tightly controlled by the Ministry of Interior under Sadeq Mahsouli, a general of the Iranian Revolutionary Guards Corps and a senior aide to Ahmadinejad. Amid charges of widespread voter fraud and irregularities, Ahmadinejad won, with 24,527,516 votes (62.6 percent) to Mousavi's 13,216,411 (33.75 percent). The two other candidates together garnered only 1,011,875 votes. There was no independent election commission, no secret balloting, no observers to supervise the counting of the votes, and no mechanism for verification. Ahmadinejad was credited with more votes than anyone in Iran's history. He won in all thirty provinces, and among all social and age categories. His three rivals all lost even in their own hometowns. The state-owned Fars News Agency declared Ahmadinejad the winner, even before the first official results had been tabulated by the Interior Ministry!

In Lebanon, the Islamic fundamentalist terrorist group Hezbollah now operates as a full-fledged political party in that country. The formation of a national unity government in 2008, gave Hezbollah and its allies control of eleven of thirty cabinets seats in the government, with effective veto power to block any moves or legislation it did not like. On June 13, 2011, Hezbollah became part of the Lebanese government, without even the charade of an election.

Likewise, in Tunisia, in 2011, the Islamist Ennahda Movement emerged as the dominant force in the government of that country. In Libya, on October 24, 2011, the National Transition Council Chairman Mustafa Abdul Jalil announced that existing laws that contradicted the teachings of Islam would be nullified, stating that shari'a law would be the basis of legislation. Abdul Jalil outlined several changes to be made including the lifting of restrictions on the number of wives a man can take.[12] Later, on August 9, 2012 the National Assembly (not the people) selected Mohamed el-Megaref, an Islamist leader of the National Front to be the head of state.

In the lead-up to the Egyptian parliamentary elections of November 2011–January 2012, as well as the lead-up to the June 2012 Egyptian presidential election, Raymond Ibrahim of the Middle East Forum would observe and note that Islamic clerics, including influential ones like Yusuf al-Qaradawi, "declared that it was mandatory for Muslims to cheat during elections—if so doing would help Islamist candidates win; that the elections were a form of jihad, and those who die are 'martyrs' who will attain the highest levels of paradise." Top Islamic institutions and influential clerics "issued *fatwas* decreeing that all Muslims were 'obligated' to go and vote for those candidates most likely to implement shari'a law, with threats of hellfire for those failing to do so,"[13] so much for the concept of "free democratic elections."

Accordingly, Islamist forces came to power in Egypt, with the victory of Mohamed Morsi, in the presidential election of June 16 and 17, 2012. This was hailed at the time as the first "free and democratic election" in Egypt's history. Within five months, there were charges of numerous irregularities and violations with "specific instances of alleged forgery, such as rigging ballots and importing pens with erasable ink to invalidate them."[14] Dr. Saad Eddin Ibrahim, a professor of political science and head of Egypt's Ibn Khaldun Center, at the American University of Cairo, closely monitored the elections. Ibrahim, who was imprisoned under the Mubarak regime as a political dissident, declared that based on research, "We here at the Ibn Khaldun Center, through 7,000 field monitors, monitored the elections, and, according to our data, [the secular candidate and former Egyptian Vice President Ahmed] Shafiq won these elections, by a margin of 30,000 votes."[15] Additionally, the results of that election were not announced for three days. It was precisely during those three days that US Secretary of State Hillary Clinton pressured the military to surrender power and portrayed any delay to proclaim a winner as "clearly troubling."[16]

Thus, Mohamed Morsi who rose through the ranks of the Muslim Brotherhood, was sworn in as Egypt's president on June 30, 2012. He then swiftly consolidated power in a *de facto* coup against the military council running the country, on August 12, 2012. Morsi fired his military commanders, abrogated the Constitution, and assumed dictatorial powers greater than those possessed by his predecessor, Hosni Mubarak. Morsi attempted to place Muslim Brotherhood officials in key leadership positions in the government, the Army and the security forces. Thus, he transformed Egypt into an Islamist state. On November 22, Mohamed Morsi issued a decree granting him sweeping powers and shielding his government from judicial oversight. Morsi finally rescinded the decree on December 8, in the face of massive public protests. The two part referendum (December 15 and 22, 2012) that approved the new Islamic constitution, insured Morsi's and the Muslim Brotherhood's dictatorial rule. Once again, an election did not produce a true democracy. In fact, in the case of Egypt, the Morsi regime lasted little more than a year. Unpopular moves (as mentioned below) quickly built opposition, which only grew during the year 2012 to 2013.

Morsi appointed extremist governors throughout the country, including in June 2013, Adel el-Khayat, a member of Al-Gama'a al-Islamiyyaa—a terrorist group—as a governor of Luxor district. Luxor was the target of the group's terror attack on November 17, 1997, in which sixty-two foreign tourists were killed and twenty-eight others were injured. Islamist Brotherhood militias were allowed to grow, as did attacks on Egyptian Copts. Ties with and support for Muslim Brotherhood groups in Tunisia, Libya and Syria were strengthened. The economy was mismanaged despite financial aid from Qatar, the United States and Western Europe. This political and economic downward spiral culminated in massive street demonstrations in major Egyptian cities that started on June 28 and continued until July 3, numbering over 22 million. Statistically, this was the largest demonstration in history to that date. On July 3, 2013, the Egyptian military on behalf of those people, staged a coup and ousted Morsi and the Brotherhood. It remains to be seen if the Brotherhood, which had struggled for 85 years to achieve power will go quietly into the night—probably not. Egypt may yet face a brutal civil war, between more secular and Islamist forces, as the one that wracked Algeria from 1991 to 2000, and Syria from 2011 to date. One thing is certain; Western-style true legitimate democracy has a long road to travel before it comes to Egypt and the rest of the Arab/Muslim Middle East.

Middle East "democracy" in effect means one man, one vote, one time. The election of an Islamist regime is not a victory for democracy, even if a real majority voted for it. It is usually the first and last free election in such a country. This type of government perpetuates their totalitarian regime thereafter without regard to any democratic principles or human rights. In Tunisia, Egypt and Libya thus far, the people voted for Islamic supremacists whose definition of "democracy" is far different from that of the West. Hence, Middle Eastern style of "democracy" threatens not just the West's security but also its civilization.

In Middle East politics (with Israel being the sole exception), it is not the people who determine an election, the shape of government and its policies, but rather the unelected head of the tribe, group or clique (in the Iranian case, Supreme Leader Ali Khamenei) who carefully staged-managed a scripted election. These illustrative examples in Egypt, Iran, and Algeria, all re-affirmed the premise that an election does not make a democracy. To claim that if an Arab/Muslim country holds popular elections and elects totalitarian Islamists, it is a "democracy" is a political falsehood of major proportions. It is nothing more than a sham and is just an attempt to gain democratic legitimacy.

Thus, it cannot be underscored enough that true real democratization requires more than plebiscites. It is an evolutionary process towards a constitutional government, which requires the incorporation and acceptance of principals such as individual liberty, a free, pluralistic, and secular society, human rights guarantees, equal rights for women as well as ethnic and religious minorities. True legitimate democracies have built-in safe guards, such as separation of church and state, transparency, freedom of expression, institutional checks and balances, limited terms for elected officials, rule of law, and a separate independent judiciary, as well as the desire to live at peace with other nations, among other factors.

True democracies that consist of these features and values are not created by elections alone. Adherents of true democracy do understand that fact. The Arab/Muslim world needs exposure to this true democracy and then change needs to evolve from within the society itself, not have it imposed from the outside, which requires years, more likely decades, of patient, disciplined, and often unpopular work, especially in a region where nothing resembling democracy has ever existed. In the case of the Arab/Muslim world, the teachings of the Qur'an and the dictates of shari'a law are opposed to true democracy. Therefore, their people will probably never experience true democracy because of these insurmountable obstacles.

36. Assassination, an accepted means of political activity in most Arab/Muslim countries, is often used to replace key political leaders in the Middle East.

While the practice pre-dates Islam, it is increasingly found after the death of Muhammad. In fact, the very word "assassin" has its origin in the Middle East. The *Hashshashin*—the Assassins—were active from the eighth to the fourteenth century. They launched terrorist attacks not only against the Christian Crusaders, but also against Muslim rulers. Since that time, heads of state and prime ministers have been murdered. Other public figures, political leaders, and military officers have been eliminated. There have been numerous unsuccessful attempts on the lives of Arab/Muslim political leaders. Significantly, the endemic instability of the Arab/Muslim Middle East makes the conclusion of any agreement a risky proposition. Any leader is but a pistol/rifle shot or bomb blast away from removal. Furthermore, there is little guarantee that his successor will honor previous commitments. The table indicates many cases of assassination and major assassination attempts.

ASSASSINATIONS	
(Events listed within modern-day boundaries)	
ALGERIA	
Date	**Event**
April 11, 1963	Foreign Minister Muhammad Khemish was assassinated.
January 3, 1967	Former National Liberation Front (FLN) leader Muhammad Khidr was assassinated while in exile in Madrid, Spain.
April 25, 1968	President Houari Boumédiènne was slightly wounded in an unsuccessful assassination attempt.
October 20, 1970	Former Prime Minister Abdel Karim Belkassem, an opponent of President Boumédiènne, was assassinated while in exile in Frankfurt, Germany.
February 3, 1987	Mustafa Bouyali, leader of the Algerian Islamic Armed Movement, was assassinated by Algerian government security forces.
June 29, 1992	Muhammad Boudiaf, Chairman of the High Council of the State of Algeria, was shot to death by an Islamist bodyguard in Annaba.
August 22, 1993	Kasdi Merbah, former Prime Minister, was assassinated.
November 22, 1999	Abdelkader Hachani, a founder of the Islamic Salvation Front, was assassinated in Bab-el-Oued, a suburb of Algiers, by Algerian security forces.
COMOROS	
Date	**Event**
May 29, 1978	Ali Soilih, the former President of Comoros, was killed while "trying to escape."
November 26, 1989	President Ahmed Abdallah was assassinated as a prelude to a coup in Moroni, the capital.
November 6, 1998	President Muhammad Taki Abdul Karim was poisoned under mysterious circumstances.
EGYPT	
Date	**Event**
December 11, 1121	Al-Afdal Shahanshah, vizier to the Fatimid caliphs, was assassinated on the orders of the Caliph Manṣūr al-Āmir bi'Aḥkāmi'l-Lāh.
October 7, 1130	The tenth Fatimid caliph, Manṣūr al-Āmir bi'Aḥkāmi'l-Lāh was assassinated, due in part to his loss of Tyre to Crusader forces.
October 24, 1260	Saif ad-Din Qutuz, third Mameluke Sultan of Egypt, was assassinated by dissident Mamelukes.
June 14, 1800	Jean Baptiste Kléber, French general and commander of French Napoleonic forces in the Middle East (present-day Egypt, Israel and Syria) was assassinated by a Syrian nationalist living in Cairo.
February 20, 1910	Boutros Ghali, pro-British Prime Minister, was assassinated by an Egyptian nationalist.
November 19, 1924	Sir Lee Stack, Governor-General of the Anglo-Egyptian Sudan was assassinated in Cairo, Egypt by Egyptian nationalists.

November 1937	A member of Misr el Fatat (Young Egypt), an extreme nationalist party modeled after the Italian fascist party, attempted to assassinate Egyptian Prime Minister Mustafa el-Nahhas, in part for his support of the Anglo-Egyptian Treaty of August 12, 1936.
February 24, 1945	Prime Minister Ahmed Maher Pasha was assassinated in the Parliament building in Cairo, by an Egyptian nationalist. Maher was pro-British, against the Muslim Brotherhood, and had declared war against the Axis, all unpopular moves in many circles.
December 28, 1948	Egyptian Prime Minister Mahmoud Fahmi a Nukrashi Pasha was assassinated by the Muslim Brotherhood, in part for Egypt's losses in its war against Israel.
February 12, 1949	Hassan al-Banna, founder and leader of the Muslim Brotherhood, was assassinated by Egyptian security forces, in retaliation for the assassination of Prime Minister Mahmoud an-Nukrashi Pasha.
October 26, 1954	The Muslim Brotherhood attempted to assassinate Egyptian President Gamal Abdel Nasser in Alexandria, Egypt. The attempt failed and Nasser banned the Brotherhood, and imprisoned thousands of its members, many being tortured and held for years in prisons and concentration camps.
ca. 1975	El Leithy Nassif, former head of President Anwar el-Sadat's Presidential Guard, who assisted him in the "Rectification (or Corrective) Revolution" of May 15, 1971, against Sadat's opponents, died after being thrown off his balcony at his London apartment. To date, the murder remains unsolved.
October 6, 1981	Egyptian Islamic Jihad, an offshoot of the Muslim Brotherhood, assassinated Egyptian President Anwar el-Sadat, while he reviewed a military parade in Cairo. He was killed for concluding a peace treaty with Israel.
October 12, 1990	Rifaat al-Mahgoub, Speaker of the Egyptian Parliament was assassinated by Islamic fundamentalists in his automobile in Cairo.
June 8, 1992	Farag Foda, a journalist sharply critical of Islamic fundamentalism, was assassinated in Cairo by members of *Al-Gama'a al-Islamiyya*, an Islamic fundamentalist group.
April 20, 1993	The Egyptian Information Minister Safwat Sherif, though wounded, escaped an assassination attempt by Islamic fundamentalists near his home in Heliopolis, Egypt.
June 26, 1995	Egyptian Islamic Jihad, working with Egyptian *al-Gama'a al-Islamiyya* and assisted by Sudan's intelligence service[17] attempted to assassinate President Hosni Mubarak by firing RPGs at the presidential convoy on its way from the Addis Ababa airport to the venue of Organization of African Unity summit in the Ethiopian capital. The grenade launcher malfunctioned and Mubarak escaped unharmed.
June 21, 2001	Notable Egyptian actress Suad Hosni was found dead beneath the balcony of her London apartment. She was preparing her biography, which was said to contain material that would have hurt important public figures in Egypt. Her manuscript was taken and to date the murderers have not been apprehended.

June 27, 2007	Egyptian billionaire businessman Ashraf Marwan was murdered when he was thrown from his fifth floor balcony of his London apartment in the United Kingdom. He was the son-in-law of Egyptian President Gamal Abdel Nasser. Later he was chief of staff of Egyptian President Anwar el-Sadat. Marwan had been hailed as both Israel's greatest spy in Egypt—code-named "the Angel"[18]—and by Egyptians as their most effective double agent, helping in the *taqiyya* in the days leading up to the start of the October 1973 Yom Kippur War.[19] To this day his murderers have not been apprehended, nor has the question been definitively answered—Who was Marwan really spying for? However, recent analysis seemed to indicate he was one of Israel's best spies.
September 5, 2013	An assassination attempt was made on the Egyptian Interior Minister Mohamed Ibrahim Moustafa. A massive car bomb detonated in his convoy as it traveled through Nasr City, a part of Cairo and his armored car was riddled with bullets, but he escaped unhurt. The blast killed one civilian and injured at least twenty-one. Supporters of the ousted Muslim Brotherhood president, Mohamed Morsi, were believed behind the attempt.

IRAN	
Date	**Event**
651 C.E.	Yazdegerd III, the last Sassanid king of Persia, was assassinated as Arab Muslim forces completed their conquest of Persia. Yazdegerd was murdered in Merv (in present day Turkmenistan).
October 14, 1092	Nizam al-Mulk, vizier to the Seljuk rulers of Persia, was assassinated en route from Isfahan to Baghdad by a member of the *Hashshashin*.
June 19, 1747	Nader Shah, Shah of Iran and founder of the Afsharid Persian Empire, was assassinated by dissident officers at Fathabad in Khorasan.
June 17, 1797	Persian Shah Aga Muhammad Khan was assassinated by his servants and succeeded by his nephew, Fath Ali Shah.
1852	An attempted assassination of Nasir al-Din Shah of Persia, by followers of the Babi movement, failed.
May 1, 1896	Nasir al-Din Shah was assassinated by an Iranian revolutionary and Pan-Islamic follower of Jamal-al-Din Afghani.
August 31, 1907	Persian Prime Minister Amin al-Sultan was assassinated by a terrorist.
June 30, 1930	Ismail Agha Shikak, also known as Simko Shikak, Iranian Kurdish politician and nationalist, was assassinated by the Iranian military in Oshnaviyeh (Ushno).
October 3, 1933	Abdolhossein Teymourtash, first Minister of the Court of Shah Reza Khan and diplomat, was murdered while in prison.
April 1937	Prince Firouz Mirza Nosrat-ed-Dowleh III, former Iranian Foreign Minister, and member of the Qajar dynasty deposed in 1921, was murdered on the orders of Shah Reza Khan.
February 4, 1949	The Tudeh Party attempted to assassinate Shah Mohammed Reza Pahlavi at a ceremony to commemorate the founding of Tehran University. He was wounded but survived.

March 7, 1951	Iranian Prime Minister General Ali Razmara was assassinated by Khalil Tahmasebi, a member of an Islamist terrorist group, *Fedaiyan Islam,* while attending a mosque service.
January 22, 1965	Iranian Premier Hassan Ali Mansur was shot by an assassin—a member of the religious fundamentalist *Fedayan Islam*—and died five days later.
April 10, 1965	A second attempt was made on the life of Shah Mohammed Reza Pahlavi. A soldier shot his way through the Marble Palace in Tehran. The assassin was killed before he reached the Shah's quarters. Two civilian guards died protecting the Shah.
August 12, 1970	The first head of Iran's Organization for Intelligence and National Security (SAVAK), General Teymur Bakhtiar, was assassinated while in exile in Iraq by SAVAK agents.

With the establishment of the Islamic Republic in February 1979, Supreme Leader Ayatollah Ruhollah Khomeini issued a *fatwa* identifying 500 individuals he wanted dead. The killings began. Khomeini died in 1989 but his successor, Ayatollah Ali Khamenei and his associates, continued to carry out assassinations globally. At the time of Khomeini's *fatwa* for the murdering of the opposition, Ali Khamenei was head of the "Committee for Special Operations," along with President Hashemi Rafsanjani; Minister of Intelligence Ali Fallahian, known as "the Butcher" for his appetite for summary executions; and Foreign Minister Ali Akbar Velayati.

Date	Event
May 1979	Ali Akbar Hashemi Rafsanjani was nearly assassinated by the Furqan group.
July 18, 1980	An attempted assassination of former Iranian Prime Minister and opposition leader, Shahpur Bakhtiar took place in a Parisian suburb. It failed.
1980	The left-wing *Mujahedin-e Khalq* attempted to assassinate the Chairman of the Iranian *Majlis* (parliament) Ali Akbar Hashemi Rafsanjani, but while seriously injuring him, did not succeed in killing him.
June 28, 1981	Ayatollah Mohammad Beheshti, Secretary-General of the Islamic Republic Party and head of the judicial branch of government, was assassinated by a massive bomb blast in Tehran by *Mujahedin-e Khalq* terrorists. Seventy-one others were also killed in the blast.
August 30, 1981	Mohammad Ali Rajai, President of Iran and Prime Minister Mohammad Javad Bahonar, Secretary-General of the Islamic Republic Party, were assassinated by a bomb blast during a meeting of Iran's Supreme Defense Council. The *Mujahedin-e Khalq* was later found responsible. During all of 1981, the *Mujahedin-e Khalq* assassinated some 1,200 religious and political leaders, many from the top echelons of the Islamic regime.[20]
April 7, 1982	Former Iranian Foreign Minister, Sadegh Ghotbzadeh, was arrested for plotting to assassinate Iranian Supreme Leader Ayatollah Ruhollah Khomeini. Ghotbzadeh was executed September 15, 1982.
July 13, 1989	Iranian separatist Kurdish politician and Secretary-General of the Kurdistan Democratic Party of Iran, Abdul Rahman Ghassemlou, was assassinated in Vienna, Austria, allegedly by Iranian agents of the Islamic Republic.

August 7, 1991	Former Iranian Prime Minister and opposition leader, Shahpur Bakhtiar, living in exile in Paris, was assassinated by three Iranian agents of the Islamic Republic.
September 17, 1992	Sadegh Sharafkandi, Kurdish separatist, and Secretary-General of the Kurdistan Democratic Party of Iran, was assassinated with three others in the Mykonos restaurant in Berlin, Germany, by Iranian agents acting upon the orders of the Iranian intelligence ministry.
January 19, 1994	Bishop Haik Hovsepian Mehr, of the *Jama'at-e Rabbani* church, part of the Assemblies of God church movement, was brutally assassinated in Tehran. His body was found later, with 26 stab wounds, buried in a Muslim graveyard. He had been an outspoken Christian rights advocate and publicized the plight of Iranian Christians. It is widely believed that he was murdered by Iranian security agents.
February 1, 1994	An assassination attempt against the Iranian President, Ali Akbar Hashemi Rafsanjani, failed.
June 24, 1994	Two Protestant clergymen, Tedhis Mikhailyan and Mehdi Dibaj were abducted and assassinated in Tehran. They had been Christian converts from Islam.
November 22, 1998	Dariush Forouhar, founder and head of the Nation of Iran party and outspoken critic of the Islamic Republic was assassinated together with his wife, Parvaneh.
December 1998	Dissident writers, Muhammad Ja'far Puyandeh, Majid Sharif, and Mohammad Mokhtiari, were assassinated. During the 1990s, over eighty writers, translators, poets, and political activists were murdered for their opposition to the Islamic regime.
February 5, 2000	A bomb intended for the residence of Supreme Leader Ayatollah Ali Khamenei, exploded and killed three and injured six in Tehran in a failed assassination attempt.
March 12, 2000	The attempted assassination of political reformer and journalist, Saeed Hajjarian took place in Tehran. Though not killed, the bullet paralyzed him.
January 15, 2007	Ardeshir Hosseinpour, an authority on electromagnetism and who worked at the nuclear site at Isfahan, was killed in an alleged radioactive poisoning. The perpetrators were never apprehended. Iran accused Israeli operatives of the assassination. Recent revelations by the scientist's sister, Mahboobeh Hosseinpour, stated that her brother was murdered—"gassed"—by Iran's Revolutionary Guards Corps because he would not cooperate with its efforts to divert nuclear work from peaceful purposes to building an atomic bomb. The planned bomb was alleged to be twelve times more powerful than the Hiroshima bomb.[21]
December 27, 2009	Ali Habib was assassinated as he left his home in Tehran. He was the nephew of Iranian opposition leader and June 2009 presidential candidate Mir Hossein Mousavi. The assassination came in the midst of massive anti-regime demonstrations protesting the Islamic leadership and its harsh policies. His death was meant as a signal that the regime would physically eliminate opposition leaders.

January 12, 2010	Another scientist, Masoud Ali Mohammadi, an elementary-particle nuclear physicist who taught at Tehran University, an important hub of nuclear research,[22] was killed by a bomb blast. The bomb detonated by remote control, had been attached to a motorcycle that exploded in front of his house in Tehran. Iranian dissidents claimed that Mohammadi had been killed by the regime because he was a supporter of reformist candidate Mir Hossein Mousavi, whom many believe actually won the 2009 Iranian presidential election before vote tampering led to Ahmadinejad's victory. Iranian government officials however, accused the United States and Israel of being behind the attack. Recent additional evidence seemed to indicate that Iranian intelligence agents might have been the real assassins.[23]
August 1, 2010	Reza Baruni, the father of Iran's military Unmanned Aerial Vehicle (UAV) program, died in an explosion that demolished his home, in Ahwaz, Khuzestan. The assailants remain unknown.
August 4, 2010	An assassination attempt was made on Iranian President Mahmoud Ahmadinejad, when a bomb was thrown at his armored convoy as it drove through Hamadan, in northern Iran. He escaped unhurt, though several bystanders were wounded.
October 8, 2010	*Jundallah*, (the People's Resistance Movement of Iran), based in Baluchistan, and fighting for Sunni rights in Iran, abducted Amir Hossein Shirani, a scientist employed for three years at the Isfahan nuclear facility. In late November, the kidnapped man appeared on the Saudi TV station *Al Arabiya* and described his nuclear work.[24] On December 22, 2010, *Jundallah* threatened to execute Shirani, if the Iranian government did not release some 200 Balochi political prisoners.[25]
November 29, 2010	Iranian scientist, Professor Majid Shahriari, who was responsible for developing the technology to design a nuclear reactor core, was killed as he drove through northern Tehran. He was the Iranian nuclear program's top expert on computer codes and cyber war and headed the team Iran established for combating the Stuxnet virus rampaging through its nuclear and military computer networks. His wife was injured in the attack. On the same day, another Iranian nuclear scientist, Professor Fereydoon Abbasi-Davani and his wife were seriously injured but survived a second coordinated bomb attack as they drove to work in Tehran. He was a high-ranking Iranian Defense Ministry official who was involved in Iran's nuclear and ballistic missile programs. Abbasi-Davani was Vice President for nuclear affairs and Chairman of the Atomic Energy Organization. Witnesses said each car was approached by a group of men on motorcycles, who attached explosives to the vehicles and detonated those seconds later.[26] Some sources suggest that this double attack may have been the work of *Jundallah*.
July 23, 2011	Darioush Rezaeinejad, a rising star among Iranian nuclear scientists, was shot to death by two motorcyclists, in front of his home in Tehran. He was attached to one of the most secret teams of Iran's nuclear program, employed by the defense ministry to construct detonators for the nuclear bombs and warheads at the top-secret Parchin nuclear and military laboratories nineteen miles southeast of Tehran.[27]

November 12, 2011	Massive multiple explosions hit the major Iranian Revolutionary Guard Corps base at Al-Ghadir, killing Major General Hassan Moghadam, the head of the IRGC missile development program, along with 36 others. Iranian supreme leader, Ayatollah Ali Khamenei, along with many other high-ranking Iranian officials, were supposed to be present at a ceremony at the explosion site, but unexpectedly cancelled at the last moment. This may have been an attempt to assassinate the supreme leader and his closest advisers. Many IRGC members, including commanders and even officers at the supreme leader's office, were arrested and investigated.
January 11, 2012	In the fifth, such attack in two years on Iranian nuclear scientists, Professor Mostafa Ahmadi Roshan, was killed by a magnetic bomb planted on his car by two motorcyclists. It exploded near the Sanati Sharif University of Technology in northern Tehran. Roshan was the deputy director for commercial affairs at the Natanz uranium enrichment facility in northern Isfahan province. Iran blamed the Israeli Mossad, but the assailants could have been anti-regime elements of the IRGC.
January 30, 2013	Hassan Shateri, also known by his alias Hush Husam Nawis, a general in the Iranian Revolutionary Guards Corps was killed in Syria. Shateri was one of the leaders of the elite Quds Force within the IRGC commanding all of its and Iran's overseas undercover activities. He acted additionally as the vital Iranian link in the military partnership between Syrian President Bashar al-Assad and the Lebanese Hezbollah leader Hassan Nasrallah. General Shateri was in the process of rapidly establishing a small guerrilla army of 5,000 IRGC fighters and 5,000 Hezbollah operatives for strengthening the defensive ring around Assad's governing institutions in Damascus and its outskirts, secure the main Syria–Lebanon road routes and keep them open to free military movement between the two countries. He served as Iranian President Mahmoud Ahmadinejad's personal emissary to Lebanon and headed the Iranian operation to rehabilitate the southern region of that nation. Additionally, he served as part of Hezbollah's central command and assisted with planning their activities. It was believed that he was killed in the alleged Israeli air strike against a Syrian military complex and arms convoy destined for Hezbollah in Lebanon.
September 28, 2013	The body of General Mojtaba Ahmadi was found in a wooded area near the town of Karaj, northwest of Tehran on September 30. He was shot to death in a suspected assassination. Ahmadi was commander of Iran's Cyber War Headquarters. To date his assailants are unknown.
November 10, 2013	Iranian Deputy Industry Minister Safdar Rahmat Abadi was assassinated while in his car in an eastern neighborhood of Tehran. He was the first central government official killed in many years. He was shot twice in the head and chest from within the vehicle. His attackers were not identified. No organization claimed responsibility, and the motivation for the killing was unknown.

	IRAQ
Date	**Event**
January 27, 661 C.E.	Ali ibn Abi Talib, cousin and son-in-law of Muhammad, as well as the fourth Caliph, was assassinated in Kufa (in present day Iraq). The Umayyad family then claimed rule of the caliphate. This event marked the beginning of the split between Sunnis and Shi'ites in Islam.
August 11, 1937	General Bakr Sidqi, Iraqi Chief of Staff, and Mohammad 'Ali Jawad, the commanding officer of the Iraqi Royal Air Force, were both assassinated in Mosul, by dissident Kurdish army officers.
April 4, 1939	King Ghazi bin Faisal was killed in a mysterious automobile accident, possibly for harboring pro-Nazi sympathies as well as for claiming Kuwait. Iraqi Prime Minister Nuri as-Sa'id may have been behind the "accident." Ghazi was succeeded by his three-year old son, Faisal II. Faisal's uncle 'Abd al-Ilah served as regent until he came of age in 1953.
July 14, 1958	During the military coup that day, King Faisal II, Crown Prince 'Abd al-Ilah, and members of the royal household in the palace were murdered by Arab Nasserite nationalists. The next day, July 15, Iraqi Prime Minister Nuri as-Sa'id was tortured to death. Two Jordanian Ministers in Baghdad at the time, former Jordanian Prime Minister Ibrahim Hashem and Sulaiman Tuqan, were also executed. The total elimination of the entire Iraqi royal family was reminiscent of the Bolshevik execution of Tsar Nicholas II and his entire family in Yekaterinburg on July 17, 1918, during the Russian Civil War. Iraqi coup-leader Colonel Abdel Karim Qassem became the nation's new head of state.
October 11, 1958	An unsuccessful assassination attempt was made on Prime Minister, Abdel Karim Qassem by Abdul Salam Aref at the Ministry of Defense in Baghdad.
October 7, 1959	Prime Minister, Abdel Karim Qassem, was wounded in an attempted assassination as he rode in his car in Baghdad. One of the assassins was Saddam Hussein, who escaped.
February 8, 1963	Prime Minister, Abdel Karim Qassem was executed during a military coup.
April 13, 1966	President Abdul Salam Aref was killed in a helicopter crash in southern Iraq. It is believed that Ba'ath Party members sabotaged the aircraft.
November 6, 1968	Former Foreign Minister Dr. Nasser el Hani was assassinated by Iraqi security agents.
January 27, 1969	Veteran Ba'ath Party leader Colonel Mustafa Nusrat, identified with the Syrian wing of the Ba'athist Party, was assassinated in Baghdad.
June 1969	Sheikh Abd el-Aziz el Badri, prominent Shi'ite leader, was assassinated by Iraqi security agents.
July 1969	Abdelsatr a Khidr, a member of the Central Committee of the Iraqi Communist Party, was murdered.
April 8, 1970	General Abdelghani ar-Rawi, leader of an abortive coup, was assassinated by Iraqi agents in Tehran, Iran.
May 14, 1970	Ali Said, former Iraqi ambassador to Afghanistan, was assassinated in the Iraqi Consulate General in Bombay, India.

March 30, 1971	Hardan al-Takriti, former Vice-President and Minister of Defense, was assassinated in Kuwait.
July 14, 1971	An attempt to assassinate President Ahmed Hassan al-Bakr was thwarted.
September 29, 1971	Nine gunmen hired by the Iraqi government and disguised as Muslim clerics, unsuccessfully tried to assassinate Kurdish leader, Mustafa Barzani.
December 15, 1971	Former Minister of Development, Fuad al Rikabi, was assassinated.
February 18, 1972	An unsuccessful assassination attempt was made on former Iraqi Prime Minister Abd ar-Razzaq al-Naif, in exile in London.
February 27, 1972	Another unsuccessful assassination attempt was made on former Iraqi Prime Minister Abd ar-Razzaq al-Naif, in Cairo, Egypt.
July 3, 1972	The Governor of Sanjar Province in northern Iraq was assassinated.
July 15, 1972	A second unsuccessful attempt was made to assassinate Kurdish leader Mustafa Barzani.
October 12, 1972	Former Foreign Minister Hashem Jawd was assassinated in Beirut, Lebanon.
November 28, 1972	The body of exiled Colonel Salah el-Samarri was found in a Lebanese village, the victim of an assassination.
June 30, 1973	Defense Minister Hamed Shihab was killed and Minister of the Interior General Saddam Ghidan was wounded in an ambush set by the chief of the Iraqi security forces.
July 9, 1978	Former Iraqi Prime Minister Abd ar-Razzaq al-Naif was assassinated in London on orders from Iraqi strongman Saddam Hussein.
April 1, 1980	An Iranian assassination attempt was made on Iraqi Deputy Prime Minister Tariq Aziz, in Baghdad. It failed.
April 15, 1980	Iranian agents made an unsuccessful attempt to murder Iraqi Minister of Information, Latif Nusseif al-Jasim. In April 1980, at least twenty Iraqi officials were killed by Iranian-inspired Shi'ite underground organizations. Iraq retaliated by expelling some 100,000 Shi'ites from the country.[28]
July 8, 1982	An unsuccessful assassination attempt against President Saddam Hussein led to the massacre of nearly 150 Shi'ite Muslims in the town of Dujail. Some 1,500 other residents were jailed and tortured.
October 4, 1982	Ahmed Hassan al-Bakr, President of Iraq (1968–79) was assassinated in Baghdad, most probably on the orders of Saddam Hussein.
May 5, 1989	Iraqi Defense Minister General Adnan Khairallah was killed in a helicopter crash, the third general to die in that fashion within the preceding nine months. It is widely believed that a falling out with Saddam Hussein led to his death.
January 13, 1993	Dr. Raji al-Tikriti, personal physician to President Saddam Hussein was murdered after being implicated in a coup attempt against the Iraqi leader.
July 1996	An assassination plot against President Saddam Hussein by dissident army officers was thwarted.

December 12, 1996	A four-man cell of the "15 Shaaban" Shi'ite resistance movement attempted to assassinate Uday Hussein, the Iraqi president's elder son and heir-apparent. Uday was severely wounded when he was struck by seventeen bullets while driving his Porsche in Mansour, an upscale suburb of Baghdad. He sustained permanent injuries for the rest of his life, and, according to popular belief, rendered impotent (a special kind of justice, because of Uday's reputation for brutal womanizing), but he survived.[29]
February 19, 1999	Grand Ayatollah Mohammad Sadeq al-Sadr, a prominent Shi'ite cleric, and his two sons were assassinated in Najaf by gunmen connected with the Ba'athist regime of Saddam Hussein.
August 19, 2003	Sérgio Vieira de Mello, UN Special Representative in Iraq, was killed in a suicide truck bomb blast at the Canal Hotel, which killed 21 others.
August 29, 2003	Ayatollah Sayed Mohammed Baqir al-Hakim, a prominent Shi'ite cleric was assassinated by a car bomb as he left the Imam Ali Mosque in Najaf. As many as 125 others were also killed in the blast.
September 21, 2003	Aqila al-Hashimi, female member of the Iraqi Governing Council was ambushed and shot by supporters of deposed dictator Saddam Hussein. She died of her wounds five days later.
May 17, 2004	Ezzedine Salim, head of the Daawa Islamic Party, and President of the Iraqi Governing Council, was killed by a car bomb.
November 1, 2004	Hatem Kamil Abdul Fatah, deputy governor of the Baghdad Governate, was assassinated by gunmen in Baghdad. He had challenged claims that Al-Qaeda terrorist mastermind Abu Musab al-Zarqawi was actually in Iraq.
February 8, 2005	The two sons, Ayman, and Gamal, as well as a bodyguard, of the Democratic Party of the Iraqi Nation leader, Mithal al-Alusi, were ambushed and murdered by terrorists in a suburb of Baghdad. The reason for their assassination was that al-Alusi had become the chief Iraqi advocate for liberal values including a free market, free press, religious pluralism, cooperation among democracies in fighting terror, and human—including women's—rights. Al-Alusi had also traveled to Israel and called for the normalization of relations and peace between Iraq and Israel.
June 28, 2005	Sheikh Dhari Ali al-Fayadh, a member of the Iraqi Parliament was assassinated along with his son and bodyguards by a car bomb. The attack was by terrorists working for Abu Musab al-Zarqawi, the head of Al-Qaeda in Iraq.
September 13, 2007	A bomb killed Sheik Abdul Sattar Abu Risha, a Sunni Arab ally of the United States and the Iraqi government.
June 12, 2009	Imam Harith al-Ubaidi, a prominent Sunni leader, head of the Iraqi Accordance Front and deputy head of the Iraqi parliament's Human Rights Committee, was assassinated at the al-Shawaf Mosque in Baghdad. Three other worshippers were also killed in the attack. Iranian and Iraqi Shi'ite extremists were suspected of the murder.

February 13, 2012	A second attempt was made to assassinate Iraqi Human rights advocate and former parliamentarian, Mithal al-Alusi. Two gunmen fired shots at al-Alusi but were driven off by his security detail. Iran was suspected as being behind the attack.
June 8, 2012	While on a visit to Sulaymaniyah, in Iraqi Kurdistan, Mouloud Anfand, the editor-in-chief of the Israel-Kurd Institute's magazine, vanished. The magazine, published in Iraqi Kurdistan, supports Israel, has writers working out of Israel and publishes interviews with senior Israeli officials. There are suspicions that he was kidnapped by Iranian intelligence agents, because of those pro-Israel activities.[30] He has not been seen or heard from since.

JORDAN	
Date	**Event**
July 20, 1951	Jordanian King Abdullah I was assassinated by one of the Grand Mufti Hajj Amin al-Husseini's men at the doorway of Al-Aqsa Mosque in Jerusalem. The main reason for the murder was that Transjordan, in March 1950, had initialed a separate peace with Israel. The King's fifteen year-old grandson, Prince Hussein, was at his side and was hit. A medal that had been pinned to Hussein's chest deflected the bullet and saved his life. Hussein, who would become Jordan's king on August 11, 1952, would survive at least eleven assassination attempts on his own life (some of the most notorious are outlined below).
Early July 1958	A military cadet, Ahmad Yusif al-Hiyari, planned to assassinate King Hussein in a grenade attack, but his plot was foiled.
November 10, 1958	Two UAR/Syrian MiG-17 fighter jets intercepted and attempted to shoot down a DeHavilland Dove civilian aircraft being piloted by King Hussein, in an assassination attempt. Hussein, a skilled pilot, eluded the attackers and the attempt failed.
April 1, 1960	A plot to assassinate Prime Minister Hazza al-Majali and the King's uncle Sharif Nasser was thwarted. Former Prime Minister Abdallah Rimawi was implicated in the plot.
Early August 1960	A Syrian-recruited agent planned to shoot Prime Minister Hazza al-Majali, but was betrayed by his father's alert to the authorities.
August 29, 1960	Prime Minister Hazza al-Majali and twelve others were murdered by an explosive charge planted by pro-UAR-Syrian agents in his office. Forty minutes later a second explosion rocked the same site. The assassins hoped King Hussein would rush to the site of the first explosion and be killed in the blast of the second, but the king had been delayed.
Fall? 1960	Two further attempts were made on King Hussein's life. In the first, an assassin infiltrated the palace and placed deadly acid in the king's nose drops' bottle. In the second, a cook at the palace was to poison the king's food. Both attempts were discovered before they proved fatal.
August 6, 1962	Three men were arrested in Morocco and charged with plotting to assassinate King Hussein during his imminent visit to that country.

October 6, 1969	The Jordanian government announced the uncovering of a plot to assassinate King Hussein.
June 9, 1970	An unsuccessful attempt was made on the life of King Hussein as he drove to Amman.
September 1, 1970	Another unsuccessful attempt was made on the life of King Hussein. It was planned as the opening event of what came to be known as Black September, the attempt to overthrow the Hashemite monarchy which triggered the Jordanian Civil War.
November 28, 1971	Jordan's Prime Minister Wasfi al-Tal was murdered in broad daylight by four Black September terrorists as he entered the lobby of the Sheraton Hotel in Cairo. While Tal lay dying, one of the assassins knelt and lapped with his tongue the blood flowing across the marble floor. That grisly scene, reported in the *Times of London* and other major newspapers, created an image of uncompromising violence and determination that was exactly what PLO chief Yasser Arafat (who claimed responsibility for the killing) both wanted and needed. The four gunmen were subsequently released by the Egyptian government and left that country.
December 15, 1971	Black September terrorists made an unsuccessful attempt to assassinate Zaid Rifai, Jordan's ambassador to the United Kingdom. At the same time, a failed attempt to assassinate the Jordanian ambassador to Switzerland, in Geneva, took place.
November 18, 1972	Another unsuccessful attempt was made to assassinate King Hussein by a dissident air force officer.

KUWAIT	
Date	**Event**
March 30, 1971	While in exile in Kuwait, Hardan 'Abdul Ghaffar al-Tikriti, former Iraqi Minister of Defense, and Deputy Premier, was assassinated. He had been a critic and rival of Iraqi deputy chairman of the Ba'athist Revolutionary Command Council, Saddam Hussein. Hardan was murdered by agents sent by Hussein.
May 2, 1985	Emir Jaber III al-Ahmad al-Jaber al-Sabah, ruler of Kuwait, escaped a suicide car-bomb assassination attempt with only minor injuries.

LEBANON	
Date	**Event**
April 28, 1192	Conrad of Montferrat (Conrad I), King of Jerusalem, was assassinated in Tyre, two days after his title to the throne was confirmed by election. The killing was carried out by the *Hashshashin*.
March 17, 1270	Philip of Montfort, Lord of Tyre, was murdered by a member of the *Hashshashin*.
March 1950	An unsuccessful assassination attempt was made on Prime Minister Riad al-Solh by members of the Syrian Social Nationalist Party.

July 17, 1951	Riad al-Solh, former Prime Minister of Lebanon, was assassinated at Marka Airport in Amman, Jordan, after holding discussions with Jordanian King Abdullah about making peace with Israel. Three days later, on July 20, King Abdullah himself was assassinated for the same reason. The three gunmen who killed al-Solh were agents of the Grand Mufti, Hajj Amin al-Husseini and linked to the Syrian Social Nationalist Party. An additional motivation may have been to avenge the execution of Anton Saadeh; one of the party's founding leaders.
May 7, 1958	Nesib Metni, editor of Lebanon's *Al-Telegragf* newspaper, was murdered by Syrian agents. His death along with several others, helped trigger the First Lebanese Civil War.
July 28, 1959	Former Minister Naim Mughabghab was murdered.
May 16, 1966	Kamel Mrowa, editor of the Beirut newspapers, *Al-Hayat* and *The Daily Star,* was murdered in his office while checking the final proofs of the next day's issue. He was a critic of Egyptian President Gamal Abdel Nasser, the Arab nationalist movement, and radical military regimes. The assassin, Adnan Sultani, was linked to the Lebanese Independent Nasserite Movement.
May 31, 1968	Former President Camille Chamoun was wounded in an assassination attempt by Syrian Ba'athist agents.
September 1976	Edouard Saeb, editor-in-chief of *L'Orient le Jour* and correspondent to *Le Monde,* was shot down by PLO gunmen while crossing Beirut's "Green Line"—the line that divided Beirut (from 1975 to 1990) between Muslim-controlled West Beirut and Christian-controlled East Beirut.
March 16, 1977	Kamal Jumblatt, leader of Lebanon's Druze population and member of the Lebanese parliament, was assassinated in the Shouf area, during the Second Lebanese Civil War. Prime suspects included the Syrian Social Nationalist Party, which Jumblatt had legalized as interior minister several years earlier, Rifaat al-Assad, brother of the Syrian President Hafez al-Assad and the Syrian *Mukhabarat*—intelligence agency.
June 13, 1978	Lebanese politician Tony Franjiyeh, his wife, daughter and thirty-two supporters, were assassinated at his home in Ehden, north Lebanon. The victims died during a raid by the Phalange—or Kata'eb—militia of Bashir Gemayel, a political rival.
August 31, 1978	Iman Musa al-Sadr, the leader of the Lebanese Shi'ite community and founder of the Movement of the Disinherited (a precursor of Hezbollah), mysteriously disappeared. Al-Sadr and two companions, Sheikh Muhammad Yaacoub and journalist Abbas Badreddine departed for Libya August 25, and were never seen again. It is widely believed that Libyan leader Muammar Qadhafi ordered their murder for reasons unknown.

February 25, 1980	Salim Lawzi, a Sunni, owner of the independent Lebanese Arabic weekly *Al-Hawadess*, was a fierce critic of Syrian president Hafez Assad and of the PLO. Lawzi moved his newspaper to London in 1977. Three years later, Lawzi returned to Lebanon to attend his mother's funeral. On February 24, 1980, while driving back to Beirut airport to board a flight to London, Lawzi was stopped and kidnapped near a Syrian army checkpoint, by PLO-affiliated As-Sa'iqa terrorists. This, despite Lawzi having a "safe conduct" pass from Lebanese Prime Minister Salim al-Hus. He was held and gruesomely tortured in the PLO-controlled village of Aramoun. His right arm was broken and dislocated. The fingers of his hands were cut off joint-by-joint and burned with acid. Pens were pierced into his abdomen and intestines, and he was shot in the head. Lawzi was subsequently dismembered and on March 4, 1980, the remnants of his body were found discarded around the town.
March 13, 1980	Syrian agent Hussein Mustafa Teliass attempted to assassinate former President Camille Chamoun with a car bomb. The attempt failed.
July 22, 1980	Riad Taha, a publisher and for thirteen years the president of the Lebanese Publishers' Association, was machine-gunned to death with his chauffeur in front of Beirut's Hotel Continental after a chase through the city. He was a strong critic of the Syrian occupation of Lebanon. The Syrian *Mukhabarat* was believed to be behind the murders.
April 1982	Sunni Sheikh Ahmad Assaf, Director of the Union Islamic Associations and Institutions in Lebanon, was assassinated. It is believed that Shi'ite Hezbollah was behind the murder.
September 14, 1982	Lebanon's President-elect, Christian Maronite leader Bashir Gemayel, was assassinated by a bomb blast, which demolished the building housing his Phalange Party headquarters in East Beirut. Shi'ite Hezbollah terrorists linked to Syria and Iran were behind the blast. During the Second Lebanese Civil War, Gemayel secretly accepted military supplies from Israel, and was ready to sign a peace treaty with the Jewish state.
October 1986	Sunni Sheikh Subhi al-Salih, the head of the Supreme Islamic Shari'a Council of Lebanon, was murdered after criticizing Syria's role in fanning sectarian violence. It is believed that Hezbollah agents carried out the assassination.
January 7, 1987	Former President Camille Chamoun survived yet another assassination attempt as a car bomb killed forty others.
May 18, 1987	Hassan Hamdan, also known as Mahdi Amel, was the ideologue and a member of the Central Committee of the Lebanese Communist Party. He was assassinated near his home in the area of Al-Mulla in Beirut, while on his way to the Institute of Social Sciences at Lebanese University where he taught. It is widely believed he was murdered by Hezbollah agents.
June 1, 1987	Lebanese Prime Minister Rashid Karami was assassinated by a bomb placed in his army helicopter that was carrying him from Tripoli to Beirut, Lebanon. Interior Minister Abdullah al-Rasi and three others were wounded. The attack was carried out by the Lebanese Forces, a Christian militia. Karami had been backed by Syria, then occupying Lebanon.

August 2, 1987	Dr. Muhammad Shoukeir, special advisor to President Amin Gemayel, was assassinated by Syrian agents in his home in West Beirut.
May 16, 1989	The Sunni Grand Mufti of Lebanon, Sheikh Hassan Khalid, was assassinated by a 300-pound car bomb as he drove through West Beirut's Aishe Bakkar neighborhood. His son-in-law and twenty other people were also killed and eighty were injured. Khaled was a moderate, advocating coexistence between Lebanon's numerous factions and the replacement of the Syrian military presence in Lebanon by a Gulf Cooperation Council-led force. The assassination was widely believed to be the work of Syria using Hezbollah agents.
September 22, 1989	Nazem el Qadri, a Sunni Muslim member of Lebanon's Parliament for thirty-eight years, was gunned down by three assassins as he left a barbershop on Beirut's Verdun Street. Also killed was el Qadri's driver. Lebanese legislators at the time were preparing to negotiate an agreement in Taif, Saudi Arabia, to end the Second Lebanese Civil War and set a deadline for Syrian occupation to end. El Qadri was critical of the Syrian presence. His assassination, though never investigated, was likely Syria's signal to other legislators not to press for a Syrian withdrawal.
November 22, 1989	Lebanese President Rene Moawad, a Maronite Christian in office only seventeen days, was killed by a huge bomb blast under his motorcade in West Beirut. He was returning from Independence Day ceremonies in West Beirut. Twenty-three other people were killed in the blast. Moawad wanted to establish a unity government to end the Second Lebanese Civil War, then in its fourteenth year.
October 12, 1990	Syrian agent, François Halal, following a plan supervised by the Secretary-General of the Lebanese Ba'ath Party, Abdallah Alamin, attempted to assassinate General Michel Aoun at the Baabda Presidential Palace.
October 21, 1990	Dany Chamoun, chairman of the National Liberal Party, son of former President Camille Chamoun, and former Maronite Christian militia leader was assassinated at his home in East Beirut by Syrian agents posing as Lebanese army soldiers. His wife and two sons were also murdered in the attack. Chamoun was an ally of General Michel Aoun, the renegade army general who opposed the Syrian-backed government of President Elias Hrawi.
February 16, 1992	Abbas Mussawi, the leader of the Hezbollah terrorist group, and four bodyguards were killed by an Israeli helicopter ambush near the village of Jibsheet in southern Lebanon.
August 31, 1995	Sheikh Nizar Al-Halabi, leader of Al-Ahbash, was assassinated. His group was linked to the Syrian regime, and was opposed to Islamic fundamentalism.
January 24, 2002	Elie Hobeika, former minister and leader of the Phalange and Lebanese Forces—a Christian militia—was assassinated by car bomb in Hazmiyeh, a suburb of Beirut. Hobeika played a leading role in the September 16, 1982, massacre of Palestinian Muslims in the Sabra and Shatila refugee camps in West Beirut.

May 7, 2002	Ramzi Albert Irani, a prominent member of the Lebanese Forces Party, was kidnapped by Syrian agents on his way home, in West Beirut. His dead mutilated body was found seventeen days later in the trunk of his automobile.
May 20, 2002	Mohammed Jihad Ahmed Jibril, son of the founder of the Popular Front for the Liberation of Palestine-General Command (PFLP-GC) Ahmed Jibril, was assassinated by a car bomb in Beirut. The younger Jibril was commander of the military wing of the PFLP-GC. Both Lebanese Christian militia and Israeli agents were suspected of the killing.
July 19, 2004	Hezbollah member, Ghaleb Awali, was killed when a bomb exploded outside his home in Beirut. Among other activities, Awali had worked on Palestinian operations against Israel. A Sunni group, *Jund al-Sham* ("Soldiers of Greater Syria"), claimed responsibility for the assassination. Nevertheless, Hezbollah blamed Israel.
February 14, 2005	Lebanon's former Prime Minister, Rafik Hariri, was assassinated by a massive 1,000-pound truck bomb that exploded as his automobile convoy travelled near the St. George Hotel in the Hamra district of Beirut. Also killed were twenty-one others. The perpetrators were Hezbollah terrorists. Hariri, a Sunni, was pro-Saudi, pro-Western and was viewed as a major obstacle to Hezbollah's domination of Lebanese politics. On August 17, 2011, a UN-mandated court indicted four Hezbollah operatives: Mustafa Badreddine, Salim al-Ayyash, Hasan Aineysseh and Asad Sabra. On January 16, 2014, the trial opened in the Hague, with the four suspects still on the run. Hariri, a Sunni Muslim, was a staunch critic of Syria's occupation of Lebanon. His assassination triggered massive rallies and prompted the "Cedar Revolution," which in turn led to the withdrawal of Syrian military forces that spring, after a 29-year occupation.
June 2, 2005	Anti-Syrian journalist Samir Kassir was assassinated when a bomb detonated in his car outside his home in East Beirut's Ashrafiyeh district. Kassir was a front-page columnist for the *al-Nahar* newspaper, where he wrote columns criticizing the pro-Syrian regime. It is believed that Syrian or Lebanese security forces were behind the assassination.
June 21, 2005	George Hawi, former Secretary-General of the Lebanese Communist Party and a resolute critic of Syria and its intelligence service, died when his car exploded as he was driving through Beirut's Wata Musaitbi district.
December 12, 2005	Gebran Tueni, member of Parliament and former editor-in-chief of *An-Nahar*, a Beirut daily newspaper, was assassinated by a car bomb that killed three others and wounded ten. The explosion blew up his armored SUV near his residence east of Beirut. He was well known for his 2000 "Open Letter" to Syrian president Bashar al-Assad, in which he criticized Syrian interference in and occupation of, Lebanon. Tueni's assassination coincided with the release of the second progress report of a United Nations inquiry into Syria's involvement in the assassination of Rafik Hariri.

November 21, 2006	Lebanese Minister of Industry, Pierre Gemayel, Phalange Party leader, was assassinated in an auto ambush in the Sin El Fil suburb of Beirut. His murder took place in the midst of a standoff between lawmakers calling for the UN tribunal to investigate Hariri's assassination and Syrian-allied members, led by Hezbollah, seeking to block it. March 14 Alliance party members accused Syria of the assassination. The March 14 Alliance was a collection of parties united by their opposition to Syrian involvement in Lebanon. Gemayel was the son of former Lebanese president Amin Gemayel (whose brother, Bashir, was assassinated in 1982, days before becoming president), and the grandson of Pierre Gemayel, founder of the right-wing Christian Phalange Party.
June 13, 2007	Walid Eido, a Sunni member of the Lebanese Parliament and a member of the Future Movement headed by Saad Hariri (the son of Rafik Hariri) was assassinated by a car bomb as he drove near Beirut's waterfront. He was a harsh critic of Syria. His son, two bodyguards and six others also died in the attack.
September 19, 2007	Antoine Ghanem, a Christian member of the Lebanese Parliament, and a member of the Phalange Party, was assassinated by a car bomb in Sin el-Fil, a Christian suburb of Beirut. Six others were killed and seventy were injured in the attack. Ghanem was a member of the anti-Syrian March 14 Alliance and fled Lebanon in fear for his life, returning just two days before the assassination.
December 12, 2007	A seventy-seven-pound car bomb killed Major General François al-Hajj, Lebanese Army Chief of Operations, and four others in Baabda, Lebanon, as he drove to work at the Defense Ministry. Al-Hajj was one of the commanders of the battle of Nahr el-Bared, where the Lebanese army defeated *Fatah al-Islam*, an Islamist militant group in the Palestinian refugee camp near Tripoli, Lebanon. Al-Hajj was to succeed General Michel Suleiman, the army chief who became Lebanon's president in 2008.
January 25, 2008	A car bomb killed Wissam Eid, a captain in Lebanon's Internal Security Forces. Eid was collecting evidence regarding the mobile communication equipment used by the Hezbollah hit men in the assassinations of Rafik Hariri and others.
October 19, 2012	The anti-Syrian, anti-Hezbollah, head of Lebanon's Internal Security Forces intelligence branch, Brigadier General Wissam al-Hasan, was killed in a massive car bomb blast in East Beirut's Ashrafiya district. Seven others were killed and seventy-three injured in the explosion. The previous August, General Al-Hasan uncovered a Syrian plot to destabilize Lebanon by a bombing campaign and arrested the pro-Syrian politician and ex-information minister Michel Samaha for complicity in the plot. He also led the investigation that implicated Damascus in the 2005 bombing atrocity that killed former Prime Minister Rafik Hariri.

August 22, 2013	Hassan al-Mouri, a Sunni militia leader, was shot to death by gunmen on motorbikes, along with a security official and a bystander, in Tripoli, Lebanon. Hassan and his family were supporters of the Shi'ite Hezbollah as well as Syria and Iran. A Sunni terrorist group, the Company of Aisha Umm al-Muminin, claimed responsibility for the assassination, in revenge for Hezbollah participation in the killing of Sunnis in Syria.
December 4, 2013	Hassan al-Laqqis, Hezbollah's chief military procurement officer was assassinated when gunmen shot him in the head as he arrived at his home in the Hadath suburb of Beirut, Lebanon. A militant Sunni group, *Ahrar al-Sunna Baalbek Brigade* claimed responsibility for his murder, though Hezbollah blamed Israel. Israel denied any involvement in the matter.
December 27, 2013	A car bomb in downtown Beirut killed former Minister of Finance and ambassador to the United States, Mohamad Chatah, a senior aide to former Lebanese Prime Minister Rafik Hariri. Chatah was a staunch critic of Iranian-backed Hezbollah, as well as Syrian President Bashar al-Assad. Five others were killed and at least seventy were injured.

LIBYA	
Date	**Event**
May 8, 1984	Members of the National Front for the Salvation of Libya attacked Muammar Qadhafi's headquarters at Bab al-Aziziyah barracks near Tripoli in an attempt to assassinate the Libyan leader. The attack was foiled.
June 1, 1998	An assassination attempt on Qadhafi's life failed, though a Libyan Islamic opposition group claimed it had killed four bodyguards and wounded Qadhafi in the attack.[31]
July 27, 2011	General Abdel Fatah Younis, commander of the Libyan rebel forces fighting Muammar Qaddafi, during the 2011 civil war, was put to death on the orders of Mustapha Abdul Jalil, head of the rebel Transitional National Council. Jalil was fearful Younis would emerge as a key leader in a post-Qadhafi government.
September 11, 2012	To mark the eleventh anniversary of the al-Qaeda attack on the US mainland, Libyan Ansar al-Shari'a terrorists affiliated with Al-Qaeda, in Benghazi, killed the US Ambassador to Libya, Christopher Stevens, and three other American diplomats during a violent attack on the US consulate there.
August 29, 2013	Libya's military prosecutor, who was in charge of cases involving Qadhafi-era regime officials, Colonel Yussef Ali al-Asseifar died when a bomb placed under his car exploded. The prosecutor's brother was also killed in the blast.
June 26, 2014	Salwa Bugaighis, lawyer, and prominent female activist was assassinated in her home in Benghazi by gunmen who killed her and abducted her husband. It is believed that one of the many Islamist militias in the city were responsible for her death.

MOROCCO	
Date	**Event**
October 29, 1965	Mehdi Ben Barka, exiled leader of the left-wing opposition National Union of Popular Forces, was kidnapped and vanished in Paris, France, by Moroccan agents directed by Moroccan Interior Minister Muhammad Oufkir. Ben Barka's body was never found.
July 10, 1971	During an attempted coup by dissident army officers, an unsuccessful assassination attempt was made on King Hassan II while he was celebrating his forty-first birthday at his palace. The plot failed but the ensuing bloodbath resulted in the death of 97 guests and 157 others were wounded. Ten high-ranking military officers were publicly executed and hundreds of other people were imprisoned.
August 16, 1972	A second unsuccessful assassination attempt to murder King Hassan II was made by dissident Moroccan Air Force officers flying F-5 jets. They attempted to shoot down his Boeing 727 aircraft as he returned from a trip to France. The assassination attempt was organized by General Muhammad Oufkir, Minister of the Interior, who was found shot to death later that same day.
OMAN	
Date	**Event**
April 26, 1966	An unsuccessful assassination attempt was made on the life of Sultan Sa'id ibn Taimur III.
SAUDI ARABIA	
Date	**Event**
November 3, 644 C.E.	The second caliph of the Rashidun dynasty, Umar bin al-Khattab, was attacked by Pirouz Nahavandi, a Persian Zoroastrian assassin in Medina. Umar died of his multiple knife wounds four days later.
July 17, 656	Uthman ibn Affan, the third caliph of the Rashidun dynasty, was assassinated in Ta'if by opponents of his rule. This event triggered an Islamic civil war.
March 25, 1975	King Faisal of Saudi Arabia was assassinated by his nephew who had a history of mental illness. The nephew was beheaded in June 1975.
August 27, 2009	Prince Muhammad bin Nayef, Saudi deputy Interior Minister in charge of counter terrorism, who spearheaded the kingdom's crackdown on Al-Qaeda, was slightly injured, when an Al-Qaeda suicide bomber blew himself up at an open Ramadan gathering in Jeddah. Nayef was the son of Minister of Interior Nayef bin Abdul Aziz and a nephew of Saudi King Abdullah. His assailant, Abdullah Hassan Tali al-Asiri, known as Abul Khair, was a mole for Al-Qaeda and smuggled the explosive into Nayef's palace concealed in his underwear. The bomber was killed in the explosion but his body protected Prince Nayef from the full force of the explosion.[32]
SOMALIA	
Date	**Event**
October 15, 1969	President Abdirashid Ali Shermarke was assassinated in Las Anod, Somalia, by one of his own bodyguards.

SUDAN	
Date	**Event**
May 9, 1968	William Deng, a southerner and founder of the Sudan African National Union, and six of his group were assassinated in Lakes State. He favored autonomy for southern Sudan. The Sudanese army was responsible for the deaths.
March 27, 1970	There was an unsuccessful attempt to assassinate President Jaafar Nimeiry by followers of the Al-Ansar religious sect, led by Imam al-Hadi al-Mahdi.
March 31, 1970	During a government-organized massacre of the Al-Ansar sect, Imam al-Hadi al-Mahdi and his son were murdered trying to escape to Ethiopia.
March 2, 1973	An eight-man Black September hit squad kidnapped two American diplomats, from the Saudi Embassy in Khartoum. They demanded the release of Sirhan Sirhan, the Palestinian assassin of US Senator Robert F. Kennedy. Under orders (secretly recorded by the CIA) from Yasser Arafat, they executed US officials Cleo A. Noel, Jr., and G. Curtis Moore, as well as a Belgian diplomat, Guy Eid.
July 30, 2005	John Garang, President of the Government of Southern Sudan, First Vice-President of Sudan and former leader of the rebel Sudan People's Liberation Army, died in a suspicious helicopter crash in Uganda.
January 1, 2008	John M. Granville, a US diplomat working in the Southern Sudan was assassinated by terrorists in Khartoum.

SYRIA	
Date	**Event**
September 14, 1146	Imad ad-Din Atabeg Zengi, Islamic governor of Mosul, Aleppo, Hama and Edessa, who fought the Christians and triggered the Second Crusade, was assassinated by a slave.
May 22, 1176	Kurdish Muslim leader, Saladin, survived an assassination attempt by the *Hashshashin* near Aleppo, Syria.
July 6, 1940	Syrian nationalist and founder of the People's Party, Abd al-Rahman Shahbandar, was assassinated by opponents from the Syrian National Bloc.
August 14, 1949	President Husni al-Za'im and Prime Minister Mushin al-Barazi were assassinated.
July 31, 1950	The commander of the Syrian Air Force, Colonel Muhammad Hassan Nasser, was murdered.
October 29, 1950	General Sami Hinnawi, former military ruler of Syria, was assassinated while in exile, in Beirut, Lebanon.
April 22, 1955	Colonel Adnan al-Maliki, Syria's Deputy Chief of Staff, was assassinated.
September 27, 1964	Former President Adib Shishakli, was assassinated while in exile at Ceres, Brazil, by Nawaf Ghazaleh, a Syrian Druze. Ghazaleh sought revenge for the bombardments of Jabal al-Druze during Shishakli's rule in the early 1950s.
June 11, 1966	Tama Oudah-Allah, a former Minister, was murdered while in exile in Cairo, Egypt.
June 4, 1970	Political leader, Mustafa Samana, was assassinated in Aleppo, Syria.

March 4, 1972	The former Minister of Defense, Muhammad Umran, was murdered while in exile in Tripoli, Lebanon.
July 10, 1973	President Hafez al-Assad was wounded in an attack by a would-be assassin.
June 25, 1980	Syrian President Hafez al-Assad survived a machine gun and hand grenade assassination attempt, made by the Sunni Muslim Brotherhood in Damascus. The Brotherhood sought to destabilize and overthrow the Shi'ite Alawi Assad regime, using assassinations and urban guerrilla warfare. As a result, in July 1980, Assad had the Syrian parliament pass Law No. 49 which declared membership in the Muslim Brotherhood a capital offense. These events would lead to the Hama Massacre.
July 21, 1980	Salah al-Din Bitar, Syrian politician, prime minister of Syria (1963–66), foreign minister (1956–57) and one of the three founders of the Ba'ath Party was assassinated in Paris, France. He was an outspoken opponent of Syrian President Hafez al-Assad, and his predominantly Alawite government. It is widely believed that an Alawite gunman was behind his murder.
January 1, 1994	Basil Assad, heir-apparent and eldest son of President Hafez al-Assad was killed in an automobile accident. There was suspicion in some quarters that he was assassinated and the Syrian media have referred to him as "Basil the Martyr."
August 1, 2008	General Muhammad Suleiman, security advisor to President Bashar al-Assad, and liaison officer to Hamas and Hezbollah, was assassinated by an unknown sniper at a resort near Tartus. Suleiman also participated in the secret Syrian nuclear project. American intelligence sources tied Suleiman to the transfers of chemical weapons from Iraq to Syria in 2003, on the eve of the US invasion of Iraq.[33] Suleiman may have been the victim of an internal power struggle. The assailant remains unknown.
August 9, 2011	During the anti-regime violence that engulfed Syria, former Syrian Defense Minister Ali Habib was shot to death hours after President Bashar Assad fired him. Assad suspected Habib of plotting with dissident officers to launch a coup against him and had Habib murdered.
October 2, 2011	Anti-regime gunmen, murdered both Sariya Hassoun, the son of Syria's Grand Mufti Ahmad Hassoun, a high profile Assad supporter, and Mohammad al-Omar, a senior university professor as they rode in a car on the road between Idlib and Aleppo.
October 7, 2011	In reprisal, Mashaal Tammo, the founder of the Kurdish Future Party, former member of parliament and opposition leader in the protests against the Assad regime, was assassinated by masked men who burst into his apartment in Qamishli, in northern Syria. It was believed that the killing was the work of a death squad run by the Syrian Air Force Intelligence Directorate, whose main function was safeguarding the Assad family at home and abroad.
July 18, 2012	Syrian Defense Minister General Dawoud Rajiha, the Deputy Defense Minister, Assef Shawkat (President Bashar Assad's brother-in-law), General Hasan Turkmani, Assistant to the Vice President and former Defense Minister, as well as Hisham Ikhtiyar, Syria's Intelligence and National Security Chief, were all killed after a suicide bomber struck the National Security headquarters in Rawda Square, Damascus.

April 29, 2013	Syrian Prime Minister Wael al-Halaqi survived a car bombing attack that targeted his convoy in the Mazzeh district in central Damascus. At least one person was killed in the assassination attempt.

TUNISIA	
Date	**Event**
August 12, 1961	Former Minister Salah Ben Yusef, exiled opponent of President Habib Bourguiba, was assassinated in a hotel in Frankfurt, Germany. Egypt's President Gamal Abdel Nasser publicly accused President Bourguiba of having ordered the killing.
October 9, 1971	Omar Suheimi, an Iraqi sentenced to death *in absentia* by a Tunisian court for plotting to assassinate President Bourguiba, was murdered in Beirut, Lebanon.
April 16, 1988	Khalil al-Wazir, also known as Abu Jihad, military chief of the PLO was assassinated at his home in Tunis. Wazir had planned many murderous attacks on Israelis. On November 2, 2012, Israel admitted responsibility for his death.
January 14, 1991	Salah Khalaf, also known as Abu Iyad, intelligence chief of the PLO, second in command to Yasser Arafat's Fatah terrorist group and Black September organizer, was assassinated in Tunis, by a rival Abu Nidal terrorist.
February 6, 2013	Opposition leader and head of the secular leftists Democratic Patriots party Chokri Belaid, was shot dead outside his home in n El Menzah, close to the capital, Tunis. He was a vocal critic of the Ennahda Movement as well as the Islamist-led Tunisian government. The Salafist Ansar al-Shari'a terrorist group was blamed for the assassination.
July 25, 2013	Opposition leader Mohamed Brahmi was shot dead in his car outside his home in Tunis. He was the founder and leader of the People's Movement. Brahmi was shot with the same pistol that killed Chokri Belaid the previous February. The Salafist Ansar al-Shari'a, a terrorist group was blamed for the assassination.

TURKEY	
Date	**Event**
October 11, 1579	Sokollu Mehmed Pasha, Grand Vizier to Sultan Murad III, was assassinated by a Dervish (a Sufi Muslim ascetic).
May 20, 1622	Sultan Osman II was assassinated by disgruntled palace janissaries (bodyguards).
April 6, 1909	Hassan Fehmi Bey, anti-Unionist journalist and editor of the *Serbesti,* was assassinated by government agents. Since his murder, at least sixty-four journalists were assassinated in Turkey as of 2010.
June 11, 1913	Mahmud Şevket Pasha, Grand Vizier to Sultan Mehmed V, was assassinated in Istanbul.
February 1, 1979	Abdi Ipekçi, journalist, editor-in-chief of the newspaper *Milliyet,* and human rights activist was killed by members of the ultranationalist and neo-fascist "Grey Wolves" (Idealist Youth) movement, in Istanbul. One of the two assassins was Mehmet Ali Agca, who later shot Pope John Paul II.

July 19, 1980	Former prime minister, Nihat Erim, was assassinated by gunmen of the radical leftist *Dev Sol* (Revolutionary Left) group.
January 31, 1990	Muammer Aksoy, law professor, politician, democratic reformer and advocate of a secularist Turkey, was assassinated by Islamic fundamentalist terrorists in Ankara.
October 6, 1990	Bahriye Ucok, former member of parliament, politician, and women's rights advocate, was assassinated by Islamic fundamentalist terrorists.
June 28, 1992	Admiral (ret.) Kemal Kayacan, former commander of the Turkish Navy, was assassinated.
January 24, 1993	Ugur Mumcu, investigative journalist for the Turkish newspaper, *Cumhuriyet,* and human rights advocate, was murdered by a bomb placed in his car.
October 21, 1999	Ahmet Taner Kislali, former Minister of Culture, journalist (also for *Cumhuriyet*) and politician, was assassinated by a bomb believed planted by Islamic fundamentalist terrorists.
May 17, 2006	Mustafa Yucel Ozbilgin, Turkish Supreme Court judge, was assassinated in Ankara. Four other judges were wounded in the attack.
July 6, 2006	Hikmet Fidan, a Kurdish politician trying to form the Patriotic Democratic Party promoting non-violent action for the Kurds, was shot dead by PKK gunmen, in Diyarbakır, in southeastern Turkey.
January 19, 2007	Hrant Dink, journalist, editor of *Agos,* human and minority rights advocate and campaigner for Turkish-Armenian reconciliation, was assassinated in Istanbul by Ogün Samast, a 17-year old Turkish nationalist. Turkish security forces may have been complicit in his death.

UNITED ARAB EMIRATES	
Date	**Event**
January 24, 1972	During a bloody attempted palace coup, the ruler of the Emirate of Sharjah (now part of the United Arab Emirates), Sheikh Khalid III ibn Muhammad al-Qasimi was assassinated. The coup failed.
October 25, 1977	Minister of State, Saif Ibn Said al-Ghubash was assassinated during an attempt on the life of the visiting Syrian Foreign Minister, Abdel Halem Khaddam.
April 16, 1985	The UAE oil minister escaped an assassination attempt.

YEMEN (includes events in the former Aden colony, Aden Protectorate, the Mutawakkilite Kingdom of Yemen, the Yemen Arab Republic and the People's Democratic Republic of Yemen, as well as the unified Republic of Yemen)	
Date	**Event**
February 17, 1948	The King of Yemen, Imam Yahya Hamid ed-Din, three of his sons and his Prime Minister Abdullah Al-Amri, were all assassinated during a motoring excursion outside the capital. Abdullah al-Wazir, an accomplice to the crime, took over as ruler.
March 1948	Abdullah al-Wazir was overthrown and he was beheaded.
March 26, 1961	An attempted assassination of Imam Ahmed at the hospital at Hodeida failed, though he was wounded. One would-be assassin shot himself. Two others were caught and beheaded.

April 1, 1965	Muhammad Mahmud al-Zube'eri, moderate political leader was murdered.
April 13, 1966	The Minister for Local Administration, Qadi Abdullah el Iryani, was assassinated in Sana'a.
June 24, 1966	Ali Hussein Qadi, President of the Aden Council of Labor Federations, was murdered.
October 6, 1966	Miakram Ghaleb, former General Secretary of Aden's Al-Umah Party, was assassinated.
February 26, 1967	A former minister in then-Aden colony, Said Muhammad, was murdered.
January 25, 1969	Colonel Abd Arraqib Abdel Wahab, former chief of staff of the Yemen Arab Republic (YAR) Army, was assassinated.
July 25, 1969	Emir Abdullah Ben Hassan, a member of the deposed Yemeni royal family, was assassinated while praying in the mosque of Saada.
April 3, 1970	Faysal al-Shaabi, former Prime Minister of the PDRY, was murdered while "attempting to flee his detention camp."
May 22, 1972	An unsuccessful assassination attempt was made on PDRY Prime Minister Muhammad Ali Haitham.
August 14, 1972	An assassination attempt was made on YAR former Prime Minister Hassan al-Amri. It was unsuccessful.
October 9, 1972	Ismail Ben Ahmed al-Marhabi, a member of the YAR Presidential Council, was assassinated.
March 20, 1973	Sources in Beirut, Lebanon, reported that forty PDRY opposition leaders were invited to attend discussions with PDRY government officials and were killed during the meeting in a mass assassination.
May 30, 1973	A second member of the YAR Presidential Council, Sheikh Muhammad Ali Uthman, was murdered by PDRY Marxists.
October 11, 1977	YAR President Ibrahim al-Hamdi was assassinated by Saudi Arabian-funded agents looking to delay the YAR's unification with the PDRY.
June 24, 1978	YAR President Ahmed al-Ghashmi was assassinated by means of a suitcase-bomb, while meeting with an envoy from the PDRY at a conference in Beirut, Lebanon.
June 26, 1978	PDRY President Salim Ali Rubai was deposed and immediately executed after a coup by the pro-Soviet National Liberation Front.
January 13, 1986	PDRY President Ali Nasir Muhammad attempted a gangland-style massacre of his rivals on the 15-member Politburo of the ruling Yemeni Socialist Party. Vice President Ali Antar, who was considered the president's main rival, Defense Minister Saleh Muslih Qassem and party disciplinary chief, Ali Shayi Hadi were all killed. The multiple murders triggered fierce fighting between rival Marxist factions in Aden, which led to Ali Nasir Muhammad's ouster on January 24, 1986.
December 28, 2002	Jarallah Omar, deputy secretary-general of the Yemen Socialist Party, and a secular Marxist, was murdered in Sana'a by an Islamic fundamentalist assassin.
June 3, 2011	There was an assassination attempt on President Ali Abdullah Saleh, when a bomb exploded in the mosque in the presidential palace. Saleh was seriously injured but survived.

September 27, 2011	An Al-Qaeda in the Arabian Peninsula suicide bomber drove a bomb-laden car into the convoy of Yemeni Defense Minister Mohamed Nasser Ali in an attempted assassination. The minister survived the blast but several of his bodyguards did not.

Additionally, there have been other notable Middle East-related assassinations in history, both within and out of the region. These include, but are not limited to, those listed in the table below.

OTHER ASSASSINATIONS RELATED TO THE MIDDLE EAST	
EGYPT	
Date	**Event**
November 6, 1944	Walter Guinness, Lord Moyne, the British Resident Minister in Egypt, was assassinated in Cairo by *LEHI*, due to his public opposition to Jewish immigration to Palestine during World War II. Moyne was one of the British officials held responsible for, among other things, the *Struma* disaster. The MV *Struma,* was a dilapidated ship—actually a 75-year-old cattle boat—carrying Jews fleeing the Holocaust from Romania. The British steadfastly refused visas to the passengers and did not let the ship proceed to Palestine, even after it broke down. Furthermore, the British persuaded Turkey not to allow the passengers to disembark. Under British pressure, the *Struma* was ejected by the Turks from Istanbul harbor and towed into the Black Sea. The *Struma* was sunk (possibly by accident), February 24, 1942, by a Soviet submarine, *Shch-213,* killing 781 men, women and children, as well as 10 crewmen, with only one survivor, a 19 year old man, David Stoliar. Even in the wake of the *Struma* disaster, the British War Cabinet, on March 5, 1942, reaffirmed its determination not to let "illegal" Jewish refugees enter Palestine. Moyne had claimed (falsely, as later events proved) that Palestine (in 1942) was too small and too crowded to accept millions of Jewish refugees attempting to flee for their lives from the Holocaust then in full swing in Nazi-occupied Europe.
IRAN	
Date	**Event**
Fall 1954	Tudeh Party dissidents plotted the assassination of Shah Mohammad Reza Pahlavi as part of a planned coup. The plot was discovered and crushed.
May 30–31, 1972	The left-wing *Mujahedin-e Khalq* failed to assassinate General Harold Price, head of the US Military Mission in Iran.
June 2, 1973	The *Mujahedin-e Khalq* assassinated Colonel Lewis Hawkins, the deputy chief of the US Military Mission in Iran.
July 22, 1980	Ali Akbar Tabatabaei, the former Iranian press attaché (under the Shah) at the Iranian Embassy in Washington, DC, was shot to death at his home in Bethesda, Maryland. Tabatabaei was a critic of Ayatollah Khomeini and was president of the Iran Freedom Foundation. The assassin was Dawud Salahuddin, an American Muslim convert, who escaped to Iran.

February 14, 1989	Iran's Supreme Leader, Ayatollah Ruhollah Khomeini sentenced British Indian author Salman Rushdie, to death for publishing his novel, *The Satanic Verses,* inspired in part by the life of Muhammad. Khomeini called for the assassination of Rushdie and "all those involved in the publication who were aware of its contents"[34] by any "good Muslim." Khomeini's edict marked the start of "creeping shari'a" or stealth jihad against the West.
December 9, 2006	Former Iranian Deputy Defense Minister Brigadier General Ali-Reza Asgari vanished after he arrived in Istanbul, Turkey. He was never seen again. Some claim he defected to the West. According to the *Sunday Times,* Asgari was described as a "gold mine for western intelligence."[35] Iran charged first, that Western intelligence agencies kidnapped him, naming the British, German and Israeli secret services. Then, Iran claimed the American CIA had a role in his disappearance. Still later, Iran charged that the Israeli Mossad abducted him and he died, while in their hands, at Ayalon Prison.[36]
May 16, 2010	General Khalil Sultan, of the Iranian Revolutionary Guard Corps al Qods section, was killed at his home in the Al Mezzeh district of Damascus. The Al Qods branch operated in Damascus and Beirut, eliminating anti-Iranian elements in Syria and Lebanon. To date, his assailants are unknown.

ISRAEL	
Date	**Event**
September 26, 1937	Lewis Yelland Andrews, the British district commissioner for the Galilee, along with a deputy and a bodyguard were on their way from attending services at the Anglican Christ Church, Nazareth, when they were gunned down by four Arabs linked to Sheikh Izzedine al-Qassam, the Grand Mufti of Jerusalem, Hajj Amin al-Husseini, and the Arab Higher Committee. Andrews died on the spot and his deputy a short while later. Legally, Andrews transferred tens of thousands of dunams of land to Jewish ownership, and helped establish dozens of Jewish communities in the Hula Valley region, the Beit She'an Valley and the Hefer Valley. He supported the report of the Peel Commission, which favored the partition of the British Mandate of Palestine, for which he was branded as anti-Arab and targeted for assassination. Additionally, during the Arab Revolt of 1936–39, he prevented the demolition of Rachel's Tomb in error by British troops who thought it was an abandoned ordinary structure. On October 1, five Arab leaders were arrested and deported to the Seychelles, and the Arab Higher Committee was outlawed. The Grand Mufti Hajj Amin al-Husseini was deposed from the presidency of the Muslim Supreme Council, and fearing arrest, fled to Beirut, Lebanon.

September 17, 1948	The *LEHI* assassinated Count Folke Bernadotte in Jerusalem. Bernadotte, who was appointed by the UN to mediate between the Arabs and Jews, had without authority, unilaterally changed the provisions of the UN Partition plan of 1947, which had been passed by a majority of the General Assembly. Bernadotte's proposal was for a gutted and shrunken Jewish state, a forced Arab–Jewish union, Arab sovereignty over Jerusalem, detachment of the Negev desert from Israel, and after two years of unlimited Jewish immigration, all future Jewish immigration to be regulated by the Arab majority—in effect slamming the door shut permanently to future Jewish immigration to Israel.
January 18, 1968	King Hussein of Jordan warned Israel via the US Embassy in Amman, of a PLO terrorist plot to assassinate Israeli officials, most prominently, Moshe Dayan.[37]
May 23, 1971	Efraim Elrom, Israeli Consul General to Turkey, was assassinated in Istanbul, by terrorists of the Turkish People's Liberation Army, which was affiliated with the PLO.
September 19, 1972	Israeli Agricultural counselor/attaché, Ami Shechori, was killed by the explosion of a letter bomb sent to him at the Israeli Embassy in London, the United Kingdom. Black September terrorists claimed responsibility.
July 1, 1973	Israeli Air Force attaché, Yosef Allon, was assassinated outside his home in Washington, DC.
November 13, 1979	An unsuccessful assassination attempt was made on Ephraim Eldar, the Israeli ambassador to Portugal, in Lisbon. Nevertheless, he was wounded, a guard was killed and two others were injured.
April 3, 1982	Israeli attaché, Yakcov Bar Simantov, was assassinated in Paris, France. The Revolutionary Armed Factions of Lebanon claimed responsibility.
June 3, 1982	Israel's Ambassador to the United Kingdom, Shlomo Argov, was gravely wounded when terrorists from Abu Nidal's Palestinian Fatah group attempted to assassinate him outside the Dorchester Hotel in central London. This event was the spark that triggered the Israeli invasion of Lebanon—Operation *Peace for Galilee*—June 6, 1982, to wipe out PLO bases in Lebanon. Argov died in 2003, at age 73, from injuries sustained in the attack.
March 4, 1988	A car filled with 100 pounds of explosive was found abandoned after its driver crashed into a utility pole. Fatah claimed credit for the failure and announced that US Secretary of State George Shultz, who was staying in the Jerusalem Hilton Hotel, had been the intended target.
March 7, 1992	Ehud Sadan, security chief at the Israeli Embassy in Ankara, Turkey, died in a car bomb attack. The Islamic Jihad terrorist group claimed responsibility.
November 4, 1995	Israeli Prime Minister Yitzhak Rabin was mortally wounded by an assassin while at a peace rally in Tel Aviv. The assassin was presumably protesting the continued Arab terrorist attacks, including suicide bombings against Israel, which Rabin's Oslo Accords with PLO chief Yasser Arafat were supposed to stop.

December 31, 2000	Binyamin Ze'ev Kahane, son of Rabbi Meir Kahane, and founder of the Kahane Chai Party, was assassinated along with his wife Talia, near Ofra. The couple was murdered by Palestinian terrorist Mustafa Muslimani of the Fatah Force 17.
October 17, 2001	Israeli Minister of Tourism, former general and founder of the Moledet Party, Rehavam Ze'evi was assassinated in the Jerusalem Hyatt hotel by four PFLP terrorists.
April 2005	Members of the PFLP plotted to assassinate the co-founder and spiritual head of the Shas party Rabbi Ovadia Yosef, in Jerusalem. Yosef was the former Chief Sephardic Rabbi of Israel. Israeli security services foiled the plot in April 2005.
August 31, 2009	Rawi Sultani, an Israeli Arab and Hezbollah agent, was arrested and indicted for planning to assassinate IDF Chief of Staff Lt.-General Gabi Ashkenazi and other senior Israeli officials.
October 29, 2014	Rabbi Yehuda Glick was the victim of an attempted assassination as he left the Menachem Begin Heritage Center in Jerusalem. He was shot three times at point-blank range by Muataz Hijazi, a member of the Islamic Jihad terrorist group. Glick was targeted because he was a vocal and political activist seeking to restore the rights of Jewish worship on the Temple Mount and sought to expand Jewish access to the area. The assassin was tracked down and killed. Glick survived.

JORDAN	
Date	**Event**
October 28, 2002	Laurence Foley, diplomat and Supervisory Executive Officer of USAID in Jordan was assassinated in Amman by agents of Abu Musab al-Zarqawi, who headed the al-Tawhid wal-Jihad terrorist group. In late 2004, al-Zarqawi would be named as Al-Qaeda leader in Iraq.

KUWAIT	
Date	**Event**
April 14–16, 1993	A thwarted assassination attempt was made against former US President George H.W. Bush during a visit to Kuwait. On June 26, 1993, the United States launched a missile attack targeting Iraq's Baghdad intelligence headquarters in retaliation for its role in the attempt.

LEBANON	
Date	**Event**
June 16, 1976	Frances E. Meloy, US ambassador in Lebanon, Robert O. Waring, US Economic Counselor, and their driver, were shot to death by PFLP terrorists in Beirut.
September 3, 1981	Syrian agents assassinated the French ambassador to Lebanon, Louis de Lamar.
November 21, 2002	A Syrian agent assassinated 31-year-old Bonnie Penner-Witheral, an American missionary, in her pre-natal clinic in Sidon.

QATAR	
Date	**Event**
February 13, 2004	Zelimkhan Yandarbiyev, acting President of the breakaway Chechen Republic of Ichkeria, was assassinated by a bomb blast in Doha, capital of Qatar. Russian security forces were suspected of the attack.

SYRIA	
Date	**Event**
May 1, 1981	Heinz Nittel, a leader of the Austrian Socialist party and the president of the Austrian-Israeli Friendship League, was shot to death outside his home in Vienna by Hesham Mohammed Rajeh, of the Abu Nidal terrorist group, under Syrian auspices.
February 12, 2008	Hezbollah military mastermind and operations officer, Imad Mughniyah was killed in a massive car bombing in the parking lot of Kfar Suseh neighborhood of Damascus, Syria. Mughniyah was involved in carrying out some of Hezbollah's most spectacular terrorist attacks. He was reputed to be the commander of Islamic Jihad. Mughniyah orchestrated many terrorist attacks against the United States, France, Kuwait, Israel and Jewish targets worldwide, killing hundreds of Americans, Israelis, and others. The US FBI maintained Mughniyah was responsible for "all but eliminating the US military presence in Lebanon."[38] Prior to September 11, 2001, Mughniyah was considered the terrorist credited with having slain the most Americans (over 350) and topped the FBI Most Wanted Terrorist list with a US $20 million bounty on his head. These acts of terrorism included the following:<ul><li>The April 18, 1983 car bombing of the US Embassy in Beirut, Lebanon, which killed eighty-three persons, seventeen of whom were Americans. It was the deadliest attack on a US diplomatic mission up to that time.</li><li>The October 23, 1983, bombings in Beirut, Lebanon, of the US Marines barracks killing 241 US service members, and the French barracks, killing 58 French servicemen and six civilians.</li><li>The April 12, 1984, attack on a restaurant near the US Air Force Base in Torrejon, Spain. The bombing killed eighteen US servicemen and injured eighty-three people.</li><li>The September 20, 1984, car bombing of the US Embassy annex building in East Beirut, Lebanon, in which sixteen were killed and the US ambassador was injured.</li><li>The June 14, 1985, TWA Flight 847 hijacking (to be fully discussed later—*see* "Basic Principle 52"). Mughniyah was indicted for the murder of US Navy diver Robert Stethem, murdered during that hijacking.</li><li>The April 5, 1988, hijacking of Kuwait Airways Flight 422, in which two Kuwaiti passengers were murdered at Larnaca, Cyprus.</li></ul>

- Mughniyah was also linked to the kidnappings of more than fifty Americans, Frenchmen, Britons, Germans and other foreigners who were abducted during the Second Lebanese Civil War (1975–90). These included, most notably: William Buckley, the CIA station chief in Beirut, kidnapped on March 16, 1984, who was hideously tortured and eventually murdered; Terry Anderson, chief Middle East correspondent for the Associated Press, abducted March 16, 1985, and only released on December 4, 1991; Terry Waite, Anglican Church negotiator, taken hostage himself on January 20, 1987 and held 1,763 days until his release on November 18, 1991; and US Marine Corps Colonel William Richard "Rich" Higgins, who, while serving with the UN Military Observer Group, was kidnapped on February 17, 1988, tortured and subsequently murdered. A year and a half after his abduction, images of his body, hung by the neck, was televised around the world, from a videotape released by Hezbollah. The exact date of Colonel Higgins' murder is uncertain; he was declared dead on July 6, 1990.

- Mughniyah was formally charged by Argentina with participating in the March 17, 1992 bombing of the Israeli Embassy in Buenos Aires. The massive explosion destroyed the embassy, a Catholic church, and a nearby school building. Among the casualties, several were Israelis, but most of the victims were Argentine civilians, many of them children. The blast killed twenty-nine and wounded 242.

- Additionally, Mughniyah was formally charged with the July 18, 1994, Hezbollah car bomb attack on the *Asociación Mutual Israelita Argentina* (AMIA) Jewish Community Center in Buenos Aires. The attack resulted in ninety-six people killed and over 200 injured.

- Mughniyah was linked to the June 25, 1996, Khobar Towers truck bombing. The Khobar Towers was a housing complex at Al-Khobar, near Dhahran, Saudi Arabia. The attack killed nineteen US Air force personnel, and one Saudi. Three hundred seventy-two Americans and Saudis were injured.

- Mughniyah was believed to be behind the October 7, 2000 abduction of three Israeli soldiers at Har Dov, in northern Israel. This abduction was aided and abetted by UNIFIL forces. UNIFIL turned a blind eye to the kidnapping, and it is believed they provided Hezbollah with UN uniforms, insignia, and vehicles.

- In mid-October, Hezbollah leader Nasrallah announced the group had also kidnapped an Israeli businessman, Elchanan Tenenbaum. In 2004, Israel freed over 400 Arab terrorist prisoners in exchange for Tenenbaum and the bodies of the three soldiers.

- On July 12, 2006, Hezbollah launched a cross-border attack, killing eight Israeli soldiers and abducting two, Ehud Goldwasser and Eldad Regev. This triggered the Second Lebanon War between Hezbollah and Israel. Goldwasser and Regev were subsequently murdered and their bodies were returned to Israel on July 16, 2008.

TURKEY	
Date	**Event**
March 15, 1921	Mehmed Talat, former Grand Vizier and Minister of the Interior, was assassinated while in exile in Berlin, in revenge for his role in the Armenian Genocide. His death was part of Operation *Nemesis* launched by the Armenian Revolutionary Federation. It was a covert operation in the 1920s to assassinate the Turkish planners of the Armenian Genocide. Some of those individuals are listed below.
December 6, 1921	Said Halim Pasha, former Grand Vizier during World War I, was assassinated in Rome as part of Operation *Nemesis*.
April 7, 1922	Both Bahattin Şakir and Jemal Azmi were assassinated in Berlin as part of Operation *Nemesis*. Şakir was claimed to be one of the leaders of a Turkish special forces unit—*Teskilat-i Mahsusa*—which carried out executions of Arabs and Armenians. Azmi, was responsible for the deaths of thousands of Armenians.
July 25, 1922	Ahmed Djemal, commonly known as Cemal Pasha, former Turkish Minister of Marine and Fifth Army commander, was assassinated in Tbilisi (in present-day Georgia) as part of Operation *Nemesis*.
August 14, 1922	Ismail Enver, known as Enver Pasha, former Minister of War, was killed near Dushanbe, Tajikistan, by a unit of Red Army cavalry commanded by an Armenian. This too, was part of Operation *Nemesis*.
January 28, 1982	Turkish Consul General Kemal Arikan was shot to death in Los Angeles, California. The Justice Commandos of Armenian Genocide claimed responsibility.
January 9, 2013	Sakine Cansiz, a founder of the Kurdistan Workers' Party (PKK), was shot to death, execution-style, along with Fidan Dogan, a representative in France of the Brussels-based Kurdistan National Committee, a lobbying group and Leyla Soylemez, a young Kurdish activist. The three women were murdered, at the Kurdish Institute of Paris, France. It is suspected that either dissident factions within the PKK or Turkish nationalists were behind the assassinations.
UNITED ARAB EMIRATES	
Date	**Event**
January 19, 2010	Mahmoud al-Mabhouh, co-founder of Hamas, one of the founders of and military commander of the Izz ad-Din al-Qassam Brigades (the military wing of Hamas) as well as a key liaison between the Hamas government in Gaza and the Al-Quds Force of Iranian Revolutionary Guard Corps, was killed in the Al Bustan Rotana Hotel in Dubai, UAE. Al-Mabhouh, an al-Qassam Brigades operative, was involved in several armed actions targeting Israel, including the abduction and killing of two Israeli soldiers in 1989.[39] Later, Mabhouh was also in charge of logistics and smuggling weapons,[40] as well as being responsible for procuring rockets from Iran to Gaza through Sudan and Egypt. It is widely believed that an eleven-man Israeli Mossad team assassinated him,[41] although Egypt, and Jordan, also had outstanding arrest warrants for Mabhouh.

November 12, 2011	Ahmed Rezaie, the son of Mohsen Rezaie, was found dead in the Gloria Hotel in Dubai. The elder Rezaie was secretary of the powerful Iranian Expediency Council and former IRGC commander. The manner of Ahmed's death bore similarities to that of Mahmoud al-Mabhouh, almost two years earlier. In 1999, Ahmed gave interviews to American and Western media, including the Voice of Israel's Farsi station, in which he openly criticized Iran's rulers, especially Supreme Leader Ayatollah Ali Khamenei. Ahmed may have been assassinated as a warning to his father, who has a close relationship with former president turned opposition leader, Hashem Rafsanjani.
OTHER	
Date	**Event**
May 13, 1981	Pope John Paul II was shot and seriously wounded in St. Peter's Square, Rome, Italy, by Turkish Muslim assailant Mehmet Ali Agca. The Pope survived the assassination attempt.
April 10, 1983	After criticizing the PLO for its defeat in the 1982 Israel–PLO War in Lebanon, and favoring negotiations with Israel, PLO moderate, Issam Sartawi, was shot and killed in the lobby of the Montechoro Hotel in Albufeira, Portugal. He was attending a meeting of the Socialist International. His assassination was later claimed by the Abu Nidal Organization.
July 22, 1987	Palestinian cartoonist Naji al-Ali, was shot in the face outside his office in London and mortally wounded. Al-Ali had been critical of the PLO and various Arab regimes. It is believed that Fatah military branch commander, Kahlil al-Wazir, also known as Abu Jihad, ordered his murder. Al-Ali died of his wounds on August 29, 1987.
November 5, 1990	Rabbi Meir Kahane, founder of the Kach Party, former Israeli Member of Knesset, and founder of the Jewish Defense League, was assassinated in a New York City hotel, by El Sayyid Nosair, an Egyptian immigrant. Nosair was a follower of Sheikh Omar Abdul-Rahman ("the Blind Sheikh") who later launched the first attack on the World Trade Center on February 26, 1993.
November 2, 2004	Dutch filmmaker, Theodoor "Theo" van Gogh was assassinated by Mohammed Bouyeri in Amsterdam, the Netherlands, for his production of the film *Submission,* which dealt with violence against women in some Islamic societies. The killer, an Islamic fundamentalist, shot van Gogh eight times, slashed his throat nearly decapitating him and nailed with a knife into his chest, a five-page note threatening the West with more of the same for "insulting" Islam.

For the sake of the historical record, attention must also be called to the alleged Israeli use of assassination. Unlike its Arab/Muslim neighbors, democratic Israel does not use assassination as a method for instituting political change at home. Additionally, Israel is often blamed for killings that are the responsibility of others. If selective assassinations have been used, they were/are against terrorists with blood on their hands. The State of Israel has a policy that it never confirms or denies its participation in selective assassinations.

It should be further noted that targeted killing has been used by governments around the world, and has become a frequent tactic of the United States and Israel against terrorists. Two examples carried out by the former were the September 14, 2009 assassination of Saleh Ali Saleh Nabhan, a top Al-Qaeda leader in Africa, killed in a helicopter raid in southern Somalia by US Navy SEALs.[42] A more noted illustration was the killing—Operation *Neptune Spear*—of former Al-Qaeda leader Osama bin Laden, on May 2, 2011, in Abbottabad, Pakistan, by US Navy SEALs of the US Special Operations Command. As for the Israelis, the IDF uses the term "focused foiling" (*sikul memukad* in Hebrew) to describe such targeted assassinations. Israel has consistently tried to avoid the loss of civilians when engaged in this tactic. The list below, by its very definition, cannot be all-inclusive. It is representative of who those individuals were and why they were targeted.

ALLEGED OR ATTRIBUTED ISRAELI RETALIATORY ASSASSINATIONS [43][44]	
Date	**Event**
July 11, 1956	From 1951 to 1956, Colonel Mustafa Hafez was the Egyptian commander of military intelligence in the Gaza Strip. He was responsible for all the Egyptian *fedayeen* activities against Israel, with the object to murder and terrorize, mainly civilians. He was killed by a parcel bomb in his Gaza office.
July 12, 1956	Lieutenant-Colonel Salah Mustafa was Egyptian military attaché in Amman, Jordan, who worked for Mustafa Hafez and dispatched *fedayeen* via Judea and Samaria (the Jordanian-occupied West Bank) to Israel on terror missions. Interestingly, he took no precautions even as news told of his superior's death the day before. Mustafa opened a parcel containing an explosive device hidden in a book, in his car immediately after retrieving it from the East Jerusalem post office. He was killed by the blast.
August 1962–early 1963	German rocket and jet propulsion scientists, several of whom were former Nazis, working in Egypt and building a missile program, were killed by parcel bombs, simply vanished or were scared away, forcing the end of the project (for further details *see* "Project *Ibis*" in "Basic Principle 55").
July 8, 1972	Ghassan Kanafani, one of the PFLP's major planners behind the Lod Airport Massacre in Israel, was killed by a car bomb in Beirut, Lebanon. Kanafani had recruited the Japanese Red Army terrorists to perpetrate the attack on the airport.

The Lod Airport Massacre occurred on May 30, 1972, when three members of the Japanese Red Army (a Japanese terrorist group) recruited and trained by the Popular Front for the Liberation of Palestine-External Operations (PFLP-EO), attacked Tel Aviv's Lod airport (now Ben Gurion International Airport). In a plan masterminded by Wadie Haddad, Israeli security personnel were caught unprepared for an attack by Japanese nationals, arriving on an Air France plane from Rome at 10 P.M. The attackers using assault rifles and grenades killed 26 people (including 17 Christian pilgrims from Puerto Rico) and injured 80 others. Two of the attackers were killed, while Kozo Okamoto was captured after being wounded.

July 25, 1972	PLO information officer and adviser to Yasser Arafat, Bassam Abu Sharif, who was the PFLP mastermind behind the Dawson's Field (near Zarka, Jordan) quadruple air hijackings on September 6, 1970, was the victim of an attempted assassination, via a book bomb, in Beirut, Lebanon. He lost four fingers, hearing in one ear and the sight of one eye, but survived. It is to be recalled that the Dawson's Field hijackings triggered the events of Black September and the Jordanian Civil War. It is possible that either Jordanian intelligence or the Israeli Mossad was responsible for the attempt on his life.
October 16, 1972	Abdel Wael Zwaiter, PLO terrorist and officially a translator at the Libyan Embassy in Rome, was tied to Black September and the Munich Olympic Games massacre of eleven Israeli athletes. He was shot twelve times at the doorway to his apartment building in Rome, Italy as part of Operation *Wrath of God.*
December 8, 1972	Mahmoud Hamshari, PLO representative in France, and a coordinator of the Munich Olympic Games massacre, was blown up by a bomb in his telephone, in Paris, France, as part of Operation *Wrath of God.*
January 24, 1973	Hussein Al Bashir, PLO-Fatah representative in Nicosia, Cyprus, was killed by a bomb in his hotel room bed. He was believed to be head of Black September in Cyprus. His death may have been part of Operation *Wrath of God.*
April 6, 1973	Basil Al-Kubaissi, PFLP member, was killed by two gunmen in a Paris, France, street. The killing was part of Operation *Wrath of God.*
April 9–10, 1973	The assassination of three PLO-Fatah-Black September commanders and operations officers took place as part of Operation *Spring of Youth.* Muhammad Youssef Al-Najjar, PLO "foreign minister," Kamal Adwan, PLO Chief of Operations and chief of PLO terror attacks within Israel, and Kamal Nasser, PLO spokesman, were shot to death in their apartments in Beirut, Lebanon, by IDF *Sayeret Matkal* Special Forces. The Special Forces were led by Ehud Barak (future Israeli Prime Minister) dressed in civilian clothes as a woman.
April 11, 1973	Zaiad Muchasi, PLO representative in Cyprus, was killed in his hotel room in Athens, Greece.
June 28, 1973	Black September director of operations in France, Mohammad Boudia, was killed by a pressure mine under his car seat in Paris, France, as part of Operation *Wrath of God.*
July 21, 1973	The attempted killing of Ali Hassan Salameh, mastermind of the Black September Munich Olympic Games massacre, was made in Lillehammer, Norway, as part of Operation *Wrath of God.* Unfortunately, in error, the hit team killed an innocent Moroccan waiter, Ahmed Bouchiki.
1976	The attempted assassination, by poisoned envelopes, of Wadie Haddad, head of the PFLP military wing and later his own group, PFLP-EO (External Operations) and its sub-group, PFLP-SOG (Special Operations Group). Haddad was responsible for several airplane hijackings, including an El Al Israel Airlines plane in July 1968, the Dawson's Field hijackings in 1970, as well as the hijacking of Air France Flight 139 to Entebbe, Uganda, in June 1976. He was also the mastermind behind the Lod Airport Massacre of May 30, 1972.

March 28, 1978	Wadie Haddad, died in an East German hotel about a month after eating Belgian chocolates coated with a slow-acting and undetectable poison.[45]
January 22, 1979	Ali Hassan Salameh, also known as "The Red Prince," and four bodyguards, were assassinated in Beirut, Lebanon, by a remotely detonated car bomb. He was operational chief in executing the Black September Munich Olympics Games massacre of eleven Israeli athletes in September 1972.
July 26, 1979	Zuheir Mohsen, the leader of the pro-Syrian as-Sa'iqa terrorist group, was shot to death in front of a casino in Cannes, France. As-Sa'iqa was involved, not only in attacks on Israel, but was also responsible for the Damour Massacre of Lebanese Christians on January 20, 1976, during the Second Lebanese Civil War. The Abu Nidal group, Lebanese Christians, Iraq or Israel may have been responsible for his assassination.
June 13, 1980	The Egyptian-born head of Iraq's nuclear program, Yehia El-Mashad, was killed in his hotel room in Paris, France, as part of Operation *Sphinx*. He had worked on Saddam Hussein's nuclear weapons program.
August 21, 1983	Top PLO Fatah official, Mamoun Meraish, was shot dead in his car by two men on a passing motorcycle, in Athens, Greece. Meraish was on his way to the Greek port of Piraeus to visit a ship he purchased for $450,000 that police believed he had intended to use for secret PLO shipping operations.
April 16, 1988	The deputy head of the PLO, and Yasser Arafat's right hand man, Khalil al-Wazir, also known as "Abu Jihad," was shot dead, while in bed with his wife in Tunis, Tunisia. One of the founders of Fatah in 1964, he was instrumental in planning many operations against Israeli targets. The Savoy Hotel attack in Tel Aviv, of March 4–5, 1975, and the Coastal Road Massacre of March 11, 1978, were among many operations he planned. Furthermore, he orchestrated attacks on Jordanians during Black September in 1970, and Lebanese during the Second Lebanese Civil War that began in 1975. He was the key planner of the first Palestinian *intifada*. Al-Wazir was killed during a joint Mossad and IDF *Sayeret Matkal* Special Forces raid on his home. His wife, lying next to him, was unharmed. The Israeli operation involved some twenty-six Israeli commandos, operating from an Israeli ship in the Mediterranean Sea off the Tunisian coast.[46]
March 22, 1990	Gerald Bull, Canadian engineer and artillery expert was shot and killed outside his apartment in Brussels, Belgium. Bull assisted the Iraqi government of Saddam Hussein during the Iran–Iraq War with long range artillery development. Additionally, after that conflict, Bull designed and constructed superguns for Iraq as part of its Project *Babylon*. The planned superguns would have barrels of 512 feet. The guns would be able to fire 600-kilogram projectiles to a range of some 620 miles, or 2,000-kilogram rocket-assisted projectiles into orbit. The superguns were potentially capable of firing chemical, biological and nuclear weapons. After his death, the project stopped and parts of the superguns were seized by British Customs in transit around Europe in November 1990. Following the 1991 Gulf War, UN teams destroyed one 350 mm supergun, components of a 1,000 mm supergun, and supergun propellant.

February 16, 1992	The co-founder and Secretary General of Hezbollah, Abbas Moussawi was assassinated in southern Lebanon, when his motorcade was hit by missiles fired from IAF Apache helicopters. He had been the former head of both the Hezbollah Security Apparatus and the Islamic Resistance, Hezbollah's military wing. As such, he had ordered operations (including hostage taking) against American, Lebanese and Israeli targets.
June 8, 1992	Atef Bseiso, PLO official involved in the Munich Olympic Games massacre, was shot in the head at point blank range in his hotel in Paris, France, as part of Operation *Wrath of God*.

During the 1991 Gulf War, Israel complied with the US request not to retaliate against Iraq, which for some six weeks, fired thirty-nine Scud missiles against the Jewish state, resulting in fourteen Israeli deaths, and some 230 wounded, though Israel was not a belligerent in that conflict.

Nevertheless, under then Israeli Prime Minister Yitzhak Shamir, Israel began planning a delayed response—a bold, top-secret plan to assassinate Iraqi leader, Saddam Hussein, code-named Operation *Bramble Bush*. There was concern that the Iraqi leader could develop more weapons of mass destruction, as indeed he attempted to do, despite UN restrictions. As IDF Chief of Staff Ehud Barak would tell ABC News, "This guy was a distorted character that presented, in my judgment, a profound, long-term, critical kind of threat to the State of Israel as well as to the whole region."[47]

The plan was to hit Saddam in Tikrit, his hometown, when he attended the funeral of his father-in-law, Khairallah Tilfah.[48] Tilfah, whose daughter Sajida married Saddam, was dying of complications from diabetes at the time.[49] Members of the IDF's elite Special Forces—*Sayeret Matkal*—would use C-130 Hercules aircraft, (other sources claim the special forces would come by helicopters[50]) flying low to avoid radar, to secretly drop commandos and jeeps deep in Jordan from where they would enter Iraq. The teams equipped with missiles would drive to a point about seven and one-half miles from the cemetery at al-Ouja. Scouts would move much closer, dig in and wait. When Saddam arrived, they would give the signal to fire the TV-guided "Midras" missiles.[51][52] The operation was approved by then Israeli Prime Minister Yitzhak Rabin and set for the night of November 7, 1992.[53]

The operation ended on November 5, 1992 (two days before the scheduled launch date), during one of the final rehearsals of the exercise. A model of the cemetery at al-Ouja was built at the Tze'elim training base in the southern Negev desert. Five of the elite soldiers acted as Saddam and his bodyguards. For reasons never fully established but thought to include fatigue, a captain ordered the firing of live, instead of dummy missiles leading to the death of the five soldiers.[54][55] Israeli military censors' suppressed publication until December 16, 2003, three days after US forces captured the former dictator hiding in a spider hole.[56]

In late 1998, the plan to assassinate Saddam was revived and approved by then Prime Minister Benjamin Netanyahu, as Operation *Bramble Bush II*. The Israeli Mossad learned that Saddam followed a predictable pattern after leaving the home of his mistress going to a secret military site nearby, a trip of some 15–20 minutes. The Mossad claimed to have a source who knew in advance when Saddam would visit his mistress.[57] The plan called for elite forces to be inserted into Iraq, break into two teams, the larger to remain some six miles away from the target, and the smaller team to move to within 200 to 300 meters from the target. Once Saddam was spotted, the order for missiles to be launched would be given.

Israeli sources said the operation was canceled because the schedule for the attack coincided with the four-day American and British bombing campaign against Iraq—Operation *Desert Fox,*

December 16–19, 1998—and because then Foreign Minister Ariel Sharon and then Defense Minister Yitzhak Mordechai doubted the accuracy of Mossad's information.[58]

Date	Event
October 26, 1995	The head of the Damascus-based Palestinian Islamic Jihad, Fathi Shiqaqi, was shot to death in front of his hotel in Sliema, Malta. Shiqaqi was behind the January 22, 1995, massacre of twenty-two Israelis, mostly soldiers, who were killed and sixty-nine others injured when two Palestinian suicide bombers detonated themselves at the Beit Lid Junction near Netanya, Israel.
January 5, 1996	Yahya Ayyash, also known as *Al-Muhandis* ("The Engineer"), was the main Hamas bomb maker. The bombings he orchestrated, during the 1990s, caused the deaths of at least ninety Israelis, with hundreds more wounded. He was killed by a remotely detonated cell phone in the Gaza Strip.
September 25, 1997	A failed attempt to assassinate Hamas political leader, Khaled Meshal took place in Amman, Jordan. The assassination was intended as retaliation to the 1997 Mahane Yehuda Market bombings in Jerusalem. Two operatives squirted a fast-acting poison in Meshaal's ear, but were chased down by his bodyguards and arrested. Under pressure from both the United States and Jordan, Israel handed over the antidote. A prisoner release by Israel secured the release of the jailed Israeli agents.
November 9, 2000	Hussein Abayat, Tanzim leader and local head of the Al-Aqsa (Second) *Intifada* was killed when an Israeli helicopter gunship blasted his car near Bethlehem, Judea.
November 22, 2000	The head of Tanzim, Fatah's military wing, Jamal Abdel Raziq, was killed with his driver in his car, after being fired on by IDF troops in the Gaza Strip. Tanzim's specialty was "drive-by shootings of Jewish motorists"[59] on Israeli highways and roads.
July 31, 2001	Hamas political leader, Jamal Mansour, was killed when missile fire hit his office in Nablus, Samaria. Mansour was part of the Hamas leadership responsible for attacks against Israeli civilians including the June 1, 2001 suicide bombing of the Dolphinarium discotheque in Tel Aviv that killed 21 people and wounded 132.
August 27, 2001	Secretary General of the PFLP, Abu Ali Mustafa, was killed when missile fire hit his office in Ramallah, Samaria. He was personally responsible for at least ten separate car bomb attacks in Israel.
October 14, 2001	Abed Rahman Hamad, a senior member of the Hamas military wing, was shot by snipers at his home in Qalqilya, Samaria. Hamad was part of the Hamas leadership responsible for attacks against Israeli civilians including the June 1, 2001, suicide bombing of the Dolphinarium discotheque in Tel Aviv.
October 18, 2001	Atif Abayyat, a member of Tanzim was killed along with two others when a car exploded in Beit Sahour. This followed the assassination of Israeli Cabinet Minister Rehavam Ze'evi by the PFLP in Jerusalem.

November 23, 2001	Mahmoud Abu Hanoud, a senior Hamas commander in Judea and Samaria was killed by IAF missile fire near Nablus. Hanoud's deputy, Ayman Hashaykah and Hashaykah's brother, a lower-ranking Hamas activist were also killed. Hanoud was part of the Hamas leadership responsible for attacks against Israeli civilians including the June 1, 2001 suicide bombing of the Dolphinarium discotheque. Additionally, he also planned the attack on a Sbarro pizzeria in Jerusalem on August 9, 2001. Fifteen people were killed in that attack, seven of them children, and 130 were wounded.
January14, 2002	Raed Karmi, a commander of the Tanzim was killed by a bomb blast in Tulkarem, Samaria. Karmi was responsible for the death of nine Israelis in Judea and Samaria.
March 5, 2002	Mohand Said Muniyer Diriya, a member of Force 17 and the operations officer for Tanzim, along with two other members of Force 17, Fawzi Hamdi Mustafa Maher and Oman Kaidan, were all killed by a missile strike on their car, in Ramallah, Samaria. Dirya and the others were responsible for at least fourteen attacks on Israelis between October 2000 and February 2002, resulting in the deaths of ten, including a Greek monk.
March 14, 2002	Mutasen Hamad, a leader of the Al-Aqsa Martyrs Brigades, and his assistant Fatah activist Maher Balbiti were killed by an IAF missile strike on their workshop for building bombs at a chicken farm next to the village of Anabta.[60] Hamad was considered a top bomb maker for Tanzim.
April 22, 2002	Tanzim leader in Hebron, Marwan Zaloum, and his top aide, Samir Abu Rajoub, a member of Force 17, were killed in a missile strike. Zaloum was believed to be responsible for numerous shooting attacks and bombings, including the March 26, 2001, killing of Shalhevet Pass, a ten-month-old infant, in a sniper attack in Hebron.
June 30, 2002	Hamas master bomber Muhaned Taher and his deputy Imad Draoza were killed in a raid in Nablus by IDF naval commandos. Taher, known as "the Engineer 4," was responsible for supplying the bombs used in the June 18, 2002, Jerusalem Egged No. 32 bus bombing that killed 19 and wounded 74, and in the June 1, 2001, Dolphinarium discotheque in Tel Aviv.
July 22, 2002	Salah Shehade was killed in an IAF F-16 air strike in Gaza City, which killed fourteen others including his wife and daughter. From 1996 to 2002, he was a top leader of the Izz ad-Din al-Qassam Brigades and instrument in organizing the suicide bombing campaign against Israeli civilian and soldiers, which killed hundreds of Israeli civilians, as well as the manufacture of Qassam rockets to fire against Israel.
March 8, 2003	Hamas terrorist, Ibrahim al-Makadmeh and three associates were killed by a missile strike on their car, in Gaza City. All were connected with the deaths of twenty-eight Israelis. Al-Makadmeh was number two in the Hamas leadership and the leader of its military wing.
April 9, 2003	Senior Islamic Jihad commander and bomb maker Mahmoud Zatma, was killed when a missile fired by an IAF Apache helicopter hit the car he was driving in Gaza City. It was believed he was behind the January 22, 1995, Beit Lid Junction suicide bombings.

June 11, 2003	Two members of the Hamas military wing, Tito Massoud and Soffil Abu Nahez, were killed when missiles fired from a helicopter hit their car in Gaza City. This was in part retaliation for the May 18, 2003, Hamas suicide attack on Egged No. 6 bus in Jerusalem, in which six people were murdered and twenty were wounded.
June 12, 2003	Yasser Taha, a senior member of the Hamas military wing and Jihad Srour were killed by missiles fired from an IAF helicopter at their car in Gaza City. This was in part a response to the Hamas bombing, on June 11, of an Egged No. 14 bus on Jaffa Road in Jerusalem. A suicide bomber dressed as an ultra-Orthodox Jew, detonated a device packed with nails and metal fragments, killing 17 and wounding over 100.
August 21, 2003	Senior Hamas leader Ismail Abu Shanab and two bodyguards were killed by a missile strike on his station wagon. Abu Shanab was in close contact with Hamas leader, Sheikh Ahmed Yassin and acted as deputy Hamas leader when Yassin was abroad. Abu Shanab was responsible for policy decisions as well as directing and approving military operations against Israelis. He admitted to being involved in planning and carrying out the kidnapping and murder of an Israeli soldier, Ilan Sa'adon. Israel responded only after the August 12, 2003, Hamas suicide bombing of a gas station at the entrance to Ariel where one Israeli was murdered and three others injured. This was also in retaliation for the August 19, 2003, Hamas suicide bombing on Egged No. 2 bus in central Jerusalem, in which 22 people were murdered and 115 were wounded including many children and babies.
September 9, 2003	The leader of Hamas in Hebron, Ahmed Uthman Muhammad Badr and a deputy, Izedin Hadr Shams-Edin Misq, were both killed by a shell fired into Badr's apartment. The Hamas infrastructure headed by Badr and Misq was responsible for terrorist attacks in which 85 Israelis were murdered and over 260 were wounded from April 2002 until their deaths.
February 2, 2004	Bethlehem-area Izz ad-Din al-Qassam Brigades leader Muhammad Abu Ouda was killed in an attempted ambush of IDF troops at his home. Ouda was behind the January 29, 2004, suicide attack in Jerusalem outside the Prime Minister's residence, in which eleven people were murdered and over forty were wounded. Abu Ouda was a member of the Hamas military infrastructure led by Ali Alaan, which perpetrated many attacks, including the November 21, 2002, suicide bombing of No. 20 bus in the Kiryat Menachem neighborhood of Jerusalem. In that attack, eleven people were murdered and forty-five were wounded.
March 22, 2004	Hamas founder and leader, Sheikh Ahmed Yassin was assassinated by an IAF helicopter gunship missile strike in Gaza City. Yassin was directly responsible for the rocket attacks on Israel, but moreover the numerous suicide attacks that resulted in the deaths, wounding and maiming of hundreds of Israeli civilians.
April 17, 2004	Abdel Aziz al-Rantissi, his son and a bodyguard, Akram Nassar, were killed by a missile strike on their van, near his home in Gaza City. He was the co-founder and leader of Hamas, and successor of Ahmed Yassin as leader of Hamas, after the death of the latter.

May 30, 2004	Wa'el Nassar, a senior leader of the Izz ad-Din al-Qassam Brigades, the military wing of Hamas, along with his assistant, Mohammed Sarsour, were killed by an IAF missile strike on the motorcycle they were riding. He was active in terrorist activities from 1992. From 2000 until his death, Nassar directed terrorist operations that claimed the lives of at least twenty-seven Israelis. Nassar headed the Qassam rocket section of Hamas. He also masterminded several terrorist attacks including the suicide bombing carried out by Reem El-Reyashi on January 14, 2004, the first ever Hamas' female suicide bomber, which killed four Israeli soldiers at the Erez checkpoint north of the Gaza Strip. In a particularly heinous operation, Nassar ordered the attack on an IDF armored personnel carrier in Gaza City's Zeitun neighborhood. Detonating a powerful bomb, six IDF soldiers were killed on May 11, 2004. Nassar's cell, as well as members of Islamic Jihad, then collected body parts of the killed soldiers[61] and exchanged them to Israel following their display in a video.
June 26, 2004	The commander of Tanzim, Nayef Abu Sharkh, a commander of Hamas, Jafer el-Massari, a commander of Islamic Jihad, Fadi Bagit, and Sheikh Ibrahim, Islamic Jihad's top commander in Judea and Samaria were killed in an IDF ambush in Nablus, Samaria.
July 22, 2004	An IDF missile strike killed two members of Islamic Jihad, including Hazem Rahim, a local commander who seized the body parts of Israeli soldiers killed when a roadside bomb destroyed their armored personnel carrier on May 11. The Hamas and Islamic Jihad terrorists paraded through the streets with body parts, and video footage flashed on Arab television showed two masked Islamic Jihad activists taking responsibility and displaying the head of an Israeli soldier on a table in front of them.[62]
July 29, 2004	Amr Abu Suta, the commander of the Abu al-Rish Brigades terror faction, and his deputy, Zaki Abu Rakha, were both killed when their car was hit by IAF missile fire in Rafah in the Gaza Strip. The Abu al-Rish Brigades is an extreme offshoot of Yasser Arafat's Fatah movement. They were responsible for the deaths of Israeli civilians dating back to 1992.
September 19, 2004	Hamas terrorist Khaled Abu Shamiyeh was killed by an IAF missile strike in Gaza City. He was a key figure in the production of rockets fired by Hamas at civilians in the Israeli town of Sderot.
October 21, 2004	Second in command in Hamas in the Gaza Strip, and a weapons expert, Adnan al-Ghoul and Imad Abbas, a senior member of the Izz ad-Din al-Qassam Brigades, were killed by an IDF missile strike on their car in Gaza City. Al-Ghoul was responsible for making Qassam and other rockets to fire at Israeli civilian towns and for manufacturing the group's most powerful explosives
September 25, 2005	Senior Islamic Jihad terrorist Sheikh Mohammed Khalil and his deputy were killed in an IAF missile strike in the Gaza Strip. He masterminded the May 2, 2004, shooting at point blank range, of Tali Hatuel, an Israeli mother who was eight months pregnant, murdering her along with four of her daughters, at the Kissufim Crossing in Israel.

October 27, 2005	Local Islamic Jihad leader, Shadi Muhana was killed by a missile strike on his car, outside Jabalya near Gaza City. His aide was also killed. This was in retaliation for the suicide bombing in Hadera, Israel, on October 26, 2005, which killed five civilians.
November 5, 2005	Hassan Madhoun, a leader of the Al-Aqsa Martyrs Brigade, and Fawzi Abu Kara of Hamas, a specialist in the manufacture of rockets and explosives were both killed when their car was hit by an IDF missile strike in the Gaza Strip. Madhoun was responsible for many lethal attacks against Israel, including the double suicide bombing attack in the port of Ashdod on March 14, 2005, in which ten Israelis were killed and twelve were wounded. Additionally, he was behind the shooting and suicide bombing attacks at the Karni crossing point on January 13, 2005, which resulted in the deaths of ten Israelis.
December 8, 2005	Iyyad Al-Najar and Ziad Qaddas, members of the Al-Aqsa Martyrs Brigades were killed in an IAF missile strike on the house that had been used in planning attacks on Israel. This was in retaliation for the suicide bombing at a shopping mall in Netanya, on December 5 that killed five and wounded over forty Israelis.
March 6, 2006	Islamic Jihad terrorists, Munir Mahmed Sukhar and Iyad Abu Shalouf, were killed by an IAF missile strike on their car in the Gaza Strip. Both were involved in rocket attacks against Israel and in attempts to smuggle terrorists armed with explosive belts from the Gaza Strip into Israel, via the Sinai Peninsula, with the purpose of carrying out terror attacks against Israeli civilians.
May 25, 2006	Mahmoud al-Majzoub, the leader of Palestinian Islamic Jihad in Lebanon, was injured by a car bomb in Sidon, Lebanon, and died the next day. His brother, Nidal, also died in the explosion. Active since August 1987, Islamic Jihad perpetrated many heinous terrorist attacks against Israel. These attacks included the following:<ul><li>The January 22, 1995, Beit Lid Junction double suicide bombings against a highway junction soldiers' pick-up station. Twenty-two were killed and sixty-nine injured.</li><li>The March 4, 1996, suicide bombing of a Tel Aviv shopping mall, which resulted in twenty, killed and seventy-five wounded.</li><li>The June 1, 2001 suicide bombing of the Dolphinarium Disco in Tel Aviv, which resulted in the death of twenty-one people.</li><li>The June 5, 2002, car bomb attack on a bus near Afula, killing seventeen and injuring thirty-eight.</li><li>The August 19, 2003, suicide bombing of a Jerusalem bus, which killed twenty-three persons and wounded over 100.</li><li>The October 4, 2003, suicide bombing of the Maxim Restaurant in Haifa, in which twenty-two persons were killed and sixty were injured.</li><li>The April 17, 2006, suicide bombing at a Tel Aviv restaurant targeted previously, killing eleven other people and wounding over fifty.</li></ul>

February 12, 2008	As has previously been detailed, Imad Mughniyah, a founder of the Hezbollah terrorist organization, and its security chief, was killed by a car bomb in a parking lot in Damascus, Syria. He had just left a reception marking the twenty-ninth anniversary of the Iranian Revolution. A bomb planted in a spare tire on the back of a parked SUV was detonated, killing him.[63] It was recently reported[64] that Mughniyah was killed in a joint US CIA and Israeli Mossad operation. The US military built the device used. Mugniyeh eluded US and Israeli agents for decades, even with a $20 million bounty on his head. Israeli agents tried twice to kill him in Beirut, killing his brother by mistake in 2004. Israel took no credit for the Damascus bombing. US State Department spokesperson Sean McCormack declared, "The world is a better place without this man in it. He was a cold-blooded killer, a mass murderer and terrorist responsible for countless innocent lives lost. One way or another he was brought to justice," McCormack said.[65] A US intelligence official said, "This is someone who has caused the United States considerable pain over probably a quarter of a century. This should indicate that terrorists can run but they can't hide."[66] "He was one of the most dangerous terrorists ever on Earth," said Danny Yatom, former head of Israel's Mossad.[67]
November 3, 2010	Mohammed Namnam was assassinated by a car bomb outside the headquarters of the Hamas security forces in Gaza City. Namnam was a top operative with the Army of Islam, a radical Palestinian terror group affiliated with Al-Qaeda. The Army of Islam was responsible for a series of terror attacks against Western institutions, Christians and other Palestinians in the Gaza Strip. Namnam was involved in the June 25, 2006, abduction of IDF soldier Gilad Shalit.[68] The Army of Islam was also behind the kidnapping of BBC correspondent Alan Johnston on March 12, 2007. Namnam was in the midst of planning attacks against American and Israeli targets in the Sinai Peninsula at the time of his death.
April 9, 2011	A key figure in Hamas, Tayser Abu Snima, was killed in an IAF strike on a car along the Gaza-Egyptian border. He was directly and physically involved in the kidnapping of Israeli soldier Gilad Shalit on June 25, 2006, in a Hamas attack near Kibbutz Kerem Shalom, Israel.
March 9, 2012	Zuheir al-Qaisi, the Secretary-General of the Popular Resistance Committees in Gaza, was killed, along with fellow member Mahmud Hanani, as their car was travelling in the Tel El-Hawa neighborhood west of Gaza City. Al-Qaisi was in the final stages of planning another major terrorist attack against Israel from Egyptian Sinai. His group gained notoriety for the 2006 abduction of Israeli soldier Gilad Shalit. Al-Qaisi was also involved in a 2008 attack on a terminal for pumping fuel from Israel into the Gaza Strip, in which two Israeli civilians were killed. Additionally, he was wanted for his role in setting up the August 18, 2011, Eilat Highway 12 ambush, which killed eight Israelis and wounded some forty others.

November 14, 2012	Ahmed al-Jabari, commander of Hamas's military wing, the Izz ad-Din al-Qassam Brigades, died along with a passenger after their car was targeted by an IAF air strike, acting on information provided by the *Shin Bet*. He was the leader in the Hamas takeover of the Gaza Strip in June 2007, in a bloody coup d'état. Additionally, he ordered the firing of Qassam rockets into southern Israeli towns and cities on almost a daily basis. Furthermore, he was responsible for numerous terrorist attacks against Israel that included the kidnapping of IDF soldier Gilad Shalit and the murder of two other IDF soldiers, in 2006.
December 3, 2013	Hezbollah official Hassan Lakkis was shot dead near his home in Hadath, some 4 miles from Beirut, Lebanon. Lakkis was a weapons expert and a close aide of Hezbollah chief Hassan Nasrallah. While Hezbollah blamed Israel for the assassination, there is reason to believe that Saudi Arabia was behind the killing since that Sunni state opposed the Iranian-Hezbollah Shi'ite support for the Assad regime in the Syrian Civil War.
August 21, 2014	The IAF demolished a four-storey house in the Tel Sultan neighborhood of Rafah killing three top officials of the military wing of Hamas, the Izz ad-Din al-Qassam Brigades. All three men were high-ranking officials who developed and improved Hamas' capabilities at weapons manufacture and supplies as well as digging attack tunnels into Israel. They were: • Muhammad Abu Shamalah—the commander of the Southern Brigade responsible for operations in all of Rafah and Khan Yunis—who was involved in carrying out and orchestrating dozens of attacks on Israel. These included the murder of an IDF officer in Rafah in 1994, an attack that killed six soldiers and wounded ten with bomb-laden tunnels in 2004, and orchestrating a bombing of the Kerem Shalom border crossing in 2008, in which booby trapped jeeps were used. Thirteen soldiers were injured in that attack. He was one of the main planners of the Kerem Shalom tunnel attack in 2006, in which two IDF soldiers were killed and Gilad Shalit was kidnapped. During the Third Gaza War, he was responsible for overseeing the infiltration of thirteen Hamas terrorists into Israel via a tunnel in the Kibbutz Sufa area. • Ra'ad Atar—the Hamas Rafah brigade commander in southern Gaza. He took part in a long series of deadly attacks on IDF soldiers over the past twenty years. These included an attack in July 2004 on the Israeli–Egyptian border that killed an IDF officer, planning and carrying out a plot to bomb an IDF post, which killed four soldiers, and taking part and planning an infiltration of an IDF post near Kerem Shalom that killed four soldiers. • Muhamad Barhoum—a key figure in arms smuggling on behalf of Hamas' Rafah brigade. He took part in raising terrorist finances and spent years in Syria.
August 24, 2014	Hamas' "finance minister" Mohammed al-Ghoul was targeted and killed in an IAF air strike in the al-Wahda neighborhood in the northern part of Gaza City. He supervised the funds used for purchasing weapons and for paying members of Hamas' military wing, the Izz ad-Din al-Qassam Brigades.

| January 18, 2015 | A combined Hezbollah and Iranian advance guard conducting reconnaissance and planning on the Syrian side of the Golan Heights, was targeted by an IAF helicopter missile strike. Hezbollah and Iran were planning to establish a Hezbollah military presence on the Syrian side of the Golan Heights buffer zone as a second front for launching a two-pronged simultaneous attack on Israel. The goal was to seize Israeli territory and hostages (via underground tunnels from Lebanon). The missile strike caused the deaths of six members of Hezbollah, including the Lebanese militant group's Golan coordinator, Jihad Mughniyeh, as well as six Iranian Revolutionary Guard officers, including Iranian General Mohammad Ali Allahdadi. |

In conclusion, it must be emphasized that there is no moral equivalency in contrasting the actions taken by terrorists and the actions taken in defense of a sovereign state. Terrorists, no matter what euphemism is used to describe them (e.g. "resistance," "militants," and "freedom fighters") to "justify" their actions, are brutal, ruthless individuals or groups, who terrorize, murder, and maim civilians—men, women, children and even infants.

37. Since before World War II, "revolutions" and military takeovers—coups d'état—have been the most prevalent means of seizing political power throughout the Arab/Muslim world.

The term "revolution" is freely used in the Middle East. Starting with the Egyptian military coup d'état of July 23, 1952, "revolution" became a more widely used euphemism to describe the military takeovers in the Middle East. Thus, the military coups that toppled the monarchies of Egypt, Iraq and Libya came to be called the "23 July [1952] Revolution," "14 July [1958] Revolution," and the "1 September [1969] Revolution," respectively. Over time, the term was applied not just to coups that overthrew monarchies, but also to such events as the Ba'athist coups in Iraq, the "14 Ramadan [February 8, 1963] Revolution, "and the later "17 July [1968] Revolution" that witnessed the emergence of strong man Saddam Hussein. In neighboring Syria coups were portrayed as the "8 March [1963] Revolution," that brought the Ba'athist Party to power as well as the later "Corrective Revolution [of November 13, 1970]" that resulted in the Assad dynasty taking power in that country.

It should be noted however, that not all Middle East coups are the same. The results do not have to be the emergence of a repressive military regime. The Turkish military coup of November 1, 1922, brought into existence a more secular, Westernized state. This may well be repeated in Egypt because of the July 3, 2013 coup—termed by some a peoples' "revolution."[69]

The Arab populist uprisings of late 2010 and early 2011, which turned into massive protests and led to the ouster of several long-time dictators* across the region were dubbed the "18 December [2010] Revolution [in Tunisia]," the "25 January Revolution [in Egypt]," the "27 January Revolution [in Yemen]," and the "17 February Revolution [in Libya]." With the Syrian Civil War still raging into its fifth year and swift rise and subsequent fall of the Muslim Brotherhood regime in Egypt and Tunisia, it is still too early to determine if these uprisings will become true revolutions as defined below.

While the perpetrators of such coups d'état call these events "revolutions," in fact they are not. It is a much misused term. A true revolution changes a country's political, economic, and even social

---

* Tunisian President Zine El Abidine Ben Ali, Egyptian President Hosni Mubarak, Yemeni President Ali Abdullah Saleh, and Libyan leader Muammar Qadhafi.

structure. There are very few true revolutions—the American (1775), French (1789), Mexican (1910), Russian (1917 and 1991), Chinese (1949), and Cuban (1959)—but in the Arab/Muslim world, only the Algerian Revolution (1954), and the Iranian Revolution (1979) may qualify for such a designation. The table below reflects both the successful and unsuccessful coups in the region. The number of failures is more difficult to determine, since unsuccessful coups d'état often go unreported.

REVOLUTIONS AND COUPS D'ÉTAT IN THE MIDDLE EAST			
(listed within modern-day country boundaries)			
ALGERIA			
Date	Instigated By	Directed Against	Result
July 2–3, 1962	Colonel Tahar Zbiri and dissident officers	President of the Provisional government, Abdur Rahman Farès	Success
September 29–October 12, 1963	Colonel Mohand Ou el Hadj, Hocine Aït Ahmed, members of the Socialist Forces Front and Berbers in the Kabylia Mountains	President Ahmed Ben Bella	Failure
June 30, 1964	Colonel Muhammad Chaabani	President Ahmed Ben Bella	Failure
June 19, 1965	Colonel Houari Boumédiènne	President Ahmed Ben Bella	Success
December 15–16, 1967	Chief of Staff Taher Zbiri and dissident military elements	President Houari Boumédiènne	Failure
January 8, 1992	Minister of Defense Khaled Nezzar and dissident military officers	President Chadli Bendjedid	Success
BAHRAIN			
Date	Instigated By	Directed Against	Result
December 16, 1981	Islamic Front for the Liberation of Bahrain and Shi'a fundamentalists The coup attempt was financially supported by Iran.	Sheikh Isa bin Sulman al-Khalifa	Failure
COMOROS			
Date	Instigated By	Directed Against	Result
August 3, 1975	Ali Soilih, Bob Denard and mercenaries supported by France	President Ahmed Abdullah	Success
January 1976	Ali Soilih	Said Muhammad Jaffa	Success
January 1976–May 1978	Seven attempted coups by dissident elements	President Ali Soilih	Failed

May 13, 1978	Bob Denard and mercenaries Denard re-installed Ahmed Abdullah as president. Denard was made commander of the Presidential Guard and supported by the white regimes in South Africa and Rhodesia. Denard converted to Islam and took the name Said Mustapha Mahdjoub.	President Ali Soilih	Success
March 8, 1985	Dissident Presidential Guard	President Ahmed Abdullah	Failure
November 1987	Dissident elements	President Ahmed Abdullah	Failure
November 29, 1989	Bob Denard and the Presidential Guard	President Ahmed Abdullah	Success
September 26, 1992	Lieutenant Said Mohamed and dissident army elements	President Said Mohamed Djohar	Failure
September 27, 1995	Bob Denard and mercenaries The attempted coup was code-named Operation *Kaskari*. The French government sent 900 troops— Operations *Azalee*—October 3, 1995, to stop Denard, though other French officials may have known and supported his activities.	President Said Mohamed Djohar	Failure
April 30, 1999	Colonel Azali Assoumani	Tadjidine Ben Said Massounde	Success
August 9, 2001	Mohamed Bacar and dissident army and navy officers	Said Abeid	Success
September ? 2001	Dissident elements	Mohamed Bacar	Failure
November ? 2001	Said Abeid	Mohamed Bacar	Failure

EGYPT			
Date	**Instigated By**	**Directed Against**	**Result**
July 23, 1952	Muhammad Naguib, Gamal Abdel Nasser and the Free Officers Movement, which included Anwar el-Sadat and Abdul Hakim Amer. The monarchy was abolished and a republic was established.	King Farouk	Success
January 16, 1953	Colonel Rashad Muhanna and dissident officers	Revolutionary Command Council	Failure
March 30, 1953	Lt. Col. Muhammad Husni al-Damanhuri and dissident officers	Revolutionary Command Council	Failure
February 1953	Police officer Ra'fat Chelebi	Revolutionary Command Council	Failure

February 26, 1954	Khalid Muhieddin, armored corps officers and liberal elements in the military. They demanded the return to power of General Naguib.	Prime Minister Gamal Abdel Nasser	Success
March 26, 1954	Gamal Abdel Nasser, Abdul Hakim Amer, "Young Officers" and elements of the National Guard	President Muhammad Naguib	Success
April 28, 1954	Dissident officers	Gamal Abdel Nasser	Failure
April 1957	Dissident officers	President Gamal Abdel Nasser	Failure
July 2, 1965	The Muslim Brotherhood The coup was planned for August 29, 1965.	President Gamal Abdel Nasser	Failure
April 1, 1966	Dissident military officers	President Gamal Abdel Nasser	Failure
August 26, 1967	Field Marshal Abdel Hakim Amer and dissident military officers	President Gamal Abdel Nasser	Failure
May 2, 1968	Eight dissident military officers	President Gamal Abdel Nasser	Failure
June 1968	Thirty-five dissident army and police officers	President Gamal Abdel Nasser	Failure
May 2, 1971	Vice President Ali Sabry, and War Minister Muhammad Fawzi	President Anwar el-Sadat	Failure
May 15, 1971	President Anwar el-Sadat This was called the "Rectification (or Corrective) Revolution."	Vice President Ali Sabry, liberals, Islamists and pro-Nasserists.	Success
May 1972	Dissident elements	President Anwar el-Sadat	Failure
November 15, 1972	Dissident elements	President Anwar el-Sadat	Failure
April 18, 1974	Dissident elements	President Anwar el-Sadat	Failure
January 1975	Leftists	President Anwar el-Sadat	Failure
August 1975	Communists	President Anwar el-Sadat	Failure
March 1976	Pro-Libyan elements	President Anwar el-Sadat	Failure
July 1977	Pro-Libyan elements	President Anwar el-Sadat	Failure
November 2008	Sami Shahab, Hezbollah agents, pro-Shi'ite Iranian elements and Muslim Brotherhood supporters	President Hosni Mubarak	Failure
February 11, 2011	Supreme Council of the Armed Forces headed by Defense Minister Mohammed Tantawi, Intelligence chief, General Omar Suleiman, and Chief of Staff Lt. Gen. Sami Al-Anan	President Hosni Mubarak	Success

August 12, 2012	President Mohamed Morsi supported by pro-Muslim Brotherhood elements of the Egyptian military headed by General Abdel-Fattah El-Sisi. (Morsi pre-empted a planned military coup led by Field Marshall Hussein Tantawi and anti-Muslim Brotherhood elements, scheduled for August 24. Morsi, in effect, carried out a civilian coup.	Supreme Council of the Armed Forces headed by Defense Minister Mohammed Tantawi, Chief of Staff Lt. Gen. Sami Al-Anan, Air Force chief Rezza Abd al-Megid, Navy commander Mahab Muhamed Mamish and Air Defense chief Abd Al-Aziz Muhamed Seif.	Success
July 3, 2013	Defense Minister Gen. Abdul Fatah Al-Sisi, the army, police, the security service, the intelligence agency, Christian, secular opposition, as well as various civilian groups calling themselves the Tamarod ("Rebel") Movement. This was called the "Corrective Revolution."	President Mohamed Morsi and the Muslim Brotherhood	Success
IRAN			
Date	**Instigated By**	**Directed Against**	**Result**
February 20–21, 1921	Reza Khan, commander of the Iranian Cossacks The coup led to the end of the Qajar dynasty, October 31, 1925. On December 12, 1925, Reza Khan was placed on the throne by his fellow officers, while the *Majlis*, convening as a constituent assembly declared him the Shah.	Prime Minister Fathollah Khan Akbar Sepahdor	Success
August 16, 1953	Prime Minister Mohammed Mossadeq, supported by the Tudeh (communist) party	Shah Mohammad Reza Pahlavi The Shah flew into exile, first in Baghdad and then Rome.	Success
August 19, 1953	General Fazlollah Zahedi and pro-monarchy military elements The coup had the assistance of the US Central Intelligence Agency and led to the return of the Shah on August 22, 1953.	Prime Minister Mohammed Mossadeq	Success
Fall 1954	Some 600 Tudeh (communist) Party military dissidents	Shah Mohammed Reza Pahlavi	Failure

Feb. 11, 1979	Ayatollah Ruhollah Khomeini and Shi'ite Islamic fundamentalists The coup was called the "Islamic Revolution" and Khomeini became the "Supreme Leader." The monarchy was abolished and an Islamic Republic was proclaimed.	Shah Mohammed Reza Pahlavi	Success
IRAQ			
Date	**Instigated By**	**Directed Against**	**Result**
October 29, 1936	General Bakr Sidqi This was the first modern military coup d'état in the Arab world against a government.	Premier Yasin al-Hashimi	Success
August 11, 1937	Aziz Yamulki, Fahmi Sa'id, Mahmud Hindi and Muhammad Khorshid This was a counter-coup to the first one.	Bakr Sidqi military dictatorship	Success
December 24, 1938	"The Circle of Seven," a group of Sunni Arab nationalist military officers with pro-German sympathies	Prime Minister Jamil al-Madfa'i	Success
April 5, 1939	"The Circle of Seven"	Regent Crown Prince Abd al-Ilah	Success
February 21, 1940	"The Golden Square" It was comprised of four army colonels—Colonel Salah al-Din al-Sabbagh, Colonel Kamal Shabib, Colonel Fahmi Said, and Colonel Mahmud Salman—who were members of the "Circle of Seven." All were anti-British and pro-German.	Regent Crown Prince Abd al-Ilah	Success
February 1, 1941	"The Golden Square"	Regent Crown Prince Abd al-Ilah	Success
April 1, 1941	"The Golden Square" and Rashid Ali al-Gailani The coup received Nazi support and financing, It established a pro-Axis and pan-Arab regime.	Regent Crown Prince Abd al-Ilah Prime Minister Taha al-Hashimi	Success

May 2–31, 1941	A British-led counter-coup was launched, designed to return to power the pro-British Hashemite government of the Regent Crown Prince 'Abd al-Ilah. It involved British and Commonwealth military forces and is also known as the Anglo-Iraq War, part of the Middle East campaign of World War II.	"The Golden Square" and Rashid Ali al-Gailani	Success
February 11–12, 1950	Chief of Police, Ali Khaled al-Hijazi	Prime Minister Tawfiq Suweidi	Failure
July 14, 1958	Brigadier General Abdel Karim Qassem and Colonel Abdul Salam Aref and the "Free Officers" The coup abolished the monarchy and established a republic.	King Faisal II	Success
December 8, 1958	Rashid Ali al-Gailani and Abdul Salam Aref	Brigadier General Abdel Karim Qassem	Failure
March 8–13, 1959	Colonel Abdul Wahab Shawaf and senior officers in Mosul The coup plotters sought union with the UAR.	Brigadier General Abdel Karim Qassem	Failure
July 14–19, 1959	Communist Party	Brigadier General Abdel Karim Qassem	Failure
February 8, 1963	Colonel Abdul Salam Aref, pro-Nasserist officers and the Ba'ath Party The coup was named the "14 Ramadan Revolution."	Brigadier General Abdel Karim Qassem	Success
May 25, 1963	Pro-Nasserist elements	Colonel Abdul Salam Aref	Failure
July 3, 1963	Communists	Colonel Abdul Salam Aref	Failure
November 10–11, 1963	Commander of the National Guard Mundher Wandawi and fourteen other Iraqi Army officers along with pro-Nasserist elements	President Abdul Salam Aref, Prime Minister Ahmed Hassan al-Bakr and the Ba'athist regime	Success
November 18, 1963	General Abdul Salam Aref	National Guard and pro-Nasserist elements	Success
September 4, 1964	Pro-Ba'athist elements	President Abdul Salam Aref	Failure
September 15–16, 1965	Prime Minister Abdul Razzaq and senior military officers The coup plotters sought union with Egypt.	President Abdul Salam Aref	Failure

October 29, 1965	Dissident officers in favor of union with Egypt	President Abdul Salam Aref	Failure
Early March 1966	Ba'athist elements	President Abdul Salam Aref	Failure
June 30, 1966	Brigadier Abdul Razzaq The coup plotters sought union with Egypt.	President Abdul Rahman Aref	Failure
July 17, 1968	Colonels Ibrahim Daoud, Abdul Razzaq Nayef and Ahmed Hassan al-Bakr The coup was named the "17 of July Revolution." The Ba'athists remained in power until March 2003.	President Abdul Rahman Aref	Success
July 30, 1968	Ahmed Hassan al-Bakr* and Ba'athist elements	Colonels Ibrahim Daoud, Abdul Razzaq Nayef	Success
January 22, 1970	Muhammad al-Numayri and dissident right-wing military and civilian elements	President Ahmed Hassan al-Bakr	Failure
July 1, 1973	Director of Internal Security Nazim Kazzar and a civilian dissident faction of the Ba'athist Party	President Ahmed Hassan al-Bakr and Vice President Saddam Hussein	Failure
1978	Communist elements	President Ahmed Hassan al-Bakr	Failure
July 16, 1979	Vice-President Saddam Hussein Hussein became Chairman of the Revolutionary Command Council and President of Iraq, when al-Bakr resigned for reasons of "ill health."	President Ahmed Hassan al-Bakr	Success
August 1979	Dissident elements allegedly aided by the Soviet Union[70]	President Saddam Hussein	Failure
November 1988	General Adnan Khairallah and dissident military elements	President Saddam Hussein	Failure
September 1989	Dissident military elements	President Saddam Hussein	Failure
January 1990	Members of the Jubur tribe	President Saddam Hussein	Failure
February–June 1991	There were three attempted coups during this period. The last led to the dismissal of the Chief of the General Staff, Hussein Rashid al-Takriti, one of Saddam Hussein's clansmen.	President Saddam Hussein	Failure

---

* Al-Bakr was named President of Iraq by the Revolutionary Council. Twenty-seven years earlier, in 1941, he had participated in the pro-Nazi, Rashid Ali al-Gailani revolt against the United Kingdom.

October 1991	Another coup attempt This led to the shake-up in Saddam Hussein's inner circle. Hussein dismissed his son-in-law the Minister of Defense, Hussein Kamel al-Majid, and reshuffled other key officials.	President Saddam Hussein	Failure
Late June 1992	This coup was attributed to dissident army elements—a mechanized brigade of Iraq's elite Republican Guards. It may have been part of a plan by Saddam Hussein to fool US forces into allowing his continued use of helicopter gunships, to put down the alleged "coup," but in reality used them to crush the Shi'ite rebellion in southern Iraq.	President Saddam Hussein	Failure
July 1993	Raji al-Tikriti and dissident military elements	President Saddam Hussein	Failure
March 1995	Members of the Iraqi National Congress	President Saddam Hussein	Failure
June 14, 1995	Army mutineers	President Saddam Hussein	Failure
June 1996	Ayad Allawi and dissident army elements	President Saddam Hussein	Failure

JORDAN			
Date	**Instigated By**	**Directed Against**	**Result**
Early September 1951	Colonel Habis al-Majali, Commander of the Hashemite regiment of the Arab Legion attempted a coup. He favored Regent Prince Nayef (the second son of Abdullah I), and opposed Talal, who had been named as the new king of Jordan.	King Talal Regent Prince Nayef	Failure
January 7, 1956	Egyptian and Saudi instigated dissidents This was in opposition to Jordan joining the Baghdad Pact.	King Hussein	Failure
April 8, 1957	General Ali Abu Nuwar, pro-Nasserist and pro-Soviet military elements	King Hussein	Failure
April 13, 1957	General Ali Abu Nuwar, pro-Nasserist and pro-Soviet military elements This was known as the "Zarqa incident."	King Hussein	Failure

February 1958	Pro-UAR advocates	King Hussein	Failure
July 17, 1958	Pro-UAR elements This attempted coup was originally planned for July 14, to coincide with the successful coup in Iraq.	King Hussein British military forces intervened in support of the legitimate government, July 17, 1958.	Failure
March 1959	General Sadeq al-Shara and dissident military officers	King Hussein	Failure
July 25, 1960	UAR/Syrian Deuxième Bureau (Syrian intelligence service)	King Hussein	Failure
April 17–early May 1963	Pro-Egyptian, pro-Syrian Ba'athist and pro-Iraqi Ba'athist elements	King Hussein	Failure
October 1969	Taqi el-Din Nabhabi and "Liberation Party" members	King Hussein	Failure
September 1, 1970	Palestinian guerrilla groups The attempted coup triggered the events of Black September and the subsequent Jordanian Civil War (*see* the "Jordanian Civil War, 1970–71" map).	King Hussein	Failure
Early November 1972	Libyan-backed PLO elements	King Hussein	Failure
LEBANON			
Date	**Instigated By**	**Directed Against**	**Result**
July 3–4, 1949	Antun Saadeh and Syrian Social Nationalist Party The coup favored the unity of the Fertile Crescent (i.e. Syria and Iraq).	President Sheikh Bishara al-Khoury	Failure
September 9–18, 1952	An amalgam of dissident politicians, and political parties It was a non-violent and bloodless coup.	President Beshara al-Khouri	Success
May 10–end of July 1958	Sabri Hamadeh, Ahmad al-Asaad, Rashid Karami, Kamal Jumblatt, Shebli al-Aryan, Saeb Salam, Adnan HakinAbdallah Yafi, Abdalah Mashnuq, Hamid Franjiyeh and Paul Meouchi, as well as mostly Muslim, and pro-UAR elements	President Camille Chamoun US military forces intervened in support of the legitimate government, July 15, 1958.	Failure
December 31, 1961	Captains Fuad Awad and Shawqi Khairallah, dissident military officers, as well as Syrian Social National Party members	President Fuad Chehab	Failure

October 20–November 2, 1969	PLO forces	President Charles Helou	Failure

LIBYA			
Date	**Instigated By**	**Directed Against**	**Result**
July 1958	Pro-UAR advocates	King Idris I British military forces intervened in support of the legitimate government, July 19, 1958.	Failure
September 1, 1969	Colonel Muammar Qadhafi The monarchy was abolished and a republic proclaimed.	King Idris I	Success
December 10, 1969	Defense Minister Colonel Adam Hawaz, Interior Minister Colonel Musa Ahmad and dissident military officers The coup was planned for December 7, 1969.	Chairman of the Revolutionary Command Council, Colonel Muammar Qadhafi	Failure
July 1970	Cyrenaican Defense Force dissidents	Chairman of the Revolutionary Command Council, Muammar Qadhafi	Failure
August 1975	Abdullah Meheishi	Chairman of the Revolutionary Command Council Muammar Qadhafi	Failure
February 1979	Dissident army units	Chairman of the Revolutionary Command Council and General Secretary of the General People's Congress, Muammar Qadhafi	Failure
August 18, 1980	Driss Chehaibi and dissident air force officers	Leader and Guide of the Revolution, Muammar Qadhafi	Failure
May 22, 1981	Magarha tribesmen	Leader and Guide of the Revolution, Muammar Qadhafi	Failure
December 19, 1981	Colonel Khalifa Khadir	Leader and Guide of the Revolution, Muammar Qadhafi	Failure
January 9, 1982	Dissident military officers	Leader and Guide of the Revolution, Muammar Qadhafi	Failure
May 8, 1984	Dissident army officers	Leader and Guide of the Revolution, Muammar Qadhafi	Failure
April 1985	Dissident army officers	Leader and Guide of the Revolution, Muammar Qadhafi	Failure
August 31, 1985	Dissident army officers	Leader and Guide of the Revolution, Muammar Qadhafi	Failure

MAURITANIA			
Date	**Instigated By**	**Directed Against**	**Result**
March 29, 1962	Dissident army officers	President Moktar Ould Daddah	Failure
July 10, 1978	Army commander Colonel Mustafa Ould Salek	President Moktar Ould Daddah	Success
April 6, 1979	Colonels Ahmed Ould Bousseif and Muhammad Khouna Haidallah	Head of the Military Committee for National Recovery, Mustafa Ould Salek	Success
January 4, 1980	Prime Minister Muhammad Khouna Haidallah	Head of State Muhammad Mahmoud Ould Luly	Success
March 18, 1981	Ahmed Salem Ould Sidi, Muhammad Abdelkader and pro-Moroccan members of the Alliance for a Democratic Mauritania	Head of State Muhammad Khouna Haidallah	Failure
February 1982	Dissident armed forces	Head of State Muhammad Khouna Haidallah	Failure
January 1983	Pro-Libyan dissidents	Head of State Muhammad Khouna Haidallah	Failure
December 12, 1984	Colonel Maaouiya Ould Sid Ahmed Ould Taya	Head of State Muhammad Khouna Haidallah	Success
June 8, 2003	Colonel Salah Ould Hananna, former minister Mohammed Ould Cheikhna and hard-line Islamists as well as disgruntled army officers	President Maaouiya Ould Sid Ahmed Ould Taya	Failure
August 3, 2005	Director of the National Police Ely Ould Mohamed Vall	President Maaouiya Ould Sid Ahmed Ould Taya	Success
August 6, 2008	Army Chief of Staff General Mohamed Ould Abdel Aziz, Generals Muhammad Ould al-Ghazwani, Philippe Swikri, Ahmad Ould Bakri and other dissident military officers	President Sidi Mohamed Ould Cheikh Abdallahi	Success
MOROCCO			
Date	**Instigated By**	**Directed Against**	**Result**
January 1971	Dissident military officers and leftist elements	King Hassan II	Failure
July 10–11, 1971	Commandant of the Skhirat Military Academy and pro-Libyan dissident army officers	King Hassan II	Failure
August 16, 1972	Defense Minister General Muhammad Oufkir and pro-Libyan dissident air force officers The coup planned to abolish the monarchy and establish a republic.	King Hassan II	Failure

OMAN			
Date	**Instigated By**	**Directed Against**	**Result**
July 23, 1970	Crown Prince Qabus bin Said	Sultan Said bin Taimur	Success

QATAR			
Date	**Instigated By**	**Directed Against**	**Result**
February 22, 1972	Prime Minister and Crown Prince Sheikh Khalifa bin Hamad al-Thani	Sheikh Ahmed bin Hamad al-Thani	Success
June 26, 1995	Crown Prince and Minister of Defense Sheikh Hamad bin Khalifa Al-Thani	Sheikh Khalifa bin Hamad al-Thani	Success

SAUDI ARABIA			
Date	**Instigated By**	**Directed Against**	**Result**
May 26, 1956	"Free Officers Association"	King Saud bin Abdul-Aziz Al Saud	Failure
August 3, 1956	Dissident military officers	King Saud bin Abdul-Aziz Al Saud	Failure
April 21, 1967	Dissident elements The coup was organized by an Egyptian military attaché.	King Faisal	Failure
July 1967	Dissident elements	King Faisal	Failure
May 6, 1969	"The Union of the People of the Arabian Peninsula"	King Faisal	Failure
September 1969	The Arab Nationalist Movement, Nasserists, and members of the PFLP The coup was planned to coincide with the successful coup in Libya.	King Faisal	Failure
July 1977	Pro-Libyan elements	King Khalid	Failure
November 20–December 4, 1979	Juhayman Saif al-Utaibi, Abdullah Hamid Muhammad al-Qahtani and some 500 Islamic fundamentalist dissidents The Grand Mosque in Mecca was seized and held for over two weeks. The extremists wanted to establish an Islamist theocracy.	King Khalid	Failure

SOMALIA			
Date	**Instigated By**	**Directed Against**	**Result**
December 9–10, 1961	Dissident officers in Hargeisa	President Aden Abdulle Osman Daar	Failure
October 21, 1969	General Muhammad Siad Barre	Prime Minister Muammad Ibrahim Egal	Success
May 5, 1971	Dissident army officers	President Muhammad Siad Barre	Failure

April 9, 1978	Dissident army officers	President Muhammad Siad Barre	Failure
April 1982	Dissident army officers	President Muhammad Siad Barre	Failure
January 26, 1991	General Mohamed Farrah Aidid	President Muhammad Siad Barre	Success

SUDAN			
Date	**Instigated By**	**Directed Against**	**Result**
June 12, 1957	Dissident officers	Prime Minister Abdullah Khalil	Failure
November 17, 1958	General Ibrahim Abboud	Prime Minister Ahmed Ismail al-Azhari	Success
March 2, 1959	Generals Abdallah and Shannan	General Ibrahim Abboud	Failure
March 4–9, 1959	Generals Abdallah and Shannan as well as other dissident officers	General Ibrahim Abboud	Failure
May 22, 1959	Generals Abdallah and Shannan as well as A.R. Shinan and B.A. Hamid	General Ibrahim Abboud	Failure
May 27, 1959	Generals Abdallah and Shannan	General Ibrahim Abboud	Failure
November 9, 1959	Members of the Revolutionary Council, military cadets and junior officers including Ali Hamid	General Ibrahim Abboud	Failure
October 26–30, 1964	Military elements, trade unionists and politicians	General Ibrahim Abboud	Success
November 8, 1964	Pro-Egyptian elements	General Ibrahim Abboud	Failure
December 28, 1966	Lieut. Khalid Husayn Uthman and leftist junior officers	Prime Minister Sadiq al-Mahdi	Failure
May 25, 1969	Colonel Jaafar Nimeiry and left-wing military officers	Prime Minister Sadiq al-Mahdi	Success
March 27, 1970	Imam Sayyid al-Hadi al-Mahdi, and Ansar Movement dissidents on Aba Island	President Jaafar Nimeiry	Failure
July 19, 1971	Major Hashem al-Atta and pro-communist left-wing officers	President Jaafar Nimeiry	Success
July 22, 1971	President Jaafar Nimeiry	Major Hashem al-Atta	Success
June 1975	Communist elements	President Jaafar Nimeiry	Failure
September 5, 1975	Colonel Hassan Osman	President Jaafar Nimeiry	Failure
July 2, 1976	Pro-Libyan elements	President Jaafar Nimeiry	Failure
February 2, 1977	Dissident air defense units	President Jaafar Nimeiry	Failure
March 20, 1979	Dissident military elements	President Jaafar Nimeiry	Failure
April 10, 1979	Dissident military elements	President Jaafar Nimeiry	Failure

March 15, 1981	Pro-Syrian elements	President Jaafar Nimeiry	Failure
February 18, 1983	Pro-Libyan elements	President Jaafar Nimeiry	Failure
March 31, 1984	Dissident army officers	President Jaafar Nimeiry	Failure
October 29, 1984	Pro-Libyan elements	President Jaafar Nimeiry	Failure
April 6, 1985	General Abdel Rahman Swar al-Dahab	President Jaafar Nimeiry	Success
September 27, 1985	Philip Abbas Gaboush	President Abdel Rahman Swar al-Dahab	Failure
April 3, 1986	Supporters of ex-President Jaafar Nimeiry	President Abdel Rahman Swar al-Dahab	Failure
June 30, 1989	Colonel Omar al-Bashir and the National Islamic Front	Prime Minister Sadiq al-Mahdi	Success
April 23, 1990	Dissident military officers	President Omar al-Bashir	Failure
September 11, 1990	Dissident military officers	President Omar al-Bashir	Failure
November 22, 2012	Salah Abdallah Gosh, former director of Sudan's National Security and Intelligence Services and dissident senior military and security officers	President Omar al-Bashir	Failure

SYRIA			
Date	**Instigated By**	**Directed Against**	**Result**
March 30, 1949	Colonel Husni Zaim and the Army High Command The coup was CIA-supported and led to a rapprochement with France.	President Shukri al-Quwatli	Success
August 14, 1949	Colonel Sami Hinnawi and dissident military officers The coup was pro-Hashemite and pro-British.	President Husni al-Zaim and Prime Minister Muhsin al-Barazi Both men were executed.	Success
December 19, 1949	Colonel Adib Shishakli	Colonel Sami Hinnawi	Success
September 27, 1950	Jordanian-inspired military dissidents	Colonel Adib Shishakli	Failure
November 21, 1951	Colonel Adib Shishakli	President Hashem el-Atassi	Success
October 1952	Brigadier Jamil Burhani as well as dissident military and police officers	Strongman Colonel Adib Shishakli and President Fawzi Selu	Failure
December 1952	Akranm Hourani	Strongman Colonel Adib Shishakli and President Fawzi Selu	Failure

February 25, 1954	Lt. Col. Faisal Atassi, Col. Amin Abu Assaf, Ghassan Jedid, Lt. Abdul Hamid Sarraj, and Capt. Mustafa Hamdun as well as dissident Druze, Ba'athists, and communists	President Adib Shishakli	Success
December 22, 1956	Pro-Western elements	Prime Minister Sabri al-Assali	Failure
August 12, 1957	Dissident military elements. The failed coup led to widespread arrests and show trials. Colonel Afif Bizri and a leftist junta gained control of the government in a partial coup.	Prime Minister Sabri al-Assali	Failure
January 14, 1958	Colonel Abdul Hamid Sarraj and other military officers The coup plotters favored unity with Egypt.	Prime Minister Sabri al-Assali	Success
September 28, 1961	Colonels Abdul Karim Nahlawi, Muhib al-Hindi, Haidar Kuzbari, and "The Military Committee" The coup marked Syria's secession from the United Arab Republic, effectively ending the union between Egypt and Syria.	UAR/Egyptian President Gamal Abdel Nasser	Success
March 28, 1962	Colonel Abdul Karim Nahlawi, Abdel Karim Zahr al-Din and pro-Nasserist military officers	President Nazem Qudsi	Success
March 31– April 1, 1962	Colonels Jasim Alwan, Luay Atassi and Nasserist elements in Aleppo The coup sought union with Egypt.	President Nazem Qudsi and military regime in Damascus	Failure
January 13, 1963	Colonel Abdul Karim Nahlawi and dissident junior officers	President Nazem Qudsi and his military regime	Failure
March 8, 1963	Colonels Ziad Hariri, Luay Atassi, Amin el-Hafez, pan-Arab Nasserist officers, Druze, Alawite, and Ismaili Shi'ite officers as well as the Military Committee of the Ba'ath Party	President Nazim al-Qudsi and military regime	Success
May 22, 1963	Pro-Nasserist elements	General Luay Atassi, Chairman of the National Revolutionary Command Council and the Ba'athist regime	Failure

July 18, 1963	Ex-Colonel Jasim Alwan, ex-General Muhammad Jarrah, ex-Colonel Akram Safadi and Nasserist elements The coup plotters sought union with Egypt.	General Luay Atassi, Chairman of the National Revolutionary Command Council, General Amin el-Hafez and the Ba'athist regime	Failure
December 19, 1965	Major General Salah Jedid and the military regional command	Chairman of the Presidential Council General Amin el-Hafez	Failure
February 23, 1966	General Salah Jadid, Salim Hatum, and the extreme left-wing of the Ba'ath Party	Chairman Amin al-Hafez, Salah Baytar and the moderate wing of the Ba'ath Party	Success
September 8, 1966	Colonels Salim Hatum, Talal Abu Asli, and Fahd al-Sha'ir	Strongman General Salah Jadid, Head of State, Nureddin al-Atassi and the extremist Ba'athist regime	Failure
March 1, 1969	General Hafez al-Assad	Strongman General Salah Jadid and Head of State, Nureddin al-Atassi	Success
February 28, 1969	General Hafez al-Assad This was a bloodless semi-coup.	Head of State, Nureddin al-Atassi	Success
November 13, 1970	General Hafez al-Assad The coup was named the "Corrective Revolution."	Strongman, Deputy Secretary-General of the Ba'ath Party, Salah Jadid and the ultra-leftist wing of the Ba'ath Party	Success
June 11, 1971	Supporters of the previous regime	President Hafez al-Assad	Failure
March 5–16, 1980	Dissident elements	President Hafez al-Assad	Failure
December ? January 1982	Dissident Sunni officers.	President Hafez al-Assad	Failure
February 2008	Military intelligence chief, Assef Shaukat and dissident elements	President Bashar al-Assad	Failure
TUNISIA			
Date	**Instigated By**	**Directed Against**	**Result**
1959	Dissident elements	President Habib Bourguiba	Failure
December 24, 1962	Major Saleb Ben Said and Captain Kebair Mehrezi	President Habib Bourguiba	Failure
1963	Dissident elements	President Habib Bourguiba	Failure
March 1976	Pro-Libyan elements	President Habib Bourguiba	Failure
January 26, 1980	Pro-Libyan elements	President Habib Bourguiba	Failure
August 3, 1987	The fundamentalist Islamic Tendency Movement	President Habib Bourguiba	Failure
November 7, 1987	Prime Minister Zine El Abidine Ben Ali	President Habib Bourguiba	Success

December 18, 2010–January 14, 2011	Labor unions, students, Islamists, and military elements	President Zine El Abidine Ben Ali	Success

TURKEY			
Date	**Instigated By**	**Directed Against**	**Result**
July 23, 1908	The *Vatan ve Hürriyet* ("Fatherland and Freedom") group of military officers, including Mustafa Kemal They sought reforms within the Ottoman Empire.	Sultan Abdul Hamid II	Success
April 13, 1909 (March 31, 1909 O.S.)	Sultan Abdul Hamid II and reactionary military officers of the Muhammadan Union	Committee of Union and Progress	Success
April 23, 1909	Mahmud Şevket Pasha and the Third Army Corps	Sultan Abdul Hamid II	Success
November 1, 1922	Mustafa Kemal and the Grand National Assembly The coup abolished the sultanate and a republic was proclaimed on October 23, 1923.	Sultan Mehmed VI Vahideddin	Success
May 27, 1960	General Cermal Gursel and the army Power was returned to a civilian government in October 1961.	President Celal Bayar, Prime Minister Adnan Menderes and the government of the Democratic Party.	Success
February 22, 1962	Colonel Talaat Aydemir and dissident cadets of the *Kara Harp Okulu*— the Turkish Military Academy	President Cemal Gursel and Prime Minister Ismet Inonu	Failure
March 21, 1963	Colonel Talaat Aydemir and dissident cadets of the *Kara Harp Okulu*— the Turkish Military Academy	President Cemal Gursel and Prime Minister Ismet Inonu	Failure
March 12, 1971	Chief of Staff, General Memduh Tagmac The coup, against anti-Kemalist forces, was known as the "Coup by Memorandum."	Prime Minister Suleyman Demirel	Success
September 12, 1980	Chief of General Staff, General Kenan Evren and the National Security Council The coup was originally planned for July 11, 1980.	President Fahri Koruturk and Prime Minister Suleyman Demirel	Success
February 28, 1997	Military and anti-Islamist elements The coup came to be known as the "post-modern coup."	Prime Minister Necmettin Erbakan	Success

2003	326 active and retired military officers, in a plot code-named *Balyoz*, or "Sledgehammer"*	Prime Minister Recep Tayyip Erdoğan and the Justice and Development Party (AKP)	Failure
2004	Military and anti-Islamist elements Two coup attempts, code-named *Sarıkız* and *Ayışığı* were planned.*	Prime Minister Recep Tayyip Erdoğan	Failure
April 27, 2007	Military and anti-Islamist elements.*	Prime Minister Recep Tayyip Erdoğan	Failure
February 22, 2010	Forty-nine former air force, navy and First Army commanders.*	Islamist government of Prime Minister Recep Tayyip Erdoğan	Failure

UNITED ARAB EMIRATES			
Date	**Instigated By**	**Directed Against**	**Result**
June 24, 1965	Council of the ruling Qawasim family with British support	Sharjah Sheikh Saqr III ibn Sultan al-Qasimi	Success
January 24, 1972	Deposed Sheikh Saqr III ibn Sultan al-Qasimi and a small group of supporters	Sharjah Sheikh Khalid III ibn Muhammad al-Qasimi	Failure
June 16, 1987	Sheikh Abd al Aziz Al Qasimi, brother of the ruler, declared that Sultan III had abdicated because he had mismanaged Sharjah's economy. Abu Dhabi supported this move. Dubai opposed Sultan III's removal and he was restored to power June 23, 1987.	Sheikh Sultan III ibn Muhammad al-Qasimi	Failure

YEMEN			
(includes events in the Mutawakkilite Kingdom of Yemen, the Yemen Arab Republic and the People's Democratic Republic of Yemen, as well as the unified Republic of Yemen)			
Date	**Instigated By**	**Directed Against**	**Result**
February 17, 1948	Abdullah al-Wazir	Imam Yahya ibn Muhammad	Success
March 13, 1948	Crown Prince Ahmed	Imam Abdullah al-Wazir	Success
February 1950	Prince Ismail, brother of the Imam	Imam Ahmed	Failure
April 2, 1955	Prince Said al-Islam Abdallah, brother of the Imam, and Lt. Col. Ahmad al-Thalaya	Imam Ahmed	Failure
September 1958	Dissident royal bodyguards	Imam Ahmed	Failure
March 26, 1961	Brig. General Abdullah al-Sallal	Imam Ahmed	Failure

---

* Critics accuse the government of Prime Minister Recep Tayyip Erdoğan of fabricating these alleged coup plots, in order to undermine Turkey's once all-powerful military. In all these cases, charges were controversial, with many discrepancies in the plans the plotters supposedly drew up.

September 26, 1962	Brig. General Abdullah al-Sallal The coup led to the establishment of a republic and triggered a civil war (1962–70).	Imam Muhammad al-Badr	Success
November 5, 1967	Abdul Rahman al-Iryani, Ahmad Numan, and Muhammad Ali Uthman The coup produced a regime free of Egyptian influence.	President Abdullah al-Sallal	Success
March 20, 1968	Extreme leftist elements of the National Liberation Front The coup took place in the separate People's Republic of Southern Yemen, which had declared its independence on November 30, 1967.	President Qahtan al-Shaabi	Failure
March 22, 1968	Leftist extremists	President Abdul Rahman al-Iryani	Failure
May 1968	Muhammad ibn al-Hussein The coup was within the Royalist regime, still entrenched in northeastern Yemen.	Imam Muhammad al-Badr	Success
August 27–28, 1968	Abdul Wahab al-Raquib and dissident military officers	President Abdul Rahman al-Iryani	Failure
Late January 1969	Dissident military officers	President Abdul Rahman al-Iryani	Failure
June 22, 1969	Extreme leftist elements of the National Liberation Front The coup took place in the People's Republic of Southern Yemen.	President Qahtan al-Shaabi	Success
June 12, 1974	Lt. Colonel Ibrahim al-Hamdi The coup was called the "Corrective Movement."	President Abdul Rahman al-Iryani	Success
August 1975	Sheikh Bazel al-Wajih and pro-Royalist elements	President Ibrahim al-Hamdi	Failure
May 1978	Major Abdullah Abdel Alim, commander of the Paratroop Corps	President Ahmed al-Ghashmi	Failure
June 25, 1978	Salim Rubai Ali The attempted coup was in the then separate PDRY.	Abdel Fattah Ismail	Failure
June 26, 1978	Abdel Fattah Ismail The coup was in the then separate PDRY.	President Salim Rubai Ali	Success
October 15, 1978	Mujahid al-Kuhali and Nasserist and pro-Ba'athist elements	President Ali Abdullah Saleh	Failure
May 1979	Dissident army officers	President Ali Abdullah Saleh	Failure

April 21, 1980	Ali Nasir Muhammad The coup was in the then separate PDRY.	President Abdel Fattah Ismail	Success
January 13–29, 1986	Ex-president Abdel Fattah Ismail and his supporters The coup was in the then separate PDRY. It led to a short, but fierce, civil war.	President Ali Nasir Muhammad	Success
May 4, 1994	Ali al-Baidh and supporters The attempted coup sought the secession of the former PDRY as the "Democratic Republic of Yemen." A short civil war ensued May 21–July 7, 1994.	Chairman of the Presidential Council Ali Abdullah Saleh	Failure
January 19, 2015	Abduk Nalek al-Houthi, Houthi Shi'ite Zaydi rebels and supporters of former President Ali Abdullah Saleh	President Abed Rabbo Mansour Hadi	Success

38. The power that dominates the Nile Valley has been and continues to be the rival of the power that controls the Tigris–Euphrates Valley.

The table provides the most notable historic examples.

POWER RIVALRY BETWEEN THE NILE VALLEY AND TIGRIS–EUPHRATES VALLEY		
Era	**The Nile Power**	**The Tigris-Euphrates Power**
2000–1600 B.C.E.	Egypt*	Babylonia
600 B.C.E.	Egypt*	Assyrian Empire
590 B.C.E.	Egypt*	Chaldean Empire
520 B.C.E.	Egypt*	Persian Empire
192 B.C.E.	Egyptian Ptolemaic Kingdom*	Seleucid Kingdom
66 B.C.E.–217 C.E.	Roman Empire	Parthian Empire
1100–71	Fatimid Caliphate	Ayyubid Empire
1805	Mohammad Ali	Ottoman Turkey
1882–1918	The United Kingdom.	Ottoman Turkey
1945–54	Egypt under King Farouk.	Iraq under Nuri as-Sa'id.
1954–90s	Egypt under Gamal Abdel Nasser, Anwar el-Sadat, and Hosni Mubarak.	Iraq under Abdel Karim Qassem and Saddam Hussein.
1979–2011	Egypt under Hosni Mubarak.	Iran under the theocratic autocracy, which sought to export the Islamic revolution to Muslim countries. Since 2012, Iran increased its influence over Iraq.
2012–to date	Egypt under the Sunni Morsi (Muslim Brotherhood) regime and then the more secular El-Sisi government.	Iran under the control of the Shi'ite theocracy along with its satellite state of Shi'ite Iraq.

FAMOUS KINGS, QUEENS AND PHARAOHS OF EGYPT		
King or Pharaoh	**Years of Reign**	**Key Facts**
ARCHAIC PERIOD	ca. 3100–2770 B.C.E.	First through second dynasty
Menes also known as Narmer	3110–2884 B.C.E.	King of Upper Egypt, Menes conquered Lower Egypt and united the two kingdoms. He founded the first dynasty. His capital was at Memphis
OLD KINGDOM	2700–2160 B.C.E.	Third through sixth dynasty Worship of kings began. Age of the pyramids.

---

* For the most prominent rulers of Egypt during this period see table that follows immediately.

Khufu or Cheops	2680–2565 B.C.E.	Khufu built the largest of the Great Pyramids at Giza. The largest pyramid ever built, it was 481 feet high, 756 feet long on each side, covering thirteen acres, made of 2,300,000 blocks each averaging 2 ½ tons, with the largest weighting 15 tons. According to Herodotus, it took 100,000 men twenty years to build it. It is considered one of the Seven Wonders of the Ancient World.
FIRST INTERMEDIATE PERIOD	2200–2050 B.C.E.	Seventh through tenth dynasty
MIDDLE KINGDOM	2134–1786 B.C.E.	Eleventh through thirteenth dynasty
SECOND INTERMEDIATE PERIOD	1786–1560 B.C.E.	Fourteenth through seventeenth dynasty
NEW KINGDOM– THE EMPIRE	1575–1087 B.C.E.	Eighteenth through twentieth dynasty The capital was moved to Thebes.
Ahmose I	1580–1557 B.C.E.	Ahmose I defeated and ousted the Hyksos from Egypt. He was the founder of the Eighteenth Dynasty and the New Kingdom. He was first to assume the title "pharaoh."
Hatshepsut	1486–1468 B.C.E.	Hatshepsut was the first great woman ruler in history. She increased women's rights in Egypt. Her reign was peaceful. She developed Egypt's resources and expanded foreign trade.
Thutmose III	1468–1436 B.C.E.	Thutmose conquered many lands in southwestern Asia and build a great empire that reached to the Euphrates River. He adopted new techniques of warfare and is considered the "Napoleon of Egypt."

Amenhotep IV or Akhenaton	1375–1358 B.C.E.	Akhenaton introduced monotheism to Egypt. He wanted the Egyptians to worship only one God, the sun-disk god Aton. His wife was the beautiful Queen Nefertiti. He built a new capital, Akhetaten. He may have been murdered.
Tutankhamun III	1361–1352 B.C.E.	King Tut died as a youth. His tomb was discovered in 1922 by British archaeologist Howard Carter. It yielded rich art treasures made of gold, ivory, and precious stones.
Ramses II	1279–1213 B.C.E.	Ramses was probably the pharaoh of the Exodus, when Moses led the Hebrew people out of Egypt. Ramses built a new capital at Tanis (called Ramses), built many temples, and erected large statues of himself.
Ptolemy I	323–284 B.C.E.	Ptolemy founded the great library at Alexandria.
Cleopatra	69–30 B.C.E.	Cleopatra formed an alliance with Julius Caesar of Rome. Caesar helped her win the kingdom from her brother. Later she allied with Marc Antony. She was the last pharaoh of Egypt.

Aside from the historic rivalry between the power that dominates the Nile Valley and the power that controls the Tigris-Euphrates Valley, there have been other long-standing rivalries, indicative of the instability and unpredictability of the Middle East. One such is the hostility between historic Syria and historic Iraq. The table provides the most notable examples.

SYRIA–IRAQ RIVALRY	
Time Period	**Sides involved in the rivalry**
750 C.E.	The Damascus-based Umayyad Caliphate (661–750 C.E.) lost the military battle for intra-Muslim leadership to the Baghdad-based Abbasid Caliphate (750–1258).

1920–1946	Intense rivalry between the French Mandate of Syria (which included Lebanon) and the British Mandate of Iraq, each power seeking dominance in the Fertile Crescent. Arab nationalists in both, played off the two colonial powers against each other, which was further complicated by ethnic, sectarian and religious rivalries.
1946–58	The revolutionary, radical, republican, pan-Arab regimes in Syria (e.g. Shishakli regime) were constantly at loggerheads with the conservative, monarchical, Hashemite, pro-western government in Iraq.
1966–2003	The two nations quarreled over use of Euphrates River water, as well as oil-transit fees. Additionally, during the lengthy Iran–Iraq War (1980–88) Syria supported Persian Iran rather than Arab Iraq. Syrian military forces were part of Operation *Desert Storm*, in freeing Kuwait from Iraqi occupation in 1991. Furthermore, Syria supported ethnic, tribal, religious and ideological groups that opposed whatever Iraqi regime ruled in Baghdad.
2003–11	The Syrian Assad regime armed, trained and gave sanctuary to pro-Saddam Sunni terrorists, who were active in Iraq and undermining the stability of the Iraqi regime of Prime Minister Nouri al-Maliki.
2011–to date	In a dramatic shift, more reflective of the Sunni–Shi'ite rift, the Shi'ite Iraqi regime of Prime Minister Nouri al-Maliki supported the Assad regime in its nation-wide battle against Syria's Sunni majority. The latter represented by the Muslim Brotherhood and the Sunni Islamic supremacist forces of Al-Qaeda—as represented by its Al-Nusra Front (*Jabhat al-Nusra*), and the dissident offshoot, the Islamic State of Iraq and the Levant, among others. It is the Islamic State of Iraq and the Levant, abbreviated as ISIL, that made dramatic military gains in 2014, in both Syria and Iraq, in their quest to establish an Islamic caliphate that is transnational and straddles the border of both Syria and Iraq.

39. The goal of pan-Arab unity has been largely illusory, akin to a mirage in the desert.

Through much of the latter half of the twentieth century, there have been numerous attempts at pan-Arab unity—*al wahdah al arabiya*—made by various Arab states. The pan-Arab ideology is the insistence on the creation of a vast unified empire "from the Atlantic Ocean to the Arab Gulf" (as the pan-Arabists have named the Persian Gulf). The most noted historic attempts at unity are depicted in the table below.

ATTEMPTS AT PAN-ARAB UNITY		
Date	**Countries Involved**	**Outcome**
February 1, 1958	Egypt and Syria formed the United Arab Republic (UAR).	Syria seceded from the UAR, September 28, 1961.*
February 14, 1958	Iraq and Jordan formed the Arab Federation.	Iraq withdrew, July 15, 1958.
March 8, 1958	The United Arab Republic (Egypt and Syria) and Yemen formed the United Arab States (UAS).*	Syria seceded, September 28, 1961. Egypt terminated the UAS, December 26, 1961.
February 11, 1959	Audhali, Beihan, Dhala, Fadhli, Lower Yafa, and Upper Aulaqi Sheikhdom formed the Federation of Arab Emirates of the South.	This was a British-sponsored federation. It was succeeded by the Federation of South Arabia.
April 4, 1962	Federation of Arab Emirates of the South and Alawi, Aqrabi, Dathina, Haushabi, Lahej, Lower Aulaqi, Maflahi, Shaib, Wahidi (Wahidi Balhaf) joined to form the Federation of South Arabia. Aden joined on January 18, 1963. Upper Aulaqi Sultanate joined in June 1964.	The British-sponsored federation was opposed by nationalist forces. The federation was abolished with the independence of the People's Republic of Southern Yemen on November 30, 1967.
April 17, 1963	Egypt, Syria, and Iraq formed the United Arab Republic.	Egypt repudiated the union on July 22, 1963.
September 2, 1963	Syria and Iraq	Canceled
May 26, 1964	Egypt and Iraq	Canceled
July 13, 1964	Egypt and the Yemen Arab Republic	Canceled
November 8, 1970	Egypt, Syria, Libya, and Sudan	Canceled
April 19, 1971	Egypt, Syria, and Libya formed the Federation of Arab Republics	Egypt abrogated the union on October 3, 1984.

---

* After Syria's secession Egypt retained the name "United Arab Republic" hoping to re-create the union wiht Syria and/or other Arab states. Only on September 2 1971, did the UAR officially take the name "Arab Republic of Egypt."

December 2, 1971	Abu Dhabi, Ajman, Dubai, Fujairah, Sharjah, and Umm al-Qaiwain formed the United Arab Emirates. Ras al Khaimah joined February 11, 1972 (*see* "Strait of Hormuz and the UAE" map).	Successful to date.
August 2, 1972	Egypt and Libya	Canceled
November 28, 1972	The Yemen Arab Republic and the PDRY	Canceled
January 12, 1974	Libya and Tunisia formed the Arab Islamic Republic	Tunisia repudiated the union on January 15, 1974.
December 8, 1976	Syria and Jordan	Canceled
December 21, 1976	Egypt and Syria	Canceled
January 28, 1979	Syria and Iraq	Canceled
March 30, 1979	The Yemen Arab Republic and the PDRY	Canceled
September 10, 1980	Libya and Syria	Canceled
January 6, 1981	Libya and Chad	Canceled
August 14, 1984	Libya and Morocco formed the Arab-African Federation	Morocco repudiated the union on August 29, 1986.
October 1988	Libya and Sudan	Canceled
February 17, 1989	Libya, the Yemen Arab Republic, the PDRY, Oman, and Djibouti were to form an Arab Sahel State.	This was a proposal by Libya, which did not come to fruition.
May 23, 1990	The Yemen Arab Republic, and the PDRY established the Republic of Yemen.	Rebel PDRY forces attempted to secede from the union, May 4, 1994. They were defeated in a short, but furious civil war that ended July 7, 1994. The January 19, 2015 Houthi Shi'ite Zayid rebel takeover of Sana'a intensified a growing civil war. Thus, the future of a united Yemen is in doubt.
August 8, 1990	Iraq invaded Kuwait on August 2–4, 1990 and forcibly annexed and unified with Kuwait, declaring it the nineteenth province of Iraq.	As a result of Operation *Desert Storm*, Kuwait was liberated by February 28, 1991 and its independence was restored.

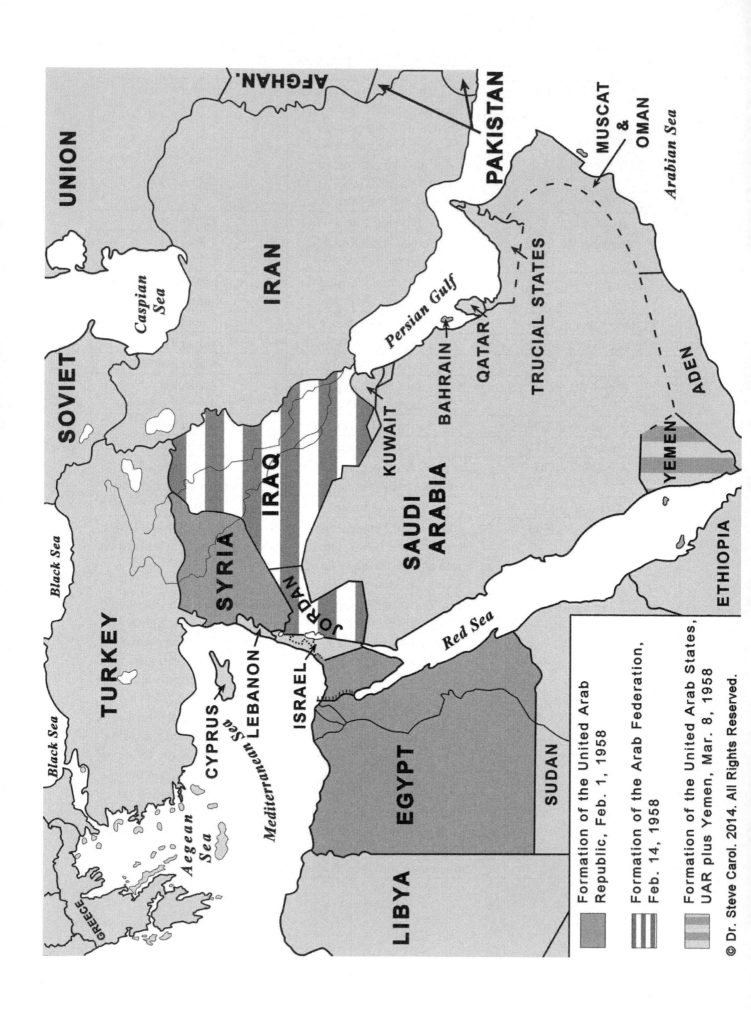

SOVIET UNION

TURKEY

GREECE

Black Sea

Aegean Sea

Caspian Sea

CYPRUS

Mediterranean Sea

LEBANON

ISRAEL

SYRIA

JORDAN

IRAQ

IRAN

AFGHAN.

PAKISTAN

KUWAIT

Persian Gulf

BAHRAIN

QATAR

TRUCIAL STATES

MUSCAT & OMAN

Arabian Sea

SAUDI ARABIA

ADEN

YEMEN

Red Sea

ETHIOPIA

SUDAN

EGYPT

LIBYA

Formation of the United Arab Republic, Feb. 1, 1958

Formation of the Arab Federation, Feb. 14, 1958

Formation of the United Arab States, UAR plus Yemen, Mar. 8, 1958

Pan-Arab ideology refused to accept anything less than a unified Arab state. Nonetheless, one of the most important underlying developments in the Arab world was the creation of separate countries. This was a relatively new idea in the region's long history. Many Arabs resent the arbitrarily drawn artificial boundaries for they intensify ethnic and sectarian violence. These boundaries were established by the Western European colonial powers—the United Kingdom, France and Italy. The enmity towards the Western European powers, which after World War II, *de facto* included the United States (as Western Europe's prime ally and supporter), superseded any antagonism against Arab imperialism. Thus, the Moroccan occupation of Western Sahara, the Iraqi conquest and annexation of Kuwait (the sole example of a forced "unity"), or the Syrian *de facto* occupation of Lebanon were not as great an issue.* Yet, despite the European-drawn boundaries, these countries put down roots, developed specific identities, and a sense of nationalism. It became evident that a major obstacle to attempts at unity was the fact that no Arab leader was willing to cede any power for the greater good of the union. Each claimant to the leadership of the pan-Arab movement—be it Gamal Abdel Nasser, Muammar Qadhafi, Hafez al-Assad or Saddam Hussein—wanted total control and leadership of the new pan-Arab entity they were endeavoring to create.

A prime example of this phenomenon took place in Iraq in 1958. The violent and bloody coup that removed the Hashemite monarchy of King Faisal II was largely instigated, encouraged, and supported by United Arab Republic President Gamal Abdel Nasser. Nasser's expectation was that Iraq would immediately join the UAR. This would bring added territory, prestige and most importantly, oil-revenues to the newly unified Arab state. However, Iraqi coup leader Abdel Karim Qassem quickly realized that merger into the UAR would at best bring him a regional governorship, whereas staying a separate independent country would bring him all the power and perks of a national head of state. Iraq therefore never joined the UAR. Thus, in this case as with others, nationalism has proven stronger than the drive towards pan-Arab unity. Hence, the concept of one pan-Arab unified nation has thus proven elusive, constantly coming into conflict with state interests.

All attempts at Arab unity have failed, with the exceptions of the establishment of the United Arab Emirates and the Republic of Yemen at least through 2015, in the case of the latter. In the case of the United Arab Emirates there was high motivation to succeed because each emirate was tiny in size and relatively weak and vulnerable. Unity was fostered by the concept of strength in numbers. Additionally, the UAE was a federal entity with each emirate retaining much power and remaining a separate unit. In the case of the Republic of Yemen, it was more an issue of obliterating an artificially drawn British colonial boundary and reuniting a historic nation. However, in the case of Yemen, unification was marred by the violent civil war of 1994. Rebellions continue to the present in the north, and there is on-going political dissatisfaction in the south. With the seizure of the Yemeni capital Sana'a by Houthi Shi'ite Zaydi rebels in January 2015, the intensification and internationalization of the Yemeni Civil War (2004 to date) with competing ethnic, tribal, religious and political factions, the future of the unified Republic of Yemen is in serious doubt.

The vehement Arab opposition to the reestablishment of a sovereign Jewish state, of any size, in what the Arabs perceive as their exclusive region is the only issue—albeit a negative one—that creates a semblance of Arab unity. Rather than Arab unity, during the last half of the twentieth century and into the twenty-first century, the Arab world has been beset by division. This Arab cold war saw the emergence of two, sometimes three, rival camps. The heightened inter-Arab rivalry was marked by plots to overthrow competing regimes, assassination attempts, support for opposing sides in the Yemen Civil War (1962–70) and the Syrian Civil War (2011 to date) as well as vicious media attacks.

---

* The Syria–Lebanon Treaty of Cooperation of May 20, 1991, codified the absorption of Lebanon by Syria.

DIVISIONS IN THE ARAB/MUSLIM MIDDLE EAST

PRIOR TO 1958		
PRO-HASHEMITE	**GREATER SYRIA**	**ANTI-HASHEMITE**
Iraq	Syria	Egypt
Jordan		Lebanon
		Saudi Arabia

1958–73	
"CONSERVATIVE"	**"PROGRESSIVE"**
Jordan	Egypt
Saudi Arabia	Syria
Lebanon	Iraq
Kuwait	Yemen (after 1962)
Morocco	Algeria
Tunisia	Sudan
Bahrain	Libya (after 1969)
Qatar	PDR Yemen
Oman	
United Arab Emirates	

1974–93		
"MODERATE"	**"CONSERVATIVE"**	**"REJECTIONIST FRONT"**
Egypt	Jordan	Iraq
Sudan	Saudi Arabia	Libya
Oman	Yemen	Algeria
Morocco	Lebanon	Syria
Tunisia	Kuwait	PDR Yemen
	Bahrain	Palestinian Liberation Organization
	Qatar	
	United Arab Emirates	

1993–2003	
"MODERATE"	**"RADICAL" & ISLAMIC FUNDAMENTALIST**
Algeria	Iraq
Bahrain	Lebanon
Egypt	Libya

Jordan	Sudan
Kuwait	Syria
Morocco	Iran*
Oman	
Palestinian Authority (PLO/PA)	
Qatar	
Saudi Arabia	
Tunisia	
United Arab Emirates	
Yemen	

2003–11		
"MODERATE"	?	"RESISTANCE BLOC" & ISLAMIC FUNDAMENTALIST
Algeria	Iraq	Gaza (Hamas-dominated since 2006)
Bahrain	Jordan	Iran*
Egypt	Libya	Lebanon (Hezbollah-dominated since 2006)
Kuwait	Oman	PFLP-GC and other terrorist groups
Morocco		Qatar
Palestinian Authority (PLO/PA)		Somalia
Saudi Arabia		Sudan
Tunisia		Syria
United Arab Emirates		Turkey†
Yemen government		Yemen–Houthi rebels

2011 TO 2013		
CONSERVATIVE "MODERATE" MONARCHIES	SALAFI SUNNI ISLAMIC FUNDAMENTALISTS	"REVOLUTIONARY CAMP" SHI'ITE ISLAMIC FUNDAMENTALIST
Bahrain	Egypt	Gaza–Islamic Jihad, which is fully financed and outfitted by Iran.
Jordan	Gaza (Hamas-dominated	Iran
Kuwait	Libya	Iraq

---

* While not an Arab state, Iran since 1979, is an Islamic fundamentalist state and a supporter of this camp.

† While not an Arab state, Turkey since 2003 has steadily moved towards becoming an Islamist state, replacing many of the secular features of the republic instituted by Mustafa Kemal Atatürk, over eight decades earlier. It has sided with Iran on many international issues, yet opposed Iran's Syrian ally the Bashar al-Assad regime during the Syrian Civil War. It became openly hostile to Israel, and protested various NATO moves.

Morocco	PFLP-GC and other terrorist groups	Lebanon (Hezbollah-dominated)
Oman*	Qatar	Syria
Saudi Arabia	Tunisia Ennahda Party	Yemen–Houthi rebels
United Arab Emirates	Turkey	

2013 TO DATE		
SUNNI CONSERVATIVE "MODERATES" and MONARCHIES	**SALAFI SUNNI ISLAMIC FUNDAMENTALISTS**	**"REVOLUTIONARY RADICAL CAMP" SHI'ITE ISLAMIC FUNDAMENTALIST**
Bahrain (government)	Al-Qaeda in the Arabian Peninsula	Bahrain (Al-Wefaq National Islamic Society)
Egypt	Ansar al-Sharia (Egypt) Ansar Bayt al-Maqdis and Majlis Shura al-Mujahideen (both in Egyptian Sinai)	Gaza–Islamic Jihad, which is fully financed and outfitted by Iran.
Jordan	Gaza–Hamas† (an arm of the Muslim Brotherhood)	Iran
Kuwait	Islamic State of Iraq and the Levant	Iraq (Shi'ite government)
March 14 Alliance in Lebanon (various Sunni and Christian Lebanese parties)	Libya	Lebanon (Hezbollah-dominated)
Morocco	Muslim Brotherhood (including Muslim Brotherhood militias in Iraq, Libya and Syria)	Syria
Oman	PFLP-GC and other terrorist groups	Yemen–Houthi rebels
Pakistan‡	Syria (al-Nusra Front)	
Qatar	Tunisia	
Saudi Arabia	Turkey (often)	
Sudan		
United Arab Emirates		
Yemen government		

---

* Most Omanis do not belong to Sunni or Shi'ite Islam. They follow a third way, Ibadism, an offshoot of Kharijism.

† Despite being Sunni, Hamas received Iranian military material support, technology and training with which to wage war against Israel, as in the Third Gaza War of 2014.

‡ Although not a Middle Eastern state, Pakistan by virtue of its close military, nuclear and security ties to Saudi Arabia increasingly has played a role in Middle East affairs.

In summation, the old ideologies—Nasserism, Arab Socialism, and Ba'athism—have proven to be bankrupt and incapable of solving the fundamental political, economic and social problems of Arab societies. Some Arabs have realized that Arab unity was a utopian dream, incompatible with their reality. This has produced cynicism and a sense of impotence. That in turn has created a wide opening for frustration. There is an ideological vacuum across the Arab world, a feeling that all the political solutions have been tried and none of them have worked. The increasingly violent rivalry between Saudi Arabia and Iran was intensified by the withdrawal of the United States from its dominant position in the region. As Syria, Iraq, Libya, and Yemen imploded, each into rival ethnic and sectarian regions, the Middle East faces increased conflict and war.

The era of Arab nationalism and the quest for pan-Arab unity ended after six decades of rule by the military in countries including Somalia, Iraq, Tunisia, Libya, and Yemen. Even non-Arab Turkey, after nine decades of secular government, supervised by the military, shifted course albeit gradually, under the direction of the Islamist Freedom and Justice Party (AKP) of Recep Tayyip Erdoğan. The void in the Arab/Muslim world is now being filled by a jihadist Islamic fundamentalism, which offers a messianic solution that secular politics failed to deliver. Thus, as Pan-Arabism declined, Pan-Islamism rose in its place.

With the advent of the Islamic Republic of Iran, pan-Islamism became a stronger and more widespread force in the greater Middle East and beyond. Ayatollah Ruhollah Khomeini railed against nationalism, "Those who say that we want nationality, they are standing against Islam. We have no use for the nationalists. Islam is against nationality." The second decade of the twenty-first century saw widespread protests sweeping the Arab world and the emergence of the transnational Muslim Brotherhood as a political force in several nations. This seemed to confirm that pan-Islamism—a transnationalist theological ideology—is in the ascendency in the region.

Growing out of the resentment of the rise of Shi'ite power in Iraq (after the decades-long suppression of that sect by the minority Sunnis), various Sunni militant jihadist groups began fighting in Iraq to overthrow the Shi'ite government and to resist the US-led coalition forces assisting Iraq. Among these groups was the *Jamā'at al-Tawḥīd wa-al-Jihād*, ("The Organization of Monotheism and Jihad"), founded in early 2004. Over the years, the group has used several different names as it eliminated rivals and consolidated its power. On April 9, 2013, the group adopted the name *ad-Dawla al-Islāmiyya fi al-'Irāq wa-sh-Shām*—the Islamic State of Iraq and the Levant (ISIL). The name was deliberately chosen, as its proclaimed goal is a transnational Islamic caliphate that will incorporate Iraq and the Levant. The Levant is a geographic and cultural region consisting of the eastern Mediterranean littoral (shoreline and hinterlands) between Anatolia (the bulk of Turkey) and the Sinai Peninsula. The Levant today consists of the island of Cyprus, part of southeastern Turkey, Lebanon, Syria, Israel, and Jordan. Beginning early in 2013, ISIL expanded into and intervened in the Syrian Civil War against the Assad regime. It also fought to decimate other rival anti-Assad Sunni groups to emerge as the dominant force in northern and northeastern Syria.

Just days after ISIL captured Fallujah, Iraq (about 43 miles west of the capital, Baghdad), ISIL proclaimed independence, on January 3, 2014. By June 10, 2014, ISIL was able to seize control of Mosul, Iraq's second largest city, and then moved south and captured Tikrit, the hometown of former dictator Saddam Hussein. This was followed by the seizure of Saadiyah, Jalawla, and Tel Afar. In the territory it controls, ISIL immediately implemented strict shari'a law. By the end of June 2014, Iraq was effectively divided into a Shi'ite south and center, including Baghdad, a Sunni, ISIL-dominated west and a Kurdish-ruled north. However, it is doubtful if ISIL will curtail its drive to reestablish a caliphate. One of the first moves by ISIL was to bulldoze away the border between the sections of

Syria and Iraq that they control. Led by Abu Bakr al-Baghdadi, ISIL's dramatic and swift victories may herald the start of a new pan-Islamic unified caliphate, especially if not challenged by sufficient military force. With the proclamation of, and rapid military expansion of ISIL, the idea of a twenty-first century caliphate (*khilafa*) is no longer in the realm of the theoretical—it is a harsh reality. On June 29, 2014, which coincided with the first day of Ramadan (1435 A.H.) ISIL proclaimed its leader, Abu Bakr al-Baghdadi as "the imam and *khalifa* (caliph) for Muslims everywhere." ISIL also said that with the establishment of the caliphate, the group was changing its name to just the Islamic State, dropping the mention of Iraq and the Levant. The proclamation concluded, "The legality of all emirates, groups, states and organizations becomes null by the expansion of the caliph's authority and the arrival of its troops to their areas. Listen to your caliph and obey him. Support your state, which grows every day."[71] Daily new recruits stream to its black banner from across the Muslim world, as the map of the Middle East undergoes dramatic change. It remains to be seen if Al-Qaeda and other Islamic supremacist groups will obey the call of the Islamic State. On the other hand, in the case of Egypt, the popular revolution that preceded the military intervention of July 3, 2013, seems to indicate that the Muslim Brotherhood tide, at least in that nation, was stoppable. Time will tell if the Muslim Brotherhood can be halted elsewhere.

Not to be forgotten nor ignored is the reality of 1,400 years of Muslim sectarianism. Sunnis versus Shi'ites, Sufis versus Salafis, Arabs versus Persians, and Africans versus Asians are but some of the divisions within the Muslim world. Additionally thus far, there has been no overarching Islamic solidarity transcending the multitude of parochial loyalties—to one's family, clan, tribe, village, or country. Thus for example, not only do Arabs consider themselves superior to all other Muslims, but the inhabitants of Hejaz, the northwestern part of the Arabian Peninsula and Islam's birthplace, regard themselves the only true Muslim Arabs, and tend to be highly disparaging of all other Arabic-speaking communities. In fact, until the twentieth century, the Arabs of Arabia did not regard Egyptians as Arabs. Nevertheless, two factors unite many of the world's Muslims. The first is resistance to the West in general and the United States and Israel, in particular. The second factor is an absolutist, non-negotiable commitment that the region will be dominated and controlled by them alone.

If there is a positive hope that can be generated from all the recent turmoil, violence and boundary-eradication, it is the fact that as the artificial borders established by the Sykes-Picot Agreement fades away, in their place we may soon see the emergence of true nation-states, largely homogeneous and steeled in the determination to preserve their national identity and sovereignty. One such state has existed for some 67 years—it is Israel. Others may soon include Kurdistan, a revival of Jabal al-Druze—a Druze state—(which existed earlier from 1921 to 1936), an Alawite State (which existed earlier from 1920 to 1936) and perhaps an *Imazighen* (Berber) state. A common factor shared by all is their experience of dealing with and suffering under the rule of Sunni Islamic states.

EVER SHIFTING ALLIANCES

[A nation] … has no eternal friends … no perpetual enemies …
only eternal and perpetual interests.
Henry John Temple, 3rd Viscount Palmerston, British Foreign Secretary, 1848

When promises are not observed, there can be no leagues or alliances.
David Hume, Scottish philosopher and historian.

The Middle East has been a region of shifting alliances, both formal and informal. Sometimes those alliances make for strange bedfellows. Most of these alliances are built on cynical pragmatism. However, Turkey, for over three centuries always maintained a policy of opposing Russia.

40. For most of its modern history, Israel has been one of the most steadfast allies of the United States, though no formal alliance exists between the two nations.

Throughout over six decades since the reestablishment of Israel, an often repeated claim is made that Israel is a draining liability—a burden—on the United States. This claim is bogus. Exacerbating this calumny were statements made by and the conduct of, Israel's leftist leaders since 1993, which created the false impression that Israeli-American ties constituted a one-way relationship. The impression was given that the United States gave and Israel merely received and thus must constantly bow to "American pressure" as personified by the US State Department.[*] The noted Israeli historian, author and Knesset member, Shmuel Katz summarized this danger best, "There exists … among many Americans, a conviction of Israeli dependence on the United States. What is worse, many Israelis have a sense of dependence; worst of all, it is a sense that exists also among Israeli leaders."[1] The truth is that the relationship is a two-way partnership. An examination of the facts will consign these charges to the trash-heap of history where they belong.

First, Israel is a beacon of Western civilization in a volatile, dangerous and troubled region, the Middle East. It is a kindred Western democracy. This means that its relationship with the United States reflects the will of the Israeli people. As such, it remains a constant, reliable, permanent US ally regardless of who is the Prime Minister. In contrast, the remainder of countries in the Middle East are one-leader states, with little or no reflection of the will of the people. That leader may be an American "ally," but is just a bullet, coup or revolution away from being replaced by a new anti-American regime. Recall that this is what happened in Iraq in 1958 under King Faisal II, and in Iran under the Shah, which until 1979, was the US's most important ally in the Persian Gulf region. Similarly, since 2002, the Islamist government of Recep Tayyip Erdoğan has encouraged anti-Americanism within Turkey and shifted that nation away from its alignment with Europe, its NATO ally the United States and its *de facto* strategic partner for over twenty years, Israel. Furthermore generally speaking, it should be noted, that for the past almost 100 years, the Arab states have supported the enemies of the United States, and the West in general. During the 1930s and 1940s, they supported the Nazi and fascist regimes in Germany and Italy, respectively. From the 1950s through the 1990s, they backed

---

[*] Note: It has always been the policy of the US State Department to force Israel to return any territories gained in legitimate wars of self-defense.

the Soviet communist bloc. Beginning in the late 1970s, many Arabs supported the Islamic regime of Iran and since the 1990s, they have backed the transnational anti-American groups such as Al-Qaeda, the Muslim Brotherhood and Islamic State. The blunt reality is that Israel is the only nation in the Middle East that shares the values, interests, and enemies of the United States.

Israel contributes substantially to the United States in the domains of hard security (defense and intelligence) and soft security (economic competitiveness, sustainability, and in other non-military sectors). Israel is the only US ally in the Middle East that always fights its own battles. Israel has never requested, nor expects, American armed forces to fight to preserve and protect the Jewish state. In contrast, the governments of Iran (in 1953), Lebanon (in 1958), Saudi Arabia (in 1963 and again in 1990–91), Jordan (in concert with Israel and the United Kingdom in 1970), Kuwait (in 1987 and 1991), Iraq (2003 to 2011), and Libya (in 2011), all needed US military intervention and support in order to survive against both internal and external threats. Additionally, American military forces assisted the Muslims in Bosnia, Kosovo, Somalia, and Afghanistan. In fact, with the exception of Kuwait, the United States has never presented a bill for its efforts. Furthermore, when asked to leave, the United States has done so. Since the United States and Israel share the same regional foes, when Israel is called upon to fight its enemies, its successes have an effect that benefits the United States. Among the Israeli contributions to the United States were several notable examples.

In May 1951, Israeli Prime Minister David Ben-Gurion, on an unofficial trip to Washington, DC, held a clandestine meeting with General Walter Bedell-Smith, the head of the CIA. As a result of his trip, Israel concluded a secret agreement—Operation *Balsam*—with the United States to share intelligence on security matters. In 1952, the Chairman of the Joint Chiefs of Staff, General Omar Bradley assessed that only Britain, Turkey, and Israel could help the United States with their air forces in the event of a Soviet attack in the Middle East. Bradley called for the integration of Israel into Mediterranean Basin area defense planning, in light of the country's location and unique capabilities.[2]

On February 25, 1956, Soviet Premier Nikita Khrushchev, in a five-hour secret speech, denounced his predecessor, Joseph Stalin and his "cult of personality" at the Twentieth Party Congress of the Communist Party of the Soviet Union. By April 13, Israeli intelligence—the *Shin Bet*—obtained a copy of the speech via a Polish journalist, Viktor Grayevsky. It was the greatest intelligence-gathering achievement for Israeli intelligence to that time. Israel's CIA liaison was James Jesus Angleton, the head of counterintelligence. The speech, in photographic format, was delivered to him. On April 17, 1956, the photographs had reached the CIA chief Allen Dulles, who quickly informed US President Dwight D. Eisenhower. After determining that the speech was authentic, the CIA leaked the speech to *The New York Times* in early June 1956.[3] The speech became a central propaganda tool in American foreign policy, with dramatic repercussions throughout the Soviet bloc as well as on Sino-Soviet relations. During the Cold War, the United States and Israel had a joint strategic interest in defeating aggressors in the Middle East seeking to invade their neighbors and disrupt the *status quo,* especially if they had the backing of the Soviet Union. This became the essence of the United States–Israel alliance in the Middle East.

In July 1958, Egypt's Nasser sought to topple the governments of Lebanon, Jordan, Libya and Iraq, (*see* "Nasser's Ambitions–Hegemony in the Arab World" map) prompting Western intervention. US military forces were deployed to Lebanon—Operation *Blue Bat*—under the Eisenhower Doctrine (*see* Appendix 7). President Eisenhower wanted US troops to be present all at once in full force, and thus had them storm a beach near Beirut, rather than disembark at the harbor. The display of overwhelming odds precluded any Nasserist resistance. British troops were sent to Jordan and Libya, to support the legitimate governments of those countries. Israel played an essential role in saving the Hashemite monarchy of Jordan. When Jordan's erstwhile ally, Saudi Arabia, refused to allow oil deliveries to over-fly Saudi airspace,[4] the United States requested that Israel allow American oil deliveries and supplies to over-fly Israel. The United Kingdom urgently needed to bring troops into Jordan to support the regime, Israel again cooperated and allowed British over-flights that ferried some 3,000 troops into Amman to support King Hussein. An Anglo-American airlift over Israel into Jordan continued from July 17 to August 4, 1958 (*see* "Western Intervention Saves Moderate Regimes" map). As King Hussein would later write in his memoirs, "Every gallon had to be flown over the skies of Israel, the mortal enemy of all Arab states. Where an Arab nation refused, an enemy agreed."[5]

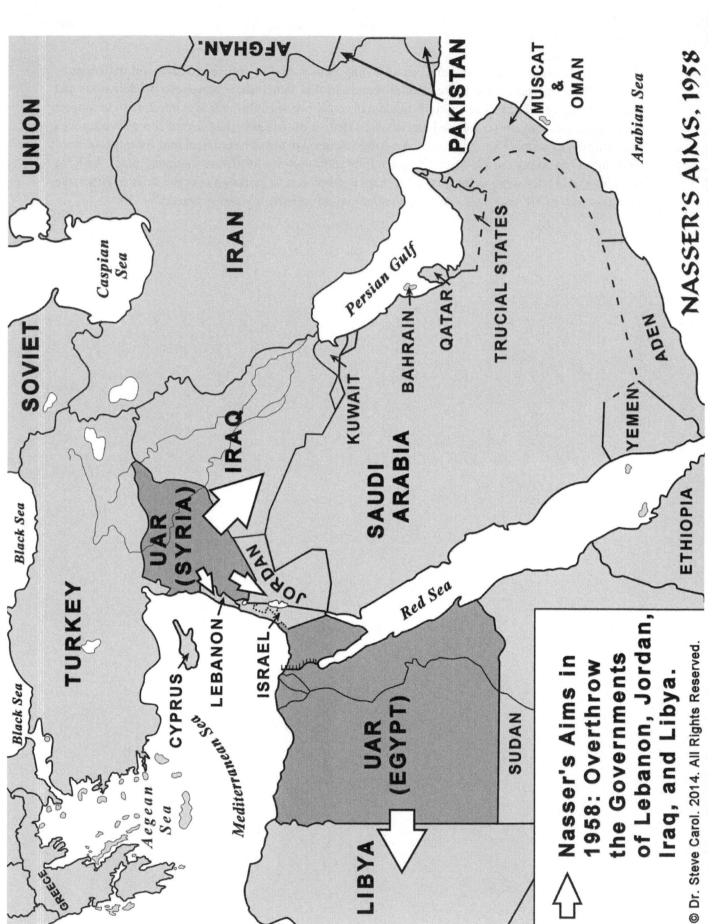

NASSER'S AIMS, 1958

Nasser's Aims in 1958: Overthrow the Governments of Lebanon, Jordan, Iraq, and Libya.

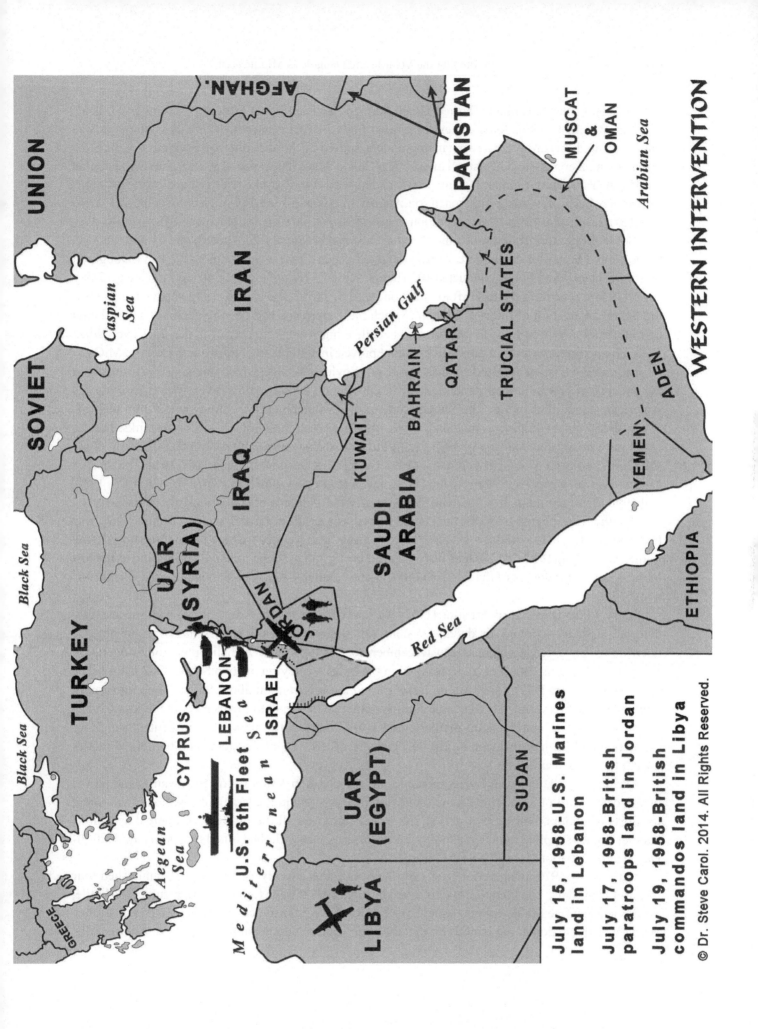

WESTERN INTERVENTION

July 15, 1958-U.S. Marines
land in Lebanon

July 17, 1958-British
paratroops land in Jordan

July 19, 1958-British
commandos land in Libya

© Dr. Steve Carol. 2014. All Rights Reserved.

President John F. Kennedy hosted Israeli Foreign Minister Golda Meir, on December 27, 1962, in Palm Beach, Florida, for a review of United States–Israel relations. Kennedy's language was unprecedented. According to a secret memorandum drafted by the attending representative of the State Department, Kennedy told his Israeli guest, "The United States has a special relationship with Israel in the Middle East really comparable only to what it has with Britain over a wide range of world affairs."[6]

As has been previously mentioned, on August 16, 1966, an Iraqi pilot flew his MiG-21F-13 to Israel as a result of a covert Israeli operation. It was the first time such a sophisticated (then) top-of-the-line Soviet-built aircraft had fallen into Western hands. On January 23, 1968, Israel loaned the MiG to the United States for evaluation, sharing the intelligence on the aircraft, under the Have Doughnut program. The United States conducted 102 flights, some 77 flying hours, in 40 days during a 75-day period before returning the aircraft to Israel on April 8, 1968.[7] The transfer helped pave the way for the Israeli acquisition of the F-4 Phantom, which the Americans had been reluctant to sell to Israel up to that point. The MiG-21 at that time was challenging American aircraft in the skies over North Vietnam and the information provided by Israel proved invaluable in combating the hostile MiGs.

In June 1967, Israel defeated a radical Arab, pro-Soviet offensive, which threatened to bring about the collapse of pro-American Arab regimes and disrupt oil supplies, thus severely undermining the American standard of living. The United States gained valuable military information from analysis of captured Soviet equipment, including SA-2, Mig-21 aircraft, and Soviet T-54 battle tanks. In fact, Israel gave an entire squadron of MiG-21s to the United States, which was dubbed the "Top Gun" squadron, and used by US air and naval forces for training purposes. Since 1967, Israel transferred captured Soviet weapons systems to the US Pentagon after every conflict: 1967, 1967–70, 1973, 1982, and 1990 (Scud remnants from the Gulf War), and 2006 (remnants of Iranian-supplied missiles).

Another unexpected gain, for the United States, as a result of Israel's victory in June 1967, was that it forced Egypt to withdraw its expeditionary army from Yemen—where it had intervened in the Yemen Civil War (1962–70)—which also removed the Egyptian threat to Saudi Arabia and to the rest of the Arab oil-producers of the Persian Gulf (*see* the "Yemen Civil War–Stalemate and Conclusion" map).

In the 1,000-Day War of Attrition (1967–70), the IDF armed with American aircraft successfully defeated a Soviet-supplied air defense system, pointing out the deficiencies in Soviet air-defense doctrine to US defense planners. On December 26–27, 1969, an IDF helicopter raid—Operation *Rooster 53*—on Ras Gharib, Egypt, resulted in the Israelis carrying off two Soviet T-62 main battle tanks and a Soviet P-12 radar system. Israel shared the information about the captured equipment with the US military. Indeed, it became common practice for Israel to furnish whole Soviet weapons systems—like 122 and 130-mm artillery, and a T-72 main battle tank—to the United States for evaluation and testing, influencing the development of US weapons systems and battlefield tactics during the Cold War.[8]

On January 22, 1970, an IDF commando raid—Operation *Rhodes*—on Shadwan Island (at the mouth of the Gulf of Suez where it meets the Red Sea) resulted in the Israeli occupation of the island for thirty-six hours. During that period, the Israelis removed all the military equipment as well as another Soviet-supplied radar system sharing the information with the United States (*see* the "1,000-Day War of Attrition–Israeli Actions" map).

On July 30, 1970, in an aerial clash over the Suez Canal, twenty Soviet MiG-21s ambushed four IAF F-4 Phantoms. The Phantoms were joined by eight IAF Mirage fighters. As a result of the battle, the Soviets lost five MiGs, with no Israeli losses. It was the first instance of Soviet aerial combat since World War II. No doubt, the Israelis briefed the Americans about the tactics employed. Additionally, the Israeli achievement proved the ineffectiveness of the military umbrella the Soviets provided its Arab clients in exchange for Soviet basing arrangements.

During the events of Black September 1970, in coordination with the United States, (which was tied up by wars in Vietnam, Laos, and Cambodia)[9] Israel brought about the withdrawal of invading Syrian forces from Jordan. This action prevented the fall of the pro-American Hashemite government of King Hussein, and the installation of a pro-Soviet radical Palestinian terrorist regime with its accompanying threat to US interests in the region.

In October 1973, thanks to US resupply of armaments, but without US forces, Israel defeated Soviet-trained and equipped Egyptian and Syrian forces. Israel again shared captured Soviet equipment, including T-62 battle tanks with the United States. Israel emerged as the only reliable ally in the entire Middle East region, where US troops could land, where US equipment could be pre-positioned, and where the United States has friendly port facilities (in Haifa and Ashdod). This saved the United States billions of dollars.

In 1977, Israel began to provide port services to the US Sixth Fleet in the Mediterranean, in part to offset the Soviet use of Tartus and Latakia, Syria as main bases for the Soviet Mediterranean Squadron. By 1992, the number of US Navy ship visits to Haifa had reached fifty per year. Admiral Carl Trost, the former Chief of Naval Operations, commented that with the end of the Cold War and the shifting American interest in power projection to the Middle East, the Sixth Fleet's need for facilities in the Eastern Mediterranean had actually increased. There were emerging threats that cemented United States–Israel ties. Six years later in 1998, the United States and Israel specifically added the proliferation of weapons of mass destruction and intermediate-range missiles to their security agenda in a new United States–Israel Memorandum of Understanding.[10]

In 1980, it was Presidential candidate Ronald Reagan who first explicitly described Israel as a strategic asset when he declared, Israel "serves as a vital strategic asset with its highly trained and experienced military forces, and is a deterrent to Soviet expansion in that troubled part of the world."[11] On November 30, 1981, the United States and Israel signed a Memorandum of Understanding on Strategic Cooperation. This provided for joint military—land, sea and air—exercises, planning for the establishment and maintenance of joint readiness activities, and joint working teams dealing with specific military issues. Though briefly suspended due to political differences between the two countries, strategic cooperation was then fully resumed in 1983 after the Israel–PLO War in Lebanon. This included for example, contingency plans for the rescuing of downed pilots in the region.

Israel bombed the Iraqi nuclear reactor at Osirak, on June 7, 1981, delaying Saddam Hussein's quest for nuclear weapons and severely reducing Iraqi military strength. It thus provided the United States with the option of engaging in conventional wars with Iraq in 1991 and 2003. It spared the United States and the world a nuclear confrontation, along with its massive human losses and multi-billion dollar cost. In fact, in October 1991, then Secretary of Defense Richard Cheney thanked Israel for its "bold and dramatic action" ten years earlier in taking out the Osirak facility, adding, and "strategic cooperation with Israel remains a cornerstone of US defense policy." Cheney reportedly gave Israeli Major General David Ivri, then the commander of the Israeli Air Force, a framed satellite photo of the Iraqi nuclear reactor destroyed by US-built Israeli aircraft. On the photo, Cheney penned, "With thanks and appreciation for the outstanding job you did on the Iraqi nuclear program in 1981, which made our job much easier in Desert Storm!"[12]

During the Israel–PLO War in Lebanon (1982), in a 46-hour campaign, June 9–11, 1982, Israel's air force, in Operation *Mole Cricket 19,* attacked 23 most advanced Soviet surface-to-air missile (SAM) batteries employed by Syria and considered impregnable. Nineteen SAM batteries (SA-2s,

SA-3s, and SA-6s) were destroyed and four others were severely damaged—all within two hours without losing an IAF airplane. In subsequent air battles involving some 150 aircraft, Israel downed 86 Syrian MiG-21s, MiG-23s, and Sukhoi-22s without IAF loss.[13] Additionally, Israel's military was the first to make widespread use of drones during this conflict.

The magnitude of Israel's victories in the Bekáa Valley operation (*Mole Cricket 19*) shocked Soviet military leaders. Top Soviet systems had been trounced. Knowing that Israel shared military information and technology with the United States, there was concern that NATO forces in Europe could emulate these victories against Soviet forces in Eastern Europe. An unforeseen benefit, occurred in 1991, when it was revealed by a Czech general (who had been serving in Moscow in 1982) that the Bekáa Valley air war made the Soviets understand that Western technology was superior to theirs, and in this Czech general's view, the blow to the Bekáa Valley SAMs was part of the cascade of events leading to the collapse of the Soviet Union.[14]

Israel's battle tactics and operational lessons, electronic warfare and other technological innovations have been shared with the United States, the value of which was estimated to be worth billions of dollars. US–Israeli defense cooperation, during the early 1980s, focused on the Eastern Mediterranean. IDF Major General (res.) Avraham Tamir, who served as the National Security Advisor to Israel's Minister of Defense, revealed that both countries were focused on Soviet military moves into Syria and Libya as well as an Israeli "air umbrella" to protect US troop movements that would seek to counter that scenario.[15]

The vice president of General Dynamics Corporation, which produced the F-16 Fighting Falcon fighter jets, stated that Israel was responsible for 600 improvements in the plane's systems, modifications estimated to be worth billions of dollars, which spared the United States dozens of research and development years. Israel upgraded the Hawkeye spy plane and the MD-500 helicopter, which helped convince US allies, Japan and the Republic of (South) Korea, to purchase those upgraded versions of the two aircraft over comparable British and French aircraft.

Former Secretary of State and NATO forces commander Alexander Haig stated that he was pro-Israeli because "Israel is the largest American aircraft carrier in the world that cannot be sunk, does not carry even one American soldier, and is located in a critical region for American national security."[16] As such, Israel helps maintain the US's capacity to project American power in the region, which in turn insures the smooth flow of oil from the Persian Gulf to the rest of the world. Israel also acts as a brake to check the attempts of radical regimes and terrorist groups to upset the status quo in the region.

The first visit to Israel of a chairman of the Joint Chiefs of Staff, General John W. Vessey, Jr., took place in early 1984.[17] Joint air and naval exercises between the two countries became increasingly frequent. The US Marine Corps engaged in live-fire exercises and practiced beach assaults in Israel as well.[18] On August 31, 1984, US Navy Secretary John Lehman, Jr., announced that the US would lease twelve Israeli Kfir C1 fighters (re-designated F-21A Kfir by the Navy) from Israel Aircraft Industries for a period of three and a half years,[19] for the Navy's "Aggressor Squadron"—Fighter Squadron 43. The Kfirs were used to train US pilots in aerial mock dog fighting tactics against Soviet aircraft. The Kfir, superior in speed and maneuverability, simulated the Soviet-made MiG-21 in training exercises. Speaking at a ceremony accepting the delivery of the first three Kfirs at Oceana Naval Air Station near Virginia Beach, Virginia, Secretary Lehman acknowledged, "the Israeli Government has made three aircraft available to us at no cost to the US taxpayer."[20] Safe ports for US Navy ships (e.g. Haifa and Ashdod), components for tank systems, and hardware for the US Marines were also mentioned by Lehman. "There are quite a few other innovative things we [the US] find we can avoid investing money in, things already done in Israel, to apply to our own country to cut the cost of defense,"[21] he added. Illustrative of his last statement was the US purchase of Israeli-made Mastiff remotely piloted vehicles (RPV) in June 1984[22] and Samson air decoys later that same year. By 1989, Israel's Defense Minister Yitzhak Rabin would reveal that the United States and Israel had conducted 27 or 28 combined exercises, and that US Marine Corps exercises were being held at the battalion level.[23]

In 1985, the Reagan administration invited Israel, along with other allies, to take part in the Strategic Defense Initiative (SDI), in order to develop an effective defensive anti-missile shield against ballistic missiles. Eventually, the United Kingdom, Germany, and Israel emerged as the largest foreign participants in the program.[24] Only Israel developed the first land-based missile defense system in the world, utilizing the Arrow anti-ballistic missile system, whose development came out of this joint program. As a result of the Arrow program, Israeli technological breakthroughs in missile defense were fully shared with the United States.

In 1986, General George F. Keegan, former head of US Air Force Intelligence, publicly declared to correspondent Wolf Blitzer, that he could not have obtained the same intelligence that he received from Israel if he had "five CIAs."[25] He further stated that between 1974 and 1990, Israel received $18.3 billion in US military grants. During the same period, Israel provided the United States with some $50 to 80 billion in intelligence, research and development savings, and Soviet weapons systems captured and transferred to the United States. He added, "The ability of the US Air Force in particular, and the Army in general, to defend whatever position it has in NATO owes more to the Israeli intelligence input than it does to any single source of intelligence, be it satellite reconnaissance, be it technology intercept, or what have you."[26]

President Ronald Reagan and Israeli Prime Minister Yitzhak Shamir signed a Memorandum of Agreement for Joint Political, Security, and Economic Cooperation, on April 21, 1988. Its purpose was to coordinate planning against threats faced by both nations in the Middle East. The five-year agreement called Israel "a major non-NATO ally of the United States."[27] It was the first formal expression of this fact that had been obvious to the world.

Additionally in 1989, Joseph Sisco, a former US Assistant Secretary of State, assistant to Secretary of State Henry Kissinger during the latter's shuttle diplomacy, told the Israeli author and military expert, Shmuel Katz, "I want to assure you, Mr. Katz, that if we were not getting full value for our money, you would not get a cent from us." Not to be overlooked is the fact that for many decades Israel shared its civil aviation security expertise with the United States.

During the Persian Gulf War in 1991, Israel provided invaluable intelligence, an umbrella of air cover for military cargo, and had personnel planted in the Iraqi desert to pick up downed American pilots. Additionally, Israel was ready to provide emergency medical services or even air support if necessary. There was nothing, which prohibited the use of US weapons stockpiles that had been pre-positioned in Israel during the 1990s for Gulf contingencies from 1991 through the US-led coalition's invasion of Iraq in 2003, if the need arose.

Moreover, on April 30, 1996, a Counterterrorism Cooperation Accord between the United States and Israel was signed. On October 31, 1998, a United States–Israel Security Memorandum of Agreement was signed. Furthermore, in April 2001, the US Air Force joined the IAF and held their first-ever joint maneuvers in the Negev Desert involving mid-air refueling, dog fighting, and air-to-ground attacks.[28]

During the war against Islamic supremacism, the US military effort against Al-Qaeda and the Taliban was based on a doctrine developed by Israel. The IDF was a global leader in targeting terrorists from the air. When Israel embarked on its assassinations policy in the summer of 2001, the United

States condemned it. Several weeks later, the World Trade Center was brought down in an Al-Qaeda terrorist attack and Washington's approach changed. Instead of condemning Israel, the Americans simply copied its methods, foreign sources say. Israel developed the first modern unmanned aerial vehicles (pilotless aircraft also known as drones). These aircraft were the lead force in the US campaign against Al-Qaeda and the Taliban. US unmanned combat air vehicles armed with missiles, started being used to kill terrorists, first in Yemen and later in Afghanistan as well as in Pakistan.[29]

Additionally, in the first decade of the twenty-first century, Israel shared with the United States, its battle-tested experience and expertise in combating Palestinian and Hezbollah terrorism, which were the role models of anti-US Islamic terrorism in Iraq, Afghanistan and elsewhere. US GIs benefited from Israel's battle tactics in urban warfare, and in dealing with improvised explosive devices (IEDs), car bombs, booby-traps, anti-tank missiles and suicide bombers. Israel relayed to the US lessons of battle (during the Cold War it was lessons about Soviet military doctrine) and counter-terrorism (including aircraft security, suicide bombings, manning of roadblocks and checkpoints, as well as interrogation of terrorists), which reduced American losses in Iraq and Afghanistan, prevented attacks on US soil, upgraded American weapons, and contributed to the US economy. Without Israel, the United States would have been forced to deploy tens of thousands of American troops in the eastern Mediterranean basin, at a cost of billions of dollars a year.

In 2005, Israel provided America with the world's most extensive experience in homeland defense, warfare against suicide bombers and car bombs. American soldiers trained in IDF facilities and Israeli-made drones flew above the "Sunni Triangle" in Iraq, as well as in Afghanistan, providing US Marines with vital intelligence.

In testimony given in 2005, Senator Daniel Inouye argued Israeli information regarding Soviet arms saved the US billions of dollars. "The contribution made by Israeli intelligence to America is greater than that provided by all NATO countries combined," he said. Yet another United States–Israel Memorandum of Understanding was signed on February 7, 2007, which formalized cooperation on homeland security.

Moreover, on March 15, 2007, in testimony before the House Armed Services Committee on the United States European Command (USEUCOM) commander General Bantz J. Craddock stated, "in the Middle East, Israel is the US's closest ally that consistently and directly supports our interests through security cooperation and understanding of US policy in the region." He added, "Israel is a critical military partner in the difficult seam of the Middle East."[30] Several months later, on May 21, 2007, US ambassador to Israel, Richard H. Jones told the Begin-Sadat Center for Strategic Studies conference on United States–Israel relations, that Israeli technologies were being used by the US armed forces in Iraq to protect American troops from improvised explosive devices, which had been responsible for most of the US casualties in the Iraq War.[31] He added that Israel was America's "closest ally" in the Middle East and that it "consistently and directly" supported US interests.[32]

In September 2007, the IAF destroyed a Syrian-DPRK nuclear plant. In effect, it was the US's surrogate in controlling nuclear proliferation by two rogue regimes. It provided the United States with vital information on Russian air defense systems, which are also employed by Iran. It bolstered the US posture of deterrence and refuted the claim that US-Israel relations have been shaped by political expediency.

Israel's utilization of American arms guarantees its existence, but at the same time gives US military industries, such as Boeing, General Dynamics, Lockheed Martin, and Sikorsky a competitive edge compared to European industries, while also boosting American military production and improving America's national security. American industries want US aid to Israel to continue. At least

74 percent of the $1.8 billion in annual US military aid to Israel must be spent in the United States. That provides jobs for some 50,000 US workers. Virtually all of the $1.2 billion in annual economic aid goes for repayment of debt to the United States, incurred from military purchases dating back many years. This debt is now close to being liquidated.

Innovative Israeli technologies have a similar effect on the American civilian sector, including but not limited to computer-related industries and agricultural industries. It should not be forgotten that most microprocessors for computers, developed by Intel, were originally invented in Israel, whereas Apple uses a flash memory invented in Israel. US firms have established research and development (R&D) centers in Israel to take advantage of its leadership in the following fields (2012 rankings):

- First in engineers/scientists per capita
- First in quality of scientific research institutions
- First in R&D as percentage of GDP
- First in wastewater recycling (80 percent)
- Second in clean-tech innovation
- Fourth in patents per million population
- Fifth in scientific publications per capita[33]

In contrast to US commitments to the Republic of (South) Korea, Japan, Germany and other parts of the world, not a single American serviceperson needs to be stationed in Israel. Considering that the cost of one serviceperson per year—including backup and infrastructure—is estimated to be about $200,000 per year, and assuming a minimum contingent of 25,000 troops, the cost savings to the United States on that score alone are on the order of $5 billion a year.

In a report entitled "Israel: A Strategic Asset for the United States," written for the Washington Institute for Near East Policy in late 2011, Robert D. Blackwill and Walter B. Slocombe reemphasized Israel's value as a strategic ally of the United States. Blackwill, was Deputy National Security advisor for Strategic Planning in the administration of George W. Bush, while Slocombe was Undersecretary of Defense for Policy in the Clinton administration. Despite its differences with the Obama administration, Israel continued to advance US national interests. "The United States has benefited in the areas of counterterrorism, intelligence and experience in urban warfare," they wrote. "Increasingly, US homeland security and military agencies are turning to Israeli technology to solve some of their most vexing technical and strategic problems."[34]

Currently, Israel provides the US with improvements in airport security techniques. Israeli-developed defense equipment, some of which benefited from generous US aid, was and is used by the US military and include some 1,000 targeting pods on Air Force, Navy and Marine strike aircraft, a revolutionary helmet-mounted sight that is standard in nearly all (2,500) frontline Air Force and Navy fighter aircraft, lifesaving armor installed in over 15,000 MRAP armored vehicles[35] used in Iraq and Afghanistan and a gun system for close-in defense of naval vessels against terrorist dinghies and small-boat swarms. Moreover, American and Israeli companies are working together to produce Israel's short range (2.5 to 44 miles) Iron Dome anti-rocket and missile system (combat proven since 2011), as well as both the David's Sling and the Arrow anti-ballistic missile systems (the latter jointly produced and funded by Israel Aerospace Industries and Boeing). David's Sling is intended to bridge the gap between the shorter-range Iron Dome system and the Arrow anti-ballistic missile systems. David's Sling and the Stunner missile used by that system is being developed as a replacement for the American Patriot system.

David's Sling is designed to intercept medium- to long-range rockets and cruise missiles, fired at ranges of 24.85 miles (40 kilometers) to 186.4 miles (300 kilometers). The system has a longer range and better capabilities than Patriot does. On November 25, 2012, Israel announced the successful test of a David's Sling two-stage intermediate anti-missile system at an undisclosed desert location in southern Israel. A second successful test took place on November 20, 2013. On April 1, 2015, Israel announced that its David's Sling system successfully passed new tests, successfully intercepting multiple targets, and was expected to become operational by mid-2015.[36] It is being developed jointly by Rafael, an Israeli defense contractor and the US Raytheon Company.[37] Israel successfully tested its Arrow 3 long-range anti-missile interceptor on February 25, 2013. A second successful test took place on January 3, 2014. The Arrow 3 will be able to intercept ballistic missiles with longer ranges than the ones that Arrow 2 can bring down (56–92 miles), and it will do so at higher altitudes. The Arrow 3 system is due to become operational in 2015. These Israeli developed techniques, modifications and improvements have been shared with the United States. Blackwill and Slocombe added:

> Israel's national missile defenses—that include the US deployment in Israel of an advanced X-band radar system and the more than 100 American military personnel who man it—will be an integral part of a larger missile defense spanning Europe, the eastern Mediterranean and the Persian Gulf to help protect US forces and allies.[38]

Without providing details, the authors said that Israeli cooperation with the US military has worked "to advance their common interest in defeating the terrorism of Hamas, Hezbollah and Al-Qaeda and its affiliate groups, and preventing nuclear proliferation in the region." For example, Israel's passed on to the United States "conclusive photographic evidence in 2007, that Syria with North Korean assistance, had made enormous strides toward 'going hot' with a plutonium-producing reactor."[39]

Recently, US aircraft manufacturer, Lockheed Martin, announced on October 12, 2013, that it chose to only manufacture a pilot's helmet co-developed by Elbit Systems, an Israeli company, for use with its advanced F-35 stealth fighter jets. "In 2011, program and industry officials acknowledged that there were technical issues facing the principle helmet system.... The government's decision to proceed exclusively with the principle helmet is indicative of their confidence in the helmet's performance and the successful resolution of previously identified technical challenges," said Lorraine Martin, Lockheed Martin executive vice president and general manager of the F-35 Lightning II program. The "Helmet Mounted Display Systems" provide pilots with unprecedented situational awareness. All the information pilots need to complete their missions—in all weather day or night—is projected on the helmet's visor. Lockheed Martin said the decision to only focus on making the "Rockwell Collins Elbit Systems of America Vision Systems Generation 2 (Gen 2) helmet currently used in training and testing "will save the company $45 million it had "originally allocated for the development of the alternate helmet."[40] Israel will receive its first F-35 joint strike fighter jets in the second half of 2016. Israel has ordered nineteen F-35s, for a total cost of $2.75 billion, and has the option to purchase seventy-five F-35s. While on the subject of the F-35, in mid-March 2014, Israeli Defense Minister Moshe Ya'alon revealed "the wings of the F-35 stealth fighter—we invented."[41] On November 4, 2014, Israel Aerospace Industry (IAI) inaugurated a production line to provide wings for the F-35. Under a $2.5 billion industrial cooperation deal, the new facility at IAI will produce up to 811 wing sets through 2030 at a rate of four per month.[42]

The on-going United States–Israel partnership was given a further boost when on March 5, 2014 the US House of Representatives voted 410-1 to upgrade Israel from a "major non-NATO ally" to a "major strategic partner of the United States."[43] This significantly expands the mutually beneficial United States–Israel strategic cooperation in the areas of national security, technology, defense industries, missile defense, space satellites, intelligence, energy, and irrigation, to name the most prominent fields. Moreover, the legislation called for increased United States–Israel "cooperative research pilot programs with Israel for: (1) border, maritime, and aviation security, (2) explosives detection, and (3) emergency services."[44] Additionally, the legislation required "the President to report to Congress regarding the status of Israel's qualitative military edge every two years (such report is currently due every four years)." The bill further directed "the Secretary of State to report to Congress regarding the range of cyber and asymmetric threats posed to Israel by state and non-state actors, and joint US–Israel efforts to address such threats."[45] The Senate is expected to support overwhelmingly this United States–Israel Strategic Partnership Act of 2014, H.R 938.

Caroline B. Glick, deputy managing editor of the *Jerusalem Post* and Senior Fellow for Middle East Affairs of the Center for Security Policy, would summarize the United States–Israel strategic relationship succinctly, "US support for Israel over the years has been *the most cost-effective* (emphasis in the original) national security investment in post-World War II US history."[46] To this, one may add that US support of Israel is morally right, ethically right, and most importantly advances the national and strategic interests of the United States. The United States can only benefit from having a reliable regional ally, Israel, whose military and intelligence capabilities can supplement America's own.

41. The maxim "the enemy of my enemy is my friend" applies in many cases to Middle Eastern history and politics.

From the outset, it must be stipulated that there are notable exceptions to this principle as it applies to the Middle East. The two most prominent exceptions are Sunnis versus Shi'ites and Arabs versus Persians, where the converse of the maxim is true, "The enemy of your enemy is not necessarily your friend." Just because the Sunnis and the Shi'ites, as well as the Arabs and Persians relate to each other with hostility and hatred, that doesn't result in love for Israel. Each pair of antagonists has and will continue to cooperate to work to destroy the "Zionist enemy" and the Jewish presence in the Middle East.

For much of the nineteenth century, both the United Kingdom and France were rivals of Russia. From an even earlier period, (*see* "Basic Principle 42") Muslim Ottoman Turkey was an enemy of the Christian Russian Empire. During the Crimean War (1853–56), the United Kingdom and France allied themselves with the Muslim Ottoman Turkish Empire to keep the Ottomans from falling under Russian hegemony. The Turks relied on Western military and economic assistance to survive.

A second example was the relationship that grew into the Franco-Israeli *de facto* alliance in 1954. At that time, France fought Arab rebels in French Algeria, who were aided by Egypt's President Gamal Abdel Nasser. Nasser in turn, was also the mortal enemy of Israel. He sponsored the *fedayeen* raids into the Jewish state, blockaded the Straits of Tiran, and engaged in a massive arms buildup, with which to confront Israel. Hence, France and Israel drew closer together to deal with the common enemy which culminated in the Sinai-Suez War of 1956 (*see* "Causes of the Sinai-Suez War" map).

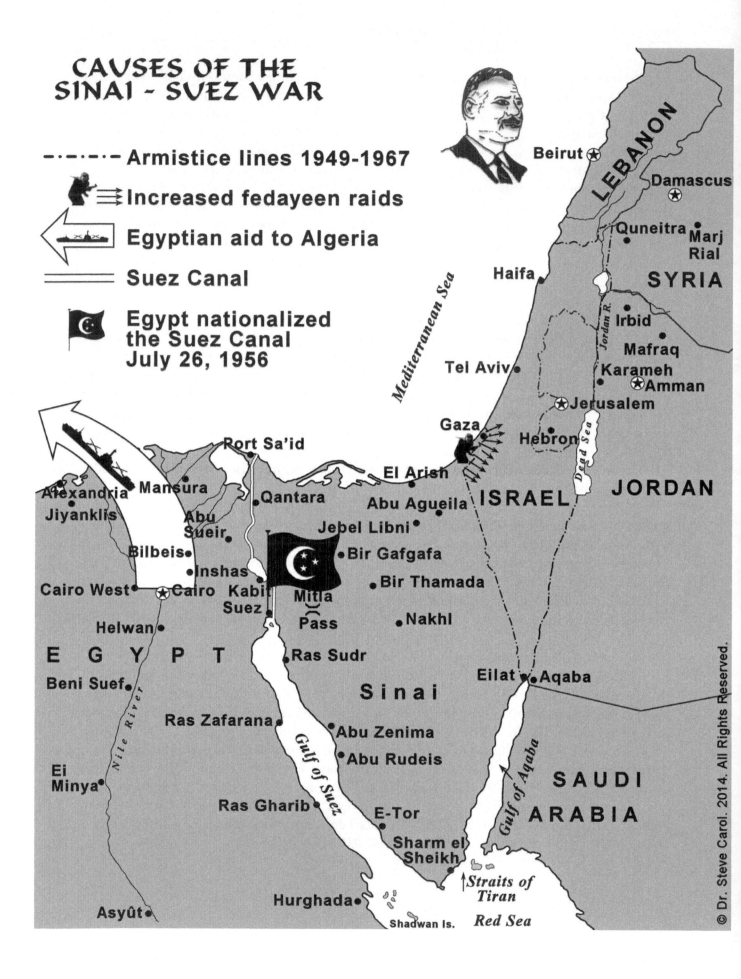

CAUSES OF THE SINAI - SUEZ WAR

- **- · - · - · -** Armistice lines 1949-1967
- Increased fedayeen raids
- Egyptian aid to Algeria
- Suez Canal
- Egypt nationalized the Suez Canal July 26, 1956

LEBANON

Beirut

Damascus

Quneitra Marj Rial

Haifa

SYRIA

Irbid

Mafraq

Tel Aviv Karameh Amman

Mediterranean Sea

Gaza Jerusalem

Hebron

Port Sa'id El Arish ISRAEL JORDAN

Alexandria Mansura Qantara Abu Agueila

Jiyanklis Abu Jebel Libni

Bilbeis Sueir Bir Gafgafa

Cairo West Inshas Bir Thamada

Helwan Cairo Kabit Mitla Nakhl

Suez Pass

E G Y P T Ras Sudr

Beni Suef S i n a i

Eilat Aqaba

Ras Zafarana Abu Zenima

Abu Rudeis

Ei Minya SAUDI

Ras Gharib E-Tor ARABIA

Sharm el Sheikh

Hurghada Straits of Tiran

Asyût Shadwan Is. Red Sea

Nile River

Jordan R.

Dead Sea

Gulf of Suez

Gulf of Aqaba

A further illustration of this principle, took place during the Yemen Civil War of 1962–70, when Israel clandestinely assisted the Royalist forces battling an Egyptian military expeditionary corps, which had intervened in support of the Yemeni Republican regime. The Egyptians provided heavy weapons, tanks, jet fighters and bombers and used poison gas (to be discussed more fully below, *see* Basic Principle 55) against the Royalists. Following the maxim "the enemy of my enemy is my friend," Israel provided, starting in March 1964, light weapons, ammunition, communication gear and medical supplies. Via a covert airlift, code-named Operation *Rotev* ("Gravy") and subsequently renamed Operation *Durban* ("Porcupine"),[47] Israeli and British operatives using an Israeli Boeing C-97 Stratofreighter cargo transport made airdrops to the Royalists. The plane refueled in French Somaliland (now Djibouti) before returning to Israel. This assistance continued until the end of 1966, during which the Stratofreighter carried out fourteen nighttime sorties from Tel Nof air base in Israel to Yemen.[48] By assisting the Royalist Yemenis, Israel was able to keep Egyptian troops bogged down in Yemen; it became Nasser's "Vietnam," and thus alleviated the Egyptian military pressure on Israel before the Six-Day War.

Yet another example occurred between the southern Sudanese and the Israelis. Even before the Six-Day War of 1967, Sudan began to take a more active role in the Arab confrontation against Israel. Sudanese Defense Minister Ahmed Abdulrahman al-Mahdi, while on a visit to Mogadishu, Somalia, April 9, 1967, called for concerted efforts "against the plots of world Zionism and the challenge and designs of imperialism."[49] With the outbreak of the Six-Day War on June 5, 1967, Sudanese Prime Minister Muhammad Mahgoub announced that Sudanese troops would be sent "to join the Arab ranks" on June 7.[50] Sudanese units arrived and took part in the fighting on the Sinai front. In addition, after the Six-Day War, Sudanese units participated in the 1,000-Day War of Attrition along the Suez Canal from 1967 to 1970. Furthermore, Sudanese belligerency was evidenced by the urging of the Deputy Prime Minister and Foreign Minister of Sudan, Ali 'Abd ar-Rahman, that Sudanese political parties and organizations were obligated to persuade Sudanese youth to "join the [PLO] commandos" that were conducting guerrilla war against Israel.[51]

In an effort to offset Sudanese participation in the Arab-Israeli conflict, Israel began to support forces in the southern Sudan that were fighting for autonomy from the central Sudanese government since 1955. Chief among the forces in opposition to Khartoum was the *Anya Nya* ("snake venom" in the Madi language), who were a guerrilla force, led by Joseph Lagu, fighting the Sudanese government since 1963. The *Anya Nya* was a separatist group made up largely of Christians and animists who resented the domination, Arabization and Islamization of the south by the Sudanese central government. Some *Anya Nya* favored independence as the nation tentatively called *Azania,* while others sought autonomy for the south.

In a classic case of the enemy of my enemy is my friend, Israel and the southern Sudanese came together against their common Arab foes. Shortly after the Six-Day War, Joseph Lagu, the founder and commander of the *Anya Nya,* sent a personal letter to the Israeli Prime Minister Levi Eshkol. Lagu wrote, "Dear Prime Minister: Congratulations for your victory against the Arabs. You are God Almighty's chosen people."[52]

In his letter to Eshkol, Lagu offered the Israelis a deal. If Israel would support *Anya Nya,* Lagu promised to tie down the Sudanese government forces, to prevent them from joining the Egyptians and other Arabs fighting Israel during the 1,000-Day War of Attrition as well as in the future. To say the least, the Israelis were interested in the proposal. "I waited for a response, but the problem was that Eshkol died. He never even saw that letter," said Lagu. The next Israeli Prime Minister, Golda Meir found Lagu's letter and invited him to Israel. In 1969, Lagu travelling under several aliases and taking a roundabout route reached Israel, where he met the new Israeli Prime Minister. Lagu told her, "We have a common concern, and that is fighting the Arabs."[53] As a result of Lagu's visit, he returned to the southern Sudan with Prime Minister Meir's promise of weapons and training.

The head of *Anya Nya's* political wing was Joseph Oduho. It was Oduho who introduced Lagu to the Israeli ambassador and political attaché in Kampala, Uganda. There was a growing Israeli presence in Uganda and that nation would serve as the land corridor to southern Sudan. Soon after, a shipment from Israel of Soviet-made weapons reached Juba in southern Sudan. These were mainly two- and three-inch mortars, anti-tank missiles and light machine guns taken from enemy Arab countries during the 1967 war. As Lagu explained, "They did not give us new weapons, or ones that were manufactured in Israel, as they did not want to be publicly known to be helping us."[54] The Israelis trained Lagu, who emerged as the undisputed leader of the *Anya Nya* forces.[55] Later, three Israeli advisors arrived and joined the *Anya Nya* rebels in the bush: a military advisor, a technician and a doctor. While other arms were coming in from other sources, the Israeli assistance, Lagu explained, was what tipped the scales, "This helped transform my movement, and we became a force to be reckoned with. We began to make a real impact in the fighting against Khartoum."[56]

Israel provided "training and [supplied] captured Soviet and Chinese weapons through its military missions in Kenya, [and] Uganda."[57] Southwestern Ethiopian airfields were reportedly used to supply the rebels[58] (for a more complete coverage of Israel's role in East Africa, *see* the author's book, *From Jerusalem to the Lion of Judah and Beyond*). Military aid arrived at Owing-Ki-Bul in an unmarked DC-3 aircraft[59] on an average of one planeload a week.[60] This critical assistance helped the *Anya Nya* fight the Khartoum government to a stalemate and paved the way for a ceasefire agreement, albeit one that only lasted eleven years.

An unexpected consequence of the severance of Ugandan-Israeli relations in 1972, was the end of Israeli assistance to the southern Sudanese *Anya Nya* movement. With the expulsion from Uganda of all Israelis (including military advisors) came the end to the use of Uganda as the main route for running arms to southern Sudan. The only other method was an expensive airdrop into southern Sudan by planes flying over Ethiopia and refueling in Kenya.

At that same time, the *Anya Nya* and the Sudanese central government signed the Addis Ababa Agreement in 1972. This was a peace accord brokered by Ethiopia's Emperor Haile Selassie, in which the south promised to stop fighting in return for a great deal of religious and cultural autonomy. The Arab central government in Khartoum insisted that all connection with the Israelis end immediately and that is what happened.

However, as is well known, there are no absolutes in foreign policy. Regimes change, alliances shift, old bonds are restored or new ones formed. In January 1986, the new Ugandan government of Yoweri Museveni accepted Israeli military assistance. This in turn, opened the door once again for Israeli military assistance to flow to the Sudanese People's Liberation Army, the successor to the *Anya Nya,* fighting the central government in Khartoum. Earlier the Second Sudanese Civil War erupted by September 1983. In fact, after a failed eleven-year ceasefire, it was a continuation of the First Sudanese Civil War with the same causes.

The Israeli arms pipeline to southern Sudan via Uganda, continued into the twenty-first century. According to Ugandan sources, Israel supplied the SPLA arms including rocket launchers, anti-aircraft weapons, armored vehicles, and surface-to-air missiles. Furthermore, Israel was also reported to be helping to establish and train a new South Sudan intelligence agency. Israeli instructors provided helicopter flight training to southern Sudanese pilots.[61] The Second Sudanese Civil War went on for a full twenty-two years from 1983 to 2005. The war ended when the two sides signed a comprehensive peace agreement, the Nairobi Peace Agreement of January 9, 2005. Among its provisions were that the south would have autonomy for six years, followed by a referendum in which it would decide whether to secede from Sudan and create an independent nation, or remain as one country.

A UN-monitored referendum was held January 9–15, 2011, in southern Sudan. It resulted in an overwhelming vote (98.83 percent) of the 3.8 million voters, in favor of secession from Sudan and independence. The Republic of South Sudan declared its independence on July 9, 2011. As Joseph Lagu reflected, "[the Israeli assistance] … set us on the path to where we are today, and that will never be forgotten. When we are independent, we will forge relations with whomever we want to," Lagu stated. "And we still remember who our old friends are."[62] As was expected Israel recognized the new Republic of South Sudan on July 10, 2011, and established full diplomatic relations.[63]

One might assume, from studying the history of conflicts in the Middle East, that Muslims would always be aligned together. This is not true. There are many cases where pragmatic cutting across religious lines were arranged and *de facto* alliances made. During the Crusades, Christian and Muslim rulers freely collaborated across the religious divide, often finding themselves aligned with members of the rival religion against their co-religionists. While the Ayyubidi leader, Saladin, was busy eradicating the Crusader Latin Kingdom of Jerusalem, he was closely aligned with the Byzantine Empire, the richest and most influential center of Christendom.

During the First Lebanese Civil War (1958), the two opposing sides were the largely Maronite Christian government against the Muslim anti-government forces. However, the "Muslim side" was comprised of many elements including Sunni, Shi'ite, Druze, as well as the Maronite Patriarch, Paul Méouchi, and Hamid Franjiyeh, the Christian leader of Zgharta.

As a result of the 2006 Memorandum of Understanding Hezbollah, the Shi'ite terrorist organization and the Free Patriotic Movement, a Maronite Christian group came together to combat Sunni political, financial and business power in Lebanon. This association of strange political bedfellows was due in large part to the historic suffering of both groups—Shi'ite and Christian—as minorities under Sunni rule. This discrimination dates back to Sunni Ottoman rule of the region. At that time, the Ottoman Turks did not even recognize the Shi'ites as a separate community. Thus, the Shi'ite-Maronite linkage was based on practicality against a common adversary, the Sunnis.

Muslim and Arab rulers have always sought the support and protection of the infidel (non-believing outside) powers they so vilify. Egypt's President Gamal Abdel Nasser, the champion of Pan-Arabism who had built his reputation on standing up to "Western imperialism," allied himself and Egypt to the infidel Soviet Union, not only for military equipment and training, but also for economic aid, including the financing and construction of the Aswan High Dam. In fact, in 1970, when Nasser's 1,000-Day War of Attrition against Israel was stymied and Israel began to inflict effective reprisals humiliating his regime, Nasser allowed Soviet and communist bloc personnel to be stationed in Egypt, to protect Egypt, fly combat patrols for Egypt, and have exclusive naval and air base facilities.

Similarly, Ayatollah Khomeini bought weapons from even the "Great Satan," the United States. Saddam Hussein used Western support to survive his war against Iran from 1980 to 1988. Even Osama bin Laden and the rest of the Afghan *mujahedeen* accepted weapons and financing from the United States, with the Islamic Republic of Pakistan as the middleman, in their struggle against the Soviet occupation of Afghanistan from 1979 to 1989.

42. Turkey usually allies itself with whichever power opposes Russia. Additionally, Turkey has always been a regional rival of Persia/Iran.

Since 1568, Turkey has fought the Russians seventeen times. In part, this hostility was a continuation of Sunni Muslim–Christian Orthodox religious conflict. As a consequence of these on-going clashes, Turkey always sought to align with those nations that stood opposed to Russia. This is what happened in the Crimean War, World War I and the Cold War.

RUSSO-TURKISH CONFLICTS					
Date	Name of Conflict	Belligerents		Victor	Treaty
1568–69	Russo-Turkish War	Russia	Ottoman Turkey and the Crimean Khanate	Russia	–
1571–74	Russo-Turkish War	Russia	Ottoman Turkey and the Crimean Khanate	Russia	–
1676–81	Russo-Turkish War	Russia and Ukraine	Ottoman Turkey and the Crimean Khanate	Russia	Bakhchisarai
1687	Russo-Turkish War	Russia	Ottoman Turkey	Ottoman Turkey	—
1689	Russo-Turkish War	Russia	Ottoman Turkey	Ottoman Turkey	—
1695–96	Russo-Turkish War, (part of the Great Turkish War)	Russia, Habsburg Austria, Poland-Lithuania, and Venice	Ottoman Turkey and the Crimean Khanate	Russia	Constantinople (1700)
1710–11	Russo-Turkish War	Russia and Principality of Moldavia	Ottoman Turkey	Ottoman Turkey	Pruth
1736–39	Russo-Turkish War	Russia and Austria	Ottoman Turkey	Draw	Niš
1768–74	Russo-Turkish War	Russia	Ottoman Turkey	Russia	Küçük Kaynarca
1787–92	Russo-Turkish War	Russia	Ottoman Turkey	Russia	Jassy
1806–12	Russo-Turkish War	Russia	Ottoman Turkey	Russia	Bucharest

1827	Greek War of Independence	Greece with naval assistance from Russia, the United Kingdom and France	Ottoman Turkey	Greece and Russia	Constantinople (1832)
1828–29	Russo-Turkish War	Russia	Ottoman Turkey	Russia	Adrianople (Edirne)
1853–56	The Crimean War	Ottoman Turkey, the United Kingdom, France and Sardinia— the Allies	Russia	The Allies	Paris (1856)
1877–78	Russo-Turkish War	Russia, Serbia, Romania and Montenegro	Ottoman Turkey	Russia	San Stefano
1914–18	Caucasus Campaign (part of World War I)	Russia and the Allied Powers	Ottoman Turkey and the Central Powers	Inconclusive in the Caucasus, but the Allies won the war	Moscow (1921)
1917–18	Turkish intervention in the Russian Civil War	Soviet Russia	Ottoman Turkey and anti-communist White (Russian) armies	Soviet Russia	Kars

Mustafa Kemal Atatürk established the Turkish Republic on October 29, 1923. He implemented a series of reforms—"Kemalism"—whereby Turkey became modernized, Westernized, secularized, democratized and Europe-oriented. He urged Turks to adopt purely Turkish names and family surnames. Atatürk abolished:

- The Sultanate (1922) and established a republic.
- The Caliphate (March 3, 1924).
- Shari'a law (1926) and replaced it with Swiss civil and Italian penal codes.
- The Islamic calendar (1926).
- The Arabic alphabet (1928) and replaced it with the Latin alphabet.
- Turkish titles e.g. bey, dey, pasha (1934).
- Turkish attire for men (1925) e.g. the fez was replaced by the Western flat cap.
- Polygamy and the veil for women. Women were given the right to vote in 1934.
- Madrasas (Islamic religious schools), which were replaced by universal and free education.
- Friday as the Sabbath day of rest. It was replaced by the European weekend.

- Non-Turkish words, i.e. Arabic and Persian ones. Many place names were also changed, e.g. Smyrna to Izmir, Adrianople to Edirne, Angora to Ankara, and Constantinople to Istanbul.

Additionally, the Islamic call to prayer—the *adhān* (called *ezan* in Turkish)—was officially changed from Arabic to Turkish on July 18, 1932 in all mosques across the country and the practice was continued for a period of 18 years. On July 16, 1950, a new government under Adnan Menderes restored Arabic as the liturgical language. Atatürk even proposed placing pews in mosques.[64] Starting almost immediately after his death in 1938, a reversal from his secularism began.

Nevertheless, Turkey's secular standing was protected by the military, which intervened four times—1960, 1971, 1980, and 1997—to insure that status. The republic of Turkey's foreign policy was Western-oriented. After World War II, it was based on alliance with the United States, membership in the NATO, orientation towards the Euro-Atlantic community and the prospect of European Union membership.

The historic animosity between Turkey and Russia (then the Soviet Union) explained why Turkey became part of NATO in 1952, as the United States and its allies stood opposed to the Soviet Union and its allies, during the Cold War (1945–91). While the Soviet Union imploded in 1991, and the Cold War ended, Russian power lessened only for about a decade. Two wars in Chechnya, followed by the Russian invasion of Georgia in 2008, and the Russian takeover of Crimea in 2014, demonstrated a resurgence of Russian power in the region north of Turkey. At roughly the same time, though still nominally a NATO ally, the relationship between Turkey and NATO began to change in 2002.

In November 2002, the Justice and Development Party (*Adalet ve Kalkinma Partisi,*—AKP) came to power in Turkey, led by Recep Tayyip Erdoğan. Since that time, Erdoğan has systematically moved Turkey away from its secular past and close ties with the West towards an Islamic-oriented state. The AKP has pursued a successful policy of creeping Islamization domestically. Erdoğan cracked down and purged the military, judiciary, and Turkey's secular media—the three pillars of the secular Kemalist ideology. Additionally, Erdoğan shifted Turkey's foreign policy accordingly to one of orientation towards the Arab/Muslim Middle East. Turkey now seeks to recapture its past status as, at least, a regional hegemonic power, if not return to great power status, as Turkey was during the Ottoman period (July 27, 1299 to October 29, 1923).

Historically, Turkey's main rival for hegemonic regional power was Persia/Iran. Second only to the number of wars fought with Russia, was the number—ten—fought between Turkey and Persia/Iran. In large part, Sunni Turkish versus Shi'ite Persian religious animosity fueled these conflicts as well as regional ambitions.

TURCO-PERSIAN CONFLICTS				
Date	**Belligerents**		**Victor**	**Treaty**
1473*	Ottoman Turkey	Timurid Persia	Ottoman Turkey	–
1514–16	Ottoman Turkey	Safavid Persia	Ottoman Turkey	–
1526–55	Ottoman Turkey	Safavid Persia	Ottoman Turkey	Amasya
1578–90	Ottoman Turkey	Safavid Persia	Ottoman Turkey	Constantinople
1603–12	Ottoman Turkey	Safavid Persia	Safavid Persia	Nasuh Pasha
1616–18	Ottoman Turkey	Safavid Persia	Safavid Persia	Serav

* As part of the Turkish-Venetian War of 1463–79.

1623–38	Ottoman Turkey	Safavid Persia	Ottoman Turkey	Zuhab
1730–36	Ottoman Turkey	Afsharid Persia	Afsharid Persia	Ganja
1743–47	Ottoman Turkey	Afsharid Persia	Afsharid Persia	Kerden
1821–23	Ottoman Turkey	Qajar Persia	Qajar Persia	Ezurum

Between 1555 and 1918, Ottoman Turkey and Persia signed no less than eighteen treaties regarding their disputed border. After World War I, during the period of the secular republic, there were good relations between Turkey and Iran. This was evidenced by the Saadabad Pact, which was in effect from July 9, 1937 through 1948, and linked Turkey with Iraq, Iran, and Afghanistan. Additionally, Turkey and Iran were formal military allies in both the Baghdad Pact (1955–58) and CENTO (1959–79).

Relations with the United States began to chill with Turkey's refusal to allow US and coalition forces to be positioned on its territory for the March 2003 invasion of Iraq. As Turkey increased its Islamization, the United States and other NATO members began to question its reliability as an ally. On the other hand, as United States resolve weakened in the region, with its declared intention of leaving Iraq and Afghanistan, Turkey sought to enlarge its regional status.

Since the rise of the AKP, Turkey has reoriented its foreign policy toward the Islamic Middle East, distancing itself from Europe, in part due to its failure to acquire European Union membership, and in part, because of its continued occupation of northern Cyprus. Additionally, at the same time, long-standing Turkish-Israeli ties deteriorated to the breaking point. This process was accelerated by Turkey, especially since 2009, when Israel reacted to Hamas rocket attacks from the Gaza Strip by launching Operation *Cast Lead*. Turkey then, abandoned its decade-long military relationship with Israel. Lastly, the AKP entertains Pan-Turkic and neo-Ottoman expansionist dreams, especially with regard to the Middle East, the Caucasus, Central Asia, the Balkans, and the eastern Mediterranean region.

Under AKP leadership, Turkey launched a period of rapprochement with Iran, which lasted from 2002 to 2011. Turkey and Iran signed a secret military pact, on October 28, 2009. Among other provisions, it required Turkey's military intelligence, its air force and navy to help Iran repel a possible Israeli attack on Iran's nuclear facilities. It included a provision for the sharing of any data and technology on Israeli weapons systems in Turkish possession, which the IDF might use for a potential strike. Since that pact was signed, Israel has cut off all advanced weapons supplies to the Turkish armed forces.

In a like fashion, from 2002 to 2011, Turkey instituted a warm rapprochement with Syria, Iran's main Arab ally, signing forty-six treaties of cooperation on a variety of issues including trade, open borders, and military training. However, the eruption of anti-Assad regime riots and violence, which morphed into a nationwide uprising and ultimate civil war in Syria starting in January 2011, ended the Turkish-Syrian reconciliation. Turkey now favors the removal of Assad, which also puts it at loggerheads with Iran. Additionally, Turkey disagreed with Iran over Iraqi politics reflective of the Sunni-Shi'ite divide. Turkey, being Sunni, and Iran, being Shi'ite religiously stand opposite each other. Deterioration of relations between Turkey and Iran became evident in March 2011, when Turkey informed the UN Security Council that it had found weapons and ammunition aboard an Iranian cargo plane bound for Syria. The cargo included rocket launchers, mortars, rifles, explosive materials and ammunition—a breach of UN resolutions banning Iran from exporting arms.[65] That was followed by Turkey's denunciation of the Assad regime's slaughter of opponents, which Iran deemed "terrorists." Through Sobh'eh Sadegh, one of Iranian Revolutionary Guards' media outlets, Iran sternly warned Turkey that Iran would choose Syria over Turkey, if it had to choose.[66] The Turco-Iranian rift was evident by September 2011, when Turkey agreed to install NATO radar facilities to detect missiles launched from Iran. The radar will be placed at a Turkish installation about 435 miles from Iran.[67]

Under the continued leadership of the AKP, Turkey's neo-Ottoman* regional ambitions will collide with Iran's regional ambitions in the Middle East, as the latter is determined to influence Iraq, Syria, Lebanon and even the Gaza Strip. A Shi'ite pro-Iranian regime already governs Iraq and the Iranian-backed Shi'ite Hezbollah dominates Lebanon. This Turkish-Iranian friction is due in part, to Sunni-Shi'ite religious animosity, between largely Sunni Turkey and Shi'ite Iran. Turkish Sunnis comprise some 75 percent of the population, while 20 percent view themselves as Shi'ite. If Iran achieves nuclear weapon capability, Turkey will certainly seek to obtain nuclear weapons of its own. With such weapons, Turkey will feel more confident in facing its two historic opponents, Russia and Iran.

By the summer of 2012, Turkey was again aligned against its historic foe, Russia. Turkey was opposed to the Assad regime in Syria. On June 22, 2012, Syria shot down a Turkish Air Force F-4 Super Phantom on a reconnaissance flight over the Syrian port of Latakia. It used an advanced Russian-supplied self-propelled medium range anti-aircraft Pantsyr-1 missile. Since the sophisticated weapon system was delivered to the Assad regime only weeks earlier, it can be assumed that local Syrian missile crews had not finished training in their use, and would have had to rely on help from their Russian military instructors to fire one.[68]

Additionally, the Russians hedging their bets on the survival of the embattled Assad regime took steps to position themselves in an alternative location in the eastern Mediterranean. Russia has cultivated a relationship with the government of Cyprus. That island nation is part of the Eurozone, which is wracked by economic troubles. In December 2011, Russia granted Cyprus a €3 billion loan. More than happy to have Russian financial assistance is Cypriot President, Demetris Christofias, and Europe's only communist head of state. Christofias has also supported the closure of the British sovereign military bases on Cyprus—Akrotiri and Dhekelia.[69]

In light of the possible loss of its long-standing naval facilities at Latakia and Tartus, Syria, the Russians would seek an alternative site. Cyprus is an ideal location. If the Christofias government succeeded in ousting the British from their bases, those facilities would be ready made, complete with infrastructure, for the Russian Mediterranean naval squadron, which has had a presence in the eastern Mediterranean since 1964.

Furthermore, Cyprus wants to begin development of the extensive gas fields that lie, off the southern Cypriot coast. Russian technical assistance may speed that process. In light of Turkish threats against any unilateral Cypriot gas field development, Cyprus would feel more secure with a Russian ally on its side. There is also, a religious component as well. Most Greek-Cypriots as well as most Russians belong to the Eastern Orthodox Church. Many Russians live and vacation in Cyprus. As Cypriot-Russian political, financial and strategic bonds grow, it will prove an attractive alternative model for economic assistance to embattled Greece, hard hit by financial collapse. A financial bailout from the Russians could have fewer demands on Greece, than those proposed by the European Union.

With northern Cyprus still occupied by Turkish troops and transplanted settlers, a Russian-Cypriot-Greek cooperative grouping benefitted the latter three states and aligns them opposite the Turkish government of Tayyip Recep Erdoğan. Once again, Turkey would be opposed to Russian moves, reverting to its historic pattern.

---

* Neo-Ottomanism is a Turkish political ideology that in its broadest sense, promotes greater Turkish engagement with areas formerly under the Ottoman Empire.

ASPECTS OF WAR

By ruses shall thou wage war, and victory comes with much planning by advisors.
Proverbs 24:6

In war, then, let your great object be victory, not lengthy campaigns.
Sun Tzu

Si vis pacem, para bellum.
("If you want peace, prepare for war.")
Publius Flavius Vegetius Renatus

The pursuit of victory without slaughter is likely to produce slaughter without victory.
John Churchill, 1st Duke of Marlborough

*No government, if it regards war as inevitable, even if it does not want it, would be
so foolish as to wait for the moment which is most convenient for the enemy.*
Otto von Bismarck

*If you will not fight for the right when you can easily win without bloodshed; if you
will not fight when your victory will be sure and not too costly; you may come to the
moment when you will have to fight with all the odds against you and only a precarious
chance of survival. There may even be a worse case. You may have to fight when
there is no hope of victory, because it is better to perish than to live as slaves.*
Winston S. Churchill

*You ask, what is our aim? I can answer in one word. It is victory, victory
at all costs, victory in spite of the terror, victory, however long and hard
the road may be; for without victory, there is no survival.*
Winston S. Churchill

*The history of failure in war can almost be summed up in two words: too late.
Too late in comprehending the deadly purpose of a potential enemy; too late
in realizing the mortal danger; too late in preparedness; too late in uniting all
possible forces for resistance; too late in standing with one's friends.*
Douglas MacArthur

In war, there is no substitute for victory.
Dwight D. Eisenhower

In the Middle East, war frequently has been an end unto itself. War has been waged on many levels
and using different methods, often simultaneously. Among these different techniques of conflict
are military (including guerrilla war, asymmetrical war, and the use of terror), political, ideological,

economic, diplomatic, media/propaganda warfare, and religious war. Increasingly these conflicts involve the deliberate use of civilians—men, women and children of all ages. They are employed as human shields or as collateral damage to be used in manipulating public opinion and the Western media. Even corpses from the morgue have been utilized as "weapons" in the propaganda war. Furthermore, military forces, as well as terrorists, disguise themselves in civilian garb as noncombatants to murder opposing soldiers, and often civilians.

The use of human shields is not a recent phenomenon nor used only by terrorist groups. During the Israeli War of Independence for example, Iraqi troops used Arab civilians as human shields at Deir Yassin. During the Six-Day War of 1967, as the IDF entered Jerusalem, they encountered Jordanian Arab Legionnaires using civilian homes, churches and mosques as military positions from which to fire on Israeli forces. Arab soldiers used civilians—men, women and children—as human shields in their confrontations with Israeli troops.[1]

These wars are often not continual, as was the case with such conflicts as the American Revolution, the Napoleonic Wars and World War II. Often, there are pauses in the overall conflicts, be they called *hudnas* (truces), armistices, or ceasefires. Some of these Middle East conflicts have been on going for decades and one of them, the Arab/Muslim war against the Jews in the Land of Israel, has been fought for 140 years. Moreover, after their defeat in such wars (which it should never be forgotten were started by Arab/Muslim aggression) the Arab/Muslim side has claimed to be the victim of such conflicts and are entitled to compensation and other rewards. Likewise, the longest-lasting conflict, Islam's war against the West, has continued intermittently for some 1,400 years. Counter-intuitively, in the Middle East, wars have been started by forces that understand they will lose militarily, but persist, knowing they can reap political gains, despite the military loss. The Egyptian attack in the Yom Kippur War of 1973 is a prime example. Furthermore, military defeat can be turned into political victory by skillful use of propaganda. This was exemplified by Egypt's defeat in the Sinai-Suez War of 1956, the PLO defeat at Karameh, Jordan on March 21, 1968, as well as the PLO defeat and expulsion from Lebanon in 1982.

Some wars were inconclusive because they stopped too soon, or were halted by international pressure and not prosecuted until the end. Due to these circumstances, these hostilities resumed years later, in order to deal with the root cause of the original conflict, albeit at an exponentially higher cost in both blood and treasure. Examples of such Middle East wars included the Israeli conflict against the PLO in Lebanon; with an inconclusive first round, occurring in 1978 and Israel forced to return to deal with the PLO in 1982. A second illustration was the Gulf War of 1991. While Kuwait was liberated from Iraqi occupation, Saddam Hussein remained in power in Iraq, a scourge to his people, his neighbors and the region. Thus, it was necessary to return to topple his regime in 2003. Similarly, Israel's inconclusive conflict with the Hamas terrorist organization in the Gaza Strip in 2008–09, led to another conflict in 2012, which was also inconclusive, to be followed by yet another round in 2014. In a like manner, Israel's 2006 battle with the Hezbollah terrorists in Lebanon was militarily inconclusive and will resume, when Hezbollah receives the "go" signal from its Iranian patron. Israel's task is to break out of the cycle of tolerating Arab/Muslim attack up to a point and then retaliating, only to be stopped by world criticism that morally equivocates Israeli civilian lives with those of the terrorist murderers that started the conflict to begin with.

There have also been horrific civil wars in the region, some of which went on, not only for years, but for decades. Over the past seven decades these include (but are not limited to) civil wars in Sudan, Yemen, the PDRY, Lebanon, Somalia, Algeria, Iraq, Libya and Syria. Finally, there are some conflicts in the Middle East, which have no "solution" short of one side being totally defeated and surrendering to the other. The ongoing Arab/Muslim war against the Jewish people and Jewish sovereignty in the Land of Israel is a case in point.

43. In the Middle East, weakness guarantees aggression.

In the Middle East, weakness begets indifference and then scorn and contempt. It is then a short step to encouraging an aggressor—be it a state actor or terrorist group—to attack. There are numerous examples of this principle during the twentieth century and extending into the twenty-first century. During World War I the perception (as well as the fact) that Ottoman Turkey was weak—the "sick man"[*] of Europe—encouraged Sharif Husayn, Guardian of Mecca and Medina, and his Hashemite dynasty from Hejaz, to guardedly launch a revolt. This uprising was mythologized[2] as well as popularized by T.E. Lawrence, "Lawrence of Arabia," as the Great Arab Revolt of 1916.

The perception of weakness and the policy of appeasement by the United Kingdom over various crises in Ethiopia, Spain and later the Sudetenland region of Czechoslovakia, encouraged the Arab Revolt of 1936–39 in the British Mandate of Palestine. The United Kingdom's noticeable weakness as it desperately tried to survive the Nazi onslaught in 1940–41, encouraged the pro-Axis coup in Iraq, led by Rashid Ali al-Gailani.

The apparent weakness of the *Yishuv*—the Jewish community in the British Mandate of Palestine—numbering only 650,000 people and deprived of assistance from any quarter, encouraged the Arab aggression of 1947–49 against the reemerging Jewish state. The seven-member Arab League declared war on Israel which was invaded by troops of five Arab armies—Egyptian, Lebanese, Syrian, Iraqi, and Transjordanian. The Arab population totaled 37.4 million inhabitants to which must be added the 1.2 million Arabs in Mandatory Palestine for a grand total of 38.58 million.

ARAB POPULATION VERSUS JEWISH POPULATION, 1948	
Country or Group	**Population[3]**
Egypt	19,529,000
Iraq	4,965,000
Lebanon	1,320,000
Saudi Arabia	3,106,000
Syria	3,068,000
Transjordan	1,188,000
Yemen	4,211,000
Arabs in the British Mandate of Palestine	1,200,000
TOTAL	**38,587,000**
The *Yishuv*—Jewish community in Mandatory Palestine	650,000

Later, in the late spring of 1967, the Arab states and the Soviet Union viewed Israel, as weak and in the words of the Soviet Ambassador to Israel, "morale … is at its lowest point. All that's left in this country [Israel] is the espresso generation and a bunch of pimps."[4] This view influenced Egyptian

---

[*] Quoted in British diplomatic correspondence in 1853, during the run up to the Crimean War, quoting Tsar Nicholas I of Russia.

President Gamal Abdel Nasser to rapidly escalate moves towards what he believed would be a final confrontation with the Jewish state. In a like manner, the weakness of Lebanon, wracked by civil war in 1975, encouraged Syria to intervene and then occupy Lebanon from 1976 to 2005. The Iraqi attack on Iran, in September 1980, was in part based upon Iran's perceived weakness after the internal convulsions of the Islamic Iranian Revolution of the preceding year. In a similar manner, the Iraqi invasion and occupation of Kuwait in 1990, was based in part on the weakness of the United States commitment to Kuwait.

The Hezbollah attacks on Israel in June and July 2006, that triggered the Second Lebanon War, was due to the perception of Israeli weakness. This feebleness was manifested in the unilateral Israeli withdrawal from southern Lebanon completed on May 24, 2000, and the release of terrorist prisoners, many with blood on their hands, all without any Israeli counter-demands. Furthermore, statements made by various high Israeli government officials accentuated the perception of weakness. In an astonishing public display of lack of resolve, then Israeli Deputy Prime Minister Ehud Olmert, in an address to the Israel Policy Forum in New York, on June 9, 2005, declared, "We are tired of fighting, we are tired of being courageous, we are tired of winning, we are tired of defeating our enemies. We want to be able to live in an entirely different environment of relations with our enemies."[5]

The Olmert government's reluctance to commit ground troops into battle during the Second Lebanon War also signaled weakness. The errors made by the Israeli leadership left Hezbollah still standing after confronting the larger, better-equipped IDF. Hezbollah continued to fire missiles at northern Israel until a ceasefire. For the first time in its history, it was Israel that sought a UN Security Council Resolution (1701) to end the fighting. This supplemented the view that Israel had not won the conflict, and having not won, it therefore "lost." Hezbollah immediately claimed "victory" and rapidly rearmed to pose an even greater threat to Israel. Israel squandered an important opportunity to deal Hezbollah a decisive military blow, and even eliminate Syria's long-range missile threat. Failure to achieve an overwhelming military victory makes another conflict with Hezbollah inevitable. Additionally, Israel's poor showing, militarily, politically, and diplomatically in the Second Lebanon War, only encouraged Hamas, in the Gaza Strip, to escalate its violence against the Jewish state.

The Hamas rocket and mortar attacks from Gaza starting in 2005 and still ongoing were similarly encouraged by the unilateral Israeli withdrawal from the Gaza Strip and northern Samaria in August 2005. This unilateral Israeli retreat uprooted twenty-five Jewish communities without Israeli counter-demands for a cessation of the attacks, violence, terrorism, and incitement from the Hamas-controlled area. Israel made matters worse when under pressure from US Secretary of State Condoleezza Rice, it also withdrew from the Philadelphi Corridor. The Philadelphi Corridor was a 8.7 mile long, 109-yard wide (a 14-kilometer long and 100-meter wide) security and buffer zone along the Egyptian–Gaza border, and left it to Egypt to prevent the smuggling of weapons, ammunition, personnel and illegal drugs into the strip.* That policy also failed miserably. The Israeli withdrawal from the Gaza Strip and Philadelphi Corridor was an egregious error. Israel further multiplied its mistake by wrongly assuming that the Egyptian regime of Hosni Mubarak would always be in power, and would secure the border. As events proved, Mubarak did not secure the border. According to the *Shin Bet* director Yuval Diskin, in the three months after Israel withdrew from Gaza, the Palestinians smuggled more weapons into the

---

* Under the provisions of the Egypt–Israel peace treaty, the Philadelphi Corridor was controlled and patrolled by the IDF. After the 1995 Oslo Accords, Israel was allowed to retain the corridor along the border to prevent the movement of illegal materials, weaponry and people between Egypt and the Gaza Strip. The Palestinians, in cooperation with some Egyptians, built smuggling tunnels under the Philadelphi Corridor to move these prohibited items into the Gaza Strip.

Gaza Strip from Egypt than they had in the previous 38 years, when Israel controlled the border. Less than six years after Israel's withdrawal, Mubarak himself was gone, ousted in a popular uprising, and at first, replaced by a Muslim Brotherhood regime, the ideological parent of Hamas in the Gaza Strip.

Israel should have kept as a minimum, the northern five miles of the Gaza Strip where the Jewish communities of Gush Katif were located, as well as the Philadelphi Corridor. These areas were a minimal necessity to maintaining Israeli security, and set the precedent that not all disputed territories would be returned to the Arab aggressors, which perpetrated the Six-Day War in the first place. A price had to be paid for aggression. Instead, Israel left the Gaza Strip completely and it was utilized by a terrorist group sworn in its charter, to Israel's total destruction. This blunder was to lead to the Second Gaza War of November 2012, and the Third Gaza War of July–August 2014. In both, Hamas unleashed a more numerous rocket and mortar barrage against Israel with increased numbers in each conflict. By the Third Gaza War, rockets from Gaza reached northern Israel almost to the border with Lebanon, hitting such Israeli cities as Tel Aviv, Haifa and Nahariya. These missiles also targeted Jerusalem, Beersheba and Dimona—the latter being the site of Israel's main nuclear research center. Shorter range missiles were domestically produced utilizing dual-use materials such as steel pipe and ball bearings. Hamas also domestically produced the Iranian Fajr-5 missile for its long-range strikes. Additionally, unbeknownst to the Israelis, some 800,000 tons of concrete was used to construct a mammoth tunnel network with over thirty-two terrorist attack tunnels, burrowed under the Israeli frontier. Hamas planned a major multiple terror attack on the Israeli villages along the frontier with the purpose of causing thousands of casualties, killing kindergarten children and abducting, sedating and spiriting back to Gaza, hundreds of Israeli hostages. The attack was planned for on or about Rosh Hashana, the Jewish New Year (September 24, 2014). Such were the results, thus far, of the Israeli total withdrawal from the Gaza Strip.

Whereas the Iron Dome short-range anti-missile system successfully protected Israel (destroying 90 percent of missiles it targeted) during the Second and Third Gaza Wars one must not forget a basic rule of war that an offensive posture is always better than a defensive one. Many thought defensive lines would provide security and warning time before an attack. History revealed that the Maginot Line of 1940, the Mareth Line of 1943, the Siegfried Line of 1944–45, and the Bar Lev line of 1973 all failed, and were overcome by new tactics and technologies, so too will be the fate of Iron Dome. It was successful in these two conflicts, given the fact that there were only four batteries operational (in the Second Gaza War) and nine batteries operational in the Third Gaza War. Israel needs fifteen Iron Dome batteries to protect the entire country. In November 2012, Israeli Defense Minister Ehud Barak asked for funding for additional batteries, but a total of nine is a far cry from the fifteen needed.

US funding for the Iron Dome system cannot be relied on. Whereas President Obama made news proclaiming his support of Iron Dome, in fact Obama's 2012 budget cut funding for Israel's missile defense systems (all missile defense systems, which also included the Iron Dome) while the US Congress did the opposite by increasing financing, doubling the amount. In comparison, President George W. Bush's 2007 $30 billion, 10-year military aid package for Israel helped fund Iron Dome. Finally, Iron Dome or any other missile defense system cannot be a substitute for territorial defense in depth. Any security provided by Iron Dome cannot be a reason for further Israeli territorial concessions such as a retreat to the 1949 Armistice lines.

A most recent example of projected weakness encouraging aggression was the announced retreat policy of the Obama administration from Iraq (in 2011) and Afghanistan (in 2014). Announcing US military total withdrawal beforehand only encouraged the already defeated Sunni jihadists in Iraq and the Taliban in Afghanistan to hang tough, make no concessions to the Americans, then claim victory when the Americans withdrew. American pressures on old traditional allies—Egypt and Israel in particular—merely added to the conviction of the Islamic supremacists that the United States is weak and in full retreat. Additionally, though Libya was neutered by the United States in 2004, the Obama administration in an unnecessary use of military force toppled the Qadhafi regime. This in turn led to chaos and rival militias vying for power. The attack on the US Consulate in Benghazi, Libya on September 11, 2012, without any American response other than a feeble excuse that it was caused by an internet video, solidified in the minds of the Islamist supremacists that the United States had no stomach for maintaining its interests in the region. Furthermore, the Obama administration's threat to use military force against the Assad regime in Syria for its use of chemical weapons and its subsequent sudden abandonment of that option, added to the supremacists belief.

Moreover, the US policy of talking much and doing little to definitively stop Iran's steady drive towards attaining nuclear weapons and long-range missiles capable of delivering such weapons, virtually proclaimed to opponents and allies alike, that the United States abdicated its leadership in the Middle East and beyond. Despite UN Security Council resolutions, the Obama administration in effect, provided over six years for Iran to continue its nuclear weapons program before it began to engage in a diplomatic talk-a-thon that continued well into 2015. With this disastrous policy, the sudden military gains by the Islamic State in Iraq and the Levant proved yet again, that weakness and appeasement led to aggression. As the situation unfolds, it is unknown as to what ultimate price the United States and its old allies, Egypt, Jordan, Saudi Arabia, the Gulf States, and Israel, will have to pay in dealing with Shi'ite Iran and the Sunni Islamic supremacists of the Islamic State because of the continued projection of weakness by the Obama administration.

44. The constant reference to the "Israeli-Palestinian conflict" is based on a false premise that historically the conflict was only between Israel and the Palestinian Arabs.

After the Six-Day War of 1967, the Arab world realized that the continuous pan-Arab assault on tiny Israel won the Jewish state world sympathy. Therefore, the Arabs redefined the conflict as no longer being between Israel and the Arab states, but rather solely between Israel and the Palestinian Arabs. The PLO redefined their terrorist movement and cause. The "Arab refugees" (so referred to up to that time in all UN official documents) were transformed into the "Palestinian people." Repetition of this bogus idea made the conflict seem smaller in the overall context of the Middle East, while at the same time emphasized the centrality of the "Palestinian problem." Thus, the Arab/Muslim side skillfully altered their image, which better served their propaganda efforts. The Palestinian Arabs are portrayed as a tiny, impoverished, out-gunned, homeless people fighting, with rocks and slingshots as modern-day "Davids," against the heartless, massive Israeli military "Goliath." The mass media picked up this refrain and the gullible Western public, ever ready to support the apparent "oppressed underdog," did not understand what was going on and had little inclination to seek the truth. However, once the historic evidence and facts are examined the truth becomes quite evident.

In fact, this is nothing more than a role reversal of the historic reality of miniscule democratic Israel continually being attacked. The Arab–Israeli conflict has grown larger over the years, in number of countries participating, not smaller. In 1947, when the Arab states rejected the UN Partition plan for Palestine, there were seven Arab League states, which engaged in a military attack to destroy the reemerging Jewish state. It was truly a "Goliath versus David" struggle with Israel as "David." Today there are twenty-one sovereign Arab states that are largely oil rich countries, with a huge population and land mass. There are twenty-two Arab states, according to the Arab League membership roster, which lists the non-existent "State of Palestine." Thus, the Arab states constitute an even larger "Goliath" than in the past. Furthermore, by February 2015 the Arab/Muslim side grew larger with the addition of Afghan and Pakistani Shi'ite fighter participating in Hezbollah deployments on the Golan Heights opposite Israel.[6] Afghanistan and Pakistan are neither Arab nor part of the Middle East. The Arabs frankly admitted that they had to portray the conflict with Israel with the latter in the "Goliath" role. This was made abundantly clear by the Egyptian journal *Al-Musswar* in December 1968, "[The Arabs must advance] a plan for rousing world opinion in stages, as it [the world] would not be able to understand or accept a war by a hundred million Arabs against a small state [i.e. Israel]."[7]

THE LEAGUE OF ARAB STATES			
FORMED: March 22, 1945		**HEADQUARTERS:** Cairo, Egypt	
CHARTER MEMBERS: Egypt, Iraq, Jordan (originally Transjordan), Lebanon, Saudi Arabia, Syria,* and Yemen			
ADDITIONAL MEMBERS OF THE ARAB LEAGUE†			
Country	**Date of Entry**	**Country**	**Date of Entry**
Libya‡	March 28, 1953	Oman	September 29, 1971
Sudan	January 9, 1956	United Arab Emirates	December 6, 1971
Morocco and Tunisia	October 1, 1958	Mauritania	November 28, 1973
Kuwait	July 20, 1961	Somalia	February 14, 1974
Algeria	August 16, 1962	"Palestine"(PLO)	September 6, 1976
PDRY§	December 12, 1967	Djibouti	September 4, 1977
Bahrain and Qatar	September 11, 1971	Comoros	November 20, 1993

Since 1964, the Arab League held summit conferences in an attempt to show Arab unity on various issues of common interest. These summits reflect the state of affairs in the Arab world. The main thrust of these summit conferences was directed against combating Israel and eventually eliminating the Jewish state. The methods included direct warfare, asymmetric warfare (terrorism and *intifada*), economic boycott, and water diversion, negotiation strategies (the Phased Plan or strategy of stages) and Arab-sponsored "peace plans." The summits were only partially successful in resolving inter-Arab conflicts, including Lebanon, Kuwait, the Western Sahara, Yemen and a host of inter-Arab territorial disputes.

---

* Syria was suspended from the Arab League on November 16, 2011. This was due to the ongoing harsh repression by the Assad regime of the Syrian citizenry as well as the Syrian Civil War.

† Eritrea was given observer status at the Arab League in January 2003.

‡ On October 25, 2002, Libya withdrew from the Arab League. This would have been effective one year later; however Libya cancelled (January 16, 2003), reaffirmed (April 3, 2003), and again cancelled (May 25, 2003) the decision to withdraw. On February 22, 2011, Libya's membership was suspended following the use of its military forces against Libyan civilians. With the victory of the Libyan rebels against the Qadhafi regime, Libya was readmitted to Arab League membership on August 27, 2011.

§ May 22, 1990–Yemen and the PDRY unified into the Republic of Yemen.

ARAB SUMMIT CONFERENCES		
Date	**Conference Location**	**Primary Actions Taken**
January 13–17, 1964	First Summit Cairo, Egypt	The summit called for the establishment of a Palestine Liberation Organization (PLO) and a Palestine Liberation Army as spearhead of a reactivated concerted campaign "to liberate Palestine."* It implemented a plan to divert the waters of the sources of the Jordan River on Syrian and Lebanese territory and deny its use by Israel. It established a unified Arab military command.
September 5–11, 1964	Second Summit Alexandria, Egypt	The summit formally allocated substantial funds to increase Arab military capability, which led to increased guerrilla activity against Israel, beginning January 1, 1965. A Joint Arab Defense Pact was signed. The summit pledged a common struggle against British imperialism in the Arabian Peninsula and the "Arabian Gulf."
September 13–17, 1965	Third Summit Casablanca, Morocco	The summit pledged "Arab solidarity" and to desist from further hostile propaganda against each other. There was an Egyptian-Saudi agreement to end hostilities in Yemen, and thus concentrate on the enemy (i.e. Israel). Tunisia boycotted the summit.
August 29– September 1, 1967	Fourth Summit Khartoum, Sudan	In the aftermath of the Arab defeat in the Six-Day War, the Arab states pledged "no peace with Israel, no recognition of Israel, no negotiations with Israel." The oil-rich states pledged financial assistance to the "confrontation states" (i.e. Egypt, Jordan and Syria) as well as to "help them rebuild their military forces." Egypt agreed to withdraw from Yemen.
December 20–24, 1969	Fifth Summit Rabat, Morocco	The summit called for an end to hostilities between the Jordanian armed forces and the PLO. Marked by disagreement, the summit ended in disarray.

---

* The PLO was founded on May 28, 1964, three years before the Six-Day War, and before there were any "occupied territories." Thus, the obvious question: Just what then, was the PLO actually trying to "liberate"? The simple answer is all of the Jewish state of Israel within its 1949 Armistice lines.

September 22–27, 1970	First Emergency Summit Cairo, Egypt	The Cairo Agreement obtained a ceasefire in the Jordanian Civil War between Jordanian and PLO forces. The summit was boycotted by Algeria, Iraq, Morocco and Syria. Unexpectedly, UAR President Gamal Abdel Nasser died within hours of the end of the summit.
November 26–28, 1973	Sixth Summit Algiers, Algeria	The summit discussed the Arab Phased Plan or strategy of stages in the conflict with Israel. It pledged continuation of restrictions and embargoes on export of oil. Oil concessions were promised to Europe and Japan in return for diplomatic good behavior (i.e. following a pro-Arab policy at international forums). The summit was boycotted by Iraq and Libya.
October 26–29, 1974	Seventh Summit Rabat, Morocco	The summit proclaimed the PLO as the "sole legitimate representative of the Palestinian people on any Palestinian land that is liberated." The Arab League leased Perim Island from the PDRY for ninety-nine years.
October 17–18, 1976	Second Emergency Summit Riyadh, Saudi Arabia	The summit attempted to deal with the escalating second civil war in Lebanon. It was attended by only five Arab states (Egypt, Kuwait, Lebanon, Saudi Arabia, and Syria) and the Palestinian Liberation Organization. The summit called for an end to the civil war and for the PLO to respect Lebanese sovereignty. It arranged a ceasefire in the conflict and the establishment of an Arab Deterrent Force to supervise the truce.
October 25–26, 1976	Eighth Summit Cairo, Egypt	The summit dealt with the deteriorating situation in Lebanon plagued by its second civil war. The summit approved a Syrian military presence and hegemony in Lebanon.
December 1–4, 1977	"Rejectionist Summit" Tripoli, Libya	The summit was opposed to Egyptian President Sadat's visit to Israel and direct Egyptian-Israeli negotiations. It established the "Steadfastness and Confrontation Front" consisting of Algeria, Iraq, Libya, the PDRY, Syria, and the PLO.
November 2–5, 1978	Ninth Summit Baghdad, Iraq	The summit opposed the Camp David Accords and movement towards an Egypt–Israel Peace Treaty. Egypt was suspended by the Arab League and the latter's secretariat was moved out of its Cairo headquarters to Tunis, Tunisia.

November 20–22, 1979	Tenth Summit Tunis, Tunisia	The summit discussed the Lebanon–PLO situation in southern Lebanon. It pledged financial aid for Lebanon's rehabilitation. It reiterated the collective Arab stance against Egypt and its peace moves with Israel.
November 25–27, 1980	Eleventh Summit Amman, Jordan	The summit rejected the Camp David Accords and the Egypt–Israel Peace Treaty. It reaffirmed the PLO as the legitimate representative of the Palestinian people. The summit discussed the Iran–Iraq War. It declared support for Iraq and Lebanon. The summit was boycotted by Algeria, Lebanon, Libya, the PDRY, Syria, and the PLO.
November 29, 1981	Twelfth Summit (Part 1) Fes, Morocco	The Saudi (Fahd) peace plan for the Middle East was unveiled. The summit collapsed after five hours, over the peace plan.
September 6–9, 1982	Twelfth Summit (Part 2–Conclusion) Fes, Morocco	The summit strongly condemned Israeli aggression against Lebanon. It approved the eight-point Saudi plan calling for Israeli return to pre-1967 borders (the 1949 Armistice lines), creation of an independent Palestinian state and a United Nations Security Council guarantee among "all states of the region." The summit called for compensation of Palestinian refugees who did not wish to return to hometowns occupied by Israel. It reiterated support for Iraq in its war with Iran. The summit was boycotted by Libya.
August 7–9, 1985	Third Emergency Summit Casablanca, Morocco	The summit failed to make progress on "issues dividing the Arabs" (Jordan–Syria, Syria–Iraq, Libya–Iraq, and Libya–PLO relations as well as inter-Arab terrorism). Egypt was barred from attending the summit. It condemned Iran for its war with Iraq. The summit was boycotted by Algeria, Lebanon, Libya, Syria, and PDRY.
November 8–11, 1987	Fourth Emergency Summit Amman, Jordan	The summit again endorsed Iraq's position in the Iran–Iraq War. It allowed any Arab League member to restore diplomatic relations with Egypt. Collective aid to Jordan, Syria, and the PLO was ended.

June 7–9, 1988	Fifth Emergency Summit Algiers, Algeria	The summit approved a resolution to provide "all possible support by all possible means" to the Palestinian *intifada* in Judea and Samaria (also known as the "West Bank") and the Gaza Strip. It called for an international conference on peace in the Middle East. The summit was boycotted by Libya.
May 23–26, 1989	Sixth Emergency Summit Casablanca, Morocco	The summit readmitted Egypt to League activities. It discussed the Palestinian *intifada* and the situation in Lebanon. The summit implicitly recognized Israel by endorsing UN Resolutions 242 and 338.
March 28–30, 1990	Seventh Emergency Summit Baghdad, Iraq	The summit failed to settle outstanding disputes between Iraq and Kuwait. It discussed the implications of Russian Jewish immigration to Israel. The summit considered Iraqi, Jordanian, and PLO needs for additional financial aid. The summit was boycotted by Libya.
August 31, 1990	Eighth Emergency Summit Cairo, Egypt	The summit failed to convince Iraq to pull its troops out of Kuwait. It condemned the invasion and at the request of Riyadh agreed to send Arab troops to Saudi Arabia. The summit deliberated about the implications of international military intervention over Kuwait. It was boycotted by Libya. With all these failures, the summit shattered the myth of Arab solidarity.
June 21–23, 1996	Ninth Emergency Summit Cairo, Egypt	The summit called on Israel to withdraw from all occupied Arab lands and to permit the Palestinians to establish an independent state with East Jerusalem as its capital. The summit declared peace with Israel as an Arab strategic choice.
October 21–22, 2000	Tenth Emergency Summit Cairo, Egypt	The summit adopted an amendment to the Arab League charter stipulating an annual Arab summit in March in commemoration of the founding of the Arab League on March 22, 1945. It discussed the second Palestinian *intifada*. It was attended by fifteen Arab leaders. The Libyan delegation walked out, angry over signs the summit would stop short of calling for breaking all ties with Israel.

March 21–22, 2001	Thirteenth Summit Amman, Jordan	The summit supported the on-going second *intifada*. It narrowed differences among Iraq, Kuwait, and Saudi Arabia. Libya proposed a single secular state of "Israetine."
March 27–28, 2002	Fourteenth Summit Beirut, Lebanon	The summit unveiled the Saudi (Crown Prince Abdullah) peace plan to end the Israeli–Palestinian conflict. It proposed diplomatic relations with Israel in exchange for full withdrawal from all Arab territories acquired in the 1967 war, creation of a Palestinian state with East Jerusalem as its capital, and return of all the Palestinian refugees to what is Israel. At the same time, the Arab leaders vowed to continue to support the second *intifada*. They further demanded that Israel sign the Non Proliferation Treaty and put its nuclear installations under international supervision. The summit was boycotted by Libya.
March 1, 2003	Fifteenth Summit Sharm el-Sheikh, Egypt	The summit convened less than three weeks before the US-led coalition invasion of Iraq. The summit adopted a set of resolutions calling on member states to refrain from assisting the foreign occupation of Iraq, at a time when neighboring Gulf states were hosting the troops that were preparing to attack Iraq. The summit failed to address a proposal of the United Arab Emirates that then Iraqi President Saddam Hussein resign and leave Iraq to avoid the invasion of his country. The summit also discussed the American-sponsored road map to peace and called for a Palestinian state. The Arab leaders rejected normalization of ties with Israel.
May 22–23, 2004	Sixteenth Summit Tunis, Tunisia	Due to inter-Arab differences, the March meeting was postponed by Tunisian President Zein Al-Abidine Bin Ali and reconvened in May. Differences remained and Libya walked out of the summit.
March 22–23, 2005	Seventeenth Summit Algiers, Algeria	The summit celebrated the Sixtieth anniversary of the Arab League and called for closer Arab ties. It pledged aid to Somalia.

March 28–30, 2006	Eighteenth Summit Khartoum, Sudan	The summit supported Sudan in its defiance of a United Nations Security Council resolution calling for the dispatch of UN troops to replace the undermanned and underfinanced African Union peacekeepers in Darfur. Syria received full backing from the summit in the face of US sanctions against Syria over the murder of Lebanese Prime Minister Rafik Hariri. The summit also reiterated the demand that Iran return three disputed islands (Abu Musa and the Tunb Islands) to the United Arab Emirates. It also expressed solidarity with the Iraqi people and denounced Israel's security barrier.
March 27–28, 2007	Nineteenth Summit Riyadh, Saudi Arabia	The summit sought to relaunch the Saudi peace plan for ending the Israeli-Palestinian conflict.
March 29–30, 2008	Twentieth Summit Damascus, Syria	The summit was marred by differences over Lebanon, with Egypt and Saudi Arabia clashing with Syria. Egypt and Saudi Arabia only sent low-level representatives to the summit. Lebanon boycotted the meeting altogether.
March 29–30, 2009	Twenty-first Summit Doha, Qatar	Libyan-Saudi differences erupted and were papered over. The summit discussed the Israeli Operation *Cast Lead* into the Gaza Strip. The Arab leaders in attendance defied the International Criminal Court by welcoming Sudanese President Omar al-Bashir, on who the Court placed a warrant for war crimes in the genocide in Darfur. The summit split between those states that supported Hamas in Gaza (Qatar and Syria), and those who supported the Palestinian Authority (Egypt and Saudi Arabia).
March 27–28, 2010	Twenty-second Summit Sirt, Libya	The summit pledged no recognition of Israel under any conditions. Attendees agreed to continued "armed resistance" (better known as terrorism) against Israel. They further agreed not to condemn genocide in Darfur, Sudan. They continued demands for an Arab Jerusalem.
March 27–29, 2012	Twenty-third Summit Baghdad, Iraq	The summit discussed the proposed Arab Union as well as the uprising in Syria.

March 27–28, 2013	Twenty-fourth Summit Doha, Qatar	The summit discussed the on-going Syrian Civil War. It saw a division of support for various factions in the conflict between two blocs with Qatar and Turkey (a non-member) on one side and Saudi Arabia, the Gulf states and Jordan on the other. The Sunni Arabs refused a rapprochement with Turkey. The Saudi faction was opposed to the Muslim Brotherhood or Al-Qaeda gaining control of Syria. Saudi Arabia announced it was supplying heavy weapons to the faction it favored.
March 25–26, 2014	Twenty-fifth Summit Kuwait City, Kuwait	The summit totally rejected the call to recognize Israel as a Jewish state. The summit denounced Israeli settlements and what it called the "judaization" of Jerusalem.
March 28–29, 2015	Twenty-sixth Summit Sharm El Sheikh, Egypt	The summit dealt with the Iranian-supported Houthi seizure of many towns in Yemen. The League agreed to Saudi-led military intervention in Yemen in support of the legitimate Yemeni government. It also discussed the threat posed by the Islamic State as well as the on-going Syrian Civil War. The Arab leaders also agreed to form a unified military force to counter growing regional security threats.

To the Arab League must be added all the various terrorist organizations, which include Fatah, the Popular Front for the Liberation of Palestine (PFLP), Palestine Islamic Jihad (PIJ), Hamas, and Hezbollah et al. Thus, there is a much larger Arab Goliath. Add to this list of Israel's enemies, the non-Arab Muslim states. These include Iran (since 1979), Pakistan (sharing nuclear and missile technology with other Arab and Islamic states), and Turkey (increasingly hostile towards the Jewish state). The latter three are part of the fifty-seven members of the Organization of Islamic Cooperation (OIC), which has demonstrated open hostility to Israel, following the dictates of the Qur'an to destroy the Jews and liberate all of "Palestine." The OIC is the largest voting bloc at the United Nations, a virulent propaganda machine, as well as a source for funds, "volunteers" and more. There should be no doubt that there is an overwhelming accumulation of forces aligned against Israel, which stands alone, now as before as the true "David" in the Middle East.

45. The Arab/Muslim exaggerated emphasis on the "Palestinian-Israeli conflict" has by and large, obscured the far worse conflicts, ethnic and sectarian cleansings, murders, assassinations and destruction perpetrated within the Islamic world as well as jihadist attacks worldwide against the West.

MODERN CONFLICTS IN THE MIDDLE EAST/MUSLIM WORLD (excluding the Arab–Israeli Conflict)	
Date	**Conflict**
1766–March 16, 2001	There was a 235 year-long Qatar–Bahrain maritime and territorial dispute over Zubarah, the Hawar Islands, Qit'at Jaradah, and the Janan Islands.
1895–96, 1914–18, 1922–25	The Ottoman Turkish government as well as the Young Turks movement, perpetrated attacks against the Assyrian (also known as the Syrian, Syriac, Nestorian, and Chaldean) Christian communities in the eastern provinces of the Ottoman Empire (an area divided after World War I among Turkey, Iran and Iraq). The massive killing and deportations, in effect ethnic and sectarian cleansing, came to be known as the Assyrian Genocide.
1902–32	Abd al-'Aziz ibn Abdur Rahman Al-Feisal Al Sa'ud (commonly known as Ibn Saud) conquered and forcibly annexed territories to create the Kingdom of Saudi Arabia. These included the Emirate of Riyadh (1902), the Emirate of Ha'il (1906 and again in 1921), Al Hasa and Qatif (1913), Hejaz (1925), and Asir (1930). Between 8,000 and 9,000 died in these wars.
1915–23	Turkish Muslim genocide was perpetrated against 1.5 million Christian Armenians, 750,000 Assyrians, and 400,000 Greeks.
1918–30	Ismail Agha Shikak, also known as Simko Shikak, led a Kurdish revolt against Persia.
May 19, 1919–July 24, 1923	The Turkish War of Independence saw Turkey successfully defeat the Allies in their attempt at partitioning Turkey. During the conflict, Turkey fought Greek, Armenian, French and British Empire forces.
1923 to date	There was an on-going Turkey–Iraq border dispute, which included the disposition of Mosul and disputed water rights.
1924 to date	There is an ongoing Jordan–Saudi Arabia dispute over the claim of suzerainty maintained by the Hashemite dynasty of Jordan over the Saudi province of Hejaz. Hejaz, on the western coast of the Arabian Peninsula, is where the holy cities of Mecca and Medina are located.
August 23, 1925–June 1927	The Great Druze Revolt erupted in the Mandate of Syria against French rule. Joined by Syrian Sunni nationalists and Maronite Christians, the fighting raged across large swaths of both Syria and Lebanon before being ruthlessly suppressed by French military forces.
October 28, 1927–September 17, 1930	The Kurds in southeastern Turkey, began a war of independence, and declared the Republic of Ararat. Turkish armed forces crushed the rebellion and the short-lived country ceased to exist. The estimated number of casualties varies widely, from 4,500 to 47,000.
August 7–11, 1933	The Simele Massacre, at Simele near Mosul, was the first of many massacres committed by the Iraqi Government during the systematic targeting of Assyrian Christians of northern Iraq. The massacre was not restricted to Simele, but also was perpetrated among sixty-three Assyrian villages in the Dohuk and Mosul districts that led to the deaths of between 600 and 3,000 Assyrians. These attacks culminated in an Assyrian exodus of some 50,000 from Iraq.

April 7–May 20, 1934	A Saudi Arabia–Yemen war was fought over Asir, in the southwestern corner of the Arabian Peninsula. The region had been annexed by Saudi Arabia, but the Imamate of Yemen claimed it. There were over 2,000 casualties. The Treaty of Ta'if was signed, with Saudi Arabia retaining Asir.
1937	Seyid Riza launched and led a Kurdish uprising against the Turkish government in the Dersim region of eastern Turkey. This Dersim Rebellion was crushed by the Turkish military, with some 40,000 people killed.
1936–74	Iran and Iraq fought a series of wars for control of the Shatt al-Arab (known as Arvand Rud in Iran) border estuary.
1943 to date	There has been a long-standing dispute between Syria and Lebanon over lack of Syrian recognition of Lebanon as a separate independent state. Syria notoriously claims the entirety of Lebanon as part of "Greater Syria."
December 1945–December 1946	In response to the establishment of the "Azerbaijan People's Government" (December 12, 1945) and the Kurdish Republic of Mahabad (December 15, 1945), Iran used a combination of diplomacy, US-UN pressure and military force to crush both secessionist movements by December 11 and December 15, 1946, respectively.
1945 to date	There has been an Iran–Afghanistan dispute over the issue of water rights of the Helmand River.
1947	The partition of the Indian Subcontinent—into India and Pakistan—resulted in between 800,000 and 1,000,000 Muslims and Hindus killed.
1947–48; 1958–59; 1963–69; 1973–77; 2004–to date	There is an insurgency in Baluchistan, straddling the Iran–Pakistan border. Over the years, the Baloch fought about a range of issues including human rights abuses, greater autonomy, increased royalties from natural resources and provincial revenue, and in some cases, full independence. The conflict has been fought primarily in Pakistan and to a lesser extent in Iran. Most Baloch are Sunni, and they are viewed as heretics by predominantly Shi'ite Iran. In Pakistan, now officially an Islamic state governed by shari'a law, the Baloch is viewed as not Muslim compliant.
1949	An insurrection was suppressed in Lebanon.
1949–August 21, 1974.	Rival claims and border clashes occurred between Saudi Arabia and Oman, as well as Saudi Arabia and Abu Dhabi (now part of the United Arab Emirates) over the Buraimi Oasis.. The dispute was resolved by the Treaty of Jeddah, but to date the UAE has not ratified the treaty.
Summer of 1953–February 25, 1954	The Syrian regime of Colonel Adib Shishakli viewed the Druze in his country as being the head of opposition to his rule. He curbed their autonomy, reduced their role in the government, purged the military of Druze officers, and severely hampered their economy. Convinced that they had been singled out for persecution the Druze revolted. Shishakli dispatched 10,000 regular troops to occupy the Jabal al-Druze. Several towns were bombarded with heavy weapons, killing scores of civilians and destroying many houses. According to Druze accounts, Shishakli encouraged neighboring Bedouin tribes to plunder the defenseless population and allowed his own troops to run amok. The carnage stopped only with the overthrow of Shishakli by a military coup on February 25, 1954.

1954, 1957–59	Imam Ghalib bin Ali al Hinai led an insurrection—the Jebel Akhdar Rebellion—against the Sultanate of Oman (then known as Muscat and Oman). British intervention, in support of the Omani government, was necessary to quell the rebellion.
1954–62	The French-Algerian National Liberation Front (FLN) conflict saw 675,000 mostly Muslims killed by both the French and the Muslim FLN. In addition, between 50,000 and 150,000 *harkis* (pro-French Muslim Algerians) were killed by the FLN.
April 1, 1955–March 31, 1959	An armed rebellion by the *Ethniki Organosis Kyprion Agoniston* ("National Organization of Cypriot Fighters"), or EOKA, began in the British protectorate of Cyprus. EOKA favored self-determination and *enosis* or union of Cyprus with Greece. The conflict became more complex as the Turkish Cypriot community favored *taxim* or partition of the island. In 1957, a rival paramilitary organization—the Turkish Resistance Organization (TMT)—came into existence. It served Turkish interests and clashed violently on occasion, with the EOKA.
August 18, 1955–February 27, 1972	The First Sudanese Civil War waged in southern Sudan, saw between 500,000 and 600,000 mostly Christians and animists killed.
1956–60	King Ahmad bin Yahya of Yemen, who was also the imam of the ruling Zaydi branch of Shi'a Islam, supported tribal and religious violence in the neighboring British Aden Protectorate. He was fearful of Sunni power in Aden and its spillover effect into Yemen, as the British sought to federate various tribes in Aden into a stronger political entity.
1957–58	Border clashes took place between Morocco and Mauritania (then French) as the former claimed all or large parts of the latter, as part of "Greater Morocco."
October 23, 1957–April 2, 1958	The Ifni War was waged by Moroccan forces seeking to gain control of the Spanish enclave of Ifni, located within Moroccan territory. While the Moroccans failed to capture Ifni, the conflict ended with the April 2, 1958, Angra de Cintra Agreement. Over 8,000 were killed on both sides. Under the terms of the agreement Cape Juby (lying adjacent to Morocco's territory to the south) was given to Morocco in June 1958. Ifni was ceded to Morocco on January 4, 1969.
February–July 1958	Civil strife occurred in Jordan including intervention by the United Arab Republic which sought to topple the Hashemite monarchy of King Hussein (*see* the "1958 Crisis, Iraqi Revolution" map).
May–July 1958	The First Lebanese Civil War erupted between largely Christian and Muslim groups with intervention by the United Arab Republic (*see* the "1958 Crisis, Iraqi Revolution" map).
July 14, 1958	A violent revolution in Iraq overthrew the Hashemite monarchy and caused the collapse of the Baghdad Pact (*see* the "1958 Crisis, Iraqi Revolution" map).

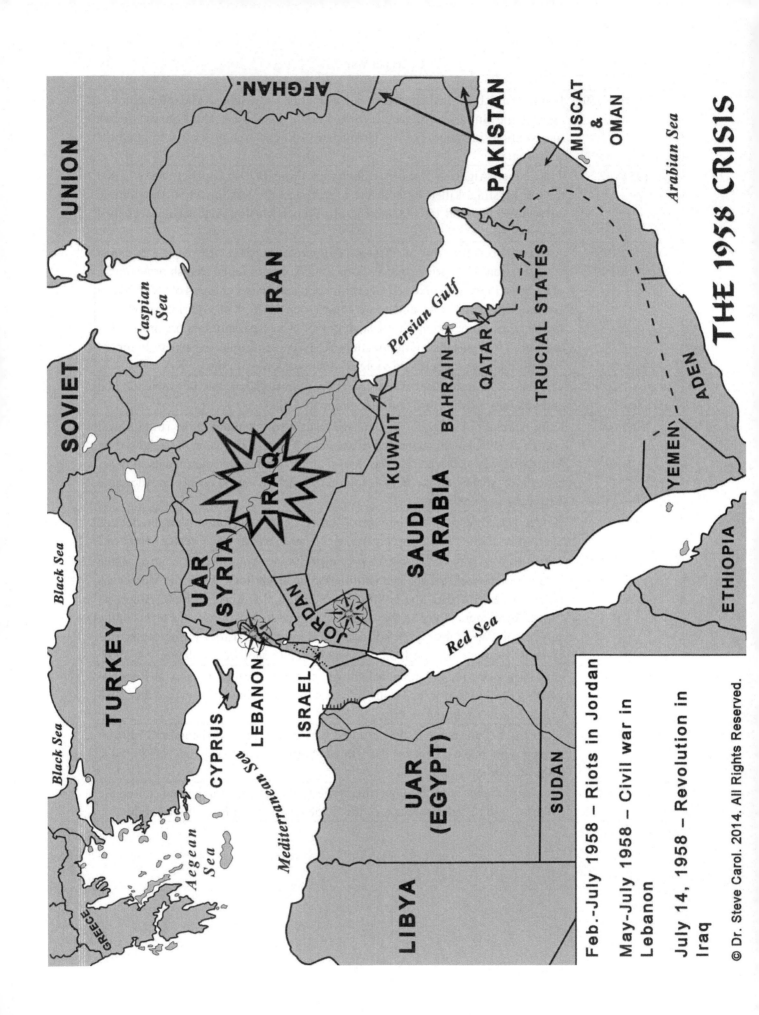

THE 1958 CRISIS

Feb.–July 1958 – Riots in Jordan

May-July 1958 – Civil war in Lebanon

July 14, 1958 – Revolution in Iraq

© Dr. Steve Carol. 2014. All Rights Reserved.

Date	Conflict
March 8–13, 1959	A failed Nasserist coup in Iraq triggered a communist rampage, where some 3,000 were killed.
July 14–19, 1959	The Iraqi communists and Kurds attacked the Turkmen population in Kirkuk. Some 300 people were killed or injured.
1961–70, 1973–75, 1980–91	A long, though intermittent, bloody Kurdish revolt took place against the Arab government in Iraq.
1962–63	There was a rebellion by the Socialist Forces Front in the Kabylie region of Algeria, against the central government.
1962–64	A Tuareg rebellion took place in northern Mali, amidst Tuareg demands for a separate Tuareg and Berber state in the Sahara. Though Mali is 90 percent Muslim including the Tuaregs, the latter is a distinct ethnic group.
1962–70	A civil war in Yemen, triggered by a UAR-inspired coup, was followed by the 1962–67 UAR (Egyptian) military intervention in that country. The war resulted in an estimated 100,000 to 150,000 killed. This conflict included the use of poison gas—confirmed by the International Red Cross (*see* the "Yemen Civil War–Coup and Egyptian Intervention" map).

THE YEMEN CIVIL WAR
1962–1970

----- Roads

Sept. 26 1962 - Army coup, by Colonel A. Al-Sallal ousted Imam M. Al-Badr. Yemen Arab Republic (YAR) established.

Egyptian aid to YAR and intervention by 70,000 troops.

Nasser's Aim: Pressure on Saudi Arabia and on the British in South Arabia.

Oct. 14, 1963 Beginning of NLF revolt in Aden.

Aid to Royalists from Saudi Arabia, Jordan and South Arabia.

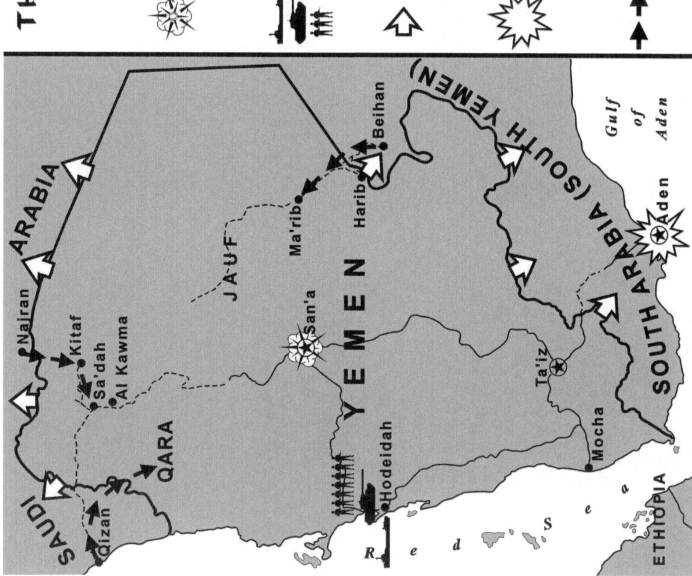

SAUDI ARABIA

Qizan
Najran
Kitaf
Sa'dah
Al Kawma
QARA
JAUF
San'a
Ma'rib
Harib
Beihan
Hodeidah
YEMEN
Ta'iz
Mocha
Red Sea
SOUTH ARABIA (SOUTH YEMEN)
Aden
Gulf of Aden
ETHIOPIA

Date	Conflict
1962–76	A separatist insurgency in Dhofar Province was fought against the central government of the Sultanate of Oman.
1962–92	A civil war in Ethiopia between mainly Muslim Eritrean secessionist rebels and the Ethiopian central government, resulted in 1,400,000 Muslims and Christians killed.
February 8–10, 1963	The 14 Ramadan Revolution in Iraq resulted in Ba'athists battling communists where some 1,000 to 5,000 were killed.
October 1963	A three-week Moroccan-Algerian border war was fought as Morocco sought unsuccessfully, to annex the Algerian territories of Bechar and Tindouf.
December 10, 1963–November 30, 1967	An Arab nationalist uprising in Aden, then known as the Federation of South Arabia, took place against British rule. The Radfan uprising (1963–64) was part of the violence during this period. The conflict also included fighting between two rival nationalist groups, the National Liberation Front (NLF) and the Front for the Liberation of Occupied South Yemen (FLOSY). They attacked each other as well as the British. By November 1967, the British withdrew and a radical Marxist wing of the NLF emerged victorious.
December 21, 1963–August 9, 1964	Cyprus' attainment of independence on August 16, 1960 did not stop the on-going Greek-Turkish communal tension and occasional violence on the island. Demographically, 78 percent of the population was Greek and 18 percent was Turkish[8] (*see* "Demography of Cyprus prior to 1974" map). In late 1963, serious fighting erupted between the two communities (*see* "Cyprus-Clashes of 1963–64, 1967 and UNFICYP" map).
January 12, 1964–February 3, 1964	A revolution in Zanzibar, by mainly Muslim Africans, resulted in some 17,000 killed, mostly Muslim Arabs in the revolution and its aftermath.
1965–66	As a result of an attempted communist coup in Indonesia and its aftermath, some 500,000 Muslims were killed.
November 15–30, 1967	Communal violence again flared on Cyprus between Greek and Turkish communities threatening to expand into a Greco-Turkish war (*see* "Cyprus-Clashes of 1963–64, 1967 and UNFICYP" map).

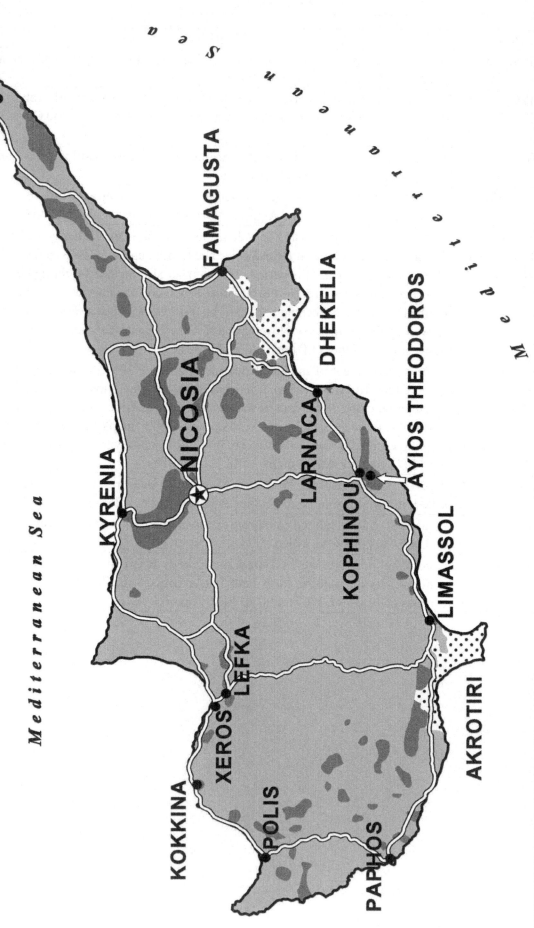

DEMOGRAPHY OF CYPRUS PRIOR TO 1974

Mediterranean Sea

Mediterranean Sea

RIZOKARPASO

FAMAGUSTA

DHEKELIA

AYIOS THEODOROS

NICOSIA

KYRENIA

LARNACA

KOPHINOU

LIMASSOL

LEFKA

XEROS

KOKKINA

POLIS

AKROTIRI

PAPHOS

Roads

Predominately Greek

Predominately Turkish

British sovereign bases

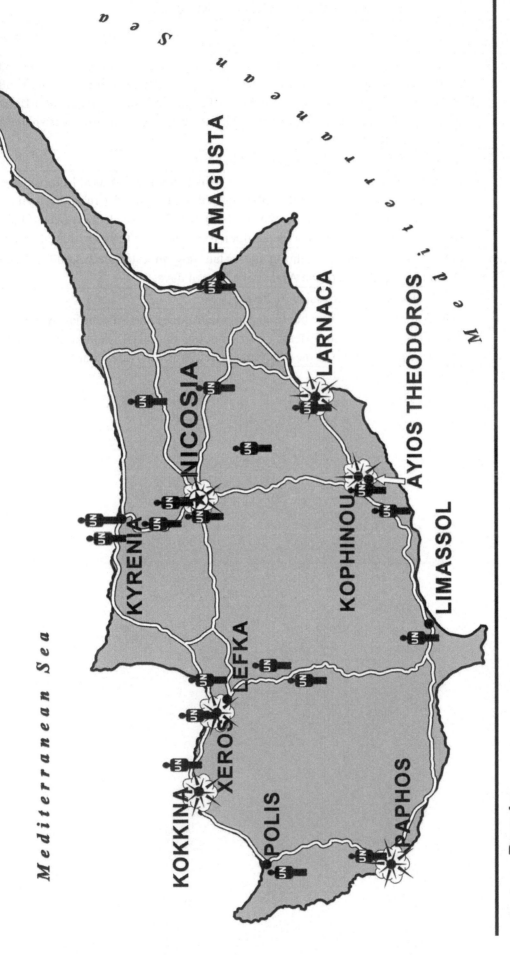

CYPRUS - CLASHES OF 1963-64, 1967 and UNFICYP

Mediterranean Sea

RIZOKARPASO

FAMAGUSTA

NICOSIA

LARNACA

KYRENIA

AYIOS THEODOROS

LEFKA

KOPHINOU

XEROS

LIMASSOL

KOKKINA

POLIS

PAPHOS

Mediterranean Sea

Roads

Dec. 21, 1963-Aug. 9, 1964 and Nov. 15-30, 1967 communal clashes

United Nations Forces in Cyprus (UNFICYP)

Date	Conflict
1968–2003	The Iraqi regime of Saddam Hussein engaged in the murderous repression and ethnic cleansing of the Kurdish people. This resulted in the deaths of over 200,000 to 300,000 Kurds—overwhelmingly Muslim. Over 1 million Iraqis of different ethnic and religious backgrounds died during this period, the overwhelming majority of them, Muslims.
1969, 1973	Saudi Arabia and the PDRY engaged in border clashes.
1969–75	A PDRY–Oman border war was fought. It included PDRY-based Marxist rebels from the Popular Front for the Liberation of the Occupied Arab Gulf trying to seize control of the Omani province of Dhofar. The war claimed over 100,000 lives and produced almost a half-million refugees on both sides of the border.
September 16,–27, 1970	The Black September fighting in Jordan saw an estimated 3,000 to 5,000 Jordanians and Palestinian Arabs killed in ten days.
September 1970	There was a Syrian invasion of Jordan.
1970–71	The Jordanian Civil War between Jordanian forces and Palestinian Arabs—all Muslims—resulted in a death toll (including the Black September conflict) estimated at 25,000 (*see* the "Jordanian Civil War, 1970–71" map).

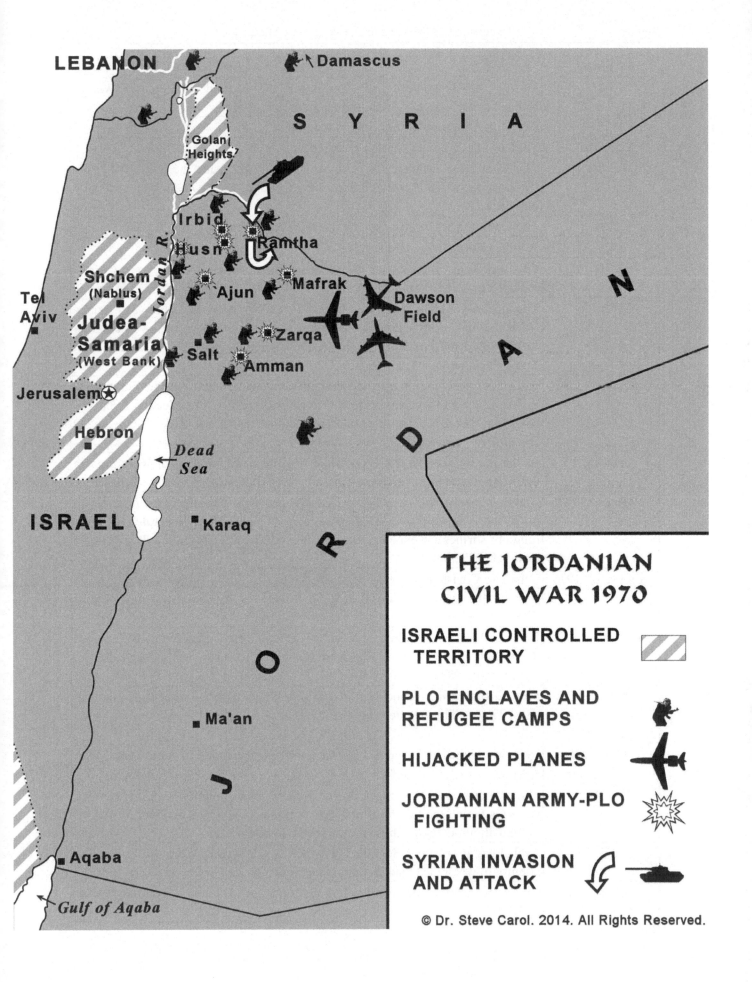

LEBANON

Damascus

S Y R I A

Golan
Heights

Irbid

Ramtha

Husn

Shchem
(Nablus)

Ajun

Mafrak

Tel
Aviv

Judea-
Samaria
(West Bank)

Salt

Zarqa

Dawson
Field

Jordan R.

Jerusalem ☆

Amman

J

Hebron

O

R

Dead
Sea

D

A

N

ISRAEL

Karaq

O

Ma'an

J

Aqaba

Gulf of Aqaba

THE JORDANIAN
CIVIL WAR 1970

**ISRAELI CONTROLLED
TERRITORY**

**PLO ENCLAVES AND
REFUGEE CAMPS**

HIJACKED PLANES

**JORDANIAN ARMY-PLO
FIGHTING**

**SYRIAN INVASION
AND ATTACK**

Date	Conflict
1971	During the Bangladesh secession from Pakistan and Bangladeshi War of Independence, some 1,250,000 Muslims were killed.[9]
1972–75	On-going Iraq–Iran border clashes took place.
October 1972–73	Yemen–PDRY border clashes occurred.
March 20, 1973	The Iraqi army invaded and occupied El-Samitah inside the Kuwaiti border. Under pressure and financial inducements by Saudi Arabia, the Iraqis eventually withdrew.
1973	There were sporadic uprisings by the Kurds in Turkey.
1973–75	Another Kurdish revolt took place in Iraq.
July 20, 1974 to date	The Turkish invasion—Operation *Attila*—and occupation of northern Cyprus took place (*see* "Cyprus-Crisis of 1974, Turkish Invasion and Occupation" map).
1975–90	The fifteen-year-long Second Lebanese Civil War was fought between largely Christian and Muslim groups. Also involved were elements of the PLO. Over 130,000 died and over 500,000 Christians fled Lebanon (*see* the "Lebanese Civil War 1976" map).
December 6, 1975	A series of massacres and armed clashes between Christian and Muslim groups, including the PLO, began in Beirut, Lebanon, triggering the Second Lebanese Civil War. These actions were collectively called "Black Saturday." Between 200 and 600, mostly Muslims, were killed.
January 18, 1976	In the predominantly PLO-controlled Muslim neighborhood of Karantina in Christian East Beirut, Lebanese Christian forces massacred some 1,500 residents.
January 20, 1976	The PLO massacred some 584 civilians in the Christian town of Damour, south of Beirut, in reprisal for the Karantina massacre. The PLO desecrated the local religious shrines and expelled some 25,000 of the residents (for details *see* "Basic Principle 22" above).
August 12, 1976	Lebanese Christian militias backed by the Syrian army, massacred some 3,500 Palestinians, mostly civilians, in the Tel al-Zaatar refugee camp in northeast Beirut.
October 19, 1976	Dozens of women, children, and elderly persons were massacred by PLO forces in the Lebanese Christian village of Aishiya. The survivors fled and did not return until 1982.
December 7, 1975–September 20, 1999	Muslim Indonesian genocide was committed against Christians in Timor Este (East Timor). This resulted in some 200,000 to 300,000 killed.
1976–2005	Syria intervened and occupied Lebanon during the Second Lebanese Civil War.
1976 to date	A Morocco–Algeria conflict began over the status of the Western Sahara.
July 21–24, 1977	A short but intense Egyptian-Libyan border war was fought over Sadat's policy vis-à-vis Israel, the failure of unification between Libya and Egypt, as well as mutual attempts to overthrow each other's government.
1977–78	Arab League member Somalia, launched a war against Ethiopia in a failed attempt to wrest the Ogaden region from the latter.
1977 to date	Civil war, anarchy and nearly continual conflict in Somalia resulted in over 550,000 killed.

January 1978–February 1979	An Islamic Revolution in Iran, overthrew the government of Shah Mohammad Reza Pahlavi and established an Islamic republic.
Late January–early February 1978	A short border conflict erupted between Saudi Arabia and the PDRY at Wadia Oasis in the Rub' al Khali (Empty Quarter) desert. In one severe clash, four Saudi Lightning fighters were shot down by PDYR MiG-21s flown by Yemeni or Cuban pilots.[10]
1978, 1979, 1980–81, 1983–87	Libya intervened in the civil war in Chad, providing aid and training to the *Front de Libération Nationale* (FROLINAT) that sought to topple the legitimate government of President François Tombalbaye. Furthermore, Libya invaded and occupied (in 1974) the 300-mile deep Aouzou Strip—rumored to be rich in uranium—that lay along the Libyan–Chadian border. Libya annexed the Aouzou Strip, some 37,000 square miles, in May 1975. Chadian resistance, French military intervention in 1978, 1983 and 1986, as well as US assistance helped drive the Libyans out by August 1987. Over 8,500 were killed on all sides.
February 23–March 4, 1979	There was another short Yemen–PDRY border war.
1979 to date	There is an on-going Iran–Pakistan dispute over territorial waters in the Arabian Sea.
November 20–December 4, 1979	Some 400 to 500 Islamic extremists seized and occupied the Grand Mosque in Mecca, Saudi Arabia. After two weeks, Saudi forces assisted by Pakistani and French troops were able to retake control of the mosque. Some 127 pilgrims and Saudi troops were killed and 451 wounded. Islamic extremist losses were 117 killed and 63 beheaded afterwards.[11]
November 1979 and February 1980	Iranian-inspired, widespread riots erupted in the Shi'ite towns of Saudi Arabia's oil-rich Eastern Province.
April 1979–1983.	A Kurdish-Iranian conflict resulted in over 40,000 casualties—most overwhelmingly Muslim.
1979–99	The Afghanistan Civil War, resulted in some 2,400,000 Muslims killed.
September 22,1980–August 20, 1988	The Iran–Iraq War, resulted in between 1,000,000 and 1,600,000 Muslims killed on both sides. There was some two million wounded as well as catastrophic damage to the economic infrastructure, amounting to $500 billion on each side.
February 2–28, 1982	Syrian President Hafez al-Assad sent 12,000 troops supported by tanks and artillery to root out Muslim Brotherhood members in the city of Hama. In the operation that lasted for some two weeks, large parts of the old city were leveled, cyanide gas was used and an estimated 7,000 to 38,000 were killed, including some 1,000 soldiers.[12] The event became known as the Hama Massacre. The attack was described as possibly being "the single deadliest act [to that date] by any Arab government against its own people in the modern Middle East."[13]
September 16–18, 1982	After the assassination of Lebanese President-elect Bashir Gemayel, as well as in revenge for the earlier massacre of Christians in the Lebanese coastal city of Damour, the Christian Phalange (Kata'eb) Party militia slaughtered hundreds of Palestinian and Lebanese Muslims in the refugee camps of Sabra and Shatila in West Beirut. The number of victims of the massacre is disputed and varies from 460 to 3,500. This was part of the on-going sectarian violence of the Second Lebanese Civil War (1975–90).

1982–84	US-French-Italian peacekeeping forces in Lebanon, were attacked, killed and forced to withdraw from that country by Hezbollah terrorists, under the direction of Iran. This included the suicide bombings of the US Marine Corps and French barracks in Beirut on October 23, 1983, resulting in 241 killed US servicemen and 58 dead French paratroopers.
1983	There was a PLO civil war in Lebanon.
1983–January 9, 2005	After an eleven-year ceasefire that failed to resolve the differences between northern and southern Sudan, as well as the north's proclamation of Sudan as an Islamic state, the Second Sudanese Civil War (erupted in 1983). The conflict resulted in some 1,900,000 killed before its conclusion with a peace agreement that led to a referendum and independence of South Sudan on July 9, 2011.
1984	A Kurdish revolt in Iran took place.
August 15, 1984–September 1, 1999; June 1, 2004 to date.	An on-going Kurdish-Turkish conflict raged between on the one hand, various Kurdish rebel groups, chief of which is the Kurdistan Workers' Party (PKK) and the Turkish government in southeastern Turkey. The Kurds seek an independent Kurdistan.
January 13–February 1986	Civil War raged in PDRY, resulting in an estimated 10,000 casualties.
April 26, 1986	There was a Qatar–Bahrain border clash over the Fasht al-Dibal reef.
1986–89	Iraqi ethnic cleansing of the Kurds during the *Al-Anfal* campaign resulted in 50,000 to 182,000 killed.
1987–88	During the Iran–Iraq War, Iran attacked Kuwait on two occasions. It fired a missile at Kuwait on September 4, 1987, and attacked Kuwait's Bubiyan Island on March 19, 1988.
March 16, 1988	The Iraqi government used poison gas on Muslim Kurds in Halabja. Between 3,000 and 5,000 perished.
1988	The Iranian government executed over 5,000 "political prisoners," most of them Muslim.
1988	Iran acting to ensure its hold over the oil-rich province of Khuzistan began the ethnic cleansing of Arabs from that area. Khuzistan, which the Arabs called "Arabistan," was the object of a pan-Arab campaign, starting in the 1970s, to claim the region as part of the "Arab homeland."
1990 to date	There is a Yemen–Oman boundary dispute.
1990–91	Iraq invaded, conquered and annexed Kuwait. After Kuwait's liberation, in one week in March 1991, some 450,000 Palestinian Arabs were forcibly expelled from Kuwait.[14] In a like manner, Saudi Arabia expelled 800,000 Yemenis, due to Yemen's opposition to the liberation of Kuwait.
1990–95	Another Tuareg rebellion swept areas of northern Mali and Niger with the goal of achieving autonomy or forming their own nation-state.
March 1, 1991–end of March.	A Shi'ite uprising in southern Iraq was harshly repressed by the Sunni Iraqi government resulting in some 200,000 Muslims killed.
March 4, 1991–April 3, 1991	A Kurdish uprising in northern Iraq was brutally suppressed by the Iraqi regime.

November 1991–December 26, 1994	The Djiboutian Civil War was fought by the Front for the Restoration of Unity and Democracy, a group comprised mainly of Afar people, against the Issa-dominated People's Rally for Progress government. The government prevailed.
December 26, 1991–2006[15]	The Algerian Civil War, between the Algerian government and various Islamist groups occurred. The war left 200,000 Algerians dead and approximately 15,000 forcibly disappeared.[16]
1991 to date	A civil war in Somalia among rival clans and Islamist groups has raged in that Horn of African country. Some 300,000[17] to 500,000[18] were killed thus far.
May 1992–June 26, 1997	A civil war in Tajikistan was fought between the central government and a group of various opposition forces including Islamist militant groups. Between 50,000 and 100,000 were killed and 1.2 million were made refugees both within and outside the country.[19]
September 30, 1992–December 1992	A Saudi Arabia–Qatar border dispute resulted in a military clash. It was mediated by Egypt.
1992–95	The war in Bosnia left 102,622 dead, according to the 2004 research of the International Criminal Tribunal. At least, 63,994 fatalities were Muslims and of those, some 38,000 were civilians.
May 4–July 7, 1994	A short violent civil war raged in Yemen as southern Yemeni army units and political factions sought to secede from the unified Republic of Yemen. The secessionists were crushed with a resulting death toll estimated at between 7,000 and 10,000 for both sides.[20]
1994–96	The First Chechen War, resulted in an estimated 53,000 to 103,000, mainly Muslims, killed.
June 1994–2000	Violence erupted in Bahrain caused by Shi'ite Islamists and anti-government elements. Saudi troops entered Bahrain to support the Sunni royal government and help quell the unrest.
September 1, 1995–early 1997.	Libyan leader Muammar Qadhafi announced the expulsion of some 30,000 Palestinians living and working in Libya. Later Qadhafi agreed to suspend the expulsion for six months, until April 1996. Libya created a refugee camp on the Libyan-Egyptian border that held 1,000 Palestinians in tents in mid-October 2006. No Arab state opened its doors to allow in these refugees. Lebanon banned even maritime traffic from Libya lest some arrive. Under military escort, Egypt allowed only those with Israeli permits to enter the PA-controlled Gaza Strip. Thousands were left stranded in the desert. Eventually, some were allowed to remain in Libya when Qadhafi rescinded his decision in early 1997.[21]
December 15–17, 1995	There was an Eritrean-Yemeni conflict over the disputed Hanish Islands at the southern end of the Red Sea.
1996–99	The war in Kosovo resulted in an estimated 7,449 to 13,627, mainly Muslims, killed as well as the loss of over 1,000 Christian Serbs.
1996 to date	There is a Qatar–Saudi Arabia dispute over the oil-rich area of Khor al-Udaid.
May 6, 1998–June 18, 2000	The Eritrean-Ethiopian War broke out as Eritrean forces entered the disputed Badme region of Ethiopia triggering a two-year war.
1998–2000	Ethiopian-Somali border clashes during the chaotic warlord era in Somalia.

August 26, 1999–April 16, 2009	Some 20,000 to 105,000 persons, mainly Muslims, were killed in the first four years of the Second Chechen War.
2003	There was an Egyptian-Sudanese border dispute over the Halaieb territory.
May 2003–June 25, 2008	An Islamic supremacist anti-government insurgency occurred in Saudi Arabia.
2003 to date	An insurgency began in Iraq by Ba'athist party remnants of the former Iraqi regime. The insurgents were assisted by foreign jihadist volunteers against the legitimate government of Iraq and US-led coalition forces.
2003 to date	Sudanese Islamist government forces assisted by nomadic, self-identifying Arab Muslim *janjaweed* militias perpetrated ethnic cleansing against non-Arabs in Darfur. Over 400,000 were killed and close to three million were displaced as refugees.
June 18, 2004 to date	The anti-government Houthi Rebellion erupted in the Marran Mountains in the northwestern part of Yemen, in Sa'ada Province near the Saudi Arabian border. The Houthis are members of the Al-Houthiun tribe. They are Zaydis who claim they adhere to the purest form of Shi'ite Islam. They sought to restore the Zaydi imamate overthrown in 1962. They are armed. supported, and trained by Iran. The Saudis intervened in 2009 in support of the Yemeni government. Over 2,000 died and internal refugees swelled to over 300,000 by 2010.[22] In January 2015, the Houthis seized control of Yemen's capital, Sana'a and ousted the Yemeni government. By April 2015, Houthi forces reached the outskirts of Aden. Saudi Arabia and other members of the Gulf Cooperation Council (GCC) intervened with airpower to stem the Houthi takeover of the entire country.
2005–06	There was a Chadian-Sudanese border war.
2005 to date	Iraq's democratically elected parliament has yet to put aside Iraqi claims against the Kuwaiti islands of Warbah and Bubiyan as well as the southern portion of the Rumaila oilfield granted to Kuwait by the UN. The uncertainty has forced Kuwait to postpone its ambitious plans for developing Bubiyan into a free-trade zone. Tourist projects in Warbah and in the nearby island of Failakah have also been frozen. To keep the Iraqis out, Kuwait built a series of fortifications along the border, including electrified ditches, anti-tank traps, and a no-man's land 10 miles-deep.
December 15, 2006–June 17, 2007	A vicious civil war in the Gaza Strip took place between Fatah and Hamas Palestinian terrorist groups. Approximately 350 were killed and over 1,000 wounded on both sides, as Hamas emerged victorious.
December 2006 to date	An on-going war in Somalia between Ethiopian troops (later replaced by troops from the African Union) assisting Somali Transitional Government forces, against the Islamic Courts Union and Al-Shabaab Islamic supremacist terrorists.
February 2007–May 2009	Another Tuareg rebellion flared across northeastern Mali and northern Niger.
May 19, 2007–September 7, 2007	Fighting raged between Fatah al-Islam, an Islamic militant group and the Lebanese Army in and around Nahr al-Bared refugee camp, near Tripoli in northern Lebanon. Nearly 450 on both sides were killed, including civilians.

May 7–14, 2008	Fighting took place between the Lebanese Army and Hezbollah over the latter's military telecommunications network as well as security at Beirut's airport.
June 10–13, 2008	A short Djiboutian-Eritrean border war was fought.
July 25–September 23 2008	Fighting erupted in Tripoli, Lebanon, between Salafist Sunnis and Shi'ite Alawites.
April 28, 2009 to date	Southern separatists began another insurgency against the central government of Yemen.
October 17, 2009 to date	An on-going Pakistani-Taliban conflict erupted in Waziristan, on the north central border with Afghanistan.
November 4, 2009 to date	Saudi Arabia militarily intervened in the Yemeni Civil War between the Yemeni government and Zaydi Shi'ite Houthi rebels.
June 2010	Violent clashes between ethnic Kyrgyz and Uzbeks, erupted in southern Kyrgyzstan. Both groups are Sunni Muslim. The violence began in the cities of Osh and Jalal-Abad, in the aftermath of the ouster, on April 15, 2010, of former President Kurmanbek Bakiyev. An estimated 2,200 people were killed, over 1,900 injured and some 400,000 fled into neighboring Uzbekistan.
June–July 2010	Syrian army units attacked Kurdish population centers in northern Syria along Syria's border with Turkey. The Turkish military coordinated with the Syrians in the operation. An estimated 300 people were killed and over 1,000 injured. Prisoners captured were turned over to the Turkish military.
November–December 2010	Warfare erupted between Al-Qaeda in the Arabian Peninsula (a Sunni group) and the Zaydi Shi'ite Houthi rebels in Yemen.
2011	Berber tribes, seeking independence, rose up in revolt against the Libyan regime of Muammar Qadhafi. The uprising centered in the towns of Gharyan, Yifrin, Kabaw, Nalut and Ziztan in the Nafusa Mountains in central western Libya.
December 18, 2010–October 23, 2011	Nation-wide popular protests and rioting, which came to be known in Tunisia as the "Dignity Revolution," led to the resignation of President Zine El Abidine Ben Ali, on January 14, 2011, after ruling for twenty-three years. On October 23, 2011, a new Islamist government, led by the Ennahda (Renaissance) Party, came to power in elections for the Constituent Assembly. Over 2,000 were killed or injured during the violence.
January 15, 2011–February 25, 2012	Nation-wide popular protests and rioting swept Yemen, already beset by the Houthi Rebellion in the north and a separatist insurgency in the south. The violence that claimed over 2,000 killed and some 22,000 injured,[23] led to the ouster, by February 25, 2012, of President Ali Abdullah Saleh after ruling Yemen for thirty-three years.
January 25, 2011–February 11, 2011	Nation-wide popular protests and rioting swept Egypt and led to the ouster of President Hosni Mubarak after thirty years as president. At least 846 were killed and over 6,400 were injured.[24]

January 26, 2011 to date	Nation-wide popular protests and rioting swept Syria, with public demands for reforms. The protests escalated into an uprising and quickly became a civil war, with opposition forces demanding the resignation of President Bashar al-Assad, the overthrow of his regime, and an end to five decades of Ba'ath Party rule. To date over 230,000 were killed, including 11,500 children.[25] Tens of thousands more were injured or were held in Syrian prisons.[26] Over 9,000,000 (half the population of Syria) were dispossessed and many made refugees fleeing into neighboring Turkey, Lebanon and Jordan.
February 14, 2011–March 18, 2011	Nation-wide popular protests and rioting swept Bahrain with the demonstrators calling for greater political freedom and equality for the majority Shi'a population as well as an end to the two century-long rule of the Al Khalifa dynasty. Iran instigated and provided logistical support to Shi'ite groups in Bahrain. Starting on March 14, Bahraini security forces cracked down on the demonstrators. The security forces were supported by the military intervention by some 4,000 Saudi and other Gulf Cooperation Council troops as well as some forces from Pakistan.
February 15–October 20, 2011	Civil war swept Libya pitting the government forces of Muammar Qadhafi against an opposition coalition seeking to oust him and his regime, which had ruled Libya for forty-two years. NATO intervention enabled the opposition forces to defeat Qadhafi, who was caught and subsequently shot on October 20, 2011. Some 25,000 were killed and over 60,000 injured.[27] Conflict continued in the country between competing armed militias and rival govenments, one in Tripoli, the other in Benghazi, each vying for political control.
January 17, 2012 to date	A Tuareg separatist insurgency, led by the National Movement for the Liberation of Azawad, began a rebellion against the central government of Mali. On April 6, 2012, the group proclaimed the "Independent State of Azawad" seceding from Mali. A truce was reached on June 18, 2013, but fighting resumed two months later.
March 26, 2012 to date	On-going disputes between Sudan and South Sudan over the use of the Greater Nile Oil Pipeline as well as the disputed oil-rich Abyei region led to fighting which included the Heglig oil field.
January 2014 to date	The Sunni Islamic State of Iraq and the Levant, which proclaimed an Islamic caliphate conducted religious sectarian cleansing of Shi'ites, Christians, Yazidis and other minority groups throughout the areas of Iraq and Syria they conquered, with beheadings, crucifixions, killings, rape and other violence as they imposed shari'a law.

In over forty-five conflicts over territory and resources in the Middle East in recent history, none had anything to do with Israel and its conflict with the Arabs. These forty-five international disputes are quite apart from the uninterrupted string of domestic clashes, civil wars, ethnic cleansings, military coups, acts of sectarian and ethnic vengeance, factional terrorism, assassinations, and other internal conflicts that have characterized the region, attaining impressive heights of cruelty (including the use of poison gas) and despoliation. The almost daily Muslim against Muslim violence can be illustrated by the terrorist attacks perpetrated in Pakistan, the third largest Muslim-majority country in the world. Data gathered by the New Delhi-based Institute for Conflict Management revealed the following:

FATALITIES IN TERRORIST VIOLENCE IN PAKISTAN 2003–14[28]				
Year	Civilians	Security Force Personnel	Terrorists/ Insurgents	Total
2003	140	24	25	189
2004	435	184	244	863
2005	430	81	137	648
2006	608	325	538	1,471
2007	1,522	597	1,479	3,598
2008	2,155	654	3,906	6,715
2009	2,324	991	8,389	11,704
2010	1,796	469	5,170	7,435
2011	2,738	765	2,800	6,303
2012	3,007	732	2,472	6,211
2013	3,001	676	1,702	5,379
2014	534	180	355	1,069
Total*	18,690	5,678	27,217	51,585

* Data through March 23, 2014.

In a 2007 research study, Gunnar Heinsohn from the University of Bremen and Daniel Pipes, director of the Middle East Forum, discovered that some 11 million Muslims were violently killed since 1948, of which 35,000, (0.3 percent) died during the (then) sixty years of Arab wars against Israel, or one out of every 315 fatalities. In contrast, over 90 percent who perished were killed by fellow Muslims.[29]

As retired Israeli ambassador Yoram Ettinger astutely observed, the root causes of Middle East regional turbulence are "inherent fragmentation, instability, unpredictability, volatility, violence, terrorism, hate education, and tenuous policies, commitments, and alliances. None of these 1,400-year-old root causes is related to the Palestinian issue, which is less than 100 years old."[30] With the exception of Israel, the entire Middle East lacks a culture of conflict resolution, let alone the necessary mechanisms of meaningful compromise. In the West, it is believed that people in the Middle East yearn for peace, compromise, and conciliation. When they do not get it, they use violence. This belief however, has nothing to do with reality. The problem is that in the Arab/Muslim Middle East, the concepts of peace, compromise, and conciliation are equated with weakness, heresy, treason, and surrender.

46. The Arab proverb, "I against my brother, I and my brothers against my cousins, I and my brothers and my cousins against the world," is taken and practiced literally through much of the Muslim world.

A nineteenth century witness to this adage was Winston Churchill. As a young man Churchill was dispatched to the Swat Valley of northwest British India (today's Pakistan) as a war correspondent for *The Daily Telegraph* assigned to cover the Pashtun Revolt of 1897. He witnessed this basic principle, so prevalent in the Arab/Muslim world and wrote about it in his first book *The Story of the Malakand*

Field Force: An Episode of Frontier War (1898). Churchill observed that within the Pashtun tribes, "every man's hand is against the other, and all against the stranger."

A mid-twentieth century example of this maxim was the Saudi and Jordanian assistance to the Yemeni Royalist forces battling an Egyptian military intervention in Yemen from 1962 to 1967. Another illustration was the Saudi-Kuwaiti cooperation and assistance against Iraq, in Operation *Desert Storm* (the US-led coalition effort to liberate Kuwait from Iraqi occupation). A third instance was the 2007 Saudi attempt to build an Arab coalition against Iran's acquisition of nuclear weapons, while at the same time supporting Syria, Iran's ally, in its continued subversion and domination of Lebanon.

47. Arab/Muslim states can always set aside their rivalries and differences for common action against Israel.

The classic example of this dictum in practice occurred in relations between Jordan and Egypt. Between 1957 and 1967, through coup plots, riots, and assassination attempts, Egyptian President Gamal Abdel Nasser tried to topple the Hashemite dynasty of Jordan's King Hussein. During this conflict, the media of both nations were waging a vitriolic propaganda war against each other. This reached a crescendo in May 1967 as Egypt's Voice of the Arabs referred to the Jordanian monarch as the "Hashemite dwarf," "the dwarf king," the "treacherous dwarf,"[31] the "Hashemite whore,"[32] the "Hashemite harlot," and the "Hashemite hyena" all in reference either to King Hussein's small physical stature or his pro-western policy of accepting aid from both the United Kingdom and the United States.

In retaliation, Radio Amman, mocked Egypt's Nasser for "hiding behind the skirts" of the United Nations Emergency Force (UNEF) in the Sinai Peninsula, a major affront to Arab male pride—accusing one of hiding behind a woman. Yet, despite all of this and more, on May 30, 1967, as Nasser gathered Arab armies for the final anticipated destruction of Israel, King Hussein flew to Cairo and reconciled with Nasser on the tarmac at the Cairo airport, kissing him on the cheeks, and signing a treaty of common defense, which placed Jordanian forces under Egyptian military command.

Even the split between Sunni and Shi'a branches of Islam does not stand in the way of confronting Israel. Upon attaining power in the summer of 2011, the Sunni Muslim Brotherhood government of Egyptian President Mohamed Morsi sought a rapprochement with the Shi'ite Islamic Republic of Iran. Historically, the Muslim Brotherhood in Egypt has downplayed religious differences between Sunni and Shi'a. The Brotherhood has argued that Twelver Shi'ism should be recognized as an acceptably orthodox school of Islamic jurisprudence. It should be recalled that the Fatimids, a Shi'ite dynasty, ruled North Africa and the Levant including Egypt (which was conquered in 969 c.e.). This Fatimid Caliphate ruled until 1171, when Saladin became Sultan of Egypt, and began the Ayyubid Sultanate of Egypt and Syria. Additionally, a July 6, 1959 Al-Azhar *fatwa,*[33] held Shi'a Islam was as valid for a Muslim to follow as Sunni. Moreover, for its part, the Islamic Republic of Iran's Constitution recognized the Four Schools of Sunni jurisprudence (*fiqh*): Hanafi, Maliki, Shafi'i, and Hanbali. From an Iranian viewpoint, the Brotherhood effectively serves as a counterbalance to the Saudi Wahhabist/Salafist-led campaign to vilify Shi'ism in Iran and among the restive Shi'ite populations of the Gulf states. In this way, the Brotherhood's ecumenical approach has helped make Sunni society increasingly more open to Shi'ite religious proselytizing. Hence, there is no religious barrier to prevent a Sunni Muslim Brotherhood-dominated Middle East from allying with Shi'ite Iran to deal with their common enemy, Israel. Thus, pan-Islamism trumps the Sunni-Shi'a split, especially when it comes to dealing with the Jewish state.

48. In addition to its continued military, diplomatic, and propaganda war against Israel, the Arab League for over a half-century waged economic warfare against the Jewish state.

The Arabs used a widespread economic boycott against the *Yishuv,* albeit irregular, sporadic, and largely ineffective, from the start of the British Mandate of Palestine in 1922. In that year, the Fifth Palestine Arabs Congress meeting in Nablus passed a resolution calling on Arabs to boycott Jewish businesses. In 1929, following the Arab riots of that year, a short-lived boycott was imposed on the Jewish economy and services. The Arab Executive Committee of the Syria–Palestine Congress called for a boycott of Jewish businesses in March 1933 and in October 1934, the Arab Labor Federation conducted a boycott as well as an organized picketing of Jewish businesses.[34] A complete boycott in 1936, at the outset of the Arab revolt in Palestine, was directed against Palestinian Jewish products and services. At times, the boycott was enforced by acts of violence. However, many Palestinian non-Jewish residents—Arab and non-Arab alike—ignored the boycott and continued to use Jewish products and especially services, such as doctors, hospitals and lawyers.

The Arab League launched its first official all-Arab boycott of the *Yishuv,* on December 2, 1945, with a declaration calling on all Arab "institutions, organizations, merchants, commissions agents and individuals [be they citizens of independent Arab states or not] to refuse to deal in, distribute, or consume Zionist products or manufactured goods."[35] The declaration was effective from January 1, 1946. Jewish protests to the British authorities to prevent the boycott because it contravened existing trade agreements between Palestine and neighboring countries fell on deaf ears.

In May 1948, the boycott was automatically applied to the State of Israel. Its purpose was to inhibit, cripple and otherwise weaken the economic growth of Israel, to discourage immigration to the Jewish state, and ultimately destroy its chances of survival in the region. In May 1951, a Central Boycott Office (CBO) of the Arab League was established in Damascus, Syria, to supervise and implement the boycott. In addition, each participating Arab state had its own national boycott office. Over the years, the boycott has undergone constant development and sophistication in order to increase its effectiveness.

The boycott operates on three levels. The primary boycott was directed against all Israeli businesses and products. No Arab country should import Israeli goods or export goods to the Israeli market, directly or indirectly. The boycott cut communication and trade between Israel and its Arab neighbors—its natural trading area. Under international law, this type of boycott is perfectly legitimate. Some Israeli products did reach Arab markets camouflaged under foreign labels or smuggled in without Israeli labels. An example would be Israeli Jaffa oranges shipped via Romania to Kuwait and the Arab Gulf states, without the label "Jaffa" stamped on the oranges. Overall, despite many restrictions, the boycott did not have its intended effect. To the contrary, the Israeli economy as well as its population grew.

When Israel gained control of Judea, Samaria, Gaza and the Golan Heights in 1967, it became more difficult to prevent Israeli goods from entering Arab countries due to the open bridges program. Israeli goods entered, for the most part, unlabeled, as "Palestinian" goods. Israel's policy of the "good fence" enabled Israeli products to enter southern Lebanon from 1978 to 2000, while Lebanese from that region could avail themselves of Israeli services in Israel itself.

The main effort of the Arab boycott office was the implementation of a secondary boycott. The secondary boycott sought to prevent private and public companies in non-Arab countries, from doing business with Israel. Under international law, this is an act of aggression. Boycott offices requested foreign firms not to trade with Israel, invest in Israel, build plants in Israel, and grant franchises in Israel. These companies were compelled to supply the boycott offices with detailed information about their transactions with Israel, and about Jews among their employees, directors and shareholders.[36] Business enterprises that violated the instructions of the boycott offices were blacklisted and threatened with boycott themselves.

The Arab League also instituted a tertiary boycott, which sought to prevent overseas suppliers from doing business with each other, if one of them had links to Israel or happened to be blacklisted. Companies were pressured into a "voluntary self-imposed boycott," for fear of losing their share of lucrative trade with the Arab world market if they were known to have any contacts with Israel. Iran, though not an Arab country, has attempted to enforce secondary and tertiary boycotts of Israel since the Islamic revolution of 1979. A recent example occurred on June 30, 2010, when the Iranian regime announced a new boycott against "Zionist" products. Iranian President Mahmoud Ahmadinejad signed a law outlawing the use of products from such "Zionist" companies as Intel, Coca Cola, Nestlé and IBM. The law also banned the airing of advertisements for "Zionist companies." The blacklist of prohibited companies is comprised mainly of international companies, mainly American, owned by Jews or that operate branches in Israel.[37]

The CBO in Damascus maintains and updates a blacklist of firms not in compliance with Arab demands. It is estimated to include as many as 10,000 firms or individuals.[38] Each Arab nation drew up boycott lists that numbered in the thousands of firms in over eighty countries. The overall Arab boycott became more powerful with the growth of multi-national corporations, who parceled out work to hundreds of smaller companies. Those known to do business with Israel did not get subcontracts. Additionally, the growing political and economic clout of the Arab oil-producing states after 1973, gave the Arabs tremendous additional leverage over both nations and companies. Both were afraid to alienate as well as endanger their access to the entire Arab/Muslim world and its large market. Most governments tolerated the choices made by domestic companies to avoid commercial relations with Israel. Most multinational firms chose to stay out of the Israeli market in order to continue business relations with the Arab world.

Any company in the world may be singled out for discriminatory attack, according to Arab boycott guidelines, the blacklisted companies were (but not limited to) those, which:

- Had a main or branch office in Israel.
- Had an assembly plant in Israel.
- Joined in licensing agreements with Israeli companies.
- Held shares in Israeli companies.
- Carried out consultative services for Israeli firms.
- Had as directors, members of joint foreign-Israeli Chambers of Commerce.
- Acted as agents for Israeli firms or as principal importers of Israeli goods.
- Prospected for natural resources in Israel.
- Refused to answer questionnaires from the Central Boycott Office regarding relationship with Israel.
- Used products from Israel.
- Shipped products to or from Israel.
- Transported any Israeli products anywhere.
- Transported Jewish immigrants to Israel.
- Sent ships to Arab and Israeli ports on the same round trip.

- Incorporated within its own product components of a blacklisted company.
- Carried out insurance business with Israel.
- Used blacklisted insurance or shipping companies.
- Gave loans or subsidies to Israeli public or private firms.
- Distributed or promoted Israeli Government Bonds.
- Made films in the Israeli interest or against that of the Arabs.
- Employed actors of Israeli nationality in films.
- Photographed films on location in Israel.[39]
- Were pro-Zionist or employed pro-Zionists.
- Participated in Jewish organizations or contributed funds to pro-Israeli groups. [40]

There were cases where a company would cancel its business in Israel, believing the much larger Arab market would be more profitable. In 1956, American Express stopped selling traveler's checks in Israel, claiming that these suddenly became unprofitable. Later, the company reversed its position. In July 1957, both British Petroleum and Shell Oil withdrew from Israel under the pressure of Arab oil producers. The French car manufacturer Renault, and British Leyland both submitted to the boycott and closed plants in Israel. Pepsi Cola submitted to the boycott for forty years. In August 1987, Cadbury Schweppes, the British soft-drink company considered pulling out of Israel, where it did $30 million of business annually in order to get off the Arab blacklist. However, after this planned move was made public, Cadbury Schweppes reversed course, negotiated a new agreement with Israel and said, "That production in Israel for the foreseeable future will be assured."[41]

Japanese companies, including Mitsubishi, Mitsui, Mazda, Toyota (until 1991[42]), Honda, Nissan, Sumitomo (metals), Suzuki and Yamaha (motorcycles), Shiba, Hayakawa, Matsushita (Panasonic), and Nippon Electric (radio and TV sets), as well as all Korean automakers avoided trade and investment opportunities in Israel from 1948 to 1993 (with some exceptions).[43] The main reason for this was that Japan obtained most of its oil from Arab countries.

The boycott was also applied to international shipping and aviation. Ships and planes calling at Israeli ports were barred from ports, though some exceptions were made for some cruise ships. After April 1950, foreign shippers carrying goods or immigrants to Israel were warned that they were subject to blacklisting in Arab states and would be denied access to Arab port facilities.

Japan Airlines, Iberia, Spain's air carrier (until 1987) and Qantas, Australia's airline, refused to fly to Tel Aviv. *Transportes Aereos Portugueses,* the Portuguese airline, was on the boycott list until April 2002. Planes en route to, or from Israel, were prohibited from flying over Arab territory. Several airlines however, defied the boycott and flew to both Arab destinations and Israel, for example TWA, which flew to both Egypt and Israel before the 1979 peace treaty between the two countries.[44] British Airways, KLM, and Air France were other airlines that flew to both Arab destinations and Israel. The author observed that some airlines had two sets of route maps. One, showed a route to Israel, which was used on flights to Tel Aviv. The other avoided depiction of any route to Israel on those same airlines' flights to other destinations, especially in the Arab world.

In one of the few instances of public access to the Arab League boycott list, *The New York Times* published an extensive listing of American business concerns, organizations, individuals and trademarks on the 1970 list[45] that encompassed a cross-section of the US economy. Among the thousands listed were:

Allstate Insurance	Loft candy
Burlington	Lord & Taylor
Botany	Merrill Lynch ("watch list" 2007)
Bonwit Teller	Miles Laboratories
Bulova Watch	Minkus Publications
Chemstrand	Minute Maid
Calvert	Monstano
Coca-Cola	Motorola
CBS	NBC
Cat's Paw	Noxon
Dupont Emerson	Owens-Illinois
E.J. Korvette	Pratt & Whitney
Encyclopedia Judaica	RCA
Empire Pencil	Republic Productions
Ford	Republic Steel
Four Roses	Revlon
General Tires	Sears Roebuck
Gristedes	Topps Chewing gum
Hartz Pet foods	Tip Top
Helena Rubenstein	Welbilt
Helene Curtis	Willys Overland
Hertz	Whirlpool
Kaiser Aluminum	Xerox
Knopf	Zenith

It must be stressed that the above represents only a tiny fraction of American individuals (*see* below) and companies listed. Additionally, such lists were maintained for numerous other countries around the world. For example, until 2007, the Marks & Spencer British retail chain was on the Arab boycott list. Furthermore, such lists were rarely made public and the general population was and continues to be unaware of the vast scope of these boycotts.

In part, due to the increased publicity about the Arab boycott, the US Congress enacted anti-boycott legislation in the form of the 1976 Ribicoff Amendment to the Internal Revenue Reform Act and the 1977 and 1979 boycott amendments to the Export Administration Act. Under the Ribicoff legislation, companies which gave in to boycott demands lost certain tax benefits in their foreign transactions, while under the 1977 and 1979 legislation, companies found to have given in to boycott demands were fined of up to $50,000 or five times the value of the exports involved[46] or jailed for a term of up to ten years.[47] However, these laws did not restrict the ability to engage in disinvestment campaigns, which has been a new tactic employed against Israel for over the past twenty years.

In the first half of 1987, over $750,000 in fines were levied and Safeway faced a fine of up to $4.5 million if found guilty of cooperating with the boycott in the stores it managed in Kuwait and Saudi Arabia.[48] *The Washington Post* reported that on August 30, 1995, the cosmetics company L'Oreal, SA agreed to pay $1.4 million in penalties to settle allegations by the US Commerce Department that it cooperated with the Arab League's economic boycott of Israel. The firm denied the charges, but said would prefer to pay the fine and avoid a costly legal defense. After the Arab League placed L'Oreal on its blacklist, the company's headquarters asked a US affiliate—Parbel of Florida, Inc.—to send information to Paris about its previous activities in Israel. The US Commerce Department alleged that the subsidiary violated US law by providing information about operations in Israel and by failing to report the request for information to the federal government. This was one of the largest penalties ever assessed by the Office of Antiboycott Compliance.[49] Despite the fines, there were some American companies (like McDonald's) which preferred to pay the fine than break the boycott and endanger loss of business with the Arab world.

The boycott offices also banned foreign authors, artists, actors, directors, producers, writers, filmmakers, and musicians as well as barred their books, films, recordings or live appearances, if they were deemed to have too close ties to Israel or show Israel and even Jews in a favorable light. There was blatant misojudaism (hatred of Jews) as foreign Jews' works were excluded as well. A few examples include:

French journalist and author Emile Zola, was boycotted because he came to the defense of Jewish French Army Captain Alfred Dreyfus, during the Dreyfus Affair in 1898. *Strange Lands and Friendly People,* by US Supreme Court Justice William O. Douglas, *The Talisman,* by Sir Walter Scott, and *Exodus,* by Leon Uris were also prohibited. Additionally, any books by Israelis were banned, e.g. David Ben-Gurion, Chaim Weizmann, Moshe Dayan, Golda Meir, and Ariel Sharon among many others. The book, *Winds of War* (as well as the TV miniseries) was excluded because the author, Herman Wouk, was Jewish. In 1991, the publisher of the *New York Daily News,* Robert Maxwell, was added to the boycott list because his company had purchased one-third of the Israeli daily, *Ma'ariv* in 1988.[50]

Some of the artists banned include,

Alan King	Elizabeth Taylor
Danny Kaye	Joanne Woodward
Eddie Cantor	Audie Murphy
George Jessel	David Janssen
Jerry Lewis	Kirk Douglas
Phil Silvers	Burt Lancaster
Steve Allen	Roger Moore
Theodore Bikel	Richard Dreyfuss
Chaim Topol	Harry Belafonte
Shelly Winters	Leonard Cohen
Laurence Harvey	Rod Stewart
Jack Lemmon	Morgan Freeman
Peter Finch	Steven Spielberg (since 2007)
Gene Wilder	Paul McCartney
Frank Sinatra	Elton John

Sammy Davis Jr.	Mick Jagger
Lee Marvin	Madonna
Charles Bronson	Rihanna
Chuck Norris	The Pixies
John Garfield	Alicia Keys
Lee J. Cobb	Black Eyed Peas
Jack Benny	Depche Mode
Tony Randall	Moby
Paul Newman	Deep Purple
Edward G. Robinson	Pet Shop Boys
Richard Boone	Aerosmith USA
Tony Curtis	Justin Bieber
Lauren Bacall	Paul Simon
Joey Bishop	Morrissey
Rodney Dangerfield	Lady Gaga
Otto Preminger	Justin Timberlake
Isaac Stern	Jethro Tull
Van Cliburn[51]	Ozzy Osborne
Judy Holliday	Red Hot Chili Peppers
Julio Iglesias	

Raquel Welch was placed on the list and then removed in 1973, when it was "discovered" that she was not an Israeli. Sophia Loren was on the list, but then removed after she promised not to make any more films in Israel. Nevertheless, many artists and performers refused to be intimidated— even when some received death threats— by the risk of boycott. Among notable examples are Paul McCartney, Michael "Mick" Jagger, Madonna, Elton John, Rod Stewart, Paul Simon and Roger Moore—all defied the Arab embargo and made appearances in Israel.

The inclusion of Elizabeth Taylor on the boycott list provides a useful illustration of unintended consequences. When she converted from Christianity to Judaism, her films were prohibited in the Arab world. Thus, Egyptians never saw her film *Cleopatra* that extols the greatness and splendor of ancient Egypt. Few Westerners can comprehend the degree to which hatred of Jews permeates every aspect of Arab/Muslim culture.

Numerous films were banned in the Arab world, due to the stars that appeared in them, because they were filmed in Israel, or for misojudaic reasons. A small sampling of such films include Walt Disney's classic movie, *Snow White*, because it contained a horse named "Samson." Syria demanded the horse's name be changed to "Simpson" but Disney refused. *The Big Red One, Delta Force,* and *I Love You Alice B. Toklas,* all were banned because they were filmed in Israel. *Voyage to the Bottom of the Sea* was banned because it showed Arabs in an unfavorable light according to the Central Boycott Office. *Independence Day,* was released in Lebanon, only after all signs of the momentary appearance of Israeli and Arab military cooperation at a desert outpost and references to the hero being Jewish—including a skullcap and a Hebrew prayer—had been cut from the film.[52] *Exodus,*

Cast a Giant Shadow, Raid on Entebbe, Victory at Entebbe, and *Schindler's List*[53]—all were banned because they depicted Jews and Israel in a favorable light. Various TV series, such as *The Phil Silvers Show, the Saint, and Return of the Saint, Route 66,* and *Vengeance Unlimited* were banned because some episodes were filmed in Israel or showed Jews and Israelis in a favorable way. In April 2013, Lebanese authorities banned Lebanese director Ziad Doueiri's award-winning film *The Attack* from being shown in his home country because it was partly shot in Tel Aviv using Israeli actors.

There were some absurdities in the boycott process. The US Navy chartered a ship SS *National Peace,* to carry oil from Saudi Arabia to the Philippines. It emerged that the same ship had once, under a different name—SS *Memory*—and on charter to a different US government agency, handled trade with Israel. That was enough for the Saudis, who refused it permission to land at Ras Tanura. In 1983, the Jordache Company, which made a popular line of jeans, was blacklisted because its President Joseph Nakash was an Israeli-American. In March 2001, Saudi Arabia banned Pokemon cards and games because symbols included "the Star of David, which everyone knows is connected to international Zionism and is Israel's national emblem."[54]

In addition to goods and businesses, many Arab states and some non-Arab Muslim states (e.g. Bangladesh, Brunei, Iran, Malaysia, and Pakistan) refuse to allow entrance to anyone who uses an Israeli passport or who has any Israeli visa stamp in his or her passport. The stamp may be a visa stamp, or a stamp on entry or departure. It can also include a stamp of another country, which indicates that the person has entered Israel. For example, if an Egyptian departure stamp is used in any passport at the Taba Crossing that is an indication that the person entered Israel. Similarly, a Jordanian stamp issued at the Arava Crossing between Aqaba and Eilat would be an indication of a visit to Israel.

Some companies showed strength and ignored the boycott. Among them was Ford Motor Company, which in 1966, closed its plant in Alexandria, Egypt, rather than submit to the boycott because it had a franchise agreement in Israel. The Arab League boycott of Ford backfired as it cost jobs for Arab workers across the Middle East, some 6,000 jobs in Lebanon alone,[55] when Ford was expelled. Ford was later invited back to Egypt. Others included McDonnell Douglas, General Electric, United Aircraft, Hughes Aircraft, Raytheon (which sold HAWK anti-aircraft missiles to both Israel and Saudi Arabia), Barclays Bank (the United Kingdom's largest), IBM, Hewlett Packard, Hilton (which maintained hotels in Tel Aviv, Jerusalem, Cairo, Alexandria, Luxor, Rabat and Dubai), Mercedes-Benz, Citibank, and Avis. The Arab governments realized that some of these companies were essential to Arab defense establishments, financial dealings, and in bringing tourist dollars to the Arab world. Thus, the Central Boycott Office decided to make some exceptions with regard to the boycott. This resulted from the realization that ending commercial relations with some important companies and other major ones would have hurt the Arab economies by causing unemployment, higher prices for substitute products and lower quality goods. Thus, over the years, implementation of the boycott regulations by the Arab states varied substantially from country to country and from time to time.

One company that the boycotting countries apparently did not find essential was Coca-Cola.[56] In 1966, Coca-Cola refused to grant a franchising request to an Israeli bottling company because of business relations it had in the Arab world. Word quickly spread throughout the United States via the Anti-Defamation League, an organization designed to fight misojudaism and other forms of bigotry. As more Americans refused to purchase Coca-Cola, the company made a decision to grant the Israeli bottling company a license. In 1968, Coca-Cola was blacklisted by the Arab League. Coca-Cola stated that ultimately it made the right economic decision to do business in Israel, as it did not want to stain its brand name in the United States. Coca-Cola was able to re-open a plant in Egypt in July

1979 (after the Egypt–Israel Peace Treaty was concluded the previous March), and was removed from the blacklist in May 1991. Bahrain, Oman, and the United Arab Emirates also allowed Coca-Cola to open bottling plants in their countries.[57]

In March 1979, Egypt pledged to lift its 30-year old boycott of Israel, as part of the Egypt–Israel Peace Treaty. Similar pledges were undertaken by the PLO in September 1993, as part of the Oslo Accords, and by Jordan in October 1994, as part of the Israel–Jordan Peace Treaty. However, not all economic, social and cultural manifestations of the Arab boycott were abolished. Constructive economic relations between Israel and the Arab states as well as the PLO, remained very dependent on the ever-changing political situation in the region.

An Arab boycott meeting was held in Damascus, Syria, in July 1990, at the request of the PLO. The PLO demanded that the boycott be expanded to include any companies that assisted Soviet Jews to reach and settle in Israel. That included transportation, housing, construction, and insurance companies as well as hotels that provided temporary housing for the immigrants.

As a result of the 1993 Oslo Accords, the Gulf Cooperation Council (GCC) announced its support for an end to the boycott and encouraged other members of the Arab League to normalize trade relations with Israel. The move prompted a surge of trade and investment in Israel by European and Asian companies and the initiation of a number of cooperation projects between Israel and Arab countries. However, the intentions of the GCC were more words than action. Despite issuing a declaration on October 1, 1994, the GCC did not lift the boycott.

The Swiss-owned Nestlé Company began investment in Israel in 1995. By May 1996, the Central Boycott Office added Nestlé to the boycott list. It was a classic case of cutting off one's nose to spite one's face. Nestlé, in refusing to submit to Arab demands to cut ties with Israel, pointed out that it employed around 23,000 people in 51 factories and 151 sales and distribution offices in Muslim countries around the world. The company added that with a total turnover of Swiss franc 3.3 billion and investments of more than one billion over time, Nestlé contributed significantly to the prosperity and well-being of the general population in those countries.[58]

Syria, in recent years, expanded the boundaries of the boycott by maintaining that while the boycott was economic in the first place, "it was also a boycott of all forms of normalization with the Zionist enemy and the patterns of American culture which the [US] tries to impose in the name of globalization on the peoples of the earth, seeking to obliterate their identity, history and culture because America is short on all of these."[59]

In 2002, several US companies were again targeted for opening branches, franchises or seemingly supporting Israel. The Central Boycott Office at the urging of Arab student groups across the Arab world blacklisted Starbucks, Coca-Cola, Johnson & Johnson and Burger King among others. Calls were made for the boycott to be extended to AOL Time Warner, Disney, Estée Lauder, Nokia, Revlon, Marks & Spencer, Selfridges and IBM.[60]

After Israel evicted its own citizens and unilaterally withdrew from the Gaza Strip in mid-2005, the Persian Gulf Kingdom of Bahrain pulled out of the Arab boycott of the Jewish state. However, the Bahraini parliament voted for a non-binding resolution asking for Bahrain to return to participating in the boycott. The US Department of Treasury issued a list (as of December 2008) of countries that may or may not require participation in, or cooperation with, the international boycott of Israel. Those countries were Kuwait, Lebanon, Libya, Qatar, Saudi Arabia, Syria, United Arab Emirates, and Yemen. Iraq was not included on the list, as its status remained under review by the Department of the Treasury.[61]

In September 2009, leading Democratic and Republican congressional representatives expressed outrage following a report in the *Jerusalem Post* that Saudi Arabia was violating its promise to the United States to stop enforcing the Arab League boycott of Israel. As part of an agreement for US support for Saudi entry into the World Trade Organization (WTO) in November 2005, Saudi Arabia had agreed to drop the boycott of Israel. To the contrary, the Saudis steadily intensified their enforcement of the anti-Israel trade embargo. Saudi Arabia became a full WTO member on December 11, 2005. US Commerce Department figures showed that the number of boycott-related and restrictive trade-practice requests received by American companies from Saudi Arabia increased, rising by more than 76 percent between 2006 and 2008. In short, Saudi Arabia played the United States for a sucker. US law bars American companies from complying with such demands, and requires them to report any boycott-related requests to the federal government.[62]

Despite the Arab boycott, full or partial, Israel was able to develop a world-class high tech economy and became a global technological power. In terms of accomplishments in science and technology, medicine and genetics, AIDS treatment, biotechnology, agricultural science and water purification as well as information technology, Israel's record of performance is virtually unmatched worldwide. The globalization of the world economy is Israel's strongest ally and the boycott's biggest barrier. The application of a boycott, particularly at the secondary and tertiary levels, is all but impossible in the age of globalization. In the field of technology, in particular, insisting on a boycott policy is not enforceable and self-defeating. A commercial airplane, whether it is the frame, the engine or the avionics, is made up of thousands of parts supplied by hundreds of contractors and sub-contractors, and Israel may be one of them. It would be utterly beyond reason to demand a certificate of origin for every part of the plane and expect the manufacturer to comply.[63]

Nevertheless, to date, no country has completely outlawed submission to boycott demands. The Arab economic boycott of Israel continues. It can be tightened and loosened at will. It remains a significant factor to be reckoned with, causing Israel certain economic difficulties. Despite a peace treaty between Israel and Jordan, the latter has engaged in a quasi-official boycott of Israeli goods. The new boycott was launched on May 10, 2010, by Jordan's trade unions. Dr. Ahmed Armouti, chair of the Trade Unions Organization, stated at a press conference that the campaign was conceived to mark sixty-two years of Israel's existence. In addition to the dissemination of lists of Israeli-made products so that Jordanians could know what not to buy, a mass public burning of Israeli fruits and vegetables was held on May 15, 2010, in Amman. The event was organized by a body called the Committee to Make War on Normalization (with Israel).[64] Thus, despite peace treaties, the war against Israel continues.

49. The Arabs have practiced limited liability war against the Jews in the Land of Israel for some eighty years.

Under the concept of limited liability war, the Arabs reject any offered compromise, gamble on winning everything by resorting to war in all its forms, in the comfortable knowledge that even in defeat they will lose nothing. If they lose the war, then they would insist on reinstating the original compromise and claim rights under it. When negotiations would resume, they are based on the original compromise, and the Arabs claim that additional concessions should be added to them.

In an effort to stop the on-going Arab violence against the *Yishuv* in the British Mandate of Palestine, which exploded in the Arab Revolt of 1936–39, the British attempted to partition Palestine for a second time according to the recommendations of the Peel Commission. In a gesture meant to appease the Arabs, the recommendation was made to give only 18.4 percent of Western Palestine to the Jews and 81.6 percent to the Arabs. The Arabs rejected the plan and continued their violence, which was suppressed by British military forces. Later, some Arab leaders sought to go back to the Peel Plan, when the United Nations Partition Plan of 1947, provided the Jews more territory.

When the United Nations Partition Plan of 1947 was adopted, the Arab states opted for war, vowing to annihilate the Jewish community in Palestine. The Arab attack nullified the partition plan, which was a legally non-binding General Assembly resolution. The Arabs lost the war, and additional territory was gained by Israel. At that point some Arabs demanded that Israel return to the 1947 partition plan lines.

In another example of return to the *status quo ante,* at the conclusion of the Sinai-Suez War, Israel was in possession of over 95 percent of the Sinai Peninsula. Egyptian President Nasser would not agree to reopen the Suez Canal nor give his agreement for the placement of a UN peacekeeping force on Egyptian soil until Israeli forces withdrew completely, not only from the Sinai Peninsula but also from the previously Egyptian-militarily administered Gaza Strip.

Almost immediately after the conclusion of the Six-Day War, and Israel's victorious acquisition of Judea and Samaria, the Gaza Strip, the Sinai Peninsula and the Golan Heights, (*see* "Six-Day War Ceasefire lines–Israeli administered territories" map) the Arab states began a campaign for Israel to withdraw to the 1949 Armistice lines—the pre-war lines that existed on June 4, 1967—as a precondition for negotiations.

The conclusion of the Yom Kippur War of 1973 found the IDF in control of a large portion of the western side of the Suez Canal, with the Egyptian Third Army cut off and trapped on the eastern side of that waterway (*see* the "Yom Kippur War Ceasefire Lines, 1973" map). Negotiations for disengagement of the forces would not commence until the Israelis agreed to withdraw to the eastern side of the canal, in fact retreating eastward into the Sinai.

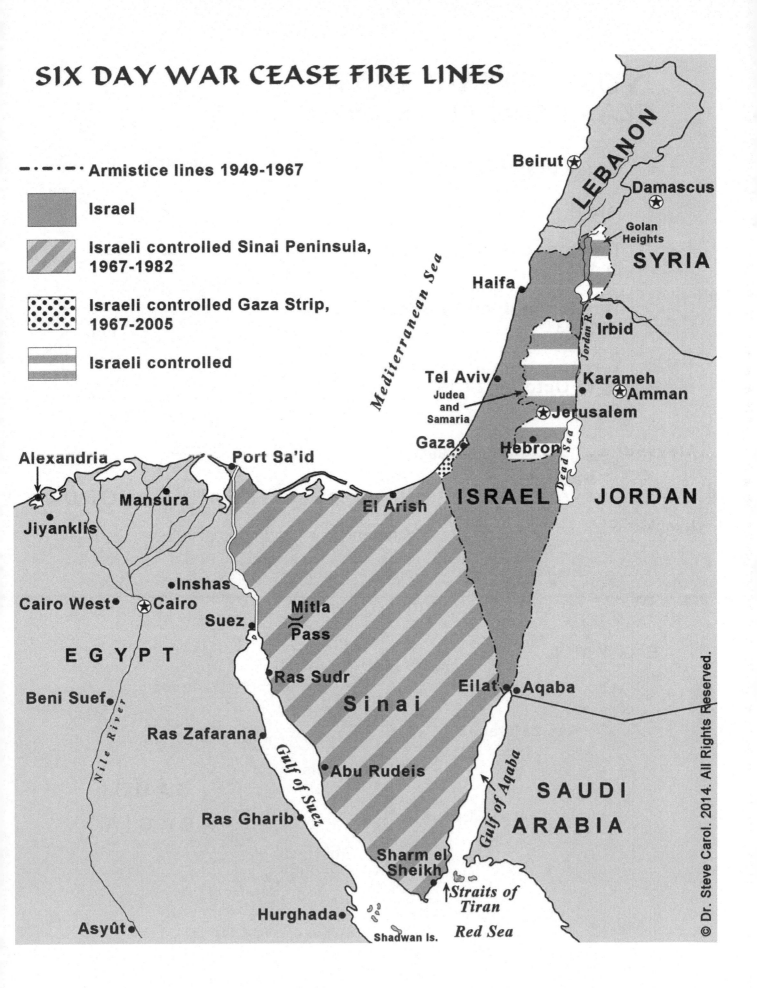

SIX DAY WAR CEASE FIRE LINES

Armistice lines 1949-1967

Israel

Israeli controlled Sinai Peninsula, 1967-1982

Israeli controlled Gaza Strip, 1967-2005

Israeli controlled

LEBANON

Beirut

Damascus

Golan Heights

SYRIA

Haifa

Mediterranean Sea

Irbid

Jordan R.

Tel Aviv

Judea and Samaria

Karameh

Amman

Jerusalem

Gaza

Hebron

Dead Sea

ISRAEL

JORDAN

Alexandria

Port Sa'id

Jiyanklis

Mansura

El Arish

Cairo West

Inshas

Cairo

Suez

Mitla Pass

E G Y P T

Ras Sudr

Beni Suef

Nile River

S i n a i

Eilat

Aqaba

Ras Zafarana

Gulf of Suez

Abu Rudeis

Gulf of Aqaba

SAUDI ARABIA

Ras Gharib

Sharm el Sheikh

Hurghada

Straits of Tiran

Shadwan Is.

Red Sea

Asyût

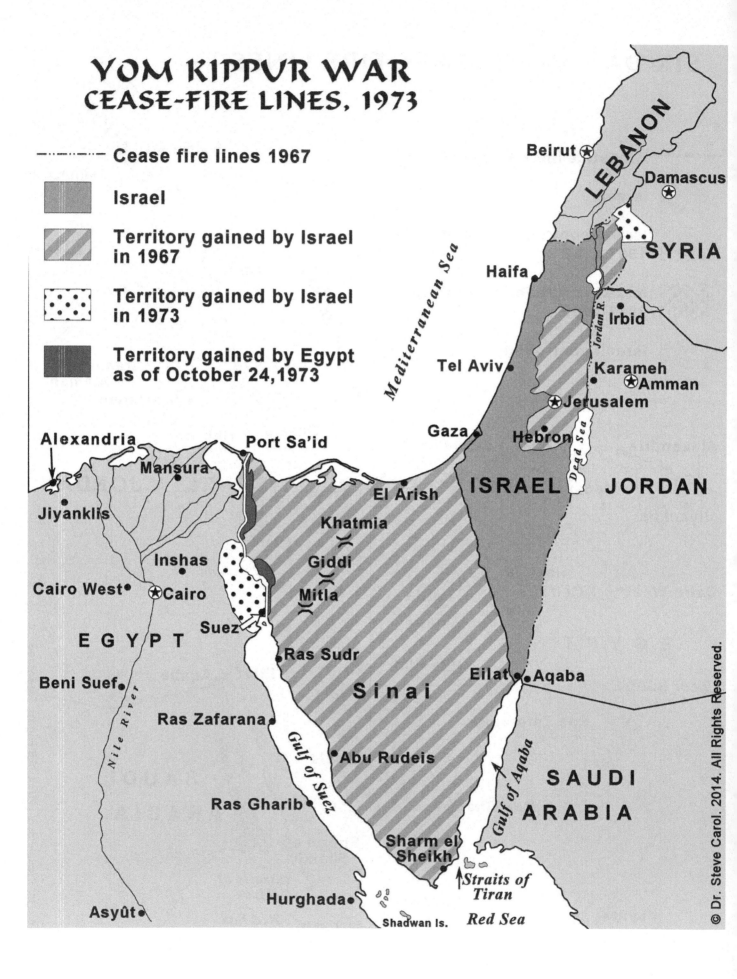

YOM KIPPUR WAR
CEASE-FIRE LINES, 1973

------ Cease fire lines 1967

Israel

Territory gained by Israel in 1967

Territory gained by Israel in 1973

Territory gained by Egypt as of October 24, 1973

Mediterranean Sea

LEBANON
Beirut
Damascus
SYRIA
Haifa
Irbid
Jordan R.
Tel Aviv
Karameh
Amman
Jerusalem
Gaza
Hebron
Dead Sea
ISRAEL
JORDAN

Alexandria
Mansura
Port Sa'id
El Arish
Jiyanklis
Khatmia
Inshas
Giddi
Cairo West
Cairo
Mitla
Suez
Ras Sudr
Sinai
Eilat
Aqaba
Beni Suef
Nile River
Ras Zafarana
Gulf of Suez
Abu Rudeis
Ras Gharib
Gulf of Aqaba
SAUDI
ARABIA
EGYPT
Sharm el Sheikh
Straits of Tiran
Hurghada
Asyût
Shadwan Is.
Red Sea

50. Throughout the ongoing Arab/Muslim conflict against Israel, the Jewish state has been forced by foreign and domestic pressures to return territory acquired in defensive wars.

At the conclusion of the Israeli War of Independence in 1949, Israel was forced to return territory in northern Sinai and southern Lebanon. In fact, during the conflict, on December 31, 1948, the United Kingdom issued an ultimatum to Israel threatening to intervene on behalf of Egypt, one of the Arab states that committed aggression against Israel, if Israel did not halt its operations in the northern Sinai and the Gaza Strip. In a like manner, following the ceasefire that ended the Sinai-Suez War, Israel was forced to withdraw from all of Sinai and the Gaza Strip in 1957, after US threats of economic sanctions.

Israel was similarly pressured to pull back from the Bashan salient (east of the Golan Heights) and the Egyptian western shore of the Suez Canal after the Yom Kippur War. Israel retreated from all of Sinai, without Egyptian recognition of Jerusalem as Israel's capital, in a phased withdrawal between 1974 and 1982. Under international pressure, Israel retreated from most of Lebanon in July 1985, and its security zone in southern Lebanon in May 2000.

Israel is the sole exception where the international legal principle of *ex injuria jus non oritur* (right cannot originate from wrong) has not been applied. At the end of World War I, aggressor states, Germany, Austria-Hungary, Bulgaria and Turkey, all lost territory permanently. Similarly, after World War II, Germany, Italy, Japan, Romania, Hungary, and Finland lost territory permanently. Only in Israel's case has territory won in a legitimate war of self-defense been removed from the control of a victorious nation.

With the advent of the twenty-first century, the Sinai Peninsula became a haven for terrorists that threatened both Egypt and Israel. The situation worsened with the massive demonstrations that toppled Egyptian President Hosni Mubarak from power on February 11, 2011. There was increased terrorist activity from Gaza-based Hamas, Al-Qaeda operatives and even local Bedouin gangs joining forces to hit targets, both in Sinai and across the border into Israel.

In the period from October 7, 2004 to September 21, 2012, popular tourist sites in Sinai, including the Taba Hilton Hotel, the Ras al-Shitan camp sites (near Nuweiba), the Old Market bazaar and two hotels at Sharm el-Sheikh as well as tourist gathering places in Dahab, were hit by savage terrorist attacks. Sinai also became the staging area as well as the launching point for terrorist attacks, including rocket strikes, on southern Israel, particularly Eilat, and the Jordanian port of Aqaba. Additionally, the Egyptian East Mediterranean Gas Company Pipeline in northern Sinai that delivered gas to Israel and Jordan, was attacked and blown up some fifteen times by Hamas terrorists operating from the Gaza Strip in coordination with other terrorist groups like Al-Qaeda, the Gaza-based Popular Resistance Committees, and the Ansar Bayt al-Maqdis ("Supporters of the Holy House") group. Egyptian gas provided about 45 percent of Israel's consumption and fueled 90 percent of Jordan's power supply. Furthermore, these same terrorist groups attacked the capital of Sinai, El Arish, hitting a police station with rockets and a battery of five mortars. In addition, they took time, using a bulldozer to damage a statue of former President Anwar el-Sadat. The attackers shot up the town with heavy machine guns, rocket-propelled grenades, mortars and automatic rifles occupying the town for some six hours. Moreover, a base camp of the Multinational Force and Observers (MFO) peacekeeping group was stormed by Salafi Bedouin linked to Al-Qaeda. The attack, at El Gorah base southwest of El Arish in northern Sinai, was well planned with the terrorists using fifty Toyota trucks, grenades, mortars and automatic guns to carry out their assault. The terrorists torched the facility, plundered its arms and ordnance stores and hoisted the black Al-Qaeda flag. Sinai became a lawless no man's land controlled by a myriad of terrorist groups, including members of the Islamic State, and smuggling gangs. With no mandate to fight Islamic and other terrorists in the peninsula, the MFO became largely superfluous.

The attacks emanating from Sinai or Gaza via Sinai in 2011, escalating in 2012, and continuing well into 2015, not to mention the ouster of two Egyptian governments—the Mubarak and Morsi regimes—raised serious questions. Does Egypt lack the will or the capability (or both) to police its own borders? Does Egypt want to maintain security along the Egypt–Israel border? The cycle of attacks were followed by Egyptian requests to Israel for exemptions to the demilitarization clauses of the Egypt–Israel Peace Treaty. Israel agreed to the upgrading of Egyptian forces in Sinai for the purpose of counterterrorism operations. Going forward, will Egypt ask for equipment that is even more sophisticated to be allowed into Sinai—such as tanks, anti-aircraft missiles and aircraft? At some point in the future, especially if there is another change of government in Cairo, would this be a way to circumvent the peace treaty and present Israel at a given moment with a well armed Egyptian army on its very doorstep?

After the first gas-pipeline bombing, Israel, for the first time since the peace treaty's signing, allowed Egypt to move military forces into Sinai. Though the two Egyptian battalions were supposed to put a lid on the growing anarchy, just days later, Israel turned down an Egyptian request to deploy additional forces, fearing "a complete breakdown of the peace treaty with Cairo." Despite Israel's willingness to overlook the agreement, Egyptian forces were not able to protect the pipeline. For Israel, allowing any Egyptian military forces into Sinai is fraught with danger and a major security concern.

Meanwhile, even prior to these events, calls emanated from Egypt for a severing of relations with Israel or at a minimal, reevaluating the provisions of the Egypt–Israel Peace Treaty of 1979. Even before Mubarak's fate was known, in an interview with the Russian *Ria Novosti*, Rashad al-Bayoumi, a leader of the Muslim Brotherhood said that, "After President Mubarak steps down and a provisional government is formed, there is a need to dissolve the peace treaty with Israel."[65] Following Mubarak's resignation, Muhammad Ghannem, a leader of Egypt's Muslim Brotherhood, told the Iranian news network *Al-Alam* that the Egyptian people need to prepare for war with Israel.

There were calls for the end to the peace treaty from the Islamist camp in Egypt, as well as calls from secular leaders. Ayman Nour, a former lawmaker and chairman of the *Ghad* ("Tomorrow") party, told an Egyptian radio station, "The Camp David Accords are finished. Egypt has to at least conduct negotiations over conditions of the agreement."[66] An April 2011 Pew Global Attitudes Research Poll revealed that 54 percent of Egyptians wanted to annul the peace treaty with Israel, while only 36 percent of Egyptians polled sought to maintain it.[67]

In an interview with the *Al-Watan* newspaper, former IAEA head, and candidate for president, a so-called "moderate," Mohamed ElBaradei said, "If Israel attacked Gaza we would declare war against the Zionist regime." ElBaradei, who assured the world that Iran was not seeking to construct nuclear weapons, added, "In case of any future Israeli attack on Gaza, as the next president of Egypt, I will open the Rafah border crossing and will consider different ways to implement the joint Arab defense agreement."[68]

ElBaradei's statement, (and he by no means was alone in this view) poses a dilemma for Israel. If it exercises its legitimate right of self-defense to stop the increasing and longer-ranged rocket attacks on Israel, as well as other terrorist activities directed at Israel from the Gaza Strip, as it did in the 2008–09

Operation *Cast Lead,* the November 2012 Second Gaza War, and the Third Gaza War of July–August 2014, it could face war with Egypt as the peace treaty will have been unilaterally abrogated by Egypt.

Another voice echoed Nour and ElBaradei. On May 29, 2011, Muslim Brotherhood Sheikh Hazem Abu Ismail announced his candidacy for the presidency of Egypt, promising to transform Egypt into an Islamic state and go to war with Israel, "The Camp David peace treaty is insulting to the Egyptian people, so it must be canceled, and I will do my best to convince people to cancel it."[69]

Public protests against Israel continued through the summer of 2011. On August 26, 2011, demonstrators in front of the Israeli Embassy in Cairo not only called for the cancellation of the Egypt–Israel Peace Treaty, and for the expulsion of the Israeli Ambassador, as well as for the opening of "borders to the Egyptian people" for jihad against Israel, but also called for the destruction of the Jews. The protesters (quite reminiscent of the frenzied crowds that filled Egyptian streets in May 1967) shouted the following, "Jews, remember the Battle of Khaybar, the Army of Muhammad is already here." They added, "Oh Zionists, please be patient, there's an Egyptian digging your grave," and "There is no god but Allah, Zionism is the enemy of Allah and so are the Americans."[70]

Mobs, estimated at 5,000, whipped up by the Muslim Brotherhood, attacked the Israeli Embassy in Cairo, on September 10, 2011. Using sledgehammers they smashed through the wall enclosing the building, broke in, seized classified papers and destroyed numerous others, as well as tore down the Israeli flag. In fact, the young man that tore down the flag, Ahmed al-Shahat, was later honored by the Egyptian military government and rewarded with both a job and an apartment.[71] The mob was led by the terrorist *Jama'a al-Islamiya,* the Egyptian founding branch of Al-Qaeda. At least five Egyptian soldiers were killed and more than 500 police and demonstrators were injured in the violence. Israeli Ambassador Yitzhak Levanon, his family and eighty embassy staff members were taken from their homes to Cairo airport and flown back to Israel aboard two Israeli military planes.[72] Several hours elapsed before Egyptian police and military forces firing tear gas moved in to try to disperse the protesters from around the embassy.

Just days after the attack on the Israeli Embassy, Egypt's Prime Minister, Essam Sharaf, in an interview with Turkish television on September 15, publicly declared, "The Camp David agreement is not a sacred thing and is always open to discussion with what would benefit the region and the case of fair peace. We could make a change if needed."[73] The timing of the remarks, so soon after the embassy attack, heightened concerns in Israel, that the days of the peace treaty were numbered.

Shortly thereafter, on October 13, 2011, Egyptian Air Force Chief General Reda Hafiz told the official MENA news agency, "Sinai is our land and we do not need permission to increase our forces on our land." That statement recalled Adolf Hitler's similar pronouncements regarding his right to change the status of and reoccupy the then demilitarized Rhineland in 1936. Hafiz added, "Egyptian planes conduct patrols to secure Egypt's borders, including the eastern [Israeli] border."[74] These moves are all in direct breach of the peace treaty, which demilitarized the Sinai Peninsula.

At the end of 2011, Rashad Bayoumi, Deputy General Guide of the Egyptian Muslim Brotherhood, openly stated that the Brotherhood would not recognize Israel's legitimacy "under any circumstance" and that "no Muslim Brotherhood members w[ould] engage in any contact or normalization with Israel." In an interview with the London-based *al-Hayat* Arabic daily, Bayoumi asserted that normalization was also "not an option" as "[Israel] is an occupying criminal enemy." The deputy leader also stressed that no Muslim Brotherhood members would ever negotiate with Israelis, and that the Brotherhood plans to initiate legal procedures towards cancelling the 1979 Egypt–Israel Peace Treaty, "The Brotherhood respects international conventions, but we will take legal action against the peace treaty with the Zionist entity,"[75] he told the newspaper.

According to the Egypt–Israel Peace Treaty, Annex I, Article II,[76] Sinai is to be demilitarized by dividing it into several zones.

> Zone A (along the eastern bank of the Suez Canal): Egypt is permitted a mechanized infantry division with up to 126 artillery pieces, up to 230 tanks, as well as up to 480 armored personnel vehicles with up to a total of 22,000 personnel.

> Zone B includes central Sinai between Zones A and C and includes the city of El Arish, the capital of Sinai. Egypt is permitted four border security battalions, no more than 4,000 personnel, to support the civilian police in Zone B.

> Zone C, is adjacent to the 150 mile-long (242 kilometer) border with Israel and the Gulf of Aqaba. In Zone C, the Egyptians are allowed to deploy only police. Only the Multinational Force and Observers (MFO) and the Egyptian civilian police are permitted within Zone C. However, in 2007, an agreement was reached to allow 750 security forces along the border town of Rafah, ostensibly to fight smuggling, but also to ensure that the Palestinians from the Hamas-controlled Gaza Strip did not seep into Egyptian territory.

> There is also a tiny Zone D along the Israeli-Egyptian border, near the Philadelphi Corridor, on the Israeli side of the border. Israel is permitted four infantry battalions, up to 4,000 personnel, but no tanks, or artillery.

The eastern Sinai is patrolled by the Multinational Force and Observers (MFO), which has its main base at El Gorah, 23 miles to the southeast of El Arish. The MFO was established on August 3, 1981, to monitor the Sinai demilitarization provisions of the Egypt–Israel Peace Treaty. Attached to the force are 1,656 soldiers from twelve nations.[77] The MFO does not get involved in any domestic quarrels in Sinai; hence, large portions of the peninsula are controlled by various terrorist groups including the Muslim Brotherhood, al-Qaeda and assorted smuggling gangs. Additionally, as of this writing, Sinai is now being used as a launching pad for attacks against both Egypt and Israel, by Ansar Bayt al-Maqdis, a group that in November 2014, swore allegiance to the Islamic State as Vilayet *Sina* ("Province of Sinai")—a "province" of the Islamic caliphate.

On March 12, 2012, Egypt's Islamist-dominated People's Assembly—the lower house of parliament—unanimously voted in support of "the expulsion from Egypt of the Israeli ambassador and the recall of Egypt's envoy from Tel Aviv."[78] They also demanded the halt of gas exports to the Jewish state. The motion was largely symbolic, because only the ruling military council could make such decisions at the time. Nevertheless, it signaled the dramatic change in Egypt after the ouster of the Mubarak regime in 2011. A parliamentary report declared, "Revolutionary Egypt will never be a friend, partner or ally of the Zionist entity [Israel], which we consider to be the number one enemy of Egypt and the Arab nation," the report said. "It will deal with that entity as an enemy, and the Egyptian government is hereby called upon to review all its relations and accords with that enemy." Additionally, the newly elected Egyptian parliament revived claims to Umm Rashrash,[79] an Egyptian police post (captured by Israel during its 1948–49 War of Independence) that later became the Israeli port city of Eilat. However, by the terms of the 1979 peace treaty Egypt gave up all claims to Eilat (Umm Rashrash).

A little over a month later, on April 22, 2012, Egypt's state-run gas company terminated its contract to supply natural gas to Israel. The original agreement was reached in 2005, between the Israeli and Egyptian governments under which Egypt allocated 7 billion cubic meters of Egyptian gas to the Israeli market for 20 years, with an option to double the supply. The cancellation of the gas deal put Egypt in violation of an economic annex of the Egypt–Israel Peace Treaty.

The calls for change or abrogation of the peace treaty continued. On April 30, 2012, former Secretary-General of the Arab League, Amr Moussa criticized the peace agreement between Egypt and Israel. Moussa declared, "The Camp David agreements do not exist anymore. They are an historic document whose place is on the shelf. The purpose of the agreement with Israel was to establish an independent Palestinian government, whereas today we are talking about an independent Palestinian state." This was not the first time that Moussa came out against the peace treaty. He previously said, "the Camp David agreement is not worth the ink and paper it was written on and signed since it has already expired."[80] Moussa's statement was factually erroneous. First, there was no expiration date to the peace treaty. Additionally, nowhere in the 1979 peace treaty is there any agreement to establish a Palestinian state.

As a result of the Egyptian presidential election, Mohamed Morsi, a member of the Muslim Brotherhood, was proclaimed the victor on June 24, 2012 (he assumed office June 30). Morsi in mid-August announced he wanted to end the demilitarization of the Sinai Peninsula, which is the centerpiece of the treaty. Morsi's legal adviser Mohammed Gadallah said the Islamist president wanted to restore Egyptian sovereignty throughout the peninsula.[81] Yet, Egypt already has sovereignty over Sinai since 1982. What is being called for is the remilitarization of the Sinai, which is a major violation of the Egypt–Israel Peace Treaty.

On August 14–15, 2011, having obtained prior approval from Israel's government, Egypt deployed 2,500 troops and 250 armored personnel carriers into the normally demilitarized zones B and C as part of Operation *Eagle*. This operation and its successor, Operation *Sinai*, were designed to dismantle the widespread terrorist infrastructure in the Sinai Peninsula. Several days earlier, on August 8, Egyptian forces employed missile-firing helicopter gunships to stop a Salafist attack on Egyptian positions at Sheikh Zuwayed east of El Arish. It was the first time in the 39 years since the October 1973 Yom Kippur War that Egyptian warplanes were deployed in the skies over Sinai. However, Egypt also began deploying tanks without coordination from Israel and in clear violation of the peace treaty. Nevertheless, by the end of August, the Egyptian government declared, "Egypt will also take protective measures and strengthen security at the border with the necessary forces capable of deterring alleged infiltrators as well as responding to any activity by the Israeli military."[82] All these statements and moves represented qualitative steps towards the cessation of peaceful relations and a *de facto* abrogation of the Egypt–Israel Peace Treaty.

This puts Israel in a dilemma. If it agrees to deployments of Egyptian military forces, it will be Israel that violates the core military principle on which the treaty was originally based, namely that the entire Sinai be demilitarized. Additionally, it places the onus of treaty revision on Israel, thus making it easier for a subsequent Egyptian abrogation of the agreement. This is the case because Israel itself will be on record acknowledging that the treaty did not meet its current needs. Furthermore, once Egyptian military forces are deployed into Sinai, there is little likelihood that they would ever be withdrawn. If the treaty were abrogated immediately, it would jeopardize Israeli use of the Suez

Canal and the right of free passage through the Gulf of Aqaba and the Straits of Tiran. Moreover, the historic clock would have been turned back to September 12, 1955 and the second similar occurrence on May 23, 1967, both of which increased the chance of, and then triggered war with Egypt—the Sinai Campaign of 1956 and the Six-Day War of 1967, respectively.

Despite the toppling of the Morsi/Muslim Brotherhood government by massive popular demonstrations and the military coup of July 3, 2013, there are still calls for revision or abrogation of the Egypt–Israel Peace Treaty. For example, the Tamarod ("Rebellion") movement called for a reversal of the 1979 peace agreement with the "Israeli entity." They gathered over 300,000 signatures (by late summer 2013) on a petition demanding the revision of the treaty. Tamarod, it should be noted was one of the groups that helped topple the Morsi/Muslim Brotherhood regime.

For the short term, the Egyptian military government may uphold only enough parts of the peace treaty with Israel to secure continued US financial aid for Egypt, but the Brotherhood has convinced the Egyptian public that the peace treaty harms Egyptian national security and threatens internal Egyptian stability. Their true objective is to bring the Egypt–Israel Peace Treaty to a national referendum, with the ultimate intention of terminating it.

It is also important to note that there is within the peace treaty a loophole that provides what could be termed an escape clause. A supplement to Article 6 of the Egypt–Israel Peace Treaty denudes it of any coherent meaning.

> Article VI (5)
>
> It is agreed by the Parties that there is no assertion that this Treaty prevails over other Treaties or agreements or that other Treaties or agreements prevail over this Treaty. The foregoing is not to be construed as contravening the provisions of Article VI (5) of the Treaty, which reads as follows: subject to Article 103 of the United Nations Charter, in the event of a conflict between the obligations of the Parties under the present Treaty and any of their other obligations, the obligation under this Treaty will be binding and implemented.'[83]

In short, if one or more Arab League members went to war with Israel (and aside from Egypt and Jordan, all have been in a formal state of war against the Jewish state since 1948), then Egypt as a signatory of the Arab League Treaty, could join in without violating the Egypt–Israel Peace Treaty. That loophole notwithstanding, any Egyptian unilateral abrogation of the treaty would be in violation of the Vienna Convention on the Law of Treaties, the governing "treaty on treaties." However, in a practical sense there would be very little that either Israel or the international community would be able to do in response (for a more detailed examination of the effectiveness of the international community and "guarantees" in the Middle East, *see* "Basic Principle 69" and "Basic Principle 70").

For the short term, Egypt faces the challenges of on-going violence against the El-Sisi regime by the Muslim Brotherhood and its Islamist supporters, despite its being outlawed, as well as al-Qaeda and Ansar Bayt al-Maqdis Islamic supremacists, all roaming the Sinai Peninsula. Secondly, Egypt must cope with an ever growing population base and a stagnant economy—bereft of foreign investment, gas revenues, and tourist dollars. If the overall situation does not improve, Egypt may well face civil war on a similar level with what has happened in Syria, Iraq, Libya and Yemen. In this atmosphere, the future of the Egypt–Israel Peace Treaty rests on a shaky foundation of quicksand.

This raises several legitimate legal questions. If Egypt unilaterally breaks the peace treaty with Israel, shouldn't Israel demand the return of the Sinai Peninsula? Will the US act in accordance with its role as guarantor of the peace and demand that the new Egyptian government give the Sinai Peninsula back to Israel? Lastly, though unlikely, if Egypt wants merely to renegotiate the peace treaty, then shouldn't the negotiations start at the beginning, which was when Israel was in *de facto* control of all of the Sinai Peninsula?

It is necessary at this point, to review the geography and history of Sinai. The Sinai Peninsula is a triangular land bridge that both joins and separates Africa and Asia. Some 23,552 square miles in size, the northern third is mainly drifting sand desert, the central third is desert plateau, while the southern third is mountainous, with peaks reaching 8,000 feet.

Throughout history, because of its location as well as the nature of its terrain, the Sinai Peninsula was always of strategic importance. In fact, much of its ancient history is linked to the Jewish people. Sinai entered recorded history through biblical accounts of the forty year wanderings of the people of Israel after their Exodus from Egypt in the thirteenth century B.C.E. It was in Sinai that the Ten Commandments were given to Moses, and there Israel became a nation. The Talmud (Shabbat 89b) asks, "What is the meaning of Sinai?" and replies "the mountain from which *sin'ah* [hatred] towards idolatry descended." Other scholarly opinions maintain that Sinai probably derived its name from the Akkadian moon god "Sin," or perhaps from the Hebrew word *sneh* ("thorn bush").

Since ancient times the Sinai Peninsula was a no man's land, a buffer zone between competing empires, an invasion and transit route for armies and traders from Africa to Asia and vice versa. Not less than fifty-two invading armies marched across Sinai.[84] The Muslim caliph Umar, for example, used the northern coastal road of Sinai for his invasion of Egypt, 639–40 C.E. Sinai is an inhospitable region where few live. It must be emphasized that Sinai has not been Egyptian since time immemorial. Egypt never had more than a weak historical connection to Sinai. At times Egypt controlled it, not as part of Egypt but for the purposes stated.

At the beginning of the modern era in 1517, the Ottoman Turkish Sultan Selim I took the Sinai route to conquer Egypt, initiating more than 400 years of Turkish suzerainty. An Egyptian Pasha appointed by the Sultan ruled Egypt and pieces of Sinai. Ottoman documents show that the exact status of Sinai within the empire was not at all certain. The whole of Sinai was apparently part of the Vilayet of Hejaz.[85] Orders from the Sultan to the governor of the Vilayet of Damascus in 1577 and another document (1594) referred to the fortress of El Arish (north Sinai) as part of Egypt. Still other evidence linked northern Sinai with the Sanjak of Gaza.[86] Thus, there was no precise linkage with a specific part of the empire.

An eighteenth century traveler describing the geographical extent of southern Syria, which then included Palestine, depicted Sinai as "this desert which is the boundary of Syria to the south."[87] It was from the desert of Sinai, a lawless area that Arabs of three Bedouin tribes raided into and plundered southern Syria, also known as Palestine.[88] Thus, we may conclude from the historic evidence cited above, that Sinai as such was never in any effective sense a part of Egypt. While certain areas—the Mediterranean northern coast and the coastal area of the southwest—may have had close connections with Egypt, the precise legal and political relationship of the peninsula with Egypt was altogether indeterminate. At the end of the eighteenth century Sinai was *terra nullius*—no man's land—in which no political interest was shown.

In October 1831, the forces of Pasha Muhammad Ali marched out of Egypt, seeking an empire in the Levant, Syria and Anatolia. This triggered two Turco-Egyptian Wars, 1831–33, and 1839–41. There was fear among the European powers, led by the United Kingdom, that Muhammad Ali's army would topple the Ottoman government. This in turn prompted European intervention. In 1841, Muhammad Ali's army was forced back to Egypt. To compensate Ali for relinquishing his administration of the island of Crete, the Ottoman Sultan permitted Egypt to administer the northwestern wedge of Sinai establishing a frontier line, which ran from Rafah to Suez City. This was the first defined frontier between Egyptian-administered Sinai and Turkish Sinai. Nevertheless, it was accepted by all parties, that whoever "ruled" Egypt as a vassal of the Ottoman Sultan and not in any formal sense as an independent sovereign, that Ottoman suzerainty remained in force.

The importance of Sinai changed with the construction of the Suez Canal, completed in 1869. Once the United Kingdom purchased a major interest in the Suez Canal in 1875, and began its "temporary" occupation of Egypt in September 1882 (which would last until the departure of the last British troops in June 1956), the British viewed Sinai as a necessary buffer to protect their interests in both the Canal and Egypt. Hence, the United Kingdom exerted pressure on a weak Ottoman Turkish Empire to draw a boundary line between British and Turkish interests. Historically, both the Turks and the British used Sinai as a vehicle for their imperial conquests.

On April 13, 1892, Evelyn Baring, 1st Earl of Cromer and British Consul-General in Egypt, proposed that the delineation line between British and Turkish territories run from east of El Arish to the head of the Gulf of Aqaba. Thus, the Sinai Peninsula, while nominally under Turkish rule, would in fact be governed by the United Kingdom. The United Kingdom's unilateral assertion of a new frontier line was neither assented nor objected to by the Ottoman government.[89] Turkey offered a counterproposal of a delineation line running from Rafah, westward to Suez City, and then back eastward to Aqaba. This suggestion was rebuffed by the British. The Turks regarded the frontier line issue as remaining an open question.

In 1905, Turkey offered a "compromise" proposal with a line drawn from El Arish in the north, to Ras Muhammad at the southern tip of Sinai. This still was not satisfactory to the British Empire. Thus, after a British ultimatum on May 3, 1906, the presence of two British gunboats, and an implicit threat of war, the Separating Administrative Line of October 1, 1906, was agreed upon by the Turkish Sultan. This transferred administration of Sinai to the British-controlled Egyptian government. The border imposed by the British ran in an almost straight line from Rafah on the Mediterranean Sea, to Taba on the eastern shore of the north end of the Gulf of Aqaba. This line was not a border in the classical sense. Egypt was still part of the Ottoman Empire. The line merely separated the Ottoman area from the Anglo-Egyptian administered area.

When World War I began in 1914, the United Kingdom moved to strengthen the Sinai buffer between the Turkish enemy and the Suez Canal. The British announced on December 16, 1914, that the "suzerainty of Turkey over Egypt was terminated" and that Egypt was a British protectorate. However, the protectorate was in fact imposed unilaterally and while *de facto* Turkish sovereignty was suspended, *de jure* it remained in effect.

On February 3, 1915, Turkey launched an attack across Sinai against the Suez Canal breaching that waterway temporarily. The Turks were repulsed by British-officered Indian troops and retreated across the peninsula. The British began a slow counteroffensive across northern Sinai, specifically along the Mediterranean coast, only capturing El Arish on December 21, 1916. The conquest and occupation by British forces under General Edmund Allenby was accomplished without the participation of Egyptian forces.[90] After the British conquest of Ottoman Palestine, Sinai became part of the Occupied Enemy

Territory Administration, i.e. occupied Palestine. If Sinai was indeed part of Egypt, this arrangement was highly contradictory.

After the war, under British and Egyptian influence, Sinai was viewed as a burden. The British governor of Sinai, C.S. Jarvis, (after it was attached to Egypt) described the Frontiers Administration of Sinai as:

> the illegitimate offspring of the British Army…and the Egyptian Ministry of Finance was asked to accept paternity. This they never did willingly. The Sinai administration having been conceived and brought into the world by purely British influence … was treated by the Egyptian Government from the first with studied neglect, and the attitude … [was] still noticeable even after … [many] years.[91]

Sinai was not part of the British Mandate of Palestine in 1922, nor was it part of Egyptian territory on February 28, 1922, when Egypt was granted its independence by the United Kingdom. Sovereignty rested with Turkey until July 24, 1923, when the latter renounced all non-Turkish territories including Sinai in the Treaty of Lausanne. The treaty included its renunciation of "all rights and titles over Egypt." However, that created a diplomatic void because there was no formal disposition of Turkish sovereignty over Sinai, either by cession or annexation or in any other formal manner as happened with other Turkish territories, which were placed under a number of mandates or otherwise legally disposed of. Sinai was thus an open territory with sovereignty not fixed to any specific nation by any formal international understanding. By default along with Egypt, the United Kingdom "inherited" the Sinai Peninsula. The Egyptians in turn, inherited it from the British again by default, but sovereign title to Sinai remained outstanding. The British themselves affirmed this state of affairs. Thus, the Mandate of Palestine-Egypt administrative frontier line, remained in place from 1917 to 1948.

On May 15, 1948, Egypt attacked the nascent State of Israel, with its forces advancing as far as the southern neighborhoods of Jerusalem and the approaches to Tel Aviv before being stopped by the IDF. Israel in its counterattack, entered Sinai where it gained control of an important portion of northern Sinai—territory from the outskirts of El Arish (Sinai's capital), to Abu Agueila, and Qusseima. Israel held this territory from December 28, 1948 until March 23, 1949. Israel's position was challenged, not by Egypt, but by the United Kingdom and forced to withdraw (*see* Armistice Lines, 1949, map).

Nevertheless, as the victim of an aggressive attack, Israel had a strong legal claim, especially to this region whose legal status was so murky. The fighting resulted only in the establishment of an armistice line. Article V (2) of the February 25, 1949, Egyptian-Israeli Armistice Agreement expressly stated, "The Armistice Demarcation Line is not to be construed in any sense as a political or territorial boundary, and is delineated without prejudice to rights, claims and positions of either Party to the Armistice as regards ultimate settlement of the Palestine question."[92] Furthermore, the 1949 Egyptian-Israeli Armistice left the boundaries of Sinai undetermined. Egypt never had any clear legal claim in its own independent right to Sinai. Reviewing history, the most that could be said is that Egypt's connection to the northern Mediterranean coast was a close one. However, the same can be said for the political entities to the northeast, be those the Ottoman Empire, the British Mandate of Palestine or Israel. As has been stated, for the largest part of history the Sinai Peninsula was *terra nullius*—no man's land.

Egypt, as successor to the British-administered Egypt, and Israel as the successor to the British Mandate of Palestine needed to negotiate the final status of that armistice line. Israel did not forcefully push its claim, acquiescing to the Egyptian position that the Rafah–Aqaba line was the frontier and according to Egyptian definition, Sinai was "occupied" from 1967 to 1982. However, with a unilateral abrogation of the Egypt–Israel Peace Treaty by Egypt, all these issues may be legitimately raised again.

With the advent of armored warfare in the early twentieth century, the northern two-thirds of Sinai was easily converted in wartime, into a huge arena for the rapid deployment of troops, tanks, artillery and other armored vehicles. From 1948 until 1967, the Sinai was used almost exclusively by the power that controlled it, Egypt, to make war upon Israel.

After the 1952 Egyptian Revolution that brought Gamal Abdel Nasser to power, the Sinai was turned into an armed camp, with *fedayeen* terrorists entrenched in the northern part of the peninsula from which they launched attacks directly or via the Gaza Strip, into Israel. The Egyptian military positioned artillery at Ras Nasrani, near the southern tip of Sinai blockading—an act of war—the Straits of Tiran against maritime traffic to and from the Israeli port of Eilat (*see* "Straits of Tiran" map). From 1955 onwards, Nasser began positioning his newly acquired Soviet arms, including tanks and jet bombers in Sinai for his coming confrontation with the Jewish state. The IDF's seven-day campaign, Operation *Kadesh,* part of the Sinai-Suez War in October–November 1956, shattered the Egyptian war machine, destroyed the *fedayeen* bases and reopened the blockaded Straits of Tiran as well as the Gulf of Aqaba to Israeli and international shipping. The cease-fire found the IDF in control of all of the Sinai Peninsula, save a tiny nine-mile-wide strip adjacent to the Suez Canal (*see* "Sinai-Suez War Ceasefire Lines" map). Once again, Israel was forced to withdraw from the Sinai mainly by US pressure but with assurances that the Straits of Tiran would be kept open and terrorist attacks originating from Sinai and Gaza would be prevented. For these purposes, the United Nations Emergency Force (UNEF) was created and stationed in the peninsula.

Colonel Richard Meinertzhagen was a military advisor and intelligence officer in the Middle East Department of the British Colonial Office. In fact, he was a friend of and shared a room with T.E. Lawrence ("Lawrence of Arabia"). In the aftermath of the Sinai-Suez War of 1956, with pressure being applied on Israel to withdraw from Sinai, Meinertzhagen wrote a letter to the *Times* of London on February 9, 1957, to clarify the peninsula's status. "Sir, [Israeli Prime Minister] Mr. Ben-Gurion [is quoted] as saying that he did not attack Egypt proper. That assertion is perfectly true. The Israeli army attacked and occupied no man's land. In 1926, Lord Lloyd asked the Foreign Office if the 1906 agreement was still valid and was told that it was. This was personally confirmed to me by Lloyd in 1928. Egypt's only rights in Sinai are administrative and these have been abused by using Sinai as a base for *fedayeen* raids and erecting coastal batteries at the mouth of the Gulf of Akaba." Nevertheless, as related earlier, in May 1967, Egypt's Nasser ordered the UNEF to leave Egypt, again imposed a blockade at the Straits of Tiran and called for war with Israel. Troops, tanks, artillery, planes and military equipment from across the Arab world flooded into the peninsula. These events triggered the Six-Day War.

In a masterful manipulation of available evidence to the contrary, Egypt's Anwar Sadat claimed that Israeli possession of Sinai spurred him to go to war in October 1973. However, the historic fact remained that Egypt was already in an on-going war with Israel since 1948. Egypt, having failed to achieve total victory over Israel in 1948, 1967, and 1967–70, tried again in 1973. Under Israeli administration from 1967 to 1973, both the Sinai Peninsula, as well as the Golan Heights, acted as buffer zones. These areas provided Israel with crucial protection from military buildups of hostile forces in proximity to vital civilian and industrial concentrations.

In October 1973 during the opening days of the Yom Kippur War, and despite a surprise Egyptian-Syrian attack, (due to several factors on the Israeli side), the Sinai Peninsula and the Golan Heights, served their primary purpose for Israel. Both areas provided the IDF with territorial defense in depth and thus the IDF was able to keep the invading Egyptian and Syrian forces at bay and protect the Israeli heartland from direct attack. During their initial attack, Egyptian forces penetrated some 8 miles eastward into the Sinai, with commando forces reaching upwards of 15 miles. On the Golan Heights, Syrian forces breached Israeli defenses to a depth of over 14 miles, and nearly reached the Bnot Ya'akov Bridge that spans the Jordan River. Nevertheless, Israel traded space for time while it mobilized and deployed its reserves and then went on the counteroffensive, crossing the Suez Canal in a westward drive. As a result, the IDF stopped and trapped the Egyptian Third Army on the east bank of the Suez Canal.

History provides examples of territorial depth that bought time to repel an aggressor. The Russians during the Napoleonic invasion of 1812 retreated all the way to Moscow. The United States during the War of 1812, withdrew from its national capital during the British invasion of 1814. Trading space for time was utilized by both Russia and China during World War II. In a like manner, Israel used this tactic during the opening days of the Yom Kippur War. However, the United States, Russia and China are nations with great territorial depth. Such land can be ceded temporarily to an invading enemy force, while a counteroffensive is prepared. Israel on the other hand, is miniscule and reduced to the 1949 Armistice lines faces catastrophic, existential danger. If the Yom Kippur War began, not on the June 10, 1967 (Six-Day War) ceasefire lines—the so-called "Purple Line"—but rather on the 1949 Armistice lines—the "Green Line"—then Israel would have been chopped into fragments. Using the actual figures cited above, Egypt would have seized the port of Ashdod and reached the outskirts of metropolitan Tel Aviv. The southern tip of the Negev including Israel's southern port city of Eilat, would have been cut off and lost. If in the north Syrian forces started from the 1949 Armistice lines, then they would have captured the Upper Galilee and penetrated into the Lower Galilee. Eshed Kinrot (the beginning of the Israel National Water Carrier from the Sea of Galilee), Safed, and Tiberius, all would have been seized. If the Jordanians, instead of fighting on the Golan Heights as they did in 1973, would have (as they did in 1967), attacked in the central sector, then Jordanian forces would have reached the Mediterranean Sea. Beersheba, capital of the Negev would have been captured, Ben-Gurion international airport (Israel's sole international airport), as well as all of Jerusalem would have been lost (see "Israel–Insecure Borders–Distances" map). Under those circumstances, it is doubtful, that Israel would have survived as an independent nation.

In this context, what actually happened to Kuwait in 1990 provided a vivid illustration of a small nation, with no defensible borders, succumbing to aggressive onslaught. The bulk of Kuwait (total area: 6,880 square miles) which is 80 percent of Israel's size (8,522 square miles) was overrun in six hours, and the entire country was swallowed up by invading Iraqi forces in less than two days. Thus, Israel took great risks for peace in 1979, by relinquishing the entire Sinai Peninsula as the price to conclude a peace treaty with Egypt. That price included:

- Israel relinquished strategic depth vital for its defense against any future aggression. The Sinai is five times the size of Israel in its pre-1967 borders. That depth was not only important in relation to Egypt, always Israel's most formidable antagonist, but in relation to its other Arab foes.
- Israel gave up direct control of its shipping lanes, through the Straits of Tiran and the Gulf of Aqaba, to and from its port of Eilat.
- Israel relinquished vital airspace as well as eight of the world's most advanced airfields–including Eitam, Refidim, Etzion, and Sharm el-Sheikh. All were turned over to Egypt.

- Strategic naval bases at A Tur, Alma and Sharm el-Sheikh were handed over.
- Israel gave up oil fields at Abu Rudeis and Alma, as well as the Sadot gas field, all valued at more than $100 billion. These oil and gas fields had made Israel all but self-sufficient in petroleum.
- Sixteen towns and villages, including Avshalom, Dikla, Haruvit, Holit, Naot Sinai, Netiv HaAsara, Nir Avraham, Ogda, Priel, Sadot, Sufa, Talmei Yosef, Yamit, DiZahav, Neviot, and Ofira were either vacated or demolished.
- More than 7,000 Israelis, who had made the desert bloom, were forcibly evacuated.

It is of interest to note, that the Bedouin tribes in Egypt's Sinai Peninsula implied that they were better off living under Israeli rule and that they suffered since Israel withdrew from the region in 1982, as part of the peace agreement with Egypt. This declaration was made in the Egyptian daily *Al-Ahram,* on May 16, 2013. The newspaper reported that many Sinai residents sought to revenge themselves on security forces after years of heavy-handed security policies under Egyptian interior minister Habib El-Adly, who many accuse of failing to respect human rights and tribal traditions during the Mubarak era. The Mohamed Morsi regime (2012–13) continued the repressive policies. Mohamed El-Asati, from Sinai's Aleiqat tribe, told *Al-Ahram* "the Bedouin have already paid a heavy price for the return of the land in the October 1973 War." He added, "the interior ministry wants to return to its old ways, but this is unacceptable after the [2011] revolution."[93]

Returning the Sinai Peninsula to Egypt three times—under British pressure in 1949, under US pressure in 1957, and by its own choice in 1979—did not end Israel's pariah status in the eyes of the Egyptian people. In exchange for Sinai, Israel did not get the "peace, cooperation and friendship" that Egypt pledged in the 1979 treaty. It got a "cold peace." After April 1982, once Egypt had the entire Sinai, they no longer had any use for the peace treaty, vis-à-vis Israel, and proceeded to ignore its other provisions. The major factor for Egyptian President Mubarak for continuing this "cold peace" was the influx of yearly US aid (some $1.75 billion, mostly military aid in 2010 alone). The Americans provided Egypt with top-of-the-line military equipment, in effect, "buying" a continuation of the "peace." Instead of a real peace, Egypt actively discouraged Egyptian reconciliation with Israel. There were no cultural relations, no tourism from Egypt, and Egyptian professional organizations banned and imposed penalties for contacts with Israel.

The peace treaty did not diminish Egyptian hatred of Jews and Israel one iota. Egypt continued as the world's most prolific producer of misojudaic ideas and attitudes. A virulent continuous and escalating stream of misojudaic invective permeated the Egyptian media. Only the Islamic Republic of Iran could compete with Egypt as world center for the publication and dissemination of both new and "classic" misojudaic literature. Egypt's educational system and media are replete with vehement misojudaic Nazi-style propaganda directed at the Jews and the Jewish state. The misojudaic cartoons match if not exceed anything drawn by Philipp Rupprecht in Julius Streicher's infamous Nazi newspaper, *Der Stürmer.* Typical of the misojudaic invective was the comment by Ahmad Regev, a journalist writing in *Al-Akhbar,* Egypt's second largest state-controlled newspaper, April 18, 2001, "Our thanks go to the late Hitler who wrought, in advance, the vengeance of the Palestinians upon the most despicable villains on the face of the earth. However, we rebuke Hitler for the fact that the vengeance was insufficient."[94] For decades Hitler's autobiography, *Mein Kampf* ("My Struggle") has long been a best seller in Egyptian and other Arab bookstores under its Arabic title *My Jihad.*

Schoolchildren in Egypt are taught that the Jews are the source of all the evil in the world. The most spurious lies are printed and distributed as "facts." To illustrate, Israel was accused in the

Egyptian press of introducing AIDS to Egypt (*Roz Al-Yusuf,* July 2, 1990), polluting the entire globe (*Roz Al-Yusuf,* June 15, 1992), causing earthquakes in Egypt (*Al-Wafd,* December 27, 1992), and of the first bombing of the World Trade Center and throwing the blame on Arabs (*Al-Jumhuriyah,* April 5, 1993). The traditional misojudaic blood libel is still in wide circulation in Egypt. All this is being reinforced by television productions. To illustrate, an Egyptian satellite television channel created "Horse Without a Horseman," a forty-one-episode series to broadcast nightly through the Islamic holy month of Ramadan with a potential audience in the tens of millions. The producers acknowledged that the series incorporated ideas from *The Protocols of the Elders of Zion*, a Tsarist Russian forgery more than 100 years old. *The Protocols of the Elders of Zion* may be in wider distribution in Egypt than anywhere in the world. "Horse Without a Horseman" traced the history of the Middle East from 1855 to 1917 from the point of view of an Egyptian who fought British occupiers and the Zionist movement.[95]

Egyptian school maps substitute "Palestine" for Israel. No map printed in Egypt (or, for that matter, in any other Arab country and most Muslim nations) depicts Israel. Though an Israeli flag flew over the building of the Israeli Embassy in Cairo until it was ransacked by a mob in September 2011, no schoolchild in Egypt ever sees "Israel" in his atlas. Little to nothing is taught about the 1978 Camp David Accords or the 1979 Egypt–Israel Peace Treaty.

Egypt joined and at times led the unremitting stream of attacks on Israel at the United Nations and at other international forums. To cite several examples: In 1992, Egypt headed the unsuccessful campaign to keep the "Zionism is racism" Resolution 3379, intact. Beginning in 1994, Egypt led the international campaign to disarm Israel of its nuclear option. At the UN anti-racism conference in Durban, South Africa in 2002, Egypt led the largely successful effort to turn the conference into an assault on Israel. Cultural exchanges, tourism and trade between the two countries reached a virtual standstill. It should be emphasized that all of these actions were taken by the "moderate" Egyptian government of President Mubarak. Any future Muslim Brotherhood-dominated government can only be worse, given their long standing opposition to the idea of an independent sovereign Jewish state in the Middle East. In short, Israel traded key strategic and economic assets as well as vital principles for paper. In fact, President Anwar Sadat was proud of his achievement. On October 19, 1980, in a *New York Times* interview, Sadat boasted, "Poor Menachem [Begin], he has his problems ... After all, I got back ... the Sinai and the Alma oil fields, and what has Menachem got? A piece of paper."

Thus, Egypt turned the promise of normal, friendly relations into a frigid relationship, violating both the letter of the treaty and the spirit of the Camp David Accords. A non-belligerency agreement would be a better descriptor for the state of Egypt–Israel relations since 1979. The contrast between what the agreements promised and what was actually delivered revealed that the treaty with Egypt was an empty shell. Sinai has been transformed into a staging area for anti-Israel smuggling and terrorism, as well as a military platform from which to launch aggression against Israel again. The Sinai Peninsula served as a springboard for Arab aggression against Israel and a battlefield. Israel was threatened with attack and/or annihilation from Sinai five times (1948–49, 1956, 1967, 1967–70, and 1973). It militarily conquered all or parts of Sinai in legitimate wars of self-defense. Nevertheless, it returned all of Sinai to Egypt from 1974 to 1982, in exchange for full and lasting peace. There is no precedent for such an action in the history of international relations. An international agreement remains valid only as long as there has been no fundamental change in the substantive circumstances prevailing at the time of signing. In international law, this principle is known as *rebus sic stantibus*. These circumstances will change, with any future Egyptian abrogation of the peace treaty. Egyptian–Israeli relations will deteriorate rapidly, radically and in a disrespectful and mocking manner.

Not to be forgotten, is that Israel has a second peace treaty with an Arab state—Jordan. In light of the uprisings that swept Egypt from 2011 to 2013, it would be foolhardy for Israel to believe its peace treaty with the Hashemite Kingdom of Jordan is inscribed in stone, impervious to change or outright repudiation. The future stability of Jordan is threatened from many quarters. The Palestinian majority has long been restless and resentful of their discrimination in the government and other sectors of society. The regime is losing the backing of its traditional Bedouin supporters. With the ascendency of Islamist supremacist forces across the Middle East, the monarchy faces a twin religious and ideological threat. The Muslim Brotherhood has been long entrenched in the kingdom. The long Syrian Civil War has forced tens of thousands of refugees to flee southward into Jordan (nearly 600,000 by the end of 2013) where they pose both a humanitarian and financial burden on Jordan as well as a political threat, depending on the affiliations of the refugees. To add to the explosive mix erupting around Jordan, Iraq is crumbling into Shi'ite–Sunni civil war, with Al-Qaeda and its various affiliates making significant military and political gains. Iraq has long had a dominant influence over Jordan, from the days of rule by the two Hashemite cousins (King Faisal II and King Hussein in Iraq and Jordan respectively), to the decades of influence and pressure by Iraq's Saddam Hussein over his weaker western neighbor, as exemplified by Jordan's support of Iraq in both the Iran–Iraq War (1980–88), and the latter's invasion and occupation of Kuwait (1990–91). The situation became worse in 2014, with the emergence of the Islamic State of Iraq and the Levant (ISIL) and the proclamation of the Islamic State and a new caliphate. The Islamic State has openly declared that Jordan is in its crosshairs and the Hashemite monarchy of King Abdullah II must go. In short, Jordan faces perilous pressures from both the north and east. This could lead to an overthrow of the monarchy, and certainly a re-alignment vis-à-vis its peace treaty with Israel. Thus, the days of the Israel–Jordan Peace Treaty may well be numbered.

In retrospect, Israel's total withdrawal from the Sinai Peninsula was a mistake. It set the precedent of total withdrawal for all other areas claimed by the Arab/Muslim side whether it was Judea, Samaria, Gaza, Jerusalem, the Galilee, the Negev, or any other part of Israel. This concept of "total withdrawal" is now expected not only by the Arab/Muslim states, but also by the European Union, the majority of UN members and by some in the US government. The 1979 Egypt–Israel Peace Treaty also did Israel military harm. It provided Egypt access to American weaponry, as well as funding to purchase the latest military equipment in the US arsenal, including F-16 fighter jets; Apache attack helicopters, Abrams tanks and other hardware. As a result, for the first time in the history of the Arab–Israeli conflict, an Arab armed force—Egypt, the Arab world's largest military force—may have reached parity with its Israeli counterpart. Despite a peace treaty, for over thirty-five years the Egyptian armed forces trained for war with one enemy declared by name—Israel. Egypt benefitted not only from gaining access to the American military pipeline, but also from the reopening of the Suez Canal, which had been blocked and closed by Egypt for eight years. It was an American-led effort that cleared the canal of mines, debris and other obstructions. Quite importantly for Egypt, the peace treaty increased foreign, especially Western, investment in Egypt and brought it out of the Soviet orbit. However, the Obama administration's policy of full support for the short-lived Morsi/Muslim Brotherhood regime 2011–13, provided an opportunity for both the new Egyptian Abdel Fattah El-Sisi regime and Russia to sign a $2 billion arms deal. This deal may lead to the reestablishment of the favorable Russian position in Egypt, as was the case in the heyday of Soviet–Egyptian relations, 1955 to 1974.

On one hand, Egypt has a desire to maintain its relationship with the United States, which is its main arms supplier as well as giving Egypt $2 billion annually in foreign aid. However, if the El-Sisi regime is toppled and a new Islamist government emerges, it will put ideology ahead of foreign investors and tourist dollars in order to confront the Jewish state. It must be understood that in the Middle East, hatred is often stronger than logic.

The harsh reality is that Islamic supremacist forces like the Sinai-based Salafist terrorist organization Ansar Bayt al-Maqdis ("Supporters of the Holy House")—active since 2011—and others throughout the Middle East, like Al-Qaeda, the Muslim Brotherhood and the Islamic State, are committed not only to ultimately revoking the Egypt–Israel as well as Israel–Jordan peace treaties, but are more importantly, committed to wiping the "Zionist entity" off the face of the map. Their motives stem not merely from Arab nationalist xenophobia but are deeply rooted in extremist Islamic supremacist ideology, which is transnational and infinitely more intense as well as inflexible. Like the precedent established by Muhammad in his signing of the Treaty of Hudaybiyyah (*see* "Timeline of Islam, Muslim Conquests and Setbacks" table) any peace with Israel will be contemptuously scrapped—once capability permits. As has been stated earlier, Islamic doctrine permits temporary truces with an enemy that cannot be defeated for the moment by force of arms. A cold Egypt–Israel peace that is 35 years old, an Israel–Jordan peace that is but 20 years old, and any future "peace" with the PLO/PA are but "moments" in the overall 1,400 year history of Islamic conquests.

With the history of Sinai and the events of 2011–15 in mind, Israel must draw the appropriate lessons in order not to repeat its mistakes in planning its future. Over thirty years of territorial withdrawals from Sinai, Gaza, Judea and Samaria, as well as southern Lebanon, have not brought Israel closer to a real meaningful peace. For Israel, the immediate challenge is to increase security both on its southwestern and eastern borders. This is being done in part with the completion of the Egypt–Israel security barrier, the June 30, 2014 call by Israeli Prime Minister Benjamin Netanyahu for a similar barrier along the entire 250-mile-long Israel–Jordan border from the Golan Heights to the Gulf of Aqaba (*see* "Security Barriers Around the World" table), an increased IDF presence on those borders as well as no doubt, the preparation of tactics and strategies for a possible reconquest (for the fourth time) of the Sinai Peninsula.

The thirty-one years of war (1948–79) were followed by thirty-six years of cold peace (1979–2015). Egypt, Jordan and only on paper the PLO, recognized the "fact" of Israel's existence. However, realities on the ground, as the events of 2011–15 prove, can change in a very short period. One fact is certain; a remilitarized Sinai Peninsula would change the strategic balance between Egypt and Israel. The fact that Egypt had three different leaders in the space of two years (2011–13), is proof that there is no telling who will run Egypt and for that matter Jordan, a year, two, or a decade from now or whether that leader/government will feel bound to preserve bilateral relations with Israel. If Israel no longer exists, there is no "fact" to recognize.

With any unilateral abrogation of the Egypt–Israel Peace Treaty, or for that matter, the Israel–Jordan Peace Treaty, the region likely will witness, once again, an Arab/Muslim war against Israel greater in severity than any previous conflict. If Israel prevails, and it must in order to survive as a state, the principle in international law of *ex injuria jus non oritur* must be applied in Israel's favor and all of the Sinai Peninsula should be under Israeli control, or *in extremis* be rendered uninhabitable and unusable by forces committed to Israel's destruction.

51. Arab/Muslim forces have historically relied on terrorist and unconventional warfare, primarily against civilians, especially when confronting a militarily superior foe.

An Arab proverb states, "Victory is gained not by the number killed but by the number frightened." The primary purpose of terrorists, no matter what they call themselves, is to instill fear, anxiety, helplessness, uncertainty, and depression in the society they wish to destroy. Attacks are often indiscriminate with civilians—men, women, children and even infants—selected as key targets. The results of such attacks were always people killed, maimed or traumatized forever. Historically this has been put into practice as outlined below.

As has previously been mentioned, the *Hashshashin*—the "Assassins"—were active from the eighth to the fourteenth century. They were followed by the Ainsarii, a sect of the Ismaili Assassins who survived the 1256 destruction of the stronghold of Alamut, their mountain fortress located in the central Elburz Mountains, south of the Caspian Sea, in present-day Iran.

The Muslim Brotherhood has long been involved in acts of terrorism. The movement's logo exhibits a Qur'an, with two crossed swords underneath; below that, the word *Aedou,* which means "prepare"—from the Qur'an 8:60 which declares, "Prepare against them [the enemy] whatever you are able of power and horses by which you may strike terror into the [hearts of] the enemy of Allah, and your enemy and others besides them whom you do not know [but] whom Allah knows."[96] Thus, the logo itself, usually sanitized and toned down in English translations, promotes terrorism as a virtue.

The Muslim Brotherhood was against Arab regimes, be they monarchies, or presidential republics, that adopted Western ideas and culture. In short, it was anti-Western. The defeat of the Arab states in their war against Israel, 1947–49, became a rallying cry for the Muslim Brotherhood against the Western-oriented Egyptian regime of King Farouk. Their anti-monarchy, anti-Western animus manifested itself in the December 28, 1948 assassination of Egyptian Prime Minister Mahmud Fahmi al-Nuqrashi, by members of the Brotherhood, in part for Egypt's losses in its war against Israel. In apparent retaliation, Muslim Brotherhood founder Hassan al-Banna was assassinated by Egyptian government agents on February 12, 1949. Sayyid Qutb, the Muslim Brotherhood's key theoretician, assumed the leadership of the Brotherhood in 1951. Qutb's radical writings attracted many to the Brotherhood, and are quoted to this day by Al-Qaeda. After the military coup that overthrew the monarchy in July 1952, the Brotherhood ran afoul of the new Egyptian strongman, Gamal Abdel Nasser. Nasser's government dissolved the Brotherhood and six of its top leaders were hanged publically. In retaliation, the Brotherhood attempted to assassinate Nasser on October 26, 1954. In retribution, Nasser ordered the Brotherhood's headquarters burned down, and arrested some 15,000 members, leaving many to rot in prison. Many of the remaining members fled Egypt. Sayyid Qutb and other leaders of the Brotherhood were arrested, imprisoned, and after a show trial, executed on August 29, 1966. Nevertheless, the Brotherhood continued thriving underground.

As has also been mentioned, on June 25, 1980, the Brotherhood attempted to assassinate Syrian President Hafez al-Assad. The attempt, while bloody, was unsuccessful. The Brotherhood viewed the ruling Shi'ite-linked Alawite class as heretics, influenced by Western culture. As a result of this attempt on his life, in July 1980 Assad had the Syrian parliament pass Law No. 49 which declared membership in the Muslim Brotherhood a capital offense. In a further example of their enmity towards more secularized rulers, the Brotherhood literally turned their guns on a prominent pro-Western Arab leader. On October 6, 1981, members of an offshoot of the Muslim Brotherhood, the Egyptian Islamic Jihad, assassinated Egyptian President Anwar el-Sadat in Cairo. This was due in large part, to his signing a peace treaty with Israel and his crackdown on Islamist groups. Returning to the situation in

Syria, the Brotherhood chafing under the restrictions imposed by Hafez al-Assad rebelled against his Westernized Alawite regime in the city of Hama, a stronghold of their movement. Assad's response was to indiscriminately bombard the city with tank and artillery fire as well as use poison gas, from February 2 to 28, 1982. Hama was largely leveled. An estimated 7,000 to 38,000 were killed. This massacre explains the Muslim Brotherhood's continued opposition to the Bashar al-Assad regime during the Syrian Civil War.

In 2004, US FBI discovered a copy of the 1991 Muslim Brotherhood document entitled, "An Explanatory Memorandum,"[97] during a search of the Annandale, Virginia home of a leading Hamas official and Muslim Brother, Ismail Elbarasse. This is the strategic document for the Muslim Brotherhood in North America, and is approved by the Muslim Brotherhood's Shura Council and Organizational Conference. This document was entered into evidence during the Holy Land Foundation trial and stipulated to by the defense that it was what it purports to be—the Muslim Brotherhood's strategy document for North America. The memorandum, written by Mohamed Akram, described a "civilization jihad" aimed at North America. It stated, "The *Ikhwan* must understand that their work in America is a "kind of grand Jihad in eliminating and destroying the Western civilization from within and sabotaging its miserable house by their hands and the hands of the believers so that it is eliminated and God's religion is made victorious over all other religions."[98] In the wake of the popular uprising supported by the Egyptian military that toppled the Morsi regime in July 2013, the Brotherhood was subsequently declared a terrorist group, a threat to Egypt's security, and banned on December 24, 2013.

Additionally, the Brotherhood was declared a terrorist group in Saudi Arabia on March 7, 2014. This move stemmed in part, because the Sunni Islamist Brotherhood doctrines challenge the Saudi principle of dynastic rule, and in part, because the Brotherhood tried to build support inside the kingdom since the 2011 Arab uprisings. Furthermore, some 1,200 Saudis have received training, and fought in the Syrian Civil War, with various anti-Assad groups including the Brotherhood. Two additional groups, the Nusra Front (*Ansar Jabhat al-Nusra li-Ahl al-Sha'm*), and the Islamic State in Iraq and the Levant, considered the Syrian branch and the Iraqi branch of Al Qaeda respectively, were also designated as terrorist organizations. The Saudis fear that these fighters may return home to undermine the Saudi government.[99]

From 1949 to date, Muslim terrorists attacked India from Pakistani-controlled Kashmir. A most horrific example was the November 26–29, 2008 terrorist attack in Mumbai (Bombay), India. Ten Islamic terrorists, calling themselves *Deccan Mujahideen*, hit eleven Indian and Jewish sites frequented by tourists in the city. The terrorists struck Chhatrapati Shivaji Terminus or Victoria Terminus railway station, and then another target every fifteen minutes for the next two hours. Targets included the Mumbai headquarters of Chabad Lubavitch Center, (where at least five people were killed, including a rabbi and his pregnant wife), a tourist restaurant, the Oberoi and Taj hotels, and two attacks on hospitals. The attackers were explicitly told to seek out Israeli and Jewish targets. In all, over 600 people were held hostage, many of them foreigners. 164 civilians and security personnel were killed and 308 wounded.[100] Some 610 hostages were rescued. Among those killed were three top police officials, including Mumbai Police Anti-Terrorism Squad (ATS) chief Hemant Karkare. The one surviving terrorist captured at the end of the 60-hour ordeal claimed that the terrorist group, *Lashkar e-Taiba,* was behind the attacks. This Kashmiri group has links to both al-Qaeda and the Pakistani Inter-Services Intelligence agency.

From 1949 to 1956, Israel faced constant attack by Arab terror groups operating from the Egyptian-occupied Gaza Strip, Jordanian-occupied Judea and Samaria, as well as bombardment from the Syrian-controlled Golan Heights (*see* the "Golan Heights" map). Collectively these terrorists called themselves *fedayeen* from the Arabic *fidā'ī,* which means men of self-sacrifice. Similarly, from 1957 to 1967, Israel again was subjected to Arab terror attacks by groups operating mainly from Jordanian-controlled Judea and Samaria, and occasionally from Syria and Lebanon (*see* "Israel–Insecure Borders–*Fedayeen* attacks and Israeli reprisals" map). This was due to Israel's insecure borders, the 1949 Armistice lines also known collectively as the "Green Line."*

---

* It should be emphasized that the "Green Line," between Israel and its Arab neighbors, has no basis and never existed in the history of the world before 1949. It did not follow any topographical features, nor represent any demographic, political, or historic precedent. It merely represented how far the IDF repulsed the invading Arab armies. It simply was where the opposing armies were when they agreed to an armistice and the ceasefire took effect.

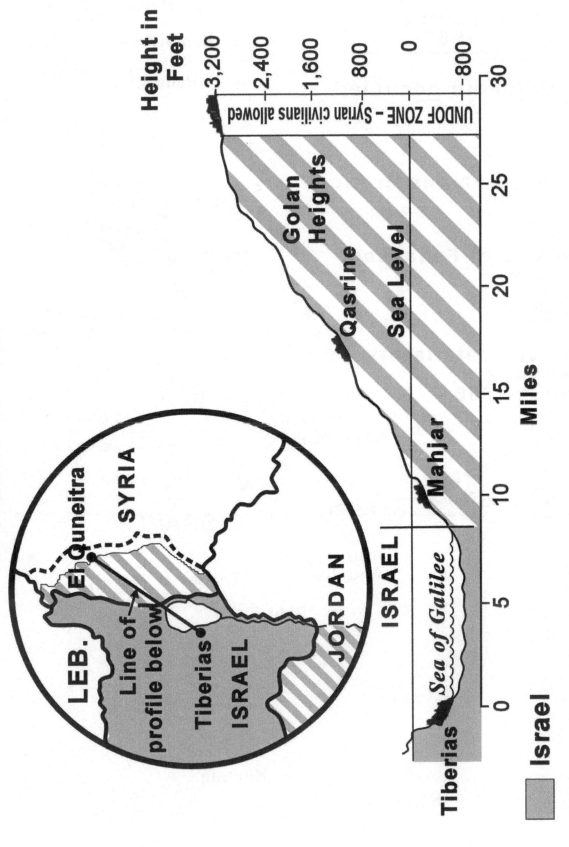

STRATEGIC IMPORTANCE OF THE GOLAN HEIGHTS

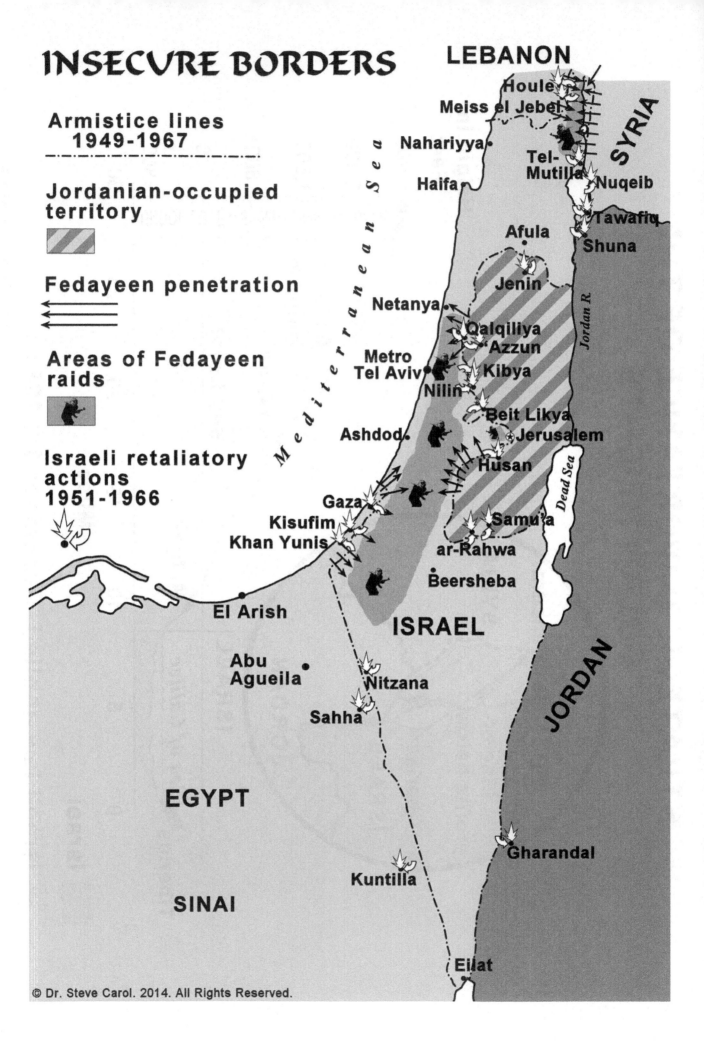

During the mid-1960s, and especially after the 1967 Six-Day War, Arab terror groups gained notoriety on a worldwide basis thanks to print media, radio, television, social media and Internet coverage. Among the many groups involved was the PLO, an umbrella organization of Palestinian Arab terror groups. The PLO was founded on May 28, 1964. It cannot be stressed often enough that this was three years before the Six-Day War, and three years before "occupied territories" became a cause célèbre. So what was the PLO trying to "liberate"? The simple answer was all of the Jewish state of Israel within its 1949 Armistice lines!

The first head of the PLO was Ahmed Shukairy, who held office from June 10, 1964 to December 24, 1967. Of interest is the fact that he was not "Palestinian" but rather a Lebanon-born politician of mixed Egyptian, Hejazi, and Ottoman Turkish descent.[101] Just prior to the Six-Day War in May 1967, Shukairy venomously vowed to drive the Jews into the sea! He was succeeded on December 24, 1967 by Yahya Hamuda, who held the PLO leadership position until February 4, 1969. At that time Muhammad Abdel Rahman Abdel Rauf Arafat al-Qudwa al-Husseini was elected PLO leader by the 11-man executive committee of the PLO.[102] He shortened his name to Yasser Arafat to conceal his relationship to the infamous Hajj Amin al-Husseini, the Grand Mufti of Jerusalem during the British Mandatory period. Recall that Hajj Amin openly collaborated with Adolf Hitler and the Nazi regime during World War II and planned for a holocaust of the Palestinian Jews in the British Mandate of Palestine. Arafat would follow in the footsteps of his relative al-Husseini in his fervent hatred of the West in general and Israel and the Jews in particular. Arafat led the PLO until his death on November 11, 2004. According to his cousin as well as Israeli intelligence and several experts, Arafat was not a "Palestinian" but was born in Cairo, Egypt, on August 24, 1929. Arafat himself sometimes claimed he was born in Gaza, at other times in Jerusalem. Alan Hart, his official biographer, says he was born in Cairo. Thus, in addition to his being a liar, Arafat was an Egyptian.[103] Arafat was succeeded by Mahmoud Abbas (also known as Abu Mazen).

The PLO contained many separate groups including:

- Fatah, established on October 10, 1959, in Kuwait.
- Hawari, active from the 1980s to 1991.
- Ahmed Abu Reish Brigade, an extremist off-shoot of Fatah.
- The Popular Resistance Committee.
- Al-Aqsa Martyrs Brigades, formed in 2000, during the second *intifada*. It was made up of Arafat's elite guards. On December 18, 2003, Fatah asked the leaders of the al-Aqsa Martyrs Brigades to join the Fatah Council, recognizing it officially as part of the Fatah organization.[104]
- The Popular Front for the Liberation of Palestine (PFLP), established in 1967. It was a secular Marxist-Leninist group, headed by Dr. George Habash, and sponsored by Syria. Dr. Wadie Haddad was the leader of the military wing of the PFLP.
- The Democratic Front for the Liberation of Palestine (DFLP), established in 1969, and led by Nayef Hawatmeh.
- Fatah Revolutionary Council, known popularly as the Abu Nidal organization, established in 1974, headed by Sabri al-Banna, and linked to Libya.

Some groups had subdivisions with different names and purposes. For example, Fatah was subdivided into Tanzim, the Fatah military wing, established in 1995, and Force 17, Fatah's elite forces, established in the early 1970s.

There are also Palestinian Arab terrorist groups that are not affiliated with the PLO, including:

- The Popular Front for the Liberation of Palestine-General Command (PFLP-GC), established in December 1968, after splitting with the PFLP. It was backed and controlled by Syria. The PFLP-GC was led by a former Syrian army officer, Ahmed Jibril and it left the PLO in 1974.
- The Popular Front for the Liberation of Palestine External Operations (PFLP-EO) was formed by Dr. Wadie Haddad, after he was expelled from the PFLP after the September 1970 multiple hijackings to Dawson's Field in Jordan.
- The Popular Democratic Front for the Liberation of Palestine (PDFLP) which split from the PFLP in 1969.
- The Arab Liberation Front, established in 1969, and backed by the Iraqi Ba'athist party.
- As-Sa'iqa, which was essentially an integral Syrian force with only a nominal Palestinian identity.
- The Popular Revolutionary Front for the Liberation of Palestine (PRFLP) was formed in February 1972, after splitting off from the PFLP. Led by Abu Shibab, it was supported by Arafat's Fatah group.
- The Popular Struggle Front and the Abu Musa organization both linked to Syria.
- The Palestine Liberation Front.
- Fatah al-Intifada was founded in 1983, when it broke away from Fatah. Led by Colonel Said al-Muragha, better known as "Abu Musa," the group came to be known as the "Abu Musa Faction."
- Palestinian Islamic Jihad, created as an offshoot of the Egyptian Islamic Jihad. Its major financial supporter is Iran and it is linked to Hezbollah, as well as Syria.
- Izz ad-Din al-Qassam Brigades is the military wing and a subdivision of the Islamic Resistance Movement, better known by its Arabic acronym, Hamas, in the Gaza Strip.
- Jund al-Sham, active since 2004, it is a Sunni Salafist group of Islamists based mainly in Ain al-Hilweh Palestinian refugee camp near Sidon, Lebanon. It is opposed to the mainstream Palestinian Fatah movement, the Syrian regime and Shi'ite Hezbollah in Lebanon.
- Fatah al-Islam, formed in November 2006 in the Nahr al-Bared UNRWA Palestinian refugee camp in Lebanon.

Often a terrorist group would appear and after some villainous and heinous deed its name would change to protect the perpetrators. An example of this would be the Black September group, which committed the infamous massacre of Israeli athletes at the 1972 Munich Olympics. Many of these groups continue their operations to date albeit under different names. Furthermore, the operational range and scope of these terrorist attacks spread out from the Middle East. They increased over the years and became a global phenomenon. The list below is just a sampling:

- 1967 to 1970–Terrorist attacks on Israel were launched from Jordan.
- 1970 to 1982–PLO terrorist attacks were launched against Israel from Lebanon.
- 1970s to date–The Al-Qaeda terror network conducted activities worldwide.
- 1971 to1983–A Marxist-leaning terrorist group (founded in 1971, and based in Tehran) known as the *fadayian* (*fedayeen* in Persian) carried out a number of political assassinations over the course of the struggle that culminated in the Iranian Islamic Revolution of 1979.
- In what proved to be a misguided attempt by Israel to use one group of Arabs as a counterweight to the PLO, in 1973 the Israeli authorities permitted the establishment of an Islamic charity,

Mujama al-Islamiya. Led by Sheikh Ahmed Yassin, it was allowed to operate in the Israeli-controlled Gaza Strip. It ran health clinics, blood banks, day care centers, and social care facilities. It was officially approved by Israel in 1979. Subsequently, the charity also built schools, mosques, youth clubs and a library. At first it was encouraged by the Israelis who saw it as being violently opposed to the PLO and various Arab communist groups.* However, this was a classic case of unanticipated consequences. In 1984, the IDF discovered an arms cache within one of the group's mosques, arrested and jailed Sheikh Yassin. A year later he was released. In December 1987, he founded the Islamic Resistance Movement—Hamas—as an outgrowth of the Muslim Brotherhood. It is a political party as well as a terrorist group active against Israel. Hamas launched numerous mortar and rocket bombardments as well as suicide attacks against Israeli civilians from the Gaza Strip, over which it gained total control in a June 2007 military putsch. Hamas initiated the First Gaza War (2008-09), the Second Gaza War (2012), and the Third Gaza War (2014) with ever increasing mortar, rocket and missile bombardment of all of Israel as well as other terrorist acts against the Jewish state.

- Egyptian Islamic Jihad, an offshoot of the Muslim Brotherhood, came to prominence with the assassination of Egyptian President Anwar el-Sadat on October 6, 1981.
- 1983 to date–Hezbollah launched attacks on Israel from Lebanon and against Jewish targets globally.
- 1994 to date–Attacks were launched on Israel from the Gaza Strip, at first by the PLO/PA (since 2005) and after 2007 by Hamas, as well as from PLO/PA-controlled areas of Judea and Samaria..
- Since 2003–Shi'ite, Sunni, Al-Qaeda and foreign terrorist attacks were launched on US-led coalition forces (until their withdrawal in 2011) as well as against Iraqis within Iraq.

All the terrorist groups and the nations that assisted them militarily, politically, diplomatically, and financially, have totally ignored the "Additional Protocol 1, Article 51 to the 1949 Geneva Conventions" which states, "The civilian population as such, as well as individual civilians, shall not be the object of attack. Acts or threats of violence the primary purpose of which is to spread terror among the civilian population are prohibited."[105]

In light of all the above, former US Secretary of State Henry Kissinger's statement in June 1982 (at the time of Israel's operation into Lebanon to eliminate threats to its population, towns and cities), is as true today as when Kissinger made it, "No sovereign state can tolerate indefinitely the buildup along its borders of a military force dedicated to its destruction and implementing its objectives by periodic shelling and raids."[106]

52. Throughout the greater Middle East and beyond, Middle Eastern-related airplane, bus, train, and ship hijackings—sometimes coupled with the destruction of aircraft—have been a method of waging war against the West. Holding passengers and crews

---

* Like Israel, the United States learned the hard way what can result from dealing with Islamic extremists, and using them as proxies in coping with another perceived larger threat. The Americans armed and funded the *mujahadeen* fighting the Soviets in Afghanistan in the 1980s. After Soviet forces were defeated and retreated back home, the Islamic terrorists turned their weapons on the Americans, and under the name of the Taliban and al-Qaeda eventually attacked the US homeland on September 11, 2001.

hostage, and seizing cargoes, all to be held for ransom, have been historic practices of some countries and various terrorist groups.

Hijackings however, were not recent phenomena that suddenly appeared in the late 1960s throughout the Middle East. They were a far older scourge faced by the Western world since the seventh century. It affected the American people since the earliest days of the republic. More importantly, it was an adjunct of the nefarious Arab and Islamic slave trade, which was international in scope.

Consequently, it is necessary to have an understanding of the scope of the Arab/Muslim slave trade. The religiously-sanctioned Islamic slave trade is one of the oldest slave trades, predating the European transatlantic slave trade by 700 years. It was initiated, implemented, institutionalized, and perpetuated by Muslim Arabs and later aided and abetted by African converts to Islam. It had a wide geographical sweep. Arabs supplied African slaves to the entire Muslim world, from Iberia and North Africa in the west to the Indian subcontinent and China in the east, via the trans-Saharan trade, the Red Sea trade, and the Indian Ocean trade. In fact, the Arabic word for "black African" and "slave" is the same—*abed.*

Historians estimate that the transatlantic slave trade, which operated between 1442 and 1870, involved 9.5 million people.[107] The Islamic slave trade was quantitatively much larger. Between 650 C.E. and 1905 it is estimated that some 17 million[108] to more than 28 million[109] were enslaved. Millions more died in the slave raids to capture slaves, as well as the long-treks—Trans-Sahara or to the east coast of Africa—to the slave markets. Thus, the Islamic slave trade brought suffering to a larger number of people than the transatlantic trade and yet its history is virtually ignored.

Slaves were under constant pressure to convert to Islam. Two women for every man were enslaved in the Arab/Muslim slave trade. Female slaves were used as household servants, cooks, wet-nurses, child-minders, and sex slaves, i.e. concubines. Male slaves were utilized as plantation field hands, farmers, salt-miners, fishermen, pearl-divers, and as expendable military troops. A significant portion of male slaves was castrated, usually performed on boys aged between eight and ten. Whereas the castration of white slaves involved the removal of the testicles, the castration of blacks, involved the complete amputation of the genitalia,[110] This resulted in a 70 to 80 percent mortality rate.[111] Such castrated black Africans were used as eunuchs, to guard the harems and to serve as attendants at Islamic holy places.

Islamic slavery continued well into the twenty-first century. Slavery was openly practiced in Ottoman Turkey[112] and Qajar (Shi'ite) Iran.[113] Slavery was not formally abolished in Saudi Arabia until 1962.[114] It was officially abolished even later in 1970, in both Oman and Yemen.[115] Mauritania abolished slavery several times: in 1905, on July 15, 1980, and again most recently in August 2007, when it was criminalized.[116]* Nevertheless, SOS Slavery, a Mauritanian advocacy group, stated there could be up to 600,000 slaves—men, women and children—in Mauritania.[117] In fact, since 1983, slavery and the slave trade were revived in Sudan.[118] When Omar al-Bashir came to power in Sudan, as a result of the military coup of June 30, 1989, he embarked on the Islamization and Arabization of

---

* However in 2009, the UN Special Rapporteur on Contemporary Forms of Slavery stated slavery still existed in Mauritania and the law suffered from a lack of implementation. The 2007 Anti-Slavery Law is further undermined by its requirements that slaves must file a legal complaint before any prosecution can be pursued. Many slaves are illiterate and are unable to complete such paperwork which is further compounded by laws barring NGOs from filing complaints on behalf of the slave. With no support programs to assist victims with the filing of complaints slaves have very few options to bring their cases to light.

the country by means of jihad. For the first time since the nineteenth century, slavery in Sudan became an instrument of a state-sponsored jihad. In Niger, which didn't abolish slavery until 2004, the ban is widely ignored, and according to a Nigerien study, as many as one million people remain in bondage there.[119] The capture and selling of women as sexual slaves continues to the present. In September and October 2014, Islamic State jihadists captured thousands of women from the Iraqi Yazidi minority and sold them into sex slavery, citing theological reasons for the action.[120]

Aside from black Africans, Islamic slave gathering cast a wide geographic net over the centuries. There were Islamic (Arab) slave raids, i.e. *razzias,* into Western Europe, along the northern Mediterranean coast, and the Indian subcontinent (from the seventh century to the early eighteenth century). The Seljuk Turks enslaved the peoples of Anatolia and the Levant (mainly from the eleventh to the fourteenth century). The Safavids (Shi'ite) raided deep into Persia, Armenia and Georgia (from the start of the sixteenth century into the first quarter of the eighteenth century). The Ottoman Turks and Tartars too, raided into Central and Eastern Europe and the Russian heartland (from the mid-fifteenth to late eighteenth century (1463 to 1794).[121]

Returning to the issue of hijackings and hostage taking, between 1530 and 1789, some 1.5 million European Christians and Jews, including American sailors and travelers, were kidnapped and enslaved in Islamic North Africa.[122] This was part of *al-jihad fi'l-bahr* ("holy war at sea"). The table indicates some of the more infamous instances of this nefarious practice.

HIJACKINGS (Setbacks for the hijackers are italicized)	
Eighteenth Century	
Date	**Event**
October 11, 1784	Without any national navy to uphold its freedom of the seas, American ships fell prey to the vessels of the North African states: Morocco, Algiers, Tunis and Tripoli. The American brig, *Betsy* out of Boston was seized by Moroccan vessels. The United States paid $20,000 for the ship's release. Almost immediately the ship was once again seized and retained, this time by Tunis, and renamed *Mashuda.*
January 1785	The Dey of Algiers, Muhammad V bin Uthman declared war on the United States and began to prey on American shipping. The American vessels *Maria* and *Dauphin,* were seized by Algerian corsairs, and the crews imprisoned. Some were forced into slavery, and their ransom set at $60,000.
June 28, 1786	To halt attacks by Morocco against American shipping, the United States agreed to pay $10,000 in "gifts" i.e. tribute (in modern parlance protection money), to the Sultan of Morocco.
Fall 1793	The Algerians seized eleven US merchant ships and enslaved more than 100 Americans.

March 27, 1794	*The attacks by the North African states, led the US Congress to authorize the construction of six warships. By 1797, the first three—the USS* United States, *USS* Constellation *and USS* Constitution—*joined the revitalized US Navy. This in turn, led to an American naval presence in the Mediterranean Sea, which has continued intermittently to the present.*
September 5, 1795	The United States agreed to pay $1,000,000 for the ransom of 115 seamen held prisoner by the Dey of Algiers. Some of the prisoners had been held for over ten years. Annual tribute payments, including $21,600 in naval stores, were to follow. Additionally, the United States gave a 36-gun frigate, the *Crescent,* to the Algerine navy. This sent the perverse message that the United States would not build warships to defend its maritime rights but would supply a warship to a hostile power that sought to attack those rights.
November 4, 1796	In order to halt the seizure of American vessels and the imprisonment of American seamen, the United States agreed to pay ransom and annual tribute to the Dey of Tripoli. The payment included "forty thousand Spanish dollars, thirteen watches of gold, silver and pinsbach, five rings, of which three of diamonds, one of sapphire and one with a watch in it, one hundred and forty piques of cloth, and four caftans of brocade."[123] An additional payment of $18,000 was also made.
August 28, 1797	To safeguard US shipping in the Mediterranean Sea, the United States agreed to pay Hammuda ibn Ali, the Bey of Tunis, a tribute even higher than that promised to Tripoli the year before.
July 11, 1798	*The US Marine Corps was resurrected as a separate military force, in part to deal with the undeclared war with France but also to cope with the North African Islamic states that were preying on US shipping. In clashes with the latter group, the Marines obtained their nickname—Leathernecks. The term derived from the stiff leather collar, called* The Stock, *which was worn from 1798 until 1872 as protection for one's neck and jugular vein from sword, scimitar, and cutlass slashes by hostile attackers. No doubt this addition to Marine attire was due in part to the verse in the Qur'an, which read, "I shall cast terror into the hearts of the infidels. Strike off their heads; strike off the very tips of their fingers." The translation is also rendered as, "I will instill terror into the hearts of the Unbelievers: smite ye above their necks and smite all their finger-tips off them" (8:12).*
September 25, 1800	As a means of pressuring the United States into paying additional tribute of $100,000, Tripoli captured the ship, *Catherine,* robbed its crew and plundered its cargo. Tunis soon followed with increased demands–forty cannon, 10,000 muskets, and a 36-gun warship! For the fledgling nation, the level of tribute demanded began to reach 10 percent of the American national budget, with no guarantee that greed would not increase that percentage.
October 19, 1800	The Dey of Algiers, Mustapha VI bin Ibrahim, forced American Captain William Bainbridge, to carry the Dey's emissary and presents to the Ottoman Sultan at Constantinople, Turkey, aboard the USS *George Washington*. The *George Washington* returned to Algiers on January 21, 1801.

| Nineteenth Century ||
Date	Event
May 10, 1801	The Tripolitan War also known as the "First Barbary War" began as the Dey of Tripoli (present-day Libya), Yusuf Karamanli, declared war on the United States for the latter's refusal to pay additional tribute money for the right to sail the Mediterranean Sea. The Dey declared war on the United States not through any formal written documents but by chopping down the flagpole at the US consulate. It would be the first war the United States fought against Islamic jihadists.
August 1, 1801	*The first shots in the Tripolitan War were fired as the USS* Enterprise *defeated the* Tripoli *without damage or casualties to the American vessel.*
June 1802	Despite a US blockade, Tripolitan vessels were able to capture the American merchantman *Franklin*. The ship's captain, Andrew Morris, and four Americans of his eight-man crew were later ransomed for $6,500.[124]
October 31, 1803	During the Tripolitan War the frigate USS *Philadelphia* commanded by William Bainbridge and its entire 305-man crew was captured by the enemy in Tripoli Harbor, when the ship ran aground on a reef.
February 16, 1804	*As a follow up to the capture of the* Philadelphia *Lieutenant Stephen Decatur, aboard USS* Intrepid, *led a raid into Tripoli harbor to seize and burn the Navy frigate USS* Philadelphia, *denying its use by Tripoli. British Admiral Lord Nelson is said to have called the raid "the most bold and daring act of the age," and Pope Pius VII declared that the United States "had done more for the cause of Christianity than the most powerful nations of Christendom have done for ages."*
August–September 1804	*The American naval squadron under the command of Commodore Edward Preble bombarded the city of Tripoli in a series of five unrelenting attacks.*
April 27, 1805	*After marching 500 miles from Egypt an American-led force of US Marines under the command of First Lieutenant Presley N. O'Bannon, as well as a force of Arab, Greek and Berber mercenaries captured the city of Derna, on the shores of Tripoli, deposing Yusuf Karamanli, the ruling pasha. They installed his brother Hamet on the throne. This event was immortalized in the second line of the Marine Corps Hymn.[125]*
June 10, 1805	*In order to regain his throne Pasha Yusuf Karamanli defeated by US forces signed a peace treaty ending the Tripolitan War. Nevertheless the United States paid $60,000 for the release of the crew of the USS* Philadelphia. *It was a one-time payment and no further tribute would be paid to Tripoli.*
1807	Claiming that US tribute due was two years in arrears, Algiers seized the schooner *Mary Ann*, the brig *Violet*, and the ship *Eagle*.
1812–15	Taking advantage of the US preoccupation with its war with the United Kingdom and claiming he did not receive enough tribute from the United States, the Dey of Algiers, Hadji Ali bin Khrelil, resumed attacks on American vessels.

August 25, 1812	The American brig *Edwin* sailing from Malta to Gibraltar was seized by Algiers. Its cargo was sold and Captain George C. Smith and his ten-man crew were made prisoners. The crew was "subject to the well known horrors of Algerine slavery."[126]
March 3, 1815	*The US Congress authorized the use of force against Algiers.*
June 17, 1815	*A ten-ship squadron under the command of Captain Stephen Decatur seeking Algerian vessels, engaged the frigate* Mashuda, *flagship of the Algerian fleet, in the Battle off Cape Gata. Decatur captured the ship and killed the fleet's commander, Admiral Ra'is Hammidia.*
June 19, 1815	*Decatur's squadron captured the brig* Estido, *towed it as well as the* Mashuda *into Algiers harbor, and threatened to bombard the city.*
June 30, 1815	*As a result of US military actions the new Dey of Algiers, Umar ben Muhammad, signed a treaty with the United States. The treaty provided for no tribute in the future, the instant release of American captives, the restoration of American property seized by the Dey, the payment of $10,000 as indemnity for the seizure of the brig* Edwin, *the emancipation of every Christian slave to be released to an American man-of-war, and the treatment of captives, in case of a future war, not as slaves but as prisoners of war exempt from labor.*
July 26, 1815	*Decatur concluded a similar treaty with Tunis. Tunis was also required to pay restitution for American vessels it allowed the British to seize as prizes during the War of 1812.*
August 5, 1815	*Decatur concluded a treaty with Tripoli similar in provisions to the treaty with Tunis.*
January 19, 1839	*The British Royal Marines landed at Aden to stop Arab raiders from attacking British shipping to and from India. Aden was to remain under British control until 1967.*
Twentieth Century[127]	
Date	**Event**
July 23, 1968	El Al Israel Airlines Flight 426, en route from Rome to Tel Aviv, was hijacked by three Popular Front for the Liberation of Palestine (PFLP) terrorists and diverted to Algiers. After over a month of negotiations both the hostages and hijackers were released.
August 29, 1969	Two PFLP terrorists, including Leila Khaled, hijacked TWA Flight 840, a plane they assumed carried Yitzhak Rabin, then the Israeli ambassador to the United States. Rabin however was not on the plane. The hijackers forced it to land in Damascus, Syria, and after the passengers and crew deplaned, the terrorists blew the plane up. Six Israeli passengers were held hostage for three months when they were exchanged for thirteen Syrian military prisoners being held by Israel. It was the first time that the PFLP targeted a non-Israeli aircraft.
July 22, 1970	Six Palestinians hijacked an Olympic Airways plane to Beirut.

September 6, 1970	Palestinian PFLP terrorists planned to hijack several aircraft simultaneously on the same day. Attempts were made on four civilian airliners: Pan Am Flight 93, TWA Flight 741, Swissair Flight 100, and El Al Israel Airlines Flight 219 (*see* below). The latter hijacking was thwarted. Therefore, on September 9, BOAC Flight 775 was hijacked. The Pan Am plane landed in Cairo, Egypt. The three others—TWA, Swissair, and BOAC—landed at Dawson's Field, near Zarka, Jordan, where all were blown up (on September 12) and the passengers were held hostage. The hostages were split into groups and held in various Palestinian-controlled areas of Jordan. This triggered the events of Black September, the Jordanian Civil War and the expulsion of the PLO from that country (*see* the "Jordanian Civil War, 1970–71" map).
September 6, 1970	*The PFLP attempted to hijack El Al Israel Airlines Flight 219 bound from Amsterdam to New York. Originally there were to be four hijackers, but two of them bearing Senegalese diplomatic passports and who bought last minute first class tickets, were not allowed to board the jet following an Israeli security officer's suspicions. The two terrorists who were able to board, were Leila Khaled who had undergone multiple plastic surgeries to alter her appearance, and Patrick Arguella of Nicaragua, a member of the Carlos international terrorist group. An Israeli air steward was shot by Arguella and badly wounded but later recovered. As the El Al captain dove the aircraft sharply, producing negative G, Israeli security men overpowered Khaled and killed Arguella. The plane landed safely at Heathrow airport in London. Khaled spent only twenty-eight days in jail, before the United Kingdom released her as part of an exchange for hostages taken by other terrorists. The British lamely claimed that she was released because the hijacking had occurred outside British jurisdiction. Khaled returned to Beirut where she taught "how to hijack aircraft" classes to PFLP recruits.*
July 28, 1971	*An attempt to blow up an El Al Israel Airlines plane bound from Rome to Lod with booby-trapped luggage failed. The bomb was given to a woman by her Arab "boyfriend" before she boarded the plane.*
August 23, 1971	*In retaliation for King Hussein's crackdown on Palestinian terror groups in Jordan, Black September targeted an Alia-Royal Jordanian Airlines Boeing 707, which was to be blown out of the sky. The plane en route from Amman to Madrid via Istanbul, Turkey, was carrying the King's mother, Queen Zien. Perhaps due to a faulty mechanism, the bomb exploded after the plane landed at Madrid, damaging the tail fuselage. The Queen Mother had already disembarked at Istanbul.*
September 20, 1971	*A similar attempt to blow up an El Al Israel Airlines plane bound London to Lod, Israel, failed again, after a bomb was given to a woman by an Arab "boyfriend."*

February 22, 1972	A Lufthansa Boeing 747, Flight 649, en route from New Delhi to Frankfurt, was hijacked by five Palestinian terrorists claiming to be members of the "Organization of Victims of Zionist Occupation." The five terrorists boarded at several airports: the first at Hong Kong; two more at Bangkok; the last two at Delhi. The plane was diverted to Aden in the PDR (South) Yemen. The hijackers obtained the release of fifteen Palestinians held in Israel in exchange for the 186 hostages. The terrorists were also paid $5 million by German authorities in exchange for the aircraft.
May 8, 1972	*Four Palestinian Black September terrorists hijacked Sabena Flight 571 on its Vienna to Tel Aviv run and flew it to Lod Airport in Israel. The terrorists demanded the release of 317 terrorists held in Israeli prisons and threatened to blow up the plane with its 109 passengers and crew if their demands were not met. On May 9, the Israelis launched Operation Isotope whereby a team of sixteen IDF Sayeret Matkal Special Forces, led by Ehud Barak and including Benjamin Netanyahu, both future Israeli Prime Ministers, stormed the plane, overpowered the terrorists, killing two male terrorists and imprisoning the two female terrorists. One passenger died of wounds suffered during the rescue raid and two others were injured.*
August 16, 1972	*A booby-trapped tape recorder exploded in the luggage compartment of an El Al Israel Airlines plane, carrying 148 passengers and crew, bound from Rome to Tel Aviv. The bomb, equipped with barometric detonator exploded over Rome, but failed to blow the plane out of the sky, since its luggage compartment had been strengthened, making it blast-resistant. The explosion caused slight damage to the rear door and hole in the baggage compartment. Two PFLP-GC members who had given the recorder to two unsuspecting British women were released by Italian authorities after a short detention.*
October 29, 1972	A Lufthansa Boeing 727, Flight 615, en route from Damascus to Frankfurt to Munich, was hijacked and diverted to Zagreb, Yugoslavia, by two Black September terrorists. The terrorists threatened to fly the jet to Munich or Tel Aviv and blow it up if their demands for the release of the three surviving terrorists of the Munich Olympic Massacre of Israeli athletes were not freed. Germany capitulated and the three terrorists were released and flown to Zagreb and then to Libya.
July 23, 1973	Japan Air Lines Flight 404, a 747 jumbo jet, carrying 155 passengers and crew, en route from Amsterdam to Tokyo, was hijacked to Dubai and then Benghazi, Libya. The lead terrorist was Osamu Maruoka, a member of the Japanese Red Army. The four others were members of the PFLP. The terrorists sought the release of Kozo Okomoto of the Lod Airport Massacre in Israel (on May 30, 1972) as well as $5 million ransom. One PFLP woman terrorist was killed when the hand grenade she was carrying went off also injuring a crew member. Four days later, the passengers were released and the aircraft was blown up. None of the other terrorists was brought to trial after being released by Libya.

September 28–29, 1973	Arab As-Sa'iqa (pro-Syrian) terrorists hijacked a Moscow-Vienna train carrying Jewish immigrants at the Czechoslovak-Austrian border. As the terrorists boarded the train in Czechoslovakia, the communist authorities there were complicit in the attack. Three to seven Jewish emigrants were taken hostage. The terrorists gave the Austrian government an ultimatum to close the Schönau Castle transit center or they would execute the hostages. The Austrian government swiftly granted the request, which caused a diplomatic crisis with Israel. Israeli Prime Minister Golda Meir personally went to Austria to intercede, to no avail. The terrorists were arrested, then freed and flown to Libya. The entire incident captured the attention of the Israeli government, media and public, when they should have been focusing on the Egyptian and Syrian military build-up. This action was part of the diversionary tactics employed by the Arabs during the days that preceded the Yom Kippur War, which erupted October 6, 1973.
November 25, 1973	KLM Flight 861, with 264 passengers and crew, was hijacked en route from Amsterdam to Tokyo, by three members of the Arab Nationalist Youth for the Liberation of Palestine. After they were refused permission to land in Syria, Cyprus, and Libya, the terrorists threatened to blow up the aircraft. Subsequently, they were allowed to land in Malta, where most of the passengers and eight of the crew were released. The remaining eleven passengers and the terrorists then flew to Dubai in the UAE, where the incident ended with the release of the remaining hostages and the escape of the terrorists.
March 3, 1974	Two members of the Arab Nationalist Youth for the Liberation of Palestine hijacked a British Overseas Airways Corporation VC-10 jet, with 102 passengers and crew aboard, en route from Bombay to London via Beirut. The aircraft was diverted to Amsterdam's Schiphol airport, where the passengers and crew were released and the aircraft was torched by the terrorists with flammable fluid. They were caught fleeing the scene.
June 27, 1976	*Air France Flight 139 (Tel Aviv–Athens–Paris), with 258 passengers and crew was hijacked en route to Paris by the PFLP-SOG (Special Operations Group) and the German* Revolutionäre Zellen *("Revolutionary Cells"), and redirected to Entebbe, Uganda, where Jewish and Israeli hostages were held. During July 3–4, in what initially was called Operation* Thunderbolt *and later came to be called Operation* Yonatan, *Israeli* Sayeret Matkal *Special Forces successfully carried out a daring mission and rescued 101 passengers and Air France crew members, being held hostage at the Old Terminal at Entebbe International Airport. The Israeli commander—Yonatan Netanyahu—and four hostages were killed during and after the operation. Seven hijackers were killed.*

October 13, 1977	*Four PFLP-SOG terrorists, on behalf of the Red Army Faction (Baader-Meinhof Group), hijacked Lufthansa Flight 181, a Boeing 737 with ninety-one passengers and crew, en route from Palma de Mallorca to Frankfurt, Germany. The plane was eventually diverted to Mogadishu, Somalia. The pilot was shot dead in front of the passengers after the terrorists learned that he had managed to pass essential information about the number of hijackers (two male and two female hijackers). Afterward, his body was dumped on the runway. This information was vital for the rescue operation that was to follow. On October 18, Federal Republic of (West) German GSG-9 commandos stormed the hijacked plane on the ground—Operation Feuerzauber ("Magic Fire")—freeing all ninety hostages and killing three of the four hijackers. Another four passengers and one German officer were injured during the rescue.*
March 11, 1978	Eleven heavily armed Fatah terrorists, led by Dalal Mughrabi, a woman, infiltrated Israel by sea, coming ashore between Haifa and Tel Aviv, where they first killed an American nature photographer, Gail Rubin, niece of US Senator Abraham Ribicoff (D-CT), and a taxi driver. They then hijacked two busses on the coastal road, filled with adults and children, forced all seventy-one into one bus, and attempted to take it to Tel Aviv. Along the way, they machine-gunned motorists and some of the passengers. Bodies were dumped on the highway. When Israeli forces finally stopped the bus by shooting out the tires, the terrorists killed as many people as they could and set the bus aflame before being killed themselves. The massacre left thirty-eight people dead on the bus, including thirteen children, and 100 injured. This Coastal Road Massacre, was the worst terror attack to date, in Israel's history.
April 12, 1984	Four PFLP terrorists hijacked Egged Bus No. 300 en route from Tel Aviv to Ashkelon with forty-one passengers and forced it to drive to the Gaza Strip. The hijackers demanded the release of some 500 PLO members held in Israeli jails. The IDF stormed the bus. As a result, one young woman soldier was killed and seven passengers were wounded in the course of the operation. Two of the gunmen were killed inside the bus. The other two reportedly were wounded and died en route to a hospital.
December 4, 1984	Four Lebanese Shi'a terrorists hijacked Kuwaiti Airlines Flight 221, en route Kuwait City to Karachi, Pakistan, and diverted the plane to Tehran, Iran. They demanded the release of terrorists jailed in Kuwait. The hijackers executed two American passengers, officials from the US Agency for International Development, Charles Hegna and William Stanford, and dumped their bodies on the tarmac. Iranian security forces stormed the plane to free the remaining hostages.
April 1, 1985	A Lebanese Middle East Airlines, Boeing 707, was hijacked by Amal Lebanese Shi'ite terrorists en route from Beirut to Jeddah, Saudi Arabia. They demanded funds for the anti-Israel resistance and subsequently surrendered.

June 14, 1985	A TWA Boeing 727 airliner, Flight 847, was hijacked on an Athens to Rome flight by two Hezbollah Lebanese Shi'ite terrorists. Aboard the aircraft were 153 passengers and crew. After shuttling between Algiers (landing there twice) and Beirut (landing there three times), the plane stopped in Beirut. Ten additional terrorists came aboard the aircraft. Groups of hostages were released in Algiers and Beirut as the terrorist demands for release of jailed terrorists were met. A US Navy diver, Robert Stethem, was viciously tortured, and then executed and his body was dumped on the tarmac. Thirty-nine Americans and the three man crew were held hostage for seventeen days. On July 1, 1985, Lebanese Amal Shi'ite leader, Nabih Berri, negotiated the release of the remaining TWA hostages. Israel was pressured to free some 300 jailed prisoners, including Kozo Okamoto, one of the Japanese Red Army terrorists who perpetrated the Lod Airport Massacre of May 30, 1972. Israel released an additional 450 terrorists in batches during July, August and September that year while maintaining that the prisoners' release was not related to the hijacking.
October 7, 1985	Palestine Liberation Front (PLF) terrorists hijacked the Italian cruise ship MS *Achille Lauro* in the Mediterranean Sea, while sailing from Alexandria to Port Sa'id, Egypt, and threatened to blow it up unless Israel freed fifty Palestinian prisoners. There were 511 passengers and crew aboard the ship. The PLF terrorists killed a retired New York Jewish-American businessman, 69-year-old wheelchair-bound Leon Klinghoffer, who was celebrating his thirty-sixth wedding anniversary with his wife, Marilyn. Klinghoffer was shot to death and his body and wheelchair flung overboard into the sea. During a news conference in Algiers in 1988, the mastermind and terrorist leader, Muhammad Zaydan, better known as Abu Abbas, callously dismissed Klinghoffer's death, remarking, "Maybe he was trying to swim for it."[128] Israeli intelligence later showed that the terrorists were in contact, via the ship's radio telephone, with a PLF coordinator in Genoa, who in turn was in touch with PLO headquarters in Tunis for final instructions. The hijackers surrendered in Port Sa'id two days later. US Navy F-14 Tomcat fighter jets intercepted an Egyptian plane carrying the hijackers and forced it to land at a NATO base in Sigonella, Sicily, where the Palestinian terrorist gunmen were taken into Italian custody. Four were sentenced to prison terms. Abu Abbas was allowed to leave Italy without being arrested. He was captured by US forces in Iraq on April 15, 2003 and died of natural causes while in US custody on March 8, 2004.
November 23, 1985	Five terrorists from the Abu Nidal group hijacked EgyptAir Flight 648 over the Mediterranean Sea on an Athens to Cairo flight. The plane carried ninety-two passengers and a crew of six. It was diverted to Malta. The terrorists shot two Israeli women and three Americans, of which only two survived. An Egyptian sky marshal was murdered after he killed the terrorist leader, Shakuri Salah Salim. Egyptian commandos attempted to rescue the passengers on November 23, 1985, in a botched raid that left fifty-eight dead, of which two were terrorists. Of the fifty-six passengers killed following the raid, four were killed as a result of commando gunfire, the rest died of suffocation resulting from poisonous gases released after the jet caught fire, due to the explosive charges set off during the attack. Thirty-five other passengers were injured.

September 5, 1986	Four Abu Nidal Palestinian terrorists, disguised as security personnel, hijacked a Pan Am 747, Flight 73, on the ground in Karachi, Pakistan. Later, a fifth terrorist joined the others. It was due to fly on to Frankfurt, Germany and then New York City. Twenty-two passengers and crew out of 379 on board died when the hijackers opened fire after the aircraft cabin lights went off, following the malfunction of the generator. Pakistani commandoes then stormed the plane. Some 150 others sustained wounds and injuries as passengers fled down emergency exits. Libya was accused of funding the hijacking. It was believed that the terrorists had planned to fill the plane with explosives and crash the jet into the center of Tel Aviv.
December 25, 1986	An Iraqi Airways Boeing 737, Flight 163, en route from Baghdad, Iraq, to Amman, Jordan, with 106 passengers and crew aboard was hijacked by four Hezbollah terrorists. On board were six undercover Iraqi officers. When one of them tried to oppose the hijackers, a grenade was thrown into the passenger cabin and another into the cockpit. The injured pilot tried to make an emergency landing near Arar, Saudi Arabia, but the plane on fire crashed. Forty-three survived the crash. Iraq accused Iran of being behind the attack, as the two nations were in the midst of their long war (1980–88).
March 7, 1988	*Three PLO terrorists hijacked a civilian bus carrying workers to the nuclear research facility at Dimona, Israel. While some passengers escaped during the attack, the terrorists were able to capture one man and ten women. Two hostages (the man and a woman) were killed and one other woman was murdered as Israeli elite police forces stormed the bus and killed all three terrorists.*
April 5, 1988	Kuwait Airways Flight 422 was hijacked from Bangkok to Kuwait with 111 passengers and crew aboard. The plane was forced to fly to Iran, then Cyprus, and finally Algiers. The Lebanese Shi'ite Hezbollah terrorists demanded the release of seventeen Shi'ites held in Kuwait. After sixteen days and the murder of two Kuwaiti passengers, the ordeal ended with the remaining hostages released and the hijackers were allowed to escape.

December 24, 1994	Four terrorists from the Algerian *Groupe Islamique Armee* (GIA)—Armed Islamic Group—disguised as presidential police personnel, boarded Air France Flight 8969, and seized the plane on the ground at Houari Boumédiènne Airport, Algiers, Algeria. There were 232 passengers and crew aboard. The terrorists called themselves the "Soldiers of Allah" and shouted *Allahu akbar* ("Allah is greater") during the hijacking and quoted passages of the Qur'an over the aircraft's speaker system. One ten-stick dynamite pack was placed in the cockpit and a second in the center of the passenger cabin. By the end of the day, sixty-three Algerian passengers were freed. Early in the morning of December 26, the Airbus A-300 was flown to Marseilles, France. There, the hijackers demanded a refueling of the aircraft to its maximum—some 27 tons of fuel. In an eerie precursor of the September 11, 2001 attacks, intelligence reports revealed that the hijackers intended to fly the plane into the Eiffel Tower in Paris, or blow it up over the city. A maximum fuel load would make the Airbus into a flying bomb. This was the first known hijacking where the intention was to destroy the aircraft and passengers, and use the fuelled aircraft as a missile to destroy ground targets, rather than to achieve political and publicity goals. On December 26, after three passengers were murdered, the French National Gendarmerie Intervention Group (GIGN), a special military force, stormed the plane in Marseilles, killing all four hijackers. Twenty-five others (passengers, crew and GIGN members) were injured during the rescue.
January 16, 1996	Nine Muslim militants, in support of Chechen rebels, seized the *Avrazya*, a ferry that ran between Trabzon, Turkey and Sochi, Russia. The ship had 177 passengers and 55 crew. The terrorists sailed for Istanbul, Turkey and threatened to blow up the ship along with 114 of the passengers who were Russian. After four days of negotiations, the terrorists surrendered.
June 9, 1997	Air Malta Flight KM 830, en route to Istanbul, Turkey, was hijacked by two Turkish gunmen. The plane was diverted to Cologne, Germany, where the hijackers demanded the release of Turkish gunman Mehmet Ali Agca, then serving a life sentence for the attempted assassination of Pope John Paul II on May 13, 1981. Negotiators convinced the hijackers to surrender.
October 29, 1998	*On the seventy-fifth anniversary of the establishment of the Turkish Republic, a Turkish Airlines Boeing 737, Flight 487, was hijacked en route from Adana to Ankara, Turkey, on a domestic flight. The hijacker was a Kurd, protesting Turkey's war against the Kurds. He demanded the plane be flown to Lausanne, Switzerland, but was persuaded by the pilot to land in Sofia, Bulgaria for refueling. Instead the pilot tricked the hijacker and landed at Ankara Esenboga airport, where Turkish special forces stormed the plane and killed the hijacker.*

It should be noted that at the Camp David Summit meeting in 2000, Israel insisted on its control of the airspace over Judea and Samaria, from the Jordan River to the Mediterranean Sea, claiming it was essential to prevent the threat of a suicide attack by a civilian aircraft laden with explosives on a major Israeli city. The American mediators mocked the Israeli position responding that the Israelis had a vivid imagination, which the Israelis employed to justify exaggerated security demands. Then came the aerial terrorist attacks on the US homeland on September 11, 2001.[129]

Twenty-first Century	
Date	**Event**
September 11, 2001	Four passenger airliners were hijacked in the United States by Islamic Al-Qaeda suicide terrorists.* American Airlines Flight 11 out of Boston was deliberately crashed into the north tower of the World Trade Center (WTC) in New York City. United Airlines Flight 175, also from Boston, was deliberately crashed into the south tower of the WTC. The two crashes caused the 110-story twin towers to collapse. A third aircraft, American Airlines Flight 77, was hijacked after leaving Dulles Airport outside Washington, DC, and was deliberately smashed into the Pentagon in Arlington, Virginia. The fourth plane, United Airlines Flight 93 was hijacked after leaving Newark, New Jersey. The goal of those hijackers was to crash into the US Capitol Building or White House in Washington DC. This plane crashed instead into a field in Shanksville, Pennsylvania, as passengers fought to regain control of the aircraft. In total, 2,974 people, including 343 firefighters, were killed both aboard the four aircraft and on the ground. It was the single worst act of terrorism committed on US homeland to date.
2005 to date	Somali "pirates" hijacked numerous ships, including cargo vessels, bulk carriers, oil tankers, chemical tankers, fishing vessels, tug boats, and yachts. In Arabic, they are referred to not as "pirates" but as *qursaan*, which derives from "corsairs," the French privateers of the late Middle Ages. Many of the ships were released after the payment of a huge ransom. Among those captured in the fall of 2008 were MV *Stolt Valor*, MV *Stolt Strength*, MV *Karagöl*, MV *Delight*, and MV *Sirius Star*. The supertanker, *Sirius Star*, was hijacked on November 15, 2008, 450 nautical miles off the coast of Kenya. It was released January 9, 2009, after payment of ransom. Typical of the ransoms paid was the case of an oil tanker MV *Maran Centaurus*, hijacked on November 30, 2009, and released January 19, 2010, after a ransom payment of between $5.5 and 7 million. More than accumulating ransom, these "pirates" sought to control the vital maritime passages from the oil-rich Persian Gulf to the Mediterranean Sea via the Suez Canal, as well as parts of the East African alternative routes that avoid the canal, via East African waters to Cape Town, South Africa. This gives the "piracy" a regional and international dimension. By holding these maritime routes hostage, the "pirates" as well as their backers, which includes Al-Qaeda, forced global negotiations. This "piracy" is nothing more than a maritime jihad against the West to bring about a change in the balance of power.
November 5, 2005	*A cruise ship, MV* Seabourn Spirit, *bound for Mombasa, Kenya, successfully repelled a Somali pirate attack using sound waves from a long range acoustic device (LRAD) and running over one pirate craft.*

---

* Al-Qaeda holds to the belief that devastating attacks on big US cities are the key to smashing America's wealth and strength. Al-Qaeda makes it perfectly clear that, short of submitting to Islamic hegemony, the non-Muslim world is the enemy.

August 22, 2008 to date	*A Maritime Safety Patrol Area was established in the Gulf of Aden to help stop and deter piracy. A multi-national naval force—Combined Task Force 151—patrolled the area as well as off the coast of Somalia. This international flotilla included ships from Australia, Bulgaria, Canada, China, Denmark, France, Germany, Greece, India, Iran, Italy, Japan, Malaysia, Netherlands, New Zealand, Norway, Pakistan, Portugal, the Republic of (South) Korea, Russia, Saudi Arabia, Singapore, Spain, Sweden, Turkey, the United Kingdom, and the United States.*
September 25, 2008	Somali pirates seized the MV *Faina*, a cargo ship off the East African coast. The ship was carrying weapons from Ukraine, including thirty-three T-72 tanks, rocket-propelled grenades, anti-aircraft guns, and thousands of rounds of ammunition[130] bound for Mombasa, Kenya. However, the ultimate destination for the weapons was southern Sudan via Kenya and/or Uganda. On February 5, 2009, the ship was ransomed for a reported $3.2 million and released the next day.
November 11, 2008	*Somali pirates attempted to board both the MV* Jag Arnav, *a bulk carrier, and MV* Timaha, *a cargo ship. Both attempts failed due to the intervention of the Indian Navy's INS* Tabar. *In 2008, 111 vessels were targeted by Somali pirates resulting in forty-two hijackings.*[131]
December 16, 2008	The UN Security Council adopted Resolution 1851, which authorized member states to carry out land-based operations in Somalia against piracy and called for deployment of ships and aircraft as well as for the seizure of pirates' vessels and weapons.
April 8–12, 2009	*The American container ship, MV* Maersk Alabama, *was boarded by Somali pirates who were unsuccessful in their attempt to take control of the ship and crew. The pirates took the captain, Richard Phillips, hostage and left in a lifeboat from the ship. The captain was rescued on April 12 when Navy SEAL snipers from the USS* Bainbridge *shot and killed three pirates.*
November 18, 2009	*Somali pirates attacked the MV* Maersk Alabama *again, but were repelled by armed security guards aboard the ship.*
March 24, 2010	*The Israeli-owned ZIM ship* Africa Star *en route from Mombasa, Kenya, to Djibouti, was fired upon by a pirate boat off the Somali coast. The pirates were unable to board the ship, which escaped. Three days later on March 27, two pirate boats approached the ship again and opened fire on it but were driven off by security guards aboard the* Africa Star, *foiling the pirating attempt.*
April 1, 2010	*The USS* Nicholas *captured five pirates, sank their small craft and then captured their mother ship off the Kenya–Somalia coast.*

July 28, 2010	The MV *M. Star*, a Japanese tanker carrying 270,000 tons of oil, bound from Das Island, UAE, to Chiba, Japan, was attacked by a boat loaded with explosives[132] while in Omani waters west of the Strait of Hormuz. An explosion caused some hull damage, but the ship was able to proceed under its own power to the port of Fujairah[133] for inspection. It was believed that the attack was staged by a Saudi terrorist operating out of Iran under the orders of the Iranian Revolutionary Guard Corps.[134] Additionally, the Abdullah Azzam Brigades, a terrorist group linked to Al-Qaeda in the Arabian Peninsula, claimed responsibility. The group claimed it carried out the attack "to weaken the infidel global order which is thrust unto Muslim lands and which loots its resources."[135] The incident pointed out the vulnerability of the Strait of Hormuz to Iranian and terrorist attack.
January 15, 2011	*The chemical freighter* Samho Jewelry *was seized by thirteen Somali pirates in the Gulf of Aden, en route UAE to Sri Lanka. The pirates held the twenty-one crew members hostage. On January 22, 2011, fifteen Republic of Korea Naval Special Warfare forces stormed the ship, killing eight pirates, capturing the others, and rescuing the crew during a three-hour firefight.*

The International Maritime Bureau's report on the piracy incidents of 2009, revealed the significant level of activity off the Somali coast over the twelve-month period. There were some 214 attacks, of which 47 resulted in a hijacking. In terms of human cost, 867 ordinary crew members were held hostage by pirates during that period.[136]

Though airline security was tightened, it was not foolproof and some nations and terrorist groups resorted to attempts to blow up aircraft in the air or on the ground. Similarly, there have been attacks on ships with the intention of sinking them.

AIRCRAFT BLOWN UP, ATTACKED ON THE GROUND AND SHIPS ATTACKED (Setbacks for the attackers are italicized)	
Date	**Event**
December 26, 1968	The PFLP attacked El Al Israel Airlines Flight 253, as it taxied down the runway to take off at Athens, Greece airport. The PFLP terrorists, raked the plane with automatic weapons fire and threw grenades, damaging the aircraft, which caught fire. One passenger was killed and a stewardess was seriously wounded. The two attacking terrorists were trained and arrived from Lebanon. They were captured and jailed but then freed after a Greek plane was hijacked and flown to Beirut, Lebanon on July 22, 1970.
December 27–28, 1968	*In response to the PFLP attack, the IDF launched Operation* Reward. *Its* Sayeret Matkal *Special Forces raided Beirut International Airport and blew up thirteen civilian airliners belonging to Lebanon's Middle East Airlines. The planes were empty and there were no casualties (see the "1,000-Day War of Attrition–Israeli Actions" map).*

February 18, 1969	Four PFLP terrorists attacked El Al Israel Airlines Flight 432 about to take off from Zurich's Kloten airport in Switzerland, raking the plane with automatic weapons fire. Six persons were injured and the co-pilot was seriously wounded, dying of his injuries a month later. An Israeli security guard aboard the aircraft did battle with the terrorists and killed their leader, engaging the three others until Swiss security forces arrived and took them into custody. Ironically, the Israeli security officer who killed the terrorist was charged in Swiss court with murder, imprisoned for several months, but was later released following intensive diplomatic pressure. The three terrorists were sentenced to twelve years in prison, but were freed less than two years later in exchange for the passengers aboard the hijacked Swissair jet at Dawson Field, Jordan.
February 10, 1970	A bus carrying El Al Israel Airlines passengers was attacked in Munich, Germany by two Egyptians and a Jordanian. The terrorists were part of a joint operation by the Action Organization for the Liberation of Palestine and the Popular Democratic Front for the Liberation of Palestine. One passenger was killed, and eleven were wounded.
February 21, 1970	The PFLP-GC blew up Swissair Flight SR 330 en route Zurich to Tel Aviv, Israel, using a bomb in the cargo compartment. All forty-seven passengers and crew were killed. Similarly, on that same day, the PFLP-GC attempted to blow up an Austrian Airlines, Caravelle SE-210, en route from Frankfurt to Tel Aviv. A bomb was packed tightly between layers of newspapers, which absorbed most of the blast, enabling the jet to land with no casualties.
April 9, 1973	*Four terrorists belonging to the Arab Nationalist Youth for the Liberation of Palestine attacked an Arkia Israel Airlines plane on the ground at Nicosia airport Cyprus. The terrorists crashed through the gates driving on the tarmac in two vehicles, shooting at the aircraft with machine guns. Fortunately, all the passengers had already disembarked. Two terrorists were killed, the others captured. The aircraft suffered damage after a collision with one of the terrorist vehicles.*
September 5, 1973	*Thanks to intelligence information, Italian police raided an apartment overlooking the airport runway at Fiumicino Airport in Rome and arrested five Palestinian Black September terrorists. They were caught just as they were about to launch SA-7 missiles at an El Al Israel Airlines Boeing 707, taxiing into position for take-off. It was the first reported attempt to use MANPADS against a civilian aircraft.*
December 17, 1973	Five members of the Arab Nationalist Youth for the Liberation of Palestine terrorist organization attacked Pan Am Flight 110 with phosphorus grenades while at the gate in Leonardo da Vinci airport in Rome, Italy. Of the 69 passengers and crew, 30 were killed and 18 injured. The aircraft was destroyed. The terrorists then attacked a Lufthansa Boeing 737 also on the ground, killing two passengers and an Italian customs agent. They forced the plane to take off and fly via Athens, and Damascus, to Kuwait City, Kuwait. At Athens they killed another passenger and dumped his body on the runway. In Kuwait they were turned over to the PLO and were subsequently released.

September 8, 1974	TWA Flight 841 flying Tel Aviv via Athens and Rome to New York, exploded while over the Ionian Sea near northern Greece. All eighty-eight passengers and crew aboard were killed. Arab terrorists linked to the Abu Nidal group planted a bomb in the aft cargo hold, which was detonated by an Arab passenger on a suicide mission.
January 13, 1975	*A Black September terrorist assisted by arch-terrorist Illich Ramirez Sanchez, known as Carlos, "the Jackal," fired two RPG-7 rockets at an El Al Israel Airlines, Boeing 707, sitting on the tarmac at Orly Airport in Paris, France. The rockets missed the Israeli plane but one struck a Yugoslavian JAT DC-9 airliner, injuring three of its passengers. It was the first time that RPG-7 rockets were fired at a civilian aircraft by terrorists.*
January 1, 1976	A terrorist bomb in the cargo hold of Middle East Airlines Flight 438, en route from Beirut to Dubai, exploded causing the aircraft to crash near Al Qaysumah, Saudi Arabia. All eighty-one persons aboard the plane were killed. As Lebanon was in the midst of a civil war that lasted fifteen years (1975–90), any one of numerous groups could have been guilty of planting the bomb on the aircraft.
January 18, 1976	*An El Al Israel Airlines Boeing 707 with 110 passengers, inbound to Nairobi's Embakasi Airport in Kenya, on its Johannesburg, South Africa-Tel Aviv, Israel run was the target of a terrorist attack. Three terrorists, members of the Popular Front for the Liberation of Palestine-Special Operations Group (PFLP-SOG), planned to fire Strela SA-7 heat-seeking missiles at the El Al plane as it approached for a landing. The plan was the work of PFLP-EO mastermind, Wadie Haddad. The terrorists' weapons, including pistols, grenades, machine guns, SA-7 missiles and their launchers were smuggled into Kenya with the knowledge of Ugandan President Idi Amin. An hour before the El Al plane was due to arrive, agents of Kenya's security services—General Service Unit (GSU)—tipped off by the Israeli Mossad, arrested them crouching by the airport perimeter fence. On the grass beside them were two missile launchers, loaded and ready to be fired. A few days later two West Germans connected with the* Revolutionäre Zellen *were sent to find out what had happened to their Arab colleagues were also arrested, apparently as a result of another tip by the Mossad to the Kenyan GSU. The female German had instructions written on her stomach in invisible ink ordering the terrorists to carry out their attack.[137] The plan was to use PFLP-SOG terrorists, assisted by Germans from the* Revolutionäre Zellen *terrorist group, as well as the cooperation of Ugandan leader Idi Amin. This was a precursor of the Entebbe hijacking of Air France Flight 139 some six months later. That is why, along with many other demands, the hijackers of the Air France flight demanded the release of the five terrorists—their comrades—held by Kenya.*
August 11, 1976	PFLP terrorists launched an attack on an El Al Israel Airlines terminal at the Istanbul, Turkey airport. Four civilians, including an American, Harold Rosenthal of Philadelphia, Pennsylvania, were killed and twenty-one were wounded.
April 21, 1980	*An attempt was made to bomb an El Al Israel Airlines aircraft out of the sky, during its Zurich, Switzerland–Tel Aviv run. The bomb was hidden in the luggage of an unwitting West-German citizen and was discovered by Israeli security officers at the airport. Subsequently, the bomb exploded in a police lab before it was defused.*

August 11, 1982	*Pan Am Flight 830, a Boeing 747 with 274 passengers and crew, en route from Tokyo to Honolulu, was damaged by a bomb placed on board by a Jordanian terrorist, Mohammed Rashid, member of the 15 May Organization. The bomb was hidden in a cigarette carton. Its detonator was of a pressure type activated when someone sat on the seat. Fortunately, a mistake was made by the bomb-builder, causing the shock waves to go to the front and rear, rather than to the side and down, a fact that could cause far more damage to the jet fuselage. A Japanese teenager was killed and fifteen others injured (including his parents) by the blast. Luckily the plane was able to make an emergency landing despite the damage to the fuselage.*
September 23, 1983	The Abu Nidal terrorist group planted a bomb in the cargo hold of Gulf Air Flight 771 en route Karachi, Pakistan, to Abu Dhabi, UAE. The bomb exploded as the aircraft was approaching Abu Dhabi airport. All 111 aboard died.
April 4, 1985	*An Alia Royal Jordanian Airlines Boeing 727 was attacked on the ground at Athens airport, Greece. The Abu Nidal group and Black September fired two RPG-7 rockets at the aircraft, which failed to explode. Minor damage was caused to the aircraft.*
April 2, 1986	The Arab Revolutionary Cells linked to the Abu Nidal terrorist group, one of several heavily sponsored by Libya, detonated a bomb aboard TWA Flight 840 flying from Rome, Italy, to Athens, Greece. Of the 121 people on board, the explosion killed four American passengers (one was an infant) blown out of the aircraft and injured seven others. Although the plane suffered rapid decompression, the pilot managed to land the plane safely at Athens.
April 17, 1986	*A Jordanian-Palestinian, Nizar al-Hindawi in the employ of Syrian intelligence, gave an explosive-laden suitcase to his pregnant Irish Catholic fiancé, Anne-Marie Murphy, and booked her a seat on El Al Israel Airlines Flight 016 bound from London to Tel Aviv. He gave her a "calculator" which in reality was a timer-detonator set to trigger the bomb. An alert El Al security screener at Heathrow Airport in London had the suitcase searched. A false bottom was discovered underneath which lay a sheet of Semtex explosive weighing 3.3 pounds. The false bottom was clearly unknown to the young pregnant girl. Unbeknownst to Murphy, her fiancé Hindawi, in one of the most callous acts of all time, had intended to kill her and their unborn child along with 375 fellow passengers on the plane. Hindawi was apprehended, tried and sentenced to 45 years imprisonment. An identical bomb was used in the downing of Pan Am Flight 103 over Lockerbie, Scotland in 1988.*
June 26, 1986	*An attempt to blow up an El Al Israel Airlines 747 failed when the bomb malfunctioned and detonated on the ground at Madrid's Barajas Airport. A passenger was given a suitcase that he believed contained drugs. It was being examined by Israeli security personnel near the El Al check-in counter, when it exploded. A security officer suffered burns and thirteen passengers were injured. The Syrian-backed Abu Mussa group working with Libya was behind the attempt.*

December 21, 1988	Pan Am Flight 103 en route London to New York exploded over Lockerbie, Scotland, killing all 259 people aboard and eleven on the ground. Another five on the ground were injured. Libyan agents planted an unaccompanied Samsonite suitcase bomb which had been routed via the interline baggage system onto Pan Am Flight 103 from Malta. The bomb containing 350 grams of Semtex, was equipped with a timer hidden in a Toshiba Bombeat radio cassette player, placed in the suitcase. The suitcase in turn was placed in the cargo compartment and exploded in mid-air at a height of 31,000 ft. The terrorists' intention was to bomb the jet out of the sky over the ocean, where the aircraft would disappear without a trace. Due to a late departure the aircraft exploded over land. It was the largest terrorist attack on Americans before the attack of September 11, 2001. A Libyan intelligence operative, Abdel Basset Ali al-Megrahi (the sacrificed pawn), was tried by a Scottish court and convicted of the bombing on January 31, 2001. Al-Megrahi was sentenced to life imprisonment, which made him eligible for parole after twenty-seven years. On August 15, 2003, Libya's UN ambassador, Ahmed Own, submitted a letter to the UN Security Council formally accepting "responsibility for the actions of its officials" in relation to the Lockerbie bombing. Five years later, on August 14, 2008, a US–Libya compensation agreement was signed in Tripoli by US Assistant Secretary of State David Welch and Libya's Foreign Ministry head of America affairs, Ahmed al-Fatroui. The deal compensated all victims of bombings involving the two countries[138] including victims of the 1988 Lockerbie bombing, the bombing of the La Belle discotheque in West Berlin on April 5, 1986, the US bombing of Tripoli and Benghazi, on April 15, 1986, as well as the American victims of Union de Transportes Aériens (UTA) Flight 772 blown out of the sky over northern Niger, on September 19, 1989 (see below). In October 2008, Libya paid $1.5 billion into a compensation fund for the US families and the United States paid $300 million for the Libyan families.[139] Al-Megrahi was released on "compassionate" grounds from a Scottish prison on August 20, 2009, only eight years after his conviction. His release was precipitated by doctors' reports that he would die of terminal prostate cancer in three months or less. However, according to leaked US diplomatic memos Libya put enormous pressure on the United Kingdom to release him, warning that if the ailing Megrahi died in a Scottish prison all British commercial activity in Libya would be cut off and a wave of demonstrations would erupt outside British embassies. The Libyans even implied "that the welfare of UK diplomats and citizens in Libya would be at risk."[140] Thus, al-Megrahi was freed. When he returned to Libya he received a hero's welcome at the Tripoli airport from a crowd waving Libyan and Scottish flags. The reports of the mass murderer's imminent death were greatly exaggerated. Al-Megrahi lived comfortably in a villa on the $2.69 million deposited in a Swiss bank, which he was paid by Libya even before his conviction. Al-Megrahi died on May 20, 2012, some three years after his release.[141] During the uprising against the Qadhafi regime in February 2011, former Libyan justice minister Mustafa Mohamed Abdel-Jalil declared that Qadhafi personally ordered the Pan Am Lockerbie bombing.[142]

September 19, 1989	A bomb in the cargo hold of a UTA DC-10, Flight 772 en route Brazzaville, Congo, via N'Djamena, Chad, to Paris, France, exploded, destroying the aircraft over the Sahara in northern Niger, killing all 170 passengers and crew aboard. The bomb, made of Semtex, was hidden in a radio-tape player placed in a Samsonite suitcase similar to the bomb that destroyed Pan-Am Flight 103. A Congolese student recruited by the Libyan People's Bureau, placed the suitcase aboard the aircraft in Brazzaville, Congo, and he then disembarked at Ndjamena, Chad. Libya resented French assistance to Chad in defeating Libyan forces occupying Chad and shattering Qadhafi's dream of a Libyan-dominated African empire. In 1999, a French court tried six Libyans in absentia and they were convicted for their part in the attack.
November 23, 1996	Ethiopian Airlines Flight 961 was commandeered shortly after take-off from Addis Ababa en route to Nairobi, Kenya, with 163 passengers and 12 crew members. According to the version widely circulated in the West, the aircraft was commandeered by a group of what were later described as drunken, dissident Ethiopian "students," allegedly demanding to be flown to Australia for political asylum. This "official version" is disputed. There are many unanswered questions about this event.[143] Initial reports claimed the actual number of hijackers was between eight and twelve. The three hijackers claimed there actually were eleven on board the aircraft. The hijackers were members of the Al-Qaeda Actions in East Africa network, which was headed by Fazul Abdullah Mohammed who planned the attack. Aboard the aircraft were eight Israelis, (five top personnel of Israel Aircraft Industries [IAI], an executive of ECI Communications, a member of an elite anti-terrorist unit, and an Israeli security guard), CIA officer Leslie Ann Shedd, head of the US Horn of Africa operation, the head of Ukraine military intelligence as well as the deputy commander of the Ukrainian air force.[144] The group secretly was on its way to a meeting in Jerusalem, Israel. They were to have discussed a deal whereby the Ukraine would supply Ethiopia with fighter jets, which Israel would upgrade, and the United States would pay for. One of the terrorists' first actions was to separate the CIA agent, the Israelis and the Ukrainians from the other passengers. In the exchange of fire between the hijackers and the Israeli security men, Leslie Ann Shedd and all the IAI directors were shot dead together with the Ukrainian intelligence chief. The deputy air force commander and one Israeli guard survived with serious injuries. It is not known if the latter two survived the plane crash. Approaching the Comoros Islands, the aircraft began to run out of fuel. The pilot attempted to carry out a controlled ditching in the shallow, sheltered waters at the northern end of Grande Comoro Island. The left engine and wingtip struck the water, causing the aircraft to cartwheel, and break up as it crashed. Numbers of survivors are disputed. Bodies of the hijackers, if there were some, could not be identified by survivors of the crash. To this day none of the governments concerned, Ethiopian, American, Israeli and Ukrainian, admits the Ethiopian Airways hijack was a well-planned Al-Qaeda attack, and that there was a firefight aboard the airliner and the victims were deliberately murdered.[145] All four governments have maintained a tight blackout on the terrorist attack because they have never discovered how Fazul obtained the top secret information about the passengers on the flight and their mission.[146]

October 12, 2000	The USS *Cole*, a US Navy destroyer (DDG 67), was attacked by an Al-Qaeda suicide team using an explosive-laden speedboat while the *Cole* was anchored and refueling in Aden, Yemen. Seventeen American sailors were killed, along with the two perpetrators of the attack. Thirty-nine American seamen were injured. The attack was the deadliest against a US naval vessel since 1987.
October 6, 2002	The French 157,000-ton crude oil tanker, SS *Limburg*, exploded in flames after it was rammed outside the Yemeni port of Mukallah, east of Aden. Both of its new armored double-walls, installed as a precaution against terror attack, were pierced. One crewman died and there was a spillage of nearly 90,000 barrels of oil.
November 18, 2002	*An El Al Israel Airlines Boeing 757, Flight 581, carrying 179 passengers and crew, was hijacked by a single Israeli-Arab wielding a knife, en route from Tel Aviv to Istanbul, Turkey. The hijacker was overpowered by the aircraft's security man.*
November 28, 2002	*An Al-Qaeda Actions in East Africa terrorist squad fired two SA-7 Strela-2 surface-to-air missiles at Arkia Israel Airlines Flight 582, just taking off (it was about 500 feet above ground) from Moi International Airport in Mombasa, Kenya. The plane with 271 passengers and crew on board was bound for Tel Aviv. Both missiles missed, and it is believed that flare-based countermeasures were deployed by the Boeing 757 aircraft. Israel had been working on methods of protecting civilian jets from missile attacks since the early 1970s.[147] Later, Kenyan police found two Strela-2 surface-to-air missiles launchers at a farm some six miles from the airport.[148]*
December 25, 2009	*Umar Farouk Abdulmuttalab, a Nigerian Muslim, attempted to blow up Northwest Flight 253, bound Amsterdam-Detroit, as it approached the Detroit airport. Abdulmuttalab tried to ignite explosive chemicals sewn into his underwear, with a syringe. He was stopped by an alert passenger and the cabin crew. He was trained for his mission in Yemen by Al-Qaeda in the Arabian Peninsula.*

Historically, as the Jewish sages tell us, "When evil comes to the world, Jacob [Israel] is the first to know it." The experiences of modern Israel in dealing with major threats and evils in the world—including such dangers as hijacking of civilian aircraft, the need for increased airport security, terrorism, suicide bombers, as well as the threat of rogue regimes and terrorist groups acquiring WMDs—is the harbinger of what would befall the West. The overall Arab/Muslim war on Israel and the Jews is the microcosm of the ever-growing global clash between Western civilization and Islamic supremacism.

53. The use of human shields is a favored tactic of the Arab/Muslim side in their conflicts with the West.

The use of human shields has both a military and political value. Non-combatants are placed in or around combat targets to deter an enemy from attacking those targets. In a like manner, non-combatants are literal shields to protect the combatants during attacks, by forcing the non-combatants—at times women and children—to march in front of the combatants. This is done in the hope that the other party will be reluctant to attack them. Furthermore, if the other party attacks these targets anyway, the resulting non-combatant casualties have propaganda value. Using these techniques, for example taking hostages for use as human shields, increases the non-combatant casualty rate and is illegal by any nation that is party to the Fourth Geneva Convention. These tactics have not only been used against the IDF, but also against US and other Western forces in Somalia, Iraq and Afghanistan. Arab/Muslim terrorists essentially and continually commit a double war crime as they strike innocent Israeli civilians while embedding their fighters and launching facilities among their own population centers, hoping they are hit in any Israeli retaliation. Hence, Israel's enemies are not only indifferent to the suffering of their own people, but welcome it for its propaganda value. As such, those who use human shields are both legally and morally responsible for any deaths that are caused.

The contemptuous use of children in active warfare increased in the last four decades, throughout the Middle East. Rather than protect children as most nations, including Israel do, Middle East tyrants, be they Ayatollah Ruhollah Khomeini or PLO chief Yasser Arafat used them as weapons and placed them in harm's way. Thus, it became standard practice to use children to throw stones, ignite explosives, wear suicide bomb-belts, and create a live shield behind which adults fire with guns and rifles at the enemy. There is daily praise of jihad on radio, television, in newspapers, social media as well as on the Internet. Children, starting in kindergarten, are taught that to be a *shaheed* ("martyr")[*] who murders Jewish men, women and children indiscriminately, is a virtue. Article 77, Paragraph 2 of the Protocols to the Geneva Convention of 1949, stipulate, "The parties to the conflict shall take all feasible measures in order that children who have not attained the age of fifteen years do not take a direct part in hostilities and, in particular, they shall refrain from recruiting them into their armed forces."[149] Article 38 of the United Nations Convention on the Rights of the Child provides that "State Parties shall take all feasible measures to ensure that persons who have not attained the age of fifteen years do not take a direct part in hostilities."[150]

During the Iran–Iraq War (1980–88), the Islamic Republic of Iran dispatched children to the front line and encouraged them to walk through Iraqi minefields. The first "human wave" attack occurred on November 29–30, 1981, during the Iranian attack to retake the city of Bostan. The children lacked military training. Boys as young as nine were reportedly used as minesweepers and cannon fodder in human wave attacks during the war.[151] Some 36,000 school age children were killed and 2,853 injured, while 2,433 were taken prisoner. Over 550,000 students (mostly pre-teens and teenagers) were sent to the front, often with a golden plastic "key to paradise"[152] hanging around their necks and the promise that they would automatically go to paradise—*al-Janna*— if they died in battle. Iran imported 500,000 such keys from Taiwan during the war.[153] These statistics were revealed by Iranian Brigadier General Mohammad-Saleh Jokar, head of the Students Basij, in an interview with the Fars news agency, in October 2009.[154]

In many cases, terrorists seek to use their own people as targets as well as shields. Dead civilians are the goal of the terrorist organizations. According to Hamas' thinking, the more Palestinian victims there are, the more the international community will try to pressure Israel to avoid any further military operations. Such ruthless calculations proved effective in gaining international support against Israel during the First Gaza War (2008–09), the Second Gaza War (November 2012), and the Third Gaza War (2014).

---

[*] Someone who wishes to lay down their life in the name of jihad, e.g. Muslim suicide bomber, or has done so. In Iran, they are termed *estesh-hadiyun* ("martyrdom-seekers").

It must be emphasized at the outset that according to shari'a there are only four ways to deal with infidel hostages: 1) execution, 2) enslavement, 3) exchange for Muslim prisoners, or 4) exchange for ransom. Thus, any hostages who have not been executed are living as slaves to their captors. The term *ghanima* ("spoil") is applied specifically to property (spoils of war) acquired by force from non-Muslims. It includes however not only property (movable and immovable) but also persons, whether in the capacity of *asra*—prisoners of war—or *sabi*—women and children). If the slave were a woman, the master was permitted to have sexual relations with her as a concubine.[155]

A shocking example of this principle occurred in September 2008, when Canadian journalist Amanda Lindhout was kidnapped in the outskirts of Mogadishu, Somalia, by Islamist forces who held her for $2.5 million in ransom. After her abduction, she was raped and impregnated by one of her captors. She was his slave—"whomever your right hand possesses"—and his property. This is justified in several passages in the Qur'an (e.g. 4:3). Additional passages include 23:5–6, 33:50, and 70:29–30, all of which allows sex with slaves; 4:24 which allows sex with married slaves; 24:32 breeding slaves; and 2:178 which explains the actual human value of a slave—less than half that of a non slave, with females valued even less. Ms. Lindhout was *ma malakat aymankum,* human "property," conquered and possessed by jihadists. On November 25, 2009, fifteen months after being kidnapped, Lindhout was released along with another hostage after their families paid a $600,000 ransom.

In the Middle East there have been several notable examples of the use of human shields. In 1948, it was Iraqi forces operating in the British Mandate of Palestine disguised as women and hiding behind civilians, who initiated the fighting at Deir Yassin, April 9, 1948. Later on, the Arabs would portray Deir Yassin as an Israeli "massacre." According to Menachem Begin, head of the National Military Organization in the Land of Israel—commonly known as the *Irgun*—(and later Prime Minister of Israel, 1977–83):

> The hostile propaganda disseminated throughout the world, deliberately ignored the fact that the civilian population of Deir Yassin was actually given a warning by us before the battle began. One of our tenders [ancillary vehicle] carrying a loud speaker was stationed at the entrance of the village and it exhorted in Arabic, all women and children and aged to leave their houses and to take shelter on the slope of the hill. By giving this humane warning our fighters threw away the element of complete surprise, and thus increased their own risk in the ensuing battle.[156]

Jerusalem *Haganah* intelligence officer Mordechai Gihon led two reconnaissance sorties into Ein Kerem, adjacent to Deir Yassin, and returned with documents revealing regular contacts between Deir Yassin and the bases of Syrian and Iraqi volunteer soldiers in Ein Kerem. On March 30, 1948, Gihon reported to his superiors "150 men, mostly Iraqis, entered Deir Yassin."[157] Some of the *Haganah's* information about developments in Deir Yassin was coming directly from inside the village itself. A *Haganah* agent code-named *Ovadia,* working in the Jerusalem area for the *Haganah's* Arabic Department, met regularly with Deir Yassin residents as well as their *mukhtar,* or village chief, who was a paid *Haganah* informant.[158]

In 1969, Israel's leftist Labor government (hardly sympathetic to Begin's right-wing Herut party) issued an extensive rebuttal of the 1948 accusations of a "massacre"[159] at Deir Yassin. The Information Division of the Foreign Ministry, at that time under Foreign Minister Abba Eban, issued a nine-page pamphlet on the battle of Deir Yassin. The 1948 accusations were made at the time of the alleged "massacre," by the Arabs, their supporters and the Labor Zionist-controlled Jewish Agency as well as the *Haganah* out to score some political points, to discredit the *Irgun* and *LEHI*, Labor's right-wing political rivals.

The pamphlet began by denouncing the massacre accusation as a "fairy-tale" and as "the 'big lie' of Deir Yassin."[160] Additionally, the pamphlet described how the *Irgun* fighters issued Arabic-language announcements, prior to the attack, urging the residents to flee. "Some two hundred villagers did come out and took shelter on the lower slopes of the hill on which Dir [Deir] Yassin was perched," the pamphlet reported. "None of them, during or after the fighting, was hurt or molested in the slightest, and all were afterwards transported to the fringe of the Arab-held fifth of East Jerusalem and there released."[161] The battle was dominated by "fierce house-to-house fighting," the pamphlet noted. "Most of the stone buildings were defended hotly and were captured only after grenades were lobbed through their windows."

According to Begin:

> Our men were compelled to fight for every house, to overcome the enemy [and] they used large numbers of hand grenades. The civilians who had disregarded our warnings, suffered inevitable casualties." [Begin emphasized] "The education which we give our soldiers throughout the years of the revolt was based on the observance of the international laws of war. We never broke them unless the enemy first did so and thus, forced us, in accordance with the accepted custom of war, to apply reprisals.[162]

> [Some Arabs] attempted to escape in women's dress. When approached, they opened fire. They were discovered to be wearing Iraqi military uniforms under the disguise. Inside the house, the Jewish fighters were horror-stricken to find that, side-by-side with those of combatant Palestinians and Iraqis, were the bodies of women and children. Either these luckless villagers had trusted in the Arab soldiers to beat off the attack or had been prevented from leaving the village with the others when the opportunity was given before the fighting began or perhaps had been afraid to go. Whatever the reason, they were the innocent victims of a cruel war and the responsibility for their deaths rests squarely upon the Arab soldiers whose duty it was under any rule of war to evacuate them the moment that they turned Dir Yassin into a fortress. This was no massacre of an unarmed, peaceful village population by a military unit as Arab propaganda pretends; the *Irgun* fought and won a battle, there was no aftermath of outrage or brutal excess.[163]

In a direct rebuke to what Labor Zionist leaders had claimed twenty-one years earlier, the 1969 Foreign Ministry pamphlet emphasized that while Arab propagandists had made much use of the statements issued by the Jewish Agency and the *Haganah* in 1948, in fact "the Agency and the *Haganah* were in no position to 'admit' or 'contradict' anything [concerning the massacre allegation], as their defense units did not take part in the battle nor could they have known at first-hand of the circumstances in which civilian casualties had been caused."[164]

Despite their having the initiative and advantage of a surprise attack, Egypt and Syria, aided by the forces of other Arab states, were militarily defeated by the IDF in the Yom Kippur War of October 1973. With that in mind, terror attacks against civilians became the weapon of choice for Israel's enemies—the Arab/Muslim states and the terrorist organizations they sponsored.

The PLO pioneered the tactic of operating in civilian surroundings during the Israel–PLO War in Lebanon in 1982. Testimony of this exploitation of innocent civilians came from the Lebanese who in effect were the hostages, "Palestinian fighters took their guns and placed them next to our [Lebanese civilian] homes, next to apartment blocks and hospitals and schools. At their own Ayn Hilweh camp the Palestinians actually put their guns on the roof of the hospital." Such tactics are in clear violation of the Geneva Convention. Article 58–Precautions against the effects of attacks stipulates:

> The Parties to the conflict shall, to the maximum extent feasible:
>
> (a) Without prejudice to Article 49 of the Fourth Convention, endeavor to remove the civilian population, individual civilians and civilian objects under their control from the vicinity of military objectives;
>
> (b) Avoid locating military objectives within or near densely populated areas
>
> (c) Take the other necessary precautions to protect the civilian population, individual civilians and civilian objects under their control against the dangers resulting from military operations.[165]

After Iraq's attack on, conquest of, and illegal annexation of Kuwait in 1990, Iraqi President Saddam Hussein employed the use of human shields to protect himself from a "decapitating" attack on himself and his government, as well as shields around Iraqi military and industrial installations. Hundreds of Western hostages were detained. On November 29, 1990, the UN Security Council passed United Nations Security Council Resolution 678, which authorized "use [of] all necessary means to uphold and implement" United Nations Security Council Resolution 660 "to restore international peace and security" if Iraq did not withdraw its forces from Kuwait and free all foreign hostages by January 15, 1991. This was the UN authorization for the Gulf War that ensued.

Thus, what was started in Lebanon in 1982 became a long-standing practice. It was the placement of terrorist fighters dressed in civilian garb within densely populated civilian areas and structures, using heretofore off limit positions such as hospitals, clinics, kindergartens, schools, playgrounds, mosques, and UN facilities. Hidden behind, adjacent to and within these structures were weapons positions, rocket launching sites, munitions storage facilities, as well as command and control centers. This all became a definitive, deliberate, and systematic policy among some Middle East regimes and virtually all terrorist organizations fighting the United States, NATO, and Israel.

Hezbollah copied and improved the tactic in southern Lebanon and put it into practice very effectively during the Second Lebanon War of 2006. Hamas in the Gaza Strip, tutored by Hezbollah and Iran, followed suit during the First (2008–09), Second (2012) and Third (2014) Gaza Wars. The United States faced these tactics in Iraq and Afghanistan. Islamic supremacists have long hid among civilians, knowing of Israeli and American reluctance to cause collateral damage. Thus, endangering civilians has become central to their strategy. When civilians are killed as inevitably some will be, or even when some pretend to be dead for propaganda purposes, their pictures are put on television and the Internet as proof of the West's ferocity, barbarism and heartlessness. The weapon of "world opinion" is unleashed to curb the forces fighting the terrorist aggression and evil.

During the Second Lebanon War of 2006, Hezbollah used human shields to protect installations and key personnel. Hezbollah used high-density residential areas as launch pads for rockets and heavy-caliber weapons. Dressed in civilian clothing so they could quickly disappear, the terrorists carried automatic assault rifles and rode in trucks mounted with cannon. Photos were taken by Australian journalist Chris Link who reported several incidents of the use of human shields in the Christian area of Wadi Chahrour in East Beirut. These included a group of men and youths preparing to fire an anti-aircraft gun yards from an apartment block with sheets hanging out on a balcony to dry. Another photo depicted the remnants of a Hezbollah Katyusha rocket in the middle of a residential block blown up in an Israeli air attack. [166]

Moreover, Iran used the cover of the Iranian Red Crescent to smuggle intelligence agents and missiles into Lebanon during the Second Lebanon War, according to a leaked US Embassy cable dated October 2008. The cable, which originated in Dubai, was based on a meeting between a US diplomat and an unnamed source. According to the cable, the Iranian Revolutionary Guard Corps smuggled officers into Lebanon during the 2006 war with Hezbollah under the guise of Red Crescent officials.[167] At the conclusion of the 2006 Second Lebanon War, Hezbollah immediately began to rearm and reconstruct its military infrastructure. The use of densely populated civilian areas as sites for bunkers, strong points and weapons caches continued. In mid-2010, it was revealed that Hezbollah even established military positions in a home for mentally handicapped children, in the southern Lebanon village of Aita al-Shaab.[168]

The Hamas terrorist group in the Gaza Strip used UN ambulances to evacuate armed terrorists from clashes with Israeli forces. Article 38, paragraph 1, of Protocol 1 of the Geneva Convention clearly states, "It is prohibited to make improper use of the distinctive emblem of the Red Cross, Red Crescent or Red Lion and Sun or of other emblems, signs or signals provided for by the Conventions or by this Protocol."[169]

In a much-noted case, on May 24, 2004, a video tape filmed by Reuters, broadcast on numerous television networks worldwide, showed two ambulances arriving at the site where an exchange of fire took place between the IDF and terrorist operatives during an IDF action in the Gaza Strip. One of the ambulances was clearly marked with a Red Crescent and "UN," and flying a UN flag. The ambulances, which belonged to UNRWA evacuated two terrorists wearing uniforms accompanying a wounded terrorist who was armed and in uniform. Two other armed terrorists (one masked), apparently unconnected to the wounded man, could also be seen getting into the ambulance after them, using it to escape. It should be noted that this occurred a full year before Israel's total withdrawal from the Gaza Strip.

During the 2008–09 First Gaza War, Hamas used human shields again. Indeed, Fathi Hamad, a Hamas member of parliament, proudly told Al-Aqsa TV (the Hamas-controlled station) that it was Hamas policy to use "women, children and the elderly" as "human shields."[170] Several examples provide evidence of this. One example was from a correspondent for Australia's *Sydney Morning Herald* who interviewed a Gazan ambulance driver who described how Hamas operatives tried to force him to use his ambulance to evacuate them from a battle zone.[171] Another correspondent for the *New York Times* quoted a source close to Hamas who described rocket fire from close proximity to residential buildings and in alleys. Yet another example involved an Italian journalist, Lorenzo Cremonesi, a correspondent for Italy's *Corriere della Sera*, talk to Gazans who testified about rocket fire from the roofs of private houses and about Hamas operatives who sought shelter in a hospital.

Members of a Gaza family whose farm was turned into a "fortress" by Hamas fighters reported that they were helpless to stop Hamas from using them as human shields. As reported in the official PLO/PA daily, *Al-Hayat Al-Jadida*:

> The Abd Rabbo family kept quiet while Hamas fighters turned their farm in the Gaza strip into a fortress. Right now they are waiting for the aid promised by the [Hamas] movement after Israel bombed the farm and turned it into ruins.

> The hill on which the Abd Rabbo family lives overlooks the Israeli town of Sderot, which turned it into an ideal military position for the Palestinian fighters, from which they have launched hundreds of rockets into southern Israel during the last few years. Several of the Abd Rabbo family members described how the fighters dug tunnels under their houses, stored arms in the fields and launched rockets from the yard of their farm during the nights.

> The Abd Rabbo family members emphasize that they are not [Hamas] activists and that they are still loyal to the Fatah movement, but that they were unable to prevent the armed squads from entering their neighborhood at night. One family member, Hadi (age 22) said: 'You can't say anything to the resistance [Hamas], or they will accuse you of collaborating [with Israel] and shoot you in the legs.[172]

During the Israeli retaliation for the incessant rocket fire—Operation *Cast Lead*—Hamas operatives made several attempts to commandeer the Al-Quds Hospital's (located in the Tel al-Hawa neighborhood in Gaza City) fleet of ambulances to move terrorists, thus copying their tactics from 2004. Ambulances and vehicles belonging to international organizations were used during fighting to evade being examined and to exploit the freedom of movement the IDF gave such vehicles. Armed Hamas operatives used them to leave battle zones and move these terrorists to wherever the wounded were taken. In addition, during Operation *Cast Lead* Hamas terrorists operated from hospitals—including Shifa Hospital (the largest) in Gaza,[173]—mosques, schools, private residences and numerous other civilian installations, correctly assuming that the Israeli security forces would not enter medical institutions and would abstain from attacking these civilian installations. These practices made distinguishing between civilians and combatants extremely difficult for the IDF.[174]

Hamas used Palestinian children in combat-support roles, according to accounts by the children themselves. The Israeli-Arab newspaper *Kul-Al-Arab* published an interview with a child from Gaza on January 9, 2009, during Operation *Cast Lead,* in which the child described how he helped Hamas fighters during their operations, "We the children, in small groups and in civilian clothes, are fulfilling missions of support for the [Hamas] Resistance fighters, by transmitting messages about the movements of the enemy forces, or by bringing them ammunition and food."[175] Furthermore, in the case of the Gaza Strip, since 2005 Hamas used child labor to help build the smuggling and attack tunnels. Some 160 Palestinian children died during this tunnel construction.[176]

Hamas fired rockets and mortars from built up areas amidst the civilian population of the Gaza Strip.[177] Weapons were also hidden in mosques, schoolyards and civilian houses, and the leadership's war room was a bunker beneath Gaza's Shifta (its largest) hospital. The Hamas terrorists fought in civilian clothes and the police were ordered to take off their uniforms.[178]

A journalist for *Newsweek* described one such incident, "It was 11:30 p.m. on January 17, in a complex of apartment buildings at the Nuseirat refugee camp in the Gaza Strip ... then suddenly there was a terrific whoosh, louder even than a bomb explosion. It was another of Hamas' homemade Qassam rockets being launched into Israel—and the mobile launch pad was smack in the middle of the four buildings, where every apartment was full."[179] [180] It should be noted that far from being just "homemade" rockets (as if they were some sort of toy), the Qassams carry a payload of 20 pounds of TNT and were packed with some 7,000 ball bearings, designed to riddle bodies in order to maim, cripple and kill.[181]

Additional confirmation of Hamas's use of civilians and homes was revealed in a detailed 500-page report written by the Intelligence and Terrorism Information Center (Malam), a small research group led by Col. (res.) Reuven Erlich, a former Military Intelligence officer who works closely with the IDF.[182] The report was released March 15, 2010, which included declassified videos. Hamas terrorists used Palestinian children as human shields, fired rockets next to schools and medical facilities as well as civilian homes serving as command centers during Operation *Cast Lead*. An entire section of the report explained how Hamas's police and internal security forces were involved in military-terrorist activities and were not, as the Goldstone Report claimed, civilian entities whose only duty was enforcing law and order. [183] Furthermore, Hamas established Qassam rocket launch pads in and near more than 100 mosques. The report also revealed the extensive deployment of improvised explosive devices (IEDs) and snipers inside and adjacent to civilian homes. Moreover, Hamas fired at IDF troops from positions adjacent to as well as hid weaponry and senior operatives inside at least eight hospitals.[184] The IDF and the *Shin Bet* ("General Security Service") cooperated with the report's authors and declassified hundreds of photographs, videos, prisoner interrogations and Hamas-drawn sketches as part of an effort to counter the criticism leveled at Israel in the UN-sponsored Goldstone Report. Thus, there should be no question as to who was responsible for the civilian deaths during the IDF operation. It was Hamas who by its cold-blooded calculations helped kill the Palestinian people who had entrusted their safety and welfare to them.

According to aerial photographs taken during the Second Gaza War, in November 2012, an Iranian-manufactured and supplied Fajr-5 missile launch pad was established in the heavily populated Zeitoun district of Gaza. The site was set up by Hamas just half a block from a mosque and children's playground, as well as about a half a block away from two civilian factories and a gas station.[185]

During the Third Gaza War (2014), photos once again revealed that Hamas continued the long-standing practice of placing rocket launching sites, munitions storage facilities, as well as command and control centers within densely populated civilian areas and structures. These included hospitals, clinics, kindergartens, schools, playgrounds, mosques, and UN facilities. These photos revealed that such was the case at Al-Wafa Hospital (photo revealed a Grad rocket), the Abu Ayn mosque (M75 rocket), a children's playground (M75 rocket) and even the Tufa Cemetery (unidentified but clearly visible rocket) — in the eastern Gaza City neighborhood of Shuja'iyya.[186] It should be noted that Al-Wafa hospital was the entry of a Hamas attack tunnel that extended over one mile to Kibbutz Kfar Aza on the Israeli side of the border. Five other attack tunnels in the immediate area were also to facilitate Hamas attacks on Nahal Oz and Sa'ad—two other towns on the Israeli side of the frontier.[187] As mentioned previously over forty attack tunnels were constructed with the aim of a mass terror attack against Israeli towns scheduled on or about the Rosh Hashana (Jewish New Year) holiday on September 24, 2014. The purpose was to kill and kidnap as many Israeli civilians as possible—men, women, and children (including kindergarteners). All these examples were but the tip of the iceberg.

Turning to Iran, it was revealed in September 2009, that the regime had hidden several of its nuclear weapons production facilities within or near large urban areas. One of those sites is in an east Tehran suburb, another beyond Teheran itself. A major enrichment site Fordow was discovered in a mountain, near Qom, Iran's holiest city. Iran's leadership dispersed their nuclear program across urban areas and deep underground. It would be impossible to strike these sites effectively without inflicting thousands of civilian casualties. If the plant near Qom were attacked, it would be viewed as a direct attack on Shi'a Islam for violating a holy city. A strike on those Tehran detonator factories would result in severe collateral damage—and the probable spread of radioactive material, an instant "dirty bomb."[188]

During the Libyan Civil War of 2011, Libyan leader Muammar Qadhafi assembled his people at potential targets of expected coalition bombing raids. Furthermore, he moved troops in civilian vehicles around his nation to avoid them being struck. On March 20, 2011, during the second day of Operation *Odyssey Dawn*, a British general reported the allies called off a bombing raid for fear that it would strike civilians, 300 of whom formed a human shield around Muammar Qaddafi's compound in Tripoli, Libya.[189] As the Libyan Civil War continued, NATO reported that Qadhafi's forces were using human shields in the war-torn town of Misrata including the use of civilian vehicles and hiding heavy armor within densely populated civilian areas.[190]

Since 1948, Israel's enemies and detractors have sought to eliminate Israel through multiple strategies: conventional war, perpetual acts of terror, economic boycott, isolation, and threats of WMDs. They seek to engulf Israel demographically and wage an ongoing international campaign to denounce, defame, denigrate, demonize and delegitimize the Jewish state with charges of "human rights" violations and attacks on Arab civilians. Israel's enemies seek to deny Israel's legitimate right of self-defense and its use of military force to defend its citizens from attack. The international community was treated to a most eloquent testimony by a non-partisan (in the Arab-Israeli conflict), testifying at the United Nations Human Rights Council (UNHRC) about Israel's actions in conflict. Colonel Richard Kemp, the former British commander in Afghanistan delivered the following oral testimony to the UNHRC on October 16, 2009:

Thank you, Mr. President.

I am the former commander of the British forces in Afghanistan. I served with NATO and the United Nations; commanded troops in Northern Ireland, Bosnia and Macedonia; and participated in the Gulf War. I spent considerable time in Iraq since the 2003 invasion, and worked on international terrorism for the UK Government's Joint Intelligence Committee.

Mr. President, based on my knowledge and experience, I can say this: During Operation *Cast Lead*, the Israeli Defense Forces did more to safeguard the rights of civilians in a combat zone than any other army in the history of warfare.

Israel did so while facing an enemy that deliberately positioned its military capability behind the human shield of the civilian population.

Hamas, like Hezbollah, are expert at driving the media agenda. Both will always have people ready to give interviews condemning Israeli forces for war crimes. They are adept at staging and distorting incidents.

The IDF faces a challenge that we British do not have to face to the same extent. It is the automatic, Pavlovian presumption by many in the international media, and international human rights groups, that the IDF are in the wrong, that they are abusing human rights.

The truth is that the IDF took extraordinary measures to give Gaza civilians notice of targeted areas, dropping over 2 million leaflets, and making over 100,000 phone calls. Many missions that could have taken out Hamas military capability were aborted to prevent civilian casualties. During the conflict, the IDF allowed huge amounts of humanitarian aid into the Gaza Strip. To deliver aid virtually into your enemy's hands is, to the military tactician, normally quite unthinkable. But the IDF took on those risks.

Despite all of this, of course innocent civilians were killed. War is chaos and full of mistakes. There have been mistakes by the British, American and other forces in Afghanistan and in Iraq, many of which can be put down to human error. But mistakes are not war crimes.

More than anything, the civilian casualties were a consequence of Hamas' way of fighting. Hamas deliberately tried to sacrifice its own civilians.

Mr. President, Israel had no choice apart from defending its people, to stop Hamas from attacking them with rockets.

And I say this again: the IDF did more to safeguard the rights of civilians in a combat zone than any other army in the history of warfare.[191]

Thank you, Mr. President. [192]

Unfortunately, while the UNHRC listened to Colonel Kemp, they did not get the message nor act upon it. During the Third Gaza War Hamas once again reverted to all the practices described above to portray Israel, the victim of aggression, as the uncaring aggressor and Hamas, the aggressor as the "victim" of legitimate Israeli self-defense. Furthermore, it must be stressed, that for the entire history of the Arab/Muslim onslaught against Israel, increasingly so during the past five decades, there has been a perverse fallacious moral equivalency made between unintentional civilian casualties and intentionally targeted civilians. Though civilians unfortunately wind up dead in either case, intent is everything where morality is concerned. In fact, no other country in the history of warfare has gone to such lengths as Israel, to avoid harming an enemy civilian population.

54. Since 1973, every Arab state or terrorist organization that has gone to war against Israel has benefited from their aggression.

After the Arab-initiated Yom Kippur War of 1973, Israel gradually but totally withdrew from the Sinai Peninsula, and from the eastern salient of the Golan Heights (*see* "Disengagement, 1974" and "Disengagement, 1975" maps).

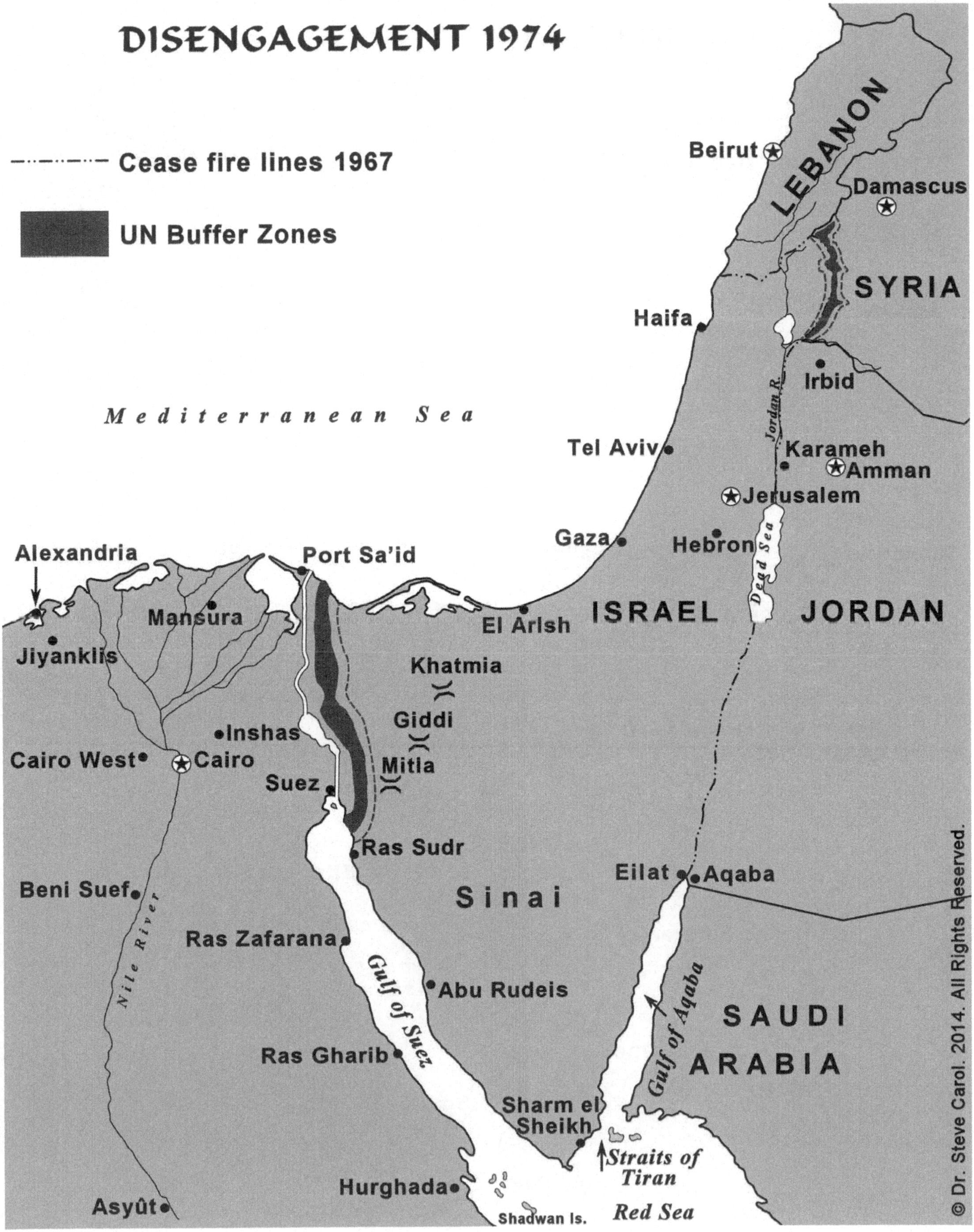

DISENGAGEMENT 1974
Cease fire lines 1967
UN Buffer Zones
Mediterranean Sea
LEBANON
Beirut
Damascus
SYRIA
Haifa
Irbid
Jordan R.
Tel Aviv
Karameh
Amman
Jerusalem
Gaza
Hebron
Dead Sea
Alexandria
Port Sa'id
Mansura
El Arish
ISRAEL
JORDAN
Jiyanklis
Khatmia
Giddi
Inshas
Cairo West
Cairo
Mitla
Suez
Ras Sudr
Eilat
Aqaba
Beni Suef
Sinai
Nile River
Ras Zafarana
Gulf of Suez
Abu Rudeis
Gulf of Aqaba
SAUDI
ARABIA
Ras Gharib
Sharm el Sheikh
Straits of Tiran
Hurghada
Asyût
Shadwan Is.
Red Sea
© Dr. Steve Carol. 2014. All Rights Reserved.

DISENGAGEMENT 1975

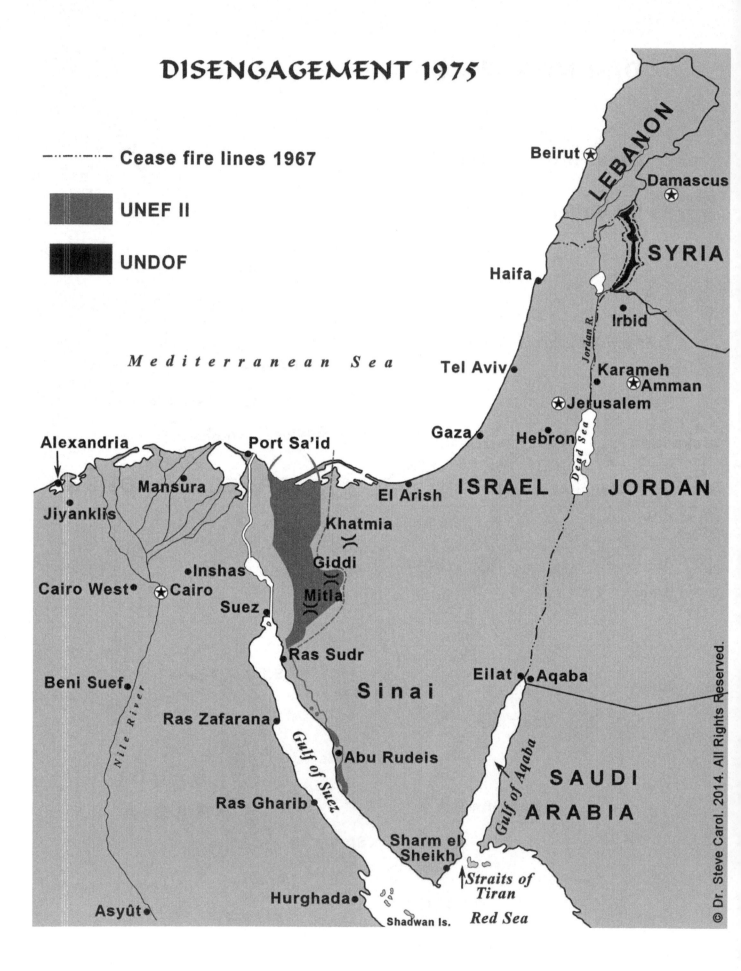

------ Cease fire lines 1967

UNEF II

UNDOF

Mediterranean Sea

LEBANON

Beirut ✪

Damascus ✪

SYRIA

Haifa

Irbid

Jordan R.

Tel Aviv

Karameh

✪Amman

✪Jerusalem

Gaza

Hebron

Dead Sea

ISRAEL

JORDAN

Alexandria

Port Sa'id

Mansura

El Arish

Jiyanklis

Khatmia

Giddi

Inshas

Mitla

Cairo West ✪ Cairo

Suez

Beni Suef

Ras Sudr

Eilat ● Aqaba

S i n a i

Ras Zafarana

Nile River

Gulf of Suez

Abu Rudeis

Gulf of Aqaba

SAUDI

ARABIA

Ras Gharib

Sharm el
Sheikh

Hurghada

↑*Straits of
Tiran*

Asyût

Shadwan Is.

Red Sea

After the 1982 PLO war against Israel in Lebanon, Israel withdrew from most of Lebanon in July 1985 and from its security zone in southern Lebanon by May 2000. After the Oslo Accords of 1993, Israel withdrew from Jericho, Gaza City, (both in 1994) and later from other major Arab cities in Judea and Samaria. Between 1995 and 1997, the Palestinian Authority was given civilian control over 98 percent of the Palestinian Arab population of the Gaza Strip, as well as Judea and Samaria. Israel did this because of Palestinian Arab pledges to stop terrorism and attacks on Israel and its citizens. This process culminated in a total Israeli withdrawal from the entire Gaza Strip in August 2005. For its trouble, Israel was attacked which resulted in four wars, suicide bombings and continued terrorism.

55. Since the early 1960s, several Arab/Muslim states have engaged in development of, threats to use, and actual usage of biological, chemical and nuclear weapons— weapons of mass destruction—WMDs.

Given the close proximity of countries as well as various ethnic and religious groups, it would seem obvious that many unintended and innocent people would become victims of any use of WMDs in the region. The Qur'an stipulates and sanctions (3:140–141) that anyone killed by accident or incident during an attack on unbelievers (including Jews, Christians, Hindus, Sikhs, Buddhists, Zoroastrians, Bahá'ís, animists and others) is automatically a martyr, with all the benefits of martyrdom. Thus, any such collateral damage to other Muslim states or individuals, which occurs during an attack on Israel, for example, is more than justified by the horrors happening to the Jews and Israel.

EGYPT

Some of the earliest attempts to acquire WMD occurred in Egypt in the late 1950s. One was code-named Project *Ibis,* which sought to produce warheads containing radioactive material. A second project, code-named *Cleopatra,* was geared to producing nuclear warheads. In mid-1959, the Egyptian military established the Bureau of Special Military Programs,[193] charged with developing both missiles and jet fighters. General Mahmoud Khalil, former head of intelligence of the Egyptian Air Force, a close friend of Egypt's President Gamal Abdel Nasser, was placed in charge of this bureau and secretly recruited German technicians, engineers and scientists (including ex-Nazis) to build aircraft factories, missile production facilities and other "projects" in Egypt. Nasser was determined to confront and destroy Israel. He failed in 1956. These new projects he believed would give him the edge and lead to victory. By this display of power, Nasser also hoped to unify the Arab world under Egyptian hegemony (*see* "Nasser's Ambitions–Hegemony in the Arab World" map). While achieving a short-lived union with Syria (1958–61) Nasser tried a grand slam regional bid at "unification" in mid-1958, but was stymied by the intervention of the United States and the United Kingdom (*see* "Western Intervention Saves Moderate Regimes, 1958" map).

On November 29, 1959, Willy Messerschmitt, aircraft designer and manufacturer of World War II fame, agreed to build a jet plane factory in Egypt. This would enable Nasser to continue not only to purchase weapons from the Soviet Union, but also to produce far more planes with which to overwhelm Israel by sheer numbers. In 1964, Messerschmitt produced Egypt's first domestically manufactured jet fighter, the Hulwan 300 (HA-300). However, as Egypt ran out of money it could ill afford to try to produce its own domestic jet fighters, besides the Soviet Union was a dependable source of such aircraft acquired by barter, rather than cash.

German scientists began arriving in Egypt, during the spring of 1960. Eventually some forty-four would be there. These included Dr. Paul Görke, whose specialty was radar and infrared rays, Dr. Eugene Sänger of the Institute of Research on Jet Propulsion in Stuttgart, Dr. Hans Kleinwachter, an electronics expert who had worked on V-2 rockets, and Dr. Wolfgang Piltz, a rocket designer and propulsion expert. Piltz had also worked on the V-2 at Peenemünde, Germany, during World War II for Hitler and would head Nasser's missile program. These scientists were joined by some 200 engineers and technicians.

In the meanwhile, the Israeli Mossad had learned of the Egyptian recruitment plans and sought to gather further information on the significance of all of these Egyptian covert activities. Isser Harel, then the head of Mossad (and captor of Nazi war criminal, Adolf Eichmann on May 11, 1960), viewed the Egyptian missile program, aided by the German scientists, as an existential threat to the Jewish state. At the time, the Mossad had at least one agent in Egypt—blond, blue eyed, six-foot tall Wolfgang Lotz. Lotz, a Jew of German birth, appeared on the social scene in Europe late in 1960, seemingly a wealthy man on "grand tour" of the European capitals. When he arrived in Paris, he was given the assignment to find out what the secret Egyptian projects were and to try to keep tabs on the German scientists. By 1961, Israeli spy Lotz had settled in Cairo, Egypt, where he was able to penetrate the small German community living there. He was also able to keep in contact with Mossad back in Tel Aviv.

The Egyptians set up a series of covert companies in order to purchase the materials and other essential products needed for these programs. From mid-1958, Hassan Sayed Kamil, an Egyptian-Swiss arms dealer, provided Egypt with material and recruits from West Germany, Austria and Switzerland. He was the director and joint owner of two front companies, MECO (Mechanical Corporation) and MPT (Motors, Turbines and Pumps), in Zurich, Switzerland, that procured important hardware for Nasser's rocket and jet fighter programs. Another bogus company was "Intra-Handel" based in Munich and Stuttgart that was headed by Dr. Heinz Krug. It was the front company for Factory 333. Three secret factories were built out in the Egyptian desert. They were, "Factory 36" where supersonic jet fighters were to be constructed, "Factory 135" where jet engines were to be produced, and "Factory 333" erected ten miles east of Cairo, where medium-range liquid-fueled missiles were to be made. In less than one year, "Factory 333" produced two liquid-fueled ballistic missiles: Al-Zafir ("The Victor"), which could carry a 400 lb. warhead at a range of 230 miles, and Al-Kahir ("The Conqueror") which could carry a one-ton warhead at a range of 372 miles. On the drawing boards and planned was a two-staged missile, Al-Ared ("The Vanguard") which would have a range of 590 miles.

On July 21, 1962, Egypt successfully test-fired four missiles for the public—two Al-Zafirs and two Al-Kahirs. Two days later on July 23, 1962—the Tenth Anniversary of Egypt's Revolution (the military coup that brought Gamal Abdel Nasser to power)—these missiles were displayed during the traditional military parade honoring the event. Nasser boasted, "Our missiles can reach any point south of Beirut," which of course included all of Israel. On September 1, 1962, Egypt released a postage stamp honoring its new rocket arsenal, with a rocket (emblazoned with the UAR flag) featured prominently on the stamp. Alongside the rocket was an atomic symbol, the meaning of which was clear.

In light of the growing Egyptian missile threat, as well as the flow of Soviet aircraft into Nasser's arsenal, Israel requested from the Eisenhower Administration in its last year, to purchase the HAWK surface-to-air missile for defense. While Secretary of State Christian A. Herter looked favorably on the sale, the State Department and Pentagon opposed it, fearful that it would inflame US–Arab relations and that US military equipment might fall into Soviet hands. Thus, the Israeli request was denied. However, perhaps as a consolation prize, the Eisenhower administration sold Israel 100 recoilless rifles. It was the first time that the United States decided to sell arms to Israel. Israel renewed its request for the HAWKs, with the new Kennedy Administration in 1961. President John F. Kennedy authorized the sale of HAWKs to Israel in August 1962. The United States tried to link the purchase to an Israeli *quid pro quo* that Israel would give a sympathetic hearing to a Palestinian Arab repatriation plan, then being debated on the unrealistic premise that most of the Arabs would turn it down. It was however, only in March 1965, that the first HAWK missile batteries were deployed in Israel.

Nevertheless, the US government under State Department pressure, continued to try to appease Nasser, with economic aid and by appointing an Arabist as US ambassador to Cairo. Kennedy was fooled by Nasser into acquiescing to the Egyptian-sponsored coup in Yemen in September 1962, as well as Egypt's subsequent open military intervention and support of the Republican regime against Royalist forces (*see* the "Yemen Civil War–Coup and Egyptian Intervention" map). The Egyptian support included the use of poison gas by the Egyptians on Yemenite towns and villages, as listed in the next table.

The real goal of Project *Ibis* however was not missile or aircraft production. The missiles that Egypt produced with German assistance lacked the electronic navigations systems needed for teleguidance. As such, they would not be suited for precision bombardment of military targets, but were excellent when fired at urban targets—it did not matter what block of a city was hit—they were "city busters." Then again, if this was Egypt's aim they could have more easily employed the Ilyushin jet bombers that the Soviet Union was supplying to the Egyptian Air Force, which could carry a larger tonnage of explosives. Nasser's long-range goal was to arm the missiles with atomic warheads, but for the moment, he had another plan that could be implemented sooner.

The core concept of Project *Ibis* was to arm 900 missiles of both types, with radioactive warheads. Egypt began purchasing large quantities of radioactive Cobalt 60 for "medical experiments." Ultimately, $4 million worth was purchased on the world market. The amount purchased was three times the amount needed to destroy Israel's entire population and render the country uninhabitable for five years. This without doubt, categorizes the Project *Ibis* plan as one of the first WMD attempts in the Middle East.

By 1962 Israeli spy, Lotz was able to establish the extent of the Egyptian missile program and passed the details on to Israel. Israel quietly appealed to the (West) German government to put pressure on the German scientists to leave Egypt. This was of no avail. On August 20, 1962, Israeli Foreign Minister Golda Meir then appealed to US President John F. Kennedy to put pressure on the German government. Again, nothing happened. Having tried diplomacy the Israelis decided to act on their own. Lotz had already furnished the Mossad with a complete list of the forty-four German scientists and engineers working in Egypt. In August 1962, the Mossad began a campaign—Operation *Damocles*—to scare away and failing that, to kill the German scientists.

In early July 1962, Hassan Sayed Kamil, the arms dealer and German "recruiter," hired a private jet to fly himself and his wife Helene, the Duchess of Mecklenburg, from their vacation on the island of Sylt in Schleswig-Holstein to Düsseldorf. At the last moment he could not go. The plane crashed on July 7, 1962 at Risenbeck,[194] and both Helene and the pilot were killed. It may be just a freak coincidence that the crash came at the time Operation *Damocles* went into effect. The official investigation declared the cause to be mechanical failure, but there was nevertheless some suspicion that the Mossad was behind the accident.

Dr. Heinz Krug, director of Intra-Handel, simply vanished in Munich on September 11, 1962.[195] He was never seen again and was presumed murdered. Rocket scientist Wolfgang Pilz received a package bomb, which exploded on November 27, 1962, severely injuring his secretary. The next day another parcel bomb sent to the Heliopolis rocket factory killed five Egyptian workers. The following day, November 29, two more parcel bombs were intercepted in the Egyptian post office. Dr. Hans Kleinwachter, another rocket scientist with a specialty in electronics, was targeted for assassination on February 12, 1963, while home from Egypt on a visit in Lörrach, Germany, but narrowly escaped when his assassin's weapon malfunctioned.

In mid-February 1963, twenty-five-year-old Heidi Görke, the daughter of radar and infrared rays expert, Dr. Paul Görke, was threatened by Mossad agents near her home in Frieberg, Germany. They urged her to persuade her father to stop his work in Egypt and return home or else it was intimated he would be killed. The Mossad agents were lured into a trap in Switzerland, arrested on March 2, 1963, and stood trial in June. The arrest and trial generated much publicity and put additional pressure on both the West German government and the German scientists. The two Mossad agents were found guilty of attempted coercion, they were sentenced to time served and released.[196] At the same time, West Germany was persuaded to offer the remaining scientists higher paying jobs at home as an inducement to leave Egypt. The Germans got the message and most left Egypt by the end of 1963, though a good number went to Syria. Pilz returned to West Germany in 1965. Lacking skilled scientists, Egypt abandoned the project.

Mossad chief, Isser Harel resigned his position in 1963, in a disagreement with Israeli Prime Minister David Ben-Gurion and Deputy Defense Minister Shimon Peres over Harel's method of dealing with the scientists and the fear of damaging Israel's relations with West Germany. Nevertheless, the combination of the death threats and diplomatic pressure successfully drove the scientists away from Egypt by the end of 1963.

What became of the Cobalt 60? Cobalt 60 has a half-life of five and one-quarter years, so it soon became useless. What became of Wolfgang Lotz? He was captured by the Egyptians in 1965 and imprisoned. After Egypt's massive defeat in the Six-Day War of 1967, Lotz and five other Israeli agents, along with eight Israeli soldiers, were exchanged for some 6,000 Egyptian POWs in Israeli hands.[197]

Chemical Weapons

Turning to chemical WMD, although Egypt acceded to the Geneva Protocol against the use of poison gas on December 6, 1928, Egypt disregarded its provisions during its intervention in Yemen.[198] Beginning in 1963, Egypt used chemical agents i.e. poison gas, against the Royalist regime in the Yemen Civil War (*see* the "Yemen Civil War–Use of Poison Gas and Placement of UNYOM" map). It was the first time that chemical weapons were used in war since the Italians used poison gas against Ethiopia in December 1935. The CIA claimed that the Soviet Union supplied Egypt with new chemical agents and munitions in the early to mid-1960s.[199] Beginning in 1963 and continuing until 1967, Egypt used such weapons on several occasions. The table indicates some of the most noted occurrences.

EGYPTIAN USE OF POISON GAS IN THE YEMEN CIVIL WAR, 1963–67	
Date	**Event**
June 8, 1963	The Egyptians attacked Al-Kawma in northern Yemen. Seven were killed and twenty-five others were injured. This seems to have been an experimental attack. The world learned of the attack through a dispatch by Richard Beeston of the London *Daily Telegraph* on July 8, 1963.
June–July 1963	Eight villages, including al Darb, al Jaraishi, Hasan Bini Awair, al Ashash, and al Kawma, all south of Sadah, were subjected to gas attack.[200]
January 1965	There was an attack on Beit Marran, where the chemical agent caused "eye injuries" to some eighty inhabitants. Attacks were also made on the Jabal Urush region.[201]
March–July 1965	There were several attacks across northern Yemen, including on al-Dhanoob and Sharazeih. Independent journalists stated that it was during this period that the first mustard and phosgene gases were employed.[202]
December 11, 1966	There was an attack on Halbal. Two were killed and thirty-five injured.
December 27–29, 1966	Attacks were made in the Jabal Iyal Yazid region (north of Sana'a). The agent used caused "eye and skin injuries," and there were "scores of victims."[203]
January 4, 1967	There was an attack on Hadda.
January 5, 1967	An attack on Kitaf resulted in over 270 casualties, of which 146 were killed as well as all animals. Immediately following the Kitaf attack, villages in the al Ans area (south of Sana'a), the Bani Matar and al Haymatain areas (west of Sana'a) were subject to gas attack.[204]
January 6, 1967	Gas attacks occurred on Beit Michlaf Doran and Beit Beni Salamah, which killed livestock.
January 7, 1967	An attack on Katar utilized agents that caused "eye and lung injuries," and resulted in 125 dead and over 225 injured.[205]
January 17, 1967	Another attack occurred on the Jabal Iyal Yazid region.
February 9, 1967	An attack on Beni Salamah resulted in seventy dead. The ineffectiveness of the UN was demonstrated on March 1, 1967, when UN Secretary-General U Thant, declared that he was "powerless" to deal with the matter.[206]
April 1967	There was a mustard gas attack on three villages held by Royalist forces in Yemen.[207]
May 3, 1967	A poison gas attack was unleashed on Bassi.
May 7, 1967	An attack was made on the Arhab tribal region, which resulted in 200 killed.[208]

May 10, 1967	Attacks on Gahar and Gadafa took place. In the former, seventy-four were killed along with 200 livestock. At Gadafa, twenty-four were killed. The Egyptians used agents which caused "eye, skin and lung injuries." It was during this period that the Saudi towns of Najran and Qizan, close to the Yemen border were also bombed. Casing from a "gas bomb" used was stamped in Cyrillic alphabet, meaning the chemical agents were supplied by the Soviet Union. Scientists reportedly tested the agent to determine whether it was a new nerve agent. No results were announced.[209] These attacks were verified by the International Red Cross, which did little more than issue a statement of "concern" from its Geneva headquarters on June 2, 1967. Earlier on May 15, 1967, Egyptian bombers attacked two Red Cross vehicles en route to investigate the gassed villages. All the Red Cross equipment was destroyed.[210]
May 17, 1967	A second gas attack on Gadafa killed ninety-six people hiding in a cave.[211]
May 23, 1967	Gas attacks were made on Beit Gadr, Beit Gabas, and Nofal, which resulted in 143 dead. Sirwah, near Marib, was also struck resulting in fifty fatalities.[212]
May 28, 1967	Sirwah was attacked a second time. This resulted in a "large number of casualties," and seventy-two killed. Thirty of the injured were taken to Saudi Arabia for treatment.[213]
June 5–6, 1967	Attacks were made on several villages: Sirwah, Kutat, Boa, Immad, and the Beni Hu-Shaysh district.[214]
July 1967	Despite Egypt's defeat in the Six-Day War, the poison gas attacks resumed: Beni Saham, on July 2, resulting in forty-five killed; Darb Ascar on July 4; Hajjah on July 15, where agents caused "eye and lung injuries," resulting in between 425 and 520 casualties, of which 50 to 150 were fatalities; as well as Mabian and Nejra on July 16, where a total of 217 were killed.[215]

THE YEMEN CIVIL WAR 1962–1970

— Roads

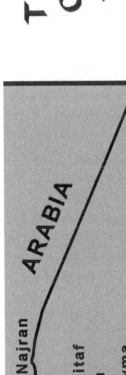

July 4, 1963–Sept. 4, 1964
United Nations Yemen
Observation Mission
(UNYOM)

1963–1967
Egyptian poison gas
attacks

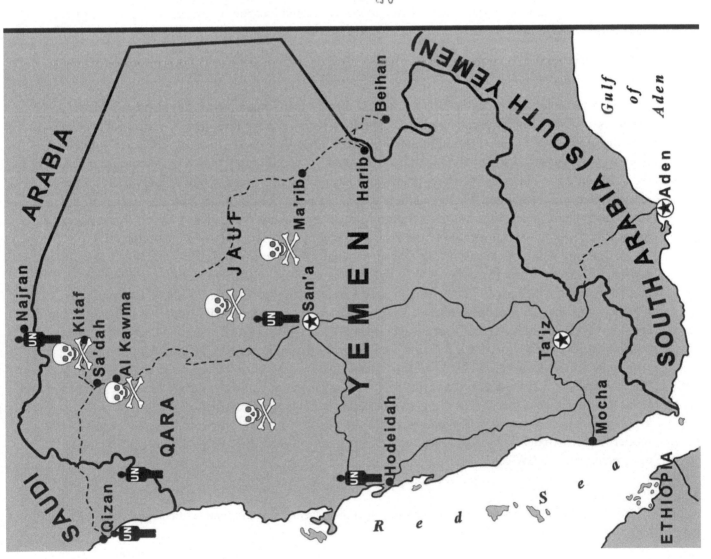

The Egyptian use of various poison gases, including mustard and phosgene gas, in nearly fifty attacks in Yemen resulted by conservative estimates in 1,500 fatalities and 1,500 injuries. There was neither world outcry nor condemnation. As a result, Saudi Arabia was fearful of Egyptian gas attacks on its own territory, since it was aiding the Royalist cause in Yemen. With the major gas attacks coming in May and June 1967, it is reasonable to believe that these were trial runs to measure the effectiveness of both the delivery systems and the results of such attacks, as well as to gauge world reaction—there was virtually none. Recall that Nasser staged-managed the May 1967 lead-up to the planned war with Israel, believing he was in control and had calculated all the angles for a massive Arab victory. Therefore, there can be little doubt that given the chance, Egypt's Nasser would have ordered gas attacks on Israel during his planned destruction of the Jewish state. Egypt's rapid defeat in the Six-Day War temporarily ended that threat.

Prior to the Yom Kippur War of 1973, Egypt actively pursued scientific research and development for the production and improvement of chemical weapons through a host of institutions. The Central Military Chemical Laboratories of the Egyptian Army researched sulfur and nitrogen mustard blister agents, as well as organophosphorous nerve agents such as sarin and VX-related compounds.[216] In 1983, the CIA alleged that Egypt received chemical weapons training, indoctrination and material from the Soviet Union. In recent years, Western intelligence reports asserted that Egypt retains a significant CW program that included blister, blood, nerve and incapacitating agents. To date, Egypt has refused to sign the Chemical Weapons Convention.[*]

Biological weapons

Going on to biological weapons (BW), the first official confirmation that Egypt possessed such weapons or was capable of producing them, came from then Egyptian President Anwar el-Sadat. At a meeting of the Arab Socialist Union National Congress Sadat answered a question about an Egyptian response to a hypothetical Israeli BW attack. He stated, "The only reply to biological warfare is that we too should use biological warfare. Briefly, we have the instruments of biological warfare in the refrigerators and we will not use them unless they [the Israelis] begin to use them."[217] In June of the same year, the Egyptian Minister of the Interior stated "the enemy, [presumably Israel] would never use BW because they are aware that Egypt has adequate means of retaliating without delay."[218]

While Egypt signed, the Biological Weapons Convention on April 10, 1972, to date it has not ratified that treaty. Reconfirmation of Egypt's BW potential was reaffirmed by the US Arms Control and Disarmament Agency (ACDA), which issued a series of reports in the mid-1990s, in compliance with international arms control treaties. These reports regularly noted, "the United States believed that Egypt developed biological warfare agents by 1972. There is no evidence to indicate that Egypt eliminated this capability and it remains likely that the Egyptian capability to conduct biological warfare continues to exist."[219] This statement did not allude to any new evidence since 1972 suggesting the existence of a BW program, nor did it provide evidence of any ongoing BW activities. What is certain however is that Egypt does have basic biotechnology infrastructure that could serve as a potential base for a covert BW program. On the basis of this presumption, Egyptian efforts to modernize or expand its biotechnology and pharmaceutical industries were seen as confirming or even increasing its BW capabilities.

---

[*] Officially named the Convention on the Prohibition of the Development, Production, Stockpiling and Use of Chemical Weapons and on their Destruction.

Missile delivery systems

Egypt began to receive Scud missiles from the Soviet Union in August 1973,[220] in preparation for the Yom Kippur War planned for October of that year. Egypt however did not give up its quest to produce its own missiles. In the 1980s, Egypt cooperated with Iraq and Argentina to develop a 500 to 625-mile range solid-fueled missile, which was designated Condor-II in Argentina, Badr-2000 in Iraq, and Vector or Delta in Egypt.[221] By 1990, pressure from Missile Technology Control Regime (MTCR) member states and financial setbacks resulted in the program's collapse.[222] Since then Egypt has focused on its indigenous Scud-B and Scud-C manufacturing capabilities. With DPRK assistance, Egypt developed a Scud-B production capability, and may have developed an enhanced Scud-C missile.[223] In 2001, Egypt reportedly attempted to acquire 500 to 625-mile range Nodong missiles from the DPRK.[224]

Nuclear weapons

Egypt's efforts to develop nuclear technology began in 1954, when President Gamal Abdel Nasser founded the Egyptian Atomic Energy Commission (now called the Atomic Energy Authority or AEA). Egypt's first (2MW) research reactor, the ETRR-1, was built by the Soviet Union at Inshas in the Nile Delta between 1954 and 1961. As a result of Israel's disclosure of its nuclear facility at Dimona in December 1960, Egypt made intensive efforts to develop nuclear weapons capability or acquire them. The Soviets controlled the disposal of spent fuel from the ETRR-1 reactor, which was in any event not capable of producing a significant amount of weapons-grade material.[225] Nevertheless, Nasser had vowed in 1961, that if Israel acquired such weapons, "we will secure atomic weapons at any costs." Egypt attempted unsuccessfully to obtain nuclear weapons or assistance in making them from the Soviet Union, both before and after the Six-Day War of 1967, as well as from China and India. Nasser received from the Soviets a questionable nuclear guarantee instead and declared that Egypt would develop its own nuclear program.

Although Egypt signed the Nuclear Non-Proliferation Treaty (NPT) in 1968, it did not ratify the treaty. In 1975, the US agreed in principle on a program to supply Egypt with eight nuclear power plants and the necessary cooperation agreements were signed. The plan was subject to a trilateral safeguards agreement signed by the United States, the International Atomic Energy Agency, and Egypt. In the late 1970s, the United States unilaterally revised the bilateral agreements and introduced new conditions that were unacceptable to the Egyptian government.[226] It was at that point that Egypt decided to ratify the NPT on February 26, 1981, with one goal in mind—the implementation of a nuclear power program. In early 1992, a deal was made for Argentina to deliver and install the ETRR-2, a larger (22.5MW) open pool research reactor and it was up and running by 1998. It is a light water reactor capable of producing 6 kilograms of plutonium—enough for one nuclear weapon—per year.

By the early twenty-first century the Egyptian government after decades of indifference, was again strongly interested in investing in a nuclear power program. In late 2004, the IAEA charged Egypt with failing to report uranium irradiation experiments conducted between 1990 and 2003, and to include imports of uranium material in its initial inventory.[227] The IAEA reported the discovery of traces of highly enriched uranium at Egypt's facilities, and in early 2005, it determined that Egypt's nuclear authority had not disclosed either the import of uranium or the experiments. The items found suggested at least the possibility of a secret uranium enrichment program that could be used to produce weapons. Subsequently, the IAEA's then-director, Egyptian Mohamed ElBaradei, did not take action against Egypt for its covert behavior, which the agency treated as minor.

The IAEA found still more traces of highly enriched uranium (HEU) from unreported activity at Inshas in 2007 and 2008. That discovery prompted Pierre Goldschmidt of the Carnegie Endowment for International Peace to write in 2009, "One should remember that the HEU particles found in Iran originated from illicit nuclear trade with Pakistan and were connected with unreported uranium enrichment activities."[228] Again, although it issued a one-page report on the matter in 2008 and kept the investigation open, the agency took no further action.

Early indications of official interest in relaunching Egypt's civilian nuclear power program included Gamal Mubarak's call for Egypt to pursue nuclear energy during a September 2006 National Democratic Party conference.[229] This was followed by his father's (President Hosni Mubarak) announced plans in 2007, to construct four nuclear power plants under IAEA supervision.[230] On August 25, 2010, President Mubarak announced that with IAEA approval, Egypt would build its first nuclear plant at El Dabaa, west of Alexandria on the Mediterranean coast. The estimated operational date is 2019.[231] However, the 2011 political upheaval in Egypt and Mubarak's subsequent removal from power have put these plans on hold. Meanwhile, the determination of Iran to emerge as a nuclear power has triggered similar ambitions within Turkey, Egypt, Saudi Arabia, and the Gulf states.

Despite the ouster of the Morsi government in June 2013, the Egyptian government continued to move ahead in the field of nuclear development. On October 6, 2013, Egypt's interim president, Adly Mansour announced that construction of a 1,000 MW light-water reactor to generate electricity at El-Debaa, 75 miles west of Alexandria, would go ahead. It would be the first of four reactors planned in the country. On November 26, 2013, the respected Middle East news site Al-Monitor reported that Egypt expected to generate $4 billion in grants from interested international companies to finance the project.[232] Egypt's 60-year-old nuclear program is already the third largest in the region, after those of Israel and Iran.

IRAQ

In all the years of Arab/Muslim war against Israel since 1948, Iraq never accepted a ceasefire or armistice with the Jewish state. Iraq participated in three of the early wars against Israel. In 1948, four brigades of the Iraqi army together with artillery, armored vehicles and aircraft deployed west of the Jordan River. They fought Israeli forces, penetrating at one time to within twelve miles of Tel Aviv. During and after the Six-Day War Iraq attacked Israel. On June 5, Iraqi aircraft attacked towns in the Jezreel Valley, Afula and Netanya on the Mediterranean coast. Seven days later on June 11, 1967, to demonstrate its rejection of the United Nations-sponsored ceasefire (which went into effect on June 10), the Iraqis launched an air attack against Israel some thirty hours after the ceasefire went into effect causing civilian casualties. In the Yom Kippur War the Third Iraqi Armored Division, consisting of two brigades of 130 tanks each and a mechanized brigade of 50 tanks, attacked Israeli forces on the Golan Heights on October 12, 1973. Additional Iraqi tanks and forces participated in the fighting until the ceasefire. Thus, there is ample historic proof of Iraq's hostility towards Israel. From the time of his accession to power in 1968, Iraqi strongman Saddam Hussein spurred Iraq's quest for WMD—chemical, biological and nuclear weapons, as well as the means to deliver them.

Chemical weapons

Iraq acceded to the Geneva Protocol banning the first use of chemical weapons in September 1931. Despite its concurrence, Iraq did not ratify that protocol and began working on chemical weapons (CW) capability. Iraq established a Chemical Corps in the mid-1960s, tasked with the nuclear, biological and chemical protection of troops and civilians. The Corps developed a laboratory-scale facility in the early 1970s to gain practical experience in synthesizing CW agents and evaluating their properties. The laboratory's work constituted a necessary step in the training of a core group of laboratory personnel for future research and production of offensive CW. In addition, it contributed to the creation of a support infrastructure and acquisition system for equipment and materials.[233] Iraq's capacity to develop chemical weapons was greatly assisted by its ability to import precursor chemicals, production equipment and obtain technical support from Western suppliers. Iraq succeeded in producing a mustard blister agent as well as the nerve agents tabun, sarin, cyclosarin and VX.

Without a declaration of war, Iraq attacked and invaded Iran on September 22, 1980. The first allegations of Iraqi CW attacks came in November 1980, when Tehran Radio reported Iraqi CW attacks at Susangerd.[234] However, after limited initial successes Iraq experienced a series of military defeats in 1981 and 1982. Thus, Iraq began to employ CW against Iranian forces. It was under the directive of Ali Hassan al-Majid, a first cousin of Iraqi dictator Saddam Hussein, that chemical weapons were used against Iran. Later during the 1991 uprisings, they would be employed against the Kurds in northern Iraq, and the mainly Shi'a Muslim marsh Arabs in southern Iraq.[235] These war crimes earned him the sobriquet of "Chemical Ali." Al-Majid was Iraq's Defense Minister, Interior Minister and head of the Iraqi Intelligence Service—the *Mukhabarat*.

On November 3, 1983, Iran made its first official complaint to the United Nations regarding Iraqi CW attacks.[236] During the Iranian offensive into Iraq of February 14 to March 19, 1984—Operation *Kheibar*—the Iraqis employed both mustard gas and sarin nerve gas[237] to stop the Iranian forces. In March 1985, during the Iranian offensive—Operation *Badr* (1985)—Iraq used the same chemical agents as well as tabun and cyanide.[238] Iraq used chemical agents again in February 1986, during its attempt to retake the Fao Peninsula, then occupied by Iranian forces. In mid-May 1986, Iraq utilized poison gas yet another time in its capture of the Iranian town of Mehran.[239] The use of CW resulted in over 100,000 Iranian casualties.[240] Of that number, "nerve gas killed about 20,000 Iranian soldiers immediately, according to official reports. Of the 90,000 survivors, some 5,000 … [sought] medical treatment regularly and about 1,000 … [were] still hospitalized with severe chronic conditions."[241] Not counted in the totals were civilian casualties in villages along the battlefront. Iraqi use of these weapons was confirmed by the United States in February 1984. Among the weapons used by Iraq was the nerve agent VX, one of the most lethal ever developed.

As has been mentioned above, on March 16–17, 1988, Iraq used poison gas and nerve agents against the Kurdish town of Halabja. Saddam Hussein's forces employed the gas against Kurdish separatists, killing approximately 5,000 civilians. It was the biggest use of chemical weapons against a civilian populated area in history, to that date. By the late 1980s, Iraq not only attempted to develop all categories of WMDs and the systems to carry them, but also actually used such weapons, both against a foreign enemy, Iran, and against its own citizens, Kurds and Arabs. Iraqi Air Force General Georges Hormiz Sada confirmed this chronology stating, "I want to make it clear, very clear to everybody in the world that we had the weapon[s] of mass destruction in Iraq, and the regime used them against our Iraqi people. It was used against Kurds in the north, [and] against Arabs—marsh Arabs in the south."[242]

In the lead up to his invasion of Kuwait, Saddam Hussein boasted on Iraqi TV on April 1, 1990, "We do not need an atomic bomb. We have the dual chemical." He warned the United States, the United Kingdom, and Israel, that Iraq possessed advanced chemical weapons. He boasted of having the "dual chemical" weapon, by which he meant advanced form of binary chemical weapons. Furthermore, he threatened, "we will make the fire eat up half of Israel if it tries to do anything against Iraq."[243] Iraq at that time was capable of producing between 3,000 and 13,000 tons of chemical weapons, including mustard gas and various nerve gases, each year.[244] US experts confirmed within days that Iraq had this capability.[245]

Following the liberation of Kuwait and Iraq's defeat by the United States and allied forces in 1991, Iraq declared to UN inspectors that between 1982 and 1990 it produced 3,859 tons of CW agents and more than 125,000 filled and unfilled special munitions. Most of these special munitions were stored at the Muthanna State Establishment, Iraq's primary CW production, filling, and testing facility. This declaration served as the basis for the United Nations Special Commission (UNSCOM) inspectors' subsequent efforts to verify the destruction of all Iraqi CW agents. However, Saddam never abandoned his intentions to resume a CW effort when sanctions were lifted and conditions were judged favorable.

In the aftermath of the 1991 Persian Gulf War, Iraq admitted to the United Nations that it possessed a large chemical weapons arsenal and that much of it had survived the war. Iraq stated it had nearly 10,000 nerve-gas warheads, more than 1,000 tons of nerve and mustard gas, nearly 1,500 chemical weapons bombs and shells, and 52 Scud missiles armed with 30 chemical and 23 conventional warheads. The United States maintained that the Iraqis underestimated their stockpiles.[246]

According to a document obtained by an UNSCOM inspector in 1998, taken by Iraq and then retrieved by the United Nations Monitoring, Verification and Inspection Commission (UNMOVIC), 13,000 chemical bombs were dropped by the Iraqi Air Force between 1983 and 1988 on Iran. Yet, Iraq declared that 19,500 bombs were consumed during this period. Thus, there was a discrepancy of 6,500 bombs. The amount of chemical agent in those bombs would be in the order of about 1,000 tons of chemical agent. In the absence of evidence to the contrary, it has to be assumed that these were unaccounted quantities.[247]

By December 1998, UNSCOM inspectors had destroyed 38,537 filled and unfilled chemical munitions, 690 metric tons of CW agents, more than 3,275 metric tons of precursor chemicals, over 425 pieces of key production equipment, and 125 pieces of analytical instruments. Taking into account items unilaterally destroyed by Iraq prior to the beginning of inspections, UNSCOM was able to account for the destruction of 88,000 filled and unfilled chemical munitions, over 690 metric tons of weaponized and bulk CW agents, approximately 4,000 metric tons of precursor chemicals, 980 pieces of key production equipment, and 300 pieces of analytical instruments.[248]

UNSCOM's final report to the United Nations Security Council noted a number of outstanding issues arising from efforts to verify the accuracy of Iraq's declarations. These included discrepancies regarding Iraq's use of chemical weapons during the 1980s resulting in UNSCOM being unable to satisfactorily account for 550 artillery shells filled with mustard agent declared to have been lost shortly after the Gulf War and approximately 500 R-400 aerial bombs. UNSCOM was also concerned over a lack of information regarding Iraq's production of VX agent.[249]

In August 1998, Iraq unilaterally declared that all outstanding CW-related disarmament issues had been resolved and effectively ceased to cooperate with UNSCOM. UNSCOM withdrew in December 1998. Operation *Desert Fox* followed this, December 16–19, 1998, in which the United States and the United Kingdom bombed a number of facilities thought to be associated with reviving Iraq's WMD programs. However, the stated purpose of the operation was to "degrade" Iraq's ability to manufacture and use WMD, not to eliminate it.

Recall that one of the justifications for the US-led March 2003 invasion of Iraq was to eliminate the WMD thought to be in Iraq's hands. This goal was supported by the belief that the country had clandestinely amassed large stockpiles of chemical weapons including VX, sarin and mustard blister agent, among other WMD that it had successfully concealed from the United Nations.

With that in mind, on February 3, 2003, US Secretary of Defense Donald Rumsfeld, recommended a military strike on a site near Khurmal in northern Iraq close to the Iranian border. It was operated by Ansar al-Islam, a Sunni jihadist group with ties to Abu Musab al-Zarqawi, a Jordanian extremist who later led the Iraq branch of the Al-Qaeda terrorist network. Evidence showed it was a chemical weapons production facility. Rumsfeld wanted the strike on February 5, 2003, before US Secretary of State Colin Powell made the case for war against the regime of Saddam Hussein at the United Nations.[250] The strike however was not carried out (the site was named in Powell's speech) and the terrorists fled taking with them no doubt, the evidence of WMD.

In April 2003 at an ammo dump near the northern Iraqi town of Bai'ji, elements of the US Fourth Infantry Division (Mech) discovered 55-gallon drums of a substance that mass spectrometer testing confirmed was cyclosarin and an unspecified blister agent. When mixed together these components form nerve gas. A mobile laboratory was also found nearby that could have been used to mix chemicals at the site. Only yards away, surface-to-surface missiles (which had been configured to carry a liquid payload), surface-to-air missiles, as well as gas masks were found.[251]

From 2003, an insurgency swept Iraq against US-led forces, as well as sectarian and ethnic fighting. The insurgents attempted to produce CW or alternatively use industrial chemicals as weapons. Perhaps too, some of these forces knew of still hidden CW stockpiles that UN inspectors had not discovered in a nation the size of California. For example, on March 16, 2007, at least 250 people were injured after exposure to a chlorine gas cloud. Although a small number of victims were hospitalized, no deaths were caused by the released gas. Chlorine gas attacks ended shortly afterwards, but security forces continued to discover chlorine gas canisters in insurgent arms caches as late as early 2008.

US troops found approximately 5,000 chemical warheads, shells, or aviation bombs in the years following the 2003 invasion of Iraq. The agents were discovered around the Muthanna State Establishment northwest of Baghdad, which had been a center of chemical weapons production in the 1980s. A six-line declassified summary of a more than thirty-five page document by the US Army's National Ground Intelligence Center was released on June 1, 2006. It confirmed evidence of WMD in Saddam's Iraq, including both degraded and possibly lethal chemical agents. According to the document, coalition forces recovered some 500 weapon munitions sites since 2003 that contained degraded mustard or sarin nerve agents. The shells dated from the 1980s—during the Iran–Iraq War—and the number of weapons found would not have posed much of a threat to protected troops, but could be devastating to civilians (Saddam used fewer than twenty such munitions to kill the estimated 5,000 Kurds at Halabja in 1988). Army Colonel John Chu told the House Armed Services Committee, "These are chemical weapons as defined under the Chemical Weapons Convention, and yes … they do constitute weapons of mass destruction."[252] The munitions found contained sarin and mustard gases, said Army Lt. Gen. Michael D. Maples, director of the Defense Intelligence Agency. Sarin attacks the neurological system and is potentially lethal. General Maples said, "Mustard is a blister agent [that] actually produces burning of any area [where] an individual may come in contact with the agent." It also is potentially fatal if it gets into a person's lungs.[253] Other key points were that these chemical agents could be used outside Iraq. Most significant was the assertions that while agents degrade over time, "chemical warfare agents remain hazardous and potentially lethal," according to the released document. Maples added that he did not believe Iraq was a "WMD-free zone."[254] Iraq completed the domestic legislative requirements for accession to the Chemical Weapons Convention (CWC) in November 2007. On January 13, 2009, Iraq submitted its accession document to the United Nations and became the 186th CWC member nation on February 12, 2009.[255]

Nevertheless, as late as 2010, Iraqi troops discovered chemical weapons that appeared to have been collected elsewhere by US or Iraqi army units and had not been secured properly. The Muthanna State complex has been held by ISIL jihadist forces since June 2014 and it was estimated that some 2,500 chemical rockets containing sarin gas and mustard gas fell into ISIL hands.[256] In early July 2014, evidence indicated that some of these chemical weapons were used by ISIL against Kurdish forces protecting the town of Kobanê, Syria.[257] These revelations leave no doubt. Iraq had and still has WMD. Now in the hands of a terrorist army, who knows how many will die?

Biological weapons

Despite its 1972 signing of the Biological and Toxic Weapons Convention that prohibited the development, production and stockpiling of biological weapons, Iraq began an offensive biological weapon (BW) program in 1985. By 1990, this program had produced 25 missile warheads and 166 four hundred-pound aerial bombs that were filled with anthrax, botulinum toxin or aflatoxin. Furthermore, Iraq acknowledged production of approximately 20,000 liters of botulinum toxin solution, 8,425 liters of anthrax solution, and 2,200 liters of aflatoxin. Iraq also admitted to having researched the weapons potential of the camelpox virus, human rotavirus, enterovirus 17, and the toxin ricin.

During the Persian Gulf War of 1991, US forces discovered a supposed "baby-food" factory at Al Hakam, 30 miles southwest of Baghdad that contained fermentation equipment suitable for the production of bacteriological weapons. Al Hakam was the principal facility in Iraq's biological weapons program. Iraq already possessed anthrax, aflatoxin, and botulinus toxin and had purchased some 30 tons of bacteria growth medium from British and German companies.[258]

Iraq used tactics of deception to hide its WMD work. These included underreporting, concealment, and unilateral destruction of biological and chemical weapons during the eight years of UN inspections from 1991 to 1998. Therefore, it was difficult to estimate the true magnitude of BW weapons remaining in Iraq. UN inspectors suspected that the Iraqis actually produced two-to-four times more agent than the Iraqis declared.[259]

Missile delivery systems

The Iraqi regime consistently sought to develop a long-range ballistic missile capability for both conventional purposes and the delivery of WMD.[260] Iraq began arming itself with short-range ballistic missiles in 1974, purchasing 819 Scud-B short-range (190 miles) ballistic missiles and 11 MAZ-543 transporter-erector-launchers (TELs) from the Soviet Union.[261]

At the start of the Iran–Iraq War on October 8, 1980, Iraq fired its first FROG-7A unguided, short-range (43 miles) Soviet-supplied artillery rockets against Iran. In January 1983, Iraq and the Soviet Union concluded a $2 billion arms deal,[262] which included Scud-B and SS-21 surface-to-surface missiles. On October 15, 1983, Iraq fired its first Scud-B missiles against Iran. Nevertheless, Iraq found itself at a disadvantage. Iran's Scud-Bs could hit Baghdad but Iraq's Scuds could not reach Tehran, which lay much farther from their common border. Thus, Iraq began to reverse-engineer

Scud-Bs in 1987 (in what was named "Project 144"). As a result Iraq produced a modified missile known as the Al Hussein that could fly over 400 miles, far enough to reach Tehran. The first Al Hussein was reportedly fired at Tehran on February 29, 1988.[263] Iraq had closed the "missile gap."

During the latter years of the Iran–Iraq War because of military stalemate, both nations resorted to the strategic bombing of enemy cities by missiles and supplemented by conventional air power. These attacks became known as the "war of the cities." There were five "war of the cities" campaigns:

- The first "war of the cities" was waged from February 7 to 22, 1984.
- The second "war of the cities" occurred from March 22 to April 8, 1985.
- The third "war of the cities" took place from January 17 to 25, 1987.
- The fourth "war of the cities" spanned the period from February to April 1987.
- The fifth "war of the cities" was fought from February 29 to April 30, 1988.

Initiated by Iraq, the last—the fifth—"war of the cities," witnessed the launching of some 193 missiles including many Al-Hussein missiles against Tehran, Qom, and Isfahan, battering those cities badly. War-weariness and this missile bombardment cracked Iranian morale and pushed the Iranian regime to accept a UN ceasefire on July 18, 1988, with hostilities formally ending on August 20. During the entire war, Iraq fired more than 516 Scud-Bs and Al-Hussein missiles at Iran.[264] In short, Iran and Iraq exchanged more ballistic missile attacks than occurred in any other conflict to that date, since Germany launched V-2 missile attacks during World War II against the United Kingdom, France, Belgium and the Netherlands. The most important and dangerous development for the world as a whole, and the Middle East in particular, was that sophisticated weapons in the form of ballistic missiles as well as chemical warfare agents were now well established in Third World countries, and there was little hesitation about using them. This bodes ill for the entire Middle East region as well as the world in general.

In February 1990, before the Iraqi invasion and occupation of Kuwait, Iraq positioned six Scud missile launchers near its western border with Jordan, to give it the ability to strike Israel.[265] During the Persian Gulf War of 1991, some ninety-three Al-Hussein (range 375 to 405 miles) and Al-Hijarah (range 470 miles) missiles were fired at coalition forces, Israel and Saudi Arabia.[266] The Iraqis claimed to have fired 50 ballistic missiles at coalition forces and 43 at Israel.[267] The deadliest strike was at Al Kohbar, near Dhahran, Saudi Arabia, where a Scud strike, on February 25, 1991, hit a US Marine Corps barracks, killing 28 and wounding more than 100 Marines.[268]

It was with the Iraqi Scud threat of the 1991 Gulf War in mind that pre-emptive action was taken on March 17, 2003, prior to the launching of Operation *Iraqi Freedom*. Two days before the invasion, while the British Parliament prepared to authorize the UK's participation, commandos from Britain's elite Special Air Service (SAS) units were already "involved in fierce fighting" behind enemy lines as part of Operation *Row*. Their mission was to destroy Scud launchers. Sixty commandos (D squadron 22 SAS) were flown in six Chinook CH-47 helicopters to a location some 75 miles inside Iraq near the town of Al-Qa'im in the country's northwest where it was believed chemical weapons were ready to be deployed.[269] A day later, an additional sixty SAS soldiers (B squadron) arrived in Land Rover vehicles having crossed from Jordan. This area was where missiles had been fired at Israel in the 1991 Gulf War and was a site of strategic importance for WMD material. The mission's objective was to prevent the launching of Scud missiles armed with chemical warheads toward Israel.[270] To date it is not known exactly what was discovered and destroyed by Operation *Row*.

Nuclear weapons

Iraq began limited work in the civilian nuclear field in 1956 and acquired a 2MW research reactor from the Soviet Union in 1962. In the late 1960s, then Vice President, (but the real strongman of the regime) and head of the Iraq Atomic Energy Commission (IAEC), Saddam Hussein ordered the establishment of a nuclear weapons program. As part of Saddam's ongoing attempts to hide his quest for nuclear weapons, Iraq ratified the Nuclear Non-Proliferation Treaty (NPT) in 1969.

In 1974, an Iraqi delegation traveled to Paris, France, to negotiate the purchase of a reactor similar to the French Osiris reactor. On September 8, 1975, French Premier Jacques Chirac and then Iraqi Vice-President Saddam Hussein initialed a nuclear cooperation agreement. By November, the details of the agreement had been worked out. France agreed to purchase Iraqi oil and sell Iraq military weapons as well as a nuclear reactor costing $275 million. The project was named after the Babylonian month of "Tammuz," the very same month that King Nebuchadnezzar II began his attack on the Jewish people in the Land of Israel in 586 B.C.E. A key question was raised at the time of the signing of the agreement. Why did oil-rich Iraq need atomic power for peaceful purposes? Iraqi ruler Saddam Hussein provided the answer. Upon the signing of the Franco-Iraqi agreement he stated, "This is the beginning of the Arab atomic bomb." He knew that two to three bombs would be enough to destroy Israel.

In any event, the type of reactor that France sold to Iraq was *not* designed to produce energy. The reactor was a replica of a French research reactor called Osiris, for classical reasons. The Iraqis complained that the name appeared to give prestige to Egypt. Thus, the name of the Iraqi reactor was changed to Osirak. Osirak was a 70-megawatt research reactor fueled with 93 percent enriched uranium. This fuel was suitable for use in the manufacture of atomic bombs. By the mid-1970s, assisted by European suppliers, Saddam Hussein had an active program under way. On January 5, 1980, Brazil and Iraq concluded a nuclear agreement whereby Brazil was to furnish natural and lightly enriched uranium to Iraq in exchange for Iraqi oil.

On September 30, 1980, only nine days after Iraq initiated the Iran–Iraq War, during an Iranian attack on Iraqi electrical power plants, two US-supplied Iranian F-4 Phantom fighter aircraft bombed Iraq's Osirak nuclear research center. According to French embassy officials in Baghdad, the attack damaged some auxiliary buildings at the site but did not damage the French-built Tammuz-1 power reactor.[271] Days later on October 4, 1980, an official Baghdad newspaper *Al Thawra,* declared, "The Iranian people should not fear the Iraqi nuclear reactor which is not intended to be used against Iran, but against the Zionist enemy." This raises an immediate additional question: What does "to be used against" mean? Nevertheless despite the newspaper's assurance, Iran launched an unsuccessful air attack against the Iraqi nuclear research reactor at Tuwaitha on November 30, 1980.

Brazil secretly aided the Iraqi nuclear weapons program by supplying natural uranium dioxide between 1981 and 1982 without notifying the IAEA. About 100 tons of mustard gas also came from Brazil. On January 14–15, 1981, two Iraqi planes, a Boeing 727 and an Ilyushin IL-76, left an airfield outside of Sao Paulo, Brazil, loaded with arms for Iraq. The IL-76 also carried eight tons of uranium oxide. This was a violation of the International Atomic Energy Agency, which called for safeguards and inspections of all such shipments. The Soviet-built IL-76 never reached Iraq. It was intercepted by an unidentified nation over Africa, the uranium unloaded, and the plane then allowed to proceed. In addition, Portugal (1980, 1982) and Niger (1981–82) also supplied uranium ore to Iraq.[272]

By 1981, Iraqi scientists were on the verge of gaining access to a plentiful source of nuclear fuel from their reactor at Osirak. However, Iraq's nuclear development program was set back by the anticipatory self-defense* preemptive Israeli air strike on the Iraqi reactor at Osirak on June 7, 1981, after Saddam Hussein's repeated public declarations to build such a weapon and destroy Israel. For example, prior to his Paris trip in September 1975, Saddam told the Lebanese news magazine *Al-Usbu al-Arabi* that Iraq's agreement with the French would be "the first concrete step toward the production of the Arabic atomic weapon."[273] Iraq responded to the Israeli pre-emptive strike by reconstituting its secret program, dispersing facilities widely and placing key technology in hardened shelters.

Saudi Arabia was alleged to have provided funding for the Iraqi nuclear weapons program. According to former Saudi diplomat, Mohammed Khilewi's account, Saudi Arabia gave $5 billion to the Iraqi nuclear research program between 1985 and the start of the Persian Gulf War.[274] This funding was provided as part of a broader Saudi effort to aid Iraq in its war against Iran.[275] Khilewi maintained that the Saudi funds were provided with the understanding that Saudi Arabia would gain control of several Iraqi nuclear weapons if the armaments were ever built.[276]

Covertly, Saddam Hussein also embarked on a "dirty nuke" project, i.e. to build radiation or radiological weapons. Such weapons used conventional high explosives to scatter highly radioactive materials to poison targets rather than destroying them with blast and heat. By 1987, Iraq had developed such a bomb some twelve feet long and weighing more than a ton. The weapon was tested three times in 1987. The first test sought to see if the thick lead case holding the irradiated charge could be blown apart, in order to discharge, it did. The second test was of a bomb sitting on the ground, which was also successful, spreading a radioactive cloud some 600 feet into the air. In the third test, the Iraqi Air Force dropped two bombs, again producing huge clouds. Such bombs were meant to cause vomiting, cancer, birth defects, and slow death within two to six weeks. While the weapon worked, it had a few limitations. The irradiated charge had to be used within a week, as it lost strength quickly. Additionally, calm weather was essential.[277] Nevertheless, this program proved that Saddam Hussein's regime was determined to clandestinely acquire and build WMDs.

On March 28, 1990, British customs officials in London arrested five people accused of trying to smuggle to Iraq, electrical capacitors designed to help detonate nuclear weapons.[278] These nuclear triggers were evidence of Iraq's nuclear weapons intentions. Although the program's existence was widely suspected, International Atomic Energy Agency (IAEA) inspectors came and went without uncovering evidence that radioactive materials were either being diverted from civilian reactors, or being acquired by other means. Had Saddam not invaded Kuwait in 1990, inviting both the increased scrutiny of the international community and the 1991 Persian Gulf War, Iraq might have succeeded in clandestinely developing nuclear weapons.

After invading Kuwait in August 1990, Iraq began an eight-month crash program to make a nuclear weapon by April 1991, according to UN inspector Rolf Ekeus.[279] Had Iraq achieved its goal, the Allied effort to liberate Kuwait may not have taken place or certainly been far more costly. The Allied bombing campaign in January 1991 destroyed many of Iraq's facilities and set back the program. Only in the aftermath of the 1991 Gulf War did the scope and scale of Iraq's prewar efforts become evident. On April 3, 1991, the United Nations Security Council adopted Resolution 687, which declared

> That Iraq shall unconditionally accept the destruction, removal, or rendering harmless, under international supervision, of:

---

* A comprehensive explanation of anticipatory self-defense will be found within "Basic Principle 58."

(a) All chemical and biological weapons and all stocks of agents and all related subsystems and components and all research, development, support and manufacturing facilities;

(b) All ballistic missiles with a range greater than 150 kilometers [95 miles] and related major parts, and repair and production facilities. The forming of a Special Commission, which shall carry out immediate on-site inspection of Iraq's biological, chemical and missile capabilities, based on Iraq's declarations and the designation of any additional locations by the Special Commission itself; Iraq shall unconditionally agree not to acquire or develop nuclear weapons or nuclear-weapons-usable material or any subsystems or components or any research, development, support or manufacturing facilities related to the above; to submit to the Secretary-General and the Director-General of the International Atomic Energy Agency … the locations, amounts, and types of all items specified above; to place all of its nuclear-weapons-usable materials under the exclusive control, for custody and removal, of the International Atomic Energy Agency.[280]

However, while the UN placed restrictions on these types of weapons and delivery systems, Iraq retained both the scientists and infrastructure needed to continue these programs. Furthermore, while Iraq's missile production was limited to missiles with a maximum 95-mile range, only on-going UN monitoring would verify that Iraq had not illicitly restarted its long-range missile programs.

Iraq's initial cooperation with the IAEA was minimal, as early declarations did not disclose the full extent of the nuclear program. Iraq's first declaration to the IAEA in April 1991, did not report all of the nuclear program's facilities. Nevertheless, inspections revealed much of the program and forced Iraq to admit its weapons aspirations, including research at Al Tuwaitha and Al Atheer.[281] The UN inspectors obtained information that Iraq was concealing both nuclear weapons information and materials.[282]

Yet, Iraq did not cease its activity to build WMDs. The United Nations attempted to monitor Iraq's nuclear program without much success. Only after the IAEA initiated special on-site inspections did Iraq begin to release significant information, even then omitting important details and either blocking IAEA access to key sites or hurriedly removing nuclear-related equipment from locations that inspectors were likely to visit. On March 11, 1993, UN inspection teams reported that Iraq had rebuilt its nuclear installations. Additionally on July 4, 1993, Iraq signed an agreement to buy a nuclear power plant from China.

The full scope of the Iraqi effort became evident only when the IAEA stumbled on a collection of classified documents. The documents revealed that the Iraqis under the noses of IAEA inspectors, had constructed what Hans Blix, then the head of the agency, regretfully admitted was a "vast unknown, undeclared uranium-enrichment program in the billion-dollar range," constituting an essential part of "an advanced nuclear-weapons development program."[283] Among other things, Iraq was in possession of some 400 tons of previously undisclosed radioactive materials, including six grams of clandestinely produced plutonium and more than thirty-five kilograms of highly enriched uranium—not yet bomb-grade material but of "high strategic value." Iraq had also acquired a large number of calutrons for enriching uranium. These electro-magnetic devices, used by the United States in constructing its first atomic bombs but subsequently abandoned in favor of more efficient means, were extremely well suited for a clandestine program like Iraq's.[284]

UNSCOM conducted some 260 inspections in Iraq over its nine-year (1991–99) existence. UNSCOM inspectors uncovered a complex of secret sites in which virtually every kind of weaponry of mass destruction was being fabricated. Iraq had purchased giant magnets and centrifuges for enriching uranium, had imported German components to enhance the range of Scud missiles purchased from the Soviet Union, had bought plants for producing chemical and biological agents, and had actually loaded those agents into warheads.[285] Although UNSCOM conducted some surprise visits with no advance notice, Iraq's intelligence agents defeated these moves more often than not. Only about a half-dozen of the surprise inspections actually succeeded.

Further evidence of Iraq's determination to acquire nuclear weapons came in 1995 when Hussein Kamel, Saddam Hussein's son-in-law defected to Jordan, bringing with him information about a well-funded and continuing program to produce nuclear warheads to be fitted to intermediate-range ballistic missiles, as well as efforts to turn highly enriched uranium into fuel for a nuclear bomb.[286]

Recalling the Israeli air strike of June 1981, Iraq was determined not to put all of its WMD "eggs" into one basket. WMD experimentation and production sites were scattered. Additionally, Iraq, at considerable expense, made its secret weapon efforts mobile. Laboratories, components, and materials were ready to hit the road at a moment's notice. During the days when UNSCOM was conducting inspections, this mobility was revealed graphically in U-2 photos of a suspect site. The pictures were taken in sequence as soon as an inspection team left its headquarters. The first photos showed no activity at the site. A slightly later sequence revealed a large number of vehicles leaving the site, then there was no activity again and finally the vehicles of the inspectors arrived,[287] but by then any incriminating evidence had been removed.

On May 28, 1998, Pakistan tested its first atomic weapon becoming the world's eighth nuclear power and the first Islamic nation to possess the bomb. Abdul Qadeer Khan was the founder of Pakistan's nuclear program. In January 2004, Khan confessed to having been involved in a clandestine international network of nuclear weapons technology proliferation from Pakistan to Libya, Iran and the DPRK.[288] Previously, Khan had offered Iraq critical nuclear weapons technology and components in the months leading up to the 1991 Persian Gulf War—an offer Iraq turned down fearing it was a sting operation run by the United States.[289]

In October 1998, Saddam expelled the UNSCOM weapons inspectors. From 1999 to 2002, there were no inspections, Iraq's clandestine WMD, and missile programs continued unabated. For example, Iraq was prohibited from making missiles that exceeded a 95-mile range. Despite this limit, in 2001 Iraq produced the Al-Samoud II, and increased its range beyond the limits set, conducting thirteen test flights of the improved missile.[290] Prior to the 2003 US-led invasion, the UN ordered the destruction of the Al-Samoud II missiles, and subsequently supervised the destruction of seventy-two missiles and three launchers.[291] However, inconsistencies in Iraqi reporting left open the question as to how many additional missiles were not reported.

Iraq refused to allow UNSCOM weapons inspections to resume until November 2002. In the interim, the United Nations Security Council had created, on December 17, 1999, a new inspection regime, the United Nations Monitoring, Verification and Inspection Commission (UNMOVIC) but it was denied access to Iraq. Throughout this period, Iraq maintained its nuclear expertise, including design information, scientists and engineers, and a powerful and effective concealment apparatus.

Meanwhile in 1999, Saddam sent agents to Niger to negotiate the purchase of enriched uranium ore. Iraq also purchased large quantities of uranium ore from Portugal. Iraq threatened to cut off oil shipments to Portugal unless uranium ore was supplied. The Niger purchase was later cited by

President George W. Bush in his 2003 State of the Union address, "The British government has learned that Saddam Hussein recently sought significant quantities of uranium from Africa."

A large-scale Iraqi-Syrian smuggling system had been set in place as a means for Iraq to circumvent UN sanctions. According to *The Times* of London, intelligence sources assigned to monitor Iraq's air traffic raised suspicions that Iraqi authorities smuggled centrifuge components out of Syria in June 2002. The parts were initially stored in the Syrian port of Tartus before being transported to Damascus International Airport. The transfer allegedly occurred when Iraqi authorities sent twenty-four planes with humanitarian assistance into Syria after a dam collapsed in June 2002, killing twenty people and leaving some 30,000 others homeless.[292] Intelligence officials did not believe these planes returned to Iraq empty.

Regardless of the merits of this one particular episode, it is well documented that Syria became the main conduit in Saddam Hussein's attempt to rebuild his military under the 1990–2003 United Nations sanctions,[293] and so the necessary contacts between regimes and along the border would already have been in place. This Iraqi-Syrian connection would later be used in reverse-flow to move Iraqi WMD components out of Iraq in the months prior to Operation *Iraqi Freedom.*

In the National Intelligence Estimate (NIE) of October 2002 (released July 18, 2003), where the collective views of fifteen US intelligence agencies (including the CIA), were summarized, one of the conclusions offered with "high confidence" was that "Iraq is continuing, and in some areas expanding its chemical, biological, nuclear, and missile programs contrary to UN resolutions."[294] The intelligence agencies of the United Kingdom, Germany, Russia, China, Israel, and France all agreed with this judgment.

Even Hans Blix, who headed the UN team of inspectors, tried to determine whether Saddam had complied with the demands of the Security Council that Iraq get rid of the weapons of mass destruction it was known to have had in the past. This lent further credibility to the case in a report Blix issued on January 27, 2003, only a few months before the US-led invasion of Iraq:

> The discovery of a number of 122-mm chemical rocket warheads in a bunker at a storage depot 170 km southwest of Baghdad was much publicized. This was a relatively new bunker, and therefore the rockets must have been moved there in the past few years, at a time when Iraq should not have had such munitions.... They could also be the tip of a submerged iceberg. The discovery of a few rockets does not resolve but rather points to the issue of several thousands of chemical rockets that are unaccounted for.[295]

Under the rubric of "unaccounted for," Blix cited 6,500 chemical bombs, stocks of VX nerve agents and anthrax, 3,000 tons of precursor chemicals, 360 tons of bulk agents for chemical weapons, and thousands of munitions for delivering such agents.[296] Thus, there can be no doubt that Iraq, under the rule of Saddam Hussein, consistently sought to acquire, produce and use WMDs. The US-led invasion of Iraq—Operation *Iraqi Freedom*—in March 2003, toppled Saddam's regime and ended the Iraqi WMD—chemical, biological, and nuclear programs.

The questions that arose shortly after the liberation of Iraq from Saddam's despotism, included, "If Saddam produced such weapons where are they now?" "Where is the proof, indeed, that he ever had them?" Did the Iraqi dictator order the program transferred to new and as yet undiscovered locations within Iraq, a country the size of California? Did Iraq transfer WMD components to Syria and the Bekáa Valley of Lebanon, as both US satellite and Russian intelligence reports indicated?

The process of searching for evidence of Iraqi WMD programs was greatly complicated. This was due first, by the total collapse of Iraq's governing structures, second by the country's large size, and lastly by the ongoing insurgency that made unescorted travel extremely dangerous. Additionally, all this was exacerbated by the destruction of most official Iraqi government archives in the closing stages of the 2003 war.

What is known is this: Several different intelligence sources reported suspicious truck convoys from Iraq to Syria in the days, weeks, and months prior to the March 2003 invasion of Iraq.[297] The movement of WMD components into Syria first was made public when, on December 23, 2002, Israel's Prime Minister Ariel Sharon stated on Israeli television, "Chemical and biological weapons which Saddam is endeavoring to conceal have been moved from Iraq to Syria."[298] About three weeks later, Israel's foreign minister Benjamin Netanyahu, repeated the accusation.[299] The US, British, and Australian governments issued similar statements.[300] "We've had six or seven credible reports of Iraqi weapons being moved into Syria before the war," a senior administration official told reporter Kenneth Timmerman. In December 2005, IDF Chief of Staff Lt.-General Moshe Ya'alon said Iraq transported WMDs to Syria six weeks before Operation *Iraqi Freedom* began.[301] In a briefing for reporters in October 2003, retired Air Force Lt. Gen. James Clapper Jr., who was head of the National Geospatial Intelligence Agency when the Iraq war began, said satellite imagery showed a heavy flow of traffic from Iraq into Syria just before the American invasion. "I think the people below Saddam Hussein and his sons' level saw what was coming and decided the best thing to do was to destroy and disperse," Lt. Gen. Clapper said.[302]

On January 4, 2004, Nizar Nayuf, a Syrian journalist who defected to an undisclosed European country, told the Dutch newspaper, *De Telegraaf,* he knew of three sites in the western part of central Syria—an area where support for the Assad regime was strong—where Iraq's WMD were being kept. They were in tunnels dug near Al-Baydah, less than 5 miles from Al-Masyaf near the city of Hama in northern Syria, (being part of a secret underground factory built by the DPRK for Scud missiles and chemical weapons storage), the Syrian air force base near the village of Tal as-Sinan north of Salamija, and near the city of Shanshar, south of Homs, on the border with Lebanon, where Brigade 661 of the armed air forces patrolled a large bunker facility.[303]

Later that month on January 25, 2004, Dr. David Kay, the first head of the Iraq Survey Group (ISG), which conducted the search for Saddam's WMD, told a British newspaper, the *Sunday Telegraph,* there, was evidence that unspecified materials had been moved to Syria from Iraq shortly before the war. "We know from some of the interrogations of former Iraqi officials that a lot of material went to Syria before the war, including some components of Saddam's WMD program. Precisely what went to Syria, and what has happened to it, is a major issue that needs to be resolved," Dr. Kay said.[304] Although a subsequent report in March 2005, declared, "ISG judged that it was unlikely that an *official* (emphasis added) transfer of WMD material from Iraq to Syria took place. However, the ISG was unable to rule out *unofficial* (emphasis added) movement of WMD-related materials."[305]

Therefore, if the United States and several other nations knew that large parts of Iraq's WMD programs were moved into Syria, the question arises, "Why didn't the Bush administration proceed to get them?" There were several reasons. First, with one war (Iraq) in the works, the United States did not want to involve itself in a second war with Syria. The initial military phase of the US-led invasion of Iraq ended on April 30, 2003, but Iraq was not fully secure as Saddam Hussein and many of the Ba'athist hierarchy had not yet been captured. Secondly, the United States at that time was engaged in an attempted rapprochement with the Syrian regime hoping for a US–Syrian dialogue. In fact, Secretary of State Colin Powell visited Damascus (May 3-4, 2003) to push this agenda. While the

United States was primarily interested in closing down the offices in Damascus of various terrorist groups including Hamas, Islamic Jihad and the Popular Front for the Liberation of Palestine (PFLP), the Assad regime wanted pressure exerted on Israel to relinquish the Golan Heights. While it is not known if Powell raised the issue of Iraqi WMD components being hidden in Syria, the Assad regime realized it need not fear a US military strike. That assurance came from Powell's own words as he declared that the use of military force against Syria was "not on the table."[306]

Retired Marine Lt. Gen. Michael DeLong was deputy commander of CENTCOM during Operation *Iraqi Freedom*. In September 2004, he told WABC Radio's Steve Malzberg that, "I do know for a fact that some of those weapons went into Syria, Lebanon and Iran. Two days before the war on March 17 [2003], we saw through multiple intelligence channels—both human intelligence and technical intelligence—large caravans of people and things, including some of the top fifty-five [most wanted] Iraqis, going to Syria," General DeLong explained. "We also know that before then, they buried some of the weapons of mass destruction," he added.[307] It must also be stressed that Charles Duelfer, who headed the ISG searching for WMDs, acknowledged his group examined less than 0.25 percent of the more than 10,000 known weapons storage sites in Iraq.[308]

In March 2005, to *News Max* reporter Charles Smith[309], and again on February 18, 2006, in an interview with Kenneth Timmerman, John Shaw, a former Deputy Undersecretary of Defense for International Technology Security, revealed what had happened to Iraq's WMDs. Shaw said, "They were moved by Russian *Spetsnaz* (special forces) units out of uniform, that were specifically sent to Iraq to move the weaponry and eradicate any evidence of its existence."[310] The WMD materials were moved to Syria and Lebanon's Bekáa Valley. "While in Iraq I received information from several sources naming the exact Russian units, what they took and where they took both WMD materials and conventional explosives," Mr. Shaw added.[311] The evacuation of Saddam's WMD stockpiles was "a well-orchestrated campaign using two neighboring client states with which the Russian leadership had a long time security relationship."[312] The British, Ukrainian and American secret services all believed that the Russians had organized a last minute evacuation of chemical and biological weapons stockpiles from Baghdad to Syria.[313]

On January 24, 2006, Iraqi Air Vice-Marshall Georges Sada, the former Iraqi National Security adviser, announced the publication of his book entitled *Saddam's Secrets: How an Iraqi General Defied and Survived Saddam Hussein,* with the tagline "An insider exposes plans to destroy Israel, hide WMDs and control the Arab world." In the book, Sada claimed that Saddam Hussein ordered to fly portions of the WMD stockpiles to secret locations in Syria. Baghdad and Damascus may have long been rivals, but there was precedent for such Iraqi cooperation with regional competitors when faced with an outside threat (*see* "Basic Principle 47"). In the run-up to the 1991 Operation *Desert Storm* and the liberation of Kuwait, the Iraqi regime flew many of its jets to safety from coalition attack, to Iran with which, just three years previous, it had been engaged in bitter trench warfare.[314]

Sada told the *New York Sun* that special Iraqi Republican Guard brigades loaded yellow barrels with the skull and crossbones sign on each barrel onto two Iraqi Airways Boeings [747 jumbo jets] from which the seats were removed. There were fifty-six flights in all. "Saddam realized this time the Americans are coming," General Sada told the *New York Sun,* one of a handful of news organizations, which took note of what he said. Sada said he was told of the WMD transfer by the pilots of the two airliners, who approached him after Saddam was captured. The pilots said there was also a ground convoy of trucks.[315]

John Loftus, President of the International Intelligence Summit, a non-profit non-partisan educational forum focusing on global intelligence affairs, made an extensive study of what happened to Iraq's WMDs. His research was based on examination of captured photographs, documents and tapes that fell into US hands after the coalition invasion of Iraq. According to this research, roughly one quarter of Saddam's WMD was destroyed under UN pressure during the early to mid 1990s. Saddam sold approximately another quarter of his weapons stockpile to his Arab neighbors during the mid to late 1990s. The Russians insisted on removing another quarter in the last few months before the war. The last remaining WMD, the contents of Saddam's nuclear weapons labs, were still inside Iraq on the day when the coalition forces arrived in 2003. His nuclear weapons equipment was hidden in enormous underwater warehouses beneath the Euphrates River.[316]

Among the captured documents and tapes was tape ISGQ-2003-M0007379 in which Saddam was briefed on his secret nuclear weapons project. This meeting clearly took place in 2002 or afterwards—almost a decade after the State Department claimed that Saddam had abandoned his nuclear weapons research. The tape also describes a laser enrichment process for uranium that had never been known by the UN inspectors even to exist in Iraq, and Saddam's nuclear briefers on the tape were Iraqi scientists who had never been on any weapons inspector's list. The tape explicitly discussed how civilian plasma research could be used as a cover for military plasma research necessary to build a hydrogen bomb.[317]

Saddam's nuclear documents compel any reasonable person to the conclusion that, more probably than not, there were in fact nuclear WMD sites, components, and programs hidden inside Iraq at the time the coalition forces invaded. In view of these newly discovered documents, it can be concluded that Saddam did have a nuclear weapons program in 2001–02, and it is reasonably certain that he would have continued his efforts towards making a nuclear bomb in 2003 had he not been stopped by the US-led coalition forces. Ninety percent of the Saddam files have never been read, let alone translated.[318] There is a need for the sake of historical accuracy to translate them.

One of the last major remnants of Saddam Hussein's secret nuclear program, a huge (550 metric tons) stockpile of concentrated natural uranium oxide—yellowcake—was moved from Iraq to Canada for disposal, reaching a Canadian port on July 5, 2008.[319] This completed a secret US operation that included a two-week airlift from Baghdad and a ship voyage crossing two oceans. This yellowcake is not something from a Betty Crocker cake mix. It is the raw material, which can be converted into highly toxic uranium hexafluoride. Uranium hexafluoride in turn, is a compound used in the uranium enrichment process that produces fuel for nuclear reactors and nuclear weapons. Again, it must be stated that there should no longer be any doubt that Saddam Hussein's Iraq was seeking to build nuclear weapons. To date, the post-Saddam Iraqi government has adhered to the nonproliferation regime and has shown little interest in pursuing even a civil nuclear program. However, with the withdrawal of US forces from Iraq, completed on December 18, 2011, the descent of that country into virtual Sunni-Shi'ite civil war and the emergence of the Islamic State, a Sunni Islamic supremacist movement that proclaimed a caliphate, there is no guarantee that a new regime may yet again engage in the quest for WMDs. Of note was the fact that the Islamic State captured both Scud missiles and chemical stockpiles during 2014.

SAUDI ARABIA
Missile delivery systems

Saudi Arabia procured approximately thirty-six Dongfeng-3 ("East Wind") intermediate-range liquid-fueled ballistic missiles from China in 1986. These missiles (NATO code-named, CSS-2) were configured with conventional high-explosive warheads and have a range of 1,865 miles. They can carry a payload of 4,730 pounds and can carry a nuclear warhead. While the DF-3s are old and relatively inaccurate, Saudi Arabia chose to display them for the first time at a Saudi military parade on April 29, 2014, in the eastern military town of Hafar Al-Batin, at the junction of the Saudi-Kuwaiti-Iraqi borders.[320] The missiles are based at the Al-Kharj air base, south of Riyadh, and at the As-Sulayyil Oasis, southwest of Riyadh.[321] The Saudis agreed to sign the NPT in 1988 in exchange for keeping the missiles. King Fahd also sent the United States a written pledge that Saudi Arabia would only use these missiles with conventional payloads, not nuclear or chemical ones, and would not use the DF-3s to carry out first-strike attacks.[322] However, given the Obama administration's rush to conclude a nuclear deal with Iran in 2014, which in reality will acknowledge Tehran's status as a pre-nuclear power with the ability to continue its nuclear weapons program, it is now doubtful that the Saudis will adhere to its 25-year-old pledges.

Another supplier is Pakistan, which has already sent the Saudis its latest version of the Ghauri-II missile after extending its range to 1,430 miles. Those missiles are tucked away in silos built in the underground city of Al-Sulaiyil, south of the capital Riyadh.[323] Other Pakistani missiles may be available to the Saudis. As of 2008, nuclear-capable ballistic missiles in Pakistan's arsenal included the Ghaznavi (range 250 miles), Shaheen-I (range 280 miles), and the Ghauri (range 750 miles).[324] Missiles under development include the 1,250 to 1,555-mile range Shaheen-II, which was first tested in 2004, improved and successfully tested again on November 13, 2014.

Saudi Arabia bought two-stage, solid-fueled, Dongfeng 21 (DF-21), NATO code named CSS-5, medium-range ballistic missiles (MRBM) from China in 2007. The US agreed to the purchase on the condition that CIA technical experts could verify they were not designed to carry nuclear warheads.[325] While the DF-21s have a shorter range, 1,554 miles, they have greater accuracy, making them more useful against high-value targets in Iran or Israel. In 2010, a new headquarters for the Saudi Strategic Missile Force was constructed in Riyadh. This was followed, in early 2012, of reports that China supplied older liquid-fueled nuclear-capable DF-5A (NATO CSS-4) three-stage ICBMs to the Saudis.[326] More recently, it was reported in early July 2012, that Chinese President Hu Jintao agreed to send Chinese nuclear engineers and technicians to help Saudi Arabia develop uranium enrichment and other nuclear production capacities.[327] Work is already in progress at the King Abdulaziz City for Science and Technology near Riyadh, as well as a base of operations for the missiles near Riyadh.[328]

In early July 2013, a previously undisclosed surface-to-surface missile base was revealed deep in Saudi Arabia at al-Watah, some 125 miles southwest of Riyadh. It was built within the last five years but was unknown until satellite images were analyzed by experts at IHS Jane's Intelligence Review. Observed were two launch pads with markings pointing northwest towards Tel Aviv, Israel, and northeast towards Tehran, Iran. The pads are designed for Saudi Arabia's arsenal of truck-launched Chinese-supplied Dongfeng DF 3 missiles, which have a range of 1,500 to 2,500 miles and can carry a two-ton payload. The DF-3 is capable of carrying a nuclear device. The missiles are stored in an underground facility built into a rocky hillside.[329]

In addition to ballistic missiles, cruise missiles are increasingly part of Pakistan's nuclear delivery plans. Its main cruise missile—the Babur—has a range of from 310 to 435 miles and was first tested in

August 2005. Two years later, in August 2007, Pakistan tested a second nuclear-capable cruise missile, the air-launched Ra'ad.[330] Another successful test launch of the Babur missile, which flew some 360 miles, was made on February 10, 2011.[331] In light of the Saudi acquisition of Pakistani nuclear weapons, it may be assumed that Saudi Arabia can and may have acquired any or all of these missiles. With warheads deliverable on demand from Pakistan, and mounted on the missiles, the desert kingdom can acquire an effective modern missile delivery system more quickly than most realize.

Nuclear weapons

Saudi Arabia started a nuclear weapons research program in 1975, according to Mohammed Khilewi, a Saudi diplomat who worked on nonproliferation issues at the Saudi mission to the United Nations in New York. After Khilewi defected to the United States in 1994, he provided the US government and media sources with accounts and documents to substantiate his claims.[332] The program was apparently under the command of Crown Prince Sultan bin Abdul Aziz al Saud, the Saudi Minister of Defense, and was run from the Al-Khari nuclear research center, at a military base south of Riyadh.[333] Saudi scientists allegedly received training on how to build weapons in Iraq and Pakistan. Saudi officials attempted to buy a miniature neutron source nuclear reactor from China in 1989, but the deal was not finalized.[334]

Additionally, Robert Baer a former US Central Intelligence Agency analyst confirmed that Saudi Arabia spent $2 billion dollars helping Pakistan develop an "Islamic bomb" in the 1970s and 1980s.[335] Saudi Arabia viewed the Pakistani "Islamic bomb" as something that would contribute to Saudi Arabia's own security.[336] This assistance is rumored to have continued even after 1998, when Pakistan first tested its nuclear weapons. For instance, Sultan Bin Abdul Aziz, the Saudi Minister of Defense, allegedly traveled to two facilities related to Pakistan's nuclear weapons program—a missile assembly plant and uranium enrichment facility—during a visit to Pakistan in 1999.[337]

On June 16, 2005, the International Atomic Energy Agency approved a deal with Saudi Arabia that keeps nuclear inspectors out of the desert kingdom. The IAEA approved the deal despite serious misgivings about such arrangements in this era of heightened proliferation fears. The Saudis qualified for a "small quantities protocol," which frees countries from reporting the possession of up to 10 tons of natural uranium—enough to make a bomb—or up to 20 tons of depleted uranium, depending on the degree of enrichment, and 2.2 pounds of plutonium.[338]

Growing Saudi domestic energy needs has pushed the kingdom to reexamine its view on nuclear power for its energy requirements. In December 2011, Saudi Arabia announced its intention to build sixteen nuclear plants to generate electricity in different parts of the country. The plants are to be constructed over the next 20 years at a cost of more than $80 billion, with the first reactor on line in 2022.[339] However, it should be recalled that once such civilian plants get nuclear materials, these materials could be converted in the future to weapons of mass destruction.

Saudi Arabia can acquire these nuclear materials with the assistance of Pakistan. This could include securing a foreign source of highly enriched uranium or plutonium, gaining training from Pakistani nuclear scientists, or even jointly developing weapons with Pakistan.[340] Saudi Arabia certainly possesses enough funds, i.e. petrodollars, to carry out a nuclear weapons undertaking. With Saudi Arabia being the center of Sunni Islam and Iran being the center of Shi'a Islam, if Iran obtains nuclear weapons capability, the Saudis will spare no expense to obtain nuclear weapons for themselves. A report to the US Senate Foreign Relations Committee concluded that if Iran obtained nuclear weapons, Saudi Arabia would be compelled to follow.[341] Diplomatic cables obtained by

WikiLeaks revealed that King Abdullah privately warned the United States in 2008 that if Iran developed nuclear weapons, Saudi Arabia would do the same.[342]

However, not waiting for an Iranian nuclear breakthrough, in late December 2010, Saudi Arabia became a *de facto* nuclear power. It was revealed that Saudi Arabia had arranged to have available for its use, two Pakistani nuclear bombs or guided missile warheads. They are most probably held in Pakistan's nuclear air base at Kamra in the northern district of Attock. At least two giant Saudi transport planes sporting civilian colors and no insignia are parked permanently at Pakistan's Kamra base with aircrews on standby. They would fly the nuclear weapons home upon receipt of a double coded signal from Saudi King Abdullah and the Director of General Intelligence Prince Muq-rin bin Abdel Aziz. A single signal would not be enough.[343] In this manner, Saudi Arabia may become the world's first nation to acquire, rather than develop nuclear weapons. It should be noted that Pakistan is not a signatory to the Non-Proliferation of Nuclear Weapons Treaty. The International Panel on Fissile Materials concluded in January 2013, that Pakistan had stockpiled about 3 tons of highly enriched uranium.[344] US intelligence estimates in 2011 concluded that the number of nuclear weapons deployed by Pakistan ranged from the mid-90s to higher than 110.[345] Moreover, according to the IFPM's report, Pakistan has a stockpile of more than 200 nuclear weapons.[346] Given the above facts, it is likely that Saudi Arabia could acquire several additional weapons quickly.

At the end of March 2011, Prince Turki al-Faisal, former longtime director of Saudi intelligence and former ambassador to Washington, and at that time chairman of the King Faisal Center for Research, called on the Gulf Cooperation Council (GCC) member states to acquire nuclear weapons. Prince Turki, speaking at the annual conference of the Emirates Center for Strategic Studies, called for a joint GCC army "acquiring the nuclear might to face that of Iran."[347] Prince Turki repeated Saudi Arabia's concern that the existence of an Iranian bomb "would compel Saudi Arabia ... to pursue policies [with] possibly dramatic consequences."[348] In February 2012, the London *Times* quoted a "senior Saudi official" as saying Riyadh would launch a "twin-track nuclear weapons program" should Iran realize its nuclear ambitions. "Politically, it would be completely unacceptable to have Iran with a nuclear capability and not the kingdom."[349]

In mid-2012, it was confirmed that Saudi Arabia would seek to acquire nuclear weapons when former senior US Middle East diplomat Dennis Ross, revealed that Saudi King Abdullah explicitly warned the US that if Iran obtains nuclear weapons Saudi Arabia would seek to do so as well. According to Ross, during an April 2009, meeting with Abdullah, the Saudi monarch vowed, "if they [Iran] get nuclear weapons, we will get nuclear weapons." Ross' direct quote of the Saudi king is the first public affirmation by a current or former US official of the Saudi position and of the threat of a Middle East nuclear arms race if Tehran acquires an atomic bomb.[350]

The Obama administration's demonstrable retreat from the Middle East as well as its great reluctance, even unwillingness to use military force in dealing with Syria's use of poison gas in August 2013, coupled with the never-ending diplomatic discussions with Iran over its nuclear weapons program, while the latter continues to sprint to the nuclear finish line, has caused Saudi Arabia to reassess its options for acquiring a nuclear arsenal for its own defense. If Iran as seems likely, acquires a nuclear weapons capability, overnight it would become the paramount power of the Persian Gulf. Iranian hegemony would lead to dictation and control of the oil reserves of the region. Iranian incitement and radicalization of the Shi'ite minorities living in Saudi Arabia, the UAE, Bahrain and other Gulf states, could cause great internal pressures and upheavals in those states, threatening the ruling families. A shocking example was the February 2011 Shi'ite uprising in Bahrain. Due only to Saudi military intervention with Pakistani assistance, was the uprising contained, suppressed, and the ruling Sunni Bahraini government kept in power. All these developments can only spur and accelerate the Saudi desire to become a nuclear power in its own right. On January 1, 2013, Saudi Crown Prince Salman, deputy premier and defense minister, traveled to Islamabad and commissioned Pakistan to build nuclear weapons for a multibillion dollar fee. Those weapons were assembled in Pakistan and held ready for transfer to Saudi Arabia at a moment's notice.[351] Meanwhile, Saudi Arabia urged the other members of the Gulf Cooperation Council (Bahrain, Kuwait, Oman, Qatar and the United Arab Emirates) on April 23, 2014, that they should work on acquiring nuclear know-how to balance any threat from Iran.[352]

LIBYA
Chemical weapons

Chronologically speaking Libya began to build an offensive chemical warfare (CW) program in the mid-1980s,[353] more than a decade after the start of its quest to obtain nuclear weapons. Nevertheless once started, the two programs ran simultaneously. During the mid to late 1980s, Libya began the construction of three chemical weapons facilities. The first was located 75 miles south of Tripoli at a site called Rabta. The facility named "Pharma-150" posed as a pharmaceuticals complex to conceal the nature of its offensive chemical weapons program. Construction at Rabta was completed in 1988, after which the facility was able to manufacture at least 100 metric tons of blister and nerve agents over the next three years.[354] Libya built the second facility called "Pharma-200" underground at an army base 650 miles south of Tripoli at Sebha. It was at Sebha that Qadhafi established a whole range of subterranean military facilities. The third chemical weapons complex built in Libya during the 1980s was "Pharma-300" or Rabta II located south of Tripoli at Tarhuna. This site promised protection from air attacks by building two 200 to 450 foot-long tunnels covered by 100 feet of sandstone shields and lined with reinforced concrete.[355]

The United States among other nations including France and Israel became increasingly concerned with Libya's willingness to utilize chemical weapons. Libya resorted to chemical warfare on a small scale as an asymmetric response to conventional military inferiority. In September 1987, Libya's military operations in Chad were near defeat following a series of dramatic reversals. When Chadian forces, with French support, launched a surprise attack on Ma'atan-as-Sarra air base inside Libya on September 5, Libyan leader Muammar Qadhafi ordered his forces to attack the Chadian troops by dropping Iranian-supplied bombs[356] containing sulfur mustard from an AN-26 transport aircraft.[357] Although this use of chemical weapons was not extensive enough to be militarily decisive, it demonstrated Libyan willingness to ignore international norms and was sufficient to alarm the international community.

American analysts asserted that the Libyan project was the largest chemical weapons factory in the developing world. They claimed its potential daily output was between 22,000 and 84,000 pounds of mustard gas and nerve agents such as sarin and tabun.[358] Therefore, the United States prepared to launch a preemptive air strike to destroy the facility.[359] It is not known why the United States did not carry out the intended strike. Perhaps it was related to the suspicious fire that broke out there in March 1990.[360]

During the late 1980s, the involvement of foreign companies in supplying Libya's chemical weapons program with materials, technology, contractor services and technical expertise began to be exposed. In January 1989, it was revealed that Imhausen-Chemie, a West German chemical company, had been serving as the prime contractor for the facility at Rabta[361] since April 1980, while several other West German companies had been involved in the program to lesser degrees.[362] These revelations made the Federal Republic of (West) Germany the focus of international criticism, even though countries such as Belgium, China, Denmark, France, the (East) German Democratic Republic, Hungary, Italy, Japan, Switzerland, Thailand, the United Kingdom, the United States, and Yugoslavia had also participated in the development and equipping of Libya's chemical weapons program. By October 2003, Libya consented to US and British investigators examining laboratories and military facilities to verify the state and extent of Libya's CW program.

After 2003, Libya closed its chemical weapons research and production facilities and destroyed 3,500 unfilled chemical shells used to deliver them on the battlefield. Such weapons were used against Chad in 1987. Between February 27 and March 3, 2004, Libya destroyed 3,200 chemical weapon artillery shells under the supervision of the Organization for the Prohibition of Chemical Weapons. On March 5, 2004, Libya declared a stockpile of 23 tons of mustard gas as well as precursors for sarin and other chemicals. Libya officially acceded to the Chemical Weapons Convention in June 2004. However, the scheduled destruction of the mustard gas didn't start until 2010 and was only halfway finished when the system used in the destruction broke, said Paul Walker of the environmental group Global Green, which closely monitors chemical weapons.[363] The remaining mustard agent was stored inside a domed concrete bunker a few hundred miles south of Tripoli. Some were thought to have decayed over the years. With the political upheaval of 2011 and subsequent Libyan Civil War that led to the ouster and death of Muammar Qadhafi, there is continued international concern that some of these materials may fall into the hands of rival militias and terrorists.

Nuclear weapons

Libya's quest for nuclear weapons began shortly after Colonel Muammar Qadhafi assumed power in a military coup on September 1, 1969. The Libyan leader attempted to purchase an atomic bomb from China twice (in 1970 and again in 1971),[364] as well as from India and Pakistan.[365] In 1974, Qadhafi offered France a $1 billion arms deal if France included an atomic bomb as part of the transaction. None of these countries sold such a weapon to him. Subsequently, Libya embarked on programs to develop nuclear, chemical, and biological weapons as well as their delivery systems. During the 1970s and 1980s, Libya decided to pursue both the uranium- and plutonium-based pathways to nuclear weapons.

Steps were taken in the 1970s to gain access to uranium ore, uranium conversion facilities, and enrichment technologies that together would have allowed Libya to produce weapons-grade uranium. This activity was conducted covertly and in violation of IAEA safeguards. Libya purchased uranium ore from French-controlled mines in Niger, some of which went to Pakistan for its nuclear weapons program. Libya admitted to the IAEA in 2004, that it had actually imported 2,263 metric tons of uranium ore concentrate from 1978 to 1981, but only declared the import of 1,000 metric tons.[366]

Meanwhile, the Soviet Union completed construction of a 10 MW research reactor at Tajura, in 1979. This facility, which came on line in 1981, enabled Libya, to explore plutonium production technology, which it did, while evading IAEA safeguards intended to detect such activities. In 1984, Libya clandestinely acquired a pilot-scale uranium conversion facility. This was only admitted to the IAEA in 2004. Unknown to date is the identity of the country that supplied Libya with this facility.[367]

In the early 1990s, Libya sought to benefit from the implosion of the Soviet Union by trying to gain access to former Soviet nuclear technology, expertise, and materials, as well as recruit ex-Soviet nuclear experts. In 1992 for example, an official of the Kurchatov Institute in Moscow, one of Russia's leading nuclear research centers, claimed that Libya had unsuccessfully tried to recruit two of his colleagues to work at the Tajura Nuclear Research Center in Libya.[368] Throughout the 1990s, Qadhafi renewed calls for the production of nuclear weapons in Libya[369] and pursued new avenues for nuclear technology procurement from China, Russia, Iraq, and Ukraine,[370] while publicly supporting the nuclear nonproliferation regime.

In 1997, Pakistani nuclear scientist Abdul Qadeer Khan sold Libya plans for establishing nuclear weapons production facilities including manufacture of atomic warheads. According to a 2008 IAEA report that sums up a four-year investigation into Libya's nuclear weapons program, Libya received nuclear bomb blueprints from the A.Q. Khan network electronically. The documents also included information on centrifuges for uranium enrichment. While there was no evidence that Libya transferred these materials to anyone, the revelation raised the concern that other rogue states could acquire the same blueprints with ease. The report stated, "A substantial amount of sensitive information related to the fabrication of a nuclear weapon was available to members of the network," including a document on how to cast uranium metal into warheads.[371] The cooperation between Khan and Libya continued until the autumn of 2003, when Khan's clandestine collaboration with several countries became public following Libya's disclosures about its efforts to build nuclear weapons. Aside from Libya, Khan was a proliferator of nuclear technologies to several other countries, including Iran and the DPRK (North Korea). Khan's information was valuable as was proved on May 28, 1998, when Pakistan conducted a series of nuclear tests.

Libya also renewed its nuclear cooperation with Russia in late 1997, and in March 1998, Libya signed a contract with the Russian company *Atomenergoeksport* for a partial overhaul of the Tajura Nuclear Research Center.[372] In late 2000, Libya's nuclear activities accelerated. Libyan authorities informed the IAEA that at that time, Libya began to order centrifuges and components from other countries with the intention of installing a centrifuge plant to make enriched uranium. Libya also imported equipment for a large precision machine shop (located at Janzour) and acquired a large stock of special steel and high strength aluminum alloy to build a domestic centrifuge production capability.[373] Libya sought not only the capability to enrich uranium to weapons-grade but also the know-how to design and fabricate nuclear weapons.[374]

It was subsequently revealed (in 2005) that a US Department of Energy report stated that Turkish firms supplied Libya with 6,992 centrifuge motors, 912 bottom magnets, and 19,447 ring magnets, which could have been used to produce up to seven nuclear weapons per year. Turkish officials stated that the parts supplied to Libya were exported to the Gulf Technical Firm in Dubai, then to Pakistan, and then to Libya, which provides evidence of a strong link to the Abdul Qadeer Khan network.[375] Furthermore, in his 2006 book *In the Line of Fire,* Pakistan's President Pervez Musharraf claimed that A.Q. Khan transferred about eighteen tons of centrifuges, parts, materials, and drawings to Iran and Libya through Dubai.[376]

In either late 2001 or early 2002, A.Q. Khan provided Libya with the blueprint of an actual fission weapon. US intelligence analysts believed the documents included a nuclear weapon design that China tested in the late 1960s and later shared with Pakistan. Apparently, the design documents produced by Libya were transferred from Pakistan and contained information in both Chinese and English, establishing their Chinese lineage. The weapon blueprint set forth the design parameters and engineering specifications for constructing an implosion weapon weighing over 1,000 pounds that could be delivered using aircraft or a large ballistic missile. Since then, Pakistan has most likely graduated to building nuclear weapons that are more advanced.[377]

The US-led invasion of Iraq in March 2003, and the removal of Saddam Hussein's Ba'athist regime sobered Qadhafi into understanding that a similar fate could await him because Libya possessed WMD. Furthermore, in October 2003, according to BBC reports, the United States intercepted a German-owned ship carrying a cargo of Pakistani-designed centrifuge parts manufactured in Malaysia, bound for Libya.[378] These two factors, more than any others, was what probably triggered Qadhafi's move to renounce his WMD program. Qadhafi's personal envoys contacted President George W. Bush and British Prime Minister Tony Blair about Libya's willingness to dismantle all WMD programs. Subsequently at Qadhafi's direction, Libyan officials provided US and British officers with documentation and additional details on Libya's nuclear, chemical, biological, and ballistic missile activities.[379]

Therefore, on December 19, 2003 (a mere six-days after the capture of Saddam Hussein), Libya made a surprise announcement that it had weapons of mass destruction and missile programs, which it would now abandon. Libyan government officials were quoted as saying that Libya bought nuclear components from various black market dealers, including Pakistani nuclear scientists. US officials who visited the Libyan uranium enrichment plants shortly afterwards reported that the gas centrifuges used there were very similar to the Iranian ones. After agreeing to disclose and dismantle all WMD programs in 2003, Qadhafi's government fully cooperated with American and British experts to do so, with dismantlement of the nuclear program completed and verified by the IAEA in 2004.

However, since 2007, there has been some suspicion that Libya may have kept a nuclear and chemical weapons plant secret from the international community. The facility allegedly was run by DPRK experts at Jabal Haruj, near Al-Sabah field.[380] In part these suspicions seem true, for on October 31, 2011, Libyan National Transitional Council head Mahmoud Jibril, announced that both nuclear material and chemical weapons were found in Libya after the ouster of Qadhafi and that IAEA inspectors were scheduled to arrive in Libya later to investigate the matter.[381] Additionally, Libya's Tajura research reactor continued to stock large quantities of radioisotopes, radioactive waste and low-enriched uranium fuel after three decades of nuclear research and radioisotope production. The materials at Tajura could be used as ingredients for dirty bombs.[382] With the emergence of an Islamist government in Tripoli, a rival government in Benghazi, and continued violence by various armed militias, Libya may again covertly begin these programs, no doubt encouraged by Iran's defiance of the UN and weak sanctions designed to curtail such a program.

SYRIA
Chemical weapons

Syria was widely believed of having one of the most advanced chemical warfare (CW) capabilities in the Middle East. According to a secret CIA report, Syria was "a major recipient of Soviet chemical weapons assistance," to the degree that it achieved "the most advanced chemical warfare capability in the Arab world, with the possible exception of Egypt."[383] Syria's initial CW capability was provided by both Czechoslovakia and the Soviet Union, which supplied "the chemical agents, delivery systems, and training."[384] Components may have come via Egypt in 1972 or 1973 as part of the two countries' preparations for their joint attack on Israel in October 1973.[385] Reports that Israeli troops captured stockpiles of Syrian chemical weapons support the view that these weapons were made available to combat units during the Yom Kippur War.[386] It is notable that although Syrian forces were severely defeated by the end of the Yom Kippur War, at no point did they make use of their CW capability. This perhaps can be best explained by the Israeli nuclear alerts during that conflict (*see* "Basic Principle 61").

During the Hafez Assad regime's suppression of the Muslim Brotherhood in the city of Hama, from February 2 to 15, 1982, it is widely believed that Syria used cyanide gas against its own citizens in what came to be known as the Hama Massacre. An estimated 7,000 to 38,000 persons were killed, including some 1,000 soldiers,[387] though the exact number killed by CW is unknown.

Since then, Syria acquired an indigenous capability to develop and produce chemical weapons agents including mustard gas, sarin and VX nerve agent. It possessed the biggest stockpile of these agents in the Middle East. In the midst of the Iran–Iraq War, Syria supplied CW warheads to Iran. In 1994, reports surfaced that Syria was cooperating with Iran in the development of ballistic missiles designed to carry chemical warheads.[388] In 2006, the Office of the Director of National Intelligence stated that, "Syria is developing the more toxic and persistent nerve agent VX."[389] Chemical weapons agents have been produced since the mid-to-late 1980s at facilities located near Hama, Homs, and Al-Safira in the Aleppo region. By 1987, Syria was able to fit sarin-filled warheads on some of its Scud-B and Scud-C ballistic missiles creating a limited long-range CW strike capability.

Iran was a major source of Syrian requirements for CW-related supplies. Syria signed an agreement with Iran in 2005 that specifies among other things, the provision of training and technical assistance to Syrian scientists and technicians and the construction of five chemical pilot plant facilities for developing and producing precursor chemicals. Mohsen Fakhrizadeh-Mahabadi, who experts believed was the head of Iran's secret "Project 111" for outfitting Iranian missiles with nuclear warheads, visited Damascus in 2005. Iranian President Mahmoud Ahmadinejad traveled to Syria in 2006, where he was believed to have promised the Syrians more than $1 billion in assistance and urged them to accelerate their efforts.

It would be a logical assumption to believe that Syria utilized most of the WMD materials that was ferried out of Iraq prior to Operation *Iraqi Freedom* in 2003. Those components were certainly of no use to a post-Saddam Iraq under American occupation. The Iraqi components were likely integrated into, facilitated and perhaps speeded up, Syria's own chemical, biological and nuclear programs. Syria already had its own chemical weapons and secretly constructed a nuclear facility. There was also intense cooperation between Syria and the DPRK.

The director of the CIA, George Tenet, testified before the Senate Armed Services Committee, in March 2004, stating, "Damascus has an active CW development and testing program that relies on foreign suppliers for key controlled chemicals suitable for producing CW."[390] In 2005, the authoritative *Jane's Defense Weekly,* as well as *Jane's Intelligence Review,* repeatedly indicated that Syria was engaged in efforts to upgrade or enhance its CW capabilities, mainly in the area of production technology, in cooperation with Iran.[391]

It was reported by the authoritative *Jane's Intelligence Review,* in February 2009, that Syria was constructing a chemical weapons facility—designated as a "chloride factory"—at Al Safir, east of Aleppo, in northwest Syria. The information, gathered from 2005 to 2008, was obtained by satellite images from DigitalGlobe's WorldView-1 satellite and GeoEye's IKONOS satellite. The images showed that the site contained not only a number of the defining features of a chemical weapons facility, but also that significant levels of construction had taken place at the facility's production plant and adjacent missile base. The Al Safir facility emerged as the most significant chemical weapons production, storage and weaponization site in Syria. It also housed Syrian Scud D missiles armed with chemical warheads targeted at Israel. There was a second facility at Jabal Kalamon, as well as three others.

Regarding this issue, two senior American officers, Marine Gen. James Mattis, (head of the US Central Command which covers the Middle East and Gulf region), and Admiral William McRaven, (head of the US Special Operations Command), testified to the Senate's Armed Services Committee, on March 6, 2012. Gneral Mattis said, "Syria has a substantial' chemical and biological weapons capability and thousands of shoulder-launched missiles."[392] Admiral McRaven also spoke to the committee about Syria's weapons of mass destruction and American preparations to deal with this menace. Those briefings were the first assessments of Syrian chemical and biological weapons capabilities to be given publicly by the heads of America's armed forces. The deadly chemicals were successfully "weaponized," meaning that conventional missile warheads were mounted with delivery systems for VX gas, including Scud B, C and D missiles. These missiles were capable of hitting any target inside Israel, and "they [were] capable of spreading VX gas in bomblets similar to those seen in cluster munitions."[393] Syria's chemical weapons are under the control of a secretive Syrian air force organization called Unit 450, a highly vetted outfit that is deemed one of the most loyal to the Assad government given the importance of the weapons.[394]

Until the on-set of the uprising against the Assad regime in 2011 and the subsequent Syrian Civil War,[395] the chemical warfare storage silos were spread out among Al Safir, the main Syrian missile base in the north; Cerin, a biological research center on the Mediterranean shore; military facilities at Hama and Homs; the Syrian naval base leased to the Russians at Latakia; and Palmyra, on the highway between Homs and Aleppo. There was great concern that if the Assad regime collapses some or most of these stores would fall into the hands of such terrorist groups as the Islamic State of Syria and the Levant (ISIL), the Nusra Front, (considered the Syrian branch of Al Qaeda), Hezbollah or the Muslim Brotherhood rebels.

In January 2013, a secret US State Department assessment disclosed that forces loyal to Syrian president Bashar al-Assad had used chemical weapons. The State Department cable, signed by the US consul in Istanbul and based on interviews with doctors, defectors from the Syrian Army, and activists, made what one unnamed administration official called a "compelling case" that the Syrian military had used Agent 15, or BZ gas, in Homs in December 2012, against the Sunni-majority opposition.[396]

During March 2013, the Assad regime repeatedly used chemical weapons against the various rebel groups seeking to topple the Syrian government. Independently, the United Kingdom, France, and Israel reached this conclusion, citing as evidence the March 19, 2013, chemical attack on the town of Khan al-Assal, west of Aleppo, Syria.[397] Evidence of the use of chemical weapons was presented to the United States, but the Obama administration did not fully accept the analysis. To do so would mean the "red line" set by the Obama administration was crossed and the United States would be forced to take action. It was believed that the attack involved the use of sarin gas, the same agent used in a 1995 attack in the Tokyo subway system that killed thirteen. In the March 19 attack, twenty-six died including Syrian soldiers.[398] This chemical strike was followed by other attacks on March 19, at Al-Otaybeh, and March 24, at Adra—both near Damascus, as well as on April 13, at Sheikh Maqsoud, and April 29, at Saraqeb—both near Aleppo.[399] The Assad regime continued to deploy chemical weapons, in part no doubt because of the failure of the international community's lack of response to the March 19 attack. At the time, Syria was estimated to have a massive arsenal of more than 1,000 tons stockpiled within the country. As a result of the continued fighting, the Syrian regime[400] consolidated the chemical stockpiles into fifteen to twenty sites.

However, as the Syrian Civil War raged on, in December 2012, in response to a demand from Russia, the Assad regime consolidated its chemical assets in three depots—Mount Kalmun army base south of Damascus, Dummar, a suburb 3 miles outside Damascus, and the Al-Safira air base, west of Aleppo. On August 21, 2013, it was alleged that the Assad regime fired sarin poison gas shells at rebel positions in the Ghouta region east of Damascus. The poison gas was fired from the Mount Kalmun army base south of the capital. Rebel sources gave an unconfirmed death toll estimated to be from 300[401] to 1,729.[402] Yet, the medical humanitarian group, *Médecins Sans Frontières* (MSF)—"Doctors Without Borders"—on August 24, 2013, declared that hospitals it supported in Syria treated about 3,600 patients with "neurotoxic symptoms," i.e. symptoms related to a poison gas attack, of whom 355 died. MSF stated it could not "scientifically confirm" the use of chemical weapons.[403] Nevertheless, the intelligence services of the United States, the United Kingdom, France and Germany concluded that the Assad regime was responsible for the attacks, accusations that were supported by a UN inspection team's report.[404] In his statement, US Secretary of State John Kerry held the Syrian government responsible for firing such weapons at eleven separate sites in and around Damascus, launching them from regime-held areas against rebel-controlled neighborhoods. At least 1,429 Syrians died in the attack, 426 children among them.[405] Kerry made the claim to justify possible US military strikes against the Assad regime. It was far from clear whether it was the Assad regime or the rebels, which used the chemical weapons in the August 21 attack. Further complicating the search for the truth was the claim that Iran developed a special formula mixture for use in such gas shells. Those shells contain only tiny quantities of sarin mixed with a large amount of riot control agents. In this manner, Iran, Syria and their proxies attempted to camouflage the use of chemical weapons.[406] By mid-2013, Syria was thought to have somewhere between 500 and 1,000 tons of chemical munitions.

The United States did not launch any military strikes, as domestic protest grew in opposition to such action. Days passed as rumors grew of the chemical agents being moved (to Iraq, to Hezbollah in Lebanon, and scattered across Syria), while the Obama administration talked of only pinprick military strikes. Russia, quick to exploit the situation, brokered an arrangement, in which Syria agreed to dismantle its CW stockpiles. Thus, on September 14, 2013, a "Framework for Elimination of Syrian Chemical Weapons," (also known as the Kerry-Lavrov pact) was signed. It called for the elimination of Syria's chemical weapon stockpiles by mid-2014. As part of the US–Russia agreement, Syria acceded to the Chemical Weapons Convention. However, in its rush to conclude an agreement and avoid taking military action, the Obama administration knew that the list of chemical substances, which the Kerry-Lavrov accord listed for removal, covered at best 70 to 75 percent of Assad's chemical arsenal. This left the Assad regime a huge loophole, which it was quick to exploit as circumstances, dictated.

The Kerry-Lavrov arrangement was confirmed by UN Security Council resolution 2118, passed unanimously on September 27, 2013, that called "for the expeditious destruction of the Syrian Arab Republic's chemical weapons program and stringent verification thereof." In the text, the Council underscored "that no party in Syria should use, develop, produce, acquire, stockpile, retain, or transfer chemical weapons." In reality, the resolution is toothless, devoid of penalties for non-compliance. Any possible use of force in the future under Chapter 7 would require a new resolution, which could be vetoed by Russia and/or China.

The UN Organization for the Prohibition of Chemical Weapons (OPCW) began preliminary inspections of Syria's chemical weapons arsenal on October 1, 2013, [407] and actual destruction began on October 6. Under OPCW supervision, Syrian military personnel began "destroying munitions such as missile warheads and aerial bombs and disabling mobile and static mixing and filling units." Ahmet Uzumcu, the Director General of the Organization for the Prohibition of Chemical Weapons, reported on October 28, that Syria declared forty-one facilities at twenty-three chemical sites where it stored approximately 1,300 tons of chemical precursors and agents and 1,230 unfilled munitions. The inspectors, however, corroborated information at only 37 of the 41 facilities.[408] Syria disclosed to international inspectors a previously undeclared research and development facility as well as a laboratory to produce ricin poison.[409] The destruction of Syria's declared chemical weapons production, mixing, and filling equipment was successfully completed by the October 31 deadline.

However, the destruction of the chemical weapons themselves fell behind schedule. The entire chemical weapons stockpile was scheduled to be completely removed from the country by February 6, 2014. As of March 21, Syria removed or destroyed more than half of its declared chemical stockpile, and proposed a new removal completion target date of April 27, 2014. By June 23, 2014, all of Syria's chemical weapons production facilities were rendered inoperable and all reported, i.e. listed, chemical weapons and their precursors were removed from the country.[410] On July 7, 2014, the United States began neutralizing the chemical components aboard the MV *Cape Ray* cargo ship, which was outfitted with two Field Deployable Hydrolysis Systems designed to neutralize chemical weapons.[411] An additional 200 tons of various chemical precursors were sent to the UK for destruction.[412] By August 18, 2014, some 581.5 metric tons of DF, a sarin precursor chemical, and 19.8 metric tons of HD, an ingredient of sulfur mustard had been neutralized.[413]

However, circumventing the Kerry-Lavrov pact Syria employed a new chemical weapon, which was not on the proscribed list of banned weapons. The new weapon is made of Chinese-manufactured chlorine gas canisters rigged with explosive detonators. Iran bought the chlorine for its Syrian ally, from a Chinese company in Hangzhou. The chlorine product is advertised over the Internet for $1,000 per ton and the company could supply quantities from 50 to 30,000 canisters. Iran initially ordered 10,000 canisters. They were delivered by Iranian military transports to Damascus military airfield where Iranian technicians repackage the chlorine in containers suitable for dropping by aircraft.[414]

Hence, on March 27, 2014, the Assad regime launched two chemical attacks against rebel forces in the Harasta neighborhood of Damascus. Both the US and UK investigated the attack.[415] This was followed on April 11, as Syrian aircraft dropped the chlorine canisters on Kafr Zita near Hama. Since then, British and French intelligence sources reported at least, four such attacks against the northern towns of Idlib and Homs and the Harasta and Jobar districts outside Damascus.[416] The Obama administration knew of these violations but kept quiet to prove the Kerry-Lavrov pact was working.

It should be noted that the use of chlorine as a weapon of war was banned by the Geneva Protocol. The protocol was promulgated after the widespread use of chlorine and mustard gas in World War I by the German army to gas hundreds of thousands of Allied troops during the Second Battle of Ypres in 1915. The protocol called for the prohibition of the use in war of asphyxiating, poisonous or other gases, and of bacteriological methods of warfare. It was signed June 17, 1925. The Geneva Protocol was augmented by the Chemical Weapons Convention of which Syria is a signatory.

Israel believes Syria has retained caches of combat-ready chemical weapons even after giving up raw materials used to produce such munitions. While Syria did relinquish those chemical agents on a declared list, it kept some missile warheads, airdropped bombs and rocket-propelled grenades primed with toxins like sarin.[417] It is believed that Israel knows the location of the sites where the Syrian regime's remaining chemical stockpiles are located. The immediate concern is if ISIL or some other Syrian rebel force, like the Nusra Front would gain access to any of these sites.

Syria, supported by its patron Iran, cheated with regard to the Kerry-Lavrov pact, with complete impunity. This end run around an international agreement is an important object lesson. There can be little doubt that having fooled the West on the Syrian chemical weapons issue, Iran will find ways to evade even the most stringent nuclear accord it concludes with the world powers and continue to finish production of its main goal—nuclear weapons.

Biological weapons

While Syria signed the Biological Weapons Convention on April 14, 1972, it never ratified the treaty and is not expected to do so anytime soon. Syria has a large pharmaceutical infrastructure that could support a biological weapons (BW) program. It began its BW program in 1983 by purchasing dual-use technologies from several countries including Egypt, France, Germany, the Netherlands, Russia, the United Kingdom, and the United States. Syria possesses a variety of biological weapon toxins. These include ricin, a very lethal toxin produced from the common castor oil plant. One kilogram of ricin can cause the same damage as eight tons of anthrax bacteria, which Syria possesses as well. Anthrax is regarded as a fairly common and easy to produce biological weapon. Syria also possesses the smallpox virus, which tops the list of the world's most lethal contaminants. Prior to 2003 Syria gained information and assistance from Iraq's biological weapon industry and there is reason to believe that components of the Iraqi program were moved to Syria just prior to Operation *Iraqi Freedom*. Since the late 1990s, both Iran and Sudan are active partners with Syria in the development of chemical and biological weapons, and—according to NATO intelligence sources—Sudan provided the grounds for field trials of chemical and biological weapons.[418]

Missile delivery systems

During the Yom Kippur War of 1973, Syria fired some 25 FROG-7 missiles at Israel. Syria is currently believed to deploy between 100 and 200 Scud missiles fitted with sarin warheads. Some of these missiles may be fitted with VX warheads. In addition, Syria is believed to have stockpiled several hundred tons of sarin and mustard agents for tactical uses in the form of artillery shells and airdropped munitions.

During the late 1980s, Syria applied an upgrade from the DPRK Hwasong-6 to its Scud-B inventory. According to *Janes,* the Hwasong-6, also known as the Scud-C, was developed by the DPRK in 1984 as an improvement of the Scud-B (R-17 SS-1) missile, which it had received from Egypt. Among the changes made by the DPRK was an expansion of the missile's range from its original 186 miles to 373 miles.

Since the late 1980s, Syria sought to increase the range and effectiveness of its missiles' strike capability by obtaining longer-range missiles from foreign suppliers such as Iran and the DPRK and by improving the sophistication of the warheads.[419] Syria reportedly purchased 150 Scud-C missiles from the DPRK in 1991.[420] By 2000, the DPRK was believed to have delivered fifty Scud-D missiles to Syria. These missiles have a range of approximately 435 miles. Today, Syria has the ability to produce liquid-fueled Scud missiles in its own facilities. Furthermore, Syria with the aid of foreign governments, such as Iran and the DPRK, seeks to develop the indigenous capability to produce solid-fueled ballistic missiles. Syria now possesses the ability to strike targets throughout Israel from fortified missile sites set deep within its territory.

In a move designed to outflank Israel in mid-April 2010, Syria positioned both Scud A and SS-1B missiles on the border with Lebanon ready for transit at a moment's notice to Hezbollah forces in Lebanon. Subsequent reports claimed that Syria actually sent the Scuds into Lebanon broken down to be reassembled upon arrival.[421] Syria trained two Hezbollah brigades in their use. The Kuwaiti newspaper *Al Rai* reported that Syria was arming Hezbollah with Scuds, a report Syria denied but both the United States and Israel later confirmed the information. Google Earth photos, taken March 22, 2010, and made public October 8, 2010, by the Israeli daily *Ha'aretz,* showed Scud missiles ready for deployment at a Syrian base at Adra, near Damascus. The photos showed five 11-meter-long

Scuds, the length of both Scud-Bs and Scud-Cs. Hezbollah sources told *Al Rai* that the group had the capability to launch 15 tons of explosives at Israel every day in the case of another war between the two sides. *Al Rai* went on to claim that Hezbollah possesses a wide range of missiles with a heavy payload, including the 1-ton Zilzal missile and half-ton Fateh 110 and M600 missiles.[422] The M600 is the Syrian version of the Scud-D missile. Their range is 435 miles placing virtually all of Israel much of Jordan and parts of Turkey within range.

These were not like the Scuds Saddam Hussein fired at Israel and Saudi Arabia during the Persian Gulf War in 1991, but dramatically improved versions of the earlier Scuds. They are self-propelled and therefore highly mobile, maneuverable and required relatively small teams and few vehicles for their operation. While lacking precision, their reach enables Hezbollah, for the first time, to hit the big Israeli air bases in the southern Negev Desert, twice as far from the Lebanese border as Tel Aviv. This would render their Hezbollah operators less susceptible to Israeli air attack. For Israel this development is equivalent to, but more dangerous than, the Cuba Missile Crisis of 1962. In that earlier crisis, the Soviet Union dispatched offensive missiles to Cuba, but they remained under firm Soviet control for the duration of the crisis. Syria in this case, is prepared to turn the missiles over to an Iranian-supported terrorist group, Hezbollah.

In May 2010, the *Sunday Times* reported that shipments of weapons from the Adra base were going to Hezbollah, and that Iran was sending missiles and other weapons to that base via Damascus airport nearby. The paper also said Hezbollah was given a section of the base for barracks, warehouses and a fleet of trucks to transport weapons to the Lebanese border, which is just 25 miles away.[423] It was announced that Syria had deployed its M-600 missile in Lebanon giving these weapons to Hezbollah. The M-600 carries a 1,100-pound conventional or unconventional warhead, and is a Syrian improvement to Iran's Fateh-110 missile, which has a range of some 150 miles. According to an article published in the May 17, 2010 issue of *Aviation Week*, the latest Syrian variant of the Scud missile is equipped with a 500-meter CEP (complex event processing) system—meaning that the missile can identify and proceed to the most meaningful target among thousands of possible options within a 500-meter range. The same article noted that the CEP of the M-600 was approximately 200 meters—nearly Scud class.[424] Furthermore, being solid-fueled, the M-600 can be fired without preparation, as opposed to the Scud missile, which must be protected from air strikes during fueling because it requires liquid fuel. Deployed north of Lebanon's Litani River, the M-600 can hit all of Israel, including Tel Aviv, Jerusalem and its ports as far south as Ashkelon.[425]

Despite promises not to do so (to two US Presidents, George W. Bush and Barak Obama), on December 5, 2012, Russia delivered a dozen mobile batteries of Iskander 9K720 (NATO code-named SS-26 Stone) cruise missiles to Syria. Each battery carries a pair of the missiles, which are designed for theater level conflict. The cruise missile flies at a hypersonic speed of more than 1.3 miles per second with a 280-mile-range and a 1,500-pound warhead, which destroys targets with pinpoint accuracy.[426] The Iskander is excessively maneuverable in the terminal phase of the flight and releases decoys. These features were designed to overcome enemy air defense systems. In some cases, this ballistic missile can be used as an alternative to precision bombing. The Iskander has several different conventional warheads, including cluster, fuel-air explosive, bunker-busting and electro-magnetic pulse types.[427] It is also nuclear-capable.

Nuclear weapons

Syria embarked on a nuclear program in the 1970s. At various times it sought assistance from different nations to acquire a reactor—including Argentina, Belgium, France, India, Switzerland and the Soviet Union—all to no avail. In 1982 and then again in 2002, the Syrian government approached Dr. Abdul Qadeer Khan, the father of Pakistan's nuclear program, in an attempt to enlist his help with their clandestine nuclear program. Khan rebuffed the Syrian request on both occasions.[428] Khan denied supplying the Syrians with any information. However, evidence seems to indicate he was less than honest. Earlier, Khan assisted Libya when Muammar Qadhafi was pursuing a nuclear weapons program, including the design and layout of a uranium enrichment plant. In the meanwhile, in 1991 China began construction of a SRR-1 research reactor as a part of an IAEA technical assistance project. China supplied the uranium.[429] The SRR-1 reactor went critical in 1996.[430]

On November 1, 2011, the International Atomic Energy Agency disclosed that a cotton-spinning factory built in the northeastern Syrian town of Al Hasakah in 2003, was in fact designed for developing nuclear weapons from enriched uranium.[431] The layout at Al Hasakah matched the plans used in Libya almost exactly, with a large building surrounded by three smaller workshops in the same configurations. Investigators were struck that even the parking lots had similarities, with a covered area to shield cars from the sun.[432] The IAEA sources revealed that the Syrian government worked on the secret Al-Hasakah complex with A.Q. Khan, basing it on the same technology he designed for Libya's nuclear bomb project. They also disclosed correspondence between Khan and a Syrian government official Muhidin Issa, after Pakistan's nuclear test in 1998, requesting scientific cooperation and asking to visit Khan's laboratories.[433]

Not to be forgotten was the fact that Syria procured the enriched uranium and equipment for the plant from Iraq when Saddam Hussein in early March 2003, decided to dispose of the bulk of his nuclear plant and weapons of mass destruction by spiriting them out to Syria in advance of the US-led Operation *Iraqi Freedom*. It is reported that some 50 trucks crossed the border on March 10, 2003, and sources in Syria confirmed they carried WMD.[434] Additionally, "Russian SPETSNATZ* units helped moved WMD out of Iraq before the war," according to John Shaw, the former US deputy undersecretary for international technology security.[435]

In 2004, US intelligence agents picked up unusual conversations between Syria and the DPRK regarding cooperation in the nuclear sphere. Syria and the DPRK already had developed strong ties including the sale of DPRK missiles to the Syrian regime. The information was related to Israel, and the IDF set up monitoring antennae aimed at Al Kibar. In 2006, Mossad agents in London were able to install a program on a Syrian official's computer and collected information on construction plans and photographs showing pipes that led to a pumping station at the Euphrates River. A building complex was erected at Al Kibar, near the town of Tal al-Abyad in the Deir Ez-Zour region in northeastern Syria, near the Euphrates and Syria's border with Turkey. The building complex was the site of a previously undisclosed Syrian nuclear reactor installation.

As was subsequently revealed, the facility housed a partially completed 25MWth gas-cooled graphite-moderated nuclear reactor, which would have been capable of producing enough plutonium for one or two weapons per year.[436] According to the US Institute for Science and International Security, the Al Kibar site matched the DPRK's Yongbyon reactor in its layout and technical design, which included heavily, sealed reinforced-concrete rooms for heat exchanges and a spent fuel holding pool.[437] The Al Kibar facility was to be a backup plant for the 40-megawatt heavy-water reactor under

---

* SPETSNAZ is the Russian acronym for "special purpose forces" assigned to special tasks.

construction near the Iranian city of Arak, designed to provide plutonium to build a bomb if Iran did not succeed in constructing a weapon using enriched uranium.[438] However, more confirmation was needed.

Thus, in March 2007, Mossad agents raided the Vienna, Austria, home of Ibrahim Othman, the head of the Syrian Atomic Energy Commission. The agents retrieved nearly 40 dozen color photographs of inside the building. The photos indicated the complex was hiding a uranium nuclear reactor. The reactor from the inside had many of the same engineering elements as the DPRK reactor at Yongbyon. The photos reinforced the view that the facility was a nuclear reactor, meant to yield bomb-grade plutonium, developed with DPRK assistance.[439] The Israeli government informed the United States in April 2007, but the Bush administration concluded there was not enough substantive evidence to justify a military attack. Therefore, Israel decided to act alone.[440]

Sometime between 12:40 and 12:53 A.M. on September 6, 2007, four Israeli Air Force (IAF) F-15s and four F-16s—in Operation *Orchard*—struck the Al Kibar facility, dropping 17 tons of explosives,[441] destroying the complex. Israel had informed the United States of its intention to do so. Due to Israel's action, Syria's clandestine nuclear weapons facility was revealed to the world and perhaps more importantly that Syria was trying, by two separate development methods—uranium as well as plutonium—to get a nuclear bomb.[442] The IAF strike severed the Syrian-Iranian-DPRK nuclear link before it took physical shape and began turning out plutonium for Iran's nuclear program.

At the very time of the Israeli attack on the Al Kibar facility, a ship from the DPRK carrying forty-five tons of yellowcake—enough to build several nuclear weapons—was headed for Syria. After the attack, Syrian President Bashar al-Assad advised DPRK leader Kim Jong-Il to reverse course, lest the United States or Israel intercept the ship when it entered the Mediterranean Sea. Furthermore, Iran and the DPRK realized that they had to cut Syria out of their nuclear plans because its proximity to Israel made any nuclear site a relatively accessible target.

It should be noted that in the summer of 2009, that same yellowcake consignment was secretly reshipped to Iran, attesting to the integral nuclear partnership between Iran and Syria.[443] Syria quickly leveled what remained of the Al Kibar site and built over it, only three days after the airstrike. Syria allowed the United Nations' International Atomic Energy Agency (IAEA) investigators to visit the site only once in June 2008 and stonewalled all further requests for access. Satellite images at the end of July 2008, showed suspicious activity in the area. The Syrians did not produce the requested explanations to the IAEA.

Syria and Iran, in their strategic alliance agreed to a division of labor in any potential war against Israel: The Syrian reactor would produce "dirty weapons," while Iran would build a nuclear bomb. Iran funded the DPRK reactor in Syria. The radiological weapons made there were to be distributed to the terrorist organizations fighting Israel. Intelligence briefings during US Congressional hearings substantiated this in late April 2008. On February 19, 2009, the IAEA announced that its investigators found new traces of uranium in samples taken from the site of the Israeli air strike on Al Kibar. In addition to discovering more uranium traces, the agency's experts found graphite particles. Graphite had not been found at the site previously. The presence of this form of carbon was evidence of the type of reactor.

Despite the Israeli air strike of 2007, Syria continued to pursue a nuclear weapons capability in collusion with both Iran and the DPRK. It was believed to have established several secret nuclear development facilities that have yet to be exposed. According to the former US representative to the IAEA, Gregory Schulte, the Syrians refused to grant the IAEA access to several suspected nuclear facilities in the country. Damascus "claimed they were military sites," he said during an interview with Israel's Channel 10 news on September 10, 2009.[444] It was revealed in October 2009, by the US Congressional Research Service, that Iran helped Syria obtain "various forms of weapons of mass destruction" and missiles, as well as buying midget submarines—all from the DPRK. There has been much activity around the village of Al-Baida, in the area around Masyaf.

On November 30, 2009, IAEA inspectors visited the bombed Syrian-DPRK facility Al Kibar site at Dir a-Zur and discovered traces of highly processed plutonium. The soil samples the inspectors collected confirmed an earlier discovery of uranium used in separating out bomb-grade plutonium from spent nuclear fuel, which the United States believed, was supplied by Iran. This is hard evidence of Iran's covert nuclear activities and proliferation. As has been mentioned, Iran and Syria have close military and nuclear development programs, and cooperation between the two countries has been intense. Iran was directly involved in the planning and construction of the demolished Syrian reactor. Iran supplied Syria with the nuclear materials and technology for its operation as part of its own program to attain a nuclear weapons capability.

Since 2008, a Western company, allegedly a front for a Western intelligence agency, has ordered photographs on at least sixteen separate occasions (the last two in January 2010), of the region in question, from DigitalGlobe, a satellite imaging service. The photos are available at Google Earth. The images depict at least five guarded installations whose purpose is unclear. In the center is a new residential complex with at least forty multistory buildings whose shape and structure are distinct from the architecture in the rest of the town.[445] A number of Google Earth users said they saw passageways to bunkers leading to installations underneath the mountains surrounding Masyaf. DigitalGlobe refused to say who requested the satellite photos. Two weeks before the September 2007 destruction of the nuclear reactor in northeast Syria, the company placed an order for numerous photographs of the installation. *Yedioth Ahronoth* reported that the photos were ordered by Israel so that it could show them to the press after the bombing. According to the newspaper, Israel sought to demonstrate its military capabilities without revealing its sources.[446]

Western intelligence agencies, on the basis of satellite photos, detected another smaller nuclear plant in a suburb of Damascus. A German newspaper, the *Süddeutsche Zeitung (SZ)*, broke the story in February 2011, and has copies of the photos. The small, two-building complex reported by the German paper is located in Marj al-Sultan, adjacent to a military base about 9.5 miles east of Damascus. *SZ* reported that the photos led analysts to believe that it is a uranium conversion plant for the production of fuel rods. It further stated that the IAEA, in Vienna, refused to comment on the photos. The images of the smaller building showed chemical equipment apparently made of stainless steel, as "would be expected in a uranium conversion plant," according to Western intelligence officials. Similar technology for the removal of impurities from the uranium is in use in the Iranian conversion plant at Isfahan, Iran. Photos of the larger building showed specialized equipment for filtering out uranium particles and hazardous chemicals resulting from the production process.

Western intelligence sources declared there are "links" between the Al Kibar site and Marj al-Sultan. Apparently, the same people were seen at both locations and/or transports between the plants were observed. In addition, the US Institute for Science and International Security published photos on February 23, 2011, of one of three more sites that were believed to be connected to the Al Kibar facility.[447] It was only in June 2011, in part due no doubt, to negative world reaction to the Syrian regime's brutal and violent suppression of its own people engaged in demonstrations for regime change that the IAEA finally decided to report Syria to the UN Security Council over its alleged covert nuclear program.[448]

Late in 2012, during the Syrian Civil War, concern was heightened over the possible existence and whereabouts of up to 50 tons of enriched uranium produced at the Marj al-Sultan uranium conversion facility. The *Financial Times* of London reported that the uranium stockpile was large enough for the production of five atomic bombs. According to anonymous officials quoted, "Syria is almost certainly in possession of good quality uranium of the type that Iran has been trying to acquire on the international market for years. It would certainly be possible to transfer this from Syria to Iran by air."[449]

With the rapid military conquest of vast swaths of Syrian and Iraqi territory by the Islamic State of Iraq and the Levant (ISIL), as well as its seizure of military equipment from both nations, there is genuine concern that ISIL may have acquired various components of Syria's clandestine nuclear program. ISIL already has a potential delivery system as evidenced by its parading of a captured Scud D surface-to-surface missile through the streets of Raqqa, Syria on July 1, 2014; though experts claim the missile is probably inoperable.[450]

IRAN

Religion and national pride fuel the Islamic Republic of Iran's aggressive foreign policy. Iran seeks hegemonic dominance of the Middle East. Iranian Islamic theologians think Islam should rule the world, and that their particular Shi'a denomination should dominate Islam. Additionally, ethnic Persians think Arabs are inferior, and ought to pay them proper respect. Not to be forgotten is the surprise attack on Iran made by Iraq on September 22, 1980, triggering a long and very costly 8-year war in terms of both lives lost and expenditure. For these reasons, Iran sought to obtain WMDs.

Chemical weapons

Iran is one of the few countries in the world since the end of World War I, which has encountered chemical warfare (CW) on the battlefield. As was previously discussed, Iran suffered chemical weapons attacks during the Iran–Iraq War of 1980–88. Beginning in 1983, Iran suffered the effects of increasingly effective Iraqi CW attacks, initially using blister (mustard) but later including nerve agents such as tabun and sarin. By the end of the war, Iran suffered as many as 100,000 chemical warfare casualties, of whom perhaps 5,000 died with many others, suffering debilitating long-term health effects.[451] Therefore, with good reason, Iranian officials concluded that their country had to develop the ability to retaliate in kind in order to deter chemical weapons use against it. Iran allegedly used CW against Iraqi forces on a limited scale beginning in 1984 or 1985. Iran was believed to conduct initial CW attacks by firing captured Iraqi CW munitions at Iraqi forces. However, by the end of the war Iran reportedly employed domestically produced CW munitions against Iraqi soldiers.[452] In mid-1996, the CIA reported that Iran had vast stockpiles of CW agents.[453] Iran joined the Chemical Weapons Convention (CWC) on April 29, 1997, but retained its CW capabilities.

The scope and status of Iran's chemical and biological weapons programs are unknown. Though there is no concrete evidence that Iran is currently developing CW, there were several instances where CW precursors were purchased from foreign sources in the past. In 1989, US authorities found Alcolac International Inc., a pharmaceutical firm based out of Baltimore, Maryland, guilty of illegally shipping almost 120 tons of thiodyglycol (a mustard gas precursor) to Iran. The same year, the US Department of Commerce put export controls on twenty-three specific chemicals that could aid CW proliferation. Also in 1989, the State Trading Corporation of India admitted that it had sold Iran over 60 tons of thionyl chloride (a nerve agent precursor) and that its supplier was planning to ship an additional 257 tons of the chemical to Iran. In 1997, under a reported multi-million dollar deal, India agreed to construct a "sophisticated chemical plant at Qazvim, on the outskirts of Tehran."[454] In 1998, China reportedly agreed to sell Iran 500 tons of phosphorus pentasulfide, a dual-use chemical, used in the production of pesticides as well as the nerve agent VX.[455] Despite its acquisition of precursors from abroad, Iran is allegedly working to develop an indigenous CW production capability. As of 1996, the US Department of Defense claimed that Iran had stockpiled almost 2,000 tons of toxic chemical agents and was continuously working on expanding its CW program. In 2000, the CIA reported that, "Teheran is rapidly approaching self-sufficiency and could become a supplier of CW-related materials to other nations."[456] It was claimed in 2005 that, with the help of Russian experts, Iran was "in the advanced research and development phase" of weaponizing chemical toxins and living organisms.[457]

These moves are in violation of the Chemical Warfare Convention, which outlaws the production, stockpiling and use of chemical weapons. In Iran there are two plants for the production of chemical weapons, the Aghajeri chemical plant, situated between Al-'Amidiyya and Behbahan, and the Shaznad plant, situated next to the Arak factories in northern Ahwaz. Ahwaz is the capital of Khuzistan Province in southwestern Iran close to the Iraqi border. Iran's stockpile of CW agents reportedly includes cyanide, mustard, phosgene and possibly sarin nerve agent.

According to an intelligence report released on July 14, 2009, by the Ahwazi Islamic Sunni Organization[458] echoing Western reports, Iran transferred its first sea transport of chemicals as part of its missile program, including missiles installed on warplanes, which Iran was trying to adapt for carrying chemical warheads. The organization further claimed that Iran was trying to obtain sulfur for military use. In 2005, chemicals were transported to Ahwaz for the purposes of burying the waste from their manufacture.[459] Additionally, as Iran prepared its options for eliminating Israel, it transshipped gas masks and chemical weapons through Syria to Hezbollah its Lebanese proxy, for possible future attacks on Israel.[460]

With such threats in mind, one is led to wonder if the explosions on May 7, 2013, were accidental or an act of sabotage. On that day, explosions ripped through a facility, which developed chemical weapons and produced fuel for surface-to-surface missiles. The facility—the Raja-Shimi chemical industrial complex—is in the Bidganeh area west of Tehran. It is affiliated with the Iranian Ministry of Defense and deals in the production of chemical materials for military use.[461]

Biological weapons

While Iran joined the Biological and Toxin Weapons Convention (BTWC) in 1973, Western sources believe it developed BW during the Iran–Iraq War. Iran showed an interest in acquiring BW agents from foreign sources. The speaker of the Iranian parliament publicly stated in 1988 "we should fully equip ourselves in defensive and offensive use of chemical, bacteriological, and radiological weapons."[462] Iran has a very sophisticated biotechnology infrastructure that includes leading research facilities and trained personnel. Thus, Iran has the potential to divert dual-use agents for illicit BW purposes. Iran possesses the technical capability to pursue actively a basic BW program. According to the CIA and experts in the field, Iran is trying to develop sophisticated biological weapons.[463] Cuba has reportedly transferred Cuban biological and chemical warfare information to Iran.[464] Iran also has a delivery system for such weapons. The Iranian Shahab missile is reportedly capable of carrying biological warheads.[465]

In mid-December 2012, it was revealed that Russian scientists assisted Iran in producing several microbial agents for bombs, which the Islamic regime has used to arm at least thirty-seven launch-ready missiles. The secret work was done at a plant named Shahid Bahonar near the city of Marzanabad adjacent to the Caspian Sea. The facility is under the supervision of the Atomic Energy Organization of Iran and is headed by Dr. Esmaeil Namazi, who oversees twenty-eight Iranian and twelve Russian scientists. The scientists have thus far developed several substances that can be weaponized, arming missile warheads with microbial agents. These include:

- Bacillus anthracis (anthrax). This bacteria was developed by the United States during World War II and through espionage was obtained by the Soviet Union, which has long mastered the production. Russian scientists have helped the Iranians to produce anthrax.
- Encephalitis. The blueprint of this virus, Venezuelan Equine Encephalitis, was provided by Venezuelan President Hugo Chavez in a 2010 agreement with the Islamic regime.
- Yellow grain. This third agent, developed with the help of the DPRK but named "yellow grain" by the Iranians, has no smell and upon impact will destroy the body's defensive system. Victims would have a hard time walking or breathing within hours and slowly their digestive systems would be destroyed, likely followed by death within 48 hours.[466]

Such missile-borne warheads do not create an explosion but spray a large area killing tens of thousands of people quickly. Iran has provided yellow grain to the terrorist group Hezbollah to use in artillery shells and rockets, and has armed cluster bombs with it for any confrontation with Israel and the United States.[467] "It is no secret that Iran, in addition to pursuing nuclear weapons, has major programs for biological and chemical weapons, in defiance of the Biological and Chemical Weapons Convention that supposedly bans such weapons worldwide,"[468] said Dr. Peter Vincent Pry, executive director of the Task Force on National and Homeland Security, an advisory board to the US Congress.

Missile delivery systems

At the start of the Iran–Iraq War (1980–88), Iran's use of rockets and missiles was limited. Iraq used missiles against Iranian cities. Iran reciprocated in kind, but did not have substantial quantities of missiles. This situation changed significantly after 1985. Iran was able to obtain approximately twenty to thirty Scud-Bs from Libya during January–February 1985.[469] These were fired March 13–16, 1985, just prior to the second "war of the cities" from March 22 to April 8, 1985, to strike at Baghdad. In mid-June 1985, Ali Akbar Hashemi-Rafsanjani, the Speaker of the *Majlis* (Iran's parliament), led a high-level delegation to China and the DPRK in order to conclude agreements to sell Iran ballistic missiles and engage in missile technology exchanges. These were followed by a second agreement in 1985 valued at $500 million, between Iran and the DPRK. Iran immediately acquired 90 to 100 Hwasong-5 missiles and the DPRK provided technical assistance in the establishment of a factory to assemble the Hwasong-5 missiles, thus helping Iran establish a production line. The Hwasong-5 was called Scud by NATO forces. In Iran, the Hwasong-5 was produced as the Shahab-1.[470] It had a range of 200 miles.

Iran responded to the Iraqi-initiated fifth "war of the cities" by striking at Baghdad and Kirkuk. Iran even fired a Scud-B ballistic missile at Kuwait on April 20, 1988. The missile landed near the Wafra oil field, but caused no damage. This fifth "war of the cities" lasted sixty-two days until April 30, 1988. During this last "war of the cities," some 532 rockets and missiles were launched by both sides. Iran launched approximately 339 (of which 80 were Shahab-1s) and Iraq launched about 193 (189 Al-Husseins and four Scud-Bs).[471] Iraq's missiles with high explosive warheads killed about 2,000 Iranians and injured 6,000. The Iraqi bombardment caused widespread demoralization. Over a quarter of the population of ten million fled Tehran. Simultaneously, there was a continuing string of Iraqi ground victories, most notably the Iraqi recapture of the Fao Peninsula, April 18–19, 1988. All these factors and the threat of the Iranian capital being hit with missiles capable of carrying chemical warheads forced Iran to accept a ceasefire.

On August 8, 1988, after eight years of bitter fighting and between 1,000,000 and 1,600,000 killed on both sides, UN Secretary-General Pérez de Cuéllar announced a ceasefire effective August 20. The Iran–Iraq War came to a formal end. Iran had not only been defeated on the battlefield, it had more significantly, been defeated at home. Its economy was depleted; its civilian industry near collapse, and its population was simply exhausted from the war.

Nevertheless, after the war, Iran acquired additional Scud-B/Hwasong-5 (as mentioned renamed Shahab-1) and Scud-C/Hwasong-6 missiles and production lines from the DPRK. The latter was renamed Shahab-2.[472] Tehran commenced producing considerable quantities of the missiles shortly thereafter.[473] Iran's limited missile achievements during the Iran–Iraq War only served to reinforce its desire to possess and produce ballistic missiles. Its missile program was thus assigned a national priority at least equal to that of its nuclear program.

Iran is not a member of the Missile Technology Control Regime, and is actively working to acquire, develop, and deploy a broad range of ballistic missiles and space launch capabilities. Corresponding to the proliferation of WMD information mentioned above, was the development and sharing of missile technology by the same three states—Iran, the DPRK, and Syria*—trading technical information on avionics, propulsion systems and other missile components, to create delivery systems for the WMDs in development.[474] The DPRK maintained a permanent mission of nuclear and missile scientists in Iran, whereas Iranian experts were in regular attendance at the DPRK's nuclear and missile tests. Between the two nations, there is an agreement for a division of labor regarding the nuclear and missile fields. Their arrangement assigns to Iran the development of small nuclear warheads for delivery by missiles and to the DPRK the development of ballistic missiles able to land a warhead at any point on earth.

On July 22, 1998, Iran successfully tested a single-stage liquid fueled missile—the Shahab-3 (a variant of the No Dong 1 missile first provided to it by the DPRK[475])—with a range of 930 miles.[476] On February 7, 1999, Iran's Defense Minister Ali Shamkani "confirmed that the Shahab-3 is now in production, and that no further flight tests are needed."[477] Iran began producing the Shahab-3 in early 2001 based upon the model used during the second Shahab-3 test in 2000.[478] The Shahab-3 is capable of carrying a nuclear warhead weighing from 1,100 pounds to 1 ton.[479] It is domestically produced within Iran and can threaten either Tel Aviv or Riyadh from the same launch point. An improved Shahab 3ER, with its 1,300-mile range, can reach Ankara, Turkey, Alexandria, Egypt, or Sana'a, Yemen[480] from one single launch point deep within Iran. Thus, Iran does not have to move its launchers to project power, making its missile arsenal more survivable.

During a September 22, 2003 military parade, authorities displayed a Shahab-3 missile draped with a banner reading, "Israel must be uprooted and erased from history."[481] Iranian engineers moved forward developing the Shahab-4 and Shahab-5 (based on the DPRK Taepodong-2), with ranges of about 2,000 and 3,100 miles respectively. These missiles would allow Iran to strike targets as far as Germany, Italy or Moscow, Russia.[482] Brigadier General Safavi, who headed Iran's Revolutionary

---

* The DPRK and Syria are also not members of the Missile Technology Control Regime.

Guard Corps, declared in 2003, "Iranian missiles can cause irreparable damage to either Israel or the United States." It was in response to this looming threat that the United States and Israel developed the Arrow anti-ballistic missile system.

In 2003 or 2004, Iran purchased a dozen Kh-55 air-launched cruise missiles from Ukraine. In 2005, Ukrainian president Viktor Yushchenko confirmed the sale of the Kh-55 missiles to Iran and China—by his predecessor, Leonid Kuchma. Israeli intelligence estimated that they were sold to Iran without nuclear warheads but with attached diagrams and specifications, so providing the technology to help Iran leapfrog into its delivery systems program. These missiles, referred to by NATO as the AS-15 "Kent," were capable of carrying conventional or nuclear warheads. At the same time as the Kh-55 cruise missile sale, a shipment of six to ten "nuclear suitcases" was delivered to Iran. The nuclear suitcases were apparently sold without nuclear explosives, but with diagrams and specifications. This means Iran had an additional method of delivering a nuclear device to a target starting over a decade ago.[483]

By May 2010, Iran was producing its own upgraded version of the Kh-55. Iranian scientists worked on lengthening the nuclear-capable, long-range cruise missile's range beyond its regular 1,550 miles and developing a version for use by fighter-bombers. This would enable Iranian warplanes to shoot missiles against targets not only in Israel but also as far away as Central Europe.[484] Covert co-operation between Cuba and Iran led to the development and testing of electromagnetic weapons ("e-bombs") able to disrupt telecommunication and power supplies and to wage cyberwarfare. These weapons can be delivered by cruise missiles, unmanned aerial vehicles or aerial bombs against the communication and military infrastructure of target countries, notably the United States.[485] From China, Iran obtained Chinese-made anti-ship surface-to-surface C-801 and C-802 missiles (the latter with a 72-mile range), which pose a potential threat to Persian Gulf and Mediterranean shipping, particularly US and Israeli naval vessels in the region.[486]

During a military parade in Tehran in September 2007, Iran displayed another new missile, Ghadr-1, with a claimed range of 1,120 miles. This was followed on November 27, 2007, by the announcement of the 1,250-mile Ashura missile.[487] Both missiles were further evidence of Iran's determination for a strategic reach well beyond its immediate frontiers.

In December 2007, Russia agreed to sell Iran the long-range S-300 anti-aircraft missile defense system. The system contains 40 to 60 launchers with four missile tubes each, radars, and control stations. The deal was worth some $1 billion. The highly advanced truck-mounted SA-20 anti-aircraft missile (which is the core of the system) can detect and shoot down any incoming aircraft within a 75-mile range. Together with the shorter-range Tor M1 missile defense system[488] and the older super-long-range S-200 systems already provided by Russia, Iran could build a solid anti-aircraft shield able to defend its nuclear facilities against a possible US or Israeli assault, and inflict serious damage to the attacking force. In March 2007, the Russian investigative journalist Ivan Safronov died mysteriously after learning that Moscow's military-industrial complex was planning to transfer S-300 missiles to Iran via Belarus.[489] However, on June 11, 2010, Moscow announced that the S-300 deal was forbidden by new UN sanctions against the Islamic Republic. In early October 2010 Sergei Chemezov, the head of Russia's state-controlled arms manufacturer, confirmed that Russia would return only Iran's advance payment of $166.8 million for air defense missiles.[490] Despite the June and October announcements, Iran received four S-300 systems via Belarus and another country.[491] Furthermore, Iran may have established a circuitous method of obtaining the S-300 systems. On October 14, 2010, Venezuela's President Hugo Chavez offered to purchase the same five advanced S-300PMU-1 air defense missile battalions Russia withheld from Iran. Venezuela and Iran are *de facto* allies. A Russian sale of the missiles to Venezuela would accomplish an end run around UN sanctions that stopped the direct Russia–Iran deal.

Iran successfully tested the Sejil-2, a new two-stage solid fueled ballistic missile, with a range of between 1,200 and 1,500 miles, on November 12, 2008. The Sejil-2 is capable of reaching Israel and parts of Europe. Though the range of this rocket is comparable to the liquid-fueled Shahab-3, a solid-fuel rocket is easier to use on short notice, easier to hide from attack, and more accurate. In late 2012, it was claimed that the Iranian regime has 170 ballistic missiles pointed at Tel Aviv alone, some armed with biological warheads.[492] It is also claimed that 500 ballistic missiles are pointed at Israel and that several other countries are on Iran's target list.[493]

Iran continued to work on producing longer-range missiles with the goal of achieving intercontinental capability. Thus on February 2, 2009, Iran successfully launched its first spy satellite—Omid ("Hope")—into space orbit utilizing a two-stage Safir 2 rocket, modified from the Shahab-3. The launch of Omid made Iran the ninth country to develop an indigenous satellite launch capability. This was followed on June 15, 2011 by the launch of Rasad 1("Messenger"), Iran's second satellite. With space launch capable missiles, Iran has the capability to deliver a nuclear warhead that can hit not only Israel, but also all of Europe and much of North America. Meanwhile the DPRK, which shared this technology with Iran, also launched such a missile, which can hit the Western United States.[494]

There were unverified reports that the Russians transferred rocket engine technology for this program and even some speculation that Moscow is helping Tehran with a missile that will have a 6,300-mile range, enabling it to reach the eastern seaboard of the United States.[495] On February 3, 2012, the 50kg Navid satellite was launched by an upgraded Safir 2 rocket with 20 percent more thrust. Such a missile can be easily transformed into an intercontinental ballistic missile. Western analysts didn't believe that Iran would have this capability until 2015. Historically, orbiting a satellite is the criterion for crediting a nation with ICBM capability. Iran's ultimate goal is to have the ability to strike anywhere including the United States. The Center for Strategic and International Studies looked at Iranian research plans. They noted that

> Iran is attempting to create a Shahab-5 and a Shahab-6, with a 3,000 to 5,000 kilometer [1,900 to 3,100 mile] range. These missiles would be three-stage rockets. If completed, the Shahab-5 and the Shahab-6 would take Iran into the realm of limited range ICBMs, and enable Iran to target the US eastern seaboard.[496]

Iran successfully tested the Sejil-2, for the second time on May 20, 2009. The United States declared that the test of the Sejil-2 was "a significant step" and indicated that Iran was enhancing its weapons delivery capability. "This is the first time they have successfully launched [a solid-fuel missile] of this range," remarked an anonymous American official.[497] A fourth test of a second generation Sejil-2 was conducted at the conclusion of a military exercise called the *Great Prophet IV,* on September 28, 2009.[498] It was announced that the Sejil-2 has radar-evading capability and Iranian officials claimed it was brought into mass production earlier in 2009.[499] Yet another successful test of the Sejil-2, occurred on December 16, 2009. The test was regarded as a move that appeared aimed to discourage a military attack on its nuclear sites and to defy Western pressure over its nuclear program.

In early 2010, security news sites *Defense Update* and *Jane's HIS* displayed photos revealing that Iran was developing a missile launch facility in the northern province of Semnan, as well as a new missile the Simorgh, both probably with DPRK assistance. The Simorgh, unveiled in early February

2010, is officially intended as a space-launch vehicle, but it could be converted for launching long-range ballistic missiles for military purposes. The platforms seen on the Semnan launch pad's new gantry tower—a multi-level tower for servicing missiles before launch—resembled those seen on the gantry tower at the DPRK's new Tongchang launch pad. Additionally, the first stage of the Simorgh missile strongly resembled the DPRK Unha-2 missile with four clustered engines and near-identical dimensions.[500] *Defense Update* also reported that east of the active site, "the Iranians are constructing a new facility that could be supporting the Iranian solid rocket propulsion development, associated with the Sejil and Ashura missiles or even larger missiles," and noted that "according to *Jane's* Intelligence analysts, the site could be associated with the next-generation Simorgh rocket."[501]

Of additional concern to the United States and other Western nations are the reports of Iranian missile tests in the Caspian Sea where shorter ranged missiles were launched from freighters. Such vessels could approach any coast and in a short time launch its missile at a target. During one such test in 1998, Iran fired a missile from a barge in the Caspian Sea that exploded a hundred miles above the surface.[502] It may have been a preliminary test towards developing an electromagnetic pulse (EMP) weapon and delivery system.

An EMP causes non-lethal gamma energy to react with the magnetic field and produces a powerful electromagnetic shock wave that causes instant blackouts and that can destroy electronic devices. The shock wave would knock out a country's power grid and communications systems for transport and financial services, leading to economic collapse.

Both the United States and the old Soviet Union conducted successful EMP test-attacks in the early 1960s. The United States conducted an EMP test code-named *Starfish Prime,* on July 9, 1962, at Johnson Island in the Pacific. A nuclear device was detonated in near space, 260 miles above the island, and instruments monitored effects on the ionosphere. When the 1-megaton explosion flared, there was no radiation or blast felt on the island below. Instead, a man-made aurora borealis appeared and an electromagnetic pulse (EMP) knocked out streetlights and a communications microwave link in Hawaii, 930 miles away.[503] The Soviets, worried about underground bunkers built to house the government and command centers in the event of a nuclear war, conducted their own K-3 test, on October 22, 1962.

Even without EMP, the destruction of a country's power grid could be catastrophic. On June 9, 2014, Al Qaeda in the Arabian Peninsula used mortars and rockets to destroy transmission towers, plunging into darkness all of Yemen, a country of 16 cities and 24 million people. It is the first time in history that terrorists have put an entire nation into blackout. The combined use of computer viruses, hacking, sabotage and kinetic attacks, and nuclear EMP attack to blackout electric grids, and collapse critical infrastructures, to defeat—or render extinct—entire nations, has been dubbed by Peter Vincent Pry, "the Blackout War."[504]

Returning to the issue of Iranian missile development, of further and greater concern was the announcement, in April 2010, that Russia began marketing the Club-K cruise missile, which is launched from a forty-foot freight container. This is a relatively cheap ($15 million each), extra-smart, easy-to-use missile system, that can be launched from a prepositioned or moving land or sea platform. It is virtually undetectable by radar until activated. Iran and Venezuela both are interested in the new system. Western military experts call the Club-K system a "real maritime fear for anyone with a waterfront." The carriers of such containers are capable of surreptitiously approaching Israeli, Egyptian, Iraqi, Saudi and any other coastlines in the region, and send missiles flying against an American, Arab or Israeli strategic or military target before their targets know they are under attack. The missile container can be carried by a ship, fishing vessel, train or truck, approach a targeted coast, highway or international railway and strike behind the target's missile defenses without alerting radar monitors or even surveillance drones and satellites. In Iranian hands, it would make the targeting of its nuclear facilities very difficult and enable Iran to wipe out an aircraft carrier up to 250 miles away. The sale of the Club-K system to Iran or Syria and their transfer to Hezbollah would give them a substantial edge and shift the balance of power away from Israel, as well as pose a dire threat to the United States presence in the region.[505]

Iran's growing partnership with Venezuela poses an additional strategic threat to the United States. That threat did not take long in manifesting itself. On October 19, 2010, an agreement was signed between Iran and Venezuela. Iran paid cash to the Chavez government for the construction of a missile complex. To be built are Medium Range Ballistic Missiles (MRBM) and Intermediate Range Ballistic Missiles (IRBM) missile launch pads, missile silos and command and control facilities on the Paraguaná Peninsula on the northern coast of Venezuela, some 75 miles from the Colombian border. Engineers from an Iranian construction firm, Khatam al-Anbia owned by the Iranian Revolutionary Guard Corps, visited the Paraguaná site in February 2011. Amir al-Hadschisadeh, the head of the Guard's Air Force, participated in the visit. According to the German newspaper, *Die Welt,* the clandestine agreement between Venezuela and Iran would mean the Chavez government would fire rocket at Iran's enemies should the Islamic Republic face military strikes.[506] The placement of Iranian Shahab-3 or longer-range missiles in Venezuela, would pose a threat to the US mainland no less than that of the Soviet Union's attempt to place MRBMs and IRBMs in Cuba in the autumn of 1962.

By 2011, Iran was working at top speed on at least three new operational ballistic surface missiles with longer ranges. They were Shahab-4 (for targets at a distance of 1,990 to 2,486 miles), the Sejil, (with a range 1,555 miles) and the Ashura-Ghadr 110A, (1,865 miles). Shahab-4 and the improved Ashura/Ghadr 110A are quite capable of hitting central and Western Europe. Furthermore, Iran is developing intercontinental ballistic missiles—the Shahab-5, with a range of 3,100 miles and the Shahab-6, a variant of the DPRK Taepodong-2C/3, with a range of over 3,700 miles, placing North America within range.[507]

On June 29, 2011, British Foreign Secretary William Hague became the first Western leader to acknowledge publicly that Iran was working toward attaining nuclear weapons and suitable delivery systems. Hague said, "Iran has also been carrying out covert ballistic missile tests and rocket launches, including testing missiles capable of delivering a nuclear payload in contravention of UN [Security Council] Resolution 1929, and it has announced that it intends to triple its capacity to produce 20 percent enriched uranium."[508] Three of those missile tests, four in all, were carried out between October 2010 and February 2011, and the fourth on June 28, in the course of the Prophet Muhammad war games.

Setbacks however plagued the Iranian missile program. In November 2011, a blast rocked the military complex near the village of Bidganeh, the location of the Revolutionary Guards' Fifth Missile division, responsible for the launching of Shahab-3 and Shahab-4 missiles. The blast, which was caused during an advanced solid engine fuel test, demolished the center and resulted in the deaths of seventeen of the center's personnel, including General Hassan Tehrani, the head of Iran's missile program.[509] Whether the explosion was the result of sabotage remains unknown. Tehran said the blast was caused by an accident while weapons were being moved.

Despite international pressure and a UN-imposed ban on such missile testing, the DPRK successfully launched a satellite into space on December 12, 2012. The successful launch indicated that the DPRK achieved intercontinental ballistic missile (ICBM) capability. Given the close cooperation on both nuclear and missile technology issues between the DPRK and Iran, the successful test only sped up a similar test by the Islamic regime of an Iranian ICBM. On January 28, 2013, using a Kavoshgar rocket dubbed *Pishgam* ("Pioneer" in Farsi); Iran launched a capsule containing a monkey into space. The capsule attained an altitude of 75 miles and allegedly returned to earth. This event was followed shortly by the DPRK's third nuclear test on February 12, of a lighter "miniaturized atomic bomb."[510] That fact combined with Iran's ability to launch a capsule with a monkey payload into orbit, added up to Iran having a payload capability to enable it to fire a nuclear-armed missile—in effect, an ICBM—at any point on Earth. This poses a strategic threat to the United States and the entire Free World. Iran sent its second monkey into space on December 14, 2013. The rocket dubbed *Pajohesh* ("Research"), was Iran's first use of liquid fuel as a propellant and reached a height of 72 miles. The monkey, named *Fargam* ("Auspicious") was returned to earth safely.

On July 12, 2013, the US National Air and Space Intelligence Center released a declassified report, "Foreign Ballistic and Cruise Missile Threat Assessment," which stated that Iran could develop and test an intercontinental ballistic missile capable of reaching the United States by 2015. The report was prepared with significant contributions from the Defense Intelligence Agency Missile and Space Intelligence Center and the Office of Naval Intelligence. The report stated that since 2008, Iran has conducted multiple successful launches of the two-stage Safir space launch vehicle and has also revealed the larger two-stage Simorgh SLV, which could serve as a test bed for developing ICBM technologies. Furthermore, since 2010, Iran has revealed the Qiam-1 Short-range ballistic missile (SRBM), the fourth generation Fateh-110 SRBM, and claims to be mass-producing anti-ship ballistic missiles. Iran has modified its Shahab 3 medium-range ballistic missile to extend its range and effectiveness and claims to have deployed the two-stage solid-propellant Sejil MRBM.[511]

Incredibly, the ongoing P5+1 nuclear talks, with a deadline of June 30, 2015, fail to address Iran's missile program—the very program designed to deliver such weapons. As James R. Clapper, Director of National Intelligence, already testified in 2013, Iran "has the largest inventory of ballistic missiles in the Middle East, and it is expanding the scale, reach, and sophistication of its ballistic missile arsenal."[512] The United States and its traditional allies will pay dearly for this lack of action.

Nuclear weapons

Iran's nuclear program began in the 1950s, under Shah Mohammad Reza Pahlavi but was slow to progress. For the Shah, a nuclear program was the ultimate affirmation of Iran's imperial grandeur. By the time of the 1979 Islamic revolution Iran had developed an impressive baseline capability in nuclear technologies. Much of Iran's nuclear talent fled the country in the wake of that revolution.[513] This loss was compounded by Ayatollah Ruhollah Khomeini's opposition to nuclear technology and resulted in the near disintegration of Iran's nuclear program post-1979.

Fearful of future Iranian nuclear weapons production, Iraq during the Iran–Iraq War struck at Iran's Bushehr nuclear power complex on several occasions: March 24, 1984, February 12, 1985, March 4, 1985, November 17, 1987, and on July 18, 1988, the day Iran announced its willingness to accept a ceasefire ending that conflict.[514] In response to these Iraqi attacks, in 1984 Ayatollah Ruhollah Khomeini changed his mind and expressed a renewed Iranian interest in nuclear power seeking the assistance of international partners to complete construction at Bushehr,[515] as well as to lay the groundwork for a nuclear weapons capability. The semi-official Iranian weekly newspaper, *Panjereh,* disclosed on April 24, 2010, that former Iranian foreign minister Ali Akbar Velayati brought Iran its first centrifuges for uranium enrichment in 1986, escorting them on the flight from Pakistan aboard the private plane of Ayatollah Khomeini. The centrifuges were purchased for approximately

$30 million from Abdul Qadeer Khan, father of the Pakistani nuclear bomb.[516] Thus since that time, in addition to its quest for chemical and biological weapons, the Islamic Republic of Iran sought a nuclear weapons capability as well. Iran developed its clandestine nuclear weapons program by deceptive techniques—*taqiyya*—and proved it could outmaneuver both United States and European diplomats as well as IAEA inspectors.

Despite claims of the need for nuclear power for its developing economy, Iran is the second-largest oil producer in the Middle East, and the world's fourth-largest producer. Thus, there is great doubt that Iran needs peaceful nuclear power for energy purposes. In 2006 for example, Tehran pumped out more than 4.12 million barrels of oil a day.[517] Experts say its oil reserves should last at least eighty more years. Additionally, Iran has the world's second-largest reserves of natural gas after Russia, and currently is the Middle East's largest natural gas producer.[518]

To the contrary, Iran for decades has sought nuclear technology for military purposes. Iran signed long-term nuclear cooperation agreements with Pakistan and China, in 1987 and 1990 respectively. Accords with both countries involved the training of Iranian personnel.[519] Since the 1990s, Iran employed a strategy of deception, defiance and concealment, to gain time for developing nuclear weapons. In the 1990s, Iran began pursuing an indigenous nuclear fuel cycle capability by developing a uranium-mining infrastructure and experimenting with uranium conversion and enrichment. Additionally, Iran tried to use third countries as transshipment points for obtaining controlled nuclear-related equipment. For example, in early 2009, a Chinese company placed an order with a Taiwanese agent for 108 nuclear-related pressure gauges. The Swiss manufacturer and the Swiss government were duped, a Chinese company went around its own government's prohibition on moving nuclear-related equipment to Iran, and Taiwanese authorities showed themselves unwilling or unable to get into step with the international community. Iran received the pressure gauges. Nuclear experts stated the large size of the order suggested very strongly that they were for centrifuges to churn out enriched uranium.[520] Furthermore, Iran has already identified one of its intended targets—Israel. Between 2000 and 2005, the Iranian government took its hard currency reserves and invested almost 70 percent of it in military equipment and its covert nuclear program.[521]

The Iranian government is a master of strategic moves. Recall that historically it was in ancient Persia (now Iran) that the strategic game of chess was modernized and perfected from its early Indian precursors. Furthermore, like their Arab counterparts, the use of *taqiyya* and *kitman* is a technique inherent in Iranian statecraft and nuclear negotiations with Americans, Europeans and other Westerners. Iranian officials are masters of these techniques.

An admission of this practice came on June 14, 2008, when Abdollah Ramezanzadeh, spokesman for Iran's former (fifth) president, Muhammad Khatami, revealed, "We had one overt policy, which was one of negotiation and confidence building, and a covert policy, which was continuation of the [nuclear weapon production] activities."[522] This tactic was echoed by a top adviser to Supreme Leader Ayatollah Ali Khamenei, former Vice Minister of Foreign Affairs Mohammad Javad Larijani, who declared, "diplomacy must be used to lessen pressure on Iran for its nuclear program ... [it is] a tool for allowing us to attain our goals."[523]

Hence, Iran engaged the West in negotiations. It is important to note that the Western view of negotiations is an instrument that may lead to compromise, peace and stability. The Iranian/Arab/ Muslim concept is fundamentally different. In the Iranian/Arab/Muslim world, it is a method of gaining benefits without concrete concessions, and the use of delay to buy time needed to reach one's goal. It is the same tactic employed by other authoritarian regimes such as the DPRK during the 1990s, as it sought and achieved its goal of becoming a nuclear power on October 9, 2006, Iran's goal is no less. Attaining nuclear weapons is the ultimate means for achieving Iranian hegemony over the Persian Gulf, the wider Middle East and beyond. Possessing nuclear weapons is the insurance policy that guarantees the Islamic regime's grasp on political power domestically. Thus, for over thirty years the Islamic Republic of Iran maintained a careful balance between bellicosity and fake rapprochement in order to move closer towards its desired goal—becoming the world's tenth nuclear power.

Through the end of the twentieth century and start of the twenty-first century, Iranian deception worked, at least until 2002. On August 14, 2002 and again in 2003, the National Council of Resistance of Iran, an opposition group based in Paris, revealed the existence of undeclared Iranian nuclear facilities and the names of various individuals and front companies involved with the nuclear program.[524] These accusations were confirmed by December 2002 satellite images. The photos proved that the Iranian government was building an undeclared uranium enrichment plant at Natanz, about 130 miles south of Tehran, and a heavy water plant at Khondab, about 32 miles northwest of the town of Arak.[525]

In February 2003, the International Atomic Energy Agency (IAEA) sent a team of inspectors to confirm Iranian statements that "the activities of the Islamic Republic are totally transparent, clear, and peaceful."[526] Their subsequent report showed the depth of Iranian deception. Iran completed 164 centrifuges, worked on 1,000 more and designed a facility to house at least 50,000. Furthermore, the inspection revealed that Tehran had not acknowledged import of almost a ton of uranium from China, nor could the Iranian nuclear agency account for some missing processed uranium.[527] The Iranian government's initial claims that its program was indigenous and entirely peaceful were false.

Furthermore, reports emerged in August 2003, of Pakistani dealings with Iran. It was claimed that Pakistani nuclear scientist Abdul Qadeer Khan offered to sell nuclear weapons technology to that country as early as 1989. The Iranian government came under intense pressure from the United States and the European Union to make a full disclosure of its nuclear program. To avoid referral to the United Nations Security Council, Iran entered into negotiations with the EU-3 (France, Germany, and the United Kingdom), and agreed in October 2003 to cooperate with the IAEA and suspend conversion and enrichment activities.[528] However, Iran exploited ambiguities in the definition of "suspension" to continue to produce centrifuge components and carry out small-scale conversion experiments.[529] Faced with renewed threats of sanctions, Iran concluded the Paris Agreement with the EU-3 on November 15, 2004.[530] Tehran agreed to continue the temporary suspension of enrichment and conversion activities, including the manufacture, installation, testing, and operation of centrifuges, and committed to working with the EU-3 to find a mutually beneficial long-term diplomatic solution.[531]

The IAEA discovered in early 2004 that Iran hid from its inspectors, blueprints obtained in 1994, for a more advanced P-2 centrifuge and a document detailing uranium hemisphere casting.[532] The IAEA called on Iran to be more cooperative and to answer all of the agency's questions about the origins of its centrifuge technology.[533] In November 2007, Iran amended its previous declaration and admitted that it had clandestinely imported gas centrifuges based on Pakistani designs, which were obtained "from a foreign intermediary in 1987." The intermediary was not named but many diplomats and analysts pointed to Pakistan and specifically, to Khan, who was said to have visited Iran in 1986.[534] The Iranians turned over the names of their suppliers and the international inspectors quickly identified the Iranian gas centrifuges as P-1s, the model developed by Khan in the early 1980s.

In April 2004, the IAEA found traces of bomb-grade uranium at other Iranian sites.[535] Iran had lied again. As a result, on September 24, 2004, the IAEA Board of Governors met in Vienna, Austria, and after recalling a litany of Iranian lies, found that "Iran's many failures and breaches of its obligations to comply with its NPT [Non-Proliferation Treaty] Safeguards Agreement ... constitute non-compliance."[536] Continuing to defy the UN, Iran announced in April 2005, that it would resume uranium conversion. Accordingly, on August 1, 2005, Iranian officials removed UN seals on the uranium processing equipment at its Isfahan reactor and unilaterally made the plant fully operational.[537] In February 2006, Iran resumed enrichment at Natanz.

Iran between 2005 and 2008, flouted five Security Council resolutions about its clandestine nuclear weapons program. The first was United Nations Security Council Resolutions 1696, passed by a vote of 14 to 1 (Qatar) on July 31, 2006. It demanded that Iran suspend enrichment activities, banned international transfer of nuclear and missile technologies to Iran and froze the foreign assets of twelve individuals and ten organizations involved with the Iranian nuclear program.[538] Iranian President Ahmadinejad vowed to ignore the UNSC resolution and continue enrichment. That same month, Iran inaugurated a heavy water production plant at Arak. That prompted another United Nations Security Council Resolution 1737, adopted on December 27, 2006.[539] Continued efforts at negotiations all provided Iran with time to press forward with its nuclear program, as well as missile development. Two additional United Nations Security Council resolutions were passed—1747 (March 24, 2007) and 1803 (March 3, 2008). Iran's continued non-compliance and defiance, exemplified by Supreme Leader Ayatollah Ali Khamenei's declaration that Iran would "continue with its path" of nuclear development,[540] led to a fifth United Nations Security Council Resolution 1835 of September 27, 2008.[541] All these resolutions called for Iran to suspend its uranium enrichment and reprocessing activities and comply with its IAEA obligations and responsibilities. Nevertheless, Iran ignored and defied all of them and pressed on with its programs. Iran was threatened with the use of sanctions. However, for Iran, the long-term advantages of obtaining nuclear weapons have always outweighed the temporary disadvantage of economic sanctions.

The use of diplomatic and economic sanctions however, has a poor historic record. In case after case, sanctions have proven not to be an effective tool of geo-economic power. They rarely if ever work. They are a diplomatic shuffle designed to give the appearance that something is being done, when the only alternatives are capitulation by doing nothing, or exercising the military option. Sanctions are only effective if they are comprehensive, swiftly applied and rigorously enforced. There must be total worldwide compliance, which is an extremely unattainable prospect. Various nations, non-governmental institutions, businesses and individuals have found methods to circumvent sanctions.

In 1917, the Western powers employed a *cordon sanitaire* (a political, diplomatic and economic barrier) against the new Bolshevik (communist) regime in Russia. That lasted only six years. The regime did not collapse, nor did it modify its revolutionary agenda. In 1935, the League of Nations invoked economic sanctions against fascist Italy for its aggressive attack on Ethiopia. They did not deter the Italian conquest of that Horn of Africa nation, nor from subsequently annexing Albania. US sanctions against the People's Republic of China lasted from 1949 to 1972 and after 21 years had not changed the regime, its policies, or agenda. The over sixty years of sanctions against the DPRK did not deter or modify its aggressive policies nor stop its ultimately successful quest for nuclear weapons. Over fifty years of sanctions on Cuba have not changed the ideology or policy of the Castro regime.

Since the March 2, 1962, military coup in Burma (now Myanmar), 50 years of varying sanctions failed to modify the actions of the various regimes that controlled that southeast Asian nation. United Nations sanctions against South Africa began on August 7, 1963, with a voluntary arms embargo against South Africa. This and subsequent additional sanctions, economic as well as political, (including the OAPEC 1973 oil embargo, and direct US sanctions starting in late 1985) did not force the minority apartheid regime to change its policies. Similarly, Rhodesia's tiny white minority population of some 250,000 defied UN, US, British Commonwealth and French sanctions from 1965 to 1980. The fact that Rhodesia could defy these sanctions for 15 years confirms the limited effectiveness of sanctions. Additionally, in all these cases, economic sanctions were counter-productive in that they stiffened the resolve of the hard-line regimes and rallied popular support of the governments targeted. In short, sanctions in the last quarter of the twentieth century against South Africa, Rhodesia, Libya, Iraq, and Iran, to name but a few examples, may have caused some discomfort for those regimes but hardly caused them to stop their policies. The use of sanctions generally does not bring about the desired results, and certainly not quickly.

In a like manner since 1979, numerous nations and multinational entities imposed sanctions and applied diplomatic pressure on the Islamic Republic of Iran. These have not deterred Iran from pursuing its quest for nuclear weapons. Iran has already anticipated sanctions. It has taken steps to circumvent them or minimize their impact, for example by stocking and rationing gasoline and planning alternative source acquisitions from Russia, Azerbaijan and Turkmenistan. Additionally, Iran has circumvented banking and currency restrictions by accepting payments in Indian, Chinese, Korean, and Japanese currencies. It established accounts in Russian and Chinese banks, for example the Bank Kunlun, to transfer funds from the Central Bank of Iran to companies linked with its army, as well as for purchasing Chinese and other goods. Such transfers help to finance international operations of the Iranian Revolutionary Guards Corps' elite Quds Force. The Quds Force provides arms, aid and training for pro-Iranian groups in the Middle East, such as Hezbollah, Hamas and Shi'ite Muslim militias in Iraq, as well as to the Assad regime fighting its opposition in the Syrian Civil War.[542] All this is in violation of a UN arms embargo and other sanctions. The United States designated the Quds a supporter of terrorism in 2007 and the European Union sanctioned them in 2011. Of interest too, is the fact that the Iranian Revolutionary Guard Corps control the smuggling networks designed to circumvent sanctions. These networks brought lucrative profits in the billions to the IRGC, which in turn is heavily involved in both the nuclear and missile development programs. Sanctions against Iran now are too little, too late. Time is something the West does not have, for Iran continues to press ahead with its WMD programs.

Nevertheless, on June 24, 2010, the US Congress by a vote of the House (408 to 8) and Senate (99-0) passed the Comprehensive Iran Sanctions, Accountability, and Divestment Act of 2010. The act applied further sanctions on the government of Iran over and above the weak sanctions passed by UN Security Council Resolution 1929 of June 9, 2010. The legislation penalized companies supplying Iran with gasoline as well as international banking institutions involved with Iran's Islamic Revolutionary Guard Corps, its nuclear program and its support for terrorist activity. It would effectively deprive foreign banks of access to the US financial system if they do business with key Iranian banks or the Revolutionary Guards.[543] President Obama signed the legislation into law on July 1, 2010. However, the US has not fully implemented its own sanction bills and executive orders—in May 1995 (under the Clinton administration), June 2010, November 2011, February 2012, and July 2012 (all under the Obama administration). Each was replete with commerce-driven waivers and exemptions, which render them ineffective and counter-productive. Meanwhile, over the past twelve years, while negotiations continued and continued, Iran built a broad and deep infrastructure for its weapons program. It dispersed and hid its facilities, many of them underground. Despite numerous rounds of incessant talks, no agreement was reached. In short, Iran was playing for time, time to complete its nuclear weapons program.

Any military strike option would be an arduous undertaking, but both the United States and Israel have the capacity for such action. While any military strike cannot guarantee the total destruction of all of Iran's WMD facilities, it is better than the alternative—letting Iran become the world's tenth nuclear weapons power. Such strikes will delay Iran's WMD efforts for three or more years (estimates vary). That might be sufficient for the short term, but any military action should be followed by an active campaign for regime change, which should be encouraged and aided. Domestic opposition to the Islamic Republic has grown over the past three decades and was demonstrated repeatedly in 2009 during the fraudulent elections of June, which were followed by other demonstrations in September and December. Unfortunately, the Obama administration did nothing to encourage regime change. To the contrary, the Obama administration steadily sought a deal with Iran, and shifted US Middle East policy, much to the consternation of its traditional friends in the region, Egypt, Jordan, Saudi Arabia, the Persian Gulf states and Israel.

Subsequently, the Obama administration embarked on withdrawal from the region. Despite any rhetoric to the contrary, the military option for the US is off the table and the Iranians know it. That was confirmed by the dismal display of lack of resolve in the crisis over Syrian chemical weapons use in August–September 2013. Diplomatic engagement, also known as appeasement, seemed the vehicle of choice for the Obama administration. When former US Ambassador to the United Nations John Bolton was asked about the chances that President Obama would order an attack on Iran, he responded skeptically, "It would take a character transplant for Obama to order a US attack."[544]

If the United States does nothing militarily and Iran gains the status of a nuclear weapons power, it is an encouragement for several nations (e.g. Turkey, Egypt, Saudi Arabia, the Gulf States, Venezuela, Argentina, and Brazil, among others) to defy the world and acquire, one way or another, nuclear weapons. Furthermore, as the Obama administration continues to press ahead with unilateral nuclear disarmament and in the absence of a safe, reliable and credible American "nuclear umbrella," it is inevitable that global proliferation and instability will increase. States like Taiwan, the Republic of (South) Korea and Japan can and will quickly become nuclear powers. The world will become far more dangerous with some 15 to 20 nuclear powers, not to mentioned the increased likelihood of terrorist groups—the Islamic State, Hamas, Hezbollah, and the various Al-Qaeda affiliates immediately come to mind—stealing, buying or otherwise obtaining such weapons.

Iran at 636,293 square miles is slightly larger than the state of Alaska (591,004 square miles). Iran's WMD and missile development sites are spread across that nation, with many being underground in reinforced structures. Iran has hidden both materials and technicians in secret facilities not open to IAEA inspectors. There may also be sites unknown to American, Israeli and other Western intelligence services. In view of the dispersal of these sites, a military strike against Iran will not be a single strike event, such as the Israeli strikes against Iraq in 1981 and Syria in 2007. Iran's WMD sites might need to be bombed more than once to persuade the regime to abandon its pursuit of such weapons. Various lists of potential nuclear development and delivery systems sites include, but are not limited to, all of the following:[545]

- Abbas-Abad: This site is about 3 miles south of Natanz in the Siah mountains. The complex consists of a sprawling underground area with two tunnels, which run under two mountains connected to Natanz. The tunnel entrance is six meters wide.
- Abyek: Iran is building a uranium enrichment plant at Abyek, 75 miles west of the capital. Construction began in 2005, and as of September 2010, it was about 85 percent complete.[546]

- Arak/ Khondab (near the city of Arak): It is a site housing a 40MWt heavy water reactor, known as IR-40, as well as a heavy water production plant. Construction began in 2004 based on designs provided by Russia, according to former UN officials.[547] Testing at the facility began in late 2013, and was fully operational by the first half of 2014.[548] The reactor is able to produce plutonium for nuclear bombs from the reactor's spent fuel rods, a method used by India, Pakistan and the DPRK to produce their nuclear arsenals. A large surface reactor, like that at Arak, is an easier target to hit with a military strike than the underground facilities at Fordow that house Iran's uranium-enrichment facilities.
- Ardakan: It is the site of a uranium milling plant, where more uranium enrichment facilities are located, including the Shahid Rezaeinejad yellowcake plant.
- Bonab, Moallem Kalayeh, and Gorgan, all are sites of research and development facilities.
- Bushehr: Located at Hellieh, on the Persian Gulf coast, is where two Russian-built, light water nuclear reactors are located. One of these is 1,000MWe, and is Iran's largest. It produces 20 percent plutonium that is, 20 percent of its eighty-two-ton payload. The plant was completed and started operation on August 22, 2010.
- Chalus is the location of a weapons development facility.
- Damavand: Site of a plasma physics research facility.
- Darkhovin: Is a site southwest of Tehran near the Iraqi border. A 360MWe nuclear power plant is due to be built there.
- Fasa is the site of a uranium conversion facility.
- Fordow: This secret nuclear development site was revealed by the Iranian government on September 21, 2009.[549] The facility is located in an underground tunnel complex on the grounds of an Iranian Revolutionary Guards Corps base near the holy city of Qom. It was built as an enrichment plant and houses 3,000 fast centrifuges of the new IR-4 type. It is designed to produce 90 percent (weapons-grade) enriched uranium in an amount sufficient for two to three bombs a year. The site in fact, was known to intelligence services, including the CIA, as far back as 2004.
- Gachine, located just north of Qeshm Island near the Strait of Hormuz, it is the site of more uranium mines and enrichment facilities.
- Isfahan: Four nuclear research reactors are located there, as well as an uranium conversion facility. It is also the location of a fuel fabrication laboratory, a fuel manufacturing plant and a zirconium processing plant. The Isfahan uranium conversion facility is where yellowcake is converted into highly toxic uranium hexafluoride. As has been mentioned, uranium hexafluoride in turn, is a compound used in the uranium enrichment process that produces fuel for nuclear reactors and nuclear weapons. From 2003 to 2005, this facility produced enough yellowcake for five atomic bombs.[550] Iran's largest missile-assembly plant and major chemical weapons facilities are also located there.
- Jabr Ibn Hagan is the location of a nuclear enrichment and conversion plant.
- Karaj is the site of a cyclone accelerator research and waste storage facility.
- Lashkar A'bad is the site of secret uranium laser enrichment plants.
- Lavizan-Shian is a new facility built in the province of Isfahan on the outskirts of the small city of Najafabad. The site was built below the Abu Reyhan medicine factory.[551] The facility beneath the factory has three levels, with two underground entrances away from the facility.
- Narigan and Zarigan: The site of uranium mines.

- Natanz: It is the location of a main nuclear enrichment facility where some 10,000 centrifuges are installed. A large-scale commercial heavy water plant is also situated there.
- Parchin is the military research site for nuclear-trigger development, nuclear implosion tests, and military laboratories. It is believed to be the place where Iran is combining the enriched uranium and other components of its nuclear program and building its actual arsenal. Since 2005, Iran has refused access to nuclear inspectors from the United Nations' International Atomic Energy Agency (IAEA) to Parchin. In January and February 2012 and again in August 2014 Iran reiterated that it would not allow IAEA inspectors to visit the site.
- Qazvin, located 93 miles northwest of Tehran. It is believed to be the location of an unreported nuclear site that contains stored uranium.
- Quds: A new underground nuclear complex located 15 miles northwest of Fordow. The buried facility has the capacity to house 8,000 uranium enrichment centrifuges.
- Saghand is Iran's main uranium mining area in the Yazd region southeast of Tehran. It became operational in March 2005. Two new uranium mines—Saghand 1 and 2 were inaugurated in April 2013.
- Tabriz is the site of an engineering and defense research complex.
- Tehran is the location of the Atomic Energy Agency of Iran research center.
- Tehran is also the location of the Shahud Hemmat Industrial Group, which develops ballistic, and cruise missiles.
- Tehran is additionally the site of the Kalaye Electric Company, which produces centrifuge parts, and is involved in uranium enrichment.
- Tehran is the venue of the Nuclear Research Center at Sharaif University. It includes a research reactor, Jabar Ibn Hayan multipurpose laboratories, radiochemical laboratory, laser research center, and plasma physics laboratories.
- Yazd is the location of a milling plant.

To freely monitor, or for that matter attack all these sites would be a formidable task to say the least.

In 2007, *Aviation Week* reporter Craig Covault cited intelligence reports over two decades of "detailed and ongoing collaboration between Iran and the DPRK. They have engaged in a steady, uninterrupted march toward acquisition of nuclear weapons and the capability to deliver them effectively on target." Charles Vick, an analyst at *Global Security,* wrote, "It cannot be stated strongly enough how closely related the DPRK and Iranian strategic space, ballistic missile and nuclear weapons programs appear to be, based on the observed trends." When one adds the collaboration between Syria and Iran as well as the collaboration between Syria and the DPRK, the world now faces a nuclear axis of evil.

It is instructive to note that both the DPRK and Iran pursued similar routes towards the attainment of nuclear weapons, though to date the latter has not yet attained that goal. On October 21, 1994, the Clinton administration and the DPRK signed an interim Agreed Framework, a deal intended to halt the DPRK's illicit nuclear weapons program while the DPRK sought economic sanctions relief. The objective of the agreement was the freezing and replacement of the DPRK's indigenous nuclear power plant program with more nuclear proliferation resistant light water reactor power plants, and the step-by-step normalization of relations between the US and the DPRK. The DPRK pursued a policy of continued talks to stall, demands for sanctions relief, hints at wanting to improve relations with the United States and other powers, making minimal concessions, all coupled with refusals to compromise on scaling back or stopping work towards achieving nuclear weapons capability or allowing international inspections. Additionally, in 2001, the DPRK promised not to produce, test or deploy missiles with a range of more than 300 miles, as well as halt the sale of missiles, missile components, technology and training. The DPRK violated all these undertakings.

The DPRK withdrew from the Nuclear Non-Proliferation Treaty on January 10, 2003, effective ninety days later. On February 10, 2005, the DPRK finally declared that it had manufactured nuclear weapons as a "nuclear deterrent for self-defense."[552] The DPRK subsequently became the world's ninth nuclear power on October 9, 2006 with a test detonation north of Hwaden, near Kiliju. Additional tests followed in 2009 and 2013. For committing all these violations and fooling the world, there were no serious consequences for the DPRK from either the United States or the United Nations. Thus, the precedent for Iran was set.

Ironically, the same US chief negotiator in the talks with the DPRK, Wendy Sherman, would later be the Obama administration's chief negotiator with Iran. In 2011, former US Ambassador to the UN John Bolton said that Wendy Sherman had been central in forming a policy on the DPRK that was "nothing less than appeasement."[553] Iran, following the pattern of its North Korean ally also engaged in denial of a nuclear weapons program and enhancement of missile technology. Likewise, it defied the international community all the while engaging in covert activities designed expressly to gain nuclear weapons capability.

Scientists at the Institute for Science and International Security, based in Washington DC, estimated in August 2009, that Iran had the capability to produce enough weapons-grade uranium for at least two nuclear warheads within six months. Whether or not this has occurred is unknown. The estimate was based on a June 2009 report by the IAEA. According to the IAEA, by May 2009 nearly 5,000 uranium enrichment centrifuges were installed and operating at the Natanz nuclear facility.[554] It should be recalled that in the summer of 2009, the 45 tons of yellowcake shipped by the DPRK and originally intended for Syria reached Iran, giving it an additional source for nuclear weapon production.[555] In early June 2010, the IAEA confirmed that Iran had amassed more than two tons of enriched uranium. Two tons of uranium would suffice for two nuclear warheads.[556]

A report from the *Times* of London on December 14, 2009, revealed that Iran had been testing a neutron initiator, the component that triggers the explosion of a nuclear bomb, and "has no possible civilian or military use other than in a nuclear weapon."[557] Mark Fitzpatrick, senior fellow for non-proliferation at the International Institute for Strategic Studies in London, said, "The most shattering conclusion is that, if this was an effort that began in 2007, it could be a *casus belli*. If Iran is working on weapons, it means there is no diplomatic solution."[558] Mr. Fitzpatrick said, "Is this the smoking gun? People should be asking that question. It looks like the smoking gun. This is smoking uranium."[559] In early 2010, French President Nicolas Sarkozy definitively stated that he was "convinced that Iran is pursuing a nuclear program and [that] Israel will not abide [by] that," the London-based Arabic-language newspaper *al-Hayat* reported. Sarkozy said France had proof that Tehran was developing a nuclear bomb and that Israel may choose to take action to neutralize the threat.[560]

Germany's *Die Welt* newspaper reported on March 4, 2012, that in mid-April and around May 11, 2010, the DPRK carried out two secret small nuclear tests that caused explosions equivalent to 50–200 tons of TNT. These tests employed enriched uranium, which heretofore the DPRK had not used in its weapon program. The newspaper report was attributed to Western intelligence reports (including German and Japanese) as well as the conclusions of two respected analysts, Swedish nuclear physicist Lars-Erik de Geer, of the Swedish Defense Research Agency in Stockholm, and Hans Rühle, who headed the German Defense Ministry's policy planning staff from 1982 to 1988. The DPRK was a acknowledged nuclear power since its first test north of Hwaden, near Kiliju, on October 9, 2006. So why should the DPRK keep the nuclear tests secret? The conclusions reached by several nuclear experts are that the DPRK conducted the tests for Iran.[561] Another source claimed that in late April 2010, Iran shipped to Pyongyang a large quantity of uranium enriched to over 20 percent—apparently for use in the May test. Furthermore, immediately after the May test, the Central Bank of Iran transferred $55 million to the account of the DPRK's Atomic Energy Commission. The size of the sum suggested that it covered the fee to the DPRK, for the two tests—the first a pilot and the second, a full-stage test.[562] Thus, Iran may well be much closer to its goal of becoming the world's tenth nuclear power.

An additional factor that must be considered is that the Islamic Republic of Iran armed with atomic weapons, like its DPRK ally, would engage in nuclear extortion, by periodically sounding lunatic, threatening its neighbors and promising a conflagration in the region—if not eventually in the United States and Europe. This is precisely what the DPRK did in April 2013, when it threatened nuclear attack on the United States, the Republic of (South) Korea, and Japan. For its menacing behavior, the DPRK was rewarded with additional economic inducements to "behave." Using such tactics Iran can gain, additional foreign aid and attention that is more global as well as recognition of its status as a regional power—now nuclear armed.

Various obstacles slowed Iran's progress in its nuclear weapons program. One problem it faced in January 2009 was that its stockpile of uranium yellowcake, produced from uranium ore, was close to running out and could be exhausted within months.[563] The IAEA said that 70 percent of the uranium had been converted into uranium hexafluoride gas, the step before insertion into the centrifuges for enrichment. About 200 tons of uranium is needed to operate a single 1,000-megawatt power station every single year and Iran declared its intention to build twenty of them. The Iranians increased production at its mine near Bandar Abbas but it was only processing about twenty-one tons per year and the site at Ardakan only provided fifty more tons per year. The Bandar Abbas site, off-limits to IAEA inspectors, could supply enough uranium for two nuclear bombs per year but its deposits were said to be of poor quality and were not nearly large enough to accommodate an energy program.[564] Thus, Iran needed to acquire uranium abroad in order to keep its nuclear program going. The Islamic Republic engaged in a worldwide quest for additional uranium ore supplies approaching countries in Africa, Latin America and Asia.

In Africa, a United Nations investigation, in July 2006, reported that Tanzania intercepted a shipment of uranium-238, the fissile material necessary for nuclear enrichment, bound for Iran that originated in the Democratic Republic of the Congo's Lubumbashi mines.[565] Iran also approached other African countries such as Nigeria and Senegal. In March 2010, Iran concluded a secret deal to trade oil for enriched uranium from Zimbabwe.[566]

In Latin America, Iran approached both Bolivia and Venezuela. An Israeli report of May 2009 concluded that Bolivia and Venezuela were supplying Iran with uranium for its nuclear program. The three-page document about Iranian activities in Latin America was prepared for a visit to South America by Israeli Deputy Foreign Minister Danny Ayalon before a conference of the Organization of American States in Honduras. "There are reports that Venezuela supplies Iran with uranium for its nuclear program," the Israeli Foreign Ministry document stated, referring to previous Israeli intelligence conclusions. It added, "Now we have evidence that also Bolivia supplies uranium to Iran."[567] In September 2009, Venezuela admitted that it allowed Iran to survey its deposits. It has been estimated that Venezuela is home to 50,000 tons of uranium, some of which may be of high quality.

In Asia, the DPRK and Myanmar (Burma) are two other uranium sources for Iran. As mentioned, the North Koreans had no qualms about providing Iran with WMD technology. Forty-five tons of DPRK uranium went from Syria to Iran after Israel bombed the Syrian nuclear reactor in September 2007. Myanmar also is working on a nuclear weapons program and has uranium deposits. Elsewhere in Central Asia in late 2009, the Associated Press cited an intelligence report, which stated that Kazakhstan was about to sell 1,350 tons of purified uranium to Iran for $450 million. Both sides denied the report.[568] Iran's pursuit of nuclear weapons will require help from friends. Unfortunately, there is no shortage of countries willing to give Iran the uranium it needs to threaten their common enemies in the West. The postponement of military action against Iran merely provided it with a window to expand, disperse and harden its nuclear facilities against attack, and indeed this occurred during the period 2009 to 2015. Given the Obama administration policies of endless negotiations, postponements, sanctions lifting and various attempts a achieving a grand bargain, Iran has in effect been given a green light to proceed at full speed to complete its nuclear weapons program within the remaining eighteen months of the Obama administration.

For the short term, it seemed that some covert action—either by the Israeli Mossad and/or the American CIA—began against the suspected Iranian nuclear program including, but not limited to, crippling computer viruses, the assassination of Iranian nuclear scientists, and a series of mysterious explosions that have killed high-level targets and damaged facilities. In April 2006, for example, sabotaged power-supply units exploded at the Natanz uranium fuel enrichment plant, destroying fifty centrifuges.[569] There were six attacks on Iranian nuclear scientists in Tehran during the period 2007–12 (for details see the "Iran section in "Basic Principle 36"). None of the perpetrators was apprehended. Iran accused both the Israeli Mossad and the American CIA of the acts, though internal opponents of the regime could also have committed these deeds. The similarities of some of the attacks suggested that a covert campaign to attack Iranian scientists was under way. This campaign was reminiscent of the Aman (Israeli Directorate of Military Intelligence) and Mossad campaigns from the early 1950s through the early 1960s in Egypt. Those campaigns were directed against German personnel comprising of many former Nazis including members of the SS paramilitary forces, the Gestapo (secret police), the Wehrmacht (Nazi armed forces) and scientists, all working for the Egyptian government of Gamal Abdel Nasser. At that time, as has been related above, the Mossad sought to intimidate or liquidate the brains behind WMD programs and curtail progress in those programs. This may very well be occurring against Iran.

In its annual report to Congress in the spring of 2010, the CIA reported Iran's determination to work towards the completion of its nuclear weapons program. The report stated that Iran was poised to begin producing nuclear weapons after its uranium program expansion in 2009, despite some difficulties with its centrifuges. "Iran continues to develop a range of capabilities that could be applied to producing nuclear weapons, if a decision is made to do so," the report stipulated. The CIA document came hard on the heels of IAEA information, released on March 3, 2010, warning that continuing nuclear activities in violation of UN resolutions raised "concerns about the possible existence in Iran of past or current undisclosed activities related to the development of a nuclear payload for a missile."[570]

On June 9, 2010, the UN Security Council passed Resolution 1929 calling for a fourth round of new yet weakened, sanctions against Iran by a vote of 12 nations in favor, 2 against (Brazil and Turkey) and 1 abstention (Lebanon). The sanctions demanded that Iran comply with international demands, cease uranium enrichment, including enrichment to a level of 20 percent, stop construction of the facility at Qom, cooperate fully with the IAEA inquiry into the military dimension of the nuclear program, and give the agency full access to its facilities. The sanctions resolution targeted Iran's banking and shipping industries, but omitted additional measures against its oil and gas sector.

Within days, there was a response from a defiant Iran. Ali Akbar Salehi, head of Iran's nuclear program announced the construction of a new uranium enrichment plant by March 2011. Additionally, Iran's government approved plans for ten new enrichment facilities that could process uranium gas into fuel for nuclear power plants. The United States and other nations feared Iran's expansion of the technology because it can also be used to make material for nuclear weapons.[571] On November 8, 2011, the IAEA declared that Iran was working on a nuclear weapon.[572]

In retrospect, it seems that the last moment for the United States and Israel, separately or together, to have destroyed most if not all of Iran's nuclear program went by without action in 2007.[573] After that date, Iran began a massive effort to move the most important elements of its nuclear weapons program, underground or buried deep within mountains. Today, the best they can achieve is temporarily to hold Iran back from building a bomb—the Israelis, perhaps for two to four years and the Americans three to five years.

On October 16, 2012, the US Air Force and the Boeing Company successfully tested an EMP missile over a military site in the Utah desert. The test was code-named CHAMP—Counter-Electronics High Power Advanced Missile Project—and was the first time a real EMP missile was tested with positive real world results.[574] An EMP can destroy the electronic devices, especially those used in Iran's nuclear plants. Underground facilities with blast proof doors would be sealed and not easily opened. The shock wave would knock out Iran's power grid and communications systems for transport and financial services, leading to economic collapse.

Israel also has EMP capability. If Israel were to use one of its Jericho-3 missiles to detonate such a weapon above north central Iran there would be no blast or radiation effects on the ground. In fact, if the strike was at noon on a sunny day the people below would not know it happened except their lights would go out, cars stop, refrigerators die, power line transformers short out, computers would fry, refineries shut down, and yes, those uranium enrichment centrifuges in caverns would stop spinning too.

In June 2010, Iran came under the first full scale cyber-attack on a state, by Stuxnet. Stuxnet was a self-perpetuating malware worm first detected in June when it was introduced into the control system of Iran's P-1 centrifuge cascade used for the enrichment of uranium. Almost immediately, the Iranian facilities at Natanz and Bushehr were partially crippled by the ever-expanding worm. Bushehr was to go on line fully at the end of August 2010, but that was delayed by the cyber attack. Since August 2010, American and UN nuclear watchdog sources reported a slowdown in Iran's enrichment processing due to technical problems which knocked out a large number of centrifuges and which its nuclear technicians were unable to repair at the time. It is estimated that at Natanz alone, 3,000 centrifuges were idled.

Iran admitted on September 27, 2010, that it was under full-scale cyber attack. The official IRNA news agency quoted Hamid Alipour, deputy head of Iran's government Information Technology Company, as saying that the Stuxnet computer worm "is mutating and wreaking further havoc on computerized industrial equipment." Stuxnet was no normal worm he said, "The attack is still ongoing and new versions of this virus are spreading." Iran admitted that 30,000 computers belonging to classified industrial units were infected and disabled by the Stuxnet virus.[575] It is not known which nation or nations initiated the cyber attack. The United States, the United Kingdom, Israel, France, Germany, Russia and China all have that capability.

On October 8, 2010, Ali Akbar Salehi head of Iran's Atomic Energy Organization admitted that Iran put to death a number of atomic scientists and technicians suspected of helping plant the Stuxnet virus in its nuclear program. The Bushehr reactor faced one delay after another since it was inaugurated at the end of August and other nuclear plants were functioning only partially since the virus first surfaced in June. Salehi accused Iranian personnel of making it possible for Western agencies to use items purchased overseas as Stuxnet carriers.[576]

Soon thereafter, Iran was beset by another setback in its drive for nuclear weapons and delivery systems. On October 12, 2010, a triple explosion wracked the Imam Ali Base located near Khorramabad in the Zagros Mountains of western Iran. The facility was where most of the Shahab-3 medium-range missile launchers were stored. Iran stocked them there for striking both US forces in the Middle East and Israel. Some of the missiles had triple warheads (tri-conic nosecones). Officially, eighteen soldiers were killed and fourteen were injured. They belonged to the Iranian Revolutionary Guards Corps (IRGC) main missile arm, the Al-Hadid Brigades. The base lies 250 miles from Baghdad and primary American bases in central Iraq located there at the time, as well as 790 miles from Tel Aviv and central Israel. Both are well within the Shahab-3 missile's 1,120–1,555 miles operational range. Iran spent hundreds of millions of dollars to build one of the largest subterranean missile launching facilities of its kind in the Middle East or Europe. Burrowed under the Imam Ali Base was an entire network of wide tunnels deep underground. Somehow, someone rigged three blasts in quick succession deep inside those tunnels, destroying a large number of launchers and causing enough damage to render the facility unfit for use.[577] It is possible that opponents of the Islamic Republic, the Israeli Mossad or another Western intelligence service were behind the explosions. An applicable quote from Proverbs 24:6 comes to mind, "By ruses shall thou wage war, and victory comes with much planning by advisors."

Some six months later, on April 25, 2011, Iranian civil defense commander Gholamreza Jalali announced that Iran's nuclear program had been attacked by a second computer virus called "Stars." Jalali did not specify the target of "Stars" or its intended effect. Jalalai said the introduction of the new virus is being investigated while admitting Stuxnet still posed a risk. He added, "We should know that fighting the Stuxnet virus does not mean the threat has been completely tackled, because viruses have a certain life span and they might continue their activities in another way."[578] Thus, he admitted that Stuxnet still had not been eliminated from Iranian nuclear-related computer systems.

While the Stuxnet and Stars cyber attacks, the explosions at the Iman Ali missile base and the August 17, 2012 explosions that cut the electric power lines from the city of Qom to the underground uranium enrichment site at Fordow,[579] certainly delayed Iran's quest for nuclear weaponry, by no means did they halt the Iranian effort or cause the Iranian regime to consider bringing it to a close. Iran moved forward when in mid-October 2010, Iran started to load 163 fuel rods into the Bushehr nuclear plant. The Western democracies still faced the looming threat of a nuclear Iran. With a cyber attack already a historic fact, it seems logical that the next step would be an EMP attack. That would freeze Iran for decades, but as of mid-2015 that had not occurred.

In its report released June 2, 2011, the Wisconsin Project on Nuclear Arms Control (America's scientific watchdog on world nuclear weapons production), estimated that by December 2008, Iran had accumulated enough U-235 to fuel one nuclear bomb; by 2009, enough for a second, by August 2010 material for a third bomb and by April 2011, enough enriched uranium for a fourth bomb. These estimates presuppose an Iranian decision to further process low-enriched material to weapons grade—a process taking no more than a couple of months. As Iran increases its stockpile of low-enriched uranium, it will consolidate its status as a "virtual" nuclear weapon state.[580] Then Iranian President Mahmoud Ahmadinejad made Iran's goal clear by stating, "Iran's nuclear train has no brake and no reverse gear."[581]

There should be no doubt that the Islamic Republic is determined no matter what the obstacles, to achieve nuclear weapons capability. This was illustrated in early December 2010, when it was reported that the DPRK was planning to transfer to Iran nuclear weapons systems parts and extra-fast centrifuges for uranium enrichment that could help Tehran go into bomb production in the first half of 2011.[582] One nuclear rogue regime assisting another rogue regime attain nuclear capability was being played out in front of the world.

On August 29, 2011, Fereydoon Abbas, head of Iran's atomic energy agency, announced that Iran's nuclear fuel production had already far exceeded its needs. This was the first public announcement of Iran's capabilities. It meant that Tehran was about to move on from 20 percent enriched uranium to 60 percent—the last step before the 90 percent enrichment needed for weapons-grade fuel. Iran had already stocked 4,500 kilograms of low-enriched uranium, which would be enough for four nuclear weapons after further enrichment. Abbas pronounced "dead" the 2009 proposal for the West to supply Iran with new fuel for its small research reactor in return for an end to Iranian production of the fuel. "We will no longer negotiate a fuel swap and a halt to our production of fuel," he said. Abbas also revealed the imminent transfer of Iran's critical enrichment facilities from Natanz to a heavily fortified subterranean facility near the holy city of Qom at Fordow, to keep it safe from air, missile and cyber attack. The facility would not be open to international inspection. With these developments in mind, Western intelligence sources estimated on September 4, 2011, that Iran's advances had brought forward to the spring of 2012 the potential completion of between two and four bombs and the ability to conduct a nuclear test.[583] Iran announced that Bushehr went on line as part of its national power grid on September 3, 2011.

The sabotage of the Fordow uranium enrichment facility's power lines on August 17, 2012, gave Israeli Prime Minister Netanyahu extra leeway to move his original red line for Iran from late September 2012 to the spring or early summer of 2013. The disruption of the underground enrichment plant's power supply caused several of the advanced IR-1 and IR-4 centrifuges producing the 20-percent grade uranium to burst into flames. Work was temporarily halted and the accumulation of 240 kilos for Iran's first nuclear bomb slowed down by at least six months.[584]

Nevertheless, in early October 2012, it was revealed that a secret nuclear site, code name Valayat 1, had been constructed at an underground facility in the outskirts of Najafabad in Isfahan Province. Iranian scientists there were working on a neutron detonator and implosion system along with separating plutonium for an implosion-type fission bomb.[585] Thus, like Libya before it, Iran decided to pursue both the uranium- and plutonium-based pathways to nuclear weapons.

The IAEA released a report on November 16, 2012, which stated Iran since August 2012, installed 700 more centrifuges at its Fordow underground facility for operation, doubling the plant's enrichment capacity. The report said Iran installed 2,800 centrifuges at Fordow, the total the facility is designed to hold. If all of them produced 20 percent enriched uranium, which could be improved to bomb grade with relative ease, it would cut to about three months, down from six, the time needed to accumulate enough fissile material for a nuclear bomb.[586] At the same time, the number of centrifuges in Natanz was doubled to 6,000 to expand substantially its output of medium-grade enriched uranium. In late November 2012, it was revealed in an Associated Press report that the IAEA obtained diagrams during an inspection visit to Iran, which showed the Islamic Republic was planning to build a nuclear bomb with, at least triple the force of the bomb that destroyed Hiroshima, Japan, in the final days of World War II. The diagrams showed a scientific calculation of the expected yield of a nuclear device, with a maximum force of 50 kilotons. In comparison, the bombs used against Hiroshima and Nagasaki, Japan, in 1945, were only 15-kiloton devices.[587]

Meanwhile in Iran, the Fordow underground uranium enrichment plant suffered a large explosion in its third centrifuge chamber at 11:30 A.M. on January 21, 2013. The facility then had 2,700 centrifuges turning out 20 percent enriched uranium. Located about 300 feet under a mountain, the facility allegedly is immune to airstrikes and most bunker-buster bombs. At the time of the explosions, 203 Iranian scientists and technicians along with 16 North Koreans were logged in at the site. The blasts killed at least 76 people, including North Koreans. The bodies of 11 of the technicians and scientists were beyond recognition.[588] The report was first published by Reza Kahlil, who is described as a former Iranian Revolutionary Guards officer who worked undercover as a double agent for the CIA until he escaped to the United States. The report was later confirmed by Israeli intelligence. This was corroborated by the German newspaper, *Die Welt,* with sources close to the German intelligence agency BND (*Bundesnachrichtendienst*), as well as *Welt am Sonntag* (a well-respected German Sunday newspaper). Khalil cited his source as Hamidreza Zakeri, a former Iranian Intelligence Ministry agent, who said the regime believes the blast was sabotage and the explosives could have reached the area disguised by the CIA as equipment imported for the site or defective machinery. None of the information about an explosion at Fordow was verified by either US officials or the Iranian regime.[589] Undeterred, Iran announced on February 13, 2013, that it would install a new generation of some 3,000 faster centrifuges at its Natanz and other facilities to produce significantly more nuclear fuel.[590]

The Iranian presidential election of June 14, 2013, and the selection of Hasan Rouhani did not slow Iran's drive for nuclear weapons one bit. On July 30, 2013, David Albright and Christina Walrond at the Institute for Science and International Security in Washington, DC, published a deeply disturbing report, which declared:

> Iran is expected to achieve a critical capability in mid-2014. [Albright and Walrond defined critical capacity as] the technical capability to produce sufficient weapon-grade uranium from its safeguarded stocks of low enriched uranium [LEU] for a nuclear explosive, without being detected.[591]

On October 24, 2013, a report released by the US Institute for Science and International Security provided its most up-to-date assessment of when Iran could produce enough weapons-grade uranium for a nuclear bomb. The report indicated that "sufficient quantity (SQ) [could be amassed] in as little as approximately 1.0-1.6 months, if it uses all its near 20 percent low enriched hexafluoride stockpile. If Iran used only 3.5 percent LEU, Iran would need at least 1.9 to 2.2 months."[592] Additionally, Iran's stockpile of highly enriched uranium nearly doubled in a year's time (from October 2012 to October 2013) and its number of centrifuges expanded from 12,000 in 2012 to 19,000 in 2013, at both its Fordow and Natanz gas centrifuge plants.[593] In fact in November 2013, Iranian Foreign Minister Javad Zarif boasted of his country's ability to forge ahead with its nuclear weapons program despite years of UN resolutions and sanctions, "Instead of 160 centrifuges that were spinning ten years ago [2003] or eight years ago [2005], today we have 19,000 centrifuges."[594] Furthermore, during 2013 Iran started installing a thousand of its more efficient second generation centrifuges—the IR-2M centrifuge—at its Natanz fuel enrichment plant. These new centrifuges allowed Iran to transform

3.5 percent enriched uranium to bomb-grade material (enriched to 90 percent) as quickly as its old centrifuges were capable of transforming 20 percent enriched uranium to weapons-grade levels. So today, 3.5 percent enrichment is as comfortable a jumping-off point for the Iranian weapons program as 20 percent enrichment was a few years ago. These second-generation centrifuges would enable Iran to produce enough nuclear fuel for a bomb with far fewer centrifuges needed—between 2,000 and 3,300 of them—and they could be concealed in a small warehouse.[595] The report concluded that assuming Iran possessed covert nuclear facilities with "optimized cascade structure and very good centrifuge performance, it is possible that Iran could use a covert plant to break out in as little as approximately one to two weeks."[596]

Shortly thereafter, during the last week of October 2013, there was an explosion at the heavy water IR-40 reactor under construction at Arak in western Iran. Recall that once operational, it is capable of producing plutonium for use in nuclear bombs as an alternative to the enriched uranium method. Speculation as to the cause of the explosion included: Sabotage, a virus planted in the computers that control the system, an error in engineering calculations in the design of the coolant containers which underestimated their strength for standing up to the required level of pressure, and/or the deliberate sale to Iran of inferior steel materials that were not strong enough to withstand such pressure. In any event, the explosion certainly delayed the start-up date of the Arak facility.[597]

On February 9, 2014, speaking to Iran's ISNA news agency, Behrouz Kamalvandi, a spokesman for Iran's atomic energy agency, stated that Iran would not allow International Atomic Energy Agency (IAEA) inspectors to visit the Parchin military nuclear complex. Whenever the IAEA applied for permission to inspect the facility in the previous three years, it was deceived by Iran with the pretext that Parchin was strictly a military base, which did not host any nuclear activity. It therefore did not qualify for international inspection. The IAEA monitors wanted to investigate suspected nuclear explosive tests there. It was not a listed facility in the Geneva interim agreement on Iranian nuclear program that Secretary of State John Kerry rushed to conclusion on November 24, 2013. This was a major error on Kerry's part. Once again, like the Kerry-Lavrov accord on Syria's chemical weapons, a major loophole was exploited. In both agreements, the Western powers thought they were getting an agreement to limit or stop Syria's used of chemical weapons and Iran's march towards acquiring nuclear weapons and in both cases, the West was outmaneuvered by Syria and Iran respectively. Such flawed international agreements riddled with loopholes, were bound to fail sooner or later. So, while publicly declaring it was "reducing its stocks of 20 percent enriched uranium," Iran suddenly increased its production of low, 5 percent grade enriched uranium and then covertly smuggled this new stock to the Parchin facility for secret upgrade to 20 percent, a level which can be rapidly enriched to weapons grade. Some 1,300 kilograms of low-grade material was transferred to Parchin and 1,630 advanced centrifuges were installed there for rapid upgrade work.[598] Thus, US Secretary of State Kerry, speaking on behalf of the Obama administration to a US Senate committee on April 8, 2014, was forced to admit that Iran had the ability to produce fissile material for a nuclear bomb in two months, if it so decided. Iran's "break-out" time is defined as how long it would take it to produce fissile material for one nuclear weapon, if it decided to build such weapons of mass destruction.[599] It should be noted that there are different perceptions of the precise point at which Iran may be considered as having "gone nuclear." The US Obama administration defines it as the point at which the Iranians can place a nuclear warhead on a missile. The Gulf States and Israel see it as the point at which Iran becomes able to use enriched uranium to build a nuclear device of any kind. The latter is imminent and in fact, may already have been reached. Thus, while Iran, the nation that perfected the game of chess, continues to be a master of that game, the Obama administration is still playing marbles. As Mark Dubowitz of the Foundation for the Defense of Democracies observed in an article in the *Wall Street Journal* in late September 2014:

> The Iranian nuclear game is to compromise on the elements of the program they've already perfected in order to gain time on the elements they haven't. They've perfected enrichment so they can suspend it for the time being. What they've gained in exchange is time to work on advanced centrifuge R&D. The more efficient the centrifuges, the fewer they need; the fewer they need, the easier they are to hide.[600]

Therefore, the deception and talks go on and on and on—as they have since 2003[*] and will end it seems, only when Iran announces (or demonstrates with a nuclear test in the Iranian desert) that it is the world's tenth nuclear power.

Yet once again, a possible act of sabotage struck the very same Parchin facility that Iran refused to open to IAEA inspection. At least two people (the exact number may never be known)—an unnamed nuclear expert was among the dead—died in a lethal massive explosion, October 5, 2014, at a military explosives factory that is part of Iran's Parchin nuclear complex some 18.5 miles southeast of Tehran. Images taken by the French satellite Pleiades on October 7 and released the next day, showed "extensive damage consistent with an attack against bunkers in a central locality within the military research complex at the Parchin military compound" and more specifically in an area of the base where trials were conducted involving "controlled detonation of [fuses] intended to serve as triggers for nuclear devices." The area where the explosion occurred was "simply eliminated" by the blast.[601]

Reports from the site began filtering into media by Monday, October 6. The BBC quoted Saham news as saying the explosion was "so intense that windows of buildings nine miles away were shattered," in a southeasterly direction. "The glare from the blast could also be seen from a great distance away."[602] Iran has admitted it had "tested fast functioning detonators, known as 'exploding bridge wires'"[603] at Parchin. Exploding bridge wires act to trigger simultaneously the conventional explosives components of a nuclear bomb, to create the right condition for the nuclear core to detonate fully in a nuclear reaction. Iran has not explained to the IAEA its own need or application for such detonators. "Given their [EBWs'] possible application in a nuclear explosive device, and the fact that there are limited civilian and conventional military applications for such technology, Iran's development of such detonators and equipment is a matter of concern,"[604] warned the IAEA. The explosion at Parchin makes one thing clear; the nuclear weapons program Iran has long denied is real.

Iran's intended target for its future nuclear arsenal was publicly enunciated on numerous occasions. The Islamic Republic has shown nothing but unremitting hostility to the Jewish state since the proclamation of the former. To a crowd chanting "death to Israel" on December 14, 2001, former Iranian president Ayatollah Ali Akbar Hashemi Rafsanjani infamously declared, "The use of an atomic bomb against Israel would totally destroy Israel, while the same against the Islamic world would only cause damage. Such a scenario is not inconceivable."[605] *Iran Emrooz* (Iran Today) quoted Ayatollah Mohammad Baqer Kharrazi, secretary-general of Iranian Hezbollah, as saying in a February 14, 2005, speech, "We are able to produce atomic bombs and we will do that. We shouldn't be afraid of anyone. The United States is not more than a barking dog."[606] On October 26, 2005, Iranian President

---

[*] Negotiations with Iran began in 2003, when Iran had about 100 centrifuges. Today (mid-2015) it has at least 19,000 with new upgraded centrifuges ready to come on line.

Mahmoud Ahmadinejad proclaimed to 4,000 attendees at an Islamic Student Associations conference on "The World Without Zionism" that:

> The establishment of the occupying [Zionist] regime of Qods [Jerusalem] was a major move by the world oppressor [the United States] against the Islamic world. Many … say it is not possible to have a world without the United States and Zionism. But you know that this is a possible goal and slogan. Imam [Ruhollah Khomeini] said: 'This regime that is occupying Qods [Jerusalem] must be eliminated from the pages of history'*[607] and this was a very wise statement. [We] cannot allow this historical enemy [Israel] to exist in the heart of the Islamic world.[608]

In February 2008, the Iranian Revolutionary Guard Corps commander, General Mohammed Ali Jafari declared that "in the near future, we will witness the destruction of Israel, the aggressor, this cancerous microbe Israel, at the [cap]able hands of the soldiers of the community of Hezbollah" which has been heavily armed by Iran and acts as its surrogate in Lebanon.[609] These pronouncements were typical of the on-going torrent of vows to "wipe Israel off the map."

In early February 2012, the Iranian government, through a website proxy, laid out the legal and religious justification for the destruction of Israel and the slaughter of Jews worldwide. The doctrine was announced on the Iranian website Alef, and was written by Alireza Forghani, an analyst and a strategy specialist for Iran's supreme leader Ayatollah Ali Khamenei. It called for the destruction of Israel and the slaughter of its people, including wiping out Israeli assets and Jewish people worldwide. The article was run on most Iran state-owned sites, including the Revolutionary Guards' Fars News Agency, showing that the regime endorsed this doctrine. It cited a major speech at prayers on February 12, 2012, in which Khamenei announced that Iran would support any nation or group that attacks the "cancerous tumor" of Israel. Using its Shahab 3 and Ghadr missiles, the article claimed that Israel could be destroyed in less than nine minutes and that Khamenei, as supreme religious authority also believed that Israel and America not only must be defeated but annihilated.[610] Thus, Iran continued to violate Article 2, clause 4, of the United Nations Charter, "All Members shall refrain in their international relations from the threat or use of force against the territorial integrity or political independence of any state, or in any other manner inconsistent with the Purposes of the United Nations."

Among Israeli targets specified named in Forghani's article were three cities, Tel Aviv, Jerusalem and Haifa, which contain over 60 percent of the Jewish population of Israel. Also named were important Israeli facilities including: the Rafael nuclear plant, which is the main nuclear engineering center of Israel; the Eilun nuclear plant; another Israeli reactor in Nebrin; and the Dimona reactor at the Negev Nuclear Research Center, the most critical nuclear reactor in Israel because it produces 90 percent enriched uranium for Israel's nuclear weapons. Other targets cited included airports and air force bases such as the Sedot Mikha Air Base, which contains Jericho ballistic missiles and is located southwest of the Tel Nof Air Base, where aircraft equipped with nuclear weapons, are located. Secondary targets include power plants, sewage treatment facilities, energy resources, and transportation and communication infrastructures, as well as urban centers. Such bombardment would continue until all the Israelis were wiped out.[611] Thus, it was not without good reason that already in

---

* The Islamic Republic News Agency (IRNA) reported Ahmadinejad's speech and the quotation from Ayatollah Khomeini. *The New York Times,* the BBC, *TIME* Magazine, and Al-Jazeera television station, all rendered the translation of Khomeini's quote as (which was not in the original) "that the occupying regime [Israel] must be *wiped off the map* (emphasis added)."

July 2004, Israeli Prime Minister Ariel Sharon called Iran's nuclear program "the biggest threat to the existence of Israel" and that "Israel will not allow Iran to be equipped with a nuclear weapon."[612]

Before and after Al Quds (Jerusalem) Day, August 17, 2012, a stream of top Iranian leaders repeated their violent invective to destroy Israel. To the cheering crowds of half a million or more in Tehran, the message was simply this: Israel must be destroyed, irrespective of whether or not it attacks the Islamic Republic. As the demonstrators shouted "Death to Israel! Death to America!" and burned American and Israeli flags, President Mahmoud Ahmadinejad called "the Zionist regime's existence an insult to all humanity" and for the removal of the "Zionist black stain."

Ahmadinejad added that "the Zionist regime is a tool to dominate the Middle East," as well as that world powers are "thirsty for Iranian blood." He declared, "the Zionist regime and the Zionists are a cancerous tumor. Even if one cell of them is left in one inch of [Palestinian] land, in the future this story [of Israel's existence] will repeat." Ahmadinejad further stated, "the nations of the region will soon finish off the usurper Zionists in the Palestinian land. A new Middle East will definitely be formed. With the grace of God and help of the nations, in the new Middle East there will be no trace of the Americans and Zionists."[613] Nor was Ahmadinejad the only Iranian leader to call for the politicide (i.e. the extermination of an entire independent nation)[614] of the Jewish state. The regime's supreme leader Ayatollah Ali Khamenei, in August 2012, promised, "the superfluous and fake Zionist regime will disappear from the landscape of geography."[615] In a like manner four months later a senior Iranian cleric, Ayatollah Ahmad Khatami warned that Tel Aviv "will burn to ashes,"[616] Islamic Revolutionary Guard Corps Aerospace Force Chief, Brig. General Amir Hajizadeh said an Israeli attack would be welcome "as a pretext to get rid of Israel for good."

The Iranian leadership's tone did not change one iota after their presidential election of June 14, 2013. Despite the Western media's campaign to portray the new Iranian president, Hasan Rouhani as a "moderate," he was quoted by Iran's semi-official ISNA news agency on the eve of his inauguration August 2, 2013, that "the Zionist regime has been a wound on the body of the Islamic world for years and the wound should be removed."[617] The election of Rouhani was designed in part to replace the bombastic demagogic Ahmadinejad, with a quiet-spoken leader who would negotiate with the West. It was designed to lull the West into a false sense of security, more negotiations, and the lifting of sanctions on Iran, as a "good will gesture." Subsequent events proved the Iranian leadership calculated correctly. Former US Ambassador to the UN, John Bolton would aptly sum it up, "The idea that Rouhani will negotiate seriously shows that this [Obama] administration is on a different planet."[618] The main difference between the two men is rhetorical. Inevitably, this will lead to the same end as the years of negotiations with the DPRK, leading to the emergence of a new nuclear power—Iran.

The anti-Israel and misojudaic vitriol continued even as the Western powers, led by the Obama administration concluded an interim agreement with Iran in Geneva, Switzerland on November 24, 2013. The deal was largely symbolic on the part of Iran and substantive on the part of the P5+1 powers (the five permanent members of the UN Security Council—the United States, the United Kingdom, France, Russia, and China—plus Germany). While the former promised a short-term freeze of portions of its nuclear program, the latter agreed to decrease economic sanctions on Iran. Just four days earlier, during a speech in Tehran to a large crowd of the paramilitary Basij group, screaming "Death to America," on November 20, 2013, Iranian Supreme Leader Ali Khamenei referred to the Jewish state as being "doomed to collapse," "the rabid dog" of the Middle East, and in a repetition of the old misojudaic canard of Jews controlling money, Khamenei ranted "because of their economic network" Israelis "should not be called humans."[619] Even as the P5+1 powers attempted to negotiate a framework for a final nuclear weapons deal with Iran in late March 2015, the commander of the

Basij militia of Iran's Revolutionary Guards, Mohammad Reza Naqdi said that "erasing Israel off the map" is "nonnegotiable."[620] We would do well to remember Holocaust survivor Elie Wiesel's timeless warning, "Always believe the threats of your enemies, and not the promises of your friends."

As for Israel, no country can be required to become complicit in its own annihilation. Given the lack of serious diplomatic progress, and meaningful early-on strong sanctions, the international community has failed to deter Iran. It is certainly no understatement to declare that a nuclear Iran would affect a fundamental shift in the strategic balance in the Middle East. Israel will again be faced with *ayn breira*—"no alternative"—in dealing with this existential threat to its survival from Iran. Israel will have to exercise anticipatory self-defense—military preemptive action—in order to survive. Israel was forced to do this in 1956, 1967, 1981, and 2007. Bear in mind that if Israel's enemies lay down their arms, there would be immediate peace. If Israel lays down its arms, there would be an immediate Holocaust 2.0.

In dealing with Iran, Israel faces a state enemy whose open preparations for attacking the Jewish state are authentically genocidal, and which may not always remain rational. Israel does not have the luxury of distance or land mass, recall it is the size of New Jersey, and as a point of comparison, Israel's population is less than the nine million people who live in New York City. A single Iranian nuclear missile or device delivered by Hezbollah, Hamas or other such proxy—for example via truck or speedboat—slipping through various ballistic missile defense systems would be a catastrophe. Unlike other rational nuclear powers—the United States, the United Kingdom, France, Russia, China and India—Israel does not possess either the massive population or territorial expanse to withstand a nuclear strike by an enemy.

Furthermore, once Iran has nuclear weapon-making capabilities, it will not be necessary for Iran immediately to use such weapons. A threatening nuclear Iran would inject the uncertainty of "if" or "when" it might strike Israel. That will have a detrimental military, economic and societal effect on Israel. Since the world will know that Iran has the bomb, certain harmful consequences will impact Israel such as:[621]

- It will erode Israel's geostrategic status.
- It will put the IDF in a hair-trigger response mode with little time for error.
- Immigration to Israel will cease.
- Tourism will cease.
- It will encourage emigration of many thousands of Israelis, especially those with marketable skills.
- It will weaken the Israeli economy. Foreign investments and the Gross Domestic Product will dwindle.
- Unemployment will increase.
- The ratio of expenditures on social services vis-à-vis military expenditures will fall.
- Physical and mental health will decline.
- The Jewish birth rate will decline.
- The relative Arab birth rate will increase resulting in an increase of Arab members in the Knesset.
- The ability of the government to enact legislation conducive to Jewish causes will decline.
- Arab terrorism will increase.
- The ability of the government to function will decline.

The question has been raised, as to whether a nuclear Iran could be deterred. The concept of deterrence that worked successfully during the Cold War simply will not work against a nuclear-armed theocratically-driven, messianic and apocalyptic end-of-times Islamic Iranian regime dedicated to its own self-preservation. The Iranian Islamic leadership is convinced that by obliterating Israel with nuclear weapons, it will hasten the coming of the Mahdi and obtain heavenly rewards for its adherents. Thus, Islamist Iran is unlikely to be deterred out of fear that its people would also be incinerated. One must recall that this is a regime that had no second thoughts in dispatching tens of thousands of its children as human detonators to clear minefields during the Iran–Iraq War. Islamic historian Bernard Lewis commented on the subject of deterrence:

> MAD, mutual assured destruction, [was effective] right through the Cold War. Both sides had nuclear weapons. Neither side used them, because both sides knew the other would retaliate in kind. This will not work with a religious fanatic [like Supreme Leader Ayatollah Ali Khamenei or former President Mahmoud Ahmadinejad]. For him, mutual assured destruction is not a deterrent, it is an inducement. [I]f they kill large numbers of their own people; they are doing them a favor. They are giving them a quick free pass to heaven and all its delights.[622]

This sentiment was clearly expressed early in the Islamic Republic's history by Ayatollah Khomeini, "We do not worship Iran, we worship Allah. For patriotism is another name for paganism. I say let this land [Iran] burn. I say let this land go up in smoke, provided Islam emerges triumphant in the rest of the world."[623] The Islamic Republic of Iran's short-term strategic objective is hegemonic domination of the Middle East and its long-term goal is the imposition of Islam all over the world. In fact, the Qur'an stipulates and sanctions (*Sura* 3, *ayahs* 140–141) that anyone killed by accident or incident during an attack on unbelievers (that includes Jews, Christians, Hindus, Sikhs, Buddhists, Zoroastrians, Bahá'ís, Yazidis, animists and others) is automatically a martyr, with all the benefits of martyrdom. Thus, any such collateral damage to other Muslim states or individuals (e.g. Palestinians, Jordanians, Syrians, Lebanese, Egyptians, or Saudis, to name a few in the area) which occurs during an attack on Israel for example, is more than justified by the horrors happening to the Jews and Israel. The longer Israel waits to attack Iran's command and control centers, the more difficult will it be to neutralize this Islamic successor of Nazism and to prevent the proliferation of nuclear weapons in the Middle East.

Facing the future, Israel must immediately strengthen its nuclear deterrence posture. To be deterred, a rational adversary would need to calculate that Israel's second-strike forces are plainly invulnerable to any first-strike aggressions. Israel has created such a second-strike force, with the acquisition of six *Dolphin*-class submarines,[624] capable of launching retaliatory nuclear missiles. With any non-rational adversary however, all Israeli deterrents are ineffective. A non-rational adversary would be one that does not value its own continued survival more highly than all other preferences. Simply put, a nuclear non-rational adversary is very dangerous and evil.

As the famous Soviet dissident and current Israeli minister Natan Sharansky has said, "In dictatorships you need courage to fight evil; in the free world, you need courage to see the evil."[625] For, as another famous Soviet dissident Alexander Solzhenitsyn, author of the *Gulag Archipelago*, observed, "In keeping silent about evil, in burying it so deep within us that no sign of it appears on the surface, we are implanting it, and it will rise up a thousand-fold in the future."[626]

Israel has the capability of striking Iran. It has aerial refueling ability and its air force has practiced traveling long-distances (e.g. the May 2009, highly publicized IAF training flight to Gibraltar and back, which included mid-air refueling[627]) equal to the distance to Iran. Additionally, the IAF has practiced operations in difficult mountainous terrain in Romania in August 2011.[628] However, due to Iran's size and the scattering of many nuclear-related targets, Israel cannot successfully continually attack Iran with conventional weapons or aircraft for a long sustained campaign, which would be necessary. The distance is great—Iran is the size of Alaska—the defenses formidable, and the casualties would be very high. Furthermore, the manned Israeli Air Force (IAF) would be needed at home to deal with the Iranian response, via its proxies and allies, Hezbollah, Hamas, and Syria (even though the latter is plagued by civil war), all of which would bombard the Israeli homeland with conventional and perhaps chemical weapons. The manned IAF would be needed to suppress those threats as rapidly as possible. However, the IAF now has a few other options, the first being the use of unmanned aircraft. In February 2010, the IAF revealed its fleet of unmanned *Heron TP* drones, which can remain in the air for a full day and could fly as far as the Persian Gulf, putting Iran within its range. The largest unmanned drone in Israel's military arsenal, the *Heron TP* is the size of a Boeing 737. Another military option for dealing with Iran would be the use of land-based and submarine-launched missiles. The Israeli missile arsenal is formidable with the Jericho and Popeye series available. Its *Dolphin*-class submarines have been modified for missile launch. (*see* "Basic Principle 59"). At this juncture, any Israeli strike would probably be limited to targeting key elements in the Iranian nuclear weapons development chain. As former US Ambassador to the United Nations John Bolton outlined in an Op-ed piece in the *New York Times*, key facilities that should be rendered inoperable are the Natanz and Fordow uranium-enrichment installations and the Arak heavy-water production plant and reactor as well as the uranium-conversion facility at Isfahan. An attack need not destroy Iran's entire nuclear infrastructure, but by breaking key links in the nuclear-fuel cycle, it could set back its program by three to five years.[629] In the interim the Obama administration would leave office, regime change might occur in Iran and new, better opportunities would present themselves in dealing with the Iran nuclear issue.

Any Israeli military strike would have to be innovative to succeed. Recall the Israeli westward crossing of the Suez Canal (in 1973), its commando rescue mission to Entebbe, Uganda (1976), its long-range bombing of PLO headquarters in Tunis (1985), as well as its strikes against Iraq's (1981) and Syria's (2007) nuclear facilities. Of course, there are many Western nations, including officials within the United States, that favor letting Israel do the dirty work to avoid fueling anti-Western sentiments in the Islamic world. Even the Sunni Arab states would be relieved if Israel carried out such a mission against the Shi'ite Iranian threat.

The question has also been raised as to would Israel use nuclear weapons in a preemptive strike on Iran. It must be emphasized that Israel has the residual national right to threaten or even use nuclear weapons in order to survive. The UN's International Court of Justice enshrines that principle jurisprudentially in the 1996 Advisory Opinion on Nuclear Weapons.[630] The answer to the above question is unknown but is a possibility, since Israel possesses several delivery systems for such weapons. There is also another option—an EMP weapon. Any military action must take into account Iran's possible reactions. Given the Obama administration's penchant for diplomacy, Iran might apply pressure on the United States, in order for the latter to pressure Israel to cease its military actions. Iran could retaliate directly by blocking the Strait of Hormuz. While the strait is not well suited for mining because of depth, width, and its hydrographic features, maritime traffic can be interdicted by the use of missiles, naval forces, suicide naval vessels and suicide aircraft, as well as the use of scuttled ships.

Iran could aid America's opponents in Iraq, Syria, and Afghanistan, but it does that anyway. It could unleash indirect retaliation by using its allies and proxies, including Syria, Lebanon, Hezbollah, and terrorist networks, including Al-Qaeda.[631] However, any Iranian escalation would certainly invite a stronger counter-escalation. Thus, military action might ignite a regional war, but the alternative of doing nothing would be worse. One of the most important repeated lessons of history is to use a little force early in order to avoid the use of greater force later. Diplomacy is not a substitute for the use of force, to be used only if diplomacy fails. In fact, diplomacy will fail unless it is backed by force. In addition, when negotiations fail, much more force is needed at a greater expenditure of blood and treasure.

It must be stressed, that the intelligence is solid and there is no doubt Iran wants nuclear weapons. It does not intend to stop its nuclear weapons quest. Iran can be stopped. All that is needed is national will by one or more of the Western democracies. We get an indication of what Israel's response must be from Israeli Prime Minister Netanyahu when he addressed a gathering of dignitaries at Auschwitz-Birkenau in 2010. They were there for the sixty-fifth anniversary of the Nazi death camp's liberation by the Soviet Red Army on January 27, 1945 (now recognized as International Holocaust Remembrance Day). Netanyahu said, "The most important lesson from the *Shoah* [Holocaust] is that murderous evil must be stopped as soon as possible, before it can realize its schemes."[632] If Iran would take the foolhardy step of actually striking Israel with nuclear weapons, Iran would cease to exist as a viable nation-state, but that will give the Israelis that survive an Iranian first strike little solace, amidst a (God forbid) nuked Israel. The harsh truth that faces the West in general and Israel in particular, is the choice between a conventional military strike/conflict now and nuclear strikes/war later.

With the current US administration already having announced when it intends to leave the region, Iran has become emboldened, worse empowered. It has reasserted its claim to Bahrain,[*] and pressed its dispute over offshore gas fields with Qatar. It is a staunch supporter of the Assad regime in Syria, despite some four years of civil war in that nation. It is fully and malevolently active in Iraq and Yemen. Iran's objective is to drive the United States out of the Middle East. Iran works with both Al-Qaeda and the Taliban to do so.

In fact, between the two, Al-Qaeda and Iran can control the core of the Middle East in a giant pincer. Al-Qaeda is seeking control of a "southern crescent" made up of Afghanistan, Pakistan, and Somalia—while Iran dominates a "northern crescent" made up of Iran, Iraq, Syria, and Hezbollah-controlled Lebanon, with perhaps the addition of an Islamist Turkey. This is a bit reminiscent of the Molotov-Ribbentrop Pact of August 23, 1939, that saw Nazi German and Soviet pincers surround and then divide Eastern Europe between them. We may well see the revival and expansion of the Saadabad Pact of July 8, 1937, that linked secular Turkey with Iraq, Iran, and Afghanistan. A new such grouping would also include Syria, Hezbollah-controlled Lebanon and the Hamas-controlled Gaza Strip. This would be an Islamist version of that earlier pact, well expanded. If one adds to that Al-Qaeda-controlled Pakistan, and Somalia, it is a formidable alliance, especially if nuclear-armed.

A nuclear Iran will trigger, indeed it has already commenced, a nuclear arms race in the Middle East, as nations such as Egypt, Saudi Arabia, and Turkey seek a deterrent force to oppose growing Iranian hegemony. This was predicted in 2006 by a classified Israeli document, which claimed that if Iran succeeds in creating a nuclear weapon, it could cause a domino effect with other Middle Eastern

---

* In November 1957, under Shah Mohammed Reza Pahlavi, the Iranian *Majlis* passed a resolution declaring Bahrain to be Iran's fourteenth province, citing Persia's conquest of the island in 1602.

countries following suit.[633] Iran aims to spread its Islamic revolution beyond its borders. Early in the Islamic Republic's history, Ayatollah Ruhollah Khomeini proclaimed, "The Iranian revolution is not exclusively that of Iran, because Islam does not belong to any particular people. The struggle will continue until the calls 'there is no god but Allah and Muhammad is the messenger of Allah' are echoed all over the world."[634] Iranian President Ahmadinejad reemphasized Khomeini's words when he pledged on February 23, 2010, "The Islamic revolution's final objective is global revolution." As has been noted above, Saudi Arabia has already made provision to acquire nuclear weapons in an emergency. Trying to dismiss the threat of a nuclear Iran is foolhardy. As Herman Kahn wrote of nuclear war, refusal to think about the unthinkable makes the unthinkable not only thinkable, but also likely. The United States, Israel and the other Western democracies would do well to heed the warning issued by the Prophet Ezekiel:

> The word of the Lord came to me: O mortal, speak to your fellow countrymen and say to them: When I bring the sword against a country, the citizens of that country take one of their member and appoint him their watchman. Suppose he sees the sword advancing against the country, and he blows the horn [shofar] and warns the people. If anybody hears the sound of the horn but ignores the warning, and the sword comes and dispatches him, his blood shall be on his own head. Since he heard the sound of the horn but ignored the warning, his bloodguilt shall be upon himself; had he taken the warning, he would have saved his life. But if the watchman sees the sword advancing and does not blow the horn, so that the people are not warned, and the sword comes and destroys one of them, that person was destroyed for his own sins; however, I will demand a reckoning for his blood from the watchman. Now, O mortal, I have appointed you a watchman for the House of Israel.[635]

The acceptance by the United States of Iran as a nuclear weapons power will be understood throughout the entire Middle East as the end of the American ability to determine, or at least to influence, matters in the region. Globally, it will be seen as the nadir of the United States as a superpower, consigning it to a status similar to the United Kingdom or France, two other Western nuclear powers.

The Western democracies face grave risks from a nuclear Iran. A nuclear Iran involves the merger between radical Islam and nuclear weapons technology. A nuclear Iran will be able to offer a protective, nuclear umbrella over Syria, Shi'ite-controlled Iraq, Lebanon and Yemen as well as any terrorist group be it Hamas, Hezbollah, Al-Qaeda, or any other group, allowing it to strike with impunity. A nuclear Iran will dramatically and totally alter the international security situation, setting the stage for a new scale of terrorist threats that the world has not yet witnessed. Irrespective of Israel, a nuclear Iran poses an existential threat to the United States and the Western world.

56. The principle in international law of *ex injuria jus non oritur*—"right cannot originate from wrong"—i.e. the aggressor must be punished and penalized, applies globally, but has been unjustly denied to Israel.

Under international law, the principle of *ex injuria jus non oritur* calls for the punishment of an aggressor state. For aggressive attacks on neighboring countries, history provides several examples of this principle. For years, attacks emanating from the Spanish Floridas against the southeastern

United States were not curtailed by the Spanish authorities. In response to these acts of aggression, the United States forced Spain to agree to the Adams-Onis Treaty of 1819, which ceded the Floridas to the United States.*

At the conclusion of World War I, Germany had to return Schleswig-Holstein to Denmark for its attack on Denmark in 1864. Austria–Hungary was stripped of the Southern Tyrol, which was given to Italy. At the same time, Austria–Hungary also lost Slavonia to Yugoslavia.

At the end of World War II, Germany permanently lost Silesia, Pomerania, and southern East Prussia to Poland, as well as northern East Prussia to Russia (then the Soviet Union). In fact, northern East Prussia, which was renamed the Kaliningrad Oblast, is 5,830 square miles in area and non-contiguous to Russia. The Sudetenland was taken from Germany and returned to Czechoslovakia. Moreover, for its aggression against Greece in 1941, Italy forfeited the Dodecanese Islands to the former. In Asia, Japan was stripped of Korea, which became two independent states. Additionally, Japan was also stripped of Manchuria, Taiwan, and the Pescadores Islands, all of which were given to China. In all of these cases, the costs of starting an aggressive war and losing included the displacement of the losers. Furthermore, Japan permanently lost the Southern Kurile Islands (Iturup/Etorofu Island, Kunashir/Kunashiri Island, Shikotan Island, and the Habomai Islands) to Russia (then the Soviet Union).

Additionally, despite the fact that the primary aggressor nations of World War II—Japan and Germany—had been totally devastated, defeated and occupied after the conflict, the United States retained control of the Ryukyu Islands, including Okinawa (1945–72). Similarly, Russia (then the Soviet Union) retained control and influence over East Germany (1945–90)—with the acquiescence of the United States. In both cases, this was done in large part, to prevent renewed aggression by Japan and Germany, respectively. Furthermore, it must be noted that both Japan and Germany were sovereign states, whereas Judea and Samaria as well as Gaza were never part of any sovereign entity.

Syria directly launched aggressive war against Israel three times, in 1948, 1967 and 1973. It committed acts of war from 1949 to 1967 from the Golan Heights (451 square miles), which overlooked Israel's Hula Valley and the Sea of Galilee. As mentioned earlier there is even some question as to the region's legal status as part of Syria. By those aggressive acts, Syria has forfeited any claim to the Golan Heights as surely as the examples cited above.

Despite its moral, legal and historic right to the recovered territories, Israel for over four decades has been called upon to return territories obtained in wars of self-defense. However more importantly than acquisition as a result of a war of self-defense, is the fact that Israel's presence in Judea and Samaria is legally justified by the binding international agreement that was concluded at the San Remo Peace Conference between the United Kingdom, France, Italy and Japan (with the United States as an observer), as embodied in the San Remo Resolution that established Palestine as the Jewish National Home and future independent Jewish state. These calls for the return of territories, (or in the Arab fabrication, "all the territories") began almost immediately after the conclusion of the Six-Day War of 1967, when these territories were recovered from Egyptian and Jordanian occupation. These territories are not "disputed territories" either, because the Arab claim to them is not of equal juridical weight to the Jewish legal right to them. Reflecting on this, Israeli ambassador to the UN Abba Eban remarked, "I think that this is the first war [the Six-Day War] in history that on the morrow the victors sued for peace and the vanquished called for unconditional surrender."[636] Immediately after the Six-Day

---

* Contrary to popular misconception, the United States did not "buy" the Floridas for $5 million. The US did agree to pay $5 million to US citizens who had claims against Spain for damages to their property. Spain got not a nickel.

War, the Arab states that launched aggression from these very territories, assumed the role of the aggrieved party and demanded the return of those lands. There is no precedent for that in the history of international relations.

57. Throughout the conflict between Arab/Muslim forces and the Jewish people in Israel, the Arab/Muslim side voiced its opposition to Zionism, tried to equate Zionism with racism, and brand it a colonizing imperialistic ideology.

Zionism is one of the oldest national liberation movements of the modern age. It is the national liberation movement of the Jewish people. Zionism is the recognition of the historical connection between the Jewish people and the Land of Israel. Zionism's goal was to regain and maintain Jewish sovereignty over the ancient Jewish homeland in the Land of Israel. The core of Jewish national identity, religion and culture is indisputably rooted exclusively in the Land of Israel, and is the primary basis for the State of Israel's current existence. The central objective of the Jewish people during its exile, which lasted nearly two millennia, was the retrieval of Jewish sovereignty and since 1948, the aim is to secure that sovereignty. As history shows, that goal is an on-going and difficult task. The term "Zionism" was coined by writer, journalist, and Jewish nationalist, Nathan Birnbaum. It was popularized by Theodor Herzl.

Zionism today depends on Jewish military capacity to defend itself. Additionally, the fate of both the Jewish state and the Jewish Diaspora are inexorably and indivisibly bound together. The influx of Jews to their ancient homeland is the fulfillment of ancient political aspirations expressed in prophesies and prayer. Zionism began with the first loss of Jewish sovereignty over their homeland in 586 B.C.E., more than 2,500 years ago (*see* "Jewish National Sovereignty in the Land of Israel" table). Zionism is intrinsic in Jewish tradition, nationality and religion. Zionism is an integral part of Judaism and to be hostile to Israel or Zionism is to be hostile to Judaism. The Zionist ideology advocated regaining sovereignty over the land of their ancestors. Mount Zion is the eastern hill of Jerusalem near where the citadel captured by King David once stood. It is southwest of the Temple Mount. This name became synonymous with Jerusalem, hence Zionism. Contrary to the beliefs of some, Zionism was not invented at the end of the nineteenth century. Psalm 137:1 states, "By the rivers of Babylon, there we sat down, yea, we wept when we remembered Zion." Psalm 137:5–6 continues, "If I forget thee, O Jerusalem, let my right hand forget her cunning. If I do not remember thee, let my tongue cleave to the roof of my mouth; if I prefer not Jerusalem above my chief joy." These are both twenty-five hundred year-old expressions of Zionism.

Many Jews though not all, were exiled from the Land of Israel by brutal military conquests. There were two such exiles in Jewish history. The first occurred in 586 B.C.E. after the Chaldean, also known as New Babylonian, conquest. The second exile occurred in 70 C.E. after the Roman conquest. These two exiles were associated with the total destruction of the ancient Jewish capital, Jerusalem, and the demolition of its Holy Temple. There was an additional dispersion in 135 C.E., because of the Roman defeat of the Bar Kokhba Rebellion. During that uprising, Jerusalem was recaptured but the rebellion was crushed before the Holy Temple could be reconstructed. It should be noted that the Jews were expelled from Jerusalem six times in history: by the Chaldeans (New Babylonians) in 586 B.C.E., the Romans in 70 C.E., the Romans again in 135 C.E., the Muslim Arabs in 638, the Christian Crusaders in 1099, and from the Old City of Jerusalem by the Jordanian Arab Legion in 1948. Each time Zionism compelled the Jews to return. Similar to the reconstruction of the Holy Temple in Jerusalem and the refortification of the city in the fifth century B.C.E., when the sovereign Jewish state was reestablished in 1948, Zionism mandated its preservation in perpetuity in its ancient homeland. Any anti-Zionist rhetoric and propaganda is merely camouflage and subterfuge for the vehement enmity that is misojudaism.

A Zionist is any person—regardless of race, creed or nationality—who supports the national movement to establish and maintain Jewish sovereignty over the ancient Jewish homeland in the Land of Israel. The Jewish prophet Nehemiah was one of the earliest Zionists and his autobiography is the Book of Nehemiah. He gave up a high position in the Persian court to journey to Jerusalem in ca. 440 B.C.E. He rebuilt the walls around Jerusalem and fortified the city to make it militarily defensible and politically autonomous (a symbol of sovereignty) within the Persian Empire. However, to paraphrase one of the most famous American advertising slogans of the 1960s[*][637] "You don't have to be Jewish to be a Zionist." Some of the more notable Christian Zionists are mentioned below.

Napoleon Bonaparte was a Zionist. When the French army was in Ottoman-controlled Palestine, and besieging the city of Acre in 1799, Napoleon had already prepared a proclamation making the area a national Jewish state. He felt confident that he could occupy Acre and then enter Jerusalem, and from there issue his proclamation. He was unable to realize this project because of the intervention of the British. This proclamation was printed and dated April 20, 1799, but his unsuccessful attempt to capture Acre prevented it from being issued.[638]

The second President of the United States, John Adams was a Zionist. After he left office, he wrote in 1818, to Major Mordechai Noah, "Farther I could find it in my heart to wish that you had been at the head of a hundred thousand Israelites... & marching with them into Judea & making a conquest of that country & restoring your nation to the dominion of it. For I really wish the Jews again in Judea an independent nation. Once restored to an independent government, and no longer persecuted, they would soon wear away some of the asperities and peculiarities of their character."[639]

President Abraham Lincoln was a Zionist. In 1863 during the Civil War, in a meeting with Canadian Christian Zionist, Henry W. Monk, Lincoln said, "restoring the Jews to their homeland is a noble dream shared by many Americans," and that the United States could work to realize that goal once the Union prevailed. Lincoln reportedly also wanted to visit Jerusalem after his presidency.[640]

Jean-Henri Dunant was a Zionist. He was the founder of the International Red Cross and felt that the Jews should return to the Land of Israel as part of his plan to revive the Middle East. It was for Dunant that, in his closing speech to the First Zionist Congress in 1897, Theodor Herzl coined the phrase "Christian Zionist."

On March 5, 1891, under the impact of the Russian pogroms directed against Jews, the Reverend William E. Blackstone, a clergyman of national standing, presented a Memorial to President Benjamin Harrison and Secretary of State, James G. Blaine. The Memorial petitioned that the President and Secretary of State use their good offices and the influence of the United States for the holding of an international conference "to consider the Israelite claim to Palestine as their ancient home and to promote in all other just and proper ways, the alleviation of their suffering condition." The Blackstone Memorial asked the question, "Why not give Palestine back to [the Jews] again? According to God's distribution of nations it is their home, an inalienable possession from which they were expelled

---

[*] In 1960, the New York City-based Levy's Rye Bread Company launched an advertising campaign with the simple slogan, "You don't have to be Jewish to love Levy's Real Jewish Rye." Brooklynite Judy Protas wrote the iconic advertising slogan. The campaign stretched into a series of posters which were placed in subways, which featured images of individuals of various ethnic groups enjoying the bread as the main visual. These included an American Indian in braids, a Chinese man, a robed choirboy, a black child, a Japanese boy, an Irish cop, an Italian grandmother and silent screen movie star Buster Keaton.

by force." The 413 signatories to this petition included not only outstanding official personalities, including members of Congress, but also a long list of eminent leaders of thought, heads of leading newspapers and press associations, as well as eminent representatives of business and the leading professions. They included:

- Melville W. Fuller, Chief Justice of the US Supreme Court
- Chauncey M. Depew, US Senator from New York
- Thomas B. Reed, Speaker of the House of Representatives
- Robert R. Hitt, Chairman of the House Committee on Foreign Affairs
- Sereno E. Payne, Chairman of the Ways and Means Committee
- Congressman William McKinley, of Ohio (later US President)
- William E. Russell, Governor of Massachusetts
- Hugh J. Grant, Mayor of New York
- DeWitt C. Cregier, Mayor of Chicago
- N. Matthews, Jr., Mayor of Boston
- John D. Rockefeller, oil industrialist
- Charles Scribner, publisher
- J. Pierpont Morgan, financier

All of these men as well as a number of other Members of Congress, judges, and Federal and State officials can be considered Zionists.

T.E. Lawrence, "Lawrence of Arabia," was a Zionist. The popular image of Lawrence, fed by Peter O'Toole's portrayal in David Lean's film classic *Lawrence of Arabia,* is that of an Arabophile. British historian Sir Martin Gilbert discovered documents showing that Lawrence was in fact a "serious Zionist." Lawrence, working for Churchill in 1921, clearly identified "the area of Palestine from the Mediterranean to the Jordan River "as the "Jewish National Home."[641]

Winston Churchill was a Zionist. From 1894, when he supported French Army Captain Alfred Dreyfus and spoke out against the prejudices that led to Dreyfus' conviction, Churchill was a supporter of Jewish rights and Zionism, including the Balfour Declaration of 1917. Although as Colonial Secretary he helped partition the Palestine Mandate for the first time, creating Transjordan on 77.5 percent of the territory, Churchill envisioned a Jewish homeland from the Jordan River to the Mediterranean Sea. As he told an audience during his visit to Jerusalem on March 29, 1921, "The hope of your race for so many centuries will be gradually realized here, not only for your own good, but for the good of all the world."[642] He consistently advocated the right of Jewish immigration to the British Mandate of Palestine, even as the British government in the 1930s adopted a pro-Arab appeasement policy. Churchill rebuked the Peel Commission for wanting to limit Jewish immigration and opposed the commission's proposed lop-sided partition plan. In May 1938 he stated, "You [the Jews] have prayed for Jerusalem for 2,000 years, and you shall have it."[643] As the clouds of European war gathered, Churchill dramatically spoke out against the May 19, 1939, MacDonald White Paper issued by the British government restricting Jewish immigration and effectively ending Jewish land purchases in Mandatory Palestine. "We're groveling to these people [the Arabs] because they're threatening us, but we've given our pledge to the Jews. How will they react? How will Hitler react if we renege on our pledge to the Jews? What value will there be in our commitments if we don't honor this one?"[644]

Orde Wingate was a Zionist. In 1936, he was assigned to a British Army Intelligence post in the British Mandate of Palestine. He viewed the establishment of a Jewish state in Palestine as being a religious duty toward the literal fulfillment of Christian prophecy. A military genius, he would shape what became Israeli military doctrine. For Wingate the best defense was a good offense, when fighting a numerically superior enemy "offense meant fighting deep inside enemy territory where the opposition was most vulnerable."[645] For this purpose, Wingate created the Special Night Squads of the *Haganah*. He trained such future Israeli military leaders as Moshe Dayan. Wingate would eventually become a hero of the *Yishuv*.

Dr. Martin Luther King, Jr., was a Zionist. The famed civil rights leader expressed himself clearly about the Jews and Israel on several occasions. "I cannot stand idly by, even though I happen to live in the United States and even though I happen to be an American Negro and not be concerned about what happens to the Jews in Soviet Russia. For what happens to them happens to me and you, and we must be concerned."[646] King further declared, "I solemnly pledge to do my utmost to uphold the fair name of the Jews -- because bigotry in any form is an affront to us all" as well as "When people criticize Zionists they mean Jews, you are talking anti-Semitism."[647] On March 25, 1968, less than two weeks before his tragic death, he spoke out with clarity and directness stating, "peace for Israel means security, and we must stand with all our might to protect its right to exist, its territorial integrity. I see Israel as one of the great outposts of democracy in the world, and a marvelous example of what can be done, how desert land can be transformed into an oasis of brotherhood and democracy. Peace for Israel means security and that security must be a reality."[648]

The historic Arab/Muslim hostility toward Judaism and the Jewish people, besides the hostility mandated in the Qur'an and other Islamic sacred texts, stemmed also from a new source starting after the late nineteenth century, modern Zionism. This new excuse for continued misojudaism began with the advent of modern Zionism and continued with the reestablishment of Jewish sovereignty in the Land of Israel in 1948. Israel represented the new soul of the Jewish people who had never lost their dignity. Jews regained not only their dignity but also their national sovereignty and the pride that comes with it, and in large measure, it represented the strength and determination shown in their ability successfully to defend themselves. This new attitude on the part of Jews indeed was the antithesis of *dhimmitude*. Hence, the Arab/Muslim hatred of Zionism, which they have branded as a form of "racism" in order to delegitimize the Jewish state and the Jewish people. It has been used as camouflage for their continued misojudaism including the "justification" for the murder of Jews.

58. Throughout its modern history, the State of Israel, time and again at the last possible second before the stroke of disaster, has relied on a policy of *ayn breira*—"no alternative"—in dealing with threats to its existence.

On numerous occasions, Israel has had no choice but to deter if it can, and to fight if it must. After a fact-finding mission to the British Mandate of Palestine on August 31, 1947, the United Nations Special Committee on Palestine (UNSCOP) issued a report calling for the second partition of the region into an Arab state and a Jewish state. UNSCOP by a majority vote on September 3, 1947, recommended partition to the United Nations General Assembly.

In an effort to influence the forthcoming UN General Assembly vote, a pan-Arab summit was held in the Lebanese town of Aley on October 11, 1947. The summit was covered by the Egyptian newspaper *Akhbar al-Yom*. Mustafa Amin, the paper's editor conducted an interview with the Secretary-General of the Arab League, Abdul Rahman Azzam. It was during this interview that Azzam made an existential threat against any proposed Jewish state. "This will be a war of extermination and momentous massacre which will be spoken of like the Tatar* [i.e. Mongol] massacre or the Crusader wars."[649] Azzam further noted that volunteers were streaming into the Arab states bordering the British Mandate of Palestine, from places as far away as India, Afghanistan and China,[650] to take up arms against the *Yishuv*.

Arab warfare against the Jewish community intensified after the UNSCOP report was released. In an attempt to influence the voting in the General Assembly, on November 24, 1947, Jamal al-Husseini, spokesman for the Palestine Arab Higher Committee, warned the UN, "The partition line proposed shall be nothing but a line of fire and blood." By the time the United Nations General Assembly voted on this second partition of Palestine, November 29, 1947, (*see* "UN Partition Plan, November 29, 1947" map) full scale war engulfed the British Mandate of Palestine, which continued unabated into the following spring and did not end until armistice agreements were signed between Israel and some of the Arab states, February–July 1949.

---

* Tatar is used loosely in Arabic to mean Mongol, a reference to the thirteenth-century invasions.

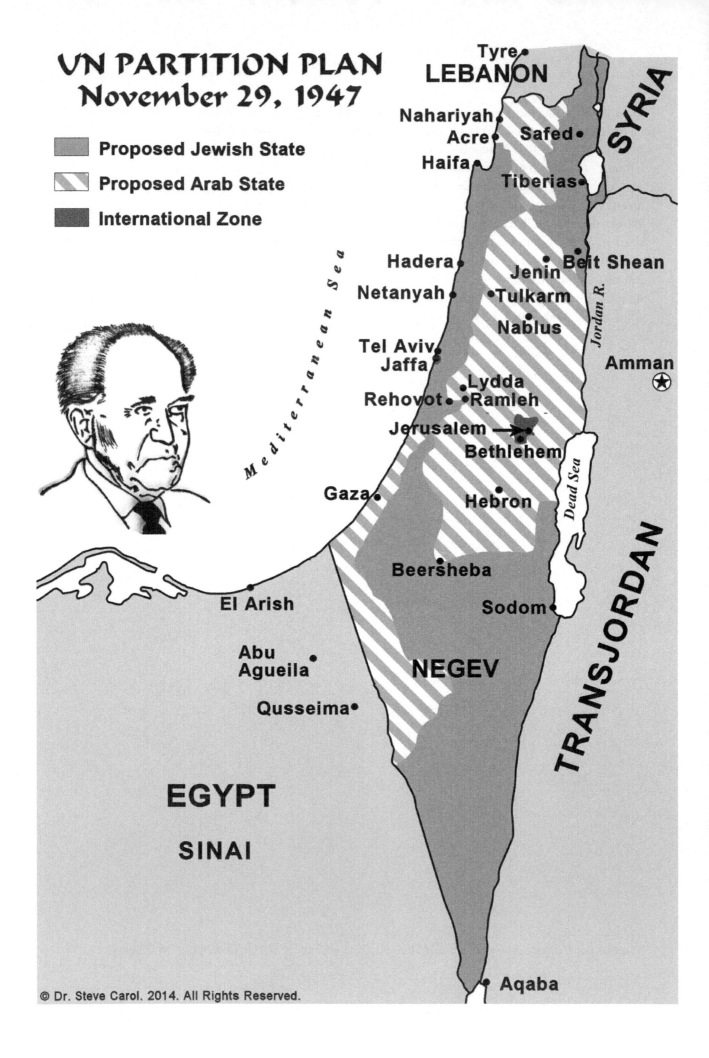

As has previously been mentioned but needs to be reemphasized, the *Yishuv* (Jewish community) in the British Mandate of Palestine, by May 1948, numbered just 650,000 people. The Jews, deprived of assistance from any quarter, were attacked by local Arabs, numbering 1,200,000, in the form of the Army of the Holy War and the Arab Liberation Army. These were soon joined by the combined military forces from the (then) seven-member Arab League whose combined populations were 37.4 million, for a grand total of 38.6 million Arabs arrayed against the *Yishuv*. Additionally, on December 5, 1947, the US imposed an arms embargo* and threatened to add economic sanctions, in order to force soon-to-be Israeli Prime Minister David Ben-Gurion to refrain from a declaration of independence and to accept a UN Trusteeship. Nevertheless, on May 14, 1948, the State of Israel proclaimed its independence, reestablishing Jewish sovereignty in the Land of Israel after 1,875 years. Arab forces had already engaged in warfare since November 29, 1947 and by June 1, 1948, the situation for Israel seemed disastrous (*see* "Arab Attack on Israel as of June 1, 1948" map).

---

* While the US arms embargo was proclaimed for the entire region, it effectively impacted only the *Yishuv* and the new State of Israel, since the United Kingdom was already providing military equipment to Libya, Egypt, Sudan, Transjordan, Iraq, and several of the Gulf states, while France supplied both Syria and Lebanon.

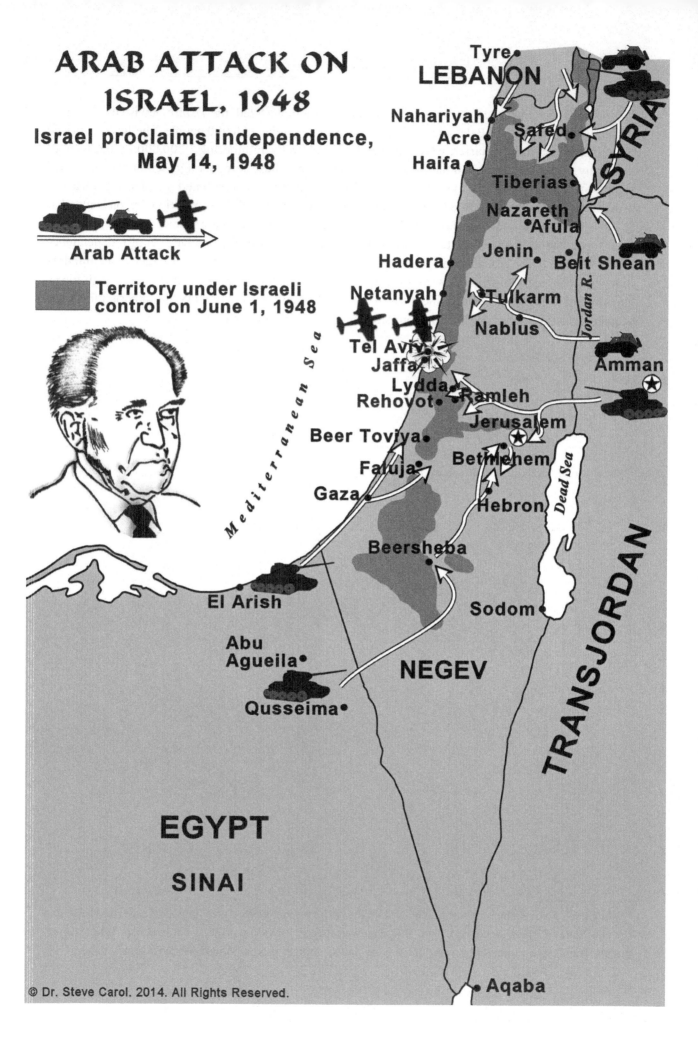

ARAB ATTACK ON ISRAEL, 1948

Israel proclaims independence, May 14, 1948

Arab Attack

Territory under Israeli control on June 1, 1948

LEBANON

SYRIA

TRANSJORDAN

EGYPT

SINAI

NEGEV

Mediterranean Sea

Dead Sea

Jordan R.

Tyre
Nahariyah
Acre
Haifa
Safed
Tiberias
Nazareth
Afula
Jenin
Beit Shean
Hadera
Netanyah
Tulkarm
Nablus
Tel Aviv
Jaffa
Amman
Lydda
Rehovot
Ramleh
Jerusalem
Beer Toviya
Bethlehem
Faluja
Hebron
Gaza
Beersheba
El Arish
Sodom
Abu Agueila
Qusseima
Aqaba

Recall the 1947 UN Partition Plan for Palestine was a non-legally binding General Assembly resolution. The plan provided no mechanism for implementation, nor did it ensure the establishment of either the Arab or Jewish states. With no United Nations condemnation of, or sanctions against Arab aggression, the re-emerging Jewish state had no alternative—*ayn breira*—but to fight a costly (losses amounted to 6,373 killed—i.e. 1 percent of the population) war of survival and independence.

In mid-February 1955, Czechoslovakia, then a Soviet satellite state, and Egypt concluded an arms agreement whereby Egypt would receive Soviet arms, including tanks, jet fighters and bombers. In October, the Soviet Union concluded a similar agreement with Syria. The United Kingdom in the meanwhile, was supplying modern weaponry to both Iraq and Jordan. Repeated Israeli requests to purchase arms from the United States to balance the Soviet sales to Egypt and Syria, were rejected. President Dwight D. Eisenhower opposed US arms sales to Israel because it would lead to an "Arab-Israeli arms race." However, since the Arab states were receiving arms from at least two major powers, the Israelis felt pressed to the wall desperate to maintain some type of arms equilibrium. The president's statement notwithstanding, an arms race began.

EGYPTIAN-ISRAELI ARMS EQUILIBRIUM, 1949–55	
EGYPT	**ISRAEL**
100 ± light tanks	100 ± light tanks
50 propeller-driven aircraft	40 to 50 propeller-driven aircraft

THE ARMS RACE BEGINS (by the summer of 1955)	
EGYPT	**ISRAEL**
200 tanks (Sherman MK 111 and Centurion)	200 tanks (could not buy Centurions)
80 jet fighters	50 jet fighters
20 bombers	–
150mm guns	–
120mm mortars	–
40 AMX-13 light tanks	–
200 tank destroyers	–
2 naval destroyers	2 naval destroyers
2 Hunt-class frigates	–
2 Colony-class frigates	–

With his new weapons arriving from the Communist bloc, Egypt's President Gamal Abdel Nasser elected to escalate his confrontation with Israel. Egypt intensified terrorist attacks from the Egyptian-occupied Gaza Strip. The Chief of Staff of the United Nations Truce Supervisory Organization (UNTSO), Lieutenant-General E.L.M. Burns wrote, "I felt that what the Egyptians were doing in sending these men, who they dignified with the name of *fedayeen* or commandos, into another country with the mission to attack men, women, and children indiscriminately was a war crime."[651] On September 12, 1955, Nasser announced the tightening of the air and sea blockade of the Gulf of Aqaba at the Straits of Tiran, forbidding passage of all Israeli-bound planes and ships. Egypt was viewed as Israel's main threat as the new Soviet war material was being stockpiled in the Sinai Peninsula on the Egyptian-Israeli frontier. Egyptian bombers would be within minutes flying time from the Israeli population centers in its heartland.

| THE EGYPTIAN-ISRAELI ARMS RACE BY OCTOBER 1956 ||
EGYPT	ISRAEL[*]
430 T-34 tanks	300 medium tanks (including M4 Sherman and Super-Sherman)
–	100 AMX-13 light tanks
200 Armored troop carriers	–
100 SU-100 self-propelled guns	60 self-propelled guns
200 Archer tank-destroyers	–
–	20 tank transporters
200± Bren carriers	200 semi-armored M3 half track carriers
–	300 four-wheel drive trucks
120 MiG-15 jet fighters	60 Mystère IVA jet fighters[†]
85 older type jet fighters	50 older (22 Ouragan and the rest Meteor) jet fighters
50 Ilyushin Il-28 jet bombers	–
20 older (Halifax and Lancaster) bombers	–
20 IL-14 jet transports	–
40 older (Dakota and Commando) transports	20 Dakota and Nord transports
15 helicopters	
2 *Skoryi* class destroyers (ex-Soviet)	–
2 Z class destroyers (ex-British)	2 destroyers
5 frigates (ex-British; ex-American, 1 Soviet)	–
2 corvettes (ex-British)	–
4 minesweepers (ex-Soviet)	–
30 motor torpedo boats (12 Italian and British; 12 Soviet; 6 Yugoslav)	9 motor torpedo boats
2 submarines (delivered after October 1956)	–
–	2 landing craft

As Nasserism swept the Arab world, and pro-Egyptian governments were formed in Syria and Jordan, Egypt concluded a military alliance with these states on October 22, 1956, and placed the troops of all three countries under the command of Egyptian General Abdel Hakim Amer. Nasser declared in the last days of October 1956, that Egypt would choose the time and the place for the final assault against Israel. Israel had to wait passively for the moment of his selection. For a second time in its modern history, Israel had reached the point of no alternative—*ayn breira*. Though militarily weak,

---

[*] Approved, but most not yet delivered.

[†] Ordered in August 1954; the first shipment of eight planes took place on April 12, 1956. By October, Israel had sixteen Mystères in its possession, the rest to be delivered.

it joined the Anglo-French plan to cripple Nasser's war machine, possibly topple him from power, and for Israel stop the terrorist raids as well as open the Straits of Tiran. This Israel did beginning on October 29, 1956, with Operation *Kadesh,* successfully achieving its military goals (*see* "Sinai-Suez War" map).

Israel learned some important lessons because of its Sinai Campaign. It could not depend on other nations for its security. Dependency on other countries for direct military assistance was risky. At the time of the Sinai-Suez War, Israel had to rely on French air cover over Israel, as well as French naval protection of its seacoast, while it committed the bulk of its forces into action in the Sinai. Needed equipment arrived at the last moment and much remained to be delivered. Dependency on other countries might also result in their reneging on military pledges made, as France did in 1967. The Sinai Campaign strengthened the Israeli predisposition for preemptive attack. Israel would begin to acquire its reputation of not waiting until a potential danger became an actual danger, though subsequent events would prove Israel had some very close calls.

In the spring of 1967, Israel was perceived as weak. The Soviet Union's rationale and role in encouraging an Arab attack on Israel has been discussed above (*see* "Basic Principle 26"). All this convinced Egyptian President Gamal Abdel Nasser to rapidly escalate a confrontation with Israel which included removal of the United Nations Emergency Force (UNEF), blockading once again, the Straits of Tiran to both Israeli air and maritime traffic, and uniting the Arab world to go to war with Israel (*see* "Causes of the Six-Day War, 1967" map). On May 26, 1967, Mohamed Heikel, Egyptian journalist, close advisor and confidant to Egyptian President Nasser summed up the Egyptian position on closing the Straits of Tiran, emphasizing its intention to incite a war with Israel, in Egypt's government-sponsored newspaper, *Al-Ahram*, "Let Israel begin! Let our second blow then be ready! Let it be a knockout!"[652]

By June 4, Arab forces from not only Egypt, Syria, and Jordan were mobilized on Israel's vulnerable armistice lines, but additional military forces began streaming to the potential war fronts from other Arab states including Algeria, Sudan, Iraq, Kuwait, Lebanon, and Saudi Arabia. On that same day, Ahmed Shukairy, then head of the PLO was asked what would happen to native born Israelis after the Arab conquest of the Jewish state. He replied, "Those who survive will remain in Palestine, but I estimate that not many of them will survive." For Israel, the issue was increasingly less the blockade of the Straits of Tiran, but the growing number of Arab troops, tanks, jet fighters and bombers amassing on its frontiers. This belief was reinforced by large numbers of Iraqi troops moving into Jordan that day. Israel estimated that if the Arabs began the war, Israel would win, but lose some 10,000 of its citizens. Once again—*ayn breira*—"no alternative" was left. Since Egypt's blockade itself was an act of war, Israel exercised a law-enforcing expression of anticipatory self-defense, which is when the danger posed by an emerging threat is observably "instant" and "overwhelming."[653] Such military preemptive action is carried out in order to survive. Israel preempted the Arab land attack with a devastating air strike on June 5, 1967—Operation *Moked* ("Focus")—which destroyed 304 out of 419 Egyptian aircraft on the ground, 57 out of 112 Syrian planes, Jordan's entire 30 plane air force and 10 planes on the ground at Iraq's westernmost base, H3, at Habbaniya (*see* the "Six-Day War, June 5–10, 1967—Israeli Attack" map).

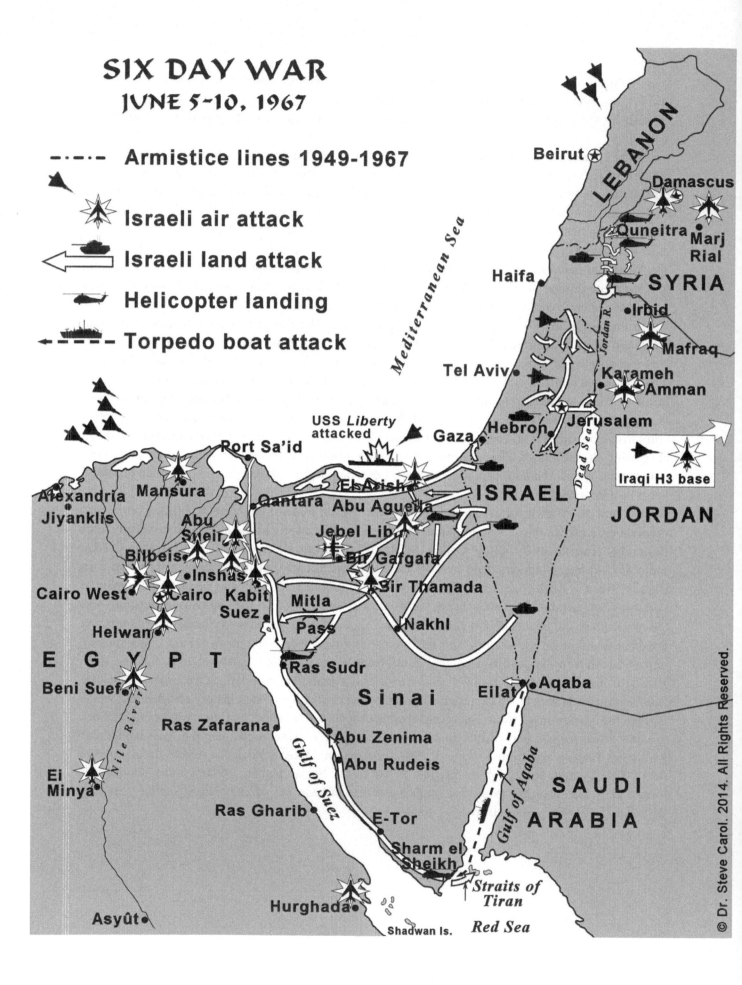

SIX DAY WAR
JUNE 5-10, 1967

–·–·–	Armistice lines 1949-1967
	Israeli air attack
	Israeli land attack
	Helicopter landing
	Torpedo boat attack

LEBANON

Beirut

Damascus

Quneitra

Marj Rial

Haifa

SYRIA

Irbid

Mafraq

Mediterranean Sea

Tel Aviv

Karameh

Amman

USS *Liberty* attacked

Gaza

Hebron

Jerusalem

Jordan R.

Dead Sea

ISRAEL

Iraqi H3 base

JORDAN

Port Sa'id

El Arish

Alexandria

Mansura

Qantara

Abu Agueila

Jiyanklis

Abu Sueir

Jebel Lib.

Bir Gafgafa

Bilbeis

Inshas

Bir Thamada

Cairo West

Cairo

Kabit

Mitla Pass

Nakhl

Suez

Helwan

Ras Sudr

E G Y P T

S i n a i

Beni Suef

Eilat

Aqaba

Ras Zafarana

Abu Zenima

Ei Minya

Abu Rudeis

SAUDI

Nile River

ARABIA

Gulf of Suez

Ras Gharib

E-Tor

Gulf of Aqaba

Sharm el Sheikh

Straits of Tiran

Asyût

Hurghada

Shadwan Is.

Red Sea

The right of anticipatory self-defense under international law was established by Hugo Grotius in Book II of *The Law of War and Peace* (1625). Here, Grotius indicates that self-defense is permissible after not only an attack has already been suffered, but also in advance— "where the deed may be anticipated." Alternatively, as he says later in the same chapter, "It be lawful to kill him who is preparing to kill." A similar argument is offered by Samuel Pufendorf in his treatise, *On the Duty of Man and Citizen According to Natural Law* (1672).[654]

Israel's use of anticipatory self-defense—its famous preemptive air strike of June 5, 1967, was not the first in history. There were several famous earlier historic examples. In the War of Spanish Succession, known in North America as Queen Anne's War (1702–13), Great Britain seeking to protect itself from the perceived threat of Spain and France joining under a Bourbon king, initiated the war.

Another example of a preemptive strike occurred during the Napoleonic Wars on April 2, 1801, when Vice Admiral Horatio Nelson of the Royal Navy, defying orders attacked the combined Danish-Norwegian fleet in the Battle of Copenhagen. The British feared the growing strength of the League of Armed Neutrality, comprised of Denmark–Norway, Prussia, Russia, and Sweden. The combined naval forces of these nations posed a threat to British naval supremacy and its blockade of French-controlled Europe. To prevent the amassing of the combined fleets of the League, the United Kingdom struck preemptively.

A third example occurred on July 3, 1940, when the British Royal Navy attacked the French fleet at Mers-el-Kébir, Algeria. France and the United Kingdom were not at war with one another, but rather as allies had been fighting Nazi Germany, whose forces rapidly overran Western Europe in the spring of 1940. France had signed an armistice with Germany and the British feared that the French fleet would fall into German hands. Prime Minister Winston Churchill ordered the attack, which sank or heavily damaged three French battleships, four destroyers and saw the loss of 1,297 French servicemen killed.

Prior to the outbreak of the Yom Kippur War of 1973, the capabilities of Egypt and Syria were well known, but their intentions were completely misread by Israel's Directorate of Military Intelligence, abbreviated as "Aman," which failed to assess the situation correctly. This came to be known as the *Mechdal* ("The Failure"). On October 6, 1973, Egypt and Syria attacked. The Egyptians crossed the Suez Canal, overwhelmed the Bar-Lev line, and moved seemingly effortlessly into the Sinai Peninsula. The Syrians nearly overran the Golan Heights completely (*see* the "Yom Kippur War–Arab Attack" map). As Soviet resupply to the Arab states began even before the commencement of hostilities (*see* the "Yom Kippur War–Soviet Supply to Egypt and Syria" map), Israel took heavy losses in the first week of the conflict. Encouraged that Israel was faltering, other Arab states—Morocco, Algeria, Libya, Tunisia, Sudan, Saudi Arabia, Kuwait, Iraq, and Jordan—began to stream men and material to the Egyptian and Syrian fronts. Israel again was faced with no alternative—*ayn breira*. Orders were given to prepare thirteen atomic bombs for possible use against the Arab enemy. However, thanks to changing fortunes on the battlefield, including an Israeli counter-attack westward across the Suez Canal, a thrust deep into Syria (*see* the "Yom Kippur War–Israeli Counterattack" map) and a massive American resupply airlift (*see* the "Yom Kippur War–US Resupply to Israel" map), Israeli forces succeeded in forcing both the Egyptians and Syrians to agree to a ceasefire (*see* the "Yom Kippur War Ceasefire lines" map).

On June 27, 1976, Air France Flight 139 scheduled to fly from Athens, Greece, to Paris, France, was hijacked to Entebbe, Uganda by Palestinian and German terrorists. The terrorists were aided by the governments of both Libya and Uganda. The terrorists copied a grim page from Nazi history—*selektzia*—separating Israelis and persons with Jewish sounding names from the rest of the hostage passengers. *Selektzia* was the process whereby the Nazi "Angel of Death," Dr. Josef Mengele at Auschwitz, chose those who would live and those who would die! While the world did little but talk and urged Israeli concessions, the Israeli government was yet again faced with no alternative—*ayn breira*. The Israel Defense Forces launched a dramatic 2,500-mile rescue raid, which succeeded in freeing 101 of the 105 hostages, and killing all the terrorists. The Israelis lost their military commander, Lieutenant Colonel Yonatan Netanyahu (the older brother of Israel's later Prime Minister Benjamin Netanyahu) and four hostages during and after the raid.

As was related earlier (*see* "Iraq: Nuclear weapons" in "Basic Principle 55"), Iraq purchased a French nuclear reactor in November 1975, with the aim of producing nuclear weapons. Iraq methodically moved forward to complete its Osirak reactor as quickly as possible. Equipment was purchased from several European countries, and uranium ore from African states. Israel's efforts to arouse the international community to take action to halt this process proved of no avail. On June 1, 1981, the French newspaper *Le Point* announced the reactor was completed. It would become fully operational in a few months. Israel again was faced with no alternative—*ayn breira*. Therefore, Israel launched a dramatic and effective preemptive air strike—Operation *Opera*—on the Tammuz-1 reactor at Osirak. The attack, carried out by eight F-16s accompanied by six F-15s punched a hole in the concrete reactor dome before the reactor began operation. It delivered fifteen delay-fused 2,000 pound bombs deep into the reactor structure (the sixteenth bomb hit a nearby hall). The blasts shredded the reactor and blew out the dome foundations, causing it to collapse on the rubble, destroying it.[655] This was the world's first attack on a nuclear reactor. One of the Israeli pilots was Amos Yadlin, (later Chief of Staff of the Israeli Air Force and then head of the IDF Military Intelligence Directorate [Aman]). The last Israeli plane was piloted by Ilan Ramon, the Israeli astronaut who subsequently perished along with the crew of the space shuttle *Columbia,* on February 1, 2003.

During the summer of 2007, the Israeli Mossad detected construction of a nuclear reactor for the production of plutonium in a remote part of Syria, with the assistance of the DPRK (*see* "Syria: Nuclear weapons" in "Basic Principle 55"). This was corroborated by photographs of the facility. It should also be recalled that many in the intelligence community believed that components of Iraq's attempts to build nuclear weapons again, were moved to Syria when the US-led coalition forces invaded Iraq in March 2003. By August 2007, the Syrian reactor was weeks away from functioning. Syria at no time informed the UN's International Atomic Energy Agency about the construction of the reactor, while the DPRK violated pledges to both the IAEA and the United States not to proliferate. Quiet diplomatic efforts to check on this facility proved to no avail. For tiny Israel, even a single nuclear strike on its heartland would be catastrophic. Thus again, Israel was confronted with no alternative—*ayn breira*. Therefore, on September 6, 2007, the IAF struck the Syrian nuclear complex, which was obliterated in the raid. US members of Congress heard testimony as to all these events on April 24, 2008, at which time White House spokeswoman Dana Perino stated, "We have good reason to believe that reactor, which was damaged beyond repair on September 6 of last year, was not intended for peaceful purposes. The construction of this [Syrian] reactor was a dangerous and potentially destabilizing development for the region and the world."[656] As these examples illustrate, Israel must grasp the reality that it is a nation and a people who stand alone and can depend on no one but themselves to deter its adversaries.

59. Israel has long been known to have nuclear warfare capacity. However, though under constant attack and threat of annihilation, it has never threatened any nation with its nuclear arsenal.

Israel's doctrine of nuclear opacity was formulated in the early 1960s, by then Israeli Prime Minister Levi Eshkol. Thus, the official Israeli position on nuclear weapons has been, "Israel will not be the first country to introduce nuclear weapons into the Middle East." Yigal Allon highlighted this point by adding the caveat that Israel would not be the second country either.[657] This became Israel's doctrine of nuclear opacity for years to come.[658] However, since the United States introduced nuclear weapons into the Middle East as part of its Sixth Fleet deployment in the early 1950s, as well as deployment of nuclear-armed Strategic Air Command bombers deployed at Middle Eastern airfields during that same period, the Israeli statement is a moot point. It should be noted that in mid-February 2015, the Obama administration declassified a 386-page top-secret document titled "Critical Technological Assessment in Israel and NATO Nations," which publicly revealed that Israel has nuclear weapons including hydrogen bombs. The report was written in 1987 by the Institute for Defense Analysis, an agency working in association with the Pentagon. That the Obama administration released this information publicly about Israel's capabilities (whereas it did not release information in the report about Germany, Italy and other NATO allies) showed the animus that the Obama administration had for the Jewish state. Its release was timed to deflect increased criticism of Obama administration negotiations for a nuclear-deal with Iran.

The Israeli nuclear weapons program grew out of the conviction that the Holocaust and global misojudaism justified any measures Israel took to ensure its survival. National security has always been the overriding concern of the Jewish state, as it should be of any nation. In Israel, this is referred to as *kadushat habitachon* ("the sanctity of security"). Israeli efforts to develop an indigenous nuclear-weapons capability was driven by deep suspicion of foreign powers' commitments to defend the Jewish people, extreme vulnerability to an enemy first strike, and an accompanying vulnerability even to a false alarm. History has demonstrated these fears to be accurate as was proven in 1948, 1967, and 1973. The Arab states have continually made threats and efforts to destroy Israel since its inception. Additionally since the late 1950s, Egypt, followed by other Arab states has sought to acquire nuclear weapons of various types. Iran, since the establishment of the Islamic Republic, has issued threats to wipe Israel off the map.[659] Thus, Israel embarked early on a program to attain military nuclear capacity.

With the establishment of the Israel Defense Forces (IDF), came the creation of *Cha'il Mada*—the IDF's Science Corps—known by the Hebrew acronym HEMED.[660] In 1949, a special unit of HEMED, HEMED *Gimmel* began a two-year geological survey of the Negev Desert to discover uranium deposits. Although no significant sources of uranium were found, recoverable amounts were located in phosphate deposits near Beersheba and Sodom. However, extracting uranium from phosphate proved too costly. HEMED *Gimmel* also worked on a method of heavy water production.[661]

In 1949, Israel and France began nuclear research cooperation. Francis Perrin, a member of the French Atomic Energy Commission and a nuclear physicist, visited the Weizmann Institute of Science in Israel. He invited Israeli scientists to the new French research facility at Saclay and a joint research effort was subsequently set up between the two states.[662] This nuclear research cooperation continued until the mid-1960s.

The Israel Atomic Energy Commission (IAEC) was established in 1952. Its chairman, Ernst David Bergmann, had long advocated an Israeli bomb as the best way to ensure "that we shall never again be led as lambs to the slaughter."[663] Bergmann was also head of the Ministry of Defense's Research and Infrastructure Division (known by its Hebrew acronym EMET ["truth"]), which had taken over the HEMED research centers (HEMED *Gimmel* among them, now renamed *Machon 4*) as part of a reorganization. Under Bergmann, the line between the IAEC and EMET blurred to the point that *Machon 4* functioned essentially as the chief laboratory for the IAEC. By 1953, *Machon 4* had not only perfected a process for extracting the uranium found in the Negev Desert, but had also developed a new method of producing heavy water, providing Israel with an indigenous capability to produce some of the most important nuclear materials.[664]

Cooperation between Israel and France increased in the early 1950s. Technical exchanges between the IAEC and the French Commissariat of Atomic Energy (CEA) began, in 1953, and a formal nuclear research agreement was signed between the two nations.[665] By 1955, France had become Israel's chief arms supplier. In addition to supplying planes, tanks, trucks, and munitions, France agreed to construct an 18 Megawatt reactor in Israel. On September 21, 1956, Israeli Director-General of the Defense Ministry Shimon Peres met with French Foreign Minister Maurice Bourges-Maunoury, who agreed to provide Israel with a nuclear reactor.[666] This was in exchange for Israeli participation in Operation *Musketeer,* the Anglo-French planned invasion of the Suez Canal Zone. While the Sinai-Suez War of 1956 resulted in Israel attaining its military goals, when Israel was threatened with Soviet rocket attack, it was abandoned politically by its allies, the United Kingdom and France. As a result, the Israelis confirmed that independent nuclear capability was needed to prevent reliance on potentially unreliable allies. On October 3, 1957, France agreed to build a larger 24 Megawatt reactor (although the cooling systems and waste facilities were designed to handle three times that power), and in protocols that were not committed to paper, France also agreed to build a chemical reprocessing plant. This complex was constructed in secret, and outside the IAEA inspection regime, by French and Israeli technicians at Dimona, in the Negev Desert. From this point on, French and Israeli scientists collaborated towards the development of their respective nuclear weapons programs. Construction of the Dimona facility was detected by the United States, via U-2 aerial reconnaissance flights in 1958.

Several nations knowingly or not, helped supply Israel with necessary components towards attaining its nuclear capabilities. These included, France, Argentina, the United Kingdom, Norway and the United States. In a report published on August 3, 2005, the BBC revealed evidence from the British National Archives that showed that the United Kingdom sold 20 tons of heavy water, essential to the operation of the Dimona reactor, to Israel for £1.5 million. Heavy water or deuterium oxide is used to allow nuclear reactors to run on natural uranium, which is widely available, rather than on enriched uranium fuel, which is scarce and tightly controlled. A byproduct of nuclear reactors is plutonium, which can be used to make nuclear bombs.

The entire transaction began in 1956, when the United Kingdom purchased 20 tons of heavy water from Norway. The British later decided it was surplus to their own needs. Then, they decided to sell the heavy water to Israel in 1958, but for political purposes, a cover story was needed. Furthermore, the British did not want the Americans to know of the sale.[667] Thus Noratom, a Norwegian company, was formed to purchase the heavy water and ship it to Israel for use in Israel's Dimona reactor. The sale was presented as a direct deal between Norway and Israel.[668] The heavy water came in two 10 ton shipments, the first in June 1959, and the second in June 1960. The export license was through Norway, yet the shipments were shipped directly from a British port on Israeli ships. British officials never asked for an Israeli guarantee that the heavy water be only intended for peaceful purposes.[669]

Norway insisted on the right to inspect the heavy water for thirty-two years, but did so only once, in April 1961, while it was still in storage barrels at Dimona.[670] Israel simply promised that the heavy water was for peaceful purposes. In addition, quantities much more than what would be required for the peaceful purpose reactors were imported. Norway either colluded or at the least was very slow to ask to inspect as IAEA rules required. Later, Norway and Israel concluded an agreement in April 1990, for Israel to return 10.5 of the 21 tons it had imported (one more ton was shipped to Israel in 1970).[671] In late 1991, Israel returned 10.5 tons of heavy water to Norway, exactly half the amount it purchased in 1959 and 1971. Israeli officials said that the remaining 10.5 tons had been lost through waste and evaporation over the years.[672] Recent calculations revealed that Israel used two tons and would retain eight tons more. It has been claimed that when the reactor started operation, the United States supplied four more tons of heavy water to Israel.[673] The United Kingdom also supplied Israel with a number of other vital materials during the 1950s and 1960s that sped up the process allowing Israel to develop nuclear weapons. Some of these materials included uranium-235, beryllium and lithium-6, which are used in making atom and even hydrogen bombs.[674]

France became the world's fourth acknowledged nuclear power on February 13, 1960, when it detonated a nuclear device at Reggan, Algeria. It is believed that collaboration between French and Israeli scientists was so extensive that the test represented the emergence of two nuclear powers.[675] Israel also supplied essential technology and hardware.[676] Israeli observers were granted "unrestricted access to French nuclear test explosion data."[677]

In mid-1960, the CIA told President Eisenhower that what was being constructed in the Negev Desert at Dimona was a large nuclear reactor with the potential for producing fissionable material in quantities sufficient to produce nuclear weapons—about 1-2 per year.[678] The information had been gathered by the CIA by both on the ground photos and U-2 aerial reconnaissance photos. President Eisenhower had known what the purpose of the Dimona reactor was from the beginning and wanted the Israelis to have the bomb for two reasons: to keep the Arabs at bay and to serve as a warning to the Soviet Union.[679]

Nevertheless, Israeli Prime Minister David Ben-Gurion attempted to camouflage its identity by calling it a "textile factory" and at other times, it was described as an "agricultural pumping station," and a "metallurgical research facility."[680] However, these ruses were exposed on December 2, 1960, when the US State Department issued a statement revealing Israel's secret nuclear installation.[681] This was followed by a December 8, 1960 CIA report outlining Dimona's implications for nuclear proliferation.[682] Precipitated by a *TIME* magazine article alleging that a "small power … neither of the communist nor the NATO bloc" was developing a nuclear weapons capability, the London *Daily Express* named Israel as the state, adding, "British and American intelligence authorities believe that the Israelis are well on their way to building their first nuclear bomb." Two days later AEC Chairman John McCone appeared on the television program *Meet the Press* to confirm that Israel was building a nuclear reactor and that the United States had inquired with the Israeli government about it. The following day's *New York Times* also ran a similar exposé on Israel's secret nuclear program.[683] With the information made public, on December 21, 1960 Ben-Gurion was forced to admit that the Dimona complex was a nuclear research center, with a 24 megawatt reactor.[684] He told the Israeli Knesset, that no bombs were being built and that the complex was "designed exclusively for peaceful purposes."[685] In 2005, a declassified US national intelligence assessment from 1961 indicated that Washington knew Israel was pursuing a nuclear weapons path. The document estimated Israel would be capable of producing a nuclear bomb by 1965–66 and had the capability to deliver the weapon to a range of 550 miles via a jet fighter-bomber.[686]

The Dimona facility became operational, on December 26, 1963.[687] Interestingly, a shipment of four metric tons of heavy water from the United States arrived in Israel just before the reactor went on line.[688] The security at Dimona (officially the Negev Nuclear Research Center) was particularly stringent. For straying into Dimona's airspace, the Israelis shot down one of their own Mirage III fighters during the Six-Day War in June 1967. On February 21, 1973, a Libyan airliner, en route Benghazi to Cairo, overshot the bulk of Egypt and apparently got lost over the Sinai Peninsula. The Israelis, fearing a kamikaze-style attack against Dimona, attempted to turn it back, but not receiving any response from the plane, shot it down with the loss of 104 of 113 aboard.

Uranium supplies were obtained from the former French colonies of Gabon, Niger, and the Central African Republic. However, by mid-1962, France had granted Algeria independence and began to mend its relationship with the Arab world, while at the same time began putting distance between itself and Israel. This cooling of the Franco-Israeli relationship also impacted on its former French African colonies (these supplies were cut off in 1967 by the French embargo against Israel). Israel began to look for other sources, particularly of yellowcake. On November 19, 1963, Israel concluded an agreement with Argentina for the purchase of 80 tons of yellowcake, which it is claimed represented Argentina's entire production of yellowcake for the next three years.[689] Additionally, Israel obtained yellowcake from South Africa and perhaps Portugal.[690]

By the mid-1960s, the CIA station in Tel Aviv determined that the Israeli nuclear weapons program was an established and irreversible fact. Under American pressure, United States inspectors visited Dimona seven times during the period 1962 to 1969, but they were unable to obtain an accurate picture of the activities carried out there, largely due to tight Israeli control over the timing and agenda of the visits.[691] The Israelis went so far as to install false control room panels and to brick over elevators and hallways that accessed certain areas of the facility. The inspectors were able to report that there was no clear scientific research or civilian nuclear power program justifying such a large reactor–circumstantial evidence of the Israeli bomb program, but found no evidence of "weapons related activities" such as the existence of a plutonium reprocessing plant.

Although the United States government did not encourage or approve of the Israeli nuclear program, it also did nothing to stop it. Walworth Barbour, US ambassador to Israel from 1961 to 1973—the bomb program's crucial years—primarily saw his job as being to insulate the President from facts, which might compel him to act on the nuclear issue, allegedly saying at one point that, "The President did not send me there to give him problems. He does not want to be told any bad news." After the 1967 war, Barbour even put a stop to military attachés' intelligence collection efforts around Dimona. Even when Barbour did authorize forwarding information, as he did in 1966 when embassy staff learned that Israel was beginning to put nuclear warheads on missiles, the message seemed to disappear into the bureaucracy and was never acted upon.

Mention should be made of what came to be called the "Apollo Affair." Between 1963 and 1965, it was claimed that 206 pounds of enriched uranium (enough for ten Hiroshima-type bombs) disappeared from the Nuclear Materials and Equipment Corporation (NUMEC), a small processing plant in Apollo, Pennsylvania. The US government accused Zalman Shapiro, president of NUMEC, of "losing" the highly enriched uranium. Investigations by the Central Intelligence Agency, Federal Bureau of Investigation, and the Atomic Energy Commission were inconclusive. Some alleged that the misplaced uranium eventually found its way to the Israeli nuclear program. In 1977, the US government discounted the allegations of an Israeli theft of the material.[692] The decommissioning of NUMEC in the early 1980s also cast doubt on such allegations when over 100 kilograms, i.e. 220 pounds, of unaccounted for uranium were discovered throughout the facility.[693]

Some Western intelligence experts believed that Israel conducted an underground nuclear test in the Negev Desert in 1963, and that preparation of nuclear material for assembly into atomic bombs began soon thereafter.[694] The Egyptian Air Force claimed to have first flown over Dimona and recognized the existence of a nuclear reactor in 1965.[695] Half of the fifty HAWK antiaircraft missiles provided to Israel by the United States were reportedly positioned around the Dimona complex.[696] According to some Western sources, Israel conducted some type of non-nuclear test, perhaps a zero yield or implosion test underground on November 2, 1966, at Al-Naqab in the Negev Desert.[697] By 1967, it is probable that Israel became the world's sixth nuclear power after the United States (1945), Soviet Union (1949), the United Kingdom (1952), France (1960), and China (1964). With a small population base and economy, Israel "took 10 years and $40 million"[698] to achieve nuclear weapons status.

As Egyptian President Gamal Abdel Nasser propelled the region towards war in mid-May 1967, Israel considered the Egyptian high-altitude overflights of May 16, 1967 as possible pre-strike reconnaissance of its nuclear facility at Dimona.[699] Egyptian maps and contingency plans for offensive operations, found at air bases in the Sinai (by Israel after the war), confirmed that aerial bombing of Dimona was a primary Egyptian objective. It was at this time that Israeli Defense Ministerial Committee member Yigal Allon amended his 1959 list of situations that would justify Israel in launching a preemptive war in anticipatory self-defense to include "an aerial attack on nuclear reactors and scientific institutions" in Israel.[700] The crisis escalated rapidly and by the last days of May, Israel stood alone facing the ever increasing (in numbers) armies from across the Arab world, massing at its frontiers. Thus, on the eve of the Six-Day War, May 26, 1967, Israeli Prime Minister Levi Eshkol ordered two nuclear devices armed in Israel's first nuclear alert.[701]

A word about the Nuclear Non-Proliferation Treaty (NPT). The NPT signed on July1, 1968, became effective on March 5, 1970. Three countries never signed the NPT, India, Pakistan, and Israel. As non-signatories, all three had the right to develop a nuclear program and all three did. The DPRK, which originally signed the NPT, continued a clandestine program to develop nuclear weapons. It withdrew from the NPT on January 10, 2003. Libya, which signed in 1968, nevertheless engaged in a clandestine nuclear weapons program until it announced its willingness to dismantle all WMDs on December 19, 2003. Iran, which also signed the NPT has ignored its provisions and proceeded rapidly to build nuclear weapons. Syria, yet another signatory of the NPT, attempted to construct a clandestine nuclear weapons reactor, until the facility was bombed by Israel on September 6, 2007.

Having lost its uranium supply from France, in late 1968 Israel executed Operation *Plumbat,* a clandestine action carried out by the Mossad to gain new supplies. On November 17, 1968, a Liberian-flagged German freighter, the *Scheersberg A,* owned by Mossad, carrying a cargo of 200 tons of uranium oxide—yellowcake—loaded in 560 drums mislabeled "plumbat" (a lead derivative) left Antwerp, Belgium bound for Genoa, Italy, after a stop in Rotterdam. The ship and its cargo never reached its planned destination. It is believed an Israeli crew brought in at the last moment, sailed to a rendezvous point between Cyprus and Turkey where the cargo was transferred to an Israeli ship in the dead of night.[702] On December 2, 1968, the *Scheersberg* docked at Iskenderun, Turkey, riding high in the water. Its uranium cargo had vanished. The uranium was covertly purchased in what was then West Germany by Israel. It is believed it ended up in Israel and was enough for the production of thirty atomic bombs.[703]

The *Scheersberg A* was used again on December 25, 1969, to refuel five missile boats in the Bay of Biscay, off the coast of France, after they had been spirited out of Cherbourg harbor, by Israeli agents.

The sinking of the INS *Eilat* on October 21, 1967, by Egyptian missile boats, galvanized the Israeli Navy into seeking out more and better naval craft, more suited to the modern conditions of missile combat. The loss of the INS *Eilat* was the first occasion in history of a warship sunk by missile fire (*see* the "1,000-Day War of Attrition–Arab Attacks" map). Israel had ordered and paid for twelve new *Saar* class missile boats from the shipyards of *Chantiers de Construction de Mécanique de Normandie* in Cherbourg. Seven boats were delivered before French President Charles de Gaulle ordered a total embargo of arms sales to Israel, which went into effect on December 28, 1968. The remaining five missile boats were spirited out of Cherbourg and met by the *Scheersberg A.*

In early 1968, the CIA reported that Israel had successfully produced four nuclear weapons. This assumption was based on conversations between Carl Duckett, head of the CIA's Office of Science and Technology, and Edward Teller, father of the hydrogen bomb. Teller said that, based on conversations with friends in the Israeli scientific and defense establishment, he concluded that Israel was capable of building a nuclear weapon. Teller also asserted that Israel would not publicly test a nuclear device.[704] Having worked closely with French nuclear scientists, Israelis probably were present at French nuclear tests, and were given access to French nuclear test data. Thus, the Israelis most likely did not have to test a device to know that it worked. In 1968, Israel also began construction of a plutonium separation plant.[705]

Furthermore, the CIA allegedly told President Lyndon Johnson that Israel had nuclear bombs, whereupon he instructed the agency not to tell anyone else, not even the Secretaries of State or Defense.[706] The CIA also had information regarding a specific type of bombing practice that Israel was conducting with its A-4 Skyhawk fighter-bombers, which would not have made any sense unless it was to deliver a nuclear payload.[707] Although denied at the time, on September 5, 1969 the United States delivered F-4E Phantom fighter-bombers to Israel, with nuclear capable delivery hardware intact.[708]

Israel's first research rocket, the Shavit-2 ("Comet) was launched July 5, 1961, some 75 miles into space for meteorological research.* Israel began its ballistic missile program in April 1963, when it signed a contract with Dassault Aviation of France to produce the MD-620 missile, named "Jericho-1" by the Israelis. By 1966, France successfully tested and produced such a missile with a 280-mile range. France ultimately delivered fourteen complete Jericho-1 missiles to Israel.[709] Franco-Israeli military arms sales ended in the aftermath of the Six-Day War. By December 1968, France suspended all arms deliveries to Israel. Israel then embarked on its own domestic missile production program, and by 1971 produced Jericho-1 missiles at the rate of three to six missiles per month.[710]

As early as 1966, the Israeli defense establishment began articulating the "red lines" whose crossings could trigger the use of nuclear weapons. Several specific scenarios could lead to nuclear use. Today, these concerns remain and are heightened. The question certainly should be asked, "Why exactly, does Israel need its nuclear weapon arsenal? The response would include all of the following:

- To deter a large conventional Arab military penetration into populated areas within Israel.
- To deter the exposure of Israeli cities to massive and devastating air attacks or all levels of unconventional (chemical, biological, and nuclear) attacks.
- To preempt enemy biological and nuclear attacks.
- To support conventional preemption against enemy biological and nuclear assets.

---

* The Shavit research rocket is distinct from the later Shavit space launch vehicle also produced by Israel to launch Ofek reconnaissance satellites into low earth orbit beginning in September 1988.

- To support conventional preemption against enemy non-nuclear (conventional, chemical, and biological) assets.
- To offset the destruction of the Israeli Air Force.
- For nuclear war interchange if nuclear weapons are used against Israeli territory.
- For the "Samson Option" (last resort destruction).[711]

Israel faces extreme vulnerability to a nuclear first strike and an accompanying vulnerability even to a false alarm.[712] For Israel, the short term nuclear threats that it faces include:

- Iran's acquisition of nuclear warfare capability will occur shortly. Current Iranian missile range is as far west as Portugal.
- Terrorist groups might be supplied with biological/nuclear warfare devices from any of several sources, directly or by theft—from Iran, Pakistan, Syria or the new regimes in Libya and elsewhere in the Arab/Muslim world.
- Syria, which already possesses chemical weapons and warheads,[713] seeks nuclear weapons capability and has already undertaken secret projects towards that goal. Despite the Israeli strike in 2007 as well as the flawed 2013 agreement to rid itself of chemical weapons, Syria may try again, just as Saddam Hussein did after the 1981 IAF strike at Osirak. Additionally, Syria, a close ally of Iran, has missile capability to strike all of Israel.
- Libya, under an al-Qaeda-influenced regime, needs continual verification that it will not restart its biological, chemical, and nuclear weapons programs.
- Saudi Arabia already has missile capability. It has a nuclear arrangement with Pakistan (as described earlier) and may seek additional nuclear weapons capability when Iran goes nuclear.
- Pakistan is already a nuclear weapons power. It has supplied weaponry and technology to several nations, including Libya, Syria, Saudi Arabia, Iraq and the DPRK. Additionally, the Pakistani government faces many internal, as well as external threats, and thus the security of its existing nuclear arsenal is always in question.

At a summit between President Nixon and Israeli Prime Minister Golda Meir, on September 25, 1969, a secret nuclear understanding was reached between the United States and the Jewish state. The understanding was that the United States passively accepted Israel's nuclear weapons status as long as Israel did not declare publicly its capability or test a weapon.[714] There is no formal record of the agreement or have Israeli or American governments ever publicly acknowledged it.

However, the Nixon library declassified a July 19, 1969, memo from national security adviser Henry Kissinger in November 2007 that came closest to articulating US policy on the issue. That memo said, "while we might ideally like to halt actual Israeli possession, what we really want at a minimum may be just to keep Israeli possession from becoming an established international fact."[715] It was at its core, a "don't ask, don't tell" policy. That "don't ask, don't tell" policy ended when (as mentioned above) in mid-February 2015, the Obama administration publicly disclosed a 1987 report revealing Israel's nuclear status.

It was reported in 1972, that two Israeli scientists, Isaiah Nebenzahl and Menachem Levin, developed a cheaper, faster uranium enrichment process. It used a laser beam for isotope separation. It reportedly could enrich seven grams of Uranium 235 to some 60 percent in one day. Sources later reported that Israel was using both centrifuges and lasers to enrich uranium.[716]

At 1:55 P.M. local time (five minutes ahead of schedule), on October 6, 1973, Egypt and Syria launched simultaneous massive surprise attacks—Operation *Badr* (1973)—against Israel, initiating the Yom Kippur War. One hundred thousand Egyptian troops, heavily armed with RPG and Sagger anti-tank missiles, supported by 1,550 tanks, and a sophisticated air defense system made up of Soviet-supplied SA-2, SA-3, and SA-6 missiles, easily surged across the Suez Canal, overwhelming the IDF—435 soldiers and 249 tanks stretched along the Bar Lev Line. The Syrians threw 28,000 troops and 1,500 tanks against the IDF's 1,000 men and eighty tanks on the Golan Heights (*see* the "Yom Kippur War, October 6–24, 1973—Arab Attack" map).

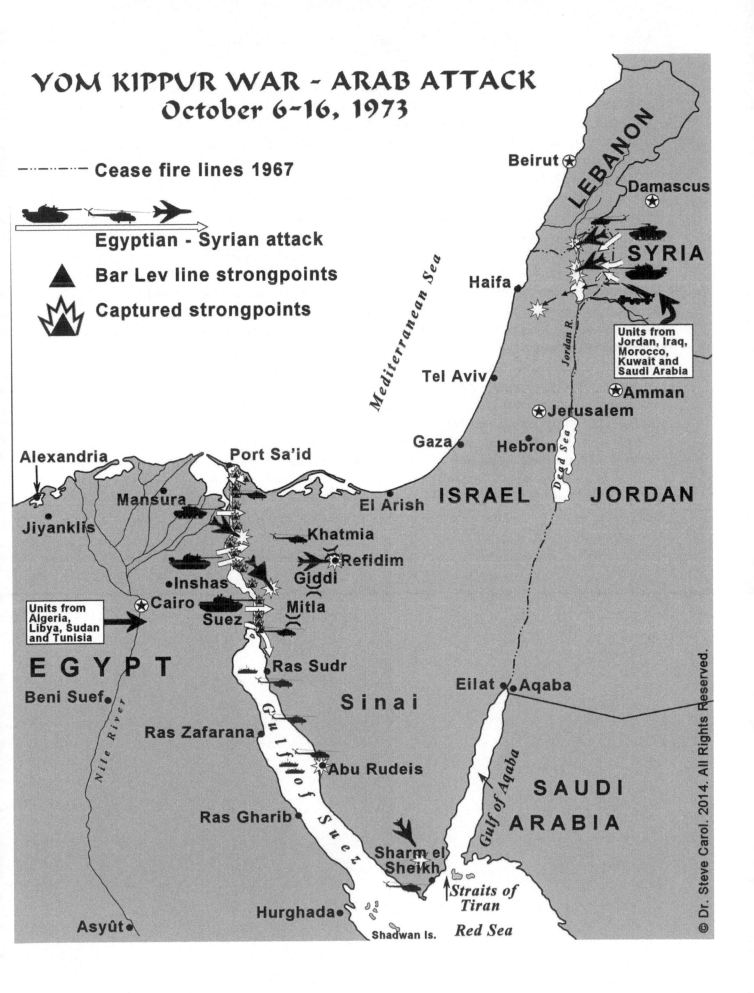

YOM KIPPUR WAR - ARAB ATTACK
October 6-16, 1973

Cease fire lines 1967

Egyptian - Syrian attack

▲ **Bar Lev line strongpoints**

Captured strongpoints

Mediterranean Sea

Beirut

Damascus

LEBANON

SYRIA

Haifa

Units from Jordan, Iraq, Morocco, Kuwait and Saudi Arabia

Tel Aviv

Amman

Jerusalem

Jordan R.

Gaza

Hebron

Dead Sea

ISRAEL

JORDAN

Alexandria

Port Sa'id

El Arish

Mansura

Jiyanklis

Khatmia

Refidim

Inshas

Giddi

Cairo

Mitla

Units from Algeria, Libya, Sudan and Tunisia

Suez

EGYPT

Ras Sudr

Sinai

Eilat Aqaba

Beni Suef

Nile River

Gulf of Suez

Ras Zafarana

Gulf of Aqaba

SAUDI

Abu Rudeis

Ras Gharib

ARABIA

Sharm el Sheikh

Hurghada

Straits of Tiran

Asyût

Shadwan Is.

Red Sea

© Dr. Steve Carol. 2014. All Rights Reserved.

Israel hastily mobilized and sent reinforcements to both fronts. By early afternoon on October 7, no effective Israeli forces were in the southern Golan Heights and Syrian forces had reached the edge of the plateau overlooking the Jordan River. By the end of the second day of the war, the Israelis had suffered 2,000 killed, 340 captured, 49 aircraft lost and some 500 tanks destroyed. In comparison, Israel suffered 850 fatalities in the entire Six-Day War in 1967.

On October 8, Israeli Defense Minister Moshe Dayan warned Israeli Prime Minister Golda Meir "this is the end of the Third Temple."[717] "Temple" was also the code word for nuclear weapons. Meir and her "kitchen cabinet" made the decision that night October 8, 1973, to issue Israel's second nuclear alert. The Israelis assembled thirteen 20-kiloton atomic bombs.[718] According to several sources, "Never Again!" was reportedly welded on the first Israeli nuclear bomb.[719] Although most probably plutonium devices, one source reports they were enriched uranium bombs. The Jericho-1 missiles at Hirbat Zachariah and the nuclear strike F-4 Phantoms at Tel Nof were armed and prepared for action against Syrian and Egyptian targets. US Secretary of State Henry Kissinger was notified of these developments hours later on October 9. As IDF reserves reached the battlefields on October 8 and 9, the military situation stabilized. The IDF counterattacked on the Golan Heights on October 11 and westward across the Suez Canal into Africa, from October 15 to 16—Operation *Abirey-Halev* (Stouthearted Men). Rapidly, the IDF encircled the Egyptian Third Army and it was faced with annihilation on the east bank of the Suez Canal, with no protective Egyptian forces remaining between the IDF and Cairo. On the Golan Heights, the IDF recaptured the entire Golan and punched eastward towards Damascus, the Syrian capital, gaining a salient of new territory from the Syrians. The tide of battle on both fronts thus turned in Israel's favor and the need for nuclear weapons receded. The number of nuclear weapons, and in fact the entire story was later leaked by the Israelis as a great psychological warfare tool (*see* the "Yom Kippur War, October 6–24, 1973—Israeli Counterattack" map).

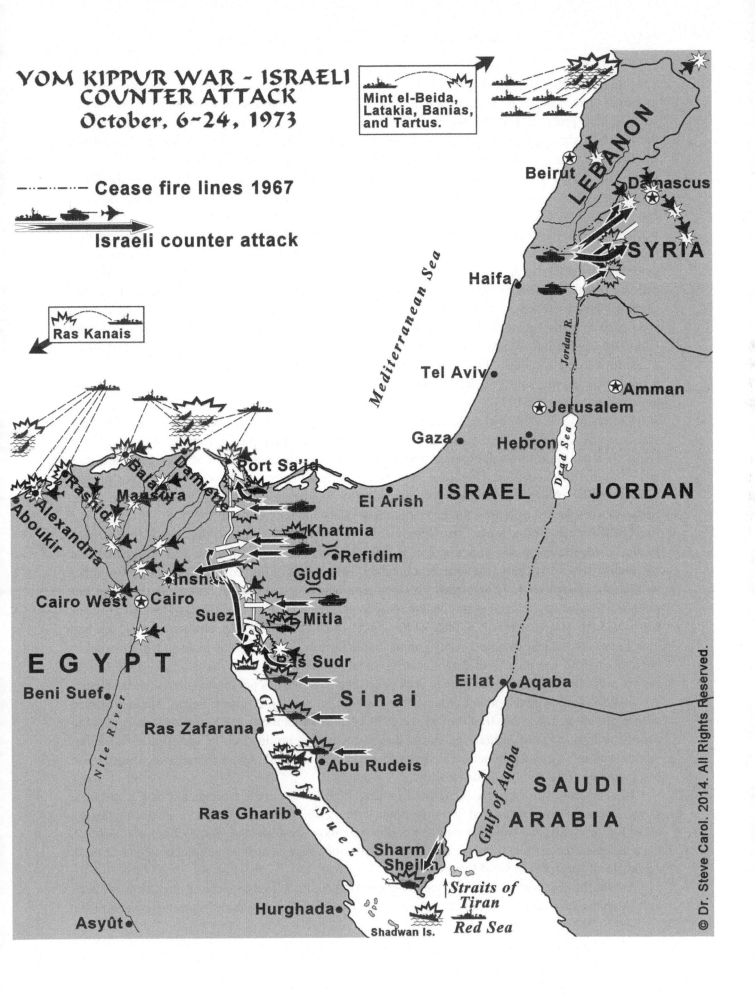

YOM KIPPUR WAR - ISRAELI COUNTER ATTACK
October, 6-24, 1973

Mint el-Beida, Latakia, Banias, and Tartus.

-----·----- Cease fire lines 1967

Israeli counter attack

Ras Kanais

Mediterranean Sea

LEBANON
Beirut
Damascus
SYRIA
Haifa

Tel Aviv
Jordan R.
Amman
Jerusalem
Gaza
Hebron
Dead Sea
ISRAEL   JORDAN

Port Sa'id
El Arish
Balaa
Damietta
Rashid
Mansura
Khatmia
Refidim
Alexandria
Aboukir
Giddi
Insha
Cairo West   Cairo
Suez
Mitla
EGYPT
Ras Sudr
Beni Suef
S i n a i
Eilat Aqaba
Ras Zafarana
Abu Rudeis
SAUDI
Ras Gharib
Gulf of Suez
Gulf of Aqaba
ARABIA
Nile River

Sharm el Sheikh
Straits of Tiran
Hurghada
Red Sea
Asyût
Shadwan Is.

Since the 1960s, it had long been US policy to supply Israel with conventional weaponry, so that in a crisis Israel would be strong enough to defend itself without having to escalate to the nuclear stage.[720] This probably was one key factor in President Nixon's order to resupply rapidly the IDF in the October war, especially after heavy initial Israeli losses. However, using a Soviet *Cosmos* spy satellite, the Soviet Union learned of Israel's nuclear alert. Therefore, on October 13, 1973, the Soviet Union dispatched nuclear warheads from Nikolayev, one of its naval bases at Odessa on the Black Sea, bound for Alexandria, Egypt. They were to be fitted on Russian Scud missiles already based in Egypt. Those missiles were delivered the previous August. The United States detected these Soviet warheads as they passed through the Straits on October 15. The Soviet ship arrived in Alexandria on October 18, 1973, with its nuclear warhead cargo. Their presence was to counterbalance and deter Israeli nuclear weapons. On October 25, 1973, *Aviation Week and Space Technology* magazine claimed that the two Soviet Scud brigades deployed in Egypt each had a nuclear warhead. American satellite photos seemed to confirm this. The United States passed to Israel images of trucks of the type used to transport nuclear warheads, parked near the launchers. The previous day, the Soviet Union threatened intervention in the war. President Nixon's response was to bring the United States to worldwide nuclear alert—DEFCON 3—whereupon Israel went to nuclear alert a third time. Some sources claimed the Soviet nuclear warheads were not unloaded and remained aboard until the ship departed in November 1973.[721]

Shortly after the 1973 Yom Kippur war, Israel allegedly fielded considerable nuclear artillery consisting of American 175 mm and 203 mm self-propelled artillery pieces, capable of firing nuclear shells. If true, these low-yield tactical nuclear artillery rounds could reach at least 25 miles, thus targeting the Syrian capital, Damascus. The Israel Defense Forces did have three battalions of the 175mm artillery (thirty-six tubes), reportedly with 108 nuclear shells and more for the 203mm tubes. Some sources described a program to extend the artillery range to 45 miles.

The CIA released a report on September 4, 1974, which concluded that Israel had already produced atomic weapons with uranium it obtained "by clandestine means."[722] It estimated that between fifteen and twenty Israeli nuclear bombs existed.[723] Unconfirmed reports pushed the number to 150. On December 1, 1974, Israeli President Ephraim Katzir declared, "It has always been our intention to develop a nuclear potential. We now have that potential."[724] In 1976, Deputy CIA Director Carl Duckett, at an unclassified state of the world intelligence briefing, declared that Israel had "ten to twenty nuclear weapons ready and available for use."[725] During his historic trip to Israel in November 1977, Egyptian President Anwar el-Sadat confided to the Israelis that one of the factors for his precedent-shattering decision to seek peace had been Israel's possession of a nuclear arsenal.

In 1977, formal development of Israel's medium-range Jericho-2 missile began.[726] Israel worked with other nations, notably Iran (before the 1979 Islamic Revolution) and South Africa, in part "to offset the high costs of military research, development, and production."[727] Israel provided South Africa with missile and production facilities designs, and that South Africa in exchange staged three test launches of the Jericho-2 for Israel.[728]

The Jericho-2 was improved since its first test firing in May 1987, when it had only a 500-mile range.[729] It now has an estimated 900-mile range with a 2,200 pound payload, a range encompassing all of Egypt, Syria, and Iraq, but only the border regions of western Iran. Some observers however, have assessed the missile to possess a 2,200–2,450-mile range, which would reach the entire Arab world, all of Iran, plus most of Europe.[730]

As was the case with missile development, Israel and South Africa cooperated on nuclear research and weapons development in the 1970s and 1980s. Both nations were under assault by much of the international community. Confirmation of this cooperation appeared years later in the Israeli daily *Ha'aretz*, which reported that former South African Deputy Foreign Minister Aziz Pahad, confirmed such joint efforts. The article also quoted South African General Constand Viljoen, "We wanted to get nuclear knowledge from whoever we could, also from Israel."[731]

On September 22, 1979, the bhangmeter (a device for detecting the yield of an atomic explosion in the atmosphere) on an American VELA 6911 satellite, detected a brief intense double flash of light[732] over the south Indian Ocean, about half-way between South Africa and Antarctica. It was believed to be a South African-Israeli joint nuclear test. It was according to some, the third test of a neutron bomb. The first two were hidden in clouds to fool the satellite and the third was an accidental detection by the satellite as the weather had cleared. The explosion was almost certainly an Israeli bomb, tested at the invitation of the South Africans. It was more advanced than the "gun type" bombs developed by the South Africans.[733] On February 22, 1980, Israeli Defense Minister Ezer Weizman denied the report of such a joint Israeli-South African nuclear test.[734] Yet, two 1997 articles in the Israeli newspaper, *Ha'aretz* claimed there was such a test. In the first article, South African Deputy Foreign Minister Aziz Pahad, corroborated for the first time that the September 22, 1979 event was from a nuclear test. This statement was confirmed by the American Embassy in Pretoria, South Africa, as an accurate account of what Pahad officially acknowledged. The article said that Israel helped South Africa develop its bomb designs in return for 550 tons of raw uranium and other assistance.[735] The second article also quoted Pahad, as verifying it was an Israeli test with South African logistical support.[736]

In the aftermath of the Israeli air strike at the Iraqi nuclear reactor at Osirak, on June 24, 1981, former Israeli Defense Minister and then Foreign Minister Moshe Dayan stated at a news conference that Israel had the capacity to produce nuclear weapons:

> We don't have any atomic bombs now. But, we have the capacity; we can do that in a short time. We are not going to be the first ones to introduce nuclear weapons into the Middle East, but we do have the capacity to produce nuclear weapons.[737]

In the early 1980s, Israel began development of the Popeye cruise missile designed for precision strikes against high-value ground targets such as airfields, bridges, and bunkers.[738] Production began in 1989. The Popeye-2 was designed with reduced weight and size and thus deployable on IAF F-16s.

A story in the London *Sunday Mirror,* September 28, 1986, revealed that Israel was the sixth largest nuclear power. Detailed coverage was provided by the London *Sunday Times* on October 5, 1986, which based its story on the information gathered from Mordechai Vanunu, an Israeli technician who had worked at Israel's nuclear facility at Dimona for nearly ten years.[739] Vanunu, who lost his job in November 1985, secretly took photographs of the Dimona facility, immigrated to Australia and published some of his material in the *Sunday Times.* He was subsequently kidnapped by Israeli agents, tried and imprisoned. Vanunu, a Jewish convert to Christianity, was sentenced to eighteen years in prison.[740] On April 21, 2004, Vanunu was released. He was forbidden from leaving Israel. He has since been indicted on charges of violating the terms of his release.

Vanunu's information revealed a sophisticated nuclear program consisting of over 200 bombs, with boosted devices, neutron bombs, F-16-deliverable warheads, and Jericho warheads.[741] The boosted weapons shown in the Vanunu photographs depicted a sophistication that inferred the requirement for testing. He revealed for the first time, the underground plutonium separation facility where Israel was producing forty kilograms annually—several times more than previously estimated. Photographs also showed sophisticated designs, which scientific experts said, enabled the Israelis to build bombs with as little as four kilograms of plutonium. These facts have increased the estimates of total Israeli nuclear stockpiles to between 100 and 200 nuclear devices.[742] In the words of one American, "[the Israelis] can do anything we or the Soviets can do." Vanunu not only made the technical details of the Israeli program and stockpile public, but in his wake, Israel began veiled official acknowledgment of the potent Israeli nuclear deterrent. They began bringing the bomb up the basement stairs if not out of the basement. Nevertheless, the Israeli policy of deliberate ambiguity continued.[743]

Israel launched its own satellite reconnaissance system from Palmachim Airbase on its Mediterranean coast on September 19, 1988,.[744] This was done in part to decrease reliance on US sources. On that day, the Ofek-1 ("Horizon") spy satellite was launched on the Shavit booster, a system closely related to the Jericho-2 missile.[745] In 1995, one US official stated, "the Jericho-2 is a Shavit minus the upper stage, which is replaced by a warhead."[746] In 2001, a spokesman for the IDF admitted that the "Shavit is Jericho."[747] The Israelis launched Ofek-1 to the west away from the Arabs and against the earth's rotation, requiring even more thrust, thus it was a test of the missile booster as well. Ofek-2 was launched on April 3, 1990. After a failed launch of Ofek-3 on September 15, 1994, the satellite was successfully put into orbit on April 5, 1995. Its orbital path which takes ninety minutes to complete, put Ofek-3 in a position to transmit in real time, photographs and data on Syria, Iraq, Iran and other Arab/Muslim nations. Its orbit ranged from 185 to 435 miles above the earth. Ofek-4, launched January 22, 1998, did not achieve earth orbit due to a launcher failure and was lost. On May 28, 2002, Ofek-5 was launched. Some observers believed that the 660-pound weight of the satellite, combined with the additional propulsive requirements of the retrograde orbit, constituted a *de facto* demonstration of the Shavit's ICBM potential. Ofek-6, launched September 6, 2004 also failed. Ofek-7 was successfully launched on June 11, 2007. On January 21, 2008, Israel launched an advanced spy satellite–TecSAR, also known as Ofek-8. The satellite fabricated by Israel Aerospace Industries was equipped with a SAR (Synthetic Aperture Radar) payload that gives it the ability to see through clouds and carry out day and night all weather imaging and reconnaissance.[748] The TecSAR (Ofek 8) was propelled into orbit by an Indian Polar Satellite Launch Vehicle rocket from the Satish Dhawan Space Centre at Sriharikota in southeastern India[749] into a sun synchronous orbit. This was necessary since Israel was not able to launch the satellite from its own territory because of geopolitical and gravitational considerations. Ofek-9 was launched on June 22, 2010, using an improved version of its Shavit launcher. Ofek-9's resolution is "much better than" a half-meter (20 inches).[750] The satellite was also able to detect objects carrying people anywhere in the Middle East.[751] On April 9, 2014, Israel launched its improved Ofek-10 spy satellite. Ofek-10's improved surveillance capabilities include high-resolution cameras able to distinguish between objects of half a meter and operate in varying lighting and weather conditions. By the next morning, it was circling in earth orbit every 99 minutes from an altitude of 375 miles.

More than twenty years after Israel became a nuclear power, it may be assumed that Israel sought thermonuclear capability as well. Confirmation of this fact was made by a May 1989 statement by William H. Webster, Director of the CIA, who indicated that Israel might be seeking to construct a thermonuclear weapon.[752] Further claims were made by Mordechai Vanunu, that "in 1986 the Israelis began producing … the hydrogen bomb."[753]

Israel went on full-scale nuclear alert again on the first day of Operation *Desert Storm,* January 18, 1991, when eight Iraqi Scud missiles were fired against the cities of Tel Aviv and Haifa by Iraq (only two actually struck Tel Aviv and one hit Haifa). This alert lasted for the duration of the war, forty-three days. The Iraqi Scud strikes on Israel confirmed the capability of Arab and Muslim states (e.g. Iran and Pakistan) which did not have a border with Israel, to attack Israel with ballistic missiles. This reinforced Israel's need for a robust first strike nuclear capability.[754]

Over the course of the war, Iraq launched thirty-nine missiles in seventeen separate attacks at Israel starting January 18, 1991. This was confirmed later by Iraqi General Abderrazzak Al-Ayubi, who told the Iraqi newspaper *Al-Jumhuriyah* "ten Iraqi missiles were fired at hostile targets in Haifa, twenty-eight on other targets in Tel Aviv, and five at Dimona."[755] Luckily, fatalities were low: two killed directly, eleven indirectly (from heart attacks and strokes), with heavy property damage and life disrupted for some 4,000 people. Several landed in the Negev Desert, including near Dimona, one of them a close miss.[756] The Israeli government threatened retaliation if the Iraqis used chemical or gas warheads against Israel. This was interpreted to mean that Israel would launch a nuclear strike if chemical or gas attacks occurred. One Israeli commentator recommended that Israel should signal Iraq "any Iraqi action against Israeli civilian populations, with or without gas, may leave Iraq without Baghdad."[757] Shortly before the end of the war the Israelis tested a "nuclear capable" missile which prompted the United States into intensifying its Scud hunting in western Iraq to prevent any Israeli response.[758] For its part, the IAF set up dummy Scud sites in the Negev Desert for pilots to practice on—"they found it no easy task."[759] Mobile Scud units in the field proved difficult to detect and destroy. The US promised Israel it would eliminate the Scuds. What became known as "the Great Scud Hunt" had questionable operational effectiveness. As the United States Gulf War Air Power Survey noted, the Iraqis fooled allied reconnaissance with decoys and thus the US was unable to confirm even a single kill, though some 100 mobile launchers were reported struck by coalition aircraft.[760] The US government made additional commitments to Israel for not attacking Iraq. Aside from the deployment in Israel of Patriot missile batteries, they included:

- Allowing Israel to designate 100 targets inside Iraq for the coalition to destroy;
- Satellite downlink to increase warning time on the Scud attacks (present and future);
- Technical parity with Saudi jet fighters in perpetuity.[761]

In reaction to the Arab targeting of Dimona, as well as attempts to hit the facility during the 1967, 1973, and 1991 wars, Israel shut down the Dimona facility during those conflicts. This was confirmed by the testimony of former Israeli cabinet minister and physics professor Yuval Neeman in January 2002, speaking to a symposium at Tel Aviv University that reactor shut down was "one of the first things done in war time."[762]

In November 1994, *Jane's Intelligence Review* estimated that Israel had seven nuclear facilities and as many as 200 nuclear weapons in a detailed review based on satellite images of Israel. The report also indicated that Nachal Soreq was the installation where Israel conducted research on nuclear weapons design, and claimed that nuclear weapons were assembled at a facility in Yodefat.[763] Seeming confirmation of Israel's nuclear status came from then Prime Minister Shimon Peres, who on December 22, 1995 while speaking to a group of Israeli newspaper and magazine editors, said publicly "give me peace, and we'll give up the atom. That's the whole story."[764] As early as February 1997, it was estimated that Israel had 400 thermonuclear and nuclear weapons of all types including neutron bombs, nuclear mines, suitcase bombs, and submarine-borne types.[765] Other sources put the estimate at between 78 and 130 nuclear weapons.[766] There may have been an underground test near Eilat, Israel, on May 28, 1998. Two members of the Knesset claimed that the alleged test might have triggered an earthquake in the region. The allegations were denied by Israeli Deputy Defense

Minister Silvan Shalom who told the Knesset that rumors of Israel having tested a nuclear device were "absolutely without foundation."[767]

In response to growing threats from Iraq, Iran, and other Muslim states, Israel developed a triad delivery system of IAF aircraft, land-based missiles and submarine-launched missiles for its nuclear arsenal. Thus, with nuclear-capable medium-range and intermediate-range ballistic missiles (MRBM and IRBM), short-range subsonic cruise missiles with advanced capabilities, and significant defensive missile capabilities,[768] Israel acquired a second-strike capability. In June 2000, Israel successfully tested a submarine-launched cruise missile near Sri Lanka, capable of carrying a nuclear warhead. The missile successfully hit its target over 900 miles away.[769] Some speculate that Israel tested an upgraded Popeye Turbo, a missile capable of carrying a nuclear warhead.[770] The National Air and Space Intelligence Center declared the Popeye Turbo operational in 2002.[771] However, as of 2012, Jane's does not list the Popeye Turbo in Israel's missile inventory.[772]

Additionally, Israel purchased six *Dolphin*-class, U-212 diesel submarines from the German firm of Thyssen-Nordseewerke. The submarines are able to launch nuclear-capable cruise missiles, an essential component of Israel's second-strike capacity.[773] The submarines have a range of 2,800 miles.[774] In October 2003, Bush administration officials as well as one Israeli official confirmed that Israel modified American-supplied *Harpoon* cruise missiles to carry nuclear warheads. This report confirmed Israel's triad ability to launch a nuclear strike from land, air, or sea, as well as its second-strike capability.[775] It was announced in early summer of 2010 that Israel intended to deploy three of the submarines—INS *Dolphin,* INS *Leviathan* and INS *Tekuma*—in the Persian Gulf near the Iranian coastline. The fourth submarine, INS *Tannin,* began operations in mid-2015. The fifth submarine— INS *Rahav*—is scheduled to arrive from Germany in mid-2015, followed by a sixth submarine, to be delivered by 2017, and Israel has even been reported to be interested in ordering three more.[776] Back in February 2013, then-Israeli Defense Minister Ehud Barak signed an agreement with Germany for the construction and delivery of a sixth Dolphin-class submarine. A name has yet to be chosen for this submarine and it is not expected to arrive in Israel until around 2019. Israel planned to have a permanent presence in the Gulf with at least one submarine on station at all times.[777]

Israeli Prime Minister Ehud Olmert in an interview on German SAT1 television, on December 11, 2006, intentionally or inadvertently, confirmed the long held belief that Israel was a nuclear power, violating Israel's longstanding policy of nuclear ambiguity. Olmert said, "Israel is a democracy, Israel doesn't threaten any country … The most that we tried to get for ourselves is to try to live without terror, but we never threaten another nation with annihilation. Iran openly, explicitly and publicly threatens to wipe Israel off the map. Can you say that this is the same level, when they [Iran] are aspiring to have nuclear weapons, as America, France, Israel, and Russia?"[778] This apparent slip of the tongue was interpreted as an admission that Israel possessed nuclear weaponry, and aroused a storm of protest within the Israeli government over the loss of Israel's traditional policy of nuclear ambiguity.[779] However, as has been outlined, this was the fourth high-ranked Israeli official over a period of several decades that has alluded to Israel being a nuclear power.

At the end of December 2006, Israel signed the United Nations Convention for the Suppression of Acts of Nuclear Terrorism. The convention dealt with the unlawful possession of nuclear devices by non-state actors, called for states to investigate alleged offenses, and to arrest, prosecute or extradite offenders. The convention also placed emphasis on international cooperation with nuclear terrorism investigations and prosecutions through information sharing and extradition of detainees.[780]

In the autumn of 2013, US experts estimated the size of Israel's nuclear arsenal at 80 nuclear warheads. Their assessment was included in the September/October issue of the *Bulletin of the Atomic Scientists*. These specialists said Israel stopped production on nuclear weapons in 2004, but kept enough fissile material to create up to 190 warheads. These experts estimated that in 1999, Israel had 70 warheads, a number lower than previous guesses at the size of Israel's nuclear arsenal. A 2009 report from the Center for Strategic and International Studies put Israel's nuclear arsenal at anywhere from 70 to 400 warheads. In April 2013, an Arms Control Association report estimated the size of Israel's alleged nuclear arsenal at 75 to 200 warheads.[781]

Israel continued to develop missile delivery systems and in January 2008, Israel test launched the Jericho-3 missile.[782] The Jericho-3 has an estimated maximum range between 3,000 and 4,000 miles and a 2,200 to 2,860 pound payload. Thus, the Jericho-3 provides Israel with an intermediate-range nuclear strike capability.[783] On November 2, 2011, Israel announced the successful test launch from its Palmachim base of a new, intercontinental ballistic missile capable of carrying a 1,650-pound nuclear warhead to a distance of 4,350 miles—further, over 6,210 miles (10,000 kilometers)[784] if fitted with a smaller warhead. Foreign sources identified the ICBM as an upgraded Jericho-3 missile. Western intelligence experts estimate that forty-two missiles with conventional warheads are enough to disable seriously Iran's main nuclear facilities in Natanz, Isfahan and Arak. In the third week of September 2011, the United States supplied Israel with GBU-28 bunker buster bombs. At the same time, Israel's government was debating whether to go public and reveal Israel's nuclear capabilities, abandoning its long-held policy of nuclear ambiguity.[785]

One of the world's foremost experts on nuclear weapons and warfare, Professor Louis René Beres, made important recommendations for Israel as soon as it is officially confirmed that Iran has crossed the nuclear threshold. Israel should immediately announce what much of the world knows, that it is a nuclear power and has been since the 1960s. Professor Beres declared, "When this critical moment arrives, Israel should already have configured (1) its optimal allocation of nuclear assets; and (2) the extent to which this particular configuration should now be disclosed. This would importantly enhance the credibility of its indispensable nuclear deterrence posture."[786]

Israel may well be compelled to adopt a "launch-on-warning" posture for both its conventional and nuclear forces. Thus in any future crisis, at the first hint from satellite intelligence or some other means that a missile fusillade was being prepared from, Iran or an Arab state, Israel to protect its populace, would have to strike first. And it would have to strike not only at missile sites, some of which it might well miss, but at a broader range of targets—communications facilities, air bases, storage bunkers, and all other critical nodes—so as to paralyze the enemy and thus rule out the possibility of attack. These are the implications of launch-on-warning.

If as is widely assumed, Israel has been a nuclear power since before 1967, it has been a most responsible one. Like the United States, the United Kingdom, France, India, and even China, it has reserved the use of nuclear weapons, as weapons of self-defense and last resort to guarantee Israel's survival. Thus far, Israel's alleged possession of nuclear weapons has not led to a regional nuclear arms race. Israel has not threatened any nation with atomic attack, nor has it vowed to wipe any country off the map. Unlike Russia, which may have "lost" some nuclear devices during the collapse of the Soviet Union, Israel is in complete control of its arsenal. In contrast to the DPRK, Pakistan and Iran, Israel does not support terrorist organizations nor is a nuclear proliferator. With the possibility of an unexpected change in the Pakistani government, what would become of its nuclear arsenal if the

Taliban gained power in that country? Israel stands in comparison as a stable democratic government and a rational nuclear power that needs nuclear weapons for survival. Nevertheless, there may come a time when Israel must make it clear to the world that it would be willing to employ its nuclear weapons in certain very precise and readily identifiable situations.

Israel should demonstrate a willingness to take strategic risks, including even existential risks, with its nuclear arsenal, as an additional factor for deterring its enemies. In an earlier period, Israeli Minister of Defense Moshe Dayan had understood and openly embraced this particular form of logic, "Israel must be like a mad dog, too dangerous to bother."[787] It can sometimes be rational to pretend irrationality. However, it must be emphasized, the deterrence benefits of any Israeli modifications of deliberate ambiguity would be altogether limited to rational adversaries. If after all, enemy decision-makers might sometime value certain national, ideological or religious preferences more highly than their own country's physical survival, they would not be deterred by any enhanced forms of Israeli nuclear deterrence.

Until there is real peace in the Middle East, (not "peace" agreements that are likely to be broken or not implemented) and until there is a foolproof international inspection regime to guarantee that countries are not cheating and hiding nuclear capabilities, Israel must keep a nuclear option. Israel will be unwilling to compromise its nuclear capability in international negotiations. Given the religiously motivated extremism emanating from the Islamic world and prevalent globally, there is no guarantee that Israel's nuclear arsenal can be a deterrent, but thus far, it has served the Jewish state well. For the future, Professor René Beres astutely observes *Si vis pacem, para bellum atomicum* ("If you want peace, prepare for atomic war.") However reluctantly, this must be Israel's overriding strategic mantra in the years ahead.[788]

PERPETUAL NEGOTIATIONS

No peace with Israel, no recognition of Israel, no negotiations with it.
Fourth Arab Summit Conference, Khartoum, Sudan, August 29–September 1, 1967

The Middle East is … a powder keg, very explosive. It needs to be defused.
Richard Nixon

To be or not to be is not a question of compromise. Either you be or you don't be.
Golda Meir, December 12, 1974

Our neighbors want to see us dead. This is not a question
that leaves much room for compromise.
Golda Meir, December 9, 1978

No to Israel as a Jewish state, no to interim borders, no to land swaps.
PLO and PA head Mahmoud Abbas, Fifth Fatah Revolutionary Council Convention,
December 11–12, 2010

Recall that historically, it was in the Middle East, in ancient Persia (now Iran) that the strategic game of chess was modernized from its early Indian precursors. Bluff, deception and diversion are long-standing negotiating techniques. It was also from this region that the term "Byzantine politics" originated. The term usually refers to something that is complicated, intricate and full of deception. Furthermore, it should be understood that in diplomacy some words are for public consumption only. In reality, often those words may be taken to mean the opposite of what they say. While many people use language to communicate their intentions, diplomats use it to conceal theirs.

Arab negotiations with Israel mean acceding to the conditions for accepting Arab demands. There are no compromises in the Western sense of the term. Rather the concept is, what is mine is mine and what is yours is negotiable. Any "compromise" has to come from the Israeli side. For example Israel, which emerged militarily victorious from the Yom Kippur War of 1973, had to "compromise" by agreeing to withdraw from the Sinai Peninsula in stages from 1974 to 1982. Moreover, it must also be understood that in the West, peace treaties are made between countries and continue no matter what government is in power. In contrast, in the Middle East the "peace" agreements that have been made are between Israel and an Arab regime (Egypt, 1979; Lebanon, 1983; the PLO, 1993; and Jordan, 1994). If the regime falls (e.g. due to coup, or assassination), the "peace" agreement is in danger of becoming a hollow shell and not worth the paper on which it is written. Furthermore, there are different meanings given to key negotiating terms such as "self-determination," "terrorism," "peace," "justice," and "recognition."

60. Israeli control of recovered territory is legal, and pales by comparison to occupation of territories by other nations.

In order to give proper perspective to the issue of "occupation" in the historic context of the greater Middle East it is important to stress that much of the Arab/Muslim world was taken by conquest, force, jihad and the sword from the indigenous peoples starting in the seventh century. These areas therefore, remain occupied by Muslim regimes. Those indigenous areas included Imazighen (Berber) North Africa, Coptic Egypt, Assyrian (Chaldean) Syria and Iraq, Zoroastrian Persia, and the Byzantine Empire to name but a few of the most prominent examples.

As has been previously mentioned, during Israel's War of Independence Egypt occupied (unlawfully, according to international law) the Gaza Strip, and Transjordan occupied (likewise unlawfully) Judea and Samaria.[1] Leading international law scholars opined that Israel since 1967 was in lawful control of Judea, Samaria, as well as the Gaza Strip. No other state could show better title than Israel to these territories, and that these territories were not "occupied" in the sense of the Geneva Convention, since those rules are designed to assure the reversion of the former legitimate sovereign, which in this case, does not exist.[2] Transjordan was not the legal sovereign of Judea and Samaria and likewise, Egypt was not the legal sovereign of the Gaza Strip.

Judge Stephen M. Schwebel, the former President of the International Court of Justice (ICJ) in The Hague, stated after the Six-Day War ended:

> (a) a state [Israel] acting in lawful exercise of its right of self-defense may seize and occupy foreign territory as long as such seizure and occupation are necessary to its self-defense;

> (b) as a condition of its withdrawal from such territory, that State may require the institution of security measures reasonably designed to ensure that that territory shall not again be used to mount a threat or use of force against it of such a nature as to justify exercise of self-defense;

> (c) Where the prior holder of territory had seized that territory unlawfully, the state, which subsequently takes that territory in the lawful exercise of self-defense has, against that prior holder, better title.

> As between Israel, acting defensively in 1948 and 1967 on the one hand, and her Arab neighbors, acting aggressively in 1948 and 1967 on the other, Israel has the better title in the territory of what was known as Palestine, including the whole of Jerusalem, than do Jordan and Egypt.[3]

Eugene V. Rostow, Professor of Law and Public Affairs, Yale University, (who in 1967 had been US Under-Secretary of State for Political Affairs) reiterated this view in 1991. "Israel has a stronger claim to [Judea and Samaria] the West Bank than any other nation or would-be nation because, under the League of Nations Mandate, Israel has the same legal right to settle the West Bank, Gaza Strip and East Jerusalem that it has to settle Haifa or West Jerusalem."[4]

Although Israel unilaterally and totally withdrew from the Gaza Strip in 2005, the UN continued to refer to the Gaza Strip as "occupied" territory. A recent example was a September 22, 2011, report put out by the Office of the UN Secretary-General, which spoke of a UN mission's visit to the "Occupied Palestinian Territory, specifically the Gaza Strip."[5] The UN's insistence on designating Gaza as "occupied" is unfounded and proved yet again, that the UN is a morally bankrupt and politically biased as well as hostile organization. In an article in the American University International Law Review, legal scholar Elizabeth Samson[6] explained that under the Geneva Conventions and international judicial precedents, the Gaza Strip can no longer be considered occupied as Israel no longer exercises "effective control." The Israeli Supreme Court also ruled on January 30, 2008, that Israel had disengaged from the Gaza Strip and had "no effective control over what occurred there."

A review of the historic record of some modern occupations is in order.

SOME MODERN OCCUPATIONS			
Area	**Square Miles**	**Occupying Country**	**Status From/To**
Estonia	17,462	Soviet Union	1940–91
Latvia	24,938	Soviet Union	1940–91
Lithuania	25,174	Soviet Union	1940–91
Gaza Strip	139	Egypt	1948–67
Judea and Samaria ("West Bank")	2,263	Jordan	1948–67
Tibet	471,700	China	1950 to date
West Papua	162,371	Indonesia	1963 to date
Sinai Peninsula	23,552	Israel	1967–82
Abu Musa and the Tunb Islands	9.5	Iran	1971 to date
Aouzou Strip	37,000	Libya	1973–94
Northern Cyprus	1,295	Turkey	1974 to date
East Timor	5,794	Indonesia	1975–99
Western Sahara	102,600	Morocco	1976 to date
Lebanon	4,015	Syria	1976–2005*
Southern Lebanon	328	Israel❖	1985–2000
Transnistria (part of Moldova)	1,607	Russia	1992 to date
Abkhazia (part of Georgia)	3,336	Russia	2008 to date
South Ossetia (part of Georgia)	1,506	Russia	2008 to date
Abyei	4,072	Sudan	2011 to date
Crimea	10,038	Russia	2014 to date

---

* On May 21, 1991, a treaty of "Brotherhood, Cooperation, and Coordination" was signed between Syria and Lebanon which formalized the Syrian occupation of Lebanon and turned the latter into a political satellite of Syria.

Gaza Strip	139	Israel▲	1967–2005
Judea and Samaria ("West Bank")	2,263	Israel▲	1967 to date
Golan Heights	451	Israel◆	1967 to date

❖ On May 17, 1983, a peace treaty was concluded between Israel and Lebanon. Among the provisions was joint Israeli-Lebanese control of the region to prevent its use by terrorist groups. Massive Syrian pressure forced the Lebanese government to suspend the treaty. When the treaty collapsed, the Israelis elected to control the region on their own with the support of the South Lebanese Army (SLA).

▲ As Professor Eugene Kontorovich of Northwestern University's School of Law and a specialist in international and constitutional law, recently explained, "When new countries emerge from old ones or from colonial empires, the last official international borders constitute the new boundary lines. It has been applied to the borders of new states around the world and recognized as a basic principle of international law by the International Court of Justice."[7] Thus in international law, Israel is the successor state to the British Mandate of Palestine. Under the San Remo Resolution, Israel has the international basis for possession of this land. The Gaza Strip, Judea and Samaria are recovered territories—liberated from Egyptian and Jordanian occupation—not a nation or parts of a nation that can be "occupied."

◆ The documents establishing the Palestine Mandate (under the League of Nations) signed by the United Kingdom as the Mandatory, and the League of Nations, became a binding treaty in international law. The resolution of the League of Nations creating the Palestine Mandate included the following significant statement:

> Article 5. The Mandatory shall be responsible for seeing that no Palestine territory shall be ceded or leased to, or in any way placed under the control of the Government of any foreign Power.

The Golan Heights was part of the historical British Mandate of Palestine rather than of historical Syria. This territory was excluded improperly and illegally from the borders of mandated Palestine in the Demarcation Agreement initialed on February 3, 1922, and finally ratified a year later on March 7, 1923. At that time, the United Kingdom unilaterally approved the transfer of the Golan Heights from the British Mandate of Palestine to the French Mandate of Syria under a Franco-British agreement delineating the boundary between the two mandates. This was in clear violation of Article 5 of the San Remo agreement establishing the British Mandate for Palestine and mentioned above. Thus, there is a legal question as to the status of the Golan Heights belonging to Syria. Israel is the legal successor state to the British Mandate of Palestine.

Furthermore, France on June 30, 1939, detached the Sanjak of Alexandretta from Syria and ceded it to Turkey, which renamed it Hatay. To date Syria has never recognized this transfer of territory terming it illegal. The Syrians cannot have it both ways. If they insisted on return of Alexandretta, then Israel had the right and strong legal case to insist on return of the Golan Heights, which is an area in dispute and not occupied.[8]

Israel's control of Judea, Samaria and until 2005, the Gaza Strip, has been among the most beneficial and least intrusive of any nation's control of territory. A comparison helps prove the point.

A COMPARISON OF TWO NATIONS' CONTROL[9]		
Categories	**Chinese Occupation of Tibet**	**Israeli Control of Gaza, Judea and Samaria**
Year Begun	1950	1967
Inhabitants Killed	1,000,000 Using the Arab guidelines this means 100 "Holocausts"	10,000 Arabs claim this is a "Holocaust"
Migrants into Region	Chinese migrants now vastly outnumber local Tibetans The Chinese are not referred to as "settlers."	Israeli inhabitants are a minority in the Arab illegal (gained in aggressive war) occupation of Judea and Samaria as well as the Gaza Strip. Since 2005, there has been no Israeli "occupation" of Gaza at all.
Religious Sites Destroyed	6,000 Tibetan monasteries	Approximately zero mosques
International Reaction	Virtually none	Overwhelming and continual condemnation of Israel

While the issue of Israeli "occupation" of Judea, Samaria, the Gaza Strip, the Golan Heights, and until 1982, the Sinai Peninsula, was brought up repeatedly at the United Nations and other international forums like the Organization of African Unity (now the African Union), most of the other occupations were rarely if ever discussed, despite those occupations lasting for longer periods of time and involving larger areas of territory. Clearly, a double standard is at work. The Arabs claim the core of the Middle East conflict is Israeli "occupation." It is not the "occupation" of various territories that is the issue, but rather the Arab/Muslim pre-occupation with destroying the Jewish state, no matter what borders it has.

61. The historic experience of Arab (Jordanian) occupation of Jerusalem, from 1948 to 1967, and its demonstrated blatant disregard for Jewish and Christian religious sentiments by Muslims, is likely to be repeated if Jerusalem is ever divided again.

At the end of the first Arab war against the State of Israel—the Israeli War of Independence—Jerusalem was divided, with East Jerusalem and the walled Old City of Jerusalem, under Jordanian occupation from May 1948 to June 1967, and cut off from Israeli Jerusalem. Thus, the Jordanians controlled thirty-six out of the thirty-nine holy sites in Jerusalem, sacred to Judaism, Christianity, and Islam (*see* "Divided Jerusalem, 1948–67" map).

The Jordanian occupation of Jerusalem was recognized by only one nation, Pakistan. Despite the 1949 UN resolution that called for all of Jerusalem to be "under a permanent international regime" no action was taken to end the Jordanian occupation. No Arab state recognized Jordan's subsequent annexation of the Old City of Jerusalem in 1950. The April 3, 1949 Israel–Jordan Armistice Agreement (Article VIII), provided for and guaranteed free movement of traffic on roads, including the Bethlehem and Latrun-Jerusalem roads; resumption of the normal functioning of the cultural and humanitarian institutions on Mount Scopus and free access thereto; free access to the Holy Places and cultural institutions and use of the cemetery on the Mount of Olives.

The Mount of Olives is a mountain ridge east of Jerusalem that, from Biblical times until today, was used as a cemetery. Access was also assured for Jews to visit the Western Wall. However, in fact, Jordan denied access to the Old City of Jerusalem. Any visitor, no matter what their nationality or religious affiliation, with an Israeli visa stamp in their passport was refused entry.

Neither Israeli Jews, nor Israeli Christians (except for a few hours on Christmas Day and Easter), nor Israeli Muslims, were allowed access to any of their holy places.

The Jordanian Arab Legion illegally expelled the Old City of Jerusalem's ancient Jewish community—a most thorough ethnic cleansing. The world watched unmoved (three years after the Holocaust). It could not be bothered (less than a decade after *Kristallnacht*) when the Jordanians desecrated and destroyed the Jewish Quarter of the Old City of Jerusalem. Its name was stricken from maps, renamed the "Al Munadeleen Quarter", and populated with Arab refugees.

Jewish academies, libraries, and no fewer than seventy-four synagogues including the famous Tiferet Yisrael and Rabbi Yehuda Hahasid synagogues, were razed. The ruined remnants of some synagogues were converted into donkey stables, cowsheds, and public lavatories. Hundreds of Torah scrolls and thousands of prayer books were burned. The Tomb of Simon the Just was desecrated and used as a stable. The Western Wall desecrated by slums, became an outdoor public urinal. On the Mount of Olives, the oldest Jewish cemetery in the world was desecrated as Jordan's King Hussein permitted the construction of a motor road through the cemetery, to the Intercontinental Hotel that was built atop the mount.

No less than 75 percent (38,000 of 50,000) of the tombstones in the Mount of Olives Cemetery were ripped out, vandalized, and stolen. Many ended up in the Jordanian Army camp in Bethany, where they were used as building material in barracks; retaining walls, pathways and latrines. Some were used to construct public urinals near the Western Wall. These actions were not the results of war but deliberate abuse intended to degrade. On Mount Scopus, the Hadassah Hospital and the Hebrew University campus were unused as the Jordanians refused to permit educational and cultural activities on the site, despite a clause in the Armistice agreement, to do so.

Christian pilgrims to the Holy Land from around the world, who wanted to visit the holy sites connected with Jesus, e.g. Nazareth, the Sea of Galilee, and the Mount of Beatitudes were forced to go to Jordan first, to visit the holy sites under Jordanian control. They then were permitted only one-way passage out of Jordanian-occupied territory via one exit, the Mandelbaum Gate, to enter Israel or what the Arabs/Jordanians labeled on their maps and called the "occupied territory of Palestine."[10] What that nomenclature referred to was 1948–67 pre-Six-Day War, Israel. Such pilgrims could not enter from Israel to Jordan. Israeli Christians were only allowed to visit Jordanian-occupied Jerusalem and Bethlehem on Christmas Day, and Easter,[11] but only for a few hours. They needed a baptismal certificate to gain access (*see* the "Old City of Jerusalem under Jordanian occupation, 1948–67" map).

Christians under the Arab-Jordanian occupation of Judea and Samaria, including the Old City of Jerusalem, fared not much better. In 1953 and 1965, Jordan adopted laws abrogating the right of Christian religious and charitable institutions to acquire real estate in Jerusalem. In 1958, Jordanian legislation required all members of the Brotherhood of the Holy Sepulcher to adopt Jordanian citizenship. In 1965, Christian institutions were forbidden to acquire any land or rights in or near

Jerusalem.[12] In 1966, Christian schools were compelled to close on Fridays instead of Sundays.[13] Jordan passed additional laws imposing strict government control on Christian schools, including restrictions on the opening of new schools. There was state control over school finances and appointment of teachers. There were requirements that the Qur'an be taught. Due to these repressive policies, many Christians emigrated from Jerusalem, leading their numbers to dwindle from 25,000 in 1949 to less than 13,000 just before the Six-Day War of June 1967.[14]

62. The Jews/Israelis have consistently attempted to reach a compromise with their hostile Arab/Muslim neighbors only to be rejected time and time again.

Since 1913 there have been numerous compromise offers made for an Arab state to live side-by-side with the Jewish state. These offers were put forth by the Jewish community in Israel and abroad, the British, the Americans, the United Nations, or some combination thereof. The following are the most notable examples.

Even before the advent of World War I in June 1913, the Sami Hochberg-Abdul Hamid Yahrawi understanding was reached at the First Arab Congress in Paris, France. This was followed by the 1918 Weizmann-Suleiman Bey Nassir Understanding concluded in Cairo, Egypt. At the Paris Peace Conference, that concluded the First World War, the Feisal-Weizmann Agreement was signed on January 3, 1919 (*see* Appendix 3).

As mentioned earlier, during the British Mandatory period the Peel Commission investigated the situation in Palestine, from November 11, 1936 to July 7, 1937 and then proposed a partition plan that offered 18.4 percent of Western Palestine to the Jews (1,900 square miles) and 81.6 percent (8,400 square miles) to the Arabs. Nevertheless, the Arabs rejected the plan. This was followed by the Woodhead Commission that met from April to November 9, 1938. The Woodhead Commission offered even less territory to the Jews but the Arabs rejected that offer as well and continued their attacks on the Jewish community as part of the Arab Revolt of 1936–39.

On November 17, 1947, Golda Meir, then head of the Political Department of the Jewish Agency, secretly met with Transjordanian King Abdullah I. Abdullah sought Jewish acquiescence to his annexing all of the British Mandate of Palestine. Meir insisted that the Arabs agree to the two state partition as envisioned by the United Nations. This was followed on November 29, 1947 by the United Nations General Assembly adopting a partition plan, but it was immediately rejected by the Arabs who launched attacks against the *Yishuv* even before the latter declared independence in 1948 (*see* Appendix 5). Just prior to the declaration of Israel's independence, Golda Meir again met clandestinely with King Abdullah, on May 11, 1948. It proved an abortive attempt to prevent the imminent invasion of the armed forces of the Arab states. King Abdullah had already made up his mind to join the Arab invasion. Two weeks earlier, on April 26, 1948, Abdullah announced belligerently to a visiting journalist "[A]ll our efforts to find a peaceful solution to the Palestine problem have failed. The only way left for us is war. I will have the pleasure and honor to save Palestine."[15] "Saving Palestine" was the euphemistic code phrase for annihilating the *Yishuv*.

The Rhodes Armistice talks, as well as the Lausanne, Paris, and Geneva conferences, all took place in 1949, in an attempt to turn the armistice agreements into final peace treaties. All of these talks failed to produce Arab-Israeli peace. Israel and Jordan initialed a secret draft peace agreement in March 1950.[16] Among its provisions were the freezing of the armistice lines between the two countries for five years, unresolved problems would be assigned to joint committees, there would be normal travel and trade between the two states, both peoples would be guaranteed mutual access to their holy places in both parts of Jerusalem, and Jordan would obtain a free port zone in Haifa linked by a narrow corridor to Jordan. The agreement was never concluded due to the assassination of Jordanian King Abdullah I.

In an attempt to foster peace through economic cooperation, from October 16, 1953 to October 11, 1955, the United States sponsored the Jordan Valley Unified Water Plan, commonly known as the Johnston Plan. Its aim was to share the waters of the Jordan Valley basin between the Arab states (Jordan, Syria and Lebanon) which would receive a 60 percent allocation and Israel, which would receive a 40 percent allocation. The plan included provision to resettle 200,000 Arab refugees as well. Technical teams from all parties accepted the plan on February 22, 1955, and subsequently, Israel accepted the plan in full. Nevertheless, on October 11, 1955, the plan was rejected by the Arab League on political grounds (*see* the "Johnston Water Sharing Plan" map).

THE CONFLICT OVER WATER

"JORDAN VALLEY AUTHORITY" 1953-1955

- irrigate and reclaim 308,875 acres
- provide 170 million kwh of hydroelectric power
- transport surplus water to the Negev Desert
- resettle 200,000 Palestinian Arab refugess in Jordan and Judea -Sumaria (West Bank)

Water Allocation: 60% for Arab States
40% for Israel

Feb. 22, 1955 - Technical Agreement reached by the United States, Israel, Jordan, Lebanon and Syria.

Oct. 11, 1955 - The Arab League on political grounds "postponed" the plan for "further study" in effect killing the plan.

- ·-- 1949-67 ARMISTICE LINES
- ▬ DMZ
- —— Rivers

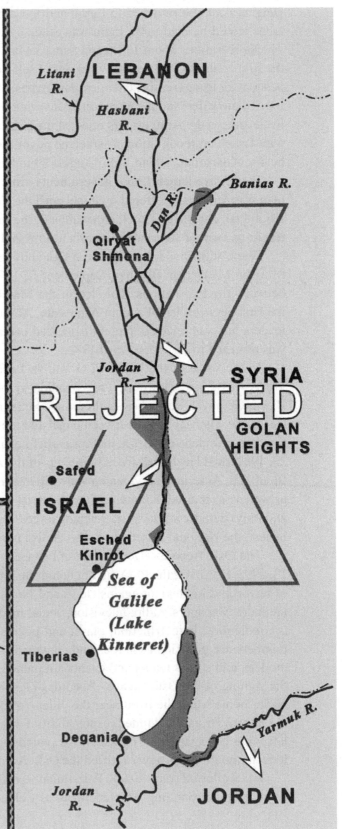

REJECTED

Immediately after the Six-Day War, on June 19, 1967, the Israel cabinet put forth a peace initiative, which was also presented at the United Nations. Israel decided the Sinai Peninsula and the Golan Heights could be returned to Egypt and Syria respectively, in return for a full peace, but that both areas would be held until, there was peace between the parties. Jerusalem would not be redivided. The deliberations about Judea and Samaria as well as the Gaza Strip were not concluded. Israel was the first country in history to win a war of self-defense and then immediately seek a compromise and peace with its aggressive enemies. The Arabs on the other hand, were the first side to lose a war and immediately demand the unconditional surrender of the winning side. All these deliberations proved irrelevant, as the Arab leaders rejected the Israeli peace overtures, emphatically stressing ""no peace with Israel, no recognition of Israel, no negotiations with it" at the Fourth Arab Summit Conference held at Khartoum, Sudan, from August 29 to September 1, 1967.

Successive Israeli Labor governments proposed the Allon Plan from 1970 on. The semi-official plan was repeatedly offered by Israel until the electoral defeat of the Labor government in 1977. The Allon Plan envisaged Israeli annexation of the Jordan Valley and areas around Jerusalem as well as a return of most of Judea and Samaria to Jordanian control. It too, was rejected by the Arabs.

The Camp David Accords were signed by Egyptian President Anwar el-Sadat and Israeli Prime Minister Menachem Begin on September 17, 1978. The accords established a "framework for peace" between the two nations. This led to the March 26, 1979 peace treaty between Egypt and Israel, the first between Israel and an Arab state. At the same time, an offer was made to Palestinian Arab leaders but was rejected. Israel dismantled communities in the Sinai and the entire Sinai Peninsula was returned to Egypt by April 1982.

In the wake of the Israel–PLO War in Lebanon in September 1982, an Israel–Lebanon Peace Treaty was signed. However, it was invalidated following the assassination of Lebanese President-elect Bashir Gemayel. Nevertheless, the United States acting as mediator facilitated another draft of a peace treaty in early May 1983, between Israel and the new Lebanese President Amin Gemayel, brother of the slain president-elect. Yet, there was stiff Lebanese parliamentary rejection of the pact. On October 23, 1983, dual Hezbollah truck bombings of the American and French barracks in Beirut took place. In all, 241 American servicemen were killed and 60 injured and 58 French paratroopers were killed as well as 15 injured. Following these terrorist attacks, the Western powers (the United States, France and Italy) withdrew their peacekeeping forces, Gemayel decided to abrogate the agreement, and at his behest, the National Assembly did so almost unanimously on March 5, 1984.

The Oslo Accords (Declaration of Principles) were signed by Israel and the PLO on September 13, 1993. However, the PLO did not honor the provisions of the accords and continued to wage a war of terror and incitement against Jews and Israel. The ongoing Palestinian incitement occurs in the media (newspapers, radio, television, social media and on the Internet), in mosques, and in schools (via polemics, indoctrination, plays, and poems). In all these venues Jews are demonized, suicide bombers are glorified as heroes and emulated. Additionally, released murderers are held up as role models, and sports teams and events are named after savage killers. In fact, only eleven days after the signing of the Oslo "peace" Accords, Yigal Vaknin was stabbed to death in an orchard near the trailer home where he lived near the village of Basra. A squad of the Palestinian Hamas Izz ad-Din al-Qassam Brigades claimed responsibility for the attack.[17] Moreover, on October 7, 1993, the Israeli left-wing newspaper *Al HaMishmar* revealed that the PLO would not ratify the Oslo Accords, and indeed, the PLO has never ratified the Oslo Accords.

Israel allowed some 70,000 Palestinian terrorists to enter the Gaza Strip, Judea and Samaria. They came from surrounding Arab countries as well as those from further afield, like Tunisia and Sudan.

Israel allowed them to be armed. The US Dayton Mission trained over 6,000 men for a PA security force, which rarely enforced security between Palestinians and Israelis.

Subsequent Israeli–PLO agreements were signed stipulating and re-stipulating that the PLO would fulfill its pledges to Israel. In each, Israel made tangible territorial concessions to obtain PLO compliance. Thus on May 4, 1994, the Cairo Agreement on the Gaza Strip and the Jericho area was concluded. It established the Palestinian Authority (PA), which was dominated by the PLO. The Oslo II Agreement (Interim Agreement) was concluded on September 28, 1995, between Israel and the PLO/PA. In that agreement, Israel handed over more than 30 percent of Judea and Samaria to the PLO/PA. The Hebron Protocol was signed between Israel and the PLO/PA on January 17, 1997. While Israel withdrew from 80 percent of Hebron retaining only a tiny enclave, the PLO/PA was to honor its previous commitments. It did not. Thus, Israel traded fundamentally irreversible tangible concessions, usually but not always territory, for theoretically reversible intangible commitments, most often promises of cessation of terrorism and incitement.

The Wye River Memorandum was signed on October 23, 1998, between Israel and the PLO/PA. It called for implementation of the earlier Oslo II Agreement (Interim Agreement). Again, the PLO/PA failed to comply. Finally, on September 4, 1999, the Sharm el-Sheikh Memorandum was signed by Israeli Prime Minister Ehud Barak and PLO Chairman Yasser Arafat. Its purpose was to implement the Oslo II Agreement (Interim Agreement) as well as to implement all other agreements between the PLO and Israel since the Oslo Accords of 1993. While Israel consistently implemented territorial withdrawals, the PLO/PA continued terrorist acts against Israel and incitement in its media, mosques and schools against Israel and Jews. Whereas, 727 Israelis were murdered by Palestinian terrorism from the end of the Six-Day War until the Oslo Accords (1967 to 1993), the signing of the Oslo Accords brought more violence, which produced 1,529 Israeli fatalities (to early 2014).[18] Oslo was supposed to bring peace and normalization. It has produced terror and death. In short, the Oslo Accords are perhaps Israel's greatest blunder and self-inflicted wound in the 67-year history of the Jewish state.

In the interim, an Israel–Jordan Peace Treaty was signed on October 26, 1994, which included an Israeli cession and recognition of Jordanian sovereignty over two areas totaling some 147 square miles. These are the Nahrayim/Baqura area at the northern end of the Israel–Jordan border where the Yarmuk and Jordan Rivers meet, and the Tzofar/Al-Ghamr area, located south of the Dead Sea in the Emek Ha'arava/Wadi Arava sector of the border. In exchange, Israel rented the land from Jordan so that Israeli landowners and their workers could continue to cultivate it. Furthermore, the landowners along with their employees and guests were permitted to go in and out as often as they wished, with no customs or immigration restrictions of any kind. In a very unusual move, the Annex declares that, while the land is under Jordanian sovereignty, the Israeli police department has jurisdiction over incidents "solely involving the [Israeli] landowners, their invitees or employees." In addition, Jordanian law does not apply to activities in which only Israelis are involved. Land purchases by non-Israelis however, can only be done with Jordanian approval.[19] Israel also agreed to give Jordan 50,000,000 cubic meters (1,765,733,335.58 cu. ft.) of water each year and for Jordan to own 75 percent of the water from the Yarmuk River.

On May 7, 2000, Israeli Prime Minister Ehud Barak and PLO/PA Chairman Yasser Arafat held a one-day summit meeting in Ramallah. After Arafat rejected the Israeli proposals as not capitulating to his maximum demands, he ordered Marwan Barghouti, the Secretary-General of Fatah and a leader of Tanzim, "Start heating things up."[20] Barghouti obeyed. On May 15, during Nakba Day commemorations, PA (Fatah) police opened fire on Israeli troops. The next day, Barghouti bragged in the newspaper that his people had fired 6,000 bullets at IDF troops. It was a trial run for what would be duplicated in September. Arafat reprimanded him for having boasted in public because he had wanted to make those planned confrontations look like a spontaneous popular uprising.[21] This event was the pattern used for what would occur after the Camp David II summit talks in July 2000.

In an attempt to move the stalled Israeli–Palestinian peace talks forward at the Camp David II summit held from July 11 to 25, 2000, Barak offered Israeli redeployment from 97 percent of the territories (95 percent of Judea and Samaria and 100 percent of the Gaza Strip). The Israeli offer included the creation of a Palestinian state in the areas of Israeli withdrawal; the removal of isolated communities and transfer of the land to Palestinian Arab control; other Israeli land exchanged for settlements remaining under Israeli control; and PA control over eastern Jerusalem, including most of the Old City. This still fell short of what Arafat wanted—100 percent of those territories. Accordingly, the Israeli offer was rejected by Arafat who launched a massive pre-planned terror war—the Al-Aqsa (Second) *Intifada*.

It should be noted that in September 2010, Mahmoud Zahar, a high-ranking Hamas' leader, told students and lecturers at the Islamic University in Gaza City, that Arafat had ordered Hamas to launch terror attacks against Israel in 2000. This marked the first time a senior Hamas official disclosed that Hamas suicide bombings during the Al-Aqsa (Second) *Intifada* were ordered by Arafat.[22] President Bill Clinton made an offer, in December 2000—the Oval Office Bridge Plan—to achieve peace during the Al-Aqsa (Second) *Intifada*. It was rejected by the PLO/PA. This was followed by an Israeli offer at the Taba Talks and at the Davos Conference, January 21–27, 2001, to reach final status talks aimed at resolving the conflict. Yasser Arafat again rejected the Israeli offer and continued the violence.

On June 24, 2002, President George W. Bush declared, "If you [the Palestinian Arabs] want your state, stop the terror." The Palestinian Arabs rejected the United States offer and continued terrorist attacks against Israel. This was followed by the Quartet's unveiling of a "Road Map" for peace on April 30, 2003. The Quartet was comprised of the United States, European Union, Russia, and the United Nations. It urged the PLO/PA to stop terrorism and incitement, but both continued. Nevertheless, the Israelis kept trying to achieve peace. Israeli Prime Minister Ariel Sharon made a unilateral offer, on April 14, 2004, of Palestinian statehood in exchange for PA compliance with all the agreements signed since Oslo in 1993. Once again, the proposed agreement was rejected by the PLO/PA.

The Sharm el-Sheikh Summit of February 8, 2005, brought together Israeli Prime Minister Ariel Sharon, Egyptian President Hosni Mubarak, King Abdullah II of Jordan, and Mahmoud Abbas PLO/PA President, in an attempt to end the violence of the Al-Aqsa (Second) *Intifada*. Sharon and Abbas explicitly included an intended cessation of all violent activity against each other's peoples, supposedly marking a formal end to the *intifada*. Incredulously a short time later, in August 2005, the Israeli government under Prime Minister Sharon (known as a right-wing hawk) unilaterally withdrew from the Gaza Strip, uprooting twenty-one Israeli communities (collectively known as Gush Katif) and forcibly relocating 9,000 of its citizens. Additionally, Israel unilaterally withdrew from and dismantled four communities in northern Samaria—Ganim, Kadum, Sa-Nur and Chomesh. As political analyst Martin Sherman, among others, has noted, "One of the most remarkable and recurring phenomena in Israeli politics is that right-wing parties running on hawkish platforms have regularly won elections, but, on winning, adopt the failed policies of their dovish left-wing rivals who were rejected at the polls."[23]

Nonetheless, not all these tangible concessions brought peace or a cessation of the violence or incitement. Instead, it fueled the violence as the PA saw a lack of Israeli resolve, continued self-abasement and appeasement as well as sensing that victory over Israel could be achieved. The Israeli concessions whetted the appetite of the Arab world for a "final solution" to the Israeli question, the elimination of the State of Israel. In this, the Arab countries will be aided by some two million Arabs within Israel to act as a Trojan horse to facilitate this goal.

At the Annapolis Conference held on November 27, 2007, a proposed two-state solution to be mutually agreed upon was made. However, further negotiations floundered over the Arab refusal to recognize Israel as the sovereign state of the Jewish people in the Middle East. As long as refusing to recognize the right of a Jewish state to exist and to accept the right of Jewish national self-determination are fundamental Arab/Muslim beliefs, so called peace negotiations will not only fail, inherently they must. A reversal of this policy in the Arab/Muslim world would require an unparalleled theological upheaval. This issue has always been at the core of the conflict.

Despite continued Arab rejections, in May 2008 via US Secretary of State Condoleezza Rice, Israeli Prime Minister Ehud Olmert offered PA Chairman Mahmoud Abbas 94 percent of Judea and Samaria, as well as shared control over Jerusalem and put an international body in charge of the holy sites. Israel also offered to allow some 5,000 Palestinian Arabs into Israel.[24] Again, this was met by Arab rejection and insistence that all their demands be met.

Israeli Prime Minister Benjamin Netanyahu attempted to jump-start negotiations by offering to demarcate temporary borders for a sovereign Palestinian state on more than 60 percent of Judea and Samaria in April 2010. The offer was rejected by PLO/PA Chairman Mahmoud Abbas, while at the same time (April 25, 2010), eight Palestinian factions rejected the two-state solution outright and called on the Palestinian Liberation Organization (PLO), of which Abbas is titular head, to halt any kind of talks with Israel.[25]

Israel has consistently made multiple and unreciprocated concessions in its efforts towards a real lasting peace. Yet successive American administrations have focused on what else Israel must do, while ignoring what it has already done, and the lessons learned from its past actions. Israeli withdrawals from parts of Judea and Samaria, southern Lebanon, and the Gaza Strip, resulted in their becoming launching pads for suicide bombers and rockets aimed at Israeli civilians. Furthermore, contrary to what the Israeli left had been claiming would happen, those withdrawals did not even improve Israel's international standing. Unfortunately, the historical reality is that every Israeli concession to the Arabs is considered both permanent and a starting point for further concessions. There is no Arab/Muslim *quid pro quo*. Arab/Muslim contempt for and hostility towards Jews in the Land of Israel, like it or not, is a reality and has been for 140 years. Islamic enmity towards Jews in general is a 1,400-year-old theological obsession. It will not go away with land concessions and economic inducements. Trying to appease the unappeasable has proven wrong—dead wrong at great cost in Jewish/Israeli blood and treasure.

For its part, the Arab/Muslim world has rejected the basic premise of a sovereign Jewish state in the Middle East since the 1880s. Long before there were the modern claims of "occupation", the Arab world sought Israel's destruction. Representative of the continuing open Arab hostility was the widely distributed statement made to the Associated Press on January 9, 1954 by Saudi Arabia's then new King Saud bin Abdul-Aziz Al Saud:

> Israel to the Arab world, is like a cancer to the human body, and the only way of remedy is to uproot it just like a cancer. Israel is a serious wound in the Arab world body, and we cannot endure the pain of this wound forever. We don't have the patience to see Israel remain occupying part of Palestine for long. We Arabs total

about 50,000,000. Why don't we sacrifice 10 million of our number and live in pride and self-respect?[26]

This declaration was less than six years after Israel had won its independence in a hard-fought war of self-defense. It was two years before the next major conflict (the Sinai-Suez War), and more than thirteen years before the Six-Day War of 1967. This theme prevails to the present. PA Chairman Mahmoud Abbas, in a speech delivered on January 17, 2010, boasted that the Arab leaders in Judea, Samaria and the Gaza Strip "have not offered [Israel] any concessions from May 1988 until today" thereby openly affirming the failure of the PA to fulfill its signed obligations under the Oslo agreements to arrest terrorists, outlaw terrorist groups and end the incitement to hatred and murder of Jews.[27] In the words of political scientist, Professor Louis René Beres, "Even by the strict legal standards of the *Convention on the Prevention and Punishment of the Crime of Genocide,* Arab actions and attitudes toward the microscopic Jewish state in their midst have remained authentically genocidal. Jurisprudentially, what they have in mind for Israel is formally called crimes against humanity."[28]

No concessions on borders, "settlements," refugees, Jerusalem, water rights, and more will suffice to appease the Arabs, unless it paves the way for the final destruction of the Jewish state. Repeated Jewish and Israeli attempts to gain peace through negotiations as indicated by the examples cited above fulfills Einstein's definition of insanity: repeating the same process over and over again, expecting a different result. Israel, long ago, had to end the dangerously, delusional doctrine of "land for peace" and the misnamed "Oslo peace process."

Despite the fact that in every agreement since the onset of the Oslo Accords, the Palestinian Arabs solemnly pledged to end the incitement against Jews and Israel on Palestinian TV, radio, and in print media, in mosques, and to purge it from Palestinian textbooks—each such undertaking has been promptly ignored. The Friday sermon delivered by a cleric at Bourin Mosque in Nablus (Shechem), on January 29, 2010, and broadcast on PA TV was typical of the incitement. It spurred misojudaic hatred and advocated violence against the Jews. In the sermon, the cleric declared "the Jews [are] the enemies of Allah and of His Messenger… [and] enemies of humanity."[29] Readers should note that the term "Jews" rather than "Israelis" are identified as the enemy, which correlates with the precepts set forth in the Qur'an. The killing of Jews as well as the use of jihad is reemphasized throughout the broadcast accusing the Jews of wishing to make war on mosques, and scheming to "kill Muslims."[30] The broadcast stressed that jihad is the only way to liberate the land and "these holy places and these mosques."[31] It should also be noted that while being a supposedly "moderate" PA TV broadcast, it quoted the main section of Article 7 of the Hamas charter wherein the rocks and trees shall call out to tell the Muslims, "Oh Muslim, Oh servant of Allah—there is a Jew behind me, come and kill him," and vowing that what they call "Palestine" "will be liberated only by means of Jihad."[32] This vehement sermon came only weeks after PLO/PA Chairman Abbas disingenuously insisted, "Today, there is no more incitement at any mosque."[33]

The Palestinians never took any of the major steps outlined by such agreements with Israel as well as US-sponsored plans, e.g. the Road Map, to stop the terrorism and end the incitement, which were preconditions for further negotiations. On a broader scale Arab/Muslim world incitement, misojudaism, violence and terror have also increased not lessened, despite Israeli concessions including territorial withdrawals. The vehement anti-Israel propaganda stemmed forth from even Egypt and Jordan, with whom Israel has formal peace treaties. Since 1993, not a single Palestinian leader has ever made a speech to his own people urging moderation and acceptance of Israel as a Jewish state. Never has a

Palestinian leader said that the Palestinians would have to give up something to get a state, and on no account urged the Arab media as well as public debate to become more moderate.

With respect to the Oslo Accords, only one side in this conflict—the Palestinian side—devotes its resources to inciting hatred and violence against Jews and Israel. The PLO/PA goes through the motions of negotiating with Israel. Hamas does not even bother with the charade of negotiations. Both groups are constantly encouraging its people to consider terrorism against Jews as an act of heroism and martyrdom. The principal failure of those pushing the implementation of the Oslo Accords and the misnamed "peace process"—the worldwide political left, mainstream media, academia, the diplomatic corps, as well as foreign governments—was their decision to ignore Palestinian incitement and give scant lip-service of condemnation to Arab acts of terrorism against Jews.

Lack of Israeli demands for compliance, which should have been backed by the international community, conveyed the message to the Palestinian Arabs that nothing is expected of them in the future. However, the fundamental fact remains: Peace cannot be obtained without a dramatic reformation of Palestinian Arab society, the abolition of incitement against Jews and Israel, and the adoption of a school curriculum based on peace, tolerance and acceptance of a sovereign Jewish state as a neighbor. One must recall the cautionary words of Israel's first Prime Minister, David Ben-Gurion, who observed, "While it is good that there be a world full of peace, fraternity, justice and honesty, it is even more important that we [Israel] be in it."

In contrast, Arab leaders consistently and skillfully have pursued the Phased Plan or strategy of stages, in dealing with Israel (*see* Appendix 9). It was first enunciated in secular form by Tunisian President Habib Bourguiba in April 1965, with the Muslim concept of temporary truces, exemplified by Muhammad's Treaty of Hudaybiyyah. Islamic doctrine permits temporary truces with an enemy that cannot be defeated for the moment, by force of arms. "If Muslims are weak, a truce may be made for ten years if necessary, for the Prophet (Allah bless him and give him peace) made a truce with the Quraysh for that long, as is related by Abu Dawud" (*Reliance of the Traveller* o9.16).[34]

Egyptian President Anwar el-Sadat pursued a phased plan or strategy of stages to destroy Israel. Sadat put it this way in an interview with *al-Anwar* on June 22, 1975, "The effort of our generation is to return to the 1967 borders.* Afterward the next generation will carry the responsibility."[35] In November 1977, Sadat journeyed to Israel and addressed the Israeli Knesset. His Israeli audience—indeed the Western world—was dazzled and mesmerized by the spectacle of an Egyptian President in the Israeli capital. Sadat's appearance and speech was designed to have a maximum impact on in the United States, Israel's major ally and military supplier. He portrayed himself as a God-fearing man, invoking the name of God ten times in the first ten sentences of his speech. In the West and Israel, many concluded that such a man certainly would not lie. Sadat was engaged in *taqiyya* (*see* "Basic Principle 66 and "Basic Principle 67"). Perhaps the Israelis and the world should have looked at Sadat more carefully, both metaphorically and physically. A famous photo[†] of the Egyptian president together with then Israeli Foreign Minister Moshe Dayan shows Sadat wearing a necktie with a

---

* There is an on-going attempt to obfuscate the 1949 Armistice lines by falsely, and misleadingly referring to them as the "1967 borders" and then using them as a basis for another Palestinian state. This is a rewriting of history as well as an effort to retroactively recognize and reward the original Arab aggression of 1947–49.

† View photos at http://4.bp.blogspot.com/_-k3RrGAJo6w/SDXnHxC9BMI/AAAAAAAACP8/2Ozodg3I05k/s400/sadat-dayan-1.jpg.

meandering pattern—a linked continual swastika design, the infamous symbol of the Nazis.* It was his way of both showing his contempt for the Israelis/Jews and telling the Arab/Muslim world that the treaty with Israel was modeled after the Treaty of Hudaybiyyah. Additionally, Sadat's words had different meanings than the way they were understood by his Israeli audience and the Western world.

From the outset, it must be understood that the term "peace" is viewed differently by the Islamic world and the West. Peace among Western democracies includes (but is not limited to) such features as a shared system of values, open borders, commerce, tourism, mutual exchange and cooperation in fields as varied as science, the environment, culture and education. There is a curtailment or outright absence of incitement and hostile propaganda, as well as an absence of military fortifications and armies standing opposite one another along a common frontier. However, this is not the peace that is achievable in the Arab/Muslim world where peace is religiously defined.

The word *salaam* is thought by many in the West, including some Israelis, to mean peace. It does not. It means an absence of conflict, non-belligerence, or in modern parlance a temporary or limited truce, armistice, or a ceasefire—a *hudna* in Arabic, an *aramesh* in Farsi (Persian). It should be understood that in the Middle East, "peace" is what you agree to when you do not think you can win a war. Such a "peace" is not a permanent relationship and will be terminated as soon as the situation changes in favor of the Muslim side. As with the Treaty of Hudaybiyyah, such a "peace" treaty can be scrapped and conflict resumed, in the blink of an eye.

The Arabic word *sulha* means dispute resolution and reconciliation. *Sulha* is closer to the Western concept of real peace, but is used only between two Muslim parties. Sadat repeatedly used the term *salaam*. It was his code message to the Arab world that he would never make *sulha* i.e. real peace, with the Jewish state of Israel. Sadat through his visit to Jerusalem shifted Arab tactics in order to reach the same goal, the elimination of the Jewish state of Israel. Through the skillful use of diplomatic duplicity, Sadat, and various Arab leaders since then (including Yasser Arafat and Mahmoud Abbas), succeeded in alienating and isolating Israel from its traditional support in the West, especially Israel's "special relationship" with the United States. Sadat and the others even divided the Israeli political establishment, playing off Israeli leftist factions against the Israeli government. Skillfully they have shifted the entire blame for the Arab–Israeli conflict and lack of peace onto Israel, the actual victim since 1948. A willfully perverse pattern emerged as Israel, the victim of terrorist violence, was accused of inciting violence against the perpetrators of the violence. This type of accusation is nevertheless commonplace in Europe and is now occurring in the United States.

Beyond the word "peace," the West must understand that other words, including "freedom," "tyranny," "liberation," and "justice" are understood differently by the Arab/Muslim world and the Western democracies. For example, the term "freedom" in the West has a political connotation as well as a legal and social one, "Freedom" as opposed to "oppression." Freedom means something different in the Islamic world. Freedom is a legal term: Freedom as opposed to slavery. Islamic society was a society in which slavery was an accepted institution existing all over the Muslim world. You were

---

* During World War II, Sadat spied for the Nazis, who he admired. As part of the "Kondor Mission," Sadat and Gamal Abdel Nasser contacted German agents at the Kit Kat, a leading Cairo nightclub in an attempt to relay aerial photographs of Egypt to German General Edwin Rommel. Sadat even located a mansion on the Rue des Pyramides that was to be used by Rommel once the field marshal arrived in Cairo. Sadat was arrested, and stripped of his rank as captain, and imprisoned. Furthermore, as Andrew Bostom states in his book *The Legacy of Islamic Anti-Semitism,* on September 18, 1953, Sadat wrote a letter to Adolf Hitler (who was rumored to still be alive at the time), that appeared prominently in the Cairo weekly newspaper *Al Musawwar,* openly praising the Nazi dictator and hoping for a similar individual to arise again (Bostom, 155).

free if you were not a slave. It was entirely a legal and social term. For the Muslim world, freedom means freedom from foreign domination or influence. Israel is viewed as foreign. It was the foreign domination, including so-called Israeli "occupation" that produced tyranny. Merriam-Webster defines "liberation" as—a movement seeking equal rights and status for a group. Readers, particularly those living in a Western society, are likely to interpret that word within this context. The word "liberation" has a very different meaning however for Arab/Muslims engaged in military conflict with Israel and the West (*see* Appendix 8 for a detailed explanation). Justice is the elimination of this tyranny, which means the elimination of Israel.

One of Sadat's favorite maxims was, "There can be no peace without justice." Justice—*'adl, 'adalah*—was regarded in traditional pre-Islamic Arab society as the redemption of one's rights which had been usurped by someone else.[36] In Muslim terms, the aim of good government is justice as opposed to injustice. In his speech to the Israeli Knesset, Sadat kept repeating that peace must be based on justice.[37] He used the word sixteen times in that one speech and defined justice as Israel's disappearance. Sadat said justice required Israel to give up all the territories taken in the 1967 conflict and the return of Palestinian Arab refugees. "We [the Arabs] insist on complete withdrawal from these territories, including Arab Jerusalem. It is no use to refrain from recognizing the Palestinian people and their right to statehood as their right of return."[38] However, the fulfillment of those conditions would guarantee that Israel would cease to exist as a Jewish state. Nevertheless, Sadat included a threat of cataclysmic war if his terms were not accepted:

> That to avoid an inevitable disaster that will befall us, you and the whole world, there is no alternative to the establishment of permanent peace based on justice [i.e. Sadat's terms]. If [the opportunity for Sadat's version of peace was] lost or wasted, the resulting slaughter would bear the curse of humanity and of history."[39]

This warning was included (akin to Hitler's threat of war at the time of the Munich Conference of 1938) to encourage the forces in both Israel and the West that favored appeasement.

Sadat also proclaimed that Jewish independence in Palestine was illegitimate in its totality stating, Israel was "on a land that did not all belong to you."[40] Sadat was following the 1956 *fatwa* signed by the leading theologians of Al-Azhar University, Egypt's center of Islamic thought and jurisprudence. That *fatwa* had declared of Israel's existence, "It is required of every Muslim to cleanse the land of this injustice." "Justice" amounts to the violent restoration and forcible maintenance of *dhimmitude* for Jews. The peace and justice, which Sadat offered Israel in his speech, was only *dhimmi* rights in a Muslim Palestine. It would be an Israeli surrender to the conditions imposed by Islam. It is in this context to which the Arab/Muslim world ascribes. There can be no diplomatic solution as long as the goal of the Arab/Muslim side remains the annihilation of the other side, Israel. This refrain has been constantly repeated. In 1990, Syrian Defense Minister Mustafa Tlass declared, "The conflict between the Arab nation and Zionism [i.e. Jewish nationalism as represented by the Jewish state of Israel] is over existence, not borders."[41]

Sadat was not the only Arab leader to openly voice the phased plan or strategy of stages. Yasser Arafat's top deputy, Salah Khalaf, also known as Abu Iyad, declared in December 1988, "Setting up a Palestinian state on a portion of the soil of Palestine is a phase towards the final objective—to establish a state in all of Palestine."[42] Even as he was about to sign a "peace accord" with Israel in September 1993, PLO chief Yasser Arafat signaled to the Arab world, that this was merely a tactic in accordance with the Phased Plan. Only twelve days before the signing of the Oslo Accords (September 13, 1993), a pre-recorded speech directed towards the Palestinian people by Arafat himself was broadcast on the Jordanian radio, in which Arafat made the following statement about the Oslo agreement, "[The Oslo agreement] will be a basis for an independent Palestinian state in accordance with the Palestinian National Council resolution issued in 1974 [the Phased Plan]. The PNC resolution issued in 1974 calls for the establishment of a national authority on any part of Palestinian soil from which Israel withdraws or which is liberated."[43]

More than a decade later, Palestinian Arab rejection of compromise was made utterly clear by three polls. The first, conducted by An-Najah University in May 2008, showed that 57.6 percent of Palestinian Arabs rejected a two-state solution—a second Palestinian Arab state alongside Israel. An earlier poll conducted by Near East Consulting (NEC) in February 2007, revealed that 75 percent of Palestinian Arabs did not think that a Jewish Israel has a right to exist! The third poll, conducted by the Palestinian Center for Policy and Survey Research, and reported in *The New York Times,* March 19, 2008, was taken just after the murder, on March 6, 2008, of eight students at Meraz Harav Yeshiva in Jerusalem by an Arab terrorist. The poll found that 84 percent of Palestinians supported the terror attack that killed the eight young students. This immediately poses the question: How can an entire Palestinian society support the murder of children? Clearly, the framing of Jews and Israelis as mortally dangerous to Palestinians has been totally successful. Israel now faces a society that is very possibly past the stage of genocide framing and at the point of seeing the killing of Israelis, even teens, as justified. All that would be necessary for the population to go along with the final script, detailed so many times by its leaders, would be the means. No matter what the Israeli concessions can there be "peace" with such an enemy?

On July 31, 2009, Saudi Foreign Minister Prince Saud al-Faisal displayed an extraordinary example of Arab "negotiating" technique. At a joint State Department news conference with Secretary of State Hillary Clinton, the Saudi Foreign Minister declared that what was required in dealing with Israel, was "a comprehensive approach that *defines the final outcome at the outset* [emphasis added] and launches into negotiations over final-status issues, including the future Palestinian state, control of Jerusalem, the return of Palestinian refugees, water and security."[44] In short, Israel had to agree in advance to accept all Arab demands for "withdrawal from *all the* [emphasis added] occupied territories."[45] By stipulating Israel's surrender on all its core issues with the Palestinians before negotiations even began the Saudis rendered those negotiations superfluous. This meant that Israel would only be asked to arrange for the technicalities and timelines for its predetermined pullback to the 1949 Armistice lines, its handover of Jerusalem to Arab control, the distribution and administration of regional water resources and the return of the refugees and their descendants to the homes they forfeited on account of the 1947–49 Arab war against the fledgling Jewish state.

Just as the Khartoum Arab Summit Conference of September 1967, resulted in the declaration of three Arab "nos"—"no peace with Israel, no recognition of Israel, no negotiations with it,"—so again forty-three years later, Israel's efforts at making a true lasting peace with its enemies was met by another trio of "nos." During the December 11–12, 2010, Fifth Fatah Revolutionary Council Convention, the ruling PLO and PA head Mahmoud Abbas enumerated the Palestinian "three nos": No to recognition of Israel as the nation-state of the Jewish people, no to dropping their demand for a Palestinian refugee "right of return," and no to agreed-upon security arrangements on the ground. It is to be reemphasized that Fatah and the PA have been dubbed the so-called "moderate" Palestinians. The militant Hamas followed suit a couple of days later. Hamas Prime Minister Ismail Haniyeh, during a mass rally in Gaza to mark the twenty-third anniversary of the Islamic movement, described Hamas' ideological refusal to recognize Israel as the homeland of the Jewish people. "Hamas will never recognize Israel, despite pressures and efforts aimed at achieving this. Hamas bears the flag of Palestinian liberation, all of Palestine, from the river to the sea. We said it five years ago and we say it now ... we will never, we will never, we will never recognize Israel."[46]

PA Chairman Mahmoud Abbas, in his September 23, 2011 speech to the United Nations General Assembly, openly revealed the true goal of Israel's Arab/Muslim enemies with one sentence. "Enough, enough, enough," Abbas declared, "63 years of ongoing tragedy must end." At the time of his speech, Jewish sovereignty in the Land of Israel as represented by the Jewish state of Israel existed for 63 years. Thus, it was clear to all that Abbas's statement was a call for Israel's demise.

Abbas's call for the elimination of Israel were echoed a year later by Hamas politburo chief, Khaled Mashaal. In a speech in Gaza on December 7, 2012, marking the twenty-fifth anniversary of the founding of the terrorist group, Mashaal defiantly declared, "Palestine is our land and nation from the [Jordan] river to the [Mediterranean] sea, from north to south, and we cannot cede an inch or any part of it." Furthermore, Mashaal stated that Hamas would never recognize the Jewish State of Israel. "Resistance is the right way to recover our rights, as well as all forms of struggle—political, diplomatic, legal and popular, but all are senseless without resistance," he said.[47] "Occupation," borders, "settlements," holy sites, water rights, refugees, and security all are of little consequence unless they are unilateral Israeli concessions to the maximalist Arab/Muslim demands. These statements again underscore the Arab/Muslim world's determination not for real give-and-take negotiations and compromise, not for genuine conflict resolution and peace, but for the elimination, eradication, and extinction of the entire Jewish State of Israel.

Whereas the PLO viewed the Oslo Accords as a tactic for obtaining tangible Israeli territorial concessions, successive Israeli governments deluded themselves into thinking the Oslo Accords were a "peace treaty" with the PLO, akin to the Egypt–Israel Peace Treaty and the Israel–Jordan Peace Treaty. Nothing could be further from the truth as the historic record of more than twenty years demonstrates. Most recently, PLO senior official Mohammad Zazeh, speaking at the international Palestinian solidarity conference "Palestine: Manifestation of Muslim Ummah's Unity" held in Karachi, Pakistan, in July 2013, said that, "Israel is an illegitimate state" that must cease to exist. "Palestine and al Quds [Jerusalem] belong to all Arabs and Muslims. This is sacred land." Zazeh said the PLO has never recognized Israel as a legitimate state, and that the 1993 Oslo Accords should not be misunderstood to have constituted Palestinian recognition of Israel.[48]

Therefore, it is patently clear from the historic record to the present that the Arab/Muslim enemies of Israel do not wish to live in true peace with Israel and its Jewish population. There are even some Israeli Arabs who consider themselves "Palestinians," and others who fight in the ranks of the ISIL and al-Qaeda jihadists. Clearly, they too are not prepared to live in peace with their Jewish neighbors. Arab/Muslim leaders have declared that any future "Palestinian" state must be *judenrein* (ethnically and religiously "cleansed of Jews"). The Palestinian state called Jordan is *judenrein* as are many of the Arab/Muslim states across the greater Middle East. While Israel, a democratic state, does not have an *Araberrein* policy, it does have 1.69 million Israeli Arabs within the 1949 Armistice lines as well as some 1.65 million Arabs in Judea and Samaria, many of whom detest the Jewish state. Despite this, Israel must continue to remain the nation-state of the Jewish people. Demographically it cannot be overwhelmed by an increased and largely hostile Arab population within its final negotiated borders. Thus, Israel should embark on a program of compensated emigration, encouraging individual Arabs (many of them would wish to leave the uncertainties of the region with its continued violence) to resettle anywhere in the world to begin new, productive and better lives. The program could also be extended to any of the 1.69 million Israeli Arabs who would wish to avail themselves of the opportunity. Additional funding for this purpose could be raised by eliminating the billions wasted on the UNRWA, which only seeks to perpetuate the so-called "refugee status" of an ever growing number of Arabs. International largesse, including Israeli contributions to a corrupt PLO/PA or Hamas leadership should be diverted to the individual Palestinians themselves. Foreign nations and NGOs, if they are truly interested in ending the humanitarian plight of these Arabs (Palestinians within the current borders of Israel as well as the millions kept virtually imprisoned in their camps) could assist financially and with resettlement.

63. The most often quoted and misunderstood United Nations Security Council resolution dealing with the Middle East is United Nations Security Council Resolution 242.

On May 19, 2011, US President Barak Obama publicly declared that a Palestinian-Israeli peace accord must "be based on the [1949 Armistice, pre-June 5,] 1967 lines with mutually agreed [land] swaps" that would result "in a sovereign and contiguous [Palestinian] state."[49] In taking this step, Obama unilaterally rejected United Nations Security Council Resolution 242 (which the United States co-wrote with the United Kingdom and to which it is a party) and endorsed the Palestinians' demand for their future state to be based on the borders that existed prior to the 1967 Middle East war. President Obama's statement is both false and misleading. There were no "borders," merely the 1949 Armistice lines, which is where the fighting ended in 1949. Despite Obama's declaration, United Nations Security Council Resolution 242 remains the definitive internationally agreed upon basis for dealing with the results of the Six-Day War of 1967. UN Resolution 242 became the basis of the entire peace process, including the 1979 Egyptian-Israeli peace treaty, the 1991 Madrid peace conference, the 1993 Oslo Accords, the 1994 Jordanian-Israeli peace treaty, and draft agreements with Syria. As such, it is important first to read what that resolution says.

UNITED NATIONS SECURITY COUNCIL RESOLUTION 242
NOVEMBER 22, 1967

The Security Council,

Expressing its continuing concern with the grave situation in the Middle East,

Emphasizing the inadmissibility of the acquisition of territory by war and the need to work for a just and lasting peace in which every State in the area can live in security;

Emphasizing further that all member States in their acceptance of the Charter of the United Nations have undertaken a commitment to act in accordance with Article 2 of the Charter;

1. Affirms that the fulfillment of Charter principles requires the establishment of just and lasting peace in the Middle East, which should include the application of both following principles:
    i)   Withdrawal of Israeli armed forces from territories occupied in the recent conflict;
    ii) Termination of all claims or states of belligerency and respect for and acknowledgment of the sovereignty, territorial integrity and political independence of every State in the area and their right to live in peace within secure and recognized boundaries free from threats or acts of force;

2. Affirms further the necessity:
    a) For guaranteeing freedom of navigation through international waterways in the area;
    b) For achieving a just settlement of the refugee problem;
    c) For guaranteeing the territorial inviolability and political independence of every State in the area, through measures including the establishment of demilitarized zones;
3. Requests the Secretary-General to designate a Special Representative, to proceed to the Middle East to establish and maintain contacts with the States concerned in order to promote agreement and assist efforts to achieve a peaceful and accepted settlement in accordance with the provisions and principles in this resolution;
4. Requests the Secretary-General to report to the Security Council on the progress of the efforts of the Special Representative as soon as possible.

Analysis

United Nations Security Council Resolution 242 was sponsored by British UN ambassador Lord Caradon, who consulted frequently with his American counterpart, Arthur Goldberg. It was an example of constructive ambiguity, i.e. formulating a position that can be accepted with equal satisfaction by both sides as a point of departure for negotiations or at least to avoid deadlock and a breakdown of talks. Every word was chosen with deliberate care.

United Nations Security Council Resolution 242 was a "package deal" as it gave something to everyone and everything to no one—in such a way, that no one knew whether they had anything. It had to be taken as a whole or not at all. Nowhere in the resolution was there any indication that Israel was an "aggressor," "invader," or an "illegal occupier" of the territories it had obtained in a legal war of self-defense forced upon it by the Arab states.

On November 22, 1967 in the United Nations Security Council, the British representative, Lord Caradon, just prior to the vote, explained

> The draft Resolution is a balanced whole. To add to it or to detract from it would destroy the balance and also destroy the wide measure of agreement we have achieved together. It must be considered as a whole as it stands. I suggest that we have reached the stage when most, if not all, of us want the draft Resolution, the whole draft Resolution and nothing but the draft Resolution.[50]

Caradon interviewed on *Kol Israel* radio on February 10, 1973, further explained:

> Question, "This matter of the (definite) article which is there in French and is missing in English, is that really significant?"

> Answer, "The purposes are perfectly clear; the principle is stated in the preamble, the necessity for withdrawal is stated in the operative section. And then the essential phrase which is not sufficiently recognized is that withdrawal should take place to secure and recognized boundaries, and these words were very carefully chosen: they have to be secure and they have to be recognized. They will not be secure unless they are recognized. And that is why one has to work for agreement. This is essential. I would defend absolutely what we did. It was not for us to lay down exactly where the

border should be. I know the 1967 border very well. It is not a satisfactory border; it is where troops had to stop in 1949, just where they happened to be that night, that is not a permanent boundary."[51]

Caradon reemphasized the issue a year later, "It would have been wrong to demand that Israel return to its positions of 4 June 1967, because those positions were undesirable and artificial. That's why we didn't demand that the Israelis return to them and I think we were right not to."[52]

Eugene V. Rostow, Professor of Law and Public Affairs at Yale University, who in 1967 was US Under-Secretary of State for Political Affairs, wrote:

> Paragraph 1 (i) of the Resolution calls for the withdrawal of Israeli armed forces 'from territories occupied in the recent conflict', and not 'from *the* [emphasis added] territories occupied in the recent conflict'. Repeated attempts to amend this sentence by inserting the word 'the' failed in the Security Council. It is, therefore, not legally possible to assert that the provision requires Israeli withdrawal from all the territories now occupied under the ceasefire resolutions to the Armistice Demarcation lines.[53]

US ambassador to the United Nations at the time, Arthur Goldberg, in the Security Council deliberations that preceded the adoption of Resolution 242 made the linkage clear:

> To seek withdrawal without secure and recognized boundaries ... would be just as fruitless as to seek secure and recognized boundaries without withdrawal. Historically, there have never been secure or recognized boundaries in the area. Neither the armistice lines of 1949 nor the ceasefire lines of 1967 have answered that description ... such boundaries have yet to be agreed upon. An agreement on that point is an absolute essential to a just and lasting peace just as withdrawal is.[54]

Years afterward, Rostow echoed this position:

> The agreement required by paragraph 3 of the Resolution, the Security Council said, should establish secure and recognized boundaries' between Israel and its neighbors 'free from threats or acts of force', to replace the Armistice Demarcation lines established in 1949, and the ceasefire lines of June 1967. The Israeli armed forces should withdraw to such lines as part of a comprehensive agreement, settling all the issues mentioned in the Resolution, and in a condition of peace.[55]

Even the Soviet delegate to the UN, Vasily Kuznetsov, who fought against the final text, conceded that the resolution gave Israel the right to "withdraw its troops only as far as the lines which it judges convenient."[56]

These essential points were clear to US President Lyndon Johnson immediately after the end of the Six-Day War, when he declared on June 19, 1967:

> There are some who have urged, as a single, simple solution, an immediate return to the situation as it was on June 4. As our distinguished and able ambassador, Mr.

Arthur Goldberg, has already said, this is not a prescription for peace, but for a renewal of hostilities.[57]

Johnson reiterated that view again within a year:

> We are not the ones to say where other nations should draw lines between them that will assure each other the greatest security. It is clear, however, that a return to the situation of June 4, 1967, will not bring peace.[58]

US bipartisan understanding of and support for Israel to have secure and recognized final borders, was on display some fifteen years after the Six-Day War, when Republican President Ronald Reagan, in a September 1, 1982, address to the American people about the Middle East declared:

> In the pre-1967 borders [*sic*] Israel was barely 10-miles-wide at its narrowest point. The bulk of Israel's population lived within artillery range of hostile Arab armies. I am not about to ask Israel to live that way again.[59]

Egypt, which had acquired the Gaza Strip by military force in 1948–49, Jordan, which had acquired the Old City of Jerusalem, Judea and Samaria, all by military force in 1948–49, and the Soviet Union, which had acquired 272,500 square miles of territory as a result of World War II (with a population two and one-half times as large as Jordan, Lebanon, Syria, and Iraq combined) were not inhibited from voting for the lofty principle of "the inadmissibility of the acquisition of territory by war" to be applied only to Israel.

Ironically, at an earlier point in history, on September 25, 1964, the Soviet government-controlled newspaper *Pravda* defended the Soviet acquisition of territory by war in these terms:

> The borders of the State have become sanctified in the efforts of the settlers in the border villages and by the streams of blood, which they have had to shed in their defense. A people which has been attacked, has defended itself and wins the war is bound in sacred duty to establish in perpetuity a political situation which will ensure the liquidation of the sources of aggression. It is entitled to maintain this state of affairs as long as the danger of aggression does not cease. A nation which has attained security at the cost of numerous victims will never agree to the restoration of previous borders. No territories are to be returned as long as the danger of aggression prevails."

That statement, which correctly described the Soviet position after World War II, just as equally applied to Israel in the autumn of 1967.

Israel is the sole exception where the international legal principle of *ex injuria jus non oritur* ("right can not originate from wrong") has not been applied. No other nation in the world acting realistically, has relinquished territories acquired from an aggressor in a war of self-defense. The fact remains that in June 1967, Judea and Samaria were recovered from illegal Jordanian occupation, the Gaza Strip was recovered from Egyptian military occupation and these territories were restored to the Jewish people and its devolvee, the State of Israel.

Turning specifically to the wording in United Nations Security Council 242, paragraph 1 (i), the actual wording is "withdrawal of Israeli armed forces from territories occupied," not "occupied territories." This should make evident that the term "occupied" referred to something "taken possession of." The term "occupied territories" preferred by Israel's enemies and others through careless usage, is a term heavy with legal meaning, as only sovereign territory can be "occupied." It was concocted arbitrarily and used by agenda-driven interpreters.

Lord Caradon's formula omitted four key words, "immediately," "unconditionally," "all" and "the." The Soviets in support of the Arabs, had attempted to insert those words in their own resolution, which was not adopted. Ambassador Goldberg made this abundantly clear:

> The notable omissions in language used to refer to withdrawal are the words *the, all,* and *the June 5, 1967 lines* [emphasis added]. I refer to the English text of the resolution. The French and Soviet texts differ from the English in this respect, but the English text was voted on by the Security Council, and thus it is determinative. In other words, there is lacking a declaration requiring Israel to withdraw from the (or all the) territories occupied by it on and after June 5, 1967. Instead, the resolution stipulates withdrawal from occupied territories without defining the extent of withdrawal. And it can be inferred from the incorporation of the words secure and recognized boundaries that the territorial adjustments to be made by the parties in their peace settlements could encompass less than a complete withdrawal of Israeli forces from occupied territories.[60]

By withholding the definitive article "the" from the word "territories", it was hoped to avoid prejudgment between contradictory Israeli and Arab positions. Thus, Caradon deliberately left open the possibility that the Israeli withdrawal might be partial rather than complete. Israel had the right to remain in the territories under international law. The use of force to disturb the Israeli presence (as would later be done in both the 1,000-Day War of Attrition of 1967–70 and the Yom Kippur War of 1973) would be a breach of the United Nations Charter and of the resolutions of the Security Council interpreting and applying it.

Despite the Soviet failure to insert the definitive article "the" into the text of the resolution, the Arab states found a round-about method of inserting it. Rather than use the original English text of the resolution, the Arab states and their supporters insisted on using the French text of the same resolution. In the French the words, "from territories" appears as *des territoires.* Translating *des* back into English, we have "from *the*" (emphasis added) magically appearing. Nevertheless, UN Resolution 242 was negotiated in English, and 10 out of 15 members of the UN Security Council were English-speaking countries. Thus, the English version of Resolution 242 was the decisive and determinative version to work with. The legally binding resolution is based on the original language in which it was first written and in the English text, there is no "the."

George Brown, British Foreign Secretary in 1967, on January 19, 1970, reemphasized this point:

> I have been asked over and over again to clarify, modify or improve the wording, but I do not intend to do that. The phrasing of the Resolution was very carefully worked out, and it was a difficult and complicated exercise to get it accepted by the United Nations Security Council. I formulated the Security Council Resolution. Before we submitted it to the Council, we showed it to Arab leaders. The proposal said 'Israel will withdraw from territories that were occupied,' and not from 'the' territories, which means that Israel will not withdraw from all the territories.[61]

Brown reiterated this section of the resolution yet again in his memoirs:

> It does not call for Israeli withdrawal from 'the' territories recently occupied, nor does it use the word 'all.' It would have been impossible to get the Resolution through if either of those words had been included, but it does set out the lines on which negotiations for a settlement must take place. Each side must be prepared to give up something; the Resolution doesn't attempt to say precisely what, because that is what negotiations for a peace treaty must be about.[62]

Caradon consistently stressed this issue. On the PBS TV program, *The MacNeil-Lehrer Report,* he emphatically repeated:

> We didn't say there should be a withdrawal to the [pre-June 5] 1967 line. We did not put the 'the' in. We did not say "all" the territories, deliberately. We all knew that the boundaries of [pre-June 5,] 1967 were not drawn as permanent frontiers, they were a ceasefire line of a couple of decades earlier. We did not say that the [pre-June 5,] 1967 boundaries must be forever.[63]

Eugene V. Rostow, by then the former dean of the Yale Law School, went on record in 1991, to make this clear:

> Resolution 242, which as undersecretary of state for political affairs between 1966 and 1969 I helped produce, calls on the parties to make peace and allows Israel to administer the territories it occupied in 1967 until a just and lasting peace in the Middle East is achieved. When such a peace is made, Israel is required to withdraw its armed forces from territories it occupied during the Six-Day War—not from the territories nor from all the territories, but from some of the territories, which included the Sinai Desert, the West Bank, the Golan Heights, East Jerusalem, and the Gaza Strip.
>
> Five-and-a-half months of vehement public diplomacy in 1967 made it perfectly clear what the missing definite article in Resolution 242 means. Ingeniously drafted resolutions calling for withdrawals from 'all' the territories were defeated in the Security Council and the General Assembly. Speaker after speaker made it explicit that Israel was not to be forced back to the 'fragile' and 'vulnerable' Armistice Demarcation Lines, but should retire once peace was made to what Resolution 242 called 'secure and recognized' boundaries, agreed to by the parties.[64]

Rostow found no legal impediment to Jewish settlement in these territories. He maintained that the original British Mandate of Palestine still applied to Judea and Samaria. He said "the Jewish right of settlement in Palestine west of the Jordan River, that is, in Israel, the West Bank [Judea and Samaria], Jerusalem, was made unassailable. That right has never been terminated and cannot be terminated except by a recognized peace between Israel and its neighbors."[65] There is no internationally binding document pertaining to this territory that has nullified this right of Jewish settlement since.

As of 2015, Israel had withdrawn from 90 percent of the territories it gained in the June 1967 Six-Day War. At that time Israel gained control of the Sinai Peninsula (23,552 square miles), the Gaza

Strip (139 square miles), Judea and Samaria (2,263 square miles), and the Golan Heights (451 square miles), for a total of 26,405 square miles (*see* "Six-Day War Ceasefire lines–Israeli administered territories" map).

As a result of the Egypt–Israel Peace Treaty of 1979, and Israel's total withdrawal from Sinai (23,552 square miles) as well as Israel's unilateral withdrawal from the Gaza Strip in 2005 (139 square miles), a total of 23,691 square miles are no longer under Israeli control. Thus, having withdrawn from 89.7 percent of the territories, Israel by 2005, had certainly complied with the spirit of withdrawal from the majority of territories. Yet, the Arab/Muslim world has not fulfilled the steps required of them as outlined in United Nations Security Council Resolution 242, "Termination of all claims or states of belligerency and respect for and acknowledgment of the sovereignty, territorial integrity and political independence of every State in the area and their right to live in peace within secure and recognized boundaries free from threats or acts of force" which certainly includes acts of incitement and terrorism.

In paragraph 1(ii), the state that was in contention, Israel was not mentioned by name. Did or did not the reference to "every State in the area" include Israel? Clearly, it was Goldberg's intention that Israeli sovereignty must be recognized. As he subsequently explained:

> [Paragraph 1(ii)] calls for respect and acknowledgement of the sovereignty of every state in the area. Since Israel never denied the sovereignty of its neighboring countries, this language obviously requires those countries to acknowledge Israel's sovereignty.[66]

Nevertheless, the Goldberg-Caradon resolution gave the Arabs the loophole of denying Israel the right to be accepted as a "State in the area." Indeed, this has been the crux of the Arab/Muslim conflict against Israel from the outset. The Arab/Muslim side has consistently refused to accept the sovereign State of Israel as the state of the Jewish people in their ancient homeland. The most important words of United Nations Security Council Resolution 242 appeared in "1(ii)": The "right to live in peace within secure and recognized boundaries free from threats or acts of force."

Two things were inextricably intertwined. One was the abstract acceptance of the State of Israel. However, what or where was this state? What boundaries did it have? Without a clear and final delineation of its boundaries, Israel's acceptance as a state could mean anything or nothing. By challenging its boundaries concretely, the Arabs could make a mockery of accepting the State of Israel abstractly.

A key concern that exists is that "secure" and "recognized" boundaries are opposing concepts given the hostile ideological character and intentions of Israel's Arab/Muslim neighbors. What Israel may reasonably regard as secure boundaries will not be recognized by its autocratic Islamic adversaries. Conversely, the boundaries which its adversaries would allegedly recognize—say the 1949 Armistice lines—can hardly be regarded as secure or defensible by Israel or by any unbiased observer.

In paragraph 2(a) reference is made to "guaranteeing of navigation through international waterways." This refers to both the Straits of Tiran and the Suez Canal. This was inserted to deal with the cause of both the Sinai-Suez War of 1956 and the Six-Day War of 1967, when the Straits of Tiran waterway was blockaded by Egypt. It also applies to the Suez Canal, from which Egypt barred Israeli ships and cargo in violation of a previous United Nations Security Council resolution of September 1, 1951.

Paragraph 2(b) calls for "a just settlement of the refugee problem." There are no qualifiers before the word "refugee." This was done deliberately to give equal application to both Arab refugees who left Israel and Arab Jews who were driven out of their countries. Any "just settlement" must deal with the claims of both groups.

In his July 14, 1967 speech to the United Nations Security Council, US Ambassador Arthur Goldberg set forth the policy of President Lyndon Johnson and the US State Department at that time: "I made it clear that the status of Jerusalem should be negotiable and that the [1949] armistice lines dividing Jerusalem were no longer viable. In other words, Jerusalem was not to be divided again."[67]

Clearly, Jerusalem was of a different status than Judea and Samaria. Furthermore, this position has been reemphasized. In 1994, the US ambassador to the UN, Madeleine Albright, announced at the Security Council that the US rejected the assertion that Jerusalem is "occupied Palestinian territory.

Arthur Goldberg, repeatedly stressed that United Nations Security Council Resolution 242 "in no way refers to Jerusalem and this omission was deliberate." In a letter he sent to the *New York Times* on March 12,1980, (in reaction to the policy of the Carter administration, which was criticizing Israeli construction practices in east Jerusalem and misrepresenting Israel's legal rights) "to set the record straight," as he put it, Ambassador Goldberg wrote:

> Resolution 242 in no way refers to Jerusalem and this omission was deliberate. I wanted to make clear that Jerusalem was a discrete matter, not linked to the West Bank [i.e. Judea and Samaria]. In a number of speeches at the UN in 1967, I repeatedly stated that the armistice lines fixed after 1948 were intended to be temporary. This of course was particularly true of Jerusalem. At no time in these many speeches did I refer to East Jerusalem as occupied territory. My speech of July 14, 1967, which Hodding Carter [President Jimmy Carter's State Department spokesman] distributed, did not say that Jerusalem was occupied territory. On the contrary, I made it clear that the status of Jerusalem should be negotiable and that the armistice lines dividing Jerusalem were no longer viable. In other words, Jerusalem was not to be divided again.[68]

At this juncture it is also worth noting that nowhere in UN Resolution 242 is there any reference to "land swaps." Nor was there any provision made for a land corridor to cross Israeli sovereign territory so that a future Palestinian state would have "territorial continuity" between what the Arabs call the West Bank and the Gaza Strip. These diplomatic innovations were thought of by diplomats in the 1990s. Israel is in no way required to agree to them according to Resolution 242.

The Yom Kippur War of October 1973 was waged by Egypt and Syria (with additional troops and military equipment coming from Morocco, Algeria, Tunisia, Libya, Sudan, Saudi Arabia, Kuwait, Iraq, and Jordan) against Israel, according to Rostow, without any provocation.[69] At the conclusion of that conflict, the United Nations Security Council passed Resolution 338, which called on the parties to implement "immediately" Resolution 242. Its text is presented below.

UNITED NATIONS SECURITY COUNCIL RESOLUTION 338
OCTOBER 22, 1973

The Security Council,

1. Calls upon all parties to the present fighting to cease all firing and terminate all military activity immediately, no later than twelve hours after the moment of the adoption of this decision, in the positions they now occupy;

2. Calls upon the parties concerned to start immediately after the ceasefire the implementation of Security Council Resolution 242 (1967) in all of its parts;

3. Decides that immediately and concurrently with the ceasefire, negotiations shall start between the parties concerned under appropriate auspices aimed at establishing a just and durable peace in the Middle East.

Just prior to the December 21, 1973 Geneva Peace Conference, the United States provided a letter of assurance to Israel that it would prevent any party from tampering with UN Security Council Resolution 242.

Although not expressly mentioned in either UNSC 242 or 338, there is no doubt that they were adopted under Chapter VI of the UN Charter, which authorizes the Security Council to make non-binding recommendations for the peaceful settlement of disputes. This is unlike the Security Council's powers to adopt binding resolutions and enforcement action under Chapter VII, to deal with threats to the peace, breaches of the peace, and acts of aggression. The six resolutions (UNSC 660, 661, 678, 686, 687, and 688) adopted against Iraq for its invasion of Kuwait, are examples of such Chapter VII resolutions.

Nevertheless, military analyst Edward N. Luttwak reminds us, in an essay that appeared in 1999 in *Foreign Affairs*, that "ceasefires and armistices have frequently been imposed under the aegis of the Security Council in order to halt fighting. But a ceasefire tends to arrest war-induced exhaustion and lets belligerents … rearm their forces. It intensifies and prolongs the struggle once the ceasefire ends—and it does usually end." This has proven to be the case at the imposed end of the 1948–49 Arab–Israel War, the 1956 Sinai-Suez War, the 1967 Six-Day War, the 1,000-Day War of Attrition of 1967 to 1970, the 2006 Second Lebanon War, the First Gaza War of 2008–09, the Second Gaza War of 2012, and the Third Gaza War of 2014.

64. Arab/Muslim countries practice bazaar diplomacy.

The rule in the bazaar is that if the vendor knows that you desire to purchase a piece of merchandize, he will raise its price. The Arabs sell words like "peace" and "security." They sign agreements including "peace treaties," and they trade with vague promises to stop terrorist acts. The Arabs demand tangible concessions such as territorial withdrawals, prisoner releases, and restrictions on access to holy places, demands for money, and arms, from eager Israeli governments seeking the intangibles mentioned above. In bazaar diplomacy, the side that first presents the terms and concessions is bound to lose. The other side builds his next set of demands using the opening offers of his opponent as the starting point. Normally in bazaar diplomacy if one bargains for a rug and the rug merchant turns down one's final offer, one is not obliged to make that into one's opening offer the next time around. However, in the world of Israeli-Arab negotiations in which Israeli concessions are routinely taken with no Arab reciprocity—no *quid pro* quo—the logic of the bazaar does not apply. Here Israel's last offer is automatically expected, indeed demanded, to be its first one whenever negotiations begin again. Furthermore, the Arab/Muslim side can and does raise non-negotiable demands as well as add additional demands that they had not previously raised.

All tangible Israeli concessions merely whet the appetite of their Arab/Muslim antagonists and raise their expectations. Israeli concessions are pocketed and then denounced as insufficient, certainly not warranting any reciprocal Arab moves. In the Arab-Israeli conflict, both sides are not discussing the same merchandise. The Israelis wish to acquire peace based on the Arab/Muslim acceptance of

Israel as a Jewish state. The objective of the Arab/Muslim side is to annihilate the Jewish state, replace it with an Arab state, and get rid of the Jews. It is essentially the strategy designed to dismantle Israel in stages. The Arab/Muslim side does not, has not, and never will accept the existence of a sovereign Jewish state in the Middle East.

In Middle Eastern bazaar diplomacy, agreements are kept not because they are signed but because they are imposed. Reciprocity in negotiations between Israel and the Arabs is impossible. It is simply foreign to the Arab world. This indicates that Arabs, unlike Jews and people in the West, lack the cultural ability to see or respect another's point of view and to moderate their demands accordingly.

An intrinsic part of negotiating is the practice of *sumud*—steadfastness. It is the practice to wait as long as it takes to wear down an opponent until they are ready to abandon the struggle. Under this practice, the Arabs/Muslims are prepared to wait decades, generations, even centuries to achieve their goals. A classic historic example is the Muslim attempts to rid the Middle East of the Christian Crusader states, which took 193 years. A more contemporary illustration of *sumud* is the ongoing process, beginning with Sadat's visit to Jerusalem in 1977, followed by Arafat's demands through the end of the twentieth century and continuing with the Saudi demands via their so-called peace plan of 2002. All three have the same goal, the return of all Arabs who claim to be Palestinian Arabs and the elimination of the Jewish State of Israel.

Western foreign policy and culture in general always is in a hurry seeking quick solutions to even complex problems. The West has been willing to settle for less in order to make a deal now. Over the years, Israel's leftist governments' political stand has been based on the principle that agreements must be reached with the Arabs at any price. To them the lack of agreements is unsustainable and considered a failure. Thus as future events proved, Israel believed somewhat naively, that the peace treaties and accords it signed would end generations of war. The Israeli left and its worldwide supporters regularly ignored not only the Palestinian leadership's declarations but also their intentions. More importantly, the left ignored the terrorism of the various Palestinian Arab groups, starting with the Al-Aqsa (Second) *Intifada* and continuing to this day.

The Israeli leftist governments were locked into a dogma which they believed "can't be wrong." In Israel, such rigid dogmas have come to be called *Ha'Conceptzia* ("the concept")*. The components of this "peace process" dogma included:

- The Israeli government was willing to give a great deal—including territory, political recognition, economic assistance and even military equipment to the Palestinians. The Israelis thought that the Palestinians would be content to accept all that and no more, and the conflict would finally be over.
- Israel thought it could have the Palestinians police themselves as well as protect the Israelis from terrorist attacks. Arafat would in effect, be their law enforcement agent, as well as governor of the autonomous region they would cede to him.
- The IDF would thus be freed of the hard and risky work of patrolling and policing the Palestinian majority areas of Judea, Samaria and the Gaza Strip.
- It was believed that as "peace" blossomed forth, both the Israelis and the Arabs would benefit from economic prosperity and a "new Middle East" would emerge.
- The Israeli public was expected to agree to territorial concessions that previous Israeli governments for 25 years had said would be suicidal.[70]

---

* A more infamous example of *Ha'Conceptzia* occurred in the months and days leading to the surprise Egyptian-Syrian attack on Israel at the start of the Yom Kippur War.

When the process began collapsing, almost immediately, the ever pernicious Israeli left felt that just sweetening the pot—a bit more territory, a piece of Jerusalem, and a second Palestinian "state"—would clinch the deal. In this assessment, the Israeli government was wrong—dead wrong. The pursuit of the illusion and false hope that is the "peace process" has cost over 1,610 Israeli fatalities (September 1993–November 2014), and thousands more wounded, crippled, maimed and psychologically scarred. The "peace process" devolved into a process of pieces—pieces of the bodies of murdered and maimed Israelis, as well as pieces of territory unilaterally relinquished by Israel to its Arab enemies for no tangible concrete concessions by the Arab side. Israel gave up Area A* in 1994, southern Lebanon in 2000 and the Gaza Strip in 2005. In return, it received suicide bombings, terror attacks, missile barrages, and continued vilification and demonization by its Arab/Muslim enemies.

The primary examples of this "peace at any price" policy came with the governments of Yitzhak Rabin and after his assassination on November 4, 1995, that of his successor Shimon Peres. It was the contention of Rabin and Peres, Israel's Labor Party prime ministers (1992–96), that the savage violence and the Oslo peace process were unrelated. Rabin and later Peres, seemingly cared little about the fact that buses, and a pizza parlor in Jerusalem as well as shopping malls in Tel Aviv all filled with their citizens were getting blown up day after day. Rabin callously dismissed their deaths as *korbanot shalom*—the "sacrifices for peace." Both men would intone, "The peace process will go on." As for Peres suffice it to recall the words of former US Secretary of State Henry Kissinger, one of the great practitioners of *realpolitik,* who remarked that Peres had "the trait of French academics who tend to believe that the formulation of an idea is equivalent to its realization."[71]

Thus, the murder of innocent men, women and children were some kind of down payment for friendship with the Palestinian Arabs, though the latter had no intention of any "peace" short of one that meant Israel's demise. Arrogantly, Rabin, Peres, Yosef Beilin and their supporters, gave no respect to anyone who gave voice to the obvious dangers inherent in this concept. After more than twenty years, the Oslo Accords, which launched the misnamed "peace process" was, in the words of Caroline B. Glick, "the largest, most destructive strategic error Israel has ever made."[72] As Benjamin Franklin pointedly remarked, "One of the greatest tragedies in life is the murder of a beautiful theory by a gang of brutal facts."

Since 1993, land conceded to the Palestinian Arabs has been transformed into a platform for terrorism and hate education, fueling the conflict. As has been said previously—and it bears repetition—the Arab/Muslim war against the sovereignty of the Jewish people in the Land of Israel has always been over the existence, and not the size, of the Jewish state. One recalls the words of Israel's seventh Prime Minister Yitzhak Shamir, "The sea is the same sea and the Arabs are the same Arabs,"[73] implying that just as the sea doesn't change, the Arabs would never accept Jewish sovereignty in the Land of Israel and make real peace with it.

However, the solution to this quandary is to walk away from the negotiating table without any agreement. Israel, like its Arab/Muslim enemies, must practice *sumud*—"steadfastness." It must avoid moral equivalence to a nonexistent "State of Palestine" and abandon the so-called "two-state solution." Israel must demonstrate the necessary strategic means and political will to do so. If Israel

---

* The Oslo Accords divided Judea and Samaria (aka the West Bank) into three areas: Area A, comprising some 18 percent of the territory, which was transferred to the Palestinian Authority—where it enjoys most governmental powers; Area B, making up 22 percent of the territory, which was divided between Israel and the Palestinians, with Israel retaining security control, and civil matters given over to the Palestinian Authority; and Area C, comprising some 60 percent of the territory—including all the settlement lands—which remained in Israeli hands.

adopted that posture and repeated it, the Arab side would realize that there would be no change unless they will genuinely compromise. Essential to Israeli "steadfastness" is the unwavering conviction of its cause including its well-documented and unique Biblical, historic and legal rights to the Land of Israel, including Jerusalem, Judea and Samaria as well as the Golan Heights.

The Third Gaza War of 2014 provided additional proof (as if it was needed) that the peace process and the "two-state" solution were dead—murdered by the hands of the PLO/Hamas and their Palestinian allies. Israel's Arab/Muslim enemies have used any respite, truce, or ceasefire to rearm, reequip and reinforce its forces for the next military round with the Jewish state. This was done from the First Gaza War through to the Third Gaza War. The latter revealed increased range for rockets fired from the Gaza Strip placing virtually all of Israel under the threat of rocket bombardment. Although the Iron Dome anti-missile system performed admirably, it is not a foolproof system. In the next round, such missiles fired from the Gaza Strip, Judea and Samaria and from Lebanon may well be equipped with global positioning system (GPS) technology. Thus, Israel must militarily crush Hamas totally. It must root out all the tunnels and prevent their reconstruction. Failure to do so will extract an even higher price in blood and treasure on Israel in the next round.

The Arabs/Muslims on the other hand know exactly what they want and are willing to wait for it. The Arab/Muslim side has not made a secret of the fact that what they meant by the word "peace" was nothing more than a temporary ceasefire or truce, a *hudna,* for a limited period. Therefore, it is most important for a nation to be prepared for war. It should never come to the negotiating table from a position of weakness. A country's adversary should always know that your nation is strong and ready for war even more than it is ready for peace. The Roman military strategist Publius Flavius Vegetius Renatus (ca. 390 C.E.) was one of the first of record to state: *Qui desiderat pacem, praeparet bellum* ("Let him who desires peace prepare for war"). Centuries later, President George Washington, in a speech to Congress, January 8, 1790, declared, "To be prepared for war is one of the most effectual means of preserving peace."

The on-going 140-year Arab/Muslim war against the Jewish people and their struggle to regain sovereignty in the Land of Israel is an irreconcilable conflict. The Arab/Muslim side does not want peace, it wants Israel to be wiped out, dead, eliminated, and erased from the map of history. The Jewish people of Israel want to preserve, protect and survive in their own nation. It is as simple as that. The conflict will end with only one winner and one loser. As a result of the conflict there will exist either exclusive Jewish sovereignty or exclusive Arab sovereignty between the Jordan River and the Mediterranean Sea. The side that will prevail is the side whose national will is the stronger and whose political vision is the sharper. In the final analysis, this is the harsh reality.

65. What the parties negotiated and promised in concluded agreements in English, French, German and other Western languages is inconsequential. What is stated publicly in Arabic or Farsi is what counts.

Several excellent illustrations of this principle involved Yasser Arafat. In a statement made to the Saudi Press Agency in Arabic, in January 1990, Arafat explained what his "peace" initiative toward Israel really meant. "The PLO offers not the peace of the weak, but the peace of Saladin."[74] As previously explained, Saladin was the great Kurdish/Muslim warrior who battled the Crusaders in the Second and Third Crusades. After his defeat by King Richard at the Battle of Arsuf, Saladin did not have the strength to continue to fight, so he concluded the Treaty of Ramla. However, Saladin's "peace" treaty was in reality, nothing more than "an armed truce" rather than true peace in the Western sense.

In fact, Saladin was using Muhammad's model, the Treaty of Hudaybiyyah (*see* "Timeline of Islam, Muslim Conquests and Setbacks" table). It was during this armed truce that Saladin built up his forces while disunity swept the Crusader camp and King Richard returned to Europe. When ready Saladin attacked with ferocity and drove the Crusaders from almost the entire Holy Land. This then was the type of "peace" Arafat offered Israel. It should be noted in modern context, that the Arab/Muslim world has long regarded Israel as a modern "Crusader state" imposed by the West on the Arab/Muslim Middle East.

One of the most demonstrative examples of this practice occurred at the time of the signing of the Israeli–PLO Declaration of Principles, also known as the Oslo Accords on September 13, 1993. The documents signed on the White House lawn by Israeli Prime Minister Yitzhak Rabin and PLO Chairman Yasser Arafat and witnessed by US President Bill Clinton, gave the impression that the world was witnessing the beginning of the end of the Israeli–Palestinian conflict. Indeed, English-language media (along with their other Western language counterparts) reported quoting from the English version of the Accords:

> [Israel and the PLO] agree that it is time to put an end to decades of confrontation and conflict, recognize their mutual legitimate and political rights, and strive to live in peaceful coexistence and mutual dignity and security and achieve a just, lasting and comprehensive peace settlement and historic reconciliation through the agreed political process.[75]

However, the very next day Arafat revealed his real intentions to the Palestinian people and the remainder of the Arab world—in Arabic:

> Since we cannot defeat Israel in war, we do this in stages. We take any and every territory that we can of Palestine, and establish sovereignty there, and we use it as a springboard to take more. When the time comes, we can get the Arab nations to join us for the final blow against Israel.[76]

Upon his return from Washington, Arafat was at first booed and hissed. When the sounds died down, he uttered the single word "Hudaybiyyah" and the people understood right away the real intent, that it was a treaty meant to be broken.[77] Furthermore, he proclaimed on television, "jihad, jihad, jihad, jihad" as the only way to gain control of all of Israel. The video clip of Arafat's pronouncement can be seen in the recent films: *Obsession: Radical Islam's War against the West* and *Farewell Israel.*

Even non-Arab but Islamic Iran, in its November 24, 2013 Geneva interim agreement with Western powers over its nuclear program referred to and invoked the meaning of the Treaty of Hudaybiyyah. After concluding the agreement with the P5+1 powers (the US, UK, France, Russia, China and Germany) Iran declared that the agreement signed was only a modern version of that treaty, a fact understood in its Islamic and historic context, made perfectly clear to all the nations in the Middle East, even if the Western powers did not grasp its significance. Mohammad Sadeq Al-Hosseini, formerly a political advisor to Iranian President Mohammad Khatami and now a TV commentator, speaking in Farsi on Syrian News TV on December 11, 2013 declared:

> We are engaged in a fierce war with the Americans on all levels. This is the Treaty of Hudaybiyyah in Geneva, and it will be followed by a conquest of Mecca. Saudi Arabia

is on its way to perdition. Its role is over. Why? Because the Iranians have reached the Mediterranean Sea. You've begun to analyze the political situation correctly. There is a change. The day Greece reached the Mediterranean coast, Persia fell to Alexander the Great for 300 years. Today, now that the Iranians are reaching the Mediterranean coast at Tyre, we are looking at 300 years of defeat for the Americans and the Westerners.[78]

Palestinian leaders including Yasser Arafat, Mahmoud Abbas and others spoke with a forked tongue. To the foreign media and Diaspora Jews they conveyed nice platitudes and words in English, French, German, and other Western languages, which were never expressed in Arabic to their constituents. To their people in Arabic, they continued to incite hatred against Israel, sanctified suicide bombers as national heroes and condemned Israel for defending itself against terrorists. They vowed they would continue the conflict until they achieved victory, meaning the total elimination of the Jewish State of Israel.

A more recent example of the difference between what is said or written in Arabic and what is broadcast to the Western world in English and other non-Arabic languages was seen in the Investigative Project on Terrorism discovery that the English version of the Muslim Brotherhood's official website no longer included its bylaws[79] and for good reason. One of these bylaws is "the need to work on establishing the Islamic State, which seeks to effectively implement the provisions of Islam and its teachings" and "defend the [Islamic] nation against its internal enemies." Another one is to "insist to liberate the Islamic nation from the yoke of foreign rule, help safeguard the rights of Muslims everywhere and unite Muslims around the world."[80] Yet another bylaw reads:

The sincere support for a global cooperation in accordance with the provisions of the Islamic shari'a, which would safeguard the personal rights, freedom of speech for active and constructive participation towards building a new basis of human civilization as is ensured by the overall teachings of Islam[81]

There are other significant differences between the Arabic and English websites as well. The home page of the English site (http://www.ikhwanweb.com/) mentions "freedom." The home page of the Arabic site (http://www.ikhwanonline.com/new/Default.aspx) has the official Muslim Brotherhood logo of two crossed swords and a Qur'an and an Arabic word that means, "Make ready." Christine Brim writes that this phrase is taken from Qur'an 8:60 that states, "Make ready for an encounter against them, all the forces and well-readied horses you can muster, that you may overawe the enemies of Allah and your own enemies and others besides them of whom you are unaware but of whom Allah is aware."[82]

66. There is an Arab proverb that states, "There is no tax on words." It succinctly expresses the negotiating style of the Arab/Muslim Middle East.

Woven into this style of negotiation is the Arab/Muslim concept of *taqiyya* and the Arab/Muslim tactic of *darura* ("necessity"). Necessity can justify even violating explicit prohibitions in Islam, as long as they are done to protect the faith. According to shari'a, deception is not only permitted in certain situations but is sometimes deemed obligatory. Many Islamic jurists have decreed that, according to Qur'an 4:29, Muslims are obligated to lie. Lying for the purpose of jihad is not only allowed, but an obligation to be proud of and even serves as a reason to blame the enemies of Islam for one's lies. Shari'a law states, "Lying is obligatory if the purpose is obligatory." The primary verse in the Qur'an sanctioning *taqiyya* vis-à-vis non-Muslims states:

> Let believers [Muslims] not take for friends and allies infidels [non-Muslims] instead of believers. Whoever does this shall have no relationship left with Allah—unless you but guard yourselves against them, taking precautions."[83]

There is widespread consensus among the *ulama* that the word *taqiyya* means lying and deception. According to Imam Tabari, whose multi-volume exegesis is a standard reference work in the Islamic world, 3:28 means, "If you [Muslims] are under their [infidels'] authority, fearing for yourselves, behave loyally to them, with your tongue, while harboring inner animosity for them." Regarding 3:28, Ibn Kathir recommends the advice of Muhammad's companion, "Let us smile to the face of some people while our hearts curse them." Any Muslim who closely observes shari'a law will always have a divinely sanctioned right to deceive, until "all chaos ceases, and all religion belongs to Allah" (Qur'an 8:39). All Muslim overtures for peace, dialogue, or even temporary truces must be seen in this light. Thus, negotiations are a method to win time. Time needed to prepare for the next round of war, time to prepare for the next terrorist onslaught. Complicating the situation is an absolute diplomatic need to maintain what pretends to be actions and policies aimed to advance negotiations, even when because of political conditions in the Arab/Muslim world there are no immediate prospects for successful negotiations.

Under Islam, lying is forbidden—but permissible to empower Islam; intentionally killing women and children is forbidden—but permissible during the jihad; sodomy is forbidden—but was used to facilitate the attempted destruction of an aircraft by the "underwear bomber; suicide is forbidden—but permissible during the jihad, called "martyrdom." Even the traditional requirements of the Five Pillars of Islam—including prayer and fasting—may be ignored during the jihad. Hence, one may lie, lie even about Islam itself, negotiate with infidels, deal with foreign women as equals (e.g. Secretaries of State Condoleezza Rice, Madeleine Albright, Hillary Clinton and Speaker of the House Nancy Pelosi), and even eat pork, all to gain the goal sought. It is the Middle Eastern version of the seventeenth century proverb, "the end justifies the means."

As has been previously mentioned, the Treaty of Hudaybiyyah concluded by Muhammad's state of Medina and the Quraysh tribe of Mecca in March 628 C.E. was the role model for all subsequent Arab/ Muslim negotiations. Muhammad needed time to build his forces for an assault on Mecca. Signing a treaty was the means to that end. In this treaty, Muhammad promised a ten-year ceasefire with the Meccans. Less than two years later, seizing on the pretext of the murder of a Muslim by an ally of the Quraysh in 630, and having in the interim gained superior strength, Muhammad's forces conquered Mecca without resistance and seized all the territory of the Quraysh. This episode has been cited by Yasser Arafat among others, as the model for later Arab/Islamic "peace agreements" with non-Islamic countries. Muhammad permitted deceit in three situations: to reconcile two or more quarreling parties, husband to wife and vice-versa, and in war.[84] The concept of *taqiyya* runs throughout Islamic history. The relevant question for the modern period immediately arises. If Muslims are permitted to lie and feign loyalty, agreeableness, even friendliness to the infidel, simply to further their war efforts—what does one make of any Muslim overtures of peace, tolerance, or dialogue? In the modern period, the list of agreements made and then broken by Arabs/Muslims to further their position included the following. They are some examples of *taqiyya* by word.

The 1949 Arab-Israeli armistice agreements included provisions for a cessation of hostilities and guaranteed free access to all holy places. Both provisions were repeatedly violated. During the Sinai-Suez War, a ceasefire was called by the Governor of Port Sa'id, Egypt in face of advancing Anglo-French forces. Within hours, it was repudiated and the Governor urged the Egyptians to fight the British and French troops.

A memorandum of understanding between Egyptian President Gamal Abdel Nasser and UN Secretary-General Dag Hammarskjold concluded at the end of the Sinai-Suez War, guaranteed free passage for Israeli shipping through the Straits of Tiran and provided guidelines as to how the United Nations Emergency Force (UNEF) would be removed in the future. That memorandum was subsequently "lost" and broken by Egypt.

From mid-1972 until the outbreak of the Yom Kippur War in early October 1973, the Egyptians spread rumors via media and other outlets, of the inadequate maintenance of and lack of spare parts for their anti-aircraft missiles and other weapons systems, while in reality they added new weapons systems to their arsenal in preparation for the forthcoming war they intended to launch. The Israel–Egypt Disengagement Agreement of 1974, limited artillery batteries to be had by both sides and allowed Israeli cargo through the Suez Canal. Egypt broke the agreement and violated both provisions but in the meanwhile Israeli forces withdrew from territory coveted by Egypt (*see* "Disengagement, 1974" map).

The Algiers Agreement between Iraq and Iran (under the Shah) signed March 6, 1975, ended their boundary dispute over the Shatt Al-Arab (known as Arvand Rud in Iran) and Iranian support for the Kurds. Five years later on September 17, 1980, Iraq abrogated the Algiers Agreement. Iraq declared the Shatt al-Arab to be a national river, completely under its sovereignty, and made it mandatory for all ships using the waterway for navigational purposes to fly only the Iraqi flag and follow Iraqi regulations. Five days later, Iraq attacked Iran beginning a bloody eight-year-long war.

During the early phases of the Iranian Revolution 1978–79, Ayatollah Ruhollah Khomeini used the deception technique of *taqiyya*—tricking an enemy into a misjudgment of one's true position. Khomeini waged a successful deception campaign from his place of exile at Neauphle-le-Chateau, just outside of Paris, France. Khomeini duped Western governments (including US President Jimmy Carter), Western intelligentsia, and the unknowing Western mainstream media. He completely hid his true intentions of what he planned to do once he would become the ruler of Iran. Khomeini kept silent about his radical views on social and legal issues. He promised the new regime would not change Iran's social structure, would maintain equal rights for women, freedom of the press, as well as not threaten oil supplies. However, he qualified his statements with phrases such as "in accordance with Islam" or "on the basis of the Qur'an."[85] Khomeini did not publicly discuss his plan to establish theocratic rule and the *velayat-e-faghih* (the rule of the head jurisprudent). The use of the term "Islamic government" was deliberately avoided. "Islamic Republic" was substituted instead in all his pronouncements. Khomeini's virulent religiously motivated misojudaism was concealed from the West. In a like manner, no mention was made of his long-standing enmity against the United States, though through the means of hundreds of thousands of underground cassettes, pamphlets and speeches the United States was constantly depicted as the "Great Satan." By the end of 1978, Khomeini came to be seen and was portrayed as a saintly old man who was determined to establish a far more just, democratic and spiritual regime than the monarchy run by the harsh, corrupt, and authoritarian Shah Mohammad Reza Pahlavi. As Khomeini later told Abol Hassan Bani-Sadr, "In Paris, I found it expedient to say certain things. In Iran, I find it expedient to refute what I said, and I do so unreservedly."[86]

Like Fidel Castro* before him, once in power in Tehran Khomeini revealed his true colors and agenda. Revolutionary courts were set up which arbitrarily arrested and executed anyone suspected of opposing the new government. A bloodbath followed as hundreds were sent before firing squads. The use of torture was resumed. Khomeini established a theocratic Islamic government—*velayat-e-faghih* (the rule of the head jurisprudent) that made him the supreme leader and source of authority in Iran.

The 1991 United Nations Mission for the Referendum in Western Sahara (MINURSO) was established as part of a settlement, which had paved the way for a ceasefire in the conflict between Morocco and the Polisario Front (as the representative of the people of the Sahrawi Arab Democratic Republic), over the contested territory of Western Sahara, the former Spanish Sahara. A referendum was to be held to determine the future of the territory. No referendum first scheduled for 1992, has been held to date due to Moroccan objections.

The Oslo Accords of August 20, 1993, signed between Israel and the PLO called for an end to terrorist attacks against Israel as well as removal of the clauses in the PLO Charter explicitly calling for Israel's destruction. These provisions were never honored by the PLO. On May 10, 1994, PLO chairman Yasser Arafat gave what he thought was an off-the-record talk at a mosque while visiting Johannesburg, South Africa. However, a South African journalist, Bruce Whitfield of 702 Talk Radio, secretly taped Arafat's remarks. Arafat cryptically alluded to his agreement with Israel. Criticized by Arabs and Muslims for having made concessions to Israel, he defended his actions by comparing them to those of the Islamic prophet Muhammad in a similar circumstance, "I see this agreement as being no more than the agreement signed between our Prophet Muhammad and the Quraysh in Mecca."[87] He further noted that although Muhammad had been criticized for this diplomacy by one of his leading companions (and the future second caliph) Umar bin al-Khattab, the prophet had been right to insist on the agreement, for it helped him defeat the Quraysh and take over their city of Mecca. In a similar manner Arafat proclaimed, "We now accept the peace agreement [with Israel], but [only in order] to continue on the road to Jerusalem."[88] In subsequent agreements with the Israelis, Arafat frequently mentioned this as a model for his own diplomacy.

The Hebron Protocol of January 17, 1997, between Israel and the PLO/PA, again called for a cessation of terrorism against Israel. Again that did not occur. The Wye River Memorandum of October 1998, once more called for the implementation of the two previous agreements including an end to terrorist attacks on Israel. Yet again, the PLO refused to honor the agreements it signed. As the twenty-first century began, *taqiyya* was also used in a verbal and written form, with great effect.

The word "Islamophobia" is used liberally as a means to paralyze and stifle all discussion concerning Islamic supremacism. While many Western media outlets are quick to condemn "Islamophobia" they stress but one of its meanings—prejudice against Islam. However, these media outlets suffer from the literal meaning of "Islamophobia" — fear of Islam — because of the violent nature of Islamist supremacism. Through self-censorship, the Western media refuses to identify an Islamist supremacist who may have committed a terrorist act, when it is evident that the act was perpetrated according to the precepts of jihad and Islamic supremacism. Thus, in the United States

---

* In waging the Cuban Revolution from 1956 to 1959, Fidel Castro was portrayed by the duped Western intelligentsia and main stream media as a freedom fighter for social justice, the "Robin Hood of the Sierra Maestra," a "man of the people" fighting the evil tyrant, Fulgencio Batista, who tortured the oppressed. However, once in power his real philosophy and agenda emerged: a Marxist-Leninist (communist) government and society, land redistribution, press censorship, and vehement anti-Americanism. This, while "peoples' courts" imprisoned "counter-revolutionaries," and the firing squads eliminated all political opposition, real or imagined.

for example, the Islamic supremacists have largely trumped the First Amendment's freedom of speech and freedom of the press.

One must recall the words of President John F. Kennedy, who emphasized, "Peace does not exist in signed documents and treaties alone, but in the hearts and minds of the people." Whereas the Israelis have long been desirous of peace, the Arab/Muslim side has sought the elimination of Israel directly or indirectly, immediately or by the Phased Plan or strategy of stages, by military means, terrorism or by negotiations.

It is necessary at this point to explain the Phased Plan or strategy of stages as practiced by the Arab/Muslim side in its ongoing war with the Jewish people in the Land of Israel. This tactic is no less than the return to the *status quo ante*. Each time the Arab/Muslim side engages in war as the "solution" to Israel's presence in the Middle East and loses, it seeks to roll the clock back to the previous offer (*see* "Basic Principle 33" on limited liability war). Currently the demand is for Israel to unilaterally retreat to the June 4, 1967 lines—what properly are called, the 1949 Armistice lines—it held prior to the outbreak of the Six-Day War. This strategy of stages was first enunciated by Tunisian President Habib Bourguiba on April 22, 1965—two years before the Six-Day War. At that time, he proposed that as a "solution" to the Arab–Israel conflict, Israel should withdraw to the 1947 UN Partition Plan lines (which would reduce Israel to three non-contiguous pieces of land connected only by a point on a map) and allow the return of all Arab refugees from the 1947–49 conflict. In fact, the return of all Arabs claiming to be refugees or their descendents to what is today Israel, has become a *sine qua non* Arab demand. It is something that Israel cannot accept and is recognized as an Arab tactic to destroy Israel demographically as well as from a security standpoint.

A *New York Times* editorial drove home the danger to Israel just weeks before the Six-Day War by declaring, "No nation, regardless of past rights and wrongs, could contemplate taking in a fifth-column of such a size. Moreover, fifth column it would be—people nurtured for 20 years [by 1967] in hatred of and totally dedicated to its destruction. The readmission of the refugees would be the equivalent to the admission to the United States of nearly 70,000,000 sworn enemies of the nation."[89] What was stated in 1967 is still true today. The hatred for Israel and the goal of its destruction is greater and more widespread today than at that time.

The Phased Plan or strategy of stages has continued since Bourguiba's proposal in 1965. The PLO formally adopted the Phased Plan on June 8, 1974, at the Twelfth Session of the Palestine National Council, which met in Cairo, Egypt (*see* Appendix 9). Sadat, Arafat, Abbas, and Saudi King Fahd among others, all have practiced a variation of this same strategy. Arab spokesmen throughout the decades have reemphasized the strategy of stages. For example on March 14, 1977, Farouk Kaddoumi, then head of the PLO Political Department in an interview with *Newsweek,* stated:

> We have to be flexible, in order to establish peace in this part of the world. So we have to accept, in this stage, that we have this [Palestinian] State on only part of our territory. But this doesn't mean that we are going to give up the rest of our rights. There are two [initial] phases to our return. The first phase to the 1967 lines, and the second to the 1948 lines … the third stage is the democratic state of Palestine. So we are fighting for these three stages.

In a like manner, Radio Damascus commented on February 15, 1977:

Let us assume just for a moment that, at Geneva, the PLO will achieve the right to create a Palestinian national entity on the West Bank and in the Gaza Strip. Israel knows full well that such a mini-state would not have a written constitution and would, therefore, not consider itself committed to any international boundaries. What this means is that the first article of the unwritten Palestinian constitution will be a call for a struggle to return the Palestinian territories on which Israel rests ... Rosh Hanikra ... Beit She'an ... Haifa and Jaffa on the coastal plain—that is, all of Palestine, from Galilee to the Negev Desert, and from the Jordan [River] to the Mediterranean.

The theme of stages—at first a small second Palestinian state, but step-by-step an ever increasing larger state—was emphasized by Salah Khalaf also known as Abu Iyad, second in command to PLO Chairman Yasser Arafat, who declared:

At first a small state; and with the help of Allah, it will be made large and expand to the east, west, north and south. I am interested in the liberation of Palestine, step by step.[90]

In April 2008, the PLO/Arab Phased Plan or strategy of stages was reemphasized by the PA representative in Lebanon, Abbas Zaki. Zaki, also known as Sharif Mash'al, was a former head of Fatah operations, stated in an interview with NBN TV:

The PLO is the sole legitimate representative [of the Palestinian people], and it has not changed its platform even one iota. The PLO proceeds through phases, without changing its strategy. Let me tell you, when the ideology of Israel collapses, and we take, at last, Jerusalem, the Israeli ideology will collapse in its entirety, and we will begin to progress with our own ideology, Allah willing, and drive them out of all of Palestine.[91]

Only four months later, in August 2008, the stages strategy was stressed yet again by Fatah MP Najat Abu-Bakr who said in a PA TV interview, that Fatah's goal remained the destruction of Israel, but that their political plan was to focus on Judea and Samaria as well as the Gaza Strip. Abu-Bakr declared, "It doesn't mean that we don't want the 1948 borders [all of Israel] ... but our current political program is to say that we want the 1967 borders."[92]

Methodically, Israel's enemies press on with the Phased plan or strategy of stages. On September 23, 2011, in an interview with *Al-Jazeera*, Abbas Zaki, by then a senior member of the Fatah Central Committee, candidly admitted the long-standing policy of stages in the final obliteration of Israel. Any interim agreement should be

based on the borders of June 4 [1967]. While the agreement is on the borders of June 4, [1967] the President [Mahmoud Abbas] understands, we understand, and everyone knows that it is impossible to realize the inspiring idea, or the great goal in one stroke. [The great and ultimate goal was always and continues to be the elimination of the State of Israel altogether. This was an outright statement to that effect.] If Israel withdraws from Jerusalem, if Israel uproots the settlements, 650,000 settlers, if Israel removes the [security] fence - what will become of Israel? Israel will come to an end. If I say that I want to remove it from existence, this will be great, great, [but] it is hard. This is not a [stated] policy. You can't say it to the world. You can say it to yourself.[93]

67. There is also *taqiyya* or *kitman*—deception applied to Arab/Muslim deeds. One of Muhammad's companions, Abu Jabir Abdullah related, "Muhammad said, 'War is deceit.'"[94]

The earliest historical records of Islam clearly confirm the prevalence of *taqiyya* as a form of Islamic warfare. The Muslim view that war is deceit has its origin in the Battle of the Trench—*khandaq* (trench or ditch). This fight is also known as the Siege of Medina, which took place from March 31 to April 26, 627 C.E.[95] This major event in the history of Islam, is related in the Qur'an (33:9–20). Arab and Jewish tribes numbering some 10,000 warriors and 600 cavalrymen, besieged Muhammad and some 3,000 of his Muslim followers in Yathrib (now Medina).[96]

According to historian Ibn Ishaq, Muhammad received a visit from Nuaym ibn Masud, an Arab leader of the Al-Ahzab tribe, who had secretly converted to Islam. Muhammad asked him to end the siege by creating discord   the use of *taqiyya*—amongst the forces aligned against the Muslims and convince them to abandon the siege. It was then that Muhammad memorably declared, "For war is deceit." Nuaym successfully sowed suspicion and fears of betrayal among the various forces aligned against Muhammad, until, thoroughly distrusting each other, they disbanded, lifted the siege from the Muslims, and saved Islam from destruction. The Battle of the Trench was the crowning victory of Islam over superior forces, which ultimately led to the taking of Mecca, then of all Arabia. Some modern examples of *taqiyya* by deed follow.

During the First Lebanese Civil War (1958), United Nations Secretary-General Dag Hammarskjold visited that nation in mid-June to ascertain firsthand, if the United Arab Republic (UAR) was intervening in the civil war and aiding the rebels seeking to overthrow the legitimate government of President Camille Chamoun. As part of his inspection, Hammarskjold was taken to the *Basta*, the Muslim section of Beirut, the capital. The *Basta* was already in the hands of the rebels and the UAR flag flew over that section of the city. However, for Hammarskjold's visit all UAR flags were removed and replaced everywhere with Lebanon's red, white and cedar tree banner. As soon as he left, UAR flags were once again hoisted. "Volunteers" from the UAR, arms, war materials, and financing continued to flow to the rebel side unopposed. Only US military intervention in July 1958 saved Lebanon from being forcibly made part of the UAR.

As previously mentioned, on July 18, 1972, Egyptian President Anwar el-Sadat publicly expelled the over 21,000 Soviet military advisers based in Egypt. The authoritative International Institute for Strategic Studies subsequently revealed that only 3,000 advisers had actually left. This was part of Sadat's grand deception in preparation for war with Israel planned for the next year. The Israelis felt that the expulsion of the Soviet military advisers significantly reduced the effectiveness of the Egyptian army. In reality, while some Soviet personnel had left Egypt because their training mission was complete, others left while new advisors took their place. It was more a military rotation of duty than an expulsion. Others were transferred to Syria as part of a three-way arrangement among the Soviet Union, Egypt, and Syria. Sadat would confirm that the "expulsion" was *taqiyya*. In an interview with the Lebanese newspaper, *Al Usbu' Al'-Arabi*, on October 7, 1974, he said:

Another part of the strategy of the deception, was the report leaked out to the West and Israel. The report said that the missiles and complicated technological weapons in the Egyptian Army had become useless with the departure of the Soviet experts. The report was backed up by detailed statements. It was so 'well served' that the West and Israel believed it. They slept peacefully, believing that we were finished technologically and that the remaining equipment in our possession was without any value or effect.

On October 24, 1975, during an interview on Egypt's Voice of the Arabs, Sadat reemphasized that the "expulsion" of the Soviet experts was "a strategic cover ... a splendid strategic distraction for our going to war." Sadat treated the Soviet "expulsion" as part of a wider Egyptian disinformation campaign.

Egypt staged massive war games on the west side of the Suez Canal in mid-May 1973. Troops were positioned, and ramps were constructed down to the water's edge—all part of the preparations for offensive war against Israel on the opposite bank of the canal. The Israelis counter-mobilized and that cost Israel $14 million. Then, Egypt stopped its preparations and seemingly reduced the number of its forces and preparations, but not in reality. Had the Israelis not counter-mobilized, what came to be known, as the Yom Kippur War would have probably erupted in the late spring rather than the early autumn. In any event, Egypt applied the same tactics in early October. On October 1, 1973, Egypt launched an extensive military exercise, *Tahrir 41,* which served as the cover for the war. Towards the culmination of this exercise the war started, code-named, *Granite 2.* This time the Israelis assumed it was just another series of war games. Israel did not want to disrupt its economy, spend the money and counter-mobilize its citizen army. Israel did nothing until it was too late and the Yom Kippur War erupted in the early afternoon of October 6, 1973, catching Israel by surprise. Egypt's Sadat was hailed throughout the Arab world as "the Master of *taqiyya*—the Master of Deception."

Deception of the enemy during war is only common sense. However, the crucial difference in Islam is that war against the infidel is a perpetual affair—in the words of the Qur'an—"until there is no more oppression and all worship is devoted to God [Allah] alone" (8:39).

On October 6, 1981, Egyptian President Anwar el-Sadat was reviewing a military parade celebrating the Egyptian successes in the Yom Kippur War. Part of the military procession was in fact, an Egyptian Islamic Jihad assassination team, which had infiltrated the Egyptian army. They caught Egyptian security by surprise and were able to kill the Egyptian leader. Sadat, the "Master of Deception," became a victim of deception.

Most recently, Al-Qaeda 9/11 conspirator, Zacarias Moussaoui rationalized his conspiratorial role in his defendant response by evoking Muhammad's assertion that "war is deceit." Asked by his lawyer why he lied, Moussaoui replied, "Because I am Al-Qaeda. The Prophet says, 'war is deceit.'" Moussaoui later told prosecutor Robert Spencer, "You're allowed to lie [*taqiyya*] for jihad. You're allowed any technique to defeat your enemy."[97]

68. In the Islamic Middle East the rational desire for peace is often perceived as weakness—a despised trait in that culture.

In their yearning for true peace, the Israelis have made territorial and other tangible concessions. Such concessions have not brought peace. In Arab/Muslim eyes, these concessions are signs of weakness. In their pursuit of peace, the Israelis have constantly demanded recognition of Israel as a

Jewish state in the Middle East, by the Arab world. However, in the case of recognition of Israel as a Jewish state, there can never be *sulha*. This has been repeated in a late 2007 interview following the Annapolis Conference, by PLO/PA Prime Minister Salam Fayad, who told *Al-Arabiya* TV that, "Israel can call itself whatever it wants, but the Palestinians will not recognize it as a Jewish state." As recently as January 19, 2014, so-called "moderate" PLO/PA Chairman Mahmoud Abbas again repeated, "Palestine can never recognize Israel as a Jewish state."[98]

Many nations have laws and practices that recognize their majority group's history, language or religion while also protecting the rights of minorities. Israeli law respects the voting, property, religious and other rights of its Arab citizens, most of them Muslims. The Druze and the Circassians can serve as an example of the successful integration of a minority group into Israeli society, mainly by virtue of their service in the IDF. With little assistance from the Israeli government, many of Israel's Christian citizens are gradually finding their way into Israeli society. Therefore, the question immediately arises: What is wrong with demanding Arab/Islamic recognition of Israel as a Jewish state? Nineteen Arab states proclaim Islam as the religion of the state, and fourteen declare their Arab ethnic identity. Arab constitutions reflect this status.

ARAB CONSTITUTIONS
(Excerpts)[99]

- ALGERIA–November 19, 1976
   Preamble: "Algeria, being a land of Islam, ... an Arab land."
   Article 2: "Islam is the religion of the state."

- BAHRAIN–February 14, 2002
   Article 1: "The Kingdom of Bahrain is a fully sovereign, independent Islamic Arab State."

- EGYPT–January 16, 2014
   Article 1, "The Arab Republic of Egypt is a sovereign state. [The Egyptian people are] part of the Arab nation and [works for] its integrity and unity. [Egypt] is part of the Muslim world."
   Article 2: "Islam is the religion of the state and Arabic its official language. Principles of Islamic Shari'a are the principal source of legislation."

- IRAQ–October 15, 2005
   Article 2: "Islam is the official religion of the State and it is a fundamental source of legislation."

- JORDAN–January 1, 1952
   Article 1: "The Hashemite Kingdom of Jordan is an independent sovereign Arab State."
   Article 2: "Islam is the religion of the state."

- KUWAIT–November 11, 1962
   Article 1: "Kuwait is an Arab State."
   Article 2: "The religion of the state is Islam and the Islamic shari'a shall be a main source of legislation."

- LEBANON–May 23, 1926
  Preamble: "b. Lebanon is Arab in its identity and in its association."

- LIBYA–National Transitional Council (draft constitution), August 2011
  Article 1: "Islam is the Religion of the State and the principal source of legislation is Islamic Jurisprudence [shari'a]."

The General National Congress (GNC) voted unanimously, December 4, 2013, that Islamic law would be the source of legislation in Libya. "Sharia is the source of legislation in Libya while all other provisions that violate it are void." All state institutions are obligated to abide by the decision.

The previous const6itution of December 11, 1969 (Provisional) declared:
  Article 1: "Libya is an Arab, democratic, and free republic."
  Article 2: "Islam is the religion of the state."

- MAURITANIA–July 12, 1991
  Article 5: "Islam shall be the religion of the people and of the State."

- MOROCCO–July 1, 2011[100]
  Preamble: "Morocco is part of the Arab-Islamic *Ummah*."
  Article 3: "Islam is the religion of the state."

- OMAN–November 6, 1996
  Article 1: "The Sultanate of Oman is an independent, Arab, Islamic, fully sovereign state."

- QATAR–April 29, 2003
  Article 1: "Qatar is an independent sovereign Arab State. Its religion is Islam and Shari'a law shall be a main source of its legislations."

- SAHRAWI ARAB DEMOCRATIC REPUBLIC–August 26–September 4, 1999
  Its very name proclaims that it is an Arab state.
  Article 2:"Islam is the state religion and source of law."
  Article 3: "The national and official language is Arabic."

- SAUDI ARABIA–March 2, 1992
  Article 1: The Kingdom of Saudi Arabia is a sovereign Arab Islamic state with Islam as its religion; God's Book [the Qur'an] and the Sunnah of His Prophet ... are its constitution."

- SOMALIA–July 20, 1961
  Article 3: "Islam shall be the state religion."

- SUDAN–July 1, 1998
  Article 1: "Islam is the religion of the majority."

- SYRIA–March 13, 1973

Article 1: "The Syrian Arab Republic is ... part of the Arab homeland ... part of the Arab nation."

Article 3: "Islamic jurisprudence is a chief source for legislation."

- TUNISIA–January 27, 2014

    Article 1: "Tunisia is a free, independent, sovereign state; its religion is Islam, its language Arabic, and its system the Republic. This article cannot be amended."

    Article 5: "The Republic of Tunisia is a part of the Arab Maghreb and works towards achieving its unity and takes all measures to ensure its realization."

    Article 73: "Running for the position of President of the Republic shall be a right entitled to every male and female voter who holds Tunisian nationality since birth, whose religion is Islam."

- UNITED ARAB EMIRATES–Provisional Constitution of July 18, 1971, made permanent in May 1996 [101]

    Article 7: "Islam is the official religion of the Union. The Islamic Shari'a shall be a main source of legislation in the Union."

    Article 110: "Union [Federal] laws shall be promulgated in accordance with the provisions of this Article and other appropriate provisions of the Constitution," renders unconstitutional any UAE law that does not take Shari'a as its source because such legislation violates the aforementioned Article 7.

- YEMEN–May 16, 1991

    Article 1: "The Yemeni People is a part of the Arab nation and the Islamic world."

    Article 2: "Islam is the religion of the state and Arabic is its official language."

    Article 3: "Islamic jurisprudence is the main source of legislation."

- Even the Constitution of the nonexistent State of Palestine, third draft, states:

    Article 5: "Arabic and Islam are the official Palestinian language and religion."[102]

Beyond the Arab states, if both the Islamic Republic of Iran and the Islamic Republic of Pakistan have those two official names and insist they be addressed and recognized as such, is there no room for a Jewish state of Israel? If you define Jewish in purely religious terms, that would mean that any state that defines itself as Islamic is, by definition, equally guilty of this discrimination. If you define Jewish in ethnic or national terms, then any state that defines itself as Arab would be equally guilty of the racism that Israel has been accused of by its enemies. There should be no double standard here. As Israeli Prime Minister Benjamin Netanyahu stated in his welcoming remarks to visiting Canadian Prime Minister Stephen Harper during a visit on January 21, 2014, "If the Palestinians expect me and my people to recognize a nation state for the Palestinian people, surely we can expect them to recognize a nation state for the Jewish people. After all, we've only been here four millennia."[103]

Not only are there the ongoing attempts to deny the Jewish nature of Israel, but the enemies of Israel, both foreign and domestic, even demand that the Jewish state remove the Star of David from its flag because it is a religious symbol. Yet, no less than sixteen Muslim nations carry the crescent moon and star, the religious symbol of Islam on their banners, including Algeria, Azerbaijan, Comoros, Egypt (1923–58), Libya (1951–69 and readopted in 2011), Malaysia, Maldives, Mauritania, Pakistan, the Sahara Arab Democratic Republic (Western Sahara), Singapore, Tunisia, Turkey, Turkish Republic of Northern Cyprus, Turkmenistan, and Uzbekistan. Saudi Arabia's flag bears the *shahada*, the Muslim affirmation of faith.[104]

Furthermore, the PLO/PA, Hamas and other enemies of Israel, desperate to denigrate the Jewish state at every turn, have additionally attacked the Israeli national flag. They claim that the two blue stripes on the Israeli flag represent the "Nile" and the "Euphrates," and that Israel's goal is to take over all the territory between those two rivers. This was most recently restated by Hamas leader Mahmoud Zahar who demanded from Gaza, that Israel must change its flag. "Israel must remove the two blue stripes from its national flag," said Zahar. "The stripes on the flag are symbols of occupation. They signify Israel's borders stretching from the River Euphrates to the River Nile."[105] This ludicrous and preposterous claim has been echoed across the Muslim world. This defamation has been debunked by both Zionist and anti-Zionist authors.[106] In reality, the Israeli flag—the Jewish flag—actually pre-dated the modern State of Israel, and is based on the Jewish *tallit* (prayer shawl).

Recent Arab use of the word "recognition" (by some Arab states, e.g. Egypt, Jordan, and Morocco, certainly not all Arab states) means simply recognizing the literal fact—*de facto* recognition—of Israel's existence rather than accepting its legal right—*de jure* recognition—to exist as a Jewish state, which is a very different matter. It must be remembered that recognition accorded Israel can always be withdrawn. The key to the ending of the 140-year-long war between the Arabs and Israel is that the Arabs and the wider Muslim world have to grasp that it is in their interests to accept Israel's existence as a Jewish state, legitimized as such under international law, and to abandon forever their attempt to remove it from the map.

Yet repeatedly, Israel's partner in the Oslo peace process—the Palestinian Arabs—refused even to grant Israel any recognition, despite pledges to the contrary at Oslo and in later reaffirmations. In an interview on July 22, 2009, in the London-based pan-Arab daily, *al-Quds al-Arabi,* Fatah Central Committee member Rafik Natsheh stated, "Fatah does not recognize Israel's right to exist, nor have we ever asked others to do so." Fatah thus continued its policy since its founding in 1964, of refusing to accept the legitimacy of the Jewish state. Natsheh declared that Fatah had never recognized Israel's right to exist and not intended ever to do so. He also served as chairman of Fatah's disciplinary "court." Natsheh, closely associated with PA President Mahmoud Abbas, said, "All … reports about recognizing Israel are false." "It's all media nonsense. We don't ask other factions to recognize Israel because we in Fatah have never recognized Israel." Natsheh stressed that neither Fatah nor the Palestinians would ever relinquish the armed struggle against Israel "no matter how long the occupation continues."[107]

Nevertheless, the Israeli government from the late 1980s was obsessed with peace. Labor Party leaders, Shimon Peres, Yitzhak Rabin and Ehud Barak envisioned a new Middle East with countries living side by side one another in peace and economic prosperity, as in modern Europe. They acted upon this vision, but instead of the theory being brought into line with reality, they attempted to move the reality in line with the theory, with disastrous results. They forgot they were not living in Switzerland with France, Germany, Liechtenstein, Austria and Italy as neighbors, but rather in one of the roughest, toughest, and most dangerous neighborhoods in the world, with "Hamastan" (the Gaza Strip), "Hezbollahland" (Lebanon), "Fatahland" in Judea and Samaria, Syria, Egypt, Jordan, Iraq, and Iran as neighbors.

These Israeli leaders deluded themselves into thinking that peace could be achieved by returning disputed lands acquired in wars of self-defense—the flawed concept of "land for peace." They believed that enhancing the economic status of the Palestinian Arabs would change their mind-set about the Israelis and Jews as well as live together in peace. These men believed, "You can only make peace with enemies." That "if it doesn't work the whole world will support us." They were wrong on both counts. They were naïve and displayed Israeli weakness again, again and again. The Oslo peace process was a leftist utopian dream based on Western values. In reality, it became the Israeli national nightmare as they were awakened by the realities of Arab/Muslim religious values as practiced in the Middle East.

It should be noted that in November 2010, documents surfaced which indicated that even Shimon Peres, one of the leaders of the Oslo peace process admitted he had erred. Peres had admitted to Benjamin Netanyahu that the Oslo process had been "based on a mistaken economic premise," and as a result, "European and US assistance to the Palestinians had gone to create a bloated bureaucracy, with PA employees looking to the international community to meet their payroll."[108]

Thus, Israel under its Labor government negotiated the Oslo Accords, which lulled the Israelis, with appropriate words, to admit a "Trojan horse" into their midst. The accords rescued defeated and discredited PLO terrorists from exile in Tunisia, bringing them back into the Land of Israel, providing them with a territorial base. The Israeli government supplied the PLO with weapons and ammunition as well as freed terrorists from Israeli prisons to rejoin their PLO comrades. The Israeli government provided an infrastructure including port facilities, airport, water, electricity, radio and television stations, even a postal system.

This was followed by the territorial withdrawals from main cities in Judea and Samaria, including Bethlehem (under Rabin and Labor Party), Hebron (under Netanyahu and the Likud Party), the retreat from southern Lebanon (under Barak and the Labor Party) and the unilateral withdrawal from the Gaza Strip (under Sharon and the Likud Party). Far from a notable achievement, Israel is the only country in the world ever to expel voluntarily its own citizens from chunks of its homeland in order to hand over the land to its enemies. Israeli Prime Minister Ariel Sharon said at the time that the Israeli pullout from the Gaza Strip "improves our international standing and promotes the chance of peace in the region."[109] These words were proved a pipe dream. Gaza had been a tactical nuisance but with the Israeli retreat became a strategic threat. As recent events have proved, Israel got neither peace nor the understanding and support of the world for their territorial withdrawals. Instead of awakening to the reality of the situation and who their enemy was, the Israeli left pushed their theory even more, insisting it would provide the desired results. The Israeli leadership seems intent on living out George Orwell's observation that "the quickest way of ending a war is to lose it."

Many Israeli governments operated on the assumption that what the West sought is proof that Israel was in the right. Israel did not learn and continued to act on the dangerously false assumption that its actions were what drove Western attitudes. It released terrorists (in hugely disproportionate numbers), froze settlement construction, removed checkpoints, withdrew from territories and destroyed thriving communities. Yet, each concession only generated new demands for still further concessions.

The West is less interested in what Israel does than what the Arab/Muslim oil-rich countries want. This policy principle expresses itself as Western pressure on Israel. The West, led by the US State Department, has consistently taken a pragmatic approach in dealing with the Arab/Muslim war against the Jewish state. Since the 1930s, there was a heavy American and Western economic investment in, and growing dependence on, the oil of the Arab states and Iran. The West had fears, dating from the mid-1950s, of an Arab oil embargo, which manifested itself in 1973–74, and feared a renewal of such a boycott, which remained a dread that influences policies to this day. Additionally, the growing fear of Arab/Muslim terror since the late 1960s propelled the Western countries into an appeasement mode, ready to sacrifice Israel in order to protect themselves. A case in point was made public in 2008. The Italian government of Premier Aldo Moro, in the mid-1970s, made an unholy agreement with Palestinian terrorist groups including the PLO and PFLP. Under the terms of the arrangement, the terrorists were allowed to act freely within Italian territory in exchange for their commitment to refrain from targeting national and international Italian sites.[110] Furthermore, there were Western commercial interests to consider. Having over 300 million potential Arab customers was preferable to being restricted to dealing only with 6 million Israelis. To these pragmatists, no matter how just Israel's case was, business was business. This in part explains the on-going success, though not total success, of the Arab economic boycott of Israel (*see* "Basic Principle 49"). Oil, commerce and fear of terrorism are what determine the greatest part of the West's Mideast policy.

Furthermore, the Israeli government encouraged the United States and the European Union to lavish billions of dollars in aid to the newly created PA. All this was given to the Arabs for Yasser Arafat's verbal promise of peace and "two states for two peoples." While the Israelis were deluding themselves, Arafat was telling the entire Arab world that this was all part of the strategy of stages. Rather than a real two-state solution to the Arab-Israeli conflict, it was a tactic for a two-state dissolution of Israel. Arafat who continued to urge jihad, jihad, jihad, jihad, claimed that Jerusalem, all of it, belonged to the Palestinian Arabs, and made it explicitly clear that peace for land did not mean security for Israel. Terrorism, a second *intifada*—the Al-Aqsa (Second) *Intifada*—and non-stop rocketing of Israel was the result. When the Al-Aqsa (Second) *Intifada* began, the IDF General Staff began to prepare a response called Operation *Thorns,* which was a plan for the retaking of the PA-controlled areas. They estimated the Israeli dead at 300; however, the Israeli government chose to do nothing. From 1993 to 2014, more than 1,610 Jews have been killed, which is more than four times the estimated combat deaths (and 17,000 injured, many maimed for life), with no apparent consequences to the terrorists' ability to inflict casualties on Israel. Is that a "peace process"? As Israelis died in suicide bombings, Israeli Prime Minister Yitzhak Rabin incredulously remarked that such Israeli deaths were the "painful price for peace."[111] This "price for peace" steadily increased, paid for in Israeli blood. Thus, the so-called "two-state solution" was exposed by historic facts and reality as little more than wishful thinking and more accurately should be called the "two-state delusion." Israeli governments had become accomplices in the Arab diplomatic offensive designed to reduce Israel territorially and demographically by the Phased Plan or strategy of stages, weakening Israel's resolve, "de-Zionizing" it, and ultimately "de-judaizing" it.

The tactics of using various forms of struggle against Israel—armed struggle and negotiating Israeli concessions—was reiterated by Fatah official, Kifah Radaydeh, Fatah Regional Committee member, in Jerusalem, on July 7, 2009:

> Fatah is facing a challenge, because [Fatah] says that we perceive peace as one of the strategies, but we say that all forms of the struggle exist, and we do not rule out the possibility of the armed struggle or any other struggle. The struggle exists in all its forms, on the basis of what we are capable of at a given time, and according to what seems right.

> What exactly do we want? It has been said that we are negotiating for peace, but our goal has never been peace. Peace is a means; and the goal is Palestine. I do not negotiate in order to achieve peace. I negotiate for Palestine, in order to achieve a state.[112]

When Palestinian groups including the PLO/PA, Fatah et al refer to "Palestine," it routinely applies to all of Israel.[113] Every segment of Palestinian society teaches that all of Israel, from the Jordan River to the Mediterranean Sea, is "occupied Palestine." This is taught and emphasized in their mosques, schools, public institutions, newspapers, speeches, on TV, and radio, as well as even in children's camps. Their maps emphasize this—Israel simply does not exist at all, within any borders! For example, on a recent episode of PA TV's "We Are Returning" program, the camera focused on a drawing of a map that depicted all of the territory of Israel, but the name "Israel" was nowhere to be seen. It was erased and covered entirely by the Palestinian flag.[114]

In historical Arab context, the harsh reality has always been that Israel represents the successful liberation of a *dhimmi* civilization. "On a territory formerly Arabized by the jihad and the *dhimma,* a pre-Islamic language, culture, topographical geography (biblical towns), and national institutions have been restored to life. This reversed the process of centuries in which the culture, social and political structures of the indigenous Jewish population … was destroyed."[115] This to the Arab/Muslim world is unacceptable.

The Phased Plan or strategy of stages policy is leading to the transition of Israelis from living in a sovereign Jewish state, to being degraded to *dhimmi* status in a Muslim state. Only a few Israelis will accept this change, while the majority will be killed or go into exile again.

So what is Israel to do? Given the nature, historic record and proclaimed goals of its Arab/Muslim enemies, Israel cannot expect "peace" in the traditional Western sense. By remaining strong and exercising swift and overwhelming military force when necessary, Israel will maintain respect and be feared by its enemies. It is the policy enunciated by President Ronald Reagan, as "peace through strength." After facing an Arab/Muslim onslaught for 140 years in the Land of Israel, the Israelis must heed the words of the Chinese military strategist and philosopher, Sun Tzu, "If you know the enemy and know yourself, you need not fear the result of a hundred battles. If you know yourself but not the enemy, for every victory gained you will also suffer a defeat."[116] In a more modern context, the Jewish citizens of Israel must recall the words of Golda Meir, of the left-of-center Labor Party and rarely considered a "hawk," who admitted, "I have never doubted for an instant that the true aim of the Arab states has always been, and still is, the total destruction of the State of Israel, or that even if we had gone back far beyond the 1967 lines to some miniature enclave, they would not still have tried to eradicate it and us. It is our duty to realize this truth. We need to [face] this truth in all its gravity, so that we may continue to mobilize from among ourselves and the Jewish people all the resources necessary to overcome our enemies."[117] For Israel, this is the reality—there is no escaping it.

ATTEMPTS AT SECURITY

Better be despised for too anxious apprehensions, than ruined by too confident security.
Edmund Burke

If you want a guarantee, buy a toaster.
Clint Eastwood

Israel's reestablishment and survival because of the Israeli War of Independence, ended with no peace with its Arab neighbors. Almost immediately, a low-intensity terrorist war was launched against Israel from across the armistice lines by Syria, Jordan and Egypt. Such belligerency forced Israel's founding fathers to adopt basic principles for survival. Israel's small territorial size (*see* "Basic Principle 3") and its tiny population precluded it from fighting long, drawn out wars of attrition with its attendant rising numbers of casualties. In order to stop such attacks, Israel needed to employ a disproportional use of force in response, especially to acts of terror. Israel's lack of territorial depth requires it to take the war to enemy territory by preemption if need be. Finally, in order to deter new rounds of hostilities from being initiated against it, Israel would have to inflict crushing military defeats on its Arab enemies. Due to continued unending Arab/Muslim enmity, Israel must continue to follow these principles.

For Israel, both in the past and still true today, certain acts constitute an automatic *casus belli* for the Jewish state.

- Diverting the waters of the Jordan River and its tributaries.
- The concentration of Egyptian (or Arab/Muslim) military power in the Sinai Peninsula.
- Closing the Straits of Tiran.
- Control of Judea and Samaria by a state or a unified Arab/Muslim military command more powerful than Jordan.
- Intensification of Arab/Muslim guerrilla war to a level, which undermines "normal" civilian life in Israel.

For the foreseeable future, Israel also faces six major threats: Iran's nuclear aspirations, missiles and rockets fired into Israel by neighbors (by both state and non-state actors), cyber warfare targeting Israel, threats to Israel's extensive off-shore gas and oil deposits, as well as the infiltration of Israel's borders and the ever-growing weapons arsenals in the region. With all these factors in mind, Israel's modern history has been focused on one indispensible and overriding concern, maintaining sovereignty as an independent Jewish state within the boundaries of the ancient Jewish homeland. The table below offers a quick summary of the shifts in Israeli policy as its political leaders sought to attain that goal.

ISRAEL'S POLITICAL AND SECURITY POLICIES			
Time Period	**Policy**	**Main events**	**Under Prime Ministers**
1948–74	Deterrence	• Israeli War of Independence • Dealing with the *fedayeen* (1949–56) • The Sinai Campaign • Blocking Nasserist move to overthrow the Jordanian monarchy (1958) • Aiding the Kurds in Iraq • Dealing with terrorism (1957–67) • Stemming Arab attempts to divert water from reaching Israel • The Six-Day War • The 1,000-Day War of Attrition • Preparing to intervene in the Jordanian Civil War (1970) • The Yom Kippur War	David Ben-Gurion (1948–53, 1955–63) Moshe Sharett (1953–55) Levi Eshkol (1963–69) Golda Meir (1969–74)
1974–81	Imposed retreats	• Withdrawing from the west bank of the Suez Canal • Withdrawing from parts of Sinai	Yitzhak Rabin (1974–77) Menachem Begin (1977–83)
1981–93	Assertiveness and regaining of deterrent posture	• IAF destruction of the Iraqi nuclear facility • The war against the PLO in Lebanon • The IAF raid on PLO headquarters in Tunis • Coping with the first *intifada*	Menachem Begin (1977–83) Yitzhak Shamir (1983–84, 1986–92) Shimon Peres (1984–86) Yitzhak Rabin (1992–95)
1993–2000	Critical concessions, retreats, wishful thinking, restraint and appeasement in the vain pursuit of peace	• The Oslo Accords • Oslo II (Taba) • The Wye River Memorandum • Camp David II • Increased terrorist attacks resulted in the deaths of 695 Israelis between 1994 and 2003[1]	Yitzhak Rabin (1992–95) Shimon Peres (1996) Benjamin Netanyahu (1996–99) Ehud Barak (1999–2001)

2000–09	Political and territorial concessions in the face of violence. Indecisiveness, unilateral retreats and waging intentional non-conclusive wars. A collapse of the deterrence policy.	• Israeli withdrawal from southern Lebanon (May 24, 2000) • Dealing with the second *intifada* • Withdrawing from the Gaza Strip • The Second Lebanon War • The First Gaza War	Ehud Barak (1999–2001) Ariel Sharon (2001–06) Ehud Olmert (2006–09)
2009–to date	Navigating through treacherous diplomatic waters and increased national security threats	• Dealing with the Obama administration • Coping with mounting international pressures • Handling the rise of Islamist fundamentalist regimes across the Arab world • The Second Gaza War • Addressing the imminent existential threat of a nuclear-armed Iran • The Third Gaza War	Benjamin Netanyahu (2009–)

As the result of pursuing policies of appeasement in the vain pursuit of peace, unilateral retreats and waging intentional non-conclusive wars Israel only made matters worse. After Hamas gained control of the Gaza Strip in January 2006, they began to shell Israel with rockets, which were described by the world media as "primitive" with the Israeli governments seemingly shrugging off the attacks as inconsequential. Thus, the international community became accustomed to regarding Palestinian missile launches against Israeli civilians as the norm, a dangerous concept to cultivate. When the Israeli government finally was obliged to act in Operation *Cast Lead* (2008–09), and Operation *Protective Edge* (2014), a world accustomed to Israeli passivity against such attacks, accused Israel of over-reacting and of using disproportionate force. What Israel was guilty of was not disproportionate use of force, but disproportionate use of restraint!

For over twenty years, Israeli governments have sought short-term fixes over long-term strategy. They have shifted from victory-driven warfare to conflict management. The Israeli governmental, academic and political elites dominated by the political left, consistently advocate that Israel, as a small nation, must comply to the wishes of the international community and that Israel's international standing is totally dependent on its being perceived as trying to make peace with the Palestinian Arabs. However, as historical events have proved irrefutably, that belief is false.

In reality, the international community is largely made up of many anti-Israel countries, at least fifty-six of which (members of the Organization of Islamic Cooperation) want to see Israel eliminated. As Israel displayed weakness, (and appeasement is a sign of weakness in the Muslim world), the anti-Israel and misojudaic voices have grown louder and more assertive in their demands. Despite the many hard facts—war, terrorism, misojudaic and anti-Israel incitement as well as educational indoctrination* and unremitting hostility—which repeatedly prove Arab unwillingness to accept a sovereign Jewish state of Israel, these leaders believe more Israeli concessions will achieve the elusive final "peace." Thus, seven successive Israeli governments pressed on, determined to disprove Einstein's definition of insanity, repeating the same process over and over again, expecting a different result. These governments believed that the only thing that stands between Israel and international pariah status was its leaders' ability to persuade the so-called international community that Israel is serious about appeasing the Arabs, specifically the Palestinians. These Israeli government elites bought into the Arab propaganda narrative that the key to "peace" in the entire region is the creation of a second Palestinian state. As has been proven earlier, this is a pipe-dream mirage in the desert.

Many who support Israel wonder why Israel had pursued this type of behavior. Israel many times has not pressed its case in the court of world public opinion. Although it is consistently the victim, Israel behaves sometimes as if it is the guilty party. In part, this is due to the psychological conditioning of some 2,000 years of exile, dispersion and persecution. Jewish passivity, weakness, submissiveness, and *dhimmitude* are traits difficult to shake. It is often said, "one can take the Jew out of the shtetl†, but one can't take the shtetl out of the Jew." To put it another way, taking the Jews out of *Galut‡* does not assure that one has cleansed the scars of exile from the Jewish soul.

However, there is an alternative to this self-destructive policy. It was voiced by Israel's first Prime Minister, David Ben-Gurion many years earlier, "it doesn't matter what the world says about Israel, it doesn't matter what they say about us anywhere else. The only thing that matters is that we can exist here on the land of our forefathers. And unless we show the Arabs that there is a high price to pay for murdering Jews, we won't survive."[2] That was true then and remains true today. The time is long overdue for Israeli leaders to tell the world that Jewish blood is not cheap, that Israel will not be a sacrificial lamb on the altar of appeasement and will do whatever it takes to insure its survival as well as that of its people.

As history shows in numerous cases, the failure to employ sufficient deterrence is a prescription for disaster and merely encourages further acts of aggression. Israel would do well to recall the words of Josiah Wedgwood, who spoke at Albert Hall in London on the occasion of the establishment of the British Mandate of Palestine on July 12, 1920. Wedgwood, a British Christian Zionist, said that the "lesson I want the new Jewish nation to learn and get by heart [is to] stand up for your rights!"[3] The lesson for Israel is to meet attacks head on, returning to the tough military responses that were successfully employed from 1948 to 1974 and again from 1981 to 1993, including anticipatory self-defense preemptive strikes. Arab/Muslim regimes need to fear Israeli military strength. Aggressors need to be convinced that there will be a stiff price to pay for acts of aggression against Israel and the

---

* If you open a math book of the fourth grade of a Palestinian school, you learn that "if a *shahid,* a martyr, on a bus can kill fifteen Jews, how many Jews can be killed by three martyrs on a train?" – as reported by Mark Tapson, "Jordan is Palestine: Arieh Eldad's Two-State Solution," FrontPage Magazine, September 30, 2011 at http://frontpagemag.com/2011/09/30/jordan-is-palestine-arieh-eldad%E2%80%99s-two-state-solution/.

† A small Jewish village or town in central or eastern Europe before the Holocaust.

‡ The Jews living outside of the Land of Israel in exile or in the Jewish Diaspora.

Jewish people—that there will be devastating consequences for such aggression. These consequences should include, but not be limited to, loss of territory, valuable resources, and regime change.

Israel needs to win wars militarily with greater effectiveness than in the past and to seek to impose its will on the enemy. It should heed the words of King David, "I pursued my enemies and overtook them; I did not turn back till I destroyed them."[4] It should have a political goal in mind and work to achieve it. This includes emphasizing its historic and legal rights to the Land of Israel, which have not changed since the San Remo Conference. Such tactics will not produce a lasting peace—peace in the sense as peace between the United States and Canada, or between Belgium and France—but will achieve periods of quiet and truces with a modicum of stability. While peace is desirable it is not a necessary condition for survival. Israel must steadfastly maintain this policy until the time that it gains recognition and respect for Jewish sovereignty and rights in the Land of Israel.

Deterrence can be achieved if Israel's Arab/Muslim opponents fear for their very survival. Concern about "world opinion" will lead Israel to become a victim of politicide, which is the gradual but systematic attempt to exterminate an independent political entity. Israelis would be wise to heed the statement of one of their early patriots, David Raziel who was commander-in-chief of the *Irgun*, from 1938 until his death on May 20, 1941. He stated, "the stories of world sympathy are stories only for fools and children."[5] Israel cannot allow itself to be treated as a banana republic, or a vassal state, or to capitulate to the major powers' whims or to be sacrificed on the altar of appeasement and political expediency, as was Czechoslovakia in 1938. While Israel should take into consideration what its friends and allies have to say, first and foremost, it is still a sovereign and independent nation that must look after its own national and security interests with national survival being paramount. Pointedly, Israel must demand and command respect from other nations. As Daniel Pipes, a recognized Middle East expert and analyst, concluded about current Israeli policies, "Israel is simply trying to cope as crises occur; its leadership lacks a strategic vision or a plan to deal with basic security issues [and] long term interests."[6] Thus, a strategic long-term vision for national survival as an independent Jewish state is an absolute necessity.

69. The United Nations has failed to maintain peace and security in the Middle East. Additionally, in a short period the UN became biased and often hostile to Israel, far from the popular image of being an impartial mediator. Furthermore, UN "peacekeeping" efforts in the greater Middle East have been far from effective.

The original purpose of the United Nations Organization established in the waning days of World War II, was to maintain peace and stability, stop aggression, engage in conflict resolution and preserve the security of its member states. The UN in short order, betrayed and fell far short of its lofty goals.

For many years, the United Nations was viewed by the public as some type of world government. This is a falsehood. It was never established as a world government. From its foundation in 1945, the United Nations has been an ever-growing organization of nations, each interested in promoting and preserving its self-interests. For that reason, from the beginning the five great powers—China, France, Russia, the United Kingdom and the United States—all insisted on having veto power in the UN Security Council.

After 1965, the United Nations General Assembly was dominated by Arab, African, Asian, communist, and leftist Latin American countries. As the group grew in number, it included European states that were subject to the pressures of the growing majority. This majority includes many autocracies, despotisms, dictatorships, and appeasement-minded states. As such, they practice repression of political opposition, are intolerant of ethnic and religious minorities and oppose a free press. This combination of states exercises what US President Gerald R. Ford, addressing the Twenty-ninth Session of the UN General Assembly on September 18, 1974, warned against—"the tyranny of the majority."[7] When it comes to acting as an honest broker or as a Middle East peacekeeper, the United Nations is an ineffective, morally bankrupt organization. From the outset, it must be emphasized that there can be no honest deal brokering if one party refuses to accept the existence of another. That is the crux of the Arab/Muslim war against the State of Israel, for Israel's only offense to those countries is its very existence, which they adamantly refuse to accept.

By 2015, there were 193 UN members and the aforementioned group easily commanded a two-thirds majority in the General Assembly. Therefore, it should come as no surprise that the UN would focus much of its attention on Israel, the one Western-style liberty-loving and tolerant nation in the Middle East. In fact, as has been mentioned, since 1948 there has been an ongoing campaign to denounce, defame, denigrate, demonize and delegitimize Israel in every international forum beginning with the United Nations. Correspondingly, the UN since 1967 has become a forum for collective legitimization of the fictional "State of Palestine."

After the passage of the 1947 UN Partition Plan, violence erupted across the British Mandate of Palestine. Armed forces of five Arab states crossed into the area on May 15, 1948, with the express purpose of extinguishing the reestablished Jewish state of Israel. For the United Nations Organization, it was the first test of overt aggression since the end of World War II. The main purpose of creating the UN was to prevent such acts of aggression. The UN failed its first test miserably. The UN did not stop the Arab aggression. There were no UN condemnations, no sanctions, or meaningful actions to punish the aggressor states. As has been mentioned above, the Arab states admitted their aggressive intent, but the UN remained docile and ineffective.

Between 1949 and 1967, the United Nations ignored both Egypt's military occupation of the Gaza Strip and Jordan's illegal occupation of Judea, Samaria and the Old City of Jerusalem. It ignored Arab destruction and desecration of holy sites, as well as restrictions on worshippers of all faiths and denial to them of access to those holy sites (*see* the "Old City of Jerusalem under Jordanian occupation, 1948–67" map). During that same period, there were no sanctions or actions taken against the many armed attacks against Israel emanating from Jordanian-occupied Judea and Samaria, the Egyptian-occupied Gaza Strip and the Syrian-controlled Golan Heights (*see* "Golan Heights" map).

The United Nations Truce Supervisory Organization (UNTSO), which monitored the Arab-Israeli armistice lines from 1949 to 1970, did little more than act as a secretarial unit reporting outbreaks of violence. In fact on June 5, 1967, UNTSO allowed Jordanian forces to occupy UNTSO positions at Government House in Jerusalem, which the Jordanians used to open fire against the Israeli-controlled parts of the city (*see* "Divided Jerusalem, 1948–67" map). Later, during the 1,000-Day War of Attrition, from 1967 to 1970, UNTSO sat at the Suez Canal failing to stop the Egyptian attacks on Israeli-controlled Sinai.

In 1951, there were no UN sanctions or actions taken to enforce the Security Council resolution, which condemned Egypt's illegal closure of the Suez Canal to Israeli ships and cargo bound to or from Israel (*see* Appendix 1). Furthermore, from 1951 to 1954, while Egypt tightened its blockade of the Straits of Tiran against Israeli ships and cargo, there was no UN action taken over the denial of the right of free passage in international waters.

The United Nations Emergency Force (UNEF) was established at the close of the Sinai-Suez War of 1956. Its mission was to maintain the peace along the Egyptian-Israeli Armistice line and keep the Straits of Tiran open to all nations, including Israel (*see* "United Nations Emergency Force

Deployment in Egypt" map). The most infamous act perpetrated by the UNEF occurred in mid-May 1967. At that time, Egyptian President Gamal Abdel Nasser mobilized his army and sent it to the Egyptian-Israeli frontier. Nasser ordered the UNEF to leave immediately and incredulously UN Secretary-General U Thant complied within three days. Thant's action was taken despite long standing international agreements that there would be lengthy deliberations if and when the UNEF had completed its mission and was to be removed. In the symbolic style of Neville Chamberlain, when the storm clouds of war appeared, the UNEF folded its umbrella and quietly stole away. The UNEF withdrawal paved the way for Nasser's blockade of the Straits of Tiran, an act of war, which in turn triggered the Six-Day War in early June 1967. Israeli Foreign Minister Abba Eban summed up the folly of relying on international peacekeepers in a June 19, 1967 speech to the UN General Assembly, when he said:

> What is the use of a fire brigade, which vanishes from the scene as soon as the first smoke and flames appear? Is it surprising that we are firmly resolved never again to allow a vital Israel interest and our very security to rest on such a fragile foundation?[8]

Syria, Jordan, and Lebanon began to divert the headwaters of the Jordan River, in February 1964, to deny Israel its main water source (*see* "Arab Attempts at Diversion of Water Resources and Israeli Response" map). Again, there was no condemnation, no sanctions, and no action taken by the United Nations.

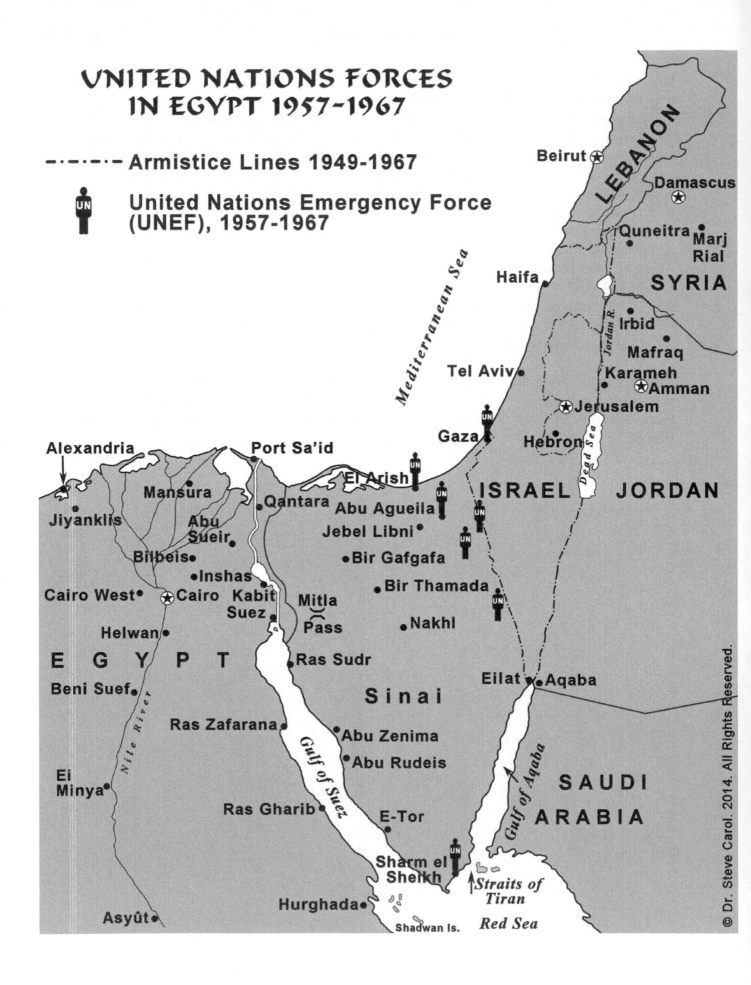

UNITED NATIONS FORCES IN EGYPT 1957~1967

- —·—·—·— **Armistice Lines 1949-1967**

United Nations Emergency Force (UNEF), 1957-1967

LEBANON

Beirut

Damascus

Quneitra Marj Rial

SYRIA

Mediterranean Sea

Haifa

Irbid

Mafraq

Tel Aviv

Karameh
Amman

Jerusalem

Gaza

Hebron

Dead Sea

Alexandria

Port Sa'id

El Arish

ISRAEL

JORDAN

Mansura

Qantara

Abu Agueila

Jiyanklis

Abu Sueir

Jebel Libni

Bilbeis

Bir Gafgafa

Cairo West

Inshas

Cairo

Kabit

Suez

Mitla Pass

Bir Thamada

Helwan

Nakhl

Jordan R.

E G Y P T

Ras Sudr

Beni Suef

S i n a i

Eilat Aqaba

Ras Zafarana

Abu Zenima

Ei Minya

Abu Rudeis

SAUDI ARABIA

Nile River

Ras Gharib

Gulf of Suez

E-Tor

Gulf of Aqaba

Asyût

Hurghada

Sharm el Sheikh

Shadwan Is.

Straits of Tiran

Red Sea

THE CONFLICT OVER WATER

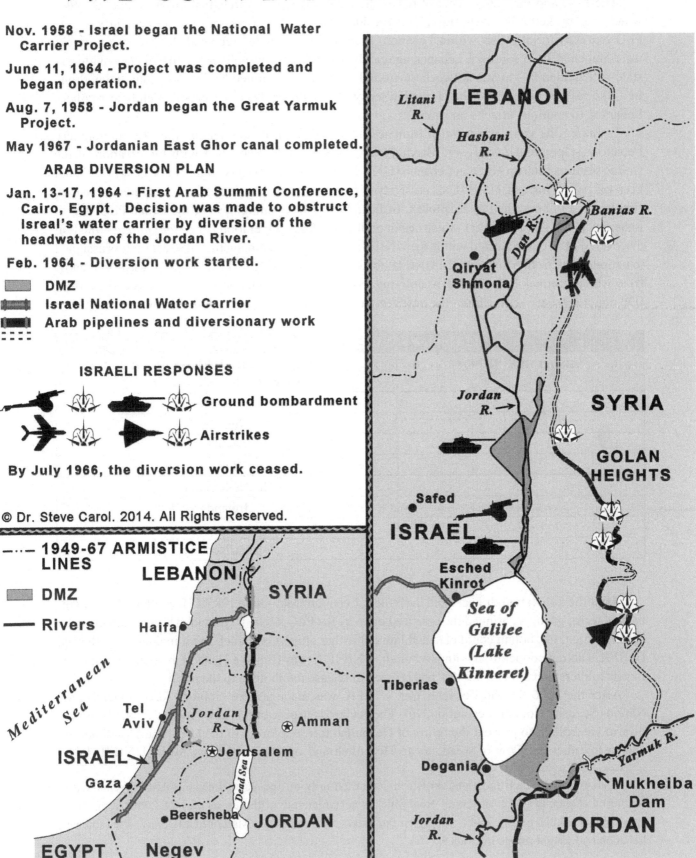

Nov. 1958 - Israel began the National Water Carrier Project.

June 11, 1964 - Project was completed and began operation.

Aug. 7, 1958 - Jordan began the Great Yarmuk Project.

May 1967 - Jordanian East Ghor canal completed.

ARAB DIVERSION PLAN

Jan. 13-17, 1964 - First Arab Summit Conference, Cairo, Egypt. Decision was made to obstruct Isreal's water carrier by diversion of the headwaters of the Jordan River.

Feb. 1964 - Diversion work started.

▭ DMZ

▤ Israel National Water Carrier

▬ Arab pipelines and diversionary work
····

ISRAELI RESPONSES

Ground bombardment

Airstrikes

By July 1966, the diversion work ceased.

—···— 1949-67 ARMISTICE LINES

▭ DMZ

— Rivers

The PLO and the government of Lebanon signed the Cairo Agreement on November 2, 1969, which was brokered by UAR (Egyptian) President Gamal Abdel Nasser. The agreement gave the PLO extraterritorial rights within Lebanon. From the early 1970s, repeated PLO terrorist attacks were launched from southern Lebanon against Israel. The PLO established a virtual state-within-a-state—"Fatahland"—to attack Israeli towns and civilians. The United Nations as usual, did nothing. In a like fashion, after 1983 the Hezbollah terrorist group established "Hezbollahland" in southern Lebanon, to continue attacks on Israel.

In the earlier case, when Israel launched a limited reprisal raid against the PLO in southern Lebanon—Operation *Litani*—on March 14–21, 1978, the UN responded with the creation of the United Nations Interim Force in Lebanon (UNIFIL). For the next twenty-eight years, UNIFIL did not keep the peace. Instead, UNIFIL sat passively as terrorist attacks continued from Lebanon into Israel, first by the PLO and then by Hezbollah. In fact, during the opening days of the Israel–PLO War in Lebanon, (First Lebanon War), which began on June 6, 1982—Operation *Peace for Galilee*—the IDF discovered PLO bases located within the UNIFIL zone, scattered among the different sectors assigned to nations, which contributed to the UNIFIL force. Thus, the PLO used UNIFIL areas as springboards from which to attack Israel as well as utilizing those personnel as human shields to protect them from IDF counterstrikes—all without the intervention of the UNIFIL forces around them.

PLO BASES WITHIN UNIFIL AREAS [9]	
Number of PLO bases	**Located within UNIFIL sector controlled by troops from**
3	Senegal
3	Nigeria
2	Ghana
4	Fiji
15	The Netherlands
2	Ireland
2	Norway
1	Ghana/Norway

After the Israeli withdrawal from the bulk of Lebanon (May–June 1985),[*] Hezbollah, the Iranian-backed terror group, continued the practice begun by the PLO. UNIFIL provided human shields from behind which, Hezbollah could plan and launch further attacks on Israel. In an incident that showed UNIFIL's actual cooperation with Hezbollah, UNIFIL troops filmed a Hezbollah abduction of three Israeli soldiers on October 7, 2000, and refused to release the footage to the public.[10]

After the 2006 Second Lebanon War, UNIFIL was made a more "robust" force under United Nations Security Council Resolution 1701. The declared purpose of this new "robust" UNIFIL was to disarm Hezbollah, to prevent the return of Hezbollah terrorist forces to the Lebanese-Israeli border, and to interdict the flow of weaponry to Hezbollah and other groups from Syria. UNIFIL failed

---

[*] A small residual Israeli force and an Israeli-supported militia—the South Lebanon Army—remained in southern Lebanon in a "security zone," from which Israel unilaterally withdrew on May 24, 2000. At that time, approximately 6,000 people, soldiers with their families—overwhelmingly Maronite Christians—fled southern Lebanon and sought refuge in Israel.

miserably on all counts as Hezbollah rearmed with more advanced weaponry to higher levels than before the 2006 war. UNIFIL not only was ineffective against the terrorist group, it restricted the actions of the victim, Israel. Far from using force to implement UN Security Council Resolution 1701, UNIFIL actually hampered Israeli efforts to monitor Hezbollah's continued violations of the arms embargo and the movement of weapons across the Lebanese-Syrian border. For example, the French commander of UNIFIL, on October 19, 2006, threatened to shoot down IAF reconnaissance flights over Lebanon that were engaged in monitoring the weapons traffic.[11] In fact, using UNIFIL as human shields to safeguard its forces from Israeli reprisals, Hezbollah grew to become the major military force in Lebanon and came to dominate Lebanon's government. As the proxies of Iran, Hezbollah enabled Iran in the latter's quest to become the regional hegemon from the borders of Afghanistan to the Mediterranean Sea. Acting as Iranian mercenaries, it intervened in the Syrian Civil War, turning the tide of that conflict in favor of the embattled Assad regime.

Today, Hezbollah has greater numbers, both in men and weaponry (over 100,000 missiles and rockets) than before the 2006 war. The flow of sophisticated armaments currently moves unimpeded from Iran and Syria into Lebanon. Hezbollah now possesses missiles (including advanced Scuds) capable of striking, not only Haifa, Tel Aviv, and the central coastal heartland, but also virtually all of Israel deep into the Negev Desert.[12] Once again, as the danger mounted in a corner of the Middle East, UN peacekeepers proved ineffective.

Furthermore, UNIFIL's actions against Israel in Lebanon set a dangerous precedent. Any possible future deployment of UN "peacekeepers" in Judea and Samaria as well as the Gaza Strip, as part of an Israel–PLO/PA "final peace accord," rather than prevent terrorist attacks against Israel, would be used to shield the terrorists in the Palestinian state and restrict the Israelis from exercising their legitimate right of self-defense.

Returning to the chronological sequence, the dismal record of UN peacekeeping in the Middle East continued. To insure a ceasefire after the Yom Kippur War Israel and Syria signed a disengagement agreement on May 31, 1974. It was based on an exchange of prisoners-of-war, Israeli withdrawal from the eastern salient (gained by the IDF during the war) to the Purple Line (the ceasefire line established after the Six-Day War), and the establishment of a 3 square mile sliver of territory—a UN separation of forces zone. On the same day, the UN Security Council adopted resolution 350, which established the United Nations Disengagement Observer Force (UNDOF) as a peacekeeping force in the zone on the Golan Heights. By 2013, UNDOF was made up of some 1,012 troops (well below its authorized strength of 1,250) from Austria, Croatia, India, Japan, and the Philippines.

During the Syrian Civil War UNDOF was largely ineffectual. Rebel forces made up of a myriad of groups including the Nusra Front linked to Al-Qaeda, the Muslim Brotherhood, Hezbollah and others began to encroach on the UNDOF zone. The Islamist Martyrs of Yarmuk militia took twenty-one UNDOF Filipino troops hostage on March 6, 2013, and held them prisoner before releasing them in Jordan three days later. This move triggered the collapse of the UNDOF force. UNDOF began disintegrating as Croatia withdrew its 100 soldiers in March 2013 amid fears it would be targeted. The commanders of the remaining 912 Austrian, Indian and Filipino troops advised their men to flee and seek sanctuary on the Israeli side of the zone if necessary. Canada and Japan had already pulled their small number of peacekeepers out in December 2012. The situation further deteriorated, after a second incident, which occurred on May 7, 2013, when four Filipino soldiers were abducted by Syrian rebels. They were released on May 12. In light of this hostage situation, the Philippine Foreign Affairs secretary Albert del Rosario recommended the total withdrawal of the entire Filipino contingent of 342 UNDOF peacekeepers.[13] On June 6, 2013, Austria announced it would withdraw its 377 peacekeepers from UNDOF after Syrian government forces and rebels battled to control a strategic crossing into the Israeli-controlled territory.[14] Aside from the Filipinos questionable continuance, there remained only 193 Indian troops in UNDOF. Despite these setbacks by 2014, UNDOF was numerically bolstered to 1,223 by troops from Fiji, Ireland, Nepal and the Netherlands. Ireland had deployed 115 peacekeepers with UNDOF in September 2013 and within two months, the Irish peacekeepers were attacked by Syrian rebels on November 29, 2013. On August 28, 2014, once again, a Syrian rebel group linked to al-Qaeda—*Jabhat al-Nusra*—detained 45 Fijian UNDOF peacekeepers, while 81 Filipino troops were besieged in two camps on the Syrian side of the frontier. They were able to escape by August 31 into Israel. Subsequently, the United Nations announced that the Philippines would pull out of UNDOF. In the interim, the Nusra Front demanded it be paid compensation for fighters killed during the confrontation with UNDOF troops, humanitarian assistance for its supporters and its removal from the UN list of terrorist organizations. On September 11, 2014, the Fijian troops were released and went to Israel. *Asharq Al-Awsat*, a London-based Arabic newspaper (owned by Faisal bin Salman, a member of the Saudi royal family), quoting Syrian opposition sources, reported September 13 that the Qatari government paid somewhere between $20 and $45 million to the Nusra Front for the release of the Fijian troops. Qatar took credit for negotiating the release, though it made no mention of a ransom.[15] On September 15, 2014, it was announced that UNDOF troops were being withdrawn from UN positions 10, 16, 31 and 37, as well as Camp Faouar, their main headquarters, on the (Syrian) side of the UNDOF zone to the Israeli-side. This was done for the UNDOF troops' safety.[16]

In light of all these developments, a paradoxical consideration might be that UN "observers" and "peacekeepers," are particularly effective when there is no fighting to observe or conflicts to resolve. A UN "peacekeeping" or "observer" force that flees in the face of danger is useless. UNDOF is rapidly collapsing and can no longer serve its purpose of enforcing a truce between Israel and Syria. Given the pullout from the force by Austria, Canada, Croatia, Japan, the Philippines and the retreat of the Fijian troops to the Israeli side of the zone, it is unlikely other countries will want to contribute troops. With the Syrian Civil War continuing unabated well into its fifth year and violent clashes occurring at the edge of the UNDOF zone, the future of UNDOF is at best "iffy"—hardly the purpose of "peacekeepers."

All of the above is but part of the United Nations bias, anti-Israel agenda and hostility towards the Jewish state. Recall that the resolutions of the UN General Assembly are legally non-binding recommendations. Nevertheless, literally hundreds of anti-Israel resolutions have come from the General Assembly, the UN Specialized Agencies and affiliated bodies. As Israeli Foreign Minister Abba Eban famously observed, "If Algeria introduced a resolution declaring that the earth was flat and that Israel had flattened it, it would pass by a vote of 164 to 13 with 26 abstentions."[17]

Using the tyranny of the majority in the UN General Assembly, the Arab/Muslim world and their allies, cunningly and incrementally created a people, gave that people international legitimacy, as well as representation at the United Nations. Many states that voted for these resolutions did not grasp the full implication of what international precedents were being created, as the following examples illustrate.

Until the adoption of United Nations General Assembly Resolution 2535 B (XXIV) of December 10, 1969, there had never been any mention of a "Palestinian Arab people" in UN resolutions, only "Arab refugees." Now, this milestone resolution spoke of "the inalienable rights of the people of Palestine."[18] This was soon followed by United Nations General Assembly Resolution 2625 (XXV) of October 24, 1970, which declared:

> Every State has the duty to refrain from any forcible action, which deprives peoples … of their right to self-determination and freedom and independence. In their actions against, and resistance to, such forcible action in pursuit of the exercise of their right to self-determination, such peoples are entitled to seek and to receive support in accordance with the purposes and principles of the [UN] Charter.[19]

With this resolution, the General Assembly asserted that "peoples" had rights superior to those of sovereign states, but moreover that states resisting the rights of "peoples" could themselves become a "threat to peace." In short, for example, Israel exercising its right of self-defense could be labeled a "threat to peace" for resisting the terrorism, violence and attacks of the "Palestinian people."

Less than two months later, United Nations General Assembly Resolution 2708 (XXV) of December 14, 1970, reaffirmed "its recognition of the legitimacy of the struggle of … peoples under alien domination to exercise their right to self-determination and independence by all the necessary means at their disposal."[20] In this manner, whereas the UN Charter permitted the use of force by member states in self-defense (Article 51), UNGA 2708 created a new category of "legitimate" force that could be used *against* (emphasis added) member states (e.g. the PLO against Israel)!

In a move that shattered diplomatic norms, on November 13, 1974, PLO chief Yasser Arafat, carrying a holstered gun, was allowed to speak at the United Nations General Assembly, becoming the first non-state leader to do so. Nine days later, on November 22, 1974, United Nations General Assembly Resolution 3236 (XXIX) specified that the Palestinian people had the "right to national independence and sovereignty," the right to use "all means" to attain these goals, as well as the right to receive support from other countries. Moreover, all states were called on to assist the Palestinian struggle.[21] On the same day, United Nations General Assembly Resolution 3237, granted "permanent observer" status to the PLO, the world's leading terrorist organization. In effect, this amounted to *de facto* member privileges, albeit without voting rights. This gave the PLO access to the resources and subdivisions of the United Nations.

The UN plunged into the depths of depravity on November 10, 1975, when it passed the infamous and abhorrent United Nations General Assembly Resolution 3379. The date was chosen deliberately by Israel's enemies, as it was the thirty-seventh anniversary of *Kristallnacht*.* Resolution 3379 equated Zionism with racism. This move was equivalent to formally declaring Israel a target. Now according

---

* *Kristallnacht,* ("Crystal Night" or "Night of the Broken Glass"—named for the broken shards of glass from shop windows) was an anti-Jewish pogrom launched by the Nazi government across Germany on November 9–10, 1938. This pogrom damaged, and in many cases destroyed, about 200 synagogues (constituting nearly all Germany and Austria had), as well as many Jewish cemeteries. More than 7,500 Jewish shops, and 29 department stores were looted and destroyed. Jewish homes were burnt down. Many Jews were physically assaulted. There was systematic public humiliation and abuse of Jews in every city and village in Nazi Germany. Some Jews were beaten to death while others were forced to watch. It was an emotionally significant open ritual of degradation and dehumanization. Some 30,000 Jews, many of them wealthy and prominent members of their Jewish communities, were arrested and deported to concentration camps at Dachau, Sachsenhausen, and Buchenwald, where they were subjected to inhumane and brutal treatment, but most were released during the following three months on condition that they leave Germany. The number of German Jews killed is uncertain. The number killed in the two-day riot is most often cited as 91. In addition, it is thought that there were hundreds of suicides. Counting deaths in the concentration camps, around 2,000–2,500 deaths were directly or indirectly attributable to the *Kristallnacht* pogrom. A few non-Jewish Germans, mistaken for Jews, were also killed. *Kristallnacht* is often referred to as the beginning of the Holocaust.

to the UN General Assembly, Israel had no rights. Israel's very existence was branded an act of aggression against the Palestinian people and a crime against international law. According to this logic, any attack on Israel was justified and any act of self-defense by Israel was illegal aggression. (For a more complete explanation of this resolution and its repeal, *see* Appendix 10).

Anti-Israel and misojudaic invective continued unabated at the United Nations. Typifying the many statements made and resolutions passed was the December 5, 1984, statement by the Saudi Arabian delegate Marouf al-Dawalibi, as he blatantly lied before the UN Human Rights Commission Conference on Religious Tolerance declaring, "The Talmud says that if a Jew does not drink every year the blood of a non-Jewish man, he will be damned for eternity."[22] Ironically, it is this UN Commission on Human Rights, replaced by the UN Human Rights Council in 2006, which is the most virulent center of anti-Israel activities in the United Nations. It has classified Israel as the principal human rights violator in the whole world. Since its inception, about 25 percent of its resolutions have condemned Israel. Censuring Israel at every turn directly affects all citizens of the world, for it constitutes a severe violation of the equality principles guaranteed by the UN Charter and underlying the Universal Declaration of Human Rights. However, that seems to matter little to the tyrannical majority.

On November 29, 2012, the UN General Assembly voted on Resolution 67/19 with the results of 138 countries in favor, nine opposed, forty-one abstentions and five nations absent, for a resolution which lifted the PLO from the status of an observer entity to a "non-member observer state". In bringing this resolution to the UN General Assembly, the PLO/PA was in unilateral violation of its obligation under the Oslo Accords (1993) and the Oslo II Agreement (Interim Agreement) of 1995. Article 31, Clause 7 of the latter clearly states, "Neither side shall initiate or take any step that will change the status of the West Bank [Judea and Samaria] and the Gaza Strip pending the outcome of the permanent status negotiations."[23]

What the UN General Assembly did flies in the face of international law. The Convention on Rights and Duties of States signed on December 26, 1933, at Montevideo, Uruguay, sets out the definition of statehood. Article 1 sets out the four criteria for statehood: (a) a permanent population; (b) a defined territory; (c) government; and (d) capacity to enter into relations with the other states.[24] The so-called state of "Palestine" has none of these.

"Palestine" lacks a "permanent population." Most of the population considers themselves not alleged citizens of a new state but perennial "refugees"—an inherited status under the unique definition applicable to Palestinians—who reject any suggestion they should form the permanent population of a new state. They consider themselves instead to be temporary residents (and UNRWA, the UN agency devoted to caring for them, is legally a "temporary" UN body) who seek to "return" to a different state, i.e. Israel, not to be permanent residents where they currently live.

"Palestine" lacks a "defined territory." A "defined territory" cannot include an area whose status and borders can only be defined, under longstanding international agreements, by negotiations. To have a defined territory, "Palestine" has to negotiate it with Israel; until then, its self-definition of territory is not a "defined territory" under the law, it is simply a negotiating position. Additionally, under international law, Judea, Samaria (what the Arabs call the "West Bank") and Gaza are disputed territories (*see* "Basic Principle 60").

"Palestine" lacks a "government." It is ruled in the Gaza Strip, by a theologically driven, ideologically motivated, fanatically dedicated hardline terrorist group—Hamas. In the Palestinian-controlled areas of Judea and Samaria (what the Arabs call "the West Bank") the territory is governed by a crafty, mainly secular, politically-slick media-savvy unelected so-called "moderate" terrorist administrative entity—the Palestinian Authority, established by the PLO. The PA's last election occurred in January 2006, and it has no capacity (much less inclination) to hold a new one. The government of each half considers the government of the other half illegitimate, and both are correct: the Hamas regime took power by a bloody coup d'état in 2007, and the PA Chairman Mahmoud Abbas, remains in power eleven years after his four-year-term expired. There is no legal governing body in either half of the purported state, much less one that governs both halves. Yet, lest the uninformed be deceived, only the tactics of Hamas and the PLO/PA are different. The strategy and final goal remains identical. This was confirmed by the words of the so-called "moderate" PLO/PA Chairman Mahmoud Abbas on official PA TV, December 31, 2009, when he called for a PLO/PA-Hamas unity agreement, "There is no disagreement between us [PLO/PA/Fatah and Hamas]: About belief? None! About policy? None! About resistance? None! So what do you [Hamas] disagree about? Why are you not signing the [reconciliation] agreement?"[25] Such "reconciliation" agreements were signed in 2011, 2012 and again on April 23, 2014. It remains to be seen if it will go into effect and which entity—the PLO/PA or Hamas—will prevail over the other.

"Palestine" lacks the "capacity to enter into relations with the other states." Mahmoud Abbas has no capacity to bind the rulers of Gaza, or even to implement his own commitments in the area in which he can at least set foot. While in office, he failed to implement his prior obligations, including the Oslo Accords, Oslo II, the Wye River Agreement, as well as Phase I of the Roadmap (which mandated the dismantling of Hamas and other terrorist groups). Furthermore, Abbas is currently an unelected official, unrecognized by half his alleged state, with no capacity to bind "Palestine" to anything.

The labeling of "Palestine" as a state is another instance of the UN's repeated attempts to redefine legal terms for political reasons. This politicized lawfare tactic was previously used when the UN redefined the legal meaning of a Palestinian "refugee" by including descendants of persons displaced, a definition never before or after used to describe refugees of any other origin (*see* 'Basic Principle 10"). In 1783, at the end of the American Revolutionary War approximately, 80,000 Loyalist refugees were driven out or left of their own accord the fledgling United States. They resettled in Canada, Australia, and the United Kingdom among other locations. Imagine if all their descendents today, numbering in the tens of millions, were to claim "refugee status," demand "compensation," as well as insist on the "right of return" to the United States.

Resolution 67/19 declared that this "state" is within the 1949 Armistice lines (falsely and misleadingly referred to as the "1967 borders") with Jerusalem again to be divided with all the major holy sites under Arab/Muslim control. With this vote, the Palestinians have buried the already dead misname "peace process," for there is nothing to negotiate. Israel, the US and the rest of the free world must stand up and declare the Oslo Accords null and void by the terrorist hands that murdered it along with just over 1,500 Israelis over the past twenty-two years!

The granting of "non-member observer state" status raises an important issue. Since the UN conferred "non-member observer state" status to a non-state terrorist organization—the PLO—Israel and other freedom-loving democratic states should demand that the UN General Assembly confer such status to each of the myriad terrorist groups in Latin America, the Provisional IRA in Northern Ireland (part of the United Kingdom), the Breton Liberation Front and the Corsican Liberation Front in France, the ETA (Basques) in Spain, the Red Army Faction in Germany, Italian Red Brigade in Italy, the ASALA (Armenian Secret Army for the Liberation of Armenia) in Turkey, the Chechen separatists in Russia, Al-Qaeda in the Arabian Peninsula, Al-Qaeda in the Maghreb, Jundallah in Iran, Lashkar-e-Taiba in Pakistan, the East Turkestan Islamic Movement in China, and Aum Shinrikyo in Japan—just to name a few. Not to be forgotten such "rights" and "membership" should be bestowed on the Islamic State caliphate, sprawling across a great expanse of Syria and Iraq. First it will give those countries named something to think about, other than what they deem the "greatest threat to world peace" i.e. Israel. By such tactics, the world gone topsy-turvy can turn the insane asylum that is the United Nations, into the world-class zoo it has become. The United States for its part should not contribute funding—not even a penny—to the United Nations.

By no means was the ineffectiveness of UN peacekeepers in the greater Middle East limited to the Arab/Muslim war against Israel. Several notable examples illustrate this chronic problem. In 1958, as Lebanon exploded into its first civil war, the government of Lebanon appealed to the United Nations complaining of Syrian aggression, infiltration and that the Syrians (then part of the United Arab Republic) were supplying weapons to the rebel forces trying to overthrow the legitimate Lebanese government. The UN responded with the United Nations Observer Group in Lebanon (UNOGIL) dispatched in June 1958 to ascertain if Syria was intervening in the domestic affairs of Lebanon. Sadly, the force contained only 166 men at its peak strength, and they were charged with monitoring the 195-mile Syrian-Lebanese border. The peacekeepers were not allowed to patrol at night and were not allowed access into rebel-held areas. As a result, it should come as no surprise that the UNOGIL report of July 4, 1958 stated that it could not find any proof of Syrian infiltration. The civil war intensified immediately as did Syrian and Egyptian intervention. Only military assistance by the United States in mid-July saved Lebanon. UNOGIL was quietly disbanded in December.

Having learned little from this previous experience, in June 1963, the United Nations Yemen Observation Mission (UNYOM) was dispatched to that civil war-torn nation. The war started when an Egyptian-sponsored coup to overthrow the legitimate Royalist government of Yemen went awry. Egyptian military intervention on behalf of the Republican forces (the coup instigators), including the first use of poison gas since World War I, was followed by Saudi assistance to the legitimate Royalist government. UNYOM's mission was to observe Egyptian and Saudi disengagement from the conflict. A force of 189 men was sent to conduct this impossible task in a 6,000 square-mile, mountainous region that rivals Afghanistan in terms of difficult terrain (see the "Yemen Civil War–Use of poison gas and placement of UNYOM" map). Far from being impartial, the Yugoslav contingent within UNYOM was hostile to the Royalist government and actually radioed the location of the Royalist positions to the Egyptian-backed Republican forces. Additionally, nothing was said or done regarding the continued use of poison gas. UNYOM's commander, Major General Carl von Horn resigned in disgust within a month of UNYOM's arrival in Yemen. In September 1964, UNYOM was terminated and forces were withdrawn from Yemen. The Yemeni Civil War continued unabated until May 1970.

In the midst of the 1963–64 communal clashes on the island of Cyprus between Greek and Turkish communities, the United Nations Security Council via Resolution 186, created the United Nations Peacekeeping Force in Cyprus (UNFICYP). Originally 3,100 men from eight countries were given the mission to prevent a recurrence of fighting between the two communities, and to contribute to the maintenance and restoration of law and order as well as a return to normal conditions (see "Cyprus-Clashes of 1963–64, 1967 and UNFICYP" map). It failed to accomplish its mission in the 1963–64 crises, which was brought to an end through the mediation efforts of the United States in the person of Dean Acheson. It failed to prevent the outbreak of a new round of fighting in 1967, which again was brought to an end through the good offices of US representative Cyrus Vance. UNFICYP was ineffective in preventing the Turkish invasion and occupation of northern Cyprus in August 1974.

Furthermore, UNFICYP did little to prevent the ethnic cleansing of Greek Cypriots from the northern portion of the island. Nevertheless, UNFICYP's mandate continues to be renewed to date.

Though both Morocco and Mauritania had historic ties to Spanish Sahara, the International Court of Justice (ICJ) ruled on October 16, 1975, that those ties did not grant those nations the right to the territory. On February 26, 1976, Spain ended its rule of the Western Sahara and withdrew its forces from that territory. Spain had already concluded the Madrid Accords (November 14, 1975) with Morocco and Mauritania, agreeing to give the territory to them—illegally according to the ICJ. The next day February 27, the Polisario Front (Popular Front for the Liberation of the Saguia al Hamra and Rio de Oro) proclaimed the independence of the territory as the Sahrawi Arab Democratic Republic. Morocco occupied and annexed the northern two-thirds of Western Sahara on April 14, 1976, and the remainder of the territory in early August 1979, following Mauritania's withdrawal. A seventeen-year long guerrilla war between Polisario and Morocco (and briefly with Mauritania before the latter's withdrawal) contesting Morocco's sovereignty ended in a September 6, 1991, UN-brokered ceasefire.

The United Nations Mission for the Referendum in Western Sahara (MINURSO)—the name is a French acronym for *Mission des Nations unies pour l'Organisation d'un Référendum au Sahara Occidental*—was established in April 1991, to monitor the ceasefire and to organize and conduct an UN-supervised referendum. This was to enable the Sahrawis of Western Sahara to choose between integration with Morocco or remain an independent state. The issue of the referendum became bogged down in a dispute over the identification of Sahrawis eligible to vote in any self-determination plebiscite. The independence referendum was originally scheduled for January 1992, but the voter eligibility issue prevented it from being held. Morocco then reneged on its promise to hold the vote, and declared it "unnecessary." In 1995, MINURSO's inability or unwillingness to act against perceived Moroccan manipulation of the process, and abuse of Sahrawi civilians, caused its former deputy chairman Frank Ruddy to deliver a strong attack on the organization.[26] Ruddy kept up his critique of what he argued was an economically costly and politically corrupt process. Years of stalemate ensued. Morocco continued to balk at any plan that explicitly offered independence.[27] Morocco instead proposed creation of a "Sahara Autonomous Region," which it updated in April 2007 with the introduction of the "Moroccan Initiative for Negotiating an Autonomy Status for the Sahara."[28] Presently, there is no plan for holding the referendum, and thus far, the ceasefire has held, but the threat of renewed conflict looms over the area. Overall, however, MINURSO was the first comprehensive UN peacekeeping mission to fail since the end of the Cold War.

There is a counterintuitive example of rare UN effectiveness in the Middle East. On December 20, 1983, the United Nations provided "safe conduct" under the UN flag for some 4,000 PLO armed terrorists from Tripoli, Lebanon, to sail to safety to Tunis, Tunisia. This action was requested by the UN Secretary General Javier Perez de Cuellar on "purely humanitarian grounds" and sanctioned by UN Security Council Resolution 543 of November 29, 1983. The UN provided protective cover for the PLO terrorists, who faced decimation, allowing them to escape. Recall it was the PLO that waged a war of terror against Israel beginning in 1964. The PLO tried violently to overthrow the Jordanian monarchy in 1970. It was the PLO that plunged Lebanon into a civil war, commencing in 1975 and lasting some fifteen years. To provide safety for armed terrorists with blood on their hands from killing, maiming and wounding thousands of innocent men, women and children claiming "humanitarian grounds" is gross hypocrisy and subverts, undermines and betrays the very principles on which the United Nations was founded in 1945.

In Somalia, on January 26, 1991, the long-standing repressive regime of Muhammad Siad Barre was toppled by an insurrection, and that Horn of Africa, Arab League country fell into an ongoing period of civil war, which continues to this day. As Somali descended into violence, mayhem and instability accompanied by several secessionist attempts, a looming humanitarian crisis resulted. A ceasefire was brokered and the United Nations Security Council, in Resolution 751, in April 1992, established the United Nations Operation in Somalia (UNOSOM) to uphold the ceasefire and assist the humanitarian aid effort.

From the outset, UNOSOM was woefully under-manned. At its maximum strength, UNOSOM had 54 military observers, 893 troops, and military support personnel. This force had to perform its duties in a nation nearly as large as Texas. Despite the presence of UNOSOM, the ceasefire was ignored, and the civil war raged on and intensified in severity. Peacekeepers were threatened and humanitarian aid supplies could not be moved. In November 1992, the leading Somali warlord General Muhammad Farrah Aided, defied the United Nations Security Council and demanded the withdrawal of UNOSOM peacekeepers. By March 1993, UNOSOM's mandate ended. Thus, the peacekeeping effort was an abject fiasco.

Undeterred, the United Nations tried again with UNOSOM II. Established by United Nations Security Council Resolution 814 of March 26, 1993, UNOSOM II began operations on May 4, 1993, with an authorized peacekeeping force of 28,000. UNOSOM II, like its predecessor UNOSOM I, was unable to restore peace, stability, law and order to Somalia. It was incapable of securing an environment to facilitate the delivery of humanitarian assistance. UNOSOM II failed to prevent or stop the Battle of Mogadishu and it began to suffer fatalities, most notably the loss of US troops (portrayed in the book: *Black Hawk Down: A Story of Modern War,* by Mark Bowden and a film of the same name). The United States and other contributing nations began to withdraw their forces from UNOSOM II. Troop strength declined rapidly to 14,968 at the time of the withdrawal of UNOSOM II forces, ordered by the United Nations Security Council in March 1995. For the second time, UN peacekeepers had failed in Somalia. The twin UN fiascos in Somalia emboldened terrorists the world over as well as triggered a rash of ship hijackings, especially off the Somalia coast.

The United Nations Mission in Sudan (UNMIS) was established by the UN Security Council Resolution 1590 of March 24, 2005.[29] Its mandate was to support implementation of the 2005 Comprehensive Peace Agreement between the government of Sudan and the Sudan People's Liberation Movement. UNMIS was deployed and equipped as a lightly armed peacekeeping operation, with troops sent primarily to protect UN staff and property, as well as to facilitate the delivery of humanitarian assistance, but was both ill-equipped and ill-disposed to engage in civilian protection efforts. The mission failed to communicate to people its capabilities as well as what its mandate dictated. There was also a general failure on the part of UNMIS forces to interact positively with the communities in which they were deployed. Thus, when violence erupted in the oil-rich Abyei region in May 2008, the populous expected UNMIS to stop it. This was beyond UNMIS capabilities. What started as a small incident between individual soldiers at a military checkpoint snowballed quickly into a full-scale military confrontation. The incident resulted in the displacement of the entire population of Abyei and its surrounding areas, and the town itself was razed to the ground by Sudan government forces. The inability and occasional unwillingness of the UNMIS military to engage with local people, led some to insist that UNMIS really stood for "Unnecessary Mission in Sudan."[30] Two referendums were scheduled for January 9, 2011: the first to ascertain if the southern Sudanese wanted independence, the second to determine if Abyei wished unification with Bar el Gazhal as part of the south, or separate status within northern Sudan. Whereas, the first referendum was held, the second regarding the status of Abyei did not take place. Disputes arose as to who was eligible to vote.

UNMIS was criticized for its failure to protect civilians. UNMIS could have devoted more resources to the protection of civilians from persistent low-intensity violence that claimed nearly 1,000 lives during the 2010–11 year, preceding the referendum.[31] On the weekend before the January 9, 2011 referendum, northern militias, on the orders of the Sudanese government, attacked pro-southern targets in the oil-rich Abyei region and killed twenty-three.[32] To date, no referendum has been held and Sudan forcibly occupies Abyei. The mandate of UNMIS ended on July 9, 2011, following the completion of the interim period set up by the Government of Sudan and SPLM during the signing of the Comprehensive Peace Agreement (CPA) on January 9, 2005. Undiscouraged by its failure with UNMIS, the UN Security Council established a new mission, the United Nations Mission in the Republic of South Sudan (UNMISS).

The UN/African Union Mission in Darfur (UNAMID) was formally approved by United Nations Security Council Resolution 1769 on July 31, 2007. It is the world's largest UN-funded peacekeeping operation to that date. Its mandate is to protect civilians in Sudan's western region of Darfur, to foster stability so that a settlement could be reached between the rebels of Darfur and the government of Sudan. However, Sudan resented international intervention in its affairs, and did little to rein in the attacks by the *janjaweed* (Sudanese Arab armed militias) against the inhabitants of Darfur. UNAMID faced continued restrictions including a requirement that peacekeepers must inform the government of Sudan before deploying on roads, including in cities. Rebel groups too, were uncooperative, denying access to rebel-controlled areas of Darfur. Nevertheless, on July 29, 2011, UNAMID's mandate was extended for one more year. In response, Sudan threatened to expel the force from its territory.

While the United Nations peacekeepers in the Middle East have supplied the world with a veritable alphabet soup of acronyms, they have conducted no real peacekeeping. The United Nations record is dismal, with the term "peacekeeping" becoming an oxymoron. Israel as demonstrated above (as well as below) has had firsthand costly experience of dealing with and trusting the United Nations, its observers and peacekeepers to insure ceasefires. Thus, Israel must continue its long-standing policy of always insisting on retaining the ability to defend itself against any threat or combination of threats. It cannot rely on international peacekeepers or international guarantees (for more on international guarantees *see* "Basic Principle 70").

70. International guarantees, especially when applied to the Middle East, are often broken and do not provide security.

The validity of this statement is proven by several notable illustrations. On May 25 1950, the United States, the United Kingdom and France issued the Tripartite Declaration (*see* Appendix 6) which pledged to control the qualitative and quantitative flow of armaments to the Middle East—to prevent any future imbalance in that region, and to guarantee the territorial *status quo* as set forth in the 1949 Armistice agreements. The three Western powers had failed to condemn the attack and aggressive war waged by the Arab states against Israel in 1948 and failed to call for sanctions. Instead of pressing for genuine peace agreements between Israel and its Arab neighbors after that war, the Western powers accepted the 1949 Armistice as an end in itself. At the time, the Soviet Union argued for peace. The West contended itself with a lesser goal, merely maintaining the armistice. They pledged that

> The three Governments, should they find that any of these states [in the Middle East]
> was preparing to violate frontiers or armistice lines, would, consistently with their

obligations as members of the United Nations, immediately take action, both within and outside the United Nations, to prevent such violation.

However, increased *fedayeen* raids from the Egyptian-occupied Gaza Strip, Jordanian-occupied Judea and Samaria as well as attacks from Syria elicited no meaningful Western response (*see* "Israel– Insecure Borders–*Fedayeen* Attacks and Israeli Reprisals" map). By 1954, the United States refused to support the Tripartite Agreement to maintain the arms balance any longer, due to the increased tensions with the Soviet Union. In November 1954, the United States offered the Egyptian regime of Gamal Abdel Nasser $27 million in military aid (along with $13 million of economic aid). The United States was selling arms to Jordan, Iraq and Saudi Arabia. The United Kingdom was supplying both Jordan and Iraq. Israeli requests to purchase arms from the United States were turned down. In short, the international guarantees provided by the Tripartite Agreement broke down. They failed to stop the increased guerrilla terrorist attacks on Israel, to maintain an arms equilibrium and to stop the slide towards war—the Sinai-Suez War—in 1956.

In 1957, in the wake of the Sinai-Suez War, (*see* "Sinai-Suez War Ceasefire lines" map) the United States pressured Israel, via the threat of economic sanctions, to withdraw from both the Sinai Peninsula and the Gaza Strip. In an *aide-mémoire* sent from US Secretary of State John Foster Dulles to Israeli Foreign Minister Abba Eban on February 11, 1957, Dulles asserted that the Gulf of Aqaba constituted an international waterway and that no nation had the right to prevent free and innocent passage in the Gulf and through the Straits of Tiran. Dulles emphasized, "the United States, on behalf of vessels of United States registry, is prepared to exercise the right of free and innocent passage and to join with others to secure general recognition of this right."[33] This was followed several days later, by public assurances, via a public address by President Eisenhower on February 20, 1957, "We should not assume that, if Israel withdraws, Egypt would prevent Israel shipping from using the Suez Canal or the Gulf of Aqaba. If, unhappily, Egypt does hereafter, violate the armistice agreements or other international obligations, then this should be dealt with firmly by the society of nations."[34]

SINAI-SUEZ WAR CEASE-FIRE LINES
November 7, 1956

— · —· · — · Armistice Lines 1949-1967

Israel

Controlled by Israel:
Israeli forces withdrew
between February 5 -
March 6, 1957

LEBANON

Beirut ✪

Damascus ✪

Quneitra • Marj Rial

Haifa

SYRIA

Mediterranean Sea

Irbid

Jordan R.

Mafraq

Tel Aviv •

Karameh

Amman ✪

Jerusalem ✪

Gaza •

Hebron •

Dead Sea

Alexandria

Port Sa'id

El Arish

ISRAEL

JORDAN

Mansura

Qantara

Abu Agueila

Jiyanklis •

Abu Sueir

Jebel Libni •

Bilbeis •

• Bir Gafgafa

• Inshas

Cairo West •

Cairo ✪

Kabit

• Bir Thamada

Mitla

Suez

Pass

• Nakhl

Helwan •

E G Y P T

Ras Sudr

Beni Suef •

Eilat • Aqaba

S i n a i

Ras Zafarana •

Abu Zenima

Ei Minya

Nile River

Abu Rudeis

Gulf of Suez

SAUDI

Ras Gharib •

E-Tor

Gulf of Aqaba

ARABIA

Sharm el Sheikh

↑ Straits of Tiran

Hurghada •

Red Sea

Asyût •

Shadwan Is.

In effect, the United States would join other countries in protecting the right of free passage through the Gulf of Aqaba. Twelve maritime states, including the United States and France issued a declaration acknowledging Israel's right to free passage. If Egypt ever used force to close the Straits of Tiran, Israel would be justified to use force (under Article 51 of the UN Charter) as an act of self-defense, to open it. On April 24, 1957, the SS *Kernhills* carrying a cargo of crude oil docked at Eilat, Israel's southern port at the head of the Gulf of Aqaba, as a symbol of United States commitment to freedom of navigation in the gulf.

Assurances were also given to Israel on several crucial issues. First, if Israel totally withdrew from the Gaza Strip, the Egyptian military would not be permitted to return. In effect, the Gaza Strip was demilitarized. Specifically the assurance stated:

> That on its withdrawal the United Nations Forces will be deployed in Gaza and that the takeover of Gaza … will be exclusively by the United Nations Emergency Force. [Furthermore,] …that the United Nations will be the agency to be utilized for carrying out the functions enumerated by the Secretary-General, namely: safeguarding life and property in the area by providing efficient and effective police protection as will guarantee good civilian administration; as will assure maximum assistance to the United Nations refugee program; and as will protect and foster the economic development of the territory and its people.'[35]

Israeli forces totally withdrew from the Gaza Strip, March 7–8, 1957. Egyptian military forces reentered the strip the next day! So much for the concept of demilitarization. Israeli Prime Minister Ben-Gurion sent Golda Meir to Washington to meet urgently with US Secretary of State John Foster Dulles. Meir asked, "What happened? Where are the promises?" Dulles replied, "Would you resume the war for this?"[36]

Most importantly, if Egypt ever attempted to remove the UNEF from its positions along the Egyptian-Israeli armistice line and at the Straits of Tiran, the UN Secretary-General would undertake lengthy deliberations to ascertain if the UNEF had completed its mission and was to be removed. This key point had been agreed to by both the United Nations in the person of Secretary-General Dag Hammarskjold and the Egyptian government and recorded in an *aide-mémoire* that formed an annex to the Secretary-General's report of November 20, 1956, endorsed by the United Nations General Assembly. The *aide-mémoire* read:

> 1. The Government of Egypt declares that, when exercising its sovereign rights on any matter concerning the presence and functioning of UNEF, it will be guided, in good faith, by its acceptance of General Assembly Resolution 1000 (ES-I) of 5 November 1956.

> 2. The United Nations takes note of this declaration of the Government of Egypt and declares that the activities of UNEF will be guided, in good faith, by the task established for the Force in the aforementioned resolutions; in particular, the United Nations, understanding this to correspond to the wishes of the Government of Egypt, reaffirms its willingness to maintain UNEF until its task is completed.[37]

Despite these pledges and guarantees, in May 1967, UAR (Egyptian) President Gamal Abdel Nasser deliberately and rapidly escalated a confrontation with Israel. In rapid succession he mobilized his army on May 14, moved his military forces eastward across the Sinai Peninsula on May 16, and demanded the withdrawal of all UNEF forces from Egypt the same day. By May 19, UNEF forces were withdrawn from the UAR-Israeli armistice line and their positions at the Straits of Tiran. By May 21, UAR forces occupied Sharm el-Sheikh and the next day, May 22, Nasser declared a blockade of the Straits of Tiran on all Israel bound ships and aircraft. The UAR blockade was an act of war against Israel. Under the UN Charter and the 1957 agreements Israel was authorized to use force in self-defense. This marked the start of what came to be called the Six-Day War. On May 22, Nasser bluntly proclaimed to the world, "Our basic aim is to destroy Israel."[38] Cairo's Voice of the Arabs echoed him that day, "The Arab people is firmly resolved to wipe Israel off the map."[39] Nasser rallied the Arab world behind him, concluding a mutual defense alliance with Syria and Jordan and accepting military forces from many other Arab states, including Algeria, Iraq, Kuwait, Lebanon, Saudi Arabia, and Sudan (*see* "Causes of the Six-Day War, 1967" map).

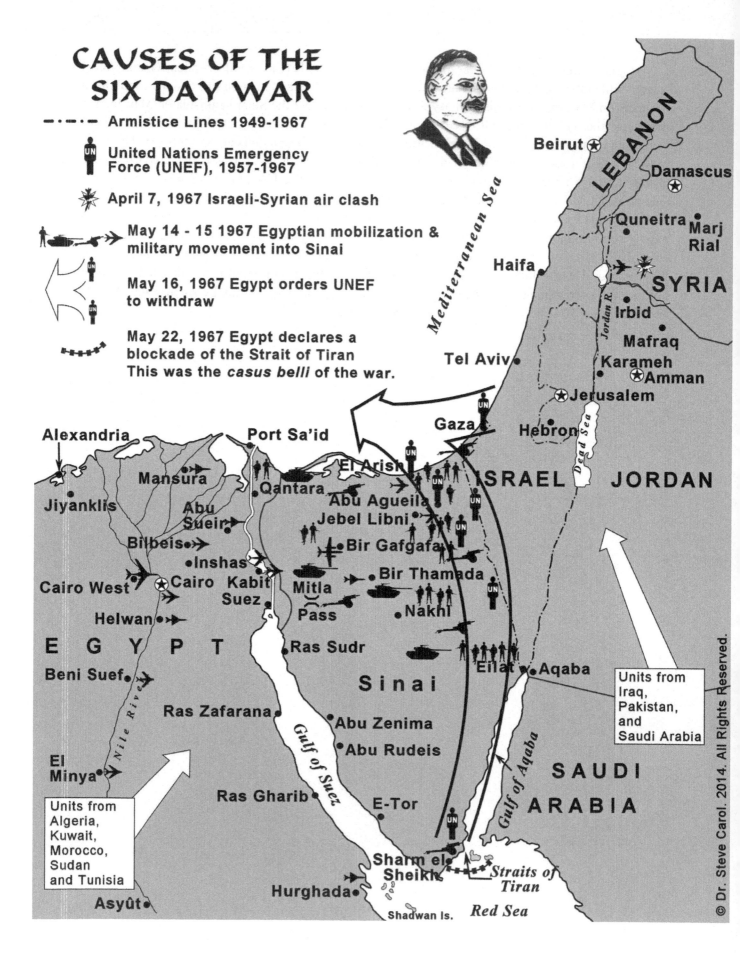

CAUSES OF THE SIX DAY WAR

- **-··-··-** Armistice Lines 1949-1967
- **UN** United Nations Emergency Force (UNEF), 1957-1967
- April 7, 1967 Israeli-Syrian air clash
- May 14 - 15 1967 Egyptian mobilization & military movement into Sinai
- May 16, 1967 Egypt orders UNEF to withdraw
- May 22, 1967 Egypt declares a blockade of the Strait of Tiran This was the *casus belli* of the war.

Mediterranean Sea

LEBANON

Beirut

Damascus

Quneitra Marj Rial

Haifa

SYRIA

Jordan R.

Irbid

Mafraq

Tel Aviv

Karameh
Amman

Jerusalem

Gaza

Hebron

Dead Sea

ISRAEL JORDAN

Alexandria

Port Sa'id

El Arish

Mansura

Qantara

Abu Agueila

Jiyanklis

Abu Sueir

Jebel Libni

Bilbeis

Bir Gafgafa

Inshas

Bir Thamada

Cairo West

Cairo

Kabit

Mitla
Pass

Nakhl

Suez

Helwan

E G Y P T

Ras Sudr

S i n a i

Beni Suef

Eilat Aqaba

Ras Zafarana

Abu Zenima

El Minya

Abu Rudeis

Gulf of Suez

Gulf of Aqaba

SAUDI
ARABIA

Units from
Iraq,
Pakistan,
and
Saudi Arabia

Nile River

Ras Gharib

E-Tor

Units from
Algeria,
Kuwait,
Morocco,
Sudan
and Tunisia

Sharm el
Sheikh

Straits of
Tiran

Hurghada

Asyût

Shadwan Is. Red Sea

The pledges and assurances to Israel made in 1957 were forgotten. The United States was unable to find the record of the meetings and discussions of the 1956 period. They subsequently turned up— but only after the war—stored in Cleveland, Ohio. Therefore, Dulles' commitments were unclear and unknown. Complete Israeli records of the conversations were readily available, and proved accurate. Moreover, on May 26, 1967, President Lyndon Johnson warned Israeli Foreign Minister Abba Eban, "Israel will not be alone unless it decides to go it alone." However, US words and its previous pledges did not stop Nasser.

Earlier on his way to Washington, DC, Eban stopped in Paris, France, to remind French President Charles de Gaulle of the French declaration and guarantee of 1957 recognizing Israel's right to defend itself physically against blockade. De Gaulle was curt and aloof. He warned Israel, "Do not make war. Do not be the first to shoot." Eban responded that Nasser had already fired the first shot by blockading the Straits of Tiran. He reminded de Gaulle that Israel agreed to withdrawn from Sharm el-Sheikh in 1957, largely on the strength of French commitments to free navigation and passage. De Gaulle replied angrily. "[He] admitted that France's declaration of 1957 on freedom of navigation was correct juridically, but this is 1967, not 1957. Look at the date. Guarantees are not absolute."[40] Additionally, during the run-up to the crisis, France embargoed the delivery of offensive weapons to the Middle East, a move severely and negatively affecting Israel because France was Israel's primary arms supplier. Among the items stopped were fifty Mirage 5 fighter-bombers, expressly built to Israeli specifications as well as five missile boats, already paid for (previously discussed—*see* "Basic Principle 59"). A phrase from the Talmud fits this historic occurrence perfectly, "Be careful with politicians, for they befriend a person only for their own needs. They appear to be friends when it is beneficial to them, but they do not stand by a person at the time of his distress."[41] As history proved, especially in Israel's case, international guarantees are no substitute for defensible borders.

Another illustration of international guarantees being violated occurred, in 1964, when Jordan requested to purchase M48 Patton tanks from the United States. President Lyndon Johnson dispatched Governor W. Averell Harriman to convince Israeli Prime Minister Levi Eshkol and Foreign Minister Golda Meir not to oppose the sale. Meir told Harriman, "But, Governor, these tanks [would be] on our threshold." Jordanian tanks in Judea and Samaria would be a scant 9 miles from the Mediterranean coast and pose an existential threat to Israel's heartland. Harriman, speaking as the representative of the US government assured Meir, "But Hussein said these tanks will never cross the Jordan River [i.e. never enter Judea and Samaria]."[42]

Despite Israeli fears, at a National Security Council meeting in February 1965, President Johnson and his advisers agreed that a tank sale to Jordan was necessary. Meanwhile, Israeli Prime Minister Levi Eshkol was informed of the pending US tank sale to Jordan. [Eshkol's] strongly negative reply increased Johnson's concern about domestic reaction to the sale of arms to Jordan."[43] Golda Meir would later recall, after the Six-Day War, "Well, since 1967 I have always been saying to American visitors: 'You want to see these tanks? We have them.'[Israel captured about 100 of the Jordanian tanks] We didn't go across the Jordan to bring them over. They just came over."[44]

This event emphasizes the need for Israel's eastern security border to be the Jordan River. It is only 42 miles from the Jordan River to the Mediterranean Sea. As has previously been mentioned, from the Jordan River Valley going westward an enemy attacking ground force would have to ascend some 4,717 feet to cross the tops of the mountain ridge that form the north-south spine of Judea and Samaria via relatively few roads, a formidable barrier. Radar arrays and electronic signals intelligence (ELINT) sites atop this mountain ridge give Israel an early warning system against attacking enemy aircraft from the east. It would take a modern fighter-bomber aircraft less than 3 minutes to cross that distance. Less than a minute and a half flying time separate the Jordan River from Jerusalem and any attacking plane would have to be shot down at least 10 miles east of Jerusalem to avoid grave damage to civilians, as well as holy sites. To do so, Israel must retain the ability to confront any attacking aircraft as soon as it crossed the Jordan River. Thus, Israeli sovereignty over Judea and Samaria is a geopolitical necessity.

A further illustration of the flouting of international pledges occurred at the conclusion of the 1,000-Day War of Attrition (1967–70). That conflict ended by an August 7, 1970 ceasefire agreement between Egypt and Israel, and guaranteed as co-signatories, by the United States and the Soviet Union. The key provision of the agreement was that

> both sides will refrain from changing the *status quo* within zones extending 50 kilometers [31 miles] to the east and to the west of the ceasefire line [the Suez Canal]. Neither side will introduce or construct any new military installations in these zones. Activities … will be limited to the maintenance of existing installations at their present sites and positions.[45]

There was to be neither movement nor increase of installations, including missile batteries. Yet, on the night of the ceasefire, Egypt and the Soviet Union violated the agreement by rapidly installing new SA-2 and SA-3 missile batteries. Within two weeks, Egypt had constructed between 20 and 30 new sites and had moved up more than 500 missiles. Egypt with Soviet connivance used the ceasefire to move the missiles to the Canal, neutralize the IAF, and threaten Israeli airspace over the western Sinai. It would be these same missile batteries that would support the Egyptian surprise attack and early successes across the Suez Canal in the opening days of the Yom Kippur War of October 1973.

The United States sought to minimize the major violation of the agreement and stressed the importance of getting talks underway. According to US Secretary of Defense Melvin Laird, "I think the important thing for us is to move forward toward negotiations, and not debate what went on 12 hours before the ceasefire and 12 hours after." Laird felt it served no purpose to discuss what occurred during the 12 hours before or after the ceasefire when intelligence was poor; there had been no Egyptian violations of the truce since the United States began reliable verification procedures, about 24 hours *after* (emphasis added) the ceasefire had gone into effect; and US intelligence was better than Israel's for detecting what was happening on the Egyptian side of the Canal.[46] *The Washington Post,* citing US officials, said that one reason the United States had been unable to confirm the Israeli charges was that its U-2 photo-reconnaissance planes did not begin flying over the Israeli-held east bank of the Canal until August 8; consequently there was a lack of pre-truce photographs against which to match the new US and Israeli-supplied photos.[47] Yet the fact remained that the violations had occurred during the first 12 hours of the ceasefire. The author has in his possession aerial reconnaissance photos of the rapid buildup of the Egyptian SAM system along the western bank of the Suez Canal.

However, belatedly on August 19, 1970, US State Department spokesman Robert McCloskey stated that the United States had concluded there was "forward deployment of surface-to-air missiles into and within the zone west of the Suez Canal around the time the ceasefire went into effect. There is some evidence that this was continued beyond the ceasefire deadline, although our evidence of this is not conclusive."[48] The United States pledged to take up the original Israeli charge of violations with Egypt and the Soviet Union. McCloskey added, "We do not now anticipate making further public statements on this matter."[49]

The US-Soviet guarantees had proved worthless. Later the United States would seek to assuage Israeli security concerns by selling it additional military equipment. In 1979, Henry Kissinger, in his memoirs *White House Years*, pointed out that the failure of the US government to pay heed to Israeli protests at the time was a grave mistake. The failure of international guarantees and the violation of the 1970 ceasefire would cost Israel a heavy toll as the IAF lost 104 aircraft and 54 aircrew servicemen,[50] nearly all due to anti aircraft artillery or surface-to-air missile fire, during the Yom Kippur War.

A further example of the failure of international guarantees in the Middle East occurred when Saudi Arabia purchased its first F-15 Eagle fighter aircraft from the United States in 1978. The Carter Administration via the Pentagon promised that they would not be deployed at Tabuk, one of Saudi Arabia's northern bases. Tabuk is just across the Gulf of Aqaba, eight minutes flying time from Israel. Tabuk is only 128 miles away from Eilat, Israel's Red Sea port. Two other Saudi bases in the northern part of the kingdom are Turayt, which is ten minutes flying time from Jerusalem, and Gurayet which is just twenty-one minutes flying time from Israel—neither were covered by the Carter pledge.

US Defense Secretary Harold Brown sought to assuage the fears of some Senators about the F-15s to be sold to Saudi Arabia—that they would be used against Israel. He explained the capabilities of these aircraft, and specified the assurances received from the government of Saudi Arabia. In a letter to Congress in 1978, before the United States approved the first F-15 deal, Brown said, "Questions have been raised concerning the possible basing of the F-15 aircraft at Tabuk air base. I would like to repeat to you the assurance given to me and other United States officials by the Saudi Arabian government that Saudi Arabia will base the F-15 aircraft, not at Tabuk, but at Dhahran, Ta'if and possibly at Riyadh or Khamis Mushait."[51] Secretary of Defense Harold Brown vowed that, should Saudi Arabia violate its commitment, the United States would withhold spare parts, and would not help the Saudis maintain the planes.[52]

In 1981, President Ronald Reagan agreed to sell the Saudi air force five sophisticated AWACS (Airborne Warning and Control System) surveillance planes, a controversial decision that was opposed by many members of Congress and only approved after some restrictions were placed on how the AWACS would be equipped and where they would be based. Reagan obtained a pledge from Riyadh not to deploy them in the kingdom's northern air bases. Saudi Arabia agreed again in 1992 (with the Clinton Administration), not to deploy the F-15s at Tabuk as one of the conditions for the purchase of additional aircraft.[53]

In March 2003, on the eve of Operation *Iraqi Freedom,* the United States asked Israel to agree to a temporary redeployment of the Saudi planes to Tabuk, until the end of the war. The Saudis flew some fifty jets to Tabuk and then refused to return them to their bases in eastern and central Saudi Arabia. The United States never once protested that the deployment violated US export terms of 1978.

In September 2003, IDF Chief of Staff Lt. General Moshe Ya'alon warned of plans by Al-Qaeda to recruit Saudi pilots to take control of several Saudi F-15s based at Tabuk and fly the fighter planes into skyscrapers in Tel Aviv, about 278 miles (less than 19 minutes flying time) from Tabuk. Israel's southern port of Eilat is only 128 miles (less than 9 minutes flying time) from Tabuk.[54]

In 2007, Boeing announced it signed a contract with Saudi Arabia, to enhance the AWACS' capabilities by installing a secure, jam-resistant, digital data link that allowed military aircraft, ships and ground units to exchange tactical pictures with each other in near real time. Forgotten was the Reagan pledge and restrictions placed on the AWACS aircraft.[55] The Saudi F-15s and AWACS remained deployed at Tabuk, Turayt, and Gurayet to this very day. Having failed to enforce the agreement, the United States sought to pacify Israel by selling it more F-15s along with additional

F-15s to Saudi Arabia. Congress was notified of the lifting of the US restrictions in early 2003. Again, international guarantees proved meaningless.

In another instance of the failure of international guarantees, the US was a party to the 1988 Wye Memorandum, which required the PA to inform the US fully of the actions the PA took to outlaw all organizations of a military, terrorist or violent character and to prevent them from operating in areas under its jurisdiction. The PA not only failed to comply, but also the United States, under successive administrations, failed to pressure the PA into fulfilling the terms of the Wye Memorandum.

71. Security barriers are not obstacles to peace.

Security barriers have been constructed throughout history, from the Great Wall of China to the security barrier between Israel and Egypt completed in 2014. Some other notable security barriers are listed below in chronological order.

SECURITY BARRIERS AROUND THE WORLD	
Barrier Location	**Specifics Regarding the Barrier**
Democratic Republic of (North) Korea (DPRK)–Republic of (South) Korea	The 151-mile-long demilitarized zone separates the two Koreas since 1953 and is the most heavily fortified border in the world.
Belfast, Derry, and other areas of Northern Ireland	The "Peace Line," is a series of barriers first constructed in the early 1970s to curb escalating violence between Catholic and Protestant neighborhoods. The barriers range from a few hundred feet to over 3 miles in length. By 2006, there were more than forty such barriers spanning a total distance of over 13 miles in Belfast, Derry, and other areas.
Oman	On June 9, 1965, a rebellion began in Oman's Dhofar Province, led by the Dhofar Liberation Front (DLF) against the central government. The guerrillas were supported by the PDRY and backing the PDRY was the Soviet Union. In response, in late 1973, the Omani government constructed the Hornbeam Line, a 31-mile barbed wire fence. As the conflict continued Oman had to construct another barrier to the southwest of the Hornbeam Line—the Damavand Line, which consisted of a double barbed wire barrier along with mines.
Cyprus	Since 1974, Turkey has constructed and maintained a 187-mile separation barrier—the Attila Line—along the 1974 ceasefire line dividing Cyprus into two parts. The barrier is made of concrete, barbed wire, watchtowers, minefields, and ditches. This was done in violation of several United Nations Security Council resolutions (*see* "Cyprus-Crisis of 1974, Turkish Invasion and Occupation" map).
Morocco–Western Sahara	This barrier called the "Berm" or "Moroccan Wall" is a series of ten-foot-high sand and stone barriers, some mined. It extends for 1,678 miles through the Western Sahara. Today there are six separate sets of walls constructed between August 1980 and April 1987. They are intended to keep Polisario Front guerrillas out of the Moroccan-occupied and controlled Western Sahara.

India–Bangladesh	In 1986, India began to construct a 2,116-mile barbed wire barrier surrounding its neighbor to prevent smuggling, illegal immigration, and infiltration by terrorists. The fence is electrified along some stretches. By March 2011, some 1,700 miles of fencing was completed but the project was subject to numerous delays.[56] The estimated cost is $1.2 billion.
India–Pakistan	In 1989, India began erecting a 330-mile separation barrier along the 460-mile disputed 1972 "Line of Control" between Indian and Pakistani-controlled Kashmir. Its purpose is to stop arms smuggling, infiltration by Pakistani-based Islamist separatists, and terrorists into Indian-controlled Kashmir. The fence is electrified barbed and concertina wire eight to twelve feet high. That barrier was completed in late 2004. According to Indian military sources, the fence reduced by 80 percent the numbers of terrorists who routinely cross into India to attack soldiers and civilians.
Kuwait–Iraq	The 120-mile demilitarized zone along this border has been manned by UN soldiers and observers since the Persian Gulf War ended in 1991. Made of electric fencing and wire, supplemented by fifteen-foot-wide trenches, the barrier extends from Saudi Arabia to the Persian Gulf. In 2006, Kuwait decided to install an additional 135-mile iron partition.
Uzbekistan–Afghanistan	The Uzbek-Afghan barrier is a separation barrier built in the early 1990s by Uzbekistan along its 130-mile border with Afghanistan. It consists of a barbed wire fence, a second taller electrified barbed-wire fence, as well as land mines.
United States–Mexico	In the mid-1990s, President Bill Clinton initiated two programs, Operation *Gatekeeper* in California and Operation *Hold the Line,* in Texas, to crack down on illegal immigration from Mexico. They produced a system of high-tech barriers, including a fourteen-mile fence separating San Diego from Tijuana. On October 26, 2006, President George W. Bush signed the Security Fence Actof 2006 into law. The law called for the construction of 700 miles of security fence along its border with Mexico. Construction on the fence began in 2006, with each mile costing the US government about $2.8 million. In 2010, the initiative was terminated due to costs after having completed 640 miles of barrier either fence or vehicle barriers.[57]
Ceuta–Morocco and Melilla–Morocco	In 1998, Spain completed two barriers around each of their North African enclaves in Morocco. Spain has 6 miles of border with Morocco around the cities of Ceuta and Melilla. The fences are two rows of high wire barricades equipped with security cameras and fiber-optic sensors, with a road running between them for police patrols. The $35 million barriers were funded in part by the European Union and were designed to stop illegal immigration and smuggling.
Thailand–Malaysia	In 2001, the two countries jointly agreed to construct a fence along their 400-mile border to reduce smuggling and stop the infiltration of Malaysian Muslim terrorist groups that led to the southern Thailand insurgency, a separatist campaign in Thailand's four southernmost provinces.

Uzbekistan–Kyrgyzstan	In 1999, Uzbekistan began construction of a barbed wire fence to secure their border with Kyrgyzstan and prevent terrorist infiltration.
Turkmenistan–Uzbekistan	On March 30, 2001, Turkmenistan's President Saparmurat Niyazov ordered his government to finish construction of the 1,007-mile fence along his country's border with Uzbekistan and Kazakhstan by the end of the year to prevent smuggling and illegal migration.
Botswana–Zimbabwe	In 2003, the government of Botswana started construction of a 300-mile ten-foot-high electric fence along its border with Zimbabwe to control the spread of hoof-and-mouth disease. Zimbabwe claimed that the fence really aimed to curb the immigration flow from troubled Zimbabwe into stable and calm Botswana.
India–Myanmar	In March 2003, India began construction of a separation barrier designed to seal off its 1,009 mile-long border with Myanmar. India hoped to curtail cross-border crime, including goods, arms and counterfeit Indian currency smuggling, drug trafficking, and insurgency. The two nations began erecting a fence along the border in March 2003.
Saudi Arabia–Yemen	In 2003, Saudi Arabia began building a ten foot-high barrier along part of its 1,118-mile border with Yemen, mainly along the vast stretches of desert east of Sa'ada Province.[58] The purpose of the fence was to prevent smuggling and terrorist infiltration. In February 2004, Saudi Arabia halted construction due to Yemeni objections that the fence violated a border treaty signed in 2000, interfering with grazing rights of the local inhabitants. However, in the summer of 2009, due to increased terrorist activities, as well as the ongoing Houthi Rebellion in Yemen, Saudi Arabia erected a high-tech razor wire fence along the border with Yemen, including Sa'ada Province.
United Arab Emirates–Oman	A separation barrier constructed by the UAE along its border with Oman is an effort to curb the flow of illegal migrants, illicit drugs, and terrorists.
Brunei–Malaysia	In 2005, Brunei built a security fence along its 12.5-mile border with Limbang, Sarawak, Malaysia, to stop smuggling and the flow of illegal immigrants.
Kazakhstan–Uzbekistan	On October 19, 2006, Kazakhstan began construction of a 28-mile separation barrier built along part of its border with Uzbekistan. The 8-foot high barbed wire fence includes searchlights and spans the Saryagash and Maktaaral administrative districts of southern Kazakhstan. It is situated along heavily populated towns and cities of eastern Uzbekistan. It is being built to curb drug smuggling across the border.
Pakistan–Afghanistan	On December 26, 2006, Pakistan announced it would fence and mine part of its 1,500-mile border to stop Islamic supremacist terrorists and drug smugglers. The Afghan government objected to the Pakistani move since it would legitimize the international recognized Durand Line (drawn in 1893 by the British).
Egypt	A security fence was built around Sharm el-Sheikh in the Sinai Peninsula to prevent future terrorist attacks on the tourist resort town.

Iran–Pakistan	Iran began construction of a separation barrier along its border with Pakistan to stop illegal border crossings, curb the flow of drugs, and stop terrorist attacks. The wall will be 3 feet thick and 10 feet high made of concrete reinforced with steel rods and will cover the 435-mile border between the two nations. Iran is constructing the barrier solely on its territory.
Saudi Arabia–Iraq	In 2006, Saudi Arabia announced plans for the construction of a high-tech razor wire security fence along the entire length of its 560-mile desert border with Iraq to secure the kingdom's borders.
Lebanon–Syria	In May 2010, Syria and the Hezbollah terrorist organization began building a fortified barrier on the western (Lebanese) slopes of Mount Hermon some 59 miles southeast of Beirut. The wall is to run from Rashaya Al-Wadi in the south, to the Lebanese Bekáa Valley town of Aita el-Foukhar, in the north,[59] creating an exclusive military zone some 14 miles long and 9 miles wide, parallel to the Lebanese-Syrian border. This area will be off-limits to the Lebanese Army. This zone is designed for several purposes. The first purpose is as an obstacle against any Israeli tank attack heading through Lebanon toward Damascus. Secondly, as a military equipment storage area as well as a weapons smuggling route across the border concealed from outside surveillance. It also deepens Syria's military presence in Lebanon, which supposedly ended in April 2005, with a Syrian military withdrawal from that nation.
Israel–Egypt	By January 2010, the Sinai Peninsula emerged as an anti-Israel terrorist base used by a myriad of groups including Al-Qaeda, Hamas, Islamic Jihad, and later ISIL. To prevent terrorist infiltration, drug smugglers, human slave traders, and a flood of illegal African immigrants (mainly Eritreans and Sudanese), Israel embarked on the construction of a security barrier along its entire border with Egypt in Sinai, from Rafah to Eilat, some 165 miles. The barrier consists of two layers of fencing. The first is a fifteen-foot, five-inch razor barbed wire fence.[60] The second layer is a steel barrier augmented by patrol roads and intelligence collecting devices such as cameras, radar and motion detectors. Construction on the fence began November 22, 2010. At a cost of $450 million, the project took three years to construct, with the final section completed in December 2013.[61]
Greece–Turkey	In January 2011, Greece announced the construction of a three meter-high security barrier along 8 miles (its land frontier) of its 128-mile border with Turkey. It is being built to stem the flow of illegal immigration. Thus far, no steps have been taken with regard to the remainder of the Greco-Turkish border along the Evros River.[62]
Israel–Syria	Starting in 2012, in reaction to the spreading Syrian Civil War with its accompanying refugee flow, illegal infiltration, as well as the increased activities of Al-Qaeda, the Islamic State, and other international terrorists, Israel began to construct a preventative security barrier along its Golan Heights border with Syria. It is similar to the one on the Egyptian-Israeli border. By early 2013, some six miles had been completed. A further 37 miles of fence is in the accelerated construction phase.

Israel–Jordan	At the end of November 2013, Israeli Prime Minister Benjamin Netanyahu gave orders for another security fence to be set up along the 105 miles of the southern section of the Israeli-Jordanian border between the Gulf of Aqaba and the Dead Sea. By June 2014, the plan had been amended to include the entire 250-mile-long Israel–Jordan border from the Golan Heights to the Gulf of Aqaba.
Egypt–Gaza Strip	As the result of a series of terrorist attacks, Egypt announced in November 2014, that it intended to create a one-kilometer (0.62 mile)— later extended to 2 kilometers (1.24 miles), 9-mile-long buffer zone along the border between Egypt and the Gaza Strip. The zone will include water-filled trenches to thwart tunnel diggers as well as a security barrier designed to stop both terrorists and smugglers.
Hungary–Serbia	It was announced in mid-June 2015 that Hungary would construct a 13-foot high barrier for 109 miles of its southern border with Serbia. The main purpose of the barrier was to stop the flow of illegal immigrants into Hungary.

In response to increased terrorism including suicide bombings after the start of the Al-Aqsa (Second) *Intifada*—the Oslo War—on September 28, 2000, Israel began construction of a security barrier as a necessary measure of passive self-defense. The barrier, along and within Judea and Samaria is planned for a total distance of 440 miles. As of June 2015, only about 273 miles (62.1 percent) of the barrier was completed. Some 35 miles (8 percent) is under construction, and 132 miles (29.9 percent) is yet to be built.[63]

While Arab supporters continuously call the Israeli barrier in Judea and Samaria, a "wall" and an obstacle to peace, in reality the vast majority of the barrier, over 385 miles is comprised of wire fences, vehicle barriers, and electronic sensors. It is 96 percent fence and only 4 percent (17.5 miles) concrete wall. The remaining 30-foot-high concrete sections being built are designed to block three areas where Arab snipers have shot at Jews: houses in border villages as well as at cars traveling on the trans-Israel highway, and around the Biblical matriarch Rachel's Tomb, just south of Jerusalem.

Thus far, the barrier has worked. Since its construction began, there has been a 90 percent decrease in terrorist attacks. When there was no security barrier, during the first three years after the start of the Al-Aqsa (Second) *Intifada*on, Israel suffered ninety-three suicide attacks that left 1,010 Israelis dead and 5,600 wounded. This would be comparable to 45,450 Americans killed and 252,000 wounded during a slightly over four-year period. In the four-year period (2006–09) since most of the fence has been completed, the number of attacks has declined to fewer than five a year, and the number of Israelis killed by terrorists has averaged fewer than ten per year.[64]

ISRAELI DEATHS BY SUICIDE TERROR ATTACKS, 2000–09[65]	
Year	**Number of Deaths**
2000	0
2001	85
2002	220
2003	142

2004	55
2005	22
2006	15
2007	3
2008	1
2009	0

In a like manner, the Israel–Egypt security barrier along their common Sinai frontier has also proven its worth, especially in stopping the flood of illegal immigrants into Israel. Only thirty-four illegal infiltrations into Israel were reported in the first half of 2013, a dramatic decrease compared to the 9,570 during the same period in the previous year.[66] Israeli barriers are not obstacles to peace. They are just some of many partitions around the world aimed at repelling invaders whether they are terrorists, smugglers, or illegal immigrants.

ROLE OF THE MEDIA

Hear now this, O foolish people, and without understanding; which
have eyes, and see not; which have ears, and hear not.
Jeremiah 5:21

My people are destroyed for lack of knowledge.
Hosea 4:6

To achieve justice, it is first necessary to call things by their right names.
Confucius

To be persuasive we must be believable; to be believable, we must be
credible; to be credible, we must be truthful. It is as simple as that.
Edward R. Murrow

Everyone is entitled to their own opinions, but they are not entitled to their own facts.
Daniel Patrick Moynihan

We are in a battle, and more than half of this battle is taking place in the battlefield of the media.
Ayman al-Zawahiri, leader of al-Qaeda

A free press—today that would include all forms of media—is one of the essential foundation stones of Western democracy. Due to the August 4, 1735, acquittal of John Peter Zenger, owner and editor of the *New York Weekly Journal,* of seditious libel charges, the principle of freedom of the press was embedded in America's democratic system and enshrined in the Bill of Rights as part of the First Amendment of the US Constitution. One should also emphasize that in Western democracies the media is the largest single factor in shaping public opinion. Public opinion has great significance because words reflect ideas and ideas motivate people. This in turn to a large extent determines public policy.

Caroline B. Glick succinctly clarified the real role of the media:

> The purpose of journalism [i.e. media] is to report on the world as it is, not as we would like it to be. [Additionally, journalism is not supposed to advance an ideological agenda.] The media are supposed to report facts, not shape perceptions. The facts, not the perceptions are supposed to inform policy. That is, they are not supposed to collaborate with policymakers, they are supposed to inform policymakers and the general public.[1]

In the Middle East however, such freedom of the press is non-existent. Save for Israel, which has a democratic and fiercely outspoken press, the media is rigidly controlled by the mélange of undemocratic tyrannies—absolute monarchies, theocracies, autocracies, and dictatorships. For them, media is just another propaganda tool. Additionally, since much of the region adheres to Islam and follows shari'a law, there is a strict prohibition against any negative criticism of that faith, precluding an open and free press. Furthermore, the media of the region are skilled in appealing to Western emotions and in telling Western audiences what they want to hear. Such "news" is related to them in English, French, German, Spanish, Italian and other languages, while revealing something quite different indicating real intent, to their home audiences in Arabic and Farsi. Unable to win decisively in the military theater of war, Israel's enemies have shifted to the media battlefield and the court of world opinion.

Moreover, it must be noted that there is a lack of journalistic preparedness among Western journalists. Many journalists have only superficial knowledge of the Middle East and its long history and nuances in its culture. They know little and understand even less. Few reporters speak Arabic, Farsi, Turkish, Kurdish, Pashto, or Hebrew and therefore they cannot independently verify and confirm information provided to them by public relations personnel of the local authorities. Likewise, understanding discussions among the handlers could readily reveal falsifications as well.

Not only does this affect American (and other Western) media coverage, but more importantly our counter-intelligence capabilities. According to its 2006 survey of instruction in foreign languages, the Modern Language Association (MLA) found American universities enrolled only 2,463 students in Arabic at the advanced level. Of those "advanced" students, perhaps one in ten would become expert. Apart from immigrants, whom intelligence agencies employ only with great caution, the prospective hiring pool of advanced students in Arabic is measured in the hundreds. The situation with regard to other languages of special interest to counterterrorism was even worse. The MLA reported the following number of students (but did not tell us how many are "advanced"): 243 Farsi, 5 Kurdish, 103 Pashto, 4 Somali, and 624 Turkish.[2]

Additionally, as large sums of Western funds streamed into the Middle East due to purchases of petroleum, the Arab/Muslim world used some of these funds to purchase interests or outright control of Western media outlets.[3] Those are in effect, propaganda organs for promoting the Arab/Muslim political and religious narrative and agenda. While it is quite legal for foreign investors to invest in the United States since the United States invests abroad, it is quite something different for foreign investors to use their investment as a propaganda weapon to be used against American interests and values.

This was openly evident at a September 2006 meeting of the 57-member Organization of Islamic Conference (now Organization of Islamic Cooperation) in Jeddah, Saudi Arabia. The information ministers called on wealthy Muslim businessmen to invest large amounts of money in Western media outlets. As OIC Secretary-General Ekmeleddin İhsanoğlu explained:

> Muslim investors must invest in the large media institutions of the world, which generally make considerable profits, so that they have the ability to affect their policies via their administrative boards. This would benefit in terms of correcting the image of Islam worldwide.[4]

Furthermore, İhsanoğlu called on Muslim countries to establish additional global networks in a variety of widely spoken foreign languages. This occurred for example, in the United States, with the launching of Al Jazeera America on August 20, 2013, to broadcast the Arab/Muslim agenda in general and the Muslim Brotherhood program in particular, to the American people 24/7 from American soil.

For the Arab/Muslim world, this is an importantF tactic to slant media coverage and convince the gullible masses in the West of the peaceful intentions of Islamic states and the righteousness of their anti-Western, anti-American, and anti-Israel causes. A prime example of such investments is those made by Saudi billionaire Prince Al Waleed bin Talal. Prince bin Talal invested billions in the Time Warner Corporation, the parent company of CNN cable news. Additionally, he purchased 7 percent in News Corp, the parent company of Fox News, making him the largest shareholder of that media giant. He influenced how news is portrayed on both CNN and Fox News. It was the same bin Talal who offered New York City Mayor Rudy Giuliani a check for $10 million during the Prince's visit to Ground Zero, the site of the September 11, 2001 World Trade Center terrorist attacks, in early October 2001. Bin Talal remarked in a written statement that, "at times like this one, we must address some of the issues that led to such a criminal attack. I believe the government of the United States of America should reexamine its policies in the Middle East and adopt a more balanced stance toward the Palestinian cause." Giuliani outraged, refused and returned the check and asserted:

> I entirely reject that statement. There is no moral equivalent for this [terrorist] act. There is no justification for it. The people who did it lost any right to ask for justification for it when they slaughtered 4,000 or 5,000 innocent people. To suggest that there is a justification for [the terrorist attacks] only invites this happening in the future. It is highly irresponsible and very, very dangerous. And one of the reasons I think this happened is because people were engaged in moral equivalency in not understanding the difference between liberal democracies like the United States, like Israel, and terrorist states and those who condone terrorism. So I think not only are those statements wrong, they're part of the problem.[5]

Middle Eastern funds are not only being used to purchase media outlets but are also used to influence important American think tanks. Foreign countries use donations to present both a favorable view of the nation involved as well as push their agendas in the international media, especially the American ones. It would be remiss to omit mentioning the recent exposé by the *New York Times* in early September 2014, whereby it was revealed that "since 2011, at least 64 foreign governments, state-controlled entities or government officials have contributed to a group of 28 major United States-based research organizations."[6] It is estimated that "a minimum of $92 million in contributions or commitments from overseas government interests [were made] over the last four years. The total is certainly more."[7] The *New York Times* report further explained that in exchange for these substantial donations the research institutions in question offered their donors two main benefits. The first "led to implicit agreements that the research groups would refrain from criticizing the donor governments" and the think tanks were "pressured to reach conclusions friendly to the government financing the research." This pushed some scholars to self-censor their research lest their findings offend the donor country. Secondly, the institution pushed "United States government officials to adopt policies that often reflect the donors' priorities."[8] While these practices are global in nature (which is beyond the scope of this book), the report listed nine Middle Eastern countries that contribute funds to nine major think tanks including these prominent ones that deal with Middle Eastern/North African issues: the Atlantic Council, Brookings Institution ($41 million received[9]), Center for Global Development, Center for Strategic and International Studies, and the Middle East Institute. Foreign funding can heavily influence a think tank's objectivity and accuracy as well as stance on crucial diplomatic issues. Specialist members of these think tanks, many of whom enter the diplomatic service, thus have dubious credibility as impartial mediators in the Arab/Muslim conflict against Israel.

Thus, think tanks are engaged in lobbying for foreign governments and in influence buying. In the past think tanks were thought of to be academically neutral but this is no longer the case. The Middle East countries named in the *New York Times* exposé include Bahrain, Kuwait, Lebanon, Libya, Morocco, Oman, Qatar, Saudi Arabia, and the United Arab Emirates.[10] Both Qatar and the United Arab Emirates[11] are heavily engaged in this practice. For example, the United Arab Emirates, a major supporter of the Center for Strategic and International Studies donated over $1 million for a new headquarters. Qatar, one of the richest countries in the Middle East, is the largest foreign donor to Brookings Institution, according to the report. In 2013 Qatar, which backs the Muslim Brotherhood and its Palestinian terrorist offshoot Hamas, paid Brookings $14.8 million over four years to fund the Doha Center in Qatar and for a special project to address relations between Muslims and the United States. Another illustration is the role of the Hariri family. They are very prominent in Lebanese politics and Middle Eastern affairs and generously donated to the Atlantic Council for the Rafik Hariri Center for the Middle East.[12] Of importance, it should be noted that despite all the calumnies spread over the years about Israeli/Jewish "influence" and "control" over the United States, Israel is *not* (emphasis added) on the list of donors to such think tanks.

Saleem Ali, formerly a visiting fellow at the Brookings Doha Center in Qatar, told the *New York Times*, "There was a no-go zone when it came to criticizing the Qatari government. It was unsettling for the academics there. But it was the price we had to pay," Ali said of the partnership, while warning members of Congress to "be aware" of Brookings reports, which he said may not contain the full truth on any given issue. The Qataris were pleased with the arrangement, which the foreign ministry touted on its website, writing, "the center will assume its role in reflecting the bright image of Qatar in the international media, especially the American ones."[13] A government official told the *Jerusalem Post*, "Qatar has been a major bankroller for Hamas and other terrorist organizations. The fact that the same Qatari government is also a major provider of funds for a respectable Washington think tank raises a whole series of questions about that think tank's relationships and impartiality."[14]

Martin Indyk, the Vice President and Director for Foreign Policy at the Brookings Institution, took a leave of absence to serve as the US Special Envoy for Israeli–Palestinian Negotiations from 2013 to 2014. Brookings, as mentioned above, was funded in generous amounts by Qatar, an ally and supporter of Hamas, a declared terrorist group sworn to the destruction of Israel and that fought three wars against Israel in pursuit of that goal. Indyk, hardly impartial or sympathetic to Israel, returned to the think tank after the negotiations failed in April 2014, to resume his position there.

Even think tank directors were not free to say or do what they pleased. In 2011, Michele Dunne, a former White House and State Department official, was appointed as the director of the Rafik Hariri Center for the Middle East at the Atlantic Council. However, in 2013 after Ms. Dunne signed a petition and testified before a US Senate Foreign Relations Committee urging the United States to suspend military aid to Egypt, calling Mr. Morsi's ouster a "military coup," Bahaa Hariri called the Atlantic Council to complain. The Hariri family was opposed to the Morsi regime and supported the new Egyptian government. Ms. Dunne resigned shortly thereafter.[15] The foreign funding of American think tanks raises a pertinent question. Should not think tanks that get funding from foreign governments register with the US Justice Department as "foreign agents" that aim to shape policy, as required by the Foreign Agents Registration Act of 1938? In light of the above, one wonders if a free, open and impartial media is possible anymore. If hostile foreign investors influence the media with political agendas, the American people will be denied access to factual truth as well as equally balanced news.

72. There is no such thing as a free press in the Arab/Muslim Middle East.

According to Freedom House, Arab media control ranges from total government oversight to mixed systems that allow some private ownership and editorial independence, but remain under the watch of government censors. In general, Arab governments seek to keep a lid on political discourse and activity—especially any that might be perceived as a threat to the established order—though the degree of control varies from country to country. All Arab states ban criticism of the ruling governments and use the media to praise their leaders and vilify their enemies. In numerous Arab states misojudaic, anti-Israel (anti-Zionist) and anti-American invective is the rule, not the exception.

Newspapers in the Arab countries can be divided into three categories: those that are government-owned (together with semi-official papers such as *al-Ahram* in Egypt, those owned by political parties, and the "independent" press. Measuring twenty countries and one non-state entity (the Palestinian Authority) in the Middle East and North Africa (including Arab states, Iran, Turkey. and Israel), Freedom House's Freedom of the Press report found one nation (Israel) free, four countries (Algeria, Tunisia, Kuwait, and Lebanon) part free, and fifteen other Arab states, as well as Turkey, and Iran, plus the Palestinian Authority, not free.[16]

According to the Islamic Mass Media Charter, adopted by the First International Islamic Mass Media Conference in Jakarta, Indonesia, September 1–3, 1980, Muslim media professionals are to "censor all material which is either broadcast or published, in order to protect the *Ummah* (the Islamic worldwide community) from influences which are harmful to Islamic character and values, and in order to forestall all dangers," and to preserve the integrity of the profession and Islamic traditions. Muslim media professionals are "committed to the propagation of *da'wah* (propagation of the faith), to elucidating Islamic issues and to the defense of the Muslim point of view."[17]

Western readers and viewers need to be apprised by mainstream media editors when reporting is about repressive, authoritarian and dictatorial regimes as well as regions controlled by terrorist groups. These editors seriously neglect their journalistic ethics and are less than honest when they fail to tell their readers/viewers when a "news" story is censored or is only favorable to that group or country and therefore is nothing more than utter propaganda.

As it stands at present, any Western news media coverage is subject to strict regulation and guidelines. Regimes, "rebel" groups and terrorist organizations establish military areas or zones into which the foreign press is not allowed. In this manner, news releases, statistics, photographs and videotape are rigidly controlled. Reporters, photographers and video crews cannot travel freely. They are directed as to what photographs or videos they can take. Additionally, they are forbidden to tell the reader/viewer that the story has been censored, unless it was censored by the Israeli government. There have been numerous cases of deliberately fabricated incidents as well as falsified photographs. More often than not, scenes are staged for the news cameras, which range from orchestrated street demonstrations and rioting to manipulated and misrepresented photographs, accompanied by highly selective editing. At times, the same photos and film footage have been recycled again and again without informing the reader/viewer that what they are seeing is stock footage, archive footage, library pictures or file footage.[18] Furthermore, journalists are dependent on Arab/Muslim handlers and fixers. These handlers either fear the various terrorist organizations and authoritarian regimes support them, or both. The journalists are guided by these handlers or minders who tell them where they can visit, who they can interview (usually individuals who will echo the party line and with open bias evident). Moreover, the Western media have engaged, at times, in the fabrication of quotes or the citation of fictitious quotes.

A more recent example of fabricated quotes occurred when Iranian President Hassan Rouhani was interviewed at the UN General Assembly meeting, September 24, 2013, by CNN's Christiane Amanpour. She asked him about the Holocaust in an attempt to portray Rouhani as a "moderate" and quite different from his predecessor, Mahmoud Ahmadinejad, an outspoken, notorious, and adamant Holocaust denier. The CNN version of Rouhani's remarks, broadcast and published on their website, was as follows:

> I've said before that I am not a historian and that when it comes to speaking of the dimensions of the Holocaust [the word "Holocaust" was added], it is the historians that should reflect on it. But in general I can tell you that any crime that happens in history against humanity, including the crime that Nazis committed towards the Jews as well as non-Jews is reprehensible [the word "reprehensible" was also added] and condemnable. Whatever criminality they committed against the Jews, we condemn.[19]"

Almost immediately, the Iranian government's FARS news agency condemned CNN's translation of his remarks about the Holocaust as largely a fabrication. FARS provided an exact translation of what he said:

> I have said before that I am not a historian and historians should specify, state and explain the aspects of historical events, but generally we fully condemn any kind of crime committed against humanity throughout the history, including the crime committed by the Nazis both against the Jews and non-Jews, the same way that if today any crime is committed against any nation or any religion or any people or any belief, we condemn that crime and genocide. Therefore, what the Nazis did is condemned, [but] the aspects that you talk about, clarification of these aspects is a duty of the historians and researchers, I am not a history scholar.[20]

When the two versions are compared it is clear that CNN expanded on what he said to help convey the impression that he was condemning Holocaust denial when it is clear that he did no such thing. In fact, in his statement Rouhani employed the old Holocaust deniers' tricks of questioning the death toll of the Holocaust, acknowledging that many others groups were also victims, and claiming that a well-established historical fact requires further examination by "historians and researchers," while repeatedly pointing out he is "not a historian."

In sum, traditional Western investigative journalism is sadly lacking and of poor and suspect quality. Since foreign media coverage in the Arab/Muslim Middle East is severely restricted, reporters depend on governmental, non-governmental organizations or terrorist groups' claims without even noting that those claims could not be verified. Any reporter (be they Western or a local "stringer") straying from the guidelines set forth by the government or group will never be allowed into that country or area again. Worse still, the journalist will suffer "serious consequences"[21] (to quote David

Schlesinger, Reuters global managing editor) including verbal threats, destruction of equipment (cameras, video cams etc.), kidnapping, beatings, long-term imprisonment even a grisly death by beheading. The use of intimidation (for example, Hezbollah had a copy of every journalist's passport[22]), harassment, and violence against the press is directed especially at those who present the Arab/Muslim view in a negative manner. In 2013, the greater Middle East remained the world's most dangerous place for reporters. According to the Committee to Protect Journalists (CPJ), 29 died in Syria, 10 in Iraq, 6 in Egypt, 5 in Pakistan and 4 in Somalia. In Syria, about 60 other journalists were kidnapped at least briefly during 2013 covering the civil war, half of whom were still missing at year's end. Most journalists who die for their work are local people covering local stories, according to CPJ research.[23]

The dangers posed to Western media personnel led to "pack-coverage" of the story in order to play it "safe." Under the "pack coverage" system, a story by a journalist from one news agency is frequently copied by others of supposedly rival news agencies. Thus, any bias is often duplicated and repeated. Such situations cause journalists to exercise self-censorship for fear of loss of access to key "newsworthy" individuals, the loss of their own job, or worse. If the situation is too dangerous the Western journalists are withdrawn, but not wishing to lose the "hot story" the media agencies rely on local "stringers." They in turn, provide not the impartial news but rather stories that reflect the party or government line, and certainly nothing unfavorable to the cause. As a result, these actions, many from the Arab/Muslim world never get printed or filmed, let alone broadcast on television.

Consequently, random "man-in-the street" interviews of local residents by Western media do not exist in any Arab/Muslim state. "Testimony" from minority groups, is rigidly controlled and monitored. What Arab Christians say for example in public, is vastly different from what they say in private. To maintain their safety and to hold up their valid loyalty as Arab patriots—be they Egyptian Copts, Iraqi Assyrians, Lebanese Maronites, or Palestinian Christians to name but a few—they must denounce Israel more vociferously at times than Muslims, otherwise they might be accused of collaborating with the "Zionist enemy." The consequences to these minorities for not cooperating with the Arab propaganda machine can be most severe including but not limited to rape of daughters and wives, torched businesses and ultimately, death by a knife or a bullet. The only testimony an ordinary Arab Christian can make on a public microphone or a television camera, is an anti-Israel statement.

Increasingly for more than forty-five years (since the Israeli victory in the Six-Day War of 1967), world media in general has been far from objective or truly impartial in its coverage of Israel. A disproportionate number of anti-Israel articles are steadily published, which is not fair and balanced journalism. To make matters worse, the opinions of the media personnel are sometimes reported as "news." This can be readily discerned by the use of numerous adjectives and adverbs in the reporting of the story (unless they are part of a direct quotation).

Many times a group of different reporters will be brought en masse to the site of an "event." The mere presence of foreign journalists, cameramen, and TV crews become the cue for an on-the-spot demonstration, spate of rock throwing, or a riot. Some Western news media willingly comply with all the Arab/Muslim restrictions and display an open, pervasive anti-Israel bias for a story they are supposed to be reporting objectively. This anti-Israel bias is reflected by the use of several techniques. Media blackouts, i.e. simply ignoring events that disturb the media's political beliefs and agenda have been used.

An additional simple tactic employed by some world news media editors is to pay the journalist only if his/her report is "suitable" in the editor's opinion. If there is a pre-disposition to report Israel in an unfavorable manner, more than likely, that is a story that will see the light of day. As Joël Kotek, a professor of political science at the Free University of Brussels as well as at France's leading university of Social Sciences, the Sciences Po in Paris explains,. Belgian "correspondents in Israel of the French-speaking Belgian press are only paid if their articles are published. So why should they waste their time and energy writing about positive events, such as an Israeli scientific discovery? The article will be rejected by the editors and they will not receive any payment."[24]

The Middle East Media Research Institute (MEMRI), the Committee for Accuracy in Middle East Reporting in America (CAMERA), HonestReporting.com and Palestinian Media Watch are media monitoring watchdog groups, created in reaction to the biased, less than objective, double-standard, anti-Israel reporting coming out of the Middle East and elsewhere. Readers are urged to check these groups in order to get a proper perspective of media stories as well as school textbooks. A conspicuous example of holding American news media accountable was the January 2014, ad placed by CAMERA (measuring three-stories high on the side of a building facing the headquarters of the *New York Times* in New York City) urging that paper to stop "Misrepresenting facts, omitting key information, skewing headlines and photos" in its reporting about Israel.[25]

Furthermore, there is a conspicuous lack of providing essential facts, context or background information in covering certain stories. Additionally, media reports frequently use facts to draw false conclusions. For example, *Teen Newsweek,* a magazine distributed to middle school students across the United States, ran a cover story in their October 23, 2000 edition, entitled, "Peace Under Fire: Palestinians and Israelis on the Brink of War." This included a chart illustrating the number of Palestinian and Israeli children killed since 1987. The Palestinian numbers, represented in bright red, many times exceed Israeli losses, shown in a less visible yellow. There is no explanation of circumstances how these children died. The implication is that there is equivalency—even though the Palestinian children were killed while attempting martyrdom in the context of violent attacks on Israeli forces, while the Israeli children were killed while sitting on a public bus or in a pizzeria, blown up by a Palestinian suicide bomber.[26]

The media is often guilty of the sin of omission or distorting historical events. Key words that reflect prejudice are substituted for words that might reflect poorly but accurately on Arab/Muslim—especially Palestinian—terrorists. The word "terrorist" is anathema to the Western press in the Middle East. Thus, readers and viewers find euphemistic substitutes, such as "assailants," "combatants," "gunmen," "militants," "insurgents," "guerrillas," "commandos," and "resistance fighters"—anything but "terrorist" when used in describing a Palestinian/Arab/Muslim terrorist. Victims of terrorist attacks are downgraded to "bystanders." Thus, the murderers are put on the same moral plane as the victims. However, the word "terrorist" is freely used to describe the actions of the Israeli government, military or citizens. While Arab leaders are usually portrayed as "moderate," Israeli leaders are labeled as "hardliners" and "warmongers." The media bias is colored by a lack of moral clarity as to what is evil. Moreover, there is an on-going refusal to mainstream Israeli views and give overwhelming emphasis of radical and critical ones. In addition, excessive credibility is given to hostile sources for outlandish news accounts.

A demonstrable example was NBC Nightly News' broadcasting of the 1982 Israel–PLO War in Lebanon. Throughout its reporting, NBC consistently refused to acknowledge PLO censorship of media coverage, while pointedly and repeatedly emphasized Israeli censorship.[27] Rarely if ever, did NBC correspondents mention to their viewers that much of the damage and devastation being filmed, of such cities as Tyre, Sidon, Damour and south Beirut had occurred earlier. This destruction actually occurred during the first part of the Second Lebanese Civil War, from 1975 to 1982, prior to the Israeli invasion.[28]

A 2011 study[*] of the dispatches from Reuters reporting the Arab-Israeli conflict, found that the news agency—the largest international news agency in the world—engaged in systematically anti-Israel-biased reporting in favor of the Arabs/Palestinians. Reuters was thus able to influence audience affective behavior and motivated direct actions along the same line.[29] These actions were in contradiction to Reuters' stated policy of strictly upholding journalistic objectivity and reflected a fundamental failure to uphold the Reuters corporate governance charter as well as ethical guiding principles.[30] The Reuters Handbook of Journalism stipulates that its correspondents uphold a strict policy of social responsibility by providing complete facts, all sides of an argument and relevant context in neutral prose.[31] As part of this responsibility, Reuters admonishes its journalists:

> We must be on alert for language that could imply support for one side of a conflict, sympathy for a point of view, or an ethnocentric vantage point. We should, for example, provide the dual names of disputed territories. We must not parrot any loaded expressions used by our sources, except in quotes and official titles. Generic references to a specific country as "the homeland" for example, are unwelcome.[32]

In reporting about the Middle East, Reuters used historical reconstruction, atrocity propaganda, vilification, mischaracterization, euphemisms, asymmetrical definitions, card stacking, non sequiturs, gross exaggeration, fauxtography, and at times, outright lies. There are also appeals to pity and to the poverty of the "poor Palestinians." Articles labeled "Analysis" were *de facto* Op-Ed pieces. Israel, the victim of Hezbollah attack and aggression was portrayed as the "aggressor."

Specific examples occurred during the 1982 Israel–PLO war in Lebanon as well as 2006 Second Lebanon War, when Reuters was accused of bias against Israel in its coverage. Among other practices, Reuters and other media outlets used edited, manipulated and staged photographs and video. A number of news photos bore concocted captions, showing something but claiming it was something else in a different location. A dramatic example occurred when the *Washington Post* published a photograph (August 2, 1982) of a baby that appeared to have lost both its arms. The UPI caption said that the seven-month-old had been severely burned when an Israeli jet accidentally hit a Christian residential area. The photo disgusted President Reagan and was one reason he subsequently called for Israel to halt its attacks. The photo and the caption however, were inaccurate. The baby in fact, did not lose its arms, and the burns the child suffered were the result of a PLO attack on East Beirut.[33] These practices came to be known in the media industry as "fauxtography." Notoriously, a Lebanese freelance photographer, Adnan Hajj[34] utilized Adobe Photoshop computer software to duplicate war scenes—at least two such photos were widely published worldwide (*see* the photos at "Adnan Hajj photographs controversy" in Wikipedia). This was done in order to exaggerate and magnify the scope of Israeli military actions. Hajj also submitted staged photos. His file at Reuters numbered 902 photos. How many of them were fabrications would never be known. As a result of public outcry, Reuters was forced to dismiss him and promptly deleted his photo file from its databank.[35] Hajj was not the only practitioner of fauxtography (for an excellent four-minute video of examples of fauxtography, Google, "Photo Fraud in Lebanon" by aish.com).

News events can be orchestrated to suit the needs of the regime. In the Arab/Muslim Middle East, in countries ruled by absolute monarchs, dictators, military strongmen, theocrats and autocrats, very little occurs by "spontaneous" actions or reactions of the "street." From demonstrations staged for

---

[*] The study examined a sample of fifty news-oriented articles related to the Middle East conflict published on the Reuters proprietary websites across a three month window.

the Western news media to attacks on foreign diplomatic missions (embassies and consulates), such "spontaneous" occurrences almost always have state approval and sponsorship, or in some cases transnational terrorist origins—witness the Al-Qaeda attack on the US Consulate in Benghazi on September 11–12, 2012. Readers should understand that attacking foreign diplomats has for centuries, been deemed a heinous violation of the law of nations, but that is willfully ignored in the Middle East. The following represents examples of such attacks on diplomatic missions.

ATTACKS ON DIPLOMATIC MISSIONS		
Year	**Diplomatic Mission**	**Location of Attack**
1829	Russia	Tehran, Iran
1979	United States	Tehran, Iran
1979	United States	Tripoli, Libya
1986	France	Tripoli, Libya
1987	Kuwait	Tehran, Iran
1987	Saudi Arabia	Tehran, Iran
1988	Soviet Union	Tehran, Iran
2006	Denmark	Beirut, Lebanon
2008	Israel	Nouakchott, Mauritania
2009	Pakistan	Tehran, Iran
2011	France	Damascus, Syria
2011	United States	Damascus, Syria
2011	Israel	Cairo, Egypt
2011	United States	Tripoli, Libya
2012	United States	Cairo, Egypt
2012	United States	Benghazi, Libya
2012	United States	Sana'a, Yemen
2012	Germany	Khartoum, Sudan
2012	United States	Cairo, Egypt
2012	Vatican City	Damascus, Syria
2012	United States	Sana'a, Yemen
2012	United States	Benghazi, Libya
2013	United States	Ankara, Turkey
2013	France	Tripoli, Libya
2013	United States	Herat, Afghanistan
2014	Turkey	Mosul, Iraq

In Iran, there is a special Press Court, which prosecutes journalists for offences such as criticizing the Supreme Leader, reporting stories that are deemed damaging to the foundations of the Islamic Republic and the government, insulting Islam or using questionable sources, i.e. Western sources, for news. Iran is a world leader in terms of jailed journalists, thirty-nine in 2009, thirty-four in 2010, and thirty-five in 2013. Turkey emerged as the world leader in 2013 with forty journalists imprisoned and currently has more reporters behind bars than any other country in the world.[36]

To illustrate just one example of the price paid by journalists seeking to report the truth in the Middle East, journalist Edouard George, then senior editor of Beirut's French-language daily *L'Orient le Jour,* compiled a list of seven foreign journalists who were murdered by the PLO between 1976 and 1981:

- Larry Buchman, correspondent for ABC Television
- Mark Tryon, Free Belgium Radio
- Jean Lougeau, correspondent for French TF-1
- Tony Italo, Italian journalist
- Graciella Difaco, Italian journalist
- Sean Toolan, correspondent for ABC Radio
- Robert Pfeffer, correspondent for *Der Spiegel*

This represents one small example of journalists who were murdered while covering only one of the many conflicts in the region, not to omit (mentioned earlier) both Daniel Pearl (2002) and James Foley (2014). Additional media personnel assassinated are listed under "Basic Principle 36".

During the first *intifada* that erupted in December 1987, foreign correspondents—including those from NBC and CNN—freely admitted that many events were staged and falsified for the media cameras. Similar activities took place during the Al-Aqsa (Second) *Intifada* that began on September 28, 2000. One of the most outrageous episodes was the alleged shooting death of twelve-year-old Muhammad al-Dura hiding behind his father Jamal, allegedly by Israeli forces, which was filmed by a France 2 crew and televised globally. This event was strategically timed for the beginning of the Al-Aqsa (Second) *Intifada*. The "shooting" and its filming was no chance coincidence, occurring on the second day of the uprising, September 30, 2000. The French producer Charles Enderlin was nowhere near the scene of the alleged killing at Netzarim Junction in the Gaza Strip. Only the sole Palestinian freelance cameraman, Talal Abu Rahma, was present, without any witnesses.[37]

An Israeli government investigative committee on the al-Dura affair was formed in 2012 by Defense Minister Moshe Ya'alon, who at the time served as strategic affairs minister. The committee examined the raw footage[38] filmed by the France 2 crew and produced by Charles Enderlin, and found that it was edited to exclude a part at the end in which the boy—declared dead by the reporter on film merely a moment earlier—is clearly seen alive, miraculously moving his body, lifting his arm, moving, and looking out, post-mortem.[39] "As opposed to the media reports that stated that the boy died of blood loss, an examination of the raw video shot by the France 2 staff shows the child alive," the investigative committee reported in May 2013. That portion of the video was never broadcast. "In addition, there is a great deal of evidence to indicate that al-Dura and his father were never hit by any bullets. Neither showed any trace of blood, nor was there any blood on the wall behind them. The picture of al-Dura's body in a Gaza morgue was that of another boy.[40] The bullet holes on the wall behind the father and son had round forms, showing they could not have come from the angled IDF position. The investigation shows that it is very unlikely that the bullet holes seen in the wall behind the two came from shots fired by IDF soldiers."[41] Importantly, instead of the gun battles purported to have happened, the footage shows Palestinian participants faking injuries, staging evacuations and choreographing "battles" in full view of dozens of reporters from leading news agencies—this, while children stroll past the alleged Israeli position, unperturbed.

Dr. David Yehuda, who was sued by France 2 for libel after he refuted claims that the boy's father was injured in the incident, and was later, cleared by a Paris court, welcomed the report's findings, saying, "This whole case was fabricated. The boy didn't die." The government review committee asked Dr. Yehuda to submit the same records and expert opinion he had presented to the French court during his trial, in which he provided proof that scars Jamal a-Dura (the father) claimed to be the result of the incident were in fact caused years earlier.[42] "I operated on [Jamal], in 1994 after he was abused by Hamas operatives who suspected he was collaborating with Israel. He was shot in the backside and his right arm was mangled from knife injuries. In 2005 and for some years after that, he presented those scars as if they were the results of that incident." Dr. Yehuda stated that the medical findings concerning the boy's injuries were also fictitious, "We know that on the day of the incident a boy named Muhammad al-Dura was pronounced dead at Shifa at 9 A.M. The boy in the report, who allegedly suffered gunshot wounds, was hit at 3 P.M. He is not Muhammad al-Dura and I have no doubt that the boy in that report is still alive.[43] We know where he is and I've asked the Shin Bet to produce him." "This case is nothing but a pile of lies and it has caused Israel tremendous damage I hope it can still be rectified," he said.[44] In short, the al-Dura story was a hoax,[45] for which Israel was castigated and pilloried worldwide, by the mainstream media.

It should be stressed that the al-Dura case, a blatant fraud, was reported as "news." There is often credible news (unfavorable to the Arab/Muslim point of view) that is dismissed by them as a hoax. Those that have visual falsehood productions have come to be called "Pallywood." This term was coined by Professor Richard Landes of Boston University in 2005. It describes the Palestinian film industry that produces staged film, video, and still photos, designed to win the public relations war against Israel. Beginning with the 1982 Israel–PLO War in Lebanon and ongoing since then, it is used by the Palestinians, other Arabs and their willing supporters. It involves specific instances of media manipulation, distortion of facts and outright fraud for use by complicit journalists. Professor Landes and his colleagues gathered extensive evidence exposing the practice of simulating injuries for Western cameras as well as "faked funerals, staged gun battles, ... professional weeping grandmothers," and bogus ambulance evacuations among other "distressing" events.[46]

Arab/Muslim news from the Middle East often includes shocking and seemingly unbelievable stories including those about Muslims seeking to legalize sex-slavery[47] or plans to destroy Egypt's Pyramids[48] or sanctioning of sodomy-suicide-missions[49] or calls to crucify infidels.[50] These seemingly impossible stories tend to be dismissed as hoaxes. However, these cited examples were not fabrications, but actual news stories. Raymond Ibrahim, Arab history researcher and author, provides us with a simple rule of thumb:

> When it comes to determining whether a story from the Muslim world is a hoax or not, first determine whether it is Islamic or not—whether it has doctrinal or historic support; whether it has some backing in the Quran and/or the Hadith.[51]

In April 2002, after nineteen months of the Al-Aqsa (Second) *Intifada*, and suffering hundreds of Israeli dead and thousands injured or maimed for life, Israel responded with Operation *Defensive Shield*. Israel deliberately chose not to bomb the terrorist sanctuaries from the air (which was standard US practice at the time in Afghanistan), in order to minimize civilian casualties, choosing instead a more costly (for the IDF) ground offensive. Israel redeployed military forces into Judea and Samaria. Its goal was to wipe out terrorist bases. Israel reoccupied Shechem (Nablus), Jenin and other cities in the region that it had ceded to Yasser Arafat, as part of the Oslo "peace process." Arafat in turn used them as havens and launching pads for terrorism.

It was during Operation *Defensive Shield* that the so-called "Battle for Jeningrad" or "Jenin massacre" took place. The Israeli army moved into that Samarian city to wipe out a nest of terrorists responsible for a particularly intense sequence of suicide bombings, murder and mayhem. A flood of foreign journalists descended on the city to document Israel's "cruelty and barbarism," and the story remained front-page news to this day. *Al-Jazeera* ran the story 24/7 with video of grieving mothers swearing revenge on the "Zionist butchers," and rumors swirled of mass graves and poison gas. The Arab League, the EU and United Nations condemned Israeli aggression—as did the editorial board of the *New York Times*. The (British) *Independent* dispatched Robert Fisk, who was embedded with the terrorists, and the newspaper's cartoonist, Dave Brown, produced an award-winning rendition of his signature theme, "Jews eating Palestinian babies."[52]

Immediately there was talk of "genocide," of "thousands" of Palestinian Arab dead, of a "siege" rivaling that of Leningrad in World War II. Palestinian Arab sources claimed a figure of 5,000 dead while Palestinian spokesman Saeb Erekat offered up an estimate of 3,000 dead. He subsequently adjusted this figure to 500, but this was still far, far from the truth. An additional claim was made that an entire "refugee camp" had been bulldozed to rubble (subsequently, before and after satellite photographs revealed that the fighting had occurred in one-tenth of one percent of the city of Jenin[53]). This charge of the total demolition of the refugee camp and the "thousands" dead, was endorsed by the UN envoy, Terje Roed-Larsen, without even conducting an investigation. Western media led by the British press, echoed the falsehood. As was subsequently demonstrated, the Israeli forces relying on tactics designed to minimize civilian casualties, killed between 46 and 52 Palestinian Arabs, most of them combatants, in days of fierce house-to-house combat. Human Rights Watch, a pro-Palestinian NGO, stated the number was 52.[54] Palestinians themselves finally confirmed 56 dead. In reality, it turned out that 45 terrorists, 9 civilians and 23 Israeli soldiers were killed in brutal house-to-house fighting.[55] Aerial views demonstrated the pinpoint nature of the Israeli operation. The Israeli strike in Jenin was far more measured and humane than other such interventions in Grozny, Russia, Serbia, and Mogadishu, Somalia. However, the propaganda damage had been done. Still today, the Jenin "massacre" endures, out of reach of rational refutation.

Another example of libelous reporting occurred on June 9, 2006, when an explosion on a Gaza beach killed seven Palestinian Arab family members. Shortly afterward, PLO/PA television released a horrific video showing a ten-year-old girl shrieking amidst the bodies. Palestinian Arab hospital workers and spokesmen angrily blamed IDF artillery fire even though no investigation had been conducted. This despite the fact the accusers had no way of knowing what caused the explosion. It was ultimately determined that the family was not killed by the IDF. Rather, Hamas had mined the area to defend their arsenal of Qassam rockets against Israeli commandos. The video was a twisted amalgam of spliced footage and questionable anachronisms. It was quite simply, a fake. The explosion occurred some ten minutes after the last Israeli shell had been fired into the area. The shrapnel in the bodies was not from Israeli ordnance. Hamas terrorists had almost certainly killed their own people but then immediately blamed Israel.

Although the 2006 Second Lebanon War was initiated by the aggressive acts of Hezbollah—first kidnapping two Israeli soldiers and then unleashing the barrage of over 4,000 missiles against Israel—Hezbollah was able through manipulation of the media, to portray itself and Lebanon as the victims of the conflict. When Israeli bombs went astray and killed civilians, as they did in the town of Qana on July 30, Hezbollah media handlers quickly descended on the scene to manage the coverage, positioning props.* These included most notoriously, a posed child's teddy bear (photographed by Sharif Karim for Reuters), a posed Minnie Mouse (by the same photographer for Reuters), and a positioned Mickey Mouse (for the Associated Press).[56] Bandaged casualties were paraded, and ashen-gray fatalities were displayed for the world media. The teddy bear, Minnie and Mickey Mouse toys were clean (therefore not at the building when it was struck) and the so-called deceased had died of other causes and had been brought to the scene from the morgue, to be displayed as alleged bombing victims. These were additional examples of the on-going fauxtography campaign. Hezbollah was thus able to turn world opinion against Israel, the real victim of the onslaught. The Lebanese Prime Minister claimed another massacre, but instead of forty dead as he claimed, only one person had died.

From December 27, 2008 to January 18, 2009, Israel launched Operation *Cast Lead* against Hamas in the Gaza Strip. The Israeli retaliatory operation was designed to halt incessant rocket fire on Israel by both Hamas and elements of Al-Qaeda and Fatah. Hamas claimed 5,000 killed and many more thousands injured. The principal source for these claims was Palestinian Arab health officials who were all employed by Hamas. It was in the interest of Hamas to minimize the number of casualties among its troops and maximize the number of civilians killed. As usual, the inflationary numbers were repeated without checking by the UN and much of the world press. Usually journalists seek two sources to verify information, but in this case, most were satisfied with one that was unreliable and likely biased. UN sources have their own bias from years of working for the benefit of the Palestinian Arabs, cooperating with Hamas and making apologies for terrorist acts directed against Jews. It was impossible to know how many of the casualties were terrorists and how many were not. Hamas ordered its fighters to take off their uniforms and to blend in with the civilian population. They hid in private homes. Hamas remorselessly used women and children as rocket crews, ammunition carriers and human bombs, while others were used as human shields (*see* "Basic Principle 54"). Thus, it was virtually impossible to know how many fatalities were innocents and how many were combatants.

According to Palestinian Arab sources, Israel murdered all the civilian dead. Nevertheless, logical questions must be asked: How many died from Hamas rockets that fell short. At least two Palestinian Arab children were killed that way. How many died when booby-traps set for Israeli troops went off in rooms full of Palestinian Arabs trapped there by Hamas terrorists? How many were killed by secondary explosions when arms caches hit by Israeli forces exploded? How many died because they were in the vicinity of rocket crews that drew Israeli fire? The truth is the people reporting casualty figures made no effort to determine the cause of death because that would limit the propaganda value of the dead.

According to the Israel Defense Forces, 700 of the dead were terrorists, mostly from Hamas, and 250 were civilians. Another 200 people were unaccounted for. If these figures are accurate, then the majority of the casualties were indeed terrorists. Israel of course, has its own bias, but it also has a record of integrity and, unlike the PLO/PA or Hamas, is an open democracy that allows its claims to be checked independently.

However, there was another independent source for an accurate accounting of casualties. An Italian journalist, Lorenzo Cremonesi, a correspondent for Italy's *Corriere della sera,* declared on Jan. 26, 2009, that the number of Palestinian Arabs killed in Operation *Cast Lead* did not exceed five or six hundred. Cremonesi based his findings on tours of hospitals in the Gaza Strip and on interviews with families of casualties. He also assessed the number of injured to be far lower than 5,000, the number quoted by Hamas. "It is sufficient to visit several hospitals [in the Gaza Strip] to understand

---

* An Arab prop man, complete with suitcase full of stuffed toys for use as props was observed and photographed in Beirut.

that the numbers don't add up," Cremonesi wrote. Only on November 1, 2010, did Hamas government Interior Minister Fathi Hamad confirm that Hamas in Gaza lost 700 fighters in Operation *Cast Lead*, 250 in the first day alone, not 50 as was first claimed.[57]

Exaggerated statistics has long been a feature of the Arab/Muslim side in the ongoing 140-year war against the Jews in the Land of Israel. Throughout, the Israelis have suffered from biased reporting, and a double standard. In fact, Israel is not the victim of a double standard, but rather the target of no standard at all. Its public relations explanations have been at times, wanting. However, as Israeli Prime Minister Golda Meir once intoned, "A bad press is better than a good epitaph."

A recent example of a "Pallywood" production occurred at the start of the Second Gaza War in November 2012. The BBC broadcasting acted as a willing accomplice to Palestinian propaganda, when they filmed a video showing an alleged "serious wounded victim" of the Israeli counter-attack on Gaza—Operation *Pillar of Cloud*—being carried away. Yet some thirty seconds later, in the unchanged video, the same man is standing on his own two feet walking away.[58]

In the Arab/Muslim Middle East, a rapid shutdown of journalistic coverage can occur quite easily. One of the reasons why Western governments, intelligence agencies, diplomats, policy makers, analysts, and academics failed to see and understand the growing popular unrest that swept Tunisia, Egypt, Jordan, Yemen, Bahrain, Libya, Syria and other areas of the Arab world from December 2010 well into 2015, was the result of a lack of information gathered by the media due to control by authoritarian regimes.

For example, during the protests, demonstrations and riots that swept Egypt from January 25 to February 11, 2011, foreign journalists were beaten, arrested and their equipment broken or stolen in attacks by supporters of Egyptian President Hosni Mubarak in Cairo, in efforts to exercise tight control as to what information got out to the world. This included, but was not limited to, journalists from CBS, ABC, CNN, Fox News, the *New York Times, Washington Post* and *Al-Jazeera*. In addition, attacks took place on journalists from Israel, Japan, France, Canada, Turkey, Denmark, Russia, Switzerland, Belgium and Greece.[59]

On the very day, February 11, 2011, that Hosni Mubarak stepped down as Egyptian president, these assaults culminated in the vicious mob attack on CBS senior correspondent Lara Logan, who suffered "a brutal and sustained sexual assault"[60] by a mob in Cairo, as they shrieked "Jew! Jew!"[61] at her, though she was not Jewish. This blatant display of misojudaic hatred permeates the Muslim world and is not covered by the mainstream media out of fear of retaliation.

A 2013 study prepared by the Almasry (Egyptian) Studies and Information Center found that hundreds of journalists were attacked since the 2011 uprising that brought the Muslim Brotherhood to power in Egypt. This included some 309 attacks, including three murders, 100 assaults, including that on Lara Logan, and 42 cases of temporary imprisonment. It is believed that undocumented attacks on journalists would push the numbers much higher. In comparison, thirteen journalists have died or been killed in Egypt during the past seventy years since 1942.[62]

During the Third Gaza War (2014), much of mainstream media engaged in the same journalistic malpractice as took place in the Second Gaza War and the Second Lebanon War. The media reported casualty figures for civilians coming from the Hamas-controlled Gaza Strip as accurate. The figures were supplied by the Hamas-controlled Gazan Ministry of Health. The Ministry of Health counted everyone not in uniform as a civilian. Most Hamas fighters did not wear uniforms. When terrorists were brought to hospitals, they were brought in civilian clothing, obscuring terrorist affiliations. The UN was sometimes sourced for the casualty figures, but the UN also got its figures from the same

Gazan Ministry of Health. Hamas released reports from the front to global media accusing the Israel Defense Forces of indiscriminate killing and targeting civilians.

Bear in mind that these fatalities included many people who were killed by Hamas rockets that fell short striking their own territory. Fourteen percent of the rockets fired by Hamas actually fell inside Gaza. That was more than 450 rockets (roughly mid-way in the conflict).[63] Therefore, there must be a calculation made of the damage inflicted by Hamas on its own people. There were also those killed by secondary explosions from booby-trapped houses, and extrajudicially killed as "collaborators," not to omit the deliberate murder of tunnel-diggers,[64] at least 160 of them children.[65] Furthermore, there is no way to know if the Gazan Ministry of Health did not count deaths from natural causes or even automobile accidents as deaths from Israeli actions. It mattered little, for both Hamas and the media, in collusion at times, had an agenda to paint Israel in the blackest of terms.

Yet, a puzzling question remains. It seems that the only time the mainstream media indulges in day-by-day casualty counts is when Israel is involved in conflict. That was not done for the numbers of civilian casualties when NATO bombed Bosnia and Herzegovina in 1995; not done when NATO bombed Yugoslavia in 1999; not done when NATO bombed Afghanistan from 2007 to 2010; not done when NATO bombed Libya in 2011; and for that matter not done when the Obama administration killed using drone strikes in Pakistan and Yemen. Once again, the anti-Israel media bias shines through.

73. Arab/Muslim indoctrination is a highly successful industry. It is well organized and is without opposition. It makes use of exaggeration, disinformation, manipulation, selective omissions, distortion of key facts, lack of context, oversimplification of complex issues and historical inaccuracy.

Many of the spokesmen in the Arab/Muslim world engage in deliberate and perverse promulgation of conflicting facts and principles, i.e. doublethink. Additionally, they engage in ambiguous, deceptive, and confusing language, i.e. doublespeak. Furthermore, the use of contradiction, evasion and circumlocution obscures true understanding of issues. Words are emptied of their normal meanings and turned into their opposites. Yasser Arafat was a master of these techniques. He showed contempt for accepted standards of honesty or morality, especially by actions that exploited the scruples of others. Thus, "terrorism," according to Arafat and the PLO, was not premeditated violence against Israeli civilians, but rather the IDF attacks in self-defense against the PLO/PA perpetrators of such attacks against civilians. This use of doublethink and doublespeak continues to the present.

News media reports frequently slant the report by presenting only one side of the story. For example, frequently the media gave coverage to Israeli responses to Arab terrorism and attacks as if the Israelis were the aggressive party. This has been going on for over forty years since the end of the Six-Day War. Barely mentioned if at all, were the facts that Israel was responding to days and weeks of unprovoked Arab attacks. Yet, the media gave ample coverage to the Israeli reprisal adding to the impression that the aggressor was Israel and that there was a tit-for-tat "cycle of violence" to which Israel contributed. Such moral equivalency between attacker and victim is proof of mainstream media bias against Israel. Yasser Arafat, Mahmoud Abbas and other PLO leaders were quick to catch on to this lop-sided coverage, constantly reframing any action Israel took in response to Palestinian terrorism as the cause of the next terrorist act.

To exemplify the exaggeration employed, during the Israel–PLO War in Lebanon (First Lebanon War), 1982—Operation *Peace for Galilee*—Israel was accused of killing 10,000 Lebanese and

Palestinians, wounding 40,000, and leaving 600,000 homeless. Later, it was learned that the figures were inventions of Yasser Arafat's brother, Dr. Fathi Arafat, who headed the Palestine Red Crescent.[66]

Arab/Muslim indoctrination permeated official government textbooks. Saudi textbooks teach many noxious lessons. A ninth grade book on the Hadith produced by the Saudi Education Ministry in 2005–06 and aimed at 13-year-olds states, "the Jews and the Christians are enemies of the believers."[67] Later in the same book it states, "The struggle against Jews and Christians will endure as long as God wills." An eighth-grade textbook says, "The Apes are the people of the Sabbath, the Jews; and the Swine are the infidels of the communion of Jesus, the Christians."[68] Vilification of Christians, Bahá'ís, secularists, unbelievers, and Western civilization is ever-present. However, the most sincere vitriol is saved for the Jews and Israel. In "Islamic History" for eighth graders, they are taught, "the whole Muslim nation is engaged in a jihad against international Zionism, manifested by the state of Jewish gangs called Israel, established on Palestinian land."[69] The twelfth grade textbook entitled "Islamic World," states "Jews will not leave Palestine except by jihad."[70]

Furthermore, Saudi texts dogmatically instruct that various other groups of "unbelievers"— apostates (which includes Shi'ites as well as Muslim moderates who reject Saudi Wahhabist ideology), and polytheists—should be killed. Under the Saudi Education Ministry's method of rote learning, these teachings amount to indoctrination, starting in first grade and continuing through high school, where militant jihad on behalf of "truth" is taught as a sacred duty. Another eighth grade text describes the duties of jihad that "the whole world should convert to Islam and leave its false religions lest their fate will be Hell."[71] These textbooks are used not only in Saudi Arabia but also in Saudi-funded schools around the world.[72] [73]

Such textbook indoctrination includes gender discrimination. For example, a text aimed at 12-year-olds and produced by the Saudi education ministry in 2005–06, called *Al-Hadith wa'l-thaqafa al-Islamiyya* ("Prophetic tradition and Islamic culture"), tells children that women complain too much, are never satisfied by their husbands' "favors," and are weak. It advises against mixing of the sexes socially (*khalwat,* which is punished in Saudi Arabia by lashes).

The Saudis pledged in writing, in July 2006, to undertake a program of textbook reform to eliminate all passages that disparage or promote hatred toward any religion or religious groups. This was to be fulfilled in time for the start of the 2008 school year. To date this reform of textbooks has not been implemented as exemplified by the above quotations. Likewise, no such reforms have been undertaken in the textbooks of Egypt and Jordan (both of which have signed peace treaties with Israel), nor in the textbooks of the Palestinian Authority, which had pledged to do so in the Oslo Accords. Elsewhere in the Arab world the incitement and hatred continues to indoctrinate new generations. We must not forget that children who are indoctrinated with such hatred are susceptible to engage in bigotry and even violence. Hate speech and publications are the precursor to genocide.

Generally, in the coverage of events in the Middle East the Arabs limit their discussion of the region to the period after the 1967 Six-Day War. Omitted from such coverage is reference to the Jordanian occupation of Judea and Samaria, the Egyptian occupation of the Gaza Strip and the Arab/Muslim desire to initiate genocide against the Jewish people. Moreover, only Arab refugees are referred to, ignoring the far larger number of Jewish refugees driven out of Arab/Muslim nations, as well as the Arab responsibility for initiating the twin refugee problem from 1947 onwards.

On September 24, 2007, then Iranian President Mahmoud Ahmadinejad told an audience at Columbia University in New York, "We don't have homosexuals like in your country. We don't have that in our country. We don't have this phenomenon; I don't know who's told you we have it."[74] At face value that may be true as they are put to death in that nation. According to the Iranian gay and lesbian rights group Homan, the Iranian government has murdered an estimated 4,000 homosexuals since 1980.[75] In fact, nine Arab/Muslim countries—Iran, Mauritania, Nigeria, Qatar, Saudi Arabia, Somalia, Sudan, United Arab Emirates, and Yemen— have made homosexuality a capital offense.

True stories that manage to appear albeit briefly in the world mainstream media that depict the Arab world unfavorably (their definition of "unfavorable") are quickly removed rarely, if ever were seen again. An excellent example of this occurred immediately after the September 11, 2001 terrorist attacks on the World Trade Center in New York City and the Pentagon in Arlington, Virginia. Rather than condemnation of these atrocities coming from within the Muslim world there was widespread celebrations. There were, for instance, views of Palestinian Arabs dancing in the streets and handing out candy to children for the brazen attack on America. When an official Foreign Press Association delegation met with PA's information minister Yasser Abed Rabbo, to protest PA threats against foreign and Palestinian free-lance photographers who took pictures of the street celebrations, Rabbo told them in no uncertain terms, "Palestinian national interests would come before freedom of the press."[76]

In a like manner, there has been a notable failure by the world media to cover Israel's immediate involvement in many international humanitarian, rescue and relief efforts. Israel sent search and rescue teams, electronic sniffers, earthmoving equipment, generators, lighting equipment, field hospitals, and even a premature-babies ward. In recent years such humanitarian assistance went to Sri Lanka, which at first refused Israeli aid, effected by the December 26, 2004 Indian Ocean basin earthquake and tsunami, Myanmar, after the cyclone of May 2, 2008, the Philippines, after the May 2009 typhoon, Haiti, in response to the January 12, 2010 earthquake, and Chile after the February 27, 2010 earthquake. Israeli humanitarian assistance was sent even to New York residents of Far Rockaway, and Long Beach, as well as the Atlantic City-Margate area along the Jersey shore, after Hurricane Sandy of October 25, 2012. Most recently, Israeli aid went to Nepal, after the twin earthquakes of April 25, and May 12, 2015. These Israeli efforts get scant or no coverage in the world press, and certainly none in the Arab/Muslim world press, lest it reflect favorably on Israel.

As stated above, there has been a long, intentional, ongoing clever and insidious international campaign to defame, denounce, demonize, delegitimize, vilify and marginalize the Jewish state. Mainstream international media for the most part have become accomplices to the activities of terrorist groups like Hamas and Hezbollah in parroting their propaganda lines in support of such groups. As a result, the world hears of Israel only after some violent retaliatory strike or some sort of alleged episode of corruption in high places. The reality is, and continues to be, that impartial journalism is a rapidly vanishing art everywhere, including in the United States, which is supposed to be the citadel of a free press.

74. The use of specific vocabulary can change reality to fiction over time. It can also obliterate history and create new truths from the fabric of the big lie technique. If someone tells a lie big enough and keeps repeating it, people will eventually come to believe it. As British Prime Minister Winston Churchill once cautioned, "A lie gets halfway around the world before the truth has a chance to get its pants on."[77]

It was the Greek historian Thucydides (ca. 460–ca. 395 B.C.E.), who first pointed out the importance of language in winning ideological battles. Noted British commentator Melanie Phillips cogently explained to a Jerusalem audience on August 27, 2014 (the day after a ceasefire ended the Third Gaza War), that "information is a strategy of war on the battleground of the mind."[78] Up to the Six-Day War of 1967, Arab rhetoric about "driving the Jews into the sea" as well as similar public declarations, only earned the Jewish state more world sympathy and support. Quickly learning how that backfired, the Arabs switched to a more subtle and sophisticated use of propaganda. For some four decades Israel's Arab/Muslim enemies have effectively deployed a psychological warfare strategy. Since 1973, the Arabs have become eminently skilled in using propaganda as a political weapon. The use of oil as a weapon was an added bonus in their arsenal against Israel as well as provided them with the almost limitless financial means to support their efforts.

The war of words is the most important semantic campaign in the battle for public opinion—at least to that segment of the public that pays attention to the media. Mainstream international media for the most part have become accomplices to the activities of terrorist groups like Hamas and Hezbollah in parroting their propaganda lines in support of such groups' agenda. The media has used terminology and definitions in a way that implies accepted fact. By doing so, it injects bias under the guise of objectivity. Illustrative of this was when the *New York Times* subtly altered its reference to the Temple Mount in Jerusalem, which unbiased historians and archaeologists have always acknowledged was the site of two Holy Jewish Temples. In apparent deference to Palestinian leaders who claim that no Jewish Temple ever stood on the Jerusalem hill toward which Jews have prayed for millennia, the *Times* began appending the phrase to include "which the Arabs call the *Haram al Sharif*." Then, a few weeks later, the *Times* referred to "the Temple Mount, which Israel claims to have been the site of the First and Second Temple." It was no longer established historical fact—but a mere "claim." Then, in a subsequent article, the *Times* described Israeli troops as having "stormed the *Haram*, holiest Muslim site in Jerusalem, where hundreds of people were at worship." No mention whatsoever of its status as the "Temple Mount" or the single holiest Jewish site.[79] It should be noted that the *Times* never referred to the Temple Mount by its Hebrew name "*Har Habayit*."

The use of particular words and phraseology is designed to apply negative connotations to American or Israeli actions. Even the subtlest of word changes can put an entirely different meaning on any descriptive phrase used. For example, in its coverage of the war in Iraq, *Al Jazeera* referred to the "war *on* (emphasis added) Iraq."[80] Similarly, Israel's response to the incessant Arab rocket bombardment of Israel—Operation *Cast Lead*—was termed the "war on Gaza" by *Al Jazeera*[81] and other Arab/Muslim media.

It is essential that all liberty-loving supporters of Israel worldwide, especially Americans and Israelis, do not use the vocabulary of Israel's enemies. If Israel's enemies control the vocabulary, they control the argument. Therefore, it is necessary to understand and use the historically correct vocabulary and resist the subversion of objective truth. With this in mind, reclaiming the historical truth must be Israel's goal, after decades of relentless distortion, falsification and omissions by Israel's Arab/Muslim enemies. The fact remains that constant negative portrayals of Israel even if false, does political damage. Political and propaganda pressure must be resisted and combated. Israel cannot leave world opinion solely to its Arab/Muslim antagonists, for it forces Israel into isolation and ultimately can compel it to yield to that international pressure.

THE WAR OF WORDS	
What the Arab/Muslim world, their supporters and most main stream media say[82]	**What is historically correct**
Six-pointed star	Star of David
"Palestinian Problem" or "Palestinian-Israeli conflict"	The on-going Arab/Muslim refusal to accept Jewish sovereignty in the Land of Israel. The Arab/Muslim war against Israel and the Jewish people as well as Israel being the frontline in the war of Islamic supremacism against the West.
"Creation of the Zionist entity (i.e. Israel)"	Reestablishment of a sovereign Jewish state of Israel in the Land of Israel.
"The *Nakba* (The Disaster)"*	The outcome of the Arab aggression of 1947–49 against the Jews in the Land of Israel. (The Israeli War of Independence)
"Palestinian refugees"	Palestinian descendents
The October (Ramadan) War, 1973	The Yom Kippur War, 1973
The Al-Aqsa (Second) *Intifada*	The Oslo War
"Palestine"	The Land of Israel—all the land between the Jordan River and the Mediterranean Sea.
"Palestinians"	The Arabs in pre-1967 Israel, Judea, Samaria, and the Gaza Strip.
"Occupied *Al Quds*" or "Occupied Arab Jerusalem"	Jerusalem
"Al-Aqsa Mosque Compound" or "Haram al-Sharif/Noble Sanctuary."	Temple Mount
Al-Buraq Wall (where Muhammad tethered his winged steed, Buraq)[83]	The Western Wall of the Second Holy Temple compound.
Mughrabi neighborhood	The Jewish Quarter of the Old City of Jerusalem
Al-Haram Al-Ibrahimi	The Cave and Tomb of the Patriarchs in Hebron, Judea.
Bilal Ibn Ribah mosque	Rachel's Tomb outside Bethlehem, Judea.
The "West Bank"	Judea and Samaria (in Hebrew *Yehuda Ve Shomron*)
"Zionist entity"	Israel (no matter what its size)
"Greater Israel"	Land of Israel—*Eretz Yisrael*
"Occupied territories"	Recovered territories

---

* The Arabs now term the reemergence of Jewish sovereignty in the Middle East—the modern State of Israel—as the *Nakba* ("the Disaster"). One of the first Arabs to coin this notion was Syrian historian Constantine Zureiq in his 1948 book, *Ma'na al-Nakba* ("The Meaning of the Disaster"). However, the term was rarely if ever, seen in the Western world for fifty years.

"1967 borders"	1949 Armistice lines
"IOF" (Israeli Occupation Forces)	IDF (Israel Defense Forces)
"activists, militants, guerrillas, freedom fighters"	terrorists, assassins, murderers
shaheed ("martyr")	suicide murderer
"armed struggle" or "resistance"	Terrorist attacks, particularly aimed at civilian targets.
"commando attacks" or "paradise operations"	suicide bombings
"collective punishment measures"	security measures
"crackdowns on Palestinian civilians"	IDF military operations
"anti-Zionist" and "anti-Zionism"	Misojudaic and misojudaism (hatred of Jews)
"colonizers"	residents, and inhabitants (While Arabs live in Israel, Arab denial of the right of Jews to live anywhere in the Land of Israel is misojudaic racism.)
"colonies" or "settlements"	Neighborhoods, communities, towns, and villages
"illegal outposts"	unauthorized housing
'the Apartheid wall'	the security fence
"peace process"	Negotiation process
"two state solution"	Arab one state solution: the eradication of the already existing State of Israel

The concept of a *Nakba* Day was inaugurated in 1998, by Yasser Arafat as another malevolent propaganda weapon and rallying point to further defame, denounce, denigrate, demonize and delegitimize the Jewish state, while eliciting worldwide sympathy for the Palestinian Arab cause. It marks the day in 1948, on which Jewish sovereignty reemerged in the Land of Israel, after 1,875 years with the proclamation of Israeli independence. To add insult to injury, the Palestinians commemorate their national disaster day every year to coincide with the Gregorian date (May 15) on which Israel was declared. Israeli Independence Day is officially celebrated on the Hebrew date, 5 *Iyar*. It is part of the Arab replacement narrative: A "Palestine," instead of an Israel; the number of so-called Palestinian refugees equaling the number of Israelis; Arab place names instead of Israeli ones; an Arab "disaster day" to replace Israeli Independence Day and the list goes on.

More importantly, a real catastrophe has been obscured. The Jews of the Middle East and North Africa were not present in any theater of war during the Arab war against Israel, 1947–49, yet in a short period, they were stripped of their citizenship and their nationality was revoked. Their assets were stolen or confiscated and they were expelled or forced to flee the Arab states from Morocco to Iraq. Where is the *nakba* remembrance for them? Where is *nakba* day for the Copts—the pre-Arab, non-Arab people of Egypt? Where is the *nakba* day for the Imazighen—the Berbers—of North Africa, non-Arab peoples that pre-date the Arab conquest by millennia? Where is the *nakba* day for the Christians of Lebanon and Bethlehem? Where is the *nakba* day for the Kurds of the Fertile Crescent and the black Africans of Darfur? All have been murdered, persecuted, victimized and subject to Arabization for generations.

Palestinian *Nakba* observance has nothing to do with historical facts, but springs solely and exclusively from their "national" impulse to express hate and malice against the Jewish people and against Israel. *Nakba* is a symbolic indication of the ongoing Arab rejection of the very idea of a sovereign Jewish state in the Middle East. If there was a disaster—a *nakba*—for the Arabs stemming from the Israeli War of Independence, it was one of their own making.

In summation, one must recall the words of King Solomon written in Proverbs 18:21, "Death and life are in the power of the tongue." The way words are used influences their meaning. The use of these obscuring, deceitful, loaded terms empowers terrorism and seeks to justify the Arab/Muslim propaganda narrative. Israel has been very negligent in waging the war of words. We serve the cause of Israel's enemies, foreign and domestic, when we use their terminology, and thereby curse ourselves. Israel has let its enemies and critics—both within Israel and without—push their hostile distorted propaganda, especially the use of specific words virtually unopposed. Israel has been relatively quiet in presenting its case about its own overwhelming moral, legal, and historic claims to the Land of Israel, over the decades of its modern existence. Additionally, it has been suggested that Israel will have to define itself to the world in a way that is at least as emotionally appealing as the Palestinians' saga of victimhood. Rather than fighting spurious accusations with impersonal facts, Israel must fight Palestinian propaganda's exploitation of public compassion with a touching but morally correct narrative of its own.[84]

75. Transliterating Arabic words and phrases into their precise English phonetic equivalents is an exercise of great complexity.

The following sampling will illustrate the problem of transliterations. The Saudi city on the Red Sea known as Jeddah may be transliterated as: Jadda, Jaddah, Jeda, Jeddah, Jidda, Jiddah, Judda, Juddah, Djiddah, Djuddah, Djouddah, Gedda, Dsjiddah, Djettah, or Dscheddah. All are acceptable! In a study of the Middle East, one will find many such different yet acceptable transliterations.

Muslim = Moslem

Qur'an = Q'run = Koran

Ramadan = Ramadhan = Ramzan

Hudaybiyyah = Hudaibiya

Abu Dhabi = Abu Zaby

Dubai = Dubayy

Al-Qaeda = el-Qaida = al-Qa'ida

Hezbollah= Hizballah = Hizbollah = Hizbullah

bedouin = badawin

Muhammad = Mohammed

Abdel = Abdul

Abdellah = Abdallah = Abd'Allah

Faisal = Feisal = Faysal

Qadhafi = Khaddafi = Gaddafi

Mecca = Makkah

Derna = Darnah

Quneitra = Qunaytirah = Kuneita

CONCLUSION

A century ago, the death of one man, Archduke Franz Ferdinand of Austria on June 28, 1914 in Sarajevo, was the spark that ignited World War I. In a like manner, the death of one man, a fruit street vendor, Mohamed Bouazizi by self-immolation on December 17, 2010, in Sidi Bouzid, Tunisia, sparked the massive popular protests and unrest that swept the Arab world from 2011 to date. Just as the main causes of the First World War were firmly implanted years earlier and included extreme nationalism, militarism, imperialism and secret alliances, so too were the causes of what came to be called the "Arab Spring" or the "Arab Awakening" which were deeply-rooted across the Arab world. These causes included the revival of Islamic supremacism, imperialism, failure of the old system of military dictatorships and autocracies, economic stagnation and perceived grievances against the West. The "Arab Spring" quickly morphed into an "Islamist Winter," with the explosion of Islamic supremacist movements across the region. However, in fact, de facto declarations of war against the West in general and the United States in particular had occurred earlier—in the late 1960s with the global export of Saudi Wahhabism funded by increased petro-dollars, advocating Sunni Islamic supremacism. In a similar fashion, the birth of the Islamic Republic of Iran in early 1979 saw the export of Shi'ite Islamic supremacism. In 1991, the Sunni Muslim Brotherhood in effect declared war on the United States with the release of their "General Strategic Goal for the Brotherhood in North America" in which they declared, "The Ikhwan must understand that their work in America is a kind of grand Jihad in eliminating and destroying the Western civilization from within and 'sabotaging' its miserable house by their hands and the hands of the believers so that it is eliminated and Allah's religion is made victorious over all other religions."[1] In all these cases, this was accompanied by massive funding, logistical and military support for sundry terrorist organizations who acted as proxies. Though efforts have been made to obscure and deny the fact that Western civilization is under attack by Islamic supremacism, to date the West seems far from successfully defending itself, let alone moving towards victory against this potent ideology.

The old political order of the Middle East established on the ruins of the Ottoman Empire at the end of World War I was swept away in Tunisia, Egypt, Yemen, Libya, and Syria (the last three ending in vicious civil wars). Similar protests affected to a lesser extent, many other Arab states from Morocco to Oman. Dictatorships were overthrown in Tunisia, Egypt, Yemen, Libya, and earlier, Iraq. The Syrian Civil War raged on into its fifth year. Past ideologies—Nasserism and Ba'athism—have proven failures, replaced by a growing demand for Islamism. Even in Turkey since 2003, the Westernizing reforms of Kemalism have been steadily eroded and replaced with a creeping Islamism under the leadership of Recep Tayyip Erdoğan.

The states of the post 1920 map—Iraq, Syria, Lebanon, Libya, and Yemen have fragmented into ethnic and sectarian components. Other states (e.g. Jordan and Saudi Arabia may follow). Smaller and more homogeneous political entities may emerge—an Alawite state, a Druze state, a Kurdish state, a central Arabian Sunni state, a central Arabian Shi'ite state, and similar Sunni and Shi'ite states in southern Arabia. Additionally, the specter of a transnational Islamic caliphate looms large in the form of the Islamic State proclaimed in April 2014, militarily conquering territory, and spreading its influence to Sinai, Libya and Algeria.

Thus, the entire region is in a state of flux, turmoil and conflict. The chances of region-wide sectarian Sunni-Shi'ite war (even nuclear war) are great, with oppressed minorities (both ethnic and religious)—Christians, Yazidis, and Kurds—caught up in the meat-grinder of such a conflict. Not to be overlooked is the distinct possibility of a war being launched by the various Muslim sects against Israel, if for no other reason than to unify these quarreling factions into an Islamic "holy war" against the despised Jewish state.

Well into the second decade of the twenty-first century the greater Middle East remains, where it has so often been in its long and tortuous history, poised on the precipice of peril. Middle Eastern violence and volatility are endemic and homegrown. The region is wracked by upheavals of a greater magnitude than before, caused by a complex mixture of tribalism, religious fundamentalism, militarism, intolerance, sexual apartheid, misojudaism, authoritarianism and centralized governmental power at the expense of individual liberty. This all is exasperated and made worse by massive amounts of petrodollars, as well as its key strategic location.

The Middle East faces the continuous challenges of the on-going obsessive determination by Arab/Muslim states as well as non-state actors, to destroy the Jewish state of Israel, most recently reemphasized by the November 9, 2014 tweet by Iran's Ayatollah Khamenei of his nine-step plan for the destruction of the Jewish state.[2] The date was deliberately chosen for its misojudaic significance, as it was the 76th anniversary of *Kristallnacht*. Looming over the Middle East and far beyond is Iran's steadfast determination to possess nuclear weapons.

After twelve years of negotiations, Iran continues to refuse a deal that would require it to curtail its nuclear weapons program. It wants a deal that allows it to become a threshold state that can go for nuclear weapons at a time of its choosing. The Obama administration has allowed the Islamic Republic some seven years (and counting) to continue its quest for nuclear weapons and the missile technology to deliver such weapons.

Unable to reach an agreement due to Iran's refusal to substantially curtail its nuclear weapons program and allow for unfettered verification, the P5+1 powers (the United States, United Kingdom, France, Russia, China and Germany) and Iran signed the "Joint Plan of Action" (November 24, 2013), to extend the negotiations for several months. Instead of tightening sanctions, the US loosened them. As a result of those negotiations, the powers reached a "Framework" agreement on April 2, 2015, at Lausanne, Switzerland, which extended yet again, negotiations paving the way for a final status deal by June 30, 2015. Thus, Iran, like its DPRK ally before it, is likely to gain enough time with never-ending negotiations to achieve its desired goal. The "Framework" agreement left more questions than answers as to what had been agreed by Iran and the P5+1 powers. The *Washington Post* (usually very sympathetic to the Obama administration) clearly laid out the faults of the "Framework" agreement:

> The 'key parameters' for an agreement on Iran's nuclear program … fall well short of the goals originally set by the Obama administration. None of Iran's nuclear facilities — including the Fordow center buried under a mountain — will be closed. Not one of the country's 19,000 centrifuges will be dismantled. Tehran's existing stockpile of enriched uranium will be "reduced" but not necessarily shipped out of the country. In effect, Iran's nuclear infrastructure will remain intact, though some of it will be mothballed for 10 years. When the accord lapses, the Islamic republic will instantly become a threshold nuclear state.[3]

Moreover, Iran adamantly refused to allow international inspectors to visit all installations Iran defined as "military."

On April 7, 2015, Iran's Foreign Minister Javad Zarif and chief of the Atomic Energy Organization of Iran (AEOI), Ali Akbar Salehi, revealed that Iran's most advanced IR-8 centrifuges would be used as soon as the final June 30, 2015 deal removing world sanctions against Iran begins. This move will enable Iran to achieve a quick turnover in producing a nuclear weapon. The IR-8 centrifuges enrich uranium 20 times faster than the current IR-1 models.[4] They want to keep their hands on their low-enriched uranium, of which they already have eight tons. If enriched to a 90 percent level, this uranium could be used to build six atomic bombs. Bottom line, Iran will be able to keep plenty of fissile material that is part of the way toward being enriched to weapons grade. Furthermore, in a step that would destroy any final deal even before it was agreed, on April 9, 2015, Iranian President Hassan Rouhani stated the Islamic Republic would not sign a deal limiting its nuclear development capacity unless all sanctions against it were lifted on the same day the deal was signed.

In effect, the "Framework" agreement rewards Iran for its past and ongoing illegal nuclear activities, whereas sanctions relief would enable Iran to wage more aggressively the conflicts it is waging and supporting across the region. Iran used the Nuclear Non-Proliferation Treaty's terms to pave the way toward nuclear weapons status, successfully defied the treaty's enforcement agency and the UN Security Council and would not be held accountable for violating its international obligations. In effect, this marks the demise of the Nuclear Non-Proliferation Treaty. Thus, Iran, like its DPRK ally before it, is likely to gain enough time with never-ending negotiations to achieve its desired goal. A nuclear arms race in the Middle East will ensue as Saudi Arabia, the Gulf States, Egypt and Turkey seek to protect their interests from a predatory Iranian Shi'ite nuclear threat. Given these factors as well as Iran's open and undiminished misojudaic animus towards the Jewish state the stark conclusion reached is that the region is being propelled towards a new more devastating and widespread war.

The Middle East is also beset by the explosive expansion (both figuratively and literally) of transnational Islamic supremacist terrorism. Furthermore, one cannot omit the multiple on-going conflicts in Libya, Syria, Iraq, Gaza, Yemen, Somalia, and Afghanistan to name a few. Ironically, Israel remains the sole relatively stable nation in the entire Middle East with freedom, liberty, and basic equality for its citizens, democratic institutions and a powerhouse of technological innovations.

Failure to learn the lessons posed by the basic principles encompassed in this work with their numerous examples to prove their validity will result in the repetition of the blunders of the past. Such failures will lead to a catastrophic calamity and worldwide chaos that will befall the West in general, including the United States, Europe, much of Africa and Asia, including Israel, as well as the peoples of the region.

As the reader by now has learned, the Middle East is a volatile, dangerous and bewildering region. It is my hope that the reader will become an advocate to speak truth to power, to present historic fact over revisionist fiction to all those who will listen. The readers concerned about the future may ask, "What can I do?" Let this book form the basis of a call to action. Use the information contained therein. Learn the historic truth! Teach the historic truth! Spread the knowledge of the historic truth! Become what I would term a "Prescott rider"—named in honor and memory of American patriot Dr. Samuel Prescott, who on that fateful night of April 18, 1775, was the only rider to reach Concord successfully to arouse the citizenry and sound the alarm. With others form a "truth force" to multiply the effect of these suggestions. It is essential, if we wish to preserve Western civilization with its Judeo-Christian values—liberty, basic freedoms, tolerance, and gender equality—that we win this conflict. A war threatens our way of life and indeed, our very existence. As I have quoted elsewhere, the Prophet Hosea (4:6) stated long ago, "My people are destroyed for lack of knowledge." I implore you to be a bearer of the flame of knowledge and truth.

Appendix 1

THE CONSTANTINOPLE CONVENTION ON FREE NAVIGATION OF THE SUEZ CANAL

(Annotated)

On October 29, 1888, Austria-Hungary, France, Germany, Italy, the Netherlands, Russia, Spain, Turkey, and the United Kingdom, signed the Convention respecting the Free Navigation of the Suez Maritime Canal. The fundamental provisions of the Convention are contained in Articles 1 and 4 as follows:

> The Suez Maritime Canal shall always be free and open; in time of war as in time of peace, to every vessel of commerce or of war, without distinction of flag. The Canal shall never be subjected to the exercise of the right of blockade. Consequently, the high Contracting Parties agree not in any way to interfere with the free use of the canal, in time of war as in time of peace.

> The Maritime Canal remaining open in time of war as a free passage, even to the ships of war of belligerents ... the High Contracting Parties agree that no right of war, no act of hostility, nor any act having for its object to obstruct the free navigation of the Canal, shall be committed in the Canal and its ports of access ... though the Ottoman Empire should be one of the belligerent Powers [in terms of the Convention the legal successor to the Ottoman Empire is Egypt].

The Convention also confirmed and completed the system of international operation embodied by the Universal Suez Canal Company, set up in 1863. Egypt nationalized the Suez Canal Company in July 1956, an act that was regarded by many users of the Canal as a contravention of the 1888 Convention. In April 1957, when the Canal was reopened to navigation after it had been obstructed by Egypt for several months, the Egyptian Government issued a declaration in which it stated its intention to respect "the terms and spirit of the Constantinople Convention and the rights and obligations arising therefrom." Despite this pledge, it continued to block Israeli flag vessels and cargo bound to or from Israel on third flag vessels until the Egypt–Israel Peace Treaty of 1979.

Appendix 2

THE BALFOUR DECLARATION

(Annotated)

Foreign Office, November 2, 1917

Dear Lord Rothschild,

I have much pleasure in conveying to you, on behalf of His Majesty's Government, the following declaration of sympathy with Jewish Zionist aspirations which has been submitted to, and approved by, the Cabinet.

His Majesty's Government view with favour *the establishment in Palestine of a national home for the Jewish people* [emphasis added], and will use their best endeavors to facilitate the achievement of this object, it being clearly understood that *nothing shall be done which may prejudice the civil and religious rights of existing non-Jewish communities in Palestine,* [emphasis added] or the rights and political status enjoyed by Jews in any other country.

I should be grateful if you would bring this declaration to the knowledge of the Zionist Federation.

Yours,

Arthur James Balfour
British Foreign Secretary

ANALYSIS

The Balfour Declaration was a deliberate act of the British Cabinet. It was part of their general foreign policy and aims in World War I. It was in part conceived to keep Eastern European and Russian Jews supporting the World War after the Bolshevik Revolution had knocked Russia out of the war. It was invested with international status when Russia, France, Italy, and the United States all gave their consent to it in advance.

The Balfour Declaration does not treat the Jews and the non-Jews mentioned, on an equal basis. The Jews were referred to in connection with regard to their "Zionist aspirations" and their "national home." The non-Jews referred to as "the existing non-Jewish communities," were entitled to enjoy "civil and religious rights"—not political ones. Arab national aspirations were recognized outside of the British Mandate of Palestine in Syria and Mesopotamia (i.e. Iraq).

The Balfour Declaration was later incorporated into the Mandate for Palestine as approved by the League of Nations council on July 24, 1922. The United Kingdom, as Mandatory Power, was responsible for the implementation of the Balfour Declaration.

In the United Kingdom and the United States as well as other countries, the press and representative spokesmen used the term "Jewish National Home" interchangeably with "Jewish Republic" and "Jewish Commonwealth." British statesmen encouraged this belief and official British documents confirmed it.[1] For example, Sir Herbert Samuel soon to be the first British High Commissioner in the British Mandate of Palestine, spoke about "a purely self-governing Commonwealth under the auspices of an established Jewish majority."[2] US President Woodrow Wilson expressed his support for the Balfour Declaration on August 31, 1918, when he stated, "I welcome an opportunity to express the satisfaction I have felt in the progress of the Zionist movement in the United States, and in the allied countries, since the declaration of Mr. Balfour."

Wilson expanded on this support in his March 2, 1919 statement, "I am persuaded that the Allied nations, with the fullest concurrence of our [US] government and people, are agreed that in Palestine shall be laid the foundations of a Jewish Commonwealth."[3] The president also referred to "the historic claims of the Jewish people in regard to Palestine."[4] In June 1919, Arthur James Balfour agreed with US Supreme Court Justice Louis D. Brandeis "Palestine should be the Jewish homeland and not merely that there be a Jewish homeland in Palestine."

Support for a Jewish homeland in Palestine was bipartisan in the United States. President Warren G. Harding declared on June 1, 1921, "It is impossible for one who has studied at all the service of the Hebrew people to avoid the faith that they will one day be restored to their historic national home and there enter on a new and yet greater phase of their contribution to the advance of humanity."[5] Harding reemphasized his views on May 11, 1922:

> I am very glad to express my approval and hearty sympathy for the effort of the Palestine Foundation fund in behalf of the restoration of Palestine as a homeland for the Jewish people. I have always viewed with an interest, which I think is quite as much practical as sentimental, the proposal for the rehabilitation of Palestine and the restoration of a real Jewish nationality, and I hope the efforts now being carried on in this and other countries in this behalf may meet the fullest measure of success.

On September 21, 1922, President Harding signed the Lodge-Fish Resolution—Joint Congressional Resolution (360) of June 30, 1922—that became law (Public Resolution No. 73). It approved the establishment of a Jewish National homeland in Palestine. The resolution read:

> Favoring the establishment in Palestine of a national home for the Jewish people.
> *Resolved by the Senate and House of Representatives of the United States of America in Congress assembled.* That the United States of America favors the establishment in Palestine of a national home for the Jewish people, it being clearly understood that nothing shall be done which should prejudice the civil and religious rights of Christian and all other non-Jewish communities in Palestine, and that the holy places and religious buildings and sites in Palestine shall be adequately protected. [Italics in the original][6]

Nevertheless, as David Ben-Gurion would state at the time of the issuance of the Balfour Declaration, "Britain has made a magnificent gesture. But only the Hebrew people can transform this right into tangible fact; only they, with body and soul, with their strength and capital, must build their National Home and bring about their national redemption." That is the way it played out in subsequent history.

Appendix 3

FEISAL-WEIZMANN AGREEMENT,
January 3, 1919
(Annotated)

His Royal Highness the Emir Feisal, representing and acting on behalf of the Arab Kingdom of Hedjaz, and Dr. Chaim Weizmann, representing and acting on behalf of the Zionist Organization, mindful of the racial kinship and ancient bonds existing between the Arabs and the Jewish people, and realizing that the surest means of working out the consummation of their national aspirations is through the closest possible collaboration in the development of the Arab State and Palestine, and being desirous further of confirming the good understanding which exists between them, have agreed upon the following Articles:

ARTICLE I

The Arab State and Palestine in all their relations and undertakings shall be controlled by the most cordial goodwill and understanding and to this end Arab and Jewish duly accredited agents shall be established and maintained in the respective territories.

ARTICLE II

Immediately following the completion of the deliberations of the Peace Conference, the definite boundaries between the Arab State and Palestine shall be determined by a Commission to be agreed upon by the parties hereto.

ARTICLE III

In the establishment of the Constitution and Administration of Palestine all such measures shall be adopted as will afford the fullest guarantees for carrying into effect the British Government's [Balfour] Declaration of the 2d of November, 1917.

ARTICLE IV

All necessary measures shall be taken to encourage and stimulate immigration of Jews into Palestine on a large scale, and as quickly as possible to settle Jewish immigrants upon the land through closer settlement, and intensive cultivation of the soil. In taking such measures the Arab peasant and tenant farmers shall be protected in their rights, and shall be assisted in forwarding their economic development.

ARTICLE V

No recognition nor law shall be made prohibiting or interfering in any way with the free exercise of religion; and further the free exercise and enjoyment of religious profession and worship without discrimination or preference shall forever be allowed. No religious test shall ever be required for the exercise of civil or political rights.

ARTICLE VI

The Mohammedan [i.e. Muslim] Holy Places shall be under Mohammedan control.

ARTICLE VII

The Zionist Organization proposes to send to Palestine a Commission of experts to make a survey of the economic possibilities of the country, and to report upon the best means for its development. The Zionist Organization will place the aforementioned Commission at the disposal of the Arab State for the purpose of a survey of the economic possibilities of the Arab State and to report upon the best means for its development. The Zionist Organization will use its best efforts to assist the Arab State in providing the means for developing the natural resources and economic possibilities thereof.

ARTICLE VIII

The parties hereto agree to act in complete accord and harmony on all matters embraced herein before the Peace Congress.

ARTICLE IX

Any matters of dispute which may arise between the contracting parties shall be referred to the British Government for arbitration.

Given under our hand at London, England, the third day of January, one thousand nine hundred and nineteen.

Chaim Weizmann
Feisal ibn-Hussein.

Feisal attached the following hand-written codicil.

RESERVATION BY THE EMIR FEISAL

If the Arabs are established as I have asked in my manifesto of January 4 addressed to the British Secretary of State for Foreign Affairs, I will carry out what is written in this agreement. If changes are made, I cannot be answerable for failing to carry out this agreement.
Feisal ibn-Hussein.

ANALYSIS

During the Allied Peace Conference in Paris, Emir Feisal, son of Hussein, Sharif of Mecca, signed the above agreement with Dr. Chaim Weizmann, leader of the Zionist movement. In a letter to Felix Frankfurter dated March 3, 1919, Emir Feisal wrote, "The Jewish movement is national and not imperialist. Our movement is national and not imperialist, and there is room in Syria [Palestine was then referred to as southern Syria[7]] for us both. Indeed I think that neither can be a real success without the other."[8]

The British promised the Arabs of the Hashemite dynasty independence after World War I. Feisal was proclaimed king of an independent "Greater Syria" on March 8, 1920, by the Syrian National Congress. It was the first modern Arab state to come into existence. However, many Arab nationalists viewed Feisal as a stooge and lackey of the British. At the same Syrian National Congress, the Arab nationalists indignantly refused to ratify Feisal's agreement with Weizmann and he had to tell the Zionists that he could agree only to limited Jewish immigration, and to a national home that would never be more than a Jewish province in a larger Arab state. One month later, the San Remo Conference (held April 18–26, 1920) assigned Syria as a mandate under French control.

The Franco-Syrian War that lasted until 1921 ensued as France used military force to take over the country. Feisal expected Zionist cooperation in helping prevent French control of much of Syria, but the Zionists were powerless to do anything. Feisal fled to the British Mandate of Iraq where he was proclaimed king on August 23, 1921, though formal independence did not occur until October 3, 1932. Feisal announced in 1931, with regard to the Feisal-Weizmann Agreement, that "His Majesty does not remember having written anything of that kind with his knowledge." Thus, the first peace agreement between Arabs and Jews was discarded.

Chaim Weizmann, in testimony to the United Nations asserted the Feisal-Weizmann Agreement was still valid in 1947:

> A postscript was also included in this treaty. This postscript relates to a reservation by King Feisal that he would carry out all the promises in this treaty if and when he would obtain his demands, namely, independence for the Arab countries. I submit that these requirements of King Feisal have at present been realized. The [then seven] Arab countries are all independent, and therefore the condition on which depended the fulfillment of this treaty, has come into effect. Therefore, this treaty, to all intents and purposes, should today be a valid document.[9]

Weizmann became Israel's first president a year later, in 1948.

Appendix 4

THE LEBANESE NATIONAL PACT OF 1943

The National Pact was an unwritten power sharing agreement concluded between Christian (largely Maronite) and Muslim (largely Sunni) communities. It was based on the 1932 census and laid the political foundation of Lebanon as a multi-confessional state.

(Annotated key sections)

- The Christians of Lebanon agreed that Lebanon would be free of any foreign (i.e. French) ties and present an Arab face to the world.
- The Muslims of Lebanon would renounce the thought of union with Syria, as part of an Islamist "Greater Syria" state.
- Arabic would be the only official language of Lebanon.
- The Christian majority would remain unchallenged but Lebanon would be identified as part of the Arab world.
- The President of Lebanon would be a Maronite Catholic.
- The Premier of Lebanon would be a Sunni Muslim.
- The Deputy Premier would be a Greek Orthodox.
- The Speaker of the National Assembly (Parliament) would be a Shi'a Muslim.
- The Deputy Speaker of the National Assembly would be a Greek Orthodox.
- In the National Assembly, Christians would outnumber Muslims by a fixed ratio of 6:5. Later, the 6:5 ratio was also applied to posts in the civil service, judiciary and military.
- The Commander of the Army would be a Maronite Catholic.
- The Governor of the Central Bank would be a Maronite Catholic.

In 1960, the number of seats in the Chamber of Deputies was increased from 77 to 99, with 54 going to Christians and 45 to Muslims, retaining the ratio of 6:5. This parliamentary adjustment lasted for twenty-nine years. Only in 1969 did the Shi'ites win separate clerical status in Lebanon. As a result of the National Reconciliation Charter (Ta'if Agreement), ratified on November 4, 1989, the number of seats in the Chamber of Deputies was raised to 128 and the ratio was altered to 5:5—parity between Christians and Muslims. While the Christians retained the presidency, the power and authority of that officer was reduced and transferred to the cabinet.

Appendix 5

UNITED NATIONS GENERAL ASSEMBLY
RESOLUTION 181
(SECOND) PARTITION OF PALESTINE
November 29, 1947

(Annotated)

BACKGROUND

While the Arabs in 1947, were a majority of the population in all of the British Mandate of Palestine (some 1,200,000), the Jews were a majority in the area allotted to them. They numbered 650,000. The Jewish state was already in existence, in all but name.

UN PARTITION OF PALESTINE, NOVEMBER 29, 1947 LAND AND PEOPLE		
Categories	**Jewish State**	**Arab State**
Percent of land	56	43
Percent of population	58	99
People left in the other state	497,000 Arabs	10,000 Jews

One percent of the land was to be a *Corpus Separatum* i.e. Jerusalem and Bethlehem (*see* "UN Partition Plan, November 29, 1947" map). From a biblical and historical perspective, the proposed Jewish state was in the "wrong" parts of the Palestine Mandate, i.e. not in the Biblical Land of Israel. Thus, biblical and historic sites such as Anathoth (Anatot), Beit Horon, Betar, Beth El, Giv'on, Hebron, Jerusalem, Modi'in, Shechem, Shiloach, and Tekoah, to name a prominent few, lay outside of the proposed Jewish state. Nevertheless, the Jews accepted the UN Partition plan for it provided a Jewish state after 1,875 years of exile and dispersion—but they would have to fight for it.

United Nations General Assembly Resolution 181 delineated a two-state solution for Jews and Arabs west of the Jordan River. Both states were to be joined in an economic union and share a joint currency. The resolution declared that Arabs and Jews would become "citizens of the State in which they are resident and enjoy full civil and political rights" and that Arabs living in the Jewish state could opt, within one year from the date of the resolution's implementation, for citizenship of the Arab state, and Jews living in the Arab state could opt for citizenship of the Jewish state.

DEMILITARIZED JERUSALEM UNDER THE UN

The city of Jerusalem was to be demilitarized and placed under a special international regime—a *Corpus Separatum*—to be administered by the United Nations through the Trusteeship Council.

However, this regime was to be limited in time. It was not to be an "international city" for all time as some have claimed.

> The Statute elaborated by the Trusteeship Council on the aforementioned principles shall come into force not later than 1 October 1948. It shall remain in force in the first instance for a period of ten years, unless the Trusteeship Council finds it necessary to undertake a reexamination of these provisions at an earlier date. After the expiration of this period the whole scheme shall be subject to examination by the Trusteeship Council in the light of experience acquired with its functioning. The residents of the City shall be then free to express by means of a referendum their wishes as to possible modifications of regime of the City.[10]

This provision for a referendum was of critical importance to the acceptance of UNGA Resolution 181 by the Chairman of the Jewish Agency, David Ben-Gurion. He knew that the Jews were in a majority within these boundaries and would be in 10 years when the referendum was to be held. Thus, he was confident that Jerusalem would return to Jewish hands.

Delineation

The Jewish state was to receive the eastern Galilee from the Hulah Basin, and the Sea of Galilee in the northeast to the crest of the Gilboa Mountains in the south. The Jewish section of the coastal plain "extends from a point between Minat El-Qila and Nabi Yunis in the Gaza Sub-District and includes the towns of Haifa and Tel Aviv, leaving Jaffa as an enclave of the Arab State." The Jews were also to receive the Negev Desert area, but without the city of Beersheba, and a strip of land along the Dead Sea.

In light of Arab attacks and aggression in 1920, 1921, 1929, 1936–39, and declarations by the Arab states as Resolution 181 was being discussed the resolution included a proviso whereby, "The Security Council determine as a threat to the peace, breach of the peace or act of aggression, in accordance with Article 39 of the Charter, any attempt to alter by force the settlement envisaged by this resolution;"[11] Whereas the Jews were ready to accept a compromise and agree to (this second) partition, the Arabs rejected it totally and immediately escalated warfare as soon as Resolution 181 passed by a vote of 33 to 13 with 10 abstentions.

Among those voting in favor of the resolution were the United States, despite a proposal to give the Negev Desert to the Arabs, the Soviet Union, and many Western European and Latin American nations. Of particular note is that Belgium resisted British pressure to vote against or abstain; Costa Rica voted "in favor" despite an Arab attempt to bribe that nation with an offer of support for a high UN position for a Costa Rican delegate.

Voting against as expected, were the six Arab members of the UN at the time—Egypt, Iraq, Lebanon, Saudi Arabia, Syria, and Yemen. They were joined by the Muslim nations of Afghanistan, Iran, Pakistan, and Turkey. Additionally India, with a very large Muslim minority voted against, as did Cuba, and Greece, the latter out of fear of Egyptian retaliation on the 150,000 Greeks in Egypt. The United Kingdom abstained, as did Argentina, Chile, China, Colombia, El Salvador, Ethiopia, Honduras, Mexico, and Yugoslavia. The delegate of Thailand (who would have voted "against") was absent, as he was recalled due to a military coup in that country.

SIGNIFICANCE

As a General Assembly resolution, UNGA 181 had no force of international law. It was a non-binding recommendation. Arab rejection of UNGA 181 and their subsequent aggressive attack on Israel rendered UNGA 181 a dead letter. The international legal basis for the Jewish state was the San Remo Resolution of April 25, 1920, which had the force of law upon its being incorporated first in the Treaty of Sèvres of August 10, 1920 and then in the 1922 League of Nations Mandate for Palestine which charged the British government with administering the area earmarked as the future Jewish state. Though the League of Nations Mandate for Palestine has expired, the rights derived from it remain in full force and effect, under both international law and Israeli law.

If anything, UN General Assembly Resolution 181 sought to legitimize illegal moves taken by the United Kingdom throughout the term of its mandate. As the League of Nations mandate made clear, the United Kingdom was supposed to preside over the territory of the British Mandate of Palestine and to foster the establishment of a Jewish state that would eventually replace the British mandatory government. UNGA Resolution 181 simply accepted an already existing national entity.

The partition plan merely expressed the willingness of two-thirds of the United Nations General Assembly to accept the establishment of a Jewish state and an Arab state in Palestine. Note, the resolution specifically called for the establishment of a "Jewish state." It did not ensure the establishment of either. Despite the call to the Security Council to keep the peace and stop the aggressor states, there was no enforcement mechanism in place to insure that the General Assembly recommendation be carried out. Indeed, even as the Arab countries attacked the newly declared Jewish state of Israel, there was no UN moves to halt the aggression, nor action to declare the Arab states, the aggressors. Israel was left to fend for itself in a life or death struggle.

As was stated earlier, but nonetheless needs to be reemphasized, the United Nations did not create Israel, despite the persistent myth that it did. The Jewish state was reborn because its foundations were laboriously laid, for several decades. By the time of the November 1947 UN General Assembly Partition Plan vote, the embryonic Jewish state had already existed, *de facto,* for upwards of a decade. The *Yishuv* had communal unity, and a resolute sense of purpose sustained by an iron-willed national tenacity. All the ingredients of statehood were present. They possessed political institutions already in place—in effect, a shadow government—led by high caliber leaders, such as David Ben-Gurion, who understood the value of sovereignty in the world of nations. There also was an extensive network of indigenous economic, financial, educational, health care, social and military institutions and services.

The Jewish people were ready to fight for their political independence. They had a military organization that would prove powerful enough to defeat the attacking Arab armies, achieving victory despite Arab hostility and belligerency. It was all these factors, not a UN General Assembly resolution, which brought about the reestablishment of a sovereign Jewish state in the Land of Israel.

This coming of age—a *bar mitzvah* so to speak—by the *Yishuv,* was achieved by fire and sword at the cost of 6,373 persons killed—1 percent of the Jewish population. UN General Assembly Resolution 181 merely reaffirmed the fact that a Jewish state already existed. The UN played no role in guaranteeing that the provisions of its resolution would be implemented. Furthermore, no people other than the Jews, has a legitimate claim to the land of Israel, whose reestablishment was exercised on behalf of this ancient people.

The Arab Palestinian state failed to emerge because no foundations had been laid for it, and its potential citizens did nothing to further its emergence. The Arabs annulled the partition plan by invading Israel in an aggressive war that sought the eradication of the fledgling Jewish state. As has been stated, because of Arab aggression, UNGA Resolution 181, the United Nations' Partition Plan, became a dead letter.

Appendix 6

THE TRIPARTITE DECLARATION
May 25, 1950

TRIPARTITE DECLARATION REGARDING THE ARMISTICE BORDERS: STATEMENT BY THE GOVERNMENTS OF THE UNITED STATES, THE UNITED KINGDOM, AND FRANCE, MAY 25, 1950[12]

The Governments of the United Kingdom, France, and the United States, having had occasion during the recent Foreign Ministers meeting in London[13] to review certain questions affecting the peace and stability of the Arab states and of Israel, and particularly that of the supply of arms and war material to these states have resolved to make the following statements:

1. The three Governments recognize that the Arab states and Israel all need to maintain a certain level of armed forces for the purposes of assuring their internal security and their legitimate self-defense and to permit them to play their part in the defense of the area as a whole. All applications for arms or war material for these countries will be considered in the light of these principles. In this connection the three Governments wish to recall and reaffirm the terms of the statements made by their representatives on the Security Council on August 4, 1949,[14] in which they declared their opposition to the development of an arms race between the Arab states and Israel.

2. The three Governments declare that assurances have been received from all the states in question, to which they permit arms to be supplied from their countries, that the purchasing state does not intend to undertake any act of aggression against any other state. Similar assurances will be requested from any other state in the area to which they permit arms to be supplied in the future.

3. The three Governments take this opportunity of declaring their deep interest in and their desire to promote the establishment and maintenance of peace and stability in the area and their unalterable opposition to the use of force or threat of force between any of the states in that area. The three Governments, should they find that any of these states was preparing to violate frontiers or armistice lines, would, consistently with their obligations as members of the United Nations, immediately take action, both within and outside the United Nations, to prevent such violation.

Appendix 7

THE EISENHOWER DOCTRINE

H.J. Res. 117–JOINT RESOLUTION TO PROMOTE PEACE
AND STABILITY IN THE MIDDLE EAST
March 9, 1957

(Annotated)

RESOLVED

That the President be and hereby is authorized to cooperate with and assist any nation or group of nations in the general area of the Middle East desiring such assistance in the development of economic strength dedicated to the maintenance of national independence.

Section 2: The president is authorized to undertake … military assistance programs, with any nation or group of nations of that area desiring such assistance … if the President determines the necessity thereof, the United States is prepared to use armed forces to assist any such nation or group of such nations requesting assistance against armed aggression from any country controlled by international communism.

Public Law 7, 85th Congress

ANALYSIS

The president was formally empowered to extend economic and military aid to the nations of the Middle East if they desired it, and was threatened by aggression from a communist-controlled country. The doctrine had two fundamental weaknesses: 1) The main threat to peace and American interests in the Middle East at the time was not open communist aggression, but the subversion of existing governments. 2) The doctrine could not be put into operation unless some government asked specifically for help.

The doctrine was utilized to assist the government of Lebanon in 1958, when it faced subversion by the United Arab Republic (UAR). Since the UAR was a client state of the Soviet Union, the terms of the Eisenhower Doctrine were stretched to meet the contingency and US forces intervened to support the legitimate Lebanese government.

Appendix 8

THE PALESTINIAN NATIONAL CHARTER

(Annotated)

BACKGROUND

The Palestinian National Charter was adopted by a gathering of 422 Palestinian activists in East Jerusalem[15] (then under Jordanian occupation) on May 28, 1964. When adopted, the document was called *Al-Mithaq al-Qawmi al-Filastini,* which was meant to reflect its origins in the Pan-Arabism of Egypt's President Gamal Abdel Nasser. Subsequently, the Palestinians claimed that *al-Qawmi* is untranslatable. It evidently implied that Palestinians were less than a nation in their own right, and are part of the Arab nation or *Ummah*. In later years, the Palestinians adopted the designation *Shaabi* for the Palestinian people.

The Six-Day War of June 1967 provided the opportunity for the PLO to claim additional territories. Thus, the charter was revised into its current form on July 17, 1968, during a meeting of the Palestine National Council. The 1964 charter was amended by adding four paragraphs and changing others. After the revision, the document was referred to as *Al-Mithaq al-Watani al-Filastini. Mithaq* was at first translated as "covenant," but later the word "charter" was adopted. Furthermore, it can be interpreted that the PLO tries to confer on its charter "sanctity" and "holiness" by calling it a "covenant," for propaganda effect. It is an effort to replace the Judeo-Christian God's biblical covenant with Abraham, which bestowed on Abraham's descendents—the Jewish nation—the Land of Israel, in perpetuity. It is another example of PLO replacement ideology.

ANALYSIS OF THE DIFFERENCES BETWEEN THE 1964 AND 1968 VERSIONS OF THE PLO CHARTER

It should clearly be noted at the outset that the Palestinian National Charter was adopted three years *before* (emphasis added) the so-called "Israeli occupation" of Judea and Samaria as well as the Gaza Strip.

Article 6 in the 1964 version of the PLO Charter declared:

> The Palestinians are those Arab citizens who were living normally in Palestine up to 1947, whether they remained or were expelled. Every child who was born to a Palestinian parent after this date whether in Palestine or outside is a Palestinian.

In 1968, Article 6 was replaced by a more explicit Article 5:

> The Palestinians are those Arab nationals who, until 1947, normally resided in Palestine regardless of whether they were evicted from it or have stayed there. Anyone born, after that date, of a Palestinian father—whether inside Palestine or outside it—is also a Palestinian.

Article 17 of the 1964 Charter expressed:

> The Partitioning of Palestine in 1947 and the establishment of Israel are illegal and false regardless of the loss of time, because they were contrary to the wish of the Palestine people and its natural right to its homeland, and in violation of the basic principles embodied in the charter of the United Nations, foremost among which is the right to self-determination.

In1968, Article 17 was deleted and replaced by Article 20, which declared:

> The Balfour Declaration, the Mandate for Palestine, and everything that has been based upon them, are deemed null and void. Claims of historical or religious ties of Jews with Palestine are incompatible with the facts of history and the true conception of what constitutes statehood. Judaism, being a religion, is not an independent nationality. Nor do Jews constitute a single nation with an identity of its own; they are citizens of the states to which they belong.

Article 24 of the original founding document, stated, "this Organization [the PLO] does not exercise any regional sovereignty over the West Bank [Judea and Samaria] in the Hashemite Kingdom of Jordan, in the Gaza Strip or the Himmah area." For the PLO *before* (emphasis added) the Six-Day War of 1967, Palestine was Israel. It was not Judea and Samaria or the Gaza Strip. Those areas, during the period 1949–67, were under the occupation of other Arab states—Jordan and Egypt respectively. The only "homeland" for the PLO in 1964, was the State of Israel. Palestinians did not object to nineteen years of Jordanian and Egyptian authority, nor does the solid Palestinian majority in Jordan today seem highly motivated to express its distinct "national identity."

In 1968, the Charter was specifically revised to remove the operative language of Article 24, thereby newly asserting a Palestinian claim of sovereignty to Judea and Samaria as well as the Gaza Strip. Since the revision, these areas are loudly claimed to comprise part of the Palestinians "ancient homeland." All of pre-1967 Israel is the remainder of what they claim. No "two state" solution is incorporated in the PLO charter nor is any contemplated at all! Additionally, whereas the PLO charter of 1964 had as one of its dominant themes, Pan-Arabism, the 1968-revised charter shifted this theme to that of emerging Palestinian nationalism, whose objective, was the creation of a sovereign Palestinian state.

Other main additions to the 1968 revised charter concern the reiterated call for armed struggle to eliminate Israel ("liberate Palestine") and the change in the attitude to Jewish rights. The original version was deliberately ambiguous:

> Article 7: Jews of Palestinian origin are considered Palestinians if they are willing to live peacefully and loyally in Palestine.

It is unclear if the above refers to Jews descended from families that lived in Palestine before the advent of Zionism, or to any Jews born in Israel, or what the status of Jews who have only one Palestinian Jewish parent. The revised 1968 version was more explicit:

Article 6: The Jews who had normally resided in Palestine until the beginning of the Zionist invasion will be considered Palestinians.

Most such Jews "of Palestinian origin" or who had "normally resided in Palestine until the beginning of the Zionist invasion" (later set by Yasser Arafat at 1881), had already died by 1968. Many of their descendants married Zionists. In any case, they are a tiny minority. About 100,000 Jews had lived in the area before 1914. Evidently, the majority of the Jews were to be expelled or murdered, but their fate is not specified.

THE PALESTINIAN NATIONAL CHARTER, REVISED 1968

The text is the English version published officially by the PLO, unabridged and unedited.[16] Note, however, that the PLO's translation sometimes deviates from the original Arabic to be more palatable to Western readers. For example, in Article 15, the Arabic is translated as "the elimination of Zionism," whereas the correct translation is "the liquidation of the Zionist presence." "The Zionist presence" is a common Arabic euphemism for the State of Israel, so this clause in fact calls for the destruction of Israel, not just the end of Zionism. Where subtleties in the original Arabic are important, the Arabic word has been inserted in parentheses.

Article 1: Palestine is the homeland of the Arab Palestinian people; it is an indivisible part of the Arab homeland, and the Palestinian people are an integral part of the Arab nation.

Article 2: Palestine, with the boundaries it had during the British Mandate, is an indivisible territorial unit.

Article 3: The Palestinian Arab people possess the legal right to their homeland and have the right to determine their destiny after achieving the liberation of their country in accordance with their wishes and entirely of their own accord and will.

Article 4: The Palestinian identity is a genuine, essential, and inherent characteristic; it is transmitted from parents to children. The Zionist occupation and the dispersal of the Palestinian Arab people, through the disasters which befell them, do not make them lose their Palestinian identity and their membership in the Palestinian community, nor do they negate them.

Article 5: The Palestinians are those Arab nationals who, until 1947, normally resided in Palestine regardless of whether they were evicted from it or have stayed there. Anyone born, after that date, of a Palestinian father—whether inside Palestine or outside it—is also a Palestinian.

Article 6: The Jews who had normally resided in Palestine until the beginning of the Zionist invasion will be considered Palestinians.

Article 7: That there is a Palestinian community and that it has material, spiritual, and historical connection with Palestine are indisputable facts. It is a national duty to bring up individual Palestinians in an Arab revolutionary manner. All means of information and education must be adopted in order to acquaint the Palestinian with his country in the most profound manner, both spiritual and material, that is possible. He must be prepared for the armed struggle and ready to sacrifice his wealth and his life in order to win back his homeland and bring about its liberation.

Article 8: The phase in their history, through which the Palestinian people are now living, is that of national (*watani*) struggle for the liberation of Palestine. Thus the conflicts among the Palestinian national forces are secondary, and should be ended for the sake of the basic conflict that exists between the forces of Zionism and of imperialism on the one hand, and the Palestinian Arab people on the other. On this basis the Palestinian masses, regardless of whether they are residing in the national homeland or in diaspora (*mahajir*) constitute—both their organizations and the individuals—one national front working for the retrieval of Palestine and its liberation through armed struggle.

Article 9: Armed struggle is the only way to liberate Palestine. This it is the overall strategy, not merely a tactical phase. The Palestinian Arab people assert their absolute determination and firm resolution to continue their armed struggle and to work for an armed popular revolution for the liberation of their country and their return to it. They also assert their right to normal life in Palestine and to exercise their right to self-determination and sovereignty over it.

Article 10: Commando action constitutes the nucleus of the Palestinian popular liberation war. This requires its escalation, comprehensiveness, and the mobilization of all the Palestinian popular and educational efforts and their organization and involvement in the armed Palestinian revolution. It also requires the achieving of unity for the national (*watani*) struggle among the different groupings of the Palestinian people, and between the Palestinian people and the Arab masses, so as to secure the continuation of the revolution, its escalation, and victory.

Article 11: The Palestinians will have three mottoes: national (*wataniyya*) unity, national (*qawmiyya*) mobilization, and liberation.

Article 12: The Palestinian people believe in Arab unity. In order to contribute their share toward the attainment of that objective, however, they must, at the present stage of their struggle, safeguard their Palestinian identity and develop their consciousness of that identity, and oppose any plan that may dissolve or impair it.

Article 13: Arab unity and the liberation of Palestine are two complementary objectives, the attainment of either of which facilitates the attainment of the other. Thus, Arab unity leads to the liberation of Palestine, the liberation of Palestine leads to Arab unity; and work toward the realization of one objective proceeds side by side with work toward the realization of the other.

Article 14: The destiny of the Arab nation, and indeed Arab existence itself, depend upon the destiny of the Palestine cause. From this interdependence springs the Arab nation's pursuit of, and striving for, the liberation of Palestine. The people of Palestine play the role of the vanguard in the realization of this sacred (*qawmi*) goal.

Article 15: The liberation of Palestine, from an Arab viewpoint, is a national (*qawmi*) duty and it attempts to repel the Zionist and imperialist aggression against the Arab homeland, and aims at the elimination of Zionism in Palestine. Absolute responsibility for this falls upon the Arab nation—peoples and governments—with the Arab people of Palestine in the vanguard. Accordingly, the Arab nation must mobilize all its military, human, moral, and spiritual capabilities to participate actively with the Palestinian people in the liberation of Palestine. It must, particularly in the phase of the armed Palestinian revolution, offer and furnish the Palestinian people with all possible help, and material and human support, and make available to them the means and opportunities that will enable them to continue to carry out their leading role in the armed revolution, until they liberate their homeland.

Article 16: The liberation of Palestine, from a spiritual point of view, will provide the Holy Land with an atmosphere of safety and tranquility, which in turn will safeguard the country's religious sanctuaries and guarantee freedom of worship and of visit to all, without discrimination of race, color, language, or religion. Accordingly, the people of Palestine look to all spiritual forces in the world for support.

Article 17: The liberation of Palestine, from a human point of view, will restore to the Palestinian individual his dignity, pride, and freedom. Accordingly the Palestinian Arab people look forward to the support of all those who believe in the dignity of man and his freedom in the world.

Article 18: The liberation of Palestine, from an international point of view, is a defensive action necessitated by the demands of self-defense. Accordingly the Palestinian people, desirous as they are of the friendship of all people, look to freedom-loving, and peace-loving states for support in order to restore their legitimate rights in Palestine, to reestablish peace and security in the country, and to enable its people to exercise national sovereignty and freedom.

Article 19: The partition of Palestine in 1947 and the establishment of the State of Israel are entirely illegal, regardless of the passage of time, because they were contrary to the will of the Palestinian people and to their natural right in their homeland, and inconsistent with the principles embodied in the Charter of the United Nations, particularly the right to self-determination.

Article 20: The Balfour Declaration, the Mandate for Palestine, and everything that has been based upon them, are deemed null and void. Claims of historical or religious ties of Jews with Palestine are incompatible with the facts of history and the true conception of what constitutes statehood. Judaism, being a religion, is not an independent nationality. Nor do Jews constitute a single nation with an identity of its own; they are citizens of the states to which they belong.

Article 21: The Arab Palestinian people, expressing themselves by the armed Palestinian revolution, reject all solutions which are substitutes for the total liberation of Palestine and reject all proposals aiming at the liquidation of the Palestinian problem, or its internationalization.

Article 22: Zionism is a political movement organically associated with international imperialism and antagonistic to all action for liberation and to progressive movements in the world. It is racist and fanatic in its nature, aggressive, expansionist, and colonial in its aims, and fascist in its methods. Israel is the instrument of the Zionist movement, and geographical base for world imperialism placed strategically in the midst of the Arab homeland to combat the hopes of the Arab nation for liberation, unity, and progress. Israel is a constant source of threat vis-à-vis peace in the Middle East and the whole world. Since the liberation of Palestine will destroy the Zionist and imperialist presence and will contribute to the establishment of peace in the Middle East, the Palestinian people look for the support of all the progressive and peaceful forces and urge them all, irrespective of their affiliations and beliefs, to offer the Palestinian people all aid and support in their just struggle for the liberation of their homeland.

Article 23: The demand of security and peace, as well as the demand of right and justice, require all states to consider Zionism an illegitimate movement, to outlaw its existence, and to ban its operations, in order that friendly relations among peoples may be preserved, and the loyalty of citizens to their respective homelands safeguarded.

Article 24: The Palestinian people believe in the principles of justice, freedom, sovereignty, self-determination, human dignity, and in the right of all peoples to exercise them.

Article 25: For the realization of the goals of this Charter and its principles, the Palestine Liberation Organization will perform its role in the liberation of Palestine in accordance with the Constitution of this Organization.

Article 26: The Palestine Liberation Organization, representative of the Palestinian revolutionary forces, is responsible for the Palestinian Arab people's movement in its struggle—to retrieve its homeland, liberate and return to it and exercise the right to self-determination in it—in all military, political, and financial fields and also for whatever may be required by the Palestine case on the inter-Arab and international levels.

Article 27: The Palestine Liberation Organization shall cooperate with all Arab states, each according to its potentialities; and will adopt a neutral policy among them in the light of the requirements of the war of liberation; and on this basis it shall not interfere in the internal affairs of any Arab state.

Article 28: The Palestinian Arab people assert the genuineness and independence of their national (*wataniyya*) revolution and reject all forms of intervention, trusteeship, and subordination.

Article 29: The Palestinian people possess the fundamental and genuine legal right to liberate and retrieve their homeland. The Palestinian people determine their attitude toward all states and forces on the basis of the stands they adopt vis-à-vis to the Palestinian revolution to fulfill the aims of the Palestinian people.

Article 30: Fighters and carriers of arms in the war of liberation are the nucleus of the popular army which will be the protective force for the gains of the Palestinian Arab people.

Article 31: The Organization shall have a flag, an oath of allegiance, and an anthem. All this shall be decided upon in accordance with a special regulation.

Article 32: Regulations, which shall be known as the Constitution of the Palestinian Liberation Organization, shall be annexed to this Charter. It will lay down the manner in which the Organization, and its organs and institutions, shall be constituted; the respective competence of each; and the requirements of its obligation under the Charter.

Article 33: This Charter shall not be amended save by [vote of] a majority of two-thirds of the total membership of the National Congress of the Palestine Liberation Organization [taken] at a special session convened for that purpose.

ANALYSIS

Israel is the only nation in the world for which a warrant for destruction exists in writing—the Palestinian National Charter. A total of thirty of the thirty-three articles in the Charter effectively deny Israel's right to exist as a Jewish state. They call for the demise of Israel either explicitly or implicitly. Articles 15, 19, 20, 22, and 23 of the Charter explicitly deny Israel's right to exist as a Jewish state. Articles 1–6, 8, 11–14, 16–18, 21, 24–26, 28, and 29 implicitly deny the State of Israel's right to exist. These articles recognize that Palestinian Arabs have the sole right to all of the land. Articles 7, 9, and 10 call all Arabs to support an armed struggle against the State of Israel. Articles 27 and 30 indirectly call for violence.

More specifically:

Article 1 proclaims, "Palestine will be an Arab State." This belies the claim that Palestine will be a secular, democratic state. Nineteen Arab states' constitutions proclaim Islam as the religion of the state. Furthermore, it means that the Jews have no rights whatsoever to this piece of land.

Article 2 declares that the "boundaries [of the Arab state of Palestine will be] … as at the time of the British Mandate … one integral unit." There will be no separate Jewish state. There can be no "two-state solution," and any talk of such a solution is merely a tactical maneuver. It has been repeatedly stressed that the *Falastin* (Palestine) the PLO seeks to create will extend *min al-nahr ila al bahr* ("from the river to the sea"). PLO leader Yasser Arafat specified the exact boundaries of this Arab Palestine in a speech at the University of Beirut, Lebanon, in December 1980, "The victory march will continue until the Palestinian flag flies in Jerusalem and in all of Palestine from the Jordan River to the Mediterranean Sea and from Rosh Hanikra [in the north] to Eilat [in the south]."[17] In short, this is a declaration of the PLO's intention to destroy Israel and "liberate" all of Palestine. It should be further noted that the phrase "boundaries [of the Arab state of Palestine will be] … as at the time of the British Mandate … one integral unit" leaves the door open for Palestinian absorption—by one method or another—of Jordan, which prior to 1921 was part of the British Mandate of Palestine.

Article 3 states that only Palestinian Arabs possess legal right to self-determination, not the Jews. Thus, it is more important for the Arabs to have a twenty-second Arab state, than for the Jews to have one Jewish state.

Article 4 sets a tone for "Palestinian" blood purity (reminiscent of the Nazis) by declaring that "the Palestinian identity is a genuine, essential, and inherent characteristic; it is transmitted from parents to children."

Article 6 pronounces that Jews who lived in Palestine before the "Zionist invasion" will be allowed to remain. However, Yasser Arafat and his minions quickly realized that such a declaration would leave too many Jews in "Palestine." Thus, in the 1968 revision of the PLO Charter this section was revised to read, "The Jews who had normally resided in Palestine until the beginning of the Zionist invasion will be considered Palestinians." At first, "the beginning of the Zionist invasion" was declared 1917, when the Balfour Declaration was issued. However, subsequently it was realized that this date would still leave too many Jews in "Palestine." Therefore, at the United Nations General Assembly on November 13, 1974, Yasser Arafat stated "the Jewish invasion began … in 1881." All others would have to go, one way or another. Thus, this is an implicit call for the expulsion or extermination of most of the Jewish population of Israel. Non-Arab Christians and non-Muslim residents of former Palestine were totally rejected as being "Palestinians." Their descendants as well as the descendants of any of the Jews who had lived in Palestine since "the beginning of the Zionist invasion" were *persona non grata* in the land of their birth. In sum, the PLO Charter proclaimed "ethnic cleansing" in advance of the deed!

Article 9, 10 and 21 expressly commits the PLO to armed struggle (i.e. terrorism) as the only way to liberate Palestine. Thus, Palestinians defined themselves—the entire population (men, women and children)—and their national movement as a violent movement directed at destroying the nation state of another people. As such, negotiations, ceasefires *(hudnas)*, "peace processes," and "road maps"—are all tactics to culminate in the politicide of Israel. Additionally, armed struggle is the overall strategy, not merely a tactical phase in the effort to destroy Israel. Of note, is the fact that the charter calls for "armed struggle" or "armed revolution" nine times throughout the document. There is no room for a peaceful means of attaining their goals. Furthermore, the Arab states are obligated to support the Palestinian war against Israel and should not deviate from the "cause" due to local interests and pressures.

Article 12 concedes that the endeavor to "safeguard … Palestinian identity" is merely a tactical and temporary stratagem meant to annul what they term "the illegal 1947 partition of Palestine" (i.e. Israel in its entirety). It reveals the Palestinians are not—and do not see themselves—as a genuinely distinct people or a cohesive nation, with a coherently defined homeland. Thus, the Palestinians not only affirm that their national demands are bogus, but that they are merely a temporary ruse. It will be transcended in favor of Arab unity in the future. This also exposes the contradiction of Palestinian "exclusiveness" and overall Arab unity.

Article 13 provides a verbal solution to the question of priority long debated throughout the Arab world: Which should come first, the liberation of Palestine or Arab unity?

Article 15 calls for the liquidation of the Zionist presence in Palestine, and defense of the Arab states.

Article 18 declares war against Israel legal. The use of any means, including terrorism is legal, but Israel's legitimate right of self-defense is illegal, since the existence of Israel itself is illegal.

Article 19 rejects UN General Assembly Resolution 181 of 1947, which called for the partition of the British Mandate of Palestine into a Jewish state and an Arab state. This reiterated the rejection of Jewish self-determination. In any event as previously noted, UNGA Resolution 181 became void and a dead letter because of the Arab invasion of and war against Israel in 1948.

Article 20 denies the historic connection of the Jewish people to the Land of Israel. Furthermore, it denies the existence of a Jewish nation (i.e. people-hood) and of the right to self-determination of the Jewish people. As is the case with other national peoples in the Middle East—including the Imazighen (the Berbers), Tuareg, Toubou, Kurds, Assyrians, Druze, Circassians, and Nubians among others—the Arab world chauvinistically demands rights for itself while denying the same rights to others.

Article 21 rejects any compromise settlement and demands nothing short of the total "liberation of all of Palestine," i.e. Israel.

Article 22 implies that there is no place for Jews anywhere. "Israel is the instrument of the Zionist movement, and geographical base for world imperialism. Israel is a constant source of threat vis-à-vis peace in the Middle East and the whole world." Thus, like the Nazis before them, trying to "save the world" from the evil Jews, the PLO would "save humanity" by ridding the world of Israel. Furthermore, the mention of 'imperialist presence' was a reference to the Kingdom of Jordan, which was created by the British and supported by them and later the United States. As noted earlier, the PLO tried to overthrow the Hashemite kingdom in 1970.

Article 23 calls on the entire world to help the Arabs destroy Israel. It set, for example, the precedent for the infamous UN General Assembly Resolution 3379 of November 10, 1975, that declared, "Zionism is Racism."

Articles 25 and 26 declare the PLO as the umbrella organization bearing the responsibility for the struggle of all the Palestinians against Israel. The PLO was not chosen it merely appointed itself.

Furthermore, it alone would decide what type of regime Palestine would have after its victory and the destruction of Israel.

Article 27 proclaims that the PLO will cooperate with all Arab states and will not interfere in the internal affairs of any Arab state. Yet, they tried to overthrow the Jordanian monarchy and take over that nation in 1970, plunged Lebanon into civil war in 1975 and fought against the legal Lebanese government until 1982, and cheered and abetted the Iraqi conquest of Kuwait in 1990.

Article 28 declares that the Palestinian movement is not the tool for any Arab state and does not accept orders from any outside authority. Yet over the years, several other "Palestinian" organizations financed and controlled by outside powers have belied this provision. They include but are not limited to the Syrian-controlled As-Sa'iqa which follows Ba'athist ideology, the Arab Liberation Front backed by the Iraqi Ba'athist party (until 2003), and the Palestinian Islamic Jihad backed by Syria, Iran and Hezbollah in Lebanon.

Article 29 legitimizes PLO terror attacks on any countries that are friendly to Israel.

The bottom line is that the Palestinian National Charter calls for the destruction of the State of Israel. The Israelis quite naturally, thought that the inflammatory language should be changed before they could consider the PLO to be a serious "partner for peace." The Charter specifically states in Article 33, that there can be no changes without the express decision of the Palestine National Council.

PLO Chairman Yasser Arafat was a master of deceit, deception and duplicity. He subsequently agreed to remove the sections of the Charter that called for Israel's destruction. Even before the Oslo Accords, on May 2, 1989, Arafat had declared in a statement in Paris, "As for the Charter, I believe there is an expression in French, *C'est caduque* ("It is null and void"). Arafat lied. On numerous occasions thereafter, he would make such claims, yet nothing was done to change the Charter.

In a letter to Israeli Prime Minister Yitzhak Rabin, dated September 9, 1993—part of the Oslo Accords—signed by Yasser Arafat as Chairman of the PLO and Fatah leader, Arafat agreed that:

> The signing of the Declaration of Principles marks a new era in the history of the Middle East. In firm conviction thereof, I would like to confirm the following PLO commitments:
>
> The PLO recognizes the right of the State of Israel to exist in peace and security.
>
> The PLO accepts United Nations Security Council Resolutions 242 and 338.
>
> The PLO commits itself to the Middle East peace process, and to a peaceful resolution of the conflict between the two sides and declares that all outstanding issues relating to permanent status will be resolved through negotiations.
>
> The PLO considers that the signing of the Declaration of Principles constitutes a historic event, inaugurating a new epoch of peaceful coexistence, free from violence and all other acts which endanger peace and stability. Accordingly, the PLO renounces

the use of terrorism and other acts of violence and will assume responsibility over all PLO elements and personnel in order to assure their compliance, prevent violations and discipline violators.

In view of the promise of a new era and the signing of the Declaration of Principles and based on Palestinian acceptance of Security Council Resolutions 242 and 338, the PLO affirms that those articles of the Palestinian Covenant which deny Israel's right to exist, and the provisions of the Covenant which are inconsistent with the commitments of this letter are now inoperative and no longer valid. Consequently, the PLO undertakes to submit to the Palestinian National Council for formal approval the necessary changes in regard to the Palestinian Covenant.[18]

Nevertheless despite the pledges, violence, incitement and terror against Israel continued. Nothing was done to change the Charter. The requirement was restated in another letter from Arafat to Rabin which accompanied the May 4, 1994 Agreement on the Gaza Strip and Jericho Area (the Cairo Agreement), but again no action was taken by Arafat and the PLO. Because the changes were not made, the 1995 Israeli PLO Oslo II Agreement (Interim Agreement) made the requirements even more specific:

ARTICLE XXXI (9): The PLO undertakes that, within two months of the date of the inauguration of the Council, the Palestinian National Council will convene and formally approve the necessary changes in regard to the Palestinian Covenant, as undertaken in the letters signed by the Chairman of the PLO and addressed to the Prime Minister of Israel, dated September 9, 1993 and May 4, 1994.

What actions were taken by the PLO to live up to its agreements?

The Oslo II agreement was signed on September 24, 1995 but the change was not made within the time period specified. On April 24, 1996, there was a vote by the PLO's Palestine National Council, meeting in Gaza. They issued a statement saying that it had become aged, and that an undefined part of it would be rewritten at an undetermined date in the future. While the English language press release stated that the PLO Charter was "hereby amended," the Arabic version of Yasser Arafat's letter on this declaration stated:

It has been decided upon:

1. Changing the Palestine National Charter by canceling the articles that are contrary to the letters exchanged between the PLO and the Government of Israel, on September 9 and 10, 1993.

2. The PNC will appoint a legal committee with the task of redrafting the National Charter. The Charter will be presented to the first meeting of the Central Council.

The governments of the United States and of Israel welcomed the vote, stating that it marked the fulfillment of the Palestinian Arab obligation on the Charter. Again, that was not actually the case. The PNC action, which has not been officially fully disclosed, only stated an intention to make changes at a future date and did not specify, in detail, the changes that would be made. The matter was referred to a legal committee for study. No such committee ever met, nor were the specific anti-Israel clauses in the Charter declared officially abrogated. Moreover, the process was incomplete because the PNC did not draft a new Charter.

Even Peace Watch, a left wing Israeli peace group that promotes the creation of a second Palestinian Arab state, issued this statement, which represents the way most Israelis feel:

> The decision fails to meet the obligations laid out in the Oslo accords in two respects. First, the actual amendment of the Covenant has been left for a future date. As of now, the old Covenant, in its original form, remains the governing document of the PLO, and will continue in this status until the amendments are actually approved. There is a sharp difference between calling for something to change and actually implementing the changes. Second, the decision does not specify which clauses will be amended.[19]

After winning the election in May 1996, Israeli Prime Minister Benjamin Netanyahu declared the failure to revise the PLO Charter to be a violation of the agreements by the Palestinian Arabs. In the 1997 Hebron Protocol, it was specifically noted again, that the PLO/PA was committed to, "Complete the process of revising the Palestinian National Charter." Thereafter, Arafat and the PLO governing bodies insisted that they were in compliance based on the PNC vote in 1996, but legal analysts do not agree. In January 1998, Chairman Arafat sent letters to President Bill Clinton and Prime Minister Tony Blair purporting to "put to rest" concerns about the PNC resolution and setting out a list of articles supposedly canceled or amended by the decision. However, personal statements by Arafat have no legal effect; only a vote of two-thirds of the PNC can amend the Charter (Article 33). On December 14, 1998, the Palestinian National Council, in accordance with the Wye River Memorandum, which required compliance with the earlier agreements, convened in Gaza in the presence of President Bill Clinton and voted to reaffirm their decision to amend the Charter. Yet again, this was insubstantial window dressing. Their action did not actually amend the Charter and the PLO/PA remained in violation of the lengthening series of agreements.

Although the Palestinian National Council (PNC) has twice taken formal decisions to revise the Palestinian National Charter (1996 and 1998) calling for Israel's destruction, the PNC Chairman, Salim Za'anoun, stated on February 3, 2001, in the official PLO/PA newspaper, *Al-Hayat Al-Jadida,* that the Palestinian Charter remained unchanged and was still in force.[20] Commenting on this lack of PLO compliance, former CIA Director James Woolsey said:

> Arafat has been like Lucy with the football, treating the rest of the world as Charlie Brown. He and the PNC keep telling everyone they've changed the charter, without actually changing it.[21]

This saga of the Charter revision is an example of the lack of good faith and compliance on the part of Arafat and the Palestinian Arabs in the course of the Oslo peace process. Farouk Kaddoumi, the PLO's "foreign minister," in an interview with the Jordanian newspaper *Al-Arab* said on April 22, 2004, that when Palestinian Authority Chairman Yasser Arafat talks about the need to pursue the struggle against Israel, he is referring to the armed struggle. Kaddoumi said the armed struggle was the only way to force Israel to accept the demands of the Palestinians. He openly admitted that the PLO charter, was *never* (emphasis added) changed.[22] The hatred and violence directed against Israel by the Palestinian Arabs does not originate with the piece of paper called the Palestinian National Charter. The original charter is still displayed by the Palestine legation to the United Nations and other Palestinian bodies. In PNA offices there is a plaque commemorating the original eighteen signers of the Charter.

CHARTER OF THE ISLAMIC RESISTANCE MOVEMENT – (HAMAS CHARTER)
August 18, 1988 [23]

(Selected excerpts annotated)

The Hamas Charter states, "Israel will rise and will remain erect until Islam eliminates it as it had eliminated its predecessors."

> Introduction: For our struggle against the Jews is extremely wide-ranging and grave, so much so that it will need all the loyal efforts we can wield, to be followed by further steps and reinforced by successive battalions from the multifarious Arab and Islamic world, until the enemies are defeated and Allah's victory prevails.

> Article 6: The Islamic Resistance Movement is a distinct Palestinian Movement which owes its loyalty to Allah, derives from Islam its way of life and strives to raise the banner of Allah over every inch of Palestine.

> Article 7: Allah bless him and grant him salvation, has said: The Day of Judgment will not come about until Muslims fight the Jews [killing the Jews], when the Jew will hide behind stones and trees. The stones and trees will say O Muslims, O Abdullah, there is a Jew behind me, come and kill him. Only the Gharkad tree, [evidently a certain kind of tree] would not do that because it is one of the trees of the Jews.[24]

Note: Article 7 is clearly misojudaic and stresses that it is the religious duty of Hamas to kill all the Jews. Islamic calls for the extermination of the Jewish people (which are not limited to the Jews of Israel alone, but rather all Jews worldwide) and the destruction of Israel dominate the mosques, seminaries, universities and media outlets throughout the Arab and Muslim worlds and increasingly in the West as well.

> Article 11: The land of Palestine has been an Islamic *Waqf* [trust] throughout the generations and until the Day of Resurrection; no one can renounce it or part of it, or abandon it or part of it.

Note: The Arab/Muslim world considers Israel *Waqf* land (under Muslim authority) and therefore they cannot and will not recognize Jewish sovereignty in the Land of Israel, under any circumstances.

> Article 13: [Peace] initiatives, the so-called peaceful solutions, and the international conferences to resolve the Palestinian problem, are all contrary to the beliefs of the

Islamic Resistance Movement. For renouncing any part of Palestine means renouncing part of the religion. There is no solution to the Palestinian problem except by jihad, for initiatives, proposals and international conferences are nothing but a waste of time and absurd nonsense.

Article 15: The day that enemies usurp part of Muslim land, Jihad becomes the individual duty of every Muslim. In face of the Jews' usurpation of Palestine, it is compulsory that the banner of Jihad be raised. 'I swear by that who holds in His Hands the Soul of Muhammad! I indeed wish to go to war for the sake of Allah! I will assault and kill, assault and kill, assault and kill *(related by Sahih Bukhari and Sahih Muslim)*.'

Thus, it is clear that "resistance" repeated throughout the charter, means genocidal jihad.

Article 22: For a long time, the enemies [i.e. the Jews] have been planning, skillfully and with precision, for the achievement of what they have attained. They took into consideration the causes affecting the current of events. They strived to amass great and substantive material wealth which they devoted to the realization of their dream. With their money, they took control of the world media, news agencies, the press, publishing houses, broadcasting stations, and others. With their money they stirred revolutions in various parts of the world with the purpose of achieving their interests and reaping the fruit therein. They were behind the French Revolution, the Communist revolution and most of the revolutions we heard and hear about, here and there. With their money they formed secret societies, such as Freemasons, Rotary Clubs, the Lions and others in different parts of the world for the purpose of sabotaging societies and achieving Zionist interests. With their money they were able to control imperialistic countries and instigate them to colonize many countries in order to enable them to exploit their resources and spread corruption there.

You may speak as much as you want about regional and world wars. They [the Jews] were behind World War I, when they were able to destroy the Islamic Caliphate, making financial gains and controlling resources. They obtained the Balfour Declaration, formed the League of Nations through which they could rule the world. They were behind World War II, through which they made huge financial gains by trading in armaments, and paved the way for the establishment of their state. It was they who instigated the replacement of the League of Nations with the United Nations and the Security Council to enable them to rule the world through them. There is no war going on anywhere, without having their finger in it.

Note: This is another misojudaic article that lays the blame for virtually all the world's ills at the feet of the Jews. Additionally, ordinary Western institutions are labeled as enemies of the Islamic Resistance.

Article 28: The Arab states surrounding Israel are required to open their borders to the Jihad fighters, the sons of the Arab and Islamic peoples, to enable them to play their role and to join their efforts to those of their brothers among the Muslim Brothers in Palestine. Israel, by virtue of its being Jewish and of having a Jewish population, defies Islam and the Muslims.

Note: Hamas makes "no distinction between Jews, Zionists and Israelis."[25]

Article 32: Today it is Palestine, tomorrow it will be one country or another. The Zionist plan is limitless. After Palestine, the Zionists aspire to expand from the Nile to the Euphrates. When they will have digested the region they overtook, they will aspire to further expansion, and so on. Their plan is embodied in the 'Protocols of the Elders of Zion,' and their present conduct is the best proof of what we are saying.

Note: Again, this is a misojudaic article based on the notorious forgery, *The Protocols of the Elders of Zion.* It was first published by the Tsarist Russian secret police in 1903, translated into multiple languages, and disseminated internationally in the early part of the twentieth century. It was utilized by (among many others) Henry Ford, who funded the printing of 500,000 copies that were distributed throughout the United States in the 1920s as well as in his weekly newspaper, the Dearborn *Independent*. Father Charles Coughlin, the radio priest of the 1930s, used the *Protocols* in his broadcasts and printed the entire text, as installments, in his weekly magazine *Social Justice,* in 1938. The Nazi regime in Germany, as well as allied fascists around the world in the 1930s and 1940s, used the *Protocols* as a primary justification for initiating the Holocaust—a "warrant for genocide."[26] The *Protocols* was republished many times since the end of World War II, most recently in numerous Arabic editions. Before his assassination in 1975, King Faisal of Saudi Arabia routinely had free copies of the *Protocols* distributed to visiting Western tourists. Given the tragedies they have abetted and their poisonous potential for more, *The Protocols of the Elders of Zion,* may be the most successful and insidious forgery in history.

Article 33: Until the Decree of Allah is fulfilled, the ranks are over-swollen, Jihad fighters join other Jihad fighters, and all this accumulation sets out from everywhere in the Islamic world, obeying the call of duty, and intoning 'Come on, join Jihad!' This call will tear apart the clouds in the skies and it will continue to ring until liberation is completed, the invaders are vanquished and Allah's victory sets in.

THE FATAH CONSTITUTION, 1964

(Excerpts)

Article 4: The Palestinian struggle is part and parcel of the worldwide struggle against Zionism, colonialism and international imperialism.

Article 7: The Zionist movement is racial, colonial and aggressive in ideology, goals, organization and method.

Article 8: The Israeli existence in Palestine is a Zionist invasion with a colonial expansive base, and it is a natural ally to colonialism and international imperialism.

Article 12: [Calls for the] Complete liberation of Palestine and eradication of Zionist economic, political, military, and cultural existence.

Article 13: Establishing an independent democratic state with complete sovereignty on all Palestinian lands, [a *Falestin* that extends *min al-nahr ila al bahr*—"From the river to the sea"] and Jerusalem is its capital city, and protecting the citizens' legal and equal rights without any racial or religious discrimination.

Article 17: Armed public revolution is the inevitable method to liberating Palestine.

Article 19: Armed struggle is a strategy and not a tactic, and the Palestinian Arab People's armed revolution is a decisive factor in the liberation fight and in uprooting the Zionist existence, and this struggle will not cease until the Zionist state is demolished and Palestine is completely liberated.

Article 22: Opposing any political solution offered as an alternative to demolishing the Zionist occupation in Palestine.

Article 23: Maintaining relations with Arab countries … with the proviso that the armed struggle is not negatively affected.

Article 24: Maintaining relations with all liberal forces supporting our just struggle in order to resist together Zionism and imperialism.

Article 25: Convincing concerned countries in the world to prevent Jewish immigration to Palestine as a method of solving the problem.

ANALYSIS

Some have labeled Fatah as "moderate" and Hamas as "extremist." That is like saying Attila the Hun is a "moderate" when measured up against Genghis Khan. It is a distinction without a difference. They are different in method, not outcome. Fatah and Hamas use different strategies towards the same goal—the elimination of Israel. Fatah, as well as the Al-Aqsa Martyrs Brigades and other terrorist groups under the PLO umbrella, are a crafty, secular, politically-slick, media-savvy group of killers, who give lip service in English to the "peace process." Hamas, Palestinian Islamic Jihad, Fatah al-Islam, et al are ideologically driven, religiously motivated, fanatically dedicated murderers, who reject "peace" altogether. Fatah/the PLO negotiate while killing Israelis, whereas Hamas murders Israelis without negotiating. PA/PLO/Fatah uses women and children as human bombs, whereas Hamas uses women and children as human shields, a distinction without a difference.

This has not changed since the founding of Fatah in 1958. In 1998, Al Fatah published a new constitution that goes beyond the Palestinian National Charter in calling for the destruction of Israel. From August 4 to 11, 2009, Fatah held its Sixth General Conference in Bethlehem. It was the first such gathering in twenty years and the first since the 1993 signing of the Oslo "Peace" Accords. There the delegates reaffirmed all parts of the Fatah Constitution.[27] The organization continues not to recognize Israel's right to exist. In fact, Fatah and other Palestinian Arab maps do not acknowledge Israel's existence at all. Fatah continues to endorse violence and terror, what the terrorist organization euphemistically call "armed struggle." It remains not a force for moderation and true peace, but rather what it has always been—a terrorist organization, an implacable enemy of Israel, dedicated to the total destruction of the Jewish state.

Appendix 9

THE PLO PHASED PLAN

(also known as the "Strategy of Stages" or the "Ten Point Program")

The PLO Phased Plan was adopted on June 8, 1974, at the Twelfth Session of the Palestine National Council, which met in Cairo, Egypt. The plan called for the simultaneous implementation of both armed struggle and diplomacy to achieve the overall goal of the PLO, which was—and continues to be—the elimination of the Jewish state of Israel.

The Palestine National Council,

On the basis of the Palestine National Charter and the Political Program drawn up at the eleventh session, held from 6 to12 January 1997, and from its belief that it is impossible for a permanent and just peace to be established in the area unless our Palestinian people recover all their national rights and, first and foremost, their rights to return and to self-determination on the whole of the soil of their homeland; and in the light of a study of the new political circumstances that have come into existence in the period between the Council's last and present sessions, resolves the following:

1. To reaffirm the Palestine Liberation Organization's previous attitude to Resolution 242, which obliterates the national right of our people and deals with the cause of our people as a problem of refugees. The Council therefore refuses to have anything to do with this resolution at any level, Arab or international, including the Geneva Conference.

2. The Palestine Liberation Organization will employ all means, and first and foremost armed struggle, to liberate Palestinian territory and to establish the independent combatant national authority for the people over every part of Palestinian territory that is liberated. This will require further changes being effected in the balance of power in favor of our people and their struggle.

3. The Liberation Organization will struggle against any proposal for a Palestinian entity the price of which is recognition, peace, secure frontiers, renunciation of national rights, and the deprival of our people of their right to return and their right to self-determination on the soil of their homeland.

4. Any step taken towards liberation is a step towards the realization of the Liberation Organization's strategy of establishing the democratic Palestinian State specified in the resolutions of the previous Palestinian National Councils.

5. Struggle along with the Jordanian national forces to establish a Jordanian-Palestinian national front whose aim will be to set up in Jordan a democratic national authority in close contact with the Palestinian entity that is established through the struggle.

6. The Liberation Organization will struggle to establish unity in struggle between the two peoples and between all the forces of the Arab liberation movement that are in agreement on this program.

7. In the light of this program, the Liberation Organization will struggle to strengthen national unity and to raise it to the level where it will be able to perform its national duties and tasks.

8. Once it is established, the Palestinian national authority will strive to achieve a union of the confrontation countries, with the aim of completing the liberation of all Palestinian territory, and as a step along the road to comprehensive Arab unity.

9. The Liberation Organization will strive to strengthen its solidarity with the socialist countries, and with the forces of liberation and progress throughout the world, with the aim of frustrating all the schemes of Zionism, reaction and imperialism.

10. In light of this program, the leadership of the revolution will determine the tactics which will serve and make possible the realization of these objectives.

The Executive Committee of the Palestine Liberation Organization will make every effort to implement this program, and should a situation arise affecting the destiny and the future of the Palestinian people, the National Assembly will be convened in extraordinary session.[28]

Appendix 10

UN "ZIONISM IS RACISM" RESOLUTION 3379

(Annotated)

There has been, since shortly after the June 1967 Six-Day War, an ongoing Arab/Muslim campaign to defame, denounce, denigrate, and delegitimize Israel in every international forum. This process accelerated after the Arab failure to defeat Israel during the Yom Kippur War of October 1973. The Arab/Muslim states chose to employ the United Nations to wage a political war against the Jewish state.

On November 10, 1975, the United Nations General Assembly (where the United States has no veto) passed a resolution (UNGA 3379) condemning and labeling "Zionism as a form of racism." Before the vote, a ballot to defer the resolution lost by only twelve votes, 67 to 55.

The final vote for Resolution 3379 was:

- 72 countries voted in favor, which included the Arab and other Islamic countries, almost all African and Asian states, as well as the Soviet Union and the communist bloc. But also voting for the resolution were:
  - India, led by Indira Gandhi, who had destroyed democracy in her own nation and who had been turned into an Arab-Soviet proxy.
  - Brazil, seeking Arab oil and investments.
  - Mexico, which voted for deferral but then voted for the resolution.
  - Iran (of the Shah), Turkey, and Cyprus all of which voted against the deferral motion and for the anti-Zionism resolution.
- 35 against which included the United States, most of Western Europe, Australia, New Zealand, and Israel.
- 32 abstentions including:
  - Japan, which voted for deferral, but which abstained on the resolution vote.
  - Jamaica and Greece both of which abstained on both votes and thus helped defeat the deferral motion.

In fact, Zionism is one of the oldest national liberation movements of the modern age. It is Zionism's bearing upon the reestablishment of Jewish sovereignty in the Land of Israel that led to the General Assembly's perverse action in passing Resolution 3379. The "Zionism is racism" resolution passed for the first time by an international organization ostensibly representing the world, vilified an entire nation—the Jewish nation—and its people. The power of such repeated calumnies must never be underestimated. Such big lies produced the Holocaust and could pave the way for a second Holocaust.

Given that racism had already been defined by the United Nations as a crime, enumerated in the Genocide Convention and numerous other instruments commonly accepted under international law, and given too, that Zionism was Israel's very *raison d'être*, this resolution in effect convicted Israel of being an outlaw state. The resolution placed Israel—the Zionist state—beyond the moral pale, and implicitly challenged its right to exist. It thereby made a mighty contribution to the campaign on the diplomatic front of the Arab/Muslim world's war against Israel.

The main objective of this campaign (spearheaded and masterminded in those days by the Soviet Union) was not to force Israel into changing this or that policy or withdrawing from this or that piece of land. It was rather, to stigmatize the Jewish state as illegitimate in its very essence. Being illegitimate, it had no right to defend itself against attack and if it did so, it was guilty of the added crime of aggression. As the then President of Egypt, Gamal Abdel Nasser, had put it shortly before the outbreak of the Six-Day War of 1967, "Israel's existence is in itself an aggression." Conversely, anyone who might launch an actual aggression of any kind against Israel, whether in the form of terrorist bombings or assault by regular military forces was, in the topsy-turvy conceptions of the United Nations, acting in self-defense and in accordance with international law.

Israel's UN ambassador Chaim Herzog noted the significance of the date:

> This night, 37 years ago, has gone down in history as the *Kristallnacht,* or the Night of the Crystals. This was the night of 10 November 1938 when Hitler's Nazi Storm troopers launched a coordinated attack on the Jewish community in Germany, burnt the synagogues in all the cities and made bonfires in the streets, of the Holy Books and the Scrolls of the Holy Laws and the Bible. It was the night when Jewish homes were attacked and heads of families were taken away, many of them never to return. It was the night when the windows of all Jewish businesses and stores were smashed, covering the streets in the cities of Germany with a film of broken glass which dissolved into millions of crystals, giving that night the name of *Kristallnacht,* the Night of the Crystals.[29]

The US ambassador to the United Nations, Daniel Patrick Moynihan, denounced the resolution in an eloquent and widely noticed speech that began and ended with a defiant sentence provided him by Norman Podhoretz of *Commentary* magazine. "The United States rises to declare before the General Assembly of the UN, and before the world, that it does not acknowledge, it will never abide by, it will never acquiesce in this infamous act." Moynihan accurately predicted that the resolution would revive misojudaism, "A great evil has been loosed upon the world. The abomination of anti-Semitism … has been given the appearance of international sanction." Later on, Moynihan proclaimed, "The lie is that Zionism is a form of racism. The overwhelmingly clear truth is that it is not."[30]

Jeanne J. Kirkpatrick, US ambassador to the UN from 1981 to 1985, made the implications of being branded a "racist" state clear. A racist state, Kirkpatrick observed, has "no rights at all, not even the right to defend itself." After 3379 was passed, Israel became "fair game for armed 'liberation' [i.e. terrorist attack]."[31] Years later, just prior to the UN General Assembly vote to consider rescinding Resolution 3379, the importance of all such resolutions was stressed by John Bolton, then Assistant US Secretary of State for International Organization Affairs, "In the UN, words take on a life of their own. To declare as 'racist' the historical and cultural underpinnings of a state is tantamount to branding that state an international criminal, for racism is a crime enumerated in the Genocide Convention and numerous other instruments commonly accepted under international law."[32]

The UN readopted UN General Assembly Resolution 3379 every year for sixteen years. It took sixteen years for the resolution to be revoked.

REPEAL OF THE UN "ZIONISM IS RACISM" RESOLUTION

On December 16, 1991, United Nations General Assembly Resolution 46/86 simply declared, "The General Assembly decides to revoke the determination contained in its resolution 3379 (XXX) of 10 November 1975." The vote was:

- 111 voted in favor, including the United States, Canada, Europe including the Soviet Union and the rest of the former Soviet bloc, including Estonia, Latvia, and Lithuania; Latin America and the Caribbean nations; many sub-Saharan African nations including Nigeria; many non-Muslim Asian nations including India, Japan, the Republic of Korea, Singapore, and Thailand; as well as Australia, New Zealand, the Pacific nations and Israel.
- 25 voted against, including Arab and Muslim states of Africa and Asia, Cuba, the DPRK, Sri Lanka, and Vietnam.
- Thirteen abstained, including Angola, Burkina Faso, Ethiopia, Ghana, Laos, Maldives, Mauritius, Myanmar, Tanzania, Trinidad and Tobago, Turkey, Uganda, and Zimbabwe.
- Fifteen nations did not vote. These included Bahrain, Chad, China, Comoros, Djibouti, Egypt, Guinea, Guinea-Bissau, Kuwait, Morocco, Niger, Oman, Senegal, Tunisia, and Vanuatu.

It should be noted, that UNGA Resolution 3379 was the only anti-Israel resolution revoked to date.

On November 10, 2005, the thirtieth anniversary of the "Zionism is racism resolution," US Ambassador to the UN, John Bolton called the resolution the UN's "single worst decision." He added, "It's incredible that it was passed to begin with" and "It's incredible that it took sixteen years to repeal it."[33]

Despite the rescinding of the "Zionism is racism" UN resolution, the damage had already been done, and could not be undone so long as the PLO exploited its status in the UN to undermine Israel. The PLO anti-Israel campaign, especially at, but not limited to the United Nations, has continued to the present day. It is Zionism's bearing upon the reestablishment of Jewish sovereignty in the State of Israel that led to the UN General Assembly's perverse actions, emulated in other international forums, like the Specialized Agencies of the United Nations. For Israel's enemies, Zionism is still viewed as an ideology to be eradicated, which, bluntly means Israel should be eliminated.

The continued anti-Zionism theme can be seen in several examples. The preamble of the African Charter on Human and Peoples' Rights, which came into effect on October 21, 1986, called expressly for the elimination of Zionism.[34] Nearly all African states have signed and ratified the treaty, and only post-apartheid South Africa qualified its 1996 accession with the reservation that the Charter fall in line with the UN's resolutions regarding the characterization of Zionism.

The UN World Conference against Racism, held at Durban, South Africa, from August 31 to September 8, 2001, effectively reinstated the UN General Assembly's definition of Zionism as racism and thus denied that Israel has the legal right to exist under international law. The UN Human Rights Council even passed a resolution endorsing Palestinian terrorism against Israel.

Furthermore, the Arab Charter on Human Rights, which was adopted[*] by the League of Arab States on May 22, 2004, and entered into force on January 24, 2008, in its preamble rejects "racism and Zionism, both of which constitute a violation of human rights and a threat to world peace." Moreover, Article 2, Section 3 denounces "Zionism, [as] a challenge to human dignity and [is] a fundamental obstacle to the human rights of peoples. It is a duty [of Arab League members] to "condemn [Zionism]

---

[*] A first version was adopted on September 15, 1994, but no state ratified it.

and to endeavor to eliminate [it]"—not a terribly subtle call for the destruction of Israel.[35] Subsequently, Louise Arbour, the High Commissioner for Human Rights, declared, "to the extent that it equates Zionism with racism ... the Arab Charter is not in conformity with General Assembly Resolution 46/86, which rejects that Zionism is a form of racism and racial discrimination."[36]

GLOSSARY

abaya	A garment—traditionally in black—worn by women that covers the whole body except the face, feet, and hands. It can be worn with the *niqab,* a face veil covering all but the eyes.
adhān (*ezan*) **in Turkish**	The Islamic call to prayer recited by the *muezzin* at prescribed times of the day. The call to prayer is given from the top of the minaret, either live or by loudspeaker.
ahl al-kitab	In Islam, this is a reference to Jews and Christians—"the people of the Book."
AKP	The Justice and Development Party (*Adalet ve Kalkınma Partisi*) in Turkey.
Alawites	A religious sect located in northwestern Syria. The Alawite faith is considered an offshoot of Twelver Shi'a Islam. Since 1970, they were the political elite and dominant force in the Syrian government.
aliyah	Literally "the act of going up" as ascending to Jerusalem. The in-gathering of Jewish exiles back to the Land of Israel; Jewish immigration to Israel.
Allahu akbar	Literally "Allah is greater," greater than all other gods. It is essentially a proclamation of Islamic superiority and supremacism.
aramesh	Farsi (Persian) term for a temporary or limited truce or ceasefire.
arkan al-Islam	The Five Pillars of Islam.
Ashkenazi Jews	Jews whose recent ancestors were of East European origin. Their lingua franca was Yiddish.
avania	"Protection money" paid for the safety and well-being of a *dhimmi*—Christian, Jew and Zoroastrian.
ayat (pl. *ayahs*)	A verse within a *sura* (chapter) in the Qur'an.
Ayatollah	The title given to the most eminent Shi'a legal experts.
ayn breira	Hebrew for "no alternative."
Basta	The Muslim section of Beirut, Lebanon.
Beta Israel	Ethiopian Jews.
Bey or Dey	The title for senior officials in the Ottoman service beneath the rank of pasha. It carried over in post-Ottoman society as a term of respect, especially in Turkey and Egypt.
BTWC	Biological and Toxin Weapons Convention.
burqa	An outer garment that covers the head and body completely worn in public by Muslim women. It is prevalent in Afghanistan, Pakistan and Saudi Arabia.
BW	Biological weapons.
caliph	The title adopted by Abu Bakr, the first caliph, as the head of the universal Islamic community. The word itself was taken from the phrase *Khalifat Rasul Allah* ("Successor to the Messenger [Muhammad] of Allah"). The Islamic state led by a supreme religious and political leader—the caliph—was/is known as a caliphate.

caliphate	An Islamic state led by a supreme religious as well as political leader known as a caliph. It is an Islamic theocracy where there is no separation of "church" (mosque) and state.
chador	A combined head covering veil and shawl worn by women, most prevalent in Iran.
CIA	United States Central Intelligence Agency.
CW	Chemical weapons.
CWC	Chemical Weapons Convention.
darura	Islamic tactic of necessity.
Dar al-Harb	House of War, i.e. the world that exists outside of Islam.
Dar al-Islam	House of Islam, i.e. those territories where Islamic law prevails.
dhimmi (pl. *dhimma*)	Non-Muslims under Islamic law who have paid a special tax—the *jizya*—and agree to a long list of strict conditions by which they are subordinated. This group includes Christians, Jews, and Zoroastrians.
Diaspora	The dispersion of the Jewish people from the Land of Israel after the Roman conquest in 73 C.E. and further brutal suppression after crushing the Bar Kokhba revolt in 135 C.E. Now applied to the Jews living outside modern Israel. Since the mid-twentieth century, the word has been commandeered by other groups, e.g. the Armenians.
DPRK	Democratic People's Republic of (North) Korea.
DTP	Kurdish Democratic Society Party (in Turkey).
EMET	Literally "truth." Hebrew acronym for *Agaf Mechkar Ve'tichun*. The organization in charge of defense research at the Israeli Ministry of Defense (1952–58).
Eretz Yisrael	Hebrew for the "Land of Israel."
Farhud	The pogrom against the Jews in Baghdad, Iraq, June 1–2, 1941.
Fatah	Arabic reverse acronym derived from *Harakat al-Tahrir [al-watani] al-Filastiniya* (Palestine National Liberation Movement). The actual acronym is *"Hataf"* meaning "sudden death." By reversing the acronym, *"Fatah"* becomes "conquest" or "victorious conquest" through holy struggle (i.e. jihad). It also refers to the rapid and violent spread of Islam during the first centuries of Islamic history, as well as being the title of *Sura* 48 in the Qur'an that details the story of the Treaty of Hudaybiyyah.
fatwa	An authoritative Islamic religious decree issued by Muslim scholars. Some *fatwas* are treated as commands from Allah, but only because the *fatwa* is popular or the imams have whipped up the masses to obey it.
fedayeen	Literally in Arabic, "men of self-sacrifice." In Islam, the term is used to describe infiltrators, fighters, and guerrilla warriors. It was the name used collectively to describe Arab terrorists who attacked Israel from the late 1940s onward.
Fertile Crescent	A geographic term historically identified as the area north of the Arabian Peninsula, extending in an arc from the Tigris–Euphrates Rivers to the Land of Israel. The region was defined to be the cradle of Western civilization. It encompasses today's Iraq, Syria, Lebanon, Jordan and Israel.

Galut	Hebrew for the Jews living outside of the Land of Israel in exile or in the Jewish Diaspora.
GCC	Gulf Cooperation Council.
Green Line	Commonly used name for the 1949 Arab-Israeli armistice lines. It was also used to describe the Attila Line that separates (since 1974) northern Turkish-occupied Cyprus from the Republic of Cyprus, in the south. It was also used to refer to the line that divided Beirut between Muslim-controlled West Beirut and Christian-controlled East Beirut from 1975 to 1990.
Hadith, hadith (pl. ahadith)	Hadith ("traditions") is a verified collection of brief stories with reference to the practices and actions as well as the sayings about and by Muhammad. Hadith are regarded by traditional Islamic schools of jurisprudence as important tools for understanding the Qur'an and in matters of Islamic law. They were written down and assembled into approved collections.
Haganah	Literally in Hebrew, "defense." The Jewish underground militia of the *Yishuv* in the British Mandate of Palestine. In 1948 after the State of Israel was established, the *Haganah* became the Israeli national army and was renamed the Israel Defense Forces (IDF).
hajj	The ritual obligation of pilgrimage to Mecca. It is one of the Five Pillars of Islam.
Halakha	*Halakha* is the collective body of Jewish religious laws, based on the Written and Oral Torah.
HaKotel HaMa'aravi	The Western Wall is the outer retaining wall of the Temple Mount compound in Jerusalem, on which stood both the First and Second Jewish Temples.
Hamas	Arabic acronym for *Harakat al-Muqawama al-Islamiya* (Islamic Resistance Movement). An Islamist Sunni Arab terror group founded in December 1987, it is the Palestinian wing of the Muslim Brotherhood in Egypt.
Haq al-Auda	The so-called right of return (to Israel) of all Arabs who claim they are "refugees."
harbi	The unbelievers, those who do not believe in Muhammad and the Qur'an. They include Christians, Jews, Hindus, Buddhists, Sikhs, Zoroastrians, Bahá'ís, animists, agnostics, polytheists, pagans, and atheists.
Hegira	The emigration of Muhammad and his followers from Mecca to Medina on July 16, 622 C.E. The event marks the year 1 of the Muslim calendar.
HEMED *Gimmel*	The HEMED unit was in charge of exploration of precious minerals and energy in Israel.
Hezbollah	Literally, in Arabic, "Party of Allah." It is a Lebanese Shi'ite terror group and political party. It is heavily subsidized and supported by the Islamic Republic of Iran and is used by Syria to maintain its influence in Lebanese politics.
hijab	A veil that covers the hair, head, neck, and chest—but reveals the face of the woman. It is particularly worn by a Muslim female beyond the age of puberty in the presence of adult males.
hilal	The very slight crescent moon that is first visible after a new moon. Muslims look for the *hilal* when determining the beginning and end of Islamic months.
Histadrut	The General Federation of Workers in the Land of Israel founded in 1920.

houris	In Islam, these are the virgins in paradise.
hudna	Arabic term for a temporary or limited truce, an armistice, or a ceasefire.
IAEA	International Atomic Energy Agency.
IAEC	Israel Atomic Energy Commission.
IAF	Israel Air Force.
iddah	In Islam, this is the period of time (three or more months) that a divorced woman must wait before she can remarry.
IDF	Israel Defense Forces (*Tzvah HaHaganah Leyisrael)*. Commonly known by the Hebrew acronym *Tzahal*.
ijtihad	Independent reasoning and interpretation of Islam. This practice ended in 1258. Currently, there are some calls for this practice to resume.
al-Ikhwan al-Muslimun	The Muslim Brotherhood.
Imam	The religious leader of Islamic public prayers. It is also the title of some Muslim rulers. In Shi'a Islam, it is the divinely guided head of the community who is regarded as infallible by virtue of his descent from Muhammad.
intifada	Literally, in Arabic, "shaking off," though it is popularly translated into English as "uprising." It is the name associated with the Palestinian Arab uprisings against Israeli rule of Judea, Samaria and the Gaza Strip, from 1987 to 1993 and from 2000 to 2002.
Irgun	The Hebrew abbreviated form for *Ha'Irgun HaTzva'i HaLe'umi BeEretz Yisrael,* "National Military Organization in the Land of Israel", commonly referred to as *Etzel*, an acronym of the Hebrew initials. The *Irgun* was a Jewish underground paramilitary group that fought the British in the British Mandate of Palestine and protected the *Yishuv* from Arab attack, from 1931 to 1948.
Islam	Submission to the will of Allah.
Janjaweed	Arab militias that sought to Arabize the largely black African sedentary peoples of Darfur, Sudan, as well as eastern Chad. The *Janjaweed* perpetrated ethnic cleansing of these people, causing the deaths of some 200,000 to 400,000 (2005-07).
jihad	Religiously sanction warfare by Muslims against non-Muslims.
jilbab	An indoor ankle-length, long-sleeved garment that leaves only the face and hands exposed, worn by Muslim women. It is similar to a caftan.
jizya	A special head tax applied to non-Muslim subjects e.g. *dhimma*, i.e. Christians and Jews, payable to the Islamic state.
JNF	Jewish National Fund.
judenrein	Ethnically and religiously cleansed of Jews.
Jundallah	Literally "Soldiers of Allah." The People's Resistance Movement of Iran is an opposition terrorist group to the current Iranian regime. It is based in Baluchistan, and fighting for Sunni rights in Iran.
Kaaba	A cube-like building in Mecca, Saudi Arabia. It is Islam's holiest shrine.

kafir (pl. *kuffar*)	*Kafir* (the original Arabic word as it appears in the Qur'an) is an abusive, derogatory, hateful, and prejudiced pejorative used to describe non-Muslims throughout the Qur'an, Sira, and Hadith. These sacred Islamic texts prescribe the political treatment of all peoples who do not believe in Islam. *Kafir*, and its plural *kuffar*, is directly used 134 times in the Qur'an, its verbal noun "*kufr*" is used 37 times, and the verbal cognates of *kafir* are used about 250 times. In Western languages it came to be translated as "unbeliever," "nonbeliever," "disbeliever," "non-Muslim," and "infidel," though the first four of these terms have a neutral connotation and appear in some translations of the Qur'an. Western translators may have interpreted it that way so as not to offend the sensibilities (political correctness at work here) of Muslims.
KDP	Kurdistan Democratic Party (active in Iran and Iraq).
Keren Kayemet LeYisrael	Hebrew for the Jewish National Fund (JNF).
KGB	Committee for State Security *(Komitet gosudarstvennoy bezopasnosti)*. It was the main internal security, intelligence, and secret police organization of the Soviet Union, 1954–91.
kharaj	A tenant tax that acknowledged Muslim land ownership.
kibbutz (pl. *kibbutzim*)	Hebrew for a collective or communal settlement based primarily on agriculture. In recent years, they have diversified into industry as well.
kitman	In Muslim doctrine, lying by omission.
Knesset	Israel's Parliament, which is composed of 120 members.
Komala	Iranian Kurdish Marxist and nationalist party, founded in 1942.
Kristallnacht	The Night of Broken Crystals or Glass was a misojudaic Nazi government pogrom in Germany that took place on November 9–10, 1938.
LEHI	Hebrew acronym for *Lohamei Herut Yisrael* ("Fighters for the Freedom of Israel"). Established on July 17, 1940, it was a small radical group that broke away from the *Irgun*, to better pursue the struggle for independence from British rule in Palestine. The British derogatorily labeled it as the "Stern Gang."
Levant	The Levant is a geographic and cultural region consisting of the eastern Mediterranean littoral (shoreline and hinterlands) between Anatolia (the bulk of Turkey) and the Sinai Peninsula. The Levant today consists of the island of Cyprus, part of southeastern Turkey, Syria, Lebanon, Israel, and Jordan.
Machon 4	Literally in Hebrew, "Institute." It was the EMET chief laboratory related to atomic energy, formerly known as HEMED *Gimmel*. It was subsequently known as the Israel Atomic Energy Commission laboratories.
madrasa	An Islamic religious school, school of theology, or religious college. Its primary purpose is the teaching of Islamic law and related religious subjects.
Mahdi	A divinely guided figure that is expected to appear in the last days and establish the rule of Islam on earth. Muhammad Ahmad assumed the title during the Mahdist Revolt (1881–99) against the British in Sudan. The conflict territorially encompassed Sudan, Egypt, Eritrea, Ethiopia, and Uganda.

mahr	In Islam, the dowry paid before marriage to the bride's nearest male relative, usually the father.
Majlis	The Iranian Parliament.
masjid	The place of worship for followers of Islam, known in the West as a mosque.
mellah	The restrictive walled Jewish quarter of cities in Morocco. In the countryside, these were segregated and restrictive—Jews only—villages. The Arab/Muslim equivalent of a ghetto.
mihrab	A *mihrab* is a crescent-shaped niche in the wall of a mosque that indicates the *qibla,* i.e. the direction of the Kaaba in Mecca and the direction that Muslims should face when praying.
minbar	A *minbar* is a raised pulpit in the mosque where the imam (prayer leader) stands to deliver sermons.
MINURSO	United Nations Mission for the Referendum in Western Sahara.
misojudaism (noun) misojudaic (adjective)	Misojudaism is a more accurate descriptor of the widespread hatred of Jews (*sin'at Yehudim* in Hebrew). Like misogyny the hatred of women, misogamy the hatred of marriage, misoneism the hatred of innovation, or misanthropy the hatred of mankind, misojudaism is a more precise term than the commonly used "anti-Semitism." Anti-Semitism is a misnomer and a racist term. Many of Israel's Arab/Muslim enemies have claimed with anthropological accuracy that they cannot be "anti-Semites," because they also are Semites. Therefore, they use the term "anti-Zionist" to camouflage their vehement misojudaic hostility.
MK	Member of the Knesset.
moshav	Hebrew for a cooperative settlement of smallholders.
Mossad	Hebrew acronym for *HaMossad LeBiyyun U'Letafkidim Meyuhadim.* ("Institute for Intelligence and Special Operations"). The national foreign intelligence agency of Israel, equivalent to the US CIA.
Mufti	An expert in Islamic law qualified to give authoritative legal opinions, i.e. *fatwas.*
mujahid (pl. *mujahadeen*)	Islamist jihad fighter, a soldier of Allah. The term was used in describing Muslim fighters in the conflicts in Afghanistan, Bosnia and Herzegovina, Chechnya, Kashmir, Iraq, Iran, Syria, and elsewhere.
mullah	Local Islamic religious leader.
mutaween	Saudi religious police.
Nakba	Literally in Arabic the "disaster" for the Arabs. It refers to the Arab view of the reestablishment of Jewish sovereignty in the Land of Israel. Historically, it was the outcome of the Arab aggression against the fledgling State of Israel, 1947–49.
niqab	A veil covering the face except for the eyes, worn by Muslim women.
NPT	Nuclear Non-Proliferation Treaty.
PA	The PLO Palestinian Authority, established May 4, 1994, to administer Palestinian areas in Judea, Samaria, and the Gaza Strip.

Palaestina or more accurately Syria Palaestina	The Roman imposed punishment name for Judea, specifically invented to humiliate the Jews Rome had just defeated in 135 C.E. It was designed also to obliterate any connection of the Jews to Judea, i.e. the Land of Israel.
Pasdaran	The Iranian Revolutionary Guards Corps officially named the Army of the Guardians of the Islamic Revolution.
Pasha	The highest Ottoman official title granted to both civilian and military commanders. Like the term "bey," it survived the Ottoman era and came to be used as a term of respect in Turkish and Arab society.
PDRY	People's Democratic Republic of Yemen, commonly known as South Yemen.
Peshmerga	The armed forces of Kurdistan.
PFLP	Popular Front for the Liberation of Palestine.
PFLP-EO	Popular Front for the Liberation of Palestine-External Operations.
PFLP-GC	Popular Front for the Liberation of Palestine-General Command.
PFLP-SOG	Popular Front for the Liberation of Palestine-Special Operations Group.
PIJ	Palestine Islamic Jihad.
PKK	Kurdistan Workers' Party, active in Turkey.
PLO	Palestine Liberation Organization. It was founded in Egypt in 1964. The PLO was reconstituted in 1968 with Fatah as its principal component and Yasser Arafat as its chairman. The PLO was recognized in 1974 by the Arab Summit in Rabat, Morocco, as the "sole legitimate representative of the Palestinian people."
PUK	Patriotic Union of Kurdistan, active in Iraq.
qibla	The direction of the Kaaba in Mecca and the direction that Muslims should face when praying.
Qur'an	The Holy book of Islam. It contains the revelations of Allah to Muhammad.
Quraysh	Muhammad's tribe. When Muhammad started to preach Islam, the Quraysh tribe forced him to leave Mecca. He subsequently was at war with the Quraysh and killed quite a few of his tribesmen and relatives. However, Muhammad did not destroy the tribe. In fact, the first four caliphs—Abu Bakr, Umar, Uthman, and Ali—were from the Quraysh.
Rashidun	The "rightly guided ones," a title given to the first four caliphs.
Reconquista	Literally in Spanish, the reconquest of Iberia (Spain and Portugal) by Christian forces after 770 years of Muslim occupation.
Rosh Hashana	The Jewish New Year.
Salafis	The *Salafis* (or *Salafists*) are ultraconservative Muslims who believe they are the direct followers of the teachings of Muhammad. They expect everyone else to emulate the piety of the *Salaf* ("the venerable predecessors" or "ancestors"), the earliest Muslims. The term *Salafist,* has been in use since the Middle Ages, but today it refers especially to a follower of a modern Sunni Islamic movement known as the *Salafiyyah,* which is related to or includes Wahhabism, so that the two terms are sometimes erroneously viewed as synonymous. In modern times both groups seek to emulate the orthodoxy and austerity of Islam's early years—the first three Muslim generations—from the time of Muhammad.

salat	The obligatory Muslim ritual prayer said five times a day. This is one of the Five Pillars of Islam.
SAM	Surface-to-air missile.
SAVAK	Farsi acronym for *Sazman-e Amniyat va Ittilaat e-Keshvar,* the State Intelligence and Security Organization of Iran, which operated under the Shah.
sawm	Fasting; the obligatory duty of all Muslims to fast from dawn to dusk during the month of Ramadan. This is one of the Five Pillars of Islam.
Sayeret Matkal	IDF Special Forces.
Sephardic Jews	Jews whose ancestors came from the Iberian Peninsula (modern Spain and Portugal). Their *lingua franca* was Ladino. Later, the term was applied to Jews from the Middle East and North Africa to distinguish them from Jews of Eastern European background.
Shabak	Hebrew acronym for *Sherut HaBitachon HaKlali.* ("General Security Service/ GSS"). It is Israel's internal security service and is commonly called the *Shin Bet.*
shahada	The obligatory Muslim declaration of faith, "I testify there is no God but Allah. I testify that Muhammad is the Prophet of Allah." It is one of the Five Pillars of Islam.
shaheed (pl. *shuhada*)	Literally, "martyr" in Arabic. Someone who wishes to lay down their life in the name of jihad, e.g. Muslim suicide bomber, or has done so.
sharaf	A Muslim man's sense of honor, pride, and self-respect.
Shari'a	Literally the "path" or "way" in Arabic. Divinely ordained Islamic law according to the Qur'an and Hadith that governs all aspects of Muslim behavior.
Sharif	Term given to individuals claiming direct descent from Muhammad.
sheikh (or *shaykh*)	A tribal leader, head of a village or a religious order. It is also a term of respect for an elder.
Shi'a	The group of Muslims that regard Ali and his descendents as the only legitimate successors to Muhammad. In the Shi'a view, Ali and his line are divinely guided Imams. The Shi'a amount to some 15 percent of the Muslim community worldwide.
Shin Bet	*See Shabak.*
shofar	A ram's horn trumpet used in Jewish religious ceremonies as well as to mark momentous events in Jewish history.
sikul memukad	Hebrew for "focused foiling," the IDF targeted killing of terrorists.
Sira	Chronological biographies of Muhammad.
SLA	South Lebanese Army.
Sufism	Islamic mysticism and asceticism.
sulha	Islamic dispute resolution and reconciliation. It is the closest to the Western concept of real and lasting peace.
Sultan	Beginning in the tenth century, the term was used to designate the temporal sovereign as distinct from the caliph. From the early sixteenth century until 1922, the Ottoman rulers united the two offices, combining in their persons the temporal power of sultan and the spiritual authority of the caliph.

sumud	Literally, "steadfastness," in Arabic. It is the Muslim practice of waiting as long as it takes to wear down one's opponent, until he is ready to abandon the struggle.
Sunnah	The customs and the practices of Muhammad and the early Islamic community that became an exemplary precedent for all Muslims.
Sunnis	Those who accept the *sunnah* and the historical succession of caliphs as opposed to the Shi'a. The Sunnis are the majority (approximately 85 percent) of the Muslim global community.
sura	A chapter in the Qur'an.
takbir	The phrase *Allahu akbar* ("Allah is greater"). It is a proclamation of Islamic superiority and supremacism.
talaq	The Muslim practice of saying, "I divorce you" three times to be divorced. It is one of the easiest of ways for Muslim men to divorce their wives.
Tanakh	The *Tanakh* is the canon of the Hebrew/Jewish Bible. The word "*Tanakh*" is a Hebrew acronym, which stands for Torah, Prophets, and Writings. It contains the Torah ("Teaching," also known as the Five Books of Moses), the Prophets (*Nevi'im*), which includes several of the historical books (Joshua, Judges, I Samuel, II Samuel, I Kings, II Kings), the three Major Prophets (Isaiah, Jeremiah, Ezekiel), and the twelve Minor Prophets (Hosea, Joel, Amos, Obadiah, Jonah, Micah, Nahum, Habakkuk, Zephaniah, Haggai, Zechariah, Malachi); and the Writings (*Ketuvim*), comprising Psalms, Proverbs, Job, the Song of Songs, Ruth, Lamentations, Ecclesiastes, Esther, Daniel, Ezra, Nehemiah, I Chronicles, II Chronicles. (This order differs significantly from the sequence in the Christian Bible).
taqiyya	Arabic term for the religiously sanctioned Muslim doctrine that allows lying and deception to conceal one's true intentions and beliefs.
tefillin	Tefillin are a set of small black leather boxes containing scrolls of parchment inscribed with verses from the Torah, which are worn by observant Jews during weekday morning prayers.
thalweg line	The middle of the main, deepest channel or downstream current of a waterway.
Torah	Judaism's founding legal and ethical religious text. It is known to Christianity as the Pentateuch, and the Five Books of Moses. The five books of the Torah in their Hebrew names are *Bereshit, Shmot, Vayikra, Bamidbar,* and *Dvarim.* In English (from the Greek), the names are Genesis, Exodus, Leviticus, Numbers, and Deuteronomy. It contains the laws God revealed to the Jews including the Ten Commandments and other comprehensive instructions on the proper ordering of state and society. The Torah also includes God's promise to Abraham that his grandson Jacob (Israel) and his descendents, the Jews (the sons of Israel), would be granted the Land of Israel in perpetuity.
Tzahal	Common Hebrew acronym for *Tzvah HaHaganah Leyisrael*—the Israel Defense Forces.
UAE	United Arab Emirates.

UAR	United Arab Republic. The short-lived union of Egypt and Syria, 1958–61. After Syria's secession Egypt retained the name "United Arab Republic" hoping to re-create the union wiht Syria and/or other Arab states. Only on September 2 1971, did the UAR officially take the name "Arab Republic of Egypt."
UDPK	United Democratic Party of Kurdistan, active in Iraq from 1958 to 1960.
ulama	Literally, in Arabic, "those learned in the ways of Islam." It is the collective term for the body of Muslim theologians, jurists and scholars.
Ummah	The Islamic worldwide community.
UNEF	United Nations Emergency Force.
UNFICYP	United Nations Peacekeeping Force in Cyprus.
UNHCR	United Nations High Commissioner for Refugees.
UNIFIL	United Nations Interim Force in Lebanon.
UNMOVIC	United Nations Monitoring, Verification and Inspection Commission (in Iraq).
UNOGIL	United Nations Observer Group in Lebanon.
UNOSOM	United Nations Operation in Somalia.
UNRWA	United Nations Relief and Works Agency for Palestine Refugees in the Near East.
UNSCOM	United Nations Special Commission (in Iraq).
UNTSO	United Nations Truce Supervisory Organization.
UNYOM	United Nations Yemen Observation Mission.
uswa hasana	An excellent model (for Muslims) of conduct, Muhammad being the perfect excellent example.
vizier	A high-ranking political adviser or minister in an Islamic government.
Waqf	A religious endowment in Islam typically denoting a building, piece of property or even cash for Muslim religious or charitable purposes.
WMD	Weapons of mass destruction—biological, chemical and nuclear weapons.
YAR	Yemen Arab Republic.
Yishuv	The Jewish community in the Land of Israel under Ottoman Turkish control as well as during the British Mandate of Palestine, 1880s–1948.
zakat	The fixed share of income or property that all Muslims must pay as an alms tax. It is one of the Five Pillars of Islam.
zunar	Wide belts and distinctive discriminatory hats and clothing mandated for *dhimma*.

ENDNOTES

INTRODUCTION

[1] Barry Rubin, Barry. *Revolution until Victory?: The Politics and History of the PLO.* (Cambridge, MA: Harvard University Press, 1994), 180.

CRITICAL GEOGRAPHIC FEATURES

[1] George Weigel, *Faith, Reason, and the War Against Jihadism: A Call to Action.* (New York: Doubleday, 2007), 17. *See also* "Judaism, Christianity and Islam," May 11, 2010, http://payingattentiontothesky.com/2010/05/11/judaism-christianity-and-islam/.

[2] For full text of the treaty, http://sam.baskent.edu.tr/belge/Montreux_ENG.pdf.

[3] Anthony Nutting, *Nasser,* (New York: E. P. Dutton & Co., 1972), 144–45.

[4] Ibid. 145.

[5] Ibid.

[6] Ibid.

[7] UN Security Council Resolution S/RES/95 (1951) S/2322 of September 1, 1951, http://unispal.un.org/unispal.nsf/f45643a78fcba719852560f6005987ad/f143ea8557419e3b852560c2006f3526?OpenDocument.

[8] Ibid.

[9] UN Security Council, S/PV.662, March 23, 1954.

[10] *Yearbook of the United Nations, 1959,* letters to the President of the Security Council, March 17 and August 31 http://unispal.un.org/unispal.nsf/9a798adbf322aff38525617b006d88d7/2aa1b0986583538a852562f500523c-1c?OpenDocument.

[11] Ibid.

[12] Rhonda Spivak, "Bypassing the Suez Canal: Israel to Have China Construct The Eilat Railway," WinnipegJewishReview.com, July 11, 2012, http://www.winnipegjewishreview.com/article_dctail.cfm?id=2692&sec=1&title=Bypassing_the_Suez_Canal:_Israel_to_Have_China_Construct_The_Eilat_Railway.

[13] "Israel-China Alliance Moves Forward With $2 Billion 'Red-Med' Freight Rail Link Alternative to Suez Canal," *Algemeiner,* March 24, 2014, http://www.algemeiner.com/2014/03/24/israel-china-alliance-moves-forward-with-2-billion-red-med-freight-rail-link-alternative-to-suez-canal/.

[14] Bernard Lewis, *The Middle East,* (New York: Scribners, 1997), 44–45.

[15] David Ben-Gurion, *ISRAEL: A Personal History,* (New York: Funk & Wagnalls, 1971), 524–25 and Ali A. Hakim, *The Middle Eastern States and the Law of the Sea,* (Syracuse, NY: Syracuse University Press, 1980), 137.

[16] "Israel-s Complaint to the Security Council Concerning Interference by Egypt with Shipping to the Israeli Port of Eilat on the Gulf of Aqaba- S-3168- Add 1- 29 January 1954," Israel Ministry of Foreign Affairs, Vols. 1-2: 1947–74, VIII. Freedom of Navigation, January 29, 1954, http://www.mfa.gov.il/MFA/Foreign+Relations/Israels+Foreign+Relations+since+1947/1947-1974/6+Israel-s+Complaint+to+the+Security+Council+Conce.htm.

[17] I.C.J. Reports 1949, A 28.

[18] Ibid.

[19] Gavriel Queenann, "Aqaba: A Bridge Too Far," Arutz 7 IsraelNationalNews.com, July 22, 2011, http://www.israelnationalnews.com/News/News.aspx/145990#.TioIF4JwtTo.

[20] "World Oil Transit Chokepoints," U.S. Energy Information Agency, November 10, 2014, http://www.eia.gov/countries/regions-topics.cfm?fips=wotc&trk=p3.

[21] Humphrey Trevelyan, *The Middle East in Revolution,* (Boston: Gambit, 1970), 261.

[22] "World Oil Transit Chokepoints," U.S. Energy Information Administration, November 10, 2014, http://www.eia.doe.gov/cabs/World_Oil_Transit_Chokepoints/Hormuz.html.

[23] Awad Mustafa, "Source: UAE, Iran Reach Accord on Disputed Hormuz Islands," *Defense News,* January 14, 2014, http://www.defensenews.com/article/20140115/DEFREG04/301150034/Source-UAE-Iran-Reach-Accord-Disputed-Hormuz-Islands.

[24] Including East Jerusalem and the Golan Heights.

[25] *Demographic Yearbook—Table 3: Population by sex, rate of population increase, surface area and density,* United Nations Statistics Division, 2006, http://unstats.un.org/unsd/demographic/products/dyb/dyb2006/Table03.pdf

[26] Howard M. Sachar, *A History of Israel From the Rise of Zionism to Our Time,* Second edition, (New York: Alfred A. Knopf, 1996), 618.

[27] Includes Moroccan-occupied Western Sahara.

[28] This includes the Golan Heights.

[29] "The Nakba of Arabic Jews," http://www.youtube.com/watch?v=dxKcFo_h5Eg.

[30] Ruth R, Wisse, "How About an Arab settlement' Freeze?" *Wall Street Journal,* March 17, 2010 http://online.wsj.com/article/SB10001424052748704743404575127542291520202.html?mod=rss_Today percent27s_Most_Popular.

[31] Roger Adelson. *London and the Invention of the Middle East: Money, Power, and War, 1902-1922.* (New Haven: Yale University Press, 1995), 22–23.

[32] "Middle East (Definition)," House of Commons Debate April 16, 1946, Vol. 421 cc2519-20 http://hansard.millbanksystems.com/commons/1946/apr/16/middle-east-definition.

[33] Roderic H. Davison, "Where is the Middle East?". *Foreign Affairs* 38 (4) 1960, 665–675.

[34] Yoram Ettinger, "Israel Needs West Bank [i.e. Judea and Samaria]," February 14, 2011, http://newmediajournal.us/indx.php/item/421.

[35] http://www.trueknowledge.com/q/distance_between_laguardia_airport_and_jfk_airport.

[36] "The San Francisco/Oakland Bay Bridge, Facts a Glance," http://www.dot.ca.gov/hq/esc/tollbridge/SFOBB/Sfobbfacts.html.

[37] Fred Barnes, *Rebel-in-chief: inside the bold and controversial presidency of George W. Bush,* (New York: Three Rivers Press, Crown Publishing, 2006), 81.

[38] "Remarks by President Obama and Prime Minister Netanyahu of Israel After Bilateral Meeting," May 20, 2011, http://www.crethiplethi.com/netanyahu-obama-remarks-following-meeting-at-white-house-may-20-2011/israel/2011/.

[39] Yoram Ettinger, "Israel Needs West Bank [i.e. Judea and Samaria]," February 14, 2011, http://newmediajournal.us/indx.php/item/421.

[40] Ibid.

[41] "For Israel, size matters," *Haaretz,* August 14, 2013, http://www.*haaretz*.com/opinion/.premium-1.541024.

[42] "Syria's historic decision to establish diplomatic relations with Lebanon and an analysis of its implications," Intelligence and Terrorism Information Center, November 5, 2008, http://www.terrorism-info.org.il/malam_multimedia/English/eng_n/html/sy_e001.htm.

[43] On October 14, 2008, Syrian President Bashar al-Assad announced the establishment of diplomatic relations between Syria and Lebanon, and the opening of embassies in their respective capitals. It remains to be seen if indeed Syria has renounced its historic claim to all of Lebanon.

[44] *See* for example, "Arabistan A Second Palestine," *Flash of Damascus* (Syria in English), No. 6, January 1972.

[45] *See* for example, "Islamic Games canceled over 'Persian Gulf' logo," YNetnews.com, January 17, 2010, http://www.ynetnews.com/articles/0,7340,L-3835670,00.html.

DEMOGRAPHICS OF THE REGION

[1] "Iran," *CIA Factbook* (2014) https://www.cia.gov/library/publications/the-world-factbook/geos/ir.html retrieved September 16, 2014.

[2] Daniel Pipes as cited in Robert D. Kaplan, "Syria: Identity Crisis," *The Atlantic,* February 1993, http://www.theatlantic.com/magazine/archive/1993/02/syria-identity-crisis/3860/.

[3] "Zaydi Islam." GlobalSecurity.org http://www.globalsecurity.org/military/intro/islam-zaydi.htm.

[4] *The CIA World Factbook, 2012.* (New York: Skyhorse Publishing, 2011).

[5] Includes Moroccan-occupied Western Sahara.

[6] Statistics as of April 22, 2015, Central Bureau of Statistics, Israel as cited in "At 67th birthday, Israel's population stands at 8.345 million," JNS, April 22, 2015, http://www.jns.org/news-briefs/2015/4/22/at-67th-birthday-israels-population-stands-at-8345-million#.VUgWKWM9Xo0=.

[7] "Persons Aged 20 and over, by Religiosity and by Selected Characteristics," CBS, Statistical Abstract of Israel 2010, 1 http://www.cbs.gov.il/shnaton61/st07_04x.pdf. For a similar study *see* "A Portrait of Israeli Jews: Beliefs, Observance, and Values of Israeli Jews, 2009, Guttman Center for Surveys of the Israel Democracy Institute for the Avi Chai–Israel Foundation, 2012, 30 http://en.idi.org.il/media/1351622/GuttmanAviChaiReport2012_EngFinal.pdf.

[8] Yaacov Yadgar and Charles Liebman, "Beyond the Religious-Secular Dichotomy: Masortiim in Israel," Berman Jewish Policy Archive, 2009, 7, http://www.bjpa.org/Publications/details.cfm?PublicationID=11931.

[9] The demographic myth has been refuted by various studies, including the Begin-Sadat Center for Strategic Studies–Bar-Ilan University's "The Million Person Gap" by Bennett Zimmerman, Roberta Seid and Michael L. Wise http://www.think-israel.org/MillionPersonGap.65.pdf or http://www.biu.ac.il/Besa/MSPS65.pdf and work undertaken by The Institute for Zionist Strategies, "Demographic Trends in the Land of Israel (1800-2007)" and "Demographic Trends in the Land of Israel (1800-2007), 2009 Update" by Yaakov Faitelson http://www.izs.org.il/eng/default.asp?father_id=114&catid=118&itemid=208.

[10] Yoram Ettinger, "The Debacle of Demographic Fatalism," Britannica Radio, December 21, 2009, http://britanniaradio.blogspot.com/2009/12/december-21-2009-debacle-of-demographic.html. *See* also Yoram Ettinger, "The demographic concept of doom," *Israel Hayom,* October 4, 2013, http://www.israelhayom.com/site/newsletter_opinion.php?id=5873.

[11] Yoram Ettinger, "It's Demographic Optimism, Stupid!," *Second Thought,* August 12, 2010, http://www.isra-pundit.com/archives/26172.

[12] Yoram Ettinger, "The demographic concept of doom," *Israel Hayom,* October 4, 2013, http://www.israelhayom.com/site/newsletter_opinion.php?id=5873.

[13] Joel Greenberg, "Palestinian Census Ignites Controversy Over Jerusalem," *New York Times,* December 11, 1997, http://www.nytimes.com/1997/12/11/world/palestinian-census-ignites-controversy-over-jerusalem.html.

[14] Begin-Sadat Center for Strategic Studies–Bar-Ilan University's "The Million Person Gap" by Bennett Zimmerman, Roberta Seid and Michael L. Wise http://www.think-israel.org/MillionPersonGap.65.pdf or http://www.biu.ac.il/Besa/MSPS65.pdf and work undertaken by The Institute for Zionist Strategies, "Demographic

Trends in the Land of Israel (1800-2007)" and "Demographic Trends in the Land of Israel (1800-2007), 2009 Update" by Yaakov Faitelson http://www.izs.org.il/eng/default.asp?father_id=114&catid=118&itemid=208.

[15] Yoram Ettinger, "The Case For Demographic Optimism," *Jewish Week,* October 18, 2009, http://www.isra-pundit.com/2008/?p=17654.

[16] Maayana Miskin, "Demographer: Beware Bibi's Plans for PA," IsraelNationalNews.com, July 10, 2009, http://www.israelnationalnews.com/News/News.aspx/132320.

[17] Yakov Faitelson, "Demographic Trends in the Land of Israel (excerpts)," January 15, 2011.

[18] Hillel Fendel, "Demographic Trend in Israel's Favor," IsraelNationalNews.com, May 31, 2010, http://www.israelnationalnews.com/News/news.aspx/137790.

[19] "New Study Claims Arab Population in Israel is Shrinking," *The Algemeiner*, December 12, 2013, http://www.algemeiner.com/2013/12/12/%E2%80%8Enew-study-claims-arab-population-in-israel-is-shrinking/.

[20] Ido Ben Porat, "Israeli Christians' New Nationality: Aramaean, not Arab, Arutz-7, September 17, 2014, http://www.israelnationalnews.com/News/News.aspx/185214#.VBuFABDlZx0.

[21] *CIA World Factbook*, June 22. 2014, https://www.cia.gov/library/publications/the-world-factbook/geos/iz.html.

[22] Ibid.

[23] Ibid.

[24] Israel Central Bureau of Statistics 2014, http://www1.cbs.gov.il/reader/shnaton/templ_shnaton_e.html?num_tab=st02_02&CYear=2014.

[25] US State Department, *International Religious Freedom Report,* 2005, http://www.state.gov/j/drl/rls/irf/2005/51602.htm.

[26] Sami Nasih Makaram, *The Druze Faith,* (Delmar, NY: Caravan Books, 1974), 105-06.

[27] Aharon Dolev, "The Druze Street in Israel: Excited and Rumbling," *Ma'ariv,* August 5 and September 14, 1983.

[28] Marsha Pomerantz, "The Druze, 1986," *Hadassah,* April 1986, 20–23.

[29] For a detailed analysis of "How Many Palestinian Arab Refugees Were There?" *see* Efraim Karsh, *Palestine Betrayed,* (New Haven, CT: Yale University Press, 2010), 264-67.

[30] Progress Report of the United Nations Mediator on Palestine, Submitted to the Secretary-General for Transmission to the Members of the United Nations General Assembly Official Records: Third Session, Supplement No. 11 (A\648), Paris, 1948, 47 and Supplement No. 11A (A\689, and A\689\Add. 1), 5.

[31] "Fact Sheet: Jewish Refugees from Arab Countries," Jewish Virtual Library, January 2013, http://www.jewishvirtuallibrary.org/jsource/talking/jew_refugees.html.

[32] Ibid.

[33] Martin Gilbert. *In Ishmael's House: A History of Jews in Muslim Lands.* (Toronto, ON: McClelland & Stewart Ltd., 2011), 329.

[34] Tzvi Ben Gedalyahu, "Gov't Wants Arabs to Pay for 1948 Pogroms against Jews," Arutz 7 IsraelNationalNews.com, December 26, 2011 http://www.israelnationalnews.com/News/News.aspx/151085#.TvijAfl-dy4.

[35] Bat Ye'or, *Islam and Dhimmitude: When Civilizations Collide,* (Madison, WI: Fairleigh Dickinson University Press, 2002), 157.

[36] "The Peel Commission Report, (July 1937)" http://domino.un.org/unispal.nsf/0/08e38a718201458b05256 5700072b358?OpenDocument.

[37] Ibid.

[38] Peel Commission Report, 93 (vi), 63, 271.

[39] Mallory Browne, "Jews in Grave Danger in All Moslem Lands," *New York Times,* May 16, 1948.

[40] Ibid.

[41] David A. Littman. "Historic Facts and Figures: The Forgotten Jewish Refugees from Arab Countries," UN Commission on Human Rights, written statement, July 17, 2003, E/CN.4/Sub.2/20003/NGO/35. *See* also Ad

Hoc Committee on Palestine – 30th Meeting," United Nations Press Release GA/PAL/84, (November 24, 1947); American Jewish Yearbook: 1958, 1969, 1970, 1978, 1988, 2001. (Philadelphia: The Jewish Publication Society of America); Arieh Avneri, *The Claim of Dispossession,* (Piscataway, NJ: Transaction Books, 1984), 276; Ben Child, "Egypt Bans Film About Jewish Community," *The Guardian,* (March 13, 2013); "Compensate Jewish Refugees from Arab Countries, Conference Urges," JTA, (September 10, 2012), http://www.jta.org/2012/09/10/news-opinion/israel-middle-east/compensate-jewish-refugees-from-arab-countries-conference-urges; Stephen Farrell, "Baghdad Jews Have Become a Fearful Few," *New York Times,* (June 1, 2008), http://www.nytimes.com/2008/06/01/world/middleeast/01babylon.html?pagewanted=all&_r=0; Hillel Fendel, "US Congress Recognizes Jewish Refugees from Arab Lands," *Arutz 7,* (February 4, 2008), http://www.israelnationalnews.com/News/News.aspx/125772#.UshUdBA0Rx1; Martin Gilbert,. *In Ishmael's House: A History of Jews in Muslim Lands.* (Toronto, ON: McClelland & Stewart Ltd., 2011), 329; House Resolution 185 (110th), "Regarding the Creation of Refugee Populations in the Middle East," https://www.govtrack.us/congress/bills/110/hres185; House Resolution 6242 (112th), "Relating to the Resolution of the Issue of Jewish Refugees from Arab Countries," https://www.govtrack.us/congress/bills/112/hr6242; "Israel Pushing for UN Summit on Jewish Refugees," *The Algemeiner,* (August 27, 2012), http://www.algemeiner.com/2012/08/27/israel-pushing-for-un-summit-on-jewish-refugees/; *Jerusalem Post,* (December 4, 2003); Gabe Kahn, "Yemeni Jew Murdered in Sana'a," Arutz 7, May 22, 2012, http://www.israelnationalnews.com/News/News.aspx/156105#.UshnqxA0Rx1; Isabel Kershner, "The Other Refugees." *Jerusalem Report,* (January 12, 20/04), http://www.jpost.com/JerusalemReport/Home.aspx; David Littman, "The Forgotten Refugees: An Exchange of Population." *The National Review,* (December 3, 2002); David Matas, and Stanley A. Urman, "Jews From Arab Countries: The Case for Rights and Redress." Justice for Jews from Arab Countries, (June 23, 2003), http://www.mefacts.org/cached.asp?x_id=10114; Aharon Mor and Orly Rahimiyan, "The Jewish Exodus from Arab Lands," Jerusalem Center for Public Opinion, (September 11, 2012), http://jcpa.org/article/the-jewish-exodus-from-arab-landstoward-redressing-injustices-on-all-sides/; "Point of no return: Information and links about the Middle East's forgotten Jewish refugees," http://www.jewishrefugees.blogspot.com/; Maurice Roumani, *The Jews from Arab Countries: A Neglected Issue.* WOJAC, 1983; Howard Sachar, *A History of Israel: From the Rise of Zionism to Our Time.* (New York: Alfred A. Knopf, Inc. 2000); David Singer, and Lawrence Grossman, Eds. *American Jewish Year Book 2003.* (New York: American Jewish Committee), 2003; Yoav Stern, "Jews of Yemen reportedly to be relocated in wake of deadly attack," *Haaretz,* December 18, 2008, http://www.haaretz.com/print-edition/features/jews-of-yemen-reportedly-to-be-relocated-in-wake-of-deadly-attack-1.259756; Norman A. Stillman. *The Jews of Arab Lands in Modern Times,* Philadelphia: Jewish Publication Society, 2003, 175; US Department of State, "International Religious Freedom Report for 2011," http://www.state.gov/j/drl/rls/irf/2011religiousfreedom/index.htm?dlid=192911#wrapper; and "Country Reports on Human Rights Practices for 2011," http://www.state.gov/j/drl/rls/hrrpt/2011humanrightsreport/index.htm?dynamic_load_id=186455#wrapper.

[42] As of 2010, the Jewish population was eight individuals. *See* Jonah Mandel, "Ezekiel unscathed!," *Jerusalem Post,* May 14, 2010, http://www.jpost.com/Jewish-World/Jewish-News/Ezekiel-unscathed.

[43] The Yemeni state media agency Saba reported that the final remnant of Yemen's ancient Jewish community, numbering about 250 people, was set to leave the country due to persecution and violence and go to Israel. Starting in July 2009, the US State Department assisted some sixty Jews to secretly escape to the United States. They traveled from their last redoubt, the town of Raida, via Sana'a, Yemen's capital.

[44] Andrew E. Harrod, "Enduring Enmity: Iran, Israel, and Islamic Anti-Semitism," Breibart, April 25, 2014, http://www.breitbart.com/Big-Peace/2014/04/25/Enduring-Enmity-Iran-Israel-and-Islamic-Anti-Semitism. *See* also "Tehran forces Iranian Jews to join anti-Israel Global March," DEBKAfile, March 23, 2012, http://www.debka.com/article/21856/.

[45] Ilan Ben Zion, "Faced with rising anti-Semitism, flagging economy, fewer than 17,000 members remain of once-burgeoning population," *The Times of Israel,* June 6, 2015, http://www.timesofisrael.com/young-turkish-jews-trickling-away-from-shrinking-community/?utm_source=The+Times+of+Israel+Daily+Edition&utm_campaign=2b04e3eccl-2015_06_06&utm_medium=email&utm_term=0_adb46cec92-2b04e3eccl-54550797.

[46] Demopoulos v. Turkey, European Court of Human Rights, Strasbourg, France, March 1, 2010.

[47] Akiva Eldar, "The ladder to climb down from the tree," *Haaretz*.com, March 11, 2010, http://www.*Haaretz*.com/hasen/spages/1155858.html.

[48] "Kuwait Population," http://countrystudies.us/persian-gulf-states/19.htm.

[49] "Angry welcome for Palestinian in Kuwait," BBC News, May 30, 2001, http://news.bbc.co.uk/2/hi/1361060.stm. *See* also *New York Times,* March 14, 1991; *USA Today,* April 3, 1991.

[50] *The Guardian,* March 13, 1991; *USA Today,* April 3, 1991.

[51] "Lebanon FM slams GCC move against Hezbollah supporters," *YaLibnan*, June 12, 2013, http://www.yalibnan.com/2013/06/12/lebanon-fm-slams-gcc-move-against-hezbollah/.

[52] "Lebanese Shi'ites fear Gulf expulsion," *Gulf News,* June 21, 2013, http://gulfnews.com/news/gulf/qatar/lebanese-shi'ites-fear-gulf-expulsion-1.1200047.

[53] Ibid.

[54] "Gulf Deports Shi'ites, 'Hezbollah Supporters,'" Nuqudy, June 12, 2013, http://english.nuqudy.com/Gulf/Gulf_Deports_Shi'ite-5799.

[55] "Saudis start deporting pro-Hizballah Lebanese and Shi'ites," DEBKAfile, June 20, 2013, http://www.debka.com/newsupdatepopup/4760/.

[56] "Palestinian Refugees–The Truth (whose responsibility?)," Maof, from the Jerusalem Cloakroom #214, June 13, 2008, http://maof.rjews.net/english/37-english/21442-palestinian-refugees--the-truth-whose-responsibility.

[57] UN Security Council Official Records, S/Agenda/58, (April 16, 1948), 19.

[58] Efraim Karsh, "Reclaiming a historical truth," *Haaretz*, June 10, 2011 http://www.*Haaretz*.com/print-edition/opinion/reclaiming-a-historical-truth-1.366893.

[59] "International: On the Eve?" *Time,* May 3, 1948, 25 http://www.time.com/time/magazine/article/0,9171,798519,00.html.

[60] John Bagot Glubb. *A Soldier with the Arabs* (London: Staughton and Hodder, 1957), 79.

[61] *Daily Mail* (London), August 12, 1948.

[62] *Sada al Janub* (Beirut), August 16, 1948.

[63] *The Daily Telegraph* (Beirut), September 6, 1948.

[64] *The Economist,* (London), October 2, 1948.

[65] *Falastin* (Jordan), February 19, 1949.

[66] "Palestinian Refugees–The Truth (whose responsibility?)," Maof, from the Jerusalem Cloakroom #214, June 13, 2008, http://maof.rjews.net/english/37-english/21442-palestinian-refugees--the-truth-whose-responsibility.

[67] *Ad-Difaa* (Jordan) September 6, 1954. *See* also Shmuel Katz, "The Mass Expulsion Lie," *Jerusalem Post,* March 14, 1986, 9.

[68] Khaled al-Azm, *Memoires* (Arabic), 3 Vols. (Al-Dar al Muttahida lil-Nahr, 1972), Vol. 1, 386–87, cited by Maurice Roumani, *The Case of the Jews from Arab Countries: A Neglected Issue.* (Jerusalem: World Organization of Jews from Arab Countries, 1975), 61.

[69] "Abu Mazen Charges that the Arab States Are the Cause of the Palestinian Refugee Problem," *Wall Street Journal,* June 5, 2003, http://www.dailyalert.org/archive/2003-06/2003-06-05.html.

[70] Alexander H. Joffe and Asaf Romirowsky, "A Tale of Two Galloways: Notes on the Early History of UNRWA and Zionist Historiography," *Middle Eastern Studies,* September 2010, http://www.romirowsky.com/7948/a-tale-of-two-galloways#_ednref56.

[71] *Convention and Protocol Relating to the Status of Refugees,* http://www.unhcr.org/3b66c2aa10.html.

[72] Joseph Schechtman, *The Refugee in the World,* A.S. (New York: Barnes and Co., 1963), 220. *See* also "Abolish UNRWA," *Jerusalem Post,* April 15, 2002, http://pqasb.pqarchiver.com/jpost/access/113737595. html?dids=113737595:113737595&FMT=ABS&FMTS=ABS:FT&date=Apr+15. percent2C+2002 &author=&pub=Jerusalem+Post&edition=&startpage=06&desc=Abolish+UNRWA.

[73] "UNRWA in figures," http://www.unrwa.org/userfiles/2011080123958.pdf.

[74] Asaf Romirowsky and Alexander Joffe, "UNRWA Keeps Quiet on Syria," *The National Interest,* November 9, 2012, http://nationalinterest.org/commentary/unrwa-keeps-quiet-syria-7716.

[75] www.un.org/unrwa/finances/index.htm.

[76] UNRWA Frequently Asked Questions, http://www.unrwa.org/etemplate.php?id=87#funding. Retrieved September 23, 2012.

[77] "Contributions to UNHCR, For Budget Year 2012, As of 31 December 2012, (Revised on: 13 June 2013), UNHCR, http://www.unhcr.org/4df1d0449.html.

[78] Josh Rogin, "Did the State Department just create 5 million Palestinian refugees?" *Foreign Policy,* May 25, 2012, http://thecable.foreignpolicy.com/posts/2012/05/25/did_the_state_ department_just_create_5_million_palestinian_refugees.

[79] John Laffin, *The PLO Connections,* (London: Corgi Books, 1983), 127.

[80] Randy Geller, "Chris Hedges, Harper's, and Israel," *CAMERA* (Committee for Accuracy in Middle East Reporting in America), November 7, 2001, http://www.camera.org/index.asp?x_context=2&x_outlet=32&x_ar- ticle=4. *See* also "Abolish UNRWA," *Jerusalem Post,* April 15, 2002.

[81] Kahn, Gabe and Rachel Hirshfeld. "US Senate Redefines 'Palestinian Refugee', IsraelNationalNews.com, May 25, 2012.

[82] *See* http://www.israelinitiative.org/Index.aspx.

[83] Maayana Miskin, "Israeli Initiative: UNRWA Has Never Helped, and Never Will," Israel National News.com, September 3, 2009, http://www.israelnationalnews.com/News/News.aspx/133246.

[84] http://www.unrwa.org/userfiles/file/financial_updates/2011/Donors%202011%20All%20Overall.pdf.

[85] "UNRWA: Caring for Refugees for Years and Still Counting," Refugees Forever? Issues in the Palestinian-Israel Conflict, *Jerusalem Post* http://info.jpost.com/C003/Supplements/Refugees/6-7.html and Judith A. Klinghoffer, "Why 'Poor Palestinians?'" Politicalmavens.com, April 27, 2008, http://politicalmavens.com/ index.php/2008/04/27/4560/?print=1.

[86] "Mount of Olives National Park," August 25, 2007, http://blog.bibleplaces.com/2007_08_01_archive.html. *See* also Yoav Zitun, "Israel's first fallen honored by family members," Ynetnews.com, April 15, 2013, http:// www.ynetnews.com/articles/0,7340,L-4368095,00.html.

[87] Yaakov Lappin, "Israel prepares to mourn 23,169 casualties of war and terrorism," *Jerusalem Post,* May 2, 2014, http://www.jpost.com/Defense/Israel-prepares-to-mourn-23169-casualties-of-war-and-terrorism-351137.

[88] http://www.icrc.org/ihl.nsf/WebART/380-600005?OpenDocument.

[89] Moran Azualy, "Bennett on Obama's speech: No occupation in our own land," Ynetnews.com, March, 21, 2013, http://www.ynetnews.com/articles/0,7340,L-4359732,00.html.

[90] Itamar Marcus and Nan Jacques Zilberdik, "PA defines "Palestine"- Tel Aviv, Haifa, Galilee, Negev, and all of Israel," Palestine Media Watch, April 14, 2011, http://palwatch.org/main.aspx?fi=157&doc_id=4899.

[91] Itamar Marcus and Nan Jacques Zilberdik, "PA TV rebroadcast of song: Jaffa, Tiberias and Haifa are in 'my country Palestine,'" Palestine Media Watch, July 25, 2011, http://palwatch.org/main.aspx?fi=157&doc_id=5323.

TRADITIONS AND THE HISTORIC RECORD

[1] Among the most historically-noted Arab family-clans are the al-Husseinis (of who Hajj Amin al-Husseini, the Grand Mufti of Jerusalem and his relative, Yasser Arafat are most notorious), the al-Tikriti clan of Iraq's Saddam Hussein and the al-Saud family-clan of Saudi Arabia.

[2] For further reference on traditions *see* Andre Servier, *La Psychologie du Musulman,* (English originally published in 1923), November 2, 2005 http://musulmanbook.blogspot.com/2005/11/preface-mind-of-musulman.html.

[3] Nahum Sokolow, *Lord Balfour's Introduction to the History of Zionism 1600-1919*, Longmans, Green and Co., London, 1919 as quoted http://www.jewishvirtuallibrary.org/jsource/Zionism/balfourintro.html.

[4] Hershel Shanks. "When Did Ancient Israel Begin?." *Biblical Archaeology Review,* Jan/Feb 2012, 59-62, 67. http://members.bib-arch.org/publication.asp?PubID=BSBA&Volume=38&Issue=1&ArticleID=11.

[5] Samuel II, 24:24.

[6] Ezra 2:64.

[7] According to the estimate of Roman consul and historian, Cassius Dio. Translation by Earnest Cary. *Roman History*, book 69, 12.1-14.3. Loeb Classical Library, 9 volumes, Greek texts and facing English translation: Harvard University Press, 1914 thru 1927.

[8] Ibid.

[9] Howard Grief. *The Legal Foundation and Borders of Israel under International Law,* (Jerusalem: Mazo Publishers, 2008), 37.

[10] "The Hebron Massacre of 1929," http://www.zionism-israel.com/Hebron_Massacre1929.htm.

[11] Matthias Küntzel, *Jihad and Jew-Hatred: Islamism, Nazism, and the Roots of 9/11,* trans. Colin Meade (New York: Telos Press, 2007), 31.

[12] Daniel Levine, *The Birth of the Irgun Zvai Leumi: A Jewish Liberation Movement,* (Jerusalem: Gefen Books, 1991), 83.

[13] Ibid., 86.

[14] Ibid., 88.

[15] The biblical phrase, "an eye for an eye" in Exodus and Leviticus (*ayin tachat ayin*) literally means "an eye under an eye" while a slightly different phrase (literally "eye for an eye") is used in another passage (in Deuteronomy) of the Jewish Bible, specifically, in the first of its three subdivisions, the Torah. For example, a passage in Leviticus states, "And a man who inflicts an injury upon his fellow man just as he did, so shall be done to him [namely,] fracture for fracture, eye for eye, tooth for tooth. Just as he inflicted an injury upon a person, so shall it be inflicted upon him."

[16] David Ben-Gurion, *The Jews in Their Land.* (London: Doubleday, 1966), 237.

[17] Steven Stotsky, "Shedding New Light on the Mufti's Alliance With the Nazis," CAMERA, July 21, 2008, http://www.camera.org/index.asp?x_context=2&x_outlet=118&x_article=1510.

[18] Barry Rubin and Wolfgang G. Schwanitz. *Nazis, Islamists, and the Making of the Modern Middle East.* (New Haven, CT: Yale University Press, 2014), 2.

[19] David G. Dalin and John F. Rothman. *Icon of Evil,* (New York: Random House, 2008), 60, 184.

[20] Ibid., 61, 184.

[21] Interview with author, January 1, 1971, Beit Jabotinsky, Tel Aviv.

[22] Ibid.

[23] Years later, on the eve of the Six-Day War, in June 1967 (after Ben-Gurion had retired from political activity and Levi Eshkol was Prime Minister), Menachem Begin joined a delegation which visited Sde Boker in order to ask David Ben-Gurion to return and accept the premiership again. After that meeting, Ben-Gurion said that if he had then known Begin as he did now, the face of history would have been different.

[24] Renzo DeFelice, *Jews in an Arab Land: Libya, 1835–1970.* (Austin, TX: University of Texas Press, 1985), 223–28, 232.

[25] The operational name was taken from two passages in the Bible: Exodus 19:4 – "Ye have seen what I did unto the Egyptians, and how I bare you on eagles' wings, and brought you unto Myself" and in the Book of Isaiah 40:31 – "But they who wait upon the Lord shall renew their strength; they shall mount up with wings as eagles; they shall run, and not be weary, and they shall walk, and not faint."

[26] Martin Gilbert, *In Ishmael's House: A History of Jews in Muslim Lands*, (Toronto, ON: McClellan & Stewart Ltd., 2011), 261.

[27] Yakhin was the name of one of the two main pillars that supported King Solomon's Temple in Jerusalem.

[28] "Arabs Create Organization For Recovery of Palestine," *New York Times,* May 29, 1964, A5.

[29] Proverbs 24:6, translated from the original Hebrew. Many English translations are mistranslated. To clarify more specifically, ruses are more than military bluffs or feints. They are acts against one's opponent by creative, clever, unorthodox means—sometimes involving force multipliers and/or superior knowledge. Their aim is to create chaos in the enemy camp that force the enemy to react in ways that were not planned for.

[30] "Golan Heights Law," Israel Ministry of Foreign Affairs, December 14, 1981, http://www.mfa.gov.il/MFA/ Peace+Process/Guide+to+the+Peace+Process/Golan+Heights+Law.htm.

[31] Lewis, George N., Steve Fetter, and Lisbeth Gronlund, "Casualties and Damage from Scud Attacks in the 1991 Gulf War," Appendix, Center for International Studies, Massachusetts Institute of Technology, Cambridge, MA, 42-50; Watson, Bruce W., "Iraqi Scud Launches During the Gulf War," Appendix C, Military Lessons of the Gulf War, George Watson and Cyr Tsouras, London, Greenhill Books, 1991, 224-25; Defense Special Missile and Astronautics Center message, subject "Mideast Conflict: Iraqi SRBM Launch Summary through 26 February 1991," 271603Z Feb 91; Bermudez, Joseph S., Jr., "Iraqi Missile Operations During 'Desert Storm' – Update," *Jane's Soviet Intelligence Review,* May 1991, 225; "11th Air Defense Artillery Brigade, Chronology of Events," undated; United States Central Command, "NBC Desk Log," February 25, 1991.

[32] "Camp David and After: An Exchange (1. An Interview with Ehud Barak)," *The New York Review of Books,* June 13, 2002, http://www.nybooks.com/articles/archives/2002/jun/13/ camp-david-and-after-an-exchange-1-an-interview-wi/?pagination=false.

[33] *Fox News,* March 27, 2008; *The Guardian* (London), April 11, 2011.

[34] *See* Exodus 13:21.

[35] Elliott Abrams. "The Gaza numbers game," *Israel Hayom*, August 7, 2014, http://www.israelhayom.com/site/ newsletter_opinion.php?id=9509.

[36] "Jerusalem Quotes" http://www.jewishvirtuallibrary.org/jsource/Quote/jeruq.html.

[37] Elie Wiesel, "For Jerusalem," *New York Times,* April 18, 2010.

[38] "Ten Top Discoveries," *Biblical Archaeology Review,* July/August/September/October 2009, http://www. bib-arch.org/bar/article.asp?PubID=BSBA&Volume=35&Issue=4&ArticleID=15.

[39] Eric H. Cline, *Jerusalem Besieged: From Ancient Canaan to Modern Israel,* (Ann Arbor, MI: University of Michigan Press, 2005).

[40] Genesis 14:18; 22:2; 22:14.

[41] Genesis 22:1-18; Qur'an 37:102–10.

[42] Nadav Shragai, "Byzantine arch found site of renovated Jerusalem synagogue," Haaretz.com, November 28, 2006, http://www.haaretz.com/news/byzantine-arch-found-at-site-of-renovated-jerusalem-synagogue-1.205622; Gil Zohar, "From Ruin to Reconstruction," Arutz 7 IsraelNationalNews.com March 17, 2010, http://www.israel-nationalnews.com/Articles/Article.aspx/9365.

[43] Moshe Dayan, *Story of My Life* (New York: Morrow and Company, 1976), 388–89.

[44] https://www.google.com/search?site=imghp&tbm=isch&source=hp&biw=1280&bih=419&q=Rabbi+Shlomo+Goren+blowing+the+shofar+at+the+Western+Wall&oq=Rabbi+Shlomo+Goren+blowing+the+shofar+at+the+Western+Wall&gs_l=img.3...2874.20199.0.20658.63.12.3.48.49.0.190.1062.9j3.12.0....0...1ac.1.45.img..40.23.1131.kPHuaI7tVFw#facrc=_&imgdii=_&imgrc=by9kZ12pMnVllM%253A%3B347PcMSw8xYmWM%3Bhttp%253A%252F%252F4.bp.blogspot.com%252F_bAaYMTUhaoU%252FRkoSnCDfHGI%252FAAAAAAAAAEc%252FO7fz9d2BUqo%252Fs400%252FRav%2BGoren%2Bshofar%2Bat%2BKotel%252C%252B67.jpg%3Bhttp%253A%252F%252Fheichalhanegina.blogspot.com%252F2007%252F05%252Fmelody-in-his-soul-dancing-man.html%3B243%3B400.

[45] "The Israeli Relinquishment of the Temple Mount," Jerusalem Center for Public Affairs, http://jcpa.org/al-aksais-in-danger-libel-temple-mount/#sthash.9xtIKvvB.dpuf. *See* also Nadav Shragai, *Har ha-merivah: Ha-maavak al Har-ha-Bayit : Yehudim u-Muslemim, dat u-politikah me-az 1967* [The Temple Mount Conflict], (Hebrew), (Jerusalem: Keter, 1995), 23, 28–38.

[46] Moshe Dayan, *Story of My Life* (New York: Morrow and Company, 1976), 388–89.

[47] Moshe Dayan, *Avnei Derech*, ("Milestones") (Hebrew), (Jerusalem: Idanim, 1976), 165, 498.

[48] For a detailed discussion of Dayan's decision, its motivations, and its implications, *see* Nadav Shragai, *Har Hamerivah* ("The Temple Mount Conflict") (Hebrew), (Jerusalem: Keter, 1995). *See* more at: http://jcpa.org/the-al-aksa-is-in-danger-libel-the-notes/#sthash.sykqG1ev.dpuf 22-27.

[49] Shlomo Goren, "The Temple Mount" (Hebrew), (Jerusalem: Ha'Idra Rabba Publications, 2005, 2nd ed.), 327.

[50] Ibid.

[51] A. Ben-Shemesh (trans.) *The Noble Quran*, (Tel Aviv: Massada, 1979). footnote 2, 231.

[52] "Moslem Claim to Jerusalem Rests on Wobbly Verse," Arutz-7, August 28, 2003, http://www.israelnationalnews.com/News/News.aspx/48845#.VHyX0GM0Rx0. *See* also Mordechai Ben-Menachem, "Middle East Nuclear Conflagration: Processes and Consequences," Human Events, November 2, 2010, http://humanevents.com/2010/11/02/middle-east-nuclear-conflagration-processes-and-consequences/.

[53] Shmuel Berkovits, *The Battle for the Holy Places* (in Hebrew), (Or Yehuda: Hed Artzi, 2000), 322.

[54] *Al-Hayat Al-Jadida* (PA), August 10, 2000; *Al-Ayyam* (PA), August 10, 2000; *Al-Quds* (Jerusalem), July 20, 2000; *Al-Hay*(London-Beriut), July 27, 2000 as quoted in Middle East Media Research Institute (MEMRI), Special Dispatch No. 121, August 28, 2000, http://www.memri.org.

[55] Yoel Cohen, "The Political Role of the Israeli Chief Rabbinate in the Temple Mount Question," *Jewish Political Studies Review,* Volume 11:1-2 (Spring 1999), http://www.jcpa.org/jpsr/s99-yc.htm.

[56] Jeremy Sharon, "Feiglin to question legal authority, legitimacy of Temple Mount Waqf," *Jerusalem Post,* September 15, 2013, http://www.jpost.com/Jewish-World/Jewish-Features/Feiglin-to-question-legal-authority-legitimacy-of-Temple-Mount-Waqf-326184.

[57] As cited in Robert Richardson, *Travels Along the Mediterranean,* London, 1922; J.M.A. Scholtz. *Biblish-Kritische Reise,* Leipzig, 1823; and John Carne, *Letters From The East,* London, 1826.

[58] "Total" includes those not classified by religion and Lebanese who were not classified by religion.

[59] According to the first official public census as cited in Eliyahu Tal, *Whose Jerusalem?,* Jerusalem: International Forum for a United Jerusalem, 1994. 94.

[60] Karl Marx, *The New York Daily Tribune,* April 1854, as related in Karl Marx, *The Eastern Question: A Reprint of Letters Written 1853-1856 Dealing with Events of the Crimean War,* (New York: B. Franklin, 1968), 322.

[61] Guide of Lievin de Hamme as cited in Eliyahu Tal, *Whose Jerusalem?,* Jerusalem: International Forum for a United Jerusalem, 1994. 94.

[62] Census conducted by the British Mandatory Government of Palestine, October 23, 1922 and 1931.

[63] Includes 495 persons of "Other faiths."

[64] Includes 52 persons of "Other faiths."

[65] Encylcopaedia Britannica as cited in Eliyahu Tal, *Whose Jerusalem?*, Jerusalem: International Forum for a United Jerusalem, 1994. 94.

[66] Statistics for 1961, 1972, 1983, 1995 are from Israel Census, Israel Central Bureau of Statistics, Statistical Abstract of Israel, 2009, http://www.cbs.gov.il/reader/shnaton/shnatone_new.htm?CYear=2009&Vol=60&CSubject=2.

[67] Statistics for 1961 are for West Jerusalem only as Eastern Jerusalem, including the Old City, was under illegal Jordanian occupation and all Jews had been driven out of that section of the city.

[68] Information from 1988 on from the Israel Central Bureau of Statistics. Until 1995 before publication of the census results, the data on those not classified by religion the Ministry of the Interior were included together with Christians.

[69] The figures for 2000 include 9,000 with no religion classified.

[70] Israeli Central Bureau of Statistics as reported to the author via e-mail, May 20, 2015.

[71] Based on the census of that year.

[72] "On Christmas Eve, Number of Christians Living in Jerusalem drops to only 2% of total population," The Jerusalem Institute for Israel Studies, December 21, 2010, http://jiis.org/index.php?cmd=newse.370&act=read&id=657.

[73] Israeli Central Bureau of Statistics as reported in Gavriel Fiske, "Capital home to 804,400, Jerusalem Day stats reveal," *The Times of Israel,* May 7, 2013, http://www.timesofisrael.com/capital-home-to-804400-jerusalem-day-stats-reveal/.

[74] *The Meaning of the Qur'an,* translated and explained by Muhammed Asad, (Bristol, England: The Book Foundation, 2003), 738.

[75] Ibid., fn 17. Cf. II Chronicles 3:10-13. *See* also fn 15, 737, Cf. II Chronicles 4.

[76] Ibid., 466. See also fn 9, 466–467.

[77] Aaron Klein, "Temple Mount '100% Islamic,' Warning: 'Any action that offends holy site will be answered by 1.5 billion Muslims,'" WorldNetDaily, June 1, 2008, http://www.wnd.com/?pageId=65919.

[78] "The PA Mufti: Jews from Germany Should Return There," MEMRI, Special Dispatch-No. 182, January 26, 2001, http://www.memri.org/bin/articles.cgi?Area=antisemitism&ID=SP18201#_edn1.

[79] Ibid.

[80] Ibid.

[81] Hillel Fendel, "Silence in the Face of Continued Temple Mount Destruction," Arutz 7, IsraelNationalNews.com, September 7, 2007, http://www.israelnationalnews.com/News/News.aspx/123622.

[82] Nadav Shragai, "Temple Mount dirt uncovers First Temple artifacts," *Haaretz,* October 19, 2006, http://www.haaretz.com/print-edition/news/temple-mount-dirt-uncovers-first-temple-artifacts-1.202828.

[83] Abdullah Kan'an, "Media Plan for Publicizing the Cause of Al Quds, Al Sharif in the West and Mechanisms for its Implementation," Protection of Islamic and Christian Holy Sites in Palestine, Second International Conference, Amman, November 23-25, 2004, ISESCO, Rabat, 2007, 195.

[84] Eric H. Close, *Jerusalem Besieged: From Ancient Canaan to Modern Israel,* (Singapore: University of Michigan Press, 2004) 12.

[85] Ibid., 33.

[86] Hillel Fendel, "PA Sheikh Denies Existence of Holy Temple," Arutz 7, IsraelNationalNews.com, August 27, 2009, http://www.israelnationalnews.com/News/News.aspx/133131.

[87] Bari Weiss, "Palestinian Leaders Deny Jerusalem's Past," *Wall Street Journal,* September 25, 2009, http://online.wsj.com/article/SB10001424052970203917304574413811883589676.html.

[88] *Al-Hayat Al-Jadida,* March 17, 2009. *See* also Itamar Marcus and Barbara Crook, "PA historian and PLO official deny Israel's history in the Land of Israel and accuse Israel of 'stealing' Palestinian symbols," *PMW Bulletin,* Palestinian Media Watch, November 3, 2009, and http://palwatch.org/main.aspx?fi=487.

[89] *Mein Kampf,* 14th edition, 1935, 197, http://quotes.liberty-tree.ca/quote_blog/Adolf.Hitler.Quote.3417.

[90] Bari Weiss, "Palestinian Leaders Deny Jerusalem's Past," Ibid.

[91] Copy of the booklet in author's library, 4.

[92] Ibid., 16. *See* also Bari Weiss, "Palestinian Leaders Deny Jerusalem's Past," Ibid.

[93] Thomas Jefferson, *The Jefferson Bible: The Life and Morals of Jesus of Nazareth Extracted Textually from the Gospels in Greek, Latin, French & English,* (Washington, DC: Smithsonian Books, 2011).

[94] *See* for example, *A Survey of Palestine,* prepared by the Anglo-American Committee of Inquiry in December 1945 and January 1946, published by the Government Printer of British Mandate authorities in Palestine, 1946, 309.

[95] UN General Assembly Resolution 181 (III) November 29, 1947.

[96] US State Department, "Military Situation – 18 July 1948," *Foreign Relations of the United States (1948),* Part II: Near East (Palestine).

[97] *Encyclopaedia Britannica,* 1961, Vol. 17, 118.

[98] Efraim Karsh, "The Palestinians, Alone," *New York Times,* August 1, 2010, http://www.nytimes.com/2010/08/02/opinion/02karsh.html?_r=1.

[99] Tacitus. *The Histories*, Book V. Translated by Alfred John Church and William Jackson Brodribb, http://classics.mit.edu/Tacitus/histories.5.v.html.

[100] Ibid.

[101] "The Palestine Mandate," The Avalon Project, Yale Law School, http://avalon.law.yale.edu/20th_century/palmanda.asp#art25.

[102] "Transjordan memorandum," Shaba,Co., http://www.shaba.co/wa?s=Transjordan_memorandum.

[103] Alan Axelrod and Charles Phillips, "United Nations Charter," Encyclopedia of Historical Treaties and Alliances, (New York: Facts on File, 2001), 648.

[104] *See* "Jews dominated the Holyland in 1695," Israpundit, October 19, 2009, http://www.israelunitycoalition.org/news/?p=4686.

[105] "Mark Twain in the Holy Land," *Zionism and the State of Israel* http://zionismandisrael.wordpress.com/2008/08/28/mark-twain-in-the-holy-land/.

[106] Bat Ye'or. *The Dhimmi,* (Cranbury, NJ: Associated University Presses), 1985, 55.

[107] Ibid, 105.

[108] Franklin Delano Roosevelt, memo to U.S. Secretary of State, May 17, 1939, Foreign Relations of the United States: Diplomatic Papers (Washington, DC: U.S. Government Printing Office, 1955), 4:757.

[109] "Robert Kennedy and Israel" Bobby Kennedy in Palestine -- 1st of 4 *Boston Post* Articles from 60 Years Ago, http://robertkennedyandisrael.blogspot.com/2008/06/bobby-kennedy-in-palestine-boston-post.html.

[110] "Hamas Minister of the Interior and of National Security Fathi Hammad Slams Egypt over Fuel Shortage in Gaza Strip, and Says: 'Half of the Palestinians Are Egyptians and the Other Half Are Saudis,'" MEMRI, Clip No. 3389, March 23, 2012, http://www.memritv.org/clip_transcript/en/3389.htm.

[111] "London-New Book: British Forces Attacked post-Holocaust Jewish Refugee Ships," September 21, 2010, http://www.vosizneias.com/64660/2010/09/21/london-new-book-british-forces-attacked-post-holocaust-jewish-refugee-ships/.

[112] The United States and Israel concluded two strategic memoranda of understandings in November 1983 and April 1988. Those agreements were signed due to Israel's unique contribution to vital US national security interests which included the war on Islamic terrorism, ballistic missile defense, restraining the Soviet Union and regional rogue regimes, sharing of critical intelligence and battle experience, and upgrading of defense and commercial industries. Haifa became an important port of call and repair facility for the United States Sixth Fleet and remained so into the 21st century. Thanks to Israel being a *de facto* strategic ally in the eastern

Mediterranean region, the US was spared the deployment of tens of thousands of US military personnel and the expenditure of billions of dollars.

[113] Avraham Sela, *The Continuum Political Encyclopedia of the Middle East,* (New York: Continuum Publishing Group, 2002), 534.

[114] Dilip Hiro, *Dictionary of the Middle East,* (New York: St. Martin's Press, 1996), 170.

[115] Sela, Ibid.

[116] Hiro, Ibid.

[117] *CIA World Factbook* gives about 15.3 million (20 percent Kurds out of 76.8 million total population) (2008 est.).

[118] Beverley Milton-Edwards, "Contemporary politics in the Middle East" *Polity,* 2006. 231, "They form a population in all four states, making 23 percent in Turkey, 23 percent in Iraq, 10 percent in Iran and 8 percent in Syria (Mcdowell, 2003, 3–4).

[119] Sandra Mackey, *The Reckoning: Iraq and the legacy of Saddam,* (New York: W.W. Norton & Company, 2002). Excerpt from 350, "As much as 25 percent of Turkey is Kurdish."

[120] Estimate based on 7 percent of 68,688,433: *World Factbook,* s.v. *Iran.*

[121] Estimate based on 15 to 20 percent of 26,783,383: *World Factbook,* s.v. *Iraq.*

[122] http://www.state.gov/r/pa/ei/bgn/3580.htm.

[123] *The Kurdish Diaspora,* (Paris: Institut Kurde de Paris, 2006), http://www.institutkurde.org/en/kurdorama/.

[124] Malcolm Cameron Lyons, and D. E. P. Jackson, *Saladin: The Politics of the Holy War,* (Cambridge, UK: Cambridge University Press, 1985), 372.

[125] Treaty of Sèvres, Section III, Articles 62-64, http://wwi.lib.byu.edu/index.php/Section_I,_Articles_1_-_260. Or http://www.hri.org/docs/sevres/part3.html.

[126] Robert W. Olson, *The Emergence of Kurdish Nationalism and the Sheikh Said Rebellion, 1880-1925,* (Austin, TX: University of Texas Press, 1989), 74.

[127] David McDowall, *A Modern History of the Kurds,* (New York: I.B. Tauris/St. Martin's Press, 2004).

[128] Pam O'Toole, "Profile: The PKK," BBC News, October 15, 2007, http://news.bbc.co.uk/2/hi/europe/7044760.stm.

[129] Carol J. Williams, "Israelis Fire on Kurds as Mob Storms Consulate," *Los Angeles Times,* February 18, 1999, http://articles.latimes.com/1999/feb/18/news/mn-9123.

[130] David Gollust, "Israel/Kurds," Voice of America, February 19, 1999, http://www.hri.org/news/usa/voa/1999/99-02-19.voa.html.

[131] Agence France-Presse, August 5, 2003.

[132] "Kurdish rebel boss in truce plea," BBC News, September 28, 2006, http://news.bbc.co.uk/2/hi/europe/5389746.stm.

[133] Daniel Steinvorth and Yassin Musharbash, "Turkey Accused of Using Chemical Weapons against PKK," *Der Spiegel,* August 12, 2010, http://www.spiegel.de/international/world/0,1518,711536,00.html.

[134] "Kurdish Group to Demand Autonomy in New Charter," *The Journal of Turkish Weekly,* January 23, 2012, http://www.turkishweekly.net/news/130375/kurdish-group-to-demand-autonomy-in-new-charter.html.

[135] Joe Parkinson and Ayla Albayrak, "Kurdish Rebels Pull Out of Turkey," *Wall Street Journal,* May 8, 2013, http://online.wsj.com/article/SB10001424127887323744604578470833747489270.html.

[136] "Turkey's Erdoğan announces Kurdish reforms," BBC.com, September 30, 2013, http://www.bbc.com/news/world-europe-24330722.

[137] "More militants surrender as Turkey's reconciliation process takes hold," Daily Sabah Turkey, March 21, 2015, http://www.dailysabah.com/nation/2015/03/22/more-militants-surrender-as-turkeys-reconciliation-process-takes-hold.

[138] David P. Goldman, "The End of Erdoğan's Cave of Wonders: An I-Told-You-So," PJ Media, December 27, 2013, http://pjmedia.com/spengler/2013/12/27/the-end-of-erdogans-cave-of-wonders-an-i-told-you-so/.

[139] Joseph Puder, "Syria, Israel and Water," http://www.kurdnas.com/en/index.php?option=com_content&task=view&id=1420&Itemid=57.

[140] Aymenn Jawad Al-Tamimi, "Syria, Turkey and the Kurds," Arutz 7 IsraelNationalNews, November 18, 2011, http://www.israelnationalnews.com/Articles/Article.aspx/10858#.Tsa4d_JKNoM.

[141] I.C. Vanly, "The Kurds in Syria and Lebanon," in *The Kurds: A Contemporary Overview,* Edited by P.G. Kreyenbroek, S. Sperl, Chapter 8, (London: Routledge, 1992), 151-152.

[142] David McDowall, *A Modern History of The Kurds,* (London: I.B. Tauris, 2009), 475.

[143] McDowall, 475.

[144] I. C. Vanly, "The Kurds in Syria and Lebanon," 163–64.

[145] Joseph Puder, "Ethnic Cleansing In Syria: The Unseen Terror," *The Evening Bulletin* (Philadelphia), July 13, 2007, http://www.frontpagemagazine.com/readArticle.aspx?ARTID=27437.

[146] Ibid.

[147] Eyal Zisser, "Bashar Under Pressure: Potential Implications of the Qamishli Riots," *IMRA Newsletter,* Tel Aviv, Notes No. 102, March 22, 2004, http://www.kokhavivpublications.com/2004/israel/03/0403221448.html.

[148] I. C. Vanly, "The Kurds in Syria and Lebanon," 163–64.

[149] Ibid.

[150] Stephen Starr, "Syria: Damascus teams up with Turkey to fight Kurdish aspirations," *Los Angeles Times,* July 8, 2010, http://latimesblogs.latimes.com/babylonbeyond/2010/07/syria-damascus-teams-up-with-turkey-to-fight-kurdish-aspirations.html.

[151] "Stateless Kurds in Syria granted citizenship," CNN World, April 7, 2011, http://articles.cnn.com/2011-04-07/world/syria.kurdish.citizenship_1_kurdish-region-kurdish-identity-stateless-kurds?_s=PM:WORLD.

[152] "Al-Watan: 37,000 stateless Kurds Applied for citizenship," *The Syria Report,* June 23, 2011, http://www.syria-report.com/news/press-review/al-watan-37000-stateless-kurds-applied-citizenship.

[153] Jonathan Spyer, "Arab World: Staying on the sidelines," *Jerusalem Post,* June 28, 2012, http://www.jpost.com/Features/FrontLines/Article.aspx?id=275683.

[154] W. G. Elphinston, *The Kurdish Question,* Journal of International Affairs, Royal Institute of International Affairs, 1946, 97 and O. Dzh. Dzhalilov, *Kurdski geroicheski epos: Zlatoruki Khan* ("The Kurdish heroic epic: Gold-hand Khan"), Moscow, 1967, 5–26, 37–39, 206.

[155] W. G. Elphinston, "The Kurdish Question," 97–98.

[156] Meiselas, Susan *Kurdistan In the Shadow of History*, (New York: Random House, 1997), 182.

[157] John H. Lorentz, *The Historical Dictionary of Iran,* Second Edition, (Lanham, MD: The Scarecrow Press, Inc., 2006).

[158] *Daily Telegraph,* (UK), November 28, 2003.

[159] Khalkhali sentenced "up to 60 Kurds a day" according to the *Daily Telegraph,* (UK), November 28, 2003.

[160] "Iran: Holy war against the humanity in Kurdistan 1979," June 12, 2009, http://shooresh1917.blogspot.com/2009/06/blog-post.html.

[161] Efraim Karsh, *The Iran–Iraq War 1980-1988,* (Oxford, UK: Osprey Publishing Ltd., 2002), 55.

[162] Natali, D., *Manufacturing Identity and Managing Kurds in Iraq, Turkey and Iran: A Study in Evolution of Nationalism,* PhD Dissertation in Political Science, University of Pennsylvania, 2000, 238.

[163] Iran: Country Reports on Human Rights Practices - 1999, Released by the Bureau of Democracy, Human Rights, and Labor, U.S. Department of State, February 23, 2000.

[164] BBC Persian language broadcast September 2, 2005.

[165] Dan Raviv and Yossi Melman, *Every Spy a Prince: The Complete History of Israel's Intelligence Community,* (Boston: Houghton Mifflin, 1990), 21.

[166] *League of Nations Official Journal,* July 1932, 13th year, No. 7., 1347–50, http://www.cogsci.ed.ac.uk/~siamakr/Kurdish/KURDICA/1999/FEB/Iraq-policy.html.

[167] Christopher Andrew and Vasili Mitrokhin, *The Mitrokhin Archive II: The KGB and the World,* (London: Allen Lane, 2005), 175.

[168] Dana Adams Schmidt, "The Kurdish Insurgency," *Strategic Review,* 2 (Summer 1974), 54.

[169] Nouri Talabany, "Who Owns Kirkuk? The Kurdish Case," *Middle East Quarterly,* Winter 2007, 75–78.

[170] Ibid.

[171] Edward Ghareeb, *The Kurdish Question in Iraq,* (Syracuse, NY: Syracuse University Press, 1981), 68.

[172] A.R. Ghassemlou, et. al., *People Without a Country: The Kurds and Kurdistan,* (London: Zed Press, 1980), 237.

[173] Yosef Gotlieb, "The Kurdish Connection," *Jerusalem Post,* December 10, 1986 and "HaMossad Ha-Israeli" (Hebrew), *HaMishpakha,* February 6, 1997, 20–24.

[174] Matthew Kalman, "Tea with a Spymaster: 'I was meeting the Shah every month'," 2008, http://www.kurdnas.com/en/index.php?option=com_content&task=view&id=1406&Itemid=57.

[175] Ian Black and Benny Morris, *Israel's Secret Wars: A History of Israeli Intelligence Services,* (New York: Grove Press, 1991), 184–85.

[176] Raviv and Melman, 142.

[177] Black and Morris, 327–28.

[178] "Senior Kurdish Politician Visited Israel with Barzani in 1968, 1973," *Al-Zaman,* Iraq, August 4, 2009, http://www.kurdnas.com/en/index.php?option=com_content&task=view&id=1407&Itemid=57.

[179] The Forty Committee was an external bureaucracy in the executive branch of the U.S. government established to oversee covert operations and thus prevent abuses.

[180] Henry Kissinger, *White House Years,* (Boston: Little, Brown and Company, 1979), 1265.

[181] William Safire, "Mr. Ford's Secret Sellout," *New York Times,* February 5, 1976, 31; "Son of 'secret Sellout,'" *New York Times,* February 12, 1976, 30; and "The CIA Report the President Doesn't Want you to read," *The Village Voice,* February 16, 1976, 70–92. The part dealing with the Kurds is entitled, "Case 2: Arms Support," 85, 87–88; hereafter cited as the "Pike Committee Report."

[182] Jack Anderson, "Israelis Infiltrate Arab Regimes," *The Washington Post,* September 17, 1972, B7. *See* also Marion Woolfson, *Prophets in Babylon: Jews in the Arab World,* (Boston: Faber & Faber, 1980), 219–20.

[183] Pike Committee Report.

[184] Kissinger, *White House Years,* 1265.

[185] Safire, Ibid.

[186] Safire, Ibid.

[187] Pike Committee Report.

[188] Ibid.

[189] Edmund Ghareeb, *The Kurdish Question in Iraq,* (Syracuse: Syracuse University Press, 1981), 140.

[190] Pike Committee Report.

[191] Pike Committee Report and Lenore G. Martin, *The Unstable Gulf: Threats From Within,* (Lexington, MA: Lexington Books, 1984), 39–40.

[192] Pike Committee Report.

[193] Ibid.

[194] Ibid.

[195] Safire, Ibid.

[196] Ibid.

[197] William E. Hazen, "Minorities in Revolt: The Kurds of Iran, Iraq, Syria, and Turkey," in R.D. McLaurin, Ed., *The Political Role of Minority Groups in the Middle East,* (New York: Praeger, 1979), 65.

[198] M. Farouk-Sluglett, P. Sluglett, J. Stork, "Not Quite Armageddon: Impact of the War on Iraq," *MERIP Reports,* July-September 1984, 24.

[199] Michael M. Gunter, *The Kurds in Turkey: A Political Dilemma,* (Boulder, CO: Westview Press, 1990), 72–73, 76, 78.

[200] Jason Morris, "Begin airs secret Israeli aid to Kurds as reminder for Iraqis," *Christian Science Monitor,* October 6, 1980, 11, http://www.csmonitor.com/1980/1006/100649.html.

[201] Michael Rubin, "Are Kurds a pariah minority?" *Social Research,* Spring, 2003, http://findarticles.com/p/articles/mi_m2267/is_1_70/ai_102140955/pg_4/.

[202] "Genocide in Iraq: The Anfal Campaign Against the Kurds," Human Rights Watch Report, July 1993, http://www.hrw.org/legacy/reports/1993/iraqanfal/.

[203] "Events a Glance," *Strategic Survey 2010,* (London: International Institute for Strategic Studies, 2010), 12.

[204] Ibid.

[205] "Ethnic Cleansing and the Kurds," http://www.jafi.org.il/education/actual/iraq/4.html.

[206] Ibid.

[207] BBC On This Day 16 March 1988, "Thousands die in Halabja gas attack," http://news.bbc.co.uk/onthisday/hi/dates/stories/march/16/newsid_4304000/4304853.stm. *See* also Efraim Karsh, *The Iran–Iraq War 1980-1988,* (Oxford, UK: Osprey Publishing Ltd., 2002), 55.

[208] Nouri Talahany. *Arabization of the Kirkuk Region.* (Uppsala, Sweden: Kurdistan Studies Press, 2011), 94.

[209] Talabany, "Who Owns Kirkuk? The Kurdish Case," 75–78.

[210] Kanan Makiya, "The Anfal: Uncovering an Iraqi Campaign to Exterminate the Kurds," *Harper's Magazine,* May 1992, 61, http://www.harpers.org/archive/1992/05/0000869.

[211] Jonathan C. Randal, "Kurdish Commander Invites Saddam Foes to Meeting in Iraq," *Washington Post,* March 27, 1991, A25, http://www.encyclopedia.com/doc/1P2-1056440.html.

[212] Michael R. Gordon and Eric Schmitt, "After the War; Much More Armor Than U.S. Believed Fled Back to Iraq," *New York Times,* March 2, 1991, A1, http://www.nytimes.com/1991/03/25/world/after-the-war-much-more-armor-than-us-believed-fled-back-to-iraq.html?pagewanted=all.

[213] Patrick E. Tyler, "After the War; Schwarzkopf Says Truce Enabled Iraqis to Escape," *New York Times,* March 27, 1991, A7, http://www.nytimes.com/1991/03/27/world/after-the-war-schwarzkopf-says-truce-enabled-iraqis-to-escape.html.

[214] "U.S. Turns Down Plea to Intervene as Kirkuk Falls," *International Herald Tribune,* March 30, 1991.

[215] United Nations S/RES/0688 (1991), April 51991, http://www.fas.org/news/un/iraq/sres/sres0688.htm.

[216] H.J. Barkey, E. Laipson, "Iraqi Kurds And Iraq's Future," *Middle East Policy,* Vol. XII, No.4, Winter 2005, 67.

[217] M. M. Gunter, M. H. Yavuz, "The Continuing Crisis In Iraqi Kurdistan," *Middle East Policy,* Vol.XII, No.1, Spring 2005, 123-24.

[218] "III: Forced Expulsions," Iraq: Forcible Expulsion of Ethnic Minorities, Vol. 15, no. 3(E), Human Rights Watch, New York, March 2003.

[219] "Repression of the Iraqi People," Saddam Hussein's Iraq, U.S. Department of State, September13, 1999 (updated February 23, 2000), accessed August 7, 2006; *Al-Hay*(London), September29, 2000.

[220] Avi Yellin, "Israel Reportedly Training Kurdish Forces," IsraelNationalNews.com, February 5, 2010, http://www.israelunitycoalition.org/news/article.php?id=5076.

[221] "Iraq's Kurds support Israel ties," Point of No Return, June 9, 2005, http://jewishrefugees.blogspot.com/2005/06/iraqs-kurds-support-israel-ties.html.

[222] "Final Draft of the Iraqi Constitution," http://portal.unesco.org/ci/en/files/20704/11332732681iraqi_constitution_en.pdf/iraqi_constitution_en.pdf.

[223] Scott Sullivan, "Bush/Sadr Contain Iran and Kurds," *Conservative Voice,* March 17, 2007.

[224] AINA.com March 13, 2007.

[225] Avi Yellin, "Israel Reportedly Training Kurdish Forces," IsraelNationalNews.com, February 5, 2010, http://www.israelunitycoalition.org/news/article.php?id=5076.

[226] "KRG statement on first oil sales through pipeline export," Kurdistan Regional Government Press Release May 23, 2014, http://www.krg.org/a/d.aspx?l=12&a=51589.

[227] Julia Payne, "Israel accepts first delivery of disputed Kurdish pipeline oil," Reuters, June 20, 2014, http://www.reuters.com/article/2014/06/20/us-israel-iraq-idUSKBN0EV0X620140620.

[228] David Sheppard, "UPDATE 1-Tanker carrying Kurdish oil reappears unladen off Israel," Reuters, August 20, 2014, http://uk.reuters.com/article/2014/08/20/iraq-security-oil-kurds-idUKL5N0QQ2YG20140820.

[229] "KRG explored [sic] 2 million barrels of oil to Israel," Kurd Press.com, June 26, 2014, http://www.kurd-press.com/En/NSite/FullStory/News/?Id=7649#Title=%0A%09%09%09%09%09%09%09%09KRG%20explored%202%20million%20barrels%20of%20oil%20to%20Israel%0A%09%09%09%09%09%09%9.

[230] Ibid.

[231] Jonathan Spyer, "Did ISIS Use Chemical Weapons Against the Kurds in Kobanê?" *Middle East Review of International Affairs,* October 12, 2014, http://www.meforum.org/4852/did-isis-use-chemical-weapons-against-the-kurds.

[232] Joseph Puder, "The Kurds and the Future of Syria," FrontpageMag, June 24, 2013, http://frontpagemag.com/2013/joseph-puder/the-kurds-and-the-future-of-syria/.

[233] Sherkoh Abbas, President of the Kurdistan National Assembly of Syria, as quoted in Joseph Puder, "The Kurds, Israel, and the Future of Syria," FrontPageMagazine.com, June 27, 2008, http://www.frontpagemag.com/readArticle.aspx?ARTID=31481.

[234] Raphael Patai, *The Arab Mind*, (New York: Hatherleigh Press, 2007), 128.

[235] *Reliance of the Traveller,* o1.2 (4), 584.

[236] *Sahih Bukhari* Hadith: Vol. 8, book 82, number 829, and *Sahih Bukhari* Hadith: Vol. 9, book 93, number 512.

[237] Harry J. Sweeney, *The Restless Wind and Shifting Sands,* (New York: iUniverse, 2009), 296.

[238] *The National Post* (Toronto), December 12, 2007.

[239] Gadi Adelman, "Exclusive: How Do You Plead, Guilty or Not Guilty? 'I Plead Muslim!'", March 8, 2010, http://www.familysecuritymatters.org/publications/id.5676/pub_detail.asp.

[240] "Girl buried alive in honor killing in Turkey," *Hurriyet Daily News and Economic Review*, February 4, 2010, http://www.hurriyetdailynews.com/n.php?n=girl-buried-alive-in-honor-killing-2010-02-04.

[241] Rob Crilly, "Children forced to watch as Pakistani couple who married for love were 'murdered as an example'," *The Telegraph* (UK), June 29, 2014, http://www.telegraph.co.uk/news/worldnews/asia/pakistan/10933481/Children-forced-to-watch-as-Pakistani-couple-who-married-for-love-were-murdered-as-an-example.html.

[242] Jonathan S. Tobin, "A World-Historic Find in Jerusalem," *Commentary,* February 2010, http://www.commentarymagazine.com/viewarticle.cfm/a-world-historic-find-in-jerusalem-15369?search=1.

[243] In the original Hebrew of the *Tanakh*, the citation is Joel 4:1-2. In several English translations of the Bible including *The Holy Scriptures of the Old Testament,* (London: British and Foreign Bible Society); *The Holy Bible: King James Version*; *Life Application Study Bible NIV*; and *Ryrie Study Bible NAS*, the above verse appears in Joel 3:1-2.

[244] Michael Angold (Ed.), *Cambridge History of Christianity: Volume 5, Eastern Christianity,* (Cambridge, UK: Cambridge University Press, 2006), 402.

[245] Abdelhak Mamoun, "Urgent: ISIL destroys Mosque of Biblical Jonah, Prophet Yunus," *Iraqi News*, July 25, 2014, http://www.iraqinews.com/features/urgent-isil-destroys-mosque-biblical-jonah-prophet-yunus/.

[246] "ISIS to Turn Biblical Prophet Jonah's Tomb into a 'Fun Park'," Artuz 9, June 22, 2015, http://www.israelnationalnews.com/News/News.aspx/197072#.VYhVi2M9Xo0.

[247] Etgar Lefkovits, "Was the Aksa Mosque built over the remains of a Byzantine church?" *Jerusalem Post,* November 16, 2008, http://www.jpost.com/Israel/Was-the-Aksa-Mosque-built-over-the-remains-of-a-Byzantine-church.

[248] Yoram Ettinger, "The Islamization of Bethlehem by Arafat," The Israel Report, December 27, 2001, http://christianactionforisrael.org/isreport/dec01/bethlehem2.html.

[249] Gertrude Emerson Sen, *The Story of Early Indian Civilization*, (India: Orient Longmans, 1964).

[250] David Miller, "Egypt's Brotherhood declares war on the bikini," *The Jerusalem Post,* August 28, 2011, http://www.jpost.com/MiddleEast/Article.aspx?id=235687&R=R3.

[251] "Hagia Sophia: Church to mosque...and back?" *The Economist,* May 10–16, 2014, 54.

[252] Ayla Jean Yackley, "Thousands of Muslims pray for Istanbul's Hagia Sophia to be a mosque again," Reuters, May 29, 2012, http://blogs.reuters.com/faithworld/2012/05/29/thousands-of-muslims-pray-for-istanbuls-hagia-sophia-to-be-a-mosque-again/.

[253] "Hagia Sophia: Church to mosque...and back?" *The Economist,* May 10–16, 2014, 54.

[254] President-elect Bashir Gemayel speech *Dayr-Salib*, Lebanon, September 4, 1982.

[255] Mordechai Nisan, *The Conscience of Lebanon: A Political Biography of Etienne Sakr (Abu-Arz),* (London: Routledge, 2003).

[256] "Palestine Facts: Israel 1967-1991, PLO in Lebanon," http://www.palestinefacts.org/pf_1967to1991_lebanon_plo.php.

[257] Amos Harel, "IDF: Palestinians building mosque on Joseph's Tomb site," *Haaretz,* October 10, 2000, http://philologos.org/bpr/files/s020.htm.

[258] Peter Hirschberg, "Israel fears Palestinian mob damage other West Bank holy sites," *The Jerusalem Report,* November 6, 2000, http://pqasb.pqarchiver.com/jrep/access/645785651.html?dids=645785651:645785651&FMT=ABS&FMTS=ABS:FT&type=current&date=Nov+06 percent2C+2000&author=Peter+Hirschberg&pub=The+Jerusalem+Report&desc=Israel+fears+Palestinian+mob+damage+at+other+West+Bank+holy-+sites&pqatl=google. *See* also Peter Hirschberg, "Israel fears Palestinian mob damage other West Bank holy sites," The Jerusalem Report, November 6, 2000, http://pqasb.pqarchiver.com/jrep/access/645785651.html?dids=645785651:645785651&FMT=ABS&FMTS=ABS:FT&type=current&date=Nov+06 percent2C+2000&author=Peter+Hirschberg&pub=The+Jerusalem+Report&desc=Israel+fears+Palestinian+mob+damage+at+other+West+Bank+holy+sites&pqatl=google.

[259] Efrat Weiss, "Joseph's Tomb compound vandalized," Ynet, April 23, 2009, http://www.ynetnews.com/articles/0,7340,L-3705477,00.html.

[260] Tzvi Ben Gedalyahu, "PA Arabs Celebrate Murder by Desecrating Joseph's Tomb," IsraelNationalNews.com, April 24, 2011, http://www.israelnationalnews.com/News/News.aspx/143680.

[261] Krishan Francis, "Maldives museum reopens minus smashed Hindu images," Associated Press, February 24, 2012, http://news.yahoo.com/maldives-museum-reopens-minus-smashed-hindu-images-143815067.html.

[262] Nadav Shragai, "What's going on underneath the Temple Mount?," *Israel HaYom,* May 31, 2014, http://www.israelhayom.com/site/newsletter_article.php?id=17877.

[263] For detailed historic background *see* Nadav Shragai, "The Palestinian Authority and the Jewish Holy Sites in the West Bank: Rachel's Tomb as a Test Case," Jerusalem Viewpoints, No. 559, Jerusalem Center for Public Affairs, Jerusalem, December 2, 2007, http://www.jcpa.org/JCPA/Templates/ShowPage.asp?DBID=1&LNGID=1&TMID=111&FID=442&PID=0&IID=1923.

264 Commission on Human Rights, Fifty-first session, E/CN.4/1995/3, April 27, 1994, http://unispal.un.org/UNISPAL.NSF/0/FB61230BEAA56BB785256A14005A30BE.

265 Maayana Miskin, "UN Org.: Rachel's Tomb is a Mosque," Arutz Sheva, October 29, 2010, http://www.israel-nationalnews.com/News/News.aspx/140345.

266 Executive Board, Hundred and eighty-fourth session, 184 EX/37, Paris, March 19, 2010, http://unispal.un.org/UNISPAL.NSF/0/8F8CBDCA74D7D20385257721007157CF.

267 "Executive Board adopts five decisions concerning UNESCO's work in the occupied Palestinian and Arab Territories," UNESCOPRESS, October 21, 2010, http://www.unesco.org/new/en/media-services/single-view/news/executive_board_adopts_five_decisions_concerning_unescos_work_in_the_occupied_palestinian_and_arab_territories/.

268 Hillel Fendel, "Reports: Iraq De-Judaizing Ezekiel's Tomb," Israel National News, January 4, 2010, http://www.israelnationalnews.com/News/News.aspx/135343.

269 Gil Ronen, "Iranian Threats of Revenge for Mordechai's 'Purim Massacre'," IsraelNationalNews.com, January 10, 2011.

270 "Iran opens three intelligence fronts against Israel," DEBKAfile, January 10, 2011, http://www.debka.com/article/20533/.

271 David Lev, "Blood Libel Alive and Well in the Muslim World," Arutz-7, March 25, 2013, http://www.israel-nationalnews.com/News/News.aspx/166544#.VBuCMBDlZx0.

272 Many examples can be found "Blood Libels," MEMRI TV, http://www.memritv.org/subject/en/362.htm.

273 "An Anti-Jewish Book Linked to Syrian Aide," New York Times, July 15, 1986, http://www.nytimes.com/1986/07/15/world/an-anti-jewish-book-linked-to-syrian-aide.html.

274 "Cartoons from the Arab World," Tom Gross MidEast Media Analysis, http://www.tomgrossmedia.com/ArabCartoons.htm.

275 Documented and translated by MEMRI and uploaded to YouTube on May 1, 2010, http://www.youtube.com/watch?v=KHqXt_JNSt8.

276 "Former Jordanian MP: Jews Use Human Blood in Passover Matzos," Arutz-7, September 18, 2014, http://www.israelnationalnews.com/News/News.aspx/185240#.VBt7FBDlZx0.

277 Ibid.

278 Raymond Ibrahim, "No 'Revolution' for Egypt's Christians," FrontPageMagazine.com, March 22, 2011, http://www.faithfulnews.com/contents/view_content2/51605/no-revolution-for-egypts-christians-front-page-christian-books-christian-book-reviews-christian-writers.

279 James P. Pinkerton, "America Needs Willpower – And the Right Leaders," FoxNews.com, July 29, 2010, http://www.foxnews.com/opinion/2010/07/29/james-pinkerton-world-trade-centre-arizona-alqaeda-wikileaks-ground-zero-mosque/.

280 Park51.org. "Park51 Issues a Statement Regarding the Name of the Planned Muslim Community Center Being Built in Lower Manhattan," September 10, 2010, http://blog.park51.org/?p=129.

281 Dan Amira, "Ground Zero Mosque Gets Less Muslim-Invasion-Sounding Name," New York, July 14, 2010, http://nymag.com/daily/intel/2010/07/ground_zero_mosque_gets_lets_m.html. See also "Commission Expected to OK Ground Zero Mosque," WCBS TV, August 2, 2011. Link now redirects to "Ground zero mosque MTA ad," CBS New York, August 10, 2010, http://newyork.cbslocal.com/2010/08/10/mta-ground-zero-mosque-ad-starts-war-of-words/ground-zero-mosque-mta-ad/ and "Cordoba Initiative," http://www.cordobainitiative.org/.

282 Joe and Bill Hutchinson, "Plan for mosque near World Trade Center site moves ahead," New York Daily News, May 6, 2010, http://www.nydailynews.com/ny_local/2010/05/06/2010-05-06_plan_for_mosque_near_world_trade_center_site_moves_ahead.html.

[283] Ed Barnes, "Muslims in NYC Planning to Build Second, Smaller Mosque Near Ground Zero," FOXNews.com, May 17, 2010, http://www.foxnews.com/us/2010/05/17/muslims-nyc-planning-build-second-smaller-mosque-near-ground-zero/.

[284] http://www.masjidmanhattan.com/.

[285] Ibid.

[286] Michelle Malkin, "Flight 93 Memorial: Seeing is Believing, September 10, 2005, http://michellemalkin.com/2005/09/10/flight-93-memorial-seeing-is-believing/. *See* also Cynthia Yacowar-Sweeney, "Under Construction – the Other 911 Mosque," CanadaFreePress.com, October 14, 2010, http://www.israelunitycoalition.org/news/?p=5945.

[287] Alec Rawls, *Crescent of Betrayal: Dishonoring the Heroes of Flight 93,* http://www.crescentofbetrayal.com/.

[288] "Flight 93 Memorial Crescent Points to Mecca," *The Classic Liberal,* October 25, 2009, http://the-classic-liberal.com/flight-93-memorial-crescent-mecca/.

[289] "Mecca mosques 'wrongly aligned,'" BBC News, April 5, 2009, http://news.bbc.co.uk/2/hi/middle_east/7984556.stm.

[290] Alec Rawls, *Crescent of Betrayal: Dishonoring the Heroes of Flight 93,* http://www.crescentofbetrayal.com/.

[291] Mike Rosen, "Rosen: Let's roll, sans crescent," Rocky Mountain News.com, September 22, 2005, http://web.archive.org/web/20051214163041/http://www.rockymountainnews.com/drmn/news_columnists/article/0,1299,DRMN_86_4102007,00.html.

[292] Qur'an 2:217, 3:118, 4:89, 9:32, 34, 47:34-5.

[293] Moshe Kohn, "The Arabs' 'Lie' of the Land," *Jerusalem Post,* October 18, 1991.

[294] "British Mandate, Anglo-American Committee," *Palestine Facts,* http://www.palestinefacts.org/pf_mandate_angloamerican_1945.php.

[295] "The Jewish flag of Palestine, 1939," November 16, 2014, http://unitedwithisrael.org/the-jewish-flag-of-palestine-1939/?utm_source=MadMimi&utm_medium=email&utm_content=Turkey+Says+Muslims+Discovered+America!+ISIS+Beheads+Former+US+Soldier&utm_campaign=20141117_m123132150_Turkey+Says+Muslims+Discovered+America!+ISIS+Beheads+Former+US+Soldier&utm_term=The+Jewish+Flag+of+Palestine+_E2_80_93+1939_21

[296] Jeanne Kirkpatrick, "How the PLO Was Legitimized," *Commentary,* July 1989, http://www.aei.org/docLib/20030829_KirkpatrickPLO.pdf.

[297] "The Jewish Channel Exclusive Interview With GOP Front-Runner and former Speaker of the House Newt Gingrich," http://newsdesk.tjctv.com/2011/12/the-jewish-channel-.

[298] *An-Nahar* (Beirut), August 24, 1972.

[299] Radio Amman, February 3, 1973 (quoted by BBC Monitoring Service).

[300] http://www.peacefaq.com/jordan.html.

[301] James Dorsey, *Wij zijn alleen Palestijn om politieke reden, Trouw,* March 31, 1977.

[302] Scan of an article by James Dorsey from the Dutch newspaper *Trouw* containing extracts of an Interview with former PLO functionary Zuheir Mohsen, spelled "Zoehair Mohsen" in the Dutch article's text, *Trouw* archives, Jacob Bontiusplaats 9, Amsterdam, 1977-03-31.

[303] *Al-Rai* (Amman), September 24, 1980.

[304] BBC Arabic service,. April 5, 1989.

[305] https://www.youtube.com/watch?v=P3n5-yG-6dU.

[306] "A Letter to Jordanian Student Congress in Baghdad," *Washington Post,* November 12, 1974. *See* also United Nations General Assembly A/31/PV.70,18 November 1976, http://unispal.un.org/UNISPAL.NSF/0/8CDEEC4F87FC841585256F58005C4891.

[307] Salah Khalaf interviewed on BBC, November 10, 1985. Cited in Benjamin Netanyahu, *A Durable Peace: Israel and Its Place among the Nations.*(New York: Warner Books, 2000)., 228.

[308] *Al-Rai* (Kuwait), December 11, 1989.

[309] Gavriel Queenann, "PA: 'If I Forget Thee, Oh Jerusalem' First Said by Crusader," Arutz 7 IsraelNationalNews.com, June 10, 2011, http://www.israelnationalnews.com/News/News.aspx/144852.

[310] Palestinian Authority President Mahmoud Abbas on Palestinian al-Fateh TV, May 14, 2011.

[311] Qur'an 3:67.

[312] *Al-Hayat Al-Jadida,* July 8, 2011.

[313] David Wenkel, "Palestinians, Jebusites, and Evangelicals," *Middle East Quarterly,* Summer 2007, 49-56, http://www.meforum.org/1713/palestinians-jebusites-and-evangelicals.

[314] Tzvi Ben Gedalyahu, "PA Declares Western Wall Was not Jewish' until 16th Century A.D.," Israel National News, November 23, 2010.

[315] Qur: al-Imran, 3:51-2; an-Nisa, 4:171; al-Maidah, 5:111.

[316] Qur'an 61:6. This quote of Jesus is not found in any Christian Scriptures.

[317] *Al-Hayat Al-Jadida,* June 24, December11, 2000, June 17, 2005, October 28, 2006, April 30, November 18, 2008; Palestinian al-Fath TV, June 9, December 24, 2009.

[318] "UNESCO converts Maimonides to Islam," July 19, 2011, http://israelmatzav.blogspot.com/2011/07/unesco-converts-maimonides-to-islam.html.

[319] "Saeb Erekat, The Guardian (UK), December 10, 2010. Also *see* "Really, really big lies: Palestinians confabulate seven million refugees," Israel Insider, December 14, 2010, http://israelinsider.net/profiles/blogs/really-really-big-lies.

[320] "Catholic Priest: Over Six Million Killed in Shoah," *Jerusalem Post,* January 14, 2010.

[321] "REMARKS BY THE PRESIDENT ON A NEW BEGINNING, Cairo University, Cairo, Egypt," Press release, THE WHITE HOUSE, Office of the Press Secretary, (Cairo, Egypt), June 4, 2009, http://www.whitehouse.gov/the_press_office/Remarks-by-the-President-at-Cairo-University-6-04-09.

[322] "The Great Game," a term usually attributed to Arthur Conolly, was used to describe the rivalry and strategic conflict between the British Empire and the Tsarist Russian Empire for supremacy in Central Asia–including Ottoman Turkey, Persia (Iran) and Afghanistan. The term was later popularized by British novelist Rudyard Kipling in his work, *Kim.* The 1950 motion picture, *Kim,* starring Errol Flynn and Dean Stockwell, as well as the made-for-television 1984 version starring John Davies and Peter O'Toole, both capture the flavor of the period and the Great Game.

[323] Jacob C. Hurewitz, (ed.), *Diplomacy in the Near and Middle East: A Documentary Record, 1914-1956,* Vol. II, (Princeton, NJ: Van Nostrand, 1956),. 90–94; Leonard Shapiro (ed.), *Soviet Treaty Series: A Collection of Bilateral Treaties, Agreements, Conventions Etc., Concluded between the Soviet Union and Foreign Powers,* Vol. I, 1917-1928. (Washington, DC: Georgetown University Press, 1950), 92–94.

[324] Kamyar Mehdiyoun. "Ownership of Oil and Gas Resources in the Caspian Sea." *The American Journal of International Law.* Vol. 94, No. 1 (January 2000), 179–189.

[325] Articles to the effect began appearing in *Filastin,* in December 1944.

[326] *Izvestia,* September 13, 1944.

[327] This information was given by President Roosevelt to Dr. Stephen Wise in March 1945. Dr. Wise was at the time the President of the World Jewish Congress and of the American Jewish Congress and Chairman of the American Emergency Zionist Council.

[328] *Jewish Chronicle,* February 23, 1945.

[329] "Cold War International History Project 1945–46 Iranian Crisis," *See* http://www.wilsoncenter.org/index.cfm?topic_id=1409&fuseaction=va2.browse&sort=Collection&item=1945 percent2D46 percent20Iranian percent20Crisis.

[330] *General Assembly, Official Records, 1st Special Session,* Vol. 1, 127-135.

[331] *General Assembly, Official Records, 2nd Session, Ad Hoc Committee on the Palestine Question,* October 3, 1947, 69–71.

[332] *General Assembly, Official Records, 1st Special Session, 1st Committee,* 51st Meeting, May 8, 1947.

[333] *Radio Moscow, May 22, 1948–British Broadcasting Corporation Summary of World Broadcasts, Part I,* May 28, 1948.

[334] "Israel-Arab conflict FAQ," http://www.interall.co.il/israel-faq.html.

[335] Rami Ginat, *The Soviet Union and Egypt, 1945–1955,* (London: Frank Cass, 1993), 85.

[336] Mordechai Namir, *Shelihut Bemoskva* ("Assignment Moscow"), (Hebrew), Tel Aviv, 1971, 109-110.

[337] *See* Jan Pelikan (ed.), *The Czechoslovak Political Trials, 1950-1954. The Suppressed Report of the Dubçek Government's Committee of Inquiry, 1968,* London, 1971, and Karel Kaplan, "Thoughts About the Political Trials," *Radio Free Europe, Czechoslovak Press Survey,* Nos. 2147, 2148, 2149, 9, 10, December 11, 1968.

[338] *Izvestia,* July 21, 1953.

[339] *General Assembly, Official Records, 2nd Session,* 125th Plenary Session, November 26, 1947, 1360.

[340] *Izvestia,* November 23, 1951.

[341] *Security Council, Official Records,* 9th Year, No. 656, January 22, 1954.

[342] *Security Council, Official Records,* 9th Year, No. 664, March 29, 1954.

[343] Richard F. Roser, *An Introduction to Soviet Foreign Policy,* (Upper Saddle River, NJ: Prentice Hall, 1969), 391–98.

[344] David Tal, *The 1956 War: Collision and Rivalry in the Middle East,* (New York: Routledge, 2001), 157.

[345] *Mezhdunarodnaya Zhizn* ("International Affairs") No. 5, Soviet Foreign Ministry Publication, 1965.

[346] Anthony Eden, *The Suez Crisis of 1956,* (Boston: Beacon Press, 1960), 199.

[347] *Keesing's Contemporary Archives,* 15219.

[348] "What the President Saw: A Nation Coming Into Its Own," Time, April 12, 2005, 5, http://www.time.com/time/magazine/article/0,9171,1048416-5,00.html.

[349] Walter Laqueur, *The Soviet Union and the Middle East,* (London: Routledge, 1959), 239.

[350] David J. Dallin, *Soviet Foreign Policy After Stalin,* (Philadelphia, PA: J.B. Lippincott Co, 1961), 406–21.

[351] *Izvestia,* July 17, 19, 1958.

[352] Aryeh Y. Yodfat, "Russia's other Middle East Pasture–Iraq," *New Middle East,* No. 38 (November 1972), 26-29.

[353] Yigal Allon, "Soviet Involvement in the Arab-Israel Conflict," *The USSR and the Middle East,* M. Corfino and S. Shamir (ed.), (Tel Aviv: Israel Universities Press, 1973), 150-151; *See also* Yitzhak Rabin, *The Memoirs of Yitzhak Rabin,* (Boston: Little Brown, 1979), 57–58.

[354] Christopher Andrew and Vasili Mitrokhin, *The Mitrokhin Archive II: The KGB and the World,* (London: Allen Lane, 2005), 175.

[355] *Pravda,* September 17, 1962.

[356] A.R. Ghassemlou, et. al., *People Without a Country: The Kurds and Kurdistan,* (London: Zed Press, 1980), 237.

[357] Radio Damascus, May 19, 1966.

[358] *Tanjug,* March 29, 1967.

[359] *New York Times,* July 10, 1967.

[360] U Thant's report to the Security Council, UN records, *Documents S/7896,* May 18, 1967 and UN records, *Documents S/PV-1342,* May 21, 1967, 26-30.

[361] *The New Times,* (Moscow edition), June 2, 1967, 1.

[362] The Lebanese newspaper, *Al-Hay*(Beirut), carried the story of Badran's trial. The headline on page 1 of the February 25, 1968 edition read, "Shams Badran: The Reports of the [Israeli] attack upon Syria were Soviet fantasies [hallucinations]." This was also reported in the Egyptian newspaper *Al Ahram* of February 24, 1968.

[363] Ian Black and Benny Morris, *Israel's Secret Wars: A History of Israel's Intelligence Service,* (New York: Grove Press, 1991, 214.

[364] TASS, August 9, 1974.

[365] *Izvestia,* December 3, 1967.

[366] *Financial Times,* May 9, 1972.

[367] Voice of the Arabs, November 19, 1967; *Al Hawadith* (Beirut), December 15, 1967; *New York Times,* December 13, 14, 15, 1967; *See* also *Times* (London), December 13, 1967. A Royalist broadcast said on December 3, 1967, that their anti-aircraft guns had shot down a Tupolev aircraft, near Sana'a with a Soviet pilot.

[368] *Al-Hayat,* November 9, 1968.

[369] *Voyenno Istorichesky Zhurnal,* (Military History Journal), Moscow, September 1970.

[370] "Ceasefire Terms," *The Jerusalem Post,* August 9, 1970.

[371] *Egypt and Union of Soviet Socialist Republics Treaty of friendship and co-operation. Signed Cairo on 27 May 1971,* United Nations Treaty Series, No. 11379 of 1971, 1–5.

[372] Ibid.

[373] Aryeh Y. Yodfat, *The Soviet Union and the Arabian Peninsula,* (New York: St. Martin's Press, 1983), 19.

[374] *Pravda,* October 26, 1979.

[375] *Le Monde* (Paris), February 1, 1972; Dubai radio, February 15, 1972.

[376] *An-Nahar,* February 17, March 11, 1972; *Al-Hayat,* February 17, April 2, 1972; Amman radio, April 25, 1972.

[377] *Al Ahram,* October 31, 1975.

[378] *The Military Balance 1972-1973,* International Institute for Strategic Studies, London, 1972. *See* also Uri Ra'anan, "The Soviet-Egypt 'Rift,'" *Commentary,* June 1976, 29-35.

[379] *Aviation Week,* November 5, 1973.

[380] Paris Radio, October 9, 1973.

[381] *Strategic Survey 1973,* International Institute for Strategic Studies, London, 1974, 27.

[382] Ibid.

[383] *Al Akhbar,* Cairo, March 5, 1976.

[384] *Aviation Week and Space Technology,* November 5, 1973.

[385] *Le Monde,* Paris, December 10, 1975.

[386] President Siad Barre's speech of November 20, 1977 as reported by Mogadishu Domestic Service, November 20, 1977.

[387] Reuters, May 15, 1977, citing *an-Nahar* of the previous week; *al-Ahram* (Cairo), May 18, 1977; President Siad Barre News Conference, as reported by *Washington Post,* May 17, 1977. *See* also Gary D. Payton, "The Soviet-Ethiopian Liaison," *Air University Review,* November-December 1979, http://www.airpower.maxwell.af.mil/airchronicles/aureview/1979/nov-dec/payton.html#payton.

[388] *Pravda,* May 6, 1977.

[389] *The Daily Telegraph,* September 3, 1977.

[390] Gebru Tareke, "The Ethiopia–Somalia War of 1977 Revisited," *International Journal of African Historical Studies,* 2000 (33), 656.

[391] *Pravda,* broadcast by Tass, November 18, 1978 (SU/5973/C1/1, November 20, 1978).

[392] *Al Hawadith* (London)March 16, 1979.

[393] Tehran Domestic Service, August 9, 1980; Foreign Broadcast Information Service (USA), South Asia, August 11, 1980, 112–14.

[394] Efraim Karsh. *The Iran–Iraq War 1980-1988,* (Oxford, UK: Osprey Publishing Ltd., 2002) 42.

[395] Ibid., 43.

[396] Robert Pear, "U.S. Says Soviets Are Expanding Base for Warships on Syrian Coast," *New York Times,* August 28, 1988.

[397] Efraim Karsh. *The Iran–Iraq War 1980-1988,* (Oxford, UK: Osprey Publishing Ltd., 2002) 43.

[398] "Kontseptsia Vneshnei Politiki Rossiyskoy Federatsii," Ministry of Foreign Affairs of Russia, June 28, 2000.

[399] Yaakov Katz and AP, "Russia confirms MiG jet sale to Syria," *Jerusalem Post,* September 3, 2009, http://www.jpost.com/servlet/Satellite?cid=1251804478577&pagename=JPost percent2FJPArticle percent2FShowFull.

[400] Aleksandr Shustov, "The U.S. military will leave Kyrgyzstan Manas Air Base in 2014," Strategic Culture Foundation Journal, December 31, 2012, http://www.strategic-culture.org/news/2012/12/31/us-military-will-leave-kyrgyzstan-manas-air-base-in-2014.html.

[401] "Ex-Soviet states form rapid reaction force," *Washington Times*, February 5, 2009, http://www.washington-times.com/news/2009/feb/05/ex-soviet-states-form-rapid-reaction-force/.

[402] "Saudis Eye Russian Air Defense System," Agence France Presse, October 1, 2009, www.defensenews.com/story.php?i=4303935&c=MID&s=TOP.

[403] Maayana Miskin, "Russia to Give Sell Lebanon Tanks, Helicopters," IsraelNationalNews.com, November 16, 2010, http://www.israelnationalnews.com/News/News.aspx/140682.

[404] Abraham Rabinovich, "Russia upgrades radar station in Syria to aid Iran," *Washington Times,* February 29, 2012, http://www.washingtontimes.com/news/2012/feb/29/russia-upgrades-radar-station-syria-aid-iran/.

[405] "At least 27 dead in Damascus bombings. Russians man Syrian air defenses," DEBKAfile, March 17, 2012, http://www.debka.com/article/21835/.

[406] "Navy Chief: Russia's Mediterranean Task Force to Include Nuclear Subs," Fars News Agency, May 12, 2013, http://english.farsnews.com/newstext.php?nn=9107169406.

[407] Egypt State Information Service, Cairo, Nov. 13, 2013; *al-Ahram*, November 19, 2013; *Daily News Egypt* (Cairo), November 20, 2013; *RIA Novosti* (Moscow), February 14, 2014.

[408] "Israel Takes out Syrian Depot Containing Russian S300 Missiles. Video: Chemical Weapons being used in Homs," *Investment Watch*, July 7, 2013, http://investmentwatchblog.com/israel-takes-out-syrian-depot-containing-russian-s300-missiles-video-chemical-weapons-being-used-in-homs/.

[409] Ariel Ben Solomon, "Syrian opposition: Israeli jets bomb missile launchers in Latakia," *Jerusalem Post,* January 27, 2014, http://www.jpost.com/Defense/Syrian-opposition-Israeli-jets-bomb-missile-launchers-in-Latakia-339465.

INFLUENCE OF ISLAM ON THE REGION

[1] "Table: Muslim Population by Country," Pew Research Religion & Public Life Project, January 27, 2011, http://www.pewforum.org/2011/01/27/table-muslim-population-by-country/.

[2] "The Future of the Global Muslim Population," Pew Research Religion & Public Life Project, January 27, 2011, http://www.pewforum.org/2011/01/27/the-future-of-the-global-muslim-population/.

[3] Ibid.

[4] Omar Sacirbey, "Sharia Law In The USA 101: A Guide To What It Is And Why States Want To Ban It," Huffingtonpost.com, July 29, 2013, http://www.huffingtonpost.com/2013/07/29/sharia-law-usa-states-ban_n_3660813.html.

[5] Richard S. Ehrlich, "Brunei Shari'a Law Announced By Sultan Hassanal Bolkiah," Huffington Post, October 22, 2013, http://www.huffingtonpost.com/2013/10/22/brunei-shari'a-law-sultan_n_4143352.html?ncid=edlinkusaolp00000003. *See* also Jeremy Grant, "Brunei imposes sharia-based penal code," ft.com, April 30, 2014, http://www.ft.com/intl/cms/s/0/b12f97d4-d043-11e3-af2b-00144feabdc0.html#axzz30NmGMbGX.

[6] "Indonesia: Shari'a-Based Laws Creep into Half of Provinces," *Christian Today, Australia,* February 9, 2009, http://au.christiantoday.com/article/indonesia-shari'a-based-laws-creep-into-half-of-provinces/5367.htm.

[7] Daniel Greenfield, "Allahu Akbar," May 14, 2011, http://sultanknish.blogspot.com/.

[8] Juan Eduardo Campo and J. Gordon Melton, *Encyclopedia of Islam,* (New York: Facts on File, 2009); 420-22.

[9] Qur'an 8:55.

[10] Qur'an 98:6.

[11] Qur'an 9:28.

[12] Qur'an 6:111.

[13] Qur'an 51:10.

[14] Qur'an 23:97.

[15] Qur'an 25:55.

[16] Qur'an 3:28; 5:51.

[17] Qur'an 6:25.

[18] *Sahih Bukhari* Hadith: Vol. 5, book 59, number 369.

[19] Qur'an 2:89; 5:59–60, 64; 33:60.

[20] Qur'an 40:35.

[21] Qur'an 83:34.

[22] Qur'an 9:29.

[23] Qur'an 37:18.

[24] Qur'an 86:15.

[25] Qur'an 3:151; 8:12.

[26] *Sahih Bukhari* Hadith: Vol. 5, book 59, number 537.

[27] Ibn Ishaq, "Life of Muhammad," 759.

[28] *Sahih Bukhari* Hadith: Vol. 5, book 58, number 148.

[29] Qur'an 4:91.

[30] Qur'an 2:191–193; 9:5; 33:60.

[31] Qur'an 5:33.

[32] Qur'an 8:12; 47:4.

[33] Qur'an 8:60; 9:29.

[34] Qur'an 6:45.

[35] Qur'an, 2:43, 2:195, 9:41; *Sahih Bukhari* Hadith: Vol. 2, book 24; and Nu Ha Mim Keller, (ed.) Reliance *of the Traveller: The Classic Manual of Islamic Sacred Law ('Umdal-Salik),* Revised Edition, (Beltsville, MD: Amana Publications, 1994), h8.17, h9.0. *Reliance of the Traveller,* carries the endorsement of Al-Azhar University in Cairo as conforming "to the practice and faith of the orthodox Sunni community."

[36] Qur'an 9:103.

[37] h8.24, page 274.

[38] Message of the Qur'an, Muhammad Asad, note 261 (Qur'an 2:273), 74. An updated version of the Abdullah Y. Ali translation, revised and edited by a committee The Presidency of Islamic Researches, IFTA, Call and Guidance (in Madinah, Saudi Arabia). Available without charge from the Royal Embassy of Saudi Arabia, Washington, DC, or you can access the online version through the website of the King Fahd Complex For the Printing of the Holy Quran in Madinah, Saudi Arabia, http://islam.about.com/gi/o.htm?zi=1/XJ&zTi=1&sdn=

islam&cdn=religion&tm=22&gps=455_61_1408_773&f=10&tt=3&bt=1&bts=1&zu=http%3A//www.quran-complex.com/Quran/Targama/Targama.asp%3FTabID%3D4%26SubItemID%3D1%261%3Deng%26t%3Deng%26SecOrder%3D4%26SubSecOrder%3D1.

[39] "The Salvation Army," http://www.directory.businessbarbados.com/charities/the-salvation-army/.

[40] Robert Spencer, "Bahrain: Bomb factory discovered in mosque," Jihad Watch, October 26, 2012, http://www.jihadwatch.org/2012/10/bahrain-bomb-factory-discovered-in-mosque.html.

[41] "What is a mosque?" markdurie.com blog, September 15, 2010, http://markdurie.blogspot.com/2010/09/what-is-mosque.html.

[42] Bill Warner, *Shari'a Law for Non-Muslims,* Center for the Study of Political Islam, 2010, 2.

[43] *Reliance of the Traveller*, o4.9.

[44] *The Wall Street Journal,* April 9, 2002.

[45] Qur'an 24:52.

[46] Col. (ret.) Dr. Jacques Neriah, "The Structure of the Islamic State (ISIS)," Jerusalem Center for Public Affairs, September 8, 2014, http://jcpa.org/structure-of-the-islamic-state/.

See also http://www.alarabiya.net/ar/arab-and-world/syria/2014/08/30/%D8%AF%D8%A7%D8%B9%D8%B4-%D9%8A%D9%81%D8%B1%D8%B6-%D9%86%D8%B8%D8%A7%D9%85%D9%87-%D8%A7%D9%84%D8%AA%D8%B9%D9%84%D9%8A%D9%85%D9%8A-%D8%AF%D9%88%D9%86-%D9%81%D9%86-%D9%88%D8%AA%D8%A7%D8%B1%D9%8A%D8%AE.html.

[47] Qur'an, 13:25, 16:94, 16:106, 33:15, *Reliance of the Traveller,* o8.0–o8.7.

[48] *Milliyet,* Turkey, August 21, 2007 Memri Turkish Media Blog http://www.thememriblog.org/turkey/blog_personal/en/2595.htm.

[49] Daniel Greenfield, "The Extremist Moderates and the Moderate Extremists, June 1, 2013, http://sultanknish.blogspot.com/2013/06/the-extremist-moderates-and-moderate.html.

[50] http://www.whitehouse.gov/news/releases/2005/10/20051028-1.html.

[51] Remarks Austin Straubel International Airport, Green Bay, Wisconsin, White House press release, August 10, 2006.

[52] Qur'an, 5:3, 32:2; *Reliance of the Traveller,* u1.0 et al, v2.0 et al, w4.5.

[53] *Sahih Bukhari* Hadith: Vol. 3, book 39, number 531, Vol. 4, book 52, number 288, Vol. 4, book 53, number 393; *Sahih Muslim* Hadith: Book 19, number 4366; *The History of Al-Tabari,* margin note 1834.

[54] Bill Warner, "The Political Violence of the Bible and the Koran," *American Thinker,* September 9, 2010, http://www.americanthinker.com/2010/09/the_political_violence_of_the.html.

[55] *Sahih Bukhari* Hadith 440 Vol. 23, Book 2, as narrated by Abu Huraira. "Then Abu Huraira recited the holy verses: 'The pure Allah's Islamic nature (true faith i.e. to worship none but Allah Alone), with which He has created human beings.'" (Qur'an 30.30).

[56] "Muslim Extremists Torch Churches in Ethiopia," March 25, 2011, http://lmliberty.us/2011/03/25/muslim-extremists-torch-churches-in-ethiopia/#axzz1HvwsTzgi. *See* also http://www.jihadwatch.org/2011/01/ethiopian-muslims-warn-christians-to-convert-leave-city-or-face-death.html.

[57] Ibid.

[58] Qur'an 60:4.

[59] Raymond Ibrahim, "Islam's doctrines of deception," Middle East Forum, October 2008, http://www.meforum.org/2095/islams-doctrines-of-deception.

[60] *Reliance of the Traveller*, r8.2, 744–745.

[61] *Reliance of the Traveller,* comment and example given by Sheik 'Abd al-Wakil Durubi, Smoothing over differences, was an example of what Muhammad had implied.

[62] Nonie Darwish, *Now They Call Me Infidel: Why I Renounced Jihad for America, Israel, and the War on Terror,* (New York: Sentinel, 2006(, 119.

[63] Ibid., 121.

[64] Ibid., 122.

[65] Michael Widlanski, "Naming and Fighting Terror," *American Thinker,* July 13, 2014, http://www.american-thinker.com/2014/07/naming_and_fighting_terror_.html.

[66] Abdullah Al Araby, "The Quran's Doctrine of Abrogation," Islam Review, http://www.islamreview.com/articles/quransdoctrine.shtml. *See also* "The Abrogation and Abrogated Qur'anic Verses," http://www.answering-islam.org/BehindVeil/btv10.html.

[67] For a thorough English translation of the Qur'an by three translators simultaneously *see* http://www.usc.edu/schools/college/crcc/engagement/resources/texts/muslim/quran/.

[68] *See* also "The Religion of Peace" Verses of Violence at http://www.thereligionofpeace.com/Qur'an/023-violence.htm.

[69] There should be no misunderstanding as to what this verse says. It is worth noting how several translators render the key word in Sura 4:34, sanctioning the beating of disobedient women, (وَاضْرِبُوهُنَّ, waidriboohunna).
Pickthall, "and scourge them,"
Yusuf Ali, "(And last) beat them (lightly),"
Al-Hilali/Khan, "(and last) beat them (lightly, if it is useful),"
Shakir, "and beat them,"
Sher Ali, "and chastise them,"
Khalifa, "then you may (as a last alternative) beat them,"
Arberry, "and beat them,"
Rodwell, "and scourge them,"
Sale, "and chastise them,"
Asad, "then beat them,"
Dawud, "and beat them."

[70] "Bible and Qur'an: equally violent?" Jihad Watch, March 14, 2009, at http://www.jihadwatch.org/2009/03/bible-and-quran-equally-violent.html.

[71] Alexis de Tocqueville, *Democracy in America,* Volume II, Chapter V, "How Religion in the United States Avails Itself of the Democratic Tendencies," http://xroads.virginia.edu/~HYPER/DETOC/ch1_05.htm.

[72] Natan Sharansky, "Antisemitism in 3-D," *The Jewish Daily Forward,* January 21, 2005, http://forward.com/articles/4184/antisemitism-in--d/.

[73] Andrew Bostom, "Text of a lecture delivered The Hudson Institute, Washington, DC, May 21, 2008," FrontPageMagazine.com, May 22, 2008, http://www.andrewbostom.org/blog/2008/05/22/hudson-institute-lecture-jihad-and-islamic-antisemitism/.

[74] Itamar Marcus and Nan Jacques Zilberdik, "PA Antisemitism: Judaism is 'distorted' and Jews have 'evil nature,'" Palestine Media Watch, June 16, 2011, citing *Al-Hayat Al-Jadida,* May 13, 2011, May 15, 2011, June 3, 2011, http://palwatch.org/main.aspx?fi=157&doc_id=5190.

[75] Dror Eydar, "'Even if you give up all the land, it won't solve the problems in the Mideast," Israel HaYon, June 28, 2013, http://www.israelhayom.com/site/newsletter_article.php?id=10309.

[76] Qur'an 98:6.

[77] Qur'an 5:60.

[78] *Sahih Bukhari* Hadith 54:524.

[79] Qur'an 4:47; 5:13.

[80] Qur'an 4:60.

[81] *See* also *Sahih Muslim* Hadith: Book 41, number 6981 through number 6985.

[82] *Sahih Bukhari* Hadith: Vol. 4, book 52, number 177.

[83] Ziad Abu-Amr, *Islamic Fundamentalism in the West Bank and Gaza: Muslim Brotherhood and Islamic Jihad,* (Bloomington: Indiana University Press, 1994), 26.

[84] This viewpoint is echoed in the Palestinian National Covenant, Article 20. (*See* Appendix 8)

[85] As related in his memoirs *Jerusalem the Holy,* (New York: BiblioBazaar, 2009, 344.

[86] Qur'an 4:89 calls for the slaying of apostates. *See* also *Sahih Bukhari* Hadith: Vol. 9, book 83, number 17 and Vol. 9, book 89, number 271.

[87] *Sahih Bukhari* Hadith: Vol. 9, book 84, number 57.

[88] Jeremy Grant, "Brunei imposes sharia-based penal code," ft.com, April 30, 2014, http://www.ft.com/intl/cms/s/0/b12f97d4-d043-11e3-af2b-00144feabdc0.html#axzz30NmGMbGX.

[89] Robert Spencer, "Brunei: Propagating religion other than Islam a crime under Sharia," Jihad Watch, February 16, 2014, http://www.jihadwatch.org/2014/02/brunei-propagating-religion-other-than-islam-a-crime-under-sharia.

[90] Thomas O. Hecht, "Islamic Imperialism: The Ongoing Tragedy on the Middle East," *BESA Perspectives,* November 25, 2009.

[91] Telephone interview with the author, September 6, 2011.

[92] Ryan Mauro, "Egypt's El-Sisi Boldly Calls For Islamic Reformation," The Clarion Project, January 22, 2014, http://www.clarionproject.org/analysis/egypts-el-sisi-boldly-calls-islamic-reformation.

[93] Linda Woodhead (Ed.), Hiroko Kawanami (Ed.), Christopher Partridge (Ed.), *Religions in the Modern World: Traditions and Transformations,* (London: Routledge, 2009), 226.

[94] Khurshid Ahmad, *Islam: Its Meaning and Message.* (London: Islamic Foundation, 1975), 37, http://www.onislam.net/english/ask-about-islam/faith-and-worship/islamic-creed/168976-a-complete-way-of-life.html; "Islam: basic principles & characteristics -II," Islamweb, http://www.islamweb.net/emainpage/index.php?page=articles&id=134357, *Islam Our Choice,* Cooperative Office for Propagation, Guidance, and Warning of Expatriates in the city of Bade'ah, 11, http://books.google.com/books?id=LJaxnolrRH4C&pg=PA11&lpg=PA11&dq=islam+provides+guidance+for+all+walks+of+life&source=bl&ots=_q_8HcPJ94&sig=N4o-Do781yEfClSLZuuGcg6hHBpM&hl=en&sa=X&ei=4JizUavPN4LPywGB3oCwAQ&ved=0CFIQ6A-EwBw#v=onepage&q=islam%20provides%20guidance%20for%20all%20walks%20of%20life&f=false.

[95] Term suggested by Daniel Pipes in his article, "Does Europe Have No-go Zones?" *The Blaze,* January 20, 2015, http://www.theblaze.com/contributions/does-europe-have-no-go-zones/.

[96] Dale Hertz, "Multicultralisme et Islam en France,: CBN News, February 17, 2011, http://www.youtube.com/embed/A3YQANdvvbY.

[97] "At least 55 Islamic No-Go Zones…in Sweden," Creeping Shari'a, November 7, 2014, http://creepingsharia.wordpress.com/2014/11/07/at-least-55-islamic-no-go-zones-in-sweden/.

[98] Soeren Kern, "European 'No-Go' Zones for Non-Muslims Proliferating – 'Occupation Without Tanks or Soldiers'," January 22, 2015, http://unitycoalitionforisrael.org/uci_2014/?p=13113.

[99] Ibid.

[100] *See* Vol. 17, 172.

[101] *Musnad Ibn Hanbal,* Vol. 2, 2992 as cited in Raymond Ibrahim, "Islam on Cows, Horses, Camels and Women," FrontpageMag, July 24, 2013, http://frontpagemag.com/author/raymond-ibrahim/.

[102] *Sunan Abu Dawud* 11, 2155.

[103] Qur'an, 2:221, 2:222, 2:223, 4:24, 4:25, 4:34, 24:31, *Reliance of the Traveller,* Book m in toto.

[104] Qur'an 2:228.

[105] Qur'an 4:34.

[106] *Sahih Bukhari* Hadith: Vol. 2, book 1, number 28.

[107] Qur'an 2:228.

[108] "Saudi Arabia Male Guardianship Policies Harm Women," Human Rights Watch, April 20, 2008, http://www. hrw.org/en/news/2008/04/20/saudi-arabia-male-guardianship-policies-harm-women.

[109] Qur'an 33:59.

[110] Daniel Pipes has described the *niqab* and *burqa* as "hideous, unhealthy, socially divisive, terrorist-enabling, and criminal-friendly garments" also calling for their ban in public places. *See* Daniel Pipes, "Niqabs and Burqas: The Threat Continues," www.Frontpagemag.com, September 1, 2009, http://www.frontpagemag.com/readArticle.aspx?ARTID=36144.

[111] "Lubna Al-Hussein, Sudanese Journalist Sentenced to Lashing for Wearing Pants: There Were Dozens of Thousands of Women Like Me," MEMRI TV, http://www.memritv.org/clip/en/2346.htm.

[112] James Calderwood, "Kuwaiti MPs propose bikini ban on beach," *The National,* November 30, 2010, http://www.thenational.ae/news/world/middle-east/kuwaiti-mps-propose-bikini-ban-on-beach. *See* also "Kuwaiti MPs propose jail time for women who wear swimsuits," Agence France-Presse, November 30, 2010.

[113] *Reliance of the Traveller* f12.4. *See* also Robert Spencer, "Islamic law: Women, don't come to mosque unless you're ugly," Jihad Watch, July 6, 2012, http://www.jihadwatch.org/2012/07/islamic-law-women-dont-come-to-mosque-unless-youre-ugly.html.

[114] *The Daily Mail* (London), April 17, 2012.

[115] "Offbeat: Barbie deemed threat to Saudi morality," *USA Today,* September 10, 2003, http://www.usatoday.com/news/offbeat/2003-09-10-barbie_x.htm.

[116] Simone Wilson, "Iran Bans Barbies; Disgruntled Little Girl Calls Replacement Dolls 'Ugly and Fat,'" LA Weekly, January 2012, http://blogs.laweekly.com/informer/2012/01/iran_bans_barbies.php.

[117] Abdullah Al-Shihri, "Saudi religious police kick off no-red-goods campaign to enforce Valentine's Day ban," The Canadian Press, February 11, 2010.

[118] "Jamat-e-Islami rallies against Valentine's Day," *The News* (Pakistan), February 12, 2013, http://www.thenews.com.pk/article-87788-Jamat-e-Islami-rallies-against-Valentines-Day.

[119] *Sahih Bukhari* Hadith: Vol. 4, book 52, number 250; and Vol. 7, book 62, number 160/

[120] "Khamenei: Islam Forbids Male-Female Chat Messages," Jewish Press News Briefs, January 7, 2014, http://www.jewishpress.com/news/breaking-news/khamenei-islam-forbids-male-female-chat-messages/2014/01/07/.

[121] *Reliance of the Traveller* e4:3, 59.

[122] Raphael Patai, *The Arab Mind,* Revised Edition, (New York: Hatherleigh Press, 2007), 34.

[123] "Islamic Law on Female Circumcision," http://answering-islam.org/Shari'a/fem_circumcision.html.

[124] Priyanka Pruthi, "New UNICEF report on female genital mutilation/cutting: Turning opposition into action," UNICEF, July 22, 2013, http://www.unicef.org/protection/57929_69881.html. *See* also "Millions risk genital mutilation: UNICEF," UNICEF, July 23, 2013, http://thenewage.co.za/102434-1020-53-Millions_risk_genital_mutilation_UNICEF.

[125] *Sunan Abu Dawud* 41:5251.

[126] Sami A. Aldeeb Abu Sahlieh, "To Mutilate in the Name of Jehovah or Allah: Legitimization of Male and Female Circumcision," *Medicine and Law,* July 1994, 575-622.

[127] Aymenn Jawad Al-Tamimi, "The Failure of Secular and Liberal Egyptians," *American Spectator,* December 16, 2011, http://spectator.org/archives/2011/12/16/the-failure-of-secular-and-lib.

[128] *Responding From Tradition: One Hundred Contemporary Fatwas from the Grand Mufti of Egypt, Fatwa 35,* December 1, 2011, Fons Vitae, 98-104.

[129] Qur'an 4:24.

[130] Qur'an 4:22–24, and 33:50.

[131] Francis Gladwyn, *The Epitome of Islamic Law*, (Calcutta, India: William Mackay, 1786), now reprinted by Gale ECCO link: http://www.gale.cengage.com/pdf/facts/ECCO.pdf.

[132] Qur'an 2:223.

[133] *Sahih Bukhari* Hadith: Vol. 3, book 31, number 129 and Vol. 7, book 62, number 81.

[134] *See* Qur'an 4:24; 23:5,6; 33:50; 70:22-30; *Sahih Bukhari* Hadith: 3, 432; 9:506; 5:637; *Sahih Muslim* Hadith: Book 2, number 3371 and number 3432; *Sunan Abu Dawud* Hadith: Book 2, number 2150 and number 2167; Tabari's History, Vol. 39, 194.

[135] Raymond Ibrahim, "Are Slave-Girls in Islam Equivalent to Animals?" Jihad Watch, December 14, 2008, http://www.raymondibrahim.com/islam/are-slave-girls-in-islam-equivalent-to-animals/.

[136] Qur'an 4:3.

[137] Aymenn Jawad Al-Tamimi, "Libya Heading Towards Islamism," *The American Spectator*, November 9, 2011, http://spectator.org/archives/2011/11/09/libya-heading-towards-islamism.

[138] "Saudi Arabia: Male Guardianship Policies Harm Women," Human Rights Watch, April 20, 2008, http://www.hrw.org/en/news/2008/04/20/saudi-arabia-male-guardianship-policies-harm-women.

[139] "Malaysia: unmarried Muslims face jail for hotel liaisons," Jihad Watch.org, January 4, 2010, http://www.jihadwatch.org/cgi-sys/cgiwrap/br0nc0s/managed-mt/mt-search.cgi?search= percent22Unmarried+Muslims+-face+jail+for+hotel+liaisons percent2C percent22+&IncludeBlogs=1&limit=20.

[140] Qur'an 65:4/

[141] Heather Murdock, "Yemen still wedded to child marriages," *The Washington Times,* December 24, 2009.

[142] Robert Spencer, "Iran: Hundreds of girls under age 10 married," Jihad Watch, August 27, 2012, http://www.jihadwatch.org/2012/08/iran-hundreds-of-girls-under-age-10-married.html.

[143] Robert Taft, "Alarm as hundreds of children under age of 10 married in Iran," *The Telegraph,* August 26, 2012, http://www.telegraph.co.uk/news/worldnews/middleeast/iran/9500484/Alarm-as-hundreds-of-children-under-age-of-10-married-in-Iran.html.

[144] According to the data of the Turkish Statistical Institute in 2012 as cited in Uzay Bulut, "The West's Dangerous Enchantment with Islam," Gatestone Institute, November 9, 2014.

[145] *Sahih Bukhari* Hadith: Vol. 7, book 62, number 88, http://www.usc.edu/schools/college/crcc/engagement/resources/texts/muslim/hadith/bukhari/062.sbt.html#007.062.088.

[146] Robert Spencer, "Iran: Hundreds of girls under age 10 married," Jihad Watch, August 27, 2012, http://www.jihadwatch.org/2012/08/iran-hundreds-of-girls-under-age-10-married.html.

[147] "Young girls seeks help as father promises her to 80 yr old, Saudi activists outraged as man marries 11 yr old," *Al Arabiya*, January 17, 2010, http://www.alarabiya.net/articles/2010/01/17/97613.html.

[148] "80-year-old man marries 14-year-old," Emirates 24/7, November 3, 2010, http://www.emirates247.com/news/region/80-year-old-man-marries-14-year-old-2010-11-03-1.312713.

[149] "Girl, 12, divorces 80-year-old husband," msnbc.com, April 22, 2010, http://www.msnbc.msn.com/id/36717454.

[150] "Raymond Ibrahim: New Saudi Fatwa Defends Pedophilia as 'Marriage'," Jihad Watch, July 21, 2011, http://www.jihadwatch.org/2011/07/raymond-ibrahim-new-saudi-fatwa-defends-pedophilia-as-marriage.html. *See* also http://www.raymondibrahim.com/from-the-arab-world/new-saudi-fatwa-defends-pedophilia-as-marriage/.

[151] Sandi Roberts, "Saudi mufti pushes for age of child brides to be 10 years old," Provo Christianity Examiner, April 19, 2012, http://www.examiner.com/article/saudi-mufti-pushes-for-age-of-child-brides-to-be-10-years-old. *See* also http://www.examiner.com/article/saudi-mufti-pushes-for-age-of-child-brides-to-be-10-years-old#ix-zz1ssjN68I3.

[152] "Yemeni 12-year-old dies in labor," Associated Press, September 12, 2009, http://www.cbsnews.com/stories/2009/09/12/ap/middleeast/main5306035.shtml.

[153] Paula Newton, "Child bride's nightmare after divorce," CNN, August 28, 2009, http://www.cnn.com/2009/WORLD/meast/08/26/yemen.divorce/index.html.

[154] Mohammed Jamjoom, "Child bride horrors last a lifetime," CNN, September 30, 2010, at http://www.cnn.com/video/#/video/world/2010/09/30/jamjoom.yemen.child.brides.cnn.

[155] Oliver Holmes, "In Yemen, women protest delay on child marriage ban," *The Christian Science Monitor,* March 23, 2010, http://www.csmonitor.com/World/Middle-East/2010/0323/In-Yemen-women-protest-delay-on-child-marriage-ban.

[156] Abdul-Aziz Oudah, "Parliamentary committee strikes down age of marriage amendment," February 10, 2009, http://www.emptyquarter.net/?p=2256.

[157] *Sahih Bukhari* Hadith: Vol. 3, book 38, number 508.

[158] Qur'an 4:34.

[159] *Sunan Abu Dawud* 11, 2142.

[160] Qur'an 4:15, 24:4, 24:6, and 24:13.

[161] Excerpt from Afghanistan's Shi'a Personal Status Law.

[162] Cited in *'Umdal-Salik,* o4.9 Classic Manual of Islamic Sacred Law.

[163] Kristen Chick, "Egyptians work to reclaim a Tahrir tainted by sexual assault," *The Christian Science Monitor,* February 1, 2013, http://www.csmonitor.com/World/Middle-East/2013/0201/Egyptians-work-to-reclaim-a-Tahrir-tainted-by-sexual-assault.

[164] Qur'an 65:4.

[165] Qur'an 4:129.

[166] Qur'an 2:232.

[167] Qur'an 2:230.

[168] Qur'an 4:11.

[169] "Saudi Arabia: Male Guardianship Policies Harm Women," Human Rights Watch, April 20, 2008, http://www.hrw.org/en/news/2008/04/20/saudi-arabia-male-guardianship-policies-harm-women.

[170] "Saudi Arabia: Where Fathers Rule and Courts Oblige," Human Rights Watch, October 18, 2010, http://www.hrw.org/en/news/2010/10/18/saudi-arabia-where-fathers-rule-and-courts-oblige.

[171] *Sahih Bukhari* Hadith: Vol. 6, book 1, number 301.

[172] Robert Taft, "Anger as Iran bans women from universities," *The Telegraph,* August 20, 2012, http://www.telegraph.co.uk/news/worldnews/middleeast/iran/9487761/Anger-as-Iran-bans-women-from-universities.html. *See* also Behrouz Samadbeighi, "77 Academic Subjects Announced Not Suitable for Women," August 7, 2012, as reported in *Roosz 1708,* August 22, 2012, http://www.roozonline.com/english/news3/newsitem/article/77-academic-subjects-announced-not-suitable-for-women.html.

[173] Qur'an 2:282.

[174] *Sahih Bukhari* Hadith: Vol. 49, book 3, number 826.

[175] *Sahih Bukhari* Hadith: Vol. 1, book 6, number 301.

[176] *Sahih Bukhari* Hadith: Vol. 9, book 88, number 219.

[177] "Baby, You Can Drive My Car," *Middle East Quarterly*, Fall 2011, 46.

[178] "Militants killing laughter and music in Pak," Reuters, February 9, 2009.

[179] "Karachi enforces ban on music in public transport," AFP, February 20, 2014, http://www.dawn.com/news/1088337/karachi-enforces-ban-on-music-in-public-transport.

[180] Interview with Kayed Al-Ghoul, member of the Political Bureau of the Popular Front for the Liberation of Palestine, *Al-Ayyam* (Gaza), September 3, 2009.

[181] "Gaza: Police ban lingerie displays in stores," Ma'an News Agency, July 27, 2010, http://www.maannews.net/eng/ViewDetails.aspx?ID=303310.

[182] There is no mention anywhere in the Qur'an of the actual number of virgins available in paradise, and the dark-eyed damsels are available for all Muslims, not just martyrs. It is in the Islamic traditions–the Hadith–that we find the 72 virgins in heaven specified: in a Hadith collected by Al-Tirmidhi (died 892 C.E.) in the Book of Sunan (Volume IV, chapters on "The Features of Paradise as described by the Messenger of Allah" [Islamic prophet Muhammad], chapter 21, "About the Smallest Reward for the People of Paradise," (number 2687). The same hadith is also quoted by Ibn Kathir (died 1373) in his Qur'anic commentary (Tafsir) of Surah Al-Rahman (55), verse 72, "The Prophet Muhammad was heard saying: 'The smallest reward for the people of paradise is an abode where there are 80,000 servants and 72 houris, over which stands a dome decorated with pearls, aquamarine, and ruby, as wide as the distance from Al-Jabiyyah [a Damascus suburb] to Sana'a [Yemen]'." Modern apologists of Islam, try to downplay the evident materialism and sexual implications of such descriptions, but, as the *Encyclopaedia of Islam* says, even orthodox Muslim theologians such as al Ghazali (died 1111) and Al-Ash'ari (died 935) have "admitted sensual pleasures into paradise." The sensual pleasures are graphically elaborated by Al-Suyuti (died 1505), Qur'anic commentator and polymath. He wrote, "Each time we sleep with a houri we find her virgin. Besides, the penis of the Elected never softens. The erection is eternal; the sensation that you feel each time you make love is utterly delicious and out of this world and were you to experience it in this world you would faint. Each chosen one [i.e. Muslim] will marry seventy [*sic*] houris, besides the women he married on earth, and all will have appetizing vaginas."

[183] Nicholas D. Kristof, "Martyrs, Virgins, and Grapes," *New York Times,* August 4, 2004.

[184] Ibn Khaldun as quoted in Bat Ye'or, *The Dhimmi,* (Rutherford, NJ: Fairleigh Dickinson University Press, 1985), 162.

[185] Majid Khadduri, *War and Peace in the Law of Islam,* (Baltimore: The Johns Hopkins Press, 1955), Reprinted (New Jersey: The Lawbook Exchange, Ltd. 2006, 2010), 53–4, 64–5, 134–36, 220–21.

[186] *Reliance of the Traveller,* o.9.0, 599.

[187] Ibid., o.9.1, 600.

[188] Dore Gold, "The West's embrace of the Muslim Brotherhood," *Israel Hayom,* June 22, 2012, http://www.israelhayom.com/site/newsletter_opinion.php?id=2105.

[189] Robert Spencer, *Yemeni cleric, "The Islamic nation will not stand by with its arms crossed in the face of these Crusades"* http://www.jihadwatch.org/2010/01/yemeni-cleric-the-islamic-nation-will-not-stand-by-with-its-arms-crossed-in-the-face-of-these-crusad.html.

[190] Leo Hohmann, "U.N. to dump flood of Muslim refugees on U.S. 'Several thousand in the pipeline, and that number will go up'," WND.com, September 16, 2014, http://www.wnd.com/2014/09/u-n-to-dump-flood-of-muslim-refugees-on-u-s/.

[191] Jerry Gordon, "An Egyptian Jew in Exile: An Interview with Bat Ye'or," *New English Review,* October 2011, http://www.newenglishreview.org/custpage.cfm/frm/98500/sec_id/98500.

[192] Newt Gingrich, "America Risk: Camus, National Security and Afghanistan," American Policy Institute, Washington, DC, July 29, 2010, http://www.aei.org/events/2010/07/29/america-at-risk-campus-national-security-and-afghanistan-event/.

[193] "Egypt Court Dissolves Muslim Brotherhood's Political Wing." Rianovost, August 9, 2014, http://en.ria.ru/world/20140809/191870783/Egypt-Court-Dissolves-Muslim-Brotherhoods-Political-Wing.html.

[194] "Charter of the Organisation of the Islamic Conference," March 14, 2008, 2, http://www.oic-oci.org/is11/english/Charter-en.pdf.

[195] http://www.news.faithfreedom.org/index.php?name=News&file=article&sid=1391.

[196] Ibn Ishaq, "Life of Muhammad," 525.

[197] Efraim Karsh, *Islamic Imperialism: A History.* (New Haven, CT: Yale University Press, 2007), 32.

[198] Bernard Lewis, AEI Annual Dinner, Irving Kristol Lecture, Washington DC, March 7, 2007.

[199] Vladimir Borisovich Lutsky, "Chapter IX Lebanon. Syria, and Palestine in the period of the Tanzimats (1840-70)," in Modern History of the Arab Countries. Progress Publishers, (1969), http://www.marxists.org/subject/arab-world/lutsky/ch09.htm.

[200] See Raymond H. Kévorkian, "The Cilician Massacres, April 1909" in Armenian Cilicia, eds. Richard G. Hovannisian and Simon Payaslian. UCLA Armenian History and Culture Series: Historic Armenian Cities and Provinces, 7. (Costa Mesa, California: Mazda Publishers, 2008), 351–53.

[201] Dilek Güven, "Riots against the Non-Muslims of Turkey: 6/7 September 1955 in the context of demographic engineering," European Journal of Turkish Studies, 12 (2011), http://ejts.revues.org/index4538.html.

[202] Asia Watch, Human Rights in Indonesia and East Timor, Human Rights Watch, New York, 1989, 253.

[203] "India revises Kashmir death toll to 47,000," Hindustan Times, November 21, 2008, http://www.hindustan-times.com/News-Feed/srinagar/India-revises-Kashmir-death-toll-to-47-000/Article1-353212.aspx.

[204] http://web.archive.org/web/20070821154629/http://www.hrvc.net/htmls/references.htm.

[205] Osama bin Laden, "Text of Fatwah Urging Jihad Against Americans," Al-Quds al-'Arabi (London in Arabic), February 23, 1998, http://www.mideastweb.org/osamabinladen1.htm.

[206] Nathaniel Allen, Peter M. Lewis and Hilary Matfess, "The Boko Haram insurgency, by the numbers," Washington Post, October 6, 2014, http://www.washingtonpost.com/blogs/monkey-cage/wp/2014/10/06/the-boko-haram-insurgency-by-the-numbers/.

[207] Lauren Ploch Blanchar, "Nigeria's Boko Haram: Frequently Asked Questions," Congressional Research Service, June 10, 2014, http://fas.org/sgp/crs/row/R43558.pdf.

[208] Robert Spencer, "Thai jihadis ring in the new year with...more jihad terror," Jihad Watch, December 31, 2009, http://www.jihadwatch.org/cgi-sys/cgiwrap/br0nc0s/managed-mt/mt-search.cgi?search=Thai+jihadis+ring+in+the+new+year+with&IncludeBlogs=1&limit=20.

[209] Sahih Bukhari Hadith: Vol. 4, book 53, number 386.

[210] Al-Siyassa, (Kuwait), June 7, 2010.

[211] Spencer Ackerman and Noah Shachtman, "Video: FBI Trainer Says Forget 'Irrelevant' al-Qaida, Target Islam," Wired, September 20, 2011, http://www.wired.com/dangerroom/2011/09/fbi-islam-qaida-irrelevant/.

[212] "Speeches to 2008 Conservative Political Action Conference," February 7, 2008, http://www.ontheissues.org/Archive/2008_CPAC_Mike_Huckabee.htm.

[213] Rowan Scarborough, "Colonel's class on radical Islam leaves career in limbo," Washington Times, October 14, 2012, http://www.washingtontimes.com/news/2012/oct/14/colonels-class-on-radical-islam-leaves-career-in-l/?page=all.

[214] "Bombshell—Pentagon Buries the Truth—Newly Revealed Document Vindicates Army Lt. Colonel Matthew Dooley In Anti-Islam Controversy," The Thomas More Law Center, December 2012. Accessed online January 4, 2013, http://us2.campaignarchive2.com/?u=adf1a83154acea60d091b413c&id=ebe19f964a&e=a2b6ac9a0c.

[215] "Statement by the President on the Garissa University College Terrorist Attack," The White House, Office of the Press Secretary, April 3, 20115, https://www.whitehouse.gov/the-press-office/2015/04/03/statement-president-garissa-university-college-terrorist-attack.

[216] "Obama Bans Islam, Jihad From National Security Strategy Document," Fox News.com, April 7, 2010, http://www.foxnews.com/politics/2010/04/07/obama-bans-islam-jihad-national-security-strategy-document/.

[217] "Syria crisis: ISIL imposes rules on Christians in Raqqa," BBC, February 27, 2014, http://www.bbc.com/news/world-middle-east-26366197.

[218] Maimonides' "Epistle to Yemen," in Isadore Twersky, A Maimonides Reader, (New York: Behrman House, 1972), 456–57.

[219] Joan Peters. From Time Immemorial: The Origins of the Arab-Jewish Conflict over Palestine, (New York: Harper & Row, 1984) 33–71.

[220] The *Farhud* was launched during the Jewish holiday of Shavuot, June 1–2, 1941. According to Martin Gilbert in his epic work, *In Ismael's House,* pro-Nazi Arab gangs killed 187 Jews, injured least 2,000, several hundred Jewish women were raped, 240 Jewish children were orphaned, 911 homes, 586 shops as well as 4 synagogues were burned and looted. It was the beginning of the end for Iraq's 2,600-year old Jewish community.

[221] Joan Peters. *From Time Immemorial: The Origins of the Arab-Jewish Conflict over Palestine.* (New York: Harper & Row, 1984) 33–71.

[222] Shmuel Trigano, "The Expulsion of the Jews from Muslim Countries, 1920-1970: A History of Ongoing Cruelty and Discrimination," November 15, 2010, http://www.israelunitycoalition.org/news/?p=6042.

[223] Martin Gilbert. *In Ishmael's House: A History of Jews in Muslim Lands.* (Toronto, ON: McClelland & Stewart Ltd.), 2011.

[224] *See* "Jonathan Kay on Muslim anti-Semitism: A hate reaching back 1,400 years," October 11, 2010, http://fullcomment.nationalpost.com/tag/jonathan-kay/#ixzz18KAJa6WY.

[225] Bat Ye'or and Andrew G. Bostom, "Andalusian Myth, Eurabian Reality," *Dhimmi Watch,* April 21, 2004, http://www.jihadwatch.org/dhimmiwatch/archives/001665.php.

[226] "Events a Glance," *Strategic Survey 2010,* (London: International Institute for Strategic Studies), 11.

[227] "Turkey's charismatic pro-Islamic leader," BBC News, November, 4, 2002, http://news.bbc.co.uk/2/hi/europe/2270642.stm.

[228] "Istanbul Mayor, an Islamist, Is Given 10-Month Jail Term," *New York Times,* April 22, 1998.

[229] Daniel Pipes, "Swiss Minarets and European Islam," *Jerusalem Post,* December 9, 2009, http://www.danielpipes.org/7808/swiss-minarets-european-islam.

[230] Caroline B. Glick, "Terrorists returning to Bethlehem and other signs of progress in the stalled peace process," Jewish World Review, December 26, 2006, http://www.jewishworldreview.com/1206/glick122606.php3.

[231] Gary Lane, "Tried by Fire: Bethlehem's Remnant," Cbn.com, October 21, 2009, http://www.cbn.com/cbnnews/181500.aspx.

[232] "Op-Ed: How Christians are Persecuted in the PA," IsraelNationalNews.com, September 30, 2014, http://www.israelnationalnews.com/Articles/Article.aspx/15731#.VC7okBA0Rx0.

[233] "Egypt: Security forces demolish church services building, assault Coptic priests, women, and children," Jihad Watch, May 1, 2009, http://www.jihadwatch.org/archives/025918.php.

[234] Chana Ya'ar, "Egyptian Muslims Burn Coptic Church in Aswan Province," Arutz 7, October 2, 2011, http://www.israelnationalnews.com/News/News.aspx/148397#.Toj3PtSb2t8. *See* also "Muslim Mob Torches Coptic Church in Egypt," Assyrian International News Agency, October 1, 2011, http://www.aina.org/news/20110930204413.htm and Raymond Ibrahim, "Egypt Destroying Churches, One a Time, Muslim Brotherhood: 'No More Churches,'" Hudson New York, October 10, 2011, http://www.hudson-ny.org/2489/egypt-destroying-churches.

[235] Ibid.

[236] Bat Ye'or, *The Dhimmi: Jews and Christians Under Islam,* (Rutherford, NJ: Fairleigh Dickinson University Press, 1985), 59.

[237] Mohammad Ibrahim, "Militants Ban School Bells in a Town in Somalia," *New York Times,* April 15, 2010, http://www.nytimes.com/2010/04/16/world/africa/16somalia.html.

[238] "French newspaper's special Muhammad issue sparks ire – and fire," *Israel Hayom,* November 3, 2011, http://www.israelhayom.com/site/newsletter_article.php?id=1678.

[239] Martin Gilbert. *In Ishmael's House: A History of Jews in Muslim Lands.* (Toronto, ON: McClellan & Stewart Ltd., 2011), 303.

[240] Haviv Rettig Gur, "Yemen's last Jews set to flee country," *Jerusalem Post,* August 14, 2009, http://www.jpost.com/servlet/Satellite?pagename=JPost percent2FJPArticle percent2FShowFull&cid=1249418604352. *See*

also "Amid mini-exodus, more Jews leave Yemen," SABA Yemen News Agency, August 12, 2009, http://www.sabanews.net/en/news191168.htm.

[241] *The Noble Qur'an*- Three esteemed translations, online: Sura 5, ay33 Yusuf Ali, "The punishment of those who wage war against Allah and His Messenger, and strive with might and main for mischief through the land is: execution, or crucifixion, or the cutting off of hands and feet from opposite sides, or exile from the land: this their disgrace in this world, and a heavy punishment is theirs in the Hereafter;" Pickthall, "The only reward of those who make war upon Allah and His messenger and strive after corruption in the land will be that they will be killed or crucified, or have their hands and feet on alternate sides cut off, or will be expelled out of the land. Such will be their degradation in the world, and in the Hereafter theirs will be an awful doom;" Shakir, "The punishment of those who wage war against Allah and His messenger and strive to make mischief in the land is only this, that they should be murdered or crucified or their hands and their feet should be cut off on opposite sides or they should be imprisoned; this shall be as a disgrace for them in this world, and in the hereafter they shall have a grievous chastisement."

[242] Bat Ye'or and Andrew G. Bostom, "Andalusian Myth, Eurabian Reality," Ibid.

[243] Sylvia Westall, "ISIL crucifies eight rival fighters, says monitoring group," Reuters, June 29, 2014, http://www.reuters.com/article/2014/06/29/us-syria-crisis-rivals-idUSKBN0F40HX20140629.

[244] Bernard Lewis, "The Return of Islam," *Commentary*, January 1976, 49. *See* also Andre Aciman, "In the Muslim City of Bethlehem," *New York Times Magazine*, December 24, 1995, http://www.nytimes.com/1995/12/24/magazine/manager-square-in-the-muslim-city-of-bethlehem.html?pagewanted=1 and Brigitte Gabriel, "Have the Presbyterians Lost Their Conscience?" *American Thinker*, June 17, 2006, http://www.americanthinker.com/2006/06/have_the_presbyterians_lost_th.html.

[245] Qur'an 4:171; 5:17, 73;

[246] Michael Angold (Ed.), *Cambridge History of Christianity: Volume 5, Eastern Christianity*, (Cambridge, UK: Cambridge University Press, 2014), 388. *See* also Father Joachim Boutros, *The History of Christianity in Egypt: Post Chalcedon and the Islamic Era*, Fort Myers, Fla.: Coptic Orthodox Diocese of the Southern United States, 2007, 21.

[247] "Mission Impossible: Sudan envoy without leverage would be an exercise in futility," Center for Security Policy, http://www.centerforsecuritypolicy.org/ and http://www.offnews.info/.

[248] Ron Prosor, "The Middle East War on Christians," *Wall Street Journal*, April 16, 2014, http://online.wsj.com/news/articles/SB10001424052702303630904579417482632439814?mg=reno64-wsj&url=http%3A%2F%2Fonline.wsj.com%2Farticle%2FSB10001424052702303630904579417482632439814.html.

[249] "Christianity by country," http://en.wikipedia.org/wiki/Christianity_by_country#By_region.

[250] "Lebanon," *The CIA World Factbook 2010*, (New York: Skyhorse Publishing, 2009), 392.

[251] Suhail Ahmad Banglori, "Pay with life for honesty," *Islam Watch*, November 9, 2006, http://www.islam-watch.org/SuhailAhmad/PayForHonesty.htm.

[252] Lawrence Solomon, "Christianity's Savior in the Middle East—Israel," *The Huffington Post*, December 23, 2013, http://www.huffingtonpost.ca/lawrence-solomon/christianity-middle-east-israel_b_4493256.html.

[253] Associated Press, as reported in Yoram Ettinger, "The Islamization of Bethlehem by Arafat," Jerusalem Cloakroom #117, Ariel Center for Policy Research, December 25, 2001. *See* also Yoram Ettinger, "Bethlehem will become a town of churches devoid of Christians," Israpundit, December 28, 2007, http://www.israpundit.com/archives/6924.

[254] Justus Reid Weiner, "Palestinian Crimes against Christian Arabs and Their Manipulation against Israel," Jerusalem Center for Public Affairs, September 19, 2008, http://jcpa.org/article/palestinian-crimes-against-christian-arabs-and-their-manipulation-against-israel/.

[255] Aaron Klein, "Media distort, fabricate Bethlehem Christmas," World Net Daily, December 23, 2013, http://www.wnd.com/2013/12/media-distort-fabricate-bethlehem-christmas/.

[256] Ibid.

[257] Khaled Abu Toameh, "The Beleaguered Christians in Bethlehem," Gatestone Institute, May 12, 2009, http://www.gatestoneinstitute.org/501/the-beleaguered-christians-in-bethlehem.

[258] Nitza Tanner, "Following the path(s) of Jesus: Bethlehem," Jerusalem Post, December 9, 2007, http://www.jpost.com/Home/Article.aspx?id=84783.

[259] Pierre Rehov, "Holy Land: The Perils Facing Christians," Gatestone Institute, September 27, 2014, http://www.gatestoneinstitute.org/4692/christians-holy-land.

[260] Dan Wooding, "Christian Groups in the Palestinian Authority (PA) to Disappear," International Christian Embassy Jerusalem, December 3, 2007, http://www.icejusa.org/site/News2?page=NewsArticle&id=6123&news_iv_ctrl=0.

[261] The Palestinian Authority's Treatment of Christians in the Autonomous Areas, Israeli Government, October 1997, translated to English by Independent Media Review Analysis (IMRA).

[262] Anthony Sadid, "Church Attack Seen as Strike at Iraq's Core," New York Times, November 1, 2010, http://www.nytimes.com/2010/11/02/world/middleeast/02iraq.html.

[263] Muhanad Mohammed, "Iraq church raid ends with 52 dead," Reuters, November 1, 2010, http://www.reuters.com/article/idUSTRE69U1YE20101101?pageNumber=1.

[264] Menelaos Agaloglou, "Victims of the Revolution," Think Africa Press (London), May 31, 2011, http://thinkafricapress.com/egypt/victims-revolution.

[265] Pierre Rehov, "Holy Land: The Perils Facing Christians," Gatestone Institute, September 27, 2014, http://www.gatestoneinstitute.org/4692/christians-holy-land.

[266] "Christmas in Bethlehem: the cross banished from souvenirs," Asia News (Italy), December 22, 2010, http://www.asianews.it/news-en/Christmas-in-Bethlehem:-the-cross-banished-from-souvenirs-shops-20318.html.

[267] Paul Merkley. Those That Bless You, I Will Bless: Christian Zionism in Historical Perspective. (Brantford, ON: Mantua Books, 2011), 216.

[268] "Demographics of Lebanon," http://en.wikipedia.org/wiki/Demographics_of_Lebanon#cite_ref-cia_15-2.

[269] "Christians Are Being Violently Pushed Out Of Middle East," January 7, 2011, http://www.disinfo.com/2011/01/christians-are-being-violently-pushed-out-of-middle-east/.

[270] The combined Syrian Catholic and Chaldean Catholic population in Mosul in 2010. "The Eastern Catholic Churches," Annuario Pontificio, 2010, http://www.cnewa.org/source-images/Roberson-eastcath-statistics/east-catholic-stat10.pdf.

[271] Frank Crimi. "Ethnic Cleansing of Syrian Christians," FrontPage Magazine, March 29, 2012, http://frontpagemag.com/2012/03/29/ethnic-cleansing-of-syrian-christians/. See also Ayaan Hirsi Ali. "The Global War on Christians in the Muslim World," Newsweek, February 6, 2012, http://www.thedailybeast.com/newsweek/2012/02/05/ayaan-hirsi-ali-the-global-war-on-christians-in-the-muslim-world.html.

[272] Nazir S. Bhatti. The Trial of Pakistani Christian Nation, 23, http://www.pakistanchristiancongress.org/ebooks/The_Trial_of_Pakistani_Christian_Nation.pdf.

[273] Frank Crimi. "Ethnic Cleansing of Syrian Christians," FrontPage Magazine, March 29, 2012, http://frontpagemag.com/2012/03/29/ethnic-cleansing-of-syrian-christians/. See also Ayaan Hirsi Ali. "The Global War on Christians in the Muslim World," Newsweek, February 6, 2012, http://www.thedailybeast.com/newsweek/2012/02/05/ayaan-hirsi-ali-the-global-war-on-christians-in-the-muslim-world.html.

[274] "Population by Religion," Central Bureau of Statistics Statistical Abstract of Israel, 2008, http://www.cbs.gov.il/reader/shnaton/templ_shnaton_e.html?num_tab=st02_02&CYear=2008.

[275] Ibid.

276 "Israel Only Safe Place for Christians in Middle East, Nazareth Priest Tells UN," September 23, 2014, http://unitedwithisrael.org/israel-only-safe-place-for-christians-in-middle-east-nazareth-priest-tells un/?utm_source=MadMimi&utm_medium=email&utm_content=Beheading+by+Muslim+in+USA+Not+Classified+as+Act+of+Terror%3F&utm_campaign=20140928_m122348864_Beheading+by+Muslim+in+USA+Not+Classified+as+Act+of+Terror%3F&utm_term=more_btn_dark_jpg.

POLITICAL PROCESSES

1 Arch Puddington, "Freedom in the World 2013: Democratic Breakthroughs in the Balance," (New York: Freedom House, 2013), 5.

2 http://www.knesset.gov.il/description/eng/eng_mimshal_yesod2.htm.

3 Jonathan Lis, "Israel raises electoral threshold to 3.25 percent," *Haaretz*, March 12, 2014, http://www.haaretz.com/news/national/1.579289.

4 "Leave the prize winners in peace," *Jerusalem Post*, May 1, 2011, http://www.jpost.com/Opinion/Editorials/Article.aspx?id=218605.

5 http://en.wikiquote.org/wiki/James_Madison.

6 Thomas Sowell, "A Bitter After-taste," Jewish World Review, June 16, 2014, http://jewishworldreview.com/cols/sowell061814.php3#.U6Cf0RDlZx0.

7 Deborah Sontag, "The Erdoğan Experiment," *New York Times*, May 11, 2003, http://www.nytimes.com/2003/05/11/magazine/the-erdogan-experiment.html?pagewanted=all&src=pm.

8 Thomas Sowell, "A Bitter After-taste," Jewish World Review, June 16, 2014, http://jewishworldreview.com/cols/sowell061814.php3#.U6Cf0RDlZx0.

9 Diana West, "Toward a 'conservative' foreign policy," *American Thinker*, January 20, 2013, http://www.americanthinker.com/2013/01/toward_a_conservative_forcign_policy.html.

10 Burak Bekdil, "Why Golda Meir was Right," *Hurriyet Daily News* (Turkey), August 23, 2011, http://cnpublications.net/2011/08/23/arabs-must-stop-hating/.

11 "Uncovering Algeria's civil war," Al Jazeera, November 18, 2010, http://www.aljazeera.com/indepth/2010/11/2010118122224407570.html.

12 Karin Laub. "Libya's declaration day." *The Advertiser* (Adelaide, Australia), October 25, 2011. 25.

13 Raymond Ibrahim. "Muslim Brotherhood 'Democracy' – Slapping, Stabbing, and Slaying for Sharia," Investigative Project on Terrorism, July 9, 2012, http://www.investigativeproject.org/3665/muslim-brotherhood-democracy-slapping-stabbing#.

14 Raymond Ibrahim. "Did the Muslim Brotherhood Really Win Egypt's Presidency?," November 9, 2012, http://www.raymondibrahim.com/from-the-arab-world/did-the-muslim-brotherhood-really-win-egypts-presidency/.

15 Ibid.

16 Ibid.

17 "Egypt and Sudan repair relations," BBC News, December 23, 1999, http://news.bbc.co.uk/2/hi/africa/576380.stm.

18 Steve Kroft, "The Perfect Spy," *60 Minutes*, CBS, May 10, 2009.

19 *See* Uri Kaufman, "Spy or Double Agent? Israel's October Surprise," *The Jewish Press*, October 2, 2007, http://www.jewishpressads.com/pageroute.do/25308/; Abraham Rabinovich, "Our mysterious man on the Nile," *The Jerusalem Post*, February 17, 2011, http://www.jpost.com/Magazine/Features/Article.aspx?id=208712; Howard Blum, "Who killed Ashraf Marwan?," *International Herald Tribune*, July 13, 2007, http://web.archive.org/web/20070715125113/http://www.iht.com/articles/2007/07/13/opinion/edblum.php; and Rajeev Syal, "Yard

probes billionaire spy's death," *The Guardian: The Observer,* October 4, 2008, http://www.guardian.co.uk/ uk/2008/oct/05/ukcrime.egypt.

[20] Karsh, *The Iran–Iraq War, 1980-1988,* (Oxford, UK: Osprey Publishing Ltd., 2002), 73.

[21] Felice Friedson, "Israel didn't assassinate Iranian physicist in 2007 – Revolutionary Guard did, sister says," *National Post* (Canada), September 30, 2014, http://news.nationalpost.com/2014/09/30/ israel-didnt-assassinate-iranian-physicist-in-2007-revolutionary-guard-did-sister-says/.

[22] "Covert war on Iran's nuclear program reaches into Tehran," DEBKAfile Special Report, January 12, 2010, http://www2.debka.com/index.php.

[23] Rachel Hirshfeld, "Did Iran Use Israel as Cover to Kill Its Own Nuclear Scientist?," Arutz 7, May 24, 2012, http://www.israelnationalnews.com/News/News.aspx/156179#.T7502nj1GJE.

[24] "Nuclear scientist killed in Tehran was Iran's top Stuxnet expert," DEBKAfile, November 29, 2010, http:// www.debka.com/article/20406/.

[25] "Jundallah is on point of executing abducted Iranian nuclear scientist," DEBKAfile, December 22, 2010, http://www.debka.com/article/20482/.

[26] Thomas Erdbrink, "Iranian nuclear scientist killed, another injured in Tehran bombings," *Washington Post* Foreign Service, November 29, 2010, http://www.washingtonpost.com/wp-dyn/content/article/2010/11/29/ AR2010112901560.html.

[27] "Slain Iranian scientist was working on a nuclear bomb detonator," DEBKAfile, July 24, 2011, http://www. debka.com/article/21146/.

[28] Efraim Karsh, *The Iran–Iraq War, 1980-1988,* (Oxford, UK: Osprey Publishing Ltd., 2002), 13.

[29] Peter Ford, "The men who shot Uday Hussein," *The Christian Science Monitor,* September 26, 2003, http:// www.csmonitor.com/2003/0926/p01s02-woiq.html.

[30] "Editor of Kurdish pro-Israel paper vanishes; Iran suspected," *Israel Hayom,* June 21, 2012, http://www. israelhayom.com/site/newsletter_article.php?id=4774.

[31] "Gadhafi Denies Claims Of Assassination Attempt," *Orlando Sentinel,* June 18, 1998, http://articles.orlan-dosentinel.com/1998-06-18/news/9806170758_1_gadhafi-assassination-attempt-moammar.

[32] "Terrorist hid explosives in his bottom," *Telegraph* (UK), September 21, 2009, http://www.telegraph.co.uk/ news/newstopics/howaboutthat/6212908/Terrorist-hid-explosives-in-his-bottom.html.

[33] Amir Kulick, "The Assassination of General Mohammed Suleiman," *Canada Free Press,* August 15, 2008, http://www.canadafreepress.com/index.php/article/4481.

[34] "On this day 14 February 1989: Ayatollah sentences author to death," BBC, http://news.bbc.co.uk/onthisday/ hi/dates/stories/february/14/newsid_2541000/2541149.stm.

[35] Uzi Mahnaimi, "Defector spied on Iran for years," *The Sunday Times,* March 11, 2007.

[36] "Yaalon: Iran's nuclear arms drive delayed. Iran: Mossad killed Iranian official," DEBKAfile, December 29, 2010, http://www.debka.com/article/20503/.

[37] A telegram from Harrison Symmes, U.S. ambassador to Jordan to the U.S. State Department.
U.S. Government. *Foreign Relations of the United States, 1964-1968, V. 20, Arab-Israeli Dispute 1967-1968.* DC: GPO, 2000.

[38] Gabe Kahn, "Syria to Air 'Israeli Confession' in Mugniyeh Hit," IssraelNationalNews.com, September 15, 2011, http://www.israelnationalnews.com/News/News.aspx/147944#.VM49vWM0Rx0.

[39] Robert Baer, "A Perfectly Framed Assassination." *Wall Street Journal,* February 27, 2010, http://online.wsj. com/article/SB10001424052748704447940457508762144 0351704.html.

[40] "Hamas aide: Leader murdered in Dubai smuggled weapons, *Gulf News,* March 3, 2010, http://gulfnews.com/ news/gulf/uae/crime/hamas-aide-leader-murdered-in-dubai-smuggled-weapons-1.591338.

[41] Duncan Gardham, "Dubai Hamas assassination: how it was planned," *The Telegraph,* February 17, 2010, http://www.telegraph.co.uk/news/worldnews/middleeast/dubai/7251960/Dubai-Hamas-assassination-how-it-was-planned.html.

[42] "Events a Glance," *Strategic Survey 2010,* (London: International Institute for Strategic Studies), 9.

[43] Yossi Melman, "Targeted killings - a retro fashion very much in vogue," *Haaretz*.com, March 24, 2004, http://www.*Haaretz*.com/print-edition/features/targeted-killings-a-retro-fashion-very-much-in-vogue-1.117714.

[44] "Israeli 'Hits' On Terrorists," Jewish Virtual Library, http://www.jewishvirtuallibrary.org/jsource/Terrorism/hits.html.

[45] "Israel used chocs to poison Palestinian," *The Sydney Morning Herald,* March 8, 2006, http://www.smh.com.au/news/World/Israel-used-chocs-to-poison-Palestinian/2006/05/08/1146940441701.html.

[46] "'I shot Abu Jihad' says Israeli commando in new interview," *Israel Hayom,* November 2, 2012, http://www.israelhayom.com/site/newsletter_article.php?id=6288.

[47] John Yang, "Israel's Secret Plan to Kill Saddam," ABC News Nightline, January 11, 2004, http://abcnews.go.com/Nightline/story?id=129003&page=1.

[48] "Israel reveals post Gulf war plan to assassinate, shelved after drill blunder," DefenceTalk | Defense & Military News, December 16, 2003, http://www.defencetalk.com/israel-reveals-post-gulf-war-plan-to-assassinate-shelved-after-drill-blunder-2074/.

[49] Ibid.

[50] Toby Harnden, "Israelis dropped assassination plan after practice run ended in disaster," *The Telegraph* (UK) December 17, 2003, http://www.telegraph.co.uk/news/worldnews/middleeast/iraq/1449688/Israelis-dropped-assassination-plan-after-practice-run-ended-in-disaster.html.

[51] John Yang, "Israel's Secret Plan to Kill Saddam," ABC News Nightline, January 11, 2004, http://abcnews.go.com/Nightline/story?id=129003&page=1.

[52] Uzi Mahnaimi, "Mossad plot to assassinate Saddam," January 17, 1999, http://www.library.cornell.edu/colldev/mideast/mossdm.htm.

[53] Association of Former Intelligence Officers, AFIO Weekly Intelligence Notes #05-99, February 3, 1999, citing the *London Times* of January 17, 1999, http://www.afio.com/sections/wins/1999/notes0599.html.

[54] "Israel reveals post Gulf war plan to assassinate, shelved after drill blunder," DefenceTalk | Defense & Military News, December 16, 2003, http://www.defencetalk.com/israel-reveals-post-gulf-war-plan-to-assassinate-shelved-after-drill-blunder-2074/.

[55] Toby Harnden, "Israelis dropped assassination plan after practice run ended in disaster," *The Telegraph* (UK) December 17, 2003, http://www.telegraph.co.uk/news/worldnews/middleeast/iraq/1449688/Israelis-dropped-assassination-plan-after-practice-run-ended-in-disaster.html.

[56] Karin Laub, "Israel Had Plot to Kill Saddam Hussein," Associated Press, December 16, 2003, http://www.democraticunderground.com/discuss/duboard.php?az=show_mesg&forum=102&topic_id=272732&mesg_id=272732.

[57] "Report says Israel dumped plan to assassinate Saddam," J Weekley.com, January 22, 1999, http://www.jweekly.com/article/full/9977/report-says-israel-dumped-plan-to-assassinate-saddam/.

[58] Association of Former Intelligence Officers, AFIO Weekly Intelligence Notes #05-99, February 3, 1999, citing the *London Times* of January 17, 1999, http://www.afio.com/sections/wins/1999/notes0599.html.

[59] Charles Krauthammer, "Land Without Peace: Why Arafat Will Not Stop His War," *Washington Post,* May, 18, 2001, http://www.freeman.org/m_online/June01/.

[60] Amos Harel, Amira Hass, "IDF kills two terrorists in West Bank on way to suicide bombing," *Haaretz*.com, March 14, 2002, http://www.*Haaretz*.com/news/idf-kills-two-terrorists-in-west-bank-on-way-to-suicide-bombing-1.50470.

[61] Nidal al-Mughrabi, "Pals kill six Israelis- Display Body Parts in Plastic Bags," May 11, 2004, http://middleeast. atspace.com/thread1865_1.html.

[62] Arthur Max, "2 killed in Israeli payback move: Palestinians defiled bodies, officials say," *The San Diego Union-Tribune,* July 24, 2004, http://www.signonsandiego.com/uniontrib/20040724/news_1n24mideast.html. *See* also Arnon Regular Haaretz Service, "PA calls on militants to return body parts of IDF troops," *Haaretz*.com, May 11, 2004, http://www.*Haaretz*.com/news/pa-calls-on-militants-to-return-body-parts-of-idf-troops-1.122042.

[63] Adam Goldman and Ellen Nakashima, "CIA and Mossad killed senior Hezbollah figure in car bombing," *Washington Post,* January 30, 2015, http://www.washingtonpost.com/world/national-security/cia-and-mossad-killed-senior-hezbollah-figure-in-car-bombing/2015/01/30/ebb88682-968a-11e4-8005-1924ede3e54a_story.html.

[64] Wills Robinson, "Revealed: CIA conducted joint operation with Mossad to kill Hezbollah leader dubbed 'Osama Bin Laden of the eighties' in a car bomb attack," *Daily Mail,* January 31, 2015, http://www.dailymail. co.uk/news/article-2934673/CIA-conducted-joint-operation-Mossad-kill-Hezbollah-leader-dubbed-Osama-Bin-Laden-eighties-car-bomb-attack.html.

[65] "World a 'better place' without Hezbollah leader: US spokesman," Agence France Press, February 13, 2008, http://afp.google.com/article/ALeqM5iQoAJbQ3bB4EqIVVj4HYlvJ-TcDg. Arthur Max, "2 killed in Israeli payback move: Palestinians defiled bodies, officials say," *The San Diego Union-Tribune,* July 24, 2004, http://www. signonsandiego.com/uniontrib/20040724/news_1n24mideast.html. *See* also Arnon Regular *Haaretz* Service, "PA calls on militants to return body parts of IDF troops," *Haaretz*.com, May 11, 2004, http://www.*Haaretz*. com/news/pa-calls-on-militants-to-return-body-parts-of-idf-troops-1.122042.

[66] "World a 'better place' without Hezbollah leader: US spokesman," Agence France Press, February 13, 2008, http://afp.google.com/article/ALeqM5iQoAJbQ3bB4EqIVVj4HYlvJ-TcDg.

[67] Anthony Shadid and Alia Ibrahim, "Bombing Kills Top Figure in Hezbollah," *Washington Post,* February 14, 2008, http://www.washingtonpost.com/wp-dyn/content/article/2008/02/13/AR2008021300494.html.

[68] Jeanette Torres, "Israel Says It Was Behind Attack of Palestinian Militant," ABC News Radio, November 4, 2010, http://abcnewsradioonline.com/world-news/2010/11/4/israel-says-it-was-behind-attack-of-palestinian-militant.html."

[69] *See* Todd Beamon and Kathleen Walter, "Ahmed Said to Newsmax: Egyptian Uprising 'Big Revolution'," Newsmax, July 4, 2013, http://www.newsmax.com/Newsfront/ahmed-said-egypt-revolution/2013/07/05/ id/513575 and Wael Nawara, "Was Morsi's Ouster a Coup Or New Egyptian Revolution?" *Al-Monitor,* July 4, 2013, http://www.al-monitor.com/pulse/originals/2013/07/was-morsi-ouster-a-coup-or-new-egyptian-revolution. html.

[70] *Al Mustaqbal* (Paris), September 1, 1979.

[71] "Sunni militants declare Islamic state in Iraq and Syria," FoxNews.com, June 30, 2014, http://www.foxnews. com/world/2014/06/30/sunni-militants-declare-islamic-state-in-iraq-and-syria/.

EVER SHIFTING ALLIANCES

[1] Shmuel Katz, "Surrender to Washington", *The Jerusalem Post,* May 20, 1983, quoted in David Isaac, "Perceived Dependence Syndrome," October 27, 2010, http://shmuelkatz.com/wordpress/?p=349&Source=email.

[2] "Military Requirements for the Defense of the Middle East" (A Briefing by the Chairman, the Joint Chiefs of Staff for the Deputy Secretary of Defense), JCS 1887/61, November 26, 1952, in Paul Kesaris (ed.), *Records of the Joint Chiefs of Staff,* Part 2, 1946–53, the Middle East.

[3] Tim Weiner, *Legacy of Ashes: The History of the CIA,* (New York: Doubleday, 2007), 123 and Yossi Melman, "Trade secrets," *Haaretz,* September 3, 2006, http://www.*Haaretz*.com/hasen/pages/ShArt. jhtml?itemNo=692298.

[4] Peter Snow, *Hussein,* (Washington, DC: Robert B. Luce, 1972), 125.

[5] Hussein. *Uneasy lies the head;: The autobiography of His Majesty King Hussein I of the Hashemite Kingdom of Jordan,* B. Ge6is Associates; distributed by (New York: Random House, 1962).

[6] "Memorandum of Conversation, Palm Beach, FL, December 27, 1962, 10:00 a.m.," in Nina J. Noring (ed.), *Foreign Relations of the United States, 1961-1963,* Volume XVIII: Near East 1962-1963, Washington, DC, U.S. Government Printing Office, 1995, 276-83.

[7] Rob Young, "Project Have Doughnut - Exploitation of the MiG-21," Foreign Technology Division, United States Air Force, retrieved March 24, 2014, http://upload.wikimedia.org/wikipedia/commons/8/8f/Project_have_doughnut_area51_49.pdf.

[8] Jeffrey T. Richelson, *The U.S. Intelligence Community,* (New York: Ballinger, 1989), 276.

[9] According to Henry Kissinger, "an analysis of our capabilities indicated that we had only four brigades capable of reaching Jordan quickly, and such an operation would enlist our entire strategic reserve." Henry Kissinger, *White House Years,* (Boston: Little Brown, 1979), 605.

[10] Gold, Ibid.

[11] Murray N. Rothbard, "The Two Faces of Ronald Reagan," *Inquiry,* 3, 13 (July 7 & 21, 1980), 16–20.

[12] Rodger W. Claire, *Raid on the Sun,* (New York: Broadway Books, 2004), 240.

[13] Chaim Herzog, *The Arab-Israeli Wars,* (New York: Random House, 1982) 347-48.

[14] Rebecca Grant, "The Bekaa Valley War," airforce-magazine.com, June 2002, http://www.airforce-magazine.com/MagazineArchive/Pages/2002/June%202002/0602bekaa.aspx.

[15] Major-General Avraham Tamir, *A Soldier in Search of Peace: An Insider's Look Israeli Strategy in the Middle East,* (New York: Harper & Row, 1988), 214.

[16] http://www.iwise.com/ygQIe.

[17] Karen L. Puschel, *US-Israeli Strategic Cooperation in the Post-Cold War Era: An American Perspective,* Jaffee Center for Strategic Studies, Tel Aviv, 1992, 88.

[18] Ibid., 89.

[19] Wolf Blitzer, "U.S. pilots to train on Kfirs," *Jerusalem Post,* September 1, 1984. *See* also "Young Lions for the Navy," *Time,* September 24, 1984.

[20] "U.S. Navy Leasing Three Israeli Jets," *New York Times,* May 1, 1985.

[21] Ibid.

[22] Ronald T. Pretty, "United States buys Israeli Mastiff RPVs," *Jane's Defence Weekly,* June 9, 1984, 900.

[23] Ibid., 106.

[24] Dore Gold, *Israel as an American Non-NATO Ally: Parameters of Defense Industrial Cooperation,* Jaffee Center for Strategic Studies, Tel Aviv, 1992, 25.

[25] Peter Grose, "Better than 5 CIAs," *New York Times,* March 9, 1986. *See* http://query.nytimes.com/gst/fullpage.html?res=9A0DE5D7143EF93AA35750C0A960948260.

[26] Ibid.

[27] Joel Brinkley, "U.S.-Israel Accord Codifies Relations, *New York Times,* April 21, 1988.

[28] Arieh O'Sullivan, "First Joint Maneuvers for IAF, USAF in Negev," *Jerusalem Post,* April 23, 2001.

[29] Aluf Benn, "Obama Learns From IDF," Israpundit, November 5, 2009, http://www.israpundit.com/2008/?p=18056.

[30] Statement of General Bantz J. Craddock, Commander, United States European Command before the House Armed Services Committee, March 15, 2007.

[31] "U.S.-Israeli Relations in the New Era," Bar-Ilan University Session on "U.S.-Israeli Strategic Glue: The Future of Security Cooperation," May 21, 2007, Embassy of the United States, Tel Aviv, Israel. *See* http://telaviv.usembassy.gov/publish/mission/amb/052107.html.

[32] Dore Gold, "Understanding the U.S.-Israel Alliance: An Israeli Response to the Walt-Mearsheimer Claim," *Jerusalem Viewpoints,* Institute for Contemporary Affairs, Jerusalem, September 2, 2007, http://www.jcpa.org/JCPA/Templates/ShowPage.asp?DBID=1&LNGID=1&TMID=111&FID=376&PID=1851&IID=1795.

[33] Michael Eisenstadt and David Pollo, "Asset Test: How the United States Benefits from Its Alliance with Israel," The Washington Institute for Near East Policy, 2013, http://www.washingtoninstitute.org/uploads/Documents/other/AssetTest_Infographic.pdf.

[34] Robert D. Blackwill and Walter B. Slocombe, "Israel: A true ally in the Middle East," *Los Angeles Times,* October 31, 2011, http://articles.latimes.com/2011/oct/31/opinion/la-oe-blackwill-israel-20111031.

[35] Michael Eisenstadt and David Pollo, "Asset Test: How the United States Benefits from Its Alliance with Israel," The Washington Institute e for Near East Policy, 2013, http://www.washingtoninstitute.org/uploads/Documents/other/AssetTest_Infographic.pdf.

[36] Avi Lewis, "Israel's new anti-ballistic missile system 'phenomenal' in testing," *The Times of Israel,* April 1, 2015, http://www.timesofisrael.com/israel-successfully-tests-new-anti-ballistic-missile system/?utm_source=The+Times+of+Israel+Daily+Edition&utm_campaign=2409baf47a-2015_04_02&utm_medium=e-mail&utm_term=0_adb46cec92-2409baf47a-54550797.

[37] "David's Sling System - First Successful Interception Test," Israel Defense, December 25, 2012, http://www.israeldefense.com/?CategoryID=483&ArticleID=1784.

[38] Ibid.

[39] Ibid.

[40] "Lockheed Martin goes with Elbit's pilot helmet for F-35 jets," *Israel Hayom,* October 13, 2013, http://www.israelhayom.com/site/newsletter_article.php?id=12549.

[41] Barak Ravid, "Defense minister leans toward Israeli operation in Iran, as Obama portrays 'weakness,'" *Haaretz*, March 18, 2014, http://www.haaretz.com/news/diplomacy-defense/.premium-1.580421.

[42] Barbara Opall, "Accent on US-Israel Alliance as IAI, Lockheed Launch F-35 Wing Line," Defense News, November 4, 2014, http://www.defensenews.com/article/20141104/DEFREG/311040028/Accent-US-Israel-Alliance-IAI-Lockheed-Launch-F-35-Wing-Line.

[43] "H.R.938 - United States-Israel Strategic Partnership Act of 2014, Section 3," Congress.Gov, March 5, 2014, http://beta.congress.gov/bill/113th-congress/house-bill/938.

[44] Ibid.

[45] Ibid.

[46] Caroline B. Glick, "The Strategic Foundations of the US-Israel Alliance," JewishWorldReview.com April 23, 2010, http://www.jewishworldreview.com/0410/glick042310.php3.

[47] Yossi Melman, "Our man in Sana'a: A Yemen president was once trainee rabbi," *Haaretz*, October 17, 2008, http://www.haaretz.com/jewish-world/2.209/our-man-in-sanaa-ex-yemen-president-was-once-trainee-rabbi-1.255745.

[48] Ibid.

[49] *Africa Report,* June 1967, 37.

[50] Radio Omdurman broadcast June 5, 1967 and BBC broadcast June 6, 1967, as reported in *Middle East Record 1967,* (Jerusalem: Israel Universities Press,1971), 222.

[51] *Middle East Record 1968,* (Jerusalem: Israel Universities Press, 1973), 235.

[52] Danna Harman, "Leaving bitterness behind," *Haaretz*.com, January 28, 2011, http://www.*Haaretz*.com/weekend/week-s-end/leaving-bitterness-behind-1.339712.

[53] Ibid.

[54] Ibid.

[55] *African Contemporary Record: Annual Survey and Documents 1971–72,* (London: Africa Research Limited, 1972), B77.

[56] Ibid.

[57] *Strategic Survey, 1970,* (London: International Institute for Strategic Studies), 53.

[58] Ibid., 52. *See* also Dick Russell, "Israeli Aid in Africa Mostly non-Military," *Jerusalem Post,* October 31, 1971.

[59] "Africa: Rumblings on a Fault Line," *Time,* March 1, 1971.

[60] Rowland Evans and Robert Novak, "Sudan: Russia's Hidden War," *The Washington Post,* January 1, 1971.

[61] "South Sudan: Africa's next major flashpoint," *The Uganda Record,* December 21, 2010, http://www.ugandarecord.co.ug/index.php?issue=74&article=909&seo=South%20Sudan:%20Africa%27s%20next%20major%20flashpoint.

[62] Danna Harman, "Leaving bitterness behind," *Haaretz*.com, January 28, 2011, http://www.*Haaretz*.com/weekend/week-s-end/leaving-bitterness-behind-1.339712.

[63] "Netanyahu announces Israeli recognition of South Sudan," *Jerusalem Post,* July 10, 2011, http://www.jpost.com/Headlines/Article.aspx?id=228654.

[64] Daniel Pipes, "How Turkey Went Bad," October 13, 2014, http://www.danielpipes.org/14988/how-turkey-went-bad.

[65] Burak-Bekdil, "Zero problems, a hundred troubles," *Hurriyet Daily News,* August 9, 2011, http://www.hurriyetdailynews.com/default.aspx?pageid=438&n=zero-problems-a-hundred-troubles-2011-08-09.

[66] Ibid.

[67] Thom Shanke, "U.S. Hails Deal With Turkey on Missile Shield," *New York Times,* September 15, 2011, http://www.nytimes.com/2011/09/16/world/europe/turkey-accepts-missile-radar-for-nato-defense-against-iran.html.

[68] "Newly-supplied Russian Pantsyr-1 anti-air missile used to down Turkish warplane," DEBKAfile, June 23, 2012, http://www.debka.com/article/22112/Newly-supplied-Russian-Pantsyr-1-anti-air-missile-used-to-down-Turkish-warplane.

[69] Helena Smith, "Cyprus elects its first communist president," *The Guardian,* February 24, 2008, http://www.guardian.co.uk/world/2008/feb/25/cyprus.greece.

ASPECTS OF WAR

[1] Steven Pressfield. *The Lion's Gate.* (New York: Sentinel, 2014), 290.

[2] *See* for example Efraim Karsh, "Seven Pillars of Fiction," The *Wall Street Journal,* August 9, 2013, http://online.wsj.com/news/articles/SB10001424127887324809004578636170899662896?mg=reno64-wsj&url=http%3A%2F%2Fonline.wsj.com%2Farticle%2FSB10001424127887324809004578636170899662896.html.

[3] Population Statistics, http://www.populstat.info/.

[4] Dmitri S. Chuvakhin, Soviet Ambassador to Israel, June 2, 1967.

[5] Tzvi Ben Gedalyahu, "Olmert Slammed For Being 'Tired of Winning'," Arutz 7, August 22, 2006, http://www.israelnationalnews.com/News/News.aspx/110547#.UZ0oR3eC1SE.

[6] "Iran airlifts thousands of Shiite fighters to boost Syria's Aleppo warfront," Osnet Daily, February 21, 2015, http://osnetdaily.com/2015/02/iran-airlifts-thousands-of-shiite-fighters-to-boost-syrias-aleppo-warfront/.

[7] Samuel Katz. *Battleground: Fact and Fantasy in Palestine.*(New York: Taylor Productions, 2002), 165.

[8] Whereas the population has grown (645,000 in 1972, 796,740 in 2009) the ration between Greeks and Turks remained fairly constant. *See Issues in the Middle East Atlas,* Central Intelligence Agency, 1973, 34 and *The CIA World Factbook 2010,* 185.

[9] Burak Bekdil, "Why Golda Meir was Right," *Hurriyet Daily News* (Turkey), August 23, 2011, http://cnpublications.net/2011/08/23/arabs-must-stop-hating/.

[10] Agence France Presse, February 26, 1978.

[11] "63 Zealots beheaded for seizing Mosque," *Pittsburgh Post-Gazette,* January 10, 1980, http://news.google.co.uk/newspapers?id=wesNAAAAIBAJ&sjid=rG0DAAAAIBAJ&pg=6824,1266876&dq=grand-mosque&hl=en.

[12] "Weapons of Mass Destruction: Hama," GlobalSecurity.org, http://www.globalsecurity.org/wmd/world/syria/hama.htm.

[13] Wright, Robin, *Dreams and Shadows : the Future of the Middle East,* (New York: Penguin Press, 2008), 243–44.

[14] "Angry welcome for Palestinian in Kuwait," BBC News, May 30, 2001, http://news.bbc.co.uk/2/hi/1361060.stm.

[15] Burak Bekdil, "Why Golda Meir was Right," *Hurriyet Daily News* (Turkey), August 23, 2011, http://cnpublications.net/2011/08/23/arabs-must-stop-hating/.

[16] "Uncovering Algeria's civil war," Al Jazeera, November 18, 2010, http://www.aljazeera.com/indepth/2010/11/2010118122224407570.html.

[17] "SOMALIA: Hundreds of thousands killed in years of war, says new president," IRINNEWS.org, November 5, 2004, http://www.globalsecurity.org/military/library/news/2004/11/mil-041105-irin03.htm.

[18] "No Running Away From Somalia," *The Nation,* Africa News, June 29, 2007, http://necrometrics.com/20c300k.htm#Somalia.

[19] Pal Kolsto, Political Construction Sites: Nation-building in Russia and the Post-Soviet States, (Boulder, CO: Westview Press, 2000), 76.

[20] "Saleh down plays Yemeni war death toll." Agence France Presse, July 12, 1994.

[21] Abbas Shiblak, "A Time of Hardship and Agony: Palestinian Refugees in Libya," *Palestine-Israel Journal*, no. 4, 1995, http://www.badil.org/en/al-majdal/item/1567-editorial.

[22] Jane Novak, "Comparative Counterinsurgency in Yemen," *MERIA Journal*, Volume 14, No. 3, September 1, 2010, http://www.israelunitycoalition.org/news/?p=6045.

[23] "Yemen says more than 2,000 killed in uprising," Associated Press, March 18, 2012.

[24] "Government fact-finding mission shows 846 killed in Egypt uprising," Associated Press and *Haaretz,* April 20, 2011, http://www.haaretz.com/news/international/government-fact-finding-mission-shows-846-killed-in-egypt-uprising-1.356885.

[25] Caroline Akoum, "Syria: Assad's forces suffer another major loss as rebels capture southern army base," *Asharq Al-Awsat* (English), June 10, 2015, http://www.aawsat.net/2015/06/article55343909/syria-assads-forces-suffer-major-loss-as-rebels-capture-southern-army-base.

[26] Press release from the London-based Syrian Observatory for Human Rights, May 12, 2013.

[27] Rory Mulholland and Jay Deshmukh. "Residents flee Gaddafi hometown," *The Sydney Morning Herald,* October 3, 2011, http://news.smh.com.au/breaking-news-world/residents-flee-gaddafi-hometown-20111003-1l49x.html.

[28] Author correspondence with Dr. Ajai Sahni, Executive Director, Institute for Conflict Management & South Asia Terrorism Portal, March 29–30, 2014, and http://www.satp.org/satporgtp/countries/pakistan/database/casualties.htm.

[29] Burak Bekdil, "Why Golda Meir was Right," *Hurriyet Daily News* (Turkey), August 23, 2011, http://www.hurriyetdailynews.com/default.aspx?pageid=438&n=why-golda-meir-was-right-2011-08-23.

[30] Yoram Ettinger, "The Palestinian fiddle," *Israel Hayom,* August 2, 2011, http://www.israelhayom.com/site/newsletter_opinion.php?id=269.

[31] http://newsgroups.derkeiler.com/Archive/Talk/talk.politics.mideast/2006-08/msg00274.html.

[32] Voice of the Arabs, May 28, 1967.

[33] "al-Azhar Verdict on the Shia," http://www.al-islam.org/encyclopedia/chapter1b/14.html.

[34] Gil Feiler, "Arab Boycott," *The Continuum Political Encyclopedia of the Middle East,* Ed. Avraham Sela, (New York: Continuum, 2002), 54–57.

[35] Dan S. Chill, *The Arab Boycott of Israel: Economic Aggression and World Reaction*, (New York: Praeger, 1976), 1.

[36] James R. Hines, Jr., *Taxed Avoidance: American Participation in Unsanctioned International Boycotts* 5, NBER Working Paper 6116, National Bureau of Economic Research, July 1997, 5, http://www.nber.org/papers/w6116.

[37] Dudi Cohen, "Iran declares boycott on Coca Cola, Intel and 'Zionists'," Ynet news.com, June 30, 2010, http://www.ynet.co.il/english/articles/0,7340,L-3913247,00.html.

[38] Dr. Nimrod Raphaeli, "The Arab Boycott of Israel in the Globalization Age," MEMRI, No. 261, January 20, 2006, http://www.memri.org/bin/articles.cgi?Page=archives&Area=ia&ID=IA26106.

[39] David Lennon, "How to make the Arab boycott list–or fight it," *Jerusalem Post Weekly*.

[40] David Leyton-Brown, ed., *The Utility of International Sanctions*, (New York: St. Martin's Press, 1987), 225.

[41] Clyde H. Farnsworth, "Arabs' Boycott of Israel Is Alive, but Hardly Flourishing," *New York Times*, August 23, 1987.

[42] Doron P. Levin, "Toyota to Sell Cars in Israel, Officials Say," *New York Times*, April 11, 1991.

[43] Gil Feiler, *From Boycott to Economic Cooperation: The Political Economy of the Arab Boycott of Israel*, (London: Frank Cass, 1998), 27.

[44] "That Arab Boycott," *Time*, July 24, 1964, http://www.time.com/time/magazine/article/0,9171,939065,00.html).

[45] "U.S. Names on Arab League's Blacklist, *New York Times*, February 27, 1975 and "Trade: The Spreading Boycott Brouhaha," *Time*, November 8, 1976, http://www.time.com/time/magazine/article/0,9171,918504-1,00.html.

[46] "Office of Antiboycott Compliance," U.S. Bureau of Industry and Security, http://www.bis.doc.gov/AntiboycottCompliance/oacrequirements.html#whatsprohibited.

[47] Adam B. Cordover, "Impact of U.S. Policy on the Arab League Boycott of Israel," http://docs.google.com/View?docid=dfhmfk5p_1fh7gbx.

[48] Clyde H. Farnsworth, "Arab's Boycott of Israel is Alive, but Hardly Flourishing," *New York Times*, August 23, 1987, http://www.nytimes.com/1987/08/23/weekinreview/arab-s-boycott-of-israel-is-alive-but-hardly-flourishing.html.

[49] Peterson Institute for International Economics, *Case Studies in Sanctions and Terrorism*, Case 76-3 (formerly 65-4) U.S. v. Arab League (1979–: Antiboycott Measures), http://www.iie.com/research/topics/sanctions/arableague.cfm.

[50] "Arabs Adding Maxwell to Company Blacklist, *New York Times*, May 6. 1991.

[51] "These Words are Rated 'No' in Jordan, *Newsday*, March 9, 1975.

[52] "'Independence Day' pro-Jewish? Lebanese think so," *Arizona Republic*, November 14, 1996. *See* also Bernard Lewis, *Semites and Anti-Semites: An Inquiry into Conflict and Prejudice.* (New York: W.W. Norton & Company, 1999), 269.

[53] *Schindler's List* was barred not only in the Arab states but in many non-Arab Muslim states. *See* Bernard Weinraub, "Islamic Nations Move to Keep Out 'Schindler's List,'" *New York Times*, April 7, 1994.

[54] "Saudis ban Pokemon cards, games," *Arizona Republic*, March 28, 2001.

[55] Alexander H. Joffe, "The Arab League and peace, after 68 years," Middle East Forum, January 9, 2014, http://www.meforum.org/3715/arab-league-peace.

[56] Mark Pendergrast, *For God, Country, and Coca-Cola: The Definitive History of the Great American Soft Drink and the Company That Makes It*, (New York: Basic Books, 2000), 285–86.

[57] "Arabs Adding Maxwell to Company Blacklist, *New York Times*, May 6, 1991.

[58] "Nestle added to Arab League boycott list," *European Jewish Press*, July 19, 2006, http://www.ejpress.org/article/9654.

[59] *Tishreen,* (Damascus, Syria), April 9, 2003.

[60] Robert Fisk, "Starbucks the target of Arab boycott for its growing links to Israel," *The Independent,* June 14, 2002, http://www.independent.co.uk/news/world/middle-east/starbucks-the-target-of-arab-boycott-for-its-growing-links-to-israel-749289.html.

[61] "List of Countries Requiring Cooperation With an International

Boycott," Department of the Treasury, Office of the Secretary, December 19, 2008, http://edocket.access.gpo.gov/2008/E8-30877.htm.

[62] Michael Freund, "'Post' report sparks congressional anger," *Jerusalem Post,* September 20, 2009, http://www.jpost.com/servlet/Satellite?cid=1253198161074&pagename=JPost percent2FJPArticle percent2FShowFull.

[63] Raphaeli, Ibid.

[64] Hillel Fendel, "Jordan Launches Campaign: 'No Zionist Enemy Products,'" IsraelNationalNews.com, May 12, 2010, http://www.israelnationalnews.com/News/News.aspx/137504.'

[65] "Muslim Brotherhood wants end to Egypt-Israeli peace deal," *Ria Novosti,* February 3, 2011, http://en.rian.ru/world/20110203/162433368.html.

[66] Oren Kessler, "Egyptian opposition figure: Rethink Camp David Accords," *The Jerusalem Post,* February 14, 2011, http://www.jpost.com/MiddleEast/Article.aspx?id=208085.

[67] "Egyptians Embrace Revolt Leaders, Religious Parties and Military, As Well:

US Wins No Friends, End of Treaty With Israel Sought," April 25, 2011, Pew Global Attitudes Project, http://pewresearch.org/pubs/1971/egypt-poll-democracy-elections-islam-military-muslim-brotherhood-april-6-movement-israel-obama.

[68] "ElBaradei: We'll fight back if Israel attacks Gaza," Ynet News.com, April 4, 2011, http://www.ynetnews.com/articles/0,7340,L-4051939,00.html.

[69] Robert Spencer, "Egypt Rushes Toward Shari'a and War," Jihad Watch, May 31, 2011, http://www.humanevents.com/article.php?id=43807.

[70] Elad Benari, "Egypt: Protesters Call for 'Destruction of Allah's Enemies," Arutz 7 Israel National News, August 26, 2011, http://www.israelnationalnews.com/News/News.aspx/147248#.TlrNRKhws60.

[71] Khaled Abu Toameh, "Egypt Rewards Violence, Paves the Way for More," Hudson New York, September 16, 2011, http://www.hudson-ny.org/2431/egypt-rewards-violence.

[72] "Cairo mob ransacks, torches Israeli embassy. Ambassador flown out," DEBKAfile, September 10, 2011, http://www.debka.com/article/21288/.

[73] Adrian Blomfield, "Egypt PM says Camp David 'not sacred,'" Sydney Morning Herald, September 17, 2011, http://www.smh.com.au/world/egypt-pm-says-camp-david-not-sacred-20110916-1kdvo.html#ixzz1Y7tOYAFj.

[74] "Egypt: Planes patrol Sinai without Israel's consent," AFP, October 13, 2011, http://www.ynetnews.com/articles/0,7340,L-4134749,00.html. *See* also "Sinai air patrol doesn't need permission: Hafez," *Daily Star* (Lebanon), October 14, 2011. 8.

[75] Jack Khoury, "Egypt's Muslim Brotherhood: Fate of Israel peace treaty may be decided in referendum," *Haaretz,* January 1, 2012, http://www.haaretz.com/news/middle-east/egypt-s-muslim-brotherhood-fate-of-israel-peace-treaty-may-be-decided-in-referendum-1.404889.

[76] Text of Egypt–Israel Peace Treaty, "Determination of Final Lines and Zones," http://www.jewishvirtuallibrary.org/jsource/Peace/egypt-israel_treaty.html.

[77] Australia, Canada, Colombia, the Czech Republic, the Republic of the Fiji Islands, France, Hungary, Italy, New Zealand, Norway, the United States and Uruguay.

[78] Associated Press, "Egypt's parliament wants Israel's ambassador out, peace cancelled," *Israel Hayom,* March 13, 2012, http://www.israelhayom.com/site/newsletter_article.php?id=3495.

[79] Gavriel Queenann, "Egyptian Parliamentarians Want Eilat," Arutz 7 Israel National News, August 26, 2011, http://www.israelnationalnews.com/News/News.aspx/147236#.TlfPc6hws60.

[80] Daniel Siryoti, "Amr Moussa: Camp David Accords 'were buried long ago,'" *Israel Hayom*, May 1, 2012, http://www.israelhayom.com/site/newsletter_article.php?id=4155.

[81] "Morsi looks to revise 1979 Egypt–Israel peace treaty," WorldTribune.com, August 15, 2012, http://www.worldnewstribune.com/2012/08/15/morsi-looks-to-revise-1979-egypt-israel-peace-treaty/. *See* also "Adviser: Morsy studying Camp David Accords amendment issue," *Egypt Independent,* Edited translation from *Al-Masry Al-Youm*, August 13. 2012, http://www.egyptindependent.com/news/adviser-morsy-studying-camp-david-accords-amendment-issue.

[82] "Israel-Egyptian peace shaken by Israel's mishandling of Palestinian terror," DEBKAfile, August 20, 2011, http://www.debka.com/article/21226/.

[83] "Peace Treaty Between Israel and Egypt, March 26, 1979," http://www.mfa.gov.il/MFA/Peace+Process/Guide+to+the+Peace+Process/Israel-Egypt+Peace+Treaty.htm.

[84] C.S. Jarvis, *Yesterday and Today in Sinai,* W. Blackwood, 1938, 63. Jarvis mentions forty-five as of 1938, to which must be added the invasions of 1948 (2), 1956, 1967 (2), 1969-1970, and 1973.

[85] L. Eckenstein, *A History of Sinai,* 1921, 135.

[86] U. Heyd. *Ottoman Documents of Palestine, 1552–1615,* 1960, 78, 126–27.

[87] M. C-F Volney, *Travels through Syria and Egypt, in the years 1783, 1784, and 1785. Containing the present natural and political state of those countries,* Vol. 2., Gale ECCO, Print Editions, 2010, 197–98, 208.

[88] Ibid. 209.

[89] Heinz Felix Frischwasser-Ra'Anan, *The Frontiers of a Nation: A re-examination of the forces which created the Palestine Mandate and determined its territorial shape,* Batchworth, 1955, 39.

[90] Richard Meinertzhagen, *Middle East Diary, 1917-1956,* Thomas Yoseloff, 1960, 18–19, 237, 324–25. Meinertzhagen even argued that sovereignty over Sinai (no man's land) was vested in the United Kingdom by conquest in World War I.

[91] C.S. Jarvis, *Three Deserts,* (New York: Dutton, 1937), 3.

[92] *American Foreign Policy, 1950-1955: Basic Documents,* Vol. 1, Department of State Publication 6446, General Foreign Policy Series 117, (Washington, DC : Government Printing Office, 1957), http://avalon.law.yale.edu/20th_century/arm01.asp.

[93] Elad Benari, "Sinai Bedouin Hint: We Were Better Off Under Israel," Arutz-7, May 18, 2013, http://www.israelnationalnews.com/News/News.aspx/168077#.UZj1n3eC1SE.

[94] Rabbi Michael Melchior, "The New Antisemitism: World Conference Against Racism - Durban," Israel Ministry of Foreign Affairs, August 20, 2001, http://www.mfa.gov.il/MFA/MFAArchive/2000_2009/2001/8/The+New+Antisemitism.htm.

[95] Daniel J. Wakin, "Anti-Semitic 'Elders of Zion' Gets New Life on Egypt TV," *New York Times,* October 26, 2002, http://www.nytimes.com/2002/10/26/world/anti-semitic-elders-of-zion-gets-new-life-on-egypt-tv.html.

[96] *See* image http://en.wikipedia.org/wiki/Muslim_Brotherhood.

[97] http://www.investigativeproject.org/document/id/20.

[98] John Guandolo, "The Muslim Brotherhood in America: Deputy National Security Advisor McDonough Meets with Hamas Support Entity," Breitbart.com, March 7, 2011, http://www.breitbart.com/Big-Peace/2011/03/07/The-Muslim-Brotherhood-in-America---Deputy-National-Security-Advisor-McDonough-Meets-with-Hamas-Support-Entity.

[99] Rania El Gamal, Maggie Fick, and Omar Fahmy, "Saudi Arabia designates Muslim Brotherhood terrorist group," Reuters, March 7, 2014, http://www.reuters.com/article/2014/03/07/us-saudi-securi-

ty-idUSBREA260SM20140307?utm_source=Sailthru&utm_medium=email&utm_term=*Mideast%20 Brief&utm_campaign=Mideast%20brief%203-7-14.

[100] "HM announces measures to enhance security," Press Information Bureau (Government of India), December 11, 2008, http://pib.nic.in/release/release.asp?relid=45446.

[101] Efraim Karsh, "Palestinian Leaders Don't Want an Independent State," *Middle East Quarterly*, Summer 2014, http://www.meforum.org/3831/palestinians-reject-statehood.

[102] "Fatah Wins Control of Palestine Group," *New York Times,* February 5, 1969; 5.

[103] Neil C. Livingsone and David Halevy, *Inside the PLO.* (New York: William Morrow, 1990), 62, citing Alan Hart, *Arafat: Terrorist or Peacemaker?* (London: Sidgwick and Jackson, 1984), 87.

[104] Aaron D. Pina, "Palestinian Factions," CRS Report for Congress, June 8, 2005, http://www.fas.org/sgp/crs/mideast/RS21235.pdf.

[105] Protocol 1, Additional to the Geneva Conventions, 1977, Part IV: Civilian Population, Section 1: General, Protection Against Effects of Hostilities, http://deoxy.org/wc/wc-proto.htm.

[106] *Washington Post,* June 16, 1982, http://www.palestinefacts.org/pf_1967to1991_lebanon_198x_backgd.php.

[107] Philip D. Curtin, *The Atlantic Slave Trade: A Census,* (Madison, WI: University of Wisconsin Press, 1969), 268. Curtin allowed for an error of plus/minus ten percent. *See* also Philip D. Curtin, Roger Antsey, and J.E. Inikori, *Journal of African History,* 17 (1970), 595-627.

[108] John Ralph Willis, *Slaves and Slavery in Muslim Africa,* (Totowa, NJ: Frank Cass, 1985), x.

[109] Peter Hammond, *Slavery, Terrorism and Islam: The Historical Roots and Contemporary Threat,* 3rd ed. (Cape Town: Frontline Fellowship, 2010), 2.

[110] R. Brunschvig, "Abd," in *Encyclopedia of Islam*, new ed., 33 as cited in John Alembillah Azumah, *The Legacy of Arab-Islam in Africa,* (Oxford, England: OneWorld Publications, 2001), 159.

[111] Gustav Nachtigal, *Sahara and Sudan,* Vol. 2, (Amherst, NY: Humanities Press, 1986), 217. *See* also J.O. Hunwick, "Black Slaves in the Mediterranean World," 22, in John Willis (ed.) *Slaves and Slavery in Muslim Africa: Volume II - The Servile Estate,* (London: Frank Cass, 1985), and Allan Fisher and Humphrey Fisher, *Slavery and Muslim Society in Africa: The Institution in Saharan and Sudanic Africa and the Trans-Saharan Trade,* (London: C Hurst & Co Publishers Ltd., 1970), 145–46.

[112] Reuben Levy, *The Social Structure of Islam,* (Cambridge: Cambridge, 1957), 88.

[113] Thomas Ricks, "Slaves and Slave Trading in Shi'a Iran, A.D. 1500–1900," *Journal of Asian and African Studies,* 36 (2001), 408.

[114] Murray Gordon, *Slavery in the Arab World,* New Amsterdam, NY, 1989, 232.

[115] Ibid., 234.

[116] "Mauritanian MPs pass slavery law," BBC News, August 9, 2007, http://news.bbc.co.uk/2/hi/africa/6938032.stm.

[117] Ibid.

[118] John Eibner, "My Career Redeeming Slaves," *Middle East Quarterly,* 4, No. 4, December 1999, 3–16, http://www.meforum.org/449/my-career-redeeming-slaves.

[119] "Mauritania: Prosecutor seeks prison for anti-slavery activists," *Jihad Watch,* August 18, 2011, http://www.jihadwatch.org/2011/08/mauritania-prosecutor-seeks-prison-for-anti-slavery-activists.html.

[120] Richard Spencer, "Thousands of Yazidi women sold as sex slaves 'for theological reasons', says Isil," *The Telegraph* (UK), October 13, 2014, http://www.telegraph.co.uk/news/worldnews/islamic-state/11158797/Thousands-of-Yazidi-women-sold-as-sex-slaves-for-theological-reasons-says-Isil.html.

[121] Alan Fisher, "Muscovy and the Black Sea Slave Trade," *Canadian American Slavic Studies* 6 (1972), 585–94.

[122] Arnaud de Borchgrave, "Commentary: Al-Qaida's navy?", August 10, 2009, http://www.upi.com/Emerging_Threats/2009/08/10/Commentary-Al-Qaidas-navy/UPI-37721249909200/.

[123] "The Barbary Treaties: Tripoli 1796 – Barlow's Receipt of Goods," The Avalon Project Yale Law School. http://www.yale.edu/lawweb/avalon/diplomacy/barbary/bar1796t.htm#t1.

[124] Joshua E. London, *Victory in Tripoli*, (Hoboken, NJ: John Wiley and Sons, 2005, 111.

[125] Hamet presented a Mameluke sword to O'Bannon, which led to adoption of the sword by all U.S. Marine officers to this day.

[126] Gardner W. Allen, *Our Navy and the Barbary Corsairs*, (Hamden, CT: Archon Books, 1965), 278.

[127] "Chronology of aviation terrorism: 1968–2004," *Skyjack Aviation Terrorism Research,* http://www.skyjack. co.il/chronology.htm.

[128] John J. Goldman, "Abbas' Arrest Ends Family's Long Wait," *Los Angeles Times,* April 17, 2003, http://articles. latimes.com/2003/apr/17/news/war-quest17.

[129] Brig.-Gen. (res.) Udi Dekel, "Defensible Borders to Secure Israel's Future: Control of Territorial Airspace and the Electromagnetic Spectrum," http://www.jcpa.org/text/security/executive_summary.pdf.

[130] Heraldscotland staff, "Pirates call all the shots," September 27, 2008, http://www.heraldscotland.com/ pirates-call-all-the-shots-1.829180.

[131] Nancy Knudsen, "IMB's Piracy Hotspots from 2009," IMB, February 16, 2010, http://www.sail-world.com/ USA/IMBs-Piracy-Hotspots-from-2009/66507.

[132] Jack Healy, "Emirates Official Says Japan Tanker Was Attacked," *New York Times,* August 6, 2010, http:// www.nytimes.com/2010/08/07/world/middleeast/07tanker.html.

[133] "Press Release: Incident involving the VLCC *M. STAR,* west of the Strait of Hormuz," Mitsui O.S.K. Lines, July 28, 2010, http://www.mol.co.jp/pr-e/2010/e-pr-1037.html.

[134] "US to sell Israel massive military fuel stocks worth $2 bn," DEBKAfile, August 28, 2010, http://www.debka. com/article/8997/.

[135] "Al-Qaeda ally claims tanker attack," Al Jazeera.net, August 4, 2010, http://english.aljazeera.net/news/mid-dleeast/2010/08/20108442348911286.html.

[136] Stephen Askins, "Piracy – a review of 2009," Ince & Co Shipping Brief, February, 2010, http://www.incelaw. com/whatwedo/shipping/article/shipping-e-brief-february-2010/Piracy-a-review-of-2009.

[137] "1976 - Islamic Terrorism Timeline," Prophet of Doom, http://prophetofdoom.net/Islamic_Terrorism_ Timeline_1976.Islam.

[138] "US–Libya compensation deal sealed," BBC News, August 14, 2008, http://news.bbc.co.uk/2/hi/ameri-cas/7561271.stm.

[139] Ibid.

[140] "Libyan convicted in Lockerbie bombing is dead, son says," *Los Angeles Times,* May 20, 2012, http:// www.latimes.com/news/nationworld/world/la-abdel-basset-ali-megrahi-libyan-convicted-in-lockerbie-bomb-ing-has-died-20120520,0,5115988.story.

[141] Ibid.

[142] Gerri Peev, "Gaddafi 'personally gave the order for Lockerbie bombing' and I have PROOF, claims dictator's former justice minister," MailOnline, February 24, 2011, http://www.dailymail.co.uk/news/article-1359910/ Libyas-Gaddafi-DID-personally-order-Lockerbie-bombing-claims-Justice-minister.html.

[143] For a more complete discussion *see* my book: *From Jerusalem to the Lion of Judah and Beyond,* (Bloomington: iUniverse, 2012),

[144] "How Much Do US Presidents Know about Terror," DEBKAfile, May 19, 2002, http://www.takeoverworld. info/Debka_Terror3.pdf and July 29, 2009, http://www.debka.com/article.php?aid=274.

[145] "Egyptian Terror-master Fazul Commanded Mombasa Attacks," November 30, 2002, http://groups.yahoo. com/group/Am-Yisrael/message/8005.

[146] "Al Qaeda's dead East Africa terror chief targeted the US and Israel," DEBKAfile, June 11, 2011, http://www.debka.com/article/21018/printversion/.

[147] Two Israeli companies have been in the forefront of aircraft protection, especially against MANPADS (Man-portable air-defense systems) which are shoulder-launched surface-to-air missiles (SAMs). Since least 2003, Elta Systems Ltd., has had "FLIGHT GUARD," a flare-based anti-missile countermeasure system. Starting in 2008, Elbrit Systems has had a laser-based Multi-Spectral Infrared Countermeasures–"MUSIC"–system (*see* video clip http://www.youtube.com/embed/uVlERTFVSpo?rel=0).

[148] "Kenyan police find Mombasa missiles," BBC News, December 6, 2002, http://news.bbc.co.uk/2/hi/africa/2552097.stm.

[149] Carrie Satterlee, "Saddam Hussein's Violations of the Geneva Convention," April 17, 2003, http://www.heritage.org/research/iraq/wm260.cfm.

[150] *Convention on the Rights of the Child,* Office of the United Nations High Commissioner for Human Rights, http://www2.ohchr.org/english/law/crc.htm.

[151] The Abuse of Human Rights in Iran, London: House of Commons, Parliamentary Human Rights Groups, 1986, 41.

[152] *New York Times Magazine,* December 2, 1984, 21.

[153] Matthias Kuentzel, "Ahmadinejad's world," July 30, 2006, http://www.crethiplethi.com/ahmadinejads-world/islamic-countries/iran-islamic-countries/2009/.

[154] Hossein Aryan, "How Schoolchildren Are Brainwashed In Iran," Radio Free Europe Radio Liberty, May 27, 2010, http://www.rferl.org/content/Commentary_How_Schoolchildren_Are_Brainwashed_In_Iran/2054304.html.

[155] Majid Khadduri, *War and Peace in the Law of Islam,* The Lawbook Exchange Ltd., 2006, 119, 131.

[156] Menachem Begin, *The Revolt,* Revised edition, (New York: Nash Publishing, 1977), 163 and interview with the author, Tel Aviv, January 1, 1971.

[157] Uri Milstein, *The War of Independence: Out of Crisis Came Decision* - Volume IV [Hebrew] (Tel Aviv: Zmora-Bitan Publishers, 1991), 257, (interview with Mordechai Gihon). Milstein found the report in the Israel Defense Forces Archives, War of Independence Collection 83/17, Reports of "Teneh," April 9, 1948. *See* also IDF Archives 500/48/29 409 - information packet paragraph 2.

[158] Milstein interview with Haganah agent Yona Ben-Sasson, November 12, 1980; also, Milstein, citing the Ben-Nur Report in the David Shaltiel Archives.

[159] "Deir Yassin: History of a Lie," March 9, 1998, http://www.deiryassin.org/denierspr-980309-99.html. As the result of this 1998 study, a total of 170 English-language history books which refer to the battle of Deir Yassin were analyzed. Only 8 of the 170 raised serious doubts as to whether or not there had been a massacre. Of the 162 books which stated definitively that a massacre had occurred, 94 of them, 58 percent gave no source whatsoever for their accusation, and an additional thirty-eight, 23.4 percent cited only secondary sources for the massacre claim. In other words, a total of 81.4 percent of the authors claiming a massacre did so without undertaking any original research to substantiate their claim.

[160] *Background Notes on Current Themes - No.6: Dir Yassin,* Ministry for Foreign Affairs, Information Division, Jerusalem, March 16, 1969, 1–2.

[161] Ibid., 4.

[162] Begin, Ibid., 164, and confirmed in an interview with the author, Tel Aviv, January 1, 1971.

[163] *Background Notes on Current Themes - No.6: Dir Yassin,* Ministry for Foreign Affairs, Information Division, Jerusalem, March 16, 1969, 5-6.

[164] Ibid., 6.

[165] "Protocol Additional to the Geneva Conventions of 12 August 1949, and relating to the Protection of Victims of International Armed Conflicts (Protocol 1) (2nd part)," Office of the United Nations High Commissioner for Human Rights, http://www2.ohchr.org/english/law/protocol1_2.htm.

[166] "Photos that damn Hezbollah," *Sunday Herald* (Australia), July 30, 2006, http://www.news.com.au/heraldsun/story/0, 19955774-5007220,00.html.

[167] Yaakov Katz, "Leak: Iran used Red Crescent to smuggle weapons," *Jerusalem Post,* November 28, 2010, http://www.jpost.com/IranianThreat/News/Article.aspx?id=197124.

[168] Maayana Miskin, "Hizbullah Hides Behind Handicapped Children," Arutz Sheva, IsraelNationalNews.com, August 16, 2010.

[169] Protocol 1, Additional to the Geneva Conventions, 1977, Part IV: Civilian Population, Article 38, paragraph 1, http://www.heritage.org/research/iraq/wm260.cfm.

[170] Itamar Marcus, Barbara Crook and Nan Jacques Zilberdik, "Eye-witnesses: Hamas used human shields in Gaza war," PMW Palestinian Media Watch, September 16, 2009, http://www.palwatch.org/main.aspx?fi=157&doc_id=1304.

[171] https://www.kintera.com/kintera_sphere/Email/New/EmailEditor.aspx#_ftnref10, Jason Koutsoukis, "Hamas tried to hijack ambulances during Gaza war," *The Sydney Morning Herald,* January 26, 2009, http://www.smh.com.au/news/world/hamas-tried-to-hijack-ambulances-during-gaza-war/2009/01/25/1232818246374.html.

[172] *Al-Hayat Al-Jadida,* January 27, 2009. *See* also "Palestinian witnesses: Hamas used civilians as human shields in Gaza war," http://www.palwatch.org/main.aspx?fi=157&doc_id=1304.

[173] https://www.kintera.com/kintera_sphere/Email/New/EmailEditor.aspx#_ftnref7 "Hamas Exploitation of Medical Institutions" Israel General Security Services, March 2009; http://www.shabak.gov.il/SiteCollectionImages/ percentD7 percentA1 percentD7 percentA7 percentD7 percent99 percentD7 percentA8 percentD7 percent95 percentD7 percentAA percent20 percentD7 percent95 percentD7 percentA4 percentD7 percentA8 percentD7 percentA1 percentD7 percent95 percentD7 percent9E percentD7 percent99 percentD7 percent9D/terror-portal/docs/english/hamasshield_en.pdf; Amir Mizroch, "Dichter: Hamas salaries paid Shifa Hospital," *The Jerusalem Post,* January 12, 2009; and http://www.jpost.com/servlet/Satellite?cid=1231424936164&pagename=JPost percent2FJPArticle percent2FShowFull.

[174] https://www.kintera.com/kintera_sphere/Email/New/EmailEditor.aspx#_ftnref2> Mizroch, Amir, "Dichter: Hamas salaries paid Shifa Hospital," *The Jerusalem Post,* January 12, 2009; http://www.jpost.com/servlet/Satellite?cid=1231424936164&pagename=JPost percent2FJPArticle percent2FShowFull "The Operation in Gaza: Factual and Legal Aspects," Israel Ministry of Foreign Affairs, July 2009, 57 and http://www.mfa.gov.il/NR/rdonlyres/E89E699D-A435-491B-B2D0-017675DAFEF7/0/GazaOperation.pdf.

[175] https://www.kintera.com/kintera_sphere/Email/New/EmailEditor.aspx#_ftnref5 Itamar Marcus and Barbara Crook, "Hamas using children in combat support roles," *Palestinian Media Watch,* January 13, 2009 and http://www.pmw.org.il/Bulletins_Jan2009.htm.

[176] Robert Spencer, "Hamas killed 160 "Palestinian" children to build jihad terror tunnels," Jihad Watch, July 25, 2014, http://www.jihadwatch.org/2014/07/hamas-killed-160-palestinian-children-to-build-jihad-terror-tunnels.

[177] https://www.kintera.com/kintera_sphere/Email/New/EmailEditor.aspx#_ftnref9, "The Operation in Gaza: Factual and Legal Aspects," Israel Ministry of Foreign Affairs, July 2009, 57 and http://www.mfa.gov.il/NR/rdonlyres/E89E699D-A435-491B-B2D0-017675DAFEF7/0/GazaOperation.pdf.

[178] Steven Erlanger and Taghreed El-Khodary, "A Gaza War Full of Traps and Trickery," *New York Times,* January 10, 2009, http://www.nytimes.com/2009/01/11/world/middleeast/11hamas.html?pagewanted=all&_r=0.

[179] https://www.kintera.com/kintera_sphere/Email/New/EmailEditor.aspx#_ftnref8, Rod Nordland, "Hamas and Its Discontents," *Newsweek,* January 20, 2009, http://www.newsweek.com/id/180691.

[180] For videos showing the use by Hamas of human shields during the Gaza War:

December 27, 2008–Footage of a civilian building in which weapons and explosives were being stored. http://www.terrorism-info.org.il/malam_multimedia/Hebrew/heb_n/video/v12b.wmv, The IDF telephoned the residents of the building, telling them to leave so they would not be harmed by the planned air strike. Numerous civilians appear on the rooftop to prevent the air strike, which was then called off to avoid harming civilians.

January 6, 2009–Footage of a terrorist shooting from a roof-top. http://www.terrorism-info.org.il/malam_multimedia/Hebrew/heb_n/video/v9.wmv; The terrorist then identifies an Israel Air Force (IAF) aircraft preparing to fire on him and calls a group of children into the house where he is located to prevent the IAF strike. He then flees the house using the children as shields.

January 8, 2009–Footage of Hamas operatives arming a rocket launcher in a school yard in Gaza http://www.youtube.com/watch?v=UN9WzUc7iB0&feature=channel_page.

January 12, 2009–Footage of a group of terrorists, one a senior operative, using children and a woman with a baby as human shields. http://www.terrorism-info.org.il/malam_multimedia/Hebrew/heb_n/video/v11.wmv, Footage includes IAF radio communications instructing the aircraft operator not to fire on the terrorists because of the woman and children among them.

For additional footage go to:

http://www.theisraelproject.org/site/apps/nlnet/content2.aspx?c=hsJPK0PIJpH&b=689705&ct=6852165.

[181] Tony Karon, "The Homemade Rocket That Could Change the Mideast," *Time,* February 11, 2002, http://content.time.com/time/world/article/0,8599,202159,00.html.

[182] Yaakov Katz, "An intelligence think-tank," JPost.com, March 15, 2010, http://www.jpost.com/MiddleEast/Article.aspx?id=170993.

[183] Yaakov Katz, "Gaza police was incorporated into Hamas military wing," JPost.com, March 15, 2010, http://www.jpost.com/Israel/Article.aspx?id=171013.

[184] Yaakov Katz, "Hamas used kids as human shields," JPost.com, March 15, 2010, http://www.jpost.com/Israel/Article.aspx?ID=171009.

[185] Aaron Klein, "PHOTO: Hamas missile launch pad next to mosque, playground. Civilian factories, gas station also half a block from Fajr-5 firing site," Klein Online, November 15, 2012, http://kleinonline.wnd.com/2012/11/15/photo-hamas-missile-launch-pad-near-mosque-playground-civilian-factories-gas-station-also-half-a-block-from-fajr-5-site/.

[186] Yaakov Lappin. "IDF shows photos of Hamas rocket sites dug into hospital, mosques." Reuters, July 22, 2014, http://unitycoalitionforisrael.org/uci_2014/?p=10352.

[187] http://dailycaller.com/wp-content/uploads/2014/07/Gaza1.jpg.

[188] Ralph Peters, "Appease-y does it for weak Prez on road to a Mideast apocalypse," *New York Post,* September 26, 2009, http://www.nypost.com/p/news/opinion/opedcolumnists/appease_does_apocalypse_for_weak_9HzomoUqSd9gZJINIwtJIL.

[189] Tzvi Ben Gedalyahu, "Mideast in Turmoil: 'Qaddafi a Legitimate Target,' Says Britain," IsraelNationalNews.com March 21, 2011.

[190] "Nato concern Libya use of human-shields in Misrata," BBC, April 6, 2011, http://www.bbc.co.uk/news/world-africa-12989878.

[191] "Debate on the Goldstone Report," United Nations Human Rights Council Emergency Session, October 16, 2009, http://www.youtube.com/watch?v=NX6vyT8RzMo&feature=player_embedded.

[192] Col. Richard Kemp delivered his oral statement under the auspices of UN Watch, a non-governmental organization based in Geneva whose mandate is to monitor the performance of the United Nations by the yardstick of its own Charter. *See* www.unwatch.org.

[193] Michael Ben-Zohar, *Spies in the Promised Land*, (Boston: Houghton Mifflin, 1972), 260.

[194] "Genealogy," The Grand Ducal House of Mecklenburg-Strelitz, http://www.mecklenburg-strelitz.org/gene-alogy.html#.U26QoRDlZx0, retrieved May 10, 2014.

[195] Richard H. Boyce, "Bonn, Israel odds over Germans in Egypt," *Pittsburgh Post-Gazette,* February 23, 1965, http://news.google.com/newspapers?nid=1144&dat=19650223&id=U4bAAAAIBAJ&sjid=Lk8EAAAAIBA-J&pg=7709,2561330. *See* also Ian Black and Benny Morris, *Israel's Secret Wars,* (New York: Grove Press, 1991), 196.

[196] "Daily News Bulletin," Jewish Telegraphic Agency, June 12, 1963, 1, http://pdfs.jta.org/1963/1963-06-13_111.pdf.

[197] Ian Black and Benny Morris, *Israel's Secret Wars,* (New York: Grove Press, 1991), 115.

[198] W. Andrew Terrill, "The Chemical Warfare Legacy of the Yemen War," *Comparative Strategy,* Vol. 10 (2), 1991, 109 and 115 passim.

[199] *Implications of Soviet Use of Chemical and Toxin Weapons for US Security Interests,* SNIE 11-17-83, Central Intelligence Agency, September 15, 1983, 10, www.foia.cia.gov. *See* also Prepared Statement of Amos A. Jordan, Acting Secretary for International Security Affairs, Department of Defense, *U.S. Chemical Warfare Policy; Hearings before the Subcommittee on National Security Policy and Scientific Developments of the Committee on Foreign Affairs; House of Representatives,* May 9, 1974, 151.

[200] SIPRI Publication: Volume 1: *The Rise of CB Weapons: The Problem of Chemical and Biological Warfare,* Almqvist & Wiskell, Stockholm, 1971, 336-341.

[201] Ibid.

[202] Ibid.

[203] Ibid.

[204] Dana Adams Schmidt, *Yemen: The Unknown War,* (New York: Holt, Rinehart and Winston, 1968), 261.

[205] *The Rise of CB Weapons: The Problem of Chemical and Biological Warfare,* 336–41.

[206] Schmidt, Ibid., 263.

[207] "How Nasser Used Poison Gas," *U.S. News & World Report,* July 3, 1967, 60 and "In New Detail–Nasser's Gas War," *U.S. News & World Report,* July 10, 1967.

[208] *The Rise of CB Weapons: The Problem of Chemical and Biological Warfare,* 336–41.

[209] Ibid.

[210] "In New Detail–Nasser's Gas War," *U.S. News & World Report,* July 10, 1967.

[211] Ibid.

[212] *The Rise of CB Weapons: The Problem of Chemical and Biological Warfare,* 336–41.

[213] Ibid.

[214] Schmidt, Ibid., 268.

[215] *The Rise of CB Weapons: The Problem of Chemical and Biological Warfare,* 336–41.

[216] Dany Shoham, "Chemical and Biological Weapons in Egypt," *The Nonproliferation Review,* Spring-Summer 1998, Vol. 5, No. 53, 49.

[217] Julian Perry Robinson, "The Problem of Chemical and Biological Warfare: Volume II: CB Weapons Today," *SIPRI,* Stockholm, 1973, 241.

[218] Ibid.

[219] *Adherence to and Compliance with Arms Control Agreements,* Government Printing Office, Washington DC, 1995, 15; *Arms Control and Disarmament Agency Annual Report,* Section VII: Adherence to and Compliance with Arms Control Agreements, Government Printing Office, Washington DC, 1996.

[220] Hanoch Bartov. *48 Years and 20 More Days,* (Hebrew, Or Yehuda: Dvir, 2002), 304-05.

[221] "Secret Egypt–Iraq Accord Collapses," *Mideast Markets,* June 12, 1989, www.lexisnexus.com.

[222] Wyn Bowen, Tim McCarthy, and Holly Porteous, "Feature, Ballistic Missile Shadow Lengthens," *Jane's International Defense Review* 2, no. 2, January 1, 1997.

[223] Bill Gertz, "Cairo's missile buys violate U.S. laws; North Korea sold Scuds, CIA says," *The Washington Times,* June 21, 1996, A1; Eli J. Lake and Richard Sale, "Egypt buys missiles from North Korea," United Press International, Washington, June 18, 2001; Bertil Lintner and Steve Stecklow, "Supply Depot: Murky Trail Shows How Arms Trade Helps North Korea," *Wall Street Journal,* February 6, 2003, A1.

[224] Eli J. Lake and Richard Sale, "Egypt buys missiles from North Korea," United Press International, Washington, DC June 18, 2000; James Hackett, "Egypt to pose a future threat?" *The Washington Times,* July 23, 2002, A19.

[225] Daniel Siryoti, "Egypt may resume civilian nuclear program, Morsi says," *Israel Hayom,* August 30, 2012, http://www.israelhayom.com/site/newsletter_article.php?id=5612.

[226] Ibid.

[227] IAEA, "Implementation of the NPT Safeguards Agreement in the Arab Republic of Egypt: Report by the Director General," February 14, 2005.

[228] Pierre Goldschmidt, "The IAEA Reports on Egypt: Reluctantly?" Carnegie Endowment for International Peace, June 2, 2009, http://www.carnegieendowment.org/2009/06/02/iaea-reports-on-egypt-reluctantly/1ztv.

[229] "Mubarak's Son Proposes Developing Nuclear Energy," Associated Press, September 19, 2006.

[230] "Egypt's Nuclear Weapons Program," Federation of American Scientists, last updated May 30, 2012, http://www.fas.org/nuke/guide/egypt/nuke/index.html.

[231] Samer al-Atrush, "Egypt announces site of planned nuclear plant," AFP, August 29, 2010, http://www.google.com/hostednews/afp/article/ALeqM5jxXcX4e6sPP56Uflfrh7XAvqCRcw.

[232] Raymond Stock, "As Obama dithers, Egypt ramps up its nuclear options," FoxNews.com, January 9, 2014, http://www.foxnews.com/opinion/2014/01/09/as-obama-dithers-egypt-ramps-up-its-nuclear-options/.

[233] "The Chemical Weapons Programme" in *Compendium of Iraq's Proscribed Weapons Programmes in the Chemical, Biological and Missile Areas,* United Nations, New York, NY, 2007, 49–76, www.un.org/Depts/unmovic/new/documents/compendium/Chapter_III.pdf.

[234] "WEAPONS & TERRORISM: Missiles, Nuclear, Biological, Chemical Weapons, and Conflict in the Middle East," http://www.terrorismfiles.org/weapons/use_of_wmd_middle_east.html.

[235] Al-Majid was tried, found guilty, sentenced to death four times for genocide and crimes against humanity, and executed on January 25, 2010. *See* "'Chemical Ali' executed in Iraq after Halabja ruling," BBC, January 25, 2010, http://news.bbc.co.uk/2/hi/middle_east/8479115.stm.

[236] Ibid.

[237] Efraim Karsh. *The Iran–Iraq War 1980-1988,* (Oxford, UK: Osprey Publishing Ltd., 2002) 42.

[238] Ibid., 47.

[239] Ibid., 49.

[240] Center for Documents of The Imposed War, Tehran.

[241] Farnaz Fassihi, "In Iran, grim reminders of Saddam's arsenal," *New Jersey Star-Ledger,* October 27, 2002.

[242] Interview on FOX News, *Hannity & Colmes,* January 25, 2006, http://usiraq.procon.org/viewsource.asp?ID=003645.

[243] *Al-Thawra* (Baghdad), April 2, 1990 as cited in Majid Khadduri and Edmund Ghareeb, *War in the Gulf, 1990-1991,* (New York: Oxford University Press, 1997), 100.

[244] Alan Cowell, "Iraq Chief, Boasting of Poison Gas, Warns of Disaster if Israel Strikes," *New York Times,* April 3, 1990.

[245] Robert Pear, "Iraq Can Deliver, U.S. Chemical Arms Experts Say," *New York Times,* April 3, 1990, A8.

[246] Elaine Sciolino, "Iraq Report Says Chemical Arsenal Survived the War," *New York Times,* April 20, 1991.

[247] Associated Press, "Text of UN chief weapons inspector statement to United Nations on Iraq," January 28, 2003, http://www.boston.com/news/packages/iraq/2003/blix_text.htm.

[248] The "Amorim report," UN Security Council Document S/1999/356, Annex 1 para. 19.

[249] The "Amorim report," UN Security Council Document S/1999/356, Annex 1 para. 21.

[250] Robert Burns, "Rumsfeld memoir: A few regrets, but not many," Associated Press, February 9, 2011, http://www.msnbc.msn.com/id/41488484/ns/politics-more_politics/.

[251] Douglas Hanson, "Pesticides, Precursors, and Petulance," *American Thinker,* April 2, 2004, http://www.americanthinker.com/printpage/?url=http://www.americanthinker.com/2004/04/pesticides_precursors_and_petu_1.html.

[252] Samantha L. Quigley, "Munitions Found in Iraq Meet WMD Criteria, Official Says," American Forces Press Service, Washington, DC, June 29, 2006, http://www.defenselink.mil/news/newsarticle.aspx?id=15918.

[253] Ibid.

[254] Ibid.

[255] *Iraq Joins the Chemical Weapons Convention,* January 14, 2009, www.opcw.org/news/news/article/iraq-joins-the-chemical-weapons-convention/.

[256] "Pentagon withheld information about decades-old chemical weapons during Iraq War, report claims," FoxNews.com, October 15, 2014, http://www.foxnews.com/politics/2014/10/15/us-troops-wounded-by-decades-old-chemical-weapons-during-iraq-war-report-claims/.

[257] Jonathan Spyer, "Did ISIS Use Chemical Weapons Against the Kurds in Kobanê?" *Middle East Review of International Affairs*, October 12, 2014, http://www.meforum.org/4852/did-isis-use-chemical-weapons-against-the-kurds.

[258] "David Kelly: Scrupulous United Nations weapons inspector who alerted the world to Iraq's biological weapons programme," *The Times* (London), July 21, 2003, http://www.timesonline.co.uk/tol/comment/obituaries/article846159.ece.

[259] *Iraq's Weapons of Mass Destruction Programs,* U.S. Central Intelligence Agency, 15.

[260] "Comprehensive Report of the Special Advisor to the DCI on Iraq's WMD," Central Intelligence Agency, No. 2, September 30, 2004, 1, http://www.cia.gov.

[261] Global Security, "Iraq Special Weapons-Scuds," http://www.globalsecurity.org.

[262] Efraim Karsh, *The Iran–Iraq War 1980-1988,* (Oxford, UK: Osprey Publishing Ltd., 2002) 43.

[263] Wisconsin Project on Nuclear Arms Control, "Iraq's Missile Program," http://www.iraqwatch.org/profiles/missile.html.

[264] Ibid.

[265] Majid Khadduri and Edmund Chareeb, *War in the Gulf, 1990-1991,* (New York: Oxford University Press, 1991), 99.

[266] United Nations Special Commission, "Report on the Status of Disarmament and Monitoring," S/1999/94, January 19, 1999, http://www.un.org.

[267] U.S. Department of Defense Information Paper, "Iraq's Scud-Ballistic Missiles," July 25, 2000, http://www.gulflink.osd.mil/ scud_info. *See* also Majid Khadduri and Edmund Ghareeb, *War in the Gulf, 1990–91: The Iraq-Kuwait Conflict and its Implications,* (New York: Oxford University Press, 1997), 171–73.

[268] U.S. Senate Select Committee on Intelligence, "Report of the Select Committee on Intelligence on the U.S. Intelligence Community's Prewar Intelligence Assessments on Iraq: Conclusions," March 29, 2005, http://www.wmd.gov/ report/ report.html #conclusion. See also "War in the Middle East," *Strategic Survey, 1990–1991,* (London: International Institute for Strategic Studies, 1991), 73.

[269] Mark Nicol, "Revealed: The SAS secret mission to kill in Iraq BEFORE MPs voted to invade," *The Daily Mail,* February 23, 2013, http://www.dailymail.co.uk/news/article-2283450/

SAS-secret-mission-kill-Iraq--BEFORE-MPs-voted-invade.html. *See also* "SAS Gulf War 2 Raid Revealed," February 25, 2013, http://www.eliteukforces.info/uk-military-news/250213-Gulf-War-2-SAS-Raid.php.

[270] Eli Leon, "'British commandos hunted for Iraqi Scuds aimed at Israel'," *Israel Hayom*, February 26, 2013, http://www.israelhayom.com/site/newsletter_article.php?id=7567.

[271] "WEAPONS & TERRORISM: Missiles, Nuclear, Biological, Chemical Weapons, and Conflict in the Middle East," http://www.terrorismfiles.org/weapons/use_of_wmd_middle_east.html.

[272] "Iraq's Nuclear Weapon Programme," IAEA, http://www.iaea.org/OurWork/SV/Invo/factsheet.html.

[273] *Al-Usbu al-Arabi,* (Arabic), Beirut, September 10, 1975.

[274] Marie Colvin and Peter Sawyer, "Saudis Bargained with Chinese for Nuclear Reactors," *Sunday Times* (London), August 7, 1994.

[275] Yana Feldman, "Country Profile 8: Saudi Arabia," *SIPRI*, July 2004, www.sipri.org.

[276] Colvin and Sawyer, 1994.

[277] William J. Broad, "Document Reveals 1987 Bob Test by Iraq," *New York Times,* April 29, 2001.

[278] Jeff Gerth, "Atom Bomb Parts Seized in Britain en route to Iraq," *New York Times,* March 29, 1990, A1.

[279] Barbara Crossette, "Iraqis Set Target of '91 for A-Bomb," *New York Times,* August 26, 1995, 1.

[280] UN RESOLUTION 687 (1991), S/RES/687 (1991), April 8, 1991, http://www.fas.org/news/un/iraq/sres/sres0687.htm.

[281] Global Security, "IAEA and Iraqi Nuclear Weapons," http://www.globalsecurity.org/wmd/world/iraq/iaea.htm.

[282] Paul Lewis, U.N. Aides Say Iraq May Be Concealing Nuclear Material, *New York Times,* June 15, 1991.

[283] Gabriel Schoenfeld, "The Terror Ahead: A nuclear attack? Be very afraid," *Wall Street Journal,* October 21, 2003, http://www.opinionjournal.com/extra/?id=110004197.

[284] Ibid.

[285] The record of these purchases can be found at http://www.IraqWatch.org.

[286] Jacques Baute, "Timeline Iraq: Challenges & Lessons Learned from Nuclear Inspections," IAEA Bulletin 46/1, June 2004.

[287] Gary Milhollin & Kelly Motz, "Iraq: The Snare of Inspections," *Commentary,* October 2002, 51–52.

[288] William J. Broad, David E. Sanger, and Raymond Bonner, "A Tale of Nuclear Proliferation: How Pakistani Built His Network," *New York Times,* February 12, 2004, A1.

[289] Robert Windrem, "Pakistan nuclear 'father's' offer to Saddam," *Nightly News with Brian Williams,* February 4, 2004, http://www.msnbc.msn.com/id/4163638.

[290] "Comprehensive Report of the Special Advisor to the DCI on Iraq's WMD," Central Intelligence Agency, No. 2, September 30, 2004, 14, http://www.cia.gov.

[291] Global Security, "Al-Samud," http://www.globalsecurity.org.

[292] *The Times,* (London) June 17, 2002.

[293] *Comprehensive Report of the Special Advisor to the DCI on Iraq's WMD* (Duelfer report), CIA, Washington, DC, September 30, 2004, http:/www.foia.cia.gov/duelfer/Iraqs_WMD_Vol1.pdf, 239.

[294] http://www.fas.org/irp/cia/product/iraq-wmd.html.

[295] Hans Blix, "The Security Council, 27 January 2003, An Update On Inspection," http://www.un.org/apps/news/printinfocusnews.asp?nid=354.

[296] Melanie Phillips, "Truth and lies over Iraq," January 17, 2006, http://www.melaniephillips.com/diary/archives/001560.html.

[297] *The Washington Times,* October 28, 2004.

[298] Israeli television Arutz 2, December 23, 2002.

[299] *Petah Tiqva,* Yoman Shevu'i supplement (Tel Aviv), February 21, 2003.

[300] "Syria's Weapons of Mass Destruction and Missile Development Program," testimony of John R. Bolton, U.S. undersecretary of arms control and international security, before the House International Relations Committee, Subcommittee on the Middle East and Central Asia, September 16, 2003; BBC News, April 14, 2003; Alexander Downer, Australian minister of foreign affairs, news conference, Canberra, June 5, 2003.

[301] "P.M. Sharon & IDF Chief Yaalon's 2002 statements on Saddam's WMDs confirmed," *Freedom News,* http://freedomist.com/2008/08/30/israel_middle_east/. *See* also Ira Stoll, "Saddam's WMD Moved to Syria, An Israeli Says," *The New York Sun,* |December 15, 2005, http://www.nysun.com/foreign/ saddams-wmd-moved-to-syria-an-israeli-says/24480/.

[302] "Missing Iraqi WMDs," February 6, 2006, http://neveryetmelted.com/categories/middle-east/lebanon/.

[303] "Iraq's Weapons in Syria: Senior Syrian Journalist," *Agence France-Presse,* January 6, 2004, http://www. freerepublic.com/focus/f-news/1259806/posts. *See* also *De Telegraaf* (Amsterdam), January 5, 2004.

[304] Con Coughlin, "Saddam's WMD hidden in Syria, says Iraq survey chief," *Sunday Telegraph,* January 25, 2004, http://www.mail-archive.com/sam11@erols.com/msg00227.html.

[305] *Addendums to the Comprehensive Report of the Special Advisor to the DCI on Iraq's WMD,* GPO, Washington, DC, March 2005, 1, www.cia.gov/library/reports/general-reports-1/iraq_wmd_2004/addenda.pdf.

[306] Duncan Campbell and Brian Whitaker, "Powell's visit to Damascus helps case tension," *The Guardian,* May 4, 2003, http://www.theguardian.com/world/2003/may/05/syria.duncancampbell.

[307] Steve Malzberg, "Ex-CENTCOM No. 2: Intel Showed Iraq Smuggled Out WMDs," *NewsMax,* September26, 2004, http://archive.newsmax.com/archives/ic/2004/9/26/161043.shtml.

[308] Jack Kelly, "Saddam's secrets — and ours," Jewish World Review, July 6, 2006, http://www.jewishworldreview.com/0706/jkelly070606.php3.

[309] Charles R. Smith, "Russia Moved Iraqi WMD," *NewsMax,* March 3, 2005, http://archive.newsmax.com/ archives/articles/2005/3/2/230625.shtml.

[310] Kenneth R. Timmerman, "Ex-Official: Russia Moved Saddam's WMD," *NewsMax.com,* February 19, 2006, http://archive.newsmax.com/archives/articles/2006/2/18/233023.shtml.

[311] Smith, Ibid.

[312] Timmerman, Ibid.

[313] John Loftus, "Shattering Conventional Wisdom About Saddam's WMD's," FrontPageMagazine.com, November 16, 2007, http://97.74.65.51/readArticle.aspx?ARTID=28874.

[314] *Los Angeles Times,* October 8, 1991.

[315] Ira Stoll, "Iraq's WMD Secreted in Syria, Sada Says," *The New York Sun,* January 26, 2006, http://www. nysun.com/foreign/iraqs-wmd-secreted-in-syria-sada-says/26514/.

[316] John Loftus, "Shattering Conventional Wisdom About Saddam's WMD's," FrontPageMagazine.com, November 16, 2007, http://97.74.65.51/readArticle.aspx?ARTID=28874.

[317] Ibid.

[318] Ibid. The full research paper on Iraqi WMD, along with the supporting documents and photographs can be found at http://www.LoftusReport.com" www.LoftusReport.com.

[319] Alissa J. Rubin and Campbell Robertson, "U.S. Helps Remove Uranium From Iraq," *New York Times,* July 7, 2008, *See* also "Last of Saddam's WMD secreted to Canada," http://www.msnbc.msn.com/id/25546334/.

[320] "Saudis parade nuclear missiles for the first time in defiance of US-Iranian nuclear accord," DEBKAfile, April 29, 2014, http://www.debka.com/article/23878/Saudis-parade-nuclear-missiles-for-the-first-time-in-defiance-of-US-Iranian-nuclear-accord.

[321] Anthony Cordesman, *Saudi Arabia Enters the Twenty-First Century,* (London: Praeger, 2003), 325.

[322] John Pike, "Missile Proliferation: Saudi Arabia," Federation of the Atomic Scientists, www.fas.org.

[323] "Two Pakistani N-bombs available to Saudi Arabia," DEBKAfile, December 30, 2010, http://www.debka.com/article/20505/.

[324] Robert S. Norris and Hands M Kristensen, "Pakistan's Nuclear Forces, 2007;" "Pakistani Nuclear Forces, 2006," Stockholm International Peace Research Institute.

[325] Jeff Stein, "Exclusive: CIA Helped Saudis in Secret Chinese Missile Deal," *Newsweek,* January 29, 2014, http://www.newsweek.com/exclusive-cia-helped-saudis-chinese-missile-deal-227283.

[326] Mark Jansson, "Conceding the Saudi Nuclear Breakout," Center for Strategic and International Studies, Washington, DC, February 21, 2012.

[327] "Morsi to shop for nuclear-capable missiles in Beijing en route for Tehran. Netanyahu, Obama meet Sept. 27," DEBKAfile, August 25, 2012, http://www.debka.com/article/22305/Morsi-to-shop-for-nuclear-capable-missiles-in-Beijing-en-route-for-Tehran-Netanyahu-Obama-meet-Sept-27.

[328] "Saudis are buying nuclear-capable missiles from China," DEBKAfile, July 4, 2012, http://www.debka.com/article/22155/Saudis-are-buying-nuclear-capable-missiles-from-China.

[329] Elad Benari, "Report: Saudis Aiming Missiles Israel and Iran," Arutz 7, July 11, 2013, http://www.israelnationalnews.com/News/News.aspx/169812#.Ud7ddndfyCA.

[330] "Pakistan Profile: Missiles" February 2010, http://www.nti.org/e_research/profiles/Pakistan/index.html.

[331] "Pakistan army says missile test is successful," *The Washington Post,* February 10, 2011, http://www.washingtonpost.com/wp-dyn/content/article/2011/02/10/AR2011021000618.html.

[332] Marie Colvin, "How an Insider Lifted the Veil on Saudi Plot for an 'Islamic Bomb,'" *Sunday Times* (London), July 24, 1994.

[333] Yana Feldman, "Country Profile 8: Saudi Arabia," *SIPRI,* July 2004, http://www.sipri.org.

[334] Marie Colvin and Peter Sawyer, "Saudis Bargained with Chinese for Nuclear Reactors," *Sunday Times* (London), August 7, 1994.

[335] Yana Feldman, "Country Profile 8: Saudi Arabia," *SIPRI,* July 2004, http://www.sipri.org.

[336] Ibid.

[337] Arnaud de Borchgrave, "Pakistan, Saudi Arabia in Secret Nuke Pact," *The Washington Times,* October 22, 2003. Originally cited in Sammy Salama, "Report Alleges Saudi Arabia Working on 'secret Nuclear Program' with Pakistani Assistance," WMD Insights, May 2006, http://www.wmdinsights.com.

[338] "Potential Threats To Israel: Saudi Arabia, 'Nuclear Ambitions?,'" GlobalSecurity.com, August 26, 2009, http://forum.globalsecurity.org/showthread.php?t=30771.

[339] "Nuclear Power in Saudi Arabia," World Nuclear Association, September 2013, http://world-nuclear.org/info/Country-Profiles/Countries-O-S/Saudi-Arabia/#.UkoPm3d-lF8.

[340] Yana Feldman, "Country Profile 8: Saudi Arabia," *SIPRI,* July 2004, www.sipri.org.

[341] "If Iran Gets Nukes, Saudi Arabia Will Follow," Media Line, March 3, 2008.

[342] *The Guardian,* June, 29, 2011.

[343] Two Pakistani N-bombs available to Saudi Arabia," DEBKAfile, December 30, 2010, http://www.debka.com/article/20505/.

[344] "Fissile Material Stocks," International Panel on Fissile Materials, January 2013, http://www.fissilematerials.org.

[345] David E. Sanger and Eric Schmitt, "Pakistani Nuclear Arms Pose Challenges to U.S. Policy," *New York Times,* January 31, 2011, http://www.nytimes.com.

[346] "Fissile Material Stocks," International Panel on Fissile Materials, January 2013, http://fissilematerials.org/countries/pakistan.html and David E. Sanger and Eric Schmitt, "Pakistani Nuclear Arms Pose Challenges to U.S. Policy," *New York Times,* January 31, 2011, http://www.nytimes.com.

[347] Arnaud de Borchgrave, "Saudi Nukes in gulf," UPI.com, March 29, 2011, http://www.upi.com/Top_News/Analysis/de-Borchgrave/2011/03/29/Commentary-Saudi-nukes-in-gulf/UPI-64781301396157/.

[348] *Haaretz,* May 30, 2012.

[349] *The Times* (London), February 10, 2012.

[350] "Wednesday's 'News of the Week in Review' Round-up," Isranet Daily Briefing, Volume XI, No. 2,833, May 30, 2012, http://www.isranet.org/wednesday%E2%80%99s-%E2%80%9Cnews-review%E2%80%9D-round-56.

[351] "Geneva fallout: Iran becomes a nuclear power, followed by Saudis. Israel loses trust in Obama," DEBKAfile, November 8, 2013, http://www.debka.com/article/23428/Geneva-fallout-Iran-becomes-a-nuclear-power-followed-by-Saudis-Israel-loses-trust-in-Obama.

[352] Rania el-Gamal and Sylvia Westall, Reuters, April 23, 2014, http://english.alarabiya.net/en/News/middle-east/2014/04/23/Saudi-prince-says-Gulf-states-must-balance-threat-from-Iran.html.

[353] Gordon M. Burck and Charles C. Flowerree, *International Handbook on Chemical Weapons Proliferation,* (New York: Greenwood Press, 1991), 267.

[354] Department of Defense, the United States of America, *Proliferation: Threat and Response,* November 1997, http://www.defenselink.mil/ pubs/prolif/me_na.html.

[355] Kenneth R. Timmerman, "Weapons of Mass Destruction: The Cases of Iran, Syria, and Libya," *Simon Wiesenthal Center Middle East Defense News,* Los Angeles, CA, August 1992, 80.

[356] Federation of American Scientists, www.fas.org/nuke/guide/iran/cw/index.html; U.S. Department of Defense, Proliferation: Threat and Response, April 1996, www.defenselink.mil/pubs/prolif/me_na.html.

[357] *Proliferation: Threat and Response,* Office of the Secretary of Defense, Washington, DC, April 1996, 26. *See also Strategic Survey, 1987–1988,* (London: International Institute for Strategic Studies, 1988), 230.

[358] Stephen Engleberg and Michael R. Gordon, "Germans Accused of Helping Libya Build Nerve Gas Plant," *New York Times,* January 1, 1989.

[359] Bill Gertz, "Chinese Move Seen as Aiding Libya in Making Poison Gas," *The Washington Times,* July 12, 1990.

[360] United Nations General Assembly Document 179 session 45 page 2, March 23, 1990.

[361] Stephen Engleberg and Michael R. Gordon, "Germans Accused of Helping Libya Build Nerve Gas Plant," *New York Times,* January 1, 1989.

[362] Timmerman, *Weapons of Mass Destruction: The Cases of Iran, Syria, and Libya,* 80.

[363] "US Fears Gadhafi Could Unleash Chemical, Nuclear WMD on Rebels, NATO," Associated Press - Newsmax.com, August 23, 2011, http://www.israelunitycoalition.org/news/?p=7122.

[364] Joseph Cirincione with Jon Wolfstahl and Miriam Rajkumar, *Deadly Arsenals: Tracking Weapons of Mass Destruction,* (Washington, DC: Carnegie Endowment for International Peace, 2002), 307; John Pike, "Libyan Nuclear Weapons," Global Security.org, http://www.globalsecurity.org;wmd/ world/ libya/ nuclear.htm.

[365] Kenneth Timmerman, "Weapons of Mass Destruction: the Cases of Iran, Syria, and Libya," *Simon Wiesenthal Center Middle East Defense News,* August 1992, 89.

[366] IAEA Board of Governors, Report by the Director General, "Implementation of the NPT Safeguards Agreement of the Socialist People's Libyan Arab Jamahiriya," 3.

[367] Ibid., 4.

[368] Jack Kelley, "Russian Nuke Experts Wooed," *USA Today,* January 8, 1992; "Libya Denies Offers to Soviets," *Washington Post,* January 11, 1992.

[369] Joshua Sinai, "Libya's Pursuit of Weapons of Mass Destruction," *The Nonproliferation Review* 4 (Spring-Summer 1997), 97.

[370] R. Jeffrey, "U.S. Complains to China About Libyan Arms Shipment," *Washington Post,* April 28, 1992; N. Mengel, *Courier-Mail,* January 20, 1992; Lee Michael Katz, "Nuclear Threat Different, Not Gone, Panel

Warned," *USA Today,* January 23, 1992; "Soviet Scientists," *USA Today,* January 23, 1992; Tom O'Dwyer, "Libya Helps Iraq Dodge Weapons Supervision," *Jerusalem Post,* November 1, 1995; and Barbara G.B. Ferguson, "Libya, Ukraine Sign Deal on Nuclear Technology Transfer," *Saudi Gazette,* June 12, 1996.

[371] Borzou Daragahi, "The World; Details told of Libya's Nuclear Bid; A UN Watchdog Agency's Report Finds the Abandoned Effort Relied on Documents put in Electronic Form," *The Los Angeles Times,* September 13, 2008; Anne Penketh, "Nuclear Bomb Blueprint on Internet, Warns UN," *The Independent,* September 13, 2008; Office of the Director General, "Implementation of the NPT Safeguards Agreement in the Socialist People's Libyan Arab Jamahiriya," Report to the IAEA Board of Governors, September 12, 2008.

[372] *Deadly Arsenals: Tracking Weapons of Mass Destruction,* Ibid., 307.

[373] "Implementation of the NPT Safeguards Agreement of the Socialist People's Libyan Arab Jamahiriya," Ibid., 6.

[374] Ibid.

[375] "They have sold materials enough for 7 nuclear weapons," *Milliyet,* December 8, 2005; "Two Turks Alleged to Nuclear Trafficking," *Sabah,* January 27, 2006.

[376] "Pakistan Nuclear Hero Wanted in Iran Cover-Up: Musharraf," Agence France Presse, September 26, 2006.

[377] Gaurav Kampani, "Proliferation Unbound: Nuclear Tales from Pakistan," CNS Research Story, February 23, 2004, http://cns.miis.edu/stories/040223.htm

[378] Samia Amin, "Recent Developments in Libya," February 10, 2004, Carnegie Endowment for International Peace website, http://www.ceip.org/ files/ projects/ npp/ resources/ Factsheets/ developemntsinlibya.htm.

[379] "President Bush: Libya Pledges to Dismantle WMD Programs," Office of the Press Secretary, The White House, December 19, 2003.

[380] Khalid Mahmoud, "Libya Denies Keeping Nuclear Plant and Washington Asserts It Has Abandoned Weapons of Mass Destruction," *Al-Sharq al-Awsat,* January 13, 2009; *Al-Sharq al-Aws*website referenced in "Libyan–Sources–Deny Nuclear Plant Allegations," *BBC Worldwide Monitoring,* January 13, 2009.

[381] Eli Leon and Associated Press, "Nuclear material found in Libya," *Israel Hayom,* October 31, 2011, http://www.israelhayom.com/site/newsletter_article.php?id=1642.

[382] Gavriel Queenann, "Where Are Qaddafi's Chemical and Nuclear Stores?," Arutz 7 Israel National News, August 25, 2011, http://www.israelnationalnews.com/News/News.aspx/147220#.TlfoZ6hws60.

[383] Jack Anderson, "Syrian Poison Gas is Going to Iran in Fight With Iraq," *Newsday,* October 2, 1985.

[384] Ibid.

[385] W. Seth Carus, "Chemical Weapons in the Middle East," *Research Memorandum* No. 9 Washington Institute for Near East Policy, Washington, DC, 1988.

[386] Statement in U.S. House of Representatives by Representative Bobbi Fielder (California), *Congressional Record,* Daily Edition, May 17, 1984, H4088.

[387] "Weapons of Mass Destruction: Hama," GlobalSecurity.org, http://www.globalsecurity.org/wmd/world/syria/hama.htm.

[388] Ahmed S. Hashim, *Chemical and Biological Weapons and Deterrence, Case Study 1: Syria,* Chemical and Biological Arms Control Institute, 1998, 9.

[389] *Unclassified Report to Congress on the Acquisition of Technology Relating to Weapons of Mass Destruction and Advanced Conventional Munitions for the period 1 January to 31 December 2006,* Office of the Director of National Intelligence, Washington, DC, 2008, 6, http://www.dni.gov/ reports/Acquisition_Technology_ Report_030308.pdf.

[390] Stoll, Ibid.

[391] Robin Hughes, "Iran aids Syria's CW Programme," *Jane's Defense Weekly,* October 21, 2005, http://www.janes.com; Robin Hughes, "Iran and Syria sign mutual assistance accord," *Jane's Defense Weekly,* December 21,

2005, http://www.janes.com; Bhupendra Jasani, "Chemical romance–Syria's unconventional affair develops," *Jane's Intelligence Review,* February 17, 2009, http://www.janes.com/news/security/jir/jir090217_1_n.shtml.

392 Lolita C. Baldor, "General warns of Syrian bioweapons, Iran threat," *The Guardian,* March 6, 2012, http://www.guardian.co.uk/world/feedarticle/10129034.

393 "Yatom: Israel could go to war over Syria's chemical weapons," *Israel Hayom*, July 12, 2012, http://www.israelhayom.com/site/newsletter_article.php?id=5035.

394 Eric Schmitt and David E. Sanger, "Hints of Syrian Chemical Push Set Off Global Effort to Stop It," *New York Times*, January 7, 2013, http://www.nytimes.com/2013/01/08/world/middleeast/chemical-weapons-showdown-with-syria-led-to-rare-accord.html?_r=0.

395 "Syria in Civil War, Red Cross Says," BBC News, July 15, 2012, http://www.bbc.co.uk.

396 Lee Smith, "The Nonexistent Red Line," *The Weekly Standard,* January 28, 2013, http://www.weeklystandard.com/articles/nonexistent-red-line_696370.html.

397 Alex Thomson, "Syria chemical weapons: finger pointed at jihadists," *The Telegraph* (UK), March 23, 2013, http://www.telegraph.co.uk/news/worldnews/middleeast/syria/9950036/Syria-chemical-weapons-finger-pointed-at-jihadists.html?fb.

398 Ibid.

399 "US has seen Syria chemical weapons evidence, says Obama," BBC News, May 16, 2013, http://www.bbc.co.uk/news/world-middle-east-22562372.

400 Jodi Rudoren and David E. Samger, "Israel Says Syria Has Used Chemical Weapons," *New York Times*, April 23, 2013, http://www.nytimes.com/2013/04/24/world/middleeast/israel-says-syria-has-used-chemical-weapons.html?pagewanted=1&_r=0.

401 Syrian Observatory for Human Rights, August 22, 2013, https://www.facebook.com/syriaohr/posts/410896459018698.

402 "Bodies still being found after alleged Syria chemical attack: opposition," *The Daily Star* (Beirut), August 22, 2013, http://www.dailystar.com.lb/News/Middle-East/2013/Aug-22/228268-bodies-still-being-found-after-alleged-syria-chemical-attack-opposition.ashx#axzz2chzutFua.

403 "MSF-backed hospitals treated Syria 'chemical victims'," BBC News, August 24, 2013, http://www.bbc.co.uk/news/world-middle-east-23827950.

404 "Syria chemical attack: Key UN findings," BBC News, September 17, 2013, http://www.bbc.co.uk.

405 "Countdown on for US strike on Syria. Kerry: Assad's chemicals killed 1,429 Syrians, 426 children," DEBKAfile, August 30, 2013, http://www.debka.com/article/23240/Countdown-on-for-US-strike-on-Syria-Kerry-Assad-s-chemicals-killed-1-429-Syrians-426-children.

406 "US rebuffs Syrian access to chemical site as 'too late to be credible'," DEBKAfile, August 25, 2013, http://www.debka.com/article/23220/US-rebuffs-Syrian-access-to-chemical-site-as-%E2%80%9Ctoo-late-to-be-credible%E2%80%9D.

407 "Press release by the Organization for the Prohibition of Chemical Weapons and the United Nations on the advance team in Syria," Organization for the Prohibition of Chemical Weapons, October 11, 2013, http://www.opcw.org.

408 Edith M. Lederer, "Chemical Watchdog: Syria Declared 41 Facilities," Associated Press, October 29, 2013, http://abcnews.go.com/US/wireStory/chemical-watchdog-syria-declared-41-facilities-20709591.

409 Dan Williams, "Israel believes Syria kept 'significant' chemical munitions," Reuters, September 19, 2014, http://www.reuters.com/article/2014/09/18/us-syria-crisis-chemicalweapons-israel-idUSKBN0HD1JX20140918.

410 "Syria Chemical Weapons Facilities 'Destroyed.'" Al-Jazeera, 1 November 1, 2013; Organization for the Prohibition of Chemical Weapons, "Announcement to Media on Last Consignment of Chemicals Leaving Syria," OPCW News, June 23, 2014, www.opcw.org.

[411] Jim Garamone, "Cape Ray Begins Neutralizing Syrian Chemical Materials," US Department of Defense News (Washington), July 7, 2014, http://www.defense.gov.

[412] "UK to Destroy More Syria Chemical Weapons," Al-Jazeera, July 9, 2014, http://www.aljazeera.com.

[413] "US ship finishes neutralizing Syrian chemical weapons," *Israel Hayom*, August 19, 2014, http://www.israel-hayom.com/site/newsletter_article.php?id=19539.

[414] "New Syrian-Iranian chlorine bombs make mockery of US-Russian chemical accord and UN monitors," DEBKAfile, April 21, 2014, http://www.debka.com/article/23857/New-Syrian-Iranian-chlorine-bombs-make-mockery-of-US-Russian-chemical-accord-and-UN-monitors.

[415] Abe Katsman, "UK and U.S. Investigating New Allegations of Syrian Chemical Attacks," Breitbart, April 11, 2014, http://www.breitbart.com/Breitbart-London/2014/04/11/U-K-U-S-Investigating-New-Allegations-of-Syrian-Chemical-Attacks.

[416] "New Syrian-Iranian chlorine bombs make mockery of US-Russian chemical accord and UN monitors," DEBKAfile, April 21, 2014, http://www.debka.com/article/23857/New-Syrian-Iranian-chlorine-bombs-make-mockery-of-US-Russian-chemical-accord-and-UN-monitors.

[417] Dan Williams, "Israel believes Syria kept 'significant' chemical munitions," Reuters, September 19, 2014, http://www.reuters.com/article/2014/09/18/us-syria-crisis-chemicalweapons-israel-idUSKBN0HD1JX20140918.

[418] Ronen Solomon "Assad's Biological Weapons," Israel Defense, February 24, 2014, http://unitycoalitionforisrael.org/uci_2014/?p=6186.

[419] Bill Gertz, "North Korean Scuds added to Syrian arsenal," *The Washington Times,* March 13, 1991, 3.

[420] "Syria's Acquisition Of North Korean Scuds," *Jane's Intelligence Review,* June 1991, 249–51

[421] "Syria sends Hizballah Scuds in disassembled batches," Debkafile.com, April 23, 2010, http://www.debka.com/article/8738/.

[422] Matthew Kalman, "Google Earth Photos Reveal Syrian Scuds," October 7, 2010, http://www.aolnews.com/world/article/google-earth-photos-reveal-syrian-scud-missiles/19666551. *See* also Avi Scharf, "Satellite images reveal: Hezbollah training in Syria missile base," *Haaretz*.com, October 8, 2010, http://www.*Haaretz*.com/print-edition/news/satellite-images-reveal-hezbollah-training-in-syria-missile-base-1.317784.

[423] Ibid.

[424] Alon Ben-David "Israel Sees Increased Hezbollah Capability," *Aviation Week*, May 18, 2010, http://www.aviationweek.com/aw/generic/story_generic.jsp?channel=defense&id=news/awst/2010/05/17/AW_05_17_2010_p28-226325.xml&headline=Israel percent20Sees percent20Increased percent20Hezbollah percent20Capability.

[425] "Hezbollah has a land-based missile range of 300 km," *Al Watan* (Syria), May 27, 2010, http://www.alwatan.sy/dindex.php?idn=80193 and translated http://translate.google.com/translate?hl=en&ie=windows-1256&langpair=auto|en&u=http://www.alwatan.sy/dindex.php percent3Fidn percent3D80193&tbb=1&rurl=translate.google.com&twu=1. *See* also Alon Ben-David, "Israel Sees Increased Hezbollah Capability," *Aviation Week,* May 18, 2010, http://www.aviationweek.com/aw/generic/story_channel.jsp?channel=defense&id=news/awst/2010/05/17/AW_05_17_2010_p28-226325.xml&headline=Israel percent20Sees percent20Increased percent20Hezbollah percent20Capability.

[426] "Assad's deadly agenda: First, chemicals, next, Iskander 9K720," DEBKAfile, December 19, 2012, http://www.debka.com/article/22625/Assad%E2%80%99s-deadly-agenda-First-chemicals-next-Iskander-9K720.

[427] Jerry Gordan, "Game changer: Russian Iskander (SS-26) Mobile Ballistic Missile Delivered to Assad's Syria," *New England Review,* December 8, 2012, http://www.newenglishreview.org/blog_direct_link.cfm/blog_id/45204.

[428] The Kyodo (Japan) News Agency claimed to have spoken directly with Khan about these matters detailed the story on December 31, 2011, which was reported by *Israel Hayom*, "Report: Syria asked Pakistani nuclear

scientist for know-how," *Israel Hayom,* January 2, 2012, http://www.israelhayom.com/site/newsletter_article. php?id=2473.

[429] International Atomic Energy Agency, "Syrian Arab Republic: Research Reactor Details-SRR-1," http:// www.iaea.org; *Nuclear Programmes in the Middle East: In the Shadow of Iran,* ed. Mark Fitzpatrick, (London: International Institute for Strategic Studies, 2008), 73–82.

[430] Ibid.

[431] "NATO squeezes Assad: A Syrian uranium enrichment plant "discovered," DEBKAfile, November 1, 2011, http://www.debka.com/article/21438/.

[432] Desmond Butler, "AP Exclusive: New signs of Syria–Pakistan nuke tie," Associated Press, November 1, 2011, http://news.yahoo.com/ap-exclusive-signs-syria-pakistan-nuke-tie-063913337.html.

[433] Ibid.

[434] "Satellite Photos Support Testimony That Iraqi WMD Went to Syria," PJ Media, June 6, 2010, http://pjmedia. com/blog/satellite-photos-support-testimony-that-iraqi-wmd-went-to-syria/.

[435] Charles R. Smith, "Russia Moved Iraqi WMD," Newsmax.com, March 3, 2005, http://archive.newsmax.com/ archives/articles/2005/3/2/230625.shtml.

[436] IAEA Board of Governors, "Implementation of the NPT Safeguards Agreement in the Syrian Arab Republic," November 19, 2008, www.iaea.org.

[437] David Albright and Paul Brannan, "ISIL Report: The Al Kibar Reactor: Extraordinary Camouflage, Troubling Implications," Institute for Science and International Security, May 12, 2008, www.isis-online.org; Anthony Cordesman, "An Overview: Syrian Weapons of Mass Destruction," Center for Strategic and International Studies, June 2, 2008, www.csis.org.

[438] Erich Follath and Holger Stark, "The Story of 'Operation Orchard,' How Israel Destroyed Syria's Al Kibar Nuclear Reactor," *Spiegel Online,* November 2, 2009, http://www.spiegel.de/international/ world/0,1518,druck-658663,00.html.

[439] David Albright and Paul Brannan, "ISIL Report: The Al Kibar Reactor: Extraordinary Camouflage, Troubling Implications," Institute for Science and International Security, May 12, 2008, http://www.isis-on-line.org; Anthony Cordesman, "An Overview: Syrian Weapons of Mass Destruction," Center for Strategic and International Studies, June 2, 2008, http://www.csis.org.

[440] David Makovsky, "The Silent Strike," *The New Yorker*, September 17, 2012, http://www.newyorker.com/ reporting/2012/09/17/120917fa_fact_makovsky.

[441] Ibid.

[442] Desmond Butler, "AP Exclusive: New signs of Syria–Pakistan nuke tie," Associated Press, November 1, 2011, http://news.yahoo.com/ap-exclusive-signs-syria-pakistan-nuke-tie-063913337.html.

[443] "North Korean yellowcake was bound for Syria when Israel struck plant," DEBKAfile Special Report February 28, 2010, http://www.debka.com/article/8621/.

[444] Nissan Ratzlav-Katz, "Military Action May Not Halt Regional Nuclear Proliferation," Israel National News, September 11, 2009, http://www.israelnationalnews.com/News/News.aspx/133384.

[445] Avi Scharf, "What is Assad hiding in his backyard? Satellite photos of secret Syrian site depict at least five guarded installations whose purpose is unclear," *Haaretz*.com, May 30, 2010, http://www.*Haaretz*.com/ print-edition/news/what-is-assad-hiding-in-his-backyard-1.292935.

[446] Ibid.

[447] Hillel Fendel, "Satellite Photos: More Nuclear Sites in Syria," IsraelNationalNews.com, February 24, 2011, at http://www.israelnationalnews.com/News/News.aspx/142508.

[448] "UN nuclear watchdog refers Syria to Security Council," BBC, June 9, 2011, http://www.bbc.co.uk/news/ world-middle-east-13717874.

[449] James Blitz, "Fears grow over Syria uranium stockpile," *Financial Times* (London), January 8, 2013, http://www.ft.com/intl/cms/s/0/a450b660-5998-11e2-88a1-00144feab49a.html#axzz2HaMdtmQh.

[450] John Hall, "ISIS leader calls on 'every Muslim' to go to the territory his group has seized to build an 'Islamic state," *The Daily Mail* (UK), July 1, 2014, http://www.dailymail.co.uk/news/article-2676347/ISIS-leader-calls-Muslim-territory-group-seized-build-Islamic-state.html.

[451] Gregory F. Giles, Iranian Approaches to Chemical Warfare, December 15, 1997, 5; Anthony Cordesman, "Creating Weapons of Mass Destruction," *Armed Forces Journal International* 126 (February 1989), 54. *See also Voice of the Islamic Republic of Iran,* July 2, 2000.

[452] "WEAPONS & TERRORISM: Missiles, Nuclear, Biological, Chemical Weapons, and Conflict in the Middle East," http://www.terrorismfiles.org/weapons/use_of_wmd_middle_east.html.

[453] Barbara Starr, "Iran Has Vast Stockpiles of CW Agents, Says CIA," *Jane's Defense Weekly,* August 14, 1996, 3.

[454] Con Coughlin Chief, "Iran in Secret Chemical Weapons Deal With India," *Sunday Telegraph,* June 24, 1996.

[455] Con Coughlin, "China Helps Iran to Make Nerve Gas," *London Daily Telegraph,* May 24, 1998, 1.

[456] Statement by Deputy Director, DCI Nonproliferation Center, A. Norman Schindler, on Iran's Weapons of Mass Destruction programs to the International Security, Proliferation and Federal Services Subcommittee of the Senate Governmental Affairs Committee, September 21, 2000, http://www.cia.gov/cia/public_affairs/speeches/2000/schindler_WMD_092200.htm.

[457] "Weapons of Mass Destruction: Biological Weapons," GlobalSecurity.org, April 28, 2005, http://www.globalsecurity.org/wmd/world/iran/bw.htm.

[458] www.sonnaalahwaz.org.

[459] "Ahwazi Organization: Iran is Planning to Attack the Gulf Countries; Iran is Producing Chemical Weapons and Burying the Waste in Ahwaz," MEMRI, October 8, 2009, http://www.israelunitycoalition.org/news/article.php?id=4652. The full report is posted http://www.sonnaalahwaz.org/Central-Archives/Al-Q/20090714-04.html.

[460] "Hezbollah Silent over Report that Group Got Chemical Weapons," *Daily Star* (Beirut), September 4, 2009.

[461] Ronen Solomon, "Explosion at Iranian Military Chemical Complex," Israel Defense, May 9, 2013, http://www.israeldefense.com/?CategoryID=483&ArticleID=2117.

[462] Gregory F. Giles, "The Islamic Republic of Iran and Nuclear, Biological, and Chemical Weapons," in Peter R. Lavoy, Scott D. Sagan, and James J. Wirtz, eds., *Planning The Unthinkable: How New Powers Will Use Nuclear, Biological, and Chemical Weapons,* Cornell (Ithaca, NY: University Press, 2000), 84.

[463] Agence France-Presse, September 14, 2006.

[464] Frederick W. Stakelbeck, "The Iran-Cuba Axis," FrontPageMagazine.com, January 18, 2006.

[465] Bill Gertz, "Iran Tests Medium-Range Missile," *The Washington Times,* July 23, 1998, 1.

[466] Reza Kahlili, "Iran making anthrax secret plant," WND, December 17, 2012, http://www.wnd.com/2012/12/iran-making-anthrax-at-secret-plant.

[467] Ibid.

[468] Ibid.

[469] Barry Schweid, "Washington News," Associated Press, January 9, 1986; Subhy Haddad, "Iraq Says it Has Pinpointed Iranian Missile Launching Base," Reuters, March 29, 1985.

[470] Pejman Peyman, "International News: Iran," UPI, September 18, 1987; John M. Broder, "Five Key Nations Sold Arms to Iran," *The Los Ange6les Times,* January 20, 1988, 5; "Pyongyang Missile Sale to Tehran Reported," *The Washington Times,* June 1, 1988, A2.

[471] "Iran's Missile Program," http://weapons.technology.youngester.com/2008/11/irans-missile-program.html. Retrieved April 15, 2014.

[472] Joseph Cirincione, Jon Wolfsthal and Miriam Rajkumar, "Iran," in *Deadly Arsenals: Nuclear, Biological, and Chemical Threats,* (Washington, DC: Carnegie Endowment for International Peace, 2005), 295.

[473] Uzi Rubin, "The Global Reach of Iran's Ballistic Missiles," The Institute for National Security Studies, November 2006.

[474] Jim Wolf, "North Korea, Iran Joined on Missile Work: U.S. General," Reuters, June 11, 2009; "Iran, North Korea Cooperating on Missile Programs, Says U.S. General," *Global Security Newswire,* June 12, 2009, http://www.nti.org.

[475] Doug Richardson, "Iran Satellite Launch Suggests Advances in Indigenous Missile Technology," *Jane's Defence Weekly,* March 5, 2009.

[476] Steve Rodan and Arieh O'Sullivan, "Iran Test Fires Shahab-3 Missile," *The Jerusalem Post,* July 24, 1998.

[477] James Hackett, "Growing missile threat from Iran," *The Washington Times,* March 2, 1999, A13.

[478] Andrew Koch and Steve Rodan, "Iran Begins Serial Production of Shahab 3," *Jane's Defence Weekly*, October 10, 2001.

[479] Yiftah S. Shapir, "Iran's Ballistic Missiles," *Strategic Assessment INSS*, Vol. 12, No. 2, August 2009, 4, http://www.inss.org.il/upload/%28FILE%291252309053.pdf.

[480] "Recognizing Iran as a Strategic Threat: An Intelligence Challenge for the United States," U.S. House Permanent Select Committee on Intelligence, Subcommittee on Intelligence Policy, Washington, DC, August 23, 2006.

[481] Michael Rubin, "The Radioactive Republic of Iran," *Wall Street Journal,* January 16, 2006, http://www.aei.org/article/23682.

[482] "Recognizing Iran as a Strategic Threat," August 23, 2006.

[483] "Netanyahu, "Iran will next hide nuclear suitcases. Bought 10 years ago from Ukraine," DEBKAfile, March 10, 2014, http://www.dcbka.com/article/23746/Netanyahu-%E2%80%9CIran-will-next-hide-nuclear-suitcases-%E2%80%9D-DEBKAfile-Bought-10-years-ago-from-Ukraine.

[484] "Iran builds nuclear-capable cruise missile able to strike Israel from afar," May 11, 2010, http://www.debka.com/article/8776/.

[485] Frederick W. Stakelbeck, "The Iran-Cuba Axis," FrontPageMagazine.com, January 18, 2006.

[486] "C-801 YJ-1/YJ-8 (Eagle Strike), CSS-N-4 SARDINE," Military Analysis Network, Federation of American Scientists, August 10, 1999; Reuters, January 19, 2010.

[487] "Iran: Continuing Impasse," *Strategic Survey 2008*, (London: International Institute for Strategic Studies, 2008), 217.

[488] In December 2005, Iran signed an arms deal with Russia which included twenty-nine Tor M1 systems to protect its Bushehr facility. *RIA Novosti,* July 13, 2006.

[489] *The Washington Post,* March 6, 2007.

[490] "Russia to return $166.8 million prepayment to Iran for S-300 missile defense system," October 7, 2010, http://en.rian.ru/russia/20101007/160869597.html. *See* also *Jerusalem Post,* October 7, 2010.

[491] "Report: Iran obtains 4 S-300 missiles," *Jerusalem Post,* August 4, 2010, http://www.jpost.com/IranianThreat/News/Article.aspx?id=183608.

[492] Reza Kahlili, "Iran aims biological warheads at Israel," WND, December 4, 2012, http://www.wnd.com/2012/12/iran-aims-biological-warheads-at-israel/.

[493] Ibid.

[494] Nazila Fathi and William J. Broad, "Iran Launches Satellite in a Challenge for Obama," *New York Times,* February 3, 2009; Borzou Daragahi, "Iran satellite launch raises alarm in West," *The Los Angeles Times,* February 4, 2009; Richard Spencer and Michael Levitin, "Iran satellite launch raises West's fears of long-range nuclear missiles," *The Daily Telegraph,* February 4, 2009.

[495] Charles P. Vick, "Weapons of Mass Destruction: Shahab-6," GlobalSecurity.org, January 26, 2009.

[496] Anthony H. Cordesman, Arleigh A. Burke and Adam C. Seitz, "Iranian Weapons of Mass Destruction: Capabilities, Developments, and Strategic Uncertainties," Center for Strategic and International Studies, October 14, 2008, 36, http://csis.org/files/media/csis/pubs/081015_iran.wmd.pdf.

[497] Martin Sieff, "Iran tests new *Sajil-2* missile that can hit Tel Aviv, Athens," United Press International, May 20, 2009; David E. Sanger and Nazila Fathi, "Launching Of Missile Shows Iran Is Advancing," *New York Times,* May 21, 2009; Nicholas Kralev, "Tehran missile test stokes debate; Weapon may reach 1,500 miles," *The Washington Times,* May 21, 2009; Doug Richardson, "Iran launches two-stage *Sejjil-2,*" *Jane's Missiles and Rockets,* June 1, 2009.

[498] Alan Cowell and Nazila Fathi, "Iran Test-Fires Missiles that Put Israel in Range," *New York Times,* September 28, 2009; William Branigin, Thomas Erdbrink, and Walter Pincus, "Iran Test-Fires Its Most Advanced Missiles," *Washington Post,* September 28, 2009; Lauren Gelfand, Allison Puccioni, and Alon Ben-David, "Iran Stands Firm on Nuclear Program Despite International Clamour," *Jane's Defence Weekly,* October 2, 2009.

[499] "Commander Underlines Role of Sejjil 2 Missiles in Boosting Iran's Power with radar-evading capability," December 19, 2009, http://english.farsnews.com/newstext.php?nn=880928149.

[500] Gil Ronen, "Satellite Photos: North Korea Assisting Iran on Missile Site," *Arutz 7,* IsraelNationalNews.com, March 7, 2010.

[501] "Massive Construction Visible Iran's Missile & Space Center Semnan," *Defense Update,* http://defense-update.com/photos/semnan_space_center_200509.html#semnan_nov09. *See* also http://press.ihs.com/photo_display.cfm?photo_id=373.

[502] "EMP: Answer to a Jewish prayer," *The Daily Caller,* March 29, 2010, http://dailycaller.com/2010/03/29/emp-answer-to-a-jewish-prayer/.

[503] "EMP: Answer to a Jewish prayer," *The Daily Caller,* March 29, 2010, http://dailycaller.com/2010/03/29/emp-answer-to-a-jewish-prayer/.

[504] Peter Vincent Pry, "Blackout War - A Revolution in Strategic Imagination," Arutz 7, November 18, 2014, http://www.israelnationalnews.com/Articles/Article.aspx/16000#.VGvtPmM0Rx0.

[505] Thomas Harding, "A cruise missile in a shipping box on sale to rogue bidders," *The Telegraph,* April 25, 2010, http://www.telegraph.co.uk/news/worldnews/europe/russia/7632543/A-cruise-missile-in-a-shipping-box-on-sale-to-rogue-bidders.html.

[506] Reza Kahlili, "Opinion: Iran is Building a Secret Missile Installation in Venezuela," Fox News Latino, May 17, 2011,
http://latino.foxnews.com/latino/news/2011/05/17/iran-building-secret-missile-installation-venezuela/. *See* also Benjamin Weinthal, "'Die Welt': Iran building rocket bases in Venezuela," *Jerusalem Post,* May 17, 2011, http://www.jpost.com/International/Article.aspx?id=220879&R=R4.

[507] "Iran tests missiles for hitting Israel, US bases, first space monkey in July," DEBKAfile, June 28, 2011, http://www.debka.com/article/21072/.

[508] "Iran testing missiles that could carry nuclear weapon, UK's Hague says," CNN, June 29, 2011, http://edition.cnn.com/2011/WORLD/meast/06/29/iran.missiles.tests/.

[509] Ronen Solomon, "Explosion at Iranian Military Chemical Complex," Israel Defense, May 9, 2013, http://www.israeldefense.com/?CategoryID=483&ArticleID=2117.

[510] David Pierson, "North Korea tested miniature nuclear device, state media says," *Los Angeles Times,* February 11, 2013, http://articles.latimes.com/2013/feb/11/world/la-fg-wn-north-korea-nuclear-20130211.

[511] Amir Mizroch, "US intel: Iran's long-range rockets could reach America by 2015," *Israel Hayom,* July 12, 2013, http://www.israelhayom.com/site/newsletter_article.php?id=10643.

[512] James R. Clapper, "Statement for the Record: Worldwide Threat Assessment of the US Intelligence Community," Senate Committee on Armed Services, Director of National Intelligence, April 18, 2013, http://

www.dni.gov/files/documents/Intelligence%20Reports/UNCLASS_2013%20ATA%20SFR%20FINAL%20 for%20SASC%2018%20Apr%202013.pdf.

[513] *Iran's Strategic Weapons Programmes: A Net Assessment,* (London: The International Institute for Strategic Studies, 2005), 9.

[514] "WEAPONS & TERRORISM: Missiles, Nuclear, Biological, Chemical Weapons, and Conflict in the Middle East," http://www.terrorismfiles.org/weapons/use_of_wmd_middle_east.html.

[515] Ibid., 12.

[516] "Pakistani centrifuges launched Iran's nuclear program 24 years ago," Debkafile.com, April 25, 2010, http://www.debka.com/article/8740/.

[517] "Top World Oil Producers, Exporters, Consumers, and Importers, 2006," Infoplease, http://www.infoplease.com/ipa/A0922041.html.

[518] "International Energy Outlook 2009," Energy Information Administration, U.S. Department of Energy, May 27, 2009, http://www.eia.doe.gov/oiaf/ieo/nat_gas.html.

[519] Joseph Cirincione, Jon Wolfsthal and Miriam Rajkumar, "Iran," *Deadly Arsenals: Nuclear, Biological, and Chemical Threats,* (Washington DC: Carnegie Endowment for International Peace, 2005), 303.

[520] Peter Enav and Debby Wu, "How nuclear equipment reached Iran," *The Washington Post* (Associated Press), February 28, 2010, http://www.washingtonpost.com/wp-dyn/content/article/2010/02/28/AR2010022801613.html.

[521] Michael Rubin, "Obama or McCain, Iran Stance Won't Change," American Enterprise Institute for Public Policy Research, October 3, 2008, http://www.aei.org/article/28718.

[522] Michael Rubin, "Iran: Recent Developments and Implications for U.S. Policy," Middle East Forum, July 22, 2009, http://www.meforum.org/2409/iran-developments-implications-us-policy.

[523] *TehranTimes,* March 3, 2009.

[524] *Iran's Strategic Weapons Programmes: A Net Assessment,* (London: The International Institute for Strategic Studies, 2005), 16.

[525] Glenn Kessler, "Nuclear Sites in Iran Worry U.S. Officials," *Washington Post,* December 14, 2002. In defiance of the United Nations, the Iranian government began operating the Khondab plant on August 26, 2006 (Ali Akbar Dareini, "Defying U.N., Iran Opens Nuclear Reactor," Associated Press, August 26, 2006).

[526] Kamal Kharrazi, as quoted by the BBC, "Iran Defiant on Nuclear Plans," December 14, 2002.

[527] IAEA, Board of Governors, "Implementation of the NPT Safeguards Agreement in the Islamic Republic of Iran GOV/2003/40, June 6, 2003.

[528] "Statement by the Iranian Government and visiting EU foreign Ministers," The International Atomic Energy Agency, October 21, 2003, http://www.iaea.org.

[529] *Iran's Strategic Weapons Programmes: A Net Assessment,* (London: The International Institute for Strategic Studies, 2005), 23.

[530] "Iran's Nuclear Program: Expanding the Nuclear Fuel Cycle; Illicit Procurement," Institute for Science and International Security, http://www.isisnucleariran.org.

[531] "Communication dated 26 November 2004 received from the Permanent Representatives of France, Germany, the Islamic Republic of Iran, and the United Kingdom concerning the agreement signed in Paris on 15 November 2004," The International Atomic Energy Agency, November 26, 2004, http://www.iaea.org.

[532] Etel Solingen, *Nuclear Logics: Contrasting Paths in East Asia and The Middle East,* (Princeton, NJ: Princeton University Press, 2007), 172.

[533] "Implementation of the NPT Safeguards Agreement in the Islamic Republic of Iran," Report by the Director General, International Atomic Energy Agency, November 15, 2004.

[534] "Implementation of the NPT Safeguards Agreement and Relevant Provisions of Security Council Resolutions 1737 (2006) and 1747 (2007) in the Islamic Republic of Iran," Report by the Director General, International Atomic Energy Agency, November 15, 2007.

[535] Louis Charbonneau, "More Bomb-Grade Uranium Found in Iran," Reuters, April 2, 2004.

[536] IAEA, Board of Governors, "Implementation of the NPT Safeguards Agreement in the Islamic Republic of Iran," GOV/2005/77, September 24, 2005.

[537] Anne Penketh, "Iran in Showdown with EU Over its Nuclear Ambitions," *The Independent,* August 1, 2005.

[538] UN Security Council Resolution 1696, adopted July 31, 2006, http://www.un.org/News/Press/docs/2006/sc8792.doc.htm.

[539] UN Security Council Resolution 1737, adopted December 27, 2006, http://www.un.org/News/Press/docs/2006/sc8928.doc.htm.

[540] Graham Bowley, "Despite Call to Halt, Iran says it will Continue its Nuclear Program," *New York Times,* July 31, 2008.

[541] UN Security Council Resolution 1835, adopted September 27, 2008, http://www.un.org/News/Press/docs/2008/sc9459.doc.htm.

[542] Ben Ariel, "Iran Using Chinese Bank to Transfer Money to its Elite Force," Arutz 7, November 19, 2014, http://www.israelnationalnews.com/News/News.aspx/187622#.VG0q-2M0Rx0.

[543] Susan Cornwell, "US Congress OKs sanctions on Iran's energy, banks," Reuters, June 24, 2010, http://www.reuters.com/article/idUSN2414825120100624.

[544] Ariel Ben Solomon, "John Bolton: Israel should have attacked Iran 'yesterday'," *Jerusalem Post*, July 16, 2013.

[545] "Iran's key nuclear sites," BBC News, September 25, 2009, http://news.bbc.co.uk/2/hi/middle_east/4617398.stm; Hussein D. Hassan, "Iranian Nuclear Sites," Congressional Research Service Report for Congress, http://ftp.fas.org/sgp/crs/nuke/RS22531.pdf.

[546] "Report: Iranian uranium enrichment site revealed," *Jerusalem Post,* September 9, 2010, http://www.jpost.com/IranianThreat/News/Article.aspx?id=187653.

[547] Jay Solomon. "Iran Seen Trying New Path to a Bomb," *Wall Street Journal,* August 5, 2013, http://online.wsj.com/article/SB10001424127887323997004578644140963633244.html?mod=WSJ_article_JasonGayHeadlines.

[548] Ibid.

[549] David Sanger and William Broad, "U.S. and Allies Warn Iran over Nuclear Deception," *New York Times,* September 25, 2009.

[550] *The Daily Telegraph* (UK), September 13, 2004.

[551] "Watch Iranians, they believe war is near, expert warns," WND.com, October 12, 2012, http://www.wnd.com/2012/10/watch-iran-they-believe-war-is-near-expert-warns/.

[552] "DPRK FM on Its Stand to Suspend Its Participation in Six-party Talks for Indefinite Period," KCNA, February 10, 2005, http://www.kcna.co.jp/item/2005/200502/news02/11.htm#1.

[553] Jennifer Rubin, "John Bolton on Wendy Sherman,: *Washington Post,* June 15, 2011, http://www.washingtonpost.com/blogs/right-turn/post/john-bolton-on-wendy-sherman/2011/03/29/AGW2ULWH_blog.html.

[554] Hana Levi Julian, "Iran Running Short of Uranium Oxide Nuke Supplies?" Arutz 7, August 25, 2009, http://www.israelnationalnews.com/News/News.aspx/133096.

[555] "North Korean yellowcake was bound for Syria when Israel struck plant," DEBKAfile Special Report February 28, 2010, http://www.debka.com/article/8621/.

[556] Associated Press, "IAEA: Iran has over 2 tons enriched uranium -2 bombs' worth," *Jerusalem Post,* June 1, 2010, http://www.jpost.com/Headlines/Article.aspx?id=177064.

[557] "Secret document exposes Iran's nuclear trigger," *The Times* (London), December 14, 2009, http://www.timesonline.co.uk/tol/news/world/middle_east/article6955351.ece.

[558] Ibid.

[559] Ibid.

[560] Roee Nahmias, "Report: Sarkozy warns Israel won't abide Iranian threat," YnetNews.com January 23, 2010, http://www.ynetnews.com/articles/0,7340,L-3838323,00.html.

[561] David P. Goldman, "Did Iran Test a Nuclear Bomb in North Korea in 2010?," Pajamas Media, March 4, 2012, http://pjmedia.com/spengler/2012/03/04/did-iran-test-a-nuclear-bomb-in-north-korea-in-2010/.

[562] "North Korea tested Iranian warhead or "dirty bomb" in 2010 for $55m," DEBKAfile, March 5, 2012, http://www.debka.com/article/21794/.

[563] Robin Pagnamenta, Michael Evans and Tony Halpin, "Iran in scramble for fresh uranium supplies," *Sunday Times*, January 24, 2009, http://www.timesonline.co.uk/tol/news/world/middle_east/article5576589.ece.

[564] George Jahn, "Iran hunts for uranium," Associated Press, February 24, 2011, http://news.yahoo.com/s/ap/20110224/ap_on_re_eu/iran_nuclear. *See* also Ryan Mauro, "Iran Scrounges For Uranium," FrontPage Magazine, March 7, 2011,

http://www.israelunitycoalition.org/news/?p=6433.

[565] "Iran Bid To Get Congo Uranium," *The Australian*, August 7, 2006; Swain, Jon, David Leppard, and Brian Johnson-Thomas, "Iran's Plot To Mine Uranium In South Africa," *Sunday Times*, August 6, 2006, http://www.timesonline.co.uk/tol/news/world/article601432.ece (April 27, 2009).

[566] "Iran, Zimbabwe strike nuke deal," AP and *Jerusalem Post* staff, April 25, 2010, http://www.jpost.com/IranianThreat/News/Article.aspx?id=173875.

[567] Anna Mahjar-Barducci, "Bolivia, Venezuela, Supply Uranium to Iran," Hudson Institute, October 6, 2010, http://www.hudson-ny.org/1585/bolivia-venezuela-supply-uranium-to-iran.

[568] "Iran dismisses reports of secret uranium deal with Kazakhstan," *RIA Novosti*, December 30, 2009, http://en.rian.ru/world/20091230/157426830.html.

[569] "Renewed Efforts to Limit Iran's Nuclear Programme," *Strategic Survey 2012*, (New York: Routledge, 2012), XII.

[570] Bill Gertz, "CIA: Iran capable of producing nukes," *The Washington Times*, March 30, 2010, http://www.washingtontimes.com/news/2010/mar/30/cia-iran-has-capability-to-produce-nuke-weapons/.

[571] The Associated Press and *Haaretz* Service, "Iran to begin work on new nuclear facility by early next year, official says," *Haaretz*, June 12, 2010, http://www.*Haaretz*.com/news/diplomacy-defense/iran-to-begin-work-on-new-nuclear-facility-by-early-next-year-official-says-1.295724.

[572] "Events A Glance," *Strategic Survey 2012: Annual Review of World Affairs*, International Institute for Strategic Studies, (New York: Routledge, 2012), 11.

[573] "Neither US nor Israel can destroy Iran's nuclear capabilities, only cause delay," DEBKAfile, August 15, 2012, http://www.debka.com/article/22276/Neither-US-nor-Israel-can-destroy-Iran%E2%80%99s-nuclear-capabilities-only-cause-delay.

[574] Tzvi Ben Gedalyahu, "Video: Doomsday for Iran? US Tests EMP Bomb," Israel National News, December 6, 2012, http://www.israelnationalnews.com/News/News.aspx/162868#.UL_efkFSQ8E.

[575] "Stuxnet worm rampaging through Iran: IT official," AFP, September 27, 2010, http://news.yahoo.com/s/afp/20100927/tc_afp/iranitcomputersecurityenergystuxnet.

[576] "Iran may have executed nuclear staffers over Stuxnet, DEBKAfile, October 10, 2010, http://www.debka.com/article/9073/.

[577] "Blasts Hit Secret Iranian Missile Launching-Pad for US, Israeli Targets," http://www.newmediajournal.us/international/1015b.htm.

[578] Gavriel Queenann, "Iranian Nuclear Program Hit By Second 'Cyber Missile' Virus," IsraelNationalNews.com, April 25, 2011, http://www.israelnationalnews.com/News/News.aspx/143692.

[579] "Iran atomic chief claims sabotage nuclear facility," TIMES Live (South Africa), September, 17, 2012, http://www.timeslive.co.za/world/2012/09/17/iran-atomic-chief-claims-sabotage-at-nuclear-facility.

[580] "Iran has secretly stocked enriched uranium for four nuclear bombs," DEBKAfile, June 3, 2011, http://www.debka.com/article/20995/.

[581] "Iran: Domestic Struggle Dims Hope of Nuclear Deal," *Strategic Survey 2011: Annual Review of World Affairs,* International Institute for Strategic Studies, (New York: Routledge, 2011), 254.

[582] "Sarkozy: North Korea to supply Iran with nuclear bomb components," DEBKAfile, December 2, 2010, http://www.debka.com/article/20414/.

[583] "Iran runs nuclear missile payload tests, moves onto 60 pc fuel enrichment," DEBKAfile, September 5, 2011, http://www.debka.com/article/21271/.

[584] "Fordow sabotage enabled Netanyahu to move Iran red line to spring 2013,"
DEBKAfile Exclusive Report - DEBKAfile, September 29, 2012, http://unitycoalitionforisrael.org/news/?p=8559.

[585] Reza Kahlili, "Iran's secret nuclear-bomb plant revealed," WND, October 8, 2012, http://www.wnd.com/2012/10/irans-secret-nuclear-bomb-plant-revealed/

[586] Paul Richter, "Iran has increased nuclear enrichment capacity, IAEA report says," *Los Angeles Times,* November 16, 2012, http://www.latimes.com/news/nationworld/world/la-fg-iran-nuclear-20121117,0,7828780.story.

[587] David Lev, "Report: Iran Building Powerful Nuclear Device," Israel National News, November 27, 2012, http://www.israelnationalnews.com/News/News.aspx/162598#.ULZTXNdSQ8F.

[588] Reza Kahlil, "North Koreans among 40 dead at Iran nuke plant," WND, February 4, 2013, http://www.wnd.com/2013/02/north-koreans-among-40-dead-at-iran-nuke-plant/?cat_orig=world.

[589] Reza Kahlil, "WND report blows Iran nuke program wide open," WND, January 28, 2013, http://mobile.wnd.com/2013/01/wnd-report-blows-iran-nuke-program-wide-open/.

[590] David Lev, "Report: Iran Tried to Upgrade Nuke Program With Chinese Magnets," Arutz-7, February 14, 2013, http://www.israelnationalnews.com/News/News.aspx/165236#.UR-7nask2iI.

[591] David Albright and Christina Walrond, "Critical Capability," Institute for Science and International Security, July 30, 2013, http://isis-online.org/isis-reports/detail/critical-capability/.

[592] "Report: Iran could build nuclear bomb within one month," *Israel Hayom,* October 25, 2013 http://isis-online.org/uploads/isis-reports/documents/Breakout_Study_Summary_24October2013.pdf.

[593] Elad Benari, "Experts' Report: Iran Could Have a Nuclear Bomb Within a Month," Arutz -7, October 25, 2013, http://www.israelnationalnews.com/News/News.aspx/173192#.Umqex3eK7d0.

[594] Karl Penhaul and Elise Labott, "Kerry heading to Geneva for Iran nuclear talks," CNN, November 7, 2013, http://www.cnn.com/2013/11/07/world/meast/iran-nuclear-talks/.

[595] Oren Dorell, "Report: Iran may be month from a bomb," *USA Today,* October 25, 2013, http://www.usatoday.com/story/news/world/2013/10/24/iran-bomb-one-month-away/3181373/.

[596] "Report: Iran could build nuclear bomb within one month," *Israel Hayom*, October 25, 2013, http://isis-online.org/uploads/isis-reports/documents/Breakout_Study_Summary_24October2013.pdf.

[597] "Mystery explosion Iran's Arak heavy water reactor," DEBKAfile, November 3, 2013, http://www.debka.com/article/23412/Mystery-explosion-at-Iran%E2%80%99s-Arak-heavy-water-reactor.

[598] "Salehi's Arak 'deal'—cover-up for 1,300 kg enriched uranium smuggled to Parchin for secret upgrade," DEBKAfile, April 20, 2014, http://www.debka.com/article/23855/Salehi%E2%80%99s-Arak-%E2%80%9Cdeal%E2%80%9D-%E2%80%93-cover-up-for-1-300-kg-enriched-uranium-smuggled-to-Parchin-for-secret-upgrade.

[599] Justyna Pawlak and Parisa Hafezi, "U.S. warns on Iran 'breakout' capability as nuclear talks start," Reuters, April 9, 2014, http://unitycoalitionforisrael.org/uci_2014/?p=8048.

[600] Mark Dubowitz, "Iran Makes the Rules," Foundation for the Defense of Democracy, cited by *The Wall Street Journal,* September 28, 2014, http://www.defenddemocracy.org/media-hit/dubowitz-mark-iran-makes-the-rules/.

[601] "Satellite photos reveal massive damage at suspected Iran nuke facility," *Times of Israel,* October 8, 2014, http://www.timesofisrael.com/massive-blast-reported-at-suspected-iranian-nuke-facility-2/.

[602] Hana Levi Julian, "'Nuclear Expert' Among Dead in Iranian Nuclear Plant Explosion, Jewishpress,com, October 6, 2014, http://www.jewishpress.com/news/breaking-news/at-least-2-dead-in-iranian-nuclear-plant-explosion/2014/10/06/. *See* also Paul Alster, "Mysterious blast Iran nuke plant proves weapons program alive, say experts," FoxNews.com, October 9, 2014, http://www.foxnews.com/world/2014/10/09/mysterious-blast-at-iran-nuke-plant-proves-weapons-program-alive-say-experts/.

[603] Oren Dorell, "Blast kills 2 at suspected Iranian nuclear site," *USA TODAY,* October 6, 2014, http://www.usatoday.com/story/news/world/2014/10/06/blast-suspected-iran-nuke-site-parchin/16808997/.

[604] Mark Langfan, "Iran Admits Testing Nuclear 'Bridge Wires' at Exploded Parchin," Arutz 7, October 10, 2014, http://www.israelnationalnews.com/News/News.aspx/186003#.VDmKjhA0Rx0.

[605] Islamic Republic News Agency, December 14, 2001.

[606] "Iranian Hardliner Says Iran Will Produce Atomic Bomb," IranMania.com, February 14, 2005.

[607] "Iranian president Tehran conference," MEMRI Special Dispatch Series, no. 1013, October 28, 2005.

[608] "Text of Mahmoud Ahmadinejad's Speech," *New York Times,* October 30, 2005, http://www.nytimes.com/2005/10/30/weekinreview/30iran.html?pagewanted=all&_r=0.

[609] "Israel to Be Destroyed by Hezbollah," *Fars News Agency* (Tehran), February 19, 2008.

[610] Reza Kahlili, "'Kill all Jews and annihilate Israel!' Iran's Ayatollah lays out legal and religious justification for attack. Israel Could Be Wiped Out in Nine Minutes, Manifesto Claims," WorldNetDaily.com, February 4, 2012, http://www.wnd.com/2012/02/ayatollah-kill-all-jews-annihilate-israel/.

[611] Reza Kahlili, "'Kill all Jews and annihilate Israel!' Iran's Ayatollah lays out legal and religious justification for attack. Israel Could Be Wiped Out in Nine Minutes, Manifesto Claims," WorldNetDaily.com, February 4, 2012, http://www.wnd.com/2012/02/ayatollah-kill-all-jews-annihilate-israel/.

[612] "Israel Targets Iran Nuclear Plant," *Sunday Times* (London), July 18, 2004.

[613] Asher Zeiger, "Ahmadinejad anticipates a 'new Middle East' with no Americans or Zionists." *The Times of Israel.* August 17, 2012, http://www.timesofisrael.com/iranians-commemorate-al-quds-day/; Full Notebook: Count on Ahmadinejad to find the right words, *National Post,* August 17, 2012, http://fullcomment.nationalpost.com/2012/08/17/full-notebook-count-on-ahmadinejad-to-find-the-right-words/; "No room for Israel in 'new Middle East': Ahmadinejad," Reuters (reprinted by the National Post on August 17, 2012, http://news.national-post.com/2012/08/17/ahmadinejad-israel/).

[614] The word "politicide" was originally coined by Israeli Foreign Minister Abba Eban in 1967.

[615] "Palestinian lands will be certainly returned to Palestinians: Leader," *Tehran Times,* August 15, 2012, http://www.tehrantimes.com/politics/100634-palestinian-lands-will-be-certainly-returned-to-palestinians-leader.

[616] Reza Kahlili, "Iran aims biological warheads at Israel," WND, December 4, 2012, http://www.wnd.com/2012/12/iran-aims-biological-warheads-at-israel/.

[617] Gil Ronen, "Rouhani: Israel an 'Old Wound' to be Removed," Arutz 7, August 2, 2013, http://trailer.webview.net/Show/0X7E253E04A986A42C4251496C23DC8AAF001E04F11E9434438186735DBD637488.htm#0_170526.

[618] Ariel Ben Solomon, "John Bolton: Israel should have attacked Iran 'yesterday'," *Jerusalem Post,* July 16, 2013, http://www.jpost.com/Iranian-Threat/News/John-Bolton-Israel-should-have-attacked-Iran-yesterday-319945.

[619] "France: Iran's 'rabid dog 'insults of Israel complicate nuke talks," The Times of Israel, November 20, 2013, http://www.timesofisrael.com/france-says-iran-comments-on-israel-complicate-nuke-talks/.

[620] Lazar Berman, "Iran militia chief: Destroying Israel is 'nonnegotiable'," *The Times of Israel,* March 31, 2015, http://www.timesofisrael.com/iran-militia-chief-destroying-israel-nonnegotiable/?utm_source=The+-Times+of+Israel+Daily+Edition&utm_campaign=37bcbb641e-2015_03_31&utm_medium=email&utm_term=0_adb46cec92-37bcbb641e-54550797.

[621] Paul Eidelberg, "Why Israel Must Destroy Iran's Nuclear Bomb-Making Facilities," October 7, 2013. With permission granted to the author for reproduction in this book.

[622] Norman Podhoretz, "The Case for Bombing Iran," *Wall Street Journal,* May 30, 2007, http://www.opinion-journal.com/federation/feature/?id=110010139.

[623] Ibid.

[624] Gil Ronen, "Germany Gives Israel Discount on Sixth Submarine, *Arutz 7* IsraelNationalNews.com, July 18, 2011, http://www.israelnationalnews.com/News/News.aspx/145809.

[625] Quoted in a review of *Londonistan,* http://www.melaniephillips.com/londonistan/.

[626] Aleksandr I. Solzhenitsyn, *The Gulag Archipelago: 1918-1956,* Part 1, (New York: Harper & Row, 1974), 178.

[627] Avraham Zuroff, "Israeli Planes Prepare for Airstrike on Iran," IsraelNationalNews.com, May 3, 2009, http://www.israelnationalnews.com/News/News.aspx/131153#.UBsJE_v1GJE.

[628] "Back to the mountain," IAF Events log, August 14, 2011, http://www.iaf.org.il/4372-37727-en/IAF.aspx.

[629] John R. Bolton, "To Stop Iran's Bomb, Bomb Iran," New York Times, March 26, 2015, http://www.nytimes.com/2015/03/26/opinion/to-stop-irans-bomb-bomb-iran.html?_r=0.

[630] Louis René Beres, "Agreement with Iran: Requiem for a nuclear Israel?", Thehill.com, April 8, 2015, http://thehill.com/blogs/congress-blog/foreign-policy/238101-agreement-with-iran-requiem-for-a-nuclear-israel.

[631] *See* Steven Emerson and Joel Himelfarb, "Would Iran Provide A Nuclear Weapon to Terrorists?," *inFocus,* Winter 2009, http://www.jewishpolicycenter.org/1532/iran-nuclear-weapon-to-terrorists.

[632] "Netanyahu Auschwitz: World must unite to confront new threats," World Holocaust Forum, January 27, 2010, http://www.worldholocaustforum.org/eng/docs/publications/2010-01/3600/.

[633] Alon Ben David, "Israel Outlines Defence Doctrine," *Jane's Defence Weekly,* May 3, 2006.

[634] Farhad Rajaee, *Islamic Values and World View: Khomeini on Man, the State and International Politics,* (Lanham, MD: University Press of America, 1983), 82–83.

[635] Ezekiel 33:1–7, *Sacred Writings: Judaism The Tanakh.* (New York: Book of the Month Club, 1992).

[636] http://www.brainyquote.com/quotes/keywords/vanquished.html.

[637] Many examples can be found at http://www.burningsettlerscabin.com/?p=7905, as well as https://www.google.com/search?hl=en&safe=off&rlz=1C1GPEA_enUS315US315&biw=1455&bih=934&tbm=isch&sa=1&q=%22you+don%27t+have+to+be+Jewish%22+Levy%27s+rye&oq=%22you+don%27t+have+to+be+-Jewish%22+Levy%27s+rye&aq=f&aqi=&aql=&gs_sm=e&gs_upl=18812l20409l0l20785l7l#q=%22you+don%27t+have+to+be+Jewish%22+Levy%27s+rye&hl=en&safe=off&rlz=1C1GPEA_enUS315US315&tbm=isch&bav=on.2,or.r_gc.r_pw.,cf.osb&fp=1&biw=785&bih=254.

[638] For text of the proclamation *see* http://www.likud.nl/ref00.html.

[639] http://www.biblicalzionist.com/Quotes.htm.

[640] Ibid., 221.

[641] Donald Macintyre, "Lawrence of Arabia was really a Zionist, historian claims," *The Independent* (London), February 24, 2007.

[642] Martin Gilbert, *Churchill and the Jews: A Life Long Friendship,* (New York: Henry Holt and Company, 2007), 57.

[643] *The Times,* London, May 5, 1938.

[644] Amy K. Rosenthal, "One of his finest hours," *World Jewish Digest,* March 2008 interview with Sir Martin Gilbert about his book: *Churchill and the Jews,* http://www.judaicaexchange.com/ME2/dirmod.

asp?sid=81E34D0AC90D4601B0A9F31C3F2D3009&nm=More+Articles&type=Publishing&mod=Publications percent3Apercent3AArticle&mid=8F3A7027421841978F18BE895F87F791&tier=4&id=9AF6147E37534A-39B3877E1AD365D805. *See* also Christian United for Israel, June 2008, http://www.c4israel.org/c4i/newspaper/june_2008/churchill_and_the_jews_by_amy_k_rosenthal.

[645] Samuel M. Katz, *The Elite,* (New York: Pocket Books, 1992), 12.

[646] Robert Spencer, "Martin Luther King, Jr. was a proud Zionist," *Jihad Watch,* January 21, 2013, http://www.jihadwatch.org/2013/01/martin-luther-king-jr-was-a-proud-zionist.html. For extensive refutation of the claim that King's statements are a hoax, *see* Martine Kramer, "In the Words of Martin Luther King...," Sandbox, March 12, 2012, http://www.martinkramer.org/sandbox/2012/03/in-the-words-of-martin-luther-king/.

[647] Seymour Martin Lipset; "The Socialism of Fools: The Left, the Jews and Israel," *Encounter magazine,* December 1969, 24.

[648] I. L. Kenen, *Israel's Defense Line,* (Buffalo, NY: Prometheus Books, 1981), 266.

[649] David Barnett and Efraim Karsh, "Azzam's Genocidal Threat," *Middle East Quarterly,* Fall 2011, 85-88. It should be noted that this quote has been reworded slightly and its date of issue was placed later in error. Barnett and Karsh definitively found the original quote and source as noted.

[650] Ibid. 87.

[651] E.L.M. Burns, *Between Arab and Israeli,* (Toronto: Clarke Irwin, 1962), 88.

[652] Michael B. Oren, *Six Days of War,* (New York: Oxford University Press, 2002), 95 and Walter Laqueur, *The Road to War,* (Baltimore: Penguin Books, 1969), 99.

[653] Louis René Beres, "Facing Iran at the margins of time," *The Jerusalem Post*, October 14, 2014, http://www.jpost.com/Opinion/Facing-Iran-at-the-margins-of-time-378862.

[654] Louis René Beres. "Striking Hezbollah-Bound Weapons in Syria: Israel's Actions Under International Law," *National Security Journal,* August 26, 2013, http://unitycoalitionforisrael.org/news/?p=9746.

[655] "Israeli Jets Destroy Iraqi Atomic Reactor; Attack Condemned by U.S. and Arab Nations," *New York Times,* June 9, 1981; Seymour Hersh, *The Sampson Option,* 216.

[656] Arshad Mohammed and Tabassum Zakaria, "U.S. says North Korea gave Syria nuclear assistance," Reuters, April 24, 2008, http://www.reuters.com/article/2008/04/24/us-korea-north-usa-idUSN2422257920080424.

[657] Avner Cohen, *Israel and the Bomb,* (New York: Columbia University Press, 1998), 236.

[658] Avner Cohen, *Israel and the Bomb,* (New York: Colombia University Press, 1998), 119.

[659] For example, former Iranian president, Ali Akbar asheni Rafsanjani, *Kayhan* (Tehran), December 15, 2001 and Iranian President Mahmoud Ahmadinejad, Islamic Republic of Iran Broadcasting, (Tehran), October 27, 2005/.

[660] Avner Cohen, *Israel and the Bomb,* Ibid., 11. *See* also Munya M. Mardor, *Rafael* (in Hebrew), (Tel Aviv: Misrad Habitachon, 1981), 72–73.

[661] Anthony Cordesman, *Perilous Prospects: The Peace Process and the Arab-Israeli Military Balance,* (Boulder, CO: Westview Press, 1996), 118.

[662] "Former Official Says France Helped Build Israel's Dimona Complex," *Nucleonics Week,* October 16, 1986, 6.

[663] Erich Marquardt, "Iran's nuke potential bedevils Israel," *Asia Times,* September 12, 2003, http://www.atimes.com/atimes/Middle_East/EI12Ak02.html.

[664] "Israel's nuclear defense history," *Los Angeles Times,* October 12, 2003.

[665] Stephen Green, *Taking Sides, America's Secret Relations with a Militant Israel,* (New York: William and Morrow Company, 1984), 149.

[666] Matti Golan, *Peres,* (Tel Aviv: Schocken Books, 1982), 54 as cited in Dan Raviv, and Yossi Melman, *Every Spy a Prince: the Complete History of Israel's Intelligence Community,* (Boston: Houghton Mifflin Company, 1990), 67–69.

[667] Michael Crick, "How Britain helped Israel get the bomb," BBC Newsnight, August 3, 2005, http://news.bbc.co.uk/2/hi/programmes/newsnight/4743493.stm.

[668] "UK helped Israel get nuclear bomb," BBC News, August 4, 2005, http://news.bbc.co.uk/2/hi/uk_news/4743987.stm.

[669] Michael Crick, "How Britain Helped Israel Get the Bomb," BBC, August 3, 2005; "UK helped Israel get nuclear bomb," BBC News, August 4, 2005, http://news.bbc.co.uk/2/hi/uk_news/4743987.stm; Ben Fenton, "Britain Secretly Sent Vital Nuclear Bomb Ingredient to Israel," Daily Telegraph, August 4, 2005. See also Robinson Freytag, "Film Sheds Light on How Israel got Heavy Water from Norway," Jerusalem Post, December 7, 2005; "UK Role in Israel's Nuclear Program Seen as 'Double Standard,'" BBC, December 12, 2005.

[670] Gary Mihollin, "Heavy Water Cheaters," Foreign Policy, (1987–88), 100–19.

[671] Gary Milhollin, "Israeli A-Bombs and Norwegian Heavy Water:
Arms Control Through Public Pressure," June 17, 1993, http://www.wisconsinproject.org/pubs/speeches/1993/speech1.html.

[672] "Israeli Heavy Water Returned to Norway," Agence France Presse, December 3, 1991; Harold Stanghelle, "Israel to Sell Back 10.5 Tons," Arbeiderbladet, Oslo, Norway, June 28,1990 as cited in Center for Nonproliferation Studies, "Nuclear Developments," June 28, 1990, 34–35. See also http://cns.miis.edu November 22, 1998.

[673] Ibid.

[674] Meirion Jones, "Secret Sale of UK plutonium to Israel," BBC, March 10, 2006; Meirion Jones, "Britain's dirty secret," New Statesman, March 13, 2006.

[675] Steve Weissman, and Herbert Krosney, The Islamic Bomb: the Nuclear Threat to Israel and the Middle East, (New York: Times Books, 1981), 114–17.

[676] Leonard S. Spector, The Undeclared Bomb, (Cambridge, MA: Ballinger Publishers, 1988), 387 (fn 22).

[677] "Post-Mortem on SNE [Special National Intelligence Estimate] 100-8-60; Implications of the Acquisition by Israel of a Nuclear Weapons Capability," Draft, January 31, 1961, Department of State Lot files, Lot No. 57D688, USNA as cited in Avner Cohen, Israel and the Bomb, (New York: Colombia University Press, 1998), 82–83; Steve Weissman, and Herbert Krosney, op. cit., 114–17.

[678] Stephen Green, Taking Sides, America's Secret Relations with a Militant Israel, 153.

[679] Dino A. Brugioni, Eyes in the Sky: Eisenhower, the CIA and Cold War Aerial Espionage, (Annapolis, MD: Naval Institute Press, 2010), 273.

[680] Ibid., 151.

[681] Avner Cohen, "Most Favored Nation," The Bulletin of American Scientists, 51, No. 1 (January-February 1995), 44–53.

[682] Anthony Cordesman, Weapons of Mass Destruction in the Middle East, Center for Strategic and International Studies, April 15, 2003.

[683] Avner Cohen, Israel and the Bomb, 88–89.

[684] "B-G reveals 'Atoms-for-Peace' reactor being built in Negev," Jerusalem Post, December 22, 1960, 1 and Avner Cohen, "Most Favored Nation," The Bulletin of Atomic Scientists, 51, No. 1 (January-February 1995), 44–53.

[685] Stephen Green, Taking Sides, America's Secret Relations with a Militant Israel, 154 and Avner Cohen, Israel and the Bomb, 91.

[686] Avner Cohen, "U.S. Knew About Nuke Plans," Yediot Aharonot (Hebrew), June 2, 2005.

[687] Ibid., 166 and Avner Cohen, Israel and the Bomb, 179.

[688] John H. Cushman, Jr., "U.S. Sent Liquid to Israel for Reactor," New York Times, November 10, 1986.

[689] William Burr and Avner Cohen, "Israel's Secret Uranium Buy," Foreign Policy, July 1, 2013, http://www.foreignpolicy.com/articles/2013/07/01/israels_secret_uranium_buy?page=0,0.

[690] Rachel Abecasis, "Iranian reportedly offered to China, Israel," Radio Renascenca, Lisbon, December 9, 1992 as quoted in Center for Nonproliferation. "Proliferation Issues," December 23, 1992, 25. *See* also http://cns. miis.edu/npr/pdfs/giulia11.pdf "Nuclear-Related Trade and Cooperation Developments for 15 States," (October–December, 1992), 77.

[691] Seymour Hersh, *The Sampson Option,* (New York: Random House, 1991), 196.

[692] Charles Mohr, "White House Discounts Allegations About Israeli Theft of Uranium," *New York Times,* October 26, 1977.

[693] Interview with a senior technical official of the Nuclear Regulatory Commission as cited in Seymour Hersh, *The Sampson Option,* 257, and Stephen Green, *Taking Sides, America's Secret Relations with a Militant Israel,* 169–179.

[694] "How Israel Got the Bomb," *Time,* April 12, 1976, 39–40.

[695] Lon O. Nordeen and David Nicolle, *Phoenix over the Nile*, (Washington, DC: Smithsonian Institute Press, 1996), 192–93.

[696] Edgar O'Balance, *The Third Arab-Israeli War,* (London: Faber and Faber, 1972), 54. *See* also Norden and Nicole, *Phoenix over the Nile,* Ibid.

[697] Anthony Cordesman, *Weapons of Mass Destruction in the Middle East,* and Warner Farr, *The Third Temple's Holy of Holies: Israel's Nuclear Weapons,* September 1999, http://www.au.af.mil/au/awc/awcgate/awc-cps.htm.

[698] Aharon Lapidot, "'Iran will not get the bomb,'" *Israel Hayom,* July 1, 2013, http://www.israelhayom.com/site/newsletter_article.php?id=10377.

[699] Michael Brecher, *Decision in Crisis. Israel, 1967 and 1973,* (Berkeley, CA: University of California Press, 1980), 104, 230–31.

[700] Avner Cohen, *Israel and the Bomb,* 270.

[701] Interview with former Israeli government official as cited in Seymour M. Hersh, *The Sampson Option,* 225, 236–37 as cited in William E. Burrows, and Robert Winderm, *Critical Mass: The Dangerous Race for Superweapons in a Fragmenting World,* (New York: Simon and Schuster, 1994), 279–80.

[702] "Uranium: The Israeli Connection," *Time,* May 30, 1977, 32–34. *See* also Raviv and Melman, *Every Spy a Prince,* 199.

[703] "The Mystery of the Missing Uranium," *The Economist,* May 7, 1977 and Steve Weissman, and Herbert Krosney, op. cit., 124–28.

[704] Anthony Cordesman, *Weapons of Mass Destruction in the Middle East,* Center for Strategic and International Studies, April 15, 2003.

[705] "How Israel Got the Bomb," *Time,* April 12, 1976, 39–40.

[706] Steve Weissman and Herbert Krosney, *The Islamic Bomb,* (New York: Times Books, 1981), 108.

[707] Ibid., 107.

[708] Leonard S. Spector, "Foreign-Supplied Combat Aircraft: Will They Drop the Third World Bomb?" *Journal of International Affairs 40,* no. 1, 1986, 145 (fn 5) and Stephen Green, *Living by the Sword: America and Israel in the Middle East 1968-1986,* (London: Faber, 1988), 18-19.

[709] Duncan Lennox, ed., "Jericho 1/2/3 (YA-1/YA-3) (Israel), Offensive Weapons," *Jane's Strategic Weapon Systems,* Issue 50, (Surrey: Jane's Information Group, January 2009), 84-86.

[710] William Beecher, "Israel Believed Producing Missiles of Atom Capability," *New York Times,* October 5, 1971, 1, 15.

[711] Louis René Beres, "Deceptions of a 'Nuclear Weapon Free Zone' for the Middle East," Purdue University, September 23, 2008. *See* also Louis René Beres, "Israel's Bomb in the Basement: A revisiting of 'Deliberate Abiguity' vs. 'Disclosure," *Between War and Peace: Dilemmas of Israeli Security,* edited by Efraim Karsh, (London: Frank Cass, 1996), 113-33. *See* also Cohen, *Israel and the Bomb,* 237.

[712] Harold Hough, "Could Israel's Nuclear Assets Survive a First Strike?" *Jane's Intelligence Review,* September 1997,.407–10.

[713] W. Andrew Terrill, "The Chemical Warfare Legacy of the Yemen War," *Comparative Strategy,* 10, 1991,.109-19.

[714] Avner Cohen, *Israel and the Bomb,* (New York: Columbia University Press, 1998), 337.

[715] David Stout, "A Mideast Nuclear Crisis, in 1969: Declassified Papers Show Nixon's bind over Israeli Program," *International Herald Tribune,* November 30, 2007 and Eli Lake, "EXCLUSIVE: Obama keeps Israel's nuke secret," *The Washington Times,* October 2, 2009, http://www.washingtontimes.com/news/2009/oct/02/president-obama-has-reaffirmed-a-4-decade-old-secr/?feat=home_cube_position1.

[716] Robert Gillette, "Uranium Enrichment: Rumors of Israeli Progress with Lasers," *Science* 183, No. 4130, March 22, 1974, 1172–74.

[717] "How Israel Got the Bomb," *Time,* April 12, 1976, 39; Seymour Hersh, *The Sampson Option,* 223.

[718] "Israel Reported to Have A-Bomb," *Facts on File World Digest News,* April 10, 1976; Seymour Hersh, *The Sampson Option,* 217, 222-226; Steve Weissman and Herbert Krosney, *The Islamic Bomb: the Nuclear Threat to Israel and the Middle East,* 107, and Erich Marquardt, "Iran's nuke potential bedevils Israel," *Asia Times,* September 12, 2003, http://www.atimes.com/atimes/Middle_East/EI12Ak02.html.

[719] Hersh, *The Sampson Option,* 180.

[720] Gerard Smith and Helena Cobban, "A Blind Eye to Nuclear Proliferation," *Foreign Affairs,* 68, no. 3, 1989, 53–70.

[721] "Officials Suspect Russians Sent Arms to Egypt," *New York Times,* November 22, 1973; "Israel Reported to Have A-Bomb," *Facts on File World Digest News,* April 10, 1976; "How Israel Got the Bomb," *Time,* April 12, 1976, 39; Edgar O'Balance, *No Victor, No Vanquished: The Yom Kippur War,* (San Rafael, CA: Presidio Press, 1978), 234–35; Shlomo Aronson, *Israel's Nuclear Options,* ACIS Working Paper No. 7. University of California Center for Arms Control and International Security, Los Angeles, CA, 1977, 15–18; Seymour Hersh, *The Sampson Option,* 231–35; and "Nuclear Weapons Reported Deployed in 1973 Middle East War," Associated Press, July 12, 1985.

[722] "Prospects for Further Nuclear Proliferation of Nuclear Weapons," Central Intelligence Agency, January 26, 1978, as cited in David Burnham, "CIA Said in 1974 Israel Had A-bombs," *New York Times,* January 27, 1978.

[723] Anthony Cordesman, *Weapons of Mass Destruction in the Middle East,* Ibid.

[724] Steve Weissman, and Herbert Krosney, op. cit., 105.

[725] Weissman and Krosney, *The Islamic Bomb,* 109.

[726] Duncan Lennox, ed., "Jericho 1/2/3 (YA-1/YA-3) (Israel), Offensive Weapons," *Jane's Strategic Weapon Systems,* Issue 50, (Surrey: Jane's Information Group, January 2009), 84–86.

[727] Gerald Steinberg, "Israel: Case Study for International Missile Trade and Nonproliferation," in William C. Potter and Harlan W. Jencks, *The International Missile Bazaar: The New Suppliers' Network* (Boulder, CO: Westview Press, 1994); 235–53; Ronen Bergman, "Treasons of Conscience," *Haaretz,* April 7, 2000.

[728] In total, analysts generally estimate that Israel provided substantial technical assistance to South Africa's Arniston missile program, including factory construction. William Burrows and Robert Windrem, *Critical Mass* (New York: Simon and Shuster, 1994), 448–55; and David B. Ottaway and R. Jeffrey Smith, "U.S. Knew of Israel-S. Africa Missile Deal," *Washington Post,* October 27, 1989, http://www.washingtonpost.com.

[729] Thomas W. Netter, "Israel Reported to Test New, Longer-Range Missile," *New York Times,* July 22, 1987, A6.

[730] Duncan Lennox, ed., "Arrow 2 (Israel), Defensive Weapons," *Jane's Strategic Weapon Systems,* Issue 50, (Surrey: Jane's Information Group, January 2009), 253–56; Duncan Lennox, ed., "Jericho 1/2/3 (YA-1/YA-3) (Israel), Offensive Weapons," *Jane's Strategic Weapon Systems,* Issue 50, (Surrey: Jane's Information Group, January 2009), 84–86; and "Jericho 2," Missilethreat.com, www.missilethreat.com.

[731] "Report: Israel Helped South Africa Develop Nuclear Weapons," Associated Press, April 20, 1997.

[732] Dino A. Brugioni, *Eyes in the Sky: Eisenhower, the CIA and Cold War Aerial Espionage,* (Annapolis, MD: Naval Institute Press, 2010), 213.

[733] "A Flash of Light," *Newsweek,* November 5, 1979.

[734] "Israel Denies It Tested Nuclear Bomb," Associated Press, February 22, 1980.

[735] *Haaretz,* April 20, 1997 as cited in "Weapons of Mass Destruction (WMD): Nuclear Weapons Testing," http://www.globalsecurity.org/wmd/world/israel/nuke-test.htm.

[736] Re'uven Pedatzur, "South African Statement On Nuclear Test Said to Serve Israel," *Haaretz*, July 29, 1997.

[737] "Dayan Says Israelis Have the Capacity to Produce A-Bombs," *New York Times,* June 25, 1981.

[738] Duncan Lennox, ed., "AGM-142 Popeye 1/2 (Have Nap/Have Lite/Raptor/Crystal Maze) (Israel), Offensive Weapons," *Jane's Strategic Weapon Systems,* Issue 50, (Surrey: Jane's Information Group, January 2009), 78–80.

[739] "Israel Called 6th Largest Nuclear Power," *Newsday,* October 6, 1986.

[740] "Revealed: The Secrets of Israel's Nuclear Arsenal," *Sunday Times* (London), No. 8,461, October 5, 1986, 1, 4–5; "Vanunu Sentenced to 18 Years in Prison," United Press International, March 27, 1988.

[741] "London Paper Reports Israel Has Built Bombs," *New York Times,* October 6, 1986.

[742] David K. Shipler, "A-Arms Capacity of Israelis: A Topic Rich in Speculation," *New York Times,* October 2, 1986.

[743] Thomas L. Friedman, "Israel and the Bomb: Megatons of Ambiguity," *New York Times,* November 9, 1986.

[744] "Notifications from Israel (Launch Year 1976-present)," United Nations Register of Objects Launched into Outer Space, United Nations Office for Outer Space Affairs, http://www.unoosa.org.

[745] John Kifner, "Israel Launches Space Program and a Satellite," *New York Times,* September 20, 1988.

[746] "Israel: How Far Can Its Missiles Fly?" The Risk Report 1, no. 5 (June 1995). 1-5.

[747] Anthony H. Cordesman, *Israel and Syria: The Military Balance and Prospects of War* (Westport, CT: Praeger Security International, 2008), 142.

[748] "Israel launches spy satellite, can view Iran through clouds and night," Associated Press, January 21, 2008.

[749] "Israeli spy satellite successfully launched from India," *Jerusalem Post,* January 21, 2008, http://www.jpost.com/servlet/Satellite?cid=1200572504264&pagename=JPost percent2FJPArticle percent2FShowFull. *See also* Mark Tran, "Israel launches new satellite to spy on Iran," *Guardian Unlimited* (London), January 21, 2008, http://www.guardian.co.uk/iran/story/0,2244324,00.html.

[750] Barbara Opall-Rome, "Israel Launches Ofeq-9 Satellite," *Defense News,* June 22, 2010, http://www.defense-news.com/story.php?i=4681651&c=AIR&s=TOP.

[751] Aviel Magnezi, "Experts: Ofek 9 will detect Iranian activity, *Ynet News,* June 24, 2010, http://www.ynetnews.com/articles/0,7340,L-3909935,00.html.

[752] Anthony Cordesman, *Weapons of Mass Destruction in the Middle East,* Center for Strategic and International Studies, April 15, 2003.

[753] "Iranian radio interviews Israeli Nuclear Whistleblower Vanunu," BBC, December 2, 2005.

[754] Aharon Levran, *Israeli Strategy after Desert Storm: Lessons from the Second Gulf War,* (London: Frank Cass, 1997), 1–10.

[755] "Iraq Tried to Hit Israeli Nuclear Plant During Gulf War," Agence France Presse, February 25, 1997.

[756] "War in the Middle East," *Strategic Survey, 1990–1991,* (London: International Institute for Strategic Studies, 1991), 72; "Iraq Says It Aimed Missiles Israeli Reactor; Says Allies Face Defeat," Associated Press, February 17, 1991; "The Gulf War: Nuclear Plant is Targeted by Iraq," *The Guardian* (London), February 18, 1991; "Iraq Lobs Two Scuds Israel," United Press International, February 25, 1991; "The Week That Was," *Jerusalem Post,* February 28, 1991; "Persian Gulf War: The revised version of the 'mother of all battles' was a dud. So, it turns out, was the coverage," *Toronto Star,* February 20, 1994. *See also* Seymour Hersh, *The Sampson Option.*

[757] Avner Cohen, and Marvin Miller, *Nuclear Shadows in the Middle East: Prospects for Arms Control in the Wake of the Gulf Crisis*, (Cambridge, MA: Massachusetts Institute of Technology, 1990), 10.

[758] Shlomo Aronson, and Oded Brosh, *The Politics and Strategy of Nuclear Weapons in the Middle East, the Opacity Theory, and Reality, 1960-1991-An Israeli Perspective*, (Albany, NY: State University of New York Press, 1992), 276.

[759] Dan Raviv and Yossi Melman, *Friend in Deed: Inside the U.S.-Israel Alliance*, (New York: Hyperion, 1994), 399.

[760] Gulf War Air Power Survey, Volume II, Part I, Washington, DC: United States Government Printing Office, 1993, 189.

[761] William E. Burrows, and Robert Windrem, *Critical Mass: The Dangerous Race for Superweapons in a Fragmenting World*, (New York: Simon and Schuster, 1994), 297fn and Martin van Creveld, *The Sword and the Olive: A Critical History of the Israeli Defense Force*, (New York: Public Affairs, 1998), 321–22.

[762] "Israeli Experts Ponder Nuclear Issues," United Press International, January 14, 2002.

[763] "Jane's: Israel Has 7 Nuclear Facilities, Up to 200 Nuclear Weapons," Associated Press, November 18, 1994; Joseph Cirincione, with Jon B. Wolfsthal and Miriam Rajkumar, *Deadly Arsenals, Tracking Weapons of Mass Destruction*, (Washington, DC: Carnegie Endowment for International Peace, 2002), 224–25.

[764] Liat Collins, "Peres: Israel ready to give up 'the atom' in peacetime. Opposition MKs call statement irresponsible," *Jerusalem Post,* December 24, 1995, http://www.highbeam.com/doc/1P1-6000295.html.

[765] Kenneth S. Brower, "A Propensity for Conflict: Potential Scenarios and Outcomes of War in the Middle East," *Jane's Intelligence Review,* Special Report No. 14, (February 1997), 14-15. Brower noted that he was making a high estimate of the number of weapons.

[766] BBC News, August 23, 2000. According to the Stockholm International Peace Research Institute's annual report released June 4, 2012, Israel has 80 nuclear warheads.

[767] "Israel Denies Conducting Nuclear Test in May," Agence France Presse, June 17, 1998.

[768] Duncan Lennox, ed., "Offensive Weapons Table," *Jane's Strategic Weapon Systems,* Issue 50, (Surrey: Jane's Information Group, January 2009), 527–32; and Duncan Lennox, ed., "Defensive Weapons Table," *Jane's Strategic Weapon Systems,* Issue 50, (Surrey: Jane's Information Group, January 2009), 535–37.

[769] "Israel Makes Nuclear Waves with Submarine Missile Test," *Sunday Times* (London), June 18, 2000. *See* also "Sri Lanka Denies Israel Cruise Missile Tests," Agence France-Presse, June 26, 2000, http://www.afp.com.

[770] "Weapons of Mass Destruction: Popeye Turbo," Globalsecurity.org, www.globalsecurity.org accessed May 12, 2011; and "Popeye Turbo – Israel Special Weapons," WMD Around the World, http://www.fas.org, accessed May 12, 2011.

[771] National Air and Space Intelligence Center, Ballistic and Cruise Missile Threat, (Wright-Patterson AFB, OH: NASIC, 2009), 29.

[772] Duncan Lennox, ed., "Weapon inventories-Offensive/defensive weapons tables, Israel," *Jane's Strategic Weapons Systems,* March 9, 2012, http://www.janes.com.

[773] Yossi Melman, "Swimming with the Dolphins," *Haaretz,* June 8, 1998; "Report: Israel to get Subs with Nuclear Strike Capability," *Jerusalem Post,* July 3, 1998; "Navy Gets New German Sub," *Haaretz*, July 26, 2000. *See* also "Israel Has Sub-Based Atomic Arms Capability," *The Washington Post,* June 15, 2002; Efraim Inbar, "Deterring the Iranian Nuclear Threat," *Jerusalem Post,* December 4, 2005; "Israeli Navy Buys Two Nuclear-Capable Submarines From Germany," *Jerusalem Post,* in FBIS Document GMP20060823738004, August 23, 2006; Ramit Plushnick-Masti, "Israel buys 2 nuclear-capable submarines," *Associated Press,* August 25, 2006; "Germany confirms sale of two ThyssenKrupp submarines to Israel," AFX News, August 25, 2006. Israel took possession of the last two submarines in September 2009. German Chancellor Angela Merkel gave

orders to speed up completion of the Israeli order, due to the increased threat from a nuclear-potential Iran. The submarines, accordingly, were delivered a year ahead of schedule.

[774] "Israel gets two more German submarines," *Agence France Presse*, September 30, 2009.

[775] "Israel Adds Fuel to Nuclear Dispute," *Los Angeles Times,* October 12, 2003.

[776] Hillel Fendel, "Germany Approves Fifth 'Special' Submarine for Israel," Arutz 7, April 13, 2015, http://www.israelnationalnews.com/News/News.aspx/193958#.VSwinGM0Rx0.

[777] Uzi Mahnaimi, "Israel stations nuclear missile subs off Iran, *The Sunday Times,* May 30, 2010, http://www.timesonline.co.uk/tol/news/world/europe/article7140282.ece.

[778] Matti Friedman, "Nuclear slip by Olmert sets off domestic political crisis," Associated Press, December 12, 2006.

[779] "Olmert Blasted for Nuclear Tongue-Slip," Arutz 7, December 12, 2006, http://www.israelnationalnews.com/News/News.aspx/117254#.UjZXlHd-nHk.

[780] "Israel Signs UN Convention Against Nuclear Terrorism," Ministry of Foreign Affairs Jerusalem, in OSC Document GMP20061228739006, December 28, 2006.

[781] Batsheva Sobelman, "Israel has 80 nuclear warheads, can make 115 to 190 more, report says," *Los Angeles Times,* September 15, 2013, http://www.latimes.com/world/worldnow/la-fg-wn-israel-nuclear-weapons-20130915,0,4117406.story.

[782] "Israel Tests a New Propulsion for 4,000 km Jericho III Missile," Defense Update, January 17, 2008, http://www.defense-update.com.

[783] "Jericho 3," Missilethreat.com, http://www.missilethreat.com, accessed May 12, 2011; and Duncan Lennox, ed., "Jericho 1/2/3 (YA-1/YA-3) (Israel), Offensive Weapons," *Jane's Strategic Weapon Systems,* Issue 50, (Surrey: Jane's Information Group, January 2009), 84–86.

[784] Avi Lewis, "Israel's new anti-ballistic missile system 'phenomenal' in testing," *The Times of Israel,* April 1, 2015, http://www.timesofisrael.com/israel-successfully-tests-new-anti-ballistic-missile system/?utm_source=The+Times+of+Israel+Daily+Edition&utm_campaign=2409baf47a-2015_04_02&utm_medium=e-mail&utm_term=0_adb46cec92-2409baf47a-54550797.

[785] "Israel tests new nuclear-capable missile, ends joint air exercise with Italy, starts missile drill," DEBKAfile, November 2, 2011, http://www.debka.com/article/21441/.

[786] Louis René Beres, "Amid the 'Arab Spring' – Reconsidering Israel's Nuclear Posture,"
May 8, 2011, http://www.israelunitycoalition.org/news/?p=6685.

[787] Ibid.

[788] Louis René Beres, "For Middle East Peace, Israel Must Prepare for Nuclear War," *U.S. News & World Report,* December 6, 2010, http://www.usnews.com/opinion/articles/2010/12/06/for-middle-east-peace-israel-must-prepare-for-nuclear-war.

PERPETUAL NEGOTIATIONS

[1] Stephen Schwebel, "What Weight to Conquest?" in: *The Arab-Israeli Conflict: Readings and Documents,* John N. Moore, ed., (Princeton, NJ: Princeton University Press, 1977), 357, 359.

[2] *See* also Jeffrey Helmreich, "Diplomatic and Legal Aspects of the Settlement Issue," *Jerusalem Issue Brief,* January 19, 2003.

[3] Schwebel, Ibid, 358–59. *See* also Professor, Judge Stephen M. Schwebel, "What Weight to Conquest," *Justice in International Law: Selected Writings,* (Cambridge, UK: Cambridge University Press, 1994), 521–25 and in the *American Journal of International Law,* April 1970, 345–47; Julius Stone, "No Peace–No War in the Middle

East," *The Arab-Israeli Conflict: Readings and Documents,* John N. Moore, ed., (Princeton, NJ: Princeton University Press, 1977), 325.

[4] Eugene V. Rostow, "Don't Strong-Arm Israel," *New York Times,* March 19, 1991, http://www.nytimes.com/1991/03/19/opinion/don-t-strong-arm-israel.html?scp=31&sq=Eugene percent20V. percent20Rostow&st=cse.

[5] "United Nations pledges to answer UN Watch's question on Gaza being 'occupied,'" January 9, 2012, http://www.youtube.com/watch?v=4Q77Nrd8WuQ.

[6] Elizabeth Samson. "Is Gaza Occupied?: Redefining the Status of Gaza Under International Law." *American University International Law Review* 25 no. 5 (2010): 915–67.

[7] Eugene Kontorovich, "Crimea, International Law, and the West Bank," *Commentary,* June 1, 2014, http://www.commentarymagazine.com/article/crimea-international-law-and-the-west-bank/.

[8] In December 2004, Turkey and Syria signed a free trade agreement that had been under negotiation for several years. The agreement was important according to a journalist, Ehud Ya'ari who accompanied the Turkish delegation, because it included a clause in which Syria ceded its claims to Alexandretta. *See* Yoav Stern, "Turkey Singing a New Tune," *Haaretz*.com, September 1, 2005, http://www.*Haaretz*.com/hasen/pages/ShArt.jhtml?itemNo=524517. However, However, Syria has made no official announcement relinquishing its rights of sovereignty and Alexandretta is still shown as Syrian territory on Syrian maps. The author possesses a Syrian map that still shows Alexandretta as Syrian. In light of the increased tensions between Turkey and Syria, caused in no small part by the Syrian rebellion and civil war that erupted in March 2011, it is doubtful that Syria will relinquish its claims.

[9] Adapted from "So, uh, when do we all start boycotting universities and denouncing the 'Apartheid' regime of Beijing?" with permission of the author, Jonathan Kay, March 18, 2008, http://politicalmavens.com/index.php/2008/03/15/so-uh-when/.

[10] "Jerusalem: Jordan, The Holy Land," Jerusalem: Middle East Trading and Commission Agency. Map in the collection of the author.

[11] Teddy Kollek, *Jerusalem,* (Washington, DC: Washington Institute for Near East Policy, 1990), 15.

[12] "Jerusalem's Eternal Truths," *Save Jerusalem,* http://www.torahohr.net/save_jerusalem/index.htm.

[13] "Israel 1948–1967, West Bank Annexed," Palestine Facts, http://www.palestinefacts.org/pf_1948to1967_jordan_annex.php.

[14] Kollek, 15.

[15] Howard Sachar, *A History of Israel,* (New York: Alfred A. Knopf, 1996), 322.

[16] Sachar, *A History of Israel,* 350.

[17] "Terrorism Against Israel: Comprehensive Listing of Fatalities (September 1993–November 2012)" Jewish Virtual Library, http://www.jewishvirtuallibrary.org/jsource/Terrorism/victims.html. *See* also "CAIR and Hamas," http://www.investigativeproject.org/documents/misc/113.pdf.

[18] "Terrorism Against Israel: Number of Fatalities (1920 - Present)," Jewish Virtual Library, retrieved March 9, 2014, http://www.jewishvirtuallibrary.org/jsource/Peace/osloterr.html.

[19] *See* Israel–Jordan Peace Treaty, October 26, 1994, Annex 1 (a), (b), (c), http://www.jewishvirtuallibrary.org/jsource/Peace/annex1.html.

[20] Dror Eydar, "The Second Intifada: A planned terror war," *Israel Hayom,* August 30, 2013, http://www.israelhayom.com/site/newsletter_opinion.php?id=5561.

[21] Ibid.

[22] Khaled Abu Toameh, "Arafat ordered Hamas attacks against Israel in 2000," *Jerusalem Post,* September 29, 2010, http://www.jpost.com/Home/Article.aspx?id=189574.

[23] Martin Sherman, "Into the Fray: A (superfluous) exercise in (inevitable) futility," *Jerusalem Post*, December 4, 2014, http://www.jpost.com/Opinion/Into-the-Fray-A-superfluous-exercise-in-inevitable-futility-383720.

[24] Elad Benari, "Rice Memoir Reveals: Olmert Offered Abbas 94%; Abbas Said No," Arutz 7, October 26, 2011, http://www.israelnationalnews.com/News/News.aspx/149084#.USpW7XeupiM/.

[25] "Eight Palestinian factions refuse two-state solutions," Kuwait News Agency, April 25, 2010, http://www.kuna.net.kw/NewsAgencyPublicSite/ArticleDetails.aspx?id=2078394&Language=en&searchtext=syria.

[26] "Smash Israel, Saud Urges," *The Charleston Daily Mail*, January 10, 1954, 1, http://newspaperarchive.com/charleston-daily-mail/1954-01-10/.

[27] Tzvi Ben Gedalyahu, "Abbas: Only Difference from Hamas Is that Fatah Is in Power," Israel National News, January 18, 2010, http://www.unitedjerusalem.org/index2.asp?id=1325698.

[28] Louis René Beres, "Mr. President There Can Be No 'Two-state solution,'" FrontPage, June 3, 2011, http://frontpagemag.com/2011/06/03/mr-president-there-can-be-no-two-state-solution/.

[29] PA TV (Fatah), January 29, 2010, translation in Itamar Marcus and Nan Jacques Zilberdik, 'PA TV sermon, "Jews are enemies of Allah and humanity–Kill them," Palestinian Media Watch, February 1, 2010, http://www.memri.org/report/en/0/0/0/0/0/0/3946.htm.

[30] Ibid.

[31] Ibid.

[32] Ibid.

[33] "Mid-East peace possible with full settlement freeze," *Mail and Guardian Online,* December 16, 2009.

[34] *Reliance of the Traveller,* o9.16 (2).

[35] *See* Y. Harkabi, *Arab Strategies and Israel's Response* (New York: Free Press, 1977), 55.

[36] Raphael Israeli, *"I, Egypt:" Aspects of President Anwar al-Sadat's Political Thought,* Jerusalem Papers on Peace Problems, 34, (Jerusalem: The Magnus Press, Hebrew University, 1981), 148.

[37] For the complete text of the speech, "President Anwar Sadat's Address to the Israeli Knesset," November 20, 1977, *see* http://www.ibiblio.org/sullivan/docs/Knesset-speech.html.

[38] Ibid.

[39] "President Anwar Sadat's Address to the Israeli Knesset," November 20, 1977, http://www.ibiblio.org/sullivan/docs/Knesset-speech.html.

[40] Ibid.

[41] Damascus Television Service, March 7, 1990.

[42] *Al-Siyassa,* (Kuwait), December 18, 1988.

[43] "Incitement to Violence Against Israel by the leadership of the Palestinian Authority," November 27, 1996, http://www.mfa.gov.il/MFA/Archive/Peace+Process/1996/INCITEMENT%20TO%20VIOLENCE%20AGAINST%20ISRAEL%20BY%20LEADERSHI.

[44] http://www.state.gov/secretary/rm/2009a/july/126829.htm.

[45] Ibid.

[46] *Globe & Mail* (Toronto), December 14, 2010 and *Jerusalem Post,* December 14, 2010.

[47] "Hamas leader calls for 'all Palestine,' national unity," *Hurriyet Daily News,* December 14, 2012, http://www.hurriyetdailynews.com/hamas-leader-calls-for-all-palestine-national-unity.aspx?pageID=238&nid=36414.

[48] "PLO Leader: Oslo Accords Not Palestinian Recognition of Israel," JNS News Service, The Jewish Press, July 25, 2013, http://www.jewishpress.com/news/breaking-news/plo-leader-oslo-accords-as-palestinian-recognition-of-israel/2013/07/25/.

[49] Jonathon M. Seidl, "Obama Sides With Palestinians—Endorses 1967 Border Demands," The Blaze, May 19, 2011, http://www.theblaze.com/stories/2011/05/19/obama-endorses-palestinian-border-demands/.

[50] S/PV 1382, 31, of 22.11.67.

[51] Lord Caradon, interviewed on *Kol Israel* ("The Voice of Israel" radio) on February 10, 1973.

[52] Lord Caradon, interview in *The Beirut Daily Star,* June 12, 1974.

[53] *American Journal of International Law,* Volume 64, September 1970, 69.

[54] S/PV. 1377, 37, of 15. 11.67.

[55] *American Journal of International Law,* Volume 64, September 1970, 68.

[56] UN S/PV. 1373, 112, of November 9, 1967. *See* also Sammy Benoit, "The Real UN Resolution 242," *The American Thinker,* June 25, 2009, http://www.americanthinker.com/2009/06/un_resolution_242_for_dummies.html.

[57] Address to the Nation, June 19, 1967. *See* "President Johnson's Five Principles for Peace in the Middle East," http://www.jewishvirtuallibrary.org/jsource/US-Israel/lbjpeace.html.

[58] Lyndon B. Johnson, Address before the 125th anniversary meeting of B'nai Brith, Washington, DC, September 10, 1968. Reprinted in the *Department of State Bulletin,* October 7, 1968.

[59] Ronald Reagan, "Address to the Nation on United States Policy for Peace in the Middle East," September 1, 1982, http://www.presidency.ucsb.edu/ws/index.php?pid=42911.

[60] Arthur Goldberg. "UN Resolution 242: Origin, Meaning, and Significance," *National Committee on American Foreign Policy,* April 2002, www.mefacts.com/cache/html/arab-countries/10159.htm.

[61] *Jerusalem Post,* January 23, 1970.

[62] *In My Way: Memoirs of Lord George Brown,* (London: St. Martin's Press, 1971), 233.

[63] *The MacNeil-Lehrer Report,* March 30, 1978.

[64] Eugene W. Rostow, "Resolved: are the settlements legal? Israeli West Bank policies," *The New Republic,* October 21, 1991, http://www.tzemachdovid.org/Facts/islegal1.shtml and http://www.bjeny.org/254.htm.

[65] Ibid.

[66] Arthur Goldberg, "The Meaning of 242," *Jerusalem Post,* June 10, 1977.

[67] Shlomo Slonim, *Jerusalem in America's Foreign Policy, 1947–1997,* (New York: Springer Publishing), 1999, 200.

[68] Howard Grief, "Security Council Resolution 242: A Violation of Law and a Pathway to Disaster," Ariel Center for Policy Research, ACPR Policy Paper No. 17, January 2008, http://www.acpr.org.il/pp/pp173-grief-E.pdf.

[69] *See* Eugene V. Rostow, "The Illegality of the Arab Attack on Israel of October 6, 1973," *The Arab-Israeli Conflict: Readings and Documents,* John N. Moore, ed., (Princeton, NJ: Princeton University Press, 1977) 458–75.

[70] Bret Stephens, "The Price of Ignoring Mideast Reality," *Wall Street Journal,* September 6, 2013, http://online.wsj.com/article/global_view.html.

[71] Henry Kissinger, *Years of Renewal,* (New York: Simon and Schuster, 1999), 376.

[72] Caroline B. Glick, "Column One: Israel's Twenty Year Nightmare," *Jerusalem Post,* September 13, 2013, http://www.jpost.com/Opinion/Columnists/Column-One-Israels-20-year-nightmare-326012.

[73] Sarah Honig, "Another Tack: The same sea," July 20, 2012, http://sarahhonig.com/2012/07/20/another-tack-the-same-sea/.

[74] United Nations Security Council, Statement by Israeli Deputy Minister for Foreign Affairs, Benjamin Netanyahu, S/PV.2923, May 29, 1990, http://unispal.un.org/UNISPAL.NSF/0/7959F6FCCFEB4D6305256516004A8944.

[75] "Declaration of Principles," Israeli Ministry of Foreign Affairs, http://www.mfa.gov.il/mfa/foreignpolicy/peace/guide/pages/declaration%20of%20principles.aspx.

[76] Jordanian television, September 14, 1993. *See* also Neil Snyder. "Palestinians Don't Want Peace with Israel and Mitt Romney was Correct to Say So," *American Thinker,* September 20, 2012, http://www.americanthinker.com/blog/2012/09/palestinians_dont_want_peace_with_israel_and_mitt_romney_was_correct_to_say_so.html.

[77] *See* video http://www.youtube.com/watch?v=eEYXAIPct_s. *See* also "Arafat would condemn [terror] operations by day while night he would do honorable things," Eye on Islam, July 27, 2009, http://eye-on-islam.blogspot.com/2009/07/arafat-would-condemn-terror-operations.html.

[78] "Iranian Political Analyst Mohammad Sadeq Al-Hosseini: If Not for the Geneva Deal, Obama Would Have Had to Kiss Nasrallah's and Khamenei's Hands to Prevent the Annihilation of Israel," MEMRI, December 11, 2013, http://www.memritv.org/clip_transcript/en/4073.htm.

[79] For original page *see* http://www.freezepage.com/1299192052LRKZCVHZXJ.

[80] "Bylaws Disappear from Brotherhood's English-language Site," IPT News, February 28, 2011, http://www.investigativeproject.org/2635/bylaws-disappear-from-brotherhood-english, and http://www.investigativeproject.org/2635/bylaws-disappear-from-brotherhood-english.

[81] Ryan Mauro, "The Muslim Brotherhood's Cover-Up, Frontpagemag.com, March 10, 2011, http://frontpagemag.com/2011/03/10/the-muslim-brotherhood%E2%80%99s-cover-up/.

[82] Christine Brim, "Muslim Brotherhood Deception: They Say Different Things in English and Arabic," Big Peace, January 30, 2011, http://bigpeace.com/cbrim/2011/01/30/muslim-brotherhood-deception-they-say-different-things-in-english-and-arabic/.

[83] Qur'an 3:28; other verses referenced by the *ulama* in support of *taqiyya* include 2:173, 2:185, 4:29, 16:106, 22:78, 40:28.

[84] See *Sahih Muslim* Hadith: Book 32, number 6303, regarded as an authentic Hadith.

[85] Amir Taheri, *The Spirit of Allah: Khomeini and the Islamic Revolution,* (Bethesda, MD: Adler & Adler, 1986), 227.

[86] Abol Hassan Bani-Sadr, *My Turn to Speak: Iran, the Revolution & Secret Deals with the U.S.*, English trans. (Washington DC: Brassey's, 1991), 2.

[87] Daniel Pipes, "Lessons from the Prophet Muhammad's Diplomacy," *Middle East Quarterly,* September 1999, http://www.danielpipes.org/316/al-hudaybiya-and-lessons-from-the-prophet-muhammads.

[88] Ibid.

[89] *New York Times,* May 14, 1967.

[90] *Al-Anba,* (Kurwait), December 18, 1988.

[91] As reported by MEMRI, April 14, 2008, http://www.memri.org/report/en/0/0/0/0/0/0/2728.htm.

[92] PA TV, August 25, 2008.

[93] "Fatah Central Committee Member Abbas Zaki Calls Netanyahu and Obama 'scumbags' and Says: 'The Greater Goal Cannot Be Accomplished in One Go,'" Al-Jazeera TV (Qatar), September 23, 2011, as monitored by MEMRI, http://www.memritv.org/clip/en/3130.htm. *See* also Chana Ya'ar, "Fatah Official: Shhh! 1949 Lines would be Israel's Doom," Arutz 7 IsraelNationalNews.com, October 3, 2011; and "PA leader: Stages plan to eliminate Israel is basis of PA policy," Palestine Media Watch, PMW Bulletin, January 6, 2014, http://palwatch.org/.

[94] *Sahih Bukhari* Hadith: Vol. 4, book 52, numbers 267–69.

[95] "The Battle of the Trench," http://www.thewaytotruth.org/prophetmuhammad/trench.html.

[96] Cyril Glasse, *New Encyclopedia of Islam: A Revised Edition of the Concise Encyclopedia of Islam,* (Lanham, MD: AltaMira Press, 2003), 81.

[97] Phil Hirschkorn, "Moussaoui: White House was my 9/11 target," CNN.com, March 27, 2006, http://www.cnn.com/2006/LAW/03/27/moussaoui/index.html.

[98] Elad Benari, "Abbas: There's No Progress, and It's All Israel's Fault," IsraelNationalNews.com, January 20, 2014, http://www.israelnationalnews.com/News/News.aspx/176491#.UuGhSxBlBWU.

[99] *International Constitutional Law,* http://www.servat.unibe.ch/law/icl/index.html

[100] "Morocco: Draft Text of the Constitution Adopted the Referendum of 1 July 2011," trans. Jefri J. Ruchti. 5, http://www.ancl-radc.org.za/sites/default/files/morocco_eng.pdf.

[101] UAE Constitution in translation, http://www.refworld.org/docid/48eca8132.html.

[102] *Draft Palestine Constitution,* March 25, 2003, http://www.mideastweb.org/palconstitution.htm.

[103] Mark Kennedy, "Stephen Harper says he won't 'single out' Israel publicly for criticism over settlements," *National Post,* January 21, 2014, http://news.nationalpost.com/2014/01/21/stephen-harper-says-he-wont-single-out-israel-publicly-for-criticism-over-settlements/.

[104] It should be noted that Iceland, Denmark, Norway, Sweden, Finland, the Faroes, Aland, England, the Dominican Republic, Georgia, Guernsey, Jersey, Jamaica, Malta, Scotland, Slovakia, and Tonga—all have Christian crosses in their flags. The United Kingdom's flag boasts two kinds of crosses.

[105] Scott Shiloh, *Mofaz: Hamas Acting Responsibly; Hamas: Israel Must Change Flag,* Arutz Sheva, January 30, 2006, http://www.israelnationalnews.com/News/News.aspx/97520.

[106] *See* for example Daniel Pipes, "Imperial Israel: The Nile-to-Euphrates Calumny," *Middle East Quarterly,* March, 1994, http://www.meforum.org/215/imperial-israel-the-nile-to-euphrates-calumny; Danny Rubinstein, "Inflammatory legends," *Haaretz*.com, November 15, 2004, http://www.*Haaretz*.com/print-edition/opinion/inflammatory-legends-1.140253; and Saqr Abu Fakhr, "Seven Prejudices about the Jews", *Al-Hayat,* November 12–14, 1997.

[107] Khaled Abu Toameh, "Fatah has never recognized Israel," *Jerusalem Post,* July 22, 2009, http://www.jpost.com/servlet/Satellite?pagename=JPost percent2FJPArticle percent2FShowFull&cid=1248277865155.

[108] Gil Ronen, "WikiLeaks: Netanyahu Would Have Used Flanking Move in Lebanon," Israel National News, November 30, 2010, http://cablegate.wikileaks.org/cable/2007/04/07TELAVIV1114.html.

[109] "Address by P.M. Sharon to Conference of Presidents," February 20, 2005, http://www.mfa.gov.il/MFA/Peace+Process/Guide+to+the+Peace+Process/Israeli+Disengagement+Plan+20-Jan-2005.htm.

[110] Menahem Gantz, "'Italy allowed Palestinian terror groups to roam free,'" Ynetnews.com, August 17, 2008, http://www.ynetnews.com/articles/0,7340,L-3583872,00.html.

[111] "Rabin's Remarks on Beit Lid Bombing, January 23, 1995," The Jewish Agency for Israel: *Speeches by Yitzhak Rabin*, http://www.jafi.org/JewishAgency/English/Jewish+Education/Compelling+Content/Eye+on+Israel/Current+Issues/Rabin/Speeches+by+Yitzhak+Rabin.htm.

[112] PA TV, July 7, 2009.

[113] The Fateh flag bears the Fateh emblem which shows the map of all of "Palestine"(i.e. Israel) over crossed rifles and PLO flags. The same emblem appears on the Fatah website, (http://rs6.net/tn.jsp?et=1102636275816&s=10484&e=001r5x73XBfBQwmhn2PfyNVdwgkvBCo_ySXTc3sr9sf9HhNs2CP4D0vPK91knkIJEMgOVB-kzFz83ukSjtsbhxKcx3FQFWokW3VSbJ5djDj16DQ=) and other official PLO/Fatah publications.

[114] *See* for example, Itamar Marcus and Nan Jacques Zilberdijk, "PA to Israelis: Go to Europe and Ethiopia because Israel is 'stolen' land, PA TV displays map portraying all of Israel as 'Palestine,'" Palestine Media Watch, May 11, 2010, http://palwatch.org/main.aspx?fi=157&doc_id=2229.

[115] Bat Ye'or, *The Dhimmi: Jews and Christians Under Islam,* (Rutherford, NJ: Fairleigh Dickinson University Press, 1985), 122.

[116] Sun Tzu, *The Art of War,* III, 18, http://www.gutenberg.org/files/132/132.txt.

[117] Golda Meir, *My Life,* (New York: G.P. Putnam's Sons, 1975), 433–34.

ATTEMPTS AT SECURITY

[1] Number died calculated from the inauguration of the Palestinian Authority on May 4, 1994, to the launching of Operation *Defensive Shield,* March 28, 2003. Numbers from IDF and Israel Foreign Ministry, which deducted those attacks perpetrated before the Palestinian Authority was given *de facto* control on the ground.

[2] As quoted by Ariel Sharon, in the documentary *Israel and the Arabs: 50 Year War*, http://en.wikiquote.org/wiki/David_Ben-Gurion.

[3] Shmuel Katz, *Lone Wolf: A Biography of Vladimir (Zeev) Jabotinsky*, (New York: Barricade Books, 1996), 666.

[4] Book of Psalms 18:38.

[5] David Raziel, "Action Defense," as cited in Daniel Levine, *The Birth of the Irgun Zvai Leumi: A Jewish Liberation Movement*, (Jerusalem: Gefen Books, 1991), 122.

[6] Dennis Mitzner and Ariel Solomon, "Daniel Pipes: 'Israel Has No Policy'," *Pajamas Media*, December 10, 2010, http://www.danielpipes.org/9168/israel-has-no-policy.

[7] Gerald Ford, "Address to the 29th Session of the General Assembly of the United Nations, September 18, 1974, http://www.presidency.ucsb.edu/ws/index.php?pid=4718#axzz1elW01T1Y. *See* also the American Presidency Project: Gerald R. Ford: Address to the 29th Session of the General Assembly of the United Nations. http://www.presidency.ucsb.edu/ws/index.php?pid=4718#ixzz1clWny3MM

[8] Shmuel Katz, "Peril in Sinai," *Jerusalem Post*, January 22, 1982 and http://www.eretzisraelforever.net/Katz/Katz_ViewArticle.asp?sAction=view&iArticleId=660794367.

[9] Raphael Israeli, *PLO in Lebanon: Selected Documents*. (London: Weidenfeld and Nicolson, 1983). xi.

[10] Amos Harel, Yossi Verter and Shlomo Shamir, "UN admits it has a videotape of soldiers' kidnap," *Haaretz Daily Newspaper - English Internet Edition*, July 6, 2001, http://www.mia.org.il/archive/010706ha_eng.html.

[11] *Yediot Aharonot*, October 20, 2006.

[12] Yoav Stern, "Report: Hezbollah's New Missiles Have Range 'Israel Can't Fathom,'" *Haaretz*, August 29, 2008.

[13] Josephine Cuneta, "Philippines Weighs Pulling Out Troops From Golan Heights," *Wall Street Journal*, May 10, 2013, http://stream.wsj.com/story/syria/SS-2-34182/SS-2-229705/.

[14] Phoebe Greenwood, "Austria to withdraw Golan Heights peacekeepers over Syrian fighting," *The Guardian*, June 6, 2013, http://www.guardian.co.uk/world/2013/jun/06/syrian-golan-crossing-israeli-military-quneitra.

[15] "Syrian rebels said to control most of the border with Israel," *Times of Israel*, September 13, 2014, http://www.timesofisrael.com/syrian-rebels-said-to-control-most-of-israel-border/.

[16] "UN pulling out peacekeepers from Syrian side of Golan Heights," *Jerusalem Post*, September 15, 2014, http://www.jpost.com/Middle-East/Report-UN-pulling-out-peacekeepers-from-Syrian-side-of-Golan-Heights-375401.

[17] As quoted in *The Guardian*, February 3, 2004.

[18] UN General Assembly Resolution 2535 B (XXIV) of December 10, 1969, http://unispal.un.org/UNISPAL.NSF/0/41F2C6DCE4DAA765852560DF004E0AC8.

[19] UN General Assembly Resolution 2625 (XXV) of October 24, 1970 at http://daccess-dds-ny.un.org/doc/RESOLUTION/GEN/NR0/348/90/IMG/NR034890.pdf?OpenElement.

[20] UN General Assembly Resolution 2708 (XXV) of December 14, 1970, http://daccess-dds-ny.un.org/doc/RESOLUTION/GEN/NR0/349/73/IMG/NR034973.pdf?OpenElement.

[21] UN General Assembly Resolution 3236 (XXIX) of November 22, 1974, http://daccess-dds-ny.un.org/doc/RESOLUTION/GEN/NR0/738/38/IMG/NR073838.pdf?OpenElement.

[22] Mitchell G. Bard, "Arab/Muslim Attitudes Toward Israel," http://www.jewishvirtuallibrary.org/jsource/myths/mf25.html.

[23] "Israeli-Palestinian Interim Agreement on the West Bank and the Gaza Strip, Washington, D.C., September 28, 1995," http://www.knesset.gov.il/process/docs/heskemb_eng.htm.

[24] Text of Convention, http://avalon.law.yale.edu/20th_century/intam03.asp.

[25] "Abbas in 2009: 'No disagreement between Fatah and Hamas about belief, policy or resistance,'" PMW Palestinian Media Watch, April 24, 2014, http://palwatch.org/main.aspx?fi=157&doc_id=11283.

[26] Frank Ruddy (1995-01-25). "Review of United Nations Operations & Peacekeeping". Washington, DC, Congress of the United States, http://www.arso.org/06-3-1.htm.

[27] "Western Sahara: Out of the Impasse," *International Crisis Group Middle East/North Africa Report,* no. 66, June 11, 2007, 3.

[28] Ibid., 6.

[29] "UNMIS, United Nations Mission in the Sudan," http://www.un.org/en/peacekeeping/missions/unmis/index.shtml.

[30] "UN Peacekeepers Slacking Over Sudan Peace Deal - Report," *The Nigerian Observer,* August 1, 2009, http://www.nigerianobservernews.com/08012009/08012009/news/foreignnews2.html.

[31] "Thousands head south for Sudan vote," Al Jazeera, January 7, 2011, http://english.aljazeera.net/news/africa/2011/01/201117131529838380.html.

[32] Caroline B. Glick, "Sudanese crossroads," *Jerusalem Post,* January 11, 2011.

[33] As quoted in "Aide-mémoire from Secretary of State Dulles to Ambassador Eban," February 11, 1957, Israel Ministry of Foreign Affairs, Foreign Relations, Historical documents, http://www.mfa.gov.il/MFA/Foreign+Relations/Israels+Foreign+Relations+since+1947/1947-1974/23+Aide-mémoire +from+Secretary+of+State+Dulles+to.htm.

[34] As quoted in "Statement to the General Assembly by Foreign Minister Meir, March 1,1957," Israel Ministry of Foreign Affairs, Foreign Relations, Historical documents, http://www.mfa.gov.il/MFA/Foreign+Relations/Israels+Foreign+Relations+since+1947/1947-1974/26+Statement+to+the+General+Assembly+by+Foreign+Mi.htm.

[35] Ibid.

[36] As quoted in "Address by Prime Minister Begin the National Defense College, August 8, 1982," Israel Ministry of Foreign Affairs, Foreign Relations, Historical documents, http://www.mfa.gov.il/MFA/Foreign percent20Relations/Israels percent20Foreign percent20Relations percent20since percent201947/1982-1984/55 percent20Address percent20by percent20Prime percent20Minister percent20Begin percent20percent20the percent20National.

[37] "Middle East: UNEF I," http://www.un.org/Depts/dpko/dpko/co_mission/unef1backgr2.html.

[38] Speech by Egyptian President Nasser at advanced UAR air base, May 22, 1967.

[39] Voice of the Arabs, May 25, 1967 as quoted in United Nations General Assembly A/PV.1526, June 19, 1967, http://unispal.un.org/UNISPAL.NSF/0/729809A9BA3345EB852573400054118A.

[40] Abba Eban, *My Country: The History of Modern Israel,* (London: Weidenfeld & Nicolson, 1972), 209; Martin Gilbert, *Israel: A History,* Chapter 21, http://www.sixdaywar.co.uk/nassers_challenge-martin-gilbert.htm. *See also* Michael Oren, *Six Days of War,* (New York: Oxford University Press, 2002), 100.

[41] The Talmud, Ethics of Our Fathers 2:3.

[42] "Golda: 'What Happened in '67,'" *Near East Report,* Vol. XX, No. 22, June 2, 1976, 97.

[43] *Foreign Relations of the United States, 1964-1968, Volume XVIII, Arab-Israeli Dispute, 1964-1967,* Office of the Historian, Bureau of Public Affairs, United States Department of State, Washington, DC, 2000, 135, 136, 138, http://www.fas.org/sgp/advisory/state/frusmide.html.

[44] "Golda: 'What Happened in '67,'" Ibid.

[45] "Ceasefire terms," *Jerusalem Post,* August 7, 1970.

[46] *New York Times,* August 17, 1970; *Washington Post,* August 17, 1970.

[47] *Washington Post,* August 18, 1970.

[48] State Department Statement, August 19, 1970 in the *Department of State Bulletin* of September 7, 1970. *See also Washington Post,* August 19, 20, 1970.

[49] Ibid.

[50] Ran Ronan. *Eagle in the Sky,* (Tel Aviv: Contento DeSemrik, 2013), 363.

[51] "King Faisal Air Base," GlobalSecurity.org, http://www.globalsecurity.org/military/world/gulf/tabuk.htm.

[52] Aluf Benn, "Worries About Saudi Planes Cloud U.S.-Israel Strategic Talks," *Daily Alert,* Jerusalem Center for Public Affairs, October 22, 2003, http://www.dailyalert.org/archive/2003-10/2003-10-22.html. *See* also "Lifting of U.S. Ban Places Israel in Saudi Arabian Danger," IsraelNationalNews.com, December 22, 2003, http://www.allbusiness.com/middle-east/israel/712891-1.html.

[53] Anthony H. Cordesman, "Iraq War Note: Saudi Redeployment of the F-15 to Tabuk," Center for Strategic & International Studies, Washington, DC, October 31, 2003, http://csis.org/files/media/csis/pubs/031031_warnote.pdf.

[54] Aluf Benn, "Worries About Saudi Planes Cloud U.S.-Israel Strategic Talks," Ibid. *See* also Melanie Phillips, "My enemy's enemy," August 2, 2007, http://www.melaniephillips.com/diary/?p=1605.

[55] "Potential Threats To Israel: Saudi Arabia," GlobalSecurity.org, July 2009, http://forum.globalsecurity.org/showthread.php?t=30771.

[56] "Bangla border fence deadline extended," *The Assam Tribune,* March 17, 2011, http://www.assamtribune.com/scripts/detailsnew.asp?id=mar1711/at09.

[57] April Reese, "U.S.-Mexico fence building continues despite Obama's promise to review effects," *New York Times,* April 16, 2009, http://www.nytimes.com/gwire/2009/04/16/16greenwire-usmexico-fence-building-continues-despite-obam-10570.html.

[58] Joshua Craze, "Saudi builds border defences as desert frontiers defy efforts to fix lines in the sand," *Islam Daily,* March 3, 2007, http://www.islamdaily.org/en/saudi-arabia/5399.saudi-builds-border-defences-as-desert-frontiers-d.htm.

[59] "Syria and Hezbullah build an apartheid wall," May 17, 2010, http://israelmatzav.blogspot.com/2010/05/syria-and-hezbullah-build-apartheid.html.

[60] Herb Keinon, "PM 'satisfied' with Egypt border fence progress," *Jerusalem Post,* March 27, 2012, http://www.jpost.com/Defense/Article.aspx?ID=263649&R=R1.

[61] Gordon Ben-zvi, "Israel Completes 245 Mile [sic], NIS 1.6 Billion Security Fence Along Sinai Border with Egypt," *The Algemeiner,* December 4, 2013, http://www.algemeiner.com/2013/12/04/245-mile-1-6-billion-shekel-security-fence-between-israel-and-sinai-completed/.

[62] "Greece considers fence on part of Turkish border,: *The Washington Post,* January 3, 2011. *See* also Henry Ridgwell, "Greece Plans to Build Controversial Border Wall, January 5, 2011, http://www.voanews.com/english/news/Greece-Plans-to-Build-Controversial-Border-Wall-112933139.html and Ariel Ungar, "It's Israel's fault: The Great Wall of Greece," IsraelNationalNews.com, January 6, 2011.

[63] "The Separation Barrier - Statistics," B" Tselem—The Israeli Information Center for Human Rights, July 16, 2012, http://www.btselem.org/separation_barrier/statistics.

[64] "Suicide and Other Bombing Attacks in Israel Since the Declaration of Principles (September 1993)," Israel Ministry of Foreign Affairs, http://www.mfa.gov.il/MFA/Terrorism-+Obstacle+to+Peace/Palestinian+terror+since+2000/Suicide+and+Other+Bombing+Attacks+in+Israel+Since.htm. *See* also "List of Palestinian suicide attacks," http://en.wikipedia.org/wiki/List_of_Palestinian_suicide_attacks and "Shin Bet: 2009 was first year in decade without suicide attacks," Haaretz.com, January 17, 2010, http://www.haaretz.com/news/shin-bet-2009-was-first-year-in-decade-without-suicide-attacks-1.261589.

[65] Ibid.

[66] Shlomo Cesana, "Only 34 illegal infiltrators enter Israel in first half of 2013," *Israel Hayom*, July 2, 2013, http://www.israelhayom.com/site/newsletter_article.php?id=10401.

ROLE OF THE MEDIA

[1] Caroline B. Glick, "About those Jews . . .," June 29, 2012,

http://www.jewishworldreview.com/0612/glick062912.php3?printer_friendly.

[2] David P. Goldman, "American Culture and American Intelligence," First Things: On the Square, July 22, 2010, http://www.firstthings.com/onthesquare/2010/07/american-culture-and-american-intelligence/david-p-goldman.

[3] For a more detailed analysis of the widespread influence, see Said Aburish, "Why is there so much Anti-Israel Bias in the Press and The American Educational System?," Disclose TV, http://www.disclose.tv/forum/why-is-there-so-much-anti-israel-bias-in-us-press-edu-sys-t72449.html.

[4] "Muslims Urged to Buy More Media Influence," Little Green Footballs, September 13, 2006, http://littlegreen-footballs.com/article/22546_Muslims_Urged_to_Buy_More_Media_Influence. See also "Muslims urged to buy influence in world media," Reuters, September 13, 2006, http://www.freerepublic.com/focus/f-news/1700846/posts.

[5] "Giuliani rejects $10 million from Saudi prince," CNN News, October 12, 2001, http://archives.cnn.com/2001/US/10/11/rec.giuliani.prince/.

[6] Eric Lipton, Brooke Williams, and Nicholas Confessore, "Foreign Powers Buy Influence Think tanks," New York Times, September 6, 2014, http://www.nytimes.com/2014/09/07/us/politics/foreign-powers-buy-influence-at-think tanks.html?_r=0.

[7] Ibid.

[8] Ibid.

[9] Ibid.

[10] Brooke Williams, Eric Lipton and Alicia Parlapiano, "Foreign Government Contributions to Nine Think tanks," New York Times, September 7, 2014, http://www.nytimes.com/interactive/2014/09/07/us/politics/foreign-government-contributions-to-nine-think tanks.html.

[11] Ibid.

[12] "The Atlantic Council Launches Rafik Hariri Center for the Middle East," PRNewswire/, September 21, 2011, http://www.prnewswire.com/news-releases/the-atlantic-council-launches-rafik-hariri-center-for-the-middle-east-130278343.html.

[13] Rick Moran, "Revealed: Brookings Shilled for Qatar," PJ Media, September 7, 2014, http://pjmedia.com/tatler/2014/09/07/revealed-brookings-shilled-for-qatar/.

[14] Herb Keinon, "Jerusalem doubts Indyk's institute after Qatar funding reports," Jerusalem Post, September 8, 2014, http://www.jpost.com/Arab-Israeli-Conflict/Jlem-doubts-Indyks-institute-after-Qatar-funding-reports-374717.

[15] Eric Lipton, Brooke Williams, and Nicholas Confessore, "Foreign Powers Buy Influence Think tanks," New York Times, September 6, 2014, http://www.nytimes.com/2014/09/07/us/politics/foreign-powers-buy-influence-at-think tanks.html?_r=0.

[16] "2014 Freedom of the Press data," Freedom of the Press, (New York: Freedom House, 2014), http://freedomhouse.org/report-types/freedom-press?gclid=CMjo9ZXDtMACFQqCfgodvyEAxQ#.U_5kuRDlZx2..

[17] Islamic Media Charter, Missouri School of Journalism, University of Missouri, http://www.rjionline.org/mas/code-of-ethics/islamic-media-charter.

[18] For example see: http://honestreporting.com/the-wretched-scandal-of-reporting-from-gaza/. See also http://www.aijac.org.au/news/article/for-propaganda-purposes-palestinian-children-in-. Regarding indoctrination, see http://palwatch.org/main.aspx?fi=157&doc_id=9308; http://www.mrctv.org/videos/us-senate-committee-palestinian-propaganda-and-child-abuse; http://www.palwatch.org/main.aspx?fi=846.

[19] Michael Moynihan, "What Hassan Rouhani Really Said About the Holocaust," The Daily Beast, September 26, 2013, http://www.thedailybeast.com/articles/2013/09/26/what-hassan-rouhani-really-said-about-the-holocaust.html.

[20] "Exclusive: CNN Fabricates Iranian President's Remarks about Holocaust," FARS News Agency, September 27, 2013, http://english.farsnews.com/newstext.aspx?nn=13920703001316.

[21] Shraga Simmons, *David & Goliath: The explosive inside story of media bias in the Israeli–Palestinian Conflict.* (Jerusalem: Emesphere Productions, 2012), 99.

[22] Christopher Allbritton. "Tales from the South, Sort of...," July 26, 2006, http://www.back-to-iraq.com/tales-from-the-south-sort-of/.

[23] "Syria, Iraq, Egypt most deadly nations for journalists," CPJ Committee to Journalists, December 30, 2013, http://www.cpj.org/reports/2013/12/syria-iraq-egypt-most-deadly-nations-for-journalis.php.

[24] Manfred Gerstenfeld, "Op-Ed: The Obsessive Belgian Anti-Israel Bias," Arutz 7, June 21, 2015, http://www.israelnationalnews.com/Articles/Article.aspx/17110.

[25] "EXCLUSIVE: New York Times Slammed for Bias on Billboard in Front of Times Square HQ," January 27, 2014, http://unitycoalitionforisrael.org/uci_2014/?p=5829.

[26] Tamar Sternthal, "*Teen Newsweek* Readers Beware!," CAMERA, November 15, 2000, http://www.camera.org/index.asp?x_context=22&x_article=187.

[27] Edward Alexander. *NBC's War in Lebanon: The Distorting Mirror.* New York: Americans For a Safe Israel, 1983, 5.

[28] Ibid., 25. *See* also John Chancellor, NBC Nightly News, June 7, 1982.

[29] Henry I. Silverman, "Reuters: Principles Of Trust Or Propaganda?" *Journal of Applied Business Research,* November/December 2011, 93–116. *See* also the full text of this study http://journals.cluteonline.com/index.php/JABR/article/view/6469.

[30] *See* "The Trust Principles," Thomson Reuters, http://thomsonreuters.com/about/trust_principles/.

[31] http://handbook.reuters.com/index.php/Reporting_about_people#Social_responsibility. Retrieved September 17, 2012.

[32] Ibid.

[33] Mitchell Bard. "Beware of Disinformation," aish.com, July 22, 2006, http://www.aish.com/jw/mo/48951491.html.

[34] Ann Scott Tyson. "Military's Killing Of 2 Journalists In Iraq Detailed In New Book," *The Washington Post,* September 15, 2009, 7.

[35] "Altered images prompt photographer's firing," NBC News.com, August 7, 2006, http://www.nbcnews.com/id/13165165/ns/world_news-mideast_n_africa/t/altered-images-prompt-photographers-firing/#.UhlSmXfxkpo.

[36] Dilay Gundogan, "New outcry as Erdoğan tells female reporter to 'know your place,'" AFP, August 8, 2014, http://news.yahoo.com/outcry-erdogan-tells-female-reporter-know-place-154626438.html.

[37] Eva Cahen, "French TV Sticks by Story That Fueled Palestinian Intifada," Crosswalk.com, February 15, 2005, http://www.crosswalk.com/1313004/.

[38] http://aldurah.com/the-al-durah-incident/the-evidence/france2-raw-footage-presented-to-court/.

[39] http://www.youtube.com/watch?v=75hiDGp89Xk.

[40] http://www.seconddraft.org/index.php?option=com_content&view=article&id=595:adfefacialrecognition-expert&catid=85:the-al-durah-case-the-videos&Itemid=250.

[41] David Lev, "Panel: Muhammad Al-Dura May be Alive," Arutz 7, May 19, 2013, http://www.israelnationalnews.com/News/News.aspx/168117#.UZqv4HeC1SE.

[42] http://www.veroniquechemla.info/2012/01/la-cour-dappel-de-paris-examine-les.html.

[43] Hillel Fendel, "French Court Grants Al-Dura Whistle-Blower Another Victory," IsraelNationalNews.com June 14, 2010. *See* also Nidra Poller, "Myth, Fact and the Al-Dura Affair," *Commentary*, September 2005 and Philippe Karsenty, "We Need to Expose the Muhammad al-Dura Hoax," *Middle East Quarterly,* Fall 2008, 57–65.

[44] Shlomo Cesana and *Israel Hayom* Staff, "Government report exonerates IDF in 2000 al-Dura shooting," *Israel Hayom,* May 20, 2013, http://www.israelhayom.com/site/newsletter_article.php?id=9389.

[45] http://www.theaugeanstables.com/al-durah-affair-the-dossier/karsenty-court-of-appeals-decision-english/.

[46] http://www.breitbart.com/Breitbart-TV/2012/11/15/Palestinians-Caught-Faking-Injuries-For-BBC%20 Cameras; http://www.nationalpost.com/news/story.html?id=48fc4069-cf42-4dbd-ab0e-857ad6142ec3; http://www.seconddraft.org./index.php?option=com_content&view=article&id=58&Itemid=63.

[47] Raymond Ibrahim, Egypt's First 'sex-Slave' Marriage," Gatestone Institute, July 5, 2012, http://www.raymondibrahim.com/11952/egypt-sex-slave-marriage.

[48] Raymond Ibrahim, "Calls to Destroy Egypt's Great Pyramids Begin," FrontPage Magazine, July 10, 2012, http://www.raymondibrahim.com/11973/calls-to-destroy-egypt-great-pyramids-begin.

[49] Raymond Ibrahim, "Sodomy 'For the Sake of Islam'," Gatestone Institute, July 12, 2012, http://www.raymondibrahim.com/11985/sodomy-for-the-sake-of-islam.

[50] Raymond Ibrahim, "Muslim Brotherhood 'Crucifies' Opponents, Attacks Secular Media," Investigative Project on Terrorism, August 15, 2012, http://www.raymondibrahim.com/12131/muslim-brotherhood-crucifies-opponents-attacks.

[51] Raymond Ibrahim, "Islam's Insanities: All Just a 'Hoax'?," FrontPageMagazine.com October 11, 2012, http://www.meforum.org/3357/islam-hoax.

[52] J. Kay, "Jenin comes to Lebanon. So where is the outcry?," *National Post,* May 29, 2007, http://www.nationalpost.com/story.html?id=96c43ca9-ec26-470a-adda-93476ff79799&k=26630.

[53] Ken Lee, "Jenin rises from the dirt," BBC News, June 24, 2003, http://news.bbc.co.uk/2/hi/middle_east/3015814.stm.

[54] "Jenin: IDF Military Operations–Civilian Casualties and Unlawful Killings in Jenin," Human Rights Watch, Vol. 14, No. 3 (E), May 2002.

[55] *See* the essays in Hersh Goodman and Jonathan Cummings, eds., *The Battle of Jenin: A Case Study in Israel's Communications Strategy* (Tel Aviv: Tel Aviv University, Jaffee Center for Strategic Studies, 2003).

[56] To see the actual photos and names of photographers who took them, go to Slublog, "The Passion of the Toys–Updated," Canada Free Press, August 11, 2006, http://www.canadafreepress.com/2006/slublog081106.htm.

[57] "Hamas Admits: Lost 700 Fighters in Cast Lead, Not 50," Arutz 7, November 1, 2010, http://www.israelnationalnews.com/News/Flash.aspx/197024#.UreQ_RA0Rx1.

[58] William Bigelow, "BBC Lies About Gaza Victim," Breitbart, November 15, 2012, http://www.breitbart.com/Big-Journalism/2012/11/15/BBC-Lies-About-Gaza-Victim.

[59] The Associated Press, February 3, 2011.

[60] Michael Shain, "CBS reporter's Cairo nightmare," *New York Post*, February 16, 2011, http://nypost.com/2011/02/16/cbs-reporters-cairo-nightmare/.

[61] Ibid.

[62] "Hundreds of journalists attacked in Egypt since revolution, study finds," Fox News, May 30, 2013, http://www.foxnews.com/world/2013/05/30/hundreds-journalists-attacked-in-egypt-since-revolution-study-finds/?test=latestnews.

[63] Elliott Abrams. "The Gaza numbers game," *Israel Hayom*, August 7, 2014, http://www.israelhayom.com/site/newsletter_opinion.php?id=9509.

[64] "Hamas reportedly executing tunnel diggers to keep locations secret," FoxNews.com, August 12, 2014, http://www.foxnews.com/world/2014/08/12/hamas-reportedly-executing-tunnel-diggers-to-keep-locations-secret/.

[65] Paul Mirengoff, "Report: least 160 children died digging Hamas' tunnels," Powerline, July 28, 2014, http://www.powerlineblog.com/archives/2014/07/report-at-least-160-children-died-digging-hamas-tunnels.php.

[66] John Corry, "TV: View of NBC Coverage of Lebanon Invasion," *New York Times,* February 18, 1984, http://www.nytimes.com/1984/02/18/movies/tv-view-of-nbc-coverage-of-lebanon-invasion.html.

[67] Adrian Morgan, "Saudi Methods of Indoctrination," Islam Watch, November 3, 2007, http://www.islam-watch.org/adrianmorgan/saudi-methods-of-indoctrination.htm. *See also* "Saudi Textbooks Incite Hate, Say Leaders in

American Publishing," The Daily Beast, October 17, 2012, http://www.thedailybeast.com/articles/2012/10/17/saudi-textbooks-incite-hate-say-leaders-in-american-publishing.html.

[68] Ibid. *see* also Nina Shea, "This is a Saudi textbook. (After the intolerance was removed.)," *Washington Post,* May 21, 2006, http://www.washingtonpost.com/wp-dyn/content/article/2006/05/19/AR2006051901769.html.

[69] Yoram Ettinger, "The Israeli-Saudi labyrinth," *Israel Hayom,* June 12, 2015, http://www.israelhayom.com/site/newsletter_opinion.php?id=12861.

[70] Ettinger, "The Israeli-Saudi labyrinth," Ibid.

[71] N.M. Guariglia, "The Saudi Indoctrination of Children," Family Security Matters, July 19, 2012, http://www.familysecuritymatters.org/publications/detail/the-saudi-indoctrination-of-children.

[72] Nina Shea and Bonnie Alldredge, "Saudi Textbooks: Still Teaching Hatred," *National Review Online,* June 29, 2010, http://article.nationalreview.com/437282/saudi-textbooksbrstill-teaching-hatred/nina-shea-bonnie-alldredge?page-1.

[73] Clarion Project, "U.S. State Department Buries Evidence of Saudi Textbook Indoctrination," Sharia Unveiled, March 29, 2014, https://shariaunveiled.wordpress.com/2014/03/29/u-s-state-department-buries-evidence-of-saudi-textbook-indoctrination/.

[74] "'No homosexuals in Iran': Ahmadinejad," Agence France Press, September 24, 2007, http://afp.google.com/article/ALeqM5hATGOzv6YSmgeMY1zdYbdpyrG2cw.

[75] Robert Spencer, "Complicity in Iran's Anti-Gay Jihad," FrontPageMagazine.com, March 17, 2008, http://archive.frontpagemag.com/readArticle.aspx?ARTID=30264.

[76] Dan Diker, "The Influence of Palestinian Organizations on Foreign News Reporting," Jerusalem Center for Public Affairs, March 27, 2003, http://www.jcpa.org/brief/brief2-23.htm.

[77] *Winston S. Churchill Quotes,* http://www.goodreads.com/author/quotes/14033.Winston_S_Churchill?page=1.

[78] "Melanie Phillips Calls for New Strategy to Present Israel's Case," Honest Reporting, August 31, 2014, http://honestreporting.com/melanie-phillips-calls-for-new-strategy-to-present-israels-case/.

[79] "7 Principles of Media Objectivity," Honest Reporting.com, http://honestreporting.com/7-principles-of-media-objectivity/.

[80] Judea Pearl, "Another perspective, or jihad TV?" *New York Times,* January 17, 2007, http://www.nytimes.com/2007/01/17/opinion/17pearl.html?pagewanted=all.

[81] http://labs.aljazeera.net/warongaza/.

[82] Bruce J. Evers, "Reporting the Israeli–Palestinian Conflict: A Personal View," in *Media Bias: Finding It, Fixing It,* (Jefferon, NC: McFarland & Company, 2007), 15, citing "Suggested Language for Talking about the struggle for self-determination," http//www.pmwatch.org/pmw/language/index.asp.

[83] Only in recent years have the Palestinian Muslims claimed the wall as an Islamic holy site, denying any Jewish connection. Official guides published by the Islamic *waqf* in 1914, 1965, and 1990 do not attribute holiness to the wall for Muslims all.

[84] Philippe Assouline "Manufacturing and Exploiting Compassion: Abuse of the Media by Palestinian Propaganda," Jerusalem Center for Public Affairs, September 9, 2013, http://jcpa.org/article/manufacturing-exploiting-compassion-abuse-media-palestinian-propaganda/.

CONCLUSION

[1] Mohamed Akram, "An Explanatory Memorandum on the General Strategic Goal for the Brotherhood in North America," The Investigative Project on Terrorism, May 19, 1991, http://www.investigativeproject.org/document/id/20. *See* also full text in Arabic followed by English http://www.investigativeproject.org/documents/misc/20.pdf.

[2] https://twitter.com/khamenei_ir/status/531366667377717248

[3] "WaPo Editorial: President Obama has Retreated From Previous Positions on Iranian Nukes," The Tower, April 3, 2015, http://www.thetower.org/1848-wapo-editorial-president-obama-has-retreated-from-previous-positions-on-iranian-nukes/.

[4] Ari Yashar, "Iran's FM, nuclear chief reveal IR-8 centrifuges 20-times faster than current ones to be used after deal signed, threatening fast breakout," Arutz 7, April 8, 2015, http://www.israelnationalnews.com/News/News.aspx/193800#.VSVmyGM0Rx0.

APPENDICES

THE BALFOUR DECLARATION

[1] However, it should be noted that the British Foreign Office rejected Zionist leader Chaim Weizmann's preferred wording of "a Jewish State."

[2] Hasan Afif El-Hasan, "Israel 60: Birthday Dedication" http://www.palestinechronicle.com/view_article_details.php?id=13807.

[3] Mitchell G. Bard, "Roots of the U.S.-Israel Relationship," http://www.jewishvirtuallibrary.org/jsource/US-Israel/roots_of_US-Israel.html.

[4] *New York Times,* March 3, 1919. *See* also Palestine Royal Commission Report, July 1937, Chapter II, 24, and http://www.jewishvirtuallibrary.org/jsource/US-Israel/roots_of_US-Israel.html.

[5] "U.S. Presidents On Israel," http://www.jewishvirtuallibrary.org/jsource/US-Israel/presquote.html.

[6] "Lodge-Fish Resolution [Joint Congressional Resolution (360)]," Office for Israeli Constitutional Law, http://www.justicenow4israel.com/lodge-fish.html.

FEISAL-WEIZMANN AGREEMENT

[7] As late as March 8, 1974, Syria's President Hafez al-Assad on Radio Damascus, referred to "Palestine" as being "not only a part of the Arab homeland but a basic part of southern Syria." Earlier, no less a figure than Ahmed Shukairy, then the Saudi delegate to the United Nations and later the first head of the Palestine Liberation Organization (PLO) told the UN Security Council on May 31, 1956, "It is common knowledge that Palestine is nothing but southern Syria." *See* Palestine Facts, "Israel 1948–1967, PLO Founding" http://www.palestinefacts.org/pf_1948to1967_plo_backgd.php.

[8] *Feisal-Frankfurter Correspondence,* (March 1919) http://www.jewishvirtuallibrary.org/jsource/History/FeisalFrankfurterCorrespondence.html.

[9] Official Records of the Second Session of the General Assembly, Supplement No. 11, United Nations Special Committee on Palestine, Report of the General Assembly, Volume III, Annex A: Oral Evidence Presented Public Meeting, Lake Success, New York, (A/364/Add.2 PV.21), United Nations, July 8, 1947, http://unispal.un.org/unispal.nsf/0/364a6ac0dc52ada785256e8b00716662?OpenDocument.

UN GA RESOLUTION 181 PARTITION OF PALESTINE

[10] "D. Duration of the Special Regime," "United Nations General Assembly Resolution 181 November 29, 1947," The Avalon Project Yale Law School http://www.yale.edu/lawweb/avalon/un/res181.htm.

[11] "United Nations General Assembly Resolution 181 November 29, 1947," The Avalon Project Yale Law School http://www.yale.edu/lawweb/avalon/un/res181.htm.

THE TRIPARTITE DECLARATION

[12] Department of State Bulletin, June 5, 1950, 886. *See* also the President's statement of May 25, 1950 (Ibid.) and the Secretary's address of May 31, 1950 (supra, 1432 - 1441).

[13] *See* the tripartite communiqué of May 13, 1950; supra, pa. 1458-1459.

[14] *See* UN Security Council, Official Records, 433rd and 434th Meetings, August 4, 1949, 20-21, 23-27, and 33–37.

THE PALESTINIAN NATIONAL CHARTER

[15] Efraim Karsh, *Arafat's War: The Man and His Battle for Israeli Conquest,* (New York: Grove Press. 2003), 36.

[16] English rendition as published in Leila S. Kadi, ed., *Basic Political Documents of the Armed Palestinian Resistance Movement* (Beirut: Palestine Research Centre, December 1969) 137–41. *See* also "The Palestinian National Charter: Resolutions of the Palestine National Council July 1-17, 1968," The Avalon Project: Documents in Law, History and Diplomacy, Yale Law School http://avalon.law.yale.edu/20th_century/plocov.asp#art33.

[17] *Sawt Falasti,*(Beirut), December 7, 1980 http://middleeastfacts.com/Articles/peace-or-piece-by-piece.php.

[18] http://www.mideastweb.org/osloletters.htm.

[19] http://www.reference.com/browse/National+Charter.

[20] *Al-Hayat Al-Jadida,* February 3, 2001, as translated by MEMRI.

[21] Joel Mowbray, "The U.N. Stand: It's always been anti-Israel," NationalReview.com, May 6, 2002, http://old.nationalreview.com/comment/comment-mowbray050602.asp.

[22] "Kaddoumi: PLO charter was never changed, "Independent Media Review Analysis, April 23, 2004 citing Khaled Abu Toameh, "Kaddoumi: PLO charter was never changed, *"Jerusalem Post,* April 22, 2004, http://www.imra.org.il/story.php3?id=20533.

HAMAS CHARTER

[23] *The Covenant of the Islamic Resistance Movement* August 18, 1988, http://avalon.law.yale.edu/20th_century/hamas.asp. *See* also Yonah Alexander. "Hamas Covenant, 1988," *Palestinian Religious Terrorism: Hamas and Islamic Jihad.* (Ardsley, NY: Transnational Publishers, 2002), 47–69.

[24] *Sahih Bukhari* Hadith: Vol.4, book 52, number 177 and *Sahih Muslim.*

[25] Ziad Abu-Amr. *Islamic Fundamentalism in the West Bank and Gaza: Muslim Brotherhood and Islamic Jihad.* (Bloomington: Indiana University Press, 1994), 26.

[26] Norman Cohn, *Warrant for Genocide: The Myth of the Jewish World-Conspiracy and the Protocols of the Elders of Zion* (New York: Harper & Row Publishers, 1966) 32–36.

THE FATAH CONSTITUTION

[27] "Fatah Conference: August 2009: A Major Opportunity Denied," The Center for Near East Policy Research, Ltd. www.israelbehindthenews.com/library/pdfs/Fatah-Conference.doc.

THE PLO PHASED PLAN

[28] "10 Point Program of the PLO (1974)," Permanent Observer Mission of Palestine to the United Nations, http://www.un.int/wcm/content/site/palestine/cache/offonce/

pid/12354;jsessionid=ED2AC7E70A82F5C7CCB42BC6357FCDEC or http://bit.ly/y2zkfZ *See* also "Political Program for the Present Stage Drawn up by the 12th PNC, Cairo, June 9, 1974," *Journal of Palestine Studies,* Summer 1974, 224-25.

UN "Zionism is Racism" Resolution 3379

[29] http://www.jewishvirtuallibrary.org/jsource/UN/herzogsp.html.

[30] "10 November 1975: Daniel Patrick Moynihan addresses the UN on Zionism," OUPblog, November 12, 2012, http://blog.oup.com/2012/11/10-november-1975-daniel-patrick-moynihan-addresses-the-un-on-zionism/. *See* filmclip http://www.youtube.com/watch?v=Z_8VqP7QKPA.

[31] Jeanne Kirkpatrick, "The U.N.'s Day of Infamy," *The Washington Post,* November 11, 1985, A23.

[32] John R. Bolton, "Zionism Is Not Racism," *New York Times,* December 16, 1991, http://www.nytimes.com/1991/12/16/opinion/zionism-is-not-racism.html.

[33] Rebecca Stoil and JTA, "NY rally marks infamous UN resolution," *Jerusalem Post,* November 11, 2005, http://www.jpost.com/International/Article.aspx?id=4466.

[34] "African (Banjul) Charter on Human and Peoples' Rights," June 27, 1981, http://www.africa-union.org/official_documents/treaties_%20conventions_%20protocols/banjul%20charter.pdf.

[35] "Arab Charter on Human Rights," UNHCR/Refworld http://www.unhcr.org/refworld/docid/3ae6b38540.html. *See* also "Arab Charter on Human Rights," http://www.acihl.org/res/Arab_Charter_on_Human_Rights_2004.pdf.

[36] "The Arab Charter on Human Rights is incompatible with international standards - Louise Arbour," International Humanist and Ethical Union, March, 11, 2008, http://www.iheu.org/node/2998.

BIBLIOGRAPHY

This bibliography is a list of books important to an understanding of Middle East history, politics, diplomacy, and culture. They contain facts and opinions of authors with different perspectives. This bibliography is not annotated so as not to bias the reader in favor or against any given book. This list is not all-inclusive. Inclusion of any book should not be construed as endorsement of its opinions and content. This list however substantiates the information represented in this book. Most are in the library of the author. Many of these works have several editions. Check Barnes & Noble.com or similar source for the latest available editions.

GENERAL OVERVIEWS OF THE MIDDLE EAST

Armajani, Yahya and Ricks, Thomas. *Middle East Past and Present.* 2d ed. Englewood, NJ: Prentice-Hall, 1986.

Cleveland, William L. *A History of the Modern Middle East.* 2d ed. Boulder, CO.: Westview Press, 2000.

Congressional Quarterly. *The Middle East.* 9th ed. Washington, DC: CQ Press, 2000.

Fisher, Sydney N., and William Ochsenwald. *The Middle East: A History.* 5th ed. 2 vols. New York. McGraw Hill, 1997.

Gale, General Sir Richard. *Great Battles of Biblical History.* New York: John Day, 1970.

Gervasi, Frank. *Thunder Over the Mediterranean.* New York: David McKay, 1975.

Hakim, Ali A. *The Middle Eastern States and the Law of the Sea.* Syracuse: Syracuse University Press, 1980.

Herzog, Chaim and Mordechai Gichon. *Battles of the Bible.* New York: Random House, 1978.

Hiro, Dilip. *Dictionary of the Middle East.* New York: St. Martin's Press, 1996.

Jefferson, Thomas. *The Jefferson Bible: The Life and Morals of Jesus of Nazareth Extracted Textually from the Gospels in Greek, Latin, French & English.* Washington, DC: Smithsonian Books, 2011.

Karlekar, Karen D. and Sarah G. Cock. eds. *Freedom of the Press, 2008: A Global Survey of Media Independence.* New York, Freedom House, 2009.

Kort, Michael G. *The Handbook of the Middle East.* Brookfield, CT: Twenty-First Century Books, 2002.

Lenczowski, George. *The Middle East in World Affairs.* 4th ed. Ithaca, NY: Cornell University Press, 1980.

Lewis, Bernard. *A Middle East Mosaic: Fragments of Life, Letters and History.* New York: Random House, 2000.

—. *The Middle East: A Brief History of the Last 2,000 Years.* New York: Scribner, 1995.

—. *The Multiple Identities in the Middle East.* New York: Schoken Books, 1998.

Long, David and Bernard Reich. eds. *The Government and Politics of the Middle East and North Africa.* Boulder, CO: Westview Press, 1986.

Mansfield, Peter. *The Middle East: A Political and Economic Survey.* London: Oxford University Press, 1973.

Ovendale, Ritchie. *The Middle East Since 1914.* 2d ed. London: Longman, 1998.

Sela, Avraham. *The Continuum Political Encyclopedia of the Middle East.* New York: Continuum Publishing Group, 2002.

Shimoni, Yaacov. *Biographical Dictionary of the Middle East.* New York: Facts on File, 1991.

The CIA World Factbook, 2010. New York: Skyhorse Publishing, 2009.

Weiner, Tim. *Legacy of Ashes: The History of the CIA.* New York: Doubleday, 2007.

Yapp. M.E. *The Near East since the First World War: A History to 1995.* London: Longman, 1996.

ISLAM

Adas, Michael. ed. *Islamic and European Expansion: The Forging of a Global Order.* Philadelphia: Temple University Press, 1993.

Ali, Abdella Yusuf. trans. *The Qur'an, Tahrike Tarsile Qur'an.* n.p. 1995.

Ankerberg, John and John Weldon. *Fast Facts on Islam: What You Need To Know Now.* Eugene, OR: Harvest House, 2001.

Arberry, J. trans. *The Koran Interpreted.* New York: Touchstone, 1955.

Asad, Muhammad. *The Message of The Qur'an.* Bilingual ed. Bristol, England: The Book Foundation, 2003.

Azumah, John Alembillah. *The Legacy of Arab-Islam in Africa.* Oxford, UK: Oneworld Publishing, 2001.

Ben-Shemesh, A. trans. *The Noble Qur'an.* Tel Aviv: Massada Publishing, 1979.

Benard, Cheryl. *Veiled Courage: Inside the Afghan Women's Resistance.* New York: Broadway Books, a Division of Random House, 2002.

Bevan, Edwyn R. and Charles Singer. eds. *The Legacy of Islam.* London: Oxford University Press, 1927.

Bostom, Andrew G. ed. *The Legacy of Jihad.* Amherst, NY: Prometheus Books, 2008.

—. *Shari'a versus Freedom: The Legacy of Islamic Totalitarianism.* NY: Prometheus Books, 2012.

Cameron Lyons, Malcolm and D.E.P. Jackson. *Saladin: The Politics of the Holy War.* Cambridge, UK: Cambridge University Press, 1985.

Campo, Juan E. ed. *Encyclopedia of Islam.* New York: Checkmark Books, 2009.

Caner, Ergun Mehmet. & Caner, Emir Fethi. *Unveiling Islam: An Insider's look at Muslim Life and Beliefs.* Grand Rapids, MI: Kregel Publications, 2002.

Darwish, Nonie. *Now They Call Me Infidel: Why I Renounced Jihad for America, Israel, and the War on Terror.* New York: Sentinel, 2006.

—. *Cruel and Usual Punishment: The Terrifying Global Implications of Islamic Law.* Nashville, TN: Thomas Nelson, 2008.

Davis, Gregory, M. *Religion of Peace?* Los Angeles: World Ahead, 2006.

Dawood, N.J. trans. *The Koran.* London: Penguin, 1999.

Esposito, John L. ed. *The Oxford Encyclopedia of the Modern Islamic World.* New York: Oxford University Press, 2001.

Fregosi, Paul. *Jihad in the West: Muslim Conquests from the 7th to the 21st Centuries.* Amherst, NY: Prometheus Books, 1998.

Glasse, Cyril. *New Encyclopedia of Islam: A Revised Edition of the Concise Encyclopedia of Islam.* Lanham, MD: Altamira Press, 2003.

Goldziher, Igantz. *Introduction to Islamic Theology and Law.* Princeton, NJ: Princeton University Press, 1981.

Guillaume, Alfred. *The Traditions of Islam: An Introduction to the Study of the Hadith Literature.* Beirut: Khayats, 1966.

—. *Islam.* New York: Penguin Books, 1978.

Hammond, Peter. *Slavery, Terrorism and Islam: The Historical Roots and Contemporary Threat.* 3rd ed. Cape Town: Frontline Fellowship, 2010.

Harris, Ellen. *Guarding the Secrets: Palestinian Terrorism and a Father's Murder of His Too-American Daughter.* New York: Scribner's, 1995.

Hirsi Ali, Ayan. *Infidel.* New York: Free Press, a division of Simon and Schuster, 2007.

Holt, Peter Malcom and Ann K.S. Lambton. eds. *The Cambridge History of Islam.* Rev. 4 vols. Cambridge, UK: Cambridge University Press, 1978.

Harrison, Lawrence & Huntington, Samuel. eds. *Culture Matters: How Values Shape Human Progress.* New York: Basic Books, 2000.

Holland, Tom. *In the Shadow of the Sword.* New York: Anchor Books, 2012.

Humphreys, R. Stephen. *Islamic History: A framework for Inquiry.* Princeton, NJ: Princeton University Press, 1991.

Ibrahim, Raymond. ed. *The Al-Qaeda Reader.* New York: Doubleday, 2007.

Karsh, Efraim. *Islamic Imperialism: A History.* New Haven, CT: Yale University Press, 2007.

Keller, Nu Ha Mim. ed. *Reliance of the Traveller: The Classic Manual of Islamic Sacred Law.* Rev. ed. Beltsville, MD: Amana Publications, 1994.

Khadduri, Majid. *War and Peace in the Law of Islam.* Clark, NJ: The Lawbook Exchange Ltd., 2006.

Khan, Muhammad Zafrullah. *The Qur'an.* Brooklyn, NY: Olive Branch Press, 1997.

Laffin, John. *The Arabs as Master Slavers.* Englewood, NJ: SBS Publishing, 1982.

Lewis, Bernard. *Islam and the West.* New York: Oxford University Press, 1993.

—. *Islam in History: Ideas, People, and Events in the Middle East.* Chicago: Open Court, 1993.

—. *The Crisis of Islam: Holy War and Unholy Terror.* New York: Modern Library, 2003.

—. *The Muslims Discovery of Europe.* New York: W. W. Norton & Company, 2001.

Manji, Irshad. *The Trouble with Islam.* New York: St. Martin Press, 2003.

Martin, Richard C. ed., *The Encyclopedia of Islam and the Muslim World,* New York: Macmillan Reference USA, 2004.

Meddeb, Abdelwahab. *The Malady of Islam.* New York: Basic Books, 2003.

Margoliouth, G. and J.M. Rodwell. *The Koran.* Mineola, NY: Dover Publications, 2005.

Muthuswamy, Moorthy S. *Defeating Political Islam: The New Cold War.* Amherst, NY: Prometheus Books, 2009.

Nagel, Tilman. *The History of Islamic Theology from Muhammad to the Present.* Princeton, NJ: Marcus Wiener Publishers, 2000.

O'Neill, John J. *Holy Warriors: Islam and the Demise of Classical Civilization.* Felibri Publications, 2010.

Peters, F.E. *Muhammad and the Origins of Islam.* Albany, NY: SUNY Press, 1994.

Pickthall, Muhammad. M. *The Meaning of the Glorious Koran.* New York: Penguin Books, 1997.

Pipes, Daniel. *In the Path of God: Islam and Political Power.* New Brunswick, NJ: Transactions Publishers, 2002.

—. *Miniatures: Views of Islamic and Middle Eastern Politics.* New Brunswick, NJ: Transactions Publishers, 2004.

Rajaee, Farhad. *Islamic Values and World View: Khomeini on Man, the State and International Politics.* Lanham, MD: University Press of America, 1983.

Rippin, Andrew. *Muslims: Their Religious Beliefs and Practices, Volume 1: The Formative Period.* London: Routledge, 1990.

Roy, Oliver. *The Failure of Political Islam.* Cambridge, MA: Harvard University Press, 1996.

—. *Sacred Writings.* Vol. 3. *Islam: The Qur'an.* Translation by Ahmed Ali. New York: Book of the Month Club, 1992.

Segal, Ronald. *Islam's Black Slaves: The Other Black Diaspora.* New York: Farrar, Straus and Giroux, 2006.

Sen, Gertrude Emerson. *The Story of Early Indian Civilization.* Andhra Pradesh, India: Orient Longmans, 1964.

Shorrosh, Anis A. *Islam Revealed: A Christian Arab's View of Islam.* Nashville, TN: Thomas Nelson Publishers, 1988.

Spencer, Robert. *Did Muhammad Exist? An Inquiry into Islam's Obscure Origins.* Wilmington, DE: ISI Books, 2012.

—. *Islam Unveiled: Disturbing Questions about the World's Fastest-growing Faith.* San Francisco: Encounter Books, 2002.

—. *Stealth Jihad: How Radical Islam is Subverting America without Guns or Bombs.* Washington, DC: Regnery Publishing, 2008.

—. *The Complete Infidel's Guide to the Koran.* Washington, DC: Regnery Publishing, 2009.

—. *The Politically Incorrect Guide to Islam and The Crusades.* Washington, DC: Regnery Publishing, 2005.

—. *The Myth of Islamic Tolerance.* Amherst, NY: Prometheus, 2005.

—. *The Truth About Muhammad: Founder of the World's Most Intolerant Religion.* Washington, DC: Regnery, 2006.

Spencer, Robert and Phyllis Chesler. *The Violent Oppression of Women in Islam.* Los Angeles: David Horowitz Freedom Center, 2007.

Sperry, Paul. *Infiltration: How Muslim Spies and Subversives have penetrated Washington,* Nashville, TN: Nelson Current, 2005.

Sultan, Wafa. *A God Who Hates: The Courageous Woman Who Inflamed the Muslim World Speaks Out Against the Evils of Islam.* New York: St. Martin's Press, 2009.

Sweeney, Harry J. *The Restless Wind and Shifting Sands.* New York: iUniverse, Inc. 2009.

Trifkovic, Serge. *The Sword of the Prophet: Islam, History, Theology impact on the World.* Boston: Regina Orthodox Press, 2002.

Warner, Bill. *Mohammed And the Unbelievers: The Sira, a Political Biography.* CSPI Publishing, 2006.

—. *Shari'a Law for Non-Muslims.* CSPI Publishing, 2010.

—. *The Hadith.* CSPI Publishing, 2010.

—. *The Islamic Doctrine of Women.* CSPI Publishing, 2010.

—. *The Life of Mohammed.* CSPI Publishing, 2010.

—. ed. *An Abridged Koran: The Reconstructed Historical Koran.* CSPI Publishing, 2006.

—. ed. *The Political Tradition of Mohammed: The Hadith for Unbelievers.* CSPI Publishing, 2006.

Warraq, Ibn. *Why I Am Not a Muslim.* Amherst, NY: Prometheus, 2003.

—. ed. *The Origins of the Koran: Classic Essays on Islam's Holy Book.* Amherst, NY: Prometheus, 1998.

—. ed. *The Quest for the Historical Muhammad.* Amherst, NY: Prometheus, 2000.

—. ed. *What the Koran Really Says: Language, Text & Commentary.* Amherst, NY: Prometheus, 2002.

—. ed. *Leaving Islam: Apostates Speak Out.* Amherst, NY: Prometheus, 2003.

Woodhead, Linda. Kawanami, Hiroko., Partridge Christopher. eds. *Religions in the Modern World: Traditions and Transformations.* London: Routledge, 2009.

Ye'or, Bat. *Eurabia: The Euro-Arab Axis.* Madison, NJ: Fairleigh Dickinson University Press, 2005.

—. *Europe, Globalization, and the Coming Universal Caliphate.* Madison, NJ: Fairleigh Dickinson University Press, 2011.

—. *Islam and Dhimmitude: Where Civilizations Collide.* Teaneck, NJ: Associated University Presses, 2002.

MUSLIM-CHRISTIAN RELATIONS

Brog, David. *Standing with Israel.* Lake Mary, FL: Charisma House, 2006.

Chafetz, Zev. *A Match Made in Heaven.* New York: Harper Collins, 2007.

Fallaci, Oriana. *The Rage and the Pride.* New York: Rizzoli International Publishers, 2002.

Hagee, John. *Jerusalem Countdown: Revised and Updated.* Lake Mary, FL: Frontline, 2007.

Ibrahim, Raymond. *Crucified Again: Exposing Islam's New War on Christians,* Washington, DC: Regnery Publishing, 2013.

Israeli, Raphael. *Green Crescent over Nazareth: The Displacement of Christians by Muslims in the Holy Land.* Portland, OR: Frank Cass, 2002.

Nicolle, David. *The Crusades.* Oxford, UK: Osprey Publishing Ltd., 2001.

Nisan, Mordechai. *Minorities in the Middle East: History of the Struggle and Self-Expression,* 2d ed., Jefferson, NC: McFarland & Company, 2002.

Spencer, Robert. *Religion of Peace? Why Christianity Is and Islam Isn't.* Washington, DC: Regnery Publishing, 2007.

Warner, Bill. *The Islamic Doctrine of Christians and Jews.* CSPI Publishing, 2010.

Weigel, George. *Faith, Reason, and the War Against Jihadism: A Call to Action.* New York: Doubleday, 2007

Ye'or, Bat. *The Decline of Eastern Christianity under Islam.* Cranbury, NJ: Associated University Presses, 1996.

Ye'or, Bat and David Maisel. *The Dhimmi: Jews and Christians under Islam.* Madison, NJ: Fairleigh Dickinson University Press, 1985.

MUSLIM-JEWISH RELATIONS

Black, Edwin. *The Farhud: Roots of the Arab-Nazi Alliance in the Holocaust.* Washington, DC: Dialog Press, 2010.

Bostom, Andrew G. ed. *The Legacy of Islamic Antisemitism: From Sacred Texts to Solemn History,* Amherst, NY: Prometheus, 2008.

Dalin, David G. and John F. Rothmann. *Icon of Evil.* New York: Random House, 2008.

Gilbert, Martin. *In Ishmael's House: A History of Jews in Muslim Lands.* Toronto, ON: McClellan & Stewart Ltd., 2011.

Katsh, Abraham I. *Judaism and the Koran.* New York: A.S. Barnes & Co, 1962.

Kressel, Neil J. *The Sons of Pigs and Apes: Muslim Antisemitism and the Conspiracy of Silence,* Washington, DC: Potomac Books, 2012.

Lewis, Bernard. *Cultures in Conflict: Christians, Muslims and Jews in the Age of Discovery.* New York: Oxford University Press, 1995.

—. *Semites and Anti-Semites: An Inquiry into Conflict and Prejudice.* New York: W.W. Norton & Company, 1999.

—. *The Jews of Islam.* Princeton, NJ: Princeton University Press, 1984.

Mattar, Philip. *The Mufti of Jerusalem.* Rev. ed. New York: Diane Publishing, 1988.

Nettlerm, Ronald L. ed. *Medieval and Modern Perspectives on Muslim-Jewish Relations.* Oxford: Harwood, 1995.

Rubin, Barry and Wolfgang G. Schwanitz. *Nazis, Islamists, and the Making of the Modern Middle East.* New Haven, CT: Yale University Press, 2014.

Shragai, Nadav. *The Al-Aksa Libel: The History of a Lie.* Jerusalem: Jerusalem Center for Public Affairs, 2012.

Stillman, Norman A. *The Jews in Arab Lands in Modern Times.* Philadelphia: Jewish Publication Soc. of America, 2003.

Ye'or, Bat. *The Dhimmi: Jews and Christians Under Islam.* Rutherford, NJ: Fairleigh Dickinson University Press, 1985.

IRAN

Clawson, Patrick and Michael Rubin. *Eternal Iran: Continuity and Chaos.* New York: Palgrave MacMillan, 2005.

Graham, Robert. *Iran: The Illusion of Power.* New York: St. Martin's Press, 1979.

Kapuscinski, Ryszard. *Shah of Shahs.* New York: Harcourt, Brace, Jovanovich, 1982.

Ledeen, Michael A. *Accomplice to Evil: Iran and the War Against the West.* New York: Truman Talley Books, 2009.

—. *The Iranian Time Bomb.* New York: St. Martin's Press, 2007.

Lorentz, John H. *The Historical Dictionary of Iran.* 2d ed. Latham, MD: The Scarecrow Press, 2007.

O'Hern, Steven. *Iran's Revolutionary Guard: The Threat that Grows While America Sleeps,* Washington, DC: Potomac Books, 2012.

Taheri, Amir. *The Spirit of Allah: Khomeini and the Islamic Revolution.* Chevy Chase, MD: Adler & Adler, 1986.

Timmerman, Kenneth R. *Countdown to Crisis: The coming Nuclear Showdown with Iran.* New York: Crown Forum, 2005.

THE KURDS

Ghareeb, Edmund. *The Kurdish Question in Iraq.* Syracuse: Syracuse University Press, 1981.

Ghassemlou, A.R., et al. *People without a Country: The Kurds and Kurdistan.* London: Zed Press, 1980.

Gunter, Michael M. *The Kurds in Turkey: A Political Dilemma.* Boulder, CO: Westview Press, 1990.

Kreyenbroek, P.G. and S. Sperl. eds. *The Kurds: A Contemporary Overview.* London: Routledge, 1992.

McDowall, David. *A Modern History of the Kurds.* 3rd rev. ed. New York: I.B. Tauris/St. Martin's Press, 2009.

Meiselas, Susan. *Kurdistan: In the Shadow of History.* 2d ed. Chicago: University of Chicago Press, 2008.

O'Ballance, Edgar. *The Kurdish Struggle, 1920-1994.* New York: Palgrave Macmillan, 1996.

—. *The Kurdish Revolt, 1961-1972.* Hamden, CT: Archon Books, 1973.

Olson, Robert W. *The Emergence of Kurdish Nationalism and the Sheikh Said Rebellion, 1880–1925.* Austin, TX: University of Texas Press, 1989.

TURKEY

Bobelian, Michael. *Children of Armenia: A Forgotten Genocide and the Century-long Struggle for Justice.* New York: Simon and Schuster, 2009.

Findley, Carter V. *The Turks in World History.* New York: Oxford University Press, 2004.

—. *Turkey, Islam, Nationalism and Modernity: A History 1789–2007.* New Haven, CT: Yale University Press, 2010.

Haniogiu, M. Sukru. *Ataturk: An Intellectual Biography.* Princeton, NJ: Princeton University Press, 2011.

Kevorkian, Raymond H. *The Armenian Genocide: A Complete History.* London: I. B. Tauris, 2011.

Kinross, Patrick Balfour, Lord Kinross. *Ataturk: A Biography of Mustafa Kemal, Father of Modern Turkey.* UK: Quill, 1992.

Lewis, Bernard. *The Emergence of Modern Turkey.* 3rd ed. New York: Oxford University Press, 2001.

Park, Bill. *Modern Turkey: People, State and Foreign Policy in a Globalized World.* New York: Routledge, 2011.

THE IRAN-IRAQ WAR - GULF WAR I

Karsh, Efraim. *The Iran–Iraq War 1980–1988.* Oxford, UK: Osprey Publishing Ltd., 2002.

McCuen, Gary. *Iran–Iraq War.* Hudson, WI: Gem Publications, 1987.

O'Ballance, Edgar. *The Gulf War.* London: Brassey's Defense Publishers, 1988.

THE ARAB WORLD & ARAB NATIONALISM General

_____. *Arabian Personalities of the Early Twentieth Century*. New York: Oleander Press, 1986.

Agwani, M.S. *Communism in the Arab East*. New York: Asia Publishing House, 1969.

Ajami, Fouad. *The Arab Predicament: Arab Political Thought and Practice since 1967*. Cambridge: Cambridge University Press, 1993.

—. *The Dream Palace of the Arabs*. New York: Vintage Books, 1999.

Bard, Mitchell. *The Arab Lobby: The Invisible Alliance That Undermines America's Interests in the Middle East*. New York: Harper Collins, 2010.

Bates, Daniel and Amal Rassam. *Peoples and Cultures of the Middle East*. Englewood Cliffs, NJ: Prentice-Hall, 1983.

Be'eri, Eliezer. *Army Officers in Arab Politics and Society*. Jerusalem: Israel Universities Press, 1969.

Carmichael, Joel. *Arabs Today*. New York: Anchor Press, 1977.

Darwish, Nonie. *The Devil We Don't Know: The Dark Side of Revolutions in the Middle East*. Hoboken, NJ: John Wiley & Sons, 2012.

Farah, Tawfic. ed. *Pan-Arabism and Arab Nationalism: The Continuing Debate*. Boulder, CO: Westview Press, 1987.

Glubb, John Bagot. *Glubb Pasha: A Soldier with the Arabs*. London: Hodder and Stoughton, 1957.

—. *The Great Arab Conquests*. London: Quarter Books, 1963.

Haddad, George M. *Revolutions and Military Rule in the Middle East, Vol. 1- The Northern Tier*. New York: Robert Speller & Sons, 1965.

—. *Revolutions and Military Rule in the Middle East, Vol. 2- The Arab States Part I–Iraq, Syria, Lebanon and Jordan*. New York: Robert Speller & Sons, 1971.

—. *Revolutions and Military Rule in the Middle East, Vol. 3- The Arab States Part 2–Egypt, the Sudan, Yemen and Libya*. New York: Robert Speller & Sons, 1973.

Halliday, Fred. *Arabia without Sultans*. New York: Vintage Books, 1975.

Hatem, M. Abdel Kader. *Information and the Arab Cause*. London: Longman, 1974.

Hitti, Philip K. *The Arabs: A Short History*. Washington DC: Regency Publishing, 1996.

Hourani, Albert. *A History of the Arab Peoples*. New York: MF Books, 1991.

Khadduri, Majid. *Arab Contemporaries: The Role of Personalities in Politics*. Baltimore: John Hopkins University Press, 1973.

Kiernan, Thomas. *Arafat: The Man and the Myth*. New York: W. Norton, 1976.

Laffin, John. *The Arabs as Master Slavers*. Englewood, NJ: SBS Publishing, 1982.

Landay, Jerry. *Dome of the Rock*. New York: Newsweek, 1972.

Lewis, Bernard. *The Arabs in History*. New York: Oxford University Press, 1993.

—. *The Assassins*. London: Weidenfeld & Nicolson, 1967.

Maalouf, Amin. *The Crusades through Arab Eyes*. New York: Schocken Books, 1985.

Mansfield, Peter. *The Arabs*. New York: Penguin Books, 1983.

—. *The Arab World: A Comprehensive History*. New York: Thomas Crowell, 1976.

Palmer, Monte. *The Arab Psyche and American Frustrations*. North Charleston, SC: CreateSpace, 2012.

Patai, Raphael. *The Arab Mind*. New York: Hatherleigh Press, 2007.

Pryce-Jones, David. *The Closed Circle: An Interpretation of the Arabs*. Chicago: Ivan R. Dee, 2009.

Rubin, Barry. *The Tragedy of the Middle East*. Cambridge, UK: Cambridge University Press, 2002.

Smith, Lee. *The Strong Horse: Power, Politics, and the Clash of Arab Civilizations*. New York: Doubleday, 2010.

EGYPT

Gershoni, Israel. *The Emergence of Pan-Arabism in Egypt.* Tel Aviv: Shiloah Center for Middle Eastern and African Studies, 1981.

Heikal, Mohamed. *The Cairo Documents: The Inside Story of Nasser and His Relationship with World Leaders, Rebels and Statesmen.* New York: Doubleday, 1973.

Hopkins, Harry. *Egypt the Crucible: The Unfinished Revolution in the Arab World.* Boston: Houghton Mifflin, 1969.

Nordeen, Lon O. and David Nicolle. *Phoenix over the Nile.* Washington, DC: Smithsonian Institute Press, 1996.

Nutting, Anthony. *Nasser.* New York: E.P. Dutton, 1972.

Stephens, Robert. *Nasser: A Political Biography.* New York: Simon and Schuster, 1971.

Vatikiotis, P.J. *The History of Egypt: From Muhammad to Sadat.* Baltimore: Johns Hopkins University Press, 1980.

IRAQ

Al-Khalil, Samir. *Republic of Fear.* New York: Pantheon Books, 1990.

Allawi, Ali. *The Occupation of Iraq: Winning the War, Losing the Peace.* New Haven, CT: Yale University Press, 2007.

Lando, Barry M. *Web of Deceit: The History of Western Complicity in Iraq from Churchill to Kennedy to George W. Bush,* New York: Other Press, 2007.

Mackey, Sandra. *The Reckoning: Iraq and the legacy of Saddam.* New York: W.W. Norton and Company, 2002.

Sassoon, Joseph. *Saddam Hussein's Ba'th Party: Inside an Authoritarian Regime,* Cambridge, UK: Cambridge University Press, 2011.

THE GULF WAR II-LIBERATION OF KUWAIT

Bulloch, John and Harvey Morris. *The Gulf War: Its Origins, History and Consequences.* London: Methuen, 1991.

Finlan, Alastair, *The Gulf War 1991.* Oxford, UK: Osprey Publishing Ltd., 2003.

Khadduri, Majid and Edmund Chareeb. *War in the Gulf 1990–91: The Iraq-Kuwait Conflict and Its Implications.* New York: Oxford University Press, 1997.

Levran, Aharon. *Israeli Strategy after Desert Storm: Lessons from the Second Gulf War.* London: Frank Cass, 1997.

Newell, Clayton R. *Historical Dictionary of the Persian Gulf War 1990–1991.* Lanham, MD: Scarecrow Press, 1998.

JORDAN

Faddah, Mohammad. *The Middle East In Transition: A Study of Jordan's Foreign Policy.* New York: Asia Publishing House, 1974.

Hussein. *Uneasy lies the head;: The autobiography of His Majesty King Hussein I of the Hashemite Kingdom of Jordan.* New York: B. Geis Associates; distributed by Random House, 1962.

Schechtman, Joseph. *Jordan: A State That Never Was.* New York: Cultural Publishing, 1968.

Sinai, Anne and Allen Pollack. eds.. *The Hashemite Kingdom of Jordan and the West Bank: A Handbook.* New York: American Academic Association for Peace in the Middle East, 1977.

Snow, Peter. *Hussein: A Biography.* Washington, DC: Robert Luce, 1972.

LEBANON

Nisan, Mordechai. *The Conscience of Lebanon: A Political Biography of Etienne Sakr Abu Arz.* London: Routledge, 2003.

O'Ballance, Edgar. *Civil War in Lebanon, 1975–1992.* New York: Palgrave Macmillan, 2002.

Vocke, Harald. *The Lebanese War: Its Origins and Political Dimensions.* New York: St. Martin's Press, 1978.

Weinberger, Naomi. *Syrian Intervention in Lebanon.* New York: Oxford University Press, 1986.

Zarmi, Meir. *The Formation of Modern Lebanon,* Ithaca, NY: Cornell University Press, 1988.

LIBYA

Cooley, John. *Libyan Sandstorm: The Complete Account of Qaddafi's Revolution.* New York: Holt, Rinehart and Winston, 1982.

First, Ruth. *Libya: The Elusive Revolution.* New York: Penguin Books, 1974.

PERSIAN GULF STATES

_____. *Area Handbook for the Peripheral States of the Arabian Peninsula.* Washington, DC: Stanford Research Institute, Superintendent of Documents, 1971.

Henderson, Simon. *The New Pillar: Conservative Arab Gulf States and U.S. Strategy,* Washington, DC: Washington Institute for Near East Policy, 2003.

Khalifa, Ali Mohammed. *The United Arab Emirates: Unity in Fragmentation.* Boulder, CO: Westview Press, 1979.

Long, David E. *The Persian Gulf.* Boulder, CO: Westview Press, 1976.

Martin, Lenore G. *The Unstable Gulf: Threats From Within.* Lexington: Lexington Books, 1984.

THE PALESTINIAN ARABS

Becker, Jillian. *The PLO: The Rise and fall of the Palestine Liberation Organization.* London: Weidenfeld and Nicolson, 1984.

Harkabi, Yehoshafat. *The Palestinian Covenant and its Meaning.* London: Vallentine Mitchell, 1979.

Kahn, Arthur and Thomas F. Murray. *The Palestinians: A Political Masquerade.* New York: Americans For a Safe Israel, 1977. A free copy is available at http://www.afsi.org/pamphlets/PalestiniansKahn.pdf.

Karsh, Ephraim. *Arafat's War: The Man and the Battle for Israel's Existence.* New York: Grove Press, 2004.

Laffin, John. *The PLO Connections.* London: Corgi Books, 1983.

Livingstone, Neil and David Halevy. *Inside the PLO.* New York: William Morrow, 1990.

Quandt, William, Fuad Jabber, and Ann Lesch. *The Politics of Palestinian Nationalism.* Berkeley, CA: University of California Press, 1973.

Rubenstein, Danny. *The Mystery of Arafat.* South Royalton, VT: Steerforth Press, 1995.

Rubin, Barry. *Revolution until Victory?: The Politics and History of the PLO.* Cambridge, MA: Harvard University Press, 1994.

Rubin, Barry and Judith Colp Rubin. *Yasser Arafat: A Political Biography.* New York: Oxford University Press, 2005.

Schechtman, Joseph. *The Refugee in the World.* New York: A.S. Barnes and Co., 1963.

Shemesh, Moshe. *The Palestinian Entity 1959–1974: Arab Politics and the PLO.* London: Frank Cass, 1988.

Taggar, Yehuda. *The Mufti of Jerusalem and Palestine Arab Politics, 1930–1937.* New York: Taylor and Francis, 1987.

SAUDI ARABIA

Baer, Robert. *Sleeping With The Devil: How Washington Sold Out Our Soul for Saudi Crude.* New York: Crown Publishers, 2003.

Cordesman, Anthony. *Saudi Arabia Enters the Twenty-First Century.* London: Praeger, 2003.

Emerson, Steven. *The American House of Saud: The Secret Petrodollar Connection.* New York: Franklin Watts, 1985.

Gold, Dore. *Hatred's Kingdom, How Saudi Arabia Supports the New Global Terrorism.* Washington, DC: Regnery, 2003.

Kelly, J.B. *Arabia, the Gulf and the West.* New York: Basic Books, 1980.

Lindey, Gene. *Saudi Arabia.* New York: Hippocrene, 1991.

Mackey, Sandra. *The Saudis: Inside the Desert Kingdom.* Boston: Houghton Mifflin, 1987.

Peterson, J.P. *Historical Dictionary of Saudi Arabia,* 2d ed. Lanham, MD: Scarecrow Press, 2003.

Weston, Mark. *Prophets and Princes: Saudi Arabia from Muhammad to the Present.* Hoboken, NJ: John Wiley and Sons, 2008.

SOMALIA

Farer, Tom. *War Clouds on the Horn of Africa: The Widening Storm.* 2d ed. New York: Carnegie Endowment for International Peace, 1979.

SUDAN

Holt, P.M. and M.W. Daly. *A History of the Sudan: From the Coming of Islam to the Present Day.* 5th ed. Harlow, England: Pearson Education, 2000.

Nelson, Harold et al. *Area Handbook for the Democratic Republic of the Sudan.* Washington, DC: Superintendent of Documents, 1973.

O'Ballance, Edgar. *Sudan, Civil War and Terrorism, 1956–1999.* New York: Palgrave Macmillan, 2000.

—. *The Secret War in the Sudan 1955–1972.* Hamden, CT: Archon Books, 1977.

SYRIA

Commins, David. *Historical Dictionary of Syria.* 2d ed. Latham, MD: The Scarecrow Press, 2004.

Maoz, Moshe. *Asad: The Sphinx of Damascus.* New York: Weidenfeld and Nicolson, 1988.

Rabinovich, Itamar. *The View from Damascus: State, Political Community and Foreign Relations in Twentieth-Century Syria.* Portland, OR: Vallentine Mitchell, 2008.

Rubin, Barry. *The Truth about Syria.* New York: Palgrave Macmillan, 2007.

Sinai, Anne and Allen Pollack. eds. *The Syrian Arab Republic: A Handbook*. New York: American Academic Association for Peace in the Middle East, 1976.

YEMEN

Nyrop, Richard et al. *Area Handbook for the Yemens*. Washington, DC: Superintendent of Documents, 1977.

O'Ballance, Edgar. *War in the Yemen*. Hamden, CT: Archon Books, 1971.

Schmidt, Dana Adams. *Yemen: The Unknown War*. New York: Holt, Rinehart and Winston, 1968.

Stookey, Robert. *Yemen: The Politics of the Yemen Arab Republic*. Boulder, CO: Westview Pres, 1978.

FOREIGN POWERS IN THE MIDDLE EAST

Allen, Gardner W. *Our Navy and the Barbary Corsairs*. Hamden, CT: Archon Books, 1965.

Andrew, Christopher and Vasili Mitrokhin. *The Mitrokhin Archive II: The KGB and the World*. London: Allen Lane, 2005.

Arens, Moshe. *Broken Covenant: American Foreign Policy and the Crisis between the U.S. and Israel*. New York: Simon and Schuster, 1995.

Ball, George and Douglas Ball. *The Passionate Attachment: America's Involvement with Israel 1947 to the Present*. New York: W.W. Norton, 1992.

Barr, James. *A Line in the Sand: The Anglo-French Struggle for the Middle East, 1914–1948*. New York: W.W. Norton & Company, 2012.

Bass, Warren. *Support Any Friend: Kennedy's Middle East and the Making of the U.S.–Israel Alliance*. New York: Oxford University Press, 2003.

Beckman, Morris. *The Jewish Brigade: An Army with Two Masters, 1944–1945*. Rockville Center, NY: Sarpedon, 1998.

Blitzer, Wolf. *Between Washington and Jerusalem: A Reporter's Notebook*. New York: Oxford University Press, 1985.

Brands, H.W. *Into the Labyrinth: The United States and the Middle East, 1945–1993*. New York: McGraw Hill, 1994.

Brugioni, Dino A. *Eyes in the Sky: Eisenhower, the CIA and Cold War Aerial Espionage*. Annapolis, MD: Naval Institute Press, 2010.

Bullard, Reader. *Britain and the Middle East: From Earliest Times to 1963*. London: Hutchinson University Library, 1964.

Cohen, Stephen P. *Beyond America's Grasp: A Century of Failed Diplomacy in the Middle East*. New York: Farrar, Straus and Girous, 2009.

Confino, M. and S. Shamir. eds. *The USSR and the Middle East*. Jerusalem: Israel Universities Press, 1973.

Copeland, Miles. *The Game of Nations*. New York: Simon and Schuster, 1969.

Dallin, David J. *Soviet Foreign Policy After Stalin*. Philadelphia, PA: J.B. Lippincott Co, 1961.

Deutschkron, Inge. *Bonn and Jerusalem: The Strange Coalition*. Philadelphia, PA: Chilton Books, 1970.

Dowty, Alan. *Middle East Crisis: U.S. Decision Making in 1958, 1970, and 1973*. Berkeley, CA: University of California Press, 1984.

Gilbert, Martin. *Churchill and the Jews*. New York: Henry Holt, 2007.

Ginat, Rami. *The Soviet Union and Egypt, 1945–1955,* London: Frank Cass, 1993.

Gold, Dore. *The Fight for Jerusalem*. Washington, DC: Regnery, 2007.

—. *Tower of Babble: How the United Nations Has Fueled Global Chaos*. New York, Three Rivers Press, 2005.

Grobman, Alex. *Nations United: How the United Nations Undermines Israel and the West.* Green Forest, AR: Balfour Books, 2006.

Hanson, Victor Davis. *Carnage and Culture: Landmark Battles in the Rise to Western Power.* New York: Anchor Press, 2002.

Heikal, Mohamed. *The Sphinx and the Commissar: The Rise and fall of Soviet Influence in the Middle East.* New York: Harper and Row, 1978.

Hirschmann, Ira. *Red Star Over Bethlehem: Russia Drives to Capture the Middle East.* New York: Simon and Schuster, 1971.

Hurewitz, Jacob C. ed. *Diplomacy in the Near and Middle East: A Documentary Record, 1535–1956.* Cambridge, UK: Archive Editions Ltd., 1987.

Karsh, Efraim and Inari Karsh. *Empires of the Sand: The Struggle for Mastery in the Middle East, 1789–1923.* Cambridge, MA: Harvard University Press, 2001.

Katz, Mark. *Russia and Arabia: Soviet Foreign Policy Toward the Arabian Peninsula.* Baltimore: Johns Hopkins University Press, 1986.

Kissinger, Henry. *White House Years.* Boston: Little Brown, 1979.

Kuniholm, Bruce. *The Origins of the Cold War in the Near East: Great Power Conflict and Diplomacy in Iran, Turkey, and Greece.* Princeton, NJ: Princeton University Press, 1980.

Laqueur, Walter. *The Soviet Union and the Middle East.* London: Routledge, 1959.

—. *The Struggle for the Middle East: The Soviet Union and the Middle East 1958–1970.* Baltimore: Penguin Books, 1972.

Lederer, Ivo and Wayne Vucinich. eds. *The Soviet Union and the Middle East: The Post World War II Era.* Stanford, CA: Hoover Institution Press, 1974.

Leiner, Frederick C. *The End of Barbary Terror.* New York: Oxford University Press, 2006.

Lewis, Bernard. *What went wrong? Western Impact and Middle Eastern Response.* New York: Oxford University Press, 2002.

London, Joshua E. *Victory in Tripoli.* Hoboken, NJ: John Wiley and Sons, 2005.

Oren, Michael B. *Power, Faith, and Fantasy: America in the Middle East 1776 to the Present.* New York: W.W. Norton, 2007.

Pennar, Jaan. *The USSR and the Arabs: The Ideological Dimension, 1917–1972.* New York: Crane, Russak and Company, 1973.

Phares, Walid. *The Lost Spring: U.S. Policy in the Middle East and Catastrophes to Avoid,* New York: Palgrave, Macmillan, 2014.

Primakov, Yevgeny. *Russia and the Arabs.* New York: Basic Books, 2009.

Pryce-Jones, David. *Betrayal: France the Arabs and the Jews.* New York: Encounter Books, 2006.

Quandt, William. *Decade of Decisions: American Policy toward the Arab–Israeli Conflict, 1967–1976.* Berkeley, CA: University of California Press, 1977.

Richelson, Jeffrey T. *The U.S. Intelligence Community.* New York: Ballinger, 1989.

Roser, Richard F. *An Introduction to Soviet Foreign Policy.* New York: Prentice Hall, 1969.

Sachar, Howard. *The Emergence of the Middle East 1914–1924.* London: Allen Lane, 1970.

—. *Europe Leaves the Middle East 1936–1954.* London: Allen Lane, 1974.

—. *Israel and Europe: An Appraisal in History.* New York: Vintage Books, 1998.

Shaked, Haim and Itamar Rabinovich, eds. *The Middle East and the United States: Perceptions and Policies.* New Brunswick, NJ: Transaction Books, 1980.

Shapiro, Leonard ed. *Soviet Treaty Series: A Collection of Bilateral Treaties, Agreements, Conventions Etc.,* *Concluded between the Soviet Union and Foreign Powers.* Washington, DC: Georgetown University Press, 1955.

Shwadran, Benjamin, *The Middle East, Oil, and the Great Powers.* New York: John Wiley and Sons, 1974.

Smolansky, Oleg. *The Soviet Union and the Arab East Under Khrushchev.* Cranbury, NJ: Associated University Presses, 1974.

Spiegel, Steven. *The Other Arab-Israeli Conflict: Making America's Middle East Policy From Truman to Reagan.* Chicago: University of Chicago Press, 1985.

Weber, Frank G. *The Evasive Neutral: Germany, Britain and the Quest for a Turkish Alliance in the Second World War.* Columbia, MO: University of Missouri Press, 1979.

Weiner, Tim. *Legacy of Ashes: The History of the CIA.* New York: Doubleday, 2007.

Yodfat, Aryeh Y. *The Soviet Union and the Arabian Peninsula.* New York: St. Martin's Press, 1983.

TWENTIETH CENTURY MIDDLE EAST

Friedman, Isaiah. *The Question of Palestine 1914–1918: British-Jewish-Arab Relations.* New York: Schocken Books, 1973.

Knox, D. Edward. *The Making of a New Eastern Question: British Palestine Policy and the Origins of Israel, 1917–1925.* Washington, DC: Catholic University of America Press, 1981.

Mack, John. *A Prince of Our Disorder: The Life of T.E. Lawrence.* Boston: Little, Brown and Company, 1976.

Trevelyan, Hunphrey. *The Middle East in Revolution.* Boston: Gambit, 1970.

Van Paasen, Pierre. *The Forgotten Ally.* Washington, DC: Top Executive Media, 2005.

Westwood, John. *The History of the Middle East Wars.* North Dighton, MA: World Publications, 2002.

Yergin, Daniel. *The Prize: The Epic Quest for Oil, Money and Power.* New York: Simon and Schuster, 1991.

Ziff, William B. *The Rape of Palestine.* Mansfield Centre CT: Martino Publishing, 2009.

ZIONISM

Ben-Sasson, H. H. ed. *A History of the Jewish People.* Cambridge, MA: Harvard University Press, 1976.

Chertoff, Mordecai. ed. *Zionism: A Basic Reader.* New York: Herzl Press, 1975.

Edelheit, Abraham and Hershel Edelheit. *History of Zionism: A Handbook and Dictionary.* Boulder, CO: Westview Press, 2000.

Eldad, Israel. *The Jewish Revolution.* Jerusalem: Gefen Publishing House, 2007.

Elon, Amos. *Herzl.* New York: Holt, Rinehardt, Winston, 1975.

Gilbert, Martin. *Churchill and the Jews: A Life Long Friendship.* New York: Henry Holt and Company, 2007.

Hertzberg, Arthur. ed. *The Zionist Idea: A Historical Analysis and Reader.* New York: Atheneum, 1972.

Katz, Shmuel. *Lone Wolf: A Biography of Vladimir (Ze'ev) Jabotinsky.* New York: Barricade Books, 1996.

Laqueur, Walter. *A History of Zionism.* New York: Holt, Rinehart & Winston, 1972.

Learsi, Rufus. *Fulfillment: The Epic Story of Zionism.* New York: Herzl Press, 1972.

Lowenthal, Marvin. ed. *The Diaries of Theodor Herzl.* New York: Grosset and Dunlap, 1962.

Medoff, Rafael and Chaim I. Waxman. *Historical Dictionary of Zionism.* Chicago: Fitzroy Dearborn Publishers. 2000.

Merkley, Paul. *Those That Bless You, I Will Bless: Christian Zionism in Historical Perspective.* Brantford, ON: Mantua Books, 2011.

Troy, Gil. *Why I am a Zionist: Israel, Jewish Identity and the Challenges of Today.* Montreal: Bronfman Jewish Education Center, 2002.

Weizmann, Chaim. *Trial and Error, The Autobiography of Chaim Weizmann.* New York: Schocken Books, 1966.

ISRAEL General

A Brief Guide to Al-Haram al-Sharif: Jerusalem. Jerusalem: Supreme Moslem Council, Moslem Orphanage Printing Press, 1924.

Auerbach, Jerold S. *Jewish State Pariah Nation.* New Orleans, LA: Quid Pro Books, 2014.

Avner, Yehuda. *The Prime Ministers.* New Milford, CT: The Toby Press, 2010.

Avriel, Ehud. *Open the Gates! A Personal Story of the "Illegal" Immigration to Israel.* New York: Atheneum, 1975.

Bar-On, Mordechai. *Moshe Dayan: Israel's Controversial Hero.* New Haven, CT: Yale University Press, 2012.

Ben-Gurion, David. *Israel: A Personal History.* New York: Funk & Wagnalls, 1971.

—. *The Jews in Their Land.* London: Doubleday, 1966.

Benziman, Uzi. *Sharon, An Israeli Caesar.* New York: Adama Books, 1985.

Black, Ian and Benny Morris. *Israel's Secret Wars: A History of Israel's Intelligence Services.* New York: Grove Press, 1991.

Bruce, F.F. *Carta's Bible History Atlas.* Jerusalem: Carta, 1982.

Cline, Eric H. *Jerusalem Besieged: From Ancient Canaan to Modern Israel.* Ann Arbor: University of Michigan Press, 2004.

Correspondents of *the New York Times, Israel: The Historical Atlas.* New York: Macmillan, 1997.

Dayan. Moshe. *Moshe Dayan: Story of My Life.* New York: William Morrow, 1976.

Derogy, Jacques and Hesi Carmel. *The Untold History of Israel.* New York: Grove Press, 1979.

Dershowitz, Alan. *The Case for Israel.* Hoboken, NJ: Wiley & Sons, 2003.

Eban, Abba. *My Country: The History of Modern Israel.* London: Weidenfeld & Nicolson, 1972.

Eisenberg, Dennis, Uri Dan, et al. *The Mossad: Inside Stories.* New York: Paddington Press, 1978.

Eidelberg, Paul. *Jewish Statesmanship: Lest Israel Fall.* Lanham, MD: University Press of America, 2002.

—. *The Myth of Israeli Democracy: Toward a Truly Jewish Israel.* 2d ed. This book can be downloaded, by request from the author, eidelberg@foundation1.org.

Elon, Amos. *Jerusalem: Battlegrounds of Memory.* New York: Kodansha International, 1995.

Evron, Yair. *Israel's Nuclear Dilemma.* Ithaca, NY: Cornell University Press, 1994.

Finkelstein, Israel and Amihai Mazar. *The Quest for the Historical Israel: Debating Archaeology and the History of Early Israel.* Atlanta, GA: Society of Biblical Literature, 2007.

Gilbert, Lela. *Saturday People, Sunday People: Israel Through the Eyes of a Christian Sojourner.* New York: Encounter Books, 2012.

Gilbert, Martin. *Exile and Return: The Emergence of Jewish Statehood.* Jerusalem: Steimatzky's Agency, 1978.

—. *Israel: A History.* New York: Harper Collins, 2008.

—. *Jerusalem: Illustrated History Atlas.* Jerusalem: Steimatzky's Agency, 1977.

—. *Jerusalem: Rebirth of a City.* New York: Viking Press, 1985.

—. *Jerusalem in the Twentieth Century.* Hoboken, NJ: Wiley & Sons, 1996.

Gilder, George. *The Israel Test.* Minneapolis, MN: Richard Vigilante Books, 2009.

Gordis, Daniel. *If a Place can Make You Cry: Dispatches from an Anxious State.* New York: Crown Publishers, 2002.

—. Menachem *Begin: The Battle for Israel's Soul*. New York: NextBook, 2014.

Grief, Howard. *The Legal Foundation and Borders of Israel under International Law*. Jerusalem: Mazo Publishers, 2008.

Herzog, Chaim. *Heroes of Israel: Profiles of Jewish Courage*. Boston: Little, Brown and Company, 1989.

Hillel, Shlomo. *Operation Babylon*. London: Collins, 1988.

Holly, David C. *Exodus, 1947*. rev. ed. Annapolis, MD: Naval Institute Press, 1995.

Karsh, Efraim. *Fabricating Israeli History: The 'New Historians*. 2d ed. New York: Routledge, 2000.

Katz, Samuel. *Soldier Spies: Israeli Military Intelligence*. Novato, CA: Presidio, 1992.

—. *The Elite*. New York: Pocket Books, 1992.

—. *Battletruth: The World and Israel*. Tel Aviv: Dvir, 1983.

Klein, Aaron. *The Late Great State of Israel*. Los Angeles: WND Books, 2009.

Kollek, Teddy. *Jerusalem*. Washington, DC: Washington Institute for Near East Policy, 1990.

Kollek, Teddy and Moshe Pearlman. *Jerusalem: Sacred City of Mankind, a History of Forty Centuries*. Jerusalem: Steinmatzky's Agency, 1968.

Kurzman, Dan. *Ben-Gurion: Prophet of Fire*. New York: Simon and Schuster, 1983.

Lau-Lavie, Naphtali. *Moshe Dayan: A Biography*. Hartford, CT: Hartmore House, 1968.

Mann, Peggy. *Golda: The Life of Israel's Prime Minister*. New York: Coward, McCann, and Geoghagen, 1971.

Meir, Golda. *My Life*. New York: G. Putnam, 1975.

Miller, Anita, Jordan Miller and Sigalit Zetouni. *Sharon: Israel's Warrior-Politician*. Chicago: Academy Chicago Publishing, 2002.

Naggar, David. *The Case for a Larger Israel*. San Francisco: Deje Publishing, 2007.

Netanyahu, Benjamin. *A Place Among the Nations: Israel and the World*. New York: Bantam Books, 1993.

Perlmutter, Amos. *The Life and Times of Menachem Begin*. New York: Doubleday & Company, 1987.

Perry, Dan and Alfred Ironside. *Israel at Fifty*. Santa Monica, CA: General Publishing Group, 1996.

Rabin, Yitzhak. *The Rabin Memoirs*. Boston: Little, Brown, 1979.

Rabinovich, Itamar and Yehuda Reinharz. eds. *Israel in Middle East, Documents and Readings on Society Politics and Foreign Relations 1948–1984*. New York: Oxford University Press, 1984.

Reich, Bernard and David H. Goldberg. *Historical Dictionary of Israel*. 2d ed. Lanham, MD: Scarecrow Press, 2008.

Rosenthal, Monroe and Isaac Mozeson. *Wars of the Jews: A Military History from Biblical to Modern Times*. New York: Hippocrene Books, 1990.

Sachar, Howard. *A History of Israel: From the Rise of Zionism to Our Time*. 2d ed. New York: Alfred Knopf, 1996.

Shamir, Yitzhak. *Summing Up*. Boston: Little, Brown, 1994.

Tal, Eliyahu. *Whose Jerusalem?* Jerusalem: International Forum for a United Jerusalem, 1994.

Thomas, Gordon. *Gideon's Spies: the Secret History of the Mossad*. New York: Thomas Dunn Books, 1999.

Thubron, Thomas. *Jerusalem*. Amsterdam: Time-Life Books, 1976.

Wasserstein, Bernard. *Divided Jerusalem*. New Haven, CT: Yale University Press, 2002.

ISRAEL'S FOREIGN POLICY

Brecher, Michael. *Decisions in Israel's Foreign Policy*. New Haven, CT: Yale University Press, 1975.

—. *The Foreign Policy System of Israel*. New Haven, CT: Yale University Press, 1972.

Carol, Steven. *From Jerusalem to the Lion of Judah and Beyond: Israel's Foreign Policy in East Africa Since 1948*. New York: iUniverse, 2011.

Curtis, Michael and Susan Gitelson. eds.. *Israel and the Third World*. New Brunswick, NJ: Transaction Books, 1976.

Dagan, Avigdor. *Moscow and Jerusalem: Twenty Years of Relations between Israel and the Soviet Union*. London: Abelard-Schuman, 1970.

Gold, Dore. *Israel as an American Non-NATO Ally: Parameters of Defense Industrial Cooperation*. Tel Aviv: Jaffee Center for Strategic Studies, 1992.

Green, Stephen.*Taking Sides, America's Secret Relations with a Militant Israel*. New York: William and Morrow Company, 1984.

Klieman, Aaron. *Israel's Global Reach: Arms Sales as Diplomacy*. Washington, DC: Pergammon Books, 1985.

Parfitt, Tudor. *Operation Moses: The Untold Story of the Secret Exodus of the Falasha Jews from Ethiopia*. New York: Stein and Day, 1985.

Puschel, Karen L. *US-Israeli Strategic Cooperation in the Post-Cold War Era: An American Perspective*. Tel Aviv: Jaffee Center for Strategic Studies, 1992.

Rafael, Gideon. *Destination Peace: Three Decades of Israeli Foreign Policy*. New York: Stein and Day, 1981.

Raviv, Dan and Yossi Melman. *Friend in Deed: Inside the U.S.–Israel Alliance*. New York: Hyperion, 1994.

THE ARAB-ISRAELI CONFLICT General

Allon, Yigal. *Shield of David: The Story of Israel's Armed Forces*. London: Weidenfeld and Nicolson, 1970.

Anbar, Michael. *Israel and its Future: Analysis and Suggestions*. New York: iUniverse, 2004.

Avneri, Arieh L. *The Claim of Dispossession: Jewish Land Settlement and the Arabs 1878–1948*. New Brunswick, NJ: Transaction Books, 1984.

Bard, Mitchell. *Myths and Facts: A Guide to the Arab–Israeli Conflict*. Chevy Chase, MD: American-Israel Cooperative Enterprise, 2002.

—. *The Arab Lobby: The Invisible Alliance That Undermines America's Interests in the Middle East*. New York: Broadside Books, 2011.

Bartov, Hanoch. *Dado: 48 Years and 20 Days*. Ma'ariv Book Guild, 1981.

Bauer, Yehuda. *From Diplomacy to Resistance: A History of Jewish Palestine, 1939–1945*. New York: Atheneum, 1973.

Ben-Tekoa, Sha'i. *Phantom Nation: Inventing the "Palestinians" as the Obstacle to Peace*. Vols. 1-3. New York: DeProgram Program, Inc., 2013.

Ben-Zohar, Michael. *Spies in the Promised Land*. Boston: Houghton Mifflin, 1972.

Betser, Muki. *Secret Soldier: The True Life Story of Israel's Greatest Commando*. New York: Atlantic Monthly Press, 1996.

Black, Ian and Benny Morris. *Israel's Secret Wars: A History of Israeli Intelligence Services*. New York: Grove Weidenfeld, 1991.

Cohen, Eliezer. *Israel's Best Defense*. New York: Orion Books, 1993.

Eitan, Raful. *A Soldier's Story: The Life and Times of an Israeli War Hero*. New York: Shapolsky Publishing, 1991.

Elazar, Daniel J. ed. *Judea, Samaria and Gaza: Views on the Present and the Future*. Washington, DC: American Enterprise Institute, 1982.

Gervasi, Frank. *The Case for Israel*. New York: Viking Press, 1967.

Gilbert, Martin. *Historical Atlas of the Arab–Israeli Conflict*. 10th ed. New York: Routledge, 2012.

Griess, Thomas. ed. *The West Point Military History Series: Atlas of The Arab–Israeli Wars, The Chinese Civil War, and the Korean War*. Wayne, NJ: Avery Publishing, 1987.

—. ed. *The West Point Military History Series: The Arab–Israeli Wars, The Chinese Civil War, and the Korean War.* Wayne, NJ: Avery Publishing, 1987.

Harkabi, Yehoshafat. *Arab Attitudes towards Israel.* Jerusalem: Israel Universities Press, 1972.

—. *Palestinians and Israel.* New York: John Wiley and Sons, 1974.

—. *Israel's Fateful Decision.* New York: Harper & Row, 1989.

Hersh, Seymour. *The Samson Option: Israel, America and the Bomb.* London: Faber and Faber, 1991.

Herzog, Chaim. *The Arab–Israeli Wars.* New York: Random House, 1982.

Honigman, Gerald A. *The Quest for Justice in the Middle East: The Arab-Israeli Conflict in Greater Perspective.* Lake Mary, FL: Creation House, 2009.

Ingrams, Doreen. *Palestine Papers 1917–1922: Seeds of Conflict.* New York: George Braziller, 1972.

Karetzky, Stephen. and Norman Frankel. eds. *The Media Coverage of the Arab–Israeli Conflict.* New York: Shapolsky Publishers, 1989.

Karsh, Efraim. *Palestine Betrayed.* New Haven, CT: Yale University Press, 2010.

Katz, Samuel. *Battleground: Fact and Fantasy in Palestine.* rev. ed. New York: Taylor Productions, 2002.

Laqueur, Walter. *The Israel–Arab Reader: A Documentary History of the Middle East Conflict.* 7th ed. New York: Bantam Books, 2008.

Levin, Kenneth. *The Oslo Syndrome.* Portland, ME: Smith & Kraus, 2005.

Levine, Daniel. *The Birth of the Irgun Zvai Leumi: A Jewish Liberation Movement.* Jerusalem: Gefen Publishing House, 1991.

Lorch, Netanel. *One Long War: Arab versus Jew Since 1920.* Jerusalem: Keter, 1976.

Moore, John N. ed. *The Arab–Israeli Conflict: Readings and Documents.* Princeton, NJ: Princeton University Press, 1977.

Narrett, Eugene. *Gathered Against Jerusalem.* Bloomington, IN: Writers Club Press, 2000.

O'Brien, Conor Cruse. *The Siege.* New York: Simon and Schuster, 1986.

Parkes, James. *Whose Land? A History of the Peoples of Palestine.* New York: Penguin Books, 1970.

Peters, Joan. *From Time Immemorial: The Origins of the Arab–Jewish Conflict over Palestine.* New York: Harper & Row, 1984.

Prittie, Terence and Walter H. Nelson. *The Economic War against the Jews.* London: Congi Books, 1979.

Raviv, Dan and Yossi Melman. *Every Spy a Prince: The Complete History of Israel's Intelligence Community.* Boston: Houghton Mifflin, 1990.

—. *Spies Against Armageddon: Inside Israel's Secret Wars.* Sea Cliff, NY: Levant Books, 2014.

Ronen, Ran. *Eagle in the Sky.* Tel Aviv: Contento De Semrik, 2013.

Rosenfeld, Alvin. *The Plot To Destroy Israel: The Road to Armageddon.* New York: G. P. Putnam's Sons, 1977.

Rubin, Barry. *The Arab States and the Palestine Conflict.* Syracuse, NY: Syracuse University Press, 1981.

Sharon, Ariel with David Chanoff. *Warrior: The Autobiography of Ariel Sharon.* New York: Simon and Schuster, 1989.

Shem-Ur, Ora. *The Challenges of Israel.* New York: Shengold Publishers, 1980.

Simmons, Shraga. *David & Goliath: The Explosive Inside Story of Media Bias in the Israeli–Palestinian Conflict.* Jerusalem: Emesphere Productions, 2012.

Sykes, Christopher. *Crossroads to Israel: 1917–1948.* Bloomington, IN: Indiana University Press, 1973.

Tessler, Mark. *A History of the Israeli–Palestinian Conflict.* Bloomington, IN: Indiana University Press, 1994.

Van Creveld. *The Sword and the Olive: A Critical History of the Israeli Defense Force.* New York: Public Affairs Press, 1998.

THE ISRAELI WAR OF INDEPENDENCE & ITS AFTERMATH

Auerbach, Jerold S. *Brothers At War: Israel and the Tragedy of the Altalena.* New Orleans, LA: Quid Pro Books, 2011.

Begin, Menachem. *The Revolt.* New York: Nash Publishing, 1977.

Bell, John Bowyer. *Terror out of Zion: Irrgun Zvai Leuni, LEHI, and the Palestine Underground, 1929–1949,* New York: St. Martin's Press, 1977.

Bercusson, David. *The Secret Army.* New York: Stein and Day, 1984.

Berkman, Ted. *Cast A Giant Shadow.* New York: Pocketbooks, 1962.

Collins, Larry and Dominique Lapierre. *O Jerusalem.* New York: Simon and Schuster, 1972.

Eldad, Israel. *The First Tithe.* Tel Aviv: Jabotinsky Institute, 2008.

Gitlin, Jan. *The Conquest of Acre Fortress.* Tel Aviv: Hadar Publishing House, 1968.

Kagan, Benjamin. *The Secret Battle for Israel.* Cleveland, OH: World Publishing, 1986.

Karsh, Efraim. *The Arab–Israeli Conflict: The Palestine War, 1948.* Oxford, UK: Osprey Publishing Ltd., 2002.

Kurzman, Dan. *Genesis 1948: The First Arab–Israeli War.* New York: World Publishing, 1970.

Larkin, Margaret. *The Six Days of Yad Mordechai.* Givatayim, Israel: Yad Mordechai Museum, 1976.

Levine, David. *The Birth of the Irgun Zvai Leumi.* Jerusalem: Gefen Publishing House, 1991.

Lorch, Netanel. *The Edge of the Sword: Israel's War of Independence, 1947–1949.* New York: G.P. Putnam's Sons, 1961.

Milstein, Uri. *History of the War of Independence Vol. I: A Nation Girds for War.* Lanham, MD: University Press of America, 1996.

—. *History of the War of Independence Vol. II: The First Month.* Lanham, MD: University Press of America, 1997.

—. *History of the War of Independence Vol. III: The First Invasion.* Lanham, MD: University Press of America, 1998.

—. *History of the War of Independence Vol. IV: Out of Crisis Came Decision.* Lanham, MD: University Press of America, 1998.

Morris, Benny. *Israel's Border Wars 1949–1956.* New York: Oxford University Press, 1993.

O'Ballance, Edgar. *The Arab–Israeli War, 1948.* New York: Hyperion Press, 1983.

Sharef, Zeev. *Three Days.* Garden City, NY: Doubleday, 1962.

Slater, Leonard. *The Pledge.* New York: Simon and Schuster, 1970.

Teveth, Shabtai. *Ben-Gurion and the Palestinian Arabs: From Peace to War.* New York: Oxford University Press, 1985.

THE ARAB BOYCOTT OF ISRAEL

Chill, Dan S. *The Arab Boycott of Israel: Economic Aggression and World Reaction.* New York: Praeger, 1976.

Feiler, Gil. *From Boycott to Economic Cooperation: The Political Economy of the Arab Boycott of Israel.* London: Frank Cass, 1998.

Leyton-Brown, David. ed. *The Utility of International Sanctions.* New York: St. Martin's Press, 1987.

Pendergrast, Mark. *For God, Country, and Coca-Cola: The Definitive History of the Great American Soft Drink and the Company That Makes It.* New York: Basic Books, 2000.

THE SINAI-SUEZ WAR & ITS AFTERMATH

Alteras, Isaac. *Eisenhower and Israel: U.S.-Israeli Relations, 1953–1960.* Gainesville, FL: University Press of Florida, 1993.

Bar-On, Mordechai. *The Gates of Gaza: Israel's Road to Suez and Back, 1955–1957.* New York: St. Martin's Press, 1994.

Bowie, Robert. *Suez 1956, International Crisis and the Rule of Law.* New York: Oxford University Press, 1974.

Dayan, Moshe. *Diary of the Sinai Campaign.* New York: Schocken Books, 1966.

Eden, Anthony. *The Suez Crisis of 1956.* Boston: Beacon Press, 1960.

Georges-Picot, Jacques. *The Real Suez Crisis.* New York: Harcourt, Brace, Jovanovich, 1978.

Golan, Aviezer. *Operation Susannah.* New York: Harper and Row, 1978.

Henriques, Robert. *100 Hours to Suez.* New York: Pyramid Books, 1957.

Lotz, Wolfgang. *The Champagne Spy.* New York: St. Martin's Press, 1972.

Love, Kennett. *Suez: The Twice Fought War.* New York: McGraw Hill, 1969.

Neff, Donald. *Warriors at Suez: Eisenhower Takes America into the Middle East.* New York: Linden Press, 1981.

O'Ballance, Edgar. *The Sinai Campaign, 1956.* New York: Frederick A. Praeger, 1960.

Shucjburgh, Evelyn. *Descent to Suez: Diaries 1951–1956.* London: Weidenfeld and Nicolson, 1986.

Tal, David. *The 1956 War: Collision and Rivalry in the Middle East.* New York: Routledge, 2001.

Thomas, Hugh. *Suez.* New York: Harper & Row, 1967.

Troen, S.I. and M. Shemesh. eds. *The Suez-Sinai Crisis, 1956: Retrospective and Reappraisal.* New York: Columbia University Press, 1990.

Varble, Derek. *The Suez Crisis 1956.* Oxford, UK: Osprey Publishing Ltd., 2003.

THE SIX-DAY WAR & ITS AFTERMATH

Brown, George. *In My Way: Memoirs of Lord George Brown.* London: St. Martin's Press, 1971.

Churchill, Randolph and Winston S. Churchill. *The Six Day War.* London: Heinemann, 1970.

Cristol, A. Jay. *The Liberty Incident: The 1967 Israeli Attack on the U.S. Navy Spy Ship.* Washington, DC: Brassey's, Inc., 2002.

Eisenberg, Dennis, Eli Landau and Menachem Portugali. *Operation Uranium Ship.* Tel Aviv: Steimatzky, 1978.

Karpin, Michael. *The Bomb in the Basement: How Israel Went Nuclear and What that Means for the World.* New York: Simon & Schuster, 2006.

Kosut, Hal. ed. *Israel and the Arabs: The June 1967 War.* New York: Facts on File, 1968.

Laqueur, Walter. *The Road to War: The Origin and Aftermath of the Arab–Israeli Conflict 1967–68.* Baltimore, MD: Penguin Books, 1968.

Marshall, S.L.A. *Swift Sword: the Historical Record of Israel's Victory, June, 1967.* New York: American Heritage Publishing. 1967.

Moskin, J. Robert. *Among Lions: The Definitive Account of the 1967 Battle for Jerusalem.* New York: Arbor House, 1982.

Neff, Donald. *Warriors for Jerusalem: The Six Days that Changed the Middle East.* New York: Linden Press, 1984.

O'Ballance, Edgar. *The Third Arab–Israeli War, 1967.* Hamden, CT: Archon Books, 1972.

Oren, Michael B. *Six Days of War: June 1967 and the Making of the Modern Middle East.* New York: Oxford University Press, 2002.

Pryce-Jones, David. *The Face of Defeat: Palestinian Refugees and Guerrillas.* New York: Holt, Rinehart and Winston, 1972.

Rabinovich, Abraham. *The Boats of Cherbourg.* New York: Seaver Books, 1988.

Safran, Nadav. *From War to War: The Arab–Israeli Confrontation 1948–1967.* New York: Pegasus, 1969.

Stevenson, William. *Strike Zion!* New York: Bantam Books, 1967.

Velie, Lester. *Countdown in the Holy Land.* New York: Funk and Wagnalls, 1969.

THE 1,000-DAY WAR OF ATTRITION

Aloni, Shlomo. *Arab–Israeli Air Wars, 1967–82.* Madrid: Osprey Aviation Series, Delprado Publishers, 2001.

Bar-Siman-Tov, Yaacov. *The Israel–Egyptian War of Attrition, 1969–1970: A Case-Study of Limited Local War.* New York: Columbia University Press, 1980.

O'Ballance, Edgar. *The Electronic War in the Middle East, 1968–70.* North Haven, CT: Shoe String Press, 1974.

O'Neill, Bard E. *Revolutionary Warfare in the Middle East: The Israelis vs. the Fedayeen.* Boulder, CO: Paladin Press, 1974.

THE YOM KIPPUR/RAMADAN WAR & ITS AFTERMATH

Adan, Avraham. *The Yom Kippur War.* New York: Drum Books, 1986.

Asher, Jerry. *Duel for the Golan: The 100 Hour Battle that Saved Israel.* New York: William Morrow, 1987.

Bar-Joseph, Uri. *The Watchman Fell Asleep: The Surprise of Yom Kippur and its Sources.* Albany, NY: State University of New York Press, 2005.

Boyne, Walter J. *The Two O'clock War.* New York: St. Martin's Press, 2002.

Brecher, Michael. *Decisions in Crisis: Israel, 1967 and 1973.* Berkeley, CA: University of California Press, 1980.

Eidelberg, Paul. *Sadat's Strategy.* New York: Americans For a Safe Israel, 1979. A free copy is available at http://www.afsi.org/pamphlets/SadatsStrategy_Eidelberg.pdf.

Herzog, Chaim. *The War of Atonement.* Jerusalem: Steinmatzky's Agency, 1975.

Heikal, Mohamed. *The Road to Ramadan.* New York: Quadrangle Books, 1975.

Insight Team of the Sunday Times. *Insight on the Middle East War.* London: Andre Deutsch, 1974.

Katz, Shmuel. *The Hollow Peace.* Israel: Dvir, 1981.

Kohler, Foy, Leon Goure and Moshe Harvey. *The Soviet Union and the October 1973 Middle East War: Implications for Détente.* Miami, FL: University of Miami, 1974.

Laqueur, Walter. *Confrontation: The Middle East and World Politics.* New York: Bantam Books, 1974.

O'Ballance, Edgar. *No Victor, No Vanquished: The Yom Kippur War.* Rafael, CA: Presidio Press, 1978.

Rabinovich, Abraham. *The Yom Kippur War: The Epic Encounter that Transformed the Middle East,* New York: Schoken Books, 2004.

Schiff, Ze'ev. *October Earthquake: Yom Kippur 1973.* Tel Aviv: University Publishing Projects, 1974.

Sobel, Lester A. ed. *Israel and the Arabs: The October 1973 War.* New York: Facts on File, 1974.

Troy, Gil. Moynihan's *Moment: America's Fight Against Zionism as Racism.* New York: Oxford University Press, 2013.

Zodhy, Badri. *The Ramadan War, 1973.* New York: Hippocrene Books, 1979.

THE ISRAEL-PLO WAR IN LEBANON

Alexander, Edward. *NBC's War in Lebanon: The Distorting Mirror.* New York: Americans For a Safe Israel, 1983. A free copy is available at http://www.afsi.org/pamphlets/NBC_war_in_lebanon_alexander. pdf.

Israeli, Raphael. ed. *The PLO In Lebanon: Selected Documents.* London: Weidenfeld and Nicolson, 1983.

Landau, Julian. *The Media: Freedom or Responsibility: The War in Lebanon1982, A Case Study.* Jerusalem: BAL Mass Communications, 1984.

Schiff, Ze'ev and Ehud Ya'ari. *Israel's Lebanon War.* New York: Simon and Schuster, 1984.

THE ISRAELI STRIKE ON IRAQ'S NUCLEAR FACILITY

Claire, Robert. *Raid on the Sun.* New York: Broadway Books, 2004.

Nakdimon, Shlomo. *First Strike.* New York: Summit Books, 1987.

Weissman, Steve and Herbert Krosney. *The Islamic Bomb.* New York: NY Times Books, 1981.

ISRAEL AND THE GULF WAR

Levran, Aharon. *Israeli Strategy After Desert Storm: Lessons from the Second Gulf War.* London: Frank Cass, 1997.

ISRAEL AND IRAN

Bostom, Andrew G. *Iran's Final Solution for Israel: The Legacy of Jihad and Shi'ite Islamic Jew-Hatred in Iran.* Washington, DC: Bravura Books, 2014.

Katz, Yaakov and Yoaz Hendel. *Israel vs. Iran: The Shadow War,* Washington, DC: Potomac Books, 2012.

TERRORISM AND JIHAD

Bar Zohar, Michael and Eitan Haber. *The Quest for the Red Prince.* New York: William Morrow, 1983.

Bawer, Bruce. *While Europe Slept: How Radical Islam is Destroying the West from Within.* New York: Doubleday, 2006.

Ben-Porat, Y., Eitan Haber and Ze'ev Schiff. *Entebbe Rescue.* New York: Dell Publishing, 1977.

Bukay, David. *Mohammad's Monsters.* Green Forest, AR: Balfour Books and the Ariel Center for Policy Research, 2004.

Burleigh, Michael. *Blood & Rage: A Cultural History of Terrorism.* New York: Harper Collins Publishers, 2009.

Dershowitz, Alan M. *Why Terrorism Works: Understanding the Threat, Responding to the Challenge.* New Haven, CT: Yale University Press, 2002.

Dietl, Wilhelm. *Holy War.* New York: Macmillan, 1984.

Dobson, Christopher. *Black September: Its Short, Violent History.* New York: Macmillan Publishing, 1974.

Dobson, Christopher and Ronald Payne. *Counterattack: The West's Battle Against the Terrorists.* New York: Facts on File, 1982.

Dunstan, Simon. *Israel's Lightning Strike: The Raid on Entebbe 1976.* Oxford, UK: Osprey Publishing Ltd., 2009.

Ehrenfeld, Rachel. *Funding Evil: How Terrorism is Financed and How to Stop it.* Chicago: Bonus Books, 2003.

Emerson, Steven. *American Jihad: The Terrorists Living Among Us.* New York: The Free Press, 2002.

—. *Jihad Incorporated.* Amherst, NY: Prometheus, 2006.

Firestone, Reuven. *Jihad: The Origin of Holy War in Islam.* New York: Oxford University Press, 1999.

Fregosi, Paul. *Jihad in the West.* Amherst, NY: Prometheus, 1998.

Frumm, David and Richard Pearle. *An End to Evil: How to Win the War on Terror.* New York: Random House, 2003.

Gabriel, Brigette. *Because They Hate: A Survivor of Islamic Terror Warns America.* New York: St. Martin's Press, 2006.

—. *They Must Be Stopped.* New York: St. Martin's Press, 2008.

Gerges, Fawas A. *Journey of the Jihadist.* Orlando, FL: Harcourt Books, 2006.

Click, Carolyn. *Shackled Warrior: Israel and the Global Jihad.* Jerusalem: Gefen Publishing House, 2008.

Hamid, Tawfik. *The Roots of Jihad.* Denver: Top Executive Media, 2006.

Habeck Mary. *Knowing the Enemy.* New Haven, CT: Yale University Press, 2006.

Huntington, Samuel P. *The Clash of Civilizations and the Remaking of World Order.* New York: Touchstone, Simon & Schuster, 1996.

Katz, Samuel M. *The Hunt for the Engineer: How Israeli Agents Tracked the Hamas Master Bomber.* Guilford, CT: The Lyons Press, 2002.

Kepel, Illes. *Jihad: The Trail of Political Islam.* Cambridge, MA: Harvard University Press, 2002.

Küntzel, Matthias. *Jihad and Jew-Hatred: Islamism, Nazism and the Roots of 9/11.* New York: Telos Press, 2009.

Laqueur, Walter. *No end to War: Terrorism in the Twenty First Century.* New York: Continuum, 2003.

—. *The Age of Terrorism.* Boston: Little, Brown and Company, 1987.

—. *The New Terrorism.* New York: Oxford University Press, 1999.

Lindsey, Hal. *The Everlasting Hatred: The Roots of Jihad.* Lake Elsinore, CA: Oracle House Publishing, 2002.

Melman, Yossi. *The Master Terrorist: The True Story behind Abu Nidal.* New York: Adama Books, 1986.

Netanyahu, Benjamin. *Fighting Terrorism.* New York: Farrar, Straus, Giroux, 1995.

—. ed. *Terrorism: How The West Can Win.* New York: Farrar, Straus, Giroux, 1986.

Netanyahu, Iddo. *Entebbe: A Defining Moment in the War of Terrorism.* Green Forest, AR: Balfour Books, 2003.

Parry, Albert. *Terrorism: From Robespierre to Arafat.* New York: Vanguard Press, 1976.

Pape, Robert A. *Dying to Win.* New York: Random House, 2005.

Peters, Ralph. *Beyond Terror: Strategy in a Changing World.* Mechanicburg, PA: Stackpole Books, 2002.

Phares, Walid. *Future Jihad: Terrorist Strategies against America.* New York: Macmillan, 2005.

—. *The Coming Revolution' Struggle for Freedom in the Middle East.* New York: Threshold Editions, Simon and Schuster, 2010.

—. *The Confrontation: Winning the war Against Future Jihad.* New York: Palgrave Macmillan, 2008.

Phillips, Melanie. *Londonistan.* New York: Encounter Books, 2006.

Pipes, Daniel. *Militant Islam Reaches America.* New York: W. W. Norton, 2003.

Poole, John H. *Tactics of the Crescent Moon.* Emerald Isle, NC: Posterity Press, 2004.

Rubin, Barry and Judith Rubin. eds. *Anti-American Terrorism and the Middle East: A Documentary Reader.* New York: Oxford University Press, 2006.

Scheuer, Michael. *Osama Bin Laden.* New York: Oxford University Press, 2011.

—. *Through Our Enemies Eyes: Osama Bin Laden, Radical Islam, and the future of America.* Washington, DC: Brassey's Inc., 2002.

Schindler, John R. *Unholy Terror: Bosnia, Al-Qa'ida, and the Rise of Global Jihad.* Minneapolis, MN: Zenith Press, 2007.

Singer, Saul. *Confronting Jihad.* Cold Spring Harbor, NY: Cold Spring Press, 2003.

Spencer, Robert. *Onward Muslim Soldiers: How Jihad still threatens the West.* Washington, DC: Regency Publishing Company, 2003.

Steyn, Mark. *America Alone: The End of the World As We Know It.* Washington, DC: Regnery Publishing, 2006.

Timmerman, Kenneth R. *Preachers of Hate: Islam and the War on America.* New York: Crown Forum, Random House, 2003.

WMDS AND THE MIDDLE EAST

Aronson, Shlomo and Oded Brosh. *The Politics and Strategy of Nuclear Weapons in the Middle East, the Opacity Theory, and Reality, 1960–1991: An Israeli Perspective* Albany, NY: State University of New York Press, 1992.

Burck, Gordon M and Charles C. Flowerree. *International Handbook on Chemical Weapons Proliferation.* New York: Greenwood Press, 1991.

Burrows, William E. and Robert Winderm. *Critical Mass: The Dangerous Race for Superweapons in a Fragmenting World.* New York: Simon and Schuster, 1994.

Cirincione, Joseph with Jon Wolfstahl and Miriam Rajkumar. *Deadly Arsenals: Tracking Weapons of Mass Destruction.* Washington, DC: Carnegie Endowment for International Peace, 2002.

Cohen, Avner. *Israel and the Bomb.* New York: Columbia University Press, 1998.

Cohen, Avner and Marvin Miller. *Nuclear Shadows in the Middle East: Prospects for Arms Control in the Wake of the Gulf Crisis.* Cambridge, MA: Massachusetts Institute Technology, 1990.

Hersh, Seymour. *The Sampson Option.* New York: Random House, 1991.

Richelson, Jeffrey T. *The U.S. Intelligence Community.* New York: Ballinger, 1989.

Robinson, Julian Perry. *The Rise of CB Weapons: The Problem of Chemical and Biological Warfare.* New York: Humanities Press, 1971.

Spector, Leonard S. *The Undeclared Bomb.* Cambridge, MA: Ballinger Publishers, 1988.

Weissman, Steve and Herbert Krosney. *The Islamic Bomb: the Nuclear Threat to Israel and the Middle East.* New York: Times Books, 1981.

THE MOVEMENT TOWARD PEACE

Ben-Meir Alon. *The War We Must Win.* Bloomington, IN: Author House, 2004.

Cohen, Raymond. *Culture and Conflict in Egyptian–Israel Relations: A Dialogue of the Deaf.* Bloomington, IN: Indiana University Press, 1990.

Cordesman, Anthony. *Perilous Prospects: The Peace Process and the Arab–Israeli Military Balance.* Boulder, CO: Westview Press, 1996.

Glick, Caroline B. *The Israeli Solution: A One State Plan for Peace in the Middle East,* New York: Crown Forum, 2014.

Kimche, Jon. *There Could Have Been Peace.* New York: Dial Press, 1973.

Marcus, Itamar and Nan Jacques Zilberdik. *Deception: Betraying the Peace Progress.* 2d ed. Jerusalem: Palestine Media Watch, 2011.

Netanyahu, Benjamin. *A Durable Peace: Israel and Its Place among the Nations.* New York: Warner Books, 2000.

Rabinovich, Itamar. *The Brink of Peace: The Israeli–Syrian Negotiations.* Princeton, NJ: Princeton University Press, 1998.

—. *The Road Not Taken: Early Arab–Israeli Negotiations.* New York: Oxford University Press, 1991.

Stone, Julius. *Israel and Palestine: Assault on the Law of Nations.* Baltimore: Johns Hopkins University Press, 1981.

Weizman, Ezer. *The Battle for Peace.* New York: Bantam, 1981.

INDEX

B

CPSIA information can be obtained at www.ICGtesting.com
Printed in the USA
BVOW10s0202110116

432467BV00001B/1/P

Contemporary Theatre, Film, and Television

ISSN 0749-064X

Contemporary Theatre, Film, and Television

A Biographical Guide Featuring Performers,
Directors, Writers, Producers, Designers, Managers,
Choreographers, Technicians, Composers, Executives,
Dancers, and Critics in the United States and Great Britain

Owen O'Donnell
Editor

Sara J. Steen
Sharon Gamboa
Associate Editors

Volume 8

 **Gale Research Inc.** · *DETROIT* · *LONDON*

STAFF

Linda S. Hubbard, *Senior Editor*

Owen O'Donnell, *Editor*

Sara J. Steen and Sharon Gamboa, *Associate Editors*

Lillie Balinova, Erin McGrath, James R. Kirkland, *Sketchwriters*

June Barnett, Dorothy Carter, Vincent Henry, Yvette Jones,
Liz Menendez, Kay Ohara, Maura Pleckaitis, Bob Van Vooris, *Editorial Assistants*

Rahadyan T. Sastrowardoyo, *Contributing Editor*

Mary Beth Trimper, *Production Manager*
Evi Seoud, *Assistant Production Manager*

Arthur Chartow, *Art Director*
C. J. Jonik, *Keyliner*

Laura Bryant, *Production Supervisor*
Louise Gagné, *Internal Production Associate*

PHOTOGRAPH CREDITS

Gerard Depardieu: Richard Delloul; James Goldman: © Barbara Goldman; Tim Luscombe: Shuhei Iwamoto;
Paul Pyant: Nicholas Richter 1988; Christian Roberts: Susan Greenhill; M. Edgar Rosenbloom: Gale Zucker.

The paper used in this publication meets the minimum requirements
of American National Standard for Information Sciences—Permanence
Paper for Printed Library Materials, ANSI Z39.48-1984.

Library of Congress Catalog Card Number 84-649371
ISBN 0-8103-2071-1
ISSN 0749-064X

Printed in the United States of America

Published simultaneously in the United Kingdom
by Gale Research International Limited
(An affiliated company of Gale Research Inc.)

Contents

Preface

The worlds of theatre, film, and television hold an undeniable appeal, and the individuals whose careers are devoted to these fields are subjects of great interest. The people both behind the scenes and in front of the lights and cameras—writers, directors, producers, performers, and others—all have a significant impact on our lives, for they enlighten us as they entertain.

Contemporary Theatre, Film, and Television Provides Broad Coverage in the Entertainment Field

Contemporary Theatre, Film, and Television (CTFT) is a comprehensive biographical series designed to meet the need for information on theatre, film, and television personalities. Prior to the publication of *CTFT*, biographical sources covering entertainment figures were generally limited in scope; for more than seventy years *Who's Who in the Theatre (WWT)*, for example, provided reliable information on theatre people. But today few performers, directors, writers, producers, or technicians limit themselves to the stage. And there are also growing numbers of people who, though not active in the theatre, make significant contributions to other entertainment media. With its broad scope, encompassing not only stage notables but also film and/or television figures, *CTFT* is a more comprehensive and, the editors believe, more useful reference tool. Its clear entry format, allowing for the quick location of specific facts, combines with hundreds of photographs to further distinguish *CTFT* from other biographical sources on entertainment personalities.

Moreover, since *CTFT* is a series, new volumes can cover the steady influx of fresh talent into the entertainment media. The majority of the entries in each *CTFT* volume present information on people new to the series, but *CTFT* also includes updated versions of previously published *CTFT* sketches on especially active figures as well as complete revisions of *WWT* entries. The *CTFT* cumulative index makes all listings easily accessible.

Scope

CTFT is a biographical series covering not only performers, directors, writers, and producers but also designers, managers, choreographers, technicians, composers, executives, dancers, and critics from the United States and Great Britain. With nearly 700 entries in *CTFT*, Volume 8, the series now provides biographies for more than 5,200 people involved in all aspects of the theatre, film, and television industries.

Primary emphasis is given to people who are currently active. *CTFT* includes major, established figures whose positions in entertainment history are assured, such as award-winning playwright Wendy Wasserstein, film producer Samuel Goldwyn, Jr., actors Gerard Depardieu and Harrison Ford, documentary filmmaker Marcel Ophuls, and the animators William Hanna and Joseph Barbera. Individuals who are beginning to garner acclaim for their work are represented in *CTFT* as well, including comedienne and television superstar Roseanne Barr; director Tim Luscombe who received the 1989 Olivier Award as Best Newcomer for his work on the London stage; Winona Ryder, the star of such recent films as *Beetlejuice, Heathers,* and *Great Balls of Fire;* Craig Safan, composer for the television series *Cheers* and the film *Stand and Deliver* among other works; and Anton Furst, 1990 Academy Award-winner for his production design on the film *Batman.*

Selected sketches also record the achievements of theatre, film, and television personalities who have recently passed away but whose work commands lasting interest. Among such notables with listings in this volume are Laurence Olivier, Irving Berlin, Bette Davis, Barbara Stanwyck, Lucille Ball, Mel Blanc, Gilda Radner, and theatre director and executive Nikos Psacharopoulos.

With its broad coverage and detailed entries, *CTFT* is designed to assist a variety of users—a student preparing for a class, a teacher drawing up an assignment, a researcher seeking a specific fact, a librarian searching for the answer to a question, or a general reader looking for information about a favorite personality.

Compilation Methods

Every effort is made to secure information directly from biographees. The editors consult industry directories, biographical dictionaries, published interviews, feature stories, and film, television, and theatre reviews to identify people not previously covered in *CTFT*. Questionnaires are mailed to prospective listees or, when addresses are unavailable, to their agents, and sketches are compiled from the information they supply. The editors also select major figures included in *WWT* whose entries require updating and send them copies of their previously published entries for revision. *CTFT* sketches are then prepared from the new information submitted by these well-known personalities or their agents. Among the notable figures whose *WWT,* seventeenth edition, entries have been completely revised for this volume of *CTFT* are actresses Pauline Collins and Gloria Foster, playwright James Goldman, and stage producer and director Woodie King, Jr. If people of special interest to *CTFT* users are deceased or fail to reply to requests for information, materials are gathered from reliable secondary sources. Sketches prepared solely through research are clearly marked with an asterisk (*) at the end of the entries.

Revised Entries

Each volume of *CTFT* is devoted primarily to people currently active in theatre, film, and television who are not already covered in the series or in *WWT*. However, to ensure *CTFT*'s timeliness and comprehensiveness, in addition to the updates of *WWT* sketches mentioned above, the editors also select *CTFT* listees from earlier volumes who have been active enough to require revision of their previous biographies. Such individuals will merit revised entries as often as there is substantial new information to provide. For example, the update of Woody Allen's entry from *CTFT*, Volume 1, included in this volume adds his most recent film work and awards; moreover, research has brought to light information about earlier stage and television work that was not included in his previous sketch. Similarly, Volume 8 provides revised entries containing significant new information on Richard Attenborough, Carol Burnett, Dick Cavett, Lee Grant, Harold Prince, Meryl Streep, and Peter Ustinov.

Format

CTFT entries, modeled after those in Gale Research's highly regarded *Contemporary Authors* series, are written in a clear, readable style with few abbreviations and no limits set on length. So that a reader needing specific information can quickly focus on the pertinent portion of an entry, typical *CTFT* listings are clearly divided into the following sections:

Entry heading—Cites the form of the name by which the listee is best known followed by birth and death dates, when available.

Personal—Provides the biographee's full or original name if different from the entry heading, date and place of birth, family data, and information about the listee's education (including professional training), politics, religion, and military service.

Vocation—Highlights the individual's primary fields of activity in the entertainment industry.

Career—Presents a comprehensive listing of principal credits or engagements. The career section lists theatrical debuts (including Broadway and London debuts), principal stage appearances, and major tours; film debuts and principal films; television debuts and television appearances; and plays, films, and television shows directed and produced. Related career items, such as professorships and lecturing, are also included as well as non-entertainment career activities.

Writings—Lists published and unpublished plays, screenplays, and scripts along with production information. Published books and articles, often with bibliographical data, are also listed.

Recordings—Cites album and single song releases with recording labels, when available.

Awards—Notes theatre, film, and television awards and nominations as well as writing awards, military and civic awards, and fellowships and honorary degrees received.

Member—Highlights professional, union, civic, and other association memberships, including official posts held.

Sidelights—Cites favorite roles, recreational activities, and hobbies. Frequently this section includes portions of agent-prepared biographies or personal statements from the listee. In-depth sidelights providing an overview of an individual's career achievements are compiled on selected personalities of special interest.

Other Sources—Indicates periodicals, serials, or books where interviews, criticism, and additional types of information can be found. Not intended as full bibliographies, these citations are provided on brief entries, sketches with sidelights, and a small number of other entries.

Addresses—Notes home, office, and agent addresses, when available. (In those instances where an individual prefers to withhold his or her home address from publication, the editors make every attempt to include at least one other address in the entry.)

Enlivening the text in many instances are large, clear photographs. Often the work of theatrical photographers, these pictures are supplied by the biographees to complement their sketches. This volume, for example, contains nearly 200 such portraits received from various individuals profiled in the following pages.

Brief Entries

CTFT users have indicated that having some information, however brief, on individuals not yet in the series would be preferable to waiting until full-length sketches can be prepared as outlined above under "Compilation Methods." Therefore, *CTFT* includes abbreviated listings on notables who presently do not have sketches in *CTFT*. These short profiles, identified by the heading "Brief Entry," highlight the person's career in capsule form.

Brief entries are not intended to replace sketches. Instead, they are designed to increase *CTFT*'s comprehensiveness and thus better serve *CTFT* users by providing pertinent and timely information about well-known people in the entertainment industry, many of whom will be the subjects of full sketches in forthcoming volumes.

Cumulative Index

To facilitate locating sketches on the thousands of notables profiled in *CTFT*, each volume contains a cumulative index to the entire series. As an added feature, this index also includes references to all seventeen editions of *WWT* and to the four-volume compilation *Who Was Who in the Theatre* (Gale, 1978). Thus by consulting only one source—the *CTFT* cumulative index—users have easy access to the tens of thousands of biographical sketches in *CTFT, WWT,* and *Who Was Who in the Theatre.*

Suggestions Are Welcome

If readers would like to suggest people to be covered in future *CTFT* volumes, they are encouraged to send these names (along with addresses, if possible) to the editors. Other suggestions and comments are also most welcome and should be addressed to: The Editors, *Contemporary Theatre, Film, and Television,* Gale Research Inc., 835 Penobscot Bldg., Detroit, MI 48226-4094.

Contemporary Theatre, Film, and Television

Contemporary Theatre, Film, and Television

* Indicates that a listing has been compiled from secondary sources believed to be reliable.

ADAMS, Casey
 See SHOWALTER, Max

*   *   *

ADDY, Wesley   1913-

PERSONAL: Born August 4, 1913, in Omaha, NE; son of John R. and Maren S. Addy; married Celeste Holm (an actress), May 22, 1966. EDUCATION—University of California, Los Angeles, B.A., 1934. MILITARY—U.S. Army, major, 1941-45.

VOCATION: Actor.

CAREER: BROADWAY DEBUT—Chorus, *Panic*, Imperial Theatre, 1935. PRINCIPAL STAGE APPEARANCES—Wedding guest, *How Beautiful with Shoes*, Booth Theatre, New York City, 1935; Marcellus and Fortinbras, *Hamlet*, Imperial Theatre, New York City, 1936; Earl of Salisbury, *Richard II*, St. James Theatre, New York City, 1937; Bernardo and Fortinbras, *Hamlet*, St. James Theatre, 1938; Hotspur, *Henry IV, Part One* and Melvin Lockhart, *Summer Night*, both St. James Theatre, 1939; Benvolio, *Romeo and Juliet*, 51st Street Theatre, New York City, 1940; Orsino, *Twelfth Night*, St. James Theatre, 1940; Haemon, *Antigone* and James Mavor Morell, *Candida*, both Cort Theatre, 1946; Benjamin Hubbard, *Another Part of the Forest*, Fulton Theatre, New York City, 1947; old Cardinal, *Galileo*, American National Theatre and Academy (ANTA) Experimental Theatre Company, Maxine Elliott's Theatre, New York City, 1947; Harry, *The Leading Lady*, National Theatre, New York City, 1948; Professor Allen Carr, *The Traitor*, 48th Street Theatre, New York City, 1949.

Supervisor of Weights and Measures, *The Enchanted*, Lyceum Theatre, New York City, 1950; Edgar, *King Lear*, National Theatre, 1950; Ladislaus Oros, S.J., *The Strong Are Lonely*, Broadhurst Theatre, New York City, 1953; Mr. Henry Brougham, *The First Gentleman*, Belasco Theatre, New York City, 1957; narrator, *Oedipus Rex*, City Center Theatre, New York City, 1959; Commander W. Harbison, *South Pacific*, City Center Theatre, 1961; Mihail Alexandrovich Rakitin, *A Month in the Country*, Maidman Playhouse, New York City, 1963; George Henderson, *Affairs of State*, La Jolla Playhouse, La Jolla, CA, 1964, then Pasadena Playhouse, Pasadena, CA, 1966; Mr. Joseph Chamberlain, *The Right Honourable Gentleman*, Huntington Hartford Theatre, Los Angeles, 1967; James Mavor Morell, *Candida*, Great Lakes Shakespeare Festival, Lakewood, OH, 1969, then Longacre Theatre, New York City, 1970.

Papa, *Mama*, Studio Arena Theatre, Buffalo, NY, 1972; Pastor Manders, *Ghosts*, Roundabout Theatre, New York City, 1973; Sam Pleasant, *And Nothing But*, Woodstock Playhouse, Woodstock, NY, 1975; Becket, *Murder in the Cathedral*, Church of the Heavenly Rest, New York City, 1977; Dr. Lucius Bingham, *The Stitch in Time*, ANTA Theatre, New York City, 1981; Forbes Marston, *Curtains!*, Westbeth Theatre Center, New York City, 1981; the Man, *With Love and Laughter*, Harold Clurman Theatre, New York City, 1982. Also appeared in *The Grass Is Greener* and *Not Even in Spring*, both Ivanhoe Theatre, Chicago, IL, 1966; *Captain Brassbound's Conversion*, Pasadena Playhouse, 1966; with the Bucks County Playhouse, New Hope, PA, 1972; in *King Lear* and *Under the Gaslight*, both Great Lakes Shakespeare Festival, 1974.

MAJOR TOURS—Dwight Babcock, *Mame*, U.S. cities, 1967-68; the Man, *With Love and Laughter*, U.S. cities, 1963; also appeared in *An Evening of the Theatre in Concert*, international cities, 1966-67; *The Irregular Verb, To Love*, U.S. cities, 1973.

FILM DEBUT—Father John Fulton, *The First Legion*, United Artists, 1951. PRINCIPAL FILM APPEARANCES—Hank Teagle, *The Big Knife*, United Artists, 1955; Pat Chambers, *Kiss Me Deadly*, United Artists, 1955; Brucker, *Timetable*, United Artists, 1956; Mr. Paul, *The Garment Jungle*, Columbia, 1957; Sulke, *Ten Seconds to Hell*, United Artists, 1959; director, *Whatever Happened to Baby Jane?*, Warner Brothers, 1962; Trowbridge, *Four for Texas*, Warner Brothers, 1963; sheriff, *Hush . . . Hush, Sweet Charlotte*, Twentieth Century-Fox, 1964; dice player, *Mister Buddwing* (also known as *Woman Without a Face*), Metro-Goldwyn-Mayer, 1966; John, *Seconds*, Paramount, 1966; Lieutenant Commander Alvin O. Kramer, *Tora! Tora! Tora!*, Twentieth Century-Fox, 1970; John P. Blandish, *The Grissom Gang*, National General/Cinerama, 1971; Nelson Chaney, *Network*, United Artists, 1976; Mr. Wentworth, *The Europeans*, Levitt-Pickman, 1979; Dr. Towler, *The Verdict*, Twentieth Century-Fox, 1982; Dr. Tarrant, *The Bostonians*, Almi, 1984.

PRINCIPAL TELEVISION APPEARANCES—Series: Dr. Hugh Campbell, *The Edge of Night*, CBS, 1958-59; Bill Woodard, *Ryan's Hope*, ABC, 1977-78; Cabot Alden, *Loving*, ABC, 1983—; also *The Days of Our Lives*, NBC, 1973. Mini-Series: Andrew Jackson, *The Adams Chronicles*, PBS, 1976. Pilots: Dr. Livingston, *The*

1

Love Boat, ABC, 1977. Episodic: Narrator, "The Brick and the Rose," *Television Workshop*, CBS, 1960; Dr. Rahm, "The Brain of Colonel Barham," *The Outer Limits*, ABC, 1965; also *Slattery's People*, CBS, 1965; *The Fugitive*, ABC, 1965; *Perry Mason*, CBS, 1966; *I Spy*, NBC, 1966; *Twelve O'Clock High*, ABC, 1966; *Love on a Rooftop*, ABC, 1967; *The Doctor* (also known as *The Visitor*), NBC; *Short, Short Drama*, NBC. Movies: Middleton, *Tail Gunner Joe*, NBC, 1977; Abner Parker, *Rage of Angels*, NBC, 1983. Specials: Mr. Smith, "Meet Me in St. Louis," *Summer Fun*, ABC, 1966.

MEMBER: Actors' Equity Association, American Federation of Television and Radio Artists, Screen Actors Guild.

ADDRESSES: AGENT—Lionel Larner Ltd., 130 W. 57th Street, New York, NY 10019.*

*   *   *

ADLON, Percy   1935-

PERSONAL: Born in 1935 in Munich, Germany; wife's name, Eleonore.

VOCATION: Director and screenwriter.

CAREER: Also see *WRITINGS* below. PRINCIPAL FILM WORK— Director: *Celeste*, New Yorker/Artificial Eye, 1982; *The Last Five Days* (also known as *Letze Funf Tage*), Bayerischer Rundfunk, 1982; *The Swing* (also known as *Die Schaukel*), Filmverlag der Autoren, 1983; (also producer) *Sugarbaby* (also known as *Zuckerbaby*), Kino International, 1985; (also producer with Eleonore Adlon) *Bagdad Cafe* (also known as *Out of Rosenheim*), Futura/Filmuerlag der Autoren/Island, 1987; (also producer) *Rosalie Goes Shopping* (also known as *Rosalie fait ses courses*), Filmverlag der Autoren, 1989, released in the United States by Four Seasons Entertainment, 1990.

PRINCIPAL TELEVISION WORK—Movies: Director, *The Guardian and His Poet*, 1979.

RELATED CAREER—Creator of more than forty television documentaries; narrator and editor of radio programs.

WRITINGS: See production details above. FILM—*Celeste*, 1982; *The Swing*, 1983; *Sugarbaby*, 1985; (with Eleonore Adlon and Christopher Doherty) *Bagdad Cafe*, 1987; *Rosalie Goes Shopping*, 1989. TELEVISION—Movies: *The Guardian and His Poet*, 1979.

AWARDS: Adolf Grimme Award in Gold (German television award), 1979, for *The Guardian and His Poet*.

OTHER SOURCES: American Film, May, 1988.*

*   *   *

AGAR, John   1921-

PERSONAL: Born January 31, 1921, in Chicago, IL; married Shirley Temple (an actress and diplomat), 1946 (divorced, 1949).

VOCATION: Actor.

CAREER: FILM DEBUT—Lieutenant Michael "Mickey" O'Rourke, *Fort Apache*, RKO, 1948. PRINCIPAL FILM APPEARANCES— Tom Wade, *Adventure in Baltimore* (also known as *Bachelor Bait*), RKO, 1949; Private First Class Conway, *The Sands of Iwo Jima*, Republic, 1949; Lieutenant Flint Cohill, *She Wore a Yellow Ribbon*, RKO, 1949; Lieutenant Joe Mallory, *Breakthrough*, Warner Brothers, 1950; Don Lowry, *The Woman on Pier 13* (also known as *I Married a Communist*), RKO, 1950; Billy Shear, *Along the Great Divide*, Warner Brothers, 1951; Ramoth, *The Magic Carpet*, Columbia, 1951; David Powell, *Woman of the North Country*, Republic, 1952; Ray Compton, *Man of Conflict*, Atlas, 1953; Ray, *Bait*, Columbia, 1954; Bill Buchanan, *The Golden Mistress*, United Artists, 1954; Tom Baxter, *The Rocket Man*, Twentieth Century-Fox, 1954; Mark Brewster, *Shield for Murder*, United Artists, 1954; Joe, *Hold Back Tomorrow*, Universal, 1955; Clete Ferguson, *Revenge of the Creature*, Universal, 1955; Dr. Matt Hastings, *Tarantula*, Universal, 1955; Sheriff Bill Jorden, *Star in the Dust*, Universal, 1956; Dr. Roger Bentley, *The Mole People*, Universal, 1956; George Hastings, *Daughter of Dr. Jekyll*, Allied Artists, 1957; Luke Random/Matthew Random, *Flesh and the Spur*, American International, 1957; Sergeant Dick Mason, *Joe Butterfly*, Universal, 1957; Jeff, *Ride a Violent Mile*, Twentieth Century-Fox, 1957; Bob Westley, *Attack of the Puppet People*, American International, 1958; Steve, *The Brain from the Planet Arous*, Howco, 1958; Jim Crayle, *Frontier Gun*, Twentieth Century-Fox, 1958; Tom Arnett, *Jet Attack* (also known as *Jet Squad*), American International, 1958; Major Bruce Jay, *Invisible Invaders*, United Artists, 1959.

Ike, *Raymie*, Allied Artists, 1960; Joe McElroy, *Lisette* (also known as *Fall Girl* and *A Crowd for Lisette*), Medallion, 1961; Alex Marsh, *Hand of Death* (also known as *Five Fingers of Death*), Twentieth Century-Fox, 1962; Don, *Journey to the Seventh Planet*, American International, 1962; Sergeant Norcutt, *Cavalry Command* (also known as *Cavalleria commandos*), Parade Pictures, 1963; Gus Cole, *Of Love and Desire*, Twentieth Century-Fox, 1963; intelligence officer, *The Young and the Brave*, Metro-Goldwyn-Mayer, 1963; Pete Stone, *Law of the Lawless*, Paramount, 1964; Dan Carrouthers, *Stage to Thunder Rock*, Paramount, 1964; Dawson, *Young Fury*, Paramount, 1965; Ed Tomkins, *Johnny Reno*, Paramount, 1966; George Gates, *Waco*, Paramount, 1966; Dr. Farrell, *Women of the Prehistoric Planet*, Real Art, 1966; Dr. Curt Taylor, *Zontar, The Thing from Venus*, Azalea, 1966; Dion O'Bannion, *The St. Valentine's Day Massacre*, Twentieth Century-Fox, 1967; Christian, *The Undefeated*, Twentieth Century-Fox, 1969; Patton, *Chisum*, Warner Brothers, 1970; Bert Ryan, *Big Jake*, National General, 1971; city official, *King Kong*, Paramount, 1976; Ivan Peter, *Miracle Mile*, Hemdale, 1989. Also appeared in *The Lonesome Trail*, Lippert, 1955; *Curse of the Swamp Creature*, American International, 1966; *Hell Raiders*, American International, 1968; *How's Your Love Life?*, 1977; *Perfect Victims*, Academy Home Video, 1988.

PRINCIPAL TELEVISION APPEARANCES—Episodic: "The Next to Crash," *Fireside Theatre*, NBC, 1952; "Desert Honeymoon," *The Unexpected*, NBC, 1952; "The Old Man's Bride," *Ford Theatre*, NBC, 1953; "The Farnsworth Case," *Fireside Theatre*, NBC, 1954; "Little War in San Dede," *Schlitz Playhouse of Stars*, CBS, 1954; "The First and Last," *Climax*, CBS, 1955; "Earthquake," *The Loretta Young Show*, NBC, 1956; "Thousand Dollar Gun," *General Electric Theatre*, CBS, 1957; *Perry Mason*, CBS, 1959; *Rawhide*, CBS, 1960; "Band of Brothers," *Best of the Post*, ABC, 1961; *Bat Masterson*, NBC, 1961; *Death Valley Days*, ABC,

1964; *The Virginian*, NBC, 1964; *Branded*, NBC, 1965; *Combat*, ABC, 1966; *Hondo*, ABC, 1967; *The Name of the Game*, NBC, 1968; *The Virginian*, NBC, 1968; also "Delaying Action," *Hollywood Opening Night*, NBC.

ADDRESSES: AGENT—William Felber and Associates, 2126 Cahuenga Boulevard, Los Angeles, CA 90068.*

*   *   *

ALBERT, Eddie   1908-

PERSONAL: Born Edward Albert Heimberger, April 22, 1908, in Rock Island, IL; son of Frank Daniel (a realtor) and Julia (Jones) Heimberger; married Maria Margarita Guadalupe Teresa Estella Bolado Castilla y O'Donnell (an actress and singer; professional name, Margo Albert), December 5, 1945 (deceased); children: Edward, Maria. EDUCATION—Attended the University of Minnesota, 1927-29. MILITARY—U.S. Navy, lieutenant.

VOCATION: Actor.

CAREER: BROADWAY DEBUT—*O, Evening Star!*, Empire Theatre, 1936. PRINCIPAL STAGE APPEARANCES—Bing Edwards, *Brother Rat*, Biltmore Theatre, New York City, 1936; Leo Davis, *Room Service*, Cort Theatre, New York City, 1937; Antipholus, *The Boys from Syracuse*, Alvin Theatre, New York City, 1938; Horace Miller, *Miss Liberty*, Imperial Theatre, New York City,

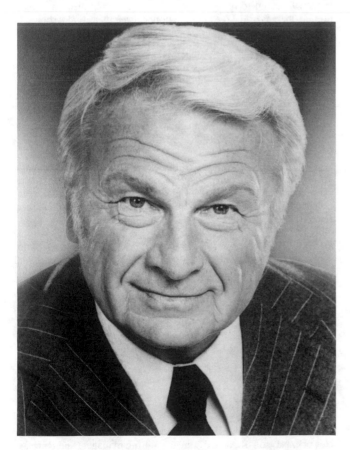

EDDIE ALBERT

1949; title role, *Reuben, Reuben*, Shubert Theatre, Boston, MA, 1955; Jack Jordan, *Say, Darling*, American National Theatre and Academy Theatre, New York City, 1958; Harold Hill, *The Music Man*, Majestic Theatre, New York City, 1960; George Bartlett, *No Hard Feelings*, Martin Beck Theatre, New York City, 1973; Martin Vanderhof, *You Can't Take It with You*, Plymouth Theatre, New York City, 1983; the Stagehand, *Parade of Stars Playing the Palace*, Palace Theatre, New York City, 1983.

FILM DEBUT—Bing Edwards, *Brother Rat*, Warner Brothers, 1938. PRINCIPAL FILM APPEARANCES—Dr. Clinton Forrest, Jr., *Four Wives*, Warner Brothers, 1939; Phil Dolan, Jr., *On Your Toes*, Warner Brothers, 1939; Peter Coleman, *An Angel from Texas*, Warner Brothers, 1940; Bing Edwards, *Brother Rat and a Baby* (also known as *Baby Be Good*), Warner Brothers, 1940; Max Stargardt, *A Dispatch from Reuters* (also known as *This Man Reuter*), Warner Brothers, 1940; Dusty Rhodes, *My Love Came Back*, Warner Brothers, 1940; Clint Forrest, *Four Mothers*, Warner Brothers, 1941; Dreamy, *The Great Mr. Nobody*, Warner Brothers, 1941; George Watkins, *Out of the Fog*, Warner Brothers, 1941; Eddie Barnes, *Thieves Fall Out*, Warner Brothers, 1941; Matt Varney, *The Wagons Roll at Night*, Warner Brothers, 1941; Leckie, *Eagle Squadron*, Universal, 1942; Terry Moore, *Lady Bodyguard*, Paramount, 1942; Bill "Panama Kid" Kingsford, *Treat 'em Rough*, Universal, 1942; Tom Hughes, *Bombardier*, RKO, 1943; Wacky, *Ladies' Day*, RKO, 1943; Chris Thomson, *Strange Voyage*, Signal, 1945; Gil Cummins, *The Perfect Marriage*, Paramount, 1946; Kip Walker, *Hit Parade of 1947*, Republic, 1947; Steve, *Smash-Up: The Story of a Woman* (also known as *Woman Destroyed*), Universal, 1947; Jake Bullard, *Time Out of Mind*, Universal, 1947; Daniel Bone, *The Dude Goes West*, Allied Artists, 1948; Bullets Booker, *You Gotta Stay Happy*, Universal, 1948.

Humphrey Briggs, *The Fuller Brush Girl* (also known as *The Affairs of Sally*), Columbia, 1950; Christopher Leeds, *Meet Me After the Show*, Twentieth Century-Fox, 1951; Lieutenant Bill Barron, *You're in the Navy Now* (also known as *U.S.S. Tea Kettle*), Twentieth Century-Fox, 1951; Orlando Higgins, "Woman of Sin" in *Actors and Sin*, United Artists, 1952; Charles Drouet, *Carrie*, Paramount, 1952; Irving Radovich, *Roman Holiday*, Paramount, 1953; Eliot Atterbury, *The Girl Rush*, Paramount, 1955; Burt McGuire, *I'll Cry Tomorrow*, Metro-Goldwyn-Mayer (MGM), 1955; Ali Hakim, *Oklahoma!*, Magna Theatres, 1955; Captain Cooney, *Attack!*, United Artists, 1956; Captain McLean, *The Teahouse of the August Moon*, MGM, 1956; Austin Mack, *The Joker Is Wild* (also known as *All the Way*), Paramount, 1957; Bill Gorton, *The Sun Also Rises*, Twentieth Century-Fox, 1957; Hanagan, *The Gun Runners*, United Artists, 1958; Major MacMahon, *Orders to Kill*, United Motion Picture, 1958; Abe Fields, *The Roots of Heaven*, Twentieth Century-Fox, 1958; Carter, *Beloved Infidel*, Twentieth Century-Fox, 1959.

Harry Davis, *The Two Little Bears*, Twentieth Century-Fox, 1961; Dr. Charles Dornberger, *The Young Doctors*, United Artsts, 1961; Colonel Newton, *The Longest Day*, Twentieth Century-Fox, 1962; Harvey Ames, *Madison Avenue*, Twentieth Century-Fox, 1962; Clint Morgan, *Who's Got the Action?*, Paramount, 1962; Colonel Bliss, *Captain Newman, M.D.*, Universal, 1963; Rider Otto, *Miracle of the White Stallions* (also known as *The Flight of the White Stallions*), Buena Vista, 1963; Ben, *The Party's Over*, Allied Artists, 1966; Charles Pether, *Seven Women*, MGM, 1966; Mr. Corcoran, *The Heartbreak Kid*, Twentieth Century-Fox, 1972; Warden Hazen, *The Longest Yard*, Paramount, 1974; Captain Ed Kosterman, *McQ*, Warner Brothers, 1974; Chief Berrigan, *The Take*, Columbia, 1974; Dr. Samuel Richards, *The Devil's Rain*,

Bryanston, 1975; Jason O'Day, *Escape to Witch Mountain*, Buena Vista, 1975; Leo Sellars, *Hustle*, Paramount, 1975; Colonel Lockyer, *Whiffs*, Twentieth Century-Fox, 1975; Pa Strawacher, *Birch Interval*, Gamma III, 1976; Alex Warren, *Moving Violation*, Twentieth Century-Fox, 1976; Eli Sande, *The Concorde—Airport' 79* (also known as *Airport '79* and *Airport '80: The Concorde*), Universal, 1979.

Daggett, *Foolin' Around*, Columbia, 1980; Max, *How to Beat the High Cost of Living*, American International, 1980; Bert Kramer, *Yesterday*, Cinepix, 1980; Samuel Ellison, *Take This Job and Shove It*, AVCO-Embassy, 1981; Henry Pollack, *Yes, Giorgio*, Metro-Goldwyn-Mayer/United Artists, 1982; Harry, *The Act* (also known as *Bless 'em All*), Film Ventures, 1984; the President, *Dreamscape*, Twentieth Century-Fox, 1984; Dean Bradley, *Stitches*, International Film Marketing, 1985; Helmes, *Head Office*, Tri-Star, 1986; Captain Danny Jackson, *Terminal Entry*, United Film, 1988; Police Chief, *Brenda Starr*, New World, 1989. Also appeared in *Rendezvous with Annie*, Republic, 1946; *This Time Forever*, 1981; *Turnaround*, Rose Productions/A-S-Major, 1987; *The Big Picture*, Columbia, 1989.

PRINCIPAL TELEVISION APPEARANCES—Series: Larry Tucker, *Leave It to Larry*, CBS, 1952; host, *Nothing But the Best*, ABC, 1953; host, *The Eddie Albert Show*, CBS, 1953; host, *Saturday Night Revue*, NBC, 1954; host, *On Your Account*, CBS, 1954-56; Oliver Wendell Douglas, *Green Acres*, CBS, 1965-71; Frank McBride, *Switch*, CBS, 1975-78. Mini-Series: Ogden Towery, *The Word*, CBS, 1978; Felix Kendrick, *Beulah Land*, NBC, 1980; Breckinridge Long, *War and Remembrance*, ABC, 1988. Pilots: Oliver Douglas, *Carol*, CBS, 1967; Bob Randall, *Daddy's Girl*, CBS, 1973; Frank McBride, *Switch* (also known as *Las Vegas Roundabout*), CBS, 1975; Carroll Yeager, *Trouble in High Timber Country*, ABC, 1980; Vincent Slattery, *Living in Paradise*, NBC, 1981; Jason O'Day, *Beyond Witch Mountain*, CBS, 1982; Bill White, *In Like Flynn*, ABC, 1985; also *Howdy*, ABC, 1970.

Episodic: Andy Thorne, "Cry of Silence," *The Outer Limits*, ABC, 1964; Mack Erickson, *Hotel*, ABC, 1985; Senator Corky McCorkindale, *Highway to Heaven*, NBC, 1986; Carlton Travis, *Falcon Crest*, CBS, 1987; Jackson Lane, *Murder, She Wrote*, CBS, 1988; Charlie Weston, *thirtysomething*, ABC, 1989; also *Teller of Tales* (also known as *The Somerset Maugham TV Theatre*), CBS, 1950; *Revlon Mirror Theatre*, NBC, 1953; "Journey to Nowhere," *Philip Morris Playhouse*, CBS, 1953; *The David Niven Theatre*, NBC, 1959; *Land of the Giants*, ABC, 1964; *Hippodrome*, CBS, 1966; *Turandot*, PBS, 1982; "1984," *Studio One*, CBS; *Your Show of Shows*, NBC; *Alcoa Premiere*, ABC; *Climax!*, CBS; *Playhouse 90*, CBS; *Schlitz Playhouse of Stars*, CBS; *Chrysler Medallion Theatre*, CBS; *Ford Theatre Hour*, NBC; *Front Row Center*, CBS; *Kraft Suspense Theatre*, NBC; *Lights Out*, NBC; *The Loretta Young Theatre*, NBC; *The Motorola Hour*, CBS; *Zane Grey Theatre* (also known as *Dick Powell's Zane Grey Theatre*), CBS; *The Alcoa Hour*, NBC; *Chevrolet Tele-Theatre*, NBC; *Dupont Show of the Week*, NBC; *Goodyear Television Playhouse*, NBC; *U.S. Steel Hour*, CBS; *The Virginian*, NBC; *Wagon Train*, NBC; *Sam Benedict*, NBC; *Wide Country*, NBC; *The Naked City*, ABC; *Dr. Kildare*, NBC; *The Lieutenant*, NBC; *The Love Boat*, ABC; *The Fall Guy*, ABC.

Movies: Dr. Thomas Spencer, *See the Man Run*, ABC, 1971; Colonel Douglas Graham, *Fireball Forward*, ABC, 1972; Pop, *Promise Him Anything*, ABC, 1975; Brian Murphy, *Evening in Byzantium*, syndicated, 1978; Captain Dunn, *Crash*, ABC, 1978; Admiral Wiley Sloan, *Goliath Awaits*, syndicated, 1981; Coach

Homer Sixx, *The Oklahoma City Dolls*, ABC, 1981; Festus, *Peter and Paul*, CBS, 1981; Reverend Harlan Barnum, *Rooster*, ABC, 1982; Joe Varon, *Mercy or Murder?*, NBC, 1987; Father Dietrich, *The Demon Murder Case*, NBC, 1983; Will Larson, *Burning Rage*, CBS, 1984; Judge Hand, *Dress Gray*, NBC, 1984; also *Nutcracker: Money, Madness, Murder*, NBC, 1987. Specials: Bumerli, *The Chocolate Soldier*, NBC, 1955; Martin Barret, *A Connecticut Yankee*, NBC, 1955; Dr. Jack Davidson, *Johnny Belinda*, CBS, 1955; host, *The Night of Christmas*, NBC, 1959; Paul Hughes, *The Ballad of Louie the Louse*, CBS, 1959; *Hollywood Sings*, NBC, 1960; Albert Warren, "The Spiral Staircase," *Theatre '62*, NBC, 1961; cameo, *Li'l Abner*, NBC, 1971; narrator, *Dr. Seuss' "The Lorax,"* CBS, 1972; Pod Clock, "The Borrowers," *Hallmark Hall of Fame*, NBC, 1973; title role, *The Lives of Ben Franklin: The Ambassador*, CBS, 1974; host, *Siegfried and Roy*, NBC, 1980; *Parade of Stars*, ABC, 1983; *Sylvia Fine Kaye's Musical Comedy Tonight III: The Spark and the Glue*, PBS, 1985; Bill Watson, "Daddy Can't Read," *ABC Afterschool Specials*, ABC, 1988.

PRINCIPAL RADIO APPEARANCES—Series: Eddie, *The Honeymooners—Grace and Eddie*, NBC, 1935.

RELATED CAREER—Founder, Eddie Albert Productions (a production company specializing in educational films), 1945; appeared in a nightclub act with Margo Albert, 1954; also singer with the Threesome, performing on radio and on stage throughout the United States; theatre manager in Minneapolis, MN.

NON-RELATED CAREER—Special World Envoy, Meals for Millions, 1963; consultant, United Nations Food Conference, Rome, Italy, 1974, and to the governor of Pennsylvania; also chairman, Eddie Albert World Trees Foundation; trustee, National Arbor Day Foundation; national conservation chairman, Boy Scouts of America; trustee, Alaska Pacific University, Anchorage, AK; director, U.S. Committee on Refugees.

AWARDS: Academy Award nomination, Best Supporting Actor, 1955, for *Roman Holiday*; Academy Award nomination, Best Supporting Actor, and National Film Critics' Award, both 1972, for *The Heartbreak Kid*; Presidential World Without Hunger Award, 1984. HONORARY DEGREES—Southern Illinois University, Doctor of Fine Arts, 1982.

MEMBER: Actors' Equity Association, Screen Actors Guild, American Federation of Television and Radio Artists, National Recreation and Parks Association (board of trustees), Bohemian Club (San Francisco).

SIDELIGHTS: RECREATIONS—Organic gardening, reading philosophical works, playing the guitar, beachcombing, designing and making movies and glass paintings, going on field trips with his son.

ADDRESSES: AGENT—Agency for the Performing Arts, 9000 Sunset Boulevard, Suite 1200, Los Angeles, CA 90069.*

*   *   *

ALEXANDER, Jason   1959-

PERSONAL: Born Jay Scott Greenspan, September 23, 1959, in Newark, NJ; son of Alex B. (an accounting manager) and Ruth M. (a nurse and health care administrator; maiden name, Simon)

Greenspan; married Daena Title (a writer), May 31, 1982. EDUCA-TION—Attended Boston University. POLITICS—Democrat.

VOCATION: Actor.

CAREER: BROADWAY DEBUT—Joe Josephson, *Merrily We Roll Along*, Alvin Theatre, 1981. LONDON DEBUT—Lino, *The Rink*, Her Majesty's Theatre, 1988. PRINCIPAL STAGE APPEARANCES—Ensemble, *Forbidden Broadway* (revue), Palsson's Theatre, New York City, 1983; Lino, Lenny, Punk, and Uncle Fausto, *The Rink*, Martin Beck Theatre, New York City, 1984; Billy, *D.*, Manhattan Theatre Club, New York City, 1985; Louis, *Personals*, Minetta Lane Theatre, New York City, 1985-86; Stanley, *Broadway Bound*, Broadhurst Theatre, New York City, 1986; emcee and various roles, *Jerome Robbins' Broadway*, Imperial Theatre, New York City, 1988-89.

FILM DEBUT—Dave, *The Burning*, Filmways, 1981. PRINCIPAL FILM APPEARANCES—Pool hustler, *Brighton Beach Memoirs*, Universal, 1986; clerk, *The Mosquito Coast*, Warner Brothers, 1986.

TELEVISION DEBUT—Pete, *Senior Trip!*, CBS, 1981. PRINCIPAL TELEVISION APPEARANCES—Series: Harold Stickley, *E/R*, CBS, 1984-85; Julian Beeby, *Everything's Relative*, CBS, 1987. Pilots: George Costanza, *The Scheinfeld Chronicles*, NBC, 1989. Episodic: Ramming, *Newhart*, CBS, 1988. Movies: Lieutenant Ernest Foy, *Rockabye*, CBS, 1986; Chris Van Allen, *Favorite Son*, NBC, 1988.

RELATED CAREER—Company member, Arena Stage, Washington, DC, 1975-76, then 1977-78.

WRITINGS: STAGE—Narrative, *Jerome Robbins' Broadway*, Imperial Theatre, New York City, 1988.

AWARDS: Drama Desk Award nomination, Best Musical Actor, 1985; Antoinette Perry Award, Drama Desk Award, and Outer Critics' Circle Award, Best Musical Actor, 1989, all for *Jerome Robbins' Broadway*.

ADDRESSES: AGENT—Bonni Allen, Bonni Allen Talent, 250 W. 57th Street, Suite 1001, New York, NY 10107.

*   *   *

ALLEN, Corey   1934-

PERSONAL: Born Alan Cohen, June 29, 1934, in Cleveland, OH. EDUCATION—Graduated from the University of California, Los Angeles, 1954; attended the University of California, Los Angeles, Law School, 1954-55.

VOCATION: Director, screenwriter, and actor.

CAREER: Also see WRITINGS below. PRINCIPAL STAGE WORK—Director, *Nite Club Confidential*, Los Angeles, 1986.

PRINCIPAL FILM APPEARANCES—Young man in town, *The Night of the Hunter*, United Artists, 1955; Buzz, *Rebel Without a Cause*, Warner Brothers, 1955; Roy, *The Big Caper*, United Artists, 1957; Gil Ramsby, *The Shadow on the Window*, Columbia, 1957; Tony

Sutherland, *Darby's Rangers* (also known as *Young Invaders*), Warner Brothers, 1958; Hal MacQueen, *Juvenile Jungle*, Republic, 1958; Cookie, *Party Girl*, Metro-Goldwyn-Mayer (MGM), 1958; magician, *Key Witness*, MGM, 1960; Duke, *Private Property*, Citations, 1960; Wash Dillon, *The Chapman Report*, Warner Brothers, 1962; Scotty, *Sweet Bird of Youth*, MGM, 1962.

PRINCIPAL FILM WORK—Director, *The Erotic Adventures of Pinocchio* (also known as *It's Not His Nose That Grows*), JLT Films, 1970; director, *Thunder and Lightning*, Twentieth Century-Fox, 1977; director, *Avalanche*, New World, 1978.

PRINCIPAL TELEVISION APPEARANCES—Series: Lieutenant Johnny Baker, *Men into Space*, CBS, 1959-60. Episodic: *Perry Mason*, CBS; *Alfred Hitchcock Presents*. Specials: "Forever James Dean," *Crazy About the Movies*, Cinemax, 1988.

PRINCIPAL TELEVISION WORK—All as director. Mini-Series: *Spies*, CBS, 1987. Pilots: *Stone*, ABC, 1979; *The Return of Frank Cannon*, CBS, 1980; *I-Man*, ABC, 1986; *J.J. Starbuck*, NBC, 1987; "Encounter at Farpoint," *Star Trek: The Next Generation*, syndicated, 1987; *Sonny Spoon*, NBC, 1988; *Road Show* (broadcast as an episode of *CBS Summer Playhouse*), CBS, 1988; *UNSUB*, NBC, 1989; also *Infiltrator*, 1987. Episodic: *Kate McShane*, CBS, 1975; *The Quest*, NBC, 1976; *Lucan*, ABC, 1978; *Chicago Story*, NBC, 1982; *Hill Street Blues*, NBC, 1984; *Jessie*, ABC, 1984; *Legmen*, NBC, 1984; *Code Name: Foxfire*, NBC, 1985; *The Otherworld*, CBS, 1985; *Dallas*, CBS, 1985 and 1986; "Song of the Younger World," *The Twilight Zone*, CBS, 1987; *Magnum, P.I.*, CBS, 1987; *J.J. Starbuck*, NBC, 1987; *Hunter*, NBC, 1988; *Sonny Spoon*, NBC, 1988; *Supercarrier*, ABC, 1988; *UNSUB*, NBC, 1989; also *Police Story*, NBC; *Movin' On*, NBC; *Police Woman*, NBC; *The Rockford Files*, NBC; *Bronk*, CBS; *Executive Suite*, CBS; *Most Wanted*, ABC; *Quincy, M.E.*, NBC; *Murder, She Wrote*, CBS; *The Family Holvak*, NBC; *Trapper John, M.D.*, CBS; *McClain's Law*, NBC; *Lobo* (also known as *The B.J./Lobo Show*), NBC; *Capitol*, CBS; *Matt Houston*, ABC; *Simon and Simon*, CBS; *T.J. Hooker*, ABC; *The Powers of Matthew Star*, NBC; *Tucker's Witch*, CBS; *The Paper Chase: The Second Year*, Showtime; *Scarecrow and Mrs. King*, CBS; *The Whiz Kids*, CBS; *High Chaparral*, NBC; *Hawaii Five-0*, CBS; *Mannix*, CBS; *Dr. Kildare*, NBC; *Streets of San Francisco*, ABC; *Ironside*, NBC; *Barnaby Jones*, CBS; *This Is the Life*. Movies: *See the Man Run*, ABC, 1971; *Cry Rape!*, CBS, 1973; (with Bob Rosenbaum) *Yesterday's Child*, NBC, 1977; *The Man in the Santa Claus Suit*, NBC, 1979; *Beverly Hills Cowgirl Blues*, CBS, 1985; *Brass*, CBS, 1985; *The Last Fling*, ABC, 1987; *Destination: America*, ABC, 1987; *The Ann Jillian Story*, NBC, 1988.

RELATED CAREER—Actor with the Players Ring and the Players Gallery, both Los Angeles; also producer (with John Herman Shaner), Freeway Circuit Theatre; director (with Guy Stockwell), Actors' Workshop.

WRITINGS: FILM—*The Erotic Adventures of Pinocchio* (also known as *It's Not His Nose That Grows*), JLT Films, 1970; (with Claude Pola) *Avalanche*, New World, 1978.

AWARDS: Emmy Award, Outstanding Directing in a Drama Series (Single Episode), 1984, for *Hill Street Blues;* Los Angeles Drama Critics' Circle Award nomination, Best Musical Direction, 1987, for *Nite Club Confidential*.*

ALLEN, Elizabeth 1934-

PERSONAL: Born Elizabeth Ellen Gillease, January 25, 1934, in Jersey City, NJ; daughter of Joseph and Viola (Mannion) Gillease; married Baron Carl Von Vietinghoff-Scheel, October 23, 1952 (divorced, 1955). EDUCATION—Attended the Traphagen School of Design, 1952-54, and Rutgers University.

VOCATION: Actress.

CAREER: STAGE DEBUT—Julie, *The Tender Trap,* summer theatre production, 1955. BROADWAY DEBUT—Juliet, *Romanoff and Juliet,* Plymouth Theatre, 1957. PRINCIPAL STAGE APPEARANCES—Ophelia, *Hamlet,* Helen Hayes Group, Brooklyn Academy of Music, Brooklyn, NY, 1956; Viola, *Twelfth Night,* Helen Hayes Group, Young Men's Hebrew Association, New York City, 1956; Portia, *The Merchant of Venice,* Helen Hayes Group, City Center Theatre, New York City 1957; Jane, *The Reluctant Debutante,* Ivy Tower Playhouse, Spring Lake, NJ, 1957; Kitty, *Where's Charley?,* Coconut Grove Playhouse, Miami, FL, 1959; ensemble, *Lend an Ear* (revue), Renata Theatre, New York City, 1959; Frenchy, *Destry Rides Again,* Starlight Theatre, Kansas City, MO, 1961; Magda, *The Gay Life,* Shubert Theatre, New York City, 1961; Nellie Forbush, *South Pacific,* Civic Arena, Pittsburgh, PA, 1964; Leona Samish, *Do I Hear a Waltz?,* 46th Street Theatre, New York City, 1965; Annie Oakley, *Annie Get Your Gun,* Sacramento Music Circus, Sacramento, CA, 1966; Maggie Cutler, *Sherry!,* Alvin Theatre, New York City, 1967; Dorothy Brock, *42nd Street,* Winter Garden Theatre, New York City, 1980. Also appeared as Martha, *Who's Afraid of Virginia Woolf?,* San Diego, CA, 1973.

MAJOR TOURS—Irene, *Say, Darling,* U.S. cities, 1959; Babe, *The Pajama Game,* U.S. cities, 1960; Nellie Forbush, *South Pacific,* U.S. cities, 1960; Julie, *Show Boat,* U.S. cities, 1963; Nellie Forbush, *South Pacific,* U.S. cities, 1963; Lois and Bianca, *Kiss Me, Kate,* U.S. cities, 1964; Nancy, *Oliver!,* U.S. cities, 1966; Stephanie, *Cactus Flower,* U.S. cities, 1967; Hannah Warren, "Visitor from New York," Diana Nichols, "Visitors from London," and Gert Franklin, "Visitors from Chicago," all in *California Suite,* U.S. cities, 1977-78; Dorothy Brock, *42nd Street,* U.S. cities, 1985; also in *My Daughter's Rated X,* U.S. cities, 1973; *Mother Is Engaged,* U.S. cities, 1974.

PRINCIPAL FILM APPEARANCES—Sage Rimmington, *From the Terrace,* Twentieth Century-Fox, 1960; Laura Beckett, *Diamond Head,* Columbia, 1962; Amelia Dedham, *Donovan's Reef,* Paramount, 1963; Miss Guinevere Plantagenet, *Cheyenne Autumn,* Warner Brothers, 1964; Mrs. MacKaninee, *Star Spangled Girl,* Paramount, 1971; Evelyn Randall, *The Carey Treatment,* Metro-Goldwyn-Mayer, 1972.

TELEVISION DEBUT—Away-We-Go girl, *The Jackie Gleason Show,* CBS, 1955. PRINCIPAL TELEVISION APPEARANCES—Series: Regular, *Jackie Gleason and His American Scene Magazine,* CBS, 1962-66; Laura Deane, *Bracken's World,* NBC, 1969-70; Martha Simms, *The Paul Lynde Show,* ABC, 1972-73; Captain Quinlan, *C.P.O. Sharkey,* NBC, 1976-77; Victoria Bellman, *Texas,* NBC, 1980-82. Episodic: Saleswoman, "The After Hours," *The Twilight Zone,* CBS, 1960; also *The Jack Paar Show,* NBC, 1959; "The Hungry Class," *Thriller,* NBC, 1960; *Tales of Wells Fargo,* NBC, 1960; *The Alcoa Hour,* ABC, 1960; *Checkmate,* CBS, 1960; *Bachelor Father,* NBC, 1960; *The Naked City,* ABC, 1960 and 1963; "The Grim Reaper," *Thriller,* NBC, 1961; *77 Sunset Strip,* ABC, 1961; *Route 66,* CBS, 1961; *Alfred Hitchcock Presents,* CBS, 1962; *The Ed Sullivan Show,* CBS, 1962; *Combat,*

ABC, 1963; *Stoney Burke,* ABC, 1963; *Burke's Law,* ABC, 1963; *Girl Talk,* ABC, 1963; *Chan Canasta,* WNEW-TV (New York City), 1963; *The Tonight Show,* NBC, 1963; *Ben Casey,* ABC, 1963 and 1965; *Slattery's People,* CBS, 1964; *The Fugitive,* ABC, 1964 and 1966; *The Man from U.N.C.L.E.,* NBC, 1966; *Dr. Kildare,* NBC, 1966. Movies: Jean Michaels, *No Other Love,* CBS, 1979. Specials: Betty Compton, *The Jimmy Walker Story,* CBS, 1960; Sergeant Juden, *Five-Finger Discount,* NBC, 1977; *Battle of the Network Stars,* ABC, 1977.

RELATED CAREER—Show girl and singer; toured in a Pontiac Industrial show, 1957.

NON-RELATED CAREER—Fashion designer and model.

AWARDS: Antoinette Perry Award nomination, Best Supporting or Featured Actress in a Musical, 1962, for *The Gay Life;* Laurel Award, Outstanding New Female Personality, 1963; *Variety* New York Drama Critics' Poll Award, Best Performance By a Female Lead in a Musical, 1965, for *Do I Hear a Waltz?*

MEMBER: Screen Actors Guild (national recording secretary, 1973 and 1975), Motion Picture Academy of Arts and Sciences (board of governors), Actors' Equity Association, American Federation of Television and Radio Artists, American Guild of Variety Artists.

SIDELIGHTS: FAVORITE ROLES—Viola in *Twelfth Night* and Annie Oakley in *Annie Get Your Gun.* RECREATIONS—Swimming, sailing, playing the guitar, sewing, and cooking.

ADDRESSES: AGENT—International Creative Management, 40 W. 57th Street, New York, NY 10019.*

* * *

ALLEN, Woody 1935-

PERSONAL: Born Allen Stewart Konigsberg, December 1, 1935, in Brooklyn, NY; legal name, Heywood Allen; son of Martin (a waiter and jewelry engraver) and Nettie (Cherry) Konigsberg; married Harlene Rosen, 1954 (divorced, 1960); married Louise Lasser (an actress), February 2, 1966 (divorced, 1969); children: Dylan Farrow (adopted daughter, with Mia Farrow), Satchel (with Farrow). EDUCATION—Attended New York University, 1953, and the City College of New York, 1953.

VOCATION: Actor, director, and writer.

CAREER: Also see *WRITINGS* below. BROADWAY DEBUT—Allan Felix, *Play It Again, Sam,* Broadhurst Theatre, 1969.

PRINCIPAL FILM APPEARANCES—Victor Shakapopulis, *What's New, Pussycat?,* United Artists, 1965; narrator, host, and voice characterization, *What's Up, Tiger Lily?,* American International, 1966; Jimmy Bond and Dr. Noah, *Casino Royale,* Columbia, 1967; Virgil Starkwell, *Take the Money and Run,* Cinerama, 1969; Fielding Mellish, *Bananas,* United Artists, 1971; Allan Felix, *Play It Again, Sam,* Paramount, 1972; Victor, Fabrizio, Fool, and Sperm, *Everything You Always Wanted to Know About Sex* (*but were afraid to ask*), United Artists, 1972; Miles Monroe, *Sleeper,* United Artists, 1973; Boris, *Love and Death,* United Artists, 1975; Howard Prince, *The Front,* Columbia, 1976; Alvy Singer, *Annie Hall,* United Artists, 1977; Isaac Davis, *Manhattan,* United Artists,

WOODY ALLEN

1979; Sandy Bates, *Stardust Memories*, United Artists, 1980; Andrew Hobbs, *A Midsummer Night's Sex Comedy*, Warner Brothers, 1982; title role, *Zelig*, Warner Brothers, 1983; title role, *Broadway Danny Rose*, Orion, 1984; Mickey Sachs, *Hannah and Her Sisters*, Orion, 1986; narrator, *Radio Days*, Orion, 1987; Mr. Alien, *King Lear*, Cannon, 1987; Sheldon Mills, "Oedipus Wrecks" in *New York Stories*, Buena Vista, 1989; Cliff Stern, *Crimes and Misdemeanors*, Orion, 1989.

PRINCIPAL FILM WORK—See production details above, unless indicated; all as director, unless indicated. Associate producer, *What's Up, Tiger Lily*, 1966; *Take the Money and Run*, 1969; *Bananas*, 1971; *Everything You Always Wanted to Know About Sex* (*but were afraid to ask)*, 1972; *Sleeper*, 1973; *Love and Death*, 1975; *Annie Hall*, 1977; *Interiors*, United Artists, 1978; *Manhattan*, 1979; *Stardust Memories*, 1980; *A Midsummer Night's Sex Comedy*, 1982; *Zelig*, 1983; *Broadway Danny Rose*, 1984; *The Purple Rose of Cairo*, Orion, 1985; *Hannah and Her Sisters*, 1986; *Radio Days*, 1987; *September*, Orion, 1987; *Another Woman*, Orion, 1988; "Oedipus Wrecks" in *New York Stories*, 1989; *Crimes and Misdemeanors*, 1989.

PRINCIPAL TELEVISION APPEARANCES—Series: Regular, *Hot Dog*, NBC, 1970-71. Episodic: Guest host, *Hippodrome*, CBS, 1966; host, "Woody Allen Looks at 1967," *The Kraft Music Hall*, NBC, 1967; also *The Dick Cavett Show*, ABC. Specials: *The Best on Record*, NBC, 1965; host, *Woody's First Special*, CBS, 1969; *The Woody Allen Special*, NBC, 1969; *Plimpton! Did You Hear the One About. . .?*, ABC, 1971; *The Sensational, Shocking, Wonderful, Wacky 70s*, NBC, 1980; *Storytellers: The P.E.N. Celebration*, PBS, 1987.

RELATED CAREER—As a gag writer, supplied jokes for such performers as Herb Shriner, Art Carney, Kaye Ballard, Buddy Hackett, and Carol Channing during the 1950s; as a stand-up comedian, appeared throughout the United States and Europe during the 1960s; plays jazz clarinet with New Orleans Funeral and Ragtime Orchestra, New York City.

WRITINGS: See production details above, unless indicated. STAGE— (Contributor) *From A to Z* (revue), Plymouth Theatre, New York City, 1960; *Don't Drink the Water*, Morosco Theatre, New York City, 1966, published by Samuel French Inc., 1967; *Play It Again, Sam*, 1969, published by Random House, 1969; *The Floating Light Bulb*, Vivian Beaumont Theatre, New York City, 1981, published by Random House, 1982.

FILM—*What's New, Pussycat?*, 1965; (with Frank Buxton, Len Maxwell, Louise Lasser, Mickey Rose, Julie Bennett, Kazuo Yamada, Julie Bennett, and Bryna Wilson) *What's Up, Tiger Lily?*, 1966; (with Rose) *Take the Money and Run*, 1969; (with Rose) *Bananas*, 1971, published in *Four Screenplays*, Random House, 1978; *Play It Again, Sam*, 1972; *Everything You Always Wanted to Know About Sex* (*but were afraid to ask)*, 1972; (with Marshall Brickman; also composer), *Sleeper*, 1973, published in *Four Screenplays*, 1978; *Love and Death*, 1975, published in *Four Screenplays*, 1978; (with Brickman) *Annie Hall*, 1977, published in *Four Screenplays*, 1978, and in *Four Films of Woody Allen*, Random House, 1982; *Interiors*, 1978, published in *Four Films of Woody Allen*, 1982; (with Brickman) *Manhattan*, 1979, published in *Four Films of Woody Allen*, 1982; *Stardust Memories*, 1980, published in *Four Films of Woody Allen*, 1982; *A Midsummer Night's Sex Comedy*, 1982; *Zelig*, 1983, published in *Three Films of Woody Allen*, Random House, 1987; *Broadway Danny Rose*, 1984, published in *Three Films of Woody Allen*, 1987; *The Purple Rose of Cairo*, 1985, published in *Three Films of Woody Allen*, 1987; *Hannah and Her Sisters*, 1986, published by Random House, 1986; *Radio Days*, 1987; *September*, 1987; *Another Woman*, 1988; "Oedipus Wrecks" in *New York Stories*, 1989; *Crimes and Misdemeanors*, 1989.

TELEVISION—Series: Staff writer, *The Colgate Comedy Hour*, NBC; staff writer, *Your Show of Shows*, NBC; staff writer, *The Pat Boone-Chevy Showroom*, ABC; staff writer, *The Tonight Show*, NBC; staff writer, *The Garry Moore Show*, CBS. Specials: (With Larry Gelbart) *The Sid Caesar Show*, NBC, 1958; (with Gelbart) *Hooray for Love*, CBS, 1960; *Woody's First Special*, CBS, 1969; (with Brickman and Rose) *The Woody Allen Special*, NBC, 1969.

RADIO—*God*, performed by the National Radio Theatre of Chicago, 1978, published by Samuel French Inc., 1975; *Death: A Comedy in One Act* (staged as *Death Knocks*), 1975, published by Samuel French Inc., 1975.

OTHER—*Getting Even*, Random House, 1971; *Without Feathers*, Random House, 1975; (illustrations by Stuart Hample) *Non-Being and Somethingness*, Random House, 1978; *Side Effects*, Random House, 1980; *The Lunatic's Tale*, Redpath Press, 1986. Also contributor to magazines such as the *New Yorker*, *Saturday Review*, *Playboy*, and *Esquire*.

RECORDINGS: ALBUMS—*Woody Allen*, Colpix, 1964; *Woody Allen, Volume 2*, Colpix, 1965; *Woody Allen: Stand-Up Comic—1964-68*, United Artists, 1978.

AWARDS: Sylvania Award, 1957, for *The Sid Caesar Show;* Emmy Award nomination, 1957; Nebula Award for Dramatic Presentation from the Science Fiction Writers of America, 1974, for *Sleeper;*

Special Silver Bear Award from the Berlin Film Festival, 1975; Academy Awards, Best Director and Best Original Screenplay, Academy Award nomination, Best Actor, British Academy of Film and Television Arts Awards, Best Film, Best Director, and Best Screenplay, National Society of Film Critics' Award, Best Screenplay, and New York Film Critics' Circle Awards, Best Director and Best Screenplay, all 1977, for *Annie Hall;* Academy Award nominations, Best Director and Best Original Screenplay, 1978, both for *Interiors;* Academy Award nomination, Best Original Screeplay, British Academy of Film and Television Arts Awards, Best Film and Best Screenplay, and New York Film Critics' Award, Best Director, all 1979, for *Manhattan;* Academy Award nominations, Best Director and Best Original Screenplay, and British Academy of Film and Television Arts Award, Best Original Screenplay, all 1984, for *Broadway Danny Rose.*

Academy Award nomination, Best Original Screenplay, British Academy of Film and Television Arts Award, Best Original Screenplay, and New York Critics' Circle Award, Best Screenplay, all 1985, for *The Purple Rose of Cairo;* Laurel Award from the Writers Guild of America, Lifetime Achievement in the Motion Picture Industry, 1986; Academy Award, Best Original Screenplay, Academy Award nomination, Best Director, British Academy of Film and Television Arts Awards, Best Director and Best Original Screenplay, British Academy of Film and Television Arts Award nomination, Best Actor, Directors Guild of America Award nomination, Outstanding Feature Film Achievement, Golden Globe nominations, Best Director and Best Screenplay, London Film Critics' Award, Best Screenplay, London Film Critics' Award nomination, Best Director, Los Angeles Film Critics' Association Award, Best Screenplay, D.W. Griffith Award from the National Board of Review, Best Director, New York Film Critics' Award, Best Director, and Writers Guild of America Award, Best Screenplay Written Directly for the Screen, all 1986, and Moussinac Prize for Best Foreign Film from the French Film Critics' Union, 1987, all for *Hannah and Her Sisters;* Academy Award nomination, Best Original Screenplay, and Writers Guild of America Award nomination, Best Screenplay Written Directly for the Screen, both 1987, for *Radio Days;* Academy Award nominations, Best Director and Best Original Screenplay, both 1990, for *Crimes and Misdemeanors.*

SIDELIGHTS: RECREATIONS—Playing jazz clarinet, poker, chess, spectator sports (especially basketball).

ADDRESSES: MANAGER—Rollins/Joffe/Morra/Brezner Inc., 130 W. 57th Street, New York, NY 10019.*

* * *

ALZADO, Lyle 1949-

PERSONAL: Full name, Lyle Martin Alzado; born April 3, 1949, in Brooklyn, NY. EDUCATION—Yankton College, B.A., 1971.

VOCATION: Actor and sports commentator.

CAREER: PRINCIPAL FILM APPEARANCES—Second assassin, *The Double McGuffin,* Mulberry Square, 1979; Bronk Stinson, *Ernest Goes to Camp,* Buena Vista, 1987; Ivan Moser, *Destroyer,* Moviestore Entertainment, 1988; Thor Alexeev, *Tapeheads,* De Laurentiis Entertainment Group, 1988; also appeared in *Who's Harry Crumb?,* Tri-Star, 1989.

PRINCIPAL TELEVISION APPEARANCES—Series: Robert Randall, *Learning the Ropes,* CTV (Toronto), then syndicated in the United States, 1988. Pilots: Deliveryman, *She's with Me,* CBS, 1982; Iron Butt, *The Highwayman,* NBC, 1987. Movies: Mamie, *The Girl, the Gold Watch, and Dynamite,* syndicated, 1981; Witkowski, *Oceans of Fire,* CBS, 1986; Reggie Diaz, *Mickey Spillane's Mike Hammer: Murder Takes All* (also known as *Mike Hammer in Las Vegas*), CBS, 1989. Specials: Host, *Yearbook: Class of 1967,* CBS, 1985; *Dom DeLuise and Friends—Part IV,* ABC, 1986; *Sportsworld Looks at Sports Humor,* NBC, 1986.

PRINCIPAL RADIO APPEARANCES—Host of a sports talk show, KWBZ, Denver, CO, 1976-77.

NON-RELATED CAREER—Professional football player with the Denver Broncos, 1971-79, Cleveland Browns, 1979-82, and the Los Angeles Raiders, 1982-85; fought Muhammed Ali in an exhibition boxing match, Denver, CO, 1979; volunteer staff member, Children's Hospital; co-chairman, Bike-a-thon and Read-a-thon for Cystic Fibrosis; honorary head coach, Special Olympic Program for Retarded Children; honorary chairman, Walk for Mankind; honorary national sports commentator and chairman of Arapahoe County Muscular Dystrophy Association; board of directors, American Cancer Society; member, Fight for Life, St. Anthony's Hospital; active in juvenile delinquent programs and the Police Athletic League of Denver.

WRITINGS: (With Paul Zimmerman) *Mile High: The Story of Lyle Alzado and the Amazing Denver Broncos,* Atheneum, 1978.

AWARDS: Earl Hartman Memorial Award from the National Football League, Outstanding Defensive Lineman, 1975; Man of the Year Award from the Denver Jaycees, 1976; Byron ''Whizzer'' White Humanitarian Award from the National Football League, Man of the Year Award from the National Football League, named All-Pro Defensive Lineman, and American Football Conference Defensive Player of the Year, all 1977; Friend of Youth Award from Optimists International, 1978.

ADDRESSES: AGENT—William Morris Agency, 151 El Camino Boulevard, Beverly Hills, CA 90212.*

* * *

ANA-ALICIA 1956-

PERSONAL: Full name, Ana-Alicia Ortiz; born December 12, 1956, in Mexico City, Mexico; father, in business; mother, a clothing manufacturing executive. EDUCATION—Received B.A., drama, from the University of Texas, El Paso; also attended Wellesley College for one year; studied law at Southwestern Law School; studied acting with Kim Stanley, Milton Katselas, and Julie Bovasso.

VOCATION: Actress.

CAREER: PRINCIPAL STAGE APPEARANCES—*Gaslight, The Odd Couple, Busybody, The Sound of Music,* and *Boeing, Boeing,* all Adobe Horseshoe Dinner Theatre, Texas, 1973-76.

PRINCIPAL FILM APPEARANCES—Janet, *Halloween II,* Universal, 1981; Arista Zelada, *Romero,* Four Seasons Entertainment, 1989.

ANA-ALICIA

PRINCIPAL TELEVISION APPEARANCES—Series: Alicia Nieves, *Ryan's Hope*, NBC, 1977-78; Melissa Agretti Cumson, *Falcon Crest*, CBS, 1982-89. Episodic: Aurora, *Battlestar Galactica*, ABC, 1979; Mary, *Moonlighting*, ABC, 1988; Samantha Ross, *Falcon Crest*, CBS, 1989; also *Buck Rogers in the 25th Century*, NBC, 1979; *Galactica 1980*, ABC, 1980; *Hotel*, ABC; *The Love Boat*, ABC; *Quincy, M.E.*, NBC; *The Hardy Boys Mysteries*, ABC; *B.J. and the Bear*, NBC; *McClain's Law*, NBC; *Lobo*, NBC; *Next Step Beyond*, syndicated. Movies: Drusilla, *Louis L'Amour's ''The Sacketts,''* NBC, 1979; Thelma Messenkott, *Condominium*, HBO, 1980; Yolanda Suarez, *Roughnecks*, syndicated, 1980; Lisa Saldonna, *The Ordeal of Bill Carney*, CBS, 1981; Violet, *Coward of the County*, CBS, 1981; Veronica, *Happy Endings*, CBS, 1983. Specials: *Battle of the Network Stars*, ABC, 1983; Philadelphia host, *CBS All-American Thanksgiving Day Parade*, CBS, 1985; Walt Disney World host, *The Second Annual CBS Easter Parade*, CBS, 1986; host, *The CBS Cotton Bowl Parade*, CBS, 1986; *Texas 150: A Celebration Special*, CBS, 1986; host, *CBS Tournament of Roses Parade*, CBS, 1988.

RELATED CAREER—Founder of Zitro Productions; company member, Twelfth Night Repertory Company.

NON-RELATED CAREER—Real estate broker; trainee with the Los Angeles Police Reserve.

AWARDS: Golden Eagle Award, Best Television Actress, 1984 and 1989.

MEMBER: Screen Actors Guild, American Federation of Television and Radio Artists, Actors' Equity Association.

SIDELIGHTS: RECREATIONS—Race car driving, motorcycle riding, scuba diving, horseback riding, and tennis.

ADDRESSES: AGENT—Ro Diamond, Century Artists, 9744 Wilshire Boulevard, Suite 308, Beverly Hills, CA 90212.

*　　　*　　　*

ANDERSON, Laurie　1947-

PERSONAL: Born in 1947 in Glenn Ellyn, IL; daughter of Arthur T. and Mary Louise (Rowland) Anderson. EDUCATION—Barnard College, B.A., art history, 1969; Columbia University, M.F.A., sculpture, 1972.

VOCATION: Performance artist and composer.

CAREER: Also see *WRITINGS* below. PRINCIPAL STAGE APPEARANCES—All performance art pieces: *For Instants, Part 5*, the Kitchen, New York City, 1977; *Handphone Table*, Museum of Modern Art, New York City, 1978; *Americans on the Move*, the Kitchen, 1979; *United States, Parts I-IV*, Brooklyn Academy of Music, Brooklyn, NY, 1983; *Empty Places*, Next Wave Festival, Brooklyn Academy of Music, 1989; also *Automotive*, Town Green, Rochester, VT, 1972; *Story Show*, 1972; *O-Range*, 1973; *Duets on Ice*, 1973; *Songs and Stories for the Insomniac*, 1975; *Refried Beans for Instants*, 1976; *Like a Stream—3, It's Cold Outside*, and *Born, Never Asked*.

MAJOR TOURS—*Home of the Brave*, U.S. cities, 1986.

PRINCIPAL FILM APPEARANCES—*Home of the Brave*, Cinecom International, 1986.

PRINCIPAL FILM WORK—Co-producer, director, and soundtrack co-producer, *Home of the Brave*, Cinecom International, 1986.

PRINCIPAL TELEVISION APPEARANCES—Series: Host, *Alive from Off Center*, PBS, 1987.

RELATED CAREER—As a performance artist and musician (electronic keyboard and electric violin), has appeared in one-woman shows at Barnard College, New York City, 1970, Harold Rivkin Gallery, Washington, DC, 1973, Artists Space, New York City, 1974, Holly Solomon Gallery, New York City, 1977, Museum of Modern Art, New York City, 1978, Holly Solomon Gallery, 1980-81, and at the Queens Museum, Queens, NY, 1984; art history instructor, City College of New York, New York City, 1973-75; artist in residence, ZBS Media, 1975; critic for such magazines as *Art News* and *Art Forum*.

WRITINGS: STAGE—All as writer, composer, and visual designer of performance art pieces, unless indicated: *Story Show*, 1972; *Automotive*, 1972; *O-Range*, 1973; *Duets on Ice*, 1973; *Songs and Stories for the Insomniac*, 1975; *Refried Beans for Instants*, 1976; *For Instants, Part 5*, the Kitchen, New York City, 1977; *Handphone Table*, Museum of Modern Art, New York City, 1978; *Americans on the Move*, the Kitchen, 1979; *United States, Parts I-IV*, Brooklyn Academy of Music, Brooklyn, NY, 1983; *Home of the Brave* (concert performance), U.S. cities, 1985; (composer only)

Alcestis, American Repertory Theatre, Cambridge, MA, 1986; *Empty Places,* Next Wave Festival, Brooklyn Academy of Music, 1989; also *Like a Stream—3, It's Cold Outside,* and *Born, Never Asked.*

FILM—Composer: (With John Cale) *Something Wild,* Orion, 1986; (also writer) *Home of the Brave,* Cinecom International, 1986; *Swimming to Cambodia,* Cinecom International, 1987.

RECORDINGS: ALBUMS—*Big Science,* Warner Brothers, 1982; (contributor) *You're the Guy I Want to Share My Money With,* 1982; *Mr. Heartbreak,* Warner Brothers, 1984; *United States Live,* Warner Brothers, 1985; *Strange Angels,* Warner Brothers, 1989.

AWARDS: New York State Council on the Arts grants, 1975 and 1977; National Endowment for the Arts grants, 1977 and 1979; Guggenheim fellowship, 1983.

MEMBER: Phi Beta Kappa.

ADDRESSES: PUBLICIST—Liz Rosenberg, Warner Brothers Records, 3 E. 54th Street, New York, NY 10022.*

*　　*　　*

ANDERSON, Michael   1920-

PERSONAL: Full name, Michael Joseph Anderson; born January 30, 1920, in London, England; son of John Lawrence (an actor) and Beatrice Gwendoline (Topping) Anderson; married second wife, Adrianne Ellis, 1977; children: David, Michael Jr., Peter, Jan (first marriage). EDUCATION—Attended the London Polytechnical Institute, 1934-36. MILITARY—Royal Signal Corps, 48th Infantry Division, 1942-46.

VOCATION: Director.

CAREER: PRINCIPAL FILM WORK—Assistant director, *Pygmalion,* Metro-Goldwyn-Mayer (MGM), 1938; assistant director, *French Without Tears,* Paramount, 1939; unit manager, *In Which We Serve,* British Lion, 1942; unit manager, *School for Secrets* (also known as *Secret Flight*), General Film Distributors, 1946; manager, *Vice Versa,* General Film Distributors, 1948; director (with Peter Ustinov), *Private Angelo,* Associated British/Pathe, 1949; director, *Hell Is Sold Out,* Eros, 1951; director, *Night Was Our Friend,* Monarch, 1951; director, *Waterfront Women* (also known as *Waterfront*), General Film Distributors, 1952; director, *The House of the Arrow,* Associated British/Pathe, 1953; director, *Will Any Gentleman?,* Stratford, 1955; director, *The Dam Busters,* Warner Brothers, 1955; director, *Around the World in Eighty Days,* United Artists, 1956; director, *Battle Hell* (also known as *Yangtse Incidents*), Herbert Wilcox, 1956; director, *1984,* Columbia, 1956; director, *Chase a Crooked Shadow,* Warner Brothers, 1958; producer and director, *Shake Hands with the Devil,* United Artists, 1959; director, *The Wreck of the Mary Deare,* MGM, 1959.

Director, *All the Fine Young Cannibals,* MGM, 1960; director, *The Naked Edge,* United Artists, 1961; director, *Flight from Ashiya* (also known as *Ashiya Kara No Hiko*), United Artists, 1964; director, *Wild and Wonderful,* Universal, 1964; director, *Operation Crossbow* (also known as *Operazione Crossbow, The Great Spy Mission,* and *Codename: Operation Crossbow*), MGM, 1965; director, *The Quiller Memorandum,* Twentieth Century-Fox, 1966;

director, *The Shoes of the Fisherman,* MGM, 1968; director, *Pope Joan* (also known as *The Devil's Imposter*), Columbia, 1972; director, *Conduct Unbecoming,* Allied Artists, 1975; director, *Doc Savage . . . The Man of Bronze,* Warner Brothers, 1975; director, *Logan's Run,* Metro-Goldwyn-Mayer/United Artists, 1976; director, *Orca* (also known as *Orca—The Killer Whale*), Paramount, 1977; director, *Dominique,* Subotsky, 1978; director, *Bells* (also known as *Murder By Phone* and *The Calling*), New World, 1981; director, *Second Time Lucky,* United International, 1984; director, *Separate Vacations,* RSL, 1986; director, *La Boutique de l'orfevre* (also known as *The Goldsmith's Shop, The Jeweller's Shop,* and *La bottega dell'orefice*), Alliance Releasing/Produzioni Atlas Consorziate, 1989; director, *Millennium,* Twentieth Century-Fox/Rank Film Distributors, 1989. Also directed *Dial 17* (short film), 1952.

PRINCIPAL TELEVISION WORK—Mini-Series: Director, *The Martian Chronicles,* NBC, 1980. Movies: Director, *Sword of Gideon,* HBO, 1986.

RELATED CAREER—Actor.

WRITINGS: FILM—(With Peter Ustinov) *Private Angelo,* Associated British/Pathe, 1949; composer, *Twelve to the Moon,* Columbia, 1960.

AWARDS: Academy Award nomination, Best Director, 1956, for *Around the World in Eighty Days.*

MEMBER: Directors Guild of America.*

*　　*　　*

ANDERSON, Richard Dean   1950-

PERSONAL: Born January 23, 1950, in Minneapolis, MN; son of Stuart Anderson (a jazz musician, school teacher, and director); mother, an artist. EDUCATION—Attended St. Cloud State College and Ohio University; studied acting with Peggy Feury.

VOCATION: Actor.

CAREER: PRINCIPAL STAGE APPEARANCES—*Superman in the Bones,* Pilgrimage Theatre, Los Angeles.

PRINCIPAL FILM APPEARANCES—Spud, *Odd Jobs,* Tri-Star, 1986; also appeared in *Young Doctors in Love,* ABC/Twentieth Century-Fox, 1982.

PRINCIPAL TELEVISION APPEARANCES—Series: Dr. Jeff Webber, *General Hospital,* ABC, 1976-81; Adam McFadden, *Seven Brides for Seven Brothers,* CBS, 1982-83; Lieutenant Simon Adams, *Emerald Point, N.A.S.,* CBS, 1983-84; title role, *MacGyver,* ABC, 1985—. Pilots: Brian Parker, *The Parkers* (broadcast as an episode of *The Facts of Life*), NBC, 1981. Episodic: *The Love Boat,* ABC. Movies: Tony Kaiser, *Ordinary Heroes,* ABC, 1986. Specials: *Battle of the Network Stars,* ABC, 1984.

RELATED CAREER—Member of the rock band Ricky Dean and Dante; street mime, jester, and juggler with an Elizabethan-style cabaret, Los Angeles; stage manager, Improvisation Theatre; writer, director, and actor at Marineland.

RICHARD DEAN ANDERSON

ADDRESSES: AGENT—Steve Dontanville, International Creative Management, 8899 Beverly Boulevard, Los Angeles, CA 90048.*

*   *   *

ANDERSSON, Harriet   1932-

PERSONAL: Born January 14, 1932, in Stockholm, Sweden; married Jorn Donner (a film director).

VOCATION: Actress.

CAREER: PRINCIPAL STAGE APPEARANCES—Title role, *The Diary of Anne Frank;* Ophelia, *Hamlet;* and in *The Beggar's Opera.* Also appeared with the Malmo City Theatre, Malmo, Sweden, 1953; Intiman Theatre of Stockholm, Stockholm, Sweden, 1956; Halsingborg Town Theatre, Halsingborg, Sweden, 1961; and the Kunigliga Dramatiska Teatern, Stockholm, during the 1980s.

FILM DEBUT—*Medan staden sover* (also known as *While the City Sleeps*), 1950. PRINCIPAL FILM APPEARANCES—Anne, *Gycklarnas afton* (also known as *The Naked Night, Sawdust and Tinsel,* and *Sunset of a Clown*), 1953, released in the United States by Times, 1956; Nix, *En lektion i karlek* (also known as *A Lesson in Love*), 1954, released in the United States by Janus, 1960; Petra, *Sommarnattens leende* (also known as *Smiles of a Summer Night*), 1955, released in the United States by Rank, 1957; Doris, *Kvinnodrom* (also known as *Journey into Autumn, Dreams* and *Women's Dreams*), 1955, released in the United States by Janus, 1960; Karin, *Sasom i*

en spegel (also known as *Through a Glass Darkly*), 1961, released in the United States by Janus, 1962; Isolde, *For att inte tala om alla dessa kvinnor* (also known as *Now, About All These Women* and *All These Women*), Janus, 1964; Louise, *Att alska* (also known as *To Love*), Prominent/L&N, 1964; Agda, *Alskande par* (also known as *Loving Couples*), 1964, released in the United States by Prominent, 1966; Ann Dobbs, *The Deadly Affair,* Columbia, 1967; Sofia Petersen, *Mennesker modes och sod musik opstar i hjertet* (also known as *Manniskor motas och ljuv musik uppstar i hjartat, People Meet and Sweet Music Fills the Heart,* and *People Meet*), 1967, released in the United States by Trans-Lux, 1969; Mathaswintha, *Der Kampf um Rom (Part One)* (also known as *Batalia pentru Roma* and *Fight for Rome*), Constantin Film, 1969.

Agnes, *Viskningar och rop* (also known as *Cries and Whispers*), New World, 1972; Monika Larsson, *Den vita vaggen* (also known as *The White Wall*), Svenska Filminstitutet, 1974; teacher's wife, *Monismanien 1995* (also known as *Monismania 1995*), Taurus/Film Edis, 1975; Sonja, *Hempa's bar* (also known as *Triumph Tiger '57* and *Cry of Triumph*), Svenska Filminstitutet, 1977; Monica, *La Sabina* (also known as *The Sabina*), Svenska Filminstitutet, 1979; Lilly, *Linus eller tegelhusets hemlighet* (also known as *Linus* and *Linus and the Mysterious Red Brick House*), Svenska Filminstituted, 1979; Justina, *Fanny och Alexander* (also known as *Fanny and Alexander*), Embassy, 1983; Cecilia Andersson, *Rakenstam* (also known as *Rakskenstam—The Casanova of Sweden* and *Casanova of Sweden*), Sandrew Film and Teater/Artisfilm/Svenska Filminstitutet, 1983; Magda, *Sommarkvallar pa jorden* (also known as *Nagra sommarkvallar pa jorden, Sommarkvallar,* and *Summer Nights*), Svenska Filminstitutet, 1987; Jasmin, *Himmel og Helvede* (also known as *Heaven and Hell*), Metronome Film/Warner Brothers, 1988.

Also appeared in *Anderssonskans Kalle* (also known as *Mrs. Andersson's Charlie*), *Motorkavalierer* (also known as *Cavaliers on the Road*), and *Tva trappor over garden* (also known as *Backyard*), all 1950; *Biffen och Bananen* (also known as *Beef and the Banana*), *Puck heter jag* (also known as *My Name Is Puck*), *Darskapens hus* (also known as *House of Folly*), and *Franskild* (also known as *Divorced*), all 1951; *Ubat 39* (also known as *U-Boat 39*), *Sabotage,* and *Trots* (also known as *Defiance*), all 1952; *Sommaren med Monika* (also known as *Monika* and *Summer with Monica*), 1953; *Hoppsan!,* 1955; *Nattbarn* (also known as *Children of the Night*) and *Sista paret ut* (also known as *The Last Couple Out* and *Last Pair Out*), both 1956; *Synnove Solbakken,* 1957; *Flottans overman* (also known as *Commander of the Navy*) and *Kvinna i leopard* (also known as *Woman in Leopardskin* and *Woman in a Leopardskin Coat*), both 1958; *Brott i Paradiset* (also known as *Crime in Paradise*) and *Noc poslubna* (also known as *Wedding Night, En Brolloppsnatt,* and *Haayo*), both 1959; *Barbara,* 1961; *Siska,* 1962; *Lyckodrommen* (also known as *Dream of Happiness*) and *En Sondag i September* (also known as *A Sunday in September*), both 1963; *For vanskaps skull* (also known as *Just Like Friends, For Friendship,* and *For the Sake of Friendship*), *Lianbron* (also known as *The Vine Bridge* and *The Vine Garden*), and *Har borjar aventyret* (also known as *Taalla Alkaa Seikkilu* and *Adventure Starts Here*), all 1965; *Ormen* (also known as *The Serpent*), 1966; *Tvarbalk* (also known as *Rooftree* and *Crossbeams*) and "Hanhon" ("He-She") in *Stimulantia,* both 1967; *Jag alskar du alskar* (also known as *I Love, You Love*), 1968; *Flickorna* (also known as *The Girls*), 1968, released in the United States by Lindgren/Sandrews, 1972; *Anna,* 1970; narrator, *Kallelsen,* 1974.

PRINCIPAL TELEVISION APPEARANCES—Movies: *I havsbandet*

(also known as *The Sea's Hold* and *On the Archipelago Boundary*), 1971; *Bebek* (also known as *Baby*), 1973.

RELATED CAREER—Music hall dancer.

AWARDS: German Film Critics' Grand Prize, 1962, for *Sasom i en spegel;* Best Actress Award from the Venice Film Festival, 1964, for *Att alska;* Swedish Film Association plaque.

ADDRESSES: OFFICE—c/o Sandrew Film and Theatre AB, Box 5612, 114 86 Stockholm, Sweden.*

*   *   *

ANDREW, Leo   1957-

PERSONAL: Born Andrew Prosser Davies, August 17, 1957, in Neath, Wales; son of Vivian (an electrician) and Dorothy Irene (a school secretary; maiden name, Prosser) Davies. EDUCATION—Received education certificate in music and drama from the West Glamorgan Institute of Higher Education, 1978; studied piano at the London College of Music.

VOCATION: Actor and choreographer.

CAREER: STAGE DEBUT—Brother, *Joseph and the Amazing Technicolor Dreamcoat,* Swansea Repertory Theatre, Swansea, Wales, 1979. LONDON DEBUT—Narrator, *Joseph and the Amazing Technicolor Dreamcoat,* Vaudeville Theatre, 1980. PRINCIPAL

LEO ANDREW

STAGE APPEARANCES—Malcolm, *Macbeth* and Amiens, *As You Like It,* both Chichester Festival Theatre, Chichester, U.K., 1983; Anatoly Sergievsky, *Chess,* Prince Edward Theatre, London, 1986. Also appeared in *Musical Chairs* and *The Final Furlong,* both Chichester Festival Theatre, 1983; as Demon, *Robinson Crusoe,* Swansea Repertory Theatre, Swansea, Wales; chorus, *Underneath the Arches,* Prince of Wales Theatre, London; clerk and member of barber shop quartet, *Poppy,* Royal Shakespeare Company, Adelphi Theatre, London; Hank J. Smith, *On Your Toes,* Palace Theatre, London; Anthony Hope, *Sweeney Todd,* Manchester Library Theatre, Manchester, U.K.; Bobby, *Company,* Palace Theatre, Westcliffe, U.K.

PRINCIPAL STAGE WORK—Assistant choreographer, *Musical Chairs,* Chichester Festival Theatre, Chichester, U.K., 1983; also assistant choreographer, *Gigi.*

MAJOR TOURS—Narrator, *Joseph and the Amazing Technicolor Dreamcoat,* U.K. cities, 1980; title role, *Jesus Christ Superstar,* U.K. cities, 1981.

TELEVISION DEBUT—Dancer, *The Max Wall Special,* Southern Television, 1980. PRINCIPAL TELEVISION APPEARANCES—Episodic: *The Agatha Christie Hour,* Thames. Specials: *The Life and Times of David Lloyd George,* BBC-Wales; "Pebble Mill at One," *Jerome Kern Special,* BBC.

RELATED CAREER—Teacher of music, drama, and English, Neath, Wales, 1978-79; entertainer on the cruise ship *S.S. Canberra;* commercial spokesman.

NON-RELATED CAREER—Tennis umpire.

MEMBER: British Actors' Equity Association, British Tennis Umpires Association.

SIDELIGHTS: RECREATIONS—Tennis and travel.

ADDRESSES: AGENT—Tano Rea, Portfolio Management, 58 Alexandra Road, London NW4 2RY, England.

*   *   *

ANDREWS, Nancy   1924-1989

PERSONAL: Full name, Nancy Currier Andrews; born December 16, 1924, in Minneapolis, MN; died of a heart attack, July 29, 1989, in New York, NY; daughter of James Currier (a hotel owner and grain executive) and Grace Ella (a drama coach; maiden name, Gerrish) Andrews; married Parke N. Bossart, 1945 (divorced, 1952); children: Tanima Cynthia. EDUCATION—Graduated from Los Angeles City College, 1940; trained for the stage at the Pasadena Playhouse College of Theatre Arts, 1940-42, at the American Shakespeare Academy, and with Ethel Chilstrom; studied piano with Dean Fletcher.

VOCATION: Actress and singer.

CAREER: STAGE DEBUT—Mistress Ford and Mistress Page, *The Merry Wives of Windsor,* Beverly Hills Shakespeare Theatre, Los Angeles, 1938. BROADWAY DEBUT—Ensemble, *Touch and Go* (revue), Broadhurst Theatre, 1949. PRINCIPAL STAGE APPEARANCES—Nicki, *Break It Up,* Theatre By the Sea, Matunuck, RI,

1950; Mrs. Sally Adams (understudy), *Call Me Madam*, Imperial Theatre, New York City, 1950; Julie, *Show Boat*, Lambertville Music Circus, Lambertville, NJ, 1951; Laura Carew, *Hazel Flagg*, Mark Hellinger Theatre, New York City, 1953; Sister Bessie, *Tobacco Road*, La Cienega Playhouse, Los Angeles, then Grist Mill Playhouse, Andover, NJ, both 1954; Emma Miller, *Plain and Fancy*, Mark Hellinger Theatre, 1955; Fauna, *Pipe Dream*, Shubert Theatre, New York City, 1956; title role, *Panama Hattie* and Lavinia, *Hit the Deck*, both Sacramento Music Circus, Sacramento, CA, 1956; Grace, *Bus Stop*, Robin Hood Theatre, Arden, DE, 1957; Mrs. Brady, *Juno*, Winter Garden Theatre, New York City, 1959; Mother Grieg, *Song of Norway*, St. Louis Municipal Opera, St. Louis, MO, 1959; Amanda, *The Glass Menagerie*, Totem Pole Playhouse, Fayetteville, PA, 1959; Mrs. Peachum, *The Threepenny Opera*, Theatre De Lys, New York City, 1959.

Auntie, *Christine*, 46th Street Theatre, New York City, 1960; Mrs. Peachum, *The Threepenny Opera*, Theatre De Lys, 1960; Mother Cadman, Madame Spig-Eye, and Irish washerwoman, *The Tiger Rag*, Cherry Lane Theatre, New York City, 1961; title role, *Madame Aphrodite*, Orpheum Theatre, New York City, 1961; Helen, *A Taste of Honey*, Emma, *Look Out, Sailor*, and Mrs. Peachum, *The Threepenny Opera*, all Red Barn Theatre, Northport, NY, 1962; Belle Poitrine, *Little Me*, Lunt-Fontanne Theatre, New York City, 1962; Mrs. Mister, *The Cradle Will Rock*, Theatre Four, New York City, 1964; Mrs. Bailie, *Say Nothing*, Jan Hus Playhouse, New York City, 1965; Dragoon, *The Day the Lid Blew Off*, Jan Hus Playhouse, 1968; Mrs. Venzenzio, *A Likely Story*, Kennebunkport Theatre, Kennebunkport, ME, 1968; Inez, *In the Summer House*, Southampton College, Southampton, NY, 1968, then Dublin International Theatre Festival, Gate Theatre, Dublin, Ireland, 1969; Marion Hollender, *Don't Drink the Water*, Bucks County Playhouse, New Hope, PA, 1969; Sister Bessie, *Tobacco Road*, Alhambra Dinner Theatre, Jacksonville, FL, 1970; Ida, *70, Girls, 70*, Starlight Theatre, Kansas City, MO, 1970; Peggy Monash, *How Much, How Much?*, Provincetown Playhouse, New York City, 1970; Aunt Demetria, *On Borrowed Time*, Bucks County Playhouse, 1973; Madame Armfeldt, *A Little Night Music*, Mall Playhouse, North Bergen, NJ, 1975; Aunt Eller, *Oklahoma!*, Jones Beach Theatre, Jones Beach, NY, 1975; Mrs. Murray, *Dearest Enemy*, Goodspeed Opera House, East Haddam, CT, 1976; Lil, *Broadway*, Wilbur Theatre, Boston, MA, 1978. Also appeared in *Hilarities*, Adelphi Theatre, New York City, 1948; as an understudy, *70, Girls, 70*, Broadhurst Theatre, New York City, 1971; in *Mademoiselle Colombe*, Playwrights Horizons, New York City, 1977; and as Miss Tweed, *Something's Afoot*, 1978.

MAJOR TOURS—Dorothy, *Gentlemen Prefer Blondes*, California cities, 1950; *Songs and Laughter* (one-woman show), European cities, 1954; Emma Miller, *Plain and Fancy*, U.S. cities, 1956; Mrs. Livingston, *Happy Hunting*, U.S. cities, 1959; Bloody Mary, *South Pacific*, U.S. cities, 1960; Madame Liang, *Flower Drum Song*, U.S. cities, 1961; Mrs. Peachum, *The Threepenny Opera*, U.S. cities, 1963; Belle Poitrine, *Little Me*, U.S. and Canadian cities, 1964, then U.S. cities, 1965; Rosie Brice, *Funny Girl*, U.S. cities, 1965-66; Marion Hollender, *Don't Drink the Water*, U.S. cities, 1970; Esther, *Two By Two*, U.S. cities, 1972.

PRINCIPAL FILM APPEARANCES—Mrs. Hudson, *The Sidelong Glances of a Pigeon Kicker* (also known as *Pigeons*), Metro-Goldwyn-Mayer/Plaza, 1970; Dr. Seaton, *Made for Each Other*, Twentieth Century-Fox, 1971; Mrs. Pat Hungerford, *Summer Wishes, Winter Dreams*, Columbia, 1973; Mrs. Captree, *Werewolf of Washington*, Diplomat, 1973; Rosie, *W.W. and the Dixie Dance*

Kings, Twentieth Century-Fox, 1975; Mrs. Logan, *Night of the Juggler*, Columbia, 1980.

TELEVISION DEBUT—*The Ed Sullivan Show*, CBS, 1950. PRINCIPAL TELEVISION APPEARANCES—Pilots: Amy Kibbe, *Kibbe Hates Finch*, CBS, 1965; Mrs. Burgess, *Kangaroos in the Kitchen*, NBC, 1982. Episodic: Aunt Hagatha, *Bewitched*, ABC, 1966; Maggie Baker, *Hawk*, ABC, 1966; Mrs. Potts, *Pistols and Petticoats*, CBS, 1966; Miss Peterson, *As the World Turns*, CBS, 1971; Mrs. Johnson, *Faith for Today*, syndicated, 1971; also *The Perry Como Show*, NBC, 1950; *The Ray Milland Show*, CBS, 1954; *Kraft Television Theatre*, NBC, 1954; *The Spike Jones Show*, NBC, 1954; *The Betty White Show*, ABC, 1954; *The Tonight Show*, NBC, 1963; *Girl Talk*, ABC, 1963, 1965, and 1969; *The Mike Douglas Show*, syndicated, 1964; *Queen for a Day*, ABC, 1964; "E.E. Cummings' Fairy Tales," *Camera Three*, CBS, 1968; *The Joe Franklin Show*, WOR-TV (New York City), 1968 and 1969; *Dinah's Diner*. Movies: Margie, *Twirl*, NBC, 1981. Specials: Nurse Carswell, "I'm with Ya, Duke," *Happy Endings*, ABC, 1975; also *TV Telethon*, Cincinnati, OH, 1962.

RELATED CAREER—Nightclub and cabaret performer, 1941-68; singer and pianist with U.S.O. shows in the Caribbean, 1943-45; also secretary and vice-president, Pasadena Playhouse Alumni Association; board of directors, Veterans Hospital Radio and Television Guild's Bedside Network.

WRITINGS. STAGE—Music and lyrics, *Bright Champagne*, Melrose Theatre, Los Angeles, 1943.

MEMBER: Actors' Equity Association, American Federation of Television and Radio Artists, American Guild of Variety Artists, Screen Actors Guild, American Federation of Musicians, National Academy of Television Arts and Sciences.

AWARDS: Theatre World Award, 1950, for *Touch and Go;* State of Israel Bonds Award.

OBITUARIES AND OTHER SOURCES: *New York Times*, July 31, 1989; *Variety*, August 2-8, 1989.*

*   *   *

ANNIS, Francesca   1944-

PERSONAL: Born May 14, 1944, in London, England.

VOCATION: Actress.

CAREER: PRINCIPAL STAGE APPEARANCES—Ophelia, *Hamlet*, Lunt-Fontanne Theatre, New York City, 1969; Isabella, *Measure for Measure*, Royal Shakespeare Company (RSC), Stratford-on-Avon, U.K., 1974; Juliet, *Romeo and Juliet*, Cressida, *Troilus and Cressida*, and Luciana, *The Comedy of Errors*, all RSC, Stratford-on-Avon, 1976; Juliet, *Romeo and Juliet* and Cressida, *Troilus and Cressida*, both RSC, Aldwych Theatre, London, 1977.

PRINCIPAL FILM APPEARANCES—Sylvia, *The Cat Gang*, Realist/CFF, 1959; Wanda, *His and Hers*, Sabre/Eros, 1961; Phyl, *West 11*, Associated British/Warner Brothers/Pathe, 1963; Annie Jones, *The Eyes of Annie Jones*, Twentieth Century-Fox, 1963; Eiras, *Cleopatra*, Twentieth Century-Fox, 1963; Jean, *Saturday Night Out*, Compton Cameo, 1964; June, *Crooks in Cloisters*, Associated

British/Warner Brothers/Pathe, 1964; Sheila Upward, *Murder Most Foul*, Metro-Goldwyn-Mayer (MGM), 1964; Gwen, *Flipper's New Adventure* (also known as *Flipper and the Pirates*), MGM, 1964; Jean Parker, *Run with the Wind*, GEFD, 1966; Sally Feathers, *The Pleasure Girls*, Times Films, 1966; Arabella Dainton, *The Walking Stick*, MGM, 1970; uptight girl, *The Sky Pirate*, Filmmakers Distribution Center, 1970; Lady Macbeth, *Macbeth*, Columbia, 1971; Kate, *Stronger Than the Sun*, BBC, 1980; Widow of the Web, *Krull*, Columbia, 1983; Lady Jessica, *Dune*, Dino De Laurentiis/Universal, 1984; Dubarry, *El rio de oro* (also known as *The Golden River*), Tesauro/Incine S.A./Federal, 1986; Mrs. Wellington, *Under the Cherry Moon*, Warner Brothers, 1986. Also appeared in *Young Jacobites*, 1959.

PRINCIPAL TELEVISION APPEARANCES—Mini-Series: Title role, *Madame Bovary*, BBC, then *Masterpiece Theatre*, PBS, 1976; Lillie Langtry, *Lillie*, London Weekend Television, then *Masterpiece Theatre*, PBS, 1979; Tuppence Beresford, "Partners in Crime," *Mystery!*, PBS, 1986; Prudence "Tuppence" Cowley, "The Secret Adversary," *Mystery!* PBS, 1987. Episodic: Tracy Conway, "Sign It Death," *Thriller*, ABC, 1974; Penelope St. Clair, *Magnum, P.I.*, CBS, 1985. Movies: Galina, *Coming Out of the Ice*, CBS, 1982; Lily Amberville, *I'll Take Manhattan*, CBS, 1987; Jacqueline Kennedy, *The Richest Man in the World: The Story of Aristotle Onassis*, ABC, 1988. Specials: Frances Derwent, *Why Didn't They Ask Evans?*, syndicated, 1981; also *The Comedy of Errors*, 1978.

AWARDS: British Academy of Film and Television Arts Award, Best Television Actress, 1978, for *Lillie* and *The Comedy of Errors*.

ADDRESSES: AGENT—Jack Gilardi, International Creative Management, 8899 Beverly Boulevard, Los Angeles, CA 90048; International Creative Management, 388-396 Oxford Street, London W1N 9HE, England.*

*   *   *

ANSPAUGH, David   1946-

PERSONAL: Born September 24, 1946, in Decatur, IN; son of Lawrence Earl (a photographer) and Marie Francis (DeMaio) Anspaugh; married Tamara Kramer, April 13, 1974; children: Vanessa Christine. EDUCATION—Indiana University, B.S., education, 1970; University of Southern California, M.F.A., cinema, 1976.

VOCATION: Director and producer.

CAREER: PRINCIPAL FILM WORK—Director, *Hoosiers*, Orion, 1987; director, *Fresh Horses*, Columbia, 1988.

FIRST TELEVISION WORK—Associate producer, *Paris*, CBS, 1979. PRINCIPAL TELEVISION WORK—Series: Associate producer, *Hill Street Blues*, NBC, 1980-81, then producer, 1981-84. Episodic: Director, *Hill Street Blues*, NBC, 1981-85; also director, *St. Elsewhere*, NBC; director, *Miami Vice*, NBC. Movies: Associate producer, *Vampire*, ABC, 1979; associate producer, *Fighting Back*, ABC, 1980; director, *Deadly Care*, CBS, 1987. Specials: Director, *The Last Leaf*, syndicated, 1984.

NON-RELATED CAREER—Teacher, Aspen, CO, 1970-74.

AWARDS: Directors Guild Award, 1982, Emmy Awards, Outstanding Drama Series, 1982 and 1983, and Golden Globes, Best Television Series—Drama, 1982 and 1983, all for *Hill Street Blues*.

MEMBER: Directors Guild of America.

ADDRESSES: AGENT—John Burnham, William Morris Agency, 151 El Camino Drive, Beverly Hills, CA 90212.

*   *   *

ANTONIO, Lou   1934-

PERSONAL: Full name, Louis Demetrios Antonio; born January 23, 1934, in Oklahoma City, OK; son of James Demetrios (a restaurant owner) and Lucille (a cashier; maiden name, Wright) Antonio. EDUCATION—University of Oklahoma, B.A., 1955; trained for the stage with Lee Strasberg, Lonny Chapman, and Curt Conway.

VOCATION: Actor, director, producer, and writer.

CAREER: STAGE DEBUT—David Slater, *The Moon Is Blue*, White Barn Theatre, Terre Haute, IN, 1955. PRINCIPAL STAGE APPEARANCES—Sidney Black, *Light Up the Sky*, Lord Byron, A. Ratt, Nursie, and the Pilot, *Camino Real*, Preacher Haggler, *Dark of the Moon*, and John Goronwyn Jones, *The Corn Is Green*, all White Barn Theatre, Terre Haute, IN, 1955; Hotspur, *Richard II* and soldier, *The Secret Concubine*, both McCarter Theatre, Princeton, NJ, 1956; Mickey Argent (understudy) and Tommy Brookman (understudy), *The Girls of Summer*, Longacre Theatre, New York City, 1956; Larrup Rule, *Saddle Tramps* and Polo, *A Hatful of Rain*, both Cecilwood Theatre, Fishkill, NY, 1957; Will Stockdale, *No Time for Sergeants*, Sergeant Gregovich, *Teahouse of the August Moon*, Brick, *Cat on a Hot Tin Roof*, Cornelius, *The Matchmaker*, and Musician-Husband, *Middle of the Night*, all Cecilwood Theatre, 1958; Woody, *The Buffalo Skinner*, Theatre Marquee, New York City, 1959; Jake Latta, *Night of the Iguana* and ensemble, *Album Leaves* (revue), both Teatro Caio Melisso, Festival of Two Worlds, Spoleto, Italy, 1959; Cliff Lewis, *Look Back in Anger*, Capri Theatre, Atlantic Beach, Long Island, NY, 1959; Nikita, *The Power of Darkness*, York Theatre, New York City, 1959.

Lieutenant Ferguson Howard, *The Golden Fleecing*, Jack, *Amazing Grace*, and Clay, *Cry of the Raindrop*, all Cecilwood Theatre, 1960; Shady One, third patron, and Lecasse, *The Good Soup*, Plymouth Theatre, New York City, 1960; Clay, *Cry of the Raindrop*, Hedgerow Theatre, Moylan, PA, 1960, then St. Mark's Playhouse, New York City, 1961; Stavros, *The Garden of Sweets*, American National Theatre and Academy Theatre, New York City, 1961; ensemble, *Brecht on Brecht* (revue), Theatre De Lys, New York City, 1962, then Playhouse-on-the-Mall, Paramus, NJ, later John Drew Theatre, East Hampton, NY, both 1963; sergeant, *Andorra*, Biltmore Theatre, New York City, 1963; Gaston, *The Lady of the Camellias*, Winter Garden Theatre, New York City, 1963; Marvin Macy, *The Ballad of the Sad Cafe*, Martin Beck Theatre, New York City, 1963; Faustus, *Tragical History of Doctor Faustus*, Phoenix Theatre, New York City, 1964; Jonas, *Ready When You Are, C.B.!*, Brooks Atkinson Theatre, New York City, 1964.

PRINCIPAL STAGE WORK—Director, *Missouri Legend*, Cecilwood Theatre, Fishkill, NY, 1960; director, *The Chalk Garden*, Elmwood Theatre, Nyack, NY, 1962; producer, *Hootsudie*, Actors' Studio West, Merle Oberon Playhouse, Los Angeles, 1972.

FILM DEBUT—Cadet, *The Strange One*, Columbia, 1957. PRINCIPAL FILM APPEARANCES—Roustabout, *Splendor in the Grass*, Warner Brothers, 1961; Abdul, *America, America* (also known as *The Anatolian Smile*), Warner Brothers, 1963; Reverend Abraham Hewlett, *Hawaii*, United Artists, 1966; Koko, *Cool Hand Luke*, Warner Brothers, 1967; Corrigan, *The Phynx*, Warner Brothers, 1970.

PRINCIPAL FILM WORK—Executive producer, *Micki and Maud*, Columbia, 1984; also production supervisor, *Private Lives*, 1983.

PRINCIPAL TELEVISION APPEARANCES—Series: Barney, *The Snoop Sisters*, NBC, 1973-74; Detective Sergeant Jack Ramsey, *Dog and Cat*, ABC, 1977; Joseph Manucci, *Makin' It*, ABC, 1979. Pilots: Sam Hatch, *Partners in Crime*, NBC, 1973; Jack Ramsey, *Dog and Cat*, ABC, 1977; also *Road to Reality*, ABC, 1960. Episodic: Lokai, "Let That Be Your Last Battlefield," *Star Trek*, NBC, 1969; also *Love of Life*, CBS, 1958 and 1960; *Tallahassee 7000*, CBS, 1959; *Naked City*, ABC, 1959 and 1963; *My True Story*, CBS, 1959-61; "A Piece of Blue Sky," *Play of the Week*, WNTA, 1960; "The Wendigo," *Great Ghost Tales*, CBS, 1961; *The Defenders*, CBS, 1961, 1962, and 1963; *Route 66*, CBS, 1963; *Breaking Point*, ABC, 1963; *Camera Three*, CBS, 1963; *The Fugitive*, ABC, 1963, 1964, 1965, and 1966; *For the People*, CBS, 1965; *Twelve O'Clock High*, ABC, 1965; *Gunsmoke*, CBS, 1965; *The Virginian*, NBC, 1966; *The Wackiest Ship in the Army*, NBC, 1966; *The Road West*, NBC, 1967; *U.S. Steel Hour*, CBS; *Studio One*, CBS; *Suspicion*, NBC; *Have Gun—Will Travel*, CBS; *The Danny Thomas Hour*. Movies: Tony, *Sole Survivor*, CBS, 1970; Hugo Jenkins, *Where the Ladies Go*, ABC, 1980; movie producer, *Agatha Christie's "Thirteen at Dinner,"* CBS, 1985; Dr. Calvin Finch, *Face to Face*, CBS, 1990. Specials: *The Power and the Glory*, CBS, 1961.

PRINCIPAL TELEVISION WORK—All as director, unless indicated. Series: Producer, *Shell Game*, CBS, 1987. Pilots: *Fools, Females, and Fun: I've Gotta Be Me*, NBC, 1974; *Fools, Females, and Fun: Is There a Doctor in the House?*, NBC, 1974; *Lanigan's Rabbi*, NBC, 1976; *The Girl in the Empty Grave*, NBC, 1977; *The Gypsy Warriors*, CBS, 1978; *Heaven on Earth*, NBC, 1979; *Boston and Kilbride*, CBS, 1979; *We're Fighting Back*, CBS, 1981; *Gabe and Walker*, ABC, 1981; *Shell Game*, CBS, 1987. Episodic: *Sons and Daughters*, CBS, 1974; *Three for the Road*, CBS, 1975; *McMillan*, NBC, 1977; *Lanigan's Rabbi*, NBC, 1977; *The Contender*, CBS, 1980; also *Gentle Ben*, CBS; *Griff*, ABC; *Owen Marshall: Counselor at Law*, ABC; *Amy Prentiss*, NBC; *Banacek*, NBC; *McMillan and Wife*, NBC; *Rich Man, Poor Man—Book II*, ABC; *Delvecchio*, CBS; *The Rockford Files*, NBC; *McCloud*, NBC. Movies: *Someone I Touched*, ABC, 1975; *Something for Joey*, CBS, 1977; *The Critical List*, NBC, 1978; *A Real American Hero*, CBS, 1978; *Breaking Up Is Hard to Do*, ABC, 1979; *Silent Victory: The Kitty O'Neil Story*, CBS, 1979; *The Star Maker*, NBC, 1981; *Something So Right*, CBS, 1982; *Between Friends*, HBO, 1983; *A Good Sport*, CBS, 1984; *Rearview Mirror*, NBC, 1984; *Threesome*, CBS, 1984; *Agatha Christie's "Thirteen at Dinner,"* CBS, 1985; *One Terrific Guy*, CBS, 1986; *Mayflower Madam*, CBS, 1987; *Pals*, CBS, 1987; (also producer) *The Outside Woman*, CBS, 1989; (also executive producer) *Dark Holiday* (also known as *Passport to Terror* and *Never Pass This Way Again*), NBC, 1989; *Face to Face*,

CBS, 1990. Specials: *The Steeler and the Pittsburgh Kid*, NBC, 1981.

RELATED CAREER—Member, Actors' Studio, 1958—.

NON-RELATED CAREER—Sports reporter, chef, waiter, ranch-hand, bricklayer's helper, junk and manure dealer, swimming-pool inspector, and Fuller Brush man.

WRITINGS: FILM—*Mission: Batangas*, Manson, 1968. TELEVISION—Episodic: *Gentle Ben*, CBS; *The Young Rebels*, ABC.

AWARDS: Theatre World Award, 1959, for *The Buffalo Skinner*; Humanitas Award and Emmy Award nomination, both 1977, for *Something for Joey*; Emmy Award nomination, Outstanding Director, 1979, for *Silent Victory: The Kitty O'Neil Story*.

MEMBER: Actors' Equity Association, Screen Actors Guild, American Federation of Television and Radio Artists, Directors Guild of America, Writers Guild of America.

SIDELIGHTS: RECREATIONS—Softball, basketball, reading, and writing.

ADDRESSES: AGENT—Triad Artists, 10100 Santa Monica Boulevard, 16th Floor, Los Angeles, CA 90067.*

*　　*　　*

ARGENTO, Dario   1940-

PERSONAL: Born September 7, 1940, in Rome, Italy; son of Salvatore Argento (a film executive); married Daria Nicolodi (an actress), 1975 (separated, 1985).

VOCATION: Director, producer, and screenwriter.

CAREER: Also see *WRITINGS* below. FIRST FILM WORK—Co-director, *Probabilita zero*, 1968. PRINCIPAL FILM WORK—Director, *The Bird with the Crystal Plumage* (also known as *L'ucello dalle piume di cristalo*, *The Phantom of Terror*, and *The Gallery Murders*), UM, 1970; director, *Cat o' Nine Tails* (also known as *Il gatto a nove code*), National General, 1971; director, *Four Flies on Grey Velvet* (also known as *Quattro mosche di velluto grigio*), Paramount, 1972; director, *Deep Red* (also known as *Profondo rosso*, *The Hatchet Murders*, *Dripping Deep Red*, and *Deep Red Hatchet Murder*), Seda Spettacoli Mahler, 1975, released in the United States by Rizzoli, 1976; director, *Suspiria*, International Classics/Twentieth Century-Fox, 1977; director, *Inferno*, Twentieth Century-Fox, 1980; director, *Sotto gli occhi dell'assassino* (also known as *Tenebrae*), Intra/Anglo-American/Bedford Entertainment/Film Gallery, 1982; producer and director, *Creepers* (also known as *Phenomena*), New Line Cinema, 1985; producer, *Demons* (also known as *Demoni*), Titanus/Ascot Entertainment Group, 1985; producer, *Demons II: The Nightmare Is Back* (also known as *Demoni II: L'incubo ritorna*), Titanus/Avatar/DAC, 1986; director, *Opera*, Columbia, 1987. Also co-producer and director, *Zombie*, 1978.

RELATED CAREER—Film critic, *Paesa Sera*.

WRITINGS: See production details above, unless indicated. FILM—(With Tonio Cervi) *Today It's Me . . . Tomorrow You!* (also known as *Oggi a me domani a te!* and *Today We Kill . . . Tomorrow We Die*), Splendid, 1968, released in the United States by Cinerama, 1971; *The Bird with the Crystal Plumage,* 1970, published in *Profondo Thrilling,* 1975; (with Marc Richards) *The Five Man Army* (also known as *Un esercito di 5 uomini*), Metro-Goldwyn-Mayer, 1970; *Cat o' Nine Tails,* 1971, published in *Profondo Thrilling,* 1975; *Four Flies on Grey Velvet,* 1972, published in *Profondo Thrilling,* 1975; (with Bernardino Zapponi) *Deep Red,* 1975; (with Daria Nicoldi; also composer) *Suspiria,* 1977; composer, *Dawn of the Dead,* United Films, 1979; *Inferno,* 1980; (with George Kemp) *Sotto gli occhi dell'assassino,* 1982; (with Franco Ferrini) *Creepers,* 1985; (with Lamberto Bava, Dardano Sacchetti, and Ferrini) *Demons,* Titanus/Ascot Entertainment Group, 1985; (with Bava, Sacchetti, and Ferrini) *Demons II: The Nightmare Is Back,* 1986; (with Ferrini) *Opera,* 1987; (with Ferrini) *The Church* (also known as *La chiesa* and *L'Eglise*), Columbia/Tri-Star, 1989. Also *Probabilita zero,* 1968; *Commandos,* 1968; *Le rivoluzione sessuale,* 1968; *La stagione dei sensi,* 1968; *Comandamenti per un gangster,* 1968; *Metti, una sera a cena* (also known as *The Love Circle*), 1969; *Le cinque giornate,* 1973; *Zombie,* 1978. TELEVISION—Series: *La porte dans l'obscurite,* 1972.*

*　　*　　*

ARGENZIANO, Carmen   1943-

PERSONAL: Surname is pronounced "Ar-jen-zi-ano" (rhymes with "piano"); born October 27, 1943, in Sharon, PA; son of Joseph Guy (a restaurateur) and Elizabeth Stella (Falvo) Argenziano. EDUCATION—Attended Youngstown University; trained for the stage at the American Academy of Dramatic Arts and the Actors' Studio; also studied with Lee Grant, Michael V. Gazzo, Milton Katselas, and Sanford Meisner.

VOCATION: Actor.

CAREER: STAGE DEBUT—Coffee house poet, *The Hairy Falsetto,* Fourth Street Theatre, New York City, 1965. PRINCIPAL STAGE APPEARANCES—John Fletcher, *El Salvador,* GNU Theatre, Los Angeles, 1988; also appeared in *A View from the Bridge,* Strasberg Institute, Los Angeles, 1981; with the Center Theatre Group, Mark Taper Forum, Los Angeles, CA, 1983; in *Last Lucid Moment* and *A Prayer for My Daughter,* both in Los Angeles; and in productions of *Sweet Bird of Youth* and *Made in America.*

PRINCIPAL FILM APPEARANCES—Student, *Cover Me Babe,* Twentieth Century-Fox, 1970; gang member, *The Jesus Trip,* Emco, 1971; Jay Kaufman, *Punishment Park,* Francoise, 1971; Flavio, *The Hot Box,* New World, 1972; (as Carmine Argenziano) second Hawk, *The Outside Man* (also known as *Un Homme est mort*), United Artists, 1973; Michael's bodyguard, *The Godfather, Part II,* Paramount, 1974; supermarket manager, *Crazy Mama,* New World, 1975; Jack McGurn, *Capone,* Twentieth Century-Fox, 1975; lieutenant, *Shark's Treasure,* United Artists, 1975; Brian, *Vigilante Force,* United Artists, 1976; Jennings, *Two-Minute Warning,* Universal, 1976; Dr. Mandrakis, *When a Stranger Calls,* Columbia, 1979; Tony Annese, *Mystique,* Telecine International/Qui, 1981; D'Ambrosia, *Sudden Impact,* Warner Brothers, 1983; Ron Bell, *Heartbreakers,* Orion, 1984; Stan, *Into the Night,* Universal, 1985; voice of Dagg, *Starchaser: The Legend of Orin* (animated), Atlantic, 1985; Matty, *Dangerously Close,* Cannon, 1986; Detective Russo, *Naked Vengeance* (also known as *Satan Vengeance*), Concorde, 1986; Lieutenant Leonard, *Under Cover,* Cannon, 1987;

CARMEN ARGENZIANO

board member, *Big Business,* Buena Vista, 1988; District Attorney Paul Rudolph, *The Accused,* Paramount, 1988; Molina, *Stand and Deliver,* Warner Brothers, 1988; Zayas, *Red Scorpion,* Shapiro/Glickenhaus Entertainment, 1989. Also appeared in *The Slams,* Metro-Goldwyn-Mayer, 1973; *Caged Heat* (also known as *Renegade Girls*), New World, 1974; *Death Force,* Capricorn Three, 1978; *Transit,* 1990.

TELEVISION DEBUT—*Judd, for the Defense,* ABC. PRINCIPAL TELEVISION APPEARANCES—Series: Dr. Nathan Solt, *HeartBeat,* ABC, 1989; Charles "Chick" Sterling, *Booker,* Fox, 1989—. Mini-Series: Adam Brand, *Once an Eagle,* NBC, 1977; also *From Here to Eternity,* NBC, 1979. Pilots: Santeen, *The 3,000 Mile Chase,* NBC, 1977; Kingston, *The Phoenix,* ABC, 1981; Varela, *Waco and Rhinehart* (also known as *U.S. Marshals: Waco and Rhinehart*), ABC, 1987; Tony, *Remo Williams,* ABC, 1988; also *Twin Detectives,* ABC, 1976. Episodic: Anarumo, *Cagney and Lacey,* CBS, 1986; Neil Robertson, *L.A. Law,* NBC, 1986; Mel, *Designing Women,* CBS, 1987; Dr. Schneider, *Hunter,* NBC, 1987; Mr. Mendez, *Coming of Age,* CBS, 1988; also *Stone,* ABC, 1980; *Scarecrow and Mrs. King,* CBS; *Cheers,* NBC; *Hill Street Blues,* NBC; *T.J. Hooker,* ABC; *Lou Grant,* CBS. Movies: Wheeler, *Search for the Gods,* ABC, 1975; lieutenant, *Kill Me If You Can,* NBC, 1977; cameraman, *Hot Rod* (also known as *Rebel of the Road*), ABC, 1979; Ed Ainsworth, *Quarterback Princess,* CBS, 1983; Rooney, *The Last Ninja,* ABC, 1983; Lieutenant Clifford, *Best Kept Secrets,* ABC, 1984; Colonel Pruett, *Fatal Vision,* NBC, 1984; Robert Walker, *Between Two Women,* ABC, 1986; judge, *Too Good to Be True* (also known as *Leave Her to Heaven*), NBC, 1988; MacDonald, *The Watch Commander* (also known as *Police*

Story: The Watch Commander), ABC, 1988; Roy Simmons, *Baja Oklahoma*, HBO, 1988; Sam Liberace, *Liberace*, ABC, 1988; also *The Man Who Fell to Earth*, ABC, 1987.

AWARDS: Drama-Logue Award, 1988, for *El Salvador;* Drama-Logue Award and *Los Angeles Weekly* Award, both for *Last Lucid Moment;* Los Angeles Drama Critics' Award and *Los Angeles Weekly* Award, both for *A Prayer for My Daughter.*

MEMBER: Academy of Motion Picture Arts and Sciences, Actors' Studio.

ADDRESSES: AGENT—Rodney Sheldon, Artists Alliance, 8457 Melrose Plaza, Suite 200, Los Angeles, CA 90069.

*   *   *

ARMITAGE, Frank
   See CARPENTER, John

*   *   *

ARMSTRONG, Curtis   1953-

PERSONAL: Born November 27, 1953, in Detroit, MI; son of Robert Leroy and Norma E. (a teacher; maiden name, D'Amico) Armstrong. EDUCATION—Attended Oakland University (Rochester, MI), 1973-75; studied acting at the Academy of Dramatic Arts.

VOCATION: Actor.

CAREER: PRINCIPAL STAGE APPEARANCES—The Boy, *The Irish Hebrew Lesson* and Cooney, *Guests of the Nation,* both Colonnades Theatre Lab, New York City, 1980; the reporter, *How I Got That Story,* Attic Theatre, Detroit, MI, 1983; also apppeared in *The Corn Is Green,* Meadow Brook Theatre, Rochester, MI, 1977; *The Caine Mutiny Court-Martial,* Meadow Brook Theatre, 1978; *The Life of Galileo,* Pittsburgh Public Theatre, Pittsburgh, PA, 1981; *Moliere in Spite of Himself,* Hartman Theatre Company, Stamford, CT, 1981; *Present Laughter,* Meadow Brook Theatre, 1985.

MAJOR TOURS—Young Charlie, *Da,* U.S. cities, 1979-80.

PRINCIPAL FILM APPEARANCES—Miles, *Risky Business,* Warner Brothers, 1983; Booger, *Revenge of the Nerds,* Twentieth Century-Fox, 1984; Dennis Gladstone, *Bad Medicine,* Twentieth Century-Fox, 1985; Charles De Mar, *Better Off Dead,* Warner Brothers, 1985; Goov, *The Clan of the Cave Bear,* Warner Brothers, 1986; Ack Ack Raymond, *One Crazy Summer,* Warner Brothers, 1986; Booger, *Revenge of the Nerds II: Nerds in Paradise,* Twentieth Century-Fox, 1987.

PRINCIPAL TELEVISION APPEARANCES—Series: Herbert Viola, *Moonlighting,* ABC, 1986-89.

RELATED CAREER—Company member, Meadow Brook Theatre, Rochester, MI, 1975-85; company member, New Jersey Shakespeare Festival, Madison, NJ, 1981; company member, Attic Theatre, Detroit, MI; co-founder, Roadside Attractions Inc.

CURTIS ARMSTRONG

ADDRESSES: AGENT—Ro Diamond, Century Artists Ltd., 9744 Wilshire Boulevard, Suite 308, Beverly Hills, CA 90212.

*   *   *

ARMSTRONG, R.G.   1917-

PERSONAL: Full name, Robert Golden Armstrong; born April 7, 1917, in Birmingham, AL. EDUCATION—Studied acting at the Actors' Studio, 1952.

VOCATION: Actor.

CAREER: PRINCIPAL STAGE APPEARANCES—Doctor Baugh, *Cat on a Hot Tin Roof,* Morosco Theatre, New York City, 1955; Chief of Police Gerald Canley, *The Long Dream,* Ambassador Theatre, New York City, 1960.

PRINCIPAL FILM APPEARANCES—Jay Lattimore, *Garden of Eden,* Excelsior, 1954; Flix, *Never Love a Stranger,* Allied Artists, 1958; Hunter Boyd, *From Hell to Texas* (also known as *Manhunt*), Twentieth Century-Fox, 1958; Asa Canfield, *No Name on the Bullet,* Universal, 1959; Sheriff Talbott, *The Fugitive Kind,* United Artists, 1960; Oramel Howland, *Ten Who Dared,* Buena Vista, 1960; Joshua Knudsen, *Ride the High Country* (also known as *Guns in the Afternoon*), Metro-Goldwyn-Mayer (MGM), 1962; Josh McCloud, *He Rides Tall,* Universal, 1964; Reverend Dhalstrom, *Major Dundee,* Columbia, 1965; Kevin McDonald, *El Dorado,*

Paramount, 1967; Mackray, *Eighty Steps to Jonah*, Motion Pictures International, 1969.

Ben Holmes, *Tiger By the Tail*, United/COM, 1970; Mel Potter, *Angels Die Hard*, New World, 1970; Quittner, *The Ballad of Cable Hogue*, Warner Brothers, 1970; Captain Dan, *The Great White Hope*, Twentieth Century-Fox, 1970; Watson, *The McMasters* (also known as *The Blood Crowd* and *The McMasters . . . Tougher Than the West Itself!*), Chevron, 1970; Clell Miller, *The Great Northfield, Minnesota Raid*, Universal, 1972; Jim Sawyer, *J.W. Coop*, Columbia, 1971; Bristowe, *Who Fears the Devil?* (also known as *The Legend of Hillbilly John* and *My Name Is John*), Jack H. Harris, 1972; Mr. Freeman, *The Final Comedown*, New World, 1972; Big Bear, *White Lightning*, United Artists, 1973; Ollinger, *Pat Garrett and Billy the Kid*, MGM, 1973; Honest John, *My Name Is Nobody*, Universal, 1974; Mayor, *Boss Nigger* (also known as *The Black Bounty Killer*), Dimension, 1974; prosecutor, *White Line Fever*, Columbia, 1975; sheriff, *Race with the Devil*, Twentieth Century-Fox, 1975; Thor Erickson, *Stay Hungry*, United Artists, 1975; Silas, *Slumber Party '57*, Cannon/Happy, 1976; Richard, *Mean Johnny Barrows*, Atlas, 1976; Amos, *The Car*, Universal, 1977; Cobb, *The Pack* (also known as *The Long Dark Night*), Warner Brothers, 1977; Sheriff T.C. Bishop, *Mr. Billion*, Twentieth Century-Fox, 1977; team manager, *Heaven Can Wait*, Paramount, 1978; Al Barber, *Fast Charlie—The Moonbeam Rider*, Universal, 1979.

Judge Simpson, *Where the Buffalo Roam*, Universal, 1980; Kellin, *Steel* (also known as *Look Down and Die*, *Men of Steel*), World Northal, 1980; Dempsey, *The Pursuit of D.B. Cooper*, Universal, 1981; government agent, *Reds*, Paramount, 1981; Rigby, *Raggedy Man*, Universal, 1981; Sarge, *Evilspeak*, Moreno, 1982; Doc, *The Beast Within*, Metro-Goldwyn-Mayer/United Artists, 1982; Lieutenant O'Mara, *Hammett*, Orion/Warner Brothers, 1982; Captain T. Tyler, *Lone Wolf McQuade*, Orion, 1983; Diehl, *Children of the Corn* (also known as *Stephen King's Children of the Corn*), New World, 1984; Scoby, *Red-Headed Stranger*, Alive, 1984; Schutte, *The Best of Times*, Universal, 1985; Coach Beetlebom, *Jocks*, Crown International, 1986; General Phillips, *Predator*, Twentieth Century-Fox, 1987; Miles Blackburn, *Bulletproof*, CineTel, 1987; Pop Luddigger, *Trapper County War* (also known as *Trapper County* and *Porter County*), Noble Entertainment Group/ Alpine Releasing Group, 1989; also appeared in *Deliver Us from Evil*, Dimension, 1975; *Dixie Dynamite*, Dimension, 1976; *Texas Detour*, 1978.

PRINCIPAL TELEVISION APPEARANCES—Series: Captain MacAllister, *T.H.E. Cat*, NBC, 1966-67; Uncle Lewis, *Friday the 13th: The Series*, syndicated, 1987. Mini-Series: Billy Soto, "Texas John Slaughter," *Walt Disney Presents*, ABC, 1958-61; General "Moose" Fitzgerald, *War and Remembrance*, ABC, 1988. Pilots: Fred Tomlinson, *The Sharpshooter* (broadcast as an episode of *Dick Powell's Zane Grey Theatre*), CBS, 1958; Ben Ritt, *Hec Ramsey* (also known as *The Century Turns*), NBC, 1972; Henry Stratemeyer, *Manhunter*, CBS, 1974; Father Reardon, *Kingston: The Power Play*, NBC, 1976; Judge Harrison Harding, *The Legend of the Golden Gun*, NBC, 1979; Mr. Fisk, *The Stockers*, NBC, 1981. Episodic: Farmer, *The Andy Griffith Show*, CBS, 1961; man, "Nothing in the Dark," *The Twilight Zone*, CBS, 1962; Zanski, *Skag*, NBC, 1980; Stanley Kazmarek, *Beauty and the Beast*, CBS, 1989; also *The Time Tunnel*, ABC, 1966; *The Invaders*, ABC, 1967. Movies: Mr. Turner, *Reflections of Murder*, ABC, 1974; General Harris, *The Time Machine*, NBC, 1978; Dunworth, *Devil Dog: The Hound of Hell*, CBS, 1978; Leland Stanford, *The Last Ride of the Dalton Gang*, NBC, 1979; Sheriff Miles Gillette, *Louis*

L'Amour's "The Shadow Riders" (also known as *The Shadow Riders*), CBS, 1982; Rusty West, *Oceans of Fire*, CBS, 1986; Samuel Johnson, *LBJ: The Early Years*, NBC, 1987; Uriah Creed, *Independence*, NBC, 1987.*

*   *   *

ARNOLD, Jeanne   1931-

PERSONAL: Born July 30, 1931, in Berkeley, CA; married William C. Stevens (a business executive), April 8, 1978. EDUCATION—Received A.B., drama, from the University of California, Berkeley; studied acting at the American Theatre Wing, with Marion Rich at the HB Studios, and with Mary Tarcai, David Craig, Fanny Bradshaw, Lehman Engel, Lee Henry, and Alan Levitt; studied singing with Amri Galli Campi and Ed Dixon.

VOCATION: Actress.

CAREER: OFF-BROADWAY DEBUT—Lucy Brown, *The Threepenny Opera*, Theatre De Lys, 1955. PRINCIPAL STAGE APPEARANCES— Ensemble, *Demi-Dozen* (revue), Upstairs at the Downstairs, New York City, 1958; ensemble, *Medium Rare* (revue), Happy Medium, Chicago, IL, 1960-61; ensemble, *Put It in Writing* (revue), Happy Medium, 1962-63; Suzanne Bonnard, *The Happy Time*, Broadway Theatre, New York City, 1968; Pignol, *Coco*, Mark Hellinger Theatre, New York City, 1969; Mrs. Peachum, *The Beggar's Opera*, Chelsea Theatre Center, Brooklyn Academy of Music, Brooklyn, NY, 1972; Mrs. Whittaker, *Marry Me! Marry Me!*, Playwrights Horizons, Westside YWCA Clark Center, New

JEANNE ARNOLD

York City, 1973; Libby, *Valentine's Day,* Manhattan Theatre Club, New York City, 1975; Mrs. Hardcastle, *She Stoops to Conquer,* Rosemary, *Picnic,* and Miss Moffett, *The Corn Is Green,* all Meadow Brook Theatre, Rochester, MI, 1977-78; Madame Arcadi, *Blithe Spirit,* Meadow Brook Theatre, 1979.

The Countess, *You Can't Take It with You,* Meadow Brook Theatre, 1980; Martha, *Arsenic and Old Lace* and Mrs. Gibbs, *Our Town,* both Meadow Brook Theatre, 1980-81; Judith Bliss, *Hay Fever,* Meadow Brook Theatre, 1981-82; grandmother, *The Children's Hour* and Esther, *Morning's at Seven,* both Meadow Brook Theatre, 1983; moderator, *Side By Side By Sondheim,* Meadow Brook Theatre, 1984; Albertine, *Toys in the Attic* and Lady Bracknell, *The Importance of Being Earnest,* both Meadow Brook Theatre, 1985; Nurse, *Romeo and Juliet* and Helene Hanff, *84 Charing Cross Road,* both Meadow Brook Theatre, 1985-86; Queen Margaret, *Richard III* and Helen Kroeger, *Pack of Lies,* both Meadow Brook Theatre, 1986-87; Big Mama, *Cat on a Hot Tin Roof,* clairvoyant, *Death Trap,* and Mrs. Chauvenet, *Harvey,* all Meadow Brook Theatre, 1987-88.

Also appeared in *The Dining Room,* Meadow Brook Theatre, 1984; as Hesione Hushabye, *Heartbreak House* and Mrs. Smith, *The Bald Soprano,* both Center Theatre Group, Los Angeles; Vera Charles, *Mame,* Civic Light Opera, Pittsburgh, PA; Mrs. Hagarty, *Hogan's Goat* and the Countess, *The Rehearsal,* both Stage Society, Los Angeles; Madame Pampinelli, *The Torchbearers,* ELT, Los Angeles; Linda Loman, *Death of a Salesman,* Charles Playhouse, Boston, MA; Lady Macbeth, *Macbeth,* Beatrice, *Much Ado About Nothing,* and Emilia, *Othello,* all San Francisco Shakespearean Theatre, San Francisco, CA; Cleopatra, *Antony and Cleopatra* and in *Six Original Plays,* both Theatre East, Los Angeles; hippie seductress, *Unemployed Saint,* New York City; ensemble, *Take Five* (revue), New York City; ensemble, *The Mad Show* (revue), New York City and Los Angeles; ensemble, *Four on the Floor* (revue), Illinois and Florida; and in productions of *Mame, The King and I, Do I Hear a Waltz?, Plain and Fancy, Flower Drum Song, The Student Prince,* and *Gigi.*

MAJOR TOURS—Pignol, *Coco,* U.S. cities, 1971.

PRINCIPAL FILM APPEARANCES—Grace Munster, *Munster Go Home,* Universal, 1966; Gertrude, *What's So Bad About Feeling Good?,* Universal, 1968; also appeared in *Dear Heart,* Warner Brothers, 1964.

PRINCIPAL TELEVISION APPEARANCES—Series: Mary Hammilmeyer, *The Cara Williams Show,* CBS, 1964-65; also Ellen Mason, *The Guiding Light,* CBS. Pilots: Mary Jones, *The Jones Boys,* CBS, 1967; Cloris, *Making It,* NBC, 1976; also *Up Pompeii.* Movies: Joan Hartlane, *Mr. and Mrs. Bo Jo Jones,* ABC, 1971. Specials: Mean stepmother, *Cinderella,* syndicated.

RELATED CAREER—Nightclub performer; actress and voiceover artist for television commercials.

RECORDINGS: ALBUMS—*The Happy Time* (original cast recording), RCA; also *Demi-Dozen* (original cast recording); *Coco* (original cast recording); *Take Five* (original cast recording).

MEMBER: Actors' Equity Association, Screen Actors Guild, American Federation of Television and Radio Artists, American Guild of Variety Artists, Theatre East Workshop (Los Angeles).

ADDRESSES: AGENT—Michael Thomas Agency, 305 Madison Avenue, New York, NY 10165.

*   *   *

ASHER, Jane   1946-

PERSONAL: Born April 5, 1946, in London, England; daughter of Richard Alan John (a doctor) and Margaret (Eliot) Asher; married Gerald Scarfe; children: three.

VOCATION: Actress and writer.

CAREER: STAGE DEBUT—*Housemaster,* Frinton Summer Theatre, Frinton, U.K., 1957. LONDON DEBUT—Muriel Webster, *Will You Walk a Little Faster,* Duke of York's Theatre, 1960. BROADWAY DEBUT—Julietta, *Measure for Measure* and Juliet, *Romeo and Juliet,* both Bristol Old Vic Company, City Center Theatre, 1967. PRINCIPAL STAGE APPEARANCES—Alice, *Through the Looking Glass,* Oxford Playhouse, Oxford, U.K., 1958; Wendy, *Peter Pan,* Scala Theatre, London, 1961; Dinah, *Level Crossing,* Theatre Royal, Windsor, U.K., 1962; title role, *Cinderella* (pantomime), New Theatre, Bromley, U.K., 1962; Cassandra, *The Trojan Women,* Edinburgh Festival, Pop Theatre, Edinburgh, Scotland, 1966; Perdita, *The Winter's Tale,* Edinburgh Festival, Pop Theatre, then Cambridge Theatre, London, both 1966; Juliet, *Romeo and Juliet* and Julietta, *Measure for Measure,* both Bristol Old Vic Company, Bristol, U.K., 1966-67; Lorette, *Summer,* Fortune

JANE ASHER

Theatre, London, 1968; Alison, *Look Back in Anger,* Royal Court Theatre, then Criterion Theatre, both London, 1968; Celia, *The Philanthropist,* Royal Court Theatre, then May Fair Theatre, London, both 1970, later Ethel Barrymore Theatre, New York City, 1971; Sally, *Old Flames,* New Vic Studio, Bristol, U.K., 1975; Ann, *Treats,* Royal Court Theatre, then May Fair Theatre, both 1976; Charlotte, *Strawberry Fields,* National Theatre Company, Cottesloe Theatre, London, 1977; title role, *Ophelia,* Oxford Playhouse, 1977; Dr. Scott, *Whose Life Is It Anyway?,* Mermaid Theatre, then Savoy Theatre, both London, 1978; title role, *Peter Pan,* Shaftesbury Theatre, London, 1978; Ruth, *Blithe Spirit,* Vaudeville Theatre, London, 1986. Also appeared in *Cleo, Great Expectations, The Happiest Days of Your Life,* and *Sixty Thousand Nights,* all Bristol Old Vic Company, 1965; *Fifty,* Oxford Playhouse, 1973; *To Those Born Later,* National Theatre Company, Cottesloe Theatre, 1977; *Before the Party,* Apollo Theatre, London, 1980, then Queens Theatre, London, 1981; *Henceforward,* Vaudeville Theatre, 1988.

PRINCIPAL STAGE WORK—Producer, *Before the Party,* Queens Theatre, London, 1981.

MAJOR TOURS—Wendy, *Peter Pan,* U.K. cities, 1972; title role, *Ophelia,* U.K. cities, 1977.

FILM DEBUT—Nina, *Crash of Silence* (also known as *Mandy*), General Film Distributors, 1952. PRINCIPAL FILM APPEARANCES—Hester Grey, *Loss of Innocence* (also known as *The Greengage Summer*), Columbia, 1961; Francesca, *The Masque of the Red Death,* American International, 1964; Lindy Birkett, *The Model Murder Case* (also known as *Girl in the Headlines*), Cinema V, 1964; Annie, *Alfie,* Paramount, 1966; Perdita, *The Winter's Tale,* Warner Brothers, 1968; Susan, *Deep End,* Paramount, 1970; Margaret, *The Buttercup Chain,* Columbia, 1971; Jane Seymour, *Henry VIII and His Six Wives,* Metro-Goldwyn-Mayer/EMI, 1972; Helen, *Runners,* Hanstall, 1983; bank manager, *Success Is the Best Revenge,* Gaumont, 1984; Mrs. Liddell, *Dreamchild,* Universal, 1985; Pauline, *Paris By Night,* Cineplex Odeon, 1989. Also appeared in *Adventure in the Hopfields,* Associated British, 1954.

PRINCIPAL TELEVISION APPEARANCES—Series: *Wish Me Luck,* ITV, 1987-90. Mini-Series: Celia Ryder, *Brideshead Revisited,* Granada, then PBS, 1982. Episodic: *Tales of the Unexpected,* syndicated. Also appeared in *Bright Smiles,* Granada; *The Mill on the Floss, The Mistress, A Voyage 'round My Father, East Lynne,* and *Love Is Old, Love Is New.*

RELATED CAREER—Company member, Bristol Old Vic Company, Bristol, U.K.; company member, National Theatre Company, London.

NON-RELATED CAREER—Trustee, Worldwide Fund for Nature; trustee, Child Accident Prevention Trust.

WRITINGS: Jane Asher's Party Cakes, Pelham, 1982; *Jane Asher's Fancy Dress,* Pelham, 1983; *Silent Night for You and Your Baby,* Pelham, 1984.

MEMBER: British Academy of Film and Television Arts, Royal Academy of Dramatic Arts (associate member).

SIDELIGHTS: RECREATIONS—Music and cooking.

ADDRESSES: AGENT—Chatto and Linnit Ltd., Prince of Wales Theatre, Coventry Street, London W1V 7FE, England.

ASHLEY, Elizabeth   1939-
(Elizabeth Cole)

PERSONAL: Born Elizabeth Ann Cole, August 30, 1939, in Ocala, FL; daughter of Arthur Kingman and Lucille (Ayer) Cole; married James Farentino (an actor), September, 1962 (divorced); married George Peppard (an actor), 1966 (divorced); married James Michael McCarthy; children: Christian Moore (second marriage). EDUCATION—Attended Louisiana State University, 1957-58; trained for the stage at the Neighborhood Playhouse with Philip Burton; studied ballet with Tatiana Semenova.

VOCATION: Actress and producer.

CAREER: STAGE DEBUT—(As Elizabeth Cole) Esmeralda, *Camino Real,* Neighborhood Playhouse, New York City, 1959. OFF-BROADWAY DEBUT—(As Elizabeth Cole) Jessica, *Dirty Hands,* Actors' Playhouse, 1959. BROADWAY DEBUT—(As Elizabeth Cole) Jane Ashe, *The Highest Tree,* Longacre Theatre, 1959. PRINCIPAL STAGE APPEARANCES—(As Elizabeth Cole) Louise, *Marcus in the High Grass,* Westport Country Playhouse, Westport, CT, 1959; Elizabeth Brown (understudy), *Roman Candle,* Cort Theatre, New York City, 1960; title role (understudy), *Mary, Mary,* Helen Hayes Theatre, New York City, 1961; Mollie Michaelson, *Take Her, She's Mine,* Biltmore Theatre, New York City, 1961; Corie Bratter, *Barefoot in the Park,* Biltmore Theatre, 1963; Maggie Train, *Ring 'round the Bathtub,* Martin Beck Theatre, New York City, 1972; Isabel, *The Enchanted,* Kennedy Center for the Performing Arts, Eisenhower Theatre, Washington, DC, 1973; Maggie, *Cat on a Hot Tin Roof,* American Shakespeare Festival, Stratford, CT, then American National Theatre and Academy Theatre, New York City, both 1974; Sabina, *The Skin of Our Teeth,* Kennedy Center for the Performing Arts, Eisenhower Theatre, then Mark Hellinger Theatre, New York City, both 1975; Betsey-No-Name, *Legend,* Ethel Barrymore Theatre, New York City, 1976; as herself, *George Abbott . . . A Celebration,* Shubert Theatre, New York City, 1976; Cleopatra, *Caesar and Cleopatra,* Kennedy Center for the Performing Arts, 1976, then Palace Theatre, New York City, 1977; Jennifer Crawford, *Hide and Seek,* Belasco Theatre, New York City, 1980; Dr. Martha Livingstone, *Agnes of God,* Music Box Theatre, New York City, 1982; Lois, *The Perfect Party,* Kennedy Center for the Performing Arts, Eisenhower Theatre, 1986; Laura Goforth, *The Milk Train Doesn't Stop Here Any More,* WPA Theatre, New York City, 1987; as herself, *Happy Birthday, Mr. Abbott!,* Palace Theatre, 1987; Isadora Duncan, *When She Danced,* Playwrights Horizons, New York City, 1990. Also appeared at the Green Mansions Theatre, Warrensbury, NY, 1960; as Mary, *Vanities,* Chicago, IL, 1977; in *Carnival of Dreams,* New Dramatists Inc., New York City, 1977; *The Madwoman of Central Park South,* New York City.

MAJOR TOURS—Dr. Martha Livingstone, *Agnes of God,* U.S. cities, 1983-84; Hannah Mae Bindler, *A Coupla White Chicks Sitting Around Talking,* U.S. cities, 1985-86.

FILM DEBUT—Monica Winthrop, *The Carpetbaggers,* Paramount, 1964. PRINCIPAL FILM APPEARANCES—Jenny, *Ship of Fools,* Columbia, 1965; Alexandria Mallory, *The Third Day,* Warner Brothers, 1965; Nan, *The Marriage of a Young Stockbroker,* Twentieth Century-Fox, 1971; Loretta, *Paperback Hero,* Rumson, 1973; Felicity, *Golden Needles* (also known as *Chase for the Golden Needles*), American International, 1974; Cora Brown, *Rancho Deluxe,* United Artists, 1975; Jeannie Carter, *92 in the Shade,* United Artists, 1975; Nancy Sue, *The Great Scout and Cathouse Thursday* (also known as *Wildcat*), American International, 1976; Mrs. Emerson, *Coma,* United Artists, 1978; Andrea Glassen, *Windows,* United Artists, 1980; Sophia Thatcher, *Paternity,* Paramount, 1981; Diana, *Split Image,* Orion, 1982; Police Commissioner Jane Kirkpatrick, *Dragnet,* Universal, 1987; Dr. Dorothy Glaser, *Vampire's Kiss,* Hemdale, 1988. Also appeared in *Lookin' to Get Out,* Paramount, 1982; *Dangerous Curves,* Vestron, 1988.

TELEVISION DEBUT—"Heaven Can Wait," *Dupont Show of the Month,* CBS, 1960. PRINCIPAL TELEVISION APPEARANCES—Mini-Series: Kate, *Sandburg's Lincoln,* NBC, 1974-76. Pilots: Sallie Baker, *The Magician,* NBC, 1973; Elizabeth Corban, *One of My Wives Is Missing,* ABC, 1976; Joann Hammil, *Tom and Joann,* CBS, 1978. Episodic: Mrs. Zal, *Cagney and Lacey,* CBS, 1985; Linda Colby, *Miami Vice,* NBC, 1987; Eleanor, *Eisenhower and Lutz,* CBS, 1988; Vera, *Murder, She Wrote,* CBS, 1989; Althea Campbell, *B.L. Stryker,* ABC, 1989; also *Run for Your Life,* NBC, 1966; *Ghost Story,* NBC, 1972; *The Defenders,* CBS; *The U.S. Steel Hour,* CBS; *The Nurses,* CBS; *Ben Casey,* ABC; *Stoney Burke,* ABC; *Sam Benedict,* CBS; *The Ed Sullivan Show,* CBS; *The Jack Paar Show,* NBC; *Mike Wallace's PM East,* WNEW (New York City); *Route 66,* CBS. Movies: Sally Dillman, *The Face of Fear,* CBS, 1971; Marian, *Harpy,* CBS, 1971; Diane Craddock, *The Heist,* ABC, 1972; Ellie Smith, *Second Chance,* ABC, 1972; Helen Connelly, *When Michael Calls,* ABC, 1972; Laurel Plunkett, *Your Money or Your Wife,* CBS, 1972; Erica Tate, *The War Between the Tates,* NBC, 1977; Sharon Allan, *A Fire in the Sky,* NBC, 1978; Eve Swiss, *Svengali,* CBS, 1983; Freddie Fox, *He's Fired, She's Hired,* CBS, 1984; Dallas, *Stagecoach,* CBS, 1986; Blanche Webster, *Warm Hearts, Cold Feet,* CBS, 1987; Babette Van Degan, *The Two Mrs. Grenvilles,* NBC, 1987; Lolly Fontenot, *Blue Bayou,* NBC, 1990. Specials: Sally Devlin, "The File on Devlin," *Hallmark Hall of Fame,* NBC, 1969; *Broadway Plays Washington! Kennedy Center Tonight,* PBS, 1982; *Blondes vs. Brunettes,* ABC, 1984; Annie, "The Rope," *American Playwrights Theatre,* Arts and Entertainment, 1989.

PRINCIPAL TELEVISION WORK—Specials: Associate producer, "Cat on a Hot Tin Roof," *American Playhouse,* PBS, 1984.

RELATED CAREER—Member, National Council of the Performing Arts, 1965-69; trustee, American Film Institute, 1968-72; professional model.

WRITINGS: (With Ross Firestone) *Postcards from the Road* (autobiography), M. Evans & Company, 1978.

AWARDS: Antoinette Perry Award, Best Supporting or Featured Actress in a Musical, Theatre World Award, and Southern Woman's Achievement Award, all 1962, for *Take Her, She's Mine.*

MEMBER: Actors' Equity Association, Screen Actors Guild, American Federation of Television and Radio Artists.

ADDRESSES: OFFICE—31 Union Square W., Suite 10-E, New York City, NY 10037. MANAGER—Raymond Katz Enterprises, 9255 Sunset Boulevard, Suite 1115, Los Angeles, CA 90069.*

ATTENBOROUGH, Richard 1923-

PERSONAL: Full name, Richard Samuel Attenborough; born August 29, 1923, in Cambridge, England; son of Frederick L. and Mary (Clegg) Attenborough; married Sheila Beryl Grant Sim (an actress), 1945; children: one son, two daughters. EDUCATION—Studied acting at the Royal Academy of Dramatic Art, 1941. MILITARY—Royal Air Force, Film Unit, 1943.

VOCATION: Actor, producer, and director.

CAREER: STAGE DEBUT—Richard Miller, *Ah! Wilderness,* Intimate Theatre, London, 1941. PRINCIPAL STAGE APPEARANCES—Sebastian, *Twelfth Night,* Ralph Berger, *Awake and Sing,* and Ba, *The Holy Isle,* all Arts Theatre, London, 1942; Andrew, *London W1,* Q Theatre, London, 1942; Leo Hubbard, *The Little Foxes,* Piccadilly Theatre, London, 1942; Pinkie Brown, *Brighton Rock,* Garrick Theatre, London, 1943; Coney, *The Way Back,* Westminster Theatre, London, 1949; Valentine Crisp, *Sweet Madness,* Vaudeville Theatre, London, 1952; Detective Trotter, *The Mousetrap,* Ambassadors' Theatre, London, 1952; David and Julian Fanshaw, *Double Image,* Savoy Theatre, London, 1956; also Toni Rigi, *To Dorothy, a Son,* 1950; Theseus, *The Rape of the Belt,* 1957.

FILM DEBUT—Young stoker, *In Which We Serve,* British Lion, 1942. PRINCIPAL FILM APPEARANCES—Tommy Draper, *The Hundred Pound Window,* Warner Brothers/First National, 1943; railway worker, *Schweik's New Adventures* (also known as *It Started at Midnight*), Coronet, 1943; English pilot, *Stairway to Heaven* (also known as *A Matter of Life and Death*), Universal, 1946; David Wilton, *Journey Together,* English Films Inc., 1946; Jack Arnold, *School for Secrets* (also known as *Secret Flight*), General Film Distributors, 1946; Pinkie Brown, *Brighton Rock* (also known as *Young Scarface*), Associated British, 1947; Ted Peters, *Dancing with Crime,* Paramount, 1947; Percy Boon, *Dulcimer Street* (also known as *London Belongs to Me*), General Film Distributors, 1948; Francis Andrews, *The Smugglers* (also known as *The Man Within*), Eagle-Lion, 1948; Jackie Knowles, *Boys in Brown,* General Film Distributors, 1949; Jack Read, *The Outsider* (also known as *The Guinea Pig*), Variety, 1949.

Jan, *The Lost People,* General Film Distributors, 1950; Pierre Bonnet, *Hell Is Sold Out,* Eros, 1951; Stoker Snipe, *Operation Disaster* (also known as *Morning Departure*), Universal, 1951; Dougall, *Father's Doing Fine,* Associated British, 1952; Dripper Daniels, *The Gift Horse* (also known as *Glory at Sea*), Independent Film Distributors, 1952; Jack Carter, *The Magic Box,* British Lion, 1954; Tom Manning, *Eight O'Clock Walk,* British Lion, 1954; Private Cox, *Private's Progress,* British Lion, 1956; George Hoskins, *The Ship That Died of Shame* (also known as *P.T. Raiders*), Continental/General Film Distributors, 1956; Knocker White, *The Baby and the Battleship,* British Lion, 1957; Henry Marshall, *Brothers in Law,* BC, 1957; Holden, *Dunkirk,* Metro-Goldwyn-Mayer (MGM), 1958; Sidney de Vere Cox, *I'm All Right, Jack,* British Lion, 1959; Stephen Leigh, *Strange Affection* (also known as *The Scamp*), Brenner, 1959; Peter Watson, *The Man Upstairs,* British Lion, 1959.

Tom Curtis, *The Angry Silence,* British Lion, 1960; Captain Bunter Phillips, *Breakout* (also known as *Danger Within*), Continental, 1960; Whitey, *S.O.S. Pacific,* Universal, 1960; Rod Hamilton, *All Night Long,* Rank, 1961; Ernest Tilley, *Jet Storm* (also known as *Killing Urge* and *Jetstream*), Britannia/British Lion, 1961; Edward

Lexy, *The League of Gentlemen*, Kingsley, 1961; Trooper Brody, *Desert Patrol* (also known as *Sea of Sand*), Universal, 1962; Gareth Probert, *Only Two Can Play*, Kingsley/Columbia, 1962; various roles, *Trial and Error* (also known as *The Dock Brief*), MGM, 1962; Roger "Big X" Bartlett, *The Great Escape*, United Artists, 1963; Regimental Sergeant Major Lauderdale, *Guns at Batasi*, Twentieth Century-Fox, 1964; Billy Savage, *Seance on a Wet Afternoon*, Artixo, 1964; Alfred Price-Gorham, *The Third Secret*, Twentieth Century-Fox, 1964; Lew Moran, *The Flight of the Phoenix*, Twentieth Century-Fox, 1965; Frenchy Burgoyne, *The Sand Pebbles*, Twentieth Century-Fox, 1966; Albert Blossom, *Doctor Dolittle*, Twentieth Century-Fox, 1967; Robert Blossom, *The Bliss of Mrs. Blossom*, Paramount, 1968; Silas, *Only When I Larf*, Paramount, 1968.

Mr. Tungay, *David Copperfield*, Twentieth Century-Fox, 1970; General Charles Whiteley, *The Last Grenade*, Cinerama, 1970; Oxford coach, *The Magic Christian*, Commonwealth, 1970; Inspector Truscott, *Loot*, Cinevision, 1971; Palmer Anderson, *A Severed Head*, Columbia, 1971; John Reginald Halliday Christie, *10 Rillington Place*, Columbia, 1971; Commander Swann, *Brannigan*, United Artists, 1975; Major Lionel Roach, *Conduct Unbecoming*, Allied Artists, 1975; Judge Cannon, *Ten Little Indians* (also known as *And Then There Were None*), AVCO-Embassy, 1975; Sloat, *Rosebud*, United Artists, 1975; General Outram, *The Chess Players* (also known as *Shatranj ke khilari*), Creative Films, 1978; Colonel John Daintry, *The Human Factor*, Metro-Goldwyn-Mayer/United Artists, 1979; narrator, *Mother Teresa*, Petrie/Productions du Daummou/CS Associates, 1985. Also narrator, *A Boy's Day*, 1964; narrator, *Don't Make Me Laugh*, 1969; narrator, *Cup Glory*, 1972; *The Village* (also known as *Il viaggio*), 1974; *Death in Persepolis*, 1974.

RICHARD ATTENBOROUGH

PRINCIPAL FILM WORK—Producer (with Bryan Forbes), *The Angry Silence*, British Lion, 1960; producer, *Whistle Down the Wind*, Pathe-America, 1961; producer (with James Woolf), *The L-Shaped Room*, Davis/Royal/Columbia, 1962; producer (with Forbes), *Seance on a Wet Afternoon*, Artixo, 1964; producer (with Brian Duffy) and director, *Oh! What a Lovely War*, Paramount, 1969; producer and director, *Young Winston*, Columbia, 1972; director, *A Bridge Too Far*, United Artists, 1977; director, *Magic*, Twentieth Century-Fox, 1978; producer and director, *Gandhi*, Columbia, 1982; director, *A Chorus Line*, Columbia, 1985; producer (with Norman Spencer and John Briley) and director, *Cry Freedom*, Universal, 1987.

PRINCIPAL TELEVISION APPEARANCES—Specials: Mr. Tungay, *David Copperfield*, NBC, 1970; *Clue: Movies, Murder, and Mystery*, CBS, 1986; *Freedomfest: Nelson Mandela's 70th Birthday Celebration*, syndicated, 1988.

RELATED CAREER—Founder (with Bryan Forbes), Beaver Films (a production company), 1959; founder, Allied Film Makers (a production company), 1960; member, Cinematograph Films Council (1967-73); chairman, Royal Academy of Dramatic Art, 1970; governor, National Film School, 1970—; member, Arts Council of Great Britain (1970-72); chairman, Capital Radio, 1973—; deputy chairman, Channel Four Television, 1980—; chairman, Goldcrest Films, 1981-85, renamed Goldcrest Films and Television, 1985—; chairman, Sussex University Arts Center Board.

NON-RELATED CAREER—Pro-chancellor, Sussex University, 1970—; trustee, Tate Gallery, London, 1976—; president, Muscular Dystrophy Group of Great Britain.

WRITINGS: In Search of Gandhi (non-fiction), New Century Publications, 1983.

AWARDS: Best Actor Awards from the Variety Club of Great Britain, 1959 and 1965; Best Actor Awards from the San Sebastian Film Festival, 1961 and 1964; British Academy of Film and Television Arts Award, Best British Actor, 1964, for *Guns at Batasi* and *Seance on a Wet Afternoon;* Golden Globe, Best Supporting Actor, 1967, for *The Sand Pebbles;* Commander, Order of the British Empire, 1967; Cinematograph Exhibitors Association Award, 1967, for Distinguished Service to British Cinema; Golden Globe, Best Supporting Actor, 1968, for *Doctor Dolittle;* Golden Globe, Best English Language Foreign Film, 1970, for *Oh! What a Lovely War;* knighted in the New Year Honours, 1976; United Nations Award, 1977; Academy Awards, Best Picture and Best Director, British Academy of Film and Television Arts Awards, Best Picture and Best Director, Directors Guild of America Award, Outstanding Directorial Achievement for Feature Films, all 1982, and Golden Globes, Best Foreign Film and Best Director, 1983, all for *Gandhi;* British Academy of Film and Television Arts Award, Film Fellowship, 1983; Martin Luther King, Jr. Non-Violent Peace Prize, 1983; Golden Globe nomination and British Academy of Film and Television Arts Award nomination, both Best Director, 1988, for *Cry Freedom;* Bancroft Medal from the Royal Academy of Dramatic Art. HONORARY DEGREES—University of Leicester, D. Litt., 1970; University of Newcastle, D.C.L., 1974.

MEMBER: British Actors' Equity Association (council member, 1949-73), British Film Institute (governor and chairman, 1982—), British Academy of Film and Television Arts (vice-president, 1971—), Actors' Charitable Trust (chairman), Garrick Club, Beefstake Club, Green Room Club.

SIDELIGHTS: RECREATIONS—Listening to music and collecting paintings.

ADDRESSES: AGENT—Martin Baum, Creative Artists Agency, 9830 Wilshire Boulevard, Beverly Hills, CA 90212.

*   *   *

AUBERJONOIS, Rene   1940-

PERSONAL: Full name, Rene Murat Auberjonois; born June 1, 1940, in New York, NY; son of Fernand (a journalist) and Laura (Murat) Auberjonois; married Judith Helen Mihalyi, October 19, 1963; children: Tessa Louise, Remy-Luc. EDUCATION—Carnegie-Mellon University, B.F.A., 1962.

VOCATION: Actor.

CAREER: STAGE DEBUT—Arena Stage, Washington, DC. OFF-BROADWAY DEBUT—Fool, *King Lear,* Lincoln Center Repertory Company, Vivian Beaumont Theatre, 1968. BROADWAY DEBUT—Marco, *Fire!,* Longacre Theatre, 1969. PRINCIPAL STAGE APPEARANCES—Witch boy, *Dark of the Moon,* Leslie, *The Hostage,* and Edmund, *Long Day's Journey into Night,* all Arena Stage, Washington, DC, 1962-64; title role, *Turtuffe,* title role, *King Lear,* Fancourt Babberley, *Charley's Aunt,* and ensemble, *Beyond the Fringe* (revue), all American Conservatory Theatre, San Francisco, CA, 1965-67; Ned, *A Cry of Players,* Lincoln

RENE AUBERJONOIS

Center Repertory Company, Vivian Beaumont Theatre, New York City, 1968; Sebastian Baye, *Coco,* Mark Hellinger Theatre, New York City, 1969; Malvolio, *Twelfth Night,* Repertory Theatre of Lincoln Center, Vivian Beaumont Theatre, 1972; Scapin, *Tricks,* Alvin Theatre, New York City, 1973; Edgar, *King Lear,* New York Shakespeare Festival, Delacorte Theatre, New York City, 1973; various roles, *The Good Doctor,* Eugene O'Neill Theatre, New York City, 1973; Jack, *The Ruling Class,* American Conservatory Theatre, 1975; John Karslake, *The New York Idea* and Solynony, *The Three Sisters,* both Brooklyn Academy of Music, Brooklyn, NY, 1977; Sandor Turai, *The Play's the Thing* and Brutus, *Julius Caesar,* both Brooklyn Academy of Music, 1978; Johann Schiml, *Break a Leg,* Palace Theatre, New York City, 1979; Ivanov, *Every Good Boy Deserves Favour,* Metropolitan Opera House, New York City, then Kennedy Center for the Performing Arts, Washington, DC, 1979.

Malvolio, *Twelfth Night* and Konstantin Sergeivich Stanislavski, *Chekhov in Yalta,* both Center Theatre Group, Mark Taper Forum, Los Angeles, 1981; Duke of Gloucester, *Richard III* and Kolya, *A Month In the Country,* both Center Theatre Group, Mark Taper Forum, 1982; Alan Squier, *The Petrified Forest,* Los Angeles Theatre Center, Los Angeles, 1985; the Duke, *Big River,* Eugene O'Neill Theatre, New York City, 1985; Mr. Samsa, *Metamorphosis,* Ethel Barrymore Theatre, New York City, 1989; Buddy Fidler/Irwin S. Irving, *City of Angels,* Virginia Theatre, New York City, 1989. Also appeared in *Chemin de Fer,* Mark Taper Forum, 1969; as Alceste, *The Misanthrope,* and in *A Flea in Her Ear* and *Twelfth Night,* all Mark Taper Forum.

PRINCIPAL STAGE WORK—Director, *Beyond the Fringe.*

FILM DEBUT—Howie, *Lilith,* Columbia, 1964. PRINCIPAL FILM APPEARANCES—Salesman, *Petulia,* Warner Brothers, 1968; Dago Red, *M*A*S*H,* Twentieth Century-Fox, 1970; lecturer, *Brewster McCloud,* Metro-Goldwyn-Mayer, 1970; Sheehan, *McCabe and Mrs. Miller,* Warner Brothers, 1971; Hugh, *Images,* Columbia, 1972; Jimmy Twitchell, *Pete 'n' Tillie,* Universal, 1972; Major Napier, *The Hindenburg,* Universal, 1975; Father Kudos, *The Big Bus,* Paramount, 1976; Bagley, *King Kong,* Paramount, 1976; Donald Phelps, *The Eyes of Laura Mars,* Columbia, 1978; Harris, *Where the Buffalo Roam,* Universal, 1980; voice of the Speaking Skull, *The Last Unicorn* (animated), ITC, 1982; Principal Horner, *3:15, The Moment of Truth* (also known as *3:15*), Dakota Entertainment, 1986; Major Siegfried Henningson, *Walker,* Universal/Northern Distribution Partners, 1987; Modoc, *My Best Friend Is a Vampire,* Kings Road, 1988; Tony Stark, *Police Academy 5: Assignment Miami Beach,* Warner Brothers, 1988; voice of Louis, *The Little Mermaid* (animated), Buena Vista, 1989.

PRINCIPAL TELEVISION APPEARANCES—Series: Clayton Endicott III, *Benson,* ABC, 1980-86; voice characterization, *The Scooby-Doo and Scrappy-Doo Show* (animated), ABC, 1980-82. Mini-Series: Dr. Eugene Lyons, *The Rhinemann Exchange,* NBC, 1977. Pilots: Andre Stryker, *Once Upon a Dead Man,* NBC, 1971; title role, *Panache,* ABC, 1976; news editor, *The TV TV Show,* NBC, 1977; Captain Sir David Edney, *The Wild Wild West Revisited,* CBS, 1979; Captain Sir David Edney, *More Wild Wild West,* CBS, 1980; Dr. Carl Jerrett, *Scalpels,* NBC, 1980. Episodic: Edgar, "King Lear," *Theatre in America,* PBS, 1974; voice characterization, *Scooby's Mystery Funhouse* (animated), ABC, 1985; voice characterization, *The Jetsons* (animated), syndicated, 1985; voice characterization, *Challenge of the GoBots* (animated), syndicated, 1985; voice characterization, *Super Powers Team: Galactic Guardi-*

ans (animated), ABC, 1985; Alvanor, *Wildfire* (animated), CBS, 1986; voice characterization, *The New Adventures of Jonny Quest* (animated), syndicated, 1987; voice characterization, *The New Adventures of the Snorks* (animated), syndicated, 1987; Harry Papazian, *Murder, She Wrote*, CBS, 1987; Captain Thorn, *Murder, She Wrote*, CBS, 1988; Mr. Richardson, *L.A. Law*, NBC, 1988; voice characterization, *Fantastic Max* (animated), syndicated, 1988; also "Camera Obscura," *Night Gallery*, NBC, 1971; *The Bob Newhart Show*, CBS, 1975; *Man from Atlantis*, NBC, 1977; *Life's Most Embarrassing Moments*, NBC, 1985; *The Mod Squad*, ABC; *McMillan and Wife*, NBC; *Love, American Style*, ABC; *Rhoda*, CBS; "The Frog Prince" and "Sleeping Beauty," *Faerie Tale Theatre*, Showtime.

Movies: Halden Brevik, *The Birdmen* (also known as *Escape of the Birdmen*), ABC, 1971; Sidney Krebs, *Shirts/Skins*, ABC, 1973; Jack Stump, *The Dark Secret of Harvest Home*, NBC, 1978; Howard, *The Kid from Nowhere*, NBC, 1982; Sumner, *The Christmas Star*, ABC, 1986; Ned, *A Smoky Mountain Christmas*, ABC, 1986; Governor Lew Wallace, *Longarm*, ABC, 1988; drunk, *Gore Vidal's "Billy the Kid,"* TNT, 1989; Merlin, *A Connecticut Yankee in King Arthur's Court*, NBC, 1989. Specials: King Louis XVI, *The Lives of Ben Franklin: The Ambassador*, CBS, 1974; Ichabod Crane, "Once Upon a Midnight Dreary," *CBS Library*, CBS, 1979; *The Screen Actors Guild 50th Anniversary Celebration*, CBS, 1984; "Death at Dinner," *The Booth*, PBS, 1985; *Emmanuel Lewis: My Very Own Show*, ABC, 1987.

PRINCIPAL TELEVISION WORK—Episodic: Director, *Marblehead Manor*, syndicated.

PRINCIPAL RADIO WORK—Specials: Director, *Oh, Dad, Poor Dad, Mama's Hung You in the Closet and I'm Feeling So Sad.*

RELATED CAREER—Company member, New Theatre for Now, Center Theatre Group, Mark Taper Forum, Los Angeles, CA, 1969-70; board of directors, California Theatre Council, 1984—; theatre panelist, National Endowment for the Arts, 1988—; founding member, American Conservatory Theatre, San Francisco, CA; founding member, Mark Taper Forum, Los Angeles; founding member, Classic Theatre Works, Los Angeles; acting teacher, University of California at Berkeley, San Francisco State University, and Juilliard School of Music and Drama.

AWARDS: Antoinette Perry Award, Best Supporting or Featured Actor in a Musical, 1970, for *Coco;* Antoinette Perry Award nomination, Best Supporting or Featured Actor in a Drama, 1974, for *The Good Doctor;* Antoinette Perry Award nomination, Best Featured Actor in a Musical, 1985, for *Big River;* also Emmy Award nomination for *Benson.*

MEMBER: Actors' Equity Association, Screen Actors Guild, American Federation of Television and Radio Artists.

SIDELIGHTS: RECREATIONS—Drawing and yoga. FAVORITE ROLES—Tartuffe and Jack in *The Ruling Class.*

ADDRESSES: OFFICE—124 W. 79th Street, New York, NY 10024. AGENT—Strain and Jennett, 1500 Broadway, Suite 2001, New York, NY 10036.

AUDRAN, Stephane   1932-

PERSONAL: Born Colette Suzanne Jeannine Dacheville, November 8, 1932, in Versailles, France; daughter of Corneille and Jeanne (Rossi) Dacheville; married Jean-Louis Trintignant (an actor; marriage ended); married Claude Chabrol (a director and writer), December 4, 1964; children: Thomas (second marriage). EDUCATION—Attended Lycee Lamartine, Paris; studied acting with Charles Dullin, Tania Balachova, Michel Vitold, and Rene Simon.

VOCATION: Actress.

CAREER: STAGE DEBUT—*La Maison carree*, Theatre Noctambules, 1955.

FILM DEBUT—*La Bonne Tisane*, 1957. PRINCIPAL FILM APPEARANCES—Ginette, *Les Bonnes Femmes*, Rome-Paris Films, 1960, released in the United States by Harold Cornsweet, 1966; Helene Hartmann, *L'Oeil du malin* (also known as *The Third Lover*), Rome-Paris Films, 1962, released in the United States by Atlantic, 1963; Fernande Segret, *Landru* (also known as *Bluebeard*), Rome-Paris Films, 1963, released in the United States by Embassy, 1963; the Wife, "La Muette" in *Paris vu par . . .* (also known as *Six in Paris*), Les Films du Losange, 1965, released in the United States by New Yorker, 1968; Jacqueline/Lydia, *Le Scandale* (also known as *The Champagne Murders*), Universal France, 1967, released in the United States by Universal, 1968; Frederique, *Les Biches* (also known as *The Heterosexuals, The Does,* and *The Girlfriends*), Films la Boetie/Alexandra, 1968, released in the United States by Jack H. Harris, 1968; Helene Desvallees, *La Femme infidele* (also known as *The Unfaithful Wife*), Films la Boetie/Cinegai, 1969, released in the United States by Allied Artists, 1969.

Helene, *La Rupture* (also known as *Le Jour des parques* and *The Breakup*), Films la Boetie/Euro International/Cinevog, 1970; Anita Caldwell, *La Dame dans l'auto avec des lunettes et un fusil* (also known as *The Lady in the Car with Glasses and a Gun*), Columbia, 1970; Helene, *Le Boucher* (also known as *The Butcher*), Films la Boetie/Euro International, 1970, released in the United States by Cinerama, 1971; the Wife, *Aussi loin que l'amour* (also known as *As Far As Love Can Go*), Columbia, 1971; Helen, *Juste avant la nuit* (also known as *Just Before Nightfall*), Films la Boetie/Columbia/Cinegai, 1971, released in the United States by Libra, 1975; Madame Alice Senechal, *Le Charme discret de la bourgeoisie* (also known as *The Discreet Charm of the Bourgeoisie*), Twentieth Century-Fox, 1972; Marie-Anne, *Un meurtre est un meurtre* (also known as *A Murder Is a Murder*), Planfilm, 1972; Helene Vallee, *Sans mobile apparent* (also known as *Without Apparent Motive*), President/Cineteleuro, released in the United States by Twentieth Century-Fox, 1972; Lucienne, *Les Noces rouges* (also known as *Wedding in Blood* and *Red Wedding Night*), Films la Boetie/Canaria Films, 1973, released in the United States by CIC, 1974; Catherine, *Vincent, Francois, Paul . . . et les autres* (also known as *Vincent, Francois, Paul, and the Others*), Gaumont, 1974; Cecile, *Comment reussir dans la vie quand on est con et pleurnichard* (also known as *How to Make Good When One Is a Jerk and a Crybaby*), Gaumont, 1974; Claire, *Le Cri du couer* (also known as *Cry of the Heart*), Films la Boetie/CIC, 1974.

Anna Kemidon, *The Black Bird*, Columbia, 1975; Ilona Bergen, *Ten Little Indians* (also known as *And Then There Were None*), AVCO-Embassy, 1975; the Wife, *Folies bourgeoises* (also known as *Twist*), Parafrance/Union Generale Cinematographique, 1976; Anne, Contessa DiSanctis, *Des Teufels Advokat* (also known as *The Devil's Advocate*), Rank, 1977; Christiane, *Mort d'un pourri* (also known as *Death of a Corrupt Man*), Adel Productions/CIC/World Northal, 1977; Mrs. Lowrey, *Les Liens de sang* (also known as *Blood Relatives* and *Blood Ties*), Societe Nouvelle de Cinema, 1978; Shireen Firdausi, *Silver Bears*, Columbia, 1978; Germaine Noziere, *Violette Noziere* (also known as *Violette*), Gaumont/New Yorker, 1978; the Widow, *Eagle's Wing*, Rank, 1979; Genevieve, *Le Soleil en face* (also known as *Face to the Sun*), Union General Cinematographique, 1979; Helene Dupre-Granval, *Le Gagnant*, World Marketing, 1979.

Jeanne, *Le Coeur a l'envers* (also known as *My Heart Is Upside-Down*), Societe Nouvelle Prodis, 1980; Walloon, *The Big Red One*, United Artists, 1980; Huguette Cordier, *Coup de torchon* (also known as *Clean Slate*), Parafrance, 1981; Edith, *Paradise pour tous* (also known as *Paradise for All*), Films A2/Parafrance, 1982; Madame Falques, *Le Choc* (also known as *The Shock*), Union Generale Cinematographique, 1982; Minon Palazzi, *La Scarlatine* (also known as *Scarlet Fever*), Union Generale Cinematographique/CAPAC/Europe 1/Films A2, 1983, released in the United States by CAPAC, 1985; Blanche, *Bay Boy*, Orion, 1984, Isabelle's mother, *Les Voleurs de la nuit* (also known as *Thieves After Dark*), Parafrance, 1984; Matrimonia, *La Cage aux folles III: "Elles" se marient* (also known as *La Cage aux Folles III: The Wedding,*), Warner Brothers/Columbia/Tri-Star, 1985; Madame Boucher, *Les Plouffe*, International Cinema, 1985; Madame Cuno, *Poulet au vinaigre* (also known as *Cop au vin*), MK2/Virgin Vision, 1985; Janice, *La Nuit magique* (also known as *Night Magic*) RSL/Spectrafilm, 1985; Brigitte, *La Gitane*, AMLF/Pathe Cinema, 1986; Babette Hersant, *Babette's gastebud* (also known as *Babette's Feast*), Walter Manley, 1987; Bernadette, *Les Saisons du plaisir* (also known as *The Seasons of Pleasure*), Bac Film/Films du Volcan, 1987; Edna Chabert, *Corps z'a corps* (also known as *Body to Body* and *Corps a corps*), Exportation Francaise Cinematographique, 1987; Sister Ananda, *Manika* (also *Une vie plus tard, Manika: The Girl Who Lived Twice, Manika Manika*, and *Une Passerelle sur le Gange*), Films du Scorpio/Twentieth Century-Fox/Manley, 1988; Florence, *Sons*, Pacific, 1989; Madame Villegran, *La Messe en si mineur* (also known as *Mass in C Minor*), FCF, 1990.

Also appeared in *Modigliani of Montparnasse* (also known as *Montparnasse 19, Montparnasse*, and *The Lovers of Montparnasse*), Franco-London Films/Astra/Pallavicini, 1957, released in the United States by Continental Distributing, 1961; *Les Cousins* (also known as *The Cousins*), Ajym Films/Societe Francaise du Cinema, 1958, released in the United States by Films-Around-the-World, 1959; *Le Signe du lion*, 1959; *Saint-Tropez blues*, 1960; provided voice dubbing for *Presentation ou Charlotte et son steak*, 1961; *Les Godelureaux*, 1961; *Le Tigre aime la chair fraiche* (also known as *The Tiger Likes Fresh Blood*), 1964; *Les Durs a cuire*, 1964; *Marie-Chantal contre le Docteur Kha* (also known as *Marie Chantal against Dr. Kha*), Rome-Paris Films/Dia/Mega and Magreb Unifilm, 1965; *La Ligne de demarcation* (also known as *The Line of Demarcation*), Rome-Paris Films/Societe Nouvelle de Cinema, 1965; *La Peau de torpedo*, 1969; *Dead Pigeon on Beethoven Street*, Bavaria Atelier Gesellschaft, 1972; *Hay que matar a B.* (also known as *B. Must Die*), 1973; *Chi dice donna dice . . . donna*, 1975; *E la donna crea l'amour*, 1976; *The Prisoner of Zenda*, Universal, 1979; *Boulevard des assassins*, 1982; *Mortelle Randonnee* (also known as *Deadly Circuit*), GEF/CCFC/Ofer Omnifilms, 1982; *Suivez mon regard* (also known as *Follow My Gaze*), Union Generale Cinematographique, 1985; *L'Isola* (also known as *The Island*), Sacis, 1986; *Les Predateurs de la nuit* (also known as *Faceless, Angel of Death, Commando Mengele*, and *L'Ange de la mort*), New World/World Marketing, 1987.

PRINCIPAL TELEVISION APPEARANCES—Mini-Series: Cara, *Brideshead Revisited*, Granada, then PBS, 1982; Paula, *Mistral's Daughter*, CBS, 1984; also *Orient Express*, French television, 1979. Movies: Georgette, *Ernest Hemingway's "The Sun Also Rises,"* NBC, 1984; Gigi, *The Blood of Others*, HBO, 1984; Pauline Rocher, *Poor Little Rich Girl: The Barbara Hutton Story*, NBC, 1987; also *Champagne Charlie*, syndicated, 1989.

AWARDS: Best Actress Award from the Berlin Film Festival, 1968, for *Les Biches;* British Academy of Film and Television Arts Award, Best Actress, 1973, for *The Discreet Charm of the Bourgeoisie;* British Academy of Film and Television Award, Best Actress, 1975, for *Just Before Nightfall;* Cesar Award, Best Actress, 1978, for *Violette Noziere.*

ADDRESSES: OFFICE—95 bis rue de Chezy, 92200 Neuilly-sur-Seine, France.*

*   *   *

AULISI, Joseph G.

PERSONAL: Full name, Joseph Garibaldi Aulisi; married Marsha L. Eck (a scenic designer).

VOCATION· Costume designer.

CAREER: PRINCIPAL STAGE APPEARANCES—Townsperson, *The Devils*, Broadway Theatre, New York City, 1965.

PRINCIPAL STAGE WORK—Costume designer: *The Ox Cart* (also known as *La Carreta*), Greenwich Mews Theatre, New York City, 1966; *The Wicked Cooks*, Orpheum Theatre, New York City, 1967; *The Man in the Glass Booth*, Royale Theatre, New York City, 1968; *Saturday Night*, Sheridan Square Playhouse, New York City, 1968; *Seven Days of Mourning*, Circle in the Square, New York City, 1969; *The Transgressor Rides Again*, Martinique Theatre, New York City, 1969; *Someone's Comin' Hungry*, Pocket Theatre, New York City, 1969; "The Son Who Hunted Tigers in Jakarta," "Sunstroke," and "The Burial of Esposito," in *Passing Through from Exotic Places*, Sheridan Square Playhouse, 1969; *Pequod*, Mercury Theatre, New York City, 1969; *The American Hamburger League*, New Theatre, New York City, 1969.

Nobody Hears a Broken Drum, Fortune Theatre, New York City, 1970; *One Night Stands of a Noisy Passenger*, Actors' Playhouse, New York City, 1970; *A Dream Out of Time*, Promenade Theatre, New York City, 1970; *Happy Birthday, Wanda June* and *Whispers on the Wind*, both Theatre De Lys, New York City, 1970; *Steambath*, Truck and Warehouse Theatre, New York City, 1970; *The Birthday Party*, Repertory Theatre of Lincoln Center, Forum Theatre, New York City, 1971; *The Shrinking Bride*, Mercury Theatre, 1971; *F. Jasmine Addams* and *The Last Analysis*, both Circle in the Square, 1971; *Inner City*, Ethel Barrymore Theatre, New York City, 1971; *The Real Inspector Hound* and *After Magritte* (double-bill), Theatre Four, New York City, 1972; *All the Girls Came Out to Play*, Cort Theatre, New York City, 1972; *Tough to Get Help*, Royale Theatre, 1972; *Ring 'round the Bathtub*, Martin Beck Theatre, New York City, 1972; *An Evening with Richard Nixon and . . .*, Shubert Theatre, New York City, 1972; *The Kid*, American Place Theatre, New York City, 1972; *The Trials of Oz*, Anderson Theatre, New York City, 1972; *The Enemy Is Dead*, Bijou Theatre, New York

City, 1973; *Rachael Lily Rosenbloom and Don't You Forget It!*, Broadhurst Theatre, New York City, 1973; *Brainchild*, Forrest Theatre, Philadelphia, PA, 1974; *Thieves*, Broadhurst Theatre, 1974; *God's Favorite*, Eugene O'Neill Theatre, New York City, 1974.

Murder Among Friends, Biltmore Theatre, New York City, 1975; *Rockabye Hamlet*, Minskoff Theatre, New York City, 1976; *Unexpected Guests*, Little Theatre, New York City, 1977; *The November People*, Billy Rose Theatre, New York City, 1978; *Marilyn: An American Fable*, Minskoff Theatre, 1983; *Precious Sons*, Longacre Theatre, New York City, 1986; *The Architect and the Emperor of Assyria*, La Mama Experimental Theatre Club, New York City, 1986; *Broadway Bound*, Broadhurst Theatre, 1986, then Center Theatre Group, Ahmanson Theatre, Los Angeles, 1987; *Barbara Cook: A Concert for the Theatre*, Ambassador Theatre, New York City, 1987; *Rumors*, Ethel Barrymore Theatre, 1988; supervising costume designer, *Jerome Robbins' Broadway*, Imperial Theatre, New York City, 1989. Also *The Milliken Breakfast Show*, 1973; *Sunset*, Buffalo, NY, 1977; *All Dressed Up*, 1986; *A Month of Sundays*, 1987; *Run for Your Wife*, New York City, 1989; with Circle in the Square at Ford's Theatre, Washington, DC, 1969-70; and with the Whole Theatre Company, Montclair, NJ, 1982-83.

MAJOR TOURS—Costume designer, *Broadway Bound*, U.S. cities, 1987.

PRINCIPAL FILM WORK—Costume designer: *The Gang That Couldn't Shoot Straight*, Metro-Goldwyn-Mayer (MGM), 1971; *Jennifer on My Mind*, United Artists, 1971; *Shaft*, MGM, 1971; *Shaft's Big Score*, MGM, 1972; *The Legend of Nigger Charley*, Paramount, 1972; *The Seven Ups*, Twentieth Century-Fox, 1973; *Death Wish*, Paramount, 1974; *Three Days of the Condor*, Paramount, 1975; (with John Buckley) *Forever Young, Forever Free* (also known as *Lollipop, Lollipop*), Universal, 1976; *Dragonfly* (also known as *One Summer Love*), American International, 1976; *Somebody Killed Her Husband*, Columbia, 1978; *Firepower*, Associated Film Distribution, 1979; *Little Darlings*, Paramount, 1980; *The Night the Lights Went Out in Georgia*, AVCO-Embassy, 1981; *Man, Woman, and Child*, Paramount, 1983; *Easy Money*, Orion, 1983; *The Buddy System*, Twentieth Century-Fox, 1984; *The Pope of Greenwich Village*, United Artists, 1984; *Slayground*, Universal, 1984; *Compromising Positions*, Paramount, 1985; *Heaven Help Us* (also known as *Catholic Boys*), Tri-Star, 1985; *Brighton Beach Memoirs*, Universal, 1986; *Off Beat*, Buena Vista, 1986; *Ironweed*, Tri-Star, 1987; *The Secret of My Success*, Universal, 1987; *Last Rites*, Metro-Goldwyn-Mayer/United Artists, 1988.

PRINCIPAL TELEVISION WORK—All as costume designer. Series: *Beacon Hill*, CBS, 1975. Pilots: *Strike Force*, NBC, 1975; *We're Fighting Back*, CBS, 1981. Episodic: "The Displaced Person," *The American Short Story*, PBS, 1977; "Paul's Case," *American Short Story*, PBS, 1978. Movies: *F. Scott Fitzgerald and "The Last of the Belles,"* ABC, 1974; *The Deadliest Season*, CBS, 1977; *The Last Tenant*, ABC, 1978; *Hollow Image*, ABC, 1979; *Too Far to Go*, NBC, 1979; *Doctor Franken*, NBC, 1980; *King Crab*, ABC, 1980; *The Gentleman Bandit*, CBS, 1981; *Senior Trip!*, CBS, 1981; *Parole*, CBS, 1982; *At Mother's Request*, CBS, 1987; *Gore Vidal's Lincoln* (also known as *Lincoln*), NBC, 1988.

AWARDS: Drama Desk Award nomination, Best Costume Design, 1989, for *Rumors;* Emmy Award nomination for *Gore Vidal's Lincoln*.*

AUTEUIL, Daniel   1950-

PERSONAL: Born January 24, 1950, in Algeria.

VOCATION: Actor.

CAREER: PRINCIPAL STAGE APPEARANCES—*Early Morning*, Theatre Nationale Populaire, Paris, France, 1970; also appeared in *Coup de chapeau* (also known as *Tribute*), Paris, 1979; *Le Garcon d'appartement*, Paris, 1980; and in productions of *Godspell* and *The Madwoman of Chaillot*, both in Paris.

PRINCIPAL STAGE WORK—Director, *Le Garcon d'appartement*, Paris, 1980.

FILM DEBUT—*L'Agression*, 1974. PRINCIPAL FILM APPEARANCES—Remy, *La Nuit de Saint Germain des Pres*, Megalo, 1977; Dede, *Monsieur Papa*, Gaumont, 1977; Daniel, *L'Amour viole* (also known as *Violated Love*), Multicine/Marin Karmitz, 1978; Jean-Bernard, *Les Heros n'ont pas froid aux oreilles* (also known as *Heroes Are Not Wet Behind the Ears*), Atya, 1978; Alain, *Bete mais discipline* (also known as *Dumb But Disciplined*), AMLF/Roissy, 1979; Jean-Yves, *Les Hommes preferent les grosses* (also known as *Men Prefer Fat Girls*), GEF/CCFC, 1981; Lum, *Que les gros salaires levent le doigt!!!* (also known as *Will the High Salaried Workers Please Raise Their Hands!!!*), Sara Films/T Films, 1982; Bertrand, *L'Indic* (also known as *The Informer*), Exportation Francaise Cinematographique/GEF/CCFC, 1983; Berg, *Les Fauves* (also known as *The Beasts*), Gaumont/ACM, 1984; Marc, *L'Amour en douce* (also known as *Love on the Quiet*), Gaumont, 1984; Lucien Morland, *Palace*, Parafrance/Exportation Francaise Cinematographique, 1984, released in United States by Third Wave Rapid, 1985; Jeannot, *Petit con*, Gaumont, 1984, released in United States by Samuel Goldwyn, 1985.

Journalist, *Le Paltoquet* (also known as *The Nonentity*), AAA/Roissy/Artificial Eye, 1986; Ugolin Soubeyran ("Galignette"), *Jean de Florette*, Roissy/AMLF, 1986, released in United States by Orion Classics, 1987; Ugolin Soubeyran, *Manon des sources* (also known as *Manon of the Spring* and *Manon of the Springs*), Roissy/AMLF, released in United States by Orion Classics, 1987; Martial, *Quelques jours avec moi* (also known as *A Few Days with Me*), Union Generale Cinematographique/Galaxy International Releasing, 1988; Romuald, *Romuald et Juliette*, Union Generale Cinematographique/President, 1988. Also appeared in *Attention les yeux*, 1975; *A nous deux* (also known as *Us Two*), AMLF, 1979; *Clara et la chic types*, 1980; *Les Sous-Doues* (also known as *The Under-Gifted*), AMLF, 1980; *La Banquiere*, 1980; *Les Sous-doues en vacances*, 1981; *Pour 100 briques, t'as plus rien maintenant* (also known as *For a Hundred Grand, You Can't Get Anything Anymore*), Union Generale Cinematographique, 1982; *L'Arbalete* (also known as *The Cross-Bow*), ACM/CCFC, 1984; *Mama, There's a Man in Your Bed*, Miramax, 1990.

AWARDS: Gerard Philipe Prize, Best Young Actor of the Year, 1979, for *Coup de chapeau;* Cesar Award and Saint Michael Award, both 1987, for *Jean de Florette*.*

AVERY, Margaret

PERSONAL: Married Robert Gordon Hunt (a director; divorced); children: Aisha. EDUCATION—Graduated from the University of California, Berkeley.

VOCATION: Actress.

CAREER: PRINCIPAL STAGE APPEARANCES—*Revolution*, Center Theatre Group, New Theatre for Now, Los Angeles, 1972; *Does a Tiger Wear a Necktie?*, Zodiac Theatre, Los Angeles, 1972; also appeared in *Sistuhs*, Los Angeles Actors' Theatre, Los Angeles.

PRINCIPAL FILM APPEARANCES—Edwina, *Terror House* (also known as *Terror at Red Wolf Inn* and *The Folks at Red Wolf Inn*), Scope III/Far West, 1972; Mercer's mistress, *Cool Breeze*, Metro-Goldwyn-Mayer (MGM), 1972; call girl, *Magnum Force*, Warner Brothers, 1973; nurse, *The Psychopath* (also known as *An Eye for an Eye*), Brentwood, 1973; Sister Jennifer, *Hell Up in Harlem*, American International, 1973; Belle Joplin, *Scott Joplin*, Universal, 1977; Annie Mae, *Which Way Is Up?*, Universal, 1977; Toby Millman, *The Fish That Saved Pittsburgh*, United Artists, 1979; Shug Avery, *The Color Purple*, Warner Brothers, 1985; Hattie Cole, *Blueberry Hill*, Metro-Goldwyn-Mayer/United Artists, 1988; Bell, *Riverbend*, Intercontinental, 1989.

PRINCIPAL TELEVISION APPEARANCES—Episodic: Nurse Sawyer, *A.E.S. Hudson Street*, ABC, 1978; Dixie, *Murder, She Wrote*, CBS, 1985; CeeCee Richards, *Rags to Riches*, NBC, 1987; Sally Cordova, *Miami Vice*, NBC, 1987; Iris Marshall, *Crime Story*, NBC, 1988; Councilwoman Slane, *Knightwatch*, ABC, 1989; also "For Us, the Living," *American Playhouse*, PBS, 1983; *Sanford and Son*, NBC; *Harry O*, ABC. Movies: Irene, *Something Evil*, CBS, 1972; Alma Rae, *Louis Armstrong—Chicago Style*, ABC, 1976; Grace, *Single Women, Married Me*, CBS, 1989; also *The Lathe of Heaven*, PBS, 1980.

RELATED CAREER—Company member, Potters Field Theatre Company, New York City, 1979; also founder (with Robert Gordon Hunt), Zodiac Theatre, Los Angeles; performer in Las Vegas with the Nicholas Brothers; as a singer toured Japan and Indonesia.

NON-RELATED CAREER—Teacher and singing waitress.

AWARDS: Los Angeles Drama Critics' Circle Award, Outstanding Performance by an Actress, 1972, for *Does a Tiger Wear a Necktie?;* Academy Award nomination, Best Supporting Actress, 1985, for *The Color Purple;* Image Award from the NAACP for *Scott Joplin;* Best Actress nomination from the Academy of Science Fiction, Fantasy, and Horror Films for *The Lathe of Heaven*.

ADDRESSES: AGENT—Beakel and De Bord Agency, 10637 Burbank Boulevard, North Hollywood, CA 91601. PUBLICIST—Mickey Freeman, Freeman and Sutton Public Relations, 8961 Sunset Boulevard, Suite 2-A, Los Angeles, CA 90069.*

B

BACHMAN, Richard
See KING, Stephen

*   *   *

BADHAM, John   1939-

PERSONAL: Full name, John MacDonald Badham; born August 25, 1939, in Luton, England; immigrated to the United States in 1945; naturalized U.S. citizen, 1950; son of Henry Lee and Mary Iola (Hewitt) Badham; married Bonnie Sue Hughes, December 28, 1967 (divorced, 1979); married Jan Speck, 1983 (divorced, 1990); children: Kelly MacDonald (first marriage). EDUCATION—Yale University, B.A., 1961, M.F.A., 1963. MILITARY—U.S. Army, 1963-64.

JOHN BADHAM

VOCATION: Director and producer.

CAREER: PRINCIPAL FILM WORK—All as director, unless indicated: *Sunshine, Part II* (also known as *My Sweet Lady*), CIC, 1975; *The Bingo Long Traveling All-Stars and Motor Kings*, Universal, 1976; *Saturday Night Fever*, Paramount, 1977; *Dracula*, Universal, 1979; *Whose Life Is It Anyway?*, Metro-Goldwyn-Mayer/United Artists (MGM/UA), 1981; *Blue Thunder*, Columbia, 1983; *WarGames*, MGM/UA, 1983; *American Flyers*, Warner Brothers, 1985; *Short Circuit*, Tri-Star, 1986; (also executive producer) *Stakeout*, Buena Vista, 1987; executive producer, *Disorganized Crime*, Buena Vista, 1989; *Bird on a Wire*, Universal, 1990.

PRINCIPAL TELEVISION WORK—All as director, unless indicated. Pilots: Associate producer, *Night Gallery*, NBC, 1969; associate producer, *Dial Hot Line*, ABC, 1970; associate producer, *A Clear and Present Danger*, NBC, 1970. Episodic: *The Senator*, NBC, 1970; *Sarge*, NBC, 1971; "The Boy Who Predicted Earthquakes," "Camera Obscura," and "Green Fingers," all *Night Gallery*, NBC, 1971; "The Girl with the Hungry Eyes," "You Can Come Up Now, Mrs. Millikan," and "The Doll of Death," all *Night Gallery*, NBC, 1972; *The Sixth Sense*, ABC, 1972; *Sunshine*, NBC, 1975; also *The Bold Ones*, NBC; *Cannon*, CBS; *Owen Marshall: Counselor at Law*, ABC; *Cool Million*, NBC; *Streets of San Francisco*, ABC; *Police Story*, NBC; *The Doctors*, NBC. Movies: Associate producer, *The Neon Ceiling*, NBC, 1971; *The Impatient Heart*, NBC, 1971; *Isn't It Shocking?*, ABC, 1973; *The Godchild*, ABC, 1974; *The Gun*, ABC, 1974; *Reflections of Murder*, ABC, 1974; *The Law*, NBC, 1974; *The Keegans*, CBS, 1976.

RELATED CAREER—President, John Badham Films Inc.; board chairman, JMB Films Inc.; president, Great American Picture Show; guest lecturer, Yale University, Loyola Marymount College, University of Alabama, Amherst College, University of Southern California, and the University of California, Los Angeles.

NON-RELATED CAREER—Mailroom worker and tour guide, Universal Studios; board of directors, Indian Spring School.

AWARDS: Emmy Award nomination, 1971, for *The Senator;* Christopher Award, 1971, for *The Impatient Heart;* Southern California Motion Picture Council Award, 1974, for *The Gun;* Emmy Award nomination, 1974, and ARD reihe 'das Film Festival Award, 1975, both for *The Law;* Image Award nomination from the NAACP, 1976, for *The Bingo Long Traveling All-Stars and Motor Kings;* Grand Prize from the International Science Fiction and Fantasy Festival of Paris and Best Horror Film Award and George Pal Memorial Award from the Academy of Science Fiction, Fantasy, and Horror Films, all 1979, for *Dracula;* Best Director Award from the Academy of Science Fiction, Fantasy, and Horror Films, 1983, for *WarGames.*

MEMBER: Directors Guild, Academy of Motion Picture Arts and Sciences, American Filmex Society, American Film Institute.

ADDRESSES: OFFICE—Universal Studios, Universal City, CA 91608. AGENT—Lee Rosenberg, Triad Artists, 10100 Santa Monica Boulevard, 16th Floor, Los Angeles, CA 90067. PUBLICIST—Nancy Seltzer and Associates, 8845 Ashcroft Avenue, Los Angeles, CA 90048.

*   *   *

BAKER, Carroll   1931-

PERSONAL: Born May 28, 1931, in Johnstown, PA; daughter of William W. and Virginia (Duffy) Baker; married Louis Ritter (a furrier), 1952 (divorced, 1952); married Jack Garfein (a director and producer), April 5, 1955 (divorced, 1969); married Donald G. Burton (an actor), March 10, 1982; children: Herschel David, Blanche Joy (second marriage). EDUCATION—Attended St. Petersburg Junior College, 1952; studied acting with Lee Strasberg at the Actors' Studio, 1953.

VOCATION: Actress and writer.

CAREER: STAGE DEBUT—*Escapade on Broadway,* Actors' Studio, New York City, 1952. BROADWAY DEBUT—*All Summer Long,* Coronet Theatre, 1954. LONDON DEBUT—Sadie Thomp-

CARROLL BAKER

son, *Rain,* 1977. PRINCIPAL STAGE APPEARANCES—Virginia Karger, *Come on Strong,* Morosco Theatre, New York City, 1962; also appeared in *A Hatful of Rain,* Actors' Studio Workshop, New York City, 1953; *Arms and the Man,* Chicago, IL, 1958; *Anna Christie,* Los Angeles, 1966; *Gentleman Prefer Blondes,* Dallas, TX, 1967; *Bell, Book, and Candle,* Atlanta, GA, 1978; *13 Rue de l'Amour,* Jacksonville, FL, 1978; *Forty Carats,* Dallas, 1979; as Lucy, *Lucy Crown,* in the U.K., 1979; *Goodbye Charlie,* Chicago, 1979; *Motive,* in the U.K., 1980; *Little Hut,* in Canada, 1981; and in *27 Wagons Full of Cotton,* in the U.K.

FILM DEBUT—Clarice, *Easy to Love,* Metro-Goldwyn-Mayer, 1953. PRINCIPAL FILM APPEARANCES—Title role, *Baby Doll,* Warner Brothers, 1956; Luz Benedict II, *Giant,* Warner Brothers, 1956; Patricia Terrill, *The Big Country,* United Artists, 1958; Eleanor Brown, *But Not for Me,* Paramount, 1959; Teresa, *The Miracle,* Warner Brothers, 1959; Gwen Terasaki, *Bridge to the Sun,* Metro-Goldwyn-Mayer (MGM), 1961; Mary Ann, *Something Wild,* United Artists, 1961; Eve Prescott, *How the West Was Won,* Cinerama, 1962; Rina, *The Carpetbaggers,* Paramount, 1964; Deborah Wright, *Cheyenne Autumn,* Warner Brothers, 1964; Catherine, *Station Six-Sahara* (also known as *Endstation 13 Sahara*), Allied Artists, 1964; Veronica, *The Greatest Story Ever Told,* United Artists, 1965; Jean Harlow, *Harlow,* Paramount, 1965; Julie Anderson, *Mister Moses,* United Artists, 1965; Sylvia West, *Sylvia,* Paramount, 1965; as herself, *Jack of Diamonds,* MGM, 1967; Deborah, *The Sweet Body of Deborah* (also known as *Il dolce corpo di Deborah, L'Adorable corps de Deborah,* and *The Soft Body of Deborah*), Warner Brothers/Seven Arts, 1969; Kathryn West, *Orgasmo* (also known as *Paranoia*), Commonwealth United, 1969.

Maude, *Captain Apache,* Scotia International, 1971; title role, *Baba Yaga—Devil Witch,* Jumbo Cinematographica/CoFiCom, 1973; as herself, *James Dean--The First American Teenager* (documentary), Coral, 1975; Laura, *La moglie di mio padre* (also known as *Confessions of a Frustrated Housewife*), Mark Associates, 1976; Mrs. Aiken, *Andy Warhol's Bad,* New World, 1977; Helen Curtis, *The Watcher in the Woods,* Buena Vista, 1980; Linda Cooper, *The World Is Full of Married Men,* New Line, 1980; Brown, *Red Monarch,* Goldcrest Films and TV Ltd., 1983; Dorothy's mother, *Star 80,* Warner Brothers, 1983; Mama Freud, *The Secret Diary of Sigmund Freud,* Twentieth Century-Fox/TLC, 1983; Mrs. Dalton, *Native Son,* Cinecom, 1986; Annie Phelan, *Ironweed,* Tri-Star, 1987. Also appeared in *L'Harem* (also known as *Her Harem*), 1968; *Honeymoon,* 1968; *Paranoia* (also known as *Una droga llamada Helen* and *A Quiet Place to Kill*), 1969; *Cosi dolce . . . cosi perversa* (also known as *Perversion, So Sweet . . . So Perverse*), 1970; *The Fourth Mrs. Anderson,* 1971; *In fondo ala piscina* (also known as *At the Bottom of the Swimming Pool*), 1971; *Il diavolo a sette face* (also known as *The Devil Has Seven Faces*), Grand National, 1971; *Il coltello di ghiaccio* (also known as *The Icepick*), 1972; *Detras del silencio* (also known as *Behind the Silence*), 1972; *Il fiore dai petali d'acciaio* (also known as *The Flower with the Deadly Sting*), P.A.B., 1973; *Take This—My Body* (also known as *Il corpo* and *The Body*), Republic, 1974; *Lezioni private* (also known as *The Private Lesson*), 1975; *Der Koder* (also known as *L'Appat* and *The Lure*), 1975; *La moglie virgine* (also known as *Valentina—The Virgin Wife* and *The Virgin Wife*), Silverstein, 1976; *Ab Morgen Sind Wir Reich un Ehrlich* (also known as *I soliti ignoti colpiscona ancore* and *Rich and Respectable*), 1977; *Ciclon* (also known as *Cyclone*), 1977; *Gipsy Angel,* 1989.

PRINCIPAL TELEVISION APPEARANCES—Episodic: Sandy Marshall, "The Next Victim," *Thriller*, ABC, 1975; also *Danger*, CBS. Movies: Gerda Hoffman, *Hitler's SS: Portrait in Evil*, NBC, 1985; Maureen Leary, *On Fire*, ABC, 1987. Specials: *The Bob Hope Show*, NBC, 1966; First Would-Be Wife, *The Bob Hope Show*, NBC, 1968; Sadie Thompson, *Rain*, BBC, 1972; *Anne Murray's Ladies' Night*, syndicated, 1979; *Bob Hope's Women I Love—Beautiful But Funny*, NBC, 1982; *What Mad Pursuit*, BBC, 1985; *Sharing Time*, Thames Television, 1985; *Sex Symbols: Past, Present, and Future*, syndicated, 1987; *The Story of Hollywood* (also known as *Talking Pictures*), TNT, 1988.

RELATED CAREER—Actress in television commercials during the 1950s; television weather reporter, 1952; assistant to magician Burling Hull, "The Great Volta," in Florida; magician and dancer with the Kemp Time Vaudeville Circuit in North Carolina; nightclub dancer and performer, New York City.

WRITINGS: Baby Doll (autobiography), Arbor House, 1983; *To Africa with Love: A Romantic Adventure* (autobiography), D.I. Fine, 1986; *A Roman Tale* (fiction), D.I. Fine, 1986.

AWARDS: Academy Award nomination, Best Actress, 1956, for *Baby Doll;* Best Supporting Actress Award from the National League Women's Press Club, 1956; San Francisco Critics' Award, Best Actress, Foreign Press Club Award, Best Dramatic Actress, Hasty Pudding Club Woman of the Year, and Film Achievement Award from *Look* magazine, all 1957; honorary Kentucky Colonel, 1962.

MEMBER: British Academy of Film and Television Arts, Academy of Motion Picture Arts and Sciences, Authors' Guild, Cheyenne tribe (honorary member).

ADDRESSES: AGENT—International Creative Management, 8899 Beverly Boulevard, Los Angeles, CA 90048.

*   *   *

BAKER, Kathy   1950-
(Kathy Whitton Baker)

PERSONAL: Full name, Kathy Whitton Baker; born June 8, 1950, in Midland, TX; children: one son. EDUCATION—Studied French at the University of California, Berkeley; also attended California Insitute of the Arts.

VOCATION: Actress.

CAREER: OFF-BROADWAY DEBUT—(As Kathy Whitton Baker) May, *Fool for Love*, Circle Repertory Theatre, 1983. PRINCIPAL STAGE APPEARANCES—(As Kathy Whitton Baker) May, *Fool for Love*, Douglas Fairbanks Theatre, New York City, 1983; (as Kathy Whitton Baker) Abbie Putnam Cabot, *Desire Under the Elms*, Roundabout Stage One Theatre, New York City, 1984; (as Kathy Whitton Baker) Lemon, *Aunt Dan and Lemon*, New York Shakespeare Festival, Public Theatre, New York City, 1986. Also appeared as May, *Fool for Love*, Magic Theatre, San Francisco, CA; and in *Under Milk Wood*, California Institute of the Arts, Valencia, CA.

PRINCIPAL FILM APPEARANCES—Louise Shepard, *The Right Stuff*, Warner Brothers, 1983; Punchy, *Street Smart*, Cannon, 1987; Martha Sinclair, *Permanent Record*, Paramount, 1988; Maggie

Gresham, *A Killing Affair* (also known as *Monday, Tuesday, Wednesday*), Hemdale, 1988; Charlie Standers, *Clean and Sober*, Warner Brothers, 1988; Martha, *Jacknife*, Cineplex Odeon, 1989; Annie, *Dad*, Universal, 1989. Also appeared in *My Sister's Keeper*, Interpictures Releasing Company/Prism Entertainment, 1986.

PRINCIPAL TELEVISION APPEARANCES—Episodic: Ariel Serra, *Mariah*, ABC, 1987; Charlene Benton, *Amazing Stories*, NBC, 1987. Movies: Lucy Stavros, *Nobody's Child*, CBS, 1986; Marcie Guilford, *The Image*, HBO, 1990.

NON-RELATED CAREER—Studied at Cordon Bleu Cooking School, Paris, France; founded her own catering service in San Francisco, CA.

AWARDS: Obie Award from the *Village Voice*, 1983, and Theatre World Award, 1984, both for *Fool for Love*.

ADDRESSES: AGENT—Tracey Jacobs, International Creative Management, 8899 Beverly Boulevard, Los Angeles, CA 90048.*

*   *   *

BAKER, Kathy Whitton
See BAKER, Kathy

*   *   *

BAKER, Kenny   1934-

PERSONAL: Born August 24, 1934, in Birmingham, England.

VOCATION: Actor.

CAREER: PRINCIPAL FILM APPEARANCES—Artoo-Detoo (R2-D2), *Star Wars*, Twentieth Century-Fox, 1977; Bungo, *Wombling Free*, Satori, 1978; plumed dwarf, *The Elephant Man*, Paramount, 1980; Artoo-Detoo (R2-D2), *The Empire Strikes Back*, Twentieth Century-Fox, 1980; dwarf, *Flash Gordon*, Universal, 1980; Fidget, *Time Bandits*, AVCO-Embassy, 1981; Artoo-Detoo (R2-D2), *Return of the Jedi*, Twentieth Century-Fox, 1983; Parody Commendatore, *Amadeus*, Orion, 1984; goblin, *Labyrinth*, Tri-Star, 1986; Brighton busker, *Mona Lisa*, Island, 1986; elf, *Sleeping Beauty*, Cannon, 1987; music performer, *Perfect Image?* (short film), Sankofa, 1989.

PRINCIPAL TELEVISION APPEARANCES—Movies: *The Hunchback of Notre Dame*, CBS, 1982. Specials: Host, *The Making of "Star Wars" as Told by C-3PO and R2-D2*, ABC, 1977.*

*   *   *

BALL, Lucille   1911-1989

PERSONAL: Born August 6, 1911, in Celoron (near Jamestown), NY; daughter of Henry D. (a telephone lineman) and Desiree (a concert pianist; maiden name, Hunt) Ball; died of cardiac arrest, April 26, 1989, in Los Angeles, CA; married Desiderio Alberto (Desi) Arnaz (an actor, producer, and bandleader), November 30,

LUCILLE BALL

1940 (divorced, 1960); married Gary Morton (a comedian), November 19, 1961; children: Lucie Desiree, Desiderio Alberto IV (first marriage). EDUCATION—Attended the Chautauqua Institute of Music and the John Murray Anderson-Robert Milton Dramatic School; also studied acting with Lela Rogers, 1935.

VOCATION: Actress and producer.

CAREER: PRINCIPAL STAGE APPEARANCES—Wildcat Jackson, *Wildcat,* Alvin Theatre, New York City, 1960.

MAJOR TOURS—Title role, *Dream Girl,* U.S. cities, 1947-48; also toured with Desi Arnaz in a vaudeville music and comedy act, U.S. cities, 1950.

FILM DEBUT—Slave girl, *Roman Scandals,* United Artists, 1933. PRINCIPAL FILM APPEARANCES—Girl at beach, *Broadway thru a Keyhole,* Twentieth Century-Fox, 1933; girl, *Bulldog Drummond Strikes Back,* United Artists, 1934; beauty operator, *Fugitive Lady,* Columbia, 1934; girl, *Jealousy,* Columbia, 1934; 1934 Goldwyn girl, *Kid Millions,* United Artists, 1934; Peggy, *Men of the Night,* Columbia, 1934; chorus girl, *Nana* (also known as *Lady of the Boulevard*), United Artists, 1934; nurse, *Carnival,* Columbia, 1935; Gwendolyn Dilley, *I Dream Too Much,* RKO, 1935; college girl, *Old Man Rhythm,* RKO, 1935; flower clerk, *Top Hat,* RKO, 1935; girl, *The Whole Town's Talking* (also known as *Passport to France*), Columbia, 1935; mannequin, *Roberta,* RKO, 1935; Miss Kelly, *Bunker Bean* (also known as *His Majesty, Bunker Bean*), RKO, 1936; Lillian Temple, *Chatterbox,* RKO, 1936; Gloria, *The Farmer in the Dell,* RKO, 1936; Kitty Collins, *Follow the Fleet,*

RKO, 1936; girl, *Winterset,* RKO, 1936; Ann Howell, *Don't Tell the Wife,* RKO, 1937; Judy Canfield, *Stage Door,* RKO, 1937; Claire Williams, *That Girl from Paris,* RKO, 1937; title role, *Affairs of Annabel,* RKO, 1938; title role, *Annabel Takes a Tour,* RKO, 1938; Christine, *Room Service,* RKO, 1938; Carol Meely, *Go Chase Yourself,* RKO, 1938; Miriam, *Having Wonderful Time,* RKO, 1938; Nancy Fleming, *Next Time I Marry,* RKO, 1938; Salina, *Joy of Living,* RKO, 1938; Jean Russell, *Beauty for the Asking,* RKO, 1939; Peggy, *Five Came Back,* RKO, 1939; Lucy, *Panama Lady,* RKO, 1939; Sandra Sand, *That's Right—You're Wrong,* RKO, 1939; Paula Sanders, *Twelve Crowded Hours,* RKO, 1939.

Bubbles, *Dance, Girl, Dance,* RKO, 1940; Joan Grant, *The Marines Fly High,* RKO, 1940; Connie Casey, *Too Many Girls,* RKO, 1940; Clara Hinklin/Mercedes Vasquez, *You Can't Fool Your Wife,* RKO, 1940; Dot Duncan, *A Girl, a Guy, and a Gob* (also known as *The Navy Steps Out*), RKO, 1941; Julie Patterson, *Look Who's Laughing,* RKO, 1941; Gloria, *The Big Street,* RKO, 1942; Terry, *Seven Days' Leave,* RKO, 1942; Christine Larson, *Valley of the Sun,* RKO, 1942; May Daly/Madame du Barry, *Du Barry Was a Lady,* Metro-Goldwyn-Mayer (MGM), 1943; as herself, *Best Foot Forward,* MGM, 1943; guest star, *Thousands Cheer,* MGM, 1943; Julie Hampton, *Meet the People,* MGM, 1944; Kitty Trimble, *Without Love,* MGM, 1945; Kathleen, *The Dark Corner,* Twentieth Century-Fox, 1946; Ricki Woodner, *Two Smart People,* MGM, 1946; Gladys Benton, *Easy to Wed,* MGM, 1946; Kay Williams, *Lover Come Back* (also known as *When Lovers Meet*), Universal, 1946; Sandra Carpenter, *Lured* (also known as *Personal Column*), United Artists, 1947; Margaret Weldon, *Her Husband's Affairs,* Columbia, 1947; Gladys O'Neill, *Sorrowful Jones,* Paramount, 1949; Anne, *Easy Living,* RKO, 1949; Ellen Grant, *Miss Grant Takes Richmond* (also known as *Innocence Is Bliss*), Columbia, 1949.

Sally Elliot, *The Fuller Brush Girl* (also known as *The Affairs of Sally*), Columbia, 1950; Agatha Floud, *Fancy Pants,* Paramount, 1950; guest, *A Woman of Distinction,* Columbia, 1950; Narah, *The Magic Carpet,* Columbia, 1951; Tracy Collini, *The Long, Long Trailer,* MGM, 1954; Susan Vega, *Forever Darling,* MGM, 1956; Kitty Weaver, *The Facts of Life,* United Artists, 1960; Angela Ballantine, *Critic's Choice,* Warner Brothers, 1963; technical advisor, *A Guide for the Married Man,* Twentieth Century-Fox, 1967; Helen North, *Yours, Mine, and Ours,* United Artists, 1968; title role, *Mame,* Warner Brothers, 1974. Also appeared in *Blood Money,* Twentieth Century-Fox/United Artists, 1933; *The Bowery,* Twentieth Century-Fox, 1933; *Moulin Rouge,* Twentieth Century-Fox/United Artists, 1934; *Bottoms Up,* Twentieth Century-Fox, 1934; *Hold That Girl,* Twentieth Century-Fox, 1934; *The Affairs of Cellini,* Twentieth Century-Fox/United Artists, 1934; *Broadway Bill* (also known as *Strictly Confidential*), Columbia, 1934; *Three Little Pigskins* (short film), Columbia, 1934; *Perfectly Mismatched* (short film), Columbia, 1934; *The Three Musketeers,* RKO, 1935; *One Live Ghost* (short film), Columbia, 1936; *So and Sew* (short film), RKO, 1936; *Abbott and Costello in Hollywood,* MGM, 1945; "Meet the Ladies" in *Ziegfeld Follies,* MGM, 1945.

PRINCIPAL TELEVISION APPEARANCES—Series: Lucy Ricardo, *I Love Lucy,* CBS, 1951-57; Lucy Ricardo, "The Lucille Ball-Desi Arnaz Show," *The Westinghouse Desilu Playhouse,* CBS, 1958-60; Lucy Carmichael, *The Lucy Show,* CBS, 1962-68; Lucy Carter, *Here's Lucy,* CBS, 1968-74; Lucy Barker, *Life with Lucy,* ABC, 1986. Pilots: Sister Hitchcock, *The Music Mart,* NBC, 1980. Episodic: "K.O. Kitty," *The Westinghouse Desilu Playhouse,* CBS, 1958; host, "The Desilu Revue," *The Westinghouse Desilu*

Playhouse, CBS, 1959; *The Phil Silvers Show,* CBS, 1959; *The Ann Sothern Show,* CBS, 1959; *The Danny Thomas Show,* CBS, 1959; *The Greatest Show on Earth,* ABC, 1963; *Make Room for Granddaddy,* ABC, 1971; *The Practice,* NBC, 1976; *The Mary Tyler Moore Hour,* CBS, 1979; also *The Tonight Show,* NBC; *The David Frost Revue,* syndicated; *The Ed Wynn Show,* CBS; *Inside U.S.A. with Chevrolet,* CBS; *Lineup,* CBS; *December Bride,* CBS; *Those Whiting Girls,* CBS; *Whirlybird,* syndicated; *The Milton Berle Show,* ABC; *Body Language.* Movies: Florabelle, *Stone Pillow,* NBC, 1986.

Specials: *The Bob Hope Show,* NBC, 1950; *Show of the Year,* NBC, 1950; *The Bob Hope Show,* NBC, 1956; *The Milton Berle Special,* NBC, 1959; *Hedda Hopper's Hollywood,* NBC, 1960; *The Bob Hope Show,* NBC, 1961; *Twelve Star Salute,* ABC, 1961; *The Bob Hope Show,* NBC, 1962; *The Bob Hope Show,* NBC, 1963; *Have Girls—Will Travel,* NBC, 1964; *A Salute to Stan Laurel,* CBS, 1965; *The Wonderful World of Burlesque I,* NBC, 1965; *Lucy in London,* CBS, 1966; *The Bob Hope Show,* NBC, 1966; *Carol + 2,* CBS, 1967; Bonnie Barton, *The Lucille Ball Comedy Hour,* CBS, 1967; *The Jack Benny Special,* NBC, 1968; *Ann-Margret: From Hollywood with Love,* CBS, 1969; *The Dinah Shore Special—Like Hep,* CBS, 1969; *Jack Benny's Birthday Special,* NBC, 1969.

Jack Benny's 20th Anniversary TV Special, NBC, 1970; *The Bob Hope Show,* NBC, 1970; *Everything You Always Wanted to Know About Jack Benny and Were Afraid to Ask,* NBC, 1971; host, *Super Comedy Bowl I,* CBS, 1971; *Swing Out, Sweet Land,* NBC, 1971; *A Salute to Television's 25th Anniversary,* ABC, 1972; *Show Business Salute to Milton Berle,* NBC, 1973; *Steve and Eydie . . . On Stage,* NBC, 1973; *The Bob Hope Show,* NBC, 1973; Norma Michaels, *Happy Anniversary and Goodbye,* CBS, 1974; Lucy Collins, *A Lucille Ball Special Starring Lucille Ball and Dean Martin,* CBS, 1975; *A Lucille Ball Special Starring Lucille Ball and Jackie Gleason,* CBS, 1975; *Bob Hope's World of Comedy,* NBC, 1976; host, *CBS Salutes Lucy—The First 25 Years,* CBS, 1976; Catherine Curtis, *A Lucille Ball Special: What Now Catherine Curtis?,* CBS, 1976; *Gypsy in My Soul,* CBS, 1976; *The Lucille Ball Special,* CBS, 1977; ringmaster, *Circus of the Stars,* CBS, 1977; *The Barbara Walters Special,* ABC, 1977; *Bob Hope's All-Star Comedy Tribute to Vaudeville,* NBC, 1977; *Lucy Comes to Nashville,* CBS, 1978; *General Electric's All-Star Anniversary,* ABC, 1978; *CBS: On the Air,* CBS, 1978; *Gene Kelly . . . An American in Pasadena,* CBS, 1978; *The American Film Institute Salute to Henry Fonda,* CBS, 1978; *Dean Martin Celebrity Roast: Jimmy Stewart,* NBC, 1978; *TV: The Fabulous '50s,* NBC, 1978; *A Tribute to "Mr. Television" Milton Berle,* NBC, 1978; *Happy Birthday, Bob!,* NBC, 1978; *Cher and Other Fantasies,* NBC, 1979.

Lucy Moves to NBC, NBC, 1980; *Sinatra—The First 40 Years,* NBC, 1980; *Bob Hope's 30th Anniversary,* NBC, 1981; *Bob Hope's Road to Hollywood,* NBC, 1983; *Happy Birthday, Bob!,* NBC, 1983; *Bob Hope's Hilarious Unrehearsed Antics of the Stars,* NBC, 1984; *Bob Hope in Who Makes the World Laugh?, Part II,* NBC, 1984; *Bob Hope Buys NBC?,* NBC, 1985; *The Night of 100 Stars II,* ABC, 1985; *All Star Party for Clint Eastwood,* CBS, 1986; *The 38th Annual Emmy Awards,* NBC, 1986; *The American Film Institute Salute to Billy Wilder,* NBC, 1986; *The Kennedy Center Honors: A Celebration of the Performing Arts,* CBS, 1986; *ABC Fall Preview Special,* ABC, 1986; *Bob Hope's High Flying Birthday Extravaganza,* NBC, 1987; *A Beverly Hills Christmas,* syndicated, 1987; *The Kennedy Center Honors: A Celebration of the Performing Arts,* CBS, 1987; *The Television Academy Hall of Fame,* Fox, 1987; *America's Tribute to Bob Hope,* NBC, 1988; *Happy Birthday Bob—50 Stars Salute Your 50 Years with NBC,* NBC, 1988; *Hollywood: The Golden Years,* Arts and Entertainment, 1988; *61st Annual Academy Awards Presentation,* ABC, 1989.

PRINCIPAL TELEVISION WORK—Series: Producer (with Desi Arnaz), *I Love Lucy,* CBS, 1951-57; executive producer and producer (with Arnaz), *The Lucy Show,* CBS, 1962-68. Pilots: Producer, *The Music Mart,* NBC, 1980; executive producer and director, *Bungle Abbey,* NBC, 1981. Specials: Producer, "The Desilu Revue," *Desilu Playhouse,* CBS, 1959; executive producer, *A Lucille Ball Special Starring Lucille Ball and Dean Martin,* CBS, 1975; executive producer, *A Lucille Ball Special Starring Lucille Ball and Jackie Gleason,* CBS, 1975; executive producer, *A Lucille Ball Special: What Now Catherine Curtis?,* CBS, 1976; executive producer, *The Lucille Ball Special,* CBS, 1977; executive producer, *Lucy Moves to NBC,* NBC, 1980.

PRINCIPAL RADIO APPEARANCES-Series: Liz Cooper, *My Favorite Husband,* CBS, 1947-51; Lucy Ricardo, *I Love Lucy,* CBS, 1952; also a regular on Phil Baker's and Jack Haley's comedy-variety shows, CBS, late 1930s and early 1940s. Episodic: *Ford Theatre,* CBS, 1948; "A Foreign Affair," *Screen Directors' Playhouse,* NBC, 1950; *The Martin and Lewis Show,* NBC; *Screen Guild Theatre,* CBS; *Suspense,* CBS; *Leave It to the Girls,* Mutual.

RELATED CAREER—Entertainer, Stage Canteen, during World War II; president, Desilu Productions, Inc., 1962-67; president, Lucille Ball Productions, 1967-89.

NON-RELATED CAREER—Waitress and soda jerk; hat model for Hattie Carnegie's salon and Chesterfield cigarettes, both 1933.

AWARDS: Motion Picture Daily Awards, Most Promising Star, 1951, Best Performer, 1952, Best Comedy Team (with Desi Arnaz), 1954, and Best Comedienne, 1955 and 1957; Emmy Awards, Best Comedienne, 1952, and Best Actress in a Continuing Performance, 1955, both for *I Love Lucy;* Emmy Awards, Outstanding Continued Performance By an Actress in a Leading Role in a Comedy Series, 1967 and 1968, both for *The Lucy Show;* Gold Medal from the International Radio and Television Society, 1971; Golden Apple Award from the Hollywood Women's Press Club, Star of the Year, 1973; Ruby Award, 1974; Entertainer of the Year Award, 1975; Friar's Club Life Achievement Award, 1977; Cecil B. De Mille Award from the Hollywood Foreign Press Association, 1978; inducted into the Television Academy Hall of Fame, 1984; Lifetime Achievement Citation from the Kennedy Center for the Performing Arts, 1986; Hasty Pudding Woman of the Year, 1988; Television Academy Citation as "First Lady of Television"; Presidential Medal of Freedom (awarded posthumously), 1989.

OBITUARIES AND OTHER SOURCES: New York Times, April 27, 1989; *Variety,* May 3-9, 1989.*

*   *   *

BALLARD, Carroll   1937-

PERSONAL: Born October 14, 1937, in Los Angeles, CA. EDUCATION—Attended the University of California, Los Angeles.

VOCATION: Director.

CAREER: PRINCIPAL FILM WORK—Art director, *Three Nuts in Search of a Bolt,* Harlequin International, 1964; second camera operator, *Star Wars,* Twentieth Century-Fox, 1977; director, *The Black Stallion,* United Artists, 1979; director, *Never Cry Wolf,* Buena Vista, 1983; director, *The Nutcracker: The Motion Picture,* Atlantic Releasing, 1986.

ADDRESSES: OFFICE—c/o Lone Dog Ltd., P.O. Box 239, Calistoga, CA 94515.*

*   *   *

BARBERA, Joseph   1911-

PERSONAL: Surname is pronounced "Bar-*bear*-uh"; full name, Joseph Roland Barbera; born March 24, 1911, in New York, NY; son of Vincente and Frances Barbera; married Dorothy Earl (divorced, 1964); married Sheila Holden; children: Lynn Meredith, Jayne Earl, Neal Francis (first marriage). EDUCATION—Graduated from the American Institute of Banking; also attended Pratt Institute, the Art Students League, and New York University.

VOCATION: Animator, producer, director, and writer.

CAREER: Also see *WRITINGS* below. PRINCIPAL FILM WORK— All with William Hanna: Animation director, *Anchors Aweigh,* Metro-Goldwyn-Mayer (MGM), 1945; animation director, *Holiday in Mexico,* MGM, 1946; animation director, *Neptune's Daughter,* MGM, 1949; animation director (also with Fred Quimby), *Dangerous When Wet,* MGM, 1953; animation director (also with Quimby), *Invitation to the Dance,* MGM, 1956; producer and director, *Hey There, It's Yogi Bear* (animated), Columbia, 1964; producer and director, *The Man Called Flintstone* (also known as *That Man Flintstone;* animated), Columbia, 1966; producer and animation director, *Project X,* Paramount, 1968; producer, *Charlotte's Web* (animated), Paramount, 1973; producer, *C.H.O.M.P.S.,* AID, 1979; executive producer, *Liar's Moon,* Crown International, 1982; producer, *Heidi's Song* (animated), Paramount, 1982; producer, *GoBots: Battle of the Rock Lords* (animated), Atlantic Releasing, 1986. Also executive producer, *The Greatest Adventure: Stories from the Bible* (home video release), 1986; producer, *Forever Like a Rose.*

Director (with Hanna) of the following short animated films: *Gallopin' Gals, Swing Social, Puss Gets the Boot,* and *Romeo in Rhythm,* all MGM, 1940; *The Goose Goes South, Midnight Snack, The Night Before Christmas,* and *Officer Pooch,* all MGM, 1941; *The Bowling-Alley Cat, Dog Trouble, Fine Feathered Friend, Fraidy Cat,* and *Puss 'n' Toots,* all MGM, 1942; *Baby Puss, Yankee Doodle Mouse, Lonesome Mouse, Sufferin' Cats,* and *War Dogs,* all MGM, 1943; *The Bodyguard, The Million Dollar Cat, The Zoot Cat, Puttin' on the Dog,* and *Mouse Trouble* (also known as *Cat Nipped* and *Kitty Foiled*), all MGM, 1944; *The Mouse Comes to Dinner* (also known as *Mouse to Dinner*), *Flirty Birdy* (also known as *Love Boids*), *Mouse in Manhattan* (also known as *Manhattan Serenade*), *Quiet, Please!,* and *Tee for Two,* all MGM, 1945; *The Milky Waif, Solid Serenade, The Cat Concerto, Springtime for Thomas,* and *Trap Happy,* all MGM, 1946; *The Invisible Mouse, Part-Time Pal* (also known as *Fair Weathered Friend*), *Cat Fishin', A Mouse in the House, Dr. Jekyll and Mr. Mouse,* and *Salt Water Tabby,* all MGM, 1947; *Kitty Foiled, Old Rockin' Chair Tom, The Little Orphan, Professor Tom, Make Mine Freedom, Mouse Cleaning,* and *The Truce Hurts,* all MGM, 1948; *Polka Dot Puss, Hatch Up Your Troubles, The Cat and the Mermouse, Heavenly Puss, Jerry's Diary, Love That Pup,* and *Tennis Chumps,* all MGM, 1949.

Framed Cat, Tom and Jerry in the Hollywood Bowl, Jerry and the Lion (also known as *Hold That Lion*), *Little Quacker, Saturday Evening Puss* (also known as *Party Cat*), *Jerry's Cousin* (also known as *City Cousin* and *Muscles Mouse*), *Texas Tom, Cue Ball Cat,* and *Safety Second* (also known as *F'r Safety Sake*), all MGM, 1950; *Casanova Cat, Cat Napping, His Mouse Friday, Jerry and the Goldfish, The Two Mouseketeers, Nit-Witty Kitty, Sleepy-Time Tom,* and *Slicked-Up Pup,* all MGM, 1951; *The Flying Cat, Cruise Cat, The Dog House, The Duck Doctor, Fit to Be Tied, Johann Mouse, Little Runaway, Push-Button Kitty, Smitten Kitten,* and *Triplet Trouble,* all MGM, 1952; *The Missing Mouse, Jerry and Jumbo, That's My Pup, Just Ducky, Two Little Indians,* and *Life with Tom,* all MGM, 1953; *Pet Peeve, Little School Mouse, Baby Butch, Mice Follies, Neapolitan Mouse, Downhearted Duckling, Posse Cat, Hic-Cup Pup* (also known as *Tyke Takes a Nap*), *Puppy Tale,* and *Touche, Pussy Cat,* all MGM, 1954; *Good Will to Men, Pup on a Picnic, Designs on Jerry, Southbound Duckling, Pecos Pest, Smarty Cat, That's My Mommie, Mouse for Sale,* and *Tom and Cherie,* all MGM, 1955; *Barbeque Brawl, The Flying Sorceress, Blue Cat Blues, Give and Take, Busy Buddies, The Egg and Jerry, Scat Cats, Down Beat Bear,* and *Muscle Beach Tom,* all MGM, 1956; *One Droopy Knight, Feedin' the Kiddie, Mucho Mouse, Timid Tabby, Tom's Photo Finish,* and *Tops with Pops,* all MGM, 1957; *Happy Go Ducky* (also known as *One Quack Mind*), *Royal Cat Nap, Robin Hoodwinked, Tot Watchers, The Vanishing Duck, Little Bo Bopped,* and *Wolf Hounded,* all MGM, 1958.

Creepy Time Pal, Tale of a Wolf, The Do-Good Wolf, Life with Loopy, Snoopy Loopy, No Biz Like Shoe Biz, and *Here Kiddie, Kiddie,* all Columbia, 1960; *Count Down Clown, Happy Go Loopy, Two-Faced Wolf, Catch Meow, Child Sock-Cology, Fee Fie Foes, Kooky Loopy, Loopy's Hare-Do, This Is My Ducky Day,* and *Zoo Is Company,* all Columbia, 1961; *Bungle Uncle, Bearly Able, Beef-for and After, Bunnies Abundant, Chicken Fracas-see, Common Scents, Rancid Ransom, Slippery Slippers,* and *Swash Buckled,* all Columbia, 1962; *Just a Wolf at Heart, Chicken-Hearted Wolf, Whatcha Watchin, A Fallible Fable, Drum-Sticked, Bear Up!, The Crook That Cried Wolf, Habit Rabbit, Not in Nottingham, Sheep Stealers Anonymous,* and *Wolf in Sheepdog's Clothing,* all Columbia, 1963; *Elephantastic, Bear Hug, Bear Knuckles, Trouble Bruin, Raggedy Rug,* and *Habit Troubles,* 1964; *Big Mouse-Take, Pork Chop Phooey, Crow's Fete,* and *Horse Shoo,* all Columbia, 1965.

PRINCIPAL TELEVISION APPEARANCES—Specials: *The 40th Annual Emmy Awards,* Fox, 1988; *Hanna-Barbera's 50th: A Yabba Dabba Doo Celebration,* TNT, 1989.

PRINCIPAL TELEVISION WORK—All as executive producer, unless indicated, with William Hanna. Series (all animated, unless indicated): Producer (also with Bob Cottle), *The Ruff and Reddy Show,* NBC, 1957-64; producer and director, *The Huckleberry Hound Show* (also featuring *Pixie and Dixie, Hokey Wolf,* and *Yogi Bear*), syndicated, 1958-62; producer and director, *Yogi Bear* (also featuring *Snagglepuss* and *Yakky Doodle Duck*), syndicated, 1958-62; producer, *The Quick Draw McGraw Show* (also featuring *Snooper and Blabber* and *Augie Doggie and Doggie Daddy*), syndicated, 1959-62; producer and director, *The Flintstones,* ABC, 1960-66; producer and director, *Top Cat,* ABC, 1961-62; producer and director, *Lippy the Lion,* syndicated, 1962; producer and director, *Touche Turtle,* syndicated, 1962; producer and director,

Wally Gator, syndicated, 1962; (also director) *The Jetsons*, ABC, 1962-63; (also director) *The Adventures of Jonny Quest* (also known as *Jonny Quest*), ABC, 1964-65; producer and director, *The Magilla Gorilla Show* (also featuring *Ricochet Rabbit* and *Punkin Puss and Mush Mouse*), syndicated, 1964-67; producer and director, *The Peter Potamus Show* (also featuring *Yippie, Yappie, and Yahooey* and *Breezly and Sneezly*), syndicated, 1964-67.

Series (continued; all animated, unless indicated): Producer and director, *The Atom Ant/Secret Squirrel Show* (also featuring *The Hillbilly Bears*, *Squiddly Diddly*, and *Precious the Dog*), NBC, 1965-68; producer, *Sinbad, Jr., the Sailor* (also known as *The Adventures of Sinbad, Jr.*), syndicated, 1966; producer and director, *The Abbott and Costello Cartoon Show*, syndicated, 1966; producer (also with Larry Harmon), *Laurel and Hardy*, syndicated, 1966-67; producer and director, *Space Kiddettes*, NBC, 1966-67; producer and director, *Space Ghost* (also featuring *Dino Boy*), CBS, 1966-68; producer and director, *Frankenstein, Jr. and the Impossibles*, CBS, 1966-68; producer, *Sampson and Goliath*, NBC, 1967-68; producer and director, *Birdman and the Galaxy Trio*, NBC, 1967-68; producer and director, *The Herculoids*, CBS, 1967-69; producer, *Moby Dick and the Mighty Mightor*, CBS, 1967-69; producer and director, *Shazzan!*, CBS, 1967-69; (also director) *The Fantastic Four*, ABC, 1967-70; *Here Come the Stars* (live-action), syndicated, 1968; producer, *The New Adventures of Huck Finn* (live-action and animated), NBC, 1968-69; producer and director, *The Wacky Races*, CBS, 1968-70; producer, *The Banana Splits Adventure Hour* (live-action and animated; also featuring *The Micro Venture, Danger Island, The Three Musketeers, The Hillbilly Bears*, and *The Arabian Knights*), NBC, 1968-70; (also director) *The Adventures of Gulliver* (also known as *The Adventures of Young Gulliver*), ABC, 1969-70; producer and director, *The Perils of Penelope Pitstop*, CBS, 1969-71; (also director) *The Cattanooga Cats* (also featuring *It's the Wolf, Around the World in 79 Days*, and *Auto Cat and Motor Mouse*), ABC, 1969-71; (also director) *Dastardly and Muttley in Their Flying Machines*, CBS, 1969-71; (also director with Charles A. Nichols) *Scooby-Doo, Where Are You?*, CBS, 1969-74.

Series (continued; all animated, unless indicated): (Also director) *Where's Huddles?*, CBS, 1970-71; (also director) *The Harlem Globetrotters*, CBS, 1970-73; (also director) *Josie and the Pussycats*, CBS, 1970-76; *Pebbles and Bamm Bamm*, CBS, 1971-72; (also director) *Help! It's the Hair Bear Bunch*, CBS, 1971-72; (also director) *The Funky Phantom*, ABC, 1971-72; producer and director, *Wait til Your Father Gets Home*, syndicated, 1972; *Sealab 2020*, NBC, 1972-73; *The Roman Holidays*, NBC, 1972-73; (also director) *The Amazing Chan and the Chan Clan*, CBS, 1972-74; (also director) *The Flintstone Comedy Hour*, CBS, 1972-74; (also director with Nichols) *Josie and the Pussycats in Outer Space*, CBS, 1972-74; *The New Scooby-Doo Movies*, CBS, 1972-74; *Speed Buggy*, CBS, 1973-74; (also director) *Butch Cassidy and the Sundance Kids*, NBC, 1973-74; producer, *Peter Puck*, NBC, 1973-74; *Inch High, Private Eye*, NBC, 1973-74; *Yogi's Gang*, ABC, 1973-75; *Jeannie*, CBS, 1973-75; *Goober and the Ghost Chasers*, ABC, 1973-75; *The Addams Family*, NBC, 1973-75; *Super Friends*, ABC, 1973-83; *Wheelie and the Chopper Bunch*, NBC, 1974-75; *The Partridge Family: 2200 A.D.*, CBS, 1974-75; *Korg: 70,000 B.C.* (live-action), ABC, 1974-75; *Hong Kong Phooey*, ABC, 1974-76; *These Are the Days*, ABC, 1974-76; *Devlin*, ABC, 1974-76; *Valley of the Dinosaurs*, CBS, 1974-76.

Series (continued; all animated, unless indicated): (Also director) *The Scooby-Doo/Dynomutt Hour*, ABC, 1976-77; *Mumbly*, ABC, 1976-77; *The Clue Club*, CBS, 1976-77; *Jabberjaw*, ABC, 1976-

78; *The Skatebirds* (also featuring *The Robonic Stooges, Wonder Wheels, Woofer and Wimper*, and *Mystery Island*), CBS, 1977-78; *The Tom and Jerry/Great Grape Ape Show*, ABC, 1977-78; (also director) *The New Super Friends Hour*, ABC, 1977-78; *Scooby's All-Star Laff-a-Lympics*, ABC, 1977-78; *Fred Flintstone and Friends*, syndicated, 1977-78; *The C.B. Bears* (also featuring *Blast Off Buzzard and Crazy Legs, Posse Impossible, Undercover Elephant, Shake, Rattle, and Roll*, and *Heyyyyyy, It's the King*), CBS, 1977-78; *The Hanna-Barbera Happiness Hour* (live-action), NBC, 1978; *Yogi's Space Race*, NBC, 1978-79; *The Galaxy Goofups*, NBC, 1978-79; *Scooby's All Stars*, ABC, 1978-79; *Challenge of the Super Friends*, ABC, 1978-79; (also director) *The World's Greatest Super Heroes*, ABC, 1978-80; *Godzilla* (also known as *Godzilla and the Super 90* and *The Godzilla Power Hour*; also featuring *Jana of the Jungle*), NBC, 1978-81; producer, *The Three Robonic Stooges*, CBS, 1978-81; *The All-New Popeye Hour*, CBS, 1978-81; *The New Shmoo*, NBC, 1979; *Fred and Barney Meet the Thing*, NBC, 1979; *Buford and the Ghost*, NBC, 1979; *Scooby-Doo and Scrappy-Doo*, ABC, 1979; *The Super Globetrotters*, NBC, 1979; *The New Fred and Barney Show*, NBC, 1979; *Casper and the Angels*, NBC, 1979-80; *Fred and Barney Meet the Shmoo*, NBC, 1979-80.

Series (continued; all animated, unless indicated): *Captain Caveman and the Teen Angels*, ABC, 1980; *Flintstone Family Adventures* (also featuring *The Frankenstones* and *Captain Caveman*), NBC, 1980-81; *The Scooby-Doo and Scrappy-Doo Show*, ABC, 1980-82; *The Drak Pack*, CBS, 1980-82; *Fonz and the Happy Days Gang*, ABC, 1980-82; *The Richie Rich Show*, ABC, 1980-82; *The Flintstones*, NBC, 1981; *Space Stars* (featuring *Space Ghost, Teen Force, The Herculoids*, and *Astro and the Space Mutts*), NBC, 1981-82; *The Kwicky Koala Show* (also featuring *Dirty Dawg, Crazy Claws*, and *The Bungle Brothers*), CBS, 1981-82; *Trollkins*, CBS, 1981-82; *Private Olive Oyl*, CBS, 1981-82; *Laverne and Shirley in the Army*, ABC, 1981-82; *The Flintstone Funnies*, NBC, 1981-84; *The Smurfs*, NBC, 1981-88; *Laverne and Shirley with the Fonz*, ABC, 1982-83; (also director) *Jokebook*, NBC, 1982; *Mork and Mindy*, ABC, 1982-83; *Scooby, Scrappy, and Yabba Doo*, ABC, 1982-83; *The Gary Coleman Show*, NBC, 1982-83; *The Little Rascals*, ABC, 1982-84; *The Shirt Tales*, NBC, 1982-84; *Pac-Man*, ABC, 1983-84; *The Biskitts*, CBS, 1983-84; (with Margaret Leosch) *Benji, Zax, and the Alien Prince* (live-action), CBS, 1983-84; *Monchhichis*, CBS, 1983-84; *The Dukes*, CBS, 1983-84; *Scooby and Scrappy-Doo*, ABC, 1983-84; *The Pink Panther and Sons*, NBC, 1984-85; *The New Scooby-Doo Mysteries*, ABC, 1984-85; *Super Friends: The Legendary Super Powers Show*, ABC, 1984-85; (also with Freddy Monnickendam) *Snorks*, NBC, 1984-86; *Challenge of the GoBots*, syndicated, 1984-86; *Scooby's Mystery Funhouse*, ABC, 1985; *The Thirteen Ghosts of Scooby-Doo*, ABC, 1985-86; *The Super Powers Team: Galactic Guardians*, ABC, 1985-86; *The New Jetsons*, syndicated, 1985-88; *The Funtastic World of Hanna-Barbera* (featuring *Yogi's Treasure Hunt, Paw Paws, Goltar and the Golden Lance*, and *The New Adventures of Jonny Quest*), syndicated, 1986-87; *The Flintstone Kids*, ABC, 1986-87; *Pound Puppies*, ABC, 1986-87; *Wildfire*, CBS, 1986-87; *Foofur*, NBC, 1986-87; *The Funtastic World of Hanna-Barbera* (featuring *Yogi's Treasure Hunt, Sky Commanders, The New Adventures of the Snorks*, and *The New Adventures of Jonny Quest*), syndicated, 1987-88; *Popeye and Son*, CBS, 1987-88; (also with Jay Wolpert) *Skedaddle* (live-action), syndicated, 1988—; *The Completely Mental Misadventures of Ed Grimley*, NBC, 1988-89.

Pilots (all live-action, unless indicated): *The Beach Girls*, syndicated, 1977; *The Funny World of Fred and Bunni* (live-action and animated), CBS, 1978; *Sergeant T.K. Yu*, NBC, 1979; (with Arthur Weinthel and W.C. Elliott) *The B.B. Beegle Show*, syndicated, 1980. Movies (all live-action, unless indicated): *Hardcase*, ABC, 1972; *Shootout in a One-Dog Town*, ABC, 1974; *The Gathering*, ABC, 1977; *The Beasts Are on the Streets*, NBC, 1978; (with William M. Aucoin) *KISS Meets the Phantom of the Park*, NBC, 1978; *The Gathering, Part II*, NBC, 1979; (with Barry Krost) *Belle Starr*, CBS, 1980; *Lucky Luke* (animated), syndicated, 1987; *Stone Fox*, NBC, 1987.

Specials (all animated, unless indicated): *Alice in Wonderland*, ABC, 1966; *Jack and the Beanstalk* (live-action and animated), NBC, 1967; *The Thanksgiving That Almost Wasn't*, syndicated, 1971; *A Christmas Story*, syndicated, 1971; producer, *Last of the Curlews*, ABC, 1972; *Yogi's Ark Lark*, ABC, 1972; *Robin Hoodnik*, ABC, 1972; *Oliver and the Artful Dodger*, ABC, 1972; *Here Come the Clowns*, ABC, 1972; *The Banana Splits in Hocus Pocus Park*, ABC, 1972; *Gidget Makes the Wrong Connection*, ABC, 1973; *Lost in Space*, ABC, 1973; *20,000 Leagues Under the Sea*, syndicated, 1973; (also director) *The Three Musketeers*, syndicated, 1973; *The Count of Monte Cristo*, syndicated, 1973; *The Crazy Comedy Concert* (live-action and animated), ABC, 1974; *The Runaways* (live-action), ABC, 1974; *Cyrano de Bergerac*, ABC, 1974; *The Last of the Mohicans*, syndicated, 1975; *Phantom Rebel* (live-action), NBC, 1976; "Davy Crockett on the Mississippi" (animated), *Famous Classic Tales*, CBS, 1976; *Taggart's Treasure* (live-action), ABC, 1976; *Five Weeks in a Balloon*, CBS, 1977; *Yabba Dabba Doo! The Happy World of Hanna-Barbera* (live-action and animated), CBS, 1977; *Energy: A National Issue*, 1977; *A Flintstones' Christmas*, NBC, 1977; *The Flintstones' Little Big League*, NBC, 1978; *Hanna-Barbera's All Star Comedy Ice Revue* (live-action and animated), CBS, 1978; "It Isn't Easy Being a Teenage Millionaire" (live-action), *ABC Afterschool Specials*, ABC, 1978; *Yabba Dabba Doo II*, CBS, 1978; *Black Beauty*, CBS, 1978; *Super Heroes Roast*, NBC, 1979; *Challenge of the Super Heroes*, NBC, 1979; *America vs. the World* (live-action), NBC, 1979; *Scooby Goes Hollywood*, ABC, 1979; *Casper's First Christmas*, NBC, 1979; *Popeye Valentine Special: The Sweethearts at Sea*, CBS, 1979; *Gulliver's Travels*, CBS, 1979; *Casper's Halloween Special: He Ain't Scary, He's Our Brother*, NBC, 1979.

Specials (continued; all animated, unless indicated): *The Gymnast* (live-action), ABC, 1980; *The Hanna-Barbera Arena Show* (live-action), NBC, 1981; *Jogging Fever*, NBC, 1981; *The Great Gilly Hopkins* (live-action), CBS, 1981; *Daniel Boone*, CBS, 1981; *Yabba Dabba Doo* (live-action and animated), CBS, 1982; *The Smurfs' Springtime Special*, NBC, 1982; *The Smurfs' Christmas Special*, NBC, 1982; *Christmas Comes to Pac-Land*, ABC, 1982; *Yogi Bear's All-Star Christmas Caper*, CBS, 1982; *My Smurfy Valentine*, NBC, 1983; *The Secret World of Og*, ABC, 1983; *The Amazing Bunjee Venture*, CBS, 1984; *The Smurfic Games*, NBC, 1984; *Smurfily-Ever After*, NBC, 1985; *Star Fairies*, syndicated, 1985; *The Flintstones' 25th Anniversary Celebration* (live-action and animated), CBS, 1986; *Ultraman! The Adventure Begins*, syndicated, 1987; *Yogi and the Magical Flight of the Spruce Goose*, syndicated, 1987; *Scooby and the Reluctant Werewolf*, syndicated, 1987; *The Jetsons Meet the Flintstones*, syndicated, 1987; *Top Cat and the Beverly Hills Cats*, syndicated, 1987; *Rockin' with Judy Jetson* (also known as *Judy Jetson and the Rockers*), syndicated, 1987; *Yogi's Great Escape*, syndicated, 1987; *Scooby-Doo and the Ghoul School*, syndicated, 1987; *Tis the Season to Be Smurfy*, NBC, 1987; *The Good, the Bad, and the Huckleberry Hound*, syndicated, 1987; *Scooby-Doo Meets the Boo Brothers*, syndicated, 1987; *Yogi and the Invasion of the Space Bears*, syndicated, 1987; *The Flintstone Kids "Just Say No" Special*, ABC, 1988;

Hanna-Barbera's 50th: A Yabba Dabba Doo Celebration (live-action and animated), TNT, 1989; also producer, *Rock Odyssey*.

RELATED CAREER—Storyboard writer and sketch artist, Van Beuren Studio, New York City, 1932-34; animator, Terrytoons, New Rochelle, NY, 1934-37; animator, director, and producer, Metro-Goldwyn-Mayer (MGM), Hollywood, CA, 1937-57; head of animation department (with William Hanna), MGM, 1955-57; founder (with Hanna) and president, Hanna-Barbera Productions, Hollywood, 1957—; also president of the board of directors, Huntington Hartford Theatre, Los Angeles; president, James A. Doolittle Theatre, Hollywood; past president, Greek Theatre Association, Los Angeles; president, Southern California Theatre Association.

NON-RELATED CAREER—Banking clerk, Irving Trust Company, New York City, 1930-32; also co-chair, Los Angeles Earthquake Preparedness Committee; board member, Greater Los Angeles Visitors and Convention Bureau; board member, St. Joseph's Medical Center; board member, Children's Village; honorary board member, Wildlife Waystation.

WRITINGS: FILM—(With William Hanna and Warren Foster) *Hey There, It's Yogi Bear* (animated), Columbia, 1964; (with Dick Robbins and Duane Poole) *C.H.O.M.P.S.*, AID, 1979; (with Robert Taylor and Jameson Brewer) *Heidi's Song* (animated), Paramount, 1982. TELEVISION—Series: (With Hanna and Douglas Widley) *The Adventures of Jonny Quest* (also known as *Jonny Quest;* animated), ABC, 1964-65.

AWARDS: All with William Hanna. Academy Award nomination, Best Animated Short Subject, 1940, for *Puss Gets the Boot;* Academy Award nomination, Best Animated Short Subject, 1941, for *The Night Before Christmas;* Academy Award, Best Animated Short Subject, 1943, for *Yankee Doodle Mouse;* Academy Award, Best Animated Short Subject, 1944, for *Mouse Trouble;* Academy Award, Best Animated Short Subject, 1945, for *Quiet, Please!;* Academy Award, Best Animated Short Subject, 1946, for *The Cat Concerto;* Academy Award nomination, Best Animated Short Subject, 1947, for *Dr. Jekyll and Mr. Mouse;* Academy Award, Best Animated Short Subject, 1948, for *The Little Orphan;* Academy Award nomination, Best Animated Short Subject, 1949, for *Hatch Up Your Troubles;* Academy Award nomination, Best Short Subject, 1950, for *Jerry's Cousin;* Academy Award, Best Animated Short Subject, 1951, for *The Two Mouseketeers;* Academy Award, Best Animated Short Subject, 1952, for *Johann Mouse;* Academy Award nomination, Best Animated Short Subject, 1954, for *Touche, Pussy Cat;* Academy Award nomination, Best Animated Short Subject, 1955, for *Good Will to Men;* Academy Award nomination, Best Animated Short Subject, 1957, for *One Droopy Knight.*

Emmy Award, Outstanding Achievement in the Field of Children's Programming, 1960, for *The Huckleberry Hound Show;* Golden Globe, Outstanding Achievement in International Television Cartoons, 1965, for *The Flintstones;* Emmy Award, Outstanding Children's Special, 1966, for *Jack and the Beanstalk;* Emmy Award, Outstanding Achievement in Children's Programming (Informational/Factual), 1973, for *The Last of the Curlews;* Emmy Award, Outstanding Informational Children's Series, 1974, for *The Runaways;* Annie Award, 1977, for *Charlotte's Web;* Christopher Award and Emmy Award, Outstanding Special—Drama or Comedy, both 1978, for *The Gathering;* Emmy Award, Outstanding Children's Entertainment Series, 1982, for *The Smurfs;* Golden Reel Award, Animation Sound Editing, and Bronze Award, Best

Children's Special, both from the International Film and Television Festival of New York, 1982, for *The Smurfs' Springtime Special;* Emmy Award, Outstanding Children's Entertainment Series, 1983, for *The Smurfs;* Bronze Award, Best Children's Special, 1984, for *The Smurfic Games;* Men of the Year Award from the National Center for Hyperactive Children, 1986; Gold Angel Award from Religion in Media, 1986, for Excellence in Media; Distinguished Service Award from the National Religious Broadcasters and Award of Excellence from the Film Advisory Board, both 1987, for *The Greatest Adventure: Stories from the Bible;* Humanitas Prize, 1987, for "Lure of the Orb" episode of *The Smurfs;* Governor's Award from the National Academy of Television Arts and Sciences, 1988.

MEMBER: National Academy of Television Arts and Sciences, Academy of Motion Picture Arts and Sciences, Cousteau Society.

ADDRESSES: OFFICE—Hanna-Barbera Productions, 3400 W. Cahuenga Boulevard, Hollywood, CA 90068.*

*   *   *

BARNETT, Ken
   See FRANCIS, Freddie

*   *   *

BARR, Roseanne   1952-

PERSONAL: Born November 3, 1952, in Salt Lake City, UT; daughter of Jerry (in sales) and Helen Barr; married Bill Pentland, 1974 (divorced, 1989); married Tom Arnold, January 20, 1990; children: Jessica, Jennifer, Jake (first marriage). RELIGION—Jewish.

VOCATION: Comedienne, actress, and writer.

CAREER: Also see *WRITINGS* below. FILM DEBUT—Ruth Patchett, *She-Devil,* Orion, 1989.

PRINCIPAL TELEVISION APPEARANCES—Series: Roseanne Conner, *Roseanne,* ABC, 1988—. Specials: *Fast Copy,* NBC, 1985; *Funny,* ABC, 1986; *Rodney Dangerfield—It's Not Easy Bein' Me,* HBO, 1986; *The Tonight Show Starring Johnny Carson 24th Anniversary Special,* NBC, 1986; *On Location: The Roseanne Barr Show,* HBO, 1987; *Lifetime Salutes Mom,* Lifetime, 1987; *The American Comedy Awards,* ABC, 1987 and 1988; *The Comedy Store 15th Year Class Reunion,* NBC, 1988; *Like Mother, Like Daughter,* Lifetime, 1988; *The Barbara Walters Special,* ABC, 1989.

PRINCIPAL TELEVISION WORK—Creative consultant, *Roseanne,* ABC, 1988—.

RELATED CAREER—As a comedienne, has appeared in comedy clubs and concert halls throughout the United States.

NON-RELATED CAREER—Window dresser and waitress.

WRITINGS: TELEVISION—Series: *Roseanne,* ABC, 1988—. Specials: *On Location: The Roseanne Barr Show,* HBO, 1987. OTHER—*Roseanne—My Life as a Woman* (autobiography), Harper and Row, 1989.

ROSEANNE BARR

AWARDS: American Comedy Award, Funniest Female Performer in a Television Special, ACE Awards, Funniest Female in a Comedy and Best Comedy Special, all 1987, for *On Location: The Roseanne Barr Show;* Golden Globe nomination, Outstanding Lead Actress in a Comedy Series, 1988, and *US* magazine Second Annual Readers Poll, Best Actress in a Comedy Series, 1989, both for *Roseanne.*

ADDRESSES: AGENT—Hal Ray, William Morris Agency, 151 El Camino Drive, Beverly Hills, CA 90212.

*   *   *

BASSETT, Linda

PERSONAL: Born c. 1950; father, a policeman; mother, a typist.

VOCATION: Actress and director.

CAREER: PRINCIPAL STAGE APPEARANCES—Shirley, Shona, Miss Cade, and Margaret, *Fen,* Joint Stock Theatre Group, London, then New York Shakespeare Festival (NYSF), Public Theatre, New York City, both 1983; doctor, House, and first girl, *Woyceck* and Mrs. Smith, *The Bald Prima Donna,* both Haymarket Studio Company, Liverpool, U.K., then Almeida Theatre, London, 1985; mother, June, and Flora, *Aunt Dan and Lemon,* NYSF, Public Theatre, then Royal Court Theatre, London, both 1985; Marylou Baines, Mrs. Etherington, and Dolcie Star, *Serious Money,* London production, then NYSF, Public Theatre, both 1987. Also appeared with the Belgrade Theatre-in-Education Company, Coventry, U.K., 1977; in *The Cherry Orchard, Medea,* and *George Dandin,* all Leicester Haymarket Studio, London; and in *Abel's Sister,* London production.

PRINCIPAL STAGE WORK—Director, Belgrade Theatre-in-Education Company, Coventry, U.K., 1977.

FILM DEBUT—Gertrude Stein, *Waiting for the Moon,* Skouras, 1987. PRINCIPAL FILM APPEARANCES—Jane Swanton, *Paris By Night,* Cineplex Odeon, 1989; also appeared in *Traffik,* Film Four International, 1989; and *Leave to Remain.*

ADDRESSES: AGENT—Megan Willis, Garricks, 7 Garrick Street, London WC2 E 9AR, England.*

*   *   *

BAUER, Rocky
See BAUER, Steven

*   *   *

BAUER, Steven   1956-
(Rocky Bauer, Rocky Echevarria)

PERSONAL: Born Steven Echevarria, December 2, 1956, in Havana, Cuba; immigrated to the United States in 1959; married Melanie Griffith (an actress), May, 1982 (divorced). EDUCATION—Studied acting at Miami-Dade Community College.

VOCATION: Actor.

CAREER: OFF-BROADWAY DEBUT—*Waiting for Lefty,* 1980. PRINCIPAL STAGE APPEARANCES—Tig, *Balm in Gilead,* Minetta Lane Theatre, New York City, 1984; Taj Mohamud, *Nanawatai,* Los Angeles Theatre Center, Los Angeles, 1985.

PRINCIPAL FILM APPEARANCES—Manny Ray, *Scarface,* Universal, 1983; Scott Muller, *Thief of Hearts,* Paramount, 1984; Frank, *Running Scared,* Metro-Goldwyn-Mayer/United Artists, 1986; Frank, *Wildfire,* Zupnik Cinema, 1988; Taj, *The Beast,* Columbia, 1988; Al Lucero, *Gleaming the Cube,* Twentieth Century-Fox, 1989.

PRINCIPAL TELEVISION APPEARANCES—Series: (As Rocky Echevarria) Private First Class Ignacio Carmona, *From Here to Eternity,* NBC, 1980; also *Que Pasa U.S.A.?,* PBS. Pilots: (As Rocky Bauer) Nick Donato, *She's in the Army Now,* ABC, 1981; (as Rocky Bauer) Buck Nichols, *Nichols and Dymes,* NBC, 1981. Episodic: Gambler, "Man from the South," *Alfred Hitchcock Presents,* NBC, 1985; also *Doctors' Private Lives,* ABC, 1979; *The Rockford Files,* NBC; *Hill Street Blues,* NBC; *One Day at Time,* CBS. Movies: (As Rocky Bauer) Dunc Widders, *An Innocent Love,* CBS, 1982; Avner, *Sword of Gideon,* HBO, 1986; Enrique "Kiki" Camarena, *Drug Wars: The Camarena Story,* NBC, 1990. Specials: Montoya, "Tales from the Hollywood Hills: A Table at Ciro's," *Great Performances,* PBS, 1987.

ADDRESSES: MANAGER—Phyllis Carlyle, Phyllis Carlyle Man-

agement, Columbia Plaza, Building 8, Room 2-B, Burbank, CA 91505.*

*   *   *

BAVA, Mario   1914-
(John Foan, John Hold, John M. Old)

PERSONAL: Born July 31, 1914, in San Remo, Italy; son of a sculptor.

VOCATION: Director, cinematographer, and screenwriter.

CAREER: Also see WRITINGS below. PRINCIPAL FILM WORK—Cinematographer, *L'elisir d'amore* (also known as *This Wine of Love*), Superfilm, 1948; cinematographer, *The Taming of Dorothy* (also known as *Her Favourite Husband*), Eagle-Lion/United Artists, 1955; cinematographer, *The Devil's Commandment* (also known as *I vampiri* and *Lust of the Vampires*), RCIP, 1956; cinematographer, *Mio figlio Nerone* (also known as *Nero's Mistress, Nero's Big Weekend,* and *My Son Nero*), 1956, released in the United States by Art Films/Manhattan Films International, 1962; cinematographer, *La morte viene dalla spazio* (also known as *The Day the Sky Exploded, Le Danger vient de l'espace,* and *Death from Outer Space*), 1958, released in the United States by Excelsior, 1961; director (as John Foan) and cinematographer, *Caltiki, the Immortal Monster* (also known as *Caltiki, il monstro immortale*), Allied Artists, 1959; cinematographer, *La tatiche de Ercole* (also known as *Hercules*), Embassy/Warner Brothers, 1959; cinematographer (with Franco Vodopivec), *Agi Murad, il diavolo bianco* (also known as *The White Warrior* and *Beli Djavo*), 1959, released in the United States by Warner Brothers, 1961.

Cinematographer, *Esther and the King,* Twentieth Century-Fox, 1960; cinematographer, *The Giant of Marathon,* Metro-Goldwyn-Mayer (MGM), 1960; cinematographer, *Ercole e la regina lidia* (also known as *Hercules Unchained*), Warner Brothers/Embassy, 1960; producer, director, cinematographer (with Ubaldo Terzano), and art director (with Giorgio Giovannini), *La maschera del demonio* (also known as *Black Sunday*), 1960, released in the United States by American International, 1961; producer, *Atom Age Vampire,* Topaz, 1961; second unit director, *The Wonders of Aladdin* (also known as *Le meraviglie di Aladino*), MGM, 1961; director and cinematographer (with Terzano), *Gli invasori* (also known as *Erik the Conquerer, La Ruee des Vikings,* and *Fury of the Vikings*), 1961, released in the United States by American International, 1963; director and cinematographer, *Ercole al centro della terra* (also known as *Hercules in the Haunted World*), 1961, released in the United States by Woolner Brothers, 1964; director, *I tre volti della paura* (also known as *Black Sabbath*), 1963, released in the United States by American International, 1964; director and cinematographer, *La regazza che sapeva troppo* (also known as *Evil Eye*), 1963, released in the United States by American International, 1964; director (as John M. Old), *La frusta e il corpo* (also known as *What!* and *Night Is the Phantom*), 1963, released in the United States by Futuramic Releasing Organization, 1965; director, *Sei donne per l'assassino* (also known as *Blood and Black Lace, Six femmes pour l'assassin,* and *Blutige Seide*), 1964, released in the United States by Allied Artists/Woolner Brothers, 1965.

Director, *Planet of the Vampires* (also known as *Terrore nello spazio, Terror en el espacio, Planet of Blood,* and *Demon Planet*), American International, 1965; director (as John M. Old), *La strada* per Fort Alamo (also known as *Arizona Bill* and *The Road to Fort Alamo*), 1965, released in the United States by World Entertainment, 1966; director, *Dr. Goldfoot and the Girl Bombs* (also known as *Le spie vengono dal semifreddo* and *I due mafiosi dell'F.B.I.*), American International, 1966; director, *Kill Baby Kill* (also known as *Operazione paura* and *Curse of the Living Dead*), Europix Consolidated, 1966; director (as John Hold), *I coltelli del vendicatore* (also known as *Knives of the Avenger* and *Raffica di coltelli*), 1967; released in the United States by World Entertainment, 1968; director, *Danger: Diabolik* (also known as *Diabolik* and *Danger Diabolik*), Paramount, 1968; director, *Hatchet for a Honeymoon* (also known as *Una hacka para la luna de miel, Il roso segno della pollias,* and *Blood Brides*), G.G.P., 1969.

Director, *Quante volte . . . quella notte* (also known as *How Often . . . That Night?*), Delfina Cinematografica, 1971; director and cinematographer, *Antefatto* (also known as *Twitch of the Death Nerve, Before the Fact—The Ecology of a Crime, Bloodbath*, and *Last House on the Left, Part II*), New Realm Distributors, 1971; director, *Baron Blood* (also known as *Gli orrori del castello de Norimberga*), American International, 1972; special effects coordinator, *Moses*, AVCO-Embassy, 1976; director and cinematographer, *Beyond the Door II* (also known as *Shock*), Film Ventures, 1979; special effects coordinator, *Inferno*, Twentieth Century-Fox, 1980. Also directed *Roy Colt e Winchester Jack*, 1970; *Reazione a catena*, 1973; *Il diavolo e il morto*, 1974; *Baby Kong*, 1977; *La venere dell'ille*, 1979.

PRINCIPAL TELEVISION WORK—Mini-Series: Special effects coordinator, *Moses—The Lawgiver*, CBS, 1975.

RELATED CAREER—Assistant cameraman.

WRITINGS: See production details above. FILM—(With Ennio De Concini, Marion Serandrei, and Marcello Coscia) *La maschera del demonio*, 1960; (with Oreste Biancoli and Piero Peirotti) *Gli invasori*, 1961; (with Alessandro Continenza, Duccio Tessari, and Franco Prosperi) *Ercole al centro della terra*, 1961; (with Marcello Fondato and Alberto Bevilacqua) *I tre volti della paura*, 1963; (with De Concini, Prosperi, Eliana De Sabata, Enzo Corbucci, and Mino Guerrini) *La regazza che sapeva troppo*, 1963; (with Marcel Fondat and Joe Barilla) *Sei donne per l'assassino*, 1964; (with Bevilacqua, Callisto Cosulich, Antonio Roman, Rafael J. Salvia, Ib Melchior, anda Louis M. Heyward) *Planet of the Vampires*, 1965; (with Romano Migliorini, Roberto Natale, and John Hart) *Kill Baby Kill*, 1966; (with Alberto Liberati and George Simonelli) *I coltelli del vendicatore*, 1967; (with Dino Mauri, Brian Degas, and Tudor Gates) *Danger: Diabolik*, 1968; (with Santiago Moncada) *Hatchet for a Honeymoon*, 1969; *Roy Colt e Winchester Jack*, 1970; also (with Carlo Reali) *Antefatto*, 1971.*

*   *   *

BAYE, Nathalie   1948-

PERSONAL: Born July 6, 1948, in Mainneville, France; children: one. EDUCATION—Graduated from the Paris Conservatory of Dramatic Art, 1972; studied classical and modern dance in New York; studied acting in Cours (Rene) Simon, France.

VOCATION: Actress.

CAREER: PRINCIPAL STAGE APPEARANCES—*Liolla*, Theatre de la Commune, France, 1974; also *The Three Sisters*, 1978.

FILM DEBUT—*Two People*, Universal, 1973. PRINCIPAL FILM APPEARANCES—Joelle, *La Nuit Americaine* (also known as *Day for Night*), Warner Brothers/Columbia, 1973; Nathalie, *La Gueule ouverte* (also known as *The Mouth Agape*), Films la Boetie, 1974; girl, *Un Jour la fete* (also known as *One Day Joy*), Union Generale Cinematographique, 1975; Martine Desdoits, *L'Homme qui aimait les femmes* (also known as *The Man Who Loved Women*), Cinema V, 1977; Janine, *Monsieur Papa*, Gaumont International, 1977; Fabienne, *Mon premier amour* (also known as *My First Love*), Gaumont, 1978; Cecilia Mandel, *La Chambre verte* (also known as *The Green Room*), New World, 1979; Judith Mesnil, *La Memoire courte* (also known as *Short Memory*), Unite Trois/Paradise, 1979.

Denise Rimbaud, *Sauve qui peut la vie* (also known as *Every Man for Himself* and *Slow Motion*), New Yorker, 1980; Brigitte, *Je vais craquer!* (also known as *The Rat Race*), CCFC, 1980; Laurence Cuers, *Une semaine de vacances* (also known as *A Week's Vacation*), Curzon Film Distributors/Parafrance, 1980; Charlotte, *Beau Pere*, New Line Cinema, 1981; Anna, *L'Ombre rouge* (also known as *The Red Shadow*), MK2, 1981; Christine, *La Provinciale* (also known as *A Girl from Lorraine*), New Yorker, 1982; Helene/Patricia, *J'ai espouse une ombre* (also known as *I Married a Shadow* and *I Married a Dead Man*), AMLF/Sara/New Yorker, 1982; Nicole, *La Balance* (also known as *The Nark*), Gala, 1983; Bertrande de Rols, *Le Retour de Martin Guerre* (also known as *The Return of Martin Guerre*), European International, 1983; Leonore, *Beethoven's Nephew* (also known as *Le Neveu de Beethoven*), Orfilm/Almaro/CBL, 1985; Francoise Chenal, *Detective*, Spectrafilm, 1985; Cecile Carline, *Lune de miel* (also known as *Honeymoon*), International Film Marketing/AAA/Revcom, 1985; Alice, *De guerre lasse* (also known as *For the Sake of Peace*), Jupiter Communications/Sara/CDF, 1987; Catherine, *En toute innocence* (also known as *In All Innocence* and *No Harm Intended*), AMLF/World Marketing, 1988; Lena Korski, *La Baule—Les Pins*, Union Generale Cinematographique, 1990. Also appeared in *Le Plein de super* (also known as *Fill It Up, Premium!* and *Fill 'er Up with Super*), Union Generale Cinematographique, 1975; *Le Derniere femme* (also known as *L'ultima donna* and *The Last Woman*), Columbia, 1975; *La jalousie*, 1975; *Le Voyage de noces* (also known as *The Honeymoon Trip*), Fox-Lira, 1976; *Mado*, Films la Boetie, 1976; *La Communion solonnelle*, 1976; *Une Etrange affaire*, 1981; *Rive Droite, Rive Gauche* (also known as *Right Bank, Left Bank*), Parafrance, 1984.

PRINCIPAL TELEVISION APPEARANCES—*Madame Sourdis*, 1979.

RELATED CAREER—Toured the United States with a dance company.

AWARDS: Cesar Award, Best Supporting Actress, 1980, for *Sauve qui peut la vie;* Cesar Award, Best Actress, 1983, for *La Balance*.*

*   *   *

BEARD, Winston
See GOLDMAN, James

BEARSE, Amanda

PERSONAL: EDUCATION—Attended Birmingham Southern College; trained for the stage with Sanford Meisner at the Neighborhood Playhouse.

VOCATION: Actress.

CAREER: PRINCIPAL FILM APPEARANCES—Soap opera actress, *Protocol,* Warner Brothers, 1984; Nicole Ferret, *Fraternity Vacation,* New World, 1985; Amy Peterson, *Fright Night,* Columbia, 1985.

PRINCIPAL TELEVISION APPEARANCES—Series: Amanda Cousins, *All My Children,* ABC, 1982-84; Marcy Rhoades, *Married . . . With Children,* Fox, 1987—. Episodic: Jean Haywood, *Hotel,* ABC, 1986. Movies: Karen, *First Affair,* CBS, 1983; Cathy, *The Goddess of Love,* NBC, 1988.

SIDELIGHTS: RECREATIONS—Motorcycling along the California coast.

ADDRESSES: AGENT—The Agency, 10351 Santa Monica Boulevard, Suite 211, Los Angeles, CA 90025.*

*   *   *

BECKMAN, John   c.1898-1989

PERSONAL: Born c. 1898 in Astoria, OR; died October 25, 1989, in Sherman Oaks, CA; father, a doctor; children: one son, one daughter. EDUCATION—Attended the University of California, Berkeley.

VOCATION: Art director and set designer.

CAREER: FIRST FILM WORK—Set designer, *Nana* (also known as *Lady of the Boulevards*), United Artists, 1934. PRINCIPAL FILM WORK—Set designer: *Kid Millions,* United Artists, 1934; *One Night of Love,* Columbia, 1934; *A Midsummer Night's Dream,* Warner Brothers, 1935; *Clive of India,* United Artists, 1935; *The Petrified Forest,* Warner Brothers, 1936; *Mr. Deeds Goes to Town,* Columbia, 1936; *Lost Horizon,* Columbia, 1937; *The Prince and the Pauper,* Warner Brothers, 1937; *The Adventures of Robin Hood,* Warner Brothers, 1938; *Juarez,* Warner Brothers, 1939; *The Roaring Twenties,* Warner Brothers, 1939; *High Sierra,* Warner Brothers, 1941; *The Maltese Falcon,* Warner Brothers, 1941; *Casablanca,* Warner Brothers, 1942; *This Is the Army,* Warner Brothers, 1943; *Arsenic and Old Lace,* Warner Brothers, 1944; *Mr. Skeffington,* Warner Brothers, 1944.

All as art director, unless indicated: Set designer, *Mildred Pierce,* Warner Brothers, 1945; set designer, *Rhapsody In Blue,* Warner Brothers, 1945; *Monsieur Verdoux,* United Artists, 1947; set designer, *Johnny Belinda,* Warner Brothers, 1948; set designer, *The Glass Menagerie,* Warner Brothers, 1950; *The Iron Mistress,* Warner Brothers, 1952; *Springfield Rifle,* Warner Brothers, 1952; *So Big,* Warner Brothers, 1953; *The System,* Warner Brothers, 1953; *Calamity Jane,* Warner Brothers, 1953; *Lucky Me,* Warner Brothers, 1953; *The McConnell Story* (also known as *Tiger in the Sky*), Warner Brothers, 1955; *Young at Heart,* Warner Brothers, 1955; *Hell on Frisco Bay* (also known as *The Darkest Hour*), Warner Brothers, 1956; *The Bad Seed,* Warner Brothers, 1956;

Toward the Unknown (also known as *Brink of Hell*), Warner Brothers, 1956; *Home Before Dark,* Warner Brothers, 1958; *Lafayette Escadrille* (also known as *Hell Bent for Glory*), Warner Brothers, 1958; *Too Much, Too Soon,* Warner Brothers, 1958; *The F.B.I. Story,* Warner Brothers, 1959; *The Helen Morgan Story* (also known as *Both Ends of the Candle*), Warner Brothers, 1959.

Art director: *Guns of the Timberland* (also known as *Stampede*), Warner Brothers, 1960; (with Lyle Wheeler) *Wake Me When It's Over,* Twentieth Century-Fox, 1960; *The Devil at Four O'Clock,* Columbia, 1961; *A Majority of One,* Warner Brothers, 1961; *Gypsy,* Warner Brothers, 1962; *Mary, Mary,* Warner Brothers, 1963; *The Trouble with Angels,* Columbia, 1966; *Who's Minding the Mint?,* Columbia, 1967; *Assignment to Kill,* Warner Brothers/Seven Arts, 1968; (with Alexander Golitzen) *In Enemy Country,* Universal, 1968; *Hook, Line, and Sinker,* Columbia, 1969; *Which Way to the Front?,* Warner Brothers, 1970.

PRINCIPAL TELEVISION WORK—All as art director. Series: *Gibbsville,* NBC, 1976; *Joe Forrester,* NBC, 1975-76; *Ryan's Four,* ABC, 1983; (with Herman Zimmerman) *All Is Forgiven,* NBC, 1986; *Designing Women,* CBS, 1986-89; also (with Bellah) *The Partridge Family,* ABC; *Call to Glory,* ABC; *Tabitha,* ABC; *Cheers,* NBC; *Webster,* ABC. Pilots: (With Ross Bellah) *Call Holme,* NBC, 1972; (with Bellah) *Matt Helm,* ABC, 1975; (with Bellah) *The Turning Point of Jim Malloy,* NBC, 1975; *The Cabot Connection,* CBS, 1977; *Mobile Medics,* CBS, 1977; (with Bellah) *Annie Flynn,* CBS, 1978; (with Bellah) *Doctors' Private Lives,* ABC, 1978; (with Bellah) *Salvage,* ABC, 1979; *Nero Wolfe,* NBC, 1979; *Modesty Blaise,* ABC, 1982. Movies: *Black Noon,* CBS, 1971; (with Bellah) *Call Her Mom,* ABC, 1972; (with Bellah) *The Dream Merchants,* syndicated, 1980; (with Bellah) *To Find My Son,* CBS, 1980; (with Bellah) *Kate's Secret,* NBC, 1986; *Miracle of the Heart: A Boystown Story,* syndicated, 1986.

RELATED CAREER—Architect, Meyer and Holler, Los Angeles; worked on interior design for Grauman's Chinese Theatre (now Mann's Chinese Theatre); designed murals for the Avalon Casino, Santa Catalina Island, CA.

OBITUARIES AND OTHER SOURCES: Hollywood Reporter, October 30, 1989; *New York Times,* October 31, 1989; *Variety,* November 1, 1989.*

*   *   *

BENNETT, Alan   1934-

PERSONAL: Born May 9, 1934, in Leeds, England; son of Walter (a butcher) and Lilian Mary (Peel) Bennett. EDUCATION—Oxford University, B.A., 1957, M.A., 1962. MILITARY—British Army, Intelligence Corps, 1952-54.

VOCATION: Playwright and actor.

CAREER: Also see *WRITINGS* below. STAGE DEBUT—Ensemble, *Better Late* (revue) Oxford Theatre Group, Edinburgh Festival, Cranston Street Hall, Edinburgh, Scotland, 1959. LONDON DEBUT—Ensemble, *Beyond the Fringe* (revue), Fortune Theatre, 1961. BROADWAY DEBUT—Ensemble, *Beyond the Fringe* (revue), John Golden Theatre, 1962. PRINCIPAL STAGE APPEARANCES—Ensemble, *Beyond the Fringe* (revue), Edinburgh Festival, Lyceum Theatre, Edinburgh, Scotland, 1959; Archbishop of

Canterbury, *Blood of the Bambergs,* Royal Court Theatre, London, 1962; Reverend Sloley-Jones, *A Cuckoo in the Nest,* Royal Court Theatre, 1964; Tempest, *Forty Years On,* Apollo Theatre, London, 1968; Mrs. Swabb, *Habeas Corpus,* Lyric Theatre, London, 1974; Anthony Blunt, "A Question of Attribution" in *Secret Spies,* National Theatre, then Queen's Theatre, both London, 1989.

PRINCIPAL FILM APPEARANCES—Neville's doctor, *Long Shot,* Mithras, 1981; voice of Mock Turtle, *Dreamchild,* Universal/Columbia/EMI/Warner Brothers, 1985; the Bishop, *Little Dorrit,* Cannon, 1987; also appeared in *Pleasure at Her Majesty's* (documentary), Roger Graef, 1976; *The Secret Policeman's Other Ball,* United International/Almi/Cinema V, 1981.

PRINCIPAL TELEVISION APPEARANCES—Series: *On the Margin,* BBC, 1966; host, *The Alan Bennett Series,* BBC, 1966-67. Mini-Series: Lord Pinkrose, *Fortunes of War,* BBC, then *Masterpiece Theatre,* PBS, 1987. Episodic: *Talking Heads,* BBC. Specials: *Beyond the Fringe* (revue), BBC, 1964. Also appeared in various roles, *My Father Knew Lloyd George,* BBC, 1965; Augustus Hare, *Famous Gossips,* 1965; *Streets Ahead,* BBC, 1966; *Alice in Wonderland,* BBC, 1967; *A Day Out,* BBC, 1972; Denis Midgley, *Intensive Care,* 1982; Shallow, *The Merry Wives of Windsor,* 1982; housemaster, *Breaking Up,* 1986.

PRINCIPAL TELEVISION WORK—Episodic: Director, "Bed Among the Lentils," *Talking Heads,* BBC, then *Masterpiece Theatre,* PBS, 1989.

PRINCIPAL RADIO APPEARANCES—Specials: *The Great Jowett,* 1980; *Dragon,* 1982.

NON-RELATED CAREER—Junior lecturer in modern history, Oxford University, 1960-62; instructor, Joint Services School for Linguists; professor of medieval history; president, North Craven Heritage Trust.

WRITINGS: STAGE—(With Dudley Moore, Peter Cook, and Jonathan Miller) *Beyond the Fringe* (revue), Edinburgh Festival, Lyceum Theatre, Edinburgh, Scotland, 1959, then Fortune Theatre, London, 1961, later John Golden Theatre, New York City, 1962, published by Souvenir Press, 1962, and Random House, 1963; *Forty Years On,* Palace Theatre, Manchester, U.K., then Apollo Theatre, London, both 1968, published by Faber and Faber, 1969; (with Carol Brahms and Ned Sherrin) *Sing a Rude Song,* Greenwich Theatre, London, 1969; *Getting On,* Theatre Royal, Brighton, U.K., then Queen's Theatre, London, both 1971, published by Faber and Faber, 1972; *Habeas Corpus,* Oxford Playhouse, Oxford, U.K., then Lyric Theatre, London, both 1973, later Martin Beck Theatre, New York City, 1975, published by Faber and Faber, 1973; *The Old Country,* Oxford Playhouse, then Queen's Theatre, both 1977, published by Faber and Faber, 1978; *Enjoy,* Richmond Theatre, Surrey, U.K., then Vaudeville Theatre, London, both 1980, published by Faber and Faber, 1980; *Kafka's Dick,* first produced in London, 1986, published in *Two Kafka Plays,* Faber and Faber, 1987; "Green Forms" and "A Visit from Miss Prothero," in *Office Suite* (double-bill), first produced in London, 1987, published by Faber and Faber, 1981; "An Englishman Abroad" and "A Question of Attribution," in *Secret Spies* (double-bill), National Theatre, then Queen's Theatre, both 1989.

FILM—*A Private Function,* Island Alive, 1985, published by Faber and Faber, 1984; *Prick Up Your Ears,* Samuel Goldwyn, 1987, published by Faber and Faber, 1987.

TELEVISION—Series: *On the Margin,* BBC, 1966; "Our Winnie," "A Woman of No Importance," "Rolling Home," "Marks," and "Say Something Happened," *Objects of Affection,* BBC, 1982, all published in *Objects of Affection and Other Plays for Television,* BBC Publications, 1982; *Talking Heads,* BBC, 1987, published by BBC Publications, 1987. Episodic: "Bed Among the Lentils" (broadcast on BBC as an episode of *Talking Heads*), *Masterpiece Theatre,* PBS, 1989. Also *A Day Out,* BBC, 1972, published in *Objects of Affection and Other Plays for Television,* 1982; *Sunset Across the Bay,* BBC, 1975; *A Little Outing,* BBC, 1977; *A Visit from Miss Prothero,* BBC, 1978, published in *Office Suite,* Faber and Faber, 1981; *Me, I'm Afraid of Virginia Woolf,* 1978, published in *The Writer in Disguise,* Faber and Faber, 1985; *Doris and Doreen,* 1978, published as *Green Forms* in *Office Suite* 1981; *The Old Crowd, Afternoon Off, One Fine Day,* and *All Day on the Sands,* all 1979, published in *The Writer in Disguise,* 1985; *Intensive Care,* BBC, 1982, published in *Objects of Affection and Other Plays for Television,* 1982; *An Englishman Abroad,* BBC-2, 1983, published in *Objects of Affection and Other Plays for Television,* 1982; *The Insurance Man,* BBC, 1986, published in *Two Kafka Plays,* Faber and Faber, 1987.

RADIO—Specials: *Uncle Clarence,* 1986.

OTHER—Contributor, *London Review of Books.*

AWARDS: *London Evening Standard* Award, Best Revue or Musical, 1961, for *Beyond the Fringe;* New York Drama Critics' Circle Award and Antoinette Perry Award, both Special Awards, 1963, for *Beyond the Fringe;* British Academy of Film and Television Arts Award, Light Entertainment Performance (television), 1967; Guild of Television Producers Award, 1967, for *On the Margin; London Evening Standard* Award, 1968, for *Forty Years On; London Evening Standard* Award, 1971, for *Getting On;* British Academy of Film and Television Arts Award—Television Writers, 1983; Broadcasting Press Guild Award, 1984; Royal Television Society Awards, 1984 and 1986; *London Evening Standard* Award, 1985.

MEMBER: British Actors' Equity Association, Actors' Equity Association, American Federation of Television and Radio Artists.

SIDELIGHTS: RECREATIONS—Medieval history.

ADDRESSES: AGENT—Anthony Jones, A.D. Peters Ltd., 10 Buckingham Street, London WC2N 6BU, England.*

* * *

BENNETT, Harve 1930-

PERSONAL: Born Harve Bennett Fischman, August 17, 1930, in Chicago, IL; son of Yale (a lawyer) and Kathryn (a journalist; maiden name, Susman) Fischman; married Carole Oettinger (an agent); children: Christopher, Susan, Callie, Samantha. EDUCATION—Received B.A., theatre arts, from the University of California, Los Angeles.

VOCATION: Producer and screenwriter.

CAREER: Also see WRITINGS below. PRINCIPAL FILM APPEARANCES—Flight recorder, *Star Trek III: The Search for Spock,* Paramount, 1984; Star Fleet commander, *Star Trek V: The Final*

Frontier, Paramount, 1989. PRINCIPAL FILM WORK—Executive producer, *Star Trek II: The Wrath of Khan,* Paramount, 1982; producer, *Star Trek III: The Search for Spock,* Paramount, 1984; producer, *Star Trek IV: The Voyage Home,* Paramount, 1986; producer, *Star Trek V: The Final Frontier,* Paramount, 1989.

PRINCIPAL TELEVISION WORK—All as executive producer, unless indicated. Series: Producer (with Tony Barrett), *The Mod Squad,* ABC, 1968-73; (also creator) *The Young Rebels,* ABC, 1970-71; *The Invisible Man,* NBC, 1975-76; *The Gemini Man,* NBC, 1976; (with Allan Balter) *The Six Million Dollar Man,* ABC, 1973-78; (with Harris Katleman) *The American Girls,* CBS, 1978; (with Katleman) *Salvage 1,* ABC, 1979; (with Katleman) *From Here to Eternity,* NBC, 1980; (with Bruce Lansbury) *The Powers of Matthew Star,* NBC, 1982-83. Mini-Series: *Rich Man, Poor Man,* ABC, 1976; (with Katleman) *From Here to Eternity,* NBC, 1979. Pilots: *The Invisible Man,* NBC, 1975; *Gemini Man* (also known as *Code Name: Minus One*), NBC, 1976; (with Katleman) *Go West, Young Girl!,* ABC, 1978; (with Katleman) *The Legend of the Golden Gun,* NBC, 1979; (with Katleman) *Salvage,* ABC, 1979; (with Katleman) *Alex and the Doberman Gang,* NBC, 1980; (with Katleman) *Nick and the Dobermans,* NBC, 1980. Episodic: Producer, *The Bionic Woman,* ABC. Movies: Producer, *The Birdmen* (also known as *Escape of the Birdmen*), ABC, 1971; producer, *The Astronaut,* ABC, 1972; producer, *Family Flight,* ABC, 1972; producer, *Death Race,* ABC, 1973; producer, *Money to Burn,* ABC, 1973; *You'll Never See Me Again,* ABC, 1973; *The Alpha Caper* (also known as *Inside Job*), ABC, 1973; *Houston, We've Got a Problem,* ABC, 1974; *Heatwave!,* ABC, 1974; *Guilty or Innocent: The Sam Sheppard Case,* NBC, 1975; *The Jesse Owens Story,*

HARVE BENNETT

syndicated, 1984. Specials: *A Woman Called Golda,* syndicated, 1982.

PRINCIPAL RADIO APPEARANCES—Series: Regular, *The Quiz Kids.*

RELATED CAREER—President, University of California, Los Angeles Theatre Arts Alumni Association, 1985-1990; also president, Bennett-Katleman Productions; associate producer and special events producer, CBS-TV; vice-president, ABC-TV; director of television commercials; newspaper columnist; drama critic; freelance writer.

NON-RELATED CAREER—Civilian aide to the Secretary of the Army, 1988-1990.

WRITINGS: FILM—*Star Trek III: The Search for Spock,* Paramount, 1984; (with Steve Meerson, Peter Krikes, and Nicholas Meyer) *Star Trek IV: The Voyage Home,* Paramount, 1986. TELEVISION—Episodic: *The Mod Squad,* ABC, 1968-73; *The Young Rebels,* ABC, 1970-71. Movies: (With Gerald DiPego, Charles Kuenstle, and Robert S. Biheller) *The Astronaut,* ABC, 1972.

AWARDS: Golden Globe, Best Dramatic Television Series, 1977, for *Rich Man, Poor Man;* Emmy Award, Outstanding Drama Special, 1982, for *A Woman Called Golda;* NAACP Image Award, Best Mini-Series, 1984, for *The Jesse Owens Story.*

ADDRESSES: OFFICE—c/o Paramount Pictures, 5555 Melrose Avenue, Los Angeles, CA 90038.

*   *   *

BENSON, Robby   1956-

PERSONAL: Born Robin Segal, January 21, 1956, in Dallas, TX; son of Jerry Segal (a writer) and Ann Benson (an actress and business promotions manager); married Karla DeVito (a singer and actress). EDUCATION—Attended the American Academy of Dramatic Arts.

VOCATION: Actor, director, producer, and writer.

CAREER: Also see *WRITINGS* below. BROADWAY DEBUT—David Hartman, *Zelda,* Ethel Barrymore Theatre, 1969. PRINCIPAL STAGE APPEARANCES—Third urchin, *The Rothschilds,* Lunt-Fontanne Theatre, New York City, 1970; Frederic, *The Pirates of Penzance,* Minskoff Theatre, New York City, 1981.

PRINCIPAL FILM APPEARANCES—Title role, *Jory,* AVCO-Embassy, 1972; Jeremy Jones, *Jeremy,* United Artists, 1973; Billy Webber, *Lucky Lady,* Twentieth Century-Fox, 1975; Billy Joe McAllister, *Ode to Billy Joe,* Warner Brothers, 1976; Henry Steele, *One on One,* Warner Brothers, 1977; priest, *The End,* United Artists, 1978; Nick Peterson, *Ice Castles,* Columbia, 1978; Emilio, *Walk Proud* (also known as *Gang*), Universal, 1979; Pinsky, *Die Laughing,* Warner Brothers, 1980; Jud Templeton, *Tribute,* Twentieth Century-Fox, 1980; Brent Falcone, "Municipalians" in *National Lampoon Goes to the Movies,* Metro-Goldwyn-Mayer/ United Artists, 1981; Danny Saunders, *The Chosen,* Contemporary, 1982; Billy Mills, *Running Brave,* Buena Vista, 1983; Howard Keach, *Harry and Son,* Orion, 1984; Carver, *City Limits,* Atlantic, 1985; Pitts, *Rent-a-Cop,* Kings Road, 1988; Scott, *White*

ROBBY BENSON

Hot (also known as *Crack in the Mirror* and *Do It Up*), Triax Entertainment/Paul International, 1989.

PRINCIPAL FILM WORK—Producer (with Mark Canton), *Die Laughing,* Warner Brothers, 1980; director, *White Hot* (also known as *Crack in the Mirror* and *Do It Up*), Triax Entertainment/Paul International, 1989.

PRINCIPAL TELEVISION APPEARANCES—Series: Bruce Carson, *Search for Tomorrow,* CBS, 1971-73; Detective Cliff Brady, *Tough Cookies,* CBS, 1986. Episodic: Ed Bolling, *Alfred Hitchcock Presents,* NBC, 1985. Movies: Leroy Small, *The Virginia Hill Story,* NBC, 1974; Frankie Hodges, *Remember When* (also known as *Four Stars in the Window*), NBC, 1974; John, *All the Kind Strangers,* ABC, 1974; Johnnie Gunther, *Death Be Not Proud,* ABC, 1975; Richie Werner, *The Death of Richie,* NBC, 1977; Nolie Minor, *Two of a Kind,* CBS, 1982; Nathan Bowzer, *California Girls,* ABC, 1985. Specials: George Gibbs, *Our Town,* NBC, 1977; *John Denver in Australia,* ABC, 1978; host, *Second Annual CBS Easter Parade,* CBS, 1986.

RELATED CAREER—Appeared in television commercials and in summer theatre productions at the age of five; film instructor, University of South Carolina; musician.

WRITINGS: FILM—(With Jerry Segal) *One on One,* Warner Brothers, 1977; (with Don Peake; also composer), *Walk Proud,* Universal, 1979; (with Segal and Scott Parker; also composer with Segal), *Die Laughing,* Warner Brothers, 1980; song composer, *The Breakfast Club,* Universal, 1985; song composer, *White Hot* (also

known as *Crack in the Mirror* and *Do It Up*), Triax Entertainment/Paul International, 1989.

ADDRESSES: OFFICE—P.O. Box 1305, Woodland Hills, CA 91364. AGENT—Sandy Bresler, Bresler-Kelly and Associates, 15760 Ventura Boulevard, Suite 1730, Encino, CA 91436.*

*   *   *

BERGERE, Lee

PERSONAL: Born April 10 in New York, NY.

VOCATION: Actor.

CAREER: PRINCIPAL STAGE APPEARANCES—Phil Gorshin, *Happiness Is Just a Little Thing Called a Rolls Royce,* Ethel Barrymore Theatre, New York City, 1968.

MAJOR TOURS—Nelson, *Mrs. McThing,* U.S. cities, 1953.

PRINCIPAL FILM APPEARANCES—Rudi Andujar, *Sullivan's Empire,* Universal, 1967; Major Maurice Miral, *In Enemy Country,* Universal, 1968; Emelio, *Bob and Carol and Ted and Alice,* Columbia, 1969; narrator, *Birds Do It . . . Bees Do It . . .* (documentary), Columbia/Warner Distributors, 1974; Zandor, *Time Trackers,* Concorde, 1989.

PRINCIPAL TELEVISION APPEARANCES—Series: George, *Hot l Baltimore,* ABC, 1975; Joseph Anders, *Dynasty,* ABC, 1981-83; also *Kitty Foyle,* NBC, 1958. Mini-Series: Nicholas Fabray, *North and South,* ABC, 1985; Papa Joe Nicollet, *Dream West,* CBS, 1986. Pilots: Stan Gorman, *The Slightly Fallen Angel* (broadcast as episode of *The Alcoa Hour*), NBC, 1959; Masha, *The Six Million Dollar Man,* ABC, 1973; Doug Braden, *Susan and Sam,* NBC, 1977. Episodic: Abraham Lincoln, "The Savage Curtain," *Star Trek,* NBC, 1969; Maxim Soury, *Murder, She Wrote,* CBS, 1987; Justin Nash, *Falcon Crest,* CBS, 1989; also "The Storm," *One Step Beyond,* ABC, 1960; *The Dick Van Dyke Show,* CBS, 1962; *Mr. Terrific,* CBS, 1967; *All in the Family,* CBS, 1976; *Wonder Woman,* CBS, 1978; *The Addams Family,* ABC; *McHale's Navy,* ABC; *The Munsters,* CBS; *My Favorite Martian,* CBS; *WKRP in Cincinnati,* CBS; *Get Smart.* Movies: Monsieur Carroll, *Evening in Byzantium,* syndicated, 1978.

ADDRESSES: AGENT—Calder Agency, 4150 Riverside Drive, Suite 204, Burbank, CA 91505.*

*   *   *

BERLIN, Irving   1888-1989

PERSONAL: Born Israel Baline, May 11, 1888, in Tyumen, Russia; immigrated to the United States in 1893; died September 22, 1989, in New York, NY; son of Moses (a cantor and shochet [meat/poultry certifier]) and Leah (Lipkin) Baline; married Dorothy Goetz, February, 1913 (died, July 17, 1913); married Ellin Mackay, January 4, 1926 (died, July, 1988); children: Irving (deceased), Mary Ellin, Linda, Elizabeth (second marriage). MILITARY—U.S. Army, Infantry, sergeant, 1917-18.

VOCATION: Composer and songwriter.

CAREER: Also see *WRITINGS* below. BROADWAY DEBUT—Ensemble, *Up and Down Broadway* (revue), Casino Theatre, 1910. PRINCIPAL STAGE APPEARANCES—*This Is the Army*, Broadway Theatre, New York City, 1942.

PRINCIPAL STAGE WORK—Producer, *Yip Yip Yaphank*, Century Theatre, New York City, 1918; producer (with Robert Sherwood and Moss Hart), *Miss Liberty*, Imperial Theatre, New York City, 1949.

MAJOR TOURS—*Show Girl*, U.S. cities, 1902.

PRINCIPAL FILM APPEARANCES—As himself, *Glorifying the American Girl*, Paramount, 1930; as himself, *This Is the Army*, Warner Brothers, 1943.

RELATED CAREER—Singer in cafes and for songwriter Harry Von Tilzer, New York City, 1902-05; singing waiter, New York City, 1905-07; staff lyricist, Ted Snyder Company (a music publishing company), New York City, 1909-13; co-founder, Waterson, Berlin, and Snyder (a music publishing company), 1913-1918; co-founder, American Society of Composers, Authors, and Publishers (ASCAP), 1914 (charter member, 1914-1989; director, 1914-18); president, Irving Berlin Inc., renamed Irving Berlin Music Corp., New York City, 1919-1989; founder (with Sam H. Harris and Joseph Schenck), Music Box Theatre, New York City, 1921; also performed in vaudeville.

WRITINGS: STAGE—All as composer of music and lyrics, unless indicated: Song contributor, *Up and Down Broadway*, Casino Theatre, New York City, 1910; song contributor, *The Ziegfeld Follies*, Jardin de Paris, New York City, 1911; *Watch Your Step*, New Amsterdam Theatre, New York City, 1914; song contributor, *Stop! Look! Listen!*, Globe Theatre, New York City, 1915, then retitled *Follow the Crowd*, Empire Theatre, London, 1916; song contributor, *The Century Girl*, Century Theatre, New York City, 1916; song contributor, *The Cohan Revue of 1918*, New Amsterdam Theatre, 1917; (also book) *Yip Yip Yaphank*, Century Theatre, 1918; song contributor, *Canary*, Globe Theatre, 1918; song contributor, *The Ziegfeld Follies*, New Amsterdam Theatre, 1919; song contributor, *The Ziegfeld Follies*, New Amsterdam Theatre, 1920; *Music Box Revue*, Music Box Theatre, New York City, 1921; *Music Box Revue*, Music Box Theatre, 1922; *Music Box Revue*, Music Box Theatre, 1923; *Music Box Revue*, Music Box Theatre, 1924; *The Cocoanuts*, Lyric Theatre, New York City, 1925; song contributor, *Betsy*, New Amsterdam Theatre, 1926; *Ziegfeld Follies*, New Amsterdam Theatre, 1927; song contributor, *Shoot the Works*, George M. Cohan Theatre, New York City, 1931; *Face the Music*, New Amsterdam Theatre, 1932; *As Thousands Cheer*, Music Box Theatre, 1933; *Louisiana Purchase*, Imperial Theatre, New York City, 1940; *This Is the Army*, Broadway Theatre, New York City, 1942; *Annie Get Your Gun*, Imperial Theatre, 1946; *Miss Liberty*, Imperial Theatre, 1949; *Call Me Madam*, Imperial Theatre, 1950; *Mr. President*, St. James Theatre, New York City, 1962; (new music and lyrics) *Annie Get Your Gun*, State Theatre, New York City, 1966.

FILM—All as composer of songs: *The Cocoanuts*, Paramount, 1929; *Hallelujah*, Metro-Goldwyn-Mayer (MGM), 1929; *Mammy*, Warner Brothers, 1930; *Reaching for the Moon*, United Artists, 1931; *Top Hat*, RKO, 1935; *Follow the Fleet*, RKO, 1936; *On the Avenue*, Twentieth Century-Fox, 1937; *Alexander's Ragtime Band*, Twentieth Century-Fox, 1938; *Carefree*, RKO, 1938; *Second Fiddle*, Twentieth Century-Fox, 1939; *Louisiana Purchase*, Paramount, 1941; *Holiday Inn*, Paramount, 1942; *This Is the Army*, Warner Brothers, 1943; *Blue Skies*, Paramount, 1946; *Easter Parade*, MGM, 1948; *Annie Get Your Gun*, MGM, 1950; *Call Me Madam*, Twentieth Century-Fox, 1953; *White Christmas*, Paramount, 1954; *There's No Business Like Show Business*, Twentieth Century-Fox, 1954.

OTHER—Composer of over 1,500 songs, including: (Lyricist) "Marie from Sunny Italy," 1907; "That Mesmerizing Mendelssohn Tune" and (lyricist with George Whiting) "My Wife's Gone to the Country" both 1909; "Alexander's Ragtime Band," "Ragtime Violin," and "Everybody's Doin' It Now," and (with Ted Snyder) "I Want to Be in Dixie," all 1911; "When I Lost You" and "When the Midnight Choo-Choo Leaves for Alabam'," both 1912; "Down in Chattanooga," 1913; "I Want to Go Back to Michigan" and "Play a Simple Melody," both 1914; "I Love a Piano" and "When I Leave the World Behind," both 1915; "Oh, How I Hate to Get Up in the Morning" and "Mandy," both 1918; "A Pretty Girl Is Like a Melody," 1919; "Say It with Music," 1921; "All Alone" and "What'll I Do?," both 1924; "Always" and "Remember," both 1925; "At Peace with the World" and "Because I Love You," both 1926; "Russian Lullaby," "Blue Skies," "The Song Is Ended," and "Shaking the Blue Skies Away," all 1927; "Marie," 1928; "Puttin' on the Ritz," 1929; "Let Me Sing and I'm Happy" and "Reaching for the Moon," both 1930; "Me!," 1931; "Let's Have Another Cup of Coffee" and "How Deep Is the Ocean," and "Say It Isn't So," all 1932; "Easter Parade," "Supper Time," and "Heat Wave," all 1933; "Cheek to Cheek" and "Top Hat, White Tie, and Tails," and "Isn't This a Lovely Day," all 1935; "Let's Face the Music and Dance," 1936; "I've Got My Love to Keep Me Warm," 1937; "Change Partners," 1938; "God Bless America," 1939; "Any Bonds Today," 1941; "This Is the Army, Mr. Jones," "I Left My Heart at the Stage Door Canteen," "Be Careful, It's My Heart," and "White Christmas," all 1942; "They Say It's Wonderful," "I Got Lost in His Arms," "There's No Business Like Show Business," "The Girl That I Marry," and "Anything You Can Do," all 1946; "Steppin' Out with My Baby," "It Only Happens When I Dance with You," and "A Couple of Swells," all 1947; "Let's Take an Old Fashioned Walk, 1949; "You're Just in Love," 1950; "Count Your Blessings," 1953; "This Is a Great Country," 1962; "An Old Fashioned Wedding," 1966.

AWARDS: Academy Award nomination, Best Music (Song), 1935, for "Cheek to Cheek" from *Top Hat;* Academy Award nomination, Best Music (Song), 1938, for "Change Partners" from *Carefree;* Academy Award nomination, Best Music (Song), 1938, for "Now It Can Be Told" from *Alexander's Ragtime Band;* Academy Award nomination, Best Music (Song), 1939, for "I Poured My Heart into a Song" from *Second Fiddle;* Academy Award, Best Music (Song), 1942, for "White Christmas" from *Holiday Inn;* Academy Award nomination, Best Writing (Original Story), 1942, for *Holiday Inn;* Medal of Merit, 1945, for *This Is the Army;* Theodore Roosevelt Distinguished Service Medal from the Theodore Roosevelt Association, 1946; Academy Award nomination, Best Music (Song), 1946, for "You Keep Coming Back Like a Song" from *Blue Skies;* French Legion of Honor, 1947; Academy Award nomination, Best Music (Song), 1954, for "Count Your Blessings" from *White Christmas;* Congressional Gold Medal of Honor, 1955, "in recognition of his services in composing many patriotic songs including 'God Bless America' "; Antoinette Perry Award, 1963, for "distinguished contribution to the musical theatre for many years"; Lifetime Achievement Award from the National Academy of Recording Arts and Sciences, 1968; Presidential

Medal of Freedom, 1977; Lawrence Langer Award for "distinguished lifetime achievement in the American theatre," 1978; Kennedy Center Honors, 1987. HONORARY DEGREES—Bucknell University, D.Mus., 1939; Temple University, D.Mus., 1954; Fordham University, D.H.L., 1969.

OBITUARIES AND OTHER SOURCES: New York Times, September 23, 1989; *Variety,* September 27-October 3, 1989.*

*   *   *

BERNARD, Jason   1938-

PERSONAL: Born Ronald Carl Johnson, May 17, 1938, in Chicago, IL; son of Milton Prentice (a minister) and Bernice Gloria (a government supervisor) Johnson; wife's name, Carole (divorced); children: Jason Kimani. EDUCATION—Received B.A. from the University of Chicago; received M.F.A. in theatre history from New York University; trained for the stage with Uta Hagen, Irene Dailey, Lee Strasberg, and Sanford Meisner. MILITARY—U.S. Army, Special Forces, Airborne Rangers.

VOCATION: Actor and director.

CAREER: STAGE DEBUT—Sydney Prince, *Light Up the Sky,* Drama Inc., Chicago, IL, 1960. OFF-BROADWAY DEBUT—John, *Day of Absence* and Klan, *Happy Ending* (double-bill), St. Mark's Playhouse, 1965. PRINCIPAL STAGE APPEARANCES—Prosecutor, *Trial of the Catonsville Nine,* Center Theatre Group, Mark Taper Forum, Los Angeles, 1971; also appeared in *MacBird!,* Village Gate Theatre, New York City, 1967; *Krapp's Last Tape, The Threepenny Opera, A Midsummer Night's Dream,* and *Henry IV, Part One,* all Seattle Repertory Theatre, Seattle, WA, 1967-69; *In a Fine Castle,* Center Theatre Group, New Theatre for Now, Los Angeles, 1972; *Seasons,* Back Alley Theatre, Van Nuys, CA; *Split Second,* Santa Monica Playhouse, Santa Monica, CA; *The Meeting,* Circle Theatre, Los Angeles; *Dream on Monkey Mountain,* Center Theatre Group; *Master Harold and the Boys,* New Mexico Repertory Theatre, Albuquerque, NM.

PRINCIPAL STAGE WORK—Director: *The Blacks* and *Blood Knot,* both Seattle Repertory Theatre, Seattle, WA, 1968-69; *Dream on Monkey Mountain, In the Wine Time,* and *Harrangues,* all Black Arts West, Seattle, 1970-73; *The Rimers of Eldridge,* New Phoenix Theatre, Waterloo, IA, 1973-75.

PRINCIPAL FILM APPEARANCES—Seldon, *Thomasine and Bushrod,* Columbia, 1974; Charles Foley, *Friday Foster,* American International, 1975; parole officer, *Car Wash,* Universal, 1976; Goose, *Uncle Joe Shannon,* United Artists, 1978; Mayor, *Blue Thunder,* Columbia, 1983; Judge Bocho, *The Star Chamber,* Twentieth Century-Fox, 1983; Captain Knewt, *WarGames,* United Artists, 1983; Tyrone Wattell, *All of Me,* Universal, 1984; Major Donovan, *No Way Out,* Orion, 1987; Benny Tate, *Bird,* Warner Brothers, 1988.

TELEVISION DEBUT—*Medical Center,* CBS, 1969. PRINCIPAL TELEVISION APPEARANCES—Series: Deputy Inspector Marquette, *Cagney and Lacey,* CBS, 1982-83; Fletch, *High Performance,* ABC, 1983; Lieutenant Ken Auriola, *Hardball,* NBC, 1989. Mini-Series: Caleb Taylor, *V—The Final Battle,* NBC, 1984. Pilots: Sergeant Lindsey Andrews, *Flatfoots* (broadcast as an episode of *Here's Boomer*), NBC, 1982; Finney Morgan, *The Faculty,* ABC,

1986; Vern Puckett, *Kingpins* (broadcast as an episode of *CBS Summer Playhouse*), CBS, 1987; Cecil Kincaid, *Heart and Soul,* ABC, 1989. Episodic: Jim Willis, *The White Shadow,* CBS, 1978; Major Sydney, *M*A*S*H,* CBS, 1982; Arnie Sandoval, *Hardcastle and McCormick,* ABC, 1985; Boswell Stokes, *The Cosby Show,* NBC, 1986; Marquette, *Cagney and Lacey,* 1986, 1987, and 1988; Hap, *Downtown,* CBS, 1986; Dexter Rollins, *Amen,* NBC, 1987; Jack Davis, *Beauty and the Beast,* CBS, 1987; Richard, *A Year in the Life,* NBC, 1987; Wilson Brickett, *Designing Women,* CBS, 1988; Officer Sweeney, *It's Garry Shandling's Show,* Showtime, 1988; Mr. Noack, *Empty Nest,* NBC, 1988; Attorney General, *Wiseguy,* CBS, 1989; Bishop Grace, *UNSUB,* NBC, 1989; Dr. Martin Luther King, Jr., "The Meeting," *American Playhouse,* PBS, 1989; Lieutenant Mulvihill, *Hardball,* NBC, 1989; also Judge Willard, *Night Court,* NBC; *Starman,* ABC; *St. Elsewhere,* NBC; *Knots Landing,* CBS; *Crazy Like a Fox,* ABC; *Hotel,* ABC.

Movies: Coach Temple, *Wilma,* NBC, 1977; Daddy Ben Ross, *A Woman Called Moses,* NBC, 1978; Dale Wrightson, *The Night the City Screamed,* ABC, 1980; Judge, *I Was a Mail Order Bride,* CBS, 1982; Everett, *Pray TV,* ABC, 1982; Caleb Taylor, *V,* NBC, 1983; Captain Sydney, *City Killer,* NBC, 1984; Sergeant Wally Rydell, *The Rape of Richard Beck,* ABC, 1985; Lieutenant Devins, *The Children of Times Square,* ABC, 1986; Sergeant Koslow, *Perry Mason: The Case of the Murdered Madam,* NBC, 1987; Lieutenant Crawford, *Gladiator School,* ABC, 1988; Dectective Mitchell, *Original Sin,* NBC, 1989.

RELATED CAREER—Acting teacher, Black Arts West, Seattle, WA, 1970-73; drama teacher, University of Northern Iowa, Cedar Falls, IA, 1973-75; artistic director, New Phoenix Theatre, Waterloo, IA, 1973-75; acting teacher and director, Hal DeWindt's Actors Studio, 1978-84.

MEMBER: Actors' Equity Association, Screen Actors Guild, American Federation of Television and Radio Artists, Academy of Motion Picture Arts and Sciences, Actors' Studio.

SIDELIGHTS: FAVORITE ROLES—Coach Temple in *Wilma,* Reverend Grace in *UNSUB,* and Martin Luther King, Jr. in "The Meeting," *American Playhouse.*

ADDRESSES: OFFICE—Cameleon Productions, P.O. Box 3811, Santa Fe, NM 87501-3811. AGENT—Larry Masser, Agency for the Performing Arts, 9000 Sunset Boulevard, Los Angeles, CA 90069.

*   *   *

BERRI, Claude   1934-

PERSONAL: Born Claude Langmann, July 1, 1934, in Paris, France.

VOCATION: Director, producer, screenwriter, and actor.

CAREER: PRINCIPAL FILM APPEARANCES—Student, "Lust" in *Les Sept peches capitaux* (also known as *I Sette peccati capitali* and *Seven Capital Sins*), Embassy, 1962; Bernard, *La Bride sur le cou* (also known as *A Briglia sciolta* and *Please, Not Now!*), Twentieth Century-Fox, 1963; Claude Avram, *Mazel Tov ou le mariage* (also known as *Marry Me! Marry Me!*), Allied Artists, 1969; Claude, *Le Sex Shop,* United Artists/New Line Cinema, 1972; Claude, *Le*

Male du Siecle, AMLF, 1975; client, *L'Homme blesse* (also known as *The Wounded Man*), Gaumont/World Marketing/Promovision International/Cinevista, 1983, released in the United States in 1985. Also appeared in *La Verite* (also known as *La Verita* and *The Truth*), Kingsley International, 1961; *J'irai cracher sur vos tombes* (also known as *I Spit on Your Grave*), Audubon, 1962; *Behold a Pale Horse*, Columbia, 1964; *Les Laches vivent d'espoir* (also known as *My Baby Is Black!*), U.S. Films, 1965; *Le Cinema de Papa*, 1971.

FIRST FILM WORK—Director, *Le Poulet* (short film; also known as *The Chicken*), Pathe Contemporary, 1963. PRINCIPAL FILM WORK—Director, *Le Vieil Homme et l'enfant* (also known as *The Two of Us*, *Claude*, and *The Old Man and the Boy*), Cinema V, 1968; producer and director, *Mazel Tov ou le mariage* (also known as *Marry Me! Marry Me!*), Allied Artists, 1969; producer and director, *Le Pistonne* (also known as *The Man with Connections*), Royal, 1970; producer (with Francois Truffaut, Mag Bodard, and Guy Benier), *L'Enfance nue* (also known as *Me* and *Naked Childhood*), Altura, 1970; producer, *L'Oeuf* (also known as *The Egg*), Columbia, 1971; producer (with Alfred W. Crown), *Taking Off*, Universal, 1971; producer and director, *Le Sex Shop*, United Artists/New Line Cinema, 1972; producer (with Christian Fechner), *Les Fous du stade* (also known as *Stadium Nuts*), CCFC, 1972; producer, *Je sais rien mais je dirai tout* (also known as *Don't Know Anything But I'll Tell All*), AMLF, 1973; executive producer, *Pleure pas la bouche pleine* (also known as *Don't Cry with Your Mouth Full*), AMLF, 1973; director, *Le Male du Siecle*, AMLF, 1975; producer (with Jacques-Eric Strauss), *Je t'aime moi non plus* (also known as *I Love You No Longer*), AMLF, 1975; producer, *Un Sac de billes* (also known as *A Bag of Marbles*), AMLF, 1975; director, *La Premiere Fois* (also known as *The First Time*), Lira/Gala Film Distributors, 1976, released in the United States by EDP, 1978; director, *Un Moment d'egarement* (also known as *A Summer Affair* and *In a Wild Moment*), Roissy/Gala Film Distributors, 1977.

Producer, *Tess*, Columbia, 1980; producer, *Inspecteur la Bavure* (also known as *Inspector Blunder*), AMLF, 1980; director and producer, *Je vous aime* (also known as *I Love You*), AMLF, 1980; producer (with Tarak Ben Ammar and Pierre Grunstein), *Deux heures moins le quart avant Jesus Christ* (also known as *A Quarter to Two Before Jesus Christ*), AMLF, 1982; producer, *L'Africain* (also known as *The African*), AMLF/Roissy, 1983; producer, *Banzai*, Roissy/AMLF, 1983; producer and director, *Tchao Pantin* (also known as *So Long, Stooge*), Roissy/AMLF/European Classics/Nelson Entertainment, 1983; producer (with Ariel Zeitoun and Marie-Laure Reyre), *L'Homme blesse* (also known as *The Wounded Man*), Gaumont/World Marketing/Promovision International/ Cinevista, 1983, released in the United States in 1985; producer (with Alain Sarde), *Garcon!* (also known as *Waiter!*), AMLF/Roissy, 1983, released in the United States in 1985; producer, *Le Vengeance du serpent a plumes* (also known as *The Vengeance of the Winged Serpent*), AMLF, 1984; producer (with Pio Angeletti and Adriano De Micheli), *Scemo di guerra* (also known as *Madman at War* and *Le Fou de guerre*), Titanus/Sergio Felicioli, 1985; director, *Jean de Florette*, Orion Classics, 1986; producer and director, *Manon des Sources* (also known as *Manon of the Springs*), Orion Classics, 1986; producer, *Hotel de France*, Films du Volcan, 1987; producer, *Trois places pour le 26* (also known as *Three Seats for the 26th*), AMLF/Gaumont/Roissy, 1988; executive producer, *A Gauche en sortant de l'ascenseur* (also known as *To the Left As You Leave the Elevator* and *The Door on the Left as You Leave the Elevator*), AMLF/Roissy, 1988; producer, *The Bear*, Tri-Star, 1989; producer (with Paul Rassam and Michael Haussman), *Valmont*, AMLF/Orion/Roissy, 1989. Also co-director, *Les Baisers*, 1964;

co-director, *La Chance et l'amour*, 1964; director, *Le Cinema de Papa*, 1971; producer and director, *Le Maitre d'ecole*.

RELATED CAREER—Owner, Renn Films.

NON-RELATED CAREER—Furrier.

WRITINGS: See production details above. FILM—(Co-writer) *Les Baisers*, 1964; (co-writer) *La Chance et l'amour*, 1964; (with Michel Rivelin and Gerard Brach) *Le Vieil homme et l'enfant*, 1968; *Mazel Tov ou le Mariage*, 1969; *Le Pistonne*, 1970; *Le Cinema de Papa*, 1971; *Le Sex Shop*, 1972; (with Jean-Louis Richard) *Le Male du siecle*, 1975; *La Premiere fois*, 1976; *Un Moment d'egarement*, 1977; *Je vous aime*, 1980; (with Alain Page) *Tchao Pantin*, 1983; (with Brach) *Jean de Florette*, 1986; (with Brach) *Manon des Sources*, 1986; also *Le Maitre d'ecole*.

AWARDS: Venice Film Festival Award, 1963, and Academy Award, Best Short Subject, 1965, both for *Le Poulet;* Academy Award nomination, Best Film, 1980, for *Tess.**

*   *   *

BERRY, Ken   1933-

PERSONAL: Born November 3, 1933, in Moline, IL; married Jackie Joseph (an actress); children: John and Jennifer (both adopted).

VOCATION: Actor.

CAREER: PRINCIPAL STAGE APPEARANCES—Ensemble, *The Billy Barnes People* (revue), Royale Theatre, New York City, 1961; Professor Harold Hill, *The Music Man*, Paper Mill Playhouse, Millburn, NJ, 1974; George M. Cohan, *George M!*, Music Circus, Sacramento, CA, 1976.

PRINCIPAL FILM APPEARANCES—Mel Cheever, *Hello Down There* (also known as *Sub-a-Dub-Dub*), Paramount, 1969; Willoughby Whitfield, *Herbie Rides Again*, Buena Vista, 1974; Zachary Moore, *Guardian of the Wilderness*, Sunn Classic, 1977; Frank, *The Cat from Outer Space*, Buena Vista, 1978; also appeared in *Two for the Seesaw*, United Artists, 1962.

TELEVISION DEBUT—*Talent Patrol*, ABC. PRINCIPAL TELEVISION APPEARANCES—Series: Woody, *The Ann Sothern Show*, CBS, 1960-61; regular, *The Bob Newhart Show*, NBC, 1962; Captain Wilton Parmenter, *F Troop*, ABC, 1965-67; Sam Jones, *Mayberry R.F.D.*, CBS, 1968-71; host, *The Ken Berry "Wow" Show*, ABC, 1972; Vinton Harper, *Mama's Family*, NBC, 1983-84, then syndicated 1986—. Pilots: *Rowan and Martin's Laugh-In*, NBC, 1967; Jack, *Letters from Three Lovers*, ABC, 1973; Ken Kelly, *Kelly's Kids* (broadcast as an episode of *The Brady Bunch*), ABC, 1974; Captain Paddy Patterson, *Over and Out*, NBC, 1976; Dr. Jim Berkley, *The Love Boat II*, ABC, 1977; Dr. Charlie Featherstone, *Featherstone's Nest*, CBS, 1979. Episodic: Sam Jones, *The Andy Griffith Show*, CBS, 1968; Dave, *Gimme a Break*, NBC, 1985; also *The Dick Van Dyke Show*, CBS, 1964; as Dr. Kapish, *Dr. Kildare*, NBC; *The Ed Sullivan Show*, CBS; *The Carol Burnett Show*, CBS; *Fantasy Island*, ABC; *Love, American Style*, ABC. Movies: Lieutenant Roger Carrington, *Wake Me When the War Is Over*, ABC, 1969; Lieutenant Parnell Murphy, *The Reluctant Heroes*, ABC, 1971; David Chase, *Every Man Needs One*, ABC, 1972. Specials: *Carol and Company*, CBS, 1966; Skip, *The*

Royal Follies of 1933, NBC, 1967; *The Fabulous Funnies,* NBC, 1968; first husband, *The First Nine Months Are the Hardest,* NBC, 1971; *L'il Abner,* NBC, 1971; Dauntless the Drab, *Once Upon a Mattress,* CBS, 1972; *Arthur Godfrey's Portable Electric Medicine Show,* NBC, 1972; *Mitzi . . . The First Time,* CBS, 1973; *Mitzi and a Hundred Guys,* CBS, 1975; *Mitzi . . . Roarin' in the Twenties,* CBS, 1976; Jimmy Valentine, *Valentine's Second Chance,* ABC, 1977; *CBS: On the Air,* CBS, 1978; *Texaco Star Theatre: Opening Night,* NBC, 1982; Phil Harper, *Eunice,* CBS, 1982.

RELATED CAREER—Toured with Horace Heidt's Youth Opportunity Caravan during the 1940s, and with the Billy Barnes Revue, 1959.

ADDRESSES: MANAGER—Richard O. Linke and Associates, 4445 Cartwright Avenue, Suite 110, North Hollywood, CA 91602.*

*   *   *

BERUH, Joseph   1924-1989

PERSONAL: Born September 27, 1924, in Pittsburgh, PA; died of a heart attack, October 30, 1989, in New York, NY; son of William Israel (a dry cleaner) and Clara (Parnes) Beruh; married Kathleen Murray (an actress), 1955 (died, August 1969); children: David Marshall and William Israel. EDUCATION—Carnegie-Mellon University, B.F.A., drama, 1950; studied acting and directing with Lee Strasberg, 1950-56, and attended the American Theatre Wing, 1951-52. MILITARY—U.S. Army, Special Services, 1943-46.

VOCATION: Producer, theatre manager, and director.

CAREER: STAGE DEBUT—Teddy Brewster, *Arsenic and Old Lace,* Rabbit Run Theatre, Madison, OH, 1946. OFF-BROADWAY DEBUT—Friend Ed, *Burning Bright,* Loft Players, Circle in the Square, 1951. PRINCIPAL STAGE APPEARANCES—Crookfinger Jake, *The Threepenny Opera,* Theatre De Lys, New York City, 1954; prison guard, drugstore clerk, waiter, and Danny Mines, *Compulsion,* Ambassador Theatre, New York City, 1957.

PRINCIPAL STAGE WORK— Director, *Missouri Legend, The Male Animal, Harvey, Peg o' My Heart, A Streetcar Named Desire, The Hasty Heart, Of Mice and Men,* and *Born Yesterday,* all Grand Teton National Theatre, Jackson Hole, WY, 1953; director, *A Sound of Hunting,* Cherry Lane Theatre, New York City, 1953; stage manager, *Compulsion,* Ambassador Theatre, New York City, 1957; producer (with Peter Kent), *Leave It to Jane,* Sheridan Square Playhouse, New York City, 1959; general manager, *The Goose,* Sullivan Street Playhouse, New York City, 1960; producer (with Lawrence Carra), *Kittiwake Island,* Martinique Theatre, New York City, 1960; general manager, *Elsa Lanchester—Herself,* 41st Street Theatre, New York City, 1961; director, *The Seven at Dawn* and general manager, *Cockeyed Kite,* both Actors Playhouse, New York City, 1961; general manager, *Hi, Paisano!,* York Playhouse, New York City, 1961; general manager, *The Long Voyage Home* and *Diff'rent* (double-bill), Mermaid Theatre, New York City, 1961; company manager, *Sunday in New York,* Cort Theatre, New York City, 1961; general manager, *Brecht on Brecht,* Theatre De Lys, 1962; company manager, *Moon on a Rainbow Shawl,* East 11th Street Theatre, New York City, 1962; general manager, *Creditors,* Mermaid Theatre, 1962; company manager, *I Can Get It for You Wholesale,* Shubert Theatre, New York City, 1962; general manager, *Anything Goes,* Orpheum Theatre, New York City, 1962;

producer, *The Cats Pajamas,* Sheridan Square Playhouse, 1962; general manager, *Riverwind,* Actors Playhouse, 1962; general manager, *The Typist* and *The Tiger* (double-bill), Orpheum Theatre, 1963; general manager, *Yes Is for a Very Young Man,* Players Theatre, New York City, 1963; general manager, *A Time of the Key,* Sheridan Square Playhouse, 1963; general manager, *Jo,* Orpheum Theatre, 1964; general manager, *Cindy* and *The Alchemist,* both Gate Theatre, New York City, 1964; general manager, *The Subject Was Roses,* Royale Theatre, New York City, 1964; general manager, *Gogo Loves You, I Knock at the Door,* and *Pictures in the Hallway,* all Theatre De Lys, 1964.

General manager, *A View from the Bridge,* Sheridan Square Playhouse, 1965; general manager, *The Day the Whores Came Out to Play Tennis* and *Sing to Me Through Open Windows* (double-bill), Players Theatre, 1965; general manager, *First One Asleep, Whistle,* Belasco Theatre, New York City, 1966; general manager (with Bill Levine), *Die Mitschuldigen (The Accomplices)* and *Woyzeck* (double-bill) and *Die Ratten (The Rats)* all Bavarian State Theatre of Munich, City Center Theatre, New York City, 1966; general manager, *That Summer—That Fall,* Helen Hayes Theatre, New York City, 1967; general manager, *Arms and the Man,* Sheridan Square Playhouse, 1967; general manager, *Fragments,* Cherry Lane Theatre, 1967; general manager, *In Circles,* Cherry Lane Theatre, 1967, then Gramercy Arts Theatre, New York City, 1968; general manager, *Love and Let Love* and *Saturday Night,* both Sheridan Square Playhouse, 1968; general manager, *Who's Who, Baby?,* Players Theatre, 1968; general manager, *The Only Game in Town,* Broadhurst Theatre, New York City, 1968; general manager, *Woman Is My Idea,* Belasco Theatre, 1968; general manager, *An Ordinary Man,* Cherry Lane Theatre, 1968; general manager, *To Be Young, Gifted, and Black* and *Love Your Crooked Neighbor,* both Cherry Lane Theatre, 1969; general manager, *A Way of Life,* American National Theatre and Academy Theatre, New York City, 1969; general manager, *God Bless You, Harold Fineberg,* Actors Playhouse, 1969; producer (with Edgar Lansbury), *Promenade,* Promenade Theatre, New York City, 1969; general manager, *Fireworks,* Village South Theatre, New York City, 1969.

Producer, *Instructions for the Running of Trains, Etc. on the Erie Railway To Go into Effect January 1, 1862* and general manager, *Golden Bat,* both Sheridan Square Playhouse, 1970; general manager, *Look to the Lilies,* Lunt-Fontanne Theatre, New York City, 1970; general manager, *The Engagement Baby,* Helen Hayes Theatre, 1970; producer (with Lansbury, Stuart Duncan, and H.B. Lutz) and general manager, *Waiting for Godot* and producer (with Lansbury, Duncan, and Nan Pearlman), *Louis and the Elephant,* both Sheridan Square Playhouse, 1971; general manager, *Do It Again!* and producer (with Lansbury, Duncan, and Jay H. Fuchs) and general manager, *Long Day's Journey into Night,* both Promenade Theatre, 1971; producer (with Lansbury and Duncan), *Godspell,* Cherry Lane Theatre, 1971, then Promenade Theatre, 1971-76, later Broadhurst Theatre, 1976, then Plymouth Theatre, 1976, then Ambassador Theatre, 1977; producer (with Lansbury and Duncan), *Godspell,* Wyndham's Theatre, London, 1971; producer (with Lansbury and Duncan), *Elizabeth I,* Lyceum Theatre, New York City, 1972; producer (with Lansbury and Duncan), *Comedy,* Colonial Theatre, Boston, MA, 1972; producer (with Lansbury), *Nourish the Beast,* American Place Theatre, Cherry Lane Theatre, 1973; producer (with Lansbury and Clinton Wilder), *The Enclave,* Theatre Four, New York City, 1973; producer (with Lansbury, Barry M. Brown, and Fritz Holt), *Gypsy,* Piccadilly Theatre, London, 1973, then Shubert Theatre, Los Angeles, later Winter Garden Theatre, New York City, both 1974; producer (with Lansbury and Ivan Reitman), *The Magic Show,* Cort Theatre, 1974; producer (with

Lansbury), *The Night That Made America Famous*, Ethel Barrymore Theatre, New York City, 1975; producer (with Lansbury), *Blasts and Bravos—An Evening with H.L. Mencken*, Cherry Lane Theatre, 1975; producer (with Lansbury), *American Buffalo*, Ethel Barrymore Theatre, then Belasco Theatre, both 1977; producer (with Lansbury and James Nederlander), *Broadway Follies*, Nederlander Theatre, New York City, 1981.

MAJOR TOURS—General manager, *The Porcelain Year*, U.S. cities, 1965; general manager, *The Subject Was Roses*, U.S. cities, 1965-66; producer (with Edgar Lansbury and Stuart Duncan), *Godspell*, U.S. and Canadian cities, 1972-74; producer (with Lansbury, Barry M. Brown, and Fritz Holt), *Gypsy*, U.S. and Canadian cities, 1974-75; producer (with Lansbury and Ivan Reitman), *The Magic Show*, U.S. cities, 1974-75.

PRINCIPAL FILM WORK—All with Edgar Lansbury: Producer, *Godspell*, Columbia, 1973; executive producer, *The Wild Party*, American International, 1975; executive producer, *Squirm*, American International, 1976; executive producer, *Blue Sunshine*, Cinema Shares, 1978; executive producer, *He Knows You're Alone*, Metro-Goldwyn-Mayer/United Artists, 1980; executive producer, *The Killing Hour*, Twentieth Century-Fox, 1983; also producer, *The Clairvoyant*, 1982.

RELATED CAREER—Owner (with Philip Minor and Gigi Cascio), Sheridan Square Playhouse, New York City, 1958-73; business manager, South Shore Music Circus, Hyannis, MA, 1960; general manager and co-producer, Gladiators Music Arena, Totowa, NJ, 1963; founder and partner (with Edgar Lansbury), Lansbury/Beruh Productions Inc., 1969-89.

AWARDS: New York Drama Critics' Circle Award, Best American Play, 1977, for *American Buffalo;* Alumni Merit Award from Carnegie-Mellon University, 1987.

MEMBER: Actors' Equity Association, Screen Actors Guild, American Federation of Television and Radio Artists, Association of Theatrical Producers and Managers, League of New York Theatres.

OBITUARIES AND OTHER SOURCES: New York Times, October 31, 1989; *Variety,* November 8, 1989.*

*   *   *

BETTI, Laura

PERSONAL: Born May 1, 1934, Bologna, Italy.

VOCATION: Actress and singer.

CAREER: STAGE DEBUT—*I Saltimbanchi* (revue), Italy. PRINCIPAL STAGE APPEARANCES—*Il ventaglio* and *Il crogiuolo*, both Italy, 1958; *Giro a vuoto* (recital), Teatro Gerolamo, Milan, Italy, 1959, then in France, and later at the Venice Biennial Exhibition; *Le donne al parlamento*, Italy, 1960; *Potentissima signora*, Italy, 1963; *Il candelaio* and *Orgia*, both in Italy, 1968; *Not I*, Italy, 1970; *Orgia*, Italy, 1984.

PRINCIPAL FILM APPEARANCES—Laura, *La dolce vita*, Astor/ American International, 1961; painter, *Labbra rosse* (also known as *Red Lips* and *Fausses ingenues*), Rotor/Gray/Orsay, 1960, released in the United States by Royal Films International, 1964;

LAURA BETTI

tourist, "Senso civico" in *Le streghe* (also known as *The Witches* and *Les Sorcieres*), Dino De Laurentiis Cinematografica, 1967, released in the United States by Lopert, 1969; maid, *Teorema* (also known as *Theorem*), Continental Distributing, 1969; Sister, *A Man Called Sledge*, Columbia, 1971; Franco's mother, *In nome del Padre* (also known as *In the Name of the Father*), Vides International, 1971; Clara, *Ritorno* (also known as *Return*), Capranica Cinematografica, 1972; Zigaina, *Sbatti il mostro in prima pagina* (also known as *Slap the Monster on Page One*), Euro International, 1972; Miss Blandish, *Last Tango in Paris*, United Artists, 1973; Donna Aparacito, *Sonny and Jed* (also known as *La banda J. and S. Cronaca criminale del far west*), Loyola Cinematography/Terra K-Tel, 1974; Tisa Borghi, *Fatti di gente perbene* (also known as *Drama of the Rich*), Produzioni Atlas Consorziate, 1974; Leonore, *La Femme aux bottes rouges* (also known as *The Woman with Red Boots*), Union General Cinematographique/Sirius, 1974, released in the United States by Gamma III, 1977.

Voice of Signora Vaccari, *Salo o le centiventi giornate di Sodoma* (also known as *Salo, or the 120 Days of Sodom, Pasolini's 120 Days of Sodom,* and *Salo*), United Artists/Cinecenta, 1975; Esther Imbriani, *Allonsanfan* Artificial Eye, 1975, released in the United States by Italtoons/Wonder Movies, 1985; Regina, *1900* (also known as *Novecento*), Paramount/United Artists/Twentieth Century-Fox, 1976; Felicia, *Le Gang*, Warner Brothers, 1976; Therese, *Vizi privati, pubbliche virtu* (also *Private Vices, Public Virtue*), Fida Cinematografica, 1976; Irina, *Il gabbiano* (also known as *The Seagull*), RAI-TV Channel 1, 1977; Jacqueline, *La Nuit tous les chat sont gris* (also known as *At Night All Cats Are Gray*), Societe Nouvelle Prodis/Exportation Francaise Cinematographique, 1977;

Madame Carrabo, *Un Papillon sur l'epaule* (also known as *A Butterfly on the Shoulder*), Gaumont, 1978; Ludovica, *La Luna,* Twentieth Century-Fox, 1979; Madame Bondi, *Il Piccolo Archimede* (also known as *The Little Archimedes*), RAI-TV Channel 2, 1979; Laura, *Lovers and Liars* (also known as *A Trip with Anita* and *Travels with Anita*), Levitt-Pickman, 1981; Virginia Capacelli, *La Nuit de Varennes,* Triumph, 1983; Carlotta Battucelli, *Retenez-moi . . . ou je fais un malheur* (also known as *To Catch a Cop*), Gaumont, 1984; Brunelda, *Klassenverhaltnisse* (also known as *Class Relations*), Artificial Eye/New Yorker, 1984; narrator, *Whoever Says the Truth Shall Die* (documentary), Minnesota Film Center, 1984.

Lidia Corradi, *Mamma Ebe,* Clemi Cinematografica, 1985; social worker, *Tutta colpa del paradiso* (also known as *Blame It on Paradise*), CEIAD, 1985; Laurie, *Corps et biens* (also known as *Lost with All Hands*), Films du Scmaphore, 1986; Miss Von Planta, *Jenatsch* (also known as *Jenach*), Films Plain Chant/Metropolis, 1987; Keli, *Noyade interdite* (also known as *Widow's Walk*), Bac, 1987; Anna's mother, *I cammelli* (also known as *The Camels*), Medusa Distribuzione, 1988; Signora Bonelli, *Courage Mountain* (also known as *A Heidi Adventure* and *The Adventures of Heidi*), Emerald Films International/Trans World Entertainment, 1989. Also appeared in *Era notte a Roma,* 1959; "La Ricotta," *Rogopag,* Arco, 1963; "Che cosa sono le nuvole?," *Capriccio all'italiana,* Dino De Laurentiis Cinematografica, 1966; *Paulina s'en va,* 1969; *Hatchet for a Honeymoon* (also known as *Una hacka para la luna de miel, Il roso segmo della pollias,* and *Blood Brides*), G.G.P., 1969; *Canterbury Tales,* United Artists, 1972; *Antefatto* (also known as *Twitch of the Death Nerve, Before the Fact—The Ecology of a Crime, Bloodbath,* and *Last House on the Left, Part II*), New Realm Distributors, 1971, then Hallmark, 1973; *Sepolta viva,* 1973; *Loin de Manhattan,* 1980; *Le ali della colomba,* RAI-TV, 1980; *La certosa di Parma,* RAI-TV, 1981; *L'Art d'aimer* (also known as *The Art of Love*), Parafrance, 1983; *Caramelle da un sconosciuto* (also known as *Sweets from a Stranger* and *Bonbons offerts par un inconnu*), Numero Uno Cinematografica, 1987; *A Futura memoria di Pier Paolo Pasolini* (also known as *In Remembrance of Pier Paolo Pasolini* and *A la memoire future de Pier Paolo Pasolini;* documentary), Pegaso Inter-Communication, 1987; *Jane B. par Agnes V.* (also known as *Jane V. by Agnes V., Birkin Double Jeu I,* and *Birkin Diptych I*), Capital Cinema/Cene-Tamaris, 1988; *Segno di fuoco,* Boa Cinematografica, 1989; *Le ros blu,* Kitchen, 1989.

PRINCIPAL TELEVISION APPEARANCES—Movies: Maria, *The Word,* CBS, 1978. Also *Venise en hiver,* French television, 1982; *Chambre d'amie,* French television, 1985.

RELATED CAREER—Singer with the Filarmonica Romana and with the Accademia Cherubini, Florence, Italy; recorded entire repertory of Bertolt Brecht and Kurt Weill songs; director, Associazione Fondo Pier Paolo Pasolini.

WRITINGS: *Teta Veleta* (fiction).

AWARDS: Coppa Volpi from the Vencie Film Festival, Best Actress, 1968, for *Teorema;* San Sebastian Film Festival Award, Best Actress, 1979; French Legion of Honor, 1984.

ADDRESSES: OFFICE—4 Via Di Montoro, Rome, Italy.

BEVERLEY, Trazana   1945-

PERSONAL: Born August 9, 1945, in Baltimore, MD; father, a brickmason; mother, a schoolteacher. EDUCATION—Graduated from New York University; studied acting with Jerzy Grotowski, Andrei Serban, Jean Erdman, and Omar Shapli.

VOCATION: Actress.

CAREER: Also see *WRITINGS* below. OFF-BROADWAY DEBUT—*Rules for Running,* 1969. PRINCIPAL STAGE APPEARANCES—Erlene and Carolyn's mother, *Les Femmes Noires,* New York Shakespeare Festival (NYSF), Public Theatre, New York City, 1974; a spectre, *My Sister, My Sister,* Little Theatre, New York City, 1974; Maxine, *Attempted Rescue on Avenue B,* Cubiculo Theatre, New York City, 1975; lady in red, *For Colored Girls Who Have Considered Suicide When the Rainbow Is Enuf,* NYSF, Public Theatre, then Booth Theatre, both New York City, 1976; Marietta Edwards, *The Brothers,* Women's Project, American Place Theatre, New York City, 1982; Iyaloja, *Death and the King's Horseman,* Vivian Beaumont Theatre, New York City, 1987; Reverend Sister Marion Alexander, *God's Trombones,* New Federal Church, Theatre of the Riverside Church, New York City, 1989. Also appeared in *The Increased Difficulty of Concentration,* Repertory Theatre of Lincoln Center, Forum Theatre, New York City, 1969; *Wedding Band,* Hartford Stage Company, Hartford, CT, 1978; *Mother Courage and Her Children,* NYSF, Public Theatre, then Center Stage Mainstage, Baltimore, MD, both 1980; *Boesman and Lena,* Northlight Theatre, Evanston, IL, 1985; as Queenie, *Show Boat;* and in productions of *Geronimo* and *Antigone.*

MAJOR TOURS—Lady in red, *For Colored Girls Who Have Considered Suicide When the Rainbow Is Enuf,* U.S. cities, 1977-78; also *The Spirit Moves* (one-woman show), U.S. cities.

PRINCIPAL FILM APPEARANCES—Dr. Ellen Baxter, *Resurrection,* Universal, 1980.

PRINCIPAL TELEVISION APPEARANCES—Movies: Johnny, *Sister Margaret and the Saturday Night Ladies,* CBS, 1987. Specials: "For Colored Girls Who Have Considered Suicide When the Rainbow Is Enuf," *American Playhouse,* PBS, 1982.

RELATED CAREER—Toured New York State prisons with the theatrical group, the Family; acting and voice production teacher, New York University School of the Arts; company member, Group Ten.

WRITINGS: STAGE—*The Spirit Moves* (one-woman show).

AWARDS: Antoinette Perry Award, Best Supporting or Featured Actress (Drama), and Audience Development Committee (AUDELCO) Award, both 1977, for *For Colored Girls Who Have Considered Suicide When the Rainbow Is Enuf.**

*   *   *

BIEHN, Michael   1957-

PERSONAL: Born in 1957; father, a lawyer.

VOCATION: Actor.

CAREER: PRINCIPAL FILM APPEARANCES—Jack, *Coach*, Crown International, 1978; Tim Warner, *Hog Wild*, AVCO-Embassy, 1980; Douglas Breen, *The Fan*, Paramount, 1981; Alexander, *The Lords of Discipline*, Paramount, 1983; Kyle Reese, *The Terminator*, Orion, 1984; Corporal Hicks, *Aliens*, Twentieth Century-Fox, 1986; Anthony Fraser, *Rampage*, DeLaurentiis Entertainment Group (unreleased), 1987; Russell Quinn, *The Seventh Sign*, Tri-Star, 1988; Garnet Montrose, *In a Shallow Grave*, Skouras, 1988; Lieutenant Coffey, *The Abyss*, Twentieth Century-Fox, 1989.

TELEVISION DEBUT—*Logan's Run*, CBS, 1977. PRINCIPAL TELEVISION APPEARANCES—Series: Mark Johnson, *Operation: Runaway*, NBC, 1978-79. Pilots: Tony, *James at 15*, NBC, 1977; Larry DeWitt, *The Paradise Connection*, CBS, 1979; Gibby Anderson, *Steeltown*, CBS, 1979. Episodic: *Hill Street Blues*, NBC; *Police Story*, NBC; *Family*, ABC. Movies: J.D., *Zuma Beach*, NBC, 1978; Tom Reardon, *A Fire in the Sky*, NBC, 1978; Daniel Allen, *China Rose*, CBS, 1983; Charles Raynor, *Deadly Intentions*, ABC, 1985. Specials: Seth, "The Terrible Secret," *ABC Afterschool Specials*, ABC, 1979.

ADDRESSES: AGENT—Ed Limato, William Morris Agency, 151 El Camino Drive, Beverly Hills, CA 90212.*

* * *

BISOGLIO, Val 1926-

PERSONAL: Born May 7, 1926, in New York, NY.

VOCATION: Actor.

CAREER: OFF-BROADWAY DEBUT—Peter, *Kiss Mama*, Actors Playhouse, 1964. PRINCIPAL STAGE APPEARANCES—Alfieri, *A View from the Bridge*, Sheridan Square Playhouse, New York City, 1965; Sergeant Carlino, *Wait Until Dark*, Ethel Barrymore Theatre, New York City, 1966; detective and Nicholas, *Victims of Duty*, Theatre for Actors and Playwrights, Colonnades Theatre, New York City, 1982. Also appeared in *They'd Come to See Charlie*, Hartford Stage Company, Hartford, CT, 1977.

MAJOR TOURS—Sergeant Carlino, *Wait Until Dark*, U.S. cities, 1967.

PRINCIPAL FILM APPEARANCES—Gangster, *The Cool World*, Cinema V, 1963; Cheech, *The Brotherhood*, Paramount, 1968; Detective Monaghan, *No Way to Treat a Lady*, Paramount, 1968; Pete Lazatti, *The Don Is Dead* (also known as *Beautiful But Deadly*) Universal, 1973; Lieutenant Lombardi, *The Hindenburg*, Universal, 1975; Finley Cummins, *St. Ives*, Warner Brothers, 1976; Frank Manero, Sr., *Saturday Night Fever*, Paramount, 1977; Chief Gray Cloud, *The Frisco Kid* (also known as *No Knife*), Warner Brothers, 1979. Also appeared in *Hot Rod Hullabaloo*, Allied Artists, 1966; *Linda Lovelace for President*, General Film, 1975.

PRINCIPAL TELEVISION APPEARANCES—Series: Captain Rocco Calvelli, *Roll Out*, CBS, 1973-74; Lieutenant Paul Marsh, *Police Woman*, NBC, 1974-76; Danny Tovo, *Quincy, M.E.*, NBC, 1976-83; Al Steckler, *Working Stiffs*, CBS, 1979. Pilots: Bendix man, *Inside O.U.T.*, NBC, 1971; Sergeant James, *Matt Helm*, ABC, 1975; Curry, *Switch* (also known as *Las Vegas Roundabout*), CBS, 1975; Papa Bagranditello, *Flying High*, CBS, 1978; Frankie Parker, *Johnny Garage*, CBS, 1983; also *The Life and Times of Barney*

Miller (broadcast as an episode of *Just for Laughs*), ABC, 1974. Episodic: Sergeant DiSalvo, *Joe Bash*, ABC, 1986; Gus Albierro, *Miami Vice*, NBC, 1986; also *The Mary Tyler Moore Show*, CBS, 1971; *All in the Family*, CBS, 1972; *Barney Miller*, ABC, 1975; *M*A*S*H*, CBS, 1981 and 1982; *Hill Street Blues*, NBC, 1985. Movies: Detective Lou Jacarrino, *The Marcus-Nelson Murders* (also known as *Kojak and the Marcus-Nelson Murders*), CBS, 1973.

RELATED CAREER—Associate producer, Colonnades Theatre Lab, New York City, 1980.

ADDRESSES: AGENT—Joshua Gray and Associates Talent Agency, 6736 Laurel Canyon Boulevard, North Hollywood, CA 91606.*

* * *

BLACQUE, Taurean

PERSONAL: Born May 10 in Newark, NJ; children: Shelby, Rodney. EDUCATION—Attended the American Musical and Dramatic Academy.

VOCATION: Actor.

CAREER: BROADWAY DEBUT—*The River Niger*, Brooks Atkinson Theatre, 1973. PRINCIPAL STAGE APPEARANCES—D.J., *Welcome to Black River* and title role, *Orrin*, both Negro Ensemble Company, St. Mark's Playhouse, New York City, 1975; Luke, *We Interrupt This Program . . .*, Ambassador Theatre, New York City, 1975; Lee, *So Nice They Named It Twice*, New York Shakespeare Festival, Public Theatre, New York City, 1975-76; Rashad, *The Meeting*, New Federal Theatre, Henry Street Settlement Playhouse, New York City, 1987.

PRINCIPAL FILM APPEARANCES—Levi, *House Calls*, Universal, 1978; lawyer, *Rocky II*, United Artists, 1979; hustler, *The Hunter*, Paramount, 1980; voice of Roscoe, *Oliver and Company* (animated), Buena Vista, 1988; Laidlaw, *Deepstar Six*, Tri-Star, 1989.

PRINCIPAL TELEVISION APPEARANCES—Series: Detective Neal Washington, *Hill Street Blues*, NBC, 1981-1987; Henry Marshall, *Generations*, NBC, 1989—. Mini-Series: *Backstairs at the White House*, NBC, 1979. Pilots: Nick, *Frankie and Annette: The Second Time Around*, NBC, 1978; Barney, *Alex and the Doberman Gang*, NBC, 1980; Carl Sebastian, *Off Duty* (broadcast as an episode of *CBS Summer Playhouse*), CBS, 1988. Episodic: *The Bob Newhart Show*, CBS, 1977 and 1978 (two episodes); *Taxi*, ABC, 1978. Movies: Jive, *The $5.20 an Hour Dream*, CBS, 1980; Oscar, *The Night the City Screamed*, ABC, 1980.

NON-RELATED CAREER—Mailman.

AWARDS: Emmy Award nomination, 1982, for *Hill Street Blues*.

ADDRESSES: AGENT—Jack Fields, Gores/Fields Agency, 10100 Santa Monica Boulevard, Suite 700, Los Angeles, CA 90067.*

BLAKE, Josh   1975-

PERSONAL: Born January 7, 1975, in Great Neck, NY; son of Frederick David (a podiatrist) and Elizabeth L. (a teacher; maiden name, Stein).

VOCATION: Actor.

CAREER: STAGE DEBUT—Ulysses Macauley, The Human Comedy, New York Shakespeare Festival, Public Theatre, New York City, 1983. BROADWAY DEBUT—Ulysses Macauley, The Human Comedy, Royale Theatre, 1984. PRINCIPAL STAGE APPEARANCES—Paperboy, For Sale, Playhouse 91, New York City, 1985; Irving Yanover, Today I Am a Fountain Pen, American Jewish Theatre Company, 92nd Street YMHA, New York City, 1985-86, then Theatre 890, New York City, 1986; David Hershkowitz, Rags, Shubert Theatre, Boston, MA, then Mark Hellinger Theatre, New York City, both 1985; also appeared in The Second Hurricane, New York City, 1984.

PRINCIPAL FILM APPEARANCES—Older boy, Fat Guy Goes Nutzoid!, Troma, 1986.

PRINCIPAL TELEVISION APPEARANCES—Series: Craig, Search for Tomorrow, NBC, 1986; Woody Greely, Once a Hero, ABC, 1987; Jake, Alf, NBC, 1988-89; Aristotle Zakalokis, The Famous Teddy Z, CBS, 1989—. Pilots: Jonathan Morgan, Father's Day, ABC, 1986. Episodic: Tony Ramos, Beauty and the Beast, CBS, 1988; Nickt Hackett, "Rock 'n' Roll Mom," Disney Sunday Movie, ABC, 1988; also voice characterization, Comic Strip (animated), 1987. Specials: Voice of child, The Life and Adventures of Santa Claus (animated), CBS, 1985.

RELATED CAREER—Actor in television commercials.

AWARDS: Goldie Award from the American Jewish Theatre, 1985.

MEMBER: American Federation of Television and Radio Artists, Screen Actors Guild, Actors' Equity Association.

SIDELIGHTS: RECREATIONS—Collecting baseball cards and rocks.

ADDRESSES: AGENT—Shirley Grant Management, P.O. Box 866, Teaneck, NJ 07666.

*   *   *

BLANC, Mel   1908-1989

PERSONAL: Full name, Melvin Jerome Blanc; born May 30, 1908, in San Francisco, CA; died of heart disease and emphysema, July 10, 1989, in Los Angeles, CA; son of Frederick and Eva (Katz) Blanc (co-managers of a women's clothing business); married Estelle Rosenbaum, 1933; children: Noel.

VOCATION: Voice specialist, actor, and producer.

CAREER: Also see WRITINGS below. PRINCIPAL FILM APPEARANCES—Voice of Gideon, Pinocchio (animated), Walt Disney, 1940; Julio, Neptune's Daughter, Metro-Goldwyn-Mayer, 1949; voice of Caesar, Champagne for Caesar, United Artists, 1950; voice characterizations, Gay Purr-ee (animated), Warner Brothers, 1962; voice of Grifter, Hey There, It's Yogi Bear (animated),

Columbia, 1964; Dr. Sheldrake, Kiss Me, Stupid, Lopert, 1964; voice of Barney Rubble and Dino, The Man Called Flintstone (also known as That Man Flintstone; animated), Columbia, 1966.

Voice characterizations, The Phantom Tollbooth (animated), Metro-Goldwyn-Mayer, 1970; voice of Barfly the Parrot, Scalawag, Paramount, 1973; voice characterizations, Journey Back to Oz (animated), Filmation, 1974; voice characterizations, Bugs Bunny, Superstar (animated), Warner Brothers, 1975; voice of Twiki and Dr. Theopolis, Buck Rogers in the 25th Century, Universal, 1979; voice characterizations, The Great American Bugs Bunny-Road Runner Chase (animated; also known as The Bugs Bunny-Road Runner Movie), Warner Brothers, 1979; voice characterizations, The Looney, Looney, Looney Bugs Bunny Movie, Warner Brothers, 1981; voice characterizations, Bugs Bunny's Third Movie—1001 Rabbit Tales (animated), Warner Brothers, 1982; voice characterizations, Daffy Duck's Movie: Fantastic Island (animated), Warner Brothers, 1983; voice of Mr. McKenzie, Strange Brew, Metro-Goldwyn Mayer/United Artists, 1983; voice of Heathcliff, Heathcliff: The Movie (animated), Atlantic/Clubhouse, 1986; voice of Daffy Duck, Howard the Duck, Universal, 1986; voice characterizations, Porky Pig in Hollywood (animated), Warner Brothers, 1986; voice characterizations, The Duxorcist (short animated film), Warner Brothers, 1987; voice characterizations, Daffy Duck's Quackbusters (animated), Warner Brothers, 1988; voice of Daffy Duck, Night of the Living Duck (short film; animated), Warner Brothers, 1988; voices of Daffy Duck, Tweety Bird, Bugs Bunny, Sylvester, and Porky Pig, Who Framed Roger Rabbit?, Buena Vista, 1988. Also provided voice characterizations for more than 850 short animated films for Warner Brothers, 1937-88.

PRINCIPAL TELEVISION APPEARANCES—Series: Regular, The Jack Benny Program, CBS, 1950-64, then NBC, 1964-65; panelist, Musical Chairs, NBC, 1955; voice characterizations, The Bugs Bunny Show (animated), ABC, 1960-62; voice of Barney Rubble and Dino, The Flintstones (animated), ABC, 1960-66; voice characterizations, The Dick Tracy Show (animated), syndicated, 1961; voice of Salty the Parrot, "Sinbad, Jr." in The Alvin Show (animated), CBS, 1961-62; voice of Hardy Har Har, Lippy the Lion (animated), syndicated, 1962; voice of Mr. Spacely and other characters, The Jetsons (animated), ABC, 1962-64; voice of Deputy Droop-A-Long, "Ricochet Rabbit," The Magilla Gorilla Show (animated), syndicated, 1964; voice of Sneezly, "Sneezly" in The Peter Potamus Show (animated), syndicated, 1964; voice characterizations, Porky Pig and Friends (animated), ABC, 1964-67; voice of Secret Squirrel, The Atom Ant/Secret Squirrel Show (animated), NBC, 1965-68; voice characterizations, The Abbott and Costello Cartoon Show (animated), syndicated, 1966; voice characterizations, The Tom and Jerry Show (animated), CBS, 1966-72; voice characterizations, The Wacky Races (animated), CBS, 1968-70; voice of Chugaboom, Yak Yak, and Bully Brothers, The Perils of Penelope Pitstop (animated), CBS, 1969-71.

Voice of Bubba McCoy, Where's Huddles? (animated), CBS, 1970; voice characterizations, The Road Runner Show (animated), ABC, 1971-72; voice characterizations, Curiosity Shop (animated), ABC, 1971-73; voice of Barney Rubble, Dino, Bronto, Zonk, and Stub, The Flintstone Comedy Hour (animated), CBS, 1972-74; voice of Speed Buggy, Speed Buggy (animated), CBS, 1973-74; voice characterizations, The Bugs Bunny Show (animated), CBS, 1975; voice of Bugs Bunny, Road Runner, and others, The Bugs Bunny/Road Runner Show (animated), CBS, 1976; voice characterizations, Sylvester and Tweety (animated), CBS, 1976-77; voice of Captain Caveman, Scooby's All-Star Laff-A-Lympics (animated), ABC, 1977-78; voice of Officer Quack-Up, The Galaxy Goof-

Ups (animated), NBC, 1978-79; voice of Quack-Up, *Yogi's Space Race* (animated), NBC, 1978-79; voice of Barney Rubble and Dino, *The New Fred and Barney Show* (animated), NBC, 1979; voice of Captain Caveman, *Captain Caveman* (animated), ABC, 1979; voice of Barney Rubble and Dino, *Fred and Barney Meet the Thing* (animated), NBC, 1979; voice of Twiki, *Buck Rogers in the 25th Century,* NBC, 1979-81; voice of Captain Caveman, *Captain Caveman and the Teen Angels* (animated), ABC, 1980; voice characterizations, *The Heathcliff and Dingbat Show* (animated), ABC, 1980-81; voice of Barney Rubble, Dino, and Chester, *The Flintstone Family Adventures* (animated), NBC, 1980-81; voice of Barney Rubble, Dino, and a pterodactyl chick, *The Flintstones* (animated), NBC, 1981; voice of Heathcliff and Spike, *The Heathcliff and Marmaduke Show* (animated), ABC, 1981-82; voice of Barney Rubble and Dino, *The Flintstone Funnies* (animated), NBC, 1984; voice characterizations, *The New Jetsons* (animated), syndicated, 1985; voice characterizations, *The Bugs Bunny/Looney Tunes Comedy Hour* (animated), ABC, 1985; voice of Captain Caveman, Dino, and Robert Rubble, *The Flintstone Kids* (also known as *Captain Caveman and Sons;* animated), ABC, 1986. Pilots: Voice of leprechaun, *Mr. O'Malley,* CBS, 1959; voice of Chickie Baby, *Murder Can Hurt You!,* ABC, 1980.

Specials: *Arthur Godfrey Loves Animals,* CBS, 1963; *Jack Benny's 20th Anniversary TV Special,* NBC, 1970; voice of Tucker the Mouse, *The Cricket in Times Square* (animated), ABC, 1973; voice of Harry the Cat, *Yankee Doodle Cricket* (animated), ABC, 1975; voice characterizations, *Bugs Bunny's Howl-oween Special* (animated), CBS, 1977; voice of Barney Rubble and Dino, *A Flintstone Christmas* (animated), NBC, 1977; voice of Bugs Bunny, Daffy Duck, Yosemite Sam, Foghorn Leghorn, and Pepe Lepew, *The Bugs Bunny Easter Special* (animated), CBS, 1977; voice of Bugs Bunny, *Bugs Bunny in Space* (animated), CBS, 1977; voice of Bugs Bunny, *How Bugs Bunny Won the West* (animated), CBS, 1978; voice characterizations, *A Connecticut Rabbit in King Arthur's Court* (animated), CBS, 1978; voice characterizations, *The Bugs Bunny Thanksgiving Diet* (animated), CBS, 1979; voice of Bugs Bunny, *Bugs Bunny's Valentine* (animated), CBS, 1979; voice characterizations, *Bugs Bunny's Looney Christmas Tales* (animated), CBS, 1979.

Voice characterizations, *The Bugs Bunny Mystery Special* (animated), CBS, 1980; voice characterizations, *Daffy Duck's Easter Show* (animated), NBC, 1980; voice characterizations, *Daffy Duck's Thanks-for-Giving Special* (animated), NBC, 1980; voice characterizations, *Bugs Bunny's Bustin Out All Over* (animated), CBS, 1980; voice characterizations, *Bugs Bunny: All American Hero* (animated), CBS, 1981; voice of Barney Rubble, second security guard, and Bulldog, *Yogi Bear's All-Star Comedy* (animated), CBS, 1982; voice of Bugs Bunny, *Bugs Bunny's Mad World of Comedy* (animated), CBS, 1985; *Bugs Bunny/Looney Tunes All-Star 50th Anniversary* (animated), CBS, 1986; voice of Barney Rubble, *The Flintstones 25th Anniversary Celebration* (animated), CBS, 1986; voice of Mr. Spacely, *Rockin' with Judy Jetson* (animated), syndicated, 1988; *Roger Rabbit and the Secrets of Toontown,* CBS, 1988; voice characterizations, *Bugs vs. Daffy: Battle of the Music Video Stars* (animated), CBS, 1988; voice of Bugs Bunny, the Crusher, Daffy Duck, Yosemite Sam, Elmer Fudd, Tweetie Bird, and Sylvester, *Bugs Bunny's Wild World of Sports* (animated), CBS, 1989; *Hanna Barbera's 50th: A Yabba Dabba Doo Celebration* (live-action and animated), TNT, 1989.

PRINCIPAL TELEVISION WORK—Producer (with others), *The Bugs Bunny Show,* ABC, 1960-62.

PRINCIPAL RADIO APPEARANCES—Series: *The Hoot Owls,* KGW (Portland, OR), 1927; various roles, *Cobwebs and Nuts,* KEX (Portland), 1933-35; *The Johnny Murray Show,* KFWB (Los Angeles), 1935-36; *The Joe Penner Show,* CBS, 1936; Professor LeBlanc, Carmichael the Bear, Sy the gardener, and train dispatcher, *The Jack Benny Program,* NBC, 1937-48; Uncle Petie and Rover, *Tommy Riggs and Betty Lou,* NBC, 1938-40; Pedro, *The Judy Canova Show,* CBS, 1940-48; Mr. Twiggs, *Major Hoople,* NBC, 1942; August Moon, *Point Sublime,* ABC, 1942-44; various roles, *Nitwit Court,* NBC, 1944; as himself and Zookie, *The Mel Blanc Show* (also known as *The Fix-It Shop* and *Mel Blanc's Fix-It Shop*), CBS, 1946-47. Also appeared on *The Al Pierce Show,* 1938-50; as host, *Are You a Genius?,* Armed Forces Radio Service; Hubert Peabody, *The Jack Carson Show,* CBS; Botsford Twink, *The Abbott and Costello Program,* NBC; Private Sad Sack, *G.I. Journal;* the Happy Postman, *Burns and Allen,* NBC; Pancho, *The Cisco Kid;* Floyd the barber, *The Great Guildersleeve;* and *Dagwood and Blondie.*

PRINCIPAL RADIO WORK—Series: Producer, *Cobwebs and Nitwits,* KEX (Portland), 1933-35.

RELATED CAREER—Professional musician playing the violin, sousaphone, and bass, 1925-30; musician with the NBC Radio Orchestra, San Francisco, CA, 1928; orchestra conductor, Orpheum Theatre, Portland, OR, 1931; member of Leon Schlesinger productions (production company for Looney Tunes and Merrie Melodies); board chairman, Blanc Communications Corporation (a production company specializing in television and radio commercials, public service announcements, and short fillers), 1960-89.

WRITINGS: RADIO—Series: *Cobwebs and Nitwits,* KEX (Portland), 1933-35. OTHER—(With Philip Bashe) *That's Not All, Folks: My Life in the Golden Age of Cartoons and Radio* (autobiography), Warner Books, 1988.

RECORDINGS: SINGLES—(With the Sportsmen) "The Woody Woodpecker Song," Capitol, 1948; "I Tawt I Taw a Puddy Tat," 1950; (with Spike Jones and His City Slickers) "Clink! Clink! Another Drink!" "Toot, Toot, Tootsie (Goodbye)." Blanc recorded comedy and children's records for Capitol Records for fifteen years.

AWARDS: Honorary mayor, Pacific Palisades, CA.

SIDELIGHTS: Mel Blanc once estimated that he supplied more than 400 different voices in approximately 3,000 cartoons between the mid-1930s and the late 1980s. Among his more familiar characterizations are those of Bugs Bunny, Porky Pig, Daffy Duck, Sylvester and Tweetie, the Road Runner, Yosemite Sam, Speedy Gonzalez, Foghorn Leghorn, Woody Woodpecker, Barney Rubble, Dino the dinosaur, Speed Buggy, Tasmanian Devil, Pepe LePew, the Frito Bandito (on television commercials), and Jack Benny's dilapidated automobile. During World War II, Blanc also provided the voice of Private Snafu for Frank Capra's wartime newsreel, *The Army-Navy Screen Magazine,* as well as voices for the Trigger Joe film series for the Army Air Forces and for a series of Navy and Marine Corps health films.

OBITUARIES AND OTHER SOURCES: The American Animated Cartoon, edited by Danny and Gerald Peary, E.P. Dutton, 1980; *Hollywood Reporter,* July 11, 1989; *New York Times,* July 11, 1989; *Variety,* July 12-18, 1989.*

BLESSED, Brian   1937-

PERSONAL: Born October 9, 1937, in Yorkshire, England; father, a coal miner; married Ann Bomann (divorced); married Hildegarde Neil (an actress); children: Catherine (first marriage); Rosalind (second marriage). EDUCATION—Trained for the stage at the Bristol Old Vic Theatre School. MILITARY—Royal Air Force, parachute regiment.

VOCATION: Actor.

CAREER: PRINCIPAL STAGE APPEARANCES—Edmund, *The Exorcism,* Comedy Theatre, London, 1975; Gorky, *State of Revolution,* National Theatre Company, Lyttelton Theatre, London, 1977; Old Deuteronomy, *Cats,* New London Theatre, London, 1981; John Freeman, *Metropolis,* Piccadilly Theatre, London, 1989. Also appeared with the Royal Shakespeare Company, Stratford-on-Avon, U.K., 1985; in *Incident at Vichy* and *Oedipus,* both in London; and in repertory at Nottingham, U.K., and Birmingham, U.K.

PRINCIPAL FILM APPEARANCES—Policeman, *The Christmas Tree,* CFF, 1966; sergeant, *Alf 'n' Family* (also known as *Till Death Do Us Part*), Sherpix, 1968; Jock Baird, *Brotherly Love* (also known as *Country Dance*), Metro Goldwyn-Mayer (MGM), 1970; Korski, *The Last Valley,* Cinerama, 1971; Tathybius, *The Trojan Women,* Cinerama, 1971; Suffolk, *Henry VIII and His Six Wives,* MGM/EMI, 1972; Pedro, *Man of La Mancha,* United Artists, 1972; Prince Vultan, *Flash Gordon,* Universal, 1980; Sulciman Khan, *High Road to China,* Warner Brothers, 1983; Geoffrey Lyons, *The Hound of the Baskervilles,* Weintraub, 1983; Exeter, *Henry V,* Samuel Goldwyn, 1989; voice of Caous (English version), *Asterix et le coup du menhir* (also known as *Asterix and the Big Fight* and *Asterix and the Stone's Blow;* animated), Gaumont/Palace, 1989. Also appeared in *Barry Lyndon,* Warner Brothers, 1975.

PRINCIPAL TELEVISION APPEARANCES—Series: *Blackadder,* BBC, 1983, then Arts and Entertainment; also *My Family and Other Animals,* BBC, then Arts and Entertainment; Constable Fancy Smith, *Z Cars,* BBC. Mini-Series: Augustus, *I, Claudius,* BBC, then *Masterpiece Theatre,* PBS, 1977; Olinthus, *The Last Days of Pompeii,* ABC, 1984; General Yevlenko, *War and Remembrance,* ABC, 1988; Long John Silver, *Return to Treasure Island,* Disney Channel, 1989; also *Cold Comfort Farm,* BBC, then *Masterpiece Theatre,* PBS, 1971; *Notorious Woman,* BBC, then *Masterpiece Theatre,* PBS, 1975. Episodic: George Briggs, "Appointment with a Killer" (also known as "A Midsummer Nightmare"), *Thriller,* ABC, 1975; Vargas, *Blake's 7,* BBC, 1978; also "Death's Other Dominion," *Space 1999,* syndicated, 1975; "The Metamorph," *Space 1999,* syndicated, 1976; "Lamb to the Slaughter," *Tales of the Unexpected,* syndicated, 1979. Movies: Abner, *The Story of David,* ABC, 1976; Captain Teach, *The Master of Ballantrae,* CBS, 1984; also *The Sweeney,* 1984. Specials: *Wine of India,* BBC, 1970; Rudolf Kammerling, *Once in a Lifetime,* BBC, then *Great Performances,* PBS, 1988; voice characterization, *Pyramid* (animated), PBS, 1988; also host, narrator, and Johann Sebastian Bach, *The Joy of Bach,* PBS; narrator, *The Natural World,* BBC. Also appeared in *Jackanory,* 1976; *The Little World of Don Camillo,* 1980; *The Three Musketeers; William the Conqueror; Lorna and Ted; Arthur of the Britons; Justice; Boy Dominic; Hadleigh; Public Eye; Brahms; The Aphrodite Inheritance; Son of a Man; Churchill's People;* and *The Recruiting Officer.*

SIDELIGHTS: RECREATIONS—Judo (black belt) and mountaineering.

ADDRESSES: MANAGER—Miller Management, 82 Broom Park, Teddington, Middlesex TW11 9RR, England.*

*   *   *

BLIER, Bernard   1916-1989

PERSONAL: Born January 11, 1916, in Buenos Aires, Argentina; died of cancer, March 29, 1989, in Paris, France; children: Bertrand, Brigitte. EDUCATION—Attended Lycee Condorcet; studied acting with Raymond Rouleau and at the Paris Conservatory with Louis Jouvet.

VOCATION: Actor.

CAREER: STAGE DEBUT—Theatre de l'Etoile, Paris, France, 1936. PRINCIPAL STAGE APPEARANCES—*L'Ecole des femmes,* Comedie Francaise, Paris, 1973; also *Le Marie, la femme, et la mort.*

FILM DEBUT—*Gribouille* (also known as *Heart of Paris*), 1937. PRINCIPAL FILM APPEARANCES—Gaston, *Le Jour se leve* (also known as *Daybreak*), 1939, released in the United States by AFE, 1940; Charbonnel, *Symphonie fantastique,* 1942, released in the United States by AFE, 1947; Remendado, *Carmen,* Super Film, 1946; Maurice Martineau, *Quai des orfevres* (also known as *Jenny Lamour*), 1947, released in the United States by Vog, 1948; Rene, *Dedee d'Anvers* (also known as *Dedee* and *Woman of Antwerp*), 1948, released in the United States by Vog, 1949; Louis, *Monseigneur,* 1949, released in the United States by Roger Richebe, 1950; Robert, *Maneges* (also known as *The Cheat* and *Riding for a Fall*), Discina International Films, 1950; Pascal Laurent, *L'Ecole buissonniere* (also known as *Passion for Life* and *I Have a New Master*), AGDC/Brandon, 1951; President, "Le Lit de la Pompadour" in *Secrets d'alcove* (also known as *The Bed* and *Il letto*), 1953, released in the United States by Pathe, 1954; Zagoriensky, *Le Joueur* (also known as *The Gambler*), Gaumont, 1958; Leader, *La Chatte* (also known as *The Cat*), Ellis Films, 1959; Capitano Castelli, *La grande guerra* (also known as *La Grande Guerre* and *The Great War*), 1959, released in the United States by Lopert, 1961; Pichon, *Archimede, le clochard* (also known as *The Magnificent Tramp*), 1959, released in the United States by Cameo International, 1962.

The Marshal, *Il gobbo* (also known as *The Hunchback of Rome*), 1960, released in the United States by Royal, 1963; police superintendent, *Crimen* (also known as *And Suddenly, It's Murder!*), 1960, released in the United States by Royal, 1964; Charles, *Le Cave se rebiffe* (also known as *The Counterfeiters of Paris* and *Money, Money, Money*), 1961, released in the United States by Metro-Goldwyn-Mayer, 1962; Mayor Leproux, *Arretez les tambours* (also known as *Women in War* and *Women and War*), 1961, released in the United States by Parade Releasing, 1965; Gregoire Duval, *Le Septieme Jure* (also known as *The Seventh Juror*), 1962, released in the United States by Trans-Lux, 1964; Torenthal, *Mathias Sandorf,* Union Generale Cinematographique, 1962; director, *Germinal,* Cocinor, 1963; Martinetti, *Il compagni* (also known as *The Organizer, The Strikers,* and *Les Camarades*), 1963, released in the United States by Continental Distributing, 1964; Monsieur Joseph, *La Bonne soupe* (also known as *Careless Love* and *The Good Soup*), International Classics, 1964; Mitch-Mitch, *Cent mille dollars au soleil* (also known as *Greed in the Sun* and *Centomila dollari al sole*), 1964, released in the United States by Metro-Goldwyn-Mayer (MGM), 1965; Reguzzoni, "Modern

People'' in *Alta infedelta* (also known as *High Infidelity* and *Haute infidelite*), 1964, released in the United States by Magna, 1965; Corna d'Oro, *Il magnifico cornuto* (also known as *The Magnificent Cuckold* and *Le Cocu magnifique*), 1964, released in the United States by Continental Distributing, 1965; Monsieur Heurtin, *La Chasse a l'homme* (also known as *Male Hunt* and *Caccia al maschio*), 1964, released in the United States by Pathe, 1965; Cafarelli, *Les Barbouzes* (also known as *The Great Spy Chase*), 1964, released in the United States by American International, 1966; commissioner, *Casanova '70*, Embassy, 1965; chief, *Le Fou du labo 4* (also known as *The Madman of Lab 4*), Gaumont, 1967; defense counsel, *Lo straniero* (also known as *The Stranger* and *L'Etranger*), Paramount, 1967; Rhome, *Peau d'espion* (also known as *To Commit a Murder, Congiura di spie,* and *Der Grausame Job*), 1967, released in the United States by Cinerama, 1970; husband, *Caroline cherie,* Mancori, 1968; Charles, *Appellez-moi Mathilde* (also known as *Call Me Mathilde*), 1968, released in the United States by Columbia, 1970; K, *Le Cri du cormoran le soir au-dessus des jonques* (also known as *The Cry of the Cormoran at Night Over the Junks*), 1969, released in the United States by Gaumont International, 1970.

Inspector, *Laisse aller, c'est une valse* (also known as *Take It Easy, It's a Waltz*), Gaumont International, 1970; Guiton, *Le Distrait* (also known as *The Daydreamer* and *Absentminded*), 1970, released in the United States by Gaumont, 1975; Webb, *Catch Me a Spy*, Rank, 1971; Chief, *Le Tueur* (also known as *The Killer*), Societe nouvelle prodis, 1971; Doctor Mezzini, *Homo eroticus* (also known as *Man of the Year*), CIDIF, 1971; Inspector, *Jo* (also known as *The Gazebo*), MGM, 1971; Bistingo, *Elle cause plus, elle flingue* (also known as *She No Longer Talks. . .She Shoots*), CIC/Films la Boetie, 1972; Boss, *Tout le monde il est beau, tout le monde il est gentil* (also known as *Everybody He Is Nice, Everybody He Is Beautiful*), CFDC, 1972; Uncle, *Moi y'en a vouloir des sous* (also known as *Me, I Want to Have Dough*), United Artists, 1972; Milan, *Le Grand Blond avec une chaussure noire* (also known as *The Tall Blond Man with One Black Shoe*), Gaumont International, 1972, released in the United States by Almi Cinema V, 1973; the President, *Les Chinois a Paris* (also known as *The Chinese in Paris*), Cine Qua Non/Production 2000/Produzioni Europee Associates, 1973; Moreu, *La Main a couper. . .* (also known as *A Hand to Cut Off*), Planfilm, 1973; Gastie-Leroy, *Je sais rien, mais je dirai tout* (also known as *Don't Know Anything But I'll Tell All*), AMLF, 1973; Frank, *Bons baisers a lundi* (also known as *Kisses Till Monday*), Films la Boetie, 1974; Mayor, *Par le sang des autres* (also known as *With the Blood of Others*), Films la Boetie, 1974, released in the United States in 1980; Priest, *Il piatto piange* (also known as *Ante Up*), Euro International, 1974; Anselme, *Ce cher Victor* (also known as *That Dear Victor*), Lugo Films, 1975; Righi, *Amici miei* (also known as *My Friends*), Cineriz, 1975; Maxine, *Le Faux-Cul* (also known as *The Phoney*), Gaumont International, 1975; Tardel, *C'est dur pour tout le monde* (also known as *It's Tough for Everybody*), Societe nouvelle de cinema, 1975; Liebard, *Le Corps de mon ennemi* (also known as *The Body of My Enemy*) AMLF, 1976; Staplin, *Serie noire* (also known as *Thriller Story*), Gaumont International/World Marketing, 1979; doctor, *Il malato immaginario* (also known as *La Malade imaginaire* and *The Hypochondriac*), Cinema International, 1979.

Police inspector, *Buffet froid* (also known as *Cold Cuts*), Interama/Gala Film Distributors, 1980; Grandfather Eugenio, *Eugenio* (also known as *Voltati Eugenio*), Intercontinental/Films du Losange, 1980; the Emir, *Petrole, petrole* (also known as *Petrol, Petrol*), IGC, 1981; Major Tarasso, *Passione d'amore* (also known as *Passion of Love*), Connoisseur, 1981, released in the United States

by Putnam Square, 1982; Mr. Bottini, *Cuore* (also known as *Heart*), RAI-TV Channel 2, 1984; Mr. Guilledou, *Ca n'arrive qu'a moi* (also known as *It Only Happens to Me*), AMLF/Sara/Films A2, 1984; Major Bellucci, *Scemo di guerra* (also known as *War Jester, Madman at War,* and *Le Fou de guerre*), Titanus/Sergio Felicioli, 1985; Paleari, *Le due vite di Mattia Pascal* (also known as *The Two Lives of Mattia Pascal*), Medusa/SACIS, 1985; J.B. Cobb, *Je hais les acteurs* (also known as *I Hate Actors*), Gaumont International, 1986; Uncle Gugo, *Pourvu que ce soit une fille* (also known as *Speriamo che sia femmina, Esperons que ce sont une fille,* and *Let's Hope It's a Girl*), Artificial Eye/President/CDE/Original, 1986; Minister, *Twist again a Moscou* (also known as *Twist Again in Moscow*), AMLF, 1986; Eva's father, *Sotto il ristorante Cinese* (also known as *Under the Chinese Restaurant* and *Below the Chinese Restaurant*), ADMV, 1987; Saltiel, *Mangeclous*, AAA, 1988; Mondoradini, *Les Fanfarons* (also known as *Una botta di vita, The Boasters,* and *A Taste of Life*), Italian International/Exportation Francaise Cinematographique, 1988; Collins, *Ada dans le jungle* (also known as *Ada in the Jungle*), FIT Productions/AAA/Hugo International, 1988; Caffarelli, *Paganini* (also known as *Kinski Paganini*), Medusa Distribuzione, 1989.

Also appeared in *Trois-six-neuf, Le Messager, La Dame de Malacca,* and *L'Habit vert,* all 1937; *Altitude 3200* (also known as *Youth in Revolt*), *Entree des artistes* (also known as *The Curtain Rises*), *Hotel du Nord, Grisou, Double Crime sur la ligne Maginot* (also known as *Treachery Within*), *Place de la Concorde,* and *Accord final,* all 1938; *L'Enfer des anges, Quartier Latin,* and *Nuit de Decembre* (also known as *Heure exquise*), all 1939; *L'Assassinat du Pere Noel* (also known as *Who Killed Santa Claus?*), *Le Pavillon brule, Premier bal,* and *Caprices,* all 1941; *La Femme que j'ai le plus aimee, Romance a trois, La Nuit fantastique, Le Journal tombe a cinq heures, Le Mariage de chiffon,* and *Marie-Martine,* all 1942; *Les Petites du quai aux fleurs, Je suis avec toi,* and *Domino,* all 1943; *Farandolle,* 1944; *Seul dans le nuit* and *Monsieur Gregoire s'evade,* both 1945; *Messieurs Ludovic* and *Le Cafe du Cadran,* both 1946; *Les Casse-pieds* (also known as *The Spice of Life*), 1948, released in the United States by Gaumont Cinemaphonic, 1954; *D'homme a hommes* (also known as *Man to Men*), 1948; *L'Invite du Mardi* and ''Tante Emma'' in *Retour a la vie,* both 1949.

Les Anciens de Saint-Loup, La Souriciere, and *Souvenirs perdus,* all 1950; *Sans laisser d'adresse* and *La Maison Bonnadieu,* both 1951; *Agence matrimoniale* and *Je l'ai ete trois fois,* both 1952; *Suivez cet homme!,* 1953; *Avant le deluge* and *Scenes de menage,* both 1954; *Le Dossier noir* and *Les Hussards,* both 1955; *Crime et chatiment* (also known as *Crime and Punishment*), *Prigionieri del male,* and *Rivelazione,* all 1956; *L'Homme a l'impermeable* (also known as *The Man in the Raincoat*), *Retour de Manivelle* (also known as *There's Always a Price Tag*), *Quand la femme s'en mele,* and *La Bonne Tisane,* all 1957; as Javert, *Les Miserables,* and in *Les Grandes familles* (also known as *The Possessors*), *Sans famille, En legitime defense,* and *L'Ecole des cocottes,* all 1958; *Marie-Octobre, Marche ou creve,* and *Les Yeux de l'amour,* all 1959.

Le Secret du Chevalier d'Eon, Le President, and *Vive Henri IV, vive l'amour!,* all 1960; *I briganti Italiani* (also known as *Les Guerilleros*), *Les Petits Matins,* and *Le Monocle noir,* all 1961; *Pourquoi Paris?* and *Les Saintes Nitouches,* both 1962; *Il magnifico avventuriero,* 1963; ''Le Jeu de la chance'' in *La Chance et l'amour,* 1964; ''La Fermeture'' in *Les Bon Vivants, Una questione d'onore* (also known as *A Question of Honor*), and *Quand passent les faisans,* all 1965; *Du mou dans la gachette, Duello nel mundo, Delitto quasi perfetto, Le Grand Restaurant,* and *Un Idiot a Paris,* all 1966; *Copain suave sa peau* and *Si j'etais un espion* (also known as *Breakdown* and *If I Were a Spy*), both 1967; *Bel Ami 2000 oder: Wie verfuhrt man einen Playboy?* (also known as *How to Seduce a Playboy* and *100 ragazze per un playboy*), Chevron, 1968; *Faut pas prendre les enfants du bon Dieu pour les canards sauvages* (also known as *Operation Leontine*), *Riusciranno i nostri eroi a trovare il loro amico misteriosamente scomparso in Africa?* (also known as *Will Your Heroes Find Their Friends Who Disappeared So Mysteriously in Africa?*), and *Elle boit pas, elle fume pas, elle drogue pas, mais elle cause*, all 1968; *Mon oncle Benjamin*, 1969.

Il furto e l'anima del commercio, 1971; *Quarta parete* and *Boccaccio*, both 1972; *Les Tontons flingueurs*, 1973; *C'est pas parce qu'on a rien a dire qu'il fermer sa gueule* and *Processo per direttissima*, both 1974; *Calmos* (also known as *Femmes fatales* and *Cool, Calm, and Collected*), AMLF, 1975; *La Nuit d'or* (also known as *Golden Night*), Union Generale Cinematographique, 1976; *Le Temoin* 1977; *Le Compromis*, 1978; *Amici miei atto III* (also known as *My Friends Act III*), Filmauro, 1985; *Billy ze kick*, AAA/World Marketing, 1985; *La famiglia* (also known as *The Family*), Vestron, 1987; *I picari* (also known as *The Picaros* and *The Rogues*), Warner Brothers, 1987; *Les Possedes* (also known as *The Possessed*), Gaumont International, 1987; *Migrations* (also known as *La Guerre la plus glorieuse*), Cinexport, 1988.

WRITINGS: FILM—(Co-writer) *Laisse aller, c'est une valse* (also known as *Take It Easy, It's a Waltz*), Gaumont International, 1970.

AWARDS: Brussels Prize, 1949; Prix Feminin de Cinema, 1950; Prix Balzac, 1973; Cesar Award, 1989; also named Chevalier of the French Legion of Honor.

OBITUARIES AND OTHER SOURCES: Variety, April 5-11, 1989.*

*   *   *

BLIER, Bertrand   1939-

PERSONAL: Surname is pronounced "Blee-ay"; born March 11, 1939, in Paris, France; son of Bernard Blier (an actor).

VOCATION: Director and screenwriter.

CAREER: Also see *WRITINGS* below. PRINCIPAL FILM WORK—Director: *Les Valseuses* (also known as *Going Places*), Societe Nouvelle Prodis/Almi Cinema V, 1973; *Calmos* (also known as *Femmes fatales* and *Cool, Calm, and Collected*), AMLF, 1975; (also producer with Georges Dancigers and Alexandre Mnouchkine) *Preparez vos mouchoirs* (also known as *Get Out Your Handkerchiefs*), New Line Cinema, 1978; *Buffet froid* (also known as *Cold Cuts*), Interama/Gala Film Distributors, 1979; *Beau-pere* (also known as *Stepfather*), Parafrance/New Line Cinema, 1981; *La Femme de mon pote* (also known as *My Best Friend's Girl*), European International/Cannon Releasing, 1984; *Notre histoire* (also known as *Separate Rooms, Our History*, and *Our Story*), AMLF/Spectrafilm, 1984; *Femmes fatales*, New Line Cinema, 1985; *Menage* (also known as *Tenue de soiree* and *Evening Dress*), Norstar/Cinecom International, 1986; (also producer) *Trop belle pour toi* (also known as *Too Beautiful for You*), AMLF, 1989, released in the United States by Orion Classics, 1990. Also directed *Hitler? Connais pas!*, 1963; *La Grimace*, 1966; *Si j'etais un espion* (also known as *Breakdown* and *If I Were a Spy*), 1967.

RELATED CAREER—Assistant director on films by John Berry, Georges Lautner, Christian-Jaque, Jean Delannoy, and Denys de la Patelliere; director of short documentary films.

WRITINGS: See production details above, unless indicated. FILM—*Hitler? Connais pas!*, 1963; *La Grimace*, 1966; (co-writer) *Si j'etais un espion*, 1967; (with Georges Lautner) *Laisse aller, c'est une valse* (also known as *Take It Easy, It's a Waltz*), Gaumont International, 1970; (with Philippe Dumarcay) *Les Valseuses*, 1973; (with Dumarcay) *Calmos*, 1975; *Preparez vos mouchoirs*, 1978; *Buffet froid*, 1979; *Beau-pere*, 1981; *Notre histoire*, AMLF/Spectrafilm, 1984; (with Gerard Brach) *La Femme de mon pote*, 1984; *Menage*, 1986; *Trop belle pour toi*, 1989.

OTHER—*Les Valseuses* (novel), 1972; *Beau-pere* (novel), 1980.

AWARDS: Academy Award, Best Foreign Film, 1978, for *Preparez vos mouchoirs;* Cesar Award, Best Screenplay, 1990, for *Trop belle pour toi.**

*   *   *

BLOCK, Larry   1942-

PERSONAL: Born October 30, 1942, in New York, NY; son of Harold (in the garment industry) and Sonia (a travel agent; maiden name, Kutcher) Block; married Jolly King (an actress), September 25, 1981; children: Zoe Lenna, Zachary Harold. EDUCATION—University of Rhode Island, B.A., English, 1964; trained for the stage with Wynn Handman. POLITICS—Liberal Democrat. RELIGION—Ethical Culture. MILITARY—U.S. Army, Special Services, specialist fourth class, 1967-69.

VOCATION: Actor.

CAREER: STAGE DEBUT—Mercutio's page, *Romeo and Juliet*, American Shakespeare Festival, Stratford, CT, 1965, for eighty performances. BROADWAY DEBUT—Understudy for Malcolm Scrawdyke, *Hail, Scrawdyke*, Booth Theatre, 1966. PRINCIPAL STAGE APPEARANCES—Boy, *La Turista*, St. Clement's Church Theatre, New York City, 1967; Jesse, *Fingernails Blue As Flowers*, American Place Theatre, New York City, 1971-72; Lucky, *Waiting for Godot*, St. Clement's Church Theatre, 1974; Johann Sebastian Fabiani (understudy) and Whimsey (understudy), *Where Do We Go from Here?*, New York Shakespeare Festival (NYSF), Public Theatre, New York City, 1974; Dromio of Ephesus, *The Comedy of Errors*, NYSF, Delacorte Theatre, New York City, 1975; Manny Alter, *Coming Attractions*, Playwrights Horizons, New York City, 1980-81; Gadshill, *Henry IV, Part One*, NYSF, Delacorte Theatre, 1981; Sir Toby Belch, *Twelfth Night*, Shakespeare and Company, Lee, MA, 1981; Leon, *The Workroom* (also known as *L'Atelier*), Center Stage, Baltimore, MD, 1981; Martin Bormann, *The Fuehrer Bunker*, American Place Theatre, 1981; Benny Silverman, *The Value of Names*, Actors Theatre of Louisville, Louisville, KY, 1983, then Hartford Stage Company, Hartford, CT, 1984; the Hotel Manager, *Souvenirs*, Cubiculo Theatre, New York City, 1984; One-Eyed, *The Golem*, NYSF, Delacorte Theatre, 1984; Sir Toby Belch, *Twelfth Night* and Mr. Fezziwig, *A Christmas Carol*, both Tyrone Guthrie Theatre, Minneapolis, MN, 1984.

Randolph, *Responsible Parties*, Vineyard Theatre, New York City, 1985; Del Bates, *The Hit Parade*, Manhattan Punch Line, New

York City, 1985; Lada I, *Largo Desolato*, NYSF, Public Theatre, 1986; Yuri Brushnik, *Coup d'Etat*, Playwrights Horizons, 1986; Censor, *Hunting Cockroaches*, Manhattan Theatre Club, New York City, 1987; Elliot Atlas, *The Square Root of Three*, Jewish Repertory Theatre, New York City, 1987; Antonio, *Two Gentlemen of Verona*, NYSF, Delacorte Theatre, 1987; Willis, *Moonchildren*, Second Stage Theatre, New York City, 1987; Cecil, *The Yellow Dog Contract*, Apple Corps Theatre, New York City, 1988; Augustin Feraillon, *A Flea in Her Ear*, Long Wharf Theatre, New Haven, CT, 1989; Herbie, *The Loman Family Picnic*, Manhattan Theatre Club, 1989. Also appeared in *Coriolanus*, *The Taming of the Shrew*, and *King Lear*, all American Shakespeare Festival, Stratford, CT, 1965; *Eh?*, Circle in the Square, New York City, 1967; *Harry, Noon, and Night* and *The Recruiting Officer*, both Theatre of the Living Arts, Philadelphia, PA, 1970; *The Last Days of British Honduras*, NYSF, 1976; *Manhattan Love Songs*, Actors' Studio, New York City, 1982; *A Tantalizing*, Actors Theatre of Louisville, 1983; *Temptation*, NYSF, Public Theatre, 1989.

PRINCIPAL FILM APPEARANCES—Springy, *Shamus*, Columbia, 1973; Peterboro referee, *Slap Shot*, Universal, 1977; Ted Peters, *Heaven Can Wait*, Paramount, 1978; Detective Burrows, *Hardcore* (also known as *The Hardcore Life*), Columbia, 1979; taxi driver, *After Hours*, Warner Brothers, 1985; bar owner, *Cocktail*, Touchstone, 1988. Also appeared in *Routed* (short film), Izar, 1989.

PRINCIPAL TELEVISION APPEARANCES—Series: Mickey Potter, *The Secret Storm*, CBS; Tom, *Sesame Street*, PBS; Cal Jamison, *General Hospital*, ABC. Mini-Series: Lasie, "Roanoak," *American Playhouse*, PBS, 1986. Pilots: Harry, *Rosetti and Ryan: Men Who Love Women*, NBC, 1977; Private Arnold Fleck, *Space Force*, NBC, 1978. Episodic: Clerk, *Tattingers*, NBC, 1988; also *M*A*S*H*, CBS, 1977 and 1978; *Miami Vice*, NBC; *One Life to Live*, ABC; *Barney Miller*, ABC; *Charlie's Angels*, ABC; *CHiPS*, NBC; *Kojak*, CBS; *Police Story*, NBC; *Baretta*, ABC; *Ellery Queen*, NBC; *Family Matters*, ABC. Movies: Springy, *A Matter of Wife . . . and Death*, NBC, 1976; Leroy Keenan, *The Last Ride of the Dalton Gang*, NBC, 1979; Kleinfeld, *Dead Man Out*, HBO, 1989; also *The Lindbergh Kidnapping Case*, NBC, 1976.

PRINCIPAL RADIO APPEARANCES—Series: Ensemble, *Work in Progress*. Episodic: "Pilot," *National Public Radio Playhouse*, National Public Radio (NPR); "Prairie du Chien," *Earplay*, NPR; *Under the Gun*, WBAI (New York City).

AWARDS: MILITARY HONORS—Commendation Medal from the U.S. Army, 1969.

ADDRESSES: AGENT—The Gage Group, 1650 Broadway, New York, NY 10019.

*   *   *

BLUM, Mark   1950-

PERSONAL: Born May 14, 1950, in Newark, NJ. EDUCATION—Studied drama at the University of Minnesota, the University of Pennsylvania, and with Andre Gregory, Aaron Frankel, and Daniel Seltzer.

VOCATION: Actor.

CAREER: OFF-BROADWAY DEBUT—Post office clerk, *The*

Cherry Orchard, Roundabout Theatre, 1976. BROADWAY DEBUT—Venetian, *The Merchant*, Plymouth Theatre, 1977. PRINCIPAL STAGE APPEARANCES—Valentine, *Two Gentlemen of Verona* and Cleante, *The Miser*, both National Shakespeare Company, Ulster County Community College, Stone Ridge, NY, 1974, then Rutgers University, New Brunswick, NJ, 1975; villager, first angel, and man, *The World of Sholem Aleichem*, Roundabout Theatre, New York City, 1976; Steve, *Say Goodnight, Gracie*, Playwrights Horizons, Manhattan Main Stage Theatre, New York City, 1978, then Actors Playhouse, New York City, 1979; younger son, *Table Settings*, Playwrights Horizons, then Chelsea Theatre Center, New York City, 1980; Michael, *Key Exchange*, Orpheum Theatre, New York City, 1981; Iago, *Othello*, Shakespeare Festival of Dallas, Dallas, TX, 1982; Johnson, *Loving Reno*, New York Theatre Studio, AMDA Studio One, New York City, 1983; Max Whitcomb, *An American Comedy*, Lee Baum, *The American Clock*, and Harry, *Wild Oats*, all Center Theatre Group, Mark Taper Forum, Los Angeles, 1983-84; Peter Austin, *It's Only a Play*, Manhattan Theatre Club, New York City, 1984; Asher, *Messiah*, Manhattan Theatre Club, Space at City Center Theatre, New York City, 1985; Ben, *Little Footsteps*, Playwrights Horizons, 1986; Ben, *The Downside*, Long Wharf Theatre, New Haven, CT, 1987. Also appeared in *Brothers*, George Street Playhouse, New Brunswick, NJ, 1976; *Close Ties*, Long Wharf Theatre, 1981; *The Cherry Orchard*, Long Wharf Theatre, 1982; *Cave Life*, Circle Repertory Theatre, New York City, 1988; in *Green Julia;* and in *Moby Dick Rehearsed*.

PRINCIPAL STAGE WORK—Stage manager, National Shakespeare Company, Ulster County Community College, Stone Ridge, NY, 1974.

PRINCIPAL FILM APPEARANCES—Intern Murphy, *Lovesick*, Warner Brothers, 1983; Gary Glass, *Desperately Seeking Susan*, Orion, 1985; George Margolin, *Just Between Friends*, Orion, 1986; Richard Mason, *Crocodile Dundee*, Paramount, 1986; Denny Gordon, *Blind Date*, Tri-Star, 1987; Arthur Peale, *The Presidio*, Paramount, 1988.

PRINCIPAL TELEVISION APPEARANCES—Series: Ken Holden, *Sweet Surrender*, NBC, 1987. Pilots: Ray Litertini, *Things Are Looking Up*, CBS, 1984. Episodic: *Miami Vice*, NBC, 1987.

ADDRESSES: AGENTS—J.J. Harris and Steve Glick, William Morris Agency, 151 El Camino Drive, Beverly Hills, CA 90212.*

*   *   *

BLUMENKRANTZ, Jeff   1965-

PERSONAL: Born June 3, 1965, in Long Branch, NJ; son of Harold David (a pharmacist) and Nancy Rachel (an interior designer; maiden name, Levy) Blumenkrantz. EDUCATION—Northwestern University, B.S., theatre, 1986. RELIGION—Jewish.

VOCATION: Actor.

CAREER: STAGE DEBUT—Zebulon and Baker, *Joseph and the Amazing Technicolor Dreamcoat*, Drury Lane Theatre, Oakbrook, IL, 1986, for fifty performances. OFF-BROADWAY DEBUT—Helper, *The Pajama Game*, Equity Library Theatre, 1986, for thirty peformances. PRINCIPAL STAGE APPEARANCES—Stewpot, *South Pacific*, New York City Opera, State Theatre, New York City,

JEFF BLUMENKRANTZ

1987; understudy for Jack, Rapunzel's Prince, and Steward, *Into the Woods,* Martin Beck Theatre, New York City, 1987-89; ensemble, *Waiting' in the Wings* (revue) Triplex Theatre, New York City, 1988; Filch, *The Threepenny Opera,* National Theatre, Washington, DC, then Lunt-Fontanne Theatre, New York City, both 1989. Also appeared in *Henry and Ellen,* Playwrights Horizons, New York City; *The Pajama Game,* Equity Library Theatre, New York City; with Civic Light Opera Company, Pittsburgh, PA; Drury Lane Oakbrook Theatre, Chicago, IL; and with Pennsylvania Center Stage.

PRINCIPAL TELEVISION APPEARANCES—Episodic: *Hothouse,* ABC, 1988; also *Sesame Street,* PBS.

RELATED CAREER—Member, B.M.I. Advanced Workshop; member, Dramatists Guild Musical Theatre Development Program.

AWARDS: Mary Martin Award from the National Institute of Music Theatre, 1988; George London grant from the National Institute for Music Theatre, 1988.

ADDRESSES: AGENT—Abrams Artists, 420 Madison Avenue, New York, NY 10017.

*　　*　　*

BOHT, Jean   1936-

PERSONAL: Surname is pronounced "boat"; born March 6, 1936, in Bebington, England; daughter of Thomas Herbert (a manufactur-

er's agent) and Edna May (MacDonald) Dance; married William P. Boht (divorced, 1970); married Carl Davis (a composer), December 28, 1970; children: Hannah Louise, Jessie Jo (first marriage). RELIGION—Church of England.

VOCATION: Actress.

CAREER: STAGE DEBUT—Liverpool Playhouse, Liverpool, U.K., 1962. LONDON DEBUT—Black straw hat girl, *St. Joan of the Stockyards,* Queen's Theatre, 1964, for twenty-one performances. PRINCIPAL STAGE APPEARANCES—Mrs. Flarty and first woman, *Hanky Park,* Mermaid Theatre, London, 1971; member of William Blake's family, *Tyger,* National Theatre Company, New Theatre, London, 1971; Mrs. Ropeen Genockey, *The Hostage,* Theatre Workshop Company, Stratford Theatre Royal, London, 1972; Eunice, *Mecca,* Open Space Theatre, London, 1977; Mrs. Moore, *In the Blood,* Theatre Upstairs, London, 1978; Sal, *Wednesday,* Bush Theatre, London, 1979. Also appeared in *The National Health,* National Theatre Company, London, 1967; *Mother Courage,* Manchester Library Theatre, Manchester, U.K., 1968; *Marie Lloyd,* Lincoln Theatre Royal, Lincoln, U.K., 1968; *Coventry Belgrade,* Royal Court Theatre, London, 1969; *Finest F' Family (Henry Livings),* Lincoln Theatre Royal, 1969; *Amphytrion,* Mermaid Theatre, 1971; *Paradise Lost,* Royal Court Theatre, 1974; *Kennedy's Children,* King's Head Theatre, London, 1974; *Homage to Been Soup,* Royal Court Theatre, 1975; *Patty Hearst,* 1976; *Interaction Rupert Street,* 1976; *The Wild Duck,* Lyric Hammersmith Theatre, London, 1980; *Touched,* Royal Court Theatre, 1980; *To Come Home to This,* Royal Court Theatre, 1981; *Birds of Passage,* Hampstead Theatre Club, London, 1983; *Lost,* Bush Theatre, 1986; *Steel Magnolias,* Lyric Theatre, London, 1989.

JEAN BOHT

PRINCIPAL FILM APPEARANCES—Mother, "Rapunzel's Story" in *Rapunzel Let Down Your Hair*, British Film Institute, 1975; Betty, *Arthur's Hallowed Ground*, Cinecom International, 1983; Mrs. Taswell, *The Girl in a Swing*, Nordisk, 1988; Aunty Nell, *Distant Voices, Still Lives*, Avenue Entertainment/British Film Institute, 1988; also appeared in *Meddle Not with Change*, 1985.

PRINCIPAL TELEVISION APPEARANCES—Series: Nellie Boswell, *Bread*, BBC-1, 1985-86. Mini-Series: Sal, *A Perfect Spy*, BBC, then *Masterpiece Theatre*, PBS, 1988; Madame Joliet, "The 4:50 from Paddington," *Agatha Christie's Miss Marple*, BBC, then *Mystery!*, PBS, 1989. Episodic: *Bergerac*, BBC-1. Also appeared in *The Boys from the Blackstuff, Sons and Lovers, Spyship, Some Mothers Do 'ave 'em, Last of the Summer Wine, Funny Man, Scully, Juliet Bravo, I Woke Up One Morning, Sweeney, Where Adam Stood, Cranford*, and *Arthur's Hallowed Ground*.

RELATED CAREER—Company member: Liverpool Playhouse, Liverpool, U.K., 1962-64; Bristol Old Vic Theatre, Bristol, U.K., 1964-65; Royal Court Theatre Company, London, 1965-66; Manchester Library Theatre Company, Manchester, U.K., 1966-67; Theatre 69, Liverpool Playhouse, 1966-67; Lincoln Theatre Royal, Lincoln, U.K., 1967-68; National Theatre Company, London, 1968-69; Joan Littlewood's Theatre Workshop, 1969-71; also co-founder and artistic director, Barnes Drama Company for Young People, 1986—.

MEMBER: British Academy of Film and Television Arts.

ADDRESSES: AGENT—Peters, Fraser, and Dunlop, the Chambers, 5th Floor, Chelsea Harbour, Lots Road, London SW10 OXF, England.

*   *   *

BRAEDEN, Eric
(Hans Gudegast)

PERSONAL: Born Hans Gudegast, April 3, in Kiel, Germany; wife's name, Dale; children: Christian. EDUCATION—Attended Montana State University.

VOCATION: Actor.

CAREER: PRINCIPAL STAGE APPEARANCES—(As Hans Gudegast) Kurt Schonforn, *The Great Indoors*, Eugene O'Neill Theatre, New York City, 1966.

PRINCIPAL FILM APPEARANCES—(As Hans Gudegast) Klaus, *Operation Eichmann*, Allied Artists, 1961; (as Hans Gudegast) radio operator, *Morituri* (also known as *The Saboteur: Code Name Morituri* and *The Saboteur*), Twentieth Century-Fox, 1965; (as Hans Gudegast) Max Eckhart, *Dayton's Devils*, Cue, 1968; (as Hans Gudegast) Von Klemme, *One Hundred Rifles*, Twentieth Century-Fox, 1969; Dr. Charles Forbin, *Colossus: The Forbin Project* (also known as *The Forbin Project* and *Colossus 1980*), Universal, 1969; Dr. Otto Hasslein, *Escape from the Planet of the Apes*, Twentieth Century-Fox, 1971; Peter Brinker, *Lady Ice*, National General, 1973; Roland, *The Ultimate Thrill* (also known as *The Ultimate Chase*), General Cinema, 1974; Bruno Von Stickle, *Herbie Goes to Monte Carlo*, Buena Vista, 1977. Also appeared in *The Adultress*, 1976.

PRINCIPAL TELEVISION APPEARANCES—Series: (As Hans Gudegast) Captain Hauptman Hans Dietrich, *The Rat Patrol*, ABC, 1966-68; Victor Newman, *The Young and the Restless*, CBS, 1980—. Pilots: Anton Granicek, *The Judge and Jake Wyler*, NBC, 1972; Emhardt, *Intertect*, ABC, 1973; Arlen Findletter, *The Six Million Dollar Man*, ABC, 1973; Kapitan Drangel, *The New. Original Wonder Woman*, ABC, 1975; Ernest Graeber, *Code Name: Diamond Head*, NBC, 1977; Stephens, *The Power Within*, ABC, 1979; Leonard Nero, *The Aliens Are Coming*, NBC, 1980. Episodic: Francis Britten, *How the West Was Won*, ABC, 1978; Nick Kincaid, *Airwolf*, CBS, 1986; Gerhardt Brunner, *Murder, She Wrote*, CBS, 1986; also *The Mary Tyler Moore Show*, CBS, 1977; *The Gallant Men*, ABC; *Combat*, ABC; *Charlie's Angels*, ABC; *Vega$*, ABC; *A Man Called Sloane*, NBC; *Project UFO*, NBC; *CHiPs*, NBC; *The Eddie Capra Mysteries*, NBC. Movies: Frederico Caprio, *Honeymoon with a Stranger*, ABC, 1969; Dr. Roan Morgan, *The Mask of Sheba*, NBC, 1970; Stoeffer, *Death Race*, ABC, 1973; Kosinsky, *Death Scream*, ABC, 1975; Ross Ford, *Happily Ever After*, CBS, 1978.

AWARDS: Daytime TV Magazine poll winner, Best New Daytime Star, for *The Young and the Restless*.

SIDELIGHTS: RECREATIONS—Boxing, soccer, running, tennis, and skiing.

ADDRESSES: AGENT—David Windsor, Irv Schechter Company, 9300 Wilshire Boulevard, Suite 410, Beverly Hills, CA 90212.*

*   *   *

BRENNAN, Eileen   1935-

PERSONAL: Born September 3, 1935, in Los Angeles, CA; daughter of John Gerald (a doctor) and Regina "Jeanne" (an actress; maiden name, Menehan) Brennan; married David John Lampson, December 28, 1968 (divorced, 1974); children: Samuel John, Patrick Oliver. EDUCATION—Attended Georgetown University; studied acting at the American Academy of Dramatic Arts, 1955-56.

VOCATION: Actress.

CAREER: OFF-BROADWAY DEBUT—Title role, *Little Mary Sunshine*, Orpheum Theatre, 1959-61. PRINCIPAL STAGE APPEARANCES—Anna Leonowens, *The King and I*, City Center Theatre, New York City, 1963; Merry May Glockenspiel, *The Student Gypsy, or The Prince of Liederkranz*, 54th Street Theatre, New York City, 1963; Irene Molloy, *Hello, Dolly!*, St. James Theatre, New York City, 1964-66; Maxine Faulk, *The Night of the Iguana*, Morris Mechanic Theatre, Baltimore, MD, 1985. Also appeared in *And Where She Stops Nobody Knows*, Center Theatre Group, Mark Taper Forum, Los Angeles, 1976; *Gethesemane Springs*, Center Theatre Group, Mark Taper Forum Laboratory Production, 1977; *Triptych*, Center Theatre Group, Mark Taper Forum Laboratory Production, 1978; *A Coupla White Chicks Sitting Around Talking*, Astor Place Theatre, New York City, 1980; and in productions of *Camelot, Guys and Dolls, Bells Are Ringing*, and *An Evening with Eileen Brennan* (one-woman show).

MAJOR TOURS—Annie Sullivan, *The Miracle Worker*, U.S. cities, 1961-62; Ellen Manville, *Luv*, U.S. cities, 1967.

EILEEN BRENNAN

FILM DEBUT—Eunice, *Divorce: American Style,* Columbia, 1967. PRINCIPAL FILM APPEARANCES—Genevieve, *The Last Picture Show,* Columbia, 1971; Darlene, *Scarecrow,* Warner Brothers, 1973; Billie, *The Sting,* Universal, 1973; Mrs. Walker, *Daisy Miller,* Paramount, 1974; Elizabeth, *At Long Last Love,* Twentieth Century-Fox, 1975; Paula Hollinger, *Hustle,* Paramount, 1975; Tess Skeffington, *Murder By Death,* Columbia, 1976; Penelope, *The Great Smokey Roadblock* (also known as *The Last of the Cowboys*), Dimension, 1976; Betty DeBoop, *The Cheap Detective,* Columbia, 1978; Mother, *FM* (also known as *Citizen's Band*), Universal, 1978; Captain Doreen Lewis, *Private Benjamin,* Warner Brothers, 1980; Gail Corbin, *The Funny Farm,* New World/ Mutual, 1982; Mrs. Peacock, *Clue,* Paramount, 1985; Stella, *Sticky Fingers,* Spectrafilm, 1988; hotel desk clerk, *Rented Lips,* Cineworld, 1988; Miss Bannister, *The New Adventures of Pippi Longstocking,* Columbia, 1988; Mrs. Wilkerson, *Stella,* Touchstone, 1990. Also appeared in *Pandemonium* (also known as *Thursday the 12th*), Metro-Goldwyn-Mayer/United Artists, 1981.

PRINCIPAL TELEVISION APPEARANCES—Series: Regular, *Rowan and Martin's Laugh-In,* NBC, 1968; Verla Grubb, *All My Children,* ABC, 1970; Ma Packer, *All That Glitters,* syndicated, 1977; Felicia Winters, *13 Queens Boulevard,* ABC, 1979; Kit Flanagan, *A New Kind of Family,* ABC, 1979-80; Captain Doreen Lewis, *Private Benjamin,* CBS, 1981-83; Kate Halloran, *Off the Rack,* ABC, 1985. Mini-Series: Annie Gray, *Black Beauty,* NBC, 1978. Pilots: Kate Halloran, *Off the Rack,* ABC, 1984; Siobhan Owens, *Off Duty* (broadcast as episode of *CBS Summer Playhouse*), CBS, 1988. Episodic: Ruth MacKenzie, *Taxi,* ABC, 1981; host, *The Shape of Things,* NBC, 1982; Brenda Babcock, *Magnum, P.I.,* CBS, 1987; Marion Simpson, *Murder, She Wrote,* CBS, 1987;

Mrs. O'Brien, *The Cavanaughs,* CBS, 1988; Corinne Denby, *Newhart,* CBS, 1988 and 1989; also *All in the Family,* CBS, 1972.

Movies: Amy, *Playmates,* ABC, 1972; Glenda, *The Blue Knight,* NBC, 1973; Mrs. Lindholm, *My Father's House,* ABC, 1975; Ann Muldoon, *The Night That Panicked America,* ABC, 1975; Carol Werner, *The Death of Richie,* NBC, 1977; Mary Jensen, *When She Was Bad . . .,* ABC, 1979; Marie, *My Old Man,* CBS, 1979; Jessy, *When the Circus Came to Town,* CBS, 1981; Sara Davis, *Incident at Crestridge,* CBS, 1981; Judith, *The Fourth Wise Man,* ABC, 1985; Mrs. Piper/Widow Hubbard, *Babes in Toyland,* NBC, 1986; Sylvia Zimmerman, *Blood Vows: The Story of a Mafia Wife,* NBC, 1987; Maude Roberti, *Going to the Chapel,* NBC, 1988. Specials: Aunt, *Kraft Salutes Walt Disney World's Tenth Anniversary,* CBS, 1982; Maggie, *Lily for President,* CBS, 1982; *Working,* PBS, 1982; *The Screen Actors Guild Fiftieth Anniversary Celebration,* CBS, 1984.

AWARDS: Page One Award from the Newspaper Guild, Theatre World Award, Obie Award from the *Village Voice,* and Kit-Kat Artists and Models Award, all 1960, for *Little Mary Sunshine;* British Academy Award nomination, Best Supporting Actress, 1972, for *The Last Picture Show;* Academy Award nomination, Best Supporting Actress, 1981, for *Private Benjamin;* Emmy Award, Outstanding Supporting Actress in a Comedy, Variety, or Music Series, 1981, and Golden Globe, Best Television Actress in a Series—Comedy or Musical, 1982, for *Private Benjamin.*

MEMBER: Actors' Equity Association, Screen Actors Guild, American Federation of Television and Radio Artists, American Guild of Variety Artists.

ADDRESSES: AGENT—David Shapira and Associates, 15301 Ventura Boulevard, Suite 345, Sherman Oaks, CA 91403.

*   *   *

BRESSON, Robert   1907-

PERSONAL: Born September 25, 1907, in Bromont-Lamothe (Puy-de-Dome), France; son of Leon and Marie-Elisabeth (Clausels) Bresson; married Leida Van der Zee, December 21, 1926.

VOCATION: Director and screenwriter.

CAREER: Also see *WRITINGS* below. PRINCIPAL FILM APPEAR-ANCES—*Mouchette,* Parc Film/Argos Films, 1967, released in the United States by Cinema Ventures, 1970; *De Weg Naar Bresson* (also known as *The Way to Bresson;* documentary), Frans Rasker/ Documentary Films, 1984.

FIRST FILM WORK—*Les Affaires publiques,* Arc Films, 1934. PRINCIPAL FILM WORK—Director: *Les Anges du peche* (also known as *Angels of the Street*), Synops/Roland Tual, 1943, released in the United States by Metro-Goldwyn-Mayer, 1950; *Les Dames du bois de Bologne* (also known as *Ladies of the Park*), Les Films Raoul Ploquin, 1945, released in the United States by Brandon, 1964; *Le Journal d'un cure de campagne* (also known as *Diary of a Country Priest*), Union Generale Cinematographique, 1951; *Un Condamne a mort s'est echappe* (also known as *Le Vent souffle ou il veut, A Man Escaped,* and *The Wind Bloweth Where It Listeth*), Societe Nouvelles des Etablissements Gaumont/Nouvelles

Editions de Films, 1956, released in the United States by New Yorker, 1957; *Pickpocket,* Agnes Delahaie, 1959, released in the United States by New Yorker, 1963; *Le Proces de Jeanne d'Arc* (also known as *Trial of Joan of Arc*), Agnes Delahaie, 1962, released in the United States by Pathe Contemporary, 1965.

Au hasard, Balthazar (also known as *Balthazar*), Argos Films/Parc Film/Athos/Svenska Filmindustri/Svenska Filminstitutet, 1966, released in the United States by Cinema Ventures, 1970; *Mouchette,* Parc Film/Argos Films, 1967, released in the United States by Cinema Ventures, 1970; *Une Femme douce* (also known as *A Gentle Creature*), Parc Film/Marianne Productions, 1969, released in the United States by New Yorker, 1971; *Quatre nuits d'un reveur* (also known as *Four Nights of a Dreamer*), Victoria Films/Albina Films/Films del'Orso, 1971, released in the United States by New Yorker, 1972; *Lancelot du lac* (also known as *Le Graal, Lancelot of the Lake,* and *The Grail*), CFDC, 1974, released in the United States by New Yorker, 1975; *Le Diable probablement* (also known as *The Devil, Probably*), Gaumont, 1977; *L'Argent* (also known as *Money*), AMLF, 1983, released in the United States by Cinecom International, 1984.

RELATED CAREER—Assistant to director Rene Clair on the film *L'Air pur,* 1939.

NON-RELATED CAREER—Painter.

WRITINGS: FILM—See production details above, unless indicated. *Ç'etait un musicien,* 1933; *Les Jumeaux de Brighton,* 1936; *Courrier sud,* 1937; (with R.P. Bruckberger and Jean Giraudoux) *Les Anges du peche,* 1943; (with Jean Cocteau) *Les Dames du bois de Bologne,* 1945; *Le Journal d'un cure de campagne,* 1951; *Un Condamne a mort s'est echappe,* 1956; *Pickpocket,* 1959; *Le Proces de Jeanne d'Arc,* 1962; *Au hasard, Balthazar,* 1966; *Mouchette,* 1967; *Une Femme douce,* 1969; *Quatre nuits d'un reveur,* 1971; *Lancelot du lac,* 1974; *Le Diable probablement,* 1977; *L'Argent,* 1983.

OTHER—*Notes sur le cinematographe,* 1976, translated by Jonathan Griffen as *Notes on Cinematography,* Urizen Books, 1977.

AWARDS: Grand Prix du Cinema Francais, 1943, for *Les Anges du peche;* Prix Louis Delluc, 1950, Grand Prix du Film d'Avant Garde, 1950, Grand Prize from the Venice Film Festival, 1951, and Grand Prix du Cinema Francais, 1951, all for *Le Journal d'un cure de campagne;* Best Director Award from the Cannes Film Festival and Best Film Award from the French Film Academy, both 1957, for *Un Condamne a mort s'est echappe;* Prix du Meillieur Film de l'Annee, 1959, for *Pickpocket;* Special Jury Prize from the Cannes Film Festival, 1962, for *Le Proces de Jeanne d'Arc;* honorary mentions from the Venice Film Festival and Panama Festival, both 1966, for *Au hasard, Balthazar;* Prix du Cinema Francais, 1967, and Panama Festival Grand Prize, 1968, both for *Mouchette;* International Film Critics' Award from the Cannes Film Festival, 1974, for *Lancelot du lac;* Grand Prix from the Cannes Film Festival, 1983, for *L'Argent;* officer, French Legion of Honor.

MEMBER: Societe des Realisateurs de Films (honorary president).

ADDRESSES: HOME—49 Quai Bourbon, Paris 4E, France.*

BRETT, Jeremy   1933-

PERSONAL: Born Jeremy Huggins, November 3, 1933, in Berkswell Grange, England; son of H.W. (a military colonel) and Elizabeth Edith Cadbury (Butler) Huggins; married Anna Massey (an actress), May, 1958 (divorced); married Joan Wilson (a television producer), 1977 (died July, 1985); children: David (first marriage); two (second marriage). EDUCATION—Trained for the stage at the Central School of Speech and Drama.

VOCATION: Actor and director.

CAREER: STAGE DEBUT—With the Library Theatre, Manchester, U.K., 1954. LONDON DEBUT—Patroclus, *Troilus and Cressida,* Old Vic Theatre, 1956. BROADWAY DEBUT—Duke of Aumerle, *Richard II,* Winter Garden Theatre, 1956. PRINCIPAL STAGE APPEARANCES—Mercury, *Amphytrion 38* and Duke of Aumerle, *Richard II,* both Library Theatre, Manchester, U.K., 1954; Malcolm, *Macbeth,* Paris, *Romeo and Juliet,* and Duke of Aumerle, *Richard II,* all Old Vic Theatre, London, 1956; Malcolm, *Macbeth,* Paris, *Romeo and Juliet,* and Troilus, *Troilus and Cressida,* all Winter Garden Theatre, New York City, 1956; Roderick, *Meet Me by Moonlight,* Aldwych Theatre, London, 1957; Ron, *Variations on a Theme,* Globe Theatre, London, 1958; William MacFly, *Mr. Fox of Venice,* Piccadilly Theatre, London, 1959; Archie Forsyth, *Marigold,* Savoy Theatre, London, 1959; Sebastian, *The Edwardians,* Saville Theatre, London, 1959.

Reverend Richard Highfield, *Johnny the Priest,* Prince's Theatre, London, 1960; title role, *Hamlet,* Strand Theatre, London, 1961; Peter, *The Kitchen,* Royal Court Theatre, London, 1961; Dunois, *Saint Joan* and Maurice Sweetman, *The Workhouse Donkey,* both Chichester Festival Theatre, Chichester, U.K., 1963; Father Riccardo Fontana, *The Deputy,* Brooks Atkinson Theatre, New York City, 1964; Gilbert, *A Measure of Cruelty,* Birmingham Repertory Theatre, Birmingham, U.K., 1965; Beliaev, *A Month in the Country,* Cambridge Theatre, London, 1965; Ronnie, *Any Just Cause,* Adeline Genee Theatre, East Grinstead, U.K., 1967; Orlando, *As You Like It* and Valere, *Tartuffe,* both National Theatre Company, Old Vic Theatre, 1967; Kent, *Edward II* and Berowne, *Love's Labour's Lost,* both National Theatre Company, Old Vic Theatre, 1968; Che Guevara, *Macrune's Guevara,* National Theatre Company, Old Vic Theatre, then Jeannetta Cochrane Theatre, London, both 1969.

George Tesman, *Hedda Gabler,* National Theatre Company, Cambridge Theatre, 1970; Bassanio, *The Merchant of Venice,* National Theatre Company, Old Vic Theatre, 1970; the Son, *A Voyage 'round My Father,* Haymarket Theatre, London, 1971; Gaston, *Traveller Without Luggage,* Thorndike Theatre, Leatherhead, U.K., 1972; John Rosmer, *Rosmersholm,* Greenwich Theatre, London, 1973; Otto, *Design for Living,* Phoenix Theatre, London, 1973; Mirabell, *The Way of the World* and Theseus and Oberon, *A Midsummer Night's Dream,* both Stratford Shakespeare Festival, Stratford, ON, Canada, 1976; Robert Browning, *Robert and Elizabeth* and title role, *Dracula,* both Ahmanson Theatre, Los Angeles, 1978; Dr. Watson, *The Crucifer of Blood,* Center Theatre Group, Ahmanson Theatre, 1980-81; Honorable William Tatham, *Aren't We All?,* Brooks Atkinson Theatre, New York City, 1985; title role, *The Secret of Sherlock Holmes,* Wyndham's Theatre, London, 1988. Also appeared as offstage narrator, *Song* (ballet), Martha Graham Dance Company, 1982.

PRINCIPAL STAGE WORK—Director, *The Tempest,* in Canada, 1982.

MAJOR TOURS—Duke of Aumerle, *Richard II*, Paris, *Romeo and Juliet*, Malcolm, *Macbeth*, and Troilus, *Troilus and Cressida*, U.S. and Canadian cities, all 1957; title role, *Dracula*, U.S. cities, 1979.

PRINCIPAL FILM APPEARANCES—Nicholas Rostov, *War and Peace*, Paramount, 1956; Malcolm, *Macbeth*, Prominent, 1963; Mullen, *The Very Edge*, British Lion/Garrick, 1963; Jordan Barker, *The Model Murder Case* (also known as *Girl in the Headlines*), Cinema V, 1964; Freddy Eynsford-Hill, *My Fair Lady*, Warner Brothers, 1964; Gilby, *Young and Willing* (also known as *The Wild and the Willing* and *The Young and the Willing*), Universal, 1964; Edward Parrish, *The Medusa Touch*, Warner Brothers, 1978.

PRINCIPAL TELEVISION APPEARANCES—Series: Title role, *The Adventures of Sherlock Holmes Series I*, Granada, then *Mystery!*, PBS, 1985; title role, *The Adventures of Sherlock Holmes Series II*, Granada, then *Mystery!*, PBS, 1986; title role, *The Return of Sherlock Holmes*, Granada, then *Mystery!*, PBS, 1987; title role, *The Return of Sherlock Holmes II*, Granada, then *Mystery!*, PBS, 1988. Mini-Series: Maxim de Winter, *Rebecca*, BBC, then *Mystery!*, PBS, 1980; Edward Ashburnham, *The Good Soldier*, Granada, then *Masterpiece Theatre*, PBS, 1983; also *Jennie: Lady Randolph Churchill*, BBC, then PBS, 1975; *Country Matters II*, Granada, then *Masterpiece Theatre*, PBS, 1979. Episodic: Peter Tower, "One Deadly Owner," *Thriller*, ABC, 1973; also *Hart to Hart*, ABC. Movies: Dr. Terrence Keith, *Madame X*, NBC, 1981; Bryan Foxworth, *Deceptions*, NBC, 1985; William Nightingale, *Florence Nightingale*, NBC, 1985. Specials: Malcolm, "Macbeth," *Hallmark Hall of Fame*, NBC, 1960; also host, *Piccadilly Circus*, PBS. Also appeared in *The Last Visitor*, BBC-2, 1982; as Danilo, *The Merry Widow*, BBC; in *Katherine Mansfield*, BBC; as Jacques, *Dinner with the Family*; Joseph Surface, *The School for Scandal*; and as title role, *The Picture of Dorian Gray*.

ADDRESSES: AGENT—William Morris Agency Ltd., 147 Wardour Street, London W1V 3TB, England.

*   *   *

BRILL, Fran

PERSONAL: Full name, Frances Joan Brill; born September 30, in Chester, PA; daughter of Joseph M. (a doctor) and Linette Brill; married Clint Ramsden, July 14, 1979 (divorced, 1983); married Francis Robert Kelly (a writer), June 17, 1988. EDUCATION—Boston University, B.F.A., 1968. RELIGION—Methodist.

VOCATION: Actress.

CAREER: STAGE DEBUT—Theatre Atlanta, 1968. BROADWAY DEBUT—Student leader, *Red, White, and Maddox*, Cort Theatre, 1969. PRINCIPAL STAGE APPEARANCES—Nancy Twinkle, *Little Mary Sunshine*, Equity Library Theatre, Master Theatre, New York City, 1970; Maggie Wylie, *What Every Woman Knows*, Roundabout Theatre, New York City, 1975; Mrs. June, *How He Lied to Her Husband* and *Overruled*, both Counterpoint Theatre Company, New York City, 1977; Ersilia, *To Clothe the Naked*, Roundabout Theatre, 1977; Lorraine, *Scribes*, Phoenix Theatre Company, Marymount Manhattan Theatre, New York City, 1977; Fish, *Dusa, Fish, Stas, and Vi*, Center Theatre Group, Mark Taper Forum, Los Angeles, 1978; Helena Charles, *Look Back in Anger*, Roundabout Theatre, 1980; Leona, *Jacob's Ladder*, WPA Theatre, New York

FRAN BRILL

City, 1980; Jenny Wilbur, *Knuckle*, Hudson Guild Theatre, New York City, 1981; Rita, *Skirmishes*, Manhattan Theatre Club, New York City, 1983; Helen, *Baby with the Bathwater*, Playwrights Horizons, New York City, 1983; Mary Hutton, *Paris Bound*, Long Wharf Theatre, New Haven, CT, 1985; Lydia, *A Delicate Situation*, Young Playwright's Festival, Playwrights Horizons, 1986; Elizabeth, *Taking Steps*, York Theatre Company, Church of the Heavenly Rest, New York City, 1986; Sybil Swensen, *Claptrap*, Manhattan Theatre Club, 1987; Betty Armstrong, *Hyde in Hollywood*, American Place Theatre, New York City, 1989.

Also appeared in *The Effect of Gamma Rays on Man-in-the-Moon Marigolds*, Washington Theatre Club, Washington, DC, 1970; *The Beaux' Stratagem*, Center Stage, Baltimore, MD, 1971; *You Can't Take It with You*, Actors Theatre of Louisville, Louisville, KY, 1972; *The House of Mirth*, Long Wharf Theatre, 1976; *The Merchant of Venice*, Meadow Brook Theatre, Rochester, MI, 1977; *Chapter Two*, Meadow Brook Theatre, 1982; *The Cherry Orchard*, Long Wharf Theatre, 1982; *Marathon of One-Act Plays '82*, Ensemble Studio Theatre, New York City, 1982; *Real Estate*, Arena Stage, Washington, DC, 1983; *Tartuffe*, Yale Repertory Theatre, New Haven, CT, 1984; *Holding Patterns*, Musical Theatre Works, New York City, 1984; *Festival of Original One-Act Comedies*, Manhattan Punch Line, INTAR Theatre, New York City, 1985-86; in *Extremities*, Japan, 1983; and in productions of *A Streetcar Named Desire*, *Otherwise Engaged*, and *A Man for All Seasons*.

PRINCIPAL FILM APPEARANCES—Sally Hayes, *Being There*, United Artists, 1979; Mrs. Sloan, *Old Enough*, Orion Classics, 1984; Dana Mardukas, *Midnight Run*, Universal, 1988; also appeared in *Reuben, Reuben*, Twentieth Century-Fox, 1983; *Routed* (short film), Izar, 1989.

PRINCIPAL TELEVISION APPEARANCES—Series: Fran Bachman, *How to Survive a Marriage*, NBC, 1974-75; also *The Jim Henson Hour*, NBC, 1989; *Sesame Street*, PBS. Episodic: Mother, "Seize the Day," *American Playhouse*, PBS, 1986; Jill, *Kate and Allie*, CBS, 1986; Joan Cahill, *Spenser: For Hire*, ABC, 1987; Katherine, *A Year in the Life*, NBC, 1988; *All My Children*, ABC, 1987; *Nurse*, CBS; *Family*, ABC; *Today's F.B.I.*, ABC; *Barnaby Jones*, CBS. Movies: Suze Winter, *Amber Waves*, ABC, 1980; also *Lip Service*, HBO, 1988. Specials: Kaye, "Oh, Boy! Babies!," *NBC Special Treat*, NBC, 1983; *Sesame Street . . . Twenty and Still Counting*, NBC, 1989; also *Look Back in Anger*, Showtime.

RELATED CAREER—Guest artist, Actors Theatre of Louisville, Louisville, KY, 1983-84; guest artist, Arena Stage, Washington, DC, 1984-85; company member, Hartman Theatre Company, Stamford, CT; company member, Parker Playhouse.

RECORDINGS: ALBUMS—*Red, White, and Maddox* (original cast recording), Metromedia Records.

AWARDS: Emmy Award, 1974, for *Sesame Street;* Drama Desk Award nomination, 1975, for *What Every Woman Knows;* Drama Desk Award nomination, 1981, for *Knuckle*.

ADDRESSES: AGENT—Writers and Artists Agency, 70 W. 36th Street, Suite 501, New York, NY 10018; Writers and Artists Agency, 11726 San Vicente Boulevard, Suite 300, Los Angeles, CA 90049.

*   *   *

BROWN, Arvin   1940-

PERSONAL: Born in 1940 in Los Angeles, CA; son of Herman S. and Annette R. (Edelman) Brown; married Joyce Ebert (an actress), November 2, 1969. EDUCATION—Stanford University, B.A., 1961; University of Bristol, certificate in drama, 1962; Harvard University, M.A., 1963; postgraduate work, Yale University, 1963-65.

VOCATION: Producer and director.

CAREER: FIRST STAGE WORK—Director, *The Stronger*, University of Bristol, Bristol, U.K. FIRST LONDON WORK—Director, *The Indian Wants the Bronx*, 1967. FIRST BROADWAY WORK—Director, *A Whistle in the Dark*, Mercury Theatre, 1969. PRINCIPAL STAGE WORK—Director: *Long Day's Journey into Night*, Long Wharf Theatre, New Haven, CT, 1966; *Misalliance, The Glass Menagerie*, and *The Rehearsal*, all Long Wharf Theatre, 1967; *A Whistle in the Dark, Don Juan in Hell*, and *The Lion in Winter*, all Long Wharf Theatre, 1968; *The Indian Wants the Bronx* and *It's Called Sugar Plum* (double-bill), *Ghosts*, and *Tango*, all Long Wharf Theatre, 1969.

Hay Fever, Helen Hayes Theatre, New York City, 1970; *Country People, Spoon River Anthology*, and *Yegor Bulichov*, all Long Wharf Theatre, 1970; *Long Day's Journey into Night*, Promenade Theatre, New York City, 1971; *You Can't Take It with You* and *The Contractor*, both Long Wharf Theatre, 1971; *Solitaire/Double Solitaire*, Long Wharf Theatre, then John Golden Theatre, New

ARVIN BROWN

York City, both 1971; *Hamlet, The Iceman Cometh, What Price Glory?, The Changing Room*, and "A Swan Song" in *Troika*, all Long Wharf Theatre, 1972; *Juno and the Paycock* and *The Widowing of Mrs. Holroyd*, both Long Wharf Theatre, 1973; *Forget-Me-Not Lane*, Long Wharf Theatre, then Center Theatre Group, Mark Taper Forum, Los Angeles, both 1973; *The Seagull*, Long Wharf Theatre, 1974; *The National Health*, Long Wharf Theatre, then Circle in the Square, New York City, both 1974; *Saint Joan*, Ahmanson Theatre, Los Angeles, 1974; *Juno and the Paycock*, Williamstown Theatre Festival, Williamstown, MA, 1974; *Ah, Wilderness!*, Long Wharf Theatre, 1974, then Circle in the Square, 1975; *Artichoke*, Long Wharf Theatre, 1975; *The Archbishop's Ceiling*, Kennedy Center for the Performing Arts, Washington, DC, 1976-77; *Privates on Parade* and *I Sent a Letter to My Love*, both Long Wharf Theatre, 1978; *Mary Barnes* and *Who's Afraid of Virginia Woolf?*, both Long Wharf Theatre, 1979; *Strangers*, John Golden Theatre, 1979; *Watch on the Rhine*, Long Wharf Theatre, 1979, then John Golden Theatre, 1980.

American Buffalo, Long Wharf Theatre, 1980, then Circle in the Square Downtown, New York City, 1981-82, later Booth Theatre, New York City, 1983-84; *A View from the Bridge*, Long Wharf Theatre, 1982, then Ambassador Theatre, New York City, 1983; *Open Admissions, The Cherry Orchard*, and *Free and Clear*, all Long Wharf Theatre, 1982; *Tobacco Road* and *Albert Herring*, both Long Wharf Theatre, 1984; *Requiem for a Heavyweight*, Long Wharf Theatre, 1984, then Martin Beck Theatre, New York City, 1985; *The Normal Heart*, Long Wharf Theatre, 1985; *Joe Egg* (also known as *A Day in the Death of Joe Egg*), Roundabout Theatre, New York City, 1984-85, then Longacre Theatre, New York City,

1985; *All My Sons,* Long Wharf Theatre, 1986, then John Golden Theatre, 1987; *Self Defense,* Long Wharf Theatre, then Joyce Theatre, New York City, both 1987; *Our Town,* Long Wharf Theatre, 1987; *Ah, Wilderness!,* Yale Repertory Theatre, New Haven, CT, then Neil Simon Theatre, New York City, both 1988; *Established Price,* Long Wharf Theatre, 1990.

PRINCIPAL TELEVISION WORK—All as director. Specials: "The Widowing of Mrs. Holroyd," *Theatre in America,* PBS, 1974; "Forget-Me-Not Lane," *Theatre in America,* PBS, 1975; "Ah, Wilderness!," *Theatre in America,* PBS, 1976; *Close Ties,* Entertainment Channel, 1983.

RELATED CAREER—Supervisor, Long Wharf Theatre Apprentice Program, New Haven, CT, 1965; director, Long Wharf Theatre Children's Theatre, 1965-67; artistic director, Long Wharf Theatre, 1967—; associate director, Williamstown Theatre Festival, Williamstown, MA, 1969; lecturer on directing, Salzburg Seminar, Salzburg, Austria, 1972; delegate, International Theatre Conference, Bulgaria, Hungary, 1979; guest lecturer, New Play Center, Vancouver, BC, Canada, 1980; guest lecturer, University of Illinois at Urbana, 1980 and 1982; also theatre advisory panel, National Endowment for the Arts.

AWARDS: Fulbright Scholarship, 1962; Vernon Rice Award, Best Off-Broadway Director, 1971, for *Long Day's Journey into Night;* *Variety* Poll Award, Best Off-Broadway Director, 1971; Antoinette Perry Award nomination, Best Director of a Play, 1975, for *The National Health;* Antoinette Perry Award nomination, Best Reproduction, 1983, for *A View from the Bridge;* Antoinette Perry Award nomination, Best Reproduction, 1984, for *American Buffalo;* Antoinette Perry Award, Best Reproduction, 1985, for *Joe Egg;* Antoinette Perry Award, Best Reproduction, 1987, for *All My Sons.* HONORARY DEGREES—University of New Haven, University of Bridgeport, and Fairfield University.

MEMBER: Theatre Communications Group (co-director, 1972-1976), International Theatre Institute, Society of Stage Directors and Choreographers, Directors Guild.

ADDRESSES: OFFICE—Long Wharf Theatre, 222 Sargent Drive, New Haven, CT 06511.*

*   *   *

BROWN, Barry M.   1942-

PERSONAL: Born August 28, 1942; son of Irving R. (a music publisher) and Hannah (Streicher) Brown. EDUCATION—University of Michigan, B.A., 1964.

VOCATION: Producer.

CAREER: PRINCIPAL STAGE WORK—Producer: (With Edgar Lansbury, Fritz Holt, and Joseph Beruh) *Gypsy,* Winter Garden Theatre, New York City, 1974; (with Holt and S. Spencer Davids) *Saturday Sunday Monday,* Martin Beck Theatre, New York City, 1974; (with Burry Fredrik, Holt, and Sally Sears) *Summer Brave,* American National Theatre and Academy Theatre, New York City, 1975; (with Fredrik, Holt, and Sears) *The Royal Family,* Helen Hayes Theatre, New York City, 1975; (with Gladys Rackmil and Holt) *Platinum,* Mark Hellinger Theatre, New York City, 1978; (with Rackmil and Holt) *The Madwoman of Central Park West,* 22

Steps Theatre, New York City, 1979; (with Lita Starr, Steven Leber, and David Krebs) *Wally's Cafe,* Brooks Atkinson Theatre, New York City, 1981; (with Allan Carr, Kenneth D. Greenblatt, Marvin A. Krauss, Steward F. Lane, James M. Nederlander, and Holt) *La Cage aux Folles,* Palace Theatre, New York City, 1983; (with Barry Weissler, Fran Weissler and Kathy Levin) *Gypsy,* St. James Theatre, New York City, 1989.

MAJOR TOURS—Producer (with Edgar Lansbury, Fritz Holt, and Joseph Beruh), *Gypsy,* U.S. and Canadian cities, 1974.

RELATED CAREER—Producing director and manager, Berkshire Theatre Festival, Stockbridge, MA, 1976.

AWARDS: Drama Desk Award, Best Revival, 1975, for *The Royal Family;* Antoinette Perry Award, Best Musical, 1984, for *La Cage aux Folles.*

MEMBER: League of New York Theatres and Producers.

SIDELIGHTS: Barry M. Brown told *CTFT* that in 1985 he, along with Fritz Holt, produced the first major AIDS benefit in the United States which raised $1.3 million at the Metropolitan Opera House in New York City.

ADDRESSES: OFFICE—250 W. 52nd Street, New York, NY 10019.

*   *   *

BRYAN, Robert   1934-

PERSONAL: Full name, Robert Hedley Bryan; born August 25, 1934, in Derby, England; son of Joseph William and Gladys (Bacon) Bryan; married Ann Daly, March 1, 1963; children: Joanna, Emma. EDUCATION—Hull University, B.Sc., education, 1957.

VOCATION: Lighting designer.

CAREER: FIRST STAGE WORK—Lighting designer, *Seagulls Over Sorrento,* Opera House, Harrogate, U.K., 1960. FIRST LONDON WORK—Lighting designer, *Mr. Whatnot,* Arts Theatre, 1963. PRINCIPAL STAGE WORK—Lighting designer: *Girlfriend,* Apollo Theatre, London, 1970; *Butley,* Criterion Theatre, London, 1971; *Forget-Me-Not Lane,* Greenwich Theatre, London, 1971; *The Little Giant* and *Liberty Ranch,* both Greenwich Theatre, 1972; *Once Upon a Time,* Duke of York's Theatre, London, 1972; *Jumpers,* National Theatre Company, Old Vic Theatre, London, 1972; *The Three Sisters* and *The House of Bernarda Alba,* both Greenwich Theatre, 1973; *The Wolf,* Apollo Theatre, then New London Theatre, London, both 1973; *Design for Living,* Phoenix Theatre, London, 1973; *Engaged,* National Theatre Company, Old Vic Theatre, 1975; *Kidnapped at Christmas,* Dolphin Theatre Company, Shaw Theatre, London, 1975; *Separate Tables,* Apollo Theatre, 1977; *Privates on Parade,* Royal Shakespeare Company (RSC), Aldwych Theatre, London, 1977; *It's All Right If I Do,* Mermaid Theatre, London, 1977; *Fire Angel,* Her Majesty's Theatre, London, 1977; *A Murder Is Announced,* Vaudeville Theatre, London, 1977, restaged in 1979; *Kismet,* Shaftesbury Theatre, London, 1978; *Night and Day,* Phoenix Theatre, 1978; *Bent,* Royal Court Theatre, London, 1979; *Undiscovered Country,* National

Theatre Company, Olivier Theatre, London, 1979; *Once in a Lifetime,* RSC, Aldwych Theatre, 1979.

Pygmalion, Shaw Theatre, 1980; *All's Well That Ends Well,* RSC, Royal Shakespeare Theatre, Stratford-on-Avon, U.K., 1981, then Barbican Theatre, London, 1982, later Martin Beck Theatre, New York City, 1983; *Henry V* and *As You Like It,* both RSC, Barbican Theatre, 1985; *Mrs. Warren's Profession,* National Theatre Company, Lyttelton Theatre, London, 1985; *Exclusive,* Strand Theatre, London, 1989; *Falstaff* (opera), Welsh National Opera, Brooklyn Academy of Music, Brooklyn, NY, 1989; *Someone Like You,* Strand Theatre, London, 1990. Also *The National Health,* National Theatre, London.

RELATED CAREER—Lighting designer, Opera House, Harrogate, U.K., 1959-60; lighting designer, Theatre Projects Ltd., London, 1960-65, then 1969-78; principal lighting designer, Glyndebourne Festival Opera, Glyndebourne, U.K., 1972-83; principal lighting designer, Royal Opera, Covent Garden, London, 1983—; also lighting designer for the Royal Ballet, London, the Australian Opera, Sydney, Australia, the Burgtheater, Vienna, Austria, and the English and Welsh National Operas; lighting designer for operas broadcast on Southern Television and the BBC.

NON-RELATED CAREER—Biology teacher, Yorkshire, U.K., 1957-60, then Nairobi, Kenya, 1965-69.

MEMBER: Society of British Theatre Lighting Designers, Association of British Theatre Technicians, Society of Television Lighting Directors.

SIDELIGHTS: RECREATIONS—Reading, squash, and walking.

ADDRESSES: OFFICE—Royal Opera House, Covent Garden, London, England. AGENT—Kenneth Cleveland Management, 34 Roland Gardens, London, England.

*   *   *

BUCK, David   1936-1989

PERSONAL: Born October 17, 1936, in London, England; died of cancer, January 17, 1989, in Esher, England; son of Joseph and Enid Marguerite (Webb) Buck; married Madeleine Smith (an actress); children: one daughter. EDUCATION—Attended Cambridge University.

VOCATION: Actor and writer.

CAREER: LONDON DEBUT—Orator, *The Chairs,* Royal Court Theatre, 1958. PRINCIPAL STAGE APPEARANCES—Captain Dann, *The Tent,* Royal Court Theatre, London, 1958; Yoshikyo, *Prince Genji,* Oxford Playhouse, Oxford, U.K., 1959; Diomedes, *Troilus and Cressida,* Royal Shakespeare Company (RSC), Stratford-on-Avon, U.K., 1960; Rosencrantz, *Hamlet,* Oliver, *As You Like It,* Tyrell, *Richard III,* and Montano, *Othello,* all RSC, 1961; Yasha, *The Cherry Orchard,* various roles, *The Caucasian Chalk Circle,* Richard, *Curtmantle,* and De Cerisay, *The Devils,* all RSC, Aldwych Theatre, London, 1961-62; title role, *Cyrano de Bergerac,* Open Air Theatre, London, 1967; Abelard, *Abelard and Heloise,* Belgrade Theatre, Conventry, U.K., 1972; Captain Plume, *The Recruiting Officer,* Haymarket Theatre, Leicester, U.K., 1973; Polydor, *The Sunset Touch,* Theatre Royal, Bristol, U.K., 1977; Simon Hench,

Otherwise Engaged, Palace Theatre, Watford, U.K., 1978. Also performed in productions at Christ's College, Cambridge University, and with the English Stage Company, London.

MAJOR TOURS—Milo, *Sleuth,* Canadian cities, 1972.

PRINCIPAL FILM APPEARANCES—Paul Preston, *The Mummy's Shroud,* Twentieth Century-Fox, 1967; Salinas, *Deadfall,* Twentieth Century-Fox, 1968; Paul Hedley, *Taste of Excitement,* Crispin, 1969; Squadron Leader David Scott, *Mosquito Squadron,* United Artists, 1970; voice of Slave Master, *The Dark Crystal,* Universal, 1982.

PRINCIPAL TELEVISION APPEARANCES—Pilots: Captain Horatio Hornblower, *Hornblower* (broadcast as an episode of *Alcoa Premiere*), ABC, 1963. Episodic: Harry Banks, "The Scarecrow of Romney Marsh," *Walt Disney's Wonderful World of Color,* NBC, 1964. Also *Mystery and Imaginaton, The Idiot,* and *1984.*

RELATED CAREER—Associate artist, Royal Shakespeare Company, Stratford-on-Avon, U.K.

WRITINGS: RADIO—Plays: *The Resurrectionists* and *The Image of God.*

AWARDS: British Academy of Film and Television Award nominations for *The Idiot* and *1984.*

OBITUARIES AND OTHER SOURCES: Variety, February 8-14, 1989.*

*   *   *

BURGE, Stuart   1918-

PERSONAL: Born January 15, 1918, in Brentwood, England; son of Henry Ormsby (an electrical engineer) and Kathleen Mary (a music teacher; maiden name, Haig) Burge; married Josephine Parker (an actress), December 21, 1949; children: Lucy, Stephen, Nicholas, Matthew, Emma. EDUCATION—Studied acting at the Old Vic School, 1936-37.

VOCATION: Director, actor, and writer.

CAREER: Also see *WRITINGS* below. STAGE DEBUT—Fourth clown, *The Witch of Edmonton,* Old Vic Theatre, London, 1936. BROADWAY DEBUT—Bates, *Venus Observed,* New Century Theatre, 1952. PRINCIPAL STAGE APPEARANCES—Player Queen, *Hamlet* and boy, *Henry V,* both Old Vic Theatre, London, 1937; company member, Bristol Old Vic Theatre, Bristol, U.K., and Oxford Playhouse, Oxford, U.K., 1939-46.

FIRST LONDON WORK—Director (with Basil Coleman), *Let's Make an Opera,* Lyric Hammersmith Theatre, 1949. PRINCIPAL STAGE WORK—Director: *Let's Make an Opera* (revival), Lyric Hammersmith Theatre, London, 1950; *The Workhouse Donkey,* Chichester Festival Theatre, Chichester, U.K., 1963; *Henry V,* Bristol Old Vic Theatre, Bristol, U.K., then Old Vic Theatre, London, both 1964; *Richard II,* Stratford Shakespeare Festival, Stratford, ON, Canada, 1964; *Othello,* Dubrovnik Festival, Dubrovnik, Yugoslavia, 1964; *Henry IV, Part One* and *Henry IV, Part Two,* both Stratford Shakespeare Festival, 1965; *Serjeant Musgrave's Dance,* Theatre De Lys, New York City, 1966; *King*

John, Nottingham Playhouse, Nottingham, U.K., 1968; *Macbeth*, *The Demonstration*, and *The Dandy Lion*, all Nottingham Playhouse, 1969; *The Ruling Class*, Nottingham Playhouse, then Piccadilly Theatre, London, both 1969; *The Alchemist*, Nottingham Playhouse, then National Theatre, London, both 1969.

The Daughter in Law and *The Idiot*, both Nottingham Playhouse, 1970; *A Yard of Sun*, Nottingham Playhouse, then National Theatre, both 1970; *Lulu*, Nottingham Playhouse, then Royal Court Theatre, London, later Apollo Theatre, London, all 1970-71; *The Rivals* and *A Close Shave*, both Nottingham Playhouse, 1971; *The Tempest* and *A Doll's House*, both Nottingham Playhouse, 1972; *The White Raven* and *The Devil Is an Ass*, both Nottingham Playhouse, 1973; *Measure for Measure*, Edinburgh Festival, Edinburgh, Scotland, 1976; *The Devil Is an Ass*, Edinburgh Festival, 1976, then National Theatre, 1977; *Fair Slaughter*, Royal Court Theatre, 1977; *Eclipse*, Royal Court Theatre, 1978; *The London Cuckolds*, Royal Court Theatre, 1979; *Curtains*, Hampstead Theatre Club, then Whitehall Theatre, both London, 1988; *The Black Prince*, Aldwych Theatre, London, 1989. Also directed *The Dock Brief* and *What Shall We Tell Caroline?* (double-bill) and *Hook, Line, and Sinker*, all 1958; *Curtmantle*, 1962; *Public and Confidential*, 1966; *The Judge* and *The Two Gentlemen of Verona*, both 1967; *Another Country*, Queen's Theatre, London.

MAJOR TOURS—Director, *Henry V*, international cities, 1964; also stage manager for Old Vic Company tours of European cities, 1939 and 1947; director with a touring repertory company, 1948.

PRINCIPAL FILM APPEARANCES—Paolo, *Malta Story*, United Artists, 1954; Head, *Little Dorrit*, Cannon, 1988.

FIRST FILM WORK—Director, *There Was a Crooked Man*, Lopert/United Artists, 1962. PRINCIPAL FILM WORK—Director: *Othello*, Warner Brothers, 1965; *The Mikado*, Warner Brothers, 1967; *Julius Caesar*, American International, 1970; *Uncle Vanya*, Arthur Cantor, 1977.

PRINCIPAL TELEVISION WORK—All as director. Movies: *The Rainbow*, BBC, then Arts and Entertainment, 1989; also *The Old Men at the Zoo*, *Breaking Up*, *Naming the Names*, *Chinese Whispers*, and *Circles of Deceit*, all BBC. Also directed *The Power and the Glory*, *The Devil and John Brown*, *Under Western Eyes*, *Luther*, *School for Scandal*, *Bill Brand*, and *Sons and Lovers*.

RELATED CAREER—Artistic director, Nottingham Playhouse, Nottingham, U.K., 1968-73; visiting professor, University of California, Davis, 1984; artistic director, Queen's Theatre, Hornchurch, U.K.; artistic director, Royal Court Theatre, London.

NON-RELATED CAREER—Civil engineer.

WRITINGS: TELEVISION—*Under Western Eyes*, *Luther*, *School for Scandal*, *Bill Brand*, and *Sons and Lovers*.

AWARDS: Commander of the British Empire, 1974; also Desmond Davis Award from the British Academy of Film and Television Arts, 1988, for Outstanding Creative Contribution to Television.

ADDRESSES: AGENT—Harriet Cruickshank, 97 Old S. Lambeth Road, London SW8 1XV, England.

BURGHOFF, Gary   1943-

PERSONAL: Born May 24, 1943, in Bristol, CT; married Janet Gale; children: Gena Gayle. EDUCATION—Attended the Music and Dramatic Theatre Academy.

VOCATION: Actor.

CAREER: OFF-BROADWAY DEBUT—Title role, *You're a Good Man, Charlie Brown*, Theatre 80 St. Mark's, 1967. PRINCIPAL STAGE APPEARANCES—Willum Cubbert, *The Nerd*, Helen Hayes Theatre, New York City, 1987; also appeared in summer theatre productions.

PRINCIPAL FILM APPEARANCES—Radar O'Reilly, *M*A*S*H*, Twentieth Century-Fox, 1970; Ted, *B.S., I Love You*, Motion Pictures International, 1971.

TELEVISION DEBUT—*CBS Television Workshop*, CBS. PRINCIPAL TELEVISION APPEARANCES—Series: Regular, *The Don Knotts Show*, NBC, 1970-71; Corporal Walter "Radar" O'Reilly, *M*A*S*H*, CBS, 1972-79. Pilots: Bill Taylor, *Casino*, ABC, 1980; Walter O'Reilly, *W*A*L*T*E*R*, CBS, 1984. Episodic: *The Good Guys*, CBS, 1969; *The Name of the Game*, NBC, 1970; *Love, American Style*, ABC, 1973; *Fernwood 2-Night*, syndicated, 1977; *Wonder Woman*, CBS, 1978; *Sweepstakes*, NBC, 1979; also *Donny and Marie*, ABC; *The Love Boat*, ABC; *Fantasy Island*, ABC. Movies: Bob Willis, *The Man in the Santa Claus Suit*, NBC, 1979. Specials: Clergyman, *Twigs*, CBS, 1975; also *Battle of the Network Stars*, ABC, 1976; *Us Against the World II*, ABC, 1978.

RELATED CAREER—Performer in nightclubs throughout the United States.

AWARDS: Emmy Award, Outstanding Continuing Performance By a Supporting Actor in a Comedy, 1977, for *M*A*S*H*.

ADDRESSES: OFFICE—c/o Robert Crystal, 146 S. Spaulding Drive, Beverly Hills, CA 90212.*

*   *   *

BURKE, Chris   1965-

PERSONAL: Born August 26, 1965, in New York, NY; son of Francis D. (a police officer) and Marian H. (a trade show manager; maiden name, Brady). EDUCATION—Attended the Kennedy Child Study Center, the Cardinal Cushing School, and the Don Cuanella School (all special education schools).

VOCATION: Actor.

CAREER: PRINCIPAL TELEVISION APPEARANCES—Series: Corky Thatcher, *Life Goes On*, ABC, 1989—. Pilots: Louis, *Desperate*, ABC, 1987.

NON-RELATED CAREER—Teacher's aide to multi-handicapped children, New York City Board of Education; volunteer at a camp for the handicapped in New York.

MEMBER: Screen Actors Guild, Association for Help of Retarded Citizens, Young Adult Institute.

CHRIS BURKE

SIDELIGHTS: Chris Burke, like his character on *Life Goes On,* suffers from Down's Syndrome, a birth defect that is a cause of mental retardation. He calls his acting career "a milestone for me and others with a handicap since I have Down's Syndrome. I have always been interested in acting and love what I am doing."

ADDRESSES: AGENT—Cynthia Katz, Abrams Artists and Associates, 420 Madison Avenue, New York, NY 10017.

*   *   *

BURNETT, Carol   1933-

PERSONAL: Born April 26, 1933, in San Antonio, TX; daughter of Jody (a movie theatre manager) and Louise (Creighton) Burnett; married Don Saroyan (an actor; divorced); married Joe Hamilton (a television producer), 1963 (divorced); children: Erin Kate, Jody Ann, Carrie Louise. EDUCATION—Attended the University of California, Los Angeles.

VOCATION: Actress and comedienne.

CAREER: OFF-BROADWAY DEBUT—Princess Winifred Woebegone, *Once Upon a Mattress,* Phoenix Theatre, 1959. BROADWAY DEBUT—Princess Winifred Woebegone, *Once Upon a Mattress,* Alvin Theatre, 1960. PRINCIPAL STAGE APPEARANCES—Hope Springfield and Lila Tremaine, *Fade Out—Fade In,* Mark Hellinger Theatre, New York City, 1964; Karen Nash, "Visitor from

Mamaroneck," Muriel Tate, "Visitor from Hollywood," and Norma Hubley, "Visitor from Forest Hills" in *Plaza Suite,* Huntington Hartford Theatre, Los Angeles, 1970; Agnes, *I Do! I Do!,* Huntington Hartford Theatre, 1973; Doris, *Same Time, Next Year,* Huntington Hartford Theatre, 1977, then Burt Reynolds' Jupiter Dinner Theatre, Jupiter, FL, 1980.

FILM DEBUT—Stella Irving, *Who's Been Sleeping in My Bed?,* Paramount, 1963. PRINCIPAL FILM APPEARANCES—Tillie Schlaine, *Pete 'n' Tillie,* Universal, 1972; Mollie Malloy, *The Front Page,* Universal, 1974; Tulip Brenner, *A Wedding,* Twentieth Century-Fox, 1978; Emily, *Chu Chu and the Philly Flash,* Twentieth Century-Fox, 1981; Kate Burroughs, *The Four Seasons,* Universal, 1981; Miss Hannigan, *Annie,* Columbia, 1982; also appeared in *Health,* Twentieth Century-Fox, 1980.

PRINCIPAL TELEVISION APPEARANCES—Series: Celia, *Stanley,* NBC, 1956-57; regular, *Pantomine Quiz,* ABC, 1958-59; regular, *The Garry Moore Show,* CBS, 1959-62; co-star, *The Entertainers,* CBS, 1964-65; host, *The Carol Burnett Show,* CBS, 1967-78; host, *Carol Burnett and Company,* ABC, 1979; host, *Carol and Company,* NBC, 1990. Mini-Series: Charlotte Kensington, *Fresno,* CBS, 1986. Episodic: Agnes Grep, "Cavender Is Coming," *The Twilight Zone,* CBS, 1962; Verla Grubb, *All My Children,* ABC, 1976; Eunice Higgins, *Mama's Family,* NBC, 1983-84; narrator, "Happily Ever After" (animated), *WonderWorks,* PBS, 1985; Susan Johnson, *Magnum, P.I.,* CBS, 1988; also *The Paul Winchell-Jerry Mahoney Show,* NBC, 1955; *The Lucy Show* (five episodes), CBS, 1966-67; *Gomer Pyle, U.S.M.C.,* CBS, 1967; *Get Smart,* NBC, 1967; *Here's Lucy,* CBS, 1969, 1970, and 1971; *The*

CAROL BURNETT

Dick Cavett Show, ABC, 1986; *The DuPont Show of the Week*, NBC; *The U.S. Steel Hour*, CBS; *The Ed Sullivan Show*, CBS; *The Jack Paar Show*, NBC; *The Jack Benny Show*, CBS; *The Tim Conway Show*, CBS; *The Muppet Show*, syndicated. Movies: Dorothy Benson, *The Grass Is Always Greener Over the Septic Tank*, CBS, 1978; Peg Mullen, *Friendly Fire*, ABC, 1979; Dori Gray, *The Tenth Month*, CBS, 1979; Beatrice O'Reilly, *Life of the Party: The Story of Beatrice*, CBS, 1982; Mary Catherine Castelli, *Between Friends*, HBO, 1983; Martha Madden, *Hostage*, CBS, 1988.

Specials: *The General Motors 50th Anniversary Show*, NBC, 1957; *American Cowboy*, CBS, 1960; *Julie and Carol at Carnegie Hall*, CBS, 1962; title role, *Calamity Jane*, CBS, 1963; Princess Winifred Woebegone, *Once Upon a Mattress*, CBS, 1964; *Carol and Company*, CBS, 1966; *Carol + 2*, CBS, 1967; *The Perry Como Christmas Show*, NBC, 1968; *Girl Friends and Nabors*, CBS, 1968; *Carol Channing Proudly Presents the Seven Deadly Sins*, ABC, 1969; *Bing Crosby and Carol Burnett—Together Again for the First Time*, NBC, 1969; *A Last Laugh at the '60s*, ABC, 1970; *Rowan and Martin Bite the Hand That Feeds Them*, NBC, 1970; *The Tim Conway Special*, CBS, 1970; *Li'l Abner*, NBC, 1971; *Julie and Carol at Lincoln Center*, CBS, 1971; *Super Comedy Bowl*, CBS, 1971; *Bing Crosby and His Friends*, NBC, 1972; *Burt Bacharach: Close to You*, ABC, 1972; Princess Winifred Woebegone, *Once Upon a Mattress*, CBS, 1972; *Keep U.S. Beautiful*, NBC, 1973; *Burt and the Girls*, NBC, 1973; *Shirley MacLaine: If They Could See Me Now*, CBS, 1974; Anne Miller, *6 Rms Riv Vu*, CBS, 1974; Emily, Celia, Dorothy, and Mother, *Twigs*, CBS, 1975; *Sills and Burnett at the Met*, CBS, 1976; *CBS: On the Air*, CBS, 1978; *Steve and Eydie Celebrate Irving Berlin*, NBC, 1978; *A Special Evening with Carol Burnett*, CBS, 1978; *Dolly and Carol in Nashville*, CBS, 1978; *The Sensational, Shocking, Wonderful, Wacky 70s*, NBC, 1980; *The Bert Convy Special—There's a Meeting Here Tonight*, syndicated, 1981; *Cheryl Ladd: Scenes from a Special*, ABC, 1982; Eunice Higgins, *Eunice*, CBS, 1982; *Texaco Star Theater: Opening Night*, NBC, 1982; *Hollywood: The Gift of Laughter*, 1982; *Burnett "Discovers" Domingo*, CBS, 1984; *The Night of 100 Stars II*, ABC, 1985; *The Kennedy Center Honors: A Celebration of the Performing Arts*, CBS, 1985; *Here's Television Entertainment*, syndicated, 1985; Alberta Johnson, *The Laundromat*, HBO, 1985; *The American Film Institute Salute to Billy Wilder*, NBC, 1986; *Neil Diamond . . . Hello Again*, CBS, 1986; "Follies in Concert," *Great Performances*, PBS, 1986; *A Carol Burnett Special: Carol, Carl, Whoopi, and Robin*, ABC, 1987; *Superstars and Their Moms*, ABC, 1987; *James Stewart: A Wonderful Life*, PBS, 1987; Karen Nash, "Visitor from Mamaroneck," Muriel Tate, "Visitor from Hollywood," and Norma Hubley, "Visitor from Forest Hills" in *Plaza Suite*, ABC, 1987; *Happy Birthday Hollywood*, ABC, 1987; *Great Moments in Disney Animation*, ABC, 1987; *Secrets Women Never Share*, NBC, 1987; *A Star-Spangled Celebration*, ABC, 1987; *Super Dave*, Showtime, 1987; *This Is Your Life*, NBC, 1987; *A Conversation with Carol*, Disney Channel, 1988; *America's All-Star Tribute to Elizabeth Taylor*, ABC, 1989; *Julie and Carol: Together Again!*, ABC, 1989; *The American Comedy Awards*, Fox, 1989.

PRINCIPAL TELEVISION WORK—Specials: Executive producer, *Plaza Suite*, ABC, 1987; executive producer, *A Conversation with Carol*, Disney Channel, 1988.

RELATED CAREER—President, Kalola Productions Inc.; Franklin D. Murphy Associate and board member, Emerson College, Boston, MA; established the "Carol Burnett Musical Competition

Award," University of California, Los Angeles, Theatre Arts School.

NON-RELATED CAREER—Restaurant hat check girl.

WRITINGS: One More Time (autobiography), Random House, 1986.

AWARDS: American Guild of Variety Artists Award, Outstanding Comedienne, and Theatre World Award, both 1960, for *Once Upon a Mattress; TV Guide* Awards, Outstanding Female Performer, 1961, 1962, and 1963, all for *The Garry Moore Show;* Emmy Award, Outstanding Performance in a Variety or Musical Program or Series, 1962, for *The Garry Moore Show;* Emmy Award, Outstanding Performance in a Variety or Musical Program or Series, 1963, for *Julie and Carol at Carnegie Hall;* Emmy Award nominations, 1968-71 and 1973-77, for *The Carol Burnett Show;* Emmy Award nomination, 1973, for *Julie and Carol at Lincoln Center;* Emmy Award nomination, 1974, for *6 Rms Riv Vu;* People's Choice Awards, Best Variety Show, for *The Carol Burnett Show*, and Favorite All-Around Female Entertainer, both 1975; People's Choice Awards, Favorite Female Television Performer and (co-winner) Favorite All-Around Female Entertainer, both 1976; voted Favorite All-Around Female Entertainer by the public in A.C. Nelson Company polls, (co-winner) 1976, 1977, 1978, and 1979; People's Choice Award, Best Musical Variety Show, 1977, for *The Carol Burnett Show;* Emmy Award nomination, Christopher Award, and Bronze Rose Award from the Montreaux Television Contest, 1977, for *Sills and Burnett at the Met;* People's Choice Awards, Favorite All-Around Female Entertainer, 1977, 1978, and 1979; National Critics' Circle Award, Outstanding Performance, 1977-78; Best Actress Award from the San Sebastian Film Festival, 1978, for *A Wedding;* Emmy Award nomination, 1979, for *The Tenth Month;* Emmy Award nomination, 1979, for *Friendly Fire.*

Women Film Crystal Award, 1980; People's Choice Awards, Favorite Female Television Performer, 1981 and 1982; American Guild of Variety Artists Award, Favorite Television Performer, 1981; Jack Benny Humanitarian Award from the March of Dimes, 1981; Humanitarian of the Year Award from Variety Clubs International, 1983; named one of the world's ten most admired women by *Good Housekeeping* magazine, 1983; Gold Medal Award from the International Radio and Television Society, 1984; Annual Cable Excellence Award, Best Actress in a Dramatic or Theatrical Program, 1984, for *Between Friends;* inducted into the Academy of Television Arts and Sciences Hall of Fame, 1985; Horatio Alger Distinguished Americans Award from the Horatio Alger Association, 1988; Woman of the Year Award from the *Los Angeles Times;* Woman of the Year Award from the Academy of Television Arts and Sciences; six Golden Globes; five Gold Medals from *Photoplay* magazine as Most Popular Television Star; four Entertainer of the Year Awards from the American Guild of Variety Artists, Best Female Comedienne; named Most Popular Television Star by the Newspaper Enterprise Association; Variety Club Award, Top Female Star; New York Friars Award, Entertainer of the Year; named one of the world's 20 most admired women in a Gallup Poll. HONORARY DEGREES—Emerson College, Doctor of Humane Letters, 1980.

ADDRESSES: AGENT—Bill Robinson, International Creative Management, 8899 Beverly Boulevard, Los Angeles, CA 90048. PUBLICIST—Rick Ingersoll Public Relations, 1659 Michael Lane, Pacific Palisades, CA 90272.

BUSFIELD, Timothy

PERSONAL: Born June 12, in Lansing, MI; married Radha Delamarter (an actress and director; divorced); married Jennifer Merwin (a fashion designer); children: Willy (first marriage); Daisy (second marriage). EDUCATION—Attended East Tennessee State University; trained for the stage at the Actors Theatre of Louisville.

VOCATION: Actor.

CAREER: PRINCIPAL STAGE APPEARANCES—Hotspur, *Richard II,* Circle Repertory Company, Entermedia Theatre, New York City, 1982; Eugene and Stanley (understudy), *Brighton Beach Memoirs,* Alvin Theatre, New York City, 1983; also appeared in *A Life,* Long Wharf Theatre, New Haven, CT, 1981.

PRINCIPAL FILM APPEARANCES—Soldier with mortar, *Stripes,* Columbia, 1981; Arnold Poindexter, *Revenge of the Nerds,* Twentieth Century-Fox, 1984; Arnold Poindexter, *Revenge of the Nerds II: Nerds in Paradise,* Twentieth Century-Fox, 1987; Mark, *Field of Dreams,* Universal, 1989.

PRINCIPAL TELEVISION APPEARANCES—Series: Mark Potter, *Reggie,* ABC, 1983; Dr. John "J.T." McIntyre, Jr., *Trapper John, M.D.,* CBS, 1984-86; Elliot Weston, *thirtysomething,* ABC, 1989—. Episodic: *AfterM*A*S*H,* CBS; also *The Paper Chase.* Specials: Host, *Don't Divorce the Children,* Lifetime, 1990.

RELATED CAREER—Company member, Actors Theatre of Louisville, Louisville, KY, 1980-81; also founder, director, and writer, Fantasy Theatre, Sacramento, CA.

ADDRESSES: AGENT—Ro Diamond, Century Artists Ltd., 9744 Wilshire Boulevard, Suite 308, Beverly Hills, CA 90212.*

*   *   *

BYRD, David

VOCATION: Actor.

CAREER: PRINCIPAL STAGE APPEARANCES—Duke of Bedford, *Henry VI, Part One,* Lord Say and Lord Hastings, *Henry VI, Part Two,* and Lord Hastings, *Richard III,* all New York Shakespeare Festival, Delacorte Theater, New York City, 1970; Raniero, *The Burnt Flowerbed,* Roundabout Theatre, New York City, 1974; Schaaf, *A Month in the Country,* Center Theatre Group, Mark Taper Forum, Los Angeles, 1983. Also appeared in *Candida* and *Arrah-Na-Pouge,* both McCarter Theatre, Princeton, NJ, 1965-66; *The Soldier's Tale* and *The Knight of the Burning Pestle* (double-bill), Long Wharf Theatre, New Haven, CT, 1974.

PRINCIPAL FILM APPEARANCES—Easy Money, *Pipe Dreams,* AVCO-Embassy, 1976; pet store owner, *Rollercoaster,* Universal, 1977; conductor, *The Turning Point,* Twentieth Century-Fox, 1977; dirty movie cameraman, *Corvette Summer* (also known as *The Hot One*), United Artists, 1978; Roy, *Sunnyside,* American International, 1979; first man, *Battlestar Galactica,* Universal, 1979; Paul Obermann, *The Formula,* Metro-Goldwyn-Mayer, 1980; doorman, *Some Kind of Hero,* Paramount, 1982; desk clerk, *The Man with Two Brains,* Warner Brothers, 1983; minister, *All of Me,* Universal, 1984; boss, *School Spirit,* Concorde/Cinema Group, 1985; Quentin, *Best Seller,* Orion, 1987; Deke, *Big Top Pee-Wee,* Paramount, 1988.

PRINCIPAL TELEVISION APPEARANCES—Series: Dr. Lester, *Highcliffe Manor,* NBC, 1979; Vincent Tully, *Mary,* CBS, 1985-86. Pilots: Bixby, *Lacy and the Mississippi Queen,* NBC, 1978. Episodic: Eines, *Amazing Stories,* NBC, 1986; Judge Shindler, *Hooperman,* ABC, 1987; Eugene, *Murphy's Law,* ABC, 1989; also *All in the Family,* CBS, 1979. Movies: Surgeon, *Deadman's Curve,* CBS, 1978; Dr. Samuels, *Transplant,* CBS, 1979; headwaiter, *Your Place or Mine?,* CBS, 1983; Leonard Mann, *Rita Hayworth: The Love Goddess,* CBS, 1983; motel manager, *Missing Pieces,* CBS, 1983; principal, *My Mother's Secret Life,* ABC, 1984; Elon, *Samson and Delilah,* ABC, 1984; Larry, *When the Bough Breaks,* NBC, 1986. Specials: Man, "If I'm Lost, How Come I Found You?" *ABC Weekend Specials,* ABC, 1978; guard, "Tales from the Hollywood Hills: The Closed Set," *Great Performances,* PBS, 1988.

RELATED CAREER—Company member, Actors Theatre of Louisville, Louisville, KY, 1972-73.

ADDRESSES: AGENT—Arthur Toretsky, ATM Associates, 870 N. Vine Street, Suite G, Los Angeles, CA 90038.*

C

CALDWELL, L. Scott

VOCATION: Actress.

CAREER: PRINCIPAL STAGE APPEARANCES—Gail, *The Daughters of the Mock*, Negro Ensemble Company, St. Mark's Playhouse, New York City, 1978; Afrodite, *A Season to Unravel* and Ruth, *Old Phantoms*, both Negro Ensemble Company, St. Mark's Playhouse, 1979; woman one and Pattie Mae Wells, *Home*, Negro Ensemble Company, St. Mark's Playhouse, 1979, then Cort Theatre, New York City, 1980; Bertha Holly, *Joe Turner's Come and Gone*, Yale Repertory Theatre, New Haven, CT, 1985, then Huntington Theatre Company, Boston, MA, 1986; Mrs. Baker, *A Month of Sundays*, Ritz Theatre, New York City, 1987; Bertha Holly, *Joe Turner's Come and Gone*, Ethel Barrymore Theatre, New York City, 1988. Also appeared in "Everyman" and "The Imprisonment" in *Plays from Africa*, Negro Ensemble Company, St. Mark's Playhouse, 1979; *Colored People's Time*, Negro Ensemble Company, Cherry Lane Theatre, New York City, 1982; *A Raisin in the Sun*, Studio Arena Theatre, Buffalo, NY, 1982; *About Heaven and Earth*, Negro Ensemble Company, Theatre Four, New York City, 1983.

PRINCIPAL FILM APPEARANCES—Janet Smith, *Without a Trace*, Twentieth Century-Fox, 1983; patron, *Exterminator 2*, Cannon, 1984.

PRINCIPAL TELEVISION APPEARANCES—Episodic: Elizabeth Connolly, *The Cosby Show*, NBC, 1988; Mrs. Hines, *TV 101*, CBS, 1989; Selma, *Tour of Duty*, CBS, 1989; Gloria Tessel, *Hunter*, NBC, 1989; also *L.A. Law*, NBC, 1989. Movies: Althea, *God Bless the Child*, ABC, 1988.

RELATED CAREER—Company member, Milwaukee Repertory Theatre, Milwaukee, WI, 1981-82.

AWARDS: Antoinette Perry Award, Best Featured Actress in a Play, 1988, for *Joe Turner's Come and Gone*.

ADDRESSES: AGENT—Bauman Hiller and Associates, 250 W. 57th Street, New York, NY 10107.*

*   *   *

CALLOW, Simon   1949-

PERSONAL: Born June 15, 1949, in London, England; son of Neil Francis and Yvonne Mary (Guise) Callow. EDUCATION—Attended Queen's University (Belfast, Ireland); trained for the stage at the London Drama Centre.

VOCATION: Actor, director, and writer.

CAREER: Also see WRITINGS below. STAGE DEBUT—*The Thrie Estates*, Assembly Hall Theatre, Edinburgh, Scotland, 1973. LONDON DEBUT—Crown Prince Maximilian, *Schippel*, Open Space Theatre, 1974. PRINCIPAL STAGE APPEARANCES—Crown Prince Maximilian, *Schippel*, Traverse Theatre, Edinburgh, Scotland, 1974; Redpenny, *The Doctor's Dilemma*, Mermaid Theatre, London, 1975; Crown Prince Maximilian, *Plumber's Progress* (previously known as *Schippel*), Prince of Wales Theatre, London, 1975; Pieter de Groot, *Soul of the White Ant*, Oliver, Jack, Putter, and Rider, *Blood Sports*, and in *Juvenalia* (one-man show), all Bush Theatre, London, 1976; Kutchevski, *Devil's Island*, Joint Stock Company, Royal Court Theatre, London, 1977; Sayers, *A Mad World, My Masters*, Joint Stock Company, Young Vic Theatre, London, 1977; Sandy, *Epsom Downs*, Joint Stock Company, Round House Theatre, London, 1977; title role, *Titus Andronicus*, Bristol Old Vic Theatre, Bristol, U.K., 1978; Boyd, *Flying Blind*, Royal Court Theatre, 1978; title role, *The Resistible Rise of Arturo Ui* and Ure, the old reaper, and a drunk, *The Machine Wreckers*, both Half Moon Theatre, London, 1978; Eddie, *Mary Barnes*, Birmingham Repertory Studio, Birmingham, U.K., 1978, then Royal Court Theatre, 1979; Orlando, *As You Like It* and Mozart, *Amadeus*, both National Theatre Company, Olivier Theatre, London, 1979; Stafford, *Sisterly Feelings*, National Theatre Company, Olivier Theatre, 1980; Guy Burgess, "An Englishman Abroad" in *Single Spies*, National Theatre Company, Queen's Theatre, London, 1989. Also appeared in repertory at Lincoln, U.K., 1973-74; in *Mrs. Grabowski's Academy*, Theatre Upstairs, London, 1975; *The Beastly Beatitudes of Balthazar B.*, Bristol Old Vic Theatre, then Duke of York's Theatre, London, 1981; *Restoration*, Royal Court Theatre, 1981; *Kiss of the Spider Woman*, Bush Theatre, 1985; and in productions of *The Relapse* and *Faust*.

PRINCIPAL STAGE WORK—Director: *The Passport*, Offstage Downstairs Theatre, London, 1985; *Jacques and His Master*, Los Angeles Theatre Center, Los Angeles, 1987; *Shirley Valentine*, Vaudeville Theatre, London, 1988, then Booth Theatre, New York City, 1989; (with Alan Bennett) "An Englishman Abroad" in *Single Spies*, National Theatre Company, Queen's Theatre, London, 1989.

PRINCIPAL FILM APPEARANCES—Emanuel Schikaneder, *Amadeus*, Orion, 1984; Handel, *Honor, Profit, and Pleasure*, Spectre Productions, 1985; Mark Varner, *The Good Father*, Skouras, 1986; Reverend Arthur Beebe, *A Room with a View*, Cinecom, 1986; Mr. Ducie, *Maurice*, Cinecom, 1987; Police Chief Hunt, *Manifesto* (also known as *For a Night of Love* and *Pour une nuit d'amour*), Cannon, 1988. Also appeared in *Gossip*, Boyd's Company, 1983.

PRINCIPAL FILM WORK—Director, *Charles Laughton: A Difficult Actor* (documentary), 1988.

PRINCIPAL TELEVISION APPEARANCES—Mini-Series: Mr. Micawber, "David Copperfield," *Masterpiece Theatre*, PBS, 1988; also *Chance of a Lifetime*. Episodic: Dr. Theodore Kemp, "The Wolvercote Tongue," *Inspector Morse*, Granada, then *Mystery!*, PBS, 1988. Also appeared in *Man of Destiny*, *La Ronde*, *All the World's a Stage*, *Wings of Song*, *The Dybbuk*, and *Instant Enlightenment*.

NON-RELATED CAREER—Box office attendant at a London theatre.

WRITINGS: STAGE—(Translator) *Jacques and His Master*, Los Angeles Theatre Center, Los Angeles, 1987. OTHER—*Being an Actor* (nonfiction), St. Martin's, 1986; *Charles Laughton: A Difficult Actor* (biography), Methuen, 1987, Grove, 1988; *Acting in Restoration Comedy*, Applause Theatre Books, 1989.

AWARDS: Drama Desk Award nomination, Best Director, 1989, for *Shirley Valentine*.

SIDELIGHTS: Regarding his careers as actor, author, and director, Simon Callow told *Vogue* magazine (May, 1989), "Of all my occupations, acting is the healthiest and offers the most release; writing is the most difficult but offers the greatest possibility of actually getting it right; and directing is probably what I do best but least enjoy."

ADDRESSES: AGENT—Marion Rosenberg, The Lantz Office, 9255 Sunset Boulevard, Suite 505, Los Angeles, CA 90069. MANAGER—Marina Martin, 7 Windmill Street, London W1, England.*

*   *   *

CAMPBELL, Cheryl 1951-

PERSONAL: Born in 1951 in Welwyn Garden City, England. EDUCATION—Graduated from the London Academy of Dramatic Art, 1972.

VOCATION: Actress.

CAREER: PRINCIPAL STAGE APPEARANCES—Jane Larr, *In the Jungle of the Cities*, Place Theatre, London, 1973; Frida Foldal, *John Gabriel Borkman* and Maggie MacFarlane, *Engaged*, both National Theatre Company, Old Vic Theatre, London, 1975; Lady Wilhelmina Belturbet, *The Amazons*, Actors' Company, Wimbledon Theatre, London, 1977; Jan, *Bedroom Farce*, National Theatre Company, Prince of Wales Theatre, London, 1978; Gloria, *You Never Can Tell*, Lyric Hammersmith Theatre, London, 1979; Diana, *All's Well That Ends Well*, Royal Shakespeare Company (RSC), Stratford-on-Avon, U.K., 1981, then Barbican Theatre, London, 1982; Nora, *A Doll's House*, RSC, Pit Theatre, Stratford-on-Avon, then Barbican Theatre, 1982. Also appeared with the Birmingham Repertory Company, Birmingham, U.K., at the Citizens' Theatre, Glasgow, Scotland, and at the Theatre Royal, Windsor, U.K.

PRINCIPAL FILM APPEARANCES—Sister Monica, *Hawk the Slayer*, ITC, 1980; Jennie Liddell, *Chariots of Fire*, Twentieth Century-

Fox, 1981; Sheila McVicar, *McVicar*, Crown International, 1982; Lady Alice Clayton, *Greystoke: The Legend of Tarzan, Lord of the Apes*, Warner Brothers, 1984; Lady Aline Hartlip, *The Shooting Party*, European Classic, 1984.

TELEVISION DEBUT—*Z Cars*, BBC. PRINCIPAL TELEVISION APPEARANCES—Mini-Series: Sarah Bernhardt, *Lillie*, BBC, 1978, then *Masterpiece Theatre*, PBS, 1979; Eileen, *Pennies from Heaven*, BBC, 1978, then PBS, 1979; Vera Brittain, *Testament of Youth*, BBC, 1979, then *Masterpiece Theatre*, PBS, 1980; Madeleine Cranmere, *Malice Aforethought*, BBC, 1979, then *Mystery!*, PBS, 1984; Griselda Clement, "The Murder at the Vicarage," *Agatha Christie's Miss Marple*, BBC, then *Mystery!*, PBS, 1989. Specials: Lady Eileen Brent, *The Seven Dials Mystery*, syndicated, 1981; *Absurd Person Singular*, BBC, then Arts and Entertainment, 1985. Also appeared in *Emma*, 1974; as Janet, *Rain on the Roof*, 1979; Lady Wellington, *The Duke of Wellington*, 1979; *The Farm*, 1982; Emma, *Affairs of the Heart*; Queen Victoria's daughter, *Edward the King*.

AWARDS: British Academy of Film and Television Arts Award, Best Television Actress, 1979, for *Testament of Youth*, *The Duke of Wellington*, and *Malice Aforethought*; British Broadcasting Press Guild Award, Best Actress, for *Testament of Youth*.

ADDRESSES: OFFICE—5 Milner Place, London N1 1TN, England. AGENT—Michael Whitehall Ltd., 125 Gloucester Road, London SW7, England.*

*   *   *

CAREY, Harry, Jr. 1921-

PERSONAL: Born May 16, 1921, in Saugus, CA; son of Harry (an actor) and Oliver (Fuller) Carey; married Marilyn Frances Fix, August 12, 1944; children: Steven, Melinda, Thomas, Cary, Patricia. MILITARY—U.S. Navy, 1941-46.

VOCATION: Actor.

CAREER: FILM DEBUT—Prentice McComber, *Pursued*, Warner Brothers, 1947. PRINCIPAL FILM APPEARANCES—Dan Latimer, *Red River*, United Artists, 1948; Jimmy Biff, *Moonrise*, Republic, 1948; William Kearney ("The Abilene Kid"), *The Three Godfathers*, Metro-Goldwyn-Mayer (MGM), 1948; Lieutenant Ross Pennell, *She Wore a Yellow Ribbon*, RKO, 1949; Lieutenant Ord, *Copper Canyon*, Paramount, 1950; Trooper Daniel "Sandy" Boone, *Rio Grande*, Republic, 1950; Sandy Owens, *Wagonmaster*, RKO, 1950; Captain Gregson, *Warpath*, Paramount, 1951; reporter, *Monkey Business*, Twentieth Century-Fox, 1952; Sergeant Shaker Schuker, *The Wild Blue Yonder* (also known as *Thunder Across the Pacific*), Republic, 1952; Griff, *Beneath the Twelve Mile Reef*, Twentieth Century-Fox, 1953; Winslow, *Gentlemen Prefer Blondes*, Twentieth Century-Fox, 1953; Hunt, *Island in the Sky*, Warner Brothers, 1953; taxi driver, *Niagara*, Twentieth Century-Fox, 1953; Dobe, *San Antone*, Republic, 1953; Jim Riley, *Sweethearts on Parade*, Republic, 1953; Bert, *The Outcast*, Republic, 1954; Johnson, *Silver Lode*, RKO, 1954; John, *House of Bamboo*, Twentieth Century-Fox, 1955; Dwight Eisenhower, *The Long Gray Line*, Columbia, 1955; Stefanowski, *Mister Roberts*, Warner Brothers, 1955; William Bensinger, *The Great Locomotive Chase* (also known as *Andrews' Raiders*), Buena Vista, 1956; Brad Jorgensen, *The Searchers*, Warner Brothers, 1956; Corporal Morrison, *Seventh Cavalry*, Columbia, 1956; Deputy Lee, *Gun the Man Down* (also known as *Arizona Mission*), United Artists, 1957; Roundtree, *Kiss Them for Me*, Twentieth Century-Fox, 1957; Chet, *The River's Edge*, Twentieth Century-Fox, 1957; Trueblood, *From Hell to Texas* (also known as *Manhunt*), Twentieth Century-Fox, 1958; Travis, *Escort West*, United Artists, 1959; Harold, *Rio Bravo*, Warner Brothers, 1959.

Dr. Joseph Mornay, *The Great Imposter*, Universal, 1960; Jim Ferguson, *Noose for a Gunman*, United Artists, 1960; Ortho Clegg, *Two Rode Together*, Columbia, 1961; Bill Martin, *A Public Affair*, Parade, 1962; Trooper Smith, *Cheyenne Autumn*, Warner Brothers, 1964; Jellicoe, *The Raiders* (also known as *The Plainsman*), Universal, 1964; Lieutenant Hudson, *Taggart*, Universal, 1964; Jenkins, *Shenandoah*, Universal, 1965; Corporal Peterson, *Alvarez Kelly*, Columbia, 1966; Ben, *Billy the Kid vs. Dracula*, Embassy, 1966; Jay C., *Cyborg 2087*, Features, 1966; Ed Mabry, *The Rare Breed*, Universal, 1966; McBee, *The Way West*, United Artists, 1967; Captain Rose, *The Devil's Brigade*, United Artists, 1968; Mooney, *Ballad of Josie*, Universal, 1968; Cort Hyjack, *Bandolero*, Twentieth Century-Fox, 1968; Reverend Rork, *Death of a Gunfighter*, Universal, 1969; Webster, *The Undefeated*, Twentieth Century-Fox, 1969; Stuart, *Dirty Dingus Magee*, MGM, 1970; Stamper, *The Moonshine War*, MGM, 1970; Pop Dawson, *Big Jake*, National General, 1971; Red, *One More Train to Rob*, Universal, 1971; Joe Pickens, *Something Big*, National General, 1971; father, *Trinity Is Still My Name*, Embassy, 1971; Hank, *Cahill, United States Marshal*, Warner Brothers, 1973; Holy Joe, *A Man from the East*, United Artists, 1974; Dumper, *Take a Hard Ride*, Twentieth Century-Fox, 1975; Dobie, *Nickelodeon*, Columbia, 1976; George Arthur, *The Long Riders*, United Artists, 1980; Dr. Emmer, *Endangered Species*, Metro-Goldwyn-Mayer/United Artists (MGM/UA), 1982; Mr. Anderson, *Gremlins*, Warner Brothers, 1984; Red, *Mask*, Universal, 1985; George Martin, *UFOria*, Universal, 1985; bartender, *Crossroads*, Columbia, 1986; Joshua Brackett, *The Whales of August*, Alive, 1987; Snappy Tom, *Cherry 2000*, Orion, 1988; Wally, *Illegally Yours*, MGM/UA, 1988; Shoes, *Breaking In*, Samuel Goldwyn Company, 1989.

PRINCIPAL TELEVISION APPEARANCES—Series: Bill Burnett, "Spin and Marty," *The Mickey Mouse Club*, ABC, 1955; Bill Burnett, "The Further Adventures of Spin and Marty," *The Mickey Mouse Club*, ABC, 1957; Bill Burnett, "The New Adventures of Spin and Marty," *The Mickey Mouse Club*, ABC, 1958. Mini-Series: Ben Jenkins, "Texas John Slaughter," *Walt Disney Presents*, ABC, 1958-61; Mr. Bond, *Black Beauty*, NBC, 1978. Pilots: Deputy Luke, *Kate Bliss and the Ticker Tape Kid*, ABC, 1978. Episodic: *Little House on the Prairie*, NBC. Movies: Fitz Bragg, *Wild Times*, syndicated, 1980; Pa Traven, *Louis L'Amour's "The Shadow Riders,"* CBS, 1982; Herald Fitch, *Once Upon a Texas Train*, CBS, 1988. Specials: *John Wayne Standing Tall*, 1989.

RELATED CAREER—Actor in summer theatre productions, Lakewood Theatre, Skowhegan, ME, 1940.

NON-RELATED CAREER—Page boy, National Broadcasting Company, New York City.*

CAREY, MacDonald   1913-

PERSONAL: Born March 15, 1913, in Sioux City, IA; son of Charles S. (a judge) and Elizabeth (Macdonald) Carey; married Christina Green; children: William, Robert, Anne, Susan, Elizabeth. EDUCATION—Attended the University of Wisconsin, 1931-32; University of Iowa, B.A, 1935, M.A., drama, 1936. MILITARY—U.S. Marine Corps Reserves, first lieutenant, 1942-45.

VOCATION: Actor.

CAREER: PRINCIPAL STAGE APPEARANCES—Charley Johnson, *Lady in the Dark*, Alvin Theatre, New York City, 1941; also appeared in *Anniversary Waltz*, Broadhurst Theatre, New York City, 1954; and in summer theatre productions.

FILM DEBUT—Dr. Timothy Kane, *Dr. Broadway*, Paramount, 1942. PRINCIPAL FILM APPEARANCES—Louie the Lug, *Star Spangled Rhythm*, Paramount, 1942; Jonathan Caldwell, *Take a Letter, Darling* (also known as *Green-Eyed Woman*), Paramount, 1942; Lieutenant Cameron, *Wake Island*, Paramount, 1942; Buzz McAllister, *Salute for Three*, Paramount, 1943; Jack Graham, *Shadow of a Doubt*, Universal, 1943; Clark Redfield, *Dream Girl*, Paramount, 1947; Jack Lindsay, *Suddenly It's Spring*, Paramount, 1947; as himself, *Variety Girl*, Paramount, 1947; J.D. Storm, *Hazard*, Paramount, 1948; Cesare Borgia, *Bride of Vengeance*, Paramount, 1949; Nick Carraway, *The Great Gatsby*, Paramount, 1949; Bruce Eldridge, *Song of Surrender*, Paramount, 1949; Lorn Reming, *Streets of Laredo*, Paramount, 1949.

Jim Bowie, *Comanche Territory*, Universal, 1950; Lane Travis, *Copper Canyon*, Paramount, 1950; Jesse James, *The Great Missouri Raid*, Paramount, 1950; Larry Wilder, *The Lawless* (also known as *The Dividing Line*), Paramount, 1950; Dr. Brett Young, *Mystery Submarine*, Universal, 1950; Jake Davis, *South Sea Sinner*, Universal, 1950; Pete Carver, *Cave of Outlaws*, Universal, 1951; Cyrus Random, Jr., *Excuse My Dust*, Metro-Goldwyn-Mayer, 1951; Hugh, *Let's Make It Legal*, Twentieth Century-Fox, 1951; Jeff, *Meet Me After the Show*, Twentieth Century-Fox, 1951; George Mason, *My Wife's Best Friend*, Twentieth Century-Fox, 1952; Doug Madison, *Count the Hours* (also known as *Every Minute Counts*), RKO, 1953; Bus Crow, *Hannah Lee* (also known as *Outlaw Territory*), Broder, 1953; Van Logan, *Fire Over Africa* (also known as *Malaga*), Columbia, 1954; Steve Stratton, *Odongo*, Columbia, 1956; Hollis Jarret, *Stranger at My Door*, Republic, 1956; Maybe Smith, *Man or Gun*, Republic, 1958; Major Malcolm Bartley, *Blue Denim* (also known as *Blue Jeans*), Twentieth Century-Fox, 1959; Patrick Henry, *John Paul Jones*, Warner Brothers, 1959.

Mr. Smith, *The Devil's Agent*, British Lion, 1962; Bill Morrison, *Stranglehold*, Rank, 1962; Dr. Wayne Bentley, *Tammy and the Doctor*, Universal, 1963; Simon Wells, *These Are the Damned* (also known as *The Damned*), Columbia, 1965; Dr James McCarey, *Foes*, Coats/Alexander/Coats, 1977; John Davis, *End of the World*, Charles Band, 1977; Hollywood actor, *American Gigolo*, Paramount, 1980; Judge Watson, *It's Alive III: Island of the Alive*, Warner Brothers, 1987.

TELEVISION DEBUT—*Studio One*, CBS, 1950. PRINCIPAL TELEVISION APPEARANCES—Series: Dr. Mark Christian, *Dr. Christian*, syndicated, 1956; Herbert L. Maris, *Lock Up*, syndicated, 1959-61; Dr. Thomas Horton, *Days of Our Lives*, NBC, 1965—. Mini-Series: Squire James, *Roots*, ABC, 1977. Pilots: Ben Forbes, *Eye for an Eye* (broadcast as an episode of *Suspicion*), NBC, 1958;

Lieutenant Duff Peterson, *Last of the Private Eyes* (broadcast as an episode of *The Dick Powell Theatre*), NBC, 1963; Eloner Pike, *The Green Felt Jungle* (broadcast as an episode of *Kraft Suspense Theatre*), NBC, 1965; Russell Lawrence, *Gidget Gets Married*, ABC, 1972; Walton Grumbly, *The Girl, the Gold, Watch and Everything*, syndicated, 1980.

Episodic: Roy Benjamin, "The Special One," *The Outer Limits*, ABC, 1964; Oscar Ramsey, *Murder, She Wrote*, CBS, 1986; Dr. Lynch, *Murder, She Wrote*, CBS, 1986; also "Yellow Jack," *Celanese Theater*, ABC, 1952; "You Be the Bad Guy," *Lux Video Theatre*, CBS, 1952; "Edge of the Law," *Ford Theatre*, NBC, 1952; *Hollywood Opening Night*, NBC, 1952; "The Sermon of the Gun," *Ford Theatre*, NBC, 1953; "The Inn of the Eagles" and "Night Call," both *Lux Video Theatre*, CBS, 1953; "Hired Mother," *General Electric Theatre*, CBS, 1953; "The Quiet Gun," *Appointment with Adventure*, CBS, 1955; "Unimportant Man" and "Deal a Blow," both *Climax!*, CBS, 1955; "Where You Love Me" and "The Hayfield," both *Stage Seven*, CBS, 1955; "Gamble on a Thief," *Climax!*, CBS, 1956; "Cry Justice," *Screen Directors Playhouse*, NBC, 1956; "Times Like These," *Twentieth Century-Fox Hour*, CBS, 1956; "Moments of Courage," *The U.S. Steel Hour*, CBS, 1956; "Easter Gift," *General Electric Theatre*, CBS, 1956; "The Kill," *Ford Theatre*, NBC, 1956; "The Plug Nickel," *Undercurrent*, CBS, 1956; "Flight into Danger," *The Alcoa Hour*, NBC, 1956; "The Chinese Game," *Climax!*, CBS, 1956; "Whereabouts Unknown," *The Kaiser Aluminum Hour*, NBC, 1957; "Broken Barrier," *Ford Theatre*, ABC, 1957; "Alibi for Murder," *On Trial* (also known as *The Joseph Cotton Show*), NBC, 1957; "Man on the Thirty-Fifth Floor," *The Jane Wyman Show* (also known as *The Fireside Theatre*), NBC, 1957; "License to Kill," *Dick Powell's Zane Grey Theatre*, CBS, 1958; *Wagon Train*, NBC, 1958; "The Lonely Stage," *Studio One*, CBS, 1958; "Natchez," *Playhouse 90*, CBS, 1958; "False Impression," *Schlitz Playhouse of Stars*, CBS, 1958; "The Vengeance," *Pursuit*, CBS, 1958; *Rawhide*, CBS, 1959; "Coyote Noon," *Alfred Hitchcock Presents*, CBS, 1959; "The Golden Deed," *Moment of Fear*, NBC, 1960; "The Devil's Ticket," *Thriller*, NBC, 1961; "Tangle of Truth," *The U.S. Steel Hour*, CBS, 1961; *Checkmate*, CBS, 1962; "House Guest," *Alfred Hitchcock Theatre*, CBS, 1962; *Mr. Novak*, NBC, 1963; "The Image Merchants," *Kraft Mystery Theatre*, NBC, 1963; *Burke's Law*, ABC, 1963, 1964, and 1965; *Arrest and Trial*, ABC, 1964; *Branded*, NBC, 1965; *Daniel Boone*, NBC, 1965; *Run for Your Life*, NBC, 1965; *Ben Casey*, ABC, 1965; *Lassie*, CBS, 1966; *Bewitched*, ABC, 1967; *The Magician*, NBC, 1973; *Owen Marshall, Counselor at Law*, ABC, 1974; *McMillan and Wife*, NBC, 1976; *Police Story*, NBC, 1976; *Buck Rogers in the 25th Century*, NBC, 1979; *Fantasy Island*, ABC.

Movies: Eliot Frost, *Ordeal*, ABC, 1973; Captain Jack Donahoe, *Who Is the Black Dahlia?*, NBC, 1975; Professor Jarvis, *Stranger in Our House*, NBC, 1978; Dr. Church, *The Rebels*, syndicated, 1979; "Mitch" Mitchell, *Top of the Hill*, syndicated, 1980; Dr. Arthur Castor, *Condominium*, syndicated, 1980. Specials: Fred Gailey, *Miracle on 34th Street*, CBS, 1955; *NBC's Sixtieth Anniversary Celebration*, NBC, 1986.

PRINCIPAL RADIO APPEARANCES—Series: Host (Mr. First Nighter), *The First Nighter*, NBC, 1938; Jason, *Jason and the Golden Fleece*, NBC, 1952-53; also Dick Grosvener, *Stella Dallas*, NBC; host and narrator, *Heartbeat Theatre*.

RELATED CAREER—Company member, Old Globe Shakespeare Company, 1936-37; member, NBC Radio Stock Company, Chicago, IL, 1937-38.

NON-RELATED CAREER—Board member, Catholic Big Brothers, 1962-64.

WRITINGS: *A Day in the Life* (poetry), 1982; *That Further Hill* (poetry), 1987.

AWARDS: Emmy Awards, Best Actor in a Daytime Drama, 1974 and 1975, and *Soap Opera Digest* Awards, Outstanding Actor in a Mature Role, 1984 and 1985, all for *Days of Our Lives;* Knight of the Holy Sepulchre (Papal Order), 1986.

MEMBER: Screen Actors Guild (vice-president, 1960), Academy of Motion Picture Arts and Sciences (assistant treasurer, 1970), American Federation of Television and Radio Artists, Actors' Equity Association, Alpha Delta Phi.

ADDRESSES: AGENT—Contemporary Artists Ltd., 132 Lasky Drive, Beverly Hills, CA 90212.*

*   *   *

CAREY, Ron   1935-

PERSONAL: Born Ronald J. Cicenia, December 11, 1935, in Newark, NJ; son of John and Fanny Cicenia; married Sharon Boyeronus, November 11, 1967. EDUCATION—Seton Hall University, B.A., 1958.

VOCATION: Actor.

CAREER: BROADWAY DEBUT—Jerry, *Lovers and Other Strangers*, Brooks Atkinson Theatre, 1968.

PRINCIPAL FILM APPEARANCES—Boston cab driver, *The Out-of-Towners*, Paramount, 1970; part of group, *Made for Each Other*, Twentieth Century-Fox, 1971; bartender, *Who Killed Mary What's 'er Name?* (also known as *Death of a Hooker*), Cannon, 1971; Devour, *Silent Movie*, Twentieth Century-Fox, 1976; Brophy, *High Anxiety*, Twentieth Century-Fox, 1977; Frankie, *Fatso*, Twentieth Century-Fox, 1980; Swiftus Lazarus, *History of the World, Part I*, Twentieth Century-Fox, 1981; Pat, *Johnny Dangerously*, Twentieth Century-Fox, 1984. Also appeared in *Dynamite Chicken*, EYR, 1972.

PRINCIPAL TELEVISION APPEARANCES—Series: Regular, *The Garry Moore Show*, CBS, 1966-67; regular, *The Melba Moore-Clifton Davis Show*, CBS, 1972; Donald Hooten, *The Corner Bar*, ABC, 1973; Frank Montefusco, *The Montefuscos*, NBC, 1975; Officer Carl Levitt, *Barney Miller*, ABC, 1976-82; Father Vincent Paglia, *Have Faith*, ABC, 1989. Pilots: Regular, *Twentieth Century Follies*, ABC, 1972; monk, *Peeping Times*, NBC, 1978; Johnny Antonizzio, *Johnny Garage*, CBS, 1983; Hugo, *Pumpboys and Dinettes on Television*, NBC, 1983. Episodic: *The New Love, American Style*, ABC; *The Jack Paar Show*, NBC; *The Johnny Carson Show*, NBC; *The Merv Griffin Show*, syndicated; *The Mike Douglas Show*, syndicated; *The Steve Allen Show*. Specials: *The Wonderful World of Aggravation*, ABC, 1972; *ABC's Silver Anniversary Celebration—25 and Still the One*, ABC, 1978.

RELATED CAREER—Stand-up comedian; appeared in over one hundred television commercials.

RECORDINGS: ALBUMS—*The Slightly Irreverent Comedy of Ron Carey,* 1966.

MEMBER: Screen Actors Guild, American Federation of Television and Radio Artists, Actors' Equity Association.*

*   *   *

CARLTON, Bob   1950-

PERSONAL: Born June 23, 1950, in Coventry, England; son of Reginald Charles (a postmaster) and Nancy Olwyn (a shop assistant; maiden name, Darlison) Carlton; married Caroline Wildi (an actress), July, 1989. EDUCATION—Hull University, B.A., drama, 1974.

VOCATION: Director and writer.

CAREER: Also see *WRITINGS* below. FIRST STAGE WORK—Director, *The Foursome,* Belgrade Theatre, Coventry, U.K. FIRST LONDON WORK—Artistic director, *They Shoot Horses, Don't They?,* Bubble Theatre, 1980. PRINCIPAL STAGE WORK—Director: *Melon,* Haymarket Theatre, London, 1987; *Lettice and Lovage,* Globe Theatre, London, 1987; *Winnie,* Victoria Palace Theatre, London, 1988; *Return to the Forbidden Planet,* Cambridge Theatre, London, 1989.

MAJOR TOURS—Director, *Cabaret,* U.K. cities, 1988-89.

FIRST TELEVISION WORK—Director, *Brookside,* Mersey Television Channel Four. PRINCIPAL TELEVISION WORK—Series: *Damon and Debbie,* Mersey Television Channel Four. Also directed *The New Shoes* (short film), Mersey Television Channel Four, 1987; *Emmerdale Farm,* Yorkshire Television.

RELATED CAREER—Assistant director, Belgrade Theatre, Coventry, U.K., 1974; associate director, Duke's Playhouse, Lancaster, U.K., 1975-78; associate director, York Theatre Royal, York, U.K., 1978-80; artistic director, Bubble Theatre, London, 1980-84; also freelance director with the Newcastle Playhouse, Newcastle, U.K., Oxford Playhouse, Oxford, U.K., Palace Theatre, Watford, U.K., and Everyman Theatre, Liverpool, U.K.

WRITINGS: STAGE—*From a Jack to a King,* Edinburgh Theatre Festival, Edinburgh, Scotland, 1985; *Return to the Forbidden Planet,* Cambridge Theatre, London, 1989; also wrote Christmas shows for the Everyman Theatre, Liverpool, U.K., 1984-88. TELEVISION—*The New Shoes* (short film), Mersey Television Channel Four, 1987.

MEMBER: British Actors' Equity Association, Agence de Corporation Culturelle et Technique.

SIDELIGHTS: RECREATIONS—Soccer, rock and roll.

ADDRESSES: AGENT—Bill Horne Personal Management.

CARPENTER, Freddie   1908-1989

PERSONAL: Born February 15, 1908, in Melbourne, Australia; died of cancer, January 19, 1989, in London, England; son of James and Jean (Dunstone) Carpenter. MILITARY—Royal Air Force, 1941-44.

VOCATION: Dancer, choreographer, and director.

CAREER: STAGE DEBUT—Chorus, *The Rise of Rosie O'Reilly,* Princess Theatre, Melbourne, Australia, 1924. BROADWAY DEBUT—Young King, *Almanac,* Erlanger Theatre, 1928. LONDON DEBUT—Dancer with Frances Mann, Palladium Theatre, 1929. PRINCIPAL STAGE APPEARANCES—Dancer: *Follow a Star,* Winter Garden Theatre, London, 1930; *Bow Bells,* Hippodrome Theatre, London, 1932; *Yours Sincerely,* Daly's Theatre, London, 1934; *That Certain Something,* Aldwych Theatre, London, 1934; *Let's Go Gay,* Embassy Theatre, then Shaftesbury Theatre, both London, 1935; *Cinderella,* Coliseum Theatre, London, 1936; *I'd Rather Be Right,* Music Box Theatre, New York City, 1937.

PRINCIPAL STAGE WORK—Choreographer, *Tulip Time,* Alhambra Theatre, London, 1935; choreographer, *The Dancing Years,* Drury Lane Theatre, London, 1939; choreographer, *Lady Behave,* His Majesty's Theatre, London, 1941; choreographer, *The Love Racket,* Victoria Palace Theatre, London, 1943; director, *Danny La Rue at the Palace,* Palace Theatre, London, 1970; director, *The Danny La Rue Show,* Prince of Wales Theatre, London, 1973; director, *Hans Andersen,* Palladium Theatre, London, 1974; director, *Irene,* Adelphi Theatre, London, 1976. Also choreographer, *Life Begins at Oxford Circus,* London, 1935; choreographer, *The Town Talks* and *Mother Goose,* both London, 1936; choreographer, *And On We Go,* London, 1937; choreographer, *Maritza* and *Bobby Get Your Gun,* both London, 1938; choreographer, *Funny Side Up,* London, 1939; choreographer, *Up and Doing* and *Present Arms,* both London, 1940; choreographer, *The Lilac Domino,* London, 1944; choreographer, *Irene, The Gaieties,* and *Big Boy,* all London, 1945; director, *Follow the Girls,* Australia, 1946; director, *The Dancing Years* and *Love Is My Reason,* both London, 1947; director, *Limelight* and *Serenade,* both London, 1948; director, *The Lilac Domino* and *The Sleeping Beauty,* both London, 1949.

Choreographer, *Dear Miss Phoebe,* London, 1952; director, *Belinda* and *Sally,* both London, 1952; director, *One Fair Daughter,* London, 1953; director, *The Billy Barnes Revue, Rose Marie,* and *A Wish for Jaime,* all London, 1960; director, *A Love for Jaime,* London, 1962; director, *How to Succeed in Business Without Really Trying,* Melbourne, Australia, 1963; director, *Never Too Late,* Melbourne, 1964; director, *A Funny Thing Happened on the Way to the Forum,* Sydney, Australia, 1964; director, *The World of Jaime,* London, 1967; director, *Let's Get Swinging* and *Queen Passionella,* both London, 1968; director, *The Corbett Follies* and *The Tommy Cooper Show,* both London, 1969; director, *Cinderella,* Manchester, U.K., 1970; director, *Charlie Girl,* Melbourne, 1971; director, *Cinderella,* Coventry, U.K., 1971; director, *No, No Nanette,* Melbourne, 1972; director, *Cowardly Custard,* South Africa, 1973; director, *Irene,* Sydney, 1974; director, *The Ronnie Corbett Revue,* Paignton, U.K., 1975; director, *Queen Daniella,* London, 1975; director, *Something's Afoot,* Hong Kong, 1978; director, *The Danny La Rue Show,* Scarborough, U.K., 1978.

MAJOR TOURS—Dancer, *Lavender,* U.K. cities, 1931; director, *The Merry Widow,* U.K. cities, 1959; director, *Kind Sir,* U.K. cities, 1961; director, *A Touch of Tartan,* U.K. cities, 1963; director, *The Danny La Rue Show,* Australian cities, 1979.

PRINCIPAL FILM APPEARANCES—Dance director, *Easy Money*, General Film Distributors, 1948.

PRINCIPAL FILM WORK—Choreographer: *Carnival*, General Film Distributors, 1946; (with George King and Leontine Sagan) *Showtime* (also known *Gaiety George*), Warner Brothers/English Films Inc., 1948; *The Winslow Boy*, Eagle-Lion, 1950; *My Heart Goes Crazy* (also known as *London Town*), United Artists, 1953.

PRINCIPAL TELEVISION WORK—Specials: Choreographer, *Sir Winston Churchill: Ninety Years On*, British television, 1964. Also associate producer, *The Noel Coward Revue;* choreographer, *The Jimmy Tarbuck Show*.

WRITINGS: STAGE—*A Wish for Jaime*, 1960.

OBITUARIES AND OTHER SOURCES: *Variety*, January 25-31, 1989.*

*   *   *

CARPENTER, John 1948-
(Frank Armitage, Martin Quartermass)

PERSONAL: Full name, John Howard Carpenter; born January 16, 1948, in Carthage, NY (some sources say Bowling Green, KY); son of Howard Ralph (a music professor) and Milton Jean (Carter) Carpenter; married Adrienne Barbeau (an actress), January 1, 1979; children: John Cody. EDUCATION—Attended Western Kentucky University; graduate work in film at the University of Southern California, 1972.

VOCATION: Director, screenwriter, and composer.

CAREER: Also see WRITINGS below. PRINCIPAL FILM APPEARANCES—Bennett, *The Fog*, AVCO-Embassy, 1980. PRINCIPAL FILM WORK—Editor, *The Resurrection of Bronco Billy* (short film), Universal, 1970; producer, director, and music director, *Dark Star*, Jack H. Harris, 1974; director, *Assault on Precinct 13*, Turtle Releasing Company, 1976; director, *Halloween*, Compass, 1978; director, *The Fog*, AVCO-Embassy, 1980; director, *Escape from New York*, AVCO-Embassy, 1981; producer (with Debra Hill), *Halloween II*, Universal, 1981; producer (with Hill), *Halloween III: Season of the Witch*, Universal, 1982; director, *The Thing*, Universal, 1982; director, *Christine*, Columbia, 1983; executive producer, *The Philadelphia Experiment*, New World, 1984; director, *Starman*, Columbia, 1984; director, *Big Trouble in Little China*, Twentieth Century-Fox, 1986; director, *Prince of Darkness*, Universal, 1987; director, *They Live*, Universal, 1988. Also director of such short films as *Revenge of the Colossal Beasts*, *Gorgo Versus Godzilla*, *Terror from Space*, *Sorcerer from Outer Space*, *The Warrior and the Demon*, and *Gorgon, the Space Monster*.

PRINCIPAL TELEVISION WORK—Movies: Director, *Someone's Watching Me!*, NBC, 1978; director, *Elvis*, ABC, 1979.

WRITINGS: See production details above, unless indicated. FILM—(Co-writer; also composer) *The Resurrection of Bronco Billy*, 1970; (with Dan O'Bannon; also composer) *Dark Star*, 1974; (also composer) *Assault on Precinct 13*, 1976; (with David Zelag Goodman) *The Eyes of Laura Mars*, Columbia, 1978; (with Debra Hill; also composer) *Halloween*, 1978; (with Hill; also composer) *The Fog*,

1980; (with Nick Castle; also composer with Alan Howarth) *Escape from New York*, 1981; (with Hill; also composer with Howarth) *Halloween II*, 1981; composer (with Howarth), *Halloween III: Season of the Witch*, 1982; composer (with Howarth), *Christine*, 1983; composer (with Howarth), *Big Trouble in Little China*, 1986; (with Desmond Nakano and William Gray) *Black Moon Rising*, New World, 1986; (as Martin Quartermass; also composer with Howarth) *Prince of Darkness*, 1987; (as Frank Armitage; also composer) *They Live*, 1988; composer (with Howarth), *Halloween 5: The Revenge of Michael Myers*, Galaxy International, 1989.

TELEVISION—Movies: (With William A. Schwartz) *Zuma Beach*, NBC, 1978; *Someone's Watching Me!*, 1978; (with Greg Strangis) *Better Late Than Never*, NBC, 1979.

MEMBER: Directors Guild of America, Writers Guild of America—West, American Society of Composers, Authors, and Publishers.

SIDELIGHTS: RECREATIONS—Helicopter piloting, music.

As a film student at the University of Southern California, John Carpenter was editor, composer, and co-wrote the screenplay for the short film *The Resurrection of Bronco Billy* which won an Academy Award in 1970 as Best Short Subject (Live Action). In 1978, his film *Halloween* became the highest grossing independently made movie of all time.

ADDRESSES: OFFICE—9454 Wilshire Boulevard, Beverly Hills, CA 90212. AGENT—International Creative Management, 8899 Beverly Boulevard, Los Angeles, CA 90048.*

*   *   *

CARR, Darleen 1950-

PERSONAL: Born in 1950 in Chicago, IL.

VOCATION: Actress.

CAREER: PRINCIPAL FILM APPEARANCES—Voice of the girl, *The Jungle Book* (animated), Buena Vista, 1967; Sidoni Riserau, *Monkeys, Go Home!*, Buena Vista, 1967; Abbey Kingsley, *The Impossible Years*, Metro-Goldwyn-Mayer, 1968; Hilda Jorgenson, *Death of a Gunfighter*, Universal, 1969; Doris, *The Beguiled*, Universal, 1971.

PRINCIPAL TELEVISION APPEARANCES—Series: Kathy, *The John Forsythe Show*, NBC, 1965-66; regular, *Dean Martin Presents the Golddiggers*, NBC, 1969; Cindy Smith, *The Smith Family*, ABC, 1971-72; Margaret Devlin, *The Oregon Trail*, NBC, 1977; Susan Winslow, *Miss Winslow and Son*, CBS, 1979; Mary Lou Springer, *Bret Maverick*, ABC, 1981-82; voice characterization, *G.I. Joe* (animated), syndicated, 1984. Mini-Series: Tommy Caldwell Damon, *Once an Eagle*, NBC, 1976-77. Pilots: Joan Chadwick McTaggart, *The Chadwick Family*, ABC, 1974; Selina Jensen, *Law of the Land*, NBC, 1976. Episodic: Marlena Lewis, *Riptide*, NBC, 1985; Trish Mercer, *Murder, She Wrote*, CBS, 1985; Beth Hartley, *Blacke's Magic*, NBC, 1986; Ginny Malcolm, *Magnum, P.I.*, CBS, 1986; Shannon McGovern, *Simon and Simon*, CBS, 1986; Sheri Strawn, *Probe*, ABC, 1988; also Jean Stone, *Streets of San Francisco*, ABC. Movies: Susan, *All My Darling Daughters*, ABC, 1972; Margot, *The Horror at 37,000 Feet*, CBS, 1973; Susan, *My Darling Daughters' Anniversary*, ABC, 1973; Carol Lerner, *Runa-*

way! (also known as *The Runaway Train*), ABC, 1973; Kathleen Kennedy, *Young Joe, the Forgotten Kennedy,* ABC, 1977; Hildy, *Rage,* NBC, 1980; Lisa Reed, *Hero in the Family,* ABC, 1986. Specials: Katey Summers, *Sleepwalker,* ABC, 1975; *Battle of the Network Stars,* ABC, 1976 and 1977; *Circus of the Stars,* CBS, 1982; voice of Mom, "Chocolate Fever," *CBS Storybreak,* CBS, 1985.

ADDRESSES: AGENT—Perry Hawthorne, CNA and Associates, 8721 Sunset Boulevard, Suite 202, Los Angeles, CA 90069.*

*   *   *

CARRIERE, Jean-Claude   1931-

PERSONAL: Born September 19, 1931, in Colombieres, France.

VOCATION: Screenwriter, actor, and director.

CAREER: Also see *WRITINGS* below. PRINCIPAL FILM APPEARANCES—Cure, *Le Journal d'une femme de chambre* (also known as *Il diario di una cameriera* and *Diary of a Chambermaid*), Cocinor, 1964; Priscillian, *La Voie lactee* (also known as *La via lattea* and *The Milky Way*), U-M, 1969; Hughes, *L'Alliance* (also known as *The Wedding Ring*), CAPAC, 1970; Chief, *Serieux comme le plaisir* (also known as *Serious As Pleasure*), Lugo, 1974; doctor, *Photo Souvenir,* FR3, 1977; psychiatrist, *Ils sont grands ces petits* (also known as *These Kids Are Grown-Ups*), United Artists/Exportation Francaise Cinematographique, 1979. Also appeared in *Insomnie,* 1963; as narrator, *Les Cocardiers,* 1967; in *Un Peu de soleil dans l'eau froide* (also known as *A Little Sun in Cold Water*), Societe Nouvelle de Cinema, 1971; *La Chute d'un corps,* 1973; Adam, *Le Jeu du solitaire,* 1976; *Le Jardin des supplices* (also known as *The Garden of Torment*), New Realm Distributors/Parafrance, 1976.

PRINCIPAL FILM WORK—Director (with Jerome Diamant-Berger and Olivier Assayas), *L'Unique* (also known as *The One and Only*), AA Revcon/Films du Scorpion, 1985; also co-director, *Rupture* (short film), 1961; co-director, *Heureux anniversaire* (short film), 1961; director, *La Pince a ongles* (short film), 1968.

WRITINGS: STAGE—*L'Aide-Memoire,* 1968; (adaptor) *The Mahabharata,* Brooklyn Academy of Music, New York City, 1989. FILM—(With Pierre Etaix) *Le Soupirant* (also known as *The Suitor*), Atlantic, 1963; (with Luis Bunuel) *Le Journal d'une femme de chambre* (also known as *Il diario di una cameriera* and *Diary of a Chambermaid*), Cocinor, 1964; (with Louis Malle) *Viva Maria!* United Artists, 1965; (with Jesus Franco) *Miss Muerte* (also known as *Dans les griffes du maniaque* and *The Diabolical Dr. Z*), U.S. Films, 1966; *Hotel Paradiso,* Metro-Goldwyn-Mayer, 1966; *Cartes sur table* (also known as *Attack of the Robots*), American International, 1967; (with Malle) *Le Voleur* (also known as *The Thief of Paris*), Lopert, 1967; (with Etaix) *Yo Yo,* Magna, 1967; (with Bunuel) *Belle de jour,* Allied Artists, 1968; (with Bunuel) *La Voie lactee* (also known as *La via lattea* and *The Milky Way*), U-M, 1969; (with John-Emmanuel Conil and Jacques Deray) *La Piscine* (also known as *La piscina* and *The Swimming Pool*), 1969, released in the United States by AVCO-Embassy, 1970.

(With Christian De Chalong) *L'Alliance* (also known as *The Wedding Ring*), CAPAC, 1970; (with Jean Cau, Claude Sautet, and Deray) *Borsalino,* Paramount, 1970; (with Milos Forman, John Guare, and John Klein) *Taking Off,* Universal, 1971; *Un Peu de soleil dans l'eau froide* (also known as *A Little Sun in Cold Water*), Societe Nouvelle de Cinema, 1971; (with Bunuel) *Le Charme discret de la bourgeoisie* (also known as *The Discreet Charm of the Bourgeoisie*), Twentieth Century-Fox/Castle Hill, 1972, published in *Avant-Scene,* April, 1973; (with Deray and Ian McLellen Hunter) *Un Homme est mort* (also known as *A Man Is Dead* and *The Outside Man*), Valoria, 1972, released in the United States by United Artists, 1973; (with Bunuel) *Le Moine* (also known as *The Monk*), Maya, 1973; (with Peter Fleischmann) *Dorothea's Rache* (also known as *Dorothea's Revenge*), Planfilm, 1973; (with Marco Ferreri) *La cagna,* 1972, released in the United States as *Liza,* CFDC/Pathe/ Oceanic/Sirius, 1976; (with Bunuel) *Le Fantome de la liberte* (also known as *The Phantom of Liberty* and *The Specter of Freedom*), Twentieth Century-Fox, 1974; (with Robert Benayoun) *Serieux comme le plaisir* (also known as *Serious as Pleasure*), Lugo, 1974; (with Jean-Claude Brialy) *Un Amour de pluie* (also known as *A Rainy Love*), Lira, 1974; (with Patrice Chereau) *La Chair de l'orchidee* (also known as *The Flesh of the Orchid*), Fox-Lira, 1974; *France Societe Anonyme* (also known as *France Incorporated*), Albina, 1974.

(With Martin Walser) *La Faille* (also known as *The Weak Spot*), Gaumont, 1975; (with Jean Curtelin and Joel Santoni) *Les Oeufs brouilles* (also known as *The Scrambled Eggs*), Columbia/Warner Distributors, 1975; (with Alphonse Boudard) *Le Gang* (also known as *The Gang*), Warner Brothers, 1976; (with Juan Bunuel, Philippe Nuridzany, Pierre Maintigneux, and Clement Biddle Wood) *Leonor,* CIC/New Line Cinema, 1977; (with Luis Bunuel) *Cet obscur objet du desir* (also known as *That Obscure Object of Desire*), CCFC/ Greenwich/Janus, 1976, released in the United States by First Artists, 1977; (with Pierre Lary and Huguette Debasieux) *Le Diable dans la boite* (also known as *The Devil in the Box*), Madeleine/ Societe Novelle de Cinema, 1977; *Julie pot de colle* (also known as *Julie Glue Pot*), Davis/Societe Nouvelle Prodis, 1977; (with Edmond Sechan) *Photo Souvenir,* FR3, 1977; (with Tonino Guerra) *Un Papillon sur l'epaule* (also known as *A Butterfly on the Shoulder*), Gaumont, 1978; (with Jean-Francois Davy) *Chaussette surprise* (also known as *Surprise Sock*) GEF/CCFC/Albatros, 1978; (with Daniel Boulanger and Joel Santoni) *Ils sont grands ces petits* (also known as *These Kids Are Grown-Ups*), United Artists/ Exportation Francaise Cinematographiques, 1979; (with Rene Gainville) *L'Associe* (also known as *The Associate*), Columbia/ Warner Distributors, 1979; (with Claude Pinoteau and Charles Israel) *L'Homme en colere* (also known as *The Angry Man*) Films Ariane/United Artists, 1979; (with Volker Schloendorff, Franz Seitz, and Gunter Grass) *The Tin Drum* (also known as *Die Blechtrommel*), United Artists/New World, 1979; (with Jean-Francois Adam, Georges Perec, and Benoit Jacquot) *Retour a la bien-aimee* (also known as *Return to the Beloved*), Societe Nouvelle Prodis/World Marketing, 1979.

(With Jean-Luc Godard and Anne-Marie Mieville) *Sauve qui peut la vie* (also known as *Everyone for Himself, Every Man for Himself,* and *Slow Motion*), Artifical Eye/MK2/New Yorker, 1980; (with Schloendorff, Margarethe Von Trotta, and Kai Hermann) *Die Falschung* (also known as *Circle of Deceit* and *False Witness*), United International/United Artists Classics, 1981; (with Carlos Saura) *Antonieta,* Gaumont/Conacina/Nuevo Cine, 1982; (with Christian Drillaud) *Itineraire bis* (also known as *Sideroads*), Films de l'Arquebuse, 1982; (with Andrzej Wajda, Agnieszka Holland, Boleslaw Michalek, and Jacek Gasiorowski) *Danton,* Triumph, 1983; (with Daniel Vigne) *Le Retour de Martin Guerre* (also known as *The Return of Martin Guerre*), European International, 1983; (with Luciano Tovoli and Michel Piccoli) *Le General de l'armee morte* (also known as *The General of the Dead Army*), World Marketing/Union Generale Cinematographique, 1983; (with Marius Constant and Peter Brook) *La Tragedie de Carmen* (also known as *The Tragedy of Carmen*), British Film Institute/MK2, 1983; (with Schloendorff, Peter Brook, and Marie-Helen Estienne) *Un Amour de Swann* (also known as *Swann in Love, Swann's Way*, and *Remembrance of Things Past*), Orion Classics, 1984; *La Jeune fille et l'enfer* (also known as *The Young Girl and Hell*), Orphee Arts/Exportation Francaise Cinematographique, 1984.

(With Jerome Diamant-Berger, Olivier Assayas, and Jacques Dorfman) *L'Unique* (also known as *The One and Only*), AA Revcon/Films du Scorpion, 1985; (with Nagisa Oshima) *Max mon amour* (also known as *Max, My Love*), Greenwich/AAA, 1986; (with Peter Fleischmann and Gianfranco Mingozzi) *Les Exploits d'un jeune Don Juan* (also known as *The Exploits of a Young Don Juan*), Exportation Francaise/AAA, 1987; (with Wajda, Holland, and Edward Zebrowsky) *Les Possedes* (also known as *The Possessed*), Gaumont International, 1987; (with Philip Kaufman) *The Unbearable Lightness of Being*, Orion, 1988; (with Nicholas Klotz) *La Nuit Bengali* (also known as *Bengali Nights* and *The Bengali Night*), Gaumont International, 1988; (with Jerzy Kawlerowicz) *Hostage of Europe*, La Societe Cine-Alliance, 1989; (with Milos Forman) *Valmont*, Orion Classics, 1989. Also *Rupture*, 1961; *Heureux anniversaire* (short film), 1961; (with Etaix) *Nous n'irons plus au bois*, 1963, re-released as *Tant qu'on a la sante*, 1965; (with Etaix) *Insomnie*, 1963; *Le Bestiaire d'amour*, 1963; *La Reine verte* (also known as *The Green Queen*), 1964; *La Pince a ongles*, 1968; *Le Grand Amour*, 1968; *Le Droit d'aimer*, 1972.

TELEVISION—Specials: (Adaptor) *The Mahabharata*, Channel Four, 1989.

OTHER—*Le Lezard*, 1957; *Monsieur Hulot's Holiday* (novelization of film), 1959; *L'Alliance*, 1963; (with Luis Bunuel) *Le Moine*, 1971; *Mon Oncle* (novelization of film), 1972; (translator) *Le Clou brulant*, 1972; *Le Pari*, 1973; (translator) *Harold et Maude*, 1974; *Le Carnaval et la politique*, 1979; (translator) *The Mahabharata*, Harper and Row, 1987; also (with Daniel Vigne) *Le Retour de Martin Guerre* (novelization of film); and contributor to journals and periodicals.

AWARDS: Academy Award nomination (with Luis Bunuel), Best Screenplay Based on Material from Another Medium, 1972, for *Le Charme discret de la bourgeoisie;* Academy Award nomination (with Bunuel), Best Screenplay Based on Material from Another Medium, 1977, for *Cet obscure objet du desir;* Academy Award nomination (with Philip Kaufman), Best Adapted Screenplay, 1989, for *The Unbearable Lightness of Being.**

*   *   *

CARSON, John David

VOCATION: Actor.

CAREER: PRINCIPAL FILM APPEARANCES—Ponce de Leon Harper, *Pretty Maids All in a Row*, Metro-Goldwyn-Mayer, 1971; Larry, *The Day of the Dolphin*, AVCO-Embassy, 1973; David, *The Savage Is Loose,* Campbell/Devon, 1974; Halsey, *Stay Hungry*, United Artists, 1976; Joe Morrison, *Empire of the Ants*, American International, 1977; Ronnie Denton, *The Fifth Floor*, Film Ventures International, 1980; Mark, *Off the Boulevard*, Touchstone,

1989. Also appeared in *The Creature from Black Lake*, Howco International, 1976; *Charge of the Model-T's*, Ry/MAC, 1979.

PRINCIPAL TELEVISION APPEARANCES—Series: Jay Spence, *Falcon Crest*, CBS, 1987-88. Pilots: Woody Guinness III, *Call Her Mom*, ABC, 1972; Tommy, "Margie Passes," *Of Men of Women*, ABC, 1973; Wilder, *Mitchell and Woods*, NBC, 1981. Episodic: Larry Burns, *Murder, She Wrote*, CBS, 1985; Billy Maddox, *Blacke's Magic*, NBC, 1986; Stafford, *The Law and Harry McGraw*, CBS, 1987; Stephen Wainwright, *Simon and Simon*, CBS, 1988; also *Fantastic Journey*, NBC, 1977; *Taxi*, ABC, 1980.

ADDRESSES: AGENT—Contemporary Artists, 132 Lasky Drive, Beverly Hills, CA 90212.

*   *   *

CARY, Falkland   1897-1989

PERSONAL: Born January 2, 1897, in Kildare, Ireland; died of a stroke, April 7, 1989, in Fleet, England; son of Henry John Litton and Katherine Frances (Boyd) Cary. EDUCATION—Received M.B. and B.A. from Trinity College (Dublin, Ireland).

VOCATION: Playwright.

CAREER: See WRITINGS below. NON-RELATED CAREER—Obstetrician.

WRITINGS: STAGE—*Burning Gold*, 1943; *Candied Peel*, 1945; *Murder Out of Tune*, 1945; *But Once a Year*, 1948; *Bed of Roses's*, 1949; (with Philip Weathers) *Madam Tic-Tac*, 1950; (with Ivan Butler) *The Paper Chain*, 1953; *Pitfall, the Owner of Redfields*, 1954; (with Philip King) *Sailor Beware!*, 1955; (with Weathers) *The Hypnotist*, 1956; (with King) *The Dream House*, 1957; (with Butler) *Danger Inside*, 1958; (with Weathers) *The Shadow Witness*, 1959; (with King) *Watch It, Sailor!*, 1960; (with Weathers) *The Proof of the Poison*, 1962; *Rock-a-Bye Sailor*, 1962; (with King) *Big Bad Mouse*, 1964; also (with Don Carrol) *Meet Aunt Mildred*.

FILM—(With Philip King) *Panic in the Parlour* (also known as *Sailor Beware!*), Distributors Corporation of America, 1957; (with King) *Watch It, Sailor*, Columbia, 1961.

TELEVISION—Specials: *The Hammer, Gentlemen at Twilight*, and *Pitfall, the Owner of Redfields*. RADIO—Plays: *Pitfall, the Owner of Redfields*.

SIDELIGHTS: Falkland Cary, author of many successful British stage comedies from the 1940s to the 1960s, began his professional career as an obstetrician. He once estimated that he delivered approximately 2,000 babies during his twenty year practice before giving up medicine to concentrate on his stage work.

OBITUARIES AND OTHER SOURCES: *Variety*, April 12-18, 1989.*

CASON, Barbara 1933-

PERSONAL: Born November 15, 1933, in Memphis, TN; married Dennis Patrick (an actor). EDUCATION—Received B.A. and M.A. in theatre from the University of Mississippi; postgraduate work in theatre at the University of Iowa.

VOCATION: Actress.

CAREER: BROADWAY DEBUT—Madame Coulmier, *The Persecution and Assassination of Jean-Paul Marat as Performed by the Inmates of the Asylum of Charenton under the Direction of the Marquis de Sade,* Majestic Theatre, 1967. PRINCIPAL STAGE APPEARANCES—Christina Chenier, *The Death of the Well-Loved Boy,* St. Mark's Playhouse, New York City, 1967; Babette, *The Firebugs,* Martinique Theatre, New York City, 1968; Miss Green, *Jimmy Shine,* Brooks Atkinson Theatre, New York City, 1968; nun, supervisor, grey lady, Mrs. Dart, landlady, and Miss Saunders, *Spitting Image,* Theatre De Lys, New York City, 1969; Mrs. Stockmann, *An Enemy of the People,* Repertory Theatre of Lincoln Center, Vivian Beaumont Theater, New York City, 1971; ensemble, *Oh Coward!* (revue), New Theatre, New York City, 1972; Claire, *A Delicate Balance,* McCarter Theatre Company, Princeton, NJ, 1982; Arkadina, *The Seagull,* Circle Repertory Company, American Place Theatre, New York City, 1983. Also appeared in "Bakers' Dozen" in *Plaza 9* (revue), 1964; *The Skin of Our Teeth,* Playhouse in the Park, Cincinnati, OH, 1966; *Hay Fever,* Hartford Stage Company, Hartford, CT, 1967; and in *Night Watch,* Morosco Theatre, New York City, 1972.

PRINCIPAL FILM APPEARANCES—Evelyn Long, *The Honeymoon Killers* (also known as *The Lonely Hearts Killers*), Cinerama, 1969; Mrs. Johnson, *House of Dark Shadows,* Metro-Goldwyn-Mayer, 1970; Letitia, *Cold Turkey,* United Artists, 1971; Mrs. Phalor, *Exorcist II: The Heretic,* Warner Brothers, 1977; also appeared in *Dear Martha.*

PRINCIPAL TELEVISION APPEARANCES—Series: Regular, *Comedy Tonight,* CBS, 1970; Miss Tillis, *The New Temperature's Rising Show,* ABC, 1973-74; Officer Cloris Phebus, *Carter Country,* ABC, 1977-79; Agnes, *Tony the Pony,* syndicated, 1979; Mrs. Shandling, *It's Garry Shandling's Show,* Showtime, 1986—, then Fox, 1988—. Pilots: Ms. Sommerville, *Delancey Street: The Crisis Within,* NBC, 1975; Roberta, *Tabitha,* ABC, 1976. Episodic: Dottie Pit, *Trapper John, M.D.,* CBS, 1980 and 1981; Elvira Fritzinger, *The Brady Brides,* NBC, 1981; Lynn LaVecque, *Madame's Place,* syndicated, 1982; Lady Di, *Hollywood Beat,* ABC, 1985; Paula, *Crazy Like a Fox,* CBS, 1985; Rebecca Winship, *Night Court,* NBC, 1986; the Lady, *Silver Spoons,* NBC, 1986; Nurse Rancid, *The Law and Harry McGraw,* CBS, 1987; Emily Goshen, *Murder, She Wrote,* CBS, 1988; also *All in the Family,* CBS, 1971 and 1975; *Scene of the Crime,* NBC, 1984. Movies: Judge A.J. White, *It Couldn't Happen to a Nicer Guy,* ABC, 1974; Greta Bennett, *Let's Switch,* ABC, 1975; Viola Andrews, *With This Ring,* ABC, 1978; Deenie Gooch, *She's Dressed to Kill* (also known as *Someone's Killing the World's Greatest Models*), NBC, 1979; Elvira Fritzinger, *The Brady Girls Get Married,* NBC, 1981; Nurse Barnes, *A Matter of Life and Death,* CBS, 1981; Rita Jean Tilford McEwan, *Memories Never Die,* CBS, 1982. Specials: Mildred Moffett, *America, You're On,* ABC, 1975; Annie, "The War Widow," *Visions,* PBS, 1976.

RELATED CAREER—Company member, Ford's TCG Theatre, 1956-62; co-founder, Front Street Theatre.

SIDELIGHTS: RECREATIONS—Flying airplanes, porcelain painting, archaeology, astronomy, and gardening.

ADDRESSES: AGENT—Bauman, Hiller, and Associates, 5750 Wilshire Boulevard, Suite 512, Los Angeles, CA 90038.

* * *

CASSIDY, David 1950-

PERSONAL: Full name, David Bruce Cassidy; born April 12, 1950, in New Jersey; son of Jack Cassidy (an actor) and Evelyn Ward (an actress and singer); married Kay Lenz (an actress), April 3, 1977 (divorced); married Meryl Tanz (a horse breeder), 1984 (divorced). EDUCATION—Studied psychology at Los Angeles City College; trained for the stage with David Craig and Milton Katselas.

VOCATION: Actor, singer, and songwriter.

CAREER: BROADWAY DEBUT—Billy, *The Fig Leaves Are Falling,* Broadhurst Theatre, 1969. PRINCIPAL STAGE APPEARANCES—Title role, *Little Johnny Jones,* Dorothy Chandler Pavilion, Los Angeles, 1981; George M. Cohan, *Parade of Stars Playing the Palace,* Palace Theatre, New York City, 1983; Joseph, *Joseph and the Amazing Technicolor Dreamcoat,* Royale Theatre, New York City, 1983. Also appeared in *And So to Bed,* Los Angeles Theatre Center, Los Angeles; *Time,* London production.

MAJOR TOURS—Title role, *Little Johnny Jones,* U.S. cities, 1981;

DAVID CASSIDY

also Joseph, *Joseph and the Amazing Technicolor Dreamcoat*, U.S. cities; *Tribute*, U.S. and Canadian cities.

PRINCIPAL FILM APPEARANCES—*Instant Karma* and *The Spirit of '76*.

PRINCIPAL TELEVISION APPEARANCES—Series: Keith Partridge, *The Partridge Family*, ABC, 1970-74; Officer Dan Shay, *David Cassidy—Man Undercover*, NBC, 1978-79. Episodic: Officer Dan Shay, "A Chance to Live," *Police Story*, NBC, 1977; also *The Survivors*, ABC; *Adam-12*, NBC; *Bonanza*, NBC; *Mod Squad*, ABC; *Ironside*, NBC; *Marcus Welby, M.D.*, SBC; *The F.B.I.*, ABC; *Alfred Hitchcock Presents*, USA. Movies: David Greeley, *The Night the City Screamed*, ABC, 1980. Specials: *The Bob Hope Show*, NBC, 1972; Keith Partridge, *Thanksgiving Reunion with the Partridge Family and My Three Sons*, ABC, 1977; *Celebrity Challenge of the Sexes*, CBS, 1977; *Parade of Stars*, ABC, 1983.

RELATED CAREER—Singer in over three hundred concert appearances.

NON-RELATED CAREER—Breeder and racer of thoroughbred horses.

RECORDINGS: ALBUMS—*Cherish*, Bell, 1972; also *Romance*, Arista. With the Partridge Family: *The Partridge Family Album*, Bell, 1970; *Up to Date*, Bell, 1971; *The Partridge Family Sound Magazine*, Bell, 1971; *The Partridge Family Shopping Bag*, Bell, 1972.

AWARDS: Golden Apple Award from the Hollywood Women's Press Club, Discovery of the Year, 1971; Emmy Award nomination, Best Actor in a Dramatic Role, 1978, for *Police Story;* also eighteen Gold Record Awards from the Recording Industry Association of America; two Grammy Award nominations.

MEMBER: Screen Actors Guild, American Federation of Television and Radio Artists, Actors' Equity Association, American Society of Composers, Authors, and Publishers.

ADDRESSES: MANAGER—Melanie Greene Management, 152 S. Roxbury Drive, Suite 5, Beverly Hills, CA 90212.

*   *   *

CASSIDY, Patrick   1961-

PERSONAL: Born January 4, 1961, in Los Angeles, CA; son of Jack Cassidy (an actor) and Shirley Jones (an actress).

VOCATION: Actor.

CAREER: BROADWAY DEBUT—Frederic, *The Pirates of Penzance*, Uris Theatre, 1981. PRINCIPAL STAGE APPEARANCES—Jeff Barry, *Leader of the Pack*, Ambassador Theatre, New York City, 1985.

PRINCIPAL FILM APPEARANCES—Randy, *Off the Wall*, Jensen Farley, 1983; Steve, *Just the Way You Are*, Metro-Goldwyn-Mayer/United Artists (MGM/UA), 1984; soldier, *Fever Pitch*, MGM/UA, 1985; Willard Freund, *Nickel Mountain*, Ziv International, 1985; Miles, *Burnin' Love* (also known as *Love at Stake*), De Laurentiis Entertainment Group, 1987.

PRINCIPAL TELEVISION APPEARANCES—Series: Terry St. Marie, *Bay City Blues*, NBC, 1983; Johnny Castle, *Dirty Dancing*, CBS, 1988. Mini-Series: Captain Hyppolyte Charles, *Napoleon and Josephine: A Love Story*, ABC, 1987. Pilots: Jack Tree, *The Six of Us*, NBC, 1982. Movies: Bob Shecky, *Angel Dusted*, NBC, 1981; David Sterling, *Midnight Offerings*, ABC, 1981; Patrick, *Choices of the Heart*, NBC, 1983; Josh Kingsley, *Christmas Eve*, NBC, 1986; David Hand, *Dress Gray*, NBC, 1986; Nick Hollander, *Something in Common*, CBS, 1986; Scott Crossfield, *Three on a Match*, NBC, 1987.

ADDRESSES: AGENTS—The Gersh Agency, 222 N. Canon Drive, Suite 202, Beverly Hills, CA 90210. MANAGER—Litke, Gale, and Associates, 10390 Santa Monica Boulevard, Suite 300, Los Angeles, CA 90025.*

*   *   *

CATES, Madelyn

PERSONAL: Born Madelyn Fagan, March 9, in New York, NY; daughter of Ben (a teacher and director) and Dorothy (Smith) Fagan; married Lou Kates (an engineer), March, 1948 (died, January, 1988); children: Mallory June, Kathryn Jane, Joshua Nathan. EDUCATION—Attended Queens College, the Waldorf School, and New York Law School; studied acting with William Hickey at the Herbert Berghof-Uta Hagen Studio, with Lee and

MADELYN CATES

Paula Strasberg at the Actors' Studio, and with Charles Nelson Reilly.

VOCATION: Actress.

CAREER: STAGE DEBUT—Adelaide, *Guys and Dolls,* Winter Park, FL, 1956, for sixteen performances. OFF-BROADWAY DEBUT—Potopovna, *Sunset,* 81st Street Theatre, 1966. BROADWAY DEBUT—Patient, *The Persecution and Assassination of Jean-Paul Marat as Performed by the Inmates of the Asylum of Charenton Under the Direction of the Marquis de Sade* (also known as *Marat/Sade*), Majestic Theatre, 1967. PRINCIPAL STAGE APPEARANCES—Bertha, *The Kitchen,* 81st Street Theatre, New York City, 1966; ensemble, *The Fourth Wall* (revue), Theatre East, New York City, 1968; Mabel Lamston, *Lemonade,* Jan Hus Playhouse, New York City, 1968; Anna, *A Patriot for Me,* Imperial Theatre, New York City, 1969; Connie, *Snowangel,* Actors Studio, then Circle Theatre Workshop, both New York City, 1972; Jeanette Fisher, *Last of the Red Hot Lovers,* Elysian Playhouse, New York City, 1975; Maquerelle, *The Malcontent,* Classic Theatre, Loretto Theatre, New York City, 1977. Also appeared in *Follies,* Studio Theatre Playhouse, Hollywood, CA, 1981; as Sadie, *Coping,* Cherry Lane Theatre, New York City; Helen, *In the Boom Boom Room,* Cubiculo Theatre, New York City; Soft Wonder, *Ecclesiazusae,* Cooper Union Theatre, New York City; Betty, *Winkelberg,* Theatre West, Hollywood; Sally Marr, *Lenny,* Charles Playhouse, Boston, MA; Connie, *A Matter of Perspective,* Theatre Exchange, North Hollywood, CA; Stella Deems, *Follies,* Mrs. Paddy, *The Curious Savage,* Mildred Harmon, *Stormless Vows,* Sally Marr, *Lenny,* and ensemble, *Side By Side By Sondheim* (revue), all the Colony, Los Angeles.

FILM DEBUT—Concierge, *The Producers,* Embassy, 1967. PRINCIPAL FILM APPEARANCES—Agnes, *A New Leaf,* Paramount, 1969; Sylvia, *The Heartbreak Kid,* Twentieth Century-Fox, 1972; Mrs. Trent, *The Devil and Max Devlin,* Buena Vista, 1981; Dr. Helen Schneider, *Jekyll and Hyde . . . Together Again,* Paramount, 1982.

TELEVISION DEBUT—Mary, *The Resurrection,* CBS, 1965. PRINCIPAL TELEVISION APPEARANCES—Pilots: Mrs. Gaskin, *The Flamingo Kid,* ABC, 1989. Episodic: Flo, *Struck by Lightning,* CBS, 1979; Evelyn Petschek, *St. Elsewhere,* NBC, 1982; Ruthie Cook, *Night Court,* NBC, 1987; also *thirtysomething,* ABC, 1989; Betty, *Archie Bunker's Place,* CBS; Flora LaRue, *Hill Street Blues,* NBC; Bella Noodleman-Chang, *Hooperman,* ABC; Mabel, *The Law and Harry McGraw,* CBS; Mrs. Dunne, *The Associates,* ABC; Mrs. Pfeiffer, *Soap,* ABC; landlady, *Hunter,* NBC; pickpocket, *Cagney and Lacey,* CBS; Mrs. Landowska, *Fame.* Movies: Zelda, *Found Money,* NBC, 1983.

RELATED CAREER—Company member, Theatre West, Hollywood, CA; company member, the Colony, Los Angeles.

AWARDS: Obie Award from the *Village Voice, Drama-Logue* Award, and Los Angeles Critics' Circle Award.

MEMBER: Actors' Equity Association (1960—), American Federation of Television and Radio Artists (1966—), Screen Actors Guild (1967—), International Women's Writing Guild.

SIDELIGHTS: RECREATIONS—Writing plays and poetry, travel.

ADDRESSES: AGENTS—Starkman Agency Inc., 1501 Broadway, New York, NY 10036; Jacobson-Wilder-Kesten, 419 Park Avenue S., New York, NY 10016; Sutton, Barth, and Vennari Inc., 8322 Beverly Boulevard, Suite 202, Los Angeles, CA 90048; Twentieth Century Artists, 3800 Barham Boulevard, Suite 303, Los Angeles, CA 90068.

*   *   *

CATTRALL, Kim   1956-

PERSONAL: Born August 21, 1956, in Liverpool, England; father, a construction engineer. EDUCATION—Graduated from the American Academy of Dramatic Arts.

VOCATION: Actress.

CAREER: BROADWAY DEBUT—Sofya, *Wild Honey,* Virginia Theatre, 1986. PRINCIPAL STAGE APPEARANCES—Masha, *The Three Sisters,* Los Angeles Theatre Center, Los Angeles, 1985; also appeared in productions of *A View from the Bridge* and *Agnes of God,* both in Los Angeles.

FILM DEBUT—Joyce, *Rosebud,* United Artists, 1975. PRINCIPAL FILM APPEARANCES—Sally Haines, *Tribute,* Twentieth Century-Fox, 1980; Ruthie, *Ticket to Heaven,* United Artists, 1981; Honeywell, *Porky's,* Twentieth Century-Fox, 1982; Karen Thompson, *Police Academy,* Warner Brothers, 1984; Dr. Helen Wickings, *City Limits,* Atlantic, 1985; Lise, *Hold-Up,* AMLF, 1985; Danny Boudreau, *Turk 182!,* Twentieth Century-Fox, 1985; Gracie Law, *Big Trouble in Little China,* Twentieth Century-Fox, 1986; Emmy, *Mannequin,* Twentieth Century-Fox, 1987; Brooke Morrison, *Masquerade,* Metro-Goldwyn-Mayer/United Artists, 1988; Lexa Shubb, *Midnight Crossing,* Vestron, 1988; Odessa, *Palais Royale,* Spectrafilm, 1988; Chris Nelson, *For Better or For Worse,* Trans World Entertainment, 1989; Justine DeWinter, *The Return of the Musketeers* (also known as *The Return of the Three Musketeers*), Universal, 1989; Aunt Eva, *Brown Bread Sandwiches,* Eagle, 1989. Also appeared in *The Other Side of the Mountain—Part II,* Universal, 1978.

PRINCIPAL TELEVISION APPEARANCES—Mini-Series: Melanie Adams, *Scruples,* CBS, 1980. Pilots: Regina Kenton, *The Night Rider,* ABC, 1979; Dina Moran, *The Gossip Columnist,* syndicated, 1980; also Amanda Tucker, *The Good Witch of Laurel Canyon,* 1982 (never broadcast). Episodic: *The Incredible Hulk,* CBS, 1979 and 1980; *Columbo,* NBC; *Family,* ABC; *The Bionic Woman,* ABC. Movies: Linda Isley, *Good Against Evil,* ABC, 1977; Anne Ware, *The Bastard* (also known as *The Kent Family Chronicles*), syndicated, 1978; Anne Kent, *The Rebels,* syndicated, 1979; Paula Bennett, *Sins of the Past,* ABC, 1984.*

*   *   *

CAVANI, Liliana   1936-

PERSONAL: Born January 12, 1936, in Capri, Italy. EDUCATION—Attended the University of Bologna and Centro Sperimentale.

VOCATION: Writer and director.

CAREER: Also see *WRITINGS* below. PRINCIPAL STAGE WORK—Director, *Iphigenia in Tauris,* Paris Opera, Paris, France, 1984.

PRINCIPAL FILM WORK—Director: *I cannibali* (also known as *The Cannibals*), Doria-San Marco, 1970; (also editor) *L'ospite* (also known as *The Guest*), RAI-TV Channel 1/Lotar, 1971; *The Night Porter* (also known as *Il portiere du notte*), AVCO-Embassy, 1974; *Milarepa,* Istituto Luce Italnoleggio Cinematografico, 1974; *Oltre il bene e il male* (also known as *Beyond Good and Evil*), United Artists, 1977; *Oltra la porta* (also known as *Beyond the Door*), Premier Releasing/Gaumont, 1982; *Interno Berlinese* (also known as *The Berlin Affair*), Cannon, 1985; *Francesco* (also known as *St. Francis of Assisi, Franciscus,* and *St. Francis*), Istituto Luce/ Italnoleggio Cinematografico/Sacis, 1989; also *La pelle,* 1981.

PRINCIPAL TELEVISION APPEARANCES—Specials: *Three Women Filmmakers,* PBS, 1987. PRINCIPAL TELEVISION WORK—Movies: Director, *Francesco d'Assisi,* 1966; director, *Galileo,* 1968. Specials: *The History of the Third Reich* (documentary) and *The Women of the Resistance* (documentary).

WRITINGS: See production details above. FILM—(With Italo Moscati) *I cannibali,* 1969; *L'ospite,* 1971; (with Moscati) *The Night Porter,* 1973, published by Einaudi, 1975; (with Moscati) *Milarepa,* 1974, published by Cappelli, 1974; (with Franco Arcalli and Moscati) *Oltre il bene e il male,* United Artists, 1977, published by Einaudi, 1977; (with Robert Katz) *La pelle,* 1981; (with Enrico Medioli) *Oltra la porta,* 1982; (with Roberta Mazzoni) *Interno Berlinese,* Cannon, 1985; (with Mazzoni) *Francesco,* 1989.

TELEVISION—(With Moscati) *Francesco d'Assisi,* 1966, published in *Francesco e Galileo: Duo film,* Gribaudi, 1970; (with Moscati) *Galileo,* 1968, published in *Francesco e Galileo: Duo film.* OTHER—(With Moscati) *Lettere dall' interno: Raconto per un film son Simone Weil,* Einaudi, 1974.*

*   *   *

CAVETT, Dick   1936-

PERSONAL: Full name, Richard Alva Cavett; born November 19, 1936, in Gibbon, NE; son of Alva B. (a teacher) and Eva (a teacher; maiden name, Richards) Cavett; married Carrie Nye McGeoy (an actress; professional name, Carrie Nye), June 4, 1964. EDUCATION—Yale University, B.A., English and drama, 1958.

VOCATION: Talk show host, writer, and actor.

CAREER: Also see *WRITINGS* below. BROADWAY DEBUT—Simon, *Otherwise Engaged,* Plymouth Theatre, 1977. PRINCIPAL STAGE APPEARANCES—Fred Allen, *Parade of Stars Playing the Palace,* Palace Theatre, New York City, 1983; narrator, *Into the Woods,* Martin Beck Theatre, New York City, 1988; Andrew Makepeace Ladd III, *Love Letters,* Promenade Theatre, New York City, 1989. Also appeared in productions in New York City and Williamstown, MA, 1958-60.

PRINCIPAL FILM APPEARANCES—As himself, *Annie Hall,* United Artists, 1977; as himself, *Power Play,* Robert Cooper, 1978; as himself, *Health* (also known as *H.E.A.L.T.H.*), Twentieth Century-Fox, 1980; as himself, *Simon,* Warner Brothers, 1980; as himself, *Acting: Lee Strasberg and the Actors' Studio* (documentary), Davida, 1981; as himself, *A Nightmare on Elm Street 3: Dream Warriors,* New Line Cinema, 1987; Bernard, *Beetlejuice,* Warner Brothers, 1988; as himself, *Moon Over Parador,* Universal, 1988;

DICK CAVETT

as himself, *Private Tutor* (also known as *Before God*), Moviestore Entertainment, 1988; as himself, *Funny,* Original Cinema, 1989; as himself, *After School,* Quest Entertainment, 1989; also appeared as himself, *CS Blues* (documentary), 1972.

PRINCIPAL TELEVISION APPEARANCES—Series: Host, *This Morning,* ABC, 1968-69; host, *The Dick Cavett Show,* ABC, 1969-74; host, *Feeling Good,* PBS, 1974-75; host, *The Dick Cavett Show,* CBS, 1975; host, *The Dick Cavett Show,* PBS, 1977-82; host, *Time Was,* HBO, 1979; host and narrator, *Yesteryear,* HBO, 1982; host, *The Dick Cavett Show,* USA, 1985-86; host, *The Dick Cavett Show,* ABC, 1986-87; host, *College Bowl,* Disney Channel, 1987—; host, *Cavett,* CNBC, 1989—. Pilots: As himself, *Nightside,* ABC, 1973. Episodic: Host, "Where It's At," *Stage '67,* ABC, 1967; as himself, *Cheers,* NBC, 1983; as himself, *Kate and Allie,* CBS, 1986; as himself, *Amazing Stories,* NBC, 1986; also *The Ed Sullivan Show,* CBS; *The Tonight Show,* NBC; *Saturday Night Live,* NBC.

Specials: *Tin Pan Alley Today,* NBC, 1967; *Plimpton! Did You Hear the One About. . .?,* ABC, 1971; host, *Funny Girl to Funny Lady,* ABC, 1975; *Dick Cavett's Backlot U.S.A.,* CBS, 1976; host, "Live from Lincoln Center: The New York Philharmonic," *Great Performances,* PBS, 1976; host, "Live from Lincoln Center: The Barber of Seville," *Great Performances,* PBS, 1976; host, "Live from Lincoln Center: Andre Watts," *Great Performances,* PBS, 1976; host and interviewer, "Live from Lincoln Center: Swan Lake," *Great Performances,* PBS, 1976; host, "Zubin Mehta, the New York Philharmonic, and Shirley Verrett," *Great Performances,* PBS, 1977; *The Marx Brothers in a Nutshell,* PBS, 1982; *Teddy Pendergrass in Concert,* HBO, 1982; *Parade of Stars,* ABC, 1983; *Bob Hope's Super Birthday Special,* NBC, 1984; host, "Live from Lincoln Center: Giselle,'' *Great Performances*, PBS, 1985; *Bob Hope Buys NBC?*, NBC, 1985; host, *Yesteryear . . . 1927*, HBO, 1985; *Harry Belafonte: Don't Stop the Carnival*, HBO, 1985; host, *The Grand Tour*, syndicated, 1985; host, *Bodywatch: In Search of the Perfect Day*, PBS, 1986; host and narrator, *Faces of Japan*, PBS, 1986; host, *Japan's Grand Kabuki in America*, PBS, 1986; *Penn and Teller's Invisible Thread*, Showtime, 1987; *The Classical Music Awards*, Arts and Entertainment, 1988; *The Designing Edge: An Aspen Journal* (also known as *For Our Times*), CBS, 1988.

RELATED CAREER—Nightclub performer, 1963-68; actor in U.S. Army training films; actor in television commercials.

NON-RELATED CAREER—Copyboy, *Time* magazine, New York City, 1960.

WRITINGS: TELEVISION—Series: Staff writer, *The Tonight Show*, NBC, 1960-62; staff writer, *The Merv Griffin Show*, NBC, 1962-63; staff writer, *The Jerry Lewis Show*, ABC, 1963; *The Dick Cavett Show*, CBS, 1975. OTHER—(With Christopher Porterfield) *Cavett* (autobiography), Harcourt, 1974; (with Porterfield) *Eye on Cavett* (autobiography), Arbor House, 1983; also contributor to such magazines as *Newsweek, Film Comment*, and *U.S. News and World Report*.

AWARDS: Emmy Awards, Best Talk Show, 1969, 1972, and 1974, all for *The Dick Cavett Show*.

ADDRESSES: OFFICE—Daphne Productions, 1 W. 67th Street, New York, NY 10023. AGENTS—Jerry Hogan, Henderson/Hogan Associates, 200 W. 57th Street, New York, NY 10019; William Morris Agency, 151 El Camino Drive, Beverly Hills, CA 90212.*

* * *

CHABROL, Claude 1930-

PERSONAL: Born June 24, 1930, in Paris, France; son of Yves and Madeleine (Delarbre) Chabrol; married Agnes Marie-Madeleine Goute, June 26, 1952 (divorced); married Stephane Audran (an actress), December 4, 1964; children: Jean-Yves, Mathieu (first marriage); Thomas (second marriage). EDUCATION—Received licencie es lettres from the Sorbonne.

VOCATION: Director and writer.

CAREER: Also see *WRITINGS* below. PRINCIPAL STAGE WORK—Director, *Macbeth*, Theatre Recamier, Paris, France, 1964.

PRINCIPAL FILM APPEARANCES—The Husband, ''La Muette'' in *Paris vu par . . .* (also known as *Six in Paris*), Les Films du Losange, 1965, released in the United States by New Yorker, 1968; Alcibiades, *La Route de Corinthe* (also known as *Who's Got the Black Box?* and *The Road to Corinth*), Films la Boetie, 1967, released in the United States by RAF, 1970; the Filmmaker, *Les Biches* (also known as *The Heterosexuals, The Does*, and *The Girlfriends*), Films la Boetie/Alexandra, 1968, released in the United States by Jack H. Harris, 1968; man in publisher's office, *Folies bourgeoises* (also known as *The Twist* and *Twist*), Union Generale Cinematographique/Parafrance, 1976; metteur en scene, *L'Animal*, Roissy/AMLF, 1977; Theodore Lyssenko, *Polar*, Films Noirs, 1982; Louis Crepin, *Les Voleurs de la nuit* (also known as

Thieves After Dark), Parafrance, 1984; Lieberman, *Je hais les acteurs* (also known as *I Hate Actors!*), Gaumont, 1986; priest, *L'Ete en pente douce* (also known as *Summer on a Soft Slope*), Allied Artists, 1987; Jacques' father, *Jeux d'artifces* (also known as *Games of Artifice* and *Fireworks*), Forum Distribution/Films du Volcan, 1987; Pierre Vergne, *Alouette, je te plumerai* (also known as *The Lark* and *Alouette plumerai*), Union Generale Cinematographique, 1988.

Also appeared in *Le Coup de berger*, 1956; *Le Beau Serge* (also known as *Bitter Reunion* and *Handsome Serge*), Ajym Films, 1958, released in the United States by United Motion Pictures, 1959; *Les Jeux de l'amour*, 1959; *A double tour* (also known as *Doppa mandata, Web of Passion*, and *Leda*), Paris-Titanus, 1959, released in the United States by Times, 1961; *Les Bonnes Femmes*, Paris-Titanus, 1960, released in the United States by Harold Cornsweet Productions, 1966; *Saint-Tropez blues*, 1960; *Les Distractions*, 1960; *Paris nous appartient* (also known as *Paris Belongs to Us* and *Paris Is Ours*), Ajym Films/Films du Carrosse, 1960, released in the United States by Merlyn, 1962; *Les Godelureaux*, 1961; *Les Menteurs* (also known as *The Liars*), Mediterrance Cinema, 1961, released in the United States by Shawn International/Ellis, 1964; ''L'Avarice'' in *Les Sept peches capitaux* (also known as *Seven Capital Sins* and *I sette pecati capitali*), Gibe/Franco-London/Titanus, 1962, released in the United States by Embassy, 1962; *Les Durs a cuire*, 1964; *Marie-Chantal contre le Docteur Kha* (also known as *Marie Chantal against Dr. Kha*), Rome-Paris Films/Dia/Mega and Magreb Unifilm, 1965; *Le Tigre se parfume a la dynamite* (also known as *An Orchid for the Tiger* and *The Tiger Uses Dynamite for Perfume*), 1965; *Brigitte et Brigitte*, 1965; *Zoe bonne*, 1966; *La Femme ecarlate*, 1968; *Et crac!*, 1969; *Version Latine*, 1969; *Le Travail*, 1969; *La Rupture* (also known as *Le Jour des parques* and *The Breakup*), Films la Boetie/Euro International/Cinevog, 1970; *Sortie de secours*, Adel Productions, 1970; *Aussi loin que l'amour* (also known as *As Far as Love Can Go*), Columbia, 1971; *Un Meurtre est un meurtre* (also known as *A Murder Is a Murder*), Planfilm, 1972; *Le Flipping*, 1973; *Les Folies d'Elodie* (also known as *The Naughty Blue Knickers*), New Realm Distributors, 1981; *Suivez mon regard* (also known as *Follow My Gaze*), Union General Cinematographique/World Marketing, 1985; *Sale destin!* (also known as *Rotten Fate!*), Allied Artists, 1987.

FIRST FILM WORK—Producer and director, *Le Beau Serge* (also known as *Bitter Reunion* and *Handsome Serge*), Ajym Films, 1958, released in the United States by United Motion Picture, 1959. PRINCIPAL FILM WORK—All as director unless indicated: (Also producer) *Les Cousins* (also known as *The Cousins*), Ajym Films/Societe Francaise de Cinema, 1958, released in the United States by Films-Around-the-World, 1959; *A double tour* (also known as *Doppa mandata, Web of Passion*, and *Leda*), Paris-Titanus, 1960, released in the United States by Times, 1961; art director and technical advisor, *A bout de souffle* (also known as *Breathless*), Societe Nouvelle de Cinema, 1960, released in the United States by Films-around-the-World, 1961; *Les Bonnes Femmes*, Rome-Paris Films, 1960, released in the United States by Harold Cornsweet, 1966; *L'Oeil du malin* (also known as *The Third Lover*), Rome-Paris Films, 1962, released in the United States by Atlantic, 1963; ''L'Avarice'' in *Les Sept peches capitaux* (also known as *Seven Capital Sins* and *I sette pecati capitali*), Gibe/Franco-London/Titanus, 1962, released in the United States by Embassy, 1963; *Landru* (also known as *Bluebeard*), Rome-Paris Films, 1963, released in the United States by Embassy, 1963; *Ophelia*, Boreal Film, 1963, released in the United States by Trans-Lux Distributing, 1964.

"Paris" in *Les Plus belles escroqueries du monde* (also known as *The Beautiful Swindlers* and *The World's Greatest Swindles*), 1964, released in the United States by Ellis/Continental Distributing, 1967; *Marie-Chantal contre le Docteur Kha* (also known as *Marie Chantal Against Dr. Kha*), Rome-Paris Films/Dia/Mega and Magreb Unifilm, 1965; *La Ligne de demarcation* (also known as *The Line of Demarcation*), Rome-Paris Films/Societe Nouvelle de Cinema, 1966; "La Muette" in *Paris vu par. . .* (also known as *Six in Paris*), Les Films du Losange, 1965, released in the United States by New Yorker, 1968; *Le Scandale* (also known as *The Champagne Murders*), Universal France, 1967, released in the United States by Universal, 1968; *La Route de Corinthe* (also known as *Who's Got the Black Box?* and *The Road to Corinth*), Films la Boetie, 1967, released in the United States by RAF, 1970; *Les Biches* (also known as *The Heterosexuals*, *The Does*, and *The Girlfriends*), Films la Boetie/Alexandra, 1968, released in the United States by Jack H. Harris, 1968; *La Femme infidele* (also known as *The Unfaithful Wife*), Films la Boetie/Cinegai, 1969, released in the United States by Allied Artists, 1969; *Que la bete meure* (also known as *This Man Must Die, Killer!*, and *Uccidero un uomo*), Films la Boetie/Rizzoli, 1969, released in the United States by Allied Artists, 1970.

La Rupture (also known as *Le Jour des parques* and *The Breakup*), Films la Boetie/Euro International/Cinevog, 1970; *Le Boucher* (also known as *The Butcher*), Films la Boetie/Euro International, 1970, released in the United States by Cinerama, 1971; technical advisor, *Eglantine*, CFDC/Union Generale Cinematographique, 1971; *La Decade prodigieuse* (also known as *Ten Days' Wonder*), Films la Boetie, 1971, released in the United States by Levitt-Pickman, 1972; *Juste avant la nuit* (also known as *Just Before Nightfall*), Films la Boetie/Columbia/Cinegai, 1971, released in the United States by Libra, 1975; *Docteur Popaul* (also known as *Scoundrel in White, High Heels*, and *Doctor Popaul*), CIC, 1972; *Les Noces rouges* (also known as *Wedding in Blood* and *Red Wedding Night*), Films la Boetie/Canaria Films, 1973, released in the United States by CIC, 1974; *Une Partie de plaisir* (also known as *A Piece of Pleasure, Pleasure Party*, and *Love Match*), Artificial Eye/Films la Boetie, 1974; *Nada* (also known as *The Nada Gang*), Films la Boetie/Italian International Film, 1974, released in the United States by New Line Cinema, 1974; *Les Innocents aux mains sales* (also known as *Dirty Hands* and *Innocents with Dirty Hands*), Films la Boetie/New Line Cinema, 1975; *Folies bourgeoises* (also known as *The Twist* and *Twist*), Union General Cinematographique/Parafrance, 1976; *Alice, ou la derniere fugue* (also known as *Alice, or the Last Escapade*), Filmel/PHPG, 1976; *Les Liens de sang* (also known as *Blood Relatives* and *Blood Ties*), Societe nouvelle de cinema, 1977; *Violette Noziere* (also known as *Violette*), Gaumont/New Yorker, 1978; *Le Cheval d'orgeuil* (also known as *Horse of Pride* and *The Proud Ones*), Planfilm, 1979.

Les Fantomes du chapelier (also known as *The Hatter's Ghost* and *The Hatmaker*), Gaumont, 1982; *Poulet au vinaigre* (also known as *Cop au vin*), MK2/Virgin Vision, 1985; *Inspecteur Lavardin*, MK2/Artificial Eye, 1986; *Le Cri du hibou* (also known as *The Cry of the Owl*), United International, 1987; *Masques* (also known as *Masks*), Cannon Releasing/MK2, 1987; *Une Affaire de femmes* (also known as *Story of Women, Women's Affairs*, and *Women's Business*), MK2, 1988, released in the United States by New Yorker, 1989; *Dr. M.*, Cori Film Distributors, 1990. Also director unless indicated: *Les Godelureaux*, 1961; supervisor, *Ples v dezju* (also known as *Dance in the Rain*), 1961; *Le Tigre aime la chair fraiche* (also known as *The Tiger Likes Fresh Blood*), 1964; (linking sequences only) *La Chance et l'amour*, 1964; *Le Tigre se parfume a la dynamite* (also known as *An Orchid for the Tiger* and *The Tiger Uses Dynamite for Perfume*), 1965; technical advisor, *Happening*,

1966; technical advisor, *Piege a pucelles*, 1972; *The Bench of Desolation* (short film), 1974; *Les Magiciens* (also known as *Initiation a la morte* and *Profezia di un delitto*), 1975.

PRINCIPAL TELEVISION WORK—All as director. Episodic: "Monsieur Bebe," "Nul n'est parfait," "Une invitation a la chasse," and "Les Gens de l'ete," all *Histoires insolites*, 1974; "De Grey" and "Le Banc de la desolation," both *Henry James*, 1974; *Madame le juge*, 1978. Movies: *The Blood of Others*, HBO, 1984.

RELATED CAREER—Film critic, *Cahiers du Cinema*, 1953-57; public relations director, Twentieth Century-Fox, Paris, 1955; president, Ajym Films (a production company), 1956-61.

WRITINGS: See production details above. FILM—*Le Beau Serge*, 1958; (with Paul Gegauff) *Les Cousins*, 1958; *Le Coup de berger*, 1959; (with Gegauff) *Les Bonnes Femmes*, 1960; (co-adaptor) *Les Godelureaux*, 1961; *L'Oeil du malin*, 1961; (with Francoise Sagan) *Landru*, 1962, published by Julliard, 1963; (with Gegauff) *Ophelia*, 1963; (with Christian Yves) *Marie-Chantal contre le Doctre Kha*, 1965; (with Colonel Remy and Daniel Boulanger) *La Ligne de demarcation*, 1966; "La Muette" in *Paris vu par . . .*, 1965; (with Gegauff) *Les Biches*, 1968; *La Femme infidel*, 1969; (with Gegauff) *Que la bete muere*, 1969; *La Rupture*, 1970; *Le Boucher*, 1970; *Juste avant la nuit*, 1971; (song only) *Docteur Popaul*, 1972; *Les Noces rouges*, 1973, published by Seghers, 1973; (with Jean-Patrick Manchette) *Nada*, 1974; (with Jean-Patrick Manchette) *Les innocents aux mains sales*, 1975; (with Ennio DeConcini, Maria Piafusto, and Norman Enfield) *Folies bourgeoises*, 1976; *Alice, ou la derniere fugue*, 1976; (with R. Sidney) *Les Liens de sang*, 1977; (with Daniel Boulanger) *Le Cheval d'orgueil*, 1979; *Les Fantomes du chapelier*, 1982; (with Dominique Roulet) *Poulet au vinaigre*, 1985; (with Roulet) *Inspecteur Lavardin*, 1986; (with Odile Barski) *Le Cri du hibou*, 1987; (with Barski), *Masques*, 1987; (with Colo Tavernier O'Hagan) *Une Affaire de femmes*, 1988; (adaptor) *Dr. M.*, Cori Film Distributors, 1990.

OTHER—Nonfiction: (With Eric Rohmer) *Hitchcock*, Editions Universitaires, 1957, translated by Stanley Hochman as *Hitchcock: The First Forty-Four Films*, Ungar, 1979; *Le Recit feminin: Contribution a l'analyse semiologique du courrier du coeur et des entrevues ou "enquetes" sur la femme dans la presse feminine actuelle*, Mouton, 1971; (with Louis Marin) *Le Recit evangelique*, Aubier Montaigne, 1974, translated by Alfred M. Johnson, Jr. as *The Gospel Narrative*, Pickwick, 1980.

AWARDS: Grand Prize from the Locarno Film Festival, 1958, for *Le Beau Serge;* Golden Bear Award from the Berlin Film Festival, 1959, for *Les Cousins.*

ADDRESSES: OFFICE—15 Quai Conti, 75006 Paris, France.*

*   *   *

CHAPMAN, Graham   1941-1989

PERSONAL: Born January 8, 1941, in Leicester, England; died of cancer, October 4, 1989, in Maidstone, England; son of Walter (a policeman) and Edith (Towers) Chapman; children: one son. EDUCATION—Cambridge University, M.A., 1962; St. Bartholomew's Hospital Medical School, M.B., B.Ch., 1966.

VOCATION: Actor and writer.

CAREER: Also see *WRITINGS* below. PRINCIPAL STAGE APPEARANCES—Ensemble, *Cambridge Circus* (revue), Plymouth Theatre, then Square East Theatre, both New York City, 1964; various roles, *Monty Python's First Farewell Tour,* Drury Lane Theatre, London, 1974; various roles, *Monty Python Live!,* City Center Theatre, New York City, 1976; various roles, *Monty Python Live at the Hollywood Bowl,* Hollywood Bowl, Hollywood, CA, 1980.

MAJOR TOURS—As a member of the comedy troupe Monty Python (with John Cleese, Terry Gilliam, Eric Idle, Terry Jones, and Michael Palin), appeared in concert tours of U.S., U.K., and Canadian cities during the 1970s.

PRINCIPAL FILM APPEARANCES—Roddy, *Doctor in Trouble,* Rank, 1970; Oxford stroke, *The Magic Christian,* Commonwealth, 1970; Fromage, *The Rise and Rise of Michael Rimmer,* Warner Brothers, 1970; news reader, *The Statue,* Cinerama, 1971; various roles, *And Now for Something Completely Different,* Columbia, 1972; King Arthur and various roles, *Monty Python and the Holy Grail,* Cinema V, 1975; Arthur Harris, *The Odd Job,* Columbia, 1978; Brian and various roles, *Monty Python's Life of Brian* (also known as *The Life of Brian*), Warner Brothers/Orion, 1979; various roles, *Monty Python Live at the Hollywood Bowl,* Columbia, 1982; title role, *Yellowbeard,* Orion, 1983; various roles, *Monty Python's The Meaning of Life,* Universal, 1983. Also appeared in *Who's There* (short film), 1971; *Pleasure at Her Majesty's,* Roger Graef, 1978; *The Secret Policeman's Other Ball,* United International/Almi Cinema V, 1982.

PRINCIPAL FILM WORK—Producer (with Mark Forstater), *The Odd Job,* Columbia, 1978.

PRINCIPAL TELEVISION APPEARANCES—Series: Regular, *At Last, the 1948 Show,* BBC, 1966-67; regular, *Monty Python's Flying Circus,* BBC, 1969-74, then PBS, 1974-82; regular, *The Big Show,* NBC, 1980. Pilots: George, *Jake's Journey,* CBS, 1988. Episodic: *The Ed Sullivan Show,* CBS. Movies: Various roles, *Pythons in Deutschland,* Bavaria Atelier, 1971; Inspector Palmer, *Still Crazy Like a Fox,* CBS, 1987. Specials: Host, *The Dangerous Film Club,* HBO, 1987; *20 Years of Monty Python, Parrot Sketch Not Included,* BBC-1, 1989.

PRINCIPAL TELEVISION WORK—Pilots: Producer, *Jake's Journey,* CBS, 1988.

RELATED CAREER—Member, Monty Python (a comedy troupe), 1969-89; co-founder and director, Python (Monty) Pictures Ltd., Python Productions Ltd., Kay-Gee-Bee Music Ltd., Sea Goat Productions Ltd., and Oversea Goats Ltd.

NON-RELATED CAREER—Physician.

WRITINGS: See production details above. STAGE—*Cambridge Circus,* 1964; *Monty Python's First Farewell Tour,* 1974; *Monty Python Live!,* 1976; *Monty Python Live at the Hollywood Bowl,* 1980.

FILM—(With Joseph McGrath, Terry Southern, Peter Sellers, and John Cleese) *The Magic Christian,* 1970; (with Cleese, Peter Cook,

and Kevin Billington) *The Rise and Rise of Michael Rimmer,* 1970; (with Bob Larbey, John Esmonde, Dave Freeman, and Barry Cryer) *The Magnificent Seven Deadly Sins,* Tigon, 1971; (with Monty Python [John Cleese, Terry Gilliam, Eric Idle, Terry Jones, and Michael Palin]) *And Now for Something Completely Different,* 1972; (with Cleese) *Rentadick,* Virgin, 1972; (with Monty Python) *Monty Python and the Holy Grail,* 1975, published by Methuen, 1977, and as *Monty Python's Second Film: A First Draft,* Methuen, 1977; (with Bernard McKenna) *The Odd Job,* 1978; (with Monty Python) *Monty Python's Life of Brian,* 1979, published in *Monty Python's Life of Brian (of Nazareth) [and] Montypythonscrapbook,* Grosset, 1979; (with Monty Python) *Monty Python Live at the Hollywood Bowl,* 1982; (with Cook and McKenna) *Yellowbeard,* 1983; (with Monty Python) *Monty Python's The Meaning of Life,* 1983, published by Methuen, 1983.

TELEVISION Series: *The Frost Report,* BBC, 1965-67; (with Cleese) *At Last, the 1948 Show,* BBC, 1966-67; *Do Not Adjust Your Set,* BBC, 1968; (with Cleese) *Marty,* BBC, 1968; (with Monty Python) *Monty Python's Flying Circus,* BBC, 1969-74. Pilots: *Jake's Journey,* CBS, 1988. Episodic: *Doctor in the House,* BBC, then syndicated, 1971; also *No, That's Me Over There,* BBC; *Mum's the Word,* BBC. Movies: (With Monty Python) *Pythons in Deutschland,* 1971. Specials: (With Cleese) *Broaden Your Mind,* 1969; (with others) *That Was the Week That Was,* ABC, 1985.

OTHER—*A Liar's Autobiography: Volume VI* (autobiography), Methuen, 1980; (contributor) *The Courage to Change: Personal Conversations About Alcoholism,* Houghton Mifflin, 1984.

With Monty Python: *Monty Python's Big Red Book,* edited by Eric Idle, published by Methuen, 1972, then Warner Books, 1975, and in *The Complete Works of Shakespeare and Monty Python,* Methuen, 1981; *The Brand New Monty Python Book,* edited by Idle, published by Methuen, 1973, then as *The Brand New Monty Python Papperbok,* Methuen, 1974, and in *The Complete Works of Shakespeare and Monty Python,* 1981; *Monty Python's Life of Brian (of Nazareth) [and] Montypythonscrapbook,* Grosset, 1979.

RECORDINGS: ALBUMS—With Monty Python: *Monty Python's Flying Circus,* BBC Records, 1969; *Another Monty Python Record,* Charisma, 1970; *Monty Python's Previous Record,* Charisma, 1972; *Monty Python's Matching Tie and Handkerchief,* Charisma, 1973, then Arista, 1975, *Monty Python Live at Drury Lane,* Charisma, 1974; *The Album of the Soundtrack of the Trailer of the Film "Monty Python and the Holy Grail,"* Arista, 1975; *Monty Python Live at City Center,* Arista, 1976; *Monty Python's Instant Record Collection,* Charisma, 1977; *Monty Python's Life of Brian,* Warner Brothers, 1979; *Monty Python's Contractual Obligation Album,* Arista, 1980; *Monty Python's The Meaning of Life,* Columbia, 1983.

TAPED READINGS—*A Liar's Autobiography,* Dove Books on Tape, 1989.

AWARDS: (With Monty Python) Golden Palm Award from the Cannes Film Festival, 1983, for *Monty Python's The Meaning of Life.*

OBITUARIES AND OTHER SOURCES: Contemporary Authors, Vol. 116, Gale, 1986; *Hollywood Reporter,* October 5, 1989; *New York Times,* October 5, 1989; *Variety,* October 11-17, 1989.*

CHAPMAN, Michael 1935-

PERSONAL: Born November 21, 1935, in New York, NY; married Amy Jones (a film editor and director).

VOCATION: Cinematographer and director.

CAREER: PRINCIPAL FILM APPEARANCES—Taxi driver, *The Last Detail*, Columbia, 1973; lawyer, *Shoot to Kill* (also known as *Deadly Pursuit*), Buena Vista, 1988.

PRINCIPAL FILM WORK—Camera operator, *End of the Road*, Allied Artists, 1970; camera operator, *The Landlord*, United Artists, 1970; camera operator, *Klute*, Warner Brothers, 1971; camera operator, *The Godfather*, Paramount, 1972; cinematographer, *The Last Detail*, Columbia, 1973; cinematographer, *The White Dawn*, Paramount, 1974; cinematographer, *The Front*, Columbia, 1976; cinematographer, *The Next Man*, Allied Artists, 1976; cinematographer, *Taxi Driver*, Columbia, 1976; production assistant, *American Boy* (documentary; also known as *American Boy: A Profile of Steve Prince*), Cinegate, 1977; cinematographer, *Invasion of the Body Snatchers*, United Artists, 1978; cinematographer, *Fingers*, Warner Brothers, 1978; cinematographer, *The Last Waltz* (concert film), Universal, 1978; cinematographer, *Hardcore* (also known as *The Hardcore Life*), Columbia, 1979; cinematographer, *The Wanderers*, Orion, 1979; cinematographer, *Raging Bull*, United Artists, 1980; cinematographer, *Dead Men Don't Wear Plaid*, Universal, 1982; cinematographer, *Personal Best*, Warner Brothers, 1982; director, *All the Right Moves*, Twentieth Century-Fox, 1983; cinematographer, *The Man with Two Brains*, Warner Brothers, 1983; director, *The Clan of the Cave Bear*, Warner Brothers, 1986; cinematographer, *The Lost Boys*, Warner Brothers, 1987; cinematographer, *Scrooged*, Paramount, 1988; cinematographer, *Shoot to Kill* (also known as *Deadly Pursuit*), Buena Vista, 1988; cinematographer, *Ghostbusters II*, Columbia, 1989.

PRINCIPAL TELEVISION WORK—Mini-Series: Cinematographer, *King*, NBC, 1978. Movies: Cinematographer, *Death Be Not Proud*, ABC, 1975; director, *The Annihilator*, NBC, 1986; cinematographer, *Gotham* (also known as *The Dead Can't Lie*), Showtime, 1988. Specials: Cinematographer, *Steve Martin: Comedy Is Not Pretty*, NBC, 1980.

RELATED CAREER—Worked on documentary films in New York City.

AWARDS: Academy Award nomination, Best Cinematography, 1981, for *Raging Bull*.*

*   *   *

CHARBONNEAU, Patricia

VOCATION: Actress.

CAREER: PRINCIPAL STAGE APPEARANCES—*My Sister in This House*, New Dramatists Inc., New York City, 1980; *Arms and the Man*, Merrimack Regional Theatre, Lowell, MA, 1983; also appeared with the Actors Theatre of Louisville, Louisville, KY, 1980-81 and 1982-83.

PRINCIPAL FILM APPEARANCES—Cay Rivvers, *Desert Hearts*, Samuel Goldwyn, 1985; Mrs. Sherman, *Manhunter*, De Laurentiis Entertainment Group, 1986; Anna, *Call Me*, Vestron, 1988; Susan Cantrell, *Shakedown* (also known as *Blue Jean Cop*), Universal, 1988; Dana Martin, *Brain Dead*, Concorde, 1990; also appeared in *Stalking Danger*, Vidmark Entertainment, 1986.

PRINCIPAL TELEVISION APPEARANCES—Series: Inga Thorson, *Crime Story*, NBC, 1986-87. Pilots: Nikki Blake, *C.A.T. Squad*, NBC, 1986; Officer Dakota Goldstein, *Dakota's Way*, ABC, 1988. Episodic: Linda Shannon, *Spenser: For Hire*, ABC, 1987; Sally Stevens, *The Equalizer*, CBS, 1987; Carole Bernstein, *Wiseguy*, CBS, 1989; Lucille Benoit, *UNSUB*, NBC, 1989; Madeline Medford, *Matlock*, NBC, 1989; Clara, *Booker*, Fox, 1990. Movies: Kathy Fitzgerald, *Disaster at Silo 7*, ABC, 1988; Emily Harris, *Desperado: Badlands Justice*, NBC, 1989.

ADDRESSES: AGENT—Steve Dontanville, International Creative Management, 8899 Beverly Boulevard, Los Angeles, CA 90048.*

*   *   *

CHAVES, Richard 1951-

PERSONAL: Born October 9, 1951, in Jacksonville, FL; father, a U.S. Marine Corps officer and drug enforcement agent. EDUCATION—Attended Occidental College; studied acting at the Film Actors' Workshop, 1976-80. MILITARY—U.S. Army, 1970-73.

VOCATION: Actor and playwright.

CAREER: OFF-BROADWAY DEBUT—*Tracers*, 1985. PRINCIPAL STAGE APPEARANCES—*Tracers*, Los Angeles, 1980; also appeared in productions of *Tracers* in Chicago and London, and in *Vietnam Trilogy*.

PRINCIPAL FILM APPEARANCES—Badman, *Cease Fire*, Cineworld, 1985; detective, *Witness*, Paramount, 1985; Poncho, *Predator*, Twentieth Century-Fox, 1987; narrator, *Dear America* (also known as *Dear America: Letters Home from Vietnam*), HBO Films, 1988.

TELEVISION DEBUT—U.S. Marine captain, *Eight Is Enough*, ABC. PRINCIPAL TELEVISION APPEARANCES—Series: Lieutenant Colonel Paul Ironhorse, *War of the Worlds*, syndicated, 1988-89. Mini-Series: Turkish lieutenant, *Onassis: The Richest Man in the World*, ABC, 1988. Episodic: Earl, *Ohara*, ABC, 1988; also *Hill Street Blues*, NBC; *Miami Vice*, NBC; *Dallas*, CBS; *St. Elsewhere*, NBC. Movies: Nolan Esherman, *Penalty Phase*, CBS, 1986; Iron Dog, *Kenny Rogers as "The Gambler" III—The Legend Continues*, CBS, 1987; also *To Heal a Nation*, NBC, 1988.

NON-RELATED CAREER—Truck driver, hotel clerk, and postal worker.

WRITINGS: STAGE—(With others) *Tracers*, Los Angeles, 1980.

AWARDS: Los Angeles Drama Critics' Circle Award (with cast), Best Ensemble, 1980, and Theatre World Award, 1985, both for *Tracers*.

SIDELIGHTS: RECREATIONS—Golf.

ADDRESSES: AGENT—Henderson/Hogan Agency, 247 S. Beverly Drive, Suite 102, Beverly Hills, CA 90212.*

* * *

CLARK, Matt 1936-

PERSONAL: Born November 25, 1936, in Washington, DC; son of Frederick William (a carpenter) and Theresa (a teacher; maiden name, Castello) Clark; married Erica Lann (an artist), 1958, (divorced, 1966); children: Matthias, Jason, Seth, Amiee.

VOCATION: Actor and director.

CAREER: Also see *WRITINGS* below. PRINCIPAL STAGE APPEARANCES—Stephen Dedalus, *A Portrait of the Artist As a Young Man,* Martinique Theatre, New York City, 1963; Timmy Cleary (understudy), *The Subject Was Roses,* Royale Theatre, then Winthrop Ames Theatre, later Helen Hayes Theatre, Henry Miller's Theatre, and Belasco Theatre, all New York City, 1964-66; also appeared in *The Trial of the Catonsville Nine,* Center Theatre Group, New Theatre for Now, Los Angeles, 1970; *One Flew Over the Cuckoo's Nest,* Burt Reynold's Jupiter Dinner Theatre, Jupiter, FL; *The Connection* and *Tonight We Improvise,* both with the Living Theatre.

MATT CLARK

PRINCIPAL STAGE WORK—Stage manager, *The Subject Was Roses,* Royale Theatre, then Winthrop Ames Theatre, later Helen Hayes Theatre, Henry Miller's Theatre, and Belasco Theatre, all New York City, 1964-66.

PRINCIPAL FILM APPEARANCES—Packy Harrison, *In the Heat of the Night,* United Artists, 1967; Romulus, *Will Penny,* Paramount, 1968; Colonel Jellicoe, *The Bridge at Remagen,* United Artists, 1969; jailer, *Macho Callahan,* AVCO-Embassy, 1970; Rufus Brady, *Monte Walsh,* National General, 1970; Bailey, *The Grissom Gang,* Cinerama, 1971; Smiley, *The Cowboys,* Warner Brothers, 1972; Pete, *The Culpepper Cattle Company,* Twentieth Century-Fox, 1972; Bob Younger, *The Great Northfield, Minnesota Raid,* Universal, 1972; Qualen, *Jeremiah Johnson,* Warner Brothers, 1972; Nick the Grub, *The Life and Times of Judge Roy Bean,* National General, 1972; Yardlet, *Emperor of the North Pole* (also known as *Emperor of the North*), Twentieth Century-Fox, 1973; coroner, *The Laughing Policeman* (also known as *An Investigation of Murder*), Twentieth Century-Fox, 1973; Deputy J.W. Bell, *Pat Garrett and Billy the Kid,* Metro-Goldwyn-Mayer, 1973; Dude Watson, *White Lightning* (also known as *McKlusky*), United Artists, 1973; Gerhard, *The Terminal Man,* Warner Brothers, 1974.

Jackson, *Hearts of the West* (also known as *Hollywood Cowboy*), Metro-Goldwyn-Mayer/United Artists (MGM/UA), 1975; Billy Bob, *Outlaw Blues,* Warner Brothers, 1977; Grover, *Kid Vengeance,* Golan-Globus/Irwin Yablans, 1977; red plainclothesman, *The Driver,* Twentieth Century-Fox, 1978; Spider, *Dreamer,* Twentieth Century-Fox, 1979; Purcell, *Brubaker,* Twentieth Century-Fox, 1980; Tom McCoy, *An Eye for an Eye,* AVCO-Embassy, 1981; Sheriff Wiatt, *The Legend of the Lone Ranger,* Associated Film Distribution, 1981; Dwayne, *Bustin' Loose,* Universal, 1981; Virgil, *Honkytonk Man,* Warner Brothers, 1982; Mickey, *Some Kind of Hero,* Paramount, 1982; Chuck Winter, *Love Letters* (also known as *My Love Letters*), New World, 1983; Secretary of Defense, *The Adventures of Buckaroo Banzi: Across the Eighth Dimension,* Twentieth Century-Fox, 1984; Tom McMullen, *Country,* Buena Vista, 1984; Uncle Henry, *Return to Oz,* Buena Vista, 1985; Stuart Hiller, *Tuff Turf,* New World, 1985; Walt Clayton, *Let's Get Harry,* Tri-Star, 1987; Dr. Tower, *The Horror Show,* MGM/UA, 1989; bartender, *Back to the Future III,* Universal, 1990; Judge Symes, *Class Action,* Twentieth Century-Fox, 1990. Also appeared in *Honky,* Jack H. Harris, 1971; *Ruckus* (also known as *The Loner*), New World, 1981.

PRINCIPAL FILM WORK—Director, *Da,* FilmDallas, 1988.

PRINCIPAL TELEVISION APPEARANCES—Series: Lieutenant Arthur Kipling, *Dog and Cat,* ABC, 1977. Mini-Series: Chief Clark, *War and Remembrance,* ABC, 1988; Chief Clark, *The Winds of War,* ABC, 1983. Pilots: Captain Kipling, *Dog and Cat,* ABC, 1977; Reynolds, *Lacy and the Mississippi Queen,* NBC, 1978; Dan O'Keefe, *The Big Easy,* NBC, 1982; Wolfe Crawley, *Highway Honeys,* NBC, 1983; Matt, *Traveling Man* (broadcast as an episode of *CBS Summer Playhouse*), CBS, 1987. Episodic: Dale Cutler, *Hardcastle and McCormick,* ABC, 1985; Peter Holden, *Midnight Caller,* NBC, 1989. Movies: Dunn, *The Execution of Private Slovik,* NBC, 1974; Georgie, *The Great Ice Rip-Off,* ABC, 1974; Charles Parimetter, *Melvin Purvis: G-Man* (also known as *The Legend of Machine Gun Kelly*), ABC, 1974; Buffalo Bill Cody, *This Is the West That Was,* NBC, 1974; Verne Miller, *The Kansas City Massacre,* ABC, 1975; George Newcombe, *The Last Ride of the Dalton Gang,* NBC, 1979; Bill Westbrook, *The Children Nobody Wanted,* CBS, 1981; Mike Raines, *In the Custody of*

Strangers, ABC, 1982; Fennie Groda, *Love, Mary,* CBS, 1985; John Hubbard, *Out of the Darkness,* CBS, 1985; Doc Shabitt, *The Quick and the Dead,* HBO, 1987; Sergeant Grinder, *Kenny Rogers as ''The Gambler'' III—The Legend Continues* (also known as *The Gambler III*), CBS, 1987; Jim Warren, *Terror on Highway 91,* CBS, 1989; also Lieutenant Shapper, *Blind Witness.* Specials: Phil Cranston, ''Andrea's Story: A Hitchhiking Tragedy'' (also known as ''A Hitchhiking Tragedy''), *ABC Afterschool Specials,* ABC, 1983; pawnshop clerk, ''Gambler,'' *CBS Schoolbreak Special,* CBS, 1988.

PRINCIPAL TELEVISION WORK—Episodic: Director, *Midnight Caller,* NBC, 1989. Specials: Director, ''My Dissident Mom,'' *CBS Schoolbreak Special,* CBS, 1987.

WRITINGS: FILM—(With Claude Harz) *Homer,* National General, 1970.

ADDRESSES: AGENT—The Kohner Agency, 9169 Sunset Boulevard, Los Angeles, CA 90069.

*   *   *

CLARKE, Caitlin   1952-

PERSONAL: Born May 3, 1952, in Pittsburgh, PA. EDUCATION—Graduated from Mt. Holyoke College and Yale University.

VOCATION: Actress.

CAREER: BROADWAY DEBUT—Title role, *Teaneck Tanzi: The Venus Flytrap,* Nederlander Theatre, 1983. PRINCIPAL STAGE APPEARANCES—Ilona and secretary, *No End of Blame,* Manhattan Theatre Club Downstage, New York City, 1982; Anita Manchip, *Quartermaine's Terms,* Playhouse 91, New York City, 1983; Ann, *Summer,* Manhattan Theatre Club Downstage, 1983; Jo, *Thin Ice,* WPA Theatre, New York City, 1984; Isabelle Rimbaud, *Total Eclipse,* Westside Arts Theatre, New York City, 1984; Madeline Arnold, *Strange Interlude,* Nederlander Theatre, New York City, 1985; Louka, *Arms and the Man* and Cherubino, *The Marriage of Figaro,* both Circle in the Square, New York City, 1985; Liz Morden, *Our Country's Good,* Center Theatre Group, Mark Taper Forum, Los Angeles, 1989. Also appeared in *Othello,* New York Shakespeare Festival, Delacorte Theatre, New York City, 1979; *Bal,* Chicago Theatre Group, Goodman Theatre, Chicago, IL, 1979; *Summer Vacation Madness,* Tyrone Guthrie Theatre, Minneapolis, MN, 1982; *Not Quite Jerusalem,* Long Wharf Theatre, New Haven, CT, 1983; with Arena Stage, Washington, DC, 1979-80; and in *Lorenzaccio.*

PRINCIPAL FILM APPEARANCES—Valerian, *Dragonslayer,* Paramount, 1981; Simone, *Crocodile Dundee,* Paramount, 1986; Sharon, *The Kid Brother,* Kinema Amerika/Yoshimura/Gagnon Toho, 1987; Carlotta, *Penn and Teller Get Killed,* Warner Brothers, 1989; Sharon, *The Big Picture,* Columbia, 1989.

PRINCIPAL TELEVISION APPEARANCES—Series: Emma Greely, *Once a Hero,* ABC, 1987. Pilots: Emma Greely, *Once a Hero,* ABC, 1987; Jessica Hildy, *The Saint* (broadcast as an episode of *CBS Summer Playhouse*), CBS, 1987. Episodic: Elaine, *Moon-*

lighting, ABC, 1987. Movies: Virginia, *The Mayflower Madam,* CBS, 1987.

ADDRESSES: AGENTS—Paul Martino and Sheila Robinson, International Creative Management, 8899 Beverly Boulevard, Los Angeles, CA 90048.*

*   *   *

CLENNON, David

VOCATION: Actor.

CAREER: PRINCIPAL STAGE APPEARANCES—Messenger to King John, *King John* and Martius, *Titus Andronicus,* both New York Shakespeare Festival (NYSF), Delacorte Theatre, New York City, 1967; Kid, *The Unseen Hand* and Emmett, *Forensic and the Navigators* (double-bill), Astor Place Theatre, New York City, 1970; Oliver, *As You Like It,* NYSF, Delacorte Theatre, 1973; boy, *Welcome to Andromeda* and narrator, *Variety Obit* (double-bill), Cherry Lane Theatre, New York City, 1973; Alfred Allmers, *Little Eyolf,* Manhattan Theatre Club, New York City, 1974; doctor, *Medal of Honor Rag,* Folger Theatre Group, Washington, DC, then Theatre De Lys, New York City, both 1976; Pyotr Sergeyevich Trofimov, *The Cherry Orchard,* NYSF, Vivian Beaumont Theatre, New York City, 1977; Jeremy M., *Talking Things Over with Chekov,* Victory Theatre, Hollywood, CA, 1987. Also appeared in ''The Golden Goose'' in *Story Theatre,* Yale Repertory Theatre, New Haven, CT, 1968; *The Blood Knot,* Long Wharf Theatre, New

DAVID CLENNON

Haven, CT, 1970; *Loot,* Hartford Stage Company, Hartford, CT, 1972; *Marat/Sade,* Actors' Theatre of Louisville, Louisville, KY, 1972; *The Seagull,* Long Wharf Theatre, 1974; *Tales from the Vienna Woods* and *Mistaken Identities,* both Yale Repertory Theatre, 1978; *S.S. Glencairn,* Long Wharf Theatre, 1978; *Beyond Therapy,* Los Angeles Public Theatre, Los Angeles, 1983; *Operation Sidewinder* and *Rosencrantz and Guildenstern Are Dead,* both Williamstown Theatre Festival, Williamstown, MA.

PRINCIPAL FILM APPEARANCES—Toombs, *The Paper Chase,* Twentieth Century-Fox, 1973; Tim, *Coming Home,* United Artists, 1977; Captain, *The Greatest,* Columbia, 1977; Lieutenant Finley Wattsberg, *Go Tell the Spartans,* AVCO-Embassy, 1978; social worker, *Billy in the Lowlands,* FIF Inc., 1978; psychiatrist, *On the Yard,* Midwest Film, 1978; Thomas Franklin, *Being There,* United Artists, 1979; Richard Fieldston, *Hide in Plain Sight,* Metro-Goldwyn-Mayer/United Artists (MGM/UA), 1980; Dave Robell, *Ladies and Gentlemen, the Fabulous Stains,* Paramount, 1981; Consul Phil Putnam, *Missing,* Universal, 1981; Geb, *Star 80,* Warner Brothers, 1982; Palmer, *The Thing,* Universal, 1982; newspaper editor, *The Escape Artist,* Orion/Warner Brothers, 1982; liaison man, *The Right Stuff,* Warner Brothers, 1983; Amnon, *Hannah K.,* Universal, 1983; Brian Gilmore, *Falling in Love,* Paramount, 1984; Randy Hughes, *Sweet Dreams,* Tri-Star, 1985; Lars, *The Trouble with Dick,* Frolix, 1986; Blanchard, *Legal Eagles,* Universal, 1986; Mason Mogan, *He's My Girl,* Scotti Brothers, 1987; Lawrence Baird, *The Couch Trip,* Orion, 1988; Jack Carpenter, *Betrayed,* MGM/UA, 1988. Also appeared in *Gray Lady Down,* Universal, 1977.

PRINCIPAL TELEVISION APPEARANCES—Series: Jeff O'Neal, *Park Place,* CBS, 1981. Pilots: Peter Karpf, *Crime Club,* CBS, 1975; David, *Marriage Is Alive and Well,* NBC, 1980; Steve Rawlin, *Reward,* ABC, 1980; Lester Brotman, *First Time, Second Time,* CBS, 1980; also *Panic in Echo Park,* NBC, 1977. Episodic: John Tate, *Alfred Hitchcock Presents,* NBC, 1985; Harold Bell, *Sledge Hammer!,* ABC, 1987; Cullen, *Beauty and the Beast,* CBS, 1988; Wilton Tibbles, *Murder, She Wrote,* CBS, 1988; Miles Drentell, *thirtysomething,* ABC, 1989 (three episodes); Mitch Duprete, *Almost Grown,* CBS, 1989; also *Barney Miller,* ABC, 1977-81 (four episodes). Movies: Tom Trimpin, *The Migrants,* CBS, 1974; Harry Jones, *Helter Skelter,* CBS, 1976; James Fitzpatrick, *Gideon's Trumpet,* CBS, 1980; Dr. Bruce Lyman, *Special Bulletin,* NBC, 1983; Reverend Werner, *Best Kept Secrets,* ABC, 1984; Phillip Murray, *Blood and Orchids,* CBS, 1986; U.S. Attorney Richard Schultz, *Conspiracy: The Trial of the Chicago 8,* HBO, 1987; also *The Day the Bubble Burst,* NBC, 1982. Specials: Medvedenko, "The Seagull," *Theatre in America,* PBS, 1975.

ADDRESSES: AGENT—Smith-Freedman and Associates, 121 N. San Vicente Boulevard, Beverly Hills, CA 90211.*

*   *   *

CLYDE, Jeremy   1941-

PERSONAL: Born March 22, 1941, in Dorney, England; children: two. EDUCATION—Attended Grenoble University.

VOCATION: Actor and singer.

CAREER: BROADWAY DEBUT—Second Lieutenant Edward Millington, *Conduct Unbecoming,* Ethel Barrymore Theatre, 1970. PRINCIPAL STAGE APPEARANCES—Sir Henry Green, *Richard II* and groom, *Macbeth,* both National Theatre Company, Old Vic Theatre, London, 1972; Clitandre, *The Misanthrope,* National Theatre Company, Old Vic Theatre, 1973. Also appeared in *Pump Boys and Dinettes,* Piccadilly Theatre, London, 1985.

PRINCIPAL FILM APPEARANCES—Monty, *The Great St. Trinian's Train Robbery,* Braywild/British Lion, 1966; Nick Topping, *Silver Bears,* Columbia, 1978; Tipping, *Ffolkes* (also known as *North Sea Hijack* and *Assault Force*), Universal, 1980; Teddy Barrington, *Invitation to the Wedding,* New Realm Distributors Ltd., 1983.

PRINCIPAL TELEVISION APPEARANCES—Series: Gessler, *Crossbow,* Family Channel, 1987—, then as *William Tell,* ITV, 1988—. Mini-Series: Edward, *Moll Flanders,* BBC, 1975, then PBS, 1980; Gerard, *The Pallisers,* PBS, 1977; David Postgate, *Campaign,* BBC, then *Dramaworks,* Arts and Entertainment, both 1988; also Charles I, "By the Sword Divided," *Masterpiece Theatre,* PBS; *The Way We Live Now,* BBC. Episodic: *The Dick Van Dyke Show,* CBS, 1965; *Batman,* ABC, 1966; *Tales of the Unexpected,* NBC, 1977; also *The Patty Duke Show,* ABC; *Hullabaloo,* NBC; *The Beverly Hillbillies,* CBS; *My Three Sons,* CBS. Movies: Andrew Parker-Bowles, *Charles and Diana: A Royal Love Story,* ABC, 1982. Specials: *The Julie London Special,* syndicated, 1968; Algernon Moncrieff, *The Importance of Being Earnest,* London Weekend Television, then PBS, 1985.

RELATED CAREER—Member of the singing duo Chad and Jeremy (with Chad Stuart), 1963-69, reformed briefly in 1982.

RECORDINGS: ALBUMS—With Chad and Jeremy: *Yesterday's Gone,* World Artists, 1965; *Before and After,* Columbia, 1965; also *The Best of Chad and Jeremy,* Capitol; *Cabbages and Kings; The Arc; I Don't Want to Lose You Baby.*

SIDELIGHTS: FAVORITE ROLES—Charles I in *By the Sword Divided.* RECREATIONS—Horseback riding.

ADDRESSES: AGENT—Joy Jameson Ltd., 7 W. Eaton Place Mews, London SW1X 8LY, England.*

*   *   *

COLE, Elizabeth
See ASHLEY, Elizabeth

*   *   *

COLE, Gary

PERSONAL: Born September 20, in Park Ridge, IL. EDUCATION—Studied theatre at Illinois State University.

VOCATION: Actor.

CAREER: PRINCIPAL STAGE APPEARANCES—Austin, *True West,* Cherry Lane Theatre, New York City, 1983; Captain Marvin

Holahan, *Landscape of the Body*, Goodman Theatre, Chicago, IL, 1987; also appeared in *Gardenia*, Goodman Theatre, 1982.

PRINCIPAL FILM APPEARANCES—Assistant coach, *Lucas*, Twentieth Century-Fox, 1986.

PRINCIPAL TELEVISION APPEARANCES—Series: Jack Killian, *Midnight Caller*, NBC, 1988—. Pilots: Gordon, *After Midnight*, ABC, 1988. Episodic: Man with a Christmas tree, "A Matter of Principle," *American Playhouse*, PBS, 1984; Daniel Gaddis, "Her Pilgrim Soul," *The Twilight Zone*, CBS, 1985; Chris Sykes, *Jack and Mike*, ABC, 1986; Alan, *Moonlighting*, ABC, 1987; Jackson, *Miami Vice*, NBC, 1987. Movies: Lee, *Heart of Steel*, ABC, 1983; Jeffrey MacDonald, *Fatal Vision*, NBC, 1984; Manny, *First Steps*, CBS, 1985; Dr. David Hayward, *Vital Signs*, CBS, 1986; Detective Jack Holtz, *Echoes in the Darkness*, CBS, 1987; Scott Grimes, *Those She Left Behind* (also known as *Daddy*), NBC, 1987.

RELATED CAREER—Co-founder and member, Remains Theatre, 1979-86; resident company member, Goodman Theatre, Chicago, IL, 1985; actor with the Steppenwolf Theatre Company, Chicago.

NON-RELATED CAREER—Bartender and house painter.

ADDRESSES: AGENT—Alan Iezman, William Morris Agency, 151 El Camino Drive, Beverly Hills, CA 90212.*

*   *   *

COLE, Olivia   1942-

PERSONAL: Born November 26, 1942, in Memphis, TN; daughter of William and Arvelia (Cage) Cole; married Richard Venture. EDUCATION—Received M.A. from the University of Minnesota; studied acting at the Royal Academy of Dramatic Art.

VOCATION: Actress.

CAREER: PRINCIPAL STAGE APPEARANCES—Sip, *The School for Scandal*, APA Repertory Company, Lyceum Theatre, New York City, 1966; Lisa, *War and Peace*, APA Repertory Company, Lyceum Theatre, 1967; title role, *Electra*, New York Shakespeare Festival, Mobile Theatre, New York City, 1969; Nerissa, *The Merchant of Venice*, Repertory Theatre of Lincoln Center, Vivian Beaumont Theatre, New York City, 1973; Nurse Lake, *The National Health*, Long Wharf Theatre, New Haven, CT, 1973, then Circle in the Square, New York City, 1974; Cariola, *The Duchess of Malfi*, Center Theatre Group, Mark Taper Forum, Los Angeles, 1975; Lena Younger, *A Raisin in the Sun*, Roundabout Theatre, New York City, 1986. Also appeared in *The Tragedy of Coriolanus, Romeo and Juliet*, and *The Taming of the Shrew*, all American Shakespeare Festival, Stratford, CT, 1965; *Six Characters in Search of an Author*, Arena Stage, Washington, DC, 1968; as Gerd, *Brand;* Beatrice, *Much Ado About Nothing;* Sabina, *The Skin of Our Teeth;* Kate, *She Stoops to Conquer;* Jenny, *The Threepenny Opera;* Electra, *The Flies;* Clea, *Black Comedy;* Adelaide, *Guys and Dolls;* and with the Seattle Repertory Theatre, Seattle, WA, 1967-68; Long Wharf Theatre, 1970-71; Williamstown Playhouse, Williamstown, MA; and the Tyrone Guthrie Theatre, Minneapolis, MN.

PRINCIPAL FILM APPEARANCES—Jane Adcox, *Heroes*, Universal, 1977; Corinne, *Coming Home*, United Artists, 1978; Jesse Keller, *Some Kind of Hero*, Paramount, 1982; Elizabeth Grimes, *Go Tell It on the Mountain*, Learning in Focus, 1984; Mrs. Newton, *Big Shots*, Twentieth Century-Fox, 1987.

PRINCIPAL TELEVISION APPEARANCES—Series: Ms. Harrison, *Szysznyk*, CBS, 1977-78; Blanche Nesbitt, *Report to Murphy*, CBS, 1982; also Deborah Mehren, *The Guiding Light*, CBS. Mini-Series: Mathilda, *Roots*, ABC, 1977; Maggie Rogers, *Backstairs at the White House*, NBC, 1979; Maum Sally, *North and South*, ABC, 1985. Pilots: Sarah Brookford, *Fly Away Home*, ABC, 1981. Episodic: Aunt Nanny, "The Fig Tree," *WonderWorks*, PBS, 1987; Ruth, *A Man Called Hawk*, ABC, 1989; judge, *L.A. Law*, NBC, 1990; also *Police Woman*, NBC, 1975. Movies: Betty Williams, *Children of Divorce*, NBC, 1980; Victorine, *Mistress of Paradise*, ABC, 1981; Ruth Walters, *Something About Amelia*, ABC, 1984; Miss Sophie, *The Women of Brewster Place*, ABC, 1989. Specials: *ABC's Silver Anniversary Celebration: 25 Years and Still the One*, ABC, 1978; *Variety '77—The Year in Entertainment*, CBS, 1978; teacher, *When, Jenny? When?*, syndicated, 1980.

AWARDS: Emmy Award, Outstanding Single Performance By a Supporting Actress in a Comedy or Drama Series, 1977, for *Roots;* NAACP Image Award; Ira Aldridge Award from the Roxbury Outreach Shakespeare Experience.

MEMBER: Actors' Equity Association, American Federation of Television and Radio Artists, Screen Actors Guild.

ADDRESSES: AGENT—Century Artists Ltd., 9744 Wilshire Boulevard, Suite 308, Beverly Hills, CA 90212.

*   *   *

COLEMAN, Jack   1958-

PERSONAL: Born February 21, 1958, in Easton, PA. EDUCATION—Graduated from Duke University.

VOCATION: Actor.

CAREER: PRINCIPAL STAGE APPEARANCES—Peter Whetworth, *The Common Pursuit*, Promenade Theatre, New York City, 1987; also company member, Globe of the Great Southwest, Odessa, TX, 1978.

PRINCIPAL FILM APPEARANCES—Stan, *The Pursuit of Happiness*, Jequerity, 1987.

PRINCIPAL TELEVISION APPEARANCES—Series: Jack Kositchek, *Days of Our Lives*, NBC, 1981-82; Steven Carrington, *Dynasty*, ABC, 1982-1989. Movies: Matt, *Bridesmaids*, CBS, 1989; Jack Devlin, *Daughter of Darkness*, CBS, 1990. Specials: *Battle of the Network Stars*, ABC, 1985.

WRITINGS: FILM—(With others) *The Pursuit of Happiness*, Jequerity, 1987.

ADDRESSES: AGENT—Howard Goldberg, Harris and Goldberg, 2121 Avenue of the Stars, Suite 950, Los Angeles, CA 90067.*

* * *

COLICOS, John 1928-

PERSONAL: Born December 10, 1928, in Toronto, ON, Canada.

VOCATION: Actor.

CAREER: OFF-BROADWAY DEBUT—Edmund, *King Lear*, City Center Theatre, 1956. BROADWAY DEBUT—De Laubardemont, *The Devils*, Broadway Theatre, 1965. PRINCIPAL STAGE APPEAR-ANCES—Lodovico, *Othello*, Gratiano, *The Merchant of Venice*, and Leonato, *Much Ado About Nothing*, all American Shakespeare Festival, Stratford, CT, 1957; Sir Edward Mortimer, *Mary Stuart*, Phoenix Theatre, New York City, 1957; Laertes, *Hamlet*, Leontes, *A Winter's Tale*, and Lysander, *A Midsummer Night's Dream*, all American Shakespeare Festival, 1958; Tullus Aufidius, *Coriolanus* and Berowne, *Love's Labour's Lost*, both Stratford Shakespeare Festival, Stratford, ON, Canada, 1961; Caliban, *The Tempest*, Petruchio, *The Taming of the Shrew*, and Comte de Guiche, *Cyrano de Bergerac*, all Stratford Shakespeare Festival, 1962; Hector, *Troilus and Cressida*, title role, *Cyrano de Bergerac*, and title role, *Timon of Athens*, all Stratford Shakespeare Festival, 1963; title role, *King Lear* and Mr. Horner, *The Country Wife*, both Stratford Shakespeare Festival, 1964; title role, *Serjeant Musgrave's Dance*, Theatre De Lys, New York City, 1966; title role, *Macbeth*, American Shakespeare Festival, 1967; Churchill, *Soldiers*, Billy Rose Theatre, New York City, 1968, then New Theatre, London, 1968. Also appeared in *Hogan's Goat*, Olney, MD, 1966.

PRINCIPAL FILM APPEARANCES—Student, *Forbidden Journey*, United Artists, 1950, Dewar, *Bond of Fear*, Eros, 1956; first man, *Murder on Approval* (also known as *Barbados Quest*), RKO, 1956; Pietro, *Passport to Treason*, Astor, 1956; Chino, *War Drums*, United Artists, 1957; Cromwell, *Anne of the Thousand Days*, Universal, 1969; Mort Dellman, *Doctors' Wives*, Columbia, 1971; Sergeant Major Al MacKenzie, *Raid on Rommel*, Universal, 1971; Jimbob Buel, *Red Sky at Morning*, Universal, 1971; Colonel Santilla, *The Wrath of God*, Metro-Goldwyn-Mayer, 1972; McLeod, *Scorpio*, United Artists, 1973; Vincent Karbone, *Breaking Point*, Twentieth Century-Fox, 1976; DeMarigny, *Drum*, United Artists, 1976; Allan Quartermain, *King Solomon's Treasure*, Canafox/Towers, 1978; Count Baltar, *Battlestar Galactica*, Universal, 1979; Count Baltar, *Mission Galactica: The Cylon Attack*, Universal, 1979; DeWitt, *The Changeling*, Associated Film Distributors, 1980; Count Baltar, *Conquest of the Earth*, Glen A. Larson, 1980; Inspector Barnes, *Phobia*, Paramount, 1980; Nick Papadakis, *The Postman Always Rings Twice*, Paramount, 1981; General Howard, *Nowhere to Hide*, New Century/Vista, 1987; Anthony Podopolis, *Shadow Dancing*, Glickenhaus, 1988.

PRINCIPAL TELEVISION APPEARANCES—Series: Count Baltar, *Battlestar Galactica*, ABC, 1978-79; Mikkos Cassadine, *General Hospital*, ABC, 1981. Mini-Series: Lord North, *The Bastard* (also known as *The Kent Family Chronicles*), syndicated, 1978. Pilots: Joe Ruby, *A Matter of Wife . . . and Death*, NBC, 1976; Major Derek Barclay-Battles, *The Paradise Connection*, CBS, 1979. Episodic: Kor, "Errand of Mercy," *Star Trek*, NBC, 1967; Lech, *Night Heat*, CBS, 1987; Kavakonis, *Night Heat*, CBS, 1988; also "Lone Survivor," *Rod Serling's Night Gallery* (also known as

Night Gallery), NBC, 1971; *Profiles in Courage*, NBC. Movies: Paul Jamison, *Goodbye Raggedy Ann*, CBS, 1971; Lester Maypole, *I'll Take Manhattan*, CBS, 1987. Specials: Lucentio, "Taming of the Shrew," *Hallmark Hall of Fame*, NBC, 1956; Tom Pettigrew, "Berkeley Square," *Hallmark Hall of Fame*, NBC, 1959; Comte de Guiche, "Cyrano de Bergerac," *Hallmark Hall of Fame*, NBC, 1962; Porthos, *The Three Musketeers*, CBS, 1960; Rawdon Crawley, *Vanity Fair*, CBS, 1961; Wentworth, *The Lives of Ben Franklin: The Ambassador*, CBS, 1971.*

* * *

COLLINS, Joan 1933-

PERSONAL: Full name, Joan Henrietta Collins; born May 23, 1933 (some sources say 1931 or 1935), in London, England; daughter of Joseph William (an agent) and Elsa (Bessant) Collins; married Maxwell Reed (an actor; divorced); married Anthony Newley (an actor, singer, director, and composer), May 27, 1963 (divorced, 1971); married Ronald S. Kass (a film producer), March, 1972 (divorced); married Peter Holm, 1985 (divorced); children: Tara Cynara, Alexander Anthony (second marriage); Katyana (third marriage). EDUCATION—Attended the Royal Academy of Dramatic Art.

VOCATION: Actress.

CAREER: STAGE DEBUT—*A Doll's House*, Arts Theatre, London,

JOAN COLLINS

1946. PRINCIPAL STAGE APPEARANCES—Appeared in productions of *Jassy, The Praying Mantis, The Skin of Our Teeth, Claudia and David, The Last of Mrs. Cheyney,* and *Murder in Mind.*

PRINCIPAL FILM APPEARANCES—Lil Carter, *Judgment Deferred,* Associated British, 1952; Pampinea, *Decameron Nights,* Film Locations, 1953; Norma, *I Believe in You,* Universal, 1953; Rene Collins, *The Slasher* (also known as *Cosh Boy*), Lippert, 1953; Mary, *The Good Die Young,* Independent Film Distributors, 1954; Stella Jarvis, *Turn the Key Softly,* Arvis, 1954; Marina, *The Woman's Angle,* Stratford, 1954; Sadie Patch, *The Adventures of Sadie* (also known as *Our Girl Friday*), Twentieth Century-Fox, 1955; Evelyn Nesbit Thaw, *The Girl in the Red Velvet Swing,* Twentieth Century-Fox, 1955; Princess Nellifer, *Land of the Pharaohs,* Warner Brothers, 1955; Frankie, *The Square Ring,* Republic, 1955; Beth Throgmorton, *The Virgin Queen,* Twentieth Century-Fox, 1955; Crystal Allen, *The Opposite Sex,* Metro-Goldwyn-Mayer, 1956; Jocelyn Fleury, *Island in the Sun,* Twentieth Century-Fox, 1957; title role, *Sea Wife* (also known as *Sea Wyf and Biscuit*), Twentieth Century-Fox, 1957; Tina, *Stopover Tokyo,* Twentieth Century-Fox, 1957; Alice Chicoy, *The Wayward Bus,* Twentieth Century-Fox, 1957; Josefa Velarde, *The Bravados,* Twentieth Century-Fox, 1958; Angela Hoffa, *Rally 'round the Flag, Boys!,* Twentieth Century-Fox, 1958; Esther, *Esther and the King,* Twentieth Century-Fox, 1960; Melanie, *Seven Thieves,* Twentieth Century-Fox, 1960; Diane, *The Road to Hong Kong,* United Artists, 1962; Jane, *One Million Dollars* (also known as *La congiuntura*), Columbia, 1965; Joanie Valens, *Warning Shot,* Paramount, 1967; Polyester Poontang, *Can Heironymus Merkin Ever Forget Mercy Humppe and Find True Happiness?,* Regional, 1969; Anne Langley, *Subterfuge,* Commonwealth United Entertainment, 1969.

Pat Camber, *Up in the Cellar* (also known as *Three in the Cellar*), American International, 1970; Sarah Booth, *The Executioner,* Columbia, 1970; Carol Radford, *Terror from Under the House* (also known as *Revenge, Inn of the Frightened People,* and *After Jenny Died*), Hemisphere, 1971; Ottilie, *Quest for Love,* Rank, 1971; Joanne Clayton, "All Through the House" in *Tales from the Crypt,* Cinerama, 1972; Molly Carmichael, *Fear in the Night,* International, 1972; Bella Thompson, "Mel" in *Tales That Witness Madness,* Paramount, 1973; Fay, *Alfie Darling,* EMI, 1974; Sarah Mandeville, *Dark Places,* Cinerama, 1974; Black Bess, *The Bawdy Adventures of Tom Jones,* Universal, 1976; Lucy, *The Devil within Her* (also known as *I Don't Want to Be Born*), American International, 1976; Marilyn Fryser, *Empire of the Ants,* American International, 1977; Agnes Lozelle, *The Big Sleep,* United Artists, 1978; Gloria, *Zero to Sixty* (also known as *Repo*), First Artists, 1978; Fontaine Khaled, *The Stud,* Trans-American, 1979; Fontaine Khaled, *The Bitch,* Brent Walker, 1979; Nera, *Sunburn,* Paramount, 1979; Nicolle, *A Game for Vultures,* New Line Cinema, 1980; Diana, *Homework,* Jensen Farley, 1982; Madame Carrere, *Nutcracker,* Rank, 1982. Also appeared in *Lady Godiva Rides Again,* Carroll, 1955; *If It's Tuesday, This Must Be Belgium,* United Artists, 1969; *The Aquarian,* 1972; *State of Siege,* Cinema V, 1973; *The Referee,* 1974; *The Great Adventure,* Pacific International, 1976; *Poliziotto senza Paula,* 1977; *Neck,* 1983; *Georgy Porgy,* 1983.

PRINCIPAL TELEVISION APPEARANCES—Series: Alexis Carrington Colby, *Dynasty,* ABC, 1981-89. Mini-Series: Avril Devereaux, *Arthur Hailey's "The Moneychangers"* (also known as *The Moneychangers*), NBC, 1976; Helene Junot, *Sins,* CBS, 1986. Pilots: Racine, *Paper Dolls,* ABC, 1982; Annie McCulloch, *The Wild Women of Chastity Gulch,* ABC, 1982. Episodic: Lorelei Circe/the

Siren, "Ring Around the Riddler" and "The Wail of the Siren," *Batman,* ABC, 1967; Edith Keeler, "The City on the Edge of Forever," *Star Trek,* NBC, 1967; also "Mission of the Dariens," *Space 1999,* syndicated, 1976; *Fantastic Journey,* NBC, 1977; *Tales of the Unexpected,* NBC, 1977; "Hansel and Gretel," *Fairie Tale Theater,* Showtime, 1982; *Fame, Fortune, and Romance,* syndicated, 1986; *The Virginian,* NBC; *Run for Your Life,* NBC; *Mission: Impossible,* CBS; *Baretta,* ABC; *Ellery Queen,* NBC; *Switch,* CBS; *Starsky and Hutch,* ABC; *Police Woman,* NBC; *Fantasy Island,* ABC; *Orson Welles' Great Mysteries,* syndicated.

Movies: Carole Bradley, *Drive Hard, Drive Fast,* NBC, 1973; Kay Dillon, *The Making of a Male Model,* ABC, 1983; Cartier Rand, *The Cartier Affair,* NBC, 1984; Pam Dugan, *Her Life As a Man,* NBC, 1984; Katrina Petrovna, *Monte Carlo,* CBS, 1986. Specials: *The Bob Hope Show,* NBC, 1959; *The Bob Hope Show,* NBC, 1962; *The Bob Hope Show,* NBC, 1966; Lorraine, "The Man Who Came to Dinner," *Hallmark Hall of Fame,* NBC, 1972; *Steve Martin—Comedy Is Not Pretty,* NBC, 1980; *Battle of the Network Stars,* ABC, 1982; *Bob Hope's Women I Love—Beautiful But Funny,* NBC, 1982; *Blondes vs. Brunettes,* ABC, 1984; *The Dean Martin Celebrity Roast: Joan Collins,* NBC, 1984; *All Star Party for Lucille Ball,* CBS, 1984; *ABC All-Star Spectacular,* ABC, 1985; *The Night of 100 Stars II,* ABC, 1985; *On Top All Over the World,* syndicated, 1985; *Hollywood Christmas Parade,* syndicated, 1987; *Secrets Women Never Share,* NBC, 1987; *All Star Party for Joan Collins,* CBS, 1987; *The 75th Anniversary of Beverly Hills,* ABC, 1989. Also appeared in *The Human Jungle.*

PRINCIPAL TELEVISION WORK—Mini-Series: Executive producer, *Sins,* CBS, 1986. Movies: Costume designer, *The Cartier Affair,* NBC, 1984; producer (with Peter Holm), *Monte Carlo,* CBS, 1986.

RELATED CAREER—Appeared in the home video release, *The Joan Collins Video Special,* 1981.

WRITINGS: *Past Imperfect: An Autobiography,* W.H. Allen, 1978, revised edition published by Simon & Schuster, 1984; *The Joan Collins Beauty Book,* Macmillan, 1980; *Katy: A Fight for Life* (biography), Gollancz, 1982; *Prime Time* (novel), Simon & Schuster, 1988.

AWARDS: Golden Apple Star of the Year from the Hollywood Women's Press Club, 1982; Golden Globe, Best Television Actress—Series (Drama), 1982, for *Dynasty.*

MEMBER: Actors' Equity Association, American Federation of Television and Radio Artists, Screen Actors Guild.

SIDELIGHTS: RECREATIONS—Travel.

ADDRESSES: AGENT—Contemporary Artists, 132 Lasky Drive, Beverly Hills, CA 90212.*

                              *   *   *

COLLINS, Pauline 1940-

PERSONAL: Born September 3, 1940, in Exmouth, England; daughter of William Henry and Mary Honora (a school teacher; maiden name, Callanan) Collins; married John Alderton (an actor);

children: four. EDUCATION—Trained for the stage at Central School of Speech and Drama.

VOCATION: Actress.

CAREER: STAGE DEBUT—Sabina, *A Gazelle in Park Lane,* Theatre Royal, Windsor, U.K., 1962. LONDON DEBUT—Lady Janet Wigton, *Passion Flower Hotel,* Prince of Wales Theatre, 1965. BROADWAY DEBUT—Title role, *Shirley Valentine,* Booth Theatre, 1989. PRINCIPAL STAGE APPEARANCES—Lou, *The Erpingham Camp,* Royal Court Theatre, London, 1967; Nancy Gray, *The Happy Apple,* Hampstead Theatre Club, London, 1967; Cecily Cardew, *The Importance of Being Earnest,* Haymarket Theatre, London, 1968; Brenda Cooper, *The Night I Chased the Women with an Eel,* Comedy Theatre, London, 1969; Rosemary and Claire, *Come As You Are,* New Theatre, London, 1970; Nancy Gray, *The Happy Apple,* Apollo Theatre, London, 1970; Judy, *Judies,* Comedy Theatre, 1974; Minnie Symperson, *Engaged,* National Theatre Company, Old Vic Theatre, London, 1975; Lucy, "Mother Figure," Paula, "Drinking Companion," Polly, "Between Mouthfuls," Milly, "Gosforth's Fete," and Beryl, "A Talk in the Park," in *Confusions,* Apollo Theatre, 1976; Yeliena Ivanovna, *The Bear,* Royal Court Theatre, 1978; Phoebe Craddock, *Romantic Comedy,* Apollo Theatre, 1983; title role, *Shirley Valentine,* Vaudeville Theatre, London, 1988.

PRINCIPAL FILM APPEARANCES—Pat Lord, *Secrets of a Windmill Girl,* Compton, 1966; title role, *Shirley Valentine,* Paramount, 1989.

PRINCIPAL TELEVISION APPEARANCES—Series: Clara Danby, *No—Honestly,* PBS, 1975; Sarah, *Upstairs, Downstairs,* London Weekend Television, then *Masterpiece Theatre,* PBS, 1974; also *Forever Green,* ITV, 1989; *Thomas and Sarah* and *Wodehouse Playhouse.* Mini-Series: Maggie Hewson, *The Black Tower,* Anglia Television, then *Mystery!,* PBS, 1988; also *Country Matters II,* Granada, then *Masterpiece Theatre,* PBS, 1979. Movies: *Knockback.*

NON-RELATED CAREER—School teacher.

AWARDS: Laurence Olivier Award, Best Actress in a New Play, 1988, Drama Desk Award, Best Actress in a Play, Antoinette Perry Award, Best Actress in a Play, Drama League of New York Award, Distinguished Performance, and special Theatre World Award, all 1989, for *Shirley Valentine;* Academy Award nomination, Best Actress, 1990, for *Shirley Valentine.*

SIDELIGHTS: RECREATIONS—Writing.

ADDRESSES: AGENT—James Sharkey Associates, 15 Golden Square, Third Floor Suite, London W1R 3AG, England.*

*   *   *

COLMAN, Henry

PERSONAL: Born September 15, in Altoona, PA. EDUCATION—Received B.S.in drama from Columbia University; also attended the University of Michigan.

VOCATION: Producer, director, and screenwriter.

CAREER: FIRST TELEVISION WORK—Associate producer, *Dr. Kildare,* NBC, 1961. PRINCIPAL TELEVISION WORK—Producer, *The Love Boat,* ABC, 1977-86; producer, "Parent Trap," *Magical World of Disney,* NBC, 1989; producer, *Top of the Hill,* CBS, 1989; also producer, *Hotel,* ABC. Pilots: Associate producer, *The Love Boat,* ABC, 1976; producer, *The Love Boat II,* ABC, 1977; producer, *The New Love Boat,* ABC, 1977; also producer, *Lame Duck.* Movies: Producer, *The Dead Don't Die,* NBC, 1975; producer, *Who Is the Black Dahlia?,* NBC, 1975; producer, *Body of Evidence,* CBS, 1988; supervising producer, *Terror on Highway 91,* CBS, 1989; producer, *The Parent Trap III,* Disney Channel, 1989.

RELATED CAREER—Guest lecturer, University of California, Los Angeles, 1980-87; guest lecturer, University of Southern California, 1980-87; guest lecturer on film and television, University of Michigan, 1987.

WRITINGS: TELEVISION—Episodic: *The Love Boat* (ten episodes), ABC; *Hotel,* ABC.

MEMBER: Writers Guild of America—West.

ADDRESSES: OFFICE—7083 Hollywood Boulevard, Los Angeles, CA 90028. AGENT—Cooper Agency, 10100 Santa Monica Boulevard, Los Angeles, CA 90067.

*   *   *

CONSIDINE, John

VOCATION: Actor and screenwriter.

CAREER: Also see *WRITINGS* below. PRINCIPAL FILM APPEARANCES—John, *The Greatest Story Ever Told,* United Artists, 1965; title role, *Doctor Death: Seeker of Souls,* Cinerama, 1973; man at bar, *California Split,* Columbia, 1974; Frank Butler, *Buffalo Bill and the Indians, or Sitting Bull's History Lesson,* United Artists, 1976; Jack Goode, *Welcome to L.A.,* United Artists, 1976; Lamar, *The Late Show,* Warner Brothers, 1977; Jeff Kuykendall, *A Wedding,* Twentieth Century-Fox, 1978; Webster, *When Time Ran Out,* Warner Brothers, 1980; Jordan Carelli, *Mystique,* Television International/Qui, 1981; Burnside, *Endangered Species,* Metro-Goldwyn-Mayer/United Artists, 1982; Dr. Ernest Greene, *Choose Me,* Island Alive, 1984; Nate Nathanson, *Trouble in Mind,* Alive, 1985; angel with tophat, *Made in Heaven,* Lorimar, 1987; General MacDonald, *Opposing Force,* Orion, 1987. Also appeared in *The Thirsty Dead* (also known as *The Blood Cult of Shangra-La*), International Amusements, 1975.

PRINCIPAL TELEVISION APPEARANCES—Series: Dr. Brian Walsh, *Bright Promise,* NBC, 1969-72; also Vic Hastings, *Another World,* NBC; Reginald Love, *Another World,* NBC. Pilots: Lou Krone, *Mickey Spillane's Margin for Murder,* CBS, 1981. Episodic: Bertram Cabot, "The Man Who Was Never Born," *The Outer Limits,* ABC, 1963; Claude Dashelle, *Hollywood Beat,* ABC, 1985; Eric, *Hardcastle and McCormick,* ABC, 1985; Philip Nordstrom, *Knight Rider,* NBC, 1985; Lean, *The A-Team,* NBC, 1986; Lieutenant Braden, *The Colbys,* ABC, 1986; Reverend Rawlinson, *Remington Steele,* NBC, 1986; John Nottingham, *Simon and Simon,* CBS, 1988; Alex Caulfield, *Highway to Heaven,* NBC, 1989; David Prescott, *Dynasty,* ABC, 1989; also *Taxi,* ABC, 1981. Movies: Larry Quinn, *See How She Runs,* CBS, 1978;

interviewer, *The Shadow Box*, ABC, 1980; Dr. Coleman, *Mother's Day on Walton's Mountain*, NBC, 1982; Frank Wells, *Marion Rose White*, CBS, 1982; Curtis Bittan, *Forbidden Love*, CBS, 1982; Steve Moss, *Dixie: Changing Habits*, CBS, 1983; Ed Judson, *Rita Hayworth: The Love Goddess*, CBS, 1983; Jack Blaine, *Passions*, CBS, 1984; Dr. Mathew Crawford, *Timestalkers*, CBS, 1987; also *Incident in San Francisco*, ABC, 1971. Specials: Richard Coburn, *Time for Elizabeth*, NBC, 1964.

WRITINGS: FILM—(With Lee Erwin, Jack A. Robinson, and Tim Considine) *Tarzan's Deadly Silence* (also known as *The Deadly Silence*), National General, 1970; (with Patricia Resnick, Allan Nicholls, and Robert Altman) *A Wedding*, Twentieth Century-Fox, 1978. TELEVISION—*Dixie: Changing Habits*, CBS, 1983.

ADDRESSES: AGENT—Susan Smith, Smith-Freedman and Associates, 121 N. San Vicente Boulevard, Beverly Hills, CA 90211.*

*   *   *

COODER, Ry   1947-

PERSONAL: Full name, Ryland Peter Cooder; born March 15, 1947, in Los Angeles, CA.

VOCATION: Composer, arranger, guitarist, and singer.

CAREER: Also see *WRITINGS* below. PRINCIPAL FILM WORK—Music arranger, *The Long Riders*, United Artists, 1980; music arranger, *Southern Comfort*, Twentieth Century-Fox, 1981. PRINCIPAL TELEVISION APPEARANCES—Specials: *Jim Henson's Ghost of Faffner Hall*, HBO, 1989.

RELATED CAREER—Guitarist with the rock band the Rising Sons, 1966-67; studio guitarist on albums by Captain Beefheart, the Rolling Stones, Randy Newman, Arlo Guthrie, John Cougar Mellencamp, and others; recording artist.

WRITINGS: All as composer. FILM—(Contributor) *Candy*, Cinerama, 1968; (contributor) *Performance*, Warner Brothers, 1970; (with Jack Nitzche) *Blue Collar*, Universal, 1978; *The Long Riders*, United Artists, 1980; *Southern Comfort*, Twentieth Century-Fox, 1981; *The Border*, Universal, 1982; *Paris, Texas*, Twentieth Century-Fox, 1984; *Streets of Fire*, Universal/RKO, 1984; *Alamo Bay*, Tri-Star, 1985; *Brewster's Millions*, Universal, 1985; *Blue City*, Paramount, 1986; *Crossroads*, Columbia, 1986; *Johnny Handsome*, Tri-Star, 1989.

TELEVISION—Series: (Theme music) *Beverly Hills Buntz*, 1987. Pilots: *Cowboy Joe*, ABC, 1988. Specials: Episodic: "Annie Oakley," *Shelley Duvall's Tall Tales and Legends*, Showtime, 1985; "The Man Who Was Death," *Tales from the Crypt*, HBO, 1989.

RECORDINGS: ALBUMS—*Ry Cooder*, Reprise, 1970; *Into the Purple Valley*, Reprise, 1971; *Boomer's Story*, Reprise, 1972; *Paradise and Lunch*, Reprise, 1974; *Chicken Skin Music*, Warner Brothers, 1976; *Show Time*, Warner Brothers, 1977; *Jazz*, Warner Brothers, 1978; *Bop Till You Drop*, Warner Brothers, 1979; *Borderline*, Warner Brothers, 1980; *The Long Riders* (original soundtrack), Warner Brothers, 1980; *Southern Comfort* (original soundtrack), Warner Brothers, 1981; *The Border* (original soundtrack), Warner Brothers, 1982; *The Slide Area*, Warner Brothers, 1982;

Paris, Texas (original soundtrack), Warner Brothers, 1984; *Alamo Bay* (original soundtrack), Warner Brothers, 1985; *Blue City* (original soundtrack), Warner Brothers, 1986; *Crossroads* (original soundtrack), Warner Brothers, 1986.

ADDRESSES: PUBLICIST—Press Relations, Warner Brother Records, 3300 Warner Boulevard, Burbank, CA 91510.*

*   *   *

COOK, Elisha, Jr.   1906-

PERSONAL: Born December 26, 1906, in San Francisco, CA; son of Elisha and Helen (an actress; maiden name, Henry) Cook; married first wife, Mary, 1929 (divorced, 1942). MILITARY—U.S. Army Air Corps, 1942-43.

VOCATION: Actor.

CAREER: STAGE DEBUT—*Lightnin'*, Chicago, IL, 1921. LONDON DEBUT—Jimmie Besant, *Coquette*, Apollo Theatre, 1929. PRINCIPAL STAGE APPEARANCES—Felix, *The Crooked Friday*, Bijou Theatre, New York City, 1925; Joe Bullitt, *Hello, Lola*, Eltinge Theatre, New York City, 1926; ensemble, *Great Temptations* (revue), Winter Garden Theatre, New York City, 1926; Dick Wilton, *Henry—Behave* and Jimmie, *Gertie*, both Nora Bayes Theatre, New York City, 1926; Algernon Simpson, *Jimmy's Women*, Biltmore Theatre, New York City, 1927; Stewart Kennedy, *Her Unborn Child*, Eltinge Theatre, 1928; Felix, *The Kingdom of God*, Ethel Barrymore Theatre, New York City, 1928; Stan Price, *Many a Slip*, Little Theatre, New York City, 1930; Emptyhead, *Privilege Car*, 48th Street Theatre, New York City, 1931; Francis Demarco, *Lost Boy*, Mansfield Theatre, New York City, 1932; Ed Martin, *Merry-Go-Round*, Provincetown Playhouse, New York City, 1932; Honey Rogers, *Chrysalis*, Martin Beck Theatre, New York City, 1932; Ed Rumplegar, *Three-Cornered Moon*, Cort Theatre, New York City, 1933; Richard, *Ah, Wilderness!*, Guild Theatre, New York City, 1933; Russell Gibbons, *Crime Marches On*, Morosco Theatre, New York City, 1935; Bird, *Come Angel Band*, 46th Street Theatre, New York City, 1936; reporter, *Lightin'*, John Golden Theatre, New York City, 1938; Guiseppe Givola, *Arturo Ui*, Lunt-Fontanne Theatre, New York City, 1963. Also appeared in *Goodbye Again*, Grossinger Playhouse, Ferndale, NY, 1933; and as Mel Frank, *Once Upon a Night*, Wilmington, DE, 1938.

MAJOR TOURS—Richard, *Ah, Wilderness!*, U.S. cities, 1934-35; also appeared in *Twelfth Night* and *When Hell Froze*, U.S. cities, both 1929.

FILM DEBUT—Stewart Kennedy, *Her Unborn Child*, 1930. PRINCIPAL FILM APPEARANCES—Herbert Terwilliger Van Dyck, *Pigskin Parade* (also known as *Harmony Parade*), Twentieth Century-Fox, 1936; Skeeter, *Two in a Crowd*, Universal, 1936; Pete, *Breezing Home*, Universal, 1937; chemist, *Danger—Love at Work*, Twentieth Century-Fox, 1937; Tony Stevens, *The Devil Is Driving*, Columbia, 1937; Ollie Stearns, *Life Begins in College* (also known as *The Joy Parade*), Twentieth Century-Fox, 1937; Egbert Eggleston, *Love Is News*, Twentieth Century-Fox, 1937; Joe Turner, *They Won't Forget*, Warner Brothers, 1937; Glen Wylie, *Wife, Doctor, and Nurse*, Twentieth Century-Fox, 1937; Waldo, *My Lucky Star*, Twentieth Century-Fox, 1938; "Professor" Pratt, *Submarine Patrol*, Twentieth Century-Fox, 1938; boy, *Three Blind Mice*, Twentieth Century-Fox, 1938; Robert Austin and Norman Hazlitt, *Grand Jury Secrets*, Paramount, 1939; Danny, *Newsboy's Home*, Universal, 1939.

Communist, *Public Deb No. 1*, Twentieth Century-Fox, 1940; Joe Briggs, *Stranger on the Third Floor*, RKO, 1940; Joe Cadd, *Tin Pan Alley*, Twentieth Century-Fox, 1940; Dicky Brown, *He Married His Wife*, Twentieth Century-Fox, 1940; cook, *Ball of Fire*, RKO, 1941; assistant director, *Hellzapoppin'*, Universal, 1941; elevator boy, *Love Crazy*, Metro-Goldwyn-Mayer (MGM), 1941; Wilmer Cook, *The Maltese Falcon*, Warner Brothers, 1941; hotel clerk, *Man at Large*, Twentieth Century-Fox, 1941; piano player, *Sergeant York*, Warner Brothers, 1941; Frank Lucas, *A-Haunting We Will Go*, Twentieth Century-Fox, 1942; genius, *A Gentleman at Heart*, Twentieth Century-Fox, 1942; Harry Williams, *I Wake Up Screaming* (also known as *Hotspot*), Twentieth Century-Fox, 1942; roadhouse customer, *In This Our Life*, Warner Brothers, 1942; Gillman, *Manila Calling*, Twentieth Century-Fox, 1942; Ernie, *Sleepytime Gal*, Republic, 1942; "Chicopee" Nevins, *Wildcat*, Paramount, 1942; Whitey, *Dark Mountain*, Paramount, 1944; Cleeve, *Dark Waters*, United Artists, 1944; Cliff March, *Phantom Lady*, Universal, 1944; Info Jones, *Up in Arms*, RKO, 1944; Kirk, *Dillinger*, Monogram, 1945; Jimmie Lobo, *Why Girls Leave Home*, Producers Releasing Corporation, 1945; Harry Jones, *The Big Sleep*, Warner Brothers, 1946; Sam, *Blonde Alibi*, Universal, 1946; Oliver S. Patch, *Cinderella Jones*, Warner Brothers, 1946; Nick, *The Falcon's Alibi*, RKO, 1946; Eugene, *Joe Palooka—Champ*, Monogram, 1946; Fly Felleti, *Two Smart People*, MGM, 1946; Marty, *Born to Kill* (also known as *Lady of Deceit*), RKO, 1947; Joe, *Fall Guy*, Monogram, 1947; Oval, *The Gangster*, Allied Artists, 1947; Frank, *The Long Night*, RKO, 1947; Roper, *Flaxy Martin*, Warner Brothers, 1949; Klipspringer, *The Great Gatsby*, Paramount, 1949.

Jonas, *Behave Yourself!*, RKO, 1951; Eddie, *Don't Bother to Knock*, Twentieth Century-Fox, 1952; Bobo, *I, the Jury*, United Artists, 1953; Torrey, *Shane*, Paramount, 1953; Standish, *Thunder Over the Plains*, Warner Brothers, 1953; Crackel, *Drum Beat*, Warner Brothers, 1954; Tulsa, *The Outlaw's Daughter*, Twentieth Century-Fox, 1954; Briggs, *The Indian Fighter*, United Artists, 1955; Punky, *Timberjack*, Republic, 1955; Finn, *Trial*, MGM, 1955; Whitey Pollack, *Accused of Murder*, Republic, 1956; George Peatty, *The Killing*, United Artists, 1956; Van Meter, *Baby Face Nelson*, United Artists, 1957; Candymouth, *Chicago Confidential*, United Artists, 1957; Willie, *The Lonely Man*, Paramount, 1957; Skeets, *Plunder Road*, Twentieth Century-Fox, 1957; Martin Schuyler, *Voodoo Island* (also known as *Silent Death*), United Artists, 1957; Watson Pritchard, *House on Haunted Hill*, Allied Artists, 1958; Larry, *Day of the Outlaw*, United Artists, 1959.

Ted Blake, *College Confidential*, Universal, 1960; Harry Nesbitt, *Platinum High School* (also known as *Rich, Young, and Deadly* and *Trouble at Sixteen*), MGM, 1960; bank teller, *One-Eyed Jacks*, Paramount, 1961; Joe, *Black Zoo*, Allied Artists, 1963; Peter Smith, *The Haunted Palace*, American International, 1963; undertaker, *Johnny Cool*, United Artists, 1963; Mr. Keith, *Papa's Delicate Condition*, Paramount, 1963; Tex, *Blood on the Arrow*, Allied Artists, 1964; father, *The Glass Cage* (also known as *Den of Doom, Don't Touch My Sister*, and *Bed of Fire*), Allied Artists, 1964; Arnold, *The Spy in the Green Hat*, MGM, 1966; Hanson, *Welcome to Hard Times* (also known as *Killer on a Horse*), MGM, 1967; Mr. Nicklas, *Rosemary's Baby*, Paramount, 1968; Jeb, *The Great Bank Robbery*, Warner Brothers, 1969.

Old convict, *El Condor*, National General, 1970; Sam, *Blacula*, American International, 1972; Bunker, *The Great Northfield, Minnesota Raid*, Universal, 1972; Gray Cat, *Emperor of the North Pole* (also known as *Emperor of the North*), Twentieth Century-Fox, 1973; Willie, *Electra Glide in Blue*, United Artists, 1973; Carl, *The Outfit* (also known as *The Good Guys Always Win*), MGM, 1973; Cody, *Pat Garrett and Billy the Kid*, MGM, 1973; Charlie, *Dead People* (also known as *Messiah of Evil, Return of the Living Dead, Revenge of the Screaming Dead*, and *The Second Coming*), Cinefilm, 1974; Wilmer, *The Black Bird*, Columbia, 1975; Eddie, *St. Ives*, Warner Brothers, 1976; Reverend Will Finley, *Winterhawk*, Howco International, 1976; Georgie, *The Champ*, Metro-Goldwyn-Mayer/United Artists MGM/UA), 1979; patron, *1941*, Universal, 1979; On-Your-Mark, *Carny*, United Artists, 1980; stable hand, *Tom Horn*, Warner Brothers, 1980; Sergeant Billy, *Harry's War*, Taft International, 1981; Mousy, "Municipalians" in *National Lampoon Goes to the Movies*, MGM/UA, 1981; Eli (the taxi driver), *Hammett*, Warner Brothers, 1982. Also appeared in *Bullets or Ballots*, Warner Brothers, 1936; *Casanova Brown*, RKO, 1944.

TELEVISION DEBUT   Coffeehead, *Dick Tracy*, ABC, 1949. PRINCIPAL TELEVISION APPEARANCES—Series: Francis "Ice Pick" Hofstetler, *Magnum, P.I.*, CBS, 1983-88. Pilots: *The Judge* (broadcast as an episode of *The Dick Powell Show*), NBC, 1963; coach, *McNab's Lab* (broadcast as an episode of *Summer Fun*), ABC, 1966; hotel clerk, *Terror at Alcatraz*, NBC, 1982; Dutch Silver, *Shadow of Sam Penny*, CBS, 1983; Eddie, *This Girl for Hire*, CBS, 1983. Episodic: Charles Pulaski, "Emergency!," *No Warning*, NBC, 1958; Samuel T. Cogley, "Court-Martial," *Star Trek*, NBC, 1967; also *The Adventures of Superman*, syndicated, 1953; "Brandenburg Gate," *TV Hour*, ABC, 1953; *Treasury Men in Action*, ABC, 1955; "Salvage," *Alfred Hitchcock Presents*, CBS, 1955; "The Trigger Finger Clue," *TV Reader's Digest*, ABC, 1956; "Round Trip," *George Sanders' Mystery Theatre*, syndicated, 1956; *The Millionaire*, CBS, 1957; *Wyatt Earp*, ABC, 1957; "Silent Ambush," *General Electric Theatre*, CBS, 1958; *Trackdown*, CBS, 1958; *Bat Masterson*, NBC, 1958; *Perry Mason*, CBS, 1958 and 1964; *Rawhide*, CBS, 1959; *Johnny Ringo*, CBS, 1959; *Gunsmoke*, CBS, 1959 and 1965.

"The Fatal Impulse," *Thriller*, NBC, 1960; *Tightrope*, CBS, 1960; "The Young Juggler," *Ford Star Time*, NBC, 1960; *The Rebel*, ABC, 1960; *Wagon Train*, NBC, 1960 and 1961; "Open House," *General Electric Theatre*, CBS, 1961; *The Real McCoys*, ABC, 1961; "Borderline," *The Dick Powell Theatre*, NBC, 1962; *Surfside 6*, ABC, 1962; *The Fugitive*, ABC, 1963; *Destry*, ABC, 1964; *Profiles in Courage*, NBC, 1965; *The Wild, Wild West*, CBS, 1966; *I Spy*, CBS, 1966; *The Road West*, NBC, 1966; *Bonanza*, NBC, 1966 and 1970; *The Monroes*, ABC, 1967; *Batman*, ABC, 1967; *McCloud*, NBC, 1971; *The Chicago Teddy Bears*, CBS, 1971; *The Persuaders*, ABC, 1972; *The Odd Couple*, ABC, 1974; *Mannix*, CBS, 1974; *Movin' On*, NBC, 1974; *Starsky and Hutch*, ABC, 1975; *S.W.A.T.*, ABC, 1975; *The Blue Knight*, CBS, 1976; *Chicago Story*, NBC, 1982; *The Motorola Television Hour*, CBS; *The Outlaws*, NBC; *Bring 'em Back Alive*, CBS. Movies: Proprietor, *Night Chase*, CBS, 1970; Willie Peanuts, *The Movie Murderer*, NBC, 1970; Mickey Crawford, *The Night Stalker*, ABC, 1972; sweeper, *Mad Bull*, CBS, 1977; Weasel, *Salem's Lot* (also known as *Salem's Lot: The Movie*), CBS, 1979; Jetter, *Leave 'em Laughing*, CBS, 1981; Mr. Bibbs, *It Came Upon the Midnight Clear*, syndicated, 1984; Novatney, *Off Sides*, NBC, 1984; Pappy Glue, *The Man Who Broke 1000 Chains*, HBO, 1987. Specials: Grandfather, *The Trouble with Grandpa*, syndicated, 1981.

RELATED CAREER—Actor in vaudeville and in summer theatre productions.

MEMBER: Actors' Equity Association, American Federation of Television and Radio Artists, Screen Actors Guild.*

*   *   *

COOKE, Alistair   1908-

PERSONAL: Full name, Alfred Alistair Cooke; born November 20, 1908, in Manchester, England; naturalized U.S. citizen, 1941; son of Samuel (a minister) and Mary Elizabeth (Byrne) Cooke; married Ruth Emerson, August 24, 1934 (divorced); married Jane White Hawkes, April 30, 1946; children: John Byrne (first marriage); Susan Byrne (second marriage). EDUCATION—Cambridge University, B.A., 1930, diploma in education, 1931; graduate work, Yale University, 1932-33, then Harvard University, 1933-34.

VOCATION: Journalist, broadcaster, and television host.

CAREER: PRINCIPAL STAGE APPEARANCES—Host, *An American Evening of Humor,* International Festival of Music and Arts, Theatre Royal, Bath, U.K., 1988.

PRINCIPAL FILM APPEARANCES—Narrator, *The Three Faces of Eve,* Twentieth Century-Fox, 1957; also narrator, *The March of Time* (newsreel), 1938-39.

PRINCIPAL TELEVISION APPEARANCES—Series: Host, *Omnibus,* CBS, 1952-56, then ABC, 1956-57, later NBC, 1957-61; host, *Masterpiece Theatre,* PBS, 1971—; narrator, *America: A Personal History of the United States,* NBC, 1972-73, then PBS, 1974; also host, *International Zone,* 1961-67. Specials: "Bacall on Bogart," *Great Performances,* PBS, 1988; *The Congress,* PBS, 1989.

PRINCIPAL TELEVISION WORK—Producer, *International Zone,* 1961-67.

PRINCIPAL RADIO APPEARANCES—Film critic, BBC, 1934-37; London correspondent, NBC, 1936-37; commentator on American affairs, BBC, 1938—; host, *Letters from America,* BBC, 1947—.

PRINCIPAL RADIO WORK—Creator, *Transatlantic Quiz,* BBC, 1944.

RELATED CAREER—Special correspondent on American affairs, *London Times,* 1938-42; American features correspondent, *London Daily Herald,* 1942-44; United Nations correspondent, *Manchester Guardian* (now known as the *Guardian*), 1945-48, then chief American correspondent, 1948-72.

WRITINGS: TELEVISION—*America: A Personal History of the United States,* NBC, 1972-73.

OTHER—Editor, *Garbo and the Night Watchmen: A Selection from the Writings of British and American Film Critics,* J. Cape, 1937, then Secker and Warburg, 1971, published as *Garbo and the Night Watchmen: A Selection Made in 1937 from the Writings of British and American Film Critics,* McGraw-Hill, 1971; *Douglas Fairbanks: The Making of a Screen Character,* Museum of Modern Art, 1940; *A Generation on Trial: U.S.A. vs. Alger Hiss,* Knopf, 1950; (contributor) *Challenge of Ideas,* Odyssey, 1950; *Letters from America* (essays), Hart-Davis, 1951; *One Man's America* (essays), Knopf, 1952; *Christmas Eve* (short stories), Knopf, 1952; *A Com-*

mencement Address, Knopf, 1954; editor, *The Vintage Mencken,* Vintage, 1955; *Around the World in Fifty Years: A Political Travelogue,* Field Enterprises, 1966; *Talk About America* (essays), Knopf, 1968; *General Eisenhower on the Military Churchill: A Conversation with Alistair Cooke,* Norton, 1970; *Alistair Cooke's America,* Knopf, 1973; *Six Men,* Knopf, 1977; *The Americans: Fifty Letters from America on Our Life and Times,* Penguin, 1979; (with Robert Cameron) *Above London,* Cameron and Company, 1980; *Masterpieces: A Decade of Masterpiece Theatre,* Knopf, 1982; *The Patient Has the Floor,* Knopf, 1986; *America Observed,* Knopf, 1988. Also writer of a weekly column in *Listener;* contributor of articles to *Theatre Arts Monthly, New Republic, Encore, Fortnightly Review,* and the *Spectator.*

AWARDS: Commonwealth Fund Fellow, Yale University, 1932-33; Commonwealth Fund Fellow, Harvard University, 1933-34; George Foster Peabody Broadcasting Award, Contribution to International Understanding, 1951, for *Letters from America;* Emmy Award, 1958, for *Omnibus;* Richard Dimbleby Award from the British Academy of Film and Television Arts, 1972; Emmy Awards, Outstanding Documentary Program Achievement (Individual—Writer) and Outstanding Documentary Program Achievement (Individual—Narrator), George Foster Peabody Broadcasting Award, and Writers Guild Award, Best Documentary, all 1973, for *America: A Personal History of the United States;* Benjamin Franklin Medal from the Royal Society of the Arts, 1973; Knight Commander, Order of the British Empire, 1973; Emmy Award, Special Classification of Outstanding Individual Achievement, 1975, for *Masterpiece Theatre;* Howland Medal from Yale University, 1977; special George Foster Peabody Broadcasting Award, 1983; Medal for Spoken Language from the American Academy of Arts and Letters, 1983; Governor's Award from the Academy of Television Arts and Sciences, 1985; named a Literary Lion by the New York Public Library, 1986; honorary fellow, Cambridge University, 1986. HONORARY DEGREES—University of Edinburgh, L.L.D., 1969; University of Manchester, L.L.D., 1973; University of St. Andrews, Litt. D., 1975.

MEMBER: National Press Club, Savile Club, Athenaeum Club, Royal and Ancient Golf Club, San Francisco Golf Club, Players Club, National Arts.

SIDELIGHTS: RECREATIONS—Golf, photography, music, playing the piano, motion pictures, beachcombing, the American West, travel, and chess.

ADDRESSES: OFFICE—1150 Fifth Avenue, New York, NY 10028.*

*   *   *

COOLIDGE, Martha   1946-

PERSONAL: Born August 17, 1946, in New Haven, CT; married Michael Backes (a producer). EDUCATION—Attended the Rhode Island School of Design, the School of Visual Arts, and Columbia University; graduate work at the New York University Institute of Film and Television.

VOCATION: Director, producer, and screenwriter.

CAREER: Also see *WRITINGS* below. PRINCIPAL FILM APPEARANCES—As herself, *Not a Pretty Picture* (documentary), Other Cinema Ltd., 1975; as herself, *Fifty Years of Action!* (documentary), Directors Guild of America Golden Jubilee Committee, 1986; as herself, *That's Adequate*, Manley/Vidmark Entertainment, 1988. Also appeared in *Calling the Shots* (documentary), World Artists Releasing/Cineplex Odeon, 1988.

PRINCIPAL FILM WORK—Producer, director, and editor, *Old Fashioned Woman* (documentary), Films Inc., 1974; producer, director, and editor, *Not a Pretty Picture* (documentary), Other Cinema Ltd., 1976; director, *Valley Girl*, Atlantic, 1983; producer and director, *The City Girl*, Moon, 1984; director, *Joy of Sex*, Paramount, 1984; director, *Real Genius*, Tri-Star, 1985; director, *Plain Clothes* (also known as *Glory Days*), Paramount, 1988. Also producer and director, *David: Off and On* (documentary), 1972; producer and director, *More Than a School* (documentary), 1973; producer and director, *Passing Quietly Through* (documentary); producer and director, *The Friendly* (short film); producer and director, *Bimbo* (short film).

PRINCIPAL TELEVISION WORK—Series: Producer, *Magic Tom*, 1968. Pilots: Director, *Sledge Hammer!*, ABC, 1987; director, *Roughhouse* (also known as "House and Home"; broadcast as an episode of *CBS Summer Playhouse*), CBS, 1988. Episodic: Director, *The Twilight Zone*, CBS, 1985.

RELATED CAREER—As an American Film Institute Academy intern, worked with director Robert Wise on *Audrey Rose*, United Artists, 1977; also co-founder, Association of Independent Video and Filmmakers Inc.; directed and appeared in the student film *Mondo Linoleum;* worked on television commercials and political documentaries; creator of an experimental video for Toyota.

WRITINGS: FILM—*David: Off and On*, 1972; *More Than a School*, 1973; *Old Fashioned Woman*, Films Inc., 1974; *Not a Pretty Picture*, Other Cinema Ltd., 1976; *The City Girl*, Moon, 1984; and *Passing Quietly Through*. TELEVISION—Series: *Magic Tom*, 1968.

AWARDS: American Film Festival Eagle Award for *David: Off and On;* CINE Golden Eagle Award for *Old Fashioned Woman;* American Film Festival Blue Ribbon Award for *Not a Pretty Picture.**

*   *   *

COOPER, Jackie   1922-

PERSONAL: Full name, John Cooper, Jr.; born September 15, 1922, in Los Angeles, CA; son of Jack Cooper (an actor); married June Horne (marriage ended); married Hildy Parks (an actress; divorced, 1951); married Barbara Kraus (an advertising executive), 1954; children: John (first marriage); Russell, Julie, Christina (third marriage). EDUCATION—Attended the University of Notre Dame. MILITARY—U.S. Navy, captain, World War II; U.S. Naval Reserve.

VOCATION: Actor, director, and producer.

CAREER: PRINCIPAL STAGE APPEARANCES—Andy Hamill, *Magnolia Alley*, Mansfield Theatre, New York City, 1949; Waldo Walton, *Remains to Be Seen*, Morosco Theatre, New York City, 1951; also appeared as Ensign Pulver, *Mr. Roberts*, London, 1951; and in *King of Hearts*, Lyceum Theatre, New York City, 1955.

JACKIE COOPER

MAJOR TOURS—Ensign Pulver, *Mr. Roberts*, U.S. cities, 1949-50.

FILM DEBUT—In a Lloyd Hamilton comedy, Educational, 1925. PRINCIPAL FILM APPEARANCES—Tenement boy, *Sunny Side Up*, Twentieth Century-Fox, 1929; Dink, *The Champ*, Metro-Goldwyn-Mayer (MGM), 1931; Skippy Skinner, *Skippy*, Paramount, 1931; Skippy Skinner, *Sooky*, Paramount, 1931; Midge Murray, *Young Donovan's Kid* (also known as *Donovan's Kid*), RKO, 1931; as himself, *Jackie Cooper's Christmas Party* (short film), MGM, 1931; Terry Parker, *Divorce in the Family*, MGM, 1932; Eddie Randall, *Feller Needs a Friend* (also known as *When a Feller Needs a Friend*), Cosmopolitan, 1932; Swipes McGurk, *The Bowery*, Twentieth Century-Fox, 1933; Ted Hackett, Jr. (as a child), *Broadway to Hollywood* (also known as *Ring Up the Curtain*), MGM, 1933; Scooter O'Neal, *Lone Cowboy*, Paramount, 1934; Bill Peck, *Peck's Bad Boy*, Twentieth Century-Fox, 1934; Jim Hawkins, *Treasure Island*, MGM, 1934; title role, *Dinky*, Warner Brothers, 1935; Stubby, *O'Shaughnessy's Boy*, MGM, 1935; "Buck" Murphy, *The Devil Is a Sissy* (also known as *The Devil Takes the Count*), MGM, 1936; Freddie, *Tough Guy*, MGM, 1936; Chuck, *Boy of the Streets*, Monogram, 1937; Larry Kelly, *Gangster's Boy*, Monogram, 1938; Ken, *That Certain Age*, Universal, 1938; Peter Trimble, *White Banners*, Warner Brothers, 1938; Timmy Hutchins, *The Big Guy*, Universal, 1939; "Rifle" Edwards, *Newsboy's Home*, Universal, 1939; Tom Allen, *The Spirit of Culver* (also known as *Man's Heritage*), Universal, 1939; Jimmy, *Streets of New York*, Monogram, 1939; Roy O'Donnell, *Two Bright Boys*, Universal, 1939; Henry Aldrich, *What a Life*, Paramount, 1939.

Byron "By" Newbold, *Gallant Sons*, MGM, 1940; Clem and Tom

Grayson, *The Return of Frank James*, Twentieth Century-Fox, 1940; William Sylvanus Baxter, *Seventeen*, Paramount, 1940; Tiny Barlow, *Glamour Boy* (also known as *Hearts in Springtime*), Paramount, 1941; Chuck Harris, *Her First Beau*, Columbia, 1941; Henry Aldrich, *Life with Henry*, Paramount, 1941; Jerry Regan, *Ziegfeld Girl*, MGM, 1941; Robert Houston Scott, *Men of Texas* (also known as *Men of Destiny*), Universal, 1942; Babe, *The Navy Comes Through*, RKO, 1942; Johnnie, *Syncopation*, RKO, 1942; Danny, *Where Are Your Children?*, Monogram, 1943; John J. Kilroy, *Kilroy Was Here*, Monogram, 1947; Ernie, *Stork Bites Man*, Universal, 1947; Skitch, *French Leave* (also known as *Kilroy on Deck*), Monogram, 1948; Lieutenant Parnell, *Everything's Ducky*, Columbia, 1961; Danton Miller, *The Love Machine*, Columbia, 1971; Raymond Couzins, *Chosen Survivors*, Columbia, 1974; Perry White, *Superman*, Warner Brothers, 1978; Perry White, *Superman II*, Warner Brothers, 1980; Perry White, *Superman III*, Warner Brothers, 1983; Perry White, *Superman IV: The Quest for Peace*, Warner Brothers, 1987; Ace Morgan, *Surrender*, Warner Brothers, 1987. Also appeared in *Fox Movietone Follies of '29*, Twentieth Century-Fox, 1929; *Scouts to the Rescue* (twelve part serial), 1939; *Going Hollywood: The War Years* (documentary), 1988.

Appeared in the following Our Gang (also know as the Little Rascals) short comedy films: *Boxing Gloves, Bouncing Babies, Moan and Groan Inc.*, and *Shivering Shakespeare*, all MGM, 1929; *The First Seven Years, When the Wind Blows, Bear Shooters, A Tough Winter, Pups Is Pups, Teacher's Pet*, and *School's Out*, all MGM, 1930; *Helping Grandma, Love Business, Little Daddy*, and *Bargain Day*, all MGM, 1931.

PRINCIPAL FILM WORK—Director, *Stand Up and Be Counted*, Columbia, 1972; also director, *Go for the Gold*, 1984.

PRINCIPAL TELEVISION APPEARANCES—Series: Socrates "Sock" Miller, *The People's Choice*, CBS, 1955-58; Charles J. "Chick" Hennessey, *Hennessey*, CBS, 1959-62; host, *The Dean Martin Comedy World*, NBC, 1974; Peter Campbell, *Mobile One*, ABC, 1975. Pilots: Host, *What's Up?*, NBC, 1971; the Widower, "Hot Machine, Cold Machine" in *Of Men Of Women*, ABC, 1972; Father, *Keeping an Eye on Denise*, CBS, 1973; Dr. Dan Morgan, *Doctor Dan*, CBS, 1974; Walter Carlson, *The Invisible Man*, NBC, 1975; Peter Campbell, *Mobile Two*, ABC, 1975; Admiral, *Operation Petticoat* (also known as *Life in the Pink*), ABC, 1977.

Episodic: Jonathan West, "Caesar and Me," *The Twilight Zone*, CBS, 1964; Neil Fletcher, *Murder, She Wrote*, CBS, 1986; Dr. Domedion, *St. Elsewhere*, NBC, 1986; also "The Invisible Killer," *Suspense*, CBS, 1952; "The Cocoon," *Tales of Tomorrow*, ABC, 1952; "Life, Liberty, and Orrin Dooley" and "A Message for Janice," *Lux Video Theatre*, NBC, 1952; "The Fall Guy," *Robert Montgomery Presents Your Lucky Strike Theatre*, NBC, 1952; "Something Old, Something New," *Ford Theatre*, NBC, 1952; "The Outer Limit," *Robert Montgomery Presents Your Lucky Strike Theatre*, NBC, 1953; "Birthright" and "Hound Dog Man," *Studio One*, CBS, 1953; "Big Jim's Boy," *Schlitz Playhouse of Stars*, CBS, 1953; "The Middle Son" and "Tour of Duty," *Armstrong Circle Theatre*, NBC, 1953; "A Reputation," *Revlon Mirror Theatre*, CBS, 1953; "The Diehard," *Kraft Theatre*, NBC, 1953; "Grand'ma Rebel" and "Twenty-Four Men to a Plane," *Medallion Theatre*, CBS, 1953; "Westward the Sun," *Motorola TV Hour*, ABC, 1953; "Towerman," *Danger*, CBS, 1953; "The 39th Bomb," *Medallion Theatre*, syndicated, 1954; "Falling Star," *The Elgin Hour*, ABC, 1954; "Yellow Jack," *Producer's Showcase*, NBC, 1955; "I Found Sixty Million Dol-

lars," *Armstrong Circle Theatre*, NBC, 1955; "A Dreamer of Summer," *Robert Montgomery Presents Your Lucky Strike Theatre*, NBC, 1954; "The Pardon-Me Boy," *Philco Playhouse*, NBC, 1955; "Yankee Peddler," *General Electric Theatre*, CBS, 1955; "It Depends on You," *Robert Montgomery Presents Your Lucky Strike Theatre*, NBC, 1955; "End of Morning" and "Really the Blues," *Robert Montgomery Presents Your Lucky Strike Theatre*, NBC, 1956; "The Old Lady Shows Her Medals," *U.S. Steel Hour*, CBS, 1956; "The Fair-Haired Boy," *Studio One*, CBS, 1958; "The Hasty Heart," *Dupont Show of the Month*, CBS, 1958; "Curtain Call," *Goodyear Theatre*, CBS, 1958; "Mid-Summer," *U.S. Steel Hour*, CBS, 1958; Hayes and Henderson, NBC, 1959; *Mrs. G. Goes to College*, CBS, 1961; "Special Assignment," *The Dick Powell Show*, NBC, 1962; "The Fourposter," *Golden Showcase*, CBS, 1962; "Thunder in a Forgotten Town," *The Dick Powell Show*, NBC, 1963; *Hawaii Five-O*, CBS, 1971; *McCloud*, NBC, 1972; "Cry of the Cat," *Ghost Story*, NBC, 1972; *Ironside*, NBC, 1972, 1973 and 1975; *Columbo*, NBC, 1973; *Hec Ramsay*, NBC, 1974; *Kojak*, CBS, 1974; *Police Story*, NBC, 1974, 1975, and 1976; *The Rockford Files*, NBC, 1975; *Starlight Theatre*, CBS; "The Hunley," *The Great Adventure*, CBS.

Movies: Lieutenant Colonel Andy Davis, *Shadow on the Land*, ABC, 1968; Ed Miller, *Maybe I'll Come Home in the Spring*, ABC, 1971; Kurt Anderson, *The Astronaut*, ABC, 1972; Steve Barker, *The Day the Earth Moved*, ABC, 1974. Specials: Host, *What's Up, America?*, NBC, 1971.

PRINCIPAL TELEVISION WORK—All as director unless indicated. Series: (Also producer) *The People's Choice*, CBS, 1955-58; (with Hy Averback; also producer with Don McGuire and Dan Cooper) *Hennessey*, CBS, 1959-62. Pilots: Producer, *Charlie Angelo*, CBS, 1962; *Keep the Faith*, CBS, 1972; (also producer) *Doctor Dan*, CBS, 1974; *Snafu*, NBC, 1976; *Having Babies III* (also known as *Julie Farr, M.D.*), ABC, 1978; *Paris*, CBS, 1979; *The White Shadow*, CBS, 1979; *Trapper John, M.D.*, CBS, 1979; *Family in Blue*, CBS, 1982; (also producer) *The Ladies*, NBC, 1987; also *The Last Detail*, 1975. Episodic: *M*A*S*H* (thirteen episodes), CBS, 1973-74; *The Mary Tyler Moore Show*, CBS, 1974; *The Texas Wheelers*, ABC, 1974; *The Rockford Files*, NBC, 1974-75; *Mobile One*, ABC, 1975; (also producer) *Holmes and YoYo*, ABC, 1976; *McMillan*, NBC, 1977; *The Feather and Father Gang*, ABC, 1977; *The Black Sheep Squadron*, NBC, 1977-78; *Lou Grant*, CBS, 1977-82; *The White Shadow*, CBS, 1979; *Glitter*, ABC, 1984; *Jessie*, ABC, 1984; "The Deacon Street Deer," *Disney Sunday Movie*, ABC, 1986; *Sledge Hammer!*, ABC, 1986 and 1987; *The Law and Harry McGraw*, CBS, 1987; *Magnum, P.I.*, CBS, 1987; *Mr. President*, Fox, 1987; *Spies*, CBS, 1987; *Ohara*, ABC, 1987; *Cagney and Lacey*, CBS, 1987 and 1988; *Simon and Simon*, CBS, 1988; *Supercarrier*, ABC, 1988; *Superboy*, syndicated, 1988; *Jake and the Fatman*, CBS, 1988; also *Quincy, M.E.*, NBC.

Movies: (Also producer) *Perfect Gentlemen*, CBS, 1978; *Rainbow*, NBC, 1978; *Sex and the Single Parent*, CBS, 1979; *White Mama*, CBS, 1980; *Rodeo Girl*, CBS, 1980; *Marathon*, CBS, 1980; *Leave 'em Laughing*, CBS, 1981; (also producer) *Rosie: The Rosemary Clooney Story*, CBS, 1982; *The Night They Saved Christmas*, ABC, 1984; *Izzy and Moe*, CBS, 1985; also *Uncommon Courage*. Specials: Producer (with Bob Finkel) of Bing Crosby and Perry Como specials, 1970-72.

RELATED CAREER—Vice-president in charge of television program production, Columbia Pictures Corporation, 1964-69; founder (with Bob Finkel), producer, and director, Cooper-Finkel

Company, 1969-73; also board of directors, Cinema Circulus, University of Southern California.

WRITINGS: (With Dick Kliener) *Please Don't Shoot My Dog* (autobiography), William Morrow, 1981.

AWARDS: Academy Award nomination, Best Actor, 1931, for *Skippy;* Emmy Award, Best Comedy Director, 1974, for *M*A*S*H;* Emmy Award, Best Dramatic Director, 1979, for pilot episode of *The White Shadow;* Film Advisory Board Awards as producer and director, 1982, for *Rosie: The Rosemary Clooney Story;* two Emmy Award nominations as Best Actor, special citation from the American Medical Association, and Public Service Medal from the United States Navy, all for *Hennessey.* Also received awards from the Academy of Motion Picture Arts and Sciences, Directors Guild of America, Writers Guild of America, Caucus for Writers, Producers, and Directors, Hollywood Radio and Television Society, American Center of Films for Children, United Funds and Community Chest, March of Dimes, American Academy of General Practice, Cinema Circulus, University of California at Los Angeles, University of Southern California, Special Olympics, International Motor Sports of America, and the Center for Improvement of Child Caring. MILITARY HONORS—Honorary Naval Aviator Wings of Gold award, 1970; Commendation Medal with citation and the Legion of Merit with citation upon retirement from the U.S. Naval Reserve, 1974; also received awards from the Pearl Harbor Survivors Association, U.S. Navy Recruiting Service, Navy League, Association of Naval Aviation, Society of Experimental Test Pilots, and the Combat Pilots Association.

MEMBER: Screen Actors Guild, American Federation of Television and Radio Artists, American Federation of Musicians, Directors Guild of America (council member and member of the national board of directors), Cinema Circulus (board of directors), Naval Aviation Society, Naval Reserve Association, Aircraft Owners and Pilots Association, VIVA to return Missing In Action Prisoners of War from Vietnam (charter member), Sports Car Club of America (former member).

SIDELIGHTS: RECREATIONS—Racing sports cars, playing the drums, skeet shooting, piloting, sailing, and cooking.

ADDRESSES: OFFICE—David Licht Associates, 9171 Wilshire Boulevard, Beverly Hills, CA 90210. AGENT—Creative Artists Agency, 9830 Wilshire Boulevard, Beverly Hills, CA 90212.*

*   *   *

COREY, Jeff   1914-

PERSONAL: Born August 10, 1914, in New York, NY; son of Nathan and Mary (Peskin) Corey; married Hope Victorson, February 26, 1938; children: Eve, Jane, Emily. EDUCATION—University of California, Los Angeles, B.A., theatre arts, 1955; trained for the stage at the Feagin School of Dramatic Art, 1930-32. MILITARY—U.S. Navy, combat photographer, 1943-45.

VOCATION: Actor, director, and teacher.

CAREER: PRINCIPAL STAGE APPEARANCES—Rosencrantz, *Hamlet,* Imperial Theatre, New York City, 1936; title role, *King Lear,* Theatre Venture '73, Beverly, MA, 1973. Also appeared in *The Life and Death of an American,* Maxine Elliott's Theatre, New

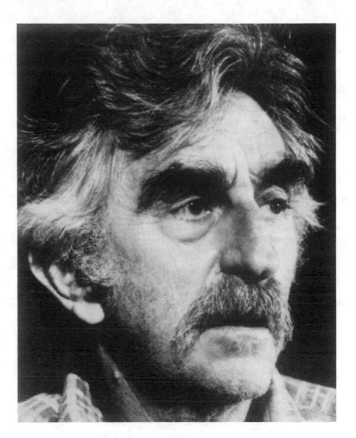

JEFF COREY

York City, 1939; *In the Matter of J. Robert Oppenheimer,* Center Theatre Group, Mark Taper Forum, Los Angeles, 1968; *Hamlet,* Center Theatre Group, Mark Taper Forum, 1973; and with the Stage Society Theatre, Los Angeles.

PRINCIPAL FILM APPEARANCES—Johann, *Third Finger, Left Hand,* Metro-Goldwyn-Mayer (MGM), 1940; Tom Sharp, *The Devil and Daniel Webster* (also known as *All That Money Can Buy, Here Is a Man,* and *A Certain Mr. Scratch*), RKO, 1941; secretary, *Paris Calling,* Universal, 1941; Henry Trotter, *Petticoat Politics,* Republic, 1941; an animator, *The Reluctant Dragon* (live-action/animated), RKO, 1941; Hector, *Small Town Deb,* Twentieth Century-Fox, 1941; Mr. Mooney, *Girl Trouble,* Twentieth Century-Fox, 1942; Coroner Larson, *The Man Who Wouldn't Die,* Twentieth Century-Fox, 1942; man, *North to the Klondike,* Universal, 1942; Harwood Green, *The Postman Didn't Ring,* Twentieth Century-Fox, 1942; orderly, *Roxie Hart,* Twentieth Century-Fox, 1942; Albert, *The Moon Is Down,* Twentieth Century-Fox, 1943; Tim Murphy, *My Friend Flicka,* Twentieth Century-Fox, 1943; man, *California,* Paramount, 1946; Sam Black, *It Shouldn't Happen to a Dog,* Twentieth Century-Fox, 1946; Blinky, *The Killers,* Universal, 1946; bank teller, *Somewhere in the Night,* Twentieth Century-Fox, 1946; freshman, *Brute Force,* Universal, 1947; brother-in-law, *The Gangster,* Allied Artists, 1947; Jed, *Hoppy's Holiday,* United Artists, 1947; reporter, *Miracle on 34th Street* (also known as *The Big Heart*), Twentieth Century-Fox, 1947; Bice, *Ramrod,* United Artists, 1947; Zu, *Alias a Gentleman,* MGM, 1948; Schwartzmiller, *Canon City,* Eagle-Lion, 1948; stranger, *The Flame,* Republic, 1948; cigarette smoker, *Homecoming,* MGM, 1948; immigration officer, *I, Jane Doe* (also known as *Diary of a Bride*), Republic, 1948; prison guard, *Joan of Arc,* RKO,

1948; Shuan, *Kidnapped,* Monogram, 1948; Union cavalry sergeant, *A Southern Yankee* (also known as *My Hero!*), MGM, 1948; Mohammad Jad, *Bagdad,* Universal, 1949; Lieutenant Macon, *City Across the River,* Universal, 1949; Collins, *Follow Me Quietly,* RKO, 1949; Beecham, *Hideout,* Republic, 1949; doctor, *Home of the Brave,* United Artists, 1949; Jed Graham, *Roughshod,* RKO, 1949; Mr. Loring, *Wake of the Red Witch,* Republic, 1949.

John Barton, *Bright Leaf,* Warner Brothers, 1950; Bart, *The Nevadan* (also known as *The Man from Nevada*), Columbia, 1950; Freddie, *The Next Voice You Hear,* MGM, 1950; Keeley, *The Outriders,* MGM, 1950; Abe Lincoln, *Rock Island Trail* (also known as *Transcontinent Express*), Republic, 1950; Richards, *Singing Guns,* Republic, 1950; Sergeant Farley, *Fourteen Hours,* Twentieth Century-Fox, 1951; Lou Brecker, *Never Trust a Gambler,* Columbia, 1951; Coyote, *New Mexico,* United Artists, 1951; Joe Harmony, *Only the Valiant,* Warner Brothers, 1951; Mokar, *The Prince Who Was a Thief,* Universal, 1951; Luke Davis, *Rawhide* (also known as *Desperate Siege*), Twentieth Century-Fox, 1951; Skee, *Red Mountain,* Paramount, 1951; Luke Benson, *Superman and the Mole Men* (also known as *Superman and the Strange People*), Lippert, 1951; Bishop, *The Balcony,* Continental, 1963; Joe, *The Yellow Canary,* Twentieth Century-Fox, 1963; the wino, *Lady in a Cage,* Paramount, 1964; Hoban, *The Cincinnati Kid,* MGM, 1965; Fryer, *Mickey One,* Columbia, 1965; Lieutenant Kebner, *Once a Thief,* MGM, 1965; Mr. Ruby, *Seconds,* Paramount, 1966; Hickock's father, *In Cold Blood,* Columbia, 1967; John Asgeirsson, *The Boston Strangler,* Twentieth Century-Fox, 1968; Sheriff Bledsoe, *Butch Cassidy and the Sundance Kid,* Twentieth Century-Fox, 1969; Wombat, *Impasse,* United Artists, 1969; Tom Chaney, *True Grit,* Paramount, 1969.

Caspay, *Beneath the Planet of the Apes,* Twentieth Century-Fox, 1970; Paul, *Cover Me Babe,* Twentieth Century-Fox, 1970; Dr. Willhunt, *Getting Straight,* Columbia, 1970; Wild Bill Hickok, *Little Big Man,* National General, 1970; Captain Marden, *They Call Me Mister Tibbs!,* United Artists, 1970; Merridew, *Catlow,* MGM, 1971; clinic doctor, *Clay Pigeon* (also known as *Trip to Kill*), MGM, 1971; trooper, *Shoot Out,* Universal, 1971; Mr. King, *Paper Tiger,* MacLean, 1975; doctor, *The Last Tycoon,* Paramount, 1976; Detective Mark Denver, *The Premonition,* AVCO-Embassy, 1976; Preacher Hagen, *Moonshine County Express,* New World, 1977; Rabbi Silverstein, *Oh, God!,* Warner Brothers, 1977; Luke Baylor, *Jennifer* (also known as *Jennifer, The Snake Goddess*), American International, 1978; Mr. Martin, *The Wild Geese,* Allied Artists, 1978; Ray Bledsoe, *Butch and Sundance: The Early Days,* Twentieth Century-Fox, 1979; Zed, *Battle Beyond the Stars,* New World, 1980; Craccus, *The Sword and the Sorcerer,* Group 1, 1982; Grand Vizier, *Conan the Destroyer,* Universal, 1984; Dean Harrington, *Creator,* Universal, 1985; Willis Beecham, *Messenger of Death,* Cannon, 1988. Also appeared in *You Belong to Me* (also known as *Good Morning Doctor*), Columbia, 1941; *Frankenstein Meets the Wolf Man,* Universal, 1943; *Unconquered,* Paramount, 1947; *Let's Live Again,* Twentieth Century-Fox, 1948; *The Wreck of the Hesperus,* 1948; narrator, *Black Shadows,* 1949; *Up River,* 1979; *Bird on a Wire,* Universal, 1990; *High Flying Lowe; Shine; Rooster; Secret Ingredient; Syncopation; The Golden Bullet; Land of the Free; Delicatessen;* and *The Judas Project.*

PRINCIPAL TELEVISION APPEARANCES—Series: Regular, *The Richard Pryor Show,* NBC, 1977; Lawyer Sam, *Hell Town,* NBC, 1985; Bill McGregor, *Morningstar/Eveningstar,* CBS, 1986. Mini-Series: William Simpson, *Testimony of Two Men,* syndicated, 1977. Pilots: Beiseker, *A Clear and Present Danger,* NBC, 1970; Captain Philip Lean, *The Fuzz Brothers,* ABC, 1973; head of

posse, *The Gun and the Pulpit,* ABC, 1974; Judge Janeway, *Banjo Hackett: Roamin' Free,* NBC, 1976; Dean Miller, *The Oath: The Sad and Lonely Sundays,* ABC, 1976; Alex Hagopian, *Roxy Page,* NBC, 1976. Episodic: Byron Lomax, "O.B.I.T.," *The Outer Limits,* ABC, 1963; Plasus, "The Cloudminders," *Star Trek,* NBC, 1969; A.J. Bancroft, *The A-Team,* NBC, 1986; Judge Robert Hirsch, *Night Court,* NBC, 1986; Hal Walker, *Starman,* ABC, 1986; Mr. Casselman, *Perfect Strangers,* ABC, 1987; Judge Ralph Colella, *Jake and the Fat Man,* CBS, 1989; salesman, *Roseanne,* ABC, 1989; Vincenzo, *Wolf,* CBS, 1989; also *The Untouchables,* ABC, 1960; "The Dead Man," *Night Gallery,* NBC, 1970; *The Bob Newhart Show,* CBS, 1973; *Barney Miller,* ABC, 1978 and 1979; *The Powers of Matthew Star,* NBC, 1982; "The Boy Who Left Home to Find Out About the Shivers," *Faerie Tale Theatre,* Showtime; Mr. Romano, *One Day At a Time,* CBS; *War of the Worlds,* syndicated; *Channing,* ABC; *The Doctors and the Nurses,* CBS; *Perry Mason,* CBS; *Gomer Pyle, U.S.M.C.,* CBS; *The Wild, Wild West,* CBS; *Run for Your Life,* NBC; *Bonanza,* NBC; *The Iron Horse,* ABC; *Judd, for the Defense,* ABC; *Garrison's Gorillas,* ABC; *Gunsmoke,* CBS; *Hawaii Five-0,* CBS; *The Bionic Woman,* ABC; *Today's F.B.I.,* ABC; *Knots Landing,* CBS; *Archie Bunker's Place,* CBS; *The New Love, American Style,* ABC; *Kojak,* CBS; *McCloud,* NBC; *Beauty and the Beast,* CBS.

Movies: Collier Landis, *The Movie Murderer,* NBC, 1970; Gehrmann, *Something Evil,* CBS, 1972; Walter Stafford, *Set This Town on Fire,* NBC, 1973; Salters, *Captains Courageous,* ABC, 1977; Aspa Soldado, *Curse of the Black Widow* (also known as *Love Trap*), ABC, 1977; Prince Feiyad, *Harold Robbins' "The Pirate,"* CBS, 1978; George, *Homeward Bound,* CBS, 1980; Riley, *Cry for the Strangers,* CBS, 1982; Lawyer Sam, *Father of Hell Town,* NBC, 1985; derelict, *Final Jeopardy,* NBC, 1985; Dr. Benjamin, *Second Serve,* CBS, 1986; Justice Harvey Sherman, *A Deadly Silence,* ABC, 1989.

FIRST TELEVISION WORK—Director, *The Psychiatrist,* NBC, 1971. PRINCIPAL TELEVISION WORK—All as director. Series: *Hawkins,* CBS, 1973-74. Episodic: *Night Gallery,* NBC, 1970-72 (ten episodes); *The Sixth Sense,* ABC, 1972; also *Police Story,* NBC; *Alias Smith and Jones,* ABC; *Meeting of Minds,* PBS.

RELATED CAREER—Instructor and director of independent actors' workshops, 1950s—; drama professor, California State University, Northridge, 1966-71; drama professor, Chapman College's World Campus Afloat, 1973; drama teacher, the Stage Society, Los Angeles; creative drama workshop founder, Los Angeles Juvenile Hall; lecturer, University of Texas, Ball State University, and University of Southern California; board of directors, Ojai Music Festivals Inc.; faculty member, American Film Institute for Advanced Film Studies.

NON-RELATED CAREER—Sewing machine salesman and speech therapist.

WRITINGS: (Contributor) *Closeups,* Workman Press.

AWARDS: MILITARY HONORS—Citation from the U.S. Navy, 1945.

MEMBER: Academy of Motion Picture Arts and Sciences (actors' executive committee, 1970—), Screen Actors Guild (board of directors), Directors Guild of America, Actors' Equity Association.

ADDRESSES: AGENT—Bauman, Hiller, and Associates, 5750 Wilshire Boulevard, Suite 512, Los Angeles, CA 90038.

COSGRAVE, Peggy

PERSONAL: Born June 23, in San Mateo, CA; daughter of John (in real estate) and Beryl Marie (a secretary; maiden name, Seeley) Cosgrave. EDUCATION—Received B.A. in drama from San Jose State College; also attended Catholic University. RELIGION—Roman Catholic.

VOCATION: Actress.

CAREER: STAGE DEBUT—Cathleen, *Long Day's Journey into Night,* Hartke Theatre, Washington, DC, 1971. OFF-BROADWAY DEBUT—Stella Mae, *Come Back to the Five and Dime, Jimmy Dean, Jimmy Dean,* Hudson Guild Theatre, 1980. BROADWAY DEBUT—Clelia Waldgrave, *The Nerd,* Helen Hayes Theatre, 1987, for 190 performances. PRINCIPAL STAGE APPEARANCES—Saunders, *Fallen Angels,* Paper Mill Playhouse, Millburn, NJ, 1977; Hannah Mae, *A Coupla White Chicks Sitting Around Talking,* Cincinnati Playhouse-in-the-Park, Cincinnati, OH, 1982; Jane, *Fallen Angels,* Coconut Grove Playhouse, Coconut Grove, FL, 1982; Zelda Spearman, *Fugue,* Long Wharf Theatre, New Haven, CT, 1986; Mrs. Hedges, *Born Yesterday,* 46th Street Theatre, New York City, 1989. Also appeared in *Straight Up* and *The Importance of Being Earnest,* both PAF Playhouse, Huntington Station, NY, 1975; *Sally's Gone, She Left Her Name,* Center Stage, Baltimore, MD, 1980; *Holiday,* Long Wharf Theatre, 1982; as Charlotte Wallace, *Beyond Therapy,* Berkshire Theatre Festival, Stockbridge, MA; Chick, *Crimes of the Heart;* Lorraine Sheldon, *The Man Who Came to Dinner;* Jessie, *'night Mother;* Mrs. West, *Member of the Wedding;* Aggie, *Love Gifts;* Reba Speldine, *A Visit to a Small Planet;* Eunice Hubble, *A Streetcar Named Desire.*

MAJOR TOURS—Hilary, *Tribute,* U.S. cities, 1980; Hannah Mae, *A Coupla White Chicks Sitting Around Talking,* U.S. cities, 1982; also Cathleen, *Long Day's Journey into Night,* U.S. cities; Rosemary, *Eccentricities of a Nightingale,* U.S. cities; Mae, *Cat on a Hot Tin Roof,* U.S. cities; Kitty, *The Royal Family,* U.S. cities; Saunders, *Fallen Angels,* U.S. cities; Blanche, *Romantic Comedy,* U.S. cities; Florrie, *Supporting Cast,* U.S. cities; Maxine and Megan, *84 Charing Cross Road,* U.S. cities; and *The Dining Room,* U.S. cities.

PRINCIPAL FILM APPEARANCES—Ticket agent, *Penn and Teller Get Killed,* Warner Brothers, 1989.

RELATED CAREER—Company member: Tyrone Guthrie Theatre, Minneapolis, MN, 1971-72; Seattle Repertory Theatre, Seattle, WA; Indiana Repertory Theatre, Indianapolis, IN; Manitoba Theatre Center, Winnipeg, MB, Canada; Bucks County Playhouse, New Hope, PA, Cleveland Playhouse, Cleveland, OH.

NON-RELATED CAREER—Volunteer, Project Hope.

AWARDS: Hartke Awards, 1969 and 1970; Helen Hayes Award nomination, Best Supporting Actress, 1986, for *Crimes of the Heart.*

MEMBER: Actors' Equity Association, American Federation of Television and Radio Artists, Screen Actors Guild, Canadian Actors' Equity Association.

SIDELIGHTS: FAVORITE ROLES—Chick in *Crimes of the Heart,* Stella Mae in *Come Back to the Five and Dime, Jimmy Dean, Jimmy Dean,* Charlotte Wallace in *Beyond Therapy,* and Cathleen in *Long Day's Journey into Night.*

Among her other credits, Peggy Cosgrave also provided the voiceover narration for the ABC-TV network's soap opera update, *Sneak Preview.*

ADDRESSES: AGENTS—Kenny Kaplan and David Kolander, Agency for the Performing Arts, 888 Seventh Avenue, New York, NY 10019.

*   *   *

PEGGY COSGRAVE

COULOURIS, George   1903-1989

PERSONAL: Born October 1, 1903, in Manchester, England; died of a heart attack, April 25, 1989, in London, England; son of Nicholas (a merchant) and Abigail (Redfern) Coulouris; married Louise Franklin (died, 1976); married Elizabeth Clarke; children: George, Mary Louise (first marriage). EDUCATION—Studied for the stage at the Central School of Speech Training and Dramatic Art.

VOCATION: Actor.

CAREER: STAGE DEBUT—Reverend William Duke, *Outward Bound,* Rusholme Repertory Theatre, Manchester, U.K., 1926. LONDON DEBUT—Sir Thomas Grey, *Henry V,* Old Vic Theatre, 1926. BROADWAY DEBUT—Friar Peter, *The Novice and the Duke,*

Assembly Theatre, 1929. PRINCIPAL STAGE APPEARANCES—Giuseppe, *Sirocco*, Daly's Theatre, London, 1927; Yank, *The Hairy Ape*, Mercutio, *Romeo and Juliet*, and Jacques, *As You Like It*, all Cambridge Festival Theatre, Cambridge, U.K., 1928; Petronius, *The Theatre of Life*, Arts Theatre, London, 1929; Jacques Bonalie, *The Black Ace*, Globe Theatre, London, 1929; Sempronius, *The Apple Cart*, Martin Beck Theatre, New York City, 1930; Tybalt, *Romeo and Juliet*, Embassy Theatre, London, 1932; the Bank Manager, *From Morn to Midnight*, Gate Theatre, London, 1932; Tallant, *The Late Christopher Bean*, Henry Miller's Theatre, New York City, 1932; Julian Mosca, *Best Sellers*, Morosco Theatre, New York City, 1933; Lord Burleigh, *Mary of Scotland*, Alvin Theatre, New York City, 1933; Lieutenant Cutting, *Valley Forge*, Guild Theatre, New York City, 1934; Dr. Shelby, *Blind Alley*, Booth Theatre, New York City, 1935; John de Stogumber, *Saint Joan*, Martin Beck Theatre, New York City, 1936; Zacharey, *Ten Million Ghosts*, St. James Theatre, New York City, 1936; Marc Antony, *Julius Caesar*, Mercury Theatre, New York City, 1937; the King, *The Shoemaker's Holiday* and Boss Mangan, *Heartbreak House*, both Mercury Theatre, 1938; Mirabeau, *Madame Capet*, Cort Theatre, New York City, 1938; Father Shaughnessy, *The White Steed*, Cort Theatre, 1939.

John Elliott, *Cue for Passion*, Royale Theatre, New York City, 1940; Teck de Brancovis, *Watch on the Rhine*, Martin Beck Theatre, 1941; title role, *Richard III*, Forrest Theatre, New York City, 1943; Waldo Cruikshank, *Bonanza Bound*, Shubert Theatre, Philadelphia, PA, 1947-48; Subtle, *The Alchemist*, the Donkey Man, *The Moon of the Caribbees*, and the Vagrant, *The Insect Comedy (or The World We Live In)*, all City Center Theatre, New York City, 1948; Jacques, *As You Like It*, title role, *Tartuffe*, Brutus, *Julius Caesar*, and Sir John Brute, *The Provok'd Wife*, all Bristol Old Vic Company, Bristol, U.K., 1950; title role, *Tartuffe*, Bristol Old Vic Company, Lyric Hammersmith Theatre, London, 1950; Ulric Brendel, *Rosmersholm*, St. Martin's Theatre, London, 1950; title role, *King Lear*, Glasgow Citizens' Theatre, Glasgow, Scotland, 1952; King James I, *Fool's Mate*, Under Thirty Group, Criterion Theatre, London, 1953; Clumber Holmes, *The Full Treatment*, Q Theatre, London, 1953; Malvolio, *Twelfth Night* and Claudius, *Hamlet*, both Embassy Theatre, 1953; Smiley Coy, *The Big Knife*, Duke of York's Theatre, London, 1954; Paul Finch, *The Ghost Writers*, Arts Theatre, London, 1955; Charles Touchdown, *Moonshine*, Q Theatre, 1955; Hawkshaw, *The Ticket-of-Leave Man*, Arts Theatre, Cambridge, U.K., 1956; John Pope, Sr., *A Hatful of Rain*, Princes' Theatre, London, 1957, then 1958; Dr. Stockmann, *An Enemy of the People*, Arts Theatre, Cambridge, 1959.

Squeezum, *Lock Up Your Daughters* and Peter Flynn, *The Plough and the Stars*, both Mermaid Theatre, London, 1962; performed in scenes from *Tartuffe* and *The Way of the World*, Georgian Theatre, Richmond, U.K., 1963; Shylock, *The Merchant of Venice*, Flora Robson Theatre, Newcastle-on-Tyne, U.K., 1963; Sir Samuel Holt, *Beekman Place*, Morosco Theatre, 1964; Father, *The Condemned of Altona*, Repertory Theatre of Lincoln Center, Vivian Beaumont Theatre, New York City, 1966; Voltaire, *The Sorrows of Frederick*, Mark Taper Forum, Los Angeles, 1967; Earl of Theign, *The Outcry*, Arts Theatre, London, 1968; Sikorski, *Soldiers*, New Theatre, London, 1968; Philip Bummidge, *The Last Analysis*, Theatre Royal, Derby, U.K., 1970; Big Daddy, *Cat on a Hot Tin Roof*, Richmond Theatre, London, 1970; Shylock, *The Merchant of Venice*, Gardner Arts Theatre, Brighton, U.K., 1973; title role, *King Lear*, Globe Playhouse, Los Angeles, 1977. Also appeared in *The Admirable Crichton*, Bristol Old Vic Company, 1950; *The Man*

in the Overcoat, Edinburgh Festival, Edinburgh, Scotland, 1950; and in stock companies, 1930-32.

PRINCIPAL STAGE WORK—Producer and director, *Richard III*, Forrest Theatre, New York City, 1943.

MAJOR TOURS—Teck de Brancovis, *Watch on the Rhine*, U.S. cities, 1941-42; Dr. Shelby, *Blind Alley*, U.S. cities, 1946-47; Smiley Coy, *The Big Knife*, U.K. cities, 1953; the General, *The Soldier and the Lady*, U.K. cities, 1954.

FILM DEBUT—Tallant, *Christopher Bean* (also known as *Her Sweetheart*), Metro-Goldwyn-Mayer, 1933. PRINCIPAL FILM APPEARANCES—Defense attorney, *The Lady in Question* (also known as *It Happened in Paris*), Columbia, 1940; Charpentier, *All This and Heaven Too*, Warner Brothers, 1940; Walter Parks Thatcher, *Citizen Kane*, RKO, 1941; Captain Holz, *Assignment in Brittany*, Metro-Goldwyn-Mayer (MGM), 1943; Andre, *For Whom the Bell Tolls*, Paramount, 1943; prosecuting attorney, *This Land Is Mine*, RKO, 1943; Teck de Brancovis, *Watch on the Rhine*, Warner Brothers, 1943; Lingley, *Between Two Worlds*, Warner Brothers, 1944; Von Beck, *The Master Race*, RKO, 1944; Dr. Byles, *Mr. Skeffington*, Warner Brothers, 1944; Jim Mordiney, *None But the Lonely Heart*, RKO, 1944; Captain Currie, *Confidential Agent*, Warner Brothers, 1945; Joachim Helm, *Hotel Berlin*, Warner Brothers, 1945; Mr. Saunders, *Lady on a Train*, Universal, 1945; Louis Pleyel, *A Song to Remember*, Columbia, 1945; Pharoah, *California*, Paramount, 1946; James Randolph, *Mr. District Attorney*, Columbia, 1946; Doc Ganson, *Nobody Lives Forever*, Warner Brothers, 1946; Superintendent Buckley, *The Verdict*, Warner Brothers, 1946; Krivoc, *Where There's Life*, Paramount, 1947; Lew Proctor, *Beyond Glory*, Paramount, 1948; Sir Robert D. Baudricort, *Joan of Arc*, RKO, 1948; Charles Vernay, *Sleep, My Love*, United Artists, 1948; Major Jack Drumman, *A Southern Yankee* (also known as *My Hero*), MGM, 1948.

Victor Sloma, *Kill or Be Killed*, Eagle-Lion, 1950; Captain Weiss, *Island Rescue* (also known as *Appointment with Venus*), Universal, 1952; Babalatchi, *An Outcast of the Islands*, British Lion, 1952; Spadoni, *The Assassin*, United Artists, 1953; the Captain, *A Day to Remember*, General Film Distributors, 1953; Briggs, *Doctor in the House*, General Film Distributors, 1954; Captain Malburn, *Duel in the Jungle*, Warner Brothers, 1954; Portuguese captain, *The Heart of the Matter*, Associated Artists, 1954; Edward Schroeder, *The Runaway Bus*, Eros, 1954; Carpenter, *Doctor at Sea*, Rank, 1955; Dallapiccola, *A Race for Life* (also known as *Handful of Dusk*), Lippert, 1955; Garvin, *The Teckman Mystery*, Associated Artists, 1955; Padre, *Private's Progress*, British Lion, 1956; Pascoe, *Doctor at Large*, Rank, 1957; Karl Brussard, *The Man Without a Body*, Eros, 1957; Carl Kraski, *Tarzan and the Lost Safari*, MGM, 1957; Colonel Sandherr, *I Accuse!*, MGM, 1958; Heinz Webber, *Kill Me Tomorrow*, Ren-Tudor, 1958; Bennie, *Law and Disorder*, RKO, 1958; Colonel Benedict, *Spy in the Sky*, Allied Artists, 1958; Commandant, *Tank Force* (also known as *No Time to Die*), Columbia, 1958; Bourdin, *The Beasts of Marseilles* (also known as *Seven Thunders*), R.F.D. Productions, 1959; Alan A. Dale, *Son of Robin Hood*, Twentieth Century-Fox, 1959; Dr. James Moran, *The Woman Eater*, Columbia, 1959.

Lacoste, *Bluebeard's Ten Honeymoons*, Allied Artists, 1960; bank manager, *The Boy Who Stole a Million*, British Lion, 1960; Petrelli, *Conspiracy of Hearts*, R.F.D. Productions, 1960; Dr. Hugo Panzer, *Surprise Package*, Columbia, 1960; camel driver, *King of Kings*, MGM, 1961; the colonel, *The Big Money*, Lopert, 1962; Forbes, *The Dog and the Diamonds*, Associated British, 1962; Francois

Lejeune, *Fury at Smugglers Bay*, Embassy, 1963; Carlos, *The Crooked Road*, Seven Arts, 1965; Dr. Londe, *The Skull*, Paramount, 1965; Ragheeb, *Arabesque*, Universal, 1966; Cardenas, *Land Raiders* (also known as *Day of the Landgrabbers*), Columbia, 1969; Swiss peasant, *The Assassination Bureau*, Paramount, 1969; Mr. Sturdevant, *No Blade of Grass*, MGM, 1970; Berigan, *Blood from the Mummy's Tomb*, Hammer, 1972; Dr. Chatal, *Papillon*, Allied Artists, 1973; Dr. Roth, *Mahler* (also known as *Mahler Lives*), Visual Programme System, 1974; Dr. Constantine, *Murder on the Orient Express*, Paramount, 1974; Dr. Powys, *The Last Days of Man on Earth* (also known as *The Final Programme*), New World, 1975; Old Man Vespucci, *The Ritz*, Warner Brothers, 1976; El Keb, *Shout at the Devil*, American International, 1976; Father Mittner, *The Tempter* (also known as *L'Anti Cristo* and *Anticristo*), AVCO-Embassy, 1978; professor, *It's Not the Size That Counts* (also known as *Percy's Progress*), Joseph Brenner, 1979; John Gurney, *Beyond the Fog* (also known as *Tower of Evil* and *Horror on Snape Island*), Independent-International, 1981; Lablache, *Vivement Dimanche* (also known as *Let It Be Sunday* and *Confidentially Yours*), Spectrafilm, 1982; Gus, *The Long Good Friday*, Embassy, 1982. Also appeared in *In the Cool of the Day*, MGM, 1963; *Too Many Thieves*, MGM, 1968; and in *I Love You, I Hate You*.

PRINCIPAL TELEVISION APPEARANCES—Mini-Series: DeBono, *Mussolini: The Untold Story*, NBC, 1985; also *Clouds of Witness*, BBC, then *Masterpiece Theatre*, PBS, 1973. Episodic: *Trials of O'Brien*, CBS, 1966; *Dundee and the Culhane*, CBS, 1967; *Search*, NBC, 1972 and 1973; also *Hart to Hart*, ABC. Movies: Max Greene, *The Stranger*, NBC, 1973; doctor, *Coffee, Tea, or Me?*, CBS, 1973. Specials: *The Suicide Club*, ABC, 1973.

PRINCIPAL RADIO APPEARANCES—Series: *To Hollywood and Back*, BBC.

RELATED CAREER—Member, Mercury Theatre Company, New York City, 1937-38.

NON-RELATED CAREER—Waiter on the ocean liner *Majestic*.

OBITUARIES AND OTHER SOURCES: New York Times, April 27, 1989; *Variety*, May 3-9, 1989.*

*   *   *

COVER, Franklin   1928-

PERSONAL: Full name, Franklin Edward Cover; born November 20, 1928, in Cleveland, OH; son of Franklin Held and Britta (Schreck) Cover; married Mary Bradford Stone (a dance company director), January 30, 1965; children: Bradford Franklin, Susan Henderson. EDUCATION—Denison University, B.A., theatre, 1951; Case Western Reserve University, M.A., 1954, M.F.A., 1955. MILITARY—U.S. Air Force, lieutenant, 1951-53.

VOCATION: Actor.

CAREER: STAGE DEBUT—With the Cain Park Theatre, Cleveland, OH, 1945. PRINCIPAL STAGE APPEARANCES—Flavius and Publius, *Julius Caesar*, Belvedere Lake Theatre, New York City, 1959; Sir Walter Blunt and Sheriff, *Henry IV, Part One*, Travers and Silence, *Henry IV, Part Two*, Dick Muggins and Jeremy, *She Stoops to Conquer*, and Captain Brennan, *The Plough and the*

FRANKLIN COVER

Stars, all Phoenix Repertory Company, Phoenix Theatre, New York City, 1960; Salem Scudder, *The Octoroon* and Marcellus and First Player, *Hamlet*, both Phoenix Repertory Company, Phoenix Theatre, 1961; Logan Harvey, *Giants, Sons of Giants*, Alvin Theatre, New York City, 1962; Roger Parkhurst, *Calculated Risk*, Ambassador Theatre, New York City, 1962; Brock Holliday, *Abraham Cochrane*, Belasco Theatre, New York City, 1964; John Cleves (understudy), *Any Wednesday*, Music Box Theatre, New York City, 1964-66, then George Abbott Theatre, New York City, 1966; prosecuting attorney, *The Investigation*, Ambassador Theatre, New York City, 1966; Charles, *A Warm Body*, Cort Theatre, New York City, 1967; Hamilton Reed, *The Freaking Out of Stephanie Blake*, Eugene O'Neill Theatre, New York City, 1967; Eddy Edwards, *Forty Carats*, Morosco Theatre, New York City, 1968-70; Howard Benedict, *Applause*, Palace Theatre, New York City, 1972; Marty, *The Killdeer*, New York Shakespeare Festival, Public Theatre, New York City, 1974; Colonel Triletzky, *Wild Honey*, Virginia Theatre, New York City, 1986; Ed Devery, *Born Yesterday*, Morris Mechanic Theatre, Baltimore, MD, 1988, then 46th Street Theatre, New York City, 1989. Also appeared with the Cleveland Playhouse, Cleveland, OH, 1954-58; and in title role, *Macbeth*, American Shakespeare Festival, Stratford, CT.

PRINCIPAL FILM APPEARANCES—Group leader, *Mirage*, Universal, 1965; Ed Wimpiris, *The Stepford Wives*, Columbia, 1975; Dan, *Wall Street*, Twentieth Century-Fox, 1987; also appeared in *What's So Bad About Feeling Good?*, Universal, 1968; *Such Good Friends*, Paramount, 1971; *The Great Gatsby*, Paramount, 1974.

PRINCIPAL TELEVISION APPEARANCES—Series: Tom Willis, *The Jeffersons*, CBS, 1975-85. Pilots: Mr. Murray, *Change at*

125th Street, CBS, 1974. Episodic: Tom Willis, *All in the Family,* CBS, 1975; Sheriff Joe Gates, *Hothouse,* CBS, 1988; Albert Blotchbinder, *227,* NBC, 1988; also *Naked City,* ABC, 1959; *The Defenders,* CBS, 1960; *Armstrong Circle Theatre,* CBS, 1960; *Play of the Week,* WNTA, 1960; *Love of Life,* CBS, 1960; *The Trials of O'Brien,* CBS, 1962; *The Doctors,* NBC, 1966; *The Edge of Night,* CBS, 1967; *The Secret Storm,* CBS, 1969; *All My Children,* ABC, 1970; *The Love Boat,* ABC, 1975; *The Jackie Gleason Show,* CBS. Movies: Conductor, *Short Walk to Daylight,* ABC, 1972; Lee Harris, *The Connection,* ABC, 1973; Hubert Humphrey, *A Woman Called Golda,* syndicated, 1982; Herbert Hoover, *The Day the Bubble Burst,* NBC, 1982. Also appeared in *What Makes Sammy Run?,* 1959; *The Investigation,* 1967.

MEMBER: Screen Actors Guild (director), American Federation of Television and Radio Artists, Actors' Equity Association, Cleveland Playhouse (honorary trustee), Players Club, English Speaking Union, Union Club (New York City), Blue Key, Kappa Sigma, Omicron Delta Kappa.

ADDRESSES: AGENT—Writers and Artists Agency, 70 W. 36th Street, New York, NY 10018.*

* * *

CRICHTON, Charles 1910-

PERSONAL: Born August 6, 1910, in Wallasey, England. EDUCATION—Attended Oxford University.

VOCATION: Director, screenwriter, and film editor.

CAREER: PRINCIPAL FILM WORK—Assistant editor, *Men of Tomorrow,* London Films, 1932; assistant editor, *Cash* (also known as *For Love or Money*), London Films, 1933; assistant editor, *The Private Life of Henry VIII,* London Films, 1933; assistant editor, *The Girl from Maxim's,* London Films, 1933; editor (with William Hornbeck), *Sanders of the River* (also known as *Bosambo*), London Films/United Artists, 1935; editor (with Francis Lyon), *Things to Come,* London Films, 1935, released in the United States by United Artists, 1936; editor (with Hornbeck), *Elephant Boy,* London Films/United Artists, 1937; editor (with Hornbeck), *Twenty-One Days Together* (also known as *Twenty-One Days* and *The First and the Last*), London Films, 1937, released in the United States by Columbia, 1940; editor, *Prison Without Bars,* London Films, 1938, released in the United States by United Artists, 1969; editor, *Old Bill and Son,* General Film Distributors, 1940; editor (with Hornbeck), *The Thief of Baghdad,* London Films/United Artists, 1940; editor, *The Big Blockade,* Ealing, 1941; associate producer and editor (with Hornbeck), *Nine Men,* Ealing, 1942, released in the United States by United Artists, 1943; director, *For Those in Peril,* Ealing, 1944; director, *The Girl on the Canal* (also known as *Painted Boats*), Ealing, 1945; director, "The Golfing Story" in *Dead of Night,* Ealing, 1945; director, *Hue and Cry,* Ealing, 1946, released in the United States by General Film Distributors, 1950; director, *Against the Wind,* Ealing/General Film Distributors, 1948; director, *Another Shore,* Ealing/General Film Distributors, 1948; director, "The Orchestra Conductor" in *Train of Events,* Ealing, 1949, released in the United States by Film Arts, 1952.

Director, *Dance Hall,* Ealing/General Film Distributors, 1950; director, *The Lavender Hill Mob,* Ealing/Universal, 1951; director, *Hunted* (also known as *The Stranger in Between*), Independent Artists/British Filmmakers, 1951, released in the United States by Universal, 1952; director, *The Titfield Thunderbolt,* Ealing, 1952, released in the United States by Universal, 1953; director, *The Love Lottery,* Ealing, 1953, released in the United States by General Film Distributors, 1954; director, *The Divided Heart,* Ealing, 1954, released in the United States by Republic, 1955; director, *The Man in the Sky* (also known as *Decision Against Time*), Ealing, 1956, released in the United States by Metro-Goldwyn-Mayer, 1957; director, *Law and Disorder,* Continental Distributing, 1958; director, *Floods of Fear,* Rank/Universal, 1958; director, *The Battle of the Sexes,* Continental, 1960; director, *The Boy Who Stole a Million,* British Lion, 1960; director, *The Third Secret,* Twentieth Century-Fox, 1964; director, *He Who Rides a Tiger,* Sigma III, 1965; director, *A Fish Called Wanda,* Metro-Goldwyn-Mayer/United Artists, 1988. Also editor, *Yellow Caesar* (also known as *The Heel of Italy*), 1940; editor, *Guests of Honour,* 1941; editor, *Young Veteran,* 1941; associate producer and editor, *Find, Fix, and Strike,* 1941; associate producer, *Greek Testament* (also known as *The Shrine of Victory*), 1942; director, *Tomorrow's Island,* 1968.

PRINCIPAL TELEVISION WORK—All as director. Series: *The Adventures of Black Beauty,* London Weekend Television, then syndicated, 1972-73; *Space 1999,* syndicated, 1975-76. Episodic: *Secret Agent,* ITV, then CBS, both 1965; *The Avengers,* ITV, 1965, then ABC, 1966; *Man in a Suitcase,* ABC, 1968; *The Strange Report,* NBC, 1971; *Shirley's World,* ABC, 1971; *The Protectors,* ATV, then syndicated, 1973; *Return of the Saint,* ATV, then CBS, 1979-80; also and *Dick Turpin.* Movies: *London—Through My Eyes,* 1970. Also directed *The Wild Duck,* British television; *The Smuggler.*

RELATED CAREER—Director of training films, Video Arts (a production company), London.

WRITINGS: FILM—(With Vivienne Knight) *Floods of Fear,* Rank, 1958; (with John Eldridge) *The Boy Who Stole a Million,* British Lion, 1960; *Tomorrow's Island,* 1968; (with John Cleese) *A Fish Called Wanda,* Metro-Goldwyn-Mayer/United Artists, 1988. TELEVISION—Episodic: (With Christopher Penford) "The Last Sunset," *Space 1999,* syndicated, 1975.

AWARDS: Academy Award nominations, Best Director and (with John Cleese) Best Original Screenplay, both 1989, for *A Fish Called Wanda.**

* * *

CRINKLEY, Richmond 1940-1989

PERSONAL: Full name, Richmond Dillard Crinkley; born January 20, 1940, in Blackstone, VA; died of cancer, January 29, 1989, in Richmond, VA; son of James Epes and Sarah Elizabeth (Beck) Crinkley. EDUCATION—University of Virginia, B.A., 1961, M.A., 1962, and Ph.D., 1966; postgraduate work, Oxford University, 1965-67.

VOCATION: Producer and theatre executive.

CAREER: PRINCIPAL STAGE WORK—Producer: *Total Eclipse, Happy Days,* and *Subject to Fits,* all Folger Theatre Group, Washington, DC, 1969-73; (with Roger L. Stevens) *The Freedom of the City,* Kennedy Center for the Performing Arts, Washington, DC, 1973, then (also with Konrad Matthaei and Hale Matthews)

Alvin Theatre, New York City, 1974; (with Stevens) *The Skin of Our Teeth*, Kennedy Center for the Performing Arts, Washington, DC, then (also with Ken Marsolais) Mark Hellinger Theatre, New York City, both 1975; (with Stevens) *Summer Brave*, Kennedy Center for the Performing Arts, then (also with Barry M. Brown, Burry Fredrik, Fritz Holt, Sally Sears, and Robert V. Straus) American National Theatre and Academy (ANTA) Theatre, New York City, both 1975; (with Stevens) *The Royal Family*, Kennedy Center for the Performing Arts, then (also with Brown, Fredrik, Holt, and Sears) Helen Hayes Theatre, New York City, both 1975; (with Stevens) *The Scarecrow, Sweet Bird of Youth, Long Day's Journey into Night, Rip Van Winkle,* and *A Texas Trilogy,* all Kennedy Center for the Performing Arts, 1975-76; (with Stevens) *The Heiress*, Kennedy Center for the Performing Arts, then (also with Steven Beckler and Thomas C. Smith) Broadhurst Theatre, New York City, both 1976; *Out of Our Father's House*, ANTA Theatre, 1978; (with Elizabeth I. McCann and Nelle Nugent) *The Elephant Man*, ANTA, Booth Theatre, New York City, 1979; *Ladyhouse Blues*, ANTA, Theatre at St. Peter's Church, New York City, 1979.

Tintypes, ANTA, Theatre at St. Peter's Church, then John Golden Theatre, New York City, both 1980; *Judgement*, ANTA, Theatre at St. Peter's Church, 1980; *The Philadelphia Story*, Lincoln Center Theatre Company, Vivian Beaumont Theatre, New York City, 1980; *The Floating Light Bulb* and *Macbeth*, both Lincoln Center Theatre Company, Vivian Beaumont Theatre, 1981; "Stops Along the Way," "In Fireworks Lie Secret Codes," and "Vivien," in *The One Act Play Festival*, Lincoln Center Theatre Company, Mitzi E. Newhouse Theatre, New York City, 1981; *Poor Little Lambs*, Theatre at St. Peter's Church, 1982; (with Eve Skina, Tina Chen, Martin Markinson, Mike Merrick, and John Roach) *Passion*, Longacre Theatre, New York City, 1983.

MAJOR TOURS—Producer (with Elizabeth I. McCann and Nelle Nugent), *The Elephant Man*, U.S. cities, 1979-81.

PRINCIPAL TELEVISION WORK—All as producer. Specials: *Out of Our Father's House*, PBS, 1978; *The Elephant Man*, ABC, 1979; *Macbeth*, ABC, 1983; also *Diary of a Madman*.

RELATED CAREER—Director of programs, Folger Shakespeare Library, and producer, Folger Theatre Group, Washington, DC, 1969-73; board member, WETA-TV, Washington, DC, 1969-73; board member, Shakespeare Quarterly, 1971-73; assistant to the chairman, John F. Kennedy Center for the Performing Arts, Washington, DC, 1973-76; executive director, American National Theatre and Academy, New York City, 1976-79; executive director, Lincoln Center Theatre Company, Vivian Beaumont Theatre, New York City, 1979-84; trustee, John F. Kennedy Center for the Performing Arts, 1981-89; founder and president, Cerberus Enterprises Inc. (a theatrical production company), 1984-89; trustee, Stage II, London; advisory board member (Washington chapter), National Society of Arts and Letters.

NON-RELATED CAREER—Assistant professor of English literature, University of North Carolina, 1967-69.

WRITINGS: *Walter Pater: Humanist*, University Press of Kentucky, 1971.

AWARDS: Fulbright fellowship, 1965-67; New York Drama Critics' Circle Award and Antoinette Perry Award, both Best Play, 1979, for *The Elephant Man*.

MEMBER: Raven Society, Phi Beta Kappa.

OBITUARIES AND OTHER SOURCES: *New York Times*, January 31, 1989.*

*   *   *

CROSBY, Denise

VOCATION: Actress.

CAREER: PRINCIPAL FILM APPEARANCES—Sally, *48 Hours*, Paramount, 1982; Bruno's moll, *The Curse of the Pink Panther*, United Artists, 1983; Enid, *The Man Who Loved Women*, Columbia, 1983; Nora Hunter, *Eliminators*, Empire, 1986; Pat, *Desert Hearts*, Samuel Goldwyn, 1985; Jill Andrews, *Arizona Heat*, Spectrum, 1988; Rachel Creed, *Pet Sematary*, Paramount, 1989. Also appeared in *The Trail of the Pink Panther*, United Artists, 1982.

PRINCIPAL TELEVISION APPEARANCES—Series: Lieutenant Tasha Yar, *Star Trek: The Next Generation*, syndicated, 1987-88. Pilots: Kim Parker, *Stark*, CBS, 1985. Movies: Teller, *Cocaine: One Man's Seduction*, NBC, 1983; Carole Lombard, *Malice in Wonderland*, CBS, 1985; Diana Dyrenforth, *My Wicked, Wicked Ways . . . The Legend of Errol Flynn*, CBS, 1985.

ADDRESSES: AGENT—Harris and Goldberg, 2121 Avenue of the Stars, Suite 950, Los Angeles, CA 90067.*

*   *   *

CROWDER, Jack
See RASULALA, Thalmus

*   *   *

CROWLEY, Pat
(Patricia Crowley)

PERSONAL: Born September 17, in Olyphant, PA; daughter of Vincent and Helen (Swartz) Crowley; married E. Gregory Hookstratten, February 2, 1958 (divorced); married A. Friendly, April 5, 1986; children: Jon, Ann (first marriage). EDUCATION—Attended the High School of the Performing Arts, New York City.

VOCATION: Actress.

CAREER: PRINCIPAL STAGE APPEARANCES—Carol Randall, *Southern Exposure*, Biltmore Theatre, New York City, 1950; Dorothy Bawke, *Four Twelves are Forty-Eight*, 48th Street Theatre, New York City, 1951; Helene Dupont, *Tovarich*, City Center Theatre, New York City, 1952.

PRINCIPAL FILM APPEARANCES—Sally Carver, *Forever Female*, Paramount, 1953; Autumn Claypool, *Money from Home*, Paramount, 1953; Susana Martinez De La Cruz, *Red Garters*, Paramount, 1954; Julie Walsh, *The Square Jungle*, Universal, 1955; Terry, *Hollywood or Bust*, Paramount, 1956; Ann, *There's Always*

Tomorrow, Universal, 1956; Mary Dennison, *Walk the Proud Land,* Universal, 1956; Ann Morrow, *Key Witness,* Metro-Goldwyn-Mayer (MGM), 1960; (as Patricia Crowley) Betty Anderson, *The Scarface Mob* (also known as *Tueur de Chicago*), Cari Releasing/Desilu, 1962; (as Patricia Crowley) Eloise, *The Wheeler Dealers* (also known as *Separate Beds*), MGM, 1963; (as Patricia Crowley) Elaine May Donaldson, *To Trap a Spy,* MGM, 1966; (as Patricia Crowley) Mary Lee McNeil, *The Biscuit Eater,* Buena Vista, 1972; Lennie Howe, *Off the Wall,* Gregory, 1977. Also appeared in *The Wild Women of Wongo,* Tropical, 1959.

PRINCIPAL TELEVISION APPEARANCES—Series: Judy Foster, *A Date with Judy,* ABC, 1951-52; Joan Nash, *Please Don't Eat the Daisies,* NBC, 1965-67; Georgia Cameron, *Joe Forrester,* NBC, 1975-76; Emily Fallmont, *Dynasty,* ABC, 1986; (as Patricia Crowley) Rebecca Whitmore, *Generations,* NBC, 1989—. Pilots: Maggie Randall, *I Remember Caviar* (broadcast as an episode of *Goodyear Theatre*), NBC, 1959; J.B., *The Rumor* (broadcast as an episode of *Stripe Playhouse*), CBS, 1959; Betty Anderson, *The Untouchables* (broadcast as an episode of *Desilu Playhouse*), CBS, 1959; Maggie Randall, *All in the Family* (broadcast as an episode of *Goodyear Theatre*), NBC, 1960; Elizabeth Williams, *The Two of Us,* CBS, 1966; Joan, *You're Only Young Twice,* CBS, 1967; Georgia Cameron, *The Return of Joe Forrester,* NBC, 1975; Maggie Haines, *The Millionaire,* CBS, 1978; Lucy Faber, *Return to Fantasy Island,* ABC, 1978; Beverly Gerber, *International Airport,* ABC, 1985; also *The World of Entertainment,* syndicated, 1982.

Episodic: Jackie Benson, "Printer's Devil," *The Twilight Zone,* CBS, 1963; Claudia Baron, *Blacke's Magic,* NBC, 1986; Edie Howard, *Murder, She Wrote,* CBS, 1987; also "Sixteen," *Television Theatre,* NBC, 1950; *Magnavox Theatre,* CBS, 1950; "The Laughing Shoes," "Fairy Tale," and "Caprice," *Armstrong Circle Theatre,* NBC, 1952; "Treasure Chest," *Television Playhouse,* NBC, 1952; "Night of Evil," *Suspense,* CBS, 1952; "The Pretext," *Video Theatre,* CBS, 1954; "Two," *The U.S. Steel Hour,* ABC, 1954; "Guilty Is the Stranger," *Goodyear Playhouse,* NBC, 1954; "Bachelor's Bride," *General Electric Theatre,* CBS, 1955; "Here Comes the Groom," *Lux Video Theatre,* NBC, 1956; "The 78th Floor," *Climax,* CBS, 1956; "Heat of Anger," *West Point,* CBS, 1956; "Girl with a Glow," *Schlitz Playhouse of Stars,* CBS, 1957; "The Deadline," *Crossroads,* ABC, 1957; "A Gun at His Back," *The Frank Sinatra Show,* ABC, 1957; "Blizzard," *The Loretta Young Show,* NBC, 1957; "Time to Go Now," *General Electric Theatre,* CBS, 1958; "The Bargain," *The Loretta Young Show,* NBC, 1958; *Maverick,* ABC, 1959; *Wanted Dead or Alive,* CBS, 1959; *77 Sunset Strip,* ABC, 1959; "Trouble in Fenton Valley," *The Loretta Young Show,* NBC, 1959; *Bronco,* ABC, 1959.

Riverboat, NBC, 1960; "Threat of Evil," *The June Allyson Show,* CBS, 1960; *Maverick,* ABC, 1960; *The Tab Hunter Show,* NBC, 1960; *Hong Kong,* ABC, 1960; *The Roaring Twenties,* ABC, 1960; *Michael Shayne,* NBC, 1961; *Hong Kong,* ABC, 1961; *Tales of Wells Fargo,* NBC, 1961; *87th Precinct,* NBC, 1961; *The Detectives,* NBC, 1961; *Dr. Kildare,* NBC, 1962; "Quick Brown Fox," *Cain's Hundred,* NBC, 1962; *Rawhide,* CBS, 1963; *Bonanza,* NBC, 1963; *The Eleventh Hour,* NBC, 1963; *The Fugitive,* ABC, 1963; *Mr. Novak,* NBC, 1963; *77 Sunset Strip,* ABC, 1963; *The Lieutenant,* NBC, 1964; *Arrest and Trial,* CBS, 1964; *Dr. Kildare,* NBC, 1964; *The Man from U.N.C.L.E.,* NBC, 1964; "Mr. Biddle's Crime Wave," *The Bob Hope Chrysler Theatre,* NBC, 1964; "A Matter of Murder," *Alfred Hitchcock Theatre,* CBS, 1964; *Judd, for the Defense,* ABC, 1968; *The Virginian,* NBC, 1968;

"Boomerang," *World of Disney,* NBC, 1968; "Love and the Wonderful Wife," *Love, American Style,* ABC, 1969; "Menace on the Mountain," *World of Disney,* NBC, 1970; *Marcus Welby, M.D.,* ABC, 1971; *Alias Smith and Jones,* ABC, 1971; *Columbo,* NBC, 1971; *The Bold Ones,* NBC, 1971; *Owen Marshall, Counselor at Law,* ABC, 1972; *Griff,* ABC, 1973; *World of Disney,* NBC, 1974; *Police Story,* NBC, 1974, 1975, and 1976; *Matt Helm,* ABC, 1975; *Police Woman,* NBC, 1976; *Streets of San Francisco,* ABC, 1976; also *The Web,* CBS; *The Chevrolet Tele-Theatre,* NBC; *The Love Boat,* ABC. Movies: Carol Long, *A Family Upside Down,* NBC, 1978.

RELATED CAREER—Child model.

NON-RELATED CAREER—Vice-president, Share Inc.; board of directors, West Lake School; board of directors, Good Shepherd School.

AWARDS: Theatre World Award, 1951.

ADDRESSES: AGENT—Light/Gordon/Rosson Agency, 901 Bringham Avenue, Los Angeles, CA 90049.*

*　　　　　*　　　　　*

CROWLEY, Patricia
See CROWLEY, Pat

*　　　　　*　　　　　*

CRUTCHLEY, Rosalie　1921-

PERSONAL: Born January 4, 1921, in London, England; daughter of Gerald and Betty (Spottiswoode) Crutchley; married Danson Cunningham (divorced); married Peter Ashmore (divorced). EDUCATION—Attended the Francis Holland School; trained for the stage at the Royal Academy of Music.

VOCATION: Actress.

CAREER: STAGE DEBUT—*Saint Joan,* Liverpool Playhouse, Liverpool, U.K., 1938. LONDON DEBUT—Angelica, *Love for Love,* Phoenix Theatre, 1943. PRINCIPAL STAGE APPEARANCES—Elizabeth, *The Circle,* Angelica, *Love for Love,* and Hippolyta, *A Midsummer Night's Dream,* all Haymarket Theatre, London, 1944-45; Goneril, *King Lear* and Beatrice, *Much Ado About Nothing,* both Bristol Old Vic Theatre, Bristol, U.K., 1946-47, then Embassy Theatre, London, 1947; Friedl von Gerhardt, *The Compelled People,* New Lindsey Theatre, London, 1949; Helen Rolt, *The Heart of the Matter,* Wilbur Theatre, Boston, MA, 1950; Madeleine, *Intimate Relations,* Arts Theatre, London, 1951; Helen Manifold, *All the Year Round,* Duke of York's Theatre, London, 1951; Marie Chassaigne, *The River Line,* Strand Theatre, London, 1953; Kristine Linde, *A Doll's House,* Lyric Hammersmith Theatre, London, 1953; Elizabeth Proctor, *The Crucible,* Royal Court Theatre, London, 1956; Dona Ana, *Don Juan* and Marcia Lissenden, *The Death of Satan,* both Royal Court Theatre, 1956. Also appeared in repertory at the Liverpool Playhouse, Liverpool, U.K., 1938-39, with the H.M. Tennent Players, 1940, in Edinburgh and Glasgow, Scotland, 1940, at the Oxford Playhouse, Oxford, U.K., 1940-42, and with the Old Vic Company, Liverpool Playhouse, 1945-46.

FILM DEBUT—Elizabeth Rusman, *Take My Life*, Eagle-Lion/Rank, 1948. PRINCIPAL FILM APPEARANCES—Julio's wife, *Salt to the Devil* (also known as *Give Us This Day*), Eagle-Lion/Rank, 1949; Carlotta, *Prelude to Fame*, Universal, 1950; Mrs. Sidney Herbert, *The Lady with a Lamp*, British Lion, 1951; Acte, *Quo Vadis*, Metro-Goldwyn-Mayer (MGM), 1951; Queen Katherine of Aragon, *The Sword and the Rose* (also known as *When Knighthood Was in Flower*), RKO, 1953; Francesca, *Flame and the Flesh*, MGM, 1954; Bella, *Make Me an Offer*, British Lion, 1954; Carmella, *Malta Story*, United Artists, 1954; Frau Bikstein, *The Gamma People*, Columbia, 1956; Mafalda Gozzi, *Miracle in Soho*, Rank, 1957; Theater Sister, *No Time for Tears*, Associated British/Pathe, 1957; Magdalena, *The Spanish Gardener*, Rank, 1957; Madame DeFarge, *A Tale of Two Cities*, Rank, 1958; Therese Blanchard, *The Beasts of Marseilles* (also known as *Seven Thunders*), Rank Film Distributors, 1959; Sister Eleanor, *The Nun's Story*, Warner Brothers, 1959.

Miriam's mother, *Sons and Lovers*, Twentieth Century-Fox, 1960; farmer's wife, *Greyfriars Bobby*, Buena Vista, 1961; Alice Byrne, *No Love for Johnnie*, Embassy, 1961; Frau Freud, *Freud* (also known as *The Secret Passion* and *Freud: The Secret Passion*), Universal, 1962; Mrs. Dudley, *The Haunting*, MGM, 1963; Teresa, *Behold a Pale Horse*, Columbia, 1964; Maude Klein, *The Model Murder Case* (also known as *Girl in the Headlines*), Cinema V, 1964; Mrs. Earnshaw, *Wuthering Heights*, American International, 1970; old crone, *Creatures the World Forgot*, Columbia, 1971; Miss Henley, *Who Slew Auntie Roo?* (also known as *Gingerbread House*), American International, 1971; Helen Dickerson, *Blood from the Mummy's Tomb*, Hammer, 1972; housekeeper, *Man of La Mancha*, United Artists, 1972; Mrs. Luke, *And Now the Screaming Starts* (also known as *Fengriffen*), Cinerama, 1973; Marie Mahler, *Mahler*, Visual Programme Systems, 1974; Somaya, *Mohammad, Messenger of God* (also known as *Al-Ris-Alah* and *The Message*), Tarik/Yablans, 1976; Josefa, *The Keep*, Paramount, 1983; Hatche's mother, *Memed My Hawk*, Focus, 1983; Grandmother, *Eleni*, Warner Brothers, 1985; Mrs. Harris, *A World Apart*, Atlantic Releasing, 1988; magnate from the bench's wife, *Little Dorrit*, Curzon Film Distributors/Cannon Releasing, 1988; Gladys, *She's Been Away*, Sales Company/BBC Enterprises, 1989. Also appeared in *Beyond This Place* (also known as *Web of Evidence*), Allied Artists, 1959; *Frederic Chopin*, 1961; *Au Pair Girls*, 1972; *House in Nightmare Park*, 1973; *The Return*, 1973.

PRINCIPAL TELEVISION APPEARANCES—Mini-Series: Catherine Parr, *The Six Wives of Henry VIII*, BBC, 1970, then CBS, 1971, later *Masterpiece Theatre*, PBS, 1972; Catherine Parr, *Elizabeth R*, BBC, then *Masterpiece Theatre*, PBS, 1972; Mother Felicity, *Smiley's People*, syndicated, 1982; Goodwife Margaret, *By the Sword Divided*, BBC, then *Masterpiece Theatre*, PBS, 1986; Goodwife Margaret, *By the Sword Divided II*, BBC, then *Masterpiece Theatre*, PBS, 1988; also *The Possessed*, BBC, then *Masterpiece Theatre*, PBS, 1971; *Cold Comfort Farm*, BBC, then *Masterpiece Theatre*, PBS, 1971; *Country Matters*, Granada, then *Masterpiece Theatre*, PBS, 1975; *Testament of Youth*, BBC, then *Masterpiece Theatre*, PBS, 1980; *The Franchise Affair*, BBC-1, 1988. Episodic: The Queen, "Checkmate," *The Prisoner*, CBS, 1968; Mrs. Lexington, "The Norwood Builder," *The Adventures of Sherlock Holmes*, Granada, then *Mystery!*, PBS, 1986; Mrs. Price-Ridley, "The Murder at the Vicarage," *Agatha Christie's Miss Marple*, BBC, then *Mystery!*, PBS, 1989; Lisa, "Death of a Ghost," *Campion*, BBC, then *Mystery!*, PBS, 1989; also "Moving on the Edge," *Play for Today*, 1982.

Movies: Simone, *The Hunchback of Notre Dame*, CBS, 1982; Mrs.

Jones, *Queenie*, ABC, 1987; Mrs. Markham, *Beryl Markham: A Shadow on the Sun* (also known as *Shadow on the Sun: The Life of Beryl Markham*), CBS, 1988. Specials: Mrs. Sparsit, *Hard Times*, Granada, then *Great Performances*, PBS, 1977; Teresa, *Monsignor Quixote*, Thames Television, then *Great Performances*, PBS, 1987; Euridice, *The Theban Plays*, BBC, then PBS, 1988. Also appeared in *Carrie's War*, 1973; *Elektra*, 1974; *North and South*, 1975; *Trilby*, 1976; *Oedipus*, 1976; *Jackanory*, 1976; *Gentle Folk*, 1977; *Horse in the House*, 1977; *Romany Rye*, 1977; *The Peppermint Pig*, 1978; *Destiny*, 1978; *Escape from the West*, 1981; *Passing Through*, 1981; *The Testament of John; Chessgame; Antigone; Brandon Chase; Cribb; Women of Troy; The Winter's Tale; The Complaisant Lover;* and *The Count of Monte Cristo.*

AWARDS: Guild of Television Award, Best Actress of the Year, 1956; International Television Award, 1970, for *The Six Wives of Henry VIII.*

ADDRESSES: MANAGER—London Management, 235/241 Regent Street, London W1A 2OT, England.*

*   *   *

CUSACK, John   1966-

PERSONAL: Surname is pronounced "*Qu*-zack"; born June 28, 1966, in Evanston, IL; son of Richard (an actor and producer) and Nancy Cusack. EDUCATION—Trained for the stage with Byrne and Joyce Piven at the Piven Theatre Workshop, Chicago, IL.

VOCATION: Actor, director, and producer.

CAREER: PRINCIPAL STAGE WORK—Director and producer, *Alagazam . . . After the Dog Wars*, Chicago, IL, 1988.

FILM DEBUT—Roscoe, *Class*, Orion, 1983. PRINCIPAL FILM APPEARANCES—Johnny Maine, *Grandview, U.S.A.*, Warner Brothers, 1984; Bryce, *Sixteen Candles*, Universal, 1984; Lane Myer, *Better Off Dead*, Warner Brothers, 1985; Harry, *The Journey of Natty Gann*, Buena Vista, 1985; Walter "Gib" Gibson, *The Sure Thing*, Embassy, 1985; Hoops McCann, *One Crazy Summer*, Warner Brothers, 1986; Denny Lachance, *Stand By Me*, Columbia, 1986; angry messenger, *Broadcast News*, Twentieth Century-Fox, 1987; Dan Bartlett, *Hot Pursuit*, Paramount, 1987; Ivan Alexeev, *Tapeheads*, De Laurentiis Entertainment Group, 1988; George "Buck" Weaver, *Eight Men Out*, Orion, 1988; Lloyd Dobler, *Say Anything*, Twentieth Century-Fox, 1989; Michale Merriman, *Fat Man and Little Boy*, Paramount, 1989.

PRINCIPAL TELEVISION APPEARANCES—Specials: *An All-Star Celebration: The '88 Vote*, ABC, 1988.

RELATED CAREER—Founder, New Crime Productions; writer and director of musicals for Evanston Township High School; appeared in industrial films and commercials.

ADDRESSES: HOME—Chicago, IL. AGENT—Ann Geddes, The Geddes Agency, 8457 Melrose Place, Los Angeles, CA 90069. PUBLICIST—Elizabeth Much, Baker/Winokur/Ryder Public Relations, 9348 Civic Center Drive, Suite 407, Beverly Hills, CA 90210.

D

DALY, Timothy   1956-

PERSONAL: Born March 1, 1956, in New York, NY; son of James Daly (an actor) and Hope Newell (an actress); married Amy Van Nostrand (an actress); children: Sam. EDUCATION—Received B.A. from Bennington College.

VOCATION: Actor.

CAREER: OFF-BROADWAY DEBUT—Trevor, Chris, Nicky, Victor, and Eddie, *Fables for Friends,* Playwrights Horizons, 1984. BROADWAY DEBUT—Leo Hart, *Coastal Disturbances,* Circle in the Square, 1987. PRINCIPAL STAGE APPEARANCES—Title role, *Oliver Oliver,* Manhattan Theatre Club, City Center Theatre Space, New York City, 1985; Leo Hart, *Coastal Disturbances,* Second Stage Theatre, New York City, 1987; also appeared in *The Fifth of July* and *Buried Child,* both Trinity Square Repertory Company, Providence, RI, 1981; *Mass Appeal* and *Bus Stop,* both Trinity Square Repertory Company; *The Glass Menagerie,* Santa Fe Festival Theatre, Santa Fe, NM; *Jenny Kissed Me,* Bucks County Playhouse, New Hope, PA.

PRINCIPAL FILM APPEARANCES—William "Billy" Howard, *Diner,* Metro-Goldwyn-Mayer/United Artists (MGM/UA), 1982; Frank, *Just the Way You Are,* MGM/UA, 1984; Tom Donnelly, *Made in Heaven,* Lorimar, 1987; Jeff Mills, *Spellbinder,* MGM/UA, 1988; also appeared in *Love or Money,* 1989.

PRINCIPAL TELEVISION APPEARANCES—Series: Dr. Edward Gillian, *Ryan's Four,* ABC, 1983; Norman Foley, *Almost Grown,* CBS, 1988. Mini-Series: Toby Amberville, *I'll Take Manhattan,* CBS, 1987. Episodic: Richard, "The Rise and Rise of Daniel Rocket," *American Playhouse,* PBS, 1986; Elliot Chase, *Midnight Caller,* NBC, 1989; also *Hill Street Blues,* NBC; *Alfred Hitchcock Presents.* Movies: Kevin Coates, *I Married a Centerfold,* NBC, 1984; Chris Philips, *Mirrors,* NBC, 1985; Guy Pehrsson, *Red Earth, White Earth,* CBS, 1989.

RELATED CAREER—Guitarist, singer, and composer in rock bands; performed in cabaret at the Williamstown Theatre Festival, Williamstown, MA, and at benefits in New York City.

AWARDS: Theatre World Award, 1987, for *Coastal Disturbances.*

MEMBER: Actors' Equity Association.*

DANIELS, Marc   c.1912-1989

PERSONAL: Born Danny Marcus, c. 1912 in Pittsburgh, PA; died of heart failure, April 23, 1989, in Santa Monica, CA; wife's name Emily; children: two daughters, one son. EDUCATION—Graduated from the University of Michigan; studied acting and directing at the American Academy of Dramatic Arts. MILITARY—U.S. Army, 1941-46.

VOCATION: Director, producer, and actor.

CAREER: Also see *WRITINGS* below. PRINCIPAL STAGE APPEARANCES—*Dead End,* Belasco Theatre, New York City; *The Yeoman of the Guard,* New York City.

PRINCIPAL STAGE WORK—Director: *Phoenix '55* (revue), Phoenix Theatre, New York City, 1955; *Copper and Brass,* Martin Beck Theatre, New York City, 1957; *Linda Stone Is Brutal,* Bucks County Playhouse, New Hope, PA, 1964; *The Girl in the Freudian Slip,* Booth Theatre, New York City, 1967; *36,* Jewish Repertory Theatre, New York City, 1980. Also assistant stage manager, *Dead End,* Belasco Theatre, New York City.

PRINCIPAL FILM WORK—Director, *Squeeze a Flower,* NLT Group W, 1970; also director, *The Big Fun Carnival,* 1957.

PRINCIPAL TELEVISION APPEARANCES—Pilots: *That's Our Sherman,* NBC, 1948.

PRINCIPAL TELEVISION WORK—All as director, unless indicated. Series: (Also producer with Jules Bricken) *Ford Theatre Hour,* CBS, 1948-51; (with Walter Hart and William Berke) *The Goldbergs,* CBS, 1949-51, then Dumont, 1954, later syndicated, 1955-56; producer, *The Nash Airflyte Theatre,* CBS, 1950-51; *I Love Lucy,* CBS, 1951-52; *My Hero* (also known as *The Robert Cummings Show*), NBC, 1952-53; (with John Rich) *Where's Raymond?* (also known as *The Ray Bolger Show*), ABC, 1953-55; (with Ernest D. Glucksman; also producer with Glucksman and Don Appel) *The Imogene Coca Show,* NBC, 1954-55; (with William A. Graham) *Witness,* CBS, 1960-61; producer, *Saints and Sinners,* NBC, 1962-63; executive producer (with Anne Marcus) and producer (with Leonard Friedlander), *The Life and Times of Eddie Roberts,* syndicated, 1980; *Life with Lucy,* ABC, 1986; creative consultant, *Can This Marriage Be Saved?,* syndicated, 1989. Pilots: *Last of the Private Eyes* (broadcast as an episode of *The Dick Powell Show;* also known as *The Hollywood Showcase*), NBC, 1963; *Assignment: Earth* (broadcast as an episode of *Star Trek*), NBC, 1968; *Prudence and the Chief,* ABC, 1970; *Planet Earth,* ABC, 1974; *Co-Ed Fever,* CBS, 1979.

Episodic: *Soldiers of Fortune,* syndicated, 1955; *Shane,* ABC,

1966; *Star Trek*, NBC, 1966-69 (fourteen episodes); *Paris 7000*, ABC, 1970; *Here We Go Again*, ABC, 1973; "One of Our Planets Is Missing," *Star Trek* (animated), NBC, 1973; *Gibbsville*, NBC, 1976; *Spencer's Pilots*, CBS, 1976; *The Andros Targets*, CBS, 1977; *Husbands, Wives, and Lovers*, CBS, 1978; *Doctors' Private Lives*, ABC, 1979; *The Life and Times of Eddie Roberts*, syndicated, 1980; *Amanda's*, ABC, 1983; *Gun Shy*, CBS, 1983; *Mr. President*, Fox, 1987 (ten episodes); also *The Survivors* (also known as *Harold Robbins' "The Survivors"*), ABC; *Hawaii Five-0*, CBS; *Ben Casey*, ABC; *Branded*, NBC; *Burke's Law*, ABC; *Love, American Style*, ABC; *Colt .45*, ABC; *Eight Is Enough*, ABC; *Apple's Way*, CBS; *Bonanza*, NBC; *Gunsmoke*, CBS (ten episodes); *Cannon*, CBS; *Alice*, CBS (eighty-six episodes); *Search*, NBC; *I Married Joan*, NBC (twenty-six episodes); *The Doris Day Show*, CBS (eleven episodes); *The Man from U.N.C.L.E.*, NBC; *The Men from Shiloh*, NBC; *Mission: Impossible*, CBS; *Owen Marshall, Counselor at Law*, ABC; *Flo*, CBS (ten episodes); *James at 15*, NBC; *The Man from Atlantis*, NBC; *Marcus Welby, M.D.*, ABC (thirty-three episodes); *Private Benjamin*, CBS; *Toma*, ABC; *Vega$*, ABC; *Saints and Sinners*, NBC; *Jigsaw*, ABC; *Hogan's Heroes*, CBS (nineteen episodes); *Dr. Kildare*, NBC; *Mickey Spillane's "Mike Hammer,"* CBS; *Crazy Like a Fox*, CBS; *The Name of the Game*, NBC; *Barnaby Jones*, CBS; *Kung Fu*, ABC; *The F.B.I.*, ABC; *East Side/West Side*, CBS; *Slattery's People*, CBS; *Fame*.

Movies: *Father Knows Best: Home for Christmas*, NBC, 1977; *He's Fired, She's Hired*, CBS, 1984; *Special People*, CBS, 1984; *Vengeance: The Story of Tony Cimo*, CBS, 1986. Specials: *Arsenic and Old Lace*, CBS, 1949; (also producer) *Jane Eyre*, CBS, 1961; *The Power and the Glory*, CBS, 1961; *The Heiress*, CBS, 1961; "Emily, Emily," *Hallmark Hall of Fame*, NBC, 1977; "Have I Got a Christmas for You," *Hallmark Hall of Fame*, NBC, 1977; *Lucy Calls the President*, CBS, 1977; "Fame," *Hallmark Hall of Fame*, NBC, 1978; (also producer) *Skinflint*, NBC, 1979. Also director, *All the Money in the World*.

RELATED CAREER—Executive officer and general manager, *This Is the Army* (World War II entertainment troup); instructor, American Academy of Dramatic Arts; director, Jane Cowl's Stock Company; senior vice-president, Theatre Network Television, which created closed-circuit broadcasts for business corporations; director of television commercials.

AWARDS: Emmy Award nomination, Outstanding Directorial Achievement in Drama, 1961, for *The Power and the Glory;* Emmy Award nomination and Directors Guild of America Award nomination, both for *Fame;* Emmy Award nomination for *Marcus Welby, M.D.;* Directors Guild of America Award nominations for *All the Money in the World* and *Alice; Variety* Showmanship Award; Director of the Year Award from the Radio and Television Editors of America.

OBITUARIES AND OTHER SOURCES: New York Times, April 29, 1989; *Variety*, May 3-9, 1989.*

*   *   *

DANO, Royal   1922-

PERSONAL: Born November 16, 1922, in New York, NY. EDUCATION—Attended New York University.

VOCATION: Actor.

CAREER: BROADWAY DEBUT—Mr. Shears, *Finian's Rainbow*, 46th Street Theatre, 1947. PRINCIPAL STAGE APPEARANCES—Ernie "Horse" Wagner, *Mrs. Gibbons' Boys*, Music Box Theatre, New York City, 1949; Ellington, *Metropole*, Lyceum Theatre, New York City, 1949; Roger, *She Stoops to Conquer*, City Center Theatre, New York City, 1950; Joe Hungry Horse, *Four Twelves Are Forty-Eight*, 48th Street Theatre, New York City, 1951; Jess Proddy, *Three Wishes for Jamie*, Mark Hellinger Theatre, New York City, 1952. Also appeared in *That's the Ticket*, Shubert Theatre, Philadelphia, PA, 1948.

MAJOR TOURS—Gus, *Barnaby and Mr. O'Malley*, U.S. cities, 1946.

PRINCIPAL FILM APPEARANCES—Moocher, *Undercover Girl*, Universal, 1950; Basra, *Flame of Araby*, Universal, 1951; tattered man, *The Red Badge of Courage*, Metro-Goldwyn-Mayer (MGM), 1951; Nugent, *Under the Gun*, Universal, 1951; captain, *Carrie*, Paramount, 1952; Corey, *Johnny Guitar*, Republic, 1954; Luke, *The Far Country*, Universal, 1955; Calvin Wiggs, *The Trouble with Harry*, Paramount, 1955; Elijah, *Moby Dick*, Warner Brothers, 1956; Lobo, *Santiago* (also known as *The Gun Runners*), Warner Brothers, 1956; Jameson, *Tension at Table Rock*, RKO, 1956; Abe, *Tribute to a Badman*, MGM, 1956; Howard Tyler, *All Mine to Give* (also known as *The Day They Gave Babies Away*), Universal, 1957; Alidos, *Crime of Passion*, United Artists, 1957; Aiken Clay, *Man in the Shadow* (also known as *Pay the Devil*), Universal, 1957; Trude, *Trooper Hook*, United Artists, 1957; Al Lees, *Handle with Care*, MGM, 1958; Trout, *Man of the West*, United Artists, 1958; Clay Ellison, *Saddle the Wind*, MGM, 1958; evangelist, *The Boy and the Bridge*, Columbia, 1959; Jake Winter, *Face of Fire*, Allied Artists, 1959; Fiddling Tom Waller, *Hound-Dog Man*, Twentieth Century-Fox, 1959; Words Cannon, *Never Steal Anything Small*, Universal, 1959; Carmichael, *These Thousand Hills*, Twentieth Century-Fox, 1959.

Sheriff, *The Adventures of Huckleberry Finn*, MGM, 1960; Ike Howes, *Cimarron*, MGM, 1960; Peter, *King of Kings*, MGM, 1961; Uncle Billy Caldwell, *Posse from Hell*, Universal, 1961; Pack Underwood, *Savage Sam*, Buena Vista, 1963; Carey, *The Seven Faces of Dr. Lao*, MGM, 1964; Ode, *Gunpoint*, Universal, 1966; Pretty Horse, *The Last Challenge*, MGM, 1967; John Bear, *Welcome to Hard Times* (also known as *Killer on a Horse*), MGM, 1967; Doctor Prather, *Day of the Evil Gun*, MGM, 1968; Carl Blair, *If He Hollers, Let Him Go*, Cinerama, 1968; Faraway, *Backtrack*, Universal, 1969; Arch Brandt, *Death of a Gunfighter*, Universal, 1969; Major Sanders, *The Undefeated*, Twentieth Century-Fox, 1969.

Zach, *Machismo—Forty Graves for Forty Guns* (also known as *Forty Graves for Forty Guns*), Boxoffice International, 1970; voice of Marley's Ghost, *Mr. Magoo's Holiday Festival* (animated), Maron, 1970; Sal Sachese, *Chandler*, MGM, 1971; John Brown, *Skin Game*, Warner Brothers, 1971; rustler, *The Culpepper Cattle Company*, Twentieth Century-Fox, 1972; Gustavson, *The Great Northfield, Minnesota Raid*, Universal, 1972; Jake, *Ace Eli and Rodger of the Skies*, Twentieth Century-Fox, 1973; MacDonald, *Cahill, United States Marshal*, Warner Brothers, 1973; coroner, *Electra Glide in Blue*, United Artists, 1973; Nick Murack, *Howzer*, URI, 1973; Reverend Johnson, *Big Bad Mama*, New World, 1974; Joseph Lang, *Dead People* (also known as *Messiah of Evil, Return of the Living Dead, Revenge of the Screaming Dead*, and *The Second Coming*), International Cinefilm, 1974; Mayor Anton

Cermak, *Capone,* Twentieth Century-Fox, 1975; Tex, *The Wild Party,* American International, 1975; Zeke Montgomery, *Drum,* United Artists, 1976; father, *The Killer Inside Me,* Warner Brothers, 1976; Ten Spot, *The Outlaw Josey Wales,* Warner Brothers, 1976; bartender, *One Man Jury,* Cal-Am Artists, 1978.

Prophet, *In Search of Historic Jesus,* Sunn Classic, 1980; Beeber, *Take This Job and Shove It,* AVCO-Embassy, 1981; Pops, *Hammett,* Warner Brothers, 1982; minister, *The Right Stuff,* Warner Brothers, 1983; Tom Fury, *Something Wicked This Way Comes,* Buena Vista, 1983; Ditto, *Teachers,* Metro-Goldwyn-Mayer/United Artists, 1984; Bailey, *Cocaine Wars,* Concorde, 1986; Gramps, *House II: The Second Story,* New World, 1987; Larn Claver, *Red-Headed Stranger,* Alive, 1987; Uncle Ned, *Ghoulies II,* Empire Entertainment, 1988; Farmer Green, *Killer Klowns from Outer Space* (also known as *Killer Klowns*), Trans World Entertainment, 1988. Also appeared in *Slingshot,* 1971; *Bad Georgia Road,* Dimension, 1977; *Hughes and Harlow: Angels in Hell,* PRO International, 1978.

PRINCIPAL TELEVISION APPEARANCES—Series: Elam Hanks, *How the West Was Won,* ABC, 1977. Pilots: Otto, *The Dangerous Days of Kiowa Jones,* ABC, 1966; Cow John, *Murder 1, Dancer 0,* NBC, 1983. Episodic: Salvation Army officer, *Amazing Stories,* NBC, 1986; Elmer Quick, *Amazing Stories,* NBC, 1986; also *Lost in Space,* CBS, 1966; "I'll Never Leave You—Ever," *Night Gallery,* NBC, 1971; *Planet of the Apes,* CBS, 1974; *Death Valley Days,* syndicated; *From Here to Eternity,* NBC. Movies: Sheriff Tackaberry, *Run Simon Run,* ABC, 1970; Tom Gurmandy, Sr., *Moon of the Wolf,* ABC, 1972; Mark Twain, *Huckleberry Finn,* ABC, 1975; Pa Bocock, *The Manhunter,* NBC, 1976; Bo Buehler, *Murder in Peyton Place,* NBC, 1977; Sutter, *Donner Pass: The Road to Survival,* NBC, 1978; Mr. Willis, *Strangers: The Story of a Mother and Daughter,* CBS, 1979; Pa Dalton, *The Last Ride of the Dalton Gang,* NBC, 1979; Ernest Farmer, *Will There Really Be a Morning?,* CBS, 1983; southern senator, *LBJ: The Early Years,* NBC, 1987; Nitro Jones, *Once Upon a Texas Train,* CBS, 1988; also *Crash,* ABC, 1978. Specials: Uncle "Sherlock" George, "My Dear Uncle Sherlock," *ABC Short Story Special,* ABC, 1977; voice, *Funny, You Don't Look 200,* ABC, 1987.

ADDRESSES: AGENT—William Morris Agency, 151 El Camino Drive, Beverly Hills, CA, 90212.*

*   *   *

DARDEN, Severn   1929-

PERSONAL: Full name, Severn Teackle Darden; born November 9, 1929, in New Orleans, LA; son of Severn T. and Geraldine (Rubenstein) Darden; married Heather Ingrid Bleackley, 1984; children: Scott Lachlan MacKinnon. EDUCATION—Attended Mexico City College, the University of Chicago, and Bard College.

VOCATION: Actor.

CAREER: BROADWAY DEBUT—Ensemble, *From the Second City* (revue), Royale Theatre, 1961. PRINCIPAL STAGE APPEARANCES—Joseph, *My Three Angels,* M.P., *Mr. Roberts,* and Corporal Shultz, *Stalag 17,* all Barter Theatre, Abington, VA, 1954; Henry Cabot Lodge, *The Hall of Mirrors,* Barter Theatre, 1956; Voltemand, *Hamlet,* Snug, *A Midsummer Night's Dream,* and officer, *The Winter's Tale,* all American Shakespeare Festival, Stratford, CT,

SEVERN DARDEN

1958; Foma Fomitch, *Friend of the Family,* Crystal Palace, St. Louis, MO, 1958; Peter, *Romeo and Juliet,* Snug, *A Midsummer Night's Dream,* Nym, *The Merry Wives of Windsor,* and French lord, *All's Well That Ends Well,* all American Shakespeare Festival, 1959; Jonathan Kobitz, *P.S. 193,* Writers' Stage Theatre, New York City, 1962; ensemble, *Seacoast of Bohemia* and *My Friend Art Is Dead* (revues), both Second City at Square East Theatre, New York City, 1962; ensemble, *To the Water Tower* (revue), Second City at Square East Theatre, 1963; Birgasse, *A Murderer Among Us,* Morosco Theatre, New York City, 1964; ensemble, *Open Season at Second City* and *A View from Under the Bridge,* (revues), both Second City at Square East Theatre, 1964; Harry, *Leda Had a Little Swan,* Cort Theatre, New York City, 1968; Sam Adams and Robinson, *The American Revolution, Part I,* Ford's Theatre, Washington, DC, 1973; ensemble, *Sills and Company* (revue), Lamb's Theatre, New York City, 1986. Also appeared in *The Second City Revue,* Chicago, IL, 1959; *Too Many Hats, The Third Program,* and *Seacoast of Bohemia* (revues), all with the Second City comedy troupe, Chicago, 1960; with the Second City comedy troupe at the Ivar Theatre, Los Angeles, 1961; *Metamorphoses,* Festival of Two Worlds, Spoleto, Italy, 1973; *Tales of the Hasidim,* New York Shakespeare Festival, Public Theatre, New York City, 1977; *The Front Page,* Long Wharf Theatre, New Haven, CT, 1982; *Sills and Company* (revue), Los Angeles, 1983-85.

MAJOR TOURS—With the Second City comedy troupe, U.S. and U.K. cities, 1957-59; *From the Second City* (revue), U.S. cities, 1965.

PRINCIPAL FILM APPEARANCES—Doctor, *Goldstein,* Montrose, 1964; H.S. Stevens, *The Double-Barrelled Detective Story,* Saloon

Productions, 1965; Miles Fisher, *Dead Heat on a Merry-Go-Round,* Columbia, 1966; doctor and Claude, *Fearless Frank* (also known as *Frank's Greatest Adventure*), American International, 1967; Vandergrist, *Luv,* Columbia, 1967; Kropotkin, *The President's Analyst,* Paramount, 1967; Shelton Quell, *P.J.* (also known as *New Face in Hell*), Universal, 1968; Henry F. Millmore, Fillard Millmore, narrator, and Millmore's Ghost, *The Virgin President,* New Line Cinema, 1968; Balthazar, *Justine,* Twentieth Century-Fox, 1969; Nate, *The Mad Room,* Columbia, 1969; portly man, *The Model Shop,* Columbia, 1969; Cecil, *They Shoot Horses, Don't They?* ABC/Cinerama, 1969; Dr. Fahrquardt, *Pussycat, Pussycat, I Love You,* United Artists, 1970; Cisco's lawyer, *Cisco Pike,* Columbia, 1971; McVey, *The Hired Hand,* Universal, 1971; mayor, *The Last Movie* (also known as *Chinchero*), Universal, 1971; J. Hovah, *Vanishing Point,* Twentieth Century-Fox, 1971; One (high priest), *Werewolves on Wheels,* Fanfare, 1971; Kolp, *Conquest of the Planet of the Apes,* Twentieth Century-Fox, 1972; Dominick, *Every Little Crook and Nanny,* Metro-Goldwyn-Mayer, 1972; hypnotist, *Play It As It Lays,* Universal, 1972; Dr. Harris, *The War Between Men and Women,* National General, 1972; Mr. Marduke, *Who Fears the Devil?* (also known as *The Legend of Hillbilly John* and *My Name Is John*), Jack H. Harris, 1972; Big Jim, *Dirty Little Billy,* Columbia, 1972; Kolp, *Battle for the Planet of the Apes,* Twentieth Century-Fox, 1973; Schwinn, *The Day of the Dolphin,* AVCO-Embassy, 1973; Sheriff Dempsey, *Jackson County Jail,* New World, 1976; Moran, *Mother, Jugs, and Speed,* Twentieth Century-Fox, 1976; Merlin Bitterstix, *Wanda Nevada,* United Artists, 1979; Maddox, *Hopscotch,* AVCO-Embassy, 1980; priest, *In God We Trust,* Universal, 1980; art editor, *A Small Circle of Friends,* United Artists, 1980; Dr. Barbour, *Why Would I Lie?* Metro-Goldwyn-Mayer/United Artists, 1980; Van Helsing, *Saturday the 14th,* New World, 1981; seminary provincial, *Young Giants,* Miracle, 1983; Dr. Meredith, *Real Genius,* Tri-Star, 1985: Dr. Barazini, *Back to School,* Orion, 1986; Max, *The Telephone,* New World, 1988. Also appeared in *Hands of the Ripper,* Universal, 1971.

PRINCIPAL FILM WORK—Producer (with Graeme Ferguson and Jim Hubbard), *The Virgin President,* New Line Cinema, 1968.

PRINCIPAL TELEVISION APPEARANCES—Series: Regular, *Story Theatre,* syndicated, 1971; Dr. Popesco, *Forever Fernwood,* syndicated, 1977-78; Foley, *Beyond Westworld,* CBS, 1980; Dr. Noah Wolf, *Take Five,* CBS, 1987. Mini-Series: Gideon, *Sandburg's Lincoln,* NBC, 1974-76; Plover, *Captains and the Kings,* NBC, 1976. Pilots: Bad guy, *The New, Original Wonder Woman,* ABC, 1975; Cap, *The Feather and Father Gang: Never Con a Killer* (also known as *Never Con a Killer*), ABC, 1977; Albert Church, *Rendezvous Hotel,* CBS, 1979; Mr. Melish, *Home Room,* ABC, 1981; Conway, *Rooster,* ABC, 1982. Episodic: *Kolchak: The Night Stalker,* ABC, 1974; *Barney Miller,* ABC, 1976; *Cheers,* NBC, 1983; and as Aploy, *The Six Million Dollar Man,* ABC. Movies: Jimmy Apache, *The Movie Murderer,* NBC, 1970; Roger, *Playmates,* ABC, 1972; Harry, *The Man Who Died Twice,* CBS, 1973; Steve Kramer, *Skyway to Death,* ABC, 1974; S.I. Gilbert, *The Disappearance of Aimee,* NBC, 1976; Moshe Meyer, *Victory at Entebbe,* ABC, 1976; Sheriff Dempsey, *Outside Chance,* CBS, 1978; Fred Hallem, *Love for Rent,* ABC, 1979; Mr. Barrington, *Orphan Train,* CBS, 1979; Hobart, *Quarterback Princess,* CBS, 1983; Paul, *A Cry for Love,* NBC, 1980; Alfredo Suero, *Evita Peron,* NBC, 1981. Specials: Marvin Simeon, *The Prison Game,* PBS, 1979; Jonathan Barnavelt, "Once Upon a Midnight Dreary," *CBS Library,* CBS, 1979; Farmer Silas, *The Princess Who Had Never Laughed,* Showtime, 1986; also *Second City Revue,* 1961.

RELATED CAREER—Monologist, Gate of Horn (nightclub), Chicago, IL, 1959.

WRITINGS: FILM—(With Graeme Ferguson) *The Virgin President,* New Line Cinema, 1968; composer, *The Last Movie,* Universal, 1971.

MEMBER: Academy of Motion Picture Arts and Sciences.

ADDRESSES: AGENT—Belson and Klass Associates, 144 S. Beverly Drive, Beverly Hills, CA 90212.

*   *   *

DaRE, Aldo
See RAY, Aldo

*   *   *

DAVID, Keith

VOCATION: Actor.

PERSONAL: Born Keith David Williams, June 4, in New York, NY; son of Lester and Delores (Dickenson) Williams. EDUCATION—Graduated from the High School of Performing Arts, 1973; received B.F.A. from the Juilliard Theatre Center; studied acting at

KEITH DAVID

the the Edith Skinner Institute and with the La Mama Repertory Company.

CAREER: STAGE DEBUT—Title role (understudy), *Othello*, New York Shakespeare Festival, Delacorte Theatre, New York City, 1979. PRINCIPAL STAGE APPEARANCES—Pirate King (understudy), pirate, and policeman, *The Pirates of Penzance*, New York Shakespeare Festival (NYSF), Delacorte Theatre, New York City, 1980; Pozzo, *Waiting for Godot* and Theseus and Oberon, *A Midsummer Night's Dream*, both NYSF, Public Theatre, New York City, 1981; Earl Dancer and narrator, *Miss Waters, to You*, AMAS Repertory Theatre, New York City, 1982; Macheath, *The Threepenny Opera*, Alliance Theatre Company, Atlanta, GA, 1984; Colline, *La Boheme*, NYSF, Public Theatre, 1984; Blue Heaven, *Ceremonies in Dark Old Men*, Ford's Theatre, Washington, DC, then Negro Ensemble Company, New York City, both 1985; Dr. Mo, *The Tale of Madame Zora*, Ensemble Studio Theatre, New York City, 1986; Ben, *Africanis Instructus*, St. Clement's Church Theatre, New York City, 1986; Tullus Aufidius, *Coriolanus*, NYSF, Public Theatre, 1988; Aaron, the Moor, *Titus Andronicus*, NYSF, Delacorte Theatre, 1989. Also appeared in *Coriolanus*, NYSF, Delacorte Theatre, 1979; *Mother Courage and Her Children*, Center Stage, Baltimore, MD, 1979; *The Haggadah: A Passover Cantata*, NYSF, Public Theatre, 1980; *Mahalia*, Hartman Theatre, Stamford, CT, 1981; *Alec Wilder: Clues to a Life*, Vineyard Theatre, New York City, 1982; *The Fantasticks*, Meadow Brook Theatre, Rochester, MI, 1983; *A Map of the World*, NYSF, Public Theatre, 1985; *Shakespeare on Broadway for the Schools*, NYSF, Belasco Theatre, New York City, 1986; *Fragments of a Greek Trilogy*, La Mama Experimental Theatre Club, New York City, 1987; *A Midsummer Night's Dream*, San Diego Repertory Theatre, San Diego, CA; and in *The Lady from Dubuque*.

PRINCIPAL FILM APPEARANCES—Childs, *The Thing*, Universal, 1982; King, *Platoon*, Orion, 1986; Alphonso, *Hot Pursuit*, Paramount, 1987; Buster Franklin, *Bird*, Warner Brothers, 1988; Frank, *They Live*, Universal, 1988; captain, *Braddock: Missing in Action III* (also known as *Braddock: An American M.I.A.*, *Missing in Action III*, and *Braddock: Missing in Action*), Cannon Releasing, 1988; Maurice, *Off Limits* (also known as *Saigon*), Twentieth Century-Fox, 1988; Teagarden, *Stars and Bars*, Columbia, 1988; Ernie Bass, *Road House*, Metro-Goldwyn-Mayer/United Artists, 1989; Powerhouse, *Always*, Universal, 1990. Also appeared in *Men at Work*.

PRINCIPAL TELEVISION APPEARANCES—Mini-Series: *Roots: The Next Generations*, ABC, 1979. Episodic: Roman Criston, *The Equalizer*, CBS, 1988; Jesse Turner, *A Man Called Hawk*, ABC, 1989. Movies: Abe Nicholson, *Ladykillers*, ABC, 1988; Martin Stover, *Murder in Black and White*, CBS, 1990. Also appeared in *Christmas in Tattertown*.

AWARDS: St. Clair Bayfield Award from Actors' Equity Association, Best Shakespearean Performance, 1989, for *Coriolanus*.

MEMBER: Screen Actors Guild, Actors' Equity Association, American Federation of Television and Radio Artists.

ADDRESSES: AGENT—Triad Artists Inc., 10100 Santa Monica Boulevard, 16th Floor, Los Angeles, CA 90067. MANAGER—Joshua Silver, MSI Entertainment, 10866 Wilshire Boulevard, 10th Floor, Los Angeles, CA 90024. PUBLICIST—Ken Amorosano, Amorosano and Associates, 3327 Deronda Drive, Los Angeles, CA 90028.

BETTE DAVIS

DAVIS, Bette   1908-1989

PERSONAL: Born Ruth Elizabeth Davis, April 5, 1908, in Lowell, MA; died of cancer, October 6, 1989, in Neuilly-sur-Seine, France; daughter of Harlow Morrell (a patent attorney) and Ruth Elizabeth (a portrait photographer; maiden name, Favor) Davis; married Harmon Oscar Nelson, Jr. (a band leader), August 18, 1932 (divorced, 1937); married Arthur Farnsworth (a businessman), December 31, 1940 (died, August 25, 1943); married William Grant Sherry (an artist), November 30, 1945 (divorced, July 4, 1950); married Gary Merrill (an actor), July 28, 1950 (divorced, 1960); children: Barbara ("BD"; third marriage); Margot and Michael (fourth marriage; both adopted). EDUCATION—Attended the John Murray Anderson School of Theatre; studied acting with Michael Mordkin, Robert Bell, George Currie, and Robert Milton; studied dance with Roshanara and Martha Graham.

VOCATION: Actress.

CAREER: Also see *WRITINGS* below. STAGE DEBUT—Broadway, Lyceum Theatre, Rochester, NY, 1928. OFF-BROADWAY DEBUT—Floy Jennings, *The Earth Between*, Provincetown Playhouse, 1929. BROADWAY DEBUT—*The Lady from the Sea*, Bijou Theatre, 1929. LONDON DEBUT—*An Informal Evening with Bette Davis*, Palladium, 1975. PRINCIPAL STAGE APPEARANCES—Elaine Bumpstead, *Broken Dishes*, Ritz Theatre, New York City, 1929; Dinah, *Mr. Pim Passes By*, Cape Players, Cape Dennis Playhouse, Cape Dennis, MA, 1930; Alabama Follensby, *Solid South*, Lyceum Theatre, New York City, 1930; ensemble, *Two's Company* (revue), Shubert Theatre, Detroit, MI, then Alvin Theatre, New York City, both 1952; Maxine Faulk, *The Night of the Iguana*, Blackstone Theatre, Chicago, IL, then Royale Theatre, New York City, both 1961; Miss Lilly Moffatt, *Miss Moffatt*, Shubert Theatre, Philadelphia, PA, 1974; *The World of Carl Sandburg* (staged reading), State Theatre, Portland, ME, 1959, then Henry Miller's Theatre, New York City, 1960; *Legendary Ladies of the Movies: An Informal Evening with Bette Davis*, Town Hall, New York City, 1973. Also appeared in *Excess Baggage, Yellow,* and *The Squall,* all George Cukor/George Kondolf Stock Company, Temple Theatre, Rochester, NY, 1928.

MAJOR TOURS—Hedvig, *The Wild Duck*, Blanche Yurka Company, U.S. cities, 1929; ensemble, *Two's Company* (revue), U.S. cities, 1952-53; *The World of Carl Sandburg* (staged reading), U.S. cities, 1959-60; *Legendary Ladies of the Movies: An Informal Evening with Bette Davis*, U.S., Canadian, and New Zealand cities, 1973-75; *Miss Bette Davis on Stage and Screen*, U.K. cities, 1975.

FILM DEBUT—Laura Madison, *Bad Sister*, Universal, 1931. PRINCIPAL FILM APPEARANCES—Janet, *Waterloo Bridge*, Universal, 1931; Margaret Carter, *Seed*, Universal, 1931; Madge Norwood, *Cabin in the Cotton*, Warner Brothers/First National, 1932; Kay Russell, *The Dark Horse*, Warner Brothers, 1932; Peggy Gardner, *Hell's House*, Capital Films Exchange, 1932; Grace Blair, *The Man Who Played God* (also known as *The Silent Voice*), Warner Brothers, 1932; Peggy, *The Menace*, Columbia, 1932; Malbro, *The Rich Are Always with Us*, Warner Brothers/First National, 1932; Dallas O'Mara, *So Big*, Warner Brothers, 1932; Ruth Westcott, *Three on a Match*, Warner Brothers/First National, 1932; Mary Lucy, *Way Back Home* (also known as *Old Greatheart* and *Other People's Business*), RKO, 1932; Norma Phillips, *Bureau of Missing Persons*, Warner Brothers, 1933; Helen Bauer, *Ex-Lady*, Warner Brothers, 1933; Alabama, *Parachute Jumper*, Warner Brothers, 1933; Jenny Hartland, *The Working Man* (also known as *The Adopted Father*), Warner Brothers, 1933; Fay, *20,000 Years in Sing Sing*, Warner Brothers, 1933; Norma Frank, *The Big Shakedown*, Warner Brothers, 1934; Lynn Mason, *Fashions of 1934* (also known as *Fashions*), First National, 1934; Arlene Bradford, *Fog Over Frisco*, Warner Brothers, 1934; Patricia Barclay and Ruth Smith, *Housewife*, Warner Brothers, 1934; Joan Martin, *Jimmy the Gent*, Warner Brothers, 1934; Mildred Rogers, *Of Human Bondage*, RKO, 1934.

Marie Roark, *Bordertown*, Warner Brothers, 1935; Ellen Garfield, *Front Page Woman*, Warner Brothers, 1935; Miriam Brady, *The Girl from Tenth Avenue* (also known as *Men on Her Mind*), Warner Brothers/First National, 1935; Julie Carston, *Special Agent*, Warner Brothers, 1935; Joyce Heath, *Dangerous*, Warner Brothers, 1936; Daisy Appleby, *The Golden Arrow*, Warner Brothers/First National, 1936; Gabrielle Maple, *The Petrified Forest*, Warner Brothers, 1936; Valerie Purvis, *Satan Met a Lady*, Warner Brothers, 1936; Joyce Arden, *It's Love I'm After*, Warner Brothers/First National, 1937; Louise "Fluff" Phillips, *Kid Galahad* (also known as *The Battling Bellhop*), Warner Brothers, 1937; Mary Dwight, *Marked Woman*, Warner Brothers, 1937; Mary Donnell, *That Certain Woman*, Warner Brothers, 1937; Julie Marsden, *Jezebel*, Warner Brothers, 1938; Louise Elliott, *The Sisters*, Warner Brothers, 1938; Judith Traherne, *Dark Victory*, Warner Brothers/First National, 1939; Empress Carlotta Von Habsburg, *Juarez*, Warner Brothers, 1939; Charlotte Lovell, *The Old Maid*, Warner Brothers/First National, 1939; Queen Elizabeth I, *The Private Lives of Elizabeth and Essex* (also known as *Elizabeth the Queen*), Warner Brothers, 1939.

Henriette Deluzy Desportes, *All This and Heaven Too*, Warner

Brothers, 1940; Leslie Crosbie, *The Letter*, Warner Brothers, 1940; nurse, *Shining Victory*, Warner Brothers, 1941; Joan Winfield, *The Bride Came C.O.D.*, Warner Brothers, 1941; Maggie Patterson, *The Great Lie*, Warner Brothers, 1941; Regina Hubbard Giddens, *The Little Foxes*, RKO, 1941; Stanley Timberlake, *In This Our Life*, Warner Brothers, 1942; Maggie Cutler, *The Man Who Came to Dinner*, Warner Brothers, 1942; Charlotte Vale, *Now, Voyager*, Warner Brothers, 1942; Katharine "Kit" Marlowe, *Old Acquaintance*, Warner Brothers/First National, 1943; as herself, *Thank Your Lucky Stars*, Warner Brothers, 1943; Sara Muller, *Watch on the Rhine*, Warner Brothers, 1943; as herself, *Hollywood Canteen*, Warner Brothers, 1944; Fanny Trellis Skeffington, *Mr. Skeffington*, Warner Brothers/First National, 1944; Miss Lilly Moffat, *The Corn Is Green*, Warner Brothers, 1945; Christine Radcliffe, *Deception*, Warner Brothers, 1946; Kate and Pat Bosworth, *A Stolen Life*, Warner Brothers, 1946; Linda Gilman, *June Bride*, Warner Brothers, 1948; Susan Grieve, *Winter Meeting*, Warner Brothers/First National, 1948; Rosa Moline, *Beyond the Forest*, Warner Brothers, 1949.

Margo Channing, *All About Eve*, Twentieth Century-Fox, 1950; Joyce Ramsey, *Payment on Demand* (also known as *The Story of a Divorce*), RKO, 1951; Janet Frobisher, *Another Man's Poison*, United Artists, 1952; Marie Hoke, *Phone Call from a Stranger*, Twentieth Century-Fox, 1952; Margaret Elliot, *The Star*, Twentieth Century-Fox, 1953; Queen Elizabeth I, *The Virgin Queen*, Twentieth Century-Fox, 1955; Aggie Hurley, *The Catered Affair*, Metro-Goldwyn-Mayer (MGM), 1956; Alicia Hull, *Storm Center*, Columbia, 1956; Catherine the Great, *John Paul Jones*, Warner Brothers, 1959; Dowager Countess de Gue, *The Scapegoat*, MGM, 1959; Apple Annie/"Mrs. E. Worthington Manville," *Pocketful of Miracles*, United Artists, 1961; Jane Hudson, *Whatever Happened to Baby Jane?*, Warner Brothers, 1962; Margaret de Lorca and Edith Phillips, *Dead Ringer* (also known as *Dead Image*), Warner Brothers, 1964; Dino's mother, *The Empty Canvas* (also known as *La Noia: L'Ennui et sa diversion* and *L'Erotisme*), Embassy, 1964; Charlotte Hollis, *Hush . . . Hush, Sweet Charlotte*, Twentieth Century-Fox, 1964; Mrs. Gerald Hayden, *Where Love Has Gone*, Paramount, 1964; title role, *The Nanny*, Twentieth Century-Fox, 1965; Mrs. Taggart, *The Anniversary*, Hammer, 1968.

Title role, *Bunny O'Hare*, American International, 1971; Wanda Fleming, *Connecting Rooms*, London Screen, 1971; millionairess, *Lo scopane scientifico* (also known as *The Scientific Cardplayer* and *The Game*), CIC, 1972; Aunt Elizabeth, *Burnt Offerings*, United Artists, 1976; Mrs. Van Schuyler, *Death on the Nile*, Paramount, 1978; Letha Wedge, *Return from Witch Mountain*, Buena Vista, 1978; Mrs. Aylwood, *The Watcher in the Woods*, Buena Vista, 1980; Libby Strong, *The Whales of August*, Alive, 1987; Miranda, *Wicked Stepmother*, Metro-Goldwyn-Mayer/United Artists, 1989. Also appeared in *Stars on Horseback* (documentary), 1943; *Second Victory Loan Campaign Fund* (short film), 1945; *A Present with a Future* (short film), 1943; *A Day at Santa Anita* (short film), Warner Brothers.

PRINCIPAL FILM WORK—Producer, *A Stolen Life*, Warner Brothers, 1946.

PRINCIPAL TELEVISION APPEARANCES—Pilots: Beatrice Enters, *Stranded* (broadcast as an episode of *Telephone Time*), ABC, 1957; the agent, *The Star Maker* (broadcast as an episode of *Studio 57*) syndicated, 1958; title role, *The Elisabeth McQueeney Story* (broadcast as an episode of *Wagon Train*), NBC, 1959; Judge Meredith, *The Judge and Jake Wyler*, NBC, 1972; title role, *Madame Sin*, ABC, 1972; Laura Trent, *Hotel*, ABC, 1983; also *Hello Mother*,

Goodbye, NBC, 1973. Episodic: Marie Hoke, "Crackup," *Twentieth Century-Fox Hour*, CBS, 1956; Dolly Madison, "Footnote on a Dolly," *Ford Theatre*, ABC, 1957; Ella Lindstrom, *Wagon Train*, NBC, 1959; Della Miller, *The Virginian*, NBC, 1962; also *Person to Person*, CBS, 1956; "With Malice Toward One," *General Electric Theatre*, CBS, 1957; "For Better, For Worse," *Schlitz Playhouse of Stars*, CBS, 1957; "The Cold Touch," *General Electric Theatre*, CBS, 1958; "Fraction of a Second," *Suspicion*, NBC, 1958; "Out There—Darkness," *Alfred Hitchcock Theatre*, CBS, 1959; "Dark Morning," *The Dupont Show with June Allyson*, CBS, 1959; *Wagon Train*, NBC, 1961; *The Andy Williams Show*, NBC, 1962; *Perry Mason*, CBS, 1963; *The Tonight Show*, NBC, 1964 and 1968; *Gunsmoke*, CBS, 1966; *The Mike Douglas Show*, syndicated, 1966; *The Milton Berle Variety Show*, ABC, 1966; *It Takes a Thief*, ABC, 1970; *The Dick Cavett Show*, ABC, 1971; *The David Frost Show*, syndicated, 1971; *This Is Your Life*, syndicated, 1972; *The Dean Martin Show*, NBC, 1973; "Directed by William Wyler," *American Masters*, PBS, 1987; *Rowan and Martin's Laugh-In*, NBC.

Movies: Mrs. Elliot, *Scream, Pretty Peggy*, ABC, 1973; Minnie Kennedy, *The Disappearance of Aimee*, NBC, 1976; Widow Fortune, *Dark Secret of Harvest Home*, NBC, 1978; Lucy Mason, *Strangers: The Story of a Mother and Daughter*, CBS, 1979; Billie Dupree, *Skyward*, NBC, 1980; Estelle Malone, *White Mama*, CBS, 1980; Elizabeth Winfield, *Family Reunion*, NBC, 1981; Alice Claypoole Vanderbilt, *Little Gloria . . . Happy at Last*, NBC, 1982; Esther Cimino, *A Piano for Mrs. Cimino*, CBS, 1982; Mini Dwyer, *Right of Way*, HBO, 1983; Carrie Louise Serrocold, *Agatha Christie's "Murder with Mirrors,"* CBS, 1985; Hannah Loftin, *As Summers Die*, HBO, 1986. Specials: "The Movie Crazy Years," *NET Playhouse*, PBS, 1971; *Johnny Carson Presents the Sun City Scandals '72*, NBC, 1972; *Warner Brothers' Movies—A Fifty Year Salute*, NBC, 1973; *The American Film Institute Salute to Henry Fonda*, CBS, 1978; *Variety '77—The Year in Entertainment*, CBS, 1978; *The American Film Institute Salute to Frank Capra*, CBS, 1982; *The Barbara Walters Special*, ABC, 1987.

PRINCIPAL RADIO APPEARANCES—Series: Host and narrator, *The Whispering Streets*, ABC, 1958. Episodic: Title role, "Elizabeth the Queen," Judith Traherne, "Dark Victory," and in "The Small Servant," *Hollywood Players*, CBS, 1946; also *Your Hollywood Parade*, NBC, 1937; *Arch Oboler's Plays*, NBC, 1939; "Of Human Bondage" and "Baby," *Everyman's Theatre*, NBC, 1940; *Plays for Americans*, NBC, 1942; Julie Marsden, "Jezebel," *Academy Award Theatre*, 1946; Linda Gilman, "June Bride" and Julie Marsden, "Jezebel," *Screen Directors' Playhouse*, NBC; "Alien Corn," *The Theatre Guild on the Air*, CBS; "Skylark," *Ford Theatre*, CBS; *Screen Guild Theatre*, CBS; "Of Human Bondage," *Everything for the Boys*, NBC; *Shell Chateau*, NBC; *Millions for Defense*, CBS; *Prudential Family Hour of Stars*, CBS; Charlotte Vale, "Now, Voyager," *Lux Radio Theatre*; "Chicago, Germany," *Treasury Star Parade; Texaco Star Theatre*. Also Tess Harding, *Woman of the Year*, 1951; Madame von Meck, *Beloved*.

RELATED CAREER—Founder and first president, Hollywood Canteen, 1942.

WRITINGS: (Author of introduction) *Bette Davis* (biography), Robinson, 1948; (with Sanford Doty) *The Lonely Life: An Autobiography*, Putnam, 1962; (author of commentary) *Mother Goddam: The Story of the Career of Bette Davis*, Hawthorn, 1974; (with Michael Herskowitz) *This 'n' That*, Putnam, 1987.

RECORDINGS: ALBUMS—*Thank Your Lucky Stars* (original soundtrack), Hollywood Soundstage, 1943; *Two's Company* (original cast recording), RCA, 1952; *Fifty Years of Film*, Warner Brothers, 1973; *Miss Bette Davis*, EMI, 1976. SINGLES—"Hush . . . Hush Sweet Charlotte," MGM, 1965.

AWARDS: Academy Award, Best Actress, 1935, for *Dangerous;* Best Actress Award from the Venice Film Festival, 1937, for *Marked Woman* and *Kid Galahad;* Academy Award, Best Actress, 1938, for *Jezebel;* Academy Award nomination, Best Actress, 1939, and *Picturegoer* Annual Gold Medal, 1940, both for *Dark Victory;* voted one of the Top Ten Money-Making Stars of 1939, 1940, 1941, and 1944 by the *Motion Picture Herald*-Fame Poll; Academy Award nomination, Best Actress, 1940, for *The Letter;* Academy Award nomination, Best Actress, 1941, for *The Little Foxes;* Golden Apple Star of the Year Award from the Hollywood Women's Press Club, 1941; Academy Award nomination, 1942, for *Now, Voyager;* Academy Award nomination, Best Actress, 1944, for *Mr. Skeffington;* Academy Award nomination, Best Actress, New York Film Critics' Circle Award, Best Female Performance, San Francisco Critics' Award, all 1950, and Best Actress Award from the Cannes Film Festival, 1951, all for *All About Eve;* Academy Award nomination, Best Actress, 1952, for *The Star;* Academy Award nomination, Best Actress, 1962, for *Whatever Happened to Baby Jane?;* Golden Apple Star of the Year Award from the Hollywood Women's Press Club, 1963.

Straw Hat Award from the Council of Stock Theatres, 1970; Sarah Siddons Award, 1973; Cecil B. De Mille Award, 1974, for Outstanding Contributions to the Entertainment Field; Life Achievement in Motion Pictures Award from the American Film Institute, 1977; Emmy Award, Outstanding Lead Actress in a Limited Series or Special, 1979, for *Strangers: The Story of a Mother and Daughter;* Emmy Award nomination, 1980, for *White Mama;* Rudolf Valentino Life Achievement Award, 1982; Louella Parsons Award, 1983; American Academy of Arts Award, 1983; Medal for Distinguished Public Service from the Department of Defense, 1983; Crystal Award from Women in Films, 1983; Cesar Award from the French Film Institute, 1986; Ordre Arts et Belles Lettres from the French Ministry of Culture, 1986; Legion of Honor from the French Ministry of Culture, 1987; Kennedy Center Honors, 1987; honors from the Film Society of Lincoln Center and the San Sebastian Film Festival, both 1989.

MEMBER: Academy of Motion Picture Arts and Sciences (president, 1941), Screen Actors Guild, Actors' Equity Association, American Federation of Television and Radio Artists.

OBITUARIES AND OTHER SOURCES: [New York] *Newsday*, October 8, 1989; *New York Times*, October 8, 1989.*

*   *   *

DAVISON, Peter

PERSONAL: Born in London, England; married Sandra Dickenson (an actress); children: Georgia. EDUCATION—Attended the Central School of Speech and Drama for three years.

VOCATION: Actor.

CAREER: PRINCIPAL FILM APPEARANCES—Policeman, *The Elephant Man,* Paramount, 1980.

TELEVISION DEBUT—*The Tomorrow People.* PRINCIPAL TELEVISION APPEARANCES—Series: Tristan Farnan, *All Creatures Great and Small,* BBC, 1977-81, then PBS; title role, *Doctor Who,* BBC, then PBS, 1982-84; title role, *Campion,* BBC, then *Mystery!,* PBS, 1989; also Dr. Steven Daker, *A Very Peculiar Practice,* BBC; *Holding the Fort,* BBC; *Sink or Swim,* BBC; *Anna of the Five Towns,* BBC; *Print-Out; Once Upon a Time.* Mini-Series: Tom, *Love for Lydia,* London Weekend Television, then *Masterpiece Theatre,* PBS, 1979; Lance, "A Pocketful of Rye," *Agatha Christie's Miss Marple,* BBC, then *Mystery!,* PBS, 1986. Episodic: Ian, *Magnum P.I.,* CBS, 1985. Specials: The Fifth Doctor Who, *Doctor Who—The Five Doctors,* BBC, then PBS, 1983.

RELATED CAREER—Actor in repertory theatres in England.

ADDRESSES: MANAGER—John Mahoney Management, 30 Chalfont Court, Baker Street, London NW1, England.*

*   *   *

DAWSON, Richard   1932-

PERSONAL: Born November 20, 1932, in Gosport, England; married Diana Dors (an actress; divorced, 1964); children: Mark, Gary.

VOCATION: Actor, comedian, and television host.

CAREER: PRINCIPAL FILM APPEARANCES—Weaver, *King Rat,* Columbia, 1965; Joey, *Munster, Go Home,* Universal, 1966; Hugh MacDonald, *The Devil's Brigade,* United Artists, 1968; Damon Killian, *The Running Man,* Tri-Star, 1987. Also appeared in *Promises, Promises* (also known as *Promise Her Anything*), NTD, 1963.

PRINCIPAL TELEVISION APPEARANCES—Series: Peter Newkirk, *Hogan's Heroes,* CBS, 1965-71; regular, *Can You Top This?,* syndicated, 1969-70; regular, *Rowan and Martin's Laugh-In,* NBC, 1971-73; Richard Richardson, *The New Dick Van Dyke Show,* CBS, 1973-74; emcee, *Masquerade Party,* syndicated, 1974-75; panelist, *Match Game, P.M.,* syndicated, 1975-78; panelist, *I've Got a Secret,* CBS, 1976; host, *Family Feud,* syndicated, 1977-85. Pilots: Friend, *Keeping an Eye on Denise,* CBS, 1973; host, *Bizarre,* ABC, 1979. Episodic: Tracy Rattigan, *The Dick Van Dyke Show,* CBS, 1963; Oliver Fair, "The Invisibles," *The Outer Limits,* ABC, 1964; guest host, *Good Morning America,* ABC, 1978; also voice characterizations, *Hong Kong Phooey* (animated), ABC; Shiperly, *The Saturday Superstar Movie* (animated), ABC. Movies: Chandler Corey, *How to Pick Up Girls!,* ABC, 1978. Specials: *All-Star Family Feud,* ABC, 1978; *David Frost Presents the Seventh Guinness Book of World Records,* ABC, 1978; *The Daytime Emmy Awards,* ABC, 1978; *Celebrity Challenge of the Sexes,* CBS, 1979; *TV's Funniest Game Show Moments,* ABC, 1984.

RELATED CAREER—Appeared in repertory theatre productions throughout the U.K.; stand-up comedian in nightclubs throughout the U.K. and U.S.

NON-RELATED CAREER—Merchant seaman.

AWARDS: Emmy Award, Best Host of a Game Show, 1978, for *Family Feud.*

ADDRESSES: OFFICE—c/o Leonard Granger, 9903 Kip Drive, Beverly Hills, CA 90210.*

*   *   *

DAY, Lynda
See GEORGE, Lynda Day

*   *   *

DENVER, John   1943-

PERSONAL: Born Henry John Deutschendorf, Jr., December 31, 1943, in Roswell, NM; son of Henry John (an officer in the U.S. Air Force) and Erma Deutschendorf; married Ann Marie Martell, June 9, 1967 (divorced, 1983); children: Zachary, Anna Kate. EDUCATION—Studied architecture at Texas Tech University.

VOCATION: Singer, songwriter, and actor.

JOHN DENVER

CAREER: PRINCIPAL FILM APPEARANCES—Jerry Landers, *Oh, God!*, Warner Brothers, 1977; narrator, *Fire and Ice*, Concorde, 1987.

PRINCIPAL TELEVISION APPEARANCES—Pilots: Jim Clayton, *Higher Ground*, CBS, 1988. Episodic: *Saturday Night Live with Howard Cosell*, ABC, 1975. Movies: George Billings, *The Christmas Gift*, CBS, 1986; Max Sinclair, *The Leftovers*, ABC, 1986; Dillard Nations, "Foxfire," *Hallmark Hall of Fame*, CBS, 1987. Specials: *The Bob Hope Show*, NBC, 1973; *The John Denver Special*, ABC, 1974; *Doris Day Today*, CBS, 1975; *John Denver's Rocky Mountain Christmas*, ABC, 1975; *The Carpenters*, ABC, 1976; *John Denver and Friend*, ABC, 1976; *The John Denver Special*, ABC, 1976; *John Denver—Thank God I'm a Country Boy*, ABC, 1977; *Sinatra and Friends*, ABC, 1977; *Grammy Awards Show*, CBS, 1978; *John Denver in Australia*, ABC, 1978; *Alaska: The American Child*, ABC, 1978; *John Denver and the Ladies*, ABC, 1979; *The Third Barry Manilow Special*, ABC, 1979; *John Denver and the Muppets: A Christmas Together*, ABC, 1980; *John Denver: Music and the Mountains*, ABC, 1981; *Two of a Kind: George Burns and John Denver*, ABC, 1981; *Bob Hope's Salute to NASA—25 Years of Reaching for the Stars*, NBC, 1983; *Salute to Lady Liberty*, CBS, 1984; *1985 Miss Universe Pageant*, CBS, 1985; *How to Be a Man*, CBS, 1985; *America Censored* (documentary), CBS, 1985; *The Twelfth Annual People's Choice Awards*, CBS, 1986; *Kraft Salutes the George Burns 90th Birthday Special*, CBS, 1986; *Liberty Weekend*, ABC, 1986; *The Special Olympics Opening Ceremonies*, ABC, 1987; *From Tahiti, Bob Hope's Tropical Comedy Special*, NBC, 1987; *Julie Andrews: The Sound of Christmas*, ABC, 1987; *John Denver's Christmas in Aspen*, CBS, 1988; *The Kennedy Center Honors: A Celebration of the Performing Arts*, CBS, 1988; *The New South Wales Royal Bicentennial Concert*, Network Ten (Australia), 1988, then Arts and Entertainment, 1989; *Our Common Future*, Arts and Entertainment, 1989; *In Performance at the White House*, PBS, 1989.

PRINCIPAL TELEVISION WORK—Pilots: Executive producer (with Jim Green and Allen Epstein), *Higher Ground*, CBS, 1988.

RELATED CAREER—Member, Chad Mitchell Trio (a folk music group), 1965-68; as a solo singer and performer since 1968, has appeared in concert halls throughout the world.

NON-RELATED CAREER—Founder, Windstar Foundation, Snowmass, CO, 1976; founder, World Hunger Project, 1977; member, Presidential Commission on World Hunger, 1978; chairman, National UNICEF Day, 1984.

WRITINGS: All as composer. FILM—(With Harold Faltermeyer, Gary Wright, Panarama, and Alan Parsons), *Fire and Ice*, Concorde, 1987. TELEVISION—Series: Theme song (with Richard L. Kniss and Michael Taylor), "Sunshine on My Shoulders," *Sunshine*, NBC, 1975. Pilots: (With Lee Holdridge) *Higher Ground*, CBS, 1988.

RECORDINGS: ALBUMS—*Rhymes and Reasons*, RCA, 1969; *Take Me to Tomorrow*, RCA, 1970; *Whose Garden Was This?*, RCA, 1970; *Poems, Prayers, and Promises*, RCA, 1971; *Aerie*, RCA, 1972; *Rocky Mountain High*, RCA, 1972; *Farewell Andromeda*, RCA, 1973; *Back Home Again*, RCA, 1974; *John Denver's Greatest Hits*, RCA, 1974; *Rocky Mountain Christmas*, RCA, 1975; *An Evening with John Denver*, RCA, 1975; *Windsong*, RCA, 1975; *Live in London*, RCA, 1976; *Spirit*, RCA, 1976; *I Want to Live*,

RCA, 1977; *John Denver's Greatest Hits, Volume 2*, RCA, 1977; *John Denver*, RCA, 1979; *A Christmas Together with the Muppets*, RCA, 1979; *Autograph*, RCA, 1980; *Some Days Are Diamonds*, RCA, 1981; *Perhaps Love*, RCA, 1981; *Seasons of the Heart*, RCA, 1982; *It's About Time*, RCA, 1983; *Collection*, Telstar, 1984; *Dreamland Express*, RCA, 1985; *One World*, RCA, 1986. With the Chad Mitchell Trio: *That's the Way It's Gonna Be*, Mercury, 1965.

AWARDS: Top Male Recording Artist Award from *Record World*, 1974-75; Entertainer of the Year Award from the Country Music Association, 1975; People's Choice Award, Favorite Musical Performer, 1975; Singing Star of the Year Award from the American Guild of Variety Artists, 1975; Male Vocalist of the Year Award from the Academy of Country Music, 1975; Golden Apple Prize from the Hollywood Women's Press Club, 1977; also received fifteen Gold Record Awards and eight Platinum Record Awards from the Recording Industry Association of America.

MEMBER: National Space Institute, Cousteau Society, Friends of the Earth, Human/Dolphin Foundation, European Space Agency, Save the Children Foundation.

SIDELIGHTS: RECREATIONS—Aviation and photography.

ADDRESSES: OFFICE—John Denver Concerts Inc., P.O. Box 1587, Aspen, CO 81612.*

*   *   *

DEPARDIEU, Gerard   1948-

PERSONAL: Born December 27, 1948, in Chateauroux, France; son of Rene (a metal worker) and Alice (Marillier) Depardieu; married Elisabeth Guignot (an actress), 1970; children: Guillaume, Julie. EDUCATION—Studied acting with Charles Dullin and Jean Laurent Cochet; also studied at the Theatre National Populaire.

VOCATION: Actor, director, and producer.

CAREER: PRINCIPAL STAGE APPEARANCES—*Boudu sauve des eaux*, 1968; *Les Garcons de la bande*, 1969; *Une Fille dans ma soupe*, 1970; *Sauves, Galapagos*, and *Clair obscure*, all 1971; *Home*, 1972; *La Chevauchee sur le lac de Constance*, 1974; *Les Insenses sont en voie d'extinction*, 1978; *Tartuffe*, 1984. PRINCIPAL STAGE WORK—Director, *Tartuffe*, 1984.

FILM DEBUT—*Le Beatnik et le minet* (short film), 1965. PRINCIPAL FILM APPEARANCES—Pierre, *Un peu de soleil dans l'eau froide* (also known as *A Little Sun in Cold Water*), Imperia, 1971; door-to-door salesman, *Nathalie Granger*, French Consulate/Moullet et Compagnie/Mouflet et Cie, 1972; postman, *Les Gaspards*, Albina, 1973; Jean-Claude, *Les Valseuses* (also known as *Going Places*), Societe nouvelle prodis/Almi Cinema V, 1973; Matriscope inventor, *Stavisky*, CCFC/Almi/Cinema V, 1974; Jean, *Vincent, Francois, Paul. . . et les autres* (also known as *Vincent, Francois, Paul . . . and the Others*), Gaumont, 1974; Pierre, *Pas si mechant que ca* (also known as *Not As Wicked As All That . . . and The Wonderful Crook*), Gaumont, 1974.

Olivier, *Maitresse* (also known as *Mistress*), Gaumont Internation-

GERARD DEPARDIEU

al, 1975; Gerard, *La Derniere Femme* (also known as *The Last Woman* and *L'ultima donna*), Columbia, 1975; Berg, *Sept morts sur ordonnance* (also known as *Seven Deaths By Prescription*), AMLF, 1975; Samson, *Barocco,* Films la Boetie, 1976; Olmo Dalco, *1900* (also known as *Novecento*), Paramount/United Artists/Twentieth Century-Fox, 1976; Michel Cayre, *Baxter, Vera Baxter,* Sunchild, 1976; man, *Le Camion* (also known as *The Truck*), Cinema 9/Films Moliere, 1977; title role, *Rene la Canne,* Rizzoli, 1977; Philibert, *La Nuit tous les chats sont gris* (also known as *At Night All Cats Are Gray*), Societe Nouvelle Prodis/Exportation Francaise Cinematographique/SAM, 1977; David Martinaud, *Dites-lui que je l'aime* (also known as *Tell Him I Love Him*), World Marketing, 1977; man with t-shirt, *Die Linkshandige Frau* (also known as *The Left-Handed Woman*), Marin Karmitz, 1977, released in the United States by New Yorker, 1980; Raoul, *Preparez vos mouchoirs* (also known as *Get Out Your Handkerchiefs*), Capac/Belga/New Line Cinema, 1978; Gerard Lafayette, *Ciao maschio* (also known as *Affentraum* and *Bye Bye Monkey*), Gaumont/Filverlag der Autoren, 1978; Raoul-Renaud Homecourt, *Le Sucre* (also known as *The Sugar*), SFP/Gaumont International/Cineproduction, 1978; Morel, *Les Chiens* (also known as *The Dogs*), World Marketing/GEF/CCFC, 1979.

Patrick, *Je vous aime* (also known as *I Love You*), AMLF, 1980; Alphonse Tram, *Buffet froid* (also known as *Cold Cuts*), Interama, 1980; title role, *Loulou,* Gaumont International/New Yorker, 1980; Roger Morzini, *Inspecteur la Bavure* (also known as *Inspector Blunder*), AMLF, 1980; Rene Ragueneau, *Mon oncle d'Amerique* (also known as *Les Somnambules*), New World, 1980; Bernard Granger, *Le Dernier Metro* (also known as *The Last Metro*), United

Artists, 1981; Bernard Coudray, *La Femme d'a cote* (also known as *The Woman Next Door*), United Artists, 1981; Mickey, *Le Choix des armes* (also known as *Choice of Arms*), Parafrance, 1983; Georges Danton, *Danton,* Triumph, 1983; as himself, *Wajda's Danton* (documentary), Cori Films International/Channel Four, 1983; Gerard Delmas, *La Lune dans le caniveau* (also known as *The Moon in the Gutter*), Columbia/Triumph, 1983; title role, *Le Retour de Martin Guerre* (also known as *The Return of Martin Guerre*), European International, 1983; Jean Lucas, *Les Comperes* (also known as *The Co-Fathers*), European International, 1984; title role, *Le Tartuffe,* Gaumont International, 1984; Charles Saganne, *Fort Saganne,* Roissy/AAA, 1984.

Campana, *La Chevre,* European Classics, 1985; Mangin, *Police,* Gaumont/TF1, 1985; Julien Chayssac, *Une Femme ou deux* (also known as *One Woman or Two*), AAA/World Marketing/Orion Classics, 1985; Jean Cadoret, *Jean de Florette,* Orion Classics, 1986; Jean Lucas, *Les Fugitifs* (also known as *The Fugitives*), Gaumont/Roissy/Buena Vista, 1986; Bob, *Menage* (also known as *Tenue de soiree*), Norstar, 1986; Dr. Lombart, *Rue du depart* (also known as *Street of Departures*), AAA/Films du Volcan/Allied Artists, 1986; Father Donissan, *Sous le soleil de Satan* (also known as *Under the Sun of Satan* and *Under Satan's Sun*), Gaumont, 1987, released in the United States by Alive Films, 1989; Marc, *Deux* (also known as *Two*), AMLF/Roissy, 1988; Auguste Rodin, *Camille Claudel,* Gaumont, 1988, released in the United States by Orion Classics, 1989; Charles, *Drole d'endroit pour une rencontre* (also known as *A Funny Place for a Meeting, A Strange Place for an Encounter,* and *A Strange Place to Meet*), Union Generale Cinematographique/Roissy, 1988; Bernard Barthelemy, *Trop belle pour toi* (also known as *Too Beautiful for You*), AMLF, 1989, released in the United States by Orion Classics, 1990; Christian Gauthier, *Je veux rentrer a la maison* (also known as *I Want to Go Home* and *Voglio tornare a casa*), Marin Karmitz, 1989; title role, *Cyrano de Bergerac,* President, 1990.

Also appeared in *Christmas Carol,* 1965; *Le Cri du cormoran, le soir au-dessus des jonques* (also known as *The Cry of the Cormoran at Night Over the Junks*), Gaumont International, 1970; *Le Tueur* (also known as *The Killer*), Societe Nouvelle Prodis, 1971; *Le Viager* (also known as *The Annuity*), United Artists, 1972; *La Scoumoune* (also known as *Killer Man*), Fox-Lira, 1972; *Au rendez-vous de la mort joyeuse,* United Artists, 1972; *L'Affaire Dominici,* Societe Nouvelle de Cinema/Imperia, 1972; *Rude journee pour la reine* (also known as *Rough Day for the Queen*), Nouvelles Editions de Films/Planfilm, 1973; *Deux hommes dans la ville* (also known as *Two Men in Town*), Valoria, 1973; *La Femme du Gange,* 1973; *Bertolucci secondo il cinema* (documentary), 1975; *Je t'aime, moi non plus* (also known as *I Love You, Me No Longer*), AMLF/Sinfonia, 1975; *Les Plages de l'Atlantique,* 1976; *Violanta,* Jordan Bojilov/Daniel Carrillo, 1977; *Reve de singe,* 1978; *L'ingorgo* (also known as *Traffic Jam* and *Bottleneck*), CineTel, 1978; *Temporale Rosy,* 1979; *Le Grand Frere,* 1982; *Rive droite, rive gauche* (also known as *Right Bank, Left Bank*), Parafrance, 1984.

PRINCIPAL FILM WORK—Co-producer, *Les Comperes* (also known as *The Co-Fathers*), European International, 1984; director, *Le Tartuffe,* Gaumont International, 1984; co-producer, *Menage* (also known as *Tenue de soiree*), Norstar, 1986; co-producer, *Jean de Florette,* Orion Classics, 1986; co-producer, *Les Fugitifs* (also known *The Fugitives*), Gaumont/Roissy/Buena Vista, 1986; co-producer, *Sous le soleil de Satan* (also known as *Under the Sun of Satan* and *Under Satan's Sun*), Gaumont, 1987, released in the

United States by Alive Films, 1989; co-producer, *Drole d'endroit pour une rencontre* (also known as *A Funny Place for a Meeting, A Strange Place for an Encounter,* and *A Strange Place to Meet*), Union Generale Cinematographique/Roissy, 1988; co-producer, *Camille Claudel,* Gaumont, 1988; co-producer, *Deux* (also known as *Two*), AMLF/Roissy, 1988; co-producer, *Je veux rentrer a la maison* (also known as *I Want to Go Home* and *Voglio tornare a casa*), Marin Karmitz, 1989; co-producer, *Trop belle pour toi* (also known as *Too Beautiful for You*), AMLF, 1989; co-producer, *Cyrano de Bergerac,* President, 1990.

PRINCIPAL TELEVISION APPEARANCES—Series: *L'Inconnu,* 1974.

AWARDS: Prix Gerard Philipe, 1973; Cesar Award, Best Actor, 1980, for *Le Dernier Metro;* Montreal World Film Festival Award (co-winner), Best Actor, 1983, for *Danton;* Best Actor Award from the Venice Film Festival, 1985, for *Police;* Fellowship Award from the British Film Institute, 1989; Cesar Award, Best Actor, 1990, for *Trop belle pour toi.*

ADDRESSES: AGENT—Art Media, 10 Avenue George V, 75008 Paris, France. PUBLICIST—Claude Davy, Conseil en Relations Publiques, 43 Rue de Lille, 75007 Paris, France.

*   *   *

DESCHANEL, Caleb   1944-

PERSONAL: Born September 21, 1944, in Philadelphia, PA; wife's name, Mary Jo (an actress); children: two daughters. EDUCATION—Attended Johns Hopkins University; studied film at the University of Southern California Film School, at the American Film Institute, and with Gordon Willis.

VOCATION: Cinematographer and director.

CAREER: PRINCIPAL FILM WORK—Camera operator, *A Woman Under the Influence,* Faces International, 1974; cinematographer, *Being There,* United Artists, 1979; cinematographer, *The Black Stallion,* United Artists, 1979; cinematographer, *More American Graffiti,* Universal, 1979; cinematographer (second unit), *Apocalypse Now,* United Artists, 1979; director, *The Escape Artist,* Orion/Warner Brothers, 1982; cinematographer, *Let's Spend the Night Together,* Ronald Schwary, 1982; cinematographer, *The Right Stuff,* Warner Brothers, 1983; cinematographer, *The Natural,* Tri-Star, 1984; cinematographer, *The Slugger's Wife* (also known as *Neil Simon's The Slugger's Wife*), Columbia, 1985; director, *Crusoe,* Island, 1989.

RELATED CAREER—Director of short films, documentaries, and television commercials.

AWARDS: National Society of Film Critics Award, Best Cinematography, 1979, for *The Black Stallion;* Academy Award nomination, Best Cinematography, 1984, for *The Right Stuff;* Academy Award nomination, Best Cinematography, 1985, for *The Natural.*

SIDELIGHTS: Regarding his career change from cinematographer to director, Caleb Deschanel told Matthew Flamm of *Premiere* (March, 1989), ''I don't see being the director as that much

different. But I've learned that I'd much rather take chances with something of my own than be on the sidelines when it fails.''

ADDRESSES: OFFICE—73 Market Street, Venice, CA 90291. AGENT—Darris Hatch, International Creative Management, 8899 Beverly Boulevard, Los Angeles, CA 90048.

*   *   *

DiCENZO, George

PERSONAL: Full name, George Ralph DiCenzo.

VOCATION: Actor.

CAREER: PRINCIPAL STAGE APPEARANCES—Frank Eaton, *Whitsuntide,* Martinique Theatre, New York City, 1972.

PRINCIPAL FILM APPEARANCES—Sergeant, *Going Home,* Metro-Goldwyn-Mayer (MGM), 1971; George, *Shoot It: Black, Shoot It: Blue,* Levitt-Pickman, 1974; Eversull, *Las Vegas Lady,* Crown International, 1976; Major Benchley, *Close Encounters of the Third Kind,* Columbia, 1977; Lieutenant ''Hardass'' Grimsley, *The Choirboys,* Universal, 1977; Darryl Diggs, *The Frisco Kid* (also known as *No Knife*), Warner Brothers, 1979; Captain Fairbanks, *The Ninth Configuration* (also known as *Twinkle, Twinkle, Killer Kane*), Warner Brothers, 1980; Hordak, *The Secret of the Sword* (animated), Atlantic, 1985; Sam Baines, *Back to the Future,* Universal, 1985; Mr. Favio, *About Last Night,* Tri-Star, 1986; DeFranco, *The Longshot,* Orion, 1986; Philadelphia ''Phil'' Horton, *Omega Syndrome* (also known as *Omega Seven*), New World, 1987; Mr. Blackhart, *The New Adventures of Pippi Longstocking,* Columbia, 1988; coach, *Eighteen Again!,* New World, 1988; Mr. Marowitz, *Sing,* Tri-Star, 1989. Also appeared in *Walk Like a Man* (also known as *Bobo* and *Bobo the Dog Boy*), Metro-Goldwyn-Mayer/United Artists, 1987; *Face of the Enemy,* Tri-Culture, 1989.

PRINCIPAL TELEVISION APPEARANCES—Series: Voices of Hercules and Sentinal One, *The Young Sentinals* (animated), NBC, 1977-78; voice of John Blackstar, *Blackstar* (animated), CBS, 1981-82; Lieutenant Edward DeNisco, *McClain's Law,* NBC, 1981-82; voice characterization, *Spider-Man and His Amazing Friends* (animated), NBC, 1981-86; voice of Lou Albano, *Hulk Hogan's Rock 'n' Wrestling!* (animated), CBS, 1985-87; voice of He-Man, *He-Man and the Masters of the Universe* (animated), syndicated, 1983—; voice of He-Man, *She Ra: Princess of Power* (animated), syndicated, 1985; voice characterization, *Goltar and the Golden Lance* (animated), syndicated, 1985; voice characterization, *Scooby's Mystery Funhouse* (animated), ABC, 1985-86; voice characterization, *Wildfire* (animated), CBS, 1986-87; also *Equal Justice,* ABC, 1989. Mini-Series: Abe Singer, *Aspen* (also known as *The Innocent and the Damned*), NBC, 1977; Anthony Orsatti, *If Tomorrow Comes,* CBS, 1986. Pilots: Zoot Lafferty, *The Blue Knight,* NBC, 1973; Suramin, *The Swiss Family Robinson,* ABC, 1975; Sam Downing, *McLaren's Riders,* CBS, 1977; Sheriff Alfredo De Vega, *The Jordan Chance,* CBS, 1978; Captain Cornworth, *To Kill a Cop,* NBC, 1978; Rudolph Ulmer, *The Tom Swift and Linda Craig Mystery Hour,* ABC, 1983; also *The Norliss Tapes,* ABC, 1973; *Equal Justice,* ABC, 1989.

Episodic: Charles, *Dynasty*, ABC, 1984 and 1985; Richard Margolis, *Alfred Hitchcock Presents*, NBC, 1985; Andy's stepfather, *Spenser: For Hire*, ABC, 1986; Johnny Blaze, *Murder, She Wrote*, CBS, 1986; Max Merrill, *Blacke's Magic*, NBC, 1986; Frank Dorgan, *The Equalizer*, CBS, 1987 and 1988; Dominic, *The Equalizer*, CBS, 1988; John Yancy, *Tattinger's*, NBC, 1988; Sergeant Kettler, *Murder, She Wrote*, CBS, 1988. Movies: Owings, *Last Hours Before Morning*, NBC, 1975; Vincent Bugliosi, *Helter Skelter*, CBS, 1976; Chief Reinhold, *The Hostage Heart*, CBS, 1977; Bennet, *High Midnight*, CBS, 1979; Cliff Barrankos, *The Night the City Screamed*, ABC, 1980; Vincent Scozzola, *Reunion*, CBS, 1980; Sam Caldwell, *Killing at Hell's Gate*, CBS, 1981; Tony Caruso, *Rivkin: Bounty Hunter*, CBS, 1981; Davis Bentlow, *Cowboy*, CBS, 1983; Bowdish, *Starflight: The Plane That Couldn't Land*, ABC, 1983; Scotty, *Warm Hearts, Cold Feet*, CBS, 1987. Specials: Voice of He-Man, *He-Man and She-Ra: A Christmas Special* (animated), syndicated, 1985.

ADDRESSES: AGENT—Ronald Leif, Contemporary Artists, 132 Lasky Drive, Beverly Hills, CA 90212.

*　　*　　*

DILLON, Kevin   1965-

PERSONAL: Born in 1965 in Mamaroneck, NY.

VOCATION: Actor.

CAREER: PRINCIPAL STAGE APPEARANCES—Appeared in productions of *Dark at the Top of the Stairs* and *The Indian Wants the Bronx*.

FILM DEBUT—Rooney, *Heaven Help Us* (also known as *Catholic Boys*), Tri-Star, 1985. PRINCIPAL FILM APPEARANCES—Bunny, *Platoon*, Orion, 1986; narrator, *Dear America: Letters Home from Vietnam*, HBO Films, 1987; Brian Flagg, *The Blob*, Tri-Star, 1988; J.J. Merrill, *The Rescue*, Buena Vista, 1988; Cosmo, *Remote Control*, Vista Organization, 1988; Skitty, *War Party*, Tri-Star, 1988; Sam, *Immediate Family*, Columbia, 1989.

TELEVISION DEBUT—*No Big Deal*, HBO. PRINCIPAL TELEVISION APPEARANCES—Movies: Rick, *When He's Not a Stranger*, CBS, 1989.

ADDRESSES: AGENT—Steve Dontanville, International Creative Management, 8899 Beverly Boulevard, Los Angeles, CA 90048.*

*　　*　　*

DINALLO, Gregory S.   1941-

PERSONAL: Born March 22, 1941, in Brooklyn, NY; son of Gregory H. (a mechanic) and Amelia L. (a school teacher; maiden name, Pisicelli) Dinallo; married Gloria Carrubba (a printmaker), June 16, 1962; children: Eric. EDUCATION—Pratt Institute, Bachelor of Industrial Design, 1962.

GREGORY S. DINALLO

VOCATION: Producer and writer.

CAREER: Also see *WRITINGS* below. PRINCIPAL TELEVISION WORK—Series: Executive script consultant, *The Powers of Matthew Star*, NBC, 1982-83; executive script consultant, *The Renegades*, ABC, 1983; producer, *Hawaiian Heat*, ABC, 1984; supervising producer, *The New Mike Hammer*, CBS, 1986-87; supervising producer, *Houston Knights*, CBS, 1987-88; also coordinating producer, *Knight Rider*, NBC.

RELATED CAREER—Writer, producer, and director of industrial and exhibit films.

NON-RELATED CAREER—Designer for the 1964, 1967, and 1970 World's Fairs.

WRITINGS: FILM—*The Cregor Find*, Buena Vista. TELEVISION—Episodic: *Switch*, CBS, 1975; *Hunter*, CBS, 1977; *The American Girls*, CBS, 1978; *The Amazing Spider-Man*, CBS, 1978; *Mrs. Columbo*, NBC, 1979; *Beyond Westworld*, CBS, 1980; *Walking Tall*, NBC, 1981; *The Renegades*, ABC, 1983; *Hawaiian Heat*, ABC, 1984; *Knight Rider*, NBC, 1985 and 1986; *The New Mike Hammer*, CBS, 1987; *Houston Knights*, CBS, 1988; also *Scarecrow and Mrs. King*, CBS; *Quincy, M.E.* CBS; *McCloud*, NBC; *Family*, ABC; *The Equalizer*, CBS; *Charlie's Angels*, ABC; *The Powers of Matthew Star*, NBC; *The Six Million Dollar Man*, ABC; *The Hardy Boys Mysteries*, ABC; *The Nancy Drew Mysteries*, ABC; *From Here to Eternity*, NBC; also *Command Five* and *Breaker's Way*. Pilots: *T.R.A.C.*, NBC. Movies: (With Scott

Swanton) *The Calendar Girl Murders*, ABC, 1984; *Ladykiller*, ABC, 1988; also *Goals*, CBS.

OTHER—*Rockets Red Glare* (fiction), St. Martin's, 1988; *In the Service of His Country* (fiction), St. Martin's, 1989.

AWARDS: Hugo Award from the Chicago Film Festival, 1972, for *Sears Cinema Circus* (industrial film).

MEMBER: Writers Guild of America—West, Mystery Writers of America, International Association of Crime Writers, P.E.N.

ADDRESSES: OFFICE—958 24th Street, Santa Monica, CA 90403. AGENT—Don Kline, Irv Schechter Company, 9300 Wilshire Boulevard, Beverly Hills, CA 90212. PUBLICIST—Jacqueline Green, Jacqueline Green Public Relations, 9230 Olympic Boulevard, Suite 202, Beverly Hills, CA 90212.

*   *   *

DIXON, Ivan   1931-

PERSONAL: Born April 6, 1931, in New York, NY.

VOCATION: Actor, director, and producer.

CAREER: PRINCIPAL STAGE APPEARANCES—Jamie, *The Cave Dwellers*, Bijou Theatre, New York City, 1957; Joseph Asagai, *A Raisin in the Sun*, Ethel Barrymore Theatre, New York City, 1959.

PRINCIPAL FILM APPEARANCES—Lathela, *Something of Value*, Metro-Goldwyn-Mayer (MGM), 1957; Jim, *Porgy and Bess*, Columbia, 1959; Tiger Blair, *Battle at Bloody Beach* (also known as *Battle on the Beach*), Twentieth Century-Fox, 1961; Asagai, *A Raisin in the Sun*, Columbia, 1961; Duff Anderson, *Nothing But a Man*, Cinema V, 1964; Mark Ralfe, *A Patch of Blue*, MGM, 1965; Soumarin, *To Trap a Spy*, MGM, 1966; naval officer, *Where's Jack?* (also known as *Run, Rebel, Run*), Paramount, 1969; Sergeant Jones, *Suppose They Gave a War and Nobody Came?* (also known as *War Games*), Cinerama, 1970; Simon, *Clay Pigeon*, MGM, 1971; Lonnie, *Car Wash*, Universal, 1976.

PRINCIPAL FILM WORK—Director, *Trouble Man*, Twentieth Century-Fox, 1972; producer (with Sam Greenlee) and director, *The Spook Who Sat By the Door*, United Artists, 1973.

PRINCIPAL TELEVISION APPEARANCES—Series: Corporal James Kinchloe, *Hogan's Heroes*, CBS, 1965-70. Mini-Series: Alan Drummond, *Amerika*, ABC, 1987. Episodic: Bolie Jackson, "The Big Tall Wish," *The Twilight Zone*, CBS, 1960; Major Harold Giles, "The Human Factor," *The Outer Limits*, ABC, 1963; Reverend Anderson, "I Am the Night—Color Me Black," *The Twilight Zone*, CBS, 1964; Sergeant James Conover, "The Inheritors," *The Outer Limits*, ABC, 1964; also *Have Gun, Will Travel*, CBS, 1961; *Cain's Hundred*, CBS, 1962; *Target: The Corruptors*, ABC, 1962; *Dr. Kildare*, NBC, 1962; *Laramie*, NBC, 1962; *Stoney Burke*, ABC, 1963; *Perry Mason*, CBS, 1963; *The Defenders*, CBS, 1963 and 1965; "The Special Courage of Captain Pratt," *Great Adventures*, CBS, 1964; "Murder in the First," *Bob Hope Chrysler Theatre*, NBC, 1964; *The Man from U.N.C.L.E.*, NBC,

1964; *The Fugitive*, ABC, 1964 and 1967; *I Spy*, NBC, 1965; "The Final War of Ollie Winter," *NET Playhouse*, WNET, 1967; *Felony Squad*, ABC, 1967; *Ironside*, NBC, 1967; *It Takes a Thief*, ABC, 1968; *The Name of the Game*, NBC, 1968 and 1969; *The Mod Squad*, ABC, 1970; *The F.B.I.*, ABC, 1970; *Love, American Style*, ABC, 1971. Movies: Joe Voit, *Fer de Lance*, CBS, 1974; judge, *Perry Mason: The Case of the Shooting Star*, NBC, 1986. Specials: "Arrowsmith," *Dupont Show of the Month*, CBS, 1960.

PRINCIPAL TELEVISION WORK—All as director. Series: *Counterattack: Crime in America*, NBC, 1982. Pilots: *Palms Precinct*, NBC, 1982. Episodic: *Khan!*, CBS, 1974; *Harris and Company*, NBC, 1979; *Tenspeed and Brownshoe*, ABC, 1980; *Legmen*, NBC, 1984; *Blue Thunder*, ABC, 1984; *Magnum, P.I.*, CBS, 1985 and 1986; *Downtown*, CBS, 1986; *Houston Knights*, CBS, 1987 and 1988; *Quantum Leap*, NBC, 1989; also *Hogan's Heroes*, CBS; *The Bill Cosby Show*, NBC; *Get Christie Love!*, ABC; *Nichols*, NBC; *Apple's Way*, CBS; *The Waltons*, CBS; *Shaft*, CBS; *Delvecchio*, NBC; *The Black Sheep Squadron* (also known as *Baa Baa Black Sheep*), NBC; *The Nancy Drew Mysteries*, ABC; *The New Adventures of Wonder Woman*, CBS; *The Rockford Files*, NBC; *The Righteous Apples*, PBS; *Palmerstown, U.S.A.*, CBS; *The Greatest American Hero*, ABC; *Bret Maverick*, NBC; *Tales of the Gold Monkey*, ABC; *Airwolf*, CBS; *The A-Team*, NBC. Movies: *Love Is Not Enough*, NBC, 1978. Specials: *The Bill Cosby Special, or ?*, NBC, 1971.

ADDRESSES: OFFICE—Bokari Productions, Inc., 3432 N. Marengo Avenue, Altadena, CA 91001.

*   *   *

DIXON, MacIntyre   1931-

PERSONAL: Born December 22, 1931, in Everett, MA. EDUCATION—Graduated from Emerson College.

VOCATION: Actor.

CAREER: BROADWAY DEBUT—Willy, *Xmas in Las Vegas*, Ethel Barrymore Theatre, 1965. PRINCIPAL STAGE APPEARANCES—Ensemble, *Stewed Prunes* (revue), Circle in the Square, then Showplace Theatre, both New York City, 1960; Tommy, "Infancy" in *Plays for Bleecker Street*, Circle in the Square, 1962; (with Richard Libertini as the Stewed Prunes) *The Cat's Pajamas* (revue), Sheridan Square Playhouse, New York City, 1962; ensemble, *The Mad Show* (revue), New Theatre, New York City, 1966; Valentine Brose, *Eh?*, Circle in the Square, 1967; Peter Smith, "Home Fires" in *Cop-Out*, Cort Theatre, New York City, 1969; various roles, *Paul Sills' Story Theatre*, Ambassador Theatre, New York City, 1970; Walrus, *Meeow!*, Cabaret Theatre, New York City, 1971; priest, "Ma" in *Twigs*, Broadhurst Theatre, New York City, 1971, then Plymouth Theatre, New York City, 1972; father, *Over Here!*, Shubert Theatre, New York City, 1974; Bub, *Lotta, Or the Best Thing Evolution's Ever Come Up With*, New York Shakespeare Festival, Public Theatre, New York City, 1973; Mr. Pard, *Rubbers*, American Place Theatre, New York City, 1975; Rudolph Kammerling, *Once in a Lifetime*, Circle in the Square, 1978; man, *Conjuring an Event*, American Place Theatre, 1978.

Burglar, *My Husband's Wild Desires Almost Drove Me Mad,* Studio Arena Theatre, Buffalo, NY, 1980; ensemble, *Tomfoolery* (revue), Village Gate Theatre Upstairs, New York City, 1981; Mad Hatter, *Alice in Wonderland,* Virginia Theatre, New York City, 1982; Blackie Caroon, *Rockaway,* Vineyard Theatre, New York City, 1982; Dr. Bourges, Pere Abbe, Dogmouth, Ducarre, doctor, critic, and announcer, *Times and Appetites of Toulouse-Lautrec,* American Place Theatre, 1985; Chubby Waters, *Broadway Bound,* Broadhurst Theatre, 1986; Simon Jenkins and Timothy Hogarth, *Room Service,* Roundabout Theatre, New York City, 1986; Carol Newquist, *Little Murders,* Second Stage Theatre, New York City, 1987; policeman, *Threepenny Opera,* Lunt-Fontanne Theatre, New York City, 1989. Also *The Quare Fellow,* Circle in the Square, 1958; *Three By Three,* Maidman Theatre, New York City, 1961; *When the Owl Screams,* Second City at Square East, New York City, 1963; *Staircase* and *Under Milk Wood,* both Actors Theatre of Louisville, Louisville, KY, 1969-70; *Ovid's Metamorphosis,* Ambassador Theatre, 1971; *People from Division Street,* Cubiculo Theatre, New York City, 1975; *Windy City,* Paper Mill Playhouse, Millburn, NJ, 1985; *Sills and Company,* Lamb's Theatre, then Actors Playhouse, both New York City, 1986; appeared with the McCarter Theatre company, Princeton, NJ, 1972-73; with the Arena Stage company, Washington, DC, 1975-76; and in productions of *The Three Sisters, His Majesty the Devil,* and *A Christmas Carol.*

PRINCIPAL FILM APPEARANCES—First deconsecration minister, *Alice's Restaurant,* United Artists, 1969; Harry Stone, *The Front,* Columbia, 1976; painter, *Fire Sale,* Twentieth Century-Fox, 1977; passenger, *Thieves,* Paramount, 1977; bartender, *Thank God It's Friday,* Columbia, 1978; courthouse reporter, *King of the Gypsies,* Paramount, 1978; counterman, *Corvette Summer* (also known as *The Hot One*), United Artists, 1978; Dan Ryan, *Starting Over,* Paramount, 1979; Cole Oyl, *Popeye,* Paramount, 1980; nature walk teacher, *Paternity,* Paramount, 1981; Carl Walters, *Reds,* Paramount, 1981; Ernie Weaver, *Dead Ringer,* Feature Film/CBS Video, 1982; DeWitt, *Batteries Not Included,* Universal, 1987; Ferguson, *The Secret of My Success,* Universal, 1987; Mayor Barclay, *Funny Farm,* Warner Brothers, 1988; Dr. Verboven, *The Dream Team,* Universal, 1989.

PRINCIPAL TELEVISION APPEARANCES—Series: Regular, *Comedy Tonight,* CBS, 1970. Pilots: Principal, *Popi,* CBS, 1975; F.B.I. official, *Big Shots in America,* NBC, 1985; also *Windows, Doors, and Keyholes,* NBC, 1978. Episodic: *All in the Family,* CBS, 1977; "The Ghost Writer," *American Playhouse,* PBS, 1984. Movies: Mr. Estes, *Delta County, U.S.A.,* ABC, 1977; post office clerk, *How to Pick Up Girls!,* ABC, 1978; Father Danzig, *Word of Honor,* CBS, 1981; reporter, *Izzy and Moe,* CBS, 1985. Specials: *We Interrupt This Season,* NBC, 1967; *I'm a Fan,* CBS, 1972.

ADDRESSES: AGENT—J. Michael Bloom, 233 Park Avenue S., New York, NY 10003.*

* * *

DODSON, Jack 1931-

PERSONAL: Full name, John S. Dodson; born May 16, 1931, in Pittsburgh, PA; son of John M. and Margaret S. Dodson; married Mary Weaver (a motion picture and television production design-

er), August 28, 1959; children: Cristina, Amy. EDUCATION—Carnegie-Mellon University, B.F.A., drama, 1953. MILITARY—U.S. Army, sergeant, 1953-56.

VOCATION: Actor.

CAREER: PRINCIPAL STAGE APPEARANCES—Father Zossima, *The Trial of Dimitri Karazamov,* Jan Hus Auditorium, New York City, 1958; man in audience, first dead man, and townsperson, *Our Town,* Circle in the Square, New York City, 1959; Blind One, *The Golem,* St. Mark's Playhouse, New York City, 1959; the General, *The Balcony,* Circle in the Square, 1960; Captain Cat, Butcher Banyon, Organ Morgan, and P.C. Attila Rees, *Under Milk Wood,* Circle in the Square, 1961; tramp, *Pullman Car Hiawatha,* Circle in the Square, 1962; the Director, *Six Characters in Search of an Author,* Martinique Theatre, New York City, 1963; the Nightclerk, *Hughie,* Royale Theatre, New York City, 1964; Paul Sycamore, *You Can't Take It with You,* Plymouth Theatre, New York City, 1983. Also appeared in *The Italian Straw Hat,* Fourth Street Theatre, New York City, 1957; *The Country Wife,* New York City, 1957; *The Quare Fellow,* Circle in the Square, 1958; *The Torchbearers,* New York City, 1960; *Plays for Bleecker Street,* Circle in the Square, 1962; *Follies of Scapin,* New York City, 1962; *Chemin de Fer,* Mark Taper Forum, Los Angeles, 1968; *Who's Happy Now?,* Mark Taper Forum, 1976; *A Penny for a Song,* New York City.

PRINCIPAL FILM APPEARANCES—Shipmate, *Munster, Go Home,* Universal, 1966; narrator, *Why Man Creates* (short documentary film), Saul Bass and Associates, 1968; Norman Gresham, *Angel in My Pocket,* Universal, 1969; Harold Clinton, *The Getaway,* National General, 1972; Llewellyn Howland, *Pat Garrett and Billy the Kid,* Metro-Goldwyn-Mayer, 1973; vault manager, *Thunderbolt and Lightfoot,* United Artists, 1974; Dr. Douglas, *Something Wicked This Way Comes,* Buena Vista, 1983.

PRINCIPAL TELEVISION APPEARANCES—Series: Howard Sprague, *The Andy Griffith Show,* CBS, 1966-68; Howard Sprague, *Mayberry R.F.D.,* CBS, 1968-71; Senator Wayne Joplin, *All's Fair,* CBS, 1976-77; Monsignor Francis X. Barlow, *In the Beginning,* CBS, 1978; Edgar "Truck" Morley, *Phyl and Mikhy,* CBS, 1980. Pilots: Wendell Henderson, *Walkin' Walter,* ABC, 1977; Mr. Bishop, *Snavely,* ABC, 1978. Episodic: Mickey Malph, *Happy Days,* ABC, 1974; Carstairs, *Cagney and Lacey,* CBS, 1985; Senator Gate, *Benson,* ABC, 1986; Carl Putnam, *Mr. Belvedere,* ABC, 1986 and 1989; Judge Farnham, *St. Elsewhere,* NBC, 1987 and 1988; Walter Johnson, *Duet,* Fox, 1988; Jack Austin, *Matlock,* NBC, 1989; also *Barney Miller,* ABC, 1975 and 1980; *The Nancy Walker Show,* ABC, 1976; *13 Queens Boulevard,* ABC, 1979; *Room 222,* ABC; *Manhunter,* CBS; *CPO Sharkey,* NBC; *Maude,* CBS; *Hawaii Five-0,* CBS; *A.E.S. Hudson Street,* ABC; *Carter Country,* ABC; *Police Story,* NBC; *Quincy,* NBC; *One Day At a Time,* CBS; *Welcome Back, Kotter,* ABC; *The Practice,* CBS; *Mork and Mindy,* ABC; *Lou Grant,* CBS; *Newhart,* CBS; *Amen!,* NBC. Movies: Chuck, *Million Dollar Infield,* CBS, 1982; Howard Sprague, *Return to Mayberry,* NBC, 1986. Specials: "Who's Happy Now?," *Theatre in America,* PBS, 1976; the Nightclerk, *Hughie,* Showtime, 1981.

ADDRESSES: OFFICE—MJD Enterprises Inc., c/o Equitable Investment Corporation, 6253 Hollywood Boulevard, Suite 1122, Hollywood, CA 90028. AGENT—STE Representation Ltd., 9301 Wilshire Boulevard, Suite 312, Beverly Hills, CA 90210.*

DONAHUE, Troy 1936-

PERSONAL: Born Merle Johnson, Jr., January 27, 1936 (some sources say January 17, 1937), in New York, NY; married Suzanne Pleshette (an actress; divorced); EDUCATION—Attended Columbia University.

VOCATION: Actor.

CAREER: PRINCIPAL FILM APPEARANCES—Frank Burnham, *The Tarnished Angels,* Universal, 1957; Artie, *Live Fast, Die Young,* Universal, 1958; Jimmy Flanders, *Monster on the Campus,* Universal, 1958; Sergeant Nickles, *The Perfect Furlough* (also known as *Strictly for Pleasure*), Universal, 1958; Sax Lewis, *Summer Love,* Universal, 1958; Tony Manza, *This Happy Feeling,* Universal, 1958; Paul Cunningham, *Voice in the Mirror,* Universal, 1958; Jesse Bascomb, *Wild Heritage,* Universal, 1958; Frankie, *Imitation of Life,* Universal, 1959; Johnny Hunter, *A Summer Place,* Warner Brothers, 1959; McVey, *The Crowded Sky,* Warner Brothers, 1960; Parrish McLean, *Parrish,* Warner Brothers, 1961; Hoyt Breckner, *Susan Slade,* Warner Brothers, 1961; Don Porter, *Rome Adventure,* Warner Brothers, 1962; Jim Munroe, *Palm Springs Weekend,* Warner Brothers, 1963; Lieutenant Matthew Hagard, *A Distant Trumpet,* Apex, 1964; Ben Gunther, *My Blood Runs Cold,* Warner Brothers, 1965; Pete Barker, *Come Spy with Me,* Twentieth Century-Fox, 1967; Gaylord Sullivan, *Those Fantastic Flying Fools* (also known as *Jules Verne's Rocket to the Moon* and *Blast Off*), American International, 1967.

Moon, *Sweet Savior,* Trans World Attractions, 1971; Merle Johnson, *The Godfather, Part II,* Paramount, 1974; Mark, *Seizure,* American International, 1974; Randall Mansfield, *Born to Kill* (also known as *Cockfighter*), New World, 1975; Donny Vinton, *Grandview, U.S.A.,* Warner Brothers, 1984; John Templeton, *Low Blow,* Crown International, 1986; Bob Jenkins, *Cyclone,* Cinetel, 1987; Don Michaelson, *Deadly Prey,* Action, 1987; Lieutenant Maxwell, *Hollywood Cop,* Peacock, 1988; Philip, *Sexpot,* Platinum/Academy Home Entertainment, 1988; Dr. Ackerman, *Dr. Alien* (also known as *I Was a Teenage Sex Mutant*), Phantom Video, 1988; Jack Barnes, *Bad Blood,* Platinum/Academy Home Entertainment, 1989; Sid Witherspoon, *Attach of the Party Nerds* (also known as *Party Nerds*), Prism Entertainment, 1989; Slim, *Terminal Force,* New World, 1989; Steve, *South Seas Massacre,* Prism Entertainment, 1989. Also appeared in *The Legend of Frank Woods,* 1977; *Tin Man,* Westcom, 1983; *Back to the Beach,* Paramount, 1987.

PRINCIPAL TELEVISION APPEARANCES—Series: Sandy Winfield II, *Surfside Six,* ABC, 1960-62; Philip Barton, *Hawaiian Eye,* ABC, 1962-63; Keefer, *The Secret Storm,* CBS, 1970. Pilots: Clint Redman, *Malibu,* ABC, 1983. Episodic: *Fantasy Island,* ABC, 1978 and 1981; *Esquire: About Men, for Women,* Lifetime, 1989; also *Wagon Train,* NBC; *77 Sunset Strip,* ABC; *Colt .45,* ABC; *Matt Houston,* ABC. Specials: *The Bob Hope Show,* NBC, 1960.

RELATED CAREER—Actor in summer theatre productions, Bucks County Playhouse, New Hope, PA.

AWARDS: Golden Globe, Most Promising Newcomer, 1960.

ADDRESSES: AGENT—Contemporary Artists, 132 Lasky Drive, Beverly Hills, CA 90212.*

DONNELLY, Candice 1954-

PERSONAL: Born January 2, 1954, in Boston, MA; daughter of James and Elinor (Di Napoli) Donnelly; children: Bronwen Boyan. EDUCATION—University of Massachusetts, B.F.A., 1975; Yale University, M.F.A., 1985.

VOCATION: Costume designer.

CAREER: FIRST BROADWAY WORK—Costume designer, *Fences,* 46th Street Theatre, New York City, 1987. PRINCIPAL STAGE WORK—Costume designer: *Chopin in Space,* Yale Repertory Theatre, New Haven, CT, 1984; *The Wonder Years,* TOMI Terrace Theatre, New York City, 1985; *Ondine,* New York Stage and Film, New York City, 1985; *Fences,* Seattle Repertory Theatre, Seattle, WA, then Goodman Theatre, Chicago, IL, both 1985-86; *Rich Relations,* Second Stage Theatre, New York City, 1986; *Dry Land,* Judith Anderson Theatre, New York City, 1986; *The Return of Pinocchio,* 47th Street Theatre, New York City, 1986; *The Skin of Our Teeth,* Classic Stage Company, New York City, 1986; *Happy Days,* Goodman Theatre, 1986; *The Maderati,* Playwrights Horizons, New York City, 1987; *Elektra,* Classic Stage Company, 1987; *The Johnstown Vindicator,* Harold Clurman Theatre, New York City, 1987; *Little Murders,* Second Stage Theatre, 1987; *Flee as a Bird* (dance piece), Joyce Theatre, New York City, 1987; *Tartuffe,* Portland Stage Company, Portland, ME, 1987; *The Milk Train Doesn't Stop Here Anymore,* WPA Theatre, New York City, 1987; *Right Behind the Flag Boys,* Playwrights Horizons, 1988; "Dirty Work" in *Three Pieces for a Warehouse,* 500 Greenwich Street, New York City, 1988; *Eastern Standard,* Seattle Repertory Theatre, then Manhattan Theatre Club, New York City, both 1988; *Loose Ends,* Second Stage Theatre, 1988; *The Film Society,* Second Stage Theatre, 1988; *Rameau's Nephew,* Classic Stage Company, 1988; *Monte* (dance piece), Joyce Theatre, 1988; *The Good Moment of Lily Baker,* New York Stage and Film, 1988; *Joe Turner's Come and Gone,* Center Stage Theatre, Baltimore, MD, 1988; *Moon Over Miami,* Yale Repertory Theatre, 1989; *Mastergate,* American Repertory Theatre, Cambridge, MA, then Criterion Theatre, New York City, both 1989; *As You Like It,* Folger Shakespeare Theatre, Washington, DC, 1989; *Rebel Armies Deep into Chad,* Long Wharf Theatre, New Haven, CT, 1989; *Baba Goya,* Second Stage Theatre, 1989; *The Merry Wives of Windsor, Texas,* St. Louis Repertory Theatre, St. Louis, MO, then Players Theatre, Columbus, OH, both 1989; *The Rose Tattoo,* Williamstown Theatre Festival, Williamstown, MA, 1989; *The Bald Soprano* and *The Chairs,* both American Repertory Theatre, 1989.

PRINCIPAL FILM WORK—Assistant designer, *Crossing Delancey,* Midwest Films, 1987; designer, *Over,* New York Stage and Film/Rebo High Definition Studio, 1988; assistant designer, *The House on Carroll Street,* HBO Films, 1988.

PRINCIPAL TELEVISION WORK—Pilots: Assistant designer, *The Clinic,* 1987.

RELATED CAREER—Assistant designer for the Michael Jackson music video, *Bad,* 1986.

ADDRESSES: OFFICE—935 St. Nicholas Avenue, Apartment 6-F, New York, NY 10032.

*   *   *

DOOHAN, James 1920-

PERSONAL: Full name, James Montgomery Doohan; born March 3, 1920, in Vancouver, BC, Canada; father, a chemist; married

JAMES DOOHAN

third wife, Wendy Braunberger, October 12, 1974; children: four (first marriage); two (third marriage). EDUCATION—Studied acting at the Neighborhood Playhouse, 1946. MILITARY—Royal Canadian Artillery, pilot captain.

VOCATION: Actor.

CAREER: PRINCIPAL FILM APPEARANCES—Bishop, *36 Hours,* Metro-Goldwyn-Mayer (MGM), 1965; Phillip Bainbridge, *One of Our Spies Is Missing,* MGM, 1966; building superintendent, *Jigsaw,* Universal, 1968; Benoit, *Man in the Wilderness,* Warner Brothers, 1971; Follo, *Pretty Maids All in a Row,* MGM, 1971; Chief Engineer Montgomery "Scotty" Scott, *Star Trek: The Motion Picture,* Paramount, 1979; Scotty, *Star Trek II: The Wrath of Khan,* Paramount, 1982; Scotty, *Star Trek III: The Search for Spock,* Paramount, 1984; Scotty, *Star Trek IV: The Voyage Home,* Paramount, 1986; Scotty, *Star Trek V: The Final Frontier,* Paramount, 1989. Also appeared in *The Wheeler Dealers* (also known as *Separate Beds*), MGM, 1963; *The Satan Bug,* United Artists, 1965; *Bus Riley's Back in Town,* Universal, 1965.

TELEVISION DEBUT—Detective, *Martin Kane, Private Eye,* NBC, 1949. PRINCIPAL TELEVISION APPEARANCES—Series: Engineer Montgomery "Scotty" Scott, *Star Trek,* NBC, 1966-69; voice of Lieutenant Montgomery Scott, Lieutenant Arex, and others, *Star Trek* (animated), NBC, 1973-75; Commander Carnarvin, *Jason of Star Command,* CBS, 1979-81. Pilots: Scrimp, *Scalplock,* ABC, 1966. Episodic: Lieutenant Branch, "Expanding Human," *The Outer Limits,* ABC, 1964; also *Hazel,* NBC, 1962; *Voyage to the Bottom of the Sea,* ABC, 1964; *Blue Light,* ABC, 1966; *Bewitched,* ABC; *Gunsmoke,* CBS; *Fantasy Island,* ABC; *Suspense,* CBS; *Bonanza,* NBC; *Ben Casey,* ABC; *The Gallant Men,* ABC; *Marcus

Welby, M.D., ABC; *The Fugitive,* ABC; *The Virginian,* NBC; *Tales of Tomorrow,* ABC; *The Man from U.N.C.L.E.,* NBC; *Then Came Bronson,* NBC; *Peyton Place,* ABC; *Daniel Boone,* NBC; *The F.B.I.,* ABC; *Thriller,* NBC; *The Twilight Zone,* CBS; *Return to Peyton Place,* NBC; *The Iron Horse,* ABC; *Magnum, P.I.,* CBS; *Shenandoah.* Specials: *53rd Annual King Orange Jamboree Parade,* NBC, 1986.

RELATED CAREER—Actor in 400 live television shows and 4,000 radio shows for the Canadian Broadcasting Corporation; actor in approximately 120 stage productions; acting teacher, Neighborhood Playhouse, New York City; speaker, college tour circuit; appeared in television commercials.

SIDELIGHTS: RECREATIONS—Carpentry and woodcarving.

ADDRESSES: AGENT—Twentieth Century Artists, 3800 Barham Boulevard, Suite 303, Los Angeles, CA 90068.*

*   *   *

DOUGLAS, Juliet 1962-

PERSONAL: Born Juliet Brown, August 18, 1962, in Redhill, England; daughter of Dennis Francis Douglas (in the garment business) and Pamela Dorothy (a teacher; maiden name, Watling) Brown. EDUCATION—Attended County Secretarial College, 1980-81; studied for the theatre at the Guildhall School of Music and Drama. RELIGION—Church of England.

JULIET DOUGLAS

VOCATION: Actress.

CAREER: STAGE DEBUT—W.P.C. Hughes, *Anagram of Murder*, Frinton Repertory Theatre. LONDON DEBUT—Valerie, *Exclusive*, Strand Theatre, 1989. PRINCIPAL STAGE APPEARANCES—Appeared in repertory theatre productions of *Blood Brothers*, *A Midsummer Night's Dream*, *Oliver*, *Equus*, *Why Not Stay for Breakfast?*, *My Cousin Rachel*, *The Big Killing*, *My Giddy Aunt*, *Intent to Murder*, *The Gingerbread Lady*, and *Pardon Me, Prime Minister*.

MAJOR TOURS—*You Never Can Tell* and *A Winter's Tale*, both in Northern Italy.

PRINCIPAL TELEVISION WORK—Episodic: *Max Headroom*, ABC. Also appeared in *Don't Wait Up*, BBC; *Call Me Mister*, BBC; *Bergerac*, BBC; *Life without George*, BBC; *Prospects*, Euston Films; *Bust*, London Weekend Television; *Piggy Bank*, Channel Four.

ADDRESSES: AGENT—Carole James Management, London, England.

*   *   *

DOWNEY, Robert

VOCATION: Director, producer, actor, and screenwriter.

CAREER: Also see *WRITINGS* below. PRINCIPAL STAGE WORK—Film sequences, *The Experiment*, Orpheum Theatre, New York City, 1967.

PRINCIPAL FILM APPEARANCES—Private Stewart Thompson, *No More Excuses*, Rogosin/Impact, 1968; as himself, *Is There Sex After Death?*, New Line Cinema, 1971; NCAA investigator, *Johnny Be Good* (also known as *Quarterback Sneak*), Orion, 1988.

PRINCIPAL FILM WORK—Director: (Also producer) *Babo 73*, Film-makers' Cooperative, 1964; (also producer) *Chafed Elbows*, Filmmakers Distribution Center, 1967; *No More Excuses*, Rogosin/Impact, 1968; *Putney Swope*, Cinema V, 1969; *Pound*, United Artists, 1970; (also producer) *Greaser's Palace*, Greaser's Palace Ltd., 1972; *Up the Academy* (also known as *Mad Magazine's Up the Academy* and *The Brave Young Men of Weinberg*), Warner Brothers, 1980; *This Is America—The Movie, Not the Country* (also known as *America*), ASA, 1986; *Rented Lips*, Cineworld, 1988. Also director, *Two Tons of Turquoise to Taos*, 1967.

WRITINGS: FILM—See production details above, unless indicated. *Babo 73*, 1964; *Chafed Elbows*, 1967; *No More Excuses*, 1968; *Putney Swope*, 1969; *Pound*, 1970; *Greaser's Palace*, 1972; (with Chuck Barris) *The Gong Show Movie*, Universal, 1980; (with Sidney Davis) *This Is America—The Movie, Not the Country*, 1986.

SIDELIGHTS: Robert Downey is the father of actor Robert Downey, Jr.

ADDRESSES: MANAGER—Loree Rodkin Management, 8600 Melrose Avenue, Los Angeles, CA 90069. PUBLICIST—Nanci Ryder, Baker/Winokur/Ryder Public Relations, 9348 Civic Center Drive, Suite 407, Beverly Hills, CA 90210.*

DRAKE, Fabia   1904-1990

PERSONAL: Full name, Fabia Drake McGlinchy; born January 20, 1904, in Herne Bay, England; died February 28, 1990; daughter of Francis Drake and Annie (Dalton) McGlinchy; married Maxwell Turner (a lawyer), 1938 (died, 1960). EDUCATION—Studied acting at the Royal Academy of Dramatic Art, 1922.

VOCATION: Actress.

CAREER: STAGE DEBUT—Tommy, *The Fairy Doll*, Court Theatre, London, 1913. PRINCIPAL STAGE APPEARANCES—Brer Rabbit, *Brer Rabbit and Mr. Fox*, Little Theatre, London, 1914; Elsie Pennithorne, *The Happy Family*, Prince of Wales Theatre, London, 1916, then Strand Theatre, London, 1917; Sarah Undershaft, *Major Barbara*, Everyman Theatre, London, 1921; Lola de la Carte, *Quarantine* and Audrey Carlton, *Secrets*, both Comedy Theatre, London, 1922; Yasmin and Pervaneh, *Hassan*, His Majesty's Theatre, London, 1923; Sylvia Latter, *The Creaking Chair*, Comedy Theatre, 1924; Monica Jesmond, *Possessions*, Vaudeville Theatre, London, 1925; Maud Leverton, *Easy Money*, St. Martin's Theatre, London, 1925; Viola, *Twelfth Night*, Fellowship of Players, Scala Theatre, London, 1925; Peggy Winton, *The Scarlet Lady*, Criterion Theatre, London, 1926; the Shingled Lady, *Escape* and Mary, *The Spot on the Sun*, both Ambassadors' Theatre, London, 1927; Lady Beryl, *The Wrecker*, New Theatre, London, 1927; Margaret Orme, *Loyalties* and Countess of Westhaven, *The Love-Lorn Lady*, both Wyndham's Theatre, London, 1928; Nancy Bird, *Young Love*, Arts Theatre, London, 1929.

Nora, *No. 17*, Royalty Theatre, London, 1930; Enid Deckle, *The World of Light*, Royalty Theatre, 1931; Lady Percy, *King Henry IV, Part One*, Viola, *Twelfth Night*, Calpurnia, *Julius Caesar*, Rosalind, *As You Like It*, Helena, *A Midsummer Night's Dream*, and Portia, *The Merchant of Venice*, all Stratford-on-Avon Company, New Stratford Memorial Theatre, Stratford-on-Avon, U.K., 1932; Mrs. Guy Daunt, *Cecilia*, Arts Theatre, 1933; Rosalind, *As You Like It*, Phoenix Theatre, London, 1933; Lulu Davenant, *Poison Flower* and Mary Lascelles, *The Rose Without a Thorn*, both Croydon Theatre, Croyden, U.K., 1934; Jennifer Lawrence, *Sixteen*, Embassy Theatre, London, then Criterion Theatre, both 1934; Elaine Taunton, *Our Mutual Father*, Repertory Players, Piccadilly Theatre, London, 1934; Princess, *Lady Precious Stream*, Little Theatre, 1934; Miss Vulliamy, *Frolic Wind*, Royalty Theatre, 1935; Lady Cynthia, *Anthony and Anna*, Whitehall Theatre, London, 1935; Frances Dane, *Indian Summer*, Arts Theatre, 1936; Ruth Wilder, *Comedienne*, Haymarket Theatre, London, 1938; Dowager Empress, *The Nightingale*, Aldwych Theatre, London, 1947. Also appeared with the Stratford-on-Avon Company, 1933; and with the Repertory Players, Play Actors, Playmates, Renaissance, and London International Theatre companies, all in the U.K.

PRINCIPAL STAGE WORK—Producer, *Much Ado About Nothing*, Aldwych Theatre, London, 1946.

MAJOR TOURS—Christina, *The Silver Cord*, U.K. cities, 1928; Lady Macbeth, *Macbeth*, Viola, *Twelfth Night*, and Beatrice, *Much Ado About Nothing*, all Stratford-on-Avon Festival Company, U.S. and Canadian cities, 1929-30.

PRINCIPAL FILM APPEARANCES—Annie Penny, *Meet Mr. Penny*, Associated British, 1938; Miss Gelding, *All Over the Town*, General Film Distributors, 1949; Lady Mercy Cotton, *Poet's Pub*, General Film Distributors, 1949; Lady Elmbridge, *The Hour of Thirteen*, Metro-Goldwyn-Mayer, 1952; Miss Farmer, *White*

Corridors, Jaro, 1952; Lady Probus, *Isn't Life Wonderful?,* Pathe, 1953; Mrs. Crabb, *Fast and Loose,* General Film Distributors, 1954; Nurse Blott, *Young Wives' Tale,* Allied Artists, 1954; opulent lady, *All for Mary,* Rank, 1956; Mrs. Tarvin, *The Good Companions,* Associated British/Pathe, 1957; Mrs. Brough, *Not Wanted on Voyage,* Renown, 1957; Sister Veronica, *Violent Stranger* (also known as *Man in the Shadow*), Amalgamated, 1957; Lady Hewitt, *Girls at Sea,* Seven Arts, 1958; Mrs. Pinner, *What a Whopper,* Regal, 1961; Arabella Parker, *My Wife's Family,* Pathe, 1962; Mrs. Piggott, *Seven Keys,* Allied Artists, 1962; Junior Commander Maddox, *Operation Bullshine,* Seven Arts/Manhattan, 1963; Miss Grimsby, *A Nice Girl Like Me,* AVCO-Embassy, 1969; Miss Gibbons, *The Devil's Widow* (also known as *Tam Lin*), British International, 1972; Aunt Olive, *Sweet Virgin* (also known as *Got It Made*), Target International, 1974; nun, *Year of the Dragon,* Metro-Goldwyn-Mayer/United Artists, 1985; Catherine Alan, *A Room with a View,* Cinecom, 1986; Madame de Rosemonde, *Valmont,* Orion, 1989. Also appeared in *Dulcimer Street* (also known as *London Belongs to Me*), General Film Distributors, 1948.

PRINCIPAL TELEVISION APPEARANCES—Mini-Series: Countess Midlothian, *The Pallisers,* BBC, then PBS, 1977; Mabel Layton, *The Jewel in the Crown,* Granada, then *Masterpiece Theatre,* PBS, 1984; Miss Henderson, "A Pocketful of Rye," *Agatha Christie's Miss Marple,* BBC, then *Mystery!,* PBS, 1986; Mrs. Jarman, "Last Bus to Woodstock," *Inspector Morse Series II,* Central Television, then *Mystery!,* PBS, 1988; also *The Rainbow,* BBC, then Arts and Entertainment, 1989. Episodic: Welfare worker, "Arrival," *The Prisoner,* CBS, 1968. Movies: Bookshop owner, *Out on a Limb,* ABC, 1987. Specials: Frances, *A Wreath of Roses,* Granada, then *Masterpiece Theatre,* PBS, 1989.

OBITUARIES AND OTHER SOURCES: New York Times, March 2, 1990.*

*   *   *

DRAPER, Polly

PERSONAL: Born June 15, in Gary, IN; married Kevin Wade (a playwright). EDUCATION—Received B.A. and M.F.A. from Yale University.

VOCATION: Actress.

CAREER: OFF-BROADWAY DEBUT—Jean, *Split,* Second Stage, 1980. PRINCIPAL STAGE APPEARANCES—Caroline Lou Bingham, *The Stitch in Time,* American National Theatre and Academy Theatre, New York City, 1980-81; Gertrude Cayce, *The Freak,* WPA Theatre, New York City, 1981, then Douglas Fairbanks Theatre, New York City, 1982; Meg, *The Actor's Nightmare* and Diane Symonds, *Sister Mary Ignatius Explains It All for You* (double-bill), Playwrights Horizons, then Westside Arts Theatre, both New York City, 1981-82; Cheryl, *Hooters,* Hudson Guild Theatre, New York City, 1982; Marlene, *Top Girls,* New York Shakespeare Festival (NYSF), Public Theatre, New York City, 1983; Blake Upton, *Mr. and Mrs.,* WPA Theatre, 1984; Lucy, "Want Ad," Danny, "Folie a'deux," Heather, "Only a Woman," and Lois, "Separate Vacation/Grounds for Divorce/Sexual History," all in *Love As We Know It,* Manhattan Punch Line, INTAR Theatre, New York City, 1985; Fiona, "The Ground Zero Club" in *The Young Playwrights Festival,* Playwrights Horizons, 1985; Linda Seward, *Rum and Coke,* NYSF, Public Theatre, 1986. Also

appeared in *Buried Child,* Yale Repertory Theatre, New Haven, CT, 1978; *As You Like It* and *Measure for Measure,* both Yale Repertory Theatre, 1979; and in *Thorn Hill,* New York City.

PRINCIPAL FILM APPEARANCES—Aileen Jones, *Seven Minutes in Heaven,* Warner Brothers, 1986; Suzy Duncan, *Making Mr. Right,* Orion, 1987; Pat, *The Pick-Up Artist,* Twentieth Century-Fox, 1987.

PRINCIPAL TELEVISION APPEARANCES—Series: Ellyn, *thirtysomething,* ABC, 1987—; also Winnie Robin, *Ryan's Hope,* ABC. Pilots: Bernadette Pascoe, *Adams Apple,* CBS, 1986. Specials: "Merrill Markoe's Guide to Glamorous Living," *Cinemax Comedy Experiment,* Cinemax, 1988.

ADDRESSES: AGENT—Jonathan Howard, Triad Artists, 10100 Santa Monica Boulevard, 16th Floor, Los Angeles, CA 90067.*

*   *   *

DUGAN, Dennis 1946-

PERSONAL: Born September 5, 1946, in Wheaton, IL; married Joyce Van Patten (an actress). EDUCATION—Studied acting at the Goodman Theatre School.

VOCATION: Actor and director.

CAREER: OFF-BROADWAY DEBUT—*The House of Blue Leaves,* Truck and Warehouse Theatre, 1971. PRINCIPAL STAGE APPEARANCES—*Rainbows for Sale,* Center Theatre Group, New Theatre for Now, Music Center of Los Angeles, Los Angeles, 1972.

PRINCIPAL STAGE WORK—Stage manager, *Rice and Beans,* International Arts Relations (INTAR) Theatre, New York City, 1979; also lighting designer, INTAR Theatre, 1979-80.

PRINCIPAL FILM APPEARANCES—Apprentice, *The Day of the Locust,* Paramount, 1975; young man, *Night Moves,* Warner Brothers, 1975; Logan, *Smile,* United Artists, 1975; Lewis, *Harry and Walter Go to New York,* Columbia, 1976; Garson Hobart, *Norman . . . Is That You?,* Metro-Goldwyn-Mayer/United Artists, 1976; Tom Trimble, *Unidentified Flying Oddball* (also known as *The Spaceman and King Arthur* and *U.F.O.*), Buena Vista, 1979; Chris, *The Howling,* AVCO-Embassy, 1981; Rob, *Water,* Rank, 1985; David Miller, *Can't Buy Me Love,* Buena Vista, 1987; Mr. Settigren, *The New Adventures of Pippi Longstocking,* Columbia, 1988; David Brodsky, *Parenthood,* Universal, 1989. Also appeared in *Night Call Nurses,* New World, 1974; *She's Having a Baby,* Paramount, 1988.

PRINCIPAL TELEVISION APPEARANCES—Series: Title role, *Richie Brockelman, Private Eye,* NBC, 1978; Ben Christian, *Empire,* CBS, 1984; Edgar "Benny" Benedek, *Shadow Chasers,* ABC, 1885-86. Mini-Series: Claude Tinker, *Rich Man, Poor Man,* ABC, 1976. Pilots: Joel Snedeger, *Alice,* CBS, 1976; title role, *Richie Brockelman: Missing 24 Hours,* NBC, 1976; Father Morgan, *Father, O Father,* ABC, 1977; Josh Fowler, *Did You Hear About Josh and Kelly?!,* CBS, 1980; Ivan Travalian, *Full House,* CBS, 1983; Marty Kessler, *Channel 99,* NBC, 1988. Episodic: Shadow, *Hooperman,* ABC, 1988; Walter Bishop, *Moonlighting,* ABC, 1988; also *M*A*S*H,* CBS, 1975 and 1983; *Scene of the Crime,* NBC, 1985; Richie Brockelman, *The Rockford Files,* NBC;

Lloyd Hoffmeyer, *Making a Living,* ABC; voice characterization, *These Are the Days* (animated), ABC. Movies: Private Becker, *Death Race,* ABC, 1973; Charlie Elliott, *The Girl Most Likely To . . .,* ABC, 1973; Officer Johnny Lucas, *Last of the Good Guys,* CBS, 1978; Daryl, *Country Gold,* CBS, 1982; Dick, *The Toughest Man in the World,* CBS, 1984. Specials: *Battle of the Network Stars,* ABC, 1978; Officer Needham, *Leadfoot,* syndicated, 1982; Andy Martin, "The Girl Who Couldn't Lose," *ABC Afternoon Playbreak,* ABC, 1975.

PRINCIPAL TELEVISION WORK—All as director. Episodic: *Hunter,* NBC, 1987; *Sonny Spoon,* NBC, 1988; *Wiseguy,* CBS, 1988; *Moonlighting,* ABC, 1988 and 1989.

ADDRESSES: AGENT—Bob Gersh, The Gersh Agency, 222 N. Canon Drive, Suite 202, Beverly Hills, CA 90210.*

*   *   *

DUNNOCK, Mildred 1900-

PERSONAL: Full name, Mildred Dorothy Dunnock; born January 25, 1900 (some sources say 1906), in Baltimore, MD; daughter of Walter (a textile merchant) and Florence (Saynook) Dunnock; married Keith M. Urmy (a banker), August 21, 1933; children: one daughter. EDUCATION—Received B.A. from Goucher College and M.A. from Columbia University; studied acting with Maria Ouspenskaya, Lee Strasberg, Robert Lewis, Elia Kazan, and Tamara Daykarhanova.

VOCATION: Actress.

CAREER: BROADWAY DEBUT—Miss Pinty, *Life Begins,* Selwyn Theatre, 1932. PRINCIPAL STAGE APPEARANCES—Woman of the congregation, *The Eternal Road,* Manhattan Opera House, New York City, 1937; Agnes Riddle, *The Hill Between,* Little Theatre, New York City, 1938; Miss Ronberry, *The Corn Is Green,* National Theatre, New York City, 1940; Miss Giddon, *The Cat Screams,* Martin Beck Theatre, New York City, 1942; Queen Margaret, *Richard III,* Forrest Theatre, Philadelphia, PA, 1943; India Hamilton, *Only the Heart,* Bijou Theatre, New York City, 1944; Rose and Flora, *Foolish Notion,* Martin Beck Theatre, 1945; Madame Tsai, *Lute Song,* Plymouth Theatre, New York City, 1946; Lavinia Hubbard, *Another Part of the Forest,* Fulton Theatre, New York City, 1946; Etta Hallam, *The Hallams,* Booth Theatre, New York City, 1948; Williams, *The Leading Lady,* National Theatre, 1948; Linda Loman, *Death of a Salesman,* Morosco Theatre, New York City, 1949; Mrs. Bayard Goodale, *Pride's Crossing,* Biltmore Theatre, New York City, 1950; Aase, *Peer Gynt,* American National Theatre and Academy (ANTA) Theatre, New York City, 1951; Gina, *The Wild Duck,* City Center Theatre, New York City, 1951; Signora Frola, *Right You Are!,* Westport Country Playhouse, Westport, CT, 1952; Mrs. Constable, *In the Summer House,* Playhouse Theatre, New York City, 1953; Big Mama, *Cat on a Hot Tin Roof,* Morosco Theatre, 1955; Constance, *King John,* American Shakespeare Festival, Stratford, CT, 1956; Susan Shepherd, *Child of Fortune,* Royale Theatre, New York City, 1956; Hera, *Maiden Voyage,* Forrest Theatre, 1957; Mary Tyrone, *Long Day's Journey into Night,* Orpheum Theatre, Montreal, PQ, Canada, 1959.

Mistress Phoebe Ricketts, *The Crystal Heart,* East 74th Street Theatre, New York City, 1960; Gertrude Povis, *Farewell, Fare-*

well, Eugene, Helen Hayes Theatre, New York City, 1960; title role, *Elizabeth the Queen,* University of Utah, Salt Lake City, UT, 1961; Mary Tyrone, *Long Day's Journey into Night,* Theatre du Nouveau Monde, Montreal, 1961; Mrs. Perpetua, *The Cantilevered Terrace,* 41st Street Theatre, New York City, 1962; Vera Ridgeway Condotti, *The Milk Train Doesn't Stop Here Anymore,* Festival of Two Worlds, Teatro Nuovo, Spoleto, Italy, then Morosco Theatre, both 1962; Hecuba, *The Trojan Women,* Festival of Two Worlds, Teatro Nuovo, then Circle in the Square, New York City, both 1963; Madame Renaud, *Traveller Without Luggage,* ANTA Theatre, 1964; Lucy Lewis, *Brother to Dragons,* American Place Theatre, New York City, 1965; Oenone, *Phedre,* Greenwich Mews Theatre, New York City, then at the American Embassy, London, both 1966; Mary Tyrone, *Long Day's Journey into Night,* Long Wharf Theatre, New Haven, CT, 1966; Amanda Wingfield, *The Glass Menagerie,* National Repertory Theatre, Oakland, CA, 1966; narrator, *Chansons de Bilitis* (ballet), Caramoor Festival, Caramoor, NY, 1967; Mrs. Edna Nichols, *Willie Doesn't Live Here Anymore,* ANTA Matinee Series, Theatre De Lys, New York City, 1967; Hecuba, *The Trojan Women,* Circle in the Square, 1967; Sido, *Colette,* Ellen Stewart Theatre, New York City, 1970; Beth, *Landscape,* Repertory Theatre of Lincoln Center, Forum Theatre, New York City, 1970; Clair Lannes, *A Place without Doors,* Stairway Theatre, New York City, then Long Wharf Theatre, both 1970, later Goodman Theatre, Chicago, IL, 1971; Emily Dickinson, *An Evening with Emily Dickinson and Robert Schumann,* Manhattan Theatre Club, New York City, 1971; the Mother, *Days in the Trees,* Circle in the Square, 1976; Madame Pernelle, *Tartuffe,* Circle in the Square, 1977. Also appeared in summer theatre productions at the Westchester County Playhouse, Mt. Kisco, NY, 1932, then 1934-38; in *Pictures in the Hallway* (staged reading), Phoenix Theatre, New York City, 1959; *Just Wild About Harry,* Festival of Two Worlds, Teatro Nuovo, 1963; with the Yale Repertory Theatre, New Haven, CT, 1967-70; Long Wharf Theatre, 1968-70, and 1972-73; *Ring 'round the Moon,* Williamstown Theatre Festival, Williamstown, MA, 1975; *What Every Woman Knows,* Long Wharf Theatre, 1975.

PRINCIPAL STAGE WORK—Director, *Graduation,* Theatre De Lys, New York City, 1965; director, *Luminosity Without Radiance: A Self-Portrait,* Manhattan Theatre Club, New York City, 1973.

MAJOR TOURS—*Herod and Mariamne,* U.S. cities, 1938; *Madam, Will You Walk?,* U.S. cities, 1941; *The Corn Is Green,* U.S. cities, 1942; Sido, *Colette,* U.S. cities, 1974.

FILM DEBUT—Miss Ronberry, *The Corn Is Green,* Warner Brothers, 1945. PRINCIPAL FILM APPEARANCES—Ma Rizzo, *Kiss of Death,* Twentieth Century-Fox, 1947; Sarah Greer, *I Want You,* RKO, 1951; Linda Loman, *Death of a Salesman,* Columbia, 1952; Dr. Marie Yeomans, *The Girl in White* (also known as *So Bright the Flame*), Metro-Goldwyn-Mayer (MGM), 1952; Senora Espejo, *Viva Zapata!,* Twentieth Century-Fox, 1952; Mrs. Golding, *The Jazz Singer,* Warner Brothers, 1953; Mrs. Mary Owen, *Bad for Each Other,* Columbia, 1954; mother, *Hansel and Gretel,* RKO, 1954; Mrs. Wiggs, *The Trouble with Harry,* Paramount, 1955; Aunt Rose Comfort, *Baby Doll,* Warner Brothers, 1956; Mother, *Love Me Tender,* Twentieth Century-Fox, 1956; Mrs. Thorton, *Peyton Place,* Twentieth Century-Fox, 1957; Sister Margharita, *The Nun's Story,* Warner Brothers, 1959; Mrs. Ellis, *The Story on Page One,* Twentieth Century-Fox, 1959; Mrs. Wandrous, *Butterfield 8,* MGM, 1960; Mrs. Gates, *Something Wild,* United Artists, 1961; Aunt Nonnie, *Sweet Bird of Youth,* MGM, 1962; Pilar, *Behold a Pale Horse,* Columbia, 1964; Mrs. Sarah Hawke, *Youngblood Hawke,* Warner Brothers, 1964; Jane Argent, *Seven*

Women, MGM, 1966; Miss Tinsley, *What Ever Happened to Aunt Alice?*, Cinerama, 1969; Mrs. Sherman, *The Spiral Staircase*, Warner Brothers, 1975; Mrs. Barrow, *One Summer Love* (also known as *Dragonfly*), American International, 1976; Nellie, *The Pick-Up Artist*, Twentieth Century-Fox, 1987.

PRINCIPAL TELEVISION APPEARANCES—Episodic: "The Last Step," *Television Theatre*, NBC, 1950; "The Handcuff," *The Web*, CBS, 1952; "On Borrowed Time," *Celanese Theatre*, ABC, 1952; "The Rose," *Gulf Playhouse*, NBC, 1952; *Broadway Television Theatre*, syndicated, 1952; "Mark of Cain," *Studio One*, CBS, 1953; "The Boy in the Front Row," "Like Father," and "Speak No Evil," *The Web*, CBS, 1953; "The Queen's Ring," *Suspense*, CBS, 1953; "The Young and the Fair," *Goodyear Playhouse*, NBC, 1953; "Miracle in the Rain," *Tales of the City* (also known as *Ben Hecht's Tales of the City*), CBS, 1953; "Game of Hide and Seek," *Goodyear Playhouse*, NBC, 1954; "Sinners," *Medallion Theatre*, CBS, 1954; "Treasure Trove," *Armstrong Circle Theatre*, NBC, 1954; "The Almighty Dollar," *Television Soundstage*, NBC, 1954; "The Worried Songbirds," *Uncle Harry*," "The Happy Journey," and "A Child Is Born," *Kraft Theatre*, ABC, 1954; "Guilty Secrets" and "The Sisters," *Inner Sanctum*, syndicated, 1954; "The Hickory Limb," *Kraft Theatre*, ABC, 1955; "A Business Proposition," *Philco Playhouse*, NBC, 1955; "President," *Alcoa Hour*, NBC, 1956; "None Are So Blind," *Alfred Hitchcock Presents*, CBS, 1956; "The Wonderful Gifts," *Kraft Theatre*, NBC, 1956; "Don't Touch Me," *Climax!*, CBS, 1957; "The Traveling Lady," *Studio One*, CBS, 1957; "Winter Dreams" and "The Play Room," *Playhouse 90*, CBS, 1957; "The West Warlock Time Capsule" and "Heart of Gold," *Alfred Hitchcock Presents*, CBS, 1957; "The Sound of Trouble," *Kraft Theatre*, NBC, 1957; "Diary of a Nurse," *Playhouse 90*, CBS, 1959; "A Trip to Cardis," *Robert Herridge Theatre*, CBS, 1960; *The Tom Ewell Show*, CBS, 1960; "The Cheaters," *Thriller*, NBC, 1960; "Night of the Story," *Dupont Theatre*, CBS, 1961; "The Mind's Own Fire," *The Investigators*, CBS, 1961; "The First Day," *Westinghouse Presents*, CBS, 1962; "Beyond the Sea of Death," *Alfred Hitchcock Theatre*, CBS, 1964; *The Defenders*, CBS, 1964; "The Hamster of Happiness," *Experiment in Television*, NBC, 1968; *The F.B.I.*, ABC, 1969; *Ghost Story*, NBC, 1972; *Camera Three*, CBS; *The Reporters*, CBS.

Movies: Mother, *A Brand New Life*, ABC, 1973; Mrs. LaCava, *A Summer Without Boys*, ABC, 1973; Lois Harrelson, *Murder or Mercy*, ABC, 1974; Serena Fox, *And Baby Makes Six*, NBC, 1979; Rose Price, *The Best Place to Be*, NBC, 1979; Serena Fox, *Baby Comes Home*, CBS, 1980; Helen, *Isabel's Choice*, CBS, 1981; as herself, *The Patricia Neal Story*, CBS, 1981. Specials: Spinster, *The Power and the Glory*, CBS, 1961; Linda Loman, *Death of a Salesman*, CBS, 1966; *Arthur Miller on Home Ground*, CBC, 1979; grandmother, *The Big Stuffed Dog*, NBC, 1980.

RELATED CAREER—Member, Actors' Studio, New York City, 1949—.

NON-RELATED CAREER—Teacher, Friends School, Baltimore, MD, then Brearly School, New York.

AWARDS: Elected to the Theatre Hall of Fame, 1984.

MEMBER: Screen Actors Guild, Actors' Equity Association (council member), American Federation of Television and Radio Artists.

ADDRESSES: AGENT—S.T.E. Representation, 9301 Wilshire Boulevard, Suite 312, Beverly Hills, CA 90210.*

DUSENBERRY, Ann

PERSONAL: Born September 13, in Tucson, AZ.

VOCATION: Actress.

CAREER: PRINCIPAL FILM APPEARANCES—Tina Wilcox (Miss Amity), *Jaws II*, Universal, 1978; Stevie, *Heart Beat*, Warner Brothers, 1979; Valerie Duran, *Cutter's Way* (also known as *Cutter and Bone*), United Artists, 1981; Dominique Corsaire, "Success Wanters" in *National Lampoon Goes to the Movies*, Metro-Goldwyn-Mayer/United Artists, 1981; Robyn Wallace, *Lies*, Alpha, 1984; Melinda, *Basic Training*, Movie Store, 1985; Page, *The Men's Club*, Atlantic Releasing, 1986. Also appeared in *Goodbye Franklin High*, Cal-Am, 1978.

PRINCIPAL TELEVISION APPEARANCES—Series: Amy March Laurence, *Little Women*, NBC, 1979; Molly Nichols Tanner, *The Family Tree*, NBC, 1983; Margo McGibbon, *Life with Lucy*, ABC, 1986. Mini-Series: Ann-Marie, *Captains and the Kings*, NBC, 1976. Pilots: Weezie Summer, *The Possessed*, NBC, 1977; Amory Osborn, *Stonestreet: Who Killed the Centerfold Model?*, NBC, 1977; Amy March, *Little Women*, NBC, 1978; Donna, *The Secret War of Jackie's Girls*, NBC, 1980; Deputy Kelly Myerson, *Fraud Squad*, ABC, 1985. Episodic: Liz Gordon, *Murder, She Wrote*, CBS, 1986; Carol Selby, *Murder, She Wrote*, CBS, 1987; Jean Merrick, *Mr. President*, Fox, 1988; Leslie Randall, *Jake and the Fatman*, CBS, 1988; Belva McPherson, *Designing Women*, CBS, 1989; Lorna, *Paradise*, CBS, 1989. Movies: Joanna Dance, *Desperate Women*, NBC, 1978; Joy Morgan and Elaine Steel, *Killjoy*, CBS, 1981; Jeannie LeMay, *Elvis and the Beauty Queen*, NBC, 1981; Jennifer, *Confessions of a Married Man*, ABC, 1983; Holly Barnes, *He's Not Your Son*, CBS, 1984; Marilyn, *Long Time Gone*, ABC, 1986. Specials: Connie, *Close Ties*, Entertainment Channel, 1983.

ADDRESSES: AGENT—Doug Warner, Agency for the Performing Arts, 9000 Sunset Boulevard, Suite 1200, Los Angeles, CA 90069.*

*   *   *

DYKSTRA, John

VOCATION: Special effects designer and producer.

CAREER: PRINCIPAL FILM WORK—Special effects designer: *Silent Running*, Universal, 1972; (also special effects cinematographer) *Star Wars*, Twentieth Century-Fox, 1977; *Avalanche Express*, Twentieth Century-Fox, 1979; *Star Trek: The Motion Picture*, Paramount, 1979; *Caddyshack*, Warner Brothers, 1980; (with Robert Shepherd, Roger Dorney, and Al Miller) *Firefox*, Warner Brothers, 1982; (with John Grant) *Lifeforce*, Tri-Star, 1985; *Invaders from Mars*, Cannon, 1986.

PRINCIPAL TELEVISION WORK—All as special effects designer. Series: (Also producer) *Battlestar Galactica*, ABC, 1978-80. Pilots: *Return of the Six Million Dollar Man and the Bionic Woman II*, NBC, 1989. Movies: *Starflight: The Plane That Couldn't Land*, ABC, 1983.

RELATED CAREER—Supervisor of special effects, Apogee Productions, Van Nuys, CA; cinematographer, National Science Foundation; special effects designer, "Voyage to the Outer Planets,"

Ruben H. Fleet Space Theatre, San Diego, CA; (with Douglas Trumbull) producer and creator of amusement park rides and aircraft simulator films; inventor, Dykstraflex camera.

AWARDS: Academy Awards, Best Visual Effects and Development of Facility Oriented Toward Visual Effects Photography, both 1977, for *Star Wars;* Academy Award nomination, Best Visual Effects, 1979, for *Star Trek: The Motion Picture;* Emmy Award, Outstanding Individual Achievement (Creative Technical Crafts division), 1979, for *Battlestar Galactica.*

ADDRESSES: OFFICE—Apogee Productions, 6842 Valjean Avenue, Van Nuys, CA 91406.*

E

ECHEVARRIA, Rocky
    See BAUER, Steven

* * *

EGGAR, Samantha   1939-

PERSONAL: Full name, Victoria Louise Samantha Marie Elizabeth Therese Eggar; born March 5, 1939, in London, England; daughter of Ralph Alfred James (a brigadier general in the British Army) and Muriel Olga (Palache-Bouman) Eggar; married Tom Stern (an actor, producer, and concert promoter) October 24, 1964 (divorced); children: Nicholas, Jenna Louise. EDUCATION—Attended the Thanet School of Art, the Slade School of Art, and the Webber-Douglas Dramatic School. RELIGION—Roman Catholic.

VOCATION: Actress.

CAREER: PRINCIPAL STAGE APPEARANCES—Appeared in British productions of *A Midsummer Night's Dream, Twelfth Night, The Taming of the Shrew,* and *Hamlet* during the 1960s; also appeared at the Oxford Playhouse, Oxford, U.K., for two seasons and at the Royal Court Theatre, London.

PRINCIPAL FILM APPEARANCES—Delia, *Doctor in Distress,* Rank, 1963; Ethel Le Neve, *Dr. Crippen,* Warner Brothers, 1963; Robin, *Psyche 59,* Columbia/Royal, 1964; Josie, *Young and Willing* (also known as *The Wild and the Willing* and *The Young and the Willing*), Universal, 1964; Miranda Grey, *The Collector,* Columbia, 1965; Fabienne, *Return from the Ashes,* United Artists, 1965; Christine Easton, *Walk, Don't Run,* Columbia, 1966; Emma Fairfax, *Doctor Dolittle,* Twentieth Century-Fox, 1967; Dany Lang, *La Dame dans l'auto avec des lunettes et un fusil* (also known as *The Lady in the Car with Glasses and a Gun*), Columbia, 1970; Mary Raines, *The Molly Maguires,* Paramount, 1970; Deborah Dainton, *The Walking Stick,* Metro-Goldwyn-Mayer, 1970; Arabella, *The Light at the Edge of the World,* National General, 1971; Myra, *The Dead Are Alive,* National General, 1972; Mary Watson, *The Seven-Per-Cent Solution,* Universal, 1977; Edina Hamilton, "Film Studio Story" in *The Uncanny,* Rank, 1977; Katherine, *Welcome to Blood City,* EMI-Famous Players, 1977; Alice Field, *Why Shoot the Teacher?,* Ambassador/Quartet, 1977; Nola Carveth, *The Brood,* New World, 1979; Dr. Megan Stewart, *The Exterminator,* AVCO-Embassy, 1980; Jennifer Baines, *Demonoid* (also known as *Macabra*), American Panorama, 1981; Samantha O'Brien, *Hot Touch,* Astral Films/Trans-Atlantic, 1982; Samantha Sherwood, *Curtains,* Jensen Farley, 1983; Julie Vickers, *For the Term of His Natural Life,* Filmco, 1985; as herself, *Directed*

by William Wyler (documentary), Tatge, 1986. Also appeared in *A Name for Evil,* Cinerama, 1970; and in *Mareth Line.*

PRINCIPAL TELEVISION APPEARANCES—Series: Anna Owens, *Anna and the King,* CBS, 1972. Pilots: Anne Roland, *The Killer Who Wouldn't Die,* ABC, 1976. Episodic: Helena Marsh, *Fantasy Island,* ABC, 1979; Mrs. Cratchit, *George Burns Comedy Week,* CBS, 1985; Nanny, *Hotel,* ABC, 1985; Sister Rachel, *Outlaws,* CBS, 1987; Camilla Rousseau, *Stingray,* NBC, 1987; Ory Palmer, "Davy Crockett," *The Magical World of Disney,* NBC, 1988; Claire Stiggs, *HeartBeat,* ABC, 1989; also *The Saint,* ABC, 1965; *Love Story,* NBC, 1973; *Lucas Tanner,* NBC, 1975; "The Man of Destiny," *Hollywood Television Theatre,* PBS, 1975; "The Hemingway Play," *Hollywood Television Theatre,* PBS, 1976; *Baretta,* ABC, 1976; *McMillan and Wife,* NBC, *Streets of San Francisco,* ABC; *Starsky and Hutch,* ABC; *Columbo,* NBC; *The Love Boat,* ABC; *Kojak,* CBS; *Hart to Hart,* ABC; *Murder, She Wrote,* CBS; *Finder of Lost Loves,* ABC; *Family,* ABC. Movies: Phyllis Dietrichson, *Double Indemnity,* ABC, 1973; Carol Ann, *All the Kind Strangers,* ABC, 1974; Billie Burke, *Ziegfeld: The Man and His Women,* NBC, 1978; Solange DuLac, *Love Among Thieves,* ABC, 1987. Specials: Evelyn Walsh McLean, "The Legendary Curse of the Hope Diamond," *Smithsonian Institution Specials,* CBS, 1975.

AWARDS: Best Actress Award from the Cannes Film Festival, 1965, Academy Award nomination, Best Actress, 1966, and Golden Globe, Best Motion Picture Actress, 1966, all for *The Collector.*

MEMBER: Screen Actors Guild, American Federation of Television and Radio Artists, Actors' Equity Association, Association of Canadian Television and Radio Artists, Academy of Motion Picture Arts and Sciences, Daughters of the British Empire, Cousteau Society, Greenpeace, Centre for Environmental Education, Special Olympics, British Olympics (entertainment committee, 1983-84), Kidney Foundation (board member, 1968-73), Young Musicians Foundation.

ADDRESSES: OFFICE—Tucker, Morgan, and Martindale, 9200 Sunset Boulevard, Los Angeles, CA 90069. AGENT—The Craig Agency, 8485 Melrose Place, Suite E, Los Angeles, CA 90069.*

* * *

ENGLUND, Robert   1949-

PERSONAL: Born June 6, 1949, in Glendale, CA; son of C. Kent (an aeronautics engineer) and Janis (McDonald) Englund; married Nancy Ellen Booth (a set designer), October 1, 1988. EDUCA-

ROBERT ENGLUND

TION—Attended Oakland University, the University of California, Northridge, and the University of California, Los Angeles; studied acting at the Academy of Dramatic Arts.

VOCATION: Actor, director, and producer.

CAREER: PRINCIPAL STAGE APPEARANCES—*The Apple Cart,* Meadow Brook Theatre, Rochester, MI, 1968; *Saint Joan,* Center Theatre Group, Ahmanson Theatre, Los Angeles, 1975; also appeared in *Godspell,* New York City, 1971; and at the Mark Taper Forum, Los Angeles, 1985.

PRINCIPAL STAGE WORK—Producer (with Cast Theatre), *Savage in Limbo,* Hollywood, CA, 1987.

FILM DEBUT—Whitey, *Buster and Billie,* Columbia, 1974. PRINCIPAL FILM APPEARANCES—Holdup man, *Hustle,* Paramount, 1975; Buck, *Death Trap* (also known as *Legend of the Bayou, Horror Hotel, Eaten Alive,* and *Starlight Slaughter*), Motion Picture Marketing, 1976; hood, *St. Ives,* Warner Brothers, 1976; Marty, *A Star Is Born,* Warner Brothers, 1976; Franklin, *Stay Hungry,* United Artists, 1976; narrator and Fly, *Big Wednesday,* Warner Brothers, 1978; Mott, *Bloodbrothers,* Warner Brothers, 1978; Beebo Crozier, *The Great Smokey Roadblock* (also known as *The Last of the Cowboys*), Dimension, 1978; Benny, *The Fifth Floor,* Film Ventures International, 1980; Harry, *Dead and Buried,* AVCO-Embassy, 1981; Ranger, *Galaxy of Terror* (also known as *Mindwarp, An Infinity of Terror, The Quest,* and *Planet of Horrors*), New World, 1981; Tripper, *Don't Cry, It's Only Thunder,* Sanrio Communications, 1982; Freddy Krueger, *A Nightmare on*

Elm Street, New Line Cinema, 1984; Freddy Krueger, *A Nightmare on Elm Street, Part 2: Freddy's Revenge,* New Line Cinema, 1985; Riley, *Never Too Young to Die,* Paul Entertainment, 1986; Freddy Krueger, *A Nightmare on Elm Street 3: Dream Warriors,* New Line Cinema, 1987; Freddy Krueger, *A Nightmare on Elm Street 4: The Dream Master,* New Line Cinema, 1988; Freddy Krueger, *A Nightmare on Elm Street 5: The Dream Child,* New Line Cinema, 1989; Eric Destler/title role, *Phantom of the Opera,* Twenty-First Century, 1989; Smiley, *Ford Fairlane,* Twentieth Century-Fox, 1989. Also appeared as Michael, *Sunburst.*

PRINCIPAL FILM WORK—Director, *976-EVIL* (also known as *Horrorscope*), New Line Cinema, 1988.

PRINCIPAL TELEVISION APPEARANCES—Series: Willie, *V,* NBC, 1984-85; Dennis Shothoffer, *Downtown,* CBS, 1986-87; Freddy Krueger (host), *A Nightmare on Elm Street—Freddy's Nightmares: The Series,* syndicated, 1988-90. Mini-Series: Willie, *V: The Final Battle,* NBC, 1984; deserter, *North and South, Book II,* ABC, 1986. Pilots: Boone, *The Mysterious Two,* NBC, 1982. Episodic: Captain Crusader, *Hollywood Beat,* ABC, 1985; Vaughn, *Hunter,* NBC, 1985; Edward Kent, *Knight Rider,* NBC, 1986; Tim Wexler, *MacGyver,* ABC, 1986; also *Police Story,* NBC; *Paris,* CBS; *Police Woman,* NBC; *Soap,* ABC. Movies: Willy, *Young Joe, the Forgotten Kennedy,* ABC, 1977; Sergeant Bell, *The Courage and the Passion,* NBC, 1978; informer, *The Ordeal of Patty Hearst,* ABC, 1979; Ted Beasly, *Mind Over Murder,* CBS, 1979; Bobby Collins, *Thou Shalt Not Kill,* NBC, 1982; Mason, *Journey's End,* Showtime, 1982; Charlie, *The Fighter,* CBS, 1983; Willie, *V,* NBC, 1983; Freddy Beenstock, *Hobson's Choice,* CBS, 1983; Scott, *Starflight: The Plane That Couldn't Land,* ABC, 1983; Sam Cooper, *I Want to Live,* ABC, 1983; Scott, *Infidelity,* ABC, 1987.

PRINCIPAL TELEVISION WORK—Episodic: Director, *A Nightmare on Elm Street—Freddy's Nightmares: The Series* (seven episodes), syndicated, 1988—.

RELATED CAREER—Resident actor, Great Lakes Shakespeare Festival, Cleveland, OH, 1970-71; resident actor, Meadow Brook Theatre, Rochester, MI, 1969-72, then guest artist, 1973.

MEMBER: Actors' Equity Association (1968—), Screen Actors Guild (1973—), American Federation of Television and Radio Artists, Directors Guild of America.

ADDRESSES: AGENT—Joe Rice, Abrams Artists, 9200 Sunset Boulevard, Los Angeles, CA 90069.

*   *   *

EPHRON, Nora   1941-

PERSONAL: Born May 19, 1941, in New York, NY; daughter of Henry (a writer) and Phoebe (a writer; maiden name, Wolkind) Ephron; married Dan Greenberg (a writer), April 9, 1967 (divorced); married Carl Bernstein (a journalist), April 14, 1976 (divorced); married Nicholas Pileggi (a writer); children: Jacob, Max (second marriage). EDUCATION—Wellesley College, B.A., 1962.

VOCATION: Writer and producer.

CAREER: Also see *WRITINGS* below. PRINCIPAL FILM APPEAR-

ANCES—Wedding guest, *Crimes and Misdemeanors*, Orion, 1989. PRINCIPAL FILM WORK—Executive producer (with Susan Seidelman and Alice Arlen), *Cookie*, Warner Brothers, 1989; associate producer, *When Harry Met Sally*, Columbia, 1989.

RELATED CAREER—Reporter, *New York Post*, New York City, 1963-68; freelance journalist, 1968-72; columnist and contributing editor, *Esquire* magazine, New York City, 1972-73, then senior editor and columnist, 1974-76; contributing editor, *New York* magazine, New York City, 1973-74.

WRITINGS: FILM—(With Alice Arlen) *Silkwood*, Twentieth Century-Fox, 1983; *Heartburn*, Paramount, 1983; (with Arlen) *Cookie*, Warner Brothers, 1989; *When Harry Met Sally*, Columbia, 1989. TELEVISION—Episodic: *Adam's Rib*, ABC, 1973. Movies: *Perfect Gentlemen*, CBS, 1978. OTHER—*Wallflower at the Orgy*, Viking, 1970; *Crazy Salad: Some Things About Women*, Knopf, 1975; *Scribble, Scribble: Notes on the Media*, Knopf, 1979; *Heartburn*, Knopf, 1983; also contributor to magazines and journals.

AWARDS: Penney-Missouri Award from the University of Missouri Journalism School and J.C. Penney and Company, 1973; Academy Award nomination (with Alice Arlen), Best Original Screenplay, 1984, for *Silkwood;* named a Literary Lion by the New York City Public Library, 1986; Academy Award nomination, Best Original Screenplay, 1989, for *When Harry Met Sally*. HONORARY DEGREES—Briarcliff College, D.H.L., 1974.

MEMBER: Writers Guild of America, Authors Guild, P.E.N., Academy of Motion Picture Arts and Sciences.

ADDRESSES: AGENT—Lynn Nesbit, International Creative Management, 40 W. 57th Street, New York, NY, 10019.*

EVERETT, Rupert   1959-

PERSONAL: Born in 1959 in Norfolk, England. EDUCATION—Attended the Ampleforth Central School for Speech and Drama; also trained for the stage at the Glasgow Citizens' Theatre.

VOCATION: Actor.

CAREER: PRINCIPAL STAGE APPEARANCES—Guy Bennett, *Another Country,* Queen's Theatre, London, 1982.

FILM DEBUT—Guy Bennett, *Another Country*, Orion Classics, 1984. PRINCIPAL FILM APPEARANCES—Tim, *Real Life*, Bedford, 1984; David Blakely, *Dance with a Stranger*, Twentieth Century-Fox, 1985; Constantine Kassanis, *Duet for One*, Cannon, 1986; Bayardo San Roman, *Chronicle of a Death Foretold* (also known as *Cronaca di una morte annunciata*), Istituto Luce-Italnoleggio Cinematografico, 1987; David Lattes, *Gli occhiali d'oro* (also known as *The Gold Spectacles* and *The Gold Rimmed Glasses*), D.M.V., 1987; James Colt, *Hearts of Fire*, Lorimar, 1987; Harry Ironminister, *The Right-Hand Man*, New World, 1987; also appeared in *Haunted Summer* and *Jigsaw*.

PRINCIPAL TELEVISION APPEARANCES—Mini-Series: George Garforth, *The Far Pavilions*, HBO, 1984. Movies: Ram Valensky, *Princess Daisy*, NBC, 1983; Lancelot, *Arthur the King*, CBS, 1985.

ADDRESSES: AGENTS—Duncan Heath Associates Ltd., Paramount House, 162-170, Wardour Street, London W1, England; Michael Black and Hildy Gottlieb, International Creative Management, 8899 Beverly Boulevard, Los Angeles, CA 90048.*

F

FAISON, Frankie

PERSONAL: Full name, Frankie Russell Faison.

VOCATION: Actor.

CAREER: PRINCIPAL STAGE APPEARANCES—(As Frankie Russell Faison) Paul, "Andrew" in *The Corner*, New York Shakespeare Festival (NYSF), Public Theatre, New York City, 1972; lord attending Duke Senior, *As You Like It*, NYSF, Delacorte Theater, New York City, 1973; understudy for Ajax, Menelaus, Aeneas, and servant, *Troilus and Cressida*, NYSF, Mitzi E. Newhouse Theatre, New York City, 1973; Sam Wilde, "Nowhere to Run, Nowhere to Hide" in *A Season-Within-a Season*, Negro Ensemble Company, St. Mark's Playhouse, New York City, 1974; Walter, *The Last Days of British Honduras*, NYSF, Public Theatre, 1974; understudy for Lennie and Crooks, *Of Mice and Men*, Brooks Atkinson Theatre, New York City, 1974; Billy, *Welcome to Black River*, Negro Ensemble Company, St. Mark's Playhouse, 1975; cabin dweller, *Io Anne!*, Theatre of the Riverside Church, New York City, 1976; Stagolee, Scagolee, and Skulleton, *The Great MacDaddy*, Theatre De Lys, New York City, 1977; Gus Washington, *Broadway, Broadway*, Forrest Theatre, Philadelphia, PA, 1978; Louis, *Black Body Blues*, Negro Ensemble Company, St. Mark's Playhouse, 1978; guard, *Coriolanus*, NYSF, Public Theatre, 1979; Bruh, "Escape from Deep Hammock During the Hurricane of '52," Bominishus, "The Organ Recital at the New Grand," and Ham Shandy, "The Men's Room" in *The Men's Room* (triple-bill), Actors Repertory Theatre, New York City, 1982; man two, *The Box*, New Directors Project, Perry Street Theatre, New York City, 1984; actor two, *District Line*, Negro Ensemble Company, Theatre Four, New York City, 1984; Gabriel, *Fences*, Goodman Theatre, Chicago, IL, 1986, then 46th Street Theatre, New York City, 1987. Also appeared *Remembrance*, NYSF, Public Theatre, 1979; *Jass* (staged reading), New Dramatists Inc., New York City, 1980.

PRINCIPAL STAGE WORK—Stage manager, *Of Mice and Men*, Brooks Atkinson Theatre, New York City, 1974.

PRINCIPAL FILM APPEARANCES—Detective Brandt, *Cat People*, RKO, 1982; electrician, *A Little Sex*, Universal, 1982; man in lobby, *Permanent Vacation*, Gray City, 1982; driver, *Hanky-Panky*, Columbia, 1982; Parker, *C.H.U.D.*, New World, 1984; Be Gee, *Exterminator II*, Cannon, 1984; Lieutenant Fisk, *Manhunter*, De Laurentiis Entertainment Group, 1986; Handy, *Maximum Overdrive*, Dino De Laurentiis, 1986; James, *The Money Pit*, Universal, 1986; eulogist, *Mississippi Burning*, Orion, 1988; landlord, *Coming to America*, Paramount, 1988; Coconut Sid, *Do the Right Thing*, Universal, 1989; also appeared in *Ragtime*, Paramount, 1981.

PRINCIPAL TELEVISION APPEARANCES—Series: Regular, *Hot Hero Sandwich*, NBC, 1979-80. Episodic: Zudo, *The Equalizer*, CBS, 1987; Mr. Carver, *A Man Called Hawk*, ABC, 1989. Movies: Intern, *Sessions*, ABC, 1983.

AWARDS: Antoinette Perry Award nomination, Best Actor in a Featured Role in a Play, 1987, for *Fences*.

ADDRESSES: AGENT—Gersh Agency, 222 N. Canon Drive, Suite 202, Beverly Hills, CA 90210; Gersh Agency, 130 W. 42nd Street, New York, NY 10036.*

*　　*　　*

FAISON, George   1947-

PERSONAL: Born in 1947 in Washington, DC. EDUCATION—Attended Howard University, 1964-66.

VOCATION: Choreographer, director, and producer.

CAREER: PRINCIPAL STAGE APPEARANCES—Dancer, *Purlie*, Broadway Theatre, then Winter Garden Theatre, both New York City, 1970, then American National Theatre and Academy Theatre, New York City, 1971; dancer (with the George Faison Universal Dance Experience), *Interludes* series, Town Hall, New York City, 1975; also dancer, *Sinner Man* (ballet), Alvin Ailey American Dance Theatre.

PRINCIPAL STAGE WORK—All as choreographer, unless indicated: *Nigger Nightmare*, New York Shakespeare Festival (NYSF), Public Theatre, New York City, 1971-72; *Don't Bother Me, I Can't Cope*, Playhouse Theatre, then Edison Theatre, both New York City, 1972; (also assistant director) *Ti-Jean and His Brothers*, NYSF, Delacorte Theatre, New York City, 1972; *Everyman and Roach*, Everyman Theatre Company, New York City, 1972; *The Wiz*, Majestic Theatre, New York City, 1975, then Broadway Theatre, New York City, 1977; *Al Green/Ashford and Simpson*, Uris Theatre, New York City, 1976; director, *Inner City*, New Theatre of Washington, Washington, DC, 1976; (with Gilbert Moses; also director) *1600 Pennsylvania Avenue*, Mark Hellinger Theatre, New York City, 1976; *Hobo Sapiens, Gazelle*, and *Suite Otis* (ballets), all Alvin Ailey American Dance Theatre, City Center Theatre, New York City, 1977; creator (with Anita L. Thomas) and director, *Fixed*, Theatre of the Riverside Church, New York City, 1977; (also director) *Up on the Mountain*, Kennedy Center Musical Theatre Lab, Washington, DC, 1980; *The Moony Shapiro Songbook*, Morosco Theatre, New York City, 1981; *Rhinestone*, Richard Allen Center, New York City, 1982; *Porgy and Bess*, Radio

City Music Hall, New York City, 1983; *The Wiz*, Lunt-Fontanne Theatre, New York City, 1984; also *Billie Holliday Ballet*, Alvin Ailey American Dance Theatre.

MAJOR TOURS—Choreographer, *The Wiz*, U.S. cities, 1978-79.

PRINCIPAL FILM APPEARANCES—The choreographer, *Driving Me Crazy*, First-Run Features, 1990.

PRINCIPAL FILM WORK—Choreographer (with Michael Smuin, Henry LeTang, Gregory Hines, Claudia Asbury, Arthur Mitchell, and Michael Meachum), *The Cotton Club*, Orion, 1984.

PRINCIPAL TELEVISION APPEARANCES—Specials: *Bill Cosby Salutes Alvin Ailey*, NBC, 1989. PRINCIPAL TELEVISION WORK—Specials: Choreographer, *The Natalie Cole Special*, CBS, 1978; creator, executive producer (with Joe Cates), and production supervisor, *Bill Cosby Salutes Alvin Ailey*, NBC, 1989; also choreographer, *The Wiz*, 1975; co-creator, *Graffiti the Great*, NBC.

RELATED CAREER—Dancer, Arthur Mitchell's Dance Company, 1966; principal dancer, Alvin Ailey American Dance Theatre, 1967-69; founder, artistic director, choreographer, and dancer, George Faison Universal Dance Experience, 1971-75; director and choreographer, Earth, Wind, and Fire concert, Madison Square Garden, New York City, 1977; choreographer with the Afro-American Total Theatre, Lincoln Center Repertory Company, Negro Ensemble Company, Capitol Ballet Company, and the Alvin Ailey American Dance Theatre; director and choreographer for concert appearances of singers Stevie Wonder, Roberta Flack, Ashford and Simpson, Dionne Warwick, Jennifer Holiday, Irene Cara, Sister Sledge, Stephanie Milles, Deniece Williams, the Supremes, and Melba Moore; choreographer of industrial shows; choreographer of more than twenty ballets; founder, Fais One Productions (a production company); costume designer for singers and for the Alvin Ailey American Dance Theatre.

AWARDS: Antoinette Perry Award, Best Choreographer, 1975, for *The Wiz*; Antoinette Perry Award nomination, Best Choreographer, 1983, for *Porgy and Bess*.

OTHER SOURCES: *Black Theatre Alliance Newsletter*, January, 1979; *New Amsterdam News*, July 16, 1975 and May 26, 1984; *New York Times*, November 27, 1977; *Washington Post*, April 20, 1980.*

*   *   *

FAISON, Matthew

PERSONAL: Full name, Matthew James Faison.

VOCATION: Actor.

CAREER: PRINCIPAL STAGE APPEARANCES—*Love's Labour's Lost*, Alabama Shakespeare Festival, Anniston, AL, 1977; *A Christmas Carol*, Alliance Theatre Company, Atlanta, GA, 1977; *Bodies*, South Coast Repertory Theatre, Costa Mesa, CA, 1982.

PRINCIPAL FILM APPEARANCES—Leonard, *Getting Even*, Quantum, 1981; executive, *Mommie Dearest*, Paramount, 1981; reporter, *True Confessions*, United Artists, 1981; Judge Stoner, *The Star Chamber*, Twentieth Century-Fox, 1983; Buzz, *The Journey of*

Natty Gann, Buena Vista, 1985; Stan, *Friday the 13th Part VI: Jason Lives*, Paramount, 1986; Sergeant Daley, *Pray for Death*, American Distribution Group, 1986; man in gay bar, *Tough Guys*, Buena Vista, 1986; judge, *Bird*, Warner Brothers, 1988.

PRINCIPAL TELEVISION APPEARANCES—Mini-Series: Dick Peterson, *Robert Kennedy and His Times*, CBS, 1985. Pilots: Dr. Igmar Nordquist, *Stephanie*, CBS, 1981; Arnie, *Happy Endings*, CBS, 1983. Episodic: Dr. Tower, *Wiseguy*, CBS, 1990; also *M*A*S*H*, CBS, 1982; *Taxi*, ABC, 1982. Movies: Association man, *Act of Violence*, CBS, 1979; Dwight Nance, *The Night the City Screamed*, ABC, 1980; Williams, *Rape and Marriage—The Rideout Case*, CBS, 1980; Packard, *Callie and Son*, CBS, 1981; Paul Clark, *A Gun in the House*, CBS, 1981; Earl Rice, *A Small Killing*, CBS, 1981; Lawrence Holmes, *Not in Front of the Children*, CBS, 1982; Dwight Curry, *Prime Suspect*, CBS, 1982; Sy Dellinger, *Take Your Best Shot*, CBS, 1982; Jack Sapunor, *M.A.D.D.: Mothers Against Drunk Drivers*, NBC, 1983; Dr. Barrett, *Anatomy of an Illness*, CBS, 1984; Dr. Bronstein, *Fatal Vision*, NBC, 1984; judge, *Something About Amelia*, ABC, 1984; judge, *Deadly Intentions*, ABC, 1985; Evan Harris, *Kids Don't Tell*, CBS, 1985; Jack Mayberry, *A Reason to Live*, NBC, 1985; Johnson, *This Child Is Mine*, NBC, 1985; George Morrison, *A Fight for Jenny*, NBC, 1986; also *Sins of the Past*, ABC, 1984; *The Richest Cat in the World*, ABC, 1986; *Go Toward the Light*, CBS, 1988; *The Case of the Hillside Strangler*, NBC, 1989. Specials: Narrator, *Carnivore*, PBS, 1976.

RELATED CAREER—Company member, National Shakespeare Festival, Old Globe Theatre, San Diego, CA, 1976; company member, Actors Theatre of Louisville, Louisville, KY, 1977; company member, Alabama Shakespeare Festival, Anniston, AL, 1977-78.

ADDRESSES: AGENT—Stone Manners Agency, 9113 Sunset Boulevard, Los Angeles, CA 90069.*

*   *   *

FAISON, Sandy

VOCATION: Actress.

CAREER: PRINCIPAL STAGE APPEARANCES—Grace Farrell, *Annie*, Alvin Theatre, New York City, 1977; Alice Kinnian, *Charlie and Algernon*, Folger Theatre Group, Washington, DC, 1979, then Helen Hayes Theatre, New York City, 1980; Alice, *You Can't Take It with You*, Plymouth Theatre, New York City, 1983. Also appeared in *La Ronde*, Syracuse Stage, Syracuse, NY, 1974; *The Collected Works of Billy the Kid*, Folger Theatre Group, 1975; *The Neighborhood Playhouse at 50: A Celebration*, Shubert Theatre, New York City, 1978; *Custer*, Hartman Theatre Company, Stamford, CT, 1980; *Loose Ends*, Cincinnati Playhouse, Cincinnati, OH, 1981; *Is There Life After High School?*, Ethel Barrymore Theatre, New York City, 1982; *The Great Magoo*, Hartford Stage Company, Hartford, CT, 1982.

PRINCIPAL FILM APPEARANCES—Suzie, *All the Right Moves*, Twentieth Century-Fox, 1983.

PRINCIPAL TELEVISION APPEARANCES—Series: Brandy Shelooe, *The Guiding Light*, CBS, 1977; Dr. Beth Corell, *The Edge of Night*, ABC, 1983-84; Mamie Grolnick, *The Days and Nights of Molly*

Dodd, NBC, 1987-88, then Lifetime, 1989—; Pamela Peyton-Finch, *Anything But Love,* ABC, 1989. Pilots: Janice, *Making It,* NBC, 1976; Susan Brenner, *Street Killing,* ABC, 1976; Pam Kowalski, *Time Out for Dad* (also known as *Kowalski Loves Ya* and *Kowalski's Way*), NBC, 1987; Felicity, *Old Money* (broadcast as an episode of *CBS Summer Playhouse*), CBS, 1988; Pamela Peyton-Finch, *Anything But Love,* ABC, 1989. Episodic: *Scarecrow and Mrs. King,* CBS. Movies: Abby Bradford, *An Eight Is Enough Wedding,* NBC, 1989.

ADDRESSES: AGENT—S.T.E. Representation, 9301 Wilshire Boulevard, Suite 312, Beverly Hills, CA 90210.*

*   *   *

FARGAS, Antonio   1946-

PERSONAL: Born August 14, 1946, in New York, NY; son of Manuel and Mildred (Bailey) Fargas; married Taylor Hustie (a fashion designer), July 13, 1979; children: Matthew, Justin. EDUCATION—Attended Fashion Industry High School, 1965; trained for the stage at the Negro Ensemble Company. POLITICS— Liberal. RELIGION—Christian.

VOCATION: Actor.

CAREER: STAGE DEBUT—George Davis, *The Toilet,* St. Mark's Playhouse, New York City, 1963. LONDON DEBUT—David, *The Amen Corner,* Saville Theatre, 1965. PRINCIPAL STAGE APPEARANCES—Scipio, *The Great White Hope,* Arena Stage, Washington, DC, 1967, then Alvin Theatre, New York City, 1968; Sampson, *Romeo and Juliet,* New York Shakespeare Festival (NYSF), Delacorte Theatre, New York City, 1968; Moustique, *The Dream on Monkey Mountain,* Negro Ensemble Company, St. Mark's Playhouse, New York City, 1971; B.B. Gunn, *The Roast,* Winter Garden Theatre, New York City, 1980; Starbuck, *The Rainmaker,* Stagewest Theatre, West Springfield, MA, 1984; Abhorson, *Measure for Measure,* NYSF, Delacorte Theatre, 1985. Also appeared in *Ceremonies in Dark Old Men,* Negro Ensemble Company, St. Mark's Playhouse, 1969; *Who's Got His Own,* Center Stage, Baltimore, MD, 1969; *Isle Is Full of Noises,* Hartford Stage Company, Hartford, CT, 1982; *Ain't Supposed to Die a Natural Death,* Theatre of Universal Images, 1983; *The Amen Corner,* Philadelphia Drama Guild, Philadelphia, PA, 1986; and with the Denver Center Theatre Company, Denver, CO, 1985-86.

MAJOR TOURS—*The Amen Corner,* international cities, 1965; also toured in *The Dream on Monkey Mountain.*

FILM DEBUT—Coolie, *The Cool World,* Cinema V, 1963. PRINCIPAL FILM APPEARANCES—The Arab, *Putney Swope,* Cinema V, 1969; Boy, *Believe in Me,* Metro-Goldwyn-Mayer (MGM), 1971; Buffalo, *Cisco Pike,* Columbia, 1971; Bunky, *Shaft,* MGM, 1971; Henry Jackson, *Across 110th Street,* United Artists, 1972; Doodlebug, *Cleopatra Jones,* Warner Brothers, 1973; Quickfellow, *Conrack,* Twentieth Century-Fox, 1974; Link Brown, *Foxy Brown,* American International, 1974; pimp, *The Gambler,* Paramount, 1974; One Eye, *Cornbread, Earl, and Me,* American International, 1975; Lindy, *Car Wash,* Universal, 1976; Bernstein, *Next Stop, Greenwich Village,* Twentieth Century-Fox, 1976; Professor (piano player), *Pretty Baby,* Paramount, 1978; Doc, *Milo Milo,* Filmverlag der Autoren, 1979; Coach, *Up the Academy* (also known as *Mad Magazine's Up the Academy* and *The Brave Young Men of Weinberg*),

Warner Brothers, 1980; taxi driver, *Firestarter,* United International, 1984; blind man, *Crimewave* (also known as *Broken Hearts and Noses* and *Broken Hearts and Bloody Noses*), Embassy, 1985; Finesse, *Streetwalkin',* Concorde, 1985; Nicky Carr, *Shakedown* (also known as *Blue Jean Cop*), Universal, 1988; Flyguy, *I'm Gonna Git You Sucka,* Metro-Goldwyn-Mayer/United Artists, 1988. Also appeared in *Pound,* United Artists, 1970; *Busting,* United Artists, 1973; *Model Behavior,* Inter-Ocean Film Sales, 1984; *The Night of the Sharks* (also known as *La notte degli squali*), VIP International, 1987.

PRINCIPAL TELEVISION APPEARANCES—Series: Huggy Bear, *Starsky and Hutch,* ABC, 1975-79; Les Baxter, *All My Children,* ABC, 1982-83. Pilots: Rick, *Hereafter,* NBC, 1975; Huggy Bear, *Starsky and Hutch,* ABC, 1975; Leonard Jones, *Adventuring with the Chopper,* NBC, 1976; Marshall Gripps, *Nurse,* CBS, 1980; Oliver, *Paper Dolls,* ABC, 1983; Frank Wilkey, *P.O.P.,* NBC, 1984. Episodic: Alejandro, *Miami Vice,* NBC, 1988. Movies: Jim Watson, *Huckleberry Finn,* ABC, 1975; Jaime Valdez, *Escape,* CBS, 1980; Vaness, *The Ambush Murders,* CBS, 1982; Clifford, *A Good Sport,* CBS, 1984; El Gato Negro, *Florida Straits,* HBO, 1986. Specials: *All Commercials—A Steve Martin Special,* NBC, 1980; *Steve Martin's The Winds of Whoopie,* NBC, 1983.

MEMBER: California Volunteers of America, Family Services of Westchester Big Brothers.

SIDELIGHTS: RECREATIONS—Restoration of colonial houses and travel abroad.

ADDRESSES: AGENT—Fred Amsel and Associates, 6310 San Vicente Boulevard, Suite 407, Los Angeles, CA 90048.*

*   *   *

FELDMAN, Corey   1971-

PERSONAL: Born July 16, 1971, in Reseda, CA; father, a musician.

VOCATION: Actor.

CAREER: PRINCIPAL FILM APPEARANCES—Boy at museum, *Time After Time,* Warner Brothers/Orion, 1979; voice of Young Copper, *The Fox and the Hound* (animated), Buena Vista, 1981; Tommy, *Friday the 13th—The Final Chapter,* Paramount, 1984; Pete, *Gremlins,* Warner Brothers, 1984; Tommy at age 12, *Friday the 13th, Part V: A New Beginning* (also known as *Friday the 13th: A New Beginning*), Paramount, 1985; Mouth, *The Goonies,* Warner Brothers, 1985; Teddy DuChamp, *Stand By Me,* Columbia, 1986; Edgar Frog, *The Lost Boys,* Warner Brothers, 1987; Dean, *License to Drive,* Twentieth Century-Fox, 1988; Bobby Keller, *Dream a Little Dream,* Vestron, 1989; Ricky Butler, *The Burbs,* Universal, 1989.

PRINCIPAL FILM WORK—Choreographer, *Dream a Little Dream,* Vestron, 1989.

PRINCIPAL TELEVISION APPEARANCES—Series: Regi Tower, *The Bad News Bears,* CBS, 1979-80; Buzzy St. James, *Madame's Place,* syndicated, 1982. Pilots: Franklin Miller, *Love, Natalie,* NBC, 1980; Rudy, *The Kid with the Broken Halo,* NBC, 1982;

Little Big Jim Malloy, *Cass Malloy,* CBS, 1982; Corey Cleaver, *Still the Beaver,* CBS, 1983; Keith Schneider, *Another Man's Shoes,* CBS, 1984; Calvin Harlan, Jr., *Rowdies,* ABC, 1986. Episodic: Radical Conrad, *Heart of the City,* ABC, 1987; Bill, "The Boss," *Trying Times,* PBS, 1989; James Fenimore Schenke, "Exile," *The Magical World of Disney,* NBC, 1990; also *Foul Play,* ABC, 1981; *Cheers,* NBC, 1983; *What's Up, Dr. Ruth?,* Lifetime, 1989; *The Love Boat,* ABC; *Father Murphy,* NBC; *Alice,* CBS; *Eight Is Enough,* ABC; *Gloria,* CBS; Billy, *Mork and Mindy,* ABC. Movies: T.C., *Willa,* CBS, 1979; Bobby, *Father Figure,* CBS, 1980. Specials: Jeff, "Fifteen and Getting Straight" (also known as "Getting Straight"), *CBS Schoolbreak Special,* CBS, 1989.

RELATED CAREER—Actor in television commercials.

AWARDS: Youth in Film Award for *The Lost Boys.*

ADDRESSES: AGENT—Chris Black, Agency for the Performing Arts, 9000 Sunset Boulevard, Suite 1200, Los Angeles, CA 90069.

*   *   *

FERRELL, Conchata   1943-

PERSONAL: Full name, Conchata Galen Ferrell; born March 28, 1943, in Charleston, WV; daughter of Luther Martin and Mescal Loraine (George) Ferrell; married Arnold A. Anderson; children: Samantha. EDUCATION—Attended West Virginia University, 1961-64, and Marshall University, 1967-68.

VOCATION: Actress.

CAREER: PRINCIPAL STAGE APPEARANCES—Maid, *The Three Sisters,* Circle Theatre, New York City, 1970; April, *The Hot l Baltimore,* Circle Theatre Company, Circle Theatre, then Circle in the Square, New York City, both 1973; Vee Talbot, *Battle of Angels,* Circle Repertory Theatre, New York City, 1974; Gertrude Blum, *The Sea Horse,* Circle Repertory Company, Westside Arts Theatre, New York City, 1974; Molly, *Elephant in the House,* Circle Repertory Company, 1975; Ann, *Wine Untouched,* 18th Street Playhouse, New York City, 1976; Helen Potts, *Picnic,* Center Theatre Group, Ahmanson Theatre, Los Angeles, 1986; also appeared in *Getting Out,* Center Theatre Group, Mark Taper Forum, Los Angeles, 1977; *Here Wait,* 1980; and in *Time Framed,* New York City.

PRINCIPAL FILM APPEARANCES—Barbara Schlesinger, *Network,* United Artists, 1976; Slugger Ann, *Deadly Hero,* AVCO-Embassy, 1976; Elinore, *Heartland,* Filmhaus, 1980; Faye Doyle, *Miss Lonelyhearts,* H. Jay Holman/American Film Institute Center for Advanced Film Studies, 1983; Mother Marta, *Where the River Runs Black,* Metro-Goldwyn-Mayer/United International, 1986; Mrs. Bobrucz, *For Keeps,* Tri-Star, 1988; Leona Valsouano, *Mystic Pizza,* Samuel Goldwyn Company, 1988.

PRINCIPAL TELEVISION APPEARANCES—Series: April Green, *The Hot l Baltimore,* ABC, 1975; Wilhelmina "The Fox" Johnson, *B.J. and the Bear,* NBC, 1979-80; Vangie Cruise, *McClain's Law,* NBC, 1981-82; Nurse Joan Thor, *E/R,* CBS, 1984-85; Kate Galindo, *Peaceable Kingdom,* CBS, 1989. Pilots: Nurse Cassidy, *Mixed Nuts,* ABC, 1977; Connie, *The Rag Business,* ABC, 1978;

Katie, *Old Money* (broadcast as an episode of *CBS Summer Playhouse*), CBS, 1988. Episodic: Harriet, *Murder, She Wrote,* CBS, 1989; Faye Doyle, "Miss Lonelyhearts," *American Playhouse,* PBS, 1983; also Frances, *Who's the Boss?,* ABC. Movies: Nurse Rhinehart, *The Girl Called Hatter Fox,* CBS, 1977; Rita Parsons, *A Death in Canaan,* CBS, 1978; Dodie Hart, *Who'll Save Our Children?,* CBS, 1978; Marge, *Before and After,* ABC, 1979; Helen, *Rape and Marriage—The Rideout Case,* CBS, 1980; Toni Owens, *Reunion,* CBS, 1980; Hazel Dawson, *The Seduction of Miss Leona,* CBS, 1980; Captain Burnside, *Life of the Party: The Story of Beatrice,* CBS, 1982; Nurse Sylvia Kaye, *Emergency Room,* syndicated, 1983; Mili Simonecu, *Nadia,* syndicated, 1984; Dr. Gardner, *The Three Wishes of Billy Grier,* ABC, 1984; Doc Norman, *North Beach and Rawhide,* CBS, 1985; Ida Sinclair, *Samaritan: The Mitch Snyder Story,* CBS, 1986; Mary, *Eye on the Sparrow,* NBC, 1987; Mononaghee, *Your Mother Wears Combat Boots* (also known as *Your Mother Wears Army Boots*), NBC, 1989; Mrs. Bixby, *Goodbye, Miss Fourth of July,* Disney Channel, 1989; also *Martin Mull in "Portrait of a White Marriage"* (also known as *Portrait of a White Marriage, Scenes from a White Marriage,* and *Martin Mull in "Scenes from a White Marriage"*), Cinemax, 1988. Specials: Mamie Trotter, "The Great Gilley Hopkins," *CBS Afternoon Playhouse,* CBS, 1981; Helen Potts, *Picnic,* Showtime, 1986; Aunt Jill, "Runaway Ralph," *ABC Weekend Specials,* ABC, 1988.

AWARDS: Obie Award from the *Village Voice,* Drama Desk Award, and Theatre World Award, all 1974, for *The Sea Horse;* Wrangler Award from the National Cowboy Hall of Fame, 1981.

MEMBER: Actors' Equity Association, Screen Actors Guild, American Federation of Television and Radio Artists, Circle Repertory Theatre West, American Civil Liberties Union, National Organization for Women.

ADDRESSES: OFFICE—Jack Fields, Gores/Fields Agency, 10100 Santa Monica Boulevard, Suite 700, Los Angeles, CA 90067.*

*   *   *

FERRIGNO, Lou   1952-

PERSONAL: Born November 9, 1952, in Brooklyn, NY; father, a police lieutenant; second wife's name, Carla (a psychotherapist and television talk show host); children: Shanna, Lou. EDUCATION—Studied acting with Milton Katselas and Howard Fine.

VOCATION: Actor.

CAREER: STAGE DEBUT—Jonathan Brewster, *Arsenic and Old Lace,* Drury Lane Theatre, Chicago, IL, 1985. MAJOR TOURS—Jonathan Brewster, *Arsenic and Old Lace,* U.S. cities.

PRINCIPAL FILM APPEARANCES—As himself, *Pumping Iron* (documentary), Cinema V, 1977; Han, *The Seven Magnificent Gladiators,* Cannon, 1982; title role, *Hercules,* Metro-Goldwyn-Mayer/United Artists/Cannon, 1983; title role, *Hercules II* (also known as *The Adventures of Hercules*), Cannon, 1983; title role, *Sinbad of the Seven Seas,* Pathe International, 1989; Zerak, *Desert Warriors* (also known as *Sand Wars*), Silver Star/Prism, 1989; Klaus, *All's Fair,* Moviestore Entertainment, 1989; Sergeant Billy Thomas, *Cage,* United Artists, 1989.

LOU FERRIGNO

TELEVISION DEBUT—Title role, *The Incredible Hulk*, CBS, 1977. PRINCIPAL TELEVISION APPEARANCES—Series: Title role, *The Incredible Hulk*, CBS, 1978-82; John Six, *Trauma Center*, ABC, 1983. Pilots: Title role, *The Incredible Hulk*, CBS, 1977; title role, *The Return of the Incredible Hulk*, CBS, 1977. Movies: Title role, *The Trial of the Incredible Hulk*, NBC, 1988; title role, *The Incredible Hulk Returns* (also known as *The Return of the Incredible Hulk*), NBC, 1988; title role, *The Death of the Incredible Hulk*, NBC, 1990. Specials: *Battle of the Network Stars*, ABC, 1976 and 1979; *Celebrity Challenge of the Sexes*, CBS, 1979; *Bob Hope for President*, NBC, 1980.

NON-RELATED CAREER—Bodybuilding instructor; lecturer on bodybuilding and fitness at seminars and universities; professional football player with the Toronto Argonauts; sheet metal worker.

RECORDINGS: VIDEOS—*Body Perfection*.

SIDELIGHTS: Lou Ferrigno, who is best known to television audiences as "The Incredible Hulk," is also an award-winning bodybuilder. In 1971 he became Teenage Mr. America and by 1974 he had won all of bodybuilding's major titles including Mr. America (1972), Mr. Universe (1973 and 1974), and Mr. International (1974).

ADDRESSES: PUBLICIST—Levine/Schneider Public Relations, 8730 Sunset Boulevard, 6th Floor, Los Angeles, CA 90069.

FISHER, Frances

VOCATION: Actress.

CAREER: PRINCIPAL STAGE APPEARANCES—May, *Fool for Love*, Douglas Fairbanks Theatre, New York City, 1984; Abbie Putnam, *Desire Under the Elms*, Hartford Stage Company, Hartford, CT, 1985; Ruth, *The Hitch-Hikers*, WPA Theatre, New York City, 1985; also appeared in *Warsaw Opera*, Actors' Studio, New York City, 1980; *The War Brides*, New Dramatists Inc., New York City, 1981.

PRINCIPAL FILM APPEARANCES—Louise, *Can She Bake a Cherry Pie?*, JagFilm, 1983; Jessica Pond, *Tough Guys Don't Dance*, Cannon, 1987; Jeannie, *Heart*, New World, 1987; Yolanda, *Patty Hearst*, Atlantic, 1988; Phyllis, *Bum Rap*, Millennium, 1988; Actress, *Heavy Petting*, Skouras, 1989; Dinah, *Pink Cadillac*, Warner Brothers, 1989; Judith Loftis, *Lost Angels*, Orion, 1989; also appeared in *The Principal*, Tri-Star, 1987.

PRINCIPAL TELEVISION APPEARANCES—Series: Deborah Saxon, *The Edge of Night*, ABC, 1976-81; Suzette Saxon, *The Guiding Light*, CBS, 1985. Pilots: Violet Coffin, *Elysian Fields* (broadcast as an episode of *CBS Summer Playhouse*), CBS, 1989. Episodic: Amanda, *The Equalizer*, CBS, 1986; Francesca, *The Equalizer*, CBS, 1987; Savannah, *Roseanne*, ABC, 1988; Libby Harcourt, *Newhart*, CBS, 1989; Nancy Proctor, *Matlock*, NBC, 1989; Tina Miller, *Top of the Hill*, CBS, 1989. Movies: Maureen Phelan, *Broken Vows* (also known as *Where the Dark Streets Go* and *Hennessey*), CBS, 1987.*

*   *   *

FISK, Jack   1934-

PERSONAL: Born December 19, 1934, in Ipava, IL; married Sissy Spacek (an actress). EDUCATION—Studied design at Cooper Union.

VOCATION: Production designer and director.

CAREER: PRINCIPAL FILM APPEARANCES—Man in the Planet, *Eraserhead*, Libra, 1978.

PRINCIPAL FILM WORK—Production designer, *Angels Hard As They Come*, New World, 1971; production designer, *Cool Breeze*, Metro-Goldwyn-Mayer (MGM), 1972; production designer, *The Slams*, MGM, 1973; production designer, *Terminal Island*, Dimension, 1973; production designer, *Badlands*, Warner Brothers, 1974; production designer, *Phantom of the Paradise*, Twentieth Century-Fox, 1974; set designer, *Darktown Strutters* (also known as *Get Down and Boogie*), New World, 1975; production designer (with William Kenny), *Carrie*, United Artists, 1976; production designer, *Vigilante Force*, United Artists, 1976; production designer, *Days of Heaven*, Paramount, 1978; production designer, *Movie, Movie*, Warner Brothers, 1978; production designer, *Heart Beat*, Warner Brothers, 1979; director, *Raggedy Man*, Universal, 1981; director, *Violets Are Blue*, Columbia, 1986.

ADDRESSES: AGENT—Creative Artists Agency, 9830 Wilshire Boulevard, Beverly Hills, CA 90212.*

FITZGERALD, Geraldine   1914-

PERSONAL: Born November 24, 1914, in Dublin, Ireland; came to the United States in 1938; naturalized U.S. citizen, 1954; daughter of Edward (an attorney) and Edith Fitzgerald; married Edward Lindsay Hogg (a songwriter), 1936 (divorced, 1946); married Stuart Scheftel (a business executive), September, 10, 1946; children: Michael (first marriage); Susan (second marriage). EDUCATION—Attended Queens College, London, and the Dublin Art School.

VOCATION: Actress and director.

CAREER: STAGE DEBUT—With the Gate Theatre, Dublin, Ireland, 1932. BROADWAY DEBUT—Ellie Dunn, *Heartbreak House,* Mercury Theatre, 1938. PRINCIPAL STAGE APPEARANCES—Rebecca, *Sons and Soldiers,* Morosco Theatre, New York City, 1943; Tanis Talbot, *Portrait in Black,* Shubert Theatre, New Haven, CT, 1945; Jennifer Dubedat, *The Doctor's Dilemma,* Phoenix Theatre, New York City, 1955; Goneril, *King Lear,* City Center Theatre, New York City, 1956; Ann Richards, *Hide and Seek,* Ethel Barrymore Theatre, New York City, 1957; Gertrude, *Hamlet,* American Shakespeare Festival, Stratford, CT, 1958; the Queen, *The Cave Dwellers,* Greenwich Mews Theatre, New York City, 1961; third woman, *Pigeons,* New Playwrights Series II, Cherry Lane Theatre, New York City, 1965; Essie Miller, *Ah, Wilderness!,* Circle in the Square, Ford's Theatre, Washington, DC, 1969.

Mary Tyrone, *Long Day's Journey into Night,* Promenade Theatre, New York City, 1971; Jenny, *The Threepenny Opera,* WPA Theatre, New York City, 1972; Juno Boyle, *Juno and the Paycock,* Hartke Theatre, Catholic University, Washington, DC, 1972; Amy, *Forget-Me-Not Lane,* Grandmother, *The Widowing of Mrs. Holroyd,* and Aline Solness, *The Master Builder,* all Long Wharf Theatre, New Haven, CT, 1973; Essie Miller, *Ah, Wilderness!,* Long Wharf Theatre, 1974, then Circle in the Square, New York City, 1975; Mary Tyrone, *Long Day's Journey into Night* and Amanda Wingfield, *The Glass Menagerie,* both Philadelphia Drama Guild, Walnut Theatre, Philadelphia, PA, 1975; Mrs. Webb, *Our Town,* American Shakespeare Festival, 1975; *Geraldine Fitzgerald in Songs of the Streets* (one-woman show), Circle in the Square, 1976; Stage Manager, *Our Town,* Williamstown Theatre Festival, Williamstown, MA, 1976; Felicity, *The Shadow Box,* Long Wharf Theatre, then Morosco Theatre, New York City, both 1977; Nora Melody, *A Touch of the Poet,* Helen Hayes Theatre, New York City, 1977.

Geraldine Fitzgerald in Streetsongs (one-woman show), Roundabout Stage One Theatre, New York City, then Pittsburgh Public Theatre, Pittsburgh, PA, both 1980; Rose Kossew, *Flight,* Royal Shakespeare Company, Other Place Theatre, Stratford-on Avon, U.K., 1986; Leonora, "I Can't Remember Anything" in *Danger: Memory!,* Mitzi E. Newhouse Theatre, New York City, 1987. Also appeared in *Everyman and Roach,* Society for Ethical Culture Auditorium, New York City, 1971; *Everyman at La Mama,* La Mama Experimental Theatre Club, New York City, 1972; *Cabaret in the Sky,* New York Cultural Center, New York City, 1974; in a concert reading, New York Cultural Center, New York City, 1975; at the Countee Cullen Great Storyteller Series, Afro-American Total Theatre, New York City, 1975; in *An Evening of Street Songs and Clown Songs,* Theatre for the New City, New York City, 1975; with the St. Nicholas Theatre Company, Chicago, IL, 1977-78; in *Darlin' June,* Long Wharf Theatre, 1976; *Out of My Father's House,* White House, Washington, DC, 1978; *I Sent a Letter to My Love,* Long Wharf Theatre, 1978; *O'Neill and Carlotta* (staged

reading), Public Theatre, New York City, 1979; *Waitin' in the Wings,* Triplex Theatre, New York City, 1986 and 1988.

PRINCIPAL STAGE WORK—Director: *Mass Appeal,* Manhattan Theatre Club, then Booth Theatre, both New York City, 1980; *The Lunch Girls,* Theatre Row Theatre, New York City, 1981; *Long Day's Journey into Night,* Theatre at St. Peter's Church, then Public Theatre, both New York City, 1981; *Mass Appeal,* Paper Mill Playhouse, Millburn, NJ, 1982; *Wednesday,* Hudson Guild Theatre, New York City, 1983; (also choreographer) *Take Me Along,* Manhattan Community College Performing Art Center, New York City, 1984; *The Return of Herbert Bracewell,* Chelsea Playhouse, New York City, 1985; *To Whom It May Concern,* St. Stephen's Church, New York City, 1985.

MAJOR TOURS—Tanis Talbot, *Portrait in Black,* U.S. cities, 1946; *Songs of the Streets* (one-woman show), U.S. cities, 1976.

PRINCIPAL FILM APPEARANCES—Peggy Summers, *Blind Justice,* Real Art, 1934; Jill, *Open All Night,* RKO, 1934; Ruth Fosdyck, *Turn of the Tide,* Gaumont, 1935; Evelyn, *The Ace of Spades,* Real Art, 1935; Jane Grey, *Department Store* (also known as *Bargain Basement*), Real Art, 1935; Joan, *The Lad,* Universal, 1935; Joan Fayre, *Lieutenant Daring, R.N.,* Butchers Film Service, 1935; Diane Morton, *Three Witnesses,* Universal, 1935; Moira O'Flynn, *Cafe Mascot,* Paramount, 1936; Peggy Mayhew, *Debt of Honor,* General Films Distributors, 1936; Ann King, *Dark Victory,* First National, 1939; Maggie Tulliver, *Mill on the Floss,* Standard, 1939; Isabella Linton, *Wuthering Heights,* United Artists, 1939; Grace Sutton, *A Child Is Born,* Warner Brothers, 1940; Bonnie Coburn, *'Til We Meet Again,* Warner Brothers, 1940; Betty Farroway, *Flight from Destiny,* Warner Brothers, 1941; Dr. Mary Murray, *Shining Victory,* Warner Brothers, 1941; Evelyn Gaylord, *The Gay Sisters,* Warner Brothers/First National, 1942; Marthe de Brancovis, *Watch on the Rhine,* Warner Brothers, 1943; Edith Wilson, *Wilson,* Twentieth Century-Fox, 1944; Virgie Alford, *Ladies Courageous,* Universal, 1944; Lettie Quincy, *Uncle Harry* (also known as *The Strange Affair of Uncle Harry*), Universal, 1945; Gladys Halvorsen, *Nobody Lives Forever,* Warner Brothers, 1946; Ellen Rogers, *O.S.S.,* Paramount, 1946; Crystal, *Three Strangers,* Warner Brothers/First General, 1946; Susan Courtney, *So Evil My Love,* Paramount, 1948.

Elizabeth, *Obsessed* (also known as *The Late Edwina Black*), United Artists, 1951; Edith Chapin, *Ten North Frederick,* Twentieth Century-Fox, 1958; Tante Maria, *The Fiercest Heart,* Twentieth Century-Fox, 1961; Marilyn Birchfield, *The Pawnbroker,* Landau Releasing/Allied Artists/American International, 1965; Reverend Wood, *Rachel, Rachel,* Warner Brothers, 1968; Mrs. Jackson, *The Last American Hero* (also known as *Hard Driver*), Twentieth Century-Fox, 1973; Jessie, *Harry and Tonto,* Twentieth Century-Fox, 1974; Sara, *Echoes of a Summer* (also known as *The Last Castle*), Cine Artists, 1976; Toland, *Ciao maschio* (also known as *Bye Bye Monkey*), Gaumont, 1978; Martha Bach, *Arthur,* Warner Brothers, 1981; Grandma Carr, *The Mango Tree,* Satori, 1981; Mrs. Monahan, *Easy Money,* Orion, 1983; Mrs. Thomason, *The Link,* Zadar, 1985; Gramma Jess, *Poltergeist II* (also known as *Poltergeist II: The Other Side*), Metro-Goldwyn-Mayer/United Artists, 1986.

PRINCIPAL TELEVISION APPEARANCES—Series: Helen Eldredge, *Our Private World,* CBS, 1965; Violet Jordan, *The Best of Everything,* ABC, 1970. Mini-Series: Rose Kennedy, *Kennedy,* NBC, 1983. Pilots: *Starr, First Baseman,* CBS, 1965; Peggy Quinn, *The Quinns,* ABC, 1977; Mabel Oberdeen, *Mabel and Max* (broadcast as an episode of *CBS Summer Playhouse*), CBS, 1987. Episodic: Grandmother, "The Widowing of Mrs. Holroyd," *Theatre in America*, PBS, 1974; Amy Bisley, "Forget-Me-Not Lane," *Theatre in America*, PBS, 1975; Essie Miller, "Ah, Wilderness!" and Mrs. Atkins, "Beyond the Horizon," both *Theatre in America*, PBS, 1976; Madame Pernelle, "Tartuffe," *Theatre in America*, PBS, 1978; Margaret Ryan, *St. Elsewhere*, NBC, 1987; Anna, *Golden Girls*, NBC, 1988; Mrs. Wilbourne, *A Year in the Life*, NBC, 1988; also "The Marble Faun," *Theatre Hour*, CBS, 1950; "To Walk the Night," *Robert Montgomery Presents*, NBC, 1951; "The Daughter" and "Fear," both *Schlitz Playhouse of Stars*, CBS, 1952; "The Gallows Tree," *Television Workshop*, CBS, 1952; "Pontius Pilate," *Studio One*, CBS, 1952; "House of Masks," *Suspense*, CBS, 1953; "Summer Tempest," *Robert Montgomery Presents*, NBC, 1953; "The Others," *Suspense*, CBS, 1953; *Theatre for You*, 1953; "Dark Possession," *Studio One*, CBS, 1954; "Love Story," *Robert Montgomery Presents*, NBC, 1954; "The Lawn Party," *Goodyear Playhouse*, NBC, 1954; "The Iron Cobweb," *Robert Montgomery Presents*, NBC, 1955; "The Secret of Emily," *Armstrong Circle Theatre*, NBC, 1955; "The Healer," *Climax!*, CBS, 1955; "Like Father, Like Son," *Studio One*, CBS, 1955; "Isobel," *Robert Montgomery Presents*, NBC, 1955; "Flower of Pride," *Studio One*, CBS, 1956; "Dodsworth," *Producer's Showcase*, NBC, 1956; *Ellery Queen*, NBC, 1959; "The Twisted Image" and "Child's Play," both *Thriller*, NBC, 1960; "The Black Sheep," *Shirley Temple Theatre*, NBC, 1960; *Naked City*, ABC, 1961; *The Nurses*, CBS, 1964; *The Defenders*, CBS, 1964; "Power of Attorney," *Alfred Hitchcock Theatre*, NBC, 1965; "Babylon Revisited," *Conflict*, 1973; "A Touch of the Poet," *Theatre in America*, PBS, 1974; *Ben Casey*, ABC; *The Desilu Playhouse*, CBS; *The Detectives* (also known as *Robert Taylor's The Detectives*), ABC; *The Dick Powell Show*, NBC; *The Rifleman*, ABC; *Route 66*, CBS; *Target: The Corrupters*, ABC; *Perry Mason*, CBS; Charlotte Vernon, *Oh Madeline*, ABC; "The Jilting of Granny Weatherall," *American Short Story*, PBS; *Wagon Train; Teller of Tales*.

Movies: Emma Talbot, *Yesterday's Child*, NBC, 1977; Sister Agnes, *Dixie: Changing Habits*, CBS, 1983; Lorraine Wyatt, *Do You Remember Love?*, CBS, 1985; Charlotte Kessling, *Circle of Violence: A Family Drama*, CBS, 1986; Abby Abelson, *Night of Courage*, ABC, 1987. Specials: Elizabeth Barrett, *The Barretts of Wimpole Street*, CBS, 1955; Amy Strickland, *The Moon and Sixpence*, NBC, 1959; Carrie Chapman Catt, "We the Women," *The American Parade*, CBS, 1974; Ella McCune, "Rodeo Red and the Runaway," *Special Treat*, NBC, 1975; *Street Songs*, PBS, 1979.

RELATED CAREER—Co-producer, Lincoln Center Community Street Festival, New York City, 1972 and 1973; member, New York State Council of the Arts, 1977; founder (with Brother Jonathan Ringkamp) and artistic director, Everyman Street Theatre, New York City, 1978—.

NON-RELATED CAREER—Painter.

WRITINGS: STAGE—(With Brother Jonathan Ringkamp) *Everyman and Roach*, Society for Ethical Culture Auditorium, New York City, 1971; (adaptor) *Hamlet*, Everyman Theatre, New York City, 1978; *Geraldine Fitzgerald in Streetsongs* (one-woman show), Roundabout Stage One Theatre, New York City, then Pittsburgh Public Theatre, both 1980.

AWARDS: Academy Award nomination, Best Supporting Actress, 1939, for *Wuthering Heights;* Vernon Rice Awards (as actress and

director) and *Variety* New York Drama Critics Poll, Best Actress in a Leading Role Off-Broadway, both 1971, for *Long Day's Journey into Night;* Handel Medallion, 1974, for the Everyman Street Theatre; National Society of Arts and Letters Lifetime Achievement Award, 1989.

MEMBER: Actors' Equity Association, Screen Actors Guild, American Federation of Television and Radio Artists.

SIDELIGHTS: RECREATIONS—Painting.

ADDRESSES: OFFICE—655 Madison Avenue, New York, NY 10021. AGENT—Iris Grossman, International Creative Management, 8899 Beverly Boulevard, Los Angeles, CA 90048. MANAGER—Alan Eichler, Alan Eichler Associates, 1524 La Baig Avenue, Los Angeles, CA 90028.*

*　　　*　　　*

FITZSIMMONS, Maureen
See O'HARA, Maureen

*　　　*　　　*

FLANAGAN, Fionnula　1941-

PERSONAL: Full name, Fionnula Manon Flanagan; born December 10, 1941, in Dublin, Ireland; immigrated to the United States in 1968; daughter of Terence Niall and Rosanna (McGuirk) Flanagan; married Garrett O'Connor, November 26, 1972. EDUCATION—Attended Fribourg University (Switzerland), 1962; trained for the stage at the Abbey Theatre School, Dublin, 1964-66.

VOCATION: Actress.

CAREER: Also see *WRITINGS* below. PRINCIPAL STAGE APPEARANCES—Mag, "Winners" in *Lovers*, Vivian Beaumont Theatre, New York City, 1968; Molly Bloom, *Ulysses in Nighttown*, Winter Garden Theatre, New York City, 1974; also *James Joyce's Women* (one-woman show), Los Angeles, 1977.

PRINCIPAL FILM APPEARANCES—Gerty McDowell, *Ulysses*, Continental Distributing, 1967; Penelope, *Sinful Davey*, United Artists, 1969; Abadaba, *Mr. Patman*, Film Consortium of Canada, 1980; Charlotte Lawless, *Reflections*, Artificial Eye, 1984; Nora Joyce, Sylvia Beach, Harriet Shaw Weaver, Gerty MacDowell, washerwoman, and Molly Bloom, *James Joyce's Women*, Universal, 1985. Also appeared in *In the Region of Ice*, 1980; *Chain Reaction*, Morning Star Productions, 1985. PRINCIPAL FILM WORK—Executive producer and producer (with Garrett O'Connor), *James Joyce's Women*, Universal, 1985.

PRINCIPAL TELEVISION APPEARANCES—Series: Aunt Molly Culhane, *How the West Was Won*, ABC, 1978-79. Mini-Series: Clothilde, *Rich Man, Poor Man*, ABC, 1976. Movies: Felicia, *The Picture of Dorian Gray*, ABC, 1973; Virginia, *The Godchild*, ABC, 1974; Bridget Sullivan, *The Legend of Lizzie Borden*, ABC, 1975; Dulcie, *Nightmare in Badham County*, ABC, 1976; Sallie White, *Mary White*, ABC, 1977; Audrey Gibson, *Young Love, First Love*, CBS, 1979; Dr. Frances Muller, *Through Naked Eyes*, ABC, 1983; Catarine Towani, *The Ewok Adventure*, ABC, 1984;

Margaret, *Scorned and Swindled*, CBS, 1984; Mrs. Wyshner, *A Winner Never Quits*, ABC, 1986.

NON-RELATED CAREER—Fellow, Study Center for Organization and Leadership Authority, 1976—; president, the Rejoycing Company, 1978—.

WRITINGS: STAGE—*James Joyce's Women* (one-woman-show), 1977. FILM—*James Joyce's Women*, Universal, 1985.

AWARDS: Antoinette Perry Award nomination, Best Supporting or Featured Actress, 1974, for *Ulysses in Nighttown;* Emmy Award, Best Supporting Actress in a Single Appearance, 1976, for *Rich Man, Poor Man;* Drama-Logue Award, Los Angeles Drama Critics' Award, and San Francisco Theatre Critics' Award, all 1977, for *James Joyce's Women;* Emmy Award nomination, 1978, for *How the West Was Won.*

MEMBER: Actors' Equity Association, Screen Actors Guild, American Federation of Television and Radio Artists, Irish Actors' Equity Association.

ADDRESSES: AGENT—Abrams, Harris, and Goldberg Ltd., 9220 Sunset Boulevard, Garden Suite B, Los Angeles, CA 90069.*

*   *   *

FOAN, John
See BAVA, Mario

*   *   *

FONDA, Bridget

BRIEF ENTRY: Born c. 1964; daughter of Peter (an actor, director, producer, and writer) and Susan Fonda. A member of one of America's most celebrated acting families, Bridget Fonda has in a brief period carved out a distinct career on her own merits, most notably in the film *Scandal* (Miramax, 1989), for which she captured critical accolades as Mandy Rice-Davies, a British showgirl involved in the 1963 sex scandal that toppled England's conservative government.

Although she grew up in a show business environment, Fonda is reluctant to credit her family background with influencing her career decision. As she noted in an interview with *US,* "It may have affected me slightly, but only because I grew up around creative people." Instead of turning to her family for an entree into the film industry, she studied at the Lee Strasberg Theatre Institute in New York City for four years and also attended acting classes taught by Harold Gruskin and David Mamet. Her first professional credits include the plays *Confession* at the Warren Robertson Workshop and *Pastels* at the Lee Strasberg Theatre Institute.

For her film debut, Fonda appeared in the erotic and sensational "Tristan and Isolde" segment of the 1988 feature *Aria* and, later that year, she displayed her comedic talents in the romantic comedy *You Can't Hurry Love.* Both films received mixed reviews, but with the release of *Scandal,* Fonda was acknowledged as a new and genuine talent, receiving a Golden Globe nomination for her performance. Her subsequent appearances have included roles in

the 1989 feature films *Shag, the Movie* and *Strapless,* on television's *21 Jump Street,* and as Louise Bradshaw in "Jacob I Have Loved" for the PBS series *WonderWorks.*

In many of her films to date Fonda has appeared in rebellious and sexually uninhibited roles, but she does not feel her career will continue along those lines. "I'm not out to do the same thing over and over again—you know, sex kitten types. I'm not that interested in playing them unless *they're* interesting. I like being thrown a challenge."

OTHER SOURCES: US, May 29, 1989.*

*   *   *

FORAY, June

PERSONAL: Born in Springfield, MA.

VOCATION: Voice specialist.

CAREER: Also see *WRITINGS* below. PRINCIPAL FILM APPEARANCES—Voice of Lucifer, *Cinderella* (animated), Walt Disney, 1950; voice of Witch Hazel, *Trick or Treat* (short animated film), Walt Disney, 1952; Marku, *The Hindu* (also known as *Sabaka*), United Artists, 1953; voice of Court Raven, *The Snow Queen* (animated), Universal, 1959; voice characterizations, *The Man Called Flintstone* (also known as *That Man Flintstone;* animated), Columbia, 1966; voice characterizations, *The Phantom Tollboth*

JUNE FORAY

(animated), Metro-Goldwyn-Mayer, 1970; voice characterizations, *The White Seal* (short animated film), Chuck Jones Enterprises, 1975; voice characterizations, *The Looney, Looney, Looney Bugs Bunny Movie* (animated), Warner Brothers, 1981; voice characterizations, *Daffy Duck's Movie: Fantastic Island* (animated), Warner Brothers, 1983; voice of Wheezy and Lena Hyena, *Who Framed Roger Rabbit?*, Buena Vista, 1988.

PRINCIPAL TELEVISION APPEARANCES—Series: Voice of Midnight the Cat and Grandie, *The Buster Brown TV Show with Smilin' Ed McConnell and the Buster Brown Gang*, NBC, 1950-51, renamed *Smilin' Ed McConnell and His Gang*, 1951-55, later renamed *Andy's Gang*, 1955-58; voice characterizations, *The Woody Woodpecker Show* (animated), ABC, 1957-58, then NBC, 1970-72; voice characterizations, *The Dick Tracy Show* (animated), syndicated, 1960; voice characterizations, *The Alvin Show* (animated), CBS, 1961-62; voice of Rocket J. Squirrel and Natasha Fatale, "Rocky and Bullwinkle," and Nell Fenwick, "Dudley Do-Right," in *Rocky and His Friends* (animated), ABC, 1959-61, then *The Bullwinkle Show* NBC, 1961-62; voice of Jerry, *The Tom and Jerry Show* (animated), CBS, 1966-72; voice of Ursula, "George of the Jungle," and Marigold and Granny, "Tom Slick," in *George of the Jungle* (animated), ABC, 1967-70; voice of Nell Fenwick, *The Dudley Do-Right Show* (animated), ABC, 1969-70.

Voice characterizations, *Curiosity Shop* (live-action and animated), ABC, 1971-73; voice characterizations, *The Bugs Bunny/Road Runner Show* (animated), CBS, 1975-88; voice of Broom Hilda and Sluggo, *The Fabulous Funnies* (animated), NBC, 1978-79; voice of Jokey Smurf and Mother Nature, *The Smurfs* (animated), NBC, 1981—; voice characterizations, *The New Jetsons* (animated), syndicated, 1985; voice of Grammi Gummi, *Disney's Adventures of the Gummi Bears* (also known as *The Gummi Bears* and *The Adventures of the Gummi Bears;* animated), NBC, 1985-89; voice characterizations, *Foofur* (animated), NBC, 1986-88; voice of Grandma Howard, *Teen Wolf* (animated), 1986-89; voice of Dweeb's mother, *The Real Ghostbusters* (also known as *Slimer! and the Real Ghostbusters;* animated), ABC, 1986 —; voice characterizations, *The Flintstone Kids* (also known as *Captain Caveman and Son;* animated), ABC, 1986—; voice of Ma Beagle and Magica Despell, *Ducktales* (also known as *Disney's Ducktales;* animated), syndicated, 1987-89; voice characterizations, *The Bugs Bunny and Tweety Show,* (animated), ABC, 1988—; voice of Ma Beagle, *Super Ducktales* (animated), syndicated, 1989—; voice of Grammi Gummi, *Disney's Gummi Bears/Winnie the Pooh Hour* (animated), ABC, 1989—; voice characterizations, *The Simpsons* (animated), Fox, 1990—.

Episodic: Voice characterizations, *Lone Ranger* (animated), syndicated; voice characterizations, *These Are the Days* (animated), ABC; Carmelita, *Green Acres,* CBS; voice of Granny, *Tiny Toons* (animated). Movies: Narrator, *You Can't Teach an Old Dog New Tricks (But You Can to a Naughty Old Man)* (animated), HBO, 1985. Specials: *Arthur Godfrey in Hollywood,* CBS, 1962; Jenny, *Death of a Salesman,* CBS, 1966; voice of Karen, *Frosty the Snowman* (animated), CBS, 1969; voice of Mother, *The Cricket in Times Square* (animated), ABC, 1973; voice of Mother, *Rikki-Tikki-Tavi* (animated), CBS, 1975; voice of Tucker the Mouse, *Yankee Doodle Cricket* (animated), ABC, 1975; voice of Mother Wolf, *Mowgli's Brothers* (animated), CBS, 1976; voice of Granny, *The Bugs Bunny Easter Special* (animated), CBS, 1977; voice of Hazel, *Bugs Bunny's Howl-oween Special* (animated), CBS, 1977; voice characterizations, *Bugs Bunny's Looney Christmas Tales* (animated), CBS, 1979; voice characterizations, *The Bugs Bunny Thanksgiving Diet* (animated), CBS, 1979; voice of Raggedy Ann and Aunt Agatha, *Raggedy Ann and Andy in "The Pumpkin Who Couldn't Smile"* (animated), CBS, 1979.

Voice of Mrs Spitznagle, "The Incredible Book Escape" (animated), *CBS Library,* CBS, 1980; voice of Duchess, "Scruffy" (animated), *ABC Weekend Specials,* ABC, 1980; voice characterizations, *Faeries* (animated), CBS, 1981; voice of Old Woman and Saturna, "Miss Switch to the Rescue" (animated), *ABC Weekend Specials,* ABC, 1981; voice of Mother, *The Chipmunk's Christmas* (animated), NBC, 1982; voice characterizations, "The Wrong Way Kid" (animated), *CBS Library,* CBS, 1982; voice of Jokey and Smurfberry Bird, *My Smurfy Valentine* (animated), NBC, 1983; voice of Jokey, *Smurfily Ever After* (animated), NBC, 1985; voice of Mrs. Sweetly, "Harry, the Fat Bear Spy" (animated), *CBS Storybreak,* CBS, 1985; voice of Vinnie, *A Chipmunk Reunion* (animated), 1985; voice of Jokey and Squirrel, *The Smurfs Christmas Special* (animated), NBC, 1986; voice of Witch Hazel, *Disney's DTV Monster Hits* (animated), NBC, 1987; voice of Aunt Alice, "The Double Disappearance of Walter Fozbek" (animated), *CBS Storybreak,* CBS, 1987; voice of Sister Mouse, "Runaway Ralph," *ABC Weekend Specials,* ABC, 1988.

PRINCIPAL TELEVISION WORK—Movies: Producer, *You Can't Teach an Old Dog New Tricks (But You Can to a Naughty Old Man)* (animated), HBO, 1985.

RADIO APPEARANCES—Series: *The Stan Freberg Show,* CBS, 1957; also *Smilin' Ed McConnell's Buster Brown Gang,* NBC; Emily Williams, *The Fitch Bandwagon,* renamed *The Phil Harris Alice Faye Show,* NBC; Junie, *Smile Time,* Mutual. Episodic: *The Halls of Ivy,* NBC; *The Jimmy Durante Show,* NBC; *The Bob Hope Show,* NBC; *The Screen Guild Theatre,* CBS; *The Great Guildersleeve,* NBC; *The Screen Directors' Playhouse,* NBC; *Suspense,* CBS; *Stars Over Hollywood,* CBS; also *Fibber McGee and Molly* and *Lux Radio Theatre.*

RELATED CAREER—Voice characterizations for children's records and television commercials; voice-over instructor, University of Southern California.

WRITINGS: TELEVISION—Movies: *You Can't Teach an Old Dog New Tricks (But You Can to a Naughty Old Man)* (animated), HBO, 1985.

RECORDINGS: ALBUMS—*Snow White,* RCA Victor; also thirty-five albums for Capitol Records.

MEMBER: Academy of Motion Picture Arts and Sciences (board of governors, 1977—), National Academy of Recording Arts and Sciences (board member).

ADDRESSES: OFFICE—c/o *The Bugs Bunny and Tweety Show,* Warner Brothers Cartoons, 3601 W. Olive Avenue, Suite 450, Burbank, CA 91505. AGENT—Joseph, Helfond, and Rix, 1717 N. Highland Avenue, Suite 414, Hollywood, CA 90028.

*   *   *

FORD, Harrison   1942-

PERSONAL: Born July 13, 1942, in Chicago, IL; first wife's name, Mary (divorced); married Melissa Matheson (a screenwriter), 1983;

HARRISON FORD

children: Willard, Benjamin (first marriage); Malcolm (second marriage). EDUCATION—Attended Ripon College.

VOCATION: Actor.

CAREER: PRINCIPAL STAGE APPEARANCES—*John Brown's Body,* Laguna Beach Playhouse, Laguna Beach, CA; also appeared in summer theatre productions in Wisconsin.

FILM DEBUT—*Dead Heat on a Merry-Go-Round,* Columbia, 1966. PRINCIPAL FILM APPEARANCES—Lieutenant Shaffer, *A Time for Killing* (also known as *The Long Ride Home*), Columbia, 1967; Willie Bill Bearden, *Journey to Shiloh,* Universal, 1968; Jake, *Getting Straight,* Columbia, 1970; Bob Flafa, *American Grafitti,* Universal, 1973; Martin Stett, *The Conversation,* Paramount, 1974; Han Solo, *Star Wars,* Twentieth Century-Fox, 1977; Kenny Boyd, *Heroes,* Universal, 1977; Lieutenant Colonel Mike Barnsby, *Force Ten from Navarone,* American International, 1978; Colonel Lucas, *Apocalypse Now,* United Artists, 1979; Tommy, *The Frisco Kid* (also known as *No Knife*), Warner Brothers, 1979; David Halloran, *Hanover Street,* Columbia, 1979; motorcycle cop, *More American Grafitti,* Universal, 1979; Han Solo, *The Empire Strikes Back,* Twentieth Century-Fox, 1980; Indiana Jones, *Raiders of the Lost Ark,* Paramount, 1981; Rick Deckard, *Blade Runner,* Warner Brothers, 1982; Han Solo, *Return of the Jedi,* Twentieth Century-Fox, 1983; Indiana Jones, *Indiana Jones and the Temple of Doom,* Paramount, 1984; John Book, *Witness,* Paramount, 1985; Allie Fox, *The Mosquito Coast,* Warner Brothers 1986; Dr. Richard Walker, *Frantic,* Warner Brothers, 1988; Jack Trainer, *Working Girl,* Twentieth Century-Fox, 1988; Indiana Jones, *Indiana Jones*

and the Last Crusade, Paramount, 1989. Also appeared in *Luv,* Columbia, 1967; *Zabriskie Point,* Metro-Goldwyn-Mayer, 1970.

PRINCIPAL TELEVISION APPEARANCES—Pilots: Mark Blackwood, *James A. Michener's "Dynasty"* (also known as *Dynasty*), NBC, 1976; Paul Winjam, *The Possessed,* NBC, 1977. Episodic: Chester Anderson, *Leave It to Beaver,* ABC; also *The F.B.I.,* ABC; *Gunsmoke,* CBS; *The Virginian,* NBC. Movies: Carl, *The Intruders,* NBC, 1970; also *The Court-Martial of Lieutenant William Calley,* 1975. Specials: Host and narrator, *Great Movie Stunts: Raiders of the Lost Ark,* CBS, 1981; also *Great Adventurers and Their Quests: Indiana Jones and the Last Crusade,* 1989; *Premiere: Inside the Summer Blockbusters,* 1989.

NON-RELATED CAREER—Carpenter, chef, pizza maker, yacht broker, and management trainee for Bullock's department store.

AWARDS: Academy Award nomination, Best Actor, 1985, for *Witness.*

ADDRESSES: MANAGER—Pat McQueeney, McQueeney Management, 146 N. Almont Drive, Los Angeles, CA 90048.*

*   *   *

FOSSEY, Brigitte   1946-

PERSONAL: Born March 11, 1946, in Tourcoing, France.

VOCATION: Actress.

CAREER: FILM DEBUT—Paulette, *Forbidden Games* (also known as *Les Jeux interdits*), Times, 1953. PRINCIPAL FILM APPEARANCES—Jane Duval, *The Happy Road,* Metro-Goldwyn-Mayer, 1957; Dominique "Waterloo" Austerlitze, *Farewell, Friend* (also known as *Adieu l'ami*), Medusa Distribuzione, 1968; Yvonne de Galais, *The Wanderer* (also known as *Le Grand Meaulnes*), Leacock-Pennebaker, 1969; young mother, *Going Places* (also known as *Les Valseuses*), Cinema V, 1974; Louise, *The Blue Country* (also known as *Le Pays bleu*), Gaumont, 1977; Genevieve Bigey, *The Man Who Loved Women* (also known as *L'Homme qui aimait les femmes*), Cinema V, 1977; Anne, *Mais ou et donc Ornicar,* Mallia, 1979; Vivia, *Quintet,* Twentieth Century-Fox, 1979; Adrienne, *Chanel solitaire,* United Film Distribution, 1981; Francoise, *La Boum,* Triumph, 1983; Yvonne, *Imperative,* Teleculture, 1985; Nicole Palazzi, *La Scarlatine* (also known as *Scarlet Fever*), CAPAC, 1985; Isabelle, *The Future of Emily* (also known as *L'Avenir d'Emile* and *Flugel und Fessein*), Mainline, 1986. Also appeared in *M comme Mathieu,* 1971; *Raphael ou le debauche,* 1971; *L'Ironie du sort,* 1974; *La Brigade,* 1974; *Femmes fatales* (also known as *Calmos*), 1975; *Le Chant de depart,* 1976; *Le Bon et les mechants* (also known as *The Good and the Bad*), 1976; *Les Fleurs du Miel,* 1976; *Les Enfants du placard,* 1977; *Die Glaserne Zelle,* 1978; *L'Affaire Suisse* (also known as *The Swiss Affair*), 1978; *Enigma,* 1983; *Le Jeune Marie,* T. Films, 1985; and in *Making It, The Triple Death of the Third Character, A Bad Son, The Party, A Bite of Living, The Party—2, Au nom de tous les Meins, A Strange Passion, A Case of Irresponsibility, The False Confidences,* and *New Cinema Paradise.**

FOSTER, Gloria   1936-

PERSONAL: Born November 15, 1936, in Chicago, IL; married Clarence Williams III (an actor), November, 1967. EDUCATION— Attended Illinois State University; studied for the stage at the University of Chicago Court Theater and with Bella Itkin at the Goodman Theatre.

VOCATION: Actress.

CAREER: OFF-BROADWAY DEBUT—*In White America,* Sheridan Square Playhouse, 1963. PRINCIPAL STAGE APPEARANCES— Ruth, *A Raisin in the Sun,* Regent Theatre, Syracuse, NY, 1961; Andromache, *The Trojan Women,* Murray Theatre, Ravinia, IL, 1965; title role, *Medea,* Martinique Theatre, New York City, 1965-66; title role, *Yerma,* Vivian Beaumont Theatre, New York City, 1966-67; Hippolyta and Titania, *A Midsummer Night's Dream,* Theatre De Lys, New York City, 1967; title role, "Sister Son/ji" in *Black Visions,* New York Shakespeare Festival (NYSF), Public Theater, New York City, 1972; Lubov Andreyevna Ranevskaya, *The Cherry Orchard,* NYSF, Public Theatre, 1973; Clytemnestra, *Agamemnon,* NYSF, Delacorte Theatre, New York City, 1977; Volumnia, *Coriolanus,* NYSF, Public Theatre, then Delacorte Theatre, both 1979; Mother Courage, *Mother Courage and Her Children,* NYSF, Public Theatre, 1980; Mary Tyrone, *Long Day's Journey into Night,* Theater at St. Peter's Church, New York City, then Public Theatre, both 1981; Molly Hoffenburg, *The Forbidden City,* NYSF, Public Theatre, 1989. Also appeared as an understudy in *Purlie Victorious,* Cort Theatre, then Longacre Theatre, both New York City, 1961-62; in *A Hand Is on the Gate,* Longacre Theatre, 1966; *A Dream Play,* Goodman Theatre, Chicago, IL, 1967; as title role, *Medea,* Oparre, *Wingless Victory,* and Sabina, *The Skin of Our Teeth,* all Goodman Theatre; and as Jocasta, *Oedipus Rex,* Hecuba, *The Trojan Women,* and Volumnia, *Coriolanus,* all Court Theatre, University of Chicago, Chicago, IL.

MAJOR TOURS—Ruth, *A Raisin in the Sun,* U.S. cities, 1962.

FILM DEBUT—Mrs. Custis, *The Cool World,* Cinema V, 1963. PRINCIPAL FILM APPEARANCES—Lee, *Nothing But a Man,* Cinema V, 1964; Mrs. Philpot, *The Comedians,* Metro-Goldwyn-Mayer, 1967; Sally, *The Angel Levine,* United Artists, 1970; Ivy Revers, *Man and Boy,* Levitt-Pickman, 1972; Medusa, *Leonard, Part 6,* Columbia, 1987.

PRINCIPAL TELEVISION APPEARANCES—Mini-Series: Camille Bell, *The Atlanta Child Murders,* CBS, 1985. Pilots: Judith, *Top Secret,* NBC, 1978. Movies: Serena, *To All My Friends on Shore,* CBS, 1972. Also appeared in *Shakespeare's Women.*

AWARDS: Obie Award from the *Village Voice* and Vernon Rice Award, both 1963, for *In White America;* Theatre World Award, 1966, for *Medea;* Alpha Kappa Alpha Award, 1966, for Outstanding Contribution in the Field of the Arts; Drama Desk Award nomination, Best Actress in a Play, 1989, for *The Forbidden City.**

*   *   *

FOWLER, Beth   1940-

PERSONAL: Born November 1, 1940, in New Jersey. EDUCATION—Graduated from Caldwell College, 1962.

BETH FOWLER

VOCATION: Actress.

CAREER: BROADWAY DEBUT—*Gantry,* George Abbott Theatre, 1970. PRINCIPAL STAGE APPEARANCES—Mrs. Segstrom, *A Little Night Music,* Shubert Theatre, then Majestic Theatre, both New York City, 1973; understudy for the role of the President's Wife, *1600 Pennsylvania Avenue,* Mark Hellinger Theatre, New York City, 1976; Julie, *Showboat,* Jones Beach Theatre, Jones Beach, NY, 1976; *Rodgers and Hart* (revue), Arlington Park Theatre, Arlington Heights, IL, 1976; Sharon McLonergan, *Finian's Rainbow,* Jones Beach Theatre, 1977; Mrs. Darling, *Peter Pan,* Lunt-Fontanne Theatre, New York City, 1979; Marie, *Preppies,* Promenade Theatre, New York City, 1983; Arlene MacNally, *Baby,* Ethel Barrymore Theatre, New York City, 1983-84; Lily Miller, *Take Me Along,* Goodspeed Opera House, East Haddam, CT, 1984, then Martin Beck Theatre, New York City, 1985; Mrs. Webb, *Our Town,* Alliance Theatre Company, Atlanta, GA, 1986; Jeannie Jeannine, *Lucky Guy,* Plaza Theatre, Dallas, TX, 1987; Edith Roosevelt, *Teddy and Alice,* Tampa Bay Performing Arts Center, Tampa Bay, FL, 1987, then Minskoff Theatre, New York City, 1987-88; Mrs. Lovett, *Sweeney Todd,* Circle in the Square, New York City, 1989-90; also appeared in *Tintypes,* Cincinnati Playhouse, Cincinnati, OH, 1981; *Georgia Avenue,* Goodspeed Opera House, 1986.

AWARDS: Drama Desk Award nomination, Best Actress in a Musical, 1989, for *Sweeney Todd.*

ADDRESSES: AGENT—Peggy Hadley Enterprises Ltd., 250 W. 57th Street, New York, NY 10107.*

FOX, Bernard

VOCATION: Actor.

CAREER: PRINCIPAL STAGE APPEARANCES—Duchotel, *13 Rue de L'Amour*, Circle in the Square, New York City, 1978.

PRINCIPAL FILM APPEARANCES—McLeod, *Spin a Dark Web* (also known as *Soho Incident*), Columbia, 1956; Shafter, *The Safecracker*, Metro-Goldwyn-Mayer (MGM), 1958; lieutenant, *The Two-Headed Spy*, Columbia, 1959; Lynch, *The List of Adrian Messenger*, Universal, 1963; room clerk, *Honeymoon Hotel*, MGM, 1964; Leslie Folliott, *Quick, Before It Melts*, MGM, 1964; policeman, *Strange Bedfellows*, Universal, 1965; Dudley, *Hold On*, MGM, 1966; Squire Moresby, *Munster, Go Home*, Universal, 1966; Jordin, *One of Our Spies Is Missing*, MGM, 1966; Ephram, *The Bamboo Saucer*, NTA, 1968; assistant to Lord Chamberlain, *Star!* (also known as *Those Were the Happy Times*) Twentieth Century-Fox, 1968; Constable Hooks, *Arnold*, Cinerama, 1973; Max, *Herbie Goes to Monte Carlo*, Buena Vista, 1977; voice of Chairman, *The Rescuers* (animated), Buena Vista, 1977; Justin, *The Private Eyes*, New World, 1980; Tarbuck, *Yellowbeard*, Orion, 1983; Horton, *Eighteen Again!*, New World, 1988. Also appeared *Home and Away*, Guest/Conquest, 1956; *$1,000,000 Duck*, Buena Vista, 1971; *House of the Dead*, 1980.

PRINCIPAL TELEVISION APPEARANCES—Series: Dr. Bombay, *Bewitched*, ABC, 1967-72; also Nigel Pennysmith, *General Hospital*, ABC. Pilots: Dr. John H. Watson, *The Hound of the Baskervilles*, ABC, 1972; Barrett, *Intertect*, ABC, 1973; Mr. Muirfield, *The Son-In-Law*, NBC, 1980. Episodic: Malcolm Merriweather, *The Andy Griffith Show*, CBS, 1963 and 1964; Jock, "The Wide Open Door," *ABC Stage '67*, ABC, 1967; Dr. Bombay, *Tabitha*, ABC, 1977; Kris Winter, *The Fall Guy*, ABC, 1985; Edgar Wyckham, *Murder, She Wrote*, CBS, 1986; Professor Stubbs, *Mr. Sunshine*, ABC, 1986; Holcomb, *Riptide*, NBC, 1986; also *The Dick Van Dyke Show*, CBS, 1964 and 1965; *M*A*S*H*, CBS, 1978; Alfie, *Make Room for Daddy*, ABC; Colonel Crittendon, *Hogan's Heroes*, CBS; Randolph Svenson, *Soap*, ABC; *Farmer's Daughter*, ABC; *The Monkees*, NBC; *F Troop*, ABC; *Love, American Style*, ABC; *The Partridge Family*, ABC. Movies: Captain Chablat, *Gauguin the Savage*, CBS, 1980.

ADDRESSES: AGENT—Joshua Gray and Associates, 6736 Laurel Canyon Boulevard, North Hollywood, CA 91606.*

*   *   *

FOX, James   1939-
(William Fox)

PERSONAL: Born May 19, 1939, in London, England; son of Robin (a theatrical agent) and Angela Fox.

VOCATION: Actor.

CAREER: PRINCIPAL FILM APPEARANCES—(As William Fox) Johnny Brent, *The Magnet*, General Films Distributors, 1950; (as William Fox) Toby Miniver, *The Miniver Story*, Metro-Goldwyn-Mayer (MGM), 1950; (as William Fox) Gregory, *The Lavender Hill Mob*, Universal, 1951; (as William Fox) busboy, *Serenade*, Warner Brothers, 1956; (as William Fox) Brinton, *The Secret Partner* (also known as *The Street Partner*), MGM, 1961; (as

William Fox) Waling, *She Always Gets Their Man*, United Artists, 1962; (as William Fox) Philip Goodwin, *What Every Woman Wants*, United Artists, 1962; Tony, *The Servant*, Landau, 1964; Oliver, *Tamahine*, MGM, 1964; Flight Lieutenant Marlow, *King Rat*, Columbia, 1965; Richard Mays, *Those Magnificent Men in Their Flying Machines, or How I Flew from London to Paris in 25 Hours and 11 Minutes*, Twentieth Century-Fox, 1965; Jason ("Jake"), *The Chase*, Columbia, 1966; Jimmy Smith, *Thoroughly Modern Millie*, Universal, 1967; Stefane, *Duffy*, Columbia, 1968; Gordon Craig, *Isadora* (also known as *The Loves of Isadora*), Universal, 1968; Giorgio, *Arabella*, Universal, 1969; Alan Richards, *No Longer Alone*, World Wide, 1978; Tom, *Runners*, Hanstall, 1983; Lord Esker, *Greystoke: The Legend of Tarzan, Lord of the Apes*, Warner Brothers, 1984; Richard Fielding, *A Passage to India*, Columbia, 1984; Henley of Mayfair, *Absolute Beginners*, Orion, 1986; Norfolk, *Comrades*, Film Four International, 1986; Patrick, *High Season*, Hemdale, 1987; Lord, *The Whistle Blower*, Hemdale, 1987. Also appeared (as William Fox) in *No Place for Jennifer*, Associated British Films/Pathe, 1950; (as William Fox) *One Wild Oat*, Eros, 1951; (as William Fox) *The Loneliness of the Long Distance Runner* (also known as *Rebel with a Cause*), Continental Distributing, 1962; *Performance*, Warner Brothers, 1970; *Pavlova—A Woman for All Time*, Poseidon, 1985; and *Finding Maubee*.

PRINCIPAL TELEVISION APPEARANCES—Mini-Series: Waldorf, *Nancy Astor*, PBS, 1984. Movies: Mansfield Markham, *Beryl Markham: A Shadow on the Sun*, CBS, 1988; also *Sun Child*, ITV, 1988. Also appeared in *The Door, Espionage, Farewell to the King, Country, New World*, and *Love Is Old, Love Is New*.

NON-RELATED CAREER—Evangelist, 1973-83.

ADDRESSES: AGENT—Michael Whitehall Limited, 125 Gloucester Road, London SW7, England.*

*   *   *

FOX, William
See FOX, James

*   *   *

FRANCIS, Freddie   1917-
(Ken Barnett)

PERSONAL: Born in 1917 in London, England; married Pamela Mann; children: Kevin. MILITARY—British Army, Kinetograph Services, 1939-46.

VOCATION: Cinematographer and director.

CAREER: PRINCIPAL FILM WORK—Camera operator (second unit), *The Macomber Affair*, United Artists, 1947; camera operator, *Mine Own Executioner*, Twentieth Century-Fox, 1947; camera operator, *Night Beat*, British Lion, 1947; camera operator, *The Small Back Room* (also known as *Hour of Glory*), British Lion, 1948; camera operator, *The Elusive Pimpernel* (also known as *The Fighting Pimpernel*), British Lion, 1950; camera operator, *Gone to Earth* (also known as *The Wild Heart* and *Gypsy Blood*), RKO/Selznick, 1950; camera operator, *Golden Salamander*, General

Film Distributors, 1950; camera operator, *Angels One Five*, Templar, 1951; camera operator, *The Tales of Hoffman*, Lopert, 1951; camera operator, *24 Hours of a Woman's Life* (also known as *Affair in Monte Carlo*), Allied Artists, 1952; camera operator, *Outcast of the Islands*, British Lion, 1952; camera operator, *Moulin Rouge*, United Artists, 1952; camera operator, *Beat the Devil*, United Artists, 1953; camera operator, *Rough Shoot* (also known as *Shoot First*), United Artists, 1953; camera operator, *Twice Upon a Time*, Fine Arts, 1953; camera operator, *Beau Brummell*, Metro-Goldwyn-Mayer (MGM), 1954; camera operator, *Monsieur Ripois* (also known as *Knave of Hearts*, *Lover Boy*, and *Lovers, Happy Lovers!*), Twentieth Century-Fox, 1954; camera operator (second unit), *Dry Rot*, Independent Film Distributors/British Lion, 1956; camera operator (second unit and special effects), *Moby Dick*, Warner Brothers, 1956; cinematographer, *A Hill in Korea* (also known as *Hell in Korea*), British Lion, 1956; cinematographer, *Time Without Pity* (also known as *No Time for Pity*), Eros/Astor, 1957; cinematographer, *Room at the Top*, Romulus, 1959; cinematographer, *Strange Affection* (also known as *The Scamp*), Brenner, 1959.

Cinematographer, *The Battle of the Sexes*, Continental, 1960; cinematographer, *Next to No Time!*, Show, 1960; cinematographer, *Sons and Lovers*, Twentieth Century-Fox, 1960; cinematographer, *Virgin Island* (also known as *Our Virgin Island*), Films-around-the-World, 1960; cinematographer, *The Horsemasters*, Buena Vista, 1961; cinematographer, *The Innocents*, Twentieth Century-Fox, 1961; cinematographer, *Never Take Candy from a Stranger* (also known as *Never Take Sweets from a Stranger* and *The Molester*), Sutton/Pathe, 1961; cinematographer, *Saturday Night and Sunday Morning*, Continental Distributing, 1961; director, *Two and Two Make Six* (also known as *A Change of Heart* and *The Girl Swappers*), Union, 1962; director, *The Day of the Triffids*, Allied Artists, 1963; director, *Nightmare*, Universal, 1963; director, *Paranoiac*, Universal, 1963; director, *The Evil of Frankenstein*, Universal, 1964; cinematographer, *Night Must Fall*, MGM, 1964; director, *Hysteria*, MGM, 1965; director, *The Brain* (also known as *Vengeance* and *Le cerveau*), Paramount, 1965; director, *Dr. Terror's House of Horrors*, Regal, 1965; director, *The Skull*, Paramount, 1965; director, *The Psychopath*, Paramount, 1966; director, *Traitor's Gate* (also known as *Das Verratertor*), Columbia, 1966; director, *The Deadly Bees*, Paramount, 1967; director, *They Came from Beyond Space*, Embassy, 1967; director, *Dracula Has Risen from His Grave*, Warner Brothers, 1968; director, *Torture Garden*, Columbia, 1968.

Director, *Mumsy, Nanny, Sonny, and Girly* (also known as *Girly*), Cinerama, 1970; director, *Trog*, Warner Brothers, 1970; director, *Gebissen wird nur Nachts—Happening der Vampire* (also known as *Vampire Happening*), Constantin Film, 1971; director, *Tales from the Crypt*, Cinerama, 1972; director, *The Creeping Flesh*, Columbia, 1972; director, *Tales That Witness Madness*, Paramount, 1973; director, *Craze* (also known as *The Infernal Idol*), Warner Brothers, 1974; director, *Son of Dracula* (also known as *Young Dracula*), Apple, 1974; director, *The Ghoul*, Rank, 1975; director (with Andre Pieters), *Golden Rendezvous*, Film Trust/Milton Okun, 1977; cinematographer, *The Elephant Man*, Paramount, 1980; cinematographer, *The French Lieutenant's Woman*, United Artists, 1981; cinematographer, *Dune*, Dino De Laurentiis/Universal, 1984; cinematographer, *The Jigsaw Man*, United Film Distribution, 1984; cinematographer, *Memed My Hawk*, Focus, 1984; cinematographer, *Code Name: Emerald*, Metro-Goldwyn-Mayer/United Artists, 1985; director, *The Doctor and the Devils*, Twentieth Century-Fox, 1985; cinematographer, *Clara's Heart*, Warner Brothers, 1988; director (as Ken Barnett) and cinematographer,

Dark Tower, Spectrafilm, 1989; cinematographer, *Her Alibi*, Warner Brothers, 1989; cinematographer, *Glory*, Tri-Star, 1989. Also camera operator, *The Sorcerer's Apprentice* (short film), 1955; director, *The Intrepid Mr. Twigg* (short film), 1968; director, *Legend of the Werewolf*, 1975.

PRINCIPAL TELEVISION WORK—Series: Director, *Star Maidens*, syndicated, 1977. Episodic: Director, *Man in a Suitcase*, ABC, 1968. Movies: Cinematographer, *The Executioner's Song*, NBC, 1982.

RELATED CAREER—Apprentice to stills photographer, Gaumont Studios, then clapper boy, B.I.P. Studios, later camera assistant, British and Dominions Studios, all 1936-39.

AWARDS: Academy Award, Best Cinematography, 1961, for *Sons and Lovers.**

*   *   *

FRANK, Richard   1953-

PERSONAL: Born January 4, 1953, in Boston, MA; son of Phillip L. and Jeanne E. (a medical secretary; maiden name, Bennett) Frank. EDUCATION—University of Michigan, B.A., speech, 1974; studied acting at the Juilliard School, 1974-78.

VOCATION: Actor and writer.

RICHARD FRANK

CAREER: STAGE DEBUT—Moritz Steifel, *Spring Awakening,* New York Shakespeare Festival, Public Theatre, New York City, 1978. BROADWAY DEBUT—Gentleman and second knight, *The Dresser,* Brooks Atkinson Theatre, 1981-82. PRINCIPAL STAGE APPEARANCES—Guard, *Salt Lake City Skyline,* New York Shakespeare Festival (NYSF), Public Theatre, New York City, 1980; Herman, *Five of Us,* Center Theatre Group, Mark Taper Forum, Taper Too, Los Angeles, 1985; Horatio, *Hamlet,* NYSF, Public Theatre, 1986; Greta, *Bent,* Coast Playhouse, Hollywood, CA, 1987; Molina, *Kiss of the Spider Woman,* Yale Repertory Theatre, New Haven, CT, 1988; Salieri, *Amadeus,* Alliance Theatre, Atlanta, GA, 1989. Also appeared in *Da,* Studio Arena Theatre, Buffalo, NY, 1979; *Moliere in Spite of Himself,* Hartman Theatre Company, Stamford, CT, 1981; *The Keeper,* Philadelphia Drama Guild, Philadelphia, PA, 1982; *The Palace of Amateurs,* Plaza Theatre, Dallas, TX, 1983; *Hang On to Me* and *Twelfth Night,* both Tyrone Guthrie Theatre, Minneapolis, MN, 1984-85.

FILM DEBUT—Father Vogler, *Amadeus,* Orion, 1985.

TELEVISION DEBUT—Stefan Mazor, *The Wall,* CBS, 1980. PRINCIPAL TELEVISION APPEARANCES—Series: Jules "Julie" Kramer, *Anything But Love,* ABC, 1989—. Pilots: Jules, *Anything But Love,* ABC, 1989. Episodic: Eli Leavitt, *Cagney and Lacey,* CBS, 1985; Jesse Morgan, *Stir Crazy,* CBS, 1985; Bailey, "Roanoak," *American Playhouse,* PBS, 1986; Biller, *Max Headroom,* ABC, 1987; Gary Fenton, *Night Court,* NBC, 1987; Frank Peterson, *Perfect Strangers,* ABC, 1987; Jason, *Newhart,* CBS, 1988; Mr. Standish, *Valerie's Family,* NBC, 1988; also *Remington Steele,* NBC; *Falcon Crest,* CBS. Movies: Resident doctor, *Cracked Up,* ABC, 1987.

RELATED CAREER—Company member, Arena Stage, Washington, DC, 1978-79; company member, Tyrone Guthrie Theatre, Minneapolis, MN, 1982-83.

NON-RELATED CAREER—Instructor, Practical Aesthetics workshop, New York University, 1982; watercolorist.

WRITINGS: STAGE—*Plato's Symposium,* Court Theatre, Los Angeles, 1987. OTHER—(Also illustrator) *The Struggling Actor's Coloring Book,* Volume 1, 1979, Volume 2, 1980.

AWARDS: Drama-Loque Award, Best Actor, 1986, for *Five of Us; L.A. Weekly* Award, Best Production, 1986, for *Plato's Symposium.*

SIDELIGHTS: FAVORITE ROLES—Molina in *Kiss of the Spider Woman.* RECREATIONS—European travel.

ADDRESSES: AGENT—Judy Schoen and Associates, 606 N. Larchmont Boulevard, Suite 309, Los Angeles, CA 90004.

*   *   *

FRANKLIN, Pamela   1950-

PERSONAL: Born February 4, 1950, in Toyko, Japan. EDUCATION—Attended Elmshurst Ballet School.

VOCATION: Actress.

CAREER: PRINCIPAL FILM APPEARANCES—Flora, *The Innocents,* Twentieth Century-Fox, 1961; Tina, *The Lion,* Twentieth

Century-Fox, 1962; Penny, *Flipper's New Adventure* (also known as *Flipper and the Pirates*), Metro-Goldwyn-Mayer (MGM), 1964; Catherine Whitset, *The Third Secret,* Twentieth Century-Fox, 1964; Julie Williams, *A Tiger Walks,* Buena Vista, 1964; Bobby, *The Nanny,* Twentieth Century-Fox, 1965; Diana Hook, *Our Mother's House,* MGM, 1967; girl, *The Night of the Following Day,* United Artists, 1969; Sandy, *The Prime of Miss Jean Brodie,* Twentieth Century-Fox, 1969; Annie, *Sinful Davey,* United Artists, 1969; Jane, *And Soon the Darkness,* EMI, 1970; Dora Spenlow, *David Copperfield,* Twentieth Century-Fox, 1970; Lori Brandon, *Necromancy* (also known as *The Witching*), Cinerama, 1972; Shelby, *Ace Eli and Rodger of the Skies,* Twentieth Century-Fox, 1973; Florence Tanner, *The Legend of Hell House,* Twentieth Century-Fox, 1973; Lorna, *The Food of the Gods,* American International, 1976.

PRINCIPAL TELEVISION APPEARANCES—Pilots: Amanda Hollister, *Intertect,* ABC, 1973; Karen Forrester, "The Forresters: Dear Karen," *The Letters,* ABC, 1973; Sheila Fielding, *Crossfire,* NBC, 1975. Episodic: Nicola Stevens, "Screamer," *Wide World of Mystery,* ABC, 1974; Abby Stevens, "Won't You Write Home, I'm Dead" (also known as "Terror from Within"), *Wide World of Mystery,* ABC, 1975; also "The Horse Without a Head," *The World of Disney,* NBC, 1963; *The Name of the Game,* NBC, 1970; *Strange Report,* NBC, 1971; *Green Acres,* CBS, 1971; *Medical Center,* CBS, 1971, 1973, and 1974; *Bonanza,* NBC, 1972; *Ghost Story,* NBC, 1972; *Sixth Sense,* ABC, 1972; *Cool Million,* NBC, 1972 and 1973; *Cannon,* CBS, 1972 and 1974; "Mirabelle's Summer," *Love Story,* NBC, 1973; *Streets of San Francisco,* ABC, 1974; *Six Million Dollar Man,* ABC, 1974; *The Magician,* NBC, 1974; *Mannix,* CBS, 1974; *Barnaby Jones,* CBS, 1974 and 1975; *Petrocelli,* NBC, 1975. Movies: Tirza, *See How They Run,* NBC, 1964; Dora Spenlow, *David Copperfield,* NBC, 1970; Elizabeth Sayres, *Satan's School for Girls,* ABC, 1973; Anna Hall, *Eleanor and Franklin,* ABC, 1976. Specials: Betsy Balcombe, "Eagle in a Cage," *Hallmark Hall of Fame,* NBC, 1965.*

*   *   *

FRELENG, Friz   1906-
(I. Freleng)

PERSONAL: Born Isadore Freleng, August 21, 1906, in Kansas City, MO.

VOCATION: Producer, director, writer, and animator.

CAREER: Also see *WRITINGS* below. PRINCIPAL FILM WORK—Animation director, *Two Guys from Texas* (also known as *Two Texas Knights*), Warner Brothers, 1948; title sequence director and animator, *The Pink Panther,* United Artists, 1963; producer and director, *The Looney Looney Looney Bugs Bunny Movie* (animated), Warner Brothers, 1981; director (with others), *Uncensored Cartoons* (animated), United American Classics, 1981; producer and director, *Bugs Bunny's Third Movie—1001 Rabbit Tales* (animated) Warner Brothers, 1982; producer and (with others) director, *Daffy Duck's Movie: Fantastic Island* (animated), Warner Brothers, 1983; director (with others), *Porky Pig in Hollywood* (animated), Warner Brothers, 1986; director, *Daffy Duck's Quackbusters* (animated), Warner Brothers, 1988.

Director of the following short animated films: *Wicked West,* Universal, 1929; *Bosko in Dutch* and *Shuffle Off to Buffalo,* both

Warner Brothers, 1933; *Buddy the Gob, Buddy and Towser, Beauty and the Beast, Buddy's Trolley Troubles, Goin' to Heaven on a Mule, How Do I Know It's Sunday?, Why Do I Dream Those Dreams?, The Miller's Daughter, The Girl at the Ironing Board, Shake Your Powder Puff, Those Beautiful Dames,* and *Pop Goes Your Heart,* all Warner Brothers, 1934; *Mr. and Mrs. Is the Name, Country Boy, I Haven't Got a Hat, Along Flirtation Walk, My Green Fedora, Into Your Dance, Country Mouse, The Merry Old Soul, The Lady in Red, Little Dutch Plate, Billboard Frolics,* and *Flowers for Madame,* all Warner Brothers, 1935; *I Wanna Play House, The Cat Came Back, I'm a Big Shot Now, Let It Be Me, Bingo Crosbyana, When I Yoo Hoo, Sunday Go to Meetin' Time, At Your Service, Madame, Toy Town Hall, Boulevardier from the Bronx,* and *Coo-Coo Nut Grove,* all Warner Brothers, 1936; *He Was Her Man, Pigs Is Pigs, The Fella with the Fiddle, She Was an Acrobat's Daughter, Clean Pastures, Streamlined Greta Green, Sweet Sioux, Plenty of Money and You, Dog Daze, The Lyin' Mouse,* and *September in the Rain,* all Warner Brothers, 1937; *My Little Buckeroo, Jungle Jitters,* and *A Star Is Hatched,* all Warner Brothers, 1938.

Confederate Honey, The Hardship of Miles Standish, You Ought to Be in Pictures, Porky's Baseball Broadcast, Little Blabbermouse, Malibu Beach Party, Calling Dr. Porky, Porky's Hired Hand, and *Shop, Look, and Listen,* all Warner Brothers, 1940; *The Fighting 69 1/2th, The Cat's Tale, Porky's Bear Facts, The Trial of Mr. Wolf, Hiawatha's Rabbit Hunt, The Wacky Worm, Sport Chumpions, Notes to You, Rookie Revue,* and *Rhapsody in Rivets,* all Warner Brothers, 1941; *Hop, Skip, and a Chump, Porky's Pastry Pirates, The Wabbit Who Came to Supper, Saps in Chaps, Lights Fantastic, Double Chaser, Foney Fables, Fresh Hare, The Sheepish Wolf, The Hare-Brained Hypnotist, Pigs in a Polka,* and *Ding Dog Daddy,* all Warner Brothers, 1942; *Fifth Column Mouse, Greetings Bait, Jack-Wabbit and the Beanstalk, Yankee Doodle Daffy, Hiss and Make Up, Daffy the Commando,* and *Slightly Daffy,* all Warner Brothers, 1943; *Little Red Riding Rabbit, Meatless Flyday, Bugs Bunny Nips the Nips, Duck Soup to Nuts, Hare Force, Goldilocks and the Jivin' Bears,* and *Stage Door Cartoon,* all Warner Brothers, 1944; *Herr Meets Hare, Life with Feathers, Hare Trigger, Ain't That Ducky,* and *Peck Up Your Troubles,* all Warner Brothers, 1945; *Baseball Bugs, Holiday for Shoestrings, Hollywood Daffy, Of Thee I Sing, Racketeer Rabbit,* and *Rhapsody Rabbit,* all Warner Brothers, 1946; *The Gay Anties, A Hare Grows in Manhattan, Tweetie Pie, Rabbit Transit, Along Came Daffy,* and *Slick Hare,* all Warner Brothers, 1947; *Back Alley Oproar, I Taw a Putty Tat, Buccaneer Bunny, Bugs Bunny Rides Again, Hare Splitter,* and *Kit for Cat,* all Warner Brothers, 1948; *Wise Quackers, Hare Do, High Diving Hare, Curtain Razor, Mouse Mazurka, Knights Must Fall, Bad Ol' Putty Tat, Dough for the Do-Do, Each Dawn I Crow,* and *Which Is Witch?,* all Warner Brothers, 1949.

Home Tweet Home, Mutiny on the Bunny, The Lion's Busy, Big House Bunny, His Bitter Half, All Bir-r-rd, Golden Yeggs, Bunker Hill Bunny, Canary Row, and *Stooge for a Mouse,* all Warner Brothers, 1950; *Canned Feud, Rabbit Every Monday, Putty Tat Trouble, A Bone for a Bone, Fair-Haired Hare, Room and Bird, His Hare Raising Tale, Tweety's S.O.S., Ballot Box Bunny,* and *Tweet, Tweet, Tweety,* all Warner Brothers, 1951; *Gift Wrapped, Foxy By Proxy, Fourteen Carrot Rabbit, Little Red Rodent Hood, Ain't She Tweet, Cracked Quack, Bird in a Guilty Cage, Tree for Two,* and *Hare Lift,* all Warner Brothers, 1952; *Snow Business, A Mouse Divided, Fowl Weather, Southern Fried Rabbit, Ant Pasted, Hare Trimmed, Tom-Tom Tomcat, A Street Cat Name Sylvester, Catty Cornered,* and *Robot Rabbit,* all Warner Brothers, 1953; *Dog Pounded, Captain Hareblower, I Gopher You, Bugs and Thugs,*

Doctor Jerkyl's Hide, Muzzle Tough, Satan's Waitin', Yankee Doodle Bugs, Sandy Claws, Goo Goo Goliath, and *By Word of Mouse,* all Warner Brothers, 1954; *Pizzicato Pussycat, Pests for Guests, Stork Naked, Sahara Hare, Hare Brush, Tweety's Circus, Lumber Jerks, This Is a Life?, A Kiddie's Kitty, Hyde and Hare, Speedy Gonzales, Red Riding Hoodwinked, Roman Legion Hare, Heir Conditioned,* and *Pappy's Puppy,* all Warner Brothers, 1955; *Tweet and Sour, Rabbitson Crusoe, Tree Cornered Tweety, Napoleon Bunny-Part, Tugboat Granny, A Star Is Bored, Yankee Dood It,* and *Two Crows from Tacos,* all Warner Brothers, 1956; *The Three Little Bops, Tweet Zoo, Tweety and the Beanstalk, Piker's Peak, Birds Anonymous, Bugsy and Mugsy, Greedy for Tweety, Show Biz Bugs, Mouse-Taken Identity,* and *Gonzales' Tamales,* all Warner Brothers, 1957; *Tortilla Flaps, Hare-Less Wolf, A Pizza Tweety Pie, A Waggily Tale, Knighty Knight Bugs,* and *A Bird in a Bonnet,* all Warner Brothers, 1958; *Trick or Tweet, Apes of Wrath, Mexicali Shmoes, Tweet and Lovely, Wild and Wooly Hare, Tweet Dreams,* and *Here Today, Gone Tamale,* all Warner Brothers, 1959.

West of the Pesos, Horse Hare, Goldimouse and the Three Cats, Person to Bunny, Hyde and Go Tweet, Mouse and Garden, From Hare to Heir, Trip for Tat, and *Lighter Than Hare,* all Warner Brothers, 1960; *Cannery Woe, D' Fightin' Ones, The Rebel without Claws, The Piped Piper of Guadalupe, Prince Violent* (also known as *Prince Varmint*), and *The Last Hungry Cat,* all Warner Brothers, 1961; *Quackodile Tears, Crow's Feat, Mexican Boarders, Honey's Money, The Jet Cage,* and *Shishkabugs,* all Warner Brothers, 1962; *Devil's Feud Cake, Mexican Cat Dance, Chili Weather,* and *The Unmentionables,* all Warner Brothers, 1963; *Nuts and Volts, Panchos's Hideaway,* and *Road to Andalay,* all Warner Brothers, 1964; *It's Nice to Have a Mouse Around the House* and *Cats and Bruises,* both Warner Brothers, 1965.

Producer of the following short animated films, all with David H. De Patie: (Also director) *Suspense Account,* United Artists, 1964 (never released); (also director with Hawley Pratt) *The Pink Phink,* United Artists, 1964; *Pink Pajamas,* United Artists, 1964; *We Give Pink Stamps, Dial "P" for Pink, Sink Pink, Pickled Pink, Shocking Pink, Pinkfinger, Pink Ice, The Pink Tail Fly, Pink Panzer, An Ounce of Pink, Reel Pink,* and *Bully for Pink,* all United Artists, 1965; *Rushing Roulette, Boulder Wham, Just Plane Beep, Chaser on the Rocks, Tired and Feathered, Harried and Hurried, Highway Runnery,* and *Run, Run, Sweet Road Runner,* all Warner Brothers, 1965; *Pink Panic, Pink Punch, Pink Piston, Vitamin Pink, The Pink Blueprint, Pink-a-Boo, Genie with the Light Pink Fur, Super Pink, Rock-a-Bye Pinky, Pink, Plunk, Plink,* and *Smile Pretty, Say Pink,* all United Artists, 1966; *Out and Out Rout, Shot and Bothered, The Solid Tin Coyote, Clippety Clobbered,* and *Never Bug an Ant,* all United Artists, 1966; *Pinknic, Pink Posies, Pink of the Litter, In the Pink, Pink Paradise, Jet Pink, Pinto Pink, Congratulations! It's Pink, Prefabricated Pink,* and *The Hand Is Pinker Than the Eye,* all United Artists, 1967; *Sky Blue Pink, Pinkadilly Circus, Psychedelic Pink, Come on In! The Water's Pink, Put-Put-Pink, G.I. Pink, Lucky Pink, The Pink Quarterback, Pinkcome Tax, Pink Valiant, The Pink Bill, Prehistoric Pink, Pink in the Clink, Tickled Pink, Little Beaux Beaux, The Pink Sphinx, Pink Is a Many Splintered Thing, The Pink Package Plot,* and *Twinkle, Twinkle, Little Pink,* all United Artists, 1968; *Fast and Furry-ous,* De Patie-Freleng Enterprises, 1968; *Pink-a-Rella, Pink Pest Control, Think Before You Pink, Slink Pink, In the Pink of the Night, Pink on the Cob,* and *Extinct Pink,* all United Artists, 1969.

Fly in the Pink, Pink Blue Plate, Pink Tuba-Dore, Pink Pranks, Psst Pink, The Pink Flea, Going with the Pink, and *Pink-In,* all

United Artists, 1971; *Pink 8-Ball,* United Artists, 1972; *Pink Aye,* United Artists, 1974; *Pink Da Vinci, Pink Streaker, Salmon Pink, Forty Pink Winks, Pink Plasma, Pink Elephant, Keep Our Forests Pink, Pink Campaign, Bobolink Pink, It's Pink But Is It Mink?,* and *The Scarlet Pinkernel,* all United Artists, 1975; *Mystick Pink, The Pink of Arabee, The Pink Pro, The Pink Piper, Pinky Doodle, Sherlock Pink,* and *Rocky Pink,* all United Artists, 1976; *Therapeutic Pink,* United Artists, 1977; *Yankee Doodle Pink, Pink of Baghdad,* and *Pinkologist,* all United Artists, 1981.

Producer (with De Patie) and director (with others) of the following short animated films: *The Ant and the Aardvark, Hasty But Tasty, The Ant from Uncle, I've Got Ants in My Plans, Technology Phooey, Mumbo Jumbo, Dune Bug, Isle of Caprice, The Tijuana Toads, A Pair of Greenbacks,* and *Go for Croak,* all United Artists, 1969; *Don't Hustle an Ant with Muscle, Hop and Chop, Never on Thirsty, A Dopey Hacienda, Scratch a Tiger, Odd Ant Out, Ants in the Pantry, Science Friction, The Froze Nose Knows,* and *The Froggy, Froggy Duo,* all United Artists, 1970; *Rough Bunch, Snake in the Gracias, Two Jumps and a Chump, Mud Squad, The Egg of Ay-Yi-Yi, A Leap in the Deep, The Fastest Tongue in the West, Croakus Pocus,* and *Serape Happy,* all United Artists, 1971; *Frog Jog* and *Flight to the Finish,* both United Artists, 1972; *Kloot's Kounty, Apache on the County Seat, The Shoe Must Go On!, A Self-Winding Side-Winder, Pay Your Buffalo Bill, Ten Miles to the Gallop,* and *Stirrups and Hiccups,* all United Artists, 1973; *Phoney Express, Giddy-Up Woe!, Gold Struck, As the Tumbleweed Turns, The Badge and the Beautiful, Strange on the Range, Big Beef at the O.K. Corral, By Hoot or By Brook, Mesa Trouble,* and *Saddle Soap Opera,* all United Artists, 1974.

PRINCIPAL TELEVISION APPEARANCES—Specials: *Bugs Bunny/ Looney Tunes All Star 50th Anniversary,* CBS, 1986; *Roger Rabbit and the Secrets of Toontown,* CBS, 1988.

PRINCIPAL TELEVISION WORK—Series (all animated, unless indicated): Producer (with David H. De Patie), *The Super Six,* NBC, 1966-69; producer (with De Patie), *Super President,* NBC, 1967-68; director of animated sequences, *My World and Welcome to It,* NBC, 1969-70; producer (with De Patie), *Here Comes the Grump,* NBC, 1969-71; producer (with De Patie), *The Pink Panther Show,* NBC, 1969-76; producer (with De Patie), *Doctor Dolittle,* NBC, 1970-72; (as I. Freleng) director (with Chuck Jones), *The Road Runner Show,* ABC, 1971-72; producer (with De Patie), *The Barkleys,* NBC, 1972-73; producer (with De Patie), *The Houndcats,* NBC, 1972-73; producer (with De Patie), *Bailey's Comets,* NBC, 1973-74; executive producer and director (both with others), *The Bugs Bunny/Road Runner Show,* CBS, 1975-85; producer (with De Patie), *Return to the Planet of the Apes,* NBC, 1975-76; producer (with De Patie), *The Oddball Couple,* ABC, 1975-77; producer (with De Patie), *The Pink Panther Laff and a Half-Hour,* NBC, 1976-77; producer (with De Patie), *What's New, Mr. Magoo?,* CBS, 1977-78; executive producer (with De Patie), *Baggy Pants and the Nitwits,* NBC, 1977-78; producer (with De Patie), *The Fantastic Four,* NBC, 1978-79; producer (with De Patie), *The All-New Pink Panther Show,* ABC, 1978-79; executive producer (with De Patie), *Spider-Woman,* ABC, 1979-80; producer (with De Patie), *Pink Panther and Sons,* NBC, 1984; director (with Jones and Bob McKimson), *The Bugs Bunny/Looney Tunes Comedy Hour,* ABC, 1985—; senior director (with Jones and McKimson), *The Bugs Bunny and Tweety Show,* CBS, 1988—. Pilots: Creator, *Philbert,* 1961 (never broadcast).

Specials (all animated, unless indicated): Producer (with Theodor Geisel, Chuck Jones, and De Patie), *Dr. Seuss' ''How the Grinch Stole Christmas,''* CBS, 1966; executive producer (with De Patie), *Dr. Seuss' ''Horton Hears a Who,''* CBS, 1970; executive producer (with De Patie), *Dr. Seuss' ''The Cat in the Hat,''* CBS, 1971; producer (with Geisel and De Patie), *Dr. Seuss' ''The Lorax,''* CBS, 1972; producer (with De Patie), ''The Incredible, Indelible, Magical, Physical Mystery Trip,'' *ABC Afterschool Specials,* ABC, 1973; producer (with De Patie), *Dr. Seuss on the Loose,* CBS, 1973; producer (with De Patie), *The Bear Who Slept Through Christmas,* NBC, 1973; producer (with De Patie), ''The Magical Mystery Trip Through Little Red's Head,'' *ABC Out-of-School Special,* ABC, 1974; executive producer (with De Patie), ''The Tiny Tree,'' *Bell System Family Theatre,* NBC, 1975; producer (with Geisel and De Patie), *Dr. Seuss' ''The Hoober-Bloob Highway,''* CBS, 1975; producer and director (with Bob McKimson and Jones), *The Bugs Bunny Easter Special,* CBS, 1977; director (with Jones), *Bugs Bunny in Space,* CBS, 1977; director (with Jones), *Bugs Bunny's Howl-oween Special,* CBS, 1977; executive producer (with De Patie), *Halloween Is Grinch Night,* ABC, 1977; executive producer (with De Patie), ''My Mom's Having a Baby,'' *ABC Afterschool Specials* (live-action), ABC, 1977; producer (with De Patie), *The Pink Panther's Christmas,* ABC, 1978; producer (with De Patie), ''Michel's Mixed-Up Musical Bird,'' *ABC Afterschool Specials* (live-action), ABC, 1978; director (with others), *Bugs Bunny's Valentine,* CBS, 1979; producer (with Jones) and director, *Bugs Bunny's Looney Christmas Tales,* CBS, 1979; director (with Jones), *The Bugs Bunny Thanksgiving Diet,* CBS, 1979; producer (with De Patie), *Dr. Seuss' ''Pontoffel Pock, Where Are You?,''* CBS, 1980; executive producer (with De Patie), ''Where Do Teenagers Come From?,'' *ABC Afterschool Specials,* ABC, 1980; producer and director, *Daffy Duck's Easter Show,* NBC, 1980; director (with Jones), *The Bugs Bunny Mystery Special,* CBS, 1980; producer (with De Patie), *The Pink Panther in Olym-Pinks,* syndicated, 1980; producer (with De Patie), *Dennis the Menace: Mayday for Mother,* NBC, 1981; director, *Bugs Bunny: All American Hero,* CBS, 1981; producer (with De Patie), *The Grinch Grinches the Cat in the Hat,* ABC, 1982; director (with Jones), *Bugs Bunny's Mad World of Television,* CBS, 1985; director (with Jones and McKimson), *Bugs Bunny's Wild World of Sports,* ABC, 1989.

RELATED CAREER—Animator, United Film Ad Service, 1924-27; animator, Walt Disney Studio, 1928-29; animator, Charles Mintz Studio, 1929-30; head animator, Warner Brothers, 1930-63, except for a brief period as animation director, Metro-Goldwyn-Mayer, 1938-39; founder (with David H. De Patie), De Patie-Freleng Enterprises, 1963—; producer of television commercials.

NON-RELATED CAREER—Office boy with Armour Packing, Kansas City, MO.

WRITINGS: FILM—See production details above. *The Looney Looney Looney Bugs Bunny Movie,* 1981; (with John Dunn and David Detigee) *Bugs Bunny's Third Movie—1001 Rabbit Tales,* 1982; (with Dunn and Detigee) *Daffy Duck's Movie: Fantastic Island,* 1983. TELEVISION—Specials: *Bugs Bunny's Looney Christmas Tales,* 1979; *Daffy Duck's Easter Show,* 1980; *Bugs Bunny: All American Hero,* 1981.

AWARDS: Academy Award nominations, both Best Short Subject (Cartoon), 1941, for *Hiawatha's Rabbit Hunt* and *Rhapsody in Rivets;* Academy Award nomination, Best Short Subject (Cartoon), 1942, for *Pigs in a Polka;* Academy Award nomination, Best Short Subject (Cartoon), 1943, for *Greetings Bait;* Academy Award nomination, Best Short Subject (Cartoon), 1945, for *Life with Feathers;* Academy Award, Best Short Subject (Cartoon), 1947, for *Tweety Pie;* Academy Award nomination, Best Short Subject (Cartoon), 1954, for *Sandy Claws;* Academy Award, Best Short Subject (Cartoon), 1955, for *Speedy Gonzales;* Academy Award, Best Short Subject (Cartoon), 1957, for *Birds Anonymous;* Academy Award, Best Short Subject (Cartoon), 1958, for *Knighty Knight Bugs;* Academy Award nomination, Best Short Subject (Cartoon), 1959, for *Mexicali Shmoes;* Academy Award nomination, Best Short Subject (Cartoon), 1960, for *Mouse and Garden;* Academy Award nomination, Best Short Subject (Cartoon), 1961, for *The Pied Piper of Guadalupe;* Academy Award, Best Short Subject (Cartoon), 1964, for *The Pink Phink;* Academy Award nomination, Best Short Subject (Cartoon), 1966, for *The Pink Blueprint;* Emmy Award, Outstanding Evening Children's Special, 1977, for *Halloween Is Grinch Night;* Emmy Award, Outstanding Animated Program, 1982, for *Grinch Grinches the Cat in the Hat.*

ADDRESSES: OFFICE—DePatie/Freleng Enterprises, 7017 Havenhurst Avenue, Van Nuys, CA 91406.*

*   *   *

FRELENG, I.
See FRELENG, Friz

*   *   *

FREWER, Matt   1958-

PERSONAL: Surname rhymes with "Brewer"; born January 4, 1958, in Washington, DC; son of Frederick Charlesley (a captain in the Canadian Navy) and Gillian Anne (German) Frewer; married Amanda Hillwood (an actress), November 10, 1985. EDUCATION—Studied acting at the Bristol Old Vic Theatre School. RELIGION—Roman Catholic.

VOCATION: Actor.

CAREER: STAGE DEBUT—Wolf, *Bent,* Theatre Royal, York, U.K., 1980, for four weeks. LONDON DEBUT—Murph, *The Indian Wants the Bronx,* Soho Poly Theatre, 1981, for three weeks. PRINCIPAL STAGE APPEARANCES—Lysander, *A Midsummer Night's Dream,* Round House Theatre, London, 1981; Prince, *Romeo and Juliet,* Shaw Theatre, London, 1982; Malcolm, *Macbeth,* Shaw Theatre, 1983; also appeared in *Deathtrap,* Northcott Theatre, Exeter, U.K., 1984; *On the Razzle,* Leeds Playhouse, Leeds, U.K., 1984.

MAJOR TOURS—Vladimir, *Waiting for Godot,* U.K. cities, 1980; the Gentleman Caller, *The Glass Menagerie,* U.K. cities, 1981; also *The Comedy of Errors, Androcles and the Lion,* and *Much Ado About Nothing,* all New Shakespeare Company, U.K. cities, 1981.

FILM DEBUT—Senior, *The Lords of Discipline,* Paramount, 1983. PRINCIPAL FILM APPEARANCES—Truck driver, *Supergirl,* TriStar, 1984; soldier, *Spies Like Us,* Warner Brothers, 1985; Tom MacWhirter, *The Fourth Protocol,* Lorimar, 1987; C.I.A. agent, *Ishtar,* Columbia, 1987; Charlie Cross, *Far from Home,* Vestron, 1989; Big Russ Thompson, *Honey, I Shrunk the Kids,* Buena Vista,

MATT FREWER

1989; Alec, *Speed Zone,* Orion, 1989; also appeared in *Monty Python's the Meaning of Life,* Universal, 1983.

TELEVISION DEBUT—American at bar, *Tender Is the Night,* BBC, 1983, then Showtime, 1985. PRINCIPAL TELEVISION APPEARANCES—Series: Edison Carter and Max Headroom, *Max Headroom,* Channel Four, 1984; Max Headroom, *The Max Headroom Show,* Cinemax, 1985; Max Headroom—host, *The Original Max Talking Headroom Show,* Cinemax, 1987; Edison Carter and Max Headroom, *Max Headroom,* ABC, 1987; Michael Stratford, *Doctor, Doctor,* CBS, 1989—. Episodic: Soldier, "Displaced Person," *American Playhouse,* PBS, 1985; Pee Wee, *St. Elsewhere,* NBC, 1987; Cliff King, *Miami Vice,* NBC, 1988. Movies: Francis Lane, *The First Olympics—Athens 1896,* NBC, 1984. Specials: Max Headroom, *The Max Headroom Christmas Special,* Cinemax, 1986; Max Headroom, *Tina Turner: Break Every Rule,* HBO, 1987. Also appeared in *Robin of Sherwood,* HTV (English television), 1984.

RELATED CAREER—As Max Headroom, commercial spokesman for New Coke.

WRITINGS: (With Amanda Hillwood) *The Fez Brothers* (juvenile).

SIDELIGHTS: RECREATIONS—Playing banjo, going to movies, and hockey.

ADDRESSES: AGENT—Harry Abrams, Abrams Artists Ltd., 9200 Sunset Boulevard, Suite 625, Los Angeles, CA 90069.

FRIELS, Colin

PERSONAL: EDUCATION—Studied acting at the National Institute of Dramatic Art (Australia), 1976.

VOCATION: Actor.

CAREER: PRINCIPAL STAGE APPEARANCES—*Sweet Bird of Youth,* Royal Haymarket Theatre, London, 1985; also appeared in *Hamlet, Macbeth,* and *The Man from Muckinupin,* all Sydney Theatre Company, Sydney, Australia; *King Lear* and *Zastrozzi,* both Nimrod Theatre Company.

PRINCIPAL FILM APPEARANCES—Mike, *Buddies,* PTY Ltd., 1983; Javo, *Monkey Grip,* Cinecom/Mainline, 1983; Rufus Dawes, *For the Term of His Natural Life,* Filmco, 1985; Adam Lucas, *The Coolangatta Gold,* Hoyts Distribution/Republic, 1985; Richard Lovat Somers, *Kangaroo,* Enterprise/Filmways, 1986; title role, *Malcolm,* Vestron, 1986; Harvey Denton, *Ground Zero,* Hoyts, 1987; Mick, *High Tide,* Hemdale, 1987; the man, *Warm Nights on a Slow Moving Train,* Filmpac Holdings, 1987; Tom Stewart, *Grievous Bodily Harm,* International Film Management, 1988. Also appeared in *Prisoners,* Endeavor Film Management, 1983.

AWARDS: Best Actor Award from the Australian Film Institute for *Malcolm.*

ADDRESSES: AGENT—Ed Limato, International Creative Management, 8899 Beverly Boulevard, Los Angeles, CA 90048.*

*   *   *

FRIENDLY, Ed   1922-

PERSONAL: Full name, Edwin S. Friendly, Jr.; born April 8, 1922, in New York, NY; son of Edwin S. and Henrietta (Steinmeier) Friendly; married Natalie Coulson Brooks, January 21, 1952; children: Brooke, Edwin S. III. MILITARY—U.S. Army, infantry, 1942-45.

VOCATION: Producer.

CAREER: PRINCIPAL TELEVISION WORK—Series: Executive producer and creator (with George Schlatter), *Rowan and Martin's Laugh-In,* NBC, 1967-69; executive producer (with Michael Landon), *Little House on the Prairie,* NBC, 1974-82; executive producer (with Earl Hamner, Jr. and Lee Rich), *The Young Pioneers,* ABC, 1978. Mini-Series: Executive producer, *Backstairs at the White House,* NBC, 1979. Pilots: Producer, *The Young Pioneers,* ABC, 1976; producer, *The Young Pioneers' Christmas,* ABC, 1976; producer, *Judgement Day,* NBC, 1981. Movies: Producer, *Peter Lundy and the Medicine Hat Stallion,* NBC, 1977; executive producer, *The Flame Is Love,* NBC, 1979; executive producer, *The Ladies,* NBC, 1987.

RELATED CAREER—Sales executive, WABC-TV, New York City, 1949-53; producer and program executive, WCBS-TV, New York City, 1956-59; vice-president of special programs, WNBC-TV, New York City, 1959-67; president, Ed Friendly Productions, Los Angeles, 1967—.

NON-RELATED CAREER—Director, Batten, Barton, Derstine, and Osborn Advertising Agency, New York City, 1946-49.

AWARDS: Special Award from the International Film and Television Festival of New York, 1967; Golden Globe, 1968, Producer of the Year Award from the Producers Guild of America, 1968, Emmy Awards, Outstanding Musical or Variety Series, 1968 and 1969, and Scout Awards, Best Weekly Series and Show of the Year, 1969, all for *Rowan and Martin's Laugh-In;* Gold Medal Award from the International Radio and Television Society, 1970; Christopher Award, 1975; Western Heritage Award from the National Cowboy Hall of Fame, 1975, for *Little House on the Prairie;* Emmy Award nomination, 1978, for *Backstairs at the White House;* Emmy Award nomination, 1977, and Western Heritage Award, 1978, both for *Peter Lundy and the Medicine Hat Stallion.*

MEMBER: Caucus for Producers, Writers, and Directors (co-chairor of steering committee).

ADDRESSES: OFFICE—8501 Wilshire Boulevard, Suite 250, Beverly Hills, CA 90211.*

*   *   *

FULLER, Samuel   1911-

PERSONAL: Full name, Samuel Michael Fuller; born August 12, 1911, in Worcester, MA; first marriage ended in divorce, 1959; married Christa Lang (an actress), July 25, 1967; children: Samantha. MILITARY—U.S. Army, First Infantry Division, 16th Regiment, corporal, 1942-45.

VOCATION: Director, producer, writer, and actor.

CAREER: PRINCIPAL FILM APPEARANCES—Policeman, *House of Bamboo,* Twentieth Century-Fox, 1955; as himself, *Pierrot le fou,* Corinth-Pathe, 1968; the director, *The Last Movie* (also known as *Chinchero*), Universal, 1971; senator, *Dead Pigeon on Beethoven Street,* Bavarian Atelier Gesellschaft, 1972; the American, *The American Friend,* New Yorker, 1977; theatre impressario, *Scott Joplin,* Universal, 1977; Interceptor commander, *1941,* Universal, 1979; old man in pool hall, *Hammett,* Warner Brothers, 1982; Charlie Felton, *White Dog* (also known as *Trained to Kill*), Paramount, 1982; Joe the cameraman, *The State of Things,* Artificial Eye, 1983; Colonel Sharp, *Slapstick of Another Kind,* International Film Marketing, 1984; Van Meer, *A Return to Salem's Lot,* Warner Brothers, 1988; also appeared in *Brigitte et Brigitte,* 1966; and in *The Young Nurses* (also known as *Nightingale*), New World, 1973.

PRINCIPAL FILM WORK—Director: *I Shot Jesse James,* Lippert, 1949; *The Baron of Arizona,* Lippert, 1950; (also producer) *The Steel Helmet,* Lippert, 1951; *Fixed Bayonets,* Twentieth Century-Fox, 1951; (also producer) *Park Row,* United Artists, 1952; *Pickup on South Street,* Twentieth Century-Fox, 1953; *Hell and High Water,* Twentieth Century-Fox, 1954; *House of Bamboo,* Twentieth Century-Fox, 1955; (also producer) *China Gate,* Twentieth Century-Fox, 1957; (also producer) *Forty Guns* (also known as *Woman with a Whip*), Twentieth Century-Fox, 1957; (also producer) *Run of the Arrow,* Universal, 1957; (also producer) *The Crimson Kimono,* Columbia, 1959; (also producer) *Verboten!,* Columbia, 1959; (also producer) *Underworld U.S.A.,* Columbia, 1961; *Merrill's Marauders,* Warner Brothers, 1962; (also producer and cinematographer with Stanley Cortez) *Shock Corridor,* Allied Artists, 1963; (also producer) *The Naked Kiss* (also known as *The Iron Kiss*), Allied Artists, 1964; *Shark* (also known as *Maneater*), Excelsior, 1970; *Dead Pigeon on Beethoven Street,* Bavarian

Atelier Gesellschaft, 1972; *The Big Red One,* United Artists, 1980; *White Dog* (also known as *Trained to Kill*), Paramount, 1982; also *Thieves After Dark* (unreleased).

PRINCIPAL TELEVISION APPEARANCES—Movies: Old man in small cafe, *The Blood of Others,* HBO, 1984.

PRINCIPAL TELEVISION WORK—Episodic: Director, ''It Tolls for Thee,'' *The Virginian,* NBC, 1962; director, ''330 Independence S.W.'' *The Dick Powell Show,* NBC, 1962; director, *The Iron Horse,* ABC, 1966 (five episodes).

NON-RELATED CAREER—Newspaper reporter for the *New York Evening Journal, New York Graphic,* and the *San Diego Sun.*

WRITINGS: See production details above, unless indicated. FILM— (With Edmund Joseph) *Hats Off,* Grand National, 1937; (with Ethel Hill and Harvey Fergusson) *It Happened in Hollywood,* Columbia, 1937; (with Wellyn Totman, Jack Townley, and Charles Francis Royal) *Gangs of New York,* Republic, 1938; (with Helen Deutsch) *Shockproof,* Columbia, 1949; *I Shot Jesse James,* 1949; *The Baron of Arizona,* 1950; *The Steel Helmet,* 1951; *Fixed Bayonets,* 1951; *Park Row,* 1952; *Pickup on South Street,* 1953; (with Russell Hughes) *The Command,* Warner Brothers, 1954; (with Jesse L. Lasky, Jr.) *Hell and High Water,* 1954; (with Harry Kleiner) *House of Bamboo,* 1955; *China Gate,* 1957; *Forty Guns,* 1957; *Run of the Arrow,* 1957; *The Crimson Kimono,* 1959; *Verboten!,* 1959; *Underworld U.S.A.,* 1961; (with Milton Sperling) *Merrill's Marauders,* 1962; *Shock Corridor,* 1963; *The Naked Kiss,* 1964; (with Harold Medford) *Capetown Affair,* Twentieth Century-Fox, 1967; (with John Kingsbridge) *Shark,* 1970; *Dead Pigeon on Beethoven Street,* 1972; (with Millard Kaufman) *The Klansman,* Paramount, 1974; *The Big Red One,* 1980; (with Curtis Hanson) *White Dog,* 1982; also *Thieves After Dark* (unreleased).

TELEVISION –Episodic: ''It Tolls for Thee,'' *The Virginian,* NBC, 1962; ''High Devil'' and (with Oliver Crawford) ''Hellcat,'' *The Iron Horse,* ABC, 1966.

OTHER—Novels: *Burn, Baby, Burn!,* Phoenix Press, 1935; *Test Tube Baby,* William Godwin, 1936; *Make Up and Kiss,* William Godwin, 1938; *The Dark Page,* Duell, Sloan & Pearce, 1944; *144 Picadilly Street,* R.W. Baron, 1971; *Dead Pigeon on Beethoven Street,* Pyramid, 1974; *The Big Red One,* Bantam, 1980; *Quint's World,* Harlequin, 1988; also *Crown of India,* 1966; *The Rifle,* 1981; *Pecos Bill and the Soho Kid,* 1986.

AWARDS: Writers Guild Award, Best Written American Low Budget Film, 1951, for *The Steel Helmet;* Bronze Lion Award from the Venice Film Festival, 1953, for *Pickup on South Street;* Creative Arts Award (Film) from Brandeis University, 1981. MILITARY HONORS—Bronze Star, Silver Star, and Purple Heart.

ADDRESSES: OFFICE—c/o Charles Silverberg, One Century Plaza, Suite 1900, 2029 Century Park E., Los Angeles, CA 90067-3088.*

*   *   *

FULLERTON, Fiona   1956-

PERSONAL: Full name, Fiona Elizabeth Fullerton; born October 10, 1956, in Kaduna, Nigeria; daughter of Bernard (a British Army

FIONA FULLERTON

officer) and Pamela Fullerton; married Simon MacCorkindale (an actor), July 10, 1976 (divorced, September, 1983). EDUCATION— Studied dance at the Elmhurst Ballet School. RELIGION—Church of England.

VOCATION: Actress.

CAREER: PRINCIPAL STAGE APPEARANCES—Title role, *Cinderella,* Palladium, London, 1976; also appeared in *The Royal Baccarat Scandal,* Haymarket Theatre, London, 1989; as Guinevere, *Camelot,* Apollo Victoria Theatre, London; Gypsy Rose Lee, *Gypsy* Haymarket Theatre; Polly Peacham, *The Beggar's Opera,* Lyric Hammersmith Theatre, London; Sally Bowles, *I Am a Camera,* Plymouth Theatre Company; Hope Langdon, *Something's Afoot,* in Hong Kong.

MAJOR TOURS—Polly Brown, *The Boyfriend,* Far Eastern and Middle Eastern cities; Jill Potts, *Caught Napping,* U.K. cities.

FILM DEBUT—Diana, *Run Wild, Run Free,* Columbia, 1969. PRINCIPAL FILM APPEARANCES—Anastasia, *Nicholas and Alexandra,* Columbia, 1971; Alice, *Alice's Adventures in Wonderland,* American National Enterprises, 1972; Elizabeth, *The Human Factor,* Metro-Goldwyn-Mayer/United Artists (MGM/UA), 1979; Pola Ivanova, *A View to a Kill,* MGM/UA, 1985.

PRINCIPAL TELEVISION APPEARANCES—Mini-Series: Elizabeth Farewell, *Shaka Zulu,* syndicated, 1985; Clarice Mannors, *The Charmer,* London Weekend Television, 1987, then *Masterpiece Theatre,* PBS, 1989; Lady Duff Twysden, *Hemingway,* syndicated,

1988; Lady Barbara Berowne, *A Taste for Death*, Anglia Television, then *Mystery*, PBS, 1989. Movies: Rachel, *Gauguin the Savage*, CBS, 1980; Skye Smith, *Hold That Dream*, syndicated, 1986; Lady Isobel Gillingham, *A Hazard of Hearts*, CBS, 1987. Also appeared as Nurse Rutherford, *Angels*, BBC; in *A Friend Indeed*, Anglia Television; *Leo Tolstoy: A Question of Faith*, BBC; *Dick Barton, Special Agent*, Southern Television.

ADDRESSES: AGENTS—Jean Diamond, London Management, 235 Regent Street, London W1, England; Mary Oreck, McCartt, Oreck, Barrett, 10390 Santa Monica Boulevard, Suite 310, Los Angeles, CA 90025.

*   *   *

FURST, Anton

PERSONAL: Born c. 1945. EDUCATION—Attended the Royal College of Art.

VOCATION: Production designer.

CAREER: PRINCIPAL FILM WORK—All as production designer, unless indicated: Assistant designer, *2001: A Space Odyssey*, Metro-Goldwyn-Mayer, 1968; *Lady Chatterley's Lover*, Prodis, 1981; *An Unsuitable Job for a Woman*, Goldcrest, 1982; *The Company of Wolves*, Cannon, 1985; *The Frog Prince* (also known as *French Lesson*), Goldcrest/Warner Brothers, 1985; *Full Metal Jacket*, Warner Brothers, 1987; *High Spirits*, Tri-Star, 1988; *Batman*, Warner Brothers, 1989.

RELATED CAREER—Founder, Holoco (a special effects studio), which has produced effects for such films as *Outland*, *Flash Gordon*, *Alien*, and *Moonraker*.

AWARDS: Academy Award, Best Art Direction, 1990, for *Batman*.

ADDRESSES: OFFICE—c/o Pinewood Studios, Iver Heath, Buckinghamshire SLO ONH, England.*

G

GAINES, Boyd 1953-

PERSONAL: Born May 11, 1953, in Atlanta, GA. EDUCATION—Graduated from the Juilliard School.

VOCATION: Actor.

CAREER: OFF-BROADWAY DEBUT—Melchior Gabor, *Spring Awakening*, New York Shakespeare Festival, Public Theater, 1978. PRINCIPAL STAGE APPEARANCES—Alcksei Belyayev, *A Month in the Country*, Roundabout Stage One Theatre, New York City, 1979; Stepan, *Barbarians*, Florizel, *The Winter's Tale*, bailiff, *Chronicle*, and cameraman and radio announcer, *Johnny on a Spot*, all Brooklyn Academy of Music, Brooklyn, NY, 1980; Gunnar Larsen, *Vikings*, Manhattan Theatre Club, New York City, 1980; double bassist, *The Double Bass*, New Theatre of Brooklyn, Brooklyn, NY, 1985; Chuck deButts, *The Maderati*, Playwrights Horizons, New York City, 1987; Peter Patrone, *The Heidi Chronicles*, Playwrights Horizons, 1988, then Plymouth Theatre, New York City, 1989. Also appeared in *Philadelphia, Here I Come!*, Philadelphia Drama Guild, Philadelphia, PA, 1980; *Love's Labour's Lost*, Center Stage Theatre, Baltimore, MD, 1982; *Oliver Oliver*, Long Wharf Theatre, New Haven, CT, 1984.

PRINCIPAL FILM APPEARANCES—Michael, *Fame*, Metro-Goldwyn-Mayer/United Artists, 1980; Coach Brackett, *Porky's*, Twentieth Century-Fox, 1982; Jason, *The Sure Thing*, Embassy, 1985; Lieutenant Ring, *Heartbreak Ridge*, Warner Brothers, 1986; Bill, *Call Me*, Vestron, 1988; Sam Logan, *Ray's Male Heterosexual Dance Hall* (short film), Fox/Lorber, 1988.

PRINCIPAL TELEVISION APPEARANCES—Series: Mark Royer, *One Day At a Time*, CBS, 1981-84. Mini-Series: Chris Bradford, *Evergreen*, NBC, 1985. Episodic: Todd Myerson, *Remington Steele*, NBC, 1985; Jim Perkins, *L.A. Law*, NBC, 1986; Lieutenant Rodger Gage, *Hotel*, ABC, 1986; Cates, *Spenser: For Hire*, ABC, 1988. Specials: "Pigeon Feathers," *American Playhouse*, PBS, 1988.

RELATED CAREER—Company member, Tyrone Guthrie Theater, Minneapolis, MN, 1981-82.

AWARDS: Theatre World Award, 1980, for *A Month in the Country*.

ADDRESSES: AGENT—J. Michael Bloom and Associates, 9200 Sunset Boulevard, Suite 710, Los Angeles, CA 90069.*

GANZ, Bruno 1941-

PERSONAL: Born March 22, 1941, in Zurich, Switzerland; married in 1965; children: one son.

VOCATION: Actor.

CAREER: PRINCIPAL STAGE APPEARANCES—*Hamlet*, Berlin, West Germany, 1967; also appeared in *Dans la jungle des villes, Torquato Tasso, La Chevauchee sur le lac de Constance*, and *Peer Gynt*, all with the Schaubuhne theatre troupe, Berlin, West Germany, 1970-76; and in *Hamlet*, Shaubuhne, 1982.

FILM DEBUT—*Chikita*, 1961. PRINCIPAL FILM APPEARANCES—Yakov Schalimov, *Sommergaeste* (also known as *Summer Guests*), Constantin/Exportfilm Bischoff and Company, 1975; Henrich Grun, *Lumiere* (also known as *Light*), Gaumont, 1975, released in the United States by New World, 1976; Gregors, *Die Wildente* (also known as *The Wild Duck*), Solaris Film Produktion/Sascha Film/Westdeutscher Rundfunk, 1976, released in the United States by New Yorker, 1977; Le Conte, *La Marquise d'O* (also known as *The Marquise of O* and *Die Marquise von O*), Gaumont, 1976; Jonathan Zimmermann, *Der Amerikanische Freund* (also known as *The American Friend*), CineGate/New Yorker, 1977; Bruno, *Die Linkshandige Frau* (also known as *The Left-Handed Woman*), Marin Karmitz/Artificial Eye, 1977, released in the United States by New Yorker, 1980; Dr. Berthold Hoffmann, *Messer im Kopf* (also known as *Knife in the Head*), New Yorker, 1978; Professor Bruckner, *The Boys from Brazil*, Twentieth Century-Fox, 1978; Thomas Rosenmund, *Schwarz und Weiss Wie Tage und Naechte* (also known as *Black and White Like Days and Nights*), Monaco/Radiant, 1978; Jonathan Harker, *Nosferatu, Phantom der Nacht* (also known as *Nosferatu, the Vampire* and *Nosferatu, the Vampyre*), Gaumont International/Twentieth Century-Fox, 1979; Kern, *Retour a la bien-aimee* (also known as *Return to the Beloved*), Societe Nouvelle Prodis/World Marketing Films, 1979.

Jakob Nuessli, *Der Erfinder* (also known as *The Inventor*), Rex Film, 1980; Jules, *Polenta*, EOS Film/SSR, 1980; Remy, *La Provinciale* (also known as *The Provincial* and *A Girl from Lorraine*), Gala Film Distributors/Cotel Films Distribution, 1980, released in the United States by New Yorker, 1982; Werner, *Oggetti Smarriti* (also known as *Lost and Found*), Twentieth Century-Fox, 1980; Georg Laschen, *Die Falschung* (also known as *Circle of Deceit* and *False Witness*), United International, 1981, released in the United States by United Artists Classics, 1982; Paul, *Dans la ville blanche* (also known as *In the White City*), Contemporary Films Ltd., 1982, released in the United States by Grey City, 1983; Faber, *System ohne Schatten* (also known as *System without Shadow* and *Closed Circuit*), Munic Film, 1983; Gustav, *De Ijssalon*, Tuschinski Film Distribution, 1985; Peter, *El Rio de Oro* (also known as *The Golden River*), Tesauaro/Incine SA/Federal, 1986; Steiner, *Der Pendler* (also known as *The Informer*), InterTeam/Metropolis, 1986; Daniel, *Der Himmel uber Berlin* (also known as *Wings of Desire* and *The Sky over Berlin*), Orion Classics/Road Movies/Argos/Westdeutscher Rundfunk, 1987; Bruno, *Bankomatt*, Pegaso Inter-Communication, 1989; Raymond Forbes, *Strapless*, Gavin Films, 1989. Also appeared in *Es Dach uberem Chopf*, 1962; as Bernard Kral, *Der sanfte Lauf*, 1967; in *5% de Risque* (also known as *5% Risk*), Gaumont, 1980; *La Dame aux camelias*, 1980; *Etwas wird sichtbar*, 1981; *Fermata Etna*, 1981; *Gedaechtnis: Ein Film fur Curt Bois und Bernhard Minetti* (documentary; also known as *Remembrance* and *Gedaechtnis*), Common Film/Westdeutscher Rundfunk, 1982; *Krieg und Frieden*, (documentary; also known as *War and Peace*), Filverlag der Autoren/New Line Cinema, 1982; as himself, *Logik des Gefuhls* 1982; in *Killer aus Florida* (also known as *Killer from Florida*), Xanadu, 1983; and in *An Italian Woman* and *Hande Hoch*.

PRINCIPAL FILM WORK—Co-director and editor, *Gedaechtnis: Ein Film fur Curt Bois und Bernhard Minetti* (documentary; also known as *Remembrance* and *Gedaechtnis*), Common Film/Westdeutscher Rundfunk, 1982.

PRINCIPAL TELEVISION APPEARANCES—Movies: Heinrich Beck, *Sins of the Fathers* (also known as *Fathers and Sons*), Showtime, 1988. Also appeared in *Geschichte einer Liebe*, 1981.

RELATED CAREER—Co-founder, Schaubuhne theatre troupe, Berlin, West Germany, 1970.

AWARDS: Federal German Prize, Best Actor, for *La Marquise d'O.**

*   *   *

GARCIA, Andy   1956-

PERSONAL: Born in 1956 in Havana, Cuba; came to the United States in 1961; father, a lawyer and businessman; wife's name, Maravi; children: Daniella. EDUCATION—Attended Florida International University.

VOCATION: Actor.

CAREER: FILM DEBUT—Ken, *Blue Skies Again*, Samuel Bronston, 1983. PRINCIPAL FILM APPEARANCES—T.J., *A Night in Heaven*, Kirkwood Fox, 1983; Ray Martinez, *The Mean Season*, Orion, 1985; Angel Maldonado, *Eight Million Ways to Die*, Tri-Star, 1986; George Stone, *The Untouchables*, Paramount, 1987; Dr. Ramirez, *Stand and Deliver*, Warner Brothers, 1988; Carlos Quintas, *American Roulette*, Film Four, 1988; Charlie Vincent, *Black Rain*, Paramount, 1989; Sergeant Raymond Avila, *Internal Affairs*, Paramount, 1990. Also appeared in *The Lonely Guy*, Universal, 1984; *Encounters of the Deep*, 1984.

PRINCIPAL TELEVISION APPEARANCES—Episodic: Alejandro, *Alfred Hitchcock Presents*, NBC, 1985; Tony Rosselli, *Foley Square*, CBS, 1986; also *Hill Street Blues*, NBC, 1981; *Brothers*, Showtime; *Archie Bunker's Place*, CBS; *From Here to Eternity*, NBC; *Que Pasa, USA?*, PBS. Movies: Clinton Earl Dillard, *Clinton and Nadine* (also known as *Blood Money*), HBO, 1988. Also appeared in *The Murder of Sherlock Holmes*.

ANDY GARCIA

RELATED CAREER—Actor in regional theatre in Florida.

ADDRESSES: AGENT—David Eidenberg, S.T.E. Representation, 9301 Wilshire Boulevard, Suite 312, Beverly Hills, CA 90210.*

*   *   *

GARSON, Greer   1908-

PERSONAL: Born September 29, 1908, in County Down, Northern Ireland; naturalized United States citizen; daughter of George and Nina Sophia (Greer) Garson; married Edward A. Snelson, 1933 (divorced, 1941); married Richard Ney (an actor), 1943 (divorced, 1947); married Elijah E. "Buddy" Fogelson, 1949. EDUCATION—Received B.A. from London University; graduate work at the University of Grenoble.

VOCATION: Actress and producer.

CAREER: STAGE DEBUT—Shirley Kaplan, *Street Scene*, Birmingham Repertory Theatre, Birmingham, U.K., 1932. LONDON DEBUT—Iris, *The Tempest*, Open Air Theatre, 1934. PRINCIPAL STAGE APPEARANCES—The Court Lady, *The Six of Calais* and courtesan, *The Comedy of Errors*, both Open Air Theatre, London, 1934; Fanny Field, *Golden Arrow*, Whitehall Theatre, London, 1935; Nina Popinot, *Vintage Wine*, Victoria Palace Theatre, London, 1935; Linda Brown, *Accent on Youth*, Globe Theatre, London, 1935; Peggy Admaston, *A Butterfly on the Wheel*, Playhouse

Theatre, London, 1935; Vivienne, *Page from a Diary*, Garrick Theatre, London, 1936; Diana, *The Visitor*, Daly's Theatre, London, 1936; Christianne Galvoisier, *Mademoiselle*, Wyndham's Theatre, London, 1936; Geraldine, *Old Music*, St. James's Theatre, London, 1937; title role, *Auntie Mame*, Broadhurst Theatre, New York City, 1958.

PRINCIPAL STAGE WORK—Producer (with Arthur Cantor), *St. Mark's Gospel*, Marymount Manhattan Theatre, Playhouse Theatre, New York City, 1978; producer (with Cantor), *The Playboy of the Weekend World*, Playhouse Theatre, 1978; producer (with Cantor), *On Golden Pond*, Hudson Theatre Guild, New Apollo Theatre, New York City, 1979, then Center Theatre Group, Ahmanson Theatre, Los Angeles, 1980.

MAJOR TOURS—Patient, *Too Good to Be True*, U.K. cities, 1932.

FILM DEBUT—Katherine Ellis, *Goodbye Mr. Chips*, Metro-Goldwyn-Mayer (MGM), 1939. PRINCIPAL FILM APPEARANCES—Linda Bronson, *Remember?*, MGM, 1939; Elizabeth Bennett, *Pride and Prejudice*, MGM, 1940; Edna Gladney, *Blossoms in the Dust*, MGM, 1941; Claire Woodruff, *When Ladies Meet*, MGM, 1941; title role, *Mrs. Miniver*, MGM, 1942; Paula, *Random Harvest*, MGM, 1942; title role, *Madame Curie*, MGM, 1943; as herself, *The Youngest Profession*, MGM, 1943; title role, *Mrs. Parkington*, MGM, 1944; Emily Sears, *Adventure*, MGM, 1945; Mary Rafferty, *The Valley of Decision*, MGM, 1945; Marise Aubert, *Desire Me*, MGM, 1947; Julia Packett, *Julia Misbehaves*, MGM, 1948; Irene Forsyte, *That Forsyte Woman* (also known as *The Forsyte Saga*), MGM, 1949; Kay Miniver, *The Miniver Story*, MGM, 1950; Jane Hoskins, *The Law and the Lady*, MGM, 1951; Calpurnia, *Julius Caesar*, MGM, 1953; Mrs. Patrick McChesney, *Scandal at Scourie*, MGM, 1953; Jan Stewart, *Her Twelve Men*, MGM, 1954; Dr. Julia Winslow Garth, *Strange Lady in Town*, Warner Brothers, 1955; as herself, *Pepe*, Columbia, 1960; Eleanor Roosevelt, *Sunrise at Campobello*, Warner Brothers, 1960; Mother Prioress, *The Singing Nun*, MGM, 1966; Mrs. Cordelia Biddle, *The Happiest Millionaire*, Buena Vista, 1967; as herself, *Directed by William Wyler* (documentary), Tatge, 1986.

PRINCIPAL TELEVISION APPEARANCES—Pilots: Aunt March, *Little Women*, NBC, 1978. Episodic: *Star Stage*, NBC; *The Love Boat*, ABC; also *Telephone Time*. Specials: Elena Krug, *Reunion in Vienna*, NBC, 1955; *The Bob Hope Show*, NBC, 1956; Regina Giddens, "The Little Foxes," *Hallmark Hall of Fame*, NBC, 1956; *The Big Party for Revlon*, CBS, 1959; Lady Cicely Wayneflete, "Captain Brassbound's Conversion," *Hallmark Hall of Fame*, NBC, 1960; Queen Mary, "Crown Matrimonial," *Hallmark Hall of Fame*, NBC, 1974; narrator, *The Little Drummer Boy, Book II*, NBC, 1975; *Dean Martin Celebrity Roast: Jimmy Stewart*, NBC, 1978; *Perry Como's Christmas in New Mexico*, ABC, 1979; *Bob Hope's Women I Love—Beautiful But Funny*, NBC, 1979; also *How He Lied to Her Husband*, BBC; *My Father Gave Me America; Holiday Tribute to Radio City Music Hall;* and *A Gift of Music*.

NON-RELATED CAREER—Worked in an advertising firm in London.

AWARDS: Academy Award nomination, Best Actress, 1940, for *Goodbye Mr. Chips;* Academy Award nomination, Best Actress, 1942, for *Blossoms in the Dust;* Academy Award, Best Actress, 1943, for *Mrs. Miniver;* Academy Award nomination, Best Actress, 1944, for *Madame Curie;* Gold Medal Award from *Photoplay* magazine, 1944-45; Academy Award nomination, Best Actress, 1945, for *Mrs. Parkington;* Academy Award nomination, Best

Actress, 1946, for *The Valley of Decision;* Sour Apple Award (with Fred MacMurray) from the Hollywood Women's Press Club, 1945; Academy Award nomination, Best Actress, and Golden Globe, Best Motion Picture Actress, both 1961, for *Sunrise at Campobello.*

ADDRESSES: AGENT—Judy Scott-Fox, William Morris Agency, 151 El Camino Drive, Beverly Hills, CA 90212.*

*   *   *

GASSMAN, Vittorio   1922-

PERSONAL: Born September 1, 1922, in Genoa, Italy; married second wife, Shelley Winters (an actress), April 28, 1952 (divorced, June 2, 1954). EDUCATION—Attended the Law University of Rome; studied acting at the Academy of Dramatic Art, Rome, with Silvio D'Amico.

VOCATION: Actor and director.

CAREER: PRINCIPAL STAGE APPEARANCES—Agamemnon, *Oresteia*, Syracuse, Greece, 1960; *Viva Vittorio!* (one-man show), Center Theatre Group, Mark Taper Forum, Los Angeles, then Promenade Theatre, New York City, both 1984. Also appeared in productions of *Hamlet, Othello, As You Like It, Troilus and Cressida, Oedipus Rex, Prometheus Bound, Ghosts, Peer Gynt, Orestes, Rosencrantz and Guildenstern Are Dead,* and *Richard III.*

PRINCIPAL STAGE WORK—Director, *Oresteia*, Syracuse, Greece, 1960; director, *Viva Vittorio!* (one-man show), Center Theatre

VITTORIO GASSMAN

Group, Mark Taper Forum, Los Angeles, then Promenade Theatre, New York City, both 1984; also director, *Irma la Douce.*

FILM DEBUT—Davide, *Preludio d'amore*, 1946. PRINCIPAL FILM APPEARANCES—Mathieu Blumenthal, *L'Ebreo errante* (also known as *The Wandering Jew*), 1947, released in the United States by Globe, 1948; Walter, *Riso amaro* (also known as *Bitter Rice*), 1948, released in the United States by Lux, 1950; Paolo Baldini, *Una voce nel tuo cuore* (also known as *A Voice in Your Heart*), 1949, released in the United States by Lupa, 1952; Vittorio, *Anna,* I.F.E., 1951; Alejandro Castillo, *Sombrero,* Metro-Goldwyn-Mayer (MGM), 1952; Peter, *The Glass Wall,* Columbia, 1953; Jory, *Cry of the Hunted,* MGM, 1953; Paul Bronte, *Rhapsody,* MGM, 1954; Mario Rossi, *Mambo,* Paramount, 1954; Giovanni, *Difendo il mio amore* (also known as *I'll Defend My Love* and *Defend My Love*), Hal Roach, 1956; Anatole Kuragin, *War and Peace* (also known as *Guerra e pace*), Paramount, 1956; Prince Piero, *La ragazza del palio* (also known as *The Love Specialist*), 1957, released in the United States by Medallion, 1959; prosecutor, *La tempesta* (also known as *The Tempest*), Paramount, 1958; Peppe, *I soliti ignoti* (also known as *Big Deal on Madonna Street*), 1958, released in the United States by United Motion Picture Organization, 1960; Guido, *The Miracle,* Warner Brothers, 1959; Giovanni Busacca, *La grande guerra* (also known as *The Great War*), 1959, released in the United States by Lopert, 1961; Peppe, *Audace colpo dei soliti ignoti* (also known as *Fiasco in Milan* and *Hold-Up a la Milanaise*), 1959, released in the United States by Avion/Trans-Universe/Jerand, 1963.

Gerardo, *Il mattatore* (also known as *Love and Larceny* and *L'Homme aux cent visages*), 1960, released in the United States by Major, 1963; Remo, *Crimen* (also known as *And Suddenly It's Murder!*), 1960, released in the United States by Royal, 1964; Sahak, *Barabba* (also known as *Barabbas*), 1961, released in the United States by Columbia, 1962; Bruno Cortona, *Il sorpasso* (also known as *The Easy Life*), 1962, released in the United States by Embassy, 1963; Mazzano, *La smania andosso* (also known as *The Eye of the Needle*), 1962, released in the United States by Eldorado, 1965; Giulio Ceriani, *Il successo,* 1963, released in the United States by Embassy, 1965; various roles, *I mostri* (also known as *Opiate '67* and *Fifteen from Rome*), 1963, released in the United States by McAbbe/Janus, 1967; various roles, *Se permettete parliamo di donne* (also known as *Parliamo di donne* and *Let's Talk About Women*), Embassy, 1964; Don Giuliano, *La congiuntura* (also known as *One Million Dollars*), 1964, released in the United States by Columbia, 1965; Perego, *La guerra segreta* (also known as *The Dirty Game*), 1965, released in the United States by American International, 1966; Prince Don Vincenzo Gonzaga, *Una vergine per il principe* (also known as *A Maiden for a Prince*), 1965, released in the United States by Royal, 1967; Belfagor Arcidiavolo, *L'arcidiavolo* (also known as *The Devil in Love* and *Il diavolo innamorato*), 1966, released in the United States by Warner Brothers, 1968; Francesco Vincenzini, *Il tigre* (also known as *The Tiger and the Pussycat*), Embassy, 1967; Cenci, *Woman Times Seven* (also known as *Sette volta donna*), Embassy, 1967; Bob Chiaramonte, *Lo scatenato* (also known as *Catch As Catch Can* and *Tutti frutti*), 1967, released in the United States by Fair Film, 1968; Pasquale Lojacono, *Questi fantasmi* (also known as *Ghosts, Italian Style* and *Three Ghosts*), 1967, released in the United States by MGM, 1969; Mario Beretti, *Una su tredici* (also known as *Twelve Plus One*), 1969, released in the United States by COFCI/CEF, 1970.

Lorenzo Santenocito, *In nome del popolo italiano* (also known as *In the Name of the Italian People*), Fida Cinematografica, 1971; title

role, *Brancaleone alle Crociate* (also known as *Brancaleone at the Crusades*), Fair Film, 1971; Prince Donati, *L'udienza* (also known as *The Audience*), Istituto Luce/Italnoleggio Cinematografico, 1972; Armando, *Senza famiglia Nullatenenti cercano affetto* (also known as *Without Family*), Interfilm, 1972; Gianni, *C'eravamo tanto amati* (also known as *Those Were the Years*), Delta Film, 1974; Captain Fausto Censolo, *Profumo di donna* (also known as *Scent of a Woman*), Curzon Film Distributors/Fida Cinematografica, 1974, released in the United States by United Artists, 1976.

Andrea Sansoni, *A mezzanotte va la ronda del piacere* (also known as *Midnight Pleasures*), Cineriz/Film Ventures, 1975; Fabio Stolz, *Anima persa* (also known as *The Forbidden Room*), Twentieth Century-Fox, 1976; Colonel Filimore, *Le Desert des tartares* (also known as *Il deserto dei tartari* and *The Desert of the Tartars*), Gaumont, 1976, released in the United States by Reggane, 1977; Tuttunpezzo, *Signore e signori, buonanotte* (also known as *Goodnight, Ladies and Gentlemen*), Titanus Distribuzione, 1977; Kardinal, Ehemann, and Kellner, *I nuovi mostri* (also known as *The New Monsters* and *Viva Italia!*), Cinema V, 1978; Luigi Corelli, *A Wedding,* Twentieth Century-Fox, 1978; Albino Millozza, *Caro Papa* (also known as *Dear Papa*), AMLF/Dean/Prospect, 1979; Mario, *La Terrazza* (also known as *The Terrace*), United Artists, 1979; Pippo Mifa, *Due pezzi di pane* (also known as *Two Pieces of Bread*), United Artists, 1979; St. Christopher, *Quintet,* Twentieth Century-Fox, 1979.

Andrea Sansoni, *The Immortal Bachelor,* S.J. International, 1980; Nino Salvatore Sebastiani, *The Nude Bomb* (also known as *The Return of Maxwell Smart*), Universal, 1980; Victor D'Anton, *Sharky's Machine,* Warner Brothers, 1981; Prince, *Il Conte Tacchia* (also known as *Count Tacchia*), Gaumont/Distributori Audiovisivi Consorziati, 1982; Alonzo, *Tempest,* Columbia, 1982; Livio, *Benvenuta,* Union Generale Cinematographique/Artificial Eye, 1983; Walter Guarini, *La Vie est un roman* (also known as *Life Is a Bed of Roses* and *Life Is a Novel*), Spectrafilm, 1984; Peppe, *I soliti ignoti vent'anni dopo* (also known as *Big Deal on Madonna Street . . . Twenty Years Later*), Medusa, 1985; Gotried, *Le Pouvoir du mal* (also known as *The Power of Evil*), Pierson/TF1/Maki/ Challenge, 1985; Carlo and Carlo's grandfather, *La famiglia* (also known as *The Family* and *La Famille*), Roissy/Vestron, 1987; baron, *I picari* (also known as *The Rogues* and *The Picaros*), Warner Brothers, 1987; Uncle Lucca, *Lo zio indegno* (also known as *The Sleazy Uncle, The Uncle,* and *The Unworthy Uncle*), Filmexport Group/Titanus Distribuzione, 1989.

Also appeared as title role, *Daniele Cortis,* 1946; Svabrin, *La figlia del capitano,* 1947; in *Le avventure de Pinocchio,* 1947; Casanova, *Il cavaliere misterioso* (also known as *Mysterious Rider*), 1948; Pietro, *Il lupo della Sila* (also known as *The Lure of Sila*), 1949; Turi, *I fuorilegge,* 1949; Giorgio, *Ho sognato il paradiso,* 1949; Yusef, *Lo sparviero del Nilo,* 1949; Mauro, *Il leone di Amalfi,* 1950; Renato Salvi, *Il tradimento,* 1951; Don Antonio, *Il sogno di Zorro,* 1951; Mauricio, *La corona negra* (also known as *La coronna nera*), 1952; Michele, *La tratta delle bianche,* 1952; Prince Sergio, *La donna piu bella del mondo* (also known as *The World's Most Beautiful Woman* and *Beautiful But Dangerous*), 1955; Giovanni d'Medici, *Giovanni delle Bande Nere,* 1956; title role, *Kean,* 1956; Michele, *La cambiale,* 1959; *Le sorprese dell'amore,* 1959; Caparra, *Fantasmi a Roma,* 1960; O'Caporale, *I briganti italiani,* 1961; Cimino, *Il giudizio universale,* 1961; *Una vita difficile,* 1961; Adriano, *Anima Nera,* 1962; Domenico Rocchetti, *La marcia su Roma,* 1962; L'Avvocato, "L'avaro" in *L'amore difficile,* 1962; Captain Nardoni, *Frenesia dell'estate,* 1963; Mario Ravicchio, *Il gaucho,* 1964; Luci Ridolfi, *Slalom,* 1965; Brancaleone da Norcia, *L'armata Brancaleone*, 1966; Bastiano da Sangallo, *Le piacevoli notti*, 1966; Pietro Breccia, *Il profeta*, 1967; Rafus, *Dove vai tutta nuda?*, 1969; Fulvio Bertuccia, *Il'arcagelo*, 1969; Filippo/Giulio, *La pecora nera*, 1969; Vittorio, *L'alibi*, 1969.

Riccardo, "La bomba alla televisione" in *Contestazione generale*, 1970; Leonardo, *Il divorzio*, 1970; title role, *Scipione detto anche l'Africano*, 1970; Guido Guidi, *Che c'entriamo noi con la rivoluzione?*, 1972; Scarpia, *La Tosca*, 1973; *The Prophet*, 1976; Franco Denza, *I Telefoni bianchi*, 1976; Antonie Mancuso, *Come una rosa al naso* (also known as *Pure As a Rose*), 1976; *We All Loved Each Other So Much*, Almi Cinema V, 1977; Achille Mengaroni, *Camera d'albergo*, 1980; *Sono fotogenico* (also known as *I'm Photogenic*), United Artists, 1980; Ciro Coppa, *Il turno*, 1981; *Di padre in figlio* (also known as *From Father to Son*), SACIS, 1983; and in *The Outlaws, Streets of Sorrow, Girls Marked Danger, The House of the Lord,* and *The Hateful Dead.*

PRINCIPAL FILM WORK—Director, *Senza famiglia nullatenenti cercano affetto* (also known as *Without Family*), Interfilm, 1972; director, *Di padre in figlio* (also known as *From Father to Son*), SACIS, 1983; also directed (with Francesco Rosi), *Kean*, 1956; and (with Adolfo Celi and Luciano Lucignani), *L'alibi*, 1969.

PRINCIPAL TELEVISION APPEARANCES—Series: Gerardo, *Il mattatore*, 1958-59. Specials: Host, *Night of Music*, Arts and Entertainment, 1990.

RELATED CAREER—Founder, Teatro Popolare Italiano (a theatre company), 1960.

WRITINGS: STAGE—*Viva Vittorio!* (one-man show), Center Theatre Group, Mark Taper Forum, Los Angeles, then Promenade Theatre, New York City, both 1984. FILM—(Co-writer) *Kean*, 1956; (co-writer) *L'alibi*, 1969; (co-writer) *Senza famiglia nullatenenti cercano affetto* (also known as *Without Family*), Interfilm, 1972; *Di padre in figlio* (also known as *From Father to Son*), SACIS, 1983. TELEVISION—Episodic: *Il attatore*, 1958-59. OTHER—*Une grande avvenire dietro le spalle*, 1981.

AWARDS: Best Actor Award from the Cannes Film Festival, 1975, for *Profumo di donna;* also received Italian awards as theatre actor of the year (four times) and film actor of the year (four times).

ADDRESSES: OFFICE—Via Flaminia 497, 00191 Rome, Italy.

*   *   *

GAYNES, George   1917-
(George Jongejans)

PERSONAL: Born George Jongejans, May 3, 1917, in Helsinki, Finland; son of Gerritt (in business) and Iya Grigorievna Gay, Lady Abdy (an artist) Jongejans; married Allyn Ann McLerie (an actress), December 20, 1953; children: one son, one daughter. EDUCATION—Graduated from the College Classique Cantonal (Lausanne, Switzerland), 1937; attended Scuola Musicale di Milano, 1938-39; trained for the stage with Lee Strasberg, 1953-58, and with John Daggett Howell, 1960. MILITARY—Royal Netherlands Navy, sub-lieutenant, 1943-45; Royal British Navy, 1945-46.

VOCATION: Actor and opera singer.

CAREER: STAGE DEBUT—(As George Jongejans) Merlin, *The Wizard* (opera), Teatro della Triennale, Milan, Italy, 1940. BROADWAY DEBUT—(As George Jongejans) Mr. Kofner, *The Consul* (opera), Ethel Barrymore Theatre, 1950. LONDON DEBUT—Jeff Moss, *Bells Are Ringing*, Coliseum Theatre, 1957. PRINCIPAL STAGE APPEARANCES—(As George Jongejans) Jupiter, *Out of This World*, New Century Theatre, New York City, 1951; Danilo, *The Merry Widow* (opera), University of Utah, Salt Lake City, UT, 1951; Bob Baker, *Wonderful Town*, Winter Garden Theatre, New York City, 1953; King David, *Absalom*, Artists Theatre, New York City, 1956; Mr. Lockit, *The Beggar's Opera*, City Center Theatre, New York City, 1957; Erno Gero, *Shadow of Heroes*, York Playhouse, New York City, 1961; ensemble, *Brecht on Brecht* (revue), American National Theatre and Academy (ANTA) Theatre Matinee Series, Theatre De Lys, New York City, 1961; Judge Aristide Forestier, *Can-Can*, City Center Theatre, 1962; Private Willis, *Iolante*, Don Alhambra de Bolero, *The Gondoliers*, and title role, *The Mikado*, all City Center Theatre, 1962; buyer, *The Lady of the Camellias*, Winter Garden Theatre, 1963; the Prisoner, *Dynamite Tonight*, York Playhouse, 1964; Don Pedro, *Beatrice et Benedict* (opera), Washington DC Opera Company, Washington, DC, 1964; title role, *The Mikado* and Sergeant Meryll, *The Yeoman of the Guard*, both City Center Theatre, 1965; John Cleves, *Any Wednesday*, Music Box Theatre, New York City, 1965, then George Abbott Theatre, New York City, 1966; the Father, *Of Love Remembered*, ANTA Theatre, 1967; the Prisoner, *Dynamite Tonight*, Martinique Theatre, New York City, 1967; Mr. Scott, *Posterity for Sale*, American Place Theatre, St. Clement's Church Theatre, New York City, 1967; Orgon, *Tartuffe*, Inner City Repertory Theatre, Los Angeles, 1967; Henry Higgins, *My Fair Lady*, Civic Light Opera, Honolulu, HI, 1968.

Jupiter, *Metamorphoses*, Center Theatre Group, Mark Taper Forum, Los Angeles, 1971; Maitre du Frene, *Gigi*, Uris Theatre, New York City, then Playhouse Theatre, Wilmington, DE, both 1973; Robert Baker, *Wonderful Town*, Dorothy Chandler Pavilion, Los Angeles, then San Francisco, CA, both 1975. Also appeared in (as George Jongejans) *La Malade imaginaire*, Maison du Peuple, Lausanne, Switzerland, 1935; (as George Jongejans) *Pulcinella* (opera), Teatro della Triennale, Milan, Italy, 1940; (as George Jongejans) in concert, Salle du Conservatoire, Paris, France, 1947; *God Bless*, Yale Drama School, New Haven, CT, 1968; and as Leporello, *Don Giovanni*, Figaro, *Le Nozze di Figaro*, and Dandini, *Cenerentola* (operas), all with the New York City Opera Company.

MAJOR TOURS—Henry Higgins, *My Fair Lady*, U.S. cities, 1964; Michael Jardeen, *A Community of Two*, U.S. cities, 1973; Maitre du Frene, *Gigi*, U.S. cities, 1974; also appeared in *Jacobowsky and the Colonel*, U.S. cities, 1967.

FILM DEBUT—*P.T. 109*, Warner Brothers, 1962. PRINCIPAL FILM APPEARANCES—Brook Latham, *The Group*, United Artists, 1966; Paul McGill, *Doctors' Wives*, Columbia, 1971; El Morocco captain, *The Way We Were*, Columbia, 1973; mission director, *Marooned*, Twentieth Century-Fox, 1973; Dr. Marderosian, *The Boy Who Cried Werewolf*, Universal, 1973; Reginald Kingsley, *Nickelodeon*, Columbia, 1976; Prince, *Harry and Walter Go to New York*, Columbia, 1976; Dr. Wissenschaft, *Altered States*, Warner Brothers, 1980; Dr. Forrest, *Dead Men Don't Wear Plaid*, Universal, 1982; John Van Horn, *Tootsie*, Columbia, 1982; Ravitch, *To Be or Not to Be*, Twentieth Century-Fox, 1983; Dr. Eugene Glztszki, *Micki and Maude*, Columbia, 1984; Commandant Lassard, *Police Academy*, Warner Brothers, 1984; Commandant Lassard, *Police Academy 2: Their First Assignment*, Warner Brothers, 1985; Commandant Lassard, *Police Academy 3: Back in Training*, Warner Brothers, 1986; Commandant Lassard, *Police Academy 4: Citizens on Patrol*, Warner Brothers, 1987; Commandant Lassard, *Police Academy 5: Assignment Miami Beach*, Warner Brothers, 1988; Commandant Lassard, *Police Academy 6: City Under Siege*, Warner Brothers, 1989. Also appeared in *Joy House* (also known as *Les Felins* and *The Love Cage*), Metro-Goldwyn-Mayer, 1964; *Ternosecco* (also known as *I'll Be Right Back, I numeri del lotto, The Numbers Game, Nini Ternosecco*, and *The Lottery Game*), Cecchi Gori Group/Fair Film, 1986; *Un tassinaro a New York* (also known as *A Taxi Driver in New York*), Italian International, 1987.

PRINCIPAL TELEVISION APPEARANCES—Series: Sam Reynolds, *Search for Tomorrow*, CBS, 1971; Frank Smith, *General Hospital*, ABC, 1980; Henry Warnimont, *Punky Brewster*, NBC, 1984-86; voice of Henry Warnimont, *Punky Brewster* (animated), NBC, 1985-87; Arthur Feldman, *The Days and Nights of Molly Dodd*, NBC, 1988, then Lifetime, 1989—. Mini-Series: Orestes Bradley, *Captains and the Kings*, NBC, 1976; Max Vincent, *Rich Man, Poor Man—Book II*, ABC, 1976-77; Brewster Perry, *Washington: Behind Closed Doors*, ABC, 1977; John Prince, *Scruples*, CBS, 1980. Pilots: David Allen, *The Girl in the Empty Grave*, NBC, 1977. Episodic: Gerald Millburn, *Hotel*, ABC, 1986; Judge Dunaway, *Matlock*, NBC, 1987; also *East Side/West Side*, CBS, 1963; *Cheers*, NBC, 1983; *The Defenders*, CBS; *Armstrong Circle Theatre*, NBC; *The U.S. Steel Hour*, CBS; *Alfred Hitchcock*, CBS; *Accent*, CBS; *Bonanza*, NBC; *Columbo*, NBC; *The Law*, NBC; *The Six Million Dollar Man*, ABC; *Mannix*, CBS; *Hawaii Five-0*, CBS; *Mission: Impossible*, CBS. Movies: Dr. Chester Ramsey, *Trilogy of Terror*, ABC, 1975; Harding, *Woman of the Year*, CBS, 1976; Wylie, *Breaking Up Is Hard to Do*, ABC, 1979; Evita's doctor, *Evita Peron*, NBC, 1981; Archangel, *It Came Upon the Midnight Clear*, syndicated, 1984. Specials: Dancing master, *The Would-Be Gentleman*, CBS, 1955; Whitelaw Savory, *One Touch of Venus*, NBC, 1955; commander, "Mom's on Strike," *ABC Afterschool Specials*, ABC, 1984; also *Hallmark Hall of Fame*, NBC.

PRINCIPAL TELEVISION WORK—Episodic: Director, *WKRP in Cincinnati*, CBS.

RELATED CAREER—(As George Jongejans) First and second basso, Opera House, Mulhouse, France, 1947-48; (as George Jongejans) first basso, Opera House, Strasbourg, France, 1948-49; (as George Jongejans) basso, New York City Opera; member, Actors' Studio, New York City, 1960—; acting teacher, Yale University, New Haven, CT, 1968-69.

MEMBER: American Guild of Musical Artists, Actors' Equity Association, American Federation of Television and Radio Artists, Screen Actors Guild.

ADDRESSES: AGENT—Jonathan Howard, Triad Artists, 10100 Santa Monica Boulevard, 16th Floor, Los Angeles, CA 90067.*

*   *   *

GAZZO, Michael V. 1923-

PERSONAL: Full name, Michael Vincente Gazzo; born April 5, 1923, in Hillside, NJ; son of Michael Basile (a bartender) and Elvira (Lunga) Gazzo; married Grace Benn, July 8, 1944; children: Peppi, Michael, Christopher. EDUCATION—Graduated from the Dramatic Workshop of the New School for Social Research, 1949; trained

MICHAEL V. GAZZO

for the stage at the Actors' Studio. MILITARY—U.S. Army Air Forces, 1942-44.

VOCATION: Actor, director, and writer.

CAREER: Also see WRITINGS below. PRINCIPAL STAGE APPEARANCES—Tripe Face, *The Aristocrats*, President Theatre, New York City, 1946; Dr. Einstein, *Arsenic and Old Lace*, Great Neck Playhouse, Great Neck, NY, 1946; Ben Hubbard, *The Little Foxes*, Shields, *Shadow of a Gunman*, Captain Boyle, *Juno and the Paycock*, Uncle, *The Trial*, and in *The Sheepwell* and *The Petrified Forest*, all with the Dramatic Workshop of the New School for Social Research, President Theatre and Rooftop Theatre, New York City, 1946-49; Destructive Desmond, *The Dog Beneath the Skin*, Cherry Lane Theatre, New York City, 1947; beggar, *Night Music*, Equity Library Theatre, American National Theatre and Academy Theatre, New York City, 1951; A. Ratt, *Camino Real*, National Theatre, New York City, 1953.

PRINCIPAL STAGE WORK—All as director, unless indicated. Associate director, *Alfred*, Great Neck Playhouse, Great Neck, NY, 1946; *Androcles and the Lion*, Great Neck Playhouse, 1946; (with Alexis Solomas) *The Dog Beneath the Skin*, Cherry Lane Theatre, New York City, 1947; *Within the Gates*, Provincetown Playhouse, New York City, 1947; *Yes Is for a Very Young Man*, Off-Broadway Inc., New York City, 1949. Also *The Imbecile* and *The Cause of It All*, both with the Dramatic Workshop of the New School for Social Research.

PRINCIPAL FILM APPEARANCES—Black suit, *The Gang That*

Couldn't Shoot Straight, Metro-Goldwyn-Mayer, 1971; Frank Pentangeli, *The Godfather, Part II*, Paramount, 1974; Muzi, *Black Sunday*, Paramount, 1977; Ben Angelelli, *Fingers*, Brut, 1978; Spiro Georgio, *King of the Gypsies*, Paramount, 1978; Harry, *The Fish That Saved Pittsburgh*, United Artists, 1979; Lobo, *Love and Bullets*, Associated Film Distribution, 1979; Police Chief Clark, *Alligator*, Group I, 1980; Rosselini, *Cuba Crossing* (also known as *Kill Castro* and *Assignment: Kill Castro*), Key West, 1980; Tazio, *Back Roads*, Warner Brothers, 1981; Frankie, *Body and Soul*, Cannon, 1981; Sonny, *Cannonball Run II*, Warner Brothers, 1984; Mike, *Fear City*, Chevy Chase Distribution, 1984; Carmine, *Cookie*, Warner Brothers, 1989. Also appeared in *On the Waterfront*, Columbia, 1954; *The Pride and the Passion*, United Artists, 1957; *A Man Called Adam*, Embassy, 1966; *Crazy Joe*, Columbia, 1974; *Sudden Impact*, Warner Brothers, 1983; *The Gun*, Columbia.

TELEVISION DEBUT—Russian officer, *Philco Television Playhouse*, NBC, 1950. PRINCIPAL TELEVISION APPEARANCES—Pilots: Banker, *Beach Patrol*, ABC, 1979. Episodic: *The Quest*, NBC, 1976; *Future Cop*, ABC, 1977; *Taxi*, ABC, 1979; *Supertrain*, NBC, 1979; *Sweepstakes*, NBC, 1979; *B.A.D. Cats*, ABC, 1980; *Small and Frye*, CBS, 1983; also *Crime Syndicated*, CBS; *Goodyear Television Playhouse*, NBC; *Danger*, CBS; *Crime Photographer*, CBS; *Robert Montgomery Presents Your Lucky Strike Theatre*, NBC; *Suspense*, CBS; *Assignment Manhunt* (also known as *Manhunt*), NBC; *The Defenders*, CBS; *Kojak*, CBS; *Medical Center*, CBS; *Baretta*, ABC; *Alice*, CBS; *Welcome Back, Kotter*, ABC; *Switch*, CBS; *Starsky and Hutch*, ABC; *Feather and Father Gang*, ABC; *Serpico*, NBC; *Columbo*, NBC; *Barnaby Jones*, CBS; *Vega$*, ABC; *Fantasy Island*, ABC; *Magnum P.I.*, CBS; *The Fall Guy*, ABC; *Cagney and Lacey*, CBS; *Darkroom*, ABC; *Ellery Queen*; *Beach Patrol*; *The Clock*; *Celebrity Time*; and *Crime of the Century*. Movies: Mario Russo, *Brink's: The Great Robbery*, CBS, 1976; Sartene, *Beggarman, Thief*, NBC, 1979; Tripoli, *Sizzle*, ABC, 1981; Johnny Masseta, *Blood Feud*, syndicated, 1983; Marullo, *John Steinbeck's "The Winter of Our Discontent,"* CBS, 1983; Sal Arcola, *First and Ten*, HBO, 1985; Joseph Salina, *Blood Ties*, Showtime, 1986.

RELATED CAREER—Acting teacher, 1950—; member, Actors' Studio, 1952—; founder, Gazzo Theatre Workshop, Los Angeles, CA.

NON-RELATED CAREER—Machinist.

WRITINGS: STAGE—*A Hatful of Rain*, Lyceum Theatre, New York City, 1955; *Night Circus*, John Golden Theatre, New York City, 1958; *The Death of the Kitchen Table in Our Fair City*, 1966; *What Do You Really Know About Your Husband?*, Shubert Theatre, New Haven, CT, 1967; *And All That Jazz* and *Like They Did the Buffalo*, both Actors' Studio, New York City, 1967; also *My Name Ain't Abe*, Dramatic Workshop, New York City. FILM—(With Alfred Hayes) *A Hatful of Rain*, Twentieth Century-Fox, 1957; *King Creole*, Paramount, 1958; *The World of Johnny Cool*, United Artists, 1964. TELEVISION—*A Hatful of Rain*, ABC, 1968.

AWARDS: *Variety* Drama Critics' Poll Award, Most Promising Playwright (tied with Paddy Chayefsky), 1955-56, for *A Hatful of Rain;* the screenplay for the film version of *A Hatful of Rain* was named One of the Best Screenplays of 1957 by *Film Daily;* Rockefeller Foundation grant, 1966, for *The Death of the Kitchen Table in Our Fair City;* Academy Award nomination, Best Supporting Actor, 1975, for *The Godfather, Part II;* Lee Strasberg Actors' Studio Award.

MEMBER: Actors' Equity Association, American Federation of Television and Radio Artist, Dramatists Guild, Screen Writers Guild, Screen Actors Guild.

SIDELIGHTS: RECREATIONS—Painting, photography, films, and sculpting.

ADDRESSES: AGENT—Mike Greenfield, Charter Management, 9000 Sunset Boulevard, Los Angeles, CA 90069.

*   *   *

GEESON, Judy   1948-

PERSONAL: Born September 10, 1948, in Arundel, England. EDUCATION—Studied acting at the Corona Stage School.

VOCATION: Actress.

CAREER: OFF-BROADWAY DEBUT—Marigold Watson, *The Common Pursuit*, Promenade Theatre, New York City, 1986. PRINCIPAL STAGE APPEARANCES—Desdemona, *An Othello*, Open Space Theatre, London, 1972; Lavinia, *Titus Andronicus*, Royal Shakespeare Company (RSC), Aldwych Theatre, London, 1973; Vivien 532, *Section Nine*, RSC, the Place, Stratford-on-Avon, U.K., 1973; Lizzie, *Next Time I'll Sing to You*, Greenwich Theatre, London, 1980; Lemon's mother, *Aunt Dan and Lemon*, Mark Taper Forum, Taper Too, Los Angeles, 1987; Zoe, *Henceforward . . .*, Alley Theatre, Houston, TX, 1987. Also appeared in *The Real Thing*, Strand Theatre, London, 1985; and in productions of *Two Gentlemen of Verona* and *An Ideal Husband*.

PRINCIPAL FILM APPEARANCES—Jane, *Wings of Mystery*, Children's Film Foundation, 1963; Angela Rivers, *Berserk*, Columbia, 1967; Pamela Dare, *To Sir, with Love*, Columbia, 1967; Sue Trenton, *Hammerhead*, Columbia, 1968; Mary Gloucester, *Here We Go Round the Mulberry Bush*, United Artists, 1968; Geraldine Hardcastle, *Prudence and the Pill*, Twentieth Century-Fox, 1968; Ella Patterson, *Three into Two Won't Go*, Universal, 1969; Jane, *Two Gentlemen Sharing*, American International, 1969; Polly Bendel, *The Executioner*, Columbia, 1970; Jacki Dewar, *Goodbye Gemini*, Cinerama, 1970; Beryl Evans, *10 Rillington Place*, Columbia, 1971; Peggy Heller, *Fear in the Night*, International, 1972; Jennifer Thatcher, *Brannigan*, United Artists, 1975; Sergeant Tilly Willing, *Carry On England*, Rank, 1976; Pamela Verecker, *The Eagle Has Landed*, Columbia, 1976; Marjorie Craven, *Dominique*, Subotsky, 1978; Dr. Fairweather, *It's Not the Size That Counts* (also known as *Percy's Progress*), Joseph Brenner, 1979; Sandy, *Horror Planet* (also known as *Inseminoid*), Almi, 1982; voice of Pekinese, *The Plague Dogs* (animated), United International, 1984; Anthea, *The Price of Life*, Discovery Program/Chanticleer, 1988. Also appeared in *Haendeligt Uheld* (also known as *One of Those Things*), Nordisk Film Kompagni, 1970; *Doomwatch*, Tigon, 1972; *Diagnosis: Murder*, Silhouette, 1974.

PRINCIPAL TELEVISION APPEARANCES—Series: Fulvia, *Star Maidens*, syndicated, 1977. Mini-Series: Caroline Penvenen, *Poldark II*, BBC, then *Masterpiece Theatre*, PBS, 1978; Susan, *Danger UXB*, Thames Television, then *Masterpiece Theatre*, PBS, 1981. Pilots: Jody Kenyon, *Sam Hill: Who Killed the Mysterious Mr. Foster?*, NBC, 1971. Episodic: Sister Ruth, *Murder, She Wrote*, CBS, 1986; Marlena, *The A-Team*, NBC, 1986; Patricia Magnuson, *Hotel*, ABC, 1986; Elena/Liane, *MacGyver*, ABC,

1988; also *Secret Agent*, CBS, 1966; "Night Is the Time for Killing," *Wide World of Mystery*, ABC, 1975; "Another Time, Another Place," *Space 1999*, syndicated, 1976. Movies: Babs, *The Secret Life of Kathy McCormick*, NBC, 1988. Specials: Helen Marlow, *Murder on the Midnight Express*, ABC, 1975.

ADDRESSES: AGENTS—Richard Stone Partnership, 25 Whitehall Street, London SW1A 2BS, England; Writers and Artists Agency, 11726 San Vicente Boulevard, Suite 300, Los Angeles, CA 90049.*

*   *   *

GEORGE, Lynda Day   1946-
   (Lynda Day)

PERSONAL: Born December 11, 1946, in San Marcos, TX; married second husband, Christopher George (an actor), May 15, 1970 (died, November 29, 1983); children: Nicky (first marriage).

VOCATION: Actress.

CAREER: PRINCIPAL FILM APPEARANCES—(As Lynda Day) Kim, *The Outsider*, Universal, 1962; (as Lynda Day) Judy Reynolds, *The Gentle Rain*, Allied Artists, 1966; (as Lynda Day) Sue McSween, *Chisum*, Warner Brothers, 1970; Terry Marsh, *Day of the Animals* (also known as *Something Is Out There*), Film Ventures, 1977; Kate, *The Amazing Captain Nemo*, Columbia/EMI/Warner, 1978; Monica, *Racquet*, Cal-Am, 1979; Barbara, *Beyond Evil*, Scope III, 1980; Eve Parsons, *Mortuary*, Film Ventures, 1983; Mary Riggs, *Pieces*, Spectacular, 1983; Beverly Carrigan, *Young Warriors*, Cannon, 1983. Also appeared in *Nitro*, 1978; *Beyond Reasonable Doubt*, Satori, 1980; and *The Junkman*, Halicki, 1982.

PRINCIPAL TELEVISION APPEARANCES—Series: (As Lynda Day) Amelia Cole, *The Silent Force*, ABC, 1970-71; Lisa Casey, *Mission: Impossible*, CBS, 1971-73; Kate Melton, *The Return of Captain Nemo*, CBS, 1978. Mini-Series: Linda Quales, *Rich Man, Poor Man*, ABC, 1976; Marge Chrysler, *Once an Eagle*, NBC, 1976-77; Mrs. Reynolds, *Roots*, ABC, 1977. Pilots: (As Lynda Day) Barbara Keeley, *The Sound of Anger*, NBC, 1968; (as Lynda Day) Lillian Crane, *The House on Greenapple Road*, ABC, 1970; (as Lynda Day) Christie, *Cannon*, CBS, 1971; Clio DuBois, *The Barbary Coast*, ABC, 1975; Lisa Manning, *Mrs. R—Death Among Friends*, NBC, 1975; Nancy Pendleton, *Twin Detectives*, ABC, 1976; Carol, *Casino*, ABC, 1980; Margo Hilliard, *Quick and Quiet*, CBS, 1981. Episodic: Nazi superwoman, *Wonder Woman*, CBS, 1976; Louise Richmond, *Blacke's Magic*, NBC, 1986; Lisa Casey, *Mission: Impossible*, ABC, 1989; also *Archie Bunker's Place*, CBS, 1981; *Fantasy Island*, ABC. Movies: (As Lynda Day) Barbara, *Fear No Evil*, NBC, 1969; (as Lynda Day) Almy Gregory, *The Sheriff*, ABC, 1971; (as Lynda Day) Molly Thornburgh, *Set This Town on Fire*, NBC, 1973; Sara Cornell, *She Cried Murder*, CBS, 1973; Mary Ellen Lewis, *Panic on the 5:22*, ABC, 1974; Louise Kennelly, *The Trial of Chaplain Jensen*, ABC, 1975; Cathy Armello, *Mayday at 40,000 Feet!*, CBS, 1976; Valerie Adams, *It Happened at Lakewood Manor*, ABC, 1977; Margo Mannering, *Murder at the World Series*, ABC, 1977; Sandra Barry, *Cruise into Terror*, ABC, 1978. Specials: Cathy Moore, *Come Out, Come Out, Wherever You Are*, ABC, 1974; *Battle of the Network Stars*, ABC, 1977; *ABC's Silver Anniversary Special—25 and Still the One*, ABC, 1978.

RELATED CAREER—Professional model.

AWARDS: Emmy Award nomination, 1981, for *Archie Bunker's Place;* also received an Emmy Award nomination for *Mission: Impossible*.

ADDRESSES: AGENT—Irv Schecter Company, 9300 Wilshire Boulevard, Suite 410, Beverly Hills, CA 90212.*

*   *   *

GOLDMAN, Bo   1932-

PERSONAL: Born September 10, 1932, in New York, NY; son of Julian (a Broadway producer and proprietor of retail stores) and Lillian (a hat model; maiden name, Levy) Goldman; married Mab Ashforth (a jewelry designer), January 2, 1954; children: Mia, Amy, Diana, Jesse, Serena, Justin. EDUCATION—Princeton University, A.B., 1953. MILITARY—U.S. Army, sergeant, 1954-56.

VOCATION: Screenwriter, producer, and director.

CAREER: Also see *WRITINGS* below. PRINCIPAL TELEVISION WORK—Series: Associate producer, *Playhouse 90*, CBS, 1958-60; producer, *NET Playhouse*, WNET, 1970-71; producer, *Theater in America*, PBS, 1972-74.

WRITINGS: STAGE—Lyricist (with Glen Paxton), *First Impressions*, Alvin Theatre, New York City, 1959. FILM—(With Lawrence Hauben) *One Flew Over the Cuckoo's Nest*, United Artists, 1975; (with Maximilian Schell and Friedrich Duerrenmatt) *Der Richter und Sein Henker* (also known as *End of the Game* and *Murder on the Bridge*), Twentieth Century-Fox, 1975; (with William Kerby and Michael Cimino) *The Rose*, Twentieth Century-Fox, 1979; *Melvin and Howard*, Universal, 1980; *Shoot the Moon*, Metro-Goldwyn-Mayer/United Artists, 1982; (with Rob Morton) *Swing Shift*, Warner Brothers, 1984; (with John Hill) *Little Nikita*, Columbia, 1988. TELEVISION—Series: *NET Playhouse*, PBS, 1970-71; *Theatre in America*, PBS, 1972-74. OTHER—Contributor of articles to the *New York Times*.

AWARDS: Academy Award, Best Screenplay Adapted from Other Material, Golden Globe Award, Best Screenplay, and Writers Guild Award, all 1976, for *One Flew Over the Cuckoo's Nest;* Academy Award, Best Original Screenplay, New York Film Critics' Award, and Writers Guild Award, all 1981, for *Melvin and Howard*.

MEMBER: Writers Guild of America-West, Academy of Motion Pictures Arts and Sciences, Dramatists Guild, American Society of Composers, Authors, and Publishers.

ADDRESSES: AGENT—Jim Wiatt, International Creative Management, 8899 Beverly Boulevard, Los Angeles, CA 90048.*

GOLDMAN, James   1927-
(Winston Beard)

PERSONAL: Born June 30, 1927, in Chicago, IL; son of Maurice Clarence (in business) and Marion (Weil) Goldman; married Marie McKeon, March 5, 1962 (divorced, 1972); married Barbara Deren (a producer and manager), October 25, 1975; children: Julia, Matthew (first marriage). EDUCATION—University of Chicago, Ph.B., 1947, M.A., 1950; post-graduate work in musicology, Columbia University, 1950-52. MILITARY—U.S. Army, private first class, 1952-54.

VOCATION: Writer.

CAREER: See *WRITINGS* below. RELATED CAREER—Associate, Department of Film, Brooklyn College, Brooklyn, NY; member, Mayor's Ad Hoc Committee on Theatre, New York City.

WRITINGS: STAGE—*They Might Be Giants,* Stratford Theatre Royal, London, 1961; (with William Goldman) *Blood, Sweat, and Stanley Poole,* Morosco Theatre, New York City, 1961, published by Dramatists Play Service, 1962; lyrics and (with William Goldman) book, *A Family Affair,* Billy Rose Theatre, New York City, 1962; *The Lion in Winter,* Ambassador Theatre, New York City, 1966, first produced in London, 1969, published by Random House, 1966; book, *Follies,* Winter Garden Theatre, New York City, 1971, published by Random House, 1971, revised version produced in Manchester, U.K., 1985, then in London, 1987.

FILM—*The Lion in Winter,* AVCO-Embassy, 1968, published by Dell, 1968; (with Edward Bond) *Nicholas and Alexandra,* Columbia, 1971; *They Might Be Giants,* Universal, 1971, published by Lancer Books, 1970; *Robin and Marian,* Columbia, 1976, published by Bantam, 1976; (with Eric Hughes) *White Nights,* Columbia, 1985.

TELEVISION—Mini-Series: (As Winston Beard; with April Smith) *Queenie,* ABC, 1987. Movies: *Oliver Twist,* CBS, 1982; (with Simon Langton) *Anna Karenina,* CBS, 1985; *Anastasia: The Mystery of Anna,* NBC, 1986. Specials: *Evening Primrose,* ABC, 1967; "Follies in Concert," *Great Performances,* PBS, 1986.

OTHER—*Waldorf* (novel), Random House, 1965; *The Man from Greek and Roman* (novel), Random House, 1974; *Myself as Witness* (novel), Random House, 1980; (contributor) *Where to Eat in America* (nonfiction), Scribners, 1987; (contributor) *Feast of Wine and Food* (nonfiction), Morrow, 1987; *Fulton County* (novel), Morrow, 1989; also contributor to such periodicals as *Atlantic Monthly, Chicago Tribune Book World, Dramatics Magazine, Harpers Bazaar, Penthouse,* and *Food and Wine.*

AWARDS: Academy Award, Best Adapted Screenplay, 1968, American Screenwriters Award, 1968, Writers Guild Award, 1968, Golden Globe nomination, 1968, British Screenwriters Award, 1969, and Zeta Plaque from the Writers Guild of Great Britain, 1969, all for *A Lion in Winter;* New York Drama Critics Award (with Stephen Sondheim), Best New Musical, 1971, and Antoinette Perry Award nomination, Best Book for a Musical, 1972, both for *Follies;* Writers Guild Award nomination, Best Teleplay, 1983, for *Oliver Twist;* Diplome d'Honneur from the Corporation des Vignerons de Champagne, 1985; *Drama* Magazine Award, *Evening Standard* Award, Olivier Award, and *Plays and Players* Award, all Best Musical, 1987, for *Follies* (revised version); Writers Guild Award nomination, Best Teleplay, 1988, for *Anastasia: The Mystery of Anna.*

JAMES GOLDMAN

MEMBER: Dramatists Guild (council member, 1966—), Authors League of America (council member, 1966—), Academy of Motion Picture Arts and Sciences, National Academy of Television Arts and Sciences, Writers Guild, Broadcast Music Incorporated, French Academy of Playwrights, National Academy of Recording Artists, P.E.N., Explorers Club (fellow), Les Compagnons du Beaujolais, New York Athletic Club.

SIDELIGHTS: RECREATIONS—Croquet, tennis, music, and reading.

ADDRESSES: AGENTS—Hal Ross and Ron Mardigian, William Morris Agency, 151 El Camino Drive, Beverly Hills, CA 90212. MANAGER—Barbara Deren Goldman, Barbara Deren Associates Inc., 965 Fifth Avenue, Penthouse, New York, NY 10021.

*   *   *

GOLDWYN, Samuel, Jr.   1926-

PERSONAL: Full name, Samuel John Goldwyn, Jr.; born September 7, 1926, in Los Angeles, CA; son of Samuel John (a film producer) and Frances (Howard) Goldwyn; married Peggy Elliott, August 23, 1969; children: Catherine, Francis, John, Anthony, Elizabeth, Peter. EDUCATION—Attended the University of Virginia. MILITARY—U.S. Army, 1944-46 and 1951-52.

VOCATION: Producer and director.

CAREER: PRINCIPAL STAGE WORK—Producer, *Gathering Storm,* London, England.

FIRST FILM WORK—Producer, *Man with the Gun* (also known as *Man Without a Gun* and *The Trouble Shooter*), United Artists, 1955. PRINCIPAL FILM WORK—All as producer, unless indicated: *The Sharkfighters*, United Artists, 1956; *The Proud Rebel*, Buena Vista, 1958; *The Adventures of Huckleberry Finn*, Metro-Goldwyn-Mayer (MGM), 1960; (also director) *The Young Lovers*, MGM, 1964; *Cotton Comes to Harlem*, United Artists, 1970; *Come Back, Charleston Blue*, Warner Brothers, 1972; *The Golden Seal*, Samuel Goldwyn Company/New Realm, 1983; executive producer, *Once Bitten*, Samuel Goldwyn Company, 1985; executive producer, *A Prayer for the Dying*, Samuel Goldwyn Company, 1987; *Mr. North*, Samuel Goldwyn Company, 1988; executive producer, *Mystic Pizza*, Samuel Goldwyn Company, 1988. Also director of *Alliance for Peace* and other documentaries for the U.S. Army.

PRINCIPAL TELEVISION WORK—All as producer, unless indicated. Series: *Adventure*, CBS, 1952-53; also *The Unexpected*, 1954. Pilots: *The Unexplained*, NBC, 1956. Specials: *59th Annual Academy Awards Presentation*, ABC, 1987; executive producer, "April Morning," *Hallmark Hall of Fame*, CBS, 1988; *60th Annual Academy Awards Presentation*, ABC, 1988.

RELATED CAREER—Writer and associate producer, J. Arthur Rank Organization; owner and chief executive officer, Samuel Goldwyn Company, Los Angeles, 1978—; trustee, American Film Institute; board of directors, Centre Theatre Group, Los Angeles.

NON-RELATED CAREER—President of the board of trustees, Fountain Valley School, CO; president, Samuel Goldwyn Foundation.

AWARDS: Emmy Award, Outstanding Variety/Music Events Programming, 1988, for *60th Annual Academy Awards Presentation;* also Edinburgh Film Festival Prize for *Alliance for Peace.*

ADDRESSES: OFFICE—Samuel Goldwyn Company, 10203 Santa Monica Boulevard, Los Angeles, CA 90067.*

*   *   *

GORDON, Bert I.   1922-

PERSONAL: Born September 24, 1922, in Kenosha, WI; wife's name, Flora; children: Susan. EDUCATION—Attended the University of Wisconsin.

VOCATION: Producer, director, special effects coordinator, and screenwriter.

CAREER: Also see *WRITINGS* below. PRINCIPAL FILM WORK—All as producer and director, unless indicated: *Serpent Island*, Medallion-TV, 1954; *King Dinosaur*, Lippert, 1955; *Beginning of the End*, Republic, 1957; (also special effects coordinator) *The Amazing Colossal Man*, American International, 1957; (also special effects coordinator) *Cyclops*, Allied Artists, 1957; (also special effects coordinator) *Attack of the Puppet People*, American International, 1958; (also special effects coordinator) *The Spider* (also known as *Earth vs. the Spider*), American International, 1958; (also special effects coordinator) *War of the Colossal Beast* (also known as *The Terror Strikes*), American International, 1958; *The Boy and the Pirates*, United Artists, 1960; producer (with Joe Steinberg) and director, *Tormented*, Allied Artists, 1960; *The Magic Sword*, United Artists, 1962; (also special effects coordinator) *Village of the Giants*, Embassy, 1965; *Picture Mommy Dead*, Embassy,

1966; (director only) *How to Succeed with Sex* (also known as *How to Succeed with the Opposite Sex*), Medford, 1970; *Necromancy* (also known as *The Witching*), Cinerama, 1972; (also cinematographer) *The Mad Bomber* (also known as *Police Connection: Detective Geronimo*), Cinemation, 1973; (also special effects coordinator) *The Food of the Gods*, American International, 1976; (also special effects coordinator with Roy Downey) *Empire of the Ants*, American International, 1977; *The Big Bet*, Golden Communications/Golden Harvest, 1986.

PRINCIPAL TELEVISION WORK—Series: Production supervisor, *The Racket Squad*, CBS, 1951-53.

RELATED CAREER—Producer of television commercials; television production supervisor.

WRITINGS: See production details above. FILM—*Serpent Island*, 1954; (with Al Zimbalist and Tom Gries) *King Dinosaur*, 1955; (with Mark Hanna) *The Amazing Colossal Man*, 1957; *Cyclops*, 1957; *The Spider*, 1958; *Attack of the Puppet People*, 1958; *Tormented*, 1960; *The Magic Sword*, 1962; *Village of the Giants*, 1965; *How to Succeed with Sex*, 1970; *Necromancy*, 1972; *The Mad Bomber*, 1973; *The Food of the Gods*, 1976; *The Big Bet*, 1986.*

*   *   *

GOULD, Harold   1923-

PERSONAL: Born Harold V. Goldstein, December 10, 1923, in Schenectady, NY; son of Louis Glen (a post office clerk) and Lillian (a clerk for the New York State Department of Health) Goldstein; married Lea Shampanier (an actress; professional name, Lea Vernon), August 20, 1950; children: Deborah, Joshua, Lowell. EDUCATION—New York State College for Teachers (now State University of New York at Albany), B.A., 1947; Cornell University, M.A., 1948, Ph.D., 1953. MILITARY—U.S. Army, 1943-45.

CAREER: Actor.

CAREER: STAGE DEBUT—Thomas Jefferson, *The Common Glory*, Amphitheatre, Williamsburg, VA, 1955. OFF-BROADWAY DEBUT—Dr. Edward Huml, *The Increased Difficulty of Concentration*, Repertory Theatre of Lincoln Center, Forum Theatre, 1969. PRINCIPAL STAGE APPEARANCES—Edmund, *King Lear* and Benedick, *Much Ado about Nothing*, both Oregon Shakespeare Festival, Ashland, OR, 1958; Old Man, *The World of Ray Bradbury*, Coronet Theatre, Los Angeles, 1964; Goldberg, *The Birthday Party*, University of California at Los Angeles Theatre Group, Los Angeles, 1966; Anselme and Harpagon, *The Miser*, Center Theatre Group, Mark Taper Forum, Los Angeles, 1968; Sosias, *Amphitryon*, Repertory Theatre of Lincoln Center, Forum Theatre, New York City, 1970; Artie Shaughnessy, *The House of Blue Leaves*, Truck and Warehouse Theatre, New York City, 1971; Glogauer, *Once in a Lifetime*, Center Theatre Group, Mark Taper Forum, 1975; Dr. Zubritsky, *Fools*, Eugene O'Neill Theatre, New York City, 1981; Jack, *Grownups*, Lyceum Theatre, New York City, 1981, then Center Theatre Group, Mark Taper Forum, 1982; Mr. Antrobus, *The Skin of Our Teeth*, Old Globe Theatre, San Diego, CA, 1983; Nat, *I'm Not Rappaport*, Seattle Repertory Theatre, Seattle, WA, 1984; Goldberg, *The Birthday Party*, Los Angeles Theatre Center, Los Angeles, 1986; Tom Garrison, *I Never Sang for My Father*, Eisenhower Theatre, Kennedy Center for the Performing Arts,

HAROLD GOULD

Washington, DC, then Center Theatre Group, Ahmanson Theatre, Los Angeles, both 1987; Beauchamp, *Artist Descending a Staircase,* Helen Hayes Theatre, New York City, 1989. Also appeared in *The Devils,* Center Theatre Group, Mark Taper Forum, 1967; *Buying Out,* Studio Arena Theatre, Buffalo, NY, 1971; *Touching Bottom,* American Place Theatre, New York City, 1978; with the Center Theatre Group, Mark Taper Forum, 1961; and in productions of *Seidman and Son, Rhinoceros, The Price,* and *Freud* (one-man show).

FILM DEBUT—*The Couch,* Warner Brothers, 1962. PRINCIPAL FILM APPEARANCES—Ponelli, *The Yellow Canary,* Twentieth Century-Fox, 1963; Arnie Tomkins, *Ready for the People,* Warner Brothers, 1964; cop, *Inside Daisy Clover,* Warner Brothers, 1965; Dr. Ostrer, *The Satan Bug,* United Artists, 1965; Ganucci's lawyer, *An American Dream* (also known as *See You in Hell, Darling*), Warner Brothers, 1966; Sheriff Spanner, *Harper* (also known as *The Moving Target*), Warner Brothers, 1966; doctor, *The Spy with My Face,* Metro-Goldwyn-Mayer, 1966; Colonel Holt, *Project X,* Paramount, 1968; Dr. Liebman, *The Arrangement,* Warner Brothers, 1969; Eric P. Scott, *The Lawyer,* Paramount, 1969; Colonel Nexdhet, *Mrs. Pollifax—Spy,* United Artists, 1971; Dr. Zerny, *Where Does It Hurt?,* Cinerama, 1972; Kid Twist, *The Sting,* Universal, 1973; mayor, *The Front Page,* Universal, 1974; Count Anton, *Love and Death,* United Artists, 1975; Dietz, *The Strongest Man in the World,* Buena Vista, 1975; Professor Baxter, *The Big Bus,* Paramount, 1976; Charles Gwynn, *Gus,* Buena Vista, 1976; Engulf, *Silent Movie,* Twentieth Century-Fox, 1976; Hector Moses, *The One and Only,* Paramount, 1978; judge, *Seems Like Old Times,* Columbia, 1980; Rockerfeller, *Playing for Keeps,* Universal, 1986; Francisco Galedo, *Romero,* August Entertainment/Four

Seasons Entertainment, 1989. Also appeared in *Two for the Seesaw,* United Artists, 1962; *Marnie,* Universal, 1964.

TELEVISION DEBUT—Hong Kong, *To Catch a Star,* 1960. PRINCIPAL TELEVISION APPEARANCES—Series: Chamberlain, *The Long, Hot Summer,* ABC, 1965-66; Norman Nugent, *He and She,* CBS, 1967-68; Martin Morgenstern, *Rhoda,* CBS, 1974-78; Harry Danton, *The Feather and Father Gang,* ABC, 1977; David Ross, *Park Place,* CBS, 1981; Jonah Foot, *Foot in the Door,* CBS, 1983; Ben Sprague, *Under One Roof,* NBC, 1985. Mini-Series: Carl Tessler, *Washington: Behind Closed Doors,* ABC, 1977. Pilots: Mr. Hunnicutt, *Under the Yum Yum Tree,* NBC, 1969; Carlson, *Ransom for a Dead Man,* NBC, 1971; Howard Cunningham, *Love and the Happy Days* (broadcast as an episode of *Love, American Style*), ABC, 1972; Dave Ryker, *Murdock's Gang,* CBS, 1973; Matthew Brandon, *Bachelor at Law,* CBS, 1973; Dr. Federicci, *Medical Story,* NBC, 1975; Samuel Quilt, *Flannery and Quilt,* NBC, 1976; Harry Danton, *Never Con a Killer,* ABC, 1977; Jack Waine, *No Complaints!,* NBC, 1985; Jack Traynor, *Tickets, Please* (broadcast as an episode of *CBS Summer Playhouse*), CBS, 1988.

Episodic: General Larrabee, "Probe 7—Over and Out," *The Twilight Zone,* CBS, 1963; radio announcer, "The Bewitchin' Pool," *The Twilight Zone,* CBS, 1964; Martin Morgenstern, *The Mary Tyler Moore Show,* CBS, 1972 and 1973; George Antrobus, "The Skin of Our Teeth," *American Playhouse,* PBS, 1983; Arnie, *The Golden Girls,* NBC, 1985; Dr. Victor Kosciusko, *Trapper John, M.D.,* CBS, 1985; Andrei Zernov, *Scarecrow and Mrs. King,* CBS, 1986; Harry Finncman, *L.A. Law,* NBC, 1986; Walter Wise, *Night Court,* NBC, 1986; Tom Garrison, "I Never Sang for My Father," *American Playhouse,* PBS, 1988; Charlie Drexel, *Midnight Caller,* NBC, 1989; also *The Invaders,* ABC, 1967 and 1968; *Police Story,* NBC, 1974; "To the Chicago Abyss," *The Ray Bradbury Theatre,* USA, 1989; *The Jack Benny Show,* NBC; *The Danny Kaye Show,* CBS; *The Red Skelton Show,* CBS; *Dennis the Menace,* CBS; *Gunsmoke,* CBS; *The Donna Reed Show,* ABC; *Hazel,* NBC; *The Dick Van Dyke Show,* CBS; *The Farmer's Daughter,* ABC; *The Big Valley,* ABC; *The Flying Nun,* ABC; *Wild, Wild West,* CBS; *Get Smart,* NBC; *I Dream of Jeannie,* NBC; *Hawaii Five-O,* CBS; *Love on a Rooftop,* ABC; *Petrocelli,* NBC; *Streets of San Francisco,* ABC; *Soap,* ABC; *Lou Grant,* CBS; *The Love Boat,* ABC; *St. Elsewhere,* NBC.

Movies: Alexander Weisberg, *A Death of Innocence,* CBS, 1971; Mr. Henshaw, *How to Break Up a Happy Divorce,* NBC, 1976; Benny Barnet, *The Eleventh Victim,* CBS, 1979; Dr. Hoxley, *Aunt Mary,* CBS, 1979; Harry Landers, *Better Late Than Never,* NBC, 1979; Dickie Dayton, *The Man in the Santa Claus Suit,* NBC, 1979; Arthur Stowbridge, *Kenny Rogers as "The Gambler,"* CBS, 1980; Louis B. Mayer, *Moviola: The Silent Lovers,* NBC, 1980; Louis B. Mayer, *Moviola: The Scarlett O'Hara War,* NBC, 1980; Mr. Campana, *King Crab,* ABC, 1980; Robert Westfield, *Born to Be Sold,* NBC, 1981; Eliot Bingham, *Help Wanted: Male,* CBS, 1982; Arthur Stowbridge, *Kenny Rogers as "The Gambler"—The Adventure Continues,* CBS, 1983; Oliver Sully, *The Red Light Sting,* CBS, 1984; Dr. Marvin Elias, *Mrs. Delafield Wants to Marry,* CBS, 1986; Nicholas Dimente, *Get Smart, Again!,* ABC, 1989. Specials: Leo Silver, "Have I Got a Christmas for You," *The Hallmark Hall of Fame,* NBC, 1977; Sol Wurtzel, *Actor,* PBS, 1978; Rabbi, *The Fourth Wise Man,* ABC, 1985; B.J., "Tales from the Hollywood Hills: The Closed Set," *Great Performances,* PBS, 1988.

RELATED CAREER—Instructor in theatre and speech, 1953-56, then assistant professor of drama and speech, 1956-60.

AWARDS: Obie Award from the *Village Voice,* 1969, for *The Increased Difficulty of Concentration;* Emmy Award nomination, 1974, for *Police Story;* Emmy Award nomination, 1977, for *Rhoda;* Emmy Award nomination, 1979, for *Moviola: The Scarlett O'Hara War;* Emmy Award nomination, 1986, for *Mrs. Delafield Wants to Marry;* ACE Award, Best Actor in a Dramatic Series, 1990, for *The Ray Bradbury Theatre;* Centennial Alumnus Award, State University of New York at Albany, National Association of State Universities and Land-Grant Colleges, 1987.

MEMBER: Academy of Motion Picture Arts and Sciences.

SIDELIGHTS: RECREATIONS—Reading, jogging, and swimming.

ADDRESSES: AGENT—Sylvia Gold, International Creative Management, 8899 Beverly Boulevard, Los Angeles, CA 90048.*

*   *   *

GRANGER, Stewart   1913-
(James Stewart)

PERSONAL: Born James Lablache Stewart, May 6, 1913, in London, England; naturalized U.S. citizen, June, 1956; son of James (an officer in the British Army) and Frederica (Lablache) Stewart; married Elspeth March (an actress), 1938 (divorced, 1948); married Jean Simmons (an actress), 1950 (divorced, 1960); married Viviane Lecerf, 1964 (divorced, 1969); children: two (first marriage); one (second marriage). EDUCATION—Attended Epsom

STEWART GRANGER

College; studied acting at the Webber-Douglas School of Dramatic Art. MILITARY—British Army, 1940-42.

VOCATION: Actor.

CAREER: STAGE DEBUT—Andrea Strozzi, *The Cardinal,* Hull Repertory Company, Little Theatre, Hull, U.K., 1935. LONDON DEBUT—Captain Hamilton, *The Sun Never Sets,* Drury Lane Theatre, 1938. PRINCIPAL STAGE APPEARANCES—Warwick, *Saint Joan,* Sir Broadfoot Basham, *On the Rocks,* Sir John Melvil, *The Clandestine Marriage,* St. John Rivers, *Jane Eyre,* General Su, *Lady Precious Stream,* Alastair, *The Millionairess,* King Magnus, *The Apple Cart,* Charles Surface, *The School for Scandal,* and Glundalca, *Tom Thumb the Great,* all Birmingham Repertory Company, Malvern Festival, Malvern, U.K., 1936-37; Lord Ivor Cream, *Serena Blandish,* Gate Theatre, London, 1938; Grand Duke Stephan, *I Am the King,* Richmond Theatre, London, 1939; Titus, *Jerusalem,* Playhouse Theatre, London, 1939; Tybalt, *Romeo and Juliet,* Leontine, *The Good-Natured Man,* Dunois, *Saint Joan,* and Anthony Anderson, *The Devil's Disciple,* all Old Vic Company, Buxton Festival, Buxton, U.K., then Streatham Hill Theatre, London, both 1939; Dr. Fleming, *Tony Draws a Horse,* Criterion Theatre, London, 1940; George Winthrop, *A House in the Square,* St. Martin's Theatre, London, 1940; Max de Winter, *Rebecca,* Lyric Theatre, London, 1949; Nikita, *The Power of Darkness,* Lyric Theatre, 1949; Clive Champion-Cheney, *The Circle,* Morris Mechanic Theatre, Baltimore, MD, then Ambassador Theatre, New York City, both 1989. Also appeared with the Hull Repertory Company, Hull, U.K., 1935-36; with the Birmingham Repertory Company, Birmingham, U.K., 1936-38; and in *Autumn,* St. Martin's Theatre, 1937.

MAJOR TOURS—Michael Davidson, *Titian Red,* U.K. cities, 1940; Robert Eden, *To Dream Again,* U.K. cities, 1942.

FILM DEBUT—(As James Stewart) *A Southern Maid,* Wardour, 1933. PRINCIPAL FILM APPEARANCES—Diner, *Give Her a Ring,* British International, 1936; Sutton, *Convoy,* Associated British, 1940; Lawrence, *So This Is London,* Twentieth Century-Fox, 1940; Larry Rains, *The Lamp Still Burns,* General Film Distributors, 1943; Peter Rokeby, *The Man in Grey,* Universal, 1943; David Penley, *Thursday's Child,* Pathe, 1943; Sub-Lieutenant Jackson, *Secret Mission,* General Films Distributors, 1944; Nino Barucci, *Madonna of the Seven Moons,* Universal, 1945; Apollodorus, *Caesar and Cleopatra,* Rank, 1946; Richard Darrel, *Caravan,* Gainsborough, 1946; Hugh Davin, *Captain Boycott,* General Film Distributors, 1947; Kit Firth, *A Lady Surrenders* (also known as *Love Story*), Universal, 1947; Paganini, *The Magic Bow,* Universal, 1947; Philip Thorn, *Blanche Fury,* Universal, 1948; Harry Somerford, *Man of Evil* (also known as *Fanny By Gaslight*), United Artists, 1948; Count Philip Koenigsmark, *Saraband* (also known as *Saraband for Dead Lovers*), Eagle-Lion, 1949; Ted Purvis, *Waterloo Road,* General Film Distributors/Eagle-Lion, 1949; Lord Terence Datchett, *Woman Hater,* Universal, 1949.

Adam Black, *Adam and Evelyn,* Two Cities, 1950; Allan Quartermaine, *King Solomon's Mines,* Metro-Goldwyn-Mayer (MGM), 1950; Sam Conride, *The Light Touch,* MGM, 1951; Private Archibald Ackroyd, *Soldiers Three,* MGM, 1951; Rudolf Rassendyll/King Rudolf V, *The Prisoner of Zenda,* MGM, 1952; Andre Moreau/title role, *Scaramouche,* MGM, 1952; Jules Vincent, *The Wild North* (also known as *The Big North*), MGM, 1952; Mark Shore, *All the Brothers Were Valiant,* MGM, 1953; Commander Claudius, *Salome,* Columbia, 1953; Thomas Seymour, *Young Bess,* MGM, 1953; title role, *Beau Brummell,* MGM, 1954; Stephen Lowry,

Footsteps in the Fog, Columbia, 1955; Rian X. Mitchell, *Green Fire*, MGM, 1955; Jeremy Fox, *Moonfleet*, MGM, 1955; Colonel Rodney Savage, *Bhowani Junction*, MGM, 1956; Sandy McKenzie, *The Last Hunt*, MGM, 1956; Tom Early, *Gun Glory*, MGM, 1957; Sir Philip Ashlow, *The Little Hut*, MGM, 1957; Harry Black, *Harry Black and the Tiger* (also known as *Harry Black*), Twentieth Century-Fox, 1958; Max Paulton, *The Whole Truth*, Columbia, 1958.

George Pratt, *North to Alaska*, Twentieth Century-Fox, 1960; John Brent, *The Secret Partner* (also known as *The Street Partner*), MGM, 1961; Captain LeBlanc, *Commando* (also known as *Marcia o crepa* and *Legion's Last Patrol*), American International, 1962; Lot, *Sodom and Gomorrah* (also known as *Sodome et Gomorrhe*, *Sodoma e Gomorra*, and *The Last Days of Sodom and Gomorrah*), Twentieth Century-Fox, 1962; Thomas Stanwood, *The Swordsman of Siena* (also known as *Le Mercenaire*, *Lo spadaccino di Sienna*, and *Il mercenario*), MGM, 1962; Surehand, *Among Vultures* (also known as *Frontier Hellcat*), Columbia, 1964; Major Richard Mace, *The Secret Invasion*, United Artists, 1964; Duke of Orgagna, *The Crooked Road*, Seven Arts, 1965; Old Surehand, *Rampage at Apache Wells*, Columbia, 1966; John "Bingo" Merrill, *Requiem for a Secret Agent*, Intercontinental/Metheus, 1966; Miles Gilchrist, *The Last Safari*, Paramount, 1967; Michael Scott, *Red-Dragon* (also known as *An 009 Mission to Hong Kong*), Woolner Brothers, 1967; Old Surehand, *Flaming Frontier*, Warner Brothers, 1968; Superintendent Cooper-Smith, *The Trygon Factor*, Warner Brothers, 1969; Sir Edward Matherson, *The Wild Geese*, Allied Artists, 1978; Dr. Martin Hoffman, *Hell Hunter*, Cinevest, 1988. Also appeared in *Over the Garden Wall*, Wardour, 1934; *Under Secret Orders*, Guaranteed, 1943; *Il giorno piu corto*, 1963; *Target for Killing*, 1966; *Spy Against the World* (also known as *Killer's Carnival*), 1966.

PRINCIPAL TELEVISION APPEARANCES—Series: Colonel Alan MacKenzie, *The Men from Shiloh*, NBC, 1970-71. Mini-Series: George Hackett, *Crossings*, ABC, 1986. Pilots: Sherlock Holmes, *Sherlock Holmes: The Hound of the Baskervilles*, ABC, 1971. Episodic: *Hotel*, ABC. Movies: Paul Dennison, *Any Second Now*, ABC, 1969; Prince Philip, *The Royal Romance of Charles and Diana*, CBS, 1982; Jason, *Chameleons*, NBC, 1989; also *A Hazard of Hearts*, CBS, 1987.

WRITINGS: *Sparks Fly Upward* (autobiography), Granada, 1981.

AWARDS: Voted one of Britain's top ten money-making stars in *Herald-Fame* motion picture polls, 1943-47 and 1949.

SIDELIGHTS: FAVORITE ROLES—King Magnus in *The Apple Cart*. RECREATIONS—Riding and shooting.

ADDRESSES: AGENTS—Jerry Martin, William Morris Agency, 151 El Camino Drive, Beverly Hills, CA 90212; David Shapira and Associates, 15301 Ventura Boulevard, Suite 345, Sherman Oaks, CA 91403.

*   *   *

GRANT, Hugh

PERSONAL: Born in London, England. EDUCATION—Attended Oxford University.

VOCATION: Actor.

CAREER: STAGE DEBUT—Nottingham Playhouse, Nottingham, U.K. PRINCIPAL STAGE APPEARANCES—*The Jockeys of Norfolk* (revue), King's Head Theatre, London, 1985; also appeared with the Oxford University Dramatic Society.

FILM DEBUT—(As Hughie Grant) Lord Adrian, *Privileged*, Oxford Film Foundation/New Yorker, 1982. PRINCIPAL FILM APPEARANCES—Clive Durham, *Maurice*, Cinecom, 1987; Hugh Dickinson, *White Mischief*, Columbia, 1988; Lord James D'Ampton, *The Lair of the White Worm*, Vestron, 1988; Harry, *The Dawning*, TVS Entertainment/Vista, 1988; Lord Byron, *Remando al viento* (also known as *Rowing with the Wind*), Ditirambo/Viking, 1988; Allan, *La Nuit Bengali* (also known as *The Bengali Night*), Gaumont, 1988.

PRINCIPAL TELEVISION APPEARANCES—Series: *The Demon Lover*, 1986; *Ladies in Charge*, 1986. Mini-Series: Apsley Cherry Garrard, *The Last Place on Earth*, Central Television, then *Masterpiece Theatre*, PBS, 1985; Bruno de Lancel, *'Til We Meet Again*, CBS, 1989. Episodic: *Shades of Darkness*. Movies: Peter Baines, *Jenny's War*, syndicated, 1985; Lord Lucius Vyne (the Highwayman), *The Lady and the Highwayman*, CBS, 1989; Charles Heidseick, *Champagne Charlie*, syndicated, 1989. Specials: William Hamilton, *Lord Elgin and Some Stones of No Value* (documentary), PBS, 1987. Also appeared in *The Detective*, *Handel*, *Dangerous Love*, and *Honour*, *Profit, and Pleasure*.

RELATED CAREER—Member of the Jockeys of Norfolk (three-man comedy troupe).

ADDRESSES: AGENT—Duncan Heath Associates, Paramount House, 162-170 Wardour Street, London W1V 3AT, England.*

*   *   *

GRANT, Lee   1931-

PERSONAL: Born Lyova Haskell Rosenthal, October 31, 1931, in New York, NY; daughter of A.W. (an educator and realtor) and Witia (a teacher; maiden name, Haskell) Rosenthal; married Arnold Manoff (a playwright; died, 1965); married Joseph Feury (a producer), 1967; children: Dinah (first marriage); Belinda (second marriage). EDUCATION—Attended the Art Student League and the High School of Music and Art; studied voice, violin, and dance at the Juilliard School of Music; attended the Metropolitan Opera Ballet School; studied acting at the Neighborhood Playhouse with Sanford Meisner and at the Actors' Studio.

VOCATION: Actress and director.

CAREER: STAGE DEBUT—Princess Ho Chee, *L'Oracolo* (opera), Metropolitan Opera House, New York City, 1933. BROADWAY DEBUT—Mildred, *Joy to the World*, Plymouth Theatre, 1948. PRINCIPAL STAGE APPEARANCES—Shoplifter, *Detective Story*, Hudson Theatre, New York City, 1949; Diane, *All You Need Is One Good Break*, Mansfield Theatre, New York City, 1950; Raina Petkoff, *Arms and the Man*, Arena Theatre, New York City, 1950; Daisy Durole, *Lo and Behold!*, Booth Theatre, New York City, 1951; Sally, *I Am a Camera*, Mount Kisco Playhouse, Mt. Kisco, NY, 1952; Amy, *They Knew What They Wanted*, Mount Kisco Playhouse, 1953; title role, *Gigi*, Mount Kisco Playhouse, 1954;

Stella, *Wedding Breakfast*, 48th Street Theatre, New York City, 1954; Eliza, *Pygmalion*, Mount Kisco Playhouse, 1956; Lizzie, *The Rainmaker*, Mount Kisco Playhouse, 1957; Mrs. Rogers, *A Hole in the Head*, Plymouth Theatre, New York City, 1957; Gittel Mosca, *Two for the Seesaw*, Booth Theatre, 1959; Rose Collins, *Captains and the Kings*, Playhouse Theatre, New York City, 1962; Solange, *The Maids*, One Sheridan Square Theatre, New York City, 1963; title role, *Electra*, New York Shakespeare Festival, Delacorte Theatre, New York City, 1964; title role, *Saint Joan*, Moorestown Theatre, Moorestown, NJ, 1966; Edna Edison, *The Prisoner of Second Avenue*, Eugene O'Neill Theatre, New York City, 1971. Also appeared in a series of one-act plays with Henry Fonda, American National Theatre and Academy Theatre, New York City, 1949; in *Liliom* and *This Property Is Condemned*, both Green Mansions Theatre, Warrensburg, NY, 1947; and as Regina, *The Little Foxes*, 1975.

PRINCIPAL STAGE WORK—Director, *The Adventures of Jack and Max*, Actors' Studio West, Los Angeles, 1968; director, *A Private View*, New York Shakespeare Festival, Public Theatre, New York City, 1983.

MAJOR TOURS—Ninotchka, *Silk Stockings*, U.S. cities, 1963; Karen Nash, "Visitor from Mamaroneck," Muriel Tate, "Visitor from Hollywood," and Norma Hubley, "Visitor from Forest Hills," in *Plaza Suite*, U.S. cities, 1968; also appeared in *Oklahoma*, U.S. cities, 1948; *The Tender Trap*, U.S. cities, 1962.

PRINCIPAL FILM APPEARANCES—Shoplifter, *Detective Story*, Paramount, 1951; Edna, *Storm Fear*, United Artists, 1956; Marilyn, *Middle of the Night*, Columbia, 1959; Carmen, *The Balcony*, Continental, 1963; Katherine McCleod, *An Affair of the Skin*, Zenith, 1964; Suzy, *Pie in the Sky* (also known as *Terror in the City*), Allied Artists, 1964; Dede Murphy, *Divorce American Style*, Columbia, 1967; Mrs. Leslie Colbert, *In the Heat of the Night*, United Artists, 1967; Miriam, *Valley of the Dolls*, Twentieth Century-Fox, 1967; Fritzie Braddock, *Buona Sera, Mrs. Campbell*, United Artists, 1968; motel resident, *The Big Bounce*, Warner Brothers/Seven Arts, 1969; Celia Pruett, *Marooned*, Columbia, 1969; Mrs. Enders, *The Landlord*, United Artists, 1970; Mrs. Bullard, *There Was a Crooked Man*, Warner Brothers, 1970; Norma Hubley, *Plaza Suite*, Paramount, 1971; Sophie Portnoy, *Portnoy's Complaint*, Warner Brothers, 1972; Jean Robertson, *The Internecine Project*, Allied Artists, 1974; Felicia Carr, *Shampoo*, Columbia, 1975; Lillian Rosen, *Voyage of the Damned*, AVCO-Embassy, 1976; Karen Wallace, *Airport '77*, Universal, 1977; Ann Thorn, *Damien—Omen II*, Twentieth Century-Fox, 1978; Ellen, *The Mafu Cage* (also known as *My Sister, My Love*), Clouds, 1978; Anne MacGregor, *The Swarm*, Warner Brothers, 1978; Clarisse Ethridge, *When You Comin' Back Red Ryder?*, Columbia, 1979.

Judge, *Little Miss Marker*, Universal, 1980; Mrs. Lupowitz, *Charlie Chan and the Curse of the Dragon Queen*, American Cinema, 1981; Deborah Ballin, *Visiting Hours* (also known as *The Fright* and *Get Well Soon*), Twentieth Century-Fox, 1981; narrator, *The Wilmar Eight* (documentary), California Newsreel, 1981; narrator, *What Sex Am I?* (documentary), Joseph Feury Productions, 1984; Mrs. Barr, *Constance*, Mirage/New Zealand Film Commission/Miramax/Enterprise, 1984; Mrs. Jones, *Trial Run*, Miracle Films/New Zealand Film Commission, 1984; Dr. Burke, *Teachers*, Metro-Goldwyn-Mayer/United Artists, 1984; as herself, *Sanford Meisner—The Theatre's Best Kept Secret* (documentary), Columbia, 1984; narrator, *Down and Out in America* (documentary), Joseph Feury Productions, 1986; as herself, *Hello Actors' Studio* (documentary), Actors' Studio, 1987; Ferguson Edwards, *The Big

Town, Columbia, 1987. Also appeared in *Arriving Tuesday*, Cinepro/New Zealand Film Commission/Walker, 1986; *Calling the Shots* (documentary), World Artists Releasing, 1988.

FIRST FILM WORK—Director, *The Stronger* (short film), American Film Institute, 1976. PRINCIPAL FILM WORK—Director: *Tell Me a Riddle*, Filmways, 1980; *The Wilmar Eight* (documentary), California Newsreel, 1981; *What Sex Am I?* (documentary), Joseph Feury Productions, 1984; *Down and Out in America* (documentary), Joseph Feury Productions, 1986; *Staying Together*, Hemdale, 1989.

PRINCIPAL TELEVISION APPEARANCES—Series: Rose Peabody, *Search for Tomorrow*, CBS, 1953-54; Stella Chernak, *Peyton Place*, ABC, 1965-66; Fay Stewart, *Fay*, NBC, 1975-76. Mini-Series: Grace Coolidge, *Backstairs at the White House*, NBC, 1979; Ava Marshall, *Bare Essence*, CBS, 1982; Rachele Mussolini, *Mussolini: The Untold Story*, NBC, 1985. Pilots: Wife, *Justice* (broadcast as an episode of *Plymouth Playhouse*), ABC, 1953; Leslie Williams, *Ransom for a Dead Man*, NBC, 1971; Diane Harper, *The Ted Bessell Show*, CBS, 1973; Meredith Leland, *Partners in Crime*, NBC, 1973; Maxine Lochman, *Thou Shalt Not Kill*, NBC, 1981; Evalyna, *The Million Dollar Face*, NBC, 1981.

Episodic: Martirio, "The House of Bernarda Alba," *Play of the Week*, WNTA, 1960; Avenging Angel, "The World of Sholem Aleichem," *Play of the Week*, WNTA, 1962; Laura, "The Love Song of Barney Kempinski," *ABC Stage '67*, ABC, 1966; also "Screwball," *The Play's the Thing*, CBS, 1950; "Zone of Quiet," *Comedy Theatre*, CBS, 1950; "Dark as Night," "Death to the Lonely," and "The Face of Fear," *Danger*, CBS, 1952; "Justice," *ABC Album*, ABC, 1953; "The Noose," *Broadway Television Theatre*, syndicated, 1953; "The Blonde Comes First," *Summer Theatre*, CBS, 1953; "Death Is a Spanish Dancer," *Ponds Theatre*, ABC, 1955; "Shadow of the Champ," *Philco Playhouse*, NBC, 1955; "Keyhole," *Playwrights '56*, NBC, 1956; "Even the Weariest River," *Alcoa Hour*, NBC, 1956; "Mooney's Kids Don't Cry," "Three Plays by Tennessee Williams," and "Look What's Going On," *Kraft Television Theatre*, NBC, 1958; *Great Ghost Tales*, NBC, 1961; "Saturday's Children," *Golden Showcase*, CBS, 1962; *The Nurses*, CBS, 1963; *East Side/West Side*, CBS, 1963; *The Defenders*, CBS, 1963 and 1965; *Slattery's People*, CBS, 1964; *Brenner*, CBS, 1964; *The Fugitive*, ABC, 1964; *Ben Casey*, ABC, 1964 and 1965; *For the People*, CBS, 1965; *Doctors/Nurses*, CBS, 1965; "The People Trap," *ABC Stage '67*, ABC, 1966; *The Big Valley*, ABC, 1967; "Deadlock," *The Bob Hope Chrysler Theatre*, NBC, 1967; *Ironside*, NBC, 1967; *Judd for the Defense*, ABC, 1968; *Mission: Impossible*, CBS, 1968; *Medical Center*, CBS, 1969; *Mod Squad*, ABC, 1970; *Name of the Game*, NBC, 1970; *Bracken's World*, NBC, 1970; *Men at Law*, CBS, 1971; *Studio One*, CBS; *Laugh-In*, NBC; *One Day at a Time*, CBS.

Movies: Lizzie, *The Respectful Prostitute*, BBC, 1964; Marjorie Howard, *Night Slaves*, ABC, 1970; Carrie Miller, *The Neon Ceiling*, NBC, 1971; Ellie Schuster, *Lieutenant Schuster's Wife*, ABC, 1972; Adele Ross, *What Are Best Friends For?*, ABC, 1973; Virginia Monroe, *Perilous Voyage*, NBC, 1976; Marion Matchett, *The Spell*, NBC, 1977; Esther Jack, *You Can't Go Home Again*, CBS, 1979; Anne Holt, *For Ladies Only*, NBC, 1981; Lillian Farmer, *Will There Really Be a Morning?*, CBS, 1983; Marilyn Klinghoffer, *The Hijacking of the Achille Lauro* (also known as *Sea of Terror*, *The Last Voyage*, and *Achille Lauro: Terror at Sea*), NBC, 1989. Specials: Florrie Sands, *Saturday's Children*, CBS, 1962; *Robert Young and the Family*, CBS, 1971; *The Wonderful World of Aggravation*, ABC, 1972; wife, "Raincheck," *Three for *the Girls,* CBS, 1973; *The Shape of Things,* CBS, 1973; Irina Arkadina, "The Seagull," *Great Performances,* PBS, 1975; hostess, *Once Upon a Time . . . Is Now: The Story of Princess Grace* (documentary), NBC, 1977; Karen Nash, "Visitor from Mamaroneck," Muriel Tate, "Visitor from Hollywood," and Claire Hubley, "Visitor from Forest Hills," *Plaza Suite,* HBO, 1982; narrator, "When Women Kill" (documentary), *America Undercover,* HBO, 1984; *Harry Belafonte: Don't Stop the Carnival,* HBO, 1985; *At Rona's,* NBC, 1989.

PRINCIPAL TELEVISION WORK—All as director. Episodic: "For the Use of the Hall," *Hollywood Television Theatre,* PBS, 1975. Movies: *A Matter of Sex,* NBC, 1984; *Nobody's Child,* CBS, 1986; *Battered,* HBO, 1989; *No Place Like Home,* CBS, 1989. Specials: (With Carolyn Raskin) *The Shape of Things,* CBS, 1973; "When Women Kill" (documentary), *America Undercover,* HBO, 1984; "Cindy Eller: A Modern Fairy Tale," *ABC Afterschool Specials,* ABC, 1985.

RELATED CAREER—Ballet dancer, Metropolitan Opera Company, New York City; company member, American Ballet Theatre, New York City.

NON-RELATED CAREER—Painter.

WRITINGS: TELEVISION—Specials: (Co-writer) *The Shape of Things,* CBS, 1973.

AWARDS: New York Drama Critics' Circle Award, 1949, for *Detective Story;* Academy Award nomination, Best Supporting Actress, 1951, and Best Actress Award from the Cannes Film Festival, 1952, both for *Detective Story;* Obie Award from the *Village Voice,* 1964, for *The Maids;* Emmy Award, Outstanding Performance By an Actress in a Supporting Role in a Drama, 1966, for *Peyton Place;* Academy Award nomination, Best Supporting Actress, 1970, for *The Landlord;* Emmy Award, Outstanding Single Performance By an Actress in a Lead Role, 1971, for *The Neon Ceiling;* Emmy Award nomination, 1971, for *Ransom for a Dead Man;* Academy Award, Best Supporting Actress, 1975, for *Shampoo;* Academy Award nomination, Best Supporting Actress, 1976, for *Voyage of the Damned;* Congressional Arts Caucus Award, Outstanding Achievement in Acting and Independent Filmmaking, 1983, for *Tell Me a Riddle;* Academy Award, Best Documentary Feature, 1986, for *Down and Out in America;* Directors Guild Award, Best Dramatic Television Special, 1987, for *Nobody's Child;* Crystal Award from Women in Film, 1988; also Emmy Award nomination for *The Bob Hope Chrysler Theatre.*

MEMBER: Actors' Equity Association, American Federation of Television and Radio Artists, Screen Actors Guild, Directors Guild of America.

ADDRESSES: AGENT—Jim Wyatt, International Creative Management, 8899 Beverly Boulevard, Los Angeles, CA 90045.*

*   *   *

GRAVES, Rupert   1963-

PERSONAL: Born June 30, 1963, in Weston-Super-Mare, England; son of Richard Harding (a musician) and Mary Lousilla (a travel coordinator; maiden name, Roberts) Graves.

VOCATION: Actor.

CAREER: STAGE DEBUT—Alistair Graham/Mr. Toad, *The Killing of Mr. Toad,* King's Head Theatre, London, 1983. PRINCIPAL STAGE APPEARANCES—Giovanni, *'Tis Pity She's a Whore,* National Theatre, London, 1988; David, "A Table for a King" and Barnby Grace, "Keeps Rain All the Night," in *A Madhouse in Goa,* Lyric Hammersmith Theatre, London, 1989; also appeared in *Sufficient Carbohydrate,* Albery Theatre, London, 1984; *Torch Song Trilogy,* Albery Theatre, 1985; Teddy, *St. Ursula's in Danger;* and in productions of *Good and Bad at Games* and *Amadeus.*

FILM DEBUT—Freddy Honeychurch, *A Room with a View,* Cinecom, 1986. PRINCIPAL FILM APPEARANCES—Alec Scudder, *Maurice,* Cinecom, 1987; John Beaver, *A Handful of Dust,* New Line Cinema, 1988.

PRINCIPAL TELEVISION APPEARANCES—Series: Tipping, *Vice Versa,* BBC, 1980-81. Mini-Series: Simon Boulderstone, *Fortunes of War,* BBC, then *Masterpiece Theatre,* PBS, 1988. Also appeared in *All for Love* and in *A Life of Puccini.*

RELATED CAREER—Worked as a clown with a traveling circus in England.

MEMBER: Pre-Raphaelite Seahorse Club (co-chairman, 1987-89).

SIDELIGHTS: RECREATIONS—Playing guitar, running, and reading.

ADDRESSES: AGENT—Jean Diamond, London Management, 235 Regent Street, London W1, England.

*   *   *

GRAY, Charles   1928-
(Oliver Gray)

PERSONAL: Born Donald Marshall Gray, August 29, 1928, in Bournemouth, England; son of Donald (a surveyor) and Maude Elizabeth (Marshall) Gray.

VOCATION: Actor.

CAREER: Also see *WRITINGS* below. STAGE DEBUT—Charles the Wrestler, *As You Like It,* Open Air Theatre, London, 1952. BROADWAY DEBUT—Henry Bolingbroke, *Richard II,* Old Vic Company, Winter Garden Theatre, 1956. PRINCIPAL STAGE APPEARANCES—Roman captain and Jupiter, *Cymbeline,* Demiwulf, *Boy with a Cart,* and title role (understudy), *Comus,* all Open Air Theatre, London, 1952; Lord Marshall, *Richard II,* Duke Frederick, *As You Like It,* Hastings, *Henry IV, Part One,* the Vinter, *Henry IV, Part Two,* the Lord, *The Taming of the Shrew,* Marullus, *Julius Caesar,* Polyxenes, *The Winter's Tale,* and Duke of Burgundy and Constable of France, *Henry V,* all Old Vic Company, Old Vic Theatre, London, 1955; Lodovico, *Othello,* chorus and Escalus, *Romeo and Juliet,* Achilles, *Troilus and Cressida,* Macduff, *Macbeth,* and Henry Bolingbroke, *Richard II,* all Old Vic Company, Old Vic Theatre, 1956; chorus and Escalus, *Romeo and Juliet,* Lennox, *Macbeth,* and Achilles, *Troilus and Cressida,* all Old Vic Company, Winter Garden Theatre, 1956; Captain Cyril Mavors, *Expresso Bongo,* Saville Theatre, London, 1958.

(As Oliver Gray) Prince of Wales, *Kean*, Broadway Theatre, New York City, 1961; Bernard Acton, *Everything in the Garden*, Duke of York's Theatre, London, 1962; Sir Epicure Mammom, *The Alchemist*, Old Vic Theatre, 1962; Maxime, *Poor Bitos*, Arts Theatre, London, 1963, then Duke of York's Theatre, 1964, later Cort Theatre, New York City, 1964; ensemble, *Hang Down Your Head and Die* (revue), Comedy Theatre, London, 1964; Sir Charles Dilke, *The Right Honourable Gentleman*, Billy Rose Theatre, New York City, 1965; Braham, *The Philanthropist*, Royal Court Theatre, then May Fair Theatre, both London, 1970; General St. Pe, *Ardele*, Queen's Theatre, London, 1975; Sheridan Whiteside, *The Man Who Came to Dinner*, Chichester Theatre Festival, Chichester, U.K., 1979. Also appeared in *The Merchant of Venice, Richard III, Antony and Cleopatra*, and *King Lear*, all with the Shakespeare Memorial Theatre Company, Shakespeare Memorial Theatre, Stratford-on-Avon, U.K., 1953.

MAJOR TOURS—Ross, *Macbeth*, U.K. cities, 1952; Henry Bolingbroke, *Richard II*, chorus and Escalus, *Romeo and Juliet*, Lennox, *Macbeth*, and Achilles, *Troilus and Cressida*, U.S. and Canadian cities, 1957; also *Antony and Cleopatra*, U.K. cities, 1954.

PRINCIPAL FILM APPEARANCES—Captain Brossard, *I Accuse!*, Metro-Goldwyn-Mayer, 1958; Lawson, *The Desperate Man*, Allied Artists, 1959; columnist, *The Entertainer*, British Lion, 1960; Gomez, *Tommy the Toreador*, Warner Brothers, 1960; Leo, *Man in the Moon* (also known as *Operation Masquerade* and *The Shabby Tiger*), United Artists, 1965; General Von Seidlitz-Gablear, *The Night of the Generals* (also known as *La Nuit de generaux*),

CHARLES GRAY

Columbia, 1967; Henderson, *You Only Live Twice*, United Artists, 1967; Mocata, *The Devil's Bride* (also known as *The Devil Rides Out*), Twentieth Century-Fox, 1968; Charles Griddon, *The Man Outside*, Allied Artists, 1968; General Cox-Roberts, *The Secret War of Harry Frigg*, Universal, 1968; Nick Harrison, "The Owl" in *The File of the Golden Goose*, United Artists, 1969; Lord Essex, *Cromwell*, Columbia, 1970; Vaughan Jones, *The Executioner*, Columbia, 1970; Air Commodore Hufford, *Mosquito Squadron*, United Artists, 1970; Blofeld, *Diamonds Are Forever*, United Artists, 1971; Cotton's father, *Bless the Beasts and Children*, Columbia, 1971; Bennington, *The Beast Must Die*, Cinerama, 1974; criminologist, *The Rocky Horror Picture Show*, Twentieth Century-Fox, 1975; Ambassador Hollander, *Seven Nights in Japan*, Paramount, 1976; Mycroft Holmes, *The Seven-Per-Cent Solution*, Universal, 1977; Charles Cook, *Silver Bears*, Columbia, 1978; Karl Liebknecht, *The Legacy*, (also known as *The Legacy of Maggie Walsh*), Universal, 1979; Bates, *The Mirror Crack'd*, Associated Film Distribution, 1980; Judge Oliver Wright, *Shock Treatment*, Twentieth Century-Fox, 1981; Sir James Chorley, *The Jigsaw Man*, United Film Distribution, 1984. Also appeared in *Wild Rovers*, Metro-Goldwyn-Mayer, 1971; *Junior Bonner*, Cinerama, 1972.

PRINCIPAL TELEVISION APPEARANCES—Series: Sir Edwin, *Upstairs, Downstairs*, London Weekend Television, then *Masterpiece Theatre*, PBS, 1974-77. Mini-Series: Mr. Calvin, *Captains and the Kings*, NBC, 1976; General Lucian Truscott, *Ike*, ABC, 1979; also *Champagne Charlie*, syndicated, 1989. Episodic: Mycroft Holmes, "The Greek Interpreter," *The Adventures of Sherlock Holmes Series II*, Granada, 1986, then *Mystery!*, PBS, 1987; Mycroft Holmes, "The Bruce-Partington Plans," *The Return of Sherlock Holmes Series II*, Granada, then *Mystery!*, PBS, 1988; also "Sanatorium" and "The Ant and the Grasshopper," both *Somerset Maugham Hour*, AR, 1961. Movies: General Lischke, *The House on Garibaldi Street*, ABC, 1979; Earl Spencer, *Charles and Diana: A Royal Love Story*, ABC, 1982. Specials: Escalus, *Romeo and Juliet*, NBC, 1957; Bounine, "Anastasia," *Hallmark Hall of Fame*, NBC, 1967; title role, *Julius Caesar*, BBC, then *The Shakespeare Plays*, PBS, 1979; Claudius, *An Englishman Abroad*, BBC, 1983, then *Great Performances*, PBS. Also appeared in *Small Backroom*, BBC, 1959; *The Big Client*, ABC, 1959; *No Hiding Place*, AR, 1959; *The First Gentleman*, Southern Television, 1960; *Tiger at the Gates*, Granada, 1961; *You Can't Escape*, BBC, 1961; *Any Other Business*, ATV, 1961; *Design for Murder*, BBC, 1961; *Voices from the Past*, BBC, 1962; *The Tycoons*, ABC, 1962; *A Matter of Principal*, ATV, 1962; *Private and Personal*, BBC, 1963; *The Perfect Friday*, ATV, 1963; *Tea Party*, BBC, 1965; and in *The Cherry Orchard, Richard III, Porterhouse Blue, Small World*, and *The Gourmet*.

WRITINGS: STAGE—*The Old Soldier*, 1971; *The Pot Plant*, 1972.

AWARDS: Clarence Derwent Award, 1964, for *Poor Bitos*.

MEMBER: Actors' Equity Association, British Actors' Equity Association.

ADDRESSES: AGENT—London Management, 235 Regent Street, London W1, England.

*   *   *

GRAY, Oliver
See GRAY, Charles

GREENHUT, Robert

VOCATION: Producer.

CAREER: PRINCIPAL FILM WORK—Unit production manager, *The Owl and the Pussycat*, Columbia, 1970; assistant director, *Panic in Needle Park*, Twentieth Century-Fox, 1971; production manager, *Born to Win*, United Artists, 1971; associate director, *Last of the Red Hot Lovers*, Paramount, 1972; executive producer and production manager, *Annie Hall*, United Artists, 1977; executive producer, *Interiors*, United Artists, 1978; associate producer and production manager, *Hair*, United Artists, 1979; executive producer, *Manhattan*, United Artists, 1979; producer, *Stardust Memories*, United Artists, 1980; producer and assistant director, *Arthur*, Warner Brothers, 1981; producer, *A Midsummer Night's Sex Comedy*, Warner Brothers, 1982; executive producer, *The King of Comedy*, Twentieth Century-Fox, 1983; producer, *Zelig*, Warner Brothers, 1983; producer, *Broadway Danny Rose*, Orion, 1984; producer, *The Purple Rose of Cairo*, Orion, 1985; producer, *Hannah and Her Sisters*, Orion, 1986; producer (with Mike Nichols), *Heartburn*, Paramount, 1986; producer, *Radio Days*, Orion, 1987; producer, *September*, Orion, 1987; producer (with James L. Brooks) and unit production manager, *Big*, Twentieth Century-Fox, 1988; executive producer (with Laurence Mark) and unit production manager, *Working Girl*, Twentieth Century-Fox, 1988; producer, *Another Woman*, Orion, 1989; producer, "Oedipus Wrecks" in *New York Stories*, Touchstone, 1989; producer, *Crimes and Misdemeanors*, Orion, 1989.

PRINCIPAL TELEVISION WORK—Movies: Associate producer, *The Silence*, NBC, 1975; associate producer, *Panic in Echo Park*, NBC, 1977.

AWARDS: Academy Award nomination, Best Picture, 1987, for *Hannah and Her Sisters.*

ADDRESSES: MANAGER— Rollins/Joffe/Morra/Brezner Inc., 130 W. 57th Street, New York, NY 10019.*

*　　*　　*

GREER, Bettejane
See GREER, Jane

*　　*　　*

GREER, Dabbs   1917-

PERSONAL: Born Robert William Greer, April 2, 1917, in Fairview, MO; son of Randall Alexander (a druggist) and Bernice Irene (a speech teacher; maiden name, Dabbs) Greer. EDUCATION—Drury College, A.B., 1939; studied acting at the Pasadena Playhouse School of Theatre.

VOCATION: Actor and director.

CAREER: STAGE DEBUT—Prince Rupert, *Cinderella*, 1924. PRINCIPAL STAGE APPEARANCES—Appeared in productions of *The Yankee*, 1926; *City and Country*, 1932; *Wild Ginger*, 1934; *Spider and the Fly*, *The Queen's Husband*, and *Outward Bound*, all 1935; *The Big Pond*, *Sky High*, *Passing of the Third Floor Back*, *Candida*,

DABBS GREER

and *You and I*, all 1936; *Wingless Victory*, 1937; *The Imaginary Invalid*, 1938; *Tonight at 8:30*, *He Who Gets Slapped*, and *The Pirates of Penzance*, all 1939; *The Nurse Wears Silk* and *The Intruder*, both 1941; *The College Widow*, *Good Gracious Annabelle*, and *Penny Wise*, all 1942; *Our Town*, *Arsenic and Old Lace*, *Intimate Strangers*, and *Monsieur Beaucaire*, all 1943; *One in Every Family*, *Personal Appearance*, *The Master Builder*, *A Christmas Carol*, *The Great Galeoto*, *Pursuit of Happiness*, *Defiance*, *Candida*, *My Sister Eileen*, *Young Man of Today*, and *It's a Wise Child*, all 1944; *The Makropolous Secret*, *Little Women*, *Autumn Crocus*, *King Lear*, *Janie*, *Spring Again*, *Tomorrow and Tomorrow*, and *Mary of Scotland*, all 1945; *Men Coming Home*, *Snafu*, *Night Must Fall*, *Hang on to Love*, *The Avon Flows*, *Lovers' Lane*, *But Not Goodbye*, and *Yankee Fable*, all 1946; *Mrs. Wiggs of the Cabbage Patch*, *The Great God Brown*, and *Years Ago*, all 1947; *Woman Bites Dog*, *Gauguin*, and *Time Is a Dream*, all 1948; *Command Decision*, *The Willow and I*, and *Pollyanna*, all 1949; *Two Blind Mice*, *The Two Mrs. Carrolls*, *Mother Is a Freshman*, and *Madam Ada*, all 1950; *Goodbye My Fancy*, 1951; *Gramercy Ghost*, 1952; *The Taming of the Shrew* and *Point of No Return*, both 1953; *Me, Candido*, 1957; *The Iceman Cometh*, 1958.

PRINCIPAL STAGE WORK—Director: *How Come Christmas* and *Time Is a Dream*, both 1937; *Dear Brutus*, 1938; *He Who Gets Slapped*, 1939; *The Late Christopher Bean* and *Penny Wise*, both 1940; *Seven Sisters* and *Air Raid*, both 1941; *Penny Wise*, *Lady Windemere's Fan*, *Our Town*, *George Washington Slept Here*, *Time Is a Dream*, and *Outward Bound*, all 1942; *Ladies Retirement*, *Arsenic and Old Lace*, *The Women*, and *Cradle Song*, all 1943; *Camille*, *The Youngest Profession*, *Sister Beatrice*, and *The Fan*, all 1944; *The Makropolous Secret, Iphigenia in Tauris, Romeo and Juliet, Autumn Crocus, The Cid, The Country Wife, The Bandersnatch, Sara Sampson,* and *Festival,* all 1945; *The Bacchae, Oedipus Rex, Uncertain Seas, It's All Been Done Before, Song with Distant Words, The Boor, Subway Circus, Young April,* and *Pierre Patelin,* all 1946; *Tournament of Roses Coronation Pageant* and *Time Is a Dream,* both 1948; *Out of the Frying Pan, Odin Against Christus, Shucks!,* and *The Willow and I,* all 1949; *Her Clothing Is Purple* and *The Traitor,* both 1950; *The Live Wire,* 1951.

FILM DEBUT—Guard at the gate, *The Black Book* (also known as *Reign of Terror*), Eagle-Lion, 1948. PRINCIPAL FILM APPEAR-ANCES—Reporter, *The Damned Don't Cry,* Warner Brothers, 1950; Mike, *The Sound of Fury* (also known as *Try and Get Me*), United Artists, 1950; police attendant, *Storm Warning,* Warner Brothers, 1950; Spud Keith, *Devil's Doorway,* Metro-Goldwyn-Mayer (MGM), 1950; communications officer, *Trial without Jury,* Republic, 1950; dealer, *California Passage,* Republic, 1950; bail-iff, *The Lady from Texas,* Universal, 1951; first man, *Weekend with Father,* Universal, 1951; aide to the Colonel, *Call Me Mister,* Twentieth Century-Fox, 1951; taxi driver, *Father's Little Divi-dend,* MGM, 1951; driver, *The Unknown Man,* MGM, 1951; reporter, *Deadline-U.S.A.* (also known as *Deadline*), Twentieth Century-Fox, 1952; Parker, *Sally and Saint Anne,* Universal, 1952; technician, *Million Dollar Mermaid* (also known as *The One-Piece Bathing Suit*), MGM, 1952; court clerk, *My Man and I,* MGM, 1952; curio shop owner, *Because of You,* Universal, 1952; intelli-gence clerk, *Diplomatic Courier,* Twentieth Century-Fox, 1952; cab driver, *Monkey Business,* Twentieth Century-Fox, 1952; scoutmaster, *Room for One More* (also known as *The Easy Way*), Warner Brothers, 1952; reporter, *The Bad and the Beautiful,* MGM, 1952; man at the bar, *Scarlet Angel,* Universal, 1952; man at Mississippi contest, *We're Not Married,* Twentieth Century-Fox, 1952; Shorty, *Take the High Ground,* MGM, 1953; jet leader, *Mission Over Korea,* Columbia, 1953; Eddie, *A Slight Case of Larceny,* MGM, 1953; a citizen, *Julius Caesar,* MGM, 1953; Haddock, *Above and Beyond,* MGM, 1953; Happy Murray, *Affair with a Stranger,* RKO, 1953; Galuppo, *China Venture,* Columbia, 1953; elevator boy, *Dream Wife,* MGM, 1953; George Payson, *Half a Hero,* MGM, 1953; Sergeant Jim Shane, *House of Wax,* Warner Brothers, 1953; Julius, *Remains to Be Seen,* MGM, 1953; Father Mahoney, *Trouble Along the Way,* Warner Brothers, 1953; fireman, *Mr. Scoutmaster,* Twentieth Century-Fox, 1953; sheriff, *Bitter Creek,* Allied Artists, 1954; Jim Langley, *The Desperado,* Allied Artists, 1954; head ranger, *Living It Up,* Paramount, 1954; bartender, *Private Hell 36,* Filmmaker, 1954; Schuyler, *Riot in Cell Block 11,* Allied Artists, 1954; committeeman, *Rose Marie,* MGM, 1954; *She Couldn't Say No* (also known as *Beautiful But Danger-ous*), RKO, 1954.

Hotel clerk, *Stranger on Horseback,* United Artists, 1955; Com-mander Holleck, *An Annapolis Story* (also known as *The Blue and the Gold*), Allied Artists, 1955; stage manager, *Hit the Deck,* MGM, 1955; minister, *At Gunpoint* (also known as *Gunpoint*), Allied Artists, 1955; bus driver, *Foxfire,* Universal, 1955; pilot instructor, *The McConnell Story* (also known as *Tiger in the Sky*), Warner Brothers, 1955; Captain Brewster, *The Scarlet Coat,* MGM, 1955; doctor, *Seven Angry Men,* Allied Artists, 1955; tutor, *The Seven Little Foys,* Paramount, 1955; Lieutenant Harrison, *Away All Boats,* Universal, 1956; Smith-Johnson, *Meet Me in Las Vegas* (also known as *Viva Las Vegas*), MGM, 1956; Potter, *The First Texan,* Allied Artists, 1956; doctor, *Tension at Table Rock,* RKO, 1956; Ephraim, *The Young Guns,* Allied Artists, 1956; Arkinson, *D-Day, the Sixth of June* (also known as *The Sixth of June*), Twentieth Century-Fox, 1956; Detective Davenport, *Hot Cars,*

United Artists, 1956; Henry, *Hot Rod Girl* (also known as *Hot Car Girl*), American International, 1956; Mac, *Invasion of the Body Snatchers,* Allied Artists, 1956; Mr. Clendening, *All Mine to Give* (also known as *The Day They Gave Babies Away*), Universal, 1957; Bonner, *Baby Face Nelson,* United Artists, 1957; Dr. Ainsley, *Chain of Evidence,* Allied Artists, 1957; Lieutenant O'Connor, *My Man Godfrey,* Universal, 1957; Brewster, *Pawnee* (also known as *Pale Arrow*), Republic, 1957; Goldsborough, *The Spirit of St. Louis,* Warner Brothers, 1957; Dr. Will Beaumont, *The Vampire* (also known as *Mark of the Vampire*), United Artists, 1957; John Clinton, *Young and Dangerous,* Twentieth Century-Fox, 1957; San Quentin captain, *I Want to Live!,* United Artists, 1958; Eric Royce, *It! The Terror from Beyond Space* (also known as *It! The Vampire from Beyond Space*), United Artists, 1959; Doc Langer, *Day of the Outlaw,* United Artists, 1959; gas station attendant, *Edge of Eternity,* Columbia, 1959; Andy, *Last Train from Gun Hill,* Paramount, 1959; Doc Jansen, *Lone Texan,* Twentieth Century-Fox, 1959.

John Burton, *Cash McCall,* Warner Brothers, 1960; aide, *Hell Is for Heroes,* Paramount, 1962; waiter, *Wives and Lovers,* Para-mount, 1963; youth leader, *Palm Springs Weekend,* Warner Broth-ers, 1963; express man, *Showdown* (also known as *The Iron Collar*), Universal, 1963; Arthur Nielsen, *Roustabout,* Paramount, 1964; Abernathy, *Shenandoah,* Universal, 1965; voice of second man, *Two Mules for Sister Sara,* Universal, 1970; Jedediah W. Willowby, *The Cheyenne Social Club,* National General, 1970; Dr. Thompson, *Rage,* Warner Brothers, 1972; Pa McKlusky, *White Lightning* (also known as *McKlusky*), United Artists, 1973; voice of Collins, *The Last American Hero* (also known as *Hard Driver*), Twentieth Century-Fox, 1975; Wally, *Chu Chu and the Philly Flash,* American International, 1981; Kyle, *Two Moon Junction,* Lorimar, 1988; Otto Klausberg, *Sundown, The Retreat of the Vampires,* Vestron, 1988. Also appeared as Lyle Phelps, . . . *And God Bless Grandma and Grandpa,* 1973; in *God Bless Dr.. Shagetz,* 1977; *Evil Town,* Trans World Entertainment, 1987.

TELEVISION DEBUT—Dr. Herdal, *The Master Builder,* 1944. PRINCIPAL TELEVISION APPEARANCES—Series: Various roles, *Fireside Theatre,* NBC, 1950-51; Sergeant Jim Ward, *Big Town,* NBC, 1954; Mr. Wilbur Jonas, *Gunsmoke,* CBS, 1955-62; Ossie Weiss, *Hank,* NBC, 1965-66; Reverend Robert Alden, *Little House on the Prairie,* NBC, 1974-82; Reverend Robert Alden, *Little House: A New Beginning,* NBC, 1982-83. Pilots: Tom Quine, *Lineup,* CBS, 1954; Sidney Bascomb, *Sally,* NBC, 1956; policeman, *Christabel* (broadcast as an episode of *Goodyear Thea-tre*), NBC, 1959; Sheriff Jim Roarke, *Checkmate* (broadcast as an episode of *Zane Grey Theatre;* also known as *Dick Powell's Zane Grey Theatre*), CBS, 1959; Professor Atkins, *Best Years,* ABC, 1962; minister, *The Brady Bunch,* ABC, 1968; theatre owner, *The Boys,* NBC, 1970; Deacon Hurd, *The Greatest Gift,* NBC, 1974; Milt Mullins, *First Impressions,* CBS, 1987; also Bill Rockwell, *Code Three,* 1954; Lee Clark, *The Marie Wilson Show,* 1956; Ted Borton, *Forest Ranger,* 1956 (unaired); Arthur Pierson, *Juvenile Court,* 1958; Mike Sampson, *Luke and the Tenderfoot,* 1958; Uncle Nabob, *The Minnie Pearl Show,* 1968; Mr. Landers, *Two Boys,* 1969; Vern Carson, *The Pink Panther,* 1989.

Episodic: Paul Marin, *Space Patrol,* ABC, 1951; Guy, *The Adven-tures of Superman,* syndicated, 1951; Shaky, *Dick Tracy,* ABC, 1951; Doc Halliday, "Let the Cards Decide," *Fireside Theatre,* NBC, 1952; Joe, *Big Town* (also known as *City Assignment*), CBS, 1952; Jeff Markworth, *This Is the Life,* Dumont, 1952; Toby Durbin, *The Lone Ranger,* ABC, 1952; John Adams, "Poor Richard," *Cavalcade of America,* NBC, 1952; Pierson, "No Gods to Serve,'' *The Visitor* (also known as *The Doctor*), NBC, 1952; Jerome McVey, "First Prize" and Saul Marcus, "Valley of the Shadow," *Fireside Theatre*, NBC, 1953; Joe Winters, *The Adventures of Superman*, syndicated, 1953; Jack, *Topper*, CBS, 1954; Johann, "Escape" and Mark Wilson, "The Saturday Story," *Cavalcade of America*, ABC, 1954; George McCadden, *Lineup*, CBS, 1954; Joe Baker, *Lassie*, CBS, 1954; George Alton, *This Is the Life*, syndicated, 1954; attendant, "Case for Father Darling," dentist, "Feeling No Pain," and Dewey Mason, "No Evil for Evil," *The Loretta Young Show*, NBC, 1954; Adams, "The After House," *Climax*, CBS, 1954; Mr. Collins, *Father Knows Best*, CBS, 1954; Merrick, "Case of the Capitol Crime," *The Man Behind the Badge*, CBS, 1954.

Keith Fowler, *The Bob Cummings Show* (also known as *Love That Bob*), NBC, 1955; Doctor Carlson, "Payment in Kind," *Henry Fonda Presents the Star and the Story* (also known as *Star and Story*), syndicated, 1955; Trusty, *Dear Phoebe*, NBC, 1955; Herb, *The Ray Milland Show*, CBS, 1955; Marshal Crawford, *The Life and Legend of Wyatt Earp* (also known as *Wyatt Earp*), ABC, 1955, Dave, "Lou Gehrig's Greatest Day" and Colonel Venable, "Grant and Lee at Appomattox," *You Are There*, CBS, 1955; Tom Denby, *Dr. Hudson's Secret Journal*, syndicated, 1955; MacGuire, "It Grows on Trees," *Lux Video Theatre*, NBC, 1955; Walter Sanger, *This Is the Life*, syndicated, 1955; Phil Harvey, *Waterfront*, syndicated, 1955; Tyler, *Dr. Hudson's Secret Journal*, syndicated, 1955; Arthur Kern, "Strange People at Pecos" and MacNamara, "Operation Flypaper," *Science Fiction Theatre*, syndicated, 1955; Tom, "Prosper's Old Mother," *General Electric Theatre*, CBS, 1955; Germy, "Gusher City," *Jane Wyman Presents the Fireside Theatre*, CBS, 1955; Ray, "Paper Gunman" and Marshal, "King of Dakota," *Frontier*, NBC, 1955; Josef, *Man Called X*, syndicated, 1955; Mr. Sayre, "Navy Corpsman," *Navy Log*, CBS, 1955; Chester Ives, "Tropical Secretary" and Les Shaw, "Ticket for May," *The Loretta Young Show*, NBC, 1955; Charlie, "Gift of Life," *Schlitz Playhouse of Stars*, CBS, 1955; Don Dogdon, *Lineup*, CBS, 1955.

Bert Keith, *The George Burns and Gracie Allen Show*, CBS, 1956; milkman, "There Was an Old Woman" and sheriff, "The Belfry," *Alfred Hitchcock Presents*, CBS, 1956; Doctor Hendricks, *The George Burns and Gracie Allen Show*, CBS, 1956; Stoolie, "The Ed Murdock Story," *The Millionaire*, CBS, 1956; Professor Reimers, "One Hundred Years from Now," *Science Fiction Theatre*, syndicated, 1956; Mr. Erwin, "We Who Love Her," *On Trial*, NBC, 1956; John Compton, "Family Affair," *Stage Seven*, CBS, 1956; Doctor English, "Call of Duty," *The West Point Story*, CBS, 1956; Nathaniel Lorne, "Johnny Tremain," *Disneyland* (also known as *Walt Disney*), ABC, 1956; Henry Blaine, "Helpmate," *Jane Wyman Presents the Fireside Theatre*, NBC, 1956; Pete Maxwell, *Dr. Hudson's Secret Journal*, syndicated, 1956; Shammy, "You Can't Escape Forever," *Lux Video Theatre*, NBC, 1956; Keever, *Mr. Adams and Eve*, CBS, 1956; Si Marsh, "Muletown Gold Strike," *Zane Grey Theatre* (also known as *Dick Powell's Zane Grey Theatre*), CBS, 1956; Joe Randolph, *Broken Arrow*, ABC, 1956; Charles Jackson, *Sheriff of Cochise*, syndicated, 1956.

Dan Malloy, *The Whirlybirds*, syndicated, 1957; Pete Maxwell, *Dr. Hudson's Secret Journal*, syndicated, 1957; Zac West, *Charlie Chan*, syndicated, 1957; Tom Nolan, *The West Point Story*, ABC, 1957; Keever, *Mr. Adams and Eve*, CBS, 1957; Germie, "The Wildcatter" and Mr. Boggs, "Roadblock," *Jane Wyman Presents the Fireside Theatre*, NBC, 1957; Cass Baker, *The Court of Last Resort*, NBC, 1957; Ethan Phelps, "Easton, Texas" and Ward Barrett, "The Witness," *Trackdown*, CBS, 1957; Haw, "The

Quill and the Gun,'' *The Web*, NBC, 1957; James Edwards, Sr., *Tombstone Territory*, ABC, 1957; Walter Harrison, "The Understanding Heart" and Mr. Blanchard, "The Accused," *The Loretta Young Show*, NBC, 1957; Sam Pike, *Meet McGraw* (also known as *The Adventures of McGraw*), NBC, 1957; Harrison Peeble/Dan Dobey, *The Adventures of Superman*, syndicated, 1957; Blandish, *How to Marry a Millionaire*, syndicated, 1957; Sam Higgens, *Man without a Gun*, syndicated, 1957; Dave Kirby, *Perry Mason*, CBS, 1957.

Jim Burdette, *The Whirlybirds*, syndicated, 1958; Ed Grines, *State Trooper*, syndicated, 1958; Sheriff Farow, *Trackdown*, CBS, 1958; Kirby, "Backfire," *Target*, syndicated, 1958; Mike Kilroy, *Trackdown*, syndicated, 1958; Ed McColl, "Handful of Ashes," Sheriff Will, "Pressure Point," and ex-Confederate, "Welcome Home a Stranger," *Zane Grey Theatre* (also known as *Dick Powell's Zane Grey Theatre*), CBS, 1958; Tom Wade, *Wanted: Dead or Alive*, CBS, 1958; storekeeper, "Texas John Slaughter," *Disneyland* (also known as *Walt Disney*), ABC, 1958; Roy Stanton, "Peligroso," *Restless Gun*, NBC, 1958; Elder Boone, *Wanted: Dead or Alive*, CBS, 1958; Joe Burton, *U.S. Marshal*, syndicated, 1958; police captain, *Colonel Flack*, syndicated, 1958; Lewis, "The Image of Fear," *Studio One*, CBS, 1958; Lester Newby, *The Ed Wynn Show*, NBC, 1958.

Franklyn Finch, *Colonel Flack*, syndicated, 1959; Jake Bender, *The Adventures of Ellery Queen*, NBC, 1959; Ben Moore, *Steve Canyon*, NBC, 1959; Amboy, *The Thin Man*, NBC, 1959; Denver Pollock, *Black Saddle*, NBC, 1959; Bryson, *Colonel Flack*, syndicated, 1959; Sheriff Jenkins, *The Rough Riders*, ABC, 1959; Clayton Beard, "The Day Before Atlanta," *Playhouse 90*, CBS, 1959; Owen Edwards, *Black Saddle*, NBC, 1959; Tanner, *Wagon Train*, NBC, 1959; Will, *Bat Masterson*, NBC, 1959; Tory Jasper, "Swampfox," *Walt Disney Presents*, ABC, 1959; John LePage, *Troubleshooters*, NBC, 1959; Hennesey's father, *Hennesey*, CBS, 1959; Marcus Trimble, *The Rifleman*, ABC, 1959; Sam Elder, *The Rifleman*, ABC, 1959; Brett Conway, *The Rifleman*, ABC, 1959; Doctor Baker, "The Red Dress" and Doctor Merrill, "The Grenade," *The Loretta Young Show*, NBC, 1959; Skeet, *Tightrope*, CBS, 1959; Ben McClaren, *Man without a Gun*, syndicated, 1959; Matty Burton, "Omaha Beach," *Alcoa-Goodyear Theatre*, NBC, 1959; bartender, *Wanted: Dead or Alive*, CBS, 1959; Scooter Jaffee, *Private Detective Richard Diamond*, CBS, 1959; Mr. Gilroy, *The Many Loves of Dobie Gillis* (also known as *Dobie Gillis*), CBS, 1959; Deacon Matthews, *Wichita Town*, NBC, 1959; Hal Kirkwood, *Perry Mason*, CBS, 1959.

Jack Scully, *The Rifleman*, ABC, 1960; Mark Twain, *Laramie*, NBC, 1960; Harvey Cleere, *Rescue Eight*, syndicated, 1960; Leo Harris, "One Man Tank" and Slim Newell, "Who's fer Divide," *Death Valley Days*, syndicated, 1960; Colby, *Laramie*, NBC, 1960; Mr. Gilroy, *The Many Loves of Dobie Gillis* (also known as *Dobie Gillis*), CBS, 1960; Farley Weaver, *The Rifleman*, ABC, 1960; Finley, *Wagon Train*, NBC, 1960; Sam, *Johnny Ringo*, CBS, 1960; Finney, *The Rifleman*, ABC, 1960; Knudsen, *Perry Mason*, CBS, 1960; Judge Blau, *Harrigan and Son*, ABC, 1960; Doc Meeker, "Night Song," *The Dupont Show with June Allyson*, CBS, 1960; Dan Reider, *Stagecoach West*, ABC, 1960; driver, *Klondike*, NBC, 1960; Ben Wilson, *Tales of Wells Fargo* (also known as *Wells Fargo*), NBC, 1960; Poe, *The Law and Mr. Jones*, ABC, 1960; nervous shepherd, "The Reluctant Dragon," *Shirley Temple's Storybook*, NBC, 1960; Lester Courtney, *The Lawman*, ABC, 1960; townsman, *Rawhide*, CBS, 1960; Helm Merriweather, *The Detectives, Starring Robert Taylor* (also known as *Robert Taylor's Detectives*), ABC, 1960.

Tom Randall, *The Untouchables*, ABC, 1961; first clerk, *The Jack Benny Show*, CBS, 1961; Sam, *Zane Grey Theatre* (also known as *Dick Powell's Zane Grey Theatre*), CBS, 1961; Al Stehl, *The Asphalt Jungle*, ABC, 1961; Ned Ferber, *The Untouchables*, ABC, 1961; Harry Cole, *This Is the Life*, syndicated, 1961; Todd Adams, "Time for Decision," Mr. Blane, "A Barrel Full of Monkeys," and Ed Foster, "The Outsider," *The Detectives, Starring Robert Taylor* (also known as *Robert Taylor's Detectives*), ABC, 1961; Ed Brandon, *Shotgun Slade*, syndicated, 1961; Foster, *Stagecoach West*, ABC, 1961; Haber, *The Aquanauts* (also known as *Malibu Run*), CBS, 1961; Henry Creasy, *Checkmate*, CBS, 1961; Reverend Forbes, *Adventures in Paradise*, ABC, 1961; Harry Wilson, *Hawaiian Eye*, ABC, 1961; Oscar Cleete, *The Aquanauts* (also known as *Malibu Run*), CBS, 1961; Hokey, *Checkmate*, CBS, 1961; Finney Tate, *Surfside Six*, ABC, 1961; Will Cass, *Bonanza*, NBC, 1961; Jefty, *Bus Stop*, ABC, 1961; Bert Taylor, *The Rifleman*, ABC, 1961; Willie Beal, *Cain's Hundred*, NBC, 1961; Mr. Willis, *Dr. Kildare*, NBC, 1961; Elmo Regis, *Laramie*, NBC, 1961; Buzz Farrell, *Perry Mason*, CBS, 1961; Mr. Halliday, *Ichabod and Me*, CBS, 1961; Councilman Dobbs, *The Andy Griffith Show*, CBS, 1961; Doc Halop, *Have Gun Will Travel*, CBS, 1961.

Mr. Berger, *The Dick Van Dyke Show*, CBS, 1962; Doctor Ellis, "All Day to Live" and Herb Raymond, "The Very Custom Special," *Alcoa Premiere*, ABC, 1962; General Fulton, *Follow the Sun*, ABC, 1962; Joe Brockway, *The Lawman*, ABC, 1962; chaplain, *The Dick Van Dyke Show*, CBS, 1962; Scanlon, "Hocus-Pocus and Frisby" and Evans, "Valley of the Shadow," *The Twilight Zone*, CBS, 1962; Gavin, "Pericles on Thirty-First Street," *The Dick Powell Theatre* (also known as *The Dick Powell Show*), NBC, 1962; hardware store clerk, *The Andy Griffith Show*, CBS, 1962; man at post office, *The Danny Thomas Show*, NBC, 1962; Joe Williams, *Empire*, NBC, 1962; Walter Horner, *Saints and Sinners*, NBC, 1962; Doctor Banner, *Stoney Burke*, ABC, 1962; Ed Crain, *The Eleventh Hour*, NBC, 1962; Fairfield, *The Fugitive*, ABC, 1962; Brower, *The Untouchables*, ABC, 1962; Jebediah Haddlebird, *Rawhide*, CBS, 1963; Charlie Piedmont, *I'm Dickens—He's Fenster*, ABC, 1963; Henshaw, *Bonanza*, NBC, 1963; Wilbur Jonas, *Gunsmoke*, CBS, 1963; Jack Tabor, *Perry Mason*, CBS, 1963; Newton Yort, "A Hero for Our Time," *Kraft Suspense Theatre*, NBC, 1963; Marshal Cloud, *Temple Huston*, NBC, 1963; Sladowski, *Grindl*, NBC, 1963; Halstead, *Perry Mason*, CBS, 1963; Charley Ward, *The Greatest Show on Earth*, ABC, 1963; Madigan, *The Rogues*, NBC, 1963.

Mr. Bishop, "The Children of Spider Country," *The Outer Limits*, ABC, 1964; E.F. Larkin, "The Inheritors," *The Outer Limits*, ABC, 1964; Naylor Sweet, *The Andy Griffith Show*, CBS, 1964; Doctor Forbes, *Destry*, ABC, 1964; Wilbur Jonas, *Gunsmoke*, CBS, 1964; Jules H. Soloman, *Arrest and Trial*, ABC, 1964; Hiram Snow, *Wagon Train*, ABC, 1964; Ossie Weiss, *Hank*, NBC, 1964; Sheriff Claypool, *The Fugitive*, ABC, 1964; Mr. Sims, *The Andy Griffith Show*, CBS, 1964; Doctor Fenner, "Prudence Crandall," *Profiles in Courage*, NBC, 1964; sheriff, *Rawhide*, CBS, 1964; filling station man, *Ninety Bristol Court*, NBC, 1964; mayor, *The Fugitive*, ABC, 1964; Mr. Clark, *The Bill Dana Show*, NBC, 1964; Orville Beaumont, *Wendy and Me*, ABC, 1964; Casey, *Lassie*, CBS, 1964; Taggart, *Peyton Place*, ABC, 1965; night court judge, *The Danny Kaye Show*, CBS, 1965; Dodson, *Perry Mason*, CBS, 1965; Taylor, "John Marshall," *Profiles in Courage*, NBC, 1965; Detective Fullmer, *The Cara Williams Show*, CBS, 1965; Mr. Waring, *The Dick Van Dyke Show*, CBS, 1965; reformed crook, *The Danny Kaye Show*, CBS, 1965; doctor,

The Virginian, NBC, 1965; Harper Caldwell, *Gomer Pyle, U.S.M.C.*, CBS, 1965; Mr. Brumley, *The Dick Van Dyke Show*, CBS, 1965.

Paul Leonard, *The F.B.I.*, ABC, 1966; Charles Fletcher, *The Fugitive*, ABC, 1966; Wilbur Jonas, *Gunsmoke*, CBS, 1966; Bill Cotton, *Perry Mason*, CBS, 1966; Ira, *Laredo*, NBC, 1966; Thomas Gimmer, *The Road West*, NBC, 1966; Roger Porter, *The F.B.I.*, ABC, 1966; Thomas, *The Fugitive*, ABC, 1966; Sam Bryant, *Bonanza*, NBC, 1966; minister, *The Invaders*, ABC, 1966; Sheriff Simmons, *Rango*, ABC, 1966; chaplain, *The Dick Van Dyke Show*, CBS, 1966; Mr. Thompson, *The Danny Kaye Show*, CBS, 1967; Sam Jensen, *The Fugitive*, ABC, 1967; Alvin Van Doyle, *The F.B.I.*, ABC, 1967; Ed Harger, *The Virginian*, NBC, 1967; Hub Dawes, *Bonanza*, NBC, 1967; Daniel Turpin, *Mannix*, CBS, 1967; Matt Carson, *The Big Valley*, ABC, 1967; motorcycle cop, *Gomer Pyle, U.S.M.C.*, CBS, 1967; Judge Quayle, *Cimarron Strip*, CBS, 1967; General Craven, *The Second Hundred Years*, ABC, 1967; Doctor Zellmer, *Judd, for the Defense*, ABC, 1967; Wilbur Jonas, *Gunsmoke*, CBS, 1967; Senator Seth Buckley, *The Wild Wild West*, CBS, 1968; Patrick Owens, *The F.B.I.*, ABC, 1968; Peck, *Petticoat Junction*, CBS, 1968; Petey O'Grady, *Mannix*, CBS, 1968; Norrie Coolidge, *The Ghost and Mrs. Muir*, NBC, 1968; Orkin, *The F.B.I.*, ABC, 1968; Captain Lyman Butler, *The Wild Wild West*, CBS, 1968; Ralph Lebow, *Judd, for the Defense*, ABC, 1968; Doc Tasker Dunkett, *Bonanza*, NBC, 1968; Norrie Coolidge, *The Ghost and Mrs. Muir*, NBC, 1969; Wilkie Coombs, *Mannix*, CBS, 1969; Thomas Gibbs, *Ironside*, NBC, 1969; sheriff, *Lancer*, CBS, 1969; Stilts, "The Boy Who Stole the Elephant," *The Wonderful World of Disney*, NBC, 1969; Arlie Sessions, *The F.B.I.*, ABC, 1969; Mr. Carew, *Ironside*, NBC, 1969; man on the bus, *Bracken's World*, NBC, 1969.

Victor Bychek, *The Name of the Game*, NBC, 1970; judge, *Bonanza*, NBC, 1970; Edgar Jarvis, *The Interns*, CBS, 1970; Howard Deal, *The F.B.I.*, ABC, 1970; Fred Smith, *Bonanza*, NBC, 1970; Jacobi, *The Young Lawyers*, ABC, 1970; Sam Dawson, *Bonanza*, NBC, 1970; Casey, *The Bold Ones*, NBC, 1971; Sal Cleary, *The F.B.I.*, ABC, 1971; Billy Jack, *O'Hara, U.S. Treasury*, CBS, 1971; Harrigan, Sr., *Nichols*, NBC, 1971; bus stop owner, *The Mod Squad*, ABC, 1972; studio guard, *The Rookies*, ABC, 1971; Harry Bell, "Earth, Air, Fire, and Water," *Ghost Story* (also known as *Circle of Fire*), ABC, 1972; Andy Spake, *Barnaby Jones*, CBS, 1972; Kelsey Waller, *The F.B.I.*, ABC, 1973; William Salter, *Cannon*, CBS, 1973; old filekeeper, *Ironside*, NBC, 1973; Dave Carson, *Adam-12*, NBC, 1973; Billy Levinson, *The Rookies*, ABC, 1973; Joe Bean, *Gunsmoke*, CBS, 1973; motel owner, *Chopper One*, ABC, 1973; Charles, *Firehouse*, ABC, 1973; Larry Parino, *Chase*, NBC, 1974; Orville Norton, *Paper Moon*, ABC, 1974; Walt Fox, *Cannon*, CBS, 1974; Harry Bell, *The Manhunter*, CBS, 1974; Seldom Seen Sam, *Shazam!*, CBS, 1975; Peter Preli, *The Rockford Files*, NBC, 1975; Rudy Zender, *Bert D'Angelo/Superstar*, ABC, 1976; watchman, *Streets of San Francisco*, NBC, 1976; Doctor Hubert Nippert, *Emergency*, NBC, 1976; Doctor Malone, *The Incredible Hulk*, CBS, 1978; Bluford Catlin, *Charlie's Angels*, ABC, 1979; *The Greatest American Hero*, ABC, 1981; Henry, *Matt Houston*, ABC, 1982; Ralph Woolsey, *Starman*, ABC, 1985; Russell, *Werewolf*, Fox, 1987; Buzz Benson, *Charles in Charge*, syndicated, 1987; Ben Farber, *Something Is Out There*, NBC, 1988; voice characterizations, *The Ann Jillian Show*, NBC, 1989; Joe, *Roseanne*, ABC, 1989; minister, *The Bradys*, CBS, 1990.

Also Paul Barrows, "Miracle at Eagle Bluff" and Max Klein, "116 E. 20th Street," *Jeweler's Showcase*, 1952; Sandy, *Mr. McNutley*, 1953; Fred Fielding, "Doc," Erwin Martin, "The Catbird Seat,"

MacIntosh, "Ask Me No Questions," and Papa Kirk, "At Mrs. Lelands," *Matinee Theatre*, 1956; Doctor Petrie, "Trigger-Finger Clue," Tad Duncan, Sr., "Courage," Doctor Rayborn, "The Old, Old Story," Paul Diamond, "Go Fight City Hall," and Captain Larsen, "The Smuggler," *Readers Digest*, 1956; Louis Johnson, *Code Three*, 1956; Melvin Sanders, *Fury*, 1956; Sheriff Barton, "Swing Your Partner, Hector," *Heinz Playhouse*, 1956; James Andrews, *Official Detective*, 1957; Mr. Boswaithe, *Anything, Incorporated*, 1957; Ben Tait, "The Party Dress," *Matinee Theatre*, 1957; Dan Seery, *Best of the Post*, 1957; John Cooper, *Grey Ghost*, 1957; Hez Crabtree, "Hickory Heart," *Matinee Theatre*, 1958; Emil Roland, *Night Watch*, 1958; George Hamlin, *This Is the Answer*, 1959; Paul Feeney, *Rogue for Hire*, 1959; Wesley, *The Plainsman*, 1959; Charlie, *Gringo*, 1959; Joe Kane, *J.P.*, 1960; Sheriff Barrett, *The Pony Express*, 1960; Sergeant Croft, *Unsolved*, 1960; Willy Medford, *Two Faces West*, 1960; Ed Morgan, *Counterintelligence Corps*, 1961; Joe Bartle, *Lone Sierra*, 1961; the Old Fox, *The Park Ranger*, 1963; Caswell, *The Lawyer*, 1964; Henry Fogle, "Secret of the Lost Creek," *Disney's Mickey Mouse Club*, 1989.

Movies: Captain John Sharke, *Dick Tracy*, syndicated, 1952; Mr. Cousins, *Green Eyes*, ABC, 1977; Ace Hutchkins, *The Winds of Kitty Hawk*, NBC, 1978; Reverend Robert Alden, *Little House: Look Back to Yesterday*, NBC, 1983; Reverend Robert Alden, *Little House: The Last Farewell*, NBC, 1984; Sills, *Bonanza: The Next Generation*, syndicated, 1988. Also appeared as Nico Van Eyden, *Time Is a Dream*, 1948.

PRINCIPAL TELEVISION WORK—Director, *Time Is a Dream*, 1948.

RELATED CAREER—Head of public schools drama department, Mountain Grove, MO, 1940-43, head of community theatre, Mountain Grove, 1941-43; instructor, director, and dean of academic studies, Pasadena Playhouse School of Theatre, 1943-50; actor in television commercials, public service messages, industrial films, and educational programs.

MEMBER: Lambda Chi Alpha.

ADDRESSES: OFFICE—P.O. Box 322 (M), Pasadena, CA 91102. AGENT—Dade, Rosen, and Schultz, 15010 Ventura Boulevard, Suite 219, Sherman Oaks, CA 91403.

*   *   *

GREER, Jane   1924-
(Bettejane Greer)

PERSONAL: Born Bettejane Greer, September 9, 1924, in Washington, DC; married Rudy Vallee (a singer and actor), 1943 (divorced, 1944).

VOCATION: Actress.

CAREER: FILM DEBUT—(As Bettejane Greer) Miss Dowling, *Pan-Americana*, RKO, 1945. PRINCIPAL FILM APPEARANCES—(As Bettejane Greer) Helen, *Two O'Clock Courage*, RKO, 1945; (as Bettejane Greer) Billie Randall, *George White's Scandals*, RKO, 1945; Judith Owens, *Dick Tracy* (also known as *Splitface* and *Dick Tracy, Detective*), RKO, 1945; Eileen Sawyer, *The Bamboo Blonde*, RKO, 1946; Lola Carpenter, *The Falcon's Alibi*, RKO,

JANE GREER

1946; Helen, *Sunset Pass*, RKO, 1946; Kathie Moffett, *Out of the Past* (also known as *Build My Gallows High*), RKO, 1947; Janice Bell, *They Won't Believe Me*, RKO, 1947; Pirouze, *Sinbad the Sailor*, RKO, 1947; Charlie, *Station West*, RKO, 1948; Joan, *The Big Steal*, RKO, 1949; Diane, *The Company She Keeps*, RKO, 1950; Ellie, *You're in the Navy Now* (also known as *U.S.S. Tea Kettle*), Twentieth Century-Fox, 1951; Julie Heldon, *Desperate Search*, Metro-Goldwyn-Mayer (MGM), 1952; Antoinette de Mauban, *The Prisoner of Zenda*, MGM, 1952; Katie McDermad, *You for Me*, MGM, 1952; Paula Henderson, *The Clown*, MGM, 1953; Diana Forrester, *Down Among the Sheltering Palms*, Twentieth Century-Fox, 1953; Katy Connors, *Run for the Sun*, United Artists, 1956; Hazel Bennet, *Man of a Thousand Faces*, Universal, 1957; Marian Spicer, *Where Love Has Gone*, Paramount, 1964; Agnes Carol, *Billie*, United Artists, 1965; Alma, *The Outfit* (also known as *The Good Guys Always Win*), MGM, 1973; Mrs. Wyler, *Against All Odds*, Columbia, 1984; Ruth Chadwick, *Just xBetween Friends*, Orion, 1986; Michael's mother, *Immediate Family*, Columbia, 1989.

PRINCIPAL TELEVISION APPEARANCES—Episodic: Kathleen Kane, *Stagecoach West*, ABC, 1960; Charlotte Pershing, *Falcon Crest*, CBS, 1984; Louise Browning, *The Insiders*, ABC, 1985; Augusta Stillman, *The Law and Harry McGraw*, CBS, 1987; Bonnie Phelps, *Murder, She Wrote*, CBS, 1988; Valerie Jeffries, *HeartBeat*, ABC, 1989; also "Look for Tomorrow," *Ford Theatre*, NBC, 1953; "Summer Dance," *Mirror Theatre*, CBS, 1953; "One Man Missing," *Playhouse 90*, NBC, 1955; "Moment of Decision," *Ford Theatre*, ABC, 1957; "A Gun for My Bride," *Zane Grey Theatre*, CBS, 1957; "Meeting in Paris," *Suspicion*, NBC, 1958; *Alfred Hitchcock Presents*, CBS, 1958; *Bonanza*, NBC, 1959; "Portrait of a Face," *Thriller*, NBC, 1961; *Burke's*

Law, ABC, 1964. Movies: Ma Traven, *Louis L'Amour's "The Shadow Riders,"* CBS, 1982.

RELATED CAREER—Professional model from the age 12; appeared as a WAC on the cover of *Life* magazine and on recruiting posters; singer with nightclub band.

ADDRESSES: AGENT—Merritt Blake, Camden Artists, 2121 Avenue of the Stars, Suite 410, Los Angeles, CA 90067.

*   *   *

GRIMALDI, Alberto   1927-

PERSONAL: Born in 1927 in Naples, Italy.

VOCATION: Producer.

CAREER: FIRST FILM WORK—Producer, *L'ombra di Zorro,* 1963. PRINCIPAL FILM WORK—All as producer unless indicated: *Faccia a faccia* (also known as *Face to Face*), Arturo Gonzales, 1967; *Per qualche dollaro in piu* (also known as *For a Few Dollars More*), 1966, released in the United States by United Artists, 1967; *Il buono, il brutto, il cattivo* (also known as *The Good, the Bad, and the Ugly*), 1966, released in the United States by United Artists, 1967; *La resa dei conti* (also known as *The Big Gundown*), Columbia, 1968; *Scusi, facciamo l'amore?* (also known as *Listen, Let's Make Love* and *Et si on faisait l'amour?*), 1968, released in the United States by Lopert, 1969; *Il mercenario* (also known as *The Mercenary* and *Salario para matar*), 1968, released in the United Artists by 1970; *Un tranquillo posto di campagna* (also known as *A Quiet Place in the Country* and *Un coin tranquille a la campagne*), 1968, released in the United States by Lopert, 1970; *Fellini Satyricon* (also known as *Satyricon*), United Artists, 1969; *Ehi, amico . . . c'e Sabata, hai chiuso* (also known as *Sabata*), United Artists, 1969.

The Bounty Hunters, P.E.A. Cinematografica, 1970; *Quemada!* (also known as *Burn!*), United Artists, 1970; *Companeros* (also known as *Vamos a matar, companeros!*), TerraFilmkunst, 1970; *Adios Sabata* (also known as *Indio Black sai che to dico: sei un gran figlio di . . .*), United Artists, 1971; *Il Decamerone* (also known as *The Decameron*), United Artists, 1971; *Oceano* (also known as *The Wind Blows Free*), P.E.A., 1971; executive producer, *Man of La Mancha* (also known as *L'uomo della Manch*), United Artists, 1972; *Last Tango in Paris* (also known as *Ultimo tango a Parigi*), United Artists, 1972; *I racconti di Canterbury* (also known as *The Canterbury Tales*), United Artists, 1972; *Trastevere,* P.E.A., 1972; *Return of Sabata* (also known as *E' tornato Sabata* and *Hai chiuso un'altra volta*), United Artists, 1972; *Storie scellerate* (also known as *Roguish Stories*), United Artists/P.E.A., 1973; *E pio lo chiamarono il magnifico* (also known as *A Man from the East* and *And Then They'll Call Him the Magnificent*), United Artists, 1974; *Il fiore delle mille e una notte* (also known as *A Thousand and One Nights* and *The Arabian Nights*), P.E.A., 1974, released in the United States by United Artists, 1980; *Salo o le centiventi giornate di Sodoma* (also known as *Salo—The 100 Days of Sodom, Pasolini's Days of Sodom,* and *Salo*), United Artists/Cenecenta, 1975; *Cadaveri eccellenti* (also known as *Illustrious Corpses* and *The Context*), Cinegate, 1975, released in the United States by United Artists, 1976; *Casanova* (also known as *Fellini's Casanova* and *Il Casanova di Federico Fellini*), Universal, 1976; *1900* (also known as *Novecento*), Paramount/United Artists/Twentieth Century-

Fox, 1976; *Lovers and Liars* (also known as *A Trip with Anita* and *Travels with Anita*), Levitt/Pickman, 1981; *Ginger et Fred* (also known as *Ginger and Fred,* Metro-Goldwyn-Mayer/United Artists, 1986.

RELATED CAREER—President, P.E.A. (Produzioni Europee Associate, S.A.S.) Films Inc; lawyer for Italian film companies.*

*   *   *

GROENER, Harry   1951-

PERSONAL: Born September 10, 1951, in Augsburg, Germany; father, a concert pianist, composer, and office clerk; mother, an opera singer; married Dawn Didawick (an actress). EDUCATION—Graduated from the University of Washington; studied dance at the San Francisco Conservatory of Ballet; studied acting at the Pacific Conservatory of Performing Arts and with the Bachelor of Fine Arts Professional Actors Training Program at the University of Washington.

VOCATION: Actor.

CAREER: BROADWAY DEBUT—Will Parker, *Oklahoma!,* Palace Theatre, 1979. PRINCIPAL STAGE APPEARANCES—Floyd Beavis, *Back Country,* Wilbur Theatre, Boston, MA, 1978; Bix Beiderbecke, *Hoagy, Bix, and Wolfgang Beethoven Bunkhaus,* Center Theatre Group, Mark Taper Forum, Los Angeles, 1980; Western Mousada, *Oh, Brother!,* American National Theatre and Academy Theatre, New York City, 1981; Munkustrap, *Cats,* Winter Garden Theatre,

HARRY GROENER

New York City, 1982; Algernon, *The Importance of Being Earnest* and Billy Bishop, *Billy Bishop Goes to War*, both Old Globe Theatre, San Diego, CA, 1982; Julian, "The Public Eye" and Brindsley, "Black Comedy," in *Light Comedies*, Center Theatre Group, Ahmanson Theatre, Los Angeles, 1983; title role, *Scapino!*, Old Globe Theatre, 1984; title role, *Sunday in the Park with George*, Booth Theatre, New York City, 1985; Edward Harrigan, *Harrigan 'n' Hart*, Longacre Theatre, New York City, 1985; Dickie Wentworth, *Girl Crazy*, Seattle Repertory Theatre, Seattle, WA, 1985; Paul, *Sleight of Hand*, Cort Theatre, New York City, 1987; Stephen Wheeler, *Eastern Standard*, Seattle Repertory Theatre, 1988; title role, *Sunday in the Park with George*, South Coast Repertory Theatre, Costa Mesa, CA, 1989. Also appeared with the Actors Theatre of Louisville, Louisville, KY, 1976-77; in *Hobson's Choice*, Long Wharf Theatre, New Haven, CT, 1977; *Journey's End*, Long Wharf Theatre, 1978; *Merton of the Movies*, Hartman Theatre Company, Stamford, CT, 1981; *Is There Life After High School?*, Ethel Barrymore Theatre, New York City, 1982; *Ghetto*, Center Theatre Group, Mark Taper Forum, 1986; and in *Beside the Seaside*.

FILM DEBUT—Dr. Campbell, *Brubaker*, Twentieth Century-Fox, 1980.

PRINCIPAL TELEVISION APPEARANCES—Series: Ralph, *Dear John*, NBC, 1988—. Mini-Series: Patrick Henry, *George Washington*, CBS, 1984; Lowell Kane, *Kane and Abel*, CBS, 1985. Episodic: Preston Hayes, *Remington Steele*, NBC, 1985; Klaus Brinkman, *St. Elsewhere*, NBC, 1987; Colin Johnson, *Jack and Mike*, ABC, 1987; George Lynwood, *Spenser: For Hire*, ABC, 1988; Michael Talbert, *Studio 5-B*, ABC, 1989; Rod Greenwood, *Matlock*, NBC, 1989; also *Star Trek: The Next Generation*, syndicated, 1990; *Captain Kangaroo*. Movies: *The Country Girl*, Showtime. Specials: *The Macy's Thanksgiving Day Parade*, NBC, 1988.

AWARDS: Antoinette Perry Award nomination, Best Featured Actor in a Musical, and Theatre World Award, both 1980, for *Oklahoma!*; Antoinette Perry Award nomination, Best Featured Actor in a Musical, 1983, for *Cats*.

SIDELIGHTS: RECREATIONS—Traveling throughout America.

ADDRESSES: AGENT—Smith-Freedman and Associates, 121 N. San Vicente Boulevard, Beverly Hills, CA 90211.

* * *

GROSS, Arye

VOCATION: Actor.

CAREER: PRINCIPAL STAGE APPEARANCES—Troilus, *Troilus and Cressida*, Globe Playhouse, Los Angeles, 1985; Second Lieutenant Rode, *The Three Sisters*, Los Angeles Theatre Center, Los Angeles, 1985; also appeared with the South Coast Repertory Theatre, Costa Mesa, CA, 1978-80.

PRINCIPAL FILM APPEARANCES—Turbo, *Exterminator II*, Cannon, 1984; Willie, *Just One of the Guys*, Columbia, 1985; Gordon Bloomfeld, *Soul Man*, New World, 1986; Jesse McLaughlin, *House II: The Second Story*, New World, 1987; Perry Kovin, *The Couch Trip*, Orion, 1988; Andy Leonard, *Tequila Sunrise*, Warner

Brothers, 1988; Wendell, *The Experts*, Paramount, 1989; Maxwell Glass, *A Matter of Degrees*, Backbeat Productions, 1990.

PRINCIPAL TELEVISION APPEARANCES—Episodic: Albert Wellington, *Remington Steele*, NBC, 1986; Otis, *Heart of the City*, ABC, 1986. Movies: Joel Baskin, *Into the Homeland* (also known as *Swallows Come Back* and *When the Swallows Come Back*), HBO, 1987.

ADDRESSES: AGENTS—Agency for the Performing Arts, 9000 Sunset Boulevard, Suite 1200, Los Angeles, CA 90069; Creative Artists Agency, 9830 Wilshire Boulevard, Beverly Hills, CA 90212.*

* * *

GUARE, John 1938-

PERSONAL: Born February 5, 1938, in New York, NY; son of Edward and Helen Claire (Grady) Guare; married Adele Chatfield-Taylor (an artist), May 20, 1981. EDUCATION—Georgetown University, A.B., 1961; Yale University School of Drama, M.F.A., 1963. MILITARY—U.S. Air Force Reserve, 1963.

VOCATION: Playwright.

CAREER: Also see WRITINGS below. PRINCIPAL STAGE WORK—Director, *In Fireworks Lie Secret Codes*, Mitzi E. Newhouse Theatre, New York City, 1981.

RELATED CAREER—Assistant to the manager, National Theatre, Washington, DC, 1960; member, Barr/Wilder/Albee Playwrights Unit, New York City, 1964; founding member, Eugene O'Neill Playwrights Conference, Waterford, CT, 1965; playwright-in-residence, New York Shakespeare Festival, New York City, 1977; seminar in writing fellow, Yale University, New Haven, CT, 1977-78, then adjunct professor of playwriting, 1978-81; vice-president, Theatre Communications Group, 1986; lecturer, New York University, New York City; fellow, New York Institute for Humanities; member of board of directors, Municipal Arts Society, New York City.

WRITINGS: STAGE—*Universe*, first produced in New York City, 1949; *Theatre Girl*, first produced in Washington, DC, 1959; *The Toadstool Boy*, first produced in Washington, DC, 1960; *The Golden Cherub*, first produced in New Haven, CT, 1962; *Did You Write My Name in the Snow?*, Yale University, New Haven, CT, 1962; *To Wally Pantoni, We Leave a Credenza*, New Dramatists Community Workshop, New York City, 1964; *The Loveliest Afternoon of the Year* and *Something I'll Tell You Tuesday* (double-bill), Caffe Cino, New York City, 1966, published by Dramatists Play Service, 1968; *Muzeeka*, first produced in Waterford, CT, 1967, then Mark Taper Forum, Los Angeles, 1967, later Provincetown Playhouse, New York City, 1968, then Open Space Theatre, London, 1969, published by Dramatists Play Service, 1968, in *Muzeeka and Other Plays*, Grove, 1969, *Off Broadway Plays*, Penguin, 1970, and in *Cop-Out, Muzeeka, Home Fires*, Grove, 1971; (also composer and lyricist) *Cop-Out* and *Home Fires* (double-bill), first produced in Waterford, CT, 1968, then Cort Theatre, New York City, 1969, published by Samuel French, 1968, in *Muzeeka and Other Plays*, 1969, *Off Broadway Plays*, 1970, and in *Cop-Out, Muzeeka, Home Fires*, 1971; *A Play by Brecht*, Broadhurst Theatre, New York City, 1969.

(Also composer and lyricist) *The House of Blue Leaves,* Truck and Warehouse Theatre, New York City, 1971, later revived at the Mitzi E. Newhouse Theatre, then Vivian Beaumont Theatre, both New York City, 1986, published as *The House of Blue Leaves: A Play,* Viking, 1972, in *Three Exposures,* Harcourt, 1982, and in *The House of Blue Leaves and Two Other Plays,* New American Library, 1987; (adaptor with Mel Shapiro and lyricist) *Two Gentlemen of Verona,* New York Shakespeare Festival (NYSF), Delacorte Theatre, then St. James Theatre, both New York City, 1971, later Phoenix Theatre, London, 1973, published by Holt, 1973; *A Day for Surprises,* Basement Theatre, London, 1971, published by Dramatists Play Service, 1970; (with Harold Stone) *Optimism, or the Adventures of Candide,* Eugene O'Neill Foundation Theatre, Waterford, CT, 1973; *Marco Polo Sings a Solo,* Cyrus Pierce Theatre, Nantucket, MA, 1973, then NYSF, Public Theatre, New York City, 1977, published by Dramatists Play Service, 1977; (also composer and lyricist) *Rich and Famous,* first produced in Lake Forest, IL, 1974, then NYSF, Public Theatre, 1976, published by Dramatists Play Service, 1977; (also composer and lyricist) *Landscape of the Body,* Academy Festival Theatre, Lake Forest, IL, then NYSF, Public Theatre, both 1977, published by Dramatists Play Service, 1978, in *Three Exposures,* 1982, and in *The House of Blue Leaves and Two Other Plays,* 1987; *Take a Dream,* produced in New York City, 1978; *Bosoms and Neglect,* Goodman Theatre, Chicago, IL, 1979, then Longacre Theatre, New York City, 1979, published by Dramatists Play Service, 1979, in *Three Exposures,* 1982, and in *The House of Blue Leaves and Two Other Plays,* 1981.

In Fireworks Lie Secret Codes, Mitzi E. Newhouse Theatre, 1981, published by Dramatists Play Service, 1981; *Lydie Breeze,* American Place Theatre, New York City, 1982, published by Dramatists Play Service, 1982; *Gardenia,* Manhattan Theatre Club, New York City, 1982, then London, 1983, published by Dramatists Play Service, 1982; (also composer and lyricist) *Hey, Stay a While,* Goodman Theatre, 1984; *Women and Water,* first produced in Los Angeles, 1984, then Arena Stage, Washington, DC, 1985; "Gluttony" in *The Show of the Seven Deadly Sins,* McCarter Theatre, Princeton, NJ, 1985; *The Talking Dog,* first produced in Urbana, IL, 1985, then in *Orchards,* Lucille Lortel Theatre, New York City, 1986, published by Knopf, 1986; *Moon Over Miami,* Yale Repertory Theatre, New Haven, CT, 1989.

FILM—(With Milos Foreman, Jean-Claude Carriere, and John Klein) *Taking Off,* Universal, 1971, published by New American Library, 1971; *Atlantic City,* Paramount, 1981. TELEVISION—Episodic: "Kissing Sweet," *Foul!,* PBS, 1969, published by Dramatists Play Service, 1970.

OTHER—(Contributor) *Showcase I: Plays from the Eugene O'Neill Foundation,* edited by John Lahr, Grove, 1969; (preface) *From Ibsen: Workshop,* Da Capo Press, 1978.

AWARDS: ABC-Yale University fellowship, 1966; Obie Award from the *Village Voice,* Distinguished Play, 1968, for *Muzeeka;* *Variety* New York Drama Critics' Poll Award, Most Promising Playwright, 1969, for *Cop-Out;* New York Drama Critics' Circle Award, Best American Play, Outer Critic' Circle Award, and Obie Award, Best New Play, all 1971, for *The House of Blue Leaves;* New York Drama Critics' Circle Award, Best Musical, Antoinette Perry Awards, Best Musical and Best Libretto, Drama Desk Awards, Best Book and Lyrics, and *Variety* New York Drama Critics' Poll Award, Best Lyricist, all 1972, for *Two Gentlemen of Verona;* Joseph Jefferson Award, 1977, for *Landscape of the Body;* Award of Merit from the American Academy of Arts and Letters, 1981; New York Film Critics' Award, Los Angeles Film Critics' Award,

National Society of Film Critics' Award, and Grand Prize from the Venice Film Festival, all Best Screenplay, and Academy Award nomination, Best Original Screenplay, all 1981, for *Atlantic City;* New York Institute of the Humanities fellowship, 1982; Antoinette Perry Award, Best Play, 1986, for *The House of Blue Leaves;* Rockefeller grant in playwriting.

MEMBER: Dramatists Guild (board of directors), Authors League of America, P.E.N. (executive board).

ADDRESSES: AGENT—R. Andrew Boose, Collyer and Boose, One Dag Hammarskjold Plaza, New York, NY 10017.*

* * *

GUDEGAST, Hans
See BRAEDEN, Eric

* * *

GUERRA, Tonino 1920-

PERSONAL: Full name, Antonio Guerra; born March 16, 1920, in Santarcangelo di Romagna, Italy; married Lora Iabloskina. EDUCATION—Received a degree in education.

VOCATION: Screenwriter.

WRITINGS: FILM—(With Michelangelo Antonioni and Elio Bartolini) *L'avventura* (also known as *The Adventure*), 1960, released in the United States by Janus, 1961, published in 1969; (with Antonioni and Ernio Flaiano) *La notte* (also known as *The Night*), Dino De Laurentiis, 1961, released in the United States by Lopert, 1962, published in *Screenplays by Michelangelo Antonioni,* 1963; (with Elio Petri, Pasquale Festa Campanile, and Massimo Franciosa) *L'assassino* (also known as *The Assassin* and *The Lady Killer of Rome*), Titanus, 1961, released in the United States by Manson Distributing, 1965; (with Antonioni, Bartolini, and Otliero Ottieri) *L'eclisse* (also known as *Eclipse* and *L'Eclipse*), Times, 1962, published in *Screenplays by Michelangelo Antonioni,* 1963; (with Damiano Damiani and Ugo Liberatore) *La noia* (also known as *The Empty Canvas, L'ennui et sa diversion,* and *L'erotisme*), 1963, released in the United States by Embassy, 1964; (with Alberto Moravia) *Le ore nude* (also known as *The Naked Hours*), Atlantica, 1964; (with Eduardo De Filippo, Renato Castellani, Leo Benvenuti, and Piero De Bernardi) *Matrimonia all'Italiana* (also known as *Marriage, Italian Style*), Embassy, 1964; (with Antonioni) *Il deserto rosso* (also known as *Red Desert* and *Le Desert rouge*), 1964, released in the United States by Rizzoli, 1965; (with Alberto De Martino, Sandro Continenza, and Natividad Zaro) *Gli invincibili sette* (also known as *The Secret Seven* and *Los invincibles*), 1964, released in the United States by Metro-Goldwyn-Mayer (MGM), 1966.

(With Petri, Ennio Flaiano, and Giorgio Salvioni) *The Tenth Victim* (also known as *La decima vittima* and *La Dixieme victime*), Embassy, 1965; (with Ottavio Jemma, Flavio Nicolini, and Marcello Baldi) *Saul e David* (also known as *Saul and David* and *Saul y David*), 1965, released in the United States by Rizzoli, 1968; (with Antonioni and Edward Bond) *Blow-Up,* Premier, 1966; (with Ruggero Maccari, Suso Lecchi D'Amico, Giorgio Salvioni, and

Rodolfo Sonego) "Fata Armenia" in *Le fate* (also known as *The Queens* and *Les Ogresses*), 1966, released in the United States by Royal, 1968; (with Raffaele La Capria, Giuseppe Patroni Griffi, and Francesco Rosi) *More Than a Miracle* (also known as *Cera, una volta, La Belle et le cavalier, Cinderella— Italian Style, Happily Ever After*, and *Once Upon a Time*), MGM, 1967; (with Franco Indovina and Luigi Malerba) *Lo scatenato* (also known as *Catch as Catch Can* and *Tutti Frutti*), 1967, released in the United States by Fair Film, 1968; (with Paolo Cavara and Moravia) *L'occhio selvaggio* (also known as *The Wild Eye*), 1967, released in the United States by American International, 1968; (with Julian Haleavy, Peter Baldwin, Ennio De Concini, Cesara Zavattini, and Vittorio DeSica) *Amanti* (also known as *A Place for Lovers* and *Le Temps des amants*), 1968, released in the United States by MGM, 1969.

(With Lucille Laks and Ken Levison) *In Search of Gregory* (also known as *Alla ricerca di Gregory*), Universal, 1970; (with Rosi and Raffaele LaCapria) *Uomini contro* (also known as *Just Another War*), Euro International, 1970; (with Elio Petri and Luciano Vincenzoni) *A Quiet Place in the Country* (also known as *Un tranquillo posto di campagna* and *Un coin tranquille a la campagne*), Lopert, 1970; (with Zavattini and Gregory Molivani) *Sunflower* (also known as *Les Fleurs du soleil* and *I girasoli*), AVCO-Embassy, 1970; (with Antonioni, Fred Gardner, Sam Shepard, and Clare Peploe) *Zabriskie Point*, MGM, 1970; (with Rosi) *Il caso Mattei* (also known as *The Mattei Affair* and *The Enrico Mattei Affair*), Cinema International, 1971; (with Iaia Fiastri, Lattuada, and Ruggero Maccari) *Bianco, rosso, e . . .* (also known as *White, Red, and . . ., White Sister*, and *The Sin*), Columbia/Warner Brothers, 1973; (with Federico Fellini) *Amarcord*, Warner Brothers/New World, 1974; (with Rosi and Lino Jannuzzi) *Re: Lucky Luciano* (also known as *Lucky Luciano* and *A proposito Luciano*), Titanus Distribuzione, 1973, released in the United States by AVCO-Embassy, 1974; (with Laks and Pierre Grimblat) *Dites-le avec les fleurs* (also known as *Say It with Flowers*), Gaumont, 1974.

(With Sergio Martino and Giorgio Salvioni) *40 gradi soto il lenzuolo* (also known as *40 gradi all'ombra del'lenzuolo* and *Sex with a Smile*), Medusa Distribuzione, 1975; (with Rosi and Jannuzzi) *Cadaveri eccellenti* (also known as *Illustrious Corpses* and *The Context*), Cinegate, 1975, released in the United States by United Artists, 1976; (with Suso Cecchi D'Amico) *Caro Michele* (also known as *Dear Michael*), Cineriz, 1976; *Letti selvaggi* (also known as *Wilde Betten*), Avis Filmverleih/Ascot Filmverleih, 1978; (with Giorgio Salvioni) *Tigers in Lipstick* (also known as *Wild Beds* and *Hijinks*), Zodiac, 1978; (with Rosi and LaCapria) *Cristo si e fermato a Eboli* (also known as *Christ Stopped at Eboli* and *Eboli*), Titanus Distribuzione/Artificial Eye, 1978; (with Jean-Claude Carriere and Jacques Deray) *Un Papillon sur l'epaule* (also known as *A Butterfly on the Shoulder*), Gaumont International/Roissy, 1978.

(With Antonioni) *Il mistero di Oberwald* (also known as *The Mystery of Oberwald*), Artificial Eye/Films sans Frontieres, 1980; (with Rosi) *Tre fratelli* (also known as *Three Brothers*), Gaumont International/Artificial Eye, 1981; (with Vittorio Taviani and Giuliani G. De Negri) *La notte di San Lorenzo* (also known as *The Night of the Shooting Stars* and *The Night of San Lorenzo*), United Artists, 1982; (with Fellini) *E la nave va* (also known as *And the Ship Sails On*), Vides, 1983; (with Antonioni and Gerard Brach) *Identificazione di una donna* (also known as *Identification of a Woman*), Gaumont, 1983; (with Andrei Tarkovsky) *Nostalghia* (also known as *Nostalgia*), Artificial Eye, 1983, released in the

United States by Grange, 1984; (with Rosi) *Bizet's Carmen* (also known as *Carmen*), Triumph, 1984; (with Paolo Taviani and Vittorio Taviani) *Kaos* (also known as *Chaos*), Cannon Film Distributors/Gala Film Distributors/Metro-Goldwyn-Mayer/United Artists Classics, 1984; (with Theo Angelopoulos and Theo Valtinos) *Taxidi stin Kythera* (also known as *Voyage to Cythera*), Greek Film Center, 1984; (with Marco Bellocchio) *Enrico IV* (also known as *Henry IV*), Gaumont, 1984, released in the United States by Orion Classics, 1985.

(With Fellini and Tullio Pinelli) *Ginger et Fred* (also known as *Ginger and Fred*), Metro-Goldwyn-Mayer/United Artists, 1986; (with Angelopoulos and Dimitris Nollas) *O Melissokomos* (also known as *The Bee Keeper*), Greek Film Center/Marin Karmitz/Artificial Eye, 1986; (with Rosi) *Cronaca di una morte annunciata* (also known as *Chronicle of a Death Foretold, Chronique d'une morte announcee, Cronica di una muerte anunciada*, and *Chronicle of a Death Announced*), Istituto Luce Italnoleggio/Virgin Vision/Gaumont/AAA/Island, 1987; (with Paolo Taviani and Vittorio Taviani) *Good Morning Babylon* (also known as *Good Morning Babilonia*), Vestron/Artificial Eye, 1987; (with Angelopoulos and Thanassis Valtinos) *Topio stin omichli* (also known as *Paysage dans le brouillard, Landscape in the Mist*, and *Paesaggio nella nebbia*), Alliance Vivafilm/Bac/ Artificial Eye/Films du Volcan, 1988; (with Gianfranco Mingozzi and Roberto Roversi) *La Femme de mes amours* (also known as *Il frutto del passero, L'Envol du moineau*, and *The Sparrow's Fluttering*), Medusa Distribuzione/AAA/Initial Groupe, 1988; (with Antonio Guerra) *Burro* (also known as *Butter*), Artisti Associati/Filmexport, 1989.

Also *Uomini e lupe* (also known as *Men and Wolves*), 1956; *Un ettaro di cielo*, 1957; *Cesta duga godinu dana* (also known as *La strada lunga un'anno*), 1958; *Le signore*, 1960; *Il carro armata dell'otto Settembre*, 1960; *I giorni contati*, 1962; "Una donna dolce dolce" in *La Donna e una cosa meravigliosa*, 1964; "Una donna d'affari" in *Controsesso*, 1964; *I grandi condottieri*, 1965; *Sissignore*, 1968; *L'invitee*, 1969; *Tre nel mille*, 1970; *Giochi particolari*, 1970; *La supertestimone*, 1971; *Gli ordini sono ordini*, 1972; *Carne per Frankenstein* (also known as *Flesh for Frankenstein*), 1973.

OTHER—*L'equilibrio*, 1967, then as *Equilibrium*, London, 1969; *I bu*, 1972; (with Federico Fellini) *Amarcord*, 1973, then as *Amarcord: Portrait of a Town*, London, 1974; *I cento uccelli*, 1974; *Il polverone*, 1978; *I guardatori della luna*, 1981; *Il miele*, 1981; *Aquilone: Una favola del nostro tempo* with *Antonioni*, 1982; *Leone dalla barba bianca*, 1983; *La pioggia tiepida*, 1984; also contributor to journals and periodicals.

ADDRESSES: OFFICE—Piazzale Clodio 32, 00195 Rome, Italy.*

*　　　*　　　*

GUINNESS, Alec 1914-

PERSONAL: Born April 2, 1914, in London, England; son of Andrew (a banker) and Agnes (Cuffe) Guinness; married Merula Salaman (an actress), June 20, 1938; children: Matthew. EDUCATION—Trained for the stage at the Fay Compton Studio of Dramatic Art, 1934, and with Martita Hunt, 1934. MILITARY—Royal Navy, lieutenant, 1941-45.

VOCATION: Actor, director, and writer.

ALEC GUINNESS

CAREER: Also see *WRITINGS* below. STAGE DEBUT—*Libel!,* Playhouse Theatre, London, 1934. PRINCIPAL STAGE APPEARANCES—Osric and Third Player, *Hamlet,* New Theatre, London, 1934; the Wolf, *Noah* and Sampson and apothecary, *Romeo and Juliet,* both New Theatre, 1935; workman and Yakov, *The Seagull,* New Theatre, 1936; Boyet, *Love's Labour's Lost,* Le Beau and William, *As You Like It,* and Old Thorney, *The Witch of Edmonton,* all Old Vic Theatre Company, London, 1936; Reynaldo and Osric, *Hamlet,* Sir Andrew Aguecheek, *Twelfth Night,* and Exeter, *Henry V,* all Old Vic Theatre Company, 1937; Aumerle and the Groom, *Richard II* and Snake, *The School for Scandal,* both John Gielgud Company, Queen's Theatre, London, 1937; Osric, Reynaldo, and Player Queen, *Hamlet,* Kronborg Castle, Elsinore, Denmark, 1937; Feodotik, *The Three Sisters* and Lorenzo, *The Merchant of Venice,* John Gielgud Company, Queen's Theatre, 1938; Arthur Gower, *Trelawny of the Wells,* title role, *Hamlet,* and Bob Acres, *The Rivals,* all Old Vic Theatre Company, 1938; Michael Ransom, *The Ascent of F.6,* Old Vic Theatre Company, 1939; Romeo, *Romeo and Juliet,* Scottish Theatre Festival, Perth, Scotland, U.K., 1939; Herbert Pockett, *Great Expectations,* Rudolf Steiner Hall, London, 1939.

Richard Meilhac, *Cousin Muriel,* Globe Theatre, London, 1940; Ferdinand, *The Tempest,* Old Vic Theatre, 1940; Lieutenant Teddy Graham, *Flare Path,* Henry Miller's Theatre, New York City, 1942; Mitya Karamazov, *The Brothers Karamazov,* Lyric Hammersmith Theatre, London, 1946; Garcin, *Vicious Circle,* Arts Theatre, London, 1946; Fool, *King Lear* and Eric Birling, *An Inspector Calls,* both Old Vic Theatre Company, New Theatre, 1946; Comte de Guiche, *Cyrano de Bergerac,* Abel Drugger, *The Alchemist,* title

role, *Richard II,* and the Dauphin, *Saint Joan,* all Old Vic Theatre Company, New Theatre, 1947; Hlestakov, *The Government Inspector* and Menenius Agrippa, *Coriolanus,* both Old Vic Theatre Company, New Theatre, 1948; Dr. James Y. Simpson, *The Human Touch,* Savoy Theatre, London, 1949; Unidentified Guest, *The Cocktail Party,* Lyceum Theatre, Edinburgh, Scotland, U.K., 1949, then Henry Miller's Theatre, 1950; title role, *Hamlet,* New Theatre, 1951; the Scientist, *Under the Sycamore Tree,* Aldwych Theatre, London, 1952; title role, *Richard III* and King, *All's Well That Ends Well,* both Stratford Shakespeare Festival, Stratford, ON, Canada, 1953; title role, *The Prisoner,* Globe Theatre, 1954; Boniface, *Hotel Paradiso,* Winter Garden Theatre, New York City, 1956.

Title role, *Ross,* Haymarket Theatre, London, 1960; Berenger the First, *Exit the King,* Edinburgh Festival, then Royal Court Theatre, London, both 1963; title role, *Dylan,* Plymouth Theatre, New York City, 1964; Von Berg, *Incident at Vichy,* Phoenix Theatre, London, 1966; title role, *Macbeth,* Royal Court Theatre, 1966; Mrs. Artminster, *Wise Child,* Wyndham's Theatre, London, 1968; Harcourt-Reilly, *The Cocktail Party,* Chichester Festival, Chichester, U.K., then Wyndham's Theatre, both 1968; John, *Time Out of Mind,* Yvonne Arnaud Theatre, Guildford, U.K., 1970; Father, *Voyage 'round My Father,* Haymarket Theatre, 1971; Arthur Wicksteed, *Habeas Corpus,* Lyric Theatre, 1973; Dudley, *A Family and a Fortune,* Apollo Theatre, London, 1975; Jonathan Swift, *Yahoo,* Queen's Theatre, 1976; Hilary, *The Old Country,* Queen's Theatre, 1977; Andrey Botvinnik, *A Walk in the Woods,* Comedy Theatre, London, 1989. Also appeared in *Queer Cargo,* Piccadilly Theatre, London, 1934; Louis Debedat, *The Doctor's Dilemma,* Richmond, 1938; *The Merchant of Venice,* Chichester Festival, 1984.

PRINCIPAL STAGE WORK—Director: *Twelfth Night,* Old Vic Theatre Company, New Theatre, London, 1948; *Hamlet,* New Theatre, 1951; *The Cocktail Party,* Chichester Festival, Chichester, U.K., then Wyndham's Theatre, London, both 1968.

MAJOR TOURS—Title role, *Hamlet,* Bob Acres, *The Rivals,* Chorus, *Henry V,* and Emile Flordon, *Libel!,* European and Egyptian cities, all 1938; Charleston, *Thunder Rock,* U.K. cities, 1940.

FILM DEBUT—Herbert Pocket, *Great Expectations,* Universal, 1946. PRINCIPAL FILM APPEARANCES—The Duke, the Parson, the Banker, the General, the Admiral, Young Ascoyne D'Ascoyne, Young Henry, and Lady Agatha, *Kind Hearts and Coronets,* General Film Distributors, 1949; George Bird, *Last Holiday,* Stratford, 1950; Prime Minister Benjamin Disraeli, *The Mudlark,* Twentieth Century-Fox, 1950; Whimple, *A Run for Your Money,* Universal, 1950; Henry Holland, *The Lavender Hill Mob,* Universal, 1951; Fagin, *Oliver Twist,* Rank/United Artists, 1951; Sidney Stratton, *The Man in the White Suit,* Rank/Universal, 1952; Edward Henry "Denry" Machin, *The Promoter* (also known as *The Card*), Universal, 1952; Captain Henry St. James, *The Captain's Paradise,* British Lion, 1953; Father Brown, *The Detective* (also known as *Father Brown*), Columbia, 1954; Peter Ross, *Malta Story,* United Artists, 1954; title role, *The Prisoner,* Columbia, 1955; Colonel Sir Edgar Fraser, *To Paris with Love,* Continental Distributing, 1955; Professor Marcus, *The Lady Killers,* Continental Distributing, 1956; Prince Albert, *The Swan,* Metro-Goldwyn-Mayer (MGM), 1956; Colonel Nicholson, *The Bridge on the River Kwai,* Columbia, 1957; Captain Ambrose, *All at Sea* (also known as *Barnacle Bill*), MGM, 1958; Gully Jimson, *The Horse's Mouth,* United Artists, 1958; Jacques De Gue and John Barrett, *The Scapegoat,* MGM, 1959.

Jim Wormold, *Our Man in Havana,* Columbia, 1960; Lieutenant Colonel Jock Sinclair, *Tunes of Glory,* Lopert, 1960; Koichi Asano, *A Majority of One,* Warner Brothers, 1961; Captain Crawford, *Damn the Defiant!* (also known as *H.M.S. Defiant*), Columbia, 1962; Prince Feisal, *Lawrence of Arabia,* Columbia, 1962; Marcus Aurelius, *The Fall of the Roman Empire,* Paramount, 1964; General Yevgraf, *Doctor Zhivago,* MGM, 1965; Herr Frick, *Situation Hopeless—But Not Serious,* Paramount, 1965; Benedict Boniface, *Hotel Paradiso,* MGM, 1966; Pol, *The Quiller Memorandum,* Twentieth Century-Fox, 1966; Major Jones, *The Comedians,* MGM, 1967; King Charles I, *Cromwell,* Columbia, 1970; Jacob Marley's ghost, *Scrooge,* National General, 1970; Pope Innocent III, *Brother Sun, Sister Moon* (also known as *Fratello Sole, Sorella Luna*), Paramount, 1973; Adolf Hitler, *Hitler: The Last Ten Days,* Paramount/Tomorrow Entertainment, 1973; Butler Bensonmum, *Murder By Death,* Columbia, 1976; Ben Obi-Wan Kenobi, *Star Wars,* Twentieth Century-Fox, 1977; Ben Obi-Wan Kenobi, *The Empire Strikes Back,* Twentieth Century-Fox, 1980; John Bigalow, *Raise the Titanic,* Associated Film Distribution, 1980; Sigmund Freud, *Lovesick,* Warner Brothers, 1983; Ben Obi-Wan Kenobi, *Return of the Jedi,* Twentieth Century-Fox, 1983; Professor Godbole, *A Passage to India,* Columbia, 1984; William Dorrit, *Little Dorrit,* Sands Films/Cannon, 1987; Mr. Todd, *A Handful of Dust,* New Line Cinema, 1988. Also appeared in the following short films: As narrator, *The Square Miles,* 1953; in *Stratford Adventure,* 1954; as narrator, *Rowlandson's England,* 1955; *The Comedians in Africa,* 1967.

PRINCIPAL TELEVISION APPEARANCES—Mini-Series: George Smiley, *Tinker, Tailor, Soldier, Spy,* BBC, 1979, then *Great Performances,* PBS, 1980; George Smiley, *Smiley's People,* BBC, then syndicated, 1982. Episodic: "The Wicked Scheme of Jebal Deeks," *Ford Startime,* NBC, 1959; performed a scene from *Dylan* on *The Ed Sullivan Show,* CBS, 1964. Movies: Earl of Dorincourt, *Little Lord Fauntleroy,* CBS, 1980. Specials: Host, *The Actor* (documentary), ABC (British television), 1968; Caesar, "Caesar and Cleopatra," *Hallmark Hall of Fame,* NBC, 1976; Father Quixote, *Monsignor Quixote,* Thames, 1985, then *Great Performances,* PBS, 1987; "Grace Kelly—The American Princess," *Crazy About the Movies,* Cinemax, 1987. Also appeared as Malvolio, *Twelfth Night,* 1969; in *Solo,* 1970; *The Gift of Friendship,* 1974; *Edwin,* 1983; *Conversation at Night; e.e. cummings;* and *Little Gidding.*

NON-RELATED CAREER—Copywriter, Arks Publicity, 1933-34.

WRITINGS: STAGE—(Adaptor) *Great Expectations,* Rudolf Steiner Hall, 1939; (adaptor) *The Brothers Karamazov,* Lyric Hammersmith Theatre, London, 1946; (creator with Alan Strachan) *Yahoo,* Queen's Theatre, London, 1976. FILM—*The Horse's Mouth,* United Artists, 1958. OTHER—*Blessings in Disguise* (autobiography), Knopf, 1985.

AWARDS: Academy Award nomination, Best Actor, 1952, for *The Lavender Hill Mob;* Commander, Order of the British Empire, 1955, created Knight Bachelor, 1959; Academy Award, New York Film Critics' Award, Golden Globe, and National Board of Review Award, all Best Actor, and British Academy of Film and Television Arts Award, Best British Film Actor, all 1957, for *The Bridge on the River Kwai;* Best Actor Award from the Venice Film Festival and Academy Award nomination, Best Adaptation, both 1958, for *The Horse's Mouth;* London *Evening Standard* Award, 1960, for *Ross;* Antoinette Perry Award, Best Actor (Dramatic), Delia Austrian Medal for Distinguished Performance from the Drama League of New York, Page One Award from the Newspaper Guild of New

York, and *Variety*-New York Drama Critics' Poll Award, Best Performance By a Male Lead in a Straight Play, all 1964, for *Dylan;* Academy Award nomination, Best Supporting Actor, 1977, for *Star Wars;* British Academy of Film and Television Arts Award, Best Television Actor, 1979, for *Tinker, Tailor, Soldier, Spy;* Special Academy Award for Contributions to Film, 1980; British Academy of Film and Television Arts Award, Best Television Actor, 1982, for *Smiley's People;* Shakespeare Prize, 1985; Ehron Baer Award for Lifetime Achievement from the Berlin Film Festival, 1988; Fellowship Award from the British Academy of Film and Television Arts Award, 1988; Academy Award nomination, Best Supporting Actor, 1989, for *Little Dorrit;* Olivier Award nomination, 1989, for *A Walk in the Woods.* HONORARY DEGREES—Boston College, D.F.A., 1962; Oxford University, D. Litt., 1978.

MEMBER: British Actors' Equity Association, Screen Actors Guild, Atheneum (London), Garrick Club.

ADDRESSES: AGENT—London Management, 235-241 Regent Street, London W1A 2JT, England.*

*   *   *

GUINNESS, Matthew   1942-

PERSONAL: Born in 1942; son of Alec Guinness (an actor) and Merula Salaman (an actress).

VOCATION: Actor.

CAREER: PRINCIPAL STAGE APPEARANCES—First workman, old sailor, wounded sailor, and Soldier N, *Lear,* English Stage Company, Royal Court Theatre, London, 1971; John Clegg, *The Changing Room,* Royal Court Theatre, London, 1971; Ross, *Macbeth,* Royal Shakespeare Company (RSC), Stratford-on-Avon, U.K., 1974; then Aldwych Theatre, London, 1975; Frank Kilb, *They Are Dying Out,* National Theatre Company, Young Vic Theatre, London, 1976; Hicks and interrogator, *Weapons of Happiness,* National Theatre Company, Lyttelton Theatre, London, 1976; sixth Roman citizen, *Coriolanus,* RSC, Stratford-on-Avon, 1977; Bonaventura, *'Tis Pity She's a Whore,* RSC, Other Place Theatre, Stratford-on-Avon, 1977, then Warehouse Theatre, London, 1978; Marquess of Montague, *Henry VI, Part Three* and Gower, *Henry V,* both RSC, Stratford-on-Avon, 1977, then Aldwych Theatre, 1978; Acres, *The Rivals* and Fool, *King Lear,* both Prospect Theatre Company, Old Vic Theatre, London, 1978; Friar Peter and Elbow, *Measure for Measure,* Riverside Studios, London, 1979; Totty, *Land Marks,* Lyric Studio Theatre, London, 1979.

PRINCIPAL FILM APPEARANCES—Denry as a boy, *The Promoter* (also known as *The Card*), Universal, 1952; Major Cusper, *The Virgin Soldiers,* Columbia, 1970; Kilgas, *One Day in the Life of Ivan Denisovich,* Cinerama, 1971; reading monk, *Luther,* American Film Theatre, 1974; first patron, *The Bride,* Columbia, 1985; soe man, *Plenty,* Twentieth Century-Fox, 1985; Randall, *Wetherby,* Metro-Goldwyn-Mayer/United Artists, 1985; Dr. Owen, *Lady Jane,* Paramount, 1986. Also appeared in *The Duellists,* Paramount, 1977.

PRINCIPAL TELEVISION APPEARANCES—Mini-Series: Hans Bethe, *Oppenheimer,* PBS, 1982. Movies: Father Byles, *S.O.S. Titanic,* ABC, 1979.*

GUNN, Bill   1934-1989

PERSONAL: Full name, William Harrison Gunn; born July 15, 1934, in Philadelphia, PA; died of encephalitis, April 5, 1989, in Nyack, NY; son of William Harrison and Louise (Alexander) Gunn. MILITARY—U.S. Navy.

VOCATION: Writer, director, and actor.

CAREER: Also see *WRITINGS* below. BROADWAY DEBUT—*The Immoralist*, Royale Theatre, 1954. PRINCIPAL STAGE APPEARANCES—Prince, *Moon on a Rainbow Shawl*, East 11th Street Theatre, New York City, 1962; Patroclus, *Troilus and Cressida*, New York Shakespeare Festival, Delacorte Theatre, New York City, 1965; also appeared in *Take a Giant Step*, Jan Hus Playhouse, New York City, 1956.

PRINCIPAL STAGE WORK—Director, *Black Picture Show*, New York Shakespeare Festival, Vivian Beaumont Theatre, New York City, 1975; director, *Rhinestone*, Richard Allen Center, New York City, 1982.

MAJOR TOURS—*A Member of the Wedding*, U.S. cities.

PRINCIPAL FILM APPEARANCES—T.P., *The Sound and the Fury*, Twentieth Century-Fox, 1959; Roscoe, *The Interns*, Columbia, 1962; Sergeant Rothschild, *Penelope*, Metro-Goldwyn-Mayer (MGM), 1966; Namana, *The Spy with My Face*, MGM, 1966; George Meda, *Ganja and Hess* (also known as *Double Possession* and *Blood Couple*), Kelly-Jordon, 1973.

PRINCIPAL FILM WORK—Director, *Ganja and Hess* (also known as *Double Possession* and *Blood Couple*), Kelly-Jordon, 1973.

PRINCIPAL TELEVISION APPEARANCES—Episodic: Homer Dobson, *The Cosby Show*, NBC, 1986; also *Look Up and Live*, CBS. PRINCIPAL TELEVISION WORK—Director, *The Alberta Hunter Story*, BBC, 1982.

WRITINGS: STAGE—*Marcus in the High Grass*, Greenwich Mews Theatre, New York City, 1960; *Johnnas*, Chelsea Theatre, New York City, 1968; *Black Picture Show*, New York Shakespeare Festival (NYSF), Vivian Beaumont Theatre, New York City, 1975, published by Reed, Cannon, 1975; *Rhinestone*, Richard Allen Center, New York City, 1982; *Family Employment*, NYSF, Public Theatre, New York City, 1985; *The Forbidden City*, NYSF, Public Theatre, 1989; also *Celebration*, Mark Taper Forum, Los Angeles.

FILM—*Fame Game*, Columbia, 1968; *Friends*, Universal, 1968; *Stop*, Warner Brothers, 1969 (unreleased); *Don't the Moon Look Lonesome*, Chuck Barris Productions, 1970; (with Ronald Ribman) *The Angel Levine*, United Artists, 1970; *The Landlord*, United Artists, 1970; *Ganja and Hess* (also known as *Double Possession* and *Blood Couple*), Kelly-Jordon Enterprises, 1973; (contributor) *The Greatest*, Columbia, 1977.

TELEVISION—Series: (With Ilunga Adell, Osa Iyaun, Michael Griffin, Gregory Robinson, and Chriz Schultz) *Watch Your Mouth*, PBS, 1978. Movies: *Johnnas*, NBC, 1972. Specials: *Sojourner*, CBS, 1975; *The Alberta Hunter Story*, BBC, 1982.

OTHER—*All the Rest Have Died* (novel), Delacorte, 1964; *Rhinestone Sharecropping* (novel), Reed, Cannon, 1981.

AWARDS: Emmy Award, 1972, for *Johnnas*; *Ganja and Hess*

named one of the Ten Best American Films of the Decade by the Cannes Film Festival, 1973; Audelco Award, Best Play of the Year, 1975, for *Black Picture Show;* Guggenheim fellowship in filmmaking, 1980.

OBITUARIES AND OTHER SOURCES: New York Times, April 7, 1989; *Hollywood Reporter*, April 10, 1989; *Variety*, April 12-18, 1989.*

*   *   *

GWYNNE, Fred   1926-

PERSONAL: Full name, Frederick Hubbard Gwynne; born July 10, 1926, in New York, NY; father, a stockbroker; married Jean Reynard, 1952; children: four. EDUCATION—Harvard University, B.A., 1951; also attended the Phoenix School of Design. MILITARY—U.S. Navy, 1944-46.

VOCATION: Actor, writer, and illustrator.

CAREER: BROADWAY DEBUT—Stinker, *Mrs. McThing*, Morosco Theatre, 1952. PRINCIPAL STAGE APPEARANCES—Bottom, *A Midsummer Night's Dream* and Silence, *Henry IV, Part Two*, both Brattle Theatre, Cambridge, MA, 1951; Dull, *Love's Labour's Lost*, City Center Theatre, New York City, 1953; Luther Raubel, *The Frogs of Spring*, Broadhurst Theatre, New York City, 1953; Polyte-le-Mou, *Irma la Douce*, Plymouth Theatre, New York City, 1960; Marvin Shellhammer, *Here's Love*, Shubert Theatre, New York City, 1963; Abraham Lincoln, *The Lincoln Mask*, Plymouth Theatre, New York City, 1972; inspector, *The Enchanted*, Eisenhower Theatre, Washington, DC, 1973; Major Michael Dillon, *More Than You Deserve*, New York Shakespeare Festival (NYSF), Public Theatre, New York City, 1974; Sir Toby Belch, *Twelfth Night*, American Shakespeare Theatre, Stratford, CT, 1974; Big Daddy, *Cat on a Hot Tin Roof*, American Shakespeare Theatre, then American National Theatre and Academy Theatre, New York City, both 1974, later Eisenhower Theatre, 1975.

Stage Manager, *Our Town* and Autolycus, *The Winter's Tale*, both American Shakespeare Festival, 1975; "The Last Meeting of the Knights of the White Magnolia" and Colonel J.C. Kincaid, "The Oldest Living Graduate," in *A Texas Trilogy*, Broadhurst Theatre, 1976; W.O. Gant, *Angel*, Minskoff Theatre, New York City, 1978; Jock Riley, *Players*, Lyceum Theatre, New York City, 1978; Otto Marvuglia, *Grand Magic*, Manhattan Theatre Club, New York City, 1979; judge, *Salt Lake City Skyline*, NYSF, Public Theatre, 1980; Claudius, *Hamlet*, American Shakespeare Festival, 1983; Inspector Bowden, *Whodunnit?*, Biltmore Theatre, New York City, 1983. Also appeared in *The Imaginary Invalid* and *Androcles and the Lion*, both Brattle Theatre.

PRINCIPAL FILM APPEARANCES—Slim, *On the Waterfront*, Columbia, 1954; Herman Munster, *Munster, Go Home*, Universal, 1966; Douglas Winter, *Luna*, Twentieth Century-Fox, 1979; Korey, *Simon*, Warner Brothers, 1980; Chairman Lincoln, *So Fine*, Warner Brothers, 1981; Frenchy Demange, *The Cotton Club*, Orion, 1984; Spender, *Water*, Rank, 1985; Uncle Hugo, *The Boy Who Could Fly*, Twentieth Century-Fox, 1986; commissioner, *Off Beat*, Buena Vista, 1986; Arthur, *Fatal Attraction*, Paramount, 1987; Oscar Reo, *Ironweed*, Tri-Star, 1987; Donald Davenport, *The Secret of My Success*, Universal, 1987; Max Green, *Disorgan-*

ized Crime, Buena Vista, 1989; Jud Crandall, *Pet Sematary*, Paramount, 1989. Also appeared in *Jack-a-Boy*, Phoenix, 1980.

PRINCIPAL TELEVISION APPEARANCES—Series: Officer Francis Muldoon, *Car 54, Where Are You?*, NBC, 1961-63; Herman Munster, *The Munsters*, CBS, 1964-66. Mini-Series: Davis LeRoy, *Kane and Abel*, CBS, 1985. Pilots: Warren Springer, *Guess What I Did Today*, NBC, 1968; Marshall Anderson, *Anderson and Company*, NBC, 1969; Judge Potter, *Sanctuary of Fear*, NBC, 1979; Jake Tekulve, *Jake's M.O.*, NBC, 1987. Episodic: Jonathan Brewster, "Arsenic and Old Lace," *The Best of Broadway*, CBS, 1955; also *The Phil Silvers Show*, CBS, 1955; "The Landlady's Daughter," *Studio One*, CBS, 1956; "Hand in Glove," *Suspicion*, NBC, 1957; "The Big Heist," *Kraft Theatre*, NBC, 1957; "The Old Foolishness," *Play of the Week*, WNTA, 1961; "Don't Shake the Family Tree," *U.S. Steel Hour*, CBS, 1963; "The Lesson," *New York Television Theatre*, WNDT, 1966; "Infancy," *NET Playhouse*, WNET, 1967; "The Police," *Hollywood Television Theatre*, PBS, 1971; "Paradise Lost," *NET Playhouse*, WNET, 1971. Movies: Long Jack, *Captains Courageous*, ABC, 1977; Herman Munster, *The Munsters' Revenge*, NBC, 1981; Waters, *The Christmas Star*, ABC, 1986; Father Macklin, *Vanishing Act*, CBS, 1986; Victor Grenville, *Murder By the Book*, CBS, 1987; Brannagan, *Murder in Black and White*, CBS, 1990. Specials: E.J. Lofgren, "Harvey," *Dupont Show of the Month*, CBS, 1958; "The Hasty Heart," *Dupont Show of the Month*, CBS, 1958; Herman Munster, *Marineland Carnival*, CBS, 1965; *It's What's Happening, Baby!*, CBS, 1965; *A Salute to Stan Laurel*, CBS, 1965; Patience, "The Littlest Angel," *Hallmark Hall of Fame*, NBC, 1969; Jonathan Brewster, *Arsenic and Old Lace*, ABC, 1969; "Dames at Sea," *Family Theatre*, NBC, 1971; E.J. Lofgren, "Harvey," *Hallmark Hall of Fame*, NBC, 1972; Charles Dickens, *Any Friend of Nicholas Nickleby Is a Friend of Mine*, PBS, 1982; Balathasar Hoffman, *The Mysterious Stranger*, PBS, 1982.

NON-RELATED CAREER—Advertising copywriter, J. Walter Thompson Agency, New York City, 1954-60.

WRITINGS: (Also illustrator) *Best in Show* (juvenile), Dutton, 1958; *What's Nude?* (humor), I. Obolensky, 1960; illustrator, *The Battle of the Frogs and the Mice: An Homeric Fable* (juvenile), Dodd, 1962; (also illustrator) *God's First World* (juvenile), Harper, 1970; (also illustrator) *The King Who Rained* (juvenile), Windmill Books, 1970; (also illustrator) *The Story of Ick* (juvenile), Windmill Books, 1971; (also illustrator) *Ick's ABC* (juvenile), Windmill Books, 1971; (also illustrator) *A Chocolate Moose for Dinner* (juvenile), Windmill Books, 1976; (also illustrator) *The Sixteen-Hand Horse* (juvenile), Windmill Books, 1980; illustrator, *The King's Trousers* (juvenile), Windmill Books, 1981; (also illustrator) *A Little Pigeon Toad* (juvenile), Simon & Schuster, 1988.

AWARDS: Obie Award from the *Village Voice*, Best Actor, 1979, for *Grand Magic*.

MEMBER: American Federation of Television and Radio Artists, Screen Actors Guild, Actors' Equity Association.

ADDRESSES: OFFICE—Triad Artists Inc., 10100 Santa Monica Boulevard, 16th Floor, Los Angeles, CA 90067.*

H

HAAS, Lukas 1976-

PERSONAL: Born April 16, 1976, in Los Angeles, CA.

VOCATION: Actor.

CAREER: STAGE DEDUT—Boy, *Waiting for Godot*, Mitzi E. Newhouse Theatre, New York City, 1988.

FILM DEBUT—Scottie Wetherly, *Testament*, Paramount, 1983. PRINCIPAL FILM APPEARANCES—Samuel Lapp, *Witness*, Paramount, 1985; Daniel, *Solar Babies*, Metro-Goldwyn-Mayer/United Artists, 1986; Frankie Scarlatti, *Lady in White*, New Century/Vista, 1988; Wendall Oler, *The Wizard of Loneliness*, Skouras, 1988; Petey Goodwin, *See You in the Morning*, Warner Brothers, 1989; Mikey Talbot, *Music Box*, Tri-Star, 1990; Horace Robedaux, *Convicts*, MCEG, 1990.

LUKAS HAAS

PRINCIPAL TELEVISION APPEARANCES—Pilots: Luke, *Brothers-in-Law*, ABC, 1985. Episodic: Brian Globe, "Ghosttrain," *Amazing Stories*, NBC, 1985; Mike, "What Are Friends For?," *The Twilight Zone*, CBS, 1986. Movies: Bobby Loeb, *Love Thy Neighbor*, ABC, 1984; Brian Mollencamp, *Shattered Spirits*, ABC, 1986; Charlie Williams, *A Place at the Table*, NBC, 1988; title role, *The Ryan White Story*, ABC, 1989. Specials: Mike Sanders, *My Dissident Mom*, CBS, 1987.

ADDRESSES: AGENT—Carol Bodie, International Creative Management, 8899 Beverly Boulevard, Los Angeles, CA 90048.

* * *

HACKETT, Buddy 1924-

PERSONAL: Born Leonard Hacker, August 31, 1924, in Brooklyn, NY; son of Philip (an upholsterer) and Anna (Geller) Hacker; married Sherry Cohen, June 12, 1955; children: Sandy Zade, Ivy Julie, Lisa Jean. MILITARY—U.S. Army.

VOCATION: Actor, comedian, and writer.

CAREER: Also see *WRITINGS* below. PRINCIPAL STAGE APPEARANCES—*Call Me Mister*, National Theatre, New York City, 1946; *Lunatics and Lovers*, Broadhurst Theatre, New York City, 1954; *I Had a Ball*, Martin Beck Theatre, New York City, 1964.

PRINCIPAL FILM APPEARANCES—Blimp Edwards, *Walking My Baby Back Home*, Universal, 1953; Smokey, *Fireman Save My Child*, Universal, 1954; Pluto, *God's Little Acre*, United Artists, 1958; Garfield, *All Hands on Deck*, Twentieth Century-Fox, 1961; Admiral John Paul Jones, *Everything's Ducky*, Columbia, 1961; Marcellus Washburn, *The Music Man*, Warner Brothers, 1962; Hans, "The Singing Bone" in *The Wonderful World of the Brothers Grimm*, Metro-Goldwyn-Mayer, 1962; Benjy Benjamin, *It's a Mad, Mad, Mad, Mad World*, United Artists, 1963; S.Z. Matts, *Muscle Beach Party*, American International, 1964; Lionel Pack, *The Golden Head*, Cinerama/Hungarofilms, 1965; Tennessee Steinmetz, *The Love Bug*, Buena Vista, 1968; townsman, *The Good Guys and the Bad Guys*, Warner Brothers, 1969; as himself, *Loose Shoes* (also known as *Coming Attractions*), Atlantic, 1980; Sammy Cohen, *Hey Babe!*, Rafal, 1984; Scrooge, *Scrooged*, Paramount, 1988; voice of Scuttle, *The Little Mermaid* (animated), Buena Vista, 1989.

PRINCIPAL TELEVISION APPEARANCES—Series: Regular, *School House*, Dumont, 1949; Stanley Peck, *Stanley*, NBC, 1956-57; regular, *The Jackie Gleason Show*, CBS, 1958-59; regular, *The*

Jack Paar Show, NBC, 1958-62; regular, *Celebrity Sweepstakes*, NBC, 1974-76; regular, *The Liar's Club*, syndicated, 1976; host, *You Bet Your Life*, syndicated, 1980. Pilots: Leonard "Boxcar" Mumfred, *There Goes the Neighborhood*, CBS, 1983. Episodic: Murray Gruen, *Murder, She Wrote*, CBS, 1987; also *The Golddiggers*, syndicated, 1971; *The New Love, American Style*, ABC, 1985; *Max Liebman Presents*, NBC; *Dan Raven*, NBC; *The Big Valley*, ABC; *Quincy, M.E.*, NBC; *The Lucy Show*, CBS; *Get Smart*. Movies: Lou Costello, *Bud and Lou*, NBC, 1978. Specials: *Variety*, NBC, 1955; *Entertainment—1955*, NBC, 1955; *The Arthur Godfrey Show*, CBS, 1961; *The All-Star Comedy Show*, ABC, 1962; *The Alan King Special*, ABC, 1969; *The Bob Hope Show*, NBC, 1969; *Plimpton! Did You Hear the One About. . .?*, ABC, 1971; *Disney World—A Gala Opening—Disneyland East*, NBC, 1971; *The Scoey Mitchlll Show*, syndicated, 1972; *Superstunt*, NBC, 1977; *Circus of the Stars*, CBS, 1979; host, *Celebrity Challenge of the Sexes III*, CBS, 1979; voice of Pardon Me Pete and Story Teller, *Jack Frost* (animated), NBC, 1980; *Buddy Hackett—Live and Uncensored*, HBO, 1983; *George Burns Celebrates 80 Years in Show Business*, NBC, 1983; *Comic Relief*, HBO, 1986; "Buddy Hackett II—On Stage at Caesar's Atlantic City," *On Location*, HBO, 1986; *Life's Most Embarrassing Moments*, syndicated, 1988.

PRINCIPAL TELEVISION WORK—Executive producer (with Ken Weinstock), *Buddy Hackett—Live and Uncensored*, HBO, 1983; executive producer, "Buddy Hackett II—On Stage at Caesar's Atlantic City," *On Location*, HBO, 1986.

RELATED CAREER—As a comedian, has performed in the Catskill resort circuit and in nightclubs throughout the United States.

NON-RELATED CAREER—Waiter.

WRITINGS: TELEVISION—*Buddy Hackett—Live and Uncensored*, HBO, 1983. OTHER—*The Truth about Golf, and Other Lies*, Doubleday, 1968; *The Naked Mind of Buddy Hackett*, Nash Publishing, 1974.

AWARDS: Donaldson Award, Best Debut Performance—Male, 1955, for *Lunatics and Lovers*.

ADDRESSES: OFFICE—800 Whittier Drive, Beverly Hills, CA 90210.*

*   *   *

HAIM, Corey   1972-

PERSONAL: Born in 1972 in Toronto, ON, Canada.

VOCATION: Actor.

CAREER: FILM DEBUT—Brian, *Firstborn*, Paramount, 1984. PRINCIPAL FILM APPEARANCES—Jake Moriarity, *Murphy's Romance*, Columbia, 1985; Jeff, *Secret Admirer*, Orion, 1985; Marty Coslaw, *Stephen King's Silver Bullet*, Paramount, 1985; Lucas Blye, *Lucas*, Twentieth Century-Fox, 1986; Sam, *The Lost Boys*, Warner Brothers, 1987; Les, *License to Drive*, Twentieth Century-Fox, 1988; Travis, *Watchers*, Universal, 1988; Dinger, *Dream a Little Dream*, Vestron, 1989.

PRINCIPAL TELEVISION APPEARANCES—Series: Matthew Wiggins,

Roomies, NBC, 1987; also *The Edison Twins*, Canadian television, 1982. Movies: Peter Weisman, *A Time to Live*, NBC, 1985.

RELATED CAREER—Actor in television commercials since the age of 10; appeared in the video *Corey Haim: Me, Myself, and I*, Twin Tower, 1989.*

*   *   *

HALSTON, Julie   1954-

PERSONAL: Born Julie Abatelli, December 7, 1954, in Flushing, NY; daughter of Rudy (a tobacco salesman) and Julia Madeline (a teacher's assistant; maiden name, Gardner) Abatelli. EDUCATION—Hofstra University, B.A., theatre, 1976; studied acting with Terry Schreiber, speech with Clyde Vinson, and dance with Carl Morris.

VOCATION: Actress and producer.

CAREER: PRINCIPAL STAGE APPEARANCES—Mrs. Tooley and Betty, *Times Square Angel*, Provincetown Playhouse, New York City, 1985-86; Enid Whetwhistle, *Sleeping Beauty, or Coma*, Provincetown Playhouse, 1986; La Condesa, *Vampire Lesbians of Sodom*, Provincetown Playhouse, 1986; Kitty, *The Lady in Question*, WPA Theatre, then Orpheum Theatre, both New York City, 1989; also appeared as Aunt Vulva, *Theodora, She-Bitch of Byzantium*, Theatre-in-Limbo, New York City; Evangeline and Mrs. Mooney, *The Dubliners*, Theatre 22, New York City; She, *My Type*, 45th Street Theatre, New York City.

JULIE HALSTON

PRINCIPAL STAGE WORK—Associate producer, *Psycho Beach Party*, Players Theatre, New York City, 1987-88; executive producer, *Sex Slaves of the Lost Kingdom*, the World, New York City, 1988; assistant to the producer, *The Lady in Question*, Orpheum Theatre, New York City, 1989.

MAJOR TOURS—*Julie Halston Speaks* (one-woman show), U.S. cities, 1984-85.

FILM DEBUT—*The Silence of the Lambs*, Orion, 1990.

RELATED CAREER—Actress in television commercials; comedy writer; member of the comedy duo, Halston and Pearl.

NON-RELATED CAREER—Registered investment counselor; librarian; council member, Fresh Air Fund; board member, Dearknows Ltd.

MEMBER: Actors' Equity Association, American Federation of Television and Radio Artists, Special Library Association.

SIDELIGHTS: RECREATIONS—Reading.

ADDRESSES: AGENT—Ambrosio/Mortimer, 165 W. 46th Street, New York, NY 10036.

*   *   *

HAMILTON, Guy   1922-

PERSONAL: Born September, 1922, in Paris, France. MILITARY—Royal Navy, 1940-45.

VOCATION: Director and screenwriter.

CAREER: Also see *WRITINGS* below. PRINCIPAL FILM WORK—Assistant director, *The Fallen Idol* (also known as *The Lost Illusion*), British Lion, 1949; assistant director, *The Third Man*, Selznick Releasing Organization, 1950; assistant director, *The African Queen*, United Artists, 1951; assistant director, *Outcast of the Islands*, British Lion, 1952; director, *The Ringer*, Regent, 1953; director, *An Inspector Calls*, British Lion, 1954; director, *The Colditz Story*, British Lion, 1955; director, *The Intruder*, British Lion, 1955; director, *Charley Moon*, British Lion, 1956; director, *Stowaway Girl* (also known as *Manuela*), Paramount, 1957; director, *The Devil's Disciple*, United Artists, 1959; director, *A Touch of Larceny*, Paramount, 1960; director, *The Best of Enemies* (also known as *I due nemici*), Columbia, 1962; director, *Goldfinger*, United Artists, 1964; director, *Man in the Middle* (also known as *The Winston Affair*), Twentieth Century-Fox, 1964; director, *Funeral in Berlin*, Paramount, 1966; director, *The Party's Over*, Allied Artists, 1966; director, *The Battle of Britain*, United Artists, 1969; director, *Diamonds Are Forever*, United Artists, 1971; director, *Live and Let Die*, United Artists, 1973; director, *The Man with the Golden Gun*, United Artists, 1974; producer and director, *Force Ten from Navarone*, American International, 1978; director, *The Mirror Crack'd*, Associated Film Distribution, 1980; director, *Evil Under the Sun*, Universal, 1982; director, *Remo Williams: The Adventure Begins*, Orion, 1985; director, *Sauf votre respect* (also known as *La Grande Fauche*, *Try This On for Size*, and *Try This One On for Size*), Films Number One/Twentieth Century-Fox/Filmexport/GCR, 1989.

RELATED CAREER—Apprentice, Victorine Studio, Nice, France, 1939.

WRITINGS: FILM—See production details above. (With Ivan Foxwell) *The Colditz Story*, 1955; (with Foxwell and William Woods) *Stowaway Girl*, 1957; (with Foxwell, Roger MacDougall, and Paul Winterton) *A Touch of Larceny*, 1960; (with Alec Medioff and Sergio Gobbi) *Sauf votre respect*, 1989.*

*   *   *

HAMILTON, Joe   1929-

PERSONAL: Full name, Joseph Henry Michael Hamilton, Jr.; born January 6, 1929, in Los Angeles, CA; son of Joseph Henry Michael and Marie (Sullivan) Hamilton; married Gloria Hartley (divorced); married Carol Burnett (an actress and comedienne), May 4, 1963 (divorced); children: Kathleen, Dana, Joseph Henry Michael III, Jeffrey, Judith, John, Jennifer, Nancy, Carrie, Jody, Erin Kate. EDUCATION—Graduated from the Los Angeles Conservatory of Music and Arts, 1951.

VOCATION: Producer.

CAREER: PRINCIPAL TELEVISION APPEARANCES—Series: As a member of the Skylarks (singing group), *The Dinah Shore Show*, NBC, 1955-57.

PRINCIPAL TELEVISION WORK—Series: Producer, *The Garry Moore Show*, CBS, 1958-64; producer, *The Entertainers*, CBS, 1964-65; producer, *The Sammy Davis, Jr. Show*, NBC, 1966; producer (with Bob Banner), *The Garry Moore Show*, CBS, 1966-67; executive producer, *The Carol Burnett Show*, CBS, 1967-78; executive producer, *The Jimmie Rodgers Show*, CBS, 1969; executive producer, *The Smothers Brothers Show*, NBC, 1975; producer, *Carol Burnett and Company*, ABC, 1979; executive producer, *The Tim Conway Show*, CBS, 1980-81; executive producer, *Mama's Family*, NBC, 1983-84, then syndicated, 1987—. Pilots: Producer, *The Primary English Class*, ABC, 1977. Movies: Producer, *The Grass Is Always Greener Over the Septic Tank*, CBS, 1978; producer, *The Tenth Month*, CBS, 1979. Specials: Associate producer, *The Ginger Rogers Show*, CBS, 1958; producer and director, *Julie and Carol at Carnegie Hall*, CBS, 1962; producer, *Carol and Company*, CBS, 1966; producer, *The Tim Conway Special*, CBS, 1970; producer, *Julie and Carol at Lincoln Center*, CBS, 1971; producer, *Once Upon a Mattress*, CBS, 1972; producer, *6 Rms Riv Vu*, CBS, 1974; producer, *Twigs*, CBS, 1975; producer, *Sills and Burnett at the Met*, CBS, 1976; producer, *Uncle Tim Wants You!*, CBS, 1977; executive producer, *A Special Evening with Carol Burnett*, CBS, 1978; producer, *Eunice*, CBS, 1982; producer, *Calamity Jane*, CBS, 1983.

RELATED CAREER—Musician and singer, 1948-51; writer and associate producer of television programs, 1951-57.

WRITINGS: TELEVISION—Pilots: Composer of theme music (with Peter Matz), *The Primary English Class*, ABC, 1977.

AWARDS: Emmy Award, Outstanding Variety Series (Musical), 1972, for *The Carol Burnett Show*; Emmy Award, Outstanding Music-Variety Series, 1974, for *The Carol Burnett Show*; Emmy Award, Outstanding Comedy-Variety or Music Series, 1975, for *The Carol Burnett Show*.

MEMBER: Bel Air Country Club, Westchester Country Club, Wialea Country Club (Maui, HI).

ADDRESSES: OFFICE—c/o EBM, Joe Hamilton Productions, 132 S. Rodeo Drive, Beverly Hills, CA 90212.

*   *   *

HAMMOND, Nicholas

VOCATION: Actor.

CAREER: PRINCIPAL STAGE APPEARANCES—Robin Rhodes, *The Complaisant Lover,* Ethel Barrymore Theatre, New York City, 1961; Second Lieutenant John Truly, *Conduct Unbecoming,* Ethel Barrymore Theatre, 1970; Sandy Tyrrell, *Hay Fever,* Center Theatre Group, Ahmanson Theatre, Los Angeles, 1984; also appeared in *Juno and the Paycock,* Center Theatre Group, Mark Taper Forum, Los Angeles, 1974; *Travesties* and *The Importance of Being Earnest,* both Center Theatre Group, Mark Taper Forum, 1976-77.

PRINCIPAL FILM APPEARANCES—Friedrich, *The Sound of Music,* Twentieth Century-Fox, 1965; Peter Lindner, *Skyjacked* (also known as *Sky Terror*), Metro-Goldwyn-Mayer, 1972; Peter Parker/Spider-Man, *Spider-Man,* Columbia-Warner Distributors, 1977; Peter Parker/Spider-Man, *Spider-Man Strikes Back,* Columbia-EMI-Warner Distributors, 1978; Peter Parker/Spider-Man, *Spider-Man: The Dragon's Challenge,* Columbia-EMI-Warner Distributors, 1980. Also appeared in *Lord of the Flies,* Continental Distributing, 1963; *Superdad,* Buena Vista, 1974.

PRINCIPAL TELEVISION APPEARANCES—Series: Peter Parker/Spider-Man, *The Amazing Spider-Man,* CBS, 1978-79. Mini-Series: Walters, *Rich Man, Poor Man,* ABC, 1976; Commander Arthur Black, *The Martian Chronicles,* NBC, 1980; John Carpenter, *The Manions of America,* ABC, 1981. Pilots: Brad Jensen, *Law of the Land,* NBC, 1976; Peter Parker/Spider-Man, *Spider-Man,* CBS, 1977; Jack Travis, *The Home Front,* CBS, 1980; Reverend Tull, *The Adventures of Pollyanna,* CBS, 1982. Episodic: Jeff Daley, *Two Marriages,* ABC, 1983; Todd Worthy, *Murder, She Wrote,* CBS, 1985; Woodward, *Mission: Impossible,* ABC, 1989. Movies: Evan Clark, *Mr. and Mrs. Bo Jo Jones,* ABC, 1971; Ron Werner, *Outrage!,* ABC, 1973; Arthur, *Trouble in Paradise,* CBS, 1989.

ADDRESSES: AGENT—The Artists Group, 1930 Century Park W., Suite 303, Los Angeles, CA 90067. MANAGER—Schumer-Oubre Management Ltd., 1697 Broadway, New York, NY 10019.*

*   *   *

HANCOCK, Herbie   1940-

PERSONAL: Full name, Herbert Jeffrey Hancock; born April 12, 1940, in Chicago, IL; son of Wayman Edward (a government meat inspector) and Winnie Belle (Griffin) Hancock; married Gudrun Meixner (a decorator and art collector), August 31, 1968; children: Jessica Dru. EDUCATION—Grinnell College, B.A., 1960; graduate work, Roosevelt University, 1960; also studied at the Manhattan School of Music, 1962, and the New School for Social Research, 1967. RELIGION—Nichiren Shoshu Buddhist.

HERBIE HANCOCK

VOCATION: Composer and musician.

CAREER: Also see *WRITINGS* below. PRINCIPAL FILM APPEARANCES—Eddie Wayne, *'Round Midnight,* Warner Brothers, 1986. PRINCIPAL FILM WORK—Music director, *'Round Midnight,* Warner Brothers, 1986.

PRINCIPAL TELEVISION APPEARANCES—Series: Host, *Rock-School,* PBS. Episodic: Gideon, *Concrete Cowboys,* CBS, 1981; also *Saturday Night Live,* NBC; *Sesame Street,* PBS; *The Mike Douglas Show,* CBS; *Phil Donahue,* NBC; *Late Night with David Letterman,* NBC. Specials: *Sun City,* MTV, 1985; "Miles Ahead: The Music of Miles Davis," *Great Performances,* PBS, 1986; *A Jazz Session--Sass and Brass,* Cinemax, 1987; host, *Showtime Coast to Coast,* Showtime, 1987; *Late Night with David Letterman Fifth Anniversary Show,* NBC, 1987; *Celebrating a Jazz Master: Thelonious Sphere Monk,* PBS, 1987; host, *The New Orleans Jazz and Heritage Festival,* Showtime, 1988; "A Duke Named Ellington," *American Masters,* PBS, 1988; *Newport Jazz '88,* PBS, 1988; *All-Star Tribute to Kareem Abdul-Jabbar,* NBC, 1989; *Grammy Living Legends,* CBS, 1989; *Our Common Future,* syndicated, then Arts and Entertainment, 1989; *The Neville Brothers: Tell It Like It Is,* Cinemax, 1989.

PRINCIPAL TELEVISION WORK—Specials: Music director, *The Neville Brothers: Tell It Like It Is,* Cinemax, 1989.

RELATED CAREER—Keyboardist with Coleman Hawkins, 1960, Donald Byrd, 1960-63, Miles Davis, 1963-68, and with the Herbie Hancock Sextet, V.S.O.P. Quintet, Chick Corea, Oscar Peterson, and various other projects, 1968—; founder, owner, and publisher, Hancock Music Company, Los Angeles, 1962—; founder, Hancock and Joe Productions, Los Angeles, 1989—; president, Harlem Jazz Music Center, New York City; as a jazz musician, has appeared in concerts throughout the world including a limited engagement with Natalie Cole and the Manhattans at the Winter Garden Theatre, New York City, in 1976.

WRITINGS: All as composer. FILM—*Blow Up,* Premier Productions, 1966; *The Spook Who Sat By the Door,* United Artists, 1973; *Death Wish,* Paramount, 1974; *A Soldier's Story,* Columbia, 1984; *'Round Midnight,* Warner Brothers, 1986; *Jo Jo Dancer, Your Life Is Calling,* Columbia, 1986; (with Michael Kamen) *Action Jackson,* Lorimar, 1988; *Colors,* Orion, 1988; *Harlem Nights,* Paramount, 1989.

TELEVISION—Specials: *Hey, Hey, Hey, It's Fat Albert,* 1969; *The George McKenna Story,* CBS, 1986.

RECORDINGS: ALBUMS—*Takin' Off,* Blue Note, 1963; *Succotash,* Pausa, 1964; *Speak Like a Child,* Blue Note, 1968; *Fat Albert Rotunda,* Warner Brothers, 1969; *Mwandishi,* Warner Brothers, 1971; *Crossings,* Warner Brothers, 1972; *Sextant,* Columbia, 1972; *Headhunters,* Columbia, 1973; *Thrust,* Columbia, 1974; *Death Wish* (original soundtrack), Columbia, 1974; *The Best of Herbie Hancock,* Blue Note, 1974; *Man-Child,* Columbia, 1975; *Secrets,* Columbia, 1976; (with V.S.O.P.) *The Quintet,* Columbia, 1977; *V.S.O.P.,* Columbia, 1977; *Sunlight,* Columbia, 1978; *An Evening with Herbie Hancock and Chick Corea in Concert,* Columbia, 1979; *Feets Don't Fail Me Now,* Columbia, 1979; *Monster,* Columbia, 1980; *Greatest Hits,* Columbia, 1980; *Lite Me Up,* Columbia, 1982; *Future Shock,* Columbia, 1983; (with Foday Musa Suso) *Village Life,* Columbia, 1985; *'Round Midnight* (original soundtrack), Columbia, 1986; *Jo Jo Dancer, Your Life Is Calling* (original soundtrack), Warner Brothers, 1986; (with Dexter Gordon) *The Other Side of 'Round Midnight,* Blue Note, 1987; *Perfect Machine,* Columbia, 1988; also *My Point of View,* Blue Note; *Maiden Voyage,* Blue Note; *Inventions and Dimensions,* Blue Note; *Empyrean Isles,* Blue Note; *The Prisoner,* Blue Note; *Herbie Hancock,* Blue Note; *Magic Windows,* Columbia; *Corea/Hancock,* Polydor; *Quartet,* Columbia; (with V.S.O.P.) *Live Under the Sky,* Columbia; *Mr. Hands,* Columbia; *Sound-System,* Columbia; (with Chick Corea) *In Concert, 1978,* Polydor.

AWARDS: Citation of Achievement from Broadcast Music Inc., 1963; Jay Award from *Jazz* magazine, 1964; *Downbeat* magazine Critics' Poll Award, Talent Deserving Wider Recognition, 1967; *Record World* magazine Award, New Artist—All-Star Band, 1968, for the Herbie Hancock Sextet; *Downbeat* magazine Critics' Poll Award, Keyboard Player of the Year, 1968, 1969, and 1970; *Downbeat* magazine Critic's Poll Award, Composer of the Year, 1971; Gold Record Award from the Recording Industry Association of America, 1973, for *Headhunters; Black Music* magazine Award, Top Jazz Artist, 1974; Grammy Award, Best R&B Instrumental Performance, 1983, for "Rockit" from *Future Shock; Rolling Stone* magazine Critics' Poll Award, Jazz Artist of the Year, and *Rolling Stone* magazine Readers' Poll Award, Jazz Artist of the Year, both 1984; Grammy Award, Best R&B Instrumental Performance, 1984, for *Sound-System;* Academy Award, Best Original Score, 1986, for *'Round Midnight;* Grammy Award, Best Jazz Instrumental Composition, 1987, for "Call Street Blues" from *'Round Midnight.* HONORARY DEGREES—Grinnell College; Berklee College of Music.

MEMBER: National Academy of Recording Arts and Sciences, American Federation of Musicians, Screen Actors Guild, American Federation of Television and Radio Artists, Pioneer Club of Grinnell College.

SIDELIGHTS: RECREATIONS—Computers and international travel.

Herbie Hancock told *CTFT* that he began playing the piano when he was seven years old and, at the age of 11, he performed with the Chicago Symphony Orchestra. Of his many compositions, Hancock noted that his favorite is "Maiden Voyage" from the album of the same name.

ADDRESSES: AGENT—Rob Light, Creative Artists Agency, 9830 Wilshire Boulevard, Beverly Hills, CA 90212. PUBLICIST—Bobbi Marcus, Bobbi Marcus Public Relations, 1616 Butler Avenue, W. Los Angeles, CA 90025. MANAGER—AGM Management, 1680 N. Vine Street, Suite 1101, Los Angeles, CA 90028.

*   *   *

HANNA, William   1910-

PERSONAL: Full name, William Denby Hanna; born July 14, 1910, in Melrose, NM; son of William John and Avice Joyce (Denby) Hanna; married Violet Blanch Wogatzke, August 7, 1936; children: David William, Bonnie Jean. EDUCATION—Studied engineering and journalism at Compton Junior College, 1929-30.

VOCATION: Animator, producer, director, and writer.

CAREER: Also see *WRITINGS* below. PRINCIPAL FILM APPEARANCES—Tyre salesman, *Roadie,* United Artists, 1980.

PRINCIPAL FILM WORK—All with Joseph Barbera: Animation director, *Anchors Aweigh,* Metro-Goldwyn-Mayer (MGM), 1945; animation director, *Holiday in Mexico,* MGM, 1946; animation director, *Neptune's Daughter,* MGM, 1949; animation director (also with Fred Quimby), *Dangerous When Wet,* MGM, 1953; animation director (also with Quimby), *Invitation to the Dance,* MGM, 1956; producer and director, *Hey There, It's Yogi Bear* (animated), Columbia, 1964; producer and director, *The Man Called Flintstone* (also known as *That Man Flintstone;* animated), Columbia, 1966; producer and animation director, *Project X,* Paramount, 1968; producer, *Charlotte's Web* (animated), Paramount, 1973; producer, *C.H.O.M.P.S.,* AID, 1979; executive producer, *Liar's Moon,* Crown International, 1982; producer, *Heidi's Song* (animated), Paramount, 1982; producer, *GoBots: Battle of the Rock Lords* (animated), Atlantic Releasing, 1986. Also executive producer, *The Greatest Adventure: Stories from the Bible* (home video release), 1986; producer, *Forever Like a Rose.*

Director of the following short animated films: *Blue Monday, What a Lion,* and *Old Smokey,* all MGM, 1938; director (with Barbera) of the following short animated films: *Gallopin' Gals, Swing Social, Puss Gets the Boot,* and *Romeo in Rhythm,* all MGM, 1940; *The Goose Goes South, Midnight Snack, The Night Before Christmas,* and *Officer Pooch,* all MGM, 1941; *The Bowling-Alley Cat, Dog Trouble, Fine Feathered Friend, Fraidy Cat,* and *Puss 'n' Toots,* all MGM, 1942; *Baby Puss, Yankee Doodle Mouse, Lonesome Mouse, Sufferin' Cats,* and *War Dogs,* all MGM, 1943; *The Bodyguard, The Million Dollar Cat, The Zoot Cat, Puttin' on the Dog,* and *Mouse Trouble* (also known as *Cat Nipped* and *Kitty Foiled*), all MGM, 1944; *The Mouse Comes to Dinner* (also known as *Mouse to Dinner*), *Flirty Birdy* (also known as *Love Boids*),

Mouse in Manhattan (also known as *Manhattan Serenade*), *Quiet, Please!*, and *Tee for Two*, all MGM, 1945; *The Milky Waif*, *Solid Serenade*, *The Cat Concerto*, *Springtime for Thomas*, and *Trap Happy*, all MGM, 1946; *The Invisible Mouse*, *Part-Time Pal* (also known as *Fair Weathered Friend*), *Cat Fishin'*, *A Mouse in the House*, *Dr. Jekyll and Mr. Mouse*, and *Salt Water Tabby*, all MGM, 1947; *Kitty Foiled*, *Old Rockin' Chair Tom*, *The Little Orphan*, *Professor Tom*, *Make Mine Freedom*, *Mouse Cleaning*, and *The Truce Hurts*, all MGM, 1948; *Polka Dot Puss*, *Hatch Up Your Troubles*, *The Cat and the Mermouse*, *Heavenly Puss*, *Jerry's Diary*, *Love That Pup*, and *Tennis Chumps*, all MGM, 1949.

Framed Cat, *Tom and Jerry in the Hollywood Bowl*, *Jerry and the Lion* (also known as *Hold That Lion*), *Little Quacker*, *Saturday Evening Puss* (also known as *Party Cat*), *Jerry's Cousin* (also known as *City Cousin* and *Muscles Mouse*), *Texas Tom*, *Cue Ball Cat*, and *Safety Second* (also known as *F'r Safety Sake*), all MGM, 1950; *Casanova Cat*, *Cat Napping*, *His Mouse Friday*, *Jerry and the Goldfish*, *The Two Mouseketeers*, *Nit-Witty Kitty*, *Sleepy-Time Tom*, and *Slicked-Up Pup*, all MGM, 1951; *The Flying Cat*, *Cruise Cat*, *The Dog House*, *The Duck Doctor*, *Fit to Be Tied*, *Johann Mouse*, *Little Runaway*, *Push-Button Kitty*, *Smitten Kitten*, and *Triplet Trouble*, all MGM, 1952; *The Missing Mouse*, *Jerry and Jumbo*, *That's My Pup*, *Just Ducky*, *Two Little Indians*, and *Life with Tom*, all MGM, 1953; *Pet Peeve*, *Little School Mouse*, *Baby Butch*, *Mice Follies*, *Neapolitan Mouse*, *Downhearted Duckling*, *Posse Cat*, *Hic-Cup Pup* (also known as *Tyke Takes a Nap*), *Puppy Tale*, and *Touche, Pussy Cat*, all MGM, 1954; *Good Will to Men*, *Pup on a Picnic*, *Designs on Jerry*, *Southbound Duckling*, *Pecos Pest*, *Smarty Cat*, *That's My Mommie*, *Mouse for Sale*, and *Tom and Cherie*, all MGM, 1955; *Barbeque Brawl*, *The Flying Sorceress*, *Blue Cat Blues*, *Give and Take*, *Busy Buddies*, *The Egg and Jerry*, *Scat Cats*, *Down Beat Bear*, and *Muscle Beach Tom*, all MGM, 1956; *One Droopy Knight*, *Feedin' the Kiddie*, *Mucho Mouse*, *Timid Tabby*, *Tom's Photo Finish*, and *Tops with Pops*, all MGM, 1957; *Happy Go Ducky* (also known as *One Quack Mind*), *Royal Cat Nap*, *Robin Hoodwinked*, *Tot Watchers*, *The Vanishing Duck*, *Little Bo Bopped*, and *Wolf Hounded*, all MGM, 1958.

Creepy Time Pal, *Tale of a Wolf*, *The Do-Good Wolf*, *Life with Loopy*, *Snoopy Loopy*, *No Biz Like Shoe Biz*, and *Here Kiddie, Kiddie*, all Columbia, 1960; *Count Down Clown*, *Happy Go Loopy*, *Two-Faced Wolf*, *Catch Meow*, *Child Sock-Cology*, *Fee Fie Foes*, *Kooky Loopy*, *Loopy's Hare-Do*, *This Is My Ducky Day*, and *Zoo Is Company*, all Columbia, 1961; *Bungle Uncle*, *Bearly Able*, *Beef-for and After*, *Bunnies Abundant*, *Chicken Fracas-see*, *Common Scents*, *Rancid Ransom*, *Slippery Slippers*, and *Swash Buckled*, all Columbia, 1962; *Just a Wolf at Heart*, *Chicken-Hearted Wolf*, *Whatcha Watchin*, *A Fallible Fable*, *Drum-Sticked*, *Bear Up!*, *The Crook That Cried Wolf*, *Habit Rabbit*, *Not in Nottingham*, *Sheep Stealers Anonymous*, and *Wolf in Sheepdog's Clothing*, all Columbia, 1963; *Elephantastic*, *Bear Hug*, *Bear Knuckles*, *Trouble Bruin*, *Raggedy Rug*, and *Habit Troubles*, 1964; *Big Mouse-Take*, *Pork Chop Phooey*, *Crow's Fete*, and *Horse Shoo*, all Columbia, 1965.

PRINCIPAL TELEVISION APPEARANCES—Specials: *The 40th Annual Emmy Awards*, Fox, 1988; *Hanna-Barbera's 50th: A Yabba Dabba Doo Celebration*, TNT, 1989.

PRINCIPAL TELEVISION WORK—All as executive producer, unless indicated; all with Joseph Barbera. Series (all animated, unless indicated): Producer (also with Bob Cottle), *The Ruff and Reddy Show*, NBC, 1957-64; producer and director, *The Huckleberry Hound Show* (also featuring *Pixie and Dixie*, *Hokey Wolf*, and *Yogi Bear*), syndicated, 1958-62; producer and director, *Yogi Bear* (also featuring *Snagglepuss* and *Yakky Doodle Duck*), syndicated, 1958-62; producer, *The Quick Draw McGraw Show* (also featuring *Snooper and Blabber* and *Augie Doggie and Doggie Daddy*), syndicated, 1959-62; producer and director, *The Flintstones*, ABC, 1960-66; producer and director, *Top Cat*, ABC, 1961-62; producer and director, *Lippy the Lion*, syndicated, 1962; producer and director, *Touche Turtle*, syndicated, 1962; producer and director, *Wally Gator*, syndicated, 1962; (also director) *The Jetsons*, ABC, 1962-63; (also director) *The Adventures of Jonny Quest* (also known as *Jonny Quest*), ABC, 1964-65; producer and director, *The Magilla Gorilla Show* (also featuring *Ricochet Rabbit* and *Punkin Puss and Mush Mouse*), syndicated, 1964-67; producer and director, *The Peter Potamus Show* (also featuring *Yippie, Yappie, and Yahooey* and *Breezly and Sneezly*), syndicated, 1964-67.

Series (continued; all animated, unless indicated): Producer and director, *The Atom Ant/Secret Squirrel Show* (also featuring *The Hillbilly Bears*, *Squiddly Diddly*, and *Precious the Dog*), NBC, 1965-68; producer, *Sinbad, Jr., the Sailor* (also known as *The Adventures of Sinbad, Jr.*), syndicated, 1966; producer and director, *The Abbott and Costello Cartoon Show*, syndicated, 1966; producer (also with Larry Harmon), *Laurel and Hardy*, syndicated, 1966-67; producer and director, *Space Kiddettes*, NBC, 1966-67; producer and director, *Space Ghost* (also featuring *Dino Boy*), CBS, 1966-68; producer and director, *Frankenstein, Jr. and the Impossibles*, CBS, 1966-68; producer, *Sampson and Goliath*, NBC, 1967-68; producer and director, *Birdman and the Galaxy Trio*, NBC, 1967-68; producer and director, *The Herculoids*, CBS, 1967-69; producer, *Moby Dick and the Mighty Mightor*, CBS, 1967-69; producer and director, *Shazzan!*, CBS, 1967-69; (also director) *The Fantastic Four*, ABC, 1967-70; *Here Come the Stars* (live-action), syndicated, 1968; producer, *The New Adventures of Huck Finn* (live-action and animated), NBC, 1968-69; producer and director, *The Wacky Races*, CBS, 1968-70; producer, *The Banana Splits Adventure Hour* (live-action and animated; also featuring *The Micro Venture*, *Danger Island*, *The Three Musketeers*, *The Hillbilly Bears*, and *The Arabian Knights*), NBC, 1968-70; (also director) *The Adventures of Gulliver* (also known as *The Adventures of Young Gulliver*), ABC, 1969-70; producer and director, *The Perils of Penelope Pitstop*, CBS, 1969-71; (also director) *The Cattanooga Cats* (also featuring *It's the Wolf*, *Around the World in 79 Days*, and *Auto Cat and Motor Mouse*), ABC, 1969-71; (also director) *Dastardly and Muttley in Their Flying Machines*, CBS, 1969-71; (also director with Charles A. Nichols) *Scooby-Doo, Where Are You?*, CBS, 1969-74.

Series (continued; all animated, unless indicated): (Also director) *Where's Huddles?*, CBS, 1970-71; (also director) *The Harlem Globetrotters*, CBS, 1970-73; (also director) *Josie and the Pussycats*, CBS, 1970-76; *Pebbles and Bamm Bamm*, CBS, 1971-72; (also director) *Help! It's the Hair Bear Bunch*, CBS, 1971-72; (also director) *The Funky Phantom*, ABC, 1971-72; producer and director, *Wait til Your Father Gets Home*, syndicated, 1972; *Sealab 2020*, NBC, 1972-73; *The Roman Holidays*, NBC, 1972-73; (also director) *The Amazing Chan and the Chan Clan*, CBS, 1972-74; (also director) *The Flintstone Comedy Hour*, CBS, 1972-74; (also director with Nichols) *Josie and the Pussycats in Outer Space*, CBS, 1972-74; *The New Scooby-Doo Movies*, CBS, 1972-74; *Speed Buggy*, CBS, 1973-74; (also director) *Butch Cassidy and the Sundance Kids*, NBC, 1973-74; producer, *Peter Puck*, NBC, 1973-74; *Inch High, Private Eye*, NBC, 1973-74; *Yogi's Gang*, ABC, 1973-75; *Jeannie*, CBS, 1973-75; *Goober and the Ghost Chasers*, ABC, 1973-75; *The Addams Family*, NBC, 1973-75; *Super Friends*, ABC, 1973-83; *Wheelie and the Chopper Bunch*,

NBC, 1974-75; *The Partridge Family: 2200 A.D.*, CBS, 1974-75; *Korg: 70,000 B.C.* (live-action), ABC, 1974-75; *Hong Kong Phooey*, ABC, 1974-76; *These Are the Days*, ABC, 1974-76; *Devlin*, ABC, 1974-76; *Valley of the Dinosaurs*, CBS, 1974-76.

Series (continued; all animated, unless indicated): (Also director) *The Scooby-Doo/Dynomutt Hour*, ABC, 1976-77; *Mumbly*, ABC, 1976-77; *The Clue Club*, CBS, 1976-77; *Jabberjaw*, ABC, 1976-78; *The Skatebirds* (also featuring *The Robonic Stooges, Wonder Wheels, Woofer and Wimper*, and *Mystery Island*), CBS, 1977-78; *The Tom and Jerry/Great Grape Ape Show*, ABC, 1977-78; (also director) *The New Super Friends Hour*, ABC, 1977-78; *Scooby's All-Star Laff-a-Lympics*, ABC, 1977-78; *Fred Flintstone and Friends*, syndicated, 1977-78; *The C.B. Bears* (also featuring *Blast Off Buzzard and Crazy Legs, Posse Impossible, Undercover Elephant, Shake, Rattle, and Roll*, and *Heyyyyyy, It's the King*), CBS, 1977-78; *The Hanna-Barbera Happiness Hour* (live-action), NBC, 1978; *Yogi's Space Race*, NBC, 1978-79; *The Galaxy Goofups*, NBC, 1978-79; *Scooby's All Stars*, ABC, 1978-79; *Challenge of the Super Friends*, ABC, 1978-79; (also director) *The World's Greatest Super Heroes*, ABC, 1978-80; *Godzilla* (also known as *Godzilla and the Super 90* and *The Godzilla Power Hour;* also featuring *Jana of the Jungle*), NBC, 1978-81; producer, *The Three Robonic Stooges*, CBS, 1978-81; *The All-New Popeye Hour*, CBS, 1978-81; *The New Shmoo*, NBC, 1979; *Fred and Barney Meet the Thing*, NBC, 1979; *Buford and the Ghost*, NBC, 1979; *Scooby-Doo and Scrappy-Doo*, ABC, 1979; *The Super Globetrotters*, NBC, 1979; *The New Fred and Barney Show*, NBC, 1979; *Casper and the Angels*, NBC, 1979-80; *Fred and Barney Meet the Shmoo*, NBC, 1979-80.

Series (continued; all animated, unless indicated): *Captain Caveman and the Teen Angels*, ABC, 1980; *Flintstone Family Adventures* (also featuring *The Frankenstones* and *Captain Caveman*), NBC, 1980-81; *The Scooby-Doo and Scrappy-Doo Show*, ABC, 1980-82; *The Drak Pack*, CBS, 1980-82; *Fonz and the Happy Days Gang*, ABC, 1980-82; *The Richie Rich Show*, ABC, 1980-82; *The Flintstones*, NBC, 1981; *Space Stars* (featuring *Space Ghost, Teen Force, The Herculoids*, and *Astro and the Space Mutts*), NBC, 1981-82; *The Kwicky Koala Show* (also featuring *Dirty Dawg, Crazy Claws*, and *The Bungle Brothers*), CBS, 1981-82; *Trollkins*, CBS, 1981-82; *Private Olive Oyl*, CBS, 1981-82; *Laverne and Shirley in the Army*, ABC, 1981-82; *The Flintstone Funnies*, NBC, 1981-84; *The Smurfs*, NBC, 1981-88; *Laverne and Shirley with the Fonz*, ABC, 1982-83; (also director) *Jokebook*, NBC, 1982; *Mork and Mindy*, ABC, 1982-83; *Scooby, Scrappy, and Yabba Doo*, ABC, 1982-83; *The Gary Coleman Show*, NBC, 1982-83; *The Little Rascals*, ABC, 1982-84; *The Shirt Tales*, NBC, 1982-84; *Pac-Man*, ABC, 1983-84; *The Biskitts*, CBS, 1983-84; *Monchhichis*, CBS, 1983-84; *The Dukes*, CBS, 1983-84; *Scooby and Scrappy-Doo*, ABC, 1983-84; *The Pink Panther and Sons*, NBC, 1984-85; *The New Scooby-Doo Mysteries*, ABC, 1984-85; *Super Friends: The Legendary Super Powers Show*, ABC, 1984-85; (also with Freddy Monnickendam) *Snorks*, NBC, 1984-86; *Challenge of the GoBots*, syndicated, 1984-86; *Scooby's Mystery Funhouse*, ABC, 1985; *The Thirteen Ghosts of Scooby-Doo*, CBS, 1985-86; *The Super Powers Team: Galactic Guardians*, ABC, 1985-86; *The New Jetsons*, syndicated, 1985-88; *The Funtastic World of Hanna-Barbera* (featuring *Yogi's Treasure Hunt, Paw Paws, Goltar and the Golden Lance*, and *The New Adventures of Jonny Quest*), syndicated, 1986-87; *The Flintstone Kids*, ABC, 1986-87; *Pound Puppies*, ABC, 1986-87; *Wildfire*, CBS, 1986-87; *Foofur*, NBC, 1986-87; *The Funtastic World of Hanna-Barbera* (featuring *Yogi's Treasure Hunt, Sky Commanders, The New Adventures of the Snorks*, and *The New Adventures of Jonny Quest*), syndicated,

1987-88; *Popeye and Son*, CBS, 1987-88; (also with Jay Wolpert) *Skedaddle* (live-action), syndicated, 1988—; *The Completely Mental Misadventures of Ed Grimley*, NBC, 1988-89.

Pilots (all live-action, unless indicated): *The Beach Girls*, syndicated, 1977; *The Funny World of Fred and Bunni* (live-action and animated), CBS, 1978; *Sergeant T.K. Yu*, NBC, 1979. Movies (all live-action, unless indicated): *Hardcase*, ABC, 1972; *Shootout in a One-Dog Town*, ABC, 1974; *The Gathering*, ABC, 1977; *The Beasts Are on the Streets*, NBC, 1978; *The Gathering, Part II*, NBC, 1979; *Lucky Luke* (animated), syndicated, 1987; *Stone Fox*, NBC, 1987.

Specials (all animated, unless indicated): *Alice in Wonderland*, ABC, 1966; *Jack and the Beanstalk* (live-action and animated), NBC, 1967; *The Thanksgiving That Almost Wasn't*, syndicated, 1971; *A Christmas Story*, syndicated, 1971; producer, *Last of the Curlews*, ABC, 1972; *Yogi's Ark Lark*, ABC, 1972; *Robin Hoodnik*, ABC, 1972; *Oliver and the Artful Dodger*, ABC, 1972; *Here Come the Clowns*, ABC, 1972; *The Banana Splits in Hocus Pocus Park*, ABC, 1972; *Gidget Makes the Wrong Connection*, ABC, 1973; *Lost in Space*, ABC, 1973; *20,000 Leagues Under the Sea*, syndicated, 1973; (also director) *The Three Musketeers*, syndicated, 1973; *The Count of Monte Cristo*, syndicated, 1973; *The Crazy Comedy Concert* (live-action and animated), ABC, 1974; *The Runaways* (live-action), ABC, 1974; *Cyrano de Bergerac*, ABC, 1974; *The Last of the Mohicans*, syndicated, 1975; *Phantom Rebel* (live-action), NBC, 1976; "Davy Crockett on the Mississippi" (animated), *Famous Classic Tales*, CBS, 1976; *Taggart's Treasure* (live-action), ABC, 1976; *Five Weeks in a Balloon*, CBS, 1977; *Yabba Dabba Doo! The Happy World of Hanna-Barbera* (live-action and animated), CBS, 1977; *Energy: A National Issue*, 1977; *A Flintstones' Christmas*, NBC, 1977; *The Flintstones' Little Big League*, NBC, 1978; *Hanna-Barbera's All Star Comedy Ice Revue* (live-action and animated), CBS, 1978; "It Isn't Easy Being a Teenage Millionaire" (live-action), *ABC Afterschool Specials*, ABC, 1978; *Yabba Dabba Doo II*, CBS, 1978; *Black Beauty*, CBS, 1978; *Super Heroes Roast*, NBC, 1979; *Challenge of the Super Heroes*, NBC, 1979; *America vs. the World* (live-action), NBC, 1979; *Scooby Goes Hollywood*, ABC, 1979; *Casper's First Christmas*, NBC, 1979; *Popeye Valentine Special: The Sweethearts at Sea*, CBS, 1979; *Gulliver's Travels*, CBS, 1979; *Casper's Halloween Special: He Ain't Scary, He's Our Brother*, NBC, 1979.

Specials (continued; all animated, unless indicated): *The Gymnast* (live-action), ABC, 1980; *The Hanna-Barbera Arena Show* (live-action), NBC, 1981; *Jogging Fever*, NBC, 1981; *The Great Gilly Hopkins* (live-action), CBS, 1981; *Daniel Boone*, CBS, 1981; *Yabba Dabba Doo* (live-action and animated), CBS, 1982; *The Smurfs' Springtime Special*, NBC, 1982; *The Smurfs' Christmas Special*, NBC, 1982; *Christmas Comes to Pac-Land*, ABC, 1982; *Yogi Bear's All-Star Christmas Caper*, CBS, 1982; *My Smurfy Valentine*, NBC, 1983; *The Secret World of Og*, ABC, 1983; *The Amazing Bunjee Venture*, CBS, 1984; *The Smurfic Games*, NBC, 1984; *Smurfily-Ever After*, NBC, 1985; *Star Fairies*, syndicated, 1985; *The Flintstones' 25th Anniversary Celebration* (live-action and animated), CBS, 1986; *Ultraman! The Adventure Begins*, syndicated, 1987; *Yogi and the Magical Flight of the Spruce Goose*, syndicated, 1987; *Scooby and the Reluctant Werewolf*, syndicated, 1987; *The Jetsons Meet the Flintstones*, syndicated, 1987; *Top Cat and the Beverly Hills Cats*, syndicated, 1987; *Rockin' with Judy Jetson* (also known as *Judy Jetson and the Rockers*), syndicated, 1987; *Yogi's Great Escape*, syndicated, 1987; *Scooby-Doo and the Ghoul School*, syndicated, 1987; *Tis the Season to Be Smurfy*, NBC, 1987; *The Good, the Bad, and the Huckleberry Hound*, syndicated, 1987; *Scooby-Doo Meets the Boo Brothers*, syndicated, 1987; *Yogi and the Invasion of the Space Bears*, syndicated, 1987; *The Flintstone Kids "Just Say No" Special*, ABC, 1988; *Hanna-Barbera's 50th: A Yabba Dabba Doo Celebration* (live-action and animated), TNT, 1989; also producer, *Rock Odyssey*.

RELATED CAREER—Animator, scriptwriter, and story editor, Warner Brothers, Burbank, CA, 1931-33; animator, scriptwriter, lyricist, and composer, Harman-Ising Animation Studios, Hollywood, CA, 1933-37; animator, director, producer, and story editor, Metro-Goldwyn-Mayer (MGM), Hollywood, 1937-57; head of animation department (with Joseph Barbera), MGM, 1955-57; founder (with Barbera) and senior vice-president, Hanna-Barbera Productions, Hollywood, 1957—.

NON-RELATED CAREER—Structural engineer.

WRITINGS: FILM—(With Joseph Barbera and Warren Foster) *Hey There, It's Yogi Bear* (animated), Columbia, 1964. TELEVISION—Series: (With Barbera and Douglas Widley) *The Adventures of Jonny Quest* (also known as *Jonny Quest;* animated), ABC, 1964-65. Specials: Composer, *The Three Musketeers* (animated), syndicated, 1973.

AWARDS: All with Joseph Barbera. Academy Award nomination, Best Animated Short Subject, 1940, for *Puss Gets the Boot;* Academy Award nomination, Best Animated Short Subject, 1941, for *The Night Before Christmas;* Academy Award, Best Animated Short Subject, 1943, for *Yankee Doodle Mouse;* Academy Award, Best Animated Short Subject, 1944, for *Mouse Trouble;* Academy Award, Best Animated Short Subject, 1945, for *Quiet, Please!;* Academy Award, Best Animated Short Subject, 1946, for *The Cat Concerto;* Academy Award nomination, Best Animated Short Subject, 1947, for *Dr. Jekyll and Mr. Mouse;* Academy Award, Best Animated Short Subject, 1948, for *The Little Orphan;* Academy Award nomination, Best Animated Short Subject, 1949, for *Hatch Up Your Troubles;* Academy Award nomination, Best Short Subject, 1950, for *Jerry's Cousin;* Academy Award, Best Animated Short Subject, 1951, for *The Two Mouseketeers;* Academy Award, Best Animated Short Subject, 1952, for *Johann Mouse;* Academy Award nomination, Best Animated Short Subject, 1954, for *Touche, Pussy Cat;* Academy Award nomination, Best Animated Short Subject, 1955, for *Good Will to Men;* Academy Award nomination, Best Animated Short Subject, 1957, for *One Droopy Knight.*

Emmy Award, Outstanding Achievement in the Field of Children's Programming, 1960, for *The Huckleberry Hound Show;* Golden Globe, Outstanding Achievement in International Television Cartoons, 1965, for *The Flintstones;* Emmy Award, Outstanding Children's Special, 1966, for *Jack and the Beanstalk;* Emmy Award, Outstanding Achievement in Children's Programming (Informational/Factual), 1973, for *The Last of the Curlews;* Emmy Award, Outstanding Informational Children's Series, 1974, for *The Runaways;* Annie Award, 1977, for *Charlotte's Web;* Christopher Award and Emmy Award, Outstanding Special—Drama or Comedy, both 1978, for *The Gathering;* Emmy Award, Outstanding Children's Entertainment Series, 1982, for *The Smurfs;* Golden Reel Award, Animation Sound Editing, and Bronze Award, Best Children's Special, both from the International Film and Television Festival of New York, 1982, for *The Smurfs' Springtime Special;* Emmy Award, Outstanding Children's Entertainment Series, 1983, for *The Smurfs;* Bronze Award, Best Children's Special, 1984, for *The Smurfic Games;* Men of the Year Award from the National Center for Hyperactive Children, 1986; Gold Angel Award from

Religion in Media, 1986, for Excellence in Media; Distinguished Service Award from the National Religious Broadcasters and Award of Excellence from the Film Advisory Board, both 1987, for *The Greatest Adventure: Stories from the Bible;* Humanitas Prize, 1987, for "Lure of the Orb" episode of *The Smurfs;* Governor's Award from the National Academy of Television Arts and Sciences, 1988.

ADDRESSES: OFFICE—Hanna-Barbera Productions, 3400 W. Cahuenga Boulevard, Hollywood, CA 90068.*

*　　*　　*

HARDWICKE, Edward　1932-

PERSONAL: Born August 7, 1932, in London, England; son of Cedric (an actor) and Helena (an actress; maiden name, Pickard) Hardwicke; married Anne Iddon (an actress), June 21, 1957 (divorced); children: Kate, Emma. EDUCATION—Trained for the stage at the Royal Academy of Dramatic Art. MILITARY—Royal Air Force, pilot officer, 1951-52.

VOCATION: Actor.

CAREER: LONDON DEBUT—*Six Characters in Search of an Author*, Arts Theatre, 1954. PRINCIPAL STAGE APPEARANCES—

EDWARD HARDWICKE

Mr. Muffle, *Wildest Dreams,* Vaudeville Theatre, London, 1961; Sam Young, *Photo Finish,* Saville Theatre, London, 1962; Tailor and Justice, *The Provoked Wife,* Vaudeville Theatre, 1963; Montano, *Othello,* National Theatre Company, London, 1964; Camille Chandebise, *A Flea in Her Ear* and Ben, *Love for Love,* both National Theatre Company, 1966; Rosencrantz, *Rosencrantz and Guildenstern Are Dead,* National Theatre Company, 1968; Anthony Witwoud, *The Way of the World* and Jacques, *The White Devil,* both National Theatre Company, 1969; Lebedev, *The Idiot* and Praed, *Mrs. Warren's Profession,* both National Theatre Company, 1970; Guido Veranzi, *The Rules of the Game,* National Theatre Company, 1971; Howard Joyce, *The Letter,* Palace Theatre, Watford, U.K., 1973; Astrov, *Uncle Vanya,* Bristol Old Vic Theatre, Bristol, U.K., 1973; Richard Halton, *On Approval,* Haymarket Theatre, London, 1975; Sir Robert Chiltern, *An Ideal Husband,* Yvonne Arnaud Theatre, Guildford, U.K., 1976; Dr. Mongicourt, *The Lady from Maxim's,* National Theatre Company, Lyttelton Theatre, London, 1977; Jack Hartnoll, *Can You Hear Me At the Back?,* Piccadilly Theatre, London, 1979; Dr. Watson, *The Secret of Sherlock Holmes,* Wyndham's Theatre, London, 1988-89; also appeared in *The Impresario of Smyrna,* Arts Theatre, London, 1954.

MAJOR TOURS—Camille Chandebise, *A Flea in Her Ear* and Ben, *Love for Love,* National Theatre Company, Canadian cities, 1967; also toured the Soviet Union with the National Theatre Company, 1965.

FILM DEBUT—George, *A Guy Named Joe,* Metro-Goldwyn-Mayer, 1943. PRINCIPAL FILM APPEARANCES—Pierre, *A Flea in Her Ear,* Twentieth Century-Fox, 1968; Montano, *Othello,* Warner Brothers, 1965; Lambert, *Otley,* Columbia, 1969; Mitchell, *The Reckoning,* Columbia, 1971; Mike McCarthy, *The Black Windmill,* Universal, 1974; Captain Paul Winter, *Full Circle,* CIC, 1977; Inspector Black, *The Odd Job,* Columbia, 1978; Lord Dunning, *Venom,* Paramount, 1982; Dr. Pierre Dubois, *Baby: The Secret of the Lost Legend,* Buena Vista, 1985. Also appeared in *Hell Below Zero,* Columbia, 1954; *Men of Sherwood Forest,* Astor, 1957; *The Day of the Jackal,* Universal, 1973.

TELEVISION DEBUT—Pat Grant, *Colditz,* BBC, 1972. PRINCIPAL TELEVISION APPEARANCES—Series: Dr. John Watson, *The Adventures of Sherlock Holmes I,* Granada, then *Mystery!,* PBS, 1985; Dr. John Watson, *The Adventures of Sherlock Holmes II,* Granada, then *Mystery!,* PBS, 1986; Dr. John Watson, *The Return of Sherlock Holmes,* Granada, then *Mystery!,* PBS, 1987; Dr. John Watson, *The Return of Sherlock Holmes II,* Granada, then *Mystery!,* PBS, 1988. Mini-Series: Biberstein, *Holocaust,* NBC, 1978; Enrico, *Oppenheimer,* BBC, 1978, then *American Playhouse,* PBS, 1982. Movies: Dieter Stahl, *The Bunker,* CBS, 1981. Specials: Gifford, *Not Guilty!,* ABC, 1974. Also appeared in *Son of Man* and *The Withered Arm.*

RELATED CAREER—Company member: Bristol Old Vic Company, Bristol, U.K., 1954-57; Old Vic Company, London, 1958-59; Oxford Playhouse, Oxford, U.K., 1959-60; National Theatre Company, London, 1964-70.

AWARDS: Clarence Derwent Award, 1966, for *A Flea in Her Ear.*

ADDRESSES: AGENT—International Creative Management, 396 Oxford Street, London W1, England.

JULIE HARRIS

HARRIS, Julie   1925-

PERSONAL: Full name, Julia Ann Harris; born December 2, 1925, in Grosse Pointe Park, MI; daughter of William Pickett (an investment banker) and Elsie (a nurse; maiden name, Smith) Harris; married Jay I. Julien (an attorney and film producer), August 16, 1946 (divorced, July, 1954); married Manning Gurian (a stage manager), October 21, 1954 (divorced, 1967); married Walter Erwin Carroll (a writer), April 27, 1977 (divorced, 1982); children: Peter Alston (second marriage). EDUCATION—Attended Yale University School of Drama, 1944-45; trained for the stage at the Perry-Mansfield School of the Dance and Theatre, 1941-43, and at the Actors' Studio.

VOCATION: Actress.

CAREER: BROADWAY DEBUT—Atlanta, *It's a Gift,* Playhouse Theatre, 1945. LONDON DEBUT—Emily Dickinson, *The Belle of Amherst* (one-woman show), Phoenix Theatre, 1977. PRINCIPAL STAGE APPEARANCES—Nelly, *The Playboy of the Western World,* Booth Theatre, New York City, 1946; White Rabbit, *Alice in Wonderland,* International Theatre, then Majestic Theatre, both New York City, 1947; Arianne, *We Love a Lassie,* Shubert Theatre, Boston, MA, then National Theatre, Washington, DC, both 1947; Weird Sister, *Macbeth,* National Theatre, New York City, 1948; Ida Mae, *Sundown Beach,* Belasco Theatre, New York City, 1948; Nancy Gear, *The Young and Fair,* Fulton Theatre, New York City, 1948; Angel Tuttle, *Magnolia Alley,* Mansfield Theatre, New York City, 1949; Felisa, *Montserrat,* Fulton Theatre, 1949; Frankie Addams, *The Member of the Wedding,* Empire Theatre, New York City, 1950; Sally Bowles, *I Am a Camera,* Empire Theatre, 1951;

title role, *Mademoiselle Colombe*, Longacre Theatre, New York City, 1954; Jeanne d'Arc, *The Lark*, Longacre Theatre, 1955; Mrs. Margery Pinchwife, *The Country Wife*, Adelphi Theatre, New York City, 1957; Ruth Arnold, *The Warm Peninsula*, Helen Hayes Theatre, New York City, 1959.

Brigid Mary Mangan, *Little Moon of Alban*, Longacre Theatre, 1960; Juliet, *Romeo and Juliet* and Blanche of Spain, *King John*, both Stratford Shakespeare Festival, Stratford, ON, Canada, 1960; Josefa Lantenay, *A Shot in the Dark*, Booth Theatre, 1961; June, *Marathon '33*, American National Theatre and Academy (ANTA) Theatre, New York City, 1963; Ophelia, *Hamlet*, New York Shakespeare Festival (NYSF), Delacorte Theatre, New York City, then Playhouse in the Park, Philadelphia, PA, both 1964; Annie, *Ready When You Are, C.B.!*, Brooks Atkinson Theatre, New York City, 1964; Teresa, *The Hostage*, Bucks County Playhouse, New Hope, PA, 1965; Georgina, *Skyscraper*, Lunt-Fontanne Theatre, New York City, 1965; Blanche Dubois, *A Streetcar Named Desire*, Falmouth Playhouse, Falmouth, MA, then Tappan Zee Playhouse, Nyack, NY, 1967; Ann Stanley, *Forty Carats*, Morosco Theatre, New York City, 1968; Anna Reardon, *And Miss Reardon Drinks a Little*, Morosco Theatre, 1971; Claire, *Voices*, Ethel Barrymore Theatre, New York City, 1972; Mary Lincoln, *The Last of Mrs. Lincoln*, ANTA Theatre, 1972; Mrs. Rogers, *The Au Pair Man*, NYSF, Vivian Beaumont Theatre, New York City, 1973; Lydia Cruttwell, *In Praise of Love*, Morosco Theatre, 1974; Emily Dickinson, *The Belle of Amherst* (one-woman show), Longacre Theatre, 1976; Gertie Kessel, *Break a Leg*, Palace Theatre, New York City, 1979; Ethel Thayer, *On Golden Pond*, Center Theatre Group, Ahmanson Theatre, Los Angeles, 1980; Clarice, *Mixed Couples*, Brooks Atkinson Theatre, 1980; Melissa Gardner, *Love Letters*, Promenade Theatre, New York City, 1989. Also appeared in *Henry IV, Part Two* and *Oedipus*, both Old Vic Company, Century Theatre, New York City, 1946; *The Women*, Repertory Theatre of New Orleans, New Orleans, LA, 1970; *Under the Ilex*, Repertory Theatre of St. Louis, St. Louis, MO, 1983, then Long Wharf Theatre, New Haven, CT, 1984; and in *Currer Bell* (one-woman show).

MAJOR TOURS—Sally Bowles, *I Am a Camera*, U.S. and Canadian cities, 1952-53; Jeanne d'Arc, *The Lark*, U.S. cities, 1956; Anna Reardon, *And Miss Reardon Drinks a Little*, U.S. cities, 1971-72; Emily Dickinson, *The Belle of Amherst* (one-woman show), international cities, 1976-77; Daisy Werthan, *Driving Miss Daisy*, U.S. cities, 1988.

FILM DEBUT—Frankie Addams, *The Member of the Wedding*, Columbia, 1952. PRINCIPAL FILM APPEARANCES—Abra, *East of Eden*, Warner Brothers, 1955; Sally Bowles, *I Am a Camera*, Distributors Corporation of America, 1955; Helen Cooper, *The Truth about Women*, Continental Distributing, 1958; Sally Hamil, *The Poacher's Daughter* (also known as *Sally's Irish Rogue*), Show Corporation of America, 1960; Grace Miller, *Requiem for a Heavyweight*, Columbia, 1962; Eleanor Vance, *The Haunting*, Metro-Goldwyn-Mayer (MGM), 1963; Miss Thing, *You're a Big Boy Now*, Seven Arts, 1966; Beth Fraley, *Harper* (also known as *The Moving Target*), Warner Brothers, 1966; Allison Landon, *Reflections in a Golden Eye*, Warner Brothers, 1967; Gladys, *The Split*, MGM, 1968; Gerrie Mason, *The People Next Door*, AVCO-Embassy, 1970; Betsie, *The Hiding Place*, Worldwide, 1975; Alice Feinchild, *Voyage of the Damned*, AVCO-Embassy, 1976; Mrs. Greenwood, *The Bell Jar*, AVCO-Embassy, 1979; Charlotte Bronte, *Bronte*, Charlotte Ltd./Radio Telefis Eireann, 1983; narrator, *Isadore Duncan: Movement from the Soul* (documentary), Geller/Goldfine, 1988; Roz Carr, *Gorillas in the Mist*, Universal,

1988. Also appeared in *Journey into Midnight*, Twentieth Century-Fox, 1968; in *Prostitute*, Connaught International, 1980; voice, *Brooklyn Bridge* (documentary), 1981.

TELEVISION DEBUT—*Actors' Studio*, ABC, 1948. PRINCIPAL TELEVISION APPEARANCES—Series: Nellie Paine, *Thicker Than Water*, ABC, 1973; Elizabeth Holvak, *The Family Holvak*, NBC, 1975; Lilimae Clements, *Knots Landing*, CBS, 1981-87. Mini-Series: Helen "Nellie" Taft, *Backstairs at the White House*, NBC, 1979; hostess, *The Prime of Miss Jean Brodie*, PBS, 1979. Pilots: Leona Miller, *The House on Greenapple Road*, ABC, 1970; Elizabeth Holvak, *The Greatest Gift*, NBC, 1974. Episodic: Catherine Sloper, "The Heiress," *Family Classics*, CBS, 1961; Margaret Hollings, *Family Ties*, NBC, 1986; Irene Culver, *The Love Boat*, ABC, 1987; also *Philco Television Playhouse*, NBC, 1948-55; "Bernice Bobs Her Hair," *Starlight Theatre*, CBS, 1951; "October Story," *Goodyear Television Playhouse*, NBC, 1951; "The Happy Rest," *Goodyear Television Playhouse*, NBC, 1953; "A Wind from the South," *U.S. Steel Hour*, CBS, 1955; "Ethan Frome," *Dupont Show of the Month*, CBS, 1960; "Turn the Key Softly," *Sunday Showcase*, NBC, 1960; "Night of the Storm," *Dupont Show of the Month*, CBS, 1961; "He Who Gets Slapped," *Play of the Week*, WNTA, 1961; *Ben Casey*, ABC, 1964; "The Robrioz Ring," *Kraft Suspense Theatre*, NBC, 1964; *Rawhide*, CBS, 1965; *Laredo*, NBC, 1965; "Nightmare," *Bob Hope Chrysler Theatre*, NBC, 1966; *The Bell Telephone Hour*, NBC, 1966; *Tarzan*, NBC, 1967; *Garrison's Gorillas*, ABC, 1968; *Run for Your Life*, NBC, 1968; *The Big Valley*, ABC, 1968; *Daniel Boone*, NBC, 1968; *Tarzan*, NBC, 1968; *Bonanza*, NBC, 1968; *Journey to the Unknown*, ABC, 1968; *Name of the Game*, NBC, 1969 and 1970; *Men from Shiloh*, NBC, 1971; *The Evil Touch*, syndicated, 1972; *Medical Center*, CBS, 1973; *Hawkins*, CBS, 1973; *The Bob Newhart Show*, CBS, 1973; *Columbo*, NBC, 1974; *Harry O*, ABC, 1975.

Movies: Katherine Colleigh, *How Awful About Allan*, ABC, 1970; Elizabeth Hall Morgan, *Home for the Holidays*, ABC, 1972; Anne Devlin, *The Gift*, CBS, 1979; Alice Warfield, *The Woman He Loved*, CBS, 1988; Margaret Berent, *Too Good to Be True* (also known as *Leave Her to Heaven*), NBC, 1988; Iris, *The Christmas Wife*, HBO, 1988; Lucille, *Single Women, Married Men*, CBS, 1989. Specials: Lu, "The Good Fairy," *Hallmark Hall of Fame*, NBC, 1956; Jeanne d'Arc, "The Lark," *Hallmark Hall of Fame*, NBC, 1957; Belinda McDonald, "Johnny Belinda" and Brigid Mary Mangan, "Little Moon of Alban," *Hallmark Hall of Fame*, NBC, 1958; Nora Helmer, "A Doll's House," *Hallmark Hall of Fame*, NBC, 1959; title role, "Victoria Regina," *Hallmark Hall of Fame*, NBC, 1961; Maria, *The Power and the Glory*, NBC, 1961; Eliza Doolittle, "Pygmalion," *Hallmark Hall of Fame*, NBC, 1963; Brigid Mary Mangan, "Little Moon of Alban," *Hallmark Hall of Fame*, NBC, 1964; Ophelia, *Hamlet*, CBS, 1964; Florence Nightingale, "The Holy Terror," *Hallmark Hall of Fame*, NBC, 1965; title role, "Anastasia," *Hallmark Hall of Fame*, NBC, 1967; *Ed Sullivan's Broadway*, CBS, 1973; Emily Dickinson, *The Belle of Amherst*, PBS, 1976; Jolene Henderson, "Stubby Pringle's Christmas," *Hallmark Hall of Fame*, NBC, 1978; *Actors on Acting*, PBS, 1984; *NBC's 60th Anniversary Celebration*, NBC, 1986; "Forever James Dean," *Crazy About the Movies*, Cinemax, 1988; Iris, "The Christmas Wife," *HBO Showcase*, HBO, 1988; voice, *The Congress*, PBS, 1989; "Harold Clurman," *American Masters*, PBS, 1989.

PRINCIPAL RADIO APPEARANCES—Episodic: "The Queen of Darkness," *WOR Mystery Theatre*, WOR (New York City), 1975.

RELATED CAREER—Member, Actors' Studio, New York City.

WRITINGS: (With Barry Tarshis) *Julie Harris Talks to Young Actors* (nonfiction), Lothrop, 1971.

RECORDINGS: *The Hostage*, Columbia, 1965; *Heroes, Gods, and Monsters of the Greek Myths*, Spoken Arts, 1968; *The Belle of Amherst*, Credo, 1976; also *Curious George, The Diary of a Young Girl*, and *Little House in the Big Woods*.

AWARDS: Theatre World Award, 1949, for *Sundown Beach;* Donaldson Award, Best Supporting Actress, 1950, for *The Member of the Wedding;* Antoinette Perry Award, Donaldson Award, and *Variety*-New York Drama Critics' Poll, all Best Actress, all 1952, for *I Am a Camera;* Academy Award nomination, Best Actress, 1952, for *The Member of the Wedding;* Sylvania Award, 1955, for "A Wind from the South," *U.S. Steel Hour;* Antoinette Perry Award, Best Actress (Dramatic), 1956, for *The Lark;* Emmy Award, Best Single Performance By an Actress, 1959, for "Little Moon of Alban," *Hallmark Hall of Fame;* Emmy Award, Outstanding Single Performance By an Actress in a Leading Role, 1962, for "Victoria Regina," *Hallmark Hall of Fame;* Antoinette Perry Award nomination, Best Actress (Dramatic), 1964, for *Marathon '33;* Antoinette Perry Award nomination, Best Actress (Musical), 1966, for *Skyscraper;* Antoinette Perry Award, Best Actress (Dramatic), 1969, for *Forty Carats;* Antoinette Perry Award, Best Actress (Dramatic), Drama Desk Award, and Outer Critics' Circle Award, all 1973, for *The Last of Mrs. Lincoln;* Antoinette Perry Award nomination, Best Actress (Dramatic), 1974, for *The Au Pair Man;* Grammy Award, Best Spoken Word Recording, and Antoinette Perry Award, Best Actress (Play), both 1977, for *The Belle of Amherst;* inducted into the Theatre Hall of Fame. HONORARY DEGREES—Mount Holyoke College, D.F.A., 1976; also received honorary degrees from Smith College, LaSalle College, Ithaca College, and Wayne State University.

MEMBER: Actors' Equity Association, Screen Actors Guild, American Federation of Television and Radio Artists, American Guild of Variety Artists.

SIDELIGHTS: RECREATIONS—Tennis, reading, gardening, knitting, and cooking.

ADDRESSES: AGENT—William Morris Agency, 151 El Camino Drive, Beverly Hills, CA 90210.*

*   *   *

HARRISON, George   1943-

PERSONAL: Born February 25, 1943, in Liverpool, England; son of Harold (a bus driver) and Louise Harrison; married Patricia Ann Boyd (a model), 1966, (divorced, 1977); married Olivia Arias, 1978; children: Dhani (second marriage). EDUCATION—Attended the Liverpool Art Institute.

VOCATION: Musician, composer, and producer.

CAREER: Also see WRITINGS below. PRINCIPAL FILM APPEARANCES—As himself, *A Hard Day's Night*, United Artists, 1964; as himself, *Help!*, United Artists, 1965; as himself (live-action sequence only), *Yellow Submarine* (animated and live-action), United Artists, 1968; as himself, *Let It Be*, United Artists, 1970; as himself, *Raga* (documentary), Apple Films, 1971; as himself, *A Concert for Bangla-Desh* (concert film), Twentieth Century-Fox, 1972; Mr. Papadopoulis, *Monty Python's Life of Brian* (also known as *The Life of Brian*), Warner Brothers/Orion, 1979; as himself, *Eric Clapton and His Rolling Hotel* (concert film), Angle Films, 1980; member of the Singing Rebel Band, *Water*, Atlantic, 1986; nightclub singer, *Shanghai Surprise*, United Artists/Metro-Goldwyn-Mayer, 1986; as himself, *Imagine* (also known as *Imagine: John Lennon* and *In My Life—The Story of John Lennon;* documentary), Warner Brothers, 1988; also appeared in *Checking Out*, Warner Brothers, 1989.

PRINCIPAL FILM WORK—All as executive producer, unless indicated: (With the Beatles [John Lennon, Paul McCartney, and Ringo Starr]) *Let It Be*, United Artists, 1970; producer (with Allen Klein) and music producer (with Phil Spector), *A Concert for Bangla-Desh*, Twentieth Century-Fox, 1972; producer (with Gavric Losey), *Little Malcolm* (also known as *Little Malcolm and His Struggle Against the Eunuchs*), Multicetera, 1974; (with Denis O'Brien) *Monty Python's Life of Brian* (also known as *The Life of Brian*), Warner Brothers/Orion, 1979; (with O'Brien) *The Missionary*, Columbia, 1981; (with O'Brien) *Time Bandits*, AVCO-Embassy, 1981; (with O'Brien) *Monty Python Live at the Hollywood Bowl*, Columbia, 1982; (with O'Brien) *Privates on Parade*, Orion Classics, 1982; (with O'Brien) *Scrubbers*, Orion, 1982; (with O'Brien) *Bullshot*, Handmade, 1983; (with O'Brien) *A Private Function*, Island Alive, 1984; *Water*, Atlantic, 1986; (with O'Brien) *Mona Lisa*, Island, 1986; (with O'Brien) *Shanghai Surprise*, Metro-Goldwyn-Mayer/United Artists, 1986; (with O'Brien) *Withnail and I*, Cineplex Odeon, 1986; (with O'Brien, John Hambley, and Johnny Goodman) *Bellman and True*, Island, 1987; (with O'Brien) *Five Corners*, Cineplex Odeon, 1987; (with O'Brien) *The Lonely Passion of Judith Hearne*, Island, 1987; *Track 29*, Island, 1987; (with O'Brien) *Pow Wow Highway*, Warner Brothers, 1988; (with O'Brien) *The Raggedy Rawney* (also known as *The Rawney*), Island, 1988; (with O'Brien) *How to Get Ahead in Advertising*, Warner Brothers, 1989; (with O'Brien) *Checking Out*, Warner Brothers, 1989; (with O'Brien) *Nuns on the Run*, Twentieth Century-Fox, 1990.

PRINCIPAL TELEVISION APPEARANCES—Episodic: *Saturday Night Live*, NBC, 1976. Specials: *Magical Mystery Tour*, BBC, 1967; *Ringo*, NBC, 1978; interviewer, *All You Need Is Cash*, NBC, 1978; *A Rockabilly Session—Carl Perkins and Friends*, Cinemax, 1986; *Sgt. Pepper: It Was Twenty Years Ago Today* (also known as *It Was Twenty Years Ago Today*), PBS, 1987; *The Prince's Trust All-Star Rock Concert*, HBO, 1987; *Rolling Stone Magazine's 20 Years of Rock 'n' Roll*, ABC, 1987.

RELATED CAREER—Guitarist with the rock and roll groups the Rebels, 1956-58, the Quarrymen, 1958-60, and the Beatles, 1960-70; founder (with the Beatles), Apple Corporation Ltd., 1968; founder, Dark Horse Records, 1976; founder, Material World Charitable Foundation; founder (with Denis O'Brien), Handmade Films (a production and financing company).

NON-RELATED CAREER—Electrician's assistant.

WRITINGS: See production details above, unless indicated. FILM—Composer: (With the Beatles) *A Hard Day's Night*, 1964; (with the Beatles) *Help!*, 1965; (with the Beatles) *Yellow Submarine*, 1968; *Wonderwall*, Cinecenta, 1969; (with the Beatles) *Let It Be*, 1970; *Time Bandits*, 1981; *Water*, 1986; *Shanghai Surprise*, 1986; *Walking After Midnight*, Festival Films, 1988; *Die Sonne Kommt* (also known as *Here Comes the Sun;* animated), German Film and Television Academy, 1988.

TELEVISION—Specials: *Magical Mystery Tour,* 1967.

OTHER—*I, Me, Mine* (autobiography), Genesis Publications, 1980.

RECORDINGS: ALBUMS—*Wonderwall Music* (original soundtrack), Apple, 1968; *Electronic Sounds,* Apple, 1969; *All Things Must Pass,* Apple, 1970; *A Concert for Bangla-Desh,* Apple, 1972; *Living in the Material World,* Apple, 1973; *Dark Horse,* Apple, 1974; *Extra Texture (Read All About It),* Apple, 1975; *33 1/3,* Dark Horse, 1976; *George Harrison,* Dark Horse, 1979; *Somewhere in England,* Dark Horse, 1981; *Gone Troppo,* Dark Horse, 1982; *Cloud 9,* Dark Horse, 1987; (with the Traveling Wilburys [Jeff Lynn, Roy Orbison, Tom Petty, and Bob Dylan]) *Traveling Wilburys, Volume One,* Wilbury Records/Warner Brothers, 1988.

With the Beatles: *Please Please Me,* EMI, 1963; *With the Beatles,* EMI, 1963; *A Hard Day's Night,* EMI, 1964; *Beatles for Sale,* EMI, 1964; *Help!,* EMI, 1965; *Rubber Soul,* EMI, 1965; *Revolver,* EMI, 1966; *Sgt. Pepper's Lonely Hearts Club Band,* EMI, 1967; *The Beatles* (also known as *The White Album*), Apple, 1968; *Yellow Submarine,* Apple, 1969; *Abbey Road,* Apple, 1969; *Let It Be,* Apple, 1970.

AWARDS: Grammy Award (with the Beatles), Best Performance by a Vocal Group, 1964, for "A Hard Day's Night"; Grammy Award (with the Beatles), Best New Artist, 1964; Order of the British Empire, 1965; Grammy Awards (with the Beatles), Album of the Year and Best Contemporary Album, both 1967, for *Sgt. Pepper's Lonely Hearts Club Band;* Academy Award (with the Beatles), Best Original Song Score, and Grammy Award (with the Beatles), Best Original Score Written for a Motion Picture or Television Special, both 1970, for *Let It Be;* Trustee Award (with the Beatles) from the National Academy of Recording Arts and Sciences, 1972; Grammy Award, Album of the Year, 1972, in *A Concert for Bangla-Desh; Rolling Stone* magazine Readers' Poll, Comeback of the Year, 1987; inducted into the Rock and Roll Hall of Fame (with the Beatles), 1988; Grammy Award (with the Traveling Wilburys), Best Rock Vocal (Duo or Group), 1990, for *Traveling Wilburys, Volume One.*

ADDRESSES: OFFICE—Handmade Films Ltd., 26 Cadogan Square, London SW1, England.*

*   *   *

HARROW, Lisa

PERSONAL: Born in New Zealand. EDUCATION—Attended the Royal Academy of Dramatic Art.

VOCATION: Actress.

CAREER: PRINCIPAL STAGE APPEARANCES—Olivia, *Twelfth Night,* Royal Shakespeare Company (RSC), Stratford-on-Avon, U.K., 1969; Lady, *Much Ado About Nothing* and Desdemona, *Othello,* both RSC, Stratford-on-Avon, 1971; Natasha, *The Lower Depths,* Pictish Princess, *The Island of the Mighty,* and Desdemona, *Othello,* all RSC, Aldwych Theatre, London, 1972; Diana, *The Great Caper,* English Stage Company, Royal Court Theatre, Lon-

don, 1974; Lady Amaranth, *Wild Oats,* RSC, Aldwych Theatre, 1976; Portia, *The Merchant of Venice,* RSC, Other Place Theatre, Stratford-on-Avon, 1978, then Warehouse Theatre, London, 1979. Also appeared in *Double Act,* London, 1988.

PRINCIPAL FILM APPEARANCES—Emily, *The Tempter,* Euro-International/Lifeguard, 1974; Helen, *All Creatures Great and Small,* EMI, 1975; Emily, *The Devil Is a Woman,* Twentieth Century-Fox, 1975; Helen, *All Things Bright and Beautiful* (also known as *It Shouldn't Happen to a Vet*), World Northal, 1979; Kate Reynolds, *The Final Conflict,* Twentieth Century-Fox, 1981; Liz Harvey, *Other Halves,* Oringham, 1985; Dr. Christine Rubin, *Shaker Run,* Mirage/Aviscom/Laurelwood, 1985; also appeared as Lady Henrietta, *Under Capricorn,* 1982.

PRINCIPAL TELEVISION APPEARANCES—Series: Liz Becker, *Star Maidens,* syndicated, 1977. Mini-Series: Title role, *Nancy Astor,* BBC, 1982, then *Masterpiece Theatre,* PBS, 1984; also *Act of Betrayal,* ITV, 1988; *Playing Shakespeare,* London Weekend Television, then PBS, 1983. Episodic: "The Testament of Arkadia," *Space 1999,* syndicated, 1975. Movies: Wanda, *From a Far Country: Pope John Paul II,* NBC, 1981. Specials: Helen Alderson, "All Creatures Great and Small," *Hallmark Hall of Fame,* NBC, 1975.

ADDRESSES: AGENTS—Julian Belfrage Associates, 60 St. James's Street, London SW1, England; Smith-Freedman and Associates, 121 N. San Vicente Boulevard, Beverly Hills, CA 90211.*

*   *   *

HARRY, Deborah   1945-

PERSONAL: Full name, Deborah Ann Harry; born July 1, 1945, in Miami, FL; daughter of Richard Smith and Catherine (Peters) Harry. EDUCATION—Centenary College, A.A., 1965.

VOCATION: Singer and actress.

CAREER: PRINCIPAL STAGE APPEARANCES—Title role, *Teaneck Tanzi: The Venus Flytrap,* Nederlander Theatre, New York City, 1983.

PRINCIPAL FILM APPEARANCES—Dee Trick, *The Foreigner,* Visions, 1978; as herself, *Roadie,* United Artists, 1980; Lillian, *Union City,* Kinesis, 1980; Nicki Brand, *Videodrome,* Universal, 1983; title role, *Forever, Lulu,* Tri-Star, 1987; Velma Von Tussle, *Hairspray,* New Line Cinema, 1988; Tina, *Satisfaction,* Twentieth Century-Fox, 1988; girl at Blind Alley, "Life Lessons" in *New York Stories,* Buena Vista, 1989; also appeared in *Mr. Mike's Mondo Video,* New Line Cinema, 1979; *Tales from the Dark Side,* 1990.

PRINCIPAL TELEVISION APPEARANCES—Pilots: *Music Central,* syndicated, 1981. Episodic: Diana Price, *Wiseguy,* CBS, 1989; also *New Visions,* VH-1, 1989; *RollerGames,* syndicated, 1989; *Saturday Night Live,* NBC; *Tales from the Dark Side,* syndicated; *The Muppet Show,* syndicated. Specials: *Blondie,* HBO, 1983; *Rapido,* BBC-2, 1989.

RELATED CAREER—Singer and songwriter with the rock group Blondie, 1975-83; also member of the folk-rock group Wind in the Willows.

RECORDINGS: ALBUMS—*Koo Koo*, Chrysalis, 1981; *Rockbird*, Geffen, 1986; *Def, Dumb, and Blonde*, Sire, 1989. With Blondie: *Blondie*, Chrysalis, 1977; *Plastic Letters*, Chrysalis, 1978; *Parallel Lines*, Chrysalis, 1979; *Eat to the Beat*, Chrysalis, 1979; *Autoamerican*, Chrysalis, 1980; *The Hunter*, Chrysalis, 1982.

SINGLES—"Backfired," Chrysalis, 1981. With Blondie: "Heart of Glass," Chrysalis, 1979; "One Way or Another," Chrysalis, 1979; "Dreaming," Chrysalis, 1979; "Call Me," Chrysalis, 1980; "Atomic," Chrysalis, 1980; "The Tide Is High," Chrysalis, 1980; "Rapture," Chrysalis, 1981; "Island of Lost Souls," Chrysalis, 1982.

WRITINGS: Ten Cents a Dance with a Nickel Change! (fiction).

AWARDS: American Society of Composers, Artists, and Publishers Award, 1979, for "Heart of Glass"; National Jewish Book Award for Fiction, 1979, for *Ten Cents a Dance with a Nickel Change!*; also recipient of Silver, Gold, and Platinum Record Awards (with Blondie) from the Recording Industries Association of America.

MEMBER: American Federation of Television and Radio Artists, Screen Actors Guild, American Society of Composers, Artists, and Publishers.

ADDRESSES: AGENT—Creative Artists Agency Inc., 9830 Wilshire Boulevard, Beverly Hills, CA 90212. MANAGER—Gary Kurfirst, Overland Productions, 1775 Broadway, New York, NY 10019.*

DEBORAH HARRY

HARRYHAUSEN, Ray 1920-

PERSONAL: Born June 29, 1920, in Los Angeles, CA; wife's name, Diana; children: Vanessa. EDUCATION—Attended Los Angeles City College. MILITARY—U.S. Army, Signal Corps.

VOCATION: Special effects designer and producer.

CAREER: PRINCIPAL FILM APPEARANCES—Man feeding elephants, *Twenty Million Miles to Earth*, Columbia, 1957; Dr. Marston, *Spies Like Us*, Warner Brothers, 1985.

PRINCIPAL FILM WORK—All as special effects designer, unless indicated: Assistant special effects designer, *Mighty Joe Young*, RKO, 1949; *The Beast from 20,000 Fathoms*, Warner Brothers, 1953; (with Jack Erickson) *It Came from Beneath the Sea*, Columbia, 1955; *The Animal World*, Warner Brothers, 1955; (with Russ Kelley) *Earth vs. the Flying Saucers* (also known as *Invasion of the Flying Saucers*), Columbia, 1956; *Twenty Million Miles to Earth*, Columbia, 1957; *The Seventh Voyage of Sinbad*, Columbia, 1958; *The Three Worlds of Gulliver* (also known as *The Worlds of Gulliver*), Columbia, 1960; *Mysterious Island*, Columbia, 1961; *Jason and the Argonauts* (also known as *Jason and the Golden Fleece*), Columbia, 1963; *First Men in the Moon*, Columbia, 1964; *One Million Years B.C.*, Twentieth Century-Fox, 1967; (also associate producer) *The Valley of Gwangi*, Warner Brothers, 1969; *Trog*, Warner Brothers, 1970; (also producer with Charles H. Schneer) *The Golden Voyage of Sinbad*, Columbia, 1974; (also producer with Schneer) *Sinbad and the Eye of the Tiger*, Columbia, 1977; (also producer with Schneer) *Clash of the Titans*, Metro-Goldwyn-Mayer/United Artists, 1981.

RELATED CAREER—Model animator, George Pal's Puppetoons, during the 1940s; creator, producer, and director of a series of animated fairy tales including *Mother Goose Presents Humpty Dumpty*, *The Story of Red Riding Hood*, *The Story of Hansel and Gretel*, and *The Story of King Midas;* creator of Dynarama (a model animation system); lecturer at college campuses and film festivals.

AWARDS: Honored at the San Jose Film Festival, 1986, for Outstanding Contribution to Fantasy in Film.

WRITINGS: Film Fantasy Scrapbook (3 volumes), 1974-81.*

*　　　*　　　*

HARWOOD, Ronald 1934-

PERSONAL: Born Ronald Horwitz, November 9, 1934, in Cape Town, South Africa; son of Isaac and Isobel (Pepper) Horwitz; married Natasha Riehle, 1959; children: Anthony, Deborah, Alexandra. EDUCATION—Trained for the stage at the Royal Academy of Dramatic Art, 1952.

VOCATION: Writer and actor.

CAREER: Also see WRITINGS below. PRINCIPAL STAGE APPEARANCES—Captain Arago, *The Strong Are Lonely*, London, 1955; also appeared in *Macbeth, The Wandering Jew, The Taming of the Shrew, Hamlet, Volpone, Twelfth Night, A New Way to Pay Old Debts, The Clandestine Marriage,* and *Henry IV, Part One*, all

Donald Wolfit's Shakespeare Company, London, 1953; *Salome*, London, 1954; and in repertory productions at Salisbury, U.K., and Chesterfield, U.K.

PRINCIPAL TELEVISION APPEARANCES—Series: Host, *Read All About It*, BBC, 1978-79.

PRINCIPAL RADIO APPEARANCES—Series: Host, *Kaleidoscope*, BBC, 1973.

RELATED CAREER—Company member, Donald Wolfit's Shakespeare Company, London, 1953; company member, 59 Theatre Company, Lyric Hammersmith Theatre, London, 1959; member of literature panel, Arts Council of Great Britain, 1973-78; artistic director, Cheltenham Festival of Literature, Cheltenham, U.K., 1975; visitor in theatre, Balliol College, Oxford University, 1986.

WRITINGS: STAGE—*Country Matters*, Sixty Nine Theatre Company, University Theatre, Manchester, U.K., 1969; (libretto) *The Good Companions*, Her Majesty's Theatre, London, 1974, published by Chappell, 1974; *The Ordeal of Gilbert Pinfold*, Royal Exchange Theatre, Manchester, U.K., 1977, then Round House Theatre, London, 1979, published by Amber Lane Press, 1983; *A Family*, Royal Exchange Theatre, then Royal Haymarket Theatre, London, both 1978, published by Heinemann, 1978; *The Dresser*, Royal Exchange Theatre, then Queen's Theatre, London, both 1980, later Brooks Atkinson Theatre, New York City, 1981, published by Amber Lane Press, 1980, then Grove Press, 1981; (with Christopher Hampton) *A Night of the Day of the Imprisoned Writer*, first produced in London, 1981; *After the Lions*, Royal Exchange Theatre, 1982, published by Amber Lane Press, 1983; *All the World's a Stage*, first produced in 1983; *Tramway Road*, Lyric Hammersmith Theatre, London, 1984, published by Amber Lane Press, 1984; *The Deliberate Death of a Polish Priest*, Almeida Theatre, London, 1985, published by Amber Lane Press, 1985; *Interpreters: A Fantasia on English and Russian Themes*, Queen's Theatre, 1985, published by Amber Lane Press, 1985; *J.J. Farr*, first produced in Bath, U.K., then London, both 1987; *Another Time*, Wyndham's Theatre, London, 1989.

FILM—*The Barber of Stamford Hill*, British Lion, 1963; (with Casper Wrede) *Private Potter*, Metro-Goldwyn-Mayer (MGM), 1963; (with Stanley Mann and Denis Cannan) *A High Wind in Jamaica*, Twentieth Century-Fox, 1965; (with Pierre Rouve and N.F. Simpson) *Diamonds for Breakfast*, Paramount, 1968; *The Girl with a Pistol* (also known as *La ragazza con la pistola*), Paramount, 1968; (with Ken Hughes) *Cromwell*, Columbia, 1970; *Sudden Terror* (also known as *Eyewitness*), National General, 1970; *One Day in the Life of Ivan Denisovich*, Cinerama, 1971, screenplay published by Sphere, then Ballantine, both 1971; *Operation Daybreak* (also known as *The Price of Freedom*), Warner Brothers, 1976; *The Dresser*, Columbia, 1983; *The Doctor and the Devils*, Twentieth Century-Fox, 1985. Also *Lost Empires*.

TELEVISION—Series: *All the World's a Stage*, 1984. Episodic: "The Way Up to Heaven," *Tales of the Unexpected*, syndicated, 1979; "Parson's Pleasure" and "The Umbrella Man," both *Tales of the Unexpected*, syndicated, 1986. Movies: *Evita Peron*, NBC, 1981; *Mandela*, HBO, 1987, screenplay published by Boxtree, then New American Library, both 1987. Specials: *The Barber of Stamford Hill*, 1960; (with Casper Wrede) *Private Potter*, 1961; *Take a Fellow Like Me*, 1961; *The Lads*, 1963; *Convalescence*, 1964; *Guests of Honour*, 1965; *The Paris Trip*, 1966; *The New Assistant*,

1967; *The Long Lease of Summer*, 1972; *The Guests*, 1972; (with John Selwyn) *A Sense of Loss*, 1978; *Breakthrough at Reykjavik* Granada Television, 1987, then as *The Summit: A Nuclear Age Drama*, PBS, 1987; *Countdown to War*, 1989.

RADIO—Plays: *All the Same Shadows*, 1971.

OTHER—*All the Same Shadows* (novel), J. Cape, 1961, published in the United States as *George Washington September, Sir!*, Farrar Straus, 1961; *The Guilt Merchants* (novel), J. Cape, 1963, then Holt Rinehart, 1969; *The Girl in Melanie Klein* (novel), Secker and Warburg, 1969, then Holt Rinehart, 1973; *Sir Donald Wolfit, C.B.E.—His Life and Work in the Unfashionable Theatre* (biography), Secker and Warburg, then St. Martin's, both 1971; *Articles of Faith* (novel), Secker and Warburg, 1973, then Holt Rinehart, 1974; *The Genoa Ferry* (novel), Secker and Warburg, 1976, then Mason/Charter, 1977; *Cesar and Augusta* (biographical novel), Secker and Warburg, 1978, then Little Brown, 1979; *One.Interior.Day.—Adventures in the Film Trade* (short stories), Secker and Warburg, 1978; editor (with Francis King), *New Stories 3* (short stories), Hutchinson, 1978; editor, *A Night at the Theatre* (essays), Methuen, 1982; *All the World's a Stage* (essays), Secker and Warburg, 1984, then Little Brown, 1985; editor, *The Ages of Gielgud: An Actor at Eighty* (biography), Hodder and Stoughton, then Limelight, both 1984; also *Dear Alec* (biography), 1989.

AWARDS: Winifred Holtby Prize from the Royal Society of Literature, 1974, for *Articles of Faith; Evening Standard* Award and Drama Critics Award, both Best Play, 1980, and Antoinette Perry Award nomination, Best Play, 1982, all for *The Dresser*.

MEMBER: Writers Guild of Great Britain (chairman, 1969), English P.E.N. (president, 1990), Royal Society of Literature, Garrick Club, Marylebone Cricket Club.

ADDRESSES: AGENT—Judy Daish, Judy Daish Associates, 83 Eastbourne Mews, London W2 6LQ, England.

*   *   *

HAUSER, Wings

PERSONAL: Married Nancy Locke (an actress; divorced).

VOCATION: Actor.

CAREER: PRINCIPAL FILM APPEARANCES—Marine driver, *Who'll Stop the Rain?* (also known as *Dog Soldiers*), United Artists, 1978; Red Dog, *Homework*, Jensen Farley, 1982; Ramrod, *Vice Squad*, AVCO-Embassy/Hemdale/Brent Walker, 1982; Stoney Cooper, *Deadly Force*, Embassy, 1983; Josh Cameron, *Night Shadows* (also known as *Mutant*), Film Ventures, 1984; Lieutenant Bird, *A Soldier's Story*, Columbia, 1984; Cliff, *Jo Jo Dancer, Your Life Is Calling*, Columbia, 1986; Mr. Havilland, *3:15, the Moment of Truth* (also known as *3:15*), Dakota Entertainment, 1986; Regency, *Tough Guys Don't Dance*, Cannon, 1987; Phil, *The Wind*, Omega, 1987; Sam Striker, *Hostage*, Noble Entertainment, 1987; John Luger, *Dead Man Walking*, Metropolis/Hit Films, 1988; Ed, *The Carpenter*, Cinepix/Capstone, 1988; Ken Griffiths, *Nightmare at Noon* (also known as *Deathstreet U.S.A.*), Omega Entertainment,

WINGS HAUSER

1988; Corporal DiNardo, *The Siege of Firebase Gloria* (also known as *Forward Firebase Gloria*), Fries Entertainment, 1989; Clete Harris, *No Safe Haven*, Overseas Filmgroup, 1989; Cavanaugh, *L.A. Bounty*, Noble Entertainment Group/Alpine Releasing Group, 1989.

PRINCIPAL FILM WORK—Associate producer, *Uncommon Valor*, Paramount, 1983.

PRINCIPAL TELEVISION APPEARANCES—Series: Greg Foster, *The Young and the Restless*, CBS, 1977-81; Lieutenant Ronald Hobbs, *The Last Precinct*, NBC, 1986. Mini-Series: *Aspen* (also known as *The Innocent and the Damned*), NBC, 1977. Pilots: Don Gerrard, *Hear No Evil*, CBS, 1982; Jack Coburn, *Command 5*, ABC, 1985; Lieutenant Ronald Hobbs, *The Last Precinct*, NBC, 1986; Sheriff Wyatt, *The Highwayman*, NBC, 1987. Episodic: Carl, *Murder, She Wrote*, CBS, 1985; Harlen Jenkins, *Airwolf*, CBS, 1985; Kyle Ludwig, *The A-Team*, NBC, 1985. Movies: Frank Carswell, *Ghost Dancing*, ABC, 1983; Wilson Mahood, *The Long, Hot Summer*, NBC, 1985; Major Frank Hollins, *Sweet Revenge*, CBS, 1984; James Rivers, *Perry Mason: The Case of the Scandalous Scoundrel*, NBC, 1987.

WRITINGS: FILM—(With Nancy Locke) *No Safe Haven*, Overseas Filmgroup, 1989.

ADDRESSES: AGENT—Stone Manners Agency, 9113 Sunset Boulevard, Los Angeles, CA 90069. MANAGER—Joel Stevens Management, 11524 Amanda Drive, Studio City Hills, CA 91604.*

HAWKESWORTH, John   1920-

PERSONAL: Born in 1920 in London, England. EDUCATION—Graduated from Oxford University; studied painting with Pablo Picasso. MILITARY—British Army, Grenadier Guards.

VOCATION: Producer, art director, and screenwriter.

CAREER: Also see WRITINGS below. PRINCIPAL FILM WORK—Production designer (with Vincent Korda and James Sawyer), *The Fallen Idol* (also known as *The Lost Illusion*), British Lion, 1949; production designer (with Korda and Joseph Bato), *The Third Man*, Korda-Selznick Releasing, 1950; production designer, *Pandora and the Flying Dutchman*, Metro-Goldwyn-Mayer (MGM), 1951; production designer (with Bato), *Breaking the Sound Barrier* (also known as *The Sound Barrier*), British Lion, 1952; production designer, *Saadia*, MGM, 1953; production designer, *The Prisoner*, Columbia, 1955; producer, *Tiger Bay*, Rank/Continental, 1959.

PRINCIPAL TELEVISION WORK—Series: Producer, *Upstairs, Downstairs*, London Weekend Television, then *Masterpiece Theatre*, PBS, 1974-77; creator and executive producer, *Q.E.D.*, CBS, 1982; producer, *The Adventures of Sherlock Holmes I*, Granada, then *Mystery!*, PBS, 1985; producer, *The Adventures of Sherlock Holmes II*, Granada, then *Mystery!*, PBS, 1986; producer, *The Return of Sherlock Holmes II*, Granada, then *Mystery!*, PBS, 1988; executive producer, *Campion*, BBC, then *Mystery!*, PBS, 1989; also producer, *The Gold Robbers*. Mini-Series: Producer (with

JOHN HAWKESWORTH

Christopher Neame), *The Flame Trees of Thika*, Euston Film, 1979-80, then *Masterpiece Theatre*, PBS, 1982; creator and producer, *The Duchess of Duke Street I and II*, BBC, 1975-76, then *Masterpiece Theatre*, PBS, 1978-80; creator and producer, *Danger UXB*, Thames Television, 1978, then *Masterpiece Theatre*, PBS, 1981; executive producer, *The Tale of Beatrix Potter*, BBC, then *Masterpiece Theatre*, PBS, 1984; creator and executive producer, *By the Sword Divided I and II*, BBC, then *Masterpiece Theatre*, PBS, 1986 and 1988; also producer, *Oscar*, 1984.

WRITINGS: See production details above, unless indicated. FILM— (With Shelley Smith) *Tiger Bay*, 1959. TELEVISION—Series: *Conan Doyle*. Mini-Series: *The Flame Trees of Thika*, 1979-80; *The Tale of Beatrix Potter*, 1984; *Oscar*, 1984. Episodic: *Upstairs, Downstairs*, 1974-77; *Danger UXB*, 1978; *The Duchess of Duke Street*, 1975-76; "The Greek Interpreter," "The Red-Headed League," and "The Final Problem," *The Adventures of Sherlock Holmes II*, 1986; *By the Sword Divided*, 1986; "The Empty House" and "The Second Stain," *The Return of Sherlock Holmes I*, Granada, then *Mystery!*, PBS, 1987; "Silver Blaze" and "The Bruce Partington Plans," *The Return of Sherlock Holmes II*, 1988; *By the Sword Divided II*, 1988; also *The Gold Robbers*, *Blackmail*, *The Hidden Truth*, and *Crime of Passion*. Also *The Million Pound Bank Note* and *The Elusive Pimpernel*.

AWARDS: Emmy Awards, Outstanding Drama Series, 1974, 1975, and 1977, and Outstanding Limited Series, 1976, all for *Upstairs, Downstairs*.

ADDRESSES: OFFICES—Flat 2, 24 Cottesmore Gardens, London W8, England; Consolidated Productions, 5 Jubilee Place, London SW3, England.

*   *   *

HEADLY, Glenne   1955-

PERSONAL: Born March 13, 1955, in New London, CT; married John Malkovich (an actor and director), August 2, 1982 (divorced). EDUCATION—Graduated from the High School of the Performing Arts; graduated from American College of Switzerland; trained for the stage at the HB Studios.

VOCATION: Actress.

CAREER: OFF-BROADWAY DEBUT—Terry, *Extremities*, Westside Arts Center, Cheryl Crawford Theatre, 1983. PRINCIPAL STAGE APPEARANCES—Emma, *Curse of the Starving Class*, Goodman Theatre, Chicago, IL, 1979; Laura Wingfield, *The Glass Menagerie*, North Light Repertory Theatre, Evanston, IL, 1982; Celia, *The Philanthropist*, Manhattan Theatre Club, New York City, 1983; Ann, *Balm in Gilead*, Steppenwolf Theatre Company, Chicago, then Circle Repertory Theatre, New York City, both 1984, later Minetta Lane Theatre, New York City, 1984-85; Raina Petkoff, *Arms and the Man*, Circle in the Square, New York City, 1985; Billie Dawn, *Born Yesterday*, Steppenwolf Theatre Company, 1988. Also appeared in productions of *Say Goodnight Gracie*, *Miss Firecracker Contest*, *Coyote Ugly*, and *Loose Ends*, all with the Steppenwolf Theatre Company.

PRINCIPAL STAGE WORK—Director, *Canadian Gothic*.

PRINCIPAL FILM APPEARANCES—Lola, *Four Friends* (also known as *Georgia's Friends*), Twentieth Century-Fox, 1981; Miss Debbylike, *Doctor Detroit*, Universal, 1983; Joan, *Eleni*, Warner Brothers, 1985; Trelis, *Fandango*, Warner Brothers, 1985; hooker, *The Purple Rose of Cairo*, Orion, 1985; Trish, *Making Mr. Right*, Orion, 1987; Renee Lomax, *Nadine*, Tri-Star, 1987; Kate, *Paperhouse*, Vestron, 1988; Janet Colgate, *Dirty Rotten Scoundrels*, Orion, 1988; Cora Gage, *Stars and Bars*, Columbia, 1988.

PRINCIPAL TELEVISION APPEARANCES—Mini-Series: Elmira Johnson, *Lonesome Dove*, CBS, 1989. Specials: Olive, "Seize the Day," *Great Performances*, PBS, 1987; voice characterization, *Santabear's Highflying Adventure* (animated), CBS, 1987.

RELATED CAREER—Company member, Steppenwolf Theatre Company, Chicago, IL; company member, St. Nicholas New Works Ensemble, Chicago, IL.

AWARDS: Theatre World Award, 1984, for *The Philanthropist*; Drama Desk Award (with company), Best Ensemble Acting, 1984, for *Balm in Gilead*; three Joseph Jefferson Awards for her work with the Steppenwolf Theatre Company, Chicago, IL.

SIDELIGHTS: RECREATIONS—Shopping. FAVORITE ROLES— Emma in *Curse of the Starving Class*.

ADDRESSES: AGENT—Brian Mann, International Creative Management, 8899 Beverly Boulevard, Los Angeles, CA 90048. MANAGER—Phyllis Carlyle Management, Columbia Plaza Production Building 8, Room 2-B, Burbank, CA 91505.*

*   *   *

HEALD, Anthony   1944-

PERSONAL: Born August 25, 1944, in New Rochelle, NY. EDUCATION—Graduated from Michigan State University.

VOCATION: Actor.

CAREER: OFF-BROADWAY DEBUT—Tom Wingfield, *The Glass Menagerie*, Lion Theatre, 1980. BROADWAY DEBUT—Wayne Foster, *The Wake of Jamey Foster*, Eugene O'Neill Theatre, 1982. PRINCIPAL STAGE APPEARANCES—Orestes, *The Electra Myth*, Equity Library Theatre, Lincoln Center Library and Museum, New York City, 1979; Jones, *Inadmissable Evidence* and Gunner, *Misalliance*, both Roundabout Theatre, New York City, 1981; Aston, *The Caretaker* and Henry Grenfel, *The Fox*, both Roundabout Theatre, 1982; Derek Meadle, *Quartermaine's Terms*, Long Wharf Theatre, New Haven, CT, 1982, then Playhouse 91, New York City, 1983; Donald, *The Philanthropist*, Manhattan Theatre Club, New York City, 1983; Fluellen, *Henry V*, New York Shakespeare Festival, Delacorte Theatre, New York City, 1984; Charlie Baker, *The Foreigner*, Astor Place Theatre, New York City, 1984; title role, *The Marriage of Figaro*, Circle in the Square, New York City, 1985; Digby Merton, *Digby*, City Center Theatre, New York City, 1985; Bill Howell, *Principia Scriptoriae*, Manhattan Theatre Club, City Center Theatre, 1986; Stephen, *The Lisbon Traviata*, Manhattan Theatre Club, 1989, then Promenade Theatre, New York City, 1989-90. Also appeared in *J.B.* and *Look Back in Anger*, both Asolo Theatre Festival, Sarasota, FL, 1968; *The Rose*

Tattoo, Hartford Stage Company, Hartford, CT, 1968; *Bonjour la Bonjour* and *The Matchmaker,* both Hartford Stage Company, 1979; *Fables for Friends,* Playwrights Horizons, New York City, 1980.

PRINCIPAL FILM APPEARANCES—Doctor, *Silkwood,* Twentieth Century-Fox, 1983; narcotics officer, *Teachers,* United Artists, 1984; Weldon, *Outrageous Fortune,* Buena Vista, 1987; man in the park, *Orphans,* Lorimar, 1987; also appeared in *Happy New Year,* Columbia, 1987.

PRINCIPAL TELEVISION APPEARANCES—Mini-Series: Kevin Kensington, *Fresno,* CBS, 1986. Pilots: Nick, *After Midnight,* ABC, 1988. Episodic: Reverend Robert Morgan, *Hard Copy,* CBS, 1987; Roger Jankowski, *Crime Story,* NBC, 1987. Movies: Dave O'Brien, *A Case of Deadly Force,* CBS, 1986.

RELATED CAREER—Company member: Asolo State Theatre, Sarasota, FL, 1968-69; Hartford Stage Company, Hartford, CT, 1968-69, then 1970-71; Milwaukee Repertory Company, Milwaukee, WI, 1969-70, then 1977-78; Actors Theatre of Louisville, Louisville, KY, 1979-80.

AWARDS: Theatre World Award, 1982, for *Misalliance.**

*   *   *

PAUL HECHT

HECHT, Paul   1941-

PERSONAL: Born August 16, 1941, in London, England; married Ingeberg Uta; children: one daughter. EDUCATION—Attended McGill University; trained for the stage at the National Theatre School of Canada, 1963.

VOCATION: Actor.

CAREER: STAGE DEBUT—*Henry IV, Part One* and *An Enemy of the People,* both with the Canadian Players Touring Company, U.S. and Canadian cities, 1963-64. OFF-BROADWAY DEBUT—The Pugnacious Collier, *Sergeant Musgrave's Dance,* Theatre De Lys, 1966. BROADWAY DEBUT—The Player, *Rosencrantz and Guildenstern Are Dead,* Alvin Theatre, 1967. PRINCIPAL STAGE APPEARANCES—Jacques Dumaine, *All's Well That Ends Well,* Friar Peter, *Measure for Measure,* and George, Duke of Clarence, *Richard III,* all New York Shakespeare Festival (NYSF), Delacorte Theatre, New York City, 1966; John Ken O'Dunc and Wayne of Morse, *MacBird!,* Village Gate Theatre, New York City, 1967; Voltore, *Volpone,* NYSF, Mobile Theatre, New York City, 1967; John Dickinson, *1776,* 46th Street Theatre, New York City, 1969.

Nathan Rothschild, *The Rothschilds,* Lunt-Fontanne Theatre, New York City, 1970; title role, *Cyrano de Bergerac,* Tyrone Guthrie Theatre, Minneapolis, MN, 1971; Marcus Antonius, *Julius Caesar* and *Antony and Cleopatra,* both American Shakespeare Festival, Stratford, CT, 1972; Mr. Brown, *The Great God Brown* and title role, *Don Juan,* both New Phoenix Repertory Company, Lyceum Theatre, New York City, 1972; Baron Tito Belcredi, *Emperor Henry IV,* Ethel Barrymore Theatre, New York City, 1973; Theodor Herzl, *Herzl,* Palace Theatre, New York City, 1976; Oronte, *The Misanthrope,* NYSF, Public Theatre, New York City, 1977; Rufio, *Caesar and Cleopatra,* Palace Theatre, 1977; Rakityin, *A Month in*

the Country, McCarter Theatre, Princeton, NJ, 1978; Dick Wagner, *Night and Day,* American National Theatre and Academy Theatre, New York City, 1979; Lloyd Dallas, *Noises Off,* Brooks Atkinson Theatre, New York City, 1985; Menenius Agrippa, *Coriolanus,* NYSF, Public Theatre, 1988; title role, *Enrico IV,* Roundabout Theatre, New York City, 1989. Also appeared in *Look After Lu Lu,* Equity Library Theatre, New York City, 1965; *The Ride Across Lake Constance,* Repertory Theatre of Lincoln Center, Forum Theatre, New York City, 1972; *The Three Sisters,* Hartman Theatre, Stamford, CT, 1986; as Dick Dudgeon, *The Devil's Disciple,* Shaw Festival, Niagara-on-the-Lake, ON, Canada; Macduff, *Macbeth,* NYSF.

PRINCIPAL FILM APPEARANCES—Rabbi Isaac Sherman, *Only God Knows,* Canart and Queensbury, 1974; Dr. Samuel Goodman, *The Reincarnation of Peter Proud,* American International, 1975; Khalid, *Rollover,* Warner Brothers, 1981; Paul, *Tempest,* Columbia, 1982; Fallaci, *Threshold,* Twentieth Century-Fox, 1983; narrator, *Ezra Pound/American Odyssey* (documentary), NYC for Visual History, 1984; Eli Seligson, *Joshua Then and Now,* Twentieth Century-Fox, 1985; Barry, *A New Life,* Paramount, 1988.

PRINCIPAL TELEVISION APPEARANCES—Series: Charles Lowell, *Kate and Allie,* CBS, 1984-86. Mini-Series: Jay Gould, *The Adams Chronicles,* PBS, 1976. Pilots: Joe Tyler, *The Imposter,* NBC, 1975; Carelli, *Street Killing,* ABC, 1976. Episodic: Fielding, *Remington Steele,* NBC; *All My Children,* ABC; *The Guiding Light,* CBS; *Another World,* NBC; *Starsky and Hutch,* ABC. Movies: Paul, *Fear on Trial,* CBS, 1975; Dr. Rufus Carter, *The Savage Bees,* NBC, 1976; Joachim, *Mary and Joseph: A Story of Faith,* NBC, 1979; Thomas Eichen, *Ohms,* CBS, 1980; Vernon

Markham, *Family Reunion*, NBC, 1981; Michel Genet, *Running Out*, CBS, 1983; Pavka Meyer, *I'll Take Manhattan*, CBS, 1987. Specials: Lieutenant F.R. Harris, "Pueblo," *ABC Theatre*, ABC, 1973; narrator, *The Selfish Giant*, CBS, 1973; Mr. Wilson, *The Haunted Mansion Mystery*, ABC, 1983; host, *Journey into Sleep*, PBS, 1989.

PRINCIPAL RADIO APPEARANCES—Series: Regular, *Hi Brown's Radio Mystery Theatre*, CBS.

RELATED CAREER—Commercial voice-over performer; also provided voices for productions by puppeteer Bil Baird.

AWARDS: Antoinette Perry Award nomination, Best Supporting or Featured Actor in a Drama, 1967, for *Rosencrantz and Guildenstern Are Dead.*

ADDRESSES: AGENT—Susan Smith, 850 Seventh Avenue, New York, NY 10036. MANAGER—Schumer-Oubre Management Ltd., 1697 Broadway, Suite 1102, New York, NY 10019.*

*   *   *

HEDISON, Al
See HEDISON, David

*   *   *

HEDISON, David   1928-
(Al Hedison)

PERSONAL: Born Albert David Heditsian, Jr., May 20, 1928 (some sources say 1930), in Providence, RI; son of Albert David and Rose (Boghosian) Heditsian; married Bridget Mori, June 29, 1968; children: Alexandra Mary, Serena Rose. EDUCATION—Attended Brown University, 1949-51; studied acting at the Neighborhood Playhouse School of Theatre, 1953.

VOCATION: Actor.

CAREER: PRINCIPAL STAGE APPEARANCES—Beliaev, *A Month in the Country*, Phoenix Theatre, New York City, 1956. Also appeared in *Are You Now or Have You Ever Been?*, 1985; *Forty Deuce*, 1985; *Clash By Night*, New York City; *Bad Bad Jo Jo*, London; *Return Engagement.*

MAJOR TOURS—*Chapter II*, U.S. cities; *Come into My Parlor*, U.S. cities.

PRINCIPAL FILM APPEARANCES—(As Al Hedison) Lieutenant Ware, *The Enemy Below*, Twentieth Century-Fox, 1957; (as Al Hedison) Andre, *The Fly*, Twentieth Century-Fox, 1958; (as Al Hedison) Jamie, *Son of Robin Hood*, Twentieth Century-Fox, 1959; Ed Malone, *The Lost World*, Twentieth Century-Fox, 1960; David Chatfield, *Marines, Let's Go*, Twentieth Century-Fox, 1961; Philip, *The Greatest Story Ever Told*, United Artists, 1965; Nick, *Kemek*, GHM, 1970; Felix Leiter, *Live and Let Die*, United Artists, 1973; King, *Ffolkes* (also known as *North Sea Hijack* and *Assault Force*), Universal, 1980; Dr. Hadley, *The Naked Face*,

Cannon, 1984; Frank Wheeler, *Smart Alec*, American Twist/Boulevard, 1986; Felix Leiter, *License to Kill*, United Artists, 1989.

PRINCIPAL TELEVISION APPEARANCES—Series: Victor Sebastian, *Five Fingers*, NBC, 1959-60; Commander/Captain Lee Crane, *Voyage to the Bottom of the Sea*, ABC, 1964-68; Sir Roger Langdon, *Dynasty II: The Colbys*, ABC, 1985-87. Mini-Series: Porcius Festus, *A.D.*, NBC, 1985. Pilots: Nick Kelton, *Crime Club*, CBS, 1973; Parker Sharon, *The Art of Crime*, NBC, 1975; Wes Dolan, *The Lives of Jenny Dolan*, NBC, 1975; David Royce, *Colorado C.I.*, CBS, 1978; Danton, *The Power Within*, ABC, 1979.

Episodic: Ed Galbin, *Crazy Like a Fox*, CBS, 1985; Miles Warner, *Trapper John, M.D.*, CBS, 1985; Vaughn, *The A-Team*, NBC, 1985; Mitch Payne, *Murder, She Wrote*, CBS, 1986; Howard Bentley, *Hotel*, ABC, 1987; Mr. Ratcliff, *Who's the Boss?*, ABC, 1987; Victor Caspar, *Murder, She Wrote*, CBS, 1989; also *Hong Kong*, ABC, 1961; *Bus Stop*, ABC, 1961; *Perry Mason*, CBS, 1962; *The Saint*, NBC, 1966; *Journey to the Unknown*, ABC, 1968; *Love, American Style*, ABC, 1969; *The F.B.I.*, ABC, 1972 and 1973; *Cannon*, CBS, 1972, 1973, and 1975; *The New Adventures of Perry Mason*, CBS, 1973; *Shaft*, CBS, 1974; *Medical Center*, CBS, 1974; *Manhunter*, CBS, 1974; *Ellery Queen*, NBC, 1976; *Family*, ABC, 1976; *Wonder Woman*, CBS, 1977; *The Bob Newhart Show*, CBS, 1978; *The Law and Harry McGraw*, CBS, 1987; Miles, *Hart to Hart*, ABC; John Taylor, *Benson*, ABC; *The Love Boat*, ABC. Movies: Roger Edmonds, *The Cat Creature*, ABC, 1973; Dr. Peter Brooks, *Adventures of the Queen*, CBS, 1975; Steven Cord, *Murder in Peyton Place*, NBC, 1977; Carson, *Kenny Rogers as "The Gambler"—The Adventure Continues*, CBS, 1983. Specials: Clay Hollinger, "Can I Save My Children?" *ABC Afternoon Playbreak*, ABC, 1974; *ABC's Silver Anniversary Special—25 and Still the One*, ABC, 1978; also *Summer and Smoke*, BBC.

AWARDS: Theatre World Award, 1956, for *A Month in the Country;* Barter Theatre Award for *Summer and Smoke.*

MEMBER: Actors' Studio.

ADDRESSES: AGENT—Triad Artists Inc., 10100 Santa Monica Boulevard, 16th Floor, Los Angeles, CA 90067.*

*   *   *

HEMION, Dwight   1926-

PERSONAL: Full name, Dwight Arlington Hemion, Jr.; born March 14, 1926, in New Haven, CT; son of Dwight Arlington and Bernice Ruby (Berquist) Hemion; married Katherine Bridget Morrissy, September 1, 1973; children: Katherine, Dwight Gustav. MILITARY—U.S. Army, Air Corps, 1944-46.

VOCATION: Producer and director.

CAREER: PRINCIPAL TELEVISION WORK—Series: Director, *Rootie Kazootie*, NBC, 1950-52, then ABC, 1952-54; director, *The Tonight Show*, NBC, 1954-56; director, *The Steve Allen Show*, NBC, 1956-60; director, *The Perry Como Show*, NBC, 1960-63; director, *The New Steve Allen Show*, ABC, 1961; producer (with

Gary Smith) and director, *The New Christy Minstrels Show*, NBC, 1964; producer (with Smith) and director, *The Roger Miller Show*, NBC, 1966-67; producer (with Smith) and director, *The Kraft Music Hall*, NBC, 1967-71; producer (with Smith) and director, *The Kopykats*, ABC, 1972; executive producer (with Smith), *The Mac Davis Show*, NBC, 1976; executive producer (with Smith), *Three Girls Three*, NBC, 1977; executive producer (with Smith and Nick Vanoff) and director, *On Stage America*, syndicated, 1984. Pilots: Director, *The Timex All-Star Jazz Show*, NBC, 1957. Episodic: Director, *Honey West*, ABC.

Specials: Director, *The Perry Como Special*, NBC, 1963; director, *Texaco Star Parade II*, CBS, 1964; director, *The Perry Como Special*, NBC, 1964; director, *The Perry Como Christmas Show*, NBC, 1964; producer (with Smith) and director, *The Frank Sinatra Show*, NBC, 1965; director, *The Perry Como Show*, NBC, 1965; director, *The Perry Como Thanksgiving Show*, NBC, 1965; director, *My Name Is Barbra*, CBS, 1965; director, *The Perry Como Christmas Show*, NBC, 1965; producer and director, *Frank Sinatra— A Man and His Music*, CBS, 1966; director, *The Perry Como Springtime Special*, NBC, 1966; director, *Perry Como's Summer Show*, NBC, 1966; producer (with Smith) and director, *The Tony Bennett Show*, ABC, 1966; director, *The Perry Como Thanksgiving Special*, NBC, 1966; director, *The Perry Como Christmas Show*, NBC, 1966; director, *The Perry Como Winter Show*, NBC, 1967; producer (with Smith) and director, *Herb Alpert and the Tijuana Brass*, CBS, 1967; director, *The Perry Como Valentine Special*, NBC, 1967; director, *The Perry Como Springtime Show*, NBC, 1967; producer (with Smith) and director, *Tin Pan Alley Today*, NBC, 1967; director, *The Perry Como Special*, NBC, 1967; producer (with Smith) and director, *Zero Hour*, ABC, 1967.

Director, *Petula*, ABC, 1970; executive producer (with Smith), *The Klowns*, ABC, 1970; producer (with Smith) and director, *The Burt Bacharach Special*, CBS, 1971; producer (with Smith) and director, *Burt Bacharach!*, ABC, 1972; producer (with Smith) and director, *Burt Bacharach: Close to You*, ABC, 1972; producer (with Smith) and director, *The Magical Music of Burt Bacharach*, syndicated, 1972; producer (with Smith) and director, *Burt Bacharach—Opus No. 3*, ABC, 1973; producer (with Smith and Joe Layton) and director, *Barbra Streisand and Other Musical Instruments*, CBS, 1973; producer (with Smith) and director, *James Paul McCartney*, ABC, 1973; producer (with Smith) and director, *Julie on Sesame Street*, ABC, 1973; producer (with Smith) and director, *Burt Bacharach in Shangri-La*, ABC, 1973; producer (with Smith) and director, *Marlo Thomas in Acts of Love—and Other Comedies*, ABC, 1973; producer (with Smith) and director, *Royal Variety Performance*, ABC, 1973; producer (with Smith) and director, *The Very First Glen Campbell Special*, NBC, 1973; producer (with Smith) and director, *The Burt Bacharach Special*, CBS, 1974; producer (with Smith) and director, *The Glen Campbell Special: The Musical West*, NBC, 1974; director, *The Sandy Duncan Show*, CBS, 1974; executive producer (with Smith) and director, *Herb Alpert and the Tijuana Brass*, ABC, 1974.

Producer (with Smith) and director, *Steve and Eydie: Our Love Is Here to Stay*, CBS, 1975; producer (with Smith) and director, *Ann-Margret Smith*, NBC, 1975; director, *Funny Girl to Funny Lady*, ABC, 1975; producer (with Smith) and director, *Ann-Margret Olsson*, NBC, 1975; executive producer (with Smith) and director, *Merry Christmas from the Crosbys*, NBC, 1975; producer (with Smith) and director, *America Salutes Richard Rodgers: The Sound of His Music*, CBS, 1976; executive producer (with Smith) and director, *Dick Cavett's Backlot USA*, CBS, 1976; producer (with

Smith) and director, *The Dorothy Hamill Special*, ABC, 1976; executive producer (with Smith) and director, *Glen Campbell . . . Down Home—Down Under*, CBS, 1976; director, *Jubilee*, NBC, 1976; executive producer (with Smith) and director, *Mac Davis Christmas Special . . . When I Grow Up*, NBC, 1976; executive producer (with Smith) and director, *Peter Pan*, NBC, 1976; producer (with Smith) and director, *America Salutes the Queen*, NBC, 1977; producer (with Smith) and director, *Steve Lawrence and Eydie Gorme: From This Moment On . . . Cole Porter*, ABC, 1977; producer (with Smith) and director, *The Neil Diamond Special*, NBC, 1977; producer (with Smith) and director, *Mac Davis . . . Sounds Like Home*, NBC, 1977; producer (with Smith) and director, *Bette Midler—Ol' Red Hair Is Back*, NBC, 1977; producer (with Smith) and director, *Ann-Margret . . . Rhinestone Cowgirl*, NBC, 1977; producer (with Smith) and director, *Bing Crosby's Merrie Olde Christmas*, NBC, 1977; producer (with Smith) and director, *Ben Vereen—His Roots*, ABC, 1978; producer (with Smith) and director, *The Kraft 75th Anniversary Special*, CBS, 1978; producer (with Smith) and director, *Lucy Comes to Nashville*, CBS, 1978; producer (with Smith) and director, *Steve and Eydie Celebrate Irving Berlin*, NBC, 1978; producer (with Smith) and director, *Elvis in Concert*, CBS, 1978; executive producer (with Smith) and director, *Mac Davis' Christmas Odyssey: Two Thousand and Ten*, NBC, 1978; executive producer (with Smith and Tom McDermott) and director, *Las Vegas Palace of Stars*, CBS, 1979; producer (with Smith), *Shirley MacLaine at the Lido*, CBS, 1979; executive producer (with Smith) and director, *The Cheryl Ladd Special*, ABC, 1979; producer (with Smith) and director, *Merry Christmas from the Grand Ole Opry*, ABC, 1979.

Producer (with Smith) and director, *Baryshnikov on Broadway*, ABC, 1980; executive producer (with Smith) and director, *Disneyland's 25th Anniversary*, CBS, 1980; executive producer (with Smith) and director, *The Eddie Rabbitt Special*, NBC, 1980; executive producer (with Smith) and director, *Linda in Wonderland*, CBS, 1980; executive producer (with Smith) and director, *Shirley MacLaine . . . Every Little Movement*, CBS, 1980; executive producer (with Smith) and director, *Ann-Margret's Hollywood Movie Girls*, ABC, 1980; producer (with Smith) and director, *Uptown*, NBC, 1980; executive producer (with Smith) and director, *Larry Gatlin and the Gatlin Brothers*, ABC, 1981; executive producer (with Smith) and director, *Walt Disney: One Man's Dream*, CBS, 1981; producer (with Smith) and director, *A Special Anne Murray Christmas*, CBS, 1981; producer (with Smith) and director, *Pavarotti and Friends*, ABC, 1982; executive producer (with Smith) and director, *Kraft Salutes Walt Disney World's 10th Anniversary*, CBS, 1982; producer (with Smith) and director, *Goldie and Kids: Listen to Us*, ABC, 1982; producer (with Smith) and director, *Christmas in Washington*, NBC, 1982; producer (with Smith) and director, *Anne Murray's Caribbean Cruise*, CBS, 1983; executive producer (with Smith), *Dorothy Hamill in Romeo and Juliet on Ice*, CBS, 1983; executive producer (with Smith and Jack Cellcio), *An Evening at the Moulin Rouge*, HBO, 1983; producer (with Smith) and director, *Sheena Easton, Act 1*, NBC, 1983; executive producer (with Smith) and director, *The Screen Actors Guild 50th Anniversary Celebration*, CBS, 1984; producer (with Smith) and director, *Anne Murray's Winter Carnival . . . From Quebec*, CBS, 1984; producer (with Smith), *Christmas in Washington*, NBC, 1984.

Producer (with Smith) and director, *Bob Hope's Happy Birthday Homecoming*, NBC, 1985; producer (with Smith) and director, *Rich Little and a Night of 42 Stars*, HBO, 1985; executive producer (with Smith) and director, *The 50th Presidential Inaugural Gala*,

ABC, 1985; director, *Anne Murray: The Sounds of London,* CBS, 1985; producer (with Smith) and director, *Christmas in Washington,* NBC, 1985; executive producer (with Smith) and director, *Here's Television Entertainment,* syndicated, 1985; director, *Andy Williams and the NBC Kids Search for Santa,* NBC, 1985; producer (with Smith) and director, *The Television Academy Hall of Fame,* NBC, 1985 and 1986; director, *Liberty Weekend,* ABC, 1986; producer (with Smith) and director, *Neil Diamond . . . Hello Again,* CBS, 1986; producer (with Smith) and director, *Barbra Streisand: One Voice,* HBO, 1986; producer (with Smith) and director, *Christmas in Washington,* NBC, 1986; producer (with Smith) and director, *Amy Grant . . . Headin' Home for the Holidays,* NBC, 1986; executive producer (with Smith), producer, and director, *We the People 200: The Constitutional Gala,* CBS, 1987; producer (with Smith) and director, *Christmas in Washington,* NBC, 1987; director, *The American Film Institute Salute to Barbara Stanwyck,* ABC, 1987; director, *Julie Andrews: The Sound of Christmas,* ABC, 1987; producer (with Smith) and director, *The Television Academy Hall of Fame,* Fox, 1987; director, *The Kennedy Center Honors: A Celebration of the Performing Arts,* CBS, 1988; producer (with Smith) and director, *America's Tribute to Bob Hope,* NBC, 1988; producer (with Smith) and director, *Christmas in Washington,* NBC, 1988; director, "Jackie Mason on Broadway," *On Location,* HBO, 1988; producer (with Smith) and director, *Neil Diamond's Greatest Hits,* HBO, 1988; executive producer (with Smith) and director, *The People's Choice Awards,* CBS, 1988 and 1989; director, *Ooh-La-La—It's Bob Hope's Fun Birthday Spectacular from Paris's Bicentennial,* NBC, 1989; director, *The 11th Annual Kennedy Center Honors: A Celebration of the Performing Arts,* CBS, 1989; producer (with Smith) and director, *From the Heart . . . The First International Very Special Arts Festival,* NBC, 1989; producer (with Smith) and director, *Christmas in Washington,* NBC, 1989; executive producer (with Smith) and director, *The Television Academy Hall of Fame,* Fox, 1989 and 1990. Also director, *The Sound of Burt Bacharach,* 1969; director, *Singer Presents Burt Bacharach,* 1970.

RELATED CAREER—Associate director, ABC-TV, New York City, 1946-49; producer and director, Yorkshire Productions, New York City, 1967-70; founder, producer, and director, Smith-Hemion Productions, Los Angeles, 1975—.

AWARDS: Director of the Year Award from the Television Directors Guild of America, 1965; Emmy Award, Outstanding Musical Program, 1966, for *Frank Sinatra—A Man and His Music;* Emmy Award, Outstanding Directorial Achievement in a Comedy, Variety, or Music Special, 1970, for *The Sound of Burt Bacharach;* Emmy Award, Outstanding Directorial Achievement in a Comedy, Variety, or Music Special, 1971, for *Singer Presents Burt Bacharach;* Emmy Award, Outstanding Directorial Achievement in a Comedy-Variety or Music Special, 1974, for *Barbra Streisand and Other Musical Instruments;* Emmy Award, Outstanding Directing in a Comedy-Variety or Music Special, 1976, for *Steve and Eydie: Our Love Is Here to Stay;* Emmy Award, Outstanding Directing in a Comedy-Variety or Music Special, 1977, for *America Salutes Richard Rodgers: The Sound of His Music;* Emmy Award, Outstanding Directing in a Comedy-Variety or Music Special, 1978, for *Ben Vereen—His Roots;* Emmy Award, Outstanding Comedy-Variety or Music Program, 1978, for *Steve and Eydie Celebrate Irving Berlin;* Emmy Awards, Outstanding Special and Outstanding Directing in a Special, both 1980, for *Baryshnikov on Broadway;* Emmy Award, Outstanding Directing in a Variety or Musical Program, 1982, for *Goldie and Kids . . . Listen to Us;* Emmy Award, Outstanding Directing in a Variety or Musical Program, 1983, for *Sheena Easton, Act 1;* Emmy Awards Outstanding

Directing in a Variety, Music, or Comedy Program, and Outstanding Directorial Achievement Award from the Directors Guild of America, both 1985, for *Here's Television Entertainment;* Outstanding Directorial Achievement Award from the Directors Guild of America, 1987, for *Julie Andrews: The Sound of Christmas;* Emmy Award, Individual Achievement in Directing for Special Events, 1989, for *The 11th Annual Kennedy Center Honors: A Celebration of the Performing Arts.*

MEMBER: Directors Guild of America, Bel-Air Country Club.

ADDRESSES: OFFICE—Smith-Hemion Productions, 1438 N. Gower, Box 15, Los Angeles, CA 90028.*

*   *   *

HENRIKSEN, Lance

VOCATION: Actor.

CAREER: PRINCIPAL STAGE APPEARANCES—Pierce, *The Basic Training of Pavlo Hummel,* Longacre Theatre, New York City, 1977; also appeared in *Saved,* Theatre Company of Boston, Boston, MA, 1971.

PRINCIPAL FILM APPEARANCES—Randy, *It Ain't Easy,* Dandelion, 1972; Murphy, *Dog Day Afternoon,* Warner Brothers, 1975; Dr. Dan Bryan, *Mansion of the Doomed* (also known as *The Terror of Dr. Chaney*), Group I, 1976; federal security agent, *The Next Man,* Allied Artists, 1976; Robert, *Close Encounters of the Third Kind,* Columbia, 1977; Sergeant Neff, *Damien—Omen II,* Twentieth Century-Fox, 1978; Raymond, *The Visitor* (also known as *Il visitatore*), International Picture Show/Marvin, 1980; Jimmy, *The Dark End of the Street,* First Run Features, 1981; District Attorney Burano, *Prince of the City,* Warner Brothers, 1981; Steve Kimbrough, *Piranha II: The Spawning* (also known as *Piranha II: Flying Killers*), Columbia, 1981; Wally Schirra, *The Right Stuff,* Warner Brothers, 1983; Ben Stryker, *Savage Dawn,* Media Home Entertainment, 1984; Vukovich, *The Terminator,* Orion, 1984; Frank Martin, *Jagged Edge,* Columbia, 1985; Brook Alistair, *Choke Canyon,* United Film Distribution, 1986; Jesse, *Near Dark,* De Laurentiis Entertainment Group, 1987; Raymond Keaton, *Deadly Intent,* Fries Distribution, 1988; Ed Harley, *Pumpkin Head,* Metro-Goldwyn-Mayer/United Artists (MGM/UA), 1988; Chris Caleek, *Hit List,* New Line Cinema, 1989; Lucas McCarthy, *The Horror Show,* MGM/UA, 1989; Rafe Garrett, *Johnny Handsome,* Tri-Star, 1989.

PRINCIPAL TELEVISION APPEARANCES—Episodic: *Scene of the Crime,* NBC, 1984. Specials: "Paul Reiser: Out on a Whim," *HBO: On Location,* HBO, 1987.

RELATED CAREER—Company member, Theatre Company of Boston, Boston, MA, 1971-73.

WRITINGS: FILM—(With James Cameron, Gale Ann Hurd, Rick Rossovich, Bess Motta, and Karl Boen) *The Terminator,* Orion, 1984.

ADDRESSES: AGENT—Bob Gersh, The Gersh Agency, 222 N. Canon Drive, Suite 202, Beverly Hills, 90210. MANAGER—Raymond Katz Enterprises, 9255 Sunset Boulevard, Suite 1115, Los Angeles, CA 90069.*

JASON HERVEY

HERVEY, Jason 1972-

PERSONAL: Born April 6, 1972; son of Alan and Marsha Hervey. EDUCATION—Trained for the stage at the Ernie Lively Actors Workshop, the Michael Cutt Actors Workshop, the Virgil Frye Actors Workshop, and with the Dupree Dance Studio.

VOCATION: Actor.

CAREER: STAGE DEBUT—Sonny, *Cat on a Hot Tin Roof,* Center Theatre Group, Mark Taper Forum, Los Angeles, 1984.

PRINCIPAL FILM APPEARANCES—Potato, *The Buddy System,* Twentieth Century-Fox, 1984; Steve, *Meatballs, Part II,* Tri-Star, 1984; Milton Baines, *Back to the Future,* Universal, 1985; Kevin Morton, *Pee-Wee's Big Adventure,* Warner Brothers, 1985; brat, *Police Academy II: Their First Assignment,* Warner Brothers, 1985; young Thornton, *Back to School,* Orion, 1986; E.J., *The Monster Squad,* Tri-Star, 1987; also appeared in *Children on Their Birthday,* American Film Institute; and in *Frankenweenie* (short film).

PRINCIPAL TELEVISION APPEARANCES—Series: Zeke, *Wildside,* ABC, 1985; Charlie Hunter, *Diff'rent Strokes,* ABC, 1985-86; Curtis Spicoli, *Fast Times,* CBS, 1986; Wayne Arnold, *The Wonder Years,* ABC, 1988—; host, *Wide World of Kids,* syndicated, 1989. Pilots: *The O'Brians.* Episodic: Little Jim, *Gun Shy,* CBS, 1983; Bobby, "The Last Electric Knight," *Magical World of Disney,* ABC, 1986; Bradley, *Simon and Simon,* CBS, 1988; also Louie as a child, *Taxi,* ABC; *A Year in the Life,* NBC; *Punky Brewster,* NBC; *Alice,* CBS; *The Love Boat,* ABC; *The Two of Us,*

CBS; *Hell Town,* NBC; *Trapper John, M.D.,* CBS; *Likely Stories,* Showtime. Movies: Jamie, *Your Place or Mine,* CBS, 1983; Todd Sweeney, *The Ratings Game,* Movie Channel, 1984; Clint, *Little Spies,* ABC, 1986; also *Gabe and Walker,* ABC. Specials: Roy, "Daddy, I'm Their Momma Now," *ABC Afterschool Specials,* ABC.

RELATED CAREER—National youth host, Jerry Lewis Muscular Dystrophy Telethon, 1988; actor in television commercials.

AWARDS: Youth in Film Award nomination, Best Young Actor in a Television Movie, for "Daddy I'm Their Momma Now," *ABC Afterschool Specials;* Youth in Film Award nomination, Best Young Actor as a Guest in a Television Series; Halo Award from *Faces* magazine.

MEMBER: Actors' Equity Association, Screen Actors Guild, American Federation of Television and Radio Artists, Variety Club.

SIDELIGHTS: RECREATIONS—Sports.

ADDRESSES: AGENT—Abrams Artists and Associates, 9200 Sunset Boulevard, Suite 625, Los Angeles, CA 90069. PUBLICIST—Freeman and Sutton, 8961 Sunset Boulevard, Suite 2-A, Los Angeles, CA 90069.

*   *   *

HIGGINS, Clare

PERSONAL: Born c. 1957 in Yorkshire, England.

VOCATION: Actress.

CAREER: PRINCIPAL STAGE APPEARANCES—Judith, *Blood Black and Gold,* Royal Exchange Theatre, Manchester, U.K., 1980; Irmgard, *Beethoven's Tenth,* Vaudeville Theatre, London, 1983; Katherine Glass, *The Secret Rapture,* National Theatre Company, Lyttelton Theatre, London, 1988; Gertrude, *Hamlet* and Hippolyta and Titania, *A Midsummer Night's Dream,* both Royal Shakespeare Company, Royal Shakespeare Theatre, Stratford-on-Avon, U.K., 1989; Gertrude, *Hamlet,* National Theatre Company, Olivier Theatre, London, 1989.

PRINCIPAL FILM APPEARANCES—Young Sophie, *1919,* British Film Institute/Channel 4, 1984; Julia Cotton, *Hellraiser,* New World, 1987; Eve, *The Fruit Machine,* Vestron, 1988; Julia Cotton, *Hellbound: Hellraiser II,* New World, 1989.

PRINCIPAL TELEVISION APPEARANCES—Mini-Series: Kitty Bennett, *Pride and Prejudice,* BBC, then *Masterpiece Theatre,* PBS, 1980; Christine Barlow, *The Citadel,* BBC, then *Masterpiece Theatre,* PBS, 1983-84; Sophie, *Cover Her Face,* Anglia Television, then *Mystery!,* PBS, 1987; Rachel Jordan, *After the War,* Granada, 1989, then *Masterpiece Theatre,* PBS, 1989-90; also *Love for Lydia,* BBC, then *Masterpiece Theatre,* PBS.*

HILL, Steven 1922-

PERSONAL: Born February 24,.1922, in Seattle, WA. EDUCA-TION—Attended the University of Washington.

VOCATION: Actor.

CAREER: PRINCIPAL STAGE APPEARANCES—Soldier, *A Flag Is Born*, Alvin Theatre, then Adelphi Theatre, later Music Box Theatre, then Broadway Theatre, all New York City, 1946; Stefanowski, *Mister Roberts*, Alvin Theatre, 1948; Thaddeus Long, *Sundown Beach*, Belasco Theatre, New York City, 1948; Bernie Dodd, *The Country Girl*, Lyceum Theatre, New York City, 1950; Lyngstrand, *The Lady from the Sea*, Fulton Theatre, New York City, 1950; Sigmund Freud, *A Far Country*, Music Box Theatre, 1961.

MAJOR TOURS—Anthony Harker, *Josephine*, U.S. cities, 1953; Thad Tale, *The Midnight Sun*, U.S. cities, 1959.

PRINCIPAL FILM APPEARANCES—Jack, *A Lady without Passport*, Metro-Goldwyn-Mayer, 1950; Benjie, *Storm Fear*, United Artists, 1956; John Tower, *The Goddess*, Columbia, 1958; Ted Widdicombe, *A Child Is Waiting*, United Artists, 1963; Mark Dyson, *The Slender Thread*, Paramount, 1965; Jacob, *It's My Turn*, Columbia, 1980; Lieutenant Jacobs, *Eyewitness* (also known as *The Janitor*), Twentieth Century-Fox, 1981; Jules Levi, *Rich and Famous*, Metro-Goldwyn-Mayer/United Artists (MGM/UA), 1981; Reb Alter Vishkower, *Yentl*, MGM/UA, 1983; Walter Rolfe, *Garbo Talks*, United Artists, 1984; Sloan, *Teachers*, United Artists, 1984; Harry, *Heartburn*, Paramount, 1986; Lamanski, *Raw Deal*, De Laurentiis Entertainment Group, 1986; Mr. Stroheim, *Brighton Beach Memoirs*, Universal, 1986; George Tyler, *On Valentine's Day* (also known as *Story of a Marriage, Part II*), Angelika/Cinecom International/J & M Enterprises, 1988; Max, *The Boost*, Hemdale, 1988; Mr. Patterson, *Running on Empty*, Warner Brothers, 1988. Also appeared in *Kiss Her Goodbye*, 1959.

PRINCIPAL TELEVISION APPEARANCES—Series: Frank Sartene, *The Greatest Show on Earth*, ABC, 1952-53; Daniel Briggs, *Mission: Impossible*, CBS, 1966-67. Episodic: George Tyler, "Story of a Marriage," *American Playhouse*, PBS, 1987; Leo Steadman, *thirtysomething*, ABC, 1988; Mr. Morosco, "Murder, Smoke, and Shadows," *Columbo*, ABC, 1989; also *Espionage*, NBC; *Actor's Studio*. Movies: Stanley Levinson, *King*, NBC, 1978; Teddy Petherton, *Between Two Women*, ABC, 1986.*

*   *   *

HILLER, Arthur 1923-

PERSONAL: Born November 22, 1923, in Edmonton, AB, Canada; son of Harry and Rose (Garfin) Hiller; married Gwen Pechet, February 14, 1948; children: Henryk, Erica. EDUCATION—University of Toronto, B.A., 1947, M.A., psychology, 1950; studied law at the University of British Columbia, 1948; also attended the University of Alberta. MILITARY—Royal Canadian Air Force, flying officer, 1942-45.

VOCATION: Director.

CAREER: FIRST STAGE WORK—Director, *Blithe Spirit*, summer theatre production, Niagara-on-the-Lake, ON, Canada, 1953.

PRINCIPAL FILM WORK—Director: *The Careless Years*, United Artists, 1957; *Miracle of the White Stallions* (also known as *The Flight of the White Stallions*), Buena Vista, 1963; *The Wheeler Dealers* (also known as *Separate Beds*), Metro-Goldwyn-Mayer (MGM), 1963; *The Americanization of Emily*, MGM, 1964; *Penelope*, MGM, 1966; *Promise Her Anything*, Paramount, 1966; *Tobruk*, Universal, 1966; *The Tiger Makes Out*, Columbia, 1967; *Popi*, United Artists, 1969; *Love Story*, Paramount, 1970; *The Out-of-Towners*, Paramount, 1970; *The Hospital*, United Artists, 1971; *Plaza Suite*, Paramount, 1971; (also producer) *Man of La Mancha*, United Artists, 1972; (also producer with Edward Rissien) *The Crazy World of Julius Vrooder* (also known as *Vrooder's Hooch*), Twentieth Century-Fox, 1974; *The Man in the Glass Booth*, American Film Theatre, 1975; *W.C. Fields and Me*, Universal, 1976; *Silver Streak*, Twentieth Century-Fox, 1976; (also producer with William Sackheim) *The In-Laws*, Warner Brothers, 1979; *Nightwing*, Columbia, 1979; *Author! Author!*, Twentieth Century-Fox, 1982; *Making Love*, Twentieth Century-Fox, 1982; *Romantic Comedy*, Metro-Goldwyn-Mayer/United Artists (MGM/UA), 1983; (also producer) *The Lonely Guy*, Universal, 1984; *Teachers*, MGM/UA, 1984; *Outrageous Fortune*, Buena Vista, 1987; *See No Evil, Hear No Evil*, Tri-Star, 1989; also *Confrontation* (short film), 1970.

PRINCIPAL TELEVISION WORK—All as director. Pilots: *Starr, First Baseman*, CBS, 1965. Episodic: "The Twisted Image" and "Child's Play," *Thriller*, NBC, 1960; also "Massacre at Sand Creek," *Playhouse 90*, CBS; *Matinee Theatre*, NBC; *Naked City*, ABC; *Ben Casey*, ABC; *The Desilu Playhouse*, CBS; *The Detectives* (also known as *Robert Taylor's Detectives*), ABC; *The Dick Powell Show*, NBC; *The Rifleman*, ABC; *Climax!*, CBS; *Target: The Corrupters*, ABC; *Gunsmoke*, CBS; *Perry Mason*, CBS; *Route 66*, CBS; *Wagon Train;* and *Alfred Hitchcock Presents*.

RELATED CAREER—Director of public service broadcasts, Canadian Broadcast Corporation, 1953-55.

AWARDS: Canadian Radio Awards, 1951 and 1952; Institute for Education Radio and Television Awards, 1952 and 1953; Emmy Award nomination, Best Director, 1962, for *Naked City;* Golden Globe, Directors Guild of America Award, New York Foreign Critics' Award, and Academy Award nomination, all Best Director, 1970, for *Love Story;* Yugoslav Film Festival Award, 1974, for *The Hospital*. HONORARY DEGREES—London Institute of Applied Research, L.H.D., 1973.

MEMBER: Academy of Motion Picture Arts and Sciences (board of governors), Directors Guild of America (president), Anti-Defamation League (regional board member), Commission on Soviet Jewry (board member).

ADDRESSES: AGENT—The Gersh Agency, 222 N. Canon Drive, Beverly Hills, CA 90212.

*   *   *

HILLERMAN, John 1932-

PERSONAL: Full name, John Benedict Hillerman; born December 20, 1932 in Denison, TX; son of Christopher Benedict and Lenora JoAnn (Medinger) Hillerman. EDUCATION—Attended the University of Texas, 1949-52; studied acting at the American Theatre Wing, 1958-59. MILITARY—U.S. Air Force, 1953-57.

JOHN HILLERMAN

VOCATION: Actor.

CAREER: PRINCIPAL STAGE APPEARANCES—*Lady of the Camellias*, Winter Garden Theatre, New York City, 1963; also *The Great God Brown*, Broadway production; and in productions of *Death of a Salesman*, *The Lion in Winter*, *The Little Foxes*, *Come Blow Your Horn*, *Caligula*, *Rhinoceros*, *The Fourposter*, *The Lark*, and *The Devil's Disciple*.

PRINCIPAL FILM APPEARANCES—Teacher, *The Last Picture Show*, Columbia, 1971; Totts, *Lawman*, United Artists, 1971; Jenkins, *The Carey Treatment*, Metro-Goldwyn-Mayer (MGM), 1972; Walter Brandt, *Skyjacked* (also known as *Sky Terror*), MGM, 1972; Mr. Kaltenborn, *What's Up Doc?*, Warner Brothers, 1972; bootmaker, *High Plains Drifter*, Universal, 1973; department store manager, *The Outside Man* (also known as *Un Homme est mort*), United Artists, 1973; Sheriff Hardin and Jess Hardin, *Paper Moon*, Paramount, 1973; Laxker, *The Thief Who Came to Dinner*, Warner Brothers, 1973; Howard Johnson, *Blazing Saddles*, Warner Brothers, 1974; Yelburton, *Chinatown*, Paramount, 1974; Carl, *The Nickel Ride*, Twentieth Century-Fox, 1974; Rodney James, *At Long Last Love*, Twentieth Century-Fox, 1975; Ned Grote, *The Day of the Locust*, Paramount, 1975; Christy McTeague, *Lucky Lady*, Twentieth Century-Fox, 1975; Scott Velie, *Audrey Rose*, United Artists, 1977; Webb, *Sunburn*, Paramount, 1979; rich man, *History of the World, Part I*, Twentieth Century-Fox, 1981; Dean Burch, *Up the Creek*, Orion, 1984; Pfarrer, *Gummibarchen Kusst Man Nicht* (also known as *Real Men Don't Eat Gummi Bears*), Tivoli Filmverleih, 1989.

PRINCIPAL TELEVISION APPEARANCES—Series: Simon Brimmer, *The Adventures of Ellery Queen*, NBC, 1975-76; John Elliot, *The Betty White Show*, CBS, 1977-78; Jonathan Quale Higgins III, *Magnum, P.I.*, CBS, 1980-88. Mini-Series: Sir Francis Commarty, *Around the World in 80 Days*, NBC, 1989. Pilots: Tree inspector, *The Last Angry Man*, ABC, 1974; Simon Brimmer, *Ellery Queen: Too Many Suspects*, NBC, 1975; John Peacock, *Beane's of Boston*, CBS, 1979; Mr. Dempster, *Gossip*, NBC, 1979; voice of IFR 7000, *Institute for Revenge*, NBC, 1979; Paul Harrison, *Battles: The Murder That Wouldn't Die*, NBC, 1980. Episodic: William Whitney, *Tenspeed and Brown Shoe*, ABC, 1980; also Claude "Al" Connors, *One Day at a Time*, CBS; *Comedy Break*, syndicated; *The F.B.I.*, ABC; *Mannix*, CBS; *Maude*, CBS; *Kojak*, CBS; *Serpico*, NBC; *Little House on the Prairie*, NBC; *The Love Boat*, ABC; *Soap*, ABC; *Lou Grant*, CBS. Movies: Medical examiner, *Sweet, Sweet Rachel*, ABC, 1971; Major Underwood, *The Great Man's Whiskers*, NBC, 1973; Thomas Q. Rachel, *The Law*, NBC, 1974; Major Walcott, *The Invasion of Johnson County*, NBC, 1976; Major Leo Hargit, *Relentless*, CBS, 1977; George Davis, *Kill Me If You Can*, NBC, 1977; Marvin, *A Guide for the Married Woman*, ABC, 1978; Victor Slavin, *Betrayal*, NBC, 1978; Greg Previn, *Marathon*, CBS, 1980; Maury Paul, *Little Gloria . . . Happy at Last*, NBC, 1982; Cyril Combs, *Assault and Matrimony*, NBC, 1987; Raymond Kepler, *Street of Dreams*, CBS, 1988. Specials: *The Dean Martin Celebrity Roast: Betty White*, NBC, 1978; *The Funniest Joke I Ever Heard*, ABC, 1984; host, *CBS All-American Thanksgiving Day Parade*, CBS, 1983-87; *Texas 150: A Celebration Special*, ABC, 1986; *Sea World's All-Star Lone Star Celebration*, CBS, 1988; *Stop the Madness*, CBS, 1989.

NON-RELATED CAREER—Company member, Theatre Club, Washington, DC, 1965-69.

AWARDS: Golden Globe, Best Supporting Actor in a Television Series, 1982, and Emmy Award, Outstanding Supporting Actor in a Drama Series, 1987, both for *Magnum, P.I.*

MEMBER: Actors' Equity Association, Academy of Motion Picture Arts and Sciences, Academy of Television Arts and Sciences, Screen Actors Guild, American Federation of Television and Radio Artists.

ADDRESSES: AGENT—McCartt, Oreck, Barrett, 9200 Sunset Boulevard, Suite 1009, Los Angeles, CA 90069. PUBLICIST—The Garrett Company, 6922 Hollywood Boulevard, Los Angeles, CA 90028.

*   *   *

HINDMAN, Earl

VOCATION: Actor.

CAREER: PRINCIPAL STAGE APPEARANCES—Marvin Hudgins, *Dark of the Moon*, Mercer-Shaw Arena Theatre, New York City, 1970; Kress, *The Basic Training of Pavlo Hummel*, New York Shakespeare Festival (NYSF), Public Theatre, New York City, 1971; Captain Martin, *The Love Suicide at the Schofield Barracks*, American National Theatre and Academy Theatre, New York City, 1972; Asa Trenchard, *The Lincoln Mask*, Plymouth Theatre, New York City, 1972; Rubin Flood, *The Dark at the Top of the Stairs*, Roundabout Theatre, New York City, 1979; Red, *Red, Red and Blue*, NYSF, Public Theatre, 1982; Exeter, *Henry V*, NYSF, Delacorte

Theatre, New York City, 1984; Owen Musser, *The Foreigner,* Studio Arena Theatre, Buffalo, NY, 1986; Gaspard Caderousse, *The Count of Monte Cristo,* Kennedy Center for the Performing Arts, Washington, DC, 1986; Big Albert Connor, *The Stick Wife,* Hartford Stage Company, Hartford, CT, 1987; T. John Blessington, *The Solid Gold Cadillac,* Yale Repertory Theatre, New Haven, CT, 1989. Also appeared in *The Rivalry,* Mummers Theatre, Oklahoma City, OK, 1970; *Henry IV, Part One,* Folger Theatre Group, Washington, DC, 1974; *The Magnificent Cuckold,* Yale Repertory Theatre, 1981; *Flint and Roses,* Alliance Theatre Company, Atlanta, GA, 1986.

MAJOR TOURS—*The Great White Hope,* U.S. cities, 1969-70.

PRINCIPAL FILM APPEARANCES—Whitey, *Who Killed Mary What's 'er Name?* (also known as *Death of a Hooker*), Cannon, 1971; Brown, *The Taking of Pelham One, Two, Three,* United Artists, 1974; Deputy Red, *The Parallax View,* Paramount, 1974; Garrity, *Shoot It: Black, Shoot It: Blue,* Levitt/Pickman, 1974; Beau Welles, *Greased Lightning,* Warner Brothers, 1977; F.B.I. agent, *The Brinks Job,* Universal, 1978; Lieutenant Hanson, *Taps,* Twentieth Century-Fox, 1981; J.T., *Silverado,* Columbia, 1985; Satch, *Three Men and a Baby,* Buena Vista, 1987; voices of Chet, Black John, and Jerry, *Talk Radio,* Universal, 1988.

PRINCIPAL TELEVISION APPEARANCES—Series: Detective Bob Reid, *Ryan's Hope,* ABC, 1975-84. Mini-Series: Lieutenant Commander Wade McClusky, *War and Remembrance,* ABC, 1988. Pilots: Rick, *Key West,* NBC, 1973. Episodic: Clayton, *Spenser: For Hire,* ABC, 1985; Findlay, *The Equalizer,* CBS, 1986; Lieutenant Elmer, *The Equalizer,* CBS, 1986 and 1987 (three episodes); Max Ordella, *Spenser: For Hire,* ABC, 1987. Movies: J.H. Potts, *Murder in Coweta County,* CBS, 1983; Detective Jake Stern, *One Police Plaza,* CBS, 1986; Danny Keeler, *Kojak: The Price of Justice,* CBS, 1987; Stern, *The Red Spider,* CBS, 1988. Specials: D. Law, "Pueblo," *ABC Theatre,* ABC, 1974; William, "A Memory of Two Mondays," *Great Performances,* PBS, 1974.

RELATED CAREER—Company member: Syracuse Repertory Theatre, Syracuse, NY, 1967; A Contemporary Theatre, Seattle, WA, 1974-75; New Jersey Shakespeare Festival, Drew University, Madison, NJ, 1976.

ADDRESSES: AGENT—Michael Hartig Agency, 114 E. 28th Street, New York, NY 10016.*

*   *   *

HINGLE, Pat   1923-

PERSONAL: Full name, Martin Patterson Hingle; born July 19, 1924, in Miami, FL; son of Clarence Martin (a building contractor) and Marvin Louise (a school teacher and musician; maiden name, Patterson) Hingle; married Alyce Dorsey, June 3, 1947 (divorced); married Julia Wright, October 25, 1979; children: Jody, Billy, Molly (first marriage). EDUCATION—University of Texas, B.F.A., 1949; trained for the stage at the American Theatre Wing, 1949-50, at the HB Studios with Uta Hagen, and at the Actors' Studio; studied voice with Albert Malver. MILITARY—U.S. Naval Reserve, 1941-46 and 1951-52.

VOCATION: Actor.

PAT HINGLE

CAREER: STAGE DEBUT—Lachie, *Johnny Belinda,* Center Playhouse, Rockville Center, NY, 1950. OFF-BROADWAY DEBUT—Harold Koble, *End As a Man,* Theatre De Lys, 1953. PRINCIPAL STAGE APPEARANCES—Fritz, *Claudia,* Lexy, *Candida,* prosecutor, *Redemption,* gentleman caller, *The Glass Menagerie,* and Sergeant Rough, *Angel Street,* all Center Playhouse, Rockville Center, NY, 1950; Dowdy, *Mister Roberts,* Cecilwood Theatre, Fishkill, NY, 1953; Harold Koble, *End As a Man,* Vanderbilt Theatre, New York City, 1953; Joe Foster, *Festival,* Longacre Theatre, New York City, 1955; Gooper, *Cat on a Hot Tin Roof,* Morosco Theatre, New York City, 1955; Jules Taggert, *Girls of Summer,* Longacre Theatre, 1956; Rubin Flood, *The Dark at the Top of the Stairs,* Music Box Theatre, New York City, 1957; title role, *J.B.,* American National Theatre and Academy (ANTA) Theatre, New York City, 1958; Howard Trapp, *The Deadly Game,* Longacre Theatre, 1960; title role, *Macbeth* and Hector, *Troilus and Cressida,* both American Shakespeare Festival, Stratford, CT, 1961; Sam Evans, *Strange Interlude,* Hudson Theatre, New York City, 1963; Parnell, *Blues for Mr. Charlie,* ANTA Theatre, 1964; Andy Willard, *A Girl Could Get Lucky,* Cort Theatre, New York City, 1964; gentleman caller, *The Glass Menagerie,* Paper Mill Playhouse, Millburn, NJ, then Brooks Atkinson Theatre, New York City, both 1965; Oscar Madison, *The Odd Couple,* Plymouth Theatre, New York City, 1966; Harry Armstrong, *Johnny No-Trump,* Cort Theatre, 1967; Victor Franz, *The Price,* Morosco Theatre, 1968.

Joseph Dobbs, *Child's Play,* Royale Theatre, New York City, 1970; Senator George W. Mason, *The Selling of the President,* Shubert Theatre, New York City, 1972; Coach, *That Championship Season,* Booth Theatre, New York City, 1973; Hermann Starr, *A Grave Undertaking,* McCarter Theatre, Princeton, NJ, 1975; Dr.

Wangel, *The Lady from the Sea*, Circle in the Square, New York City, 1976; Willy Loman, *Death of a Salesman*, Studio Arena Theatre, Buffalo, NY, 1976; Kearns, *A Life*, Morosco Theatre, 1980; Big Daddy, *Cat on a Hot Tin Roof*, Center Theatre Group, Mark Taper Forum, Los Angeles, 1983. Also appeared at Burt Reynolds' Jupiter Theatre, Jupiter, FL, 1985-86.

MAJOR TOURS—Title role, *Thomas A. Edison: Reflections of a Genius* (one-man show), U.S. cities, 1978—.

FILM DEBUT—Bartender, *On the Waterfront*, Columbia, 1954. PRINCIPAL FILM APPEARANCES—Herman Kreitzer, *No Down Payment*, Twentieth Century-Fox, 1957; Harold Knoble, *The Strange One* (also known as *End As a Man*), Columbia, 1957; Ace Stamper, *Splendor in the Grass*, Warner Brothers, 1961; Ralph, *All the Way Home*, Paramount, 1963; Homer Atkins, *The Ugly American*, Universal, 1963; Sam Brewster, *Invitation to a Gunfighter*, United Artists, 1964; narrator, *A Texas Romance, 1909* (short film), Janus, 1965; Big Foot, *Nevada Smith*, Paramount, 1966; Judge Adam Fenton, *Hang 'em High*, United Artists, 1968; Lew Haley, *Jigsaw*, Universal, 1968; Harry Mitchell, *Sol Madrid* (also known as *The Heroin Gang*), Metro-Goldwyn-Mayer (MGM), 1968; Sam Pendlebury, *Bloody Mama*, American International, 1970; Grady Fring, *Norwood*, Paramount, 1970; Bingamon, *WUSA*, Paramount, 1970; Captain Pearson, *The Carey Treatment*, MGM, 1972; Eli, *Happy As the Grass Was Green* (also known as *Hazel's People* and *A People's Place*), Martin, 1973; Captain Stewart, *One Little Indian*, Buena Vista, 1973; Henry Binghamton, *Nightmare Honeymoon* (also known as *Deadly Honeymoon*), MGM, 1973; Lieutenant Novik, *The Super Cops*, Metro-Goldwyn-Mayer/United Artists (MGM/UA), 1974; John Adams, *Independence*, Twentieth Century-Fox, 1975; Josephson, *The Gauntlet*, Warner Brothers, 1977; Vernon, *Norma Rae*, Twentieth Century-Fox, 1979; narrator, *America Lost and Found* (documentary), American Portrait Unit of Media Study/Buffalo, 1979; Lyle Striker, *When You Comin' Back, Red Ryder?*, Columbia, 1979.

Ed Reese, *Going Berserk*, Universal, 1983; Coach Easton, *Running Brave*, Buena Vista, 1983; Chief Jannings, *Sudden Impact*, Warner Brothers, 1983; Frank Boda, *The Act* (also known as *Bless 'em All*), Film Ventures, 1984; Edward Roundfield, *Brewster's Millions*, Universal, 1985; Mr. Boyce, *The Falcon and the Snowman*, Orion, 1985; Oscar Milstone, *In 'n' Out* (also known as *Gringo Mojado*), New World, 1986; Hendershot, *Maximum Overdrive*, De Laurentiis Entertainment Group, 1986; Hughes Larrabee, *Baby Boom*, MGM/UA, 1987; voice of Rooter and narrator, *The Land Before Time* (animated), Universal, 1988; Police Commissioner James Gordon, *Batman*, Twentieth Century-Fox, 1989. Also appeared in *The Long Gray Line*, Paramount, 1955; *Running Wild*, Golden Circle, 1973; and in *Deliver Us from Evil*, Dimension, 1975.

TELEVISION DEBUT—Cockney panhandler, *Dr. Jekyll and Mr. Hyde*, 1950. PRINCIPAL TELEVISION APPEARANCES—Series: Chief Gene Paulton, *Stone*, ABC, 1980; Henry Cobb, *Blue Skies*, CBS, 1988. Mini-Series: Admiral William F. "Bull" Halsey, *War and Remembrance*, ABC, 1988. Pilots: Salem Chase, *A Clear and Present Danger*, NBC, 1970; Ira Groom, *The City*, ABC, 1971; Arthur Piper, *Sweet, Sweet Rachel*, ABC, 1971; Dr. Sam Abelman, *The Last Angry Man*, ABC, 1974; Deputy Chief Gene Paulton, *Stone*, ABC, 1979. Episodic: Horace Ford, "The Incredible World of Horace Ford," *The Twilight Zone*, CBS, 1963; Sheriff Smivey, *Amazing Stories*, NBC, 1985; narrator and Sam Donohue, "Casebusters," *Disney Sunday Movie*, ABC, 1986; Barney Kale, *Murder, She Wrote*, CBS, 1986; Tom McCabe, *Matlock*, NBC, 1986; Waldo, *The Equalizer*, CBS, 1989; also *The Invaders*, ABC,

1968; *M*A*S*H*, CBS, 1980; "Noon Wine," *American Playhouse*, PBS, 1985; Dr. John Chapman, *Gunsmoke*, CBS; *Suspense*, CBS; *Studio One*, CBS; *Alcoa/Goodyear Theatre*, NBC; *Suspicion*, CBS; *Play of the Week*, PBS; *Danger*, CBS; *The Phil Silvers Show*, NBC; *Doctor Kildare*, NBC; *The Untouchables*, ABC; *Route 66*, CBS; *Kraft Television Theatre*, NBC; *Armstrong Circle Theatre*, NBC; *The Eleventh Hour*, NBC; *Alfred Hitchcock Presents*, CBS; *The Defenders*, CBS; *Lamp Unto My Feet*, CBS; *The Fugitive*, ABC; *Look Up and Live*, CBS; *Kraft Suspense Theatre*, NBC; *Eternal Light*, NBC; *Rawhide*, CBS; *Daniel Boone*, NBC; *The Andy Griffith Show*, CBS; *The Loner*, CBS; *Shenandoah*, ABC; *Mission: Impossible*, CBS; *Judd for the Defense*, ABC; *The Bob Hope Chrysler Theatre*, NBC; *Felony Squad*, ABC; *High Chapparal*, NBC; *The Bold Ones*, NBC; *Bonanza*, NBC; *Lancer*, CBS; *Medical Center*, CBS; *The Young Lawyers*, ABC; *Ironside*, NBC; *Owen Marshall, Counselor at Law*, ABC; *Trapper John, M.D.*, CBS.

Movies: Earl Crocker, *The Ballad of Andy Crocker*, ABC, 1969; sheriff, *If Tomorrow Comes*, ABC, 1971; Cecil Tabor, *Trouble Comes to Town*, ABC, 1973; Gus Reed, *The Secret Life of John Chapman*, CBS, 1976; Judge Henry Martin, *Escape from Bogen County*, CBS, 1977; Joe Hayden, *Sunshine Christmas*, NBC, 1977; Doc Hodgins, *Tarantulas: The Deadly Cargo*, CBS, 1977; John Marsh, *Disaster on the Coastliner*, ABC, 1979; Colonel Tom Parker, *Elvis*, ABC, 1979; Bob Halburton, *Wild Times*, syndicated, 1980; Jackson, *Of Mice and Men*, NBC, 1981; Senator Ross Clayton, *Washington Mistress*, CBS, 1982; Henry Banks, *The Fighter*, CBS, 1983; Jim Bartlett, *The Lady from Yesterday*, CBS, 1985; Chappy Beck, *The Rape of Richard Beck*, ABC, 1985; George Nielsen, *Manhunt for Claude Dallas*, CBS, 1986; Sam Rayburn, *LBJ: The Early Years*, NBC, 1987; George Keeler, *Kojak: The Price of Justice*, CBS, 1987; Charlie King, *The Town Bully*, ABC, 1988; Judge Munson, *Stranger on My Land*, ABC, 1988; Fire Chief James Roberts, *Everybody's Baby: The Rescue of Jessica McClure*, ABC, 1989. Specials: Ghost of Christmas Past, *Carol for Another Christmas*, ABC, 1964; Jim O'Conner, *The Glass Menagerie*, CBS, 1966; Ralph, "All the Way Home," *Hallmark Hall of Fame*, NBC, 1971; Lou, *Twigs*, CBS, 1975; *General Electric's All-Star Anniversary*, ABC, 1978; Dr. Gerald Lyman, *Bus Stop*, HBO, 1982; also narrator, *The Victims*, NET; narrator, *Let Us Now Praise Famous Men* (documentary).

PRINCIPAL RADIO APPEARANCES—*Voice of America*.

RELATED CAREER—Member, Actors' Studio, New York City, 1952—; stage director, McCarter Theatre Company, Princeton, NJ, 1977-78; also performed at the White House, 1965, and at the Library of Congress, 1984; appeared as Thomas Edison in television commercials for General Electric.

NON-RELATED CAREER—Waiter, laborer, and construction worker.

AWARDS: Antoinette Perry Award nomination, Best Supporting or Featured Actor, 1958, for *The Dark at the Top of the Stairs;* also received a Clio Award for his portrayal of Thomas Edison in General Electric television commercials. HONORARY DEGREES—Otterbein College, Doctor of Humanities, 1974.

MEMBER: Actors' Equity Association, American Federation of Television and Radio Artists, Screen Actors Guild.

ADDRESSES: AGENT—Sylvia Gold, International Creative Management, 8899 Beverly Boulevard, Los Angeles, CA 90048.

HODGE, Patricia 1946-

PERSONAL: Born September 29, 1946, in Lincolnshire, England; married Peter Owen (a music publisher); children: one son. EDUCATION—Attended the London Academy of Music and Dramatic Arts.

VOCATION: Actress.

CAREER: LONDON DEBUT—*Rookery Nook.* PRINCIPAL STAGE APPEARANCES—Clara Popkiss, *Popkiss,* Globe Theatre, London, 1972; Catherine, *Pippin,* Her Majesty's Theatre, London, 1973; Jeannie, *Hair,* Queen's Theatre, London, 1974; Jackie Page, *Happy Yellow,* Bush Theatre, London, 1977; Emma, *Then and Now,* Hampstead Theatre Club, London, 1979; Rosalind, *As You Like It,* Chichester Festival Theatre, Chichester, U.K., 1983; Gertrude Lawrence, *Noel and Gertie,* Comedy Theatre, London, 1989.

PRINCIPAL FILM APPEARANCES—Screaming woman, *The Elephant Man,* Paramount, 1980; Miss Hemmings, *Riding High,* Enterprise, 1980; Edward's wife, *Hud* (also known as *Skin*), Synchron, 1986; Emma, *Betrayal,* Twentieth Century-Fox, 1983; Christina Alperin, *Sunset,* Tri-Star, 1988; Brenda Von Falkenberg, *Just Ask for Diamond* (also known as *Falcon's Malteser*), Twentieth Century-Fox/Kings Road Entertainment, 1988.

PRINCIPAL TELEVISION APPEARANCES—Series: Phyllida Erskine-Brown, *Rumpole of the Bailey,* Thames, 1977—, then *Mystery!,* PBS, 1984—; also *Holding the Fort; Jemima Shore Investigates.* Mini-Series: Anna Quayne, *The Death of the Heart,* Granada, 1986, then *Masterpiece Theatre,* PBS, 1987; Mary Fisher, *The Life and Loves of a She-Devil* (also known as *She Devil*), BBC, then Arts and Entertainment, 1987; Lady Hilda Trelawney Hope, "The Second Stain," *The Return of Sherlock Holmes,* Granada, then *Mystery!,* PBS, 1988; also *Edward and Mrs. Simpson,* BBC, then *Masterpiece Theatre,* PBS. Pilots: Kate, *Quiller: Night of the Father,* ABC, 1975. Movies: Elizabeth Beaumont, *Behind Enemy Lines,* NBC, 1985; also *Hotel du Lac,* BBC, then Arts and Entertainment, 1986; *The Heat of the Day,* ITV; *92 Grosvenor Street.* Specials: Olivia, "The Shell Seekers," *Hallmark Hall of Fame,* ABC, 1989. Also appeared in *The Naked Civil Servant,* PBS.

ADDRESSES: AGENT—Michael Anderson, International Creative Management, 388 Oxford Street, London W1, England. MANAGER—D&J Arlon Ltd., 59-A Connaught Street, London W2, England.*

*   *   *

HODGES, Patricia

PERSONAL: Born in Puyallup, WA. EDUCATION—Graduated from the University of Washington.

VOCATION: Actress.

CAREER: PRINCIPAL STAGE APPEARANCES—Yvette, *Mother Courage and Her Children,* Regan, *King Lear,* and Edna St. Vincent Millay, Mrs. Thrale, Christina Rossetti, Charlotte Bronte, and Mrs. Cadwallader, *The Other Half,* all with the Acting Company, American Place Theatre, New York City, 1978; lady in waiting, *Twelfth Night,* American Shakespeare Theatre, Stratford, CT,

1978; understudy for the roles of Johanna, Marlies, and Ruth, *Three Acts of Recognition,* New York Shakespeare Festival, Public Theatre, New York City, 1982; Comrade and Airwoman, *No End of Blame,* Manhattan Theatre Club, New York City, 1981-82; Peggy, *Bhutan,* South Street Theatre, New York City, 1983; Sarah, *No Direction Home,* New York Theatre Studio, New Dramatists, New York City, 1984; Fanny, *On the Verge, or The Geography of Yearning,* John Houseman Theatre, New York City, 1987; Louisa, Emma Gordon, Mrs. Blackpool, and Mrs. Pegler, *Hard Times,* American Theatre Exchange, Theatre 890, New York City, 1987; also appeared with the Actors Theatre of Louisville, Louisville, KY, 1982-83; and in *The Three Sisters,* Hartman Theatre, Stamford, CT, 1986.

PRINCIPAL FILM APPEARANCES—*Heaven's Gate,* United Artists, 1980.

PRINCIPAL TELEVISION APPEARANCES—Episodic: Cookie, *Cagney and Lacey,* CBS, 1988. Movies: Liz, *Muggable Mary: Street Cop,* CBS, 1982.

ADDRESSES: AGENT—Ambrosio, Mortimer, and Associates, 165 W. 46th Street, Suite 1109, New York, NY 10036.*

*   *   *

HOLD, John
See BAVA, Mario

*   *   *

HOLDRIDGE, Lee 1944-

PERSONAL: Born March 3, 1944, in Port-au-Prince, Haiti. EDUCATION—Attended the Manhattan School of Music.

VOCATION: Composer.

CAREER: Also see *WRITINGS* below. PRINCIPAL STAGE WORK—Dance arranger, *By Jupiter,* Theatre Four, New York City, 1967; orchestrator, *The Harold Arlen Songbook,* Stage 73, New York City, 1967; conductor, *Neil Diamond One Man Show,* Winter Garden Theatre, New York City, 1972.

PRINCIPAL FILM WORK—Music director, *Mahogany,* Paramount, 1975; music director, *E'Lollipop,* Columbia-Warner Distributors, 1975; music director, *Winterhawk,* Howco International, 1976; music director, *Dead Men Don't Wear Plaid,* Universal, 1982; orchestrator, *The Beastmaster,* Metro-Goldwyn-Mayer/United Artists, 1982; orchestrator, *Mr. Mom,* Twentieth Century-Fox, 1983; music arranger and conductor, *Flashdance,* Paramount, 1983; orchestrator, *Transylvania 6-5000,* New World, 1985; orchestrator, *The Men's Club,* Atlantic Releasing, 1986; orchestrator, *Born in East L.A.,* Universal, 1987; music arranger, *A Tiger's Tale,* Atlantic Entertainment, 1988.

PRINCIPAL TELEVISION WORK—Movies: Music conductor, *Sunshine,* CBS, 1973. Specials: Music conductor (with Eddie Karam), *The John Denver Special,* ABC, 1976.

RELATED CAREER—Music arranger for Neil Diamond, 1969-73; also composer of orchestral works.

WRITINGS: All as composer of score, unless indicated. STAGE—Composer of dance music, *A Joyful Noise*, Mark Hellinger Theatre, New York City, 1966; composer of dance music, *The Education of H*Y*M*A*N K*A*P*L*A*N*, Alvin Theatre, New York City, 1968; *Into the Light*, Neil Simon Theatre, New York City, 1986.

FILM—(With Pat Williams, Edd Kaleroff, Chris Dedrick, and Warren Marley) *The Sidelong Glances of a Pigeon Kicker* (also known as *Pigeons*), Metro-Goldwyn-Mayer/Plaza, 1970; (with Joseph Brook) *Jeremy*, United Artists, 1973; (with Neil Diamond) *Jonathan Livingston Seagull*, Paramount, 1973; *Nothing By Chance* (documentary), R.C. Riddell and Associates, 1974; *Sunshine Part II* (also known as *My Sweet Lady*), CIC, 1975; *E' Lollipop*, Columbia-Warner Distributors, 1975; *Forever Young, Forever Free* (also known as *E lollipop, lollipop*), Universal, 1976; *Goin' Home*, Prentiis, 1976; *Mustang Country*, Universal, 1976; *Winterhawk*, Howco International, 1976; *The Pack* (also known as *The Long Dark Night*), Warner Brothers, 1977; *Moment By Moment*, Universal, 1978; *Oliver's Story*, Paramount, 1978; *The Other Side of the Mountain, Part II*, Universal, 1978; *French Postcards*, Paramount, 1979; *Tilt*, Warner Brothers, 1979; *American Pop*, Columbia, 1981; *The Beastmaster*, Metro-Goldwyn-Mayer/United Artists, 1982; *Mr. Mom*, Twentieth Century-Fox, 1983; *Micki and Maude*, Columbia, 1984; *Splash*, Buena Vista, 1984; *Sylvester*, Columbia, 1985; (with Alfie Kabiljo) *Transylvania 6-5000*, New World, 1985; *The Men's Club*, Atlantic Releasing, 1986; *Sixteen Days of Glory* (documentary), Paramount, 1986; *Born in East L.A.*, Universal, 1987; *Walk Like a Man* (also known as *Bobo* and *Bobo the Dog Boy*), Metro-Goldwyn-Mayer/United Artists/United International, 1987; *Big Business*, Buena Vista, 1988; *A Tiger's Tale*, Atlantic Entertainment, 1988; *Old Gringo*, Columbia, 1989.

TELEVISION—Series: (Theme music) *McCloud*, NBC, 1970-77; (theme music) *Hec Ramsey*, NBC, 1972-74; *Sierra*, NBC, 1974; (with Dick De Benedictis) *The Family Holvak*, NBC, 1975; (theme music) *Sara*, CBS, 1976; (with Mark Snow) *The Gemini Man*, NBC, 1976; *Code R*, CBS, 1977; (with George Aliceson Tipton) *Julie Farr, M.D.*, ABC, 1978-79; (with Lex DeAvezedo) *Young Maverick*, CBS, 1979-80; *Wizards and Warriors*, CBS, 1983; *The Mississippi*, CBS, 1983-84; (also theme music) *Lime Street*, ABC, 1985; (theme song) *Moonlighting*, ABC, 1985-89; (also theme music) *Beauty and the Beast*, CBS, 1987-90; *Just in Time*, ABC, 1988. Mini-Series: *John Steinbeck's "East of Eden,"* ABC, 1981. Pilots: *The Rangers*, NBC, 1974; (with Jerry Fielding) *Fools, Females, and Fun: Is There a Doctor in the House?*, NBC, 1974; (with Fielding) *Fools, Females, and Fun: I've Gotta Be Me*, NBC, 1974; (with Fielding) *Fools, Females, and Fun: What About That One?*, NBC, 1974; *Pine Canyon Is Burning*, NBC, 1977; *Having Babies III*, ABC, 1978; *Skyward Christmas*, NBC, 1981; *Two the Hard Way*, CBS, 1981; *Fly Away Home*, ABC, 1981; *This Is Kate Bennett*, ABC, 1982; *The Boys in Blue*, CBS, 1984; *Adams Apple*, CBS, 1986; *Desperate*, ABC, 1987; *My Africa* (broadcast as an episode of *CBS Summer Playhouse*), CBS, 1988; (with John Denver) *Higher Ground*, CBS, 1988. Episodic: "Young Harry Houdini," *Disney Sunday Movie*, ABC, 1987; "14 Going on 30" (also known as "Fassst Forward") *Disney Sunday Movie*, ABC, 1988; "A Mother's Courage: The Mary Thomas Story" (also known as "The Mary Thomas Story" and "Long Shot"), *The Magical World of Disney*, NBC, 1989; "Things That Go Bump in the Night," *Christine Cromwell*, ABC, 1989.

Movies: *Skyway to Death*, ABC, 1974; *To Kill a Cop*, NBC, 1978; *Like Mom, Like Me*, CBS, 1978; *Valentine*, ABC, 1979; *Mother and Daughter: The Loving War*, ABC, 1980; *If Things Were Different*, CBS, 1980; *Skyward*, NBC, 1980; *Three Hundred Miles for Stephanie*, NBC, 1981; *Freedom*, ABC, 1981; *The Day the Loving Stopped*, ABC, 1981; *For Ladies Only*, NBC, 1981; *Thou Shalt Not Kill*, NBC, 1982; *In Love with an Older Woman*, CBS, 1982; *Running Out*, CBS, 1983; *First Affair*, CBS, 1983; *Agatha Christie's "A Caribbean Mystery,"* CBS, 1983; *Thursday's Child*, CBS, 1983; (title song) *Love Is Forever*, NBC, 1983; *Legs*, ABC, 1983; *I Want to Live*, ABC, 1983; *He's Fired, She's Hired*, CBS, 1984; *Shattered Vows*, NBC, 1984; *The Other Lover*, CBS, 1985; *Letting Go*, ABC, 1985; *Pleasures*, ABC, 1986; *Miracle of the Heart: A Boystown Story*, syndicated, 1986; *Mafia Princess*, NBC, 1986; *I'll Take Manhattan*, CBS, 1987; *Eight Is Enough: A Family Reunion*, NBC, 1987; *Fatal Judgment*, CBS, 1988; *A Friendship in Vienna*, Disney Channel, 1988; *Do You Know the Muffin Man?*, CBS, 1989; *Incident at Dark River* (also known as *The Smell of Money*), TNT, 1989.

Specials: *The General*, CBS, 1974; "Power and the Presidency," *American Parade*, CBS, 1974; *We the Women*, CBS, 1974; *F.D.R.: The Man Who Changed America*, CBS, 1975; *Sojourner*, CBS, 1975; *Song of Myself*, CBS, 1976; "Stop, Thief!," *American Parade*, CBS, 1976; *With All Deliberate Speed*, CBS, 1976; (with Eddie Karam) *John Denver—Thank God I'm a Country Boy*, ABC, 1977; (with Glen D. Hardin and Doug Gilmore) *John Denver in Australia*, ABC, 1978; *John Denver: Music and the Mountains*, ABC, 1981; "The Sharks," *National Geographic Special*, PBS, 1982; *The Best Legs in the Eighth Grade*, HBO, 1984; "Graham Greene's 'The Tenth Man,' " *Hallmark Hall of Fame*, CBS, 1988; "The Explorers: A Century of Discovery," *National Geographic Special*, PBS, 1988.

RECORDINGS: ALBUMS—(With the London Symphony) *Concerto No. 2 for Violin and Orchestra/Lazarus and His Beloved*, Varese/Sarabande; (with the London Symphony) *Music of Holdridge*, Varese/Sarabande; *Beauty and the Beast* (original soundtrack), Capitol; *Moonlighting* (original soundtrack), MCA; *Old Gringo* (original soundtrack), GNP/Crescendo.

AWARDS: Circle of Friends of Music Award, Arenzano, Italy, 1972; Emmy Award, Outstanding Dramatic Underscoring, 1988, for *Beauty and the Beast*; Emmy Award, Outstanding Music and Lyrics, 1989, for *Beauty and the Beast*; Emmy Award, Outstanding Underscoring of a Documentary, 1989, for *The Explorers*.

ADDRESSES: AGENT—Bart-Milander Associates Inc., 4146 Lankershim Boulevard, Suite 300, North Hollywood, CA 91602.

*   *   *

HOLLAND, Jeffrey   1946-

PERSONAL: Born Jeffrey Michael Parkes, July 17, 1946, in Walsall, England; son of Samuel and Doris Maud (Harrison) Parkes; married Eleanor Hartopp (an actress), October 2, 1971; children: Lucy, Sam. EDUCATION—Studied acting at the Birmingham School of Speech and Drama, 1965-68.

VOCATION: Actor.

CAREER: STAGE DEBUT—Judge's clerk, *No Fear or Favour*, Alexandra Theatre, Birmingham, U.K., 1967, for fourteen performances. LONDON DEBUT—German inventor, *Dad's Army,* Shaftesbury Theatre, 1975, for more than two hundred performances. PRINCIPAL STAGE APPEARANCES—Jodelet, *Cyrano de Bergerac,* Chichester Festival Theatre, Chichester, U.K., 1975; Stephano, *The Tempest* and Snug, *A Midsummer Night's Dream,* both Assembly Halls, Edinburgh, Scotland, 1978; Spike Dixon, *Hi De Hi!—The Musical,* Victoria Palace Theatre, London, 1983-84; John Smith, *Run for Your Wife!,* Criterion Theatre, London, 1985-88, then Whitehall Theatre, London, 1989.

MAJOR TOURS—Private Walker, *Dad's Army,* U.K. cities, 1976.

TELEVISION DEBUT—Alan Hunt, *Dixon of Dock Green,* BBC, 1972. PRINCIPAL TELEVISION APPEARANCES—Series: Spike Dixon, *Hi De Hi,* BBC, 1979-87; regular, *Russ Abbot's Madhouse,* London Weekend Television, 1981-85; James Twelvetrees, *You Rang, M'Lord?,* BBC, 1988—. Mini-Series: Carter, *The Mayor of Casterbridge,* BBC, then *Masterpiece Theatre,* PBS, both 1978. Specials: Earl Marshall, *Richard II,* BBC, 1978, then PBS, 1979; William, *As You Like It,* BBC, 1979; Nym, *Henry V,* BBC, 1979.

RELATED CAREER—Company member, Belgrade Theatre, Coventry, U.K., 1968-73.

MEMBER: The Sons of the Desert.

ADDRESSES: AGENT—Jean Diamond, London Management, 235 Regent Street, London W1A 2JT, England.

*   *   *

HOMEIER, Skip 1930-
(Skippy Homeier)

PERSONAL: Full name, George Vincent Homeier; born October 5, 1930, in Chicago, IL. EDUCATION—Attended the University of California, Los Angeles.

VOCATION: Actor.

CAREER: PRINCIPAL STAGE APPEARANCES—Emil Bruckner, *Tomorrow the World,* Ethel Barrymore Theatre, New York City, 1943-44.

FILM DEBUT—(As Skippy Homeier) Emil Bruckner, *Tomorrow the World,* United Artists, 1944. PRINCIPAL FILM APPEARANCES—(As Skippy Homeier) Skippy, *Boy's Ranch,* Metro-Goldwyn-Mayer, 1946; (as Skippy Homeier) Hank Evans, *Mickey,* Eagle-Lion, 1948; Arthur Bixby, *Arthur Takes Over,* Twentieth Century-Fox, 1948; Jim, *The Big Cat,* Eagle-Lion, 1949; Hunt Bromley, *The Gunfighter,* Twentieth Century-Fox, 1950; Whitey, *Fixed Bayonets,* Twentieth Century-Fox, 1951; Mac, *Sailor Beware,* Paramount, 1951; Pretty Boy, *Halls of Montezuma,* Twentieth Century-Fox, 1951; Steve, *Sealed Cargo,* RKO, 1951; Carl Pennock, *Has Anybody Seen My Gal?,* Universal, 1952; Art Romer, *The Last Posse,* Columbia, 1953; Reynolds, *Beachhead,* United Artists, 1954; John, *Black Widow,* Twentieth Century-Fox, 1954; Roxey, *Cry Vengeance,* Allied Artists, 1954; Buddy Ferris, *Dawn at Socorro,* Universal, 1954; Cass Downing, *The Last Gun,* United Artists, 1954; Bob Dennis, *At Gunpoint* (also known as *Gunpoint*), Allied Artists, 1955; Sam Mayhew, *The Road to Denver,* Republic, 1955; Howie Stewart, *Ten Wanted Men,* Columbia, 1955; Swanson, *Between Heaven and Hell,* Twentieth Centu-

ry-Fox, 1956; Jack Sutton, *The Burning Hills,* Warner Brothers, 1956; Brank Banner, *Dakota Incident,* Republic, 1956; Clay Anderson, *Stranger at My Door,* Republic, 1956; John Railton, *No Road Back,* RKO, 1957; Billy Jack, *The Tall T,* Columbia, 1957; Howard Hayes, *Day of the Bad Man,* Universal, 1958; Joe Martin, *Plunderers of Painted Flats,* Republic, 1959; Frank, *Comanche Station,* Columbia, 1960; Caslon, *Showdown,* Universal, 1963; Gerald Winslow, *Stark Fear,* Ellis, 1963; Pink, *Bullet for a Badman,* Universal, 1964; Ollie, *The Ghost and Mr. Chicken,* Universal, 1966; Deputy Sheriff Laswell, *Tiger By the Tail,* Commonwealth, 1970; major, *The Greatest,* Columbia, 1977. Also appeared in *Thunder Over Arizona,* Republic, 1956; *Lure of the Swamp,* Twentieth Century-Fox, 1957; *Starbird and Sweet William,* 1976; and in *The Captives* and *Decision at Durango.*

PRINCIPAL TELEVISION APPEARANCES—Series: Lieutenant Dan Raven, *Dan Raven,* NBC, 1960-61; Doctor Hugh Jacoby, *The Interns,* CBS, 1970-71. Mini-Series: Ross Mantee, "Elfego Baca" (also known as "The Nine Lives of Elfego Baca"), *Walt Disney Presents,* ABC, 1958-60; Lars Haglund, *Washington: Behind Closed Doors,* ABC, 1977. Pilots: Joseph, *The Wild Wild West Revisited,* CBS, 1979. Episodic: Dr. Roy Clinton, "Expanding Human," *The Outer Limits,* ABC, 1964; Melakon, *Star Trek,* NBC, 1968; Dr. Sevrin, *Star Trek,* NBC, 1969; Dr. Jacoby, *The Interns,* CBS, 1970; Steve, "Bad Connections," *Circle of Fear,* NBC, 1973; also "The Bride Possessed," *One Step Beyond,* ABC, 1959; *The Addams Family,* ABC, 1964; *Voyage to the Bottom of the Sea,* ABC, 1965, 1966, and 1968; *The Incredible Hulk,* CBS, 1979; astronomer, "The Dark Side," *Science Fiction Theatre,* syndicated; "Autumn in New York," *Schlitz Playhouse of Stars,* CBS; *Studio One,* CBS; *Suspense,* CBS; *Playhouse 90,* CBS; *The Alcoa Hour,* NBC; *Kraft Theatre; Armstrong Circle Theatre; Alfred Hitchcock Presents.* Movies: Lyman George, *The Challenge,* ABC, 1970; doctor, *Two for the Money,* ABC, 1972; Arnold Markwell, *The Voyage of the Yes,* CBS, 1973; Judge Charles H. Older, *Helter Skelter,* CBS, 1976; Dr. Medlow, *Overboard,* NBC, 1978.

RELATED CAREER—Radio actor, 1936-43.*

*   *   *

HOPKINS, Anthony 1937-

PERSONAL: First name is pronounced "An-tony"; born December 31, 1937, in Port Talbot, Wales; son of Richard Arthur (a baker) and Muriel Annie (Yeates) Hopkins; married Petronella Barker, 1967 (divorced, 1972); married Jennifer Lynton, January 13, 1973; children: Abigail (first marriage). EDUCATION—Attended the Welsh College of Music and Drama, 1954-56; studied acting at the Royal Academy of Dramatic Art, 1961-63. MILITARY—British Army, Royal Artillery, 1958-60.

VOCATION: Actor.

CAREER: STAGE DEBUT—Mickser, *The Quare Fellow,* Library Theatre, Manchester, U.K., 1960. LONDON DEBUT—Metellus Cimber, *Julius Caesar,* Royal Court Theatre, 1964. BROADWAY DEBUT—Martin Dysart, *Equus,* Plymouth Theatre, 1974. PRINCIPAL STAGE APPEARANCES—Undershaft, *Major Barbara,* Phoenix Theatre, Leicester, U.K., 1963; Irregular Mobiliser, *Juno and the Paycock* and Etienne Plucheaux, *A Flea in Her Ear,* both National Theatre Company, Old Vic Theatre, London, 1966; Blagovo, *A Provincial Life,* Royal Court Theatre, London, 1966;

ANTHONY HOPKINS

Edgar, *The Dance of Death,* Andrei Prosorov, *The Three Sisters,* and Audrey, *As You Like It,* all National Theatre Company, Old Vic Theatre, 1966-67; Emperor, *The Architect and the Emperor of Assyria,* John Frankford, *A Woman Killed with Kindness,* and title role, *Coriolanus,* all National Theatre Company, Old Vic Theatre, 1971; title role, *Macbeth,* National Theatre Company, Old Vic Theatre, 1972; Petruchio, *The Taming of the Shrew,* Chichester Festival Theatre, Chichester, U.K., 1972; Martin Dysart, *Equus,* Huntington Hartford Theatre, Los Angeles, 1977; Prospero, *The Tempest,* Mark Taper Forum, Los Angeles, 1979; Deeley, *Old Times,* Roundabout Theatre, New York City, 1983-84; title role, *King Lear,* National Theatre, London, 1986-87; Antony, *Antony and Cleopatra,* National Theatre, 1987; Rene Gallimard, *M. Butterfly,* Shaftesbury Theatre, London, 1989. Also in *The Lonely Road,* Old Vic Theatre, 1985; *Pravda,* Olivier Theatre, London, 1985-86; and appeared with the Nottingham Repertory Company, Nottingham, U.K., Phoenix Theatre, Leicester, U.K., the Liverpool Playhouse, Liverpool, U.K., and the Hornchurch Repertory Company, Hornchurch, U.K.

PRINCIPAL STAGE WORK—Assistant stage manager, Library Theatre, Manchester, U.K., 1960.

FILM DEBUT—Brechtian, *The White Bus,* 1967. PRINCIPAL FILM APPEARANCES—Prince Richard the Lion Hearted, *The Lion in Winter,* AVCO-Embassy, 1968; Claudius, *Hamlet,* Columbia, 1969; John Avery, *The Looking Glass War,* Columbia, 1970; Philip Calvert, *When Eight Bells Toll,* Cinerama, 1971; David Lloyd George, *Young Winston,* Columbia, 1972; Torvald Helmer, *A Doll's House,* Paramount, 1973; Kostya, *The Girl from Petrovka,*

Universal, 1974; Superintendent John McCleod, *Juggernaut,* United Artists, 1974; Siegfried Farnan, *All Creatures Great and Small,* EMI, 1975; Elliot Hoover, *Audrey Rose,* United Artists, 1977; Lieutenant Colonel John Frost, *A Bridge Too Far,* United Artists, 1977; Captain Johnson, *International Velvet,* Metro-Goldwyn-Mayer/United Artists, 1978; Corky/voice of Fats, *Magic,* Twentieth Century-Fox, 1978; Adam Evans, *A Change of Seasons,* Twentieth Century-Fox, 1980; Dr. Frederick Treves, *The Elephant Man,* Paramount, 1980; Lieutenant William Bligh, *The Bounty,* Orion, 1984; Bill Hooper, *The Good Father,* Skouras, 1986; Frank Doel, *84 Charing Cross Road,* Columbia, 1987; Dafydd Llewellyn, *A Chorus of Disapproval,* Southgate Entertainment, 1987; Major Angus Barry ("Cassius"), *The Dawning,* TVS Entertainment/ Vista, 1988.

TELEVISION DEBUT—*A Heritage and Its History,* 1968. PRINCIPAL TELEVISION APPEARANCES—Mini-Series: Dr. Adam Kelno, *QB VII,* ABC, 1974; Neil Gray, *Hollywood Wives,* ABC, 1985. Movies: Dr. Michael Grant, *Dark Victory,* NBC, 1976; Bruno Richard Hauptmann, *The Lindbergh Kidnapping Case,* NBC, 1976; Yitzhak Rabin, *Victory at Entebbe,* ABC, 1976; Captain Christopher Jones, *Mayflower: The Pilgrim's Adventure* (also known as *The Voyage of the Mayflower*), CBS, 1979; Hitler, *The Bunker,* CBS, 1981; Paul, *Peter and Paul* (also known as *The Acts of Peter and Paul*), CBS, 1981; John Strickland, *A Married Man,* Channel Four, BBC, then syndicated in the United States, 1984; Quasimodo, *The Hunchback of Notre Dame,* CBS, 1982; Ravic, *Arch of Triumph,* CBS, 1985; Arthur Jamison, *Guilty Conscience,* CBS, 1985; Galeazzo Ciano, *Mussolini: The Decline and Fall of Il Duce* (also known as *Mussolini and I*), HBO, 1985; Guy Burgess, *Blunt,* BBC, 1985; Jean Louis Chavel, *The Tenth Man* (also known as *Graham Greene's "The Tenth Man"*), CBS, 1988; Abel Magwitch, *Great Expectations,* Disney Channel, 1989; also *A Company of Five,* 1968; *A Walk Through the Forest,* 1968; *The Three Sisters,* 1969; *The Peasants Revolt,* 1969; Astrov, *Uncle Vanya,* 1970; title role, *Danton,* 1970; *Hearts and Flowers,* 1970; *The Poet Game,* 1971; *The Edwardians,* 1972; title role, *Lloyd George,* 1972; Dando Hamer, "Possessions," *Childhood,* 1974; Marek, *Find Me,* 1974; title role, *Kean,* 1978; *Othello,* BBC, 1981; *Little Eyolf,* BBC, 1981; *Strangers and Brothers,* 1983; *Old Times.* Specials: Pierre Bezuhov, *War and Peace,* PBS, 1973-74; Siegfried Farnon, "All Creatures Great and Small," *Hallmark Hall of Fame,* NBC, 1975; Theo Gunge, "The Arcata Promise," *Great Performances,* PBS, 1977.

RECORDINGS: First voice, *Under Milk Wood,* 1988.

AWARDS: British Academy of Film and Television Arts Award, Best Actor, 1972, for *War and Peace;* New York Drama Desk Award and Outer Circle Award, both Best Actor, 1975, for *Equus;* American Authors and Celebrity Forum Award, 1975; Emmy Award, Outstanding Lead Actor in a Drama or Comedy Special, 1976, for *The Lindbergh Kidnapping Case;* Los Angeles Drama Critics' Award, 1977, for *Equus;* Emmy Award, Outstanding Lead Actor in a Limited Series or a Special, 1981, for *The Bunker;* Emmy Award nomination, Outstanding Lead Actor in a Limited Series or a Special, 1982, for *The Hunchback of Notre Dame;* Film Actor Award from the Variety Club, 1984, for *The Bounty;* British Theatre Association Award, Best Actor, Olivier Award, and Stage Actor Award from the Variety Club, all 1985, for *Pravda;* Best Actor Award from the Moscow Film Festival, 1987, for *84 Charing Cross Road;* Commander, Order of the British Empire, 1987.

MEMBER: Motion Picture Academy, American Film Institute, British Association of Film and Television Arts.

SIDELIGHTS: RECREATIONS—Music, playing the piano, astronomy, reading philosophy and European history.

ADDRESSES: AGENTS—Jeremy Conway Ltd., 109 Jermyn Street, London SW1, England; Harris and Goldberg, 2121 Avenue of the Stars, Los Angeles, CA 90067.

* * *

HORTON, Peter

PERSONAL: Born August 20, in Bellevue, WA; father, in the shipping business; married Michelle Pfeiffer (an actress; divorced). EDUCATION—Received degree in music composition from the University of California, Santa Barbara; also attended Principia College.

VOCATION: Actor and director.

CAREER: PRINCIPAL STAGE APPEARANCES—Butterflies Are Free, Masquers Theatre, Los Angeles; also appeared with the Lobero Repertory Company Theatre, Santa Barbara, CA.

PRINCIPAL FILM APPEARANCES—Joey Madona, Fade to Black, American Cinema, 1980; Jacob, Split Image, Orion, 1982; Dr. Burt Stanton, Stephen King's Children of the Corn (also known as Children of the Corn), New World, 1984; Father Mahoney, Where the River Runs Black, Metro-Goldwyn-Mayer/United Artists, 1986; Harry, "Hospital" in Amazon Women on the Moon, Universal, 1987. Also appeared in Serial, Paramount, 1980.

PRINCIPAL FILM WORK—Director, "Two I.D.s" in Amazon Women on the Moon, Universal, 1987.

PRINCIPAL TELEVISION APPEARANCES—Series: Crane McFadden, Seven Brides for Seven Brothers, CBS, 1982-83; Professor Gary Shepherd, thirtysomething, ABC, 1987—. Pilots: Tom Sawyer, Sawyer and Finn, NBC, 1983. Movies: Tony Smith, She's Dressed to Kill, NBC, 1979; Jack O'Callahan, Miracle on Ice, ABC, 1981; Bill, Freedom, ABC, 1981; Doug, Choices of the Heart, NBC, 1983.

PRINCIPAL TELEVISION WORK—Episodic: Director, thirtysomething, ABC, 1988 and 1989; director, The Wonder Years, ABC, 1989. Specials: Director, "One Too Many," ABC Afterschool Specials, ABC, 1985.

RELATED CAREER—Musical composer.

SIDELIGHTS: RECREATIONS—Playing classical piano.

ADDRESSES: AGENTS—Martin Bauer and Peter Benedek, Bauer/Benedek Agency, 9255 Sunset Boulevard, Suite 710, Los Angeles, CA 90069.*

C. THOMAS HOWELL

HOWELL, C. Thomas 1966-
(Tom Howell)

PERSONAL: Born December 7, 1966, in Los Angeles, CA; son of Chris Howell (a stunt coordinator); married Rae Dawn Chong (an actress).

VOCATION: Actor.

CAREER: PRINCIPAL FILM APPEARANCES—(As Tom Howell) Tyler, E.T. The Extra-Terrestrial, Universal, 1982; Ponyboy Curtis, The Outsiders, Warner Brothers, 1983; Tim Pearson, Grandview, U.S.A., Warner Brothers, 1984; Robert, Red Dawn, Metro-Goldwyn-Mayer/United Artists, 1984; Billy Carey, Tank, Universal, 1984; Michael Ryan, Secret Admirer, Orion, 1985; Jim Halsey, The Hitcher, Tri-Star, 1986; Mark Watson, Soul Man, New World, 1986; Bubber Drumm, A Tiger's Tale, Atlantic, 1987; Arturo Toscanini, Il giovane Toscanini (also known as Young Toscanini), Carthago, 1988; Raoul, The Return of the Musketeers (also known as The Return of the Three Musketeers), Universal, 1989; Monroe Clark, Side Out, Tri-Star, 1989. Also appeared in Far Out, Man, New Line Cinema/Prism Entertainment, 1989.

PRINCIPAL TELEVISION APPEARANCES—Series: Scott, Two Marriages, ABC, 1983-84; also The Little People (also known as The Brian Keith Show), NBC. Episodic: Jenner Brading, "The Eyes of the Panther," Nightmare Classics, Showtime, 1989. Movies: Tripp, Into the Homeland, HBO, 1987. Specials: Battle of the Network Stars, ABC, 1984.

RELATED CAREER—Owner and producer (with Scott Shore), Buckwheat Films.

NON-RELATED CAREER—Junior rodeo circuit champion.

ADDRESSES: AGENT—Creative Artists Agency, 9830 Wilshire Boulevard, Beverly Hills, CA 90212. PUBLICIST—Jeff Ballard Public Relations, 4814 Lemona Avenue, Sherman Oaks, CA 91413.

*   *   *

HOWELL, Tom
See HOWELL, C. Thomas

*   *   *

HUDSON, Bill   1949-

PERSONAL: Born October 17, 1949, in Portland, OR; married Goldie Hawn (an actress and producer), 1976 (divorced); married Cindy Williams (an actress). EDUCATION—Attended Portland State University.

VOCATION: Actor, producer, and musician.

CAREER: PRINCIPAL FILM APPEARANCES—Repo crew member, *Zero to Sixty* (also known as *Repo*), First Artists, 1978; Frederick, *Hysterical*, Embassy, 1983; Obie's dad, *Big Shots*, Twentieth Century-Fox, 1987.

PRINCIPAL TELEVISION APPEARANCES—Series: Co-host, *The Hudson Brothers Show*, CBS, 1974; co-host, *The Hudson Brothers Razzle Dazzle Comedy Show*, CBS, 1974-77; co-host, *Bonkers*, syndicated, 1978-79; Tom Burke, *Just Like Family*, Disney Channel, 1989—; also *A Family Tree*, Showtime. Pilots: Eddie Reardon, *The Millionaire*, CBS, 1978; Tom Burke, *Help Wanted: Kids*, ABC, 1986. Episodic: Donald Travers, *The Highwayman*, NBC, 1988; Mr. Plenn, *Doogie Howser, M.D.*, ABC, 1989. Movies: Man in KISS booth, *KISS Meets the Phantom of the Park*, NBC, 1978. Specials: Host, *National Family Safety Test*, Disney Channel, 1989.

PRINCIPAL TELEVISION WORK—Series: Producer, *A Family Tree*, Showtime. Pilots: Producer, *Joanna*, ABC, 1985.

RELATED CAREER—With brothers Mark and Brett performed as the Hudson Brothers; founder, TaylorMade Productions (a television and film production company).

WRITINGS: FILM—(With Mark Hudson, Brett Hudson, and Trace Johnston) *Hysterical*, Embassy, 1983.

ADDRESSES: AGENT—Triad Artists, 10100 Santa Monica Boulevard, 16th Floor, Los Angeles, CA 90067. PUBLICIST—Russell L. Patrick, The Disney Channel, 3800 W. Alameda Avenue, Burbank, CA 91505.*

HUDSON, Ernie

PERSONAL: Born in Benton Harbour, MI. EDUCATION—Graduated from Wayne State University; also attended the University of Minnesota; trained for the stage at the Yale University School of Drama. MILITARY—U.S. Marine Corps.

VOCATION: Actor.

CAREER: PRINCIPAL STAGE APPEARANCES—*The Cage*, Los Angeles Actors Theatre, Los Angeles, 1984; also appeared in *The Great White Hope*, Theatre-in-the-Round, Minneapolis, MN, then Los Angeles; and in *Daddy Goodness*, Los Angeles.

PRINCIPAL FILM APPEARANCES—Killer, *The Main Event*, Warner Brothers, 1979; Quinine, *The Octagon*, American Cinema Releasing, 1980; heckler, *The Jazz Singer*, Associated Film Distributors, 1980; Half Dead, *Penitentiary II*, Metro-Goldwyn-Mayer/United Artists (MGM/UA), 1982; Muhammed, *Going Berserk*, Universal, 1983; Washington, *Spacehunter: Adventures in the Forbidden Zone* (also known as *Road Gangs* and *Adventures in the Creep Zone*), Columbia, 1983; Detective Staggs, *Two of a Kind*, Twentieth Century-Fox, 1983; Mr. Porter, *Joy of Sex*, Paramount, 1984; Winston Zeddemore, *Ghostbusters*, Columbia, 1984; Bagdad, *Weeds*, De Laurentiis Entertainment Group, 1986; Dawson, *The Wrong Guys*, New World, 1988; Justin Jones, *Leviathan*, MGM/UA, 1989; Winston Zeddemore, *Ghostbusters II*, Columbia, 1989; Jefferson Carter, *Trapper County War* (also known as *Trapper County* and *Porter Country*), Noble Entertainment Group/Alpine Releasing Group/Titan, 1989. Also appeared in *Leadbelly*, Paramount, 1976; and in *Joni*, World Wide, 1980.

PRINCIPAL TELEVISION APPEARANCES—Series: Smythe, *Highcliffe Manor*, NBC, 1979; Detective Sergeant Tremaine "Night Train" Lane, *The Last Precinct*, NBC, 1986. Mini-Series: E.D. Nixon, *King*, NBC, 1978; also *Roots: The Next Generations*, ABC, 1981. Pilots: Harold "Jazzman" Malloy, *Crazy Times*, ABC, 1981; Kwame Botulo, *Almost American*, NBC, 1981; Leo Kelly, *100 Centre Street*, ABC, 1984; Detective Sergeant Tremaine "Night Train" Lane, *The Last Precinct*, NBC, 1986; also *Skag*, NBC, 1980. Episodic: "Digger" Love, *The New Mike Hammer*, CBS, 1986; Prince Gilbert Kassa-Myboto, *Gimme a Break*, NBC, 1987; Reggie "The Sandman" Martin, *Full House*, ABC, 1987; Samuel Obae, *Private Eye*, ABC, 1987; also *The Incredible Hulk*, CBS, 1979; *Taxi*, ABC, 1981; *The Insiders*, ABC, 1985; *Fantasy Island*, ABC; *Little House on the Prairie*, NBC; *Webster*, ABC. Movies: Black Bart, *Mad Bull*, CBS, 1977; El Caliph, *Last of the Good Guys*, CBS, 1978; counselor, *White Mama*, CBS, 1980; Homer Burden, *The $5.20 an Hour Dream*, CBS, 1980; Mr. Harrison, *A Matter of Life and Death*, CBS, 1981; Ernie, *California Girls*, ABC, 1985; Lamar, *Love on the Run*, NBC, 1985; Joe Hamilton, *The Dirty Dozen: The Fatal Mission* (also known as *Dirty Dozen IV*), NBC, 1988; also *Women of San Quentin*, NBC, 1983. Specials: Ted Young, *Journey Together*, CBS, 1978.

RELATED CAREER—Resident playwright, Concept East (a theatrical company), Detroit, MI.

ADDRESSES: AGENT—Bob Gersh, The Gersh Agency, 222 N. Canon Drive, Suite 202, Beverly Hills, CA 90210. PUBLICIST—Monique Moss, Levine-Schneider Public Relations, 8730 Sunset Boulevard, Sixth Floor, Los Angeles, CA 90069.

HUNT, Helen 1963-

PERSONAL: Born June 15, 1963, in Los Angeles, CA; daughter of Gordon Hunt (a director); mother, a photographer.

VOCATION: Actress.

CAREER: PRINCIPAL STAGE APPEARANCES—Jill, *Been Taken,* Ensemble Studio Theatre, New York City, 1985; Emily Webb, *Our Town,* Lyceum Theatre, New York City 1989. Also appeared in *The Good War* and *Vital Signs,* both Mark Taper Forum, Los Angeles; *Alice in Wonderland,* Los Angeles Cultural Arts Center, Los Angeles; *Gladiators,* Cast Theatre, Hollywood, CA; *Methusalem,* Wallenboyd Theatre; *The Value of Names,* Skylight Theatre.

PRINCIPAL FILM APPEARANCES—Tracy Calder, *Rollercoaster,* Universal, 1977; Lynne Stone, *Girls Just Want to Have Fun,* New World, 1985; Leena, *Trancers* (also known as *Future Cops*), Empire, 1985; Beth Bodell, *Peggy Sue Got Married,* Tri-Star, 1986; Teresa "Teri" McDonald, *Project X,* Twentieth Century-Fox, 1987; Jennifer, *Miles from Home,* Cinecom, 1988; Jessie Gates, *Next of Kin,* Warner Brothers, 1989. Also appeared in *The Frog Prince.*

PRINCIPAL TELEVISION APPEARANCES—Series: Jill Prentiss, *Amy Prentiss,* NBC, 1974-75; Helga Wagner, *The Swiss Family Robinson,* ABC, 1975-76; Kerry Gerardi, *The Fitzpatricks,* CBS, 1977-78; Lisa Quinn, *It Takes Two,* ABC, 1982-83. Pilots: Sharon McNamara, *Having Babies,* ABC, 1976. Episodic: Mary Austin, "Land of Little Rain," *American Playhouse,* PBS, 1988; also "Weekend," *American Playhouse,* PBS, 1982; Robin Trask, *Family,* ABC; Laurie Slaughter, *The Mary Tyler Moore Show,* CBS; Clancy, *St. Elsewhere,* NBC. Movies: Sarah Sergeant, *Pioneer Woman,* ABC, 1973; Susan Lindsay, *All Together Now,* ABC, 1975; Teila Rodriguez, *Death Scream* (also known as *The Woman Who Cried Murder*), ABC, 1975; Kristina Matchett, *The Spell,* NBC, 1977; Janice Hurley, *Transplant,* CBS, 1979; Lizzie Eaton, *Angel Dusted,* NBC, 1981; Naomi, *Child Bride of Short Creek,* NBC, 1981; Kathy Miller, *The Miracle of Kathy Miller,* CBS, 1981; Sandy Cameron, *Desperate Lives,* CBS, 1982; Tami Maida, *Quarterback Princess,* CBS, 1983; Jenny Wells, *Bill: On His Own,* CBS, 1983; Kathy, *Choices of the Heart,* NBC, 1983; Debbie Markham, *Sweet Revenge,* CBS, 1984; also *Why Are You Here?* Specials: *Battle of the Network Stars,* ABC, 1982.

ADDRESSES: AGENT—International Creative Management, 8899 Beverly Boulevard, Los Angeles, CA 90048.*

I

IRELAND, John   1916-

PERSONAL: Full name, John Benjamin Ireland; born January 30, 1916, in Victoria, BC, Canada; son of John Benjamin (a rancher) and Katherine (an educator; maiden name, Ferguson) Ireland; married Elaine Sheldon Gudman, 1940 (divorced, 1949); married Joanne Dru (an actress), 1949 (divorced, 1958); married Daphne Cameron Myrick, 1962; children: two sons (first marriage); Daphne. EDUCATION—Studied acting at the Davenport Free Theatre, New York City.

VOCATION: Actor and director.

CAREER: STAGE DEBUT—Robin Hood Theatre, Arden, DE, 1939. OFF-BROADWAY DEBUT—With the Irish Repertory Players, Cherry Lane Theatre, 1939. BROADWAY DEBUT—Sergeant and first murderer, *Macbeth*, National Theatre, 1941. PRINCIPAL STAGE APPEARANCES—Reporter, *Native Son*, Majestic Theatre, New York City, 1942; Krafft, *Counterattack*, Windsor Theatre, New York City, 1943; first murderer, *Richard III*, Forrest Theatre, New York City, 1943; Gustave Jensen, *A New Life*, Royale Theatre, New York City, 1943; Mr. Deane, *Doctors Disagree*, Bijou Theatre, New York City, 1943; Sir Archibald Mackenzie, *A Highland Fling*, Plymouth Theatre, New York City, 1944; Buck Carpenter, *Deadfall*, Holiday Theatre, New York City, 1955; Brutos, *Infidel Caesar*, Music Box Theatre, New York City, 1962. Also appeared in *Macbeth*, Center Theatre Group, Ahmanson Theatre, Los Angeles, 1975; *The Pleasure of His Company*, Toronto, ON, Canada, 1985; *An Evening of Samuel Beckett*, Dublin Theatre Festival, Dublin, Ireland; at the Oxford Playhouse, Oxford, U.K.; and in *Robert W. Service* (one-man show).

MAJOR TOURS—Captain Hook, *Peter Pan*, Clare Tree Children's Theatre, U.S. cities, 1940; Horatio, *Hamlet*, Lorenzo, *The Merchant of Venice*, Macduff, *Macbeth*, and Iago, *Othello*, U.S. cities, all 1940; miner, *The Moon Is Down*, U.S. cities, 1942; Dr. John Buchanan, Jr., *Summer and Smoke*, U.S. cities, 1950; Murray Burns, *A Thousand Clowns*, U.S. cities, 1963-64; *Outward Bound*, U.S. cities, 1983.

FILM DEBUT—Windy, *A Walk in the Sun* (also known as *Salerno Beachhead*), Twentieth Century-Fox, 1945. PRINCIPAL FILM APPEARANCES—Detective Engelhofer, *Behind Green Lights*, Twentieth Century-Fox, 1946; Bennie Smith, *It Shouldn't Happen to a Dog*, Twentieth Century-Fox, 1946; Billy Clanton, *My Darling Clementine*, Twentieth Century-Fox, 1946; Howard Williams, *Wake Up and Dream*, Twentieth Century-Fox, 1946; voice of police stenographer, *Somewhere in the Night*, Twentieth Century Fox, 1946; narrator, *Repeat Performance*, Eagle-Lion, 1947; Karty, *The Gangster*, Allied Artists, 1947; Reno, *I Love Trouble*, Columbia, 1947; Duke Martin, *Railroaded*, Eagle-Lion, 1947; St.

Severe, *Joan of Arc*, RKO, 1948; Paul Lester, *Open Secret*, Eagle-Lion, 1948; Fantail, *Raw Deal*, Eagle-Lion/Reliance, 1948; Cherry Valance, *Red River*, United Artists, 1948; Captain Jed Calbern, *A Southern Yankee* (also known as *My Hero!*), Metro-Goldwyn-Mayer (MGM), 1948; Jack Burden, *All the King's Men*, Columbia, 1949; narrator, *The Undercover Man*, Columbia, 1949; Danny Johnson, *Anna Lucasta*, Columbia, 1949; Bitter Creek, *The Doolins of Oklahoma* (also known as *The Great Manhunt*), Columbia, 1949; Bob Ford, *I Shot Jesse James*, Screen Guild, 1949; "Early" Byrd, *Mr. Soft Touch* (also known as *House of Settlement*), Columbia, 1949; Lednov, *Roughshod*, RKO, 1949; Frazee, *The Walking Hills*, Columbia, 1949.

Steve Conway, *Cargo to Capetown*, Columbia, 1950; Johnny, *The Return of Jesse James*, Lippert, 1950; Pete Ferreday, *The Basketball Fix* (also known as *The Big Decision*), Real Art, 1951; Lieutenant John Haywood, *Little Big Horn* (also known as *The Fighting Seventh*), Lippert, 1951; Quantrell, *Red Mountain*, Paramount, 1951; John Barrington, *The Scarf*, United Artists, 1951; Hub Fasken, *Vengeance Valley*, MGM, 1951; Jeff Waring, *The Bushwhackers* (also known as *The Rebel*), Real Art, 1952; title role, *Hurricane Smith*, Paramount, 1952; Sergeant Fletcher, *Combat Squad*, Columbia, 1953; John Williams, *The Forty-Ninth Man*, Columbia, 1953; Rochelle, *Hannah Lee* (also known as *Outlaw Territory*), Broder, 1953; Frank Webster, *The Fast and the Furious*, American Releasing, 1954; Eddie, *The Good Die Young*, Independent Film Distributors, 1954; Ralph Payne, *Security Risk*, Allied Artists, 1954; Clint McDonald, *Southwest Passage* (also known as *Lands West*), United Artists, 1954; ringleader, "The Hostages" in *The Steel Cage*, United Artists, 1954; Pel, *The Glass Tomb* (also known as *The Glass Cage*), Lippert, 1955; Judson Prentiss, *Queen Bee*, Columbia, 1955; Cane Miro, *Gunslinger*, Associated Releasing, 1956; Johnny Ringo, *Gunfight at the O.K. Corral*, Paramount, 1957; Jonas Bailey, *No Place to Land* (also known as *Man Mad*), Republic, 1958; Louis Canetto, *Party Girl*, MGM, 1958; Griff Parker, *Stormy Crossing* (also known as *Black Tide*), Eros, 1958.

Max Hammond, *Faces in the Dark*, Rank, 1960; Crixus, *Spartacus*, Universal, 1960; Phil Macy, *Wild in the Country*, Twentieth Century-Fox, 1961; Jeff Saygure, *Brushfire*, Paramount, 1962; Ray Reed, *Return of a Stranger*, WPD, 1962; prison warden, *The Ceremony* (also known as *La ceremonia*), United Artists, 1963; Johnny Greco, *Med mord i bagaget* (also known as *No Time to Kill*), Agnes DeLahaie, 1963; Sergeant Harry, *55 Days at Peking*, Allied Artists, 1963; Ballomar, *The Fall of the Roman Empire*, Paramount, 1964; Steve Marak, *I Saw What You Did*, Universal, 1965; Tom Horn, *Fort Utah*, Paramount, 1967; Dan Shelby, *Arizona Bushwhackers*, Paramount, 1968; Dave, *Villa Rides*, Paramount, 1968; detective, *Una sull'altra* (also known as *One on Top of the Other*), 1969, released in the United States by GGP Releasing, 1971.

Mr. Hadley, *The Adventurers*, Paramount, 1970; Captain O'Connor, *La dalle Ardenne all'inferno* (also known as *Dirty Heroes*), Golden Eagle, 1971; Jacob Kagan, *Habricha el hashemesh* (also known as *Escape to the Sun* and *Niet!*), Cinevision, 1972; the director, *The House of Seven Corpses*, International Amusements, 1974; Mr. Milton, *Il letto in piazza* (also known as *Sex-Diary*), Americine, 1975; Lieutenant Nulty, *Farewell, My Lovely*, AVCO-Embassy, 1975; Sheriff H. "Duke" Bingham, *Tender Flesh* (also known as *Welcome to Arrow Beach*), Warner Brothers, 1976; Dwight McGowan, *The Swiss Conspiracy*, Warner Brothers/S.J. International, 1976; Clift, *Salon Kitty* (also known as *Madam Kitty*), Trans American/American International, 1976; Sheriff Bub/High Priest, *Satan's Cheerleaders*, World Amusements, 1977; Tony Santore, *Love and the Midnight Auto Supply*, Producers Capitol, 1978; captain, *Tomorrow Never Comes*, Rank, 1978; Lucas Johnson, *Delta Fox*, Sebastian International, 1979; judge, *Bordello*, Prism Entertainment, 1979; Senator Smedley, *The Shape of Things to Come* (also known as *H.G. Wells' "The Shape of Things to Come"*), Film Ventures International, 1979.

David Cole, *Guyana, Cult of the Damned* (also known as *Guyana: El crimen del siglo* and *Guyana, Crime of the Century*), Universal, 1980; Hank Walden, *The Incubus*, Artists Releasing, 1982; priest, *El tesoro del Amazones* (also known as *The Treasure of the Amazon*), Videocine/S.A., 1985; George Adams, *Thunder Run*, Cannon, 1985; Brewer, *Martin's Day*, Metro-Goldwyn-Mayer/United Artists, 1985; Zenas Beecham, *Messenger of Death*, Cannon, 1988. Also narrator, *This Is Korea!*, 1951; appeared in *Hell's Horizon*, Columbia, 1955; *Day of the Nightmare*, Herts-Lion, 1965; *Hate for Hate* (also known as *Odio per odio*), West Film, 1967; *Caxambu!*, 1967; *Fidarsi e benem sparare e meglio* (also known as *Trusting Is Good, Shooting Is Better*), 1967; Stuart, *El "Che" Guevara* (also known as *Rebel With a Cause*), 1968; *Una pistola per cento bare*, 1968; *Tutto per tutto* (also known as *All Out*), 1968; *Corri, uomo, corri* (also known as *Run, Man, Run*), 1968; *T'ammazzo! Raccomandanti a Dio* (also known as *I Kill You and Commend You to God*), 1968; *Quel caldo maleditto giorno di fuoco* (also known as *That Damned Hot Day of Fire*), 1968; *Once Upon a Time in the West*, Paramount, 1969; *Quanto costa morire* (also known as *The Cost of Dying*), 1969; *Gli insaziabili* (also known as *Femmine insaziabili* and *Carnal Circuit*), 1969; *Zenabel*, 1969.

The Challenge of the Mackennas, 1970; *Der Wuger Kommt auf Leisen Socken* (also known as *The Strangler of Vienna* and *The Mad Butcher*), 1972; *Dieci bianchi uccidi da un piccolo Indiano* (also known as *Ten Whites Killed by One Little Indian*), 1974; *La furie du desir*, 1975; *Noi non siamo angeli* (also known as *We're No Angels*), 1975; *Quel pomeriggio maledetto* (also known as *The Perfect Killer*), JPT and Metheus/Prism Entertainment, 1977; *Maniac!* (also known as *Assault on Paradise* and *The Town That Cried Terror*), New World, 1977; *Kino, the Padre on Horseback*, Key International, 1977; *On the Air Live with Captain Midnight* (also known as *Captain Midnight*), Sebastian International, 1979; *Garden of Venus*, 1981; *Miami Golem*, Uniexport, 1986.

PRINCIPAL FILM WORK—Producer and director (with Lee Garmes), *Hannah Lee* (also known as *Outlaw Territory*), Broder, 1953; director (with Edward Sampson), *The Fast and the Furious*, American Releasing, 1954.

TELEVISION DEBUT—"Confession," *Philco Television Playhouse*, NBC, 1951. PRINCIPAL TELEVISION APPEARANCES—Series: John Hunter, *The Cheaters*, BBC, 1961; Jed Colby, *Rawhide*, CBS, 1965-66; Lyman "Shack" Shackelford, *Cassie and Company*, NBC, 1982. Pilots: Marshall Wayburn, *The Millionaire*, CBS, 1978; Joe Virgil, Sr., *Tourist*, syndicated, 1980. Episodic: Rhymes, *Buck James*, ABC, 1988; Charles Redstone, Sr., *J.J. Starbuck*, NBC, 1988; Franken, *Snoops*, CBS, 1989; also "The Man I Marry," *Schlitz Playhouse of Stars*, CBS, 1952; "A Tale of Two Cities," *Plymouth Playhouse*, ABC, 1953; "Prisoner in Town" and "Reunion at Steepler's Hill," *Schlitz Playhouse of Stars*, CBS, 1954; "Time Bomb," *Philco Television Playhouse*, NBC, 1954; *Pall Mall Playhouse*, ABC, 1955; "Lonely Man," *Studio 57*, NBC, 1955; "There's No Forever," *Damon Runyon Theatre*, CBS, 1955; "Murder in Paradise" and "Ride to the West," *Schlitz Playhouse of Stars*, CBS, 1955; "The Bridge," *The Elgin Hour*, ABC, 1955; "Dealer's Choice" and "Ordeal," *Schlitz Playhouse of Stars*, CBS, 1956; "This Land Is Mine," *Fireside Theatre*, NBC, 1956; "Prologue to Glory," *General Electric Theatre*, CBS, 1956; "Return to Nowhere," *Zane Grey Theatre*, CBS, 1956; "Without Incident" and "A Sound of Different Drummers," *Playhouse 90*, CBS, 1957; "Black Angel," *Lux Video Theatre*, NBC, 1957; "Avalanche at Devil's Pass," *Climax*, CBS, 1957; "End of Violence," *Suspicion*, NBC, 1958; *Riverboat*, NBC, 1959.

"Close Set," *Ford Star Time*, NBC, 1960; *Asphalt Jungle*, ABC, 1961; "Papa Benjamin," *Thriller*, NBC, 1961; *The Cheaters*, syndicated, 1961; "Obituary for Mr. 'X'," *Dick Powell Theatre*, NBC, 1962; "The Matched Pearl," *Alfred Hitchcock Theatre*, NBC, 1962; *Rawhide*, CBS, 1962; "A Hero for Our Times," *Kraft Suspense Theatre*, NBC, 1963; *Mr. Broadway*, CBS, 1964; *Burke's Law*, ABC, 1965; *Branded*, NBC, 1965 and 1966; *Shenandoah*, ABC, 1966; *The Man Who Never Was*, ABC, 1966; *Gunsmoke*, CBS, 1966 and 1967; *Bonanza*, NBC, 1967; *Daniel Boone*, NBC, 1967; *The Iron Horse*, ABC, 1967; *The Name of the Game*, NBC, 1969; *Men from Shiloh*, NBC, 1970; "Creatures of the Canyon," *Ghost Story*, NBC, 1972; *Mission: Impossible*, CBS, 1972; *Khan!*, CBS, 1975; *Police Story*, NBC, 1975; *Quest*, NBC, 1976; *Beverly Hills Buntz*, NBC, 1988; Sheriff Evers, *Quincy, M.E.*, NBC. Movies: Bruno Walters, *The Girl on the Late, Late Show*, NBC, 1974; Lieutenant Gifford, *The Phantom of Hollywood*, CBS, 1974; George Hunter, *The Courage of Kavik, the Wolf Dog* (also known as *Kavik the Wolf Dog*), NBC, 1980; John Huston, *Marilyn: The Untold Story*, ABC, 1980; Jonathan Aaron Cartwright, *Bonanza: The Next Generation*, syndicated, 1988; Walter Haslitt, *Perry Mason: The Case of the Lady in the Lake*, NBC, 1988; also *Crossbar*, CBS, 1979; *The Last Tycoon*, BBC. Specials: *When the West Was Fun: A Western Reunion*, ABC, 1979.

NON-RELATED CAREER—Professional swimmer.

WRITINGS: Lyricist, "No Head on My Pillow" (song).

AWARDS: Academy Award nomination, Best Supporting Actor, 1949, for *All the King's Men*.

MEMBER: Screen Actors Guild, Actors' Equity Association, Directors Guild of America, Writers Guild of America.

SIDELIGHTS: RECREATIONS—Painting, swimming, tennis, reading, and writing.

ADDRESSES: AGENT—Burton Moss Agency, 113 N. San Vicente Boulevard, Suite 202, Beverly Hills, CA 90211.*

IRVIN, John   1940-

PERSONAL: Born May 7, 1940, in England.

VOCATION: Director.

CAREER: FIRST FILM WORK—Director, *Gala Day* (documentary). PRINCIPAL FILM WORK—Director: *The Dogs of War*, United Artists, 1980; *Ghost Story*, Universal, 1981; *Champions*, Embassy, 1984; *Turtle Diary*, Samuel Goldwyn, 1985; *Raw Deal*, De Laurentiis Entertainment Group, 1986; *Hamburger Hill*, Paramount, 1987; *Next of Kin*, Warner Brothers, 1989.

PRINCIPAL TELEVISION WORK—Series: Broadcast operations, *It's Back to School*, syndicated, 1987—. Mini-Series: Director, *Tinker, Tailor, Soldier, Spy*, PBS, 1980. Specials: Director, "Hard Times," *Great Performances*, PBS, 1977; director, "Possessions," *Childhood*, Granada, then *Great Performances*, PBS, 1977.

RELATED CAREER—Worked in the cutting room at Rank Film studios.

ADDRESSES: AGENT—Jim Wiatt, International Creative Management, 8899 Beverly Boulevard, Los Angeles, CA 90048.*

*   *   *

IVEY, Judith   1951-

PERSONAL: Born September 4, 1951, in El Paso, TX; daughter of Nathan Aldean (a college president) and Dorothy Lee (a teacher; maiden name, Lewis) Ivey; married Tim Braine (a producer and television executive), May 14, 1989. EDUCATION—Illinois State University, B.S., 1973. RELIGION—Roman Catholic.

VOCATION: Actress.

CAREER: STAGE DEBUT—Jilly, *The Sea*, Goodman Theatre Center, Chicago, IL, 1974. BROADWAY DEBUT—Kate, *Bedroom Farce*, Brooks Atkinson Theatre, 1979, for one hundred forty performances. PRINCIPAL STAGE APPEARANCES—Shirley, *The Goodbye People*, Jean, *The Moundbuilders*, and various roles, *Oh, Coward!*, all Evanston Theatre Company, Evanston, IL, 1977-78; Margaret, *Much Ado About Nothing*, American Shakespeare Festival, Philadelphia, PA, 1978; Gilda, *Design for Living*, Arena Stage, Washington, DC, 1979.

Kathleen Herlihy, *Sunday Runners in the Rain* and woman in overalls, *Girls, Girls, Girls*, both New York Shakespeare Festival (NYSF), Public Theatre, New York City, 1980; Fish, *Dusa, Fish, Stas, and Vi*, Manhattan Theatre Club, New York City, 1980; Piaf and Madeleine, *Piaf*, Plymouth Theatre, New York City, 1981; Evelyn, *The Rimers of Eldritch*, La Mama Experimental Theatre Club, New York City, 1981; Melanie, *Pastorale*, Second Stage Theatre, New York City, 1982; Eileen, *Two Small Bodies*, Production Company, Theatre Guinevere, New York City, then Matrix Theatre, Los Angeles, both 1982; Joyce, *Jazz Poets at the Grotto* and Kathy, *Second Lady*, both Production Company, Theatre Guinevere, 1983; Josie, *Steaming*, Brooks Atkinson Theatre, New York City, 1983; Bonnie, *Hurlyburly*, Goodman Theatre Center, Chicago, IL, 1983, then Promenade Theatre, New York City, later Ethel Barrymore Theatre, New York City, both 1984.

JUDITH IVEY

Bea, *Precious Sons*, Longacre Theatre, New York City, 1986; Ruth, *Blithe Spirit*, Morris Mechanic Theatre, Baltimore, MD, then Neil Simon Theatre, New York City, both 1987. Also appeared in *The Philanthropist*, Goodman Theatre Center, 1974; *Mourning Becomes Electra*, Goodman Theatre Center, 1975; *Statues* and *The Bridge at Belharbour* (double bill), Goodman Theatre Center, 1976; *Design for Living*, *Don Juan*, and *The Sport of My Mad Mother*, all Goodman Theatre Center, 1976-77; *Much Ado About Nothing*, Goodman Theatre Center, 1977; *Whose Life Is It Anyway?*, Folger Theatre Group, Washington, DC, 1978; *The Dumping Ground*, Ensemble Studio Theatre, New York City, 1981; *Much Ado About Nothing*, McCarter Theatre Company, Princeton, NJ.

FILM DEBUT—Sally, *Harry and Son*, Orion, 1984. PRINCIPAL FILM APPEARANCES—Iris, *The Lonely Guy*, Universal, 1984; Didi, *The Woman in Red*, Orion, 1984; Nancy Miller, *Compromising Positions*, Paramount, 1985; Blanche, *Brighton Beach Memoirs*, Universal, 1986; Zelda, *Hello Again*, Buena Vista, 1987; Charlotte Bonnard, *Sister, Sister*, New World, 1988; Frances, *Miles from Home*, Cinecom International/Norstar Releasing, 1988.

TELEVISION DEBUT—Louise, "The Shady Hill Kidnapping," *American Playhouse*, PBS, 1982. PRINCIPAL TELEVISION APPEARANCES—Movies: Sister Margaret, *Dixie: Changing Habits*, CBS, 1983; Noel Varner, *The Long, Hot Summer*, NBC, 1985; Sister Brenda Hayes, *We Are the Children*, ABC, 1987.

AWARDS: Joseph Jefferson Award nomination, 1978, for *The Goodbye People*; *Drama-Logue* Award, 1982, for *Two Small Bodies*; Antoinette Perry Award, Best Featured Actress in a Play, Drama Critics' Award, and *Drama-Logue* Award, all 1983, for

Steaming; Antoinette Perry Award, Best Featured Actress in a Play, and Drama Desk Award, both 1985, for *Hurlyburly.*

MEMBER: Actors' Equity Association, Screen Actors Guild, American Federation of Television and Radio Artists, National Organization for Women, American Society for the Prevention of Cruelty to Animals.

ADDRESSES: AGENT—Nicole David, Triad Artists, 10100 Santa Monica Boulevard, 16th Floor, Los Angeles, CA 90067.*

J

JACKSON, Sherry 1942-

PERSONAL: Born in 1942 in Wendell, ID.

VOCATION: Actress.

CAREER: PRINCIPAL FILM APPEARANCES—Jane at age six, *You're My Everything*, Twentieth Century-Fox, 1949; Amelia, *The Breaking Point*, Warner Brothers, 1950; Susie, *Covered Wagon Raid*, Republic, 1950; girl, *Louisa*, Universal, 1950; Susie Kettle, *Ma and Pa Kettle Go to Town* (also known as *Going to Town*), Universal, 1950; girl in iron lung, *Where Danger Lives*, RKO, 1950; Musetta as a child, *The Great Caruso*, Metro-Goldwyn-Mayer (MGM), 1951; little Italian girl, *Hello God*, Flynn, 1951; Annie Ridd as a child, *Lorna Doone*, Columbia, 1951; Ruthie Reed, *When I Grow Up*, Eagle-Lion, 1951; Jenny, *The Lion and the Horse*, Warner Brothers, 1952; Susie Kettle, *Ma and Pa at the Fair*, Universal, 1952; Jacinta Marto, *The Miracle of Our Lady of Fatima* (also known as *The Miracle of Fatima*), Warner Brothers, 1952; child, *Something to Live For*, Paramount, 1952; Susan Halleck, *This Woman Is Dangerous*, Warner Brothers, 1952; Susie Kettle, *Ma and Pa Kettle on Vacation* (also known as *Ma and Pa Kettle Go to Paris*), Universal, 1953; Carole Williams, *Trouble Along the Way*, Warner Brothers, 1953; Annie, *Come Next Spring*, Republic, 1956; Mary Jane, *The Adventures of Huckleberry Finn*, MGM, 1960; young Evelyn, *A Modern Marriage* (also known as *Frigid Wife*), Monogram, 1962; Lee Sullivan, *Wild on the Beach*, Twentieth Century-Fox, 1965; Samantha, *Gunn*, Paramount, 1967; Connie Logan, *The Mini-Skirt Mob*, American International, 1968; Mona, *The Monitors*, Commonwealth United Entertainment, 1969; Jennifer Randall, *Bare Knuckles*, Intercontinental Releasing, 1978. Also appeared in *Cotter*, 1972; *The Curse of the Moon Child*, 1972; *Stingray*, AVCO-Embassy, 1978.

PRINCIPAL TELEVISION APPEARANCES—Series: Terry Williams, *The Danny Thomas Show* (also known as *Make Room for Daddy*), ABC, 1953-57, then CBS, 1957-58. Pilots: Alice Watson, *Come a Running*, CBS, 1963; Kate Valentine, *Enigma*, CBS, 1977; title role, *Brenda Starr, Reporter*, syndicated, 1979; Jennifer, *Casino*, ABC, 1980. Episodic: Comfort Gatewood, "The Last Rites of Jeff Myrtlebank," *The Twilight Zone*, CBS, 1962; Andrea, "What Are Little Girls Made Of?," *Star Trek*, NBC, 1966; Terry Johnson, *Make Room for Granddaddy*, ABC, 1970; also *Lost in Space*, CBS, 1965; "Death in Slow Motion" and "The Riddler's False Notion," *Batman*, ABC, 1966; *The Incredible Hulk*, CBS, 1978; voice characterization, *Jeannie* (animated), CBS; *Alice*, CBS; *Love, American Style*, ABC; *Gomer Pyle, U.S.M.C.*, CBS; *Bringing Up Buddy*, CBS; *The Many Loves of Dobie Gillis*, CBS; *My Three Sons*. Movies: Nancy Delacourt, *Wild Women*, ABC, 1970; Pat Clauson, *The Girl on the Late, Late Show*, NBC, 1974; Stefanie, *Hitchhike!*, ABC, 1974; Marie Derry, *Returning Home*, ABC,

1975. Specials: Joanna, "The Story of Daniel in the Lion's Den," *Greatest Heroes of the Bible*, NBC, 1978.*

* * *

JAFFREY, Saeed 1929-

PERSONAL: Born in 1929 in Maler Kotla, India; father, in the Indian Medical Service; wife's name, Madhur (an actress), 1957 (divorced); children: three. EDUCATION—Received M.A. in history from the University of Allahabad; also attended Catholic University, 1956-57; graduated from the Staff Training School, All India Radio; studied acting at the Royal Academy of Dramatic Art, 1956; and with Lee Strasberg and Elia Kazan at the Actors' Studio.

VOCATION: Actor.

CAREER: PRINCIPAL STAGE APPEARANCES—Poet, *The Eagle Has Two Heads*, Unity Theatre, New Delhi, India, 1954; father, *Blood Wedding*, Actors Playhouse, New York City, 1958; Professor Godbole, *A Passage to India*, Ambassador Theatre, New York City, 1962; merchant, "From India: A Prologue" and Haiku reader, "From Japan: Kendo," in *A Tenth of an Inch Makes the Difference*, East End Theatre, New York City, 1962; Chief Kim Bong Choy, *Nathan Weinstein, Mystic, Connecticut*, Brooks Atkinson Theatre, New York City, 1966; Osman, *Captain Brassbound's Conversion*, Cambridge Theatre, London, 1971. Also appeared in *Othello*, *The Firstborn*, *A Phoenix Too Frequent*, *Under Milk Wood*, *Auto-Da-Fe*, *The Importance of Being Earnest*, *The Cocktail Party*, and *Le Bourgeois Gentilhomme*, all Unity Theatre, New Delhi, India, 1951-56; *Twelfth Night*, Equity Library Theatre, New York City, 1960; *King of the Dark Chamber*, Jan Hus House, New York City, 1961; *India: A Dancer's Pilgrimage*, Kaufman Concert Hall, New York City, 1961; *Rashoman*, *The Little World of Don Camillo*, *Bus Stop*, *Rain*, *A Thurber Carnival*, *Witness for the Prosecution*, *Teahouse of the August Moon*, and *The Little Hut*, all summer theatre productions, 1958-64; *The Private Life of the Master Race* and *The Harmfulness of Tobacco*, both New York Public Library, New York City; *The Physician in Spite of Himself*, Theatre-in-the-Street Group, New York City; *Tagore Suite*, Jacob's Pillow, 92nd Street Y, Cooper Union; *Kindly Monkeys*, Arts Theatre, London; *A Touch of Brightness*, Royal Court Theatre, London; *The Mother Country*, Riverside Theatre, London.

PRINCIPAL STAGE WORK—Director, *Under Milk Wood* and *King of the Dark Chamber*, both Unity Theatre, Delhi, India.

MAJOR TOURS—Friar Lawrence, *Romeo and Juliet* and Gremio, *The Taming of the Shrew*, both Players Inc. Repertory Company,

U.S. cities, 1957-58; ensemble, *Brecht on Brecht* (revue), American National Theatre and Academy, U.S. cities, 1963.

PRINCIPAL FILM APPEARANCES—Murad, *The Guru,* Twentieth Century-Fox, 1969; district chief, *The Horsemen,* Columbia, 1971; Billy Fish, *The Man Who Would Be King,* Allied Artists, 1975; Dr. Anil Mukerjee, *The Wilby Conspiracy,* United Artists, 1975; Mir Roshan Ali, *Shatranj ke khilari* (also known as *The Chess Players*), Connoisseur, 1977, released in the United States by Creative Films, 1978; Sri Narain, *Hullabaloo Over Georgie and Bonnie's Pictures,* Contemporary, 1979; Selim, *Sphinx,* Warner Brothers, 1981; Sardar Patel, *Gandhi,* Columbia, 1982; Actor, *The Courtesans of Bombay* (documentary), Enterprise/New Yorker/Cinecom International, 1982; narrator, *Pandit Nehru* (also known as *Jawaharlal Nehru;* documentary), National Film Development Corporation, 1982; Hamidullah, *A Passage to India,* Columbia, 1984; Raaz, *The Razor's Edge,* Columbia, 1984; Nasser, *My Beautiful Laundrette,* Orion, 1986; Hussein, *The Deceivers,* Cinecom, 1988; Mr. Patel, *Just Ask for Diamond* (also known as *The Falcon's Malteser*), Twentieth Century-Fox/Kings Road Entertaiment, 1988; Saeed, *Partition,* Jane Balfour Films, 1988. Also appeared in *Mandi* (also known as *Marketplace*), 1983; *Jalwa,* 1987; *Tamas,* Blaze, 1987; *Manika* (also known as *Manika: Une vie plus tard, Manika: The Girl Who Lived Twice, Manika Manika,* and *Une Passerelle sur le Gange*), Films du Scorpion/Twentieth Century-Fox/Manley, 1988.

PRINCIPAL TELEVISION APPEARANCES—Series: *The Sun Rises in the East,* 1972; Rafiq, *Gangsters,* BBC; *Tandoori Nights,* Channel Four. Mini-Series: Biju, *The Far Pavilions,* HBO, 1984; Nawab, *The Jewel in the Crown,* Granada, then *Masterpiece Theatre,* PBS, 1984. Episodic: *Armstrong Circle Theatre,* CBS; *The Jack Benny Show,* CBS; *The Nurses,* CBS; *The Defenders,* CBS; *Camera Three,* CBS; *CBS Workshop,* CBS; *File Seven.* Movies: Taj, *The Last Giraffe,* CBS, 1979. Specials: Frank Bhoolabhoy, *Staying On,* Granada, then *Great Performances,* PBS, 1981. Also appeared as Musquat Singh, *A Killing on the Exchange,* Anglia Television; in *A Passage to India,* BBC; and in *The Lion of the Punjab.*

PRINCIPAL RADIO APPEARANCES—Series: *Reflections of India,* WQXR (New York City), 1961-62. Specials: All Indian roles, *The Pump,* BBC, 1973. Also disk-jockey, newscaster, and actor, All India Radio, 1951-56; United Nations Radio, 1958-60.

PRINCIPAL RADIO WORK—Series: Producer, *Reflections of India,* WQXR, 1961-62.

RELATED CAREER—Founder, Unity Theatre, New Delhi, India, 1951-56; director, All India Radio, 1951-56, also public relations director, 1955-56; program manager, director, interviewer, and actor for India's first television station, 1955-56; director of publicity and advertising, Government of India Tourist Office, United States, 1958-60; member, Actors' Studio, New York City, 1958—; advertising copywriter; actor in television and radio commercials; appeared in print advertisements; cartoonist for *New York Mirror* and *Delhi Times.*

WRITINGS: RADIO—Series: *Reflections of India,* WQXR, 1961-62. Also staff writer, All India Radio, 1951-56.

RECORDINGS: ALBUMS—Readings of Asian poems, *Adventures in Appreciation.*

AWARDS: Best Travel Advertisement citation from British Advertising Magazines, 1960.

MEMBER: Actors' Equity Association, Screen Actors Guild, American Federation of Television and Radio Artists.

ADDRESSES: AGENT—Crouch Associates, 59 Frith Street, London W1, England.*

*   *   *

JAMES, Geraldine   1950-

PERSONAL: Born July 6, 1950, in Maidenhead, England; father, a cardiologist. EDUCATION—Studied acting at the London Drama Center.

VOCATION: Actress.

CAREER: PRINCIPAL STAGE APPEARANCES—Dr. Helga Von Zandt, *The Passion of Dracula,* Queen's Theatre, London, 1978; Imogen, *Cymbeline,* National Theatre, London, 1988; Portia, *The Merchant of Venice,* Phoenix Theatre, London, 1989, then 46th Street Theatre, New York City, 1989-90. Also appeared as Jessica, *The Merchant of Venice,* Coventry, U.K., 1979; in *When I Was a Girl, I Used to Scream and Shout,* Whitehall Theatre, London; *A Betrothal,* Man in the Moon Theatre, London; *Miss Julie, The Corn Is Green, The Miracle Worker, Arms and the Man, The Entertain-*

GERALDINE JAMES

er, *The White Devil*, and *Othello*, all in repertory productions at Chester, Exeter, Coventry, and Oxford, U.K.; *If Five Years Pass* and *Grandma's Faust*, both in London; and at the Second World Arts Festival, Lagos, Nigeria.

PRINCIPAL FILM APPEARANCES—Ritchie's wife, *Bloody Kids*, Palace/British Film Institute, 1979; Pamela, *Sweet William*, World Northal, 1980; Mirabehn, *Gandhi*, Columbia, 1982; Harriet Ambrose, *She's Been Away*, Sales Company/BBC Enterprises, 1989; Mrs. Brisket, *The Wolves of Willoughby Chase*, Zenith, 1989; Carmen, *The Tall Guy* (also known as *The Tall Guys*), Vestron/Virgin Vision, 1989; also appeared in *The Storm*.

PRINCIPAL TELEVISION APPEARANCES—Mini-Series: Sarah Layton, *The Jewel in the Crown*, Granada, then *Masterpiece Theatre*, PBS, 1984; Lady Maud Lynchwood, *Blott on the Landscape*, BBC, then Arts and Entertainment, 1986; Angela O'Hara, *Echoes*, Channel Four, 1988, then Arts and Entertainment, 1989. Movies: Krista Donner, *Freedom Fighter* (also known as *Wall of Tyranny*), NBC, 1987. Specials: *Who' Who*, BBC-2, 1982. Also appeared in *Dummy*, 1977; *Night Cruiser*, 1980; *I Remember Nelson*, 1981; and *Love Among the Artists*, *The History Man*, and *Time and the Conways*.

RELATED CAREER—Dresser, Royal Shakespeare Company, Stratford-on-Avon, U.K., and London.

AWARDS: Best Actress Award from the Venice Film Festival, 1989, for *She's Been Away*.

ADDRESSES: AGENTS—Sam Cohn, International Creative Management, 40 W. 57th Street, New York, NY 10019; Julian Belfrage Associates, 60 St. James's Street, London SW1, England.

*   *   *

JAMES, John   1956-

PERSONAL: Born April 18, 1956, in Minneapolis, MN; son of Herb Oscar Anderson (a radio personality); mother, a film editor. EDUCATION—Studied acting at the American Academy of Dramatic Arts and with Richard Adelman, Doug Taylor, and Barbara Baxley.

VOCATION: Actor.

CAREER: STAGE DEBUT—Don Baxter, *Butterflies Are Free*, Tiffany's Attic Theatre, Kansas City, MO, 1978, for eighty performances. PRINCIPAL STAGE APPEARANCES—*They're Playing Our Song*, Hirschfeld Theatre, Miami, FL, 1989; also appeared in *Social Security*, Cherry County Playhouse.

MAJOR TOURS—Chuck Baxter, *Promises, Promises*, U.S. cities.

PRINCIPAL FILM APPEARANCES—Man in stands, *Back to School*, Orion, 1986.

PRINCIPAL TELEVISION APPEARANCES—Series: Tom Bergman, *Search for Tomorrow*, CBS, 1977-78; Jeff Colby, *Dynasty*, ABC, 1981-85, then 1987-89; Jeff Colby, *The Colbys*, ABC, 1985-87. Movies: Ted Barnes, *He's Not Your Son*, CBS, 1984; Eric Beckett, *Haunted By Her Past*, NBC, 1987. Specials: *Battle of the Network Stars*, ABC, 1980, 1982, and 1983; *Macy's Thanksgiving Day*

JOHN JAMES

Parade, NBC, 1986; *Philadelphia Thanksgiving Day Parade*, Lifetime, 1987; *The Second Annual Star Spangled Celebration*, ABC, 1988; *One Day in America*, syndicated, 1989.

RELATED CAREER—Actor in stage productions in New York City and in television commercials; spokesperson for Great American Savings in California; national spokesperson for Farah Clothing; also singer and songwriter.

AWARDS: Received the Belding Award as spokesperson for Great American Savings; Golden Globe nomination for *Dynasty*.

SIDELIGHTS: RECREATIONS—Tennis, skiing, traveling, scuba diving, horseback riding, trap shooting, and playing the guitar.

ADDRESSES: AGENT—Badgley and Connor, 9229 Sunset Boulevard, Los Angeles, CA 90069.

*   *   *

JOHNSON, Chas. Floyd

PERSONAL: Born Charles Johnson, February 12, in Camden, NJ; son of Orange Maull (a real property officer) and Bertha Ellen (a school principal; maiden name, Seagers) Johnson; married Sandra Brashears, June 5, 1967 (divorced, 1971); married Anne Burford (a television production executive), June 18, 1983; children: Kristin Suzanne. EDUCATION—Attended the University of Delaware,

1960-61; Howard University, B.A., political science, 1962; Howard University Law School, J.D., 1965. POLITICS—Democrat. RELIGION—Methodist. MILITARY—U.S. Army, Judge Advocate General's Corps, specialist fifth class, 1965-67.

VOCATION: Actor, producer, and writer.

CAREER: Also see *WRITINGS* below. STAGE DEBUT—*Focus on Blacks in American Theatre,* Back Alley Theatre, Washington, DC, 1967, for thirty performances. PRINCIPAL STAGE APPEARANCES—Alton Scales, *The Sign in Sidney Brustein's Window,* Theatre Lobby, Washington, DC, 1967; Bernard, *The Boys in the Band,* Morgan Theatre, Santa Monica, CA, 1972; lieutenant, *The Drumhead,* Merle Oberon Theatre, Los Angeles, 1974.

TELEVISION DEBUT—Leroy, *Toma,* ABC, 1973. PRINCIPAL TELEVISION APPEARANCES—Episodic: Corporal, *The Six Million Dollar Man,* ABC, 1973; police officer, *Kojak,* CBS, 1974. Specials: *Voices of Our People . . . In Celebration of Black Poetry,* PBS, 1982.

PRINCIPAL TELEVISION WORK—Series: Associate producer, then producer, later co-executive producer, *The Rockford Files,* NBC, 1974-80; producer (with Geoffrey Fischer), *Bret Maverick,* NBC, 1981-82; producer (with Richard Chapman), *Simon and Simon,* CBS, 1982-83; producer, *Magnum, P.I.,* CBS, 1982-84, then supervising producer, 1985-86, later co-executive producer, 1987-88; co-executive producer, *B.L. Stryker,* ABC, 1989—. Pilots: Producer, *Hellinger's Law,* CBS, 1981; producer (with Nick Thiel and Reuben Leder), *The Return of Luther Gillis,* CBS, 1984. Specials: Producer, *Voices of Our People . . . In Celebration of Black Poetry,* PBS, 1982.

RELATED CAREER—Production coordinator, Universal Television, 1971-74, then associate producer, 1974-76, producer, 1976-82, supervising producer, 1982, and executive producer, 1985-87; vice-president, Communications Bridge (a media organization for minority-training in video technology), Los Angeles; founding member and vice-president, Media Forum.

NON-RELATED CAREER—Attorney, Howard Berg Law Offices, Wilmington, DE, 1965; Courts and Boards defense counsel, U.S. Army, 1965-67; attorney, U.S. Copyright Office, Washington, DC, 1967-70; member of the American delegation, UNESCO International Copyright Conference, Paris, France, 1970; attorney, Swedish Ministry of Justice, Stockholm, Sweden, 1970.

WRITINGS: TELEVISION—Episodic: "The Deep Blue Sleep," *The Rockford Files,* NBC, 1975; "The Prisoner of Rosemont Avenue," *The Rockford Files,* NBC, 1976; "Paradise Blues," *Magnum, P.I.,* CBS, 1984; "Photoplay," *Magnum, P.I.,* CBS, 1985. Specials: *Voices of Our People . . . In Celebration of Black Poetry,* PBS, 1982. OTHER—*The Origins of the Stockholm Protocol,* U.S. Copyright Society, 1970.

AWARDS: Emmy Award, Outstanding Drama Series, 1978, for *The Rockford Files;* Alumni Achievement Award from Stony Brook College Preparatory School, 1979; Emmy Award nominations, Outstanding Drama Series, 1979 and 1980, for *The Rockford Files;* Los Angeles Area Emmy Award, Best Entertainment Special, 1981, for *Voices of Our People . . . In Celebration of Black Poetry;* Outstanding Alumnus Award from the Howard University Alumni Club of Southern California, 1982; Commendations from the California State Legislature, the California State Senate, the City of Los Angeles, and the Hawaii State Senate, all 1982; Emmy

Award nominations, 1983 and 1984, for *Magnum, P.I.;* Outstanding Alumnus Award from Howard University, 1985. MILITARY HONORS—U.S. Army Commendation Medal, 1968.

MEMBER: Screen Actors Guild, Producers Guild of America, Writers Guild of America—West, American Federation of Television and Radio Artists, National Academy of Television Arts and Sciences, American Film Institute, Omega Psi Phi.

ADDRESSES: OFFICE—c/o Glen A. Larson Productions, Universal Television, 100 Universal City Plaza, Universal City, CA 91608. AGENT—McCartt, Oreck, and Barrett, 10390 Santa Monica Boulevard, Suite 310, Los Angeles, CA 90025.

*   *   *

JONES, Jeffrey   1947-

PERSONAL: Full name, Jeffrey Duncan Jones; born September 28, 1947, in Buffalo, NY; son of Douglas Bennett and Ruth (an art historian; maiden name, Schooley) Jones. EDUCATION—Lawrence University, B.A., 1968; trained for the stage at the London Academy of Music and Dramatic Arts.

VOCATION: Actor.

CAREER: STAGE DEBUT—Chorus, *The House of Atreus,* Tyrone Guthrie Theatre, Minneapolis, MN, 1967. LONDON DEBUT—Joseph Surface, *A School for Scandal,* Logan Place Theatre, 1970,

JEFFREY JONES

for six performances. OFF-BROADWAY DEBUT—(As Jeffrey Duncan Jones) Limester, *Lotta*, New York Shakespeare Festival, Public Theatre, 1973, for sixty performances. PRINCIPAL STAGE APPEARANCES—Watch, *Much Ado About Nothing*, third murderer and messenger, *Macbeth*, officer, *The Duchess of Malfi*, and guide, *Volpone*, all Stratford Shakespeare Festival, Festival Stage, Stratford, ON, Canada, 1971; Crookfinger Jake, *The Threepenny Opera*, Stratford Shakespeare Festival, Avon Stage, 1972; (as Jeffrey Duncan Jones) Francisco, *The Tempest*, New York Shakespeare Festival (NYSF), Mitzi E. Newhouse Theatre, New York City, 1974; Ivan, *Carmilla*, Kerry, *Noon*, Baron Frank, *Frankenstein*, Matt, *The Threepenny Opera*, title role, *The Real Inspector Hound*, Feraillon, *A Flea in Her Ear*, Merlie, *The Ballad of the Sad Cafe*, and Sarge, *Female Transport*, all Actors Theatre of Louisville, Louisville, KY, 1974-75; Captain DeFoenix, *Trelawney of the Wells*, NYSF, Vivian Beaumont Theatre, New York City, 1975; Dr. Pinch, *The Comedy of Errors*, NYSF, Delacorte Theatre, New York City, 1975; Randall Underwood, *Heartbreak House*, Arena Stage, Washington, DC, 1975; Roy, *Scribes*, Phoenix Theatre, Marymount Manhattan Theatre, New York City, 1976; Sergeant Wilson, *Secret Service* and Major Thompson, *Boy Meets Girl*, both Phoenix Theatre, Playhouse Theatre, New York City, 1976; Giles Ralston, *The Mousetrap*, Seattle Repertory Theatre, Seattle, WA, 1976; Chandebise and Poche, *A Flea in Her Ear*, Hartford Stage Company, Hartford, CT, 1977; Carver (Leo), *Design for Living*, McCarter Theatre, Princeton, NJ, 1977; Tom, *The Utter Glory of Morrisey Hall*, McCarter Theatre, 1978; Harold, *They Are Dying Out*, Yale Repertory Theatre, New Haven, CT, 1979; Sherlock Holmes (understudy), *The Crucifer of Blood*, Booth Theatre, New York City, 1979.

Pinhead manager, policeman, Will, and Lord John, *The Elephant Man*, Booth Theatre, 1980; Clive and Edward, *Cloud 9*, Theatre De Lys, New York City, 1981; Karl Bodenschatz, *The Death of Von Richthofen as Witnessed from Earth*, NYSF, Public Theatre, 1982; Montjoy, *Henry V*, NYSF, Delacorte Theatre, 1984; Maurice Stapleton, *Love Letters on Blue Paper*, Hudson Guild Theatre, New York City, 1984; Hans Christian Anderson, *Rainsnakes*, Long Wharf Theatre, New Haven, CT, 1984. Also appeared in *Heartbreak House*, Philadelphia Drama Guild, Philadelphia, PA, 1976; as Donald, *Porcelain Time*, Berkshire Theatre Festival, Stockbridge, MA; Antipholus of Syracuse, *The Comedy of Errors*, Manitoba Theatre Centre, Winnipeg, MB, Canada; Tony Cavendish, *The Royal Family* and Jim, *The Glass Menagerie*, both American Stage Festival, Milford, NH; Raymond de Chelles, *Custom of the Country*, Shakespeare and Company, Lee, MA; Sarge, *Female Transport*, NYSF, Public Theatre; in *The Merchant of Venice*, Stratford Shakespeare Festival; as Sergius, *Arms and the Man*, Vancouver Playhouse, Vancouver, BC, Canada; and in *The Shoemaker's Holiday*, *The Visit*, *Harper's Ferry*, and *The Second Shepherd's Play*, all Tyrone Guthrie Theatre, Minneapolis, MN.

MAJOR TOURS—Pinhead manager, policeman, Will, and Lord John, *The Elephant Man*, U.S. cities, 1979-80.

FILM DEBUT—Fred, *The Revolutionary*, United Artists, 1970. PRINCIPAL FILM APPEARANCES—Ruteledge child, *A Wedding*, Twentieth Century-Fox, 1978; U.S. Assistant Secretary of Defense, *The Soldier* (also known as *Codename: The Soldier*), Embassy, 1982; Clive Barlow, *Easy Money*, Orion, 1983; Emperor Joseph II, *Amadeus*, Orion, 1984; Mayor Lepescu, *Transylvania 6-5000*, New World, 1985; Ed Rooney, *Ferris Bueller's Day Off*, Paramount, 1986; Dr. Jenning, *Howard the Duck*, Universal, 1986; Major Fischer, *The Hanoi Hilton*, Cannon, 1987; Charles, *Beetlejuice*, Warner Brothers, 1988; Inspector Lestrade, *Without a Clue*, Orion,

1988; Eliot Draisen, *Who's Harry Crumb?*, Tri-Star, 1989; Gercourt, *Valmont*, Orion, 1989.

TELEVISION DEBUT—*Kojak*, CBS, 1971. PRINCIPAL TELEVISION APPEARANCES—Series: Walter Kellogg, *The People Next Door*, CBS, 1989. Mini-Series: Mr. Acme, *Fresno*, CBS, 1986; also *The Adams Chronicles*, PBS, 1976. Pilots: Harry, *A Fine Romance*, CBS, 1983. Episodic: Sergeant Jones, "Secret Service," *Theatre in America*, PBS, 1977; Carl Wilkerson, "Opening Day," *The Twilight Zone*, CBS, 1985; John Baldwin, *Amazing Stories*, NBC, 1986; also Clifford Connant, *Remington Steele*, NBC; *Ryan's Hope*, ABC; *One Life to Live*, ABC. Movies: Budge Hollander, *If Tomorrow Comes*, CBS, 1986; Thomas Jefferson, *George Washington II: The Forging of a Nation*, CBS, 1986; Buffalo Bill, *Kenny Rogers as "The Gambler" III—The Legend Continues*, CBS, 1987. Specials: Voice of the Man in the Magic Mirror, *Disney's DTV Monster Hits* (animated), NBC, 1987.

AWARDS: Tyrone Guthrie Award, 1971.

MEMBER: Actors' Equity Association, American Federation of Television and Radio Artists, Screen Actors Guild.

ADDRESSES: AGENT—Marilyn Szatmary, J. Michael Bloom, 9200 Sunset Boulevard, Suite 710, Los Angeles, CA 90069.

*   *   *

JONES, Quincy   1933-

PERSONAL: Full name, Quincy Delight Jones, Jr; born March 14, 1933 (some sources say 1934), in Chicago, IL; son of Quincy Delight and Sarah Jones; married second wife, Peggy Lipton (an actress), 1974 (divorced, 1986); children: Jolie, Martina-Lisa, Quincy III (first marriage); Kidada, Rashida (second marriage). EDUCATION—Attended Seattle University, the Berklee College of Music, and studied music with Nadia Boulanger and Messiaen in Paris.

VOCATION: Composer, arranger, producer, and musician.

CAREER: Also see *WRITINGS* below. PRINCIPAL FILM APPEARANCES—*Save the Children* (documentary), Paramount, 1973; *Blues for Trumpet and Koto*.

PRINCIPAL FILM WORK—Music director, *A Dandy in Aspic*, Columbia, 1968; music supervisor, *Man and Boy*, Levitt-Pickman, 1971; music supervisor, *Come Back Charleston Blue*, Warner Brothers, 1972; music supervisor, *The Wiz*, Universal, 1978; producer (with Steven Spielberg, Kathleen Kennedy, and Frank Marshall), *The Color Purple*, Warner Brothers, 1985; executive music producer, *Fast Forward*, Columbia, 1985; executive music producer, *The Slugger's Wife*, Columbia, 1985; executive music producer, *Fever Pitch*, Metro-Goldwyn-Mayer/United Artists, 1985. Also executive producer, *Stalingrad*.

PRINCIPAL TELEVISION APPEARANCES—Episodic: Host, *Saturday Night Live*, NBC, 1990. Specials: *Duke Ellington . . . We Love You Madly*, CBS, 1973; *Diana*, CBS, 1981; *Bugs Bunny/Looney Tunes All-Star 50th Anniversary*, CBS, 1986; *The Kennedy Center Honors: A Celebration of the Performing Arts*, CBS, 1986; *Whatta Year . . . 1986*, ABC, 1986; *An All-Star Celebration Honoring Martin Luther King, Jr.*, NBC, 1986; *Mancini and Friends*, PBS,

1987; *All-Star Tribute to Kareem Abdul-Jabbar,* NBC, 1989; "Bernstein at Seventy," *Great Performances,* PBS, 1989; *The Songwriters Hall of Fame Twentieth Anniversary . . . The Magic of Music,* CBS, 1989; *The Unforgettable Nat "King" Cole,* Disney Channel, 1989; *Sammy Davis, Jr.'s Sixtieth Anniversary Celebration,* ABC, 1990.

PRINCIPAL TELEVISION WORK—Series: Music director, *The New Bill Cosby Show,* CBS, 1972-73. Pilots: Co-executive producer, *Heart and Soul,* NBC, 1988; executive producer, *Livin' Large,* ABC, 1989. Specials: Producer and music director, *Duke Ellington . . . We Love You Madly,* CBS, 1973; music director, *Show Business Salute to Milton Berle,* NBC, 1973; music director, *An All-Star Celebration Honoring Martin Luther King, Jr.,* NBC, 1986.

RELATED CAREER—Trumpeter and music arranger, Lionel Hampton Orchestra, 1950-53; music director and trumpeter, Dizzy Gillespie's Orchestra, 1956; music director, Mercury Records, 1961, then vice-president in charge of artists and repertory, 1964; founder, Qwest Records, 1981; music arranger, Disques Barclay, Paris, France; music arranger for Ray Anthony, Tony Bennett, Count Basie, Ray Charles, Peggy Lee, Johnny Mathis, Frank Sinatra, Sarah Vaughan, Dinah Washington, Andy Williams, and others; record producer for Patti Austin, George Benson, Brook Benton, Billy Eckstine, Aretha Franklin, Lesley Gore, Lena Horne, James Ingram, Michael Jackson, Al Jarreau, the Brothers Johnson, Little Richard, Rufus, Rod Temperton, USA for Africa, and others.

WRITINGS: All as composer. FILM—*Pojken i tradet* (also known as *The Boy in the Tree*), 1964; *The Pawnbroker,* Landau/Allied Artists/American International, 1965; *The Slender Thread,* Paramount, 1965; *Walk Don't Run,* Columbia, 1966; (contributor) *Made in Paris,* Metro-Goldwyn-Mayer (MGM), 1966; *Banning,* Universal, 1967; *The Deadly Affair,* Columbia, 1967; *Enter Laughing,* Columbia, 1967; *In Cold Blood,* Columbia, 1967; *In the Heat of the Night,* United Artists, 1967; *Mirage,* Universal, 1968; *The Counterfeit Killer,* Universal, 1968; *A Dandy in Aspic,* Columbia, 1968; *For Love of Ivy,* Cinerama, 1968; *The Hell with Heroes,* Universal, 1968; *Jigsaw,* Universal, 1968; *The Split,* MGM, 1968; *Bob and Carol and Ted and Alice,* Columbia, 1969; *Cactus Flower,* Columbia, 1969; *The Italian Job,* Paramount, 1969; *John and Mary,* Twentieth Century-Fox, 1969; *The Lost Man,* Universal, 1969; *Mackenna's Gold,* Columbia, 1969; *Eggs* (short film), 1970; *Of Men and Demons* (short film), 1970; *The Out-of-Towners,* Paramount, 1970; *They Call Me Mister Tibbs!,* United Artists, 1970; *Up Your Teddy Bear* (also known as *The Toy Grabbers* and *Mother*), Geneni/Richard, 1970; *The Last of the Mobile Hotshots* (also known as *Blood Kin*), Warner Brothers, 1970; *The Anderson Tapes,* Columbia, 1971; *Brother John,* Columbia, 1971; *Honky,* Jack H. Harris, 1971; *$ (Dollars)* (also known as *The Heist*), Columbia, 1971; (with Donny Hathaway) *Come Back Charleston Blue,* Warner Brothers, 1972; *The Getaway,* National General, 1972; *The Hot Rock* (also known as *How to Steal a Diamond in Four Easy Lessons*), Twentieth Century-Fox, 1972; *The New Centurions* (also known as *Precinct 45: Los Angeles Police*), Columbia, 1972; *Mother, Jugs, and Speed,* Twentieth Century-Fox, 1976; *The Wiz,* Universal, 1978; *The Color Purple,* Warner Brothers, 1985; (with Thomas Dolby) *Fever Pitch,* Metro-Goldwyn-Mayer/United Artists, 1985; also *Blues for Trumpet and Koto.*

TELEVISION—Series: *Hey Landlord,* NBC, 1966-67; *The Bill Cosby Show,* NBC, 1969-71; *The New Bill Cosby Show,* CBS, 1972-73; *Sanford and Son,* NBC, 1972-77; *Sanford Arms,* NBC, 1977; (theme music) *The Oprah Winfrey Show,* syndicated, 1989.

Mini-Series: (With Gerald Fried) *Roots,* ABC, 1977. Pilots: *Ironside,* NBC, 1967; *Split Second to an Epitaph,* NBC, 1968; *Killer By Night,* CBS, 1972.

RECORDINGS: ALBUMS—*Big Band Bossa Nova,* Mercury, 1962; *Walking in Space,* A&M, 1969; *Gula Matari,* A&M, 1970; *Smackwater Jack,* A&M, 1971; *Summer in the City,* A&M, 1973; *Body Heat,* A&M, 1974; *Mellow Madness,* A&M, 1975; *I Heard That!!,* A&M, 1976; *Quintessential Charts,* Impulse, 1976; *Sounds . . . and Stuff Like That,* A&M, 1978; *Great Wide World of Quincy Jones,* Mercury, 1981; *The Dude,* A&M, 1981; *Best of Quincy Jones,* A&M, 1982; also *Quincy Jones and Billy Eckstine,* Mercury; *You've Got It Bad Girl,* A&M.

AWARDS: Grammy Award, Best Instrumental Arrangement, 1963, for "I Can't Stop Loving You" by Count Basie; Academy Award nomination, Best Song, 1967, for "The Eyes of Love" from *Banning;* Academy Award nomination, Best Original Music Score, 1967, for *In Cold Blood;* Academy Award nomination, Best Music (Song), 1968, for the title song from *For Love of Ivy;* Grammy Award, Best Instrumental Jazz Performance (Large Group or Soloist with Large Group), 1969, for *Walking in Space;* Grammy Award, Best Pop Instrumental Performance, 1971, for *Smackwater Jack;* Grammy Award, Best Instrumental Arrangement, 1973, for *Summer in the City;* Gold Record Award from the Recording Industry Association of America, 1974, for *Body Heat;* Emmy Award, Best Music Composition, 1977, for *Roots;* Grammy Award, Best R&B Performance By a Duo or Group with Vocal, 1981, for *The Dude;* Grammy Award (as producer), Best Cast Show Album, 1981, for *Lena Horne: The Lady and Her Music Live on Broadway;* Grammy Award (with Johnny Mandel), Best Arrangement on an Instrumental Recording, 1981, for "Velas" from *The Dude;* Grammy Award (with Jerry Hey), Best Instrumental Arrangement Accompanying Vocal(s), 1981, for "Ai No Corrida" from *The Dude;* Grammy Award, Producer of the Year, 1981; Golden Note Award from the American Society of Composers, Authors, and Publishers, 1982; Grammy Award (as producer with Michael Jackson), Record of the Year, 1983 for "Beat It" by Jackson; Grammy Award (as producer), Album of the Year, 1983, for *Thriller* by Jackson; Grammy Award (as producer), Best Recording for Children, 1983, for *E.T. The Extra-Terrestrial;* Grammy Award (with Jackson), Producer of the Year, 1983; *Rolling Stone* magazine Readers' Poll, Producer of the Year, 1983; Trendsetters Award from *Billboard* magazine, 1983; Grammy Award (with Jeremy Lubbock), Best Arrangement on an Instrumental, 1984, for "Grace (Gymnastics Theme)" from *Official Music of the XXIII Olympiad in Los Angeles;* Academy Award nominations, Best Picture (with Steven Spielberg, Kathleen Kennedy, and Frank Marshall) and Best Original Musical Score, both 1985, for *The Color Purple;* Academy Award nomination, Best Song, 1985, for "Miss Celie's Blues (Sister)" from *The Color Purple;* Grammy Award (as producer), Record of the Year, 1985, for "We Are the World" by USA for Africa; Grammy Award (as record producer), Best Music Video (Short Form), 1985, for *We Are the World—The Video Event;* Humanitarian Award from the T.J. Martell Foundation 1986; French Legion of Honor, 1990; *Downbeat* magazine Critics' Poll Award; *Downbeat* magazine Readers' Poll Award; Antonio Carlos Jobim Award; German Jazz Federation Award; Edison International Award of Sweden. HONORARY DEGREES—Berklee College of Music.

ADDRESSES: OFFICE—Quincy Jones Productions, 7250 Beverly Boulevard, Los Angeles, CA 90036. AGENT—Triad Artists, 10100 Santa Monica Boulevard, 16th Floor, Los Angeles, CA 90067.*

JONGEJANS, George
See GAYNES, George

*   *   *

JOSEPHS, Wilfred 1927-

PERSONAL: Born July 24, 1927, in Newcastle-upon-Tyne, England; son of Philip and Rachel (Block) Josephs; married Valerie Wisbey, 1956; children: two daughters. EDUCATION—Attended the University of Durham at Newcastle and the Guildhall School of Music; studied composition in Paris with Max Deutsch as a Leverhulme Scholar. MILITARY—British Army, 1951-53.

VOCATION: Composer.

CAREER: Also see *WRITINGS* below. PRINCIPAL FILM WORK— Music director, *Bomb in the High Street*, Hemisphere, 1964.

WRITINGS: All as composer. STAGE—*Alice Through the Looking Glass* (opera), 1978; also *King of the Coast* (children's musical); *Rebecca* (opera).

FILM—*Cash on Demand*, Columbia, 1962; *The Webster Boy* (also known as *Middle of Nowhere*), Regal, 1962; *Bomb in the High Street*, Hemisphere, 1964; *Die, Die, My Darling* (also known as *Fanatic*), Columbia, 1965; *Twenty-Four Hours to Kill*, Seven Arts, 1966; *The Deadly Bees*, Paramount, 1967; *My Side of the Mountain*, Paramount, 1969; *Ben Gurion*, 1969; *Dark Places*, Cinerama, 1974; *A Heritage to Build On*, 1974; *All Creatures Great and Small*, EMI, 1975; *Callan*, Cinema National, 1975; *Sea Areas Forties*, 1975; *Noah* (animated), 1976; *Swallows and Amazons*, LDS, 1977; *The Uncanny*, Rank, 1977; *The Flame Moves East* (documentary), 1977; *Mannen i skuggan* (also known as *Black Sun*), Stockholm Film, 1978; *Cocoa* (documentary), 1979; *Project North Sea* (documentary), 1979; *Martin's Day*, Metro-Goldwyn-Mayer/United Artists, 1985; (with Sri Hastanto) *Mata Hari*, Cannon, 1985. Also *Sixty Years of Fashion, Seven Hundred Million, Land of Britain, Oxford, Death and the Sky Above*, and *The Inheritance* (documentary).

TELEVISION—(All for British television, unless indicated). Series: *The Somerset Maugham Series*, 1969, then 1971-72; *Grasshopper Island*, 1970; *Horizon*, BBC, 1970-74, then 1983-85; *Suspicion*, 1971-72; *The British Empire*, 1971-72; *The Guardians*, 1971-72; *Pollyanna*, 1972; *The Brontes of Haworth*, 1973; *Love Story*, 1973; *The Pallisers*, BBC, 1974, then PBS, 1977; *A Place in Europe*, 1974; *The Great War*, 1974; *The Ghosts of Motley Hall*, 1975-77; *The Enemy at the Door*, 1977; *Gammon and Spinach*, 1977; *The Avenue*, 1977; *The Voyage of Charles Darwin*, 1978; (theme music) *Diary of Britain*, 1978; *The Human Race*, 1979-80; *Quest of Eagles*, 1979-80; *Sunday at Nine*, 1982; *The Home Front*, 1982; *The Making of Britain*, 1982-83; *The Return of the Antelope*, 1986; *Newcastle University*, 1986; *Drummonds; The Brief*. Mini-Series: (Theme music) *I, Claudius*, BBC, 1976, then *Masterpiece Theatre*, PBS, 1977; *Pride and Prejudice*, BBC, then *Masterpiece Theatre*, PBS, 1980; *Disraeli*, ATV, 1977, then *Masterpiece Theatre*, PBS, 1980; *Sister Dora*, 1977; *The Norman Conquests*, Thames, then *Great Performances*, PBS, 1978. Episodic: "Catherine Cookson," *The South Bank Show*. Movies: *Robinson Crusoe*, BBC, then NBC, 1974; *All Creatures Great and Small*, NBC, 1975; *The Hunchback of Notre Dame*, BBC, then NBC, 1977; *A Married Man*, London

Weekend Television, then syndicated, 1984; *Pope John Paul II*, CBS, 1984.

Also *A Voyage 'round My Father, The Beast in the Jungle, The Fosters*, and *Pitchi Poi*, all 1969; *Sweeney Todd, The Warmonger*, and *Doc—Shadow of Progress*, all 1970; *Cider with Rosie*, 1971-72; *Cherie*, 1974; *A Provincial Lady* and *Making Faces*, both 1975; *The Inventing of America*, BBC, then NBC, 1975; *The House of Bernarda Alba*, 1976; *The Parenthood Game*, 1977; *The Moles*, both 1982; *The Atom Spies, A Case of Cruelty to Prawns, Stage Equus—the Ballet, Fanfare for Young Musicians, Carpathian Eagle*, and *Churchill and the Generals*, all 1979-80; *The Gay Lord Quex*, BBC, 1983-85; *A Crack in the Ice*, 1983-85; *People Like Us; A Walk in the Dark; The Appointment* (television opera); *Redbrick; Evil; Jumping the Queue*.

OTHER—Composer of symphonic, choral, and chamber music, including ten symphonies, a quartet, and a requiem.

NON-RELATED CAREER—Dentist.

AWARDS: First Prize, La Scala, Milan, 1963, for *Requiem;* Guardian/ Arts Council Prize, 1969, for *King of the Coast;* Golden Mercury Award from the Venice Film Festival, 1970, for *Doc—Shadow of Progress;* Harriet Cohen Commonwealth Medal. HONORARY DE-GREES—University of Durham at Newcastle, Doctor of Music, 1978.

MEMBER: Society for the Promotion of New Music Inc. (council member), Society of Musicians, Composers' Guild of Great Britain.

SIDELIGHTS: RECREATIONS—Writing music, swimming, reading, opera, theatre, and films.

ADDRESSES: OFFICE—15 Douglas Court, Quex Road, London NW6 4PT, England. AGENTS—Nigel Britten, London Management, London W1, England; Robert Lantz, The Lantz Office, 888 Seventh Avenue, New York, NY 10016.*

*   *   *

JOSEPHSON, Erland 1923-

PERSONAL: Born June 15, 1923, in Stockholm, Sweden.

VOCATION: Actor, director, producer, and writer.

CAREER: PRINCIPAL STAGE APPEARANCES—Gaev, *The Cherry Orchard*, Brooklyn Academy of Music, Majestic Theatre, Brooklyn, NY, 1988; also appeared with the Municipal Theatre, Helsingborg, Sweden, 1945-49; Gothenburg Theatre, Gothenburg, Sweden, 1949-56; Royal Dramatic Theatre, Stockholm, Sweden, 1956—; and in over one hundred plays in Sweden.

PRINCIPAL FILM APPEARANCES—Egerman, *Ansiktet* (also known as *The Magician* and *The Face*), Janus, 1959; Anders, *Brink of Life*, Nordisk Tonefilm, 1960; Baron Von Merkens, *Vargtimmen* (also known as *Hour of the Wolf*), Lopert, 1968; Elis Vergerus, *En passion* (also known as *The Passion of Anna*), Svensk Filmindustri-Cinematograph, 1969, released in the United States by United Artists, 1970; doctor, *Viskingar och Rop* (also known as *Cries and Whispers*), New World, 1972; Johan, *Scenes from a Marriage*, Cinema V, 1974; teacher, *Monismanien 1995* (also known as

Monismania 1995), Taurus/Film Edis, 1975; Dr. Tomas Jacobi, *Ansikte mot Ansikte* (also known as *Face to Face*), Paramount, 1976; Editor-in-Chief Doncker, *Den Allvarsamma Leken* (also known as *Games of Love and Loneliness* and *The Serious Game*), Svenska Filminstitutet, 1977; Friedrich "Fritz" Nietzsche, *Oltre il bene e il male* (also known as *Beyond Good and Evil*), United Artists, 1977, Films Inc., 1984; Josef, *Hostsonaten* (also known as *Autumn Sonata* and *Herbstsonate*), New World, 1978; Leo Maria, *Die Erste Polka* (also known as *The First Polka*), Bavaria Atelier/Jugendfilm Verleih, 1978; Uncle Dan, *En och En* (also known as *One and One*), Svenska Filminstitutet/Sandrew Film and Teater, 1978; Nicky, *Dimenticare Venezia* (also known as *To Forget Venice*), Quartet/Connoisseur, 1979.

Karl Henrik Eller, *Marmeladupproret* (also known as *The Marmalade Revolution, The Revolution Marmalade,* and *La Revolte des confitures*), Svenska Filminstitutet, 1980; Erland, *Karleken* (also known as *Love*), Svenska Filminstitutet, 1980; Martin Jordan, *Montenegro* (also known as *Montenegro—Or Pigs and Pearls*), New Realm/Atlantic, 1981; Max, *Bella Donna,* Von Vietinghoff Filmproduktion Westdeutscher Rundfunk/Sender Freies Berlin, 1982; Isak Jacobi, *Fanny och Alexander* (also known as *Fanny and Alexander*), Svenska Filminstitutet, 1982, released in the United States by Embassy, 1983; stranger, *La Casa del tappeto giallo* (also known as *House of the Yellow Carpet*), Gaumont/SACIS/RPA International, 1983; Domenico, *Nostalghia* (also known as *Nostalgia*), Artificial Eye, 1983, released in the United States by Grange, 1984; Erik Sander, *Un Caso di incoscienza* (also known as *A Case of Irresponsibility*), Asa Cinematografica/RAI-TV Channel 2, 1984; Gabriel Berggren, *Dirty Story,* Golden, 1984; Henrik Vogler, *After the Rehearsal,* Columbia/Triumph, 1984; Goldberg, *Angelan Sota/Angelas Krig* (also known as *Angela's War*), Jorn Donner, 1984.

Oscar Seidenbaum, *The Flying Devils* (also known as *De Flyngande Djavlarna*), Continental/Metronome, 1985; David Sprengel, *Amorosa* (also known as *Amarosa*), Sandrew Film and Teater/Curzon Film Distributors, 1986; Robert's father, *Le Mal d'aimer* (also known as *The Malady of Love, La Queue du diable, La coda del diavolo,* and *The Devil's Tail*), AAA/SACIS/Film du Volcan, 1986; Alexander, *Offret-Sacrificatio* (also known as *The Sacrifice, Le Sacrifice,* and *Offret/Sacrificatio*), Orion, 1986; Monsignor Francesco Ghezzi, *Saving Grace,* Columbia, 1986; Serra, *L'Ultima Mazurka* (also known as *The Last Mazurka*), SACIS/Istituto Luce Italnoleggio Cinematografica, 1986; Cavour, *Garibaldi—The General,* RAI-TV Channel 2/Antenne 2/Jadran, 1986; Zupanev, *Testament d'un poete Juif assassine* (also known as *Testament of a*

Murdered Jewish Poet), TFI Swan/Court de Coeur/World Marketing, 1987; the Ambassador, *The Unbearable Lightness of Being,* Orion, 1988; Maurizio, *La Donna Spezzata* (also known as *A Woman Destroyed*), SACIS, 1988; narrator (Swedish version), *Directed by Andrei Tarkovsky* (also known as *Regi: Andrej Tarkovskij;* documentary), Svenska Filminstitutet/Artificial Eye, 1988; Dr. Bettelheim, *Hanussen,* Columbia, 1988. Also appeared in *Flickorna* (also known as *The Girls*), Lindgren/Sandrews, 1972; *Variola Vera,* Art Film/Croatia Film, 1982; *Bakom Jalusin* (also known as *Behind the Shutters*), Farago/Svenska Filminstitutet, 1984; *Il giorno prima* (also known as *The Day Before* and *La Veille*), Cristaldi/Columbia Pictures Italia, 1987; *Migrations* (also known as *La Guerre la plus glorieuse*), Cinexport, 1988.

PRINCIPAL TELEVISION APPEARANCES—Mini-Series: Johan, *Scenes from a Marriage,* PBS, 1977. Movies: Hans Swanson, *Control,* HBO, 1987.

PRINCIPAL FILM WORK—Producer (with Sven Nyqvist and Bengt Forslund) and director (with Nyqvist and Ingrid Thulin), *En och En* (also known as *One and One*), Svenska Filminstitutet/Sandrew Film and Teater, 1978; director (with Nyqvist) and producer, *Marmeladupproret* (also known as *The Marmalade Revolution, The Revolution Marmalade,* and *La Revolte des confitures*), Svenska Filminstitutet, 1980.

RELATED CAREER—Director, Royal Dramatic Theatre, Stockholm, Sweden, 1966-75.

WRITINGS: FILM—(With Ingmar Bergman) *All These Women* (also known as *Now About All These Women*), Janus, 1964; *En och En* (also known as *One and One*), Svenska Filminstitutet/Sandrew Film and Teater, 1978; *Marmeladupproret* (also known as *The Marmalade Revolution, The Revolution Marmalade,* and *La Revolte des Confitures*), Svenska Filminstitutet, 1980; also *The Pleasure Garden.* OTHER—*Cirkel,* 1946; *Spegeln och en portvakt,* 1946; *Spel med bedrovade artister,* 1947; *Ensam och fri,* 1948; *Lyssnarpost,* 1949; *De vuxna barnen,* 1952; *Utflykt,* 1954; *Sallskapslek,* 1955; *En berattelse om herr Silberstein,* 1957; *Kungen ur leken,* 1959; *Doktor Meyers sista dagar,* 1964; *Kandidat Nilssons forsta natt,* 1964; *Lejon i Overgangsaldern (pjas Dromaten),* 1981.

ADDRESSES: OFFICE—Royal Dramatic Theatre, Nybroplan, Box 5037, 102 41 Stockholm, Sweden. AGENT—Paul Kohner Inc., 9169 Sunset Boulevard, Los Angeles, CA 90069.*

K

KAHN, Madeline 1942-

PERSONAL: Born Madeline Gail Wolfson, September 29, 1942, in Boston, MA; daughter of Bernard B. and Paula (Kahn) Wolfson. EDUCATION—Hofstra University, B.A., 1964; studied acting at the Warren Robertson Actors' Workshop.

VOCATION: Actress and singer.

CAREER: BROADWAY DEBUT—Ensemble, *New Faces of 1968* (revue), Booth Theatre, 1968. PRINCIPAL STAGE APPEARANCES—Cunegonde, *Candide in Concert* (opera), Philharmonic Hall, New York City, 1968; servant, *Promenade,* Promenade Theatre, New York City, 1969; Goldie, *Two By Two,* Imperial Theatre, New York City, 1970; Chrissy, *Boom Boom Room,* New York Shakespeare Festival (NYSF), Vivian Beaumont Theatre, New York City, 1973; Amalia Balash, *She Loves Me,* Town Hall, New York City, 1977; Diane McBride, *Marco Polo Sings a Solo,* NYSF, Public Theatre, New York City, 1977; Mildred Plotka and Lily Garland, *On the Twentieth Century,* St. James Theatre, New York City, 1978; Madame Arcati, *Blithe Spirit,* Santa Fe Festival Theatre, Santa Fe, NM, 1983; Shirley, *What's Wrong with This Picture?,* Manhattan Theatre Club, New York City, 1985; Billie Dawn, *Born Yesterday,* 46th Street Theatre, New York City, 1989. Also appeared in *Kiss Me Kate,* City Center Theatre, New York City, 1965; *America,* Santa Fe Festival Theatre; *La Boheme* (opera), Washington Opera Society, Washington, DC; *La Perichole* (opera), Carnegie Hall, New York City.

MADELINE KAHN

FILM DEBUT—*The Dove* (short film), Coe/Davis/Love, 1968. PRINCIPAL FILM APPEARANCES—Eunice Burns, *What's Up, Doc?,* Warner Brothers, 1972; school teacher, *From the Mixed-Up Files of Mrs. Basil E. Frankweiler* (also known as *The Hideaways*), Cinema V, 1973; Trixie Delight, *Paper Moon,* Paramount, 1973; Lili Von Shtupp, *Blazing Saddles,* Warner Brothers, 1974; Elizabeth, *Young Frankenstein,* Twentieth Century-Fox, 1974; Jenny Hill, *The Adventures of Sherlock Holmes' Smarter Brother,* Twentieth Century-Fox, 1975; Kitty O'Kelly, *At Long Last Love,* Twentieth Century-Fox, 1975; Estie Del Ruth, *Won Ton Ton, the Dog Who Saved Hollywood,* Paramount, 1976; Victoria Brisbane, *High Anxiety,* Twentieth Century-Fox, 1977; Mrs. Montenegro, *The Cheap Detective,* Columbia, 1978; El Sleezo patron, *The Muppet Movie,* Associated Film Distribution, 1979; Mrs. Constance Link, *First Family,* Warner Brothers, 1980; Bunny Weinberger, *Happy Birthday, Gemini,* United Artists, 1980; Cynthia, *Simon,* Warner Brothers, 1980; sorceress, *Wholly Moses!,* Columbia, 1980; Empress Nympho, *History of the World, Part I,* Twentieth Century-Fox, 1981; Betty, *Yellowbeard,* Orion, 1983; Caroline Howley, *City Heat,* Warner Brothers, 1984; Eliza Swain and Letitia Swain, *Slapstick of Another Kind,* Entertainment Releasing Company/International Film Marketing, 1984; Mrs. White, *Clue,* Paramount, 1985; voice of Draggle, *My Little Pony* (animated), De Laurentiis Entertainment Group, 1986; voice of Gussie Mausheimer, *An American Tale* (animated), Universal, 1986.

PRINCIPAL TELEVISION APPEARANCES—Series: Regular, *Comedy Tonight,* CBS, 1970; Madeline Wayne, *Oh Madeline,* ABC, 1983-84; Lois Gullickson, *Mr. President,* Fox, 1987-88. Pilots: *Klein Time,* CBS, 1977. Episodic: *Evening at the Improv,* syndicated, 1981; *The ABC Comedy Special,* ABC, 1986; also *The Carol Burnett Show,* CBS; *The Muppet Show,* syndicated; *Saturday Night Live,* NBC. Movies: Violet Kingsley, *Chameleon,* ABC, 1986. Specials: Miss Kelly, ''Harvey,'' *Hallmark Hall of Fame,* NBC, 1972; *The George Burns Special,* CBS, 1976; *Comic Relief,* HBO, 1986; Ellie Coleman, ''Wanted: The Perfect Guy,'' *ABC Afterschool Specials,* ABC, 1986; ''Celebrating Gershwin,'' *Great Perform-*

ances, PBS, 1987; *Irving Berlin's 100th Birthday Celebration,* CBS, 1988; *Sesame Street Special,* PBS, 1988.

RELATED CAREER—Nightclub performer, Upstairs at the Downstairs, New York City, 1966-67.

RECORDINGS: ALBUMS—*New Faces of 1968* (original cast recording), Warner Brothers, 1968; *Two By Two* (original cast recording), Columbia, 1970; *Blazing Saddles* (original soundtrack), Elektra, 1974; *Young Frankenstein* (original soundtrack), ABC, 1975; *At Long Last Love* (original soundtrack), RCA-Victor, 1975; *Frank Loesser Revisited,* Painted Smiles, 1975; *On the Twentieth Century* (original cast recording), Columbia, 1978; also *Two Revues* (original cast recording). VIDEOS—Various roles, *Scrambled Feet,* RKO, 1983.

AWARDS: Academy Award nomination, Best Supporting Actress, and Golden Globe nomination, both 1973, for *Paper Moon;* Antoinette Perry Award nomination, Best Actress in a Drama, and Drama Desk Award, both 1974, for *Boom Boom Room;* Academy Award nomination, Best Supporting Actress, 1974, for *Blazing Saddles;* First Annual Academy of Humor Award, 1975; Distinguished Service Award from the Hofstra University Alumni Association, 1975; Golden Globe nomination, 1975, for *Young Frankenstein;* Antoinette Perry Award nomination, Best Actress in a Musical, 1978, for *On the Twentieth Century;* Emmy Award, 1986, for "Wanted: The Perfect Guy," *ABC Afterschool Specials.*

ADDRESSES: AGENT—Jeffrey Richards Association, Alwyn Court, 911 Seventh Avenue, New York, NY 10019.

*   *   *

KAREN, James   1923-

PERSONAL: Born November 28, 1923, in Wilkes-Barre, PA. son of Joseph H. (a produce dealer) and Mae (Freed) Karnufsky; married Susan Reed (a folk singer), September 2, 1949 (divorced); married Alba Francesca (an actress and producer), May 14, 1989; children: son's name Reed. EDUCATION—Studied acting with Sanford Meisner at the Neighborhood Playhouse. MILITARY—U.S. Air Force, 1942-45.

VOCATION: Actor.

CAREER: BROADWAY DEBUT—*A Streetcar Named Desire,* Ethel Barrymore Theatre, 1948. PRINCIPAL STAGE APPEARANCES—Tom, *Celebration,* Six O'Clock Theatre's Studio Productions, Maxine Elliot's Theatre, New York City, 1948; townsperson, *An Enemy of the People,* Broadhurst Theatre, New York City, 1950; Chuck Robbins, *Third Best Sport,* Ambassador Theatre, New York City, 1958; Howard Merrick, *Deep Are the Roots,* St. Mark's Playhouse, New York City, 1960; Captain Moss, *A Cook for Mr. General,* Playhouse Theatre, New York City, 1961; Jerry, *The Jackhammer,* Theatre Marquee, New York City, 1962; Dean Maveeda, *A Matter of Like Life and Death,* East End Theatre, New York City, 1963; understudy for Julian, *The Cactus Flower,* Royale Theatre, New York City, 1965; understudy for Petey, *The Birthday Party,* Booth Theatre, New York City, 1967; understudy, *The Only Game in Town,* Broadhurst Theatre, 1968; Reverend Henning and job dispenser, *The Engagement Baby,* Helen Hayes Theatre, New York City, 1970; Larry, *The Country Girl,* Billy Rose Theatre, New York City, 1972; understudy for George, *Who's Afraid of*

JAMES KAREN

Virginia Woolf?, Music Box Theatre, New York City, 1976. Also appeared in *The Time of Storm,* Greenwich Mews Theatre, New York City, 1954; *Tiny Alice,* Billy Rose Theatre, 1964; *Everything in the Garden,* Plymouth Theatre, New York City, 1967; *Who's Afraid of Virginia Woolf?,* London production; and *A Moon for the Misbegotten,* Broadway production.

PRINCIPAL FILM APPEARANCES—Dr. Adam Steele, *Frankenstein Meets the Space Monster* (also known as *Mars Invades Puerto Rico* and *Frankenstein Meets the Spacemen*), Allied Artists, 1965; professor, *Hercules in New York* (also known as *Hercules: The Movie*), RAF-United, 1970; Mr. Tucker, *I Never Sang for My Father,* Columbia, 1970; child psychiatrist, *Rivals,* AVCO-Embassy, 1972; Annenberg, *Amazing Grace,* United Artists, 1974; Hugh Sloan's lawyer, *All the President's Men,* Warner Brothers, 1976; newsstand operator, *Opening Night,* Faces, 1977; Vice President Price, *Capricorn One,* Warner Brothers, 1978; Andrews, *F.I.S.T.,* United Artists, 1978; Mac Churchill, *The China Syndrome,* Columbia, 1979; Barney Callahan, *The Jazz Singer,* Associated Film, 1980; Loomis, *Take This Job and Shove It,* AVCO-Embassy, 1981; Teague, *Poltergeist,* Metro-Goldwyn-Mayer/United Artists, 1982; Judge Hillierarold, *Frances,* Universal, 1982; Wendell Rossmore, *Time Walker,* New World, 1982; Mr. Collins, *Sam's Son,* Invictus, 1984; Andrew Hardesty, *Jagged Edge,* Columbia, 1985; colonel, *Latino,* Manson International, 1985; Frank, *Return of the Living Dead,* Orion, 1985; General Wilson, *Invaders from Mars,* Cannon, 1986; Logan, *Hardbodies II,* Cinetel, 1986; Lynch, *Wall Street,* Twentieth Century-Fox, 1987; Ed, *Return of the Living Dead, Part II,* Lorimar, 1988. Also appeared in *Jeremy,* United Artists, 1973; *Kiss Me Goodbye,* Twentieth Century-Fox, 1982; *Micki and Maude,* Columbia, 1984; *The Roommate* (short film), *Asa Nisi Masa*, 1988; as narrator, *Spirit of the Eagle*, August Entertainment (upcoming); in *Vital Signs*, Twentieth Century-Fox (upcoming); *The Closer* Ion (upcoming); *Herbie*, Buena Vista.

TELEVISION DEBUT—Bob Cratchett, *A Christmas Carol*, NBC, 1948. PRINCIPAL TELEVISION APPEARANCES—Series: Lincoln Tyler, *All My Children*, ABC, 1970; Major Wymore, *The Powers of Matthew Star*, NBC, 1983. Mini-Series: Earl Silbert, *Blind Ambition*, CBS, 1979. Pilots: Powerbroker, *Institute for Revenge*, NBC, 1979; Carol's father, *Me and Ducky*, NBC, 1979; Fred Korbell, *Topper*, ABC, 1979; also *Richie Brockelman: Missing Twenty-Four Hours*, NBC, 1976. Episodic: Lawyer, *227*, NBC, 1985; Mr. Slater, *Melba*, CBS, 1986; Dr. Hightower, *Magnum, P.I.*, CBS, 1987; James Whitlow, *Who's the Boss?*, ABC, 1987; mayor, *Jake and the Fatman*, CBS, 1987; Governor E.J. LaChatte, *Sledge Hammer!*, ABC, 1988; Raymond, *Golden Girls*, NBC, 1988; Arvin Johns, *Murphy Brown*, CBS, 1989; Jack Wingate, *Booker*, Fox, 1989; Lyle Vandergrift, *Jake and the Fatman*, CBS, 1989; Mr. Simenton, *Highway to Heaven*, NBC, 1989; Nagen, *Mancuso, F.B.I.*, NBC, 1989; Robert Sanborn, *MacGyver*, ABC, 1989; Stepfield, "Wild Jack" (also known as "Jack of the Wild," "McCall!," and "McCall of the Wild"), *The Magical World of Disney*, NBC, 1989; also *Gibbsville*, NBC, 1976; *The San Pedro Beach Bums*, ABC, 1977; *The Kallikaks*, NBC, 1977; *Executive Suite*, CBS, 1977; *Rafferty*, CBS, 1977; *M*A*S*H*, CBS, 1983; *Cheers*, NBC, 1985; Elliott Randolph, *Eight Is Enough*, ABC; "The Boy Who Loved Trolls," *WonderWorks*, PBS; *Family Ties*, NBC; *Dynasty*, ABC; *Knots Landing*, CBS; *Moonlighting*, ABC; *Amazing Stories*, NBC; *Three's Company*, ABC; *Emerald Point, N.A.S.*, CBS; *Hardcastle and McCormick*, ABC; *Tucker's Witch*, CBS; *Trapper John, M.D.*, CBS; *Simon and Simon*, CBS; *Quincy, M.E.*, NBC; *The Jeffersons*, CBS; *One Day at a Time*, CBS; *The Rockford Files*, NBC; *The Love Boat*, ABC; *Family*, ABC; *Lou Grant*, CBS; *Delvecchio*, CBS; *The Blue Knight*, CBS; *Serpico*, NBC; *Police Woman*, NBC; *McMillan and Wife*, NBC; *The Streets of San Francisco*, ABC; *Starsky and Hutch*, ABC; *Hawaii Five-O*, CBS; *The Paper Chase*; *The Bionic Woman*; *Charles in Charge*; *Lassie*; *Mathnet*.

Movies: Bob Block, *The Gathering*, ABC, 1977; Dr. Sutterman, *Mary Jane Harper Cried Last Night*, CBS, 1977; Dr. Wingreen, *Something for Joey*, CBS, 1977; psychologist, *The Ordeal of Patty Hearst*, ABC, 1979; Alvin Heller, *Once Upon a Family*, CBS, 1980; Untermeyer, *Portrait of a Rebel: Margaret Sanger*, CBS, 1980; Admiral McIntire, *F.D.R.—The Last Year*, NBC, 1980; Dr. Spandler, *The Violation of Sarah McDavid*, CBS, 1981; Nathan Lassiter, *Little House: The Last Farewell*, NBC, 1984; Mr. Fairmont, *The Billionaire Boys Club*, NBC, 1987; Aide, *Drug Wars: The Camarena Story*, NBC, 1990; also *Women in White*, NBC, 1979; *Jacqueline Bouvier Kennedy*, ABC; 1981; *The Day the Bubble Burst*, NBC, 1982; *Eight Is Enough: A Family Reunion*, NBC, 1987; Mr. McCabe, *Rich Men, Single Women*, ABC, 1990. Specials: Mr. Fairchild, "Have You Ever Been Ashamed of Your Parents?," *ABC Afterschool Special*, ABC, 1983; "Buster Keaton: A Hard Act to Follow," *American Masters*, PBS, 1987.

RELATED CAREER—Actor in television and radio commercials; commercial spokesperson for Pathmark supermarkets in the New York and Philadelphia area for twenty-two years.

MEMBER: Academy of Motion Picture Arts and Sciences, Academy of Science Fiction, Fantasy, and Horror Films, Screen Actors Guild, American Federation of Television and Radio Artists, Actors' Equity Association, Players Club.

SIDELIGHTS: RECREATIONS—Sailing, antique and classic cars, and travel. James Karen informed *CTFT* that "filming abroad always interests me."

ADDRESSES: AGENTS—Mary Ellen White, M.E.W. Inc., 151 N. San Vicente Boulevard, Beverly Hills, CA 90211; Mary Oreck, 10390 Santa Monica Boulevard, Suite 310, Los Angeles, CA 90025.

*   *   *

KARINA, Anna   1940-

PERSONAL: Born Hanne Karin Blarke Bayer, September 22, 1940, in Copenhagen, Denmark; married Jean-Luc Godard (a film director, producer, and writer), March 2, 1961 (divorced, 1967); married Pierre-Antoine Fabre, 1968 (divorced); married Daniel-Georges Duval, 1978.

VOCATION: Actress.

CAREER: FILM DEBUT—*Pigen og skoene* (also known as *The Girl and the Shoes;* short film), 1959. PRINCIPAL FILM APPEAR-ANCES—Veronica Dreyer, *Le Petit Soldat* (also known as *The Little Soldier*), filmed in 1960, released by Georges de Beauregard/Societe Nouvelle de Cinema, 1963, released in the United States by West End, 1965; Angela, *Une Femme est une femme* (also known as *A Woman Is a Woman* and *La donna e donna*), Rome-Paris Films, 1961, released in the United States by Pathe Contemporary, 1961; Toni, *She'll Have to Go* (also known as *Maid for Murder*), 1961, released in the United States by Janus, 1963; actress in comedy film, *Cleo de 5 a 7* (also known as *Cleo from 5 to 7*), Rome-Paris Films, 1962, released in the United States by Zenith International, 1962; Nana, *Vivre sa vie* (also known as *My Life to Live* and *It's My Life*), Les Films de la Pleieade, 1962, released in the United States by Union/Pathe Contemporary, 1963; title role, *Sheherazade* (also known as *Scheherazade* and *La Schiavadi Bagdad*), 1962, released in the United States by Shawn International, 1965; Colombe, "The Fox and the Crow" in *Les Quatres Verites* (also known as *Le quattro verita* and *Three Fables of Love*), Janus, 1963; Giselle, *Dragees au poivre* (also known as *Confette al pepe* and *Sweet and Sour*), Pathe, 1963; chambermaid, *La Ronde* (also known as *Circle of Love*), 1964, released in the United States by STER, 1965; Odile, *Band a part* (also known as *Band of Outsiders* and *The Outsiders*), Anouchka Films, 1964, released in the United States by Royal, 1966; Helene, *De l'amour*, 1964, released in the United States by Goldstone, 1968.

Natasha Von Braun, *Alphaville* (also know as *Une Etrange Aventure de Lemmy Caution* and *A Strange Case of Lemmy Caution*), Chaumiane Productions and Filmstudio, 1965, released in the United States by Pathe, 1965; Marianne Renoir, *Pierrot le fou*, Rome-Paris Films, 1965, released in the United States by Pathe/Corinth, 1968; Suzanne Simonin, *La Religieuse* (also known as *The Nun, La Religieuse de Diderot*, and *Suzanne Simonin*), 1965, released in the United States by Altura, 1971; Paula Nelson, *Made in U.S.A.* (also known as *Made in America*), Rome-Paris Films, 1966; Miss Conversation, "Anticipation, ou L'Amour en l'an 2000" in *Le Plus vieux metier du monde* (also known as *The Oldest Profession*), Francoriz, 1966, released in the United States by Goldstone/VIP, 1968; Marie Cardona, *Lo straniero* (also known as *L'Etranger* and *The Stranger*), Paramount, 1967; Anne, *The Magus*, Twentieth Century-Fox, 1968; Maria Holz, *Before Winter Comes*,

Columbia, 1968; Margot, *Laughter in the Dark,* Lopert, 1969; Melissa, *Justine,* Twentieth Century-Fox, 1969.

Jeanne, *L'Alliance* (also known as *The Wedding Ring*), CAPAC, 1970; Elle, *Rendez-vous a Bray* (also known as *Rendezvous at Bray* and *Meeting in Bray*), CFDC/Essential Cinema, 1971; Anna Bryant, *The Salzburg Connection,* Twentieth Century-Fox, 1972; Julie, *Vivre ensemble,* Societe Nouvelle de Cinema/Imperia, 1973; Elena, *Pane e cioccolata* (also known as *Bread and Chocolate*), 1973, released in the United States by CIC/World Northal, 1978; Louise, *L'Assassin musicien* (also known as *The Musician Killer*), Sunchild, 1975; Clara, *Les Oeufs brouilles* (also known as *The Scrambled Eggs*), Columbia-Warner Distributors, 1975; Columbine, *Also es war so. . . .* (also known as *Willie and the Chinese Cat* and *Willie Eine Zauberposse*), New International Cinema, 1976; Irene, *Chinesisches roulette* (also known as *Chinese Roulette*), Cinegate/Films Moliere/New Yorker, 1977; Nathalie, *Chaussette surprise* (also known as *Surprise Sock*), GEF/CCFC/Albatros Films, 1978; mother, *Historien om en moder* (also known as *The Story of a Mother*), Statens Filmcentral, 1979.

Berthe Granjeux, *Ave Maria,* AAA, 1984, released in the United States by Greenwich, 1984; Jim's mother, *L'Ile au tresor* (also known as *Treasure Island*), Films du Passage/Cannon Releasing, 1985; Lola, *Cayenne-Palace,* Metropolis/Union Generale Cimematographique, 1987; Myrrha, *L'Ete dernier a Tanger* (also known as *Last Summer in Tangiers*), AAA, 1987; Catherine, *L'Oeuvre au noir* (also known as *The Abyss*), Union Generale Cinematographique/Twentieth Century-Fox/Philippe Dussart Productions, 1988. Also *Presentation ou Charlotte et son steak* (short film), filmed in 1953, Karina's voice dubbed onto soundtrack in 1961; *Ce soir ou jamais,* 1961; *Le Soleil dans l'oeil,* 1961; *Les Fiances du Pont Macdonald* (short film), 1961; *Le Joli Mai,* 1962; *Un Mari a prix fixe,* 1963; *Petit jour* (short film), 1964; *Le Voleur du Tibidabo* (also known as *La vida es magnifica*), 1964; *Le Soldatess,* 1965; *Zarliche Haie* (also known as *Tendres requins*), 1966; *Lamiel,* 1967; *Michael Kohlhaas—Der Rebell,* 1969; *Le Temps de mourir,* 1969; *L'Invenzione di moral* (also known as *Moral's Invention*), Mount Street Film/Alga Cinematografica, 1974; as Anna, *Just Like at Home,* 1979; in *L'Ami de Vincent* (also known as *A Friend of Vincent*), AMLF/World Marketing, 1983; *Derniere chansons* (also know as *Last Song*), La Cecilia, 1986, released in the United States by MBO/Metropolis, 1987.

PRINCIPAL FILM WORK—Director, *Vivre ensemble,* Societe Nouvelle de Cinema/Imperia, 1973.

PRINCIPAL TELEVISION APPEARANCES—Movies: *Anna,* 1965.

RELATED CAREER—Photographer's model; founder, Raska (a production company), 1972.

WRITINGS: FILM—*Vivre ensemble,* Societe Nouvelle de Cinema/Imperia, 1973; (with Denis Berry) *Derniere chansons* (also known as *Last Song*), La Cecilia, 1986, released in the United States by MBO/Metropolis, 1987. OTHER—*Golden City,* 1983.

AWARDS: Best Actress Award from the Berlin Film Festival, 1961, for *A Woman Is a Woman.*

ADDRESSES: AGENT—78 Boulevard Malesherbes, 75008 Paris, France.*

KAUFMAN, Victor A.   1943-

PERSONAL: Born June 21, 1943, in New York, NY. EDUCATION—Graduated from Queens College; New York University School of Law, J.D., 1967.

VOCATION: Film executive and attorney.

CAREER: PRINCIPAL FILM WORK—Assistant general counsel, Columbia Pictures Industries Inc., 1974, then deputy general counsel and corporate secretary, 1975, general counsel, 1976-81, vice-president, 1976-79, senior vice-president, 1979-81, and executive vice-president, 1981-83; vice-chairman, Columbia Pictures, 1981-83; chairman and chief executive officer, Tri-Star Pictures Inc., 1983-87; president and chief executive officer, Columbia Pictures Entertainment Inc., 1987—.

RELATED CAREER—Teacher of criminal law, University of California, Los Angeles, School of Law; attorney, Simpson, Thacher, and Bartlett, New York City.

ADDRESSES: OFFICE—Columbia Pictures Entertainment Inc., 711 Fifth Avenue, New York, NY 10022.

*   *   *

KECK, Michael   1946-

PERSONAL: Born December 17, 1946, in Raleigh, NC; son of Dementrious Hiawatha (a university administrator) and Thelma Inez (in public relations; maiden name, Mitchell) Keck; married Rebecca Boyd, April 26, 1966 (divorced, 1976); children: Shannon Michele. EDUCATION—St. Augustine's College, B.S., 1969; also studied at the Virginia State Music Institute, Callanwolde Fine Arts Center, and attended workshops with Eric Morris, Sylvia Mays, Steven Kent, and Joseph Chaikin.

VOCATION: Actor, sound director, and composer.

CAREER: OFF-BROADWAY DEBUT—*Hollywood Scheherazade,* 45th Street Theatre, 1989, for twenty performances. PRINCIPAL STAGE APPEARANCES—Spider Evans, *Wasted,* Seven Stages Theatre, Atlanta, GA, 1984; detective, *Tales from Edgar Allan Poe,* Atlanta Children's Theatre, Alliance Theatre Company, Atlanta, 1986; Avery Arable and Zuckerman, *Charlotte's Web,* Atlanta Children's Theatre, Alliance Theatre Company, 1987; Jodie Montgomery, *Ain't No Use in Going Home, Jodie's Got Your Gal and Gone,* Oakland Ensemble Theatre, Oakland, CA, 1989. Also appeared as Jake, *The Threepenny Opera,* Nelson, *Rising Upon the Land,* Crow, *The Tooth of Crime,* title role, *Sizwe Banzi Is Dead,* Spurlock, *Earthling,* Tonio, Victor, and Camilo, *Dreams Against the State,* Jingo, *Burning Bridges and the Troll,* and Tofie, *Kanna He Is Coming Home,* all Seven Stages Theatre; Lee Cocker, *To Gleem It Around to Show My Shine,* Alliance Theatre Company; street musician, *A Christmas Carol,* Academy Theatre, Atlanta; priest, *Roshomon* and Charlie, *Split Second,* both Theatrical Outfit, Atlanta; title role, *Puss in Boots,* Center for Puppetry Arts, Atlanta; title role, *Johnny Rucker,* Intown Theatre; Tom Robinson, *To Kill a Mockingbird,* Avalon Theatre; Magnolia, *Splendora;* narrator and local lad, *Tommy: The Rock Opera.*

MICHAEL KECK

PRINCIPAL STAGE WORK—Sound designer: *The Blacks: A Clown Show*, Seven Stages Theatre, Atlanta, GA, 1981; *Wasted*, Seven Stages Theatre, 1984; *Tales from Edgar Allan Poe*, Atlanta Children's Theatre, Alliance Theatre Company, Atlanta, 1986; *Charlotte's Web*, Atlanta Children's Theatre, Alliance Theatre Company, 1987; *Hollywood Scheherazade*, 45th Street Theatre, New York City, 1989; *Ain't No Use in Going Home, Jodie's Got Your Gal and Gone*, Oakland Ensemble Theatre, Oakland, CA, 1989; also *Burning Bridges and the Troll, Southern Comfort, Kanna He Is Coming Home, Dreams Against the State, Sizwe Banzi Is Dead, Bang Bang Uber Alles, The Tooth of Crime*, and *Black Cat Bones*, all Seven Stages Theatre; *A Christmas Carol, People of the Brick, Cyparis*, and *The Keepers*, all Academy Theatre, Atlanta; *Laundry and Bourbon, Lone Star, Fool for Love, Othello, The Hobbit, Return to Middle Earth, Lysistrata, Terra Nova, The Actor's Nightmare, Sister Mary Ignatius Explains It All for You*, and *Roshomon*, all Theatrical Outfit, Atlanta; *The Rainmaker*, On Stage Atlanta, Atlanta; *Prior Engagements, Two Masters, The Changeling, Pericles, The House of Bernada Alba*, and *Moby Dick Rehearsed*, all Theatre Emory, Atlanta; *Henry V* and *As You Like It*, both Callanwolde Fine Arts Center, Atlanta; *Gardinia, Homesteaders*, and *Waiting for the Parade*, all Horizon Theatre, Atlanta; *A Doll's House*, Alliance Theatre Company, Atlanta; *Puss In Boots*, Center for Puppetry Arts, Atlanta; *Mr. Universe*, Henry Street Settlement Theatre, New York City; *Flowers for Algernon* and *To Kill a Mockingbird*, both Avalon Theatre; *King Lear, The Taming of the Shrew*, and *A Winter's Tale*, all Georgia Shakespeare Festival; *Macbeth*, Performace Gallery; *The Andersonville Trial*, Theatre in the Square; *Sluts*, Southern Theatre Conspiracy; *Freedom for the City*, Theatre Gale; *Splendora; Tommy: The Rock Opera; Out of Florida; Sea Scape; Bananaland; Rhodes Hall (Haunted House); You Can't Judge a Book;* and for the dance pieces *Earth, Sea, and Sky*, Room to Move; *Seven Exits*, Solo to Solo with June Schneider; *Cycles* and *Plants*, both Dance South; and *Rainforest* and *Modern Art*, both Carl Ratcliff Dance Theatre.

RELATED CAREER—Appeared on tour of U.S. and Canadian cities with the Who, 1976; music instructor, theatre department, Emory University, 1983-89; artist in residence, Cornell University, department of theatre arts, 1988; actor in commercials and industrial films.

WRITINGS: STAGE—Composer: *The Blacks: A Clown Show*, Seven Stages Theatre, Atlanta, GA, 1981; *Wasted*, Seven Stages Theatre, 1984; *Tales from Edgar Allan Poe*, Atlanta Children's Theatre, Alliance Theatre Company, Atlanta, 1986; *Charlotte's Web*, Atlanta Children's Theatre, Alliance Theatre Company, 1987; *Hollywood Scheherazade*, 45th Street Theatre, New York City, 1989; *Ain't No Use in Going Home, Jodie's Got Your Gal and Gone*, Oakland Ensemble Theatre, Oakland, CA, 1989; also *Burning Bridges and the Troll, Southern Comfort, Kanna He Is Coming Home, Dreams Against the State, Sizwe Banzi Is Dead, Bang Bang Uber Alles, The Tooth of Crime*, and *Black Cat Bones*, all Seven Stages Theatre; *A Christmas Carol, People of the Brick, Cyparis*, and *The Keepers*, all Academy Theatre, Atlanta; *Laundry and Bourbon, Lone Star, Fool for Love, Othello, The Hobbit, Return to Middle Earth, Lysistrata, Terra Nova, The Actor's Nightmare, Sister Mary Ignatius Explains It All for You*, and *Roshomon*, all Theatrical Outfit, Atlanta; *The Rainmaker*, On Stage Atlanta, Atlanta; *Prior Engagements, Two Masters, The Changeling, Pericles, The House of Bernada Alba*, and *Moby Dick Rehearsed*, all Theatre Emory, Atlanta; *Henry V* and *As You Like It*, both Callanwolde Fine Arts Center, Atlanta; *Gardinia, Homesteaders*, and *Waiting for the Parade*, all Horizon Theatre, Atlanta; *A Doll's House*, Alliance Theatre Company, Atlanta; *Puss In Boots*, Center for Puppetry Arts, Atlanta; *Mr. Universe*, Henry Street Settlement Theatre, New York City; *Flowers for Algernon* and *To Kill a Mockingbird*, both Avalon Theatre; *King Lear, The Taming of the Shrew*, and *A Winter's Tale*, all Georgia Shakespeare Festival; *Macbeth*, Performace Gallery; *The Andersonville Trial*, Theatre in the Square; *Sluts*, Southern Theatre Conspiracy; *Freedom for the City*, Theatre Gale; *Splendora; Tommy: The Rock Opera; Out of Florida; Sea Scape; Bananaland; Rhodes Hall (Haunted House); You Can't Judge a Book;* and for the dance pieces *Earth, Sea, and Sky*, Room to Move; *Seven Exits*, Solo to Solo with June Schneider; *Cycles* and *Plants*, both Dance South; and *Rainforest* and *Modern Art*, both Carl Ratcliff Dance Theatre.

AWARDS: B.A.C. grants for music, 1984, 1986, and 1987; Atlanta Mayor's fellowship, 1985; C.A.C. grant from the Ford Foundation, 1986; Georgia Arts Council grants, 1986, 1987, and 1988.

MEMBER: Actors' Equity Association, American Federation of Radio and Television Artists, American Society of Composers, Authors, and Publishers.

SIDELIGHTS: RECREATIONS—Jogging, reading, roller skating, and travel.

ADDRESSES: AGENT—Theresa Holden, Western and Southern Arts Management, P.O. Box 50120, Austin, TX 78763.

KELLEY, DeForest   1920-

PERSONAL: Born January 20, 1920, in Atlanta, GA.

VOCATION: Actor.

CAREER: PRINCIPAL FILM APPEARANCES—Vince Grayson, *Fear in the Night,* Paramount, 1947; Bob Kirby, *Variety Girl,* Paramount, 1947; Smalley, *Canon City,* Eagle-Lion, 1948; Ace Martin, *Duke of Chicago,* Republic, 1949; Lieutenant Glenson, *Malaya* (also known as *East of the Rising Sun*), Metro-Goldwyn-Mayer (MGM), 1950; Fred, *Taxi,* Twentieth Century-Fox, 1953; Charlie, *House of Bamboo,* Twentieth Century-Fox, 1955; Edward Clary, *Illegal,* Warner Brothers, 1955; hotel clerk, *The View from Pompey's Head* (also known as *Secret Interlude*), Twentieth Century-Fox, 1955; medic, *The Man in the Grey Flannel Suit,* Twentieth Century-Fox, 1956; Breck, *Tension at Table Rock,* RKO, 1956; Morgan Earp, *Gunfight at the O.K. Corral,* Paramount, 1957; Southern officer, *Raintree County,* MGM, 1957; Wexler, *The Law and Jake Wade,* MGM, 1958; Curley Burne, *Warlock,* Twentieth Century-Fox, 1959; Troop, *Gunfight at Comanche Creek,* Allied Artists, 1964; Sam Corwin, *Where Love Has Gone,* Paramount, 1964; first sheriff, *Black Spurs,* Paramount, 1965; Mr. Turner, *Marriage on the Rocks,* Warner Brothers, 1965; Guy Tavenner, *Town Tamer,* Paramount, 1965; Toby Jack Saunders, *Apache Uprising,* Paramount, 1966; Bill Rile, *Waco,* Paramount, 1966; Dr. Elgin Clark, *Night of the Lepus,* MGM, 1972; Dr. Leonard "Bones" McCoy, *Star Trek: The Motion Picture,* Paramount, 1979; Dr. Leonard "Bones" McCoy, *Star Trek II: The Wrath of Khan,* Paramount, 1982; Dr. Leonard "Bones" McCoy, *Star Trek III: The Search for Spock,* Paramount, 1984; Dr. Leonard "Bones" McCoy, *Star Trek IV: The Voyage Home,* Paramount, 1986; Dr. Leonard "Bones" McCoy, *Star Trek V: The Final Frontier,* Paramount, 1989. Also appeared in *The Men* (also known as *Battle Stripe*), United Artists, 1950.

PRINCIPAL TELEVISION APPEARANCES—Series: Dr. Leonard "Bones" McCoy, *Star Trek,* NBC, 1966-69; voice of Dr. Leonard "Bones" McCoy, *Star Trek* (animated), NBC, 1973. Pilots: Jake Brittin, *333 Montgomery,* NBC, 1960; lab chief, *Police Story,* NBC, 1967; Dr. Goldstone, "I Never Said Goodbye," *ABC's Matinee Today,* ABC, 1973; Dr. Leonard "Bones" McCoy, "Encounter at Far Point," *Star Trek: The Next Generation,* syndicated, 1987; also *Johnny Risk,* NBC, 1958; *The Cowboys,* ABC, 1974. Episodic: Ike Clanton, "Gunfight at the O.K. Corral," *You Are There,* CBS; *Gunsmoke,* CBS; *Rawhide,* CBS; *Death Valley Days,* syndicated; *Dick Powell's Zane Grey Theatre,* CBS; *Bonanza,* NBC; *The Virginian,* NBC; *Silent Service,* syndicated; *Navy Log.*

ADDRESSES: AGENTS—Contemporary Artists, 132 Lasky Drive, Beverly Hills, CA 90212; Camden Artists, 2121 Avenue of the Stars, Suite 410, Los Angeles, CA 90067.*

*   *   *

KEMP, Elizabeth   1957-

PERSONAL: Born November 5, 1957, in Key West, FL; daughter of Joseph Clifton (a captain in the U.S. Navy and a business executive) and Nancy Jean (Haycock) Kemp; married Michael Margotta (an actor), January 21, 1983. EDUCATION—Attended the Art Students League of New York and the American Academy of Dramatic Arts.

ELIZABETH KEMP

VOCATION: Actress.

CAREER: STAGE DEBUT—Gabby, *The Petrified Forest,* Center Stage, Baltimore, MD, 1973. OFF-BROADWAY DEBUT—Susan, *Heat,* New York Shakespeare Festival, Public Theatre, 1974. PRINCIPAL STAGE APPEARANCES—Girl, *Lunch Hour* and Cousin, *Playing with Fire,* both Counterpoint Theatre Company, New York City, 1977; maid, woman, and script girl, *Once in a Lifetime,* Circle in the Square, New York City, 1978; Maureen Vega, *North Shore Fish,* WPA Theatre, New York City, 1987. Also appeared in *The Best Little Whorehouse in Texas,* Actors' Studio, New York City, 1977; *Bright,* New Dramatists Inc., New York City, 1977; *Tiger Tail,* Alliance Theatre Company, Atlanta, GA, 1978; *Mackerel,* Folger Theatre Group, Washington, DC, 1978; *Bus Stop, Playing with Fire, Holiday,* and *Twelfth Night,* all California Actors Theatre, Los Gatos, CA, 1978-79.

FILM DEBUT—Nancy, *He Knows You're Alone,* Metro-Goldwyn-Mayer/United Artists, 1980. PRINCIPAL FILM APPEARANCES—Virna Nightbourne, *The Killing Hour* (also known as *The Clairvoyant*), Twentieth Century-Fox, 1981; Nancy, *Sticky Fingers,* Spectrafilm, 1988; also Nancy, *Eating,* Jagfilm.

PRINCIPAL TELEVISION APPEARANCES—Series: Betsy, *Love of Life,* CBS, 1973-77. Episodic: *Police Story,* NBC; *Vietnam War Story,* HBO. Movies: Kay, *Family of Spies,* CBS, 1990.

RELATED CAREER—Member, Actors' Studio.

ADDRESSES: AGENT—Bill Treusch, 853 Seventh Avenue, Suite 9-A, New York, NY 10019.

JEREMY KEMP

KEMP, Jeremy 1935-

PERSONAL: Born Jeremy Walker, February 3, 1935, near Chesterfield, England; son of Edmund Reginald (an engineer) and Elsa May (Kemp) Walker. EDUCATION—Studied acting at the Central School of Speech and Drama, London, 1955-58. MILITARY—British Army, Gordon Highlanders.

VOCATION: Actor.

CAREER: STAGE DEBUT—Landlord, *Misery Me,* Arts Theatre, Felixstowe, U.K., 1957. LONDON DEBUT—Orator, *The Chairs,* Royal Court Theatre, 1958. PRINCIPAL STAGE APPEARANCES—Malcolm, *Macbeth,* Old Vic Theatre, London, 1958; Sergeant Lugg, *The Magistrate* and Oliver, *As You Like It,* both Old Vic Theatre, 1959; Frank Broadbent, *Celebration,* Nottingham Playhouse, Nottingham, U.K., 1960, then Duchess Theatre, London, 1961; Hector Barlow, *Afternoon Men,* Arts Theatre, London, 1963; the Major, *Incident at Vichy,* Phoenix Theatre, London, 1966; Richard Howarth, *Spoiled,* Haymarket Theatre, London, 1971; Aston, *The Caretaker,* Mermaid Theatre, London, 1972; Buckingham, *Richard III,* Olivier Theatre, London, 1979.

PRINCIPAL FILM APPEARANCES—Vince Howard, *Face of a Stranger,* Allied Artists, 1964; Drake, *Dr. Terror's House of Horrors,* Regal Films, 1965; Phil Bradley, *Operation Crossbow* (also known as *Operazione Crossbow, The Great Spy Mission,* and *Codename: Operation Crossbow*), Metro-Goldwyn-Mayer, 1965; Willi Von Klugermann, *The Blue Max,* Twentieth Century-Fox, 1966; senior British officer, *Cast a Giant Shadow,* United Artists,

1966; Hall, *Assignment K,* Columbia, 1968; Detective Sergeant Pierce, *The Strange Affair,* Paramount, 1968; Harry Riker, *A Twist of Sand,* United Artists, 1968; Galleria, *Eyewitness* (also known as *Sudden Terror*), National General, 1970; Kurt Von Ruger, *Darling Lili,* Paramount, 1970; Jim Harcourt, *The Games,* Twentieth Century-Fox, 1970; Joan's father, *Pope Joan* (also known as *The Devil's Imposter*), Columbia, 1972; Grabinski, *The Blockhouse,* Hemdale, 1974; Kendrick, *The Belstone Fox,* Rank/Twentieth Century-Fox, 1976; Baron Von Leinsdorf, *The Seven-Per-Cent Solution,* Universal, 1977; RAF briefing officer, *A Bridge Too Far,* United Artists, 1977; Dr. Smythe, *Caravans,* Universal/Ibex, 1978; Duke Michael, *The Prisoner of Zenda,* Universal, 1979; Frank, *Return of the Soldier,* Twentieth Century-Fox, 1983; Ferryman, *Uncommon Valor,* Paramount, 1983; General Streck, *Top Secret!,* Paramount, 1984; Mr. Wellbeloved, *When the Whales Came,* Twentieth Century-Fox, 1989. Also appeared in *Jamaican Gold,* 1971; *The Salzburg Connection,* Twentieth Century-Fox, 1972; *East of Elephant Rock,* Kendon, 1976; *Leopard in the Snow,* New World, 1979.

PRINCIPAL TELEVISION APPEARANCES—Series: *Z Cars* and *Colditz,* both British television. Mini-Series: Brigadier General Armin Von Roon, *The Winds of War,* ABC, 1983; General Horatio Gates, *George Washington,* CBS, 1984; General Patrick Gordon, *Peter the Great,* NBC, 1986; Brigadier General Armin Von Roon, *War and Remembrance,* ABC, 1989; also *Summer's Lease,* BBC-2. Pilots: Kleist, *Keefer,* ABC, 1978. Episodic: Minister Melnikov, *Murder, She Wrote,* CBS, 1989; also *Space 1999,* syndicated, 1976. Movies: Geoffrey Moore, *The Rhinemann Exchange,* NBC, 1977; German official, *Evita Peron,* NBC, 1981; Baron Hunyadi, *Phantom of the Opera,* CBS, 1983; Thompson, *Sadat,* syndicated, 1983. Specials: Duke of Norfolk, *Henry VIII;* Warwick, *Saint Joan;* Leontes, *The Winter's Tale;* also *King Lear.* Also appeared in *The Lovers of Florence, Brassneck, Lisa, Goodbye, Unity, The Contract, Sherlock Holmes, Slip-Up,* and *The Last Reunion.*

MEMBER: British Actors' Equity Association (council member for six years), Lords Taverners, Stage Golfing Society, Sparks.

SIDELIGHTS: RECREATIONS—"As much sport as my age will allow: skiing, cricket, tennis, swimming, hiking, etc."

ADDRESSES: AGENT—Marina Martin, 6-A Danbury Street, London NW 8JU, England.

*   *   *

KENNEDY, Mimi 1948-

PERSONAL: Born September 25, 1948, in Rochester, NY; daughter of Daniel Gerald and Nancy Helen (Colgan) Kennedy; married Lawrence Edwin Dilg, May 27, 1978; children: John Francisco, Mary Jacinta. EDUCATION—Graduated from Smith College, 1970.

VOCATION: Actress.

CAREER: BROADWAY DEBUT—Jan, *Grease,* Broadhurst Theatre, 1975. OFF-BROADWAY DEBUT—Anne Bonney, *Hot Grog,* Marymount Manhattan Theatre, 1977. PRINCIPAL STAGE APPEARANCES—Marilyn, *Grownups,* Center Theatre Group, Mark Taper Forum, Los Angeles, 1982; also appeared in *Last of the Red Hot Lovers,* 1972.

PRINCIPAL FILM APPEARANCES—Sally, *Chances Are,* Tri-Star, 1989; Eli's mom, *Immediate Family,* Columbia, 1989.

PRINCIPAL TELEVISION APPEARANCES—Series: Regular, *Three Girls Three,* NBC, 1977; Victoria Chasen, *Stockard Channing in Just Friends,* CBS, 1979; regular, *The Big Show,* NBC, 1980; Nan Gallagher, *The Two of Us,* CBS, 1981-82; Doris Winger, *Spencer* (also known as *Under One Roof*), NBC, 1984-85; Andrea Tobin, *Family Man,* ABC, 1988. Mini-Series: Pat Kennedy, *Robert Kennedy and His Times,* CBS, 1985. Episodic: Kristi Carruthers, "Aqua Vita," *The Twilight Zone,* CBS, 1986; Mrs. Parker, "Davy Crockett," *Shelley Duvall's Tall Tales and Legends,* Showtime, 1987; Miss Wagner, *Homeroom,* ABC, 1989; also "Popular Neurotics," *American Playhouse,* PBS, 1984; "The Man Who Was Death," *Tales from the Crypt,* HBO, 1989. Movies: Jenny, *Getting Married,* CBS, 1978; Arlene Gilbert, *Thin Ice,* CBS, 1981; Eloise Davis, *Bride of Boogedy,* ABC, 1987; Jane, *Baby Girl Scott,* CBS, 1987. Specials: *Battle of the Network Stars,* ABC, 1981; *I've Had It Up to Here,* NBC, 1981; Eloise Davis, *Mr. Boogedy,* ABC, 1986; voice of Mrs. Gridley, "The Mouse and the Motorcycle" (animated), *ABC Weekend Specials,* ABC, 1986.

WRITINGS: STAGE—(Contributor) *Hard Sell,* New York Shakespeare Festival, Public Theatre, New York City, 1980.

ADDRESSES: AGENT—Triad Artists, 10100 Santa Monica Boulevard, Los Angeles, CA 90067.*

*   *   *

KERNS, Joanna   1953-
(Joanna de Varona)

PERSONAL: Born Joanna de Varona, February 12, 1955, in San Francisco, CA; married Richard Kerns (a producer and director; divorced, 1985); children: Ashley.

VOCATION: Actress.

CAREER: PRINCIPAL STAGE APPEARANCES—(As Joanna de Varona) Zoe, blushing bride, nymph, pygmy, and Yew, *Ulysses in Nigthtown,* Winter Garden Theatre, New York City, 1974. PRINCIPAL STAGE WORK—Director, *What Every Woman Knows,* West Coast Ensemble Theatre, Los Angeles, 1989.

MAJOR TOURS—(As Joanna de Varona) *Two Gentlemen of Verona,* New York Shakespeare Festival, U.S. and Canadian cities, 1973.

PRINCIPAL FILM APPEARANCES—Diana, *Coma,* United Artists, 1978; Nancy, *Cross My Heart,* Universal, 1987; Katharine Watson, *Street Justice,* Lorimar, 1989.

PRINCIPAL TELEVISION APPEARANCES—Series: Pat Devon, *The Four Seasons,* CBS, 1984; Maggie Seaver, *Growing Pains,* ABC, 1985—. Mini-Series: Maria Marshall, *Blind Faith,* NBC, 1990. Pilots: Paula Saletta, *The Return of Marcus Welby, M.D.,* ABC, 1984. Episodic: Cheryl Blaste, *Hooperman,* ABC, 1988; also *Hill Street Blues,* NBC; *Laverne and Shirley,* ABC; *The Associates,* ABC. Movies: Meg, *Marriage Is Alive and Well,* NBC, 1980; Doris Marshall, *Mother's Day on Walton's Mountain,* NBC, 1982; Doris Marshall, *A Wedding on Walton's Mountain,* NBC, 1982; Doris Marshall, *A Day of Thanks on Walton's Mountain,* NBC, 1982; Andrea, *A Bunny's Tale,* ABC, 1985; Anita Parrish, *The Rape of*

Richard Beck, ABC, 1985; Lana Singer, *Stormin' Home,* CBS, 1985; Stephanie Blume, *Mistress,* CBS, 1987; Diane Pappas, *Those She Left Behind,* NBC, 1989; also *V,* NBC, 1983. Specials: *Are You a Missing Heir?,* ABC, 1978; *Lifetime Salutes Mom,* Lifetime, 1987; *The Regis Philbin Show,* Lifetime, 1987; *The National Love and Sex Test,* ABC, 1988; *Second Annual Star-Spangled Celebration,* ABC, 1988; *Like Mother, Like Daughter,* Lifetime, 1988; host, *Sea World's Miracle Babies and Friends,* ABC, 1989.

RELATED CAREER—Actress in television commercials.

NON-RELATED CAREER—Gymnast.

WRITINGS: TELEVISION—Episodic: "Guess Who's Coming to Dinner," *Growing Pains,* ABC, 1989.

ADDRESSES: AGENT—John Kimble, Triad Artists, 10100 Santa Monica Boulevard, 16th Floor, Los Angeles, CA 90067.

*   *   *

KERWIN, Brian   1949-

PERSONAL: Born October 25, 1949, in Chicago, IL. EDUCATION—Attended the University of Southern California.

VOCATION: Actor.

CAREER: OFF-BROADWAY DEBUT—*Emily,* Manhattan Theatre Club, 1988. PRINCIPAL STAGE APPEARANCES—Title role, *The Incredibly Famous Willy Rivers,* Old Globe Theatre, San Diego, CA, 1986; also appeared in *Strange Snow,* Coast Playhouse, Los Angeles, 1986.

MAJOR TOURS—Ed, *Torch Song Trilogy,* U.S. cities, 1983.

PRINCIPAL FILM APPEARANCES—T.J. Swackhammer, *Hometown, U.S.A.,* Film Ventures International, 1979; Bobby Jack Moriarty, *Murphy's Romance,* Columbia, 1985; George, *Nickel Mountain,* Ziv International, 1985; Hank Mitchell, *King Kong Lives,* De Laurentiis Entertainment, 1986; Ed, *Torch Song Trilogy,* New Line Cinema, 1988; also appeared in *Getting Wasted,* 1980; and *Soft Explosion.*

PRINCIPAL TELEVISION APPEARANCES—Series: Greg "Snapper" Foster, *The Young and the Restless,* CBS, 1976-77; Deputy Birdwell "Birdie" Hawkins, *The Misadventures of Sheriff Lobo* (also known as *The B.J./Lobo Show*), NBC, 1979-80; Deputy Birdwell "Birdie" Hawkins, *Lobo,* NBC, 1980-81. Mini-Series: Gideon Chisholm, *The Chisholms,* CBS, 1979; Malachy Hale, *The Blue and the Gray,* CBS, 1982; Dancy Cutler, *Bluegrass,* CBS, 1988. Pilots: Albie McRae, *The Busters,* CBS, 1978; Bruce Douglas, *The Paradise Connection,* CBS, 1979; Willie James, *The James Boys,* NBC, 1982. Episodic: *The American Girls,* CBS, 1978; Terence O'Casey, *St. Elsewhere,* NBC, 1986; also Birdwell "Birdie" Hawkins, *B.J. and the Bear,* NBC. Movies: Til Johnson, *A Real American Hero,* CBS, 1978; Jack Vanda, *Power,* NBC, 1980; Michael Carrington, *Miss All-American Beauty,* CBS, 1982; Nick Todd, *Intimate Agony,* ABC, 1983; Keating, *Wet Gold,* ABC, 1984; also *The Greatest Thing That Almost Happened,* CBS, 1977. Specials: *Battle of the Network Stars,* ABC, 1980 and 1981; Hal

Graham, "Tales from the Hollywood Hills: Natica Jackson," *Great Performances*, PBS, 1987.

AWARDS: Los Angeles Drama Critics' Circle Award nomination, Best Lead Performance, 1987, for *Strange Snow;* Theatre World Award, 1988, for *Emily.*

ADDRESSES: AGENT—The Lantz Office, 9255 Sunset Boulevard, Suite 505, Los Angeles, CA 90069.*

*   *   *

KING, Stephen   1947-
(Richard Bachman)

PERSONAL: Full name, Stephen Edwin King; born September 21, 1947, in Portland, ME; son of Donald (a sailor) and Nellie Ruth (Pillsbury) King; married Tabitha Jane Spruce (a writer), January 2, 1971; children: Naomi Rachel, Joseph Hillstrom, Owen Phllllp. EDUCATION—University of Maine, B.S., 1970.

VOCATION: Writer.

CAREER: Also see *WRITINGS* below. PRINCIPAL FILM APPEARANCES—Jordy, *Creepshow,* Warner Brothers, 1982; truck driver, *Creepshow 2,* New World, 1987; priest, *Pet Sematary,* Paramount, 1989, also appeared in *Knightriders,* United Film Distribution, 1981; *Maximum Overdrive,* Dino De Laurentiis Entertainment, 1986.

PRINCIPAL FILM WORK—Director, *Maximum Overdrive,* Dino De Laurentiis Entertainment, 1986; creative consultant, *A Return to Salem's Lot,* Warner Brothers, 1987.

RELATED CAREER—Writer in residence, University of Maine, Orono, 1978-79.

NON-RELATED CAREER—High school English teacher, Hampden Academy, Hampden, ME, 1971-73; also worked as a janitor, mill worker, and laundry worker.

WRITINGS: FILM—*Creepshow,* Warner Brothers, 1982; *Cat's Eye,* Metro-Goldwyn-Mayer/United Artists, 1985; *Stephen King's Silver Bullet,* Paramount, 1985; *Maximum Overdrive,* Dino De Laurentiis Entertainment, 1986; *Pet Sematary,* Paramount, 1989.

OTHER—All novels, unless indicated. *Carrie,* Doubleday, 1974; *Salem's Lot,* Doubleday, 1975; *The Shining,* Doubleday, 1977; (as Richard Bachman) *Rage,* New American Library, 1977, also published in *The Bachman Books: Four Early Novels,* New American Library, 1985; *Night Shift* (short stories), Doubleday, 1978; *The Stand,* Doubleday, 1978; *The Dead Zone,* Viking, 1979; (as Bachman) *The Long Walk,* New American Library, 1979, also published in *The Bachman Books,* 1985; *Firestarter,* Viking, 1980; (as Bachman) *Roadwork,* New American Library, 1981, also published in *The Bachman Books,* 1985; *Danse Macabre* (nonfiction), Everest, 1981; *Cujo,* Viking, 1981; (as Bachman) *The Running Man,* New American Library, 1982, also published in *The Bachman Books,* 1985; *Different Seasons* (novellas), Viking, 1982; *Creepshow* (graphic novel), New American Library, 1982; *Christine,* Viking, 1983; *Pet Sematary,* Doubleday, 1983; (with Peter Straub) *The Talisman,* Viking, 1984; (as Bachman) *Thinner,* New American Library, 1985; *Cycle of the Werewolf,* New American

Library, 1985; *Skeleton Crew,* Putnam, 1985; *Silver Bullet,* New American Library, 1985; *Maximum Overdrive,* New American Library, 1986; *It,* Viking, 1986; *The Eyes of the Dragon,* Viking, 1987; *Misery,* Viking, 1987; *The Tommyknockers,* Putnam, 1987; *The Dark Tower: The Gunslinger,* New American Library, 1988; *Nightmares in the Sky,* Viking, 1988; *The Dark Tower: The Drawing of the Three,* New American Library, 1989; *The Dark Half,* Viking, 1989.

MEMBER: Authors Guild, Screen Writers of America, Writers Guild of America, Screen Actors Guild.

SIDELIGHTS: In addition to the films noted above for which Stephen King has written the screenplay, his novels and short stories have been adapted to such other projects as *Carrie,* United Artists, 1976; *The Shining,* Warner Brothers, 1980; *The Dead Zone,* Paramount, 1983; *Cujo,* Warner Brothers, 1983; *Christine,* Columbia, 1983; *Firestarter,* Universal, 1984; *Children of the Corn,* New World, 1984; *Stand By Me,* Columbia, 1986; the made for television movie *Salem's Lot,* CBS, 1979; and the stage musical *Carrie,* produced by the Royal Shakespeare Company in 1988.

ADDRESSES: HOME—Bangor, ME.*

*   *   *

KING, Woodie, Jr.   1937-

PERSONAL: Born July 27, 1937, in Mobile, AL; son of Woodie and Ruby (Johnson) King; married Willie Mae Washington (a teacher); children: Michelle, Woodie Geoffrey, Michael. EDUCATION—Graduated from the Will-o-Way School of Theatre, 1962; graduate work in theatre at Wayne State University; also attended the Detroit School of Arts and Crafts.

VOCATION: Producer, director, writer, and actor.

CAREER: STAGE DEBUT—*Green Grow the Lilacs,* Time Community Playhouse, Detroit, MI, 1957, for twenty five performances. OFF-BROADWAY DEBUT—White, *A Study in Color,* St. Mark's Playhouse, 1964, for sixteen performances. BROADWAY DEBUT—Young Negro, *The Great White Hope,* Alvin Theatre, New York City, 1968-69. PRINCIPAL STAGE APPEARANCES—Sulk, *The Displaced Person,* American Place Theatre, St. Clement's Church Theatre, New York City, 1966-67; Ed, *The Perfect Party,* Tambellini's Gate Theatre, New York City, 1969. Also appeared in "Benito Cereno" in *The Old Glory,* St. Clement's Church Theatre, 1965; *Day of Absence,* St. Mark's Playhouse, New York City, 1966; *Who's Got His Own,* American Place Theatre, New York City, 1966; *Lost in the Stars,* Equity Library Theatre, New York City, 1967.

FIRST LONDON WORK—Director, *I Have a Dream,* University of Sussex, 1989. PRINCIPAL STAGE WORK—Producer, *A Black Quartet,* Tambellini's Gate Theatre, then Frances Adler Theatre, both New York City, 1969; producer, *Slave Ship,* Chelsea Theatre Center, Brooklyn Academy of Music, Brooklyn, NY, 1969-70, then Washington Square Methodist Church, New York City, 1970; producer (with Dick Williams), *In New England Winter,* New Federal Theatre, Henry Street Playhouse, New York City, 1971; producer, *Behold! Cometh the Vanderkellans,* Theatre De Lys, New York City, 1971; producer (with Williams), *Black Girl,* New Federal Theatre, New York City, 1972; producer (with Williams),

WOODIE KING, JR.

A Recent Killing, New Federal Theatre, 1973; producer, *What the Wine-Sellers Buy,* New Federal Theatre, 1973, then (with Joseph Papp) New York Shakespeare Festival (NYSF), Vivian Beaumont Theatre, later (also director) NYSF, Mobile Theatre, both New York City, 1974; producer, *The Prodigal Sister,* Theatre De Lys, 1974.

Producer, *The First Breeze of Summer,* Negro Ensemble Company, St. Mark's Playhouse, then Palace Theatre, both New York City, 1975; producer, *The Taking of Miss Janie,* St. Mark's Playhouse, then (with Papp) NYSF, Mitzi E. Newhouse Theatre, New York City, 1975; producer (with Paul Berkowsky and Lucille Lortel), *Medal of Honor Rag,* Theatre De Lys, 1976; director, *Sizwe Banzi Is Dead,* Pittsburgh Public Theatre, Pittsburgh, PA, 1976; producer, *For Colored Girls Who Have Considered Suicide When the Rainbow Is Enuf,* New Federal Theatre, then (with Papp), NYSF, Public Theatre, New York City, 1976, then Booth Theatre, New York City, 1976-78; director, *Cockfight,* American Place Theatre, New York City, 1977; director, *The First Breeze of Summer,* Center Stage Theatre, Baltimore, MD, 1977; director, *Siwze Banzi Is Dead,* Studio Arena Theatre, Buffalo, NY, 1977; *Daddy,* New Federal Theatre, Henry Street Playhouse, 1977; director, *Sizwe Banzi Is Dead,* Indiana Repertory Theatre, Indianapolis, IN, 1978; director, *A Raisin in the Sun,* GeVa Theatre, Rochester, NY, 1978; producer, *Hot Dishes!, Anna Lucasta, The God of Vengeance,* and *Black Medea,* all New Federal Theatre, Harry DeJur Playhouse, New York City, 1978; producer, *Take a Giant Step* and *In Splendid Error,* both New Federal Theatre, Pilgrim Theatre, New York City, 1978; producer, *Take It from the Top* and *Flamingo Flomongo,* both New Federal Theatre, Harry DeJur Playhouse, 1979; producer, *Trouble in Mind* and *Raisin in the Sun,* both New Federal Theatre, Pilgrim Theatre, 1979.

Executive producer, *Reggae,* Biltmore Theatre, New York City, 1980; producer (with Steve Tennen), *Branches from the Same Tree,* New Federal Theatre, Harry DeJur Playhouse, 1980; producer (with Tennen), *The Trial of Dr. Beck, Louis, Boy and Tarzan Appear in a Clearing, A Day Out of Time,* and *Child of the Sun,* all New Federal Theatre, Harry DeJur Playhouse, 1981; producer (with Tennen), *Things of the Heart: Marian Anderson's Story, The Dance and the Railroad, Widows, No, Steal Away, The Black People's Party,* and *Zora* and *When the Chickens Came Home to Roost* (double-bill), all New Federal Theatre, Louis Abrons Arts for Living Center, New York City, 1981; director, *Appear and Show Cause,* Pittsburgh Public Theatre, 1981; producer (with Tennen), *Dreams Deferred, Keyboard, La Chefa, Paper Angels, Love,* and *Jazz Set,* all New Federal Theatre, Louis Abrons Arts for Living Center, 1982; producer (with Tennen), *Who Loves the Dancer, The World of Ben Caldwell,* and *Portrait of Jennie,* all New Federal Theatre, Harry DeJur Playhouse, 1982; producer, *The Upper Depths,* Wonderhorse Theatre, New York City, 1982; producer (with Tennen), *Adam, Champeeen!, Trio,* and *Basin Street,* all New Federal Theatre, Harry DeJur Playhouse, 1983; producer, *Shades of Brown* and *The Trial of Adam Clayton Powell, Jr.,* both New Federal Theatre, Louis Abrons Arts for Living Center, 1983; director, *Appear and Show Cause,* Cleveland Playhouse, Cleveland, OH, 1983; producer (with others) and director, *Dinah! Queen of the Blues,* Westside Arts Center, Cheryl Crawford Theatre, New York City, 1983-84; producer, *Oh! Oh! Obesity,* New Federal Theatre, 1984.

Producer, *Long Time Since Yesterday,* New Federal Theatre, Harry DeJur Playhouse, 1985; producer, *Nonsectarian Conversations with the Dead,* New Federal Theatre, Experimental Theatre, New York City, 1985; producer and director, *Appear and Show Cause,* New Federal Theatre, Theatre Guinevere, New York City, 1985; producer, *In the House of Blues,* New Federal Theatre, Louis Abrons Arts for Living Center, 1985; director, *Love to All,* American Place Theatre, 1985; director, *Boesman and Lena,* Northlight Theatre, Evanston, IL, 1985; producer and director, *I Have a Dream,* New Federal Theatre, Louis Abrons Arts for Living Center, 1985-86; producer, *December Seventh,* New Federal Theatre, Theatre Guinevere, 1986; producer, *Williams and Walker,* New Federal Theatre, 1986; producer, *Stories About the Old Days, The Sovereign State of Boogedy Boogedy,* and *Time Out of Time,* all New Federal Theatre, Louis Abrons Arts for Living Center, 1986; producer, *Lillian Wald: At Home on Henry Street,* New Federal Theatre, Harry DeJur Playhouse, 1986; director, *Lady Day at Emerson's Bar and Grill,* Alliance Theatre Company, Atlanta, GA, 1986; producer, *Brother Malcolm,* New Heritage Repertory Theatre, New York City, 1986; producer, *Hats* and *Boogie Woogie and Booker,* both New Federal Theatre, Louis Abrons Arts for Living Center, 1987; producer, *The Meeting, From the Mississippi Delta,* and *Trinity,* all New Federal Theatre, Harry DeJur Playhouse, 1987; director, *'night Mother,* Virginia Museum Theatre, Richmond, VA, 1987; director, *Checkmates,* 46th Street Theatre, New York City, 1988; artistic consultant, *Don't Get God Started,* Longacre Theatre, New York City, 1987-88; producer, *After Crystal Night* and *Mr. Universe,* both New Federal Theatre, 1988; director, *Splendid Mummer,* American Place Theatre, 1988; director, *God's Trombones,* Shubert Theatre, Philadelphia, PA, 1988, then Ford's Theatre, Washington, DC, 1989, later Theatre of the Riverside Church, New York City, 1989.

MAJOR TOURS—Producer (with Joseph Papp), *What the Wine-Sellers Buy,* U.S. cities, 1975; producer (with Papp), *For Colored Girls Who Have Considered Suicide When the Rainbow Is Enuf,* U.S. cities, 1978; director, *Love to All,* U.S. cities, 1981; director,

Home, U.S. cities, 1981-86; director, *Appear and Show Cause*, U.S. cities, 1985-86; director, *I Have a Dream*, U.S. cities, 1986; director, *Checkmates*, U.S. cities, 1987-88.

PRINCIPAL FILM APPEARANCES—Jerry, *Together for Days* (also known as *Black Cream*), Olas, 1972; Larry, *Serpico*, Paramount, 1973. PRINCIPAL FILM WORK—Producer (with Herbert Danska) *Right On!* (documentary), Leacock-Pennebaker, 1970; producer (with St. Claire Burne) and director, *The Long Night*, Howard Mahler, 1976; producer and director, *The Black Theatre Movement: "A Raisin in the Sun" to the Present* (documentary), National Black Theatre Touring Circuit, 1978; director, *The Torture of Mothers* (documentary), Woodie King Associates, 1980; director, *Death of a Prophet*, National Black Theatre Touring Circuit, 1982.

PRINCIPAL TELEVISION APPEARANCES—Episodic: *NYPD*, ABC; *As the World Turns*, CBS. PRINCIPAL TELEVISION WORK—Specials: Producer and director, *Women of the Regent Hotel*, CBS, 1988.

RELATED CAREER—Professional model, 1955-68; drama critic, *Detroit Tribune*, 1959-62; co-founder and manager, Concept-East Theatre, Detriot, MI, 1960-63; cultural arts director, Mobilizations for Youth, New York City, 1965-70; arts and humanities consultant, Rockefeller Foundation, 1968-70; founder and director, New Federal Theatre, Henry Street Settlement, New York City, 1970—; lecturer, Yale University, New Haven, CT, 1973-77; founder, National Black Touring Circuit, 1980—; lecturer, Columbia University, New York City, 1984-86; visiting professor, Oberlin College, Oberlin, OH, 1985-86; also instructor, Penn State University, University Park, PA; founder, president, and cultural arts director, Woodie King Associates.

WRITINGS: STAGE—*The Weary Blues*, Lincoln Center Library, New York City, 1966; *Simple's Blues*, Clark Center of Performing Arts, New York City, 1967.

FILM—*Right On!*, Leacock-Pennebaker, 1970; (with Julian Mayfield) *The Long Night*, Howard Mahler, 1976; *The Black Theatre Movement: "A Raisin in the Sun" to the Present* (documentary), National Black Theatre Touring Circuit, 1978; *The Torture of Mothers* (documentary), Woodie King Associates, 1980; *Death of a Prophet* (documentary), National Black Theatre Touring Circuit, 1982; also *The Beast of Harlem, Jet!, Black Dreams, Sunday February 21: The Day Malcolm X Died*, and (with others) *Harlem Transfer*.

TELEVISION—Episodic: *Sanford and Son*, NBC, 1974; *Hot l Baltimore*, ABC, 1975.

OTHER—Editor, *A Black Quartet*, New American Library, 1970; editor (with Ron Milner), *Black Drama Anthology*, Columbia University Press, 1972, then New American Library, 1986; editor (with Earl Anthony), *Black Poets and Prophets: The Theory, Practice, and Esthetics of the Pan-Africanist Revolution*, New American Library, 1972; editor, *Black Short Story Anthology*, Columbia University Press, 1972; editor, *Black Spirits: A Festival of New Black Poets in America*, Random House, 1972; editor, *The Forerunners: Black Poets in America*, Howard University Press, 1975; *Black Theatre: Present Condition* (essays), Publishing Center for Cultural Resources, 1981; also editor, *The Pan African Movement*, 1974; editor, *New Plays for the Black Theatre*, Third World, 1988; also editor, *Short Stories By Black Writers*, New American Library. Short stories have appeared in *The Best Short Stories By Negro Writers*, Little, Brown, 1967; *Black Short Story*

Anthology, Columbia University Press, 1972; *We Be Word Sorcers*, Bantam, 1973; also *City Streets*, Bantam. Has also written for such periodicals as *Negro Digest, Black Creation, Black Scholar, Rockefeller Foundation Quarterly, Black American Literature Forum, Variety, Liberator, Black World, Drama Review, Black Theatre Magazine, New York Times*, and *Association for Study on Negro Life and History*.

RECORDINGS: ALBUMS—Producer, *New Black Poets in America*, Motown, 1972; producer, *Nation Time*, Motown, 1972.

AWARDS: John Hay Whitney Fellowship for directing at the American Place Theatre, 1965-66; International Film Critics Award, 1970, for *Right On!;* New York Drama Critics' Circle Award, Best American Play, 1975, for *The Taking of Miss Janie;* Audelco Award, Best Director, 1986, for *Appear and Show Cause;* Joseph Jefferson Award nomination, Best Director, 1986, for *Boesman and Lena;* Carbonell Award nomination, Best Director, 1985, for *Home;* NAACP Image Award, Best Director, 1987, for *Checkmates;* also received an award from the American Women in Radio and Television for *Women of the Regent Hotel;* and fourteen Audelco Awards for Best Production or Best Director.

MEMBER: Actors' Equity Association, Screen Actors Guild, Directors Guild of America, Black Filmmakers Foundation, National Theatre Conference, Society of Stage Directors and Choreographers, Audelco, Theatre Communication Group, Association for Study of Negro Life and History.

ADDRESSES: OFFICES—Woodie King Associates, 417 Convent Avenue, New York, NY 10031; New Federal Theatre, 466 Grand Street, New York, NY 10002.

*   *   *

KIRCHENBAUER, Bill   1953-

PERSONAL: Surname is pronounced "Kir-ken-bower"; born February 19, 1953, in Salzburg, Austria; son of Alfred Ellsworth (in the U.S. Army) and Hester Elaine (Andrews) Kirchenbauer; married Lynn Allison Robbins, April 25, 1987. EDUCATION—Attended St. Petersburg Junior College, 1972-73; studied improvisation and mime with Howard Storm.

VOCATION: Actor and comedian.

CAREER: PRINCIPAL FILM APPEARANCES—Doctor, *Skatetown U.S.A.*, Columbia, 1979; crazed husband, "Municipalians" in *National Lampoon Goes to the Movies* (also known as *National Lampoon's Movie Madness*), Metro-Goldwyn-Mayer/United Artists, 1981; Jack Flynn, *Full Moon High*, Filmways, 1982; Polish killer, *They Call Me Bruce* (also known as *A Fistful of Chopsticks*), Film Ventures, 1982; Gower, *Stoogemania*, Atlantic, 1986. Also appeared in *Airplane*, Paramount, 1980; *G.O.R.P.*, Filmways, 1980; *Night Patrol*, New World, 1984.

PRINCIPAL TELEVISION APPEARANCES—Series: Tony Roletti, *Fernwood Tonight*, syndicated, 1977, retitled *America 2-Night*, syndicated, 1977-78; regular, *Barbara Mandrell and the Mandrell Sisters*, NBC, 1980-82; regular, *The Book of Lists*, CBS, 1982; Angry Arnie, *The Investigators*, HBO, 1984; Coach Graham Lubbock, *Growing Pains*, ABC, 1987-88; Coach Graham Lubbock, *Just the Ten of Us*, ABC, 1988—. Pilots: Guest, *The Lisa Hartman*

BILL KIRCHENBAUER

Show, ABC, 1979; Angry Arnie, *Stopwatch: Thirty Minutes of Investigative Ticking,* HBO, 1983; *Kid's Crosswits,* NBC, 1986. Episodic: Tony Roletti, *Thicke of the Night,* syndicated, 1984; Floyd, *Mama's Family,* syndicated, 1987; also *Night Court,* NBC, 1985; *Crosswits,* NBC, 1986; *Win, Lose, or Draw,* NBC, 1988; Todd Norman Taylor, *Mork and Mindy,* ABC; *Madame's Place,* syndicated; *The Merv Griffin Show,* syndicated; *The Tonight Show,* NBC; *Late Night with David Letterman,* NBC; *Hour Magazine,* syndicated; *Make Me Laugh,* syndicated; *An Evening at the Improv,* syndicated. Movies: Nick Grady, *Jury Duty: The Comedy,* ABC, 1990. Specials: *Chevy Chase and Friends,* NBC, 1977; *Gallagher's Melon Crazy,* Showtime, 1984; *The Smothers Brothers Present the Young Comedians,* HBO, 1985; *Stand-Up Comics Take a Stand!,* Family Channel, 1989; *A Comedy Celebration: The Comedy and Magic Club's Tenth Anniversary Special,* Showtime, 1989; also *The Best of the American Comedians,* BBC; *The Dick Shawn Special.*

RELATED CAREER—As a stand-up comedian, has appeared in comedy clubs and concert halls throughout the United States and Canada.

NON-RELATED CAREER—Video electronics salesman.

WRITINGS: TELEVISION—Episodic: *Just the Ten of Us,* ABC, 1990.

AWARDS: Winner of the first Los Angeles Stand-Up Comedy Competition, 1978.

MEMBER: Screen Actors Guild, American Federation of Television and Radio Artists.

ADDRESSES: AGENT—Bernie Young Agency, 6006 Greenbelt Road, Suite 285, Greenbelt, MD 20770.

       *   *   *

KITCHEN, Michael   1948-

PERSONAL: Born October 31, 1948, in Leicester, England; children: one son. EDUCATION—Trained for the stage with the Belgrade Theatre, Coventry, U.K., 1965, with the National Youth Theatre, 1965, and at the Royal Academy of Dramatic Art, 1966-1969.

VOCATION: Actor.

CAREER: PRINCIPAL STAGE APPEARANCES—Cragge, *Skyvers,* Theatre Upstairs, London, 1971; Bando and Mask, *Big Wolf,* Royal Court Theatre, London, 1972; Will, *Magnificence,* Royal Court Theatre, 1973; Moritz Stiefel, *Spring Awakening* and Benvolio, *Romeo and Juliet,* both National Theatre Company, Old Vic Theatre, London, 1974; title role, *The Picture of Dorian Gray,* Greenwich Theatre, London, 1975; Iago, *Othello,* Macbeth II, third murderer, and Porter, *Macbeth,* and Jack Chesney, *Charley's Aunt,* all National Theatre Company, Young Vic Theatre, London, 1975; Howard Needham, *Sparrowfall,* Hampstead Theatre Club, London, 1976; Foster, *No Man's Land,* National Theatre Company, Longacre Theatre, New York City, 1976, then Lyttelton Theatre, London, 1977; Nick, *Bedroom Farce* and Trotsky, *State of Revolution,* both National Theatre Company, Lyttelton Theatre, 1977; Lenny, *The Homecoming,* Garrick Theatre, London, 1978; Mercutio, *Romeo and Juliet,* Royal Shakespeare Company (RSC), Royal Shakespeare Theatre, Stratford-on-Avon, U.K., 1986; Hogarth, *The Art of Success* and Bolingbroke, *Richard II,* RSC, Stratford-on-Avon, then Barbican Theatre, London, both 1987. Also appeared at the Forum Theatre, Billingham, U.K, 1970; King's Head Theatre, Islington, U.K., 1970; and in *On the Razzle* and *Rough Crossing,* both National Theatre Company.

PRINCIPAL FILM APPEARANCES—Bungabine, *Unman, Wittering, and Zigo,* Paramount, 1971; Greg, *Dracula A.D. 1972* (also known as *Dracula Today*), Warner Brothers, 1972; Larner, *Breaking Glass,* GTO, 1980; Peter, *Caught on a Train,* British Film Institute, 1980; Berkeley Cole, *Out of Africa,* Universal, 1985; Bricks, *Dykket* (also known as *The Dive*), Gavin, 1989. Also appeared in *Towards the Morning,* 1980; Diessen, *Pied Piper,* 1989; Quinton, *Fools of Fortune,* 1990; Clive, *The Russia House,* 1990.

TELEVISION DEBUT—*Is That Your Body, Boy?,* BBC. PRINCIPAL TELEVISION APPEARANCES—Mini-Series: William Hatchard, *Love Song,* Anglia Television, then *Masterpiece Theatre,* PBS, 1987; also Branwell Bronte, *The Brontes of Howarth.* Movies: Rochus Misch, *The Bunker,* CBS, 1981; also *The Justice Game,* BBC-1, 1989. Specials: George Newton, *Once the Killing Starts,* ABC, 1974; Ian, *Sleepwalker,* ABC, 1975; Edmund, *King Lear,* BBC-2, 1982; also *The Comedy of Errors,* 1983. Also appeared in *Brimstone and Treacle,* produced in 1976, broadcast in 1985; *Freud,* 1982; as title role, *Young Stephen Hind;* D.H. Lawrence, *Lawrence and Freda;* and in *No Man's Land, Bedroom Farce, The Long and the Short and the Tall, A Room for the Winter, Churchill's People, Fall of Eagles, The Best of Everything, Man at the Top, Ball Trap at the Cote Sauvage,* and *Benefactors.*

RELATED CAREER—Assistant stage manager, Belgrade Theatre, Coventry, U.K., 1965.

ADDRESSES: AGENT—Markham and Froggat Ltd., 4 Windmill Street, London W1, England.

*   *   *

KNOPFLER, Mark   1949-

PERSONAL: Born August 12, 1949, in Glasgow, Scotland; father, an architect; mother, a school teacher; second wife's name, Lourdes Salamone. EDUCATION—Received a degree in English literature from the University of Leeds, 1973.

VOCATION: Composer, singer, and guitarist.

CAREER: Also see *WRITINGS* below. PRINCIPAL FILM APPEARANCES—*The Secret Policeman's Third Ball* (concert film), Virgin Vision, 1987. PRINCIPAL FILM WORK—Theme song arranger, *The Princess Bride,* Twentieth Century-Fox, 1987.

PRINCIPAL TELEVISION APPEARANCES—Specials: *The Prince's Trust All-Star Rock Concert,* HBO, 1986; *A Session with Chet Atkins, Certified Guitar Player* (also known as *Chet Atkins and Friends: Music from the Heart*), Cinemax, 1987.

RELATED CAREER—Member of the rock groups Brewer's Droop and Cafe Racers, both in London; founder and lead guitarist with the rock group Dire Straits, 1977—.

NON-RELATED CAREER—Reporter and rock music critic, *Yorkshire Evening Post,* 1968-70; lecturer, Loughton College, 1973-77.

WRITINGS: All as composer. FILM—*Local Hero,* Warner Brothers, 1983; *Cal,* Warner Brothers, 1984; *Comfort and Joy,* Universal, 1984; *Lucas,* Twentieth Century-Fox, 1986; *The Princess Bride,* Twentieth Century-Fox, 1987. TELEVISION—*In Private and Public: The Prince and Princess of Wales* (documentary), British television, 1986.

RECORDINGS: ALBUMS—*Local Hero* (original soundtrack), Warner Brothers, 1983; *Cal* (original soundtrack), Warner Brothers, 1984; *Comfort and Joy* (original soundtrack), Phonogram, 1985; *The Princess Bride* (original soundtrack), Warner Brothers, 1987.

With Dire Straits: *Dire Straits,* Warner Brothers, 1978; *Communique,* Warner Brothers, 1979; *Making Movies,* Warner Brothers, 1980; *Love Over Gold,* Warner Brothers, 1982; *Twisting By the Pool,* Warner Brothers, 1983; *Alchemy,* Warner Brothers, 1984; *Brothers in Arms,* Warner Brothers, 1985.

AWARDS: Grammy Award (with Dire Straits), Best Performance by a Group, and MTV Video Music Awards (with Dire Straits), Best Group Video and Best Video of the Year, all 1986, for "Money for Nothing" from *Brothers in Arms.*

ADDRESSES: PUBLICIST—Warner Brothers Records, 3300 Warner Boulevard, Burbank, CA 91505.*

KONCHALOVSKY, Andrei   1937-

PERSONAL: Full name, Andrei Sergeyevich Mikhalkov-Konchalovsky; some sources note first name as Andron; born in 1937 in Moscow, U.S.S.R.; immigrated to the United States in 1980; son of Sergey Mikhalkov (a writer) and Natalia Konchalovskaia (a poet); married Natalya Arinbasarova (marriage ended); married second wife, 1969 (divorced); married third wife; children: two. EDUCATION—Graduated from the State Film School (VGIK), 1964, studying under Mikhail Romm; also studied piano at the Moscow Conservatoire, 1947-57.

VOCATION: Director and screenwriter.

CAREER: Also see *WRITINGS* below. PRINCIPAL FILM APPEARANCES—*Ivanovo detstvo* (also known as *My Name Is Ivan* and *Ivan's Childhood*), Mosfilm, 1962, released in the United States by Sig Shore, 1963. PRINCIPAL FILM WORK—All as director, unless indicated: Assistant director, *Ivanovo detsvo* (also known as *My Name Is Ivan* and *Ivan's Childhood*), Mosfilm, 1962, released in the United States by Sig Shore, 1963; *Dyadya Vanya* (also known as *Uncle Vanya*), Mosfilm, 1971, released in the United States by Artkino, 1972; *Siberiade* (also known as *The Siberiad*), Soviexport, 1979; *Maria's Lovers,* Cannon, 1985; *Runaway Train,* Cannon, 1985; *Duet for One,* Cannon, 1986; *Shy People,* Cannon, 1987; *Tango and Cash,* Warner Brothers, 1989; *Homer and Eddie,* Skouras, 1990. Also directed *Malchik i golub* (also known as *The Boy and the Pigeon;* short film), 1961; *Pyervy uchityel* (also known as *The First Teacher*), 1965; *Istoriya Asi Klyachinoy, kotoraya lyubila, da nye vyshla zamuzh* (also known as *The Happiness of Asya, Happy Asya, Asya's Happiness,* and *The Story of Asya Klyachina, Who Loved But Did Not Marry*), 1966; *Dvoryanskoye gnezdo* (also known as *A Nest of Gentlefolk*), 1969; *Romans a uljublennyh* (also known as *Lovers' Romance* and *The Romance of Lovers*), 1974.

PRINCIPAL TELEVISION WORK—Movies: Director, *Split Cherry Tree,* HBO, 1982.

WRITINGS: FILM—See production details above, unless indicated. (With Andrei Tarkovsky) *Katok i skripka* (also known as *Violin and Roller, The Steamroller and the Violin, The Skating-Rink and the Violin,* and *The Violin and the Roller*), Mosfilm, 1961, released in the United States by Artkino, 1962; (with Tarkovsky) *Andrey Rubliov* (also known as *Andrei Rublev*), Mosfilm, 1964; (with others) *Pyervy uchityel,* 1965; *Istoriya Asi Klyachinov, kotoraya lyubila, da nye vyshla zamuzh,* 1966; (with others) *Dvoryanskoye gnezdo,* 1969; *Tashkent—gorod khlyebny* (also known as *Tashkent—City of Bread*), 1969; *Pyesn o Manshuk* (also known as *The Song of Manshuk*), 1969; *The End of the Chieftain,* 1970; *Dyadya Vanya,* 1971; *Romans o uljublennyh,* 1974; *Siberiade,* 1978; (with Gerard Brach, Paul Zindel, and Marjorie David) *Maria's Lovers,* 1985; (with Tom Kempinsky and Jeremy Lipp) *Duet for One,* 1986; (with Brach and David) *Shy People,* 1987.

TELEVISION—Movies: *Split Cherry Tree,* HBO, 1982.

AWARDS: Special Jury Prize from the Cannes Film Festival, 1979, for *Siberiade.*

ADDRESSES: AGENT—Marty Baum, Creative Artists Agency, 9830 Wilshire Boulevard, Beverly Hills, CA 90212.*

KRISTEL, Sylvia 1952-

PERSONAL: Born September 28, 1952, in Utrecht, the Netherlands; daughter of innkeepers.

VOCATION: Actress.

CAREER: PRINCIPAL FILM APPEARANCES—Diana, *Le Jeu avec le feu* (also known as *Playing with Fire*), Union Generale Cinematographique, 1974; title role, *Emmanuelle,* Parafrance, 1974; Avril, *Un Linceul n'a pas de poches* (also known as *No Pockets in a Shroud*), Societe Nouvelle Prodis, 1974; Julia, *Der Lieberschuler* (also known as *Julia* and *Julia: Innocence Once Removed*), Cine-Media International, 1975; title role, *Emmanuelle II* (also known as *Emmanuelle—The Joys of a Woman*), Parafrance, 1976; Alice, *Alice ou le derniere fugue* (also known as *Alice, or the Last Escapade*), Filmel/PHPG, 1977; Diana, *La Marge* (also known as *The Margin* and *The Streetwalker*), Paris/New Realm Distributors, 1976; Mathilde Leroy, *Une Femme fidele* (also known as *A Faithful Woman* and *Game of Seduction*), Alpha/Spectro/Virgin Vision, 1976; Krista, *Rene la Canne* (also known as *Rene the Cane*), President/AMLF, 1977; Marie Therese, *Behind the Iron Mask* (also known as *The Fifth Musketeer*), Columbia, 1977; title role, *Goodbye Emmanuelle,* Parafrance/Columbia-Warner Distributors, 1978, released in the United States by Miramax, 1980; Isabelle, *The Concorde—Airport '79* (also known as *Airport '79: The Concorde, Airport '79,* and *Airport '80: The Concorde*), Universal, 1979; Dany Kielland, *Mysteries,* Cinevog, 1979.

Agent 34, *The Nude Bomb* (also known as *The Return of Maxwell Smart*), Universal, 1980; Constance Chatterley, *Lady Chatterley's Lover,* Prodis, 1981; Nicole Mallow, *Private Lessons* (also known as *Philly*), Jensen Farley, 1981; Ms. Regina Copuletta, *Private School,* Universal, 1983; Sylvia, *Emmanuelle IV,* Cannon, 1983; title role, *Mata Hari,* Cannon, 1985; Sophia, *Red Heat* (also known as *Rote Hitze*), TAT Filmproduction/Inter-Ocean/Miracle, 1985; Vanessa, *Dracula's Widow,* De Laurentiis Entertainment Group, 1989; Julie, *The Arrogant* (also known as *Sylvia Kristel's Desires*), Cannon, 1989. Also appeared in *Niet voor de poesen* (also known as *Because of the Cats*), Cinevog, 1972; *Frank and Eva—Living Apart Together,* Actueel, 1973; *Letti Selvaggi* (also known as *Wilde Betten*), Avis Filmverleih/Ascot Filmverleih, 1978; *Tigers in Lipstick* (also known as *Wild Bed* and *Hijinks*), Zodiac, 1978; *The Big Bet,* Golden Communications/Golden Harvest, 1986.

PRINCIPAL TELEVISION APPEARANCES—Pilots: Brett Devereaux, *The Million Dollar Face,* NBC, 1981. Movies: Maddalena, *Casanova,* CBS, 1987.

RELATED CAREER—Professional model; winner of Miss TV Europe beauty contest.

NON-RELATED CAREER—Secretary and gas station attendant.*

*   *   *

KURYS, Diane 1949-

PERSONAL: Born in 1949 in France; daughter of Daniel (a clothing store owner) and Lena Kurys.

VOCATION: Director, screenwriter, and actress.

CAREER: PRINCIPAL FILM APPEARANCES—*Casanova* (also known as *Fellini's Casanova*), Universal, 1976.

PRINCIPAL FILM WORK—Director and co-producer, *Diabolo menthe* (also known as *Peppermint Soda*), Gaumont, 1978, released in the United States by New Yorker, 1979; co-producer, *Coup de sirocco* (also known as *Sirocco Blow*), Gaumont/World Marketing, 1979; director, *Cocktail Molotov* (also known as *Molotov Cocktail*), AMLF, 1979, released in the United States by New Yorker, 1981; co-producer, *Le Grand Pardon* (also known as *The Big Pardon*), Gaumont, 1981; director, *Coup de foudre* (also known as *Entre nous, Between Us,* and *At First Sight*), Gaumont/Metro-Goldwyn-Mayer/United Artists Classics, 1983; director, *Un Homme amoureux* (also known as *A Man in Love*), Gaumont/Cinecom International, 1987; director, *La Baule—Les Pins,* Union Generale Cinematographique, 1990.

RELATED CAREER—Actress with Jean-Louis Barrault's theatre group; adaptor and translator of plays.

WRITINGS: FILM—*Diabolo menthe* (also known as *Peppermint Soda*), Gaumont, 1978; (with Phillipe Adrien and Alain LeHenry) *Cocktail Molotov* (also known as *Molotov Cocktail*), AMLF, 1979; *Coup de foudre* (also known as *Entre nous, Between Us,* and *At First Sight*), Gaumont/Metro-Goldwyn-Mayer/United Artists Classics, 1983; (with Oliver Schatzky and Israel Horovitz) *Un Homme amoureux* (also known as *A Man in Love*), Gaumont/Cinecom International, 1987; (with LeHenry) *La Baule—Les Pins,* Union General Cinematographique, 1990.

AWARDS: Prix Louis Deluc, Best Picture, 1978, for *Diabolo menthe;* Academy Award nomination, Best Foreign Language Film, 1983, for *Coup de foudre.**

L

LAKE, Harriette
See SOTHERN, Ann

*   *   *

LAMPKIN, Charles   1913-1989

PERSONAL: Born in 1913 in Cleveland, OH; died of natural causes, April 17, 1989, in San Jose, CA; children: three stepchildren. EDUCATION—Attended John Carroll University and the Cleveland School of Music.

VOCATION: Actor.

CAREER: FILM DEBUT—Charles, *Five,* Columbia, 1951. PRINCIPAL FILM APPEARANCES—Taylor, *Rider on a Dead Horse,* Allied Artists, 1962; Gus, *Toys in the Attic,* United Artists, 1963; Lafe, *One Man's Way,* United Artists, 1964; Porter, *The Rare Breed,* Universal, 1966; Edward, *Journey to Shiloh,* Universal, 1968; cashroom guard, *The Thomas Crown Affair* (also known as *Thomas Crown and Company* and *The Crown Caper*), United Artists, 1968; Dr. Catlin, *Watermelon Man,* Columbia, 1970; Big Sid, *Hammer,* United Artists, 1972; Congressman Walding, *The Man,* Paramount, 1972; Jenkins, *Cornbread, Earl, and Me,* American International, 1975; mailman, *Special Delivery,* American International, 1976; Constable, *Islands in the Stream,* Paramount, 1977; Justice Josiah Clewes, *First Monday in October,* Paramount, 1981; Butler, *S.O.B.,* Paramount, 1981; Judge Richards, *Second Thoughts,* Universal, 1983; Willie Walsh, *Swordkill,* Empire, 1984; Pops, *Cocoon,* Twentieth Century-Fox, 1985; also appeared in *Twilight of Honor* (also known as *The Charge Is Murder*), Metro-Goldwyn-Mayer, 1963; *The Great White Hope,* Twentieth Century-Fox, 1970.

PRINCIPAL TELEVISION APPEARANCES—Series: Tiger Shepin, *Frank's Place,* CBS, 1987-88. Pilots: Captain Kingsley, *Nick and Nora,* ABC, 1975; also *Deadlock,* NBC, 1969; *Jigsaw* (also known as *Man on the Move*), ABC, 1972. Episodic: Clarence Robinson, *Night Court,* CBS, 1985; Bill, *Bridges to Cross,* CBS, 1986; Ezra, *He's the Mayor,* ABC, 1986; Felix, *227,* NBC, 1987; Sam, *Webster,* ABC, 1987; also *The Untouchables,* ABC; *The Bold Ones,* NBC; *The F.B.I.,* ABC; *The Jeffersons,* CBS; *The Incredible Hulk,* CBS; *Too Close for Comfort,* ABC; *Father Murphy,* NBC; *Scarecrow and Mrs. King,* CBS; *Highway to Heaven,* NBC. Movies: Cook, *Breakout,* NBC, 1970; Wyn Stokey, *Hurricane,* ABC, 1974; George Lincoln, *Panic on the 5:22,* ABC, 1974; Irvin McDuffie, *Eleanor and Franklin: The White House Years,* ABC, 1977; Elroy, *Last of the Great Survivors,* CBS, 1984; Judge Clement Autley, *The Last Innocent Man,* HBO, 1987; also *The Law,* NBC, 1974. Specials: Davy Henderson, "A Homerun for Love," *ABC Afterschool Specials,* ABC, 1978; *Hollywood's Most Sensational Mysteries,* NBC, 1984.

RELATED CAREER—Lecturer on theater arts, music, and speech, University of the Pacific, Santa Clara, CA; stage actor with the Cleveland Playhouse, Cleveland, OH.

OBITUARIES AND OTHER SOURCES: Variety, May 10-16, 1989.*

*   *   *

LANG, Belinda   1953-

PERSONAL: Born December 23, 1953; daughter of Jeremy (an actor) and Joan (an actress; maiden name, Heal) Hawk; married Hugh Fraser (an actor), October 15, 1988. EDUCATION—Trained for the stage at the Central School of Speech and Drama for three years.

VOCATION: Actress and singer.

CAREER: STAGE DEBUT—Amanda, *Private Lives,* Frinton Summer Theatre, Frinton, U.K., 1974. LONDON DEBUT—Daphne Stillington, *Present Laughter,* Vaudeville Theatre. PRINCIPAL STAGE APPEARANCES—Dolly, *You Never Can Tell* and Polly Peachum, *The Threepenny Opera,* both Oxford Playhouse, Oxford, U.K., 1977; Gerd, *Brand* and Helena, *All's Well That Ends Well,* both Oxford Playhouse, 1978; Vickey Hobson, *Hobson's Choice,* Haymarket Theatre, London, 1982; Catherine, *The Dark River,* Orange Tree Theatre, London, 1984; Miss Sterling, *The Clandestine Marriage,* Albery Theatre, London, 1984; Ismene, *Antigone,* National Theatre, London, 1984; Melitta, *Mrs. Klein,* Apollo Theatre, London, 1989. Also appeared in *Trouble in Paradise,* Stratford Theatre Royal, London, 1984; *Rumblings,* Bush Theatre, London, 1985.

MAJOR TOURS—Dolly, *You Never Can Tell* and Polly Peachum, *The Threepenny Opera,* U.K. cities, 1977; Gerd, *Brand* and Helena, *All's Well That Ends Well,* U.K. cities, 1978.

PRINCIPAL FILM APPEARANCES—Girl in bath, *The Imitation Game,* British Film Institute, 1980.

TELEVISION DEBUT—Beth, *To Serve Them All My Days,* BBC, then *Masterpiece Theatre,* PBS, 1980. PRINCIPAL TELEVISION APPEARANCES—Series: Kate, *Dear John,* BBC, 1985 and 1987; Sheila, *Bust,* London Weekend Television, 1988. Mini-Series:

BELINDA LANG

Martha Brett, *The Bretts*, Central Television, 1986, then *Masterpiece Theatre*, PBS, 1987; Martha Brett, *The Bretts II*, Central Television, 1987, then *Masterpiece Theatre*, PBS, 1989.

RELATED CAREER—Cabaret singer.

SIDELIGHTS: RECREATIONS—Travel.

ADDRESSES: AGENT—Ken McReddie, 91 Regent Street, London W1, England.

*   *   *

LATHAN, Bobbi Jo   1951-

PERSONAL: Born Barbara Jo Lathan, October 5, 1951, in Dallas, TX; daughter of Allan Adale (a colonel in the U.S. Air Force) and Lillian Iris (a concert pianist; maiden name, Watson) Lathan; married Thanos Karris (an entertainment manager), June 6, 1976. EDUCATION—Received B.A. in English, speech, and drama from North Texas State University; studied acting with Peter Flood, Wynn Handman, and Bob McAndrew. RELIGION—Christian Scientist.

VOCATION: Actress.

CAREER: STAGE DEBUT—Ursula, *Sweet Charity*, Casa Manana Theatre, Fort Worth, TX, 1973. BROADWAY DEBUT—Doatsey

Mae, reporter, and understudy for Miss Mona Stangley, *The Best Little Whorehouse in Texas*, 46th Street Theatre, 1978-79. PRINCIPAL STAGE APPEARANCES—Billie Fenstermacher, *The Guys in the Truck*, New Apollo Theatre, New York City, 1983; Miss Lucy, *Sweet Bird of Youth*, Playhouse in the Park, Cincinnati, OH, 1983. Also appeared as Dolly, *Rainbow Dancing*, Actors' Studio, New York City; Kate, *What the Hell Nell!*, Michael Bennett Studio, New York City; Maggie Murphy, *Zapata*, Goodspeed Opera House, East Haddam, CT; Titania, *A Midsummer Night's Dream*, Casa Manana Theatre, Fort Worth, TX; Mary, *Drumwright*, Tennessee Theatre.

MAJOR TOURS—Gloria, *Everybody Loves Opal*, U.S. cities; Miss Mona Stangley, *The Best Little Whorehouse in Texas*, U.S. cities.

FILM DEBUT—Charmane, *In a Pig's Eye*, Elsinore, 1989.

PRINCIPAL TELEVISION APPEARANCES—Pilots: Party guest, *A Fine Romance*, CBS, 1983. Episodic: Susie, *Downtown*, CBS, 1986; Vera, *Simon and Simon*, CBS, 1986; State Trooper McElroy, *St. Elsewhere*, NBC, 1987; Sherri, *HeartBeat*, ABC, 1988; Ginger, *Night Court*, NBC, 1988; Donna, *In the Heat of the Night*, NBC, 1989; Lydia, *Perfect Strangers*, ABC, 1989; Angela Wilder, *Hunter*, NBC, 1989; also *Out of This World*, syndicated, 1987; *The Van Dyke Show*, CBS, 1988; *Texas*, NBC; *Capitol*, CBS; *Matlock*, NBC; *L.A. Law*, NBC; *Scarecrow and Mrs. King*, CBS; *1st and Ten*, HBO; *One Big Family*, syndicated. Movies: Christine, *Love and Betrayal*, CBS, 1989; also *The Dain Curse*, CBS, 1978; *Broken Promise*, CBS, 1981; *The Man Who Fell to Earth*, ABC, 1987.

BOBBI JO LATHAN

RELATED CAREER—Actress in television commercials, Dallas, TX; performer in a nightclub tour.

NON-RELATED CAREER—School teacher.

MEMBER: Screen Actors Guild, American Federation of Television and Radio Artists, Actors' Equity Association.

ADDRESSES: AGENT—Harry Gold and Associates, 12725 Ventura Boulevard, Suite E, Studio City, CA 91604. MANAGER—Karris/Magerman Management, 4444 Woodman Avenue, Suite 4, Sherman Oaks, CA 91423.

*   *   *

LAURANCE, Matthew

PERSONAL: Born in Hewlett, NY. EDUCATION—Received B.A. in political science from Tufts University; trained for the stage with Sanford Meisner at the Neighborhood Playhouse and with Uta Hagen at the HB Studios.

VOCATION: Actor.

CAREER: PRINCIPAL STAGE APPEARANCES—*Dream House*, Los Angeles; also appeared in productions of *Tartuffe, Guys and Dolls, Romeo and Juliet, Who's Afraid of Virginia Woolf?*, and *The Glass Menagerie*.

PRINCIPAL STAGE WORK—Assistant to director, *On Golden Pond*, New Apollo Theatre, New York City, 1979.

PRINCIPAL FILM APPEARANCES—Ronnie Ciello, *Prince of the City*, Warner Brothers, 1981; Sal Amato, *Eddie and the Cruisers*, Embassy, 1983; Ali, *Best Defense*, Paramount, 1984; Ardmore cop, *Streets of Fire*, Universal/RKO, 1984; Ron Dellasandro, *St. Elmo's Fire*, Columbia, 1985; Sal Amato, *Eddie and the Cruisers II: Eddie Lives*, Scotti Brothers, 1989. Also appeared in *Dead Men Don't Wear Plaid*, Universal, 1982.

PRINCIPAL TELEVISION APPEARANCES—Series: Regular, *Saturday Night Live*, NBC, 1981; Ben Coleman, *Duet*, Fox, 1987-89. Pilots: Tony Parese, *Popeye Doyle*, NBC, 1986. Episodic: Mark Forsch, *Foley Square*, CBS, 1985; Steve, *My Sister Sam*, CBS, 1986 and 1987; also *Taxi*, NBC, 1982; *Cagney and Lacey*, CBS; *It's a Living*, ABC. Movies: Nate, *Consenting Adult*, ABC, 1985; Dan, *The Leftovers*, ABC, 1986; Dr. Farber, *Ordinary Heroes*, ABC, 1986; Max, *Samaritan: The Mitch Snyder Story*, CBS, 1986; Marvin Bernstein, *Do You Know the Muffin Man?*, CBS, 1989.

SIDELIGHTS: RECREATIONS—Golf, basketball, softball, and reading detective novels.

ADDRESSES: AGENT—Steve Dontanville, International Creative Management, 8899 Beverly Boulevard, Los Angeles, CA 90048. MANAGER—Mike Hewitson, DeMann Entertainment, 9200 Sunset Boulevard, Suite 915, Los Angeles, CA 90069. PUBLICIST—Baker/Winokur/Ryder Public Relations, 9348 Civic Center Drive, Suite 407, Beverly Hills, CA 90210.*

ROSEMARY LEACH

LEACH, Rosemary   1935-

PERSONAL: Born December 18, 1935, in Much Wenlock, England; daughter of Sidney (a teacher) and Mary Eileen (a teacher; maiden name, Parker) Leach; married Colin Starkey (an actor), November 3, 1981. EDUCATION—Attended the Royal Academy of Dramatic Art.

VOCATION: Actress.

CAREER: STAGE DEBUT—With the Amersham Repertory Theatre, Amersham, U.K., 1955. PRINCIPAL STAGE APPEARANCES—Queen Elizabeth, *Richard III*, St. George's Theatre, London, 1976; Vera, *Just Between Ourselves*, Queen's Theatre, London, 1977; Amy Evans, *I Sent a Letter to My Love*, Greenwich Theatre, London, 1979; Rosalind, *As You Like It*, St. George's Theatre, 1979; Helene Hanff, *84 Charing Cross Road*, Ambassador's Theatre, London, 1981; Anne Wheatley, *Other Worlds*, Royal Court Theatre, London, 1983; also appeared in *The Health Farm*, King's Head Theatre, London, 1989.

MAJOR TOURS—Lettice Douffet, *Lettice and Lovage*, U.K. cities, 1990; also Daisy, *Gert and Daisy*, U.K. cities.

PRINCIPAL FILM APPEARANCES—Mary Bell, *Face of a Stranger*, Allied Artists, 1964; Kate, *Ghost in the Noonday Sun*, Columbia, 1973; Mrs. MacLaine, *That'll Be the Day*, EMI, 1974; voice of Vera, *The Plague Dogs* (animated), United International, 1984; Mrs. Inchcliff, *Turtle Diary*, Samuel Goldwyn, 1985; Mrs. Honeychurch, *A Room with a View*, Cinecom, 1986; Miss Scope,

The Children, Isolde, 1989; also appeared in *The Bride,* Columbia, 1985.

TELEVISION DEBUT—"Mr. Big," *Armchair Theatre,* ATV. PRINCIPAL TELEVISION APPEARANCES—Series: *Now Look Here,* 1973-74; *Sadie, It's Cold Outside,* 1975; *Life Begins at Forty,* 1978-79. Mini-Series: Aunt Fenny, *The Jewel in the Crown,* Granada, then *Masterpiece Theatre,* PBS, 1984; Joan Plumleigh-Bruce, *The Charmer,* London Weekend Television (LWT), then *Masterpiece Theatre,* PBS, 1989; also *Disraeli,* ATV, 1977, then *Masterpiece Theatre,* PBS, 1980. Pilots: Philippa, *To Sir, with Love,* CBS, 1974. Episodic: Sister Agnes, "Displaced Person," *American Playhouse,* PBS, 1985; also *Rumpole of the Bailey,* Thames, 1979, then *Mystery!,* PBS. Movies: Dulcinea, *The Adventures of Don Quixote,* CBS, 1973; Mrs. Gaines, *Brief Encounter,* NBC, 1974; Eleanor Trundle, *Still Crazy Like a Fox,* CBS, 1987; also *S.O.S. Titanic,* ABC, 1979. Specials: Marcelle, *The Roads to Freedom,* BBC, then PBS, 1972; Mrs. Walker, *Once in a Lifetime,* BBC, then *Great Performances,* PBS, 1988; Violet, "The Winslow Boy," *Great Performances,* PBS, 1990. Also appeared in *Germinal,* 1970; *Chariots of Fire,* 1970; *No That's Me Over Here,* 1970; *The Wild Duck,* 1970; *Cider with Rosie,* 1971; *When the Wheel Turns,* 1972; *Bermondsey,* 1972; *When Day Is Done,* 1974; *Tip Through the Tulips,* 1976; *Dad,* 1976; *Six Women,* 1976; *Hindle Wakes,* 1977; *Just Between Ourselves,* 1978; *Hands,* 1979; *All's Well That Ends Well,* 1980; *Swallows and Amazons,* 1982; *Leaving Home,* LWT, 1987; *Boon,* Central Television, 1988; *Summers' Lease,* BBC, 1989; *Othello; The Critic; The Power Game; Pleasure Where She Finds It; The Cupboard.*

RELATED CAREER—Appeared with repertory companies in Coventry, Birmingham, and Liverpool, 1955-59.

AWARDS: Society of West End Theatres Award nomination, Best Supporting Performance, 1977, for *Just Between Friends;* Olivier Award, Best Actress, 1981, for *84 Charing Cross Road.*

SIDELIGHTS: Rosemary Leach informed *CTFT* that she does not have a favorite role, but she "enjoyed playing Helene Hanff in *84 Charing Cross Road,* Lettice Douffet in *Lettice and Lovage,* and Adelaide in *Guys and Dolls.*" In addition she stated, "[I] prefer theatre and radio to other media."

ADDRESSES: AGENT—William Morris Agency, 31-32 Soho Square, London WIV 5DG, England.

*   *   *

LEAR, Norman   1922-

PERSONAL: Full name, Norman Milton Lear; born July 27, 1922, in New Haven, CT; son of Herman (in sales) and Jeanette (Seicol) Lear; married second wife, Frances A. Loeb, December 7, 1956 (divorced); married Lyn Davis; children: Ellen (first marriage); Kate, Maggie (second marriage); Benjamin (third marriage). EDUCATION—Attended Emerson College, 1940-42. MILITARY—U.S. Army Air Force, technical sergeant, 1942-45.

VOCATION: Producer, director, and screenwriter.

CAREER: Also see *WRITINGS* below. PRINCIPAL FILM WORK—All as producer, unless indicated: (With Bud Yorkin) *Come Blow Your Horn,* Paramount, 1963; *Never Too Late,* Warner Brothers,

1965; *Divorce American Style,* Columbia, 1967; *The Night They Raided Minsky's* (also known as *The Night They Invented Striptease*), United Artists, 1968; executive producer, *Start the Revolution Without Me,* Warner Brothers, 1970; (also director) *Cold Turkey,* United Artists, 1971; executive producer, *The Princess Bride,* Twentieth Century-Fox, 1987.

PRINCIPAL TELEVISION APPEARANCES—Specials: *Bob Hope's World of Comedy,* NBC, 1976; *The American Comedy Awards,* ABC, 1987; *Hollywood's Favorite Heavy: Businessmen on Primetime TV,* PBS, 1987; *The Television Academy Hall of Fame,* Fox, 1987; *Fifty Years of Television: A Golden Celebration,* CBS, 1989.

PRINCIPAL TELEVISION WORK—Series: Producer (with Ed Simmons and Karl Hoffenberg) and director, *The Martha Raye Show,* NBC, 1954-56; producer, *The Andy Williams Show,* NBC, 1965; creator and executive producer, *All in the Family,* CBS, 1971-79; creator (with Aaron Ruben and Bud Yorkin) and executive producer (with Yorkin), *Sanford and Son,* NBC, 1972-77; creator and executive producer (with Rod Parker), *Maude,* CBS, 1972-78; executive producer, *Good Times,* CBS, 1974-79; creator, *The Jeffersons,* CBS, 1975-85; producer (with Ron Clark and Gene Marcione), *Hot l Baltimore,* ABC, 1975; executive producer, *One Day At a Time,* CBS, 1975-84; creator (with Parker) and executive producer, *The Nancy Walker Show,* ABC, 1976-77; creator, *All's Fair,* CBS, 1976-77; executive producer, *Mary Hartman, Mary Hartman,* syndicated, 1976-77; creator, *All That Glitters,* syndicated, 1977; executive producer, *A Year At the Top,* CBS, 1977; creator, *Fernwood 2-Night,* syndicated, 1977; executive producer, *Forever Fernwood,* syndicated, 1977-78; creator, *Apple Pie,* ABC, 1978; executive producer, *Mr. Dugan,* CBS, 1979 (three episodes produced but never broadcast); executive producer, *Hanging In,* CBS, 1979; creator and executive producer, *The Baxters,* syndicated, 1979; creator (with Alex Haley) and executive producer (with Haley and Ronald Rubin), *Palmerstown, U.S.A.,* CBS, 1980-81; creator and executive producer, *a.k.a. Pablo,* ABC, 1984.

Pilots: Producer, *Band of Gold* (broadcast as an episode of *General Electric Theatre*), CBS, 1961; executive producer (with Jerry Weintraub), *King of the Road,* CBS, 1978; executive producer (with Richard Dorso), *P.O.P.,* NBC, 1984. Movies: Executive producer, *Heartsounds,* ABC, 1984. Specials: Producer (with Yorkin), *The Danny Kaye Show,* CBS, 1961; producer (with Yorkin), *Henry Fonda and the Family,* CBS, 1962; producer (with Yorkin), *The Andy Williams Special,* NBC, 1962; producer, *Robert Young and the Family,* 1970; executive producer (with Yorkin), *I Love Liberty,* ABC, 1982; also producer, *The TV Guide Awards Show,* 1962; creator and producer (with Yorkin), *Another Evening with Fred Astaire;* creator and producer (with Yorkin), *An Evening with Carol Channing;* creator and producer (with Yorkin), *The Many Sides of Don Rickles.*

RELATED CAREER—Worked in public relations, 1945-49; freelance comedy writer, 1950-54; founder (with Bud Yorkin), Tandem Productions, 1959; founder, T.A.T. Communications, later known as Embassy Communications, 1974; founder, Act III Communications, 1987.

NON-RELATED CAREER—President, American Civil Liberties Foundation of Southern California; co-founder, People for the American Way; board of directors: Constitutional Rights Foundation, Helsinki Watch, Los Angeles Urban League, Mexican-American Legal Defense and Education Fund, and National Women's

Political Caucus; previously worked as furniture salesman and as a sidewalk photographer (specializing in baby pictures).

WRITINGS: FILM—(With Herbert Baker, Walter DeLeon, and Ed Simmons) *Scared Stiff,* Paramount, 1953; *Come Blow Your Horn,* Paramount, 1963; *Divorce American Style,* Columbia, 1967; (with Arnold Schulman and Sidney Michaels) *The Night They Raided Minsky's* (also known as *The Night They Invented Striptease*), United Artists, 1968; *Cold Turkey,* United Artists, 1971.

TELEVISION—Series: Staff writer, *Ford Star Revue,* NBC, 1951; staff writer, *The Tennessee Ernie Ford Show,* NBC, 1955-57; head writer, *All in the Family,* CBS, 1971-72. Episodic: *a.k.a. Pablo,* ABC, 1984; also *The Colgate Comedy Hour,* NBC; *The George Gobel Show,* NBC. Pilots: *P.O.P.,* NBC, 1984. Specials: (With Hal Kanter) *The Danny Kaye Show,* CBS, 1961; (with Toni Koch) *Henry Fonda and the Family,* CBS, 1962; (with Bud Yorkin) *The Andy Williams Special,* NBC, 1962; (with Richard Alfieri, Rita Mae Brown, Rick Mitz, and Arthur Allan Seidelman) *I Love Liberty,* ABC, 1982.

AWARDS: Named one of the Top Ten Motion Picture Producers of the Year by the Motion Picture Exhibitors, 1963, 1967, and 1968; Academy Award nomination, Best Story and Screenplay Written Directly for the Screen, and Writers Guild Award nomination, both 1967, for *Divorce American Style;* Emmy Awards, 1970, 1971, 1972, and 1973, all for *All in the Family;* Showman of the Year Award from the Publicists Guild, 1971; Showman of the Year Award from the Association of Business Managers, 1972; Broadcaster of the Year Award from the International Radio and TV Society, 1973; Man of the Year Award from the National Academy of Television Arts and Sciences (Hollywood chapter), 1973; Humanitarian Award from the National Conference of Christians and Jews, 1976; Mark Twain Award from the International Platform Association, 1977; Valentine Davies Award from the Writers Guild of America, 1977; Showman of the Year Award from the Publicists Guild, 1977; Peabody Award, 1977, for *All in the Family;* William O. Douglas Public Counsel Award, 1981; First Amendment Lectureship Award from Ford Hall Forum, 1981; Gold Medal from the International Radio and TV Society, 1981; Distinguished American Award, 1984; inducted into the TV Academy Hall of Fame, 1984; Emmy Award nomination, Outstanding Drama, 1984, for *Heartsounds;* Mass Media Award from the American Jewish Committee Institute of Human Relations, 1986; International Award of the Year from the National Association of TV Program Executives, 1987; American Comedy Award, Lifetime Achievement Award, 1987. MILITARY AWARDS—Air Medal with four oak leaf clusters. HONORARY DEGREES—Emerson College, H.H.D., 1968.

MEMBER: Writers Guild of America, Screen Producers Guild (executive board member, 1968), Directors Guild of America, Producers Guild of America, American Federation of Television and Radio Artists, Caucus of Producers, Writers, and Directors.

ADDRESSES: OFFICE—Act III Communications, 1800 Century Park E., Los Angeles, CA 90067.*

*   *   *

LEIGH, Jennifer Jason   1958-

PERSONAL: Born in 1958 in Los Angeles, CA; daughter of Vic Morrow (an actor) and Barbara Turner (a television writer).

JENNIFER JASON LEIGH

VOCATION: Actress.

CAREER: PRINCIPAL STAGE APPEARANCES—Madge Owens, *Picnic,* Center Theatre Group, Ahmanson Theatre, Los Angeles, 1986; title role, *Sunshine,* Circle Repertory Theatre, New York City, 1989. Also appeared in *The Shadow Box,* Los Angeles, 1979.

FILM DEBUT—Tracy, *Eyes of a Stranger,* Warner Brothers, 1980. PRINCIPAL FILM APPEARANCES—Young girl, *Wrong Is Right* (also known as *The Man with the Deadly Lens*), Columbia, 1982; Stacy Hamilton, *Fast Times at Ridgemont High,* Universal, 1982; Allison, *Easy Money,* Orion, 1983; Candy Webster, *Grandview, U.S.A.,* Warner Brothers, 1984; Agnes, *Flesh and Blood,* Orion/Riverside, 1985; Nash, *The Hitcher,* Tri-Star, 1986; Teensy, *The Men's Club,* Atlantic Releasing, 1986; Tanille LaRoux, *Under Cover,* Cannon, 1987; Lucy Bonnard, *Sister, Sister,* New World, 1987; Carol Rivers, *Heart of Midnight,* Samuel Goldwyn, 1988; Lydia Johnson, *The Big Picture,* Columbia, 1989; Tralala, *Last Exit to Brooklyn,* AMLF/Cinecom, 1989.

PRINCIPAL TELEVISION APPEARANCES—Movies: Kristy Teeter, *Angel City,* CBS, 1980; Amy Wheeler, *The Killing of Randy Webster,* CBS, 1981; Casey Powell, *The Best Little Girl in the World,* ABC, 1981; Bonny Dillon, *The First Time,* ABC, 1982; Carol Heath, *Girls of the White Orchid,* NBC, 1983. Specials: Laurie, "I Think I'm Having a Baby," *CBS Afternoon Playhouse,* CBS, 1981; Andrea Fairchild, "Have You Ever Been Ashamed of Your Parents?," *ABC Afterschool Specials,* ABC, 1983; Madge Owens, *Picnic,* Showtime, 1986.

AWARDS: Best Actress Award from Los Angeles Valley College, 1979, for *The Shadow Box.*

ADDRESSES: AGENT—Triad Artists, 10100 Santa Monica Boulevard, 16th Floor, Los Angeles, CA 90067. MANAGER—Elaine Rich Management, 2400 Whitman Place, Los Angeles, CA 90068.*

*   *   *

LELOUCH, Claude   1937-

PERSONAL: Full name, Claude Barruck Joseph Lelouch; born October 30, 1937, in Paris, France; son of Simon and Charlotte (Abeilard) Lelouch; married Christine Cochet, 1968 (divorced); children: one son, two daughters. MILITARY—Served with Service-Cinema des Armees, 1958-60.

VOCATION: Director, producer, and screenwriter.

CAREER: Also see *WRITINGS* below. PRINCIPAL FILM APPEARANCES—Metteur en scene, *Confidences pour confidences* (also known as *Confidences for Confidences*), Exportation Francaise Cinematographique, 1979; man on train, *Happy New Year,* Columbia, 1987; also appeared as Claude, *Le Propre de l'homme* (also known as *The Right of Man*), 1960.

PRINCIPAL FILM WORK—Producer and director, *La Femme spectacle* (also known as *Night Women*), 1964, released in the United States by Olympic International, 1967; producer, director, and editor (with Claude Barrois), *Une Fille et des fusils* (also known as *To Be a Crook*), 1965, released in the United States by International/Comet, 1967; producer, director, cinematographer, and editor (with Barrois and G. Boisser), *Un Homme et un femme* (also known as *A Man and a Woman*), Allied Artists, 1966; director, camera operator, and editor, *Vivre pour vivre* (also known as *Live for Life* and *Vivere per vivere*), United Artists/Lopert, 1967; director (with others), *Loin de Vietnam* (also known as *Far from Vietnam*), 1967, released in the United States by New Yorker, 1968; producer (with Alexandre Mnouchkine and Georges Dancigers), *Les Gauloises bleues,* 1968, released in the United States by Lopert, 1969; director (with Francois Reichenbach), *13 jours en France* (also known as *Grenoble;* documentary), 1968, released in the United States by United Productions of America, 1969; director, *La Vie, l'amour, la mort* (also known as *Life Love Death*), Lopert, 1969; director and cinematographer, *Un Homme qui me plait* (also known as *Histoire d'aimer, Again a Love Story, Un tipo chimi place,* and *Love Is a Funny Thing*), 1969, released in the United States by United Artists, 1970.

Director, *Le Voyou* (also known as *The Crook*), United Artists, 1971; director and cinematographer, *Smie, Smae, Smoe,* Films 13, 1971; producer, *Ca' n'arrive qu'aux autres* (also known as *It Only Happens to Others*), GSF, 1971; director and cinematographer (with Jean Collomb), *L'Aventure c'est l'aventure* (also known as *Money, Money, Money* and *Adventure Is Adventure*), Films 13, 1972; director, "The Losers" in *Visions of Eight* (also known as *Olympic Visions;* documentary), Cinema V, 1973; producer, director, and cinematographer (with Collomb), *La Bonne Annee* (also known as *Happy New Year* and *The Good Year*), Films 13, 1973; director, *Mariage* (also known as *Marriage*), Films 13, 1974; director, *Toute une vie* (also known as *And Now My Love* and *A Lifetime*), CFDC, 1974, released in the United States by AVCO-Embassy, 1975; director and cinematographer, *Le Bon et les*

mechants (also known as *The Good and the Bad* and *The Good Guy and the Bad Guys*), Films 13, 1975; producer and director, *Le Chat et la souris* (also known as *Cat and Mouse*), Films 13, 1975, released in the United States by Quartet, 1978; producer and director, *Si c'etait a refaire* (also known as *Second Chance, If It Were to Do Over Again,* and *If I Had to Do It All Over Again*), United Artists, 1976; director, *Another Man, Another Chance* (also known as *Un Autre Homme, un autre chance*), United Artists, 1977; executive producer, *Moliere,* Gades Film International/United Artists/Films 13, 1978; director and camera operator, *Robert et Robert* (also known as *Robert and Robert*), AMLF/Films 13, 1978; producer, *Alors, Heureux?,* Films 13, 1979; director, *A nous deux* (also known as *An Adventure for Two* and *Us Two*), AMLF, 1979.

Producer and director, *Les Uns et les autres* (also known as *Bolero*), Sharp Features, 1981, released in the United States by Double, 1982; director, *Edith et Marcel* (also known as *Edith and Marcel*), Films 13/Parafrance, 1982, released in the United States by Miramax, 1984; producer and director, *Viva la vie!* (also known as *Long Live Life!*), Union Generale Cinematographique, 1984; producer and director, *Partir revenir* (also known as *Going and Coming Back* and *Departing Return*), Films 13/Union Generale Cinematographique, 1985; producer and director, *Un Homme et une femme: vingt ans deja* (also known as *A Man and a Woman: Twenty Years Later*), Warner Brothers, 1986; producer and director, *Attention Bandits* (also known as *Les Nouveau bandits, Bandits,* and *Warning, Bandits*), JP2A Audiovisuel/Grange Communications/Films 13/AAA, 1987; producer (with Jean-Paul Belmondo) and director, *Itineraire d'un enfant gate* (also known as *Itinerary of a Spoiled Child* and *Der Gluckspilz*), AFMD/JP2A Audiovisuel, 1988. Also producer, director, and editor, *Le Mal du siecle,* 1953; producer, director, and editor, *USA en vrac,* 1953; producer, director, and editor, *Quand le rideau se leve,* 1957; producer, director, and editor, *La Guerre du silence,* 1959; producer, director, and editor, *Les Mecaniciens de l'armee de l'air,* 1959; producer, director, and editor, *S.O.S. Helicoptere,* 1959; producer and director, *Le Propre de l'homme* (also known as *The Right of Man*), 1960; producer and director, *24 heures d'amant,* 1964; producer, director, and cinematographer, *Les Grands moments,* 1965; producer and director, *Jean-Paul Belmondo,* 1965; producer and director, *Pour un maillot jaune,* 1965; producer and director, *Rendez-vous,* 1976.

RELATED CAREER—Made several short films as a "cinereporter," 1956-58; founder, Les Films 13 (a film production company), 1960—; produced 250 scopitones (short musicals shown on a video jukebox), 1960-62; publicist, Films and Scopitones, 1961-62; president and director-general, General Societe les Films 13, 1966—.

WRITINGS: See production details above, unless indicated. FILM—*Le Mal du siecle,* 1953; *USA en vrac,* 1953; *Quand le rideau se leve,* 1957; *La Guerre du silence,* 1959; *Les Mecaniciens de l'armee de l'air,* 1959; *S.O.S. Helicoptere,* 1959; *Le Propre de l'homme,* 1960; *La Femme spectacle,* 1964; *24 heures d'amant,* 1964; *Les Grands Moments,* 1965; *Jean-Paul Belmondo,* 1965; *Pour un maillot jaune,* 1965; (with Pierre Uytterhoeven) *Une Fille et des fusils,* 1965; (with Uytterhoeven) *Une Homme et une femme,* Allied Artists, 1966; (with Uytterhoeven) *Vivre pour vivre,* United Artists/ Lopert, 1967; (with Uytterhoeven and Francois Reichenbach) *13 jours en France,* 1968; (with Uytterhoeven) *La Vie, l'amour, la morte,* 1969; (with Uytterhoeven) *Un Homme qui me plait,* 1969; (with Uytterhoeven) *Le Voyou,* 1971; *Smie, Smae, Smoe,* 1971; *L'Aventure c'est l'aventure,* 1972; (with Uytterhoeven) *La Bonne Annee,* 1973; (with Uytterhoeven) *Toute une vie,* 1974; (with

Uytterhoeven) *Mariage*, 1974; *Le Bon et les mechants*, 1975; *Le Chat et la souris*, 1975; *Si c'etait a refaire*, 1976; *Another Man, Another Chance*, 1977; *Robert et Robert*, 1978; *A nous deux*, 1979; *Les Uns et les autres*, 1981; (with Uytterhoeven and Gilles Durieux) *Edith et Marcel*, 1982; (with Jerome Tonnerre) *Viva la vie!*, 1984; (with Uytterhoeven, Tonnerre, and Julie Pavesi) *Partir revenir*, 1985; (with Uytterhoeven, Monique Lange, and Tonnerre) *Un Homme et une femme: vingt ans deja*, 1986; (with Uytterhoeven) *Attention Bandits*, 1987; *Itineraire d'un enfant gate*, 1988.

AWARDS: Academy Awards, Best Foreign Film and (with Pierre Uytterhoeven) Best Story and Screenplay Written Directly for the Screen, Academy Award nomination, Best Director, and Golden Palm from the Cannes Film Festival, all 1966, for *Une Homme et une femme;* Grand Prix du Cinema Francaise, 1967, for *Vivre pour vivre;* Prix Raoul Levy, 1970; chevalier, Ordre National du Merite, officier, Ordre des Arts et des Lettres.

ADDRESSES: OFFICE—15 Avenue Hoche, 75008 Paris, France. PUBLICIST—Roberta Barrows, Warner Brothers Publicity Department, 4000 Warner Boulevard, Burbank, CA 91522.*

*   *   *

LEWIS, Al   1923-

PERSONAL: Born Alexander Meister, April 30, 1923, in New York, NY; son of Alexander and Ida (Nedal) Meister; married Marge Domowitz, November 1, 1956; children: David, Theodore, Paul. EDUCATION—Graduated from Oswego State Teachers Col-

AL LEWIS

lege, 1944; Columbia University, M.A., 1947, Ph.D., 1952; studied at the Actors Workshop, 1947-55.

VOCATION: Actor.

CAREER: PRINCIPAL STAGE APPEARANCES—*The Ice Man Cometh*, Circle in the Square, New York City, 1956.

MAJOR TOURS—Bell boy, *The Best Man*, Hanna Theatre, Cleveland, OH, 1961.

PRINCIPAL FILM APPEARANCES—Machine Gun Manny, *Pretty Boy Floyd*, Continental, 1960; store owner, *The World of Henry Orient*, United Artists, 1964; Grandpa Munster, *Munster, Go Home*, Universal, 1966; Turkey, *They Shoot Horses, Don't They?*, ABC/Cinerama, 1969; Bert, *The Boatniks*, Buena Vista, 1970; messenger, *They Might Be Giants*, Universal, 1971; Judge Harrison, *Used Cars*, Columbia, 1980; Uncle Joe Russo, *Married to the Mob*, Orion, 1988; Mr. Wolfstadt, *Bum Rap*, Millennium, 1988. Also appeared in *Black Starlet*, Omni, 1974.

PRINCIPAL TELEVISION APPEARANCES—Series: Uncle Al, *The Uncle Al Show*, ABC, 1958-59; Officer Leo Schnauser, *Car 54, Where Are You?*, NBC, 1961-63; Grandpa Munster, *The Munsters*, CBS, 1964-66. Episodic: *Taxi*, ABC, 1981. Movies: Mike Jacobs, *Ring of Passion*, NBC, 1978; Grandpa, *The Munster's Revenge*, NBC, 1981; also *Save the Dog!*, Disney Channel, 1988. Specials: Grandpa Munster, *Marineland Carnival*, CBS, 1965.

NON-RELATED CAREER—Lecturer on Black history in America; restaurateur.

MEMBER: American Federation of Television and Radio Artists, Actors' Equity Association, Screen Actors Guild, American Guild of Musicians and Artists.

ADDRESSES: AGENT—Abrams Artists and Associates, 9200 Sunset Boulevard, Suite 625, Los Angeles, CA 90048 *

*   *   *

LEWIS, Edmund   1959-

PERSONAL: Born Edmund Grossman, February 12, 1959, in London, England; son of Alfred (a shopkeeper) and Vera (a landlady; maiden name, Smith) Grossman. EDUCATION—Trained for the stage at the Royal Academy of Dramatic Art.

VOCATION: Actor.

CAREER: STAGE DEBUT—Anaethetist, *Having a Ball*, Palace Theatre, Watford, U.K. LONDON DEBUT—Skylight, *Class Enemy*, Man in the Moon Theatre, 1983. OFF-BROADWAY DEBUT—Tinkler, *The Longboat*, Harold Clurman Theatre, 1987. PRINCIPAL STAGE APPEARANCES—Willie, *Without Apologies*, Hudson Guild Theatre, New York City, 1988; also appeared as Steve/Reg, *Up 'n' Under*, Hudson Guild Theatre; Tony, *A Most Secret War*, Harold Clurman Theatre, New York City; Walter Hamilton, *Saint Florence*, Capital Repertory Company, Albany, NY; Billy, *Billy Liar*, Paris, *Romeo and Juliet*, Mark, *Kiss Me Hard, Kiss Me Quick*, Kevin, *What's My Handicap?*, and various roles, *Japanese No Plays*, all in London.

EDMUND LEWIS

PRINCIPAL TELEVISION APPEARANCES—Mini-Series: Parmenas, *A.D.*, NBC, 1985.

AWARDS: Drama Desk Award nomination, Outstanding Featured Actor in a Play, 1989, for *Without Apologies;* Silver Medal from the Royal Academy of Dramatic Art; recipient of stage fighting awards.

MEMBER: Actors' Equity Association.

SIDELIGHTS: RECREATIONS—Karate and all sports.

ADDRESSES: AGENT—David Drummond Agency, 102 W. 75th Street, New York, NY 10023.

*   *   *

LICHT, Jeremy   1971-

PERSONAL: Surname is pronounced "licked"; full name, Jeremy Adam Licht; born January 4, 1971, in Los Angeles, CA; son of Dennis Howard and Trudi Marsha Licht.

VOCATION: Actor.

CAREER: PRINCIPAL STAGE APPEARANCES—David, *Lies My Father Told Me*, Westwood Playhouse, Los Angeles.

PRINCIPAL FILM APPEARANCES—Tim Johnson, *The Next One*,

All Star, 1982; Anthony, "It's a Good Life" in *Twilight Zone: The Movie*, Warner Brothers, 1983.

TELEVISION DEBUT—Tommy, *And Your Name Is Jonah*, CBS, 1979. PRINCIPAL TELEVISION APPEARANCES—Series: Mark Hogan, *Valerie*, NBC, 1986-87, retitled *Valerie's Family*, NBC, 1987-88, retitled *The Hogan Family*, NBC, 1988—. Pilots: Jed, *Skeezer*, NBC, 1982; also *Jessie*, CBS; *Close to Home*, NBC. Episodic: *Angie*, ABC; *The Phoenix*, ABC; *St. Elsewhere*, NBC; *Hotel*, ABC; *Bay City Blues*, NBC; *Finder of Lost Loves*, ABC. Movies: Jarod at age three, *The Seekers*, HBO, 1979; Paul, *The Comeback Kid*, ABC, 1980; Nick Harris, *A Cry for Love*, NBC, 1980; Byron, *Father Figure*, CBS, 1980; D.W. Demerjian, *Once Upon a Family*, CBS, 1980; Willie Carney, *The Ordeal of Bill Carney*, CBS, 1981; Michael Gibbs, *Lois Gibbs and the Love Canal*, CBS, 1982; David Maris, *Lots of Luck*, Disney Channel, 1985. Specials: Rufus, "All the Way Home," *NBC Live Theatre*, NBC, 1981; Matt Elder, "All the Kids Do It," *CBS Afterschool Special*, CBS, 1984; as himself, *Alvin Goes Back to School*, NBC, 1986.

RELATED CAREER—Actor in television commercials; model.

NON-RELATED CAREER—Honorary chairor, annual Cystic Fibrosis "Bowl-for-Breath"; spokesperson for the March of Dimes.

AWARDS: Youth in Film Award nomination, Best Actor in a Feature Film, 1984, for *Twilight Zone: The Movie;* Youth in Film Award, Best Actor in a Comedy Series, 1986, for *Valerie*.

MEMBER: American Film Institute, International Thespian Society, Extraordinary Students of America, Students Against Driving

JEREMY LICHT

Drunk, United Friends of the Children, Kidsnet, Famous Fone Friends, Purina Pet Program.

SIDELIGHTS: RECREATIONS—Bowling.

ADDRESSES: OFFICE—c/o *The Hogan Family*, Lorimar Studios, 10202 Washington Boulevard, Culver City, CA 90230.

* * *

LINNEA
See QUIGLEY, Linnea

* * *

LINVILLE, Joanne

PERSONAL: Born c. 1926, in California; father, in the oil business; married Mark Rydell (a director, producer, and actor), November 23, 1962 (divorced); children: Christopher. EDUCATION—Attended Compton Junior College; studied acting with Stella Adler.

VOCATION: Actress.

CAREER: BROADWAY DEBUT—Valeria, *Daughter of Silence*, Music Box Theatre, 1961. PRINCIPAL STAGE APPEARANCES—*Johnny Johnson*, Carnegie Hall Theatre, New York City, 1956; *Gethsemane Springs*, New Theatre for Now, Mark Taper Forum, Los Angeles, 1978.

FILM DEBUT—Joanna, *The Goddess*, Columbia, 1958. PRINCIPAL FILM APPEARANCES—Sarah Cross, *Scorpio*, United Artists, 1973; Ria Gable, *Gable and Lombard*, Universal, 1976; Freddie, *A Star Is Born*, Warner Brothers, 1976; Dr. Weston, *The Seduction*, AVCO-Embassy, 1982.

TELEVISION DEBUT—*Studio One*, CBS, 1956. PRINCIPAL TELEVISION APPEARANCES—Series: Zina Willow, *Behind the Screen*, CBS, 1981-82. Pilots: Connie Durstine, *The House on Greenapple Road*, ABC, 1970. Episodic: Daisy Sage, "The Animal Kingdom," *The Alcoa Hour*, NBC, 1957; Lavinia, "The Passerby," *The Twilight Zone*, CBS, 1961; Romulan commander, "The Enterprise Incident," *Star Trek*, NBC, 1968; Samuels, *L.A. Law*, NBC, 1988; also "The Dead Part of the House" and "Moment of Hate," *One Step Beyond*, ABC, 1959; *Route 66*, CBS, 1962; *Dr. Kildare*, NBC, 1962; *Empire*, NBC, 1962; *Gunsmoke*, CBS, 1962; *Sam Benedict*, NBC, 1962; *The Defenders*, CBS, 1962; *The Dick Powell Show*, NBC, 1962; *The Nurses*, CBS, 1962; *Ben Casey*, ABC, 1962; "The Pit," *The Invaders*, ABC, 1968; *The Kaiser Aluminum Hour*, NBC; "Mrs. 'arris Goes to Paris" and "American Primitive," *Studio One*, CBS; *U.S. Steel Hour*. CBS; *Robert Montgomery Presents*, NBC; *Suspicion*, NBC. Movies: Helen Warner, *Secrets*, ABC, 1977; Nan Forester, *The Critical List*, NBC, 1978; Elena's mother, *The Users*, ABC, 1978; Rosalind, *The Right of the People*, ABC, 1986; Dr. Anne Morgan, *From the Dead of Night*, NBC, 1989. Specials: Anvar, "The Ascent of Mount Fuji," *Hollywood Television Theatre*, PBS, 1978.

RELATED CAREER—Member, Actors Studio; dancer, Las Vegas, NV.

ADDRESSES: AGENT—Chris Black, William Morris Agency, 151 El Camino Drive, Beverly Hills, CA 90212.*

* * *

LOGAN, Nedda Harrigan   1900-1989

PERSONAL: Born in 1900 in Rumson, NJ; died of lung cancer, April 1, 1989, in New York, NY; daughter of Edward "Ned" (a composer, writer, and vaudeville performer) and Anne Theresa (Braham) Harrigan; married Walter Connolly (an actor; died, May 28, 1940); married Joshua Logan (a director, producer, and writer), 1945 (died, July 1988); children: Ann (first marriage); Harrigan and Thomas (second marriage). EDUCATION—Graduated from the National Park Seminary.

VOCATION: Actress.

CAREER: PRINCIPAL STAGE APPEARANCES—Sister, *The Childrens' Tragedy*, Greenwich Village Theatre, New York City, 1921; Lisa Toselli, *Treat 'em Rough*, Klaw Theatre, New York City, 1926; Wells, *Dracula*, Fulson Theatre, New York City, 1927; Janet Aiken, *Merry Andrew*, Henry Miller's Theatre, New York City, 1929; Fifine, *Becky Sharp*, Knickerbocker Theatre, New York City, 1929; Estelle Fenley, *Monkey*, Mansfield Theatre, New York City, 1932; Myra Crana, *Bidding High*, Vanderbilt Theatre, New York City, 1932; Frieda Chatfield, *Dangerous Corner*, Empire Theatre, New York City, 1932; Felicia Mitchell, *A Hat, a Coat, and a Glove*, Selwyn Theatre, New York City, 1934; Natalia, *Field of Ermine*, Mansfield Theatre, 1935; Donna Lucia D'Alvadorez, *Charley's Aunt*, Cort Theatre, New York City, 1940; Edith Bolling Wilson, *In Time to Come*, Mansfield Theatre, 1941. Also appeared in *A Woman of No Importance*, Fulton Theatre, New York City, 1916; *Cardinal Richelieu*, Mohawk Drama Festival, Schenectady, NY, 1940; and in *Three's a Family*, *Personal Appearance*, and other plays produced in Europe by the U.S.O. during World War II.

MAJOR TOURS—*A Woman's a Fool to Be Clever*, U.S. cities, 1938; also appeared in *Musical Moments* (revue), U.S. cities.

PRINCIPAL FILM APPEARANCES—Miss Burns, *I'll Fix It*, Columbia, 1934; Louise DeVoe, *The Case of the Black Cat*, Warner Brothers, 1936; Madame Lucretia Barelli, *Charlie Chan at the Opera*, Twentieth Century-Fox, 1936; Mrs. Tristo, *Fugitive in the Sky*, Warner Brothers, 1937; Madame Tchernov, *Thank You, Mr. Moto*, Twentieth Century-Fox, 1937; Mrs. Nelson, *Men Are Such Fools*, Warner Brothers, 1938; Countess Varloff, *A Trip to Paris*, Twentieth Century-Fox, 1938; Mrs. Burton, *The Honeymoon's Over*, Twentieth Century-Fox, 1939; Joan Trask, *On Trial*, Warner Brothers, 1939; Mrs. Long, *Castle on the Hudson* (also known as *Years Without Days*), Warner Brothers, 1940; Madame Lucien, *Devil's Island*, Warner Brothers, 1940; Seena Haynes, *Scandal Sheet*, Columbia, 1940.

RELATED CAREER—Founder, Stage Door Canteen, New York City, 1942; trustee, National Corporate Theater Fund.

NON-RELATED CAREER—Trustee, Museum of the City of New York.

AWARDS: Woman of the Year Award from the United Service Organizations (U.S.O.), 1983.

MEMBER: Actors' Equity Association, Screen Actors Guild, Actors' Fund (president, 1979-89).

OBITUARIES AND OTHER SOURCES: New York Times, April 3, 1989; *Variety,* April 5-11, 1989.*

*   *   *

LOM, Herbert   1917-

PERSONAL: Born September 11, 1917, in Prague, Czechoslovakia; son of Charles and Olga (Gottlieb) Lom; married Dina Scheu (divorced). EDUCATION—Studied acting at the Prague School of Acting, the London Embassy School, the Old Vic Theatre School, the Sadlers Wells School, and the Westminster School.

VOCATION: Actor.

CAREER: LONDON DEBUT—Dr. Larson, *The Seventh Veil,* Prince's Theatre, 1951. PRINCIPAL STAGE APPEARANCES—Pless, *The Trap,* Duke of York's Theatre, London, 1952; the King, *The King and I,* Drury Lane Theatre, London, 1953-55; Napoleon Bonaparte, *Betzi,* Haymarket Theatre, London, 1975.

PRINCIPAL FILM APPEARANCES—Napoleon, *The Young Mr. Pitt,* Twentieth Century-Fox, 1942; Torg, *The Dark Tower,* Warner Brothers, 1943; medical officer, *Secret Mission,* General Film

HERBERT LOM

Distributors, 1944; Gregory Lang, *Appointment with Crime,* British National, 1945; Monsieur Andrea Roux, *Hotel Reserve,* RKO, 1946; Keitel, *Night Boat to Dublin,* Associated British/Pathe, 1946; Dr. Larson, *The Seventh Veil,* General Film Distributors/Universal, 1946; Jules and George de Lisle, *Dual Alibi,* British National, 1947; Hendleman, *The Girl in the Painting,* Universal, 1948; Keramikos, *Snowbound,* Universal, 1949.

Anthemus, *The Black Rose,* Twentieth Century-Fox, 1950; Rahman, *Cage of Gold,* Ealing, 1950; Ranki, *Golden Salamander,* General Film Distributors, 1950; Max, *Good Time Girl,* Film Classics, 1950; Kristo, *Night and the City,* Twentieth Century-Fox, 1950; Dominic Danges, *Hell Is Sold Out,* Eros, 1951; Karl Theodor, *The Great Manhunt,* Columbia, 1951; Peter Hobart, *The Lucky Mascot* (also known as *The Brass Monkey*), Allied Artists, 1951; Ford, *School for Brides* (also known as *Two on the Tiles*), Hoffberg, 1952; Ford, *Whispering Smith Versus Scotland Yard* (also known as *Whispering Smith Hits London*), RKO, 1952; Julius de Koster, Jr., *The Paris Express* (also known as *The Man Who Watched Trains Go By*), George Schaefer, 1953; Mados, *Mr. Denning Drives North,* Carroll, 1953; Alex Leon, *Project M7* (also known as *The Net*), Universal, 1953; Maurice Meister, *The Ringer,* Regent, 1953; Peter Sandorski, *Shoot First* (also known as *Rough Shoot*), United Artists, 1953; Emil Landosh, *Beautiful Stranger* (also known as *Twist of Fate*), British Lion, 1954; Amico, *The Love Lottery,* General Film Distributors, 1954; Louis, *The Ladykillers,* Continental Distributors, 1956; Narbonne, *Star of India,* United Artists, 1956; Napoleon, *War and Peace,* United Artists, 1956; Vargas, *Chase a Crooked Shadow,* Warner Brothers, 1958; harbor master, *Fire Down Below,* Columbia, 1957; Trifon, *Action of the Tiger,* Metro-Goldwyn-Mayer (MGM), 1957; Gino, *Hell Drivers,* Rank, 1958; Major DuPaty de Clam, *I Accuse!,* MGM, 1958; Juan Menda, *Intent to Kill,* Twentieth Century-Fox, 1958; Orsini, *The Roots of Heaven,* Twentieth Century-Fox, 1958; Herod Antipas, *The Big Fisherman,* Buena Vista, 1959; Nick, *Room 43* (also known as *Passport to Shame*), Cory, 1959; Emil Saxon, *Third Man on the Mountain* (also known as *Banner in the Sky*), Buena Vista, 1959.

Van Leyden, *Flame Over India* (also known as *North West Frontier*), Twentieth Century-Fox, 1960; Anton Reger, *I Aim at the Stars,* Columbia, 1960; Tigranes, *Spartacus,* Universal, 1960; Ben Yussef, *El Cid,* Allied Artists, 1961; Waldo Zhernikov, *The Frightened City,* Allied Artists, 1961; Captain Nemo, *Mysterious Island,* Columbia, 1961; Castel Benac, *I Like Money* (also known as *Mr. Topaze*), Twentieth Century-Fox, 1962; Chong Sing, *Tiara Tahiti,* Zenith, 1962; title role, *The Phantom of the Opera,* Universal, 1962; Wilkie, *No Tree in the Street* (also known as *No Trees on the Street*), Seven Arts, 1964; Chief Inspector Charles Dreyfus, *A Shot in the Dark,* United Artists, 1964; Dr. Charles Bovard, *Return from the Ashes,* United Artists, 1965; Brinkley, *Treasure of Silver Lake,* Columbia, 1965; Mr. Casimir, *Bang, Bang, You're Dead* (also known as *Marrakesh*), American International, 1966; Shabhandar, *Gambit,* Universal, 1966; Randolph, *The Karate Killers,* MGM, 1967; Simon Legree, *Uncle Tom's Cabin,* Kroger Babb, 1968; Matt Wilson, *Assignment to Kill,* Warner Brothers, 1968; Diego, *Eve* (also known as *The Face of Eve*), Commonwealth, 1968; governor, *99 Women,* Commonwealth United, 1969; Matt Wilson, *Assignment to Kill* (also known as *The Assignment*), Warner Brothers/Seven Arts, 1969; General Huerta, *Villa Rides,* Paramount, 1968; Dr. Hassler, *Journey to the Far Side of the Sun* (also known as *Doppelganger*), Universal, 1969.

Lord Henry Wotten, *Dorian Gray* (also known as *The Secret of Dorian Gray, Das Bildnis des Dorian Gray,* and *Il dio chiamato*

Dorian), American International, 1970; Van Helsing, *Count Dracula*, Phoenix, 1971; Marot, *Murders in the Rue Morgue*, American International, 1971; Byron, *Asylum* (also known as *House of Crazies*), Cinerama, 1972; Count Cumberland, *Mark of the Devil* (also known as *Burn Witch Burn*, *Brenn Hexe Brenn*, and *Bis Aufs Blut Gequalt*), Hallmark Releasing, 1972; Henry Fengriffen, *And Now the Screaming Starts*, Cinerama, 1973; Prescott, *Dark Places*, Cinerama, 1974; Chief Inspector Charles Dreyfus, *The Return of the Pink Panther*, United Artists, 1975; Dr. Armstrong, *Ten Little Indians* (also known as *And Then There Were None*), AVCO-Embassy, 1975; ex-Chief Inspector Charles Dreyfus, *The Pink Panther Strikes Again*, United Artists, 1976; Inspector Watkins, *Charleston*, Analysis, 1978; former Chief Inspector Charles Dreyfus, *Revenge of the Pink Panther*, United Artists, 1978.

Mikhail Yaskov, *Hopscotch*, AVCO-Embassy, 1980; Dr. Hartz, *The Lady Vanishes*, Rank/Group 1, 1980; Mr. Zebra, *The Man with Bogart's Face* (also known as *Sam Marlow, Private Eye*), Twentieth Century-Fox, 1980; Charles Dreyfus, *The Trail of the Pink Panther*, Metro-Goldwyn-Mayer/United Artists (MGM/UA), 1982; Charles Dreyfus, *Curse of the Pink Panther*, MGM/UA, 1983; Dr. Sam Weizak, *The Dead Zone*, Paramount, 1983; Ali Safa Bey, *Memed My Hawk*, Focus, 1984; Colonel Bockner, *King Solomon's Mines*, Cannon Group, 1985; General Mosquera, *Whoops Apocalypse*, ITC, 1987; Mackintosh, *Going Bananas* (also known as *My African Adventure*), Cannon Releasing, 1987; Elia, *Skeleton Coast*, Nelson Entertainment, 1988; Colonel Diaz, *River of Death*, Pathe Communications/Viacom, 1989; General Romensky, *Ten Little Indians*, Cannon Group, 1989; Ludwig, *Masque of the Red Death*, Twenty First Century, 1989. Also appeared in *Mein Kempf—My Crimes*, Associated British, 1940; *Horse Without a Head*, Buena Vista, 1963; *Dragonard* (also known as *Master of Dragonard Hill*), Cannon Releasing, 1987.

PRINCIPAL TELEVISION APPEARANCES—Mini-Series: Monsieur Chardin, *Lace*, ABC, 1984. Pilots: Victor Russo, *Mr. Jerico*, ABC, 1970. Episodic: *The Errol Flynn Theatre*, Dumont, 1957. Movies: Dr. Roger Corder, *The Human Jungle*, syndicated, 1964; Barnabas, *Peter and Paul*, CBS, 1981.

WRITINGS: *Enter a Spy* (novel), Merlin Press, 1978.

MEMBER: British Actors' Equity Association, Screen Actors Guild, Reform Club.

ADDRESSES: AGENTS—Camden Artists, 2121 Avenue of the Stars, Suite 401, Los Angeles, CA 90067; Duncan Heath Ltd., 162 Wardour Street, London W1V 3AT, England.

*   *   *

LONG, William Ivey

VOCATION: Costume designer.

CAREER: PRINCIPAL STAGE WORK—Costume designer: *Two Small Bodies* and *Earth-Worms*, both Playwrights Horizons, New York City, 1977; *Conjuring an Event*, American Place Theatre, New York City, 1978; *The Vienna Notes*, Playwrights Horizons, 1979; *The Inspector General*, Circle in the Square, New York City,

1979; *Altar Boys*, Theatre Four, New York City, 1979; *The 1940's Radio Hour*, St. James Theatre, New York City, 1979; *The Impossible H.L. Mencken*, American Place Theatre, 1979 and 1980; *Passione*, Playwrights Horizons, then Morosco Theatre, New York City, both 1980; *Johnny on a Spot*, Brooklyn Academy of Music, Brooklyn, NY, 1980; *True West*, New York Shakespeare Festival (NYSF), Public Theatre, New York City, 1980; *Mass Appeal*, Manhattan Theatre Club, New York City, 1980, then Booth Theatre, New York City, 1981; *A Midsummer Night's Dream*, Alaska Repertory Theatre, Anchorage/Fairbanks, AK, 1981; *The Actor's Nightmare* and *Sister Mary Ignatius Explains It All for You* (double-bill), Playwrights Horizons, 1981; *Hunting Scenes from Lower Bavaria*, Manhattan Theatre Club, 1981; *Twelve Dreams*, NYSF, Public Theatre, 1981; *Nine*, 46th Street Theatre, New York City, 1982; *Poor Little Lambs*, Theatre at St. Peter's Church, New York City, 1982; *The Lady and the Clarinet*, Lucille Lortel Theatre, New York City, 1983; *American Passion*, Joyce Theater, New York City, 1983; *Play Memory*, Longacre Theatre, New York City, 1984; *The Tap Dance Kid*, Broadhurst Theatre, New York City, 1983, then Minskoff Theatre, New York City, 1984; *End of the World*, Music Box Theatre, New York City, 1984; *Nine*, Opera House, Kennedy Center for the Performing Arts, Washington, DC, 1984; *Hey Ma . . . Kaye Ballard*, Promenade Theatre, New York City, 1984; *After the Fall*, Playhouse 91, New York City, 1984.

A Broadway Baby, Goodspeed Opera House, East Haddam, CT, 1985; *The Marriage of Bette and Boo*, NYSF, Public Theatre, 1985; *One Man Band*, South Street Theatre, New York City, 1985; *Principia Scriptoriae*, Manhattan Theatre Club, 1986; *Hamlet*, NYSF, Public Theatre, 1986; *Smile*, Lunt-Fontanne Theatre, New York City, 1986; *Sleight of Hand*, Cort Theatre, New York City, 1987; *Laughing Wild*, Playwrights Horizons, 1987; *Wenceslas Square*, NYSF, Public Theatre, 1988; *Mail*, Music Box Theatre, 1988; *Italian American Reconciliation*, Manhattan Theatre Club, 1988; *Lend Me a Tenor*, Royale Theatre, New York City, 1989. Also *Jungle Coup*, Playwrights Horizons; *A Quiet Place* and *Trouble in Tahiti*, both Vienna Staatsoper, Vienna, Austria; *Wozzeck*, Welsh National Opera; *Men's Fugue*, Twyla Tharp Dance Company.

MAJOR TOURS—Costume designer, *Nine*, U.S. cities, 1984; costume designer, *The Tap Dance Kid*, U.S. cities, 1987.

PRINCIPAL TELEVISION WORK—All as costume designer. Episodic: "Ask Me Again," *American Playhouse*, PBS, 1989. Specials: *The 1985 Miss Universe Pageant*, CBS, 1985; *The 1988 Miss Universe Pageant*, CBS, 1988; *Miss Teen U.S.A.*, CBS, 1988; "Paul Taylor: Roses and Last Look," *Great Performances*, PBS, 1988.

RELATED CAREER—Costume designer: Yale Repertory Theatre, New Haven, CT, 1973-75; (also set designer) PAF Playhouse, Huntington Station, NY, 1977-79; Arena Stage, Washington, DC, 1978-79; American Repertory Theatre, Cambridge, MA, 1979; Goodman Theatre, Chicago, IL, 1981-82; Long Wharf Theatre, New Haven, CT, 1983-84; and with the Paul Taylor Dance Company.

AWARDS: Antoinette Perry Award and Drama Desk Award, both Best Costume Designer, and Joseph Maharam Award, all 1982, for *Nine*; Antoinette Perry Award nomination, and Drama Desk Award, both Best Costume Designer, 1989, for *Lend Me a Tenor*.*

LONSDALE, Michael
  See LONSDALE, Michel

        *   *   *

LONSDALE, Michel   1931-
  (Michael Lonsdale)

PERSONAL: Born in 1931 in Paris, France.

VOCATION: Actor.

CAREER: PRINCIPAL STAGE APPEARANCES—L'Interrogateur, *L'Amant Anglaise,* Le Treteau de Paris, Barbizon-Plaza Theatre, New York City, 1971; recorded voice, *The Human Voice,* University Theatre, New York City, 1984.

PRINCIPAL FILM APPEARANCES—(As Michael Lonsdale) Priest, *Le Proces* (also known as *The Trial, Der Prozess,* and *Il processo*), Astor, 1963; secretary, *Je vous salue Mafia* (also known as *Hail Mafia* and *Da New York: Mafia uccide*), Goldstone, 1965; Debu-Bridel, *Paris brule-t-il?* (also known as *Is Paris Burning?*), Paramount, 1966; Morane, *La Mariee etait en noir* (also known as *The Bride Wore Black*), Artistes Associes, 1968; (as Michael Lonsdale) Cardinal Maffeo Barberini (later Pope Urban VIII), *Galileo,* Fenice Cinematografica/Rizzoli/Kinozenter, 1968, released in the United States by American Film Theatre, 1975; Stein, *Detruire, dit-elle* (also known as *Destroy, She Said*), Grove, 1969; Monsieur Tabard, *Baisers voles* (also known as *Stolen Kisses*), Lopert, 1969.

Man, *Le Printemps* (also known as *Spring*), Euro Images, 1971; French narrator, *Les Annees Lumiere—1895-1900* (documentary; also known as *The Lumiere Years*), Planfilm, 1971; inspector, *Les Assasins de l'ordre* (also known as *The Assassins of Order*), Productions Belles Rives, 1971; Lucas, *Il etait un fois un flic* (also known as *There Was Once a Cop*), Gaumont, 1971; Father Henri, *Le Souffle au coeur* (also known as *Murmur of the Heart* and *Dearest Love*), Minerva/Walter Reade/Continental Distribuling, 1971; Pasteur, *La Vieille Fille* (also known as *The Old Maid*), Valoria, 1971; Polyte, *Papa les petits bateaux* (also known as *Papa the Little Boats*), CCFC, 1971; Thomas, *Out One: Noli me tangere,* Sunchild, 1971; Thomas, *Out One: Spectre* (also known as *Spectre*), Sunchild, 1972; Sergei, *Chut!,* Parafrance, 1971; Commissioner Lebel, *The Day of the Jackal,* Universal, 1973; Philippe, *La Fille au violoncelle* (also known as *The Girl with the Cello*), Albina Distribution, 1973; judge, *Glissements progressifs du plaisir* (also known as *Successive Slidings of Pleasure*), Fox-Lira, 1973; Stephane, *Les Grands sentiments font les bons gueuletons* (also known as *Big Sentiments Make for Good Sports*), Films la Boetie, 1973; Duc de Croytor, *Caravan to Vaccares,* Rank, 1974; French Vice-Consul of Lahore, *India Song,* Artificial Eye, 1974; Jean Bermans, *Le Fantome de la liberte* (also known as *The Phantom of Liberty* and *The Specter of Freedom*), Twentieth Century-Fox, 1974; Dr. Mezy, *Stavisky,* Cinemation, 1974; Carlille, *Un Linceul n'a pas de poches* (also known as *No Pockets in a Shroud*), Societe Nouvelle Prodis, 1974; judge, *Les Suspects* (also known as *The Suspects*), Valoria, 1974; painter, *Une Baleine qui avait mal aux dents* (also known as *A Whale That Had a Toothache*), Films 88, 1974.

Uncle, *Folle a tuer* (also known as *Mad Enough to Kill*), Fox-Lira, 1975; minister, *Section speciale* (also known as *Special Section*),

United Artists, 1975; President, *Les Oeufs brouilles* (also known as *The Scrambled Eggs*), Columbia-Warner Distributors, 1975; doctor, *Aloise,* Framo Diffusion, 1975; Fournier, *Serieux comme le plaisir* (also known as *Serious As Pleasure*), Lugo, 1975; David, *La Traque* (also known as *The Track*), Columbia-Warner Distributors, 1975; Morrison, *Le Telephone rose* (also known as *The Pink Telephone*), Gala Film Distributors/Gaumont International, 1975; Swan, *The Romantic Englishwoman,* New World, 1975; Pierre, *Mr. Klein* (also known as *M. Klein*), Twentieth Century-Fox/Lira/Quartet, 1976; Aberaud, *L'Imprecateur* (also known as *The Accuser* and *Der Anklager*), Exportation Francaise Cinematographique/Parafrance, 1977; Georges Aubert, *Le Diable dans la boite* (also known as *The Devil in the Box*), Madeleine/Societe Nouvelle de Cinema, 1977; storyteller (first story), *Une sale histoire* (also known as *A Dirty Story*), Films du Losange, 1977; waiter, *Die Linkshandige Frau* (also known as *The Left-Handed Woman*), Marin Karmitz/Artificial Eye, 1977, released in the United States by New Yorker, 1980; L'Huissier, *Bartleby,* Antenne 2, 1978; (as Michael Lonsdale) Alain Renoudot, *The Passage,* United Artists, 1979; (as Michael Lonsdale) Hugo Drax, *Moonraker,* United Artists, 1979.

Narrator, *Le Risque de vivre* (also known as *The Risk of Living*), Roissy, 1984; Bodley, *Enigma,* Embassy, 1983; St. Eligius, *Le Bon Roi Dagobert* (also known as *Good King Dagobert*), Gaumont, 1984; (as Michael Lonsdale) the Senator, *Erendira,* Miramax, 1984; doctor, *Le Juge* (also known as *The Judge*), GEF, 1984; Ernst Manfredi, *The Holcroft Covenant,* Universal, 1985; (as Michael Lonsdale) Commissioner Bellanger, *Billy-Ze-Kick,* AAA/World Marketing, 1985; (as Michael Lonsdale) the Abbott, *The Name of the Rose,* Twentieth Century-Fox, 1986; Tanzmann, *Der Madonna Mann* (also known as *The Madonna Man*), Radiant/Studio Hamburg/Friedlander, 1988; Xavier Lorion, *Souvenir,* Palisades, 1988; Cammerschulze, *Niezwylka Podroz Baltazara Kobera* (also known as *The Fabulous Journey of Balthazar Kober, The Tribulations of Balthazar Kobera,* and *Les Tribulations de Balthasar Kober*), Film Polski/Jeck Films/La Sept, 1988. Also appeared in *C'est arrive a Aden,* 1956; *Une Balle dans le canon,* 1958; *Les Portes claquent,* 1961; *La Main chaude,* 1960; *Adorable Menteuse,* 1961; *Les Snobs,* 1961; *La Denonciation* (also known as *The Immoral Moment*), 1962, released in the United States by Jerand Film Distributors, 1967; *Tous les enfants du monde,* 1963; *Behold a Pale Horse,* Columbia, 1964; *Jaloux comme un tigre,* 1964; *Les Copains,* 1964; *La Bourse et la vie,* 1965; *Le Judoka agent secret,* 1966; *Les Compagnons de la marguerite,* 1966; *L'Homme a la Buick,* 1967; *L'Authentique proces de Carl Emmanuel Jung,* 1967; *La Pince a ongles* (also known as *The Nail Clippers*), 1968; *L'Hiver,* 1969; *Hibernatus,* 1969; *La Rose et le revolver,* 1970; *L'Etalon,* 1970; *L'Automne,* 1971; *Jaune le soleil,* 1971; *La Grande Paulette,* 1972; *La Raison du plus fou* (also known as *The Right of the Maddest*), Gaumont International, 1972; *Les Jeux de la comtesse,* 1981; *Chariots of Fire,* Twentieth Century-Fox, 1981; *L'Eveille du pont d'Alma* (also known as *The Insomniac on the Bridge*), Citevox, 1985.

PRINCIPAL TELEVISION APPEARANCES—Mini-Series: (As Michael Lonsdale) Grigoriev, *Smiley's People,* syndicated, 1982. Movies: (As Michael Lonsdale) Martin Bormann, *The Bunker,* CBS, 1981; Detective Dubois, *Riviera,* ABC, 1987. Specials: (As Michael Lonsdale) Narrator, ''Tahiti: Fire Waters,'' *Cousteau's Rediscovery of the World,* TBS, 1988.

RELATED CAREER—Stage actor in Paris, France.

ADDRESSES: AGENTS—Plunket Greene Limited, 4 Ovington

Gardens London SW3 1LS, England; Isabelle Kloucowsky, 16 Avenue de Bretevil, Paris 7E, France.*

*   *   *

LOUGHLIN, Lori

PERSONAL: Surname is pronounced "Lock-in"; born July 28, in Long Island, NY.

VOCATION: Actress.

CAREER: PRINCIPAL FILM APPEARANCES—Susan Baxter, *Amityville 3-D,* Orion, 1983; Abby, *The New Kids,* Columbia, 1985; Toni, *Secret Admirer,* Orion, 1985; Christian, *RAD,* Tri-Star, 1986; Sandi, *Back to the Beach,* Paramount, 1987; Tara Mitchell, *The Night Before,* HBO Video/ITC Entertainment, 1989.

PRINCIPAL TELEVISION APPEARANCES—Series: Jody Travis, *The Edge of Night,* ABC, 1980-83; Rebecca Donaldson, *Full House,* ABC, 1988-89. Pilots: Linda Craig, *The Tom Swift and Linda Craig Mystery Hour,* ABC, 1983; Christie, *Brotherhood of Justice,* ABC, 1986; Tammy, *Old Money* (broadcast as an episode of *CBS Summer Playhouse*), CBS, 1988. Episodic: Jenny Morrow, *The Equalizer,* CBS, 1986 and 1987. Movies: Judith Maple at age 14, *Too Far to Go,* NBC, 1979; Candy Cassidy, *North Beach and Rawhide,* CBS, 1985; Jenny Gavin, *A Place to Call Home,* CBS, 1987. Specials: Kelly, "Babies Having Babies," *CBS Schoolbreak Special,* CBS, 1986; Kay Cork, "Tales from the Hollywood Hills: The Old Reliable," *Great Performances,* PBS, 1988; Sally, "No Means No," *CBS Schoolbreak Special,* CBS, 1988.

RELATED CAREER—Print model; appeared in television commercials.

ADDRESSES: AGENT—Alan Iezman, William Morris Agency, 151 El Camino Drive, Beverly Hills, CA 90212.*

*   *   *

LUCKHAM, Cyril   1907-1989

PERSONAL: Born July 25, 1907, in Salisbury, England; died February 7, 1989, in London, England; son of Charles Minty and Mary Emmeline (Browne) Luckham; married Violet Sylvia Lamb; children: two sons, one daughter. EDUCATION—Attended the Royal Naval College; studied for the stage with the Arthur Brough Players and at the Folkestone Dramatic School. MILITARY—Royal Navy, lieutenant.

VOCATION: Actor.

CAREER: STAGE DEBUT—Footman, *The Admirable Crichton,* Leas Pavilion, Folkestone, U.K., 1935. LONDON DEBUT—Torvald Helmer, *A Doll's House,* Arts Theatre, 1945. PRINCIPAL STAGE APPEARANCES—Leonid Gayev, *The Cherry Orchard,* St. James's Theatre, London, 1948; the Victor, *The Moment of Truth,* Adelphi Theatre, London, 1951; Aaron, *The Firstborn,* Winter Garden Theatre, London, 1952; Voinitsky, *Uncle Vanya,* Arts Theatre, London, 1952; Colonel Desmond De S. Rinder-Sparrow, *The Love*

of Four Colonels, Wyndham's Theatre, London, 1952; Major Petkoff, *Arms and the Man,* Arts Theatre, 1953; Oderbruch, *The Devil's General,* Savoy Theatre, London, 1953; the Vicar, *I Capture the Castle,* Aldwych Theatre, London, 1954; Ali, *The Impresario from Smyrna,* Arts Theatre, 1954; Fairchild, *Sabrina Fair,* Palace Theatre, London, 1954; Felix Dulay, *My Three Angels,* Lyric Theatre, London, 1955; the Honorable Gerald Piper, *The Family Reunion,* Phoenix Theatre, London, 1956; Duke Senior, *As You Like It,* King of France, *King John,* title role, *Julius Caesar,* Belarius, *Cymbeline,* and Gonzalo, *The Tempest,* all Shakespeare Memorial Theatre, Stratford-on-Avon, U.K., 1957; Friar Laurence, *Romeo and Juliet,* Feste, *Twelfth Night,* Polonius, *Hamlet,* Helicanus, *Pericles,* and Leonato, *Much Ado About Nothing,* all Shakespeare Memorial Theatre, 1958; Parolles, *All's Well That Ends Well,* Quince, *A Midsummer Night's Dream,* and Gloucester, *King Lear,* all Shakespeare Memorial Theatre, 1959; Sorin, *The Seagull,* Old Vic Theatre, London, 1960; Reginald Kinsale, *Photo Finish,* Saville Theatre, London, 1962; Dr. Wolfgang Himmelmann, *Night Conspirators,* Saville Theatre, 1963; David Lancaster, *The Vortex,* Yvonne Arnaud Theatre, Guildford, U.K., 1965; M'Comas, *You Never Can Tell,* Haymarket Theatre, London, 1966.

MAJOR TOURS—Francis Morgan, *Strip the Willow,* U.K. cities, 1960.

PRINCIPAL FILM APPEARANCES—Dr. Meinard, *The Stranger from Venus* (also known as *Immediate Disaster* and *The Venusian*), Princess Pictures, 1954; Hugh Ferguson, *The Hostage,* Eros, 1956; magistrate, *The Birthday Present,* British Lion, 1957; coroner, *How to Murder a Rich Uncle,* Columbia, 1957; doctor, *Out of the Clouds,* Rank, 1957; Colonel Harbottle, *Invasion Quartet,* Metro-Goldwyn-Mayer (MGM), 1961; doctor, *The Pumpkin Eater,* Royal/Columbia, 1964; magistrate, *Some People,* American International, 1964; Sir Carmichael Clarke, *The Alphabet Murders* (also known as *The ABC Murders*), MGM, 1966; Archbishop Cranmer, *A Man for All Seasons,* Columbia, 1966; cabinet minister, *The Naked Runner,* Warner Brothers, 1967; Prior Houghton, *Anne of the Thousand Days,* Universal, 1969; Josiah Swineyard, *Happy Deathday,* MRA, 1969; magistrate, *One More Time,* United Artists, 1970; Professor Tringham, *Cry of the Penguins* (also known as *Mr. Forbush and the Penguins*), British Lion, 1972; Dr. Mark Eddington, *Providence,* Cinema V, 1977; also appeared in *Murder in Reverse,* Four Continents, 1946.

PRINCIPAL TELEVISION APPEARANCES—Series: Lawrence Mont, *The Forsyte Saga,* BBC, then PBS, 1969-70. Mini-Series: Duke of Marlborough, *Jennie: Lady Randolph Churchill,* Thames, then PBS, both 1975; Edward Drexel, *The Omega Factor,* BBC, 1979, then syndicated, 1981; Bishop Proudie, "The Barchester Chronicles," *Masterpiece Theatre,* PBS, 1984. Movies: *Murder at the Wedding* and *Donkey's Years.* Specials: Dr. Baston, *The Potting Shed,* Yorkshire Television, then PBS, 1982; Bishop, *Mrs. Silly,* Granada, 1988, then PBS, 1989. Also appeared in *The Guardians.*

RELATED CAREER—Actor with repertory companies at Folkestone, U.K., Manchester, U.K., Bristol, U.K., Coventry, U.K., and Southport, U.K., 1935-44; company member, Liverpool Playhouse, Liverpool, U.K., and the Old Vic Company, London, 1945-51.

OBITUARIES AND OTHER SOURCES: Variety, February 15-21, 1989.*

LUCKINBILL, Laurence   1934-

PERSONAL: Full name, Laurence George Luckinbill; born November 21, 1934, in Fort Smith, AR; son of Laurence Benedict and Agnes (Nulph) Luckinbill; married Robin Strasser (an actress), November 19, 1966 (divorced); married Lucie Arnaz (an actress), June 23, 1980; children: Laurence Nicholas, Benjamin Joseph (first marriage); Simon (second marriage); Jennifer (step-daughter). EDUCATION—Attended Fort Smith Junior College, 1951-52; University of Arkansas, B.A., 1955; Catholic University of America, M.F.A., 1957; postgraduate work at New York University, 1960; trained for the stage with Uta Hagen at the HB Studios and with George Kernodle at the University of Arkansas. MILITARY— U.S. Army, Chemical Corps, first lieutenant, 1956.

VOCATION: Actor and director.

CAREER: OFF-BROADWAY DEBUT—Old shepherd, *Oedipus Rex,* Carnegie Playhouse, 1959. BROADWAY DEBUT—Will Roper, *A Man for All Seasons,* American National Theatre and Academy Theatre, New York City, 1963. LONDON DEBUT—Hank, *The Boys in the Band,* Wyndham's Theatre, 1969. PRINCIPAL STAGE APPEARANCES—George Fabry, *There Is a Play Tonight,* Theatre Marquee, New York City, 1961; Iago, *Othello,* Hotspur, *Henry IV, Part One,* and Justice Swallow, *Henry IV, Part Two,* all Great Lakes Shakespeare Festival, Cleveland, OH, 1962; title role, *Caligula,* McCarter Theatre, Princeton, NJ, 1962; Simon Holt, *Beekman Place,* Morosco Theatre, New York City, 1964; Damis, *Tartuffe,* American National Theatre and Academy, Washington Square Theatre, New York City, 1965; title role, *Galileo,* McCarter Theatre, 1965; Biff Loman, *Death of a Salesman* and Edmund, *King Lear,* both American Conservatory Theatre, San Francisco, CA, 1966; Orestes, *The Flies,* APA Repertory Theatre, New York City, 1966; Hank, *The Boys in the Band,* Theatre Four, New York City, 1968; Sensuality, *Horseman, Pass By,* Fortune Theatre, New York City, 1969.

Ted, "The Electric Map" in *The Memory Bank,* Tambellini's Gate Theatre, New York City, 1970; Dr. Prentice, *What the Butler Saw,* McAlpin Rooftop Theatre, New York City, 1970; Patrick, *A Meeting By the River,* Center Theatre Group, New Theatre for Now, Los Angeles, then Phoenix Theatre Sideshows, Edison Theatre, New York City, both 1972; Frank Elliot, *Alpha Beta,* Eastside Playhouse, New York City, 1973; Brian, *The Shadow Box,* Center Theatre Group, Mark Taper Forum, Los Angeles, 1975, then Long Wharf Theatre, New Haven, CT, 1976, later Morosco Theatre, New York City, 1977; Anton Ignatyevich Kerzhentsen and Hamlet, *Poor Murderer,* Ethel Barrymore Theatre, New York City, 1976; Simon, *A Prayer for My Daughter,* New York Shakespeare Festival, Public Theatre, New York City, 1978; title role, *Galileo,* New York Actors Theatre, Havemeyer Hall, Columbia University, New York City, 1978; George Schneider, *Chapter Two,* Imperial Theatre, New York City, 1979.

Ralph Michaelson, *Past Tense,* Circle in the Square, New York City, 1980; Ken Harrison, *Whose Life Is It Anyway?,* Wilshire Theatre, Los Angeles, 1980; Vernon Gersch, *They're Playing Our Song,* St. Louis Municipal Opera, St. Louis, MO, 1982; He (Michael), *I Do! I Do!,* Dallas Music Hall, Dallas, TX, 1983; Dick Biehm, *Dancing in the End Zone,* Ritz Theatre, New York City, 1985; David Kahn, *Social Security,* Ahmanson Theatre, Los Angeles, then Royal Poinciana Playhouse, Palm Beach, FL, both 1987. Also appeared in *Faces in the American Mirror,* 1963; *Arms and the Man,* 1965; *Sodom and Gomorrah,* Playhouse in the Park, Cincinnati, OH, 1966-67; *Tadpole,* Center Theatre Group, New Theatre

for Now, Mark Taper Forum, 1973; *Too Much Johnson,* Center Theatre Group, Mark Taper Forum, 1975; *The Guardsman,* University of Arkansas, 1983, then Paper Mill Playhouse, Millburn, NJ, 1984; and *The Fantasticks.*

PRINCIPAL STAGE WORK—Director: *Macbeth* (Arabic production), Sudan, 1961; *Our Town* (Italian production), Rome, 1961; *Old Acquaintance,* Paramus, NJ, 1967.

MAJOR TOURS—Will Roper, *A Man for All Seasons,* U.S. cities, 1963-64; Frank Bryant, *Educating Rita,* U.S. cities, 1981; He (Michael), *I Do! I Do!,* U.S. cities, 1983; and as Lyndon Johnson in a one-man show, U.S. cities, 1988.

PRINCIPAL FILM APPEARANCES—Hank, *The Boys in the Band,* Cinema Center, 1970; Richard Messenger, *Such Good Friends,* Paramount, 1971; Wayne Nesbitt, *Corky,* Metro-Goldwyn-Mayer, 1972; narrator, *Moonwalk One,* Francis Thompson, 1972; Banks, *The Money,* Calliope, 1975; Noel Crossman, Jr., *The November Plan,* CIC, 1976; Dr. Gregson, *The Promise,* Universal, 1979; Mayor Claude Franklyn, *Not for Publication,* Samuel Goldwyn/ Thorne, 1984; Mr. Mooney, *Cocktail,* Buena Vista, 1988; Homer Foxx, *Messenger of Death* (also known as *Avenging Angels*), Pathe Releasing/Trans World, 1988; Sybok, *Star Trek V: The Final Frontier,* Paramount, 1989.

PRINCIPAL TELEVISION APPEARANCES—Series: Frank Carver, *The Secret Storm,* CBS, 1967-68; Steve Prescott, *Where the Heart Is,* CBS, 1969-70; Glenn Garth Gregory, *The Delphi Bureau,* ABC, 1972-73. Mini-Series: Major Richard Arnold, *Ike* (also known as *Ike: The War Years*), ABC, 1979; narrator, *James A. Michener's "Space"* (also known as *Space*), CBS, 1985. Pilots: Howard, *Lights Out,* NBC, 1972; Glen Garth Gregory, *The Delphi Bureau,* ABC, 1972; Dr. Glickman, *Momma the Detective,* NBC, 1981; Adam Margolin, *One More Try,* CBS, 1982; also *Someone to Watch Over Me,* NBC, 1975. Episodic: Howard, *Murder, She Wrote,* CBS, 1985; Frank Bradford, *Hotel,* ABC, 1987; narrator, "Robert Frost," *Voices and Visions,* PBS, 1988; Sergeant Cooper, *Murder, She Wrote,* CBS, 1988; also *N.Y.P.D.,* ABC, 1968; *The Bold Ones,* NBC, 1970; *NET Playhouse Biography,* NET, 1971; *Bonanza,* NBC, 1971; *Mission: Impossible,* CBS, 1972; *The F.B.I.,* ABC, 1974; *Harry O,* ABC, 1974; *The Rookies,* ABC, 1974; *Barnaby Jones,* CBS, 1974; *The Mary Tyler Moore Show,* CBS, 1975; *City of Angels,* NBC, 1976.

Movies: Lawrence Lewis, *Panic on the 5:22,* ABC, 1974; Don Davies, *Death Sentence,* ABC, 1974; Bill Anderson, *Winner Take All,* NBC, 1975; Governor Hal Hoffman, *The Lindbergh Kidnapping Case,* NBC, 1976; Harry McClain, *The Mating Season,* CBS, 1980; Jim Burton, *One Terrific Guy,* CBS, 1986; Senator Bob Mathias, *To Heal a Nation,* NBC, 1988; also *Murder Impossible,* ABC, 1974. Specials: *And the Bones Came Together,* ABC, 1973; "A Special Act of Love," *ABC Afternoon Playbreak,* ABC, 1973; title role, *Lyndon Johnson,* PBS, 1987. Also appeared as Pabundren, *As I Lay Dying.*

RELATED CAREER—Manager, National Players Inc., 1957-60; drama advisor, U. S. State Department, Khartoum, Sudan, 1961; visiting lecturer, University of Rome, Rome, Italy, 1962; drama lecturer, Queensborough Community College, Queens, NY, 1967-68; founding director, New York Actors Theatre, New York City, 1978; stage carpenter.

NON-RELATED CAREER—Cannery worker.

WRITINGS: STAGE—*Roy Brightswood* (also known as *Roy Hurd*); *The Golden Gate.* OTHER—*Feature People;* also contributor to journals and periodicals.

AWARDS: *Variety* New York Drama Critics' Poll, Best Actor, 1970, for *The Memory Bank;* Distinguished Achievement Award from the Catholic University Alumni, 1976; Antoinette Perry Award nomination, 1977, for *The Shadow Box;* Arkansas Traveller Award, 1979.

MEMBER: Actors' Equity Association (council member, 1968-69), Screen Actors Guild (director, 1971-72), American Federation of Television and Radio Artists, American Civil Liberties Union, Players Club, Underwater Society, Democratic Club.

SIDELIGHTS: FAVORITE ROLE—Galileo. RECREATIONS—Writing articles about the theatre and film.

ADDRESSES: OFFICE—c/o Richard M. Rosenthal, 445 Park Avenue, New York, NY 10022. AGENT—Artists Agency, 10000 Santa Monica Boulevard, Suite 305, Los Angeles, CA 90067.*

*　　　*　　　*

LUKE, Keye　1904-

PERSONAL: Born June, 1904, in Canton, China.

VOCATION: Actor.

CAREER: PRINCIPAL STAGE APPEARANCES—Wang Chi Yang, *Flower Drum Song,* St. James Theatre, New York City, 1958-60. MAJOR TOURS—Wang Chi Yang, *Flower Drum Song,* U.S. cities, 1960.

FILM DEBUT—Shay Kee Seng, *The Painted Veil,* Metro-Goldwyn-Mayer, 1934. PRINCIPAL FILM APPEARANCES—Taki, *The Casino Murder Case,* Metro-Goldwyn-Mayer (MGM), 1935; Lee Chan, *Charlie Chan in Paris,* Twentieth Century-Fox, 1935; Dr. Wong, *Mad Love* (also known as *The Hands of Orlac*), MGM, 1935; young Chinese, *Oil for the Lamps of China,* Warner Brothers, 1935; ambassador's son, *Shanghai,* Paramount, 1935; Lee Chan, *Charlie Chan in Shanghai,* Twentieth Century-Fox, 1935; Lee Chan, *Charlie Chan at the Circus,* Twentieth Century-Fox, 1936; Lee Chan, *Charlie Chan at the Opera,* Twentieth Century-Fox, 1936; Lee Chan, *Charlie Chan at the Race Track,* Twentieth Century-Fox, 1936; Wong, *King of Burlesque,* Twentieth Century-Fox, 1936; Lee Chan, *Charlie Chan at Monte Carlo,* Twentieth Century-Fox, 1937; Lee Chan, *Charlie Chan at the Olympics,* Twentieth Century-Fox, 1937; Lee Chan, *Charlie Chan on Broadway,* Twentieth Century-Fox, 1937; elder son, *The Good Earth,* MGM, 1937; Dr. Wong, *International Settlement,* Twentieth Century-Fox, 1938; Lee Chan, *Mr. Moto's Gamble,* Twentieth Century-Fox, 1938; Ling, *Barricade,* Twentieth Century-Fox, 1939; Andrew Abbott, *Disputed Passage,* Paramount, 1939; Jimmy Riley, *North of Shanghai,* Columbia, 1939.

Man, *No, No Nanette,* RKO, 1940; Kato, *The Green Hornet* (serial), Universal, 1940; Jimmy Wong, *The Phantom of Chinatown,* Monogram, 1940; Chang Howe, *Sued for Libel,* RKO, 1940; Clancy, *Bowery Blitzkrieg* (also known as *Stand and Deliver*), Monogram, 1941; Lin Tai Yen, *Burma Convoy,* Universal, 1941; George, *Gang's All Here,* Monogram, 1941; Buck Wing, *Let's Go*

Collegiate (also known as *Farewell to Fame*), Monogram, 1941; Kumi, *Mr. and Mrs. North,* MGM, 1941; Mr. Toy, *They Met in Bombay,* MGM, 1941; steamship officer clerk, *Across the Pacific,* Warner Brothers, 1942; secretary, *Destination Unknown,* Universal, 1942; Dr. Lee Wong How, *Dr. Gillespie's New Assistant,* MGM, 1942; Jerry, *The Falcon's Brother,* RKO, 1942; surgeon, *Invisible Agent,* Universal, 1942; Japanese statesman, *Journey for Margaret,* MGM, 1942; Lao Lee, *Mexican Spitfire's Elephant,* RKO, 1942; Wellington Wong, *North to the Klondike,* Universal, 1942; Thomas Chang, *Somewhere I'll Find You,* MGM, 1942; Haru, *Spy Ship,* Warner Brothers, 1942; Ah Foo, *A Tragedy at Midnight,* Republic, 1942; Kim How, *A Yank on the Burma Road* (also known as *China Caravan*), MGM, 1942; Dr. Lee Wong How, *Dr. Gillespie's Criminal Case* (also known as *Crazy to Kill*), MGM, 1943; Flashy Logaz, *Salute to the Marines,* MGM, 1943; Captain Wing, *The Adventures of Smilin' Jack* (serial), Universal, 1943; Dr. Lee, *Andy Hardy's Blonde Trouble,* MGM, 1944; Dr. Lee Wong How, *Between Two Women,* MGM, 1944; Dr. Lee Wong How, *Three Men in White,* MGM, 1944.

Haan-Soo, *First Yank into Tokyo* (also known as *Mask of Fury*), RKO, 1945; Ah Fong, *Secret Agent X-9* (serial), Universal, 1945; Charlie Otani, *Tokyo Rose,* Paramount, 1945; as himself, *How Do You Do?,* Producers Releasing, 1946; Tal Shan, *Lost City of the Jungle* (serial), Universal, 1946; Dr. Lee Wong How, *Dark Delusion* (also known as *Cynthia's Secret*), MGM, 1947; Lee Chan, *The Feathered Serpent,* Monogram, 1948; Jimmie, *Sleep, My Love,* United Artists, 1948; Loy, *Waterfront at Midnight,* Paramount, 1948; Lee Chan, *Sky Dragon,* Monogram, 1949; Ramundo, *Young Man with a Horn* (also known as *Young Man of Music*), Warner Brothers, 1950; Pidada, *Fair Wind to Java,* Republic, 1953; Japanese officer, *South Sea Woman* (also known as *Pearl of the South Pacific*), Warner Brothers, 1953; Chief Don, *Hell's Half Acre,* Republic, 1954; Wong, *World for Ransom,* Allied Artists, 1954; Li Ching, *The Bamboo Prison,* Columbia, 1955; elder brother, *Love Is a Many-Splendored Thing,* Twentieth Century-Fox, 1955; Captain Kuo Tai, *Battle Hell* (also known as *Yangtse Incident*), Herbert Wilcox, 1956.

Gondai-San, *Nobody's Perfect,* Universal, 1968; Sen Chiu, *Project X,* Paramount, 1968; Professor Soong Li, *The Chairman* (also known as *The Most Dangerous Man in the World*), Twentieth Century-Fox, 1969; Foo Sen, *The Hawaiians* (also known as *Master of the Islands*), United Artists, 1970; cook in kitchen, *Won Ton Ton, the Dog Who Saved Hollywood,* Paramount, 1976; Chung Wei, *The Amsterdam Kill,* Columbia, 1978; Dr. Device, *Just You and Me, Kid,* Columbia, 1979; Grandfather, *Gremlins,* Warner Brothers, 1984; Ishimine, *A Fine Mess,* Columbia, 1986; Mr. Thule, *Dead Heat,* New World, 1988; Dr. Raj, *The Mighty Quinn,* Metro-Goldwyn-Mayer/United Artists, 1989. Also appeared in *Here's to Romance,* Twentieth Century-Fox, 1935; *Eight Bells,* Columbia, 1935; *Anything Goes* (also known as *Tops Is the Limit*), Paramount, 1936; *No Hands on the Clock,* Paramount, 1941; *Passage from Hong Kong,* Warner Brothers, 1941; *Around the World in Eighty Days,* United Artists, 1956; *The Hunters,* Twentieth Century-Fox, 1958; *They Call Me Bruce* (also known as *A Fistful of Chopsticks*) Film Ventures International, 1982; *Noon Sunday;* and *Their Greatest Glory.*

PRINCIPAL TELEVISION APPEARANCES—Series: Thomas Wong, *Kentucky Jones,* NBC, 1964-65; Kralahome, *Anna and the King,* CBS, 1972; Master Po, *Kung Fu,* ABC, 1972-75; voice of Charlie Chan, *The Amazing Chan and the Chan Clan* (animated), CBS, 1972-74; Dr. Fong, *Harry O,* ABC, 1976; voice characterization, *Jabberjaws* (animated), ABC, 1977-78; voice of Zoltar, *Battle of the Planets* (animated), syndicated, 1978; voice characterization, *Spider-Man and His Amazing Friends* (animated), NBC, 1981; voice characterization, *Alvin and the Chipmunks* (animated), NBC, 1983; Sabasan, *Sidekicks*, ABC, 1986-87; voice characterization, *The New Adventures of Jonny Quest* (animated), syndicated, 1987. Pilots: Master Po, *Kung Fu*, ABC, 1972; Lord Sun Ming, *Judge Dee and the Monastery Murders*, ABC, 1974; Mr. Hu, *Brothers*, CBS, 1980; Duc, *Fly Away Home*, ABC, 1981; Jimmy Yew, *Unit 4*, CBS, 1981; Tan Ng, *Cocaine and Blue Eyes*, NBC, 1983; Chang Ching-Tzu, *Blade in Hong Kong*, CBS, 1985; Sabasan, *The Last Electric Knight*, ABC, 1986.

Episodic: Charlie Lee, *The Andy Griffith Show*, CBS, 1967; Donald Cory, *Star Trek*, NBC, 1969; narrator, *Reading Rainbow*, PBS, 1982; Jimmy Wong, *Crazy Like a Fox*, CBS, 1985; Grandfather Ho, *Night Court*, NBC, 1986; Hwan Li, *Downtown*, CBS, 1986; Mitsumo, *The Golden Girls*, NBC, 1986; Mr. Shibata, *Night Court*, NBC, 1987; Master, *Beauty and the Beast*, CBS, 1988; Adam Chung, *MacGyver*, ABC, 1988; also *Texaco Star Theatre* (also known as *The Milton Berle Show*), NBC, 1950; "Task Force Smith," *Hollywood Playhouse*, 1952; "The Traitor" and "The Reign of Amelia Jo," *Fireside Theatre* (also known as *Jane Wyman Presents the Fireside Theatre*), NBC, 1954; *Crusader*, CBS, 1955; "Ring Once for Death," *Studio 57* (also known as *Heinz Studio 57*), Dumont, 1955; *Gunsmoke*, CBS, 1955; "Chinese Luck," *The Ray Milland Show*, CBS, 1955; *My Little Margie*, NBC, 1955; "Cavalry in China," *Crossroads*, CBS, 1956; "Time Bomb," *Telephone Time*, CBS, 1956; "The Smuggler," *TV Reader's Digest*, ABC, 1956; *Wire Service*, ABC, 1957; May Day," *Panic!*, NBC, 1957; "Into the Dark," *Alcoa Theatre*, NBC, 1958; *The Gale Storm Show* (also known as *Oh Susanna*), CBS, 1958; *Richard Diamond*, CBS, 1958.

Follow the Sun, ABC, 1961; *Fair Exchange*, CBS, 1962; *Target: The Corrupters*, ABC, 1962; *The Mickey Rooney Show*, ABC, 1964; *I Spy*, NBC, 1965; *The Wackiest Ship in the Army*, NBC, 1965; *Jonny Quest* (animated), ABC, 1965; *The Littlest Hobo*, 1965; *Perry Mason*, CBS, 1965; *The Smothers Brothers Show*, CBS, 1966; *The F.B.I.*, ABC, 1966 and 1967; *Family Affair*, CBS, 1968; *The Outsider*, NBC, 1968; *Big Valley*, ABC, 1968; *Hawaii Five-0*, CBS, 1969; *The New Adventures of Huckleberry Finn*, NBC, 1969; *It Takes a Thief*, ABC, 1970; *Paris 7000*, ABC, 1970; *Marcus Welby, M.D.*, ABC, 1971; *Adam-12*, NBC, 1971 and 1972; *Here's Lucy*, CBS, 1972; *Love, American Style*, ABC, 1974; *Cannon*, CBS, 1975; *Khan*, CBS, 1975; *M*A*S*H*, CBS, 1978, 1979, and 1980; *Street Hawk*, ABC, 1985; voice characterization, *Fangface* (animated), ABC; *Danger*, CBS; *December Bride*, CBS; *Soldiers of Fortune*, syndicated; *Annie Oakley*, syndicated; *Medic*, NBC; *Climax*, CBS; *The Jerry Lewis Show*, ABC; *Trackdown*, CBS; *This Is the Life*, ABC; *The Bob Hope Chrysler Show*, NBC; *Dragnet*, NBC; *Quincy, M.E.*, NBC; *How the West Was Won*, ABC; *Vega$*, ABC; *Charlie's Angels*, ABC; *Remington Steele*, NBC; *Magnum P.I.*, CBS; *Falcon Crest*, CBS; *Voyagers*, NBC; *The A-Team*, NBC; *Mickey Spillane's Mike Hammer*, CBS; *Miami Vice*, NBC; *Trapper John, M.D.*, CBS; *T.J. Hooker*, ABC; *General Hospital*, ABC; *Friday the 13th*, syndicated; *The Judge*, syndicated; *Meeting of Minds*, PBS; *Down to Earth*; *9 to 5*; *Citizen Chang*; *Never Too Young*; *The Yee Family*; *Might Man and Yukk*; *Rickety Racket*; *Reach for the Sun*; and *The Adventures of Goldie Gold*.

Movies: Thief, *The Cat Creature*, ABC, 1973; Dr. Makimura, *Blood Sport*, CBS, 1986; Master Po, *Kung Fu: The Movie*, CBS, 1986. Specials: *America Pauses for Springtime*, CBS, 1959; "Judge-

ment: The Court Martial of the Tiger of Malaya—General Yamashita," *ABC Theatre*, ABC, 1974.

NON-RELATED CAREER—Artist and poster designer, Twentieth Century-Fox and RKO Studios.*

*   *   *

LUNGHI, Cherie 1953-

PERSONAL: Born in 1953 in London, England.

VOCATION: Actress.

CAREER: PRINCIPAL STAGE APPEARANCES—Laura, *Teeth 'n' Smiles*, English Stage Company, Royal Court Theatre, London, 1975; Hero, *Much Ado About Nothing*, Royal Shakespeare Company (RSC), Royal Shakespeare Theatre, Stratford-on-Avon, U.K., 1976, then Aldwych Theatre, London, 1977; Liz and Carol, *Destiny*, RSC, Other Place Theatre, Stratford-on-Avon, 1976, then Aldwych Theatre, 1977; Cordelia, *King Lear* and Genevieve, *The Days of the Commune*, both RSC, Aldwych Theatre, 1977; Rhoda, *That Good Between Us* and Madeline and Pat, *Bandits*, both RSC, Warehouse Theatre, London, 1977; Celia, *As You Like It* and Lucy Carter, *Saratoga*, both RSC, Aldwych Theatre, 1978; Viola, *Twelfth Night*, RSC, Royal Shakespeare Theatre, 1979; Yelena Andreyevna, *Uncle Vanya*, National Theatre Company, Lyttelton Theatre, London, 1982.

PRINCIPAL FILM APPEARANCES—Guenevere, *Excalibur*, Warner Brothers, 1981; Beatrice Manceau, *Praying Mantis*, Channel Four, 1982; Mary Morstan, *The Sign of Four*, Mapleton, 1983; Michal, *King David*, Paramount, 1985; Helene, *Letters to an Unknown Lover* (also known as *Les Louves*), Channel Four/Anttene-2/Portman, 1985; Jenny Parker, *Parker*, Moving Picture Company/Virgin, 1985; Carlotta, *The Mission*, Warner Brothers, 1986; Susan, *Coast to Coast*, BBC/Britannica/Dean-Clough, 1986; Halina, *Popielusko* (also known as *To Kill a Priest*, *Le Complot*, and *Le Complot a priest*), Imperia/AMLF/Columbia, 1988.

PRINCIPAL TELEVISION APPEARANCES—Mini-Series: Una Marbury, *Ellis Island*, CBS, 1984; Margaret Van der Merwe, *Master of the Game*, CBS, 1984; also *Kean*, BBC, then *Masterpiece Theatre*, PBS, 1979. Pilots: Adriana, *Intrigue*, CBS, 1988. Movies: Nancy, *Oliver Twist*, CBS, 1982; Usta, *Harem*, ABC, 1986; Lili Gloebocka, *The Man Who Lived at the Ritz*, syndicated, 1988.

ADDRESSES: AGENT—Jeremy Conway Ltd., 109 Jermyn Street, London SW1Y 6HB, England.*

*   *   *

LUSCOMBE, Tim 1960-

PERSONAL: Born November 12, 1960, in Epsom, England; son of David William (a surveyor) and Jill Patricia (Oxley) Luscombe. EDUCATION—Received B.A. in geography from Oxford University; attended the Bristol Old Vic Theatre School as a director trainee.

VOCATION: Director.

TIM LUSCOMBE

CAREER: FIRST STAGE WORK—Director, *Hamlet,* Redgrave Theatre, Farnham, U.K., 1985. FIRST LONDON WORK—Director, *The Browning Version* and *Harlequinade,* both Royalty Theatre, London, 1988. FIRST BROADWAY WORK—Director, *Artist Descending a Staircase,* Helen Hayes Theatre, 1989. FIRST OFF-BROADWAY WORK—Director, *When She Danced,* Playwrights Horizons, 1990. PRINCIPAL STAGE WORK—Director: *Warrior,* Chichester Festival Theatre, Chichester, U.K., 1988; *When She Danced,* King's Head Theatre, London, 1988; *Easy Virtue,* Garrick Theatre, London, 1988; *Artist Descending a Staircase,* Duke of York's Theatre, London, 1988; *The Parasol,* Royal Exchange Theatre, Manchester, U.K., 1989.

MAJOR TOURS—Director, *Hamlet,* U.K. cities, 1985.

AWARDS: Olivier Award nomination, Best Newcomer, 1989, for *The Browning Version, Harlequinade,* and *Easy Virtue.*

MEMBER: British Actors' Equity Association, Society of Stage Directors and Choreographers, Directors Guild of Great Britain.

ADDRESSES: AGENT—David Watson, Simpson Fox Associates, 52 Shaftesbury Avenue, London W1V 7DE, England.

M

MacINTOSH, Joan 1945-

PERSONAL: Born November 25, 1945, in New Jersey. EDUCATION—Graduated from Beaver College; also attended New York University.

VOCATION: Actress.

CAREER: OFF-BROADWAY DEBUT—*Dionysus in '69*, Performance Group, Performing Garage Theatre, 1969. PRINCIPAL STAGE APPEARANCES—Dark Power, *Makbeth*, Performance Group, Performing Garage Theatre, New York City, 1969; Big Time Clementine, *Commune*, Performance Group, Performing Garage Theatre, 1970; Becky, *The Tooth of Crime*, Performance Group, Performing Garage Theatre, 1973; title role, *Mother Courage and Her Children* and Star, *The Marilyn Project*, both Performance Group, Performing Garage Theatre, 1975; Jocasta, *Seneca's Oedipus*, Performance Group, Performing Garage Theatre, 1977; Worker, *Saint Joan of the Stockyards*, Emcompass Theatre, New York City, 1978; Nell, *Endgame*, Manhattan Theatre Club, New York City, 1980; Ellis, *Killings on the Last Line*, American Place Theatre, New York City, 1980; *Request Concert* (one-woman show), Interart Theatre, New York City, 1981; Frances Anna Duffy Walsh and Gertrude Graham Finn (understudy), *The Curse of an Aching Heart*, Little Theatre, New York City, 1982; Suzanne, *Three Acts of Recognition*, New York Shakespeare Festival (NYSF), Public Theatre, New York City, 1982.

Jana Latvis, *Whispers*, Open Space Theatre, New York City, 1987; Elizabeth, *Almost By Chance a Woman: Elizabeth*, Yale Repertory Theatre, New Haven, CT, 1987; Mama, *A Shayna Maidel*, Westside Arts Theatre, New York City, 1987; Portia, *Julius Caesar*, NYSF, Public Theatre, 1988; lady in the box, *Our Town*, Lincoln Center Theatre Company, Lyceum Theatre, New York City, 1989; Queen, *Cymbeline*, NYSF, Public Theatre, 1989. Also appeared in *The Beard*, Performance Group, Performing Garage Theatre, 1973; *Alice in Concert*, NYSF, Public Theatre, 1978; *Dispatches*, NYSF, Public Theatre, 1979; *Plenty*, Arena Stage, Washington, DC, 1980; *Sore Throats*, Repertory Theatre of St. Louis, St. Louis, MO, 1982; *Hedda Gabler*, Tyrone Guthrie Theatre, Minneapolis, MN, 1983; *Screenplay*, Arena Stage, 1983; *The Balcony*, American Repertory Theatre, Cambridge, MA, 1985; *The Goddess Project*, Whole Theatre, Montclair, NJ; *The Three Sisters*, Tyrone Guthrie Theatre; *Consequence*, New York City; and with the Mirror Repertory Company, New York City, 1983-86.

PRINCIPAL FILM APPEARANCES—Nan Haas, *A Flash of Green*, Spectra, 1984; Evelyn, *Chain Letters*, Chain Letters Production, 1985; Larkin's mother, *Fresh Horses*, Weintraub Entertainment Group, 1988; also appeared in *Dionysus in '69*, Sigma III, 1970.

PRINCIPAL TELEVISION APPEARANCES—Episodic: *Another World*, NBC; *As the World Turns*, CBS; *One Life to Live*, ABC. Specials: Woman in graveyard, "Our Town," *Great Performances*, PBS, 1989.

AWARDS: Obie Award from the *Village Voice*, Distinguished Performance, 1971, for *Commune*; Drama Desk Award, 1981, for *Request Concert*.

ADDRESSES: AGENT—J. Michael Bloom, 233 Park Avenue S., New York, NY 10003.*

*   *   *

MacKENZIE, Philip Charles

VOCATION: Actor.

CAREER: PRINCIPAL FILM APPEARANCES—Doctor, *Dog Day Afternoon*, Warner Brothers, 1975; also appeared in *Wedding Band*.

PRINCIPAL TELEVISION APPEARANCES—Series: Midas Metcovitch, *The Six O'Clock Follies*, NBC, 1980; David Wasserman, *Making the Grade*, CBS, 1982; Donald, *Brothers*, Showtime, 1984-88; Ted Nichols, *Duet*, Fox, 1989; Ted Nichols, *Open House*, Fox, 1989—. Pilots: Jack Elmdorf, *Characters*, NBC, 1980. Episodic: Jerry Nurko, *Newhart*, CBS, 1986; also *Cheers*, NBC, 1982. Movies: Cavanaugh, *Girls of the White Orchid* (also known as *Death Ride to Osaka*), NBC, 1983; Ruber, *The Red-Light Sting*, CBS, 1984; John Pierson, *Blind Justice*, CBS, 1986. Specials: Dr. LaFleur, "Heartbreak Winner," *ABC Afterschool Specials*, ABC, 1980.

PRINCIPAL TELEVISION WORK—Episodic: Director, *Brothers*, Showtime.

AWARDS: ACE Award, Best Actor in a Comedy Series, 1985, for *Brothers*.

ADDRESSES: AGENT—Triad Artists, 10100 Santa Monica Boulevard, 16th Floor, Los Angeles, CA 90067.*

MAGGART, Brandon   1933-

PERSONAL: Born December 12, 1933, in Carthage, TN. EDUCA-TION—Graduated from the University of Tennessee.

VOCATION: Actor.

CAREER: PRINCIPAL STAGE APPEARANCES—Patroklos, *Sing Muse!,* Van Dam Theatre, New York City, 1961; Berenger, *The Killer,* Theatre 1962, Cherry Lane Theatre, New York City, 1962; Colin, *Like Other People,* Village South Theatre, New York City, 1963; ensemble, *Put It in Writing* (revue), Theatre De Lys, New York City, 1963; Carruthers, *Kelly,* Broadhurst Theatre, New York City, 1965; ensemble, *New Faces of 1968* (revue), Booth Theatre, New York City, 1968; ensemble, *Free Fall* (revue), Upstairs at the Downstairs, New York City, 1969; Buzz Richards, *Applause,* Palace Theatre, New York City, 1970-72; Bell Man, *Wedding Band,* New York Shakespeare Festival, Public Theatre, New York City, 1972; Josephus Gage, *Lorelei, or "Gentlemen Still Prefer Blondes,"* Palace Theatre, 1974; ensemble, *Straws in the Wind* (revue), American Place Theatre, New York City, 1975; Sam Williams, *We Interrupt This Program,* Ambassador Theatre, New York City, 1975; ensemble, *Potholes* (revue), Cherry Lane Theatre, 1979; Harold, *Musical Chairs,* Equity Library Theatre, Rialto Theatre, New York City, 1980; Nat and voice of Sol, *One Night Stand,* Nederlander Theatre, New York City, 1980. Also appeared in *The Long Valley,* Theatre De Lys, 1975; *Nurse Jane Goes to Hawaii,* Pennsylvania Stage Company, Allentown, PA, 1982.

PRINCIPAL STAGE WORK—Associate producer (with James Catusi and Zenon R. Mocarski Inc.), *Hay Fever,* Helen Hayes Theatre, New York City, 1970.

MAJOR TOURS—Josephus Gage, *Lorelei, or "Gentlemen Still Prefer Blondes,"* U.S. cities, 1973; ensemble, *Hellzapoppin'* (revue), U.S. cities, 1976-77.

PRINCIPAL FILM APPEARANCES—Dr. Arthur Osgood and man in cafe, *The Magic Garden of Stanley Sweetheart,* Metro-Goldwyn-Mayer, 1970; National Guard sergeant, *Hail* (also known as *Hail to the Chief* and *Washington B.C.*), Cine-Globe, 1973; Cleveland Sam, *Dressed to Kill,* Filmways, 1980; Harry Stadling, *You Better Watch Out* (also known as *Christmas Evil*), Pressman, 1980; Ernie Holm, *The World According to Garp,* Warner Brothers, 1982.

PRINCIPAL TELEVISION APPEARANCES—Series: George Elliot, *Jennifer Slept Here,* NBC, 1983-84; Lou Waters, *Brothers,* Showtime, 1984-88; Michael, *Chicken Soup,* ABC, 1989. Movies: Mule, *My Old Man,* CBS, 1979; Bert, *Running Out,* CBS, 1983; Charlie, *Dream Date,* NBC, 1989. Specials: *I'm a Fan,* CBS, 1972.

AWARDS: Theatre World Award, 1963, for *Put It in Writing.*

ADDRESSES: AGENT—International Creative Management, 8899 Beverly Boulevard, Los Angeles, CA 90048. MANAGER—Green and Siegel Management, 1140 N. Alta Loma Drive, Suite 105, Los Angeles, CA 90069.*

JOSEPH MAHER

MAHER, Joseph   1933-

PERSONAL: Surname is pronounced "Ma-*har*"; born December 29, 1933, in Westport, Ireland; son of Joseph (a school teacher) and Delia A. (O'Malley) Maher.

VOCATION: Actor, director, and playwright.

CAREER: Also see *WRITINGS* below. STAGE DEBUT—Biondello, *The Taming of the Shrew,* Canadian Players Theatre, Toronto, ON, Canada, 1959. OFF-BROADWAY DEBUT—I.R.A. officer, *The Hostage,* One Sheridan Square Theatre, 1962. BROADWAY DE-BUT—Red Gus Risto (understudy), *The Chinese Prime Minister,* Royale Theatre, 1964. PRINCIPAL STAGE APPEARANCES—Col, *Live Like Pigs,* Actors' Playhouse, New York City, 1965; Reverend Mort, *Eh?,* Circle in the Square, New York City, 1966-67; Sir Andrew Aguecheek, *Twelfth Night,* Roderigo, *Othello,* and interpreter, *All's Well That Ends Well,* all San Diego National Shakespeare Festival, Old Globe Theatre, San Diego, CA, 1967; Gordon Lowther, *The Prime of Miss Jean Brodie,* Helen Hayes Theatre, New York City, 1968; various roles, *The Local Stigmatic,* Actors' Playhouse, 1969; Canterbury, *Henry V,* American Shakespeare Festival, Stratford, CT, then American National Theatre and Academy (ANTA) Theatre, New York City, both 1969; Sir Andrew Melvil, *Mary Stuart,* Repertory Theatre of Lincoln Center, Vivian Beaumont Theatre, New York City, 1971; Gerome, *There's One in Every Marriage,* Royale Theatre, New York City, 1972; Fitzpatrick, *The Contractor,* Chelsea Manhattan Theatre, New York City, 1973; Captain, *Juno and the Paycock,* Long Wharf Theatre, New Haven, CT, 1973; Sir Augustus Ludbourne, *Who's Who in Hell,* Lunt-Fontanne Theatre, New York City, 1974; Herbert Dean, *The*

Royal Family, Kennedy Center for the Performing Arts, Washington, DC, then Brooklyn Academy Playhouse, Brooklyn, NY, both 1975, later Helen Hayes Theatre, 1975-76; Alan West, *Savages,* Center Theatre Group, Mark Taper Forum, Los Angeles, 1975; the Son, *Days in the Trees,* Circle in the Square, 1976; Alan West, *Savages,* Hudson Guild Theatre, New York City, 1977; Martin, *Black Angel,* Center Theatre Group, Mark Taper Forum, 1978; the Trick Cyclist, *Spokesong,* Long Wharf Theatre, 1978, then Circle in the Square, 1979; Geoffrey Carson, *Night and Day,* ANTA Theatre, 1979.

Ed, *Entertaining Mr. Sloane,* Westside Mainstage Theatre, then Cherry Lane Theatre, both New York City, 1981; Bernard, *Dear Daddy,* Philadelphia Drama Guild, Philadelphia, PA, 1981-82; Frank Doel, *84 Charing Cross Road,* Nederlander Theatre, New York City, 1982-83; Truscott, *Loot,* Manhattan Theatre Club, Space at City Center Theatre, then Music Box Theatre, both New York City, 1986; Ed, *Entertaining Mr. Sloane* and Truscott, *Loot,* both Center Theatre Group, Mark Taper Forum, 1987; Dr. Rance, *What the Butler Saw,* Manhattan Theatre Club, City Center Stage One Theatre, New York City, 1989. Also appeared in *Forget-Me-Not-Lane,* Long Wharf Theatre, 1973; *Saint Joan,* Center Theatre Group, Ahmanson Theatre, Los Angeles, 1974; *The National Health,* Long Wharf Theatre, 1974; *Henry V,* New York City, 1974; *Afore Night Come,* Long Wharf Theatre, 1975; *Richard III,* Long Wharf Theatre, 1976; *Absent Friends,* Long Wharf Theatre, 1977; *Live Like Pigs,* New York City, 1981; *Tales from Hollywood,* Center Theatre Group, Mark Taper Forum, 1982; *The Hostage,* Long Wharf Theatre, 1983; *The Importance of Being Earnest,* Off-Broadway production.

PRINCIPAL STAGE WORK—Director, *The Hostage,* Long Wharf Theatre, New Haven, CT, 1983.

MAJOR TOURS—Dr. Talacryn (Bishop of Caerleon), *Hadrian VII,* U.S. cities, 1971.

PRINCIPAL FILM APPEARANCES—Charlie, *It Ain't Easy,* Dandelion, 1972; Mr. Coates, *For Pete's Sake* (also known as *July Pork Bellies*), Columbia, 1974; Sisk, *Heaven Can Wait,* Paramount, 1978; Adams, *Time After Time,* Warner Brothers/Orion, 1979; Dr. Coleson, *Just Tell Me What You Want,* Warner Brothers, 1980; Fibber Geyer, *Those Lips, Those Eyes,* United Artists, 1980; Dr. Kalman, *I'm Dancing As Fast As I Can,* Paramount, 1981; Gridley, *Going Ape!,* Paramount, 1981; Duke, *Under the Rainbow,* Orion/Warner Brothers, 1981; Mulloch, *The Evil That Men Do,* Tri-Star, 1984; Dr. Lucas Budlong, *My Stepmother Is an Alien,* Columbia, 1988; Michael Sinclair, *Funny Farm,* Warner Brothers, 1988.

TELEVISION DEBUT—"Little Moon of Alban," *Hallmark Hall of Fame,* NBC, 1964. PRINCIPAL TELEVISION APPEARANCES—Series: Sylvester, *Double Dare,* CBS, 1985; St. Peter, *Second Chance,* Fox, 1987; Brian Alquist, *Anything But Love,* ABC, 1989—; also Leonard Brooks, *Another World,* NBC. Pilots: Albert Vogel, *At Your Service,* NBC, 1984; Stockwell, *Mr. and Mrs. Ryan,* ABC, 1986; Mr. Bell, *Why On Earth?* (also known as *Down to Earth*), ABC, 1988. Episodic: Mr. Dudley, *Gimme a Break,* NBC, 1987; Bob, *ALF,* NBC, 1988; Charles Van Duren, *My Two Dads,* NBC, 1988; also *M*A*S*H,* CBS, 1975; *The Cavanaughs,* CBS; *Moonlighting,* ABC; *Tattinger's,* NBC; *Wonder Woman.* Movies: Doctor, *My Father's House,* ABC, 1975; Phil Kiley, *My Old Man,* CBS, 1979; Smythe, *Little Gloria . . . Happy at Last,* NBC, 1982; doctor, *Will There Really Be a Morning?,* CBS, 1983; Jack Kendrix, *Bigfoot,* ABC, 1987. Specials: Giorgio Vasari, *I, Leonardo: A Journey of the Mind,* CBS, 1983; Smedley Cork,

"Tales from the Hollywood Hills: The Old Reliable," *Great Performances,* PBS, 1988.

RELATED CAREER—Company member: Theatre Company of Boston, Boston, MA, 1965; Charles Playhouse, Boston, 1969-70; American Shakespeare Festival, Stratford, CT, 1969, 1970, and 1972; Tyrone Guthrie Theatre Company, Minneapolis, MN, 1971-72; Alley Theatre, Houston, TX, 1972-73.

WRITINGS: STAGE—*Dance for Me, Simeon,* George Street Playhouse, New Brunswick, NJ, 1979, and A.T.A. Theatre, New York City.

AWARDS: Los Angeles Critics' Award nomination, 1975, and Obie Award from the *Village Voice,* 1978, both for *Savages;* Antoinette Perry Award nomination, Best Actor in a Featured Role in a Play, 1979, for *Spokesong;* Antoinette Perry Award nomination, 1980, for *Night and Day;* Antoinette Perry Award nomination, Best Actor in a Featured Role in a Play, Outer Critics' Circle Award nomination, and Drama Desk Award, all 1986, Los Angeles Drama Critics' Award and *Drama-Logue* Award, both 1987, all for *Loot; Drama-Logue* Award, 1987, for *Entertaining Mr. Sloane.*

MEMBER: Academy of Motion Picture Arts and Sciences.

SIDELIGHTS: FAVORITE ROLES—Captain in *Juno and the Paycock* and Alan West in *Savages.*

ADDRESSES: AGENT—Joan Scott, Writers and Artists Agency, 70 W. 36th Street, Suite 501, New York, NY 10018 and 11726 San Vicente Boulevard, Los Angeles, CA 90049.

*　　*　　*

MAKAVEJEV, Dusan　1932-

PERSONAL: Born October 13, 1932, in Belgrade, Yugoslavia; married Bojana Marijan, 1964. EDUCATION—Received a degree in psychology from Belgrade University, 1955; studied at the Academy for Theatre, Radio, Film, and Television (Belgrade). MILITARY—Yugoslavian Army, 1959-60.

VOCATION: Director and screenwriter.

CAREER: Also see WRITINGS below. PRINCIPAL FILM WORK—Director: *Ljubavni Slucaj, ili tragedija sluzbenice P.T.T.* (also known as *Love Affair, or the Case of the Missing Switchboard Operator* and *An Affair of the Heart*), 1967, released in the United States by Brandon, 1968; *Nevinost bez zastite* (also known as *Innocence Unprotected*), 1968, released in the United States by Avala/Grove Press, 1971; *WR Misterite organizma* (also known as *WR: The Mysteries of the Organism* and *WR—Misterije Organizma*), Yugoslavija Film/Cinema V, 1971; *Sweet Movie,* CFDC, 1974; *Montenegro* (also known as *Montenegro, or Pigs and Pearls*), New Realm/Atlantic, 1981; *The Coca-Cola Kid,* Cinecom International/Film Gallery, 1985; *Manifesto* (also known as *For One Night of Love* and *Pour une nuit d'amour*), Cannon Releasing, 1988; also *Covek nije tica* (also known as *Man Is Not a Bird*), 1966. Also director of the following short films and documentaries: *Jatagan Mala,* 1953; *Pecat* (also known as *The Seal*), 1955; *Antonijevo razbijeno ogledalo* (also known as *Anthony's Broken Mirror*), 1957; *Spomenicima ne treba verovati* (also known as *Don't Believe in Monuments*), 1958; *Slikovnica pcelara* (also known as *Beekeep-*

er's Scrapbook), 1958; *Prokleti praznik* (also known as *Damned Holiday*), 1958; *Boje sanjaju* (also known as *Colors Are Dreaming*), 1958; *Sto je radnicki savjet?* (also known as *What Is a Workers' Council?*), 1959; *Eci, pec, pec* (also known as *One Potato, Two Potato*), 1961; *Pedagoska bajka* (also known as *Educational Fairy Tale*), 1961; *Osmjeh 61* (also known as *Smile 61*), 1961; *Parada* (also known as *Parade*), 1962; *Dole plotovi* (also known as *Down with the Fences*), 1962; *Ljepotica 62* (also known as *Miss Yugoslavia 1962*), 1962; *Film o knjizi A.B.C.* (also known as *Film About the Book*), 1962; *Nova igracka* (also known as *New Toy*), 1964; *Nova domaca zivotinja* (also known as *New Domestic Animal*), 1964.

WRITINGS: STAGE—*New Man of the Flower Market*, Students' Theatre, Belgrade, Yugoslavia, 1962. FILM—See production details above: *Jatagan Mala*, 1953; *Pecat*, 1955; *Antonijevo razbijeno ogledalo*, 1957; *Spomenicima ne treba verovati*, 1958; *Slikovnica pcelara*, 1958; *Prokleti praznik*, 1958; *Boje sanjaju*, 1958; *Sto je radnicki savjet?*, 1959; *Eci, pec, pec*, 1961; *Pedagoska bajka*, 1961; *Osmjeh 61*, 1961; *Parada*, 1962; *Dole plotovi*, 1962; *Ljepotica 62*, 1962; *Film o knjizi A.B.C.*, 1962; *Nova igracka*, 1964; *Nova domaca zivotinja*, 1964; *Covek nije tica*, 1966; *Ljubavni Slucaj, ili tragedija sluzbenice P.T.T.*, 1967; *Nevinost bez zastite*, 1968; *WR Misterite organizma*, 1971; *Sweet Movie*, 1974; (with Bon Jonsson, Donald Arthur, Arnie Gelbert, Branko Vucicevic, and Bojana Marijan) *Montenegro*, 1981; *Manifesto*, 1988.

OTHER—*A Kiss for Komradess Slogan*, 1964.

AWARDS: Ford Foundation grant, 1968.*

*   *   *

MAKO   1932-

PERSONAL: Full name, Makoto Iwamatsu; born December 10, 1932, in Kobe, Japan; married Shizuko Hoshi (a dancer, choreographer, dance teacher, and actress); children: two daughters. EDUCATION—Attended Pratt Institute; studied for the theatre at the Pasadena Playhouse. MILITARY—U.S. Armed Forces.

VOCATION: Actor, director, and playwright.

CAREER: Also see *WRITINGS* below. BROADWAY DEBUT—The Reciter, Shogun, and Jonathan Goble, *Pacific Overtures*, Winter Garden Theatre, 1976. PRINCIPAL STAGE APPEARANCES—Taki, *A Banquet for the Moon*, Theatre Marquee, New York City, 1961; Sam Shikaze, *Yellow Fever*, Pan Asian Repertory Theatre, 47th Street Theatre, New York City, 1983; Nobu, *The Wash*, Center Theatre Group, Mark Taper Forum, Los Angeles, 1985. Also appeared in *Gold Watch*, Inner City Repertory Theatre, Los Angeles, 1972; *Station J*, East/West Players, Los Angeles, 1981; *Pacific Overtures* and *Hokusai Sketchbooks*, both East/West Players, Los Angeles; with the Inner City Repertory Theatre, Los Angeles, 1967-68.

PRINCIPAL STAGE WORK—All as director: (With Shizuko Hoshi) *The Fisher King*, Center Theatre Group, Mark Taper Forum, 1976; *The Music Lessons* and *F.O.B. (Fresh Off the Boat)*, both New York Shakespeare Festival (NYSF), Public Theatre, New York City, 1980.

PRINCIPAL FILM APPEARANCES—Po-Han, *The Sand Pebbles*,

MAKO

Twentieth Century-Fox, 1966; Kenji, *The Ugly Dachshund*, Buena Vista, 1966; Calvin Coolidge Ishimura, *The Private Navy of Sergeant O'Farrell*, United Artists, 1968; Secret Service Agent Eliot Fong, *The Great Bank Robbery*, Warner Brothers, 1969; psychiatrist, *Fools*, Cinerama, 1970; Mun Ki, *The Hawaiians* (also known as *Master of the Islands*), United Artists, 1970; Oomiak, *The Island at the Top of the World*, Buena Vista, 1974; Yuen Chung, *The Killer Elite*, United Artists, 1975; Herbert, *The Big Brawl*, Warner Brothers, 1980; James Chan, *An Eye for an Eye*, AVCO-Embassy, 1981; Nakamura, *Under the Rainbow*, Orion/Warner Brothers, 1981; friend, *The Bushido Blade* (also known as *The Bloody Bushido Blade*), Trident, 1982; Akiro the Wizard, *Conan the Barbarian*, Universal, 1982; Mike, *Testament*, Paramount, 1983; Akiro the Wizard, *Conan the Destroyer*, Universal, 1984; Akira Tanaka, *Armed Response*, CineTel, 1986; Captain Vinh, *P.O.W.: The Escape*, Cannon, 1986; Nobu, *The Wash*, Skouras, 1988; Dyama, *Silent Assassins*, Action Brothers, 1988; Jimmy Sakuyama, *Tucker: The Man and His Dream*, Paramount, 1988; Max Chin, *An Unremarkable Life*, CFG, 1989. Also appeared in *Tora! Tora! Tora!*, Twentieth Century-Fox, 1970; *Chinmoku*, 1972; *Prisoners*, 1975.

PRINCIPAL TELEVISION APPEARANCES—Series: Major Taro Oshira, *Hawaiian Heat*, ABC, 1984. Pilots: Simba, *Alfred of the Amazon*, CBS, 1967; Kenji, *Streets of San Francisco*, ABC, 1972; Tao Gan, *Judge Dee in the Monastery Murders*, ABC, 1974; Mataro Sakura, *The Last Ninja*, ABC, 1983. Episodic: Inspector Toshi, *Ohara*, ABC, 1987; Tommy Nguyen, *Spenser: For Hire*, ABC, 1987; Trahn, *Tour of Duty*, CBS, 1987; Thanarat, *The Equalizer*, CBS, 1988; Yo Tin, *Supercarrier*, ABC, 1988; Kao, *Paradise*, CBS, 1990; also *M*A*S*H*, CBS, 1974, 1976, and 1980; *The Incredible Hulk*, CBS, 1978 and 1979; *Hawaiian Eye*,

ABC; *The F.B.I.*, ABC; *Ironside*, NBC; *Hawaii Five-0*, CBS; *Mannix*, CBS; *F Troop*, ABC. Movies: Yuro, *The Challenge*, ABC, 1970; Tadashi, *If Tomorrow Comes*, ABC, 1971; Fukimoto, *Farewell to Manzanar*, NBC, 1976; Bai, *When Hell Was in Session*, NBC, 1979; Mori, *Girls of the White Orchid* (also known as *Death Ride to Osaka*), NBC, 1983; the Manchu, *Kung Fu: The Movie*, CBS, 1986; Captain Kilalo, *Murder in Paradise*, NBC, 1990.

RELATED CAREER—Founder and artistic director, East/West Players and the Children's Workshop, both Los Angeles, 1966—.

WRITINGS: STAGE—(With Dom Magwili) *Christmas in Camp*, East/West Players, Los Angeles, 1981; *There's No Place Like a Tired Ghost*, Inner City Repertory Theatre, Los Angeles, 1972.

AWARDS: Academy Award nomination, Best Supporting Actor, 1966, for *The Sand Pebbles;* Antoinette Perry Award nomination, Best Actor in a Musical, 1976, for *Pacific Overtures*.

MEMBER: Actors' Equity Association, Screen Actors Guild, American Federation of Television and Radio Artists.

ADDRESSES: AGENT—Fred Amsel and Associates, 6310 San Vicente Boulevard, Suite 407, Los Angeles, CA 90048.*

*   *   *

MALONEY, Peter

PERSONAL: Married Ellen Sandler (an actress and playwright; marriage ended); married Kristin Griffith (an actress); children: one son. EDUCATION—Graduated from Syracuse University; studied acting with Uta Hagen.

VOCATION: Actor, director, and playwright.

CAREER: Also see *WRITINGS* below. PRINCIPAL STAGE APPEARANCES—Peter Mitchell, *The Fisherman* and Goodfellow Pincher, *The Fourth Pig* (double-bill), Maidman Playhouse, New York City, 1965; sailor, *Hotel Passionato*, East 74th Street Theatre, New York City, 1965; Nicholas Tyler, *The Experiment*, Orpheum Theatre, New York City, 1967; Forensic, *Forensic and the Navigators*, Astor Place Theatre, New York City, 1970; the sheep, *The Serpent* and Clov, *Endgame*, both Open Theatre, Washington Square Methodist Church, New York City, 1970; jury member, *Twelve Angry Men*, Queens Playhouse, Queens, NY, 1972; Katar, *And They Put Handcuffs on the Flowers*, Mercer-O'Casey Theatre, New York City, 1972; Pylades and family member, *The Orphan*, New York Shakespeare Festival, Public Theatre, New York City, 1973; Charlie Hughes, *Hughie*, John Golden Theatre, New York City, 1975; fourth actor, cashier, newspaper vendor, conductor, gypsy, Francisco, and Polonius II, *Poor Murderer*, Ethel Barrymore Theatre, New York City, 1976; Soren, Bernard, and Alf, *Big and Little*, Phoenix Theatre Company, Marymount Manhattan Theatre, New York City, 1979; Mr. Webb, *Our Town*, Lincoln Center Theatre Company, Lyceum Theatre, New York City, 1988. Also appeared in *Terminal*, Open Theatre, Washington Square Methodist Church, 1970; with the Asolo State Theatre, Sarasota, FL, 1976-77; in *Candida*, Massachusetts Center Repertory Company Theatre, Boston, MA, 1977; *Hunger and Thirst*, *The Skin of Our Teeth*, and *The Merchant of Venice*, all Berkshire Theatre Festival,

Stockbridge, MA; and in productions of *No Time for Comedy* and *The Chalk Garden*.

PRINCIPAL STAGE WORK—All as director, unless indicated: Stage manager, *Doubletalk*, Theatre De Lys, New York City, 1964; *Time Trial*, New York Shakespeare Festival, Public Theatre, New York City, 1975; *The Elusive Angel*, New Dramatists Inc., New York City, 1975; *The Slab Boys*, Hudson Guild Theatre, New York City, 1980; *The New Yorkers*, Morse Center Trinity Theatre, New York City, 1984; magic consultant, *Feathertop*, WPA Theatre, New York City, 1984; *The Frog Prince*, Marathon '85, Ensemble Studio Theatre, New York City, 1985; *Mandragola*, Folger Shakespeare Theatre, Washington, DC, 1986. Also choreographer, Circle in the Square at Ford's Theatre, Washington, DC, 1971; director, Syracuse Stage, Syracuse, NY, 1977-78 and 1980-81; director, Actors Theatre of Louisville, Louisville, KY, 1979-80.

MAJOR TOURS—Charlie Hughes, *Hughie*, U.S. cities.

PRINCIPAL FILM APPEARANCES—Putney's chauffeur, *Putney Swope*, Cinema V, 1969; pharmacist, *Hi, Mom!*, Sigma III, 1970; Jake Guzik, *Capone*, Twentieth Century-Fox, 1975; doctor, *Breaking Away*, Twentieth Century-Fox, 1979; newspaper clerk, *The Amityville Horror*, American International, 1979; Martin, *A Little Romance*, Orion, 1979; Lee McHugh, *Hide in Plain Sight*, Metro-Goldwyn-Mayer/United Artists (MGM/UA), 1980; Bennings, *The Thing*, Universal, 1982; Ian, *Desperately Seeking Susan*, Orion, 1985; Dr. Dominick Princi, *Manhunter*, De Laurentiis Entertainment Group, 1986; waiter, *Bright Lights, Big City*, MGM/UA, 1988; Dr. Peter Ames, *Lost Angels*, Orion/Vestron, 1989; also appeared in *The Appointments of Dennis Jennings*, HBO Films, 1989.

PRINCIPAL TELEVISION APPEARANCES—Mini-Series: *John Steinbeck's "East of Eden,"* ABC, 1981. Pilots: Mr. Hardy, *The Four of Us*, ABC, 1977; Eli Clay, *Sanctuary of Fear*, NBC, 1979; Mustaf, *Callahan*, ABC, 1982; the Fixer, *The Saint* (broadcast as an episode of *CBS Summer Playhouse*), CBS, 1987. Episodic: *N.Y.P.D.*, ABC; *Columbo*, NBC. Movies: Veterinarian, *My Old Man*, CBS, 1979; Darryl F. Zanuck, *Moviola: This Year's Blonde*, NBC, 1980; Henry, *Revenge of the Stepford Wives*, NBC, 1980.

RELATED CAREER—Company member, Open Theatre, New York City, 1966-70; also member of Actors' Studio, New Dramatists Inc., and the Ensemble Studio Theatre.

NON-RELATED CAREER—Encyclopedia salesman.

WRITINGS: STAGE—*Amazing Grace*, New Dramatists Inc., New York City, 1977; *Bicycle Boys*, Ensemble Studio Theatre, New York City, 1978; (adaptor) *Mandragola*, Folger Shakespeare Theatre, Washington, DC, 1986; also *Bad Blood*, *Lost and Found*, *American Garage*, and *Pastorale*.

AWARDS: Burns Mantle Theatre Yearbook Award, Best Actor of the Year, 1970, for *The Serpent*.

ADDRESSES: AGENT—Writers and Artists Agency, 70 W. 36th Street, New York, NY 10018.*

MAMET, David 1947-

PERSONAL: Surname is pronounced "*Mam*-it"; full name, David Alan Mamet; born November 30, 1947, in Chicago, IL; son of Bernard Morris (an attorney) and Lenore June (a teacher; maiden name, Silver) Mamet; married Lindsay Crouse (an actress), December 21, 1977; children: Willa. EDUCATION—Goddard College, B.A., English, 1969; studied acting at the Neighborhood Playhouse, 1968-69.

VOCATION: Playwright and director.

CAREER: Also see *WRITINGS* below. PRINCIPAL STAGE WORK— Stage manager, *The Fantasticks,* Sullivan Street Playhouse, New York City, 1969-70; director, *Beyond the Horizon,* St. Nicholas Theatre, Chicago, IL, 1974; director, *The Woods,* St. Nicholas Theatre, 1977; director, "The Sancity of Marriage," "Dark Pony," and "Reunion," in *Reunion,* Circle Repertory Theatre, New York City, 1979; director, *Twelfth Night,* Circle Repertory Theatre, 1980; director, *A Sermon,* Ensemble Studio Theatre, New York City, 1981; director, *The Woods,* Second Stage Theatre, New York City, 1982; director, "Litko" in *Litko and Shoehorn* (double-bill), Hartley House Theatre, New York City, 1984.

PRINCIPAL FILM APPEARANCES—As himself, *Sanford Meisner— The Theatre's Best Kept Secret* (documentary), Columbia, 1984; Herb, *Black Widow,* Twentieth Century-Fox, 1987.

PRINCIPAL FILM WORK—Director, *House of Games,* Orion, 1987; director, *Things Change,* Columbia, 1988.

PRINCIPAL TELEVISION WORK—Specials: Executive producer (with Michael Hausman), "Lip Service," *HBO Showcase,* HBO, 1988.

RELATED CAREER—Stagehand, Hull House Theatre, Chicago, IL; actor, New England summer theatre productions, 1969; drama instructor, Marlboro College, Marlboro, VT, 1970; artist-in-residence and drama instructor, Goddard College, Plainfield, VT, 1971-73; founding member and artistic director, St. Nicholas Company, Plainfield, VT, 1972; faculty member, Illinois Arts Council, 1974; founder (with Steven Schachter, William H. Macy, and Patricia Cox) and director, St. Nicholas Players, Chicago, 1974-76; contributing editor, *Oui* magazine, 1975-76; visiting lecturer, University of Chicago, Chicago, IL, 1975, 1976, and 1979, and at New York University, New York City, 1981; teaching fellow, Yale University School of Drama, New Haven, CT, 1976-77; associate artistic director and playwright-in-residence, Goodman Theatre, Chicago, 1978-84; associate director, New Theatre Company, Chicago, 1985; co-founder, Dinglefest Theatre.

NON-RELATED CAREER—Busboy, Second City Theatre, Chicago, IL; also factory worker, real estate agent, window washer, office cleaner, taxi driver, short-order cook, and telephone salesman.

WRITINGS: STAGE—*Lakeboat,* Marlboro Theatre Workshop, Marlboro, VT, 1970, revised version produced in Milwaukee, WI, 1980, then Goodman Theatre, Chicago, IL, later Long Wharf Theatre, New Haven, CT, both 1982, published by Grove, 1981; *Duck Variations,* St. Nicholas Company, Goddard College, Plainfield, VT, 1972, then St. Clement's Church Theatre, New York City, 1975, later in *Sexual Perversity in Chicago* and *Duck Variations* (double-bill), Cherry Lane Theatre, New York City, 1976, then Regent Theatre, London, 1977, published in *Sexual Perversity in Chicago and Duck Variations,* Grove, 1978; *Sexual*

Perversity in Chicago, Organic Theatre Company, Chicago, IL, 1974, then St. Clement's Church Theatre, 1975, later in *Sexual Perversity in Chicago* and *Duck Variations* (double-bill), Cherry Lane Theatre, 1976, then Regent Theatre, 1977, published in *Sexual Perversity in Chicago and Duck Variations,* 1978; *Squirrels,* St. Nicholas Theatre, 1974, published by Samuel French, 1982; *The Poet and the Rent: A Play for Kids from Seven to 8:15,* first produced in Chicago, 1974, published in *Three Children's Plays,* Grove, 1986.

American Buffalo, Goodman Theatre, Stage Two, Chicago, 1975, then St. Clement's Church Theatre, New York City, 1976, later (revised version) Ethel Barrymore Theatre, New York City, 1977, then Cottesloe Theatre, London, 1978, later Booth Theatre, New York City, 1983, published by Grove, 1977; *Reunion,* St. Nicholas Theatre, then Actors Theatre of Louisville, Louisville, KY, both 1976, later Yale Repertory Theatre, New Haven, CT, 1977, then Circle Repertory Theatre, New York City, 1979, published by Grove, 1979; *The Woods,* St. Nicholas Theatre, 1977, then New York Shakespeare Festival (NYSF), Public Theatre, New York City, 1979, later London, 1984, published by Grove, 1979; *All Men Are Whores,* Yale Cabaret, New Haven, CT, 1977, published in *Short Plays and Monologues,* Dramatists Play Service, 1981; *A Life in the Theatre,* Goodman Theatre, Stage Two, then Theatre De Lys, New York City, both 1977, later Open Space Theatre, London, 1979, published by Grove, 1978; *The Revenge of the Space Pandas, or Binky Rudich and the Two Speed-Clock,* St. Nicholas Theatre, then Flushing Town Hall, Queens, NY, both 1977, published by Sergel, 1978, then in *Three Children's Plays,* 1986; *Dark Pony,* Yale Repertory Theatre, 1977, then in *Reunion,* Circle Repertory Theatre, later London, 1981, published by Grove, 1979; "The Sanctity of Marriage" in *Reunion,* Circle Repertory Theatre, 1979, published by Samuel French, 1982; *The Water Engine: An American Fable* and *Mr. Happiness* (double-bill), St. Nicholas Theatre, 1977, then NYSF, Public Theatre, later Plymouth Theatre, New York City, both 1978, published by Grove, 1978; *Lone Canoe, or the Explorer,* Goodman Theatre, 1979; *Shoeshine,* Ensemble Studio Theatre, New York City, 1979, published in *Short Plays and Monologues,* 1981.

A Sermon, Ensemble Studio Theatre, 1981, then London, 1987, published in *Short Plays and Monologues,* 1981; *Edmond,* Goodman Theatre, 1982, then Provincetown Playhouse, New York City, 1982, later London, 1985, published by Grove, 1983, then Methuen, 1986; *The Disappearance of the Jews,* Goodman Theatre, 1983; "Two Conversations," "Two Scenes," and "Yes, But So What," in *Five Unrelated Pieces,* Ensemble Studio Theatre, 1983, published in *Dramatic Sketches and Monologues,* Samuel French, 1985; *Glengarry Glen Ross,* National Theatre, London, 1983, then Goodman Theatre, later John Golden Theatre, New York City, both 1984, published by Grove and Methuen, both 1984; (adaptor) *Red River,* Goodman Theatre, 1983; *The Dog, Film Crew, and 4 A.M.,* all first produced in 1983, published in *Dramatic Sketches and Monologues,* 1985; "Pint's a Pound the World Around," "Deer Dogs," "Conversations with the Spirit World," and "Dowsing," in *Vermont Sketches,* first produced in New York City, 1984, published in *Dramatic Sketches and Monologues,* 1985; "Litko" in *Litko and Shoehorn* (double-bill), Hartley House Theatre, New York City, 1984, published in *Short Plays and Monologues,* 1981; *The Frog Prince,* first produced in Louisville, KY, 1984, then Marathon '85, Ensemble Studio Theatre, 1985, published in *Three Children's Plays,* Grove, 1986.

The Spanish Prisoner and *The Shawl,* both New Theatre Company, Goodman Theatre, 1985; *Prairie du Chien,* Mitzi E. Newhouse

Theatre, New York City, 1985, then London, 1986, published in *Short Plays and Monologues,* 1981; *The Shawl,* Mitzi E. Newhouse Theatre, 1985, then London, 1986, published by Grove, 1985; (adaptor) *The Cherry Orchard,* New Theatre Company, Goodman Theatre, 1985, published by Grove, 1987; "Vint" in *Orchards,* first produced in Urbana, IL, 1985, then the Acting Company, New York City, 1986, published by Knopf, 1986; *Speed-the-Plow,* Royale Theatre, New York City, 1988, published by Grove, 1988; "Where Were You When It Went Down?" in *Urban Blight,* Manhattan Theatre Club, City Center Theatre, New York City, 1988; "Bobby Gould in Hell" in *Oh, Hell,* Mitzie E. Newhouse Theatre, 1989. Also wrote *Donny March,* first produced in 1981; *Mackinac* and *Marranos,* both Saint Nicholas Theatre.

FILM—*The Postman Always Rings Twice,* Paramount, 1981; *The Verdict,* Twentieth Century-Fox, 1982; *House of Games,* Orion, 1987, published by Grove, 1987; *The Untouchables,* Paramount, 1987; (with Shel Silverstein) *Things Change,* Columbia, published by Grove, 1988; *We're No Angels,* Paramount, 1989.

TELEVISION—Episodic: *Hill Street Blues,* NBC, 1987; also *L.A. Law.,* NBC. Specials: "A Life in the Theatre," *Great Performances,* PBS, 1979.

RADIO—Specials: "The Water Engine," *Earplay,* National Public Radio, 1978; *Prairie du Chien,* National Public Radio, 1978; also *Cross Patch* and *Goldberg Street,* both 1985, published in *Dramatic Sketches and Monologues,* 1985.

OTHER—(Contributor) *The Ensemble Studio Theatre Marathon '84,* Broadway Play Publishing, 1985; *Writing in Restaurants* (essays), Viking, 1986; (with Donald Sultan) *Warm and Cold* (juvenile), Solo, 1984; (with Lindsay Crouse) *The Owl* (juvenile), Kipling, 1987; *Five Television Plays,* Grove, 1990.

AWARDS: Joseph Jefferson Award, 1975, for *Sexual Perversity in Chicago;* Joseph Jefferson Award, 1976, for *American Buffalo;* Obie Award from the *Village Voice,* Best New Playwright, 1976, for *American Buffalo* and *Sexual Perversity in Chicago;* Children's Theatre Grant from the New York State Council on the Arts, Rockefeller Grant, and CBS Creative Writing Fellow, all 1976; New York Drama Critics' Circle Award, Best American Play, 1977, for *American Buffalo;* Outer Critics' Circle Award, 1978, for "contributions to the American theatre;" Obie Award, 1983, for *Edmond;* Society of West End Theatres Award, 1983; Academy Award nomination, Best Adapted Screenplay, 1983, for *The Verdict;* Hull-Warriner Award from the Dramatists Guild, 1984; New York Drama Critics' Circle Award, Best American Play, Pulitzer Prize, Joseph Dintenfass Award, and Antoinette Perry Award nomination, Best Play, all 1984, for *Glengarry Glen Ross;* Antoinette Perry Award nomination, Best Reproduction of a Play, 1984, for *American Buffalo;* Academy-Institute Award in Literature, 1986; Golden Globe nomination, Best Screenplay, 1988, for *House of Games;* Writers Guild Award nomination, Best Screenplay Based on Material from Another Medium, 1988, for *The Untouchables.*

MEMBER: Dramatists Guild, Writers Guild of America, Actors' Equity Association, P.E.N., United Steelworkers of America, Randolph Hollister Association.

ADDRESSES: OFFICE—St. Nicholas Theatre, 2851 N. Halstead Street, Chicago, IL 60657. AGENT—Howard Rosenstone, Rosenstone/ Wender, 3 E. 48th Street, New York, NY 10017.*

MANFREDI, Nino   1921-

PERSONAL: Born Nino Saturnino, March 22, 1921, in Castro del Volsci, Italy; married Erminia Ferrari, 1955; children: two daughters, one son. EDUCATION—Studied law; also attended the Academy of Dramatic Art (Rome), 1944-47.

VOCATION: Actor, director, and screenwriter.

CAREER: Also see *WRITINGS* below. FILM DEBUT—*Monastero de Santa Chiara,* 1949. PRINCIPAL FILM APPEARANCES—Ugo Nardi, *Audace colpo dei soliti ignoti* (also known as *Holdup a la Milanaise* and *Fiasco in Milan*), 1959, released in the United States by Avion-Trans-Universe/Jerand, 1963; Nino Pasqui, *Le pillole d'Ercole* (also known as *Hercules' Pills*), Dino De Laurentiis, 1960; Quirino Filonzi, *Crimen* (also known as *And Suddenly It's Murder!*), 1960, released in the United States by Royal, 1964; Tomagra, "L'avventura di un soldato" ("The Soldier") in *L'Amore difficile* (also known as *Of Wayward Love* and *Erotica*), 1962, released in the United States by Pathe, 1964; Francesco, "Scandalosa" ("The Scandal") in *Alta infedelta* (also known as *High Infidelity* and *Haute infidelite*), 1964, released in the United States by Magna, 1965; Jose Luis, *El verdugo* (also known as *Not on Your Life* and *La ballata del boia*), 1964, released in the United States by Pathe Contemporary, 1965; Giorgio, "La telefonata" ("The Telephone Call") in *Le Bambole* (also known as *Four Kinds of Love, The Dolls,* and *Bambole!*), Columbia, 1965; Lamporecchi, *Made in Italy* (also known as *A l'Italienne*), 1965, released in the United States by Royal, 1967; Dudu, *Operazione San Gennaro* (also known as *Treasure of San Gennaro* and *Operation San Gennaro*), 1966, released in the United States by Paramount, 1968; the Doctor, *Una rosa per tutti* (also known as *A Rose for Everyone* and *Everyman's Woman*), Royal, 1967; Natalino, *Italian Secret Service,* Cineriz, 1968; Marco, *Il padre di famiglia* (also known as *Head of the Family* and *Jeux d'adultes*), Paramount, 1968, released in the United States by Allied Artists, 1970.

Benedetto Parisi, *Per grazia ricevuta* (also known as *The Cross-Eyed Saint*), Cineriz, 1970; Zilio, *La betia* (also known as *In Love, Every Pleasure Has Its Pain*), Titanus Distribuzione, 1971; title role, *Girolimoni, il mostro di Roma* (also known as *The Assassin of Rome*), Columbia, 1972; Paolo Antonazzi, *Lo chiameremo Andrea* (also known as *We'll Call Him Andrea*), Cinema International/ Verona Produzione, 1972; Carmelo Mazzullo, *Trastevere,* Produzioni Europee Associates, 1972; Nino Garafalo, *Pane e cioccolata* (also known as *Bread and Chocolate*), CIC/World Northal, 1973; Antonio, *C'eravamo tanto amati* (also known as *We All Loved Each Other So Much*), Almi/Cinema V, 1974; Marcello Ferrari, *Attenti al buffone!* (also known as *Eye of the Cat*), Medusa Distribuzione, 1975; Antonio Pecorari, "Il cavallucio svedese" in *Quelle strane occasioni* (also known as *Strange Events*), Cineriz, 1976; Giacinto Mazzatella, *Brutti, sporchi, e cattivi* (also known as *Down and Dirty* and *Ugly, Dirty, and Bad*), Gold Film, 1976; Cardinal Caprettari, "Le Soleil du Vatican" in *Signore e signori, buonanotte* (also known as *Goodnight, Ladies and Gentlemen*), Titanus Distribuzione, 1977; Don Colombo, *In nome del Papa Re* (also known as *In the Name of the Pope King*), Rizzoli, 1977; Sasa Iovine, *La mazzetta* (also known as *The Payoff*), United Artists, 1978; Mr. Parisy, *Gros Calin,* Exportation Francaise Cinematographique, 1979.

Michele, *Cafe Express,* Vides International, 1980; Bedouin, *Testa o croce* (also known as *Heads or Tails*), CIDIF/SACIS, 1982; Domenico, *Spaghetti House,* Titanus Distribuzione, 1982; Sandro, "In the Red Beret" in *Questo e quello* (also known as *This and*

That), CIDIF, 1983; Salvietti, *Grandi magazzini* (also known as *Department Store*), Columbia Pictures Italia, 1986; beggar, *I picari* (also known as *The Picaros* and *The Rogues*), Warner Brothers, 1987; Pontius Pilate, *Secondo Ponzio Pilato* (also known as *According to Pontius Pilate*), United International, 1987; Stella's father, *Helsinki Napoli All Night Long*, Cofimedia/Capital Cinema, 1988. Also appeared as Francisco, *Torna a Napoli*, 1951; in *Anema e core*, 1951; as Stornello, *Prigionera della torre fuoco*, 1952; in *Ho scelto l'amore*, 1952; *Canzoni, Canzoni, Canzoni*, 1953; *Viva il cinema!*, 1953; *Lo scapolo*, 1955; *La domenica della buono gente*, 1955; *Toto, Pepino, e la mala femmina*, 1956; as Otello, *Gli innamorati*, 1956; Paolo, *Guardia, guardia scelta brigadiere e maresciallo*, 1956; Carletto, *Tempo di villeggiatura*, 1956; in *Prigionieri del male*, 1957; *Susanna tutta panna*, 1957; *Femmine tre volte*, 1957; *Il bacto del sole*, 1958; *Pezzo, capopezzo e capitano*, 1958; as Mario, *Adorabili e bugiarde*, 1958; Nino, *Camping*, 1958; Enea Serafino, *Carporale di giornata*, 1958; Otello Cucchiaroni, *Guardia ladro e cameriera*, 1958; Toni, *Venezia, la luna, et tu*, 1958; Toto Improta, *Camela e una bambola*, 1959; *I ragazzi dei paroli*, 1959.

Nando, *L'impiegato*, 1960; in *I giudizio universale* (also known as *The Last Judgement*), 1961; as Giacinto Rossi, *A cavallo della tigre*, 1961; Franco Bartolucci, *Il carabiniere a Cavallo*, 1961; Nino Borsetti, *I motorizzati*, 1962; Omero, *Anni Ruggenti*, 1962; Nino, *La parmigiana*, 1962; Quirino, "E vissero felici" in *I cuori infranti*, 1963; Stephano Liberati, *Il gaucho*, 1963; Andrea, "Cocaina dedomenica" and Spadini, "Donna d'affair" in *Controsesso*, 1964; Nanni Galassi, "Il Vittimista" in *Thrilling*, 1965; Guido Roganelli, "Una giornata decisiva" in *I complessi*, 1965; various roles, *Questa volta parliamo di uomini* (also known as *Let's Talk About Men*), 1965; in *Io, io, io . . . e gli altri* (also known as *I, I, I . . . and the Others*), 1965; as Cianfanna, *Io, la conoscevo bene*, 1965; Franco, *Adulterio all'italiana*, 1966; Balestrini, *Straziami ma di baci saziami*, 1968; Oreste Sabatini, *Riusciranno i nostri eroi a ritrovare l'amico misteriosamente scomparso in Africa?*, 1968; various roles, *Vedu nudo*, 1969.

Cornacchia/Pasquino, *Nell'anno del signore*, 1970; title role, *Rosolino Paterno—Soldato*, 1970; "Concerto a tre pifferi" in *Contestazione generale*, 1970; Gepetto, *Le avventure di Pinocchio*, 1971; Quitilio Teramella, *Roma bene*, 1971; *Un sorriso, uno schiaffo, un baccio in bocca*, 1975; Enzo Lucarelli, "Il superiore" and Paolo Gallizzi, "L'equivoco" in *Basta che non si sappia in giro!*, 1976; in *Il Conte di Monte Cristo*, 1977; *I nuovi Mostri* (also known as *Viva Italia!* and *The New Monsters*), Filmverlag der Autoren/Cinema V, 1977; as Vittorio Barletta, *Il gioccattolo*, 1979; in *Il viaggiatori della Sera*, 1979; *Insieme*, 1979; *Nudo di donna* (also known as *Portrait of a Woman, Nude*), Cineriz, 1981; *Il tenente dei carabinieri* (also known as *The Lieutenant Carabineer* and *The Police Lieutenant*), Columbia, 1986.

PRINCIPAL FILM WORK—Director: "L'avventura di un soldato" ("The Soldier") in *L'Amore difficile* (also known as *Of Wayward Love* and *Erotica*), 1962, released in the United States by Pathe, 1964; (also producer) *Per grazia ricevuta* (also known as *The Cross-Eyed Saint*), Cineriz, 1970; *Nudo di donna* (also known as *Portrait of a Woman, Nude*), Cineriz, 1981.

RELATED CAREER—Worked on radio and in stage revues before World War II; member, Maltagliati-Gassman stage company, 1947; actor with the Piccolo Teatro di Milano, 1948; dubbed voices in Italian films.

WRITINGS: See production details above, unless indicated. FILM—

(With others) *Camping*, 1958; (with others) *Le pillole d'Ercole*, 1959; (with Fabio Carpi, Giuseppe Orlandini, and Ettore Scola) "L'avventura di un soldato" in *L'Amore difficile*, 1962; (with Dino Risi, Adriano Baracco, and Ennio De Concini) *Operazione San Gennaro*, 1966; (with Eduardo Borras, De Concini, and Franco Rossi) *Una rosa per tutti*, 1967; (with Leo Benvenuti and Piero DeBernardi) *Per grazia ricevuta*, 1970; (with Franco Brusati and Iaia Fiastri) *Pane e cioccolata*, 1973; (with Nanni Loy and Elvio Porta) *Cafe Express*, 1980; (with Agenore Incrocci ("Age"), Ruggero Maccari, and Furio Scarpelli) *Nudo di donna*, 1981; (with Loy, Franco Ferrini, Enrico Oldoini, and Renato Pozzetto) *Testa o croce*, 1982; (with Age, Scarpelli, Peter Barnes, and Giulio Paradisi) *Spaghetti House*, 1982; (with Bernardino Zapponi) "In the Red Beret" in *Questo e quello*, 1983.

AWARDS: Prize for First Work from the Cannes Film Festival, 1971, for *Per grazia ricevuta.**

*   *   *

MARLOWE, Theresa   1957-

PERSONAL: Born Theresa Aceves, July 20, 1957, in Monroe, MI. EDUCATION—Studied acting at the British Theatre Association, the Folger Theatre, and the Source Theatre; studied voice with Marion Rich and Lucille Rubin; studied singing with Bill Reed.

VOCATION: Actress.

CAREER: STAGE DEBUT—Nora, *Riders to the Sea*, WPA Theatre,

THERESA MARLOWE

Washington, DC, for twenty-five performances. OFF-BROAD-WAY DEBUT—Anthea Arlo, "Sleeping Beauty, or Coma" and Renee Vain and Tracy, "Vampire Lesbians of Sodom," in *Vampire Lesbians of Sodom*, Provincetown Playhouse, 1985. PRINCIPAL STAGE APPEARANCES—Irina, *The Three Sisters*, Source Theatre, Washington, DC, 1979; Bettina Barnes, *Psycho Beach Party*, Players Theatre, New York City, 1987; Heidi Mittelhoffer, *The Lady in Question*, Orpheum Theatre, New York City, 1989. Also appeared as Valerie Waverly, *Times Square Angel*, Provincetown Playhouse; Ashes Mercredi, *Champagne* and Jenna, *Triplets in Uniform*, both La Mama Experimental Theatre Company, New York City; Rita, *Theodora*, Theatre-in-Limbo, New York City; Angel, *Trade*, Tiffany, *Cold Rubber Room*, and Zera, *Rouge and Lace*, all Rendezvous Productions, New York City; Canada, *Summer of Education*, Meat and Potatoes Company, New York City; Chorus, *Helen*, Classic Theatre, New York City; Kath, *Entertaining Mr. Sloane*, the Writer, *Lady of Larkspur Lotion*, Curley's wife, *Of Mice and Men*, the Woman, *Talk to Me Like the Rain*, Perfect Peggy, *A Late Snow*, Kate, *The Long Voyage Home*, Maria, *The Queen and the Rebels*, and Hera, *Persephone*, all Source Theatre Company, Washington, DC; May, *Dressing for Parts*, the Wife, *Hello Out There*, and Cecelia, *Tears of My Sister*, all Rendezvous Productions, Washington, DC; third witch, *Macbeth*, Georgetown Classical Theatre; Terese, *Sherlock Holmes*, Trinity Players; Dunyasha, *The Cherry Orchard*, Georgetown Repertory; Janice Vickery, *The Effect of Gamma Rays on Man-in-the-Moon Marigolds*, Fine Line Actors Theatre; Hermia, *A Midsummer's Night Dream*, Shakespeare Summer Festival.

AWARDS: Best Actress Award from the Source Theatre, 1979, for *The Three Sisters.*

MEMBER: Actors' Equity Association.

SIDELIGHTS: RECREATIONS—Writing, aerobics, reading, and going to movies.

ADDRESSES: AGENT—Lynn Oliver Moore, Spotlight.

*   *   *

MARSHALL, William   1924-

PERSONAL: Full name, William Horace Marshall; born August 19, 1924, in Gary, IN; son of Vereen (a dentist) and Thelma (Edwards) Marshall. EDUCATION—Attended the Art Institute of Chicago, 1938-40, the Alliance Francaise, Paris, 1959-63, and New York University; studied acting at the American Theatre Wing, 1947, the Actors Studio, 1952-54, and the Neighborhood Playhouse, 1958. MILITARY—U.S. Army, 1943.

VOCATION: Actor.

CAREER: BROADWAY DEBUT—Chorus, *Carmen Jones*, Broadway Theatre, 1944. PRINCIPAL STAGE APPEARANCES—Title role (understudy), *Jeb*, Martin Beck Theatre, New York City, 1946; Joshua (understudy) and freed man, *Our Lan'*, Royale Theatre, New York City, 1947; Sad-Act, *A Long Way from Home*, Maxine Elliott's Theatre, New York City, 1948; Rolla Bennett, *Set My People Free*, Hudson Theatre, New York City, 1948; General Joe Hooker, *The Washington Years*, American Negro Theatre, New York City, 1948; Hlabeni, *Lost in the Stars*, Music Box Theatre, New York City, 1949; Cookson, *Peter Pan*, Imperial Theatre, New

York City, 1950; the Lawd, *The Green Pastures*, Broadway Theatre, 1951; Kelly, *Time to Go*, Yugoslavian Hall, New York City, 1952; title role, *Othello*, Mother Zion Church, New York City, 1953; title role, *Oedipus Rex*, Chicago Playwrights Company, Chicago, IL, 1955; title role, *Othello*, Brattle Theatre, Cambridge, MA, then City Center Theatre, New York City, 1955; Chief Uturo, *The Virtuous Island*, Carnegie Hall Playhouse, New York City, 1957; title role, *Othello*, New York Shakespeare Festival, Belvedere Lake Theatre, New York City, 1958; Henry Simpson, *Toys in the Attic*, Piccadilly Theatre, London, 1960; Bear Baiter, *When We Dead Awaken*, Gate Theatre, Dublin, Ireland, 1961; Saul, *Javelin*, Actors Playhouse, New York City, 1966; Othello, *Catch My Soul*, Center Theatre Group, Ahmanson Theatre, Los Angeles, 1968; Captain, *Leviathan 99*, Samuel Goldwyn Studios, Los Angeles, 1972; title role, *Othello*, National Shakespeare Festival, Old Globe Theatre, San Diego, CA, 1976. Also appeared in *Trial By Fire*, Blackfriars Theatre, New York City, 1947; *An Enemy of the People*, Chicago Theatre Group, Goodman Theatre, Chicago, 1979.

PRINCIPAL STAGE WORK—Producer, *Othello*, Mother Zion Church, New York City, 1953; director, *Long Voyage Home*, American Artists and Students Center, Paris, 1962.

MAJOR TOURS—Title role, *Othello*, Dublin Theatre Festival, European cities, 1962-63; also *Call Me Mister*, 1948; and (also director) *The Bear* and *The Marriage Proposal*, U.S. Air Force bases, France, 1961.

FILM DEBUT—King Dick, *Lydia Bailey*, Twentieth Century-Fox, 1952. PRINCIPAL FILM APPEARANCES—Glycon, *Demetrius and the Gladiators*, Twentieth Century-Fox, 1954; leader, *Something of Value*, Metro-Goldwyn-Mayer (MGM), 1957; Ashumen, *To Trap a Spy*, MGM, 1966; Al Poland, *The Hell with Heroes*, Universal, 1968; Edward W. Brooke, *The Boston Strangler*, Twentieth Century-Fox, 1968; attorney general, *Skullduggery*, Universal, 1970; Tatakombi, *Tarzan's Jungle Rebellion*, New General, 1970; Morrie Bronson, *Zigzag* (also known as *False Witness*), MGM, 1970; Doctor Craig Smith, *Honky*, Jack H. Harris, 1971; title role, *Blacula*, American International, 1972; Manuwalde/Blacula, *Scream Blacula Scream*, American International, 1973; Bishop Garnet Williams, *Abby*, American International, 1974; Attorney General William Klinger, *Twilight's Last Gleaming*, Allied Artists, 1977; attendant, *Curtains*, Jensen Farley, 1983; pirate captain, "Video Pirates," *Amazon Women on the Moon*, Universal, 1987. Also appeared in *Piedra de Toque*, Asturia Films, 1953; *Sabu and the Magic Ring*, Allied Artists, 1957; *The Great Skycopter Rescue*, 1982; *Vasectomy, a Delicate Matter* (also known as *Vasectomy*), Vandom International/Seymour Borde and Associates, 1986.

PRINCIPAL TELEVISION APPEARANCES—Series: Judge Marcus Black, *Rosetti and Ryan*, NBC, 1977; King of Cartoons, *Pee-Wee's Playhouse*, CBS, 1986—; also Mr. Kano, *Danger Man*, British television, 1959. Pilots: Doctor Harold Tawn, *U.M.C.*, CBS, 1969; Judge Marcus Black, *Rosetti and Ryan: Men Who Love Women*, NBC, 1977; Ubal, *Sabu and the Magic Ring* (never broadcast). Episodic: "As Adam, Early in the Morning," *Repertoire Workshop*, CBS, 1966; *Daniel Boone*, NBC, 1967; also *Alfred Hitchcock Presents*, CBS; *The Man from U.N.C.L.E.*, NBC; *Ben Casey*, ABC; *Secret Agent*, CBS; *Tarzan*, NBC. Movies: Captain Condor Sekallie, *The Mask of Sheba*, NBC, 1970; Mr. Poore, *Killer Instinct* (also known as *Over the Edge*), NBC, 1988; also *Beverly Hills Madam*, NBC, 1986. Specials: The Lawd, *The Green Pastures*, BBC, 1958; Don Cheek, "One More Hurdle,"

NBC Special Treat, NBC, 1984; King of Cartoons, *A Special Evening of Pee-Wee's Playhouse*, CBS, 1987. Also appeared as the Battler, *The World of Nick Adams*, NBC, 1957; *The Big Pride*, BBC, 1961.

PRINCIPAL RADIO APPEARANCES—Yank, *Bound East of Cardiff*, NBC, 1952; *The Lower Basin Street*, 1952; title role, *The Emperor Jones*, BBC, 1959.

RELATED CAREER—With the New York Shakespeare Festival, toured New York City schools in a performance of *Othello*, 1953; played gospel music as a disc jockey for radio station WLIB (New York City), 1956; singer at the Moulin Rouge, Paris, 1962-63.

NON-RELATED CAREER—Steel mill worker, stevedore, and commercial artist.

MEMBER: Actors' Equity Association (recording secretary, 1950-51), Avant-Garde Francaise d'Amerique, American Federation of Television and Radio Artists, Screen Actors Guild.

SIDELIGHTS: RECREATIONS—Horseback riding, swimming, dancing, and writing poetry.*

*   *   *

MARTIN, Dean   1917-

PERSONAL: Born Dino Paul Crocetti, June 17, 1917, in Steubenville, OH; son of Guy Crocetti (a barber); married Elizabeth Ann McDonald, 1940 (divorced, 1949); married Jeanne Bieggers, 1949 (divorced); married Cathy Mae Hawn, 1973 (divorced, 1976); children: Craig, Claudia, Gail, Deanna (first marriage); Dean Paul (Dino, Jr.; deceased), Ricci, Gina (second marriage); Sasha (third marriage; adopted).

VOCATION: Singer and actor.

CAREER: FILM DEBUT—Steve Baird, *My Friend Irma*, Paramount, 1949. PRINCIPAL FILM APPEARANCES—Sergeant Puccinelli, *At War with the Army*, Paramount, 1950; Steve Baird, *My Friend Irma Goes West*, Paramount, 1950; Al Crowthers, *Sailor Beware*, Paramount, 1951; Bill Baker, *That's My Boy*, Paramount, 1951; Chick Allen, *Jumping Jacks*, Paramount, 1952; as himself, *The Road to Bali*, Paramount, 1952; Bill Miller, *The Stooge*, Paramount, 1952; Joe Anthony, *The Caddy*, Paramount, 1953; Honey Talk Nelson, *Money from Home*, Paramount, 1953; Larry Todd, *Scared Stiff*, Paramount, 1953; Steve, *Living It Up*, Paramount, 1954; Pete Nelson, *Three Ring Circus* (also known as *Jerrico, the Wonder Clown*), Paramount, 1954; Bob Miles, *You're Never Too Young*, Paramount, 1955; Rick Todd, *Artists and Models*, Paramount, 1955; Slim Mosely, Jr., *Pardners*, Paramount, 1956; Steve Wiley, *Hollywood or Bust*, Paramount, 1956; Ray Hunter, *Ten Thousand Bedrooms*, Metro-Goldwyn-Mayer (MGM), 1957; Michael Whiteacre, *The Young Lions*, Twentieth Century-Fox, 1958; Dude, *Rio Bravo*, Warner Brothers, 1959; Bama Dillert, *Some Came Running*, MGM, 1959; Maury Novak, *Career*, Paramount, 1959.

Jeffrey Moss, *Bells Are Ringing*, MGM, 1960; Sam Harmon, *Ocean's Eleven*, Warner Brothers, 1960; as himself, *Pepe*, Columbia, 1960; Michael Haney, *Who Was That Lady?*, Columbia, 1960; Bo Gillis, *Ada*, MGM, 1961; Tony Ryder, *All in a Night's Work*,

DEAN MARTIN

Paramount, 1961; as himself, *The Road to Hong Kong*, United Artists, 1962; Sergeant Chip Deal, *Sergeants 3*, United Artists, 1962; Steve Flood, *Who's Got the Action?*, Paramount, 1962; bum, *Come Blow Your Horn*, Paramount, 1963; Joe Jarrett, *Four for Texas*, Warner Brothers, 1963; Julian Berniers, *Toys in the Attic*, United Artists, 1963; Jason Steel, *Who's Been Sleeping in My Bed?*, Paramount, 1963; Dino, *Kiss Me, Stupid*, Lopert, 1964; Little John, *Robin and the Seven Hoods*, Warner Brothers, 1964; Leonard Crawley, *What a Way to Go!*, Twentieth Century-Fox, 1964; Ernie Brewer, *Marriage on the Rocks*, Warner Brothers, 1965; Tom Elder, *The Sons of Katie Elder*, Paramount, 1965; Matt Helm, *Murderer's Row*, Columbia, 1966; Matt Helm, *The Silencers*, Columbia, 1966; Sam Hollis, *Texas Across the River*, Universal, 1966; Matt Helm, *The Ambushers*, Columbia, 1967; Alex Flood, *Rough Night in Jericho*, Universal, 1967; Dee Bishop, *Bandolero!*, Twentieth Century-Fox, 1968; Van Morgan, *Five Card Stud*, Paramount, 1968; David Sloane, *How to Save a Marriage—And Ruin Your Life* (also known as *Band of Gold*), Columbia, 1968; Matt Helm, *The Wrecking Crew*, Columbia, 1968; Captain Vernon Demarest, *Airport*, Universal, 1970; Joe Baker, *Something Big*, National General, 1971; Billy Massey, *Showdown*, Universal, 1973; Joe Ricco, *Mr. Ricco*, MGM, 1975; Jamie Blake, *The Cannonball Run*, Twentieth Century-Fox, 1981; Jamie Blake, *Cannonball Run II*, Warner Brothers, 1984.

TELEVISION DEBUT—*Toast of the Town*, CBS. PRINCIPAL TELEVISION APPEARANCES—Series: Host (with Jerry Lewis), *The Colgate Comedy Hour*, NBC, 1950-55; host, *The Dean Martin Show*, NBC, 1965-74; as himself, *Half Nelson*, NBC, 1985. Pilots: Host, *The Powder Room*, NBC, 1971; host, *Dean's Place*, NBC,

1975. Episodic: *Welcome Aboard*, NBC, 1948; *The Danny Thomas Show*, CBS, 1958; *Startime*, NBC, 1959 and 1960; *Rawhide*, CBS, 1964; *Vega$*, ABC, 1979; guest host, *The Big Show*, NBC, 1980; *On Stage America*, syndicated, 1984; *The Motown Revue*, NBC, 1985; *The Dom DeLuise Show*, syndicated, 1987; also *Club Oasis*, NBC.

Specials: *Show of the Year*, NBC, 1950; *The General Motors 50th Anniversary Show*, NBC, 1957; *The Dean Martin Show*, NBC, 1958; *Bing Crosby and His Friends*, CBS, 1958; *The Dean Martin Show*, NBC, 1958; *The Bob Hope Show*, NBC, 1959; *The Phil Harris Show*, NBC, 1959; *The Dean Martin Show*, NBC, 1959; *The Frank Sinatra Show*, ABC, 1959; *The Dean Martin Show*, NBC, 1960; *The Bob Hope Show*, NBC, 1961; *The Judy Garland Show*, CBS, 1962; *The Bob Hope Show*, NBC, 1963; *Favorite Songs*, NBC, 1964; *The Best on Record*, NBC, 1965; *The Wonderful World of Burlesque*, NBC, 1966; *Movin' with Nancy*, NBC, 1967; *Ann-Margret: From Hollywood with Love*, CBS, 1969; *Bing Crosby—Cooling It*, NBC, 1970; *Jack Benny's 20th Anniversary TV Special*, NBC, 1970; *Petula*, ABC, 1970; *City vs. Country*, ABC, 1971; *Swing Out, Sweet Land*, NBC, 1971; *Bing Crosby—Cooling It*, CBS, 1973; *Jack Benny's First Farewell Show*, NBC, 1973; *The Bob Hope Special*, NBC, 1974; *Dean Martin's Celebrity Roast* (a series of 28 specials), NBC, 1974-79; *A Lucille Ball Special Starring Lucille Ball and Dean Martin*, CBS, 1975; *The Don Rickles Show*, CBS, 1975; *Dean Martin's California Christmas*, NBC, 1975; *Dean Martin's Red Hot Scandals of 1926*, NBC, 1976; *The First 50 Years*, NBC, 1976; *Sinatra and Friends*, ABC, 1977; *Dean Martin's Christmas in California*, NBC, 1977; *Dean Martin's Red Hot Scandals, Part 2*, NBC, 1977; *Bob Hope's All-Star Comedy Spectacular from Lake Tahoe*, NBC, 1977; *The Stars Salute Israel at 30*, ABC, 1978; *Highlights of the Dean Martin Roasts*, NBC, 1980; *Shirley MacLaine . . . Every Little Movement*, CBS, 1980; *The Mac Davis Tenth Anniversary Special: I Still Believe in Music*, NBC, 1980; *Sinatra—The First 40 Years*, NBC, 1980; *The Dean Martin Christmas Special*, NBC, 1980; *Dean Martin's Comedy Classics*, NBC, 1981; *Ladies and Gentlemen, Bob Newhart . . . Part II*, CBS, 1981; *Dean Martin's Christmas at Sea World*, NBC, 1981; *Dean Martin at the Wild Animal Park*, NBC, 1982; *Bob Hope's Pink Panther Thanksgiving Gala*, NBC, 1982; *George Burns' 100th Birthday Party*, NBC, 1982; *Dom DeLuise and Friends*, ABC, 1983; *Dean Martin in London*, Showtime, 1983; *The Dean Martin Celebrity Roast: Joan Collins*, NBC, 1984; *Dom DeLuise and Friends, Part 2*, ABC, 1984; *The Dean Martin Celebrity Roast: Mr. T*, NBC, 1984; *All Star Party for Lucille Ball*, CBS, 1984; *The Dean Martin Celebrity Roast: Michael Landon*, NBC, 1984; *The 50th Presidential Inaugural Gala*, ABC, 1985; *Bob Hope Buys NBC?*, NBC, 1985; *All-Star Party for "Dutch" Reagan*, CBS, 1985; *Dom DeLuise and Friends, Part IV*, ABC, 1986; *Las Vegas: An All-Star 75th Anniversary*, ABC, 1987; *America's Tribute to Bob Hope*, NBC, 1988.

PRINCIPAL RADIO APPEARANCES—Series: *The Martin and Lewis Show*, NBC. Episodic: *The Big Show*, NBC.

RELATED CAREER—(As Dino Martino) Singer with Ernie McKay's Band; partner with Jerry Lewis in the comedy team of Martin and Lewis, 1946-56.

NON-RELATED CAREER—Amateur welterweight boxer under the name "Kid Crocket," gas station attendant, steel mill worker, clerk, and croupier.

RECORDINGS: ALBUMS—*Dean Martin Sings*, Capitol, 1955; *This Is Dean Martin*, Capitol, 1958; *Bells Are Ringing* (original soundtrack), Capitol, 1960; *Everybody Loves Somebody*, Reprise, 1964; *Dream with Dean*, Reprise, 1964; *The Door Is Still Open to My Heart*, Reprise, 1964; *Dean Martin Hits Again*, Reprise, 1965; *(Remember Me) I'm the One Who Loves You*, Reprise, 1965; *Houston*, Reprise, 1965; *Somewhere There's a Someone*, Reprise, 1966; *The Dean Martin TV Show*, Reprise, 1967; *Welcome to My World*, Reprise, 1967; *Gentle on My Mind*, Reprise, 1969; *I Take a Lot of Pride in What I Am*, Reprise, 1969; *My Woman, My Woman, My Wife*, Reprise, 1970; *For the Good Times*, Reprise, 1970; *You're the Best Thing That Ever Happened to Me*, Reprise, 1973; *The Nashville Sessions*, Warner Brothers, 1983.

SINGLES—"Powder Your Face with Sunshine," Capitol, 1949; "I'll Always Love You," Capitol, 1950; "If," Capitol, 1951; "You Belong to Me," Capitol, 1952; "Love Me, Love Me," Capitol, 1953; "That's Amore," Capitol, 1953; "I'd Cry Like a Baby," Capitol, 1954; "Memories Are Made of This," Capitol, 1955; "Innamorata," Capitol, 1956; "Standing on the Corner," Capitol, 1956; "Return to Me," Capitol, 1958; "Angel Baby," Capitol, 1958; "Volare (Nel Blu Dipinto Di Blu)," Capitol, 1958; "Everybody Loves Somebody," Reprise, 1964; "The Door Is Still Open to My Heart," Reprise, 1964; "You're Nobody Till Somebody Loves You," Reprise, 1965; "Send Me the Pillow You Dream On," Reprise, 1965; "(Remember Me) I'm the One Who Loves You," Reprise, 1965; "Houston," Reprise, 1965; "I Will," Reprise, 1965; "Somewhere There's a Someone," Reprise, 1966; "Come Running Back," Reprise, 1966; "In the Chapel in the Moonlight," Reprise, 1967; "Little Ole Wine Drinker, Me," Reprise, 1967; "For the Good Times," Reprise, 1970; "L.A. Is My Home," MCA, 1985.

AWARDS: Motion Picture Herald-Fame poll winner (with Jerry Lewis), One of the Top Ten Money Making Stars, 1951, 1952 (number one), 1953, 1954, and 1955; Golden Apple Star of the Year Award from the Hollywood Women's Press Club (with Jerry Lewis), 1954; Golden Globe, Best Television Star, 1967, for *The Dean Martin Show*.

ADDRESSES: AGENT—Chasin/Park/Citron Agency, 9255 Sunset Boulevard, Los Angeles, CA 90069.*

*　　　*　　　*

MARTIN, George　1926-

PERSONAL: Born January 3, 1926, in London, England. EDUCATION—Studied oboe at the Guildhall School of Music.

VOCATION: Music director, composer, and record producer.

CAREER: Also see *WRITINGS* below. PRINCIPAL FILM APPEARANCES—*Give My Regards to Broad Street*, Twentieth Century-Fox, 1984. PRINCIPAL FILM WORK—Music director: *A Hard Day's Night*, United Artists, 1964; *Ferry Across the Mersey*, United Artists, 1964; *Yellow Submarine*, United Artists, 1968; *Pulp*, United Artists, 1972; *The Optimists* (also known as *The Optimists of Nine Elms*), Paramount, 1973; *Sergeant Pepper's Lonely Hearts Club Band*, Universal, 1978; *Give My Regards to Broad Street*, Twentieth Century-Fox, 1984.

RELATED CAREER—Record producer for comedians Peter Sellers, Spike Milligan, and Flanders and Swann and for such recording artists as the Beatles, Gerry and the Pacemakers, Billy J. Kramer and the Dakotas, Cilla Black, Ringo Starr, Paul McCartney, Sea Train, Stackridge, John McLaughlin, America, and Jeff Beck.

WRITINGS: FILMS—Composer: *Yellow Submarine,* United Artists, 1968; *Live and Let Die,* United Artists, 1973; (with Elmer Bernstein) *Honky Tonk Freeway,* Universal, 1981.

AWARDS: Grammy Awards (as producer), Record of the Year and Best Contemporary Album, both 1967, for *Sergeant Pepper's Lonely Hearts Club Band* by the Beatles; Grammy Award, Best Arrangement Accompanying Vocalist, 1973, for "Live and Let Die" by Paul McCartney and Wings; *Rolling Stone* magazine Reader's Poll, Producer of the Year, 1982, for *Tug of War* by McCartney.*

*   *   *

MARTIN, Helen

PERSONAL: Full name, Helen Dorothy Martin; born July 28, in St. Louis, MO; daughter of William (a minister) and Amanda Frankie (Fox) Martin. EDUCATION—Attended Fisk University and A&I State College; studied acting at the Paul Mann Workshop.

VOCATION: Actress.

CAREER: STAGE DEBUT—With the Rose McClendon Players, New York City, 1939. BROADWAY DEBUT—Vera Thomas, *Native Son,* St. James Theatre, 1941. PRINCIPAL STAGE APPEARANCES—Honey Turner, *Deep Are the Roots,* Fulton Theatre, New York City, 1945, then Wyndham's Theatre, London, 1947; Della, *The Royal Family* and Paula, *The Petrified Forest,* both Salt Creek Theatre, Hinsdale, IL, 1951; Poppy, *Take a Giant Step,* Lyceum Theatre, New York City, 1953; Rummy Mitchins, *Major Barbara,* Greenwich Mews Theatre, New York City, 1954; Mrs. Tancred, *Juno and the Paycock,* Greenwich Mews Theatre, 1955; Jeniella, *King of Hearts,* Woodstock Theatre, Woodstock, NY, 1956; Martha Lane, *A Land Beyond the River,* Greenwich Mews Theatre, 1957; Auntie Alice, *Fever of Life,* Westport Country Playhouse, Westport, CT, 1957; Jessie, *The Ballad of Jazz Street,* Greenwich Mews Theatre, 1959.

Maude Carter, *The Long Dream,* Ambassador Theatre, New York City, 1960; Susie, *Period of Adjustment,* Helen Hayes Theatre, New York City, 1960; Felicity Trollop Pardon, *The Blacks,* St. Mark's Playhouse, New York City, 1961; Missy Judson, *Purlie Victorious,* Cort Theatre, then Longacre Theatre, both New York City, 1961; Essie, *Critic's Choice,* Colonie Theatre, Latham, NY, then Playhouse in the Park, Philadelphia, PA, both 1962; Hannah, *My Mother, My Father, and Me,* Plymouth Theatre, New York City, 1963; Adelaide Bobo, *The Blacks,* St. Mark's Playhouse, 1963; Ruby Grant, *One Is a Lonely Number,* Mermaid Theatre, New York City, 1964; Maria Pleasant, *The Cat and the Canary,* Stage 73, New York City, 1965; Sister Douglas, *The Amen Corner,* Ethel Barrymore Theatre, New York City, then Lyceum Theatre, Edinburgh, Scotland, later Saville Theatre, London, all 1965; Ann Hall, *What Do You Really Know About Your Husband?,* Shubert Theatre, New Haven, CT, 1967; Sarah Goldfine (understudy), *Something Different,* Cort Theatre, 1967; Rheba, *You Can't Take It with You,* Arena Stage, Washington, DC, 1969.

Idella, *Purlie,* Broadway Theatre, then Winter Garden Theatre, both New York City, 1970, later American National Theatre and

Academy Theatre, New York City, 1971, then Billy Rose Theatre, New York City, 1972; Mrs. Johnson, *Raisin,* Arena Stage, then 46th Street Theatre, New York City, both 1973, later Lunt-Fontanne Theatre, New York City, 1975; Sookey, *Cat on a Hot Tin Roof,* Center Theatre Group, Mark Taper Forum, Los Angeles, 1983. Also appeared as Ruby Jackson, *Striver's Row,* the Maid, *Three's a Family,* and in *Hits, Bits, and Skits* (revue), all American Negro Theatre, New York City; as the Maid, *Three's a Family* and little girl, *Mamba's Daughter,* both in New York City, 1943; in *Chicken Every Sunday,* Blackstone Theatre, Chicago, IL, 1944; *The String,* Inner City Cultural Center, Los Angeles, 1978; and in *Stevedore,* Off-Broadway production.

MAJOR TOURS—Vera Thomas, *Native Son,* U.S. cities, 1941; Honey Turner, *Deep Are the Roots,* U.K. cities, 1947; Rheba, *You Can't Take It with You,* U.S. cities, 1954-55; Millie, *Anniversary Waltz,* U.S. cities, 1955; Adelaide Bobo, *The Blacks,* U.S. cities, 1963; Millie, *Happy Anniversary,* U.S. cities, 1964; Rheba, *You Can't Take It with You,* U.S. cities, 1966; Idella, *Purlie,* U.S. cities, 1971-72.

PRINCIPAL FILM APPEARANCES—Helen Ward, *The Phoenix City Story,* Allied Artists, 1955; church sister, *Cotton Comes to Harlem,* United Artists, 1970; job applicant, *Where's Poppa?* (also known as *Going Ape*), United Artists, 1970; Alma Lee Brown, *Death Wish,* Paramount, 1974; Mrs. Bell, *A Hero Ain't Nothing But a Sandwich,* New World, 1977; Baptist, *Deal of the Century,* Warner Brothers, 1983; Mrs. Parks, *Repo Man,* Universal, 1984; Bobby's grandmother, *Hollywood Shuffle,* Samuel Goldwyn, 1987. Also appeared in *The Anderson Tapes,* Columbia, 1971.

PRINCIPAL TELEVISION APPEARANCES—Series: Luzelle Carter, *Baby, I'm Back,* CBS, 1978; Pearl Shay, *227,* NBC, 1985—. Pilots: Mother, *Big Daddy,* CBS, 1973; Grandma Johnson, *The Jerk, Too,* NBC, 1984; also *Wash and Dry,* WNYC (New York City), 1974. Episodic: Laura, *That's My Mama,* ABC, 1974-75; Shirley Luskin, *Full House,* ABC, 1989; Mrs. Johnson, "A Raisin in the Sun," *American Playhouse,* PBS, 1989; also "The Bitter Cup," *Frontiers of Faith,* NBC, 1960; *The Nurses,* CBS, 1964; *The Defenders,* CBS, 1964; Aunt Lil, *Benson,* ABC; *Police Woman,* NBC; *Starsky and Hutch,* ABC; *Sanford and Son,* NBC; *The Jeffersons,* CBS; *Maude,* CBS; *Good Times,* CBS; *Hill Street Blues,* NBC; *St. Elsewhere,* NBC. Movies: Flower lady, *Cindy,* ABC, 1978; Mrs. Cartwright, *This Man Stands Alone* (also known as *Lawman Without a Gun*), NBC, 1979; Mrs. Harrod, *Dummy,* CBS, 1979; Mrs. McKenzie, *Amos,* CBS, 1985; also *Better Late Than Never,* NBC, 1979. Specials: "Green Pastures," *Hallmark Hall of Fame,* NBC, 1959; "J.T.," *CBS Children's Hour,* CBS, 1969; *Living the Dream: A Tribute to Dr. Martin Luther King,* syndicated, 1988.

PRINCIPAL RADIO APPEARANCES—Specials: Honey Turner, *Deep Are the Roots,* BBC, 1947.

RELATED CAREER—Founding member, American Negro Theatre, New York City, 1940; disk jockey, WOV, 1953; also conductor and singer with jazz bands in Tennessee.

NON-RELATED CAREER—Factory worker, postal worker, hotel maid, elevator operator, Western Union clerk.

MEMBER: Actors' Equity Association, Screen Actors Guild, American Federation of Television and Radio Artists.*

MASINA, Giulietta 1921-

PERSONAL: Full name, Giulia Anna Masina; born February 22, 1921, in Bologna, Italy; married Federico Fellini (a director and writer), October 30, 1943. EDUCATION—Attended the University of Rome.

VOCATION: Actress.

CAREER: STAGE DEBUT—Felice Viaggio, Rome, Italy, 1939. PRINCIPAL STAGE APPEARANCES—Angelica, University of Rome, 1948.

FILM DEBUT—Paisa (also known as Paisan), Mayer/Burstyn, 1948. PRINCIPAL FILM APPEARANCES—Marcella, Senza pieta (also known as Without Pity), Lux, 1949; Melina Amour, Luci del varieta (also known as Variety Lights and Lights of Variety), 1951, released in the United States by Pathe Contemporary, 1965; Pippo, Persiane chiuse (also known as Behind Closed Shutters), Lux, 1952; Passerotto, Europa '51 (also known as The Greatest Love), 1952, released in the United States by Lux, 1954; Cabiria, Lo sceicco bianco (also known as The White Sheik), 1952, released in the United States by Janus/Api, 1956; Rosita, Donne proibite (also known as Angels of Darkness), 1953, released in the United States by Supra, 1956; Gelsomina, La Strada, 1954, released in the United States by Trans-Lux, 1956; Iris, Il bidone (also known as The Swindle), Astor, 1955, released in the United States by Pathe Contemporary, 1962; Cabiria, Le notti di Cabiria (also known as Cabiria and The Nights of Cabiria), 1956, released in the United States by Lopert, 1957; Lina, Nella citta l'inferno (also known as The Wild, Wild Women and Hell in the City), Rima, 1958, released in the United States by Trans-Lux Distributing, 1961; title role, Giulietta degli spiriti (also known as Juliet of the Spirits), Rizzoli, 1965; Gabrielle, The Madwoman of Chaillot (also known as The Madwoman of Sulpice), Warner Brothers/Seven Arts, 1969.

Title role/Mrs. Winter, Perinbaba, Omnia, 1985; title role, Frau Holle, Jugendfilm, 1985; Amelia Bonnetti (Ginger), Ginger et Fred (also known as Ginger and Fred), Metro-Goldwyn-Mayer/United Artists, 1986. Also appeared in Via Padova, 1946; Wanda la Peccatrice, 1946; Sette ore di guai, 1946; Il romanzo della mia vita, 1946; Ai margini della metropoli, 1946; Cameriera bella presenza offresi. . ., 1951; Cento anni d'amore, 1954; Buonanotte Avvocato!, 1957; Fortunella, 1958; La Grande Vie (also known as Das Kunstseidene Madchen and La gran vita), 1960; Non stuzzicate la Zanzara, 1967.

RELATED CAREER—Radio actress in Rome.

NON-RELATED CAREER—School teacher.

AWARDS: Best Actress Award from the Cannes Film Festival, 1957, for Le notti di Cabiria; also Italian Film Critics' Award, Best Supporting Actress, for Senza pieta.*

*   *   *

MASTROSIMONE, William 1947-

PERSONAL: Born August 19, 1947, in Trenton, NJ. EDUCATION—Attended Tulane University, 1966-70; Rider College, B.A., English, 1974; Rutgers University, M.F.A., 1976.

VOCATION: Playwright.

WRITINGS: STAGE—The Woolgatherer, first produced in New Brunswick, NJ, 1979, then Circle Repertory Company, Circle Repertory Theatre, New York City, 1980, later in London, 1985, published by Samuel French, 1981; Extremities, Theatre Center Philadelphia, Philadelphia, PA, 1980, then Westside Arts Center, Cheryl Crawford Theatre, New York City, 1982, later in London, 1984, published by Samuel French, 1985; A Tantalizing, 1982 Shorts Festival, Actors Theatre of Louisville, Louisville, KY, 1982, published by Samuel French, 1985; Shivaree, Seattle Repertory Theatre, Seattle, WA, 1983, published by Samuel French, 1984; The Undoing, Humana Festival of New American Plays, Actors Theatre of Louisville, 1984; Nanawatai, first produced in Bergen, Norway, 1984, then Los Angeles Theatre Center, Los Angeles, 1985, published by Samuel French, 1986; Tamer of Horses, Crossroads Theatre Company, New Brunswick, NJ, 1985, then Los Angeles Theatre Center, 1986; Cat's Paw, Poncho Forum, Seattle Repertory Theatre, 1986, published by Samuel French, 1987; The Understanding, New-Plays-in-Progess Series, Seattle Repertory Theatre, 1985; Sunshine, Circle Repertory Company, Circle Repertory Theatre, 1989.

FILM—(With Edwin Cook, Wendy Cutler, Andy Goldberg, and Roger Steffens) Extremities, Atlantic, 1986; The Beast, Columbia, 1988.

AWARDS: Los Angeles Drama Critics' Circle Award, 1982; John Gassner Award from the Outer Critics' Circle, 1983.

ADDRESSES: AGENT—George Lane, William Morris Agency, 1350 Avenue of the Americas, New York, NY 10019.*

*   *   *

MAXFIELD, James 1939-

PERSONAL: Born October 11, 1939, in Philadelphia, PA; son of C. James, Jr. (in business) and Patricia A. (Redman) Maxfield; married Leslie Patterson Wheeler, November 24, 1961 (divorced, 1974); children: Carolyn, Lesley. EDUCATION—Attended the Wharton School of Business, University of Pennsylvania, 1959-61; studied acting with Robert X. Modica, David Man, and Jacqueline Bartone; studied voice and speech with Nancy Andrews and Geoff Prysirr; attended Mary Jo Slater soap opera workshop and Weist Barron commercial courses. RELIGION—Presbyterian.

VOCATION: Actor.

CAREER: STAGE DEBUT—Policeman, You Touched Me, TRG Repertory Company, Off Center Theatre, New York City, 1980, for thirty-six performances. PRINCIPAL STAGE APPEARANCES—Allen, Something for the Boys, AMDA Studio One, New York City, 1981; Alan, Magic Time, Penta Players, Midtown Repertory Company, New York City, 1988.

PRINCIPAL FILM APPEARANCES—Governor's aide, Arthur, Warner Brothers, 1981; also appeared in Trading Places, Paramount, 1983; Wall Street, Twentieth Century-Fox, 1987; Arthur 2: On the Rocks (also known as Arthur II), Warner Brothers, 1988; Working Girl, Twentieth Century-Fox, 1988; When Harry Met Sally, Columbia, 1989; See You in the Morning, Warner Brothers, 1989; Blue Steel, Metro-Goldwyn-Mayer/United Artists, 1990.

JAMES MAXFIELD

TELEVISION DEBUT—Mr. Monteweize, *The File of Jill Hatch*, PBS, 1983. PRINCIPAL TELEVISION APPEARANCES—Series: Brad, *Another World*, NBC, 1988—; also *One Life to Live*, ABC; *As the World Turns*, CBS; *Search for Tomorrow*, CBS; *Edge of Night*, ABC. Episodic: C.I.A. agent, *The Equalizer*, CBS, 1988. Movies: *Rage of Angels*, NBC, 1983. Specials: *The Big Blonde*, PBS.

RELATED CAREER—Professional model; appeared in print advertising and television commercials.

NON-RELATED CAREER—Real estate salesman.

MEMBER: Screen Actors Guild, American Federation of Television and Radio Artists, Main Line Board of Realtors, 1973-81 (salesman of the year, 1975, and Million Round Table for Realtors), Chester County Board of Realtors, 1973-81.

*   *   *

MAXWELL, Lois   1927-

PERSONAL: Born Lois Hooker, 1927, in Canada.

VOCATION: Actress.

CAREER: PRINCIPAL FILM APPEARANCES—Julia Kane, *That Hagen Girl*, Warner Brothers, 1947; Karen Long, *The Big Punch*, Warner Brothers, 1948; Imogene, *Corridor of Mirrors*, Apollo, 1948; Ruth Collins, *The Dark Past*, Columbia, 1948; Miss McIntyre,

The Decision of Chirstopher Blake, Warner Brothers, 1948; Jane Darrin, *The Crime Doctor's Diary*, Columbia, 1949; Louise Maitlin, *Kazan*, Columbia, 1949; Erika, *Brief Rapture*, Jewel, 1952; Peggy, *Scotland Yard Inspector* (also known as *Lady in the Fog*), Lippert, 1952; Christine Ralston, *Twilight Women* (also known as *Women of Twilight*), Lippert, 1953; Thelma Tasman, *Woman in Hiding* (also known as *Man Trap* and *Man in Hiding*), United Artists, 1953; Lily, *The Great Hope* (also known as *La grande speranza*), Minerva, 1954; Amneris (sung by Ebe Stignanai), *Aida*, Eagle Films, 1954; Enid Mansell, *The Woman's Angle*, Stratford, 1954; Diane Boyd, *Passport to Treason*, Astor, 1956; Kim, *Satellite in the Sky*, Warner Brothers, 1956; Stephanie Blake, *High Terrace*, RKO/Allied Artists, 1957; Vicky Harker, *Time Without Pity*, Eros/Astor, 1957; Jill Brook, *Kill Me Tomorrow*, Ren/Tudor, 1958; Ethel Winter, *Face of Fire*, Allied Artists, 1959; Helen Kennedy, *The Unstoppable Man*, Sutton, 1961; Miss Moneypenny, *Dr. No*, United Artists, 1962; Nurse Mary Lore, *Lolita*, Metro-Goldwyn-Mayer (MGM), 1962; Gwen, *Come Fly with Me*, MGM, 1963; Miss Moneypenny, *From Russia with Love*, United Artists, 1963; Grace Markway, *The Haunting*, MGM, 1963; Miss Moneypenny, *Goldfinger*, United Artists, 1964; Miss Moneypenny, *Thunderball*, United Artists, 1965; Max, *Operation Kid Brother* (also known as *O.K. Connery*), United Artists, 1967; Miss Moneypenny, *You Only Live Twice*, United Artists, 1967; Miss Moneypenny, *On Her Majesty's Secret Service*, United Artists, 1969.

Woman at fashion show, *The Adventurers*, Paramount, 1970; Miss Moneypenny, *Diamonds Are Forever*, United Artists, 1971; Miss Moneypenny, *Live and Let Die*, United Artists, 1973; Miss Moneypenny, *The Man with the Golden Gun*, United Artists, 1974; Miss Moneypenny, *The Spy Who Loved Me*, United Artists, 1977; Mrs. Hogarth, *Age of Innocence*, Willoughby, 1977; Englishwoman, *Lost and Found*, Columbia, 1979; Miss Moneypenny, *Moonraker*, United Artists, 1979; the Director, *Mr. Patman*, Film Consortium of Canada, 1980; Miss Moneypenny, *For Your Eyes Only*, United Artists, 1981; Miss Moneypenny, *Octopussy*, Metro-Goldwyn-Mayer/United Artists (MGM/UA), 1983; Miss Moneypenny, *A View to a Kill*, MGM/UA, 1985; Monica, *The Blue Man* (also known as *Eternal Evil*), Cine 360/New Century/Seymour Borde and Associates, 1985; Edie, *Martha, Ruth, and Edie*, Simcom International/Norstar, 1988. Also appeared in *Amori e veleni* (also known as *Brief Rapture*), 1950; *Domani e troppo tardi* (also known as *Tomorrow Is Too Late*), 1950; *Endless Night* (also known as *Agatha Christie's Endless Night*), British Lion, 1971.

PRINCIPAL TELEVISION APPEARANCES—Series: Earth girl, *Stingray*, syndicated, 1965; Miss Holland, *U.F.O.*, syndicated, 1972; Nancy Williams, *Adventures in Rainbow Country*, syndicated, 1972. Episodic: *Douglas Fairbanks, Jr. Presents the Rheingold Theatre*, syndicated. Movies: Mary Smith, *Lady in a Corner*, NBC, 1989.*

*   *   *

McBRIDE, Jim   1941-

PERSONAL: Born September 16, 1941, in New York, NY; married Tracy Tynan (a costume designer); children: three sons. EDUCATION—Attended New York University.

VOCATION: Director, screenwriter, and producer.

CAREER: Also see *WRITINGS* below. PRINCIPAL FILM APPEAR-

ANCES—Man at elevator, *Hot Times,* William Mishkin, 1974; man in cantina, *The Last Embrace,* United Artists, 1979; also appeared in *My Girlfriend's Wedding,* Paradigm/New Yorker, 1969.

FIRST FILM WORK—Producer, director, and editor, *David Holzman's Diary,* Paradigm, 1968. PRINCIPAL FILM WORK—Director: (Also editor) *My Girlfriend's Wedding,* Paradigm/New Yorker, 1969; *Glen and Randa,* UMC, 1971; *Hot Times,* William Mishkin, 1974; *The Last Embrace,* United Artists, 1979; *Breathless,* Orion, 1983; *The Big Easy,* Columbia, 1987; *Great Balls of Fire,* Orion, 1989.

PRINCIPAL TELEVISION WORK—Episodic: Director, ''The Once and Future King,'' *The Twilight Zone,* CBS, 1986.

RELATED CAREER—Instructor, New York University.

NON-RELATED CAREER—Cab driver.

WRITINGS: FILM—*David Holzman's Diary,* Paradigm, 1968; *My Girlfriend's Wedding,* Paradigm/New Yorker, 1969; (with Lorenzo Mans and Rudy Wurlitzer) *Glen and Randa,* UMC, 1971; *Hot Times,* William Mishkin, 1974; *The Last Embrace,* United Artists, 1979; (with L.M. Kit Carson) *Breathless,* Orion, 1983; *Great Balls of Fire,* Orion, 1989.

AWARDS: Grand Prizes from the Manheim and Pesaro Film Festivals, both 1967, for *David Holzman's Diary.**

*   *   *

JOANNA McCALLUM

McCALLUM, Joanna

PERSONAL: Daughter of John McCallum (an actor, director, and producer) and Googie Withers (an actress).

VOCATION: Actress.

CAREER: PRINCIPAL STAGE APPEARANCES—Kitty Verdun, *Charley's Aunt,* Apollo Theatre, London, 1971; Diana Claiborne, *Friends and Romans,* Yvonne Arnaud Theatre, Guildford, U.K., 1972; Bianca, *The Taming of the Shrew,* Chorus and Prologue, *The Persians,* Rosie Probert and Mrs. Ogmore Pritchard, *Under Milkwood,* and Good Fairy, *Pinnochio,* all Crucible Theatre, Sheffield, U.K., 1972; Helena and second queen, *A Midsummer Night's Dream,* New Shakespeare Company, Open Air Theatre, Regent's Park, London, 1974; Amanda, *Mr. Whatnot* and lawyer, *I Am the Vicar,* both Belgrade Theatre, Coventry, U.K., 1974; Ophelia, *Rosencrantz and Guildenstern Are Dead,* Lady Macbeth, *Macbeth,* and Sylvia, *Two Gentleman of Verona,* all Young Vic Theatre, London, 1974; Amy Spettigue, *Charley's Aunt,* Rosalind, *As You Like It,* and Katherine, *The Taming of the Shrew,* all Young Vic Theatre, 1975-76; Princess of France, *Love's Labour's Lost,* reporter, *The Winslow Boy,* Edith, *Golden Pathway Annual,* and Gwendoline, *The Importance of Being Earnest,* all Bristol Old Vic Theatre, Bristol, U.K., 1976; Zerbinetta, *Scapino,* Katherine, *The Taming of the Shrew,* and Cynthia, *The Real Inspector Hound,* all Young Vic Theatre, 1977; Virginia Vanderpool, *Saratoga,* Royal Shakespeare Company, Aldwych Theatre, London, 1978; Ruth, *Blithe Spirit,* Thorndike Theatre, Leatherhead, U.K., 1979; Nora, *A Doll's House,* Perth Theatre Festival, Perth, Australia, 1982; Portia, *The Merchant of Venice,* Chichester Theatre Festival, Chichester, U.K., 1984; Jane Marryot, *Cavalcade* and Lady

Marguerite Blakeney, *The Scarlet Pimpernel,* both Chichester Theatre Festival, 1985, then Her Majesty's Theatre, London, 1985-86.

MAJOR TOURS—Lady Macbeth, *Macbeth,* Young Vic Theatre, Mexico and Spain, 1976; Katherine, *The Taming of the Shrew,* U.K., U.S., and Canadian cities, 1976; Elizabeth Champion-Cheney, *The Circle,* Triumph Theatre, U.K. cities, 1978.

PRINCIPAL FILM APPEARANCES—Jenny Blake, *The Nickel Queen,* Woomera, 1971; bookshop cashier, *Hopscotch,* AVCO-Embassy, 1980.

PRINCIPAL TELEVISION APPEARANCES—Mini-Series: Winifred Holtby, *Testament of Youth,* BBC, 1979, then *Masterpiece Theatre,* PBS, 1980; Mrs. Frances Neville, *By the Sword Divided,* BBC, 1984, then *Masterpiece Theatre,* PBS, 1986. Episodic: Title role, ''Barbara, of the House of Grebe,'' *Thomas Hardy,* BBC, 1973; Carol Waterlow, ''When the Bough Breaks,'' *Within These Walls,* London Weekend Television (LWT), 1974; Helen, ''Marriage Ring No. 20,'' *For Better or Worse,* Thames, 1975; Monica Becket, ''Unbecoming Habits,'' ''Deadline,'' and ''Let Sleeping Dogs Die,'' *Bognor,* Thames, 1980; ''Just Desserts,'' *Bognor,* Thames, 1981; Hilary Rogers, ''Love and War,'' *Crown Court,* Granada, 1984. Specials: Camilla, *A Wreath of Roses,* Granada, 1987, then *Masterpiece Theatre,* PBS, 1989. Also appeared as Julia Shepherd, *Last Year's Confetti,* LWT, 1971; Miss Eynsford-Hill, *Pygmalion,* BBC, 1973; Lady Macbeth, *Macbeth,* Dramacourt Ltd., 1975; the Countess, *Henry VI, Part I,* BBC, 1981; Iris Aroon St. Charles, *Good Behaviour,* BBC, 1982-83; Virgilla, *Coriolanus,* BBC, 1983; Bunty, *Struggle,* LWT, 1983; lift girl, *A Still Small*

Shout, BBC, 1985; Lady Christine Collett, *Rockliffes' Babies,* BBC, 1988; Marion Sharpe, *The Franchise Affair,* BBC, 1989; Alicia, *The Ginger Tree,* BBC, 1989.

ADDRESSES: AGENT—Joyce Edwards Representation, 275 Kennington Road, London SE11 6BY, England.

*   *   *

McCALLUM, John   1918-

PERSONAL: Born March 14, 1918, in Brisbane, Australia; son of John Neil (a theatre owner and producer) and Lillian Elsie (an actress; maiden name, Dyson) McCallum; married Googie Withers (an actress), January 24, 1948; children: Joanna, Nicholas, Amanda. EDUCATION—Trained for the stage at the Royal Academy of Dramatic Art. MILITARY—Australian Imperial Forces, 2/5 Field Regiment, 1941-45.

VOCATION: Actor, director, producer, and theatre manager.

CAREER: STAGE DEBUT—Wolsey, *Henry VIII,* Cremorne Theatre, Brisbane, Australia, 1934, for three performances. PRINCIPAL STAGE APPEARANCES—Ex-officer, *Cornelius,* Westminster Theatre, London, 1940; Baldasarre, *The Maid of the Mountains* and General Esteban, *Rio Rita,* both Theatre Royal, Sydney, Australia, 1945; Tony Macrae, *Western Wind,* Q Theatre, then Piccadilly Theatre, both London, 1949; Sir Philip Hayes, K.B.E., *View Over*

JOHN McCALLUM

the Park, Lyric Hammersmith Theatre, London, 1950; James Manning, *Waiting for Gillian,* St. James's Theatre, London, 1954; Mr. Darling, *Peter Pan,* Scala Theatre, Brisbane, Australia, 1956; Gil, *Janus,* Aldwych Theatre, London, 1957; Lord Dungavel, *Roar Like a Dove,* Phoenix Theatre, London, 1957, then Comedy Theatre, Melbourne, Australia, 1959; John Middleton, *The Constant Wife,* Albery Theatre, London, 1973; Campbell Sinclair, *As It's Played Today,* Comedy Theatre, 1974; Clive Champion-Cheney, *The Circle,* Chichester Theatre Festival, Chichester, U.K., then Haymarket Theatre, London, both 1976; Cecil, *The Kingfisher,* Comedy Theatre, 1978; Sir Oliver Surface, *School for Scandal,* Duke of York's Theatre, London, 1985; the Judge, *The Chalk Garden,* Chichester Theatre Festival, 1986; David, *Hay Fever,* Chichester Theatre Festival, 1988; General Wilkins, *The Royal Baccarat Scandal,* Haymarket Theatre, 1989. Also appeared in *Hamlet* and *Richard II,* both Scala Theatre, 1935; with the Memorial Theatre Company, Stratford-on-Avon, U.K., 1939; Francisco, *The Tempest* and the Herald, *King Lear,* both with the Old Vic Company, 1939.

PRINCIPAL STAGE WORK—All as director, unless indicated: *The Wind and the Rain,* Theatre Royal, Sydney, Australia, 1945; *Roar Like a Dove* and *The Piccadilly Bushman,* both Comedy Theatre, Melbourne, Australia, 1959; *My Fair Lady,* Her Majesty's Theatre, Melbourne, Australia, 1960; (also designer) *Plaza Suite,* Theatre Royal, Sydney, Australia, 1969; *My Fair Lady,* Her Majesty's Theatre, 1970; *As It's Played Today,* Comedy Theatre, 1974.

MAJOR TOURS—Director and appeared as Simon Foster, *Simon and Laura* and director and appeared as Freddie Page, *The Deep Blue Sea,* Australian and New Zealand cities, both 1955; director and appeared in *Relatively Speaking,* Australian cities, 1968; Cecil, *The Kingfisher,* Australian cities, 1978; Hillcrist, *The Skin Game,* Gayev, *The Cherry Orchard,* and Sir Tristam, *Dandy Dick,* U.K. cities, all 1983; David, *Stardust,* U.K. and Australian cities, 1984; Sir Oliver Surface, *School for Scandal,* British Council tour, European cities, 1985; Cecil, *The Kingfisher,* Far East and Middle East cities, 1987; General Wilkins, *The Royal Baccarat Scandal,* U.K. cities, 1988.

FILM DEBUT—Joe Bartle, *The Root of All Evil,* General Film Distributors, 1947. PRINCIPAL FILM APPEARANCES—Narrator, *Bush Christmas,* Universal, 1947; Arthur Alce, *The Loves of Joanna Godden,* General Film Distributors, 1947; Garry, *The Calendar,* General Film Distributors, 1948; store helper, *Letter from an Unknown Woman,* Universal, 1948; David Howarth, *A Boy, a Girl, and a Bike,* General Film Distributors, 1949; Nigel Hood, *Miranda,* Eagle-Lion, 1949; Tommy Swann, *It Always Rains on Sunday,* Eagle-Lion, 1949; Murray, *Five Angles on Murder* (also known as *The Woman in Question*), General Film Distributors, 1950; Reggie Pelham, *Traveller's Joy,* General Film Distributors, 1951; Tommy Dillon, *Four Against Fate* (also known as *Derby Day*), British Lion, 1952; sitter in Bath studio, *The Magic Box,* British Lion, 1952; Dr. Nils Ahlen, *Valley of Eagles,* Lippert, 1952; Detective Inspector Lowther, *The Long Memory,* General Film Distributors, 1953; Charles Armstrong, *Melba,* United Artists, 1953; John Marlowe, *Trent's Last Case,* British Lion, 1953; Charles Roberts, *Devil on Horseback,* British Lion, 1954; Malcolm, *Trouble in the Glen,* Republic, 1954; Larry Burns, *Lady Godiva Rides Again,* Carroll, 1955; Mitchell Gillie, *Port of Escape,* Renown, 1955; Rankin, *Smiley,* Twentieth Century-Fox, 1957. Also appeared in *Three in One,* Tradition, 1956.

PRINCIPAL FILM WORK—Producer and director, *The Nickel Queen,* Woomera, 1971; executive producer, *Attack Force Z* (also known as *The Z Men*), Virgin Vision, 1981; executive producer, *The Highest Honor—A True Story* (also known as *Southern Cross*), Enterprise/Nelson Entertainment, 1982.

TELEVISION DEBUT—*Alexandra Place*, BBC, 1948. PRINCIPAL TELEVISION APPEARANCES—Specials: George Musgrove, "Melba," *Great Performances*, PBS, 1989.

PRINCIPAL TELEVISION WORK—Series: Executive producer (with Bob Austin), *Skippy: The Bush Kangaroo*, syndicated, 1969; also producer, *Barrier Reef*, 1970; producer, *Boney*, 1971-72; producer, *Bailey's Bird*, 1976. Also producer, *Shannon's Mob*.

RELATED CAREER—Assistant managing director, J.C. Williamson's Theatres Ltd., Australia, 1958-60, then joint managing director, 1960-67; chairman, managing director, and executive producer, Fauna Productions Ltd., 1967—; chairman and managing director, John McCallum Productions Ltd., 1973—.

WRITINGS: STAGE—*As It's Played Today*, Comedy Theatre, Melbourne, Australia, 1974. FILM—(With Henry C. James and Joy Cavill) *The Nickel Queen*, Woomera, 1971. OTHER—*Life with Googie*, Heinemann, 1977.

AWARDS: Commander, Order of the British Empire, 1971.

MEMBER: Australian Producers and Directors Guild (president, 1970-71), Australian Film Council (founder and president, 1970-71), Lords Taverners—Australia (president); Lords Taverners—U.K., Garrick Club, Melbourne Club, Australian Club, Elanora Country Club, Royal Sydney Golf Club, MCC (U.K.), MCG (Melbourne).

SIDELIGHTS: FAVORITE ROLES—Lord Dungavel in *Roar Like a Dove* and Cecil in *The Kingfisher*. RECREATIONS—Cricket, golf, and gardening.

ADDRESSES: OFFICE—c/o Hardings, One York Street, Sydney 2000, Australia. AGENT—Larry Dalzell and Associates, Suite 12, 17 Broad Court, London WC2 B5QN, England.

*   *   *

McCLELLAND, Allan   1917-1989

PERSONAL: Born December 31, 1917, in Dunmurry, Northern Ireland; died February, 1989, in London, England; son of William and Nell (Worland) M'Clelland; married Charlotte French Cox.

VOCATION: Actor and writer.

CAREER: STAGE DEBUT—Raleigh, *Journey's End*, Playhouse Theatre, Belfast, Ireland, 1936. LONDON DEBUT—St. John Hotchkiss, *Getting Married*, Arts Theatre, 1945. PRINCIPAL STAGE APPEARANCES—Clincher, *The Constant Couple*, Laertes, *Hamlet*, and Charles Surface, *The School for Scandal*, all Arts Theatre, London, 1945; Denzil, *Call It Madness*, New Lindsey Theatre, London, 1949; Josef Lausman, *The Ivory Tower*, Vaudeville Theatre, London, 1950; Craig, *Danger, Men Working*, Lyric Hammersmith Theatre, London, 1951; Peter, *The Passing Day*, Ambassadors' Theatre, London, 1951; Christopher Wren, *The Mousetrap*, Ambassadors' Theatre, 1952; narrator, *Ulysses in Nighttown*, Arts Theatre, London, 1959; captain's secretary, *Santa Cruz*, Lyric

Hammersmith Theatre, 1966; *George Moore's Celibate Lives* (one-man show), King's Head Theatre, London, 1973; George Moore, *The Singular Life of Albert Nobbs*, New End Theatre, London, 1978.

PRINCIPAL FILM APPEARANCES—Mr. Stuart, *These Are the Damned* (also known as *The Damned*), Columbia, 1965; doctor, *The Looking Glass War*, Columbia, 1970; also appeared in *The Smugglers* (also known as *The Man Within*), Eagle-Lion, 1948.

RELATED CAREER—Appeared in numerous television plays.

NON-RELATED CAREER—Speech therapist.

WRITINGS: STAGE—*Call It Madness*, New Lindsey Theatre, London, 1949; *George Moore's Celibate Lives*, King's Head Theatre, London, 1973. OTHER—Plays and short stories for the BBC.

OBITUARIES AND OTHER SOURCES: *Variety*, February 8-14, 1989.*

*   *   *

McCLURG, Edie

PERSONAL: Born July 23, in Kansas City, MO. EDUCATION—Received degree in radio and television communications from the University of Missouri; received master's degree in communications from Syracuse University.

VOCATION: Actress and writer.

CAREER: Also see *WRITINGS* below. FILM DEBUT—*Carrie*, United Artists, 1976. PRINCIPAL FILM APPEARANCES—Gloria's mother, *Cheech and Chong's Next Movie*, Universal, 1980; Susan, *Eating Raoul*, Twentieth Century-Fox, 1982; voice of Miss Right, *The Secret of NIMH* (animated), Metro-Goldwyn-Mayer/United Artists, 1982; checkout lady, *Mr. Mom*, Twentieth Century-Fox, 1983; Queen, *Cheech and Chong's The Corsican Brothers*, Orion, 1984; Marge, *Back to School*, Orion, 1986; school secretary, *Ferris Bueller's Day Off*, Paramount, 1986; Donna, *The Longshot*, Orion, 1986; car rental agent, *Planes, Trains, and Automobiles*, Paramount, 1987; Chastity Pariah, *Elvira, Mistress of the Dark*, New World, 1988; voice of Carlotta, *The Little Mermaid* (animated), Buena Vista, 1989. Also appeared in *Cracking Up*, American International, 1977; *Pandemonium* (also known as *Thursday the 12th*), Metro-Goldwyn-Mayer, 1982; *She's Having a Baby*, Paramount, 1988.

PRINCIPAL TELEVISION APPEARANCES—Series: Regular, *Tony Orlando and Dawn*, CBS, 1976; Venus Kallikak, *The Kallikaks*, NBC, 1977; regular, *The Big Show*, NBC, 1980; regular, *The David Letterman Show*, NBC, 1980; Willamae Jones, *Harper Valley P.T.A.*, NBC, 1981; Marion, *No Soap, Radio*, ABC, 1982; Salaria, *Madame's Place*, syndicated, 1982; voice of Mrs. Seaworth, *The Snorks* (animated), NBC, 1984; voice characterization, *The 13 Ghosts of Scooby-Doo* (animated), ABC, 1985; voice characterization, *The New Jetsons* (animated), syndicated, 1985; Bonnie Brendl, *Small Wonder*, syndicated, 1985-86; Fannie, *Together We Stand* (also known as *Nothing Is Easy*), CBS, 1986; Mrs. Poole, *Valerie*, NBC, 1986-87, retitled *Valerie's Family*, 1987, later retitled *The Hogan Family*, 1988—. Pilots: Helen, *Pottsville*, CBS, 1980;

regular, *Top Ten*, NBC, 1980; Ida Antoine, *Second Edition*, CBS, 1984. Episodic: Lucille Tarlek, *WKRP in Cincinnati*, CBS; *The Richard Pryor Show*, NBC. Movies: Angela, *Bill: On His Own*, CBS, 1983; Beth Crawford, *Crash Course*, NBC, 1988; Ruth, *Dance 'til Dawn* (also known as *Senior Prom*), NBC, 1988. Specials: Esmerelda, "Hansel and Gretel," *Once Upon a Brothers Grimm*, CBS, 1977; *The Chevy Chase Show*, NBC, 1977; Esther Greene, "A Home Run for Love," *ABC Afterschool Specials*, ABC, 1978; Hermit Hattie, *The Pee Wee Herman Show*, HBO, 1981; *The Paragon of Comedy*, Showtime, 1984; *Candid Camera on Wheels*, CBS, 1989.

RELATED CAREER—Company member, Pitschel Players (an improvisation group).

NON-RELATED CAREER—Newswoman and documentary producer for National Public Radio, Kansas City, MO.

WRITINGS: TELEVISION—Series: Staff writer, *The David Letterman Show*, NBC, 1980. Specials: (With others) *The Pee Wee Herman Show*, HBO, 1981; (with John Paragon and Paul Reubens) *The Paragon of Comedy*, Showtime, 1984.

SIDELIGHTS: RECREATIONS—Bowling.

ADDRESSES: AGENT—Chris Barret, McCartt/Oreck/Barrett, 10390 Santa Monica Boulevard, Suite 310, Los Angeles, CA 90025. PUBLICIST—Paulette Cohn, Michael Dalling Company, 8150 Beverly Boulevard, Suite 203, Los Angeles, CA 90048.*

*   *   *

McCORMACK, Patty   1945-

PERSONAL: Born Patricia Ellen Russo, August 21, 1945, in New York, NY; daughter of Frank (a fireman) and Elizabeth (a professional roller skater; maiden name, McCormack) Russo; married Bob Catania (a restaurateur), 1967 (divorced); children: Bobby, Danielle. EDUCATION—Attended the Wallard Mace Professional Children's School; studied speech with Eleanor Raab.

VOCATION: Actress.

CAREER: BROADWAY DEBUT—Cathy Roberts, *Touchstone*, Music Box Theatre, New York City, 1953. PRINCIPAL STAGE APPEARANCES—Rhoda Penmark, *The Bad Seed*, 46th Street Theatre, New York City, 1954.

MAJOR TOURS—*Rumors*, U.S. cities, 1989; also Corie Bratter, *Barefoot in the Park*, U.S. cities.

FILM DEBUT—*Two Gals and a Guy*, United Artists, 1951. PRINCIPAL FILM APPEARANCES—Rhoda Penmark, *The Bad Seed*, Warner Brothers, 1956; Annabella, *All Mine to Give* (also known as *The Day They Gave Babies Away*), Universal, 1957; Kathy O'Rourke, *Kathy O*, Universal, 1958; Angel, *The Snow Queen*, Universal, 1959; Joanna, *The Adventures of Huckleberry Finn*, Metro-Goldwyn-Mayer (MGM), 1960; Janet Somers, *The Explosive Generation*, United Artists, 1961; Warden's daughter, *Jacktown*, Pictorial International, 1962; Janet, *Born Wild*, American International, 1968; Susan Hoffman, *Mary Jane*, American International, 1968; Edie, *The Mini-Skirt Mob*, American International, 1968; Deanie Donford,

The Young Runaways, MGM, 1968; Sylvia Ross, *Bug*, Paramount, 1975; Kate, *Saturday the 14th Strikes Back*, Concorde, 1988.

PRINCIPAL TELEVISION APPEARANCES—Series: Ingeborg, *Mama* (also known as *I Remember Mama*), CBS, 1953-57; Torey Peck, *Peck's Bad Girl*, CBS, 1959-60; Lisha Steele, *Young Dr. Malone*, NBC, 1962; Linda Warren, *The Best of Everything*, ABC, 1970; Kim Reynolds, *As the World Turns*, CBS, 1975-76; Anne Brookes, *The Ropers*, ABC, 1979-80; Evelyn Michaelson, *Dallas*, CBS, 1981-82. Mini-Series: Liz Coburn, *On Wings of Eagles*, NBC, 1986. Pilots: Sophie Metzman, *Night Partners*, CBS, 1983; Mrs. Brody, *The Flamingo Kid*, ABC, 1989.

Episodic: Wendy North, *Second Chance*, Fox, 1987; also *Kraft Theatre*, NBC, 1952; "The Party," *Revlon Mirror Theatre*, NBC, 1953; *Ben Hecht's Tales of the City* (also known as *Tales of the City*), CBS, 1953; "A Handful of Stars," *The Web*, CBS, 1954; "I Remember, I Remember" and "The Golden Box," *The Campbell Television Soundstage* (also known as *TV Soundstage*), NBC, 1954; "Jody and Me," *Armstrong Circle Theatre*, NBC, 1954; "Somebody Special," *Philco Playhouse*, NBC, 1954; "An Episode of Sparrows," *Climax*, CBS, 1956; "Alien Angel," *General Electric Theatre*, CBS, 1956; "The Miracle Worker," "The Clouded Image," and "Child of Trouble," all *Playhouse 90*, CBS, 1957; "Dan Marshall's Brat," *Dupont Theatre*, ABC, 1957; "We Won't Be Any Trouble," *Matinee Theatre*, NBC, 1957; "Sing a Song," *Kraft Theatre*, NBC, 1957; "The Spell of the Tigress," *Kraft Theatre*, NBC, 1958; "The Devil's Violin," *Matinee Theatre*, NBC, 1958; "The Dungeon," *Playhouse 90*, CBS, 1958; "Chain and the River," *Goodyear Theatre*, NBC, 1958; "Project Immortality," *Playhouse 90*, CBS, 1959; "Rachel's Summer," *U.S. Steel Hour*, CBS, 1959; "Make Me Not a Witch," *Alcoa Premiere Theatre*, ABC, 1959; "Summer Hero," *The Chevy Mystery Show*, NBC, 1960; *Route 66*, CBS, 1960; *Death Valley Days*, syndicated, 1960; *Route 66*, CBS, 1961; *The New Breed*, ABC, 1962; *Rawhide*, CBS, 1962; *The Doctors*, NBC, 1963; *Rawhide*, CBS, 1963; *Farmer's Daughter*, ABC, 1964; "Burning Bright," *Play of the Week*, WNTA, 1966; *The Wild, Wild West*, CBS, 1968; *Lancer*, CBS, 1969; *Police Story*, NBC, 1974; *Streets of San Francisco*, ABC, 1974; *Barnaby Jones*, CBS, 1974; *Marcus Welby, M.D.*, ABC, 1974; *Manhunter*, CBS, 1974; *Cannon*, CBS, 1975; *Wagon Train*, NBC; *Cavalcade of America*, ABC; *Freddy's Nightmares*, syndicated. Movies: Mary Peterson, *Invitation to Hell*, ABC, 1984.

PRINCIPAL RADIO APPEARANCES—Series: *The Second Mrs. Burton*.

RELATED CAREER—Child model, singer with the rock band Mikey Vee and the Imperials, and talent agent.

AWARDS: Academy Award nomination, Best Supporting Actress, 1956, for *The Bad Seed*.

MEMBER: Actors' Equity Association, Screen Actors Guild, American Federation of Television and Radio Artists.*

*   *   *

McCOWEN, Alec   1925-

PERSONAL: Full name, Alexander Duncan McCowen; born May 26, 1925, in Tunbridge Wells, England; son of Duncan and Mary

ALEC McCOWEN

(Walkden) McCowen. EDUCATION—Trained for the stage at the Royal Academy of Dramatic Art.

VOCATION: Actor, director, and writer.

CAREER: Also see *WRITINGS* below. STAGE DEBUT—Micky, *Paddy, the Next Best Thing,* Macclesfield Repertory Theatre, Macclesfield, U.K., 1942. LONDON DEBUT—Maxim, *Ivanov,* Arts Theatre, 1950. BROADWAY DEBUT—Messenger, *Antony and Cleopatra,* Ziegfeld Theatre, 1951. PRINCIPAL STAGE APPEARANCES—Georges Almaire, *The Mask and the Face* and Kitts, *Preserving Mr. Panmure,* both Arts Theatre, London, 1950; Brian, *The Martin's Nest,* Westminster Theatre, London, 1951; Hugh Voysey, *The Voysey Inheritance* and the Announcer, *The Holy Terrors,* both Arts Theatre, 1952; Daventry, *Escapade,* St. James's Theatre, London, 1953; Larry Thompson, *Serious Charge,* Repertory Players, Adelphi Theatre, London, 1953; Julian Heath, *Shadow of the Vine,* Wyndham's Theatre, London, 1954; Henri de Toulouse-Lautrec, *Moulin Rouge,* New Theatre, Bromley, U.K., 1954; Barnaby Tucker, *The Matchmaker,* Haymarket Theatre, London, 1954; Vicomte Octave de Clerambard, *The Count of Clerambard,* Garrick Theatre, London, 1955; Dr. Bird, *The Caine Mutiny Court Martial,* Hippodrome Theatre, London, 1956; Lancelot Berenson, *No Laughing Matter,* Arts Theatre, 1957; Michael Claverton-Ferry, *The Elder Statesman,* Edinburgh Festival, Edinburgh, and then Cambridge Theatre, London, both 1958; Mr. Brisk, *The Double Dealer,* Touchstone, *As You Like It,* Algernon Moncrieff, *The Importance of Being Earnest,* Ford, *The Merry Wives of Windsor,* Dauphin, *Saint Joan,* and title role, *Richard II,* all Old Vic Theatre Company, London, 1959-60.

Mercutio, *Romeo and Juliet,* Oberon, *A Midsummer Night's Dream,* and Malvolio, *Twelfth Night,* all Old Vic Theatre Company, London, 1960-61; Sebastian, *Castle in Sweden,* Piccadilly Theatre, London, 1962; ensemble, *Not to Worry* (revue), Garrick Theatre, 1962; Antipholus of Syracuse, *The Comedy of Errors* and Fool, *King Lear,* both Royal Shakespeare Company (RSC), Stratford-on-Avon, U.K., then Aldwych Theatre, London, both 1962; Father Riccardo Fontana, *The Representative* and Antipholus of Syracuse, *The Comedy of Errors,* both RSC, Aldwych Theatre, 1963; Fool, *King Lear,* RSC, Aldwych Theatre, 1964; Antipholus of Syracuse, *The Comedy of Errors* and Fool, *King Lear,* both RSC, State Theatre, New York City, 1964; Ronald Gamble, *Thark,* Yvonne Arnaud Theatre, Guildford, U.K., then Garrick Theatre, both 1965; the Author, *The Cavern,* Strand Theatre, London, 1965; Arthur Henderson, *After the Rain,* Hampstead Theatre Club, London, 1966, then Duchess Theatre, London, 1967, later John Golden Theatre, New York City, 1967; Father William Rolfe, *Hadrian VII,* Birmingham Repertory Theatre, Birmingham, U.K., 1967, then Mermaid Theatre, London, 1968, later Helen Hayes Theatre, New York City, 1969.

Title role, *Hamlet,* Birmingham Repertory Theatre, 1970; Philip, *The Philanthropist,* Royal Court Theatre, then May Fair Theatre, both London, 1970, later Ethel Barrymore Theatre, New York City, 1971; title role, *Butley,* Criterion Theatre, London, 1972; Alceste, *The Misanthrope* and Martin Dysart, *Equus,* both National Theatre Company, Old Vic Theatre, London, 1973; Professor Higgins, *Pygmalion,* Albery Theatre, London, 1974; Alceste, *The Misanthrope,* National Theatre Company, Kennedy Center for the Performing Arts, Washington, DC, then St. James Theatre, New York City, both 1975, later Old Vic Theatre, 1975; Ben Musgrave, *The Family Dance,* Criterion Theatre, 1976; Martin Dysart, *Equus,* Helen Hayes Theatre, 1977; Antony, *Antony and Cleopatra,* Prospect Theatre Company, Edinburgh Festival, then Old Vic Theatre, both 1977; *St. Mark's Gospel* (one-man show), Riverside Studio Theatre, then Mermaid Theatre, later Comedy Theatre, all London, 1978, then Marymount Manhattan Theatre, later Playhouse Theatre, both New York City, 1978; Frank, *Tishoo!,* Wyndham's Theatre, 1979.

Andrew Crocker-Harris, *The Browning Version* and Arthur Gosport, *Harlequinade* (double-bill), National Theatre, London, 1980; Captain Corcoran, *H.M.S. Pinafore,* National Theatre, 1981; *St. Mark's Gospel* (one-man show), Playhouse Theatre, 1981; Hitler, *The Portage to San Christabel of A.H.,* Mermaid Theatre, 1982; title role, *Kipling* (one-man show), Mermaid Theatre, then Royale Theatre, New York City, both 1984; Harry Rivers, *Exclusive,* Strand Theatre, 1989; *St. Mark's Gospel* (one-man show), Lambs Theatre, New York City, 1990. Also appeared in *The Silver Box,* Lyric Hammersmith Theatre, London, 1951; *A Month in the Country* and *Waiting for Godot,* both National Theatre, 1988-89; and in repertory theatre productions, 1943-49.

PRINCIPAL STAGE WORK—Director, *While the Sun Shines,* Hampstead Theatre Club, London, 1972; director, *St. Mark's Gospel* (one-man show), Riverside Studio Theatre, then Mermaid Theatre, later Comedy Theatre, all London, 1978, then Marymount Manhattan Theatre, later Playhouse Theatre, both New York City, 1978, later Playhouse Theatre, 1981, then Lambs Theatre, New York City, 1990.

MAJOR TOURS—Antipholus of Syracuse, *The Comedy of Errors* and Fool, *King Lear,* RSC, Soviet, European, and U.S. cities, 1964; also *Love in a Mist,* Indian and Burmese cities, 1945.

FILM DEBUT—*The Cruel Sea*, General Film Distributors. PRINCI-PAL FILM APPEARANCES—Ken Thompson, *The Deep Blue Sea*, Twentieth Century-Fox, 1954; Peter Crowley, *Town on Trial*, Columbia, 1956; Albert, *The Good Companions*, Associated British/Pathe, 1957; surgeon, *The Third Key* (also known as *The Long Arm*), Rank, 1957; Alec Graham, *Time Without Pity*, Eros/Astor, 1957; Redpenny, *The Doctor's Dilemma*, Metro-Goldwyn-Mayer (MGM), 1958; Cottan, *A Night to Remember*, Rank, 1958; Duty Officer Hucknall, *The One That Got Away*, Rank, 1958; Able Seaman Morgan, *The Silent Enemy*, Universal, 1959; voice of Bottom, *A Midsummer Night's Dream*, Show Corporation, 1961; Brown, *The Loneliness of the Long Distance Runner* (also known as *Rebel with a Cause*), Continental Distributing, 1962; Dickie Bayliss, *In the Cool of the Day*, MGM, 1963; Alan Bax, *The Devil's Own* (also known as *The Witches*), Twentieth Century-Fox, 1967.

Micah Hale, *The Hawaiians* (also known as *Master of the Islands*), United Artists, 1970; Chief Inspector Oxford, *Frenzy*, Universal, 1972; Henry Pulling, *Travels with My Aunt*, MGM, 1972; Freddy, *Stevie*, First Artists, 1978; Major Trumbo, *Hanover Street*, Columbia, 1979; Q/Algy, *Never Say Never Again*, Warner Brothers, 1983; J.M. Barrie, *The Young Visiters*, James Hill Productions, 1984; Father Vincent, *Forever Young*, Cinecom International/Twentieth Century-Fox, 1984; Mr. Philpott, *The Assam Garden*, Moving Picture Company, 1985; Acting High Commissioner, *Cry Freedom*, Universal, 1987; Wing Commander Morton, *Personal Services*, VIP/Vestron, 1987; Ely, *Henry V*, Samuel Goldwyn, 1989. Also appeared in *The Divided Heart*, Republic, 1955; *The Agony and the Ecstasy*, Twentieth Century-Fox, 1965.

PRINCIPAL TELEVISION APPEARANCES—Mini-Series: *The Secret Adversary*, London Weekend Television, then PBS, 1987. Episodic: "Hunted Down," *Storyboard*, Thames, 1989. Movies: *Private Lives*, 1976; *Mr. Palfrey of Westminster*, 1984. Specials: Malvolio, *Twelfth Night*, BBC, then PBS, 1980; David Hume, *Dialogue in the Dark*, BBC-2, 1989.

WRITINGS: STAGE—(Adaptor) *St. Mark's Gospel*, Riverside Studio Theatre, London, 1978. OTHER—*Young Gemini* (autobiography), 1979; *Double Bill*, 1980; *Personal Mark*, 1984.

AWARDS: Clarence Derwent Award, 1960, for *As You Like It*; *Evening Standard* Award, Best Actor, London Critics' Award, and *Plays and Players* Award, 1968, Best Actor Award from the Drama League of New York and Antoinette Perry Award nomination, Best Actor in a Play, 1969, all for *Hadrian VII*; Variety Club of Great Britain Award and Best Actor Award from the Drama League of New York, 1970, and Antoinette Perry Award nomination, Best Actor in a Play, 1971, all for *The Philanthropist*; *Evening Standard* Award, 1973, for *The Misanthrope*; Antoinette Perry Award nomination, Best Actor in a Play, 1979, for *St. Mark's Gospel*; *Evening Standard* Award, 1982; Commander, Order of the British Empire.

MEMBER: Buckstone Club.

SIDELIGHTS: RECREATIONS—Playing piano and gardening. FAVORITE ROLES—Astrov in *Uncle Vanya*.

ADDRESSES: AGENT—STE Representation, 888 Seventh Avenue, New York, NY 10019. MANAGER—Jeremy Conway, Eagle House, 109 Jermyn Street, London SW1 76HB, England.*

RODDY McDOWALL

McDOWALL, Roddy   1928-

PERSONAL: Full name, Roderick Andrew McDowall; born September 17, 1928, in London, England; son of Thomas Andrew (a merchant seaman) and Winifred (Corcoran) McDowall. EDUCATION—Attended St. Joseph's College (London); studied acting with Mira Rostova and David Craig.

VOCATION: Actor.

CAREER: STAGE DEBUT—Roger Woodley, *Young Woodley*, Westport Country Playhouse, Westport, CT, 1946. BROADWAY DEBUT—Bentley Summerhayes, *Misalliance*, City Center Theatre, 1953. PRINCIPAL STAGE APPEARANCES—Malcolm, *Macbeth*, Salt Lake City Centennial Theatre, Salt Lake City, UT, 1947; Ninian, *The First Mrs. Fraser*, La Jolla Playhouse, La Jolla, CA, 1948; Walton, *Remains to Be Seen*, Alcazar Theatre, San Francisco, CA, 1952; Daventry, *Escapade*, 48th Street Theatre, New York City, 1953; Louis Dubedat, *The Doctor's Dilemma*, Phoenix Theatre, New York City, 1955; Ariel, *The Tempest* and Octavius, *Julius Caesar*, both American Shakespeare Festival, Stratford, CT, 1955; Ben Witledge, *No Time for Sergeants*, Alvin Theatre, New York City, 1955; Yegor Gloumov, *The Diary of a Scoundrel*, Phoenix Theatre, 1956; Benjamin, *Good As Gold*, Belasco Theatre, New York City, 1957; Artie Strauss, *Compulsion*, Ambassador Theatre, New York City, 1957; Pepe, *A Handful of Fire*, Martin Beck Theatre, New York City, 1958; Marcel Blanchard, *Look After Lulu*, Henry Miller's Theatre, New York City, 1959; Tarquin, *The Fighting Cock*, American National Theatre and Academy Theatre, New York City, 1959; Mordred, *Camelot*, Majestic Theatre, New York City, 1960; Claud, *The Astrakhan Coat*, Helen Hayes Theatre, New York City, 1967. Also appeared in *Otherwise Engaged*, 1978; and as Elwood P. Dowd, *Harvey*, 1980.

MAJOR TOURS—Lachie, *The Hasty Heart*, U.S. cities, 1949-50; Richard, *The Youngest*, U.S. cities, 1951-52; also appeared in *O Mistress Mine*, U.S. cities, 1950-51; and as Fancourt Babberly, *Charley's Aunt*, U.S. cities, 1976.

FILM DEBUT—Peter Osborne, *Murder in the Family*, Twentieth Century-Fox, 1938. PRINCIPAL FILM APPEARANCES—Ginger, *Just William*, Associated British/Pathe, 1939; Albert Perkins, *Confirm or Deny*, Twentieth Century-Fox, 1941; Huw, *How Green Was My Valley*, Twentieth Century-Fox, 1941; Vaner the cabin boy, *Man Hunt*, Twentieth Century-Fox, 1941; young Bob Stoler, *You Will Remember*, British Lion, 1941; Hugh Aylesworth, *On the Sunny Side*, Twentieth Century-Fox, 1942; Ronnie Cavanaugh, *The Pied Piper*, Twentieth Century-Fox, 1942; Benjamin Blake as a boy, *Son of Fury*, Twentieth Century-Fox, 1942; Joe Carraclough, *Lassie, Come Home*, Metro-Goldwyn-Mayer (MGM), 1943; Ken McLaughlin, *My Friend Flicka*, Twentieth Century-Fox, 1943; Francis as a boy, *The Keys of the Kingdom*, Twentieth Century-Fox, 1944; John Ashwood II as a boy, *The White Cliffs of Dover*, MGM, 1944; Jimmy Graham, *Molly and Me*, Twentieth Century-Fox, 1945; Ken McLaughlin, *Thunderhead—Son of Flicka*, Twentieth Century-Fox, 1945; voice, *Hangover Square*, Twentieth Century-Fox, 1945; Stanley Owen, *Holiday in Mexico*, MGM, 1946; David Balfour, *Kidnapped*, Monogram, 1948; Malcolm, *Macbeth*, Republic, 1948; Scott Jordan, *Black Midnight*, Monogram, 1949; Alec, *Tuna Clipper*, Monogram, 1949; Jimmy, *Big Timber*, Monogram, 1950; Ted, *Killer Shark*, Monogram, 1950; Erik, *The Steel Fist*, Monogram, 1952.

Malcolm, *Midnight Lace*, Universal, 1960; Yuri Gligoric, *The Subterraneans*, MGM, 1960; Private Morris, *The Longest Day*, Twentieth Century-Fox, 1962; Octavian, *Cleopatra*, Twentieth Century-Fox, 1963; Martin Ashley, *Shock Treatment*, Twentieth Century-Fox, 1964; D.J., Jr., *The Loved One*, MGM, 1965; Gregory Benson, *That Darn Cat*, Buena Vista, 1965; Oliver Parsons, *The Third Day*, Warner Brothers, 1965; Matthew, *The Greatest Story Ever Told*, United Artists, 1965; Walter Baines, *Inside Daisy Clover*, Warner Brothers, 1965; Alan "Mollymauk" Musgrave, *Lord Love a Duck*, United Artists, 1966; CIA Agent Adam, *The Defector* (also known as *Lautlose Waffen* and *L'Espion*), Warner Brothers/Seven Arts, 1966; title role, *The Adventures of Bullwhip Griffin*, Buena Vista, 1967; Tony, *The Cool Ones*, Warner Brothers, 1967; Arthur Pimm, *It!* (also known as *Curse of the Golem*), Warner Brothers, 1967; Nick Evers, *Five Card Stud*, Paramount, 1968; Cornelius, *Planet of the Apes*, Twentieth Century-Fox, 1968; Santoro, *Angel, Angel, Down We Go* (also known as *Cult of the Damned*), American International, 1969; Nate Ashbury, *Hello Down There* (also known as *Sub-a-Dub-Dub*), Paramount, 1969; Wister, *Midas Run* (also known as *Run on Gold*), Cinerama, 1969.

Mr. Jelk, *Bedknobs and Broomsticks*, Buena Vista, 1971; Cornelius, *Escape from the Planet of the Apes*, Twentieth Century-Fox, 1971; Mr. Proffer, *Pretty Maids All in a Row*, MGM, 1971; Caesar, *Conquest of the Planet of the Apes*, Twentieth Century-Fox, 1972; Frank Gass, *The Life and Times of Judge Roy Bean*, National General, 1972; Acres, *The Poseidon Adventure*, Twentieth Century-Fox, 1972; Robert, *Arnold*, Cinerama, 1973; Caesar, *Battle for the Planet of the Apes*, Twentieth Century-Fox, 1973; Ben Fischer, *The Legend of Hell House*, Twentieth Century-Fox, 1973; Stanton, *Dirty Mary, Crazy Larry*, Twentieth Century-Fox, 1974; Bobby, *Funny Lady*, Columbia, 1975; Riley, *Embryo*, Cine Artists, 1976;

Tony Da Vinci, *Mean Johnny Barrows*, Atlas, 1976; Skateboard, *Sixth and Main*, National Cinema, 1977; Mr. Stallwood, *The Cat from Outer Space*, Buena Vista, 1978; Dr. Mellon, *Laserblast*, Irwin Yablans, 1978; Gypsy grandmother/Dr. Fishbind, *Rabbit Test*, AVCO-Embassy, 1978; White Robe, *Circle of Iron* (also known as *The Silent Flute*), AVCO-Embassy, 1979; voice of Franz Prince Fritz, *Nutcracker Fantasy* (animated), Sanrio, 1979; Jenkins, *Scavenger Hunt*, Twentieth Century-Fox, 1979; voice of robot, *The Black Hole*, Buena Vista, 1979.

Gillespie, *Charlie Chan and the Curse of the Dragon Queen*, American Cinema, 1981; Terry Corrigan, *Class of 1984*, United Film Distribution, 1982; Rex Brewster, *Evil Under the Sun*, Universal, 1982; Peter Vincent, *Fright Night*, Columbia, 1985; voice of Nugget, *GoBots: Battle of the Rocklords* (animated), Clubhouse/Atlantic, 1986; Thomas Franklin Murray, *Dead of Winter*, Metro-Goldwyn-Mayer/United Artists (MGM/UA), 1986; Andrew, *Overboard*, MGM/UA, 1986; minister, *Doin' Time on Planet Earth* (also known as *Coming Down to Earth*), Cannon Releasing, 1988; Peter Vincent, *Fright Night, Part II* (also known as *Fright Night II*), New Century/Vista, 1988; as himself, *Going Hollywood: The War Years* (also known as *Going Home*), Warner Home Video, 1988; Dr. Dante, *Cutting Class*, Republic, 1989; judge, *The Big Picture*, Columbia, 1989. Also appeared in *Hey! Hey! USA!*, General Film Distributors, 1938; *Convict 99*, General Film Distributors, 1938; *I See Ice*, Associated British, 1938; *John Halifax—Gentleman*, MGM, 1938; *Scruffy*, British Independent, 1938; *Yellow Sands*, Associated British, 1938; *Dead Man's Shoes*, Associated British, 1939; *Murder Will Out*, Warner Brothers, 1939; *Dirt*, 1939; *Brother's Keeper*, 1939; *The Outsider*, Associated British, 1940; *Saloon Bar*, Associated British, 1940; *This England* (also known as *Our Heritage*), Twentieth Century-Fox, 1941; *Poison Pen*, Republic, 1941; *Rocky*, Monogram, 1948; *Green Grass of Wyoming*, World, 1948; *Everybody's Dancin'*, Lippert, 1950; *Paris brule-t-il?*, (also known as *Is Paris Burning?*), Paramount, 1966.

PRINCIPAL FILM WORK—Co-associate producer, *Tuna Clipper*, Monogram, 1949; co-executive producer, *Killer Shark*, Monogram, 1950; director, *The Devil's Widow* (also known as *Tam Lin*), British International, 1971; executive producer, *Overboard*, MGM/UA, 1986.

PRINCIPAL TELEVISION APPEARANCES—Series: Galen, *The Planet of the Apes*, CBS, 1974; Dr. Jonathan Willaway, *The Fantastic Journey*, NBC, 1977; Bon Chance Louis, *Tales of the Gold Monkey*, ABC, 1982-83; Norman Parks, *Bridges to Cross*, CBS, 1986; Chiun, *Remo Williams*, ABC, 1988. Mini-Series: Bobby Ballard, *The Rhinemann Exchange*, NBC, 1977; Father Stone, *The Martian Chronicles*, NBC, 1980; Jason Swankle, *Hollywood Wives*, ABC, 1985. Pilots: Jeremy, *Night Gallery*, NBC, 1969; Cosmo Topper, Jr., *Topper Returns*, NBC, 1973; Dr. Peterson, *Hart to Hart*, ABC, 1979; Derek, *The Million Dollar Face*, NBC, 1981; Mr. Heller, *Judgement Day*, NBC, 1981; host, *Twilight Theatre*, NBC, 1982; Manfred Hayes, *This Girl for Hire*, CBS, 1983; Paul Fisk, *London and Davis in New York*, CBS, 1984.

Episodic: Sam Conrad, "People Are Alike All Over," *The Twilight Zone*, CBS, 1960; the Bookworm, "The Bookworm Turns While Gotham City Burns," *Batman*, ABC, 1966; Bob Cratchit, *George Burns Comedy Week*, CBS, 1985; Alger Kenyon, *Murder, She Wrote*, CBS, 1985; Christopher Hoyt, *Matlock*, NBC, 1987; Carmilla, *Nightmare Classics*, Showtime, 1989; also *Faith Baldwin's Theatre of Romance*, ABC, 1951; *Campbell Television Soundstage* (also known as *TV Soundstage*), NBC, 1953; *Ponds*

Theatre, ABC, 1955; *Oldsmobile Music Theatre*, NBC, 1959; *The Invaders*, ABC, 1967; *Wonder Woman*, CBS, 1977 and 1978; "Heart of Darkness," *Playhouse 90*, CBS; "Billy Budd," *Dupont Show of the Month*, CBS; "He's for Me," *The Alcoa Hour*, NBC; the Devil (Mephistopheles), *Fantasy Island*, ABC; *The Kaiser Aluminum Hour*, NBC; *Matinee Theatre*, NBC; *Robert Montgomery Presents Your Lucky Strike Theatre*, NBC; *Suspicion*, NBC; *Chrysler Medallion Theatre* (also known as *Medallion Theatre*), CBS; *The Elgin Hour*, NBC; *Goodyear Television Playhouse*, NBC; *Naked City*, ABC; *Arrest and Trial*, ABC; *McMillan and Wife*, NBC; *The Arthur Murray Party*.

Movies: Dr. Michael Lomas, *A Taste of Evil*, ABC, 1971; Dr. Ralph Baird, *Terror in the Sky*, CBS, 1971; Albert Soames, *What's a Nice Girl Like You. . .?*, ABC, 1971; Dr. Henry Sawyer, *Miracle on 34th Street*, CBS, 1973; Marvin Ellis, *The Elevator*, ABC, 1974; Franklin, *Flood*, NBC, 1976; Calvin Braderman, *The Immigrants*, syndicated, 1978; Hasan, *The Thief of Baghdad*, NBC, 1978; MacFarland, *The Memory of Eva Ryker*, CBS, 1980; Rene Valentine, *Mae West*, ABC, 1982; Prince John, *The Zany Adventures of Robin Hood*, CBS, 1984; March Hare, *Alice in Wonderland*, CBS, 1985; voice of Ratty, *The Wind in the Willows* (animated), ABC, 1987; Bank of England assistant, *Around the World in Eighty Days*, NBC, 1989.

Specials: Waiter, "The Good Fairy," *Hallmark Hall of Fame*, NBC, 1956; *The Best of Anything*, NBC, 1960; Ariel, "The Tempest," *Hallmark Hall of Fame*, NBC, 1960; "Not Without Honor," *Equitable's American Heritage*, NBC, 1960; Mestizo, *The Power and the Glory*, CBS, 1961; Charles, "Saint Joan," *Hallmark Hall of Fame*, NBC, 1967; voices of Mowgli, Shere Khan, Akela, Tabaqui, Bagheera, Baloo, and narrator, *Mowgli's Brothers* (animated), CBS, 1976; *An All-Star Tribute to Elizabeth Taylor*, CBS, 1977; *Circus of the Stars*, CBS, 1982; *Happy Birthday, Hollywood*, ABC, 1987; *Kennedy Center Honors: A Celebration of the Performing Arts*, CBS, 1988; *America's All-Star Tribute to Elizabeth Taylor* (also known as *America's Hope Award*), ABC, 1989; also *Ah! Wilderness*, 1951.

NON-RELATED CAREER—Photographer.

WRITINGS: Double Exposure Take Two (celebrity photo essays), Morrow, 1989; also *Double Exposure* (celebrity photo essays), 1966.

AWARDS: Star of Tomorrow, 1944; Antoinette Perry Award, Best Supporting or Featured Actor in a Play, 1960, for *The Fighting Cock;* Emmy Award, Best Supporting Actor in a Dramatic Special, 1961, for "Not Without Honor," *Equitable's American Heritage;* American Cinema Foundation Award, 1985.

SIDELIGHTS: FAVORITE ROLES—Artie Strauss in *Compulsion* and Ariel in *The Tempest*. RECREATIONS—Collecting film memorabilia.*

*   *   *

McFADDEN, Cheryl
    See McFADDEN, Gates

GATES McFADDEN

McFADDEN, Gates
(Cheryl McFadden, Jesse Stuart Gates)

PERSONAL: EDUCATION—Received B.A. in theatre arts from Brandeis University; studied acting and mime under Jacques LeCoq at the Ecole Mime et Theatre, Paris, France.

VOCATION: Actress, choreographer, director, and playwright.

CAREER: Also see *WRITINGS* below. PRINCIPAL STAGE APPEARANCES—(As Cheryl McFadden) Ellen/Mrs. Saunders and Betty, *Cloud 9*, Theatre De Lys, New York City, 1981; (as Cheryl McFadden) Gillian, *To Gillian on Her 37th Birthday*, Ensemble Studio Theatre, New York City, 1983, then Circle in the Square Downtown, New York City, 1984; (as Cheryl McFadden) Ruth, *The Homecoming*, Jewish Repertory Theatre, New York City, 1984; (as Cheryl McFadden) Annie Sutter, *The Bloodletters*, Ensemble Studio Theatre, 1984; (as Cheryl McFadden) Casey Staiger, *How to Say Goodbye*, Vineyard Theatre, New York City, 1986; (as Cheryl McFadden) Dr. Handleman, *Couch Tandem*, Women's InterArt Center, New York City, 1987; Kate, *Emerald City*, Perry Street Theatre, New York City, 1988; also appeared in (as Cheryl McFadden) Mary, *Rosario and the Gypsies*, Ensemble Studio Theatre; (as Cheryl McFadden) Mrs. Malloy, *The Matchmaker*, La Jolla Playhouse, La Jolla, CA.

PRINCIPAL STAGE WORK—(As Cheryl McFadden) Choreographer, *The Winter's Tale*, Brooklyn Academy of Music Theatre Company, Helen Owen Carey Playhouse, Brooklyn, NY, 1980; (as Cheryl McFadden) fight choreographer, *Johnny on the Spot*, Brooklyn Academy of Music Theatre Company, Brooklyn Academy of

Music, Brooklyn, NY, 1980; (as Cheryl McFadden) choreographer, *A Midsummer Night's Dream,* Brooklyn Academy of Music Theatre Company, Brooklyn Academy of Music, 1981. Also choreographer, *Yesterday Is Over,* Women's InterArt Center, New York City; director, *Bottleneck at the Bar,* Golden Lion Theatre, New York City. Also director and choreographer: *Bumps and Knots,* Lyric Hammersmith Theatre, London; *Women of Trachis, He Who Gets Slapped,* and *Old Times,* all Springold Theatre, Waltham, MA; and *Medea,* Studio Theatre, Pittsburgh, PA.

PRINCIPAL FILM APPEARANCES—(As Cheryl McFadden) Mr. Price's secretary, *The Muppets Take Manhattan,* Tri-Star, 1984; (as Cheryl McFadden) Gena, *When Nature Calls,* Troma, 1985; Caroline Ryan, *Hunt for Red October,* Paramount, 1990; Diane Conners, *Filofax,* Buena Vista, 1990. PRINCIPAL FILM WORK—(As Cheryl McFadden) Choreographer and director of fantasy sequences, *Dreamchild,* Universal, 1985; (as Cheryl McFadden) choreographer (with Charles Augins and Michael Moschen), *Labyrinth,* Tri-Star, 1986.

PRINCIPAL TELEVISION APPEARANCES—Series: Dr. Beverly Crusher, *Star Trek: The Next Generation,* syndicated, 1987-88, then 1989—; also *Beyond the Groove,* Channel 4. Pilots: Darcy Stafford, *The Wizard,* CBS, 1986. Episodic: Anita Garcia, *The Cosby Show,* NBC, 1987; also Tammy Dryden, *The Edge of Night;* Mrs. Mallory, *All My Children,* ABC; *Another World,* NBC.

RELATED CAREER—Teacher of acting and improvisation, New York University Graduate School of the Arts; full-time undergraduate and graduate lecturer and instructor at the University of Pittsburgh; assistant professor, Brandeis University Graduate School of Theatre Arts; guest artist and faculty member at numerous universities and schools, including Harvard University, Perdue University, Brooklyn College, Fairleigh Dickinson University, Lincoln Center Institute for the Arts, Nashville Institute for the Arts, and the American Academy of Dramatic Arts; founder and artistic director, New York Theatre Commotion (a touring theatre company which performed original scripts in New York City, Pittsburgh, Philadelphia, and Boston).

WRITINGS: STAGE—(As Jesse Stuart Gates) *Bottleneck at the Bar,* Golden Lion Theatre, New York City.

ADDRESSES: AGENT—Susan Smith and Associates, 121 N. San Vicente Boulevard, Beverly Hills, CA 90211 and 192 Lexington Avenue, New York, NY 10016.

*   *   *

McGUANE, Thomas   1939-

PERSONAL: Full name, Thomas Francis McGuane III; born December 11, 1939, in Wyandotte, MI; son of Thomas Francis (a manufacturer) and Alice Rita (Torphy) McGuane; married Portia Rebecca Crockett, September 8, 1962 (divorced, 1975); married Margot Kidder (an actress), August, 1976 (divorced, May, 1977); married Laurie Buffett, September 19, 1977; children: Thomas Francis IV (first marriage); Maggie (second marriage); Anne Buffett (third marriage); Heather Hume (stepdaughter). EDUCATION—Michigan State University, B.A., 1962; Yale University, M.F.A., 1965; postgraduate work at Stanford University, 1966-67; also attended the University of Michigan and Olivet College.

VOCATION: Writer.

CAREER: Also see *WRITINGS* below. PRINCIPAL FILM APPEARANCES—Cowboy in bar, *Cold Feet,* Avenue, 1989. PRINCIPAL FILM WORK—Director, *92 in the Shade,* United Artists, 1975.

RELATED CAREER—Special contributor, *Sports Illustrated,* 1969-73.

WRITINGS: FILM—*Rancho Deluxe,* United Artists, 1975; *92 in the Shade,* United Artists, 1975; *The Missouri Breaks,* United Artists, 1976; (with Bud Shrake) *Tom Horn,* Warner Brothers, 1980; (with Jim Harrison) *Cold Feet,* Avenue, 1989. OTHER—*The Sporting Club* (novel), Simon & Schuster, 1969; *The Bushwacked Piano* (novel), Simon & Schuster, 1971; *Ninety-Two in the Shade* (novel), Farrar, Straus & Giroux, 1973; *Panama* (novel), Farrar, Straus & Giroux, 1978; *An Outside Chance: Essays on Sport* (nonfiction), Farrar, Straus & Giroux, 1980; *Nobody's Angel* (novel), Random House, 1982; *Something to Be Desired* (novel), Random House, 1984; *In the Crazies: Book and Portfolio* (signed limited edition), Winn Books, 1984; *To Skin a Cat* (short stories), Dutton, 1986; *Keep the Change* (novel), Houghton Mifflin, 1989.

AWARDS: Wallace Stegner fellowship from Stanford University, 1966-67; Richard and Hinda Rosenthal Foundation Award for Fiction from the National Institute of Arts and Letters, 1971, for *The Bushwacked Piano;* National Book Award nomination, 1974, for *92 in the Shade.*

MEMBER: Mandible Club (Key West, FL).

SIDELIGHTS: A film version of Thomas McGuane's novel *The Sporting Club,* adapted by Lorenzo Semple, Jr., was released by AVCO-Embassy in 1971.

ADDRESSES: AGENT—John Hawkins Associates, 71 W. 23rd Street, Suite 1600, New York, NY 10010.*

*   *   *

McKEON, Nancy   1966-

PERSONAL: Born April 4, 1966, in Westbury, NY; father, a travel agent.

VOCATION: Actress and producer.

CAREER: PRINCIPAL TELEVISION APPEARANCES—Series: Jill Stone, *Stone,* ABC, 1980; Jo Polniaszek, *The Facts of Life,* NBC, 1980-89. Pilots: Ann, *Return to Fantasy Island,* ABC, 1978; Jill Stone, *Stone,* ABC, 1979; Beth Franklin, *High School U.S.A.,* ABC, 1983; Slugger, *Dusty,* NBC, 1983. Movies: Susan Moreland, *A Question of Love,* NBC, 1978; Jo Polniaszek, *The Facts of Life Goes to Paris,* NBC, 1982; Kimberly Downs, *This Child Is Mine,* NBC, 1985; Rhonda Malone, *Poison Ivy,* NBC, 1985; Cindy Fralick, *Firefighter,* CBS, 1986; Jo Polniaszek, *The Facts of Life Down Under,* NBC, 1987; Nikki Glover, *Strange Voices,* NBC, 1987; title role, *A Cry for Help: The Tracey Thurman Story,* NBC, 1989. Specials: Lucy, "Schoolboy Father," *ABC Afterschool Specials,* ABC, 1980; voice of Scruffy, "Scruffy" (animated), *ABC Weekend Specials,* ABC, 1980; Nancy Parks, "Please Don't Hit Me, Mom," *ABC Afterschool Specials,* ABC, 1981; *Battle of the Network Stars,* ABC, 1980, 1982, and 1983; voice characterization, *The Puppy Saves the Circus* (animated), ABC, 1981; voice of Amelia Day, "Miss Switch to the Rescue" (animated), *ABC Weekend Specials,* ABC, 1981; co-host, *Candid Kids,* NBC, 1985.

PRINCIPAL TELEVISION WORK—Movies: Executive producer (with Greg H. Sims), *Firefighter,* CBS, 1986; executive producer (with Sims), *Strange Voices,* NBC, 1987.

RELATED CAREER—As a child, worked as a model, in television commercials, and in soap operas.*

*   *   *

McKERN, Leo   1920-

PERSONAL: Born Reginald McKern, March 16, 1920, in Sydney, New South Wales, Australia; son of Norman Walton and Vera (Martin) McKern; married Jane Holland (an artist), 1946; children: two daughters. MILITARY—Australian Army, 1940-42.

VOCATION: Actor.

CAREER: Also see *WRITINGS* below. STAGE DEBUT—Chemist, *Uncle Harry,* Theatre Royal, Sydney, Australia, 1944. LONDON DEBUT—Forester, *Love's Labour's Lost,* Old Vic Company, New Theatre, 1949. PRINCIPAL STAGE APPEARANCES—Jeremy, *She Stoops to Conquer,* Old Vic Company, London, 1949; Guildenstern, *Hamlet,* Simon, *The Miser,* Feste, *Twelfth Night,* and Nightingale, *Bartholomew Fair,* all Old Vic Company, 1950; Nym and Sir Thomas Erpingham, *Henry V,* Nym, *The Merry Wives of Windsor,*

LEO McKERN

messenger, *Electra,* and confectioner, *The Wedding,* all Old Vic Company, 1951; Fool, *King Lear* and Apemantus, *Timon of Athens,* both Old Vic Company, 1952; Ulysses, *Troilus and Cressida,* Gremio, *The Taming of the Shrew,* Quince, *A Midsummer Night's Dream,* and Friar Lawrence, *Romeo and Juliet,* all Shakespeare Memorial Theatre Company, Stratford-on-Avon, U.K., 1954; title role, *Toad of Toad Hall,* Prince's Theatre, London, 1954; traveller, *The Queen and the Rebels,* Haymarket Theatre, London, 1955; Claggart, *The Good Sailor,* Lyric Hammersmith Theatre, London, 1956; Big Daddy, *Cat on a Hot Tin Roof,* Comedy Theatre, London, 1958; Tyepkin, *Brouhaha,* Aldwych Theatre, London, 1958; title role, *Rollo,* Strand Theatre, London, 1959.

The Common Man, *A Man for All Seasons,* Globe Theatre, London, 1960; Ferrante, *Queen After Death,* Oxford Playhouse, Oxford, U.K., 1961, then American National Theatre and Academy Theatre, New York City, 1961; title role, *Peer Gynt* and Subtle, *The Alchemist,* both Old Vic Company, 1962; Iago, *Othello,* Old Vic Company, 1963; Menenius, *Coriolanus* and Governor, *The Life in My Hands,* both Nottingham Playhouse, Nottingham, U.K., 1963-64; Baron Bolligrew, *The Thwarting of Baron Bolligrew,* Aldwych Theatre, 1965; title role, *Volpone,* Oxford Playhouse, then Garrick Theatre, London, 1966-67; Shylock, *The Merchant of Venice,* Oxford Playhouse, 1973; title role, *Rollo,* Royal Exchange Company, Manchester, U.K., 1978; Kelemen, *The Wolf,* Oxford Playhouse, then Apollo Theatre, later Queen's Theatre, then New London Theatre, all London, 1973; Matt Quintan, *The Housekeeper,* Apollo Theatre, 1982; James Boswell, *Boswell for the Defense,* Playhouse Theatre, Melbourne, Australia, then Playhouse Theatre, London, both 1989. Also appeared as Governor Bligh, *The Man Who Shot the Albatross* and Rollo, *Patate,* both in Melbourne, 1970-71; in *Uncle Vanya* and *Crime and Punishment,* both Royal Exchange Company, 1978; *Number One,* Queen's Theatre, 1983.

MAJOR TOURS—Arts Council tours of U.K. cities, 1947; also Confederation of Shipbuilding and Engineering Unions tour of Germany.

PRINCIPAL FILM APPEARANCES—Third knight, *Murder in the Cathedral,* Classics, 1952; Gaston Nikopopoulos, *All for Mary,* Rank, 1956; Max, *Yesterday's Enemy,* Columbia, 1959; Robert Stanford, *Time Without Pity,* Eros/Astor, 1957; McGill, *X the Unknown,* Warner Brothers, 1957; attorney general, *A Tale of Two Cities,* Rank, 1958; Benter, *The Mouse That Roared,* Columbia, 1959; inspector, *Jazz Boat,* Columbia, 1960; Tommy Kennedy, *Scent of Mystery* (also known as *Holiday in Spain*), Michael Todd, Jr., 1960; Bill Maguire, *The Day the Earth Caught Fire,* Universal, 1961; Headmaster Muche, *I Like Money* (also known as *Mr. Topaze*), Twentieth Century-Fox, 1962; Brandt, *Lisa* (also known as *The Inspector*), Twentieth Century-Fox, 1962; Simenova, *Agent 8 3/4* (also known as *Hot Enough for June*), Continental, 1963; Heibronn, *Doctor in Distress,* Rank, 1963; Professor Bowles-Ottery, *A Jolly Bad Fellow* (also known as *They All Died Laughing*), Continental Distributing, 1964; Captain O'Sullivan, *King and Country,* Allied Artists, 1964; Squint, *The Amorous Adventures of Moll Flanders,* Paramount, 1965; Clang, *Help!,* United Artists, 1965; Thomas Cromwell, *A Man for All Seasons,* Columbia, 1966; Smith, *Assignment K,* Columbia, 1968; Flannery, *The High Commissioner* (also known as *Nobody Runs Forever*), Cinerama, 1968; Cardinal Leone, *The Shoes of the Fisherman,* Metro-Goldwyn-Mayer (MGM), 1968; Captain Grimes, *Decline and Fall . . . of a Bird Watcher* (also known as *Decline and Fall*), Twentieth Century-Fox, 1969.

Tom Ryan, *Ryan's Daughter,* MGM, 1970; General Kurt Maelzer,

Massacre in Rome, National General/Compagnia Cinematografica Champion, 1973; Moriarty, *The Adventures of Sherlock Holmes' Smarter Brother*, Twentieth Century-Fox, 1975; Bugenhagen, *The Omen* (also known as *Birthmark*), Twentieth Century-Fox, 1976; Harry Bundage, *Candleshoe*, Buena Vista, 1978; Bugenhagen, *Damien: Omen II*, Twentieth Century-Fox, 1978; narrator, *The Last Tasmanian* (documentary), Artis/Australian Film Commission/Tasmanian Film Commission, 1979; Paddy Button, *The Blue Lagoon*, Columbia, 1980; Dr. Grogan, *The French Lieutenant's Woman*, United Artists, 1981; Sir Frederick Carlion, *Country*, British Film Institute, 1981; narrator, *Voyage of Bounty's Child* (documentary), Look Film Productions, 1983; Thomas, *The Chain*, Rank, 1985; Imperius, *Ladyhawke*, Warner Brothers/Twentieth Century-Fox, 1985; Frank, *Travelling North*, CEL, 1987. Also appeared in *Beyond This Place* (also known as *Web of Evidence*), 1956; as narrator, *Mikhali*, 1960; voice, *The Lion, the Witch, and the Wardrobe*, 1979.

PRINCIPAL TELEVISION APPEARANCES—Series: Horace Rumpole, *Rumpole of the Bailey*, Thames, 1977—, then *Mystery!*, PBS, 1984—. Mini-Series: Nicodemus Boffin, *Our Mutual Friend*, BBC, then *Masterpiece Theatre*, PBS, 1978; Basil Zaharov, *Reilly, Ace of Spies*, 1983, then *Mystery!*, PBS, 1984. Episodic: Number Two, "The Chimes of Big Ben," "Once Upon a Time," and "Fall Out," *The Prisoner*, CBS, 1968; also *Space 1999*, syndicated, 1976. Movies: Herod, *The Nativity*, ABC, 1978; David Ben-Gurion, *The House on Garibaldi Street*, ABC, 1979; Inspector Curry, *Agatha Christie's "Murder with Mirrors,"* CBS, 1985. Specials: Duke of Gloucester, *King Lear*, PBS, 1984; Sancho, *Monsignor Quixote*, Thames, 1985, then PBS, 1987. Also appeared in *The Boxwallah*, Yorkshire Television, 1982.

PRINCIPAL RADIO APPEARANCES—*Le Bourgeois Gentilhomme*, R3, 1982.

NON-RELATED CAREER—Engineering apprentice, 1935-37; artist, 1937-40.

WRITINGS: RADIO—Plays: *Chain of Events*. OTHER—*Just Resting* (memoir), Methuen, 1983; (introduction) *Volpone*, Longman, 1985.

AWARDS: Radio Industries Play of the Year; Officer of the Australian Order (A.O.).

MEMBER: British Actors' Equity Association, National Trust, Amnesty International, Earthcare.

ADDRESSES: AGENT—International Creative Management, 388-396 Oxford Street, London W1N 9HE, England.*

*   *   *

McKINNEY, Bill

PERSONAL: Full name, William McKinney.

VOCATION: Actor.

CAREER: PRINCIPAL FILM APPEARANCES—Steve St. John, *She Freak* (also known as *Alley of Nightmares*), Sonney, 1967; Hays, *The Road Hustlers*, American International, 1968; Shotgun, *Angel Unchained*, American International, 1970; mountain man, *Deliver-*

ance, Warner Brothers, 1972; Red Terwiliger, *Junior Bonner*, Cinerama, 1972; Fermel Parlee, *The Life and Times of Judge Roy Bean*, National General, 1972; Officer Purdy, *Cleopatra Jones*, Warner Brothers, 1973; Buck, *The Outfit* (also known as *The Good Guys Always Win*), Metro-Goldwyn-Mayer, 1973; Art, *The Parallax View*, Paramount, 1974; crazy driver, *Thunderbolt and Lightfoot*, United Artists, 1974; Cade Redman, *Cannonball* (also known as *Carquake*), New World, 1976; Terrill, *The Outlaw Josey Wales*, Warner Brothers, 1976; Cobb, *The Shootist*, Paramount, 1976; Rocky, *For Pete's Sake* (also known as *July Pork Bellies*), Columbia, 1974; Reverend Theodore Peabody, *Breakheart Pass*, United Artists, 1976; Constable, *The Gauntlet*, Warner Brothers, 1977; jail cop, *Valentino*, United Artists, 1977; Dallas, *Every Which Way But Loose*, Warner Brothers, 1978; Tommy Clark, *When You Comin' Back, Red Ryder?*, Columbia, 1979.

Dallas, *Any Which Way You Can*, Warner Brothers, 1980; Lefty LeBow, *Bronco Billy*, Warner Brothers, 1980; Dill, *Carny*, United Artists, 1980; Kern, *First Blood*, Orion, 1982; Pop McCormick, *Tex*, Buena Vista, 1982; "Big Daddy" Don Garlits, *Heart Like a Wheel*, Twentieth Century-Fox, 1983; head coach, *Against All Odds*, Columbia, 1984; Chief Wilson, *Final Justice*, Mediterranean-Arista, 1985; bartender, *Pink Cadillac*, Warner Brothers, 1989; Father Burke, *Kinjite* (also known as *Kinjite: Forbidden Subjects*), Cannon, 1989; Miller, *Under the Gun*, Magnum Entertainment, 1989. Also appeared in *St. Helens*, Parnell, 1981.

PRINCIPAL TELEVISION APPEARANCES—Series: Deputy Jim Shanks, *The Family Holvak*, NBC, 1975. Pilots: Lobo, *Alias Smith and Jones*, ABC, 1971; Mr. Brown, *The Healers*, NBC, 1974; Willie Coggins, *The Underground Man*, NBC, 1974; Badger, *Strange New World*, ABC, 1975; Deputy Stebbins, *The Highwayman*, NBC, 1987. Episodic: Dempsey, *Murder, She Wrote*, CBS, 1986; Jake Gordon, *Ohara*, ABC, 1987; Lipscombe, *Houston Knights*, CBS, 1987; Tom Warner, *Falcon Crest*, CBS, 1987; Micah, *Beauty and the Beast*, CBS, 1989. Movies: Sergeant, *The Execution of Private Slovik*, NBC, 1974; Corporal Crawley, *The Godchild*, ABC, 1974; Pratt, *The Strange and Deadly Occurrence*, NBC, 1974; Drago Wellman, *This Is the West That Was*, NBC, 1974; Willie, *Christmas Miracle in Caulfield, U.S.A.* (also known as *The Christmas Coal Mine Miracle*), NBC, 1977.*

*   *   *

McRANEY, Gerald   1948-

PERSONAL: Born August 19, 1948, in Collins, MS; married Pat Rae Moran (divorced); married Delta Burke (an actress), May 27, 1989; children: Jessica, Angus, Kate (first marriage). EDUCATION—Attended the University of Mississippi; studied acting with Jeff Corey.

VOCATION: Actor.

CAREER: PRINCIPAL FILM APPEARANCES—Wesley Stuart, *Night of Bloody Horror*, Howco, 1969; Terrance Bradford, *Women and Bloody Terror*, Howco, 1970; Bastian's father, *The Neverending Story*, Warner Brothers, 1984; Jake Wheeler, *American Justice* (also known as *Jackals*), Movie Store, 1986; also appeared in *The Brain Machine*, 1972; and *Keep Off! Keep Off!*, Gamalex, 1975.

TELEVISION DEBUT—*Night Gallery*, NBC. PRINCIPAL TELEVISION APPEARANCES—Series: Richard "Rick" Simon, *Simon and*

Simon, CBS, 1981-88; J.D. "Mac" MacGillis, *Major Dad*, CBS, 1989. Mini-Series: *Roots: The Next Generations*, ABC, 1979. Pilots: Sid Burton, *The Jordan Chance*, CBS, 1978; Jennings, *The Seal*, NBC, 1981; Rick Simon, *Shadow of Sam Penny*, CBS, 1983. Episodic: Ricky, *The Incredible Hulk*, CBS, 1978 and 1979; Dash Goff, *Designing Women*, CBS, 1988; also *Logan's Run*, CBS, 1977; *Newhart*, CBS, 1990; *The Rockford Files*, NBC; *The Dukes of Hazzard*, CBS; *Eight Is Enough*, ABC; *How the West Was Won*, ABC; *Hawaii Five-0*, CBS; *Barnaby Jones*, CBS; *Gunsmoke*, CBS. Movies: Smith, *The F.B.I. Story: The F.B.I. vs. Alvin Karpis, Public Enemy Number One*, CBS, 1974; Denny, *The Return of the Incredible Hulk*, CBS, 1977; Dr. Gus Henderson, *Women in White*, NBC, 1979; Patrolman Ashley, *The Aliens Are Coming*, NBC, 1980; Merle, *Where the Ladies Go*, ABC, 1980; Cliff Sulkes, *Rape and Marriage—The Rideout Case*, CBS, 1980; Howdy Tilford, *Memories Never Die*, CBS, 1982; Dan Evans, *The Haunting Passion*, NBC, 1983; Lieutenant Eckford, *City Killer*, NBC, 1984; Christopher Wilder, *Easy Prey*, ABC, 1986; Charlie Carson, *A Hobo's Christmas*, CBS, 1987; Jones, *Where the Hell's That Gold?!!?* (also known as *Love and Curses*), CBS, 1988; Chuck Yoman, *The People Across the Lake*, NBC, 1988; Huff, *Murder By Moonlight*, CBS, 1989; also *The Law*, NBC, 1974; *The Trial of Chaplain Jensen*, ABC, 1975. Specials: *CBS Tournament of Roses Parade*, CBS, 1985; *America Picks the All-Time Favorite Movies*, NBC, 1988.

PRINCIPAL TELEVISION WORK—Episodic: Director, *Simon and Simon*, CBS, 1986 and 1988.

RELATED CAREER—Actor in repertory theatre productions, New Orleans, LA, 1970.

WRITINGS: TELEVISION—Episodic: *Simon and Simon*, CBS, 1987.

ADDRESSES: OFFICE—c/o Michael Karg, 247 S. Beverly Drive, Beverly Hills, CA 90212.*

*   *   *

MEANEY, Colm

VOCATION: Actor.

CAREER: STAGE DEBUT—Abbey Theatre, Dublin, Ireland. PRINCIPAL STAGE APPEARANCES—Derek and Vince, *Fish in the Sea*, Half Moon Theatre, London, 1975; Lin Piao, *History of the Tenth Struggle*, Scarab Theatre, ICA Theatre, London, 1976; Kevin, *The Poker Session*, Theatre-Off-Park, New York City, 1984; Patrick O'Connor, *Diary of a Hunger Strike*, Los Angeles Theatre Centre, Los Angeles, 1985; Mick Ross, *Breaking the Code*, Kennedy Center for the Performing Arts, Washington, DC, 1987, then Neil Simon Theatre, New York City, 1987-88; also appeared in *Yobbo Nowt*, 7:84 Theatre Company, Shaw Theatre, London, 1975; *Alpha* and *The Birthday Party*, both Los Angeles Theatre Centre.

PRINCIPAL FILM APPEARANCES—Mr. Bergin, *The Dead*, Vestron/Zenith, 1987; also appeared in *Omega Syndrome* (also known as *Omega Seven*), New World, 1987.

PRINCIPAL TELEVISION APPEARANCES—Series: Transporter Chief O'Brien, *Star Trek: The Next Generation*, syndicated, 1987—. Episodic: *Remington Steele*, NBC; *Moonlighting*, ABC. Movies:

Perfect Witness, HBO, 1989; also *The Hidden Curriculum*, BBC; *Strangers*, Granada; *Nailed*, Granada.

RELATED CAREER—Company member, Great Lakes Shakespeare Festival, Cleveland, OH, 1982-83.

AWARDS: Drama-Logue Award, 1986, for *Diary of a Hunger Strike.*

ADDRESSES: AGENT—The Gage Group, 9229 Sunset Boulevard, Suite 306, Los Angeles, CA 90069.*

*   *   *

MERRILL, Dina   1925-

PERSONAL: Born Nedenia Hutton, December 29, 1925, in New York, NY; daughter of Edward F. Hutton (a stockbroker) and Marjorie Merriweather Post; married Stanley M. Rumbough, Jr., March 23, 1946 (divorced, December, 1966); married Cliff Robertson (an actor), December 21, 1966 (divorced); married Ted Hartley (a business executive), November 18, 1989; children: Stanley M., Nina, David (first marriage); Heather (second marriage). EDUCATION—Attended George Washington University, 1940-41; studied acting at the American Academy of Dramatic Arts and at the American Music and Dramatic Academy; also studied with Uta Hagen, Sanford Meisner, and David Craig. POLITICS—Republican.

DINA MERRILL

VOCATION: Actress.

CAREER: STAGE DEBUT—June, *The Man Who Came to Dinner,* Bucks County Playhouse, New Hope, PA, 1944. BROADWAY DEBUT—*The Mermaids Singing,* Empire Theatre, 1946. PRINCIPAL STAGE APPEARANCES—Title role, *Major Barbara* and aviatrix, *Misalliance,* both Shaw Festival, Niagara-on-the-Lake, ON, Canada, 1965; Mrs. Manningham, *Angel Street,* Lyceum Theatre, New York City, 1975; Lillian Hellman, *Are You Now, or Have You Ever Been,* Promenade Theatre, New York City, 1979; Mrs. Venable, *Suddenly Last Summer,* Horace Mann Theatre, New York City, 1981; Peggy Porterfield, *On Your Toes,* Virginia Theatre, New York City, then Dorothy Chandler Pavilion, Los Angeles, both 1983; Lady Bracknell, *The Importance of Being Earnest,* Samuel Beckett Theatre, New York City, 1985; also appeared in *George Washington Slept Here,* New York City, 1945; Desdemona, *Othello,* 1960; *The Torch-Bearers,* McCarter Theatre, Princeton, NJ, 1977; *Loved,* Syracuse Stage, Syracuse, NY, then PAF Playhouse, Huntington Station, NY, both 1978; *The Unexpected Guest,* Hartman Theatre Company, Stamford, CT, 1979; *The V.I.P.s,* John Drew Theatre, East Hampton, NY, 1981; with the Mirror Repertory Company, New York City, 1985; and in productions of *The Smile of the Cardboard Man,* HB Playwrights Foundation, New York City; *Surprise,* John Drew Theatre; as Olivia, *Twelfth Night;* and in *My Sister Eileen.*

MAJOR TOURS—*Voice of the Turtle,* U.S. cities, 1961; *Write Me a Murder,* U.S. cities, 1963.

FILM DEBUT—Sylvia, *Desk Set* (also known as *His Other Woman*), Twentieth Century-Fox, 1957. PRINCIPAL FILM APPEARANCES—Margie Solitaire, *A Nice Little Bank That Should Be Robbed* (also known as *How to Rob a Bank*), Twentieth Century-Fox, 1958; Ensign Benson, *Don't Give Up the Ship,* Paramount, 1959; Lieutenant Barbara Duran, *Operation Petticoat,* Universal, 1959; Emily Liggett, *Butterfield 8,* Metro-Goldwyn-Mayer (MGM), 1960; Jean Halstead, *The Sundowners,* Warner Brothers, 1960; Nikki Kovacs and Doris Delaney, *Twenty Plus Two,* Allied Artists, 1961; Karin Bell, *The Young Savages,* United Artists, 1961; Rita Behrens, *The Courtship of Eddie's Father,* MGM, 1963; Karin Grandstedt, *I'll Take Sweden,* United Artists, 1965; Velvet Green, *The Greatest,* Columbia, 1977; Antoinette Sloan Goddard, *A Wedding,* Twentieth Century-Fox, 1978; Connie Herschel, *Just Tell Me What You Want,* Warner Brothers, 1980; Cynthia Young, *Caddyshack II,* Warner Brothers, 1988; also appearaed in *Catch Me If You Can,* 1959; *Walking Major,* 1970; *Running Wild,* Golden Circle, 1973; *The Meal,* Ambassador, 1975; *Throw Out the Anchor,* 1972; *Deadly Encounter,* 1979; *Twisted,* Greenroom Entertainment.

PRINCIPAL TELEVISION APPEARANCES—Series: Estelle Modrian, *Hot Pursuit,* NBC, 1984. Mini-Series: Mrs. Hickinger, *Roots: The Next Generations,* ABC, 1979. Pilots: Beatrice Savarona, *The Lonely Profession,* NBC, 1969; Penelope Parkington, "The Parkingtons: Dear Penelope," *The Letters,* ABC, 1973; Helen Martinson, *Kingston: The Power Play,* NBC, 1976. Episodic: Calamity Jan, "The Great Escape" and Calamity Jan, "The Great Train Robbery," *Batman,* ABC, 1968; Jessica Cabot, *Hotel,* ABC, 1986; also "A Place Full of Strangers," *Four Star Playhouse,* CBS, 1955; "Return to Cassino" and "The Center of the Maze," *Playwrights '56,* NBC, 1956; "One for All," *Matinee Theatre,* NBC, 1958; "Spider Web," *Climax!,* CBS, 1958; "The Time of Your Life," *Playhouse 90,* CBS, 1958; "What Makes Sammy Run," *Sunday Showcase,* NBC, 1959; "The Fallen Idol," *Dupont Show of the Month,* CBS, 1959; "Murder Is a Private Affair," *Desilu Playhouse,* CBS, 1960; "Men in White," *Dupont Show of*

the Month, CBS, 1960; *Checkmate,* CBS, 1961; *Hong Kong,* ABC, 1961; "Brandenburg Gate," *U.S. Steel Hour,* CBS, 1961; "The Dispossessed," *Westinghouse Presents,* CBS, 1961; *The Investigators,* CBS, 1961; "Obituary for Mr. 'X' " and "The Court-Martial of Captain Wycliff," *The Dick Powell Show,* NBC, 1962; "Footnote to Fame," *Westinghouse Presents,* CBS, 1962; *Dr. Kildare,* NBC, 1962; *The Expendables,* ABC, 1962; "Bonfire," *Alfred Hitchcock Theatre,* CBS, 1962; *The New Breed,* ABC, 1962; *The Eleventh Hour,* NBC, 1963; *Burke's Law,* ABC, 1963; "The Candidate," *Bob Hope Chrysler Theatre,* NBC, 1963; *The Rogues,* NBC, 1964; *The Mickey Rooney Show,* ABC, 1964; "The Gun," *Kraft Suspense Theatre,* NBC, 1964.

The Rogues, NBC, 1965; "The Game," *Bob Hope Chrysler Theatre,* NBC, 1965; *The F.B.I.,* ABC, 1965; *Daniel Boone,* NBC, 1965; *Twelve O'Clock High,* ABC, 1966; *Daktari,* CBS, 1966; *Shenandoah,* ABC, 1966; *Bonanza,* NBC, 1966; "The Trap of Solid Gold," *Stage '67,* ABC, 1967; *Mission: Impossible,* CBS, 1969; *The Name of the Game,* NBC, 1969 and 1970; *The Bold Ones,* NBC, 1971; *The Men from Shiloh,* NBC, 1971; *Medical Center,* CBS, 1971; *The F.B.I.,* ABC, 1972; "Waiting Room," *Night Gallery,* NBC, 1972; *Cannon,* CBS, 1973; *Marcus Welby, M.D.,* CBS, 1973; "Hatred Unto Death," *Night Gallery,* NBC, 1973; *The Odd Couple,* ABC, 1974; *Ellery Queen,* NBC, 1975; *Switch,* CBS, 1976; *Hawaii Five-0,* CBS, 1976; *Quincy, M.E.,* NBC, 1976; also *The Alcoa Theatre,* NBC; *To Tell the Truth,* CBS. Movies: Brancie Hagen, *The Sunshine Patriot,* NBC, 1968; Emily Garth Pleasant, *Seven in Darkness,* ABC, 1969; Mrs. Greher, *Mr. and Mrs. Bo Jo Jones,* ABC, 1971; Florence Carlyle, *Family Flight,* ABC, 1972; Cele, *The Tenth Month,* CBS, 1979; also *Do Me a Favor—Don't Vote for My Mom* and *The Brass Ring.* Specials: *Bob Hope's Road to Hollywood,* NBC, 1983; also Nan Cooper, *The Alan King Show,* 1986.

RELATED CAREER—Fashion model, 1944-46; creative director, RKO Pavilion (a film production company); board member, American Music and Dramatic Academy.

NON-RELATED CAREER—Board of directors, E.F. Hutton, 1980—; board of directors, Continental Telecom, 1981—; vice-chairman, County of Manhattan Republican Party; president, New York Mission Society; board member, Juvenile Diabetes Foundation; board member, Joslin Diabetes Foundation; board member, New York Committee Olympic Ski Team.

ADDRESSES: AGENT—The Gersh Agency, 222 N. Canon Drive, Beverly Hills, CA 90210.*

*   *   *

MERRITT, Theresa   1922-

PERSONAL: Born September 24, 1922, in Newport News, VA.

VOCATION: Actress.

CAREER: PRINCIPAL STAGE APPEARANCES—Sister Henrietta Pinkston, *Trumpets of the Lord,* Brooks Atkinson Theatre, New York City, 1969; Ruby, *Five on the Black Hand Side,* American Place Theatre, St. Clement's Church Theatre, New York City, 1970; Berenice Sadie Brown, *F. Jasmine Addams,* Circle in the Square, New York City, 1971; Miss Maybell, *Don't Play Us Cheap,* Ethel Barrymore Theatre, New York City, 1972; Tituba,

The Crucible, Vivian Beaumont Theatre, New York City, 1972; Mammy, *Gone with the Wind,* Dorothy Chandler Pavilion, Los Angeles, then Curran Theatre, San Francisco, CA, both 1973; Evillene, *The Wiz,* Broadway Theatre, New York City, 1976; Berenice Sadie Brown, *The Member of the Wedding,* Hartford Stage Company, Hartford, CT, 1980; Mrs. Bruchinski, *Division Street,* Ambassador Theatre, Los Angeles, 1980; ensemble, *Talking With* (revue), Manhattan Theatre Club Downstage, New York City, 1982; Sarah Goldfine, *Something Different,* South Street Theatre, New York City, 1983; Ma Rainey, *Ma Rainey's Black Bottom,* Yale Repertory Theatre, New Haven, CT, 1983, then Cort Theatre, New York City, 1984; Mistress Quickly, *Henry IV, Part One,* New York Shakespeare Festival, Delacorte Theatre, New York City, 1987; Reverend Sister Rena Pinkston, *God's Trombones,* New Federal Theatre, Theatre of the Riverside Church, New York City, 1989. Also appeared in *La Dispute,* Theatre National Populaire, Lyttelton Theatre, London, 1976; *Trouble in Mind,* Pilgrim Theatre, New York City, 1979; *A Raisin in the Sun,* Studio Arena Theatre, Buffalo, NY, 1982; *Marriage,* Yale Repertory Theatre, 1985.

PRINCIPAL FILM APPEARANCES—Peggy, *They Might Be Giants,* Universal, 1977; Mrs. Crosby, *The Goodbye Girl,* Warner Brothers, 1977; Aunt Em, *The Wiz,* Universal, 1978; Arrabelle Smalls, *The Great Santini,* Orion/Warner Brothers, 1979; Jewel, *The Best Little Whorehouse in Texas,* Universal, 1982; Simone, *The Serpent and the Rainbow,* Universal, 1988.

PRINCIPAL TELEVISION APPEARANCES—Series: "Mama" Eloise Curtis, *That's My Mama,* ABC, 1974-75. Movies: *Miracle at Beekman's Place,* NBC, 1989.

AWARDS: Antoinette Perry Award nomination, Best Featured Actress in a Play, 1985, for *Ma Rainey's Black Bottom.*

ADDRESSES: AGENT—Bauman, Hiller, and Associates, 250 W. 57th Street, New York, NY 10107 and 5750 Wilshire Boulevard, Suite 512, Los Angeles, CA 90038.*

*   *   *

METCALF, Mark

PERSONAL: Born March 11, in Findlay, OH. EDUCATION— Attended the University of Michigan.

VOCATION: Actor and producer.

CAREER: OFF-BROADWAY DEBUT—Tom, *Creeps,* Folger Theatre Group, Playhouse II, 1973. PRINCIPAL STAGE APPEARANCES— Marcellus and Player King, *Hamlet,* New York Shakespeare Festival (NYSF), Delacorte Theatre, New York City, 1975; Jimmy, *The Beach Children* and Banner, *The Far-Off Sweet Forever,* both New Dramatists Inc., New York City, 1976; Leif, *Patrick Henry Lake Liquors,* Manhattan Theatre Club, New York City, 1976; Clark, then Billy, *Streamers,* NYSF, Mitzi E. Newhouse Theatre, New York City, 1976; Richard, *Mother Ryan,* New Dramatists Inc., 1977; Defense, *Salt Lake City Skyline,* NYSF, Public Theatre, New York City, 1980; Griever, *Blue Window,* Production Company, Theatre Guinevere, New York City, 1984; Jake Marlowe, *Mr. and Mrs.,* WPA Theatre, New York City, 1984; Romeo, *Romeo and Juliet,* Boat Basin Rotunda, New York City, 1984; Hank, *No Direction Home,* New Dramatists Inc., New York Theatre Studio,

New York City, 1984; Theseus and Oberon, *A Midsummer Night's Dream,* Directors Company, Musical Theatre Works, New York City, 1985; Marshall, *Trinity Site,* WPA Theatre, 1986; Dan Woodruf, *Talk Radio,* NYSF, Public Theatre, 1987; Zack, *Men in the Kitchen,* Long Wharf Theatre, New Haven, CT, 1986. Also appeared in *The Tempest,* McCarter Theatre, Princeton, NJ, 1972; *Macrune's Guevara,* Phoenix Sideshows, Playhouse II, New York City, 1975; *Long Day's Journey into Night,* Arena Stage, Washington, DC, 1975; *The Tooth of Crime,* Stagewest, West Springfield, MA, 1976; *Coyote Ugly,* Yale Repertory Theatre, New Haven, CT, 1982; *Accent on Youth,* Long Wharf Theatre, 1983; *All My Sons,* Stagewest, 1984; *Of Mice and Men,* Roundabout Theatre, New York City, 1987; with the Milwaukee Repertory Company, Milwaukee, WI, 1970-71; with the Seattle Repertory Theatre, Seattle, WA, 1974-75.

PRINCIPAL FILM APPEARANCES—Pratt, *Julia,* Twentieth Century-Fox, 1977; Doug Neidermeyer, *National Lampoon's Animal House,* Universal, 1978; Dooley, *Where the Buffalo Roam,* Universal, 1980; Jim "Ox" Connolly, *Chilly Scenes of Winter* (also known as *Head Over Heels*), United Artists, 1982; Mike, *The Final Terror* (also known as *Campsite Massacre, Bump in the Night,* and *The Forest Primeval*), Comworld/Watershed/Roth, 1983; Andrews, *Almost You,* Twentieth Century-Fox/TLC, 1984; Eric, *The Oasis,* Titan, 1984; Joe, *The Heavenly Kid,* Orion, 1985; Aguilla Beckersted, *One Crazy Summer,* Warner Brothers, 1986; George Harkness Skeel, *Mr. North,* Samuel Goldwyn, 1988.

PRINCIPAL FILM WORK—Producer (with Amy Robinson and Griffin Dunne), *Chilly Scenes of Winter* (also known as *Head Over Heels*), United Artists, 1982.

PRINCIPAL TELEVISION APPEARANCES—Episodic: David Lewis, *Teachers Only,* NBC, 1982; Brody, *Miami Vice,* NBC, 1988; Nathan Kirkpatrick, *A Man Called Hawk,* ABC, 1989.

ADDRESSES: AGENT—Agency for the Performing Arts, 9000 Sunset Boulevard, Suite 1200, Los Angeles, CA 90069.*

*   *   *

MICHAELS, Marilyn   1943-

PERSONAL: Born Marilyn Sternberg, February 26, 1943; daughter of Harold (an opera singer) and Fraydele (a performer on the Yiddish stage; maiden name, Oyshera) Sternberg; married Peter Wilk (a surgeon), March 27, 1983; children: Mark Edward. EDUCATION—Graduated from the High School of Music and Art. POLITICS—Democrat. RELIGION—Jewish.

VOCATION: Comedienne, actress, and impressionist.

CAREER: STAGE DEBUT—Fanny Brice, *Funny Girl,* State Fair Music Hall, Dallas, TX, 1965. PRINCIPAL STAGE APPEARANCES— One-woman concert, Town Hall, New York City; also appeared in *Who Does She Think Is?* (one-woman show).

MAJOR TOURS—Fanny Brice, *Funny Girl,* U.S. cities, 1965-66.

TELEVISION DEBUT—*The Ed Sullivan Show,* CBS, 1962. PRINCIPAL TELEVISION APPEARANCES—Series: Regular, *The Kopykats,* ABC, 1972; regular, *ABC Comedy Hour,* ABC, 1972. Pilots: *The Singers,* CBS, 1969. Episodic: *The Love Boat,* ABC, 1985; *On*

Stage America, syndicated, 1985; also *On Broadway Tonight*, CBS; *The Wil Schreiner Show*, syndicated; *The Tonight Show*, NBC; *Star Search*, syndicated; *Truth or Consequences*, syndicated; *Regis Philbin's Morning Show*, syndicated; *Hollywood Squares*, syndicated; *Wordplay*, syndicated; *Win, Lose, or Draw*, syndicated; *P.M. Magazine*, syndicated; *A.M. Los Angeles*. Specials: *Ed Sullivan's Broadway*, CBS, 1973; *Dean Martin Celebrity Roast: Dan Haggerty*, NBC, 1977; *Juke Box Award Show*, NBC.

RELATED CAREER—Actress and impressionist in television commercials; nightclub and cabaret performer throughout the United States, including the Riviera and Sahara, both Las Vegas, NV; the Rainbow Grill and Les Mouches, both New York City; the Improv and Hollywood's Backlot (Studio One), both Los Angeles; and at resorts in Atlantic City, Lake Tahoe, Chicago, and Miami.

NON-RELATED CAREER—Artist, paintings exhibited at the Norval Gallery, New York City, and the Gallery of Fine Arts, Palm Beach, FL.

RECORDINGS: ALBUMS—(Performer with Fradele and Moishe Oysher; also producer) *An Oysher Album* and *Sex Symbol—Superstar*.

WRITINGS: Short story published in *US* magazine.

ADDRESSES: AGENT—William Morris Agency, 151 El Camino Drive, Beverly Hills, CA 90212 and 1350 Avenue of the Americas, New York, NY 10019. MANAGER—Richard Gordon, 8401 Fountain Avenue, Los Angeles, CA 90069.

*   *   *

MICHELL, Keith   1928-

PERSONAL: Born December 1, 1928, in Adelaide, South Australia; son of Joseph (a furniture manufacturer) and Maud Alice (Aslat) Michell; married Jeannette Laura Sterke (an actress and art instructor), October 18, 1957; children: Paul Joseph, Helena Elizabeth Anne. EDUCATION—Attended Adelaide University, 1948; trained for the stage at the Old Vic Theatre School, 1949-50.

VOCATION: Actor, director, writer, and producer.

CAREER: STAGE DEBUT—Roger, *Lover's Leap*, Playbox Theatre, Adelaide, South Australia, 1947. LONDON DEBUT—Charles II, *And So to Bed*, New Theatre, 1951. BROADWAY DEBUT—Nestor and Oscar, *Irma La Douce*, Plymouth Theatre, 1960. PRINCIPAL STAGE APPEARANCES—Petruchio, *The Taming of the Shrew*, Theseus, *A Midsummer Night's Dream*, Tybalt, *Romeo and Juliet*, and Troilus, *Troilus and Cressida*, all Shakespeare Memorial Theatre Company, Stratford-on-Avon, U.K., 1954; Macduff, *Macbeth*, Master Ford, *The Merry Wives of Windsor*, Orsino, *Twelfth Night*, and Parolles, *All's Well That Ends Well*, all Shakespeare Memorial Theatre Company, 1955; title role, *Don Juan*, Royal Court Theatre, London, 1956; Benedick, *Much Ado About Nothing*, Old Vic Company, London, 1956; Proteus, *Two Gentlemen of Verona*, Antony, *Antony and Cleopatra*, and Aaron, *Titus Andronicus*, all Old Vic Company, 1957; Nestor-le-Fripe and Oscar, *Irma La Douce*, Lyric Theatre, London, 1958, then National Theatre, Washington, DC, 1960; Vicomte de Valmont, *The Art of Seduction*, Aldwych Theatre, London, 1962; Don John, *The Chances* and Ithocles, *The Broken Heart*, both Chichester Theatre Festival, Chichester, U.K., 1962; Count, *The Rehearsal*, Royale Theatre,

New York City, 1963; Robert Browning, *Robert and Elizabeth*, Lyric Theatre, 1964; Kain Sutherland, *Kain*, Yvonne Arnaud Theatre, Guildford, U.K., 1966; Henry VIII, *The King's Mare*, Garrick Theatre, London, 1966; Don Quixote, *Man of La Mancha*, Piccadilly Theatre, London, 1968, then Martin Beck Theatre, New York City, 1969.

Peter Abelard, *Abelard and Heloise*, Wyndham's Theatre, London, 1970, then Ahmanson Theatre, Los Angeles, 1971, later Brooks Atkinson Theatre, New York City, 1971; title role, *Hamlet*, Bankside Globe Theatre, London, 1972; Robert Browning, *Dear Love*, Comedy Theatre, London, 1973; the Director, *Tonight We Improvise*, title role, *Oedipus Tyrannus*, and *Keith Michell in Concert* (one-man show), all Chichester Theatre Festival, 1973; title role, *Cyrano de Bergerac* and Iago, *Othello*, both Chichester Theatre Festival, 1975, then Hong Kong Arts Festival, Hong Kong, 1976; Becket, *Murder in the Cathedral*, Chichester Theatre Festival, 1977; Magnus, *The Apple Cart*, Chichester Theatre Festival, then Phoenix Theatre, London, both 1977; Sherlock Holmes, *The Crucifer of Blood*, Haymarket Theatre, London, 1979; Oscar Jaffe, *On the Twentieth Century*, Her Majesty's Theatre, London, 1980; Pete McGynty, *Pete McGinty and the Dreamtime*, Melbourne Theatre Company, Melbourne, Australia, 1981; Rochester, *Jane Eyre*, Chichester Theatre Festival, 1986; Georges, *La Cage aux Folles*, Palace Theatre, New York City, 1984; Sir W. Gordon Cumming, *The Royal Baccarat Scandal*, Chichester Theatre, Festival, 1988, then Haymarket Theatre, 1989. Also appeared in *The First Four Hundred Years*, Comedy Theatre, Melbourne, Australia, 1964; *The Fire of London*, Mermaid Theatre, London, 1966; as Major Mathieu, *M. Perichon's Travels*, 1976; in *The Captain Beaky Christmas Show*, London, 1981-82; *On the Rocks*, Chichester Theatre Festival, 1982; and as Prospero, *The Tempest*, Brisbane, Australia, 1982.

PRINCIPAL STAGE WORK—Co-producer, *Kain*, Yvonne Arnaud Theatre, Guildford, U.K., 1966; director, *A Month in the Country* and *The Confederacy*, both Chichester Theatre Festival, Chichester, U.K., both 1973; director and designer, *Twelfth Night*, Chichester Theatre Festival, 1976; director and designer, *In Order of Appearance*, Chichester Theatre Festival, 1977.

MAJOR TOURS—Bassanio, *The Merchant of Venice*, Duckworth, *Black Arrow*, and Merrythought, *Knight of the Burning Pestle*, Young Vic Theatre Company, U.K. and European cities, 1950-51; Orlando, *As You Like It* and Hotspur, *Henry IV, Part I*, Shakespeare Memorial Theatre Company, Australian cities, 1952-53; Thomas, *The Lady's Not for Burning*, New Zealand Players Company, New Zealand cities, 1954; Magnus, *The Apple Cart* and title role, *Othello*, both Chichester Festival Company, European cities, 1977; Georges, *La Cage aux Folles*, U.S. and Australian cities, 1984-85; Augustus John, *Portraits*, U.K. cities, 1987; also appeared in *The First Four Hundred Years*, Australian and New Zealand cities, 1964; *Amadeus*, U.K. cities, 1983.

FILM DEBUT—Harry Bell, *True As a Turtle*, Rank, 1957. PRINCIPAL FILM APPEARANCES—Colonel St. Gerard, *Dangerous Exile*, Rank, 1958; Sir Paul Deverill, *The Gypsy and the Gentleman*, Rank, 1958; Cass Michaels, *All Night Long*, Rank, 1961; Jason, *The Hellfire Club*, Embassy, 1963; Malcolm Marsh, *Seven Seas to Calais*, Metro-Goldwyn-Mayer (MGM), 1963; Dr. Alan Hewitt, *Prudence and the Pill*, Twentieth Century-Fox, 1968; Hubert Morillon, *House of Cards*, Universal, 1969; Adam Booth, *The Executioner*, Columbia, 1970; King Henry VIII, *Henry VIII and His Six Wives*, MGM/EMI, 1972; voice characterization, *Grendel, Grendel, Grendel* (animated), Victorian Film Corporation, 1981;

Preston Turner, *Cross Creek*, Universal, 1983; Colonel Wilson, *The Deceivers*, Cinecom, 1988; also appeared in *Moments*, Pemini Organisation, 1974.

PRINCIPAL TELEVISION APPEARANCES—Series: *My Brother Tom*, 1987. Mini-Series: Henry VIII, *The Six Wives of Henry VIII*, BBC, 1970, then CBS, 1971, later *Masterpiece Theatre*, PBS, 1972; Captain James Cook, *Captain Cook*, 1988, then TNT, 1989. Episodic: Mark Antony, "Antony and Cleopatra," *Spread of the Eagle*, BBC, 1963; Dennis Stanton, *Murder, She Wrote*, CBS, 1988 and 1989. Movies: Jacob, *The Story of Jacob and Joseph*, ABC, 1974; King David, *The Story of David*, ABC, 1976; Matthew Poole, *The Tenth Month*, CBS, 1979; Pontius Pilate, *The Day Christ Died*, CBS, 1980. Specials: John Churchill, "Soldier in Love," *Hallmark Hall of Fame*, NBC, 1967; Mark Antony, *Julius Caesar*, BBC, then *The Shakespeare Plays*, PBS, 1979; Robin Oakapple, *Ruddigore*, PBS, 1985; also *Keith Michell in Concert at Chichester*, 1974; Grand Inquisitor, *The Gondoliers*, PBS; Major General Stanley, *The Pirates of Penzance*, PBS; *The Keith Michell Special; The Keith Michell Christmas Show; Keith Michell at the Shows*. Also appeared as Professor Higgins, *Pygmalion*, BBC, 1956; Rudolph, *Mayerling Affair*, BBC, 1956; Gaston, *Traveller Without Luggage*, ATV, 1959; Paul, *Guardian Angel*, ITV, 1960; Hector, *Tiger at the Gates*, ITV, 1960; Heathcliff, *Wuthering Heights*, BBC, 1962; Clarry, *Shifting Heart*, ITV, 1962; Cordiner, *Bergonzi Hand*, BBC, 1963; Sir Robert Chiltern, *An Ideal Husband*, 1970; in *Ring 'round the Moon*, BBC, 1964; *The Story of the Marlboroughs*, BBC; as Kain Sutherland, *Kain;* Robert Browning, *Dear Love;* Captain Beaky, *Captain Beaky and His Band;* Captain Beaky, *Captain Beaky Volume 2;* in *The Great Impersonation; Loyalties;* and *Act of Violence*.

RELATED CAREER—Artistic director, Chichester Theatre Festival, Chichester, U.K., 1972-76.

NON-RELATED CAREER—Artist and art teacher.

WRITINGS: STAGE—*In Order of Appearance*, Chichester Theatre Festival, Chichester, U.K., 1977; *Pete McGynty and the Dreamtime*, Melbourne Theatre Company, Melbourne, Australia, 1981. OTHER—*Practically Macrobiotic* (cookbook), 1987.

RECORDINGS: ALBUMS—*Ancient and Modern*, Spark; *At the Shows*, Spark; *Words, Words, Words*, Spark; also *The Sonnets and the Prophets; Captain Beaky and His Band; Captain Beaky Volume 2*.

AWARDS: London Critics' Award, Best Actor in a Musical, 1968, for *Man of La Mancha;* Society of Film and Television Arts Award, Best Actor, 1970; British Academy of Film and Television Arts Award, Best Television Actor, 1970, for *The Six Wives of Henry VIII* and *An Ideal Husband;* Emmy Award, Outstanding Single Performance By an Actor in a Leading Role, 1971, for *The Six Wives of Henry VIII;* Show Business Personality of the Year Award from the Grand Order of Water Rats, Sun Television Award, Top Actor, Special Award from the Royal Variety Club of Great Britain, and Royal Academy of Television Arts Award, Outstanding Single Performance By an Actor in a Leading Role, all 1971; British Film Award from the *Evening News*, 1973; Logie Award, 1974.

MEMBER: British Actors' Equity Association.

SIDELIGHTS: RECREATIONS—Painting, photography, swimming, and riding.

Since 1959 Keith Michell's paintings, silk screens, and lithographs have been exhibited at one-man shows in England and the United States. His work has been displayed at the John Whibley Gallery in London and the Wright-Hepburn Webster Gallery in New York City. He has also provided illustrations *Captain Beaky, Captain Beaky, Volume 2, Alice in Wonderland* (BBC presentation), *Pete McGynty*, and *Practically Macrobiotic*.

ADDRESSES: AGENT—Jean Diamond, London Management Ltd., 235 Regent Street, London W1, England.

*   *   *

MIDDLEMASS, Frank   1919-

PERSONAL: Born in 1919.

VOCATION: Actor.

CAREER: PRINCIPAL STAGE APPEARANCES—Polonius, *Hamlet*, Chorus, *Romeo and Juliet*, and Pompey, *Measure for Measure*, all Bristol Old Vic Theatre Company, City Center Theatre, New York City, 1967; Dr. Grapielkof, *Spitting Image*, Hampstead Theatre Club, London, 1968; Sir Epicure Mammon, *The Alchemist* and Fool, *King Lear*, both Nottingham Playhouse, Nottingham, U.K., 1969, then Old Vic Theatre, London, 1970; Gripe, *The Confederacy*, Chichester Festival Theatre, Chichester, U.K., 1974; Ulrik Brendel, *Rosmersholm*, Royal Haymarket Theatre, London, 1977; Major Petkoff, *Arms and the Man*, Greenwich Theatre, London, 1978; M'Comas, *You Never Can Tell*, Lyric Hammersmith Theatre, London, 1979; Boss Mangan, *Heartbreak House*, Royal Haymarket Theatre, 1983. Also appeared in *Widowers' Houses*, English Stage Company, Royal Court Theatre, London, 1970.

MAJOR TOURS—Chorus, *Romeo and Juliet*, U.S. cities, 1967.

PRINCIPAL FILM APPEARANCES—Guest, *Frankenstein Must Be Destroyed!*, Warner Brothers, 1969; Bruce, *Otley*, Columbia, 1969; Sir Charles Lyndon, *Barry Lyndon*, Warner Brothers, 1975; Dr. Windsor, *The Island*, Universal, 1980; Dr. Sunderland, *A Swarm in May*, ICA Projects, 1983; voice of Caterpillar, *Dreamchild*, Universal, 1985; also appeared in *Say Hello to Yesterday*, Cinerama, 1971; *Squaring the Circle* (documentary), TVS/Metromedia Producers Corporation/Television South/Britannic Films, 1983.

PRINCIPAL TELEVISION APPEARANCES—Mini-Series: Charles Poldark, *Poldark*, BBC, then *Masterpiece Theatre*, PBS, 1977; Henry Barnes, *A Family Affair*, Entertainment Channel, 1982; King Maajid, *Lace*, ABC, 1984; Uncle Pumblechook, *Great Expectations*, Disney Channel, 1989; also *Kean*, BBC, then *Masterpiece Theatre*, PBS, 1979; *Crime and Punishment*, BBC, then *Masterpiece Theatre*, PBS, 1980; *To Serve Them All My Days*, 1980, then *Masterpiece Theatre*, PBS; "Winston Churchill: The Wilderness Years," *Masterpiece Theatre*, PBS, 1981; *The Bretts*, Central Television, then *Masterpiece Theatre*, PBS, 1987. Pilots: Dr. Henriques, *Madame Sin*, ABC, 1972. Specials: Pompey, *Measure for Measure*, BBC, then *The Shakespeare Plays*, PBS, 1979; *Masterpiece Theatre: Fifteen Years*, PBS, 1986. Also appeared in *The Invisible Man*, 1982; *The First Part of King Henry VI*, 1983; *The Second Part of King Henry VI*, 1983; *King Lear* and *The Blue Carbuncle*.

PRINCIPAL RADIO APPEARANCES—Episodic: "Mad for the Love of Old Balconies," *Globe Theatre*, BBC Radio 4, 1989.

ADDRESSES: AGENT—Vernon Conway Ltd., 19 London Street, Paddington, London W2, England.*

*   *   *

MILIUS, John   1944-

PERSONAL: Full name, John Frederick Milius; born April 11, 1944, in St. Louis, MO; son of William Styx (a shoe manufacturer) and Elizabeth (Roe) Milius; married Renee Fabri, January 7, 1967 (marriage ended); married Celia Kaye (an actress), February 26, 1978; children: Ethan Jedediah, Marco Alexander (first marriage). EDUCATION—Attended Los Angeles City College, 1966; studied filmmaking at the University of Southern California, 1968.

VOCATION: Screenwriter, director, and producer.

CAREER: Also see *WRITINGS* below. PRINCIPAL FILM APPEARANCES—State trooper, *Deadhead Miles*, filmed in 1970, released by Paramount, 1982; also appeared in *Conan the Barbarian*, Universal, 1982.

PRINCIPAL FILM WORK—All as director, unless indicated: *Dillinger*, American International, 1973; *The Wind and the Lion*, Metro-Goldwyn-Mayer/United Artists (MGM/UA), 1975; *Big Wednesday*, Warner Brothers, 1978; executive producer, *1941*, Universal, 1979; executive producer, *Hardcore* (also known as *The Hardcore Life*), Columbia, 1979; executive producer, *Used Cars*, Columbia, 1980; *Conan the Barbarian*, Universal, 1982; producer (with Buzz Feitshans), *Uncommon Valor*, Paramount, 1983; *Red Dawn*, MGM/UA, 1984; *Farewell to the King*, Orion, 1989.

RELATED CAREER—Production assistant, American International Pictures, 1968; co-founder, American Zoetrope (a film production company), 1969; instructor of motion picture script analysis, University of Southern California, 1973, and advanced motion picture script analysis, 1974; founder, A-Team Productions, 1979.

WRITINGS: FILM—(With James Gordon White and Willard Huyck) *The Devil's 8*, American International, 1969; (with Alan Caillou) *Evel Knievel*, Fanfare, 1971; (uncredited) *Dirty Harry*, Warner Brothers, 1972; (with Edward Anhalt) *Jeremiah Johnson*, Warner Brothers, 1972; *The Life and Times of Judge Roy Bean*, National General, 1972; (with Michael Cimino) *Magnum Force*, Warner Brothers, 1973; *Dillinger*, American International, 1973; *The Wind and the Lion*, Metro-Goldwyn-Mayer/United Artists (MGM/UA), 1975; (with Dennis Aaberg) *Big Wednesday*, Warner Brothers, 1978; (with Francis Ford Coppola) *Apocalypse Now*, United Artists, 1979; (with Oliver Stone) *Conan the Barbarian*, Universal, 1982; (with Kevin Reynolds) *Red Dawn*, MGM/UA, 1984; *Farewell to the King*, Orion, 1989. TELEVISION—Pilots: (With William F. Nolan) *Melvin Purvis—G Man*, ABC, 1974. OTHER—*The Life and Times of Judge Roy Bean* (novel), Bantam, 1973.

AWARDS: National Student Film Festival Award, 1968; Heritage Wrangler Award, 1972, for *Jeremiah Johnson;* Writers Guild of America Award nomination, 1975, for *The Wind and the Lion;* National Bell Ringer Educational Award and Writers Guild of America Award nomination, both 1978, for *Big Wednesday;* Academy Award nomination (with Francis Ford Coppola), Best Screenplay

Based on Material from Another Medium, and Writers Guild of America Award nomination, both 1979, for *Apocalypse Now*.

SIDELIGHTS: RECREATIONS—History, surfing, collecting guns.

ADDRESSES: AGENT—Jeff Berg, International Creative Management, 8899 Beverly Boulevard, Los Angeles, CA 90048.*

*   *   *

MILLER, Dick   1928-

PERSONAL: Born December 25, 1928, in New York, NY. EDUCATION—Graduated from Columbia University; graduate work at the New York University School of Dramatic Arts; also attended the City College of New York. MILITARY—U.S. Navy.

VOCATION: Actor.

CAREER: PRINCIPAL STAGE APPEARANCES—Understudy, *It's a Bird . . . It's a Plane . . . It's Superman*, Alvin Theatre, New York City, 1966.

PRINCIPAL FILM APPEARANCES—Tall Tree, *Apache Woman*, Associated Releasing, 1955; Sergeant Neil, *It Conquered the World*, American International, 1956; Ben, *Carnival Rock*, Howco, 1957; Joe Piper, *Not of This Earth*, Allied Artists, 1957; Jimmy Tonto, *Gunslinger*, Associated Releasing Corporation, 1957; Shorty, *Rock All Night*, American International, 1957; Mort, *Sorority Girl* (also known as *The Bad One* and *Confessions of a Sorority Girl*), American International, 1957; Dave Royer, *War of the Satellites*, Allied Artists, 1958; Walter, *A Bucket of Blood*, American International, 1959; Fouch, *Little Shop of Horrors*, Filmgroup, 1961; Stefan, *The Terror* (also known as *Lady of the Shadows*), American International, 1963; Rills, *Wild, Wild Winter*, Universal, 1966; Zollicoffer, *A Time for Killing* (also known as *The Long Ride Home*), Columbia, 1967; Cash, *The Trip*, American International, 1967; rifleman, *Executive Action*, National General, 1973; Forgarty, *Truck Turner*, American International, 1974; Bonny, *Big Bad Mama*, New World, 1974; Wilbur Janeway, *Crazy Mama*, New World, 1975; Hugo, *Darktown Strutters* (also known as *Get Down and Boogie*), New World, 1975; Birdie, *White Line Fever*, Columbia, 1975; Walter Paisley, *Hollywood Boulevard*, New World, 1976; Mack, *Moving Violation*, Twentieth Century-Fox, 1976; Bernie, *Mr. Billion*, Twentieth Century-Fox, 1977; Palm Club owner, *New York, New York*, United Artists, 1977; Sam, *Summer School Teachers*, New World, 1977; Sergeant Bresner, *I Wanna Hold Your Hand*, Universal, 1978; Buck Gardner, *Piranha*, New World, 1978; Jerry, *Starhops*, First American, 1978; Patek, *The Lady in Red* (also known as *Guns, Sin, and Bathtub Gin*), New World, 1979; Police Chief Klein, *Rock 'n' Roll High School*, New World, 1979.

Watchman, *Heartbeeps*, Universal, 1981; Walter Paisley, *The Howling*, AVCO-Embassy, 1981; Crazy Mel, *Space Raiders* (also known as *Starchild*), New World, 1983; Walter Paisley, *Twilight Zone—The Movie*, Warner Brothers, 1983; Mr. Futterman, *Gremlins*, Warner Brothers, 1984; pawn shop clerk, *The Terminator*, Orion, 1984; waiter, *After Hours*, Warner Brothers, 1985; Charles Drake, *Explorers*, Paramount, 1985; Steve, *Armed Response*, Cinetel, 1986; Walter Paisley, *Chopping Mall* (also known as *Killbots* and *R.O.B.O.T.*), Concorde, 1986; police armorer, *Night of the Creeps*, Tri-Star, 1986; cab driver, *Inner Space*, Warner

Brothers, 1987; Max King, *Project X*, Twentieth Century-Fox, 1987. Also appeared in *The Oklahoma Woman*, American Releasing, 1956; *Naked Paradise* (also known as *Thunder Over Hawaii*), American International, 1957; *The Undead*, American International, 1957; *Attack of the Crab Monsters*, Allied Artists, 1957; *The Intruder* (also known as *The Stranger, I Hate Your Guts*, and *Shame*), Pathe-American, 1962; *Ski Party*, American International, 1965; *The Dirty Dozen*, Metro-Goldwyn-Mayer (MGM), 1967; *St. Valentine's Day Massacre* Twentieth Century-Fox, 1967; *Targets*, Paramount, 1968; *The Legend of Lylah Clare*, MGM, 1968; *The Wild Racers*, American International, 1968; *The Grissom Gang*, Cinerama, 1971; *Ulzana's Raid*, Universal, 1972; *The Slams*, MGM, 1973; *The Student Teachers*, New World, 1973; *Night Call Nurses*, New World, 1974; *Candy Stripe Nurses*, New World, 1974; *Capone*, Twentieth Century-Fox, 1975; *Hustle*, Paramount, 1975; *Cannonball* (also known as *Carquake*), New World, 1976; *Grand Theft Auto*, New World, 1977; *Corvette Summer* (also known as *The Hot One*), United Artists, 1978; *Game Show Models*, 1978; *Dr. Heckyl and Mr. Hype*, Cannon, 1980; *Used Cars*, Columbia, 1980; *Vortex*, B Movies, 1982; *White Dog* (also known as *Trained to Kill*), Paramount, 1982; *Get Crazy*, Embassy, 1983; *All the Right Moves*, Twentieth Century-Fox, 1983; *Heart Like a Wheel*, Twentieth Century-Fox, 1983; *Lies*, Alpha, 1984; *The Burbs*, Universal, 1988.

PRINCIPAL TELEVISION APPEARANCES—Series: Host (with Bobby Sherwood), *Midnight Snack*, CBS, 1950; Mr. Lou Mackie, *Fame*, Fox, 1985-87; also host, *The Dick Miller Show*, WOR-TV. Mini-Series: Drunk, *V—The Final Battle*, NBC, 1984. Pilots: Theater owner, *W*A*L*T*E*R*, CBS, 1984. Episodic: *Taxi*, ABC, 1979. Movies: Investigator Ned, *The Eleventh Victim*, CBS, 1979.

PRINCIPAL RADIO APPEARANCES—Series: *The Dick Miller Show*, WMCA (New York City).

RELATED CAREER—Producer, director, and writer of television and radio shows during the 1950s; disk jockey.

NON-RELATED CAREER—Commercial artist; psychologist at Bellevue Mental Hygiene Clinic, New York City, and Queens General Hospital Psychiatric Department, Queens, NY; semi-professional football player; boxer.*

*   *   *

MILLER, Nolan   1935-

PERSONAL: Born January 8, 1935, in Texas; son of Bert (an oil rigger) and Marie (English) Miller; married Sandra Stream, August 23, 1980. EDUCATION—Attended Chouinard Art Academy.

VOCATION: Costume designer.

CAREER: PRINCIPAL FILM WORK—Costume designer: *Harlow*, Magna, 1965; *How to Commit Marriage*, Cinerama, 1969; *Mr. Mom* (also known as *Mr. Mum*), Twentieth Century-Fox, 1983; *The Princess Academy*, Empire, 1987; *Skin Deep*, Twentieth Century-Fox, 1989.

FIRST TELEVISION WORK—Costume designer, *Matinee Theatre*, NBC. PRINCIPAL TELEVISION WORK—All as costume designer, unless indicated. Series: *The June Allyson Show*, CBS, 1959-61; *The Dick Powell Show*, NBC, 1961-63; *Burke's Law*, ABC, 1963-

66; *Green Acres*, CBS, 1965-71; *The Survivors* (also known as *Harold Robbins' "The Survivors"*), ABC, 1969-70; *Charlie's Angels*, ABC, 1976-81; *The Love Boat*, ABC, 1977-86; *Vega$*, ABC, 1978-81; *Hart to Hart*, ABC, 1979-84; *Aloha Paradise*, ABC, 1981; *Dynasty*, ABC, 1981-89; *Matt Houston*, ABC, 1982-85; wardrobe consultant, *Hotel*, ABC, 1983-88; *The Colbys*, ABC, 1985-87; wardrobe consultant, *Life with Lucy*, ABC, 1986; wardrobe consultant, *HeartBeat*, ABC, 1988. Mini-Series: *Hollywood Wives*, ABC, 1985; *Crossings*, ABC, 1985. Pilots: *Charlie's Angels*, ABC, 1976; *Lanigan's Rabbi* (also known as *Friday the Rabbi Slept Late*), NBC, 1976; *Return to Fantasy Island*, ABC, 1978; *Kate Bliss and the Ticker Tape Kid*, ABC, 1978; *Casino*, ABC, 1980; *Shooting Stars*, ABC, 1983; *Letters from Three Lovers*, ABC, 1978; *Velvet*, ABC, 1984; *No Man's Land*, NBC, 1984; *International Airport*, ABC, 1985; *Mr. and Mrs. Ryan*, ABC, 1986; wardrobe consultant, *Hope Division*, ABC, 1987; *Divided We Stand*, ABC, 1988; *The Loner*, ABC, 1988. Episodic: *Zane Gray Theatre* (also known as *Dick Powell's Zane Gray Theatre*), CBS.

Movies: *The House That Would Not Die*, ABC, 1970; *Crowhaven Farm*, ABC, 1970; *Love, Hate, Love*, ABC, 1971; *Taste of Evil*, ABC, 1971; *Say Goodbye, Maggie Cole*, ABC, 1972; *Heat of Anger*, CBS, 1972; *The Great American Beauty Contest*, ABC, 1973; *The Bait*, ABC, 1973; *The Affair*, ABC, 1973; *Hit Lady*, ABC, 1974; *The Legend of Valentino*, ABC, 1975; *Lady of the House*, NBC, 1978; *The Users*, ABC, 1978; *Wild and Wooly*, ABC, 1978; *Love's Savage Fury*, ABC, 1979; *The French Atlantic Affair*, ABC, 1979; *Murder Can Hurt You!*, ABC, 1980; *Sizzle*, ABC, 1981; *Help Wanted: Male*, CBS, 1981; *Paper Dolls*, ABC, 1982; *Bare Essence*, CBS, 1982; *The Day the Bubble Burst*, NBC, 1982; *Fantasies*, ABC, 1982; *Don't Go to Sleep*, ABC, 1982; *The Making of a Male Model*, ABC, 1983; *The Wild Women of Chastity Gulch*, ABC, 1983; *Dark Mirror*, ABC, 1984; *Malice in Wonderland*, CBS, 1985; *There Must Be a Pony*, ABC, 1986; *The Two Mrs. Grenvilles*, CBS, 1987; *Poker Alice*, CBS, 1987; wardrobe consultant, *Harry's Hong Kong*, ABC, 1987; *A Stranger Waits*, CBS, 1987; *Cracked Up*, ABC, 1987; *Peter Gunn*, ABC, 1989; *Sweet Bird of Youth*, NBC, 1989. Specials: *58th Annual Academy Awards Presentation*, ABC, 1986.

RELATED CAREER—Founder, Nolan Miller Enterprises Inc. and Nolan Miller Ltd.; costume designer for theatre and Las Vegas stage productions and for television commercials.

NON-RELATED CAREER—Worked in a florist shop, Beverly Hills, CA.

AWARDS: Emmy Award, Best Costume Design, 1983, for *Dynasty;* Emmy Award nomination, Best Costume Design, 1985, for *Malice in Wonderland;* named Designer of the Year by the Atlanta Apparel Mart, 1989.

MEMBER: Costume Designers Guild, Screen Actors Guild, Academy of Television Arts and Sciences.

ADDRESSES: OFFICE—241 S. Robertson Boulevard, Beverly Hills, CA 90211. PUBLICIST—Michelle Bega, Levine/Schneider Public Relations, 8730 Sunset Boulevard, Sixth Floor, Los Angeles, CA 90069.

LIZA MINNELLI

MINNELLI, Liza   1946-

PERSONAL: Full name, Liza May Minnelli; born March 12, 1946, in Los Angeles, CA; daughter of Vincente Minnelli (a film director and producer) and Judy Garland (a singer and actress); married Peter Allen (a singer, songwriter, and actor), 1967 (divorced, 1972); married Jack Haley, Jr. (a producer), September 15, 1974 (divorced, 1979); married Mark Gero (a sculptor and producer), December 4, 1979. EDUCATION—Attended the University of Paris (Sorbonne), 1962-63; trained for the stage at the HB Studios with Uta Hagen and Herbert Berghof.

VOCATION: Singer, actress, and entertainer.

CAREER: OFF-BROADWAY DEBUT—Ethel Hofflinger, *Best Foot Forward*, Stage 73, 1963. PRINCIPAL STAGE APPEARANCES—Lili, *Carnival!*, Mineola Playhouse, Mineola, NY, 1964; title role, *Flora, the Red Menace*, Alvin Theatre, New York City, 1965; *Liza with a Z* (concert performance), Winter Garden Theatre, New York City, 1974; Roxie Hart, *Chicago*, 46th Street Theatre, New York City, 1975; Michelle Craig, *The Act*, Majestic Theatre, New York City, 1977; Lillian Hellman, *Are You Now, or Have You Ever Been*, Promenade Theatre, New York City, 1979; *Liza Minnelli in Concert with Roger Minami and Obba Babatunde* (concert performance), Carnegie Hall, New York City, 1979; Angel, *The Rink*, Martin Beck Theatre, New York City, 1984; *Liza Minnelli* (concert performance), Carnegie Hall, 1987. Also appeared in *Take Me Along* and *Flower Drum Song*, both Cape Cod Melody Top Theatre, Hyannis, MA, 1962; title role, *The Diary of Anne Frank*, 1962; *A Star-Spangled Gala*, Metropolitan Opera House, New York City, 1976; *An Evening with Alan Jay Lerner*, State Theatre, New York City, 1989; narrator, *The Owl and the Pussycat*, Martha Graham Dance Company, Metropolitan Opera House.

MAJOR TOURS—Title role, *The Diary of Anne Frank*, U.S. and European cities, 1962; Lili, *Carnival!*, U.S. cities, 1964; *Liza with a Z* (concert performance), international cities, 1975.

PRINCIPAL FILM APPEARANCES—Eliza, *Charlie Bubbles*, Universal, 1968; Pookie Adams, *The Sterile Cuckoo* (also known as *Pookie*), Paramount, 1969; Junie Moon, *Tell Me That You Love Me, Junie Moon*, Paramount, 1970; Sally Bowles, *Cabaret*, Allied Artists, 1972; voice of Dorothy, *Journey Back to Oz* (animated), Filmation, 1974; narrator, *That's Entertainment!*, Metro-Goldwyn-Mayer/United Artists (MGM/UA), 1974; Claire, *Lucky Lady*, Twentieth Century-Fox, 1975; Nina, *A Matter of Time*, American International, 1976; as herself, *Silent Movie*, Twentieth Century-Fox, 1976; Francine Evans, *New York, New York*, United Artists, 1977; Linda Marolla, *Arthur*, Warner Brothers, 1981; as herself, *The King of Comedy*, Twentieth Century-Fox, 1983; as herself, *The Muppets Take Manhattan*, Tri-Star, 1984; narrator, *That's Dancing!*, MGM/UA, 1984; Della Roberts, *Rent-a-Cop*, Kings Road Entertainment, 1988; Linda Marolla Bach, *Arthur II: On the Rocks*, Warner Brothers, 1988. Also appeared as child, *In the Good Old Summertime*, Metro-Goldwyn-Mayer, 1949; *A Great Wind Cometh*, 1984.

PRINCIPAL TELEVISION APPEARANCES—Episodic: *Ford Star Jubilee*, CBS, 1956; "The Princess and the Pea," *Faerie Tale Theatre*, Showtime, 1983; also *Mr. Broadway*, NBC; *That's Life*, ABC; *The Keefe Brasselle Show*, NBC; *The Judy Garland Show*, CBS; *The Ed Sullivan Show*, CBS. Movies: Mary-Lou Weisman, *A Time to Live*, NBC, 1985. Specials: *The Gene Kelly Pontiac Special*, CBS, 1959; *The Arthur Godfrey Show*, NBC, 1963; Little Red, *The Dangerous Christmas of Red Riding Hood*, ABC, 1965; *The Perry Como Springtime Special*, NBC, 1966; *The Alan King Show*, NBC, 1968; *Comedy Is King*, NBC, 1968; *Movin'*, CBS, 1970; *The Anthony Newley Show*, ABC, 1971; *Liza with a Z*, NBC, 1972; *Royal Variety Performance*, ABC, 1973; *The Mac Davis Special*, NBC, 1975; host, *Jubilee*, NBC, 1976; *Gene Kelly . . . An American in Pasadena*, CBS, 1978; *Baryshnikov on Broadway*, ABC, 1980; *Goldie and Liza Together*, CBS, 1980; *Mac Davis Tenth Anniversary Special: I Still Believe in Music*, NBC, 1980; *Salute to Lady Liberty*, CBS, 1984; *Those Fabulous Clowns*, HBO, 1984; *Liberty Weekend*, ABC, 1986; *Standing Room Only: Liza in London*, HBO, 1986; *Carnegie Hall: The Grand Reopening*, CBS, 1987; *Happy Birthday Hollywood*, ABC, 1987; *In Performance at the White House*, PBS, 1987; host, *Minnelli on Minnelli: Liza Remembers Vincente*, PBS, 1987; "Celebrating Gershwin," *Great Performances*, PBS, 1987; prostitute, Max, and Norman, *Liza Minnelli in Sam Found Out: A Triple Play*, ABC, 1988; "Gregory Peck—His Own Man," *Crazy About the Movies*, Cinemax, 1988; *Frank, Liza, and Sammy: The Ultimate Event*, Showtime, 1989; *The Songwriters Hall of Fame Twentieth Anniversary . . . The Magic of Music*, CBS, 1989.

RELATED CAREER—Performer in concerts and nightclubs throughout the world.

RECORDINGS: ALBUMS—*Best Foot Forward*, Cadence, 1963; *Judy and Liza at the London Palladium*, Capitol, 1964; *Flora, the Red Menace* (original cast recording), RCA, 1965; *The Dangerous Christmas of Red Riding Hood* (original soundtrack), ABC/Paramount, 1965; *New York, New York* (original soundtrack), United Artists, 1977; *The Act* (original cast recording), DRG, 1977; *The*

Rink (original cast recording), Polydor, 1984. Also *Tropical Nights,* 1977; *Liza Minnelli at Carnegie Hall,* 1987; *Liza Minnelli,* A&M; *Come Saturday Morning,* A&M; *It Amazes Me,* Capitol; *There Is a Time,* Capitol; *Liza with a Z,* Columbia; *Liza Minnelli: The Singer,* Columbia; *Liza Minnelli: Live at the Winter Garden,* Columbia; *Foursider,* A&M; *Maybe This Time,* Capitol.

AWARDS: Theatre World Award, 1963, for *Best Foot Forward;* Best Plays Citation, Best New Performer, and Antoinette Perry Award, Best Actress in a Musical, both 1965, for *Flora, the Red Menace;* David Di Donatello Award, Best Foreign Actress of the Year, and Academy Award nomination, Best Actress, both 1970, for *The Sterile Cuckoo;* Academy Award and British Academy Award, both Best Actress, 1972, and Golden Globe, Best Actress (Musical/Comedy), 1973, all for *Cabaret;* Las Vegas Entertainment Female Star of the Year, 1972 and 1974; special Antoinette Perry Award, 1974; Antoinette Perry Award, Best Actress in a Musical, 1978, for *The Act;* Antoinette Perry Award nomination, Best Actress in a Musical, 1984, for *The Rink;* Golden Globe, Best Performance By an Actress in a Mini-Series or Motion Picture Made for Television, 1986, for *A Time to Live.*

MEMBER: American Federation of Television and Radio Artists, Actors' Equity Association, Screen Actors Guild.

ADDRESSES: AGENTS—International Creative Management, 8899 Beverly Boulevard, Los Angeles, CA 90048 and 40 W. 57th Street, New York, NY 10022.*

*   *   *

MIOU-MIOU   1950-

PERSONAL: Born Sylvette Herry, February 22, 1950, in Paris, France; father, a policeman; mother, an operator of a fruit and vegetable stand; children: Angel (with Patrick Dewaere; an actor); Jeanne (with Julien Clerc; a singer).

VOCATION: Actress.

CAREER: PRINCIPAL FILM APPEARANCES—Marie-Ange, *Les Valseuses* (also known as *Going Places*), Cinema V, 1973; Monique, *Les Granges brulees* (also known as *The Burned Barns*), Twentieth Century-Fox/Lira, 1973; girl, *La Grande Trouille* (also known as *The Big Scare*), AMLF, 1974; Anita, *Pas de probleme!* (also known as *No Problem!*), Gaumont International, 1975; Rita, *Fraiche* (also known as *Love and Cool Water*), Gaumont International, 1975; Rosanna, *Marcia Trionfale* (also known as *La Marche triomphante* and *Victory March*), Cineriz, 1975; Lucy, *Un genio, due compari, un pollo* (also known as *The Genius*), Titanus, 1976; Marie, *Jonas—Qui aura 25 ans en l'an 2000* (also known as *Jonah—Who Will Be 25 in the Year 2000*), New Yorker, 1976; friend, *On aura tout vu* (also known as *We've Seen Everything*), Gaumont International, 1976; Marie, *F comme Fairbanks* (also known as *F for Fairbanks*), Gaumont International, 1976; Juliette, *Dites-lui que je l'aime* (also known as *Tell Him I Love Him*), World Marketing, 1977; Julia, *Les Routes du sud* (also known as *The Roads of the South*), Parafrance/Trinacra, 1978; Nicole, *Au revoir, a lundi* (also known as *Goodbye, See You Monday*), Gades, 1979; Marie Mage, *La Derobade* (also known as *The Getaway*), World Marketing, 1979.

Corinne Levasseur, *La Femme Flic* (also known as *The Woman*

Cop), AMLF, 1980; title role, *Josepha,* GEF/CCFC, 1981; Julie Boucher, *Est-ce bien raisonnable?* (also known as *Is This Really Reasonable?*), AMLF, 1981; Marie, *La Gueule du loup* (also known as *The Jaws of the Wolf*), Union Generale Cinematographique, 1981; Madeleine, *Coup de foudre* (also known as *Entre Nous, Between Us,* and *At First Sight*), Metro-Goldwyn-Mayer/United Artists, 1983; Jessica, *Canicule* (also known as *Dog Day*), Union Generale Cinematographique, 1984; Laura, *Le Vol du sphinx* (also known as *The Flight of the Phoenix*), President/Distributeurs Associes, 1984; Alice, *Attention! Une Femme peut en cacher une autre* (also known as *My Other Husband*), Gaumont International/ Triumph, 1985; Monique, *Menage* (also known as *Tenue de soiree* and *Evening Dress*), AAA Classics/Cinecom International/Roissy/ Norstar, 1986; Lauda, *Les Portes tournantes* (also known as *The Revolving Doors*), Union Generale Cinematographiques/Image, 1988; title role, *La Lectrice* (also known as *The Reader*), Orion Classics, 1989.

Also appeared in *Quelques messieurs trop tranquilles* (also known as *Some Too Quiet Gentleman*), Gaumont International, 1971; *La Cavale* (also known as *On the Lam*), Prodis, 1971; *Themroc,* CIC, 1972; *Elle court, elle court la banlieue* (also known as *The Suburbs Are Everywhere*), United Artists, 1973; *The Adventures of Rabbi Jacob* (also known as *The Mad Adventures of Rabbi Jacob*), Societe Nouvelle de Cinema, 1973; *L'Ingorgo* (also known as *Bottleneck* and *Traffic Jam*), CineTel, 1978; *Blanche et Marie,* FR3/Canal Plus/G.A./Odessa, 1985; *Tendre Dracula; The Bottom Line;* and *Guy de Maupassant.*

RELATED CAREER—Co-founder and appeared in revues, Cafe de la Gare (nightclub), Paris, France.

NON-RELATED CAREER—Worked in an upholsterer's shop.*

*   *   *

MIRISCH, Walter   1921-

PERSONAL: Full name, Walter Mortimer Mirisch; born November 8, 1921, in New York, NY; son of Max and Josephine (Urbach) Mirisch; married Patricia Kahan, October 11, 1947; children: Anne, Andrew, Lawrence. EDUCATION—Attended City College of New York, 1938-40; University of Wisconsin, B.A., 1942; Harvard University, Graduate School of Business, I.A., 1943.

VOCATION: Producer.

CAREER: PRINCIPAL FILM WORK—All as producer, unless indicated: *Fall Guy,* Monogram, 1947; *I Wouldn't Be in Your Shoes,* Monogram, 1948; *Bomba the Jungle Boy,* Monogram, 1949; *Bomba on Panther Island,* Monogram, 1949; *Bomba and the Hidden City* (also known as *The Hidden City*), Monogram, 1950; *County Fair,* Monogram, 1950; *The Lost Volcano,* Monogram, 1950; *Cavalry Scout,* Monogram, 1951; *Elephant Stampede* (also known as *Bomba and the Elephant Stampede*), Monogram, 1951; *Flight to Mars,* Monogram, 1951; *Fort Osage,* Monogram, 1951; *The Lion Hunters* (also known as *Bomba and the Lion Hunters*), Monogram, 1951; *African Treasure* (also known as *Bomba and the African Treasure*), Monogram, 1952; *Bomba and the Jungle Girl,* Monogram, 1952; *Flat Top,* Allied Artists, 1952; *Hiawatha,* Monogram, 1952; *Rodeo,* Monogram, 1952; *Wild Stallion,* Monogram, 1952; executive producer, *The Maze,* Allied Artists, 1953; *An Annapolis Story* (also known as *The Blue and the Gold*), Allied Artists, 1955;

The Warriors (also known as *The Dark Avenger*), Allied Artists, 1955; (with Richard Heermance) *Wichita*, Allied Artists, 1955; *The First Texan*, Allied Artists, 1956; *The Oklahoman*, Allied Artists, 1957; *The Tall Stranger*, Allied Artists, 1957; *Fort Massacre*, United Artists, 1958; *The Gunfight at Dodge City*, United Artists, 1958; *Man of the West*, United Artists, 1958; *Cast a Long Shadow*, United Artists, 1959; *The Horse Soldiers*, United Artists, 1959; *The Man in the Net*, United Artists, 1959.

The Magnificent Seven, United Artists, 1960; *By Love Possessed*, United Artists, 1961; executive producer, *West Side Story*, United Artists, 1961; *Two for the Seesaw*, United Artists, 1962; *Toys in the Attic*, United Artists, 1963; *Hawaii*, United Artists, 1966; *Fitzwilly* (also known as *Fitzwilly Strikes Back*), United Artists, 1967; *In the Heat of the Night*, United Artists, 1967; *Sinful Davy*, United Artists, 1969; *Some Kind of a Nut*, United Artists, 1969; executive producer, *Halls of Anger*, United Artists, 1970; *The Hawaiians* (also known as *Master of the Islands*), United Artists, 1970; executive producer, *They Call Me Mister Tibbs!*, United Artists, 1970; *The Organization*, United Artists, 1971; *Scorpio*, United Artists, 1973; *Mr. Majestyk*, United Artists, 1974; *Serpico*, Paramount, 1974; *The Spikes Gang*, United Artists, 1974; *Midway* (also known as *The Battle of Midway*), Universal, 1976; *Gray Lady Down*, Universal, 1978; (with Morton Gottlieb) *Same Time, Next Year*, Universal, 1978; *Dracula*, Universal, 1979; *The Prisoner of Zenda*, Universal, 1979; (with Gottlieb) *Romantic Comedy*, Metro-Goldwyn-Mayer/United Artists, 1983.

PRINCIPAL TELEVISION WORK—Series: Producer, *Wichita Town*, NBC, 1959-60. Movies: Executive producer, *High Midnight*, CBS, 1979.

RELATED CAREER—Movie usher; management trainee, Skouras Theatres, 1938-40, and Oriental Theatre Corporation, 1940-42; executive producer, Allied Artists, 1946-57; founder (with Marvin and Harold Mirisch) and vice-president in charge of production, Mirisch Company, 1957, then president and head of production, 1969—; trustee, American Film Institute; trustee, Filmax; board member, Performing Arts Council, Los Angeles Music Center; president, Center Theatre Group of Los Angeles.

NON-RELATED CAREER—Board member, University of Wisconsin Alumni Association, 1967-73; board member, Cedars-Sinai Medical Center, Los Angeles; board member, California State University, Northridge, CA.

AWARDS: Academy Award, Best Picture, 1967, for *In the Heat of the Night;* Irving Thalberg Award from the Academy of Motion Picture Arts and Sciences, 1977; Jean Hersholt Humanitarian Award from the Academy of Motion Picture Arts and Sciences, 1982; Producer of the Year Award; Order of Arts and Letters (France).

MEMBER: Screen Producers Guild (president, 1960-61), Academy of Motion Picture Arts and Sciences (board of directors, 1962, board of governors, 1964, president, 1973-77).*

*   *   *

MITCHELL, Gregory   1951-

PERSONAL: Born December 9, 1951, in Brooklyn, NY; son of Patrick (a psychologist) and Margaret (a voice and piano teacher;

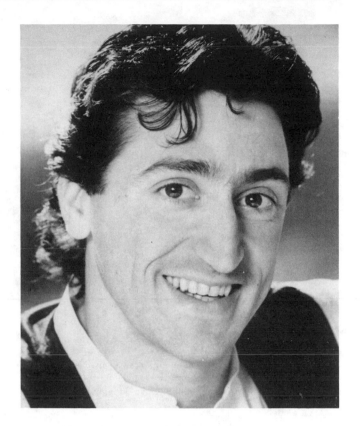

GREGORY MITCHELL

maiden name, Musto) Mitchell; married Cheryl Jones (a dancer), June 10, 1982; children: Garrett. EDUCATION—Attended the Juilliard School, 1969-75; studied acting with Uta Hagen at the HB Studios, 1986—. RELIGION—Christian.

VOCATION: Actor and dancer.

CAREER: BROADWAY DEBUT—Queen's companion, *Merlin*, Mark Hellinger Theatre, 1982. PRINCIPAL STAGE APPEARANCES—Jazz teacher, *One More Song, One More Dance*, Joyce Theatre, New York City, 1983; Escort, *Song and Dance*, Royale Theatre, New York City, 1985-86; Edouardo, *Tango Apasionado*, Westbeth Theatre Center, New York City, 1987; slavemaster and marksman, *Phantom of the Opera*, Majestic Theatre, New York City, 1988; Gregorio and Orfeo, *Dangerous Games*, Nederlander Theatre, New York City, 1989. Also appeared as Eddie Correlli, *Kicks*, Tony Milano, *The Young Strangers*, and Orfeo, *Orfeo del Campo*, all in New York City; Gregorio and Orfeo, *Dangerous Games*, American Musical Theatre Festival, Philadelphia, PA, then Spoleto Festival USA, Charleston, SC, later La Jolla Playhouse, La Jolla, CA; Leonardo, *Blood Wedding*, Great Lakes Theatre Festival, Cleveland, OH, then Old Globe Theatre, San Diego, CA, later Coconut Grove Playhouse, Miami, FL; Alexi Petrikov, *Woman of the Year*.

PRINCIPAL FILM APPEARANCES—Dancer, *A Chorus Line: The Movie*, Columbia, 1985.

PRINCIPAL FILM WORK—Assistant to the choreographer, *Naked Tango*.

PRINCIPAL TELEVISION APPEARANCES—Episodic: Bryce, *One*

Life to Live, ABC. Specials: *Dance in America,* PBS; *I Feel a Song Coming On,* PBS.

RELATED CAREER—Co-founder, past president, and board member, New York Arts Group; member, Feld Ballet Company; actor in television commercials.

MEMBER: Actors' Equity Association, American Federation of Television and Radio Artists, Screen Actors Guild.

ADDRESSES: AGENT—Abrams Artists and Associates Ltd., 420 Madison Avenue, Suite 1400, New York, NY 10017.

*   *   *

MIYORI, Kim

PERSONAL: Born in Santa Maria, CA; father, a federal corrections officer; mother, a bookkeeper and receptionist. EDUCATION—Graduated from Carnegie-Mellon University; also attended the University of Utah; trained for the stage at the Pacific Conservatory of Performing Arts; also trained in Kabuki, Japanese dancing, and swordfighting.

VOCATION: Actress.

CAREER: BROADWAY DEBUT—*Pacific Overtures,* Winter Garden Theatre, 1976. PRINCIPAL STAGE APPEARANCES—Manchuka, *Zoot Suit,* Winter Garden Theatre, New York City, 1979; Zeng Wencai, *Peking Man,* Horace Mann Theatre, New York City, 1980; Marsha, *The Wash,* Mark Taper Forum, Los Angeles, 1986; Geisha, *Teahouse of the August Moon,* Burt Reynolds Dinner Theatre, Jupiter, FL, 1987. Also appeared in *Wind Dances,* East/West Players, Los Angeles, 1982; and at Potter's Field Theatre, New York City, 1980.

PRINCIPAL FILM APPEARANCES—Kyoko Bruckner, *Loverboy,* Tri-Star, 1989; Jenny Sumner, *The Big Picture,* Columbia, 1989; also appeared in *Sergeant Pepper's Lonely Hearts Club Band,* Universal, 1978.

PRINCIPAL TELEVISION APPEARANCES—Series: Dr. Wendy Armstrong, *St. Elsewhere,* NBC, 1982-84; Paula Hershon, *Hard Copy,* CBS, 1987. Episodic: Lia, *Airwolf,* CBS, 1985; Midori Kimura, *Our House,* NBC, 1986; Gayle McGiveny, *Murder, She Wrote,* CBS, 1987; Ho Xuan, *Simon and Simon,* CBS, 1988; Dr. Triwai, *MacGyver,* ABC, 1989; also *Scene of the Crime,* NBC, 1984. Movies: Teri Tanaka, *Generation,* ABC, 1985; Yoko Ono, *John and Yoko: A Love Story,* NBC, 1985; Barbara Grayle, *Blood Sport,* CBS, 1986; Kim Hinkle, *When the Bough Breaks,* NBC, 1986; Diana Ishimura, *Island Sons,* ABC, 1987.

RELATED CAREER—Ballet teacher.

SIDELIGHTS: RECREATIONS—Community work.

ADDRESSES: AGENT—Smith-Freedman and Associates, 121 N. San Vicente Boulevard, Beverly Hills, CA 90211.*

*   *   *

MOLINA, Alfred

PERSONAL: Born c. 1953 in London, England; married Jill Gascoine (an actress). EDUCATION—Graduated from the Guildhall School of Music and Drama.

VOCATION: Actor.

CAREER: PRINCIPAL STAGE APPEARANCES—Policeman, *Destiny,* Margarelon, *Troilus and Cressida,* and Fat Gentleman and Bismarck, *The Days of the Commune,* all Royal Shakespeare Company (RSC), Aldwych Theatre, London, 1977; P.C. Boyd and Pathologist, *Bandits,* Keeper #2, Soldier #2, and San-ko, *The Bundle,* and Al, *Frozen Assets,* all RSC, Warehouse Theatre, London, 1977; Hero Aussie and Willie, *Dingo,* RSC, Warehouse Theatre, 1978; Brick, *Irish Eyes and English Tears,* Theatre Upstairs, London, 1978; Teddington Ted, *Wheelchair Willie,* Royal Court Theatre, London, 1978; the Maniac, *Accidental Death of an Anarchist,* Half Moon Theatre, London, 1979. Also appeared in *That Good Between Us,* RSC, Warehouse Theatre, 1977; *King Lear,* RSC, Aldwych Theatre, 1977; *Destry Rides Again,* Donmar

ALFRED MOLINA

Warehouse Theatre, London, 1982; *Dreyfus*, Hampstead Theatre Club, London, 1982; *Viva*, Stratford Theatre Royal, London, 1985; and in productions of *The Biko Inquest, The Taming of the Shrew, Happy End*, and *Serious Money*.

PRINCIPAL FILM APPEARANCES—Satipo, *Raiders of the Lost Ark*, Paramount, 1981; John, *Meantime*, Film Four International, 1983; Detective Constable Rogers, *Number One*, Stageforum, 1984; young Christos, *Eleni*, Warner Brothers, 1985; Cezar, *Ladyhawke*, Warner Brothers/Twentieth Century-Fox, 1985; Pierre, *Water*, Rank, 1985; Sergei, *Letter to Brezhnev*, Circle, 1986; Kenneth Halliwell, *Prick Up Your Ears*, Samuel Goldwyn, 1987; Avanti, *Manifesto* (also known as *For a Night of Love, For One Night of Love*, and *Pour une nuit d'amour*), Cannon, 1988. Also appeared in *Not Without My Daughter*, Pathe, 1990.

PRINCIPAL TELEVISION APPEARANCES—Series: *El C.I.D.*, ITV, 1990. Movies: *Drowning in the Shallow End*, BBC-2, 1990. Also appeared in *The Losers, Anyone for Dennis, Joni Jones, Blat, The Accountant*, and *Virtuoso*.

RELATED CAREER—Stand-up comic with a street theatre group.

AWARDS: *Plays and Players* Award, Most Promising New Actor, 1979, for *Accidental Death of an Anarchist*.

ADDRESSES: AGENT—Lou Coulson, 37 Berwick Street, London W1, England.

*   *   *

MOLINARO, Al   1919-

PERSONAL: Born June 24, 1919, in Kenosha, WI; father, a tavern operator; married Jackie Martin (a television time buyer), 1948; children: Michael.

VOCATION: Actor.

CAREER: PRINCIPAL FILM APPEARANCES—Drapery man, *Freaky Friday*, Buena Vista, 1976.

TELEVISION DEBUT—*Green Acres*, CBS. PRINCIPAL TELEVISION APPEARANCES—Series: Murray Greshner, *The Odd Couple*, ABC, 1970-75; Alfred Delvecchio, *Happy Days*, ABC, 1976-82; Alfred Delvecchio, *Joanie Loves Chachi*, ABC, 1982-83. Pilots: Peavey, *Great Day*, ABC, 1977; Benny, *Rosetti and Ryan: Men Who Love Women*, NBC, 1977; Casey, *A Christmas for Boomer*, NBC, 1979; Sal Ugily, *The Ugily Family*, ABC, 1980; also *Anson and Lorrie*, NBC, 1981. Episodic: *Bewitched*, ABC; *That Girl*, ABC; Agent 44, *Get Smart*. Movies: Forenzo, *Mayday at 40,000 Feet!*, CBS, 1976; sightseer, *Gridlock* (also known as *The Great American Traffic Jam*), NBC, 1980.

RELATED CAREER—Television producer in Los Angeles, 1960; also actor in television commercials and musician.

ADDRESSES: AGENTS—Michael Rosen and Ernest Dade, Dade/

Rosen/Schultz, 15010 Ventura Boulevard, Suite 219, Sherman Oaks, CA 91403.*

*   *   *

MOLINARO, Edouard   1928-

PERSONAL: Born May 13, 1928, in Bordeaux, France.

VOCATION: Director.

CAREER: Also see *WRITINGS* below. PRINCIPAL FILM APPEARANCES—Secretary, *The Season for Love* (also known as *La morte-saison des amours*), Gaston Hakim, 1963.

PRINCIPAL FILM WORK—Director: *Back to the Wall*, Chavane, 1959; *The Passion of Slow Fire*, Trans-Lux, 1962; *The Road to Shame*, Atlantic, 1962; "Envy" in *Seven Capital Sins* (also known as *Les Sept Peches capitaux* and *I sette pecati capitali*), Embassy, 1962; *A Mistress for the Summer* (also known as *Une Fille pour l'ete, Una ragazza per l'estate, Girls for the Summer*, and *A Lover for the Summer*), American, 1964; *Male Hunt* (also known as *La Chasse a l'homme* and *Caccia al maschio*), Pathe, 1965; *A Ravishing Idiot* (also known as *Une ravissante idiote, The Ravishing Idiot, Agent 38-24-36, The Warm-Blooded Spy, Adorable Idiot*, and *Bewitching Scatterbrain*), Seven Arts, 1966; *To Commit a Murder* (also known as *Peau d'espion, Congiura di spie*, and *Grausame job*), Cinerama, 1970; *Dracula and Son* (also known as *Dracula pere et fils*), Gaumont, 1976; *La Cage aux folles* (also known as *The Mad Cage* and *Birds of a Feather*), United Artists, 1979; "The French Method" in *Sunday Lovers*, United Artists, 1980; *La Cage aux folles II*, United Artists, 1981; *Just the Way You Are*, Metro-Goldwyn-Mayer/United Artists, 1984; *L'Amour en douce*, Gaumont, 1985; *Palace*, Wonderland/Third Wave/Rapid, 1985; also *Le Dos au mur*, 1957; *The Gentle Art of Seduction;* and *The Door on the Left As You Leave the Elevator*.

RELATED CAREER—Director of award-winning short technical films.

WRITINGS: FILM—See production details above. (With Maurice Clavel) *A Mistress for the Summer*, 1964; (with Andre Tabet and Georges Tabet) *A Ravishing Idiot*, 1966; (with Jacques Robert) *To Commit a Murder*, 1970; (with Jean-Marie Poire and Alain Goddard) *Dracula and Son*, 1976; (with Marcello Dannon, Francis Veber, and Jean Poiret) *La Cage aux folles*, 1979.

AWARDS: Academy Award nomination, Best Director, 1979, for *La Cage aux folles*.*

*   *   *

MOODY, Ron   1924-

PERSONAL: Born Ronald Moodnick, January 8, 1924, in London, England; name legally changed in 1930; son of Bernard (a studio

RON MOODY

executive) and Kate (Ogus) Moodnick. EDUCATION—London School of Economics, B.Sc., 1950.

VOCATION: Actor.

CAREER: STAGE DEBUT—*Intimacy at Eight,* New Lindsey Theatre, London, 1952. PRINCIPAL STAGE APPEARANCES—Vagabond student, *For Amusement Only,* Apollo Theatre, London, 1956; Pierrot, *For Adults Only,* Strand Theatre, London, 1958; Governor of Buenos Aires, *Candide,* Saville Theatre, London, 1959; Fagin, *Oliver!,* New Theatre, London, 1960; title role, *Joey, Joey,* Bristol Old Vic Theatre, Bristol, U.K., 1962; Mr. Darling/Captain Hook, *Peter Pan,* Scala Theatre, London, 1966; Aristophanes, *Liz,* Marlowe Theatre, Canterbury, U.K., 1968; Polonius and first gravedigger, *Hamlet,* Bankside Globe Theatre, London, 1971; Mr. Darling/Captain Hook, *Peter Pan,* Coliseum Theatre, London, 1972; Fagin, *Oliver!,* Dorothy Chandler Pavilion, Los Angeles, then Curran Theatre, San Francisco, CA, both 1973; Mr. Sterling, *The Clandestine Marriage,* Savoy Theatre, London, 1975; Mr. Darling/Captain Hook, *Peter Pan,* Palladium Theatre, London, 1975; title role, *The Showman,* Stratford Theatre Royal, London, 1976; Mr. Darling/Captain Hook, *Peter Pan,* Casino Theatre, London, 1977; Fagin, *Oliver!,* Aldwych Theatre, London, then Mark Hellinger Theatre, New York City, 1984; title role, *Sherlock Holmes—The Musical,* Cambridge Theatre, London, 1989. Also appeared in *Intimacy at 8:30,* Criterion Theatre, London, 1954; *Royal Command Performance,* Palladium Theatre, London, 1968;

title role, *Richard III,* Canada, 1978; *Marino Faliero,* Young Vic Theatre, London, 1982.

PRINCIPAL STAGE WORK—Director, *Saturnalia,* Belgrade Theatre, Coventry, U.K., 1971.

MAJOR TOURS—Right Honorable Sir Joseph Porter, K.C.B., *H.M.S. Pinafore,* U.S. cities, 1988; also appeared in *Move Along Sideways,* U.S. and U.K. cities.

FILM DEBUT—*Davy,* Metro-Goldwyn-Mayer, 1958. PRINCIPAL FILM APPEARANCES—Violinist, *Follow a Star,* Rank, 1959; Jelks, *Make Mine Mink,* Continental Distributing, 1960; Gabrielle, *Five Golden Hours,* Columbia, 1961; Mountjoy, *The Mouse on the Moon,* United Artists, 1963; Sid Pudney, *A Pair of Briefs,* Davis, 1963; Orlando, *Summer Holiday,* American International, 1963; Inspector, *Ladies Who Do,* Continental Distributing, 1964; H. Driffold Cosgood, *Murder Most Foul,* Metro-Goldwyn-Mayer, 1964; German, *San Ferry Ann,* British Lion, 1965; Professor Bastinado, *Seaside Swingers* (also known as *Every Day's a Holiday*), Embassy, 1965; Coach, *The Sandwich Man,* Rank, 1966; Fagin, *Oliver!,* Columbia, 1968; Uriah Heep, *David Copperfield,* Twentieth Century-Fox, 1970; Ippolit Vorobyaninov, *The Twelve Chairs,* UMC, 1970; Hawk Dove, *Flight of the Doves,* Columbia, 1971; Steps, *Dogpound Shuffle* (also known as *Spot*), Bloom, 1975; Dr. Rogers, *Dominique,* Subotsky, 1978; Merlin, *The Unidentified Flying Oddball* (also known as *The Spacemen and King Arthur* and *UFO*), Buena Vista, 1979; King Awad, *Wrong Is Right* (also known as *The Man with the Deadly Lens*), Columbia, 1982; Baron Gaspard Beersbohm, *Where Is Parsifal?,* Terence Young, 1984; voice of Prolix, *Asterix and the Big Fight* (also known as *Asterix and the Stone's Blow*), Gaumont/Palace/Extrafilm, 1989. Also appeared in *The Bed Sitting Room,* United Artists, 1969.

PRINCIPAL TELEVISION APPEARANCES—Series: Detective Inspector Roger Hart, *Nobody's Perfect,* ABC, 1980; Bon Chance Louis, *Tales of the Gold Monkey,* ABC, 1981. Mini-Series: LeBrun, *The Word,* CBS, 1978. Episodic: *Hart to Hart,* ABC, 1981; *Highway to Heaven,* NBC, 1984; *Murder, She Wrote,* CBS, 1985. Movies: Uriah Heep, *David Copperfield,* NBC, 1970; Captain Lesgate "Swann", *Dial M for Murder,* NBC, 1981; *The Caucasian Chalk Circle,* Thames, 1985; *Hideaway,* BBC, 1985. Specials: *Portrait of Petula,* NBC, 1969; *Bing Crosby's Merrie Olde Christmas,* NBC, 1977; *The David Soul and Friends Special,* ABC, 1977. Also appeared in *Winter's Tale,* 1980; as Iago, *Othello,* 1981; in *Ither Side of London,* 1983; *Is That Your Body, Boy?; Taste;* and *Baden Powell.*

WRITINGS: STAGE—(Also composer and lyricist) *Joey, Joey,* Bristol Old Vic Theatre, Bristol, U.K., 1962, then Saville Theatre, London, 1966; (also composer) *Saturnalia,* Belgrade Theatre, Coventry, U.K., 1971; *Move Along Sideways,* Stratford Theatre Royal, London, 1976; (also composer and lyricist) *The Showman,* Stratford Theatre Royal, 1976. OTHER—(Contributor) *My L.S.E.* (nonfiction), Robson Books, 1977; *The Devil You Don't* (novel), Robson Books, 1979; *Very Very Slightly Imperfect* (novel), Robson Books, 1983.

AWARDS: Academy Award nomination, Variety Club of Great Britain Award, Golden Bear Award from the Moscow Film Festival, and Golden Globe, Best Actor, all 1968, for *Oliver!*; Antoinette Perry Award nomination, Best Actor in a Musical, and Theatre World Award, both 1984, for *Oliver!*.

MEMBER: Academy of Motion Picture Arts and Sciences, Screen Actors Guild, Performing Rights Society, British Actors' Equity Association, Variety Club of Great Britain, Clowns International (president, 1984).

SIDELIGHTS: FAVORITE ROLES—Vagabond student in *For Amusement Only,* Pierrot in *For Adults Only,* governor in *Candide,* and Fagin in *Oliver!*. RECREATIONS—Writing, music, painting, theatre history, and archaeology.

ADDRESSES: OFFICE—Ingleside, 41 the Green, London N14, England.*

*   *   *

MOONBLOOD, Q.
See STALLONE, Sylvester

*   *   *

MOORE, Dudley   1935-

PERSONAL: Full name, Dudley Stuart John Moore; born April 19, 1935, in Dagenham, England; son of John and Ada Francis (Hughes) Moore; married Suzy Kendall (an actress), 1968 (divorced); married Tuesday Weld (an actress), 1975 (divorced, 1980); married Brogan Lane, February 21, 1988; children: Patrick (second marriage). EDUCATION—Oxford University, B.A., 1957, B.Mus., 1958; also attended the Guildhall School of Music, London.

VOCATION: Actor, composer, musician, writer, and producer.

CAREER: Also see *WRITINGS* below. STAGE DEBUT—With the Oxford University Drama Society, 1955. LONDON DEBUT—Ensemble, *Beyond the Fringe* (revue), Fortune Theatre, 1961. BROADWAY DEBUT—Ensemble, *Beyond the Fringe* (revue), John Golden Theatre, 1962. PRINCIPAL STAGE APPEARANCES—Ensemble, *Beyond the Fringe* (revue), Edinburgh Festival, Lyceum Theatre, Edinburgh, Scotland, 1959; Allan Felix, *Play It Again, Sam,* Globe Theatre, London, 1970; *Behind the Fridge* (two-man show with Peter Cook), Cambridge Theatre, London, 1972-73, then retitled *Good Evening,* Plymouth Theatre, New York City, 1973.

MAJOR TOURS—*Behind the Fridge* (two-man show with Peter Cook), Australian and New Zealand cities, 1971-72; *Good Evening* (two-man show with Cook), U.S. cities, 1975.

FILM DEBUT—Narrator, *The Hat* (animated), Contemporary Films, 1964. PRINCIPAL FILM APPEARANCES—John Finsbury, *The Wrong Box,* Columbia, 1966; Stanley Moon, *Bedazzled,* Twentieth

Century-Fox, 1967; Rupert Street, *Thirty Is a Dangerous Age, Cynthia,* Columbia, 1968; police sergeant, *The Bed Sitting Room,* United Artists, 1969; Lieutenant Kit Barrington, *Those Daring Young Men in Their Jaunty Jalopies* (also known as *Monte Carlo or Bust!*), Paramount, 1969; Dormouse, *Alice's Adventures in Wonderland,* American National Enterprises, 1972; Stanley Tibbets, *Foul Play,* Paramount, 1978; George Webber, *10,* Warner Brothers, 1979; narrator, *To Russia . . . With Elton* (documentary), ITC Entertainment, 1979; Harvey Orkin and Herschel, *Wholly Moses!,* Columbia, 1980; Dr. Watson, Mrs. Ada Holmes, and Mrs. Spiggott, *The Hound of the Baskervilles,* Atlantic, 1980; Arthur Bach, *Arthur,* Warner Brothers, 1981; Patrick Dalton, *Six Weeks,* Universal, 1982; Saul Benjamin, *Lovesick,* Warner Brothers, 1983; Jason Carmichael, *Romantic Comedy,* Metro-Goldwyn-Mayer/United Artists, 1983; Wylie Cooper, *Best Defense,* Paramount, 1984; Rob Salinger, *Micki and Maude,* Columbia, 1984; Claude Eastman, *Unfaithfully Yours,* Twentieth Century-Fox, 1984; Patch, *Santa Claus: The Movie,* Tri-Star, 1985; Dr. Jack Hammond, *Like Father, Like Son,* Tri-Star, 1987; Arthur Bach, *Arthur II: On the Rocks,* Warner Brothers, 1988; narrator, *Milo and Otis,* Columbia, 1989. Also appeared in *Derek and Clive Get the Horn,* 1980; *Crazy People,* Paramount, 1990.

PRINCIPAL FILM WORK—Executive producer, *Arthur II: On the Rocks,* Warner Brothers, 1988; also executive producer, *Derek and Clive Get the Horn,* 1980.

PRINCIPAL TELEVISION APPEARANCES—Series: *Not Only . . . But Also,* BBC, 1964, 1966, and 1970; *Goodbye Again,* ITV, 1968; *Here's Lulu . . . Not to Mention Dudley Moore,* BBC, 1972; also

DUDLEY MOORE

Strictly for the Birds. Episodic: *Dolly,* ABC, 1987; *The Jim Henson Hour,* NBC, 1989; *The Jack Parr Show,* NBC; *The Tonight Show,* NBC. Specials: *A Trip to the Moon,* CBS, 1964; *Royal Command Performance,* ITV, 1965; *Us Against the World II,* ABC, 1978; *The Muppets Go to the Movies,* ABC, 1981; *Bob Hope's Pink Panther Thanksgiving Gala,* NBC, 1982; *Bob Hope Special: Happy Birthday, Bob!,* NBC, 1983; *The American Film Institute Salute to John Huston,* CBS, 1983; *Comic Relief,* HBO, 1987; *Mancini and Friends,* PBS, 1987; *The American Comedy Awards,* ABC, 1988; *The 75th Anniversary of Beverly Hills* (also known as *Beverly Hills Seventy-Fifth Diamond Jubilee*), ABC, 1989; *America's All-Star Tribute to Elizabeth Taylor* (also known as *America's Hope Award*), ABC, 1989; also narrator, *Pleasure at Her Majesty's,* 1976; host, *The Comedy Club Special,* 1988.

RELATED CAREER—Composed incidental music for productions of the Royal Shakespeare Company, London, 1958-60; jazz pianist with the John Dankworth Band and with the Vic Lewis Band which toured U.S. cities in 1959; performed in concert at the Royal Festival Hall, London, 1960; composed incidental music for productions of the Gillian Lynne Dance Company, Saville Theatre, London, 1963; nightclub performer at the Establishment Club, London, 1961, the Blue Angel, New York City, 1963, the Village Vanguard and Rainbow Grill, both New York City, 1964, Small's, London, 1973, and at Michael's Pub, New York City, 1974; guest pianist with the Los Angeles Philharmonic Orchestra, 1981.

WRITINGS: STAGE—(Composer of incidental music) *Serjeant Musgrave's Dance* and *One-Way Pendulum,* both English Stage Company, Royal Court Theatre, London, 1959; (composer of incidental music) *Platonov,* English Stage Company, Royal Court Theatre, 1960; (composer of incidental music) *The Caucasian Chalk Circle,* Royal Shakespeare Company, Aldwych Theatre, London, 1962; (composer) *England, Our England,* Prince's Theatre, London, 1962; (composer of incidental music) *The Owl and the Pussycat* (ballet), Western Theatre Ballet Company, London, 1962; (with Alan Bennett, Peter Cook, and Jonathan Miller) *Beyond the Fringe* (revue), Edinburgh Festival, Lyceum Theatre, Edinburgh, Scotland, 1959, then Fortune Theatre, London, 1961, later John Golden Theatre, New York City, 1962, published by Souvenir Press, 1962, and Random House, 1963; (adaptor) *Play It Again, Sam,* Globe Theatre, London, 1970; (with Cook) *Behind the Fridge* (revue), Cambridge Theatre, London, 1972, then retitled *Good Evening,* Plymouth Theatre, New York City, 1973.

FILM—(With Cook; also composer) *Bedazzled,* Twentieth Century-Fox, 1967; (with Joseph McGrath and John Wells; also composer) *Thirty Is a Dangerous Age, Cynthia,* Columbia, 1968; (composer) *Inadmissable Evidence,* Paramount, 1968; (composer) *Staircase,* Twentieth Century-Fox, 1969; (with Cook and Paul Morrissey; also composer) *The Hound of the Baskervilles,* Atlantic, 1980; (composer) *Six Weeks,* Universal, 1982; also (composer) *Derek and Clive Get the Horn,* 1980. TELEVISION—Series: (With Cook) *Not Only . . . But Also,* BBC, 1964, 1966, and 1970. OTHER—*Dud and Pete: The Dagenham Dialogues,* 1971.

RECORDINGS: ALBUMS—*Good Evening* (original cast recording), 1973; *Beyond the Fringe* (original cast recording); *Bedazzled* (original soundtrack); *The Other Side of Dudley Moore; Today; Genuine Dud; Derek and Clive—Live; All That Jazz;* and *Dudley Moore Trio—Down Under.*

AWARDS: Special Antoinette Perry Award (with Alan Bennett, Peter Cook, and Jonathan Miller), Award, 1963, for *Beyond the Fringe;* British Academy of Film and Television Arts Award, Best

Light Entertainment Performance (Television), 1965; Grammy Award (with Cook), Best Spoken Word Recording, 1974, for *Good Evening;* Golden Apple Award, Discovery of the Year, 1979; Academy Award nomination, Best Actor, 1981, for *Arthur;* National Association of Theatre Operators (NATO) Award, Male Star of the Year, 1983; Golden Globe, Best Performance By an Actor in a Motion Picture—Comedy or Musical, 1985, for *Micki and Maude.*

MEMBER: British Actors' Equity Association, Actors' Equity Association, Screen Actors Guild, Writers Guild, Performing Rights Society.

SIDELIGHTS: RECREATIONS—Films, theatre, and music.

ADDRESSES: OFFICES—73 Market Street, Venice, CA 90291; c/o Mary Walker, 21 Hasker Street, London SW3, England. AGENTS—Louis Pitt, International Creative Management, 8899 Beverly Boulevard, Los Angeles, CA 90048; Oscar Beuselinck, Wright and Webb, 10 Soho Square, London W1, England.*

*   *   *

MOREAU, Jeanne   1928-

PERSONAL: Born January 23, 1928, in Paris, France; daughter of Anatole-Desire (a restaurateur) and Katherine (a dancer; maiden name, Buckley) Moreau; married Jean-Louis Richard (an actor), 1949 (divorced, 1951); married Teodoro Rubanis (divorced, 1977); married William Friedkin (a director), 1977 (divorced, 1980); children: Jerome (first marriage). EDUCATION—Attended Lycee Edgar-Quinet and the Conservatoire National d'Art Dramatique.

VOCATION: Actress.

CAREER: STAGE DEBUT—*A Month in the Country,* Comedie Francaise, Paris, France. PRINCIPAL STAGE APPEARANCES—Sarah Bernhardt, *Parade of Stars Playing the Palace,* Palace Theatre, New York City, 1983; Hannah Jelkes, *The Night of the Iguana,* Morris Mechanic Theatre, Baltimore, MD, 1985; also appeared in French productions of *L'Heure eblouissante (The Dazzling Hour),* 1953; *La Chatte sur un toit brulant (Cat on a Hot Tin Roof); La Chevauchee sur le lac de Constance (The Ride Across Lake Constance); La Machine infernale; Pygmalion; La Bonne Soupe; Lulu;* and *L'Intoxe.*

FILM DEBUT—*Dernier amour,* 1948. PRINCIPAL FILM APPEARANCES—Rosie Facibey, *Julietta,* 1953, released in the United States by Kingsley International, 1957; Mother, *Secrets d'alcove,* Pathe, 1954; Marianne, *Les Hommes en blanc* (also known as *The Doctors*), 1955, released in the United States by Kingsley International, 1956; Agnes, *Demoniaque* (also known as *Les Louves* and *The She Wolves*), 1956, released in the United States by Fernard Rivers S.A., 1958; *Le Dos au mur* (also known as *Back to the Wall*), 1958, released in the United States by Chavane, 1959; Jeanne Tournier, *Les Amants* (also known as *The Lovers*), 1958, released in the United States by Zenith, 1959; Florence Carala, *Ascenseur pour l'echafaud* (also known as *Frantic*), 1958, released in the United States by Times, 1961; woman with dog, *Les Quatres cents coups* (also known as *The Four Hundred Blows*), Janus, 1959; Juliette de Merteuil, *Les Liaisons dangereuses* (also known as *Relazioni pericolose* and *Dangerous Love Affairs*), 1959, released in the United States by Astor, 1961.

Ljuba, *Five Branded Women,* Paramount, 1960; Anne Desbaredes, *Moderato cantabile,* 1960, released in the United States by Royal, 1964; Lidia, *La notte* (also known as *The Night* and *La Nuit*), Dino De Laurentiis, 1961, released in the United States by Lopert, 1962; woman in bar, *Une femme est une femme* (also known as *A Woman Is a Woman* and *La donna e donna*), 1961, released in the United States by Pathe Contemporary, 1964; Catherine, *Jules et Jim* (also known as *Jules and Jim*), Janus, 1962; Miss Burstner, *Le Proces* (also known as *The Trial, Der Prozess,* and *Il processo*), 1962, released in the United States by Astor, 1963; title role, *Eva* (also known as *Eva, the Devil's Woman*), Paris Film/Interopa, 1962, released in the United States by Times, 1964; Frenchwoman, *The Victors,* Columbia, 1963; Jeanne, *Le Feu follet* (also known as *The Fire Within* and *Fuoco fatuo*), 1963, released in the United States by Governor/Gibralter, 1964; Jackie Demaistre, *La Baie des anges* (also known as *Bay of Angels*), Pathe Contemporary, 1964; Celestine, *Le Journal d'une femme de chambre* (also known as *Diary of a Chambermaid* and *Il diario di una cameriera*), Cocinor, 1964, released in the United States by International Classics, 1965; Cathy, *Peau de banane* (also known as *Banana Peel*), 1964, released in the United States by Pathe, 1965; Christine, *Le Train* (also known as *The Train* and *Il treno*), 1964, released in the United States by United Artists, 1965.

Title role, *Mata Hari Agent H-21* (also known as *Mata Hari* and *Mata Hari, agente segreto H 21*), Magna, 1965; Maria I, *Viva Maria,* United Artists, 1965; Marchioness Eloise of Frinton, *The Yellow Rolls-Royce,* Metro-Goldwyn-Mayer (MGM), 1965; title role, *Mademoiselle,* Lopert, 1966; Doll Tearsheet, *Chimes at Midnight* (also known as *Campanadas a medianoche* and *Falstaff*), Peppercorn-Wormser/U-M Film Distributors, 1967; Anna, *The Sailor from Gibraltar,* Lopert, 1967; title role, "Mademoiselle Mimi" in *Le Plus vieux metier du monde* (also known as *The Oldest Profession, L'amore attraverso i secoli,* and *Das alteste gewerbe der welt*), 1967, released in the United States by Goldstone/VIP, 1968; Julie Kohler, *La Mariee etait en noir* (also known as *The Bride Wore Black*), Artistcs Assocics, 1968; Catherine the Great, *Great Catherine,* Warncr Brothcrs, 1968; Virginie Ducrot, *Une Histoire immortelle* (also known as *The Immortal Story*), 1968, released in the United States by Fleetwood/Altura, 1969.

As herself, *Alex in Wonderland,* MGM, 1970; Martine Bernard, *Monte Walsh,* National General, 1970; Madeleine, *Comptes a rebours* (also known as *Reckonings Against the Grain*), CCFC, 1971; Myriam, *L'Humeur vagabonde* (also known as *Vagabond Humor*), Sodor Films, 1971; L'Aimie—the Other Woman, *Nathalie Granger,* French Consulate/Moullet et Compagnie, 1972; Louise, *Chere Louise* (also known as *Dear Louise*), Columbia-Warner Distributors, 1972; Renee, *La Race des "Seigneurs"* (also known as *The "Elite" Group*), Films la Boetie, 1973; Jeanne, *Les Valseuses* (also known as *Going Places*), Cinema V, 1974; Elisa Boussac, *Je t'aime* (also known as *I Love You*), Films Mutuels, 1974; Maria, *Le Jardin qui bascule* (also known as *The Garden That Tilts*), Coline Distribution, 1975; Berthe, *Souvenirs d'en France* (also known as *French Provincial* and *Inside Memories of France*), AMLF, 1975; Sylvana, *Hu-Man,* Romantique/ORTF/Camera One, 1975; Sarah Dedieu, *Lumiere* (also known as *Light*), Gaumont, 1975, released in the United States by New World, 1976; Didi, *The Last Tycoon,* Paramount, 1976; Florence, *Mr. Klein* (also known as *M. Klein*), Fox-Lira/Quartet, 1976.

Helene, *Plein sud* (also known as *Heat of Desire*), Triumph, 1980; title role, *Joanna Francesa* (also known as *Jeanne the Frenchwoman*), Unifilm/New Yorker, 1981; Lou, *La Truite* (also known as *The Trout*), Gaumont/TF1/Triumph, 1982; Lysiane, *Querelly—*

ein pakt mit dem teufel (also known as *Querelle* and *Querelle—A Pact with the Devil*), Palace, 1982, released in the United States by Triumph, 1983; the Hostess, *Le Paltoquet* (also known as *The Nonentity*), AAA/Roissy/Artificial Eye, 1986; Marie-Aude, *Sauve-toi Lola,* Onyx/AAA Classics, 1986; Sabine, *Le Miracule* (also known as *The Miracle Healing*), Films du Volcan, 1986, released in the United States by Cannon Releasing, 1987; narrator, *Hotel Terminus: Klaus Barbie, His Life and Times* (also known as *Hotel Terminus: Klaus Barbie et son temps;* documentary), Samuel Goldwyn/Orion International, 1988.

Also appeared in *Meurtes* (also known as *Three Sinners*), 1950; *Pigalle Sainte-Germain-des-Pres,* 1950; *L'Homme de ma vie,* 1951; *Il est minuit, Docteur Schweitzer,* 1952; *Dortoir des grandes* (also known as *Inside a Girls' Dormitory*), 1953; *Touchez pas au grisbi,* 1953; *Les Intriguantes,* 1954; *La Reine Margot,* 1954; *M'sieur la caille,* 1955; *Gas-Oil,* 1955; *Jusqu-au dernier,* 1956; *Le Salaire du peche,* 1956; *L'Etrange Mr. Steve,* 1957; *Trois jours a vivre,* 1957; *Echec a porteur,* 1957; *Le Dialogue des Carmelites,* 1959; *L'Amour a travers les ages,* 1967; *Le Petit Theatre de Jean Renoir* (also known as *The Little Theatre of Jean Renoir*), 1969; *Le Corps de Diane,* 1969; *Langlois* (short documentary film), 1970; *Pleurs,* 1974; *Madame Rosa,* 1978; *L'Intoxe,* 1980; *Lucien chez les barbares,* 1981; *Mille milliards de dollars,* 1982; *Au-dela de cette limite votre billet n'est pas valable* (also known as *Your Ticket Is No Longer Valid*), 1982; *The Wizard of Babylon,* New Yorker, 1983; *Jean-Louis Barrault—A Man of the Theatre* (documentary), Beta Film, 1984; *Lillian Gish* (documentary), Acapella Films, 1984; *Francois Simon—La Presence* (documentary), CSS Geneva, 1986; *Calling the Shots* (documentary), World Artists Releasing/Cineplex Odeon/Films Transit, 1988; *La Nuit de l'ocean* (also known as *The Night of the Ocean*), Forum Distribution/World Marketing, 1988; *Nikita,* Gaumont, 1990.

FIRST FILM WORK—Director, *Lumiere* (also known as *Light*), Gaumont, 1975, released in the United States by New World, 1976. PRINCIPAL FILM WORK—Director, *L'Adolescente* (also known as *The Adolescent*), Parafrance, 1978; producer and director, *Lillian Gish* (documentary), Acapella Films, 1984.

PRINCIPAL TELEVISION APPEARANCES—Specials: *The American Film Institute Salute to Lillian Gish,* CBS, 1984; *With Orson Welles: Stories from a Life in Film,* TNT, 1990.

RELATED CAREER—Member, Comedie Francaise, Paris, France, 1948-52; member, Theatre Nationale Populaire, Paris, 1953; president, Cannes Film Festival, 1975; founder (with Klaus Hellwig), Moreau Productions, 1982.

WRITINGS: FILM—*Lumiere* (also known as *Light*), Gaumont, 1975, released in the United States by New World, 1976; (with Henriette Jelinek) *L'Adolescente* (also known as *The Adolescent*), Parafrance, 1978.

AWARDS: Best Actress Award from the Cannes Film Festival, 1960, for *Moderato cantabile;* British Academy of Film and Television Arts Award, 1966, Best Foreign Actress, for *Viva Maria;* Chevalier, Legion d'honneur, Ordre Nationale du Merite et des Arts et Lettres.

SIDELIGHTS: RECREATIONS—Theatre, art, painting, books, music, sculpture, and landscapes.

ADDRESSES: OFFICE—Artmedia, 10 Avenue George V, 75008 Paris, France. AGENT—Ed Limato, William Morris Agency, 151

El Camino Drive, Beverly Hills, CA 90212. PUBLICIST—Solters/
Roskin/Friedman Inc., 5455 Wilshire Boulevard, Suite 2200, Los
Angeles, CA 90036.*

* * *

MORRIS, Anita

PERSONAL: Born in Durham, NC.

VOCATION: Actress.

CAREER: BROADWAY DEBUT—Reporter, apostle woman, tem-
ple lady, and leper, *Jesus Christ Superstar,* Mark Hellinger Thea-
tre, 1971. PRINCIPAL STAGE APPEARANCES—Citizen of New
York City, *Seesaw,* Uris Theatre, New York City, 1973; Academy
Awards guest, Stella Starfuckoff, Rachael's Ocho Rios twin, one
man girl, and Doris, *Rachael Lily Rosenbloom and Don't You Ever
Forget It!,* Broadhurst Theatre, New York City, 1973; Charmin,
The Magic Show, Cort Theatre, New York City, 1974; ensemble,
Unsung Cole (revue), Circle Repertory Company, Circle Repertory
Theatre, New York City, 1977; ensemble, *Sugar Babies* (revue),
Mark Hellinger Theatre, New York City, 1979; Eileen, *Two Small
Bodies,* Playwrights Horizons, Queens, NY, 1979; Carla, *Nine,*
46th Street Theatre, New York City, 1982. Also appeared with the
Hartford Stage Company, Hartford, CT, 1975-76.

MAJOR TOURS—Lila, *Home Again, Home Again,* U.S. and
Canadian cities, 1979.

PRINCIPAL FILM APPEARANCES—Linda Jo/May, *The Happy
Hooker,* Cannon, 1975; So Fine dancer, *So Fine,* Warner Brothers,
1981; Ronda Ray, *The Hotel New Hampshire,* Orion, 1984; Mrs.
Wynic, *Maria's Lovers,* Cannon, 1985; Dido Lament, *Absolute
Beginners,* Orion, 1986; Malvina Kerch, *Blue City,* Paramount,
1986; Carol, *Ruthless People,* Buena Vista, 1986; Phoebe,
"Rigoletto" in *Aria,* Virgin Vision, 1987; Madelyn, *Eighteen
Again!,* New World, 1988; Clair Vin Blanc, *A Sinful Life,* New
Line Cinema, 1989; Missouri Martin, *Bloodhounds of Broadway,*
Vestron, 1989; also appeared in *The Broad Coalition,* August
Films, 1972; and *What Do I Tell the Boys at the Station?,* August
Films, 1972.

PRINCIPAL TELEVISION APPEARANCES—Series: Barbara "Babs"
Berrenger-DeGava, *Berrenger's,* NBC, 1985; Barbara Whiteman,
Down and Out in Beverly Hills, Fox, 1987. Episodic: Leona
Proverb, *Miami Vice,* NBC, 1987; Madeline Keith, *Cheers,* NBC,
1987; Betty, *Who's the Boss?,* ABC, 1989; Catherine McKay,
Matlock, NBC, 1989; Leona Schumann, *Murder, She Wrote,* CBS,
1989. Movies: Lola Crane, *A Masterpiece of Murder,* NBC, 1986;
Jezebel, *A Smoky Mountain Christmas,* ABC, 1986. Specials:
Circus of the Stars, CBS, 1982, 1986, and 1988; *Eubie Blake: A
Century of Music,* PBS, 1983.

ADDRESSES: AGENT—Sylvia Gold, International Creative Management, 8899 Beverly Boulevard, Los Angeles, CA 90048.*

MORRIS, Garrett   1944-

PERSONAL: Born February 1, 1944, in New Orleans, LA; wife's
name, Freda. EDUCATION—Graduated from Dillard University;
studied music at the Juilliard School of Music, at the Manhattan
School of Music, and at Tanglewood, MA.

VOCATION: Actor.

CAREER: PRINCIPAL STAGE APPEARANCES—Leroy, *The Bible
Salesman,* Broadway Congregational Church, New York City,
1960, then Martinique Theatre, New York City, 1961; Peter, *Porgy
and Bess,* City Center Light Opera Company, City Center Theatre,
New York City, 1964; aide to Ranor, *I'm Solomon,* Mark Hellinger
Theatre, New York City, 1968; second barker, *Show Boat,* Music
Theatre of Lincoln Center, State Theatre, New York City, 1966;
Prover, *Hallelujah, Baby!,* Martin Beck Theatre, New York City,
1967; Lalu, *Slave Ship,* Brooklyn Academy of Music, Brooklyn,
NY, 1969-70, then Washington Square Methodist Church, New
York City, 1970; Mack, *Transfers,* Village South Theatre, New
York City, 1970; Blood, *Operation Sidewinder,* Repertory Theatre
of Lincoln Center, Vivian Beaumont Theatre, New York City,
1970; Crook, *In New England Winter,* Henry Street Playhouse,
New York City, 1971; Corporal Jones, *The Basic Training of Pavlo
Hummel,* New York Shakespeare Festival (NYSF), Public Theatre,
New York City, 1971; cop, *What the Wine-Sellers Buy,* NYSF,
Vivian Beaumont Theatre, then Center Theatre Group, New Thea-
tre for Now, Mark Taper Forum, Los Angeles, both 1974. Also
appeared in *Porgy and Bess,* City Center Light Opera Company,
City Center Theatre, 1961; *Finian's Rainbow,* City Center Light
Opera Company, City Center Theatre, 1967; *The Great White
Hope,* Alvin Theatre, New York City, 1968; *Ododo (Truth),* Negro
Ensemble Company, St. Mark's Playhouse, New York City, 1970;
Nigger Nightmare, NYSF, Public Theatre, 1971; *Ain't Supposed to
Die a Natural Death,* Ethel Barrymore Theatre, New York City,
1971, then Ambassador Theatre, New York City, 1971-72; *Don't
Bother Me, I Can't Cope,* Ford's Theatre, Washington, DC, 1974;
Sweet Talk, NYSF, Public Theatre, 1974; *The World of Ben
Caldwell,* New Federal Theatre, New York City, 1982; *The Unvar-
nished Truth,* Ahmanson Theatre, Los Angeles, 1985.

MAJOR TOURS—Second barker, *Show Boat,* U.S. cities, 1966.

PRINCIPAL FILM APPEARANCES—Garrett, *Where's Poppa?* (also
known as *Going Ape*), United Artists, 1970; Everson, *The Ander-
son Tapes,* Columbia, 1971; Mr. Mason, *Cooley High,* American
International, 1975; Slide, *Car Wash,* Universal, 1976; Power and
Light man, *How to Beat the High Cost of Living,* American
International, 1980; Harvey McGraw, *The Census Taker,* Seymour
Borde, 1984; Chocolate Chip Charlie, *The Stuff,* New World, 1985;
helicopter junkie, *Critical Condition,* Paramount, 1987; Dummont,
The Underachievers, Lightning, 1988; con, *Dance to Win,* Metro-
Goldwyn-Mayer/United Artists, 1989; census taker, *Husbands,
Wives, Money, and Murder,* Trans World Entertainment, 1989.

PRINCIPAL TELEVISION APPEARANCES—Series: "Wheels" Daw-
son, *Roll Out!,* CBS, 1973-74; regular, *Saturday Night Live,* NBC,
1975-80; Principal Dwight Ellis, *It's Your Move,* NBC, 1984-85;
Arnold "Sporty" James, *Hunter,* NBC, 1986—. Pilots: Janitor,
Change at 125th Street, CBS, 1974; Lieutenant Greg Larkin, *The
Invisible Woman,* NBC, 1983; Dwayne, *At Your Service,* NBC,
1984. Episodic: Asam Ali Shamba, *Scarecrow and Mrs. King,*
CBS, 1985; Gary Samuels, *The Love Boat,* ABC, 1986; Bob
Winslow, *227,* NBC, 1987; Russ, *Married with Children,* Fox,
1987 and 1989; Officer Audette, *Who's the Boss?,* ABC, 1988; also

Murder, She Wrote, CBS, 1985; "Dealer's Choice," *The Twilight Zone,* CBS, 1985; *Hill Street Blues,* NBC; *The Jeffersons,* CBS. Specials: *Things We Did Last Summer,* NBC, 1978; *Saturday Night Live Fifteenth Anniversary,* NBC, 1989.

RELATED CAREER—Singer and musical arranger with the Harry Belafonte Folk Singers.

WRITINGS: STAGE—*The Secret Place,* Playwrights Horizons, New York City, 1972; also *Daddy Picou and Marie Le Veau,* 1981.

MEMBER: American Federation of Television and Radio Artists.

SIDELIGHTS: RECREATIONS—Jogging.

ADDRESSES: AGENTS—J. Michael Bloom Ltd., 9200 Sunset Boulevard, Suite 1210, Los Angeles, CA 90069; Abrams Artists, 9200 Sunset Boulevard, Suite 625, Los Angeles, CA 90069.*

*   *   *

MORRIS, Mary   1915-1988

PERSONAL: Born December 13, 1915, in Suva, Fiji Islands; died October 14, 1988, in Aigle, Switzerland; daughter of Herbert Stanley and Sylvia Ena (de Creft-Harford) Morris. EDUCATION— Trained for the stage at the Royal Academy of Dramatic Art.

VOCATION: Actress and producer.

CAREER: LONDON DEBUT—Third old woman, *Lysistrata,* Gate Theatre, 1936. PRINCIPAL STAGE APPEARANCES—Antonia, *Squaring the Circle,* Vaudeville Theatre, London, 1941; Glasha, *Distant Point,* Westminster Theatre, London, 1941; Esther, *On Life's Sunny Side* and Anne Pedersdotter, *The Witch,* both Arts Theatre, London, 1943; Abigail Sarclet, *Duet for Two Hands,* Lyric Theatre, London, 1945; Julia, *The Day of Glory,* Embassy Theatre, London, 1946; title role, *Peter Pan,* Scala Theatre, London, 1946; Lucie, *Men Without Shadows,* Lyric Hammersmith Theatre, London, 1947; the Strange Lady, *As You Desire Me,* Embassy Theatre, 1948; Nina Moore, *If This Be Error,* Q Theatre, London, 1949, then Lyric Hammersmith Theatre, 1950; chorus, *Pericles,* Rudolf Steiner Hall, London, 1950; Elizabeth Tudor, *The Young Elizabeth,* New Theatre, London, 1952; the Stepdaughter, *Six Characters in Search of an Author,* Arts Theatre, then St. James's Theatre, both London, 1954; Lavinia Mannon, *Mourning Becomes Electra,* Arts Theatre, 1955; title role, *Electra,* Oxford Playhouse, Oxford, U.K., 1956; also appeared as Caesonia, *Caligula,* 1949.

PRINCIPAL STAGE WORK—Producer, *Beauty and the Beast,* Mercury Theatre, London, 1949; producer, *Celestina,* Embassy Theatre, London, 1951.

MAJOR TOURS—Emmy Baudine, *They Walk Alone,* U.K. cities, 1942; Kathy, *Wuthering Heights,* U.K. cities, 1943; also *The Maids,* U.K. cities, 1964.

PRINCIPAL FILM APPEARANCES—Victoria Van Brett, *Double Door,* Paramount, 1934; Duchess of Kent, *Victoria the Great,* RKO, 1937; Renee, *Prison Without Bars,* United Artists, 1939; chauffeuse, *U-Boat 29* (also known as *The Spy in Black*), Columbia, 1939; Halima, *The Thief of Baghdad,* United Artists, 1940; girl, *Major Barbara,* United Artists, 1941; Ludmilla Koslowski,

Pimpernel Smith (also known as *Mister V*), United Artists, 1942; Anna Petrovich, *Underground Guerrillas* (also known as *Undercover* and *Chetnik*), Columbia, 1944; Sarah Duboste, *The Man from Morocco,* Pathe, 1946; Lettie Shackleton, *The Agitator,* Four Continents, 1949; Anna Braun, *High Treason,* General Film Distributors/Pacemaker/Mayer/Kingsley, 1951; Louise, "The Actor" in *Train of Events,* Film Arts, 1952.

PRINCIPAL TELEVISION APPEARANCES—Mini-Series: Countess Vronsky, "Anna Karenina," BBC, then *Masterpiece Theatre,* PBS, 1978. Episodic: Number Two, "Dance of the Dead," *The Prisoner,* ITC, then CBS, 1968. Also *An Unofficial Rose, The Spread of the Eagle, Richard II, A Family Reunion, The Velvet Glove,* and *Cleopatra.*

RELATED CAREER—Founder, Strange Players (a theatrical repertory company), Oxted, U.K., 1936-37.

OBITUARIES AND OTHER SOURCES: *Variety,* November 22, 1988.*

*   *   *

MORRISSEY, Paul   1939-

PERSONAL: Born in 1939 in New York, NY. EDUCATION— Attended Fordham University. MILITARY—U.S. Army.

VOCATION: Director, producer, and screenwriter.

CAREER: Also see WRITINGS below. PRINCIPAL STAGE WORK— Director, *Man on the Moon,* Little Theatre, New York City, 1975.

PRINCIPAL FILM APPEARANCES—Party guest, *Midnight Cowboy,* United Artists, 1969; Malibu party guest, *Rich and Famous,* Metro-Goldwyn-Mayer/United Artists, 1981; as himself, *Chambre 666* (also known as *Room 666* and *Chambre 666 n'importe quand . . .*), Gray City/Classic, 1982.

PRINCIPAL FILM WORK—Producer and director, *Civilization and Its Discontents,* Film-Makers Cooperative, 1964; production assistant, *My Hustler,* Film-Makers Distribution Center/Andy Warhol Films, 1965; production assistant, *Space,* Andy Warhol Films, 1965; production assistant, *Chelsea Girls,* Film-Makers Cooperative/Film-Makers Distribution Center/Andy Warhol Films, 1966; production assistant, *More Milk Evette* (also known as *Lana Turner* and *More Milk Yvette*), Film-Makers Cooperative, 1966; production assistant, *Nude Restaurant,* Factory Films/Film-Makers Cooperative, 1967; cinematographer, *Bike Boy,* Andy Warhol Films/Film-Makers Cooperative, 1967; executive producer, *The Loves of Ondine,* Film-Makers Cooperative, 1968; executive producer, cinematographer, and editor, *Lonesome Cowboys,* Factory Films/Film-Makers Cooperative/Sherpix, 1968; director and cinematographer, *Flesh,* Sherpix, 1968; executive producer, *Blue Movie,* Andy Warhol Films, 1969; director, *Trash,* Almi Cinema V, 1970; director, *Andy Warhol's Women* (also known as *Women in Revolt*), Andy Warhol Films, 1971; director and cinematographer, *Heat,* Levitt-Pickman/Andy Warhol Films, 1972; director, *Andy Warhol's Frankenstein* (also known as *Carne per Frankenstein* and *De la chair pour Frankenstein*), CFDC/Bryanston, 1973; producer and director, *L'Amour,* Altura, 1973; director, *Blood for Dracula* (also known as *Andy Warhol's Dracula* and *Dracula vuole vivere: cerca sangue di vergine!*), CFDC/Bryanston, 1974; director, *The*

Hound of the Baskervilles, Atlantic, 1980; director, *Forty Deuce,* Island, 1982; director, *Mixed Blood* (also known as *Cocaine*), Sara/Cinevista/Promovision International, 1984; *Beethoven's Nephew* (also known as *Akaile neveu de Beethoven*), Oro Film/Almaro/CBL, 1985; director, *Spike of Bensonhurst,* FilmDallas, 1988. Also director, *Madame Wang's,* 1981.

NON-RELATED CAREER—In the insurance business.

WRITINGS: See production details above. FILM—*Flesh,* 1968; *Trash,* 1970; (with John Hollowell) *Heat,* 1972; *Andy Warhol's Frankenstein,* 1973; *Blood for Dracula,* 1974; (with Peter Cook and Dudley Moore) *The Hound of the Baskervilles,* 1980; *Madame Wang's,* 1981; (with Alan Browne) *Mixed Blood,* 1984; (with Mathieu Carriere) *Beethoven's Nephew,* 1985; (with Browne) *Spike of Bensonhurst,* 1988.*

*   *   *

MOSTEL, Josh   1946-

PERSONAL: Full name, Joshua Mostel; born December 21, 1946, in New York, NY; son of Zero (an actor) and Kathryn Celia (an actress, dancer, and writer; maiden name, Harken) Mostel; married Peggy Rajski (a producer and director), June 24, 1983. EDUCATION—Brandeis University, B.A., 1970.

VOCATION: Actor and director.

JOSH MOSTEL

CAREER: STAGE DEBUT—Joey, *The Homecoming,* Provincetown Theatre, Provincetown, MA, 1968. OFF-BROADWAY DEBUT—Ensemble, *The Proposition* (revue), Gramercy Arts Theatre, then Mercer-Shaw Theatre, both 1971. BROADWAY DEBUT—Private Larry Fishbein, "Defender of the Faith," folk singer, "Epstein," and first intern, "Eli, the Fanatic," in *Unlikely Heroes,* Plymouth Theatre, 1971. PRINCIPAL STAGE APPEARANCES—Harvey and Frank Likk, *Soft Touch,* Wilbur Theatre, Boston, MA, 1973; messenger, *An American Millionaire,* Circle in the Square, New York City, 1975; ensemble, *Straws in the Wind* (revue), American Place Theatre, New York City, 1975; Milo Crawford, "Lu Ann Hampton Laverty Oberlander" and "The Last Meeting of the Knights of the White Magnolia" in *A Texas Trilogy,* Kennedy Center for the Performing Arts, Washington, DC, then Broadhurst Theatre, New York City, both 1976; Dubois, *The Misanthrope,* New York Shakespeare Festival (NYSF), Public Theatre, New York City, 1977; Hirschel, *Gemini,* Arena Stage, Washington, DC, 1978; Louie, *Every Place Is Newark* and Orville, *The Wright Brothers,* both Aspen Playwrights Conference, Aspen, CO, 1978; Bottom, *A Midsummer Night's Dream,* Kenyon Theatre Festival, Warren, OH, 1980; Norman Bulansky, *The Boys Next Door,* Lambs Theatre, New York City, 1987; Charlie Langman, *The Road to Urga,* Lincoln Center Theatre, New York City, 1987; Matt of the Mint, *Threepenny Opera,* Lunt-Fontanne Theatre, New York City, 1989. Also appeared in *The Hostage* and *Lysistrata,* both Provincetown Theatre, Provincetown, MA, 1968; ensemble, *The Proposition* (revue), in Massachusetts, 1969; in *Curse You, Spread Eagle,* Washington Theatre Club, Washington, DC, 1971; *More Than You Deserve,* NYSF, Public Theatre, 1974; as C.K., *Men in the Kitchen,* Long Wharf Theatre, New Haven, CT.

PRINCIPAL STAGE WORK—Director, *Ferocious Kisses,* Manhattan Punchline Theatre, New York City, 1981; director, *Love As We Know It,* Manhattan Punchline Theatre, 1986.

FILM DEBUT—Borrelli, *Going Home,* Metro-Goldwyn-Mayer, 1971. PRINCIPAL FILM APPEARANCES—Frank, *The King of Marvin Gardens,* Columbia, 1972; King Herod, *Jesus Christ, Superstar,* Universal, 1973; Norman, *Harry and Tonto,* Twentieth Century-Fox, 1974; Victor, *Deadly Hero,* AVCO-Embassy, 1976; Morris Fink, *Sophie's Choice,* Universal, 1982; Duster, *Fighting Back,* Paramount, 1982; private detective, *Star 80,* Warner Brothers, 1983; David, *Almost You,* Twentieth Century-Fox, 1984; Casio vendor, *Brother from Another Planet,* Cinecom, 1984; Sol, *Windy City,* Warner Brothers, 1984; Dicky Dunck, *Compromising Positions,* Paramount, 1985; Jack Schnittman, *The Money Pit,* Universal, 1986; Howard F. Howard, *Stoogemania,* Atlantic, 1986; Mayor Cabell Testerman, *Matewan,* Cinecom, 1987; Uncle Abe, *Radio Days,* Orion, 1987; Ollie, *Wall Street,* Twentieth Century-Fox, 1987; actor, *Heavy Petting* (documentary), Skouras, 1988; Mel Gorsky, *Animal Behavior,* Cinestar, 1989. Also appeared as Russell, *Dead Ringer,* 1982.

PRINCIPAL TELEVISION APPEARANCES—Series: Jim "Blotto" Blutarski, *Delta House,* ABC, 1979; Private Maxwell, *At Ease,* ABC, 1983; Wesley Harden, *Murphy's Law,* ABC, 1988. Pilots: Nathan, *Hereafter,* NBC, 1975; Steve, *Off Campus,* CBS, 1977. Episodic: Leonard, *Spenser: For Hire,* ABC, 1986; Taurus, *The Equalizer,* CBS, 1986; Winston Erdlow, *The Equalizer,* CBS, 1987; Barney Green, *Seventh Avenue,* NBC, 1977; also *The Boy Who Loved Trolls,* PBS. Specials: *Zero Hour,* ABC, 1967.

RELATED CAREER—Operatic soprano as a child.

WRITINGS: TELEVISION—Specials: (With Mickey Lemle) *Media Probes: The Language Show.*

AWARDS: Outer Critics' Circle Award nomination, Best Actor, 1987, for *The Boys Next Door.*

ADDRESSES: AGENT—Tim Angle, Triad Artists, 10100 Santa Monica Boulevard, 16th Floor, Los Angeles, CA 90067.

*　　*　　*

MULDAUR, Diana 1938-

PERSONAL: Full name, Diana Charlton Muldaur; born August 19, 1938, in New York, NY; daughter of Charles Edward Arrowsmith and Alice Patricia (Jones) Muldaur; married James Mitchell Vickery, July 26, 1969 (died, 1979); married Robert J. Dozier, October 11, 1981. EDUCATION—Sweet Briar College, B.A., 1960.

VOCATION: Actress.

CAREER: PRINCIPAL STAGE APPEARANCES—Miss Moran, *A Very Rich Woman,* Belasco Theatre, New York City, 1965.

PRINCIPAL FILM APPEARANCES—Cynthia, *The Swimmer,* Columbia, 1968; Anne Marley, *Number One* (also known as *The Pro*), United Artists, 1969; Ruth Petrocelli, *The Lawyer,* Paramount, 1969; Katy, *One More Train to Rob,* Universal, 1971; Alexandra Perry, *The Other,* Twentieth Century-Fox, 1972; Alana Fitzgerald, *Chosen Survivors,* Columbia, 1974; Lois Boyle, *McQ,* Warner Brothers, 1974; Elaine, *Beyond Reason,* Allwyn, 1977.

PRINCIPAL TELEVISION APPEARANCES—Series: Ann Wicker, *The Secret Storm,* CBS, 1965; Belle, *The Survivors,* ABC, 1969-70; Chris Coughlin, *McCloud,* NBC, 1970-77; Joy Adamson, *Born Free,* NBC, 1974; Judge Eleanor Hooper, *The Tony Randall Show,* ABC, 1976-77, then CBS, 1977-78; Ginny Linden, *Hizzoner,* NBC, 1979; Terri Seymour, *Fitz and Bones,* NBC, 1981; Dr. Alice Foley, *A Year in the Life,* NBC, 1987-88; Dr. Katherine Pulaski, *Star Trek: The Next Generation,* syndicated, 1988-89; Rosalind Shays, *L.A. Law,* NBC, 1989—. Mini-Series: Claire Randall, *The Word,* CBS, 1978; Elizabeth Sutton, *Black Beauty,* NBC, 1978. Pilots: Chris Coughlin, *McCloud: Who Killed Miss U.S.A.?,* NBC, 1970; Carrie Donovan, *Call to Danger,* CBS, 1973; Marg, *Planet Earth,* ABC, 1974; Rachel LeMaire, *Charlie's Angels,* ABC, 1976; Edith Cole, *The Deadly Triangle,* NBC, 1977; Sandra, *Pine Canyon Is Burning,* NBC, 1977; Terri Seymour, *Terror at Alcatraz,* NBC, 1982; Claire Shelton, *Too Good to Be True,* ABC, 1983; Dr. Alice Foley, *A Year in the Life,* NBC, 1986.

Episodic: Dr. Anne Mulhall, "Return to Tomorrow" and Dr. Miranda Jones, "Is There in Truth No Beauty," *Star Trek,* NBC, 1968; also *The Americans,* NBC, 1961; *Dr. Kildare,* NBC, 1966; *Hawk,* ABC, 1966; "Dark Lady of the Sonnets," *New York Television Theatre,* WNET (New York City), 1966; *T.H.E. Cat,* NBC, 1966; *Run for Your Life,* NBC, 1967; *Gunsmoke,* CBS, 1967; *Mannix,* CBS, 1967, 1971, and 1973; *The F.B.I.,* ABC, 1968 and 1972; *I Spy,* NBC, 1968; *The Invaders,* ABC, 1968; *Outcasts,* ABC, 1968; *Bonanza,* NBC, 1968; *Felony Squad,* ABC, 1968; *The Courtship of Eddie's Father,* ABC, 1969; *Mod Squad,* ABC, 1970; *Dan August,* ABC, 1970; *Hawaii Five-0,* CBS, 1970 and 1972; *Alias Smith and Jones,* ABC, 1971; *The Name of the Game,* NBC, 1971; *Marcus Welby, M.D.,* ABC, 1971; *The Men from Shiloh,*

NBC, 1971; *Ironside,* NBC, 1971; *Banyon,* NBC, 1972; *Medical Center,* CBS, 1972; *Owen Marshall, Counselor at Law,* ABC, 1972 and 1973; *The Bold Ones,* NBC, 1973; *Hec Ramsey,* NBC, 1973; *Kung Fu,* ABC, 1973; *Search,* NBC, 1973; "Hog Wild," *The World of Disney,* NBC, 1974; *Cannon,* CBS, 1974; *Insight,* ABC, 1974; *The Rockford Files,* NBC, 1975; *Caribe,* ABC, 1975; *S.W.A.T.,* ABC, 1975; *Insight,* syndicated, 1975; *Ellery Queen,* NBC, 1976; Dr. Janet Carlisle, *Quincy, M.E.,* NBC. Movies: Kay Damian, *Ordeal,* ABC, 1973; Florence Kowski, *To Kill a Cop,* NBC, 1978; May Purcell, *Maneaters Are Loose!,* CBS, 1978; Kate Keller, *The Miracle Worker,* NBC, 1979; Sally Bingham, *The Return of Frank Cannon,* CBS, 1980; Angela Stafford, *Agatha Christie's "Murder in Three Acts,"* CBS, 1986; Chris Coughlin, *The Return of Sam McCloud,* CBS, 1989. Specials: Julie Sears, *It Can't Happen to Me,* syndicated, 1979; also "A Special Act of Love," *ABC Afternoon Playbreak,* ABC, 1973.

RELATED CAREER—Board of advisors, National Center for Film and Video Preservation, John F. Kennedy Center for the Performing Arts, Washington, DC, 1986.

NON-RELATED CAREER—Board of directors, Asthma and Allergy Foundation of America (Los Angeles chapter).

MEMBER: Academy of Motion Picture Arts and Sciences, Screen Actors Guild (director, 1978), Academy of Television Arts and Sciences (executive board member, director, president, 1983-85), Conservation Society of Martha's Vineyard Island.

ADDRESSES: AGENTS—Alexander Tucker, 10780 Santa Monica Boulevard, Suite 280, Los Angeles, CA 90025; Clarke Lilly, 333 Apolina Avenue, Balboa Island, CA 92662.*

*　　*　　*

MUMY, Bill 1954-

PERSONAL: Surname is pronounced "Moo-my"; born in 1954; son of Charles Mumy (a cattle rancher); wife's name, Eileen.

VOCATION: Actor.

CAREER: PRINCIPAL FILM APPEARANCES—Neil Bateman, *Tammy, Tell Me True,* Universal, 1961; Boom-Boom, *Palm Springs Weekend,* Warner Brothers, 1963; Alex Martin, *A Ticklish Affair,* Metro-Goldwyn-Mayer, 1963; child, *A Child Is Waiting,* United Artists, 1963; Erasmus Leaf, *Dear Brigette,* Twentieth Century-Fox, 1965; Sterling North, *Rascal,* Buena Vista, 1969; Teft, *Bless the Beasts and Children,* Columbia, 1971; Lariot, *Papillon,* Allied Artists, 1973; Tim, "It's a Good Life" in *Twilight Zone—The Movie,* Warner Brothers, 1983; member of the James Roberts Band, *Hard to Hold,* Universal, 1983.

TELEVISION DEBUT—*Romper Room,* syndicated. PRINCIPAL TELEVISION APPEARANCES—Series: Will Robinson, *Lost in Space,* CBS, 1965-68; Weaver, *Sunshine,* NBC, 1975; also voice of Matty Matel, *Matty's Funday Funnies* (animated), ABC. Pilots: Chris Williams, *The Two of Us,* CBS, 1966; Nick Butler, *The Rockford Files,* NBC, 1974; Larry, *Archie,* ABC, 1976; also Will Robinson, *Space Family Robinson.* Episodic: Anthony Fremont, "It's a Good Life," *The Twilight Zone,* CBS, 1961; Billy Bayles, "Long Distance Call," *The Twilight Zone,* CBS, 1961; Pip, "In Praise of Pip," *The Twilight Zone,* CBS, 1963; Googie, *The*

Munsters, CBS, 1965; clerk, "Bang! You're Dead," *Alfred Hitchcock Presents,* NBC, 1985; Doctor Irwin Bruckner, *Matlock,* NBC, 1988; also *Bewitched,* ABC, 1964; *The Virginian,* NBC, 1964; *I Dream of Jeannie,* NBC, 1965; *Lancer,* CBS; *Here Come the Brides,* ABC; *Riverboat,* NBC; *Have Gun, Will Travel,* CBS; *The Adventures of Ozzie and Harriet,* ABC; *Ben Casey,* ABC; *Playhouse 90,* CBS; *The Red Skelton Show.* Movies: Weaver, *Sunshine,* CBS, 1973; Weaver, *Sunshine Christmas,* NBC, 1977.

RELATED CAREER—Lead singer and musician for the rock group Bill Mumy and the Igloos.

WRITINGS: (With Miguel Ferrer) *Comet Man* (comic book), Marvel Comics, 1986.

ADDRESSES: AGENT—The Kohner Agency, 9169 Sunset Boulevard, Los Angeles, CA 90069.*

*   *   *

MURDOCH, Richard   1907-

PERSONAL: Born April 6, 1907, in Keston, England; son of Bernard (a tea broker) and Amy Florence (Scott) Murdoch; married Peggy Rawlings (an actress), 1932; children: Belinda, Jane, Timothy. EDUCATION—Attended Cambridge University. MILITARY—Royal Air Force, squadron leader, 1939-45.

VOCATION: Actor.

RICHARD MURDOCH

CAREER: STAGE DEBUT—Chorus, *The Blue Train,* King's Theatre, Southsea, U.K., 1927. LONDON DEBUT—Chorus, *The Blue Train,* Prince of Wales Theatre, 1927. PRINCIPAL STAGE APPEARANCES—Ronnie Webb, *The Five O'Clock Girl,* London Hippodrome, London, 1929; ensemble, *Cochran's 1930 Revue,* London Pavilion, London, 1930; Percy Pim, *Stand Up and Sing,* London Hippodrome, 1931; Sergeant Oliver, *Over She Goes,* Saville Theatre, London, 1936; Queen Hysteria, *Little Miss Muffet,* Casino Theatre, London, 1949; Buttons, *Cinderella,* Wimbledon Theatre, London, 1952; Bobby Denver, *As Long As They're Happy,* Grand Theatre, Blackpool, U.K., 1953; ensemble, *Happy Returns* (revue), Belgrade Theatre, Coventry, U.K., 1962; General de la Petadiere-Frenouillou, *The General's Tea Party,* Harrogate Festival, Harrogate, U.K., then Jeanetta Cochrane Theatre, London, both 1966; Aubrey Allington, *Tons of Money,* May Fair Theatre, London, 1968; William, *You Never Can Tell,* Shaw Festival, Niagara-on-the-Lake, ON, Canada, 1973; Ernest, *Bedroom Farce,* Athenaeum Theatre, Plymouth, U.K., 1979; Lord Caversham, *An Ideal Husband,* Westminster Theatre, London, 1989. Also appeared in *Ballyhoo,* Comedy Theatre, London, 1932; *Charlot's Char-a Bang, Stop-Go!, The Sleeping Beauty,* and *The Town Talks,* all Vaudeville Theatre, London, 1935-36; *Band Wagon,* London Palladium, London, 1939; the Headmaster, *Forty Years On;* and the Headmaster, *The Happiest Days Of Your Life.*

MAJOR TOURS—Philip Brown, *Oh, Letty!,* U.K. cities, 1929; Paul Daventry, *Mother of Pearl,* U.K. cities, 1933; Guy Holden, *Gay Divorce,* U.K. cities, 1936; Tommy Towers, *Tax Free,* U.K. cities, 1961; William, *You Never Can Tell,* U.S. and Canadian cities, 1973; Colonel Barstow, *Not in the Book,* South African cities, 1974; farmer, *Birds of Paradise,* U.K. cities, 1976; Sir William Boothroyd, *Lloyd George Knew My Father,* U.K. cities, 1977; Lord Caversham, *An Ideal Husband,* U.K. cities, 1989; also *Band Waggon,* U.K. cities, 1938; *Strike a New Note,* U.K. cities, 1946.

FILM DEBUT—P.C. Lewis, *The Terror,* 1935, released in the United States by Alliance, 1941. PRINCIPAL FILM APPEARANCES—Sergeant Oliver, *Over She Goes,* Associated British, 1937; Stinker, *Band Wagon,* General Film Distributors, 1940; Stinker Burton, *Charley's (Big-Hearted) Aunt,* General Film Distributors, 1940; Stinker, *I Thank You,* General Film Distributors, 1941; Teddy Deakin, *The Ghost Train,* General Film Distributors, 1941; illusionist, *You Can't Do Without Love,* Columbia, 1946; Bill Scott, *It Happened in Soho,* Associated British, 1948; Captain Wimpole, *Lilli Marlene,* RKO, 1951; sitter in Bath studio, *The Magic Box,* British Lion, 1952; David Felton, *The Gay Adventure* (also known as *Golden Arrow* and *Three Men and a Girl*), United Artists, 1953; Commander Bissham-Ryley, *Strictly Confidential,* Rank, 1959; Cabinet Minister Who Should Have Kept His Mouth Shut, *Whoops Apocalypse,* Miracle Films/Metro-Goldwyn-Mayer/United Artists, 1986.

TELEVISION DEBUT—*TV Follies,* BBC. PRINCIPAL TELEVISION APPEARANCES—Series: Uncle Tom, *Rumpole of the Bailey,* Thames, 1977—, then *Mystery!,* PBS, 1984—. Episodic: *Never the Twain,* Thames, then PBS, 1987; *The New Avengers,* CBS. Also appeared in *In the Looking Glass, The Three Kisses, Doctor's Daughters, Old Boy Network, This is Your Life, Wogan,* and *Mr. Majeika.*

PRINCIPAL RADIO APPEARANCES—*Much Murdoch,* Australian Broadcasting Commission, 1954; also in *Band Wagon, Much Binding-in-the-Marsh, The Men from the Ministry,* and in Service programs during World War II.

MEMBER: Royal Automobile Club, Stage Golfing Society, (former captain and president), Walton Heath Golf Club.

SIDELIGHTS: FAVORITE ROLES—William in *You Never Can Tell* and Sir William Boothroyd in *Lloyd George Knew My Father.* RECREATIONS—Golf and sailing.

ADDRESSES: AGENT—Essanay Ltd., 2 Bruton Street, London W1R 9TG, England.

*   *   *

MUSIC, Lorenzo   1937-

PERSONAL: Born May 2, 1937, in Brooklyn, NY; wife's name, Henrietta; children: three. EDUCATION—Graduated from the University of Minnesota.

VOCATION: Producer, writer, voice specialist, and actor.

CAREER: Also see *WRITINGS* below. PRINCIPAL FILM APPEARANCES—Cobb's writer, *Nickelodeon*, Columbia, 1976; Carlton, *Oh, Heavenly Dog!*, Twentieth Century-Fox, 1980; voice of Ralph, *Twice Upon a Time* (animated), Warner Brothers, 1983; voice of Ping Pong, *The Adventures of the American Rabbit* (animated), Atlantic/Clubhouse, 1986.

PRINCIPAL TELEVISION APPEARANCES—Series: Voice of Carlton the doorman, *Rhoda,* CBS, 1974-78; host, *The Lorenzo and Henrietta Music Show,* syndicated, 1976; voice of Super-Pac, *Pac-Man* (animated), ABC, 1984; voice of Tummi, *Disney's Adventures of the Gummi Bears* (also known as *The Gummi Bears* and *The Adventures of the Gummi Bears;* animated), NBC, 1985-1989; voice of Ozzie, *Disney's Fluppy Dogs* (animated), ABC, 1986; voice of Peter, *The Real Ghostbusters* (also known as *Slimer! and the Real Ghostbusters;* animated), ABC, 1986; voice of Tummi, *Disney's Gummi Bears/Winnie the Pooh Hour* (animated), ABC, 1989—. Pilots: Host, *The New Lorenzo Music Show,* ABC, 1976; voice of Carlton, *Carlton Your Doorman* (animated), CBS, 1980. Specials: *The Smothers Brothers Comedy Hour 20th Reunion Show,* CBS, 1988; voice of Garfield, *Here Comes Garfield* (animated), CBS, 1982; voice of Garfield, *Garfield on the Town* (animated), CBS, 1983; voice of Garfield, *Garfield in the Rough* (animated), CBS, 1984; voice of Garfield, *Garfield's Halloween Adventure* (animated), CBS, 1985; voice of Garfield, *Garfield in Paradise* (animated), CBS, 1986; voice of Garfield, *A Garfield Christmas*

(animated), CBS, 1987; voice of Garfield, *Garfield Goes to Hollywood* (animated), CBS, 1987; voice of Garfield, *Garfield: His Nine Lives* (animated), CBS, 1988; voice of Garfield, *Happy Birthday, Garfield!* (animated), CBS, 1988; voice of Garfield, *Garfield's Thanksgiving* (animated), CBS, 1989; voices of Garfield and Sam Spade, *Garfield's Babes and Bullets* (animated), CBS, 1989.

PRINCIPAL TELEVISION WORK—Series: Creator (with David Davis), *The Bob Newhart Show,* CBS, 1972-78; producer (with Davis, Allan Katz, Don Reo, and Bob Ellison), *Rhoda,* CBS, 1974-78; executive producer (with Lewis Arquette), *The Lorenzo and Henrietta Music Show,* syndicated, 1976. Pilots: Executive producer, *The New Lorenzo Music Show,* ABC, 1976; creator and producer (both with Steve Pritzker), *Friends,* CBS, 1978; producer (with Barton Dean), *Carlton Your Doorman* (animated), CBS, 1980.

RELATED CAREER—(With Henrietta Music) Performer in nightclubs and on tour with the USO; folk singer.

WRITINGS: TELEVISION—See production details above, unless indicated. Series: Composer of theme music, *The Bob Newhart Show,* 1972-78. Pilots: (With Carl Gottlieb, James L. Brooks, Jerry Davis, and Allan Burns) *The New Lorenzo Music Show,* 1976; (with Steve Pritzker) *Friends,* 1978; (with Barton Dean) *Carlton Your Doorman* (animated), 1980. Episodic: (With Davis) "The Snow Must Go," (with Davis) "1040 or Fight," and "Anchorman Overboard," all *The Mary Tyler Moore Show,* CBS, 1970; (with Davis) "The Boss Isn't Coming to Dinner," (with Davis) "I Am Curious Cooper," (with Davis) "A Girl's Best Mother Is Not Her Friend," (with Davis) "Don't Break the Chain," and (with Davis) "Ted Over Heels," all *The Mary Tyler Moore Show,* CBS, 1971; (with Davis) "Fly the Unfriendly Skies," (with Davis) "Tennis, Emily?," (with Davis) "P-I-L-O-T," and (with Davis) "His Busiest Season," all *The Bob Newhart Show,* 1972; (with Davis) "A Home Is Not Necessarily a House," *The Bob Newhart Show,* 1973; *The Lorenzo and Henrietta Music Show,* 1976; also *The Smothers Brothers Show,* CBS; *Rhoda.* Specials: *Garfield on the Town* (animated), 1983.

AWARDS: Emmy Award, Outstanding Animated Program (Special or Series), 1980, for *Carlton, Your Doorman.*

ADDRESSES: OFFICE—160 S. Windsor Boulevard, Los Angeles, CA 90004. AGENT—Sutton, Barth, and Vennari, 8322 Beverly Boulevard, Suite 202, Los Angeles, CA 90048.*

N

NADER, Michael   1945-

PERSONAL: Born February 19, 1945, in St. Louis, MO; wife' name, Robin; children: Lindsay Michelle. EDUCATION—Attended Santa Monica City College; studied acting at the Actors' Studio, the HB Studios, and with Alan Miller.

CAREER: PRINCIPAL STAGE APPEARANCES—Sterling Hayden and Jerome Robbins, *Are You Now or Have You Ever Been. . .?*, Theatre of the Riverside Church, New York City, 1973; Ron, "The Wake" in *Love-Death Plays of William Inge*, Billy Munk Theatre, New York City, 1975; also Tye McCool, *Vieux Carre*, Beverly Hills Playhouse, Beverly Hills, CA; performed in regional theater in Hawaii.

PRINCIPAL FILM APPEARANCES—Pajama boy, *Pajama Party*, American International, 1964; surfer, *Muscle Beach Party*, American International, 1964; Mike, *How to Stuff a Wild Bikini*, American International, 1965; Butch, *Beach Blanket Bingo*, American International, 1965; air police, *Sergeant Deadhead* (also known as *Sergeant Deadhead, the Astronaut*), American International, 1965; Bobby, *Ski Party*, American International, 1965; Joey, *Fireball 500*, American International, 1966.

PRINCIPAL TELEVISION APPEARANCES—Series: Peter "Siddo" Stone, *Gidget*, ABC, 1965-66; Kevin Thompson, *As the World Turns*, CBS, 1976-78; Alexi Theopolous, *Bare Essence*, NBC, 1983; Farnsworth "Dex" Dexter, *Dynasty*, ABC, 1983-89. Mini-Series: Burchardt, *The Great Escape II: The Untold Story*, NBC, 1988. Pilots: LaCroix, *Nick Knight*, CBS, 1989. Movies: Nick Scalfone, *Lady Mobster*, ABC, 1988.

RELATED CAREER—Producer of workshop theater; as a model with the Zoli Agency, appeared on magazine covers.

SIDELIGHTS: RECREATIONS—Surfing, skiing, and restoring old cars.

ADDRESSES: AGENT—Dee Dee Davidson, Gores/Fields Agency, 10100 Santa Monica Boulevard, Suite 700, Los Angeles, CA 90067.*

*   *   *

NELSON, Richard   1950-

PERSONAL: Born October 17, 1950, in Chicago, IL; married Cynthia B. Bacon, 1972; children: one daughter. EDUCATION—Hamilton College, B.A., 1972.

VOCATION: Playwright.

CAREER: Also see *WRITINGS* below. PRINCIPAL STAGE WORK—Director (with Ted D'Arms), *Between East and West*, Seattle, WA, 1984.

RELATED CAREER—Literary manager, Brooklyn Academy of Music Theatre Company, Brooklyn, NY, 1979-81; associate director, Goodman Theatre, Chicago, IL, 1980-83; dramaturg, Tyrone Guthrie Theatre, Minneapolis, MN, 1981-82.

WRITINGS: STAGE—*The Killing of Yablonski*, New Theatre for Now, Los Angeles, 1975, then PAF Playhouse, Huntington Station, NY, 1978; *Conjuring an Event*, Center Theatre Group, Mark Taper Forum, Los Angeles, 1976, then American Place Theatre, New York City, 1978, published in *An American Comedy and Other Plays*, Performing Arts Journal Publications, 1984; *Scooping*, Arena Stage, Washington, DC, 1977; *Jungle Coup*, Playwrights Horizons, New York City, 1978, published in *Plays from Playwrights Horizon*, Broadway Play Publishing, 1987; *The Vienna Notes*, first produced in Minneapolis, MN, 1978, then Playwrights Horizons, Mainstage Theatre, New York City, later Mark Taper Forum, and in Sheffield, U.K., all 1979, published in *Wordplays 1*, Performing Arts Journal Publications, 1980; (adaptor) *Don Juan*, Arena Stage, 1979.

(Adaptor) *The Suicide*, first produced in Chicago, IL, 1980; *Bal*, Chicago Theatre Group, Goodman Theatre, Chicago, 1980, published in *An American Comedy and Other Plays*, 1984; (translator with Helen Ciulei) "The Wedding" in *The Marriage Dance*, Lepercq Space, Brooklyn Academy of Music, Brooklyn, NY, 1980, then Seattle Repertory Theatre, Seattle, WA, 1984; (adaptor) *Jungle of Cities*, Playhouse Theatre, Brooklyn Academy of Music, 1981; (adaptor) *Il Campiello: A Venetian Comedy*, New York Shakespeare Festival, Public Theatre, New York City, 1981, published by Theatre Communications Group, 1981; *Rip Van Winkle or "The Works,"* Yale Repertory Theatre, New Haven, CT, 1981, published by Broadway Play Publishing, 1986; (adaptor) *The Marriage of Figaro*, Tyrone Guthrie Theatre, Minneapolis, 1982, then Circle in the Square, New York City, 1985; *An American Comedy*, Center Theatre Group, Mark Taper Forum, 1983, published in *An American Comedy and Other Plays*, 1984; *The Return of Pinocchio*, first produced in Seattle, 1983, then 47th Street Theatre, New York City, 1986, published in *An American Comedy and Other Plays*, 1984; (adaptor) *The Three Sisters*, first produced in Minneapolis, 1984; *Between East and West*, first produced in Seattle, 1984, published in *New Plays USA 3*, Theatre Communications Group, 1986; (adaptor) *The Accidental Death of an Anarchist*, Arena Stage, then Belasco Theatre, New York City, both 1984, published by Samuel French Inc., 1987; *Principia Scriptoriae*, Manhattan Theatre Club, New York City, then Royal Shakespeare

Company, London, both 1986, published by Broadway Play Publishing, 1986; (book for musical) *Chess,* Imperial Theatre, New York City, 1988; *Sensibility and Sense,* Mitzi E. Newhouse Theatre, New York City, 1989; *Some Americans Abroad,* Mitzi E. Newhouse Theatre, 1990.

TELEVISION—Episodic: *Kojak,* CBS. Movies: (With Elinor and Stephen Karpf) *Terror in the Sky,* CBS, 1971; *Houston, We've Got a Problem,* ABC, 1974.

OTHER—(Editor) *Strictly Dishonorable and Other Lost American Plays,* Theatre Communications Group, 1986.

AWARDS: Watson fellowship, 1972; Rockefeller grant, 1979; Obie Award from the *Village Voice,* 1979, for *The Vienna Notes;* Obie Award, 1980; National Endowment for the Arts fellowships, 1980 and 1985; Guggenheim fellowship, 1983; ABC Award, 1985; Playwrights USA Award, 1986; HBO Award, 1986; *Time Out* Award (London), 1987.

ADDRESSES: AGENT—Peter Franklin, William Morris Agency, 1350 Avenue of the Americas, New York, NY 10019.*

*   *   *

NEWELL, Patrick

VOCATION: Actor.

CAREER: PRINCIPAL STAGE APPEARANCES—Herbert Price, *The Ghost Train,* Old Vic Theatre, London, 1976, then Vaudeville Theatre, London, 1977.

PRINCIPAL FILM APPEARANCES—Doctor, *Night Without Pity,* Golden Era, 1962; first warder, *Trial and Error* (also known as *The Dock Brief*), Metro-Goldwyn-Mayer (MGM), 1962; King Harold, *Father Came Too,* Rank, 1964; Major Clarke, *The Unearthly Stranger,* American International, 1964; Mr. Hoskins, *Seaside Swingers* (also known as *Every Day's a Holiday*), Embassy, 1965; Cracknell, *The Alphabet Murders* (also known as *The ABC Murders*), MGM, 1966; P.C. Benson, *A Study in Terror* (also known as *Fog* and *Sherlock Holmes Grosster Fall*), Columbia, 1966; Colonel, *The Long Duel,* Paramount, 1967; victim, *The Strange Affair,* Paramount, 1968; man in hotel, *Old Dracula* (also known as *Vampira* and *Old Drac*), American International, 1975; Captain Billings, *Stand Up Virgin Soldier,* Warner Brothers, 1977; Charlie Whitlock, *The Golden Lady,* Target International, 1979; Bentley Bobster, *Young Sherlock Holmes,* Paramount, 1985; Jose Maria Gil Ramos, *Redondela,* Pedro Costa, 1987; Lester, *Consuming Passions,* Samuel Goldwyn, 1988. Also appeared in *Go for a Take,* 1972; *Dr. Fischer of Geneva,* Consolidated/BBC, 1984.

PRINCIPAL TELEVISION APPEARANCES—Series: "Mother," *The Avengers,* ABC, 1968-69; regular, *Kraft Music Hall Presents the Des O'Connor Show,* NBC, 1970. Mini-Series: Thomas, *Moll Flanders,* BBC, 1975, then PBS, 1980; Schalon, *Casanova,* syndicated, 1981. Episodic: Blessington, "The Resident Patient," *The Adventures of Sherlock Holmes,* Granada, then *Mystery!,* PBS, 1986; also *The Benny Hill Show,* syndicated. Movies: Julius Bates, *Destiny of a Spy,* NBC, 1969.*

NEWMAN, Lionel   1916-1989

PERSONAL: Born January 4, 1916, in New Haven, CT; died of cardiac arrest, February 3, 1989, in Los Angeles, CA; married Beverly Carroll; children: three daughters.

VOCATION: Composer, conductor, music director, and studio executive.

CAREER: Also see *WRITINGS* below. PRINCIPAL FILM WORK—All as music director, unless indicated: *Son of Frankenstein,* Universal, 1939; *Bill and Coo,* Republic, 1947; *Kiss of Death* and *Nightmare Alley,* both Twentieth Century-Fox, 1947; *Apartment for Peggy, Cry of the City, Deep Waters, Give My Regards to Broadway, Green Grass of Wyoming, Luck of the Irish, Road House, Scudda-Hoo! Scudda-Hay!* (also known as *Summer Lightning*), *The Street with No Name, That Wonderful Urge, Walls of Jericho,* and *You Were Meant for Me,* all Twentieth Century-Fox, 1948; *Come to the Stable, Father Was a Fullback, I Was a Male War Bride* (also known as *You Can't Sleep Here*), *It Happens Every Spring, Slattery's Hurricane,* and *Thieves' Highway,* all Twentieth Century-Fox, 1949.

Cheaper By the Dozen, I'll Get By, Love That Brute, Mister 880, Mother Didn't Tell Me, Stella, Three Came Home, Ticket to Tomahawk, Wabash Avenue, When Willie Comes Marching Home, and *Where the Sidewalk Ends,* all Twentieth Century-Fox, 1950; *As Young As You Feel, Elopement, Fixed Bayonets, Follow the Sun, The Frogmen, Golden Girl, The Guy Who Came Back, Halls of Montezuma, I Can Get It for You Wholesale* (also known as *Only the Best*), *I'd Climb the Highest Mountain, Let's Make It Legal, Love Nest, Meet Me After the Show, The Model and the Marriage Broker, Mr. Belvedere Rings the Bell, Rawhide* (also known as *Desperate Siege*), *The Secret of Convict Lake, The Thirteenth Letter,* and *You're in the Navy* (also known as *U.S.S. Tea Kettle*), all Twentieth Century-Fox, 1951; *Belles on Their Toes, Deadline—U.S.A.* (also known as *Deadline*), *Diplomatic Courier, Dreamboat, The I Don't Care Girl, Les Miserables, Lydia Bailey, Monkey Business, My Pal Gus, My Wife's Best Friend, Night Without Sleep, The Outcasts of Poker Flat, The Pride of St. Louis, Red Skies of Montana* (also known as *Smoke Jumpers*), *Return of the Texan, Something for the Birds,* and *We're Not Married,* all Twentieth Century-Fox, 1952; *A Blueprint for Murder, Down Among the Sheltering Palms, Gentlemen Prefer Blondes, The Girl Next Door, Inferno, Man in the Attic, Mr. Scoutmaster, Niagara, Pickup on South Street, Powder River, The Silver Whip, Taxi, Titanic,* and *Vicki,* all Twentieth Century-Fox, 1953; *Broken Lance, Gorilla at Large, Night People, River of No Return,* (with Alfred Newman) *There's No Business Like Show Business,* and *Three Young Texans,* all Twentieth Century-Fox, 1954.

The Girl in the Red Velvet Swing, Good Morning Miss Dove, House of Bamboo, The Racers (also known as *Such Men Are Dangerous*), *Rains of Ranchipur, Seven Cities of Gold, Soldier of Fortune, The View from Pompey's Head* (also known as *Secret Interlude*), *Violent Saturday, White Feather,* and *How to Be Very, Very Popular,* all Twentieth Century-Fox, 1955; *The Best Things in Life Are Free, D-Day, the Sixth of June* (also known as *The Sixth of June*), *The Girl Can't Help It, Hilda Crane, The Lieutenant Wore Skirts, On the Threshold of Space, The Revolt of Mamie Stover, Teenage Rebel,* and *Twenty-Three Paces to Baker Street,* all Twentieth Century-Fox, 1956; *The Harder They Fall* and *The Solid Gold Cadillac,* both Columbia, 1956; *An Affair to Remember, Desk Set* (also known as *His Other Woman*), *The Enemy Below, No Down Payment,* (with Ramon Hernandez) *The Sun Also Rises, The True*

Story of Jesse James (also known as *The James Brothers*), *The Wayward Bus*, and *Will Success Spoil Rock Hunter?* (also known as *Oh! For a Man*), all Twentieth Century-Fox, 1957; *The Gift of Love, In Love and War, Mardi Gras, The Young Lions, Ten North Frederick, Rally 'round the Flag, Boys!*, and *The Long, Hot Summer*, all Twentieth Century-Fox, 1958; *Journey to the Center of the Earth, Hound-Dog Man, A Private's Affair, The Remarkable Mr. Pennypacker, Say One for Me, The Sound and the Fury, Warlock*, and *Woman Obsessed*, all Twentieth Century-Fox, 1959.

North to Alaska, Wake Me When It's Over, and (with Earle H. Hagen) *Let's Make Love*, all Twentieth Century-Fox, 1960; music conductor, *Cleopatra*, Twentieth Century-Fox, 1963; (with Alexander Courage) *The Pleasure Seekers*, Twentieth Century-Fox, 1964; *The Sand Pebbles*, Twentieth Century-Fox, 1966; *The St. Valentine's Day Massacre* and (with Courage) *Doctor Dolittle*, both Twentieth Century-Fox, 1967; *A Flea in Her Ear* and music conductor, *Planet of the Apes*, both Twentieth Century-Fox, 1968; (with Lennie Hayton) *Hello, Dolly!*, Twentieth Century-Fox, 1969; *The Salzburg Connection* and *When Legends Die*, both Twentieth Century-Fox, 1972; music conductor, *The Omen*, Twentieth Century-Fox, 1976; *Alien*, Twentieth Century-Fox, 1979; *The Final Conflict*, Twentieth Century-Fox, 1981; music conductor, *Cross Creek*, Universal, 1983; *Unfaithfully Yours*, Twentieth Century-Fox, 1984.

PRINCIPAL TELEVISION APPEARANCES—Specials: *The Jerry Lewis Show*, NBC, 1960. PRINCIPAL TELEVISION WORK—All as music supervisor, unless indicated. Series: *Batman*, ABC, 1966-68; *Paris 7000*, ABC, 1970; *The Most Deadly Game*, ABC, 1970-71; *The Young Rebels*, ABC, 1970-71; *Arnie*, CBS, 1970-72; *M*A*S*H*, CBS, 1972-83; *The New Adventures of Perry Mason*, CBS, 1973-74; *Roll Out!*, CBS, 1973-74; *Planet of the Apes*, CBS, 1974; *The Swiss Family Robinson*, ABC, 1975-76; *Loves Me, Loves Me Not*, CBS, 1977; *Nashville 99*, CBS, 1977; *Young Dan'l Boone*, CBS, 1977; *James at Fifteen*, NBC, 1977-78; *Husbands, Wives, and Lovers*, CBS, 1978; *W.E.B.*, NBC, 1978; *The Paper Chase*, CBS, 1978-79; *Billy*, CBS, 1979; *Trapper John, M.D.*, CBS, 1979-86; *Hagen*, CBS, 1980; *Breaking Away*, ABC, 1980-81; *Ladies' Man*, CBS, 1980-81; *Jessica Novak*, CBS, 1981; *Manimal*, NBC, 1983; *Automan*, ABC, 1983-84; *Masquerade*, ABC, 1983-84; *Cover Up*, CBS, 1984-85; *Charlie and Company*, CBS, 1985-86; *Mr. Belvedere*, ABC, 1985-89. Mini-Series: *Jacqueline Susann's "Valley of the Dolls 1981,"* CBS, 1981. Pilots: *They Call It Murder*, NBC, 1971; *Big Rose*, CBS, 1974; *Time Travelers*, ABC, 1976; *The Fighting Nightingales*, CBS, 1978; music director and music conductor, *Breaking Away*, ABC, 1979; *Hunter's Moon*, CBS, 1979; *Characters*, NBC, 1980; *Jake's Way*, CBS, 1980; *Hardcase*, NBC, 1981; *Norma Rae*, NBC, 1981; *Rise and Shine*, CBS, 1981; *Adams House*, CBS, 1983; *Mr. Mom*, ABC, 1984; *W*A*L*T*E*R*, CBS, 1984; *Second Edition*, CBS, 1984; *In Like Flynn*, ABC, 1985; also *Fathers and Sons*, 1985. Movies: *The Challenge*, ABC, 1970; *Tribes* (also known as *The Soldier Who Declared Peace*), ABC, 1970; music conductor, *When Michael Calls*, ABC, 1972; *Terror on the Beach*, CBS, 1973; *The Mark of Zorro*, ABC, 1974; *The Red Badge of Courage*, NBC, 1974; *A Girl Named Sooner*, NBC, 1975; *Good Against Evil*, ABC, 1977; *Murder in Peyton Place*, NBC, 1977; *Ring of Passion*, NBC, 1978; *The Day Christ Died*, CBS, 1980; *Tourist*, syndicated, 1980; *The Rules of Marriage*, CBS, 1982; *Tomorrow's Child*, ABC, 1982; *Blood Feud*, syndicated, 1983; *Kentucky Woman*, CBS, 1983; *Ernest Hemingway's "The Sun Also Rises,"* NBC, 1984; *Love Thy Neighbor*, ABC, 1984; *Covenant*, NBC, 1985; *A Letter to Three Wives*, NBC, 1985; *Peyton Place: The Next Generaton*, NBC, 1985. Specials: *The 58th Annual Academy Awards Presenta-*

tion, ABC, 1986; *The 59th Annual Academy Awards Presentation*, ABC, 1987. Also *Goodbye Charlie*, 1985; *Sam*, 1985; *Crazy Dan*, 1986.

RELATED CAREER—Head of music department, Twentieth Century-Fox, 1970-85; vice-president and music director, Twentieth Century-Fox, 1977-82, then senior vice-president and music director of the film and television divisions, 1982-85; senior vice-president of music, Metro-Goldwyn-Mayer/United Artists Communications Company, 1988-89; also conductor and pianist with stage productions of *Earl Carroll's Vanities;* pianist for Mae West; as a guest conductor toured the United States, Canada, New Zealand, and appeared at the Royal Albert Hall, London.

WRITINGS: STAGE—Song contributor, *Earl Carroll's Vanities*. FILM—All as composer, unless indicated: Song contributor (with Arthur Quenzer), *The Cowboy and the Lady*, United Artists, 1938; (with Frank Loesser, Alfred Newman, and Mack Gordon) *Johnny Apollo*, Twentieth Century-Fox, 1940; song contributor (with Charles Henderson and Harry James), *Do You Love Me?* (also known as *Kitten on the Keys*), Twentieth Century-Fox, 1946; song contributor (with David Buttolph, Royal Foster, B.G. "Buddy" DeSylva, Lew Brown, and Ray Henderson) *Bill and Coo*, Republic, 1947; song contributor (with Dorcas Cochran), *Road House*, Twentieth Century-Fox, 1948; *The Jackpot*, Twentieth Century-Fox, 1950; (with Sol Kaplan) *Rawhide* (also known as *Desperate Siege*) and song contributor (with Eliot Daniel), *Golden Girl*, both Twentieth Century-Fox, 1951; *Bloodhounds of Broadway* and *Don't Bother to Knock*, both Twentieth Century-Fox, 1952; *City of Bad Men, Dangerous Crossing*, and *The Kid from Left Field*, all Twentieth Century-Fox, 1953; *The Gambler from Natchez, Princess of the Nile, The Rocketman, The Siege at Red River* (also known as *The Siege of Red River*), and song contributor (with Ken Darby), *River of No Return*, all Twentieth Century-Fox, 1954; *The Best Things in Life Are Free, The Last Wagon, Love Me Tender*, and *The Proud Ones*, all Twentieth Century-Fox, 1956; *The Killer Is Loose* and (also song contributor with Carroll Coates) *A Kiss Before Dying*, both United Artists, 1956; *Bernardine, The Way to the Gold*, and (also song contributor with Coates) *Kiss Them for Me*, all Twentieth Century-Fox, 1957; *The Bravados, Mardi Gras, A Nice Little Bank That Should Be Robbed* (also known as *How to Rob a Bank*), and *Sing, Boy, Sing*, all Twentieth Century-Fox, 1958; *Compulsion*, Twentieth Century-Fox, 1959; *Let's Make Love* and *North to Alaska*, both Twentieth Century-Fox, 1960; *Move Over, Darling*, Twentieth Century-Fox, 1963; *The Pleasure Seekers*, Twentieth Century-Fox, 1964; *Do Not Disturb*, Twentieth Century-Fox, 1965; *The Boston Strangler*, Twentieth Century-Fox, 1968; (with Lennie Hayton) *Hello, Dolly!*, Twentieth Century-Fox, 1969; *The Great White Hope* and *Myra Breckinridge*, both Twentieth Century-Fox, 1970; *The Salzburg Connection*, Twentieth Century-Fox, 1972; (with Irwin Kostal) *The Blue Bird*, Twentieth Century-Fox, 1976. TELEVISION—Series: Title theme (with Dorcas Cochran) *Adventures in Paradise*, ABC, 1959-62; *Valentine's Day*, ABC, 1964-65; title theme (with Vera Matson), *Daniel Boone*, NBC, 1964-70. Movies: *Fireball Forward*, ABC, 1972; *When Michael Calls*, ABC, 1972.

AWARDS: Academy Award nomination (with Arthur Quenzer), Best Music (Song), 1938, for the title song from *The Cowboy and the Lady;* Academy Award nomination, Best Music (Scoring of a Musical Picture), 1950, for *I'll Get By;* Academy Award nomination (with Eliot Daniel), Best Music (Song), 1951, for "Never" from *Golden Girl;* Academy Award nomination (with Alfred Newman), Best Music (Scoring of a Musical Picture), 1954, for *There's No Business Like Show Business;* Academy Award nomination, Best Music (Scoring of a Musical Picture), 1956, for *The Best Things in Life Are Free;* Academy Award nomination, Best Music (Scoring of a Musical Picture), 1958, for *Mardi Gras;* Academy Award nomination, Best Music (Scoring of a Musical Picture), 1959, for *Say One for Me;* Academy Award nomination (with Earle H. Hagen), Best Music (Scoring of a Musical Picture), 1960, for *Let's Make Love;* Academy Award nomination (with Alexander Courage), Best Music (Scoring of Music—Adaptation or Treatment), 1965, for *The Pleasure Seekers;* Academy Award nomination (with Courage), Best Music (Scoring of Music—Adaptation or Treatment), 1967, for *Doctor Dolittle;* Academy Award (with Lennie Hayton), Best Music (Score of a Musical Picture [Original or Adaptation], 1969, for *Hello, Dolly!*

OBITUARIES AND OTHER SOURCES: New York Times, February 8, 1989; *Variety,* February 8-14, 1989.*

*   *   *

NICHOLS, Mike   1931-

PERSONAL: Born Michael Igor Peschkowsky, November 6, 1931, in Berlin, Germany; surname legally changed in 1939; naturalized U.S. citizen, 1944; son of Nicholaievitch (a physician) and Brigitte (Landauer) Peschkowsky; married Patricia Scott (a singer), 1957 (divorced, 1960); married Margot Callas, 1963 (divorced, 1974); married Annabel Davis-Goff (a screenwriter; divorced); married Diane Sawyer (a television journalist), April 19, 1988; children:

MIKE NICHOLS

Daisy (first marriage); Max, Jenny (third marriage). EDUCATION—Attended the University of Chicago, 1950-53; trained for the stage with Lee Strasberg, 1954.

VOCATION: Actor, director, producer, and writer.

CAREER: Also see *WRITINGS* below. STAGE DEBUT—With the Playwrights Theatre Club, Chicago, IL. BROADWAY DEBUT—*An Evening with Mike Nichols and Elaine May,* John Golden Theatre, 1960. PRINCIPAL STAGE APPEARANCES—Howard Miller, *A Matter of Position,* Walnut Street Theatre, Philadelphia, PA, 1962; George, *Who's Afraid of Virginia Woolf?,* Long Wharf Theatre, New Haven, CT, 1980; also appeared in *Saint Joan,* Vancouver, BC, Canada.

PRINCIPAL STAGE WORK—All as director, unless indicated: *Barefoot in the Park,* Biltmore Theatre, New York City, 1963; *The Knack,* New Theatre, New York City, 1964; *Luv,* Booth Theatre, New York City, 1964; *The Odd Couple,* Plymouth Theatre, New York City, 1965; *The Apple Tree,* Shubert Theatre, New York City, 1966; *The Little Foxes,* Vivian Beaumont Theatre, New York City, 1967; *Plaza Suite,* Plymouth Theatre, 1968; *The Prisoner of Second Avenue,* Eugene O'Neill Theatre, New York City, 1971; *Uncle Vanya,* Circle in the Square/Joseph E. Levine Theatre, New York City, 1973; *Comedians,* Music Box Theatre, New York City, 1976; *Streamers,* New York Shakespeare Festival (NYSF), Mitzi E. Newhouse Theatre, New York City, 1976; producer, *Annie,* Alvin Theatre, New York City, 1977; (also producer with Hume Cronyn) *The Gin Game,* Long Wharf Theatre, New Haven, CT, then John Golden Theatre, New York City, both 1977, later Lyric Theatre, London, 1979; *Drinks Before Dinner,* NYSF, Public Theatre, New York City, 1978; producer (with Allen Lewis), *Billy Bishop Goes to War,* Theatre de Lys, then Morosco Theatre, both New York City, 1980; *Who's Afraid of Virginia Woolf?,* Long Wharf Theatre, New Haven, CT, 1980; *Lunch Hour,* Ethel Barrymore Theatre, New York City, 1980; *Fools,* Eugene O'Neill Theatre, 1981; producer (with Emanuel Azenberg), *Grownups,* Lyceum Theatre, New York City, 1981; *The Real Thing,* Plymouth Theatre, 1984; *Hurlyburly,* Goodman Theatre, Chicago, IL, then Promenade Theatre, New York City, later Ethel Barrymore Theatre, all 1984; producer (with Azenberg) and production supervisor, *Whoopi Goldberg,* Lyceum Theatre, 1984; *Social Security,* Ethel Barrymore Theatre, 1986; *Standup Shakespeare,* Theatre 890, New York City, 1987; *Waiting for Godot,* Mitzi E. Newhouse Theatre, 1988; also director, *The Importance of Being Earnest,* Vancouver, BC, Canada.

MAJOR TOURS—Director, *Barefoot in the Park,* U.S. cities, 1964; director, *The Prisoner of Second Avenue,* U.S. cities, 1972-73; producer (with Hume Cronyn) and director, *The Gin Game,* U.S. cities, 1978; producer, *Annie,* U.S. and Canadian cities, 1978-81.

PRINCIPAL FILM WORK—Director: *Who's Afraid of Virginia Woolf?,* Warner Brothers, 1966; *The Graduate,* Embassy, 1967; *Catch-22,* Filmways, 1970; (also producer) *Carnal Knowledge,* AVCO-Embassy, 1971; *The Day of the Dolphin,* AVCO-Embassy, 1973; (also producer with Don Devlin) *The Fortune,* Columbia, 1975; *Gilda Live,* Warner Brothers, 1980; (also producer with Michael Hausman) *Silkwood,* Twentieth Century-Fox, 1983; (also producer with Robert Greenhut) *Heartburn,* Paramount, 1986; *Biloxi Blues,* Universal, 1988; *Working Girl,* Twentieth Century-Fox, 1988.

PRINCIPAL TELEVISION APPEARANCES—Episodic: *The Jack Paar Show,* NBC, 1957; *Laugh Line,* NBC, 1959; also *The Today Show,* NBC; *The Perry Como Show,* NBC; *The Dinah Shore Show,*

NBC. Specials: *Accent on Love*, NBC, 1959; *The Fabulous '50s*, CBS, 1960; *Jack Parr Presents*, NBC, 1960; *The Jack Paar Special*, NBC, 1960; *A Last Laugh at the '60s*, ABC, 1970.

PRINCIPAL TELEVISION WORK—Series: Executive producer (with Aaron Spelling and Leonard Goldberg), *Family*, ABC, 1976-80; executive producer, *The Thorns*, ABC, 1988. Specials: Executive producer, *The "Annie" Christmas Show*, NBC, 1977; also *Broadway, An Evening with Mike Nichols and Elaine May*.

RELATED CAREER—Member, Compass Players (an improvisational theatrical company), Chicago, IL, 1955-57; performer (with Elaine May) in an improvisational comedy act, appearing in nightclubs and cabarets throughout the United States, 1957-61; performer at the Inaugural Gala for President Lyndon B. Johnson, Washington, DC, 1965; recorded albums with Elaine May.

WRITINGS: STAGE—Speical material, *The Carol Burnett Show*, Greek Theatre, Los Angeles, CA, 1966; (adaptor with Albert Todd) *Uncle Vanya*, Circle in the Square/Joseph E. Levine Theatre, New York City, 1973. TELEVISION—(With Ken Welch) *Julie and Carol at Carnegie Hall*, CBS, 1962.

AWARDS: Antionette Perry Award, Best Director, 1964, for *Barefoot in the Park;* Antionette Perry Award and *Variety*-New York Critics' Poll Award, both Best Director, 1965, for *The Odd Couple* and *Luv;* Outer Critics' Circle Award "for directing four current hits," 1965; Sam S. Shubert Foundation Award "for outstanding contributions to the New York legitimate theatre for the 1964-65 season," 1965; *Cue* magazine Award, Entertainer of the Year "for directorial achievements," 1965; Famous Fives Poll, Outstanding Director, and Academy Award nomination, Best Director, both 1966, for *Who's Afraid of Virginia Woolf?;* Academy Award, Best Director, 1967, New York Film Critics' Award, Best Director, 1967, Directors Guild of America Award, Outstanding Directorial Achievement, 1967, Golden Globe, Best Motion Picture Director, 1968, and British Academy of Film and Television Arts Award, Best Film Director, 1968, all for *The Graduate;* Antoinette Perry Award, Best Director, 1968, for *Plaza Suite;* Antoinette Perry Award, Best Director, 1972, for *The Prisoner of Second Avenue;* Antoinette Perry Award nomination, Best Director of a Drama, 1974, for *Uncle Vanya;* Antoinette Perry Award nominations, Best Director of a Play, 1977, for *Comedians* and *Streamers;* Antoinette Perry Award, Best Musical, 1977, for *Annie;* Antoinette Perry Award nomination, Best Director of a Play, 1978, for *The Gin Game;* Academy Award nomination, Best Director, 1983, for *Silkwood;* Antoinette Perry Award, Best Director of a Play, 1984, for *The Real Thing;* Academy Award nomination, Best Director, 1988, for *Working Girl.*

MEMBER: Actors' Equity Association, American Federation of Television and Radio Artists, Society of Stage Directors and Choreographers, Screen Actors Guild, American Guild of Variety Artists, Writers Guild of America.

SIDELIGHTS: RECREATIONS—Raising Arabian horses.

ADDRESSES: OFFICE—c/o Marvin B. Meyer, Rosenfeld, Meyer, and Sussman, 9601 Wilshire Boulevard, Beverly Hills, CA 90210. AGENT—Sam Cohn, International Creative Management, 40 W. 57th Street, New York, NY 10019.*

NICHOLS, Nichelle 1936-

PERSONAL: Born in 1936 in Chicago, IL; father, a mayor and chief magistrate.

VOCATION: Actress and singer.

CAREER: PRINCIPAL STAGE APPEARANCES—May, *Italian-American Reconciliation*, GNU Theatre, Los Angeles, 1987; also appeared in *No Strings*, 54th Street Theatre, New York City, 1952; *Reflections* (one-woman show), Los Angeles, 1990; as Hazel Sharp, *Kicks and Company;* title role, *Carmen Jones*, Chicago, IL; and in productions of *The Blacks, Blues for Mr. Charlie, For My People,* and *The Roar of the Greasepaint, the Smell of the Crowd.*

PRINCIPAL FILM APPEARANCES—Dancer, *Porgy and Bess*, Columbia, 1959; dice player, *Mister Buddwing* (also known as *Woman Without a Face*), Metro-Goldwyn-Mayer (MGM), 1966; Jenny Ribbock, *Doctor, You've Got to Be Kidding*, MGM, 1967; Dorinda, *Truck Turner*, American International, 1974; Lieutenant Commander Uhura, *Star Trek: The Motion Picture*, Paramount, 1979; Lieutenant Commander Uhura, *Star Trek II: The Wrath of Khan*, Paramount, 1982; Lieutenant Commander Uhura, *Star Trek III: The Search for Spock*, Paramount, 1984; Lieutenant Commander Uhura, *Star Trek IV: The Voyage Home*, Paramount, 1986; Sergeant Leona Hawkins, *The Supernaturals*, Republic Entertainment, 1987; Lieutenant Commander Uhura, *Star Trek V: The Final Frontier*, Paramount, 1989. Also appeared in *Made in Paris*, MGM, 1966.

PRINCIPAL TELEVISION APPEARANCES—Series: Lieutenant Uhura, *Star Trek*, NBC, 1966-69; voice of Lieutenant Uhura, *Star Trek* (animated), NBC, 1973-75. Episodic: Ruana, *Tarzan*, NBC, 1966; also *The Lieutenant*, NBC, 1964; *Head of the Class*, ABC, 1988. Specials: *Black Stars in Orbit*, PBS, 1990.

RELATED CAREER—Toured the United States, Canada, and Europe as a singer with the Duke Ellington and Lionel Hampton bands; nightclub performer at the Blue Note and the Playboy Club, both in New York City.

NON-RELATED CAREER—Spokesperson for the Kwanza Foundation; founder, Women in Motion (astronaut recruiting company); board member, National Space Institute; contributor to National Space Institute publications.

RECORDINGS: ALBUMS—*Dark Side of the Moon*, Americana. SINGLES—"Shoop Shoop," Twentieth Century.

AWARDS: Sara Siddons Award nominations for *The Blacks* and *Kicks and Company.*

SIDELIGHTS: RECREATIONS—Oil painting, designing clothes, reading science fiction, writing, sculpting, and sports cars.

ADDRESSES: AGENT—The Artists Group, 1930 Century Park W., Suite 303, Los Angeles, CA 90067.*

*   *   *

NITZSCHE, Jack

PERSONAL: Born Bernard Nitzsche, c. 1937, in Michigan. EDUCATION—Attended Westlake College of Music.

VOCATION: Composer, music director, and orchestrator.

CAREER: Also see *WRITINGS* below. PRINCIPAL FILM WORK—Music director, *Village of the Giants*, Embassy, 1965; music director and orchestrator, *When You Comin' Back, Red Ryder?*, Columbia, 1979. PRINCIPAL TELEVISION WORK—Specials: Music director, *Rolling Stone: The 10th Anniversary*, CBS, 1977.

RELATED CAREER—Music arranger for record producer Phil Spector, 1962-66; session musician with the Rolling Stones, 1965-66, and with Buffalo Springfield, 1967; keyboardist and producer for the music group Crazy Horse, 1970-71; keyboardist for the music group the Stray Gators, 1973; also music arranger for Specialty Records, Original Sound Records, record producer Lee Hazlewood, and for the Rolling Stones, the James Gang, Neil Young, and Ringo Starr; record producer for Neil Young, Buffy Sainte-Marie, Rick Nelson, Graham Parker, and Mink DeVille.

WRITINGS: All as composer. FILM—*Village of the Giants*, Embassy, 1965; *Performance*, Warner Brothers, 1970; *Greaser's Palace*, Greaser's Palace Ltd., 1972; *The Exorcist*, Warner Brothers, 1973; *One Flew Over the Cuckoo's Nest*, United Artists, 1975; (with Richard Hazard) *Heroes*, Universal, 1977; (with Ry Cooder) *Blue Collar*, Universal, 1978; *When You Comin' Back, Red Ryder?*, Columbia, 1979; *Hardcore*, Columbia, 1979; *Heart Beat*, Warner Brothers, 1979; *Melvin and Howard*, Universal, 1980; *Cruising*, United Artists, 1980; *Cutter's Way* (also known as *Cutter and Bone*), United Artists, 1981; *An Officer and a Gentleman*, Paramount, 1982; *Cannery Row*, Metro-Goldwyn-Mayer/United Artists (MGM/UA), 1982; *Personal Best*, Warner Brothers, 1982; *Without a Trace*, Twentieth Century-Fox, 1983; *Breathless*, Orion, 1983; *The Razor's Edge*, Columbia, 1984; *Starman*, Columbia, 1984; *Windy City*, Warner Brothers, 1984; *The Jewel of the Nile*, Twentieth Century-Fox, 1985; (with Michael Hoenig) *9 1/2 Weeks*, MGM/UA, 1986; *Stand By Me*, Columbia, 1986; *Streets of Gold*, Twentieth Century-Fox, 1986; (with Buffy Sainte-Marie) *Stripper*, Twentieth Century-Fox, 1986; *The Whoopee Boys*, Paramount, 1986; *The Seventh Sign*, Tri-Star, 1988; *Next of Kin*, Warner Brothers, 1989. TELEVISION—Series: *Starman*, ABC, 1986-87.

OTHER—Songs: (With Sonny Bono) "Needles and Pins," 1963; "The Lonely Surfer," 1963; "Gone Dead Train," 1970; (with Ry Cooder and Paul Schrader) "Hard Working Man," 1978; "No One Knows Better Than You," 1979; "I Love Her Too," 1979; "We're Old Enough to Know," 1981; (with Will Jennings and Buffy Sainte-Marie) "Up Where We Belong," 1982; "Hit and Run Lovers," 1984.

RECORDINGS: ALBUMS—*The Lonely Surfer*, Reprise, 1963; (with the London Symphony Orchestra) *St. Giles Cripplegate*, Reprise, 1972; *One Flew Over the Cuckoo's Nest* (original soundtrack), Fantasy, 1975; *Blue Collar* (original soundtrack), MCA, 1978; *The Razor's Edge* (original soundtrack), Southern Cross, 1984; *Starman* (original soundtrack), Varese/Sarabande, 1984.

AWARDS: Academy Award (with Will Jennings and Buffy Sainte-Marie), Best Song, 1983, for "Up Where We Belong" (from *An Officer and a Gentleman*).

OTHER SOURCES: The Illustrated Encyclopedia of Rock, Harmony Books, 1977; *Rolling Stone Encyclopedia of Rock & Roll*, Summit Books, 1983.*

NOONAN, Tom   1951-

PERSONAL: Born April 12, 1951, in Greenwich, CT; married Karen Young (an actress). EDUCATION—Graduated from Yale University.

VOCATION: Actor.

CAREER: OFF-BROADWAY DEBUT—Tilden, *Buried Child*, Theatre De Lys, 1978. PRINCIPAL STAGE APPEARANCES—Sepp, *Farmyard*, Theater for the New City, New York City, 1981; Rube Janik, *Spookhouse*, Playhouse 91, New York City, 1984; also appeared in productions of *The Invitational, The Breakers, Five of Us*, and *Marathon '88*, all in New York City.

PRINCIPAL FILM APPEARANCES—Man in park, *Willie and Phil*, Twentieth Century-Fox, 1980; gangster, *Gloria*, Columbia, 1980; Jake, *Heaven's Gate*, United Artists, 1980; Ferguson, *Wolfen*, Warner Brothers, 1981; Paddy, *Easy Money*, Orion, 1983; Daryl Potts, *Eddie Macon's Run*, Universal, 1983; Holtzman, *Best Defense*, Paramount, 1984; Reese, *The Man with One Red Shoe*, Twentieth Century-Fox, 1985; Varrick, *F/X*, Orion, 1986; Francis Dollarhyde, *Manhunter*, De Laurentiis Entertainment Group, 1986; Frankenstein, *The Monster Squad*, Tri-Star, 1987; man in diner, "A Ghost" in *Mystery Train*, Orion Classics, 1989. Also appeared in *Tom Goes to the Bar* (short film), Cinecom International, 1986; *Collision Course* (also known as *East/West Cop*), Recorded Releasing/Rich International, 1989.

PRINCIPAL TELEVISION APPEARANCES—Episodic: Brandon Thonton, *The Equalizer*, CBS, 1989. Movies: Bo, *Rage*, NBC, 1980.*

                    *   *   *

NOYES, Thomas   1922-1989

PERSONAL: Full name, Thomas Ewing Noyes; born October 24, 1922, in Washington, DC; died of heart failure, October 28, 1989, in Washington, DC; son of Newbold (a journalist) and Alexandra (Ewing) Noyes; married Ann Lilienthal, December 19, 1944 (divorced, 1951): married Elizabeth Ross (an actress), February 22, 1952; children: Christopher, Alexander, Victoria. EDUCATION—Yale University, B.A., 1947. MILITARY—U.S. Navy Air Corps, flight instructor, ensign, 1942-43.

VOCATION: Producer and actor.

CAREER: STAGE DEBUT—Mr. Bonaparte, *Golden Boy*, Yale University Dramatic Association, New Haven, CT, 1946. PRINCIPAL STAGE APPEARANCES—Second gendarme and second seaman, *Now I Lay Me Down to Sleep*, Broadhurst Theatre, New York City, 1950; Carter Reynolds, *The Small Hours*, National Theatre, New York City, 1951; Duncan, *Billy Budd*, Biltmore Theatre, New York City, 1951.

FIRST STAGE WORK—Producer of a season of plays for the Yale Players, Siasconset, MA, 1946. PRINCIPAL STAGE WORK—(With Ann Noyes) *The Innocents*, Pocono Playhouse, Mountainhome, PA, 1949; (with Lyn Austin) *Take a Giant Step*, Lyceum Theatre, New York City, 1953; (with Austin) *The Frogs of Spring*, Broadhurst Theatre, New York City, 1953; (with Austin) *Portrait of a Lady*, American National Theatre and Academy Theatre, New York City,

1954; (with Austin and Roger Stevens) *Blue Denim*, Westport Country Playhouse, Westport, CT, 1955; (with Austin) *Joyce Grenfell Requests the Pleasure . . .*, Bijou Theatre, New York City, 1955; (with Austin and Stevens) *The Crystal Heart*, Saville Theatre, London, 1957; (with Austin) *Copper and Brass*, Martin Beck Theatre, New York City, 1957.

PRINCIPAL TELEVISION APPEARANCES—Episodic: *Lux Video Theatre*, NBC, 1951.

PRINCIPAL RADIO APPEARANCES—Series: Host of a talk show, WRC-AM (Washington, DC), during the 1980s; commentator, *All Things Considered*, NPR.

RELATED CAREER—Consultant to the National Endowment for the Humanities and to National Public Radio, both during the 1970s.

NON-RELATED CAREER—General assigment reporter, *Long Island Press*, 1959-64; reporter and editorial writer, *Washington Evening Star*, Washington, DC, 1964-72.

OBITUARIES AND OTHER SOURCES: New York Times, October 31, 1989; *Variety*, November 8, 1989.*

O

O'BANNON, Dan 1946-

PERSONAL: Full name, Daniel Thomas O'Bannon; born September 30, 1946, in St. Louis, MO; son of Thomas Sidney and Bertha (Lowenthal) O'Bannon; married Diane Louise Lindley, January 18, 1986. EDUCATION—University of Southern California, B.F.A., cinema, 1970; also attended the Washington University School of Fine Arts, 1964-66, and MacMurray College, 1966-68.

VOCATION: Screenwriter and director.

CAREER: Also see *WRITINGS* below. PRINCIPAL FILM APPEARANCES—Pinback, *Dark Star*, Jack H. Harris, 1975. PRINCIPAL FILM WORK Editor, production designer, set decorator, special effects photographer, and special effects director (with Bill Taylor), *Dark Star*, Jack H. Harris, 1975; computer animator, *Star Wars*, Twentieth-Century Fox, 1977; animation designer (with Thomas Warkentin, Angus McKie, Richard Corben, Juan Gimenez, and Lee Mishkin), *Heavy Metal*, Columbia, 1981; director, *The Return of the Living Dead*, Orion, 1985.

WRITINGS: FILM—(With John Carpenter) *Dark Star*, Jack H. Harris, 1975; *Alien*, Twentieth Century-Fox, 1979; (with Ronald Shusett) *Dead and Buried*, AVCO-Embassy, 1981; (with Warkentin, McKie, Corben, Dan Goldberg, Len Blum, and Berni Wrightson) *Heavy Metal*, Columbia, 1981; (with Don Jakoby) *Blue Thunder*, Columbia, 1983; (with Jakoby) *Lifeforce*, Tri-Star, 1985; *The Return of the Living Dead*, Orion, 1985; (with Jakoby) *Invaders from Mars*, Cannon, 1986. TELEVISION—Episodic: *Blue Thunder*, ABC, 1984.

MEMBERS: Writers Guild of America—West.

ADDRESSES: OFFICE—c/o Jim Rogers and Associates, 8285 Sunset Boulevard, Los Angeles, CA 90046. AGENT—Morton Agency, 1105 Glendon Avenue, Los Angeles, CA 90024. PUBLICIST—Nan Herst Public Relations, 8733 Sunset Boulevard, Suite 103, Los Angeles, CA 90069.*

*   *   *

O'BRIEN, Jack 1939-

PERSONAL: Full name, Jack George O'Brien; born June 18, 1939, in Saginaw, MI; son of J. George (a business representative) and Evelyn Mae (MacArthur Martens) O'Brien. EDUCATION—University of Michigan, A.B., 1961, M.A., 1962; trained for the stage with Ellis Rabb and John Houseman.

VOCATION: Director.

CAREER: PRINCIPAL STAGE WORK—Assistant director, *You Can't Take It with You*, *War and Peace*, *Pantagleize*, and *The Cherry Orchard*, all APA Phoenix Repertory Company, Lyceum Theatre, New York City, 1967; assistant director, *Pantagleize* and *The Cocktail Party*, both APA Phoenix Repertory Company, Lyceum Theatre, 1968; assistant director, *Hamlet* and director, *Cock-a-Doodle Dandy*, both APA Phoenix Repertory Company, Lyceum Theatre, 1969; assistant director, *Hamlet*, National Shakespeare Festival, Old Globe Theatre, San Diego, CA, 1969; director, *Merry Wives of Windsor*, National Shakespeare Festival, Old Globe Theatre, 1972; director, *Dido and Aeneas* (opera), Dallas Civic Opera, Dallas, TX, 1972; associate artistic director, *The Three Sisters*, Billy Rose Theatre, New York City, 1973; director, *Much Ado About Nothing*, National Shakespeare Festival, Old Globe Theatre, 1975; director, *The Abduction from the Seraglio* (opera), San Francisco Spring Opera, San Francisco, CA, 1975; director, *The Magic Flute* (opera), San Francisco Opera, San Francisco, CA, 1975; director, *The Time of Your Life*, Harkness Theatre, New York City, 1975; director, *As You Like It* National Shakespeare Festival, Old Globe Theatre, 1976; director, *Our Town*, Old Globe Theatre, 1976; director, *Porgy and Bess*, Houston Grand Opera, Uris Theatre, then Mark Hellinger Theatre, both New York City, 1976; director, *Nefertiti*, Blackstone Theatre, Chicago, IL, 1977; director, *Hamlet*, National Shakespeare Festival, Old Globe Theatre, 1977; director, *Street Scene*, New York City Opera, State Theatre, New York City, 1977; director, *A Midsummer Night's Dream*, National Shakespeare Festival, Old Globe Theatre, 1978; director, *Tosca* (opera), Santa Fe Opera, Santa Fe, MN, 1978; director, *Aida* (opera), Houston Grand Opera, Houston, TX, 1979; director, *A Man for All Seasons*, Center Theatre Group, Ahmanson Theatre, Los Angeles, 1979; director, *The Most Happy Fella*, Majestic Theatre, New York City, 1979.

Director, *Romeo and Juliet*, National Shakespeare Festival, Old Globe Theatre, 1980; director, *King Lear* and *The Country Wife*, both National Shakespeare Festival, Old Globe Theatre, 1981; director, *Mary Stuart*, Center Theatre Group, Ahmanson Theatre, 1981; director, *The Gin Game*, *The Tempest*, and *Yankee Wives*, all Old Globe Theatre, 1982-83; director, *Porgy and Bess* Radio City Music Hall, New York City, 1983; director, *The Skin of Our Teeth*, *Twelfth Night*, and *Macbeth*, all Old Globe Theatre, 1983; director, *Othello*, *Season's Greetings*, and *The Torch-Bearers*, all Old Globe Theatre, 1984-85; director, *A Midsummer Night's Dream* and (with Tom Moore) *Fallen Angels*, both Old Globe Theatre, 1985; director, *The Lighthouse* (opera), San Diego Chamber Opera, San Diego, CA, 1986; director, *Emily* and *The Incredibly Famous Willy Rivers*, both Old Globe Theatre, 1986-87; director, *The Cocktail Hour*, Old Globe Theatre, 1988, then Promenade Theatre, New York City, 1989; director, *Up in Saratoga*, Old Globe

Theatre, 1989. Also director, *The Tavern*, Lake Forest Playhouse, 1972; director, *Il Cordovano* (opera), American Opera Center, 1976; director, *Cosi Fan Tutti* (opera), Texas Opera Theatre, 1980; director, *White Linen, Antony and Cleopatra*, and *Kiss Me Kate*, all Old Globe Theatre; executive producer, National Shakespeare Festival, Old Globe Theatre, 1983; director of productions with the American Conservatory Theatre, San Francisco, CA, 1970-71, 1972-74, 1976-77, and 1980-81, and with the Studio Arena Theatre, Buffalo, NY, 1980-81.

MAJOR TOURS—Director, *Porgy and Bess*, U.S. and European cities, 1977-78, then in fourteen opera company consortium, 1986-87.

PRINCIPAL TELEVISION WORK—All as director. Episodic: "The Time of Your Life," *Theatre in America*, PBS, 1976; "The Skin of Our Teeth," *American Playhouse*, PBS, 1983; "Painting Churches," *American Playhouse*, PBS, 1986; "All My Sons," *American Playhouse*, PBS, 1987; "I Never Sang for My Father," *American Playhouse*, PBS; 1988. Specials: "The Good Doctor," *Great Performances*, PBS, 1977; "The Most Happy Fella," *Great Performances*, PBS, 1980; also "Street Scene," *Live from Lincoln Center*, PBS.

RELATED CAREER—Theatre instructor, Hunter College, New York City, 1963-64; associate artistic director, the Acting Company, New York City, 1974-75; artistic director, Old Globe Theatre, San Diego, CA, 1981—; member, board of directors, Theatre Communications Group, 1989—; member, Opera/Musical Theatre Professional Companies Panel of the National Endowment for the Arts.

WRITINGS: STAGE—(Adaptor and translator) *Orpheus in the Underworld*, Dallas Civic Opera, Dallas, TX, and Kansas City Civic Opera, Kansas City, MO, 1968; (adaptor and translator) *Le Coq d'Or*, Dallas Civic Opera, 1971; (book with Stuart Hample and lyrics) *The Selling of the President*, American Conservatory Theatre, San Francisco, CA, 1971, then Shubert Theatre, New York City, 1972.

AWARDS: Antoinette Perry Award nomination, Best Director, 1977, for *Porgy and Bess;* Drama Desk Award nomination, Best Director, 1989, for *The Cocktail Hour*.

MEMBER: Actors' Equity Association, Society of Stage Directors and Choreographers, Directors Guild, American Society of Composers, Authors, and Publishers, National Fund for New American Plays.

ADDRESSES: OFFICE—Old Globe Theatre, P.O. Box 2171, San Diego, CA 92112. AGENT—Phyllis Wender, Rosenstone/Wender, 3 E. 48th Street, New York, NY 10017.

*   *   *

O'HARA, Jenny

PERSONAL: Born February 24, in Sonora, CA. EDUCATION—Attended the Carnegie School of Technology (now Carnegie-Mellon University).

VOCATION: Actress.

CAREER: BROADWAY DEBUT—*Dylan*, Plymouth Theatre, 1964. PRINCIPAL STAGE APPEARANCES—Louka, *Arms and the Man*, Sheridan Square Playhouse, New York City, 1967; Pookie Chapman, *The Fig Leaves Are Falling*, Broadhurst Theatre, New York City, 1969; the Tiger, *Sambo*, New York Shakespeare Festival, Public Theatre, New York City, 1969; Lucy Tyler, *My House Is Your House*, Players Theatre, New York City, 1970; Fran Kubelik, *Promises, Promises*, Shubert Theatre, New York City, 1971; Belle, *The Kid*, American Place Theatre, New York City, 1972; Pearl, *The Iceman Cometh*, Circle in the Square/Joseph E. Levine Theatre, New York City, 1973; Nelli March, *The Fox*, Roundabout Theatre, New York City, 1982; Sylvie, *The Odd Couple*, Center Theatre Group, Ahmanson Theatre, Los Angeles, 1984, then Broadhurst Theatre, New York City, 1985-86; Miss Ritter, *She Loves Me*, Ahmanson Theatre, 1987. Also appeared in *Play with a Tiger*, Renata Theatre, New York City, 1964; *Hang Your Head and Die*, Mayfair Theatre, New York City, 1964; *Kid Twist*, Center Theatre Group, Mark Taper Forum, Los Angeles, 1978; *Hello and Goodbye*, Yale Repertory Theatre, New Haven, CT, 1982; *Daughters*, Philadelphia Drama Guild, Philadelphia, PA, 1982.

PRINCIPAL FILM APPEARANCES—Betty Bendix, *Heart Beat*, Warner Brothers, 1979; first party dancer, *The Last Married Couple in America*, Universal, 1980.

PRINCIPAL TELEVISION APPEARANCES—Series: Miss Emily Mahoney, *The Facts of Life*, NBC, 1979; Rebecca, *Highcliffe Manor*, NBC, 1979; Lucy Dexter, *Secrets of Midland Heights*, CBS, 1980-81; Dixie Randazzo, *My Sister Sam*, CBS, 1986-88; Muriel Spiegelman, *Live-In*, CBS, 1989. Mini-Series: Ruth Manly, *Black Beauty*, NBC, 1978; Liz Garfield, *Blind Ambition*, CBS, 1979; resistance fighter, *V—The Final Battle*, NBC, 1984. Pilots: Dr. Joan Watson, *The Return of the World's Greatest Detective*, NBC, 1976. Episodic: Mrs. Montebello, *Family*, ABC, 1976; Miss Chase, *Family*, ABC, 1976; Lisa, *Murphy Brown*, CBS, 1988; also *Barney Miller*, ABC, 1978 and 1979. Movies: Maggie Hefner, *Brink's: The Great Robbery*, CBS, 1976; Carol Arizzio, *The Hunted Lady*, NBC, 1977; the woman, *Good Against Evil*, ABC, 1977; Ann Webster, *A Fire in the Sky*, NBC, 1978; Patty Miller, *Letters from Frank*, CBS, 1979; Deb Pierce, *The Last Song*, CBS, 1980; Rose, *Blinded By the Light*, CBS, 1980; Mrs. Martinelli, *The Women's Room*, ABC, 1980; Peggy, *Another Woman's Child*, CBS, 1983; Lisa Mason, *The Secret Life of Kathy McCormick*, NBC, 1988; Miriam, *Winnie*, NBC, 1988. Specials: Host, *Rollin' on the River*, 1971.

ADDRESSES: AGENTS—Century Artists, 9744 Wilshire Boulevard, Suite 308, Beverly Hills, CA 90212.*

*   *   *

O'HARA, Maureen   1921-
(Maureen Fitzsimmons)

PERSONAL: Born Maureen Fitzsimmons, August 17, 1921, in Milltown, Ireland; naturalized U.S. citizen, 1946; married George Hanley Brown (a director), 1939 (divorced, 1941); married Will Price (a director), 1941 (divorced, 1952); married Charles F. Blair, 1968 (died, 1978); children: one daughter (second marriage). EDUCATION—Trained for the stage at the Abbey Theatre School, the Guildhall School of Music, and the London College of Music.

VOCATION: Actress.

CAREER: FILM DEBUT—(As Maureen Fitzsimmons) Secretary, *Kicking the Moon Around* (also known as *The Playboy* and *Millionaire Merry-Go-Round*), General Film Distributors, 1938. PRINCIPAL FILM APPEARANCES—Mary Yelland, *Jamaica Inn*, Paramount, 1939; Esmeralda, *The Hunchback of Notre Dame*, RKO, 1939; Sidney Fairfield, *A Bill of Divorcement* (also known as *Never to Love*), RKO, 1940; Judy, *Dance, Girl, Dance*, RKO, 1940; Eileen O'Shea, *Little Miss Molly* (also known as *My Irish Molly*), Alliance, 1940; Angharad Morgan, *How Green Was My Valley*, Twentieth Century-Fox, 1941; Lolita, *They Met in Argentina*, RKO, 1941; Margaret Denby, *The Black Swan*, Twentieth Century-Fox, 1942; Carolyn Bainbridge, *Ten Gentlemen from West Point*, Twentieth Century-Fox, 1942; Second Lieutenant Mary Carter, *To the Shores of Tripoli*, Twentieth Century-Fox, 1942; Toni Donne, *The Fallen Sparrow*, RKO, 1943; Valentine, *The Immortal Sergeant*, Twentieth Century-Fox, 1943; Louise Martin, *This Land Is Mine*, RKO, 1943; Louisa Cody, *Buffalo Bill*, Twentieth Century-Fox, 1944; Francisca, *The Spanish Main*, RKO, 1945; Katherine Hilliard, *Do You Love Me?* (also known as *Kitten on the Keys*), Twentieth Century-Fox, 1946; Julie, *Sentimental Journey*, Twentieth Century-Fox, 1946; Odalie D'Arceneaux, *The Foxes of Harrow*, Twentieth Century-Fox, 1947; Leslie Hale, *The Homestretch*, Twentieth Century-Fox, 1947; Doris Walker, *Miracle on 34th Street*, Twentieth Century-Fox, 1947; Shireen, *Sinbad the Sailor*, RKO, 1947; Tracey, *Sitting Pretty*, Twentieth Century-Fox, 1948; Adelaide Culver, *Affairs of Adelaide* (also known as *Forbidden Street* and *Britannia Mews*), Twentieth Century-Fox, 1949; Princess Marjan, *Bagdad*, Universal, 1949; Elizabeth Cooper, *Father Was a Fullback*, Twentieth Century-Fox, 1949; Marian Washburn, *A Woman's Secret*, RKO, 1949.

Katie, *Commanche Territory*, Universal, 1950; Mrs. Kathleen Yorke, *Rio Grande*, Republic, 1950; Countess D'Arneau, *Tripoli* (also known as *First Marines*), Paramount, 1950; Claire, *At Sword's Point* (also known as *Sons of the Musketeers*), RKO, 1951; Princess Tanya, *Flame of Araby*, Universal, 1951; Spitfire Stevens, *Against All Flags*, Universal, 1952; Dell McGuire, *Kangaroo*, Twentieth Century-Fox, 1952; Mary Kate Danaher, *The Quiet Man*, Republic, 1952; Kate Maxwell, *The Redhead from Wyoming*, Universal, 1953; Elaine Corwin, *War Arrow*, Universal, 1953; Joanna Dane, *Fire Over Africa* (also known as *Malaga*), Columbia, 1954; title role, *Lady Godiva*, Universal, 1955; Mary O'Donnell, *The Long Gray Line*, Columbia, 1955; Karen Harrison, *The Magnificent Matador* (also known as *The Brave and the Beautiful*), Twentieth Century-Fox, 1955; Joan Madison, *Everything But the Truth*, Universal, 1956; Sylvia Merrill, *Lisbon*, Republic, 1956; Minnie Wead, *The Wings of Eagles*, Metro-Goldwyn-Mayer, 1957.

Beatrice Severn, *Our Man in Havana*, Columbia, 1960; Kit Tilden, *The Deadly Companions* (also known as *Trigger Happy*), Pathe/American, 1961; Maggie McKendrick, *The Parent Trap*, Buena Vista, 1961; Peggy Hobbs, *Mr. Hobbs Takes a Vacation*, Twentieth Century-Fox, 1962; Katherine McLintock, *McLintock!*, United Artists, 1963; Olivia Spencer, *Spencer's Mountain*, Warner Brothers, 1963; Moira, *The Battle of the Villa Fiorita* (also known as *Affair at the Villa Fiorita*), Warner Brothers, 1965; Martha Price, *The Rare Breed*, Universal, 1966; Elsie Waltz, *How Do I Love Thee?*, Cinerama, 1970; Martha McCandles, *Big Jake*, National General, 1971.

PRINCIPAL TELEVISION APPEARANCES—Episodic: Constance Peterson, "Spellbound," *Theater '62*, NBC, 1962. Movies: Ruth Tiflin, *The Red Pony*, NBC, 1973. Specials: *The Bob Hope Show*, NBC, 1959; *The Talent Scouts Program*, NBC, 1960; *Talent Search*, NBC, 1960; Susanna Cibber, "A Cry of Angels," *Hall-*

mark Hall of Fame, NBC, 1963; *The Andy Williams Show*, NBC, 1964; Mother Goose, *Who's Afraid of Mother Goose?*, ABC, 1967; *The Fabulous Fordies*, NBC, 1972. Also appeared in *Mrs. Miniver, The Scarlet Pimpernel,* and *High Button Shoes.*

RELATED CAREER—Radio performer from age twelve; co-founder, Price Merman Productions, 1951; also appeared in repertory with the Abbey Theatre, Dublin, Ireland.*

*   *   *

OLD, John M.
  See BAVA, Mario

*   *   *

OLIVIER, Laurence   1907-1989

PERSONAL: Full name, Laurence Kerr Olivier; born May 22, 1907, in Dorking, England; died July 11, 1989, in Steyning, England; son of Gerard Kerr (a clergyman) and Agnes Louise (Crookenden) Olivier; married Jill Esmond (an actress), 1930 (divorced, 1940); married Vivien Leigh (an actress), August 30, 1940 (divorced, 1960); married Joan Plowright (an actress), March 17, 1961; children: Simon Tarquin (first marriage); Richard Kerr, Tamsin Agnes Margaret, and Julie Kate (third marriage). EDUCA-

LAURENCE OLIVIER

TION—Attended St. Edward's School, 1921-24; studied acting with Elsie Fogerty at the Central School of Speech Training and Dramatic Art. MILITARY—Royal Navy, Fleet Air Arm, 1944.

VOCATION: Actor, director, and producer.

CAREER: Also see *WRITINGS* below. STAGE DEBUT—Policeman, *The Ghost Train,* Brighton Hippodrome, Brighton, U.K. BROADWAY DEBUT—Hugh Bromilow, *Murder on the Second Floor,* Eltinge Theatre, 1929. PRINCIPAL STAGE APPEARANCES—Suliot officer, *Byron,* Century Theatre, London, 1924; Thomas of Clarence and Snare, *Henry IV, Part Two,* Fellowship of Players, Regent Theatre, London, 1925; Tony Lumpkin, *She Stoops to Conquer* and Minstrel, *The Marvelous History of Saint Bernard,* both Birmingham Repertory Company, Kingsway Theatre, Birmingham, U.K., 1926; young man, *The Adding Machine,* Malcolm, *Macbeth,* Martellus, *Back to Methuselah,* title role, *Harold,* and Lord, *The Taming of the Shrew,* all Birmingham Repertory Company, Court Theatre, London, 1928; Gerald Arnwood, *Bird in Hand,* Royalty Theatre, London, 1928; Captain Stanhope, *Journey's End,* Stage Society, Apollo Theatre, London, 1928; Michael "Beau" Geste, *Beau Geste,* His Majesty's Theatre, London, 1929; Prince Po, *The Circle of Chalk,* New Theatre, London, 1929; Richard Parish, *Paris Bound,* Lyric Theatre, London, 1929; John Hardy, *The Stranger Within,* Garrick Theatre, London, 1929; Jerry Warrender, *The Last Enemy,* Fortune Theatre, London, 1929; Ralph, *After All,* Arts Theatre, London, 1930; Victor Prynne, *Private Lives,* Phoenix Theatre, London, 1930, then Times Square Theatre, New York City, 1931; Steven Beringer, *The Rats of Norway,* Playhouse Theatre, London, 1933; Julian Dulcimer, *The Green Bay Tree,* Cort Theatre, New York City, 1933; Richard Kurt, *Biography,* Globe Theatre, London, 1934; Bothwell, *Queen of Scots,* New Theatre, 1934; Anthony Cavendish, *Theatre Royal,* Lyric Theatre, 1934.

Peter Hammond, *Ringmaster,* Shaftesbury Theatre, London, 1935; Richard Harben, *Golden Arrow,* Whitehall Theatre, London, 1935; Romeo, then Mercutio, *Romeo and Juliet,* New Theatre, 1935; Robert Patch, *Bees on the Boatdeck,* Lyric Theatre, 1936; title role, *Hamlet,* Old Vic Theatre Company, Old Vic Theatre, London, then Kronborg Castle, Elsinore, Denmark, both 1937; Sir Toby Belch, *Twelfth Night* and title role, *Henry V,* both Old Vic Theatre Company, Old Vic Theatre, 1937; title role, *Macbeth,* Old Vic Theatre Company, Old Vic Theatre, then New Theatre, both 1937; Iago, *Othello,* Vivaldi, *The King of Nowhere,* and Caius Marcius, *Coriolanus,* all Old Vic Theatre Company, Old Vic Theatre, 1938; Gaylord Easterbrook, *No Time for Comedy,* Ethel Barrymore Theatre, New York City, 1939; Romeo, *Romeo and Juliet,* 51st Street Theatre, New York City, 1940; Button Moulder, *Peer Gynt,* Sergius Saranoff, *Arms and the Man,* and title role, *Richard III,* all Old Vic Theatre Company, New Theatre, 1944, then Comedie-Francaise Theatre, Paris, France, 1945; title role, *Oedipus* and Puff, *The Critic* (double-bill), Astrov, *Uncle Vanya,* Hotspur, *Henry IV, Part One,* and Justice Shallow, *Henry IV, Part Two,* all Old Vic Theatre Company, New Theatre, 1945; title role, *Oedipus* and Puff, *The Critic* (double-bill), Hotspur, *Henry IV, Part One,* Justice Shallow, *Henry IV, Part Two,* and Astrov, *Uncle Vanya,* all Old Vic Theatre Company, Century Theatre, New York City, 1946; title role, *King Lear,* Old Vic Theatre Company, New Theatre, 1946; Sir Peter Teazle, *The School for Scandal,* title role, *Richard III,* and Chorus, *Antigone,* all Old Vic Theatre Company, New Theatre, 1949.

Duke of Altair, *Venus Observed,* St. James' Theatre, London, 1950; Caesar, *Caesar and Cleopatra* and Antony, *Antony and Cleopatra,* both St. James' Theatre, then Ziegfeld Theatre, New York City, both 1951; Grand Duke, *The Sleeping Prince,* Phoenix Theatre, 1953; title role, *Macbeth,* title role, *Titus Andronicus,* and Malvolio, *Twelfth Night,* all Shakespeare Memorial Theatre Company, Shakespeare Memorial Theatre, Stratford-on-Avon, U.K., 1955; title role, *Titus Andronicus,* Stoll Theatre, London, 1957; Archie Rice, *The Entertainer,* English Stage Company, Royal Court Theatre, then Palace Theatre, both London, 1957, later Royale Theatre, New York City, 1958; title role, *Coriolanus,* Shakespeare Memorial Theatre Company, Shakespeare Memorial Theatre, 1959; Berenger, *Rhinoceros,* Royal Court Theatre, then Strand Theatre, London, both 1960; title role, *Becket,* St. James Theatre, New York City, 1960; Henry II, *Becket,* Hudson Theatre, New York City, 1961; Prologue and Bassanes, *The Broken Heart* and Astrov, *Uncle Vanya,* both Chichester Theatre Festival, Chichester, U.K., 1962; Fred Midway, *Semi-Detached,* Saville Theatre, London, 1962; Astrov, *Uncle Vanya,* Chichester Theatre Festival, 1963; Astrov, *Uncle Vanya* and Captain Brazen, *The Recruiting Officer,* both National Theatre Company, Old Vic Theatre, 1963; title role, *Othello,* National Theatre Company, Old Vic Theatre, then Chichester Theatre Festival, both 1964; Halvard Solness, *The Master Builder,* National Theatre Company, Old Vic Theatre, 1964.

Tattle, *Love for Love,* National Theatre Company, Old Vic Theatre, 1965; Edgar, *The Dance of Death,* National Theatre Company, National Theatre, London, 1967; Etienne, *A Flea in Her Ear,* National Theatre Company, National Theatre, 1967; A.B. Raham, *Home and Beauty,* National Theatre Company, National Theatre, 1969; Chebutikin, *The Three Sisters,* National Theatre Company, National Theatre, then Brighton Royal Theatre, Brighton, U.K., both 1969; Shylock, *The Merchant of Venice,* National Theatre Company, National Theatre, 1970; James Tyrone, *Long Day's Journey into Night,* National Theatre Company, National Theatre, 1971; Antonio, *Saturday, Sunday, Monday* and John Tagg, *The Party,* both National Theatre Company, National Theatre, 1973; holographic image, *Time,* Dominion Theatre, London, 1986. Also appeared in *Henry VIII* and *The Cenci,* both Empire Theatre, London, 1925.

PRINCIPAL STAGE WORK—Producer, *Golden Arrow,* Whitehall Theatre, London, 1935; producer (with Ralph Richardson), *Bees on the Boatdeck,* Lyric Theatre, London, 1936; producer and director (with Robert Ross), *Romeo and Juliet,* 51st Street Theatre, New York City, 1940; producer, *The Skin of Our Teeth,* Phoenix Theatre, London, 1945; director, *King Lear,* Old Vic Theatre Company, New Theatre, London, 1946; producer, *Born Yesterday,* Garrick Theatre, London, 1947; producer, *A Streetcar Named Desire,* Aldwych Theatre, London, 1949; director, *Antigone* and *The Proposal* (double-bill) and *The School for Scandal,* both Old Vic Theatre Company, New Theatre, 1949; producer, *Venus Observed* and *Captain Carvallo,* both St. James's Theatre, London, 1950; producer, *Caesar and Cleopatra, Antony and Cleopatra,* and *Othello,* all St. James's Theatre, 1951; producer (with Gilbert Miller), *The Happy Time,* St. James's Theatre, 1952; director, *Venus Observed,* New Century Theatre, New York City, 1952; producer, *Anastasia,* St. James's Theatre, 1953; producer, *Waiting for Gillian,* St. James's Theatre, 1954; producer, *Meet a Body,* Duke of York's Theatre, London, 1954.

Producer, *Double Image,* Savoy Theatre, London, 1956; producer, *The Summer of the Seventeenth Doll,* New Theatre, 1957; producer, *The Shifting Heart,* Duke of York's Theatre, 1959; producer (with others), *The Tumbler,* Helen Hayes Theatre, New York City, 1960; producer, *A Lodging for a Bride,* Westminster Theatre, London,

1960; producer (with others), *Over the Bridge*, Prince's Theatre, London, 1960; director, *The Chances, The Broken Heart*, and *Uncle Vanya*, all Chichester Theatre Festival, Chichester, U.K., 1962; director, *Hamlet*, National Theatre Company, Old Vic Theatre, London, 1963; director, *Uncle Vanya*, National Theatre Company, Old Vic Theatre, 1963; director, *The Crucible*, National Theatre Company, National Theatre, London, 1965; director, *Juno and the Paycock*, National Theatre Company, Alexandra Theatre, Birmingham, U.K., then National Theatre, both 1966; director, *The Three Sisters*, National Theatre, 1967; director (with others), *The Advertisement*, Brighton Royal Theatre, Brighton, U.K., 1968; director, *Love's Labour's Lost*, National Theatre Company, National Theatre, 1968; director, *The Three Sisters*, National Theatre Company, Ahmanson Theatre, Los Angeles, 1970; director, *Amphitryon Thirty-Eight*, National Theatre Company, New Theatre, Oxford, U.K., then National Theatre, both 1971; director, *Eden End*, National Theatre Company, Richmond Theatre, London, then National Theatre, both 1974; director, *Filumena*, St. James Theatre, New York City, 1980.

MAJOR TOURS—Richard Coaker, *The Farmer's Wife*, U.K. cities, 1926; Mr. Antrobus, *The Skin of Our Teeth*, and in *The School for Scandal* and *Richard III*, Old Vic Theatre Company, Australian and New Zealand cities, 1948; title role, *Titus Andronicus*, European cities, 1957; Henry II, *Becket*, U.S. cities, 1961; title role, *Othello* and *Love for Love*, both National Theatre Company, West German and Soviet Union cities, 1965; *Love for Love, The Dance of Death*, and Plucheux, *A Flea in Her Ear*, Canadian cities, 1967.

FILM DEBUT—Man, *Too Many Crooks*, Paramount, 1927. PRINCIPAL FILM APPEARANCES—Peter Bille, *The Temporary Widow* (also known as *Murder for Sale*), Wardour, 1930; Lieutenant Nichols, *Friends and Lovers*, RKO, 1931; Straker, *Her Strange Desire* (also known as *Potiphar's Wife*), Powers, 1931; Julian Rolfe, *The Yellow Ticket* (also known as *The Yellow Passport*), Twentieth Century-Fox, 1931; Nick Allen, *Westward Passage*, RKO, 1932; Nicholas Randall, *Perfect Understanding*, United Artists, 1933; Clive Dering, *No Funny Business*, United Artists/Principal, 1934; Orlando, *As You Like It*, Twentieth Century-Fox, 1936; Captain Ignatoff, *I Stand Condemned* (also known as *Moscow Nights*), United Artists, 1936; Michael Ingolby, *Fire Over England*, United Artists, 1937; Logan, *The Divorce of Lady X*, United Artists, 1938; Tony McVane, *Clouds Over Europe* (also known as *Q Planes*), Columbia, 1939; Heathcliff, *Wuthering Heights*, United Artists, 1939; Vincent Lunardi, *Conquest of the Air*, United Artists, 1940; Mr. Darcy, *Pride and Prejudice*, Metro-Goldwyn-Mayer (MGM), 1940; Maxim de Winter, *Rebecca*, United Artists, 1940; Larry Durrant, *Twenty-One Days Together* (also known as *Twenty One Days* and *The First and the Last*), Columbia, 1940; Johnnie, *The Invaders* (also known as *Forty-Ninth Parallel*), Columbia, 1941; Admiral Lord Horatio Nelson, *That Hamilton Woman* (also known as *Lady Hamilton*), United Artists, 1941; narrator, *This Happy Breed*, Prestige/Universal, 1944; Ivan Dimitrevitch Kouzenetsoff, *Adventure for Two* (also known as *The Demi-Paradise*), General Film Distributors, 1945; title role, *Henry V*, United Artists, 1946; title role, *Hamlet*, General Film Distributors, 1948; George Hurstwood, *Carrie*, Paramount, 1952; second Holborn policeman, *The Magic Box*, British Lion, 1952; Captain MacHeath, *The Beggar's Opera*, Warner Brothers, 1953; title role, *Richard III*, Lopert, 1956; Charles, Prince Regent, *The Prince and the Showgirl*, Warner Brothers, 1957; General "Gentleman Johnnie" Burgoyne, *The Devil's Disciple*, United Artists, 1959.

Archie Rice, *The Entertainer*, Bryanston/British Lion, 1960;

Marcus Licinius Crassus, *Spartacus*, Universal, 1960; Graham Weir, *Term of Trial*, Warner Brothers, 1962; Newhouse, *Bunny Lake Is Missing*, Columbia, 1965; title role, *Othello*, Warner Brothers, 1965; Mahdi, *Khartoum*, United Artists, 1966; prologue and epilogue narrator, *Romeo and Juliet*, Paramount, 1968; Piotr Ilyich Kamenev, *The Shoes of the Fisherman*, MGM, 1968; Air Chief Marshal Sir Hugh Dowding, *The Battle of Britain*, United Artists, 1969; Field Marshal Sir John French, *Oh! What a Lovely War*, Paramount, 1969; Mr. Creakle, *David Copperfield*, Twentieth Century-Fox, 1970; Count Witte, *Nicholas and Alexandra*, Columbia, 1971; Edgar, *The Dance of Death*, Paramount, 1971; Duke of Wellington, *Lady Caroline Lamb*, United Artists, 1972; Andrew Wyke, *Sleuth*, Twentieth Century-Fox, 1972; Dr. Chebutikan, *The Three Sisters*, American Film Theatre, 1974; Szell, *Marathon Man*, Paramount, 1976; narrator, *Gentleman Tramp* (documentary), PWE/Fox/Rank, 1976; Dr. Spaander, *A Bridge Too Far*, United Artists, 1977; Professor Moriarty, *The Seven-Per-Cent Solution*, Universal, 1977; Dr. Astrov, *Uncle Vanya*, Arthur Cantor, 1977; Loren Hardeman, Sr., *The Betsy*, Allied Artists, 1978; Ezra Lieberman, *The Boys from Brazil*, Twentieth Century-Fox, 1978; Abraham Van Helsing, *Dracula*, Universal, 1979; Julius Edmond Santorin, *A Little Romance*, Orion, 1979; Cantor Rabinovitch, *The Jazz Singer*, Associated 1980; Zeus, *Clash of the Titans*, Metro-Goldwyn-Mayer/United Artists (MGM/UA), 1981; General Douglas MacArthur, *Inchon*, MGM/UA, 1981; Pfeufer, *Wagner*, Alan Landsburg, 1983; Admiral Sir Gerald Scaith, *The Jigsaw Man*, United Film Distribution, 1984; Admiral Hood, *The Bounty*, Orion, 1984; Rudolf Hess, *Wild Geese II*, Universal, 1985; as himself, *Directed By William Wyler* (documenatary), Tatge, 1986; old soldier, *War Requiem*, Anglo International, 1989; also commentator, *Words for Battle*, 1942; narrator, *Tree of Life*, 1971.

PRINCIPAL FILM WORK—Producer (with Filippo Del Giudice) and director (with Reginald Beck), *Henry V*, United Artists, 1946; producer and director, *Hamlet*, General Film Distributors, 1948; producer (with Herbert Wilcox), *The Beggar's Opera*, Lopert, 1953; director (with Anthony Bushell) and producer, *Richard III*, Warner Brothers, 1956; producer and director, *The Prince and the Showgirl*, Warner Brothers, 1957; director (with John Sichel), *The Three Sisters*, America Film Theatre, 1974.

TELEVISION DEBUT—Title role, *John Gabriel Borkman*, BBC, 1958. PRINCIPAL TELEVISION APPEARANCES—Series: Narrator, *World at War*, syndicated, 1973. Mini-Series: Nicodemus, *Jesus of Nazareth*, NBC, 1977; Lord Marchmain, *Brideshead Revisited*, Granada, 1980-81, then *Great Performances*, PBS, 1982; Gaius, *The Last Days of Pompeii*, ABC, 1984; King William III, *Peter the Great*, NBC, 1986; Harry Burrard, "Lost Empires," *Masterpiece Theatre*, PBS, 1987. Episodic: Host and narrator, "Male of the Species," *On Stage*, NBC, 1969; also *ABC Stage '67*, ABC. Movies: Mr. Creakle, *David Copperfield*, NBC, 1970; Sir Arthur Granville-Jones, *Love Among the Ruins*, ABC, 1975; Big Daddy, *Cat on a Hot Tin Roof*, NBC, 1976; Doc Delaney, *Come Back, Little Sheba*, NBC, 1977; Mr. Joseph Halperin, *Mr. Halperin and Mr. Johnson*, HBO, 1984; old soldier, *War Requiem*, BBC, 1988. Specials: Charles Strickland, *The Moon and Sixpence*, NBC, 1959; Priest, *The Power and the Glory*, CBS, 1961; Astrov, *Uncle Vanya*, BBC, 1963, then *N.E.T. Playhouse*, PBS, 1967; James Tyrone, *Long Day's Journey into Night*, ABC, 1973; Shylock, *The Merchant of Venice*, ABC, 1974; barrister, *A Voyage 'round My Father*, 1982; title role, *King Lear*, syndicated, 1983; Henry Breasley, "The Ebony Tower," *Great Performances*, PBS, 1987. Also *The Collection, Daphne Laureola*, and *Saturday, Sunday, Monday*.

PRINCIPAL TELEVISION WORK—Movies: Producer (with Derek Granger), *Cat on a Hot Tin Roof,* NBC, 1976; artistic and creative producer, *Come Back, Little Sheba,* NBC, 1977. Also producer, *The Best Play of the Year,* 1976 and 1977; producer and director, *Hindle Wakes,* 1976; producer, *Saturday, Sunday, Monday;* producer, *The Collection.*

PRINCIPAL RADIO APPEARANCES—Specials: Title role, "Richard III," *Columbia Workshop,* CBS, 1946.

RELATED CAREER—Assistant stage manager and understudy, St. Christopher Theatre, Letchworth, U.K., 1925; artistic director (with Ralph Richardson and John Burrell), Old Vic Theatre Company, London, 1944-49; actor and manager, St. James's Theatre, London, 1950-51; president, Actor's Orphanage, 1956; artistic director, Chichester Theatre Festival, Chichester, U.K., 1961-65; founder and artistic director, National Theatre of Great Britain, London, 1963-73, then associate director, 1973; member, South Bank Theatre Board, 1967.

WRITINGS: FILM—(Adaptor with Alan Dent) *Henry V,* United Artists, 1946; (adaptor with Dent, Colley Cibber, and David Garrick) *Richard III,* Warner Brothers, 1956. OTHER—*Confessions of an Actor,* (autobiography), Simon & Schuster, 1982; *On Acting,* Simon & Schuster, 1986; also (with Michel Saint-Denis) *Five Seasons of the Old Vic Theatre Company,* 1950.

AWARDS: Academy Award nomination, Best Actor, 1939, for *Wuthering Heights;* Academy Award nomination, Best Actor, 1940, for *Rebecca;* Academy Award nomination, Best Actor, 1946, for *Henry V;* New York Film Critics' Circle Award, Best Actor, and New York Film Critics' Circle Award nominations, Best Film and Best Direction, all 1946, for *Henry V;* Academy Award, Special Citation, 1946, for "outstanding achievement as actor, producer, and director in bringing *Henry V* to the screen"; Academy Awards, Best Picture and Best Actor, Academy Award nomination, Best Director, New York Film Critics' Circle Award, Best Actor, and New York Film Critics' Circle Award nominations, Best Film and Best Direction all 1948, for *Hamlet;* British Academy of Film and Television Arts Award, Best British Film Actor, 1955, and Academy Award nomination, Best Actor, 1956, both for *Richard III;* Selznick Golden Laurel Trophy, 1956, "for contributions to international goodwill"; *Evening Standard* Drama Award, 1957, and Antoinette Perry Award nomination, Best Actor in a Play, 1958, both for *The Entertainer;* Academy Award nomination, Best Actor, 1960, for *The Entertainer;* Emmy Award, Outstanding Single Performance By an Actor in a Lead or Supporting Role, 1960, for *The Moon and Sixpence;* Olympus Award from the Taormina (Italy) Film Festival, 1962; Academy Award nomination, Best Actor, 1965, for *Othello;* Sonning Prize from Kobenhavns Universitet, 1966; Gold Medallion from the Swedish Academy of Literature, 1968; British Academy of Film and Television Arts Award, Best Supporting Film Actor, 1969, for *Oh! What a Lovely War.*

Emmy Award nomination, 1970, for *David Copperfield;* New York Film Critics' Circle Award and Academy Award nomination, both Best Actor, 1972, for *Sleuth;* Emmy Award, Outstanding Single Performance By an Actor in a Leading Role, 1973, for *Long Day's Journey into Night;* Emmy Award nomination, Outstanding Lead Actor in a Special Program, 1975, for *Love Among the Ruins;* Academy Award nomination, Best Supporting Actor, 1976, for *Marathon Man;* Albert Medal from the Royal Society of the Arts, 1976; special Academy Award, 1978, for Lifetime Achievement in Film; Academy Award nomination, Best Actor, 1978, for *The Boys*

from Brazil; Commonwealth Award from the Bank of Delaware; Emmy Award, Outstanding Supporting Actor in a Limited Series or Special, 1982, for *Brideshead Revisited;* Cecil B. De Mille Award from the Hollywood Foreign Press Association, 1983; honored by the Film Society of Lincoln Center, 1983; Emmy Award, Outstanding Lead Actor in a Limited Series or a Special, 1984, for *King Lear;* Award of Excellence from the Banff Television Festival, 1985; knighted, 1947; Commander of the Order of Dannebrog (Denmark), 1949; Chevalier of the Legion of Honor (France), 1953; Grand Officer of the Ordine al Merito della Republica (Italy), 1954; created Baron Olivier of Brighton, U.K., 1970; Order of the Yugoslav Flag with Golden Wreath, 1971. HONORARY DEGREES—Oxon University, D.Litt., 1957; Oxford University, D.Litt., 1957; Edinburgh University, LL.D., 1964; University of London, D.Litt., 1968; University of Manchester, LL.D., 1969; University of Sussex, D.Litt., 1978.

OBITUARIES AND OTHER SOURCES: New York Times, July 12, 1989; *Theatre Week,* July 24, 1989; *Variety,* July 12-18, 1989.*

*   *   *

OLMI, Ermanno   1931-

PERSONAL: Born July 24, 1931, in Bergamo, Italy; married Loredana Detto; children: three. EDUCATION—Attended Accademia d'Arte Drammatica, Milan.

VOCATION: Director, cinematographer, producer, screenwriter, and film editor.

CAREER: Also see WRITINGS below. PRINCIPAL FILM APPEARANCES—*Una storia Milanese,* 1962. PRINCIPAL FILM WORK—Director, *Il posto* (also known as *The Sound of the Trumpets* and *The Job*), Janus, 1963; producer and director, *I fidanzati* (also known as *The Fiances* and *The Engagement*), Janus, 1964; director, *. . . e venne un uomo* (also known as *A Man Named John, A Man Called John,* and *And There Came a Man*), Brandon, 1968; director, cinematographer, and editor, *L'albero degli zoccoli* (also known as *The Tree of Wooden Clogs*), Gaumont/Sacis/New Yorker, 1979; director, producer, cinematographer, art director, costume designer, and editor, *Camminacammina* (also known as *Cammina Cammina, Walking Walking,* and *Keep on Walking*), Gaumont/Grange Communications, 1983; director, cinematographer, and editor, *Milano '83* (documentary; also known as *Milan '83*), Trans World/RAI-TV Channel 3, 1983; director, cinematographer (with Maurizio Zaccoli), and editor (with Guilia Ciniselli), *Lunga vita alla Signora!* (also known as *Long Live the Lady* and *Long Life to the Mrs.*), Sacis International, 1987; director and editor, *La leggenda del Santo Bevitore* (also known as *The Legend of the Holy Drinker*), Columbia/Filmexport Group/Cecchi Group, 1988. Also production supervisor and director, *Il tempo si e fermato* (also known as *Time Has Stopped* and *Time Stood Still*), 1959; director and editor, *Un certo giorno* (also known as *One Fine Day*), 1968.

Production supervisor for the following short films and documentaries: (Also director) *La digi sul ghiaccio,* 1953; (also director) *La pattuglia di passo San Giacomo,* 1954; (also director) *Societa Ovesticino-Dinamo,* 1955; (also director) *Cantiere d'inverno,* 1955; (also director) *La mia valle,* 1955; *La tesatura meccanica della linea a 220,000 volt,* 1955; *San Massenza (Cimego),* 1955; (also director) *L'onda,* 1955; (also director) *Buongiorno natura,* 1955; *Pantano d'avio,* 1956; (also director) *Michelino la B,* 1956;

(also director) *Construzione meccaniche riva*, 1956; *Peru—Istituto de Verano*, 1956; *Fertilizzanti complessi*, 1956; *Fibre e civilta*, 1957; *Progresso in agricoltura*, 1957; *Campi sperimentali*, 1957; *Colonie Sicedison*, 1958; *Bariri*, 1958; (also director) *Tre fili fino a Milano*, 1958; (also director) *Giochi di Colonia*, 1958; *Il frumento*, 1958; (also director) *Venezia citta minore*, 1958; *El frayle*, 1959; *Fertiluzzanti produtti dalla Societa del Gruppo Edison*, 1959; *Cavo olio fludio 220,000 volt*, 1959; *Auto chiese*, 1959; *Natura e chimica*, 1959; (also director) *Il grande paese d'Acciaio*, 1960; *Il pomodoro*, 1961; *Il sacco in Plypac*, 1961; (also director) *Le grand barrage*, 1961; (also director) *Un metro lungo cinque*, 1961; *Po: forza 50,000*, 1961.

PRINCIPAL TELEVISION WORK—Movies: Director, cinematographer, editor, and art director, *I recuperanti* (also known as *The Scavengers*), RAI-TV Channel 1 (Italy), 1969; director, cinematographer, and editor, *Durante l'estate* (also known as *During the Summer* and *In the Summertime*), RAI-TV Channel 1, 1971; director, producer, cinematographer, and editor, *La circostanza* (also known as *The Circumstance*), RAI-TV Channel 1, 1974.

RELATED CAREER—Clerk, Edisonvolta S.P.A. (film production company), Milan, Italy, 1949-52, then film project director, 1952; also founder (with Tullio Kezich and others), 22 December S.P.A. (film production company).

WRITINGS: See production details above. FILM—*Il tempo si e fermato*, 1959; *Il posto*, 1963; *I fidanzati*, 1964; (with Vincenzo Labella) *. . . e venne un uomo*, 1968; *Un certo giorno*, 1968; *L'albero degli zoccoli*, 1979; *Camminacammina*, 1983; *Milano '83*, 1983; *Lunga vita alla Signora!*, 1987; (with Tullio Kezich) *La leggenda del Santo Bevitore*, 1988. TELEVISION—(With Tullio Kezich and Mario Rigoni Stern) *I recuperanti*, 1969; (with Fortunato Pasquelino) *Durante l'estate*, 1971; *La circostanza*, 1974.

AWARDS: Catholic Film Office Award from the Cannes Film Festival, 1964, for *I fidanzati*; Palme d'Or from the Cannes Film Festival, for *L'albero degli zoccoli*.*

*   *   *

OLSEN, Merlin   1940-

PERSONAL: Full name, Merlin Jay Olsen; born September 15, 1940, in Logan, UT; son of Lynn Jay and Merle (Barrus) Olsen; married Susan Wakley, March 30, 1962; children: Kelly Lynn, Jill Catherine, Nathan Merlin. EDUCATION—Utah State University, B.S., finance, 1962, M.S., economics, 1970.

VOCATION: Actor and sports analyst.

CAREER: PRINCIPAL FILM APPEARANCES—Big George, *The Undefeated*, Twentieth Century-Fox, 1969; Eli Jones, *One More Train to Rob*, Universal, 1971; Sergeant Fitzsimmons, *Something Big*, National General, 1971; Benton, *Mitchell*, Allied Artists, 1975.

PRINCIPAL TELEVISION APPEARANCES—Series: Announcer and analyst, *NFL Game of the Week*, NBC, 1977—; Jonathan Garvey, *Little House on the Prairie*, NBC, 1977-81; John Michael Murphy, *Father Murphy*, NBC, 1981-82; Buddy Landau, *Fathers and Sons*, NBC, 1986; Aaron Miller, *Aaron's Way*, NBC, 1988. Pilots: Buddy Landau, *Fathers and Sons*, NBC, 1985. Movies: Stan

MERLIN OLSEN

Webster, *A Fire in the Sky*, NBC, 1978; Todd Simms, *The Golden Moment—An Olympic Love Story*, NBC, 1980; Jake Calahan, *Time Bomb*, NBC, 1984. Specials: *Bob Hope's All-Star Comedy Look at the Fall Season: It's Still Free and Worth It!*, NBC, 1981; Jonas Wintergreen, *The Juggler of Notre Dame*, syndicated, 1982; co-host, *Children's Miracle Network Telethon*, 1983—; *Bob Hope's All-Star Super Bowl Party*, NBC, 1983; *The Dean Martin Celebrity Roast*, NBC, 1984; *The World's Funniest Commercial Goofs*, ABC, 1985; *NBC's 60th Anniversary Celebration*, NBC, 1986; host and narrator, *Lifequest*, syndicated, 1987; narrator, *The Sleeping Beauty*, PBS, 1987; *Kraft Salutes Super Night at the Super Bowl*, CBS, 1987; commentator, *Super Bowl XXIII*, NBC, 1989; host "Conquering Pain," *LifeQuest*, syndicated, 1989; host, "Diet Dilemma, *LifeQuest*, syndicated, 1989.

RELATED CAREER—Television spokesman, Florists Transworld Delivery (FTD); grand marshall, 94th Tournament of Roses Parade, Pasadena, CA.

NON-RELATED CAREER—Professional football player, Los Angeles Rams, 1962-76; worked for Allied Chemical Corporation, 1962-67; owner, Merlin Olsen Porsche-Audi, 1969—; motivational consultant, Liggett & Meyers, 1971-72; worked for Consolidated Cigar, 1972-73; public relations executive, Combined Communications Corporation, 1972-73.

AWARDS: Maxwell Trophy as Most Valuable Player from the National Football League, 1974; inducted into the College Football Hall of Fame, 1980; inducted into the Professional Football Hall of Fame, 1982; named to the National Football League/American Football League Quarter Century Team.

ADDRESSES: OFFICE—c/o NBC Sports, 30 Rockefeller Plaza, New York, NY 10020.*

* * *

OPHULS, Marcel 1927-

PERSONAL: Born Marcel Oppenheimer, November 1, 1927, in Frankfurt-am-Main, Germany; naturalized French citizen in 1938; naturalized U.S. citizen in 1950; son of Max (a film director) and Hilda (Wall) Oppenheimer; married Regine Ackerman, August 21, 1956; children: Catherine Julie, Danielle, Jeanne Dorothee. EDUCATION—Attended Occidental College, 1946-49; University of Paris (Sorbonne), License et Letters, philosophy, 1950; also attended the University of California, Berkeley. MILITARY—U.S. Army, 1946-47.

VOCATION: Director, producer, and writer.

CAREER: Also see *WRITINGS* below. PRINCIPAL FILM APPEARANCES—*Egon Schiele—Excess and Punishment*, Gamma, 1981. PRINCIPAL FILM WORK—Assistant director, *Moulin Rouge*, United Artists, 1952; assistant director, *Un Acte d'amour* (also known as *Act of Love*), United Artists, 1953; assistant director, *Lola Montes* (also known as *The Sins of Lola Montes* and *The Fall of Lola Montes*), Brandon, 1955; director (West German segment), *L'Amour a vingt ans* (also known as *Love at Twenty, Amore a vent'anni, Milosc Dwudziestolatkow*, and *Liebe Mit Zwanzig*), 1962, released in the United States by Embassy, 1963; producer and director, *Peau de banane* (also known as *Banana Peel*), Pathe, 1965; producer (with Andre Harris) and director, *Le Chagrin et la pitie* (also known as *The Sorrow and the Pity* and *The Sorrow and the Shame*; documentary), Almi/Cinema V, 1970; producer and director, *A Sense of Loss* (documentary), Contemporary/Cinema V, 1972; director, *The Memory of Justice* (documentary), CIC/Paramount, 1976; producer and director, *Hotel Terminus: Klaus Barbie, His Life and Times* (also known as *Hotel Terminus: The Life and Times of Klaus Barbie* and *Klaus Barbie et son temps;* documentary), Samuel Goldwyn/Orion International, 1988. Also assistant director, *Marianne de ma jeunesse*, 1954; director, *Matisse, or The Talent for Happiness* (short film), 1960; producer and director, *Feu a volonte* (also known as *Faites vos jeux, Mesdames*, and *Fire at Will*), 1964.

PRINCIPAL TELEVISION WORK—Series: Field producer, *20/20*, ABC, 1978—. Specials: Co-director, *Till Eulenspiegel*, German television, 1966; director, *Munich, ou La Paix pour cent ans* (also known as *Munich, or Peace in Our Time;* documentary), ORTF, 1967; director, *Clavigo*, 1970; director, *The Harvest of My Lai*, 1970; director, *America Revisited*, 1971; director, *Zwei ganze tage* (also known as *Two Whole Days*), 1971; director, *Kortnergeschichte* (documentary), German television, 1980; director, *Yorktown, le sens d'une bataille*, 1982.

RELATED CAREER—Actor with Theatre Unit, U.S. Army Occupation Forces, Tokyo, Japan, 1946; (as Marcel Wall) assistant director, French film industry, 1951-56; story editor and director, Sudwestfunk (television and radio), Baden-Baden, West Germany, 1956-59; journalist and director, *Zoom* (French television news magazine), 1966-68; reporter and director of news magazine

features, ORTF (French television), 1966-68; senior story editor, NDR (German television), 1968-71; senior visiting fellow, Council of Humanities, Princeton University, Princeton, NJ, 1973; staff producer, CBS News, then ABC News, 1975-78; advisory council, sociology department, Princeton University.

WRITINGS: See production details above. FILM—*Matisse, or The Talent for Happiness*, 1960; (West German segment) *L'Amour a vingt ans*, 1962; (co-writer) *Feu a volonte*, 1964; (with Claude Sautet and Daniel Boulanger) *Peau de banane*, 1965; (with Andre Harris) *Le Chagrin et la pitie*, 1970; *A Sense of Loss*, 1972; *The Memory of Justice*, 1976; *Hotel Terminus: Klaus Barbie, His Life and Times*, 1988. TELEVISION—(Co-writer) *Till Eulenspiegel*, 1966; *Munich, ou La Paix pour cent ans*, 1967; *The Harvest of My Lai*, 1970; *America Revisited*, 1971; *Kortnergeschichte*, 1980; *Yorktown, le sens d'une bataille*, 1982. OTHER—Contributor to periodicals and journals.

AWARDS: Prix de Dinard, Prix Georges Sadoul, British Film and Television Academy Award, Special Award from the National Society of Film Critics, all 1971, and New York Film Critics' Award, Special Citation for the Year's Best Documentary, 1972, all for *Le Chagrin et la pitie;* International Critics' Prize from the Cannes Film Festival, 1988, and Academy Award, Best Screenplay, 1989, both for *Hotel Terminus: Klaus Barbie, His Life and Times;* Knight of Arts and Letters from the French Ministry of Culture. HONORARY DEGREES—Columbia College (Chicago, IL), Doctor of Arts, 1983.

MEMBER: Societe des Gens des Lettres (board of directors), German Academy of Arts, French Authors Guild, French Directors Guild (board of directors); French Filmmakers' Society (secretary general).

ADDRESSES: HOME—10 rue Ernest Deloison, Neuilly-sur-Seine, France.*

* * *

OPPENHEIMER, Jess 1913-1988

PERSONAL: Born November 11, 1913, in San Francisco, CA; died of heart failure, December 27, 1988, in Los Angeles, CA; children: one daughter, one son. EDUCATION—Attended Stanford University.

VOCATION: Producer, writer, and director.

CAREER: Also see *WRITINGS* below. PRINCIPAL TELEVISION WORK—Series: Creator (with Madelyn Pugh and Bob Carroll, Jr.) and producer, *I Love Lucy*, CBS, 1951-56; executive producer, *Angel*, CBS, 1960-61; producer (with Pier Oppenheimer), *Here's Hollywood*, NBC, 1960-62; creator and executive producer, *Glynis*, CBS, 1963; producer, *Get Smart*, NBC, 1967-68; creator and producer, *The Debbie Reynolds Show*, NBC, 1969-70. Pilots: Producer, *The Third Commandment*, NBC, 1959; producer, *The Big Brain*, CBS, 1963; executive producer, *Hide and Seek*, CBS, 1963. Episodic: Producer, *The U.S. Steel Hour;* producer and director, *Bob Hope Presents the Chrysler Theatre*, NBC. Specials: Producer, *The General Motors 50th Anniversary Show*, NBC, 1957; producer, *The Rosalind Russell Show* (broadcast as an episode of *Ford Startime*), NBC, 1959; executive producer, *The Lucille Ball Comedy Hour*, CBS, 1967; producer and director, *For*

Love or $$$, NBC, 1968; also producer, *The Danny Kaye Special;* producer, *The Emmy Awards Show*.

PRINCIPAL RADIO WORK—Series: Producer and director, *The Baby Snooks Show*, CBS, 1943-48; producer and director, *My Favorite Husband*, CBS, 1948-51.

RELATED CAREER—Executive, NBC Television, 1956.

NON-RELATED CAREER—Fur industry worker during the 1930s; holder of more than twenty patents, including the inthelens prompter.

WRITINGS: TELEVISION—Series: (With Madelyn Pugh and Bob Carroll, Jr.) *I Love Lucy*, CBS, 1951-56. Pilots: *Hide and Seek*, CBS, 1963; (with Samuel W. Taylor) *The Big Brain*, CBS, 1963. Episodic: (Uncredited) "Oh Say Can You See," *All in the Family*, CBS, 1973. Specials: (With Abby Mann, Mike Marmer, and Orson Welles) *NBC: The First 50 Years*, NBC, 1976; *NBC: The First 50 Years—A Closer Look*, NBC, 1977.

RADIO—Series: *The Packard Hour*, 1937-39; *Screen Guild Theatre*, CBS, 1939-40; *The Sealtest Hour Starring Rudy Vallee and John Barrymore*, NBC, 1939-41; (with Everett Freeman, Bill Danch, and Jerry Seelen) *The Baby Snooks Show*, CBS, 1943-48; (with Madelyn Pugh and Bob Carroll, Jr.) *My Favorite Husband*, CBS, 1948-51; also *The Jack Benny Show*, CBS; *The Edgar Bergen and Charlie McCarthy Show* (also known as *The Chase and Sanborn Show*), NBC.

OBITUARIES AND OTHER SOURCES: Variety, January 4-10, 1989.*

*　　*　　*

O'STEEN, Michael 1962-

PERSONAL: Surname is pronounced "O-*steen*"; born January 28, 1962, in New York, NY; son of Thomas (a dance teacher) and Nora (a dance teacher; maiden name, Reho) O'Steen. EDUCATION—Received B.F.A. in acting from Carnegie-Mellon University; also studied acting with Mel Shapiro, Barbara Baxley, and Paul Rudd.

VOCATION: Actor.

CAREER: STAGE DEBUT—Newsboy, *Gypsy*, Pittsburgh Civic Light Opera, Pittsburgh, PA, 1976. BROADWAY DEBUT—Flat Top, *Starlight Express*, Gershwin Theatre, 1988. PRINCIPAL STAGE APPEARANCES—Stub, *Leave It to Jane*, Goodspeed Opera House, East Haddam, CT, 1985-86; Lon, *Meet Me in St. Louis*, Gershwin Theatre, New York City, 1989; also appeared as Tom, *No, No, Nanette*, Claridge Hotel, Atlantic City, NJ; as Riff, *West Side Story*, Jimmy, *110 in the Shade*, Rolf, *The Sound of Music*, Lewis, *Pippin*, and young Vincent, *Follies*, all Pittsburgh Civic Light Opera, Pittsburgh, PA; Nick Piazza, *Fame: The Musical*, Walnut Street Theatre, Philadelphia, PA; Don Lockwood, *Singin' in the Rain*, Coachlight Dinner Theatre, Warehouse Point, CT; Rudy, *Hamelin*, Musical Theatre Works, New York City; and Matt, *Babes in Arms*.

MAJOR TOURS—Mungojerrie, *Cats*, U.S. cities; Angie the Ox, *Guys and Dolls*, U.S. cities; Nick Piazza, *Fame: The Musical*, U.S. cities.

PRINCIPAL TELEVISION APPEARANCES—Episodic: *Ryan's Hope*, ABC.

MEMBER: Actors' Equity Association.

ADDRESSES: AGENT—Peggy Hadley Enterprises Ltd., 250 W. 57th Street, Suite 2317, New York, NY 10107.

P

PACEY, Steven 1957-

PERSONAL: Born May 6, 1957, in Leamington, England; son of Larry (a builder) and Wendy (Sykes) Pacey; married Joan Marine, November 29, 1986; children: Jessica and Laura (twins).

VOCATION: Actor.

CAREER: STAGE DEBUT—*Collapse of Stout Party*, 1969. LONDON DEBUT—Ronnie Winslow, *The Winslow Boy*, Albery Theatre, 1970. PRINCIPAL STAGE APPEARANCES—Joe, *Leave Him to Heaven*, New London Theatre, London, 1976; Jesus, *Godspell*, Duke of York's Theatre, London, 1978; Guy, *Mr. Cinders*, Fortune Theatre, London, 1983; Tony, *West Side Story*, Her Majesty's Theatre, London, 1984; Mike, *High Society*, Victoria Palace Thea-

tre, London, 1987; Brocklehurst, *The Admirable Crichton*, Haymarket Theatre, London, 1988; Dexter, *Exclusive*, Strand Theatre, London, 1989.

MAJOR TOURS—Jesus, *Godspell*, U.K. cities, 1974; Joseph, *Joseph and the Amazing Technicolor Dreamcoat*, U.K. cities, 1978.

PRINCIPAL FILM APPEARANCES—Lucius, *Julius Caesar*, American International, 1970; officer, *Aces High*, EMI, 1977; also appeared in *Conspiracy*, 1989.

TELEVISION DEBUT—*A Legacy*, BBC, 1974. PRINCIPAL TELEVISION APPEARANCES—Series: Del Tarrant, *Blake's Seven*, syndicated; also Clifford, *Troubles and Strife*; Klaus, *The Cedar Tree*. Also appeared in *Red Letter Day*, *A Gentle Rain*, *The Purple Twilight*, *The Cuckoo Waltz*, *Goodbye Darling*, and *Lovejoy*.

SIDELIGHTS: FAVORITE ROLES—Mike in *High Society*.

ADDRESSES: MANAGER—CCA Personal Management, 4 Court Lodge, 48 Sloane Square, London SW1, England.

*   *   *

STEVEN PACEY

PALMER, Geoffrey 1927-

PERSONAL: Born June 4, 1927, in London, England; son of Fredrick Charles (a chartered surveyor) and Norah Gwendolen (Robins) Palmer; wife's name, Sally; children: Charles, Harriet. MILITARY—Royal Marines, corporal instructor, 1946-48.

VOCATION: Actor.

CAREER: LONDON DEBUT—*Albertine By Moon Light*, Westminster Theatre, 1955. PRINCIPAL STAGE APPEARANCES—Edward, *West of Suez*, Royal Court Theatre, London, 1971; Elmer Penn, *Savages*, Royal Court Theatre, 1973; Victor, *Private Lives*, Globe

Theatre, London, 1974; Farrant, *Eden End,* National Theatre, London, 1974; Richard, *On Approval,* Haymarket Theatre, London, 1975; Warwick, *Saint Joan,* Old Vic Theatre, London, 1978; Layborne, *Tishoo,* Wyndham's Theatre, London, 1979; Sir John, *A Friend Indeed,* National Theatre Company, Shaftesbury Theatre, London, 1984; Sydney, *Kafka's Dick,* Royal Court Theatre, 1986.

PRINCIPAL FILM APPEARANCES—Dr. Tanfield, *Incident at Midnight,* Schoenfeld, 1966; police driver, *The Engagement,* Anglo/EMI, 1970; doctor and Basil Keyes, *O Lucky Man!* Warner Brothers, 1973; first policeman, *The Battle of Billy's Pond,* Children's Film Foundation, 1976; Colonel Wyndham, *The Outsider,* CIC/Paramount, 1979; British ambassador, *Beyond the Limit* (also known as *The Honorary Consul*), Paramount, 1983; Fallast, *A Zed and Two Noughts* (also known as *Zoo*), Skouras/Samuel Goldwyn/Artificial Eye, 1985; Canford, *Clockwise,* Universal/Cannon, 1986; judge, *A Fish Called Wanda,* Metro-Goldwyn-Mayer/United Artists, 1988; Saab salesman, *Hawks,* Skouras/Rank, 1988. Also as Sir Horace, *Smack and Thistle,* 1990.

TELEVISION DEBUT—*Round Britain,* BBC, 1950. PRINCIPAL TELEVISION APPEARANCES—Series: Jimmy Anderson, *The Fall and Rise of Reginald Perrin,* BBC, then PBS, 1978; Ben Parkinson, *Butterflies,* BBC, then PBS, 1982; Major Harry Truscott, *Fairly Secret Army,* Channel Four, then syndicated, 1987; Harold Stringer, *Hot Metal,* PBS, 1988; Donald Fairchild, *Executive Stress,* PBS, 1988; also Leo, *The Last Song,* BBC. Mini-Series: Dr. Edwin Lorimer, *Death of an Expert Witness,* Anglia Television, 1984,

GEOFFREY PALMER

then *Mystery!,* PBS, 1985; Mr. Burton, *Christabel,* BBC, then *Masterpiece Theatre,* PBS, 1989. Episodic: Major General Sir Robert Godolphin, *After the War,* Granada, 1989, then *Masterpiece Theatre,* PBS, 1989-90; also *Oxbridge Blues,* BBC, 1984, then PBS, 1985. Movies: Miss Weber, *The Insurance Man,* BBC, 1985. Specials: *Absurd Person Singular,* BBC, then Arts and Entertainment, 1985; Robert Lancaster, *Waters of the Moon,* BBC, then Arts and Entertainment, 1986; Bernard, *Season's Greetings,* BBC, then Arts and Entertainment, 1988. Also appeared in *A Prize of Arms,* 1962; *The Houseboy,* Yorkshire Television, 1982; *A Little Rococo,* 1982; *A Midsummer Night's Dream,* 1982; and in *Radio Pictures.*

ADDRESSES: MANAGER—Marmont Management, 302-308 Regent Street, London W1, England.

*   *   *

PANKOW, John

VOCATION: Actor.

CAREER: PRINCIPAL STAGE APPEARANCES—Lucentio, *The Taming of the Shrew,* Oak Park Festival Theatre Company, Oak Park, IL, 1979; cameraman, *Merton of the Movies,* Master Theatre, New York City, 1980; Hector McKenzie, *The Slab Boys,* Hudson Guild Theatre, New York City, 1980; citizen of Vienna, then understudy for Mozart and Venticello, later Wolfgang Amadeus Mozart, *Amadeus,* Broadhurst Theatre, New York City, 1980-83; Blow, *Forty-Deuce,* Perry Street Theatre, New York City, 1981; Abram, *Hunting Scenes from Lower Bavaria,* Manhattan Theatre Club, New York City, 1981; Betty and Gerry, *Cloud 9,* Theatre De Lys (renamed Lucille Lortel Theatre), New York City, 1982; Gregory, *Jazz Poets at the Grotto,* the Production Company, Theatre Guinevere, New York City, 1983; Williams, *Henry V,* New York Shakespeare Festival, Delacorte Theatre, New York City, 1984; Rocky Pioggi, *The Iceman Cometh,* Lunt-Fontanne Theatre, New York City, 1985; Alfred Martino, *North Shore Fish,* WPA Theatre, New York City, 1987; Zackerman, *Serious Money,* Royale Theatre, New York City, 1988. Also appeared in *The Time of Your Life,* Goodman Theatre, Chicago, IL, 1983-84; *Italian-American Reconciliation,* Manhattan Theatre Club, 1988; *Aristocrats,* Manhattan Theatre Club, Theatre Four, New York City, 1989.

PRINCIPAL FILM APPEARANCES—Bullie, *The Chosen,* Contemporary, 1982; youth in phone booth, *The Hunger,* United Artists, 1983; John Vukovich, *To Live and Die in L.A.,* Metro-Goldwyn-Mayer, 1985; Kovacs, *Batteries Not Included,* Universal, 1987; Fred Melrose, *The Secret of My Success,* Universal, 1987; Geoffrey Fisher, *Monkey Shines,* Orion, 1988; Chuck Dietz, *Talk Radio,* Universal, 1988. Also appeared in *Johnny Be Good* (also known as *Quarterback Sneak*), Orion, 1988.

PRINCIPAL TELEVISION APPEARANCES—Series: Danny Martin, *The Doctors,* NBC, 1981-82. Episodic: Billy Hanratty, *Spenser: For Hire,* ABC, 1987; Chuck Savin, *Leg Work,* CBS, 1987. Movies: Fred, *First Steps,* CBS, 1985. Specials: George Richie, "Life on the Mississippi," *Great Performances,* PBS, 1980.

ADDRESSES: AGENT—Arlene Forster, Triad Artists Inc., 10100 Santa Monica Boulevard, 16th Floor, Los Angeles, CA 90068.*

*   *   *

PAPAS, Irene 1926-

PERSONAL: Born Irene Lelekou, March 9, 1926, in Corinth, Greece; married Alkis Papas, 1947 (divorced, 1951); married Jose Kohn, 1957 (marriage annulled). EDUCATION—Studied acting at the Royal Drama School (Athens).

VOCATION: Actress.

CAREER: BROADWAY DEBUT—Angelina Capuano, *That Summer—That Fall,* Helen Hayes Theatre, 1967. PRINCIPAL STAGE APPEARANCES—Title role, *Medea,* Circle in the Square, New York City, 1973; Agave, *The Bacchae,* Circle in the Square, 1980; also appeared in *Orpheus Descending,* Circle in the Square, 1984; with the Greek Popular Theatre, 1958; and in productions of *Iphigenia in Aulis, The Idiot, Journey's End, The Merchant of Venice,* and *Inherit the Wind,* all in New York City.

FILM DEBUT—*Lost Angels,* 1951. PRINCIPAL FILM APPEARANCES—Yvonne, *The Man from Cairo,* Lippert, 1953; Mrs. Azzali, *Le infedeli* (also known as *The Unfaithfuls*), 1953, released in the United States by Allied Artists, 1960; Jocasta Constantine, *Tribute to a Badman,* Metro-Goldwyn-Mayer, 1956; Grune, *Attila* (also known as *Atilla, Flagello di Dio*), Lux, 1958; Maria, *The Guns of Navarone,* Columbia, 1961; title role, *Antigone,* Norma Releasing, 1962; title role, *Electra,* Lopert, 1962; Sophia, *The Moon-Spinners,* Buena Vista, 1964; the Widow, *Zorba the Greek,* International Classics, 1964; Luisa Roscio, *A ciascuno il suo* (also known as *We Still Kill the Old Way*), Lopert, 1967; Lea Weiss, *Die Zuegin aus der Hoelle* (also known as *Witness Out of Hell*), Rank, 1967; Ida Ginetta, *The Brotherhood,* Paramount, 1968; Ajmi, *Mas alla de las montanas* (also known as *The Desperate Ones* and *Beyond the Mountains*), American International, 1968; Queen Catherine of Aragon, *Anne of the Thousand Days,* Universal, 1969; Caliope, *A Dream of Kings,* National General, 1969; Helene, *Z,* Cinema V, 1969.

Housewife, *N.P. il segreto* (also known as *N.P.* and *N.P.—The Secret*), Zeta-a-Elle, 1971; Helen, *The Trojan Women,* Cinerama, 1971; Donna Raimonda, *Le faro da padre* (also known as *I'll Take Her Like a Father*), Cineriz, 1974; Hind, *Mohammad, Messenger of God* (also known as *Al-Ris-Alah* and *The Message*), Tarik/Irwin Yablans, 1976; Zipporah, *Moses,* AVCO-Embassy, 1976; Clytemnestra, *Iphigenia,* Cinema V, 1977; Simonetta Palazza, *Bloodline* (also known as *Sidney Sheldon's Bloodline*), Paramount, 1979; Giulia, *Eboli* (also known as *Cristo si e fermato a Eboli* and *Christ Stopped at Eboli*), Franklin Media, 1980; Mabrouka, *Lion of the Desert* (also known as *Omar Mukhtar* and *Omar Mukhtar—Lion of the Desert*), United Film Distribution, 1981; Mariangela, *Il disertore* (also known as *The Deserter*), Istituto Luce/SACIS, 1983; grandmother, *Erendira,* Miramax, 1984; Mother Giuseppina, *The Assisi Underground,* Golan-Globus, 1985; Shaheen Parvizi, *Into the Night,* Universal, 1985; Angela's mother, *Cronaca di una morte annunciata* (also known as *Chronicle of a Death Foretold*),

Istituto Luce/Italnoleggio Cinematographico, 1987; Penelope, *High Season,* Hemdale, 1987; Mrs. Araya, *Sweet Country,* Cinema Group, 1987. Also appeared in *Nekri Politeia* (also known as *Dead City*), 1951; *Dramma della Casbah,* 1953; *Vortice,* 1953; *Teodora, Imperatrice di Bisanzio,* 1954; *The Power and the Prize,* 1960; *Roger la Honte,* 1966; *Ecce Homo,* 1968; *Roma Bene,* 1971; *Un posto ideale per uccidere,* 1971; *Non si sevizia un paperino* (also known as *You Don't Torture Ducklings*), Medusa Distribuzione, 1972; *Once Upon a Time in New York,* 1972; *Piazza Pulita,* 1972; *Sutjeska,* 1972; *Oasis of Fear,* 1973; *Bodas de sangre* (also known as *Blood Wedding*), Artificial Eye/Almi Cinema V, 1976; *L'uomo di Corleone,* 1977; and *Un ombra nell'ombra,* 1977.

PRINCIPAL TELEVISION APPEARANCES—Mini-Series: Zipporah, *Moses—The Lawgiver,* CBS, 1975. Also appeared in *L'Odissea* (also known as *The Odyssey*), 1968.

RELATED CAREER—Singer and dancer in variety shows in Greece.

AWARDS: Salonika (Greece) Film Festival Award, Best Actress, for *Antigone* and *Electra.*

ADDRESSES: OFFICE—United Film Distribution, 115 Middle Neck Road, Great Neck, NY 11021.*

*   *   *

PARAGON, John

VOCATION: Actor and writer.

CAREER: Also see *WRITINGS* below. PRINCIPAL FILM APPEARANCES—Sy Baby, *Cheech and Chong's Next Movie,* Universal, 1980; Red carpetman, *Things Are Tough All Over,* Columbia, 1982; sexshop salesman, *Eating Raoul,* Twentieth Century-Fox, 1982; Rooster, *Going Berserk,* Universal, 1983; movie lot actor, *Pee Wee's Big Adventure,* Warner Brothers, 1985; Hugo, *Echo Park,* Atlantic, 1986; gas station attendant, *Elvira, Mistress of the Dark,* New World, 1988; Richard Fletcher, *UHF,* Orion, 1989. Also appeared in *Pandemonium* (also known as *Thursday the 12th*), United Artists, 1982.

PRINCIPAL TELEVISION APPEARANCES—Series: Regular, *The Half-Hour Comedy Hour,* ABC, 1983; the breather, *Elvira's Movie Macabre,* syndicated, 1983—; regular, *FTV,* syndicated, 1985; Jambi and Pterri, *Pee Wee's Playhouse,* CBS, 1986—. Pilots: Regular, *The Facts,* CBS, 1982; also *Welcome to the Fun Zone,* NBC, 1984. Movies: Beef, *Last of the Great Survivors,* CBS, 1984. Specials: Jambi, *The Pee Wee Herman Show,* HBO, 1981; host, *The Paragon of Comedy,* Showtime, 1984; *Cheech and Chong: Get Out of My Room,* Showtime, 1985; Jambi, *A Special Evening of Pee Wee's Playhouse,* CBS, 1987; *Pee Wee's Playhouse Christmas Special,* CBS, 1988.

WRITINGS: FILMS—(With Sam Egan and Cassandra Peterson) *Elvira, Mistress of the Dark,* New World, 1988. TELEVISION—

Series: (With others) *Pee Wee's Playhouse*, CBS, 1986—. Pilots: (With others) *The Cheech Show* (also known as *Cheech* and *Let's Party with Cheech*), NBC, 1988. Specials: (With others) *The Pee Wee Herman Show*, HBO, 1981; (with Edie McClurg and Paul Reubens) *The Paragon of Comedy*, Showtime, 1984; (with others) *Pee Wee's Playhouse Christmas Special*, CBS, 1988.

ADDRESSES: AGENT—William Morris Agency, 151 El Camino Drive, Beverly Hills, CA 90212.*

*   *   *

PARENT, Gail   1940-

PERSONAL: Born August 12, 1940, in New York, NY; daughter of Theodore (a Wall Street executive) and Ruth (Goldberg) Kostner; married Lair Parent (a television producer), June 24, 1962 (divorced, 1979); children: two sons. EDUCATION—Attended Syracuse University, 1958-60; New York University, B.S., 1962.

VOCATION: Writer and producer.

CAREER: Also see *WRITINGS* below. PRINCIPAL TELEVISION WORK—Series: Producer (with Kenny Solms), *The Smothers Brothers Show*, NBC, 1975; creator (with Ann Marcus, Jerry Adelman, and Daniel Gregory Browne), *Mary Hartman, Mary Hartman*, syndicated, 1975; producer (with Solms), *Three Girls Three*, NBC, 1977. Pilots: Executive producer, *Sheila*, CBS, 1977; executive producer (with Ann Elder), *I'd Rather Be Calm*, CBS, 1982.

NON-RELATED CAREER—Junior high school English teacher, New York City.

WRITINGS: STAGE—(Contributor) *Instant Replay* (revue), Upstairs at the Downstairs, New York City, 1968; (with Kenny Solms) *Lorelei or "Gentlemen Still Prefer Blondes,"* pre-Broadway tour of U.S. cities, 1973, then Palace Theatre, New York City, 1974.

FILM—(With Solms) *Sheila Levine Is Dead and Living in New York*, Paramount, 1975; (with Andrew Smith) *The Main Event*, Warner Brothers, 1979; (with Armyan Bernstein) *Cross My Heart*, Universal, 1987.

TELEVISION—Series: (With others) *The Smothers Brothers Show*, NBC, 1975; (with Solms) *Three Girls Three*, NBC, 1977; also (with Solms and others) *The Carol Burnett Show*, CBS. Pilots: (With others) *Hellzapoppin'*, ABC, 1972; (with Solms) *Sheila*, CBS, 1977; (with Ann Elder) *I'd Rather Be Calm*, CBS, 1982. Episodic: (With Solms) "We Closed in Minneapolis," *The Mary Tyler Moore Show*, CBS, 1971; *Sons and Daughters*, CBS, 1974; *Mary Hartman, Mary Hartman*, syndicated, 1975; also *Rhoda*, CBS. Movies: (With Solms) *Call Her Mom*, ABC, 1972. Specials: (With Solms, Bill Angelos, and Buz Kohan) *Ann-Margret: From Hollywood with Love*, CBS, 1969; (with Sheldon Keller and Solms) *Bing Crosby and Carol Burnett—Together Again for the First Time*, NBC, 1969; (with Solms, Pat McCormick, and Jack Riley) *The Many Sides of Don Rickles*, ABC, 1970; (with Solms, Gary

Belkin, Martin Charnin, Bob Ellison, Thomas Meehan, and Bob Randall) *Annie and the Hoods*, ABC, 1974; (with Solms) *Sills and Burnett at the Met*, CBS, 1976.

OTHER—Fiction: *Sheila Levine Is Dead and Living in New York*, Putnam, 1972; *David Meyer Is a Mother*, Harper, 1976; *The Best Laid Plans*, Putnam, 1980; *A Sign of the Eighties*, Putnam, 1987; also *A Little Bit Married*. Also (with Solms) nightclub revue sketch writer; contributor to periodicals.

AWARDS: Emmy Award, Outstanding Writing Achievement in a Variety or Music Series, 1973, for *The Carol Burnett Show*.

ADDRESSES: AGENTS—Creative Artists Agency, 9830 Wilshire Boulevard, Beverly Hills, CA 90212; Owen Laster, William Morris Agency, 1350 Avenue of the Americas, New York, NY 10019. PUBLISHER—Putnam Publishing Group, 200 Madison Avenue, New York, NY 10016.*

*   *   *

PARICHY, Dennis

PERSONAL: EDUCATION—Attended Northwestern University; studied lighting design at Lester Polikoff's Studio.

VOCATION: Lighting designer.

CAREER: PRINCIPAL STAGE WORK—Lighting designer: *Trainer, Dean, Liepolt, and Company*, American Place Theatre, New York City, 1968; *War Games*, Fortune Theatre, New York City, 1969; *The Transgressor Rides Again*, Martinique Theatre, New York City, 1969; *Boy on the Straight-Back Chair*, American Place Theatre, St. Clement's Church Theatre, New York City, 1969; *The Shepherd of Avenue B* and *Steal the Old Man's Bundle* (double-bill) and *The Jumping Fool*, all Fortune Theatre, 1970; *Come Back, Little Sheba*, Queens Playhouse, Queens, NY, 1974; *The Persians, Him*, and *Battle of Angels*, all Circle Repertory Theatre, New York City, 1974.

The Mound Builders, Harry Outside, The Elephant in the House, Not to Worry, and *Dancing for the Kaiser*, all Circle Repertory Theatre, 1975; *Serenading Louie, A Tribute to Lili Lamont*, and *The Farm*, all Circle Repertory Theatre, 1976; *Knock Knock*, Circle Repertory Theatre, then Biltmore Theatre, New York City, both 1976; *The Wise Woman and the King*, Manhattan Theatre Club, New York City, 1976; *My Life, Exiles*, and *Feedlot*, all Circle Repertory Theatre, 1977; *Ashes*, Manhattan Theatre Club, then Public Theatre, New York City, both 1977; *In the Summer House, The Last Street Play*, and *Chez Nous*, all Manhattan Theatre Club, 1977; *Ulysses in Traction, Glorious Morning*, and *In the Recovery Lounge*, all Circle Repertory Theatre, 1978; *Statements After an Arrest Under the Immorality Act, Scenes from Soweto, Rib Cage, Strawberry Fields*, and *The Rear Column*, all Manhattan Theatre Club, 1978; *Catsplay*, Manhattan Theatre Club, then Promenade Theatre, New York City, both 1978; *The Water Engine* and *Mr. Happiness* (double-bill), Plymouth Theatre, New York City, both 1978; *Gimme Shelter*, Brooklyn Academy of Music, Lepercq Space, Brooklyn, NY, 1978; *The Best Little Whorehouse in Texas*, Entermedia Theatre, then 46th Street Theatre, both New York City, 1978; *Grand Magic* and *Don Juan Comes Back from the War*, both Manhattan Theatre Club, 1979; *My Sister's Keeper*, Hudson Guild Theatre, New York City, 1979; *Devour the Snow*, Hudson Guild

Theatre, then John Golden Theatre, New York City, both 1979; *The Runner Stumbles*, *The Human Voice*, *Winter Signs*, *Reunion*, *Hamlet*, and *Mary Stuart*, all Circle Repertory Theatre, 1979; *Tunnel Fever, or the Sheep Is Out*, American Place Theatre, 1979; *Chinchilla*, Phoenix Theatre, Marymount Manhattan Theatre, New York City, 1979; *Talley's Folly*, Circle Repertory Theatre, then Center Theatre Group, Mark Taper Forum, Los Angeles, both 1979, later Brooks Atkinson Theatre, New York City, 1980; *Fifth of July*, Center Theatre Group, Mark Taper Forum, 1979, then New Apollo Theatre, New York City, 1980.

The Woolgatherer and *Innocent Thoughts, Harmless Intentions*, both Circle Repertory Theatre, 1980; *Banjo Dancing*, Century Theatre, New York City, 1980; *The Trouble with Europe*, Phoenix Theatre, Marymount Manhattan Theatre, 1980; *American Days* and *One Wedding, Two Rooms, Three Friends*, both Manhattan Theatre Club, 1980; *Come Back to the 5 and Dime, Jimmy Dean, Jimmy Dean* and *Summer*, both Hudson Guild Theatre, 1980; *The White Devil*, American Place Theatre, 1980; *Look Back in Anger*, Roundabout Theatre, New York City, 1980; *Crimes of the Heart*, Manhattan Theatre Club, 1980, then John Golden Theatre, 1981; *Duet for One*, Royale Theatre, New York City, 1981; *Hedda Gabler*, Roundabout Theatre, 1981; *Twelfth Night*, *The Beaver Coat*, *In Connecticut*, *Childe Byron*, *A Tale Told*, and *The Diviners*, all Circle Repertory Theatre, 1981; *Close of Play*, Manhattan Theatre Club, 1981; *Il Campiello: A Venetian Comedy*, *Waiting for Godot*, and *A Midsummer Night's Dream*, all Public Theatre, 1981; *The Best Little Whorehouse in Texas*, Eugene O'Neill Theatre, New York City, 1982; *Skirmishes*, Manhattan Theatre Club, 1982; *Lennon* and *Richard II*, both Entermedia Theatre, 1982; *Snow Orchid* and *A Think Piece*, both Circle Repertory Theatre, 1982; *Angels Fall*, Circle Repertory Theatre, 1982, then Longacre Theatre, New York City, 1983; *The Curse of an Aching Heart*, Little Theatre, New York City, 1982; *The Country Wife*, American Place Theatre, 1982; *Elba* and *Early Warnings*, both Manhattan Theatre Club, 1983; *Domestic Issues*, Circle Repertory Theatre, 1983; *The Seagull*, Circle Repertory Company, American Place Theatre, 1983; *The Cradle Will Rock*, American Place Theatre, then Douglas Fairbanks Theatre, New York City, both 1983; *Pericles*, American Place Theatre, 1983; *A Raisin in the Sun*, Goodman Theatre, Chicago, IL, 1983; *Levitation* and *Love's Labour's Lost*, both Circle Repertory Theatre, 1984; *The Miss Firecracker Contest*, Manhattan Theatre Club, then Westside Arts Center/Cheryl Crawford Theatre, both 1984; *Criminal Minds*, Theatre Guinevere, New York City, 1984; *As You Like It* and *Passion Play*, both Seattle Repertory Theatre, Seattle, WA, 1984; *In Celebration*, Manhattan Theatre Club, the Space at City Center Theatre, New York City, 1984; *After the Fall*, Playhouse 91, New York City, 1984.

Dysan, *Angelo's Wedding*, *Talley and Son*, and *Tomorrow's Monday*, all Circle Repertory Theatre, 1985; *Dancing in the End Zone*, Ritz Theatre, New York City, 1985; *As Is*, Circle Repertory Theatre, then Lyceum Theatre, New York City, both 1985; *Penn and Teller*, Westside Arts Theatre, New York City, 1985; *A New Way to Pay Old Debts*, *As You Like It*, and *The Skin of Our Teeth*, all Marymount Manhattan Theatre, 1985; *An Enemy of the People*, Roundabout Theatre, 1985; *Glengarry Glen Ross*, Syracuse Stage, Syracuse, NY, 1985; *A View from the Bridge*, Studio Arena Theatre, Buffalo, NY, then Capital Repertory Company Theatre, Albany, NY, later Syracuse Stage, all 1986; *Burn This!*, Center Theatre Group, Mark Taper Forum, 1986, then Plymouth Theatre, 1987-88; *All My Sons* and *Pancho Forum: Endgame*, both Seattle Repertory Theatre, 1985-86; *The Beach House*, Circle Repertory Theatre, 1986; *Picnic*, Center Theatre Group, Ahmanson Theatre, Los Angeles, 1986; *Caligula*, *The Mound Builders*, and *Quiet in the*

Land, all Triplex Theatre, New York City, 1986; *Ten By Tennessee*, Acting Company, Lucille Lortel Theatre, New York City, 1986; *Bloody Poetry*, Manhattan Theatre Club, 1986-87; *The Lucky Spot*, Manhattan Theatre Club, 1987; *Coastal Disturbances* Second Stage Theatre, New York City, 1987; *The Nerd*, Helen Hayes Theatre, New York City, 1987; *A Shayna Maidel*, Westside Arts Theatre, 1987; *Hedda Gabler*, Studio Arena Theatre, 1987; *Born Yesterday*, Philadelphia Drama Guild, Philadelphia, PA, 1987; *El Salvador* and *Only You*, both Circle Repertory Theatre, 1987-88; *Summer and Smoke*, Center Theatre Group, Ahmanson Theatre, 1988; *The Road to Mecca*, Promenade Theatre, 1988; *The Big Love*, New Directors Series, New York Theatre Workshop, New York City, 1988; *Cave Life*, *Borderlines*, and *V and V Only*, all Circle Repertory Theatre, 1988; *Sleuth*, Circle Repertory Theatre, then Center Theatre Group, Ahmanson Theatre, both 1988; *The Film Society*, Second Stage Theatre, 1988; *Men Should Weep*, Studio Arena Theatre, 1988; *Eastern Standard*, Manhattan Theatre Club, 1988; *Amulets Against the Dragon Forces*, *Beside Herself*, *Florida Crackers*, and *Sunshine*, all Circle Repertory Theatre, 1989; *Approaching Zanzibar*, Second Stage Theatre, 1989; *My Children! My Africa!*, Perry Street Theatre, New York City, 1989; *The Tempest*, Roundabout Theatre, 1989; *The Tenth Man*, Vivian Beaumont Theatre, New York City, 1989. Also lighting designer for *Who's Afraid of Virginia Woolf?*, Circle Repertory Theatre; *South Pacific*, Minnesota Opera; *The Cradle Will Rock*, London production.

MAJOR TOURS—Lighting designer: *Crimes of the Heart*, U.S. cities, 1983-84; *Kabuki Macbeth*, Acting Company, U.S. cities, 1988; also *Fool for Love*, Japanese cities.

RELATED CAREER—Lighting designer: Playhouse in the Park, Cincinnati, OH, 1976-77; Hartman Theatre Company, Stamford, CT, 1977-78; PAF Playhouse, Huntington Station, NY, 1979; Chicago Theatre Group, Goodman Theatre, Chicago, IL, 1979-80; GeVa Theatre, Rochester, NY, 1980-81; Tyrone Guthrie Theatre, Minneapolis, MN, 1981-82; Philadelphia Drama Guild, Philadelphia, PA, 1982; Cleveland Playhouse, Cleveland, OH, 1983-84; also electrician and stage hand, 92nd Street Y, New York City; teacher, Barnard College and Lester Polikoff's Studio.

AWARDS: Antoinette Perry Award nomination, Best Lighting Designer, 1980, for *Talley's Folly;* Obie Award from the *Village Voice*, 1981, for sustained excellence in lighting design; Antoinette Perry Award nomination, Best Lighting Designer, 1981, for *Fifth of July;* also received Joseph Maharam Award and Drama Desk Award.*

*   *   *

PARKER, Corey   1965-

PERSONAL: Born July 8, 1965, in New York, NY. EDUCATION—Attended New York University.

VOCATION: Actor.

CAREER: OFF-BROADWAY DEBUT—*Meeting the Winter Bike Rider* (also known as *Meeting the Bike Rider*), Young Playwrights Festival, New York Shakespeare Festival, Public Theatre, 1984. PRINCIPAL STAGE APPEARANCES—John, *Been Taken*, One-Act Play Marathon '84, Ensemble Studio Theatre, New York City, 1984; Corky Sutter, *The Bloodletters*, both Ensemble Studio Theatre, 1984; Patrick, *The Semi-Formal,* One-Act Play Marathon '85, Ensemble Studio Theatre, 1985; also appeared in *Red Storm Flower,* New Dramatists Inc., 1980.

PRINCIPAL FILM APPEARANCES—John Dealy, *Scream for Help,* Lorimar, 1984; Pete, *Friday the 13th, Part V: A New Beginning,* Paramount, 1985; janitor, *9 1/2 Weeks,* Metro-Goldwyn-Mayer/ United Artists, 1986; Lopez, *Something Special* (also known as *Willy/Milly* and *I Was a Teenage Boy*), Concorde/Cinema Group, 1987; Epstein, *Biloxi Blues,* Universal, 1988; Alex, *Big Man on Campus* (also known as *The Hunchback of UCLA* and *Hunchback*), Vestron, 1989; Marlon, *How I Got into College* (also known as *Admissions*), Twentieth Century-Fox, 1989.

PRINCIPAL TELEVISION APPEARANCES—Pilots: Michael Gunz, *Sons of Gunz* (broadcast as an episode of *CBS Summer Playhouse*), CBS, 1987. Episodic: Henry, *The Bronx Zoo,* NBC, 1987; Lee, *thirtysomething,* ABC, 1989 and 1990. Movies: Tony Miraldo, *Courage,* CBS, 1986; Larry Schreuder, *At Mother's Request,* CBS, 1987. Specials: David, "Don't Touch," *ABC Afterschool Specials,* ABC, 1985; Ray Thomas, "Teen Father," *ABC Afterschool Specials,* ABC, 1986.

ADDRESSES: AGENT—Diane Roberts, The Gersh Agency, 222 N. Canon Drive, Suite 202, Beverly Hills, CA 90210.*

*   *   *

PASSER, Ivan   1933-

PERSONAL: Born July 10, 1933, in Prague, Czechoslovakia; immigrated to the United States in 1969. EDUCATION—Attended the Film Faculty of the Academy of Musical Arts (Prague).

VOCATION: Director and screenwriter.

CAREER: Also see *WRITINGS* below. PRINCIPAL FILM WORK— All as director, unless indicated: Assistant director, *Lasky jedne plavovlasky* (also known as *Loves of a Blonde* and *A Blonde in Love*), Ceskoslovensky, 1965, released in the United States by Prominent/CBK Film Enterprises, 1966; *Intimni osvetleni* (also known as *Intimate Lighting*), Ceskoslovensky, 1966, released in the United States by Altura International/Fleetwood, 1969; *Born to Win,* United Artists, 1971; *Law and Disorder,* Columbia, 1974; *Crime and Passion* (also known as *An Ace Up My Sleeve*), American International, 1976; *Silver Bears,* Columbia, 1978; *Cutter's Way* (also known as *Cutter and Bone*), United Artists, 1981; *Creator,* Universal, 1985; *Haunted Summer,* Cannon, 1989. Also assistant director, *Audition,* 1961; assistant director, *Cerny Petr* (also known as *Black Peter* and *Peter and Pavla*), 1963; *Fadni odpoledne* (also known as *A Boring Afternoon*), 1965.

PRINCIPAL TELEVISION WORK—Episodic: Director, *Faerie Tale Theatre,* Showtime.

RELATED CAREER—Assistant director for Milos Forman, 1961-65.

NON-RELATED CAREER—Longshoreman, New York City, 1969.

WRITINGS: FILM—See production details above, unless indicated. (With Milos Forman) *Konkurs* (also known as *Talent Competition* and *Competition*), Ceskoslovensky, 1964, released in the

United States by Brandon, 1968; (with Jaroslav Papousek, Forman, and Vaclav Sasek) *Lasky jedne plavovlasky,* 1965; (with Papousek and Vaclav Sasek) *Intimni osvetleni,* 1966; (with Forman and Papousek) *Hori, ma panenko* (also known as *The Fireman's Ball* and *Like a House on Fire*), Ceskoslovensky, 1967, released in the United States by Cinema V, 1968; (with William Richert and Kenneth Harris Fishman) *Law and Disorder,* 1974; also (co-writer) *Cerny Petr,* 1963.

AWARDS: Special Award from the National Society of Film Critics, 1969, for *Intimni osvetleni;* Rosenthal Foundation Award from the National Society of Film Critics, 1972, for Contribution to Film Art Not Yet Recognized By the Public.*

*   *   *

PATTERSON, Dick   1929-
(Richard Patterson)

PERSONAL: Born April 12, 1929, in Clear Lake, IA; son of Grover L. (a painter) and Neva P. (a nursing home administrator; maiden name, Carlock) Patterson; married Pat Lynn Louchheim (a personal manager), May 5, 1975; children: Marlene Elizabeth, Laura Christine. EDUCATION—University of California, Los Angeles, B.A., theatre arts, 1954. MILITARY—U.S. Army, corporal, 1951-53.

VOCATION: Actor and composer.

DICK PATTERSON

CAREER: STAGE DEBUT—Ensemble, *Vintage '60* (revue), Ivar Theatre, Hollywood, CA, 1960. BROADWAY DEBUT—Ensemble, *Vintage '60* (revue), Brooks Atkinson Theatre, 1960, for eight performances. PRINCIPAL STAGE APPEARANCES—Ensemble, *The Billy Barnes People* (revue), Royale Theatre, New York City, 1961; Albert Peterson, *Bye Bye, Birdie*, Martin Beck Theatre, New York City, 1961; Rudolph Governor, *Fade Out—Fade In*, Mark Hellinger Theatre, New York City, 1964; Georges Chauvinet, *Pajama Tops*, New Locust Theatre, Philadelphia, PA, 1973-74; Mike Curtis, *Something Old, Something New*, Morosco Theatre, New York City, 1977; Roger Cooper, *Walls*, Burt Reynolds' Jupiter Theatre, Jupiter, FL, 1982, then Huntington Hartford Theatre, Los Angeles, 1983; Ted Farley, *Smile*, Lunt-Fontanne Theatre, New York City, 1986-87; Lutz, *The Student Prince*, Long Beach Civic Light Opera Company, Long Beach, CA, 1989. Also appeared in *Sweet Charity*, Coconut Grove Playhouse, Miami, FL, 1967; as Roger, *Who Gets the Drapes?*, Las Vegas, NV, 1976; in *An Evening with Dick Patterson* (one-man show), 1987; and in summer theatre productions of *The Music Man, Cactus Flower, Guys and Dolls, Flower Drum Song, Will Success Spoil Rock Hunter?, Luv, The Man Who Came to Dinner, The Owl and the Pussycat*, and *No Hard Feelings*.

MAJOR TOURS—Albert Peterson, *Bye Bye, Birdie*, U.S. cities, 1961-62; Warren, *On a Clear Day*, U.S. cities, 1975.

FILM DEBUT—Pilot, *The Absent-Minded Professor*, Buena Vista, 1961. PRINCIPAL FILM APPEARANCES—Perky, *Dondi*, Allied Artists, 1961; Rick Preston, *A Matter of Innocence* (also known as *Pretty Polly*), Universal, 1968; Mr. Rudie, *Grease*, Paramount, 1978; record store manager, *Can't Stop the Music*, Associated Film Distribution, 1980; Mr. Spears, *Grease 2*, Paramount, 1982; also appeared in *The Strongest Man in the World*, Buena Vista, 1975; *Leo and Loree*, United Artists, 1980.

TELEVISION DEBUT—"The Beatnik," *The Millionaire*, CBS, 1959. PRINCIPAL TELEVISION APPEARANCES—Series: Regular, *Stump the Stars*, syndicated, 1969. Pilots: Dr. Jerry Berry, *My Son, the Doctor*, CBS, 1966; also *Don't Call Me Mama Anymore*, CBS, 1973; *Some Like It Hot*. Episodic: Announcer, *Max Headroom*, ABC, 1987; also *The Dick Van Dyke Show*, CBS, 1964; *The Ed Sullivan Show*, CBS; *Here's Lucy*, CBS; *PDQ*, NBC; *Password*, CBS; *Hollywood Squares*, NBC; *Love, American Style*, ABC; *The Carol Burnett Show*, CBS; *Happy Days*, ABC; *Laverne and Shirley*, ABC; *The Mary Tyler Moore Show*, CBS; *CHiPs*, NBC; *General Hospital*, ABC; *The Young and the Restless*, CBS; *The Fall Guy*, ABC; *Small Wonder*, syndicated; announcer, *Celebrity Charades;* announcer, *Do It Now; Get Smart; Too Close for Comfort*. Movies: (As Richard Patterson) Ted Comden, *Roll, Freddie, Roll!*, ABC, 1974; (as Richard Patterson) Harvey Clark, *Make Me an Offer*, ABC, 1980; (as Richard Patterson) Howard Chase, *Sunset Limousine*, CBS, 1983; also *Lots of Luck*, Disney Channel, 1985.

PRINCIPAL RADIO APPEARANCES—Episodic: *The Ken and Bob Show*, KABC (Los Angeles).

RELATED CAREER—As a member of the comedy team of Bennett and Patterson, appeared in nightclubs throughout the United States; writer of material for such performers as Debbie Reynolds and Rich Little.

RECORDINGS: SINGLES—"Santa's Marching Song," RCA, 1959.

WRITINGS: Songs: "Everything's Gonna Be O.K."; (with Claude Baum) "Santa's Marching Song."

MEMBER: Pacific Pioneer Broadcasters, UCLA Theatre Arts Alumni Association, Sigma Chi.

ADDRESSES: AGENTS—First Artists Agency, 427 N. Canon Drive, Suite 203, Beverly Hills, CA 90210; (commercials) Sutton, Barth, and Vennari, 145 S. Fairfax Avenue, Los Angeles, CA 90036. MANAGER—Pat Lynn, Patco, 10525 Strathmore Drive, Los Angeles, CA 90024.

*   *   *

PATTERSON, Richard
   See PATTERSON, Dick

*   *   *

PAYNE, John   1912-1989

PERSONAL: Born May 23 (some sources say May 28), 1912, in Roanoke, VA; died of heart failure, December 6, 1989, in Malibu, CA; son of George Washington (a gentleman farmer) and Ida Hope (Schaeffer) Payne; married Anne Shirley (an actress; divorced); married Gloria DeHaven (an actress; divorced); married Alexandra (Sandy) Crowell Curtis (an actress), 1952; children: Julie Anne, Kathleen, Thomas. EDUCATION—Graduated from Roanoke College; studied acting at Columbia University and singing at the Juilliard School of Music. MILITARY—U.S. Army Air Corps, pilot, during World War II.

VOCATION: Actor.

CAREER: PRINCIPAL STAGE APPEARANCES—Understudy, *At Home Abroad* (revue), Winter Garden Theatre, New York City, 1935.

MAJOR TOURS—Bill Johnson, *Good News*, U.S. cities, 1973-74.

FILM DEBUT—Harry, *Dodsworth*, United Artists, 1936. PRINCIPAL FILM APPEARANCES—Jimmy Maxwell, *Hats Off*, Grand National, 1937; Bill Adams, *Love on Toast*, Paramount, 1937; Martin Bates, *College Swing* (also known as *Swing, Teacher, Swing*), Paramount, 1938; Don Vincente, *Garden of the Moon*, Warner Brothers, 1938; Eddie Greer, *Indianapolis Speedway* (also known as *Devil on Wheels*), Warner Brothers, 1939; Steve Nelson, *Kid Nightingale*, Warner Brothers, 1939; Jerry Harrington, *Wings of the Navy*, Warner Brothers, 1939.

Richard Lansing, *The Great Profile*, Twentieth Century-Fox, 1940; Slim, *King of the Lumberjacks*, Warner Brothers, 1940; Lee Danfield, *Maryland*, Twentieth Century-Fox, 1940; Bud Borden, *Star Dust*, Twentieth Century-Fox, 1940; Bill Morrissey, *Tear Gas Squad*, Warner Brothers, 1940; Skeets Harrigan, *Tin Pan Alley*, Twentieth Century-Fox, 1940; Rix Martin, *The Great American Broadcast*, Twentieth Century-Fox, 1941; Dan Hopkins, *Remember the Day*, Twentieth Century-Fox, 1941; Ted Scott, *Sun Valley Serenade*, Twentieth Century-Fox, 1941; Jay Williams, *Weekend in Havana*, Twentieth Century-Fox, 1941; Bill Smith, *Footlight Serenade*, Twentieth Century-Fox, 1942; Corporal James Murfin,

Iceland, Twentieth Century-Fox, 1942; Dan, *Springtime in the Rockies*, Twentieth Century-Fox, 1942; Chris Winters, *To the Shores of Tripoli*, Twentieth Century-Fox, 1942; Johnnie Cornell, *Hello, Frisco, Hello*, Twentieth Century-Fox, 1943; Harry Fox, *The Dolly Sisters*, Twentieth Century-Fox, 1945; Gray Maturin, *The Razor's Edge*, Twentieth Century-Fox, 1946; Bill, *Sentimental Journey*, Twentieth Century-Fox, 1946; Jeff, *Wake Up and Dream*, Twentieth Century-Fox, 1946; Fred Gailey, *The Miracle on 34th Street* (also known as *The Big Heart*), Twentieth Century-Fox, 1947; Rick Maxon, *Larceny*, Universal, 1948; Eric Busch, *The Saxon Charm*, Universal, 1948; title role, *Captain China*, Paramount, 1949; Eddie Rice, *The Crooked Way*, United Artists, 1949; Clayton Fletcher, *El Paso*, Paramount, 1949.

Todd Croyden, *The Eagle and the Hawk* (also known as *Spread Eagle*), Paramount, 1950; Lieutenant O'Bannon, *Tripoli* (also known as *First Marines*), Paramount, 1950; Steve Singleton, *Crosswinds* (also known as *Jungle Attacks*), Paramount, 1951; Pete Black, *Passage West* (also known as *High Venture*), Paramount, 1951; Kelly Hanson, *The Blazing Forest*, Paramount, 1952; Dick Lindsay, *Caribbean* (also known as *Caribbean Gold*), Paramount, 1952; Joe Rolfe, *Kansas City Confidential* (also known as *The Secret Four*), United Artists, 1952; Barbarossa, *Raiders of the Seven Seas*, United Artists, 1953; Rock Grayson, *The Vanquished*, Paramount, 1953; Ernie Driscoll, *99 River Street*, United Artists, 1953; Jefferson Harder, *Rails into Laramie*, Universal, 1954; Dan Ballard, *Silver Lode*, RKO, 1954; Mike Cormack, *Hell's Island* (also known as *The Ruby Virgin*, *Love Is a Weapon*, and *South Seas Fury*), Paramount, 1955; Bill Mayhew, *The Road to Denver*, Republic, 1955; Kirby Randolph, *Santa Fe Passage*, Republic, 1955; Tennessee, *Tennessee's Partner*, Filmcrest/RKO, 1955; Ben Grace, *Slightly Scarlet*, RKO, 1956; Matt Brady, *The Boss*, United Artists, 1956; Mackenzie, *Hold Back the Night*, Allied Artists, 1956; John Wiloughby, *Rebel in Town*, United Artists, 1956; Major Paul Peterson, *Bailout at 43,000*, United Artists, 1957; Mike Brent, *Hidden Fear*, United Artists, 1957; Iverson, *The Risk* (also known as *Suspect*), Kingsley, 1961; Bob Martin, *They Ran for Their Lives*, Color Vision, 1968; John, *The Savage Wild*, American International, 1970; also appeared in *The Gift of the Nile*.

PRINCIPAL FILM WORK—Director, *They Ran for Their Lives*, Color Vision, 1968.

PRINCIPAL TELEVISION APPEARANCES—Series: Vint Bonner, *The Restless Gun*, NBC, 1957-59; host, *Call of the West*, syndicated, 1969. Pilots: Britt Ponset, *The Restless Gun* (broadcast as an episode of *Schlitz Playhouse of Stars*), CBS, 1957; Torin O'Connor, *O'Connor's Ocean*, NBC, 1960; Ingalls, *Go West, Young Girl*, ABC, 1978. Episodic: "Double-Dyed Deceiver," *The Nash Airflyte Theatre*, CBS, 1950; "The Name Is Bellingham" and "Exit," *Schlitz Playhouse of Stars*, CBS, 1951; "The Deep Six," *Robert Montgomery Presents*, NBC, 1953; "Lash of Fear," *General Electric Theatre*, CBS, 1955; "Deadline," *Studio 57*, Dumont, 1956; "Until the Man Dies," *Zane Grey Theatre* (also known as *Dick Powell's Zane Grey Theatre*), CBS, 1957; "The Little Hours," *General Electric Theatre*, CBS, 1962; *Name of the Game*, NBC, 1968; *Gunsmoke*, CBS, 1970; *Cade's County*, CBS, 1971; *Columbo*, NBC, 1975. Movies: Mr. Jerome, *The Christmas Star*, ABC, 1986. Specials: C.K. Dexter Haven, "The Philadelphia Story," *The Best of Broadway*, CBS, 1954; also "Alice in Wonderland," *Hallmark Hall of Fame*, NBC, 1955.

PRINCIPAL TELEVISION WORK—Series: Executive producer, *The Restless Gun*, NBC, 1957-59. Pilots: Producer, *O'Connor's Ocean*, NBC, 1960.

NON-RELATED CAREER—Professional wrestler.

OBITUARIES AND OTHER SOURCES: [New York] *Daily News*, December 7, 1989; *New York Times*, December 8, 1989; *Variety*, December 13, 1989.*

*   *   *

PEARCE, Richard   1943-

PERSONAL: Full name, Richard Inman Pearce, Jr.; born January 25, 1943, in San Diego, CA; son of Richard Inman and Patricia (Pittman) Pearce; married Lynzee Klingman; children: Remy Elizabeth. EDUCATION—Yale University, B.A., English literature, 1965; New School for Social Research, M.A., political economics, 1974.

VOCATION: Director, cinematographer, and producer.

CAREER: PRINCIPAL FILM WORK—Cinematographer, *Interviews with My Lai Veterans* (documentary), Laser, 1969; cinematographer, *Woodstock* (documentary), Warner Brothers, 1970; cinematographer, *Marjoe* (documentary), Cinema V, 1972; cinematographer, *Let the Good Times Roll* (documentary), Columbia, 1973; associate proudcer and cinematographer, *Hearts and Minds* (documentary), Warner Brothers, 1975; camera operator assistant, *Running Fence* (documentary), Maysles/Transatlantic, 1977; cinematographer, *Baby Snakes*, Intercontinental Absurdities, 1979; additional photography, *Hair*, United Artists, 1979; cinematographer, *Rust Never Sleeps* (documentary), International Harmony, 1979; director, *Heartland*, Filmhaus, 1980; director, *Threshold*, Twentieth Century-Fox, 1983; director, *Country*, Buena Vista, 1984; director, *No Mercy*, Tri-Star, 1986; also director, cinematographer, and editor, *Campamento* (documentary), 1970; cinematographer, *America Is Hard to See* (documentary).

PRINCIPAL TELEVISION WORK—All as director. Episodic: (Also producer with Michael Hausman) "The Gardener's Son," *Visions*, PBS, 1977; *Alfred Hitchcock Presents*, NBC, 1985. Movies: *Siege*, CBS, 1978; *No Other Love*, CBS, 1979; *Sessions*, ABC, 1983; *Dead Man Out*, HBO, 1989; *The Final Days*, ABC, 1989.

RELATED CAREER—Cameraman for documentaries by D.A. Pennebaker.

AWARDS: Alicia Patterson Foundation Fellow, 1974-75; Golden Bear Award from the Berlin Film Festival, 1980, for *Heartland;* Christopher Awards, 1981 and 1984.

ADDRESSES: AGENT—William Morris Agency, 1350 Avenue of the Americas, New York, NY 10019.*

*   *   *

PENGHLIS, Thaao

PERSONAL: Born in Sydney, Australia; father, a mechanic for General Motors; mother, a housewife. EDUCATION—Graduated from the University of New South Wales; studied acting with Milton Katselas and Uta Hagen.

THAAO PENGHLIS

VOCATION: Actor.

CAREER: STAGE DEBUT—Mr. T., *Jockeys,* Promenade Theatre, New York City, 1977. PRINCIPAL STAGE APPEARANCES—*Play with Fire,* Westwood Playhouse, Los Angeles; also appeared in productions of *The Collection, The Lion in Winter, The Balcony,* and *No Exit.*

PRINCIPAL FILM APPEARANCES—Christopher, *Slow Dancing in the Big City,* United Artists, 1978; Marco, *The Bell Jar,* AVCO-Embassy, 1979; Eccheverria, *Altered States,* Warner Brothers, 1980; Colonel Richard Godowni, *Les Patterson Saves the World,* Hoyts, 1987.

PRINCIPAL TELEVISION APPEARANCES—Series: Victor Cassadine, *General Hospital,* ABC, 1981; Count Antony DiMera, *Days of Our Lives,* NBC, 1981-85; Nicholas Black, *Mission: Impossible,* ABC, 1988—. Mini-Series: Captain Albert Steinberger, *Emma: Queen of the South Seas,* syndicated, 1988. Pilots: Paul Boudea, *Power's Play,* CBS, 1986. Episodic: Philippe, *Magnum, P.I.,* CBS, 1986; Armand Ghia, *Who's the Boss?,* ABC, 1987. Movies: Antonio Moreno, *Moviola: The Silent Lovers,* NBC, 1980; Amer, *Sadat,* syndicated, 1983; Abu Ladeen, *Under Siege,* NBC, 1986.

RELATED CAREER—Assistant to acting teacher and director Milton Katselas.

NON-RELATED CAREER—Worked with Greek immigrants for the Australian diplomatic service; worked at the United Nations.

ADDRESSES: AGENT—McCartt, Oreck, Barrett, 10390 Santa Monica Boulevard, Suite 310, Los Angeles, CA 90025. PUBLICIST—Lori DeWaal, The Garrett Company, 6922 Hollywood Boulevard, Los Angeles, CA 90028.

*   *   *

PERLMAN, Ron   1950-

PERSONAL: Born April 13, 1950, in New York, NY; father, a jazz drummer; married Opal Stone (a fashion designer); children: Blake Amanda. EDUCATION—Graduated from the City University of New York; received M.F.A. from the University of Minnesota.

VOCATION: Actor.

CAREER: OFF-BROADWAY DEBUT—Emperor, *The Architect and the Emperor of Assyria,* La Mama Theatre Annex, 1976. BROADWAY DEBUT—Beadle Treitel, *Teibele and Her Demon,* Brooks Atkinson Theatre, 1979. PRINCIPAL STAGE APPEARANCES—Beadle Treitel, *Teibele and Her Demon,* Arena Stage, Washington, DC, 1979; also appeared in *Sunset,* Studio Arena Theatre, Buffalo, NY, 1977-78; *La Tragedie de Carmen,* Lincoln Center, New York City; *American Heroes, The Resistible Rise of Arturo Ui, School for Buffoons,* and *Hedda Gabler,* all in New York City; with the Classic Stage Company, New York City; and in productions of *Tartuffe, Woyzeck, Measure for Measure, House of Blue Leaves, Two Gentlemen of Verona,* and *The Iceman Cometh.*

MAJOR TOURS—Emperor, *The Architect and the Emperor of Assyria,* European cities; also *Pal Joey,* U.S. cities.

PRINCIPAL FILM APPEARANCES—Amoukar, *Quest for Fire,* Twentieth Century-Fox, 1982; Zeno, *The Ice Pirates,* Metro-Goldwyn-Mayer/United Artists, 1984; Salvatore, *The Name of the Rose,* Twentieth Century-Fox, 1986.

PRINCIPAL TELEVISION APPEARANCES—Series: Vincent, *Beauty and the Beast,* CBS, 1987-89. Movies: Jacob Schuler, *A Stoning in Fulham County,* NBC, 1988. Specials: *Starathon '90,* syndicated, 1990.

RELATED CAREER—Stand-up comedian while in high school.

AWARDS: Emmy Award nomination, Outstanding Lead Actor in a Drama Series, 1989, for *Beauty and the Beast.*

ADDRESSES: AGENT—Bagley, McQueeney, and Connor, 9229 Sunset Boulevard, Suite 607, Los Angeles, CA 90069. PUBLICIST—Levine/Schneider Public Relations, 8730 Sunset Boulevard, 6th Floor, Los Angeles, CA 90069. MANAGER—Larry Thompson Organization, 1440 S. Sepulveda Boulevard, Suite 118, Los Angeles, CA 90025.*

*   *   *

PERRY, Keith   1931-

PERSONAL: Born October 29, 1931, in Des Moines, IA; son of Ralph Brady (a watchmaker and jeweler) and Beatrice (Gooding) Perry. EDUCATION—Rice University, B.A., 1953; Fletcher School of

KEITH PERRY

International Law and Diplomacy, M.A., 1954; studied acting with Shepard Traube. MILITARY—U.S. Army, sergeant, 1954-57.

VOCATION: Actor.

CAREER: STAGE DEBUT—Constable of France, *Henry V,* American Shakespeare Festival, Stratford, CT, 1963. BROADWAY DEBUT—Jackson, *Pickwick,* 46th Street Theatre, 1965. PRINCIPAL STAGE APPEARANCES—Lieutenant Pyle, *A Recent Killing,* New Federal Theatre, New York City, 1973; Ernest, cameraman, and necktie man, *Once in a Lifetime,* Circle in the Square, New York City, 1978; Fyodr Andreyevich Lyulykov, priest, and merchant, *The Inspector General,* Circle in the Square, 1979; Mr. Wickfield, *Copperfield,* American National Theatre and Academy Theatre, New York City, 1981; Luther Kingsley, *City of Angels,* Virginia Theatre, New York City, 1989-90. Also appeared in *I'm Solomon,* Mark Hellinger Theatre, New York City, 1968; *Love Match,* Center Theatre Group, Mark Taper Forum, Los Angeles, 1969; *Oliver!,* Playhouse in the Park, Cincinnati, OH, 1976; *Mademoiselle Colombe,* Playwrights Horizons, New York City, 1977; *Room Service,* Playhouse in the Park, 1979; *The Imaginary Invalid,* Theatre By the Sea, Portsmouth, NH, 1984; *Ten Little Indians,* New Vic Theatre, New York City, 1985; *The Crucible,* Pennsylvania Stage Company, Allentown, PA, 1985; *Epicene, The Silent Woman,* off-Broadway production; at the Studio Arena Theatre, Buffalo, NY, 1968-69.

MAJOR TOURS—Carrasco, *Man of La Mancha,* U.S. cities, 1969-70; Job Anderson and Dirk, *Treasure Island,* U.S. cities, 1975; Thomson, *1776,* U.S. cities, 1975-76; Baron Van Swieten, *Amadeus,*

U.S. and Canadian cities, 1982-84; Charles Hethersett, *Me and My Girl,* U.S. cities, 1987-89.

RELATED CAREER—Television and radio awards specialist, NBC Awards Department, New York City, 1957-65.

*   *   *

PERRYMAN, Dwayne B., III   1963-

PERSONAL: Born November 30, 1963, in Brooklyn, NY; son of Beverly Ann Perryman Mitchell (a day care administrator). EDUCATION—Attended the New School for Social Research and the Borough of Manhattan Community College, 1985-87; studied acting at the Actors' Studio and with the Cecil Alonzo Players; studied comedy with Michael Hampton-Cane.

VOCATION: Actor and stage manager.

CAREER: STAGE DEBUT—Walter, *Bend, Tear, and Spindle,* Peter Rutger Theatre, Brooklyn, NY, 1981, for eight performances. PRINCIPAL STAGE APPEARANCES—Puck, *A Midsummer Night's Dream,* Riverside Ensemble, New York City, 1987; guard, *Richard III,* Actors' Studio, New York City, 1989; also appeared as Gitlow, *Purlie Victorious,* Mind Power Playhouse, New York City, 1985.

PRINCIPAL STAGE WORK—All as stage manager, unless indicated: *Four Saints in Three Acts,* Opera Ensemble Theatre, New York City, 1986; *The Tavern,* Equity Library Theatre, New York City, 1987; *The Threepenny Opera,* Riverside Opera Ensemble, New York City, 1987; *Who Does She Think She Is?,* Tomi Theatre, New York City, 1987; *Future Flight, Time of Our Life, On Off Broadway, Skin of Our Teeth, Two On an Island, The Cat Who Died of Leukemia,* and *Obscenery* (series of one-act plays), American Music Dramatic Academy, New York City, 1987; *Iowa Boys,* Ohio Theatre, then Actors' Studio, both 1988; *A Tantalizing, Fallen Angels, Beyond Therapy, Family Life, Thugs, Final Placement, Men As Trees Walking, Penguin Blues,* and *It's Still Life* (series of one-act plays), *Rasputin* and *Go-See* (staged readings), and *The Cherry Orchard,* all Actors' Studio, New York City, 1989; *Goree* New Federal Theatre, New York City, 1989; assistant technical director, *Chinese Charades,* Puerto Rican Traveling Theatre, New York City, 1989; *God's Trombones,* New Federal Theatre, Theatre of the Riverside Church, New York City, 1989; also *Cheating Cheaters,* Stepping Stone Theatre, 1987.

FILM DEBUT—Little Al, *Dance in Motion,* Abbott View, 1987. PRINCIPAL FILM APPEARANCES—Henry, *The Deranged,* 1989.

RELATED CAREER—Technical director, singer, and stand-up comic; president and director of music and horror videos, Perryman Enterprises.

AWARDS: Cecil Alonzo's Entertainers Award, Stand-Up Comedy Routine, 1985.

MEMBER: Actors' Equity Association.

SIDELIGHTS: RECREATIONS—Drawing, dancing, weight lifting, tennis, swimming, swing riding, running, and boxing.

ADDRESSES: HOME—Brooklyn, NY.

PESCI, Joe   1943-

PERSONAL: Born February 9, 1943, in Newark, NJ.

VOCATION: Actor.

CAREER: PRINCIPAL FILM APPEARANCES—Joey, *Raging Bull*, United Artists, 1980; Roger, *I'm Dancing As Fast As I Can*, Paramount, 1982; Ruby Dennis, *Dear Mr. Wonderful*, Lilienthal, 1983; Nicky, *Easy Money*, Orion, 1983; Mayakofsky, *Eureka*, United Artists, 1983; Corrado Emilio Parisi, *Tutti Dentro* (also known as *Put 'em All in Jail*), CDE, 1984; Frankie Monaldi, *Once Upon a Time in America*, Warner Brothers, 1984; David, *Man on Fire*, Tri-Star, 1987; Mr. Big, *Moonwalker*, Warner Brothers, 1988; Leo, *Backtrack*, Vestron, 1988; Leo Getz, *Lethal Weapon II*, Warner Brothers, 1989; Tommy, *Good Fellas*, Warner Brothers, 1989; Oscar, *Betsy's Wedding*, Disney, 1989. Also appeared in *Death Collector* (also known as *Family Enforcer*), Epoh, 1976; (as Joey Pesci) *Don't Go in the House*, Turbine, 1980.

PRINCIPAL TELEVISION APPEARANCES—Series: Rocky Nelson, *Half Nelson*, NBC, 1985.

AWARDS: New York Film Critics Award, American Society of Film Critics Award, and Academy Award nomination, all Best Supporting Actor, 1980, for *Raging Bull;* also Los Angeles Film Critics Award nomination, Golden Globe nomination, and British Academy Award, Best Newcomer to Film, all for *Raging Bull.*

ADDRESSES: AGENT—Jim Cota, The Artists Agency, 10000 Santa Monica Boulevard, Suite 305, Los Angeles, CA 90067.

*   *   *

PETERSEN, Wolfgang   1941-

PERSONAL: Born March 14, 1941, in Emden, Germany.

VOCATION: Director and screenwriter.

CAREER: Also see *WRITINGS* below. PRINCIPAL FILM WORK—Director: *Die Konsequenz* (also known as *The Consequence*), Almi Cinema V/Prestige, 1977; (also producer) *Einer von uns Beiden* (also known as *One or the Other*), Transocean International, 1978; *Schwarz und Weiss Wie Tage und Naechte* (also known as *Black and White Like Days and Nights*), Monaco/Radiant/Osterreichischer Rundfunk Fernsehen/Westdeutscher Rundfunk, 1978; *Das Boot* (also known as *The Boat*), Columbia, 1982; *Reifezeugnis* (also known as *For Your Love Only*), Cannon Releasing, 1982; *The Neverending Story*, Warner Brothers, 1984; *Enemy Mine*, Twentieth Century-Fox, 1985.

PRINCIPAL TELEVISION WORK—Series: Director, *Scenes of the Crime*.

RELATED CAREER—Stage director and actor, Ernst Deutsch Theatre, Hamburg, West Germany.

WRITINGS: See production details above. FILM—(With Alexander Ziegler) *Die Konsequenz*, 1977; (with Karl-Heinz Willschrei and Jochen Wedegartner) *Schwarz und Weiss Wie Tage und Naechte*, 1978; *Das Boot*, 1982; (with Herbert Lichtenfeld) *Reifezeugnis*, 1982; (with Herman Weigel) *The Neverending Story*, 1984.

AWARDS: Academy Award nominations, Best Director and Best Screenplay, both 1983, for *Das Boot.*

ADDRESSES: AGENT—The Chasin Agency, 190 N. Canon Drive, Suite 210, Beverly Hills, CA 90210.

*   *   *

PFEIFFER, Michelle   1957-

PERSONAL: Born in 1957 in Santa Ana, CA; daughter of Dick (a heating and air-conditioning contractor) and Donna Pfeiffer; married Peter Horton (an actor; divorced). EDUCATION—Studied court reporting at Whitley College; also attended Golden West College; studied acting with Peggy Feury.

VOCATION: Actress.

CAREER: PRINCIPAL STAGE APPEARANCES—Olivia, *Twelfth Night*, New York Shakespeare Festival, Delacorte Theatre, New York City, 1989.

PRINCIPAL FILM APPEARANCES—Suzi Q, *The Hollywood Knights*, Poly-Gram/Columbia, 1980; Sue Wellington, *Falling in Love Again*, International Picture of Atlanta, 1980; Cordelia Farrington III, *Charlie Chan and the Curse of the Dragon Queen*, American Cinema, 1981; Stephanie Zinone, *Grease II*, Paramount, 1982; Elvira, *Scarface*, Universal, 1983; Diana, *Into the Night*, Univer-

MICHELLE PFEIFFER

sal, 1985; Isabeau, *Ladyhawke,* Warner Brothers/Fox, 1985; Faith Healy, *Sweet Liberty,* Universal, 1986; Brenda, "Hospital" in *Amazon Women on the Moon,* Universal, 1987; Sukie Ridgemont, *The Witches of Eastwick,* Warner Brothers, 1987; Angela De Marco, *Married to the Mob,* Orion, 1988; Jo Ann Vallenari, *Tequila Sunrise,* Warner Brothers, 1988; Madame de Tourvel, *Dangerous Liaisons,* Warner Brothers, 1988; Susie Diamond, *The Fabulous Baker Boys,* Twentieth Century-Fox, 1989. Also appeared as Katya, *The Russia House,* 1990.

PRINCIPAL TELEVISION APPEARANCES—Series: Bombshell, *Delta House,* ABC, 1979; Officer Samantha "Sunshine" Jensen, *B.A.D. Cats,* ABC, 1980. Episodic: *Fantasy Island,* ABC. Movies: Tricia, *The Solitary Man,* CBS, 1979; Sue Lynn, *Callie and Son,* CBS, 1981; Jennifer Williams, *The Children Nobody Wanted,* CBS, 1981; Ginny Stamper, *Splendor in the Grass,* NBC, 1981. Specials: Jane, *One Too Many,* CBS, 1985; Natica Jackson, "Tales from the Hollywood Hills: Natica Jackson," *Great Performances,* PBS, 1987.

RELATED CAREER—Founder (with Kate Guinzburg) of a production company in association with Orion Pictures.

NON-RELATED CAREER—Check-out clerk, Vons Supermarket, Santa Ana, CA.

AWARDS: Academy Award nomination, Best Supporting Actress, 1989, for *Dangerous Liaisons;* Los Angeles Film Critics Association Achievement Award, Best Actress, 1989, D.W. Griffith Award from the National Board of Review, Best Actress, 1989, New York Film Critics Award, Best Actress, 1989, National Society of Film Critics Award, Best Actress, 1990, Golden Globe, Best Performance By an Actress in a Motion Picture—Drama, 1990, and Academy Award nomination, Best Actress, 1990, all for *The Fabulous Baker Boys.*

MEMBER: Screen Actors Guild.

ADDRESSES: AGENT—Ed Limato, William Morris Agency, 151 El Camino Drive, Beverly Hills, CA 90212.*

*   *   *

PHILLIPS, Lloyd   1949-

PERSONAL: Born December 14, 1949, in New Zealand; son of Morris (an engineer) and Hilda (a writer; maiden name, Rosenbaum) Phillips. EDUCATION—Graduated from the National Film School (England).

VOCATION: Producer.

CAREER: Also see *WRITINGS* below. FIRST STAGE WORK—Associate producer, *The Threepenny Opera,* Lunt-Fontanne Theatre, New York City, 1989.

FIRST FILM WORK—Producer, *The Dollar Bottom,* Paramount, 1981. PRINCIPAL FILM WORK—Producer, *Battle Truck* (also known as *Warlords of the Twenty-First Century*), New World, 1982; producer, *Nate and Hayes* (also known as *Savage Islands*), Paramount, 1983.

WRITINGS: FILM—(With John Hughes and David Odell) *Nate and Hayes* (also known as *Savage Islands*), Paramount, 1983.

AWARDS: Academy Award, Best Short Film (Live Action), 1980, and British Academy of Film and Television Arts Award nomination, Best Live-Action Short Subject Film, 1981, both for *The Dollar Bottom.*

MEMBER: Agence de Cooperation Culturelle et Technique (Agency for Cultural and Technical Cooperation)—English Union.

ADDRESSES: OFFICE—8981 Sunset Boulevard, Suite 307, Los Angeles, CA 90069. AGENT—International Creative Management, 8899 Beverly Boulevard, Los Angeles, CA 90048.

*   *   *

PHILLIPS, Sian   1934-

PERSONAL: Born May 14, 1934, in Bettws, Wales; daughter of David and Sally (Thomas) Phillips; married Peter O'Toole (an actor), 1960 (divorced, 1979); married Robin Sachs (an actor), December 24, 1979; children: Kate, Pat (first marriage). EDUCATION—Attended the University of Wales; studied acting at the Royal Academy of Dramatic Art.

VOCATION: Actress.

CAREER: LONDON DEBUT—Title role, *Hedda,* Duke of York's

SIAN PHILLIPS

Theatre, 1957. PRINCIPAL STAGE APPEARANCES—Title role, *Saint Joan*, Belgrade Theatre, Coventry, U.K., 1958; Masha, *The Three Sisters*, Nottingham Playhouse, Nottingham, U.K., 1958; Princess Siwan, *King's Daughter*, Hampstead Theatre Club, London, 1959; Katherine, *The Taming of the Shrew*, Oxford Playhouse, Oxford, U.K., 1960; Julia, *The Duchess of Malfi* and Bertha, *Ondine*, both Royal Shakespeare Company, Aldwych Theatre, London, 1961; Arlow, *The Lizard on the Rock*, Phoenix Theatre, London, 1962; Penelope, *Gentle Jack*, Queen's Theatre, London, 1963; Yolande, *Maxibules*, Queen's Theatre, 1964; Hannah Jelkes, *Night of the Iguana*, Ashcroft Theatre, Croydon, U.K., 1965; Myra, *Ride a Cock Horse*, Piccadilly Theatre, London, 1965; Ann Whitefield, *Man and Superman*, New Art Theatre, then Vaudeville Theatre, later Garrick Theatre, all London, 1966; strange lady, *The Man of Destiny*, Mermaid Theatre, London, 1966; Edwina, *The Burglar*, Vaudeville Theatre, 1967; Alma Winemiller, *Eccentricities of a Nightingale*, Yvonne Arnaud Theatre, Guildford, U.K., 1967; Queen Juana, *The Cardinal of Spain*, Yvonne Arnaud Theatre, 1969; Ruth Grey, *Epitaph for George Dillon*, Young Vic Theatre, London, 1972; Mrs. Elliot, *Alpha Beta*, Palace Theatre, Watford, U.K., 1973; Virginia Woolf, *A Nightingale in Bloomsbury Square*, Hampstead Theatre Club, 1974; Duchess of Strood, *The Gay Lord Quex*, Albery Theatre, London, 1975; Myra Evans, *Spinechiller*, Duke of York's Theatre, 1978; Mrs. Arbuthnot, *A Woman of No Importance* and Countess, *The Inconstant Couple*, both Chichester Festival Theatre, Chichester, U.K., 1978; Mrs. Clandon, *You Never Can Tell*, Lyric Hammersmith Theatre, London, 1979; Mrs. Patrick Campbell, *Dear Liar*, Mermaid Theatre, 1982. Also appeared in *Pal Joey*, Half Moon Theatre, London, 1980, then Albery Theatre, 1981; *Major Barbara*, National Theatre, London, 1982; *Peg*, Phoenix Theatre, 1984; *Gigi*, Lyric Theatre, London, 1985; *Love Affair*, 1984; *Paris Match*, Garrick Theatre, 1989.

MAJOR TOURS—Margaret Muir, *The Holiday*, U.K. cities, 1957; toured Wales in original Welsh plays and in classic English translations for the Welsh Arts Council, 1953-55.

PRINCIPAL FILM APPEARANCES—Wren, *The Longest Day*, Twentieth Century-Fox, 1962; Gwendolyn, *Becket*, Paramount, 1964; Ella, *Young Cassidy*, Metro-Goldwyn-Mayer (MGM), 1965; Ursula Mossbank, *Goodbye Mr. Chips*, MGM, 1969; Dr. Hayden, *Murphy's War*, Paramount, 1971; Mrs. Ogmore-Pritchard, *Under Milk Wood*, Altura Films International, 1973; Lady Ripon, *Nijinsky*, Paramount, 1980; Cassiopeia, *Clash of the Titans*, Metro-Goldwyn-Mayer/United Artists, 1981; Reverend Mother Gaius Helen Mohiam, *Dune*, Dino De Laurentiis/Universal, 1984; Annabella Rock, *The Doctor and the Devils*, Twentieth Century-Fox, 1985; Madame de Volanges, *Valmont*, Orion, 1989. Also appeared in *Laughter in the Dark*, 1968.

PRINCIPAL TELEVISION APPEARANCES—Mini-Series: Emmeline Pankhurst, *Shoulder to Shoulder*, BBC, 1974, then *Masterpiece Theatre*, PBS, 1975; Beth Morgan, *How Green Was My Valley*, BBC, 1975, then *Masterpiece Theatre*, PBS, 1976; Livia, *I, Claudius*, BBC, 1976, then *Masterpiece Theatre*, PBS, 1977; Ann Smiley, *Tinker, Tailor, Soldier, Spy*, PBS, 1980; Clementine Churchill, "Churchill: The Wilderness Years," *Masterpiece Theatre*, PBS, 1981; Ann Smiley, *Smiley's People*, syndicated, 1982; also *Crime and Punishment*, BBC, 1979, then *Masterpiece Theatre*, PBS, 1980; *Vanity Fair*, Arts and Entertainment, 1988. Movies: Charal, *Ewoks: The Battle for Endor*, ABC, 1985; Duchess of Windsor, *The Two Mrs. Grenvilles*, NBC, 1987. Specials: *Pyramid*, PBS, 1988. Also appeared in *Boudicca*, 1977; *Off to Philadelphia in the Morning*, 1977; *The Oresteia of Aeschylus*, 1978; *Sean*

O'Casey, 1980; *How Many Miles to Babylon?*, 1982; *George Barrow*, 1983; *The Achurch Papers; Lady Windermere's Fan; A Painful Case;* and *Language and Landscape*.

RELATED CAREER—Worked for BBC-Radio, Wales, during the mid-1940s, and BBC-Television, Wales, during the 1950s; newsreader, announcer, and member, BBC Repertory Company, 1953-55; member, National Eisteddfod of Caernarvon and Gorsedd of Bards, both in recognition of services to Welsh drama.

RECORDINGS: ALBUMS—*Pal Joey, Peg,* and *I Remember Mama.* SINGLES—"Bewitched, Bothered, and Bewildered."

AWARDS: New York Critics' Circle Award and the Famous Seven Critics' Award, both 1969 for *Goodbye Mr. Chips;* British Academy of Film and Television Arts Award, Best Actress, 1975, for *How Green Was My Valley;* British Academy of Film and Television Arts Award, Best Actress, and Royal Television Society Award, both 1978, for *I, Claudius.* HONORARY DEGREES—University of Wales, Doctor of Literature, 1984.

MEMBER: Welsh Arts Council, National Theatre of Wales (governor), Honorary Order of the Druids.

SIDELIGHTS: RECREATIONS—Canvas embroidery and gardening.

ADDRESSES: AGENT—Saraband Ltd., 153 Petherton Road, London N5, England.*

*　　*　　*

PIALAT, Maurice　1925-

PERSONAL: Born August 21, 1925, in Puy-de-Dome, France. EDUCATION—Attended L'Ecole des Arts Decoratifs and L'Ecole des Beaux-Arts.

VOCATION: Director, producer, screenwriter, and actor.

CAREER: See also *WRITINGS* below. PRINCIPAL FILM APPEARANCES—Police inspector, *Que la bette muere* (also known as *This Man Must Die* and *Uccidero un uomo*), Allied Artists, 1970; client, *Mes petites amoureuses* (also known as *My Little Loves*), AMLF, 1974; father, *A nos amours* (also known as *To Our Loves*), Gaumont/Artificial Eye, 1983, released in the United States by Triumph, 1984; Dean Menou-Segrais, *Sous le soleil de Satan* (also known as *Under the Sun of Satan* and *Under Satan's Sun*), Gaumont, 1987, released in the United States by Alive Films, 1989.

PRINCIPAL FILM WORK—Director: *L'Enfance nue* (also known as *Me* and *Naked Childhood*), 1968, released in the United States by Altura, 1970; *Nous ne vieillirons pas ensemble* (also known as *We Won't Grow Old Together, We Will Not Grow Old Together,* and *Break-Up*), Corona, 1972; *La Gueule ouverte* (also known as *The Mouth Agape*), Films la Boetie, 1974; *Passe ton bac d'abord* (also known as *Graduate First* and *Get Your Diploma First*), Films du Livradois/AMLF/New Yorker, 1979; *Loulou*, Gaumont/Artificial Eye, 1979, released in the United States by New Yorker, 1980; (also producer) *A nos amours* (also known as *To Our Loves*), Gaumont/Artificial Eye, 1983, released in the United States by Triumph, 1984; *Police*, Gaumont/New Yorker/Artificial Eye, 1985; *Sous le soleil de Satan* (also known as *Under the Sun of Satan* and *Under Satan's Sun*), Gaumont, 1987, released in the United

States by Alive Films, 1989. Also director *L'Amour existe* (short film), 1958.

PRINCIPAL TELEVISION WORK—Director: *Janine*, 1961; *Maitre Galip*, 1962; *La Maison des Bois*, 1971.

RELATED CAREER—Painter.

WRITINGS: FILM—See production details above: *L'Enfance nue*, 1968; *Nous ne vieillirons pas ensemble*, 1972; *La Gueule ouverte*, 1974; *Passe ton bac d'abord*, 1979; (with Arlette Langmann) *Loulou*, 1979; (with Langmann) *A nos amours*, 1983; (with Catherine Breillat, Sylvie Danton, and Jacques Feschi) *Police*, 1985; (with Dantan) *Sous le soleil de Satan*, 1987.

AWARDS: Venice Film Festival Award, 1958, for *L'Amour existe;* Prix Jean Vigo, 1967, for *L'Enfance nue;* Golden Palm Award from the Cannes Film Festival, 1987, for *Sous les soleil de Satan.**

*   *   *

PISIER, Marie-France   1944-

PERSONAL: Born May 10, 1944, in Dalat, Indochina (Vietnam); father, a French government official. EDUCATION—Received degrees in law and political science from the University of Paris.

VOCATION: Actress and screenwriter.

CAREER: Also see *WRITINGS* below. PRINCIPAL FILM APPEARANCES—Colette, *L'Amour a vingt ans* (also known as *Love at Twenty, Amore a vent'anni, Milosc Dwudziestolatkow,* and *Liebe Mit Zwanzig*), 1962, released in the United States by Embassy, 1963; Eva, *Trans-Europ-Express*, Trans American, 1968; Colette Tazzi, *Baisers voles* (also known as *Stolen Kisses*), Lopert, 1969; Sophie, *Celine et Julie vont en bateau* (also known as *Celine and Julie Go Boating*), Les Films Christian Fachner, 1974; Regina, *Souvenirs d'en France* (also known as *French Provincial* and *Inside Memories of France*), AMLF, 1975; Nelly, *Barocco*, Films la Boetie, 1976; Agathe, *Serail*, Comtemporary, 1976; Karine, *Cousin, Cousine*, Les Films Pomerey/Gaumont, 1976; Gilberte, *Le Corps e mon ennemi* (also known as *The Body of My Enemy*), AMLF, 1976; Noelle Page, *The Other Side of Midnight*, Twentieth Century-Fox, 1977; Madame Umlaut, *Les Apprentis sorciers*, Backstreet/Institut National de L'Audiovisuel/Buffalo, 1977; Charlotte Bronte, *Les Soeurs Bronte* (also known as *The Bronte Sisters*), Gaumont, 1979; Madame Tessier, *French Postcards*, Paramount, 1979.

Colette Lecoudray, *La Banquiere* (also known as *The Woman Banker*), Gaumont, 1980; Colette, *L'Amour en fuite* (also known as *Love on the Run*), Les Films du Carosse, 1980; B.B., *Miss Right*, IAP/Sony Video Software, 1981; Gabrielle "Coco" Chanel, *Chanel solitaire*, United Film Distribution, 1981; journalist, *L'As des as* (also known as *Ace of Aces*), Gaumont, 1982; Florence, *Der Stille Ozean* (also known as *The Silent Ocean*), Teamfilm/Osterreichischer Rundfunk Fernsehen/Zweites Deutsches Fernsehen, 1982; Laurence Ballard, *Le Prix de danger* (also known as *The Prize of Peril*), Brent Walker Film Distributors/Union Generale Cinematographique, 1983; Dr. Emilienne Simpson, *Hot Touch*, Astral/Trans-Atlantic Enterprises, 1982; Persephone, *Parking*, A.M., 1985; Martha, *L'Oeuvre au noir* (also known as *The Abyss*), Union Generale Cinematographique/Twentieth Century-Fox, 1988.

Also appeared in *Qui ose nous accuser?*, 1961; *La Morte d'un tueur*, 1963; *Les Yeux cernes*, 1964; *Der Zauberberg* (also known as *The Magic Mountain*), Franz Seitz Filmproduktion/Gaumont/Opera Film Produzione/Zweites Deutsches Fernsehen, 1982; *L'Ami de Vincent* (also known as *A Friend of Vincent*), AMLF/World Marketing, 1983; *Les Nanas* (also known as *The Chicks*), Union Generale Cinematographique, 1984; *44 ou les recits de la nuit* (also known as *44, or Tales of the Night*), 1985; *L'Inconnu de Vienne*, SFP, 1986.

PRINCIPAL TELEVISION APPEARANCES—Mini-Series: Lisa, *The French Atlantic Affair*, ABC, 1979; Valentine O'Neill, *Scruples*, CBS, 1980.

WRITINGS: FILM—(With Jacques Rivette, Eduardo du Gregorio, Juliet Berto, Dominique LaBourier, and Bulle Ogier) *Celine et Julie vont en bateau* (also known as *Celine and Julie Go Boating*), Les Films Christian Fachner, 1974; (with Francois Truffaut, Jean Aurel, and Suzanne Schiffman) *L'Amour en fuite* (also known as *Love on the Run*), Les Films du Carosse, 1980.

AWARDS: Cesar Award, Best Actress, 1975, for *Cousin Cousine.**

*   *   *

PLAYTEN, Alice   1947-

PERSONAL: Born August, 1947, in New York, NY. EDUCATION—Attended New York University.

VOCATION: Actress.

CAREER: STAGE DEBUT—*Wozzeck* (opera), Metropolitan Opera House, New York City, 1959. PRINCIPAL STAGE APPEARANCES—Bet, *Oliver!*, Imperial Theatre, New York City, 1963; Ermengarde, *Hello, Dolly!*, St. James Theatre, New York City, 1964; Kafritz, *Henry, Sweet Henry*, Palace Theatre, New York City, 1967; Miss U, *Promenade*, Promenade Theatre, New York City, 1969; Ingrid, "The Elevator" and Alice, "I Want to Walk to San Francisco" in *The Last Sweet Days of Isaac*, Eastside Playhouse, New York City, 1970, then Playhouse in the Park, Cincinnati, OH, 1971; ensemble, *National Lampoon's Lemmings* (revue), Village Gate Theatre, New York City, 1973; young Libby, *Valentine's Day*, Manhattan Theatre Club, New York City, 1975; Edith, *The Pirates of Penzance*, New York Shakespeare Festival, Delacorte Theatre, New York City, 1980; Meg, *The Actor's Nightmare* and Diane Symonds, *Sister Mary Ignatius Explains It All for You* (double-bill), Playwrights Horizons, then Westside Arts Theatre, both New York City, 1982; Eden, *That's It, Folks!*, Playwrights Horizons, 1983; Ronnie Roberts, *Yankee Wives*, Old Globe Theatre, San Diego, CA, 1983; Eve, *Up from Paradise*, Jewish Repertory Theatre, New York City, 1983; Emma, *Spoils of War*, Second Stage Theatre, then Music Box Theatre, both New York City, 1988. Also appeared in *A History of the American Film*, Center Theatre Group, Mark Taper Forum, Los Angeles, 1976-77; *The Admirable Crichton*, Long Wharf Theatre, New Haven, CT, 1980-81; *George M!*, Palace Theatre, New York City; and in productions of *A Visit, The Hotel Play*, and *The Sorrows of Stephen*, all in New York City.

MAJOR TOURS—Baby Louise, *Gypsy*, U.S. cities, 1961.

PRINCIPAL FILM APPEARANCES—Harriet, *Ladybug, Ladybug*, United Artists, 1963; Della Isadore, *Who Killed Mary What's 'er*

Name? (also known as *Death of a Hooker*), Cannon, 1971; Corrine, *California Dreaming,* American International, 1979; voice of Gloria, *Heavy Metal* (animated), Columbia, 1981; demon's voice, *Amityville II: The Possession,* Orion, 1982; Blix, *Legend,* Universal, 1985; voices of Baby Lickety Split and Bushwoolie, *My Little Pony* (animated), De Laurentiis Entertainment Group, 1986; Una, *Le Big Bang* (also known as *The Big Bang*), Twentieth Century-Fox, 1987.

PRINCIPAL TELEVISION APPEARANCES—Series: Regular, *Masquerade,* PBS, 1971; Alice, *The Lost Saucer,* syndicated, 1975-76; Alice, *That's Cat,* syndicated, 1977. Pilots: Sergeant "Lizard" Gossamer, *Over and Out,* NBC, 1976. Specials: Voice of Nutshell Kid, *Really Rosie: Starring the Nutshell Kids* (animated), CBS, 1975; also "Me and Dad's New Wife," *ABC Afterschool Specials,* ABC, 1976.

RECORDINGS: ALBUMS—*Hello, Dolly!* (original cast recording), RCA; *Henry, Sweet Henry* (original cast recording), ABC.

AWARDS: Theatre World Award, 1967, for *Henry Sweet Henry;* Obie Award from the *Village Voice,* 1972-73, for *National Lampoon's Lemmings;* Drama Desk Award nomination, Best Featured Actress in a Play, 1989, for *Spoils of War.*

ADDRESSES: AGENTS—Smith-Freedman and Associates, 850 Seventh Avenue, New York, NY 10019; The Gersh Agency, 222 N. Canon Drive, Suite 202, Beverly Hills, CA 90210.*

*   *   *

PLESHETTE, John   1942-

PERSONAL: Born July 27, 1942, in New York, NY. EDUCATION—Attended Brown University and Carnegie-Mellon University; studied acting with Stella Adler and Sanford Meisner.

CAREER: BROADWAY DEBUT—David Grossman, *The Zulu and the Zayda,* Cort Theatre, 1965-66. PRINCIPAL STAGE APPEARANCES—Moth, *Love's Labour's Lost,* New York Shakespeare Festival (NYSF), Delacorte Theatre, New York City, 1965; Marquess of Dorset, *Richard III* and boy, *Measure for Measure,* both NYSF, Delacorte Theatre, 1966; Ted Ken O'Dunc, *MacBird!,* Village Gate Theatre, New York City, 1967; boy, *Jimmy Shine,* Brooks Atkinson Theatre, New York City, 1968; Michael Fisch, *The Shrinking Bride,* Mercury Theatre, New York City, 1971; Jacob "Carruthers" Perew, *Green Julia,* Sheridan Square Playhouse, New York City, 1972; Jim, *Allergy,* Manhattan Theatre Club, New York City, 1974; Jigger Hannafin, *Says I, Says He,* Center Theatre Group, Mark Taper Forum, Los Angeles, 1979-80. Also appeared in productions of *It's Called the Sugar Plum* and *Sound of Silence.*

PRINCIPAL STAGE WORK—Director, *The Pornographer's Daughter,* Manhattan Theatre Club, New York City, 1975.

PRINCIPAL FILM APPEARANCES—Finkle, *End of the Road,* Allied Artists, 1970; Murray, *Parades* (also known as *Break Loose*), Cinerama, 1972; theatrical agent, *House Calls,* Universal, 1978; director, *Rocky II,* United Artists, 1979; Capitol Studios vice president, *S.O.B.,* Paramount, 1981; Hap Ludlow, *Micki and*

Maude, Columbia, 1984; Dr. Lido, *Paramedics,* Vestron, 1988. Also appeared in *Won Ton Ton—The Dog That Saved Hollywood,* Paramount, 1976; *Slap Shot,* Universal, 1977.

PRINCIPAL TELEVISION APPEARANCES—Series: Dr. Danvers, *Doctors' Hospital,* NBC, 1975-76; Richard Avery, *Knots Landing,* CBS, 1979-83. Mini-Series: Marty Cass, *Seventh Avenue,* NBC, 1977. Pilots: Nicky Holroyd, *Bell, Book, and Candle,* NBC, 1976. Episodic: Dr. Ashfield, *Simon and Simon,* CBS, 1986; Nicky Saperstein, *Murder, She Wrote,* CBS, 1986; Charley, *Highway to Heaven,* NBC, 1987; Dr. Slevin, *Hard Copy,* CBS, 1987; Lancer, *MacGyver,* ABC, 1987; Stanley, *Highway to Heaven,* NBC, 1988. Movies: Lee Harvey Oswald, *The Trial of Lee Harvey Oswald,* ABC, 1977; Kip Nathan, *The Users,* ABC, 1978; Willie Hedges, *Once Upon a Family,* CBS, 1980; Jeff McNulty, *The Kid with the Broken Halo,* NBC, 1982; Frank Vandenberg, *Burning Rage,* CBS, 1984; Al Singer, *Stormin' Home,* CBS, 1985; Tommy Gallep, *Malice in Wonderland,* CBS, 1985; David Elias, *Mrs. Delafield Wants to Marry,* CBS, 1986; John Hamill, *Welcome Home, Bobby,* CBS, 1986; Mel Erman, *Shattered Innocence,* CBS, 1988; Eddie Maltz, *Sidney Sheldon's "Windmills of the Gods,"* CBS, 1988; Wagner Thorne, *Murder in Paradise,* NBC, 1990. Specials: *Zero Hour,* ABC, 1967.

PRINCIPAL TELEVISION WORK—Episodic: Director, *Knots Landing,* CBS.

WRITINGS: TELEVISION—Episodic: *Ryan's Four,* ABC, 1983; also *Knots Landing,* CBS.

ADDRESSES: OFFICE—2643 Creston Drive, Los Angeles, CA 90068. AGENTS—McCartt, Oreck, Barrett, 10390 Santa Monica Boulevard, Suite 310, Los Angeles, CA 90025; Harris and Goldberg, 2121 Avenue of the Stars, Suite 950, Los Angeles, CA 90067.*

*   *   *

POUNDER, C.C.H.   1952-

PERSONAL: Born December 25, 1952, in Georgetown, Guyana. EDUCATION—Ithaca College, B.F.A., 1975.

VOCATION: Actress.

CAREER: PRINCIPAL STAGE APPEARANCES—Rita, *The Mighty Gents,* Mobile Theatre, New York Shakespeare Festival (NYSF), Delacorte Theatre, New York City, 1979; Valeria, *Coriolanus,* NYSF, Delacorte Theatre, then Public Theatre, New York City, both 1979; Mrs. Brewster, *Open Admissions,* Music Box Theatre, New York City, 1984. Also appeared in *S.S. Glencairn,* Long Wharf Theatre, New Haven, CT, 1978; with the Actors Theatre of Louisville, Louisville, KY, 1975-77; Arena Stage, Washington, DC, 1977-78; Milwaukee Repertory Theatre, Milwaukee, WI, 1980-81.

PRINCIPAL FILM APPEARANCES—Nurse Gibbons, *All That Jazz,* Columbia/Twentieth Century-Fox, 1979; mother, *Union City,* Kinesis/Mainline, 1980; Anne, *I'm Dancing As Fast As I Can,* Paramount, 1982; Deborah, *Go Tell It on the Mountain,* Learning in Focus, 1984; Peaches Altamont, *Prizzi's Honor,* Twentieth Century-Fox, 1985; Brenda, *Baghdad Cafe* (also known as *Out of Rosenheim*), Filverlag der Autoren/Island, 1987.

PRINCIPAL TELEVISION APPEARANCES—Series: Dawn Murphy, *Women in Prison,* Fox, 1987-88. Mini-Series: Venus Taylor, *The Atlanta Child Murders,* CBS, 1985; Ernestine Littlechap, *If Tomorrow Comes,* CBS, 1986. Pilots: Anna Mae Demsey, *The Line,* NBC, 1987; also *On the Edge,* NBC, 1987. Episodic: Vonette Timmons, *Cagney and Lacey,* CBS, 1986; Lucinda Merkle, *227,* NBC, 1989; also Yvonne, *Miami Vice,* NBC. Movies: Priscilla, *As Summers Die,* HBO, 1986; Ada Johnson, *Resting Place,* CBS, 1986; Roberta, *Leap of Faith,* CBS, 1988; Janice, *Run Till You Fall,* CBS, 1988; Julie, *Third Degree Burn,* HBO, 1989; Prue, *No Place Like Home,* CBS, 1989; also *Common Ground,* CBS, 1990. Specials: Renee Cook, ''My Past Is My Own,'' *CBS Schoolbreak Special,* CBS, 1989.

AWARDS: Image Award nomination from the NAACP, Best Actress in a Television Drama, 1986.

ADDRESSES: OFFICE—870 N. Vine Street, Suite G, Los Angeles, CA 90038.*

*   *   *

PRESLEY, Priscilla   1946-

PERSONAL: Full name, Priscilla Ann Beaulieu Presley; born May 24, 1946, in Brooklyn, NY; married Elvis Presley (a singer and actor), May 1, 1967 (divorced, 1973); children: Lisa Marie.

VOCATION: Actress and producer.

CAREER: PRINCIPAL FILM APPEARANCES—Jane Spencer, *The Naked Gun—From the Files of Police Squad!,* Paramount, 1988.

PRINCIPAL TELEVISION APPEARANCES—Series: Host, *Those Amazing Animals,* ABC, 1980-81; Jenna Wade, *Dallas,* CBS, 1983-88. Pilots: *Tom Snyder's Celebrity Spotlight,* NBC, 1980. Movies: Sandy Redford, *Love Is Forever* (also known as *Comeback*), NBC, 1982. Specials: *The Barbara Walters Special,* ABC, 1985; *Night of 100 Stars II,* NBC, 1985; host, *Elvis' Graceland,* syndicated, 1987; *The American Comedy Awards,* ABC, 1989; *Super Bloopers and New Practical Jokes,* NBC, 1989.

PRINCIPAL TELEVISION WORK—Series: Executive producer (with Rick Husky and James D. Parriott), *Elvis,* ABC, 1990. Movies: Executive producer (with Joel Stevens and Bernard Schwartz), *Elvis and Me,* ABC, 1988.

RELATED CAREER—Commercial spokesperson for beauty products.

NON-RELATED CAREER—Fashion designer.

WRITINGS: *Elvis and Me* (autobiography), Berkeley, 1985.

ADDRESSES: OFFICE—1167 Summit Drive, Beverly Hills, CA 90210.*

*   *   *

PRESNELL, Harve   1933-

PERSONAL: Born September 14, 1933, in Modesto, CA. EDUCATION—Attended the University of Southern California.

VOCATION: Actor and singer.

CAREER: BROADWAY DEBUT—Johnny ''Leadville'' Brown, *The Unsinkable Molly Brown,* Winter Garden Theatre, 1960. PRINCIPAL STAGE APPEARANCES—Johnny ''Leadville'' Brown, *The Unsinkable Molly Brown,* Coconut Grove Playhouse, Miami, FL, 1967; Frank Butler, *Annie Get Your Gun,* Jones Beach Theatre, Long Island, NY, 1978; Oliver ''Daddy'' Warbucks, *Annie II: Miss Hannigan's Revenge,* Opera House, Kennedy Center for the Performing Arts, Washington, DC, 1990. Also appeared in *Nobody Starts Out to Be a Pirate,* Whole Theatre Company, Montclair, NJ, 1983-84; as Oliver ''Daddy'' Warbucks, *Annie,* American National Theatre and Academy Theatre, then Eugene O'Neill Theatre, later Uris Theatre, all New York City.

MAJOR TOURS—Johnny ''Leadville'' Brown, *The Unsinkable Molly Brown,* U.S. cities, 1962; Billy Bigelow, *Carousel,* U.S. cities, 1965; Oliver ''Daddy'' Warbucks, *Annie,* U.S. cities, 1979.

PRINCIPAL FILM APPEARANCES—Johnny ''Leadville'' Brown, *The Unsinkable Molly Brown,* Metro-Goldwyn-Mayer (MGM), 1964; Sol Rogers, *The Glory Guys,* United Artists, 1965; Danny, *When the Boys Meet the Girls* (also known as *Girl Crazy*), MGM, 1965; Rotten Luck Willie, *Paint Your Wagon,* Paramount, 1969; also appeared in *Blood Bath,* Cannon, 1976.

PRINCIPAL TELEVISION APPEARANCES—Series: Matthew Crane, *Ryan's Hope,* ABC, 1984-85. Pilots: *The Singers,* CBS, 1969. Movies: Ballad singer, *The Great Man's Whiskers,* NBC, 1973.

RELATED CAREER—Opera singer.

AWARDS: Golden Globe, Most Promising Newcomer—Male, 1965, for *The Unsinkable Molly Brown.**

*   *   *

PRESTON, Kelly

PERSONAL: Born c. 1963 in Hawaii; father, an agricultural engineer. EDUCATION—Studied acting at the University of California, Los Angeles, at the University of Southern California, and with Milton Katselas.

VOCATION: Actress.

CAREER: PRINCIPAL FILM APPEARANCES—Roseanne, *Christine*, Columbia, 1983; Dhyana, *Metalstorm: The Destruction of Jared-Syn*, Universal, 1983; Marilyn McCauley, *Mischief*, Twentieth Century-Fox, 1985; Deborah Anne Fimple, *Secret Admirer*, Orion, 1985; Cini, *52 Pick-Up*, Cannon, 1986; Tish, *Space Camp*, Twentieth Century-Fox, 1986; Shirley Butts, *A Tiger's Tale*, Atlantic, 1987; Violet, "Titan Man" in *Amazon Women on the Moon*, Universal, 1987; Sara Lee, *Love at Stake* (also known as *Burnin' Love*), Tri-Star, 1987; Miranda Reed, *Spellbinder*, Metro-Goldwyn-Mayer/United Artists, 1988; Marnie Mason, *Twins*, Universal, 1988; Bonnie, *The Experts*, Paramount, 1989.

PRINCIPAL TELEVISION APPEARANCES—Series: Mary Lee, *For Love and Honor*, NBC, 1983; also *Capitol*, CBS. Episodic: Amy Braddock, *Blue Thunder*, ABC, 1984; guest, *The Dave Thomas Comedy Show*, CBS, 1990.

RELATED CAREER—Professional model.

NON-RELATED CAREER—In the advertising industry.*

*   *   *

PRINCE, Faith

PERSONAL: EDUCATION—Attended the Cincinnati Conservatory of Music, 1980.

CAREER: BROADWAY DEBUT—Ma, Tessie Tura, and ensemble, *Jerome Robbins' Broadway*, Imperial Theatre, 1989. PRINCIPAL STAGE APPEARANCES—Ensemble, *Scrambled Feet* (revue), Village Gate Theatre Upstairs, New York City, 1979; Audrey, *Little Shop of Horrors*, Orpheum Theatre, New York City, 1983; Miss Adelaide, *Guys and Dolls*, Seattle Repertory Theatre, Seattle, WA, 1985; various roles, *Groucho: A Life in Revue*, Lucille Lortel Theatre, New York City, 1986; ensemble, *Living Color* (revue), Don't Tell Mama Theatre, New York City, 1986; Carrie Pepperidge, *Carousel*, Kennedy Center for the Performing Arts, Opera House, Washington, DC, 1986; Delores, *Olympus on My Mind*, Actors Outlet Theatre, Paper Mill Playhouse, Millburn, NJ, 1986-87; Chicky Griffin, *Lucky Guy*, Plaza Theatre, Dallas, TX, 1987. Also appeared in *Tintypes*, Seattle Repertory Theatre, 1980, then Royal Poinciana Playhouse, Palm Beach, FL, 1981; *Leave It to Jane*, Goodspeed Opera House, East Haddam, CT, 1985; *Urban Blight*, Manhattan Theatre Club, New York City, 1988.

MAJOR TOURS—Ensemble, *Scrambled Feet* (revue), U.S. cities.

PRINCIPAL FILM APPEARANCES—Angela, *The Last Dragon*, Tri-Star, 1985.

PRINCIPAL TELEVISION APPEARANCES—Series: Rabbit, *Encyclopedia*, HBO, 1988.

AWARDS: Drama Desk Award nomination, Best Actress in a Musical, 1989, for *Jerome Robbins' Broadway*.

ADDRESSES: AGENT—211 E. 53rd Street, New York, NY 10022.*

*   *   *

PRINCE, Hal
See PRINCE, Harold S.

*   *   *

PRINCE, Harold S.   1928-
(Hal Prince)

PERSONAL: Full name, Harold Smith Prince; born January 30, 1928, in New York, NY; son of Milton A. (a stockbroker) and Blanche (Stern) Prince; married Judith Chaplin, October 26, 1962; children: Charles, Daisy. EDUCATION—University of Pennsylvania, B.A., 1948. MILITARY—U.S. Army, 1950-52.

VOCATION: Producer and director.

CAREER: PRINCIPAL STAGE APPEARANCES—*George Abbott . . . a Celebration*, Shubert Theatre, New York City, 1976.

PRINCIPAL STAGE WORK—All as producer, unless indicated: Assistant stage manager, *Tickets, Please*, Coronet Theatre, New York City, 1950; assistant stage manager, *Wonderful Town*, Winter Garden Theatre, New York City, 1953; (with Frederick Brisson and Robert E. Griffith) *The Pajama Game*, St. James Theatre, New York City, 1954; (with Brisson and Griffith) *Damn Yankees*, 46th Street Theatre, New York City, 1955; (with Brisson and Griffith) *New Girl in Town*, 46th Street Theatre, 1957; (with Griffith) *West Side Story*, Winter Garden Theatre, 1957, then Her Majesty's Theatre, London, 1958; (with Griffith) *A Swim in the Sea*, Walnut Street Theatre, Philadelphia, PA, 1958; (with Griffith and H.M. Tennent) *Two for the Seesaw*, Haymarket Theatre, London, 1958; (with Griffith) *Fiorello!*, Broadhurst Theatre, New York City, 1959.

(With Griffith) *Tenderloin*, 46th Street Theatre, 1960; (with Griffith) *A Call on Kuprin*, Broadhurst Theatre, 1961; *Take Her, She's Mine*, Biltmore Theatre, New York City, 1961; director, *A Family Affair*, Billy Rose Theatre, New York City, 1962; *A Funny Thing Happened on the Way to the Forum*, Alvin Theatre, New York City, 1962, then Strand Theatre, London, 1963; (with Sidney Gordon and Howard Erskine; also director) *She Didn't Say Yes*, Falmouth Theatre, Coonamessett, MA, 1963; (with Lawrence N. Kasha and Phillip C. McKenna; also director) *She Loves Me*, Eugene O'Neill Theatre, New York City, 1963, then Lyric Theatre, London, 1964; (with Michael Codron and Pledon Ltd.) *Poor Bitos*, Cort Theatre, New York City, 1964; *Fiddler on the Roof*, Imperial Theatre, New York City, 1964, then Majestic Theatre, New York City, 1967, later (with Richard Pilbrow) Her Majesty's Theatre, 1967; director, *Baker Street*, Broadway Theatre, New York City, 1965; *Flora, the Red Menace*, Alvin Theatre, 1965; (with Ruth Mitchell; also director) *It's a Bird . . . It's a Plane . . . It's Superman!*, Alvin Theatre, 1966; (with Mitchell; also director) *Cabaret*, Broadhurst Theatre, 1966, then Imperial Theatre, 1967, later Broadway Theatre, 1968, then (with Pilbrow) Palace Theatre,

HAROLD S. PRINCE

London, 1968; (with Pilbrow) *The Beggar's Opera,* Apollo Theatre, London, 1968; (with Mitchell; also director) *Zorba,* Imperial Theatre, 1968.

(With Mitchell; also director) *Company,* Alvin Theatre, 1970, then (with Pilbrow) Her Majesty's Theatre, 1972; (with Mitchell; also director with Michael Bennett) *Follies,* Winter Garden Theatre, 1971; *Don Juan* and (also director) *The Great God Brown,* both New Phoenix Repertory Company, Lyceum Theatre, New York City, 1972; "A Meeting By the River," in *Phoenix Theatre Sideshows,* New Phoenix Repertory Company, Edison Theatre, New York City, 1972; "Strike Heaven on the Face!" and "Games and After Liverpool" (double-bill) and "The Government Inspector," all in *Phoenix Theatre Sideshows,* New Phoenix Repertory Company, Edison Theatre, 1973; *Chemin de Fer, Holiday,* and (also director) *The Visit,* all New Phoenix Repertory Company, Ethel Barrymore Theatre, New York City, 1973; (also director) *Candide* (opera), Chelsea Theatre Center, Brooklyn Academy of Music, Brooklyn, NY, 1973, then (with Mitchell) Broadway Theatre, 1974; (with Mitchell; also director) *A Little Night Music,* Shubert Theatre, then Majestic Theatre, both 1973, later (with Pilbrow) Adelphi Theatre, London, 1975; *The Rules of the Game* and (also director) *Love for Love,* both New Phoenix Repertory Company, Helen Hayes Theatre, New York City, 1974; "The Removalists" and "In the Voodoo Parlor of Marie Leveau" in *Phoenix Theatre Sideshows,* New Phoenix Repertory Company, Playhouse II, New York City, 1974; "Pretzels" in *Phoenix Theatre Sideshows,* Playhouse II, then Theatre Four, New York City, both 1974.

The Member of the Wedding, New Phoenix Repertory Company,

Helen Hayes Theatre, 1975; "Dandelion Wine" and "Meeting Place," both in *Phoenix Theatre Sideshows,* New Phoenix Repertory Company, Playhouse II, 1975; (with Mitchell; also director) *Pacific Overtures,* Winter Garden Theatre, 1976; director, *Ashmedai* (opera), New York City Opera, State Theatre, New York City, 1976; director, *Some of My Best Friends,* Longacre Theatre, New York City, 1977; (with Mitchell) *Side By Side By Sondheim,* Music Box Theatre, New York City, 1977; director, *On the Twentieth Century,* St. James Theatre, 1978; director, *The Girl of the Golden West* (opera), Lyric Opera of Chicago, Chicago, IL, 1978, then San Francisco Opera, San Francisco, CA, 1979; director, *Evita,* Prince Edward Theatre, London, 1978, then Broadway Theatre, 1979; director, *Sweeney Todd, the Demon Barber of Fleet Street,* Uris Theatre, New York City, 1979, then Drury Lane Theatre, London, 1980.

Director, *Silverlake* (opera), New York City Opera, State Theatre, 1980; director, *Fanciulla del West* (opera), Lyric Opera of Chicago, 1980; (with Lew Grade, Martin Starger, and Robert Fryer; also director) *Merrily We Roll Along,* Alvin Theatre, 1981; director, *Willie Stark* (opera), Houston Grand Opera, Houston, TX, 1981; director, *Candide* (opera), New York City Opera, State Theatre, 1982; (also director) *A Doll's Life,* Mark Hellinger Theatre, New York City, 1982; director, *Turandot* (opera), Vienna State Opera, Vienna, Austria, 1983; director, *Girl of the Golden West* (opera), La Scala, Milan, Italy, 1983; director, *Play Memory,* Longacre Theatre, 1984; director, *End of the World,* Music Box Theatre, 1984; director, *Diamonds,* Circle in the Square Theatre, New York City, 1984.

(With others; also director) *Grind,* Mark Hellinger Theatre, 1985; director, *Roza,* Center Theatre Group, Mark Taper Forum, Los Angeles, 1986, then Royale Theatre, New York City, 1987; director, *The Phantom of the Opera,* Her Majesty's Theatre, 1986, then Majestic Theatre, 1988; director, *Sweeney Todd, the Demon Barber of Fleet Street* (opera), New York City Opera, State Theatre, 1987; director, *Cabaret,* Imperial Theatre, 1987, then Minskoff Theatre, New York City, 1988; director, *Madam Butterfly* (opera), Lyric Opera of Chicago, 1988; director, *Don Giovanni* (opera), New York City Opera, State Theatre, 1989; director, *Faust* (opera), Metropolitan Opera, Metropolitan Opera House, New York City, 1989. Also producer, *Knuckle,* New Phoenix Repertory Company, 1975.

MAJOR TOURS—All as producer, unless indicated: Director, *The Matchmaker,* New York State Council on the Arts/Phoenix Theatre, U.S. cities, 1963; *Fiddler on the Roof,* U.S cities, 1966-69; (with Ruth Mitchell; also director) *Cabaret,* U.S. cities, 1967-69; (with Mitchell; also director) *Zorba,* U.S. cities, 1968-70; (with Mitchell; also director) *Company,* U.S. cities, 1971-72; (with Mitchell; also director with Michael Bennett) *Follies,* U.S. cities, 1971-72; (with Mitchell; also director) *A Little Night Music,* U.S. cities, 1974-75; (with Mitchell) *Side By Side By Sondheim,* U.S. cities, 1977-78; director, *Sweeney Todd, the Demon Barber of Fleet Street,* U.S. and international cities, 1980-82; director, *Evita,* U.S. and international cities, 1980-83; director, *Cabaret,* U.S. cities, 1987.

PRINCIPAL FILM WORK—Director, *Something for Everyone (also known as The Rook* and *Black Flowers for the Bride),* National General, 1970; director, *A Little Night Music,* New World, 1977.

PRINCIPAL TELEVISION APPEARANCES—Specials: Intermission guest, "Candide," *Live from Lincoln Center,* PBS, 1986; also *My*

Life for Zarah Leander (documentary), 1986; "Bernstein at 70," *Great Performances*, PBS, 1989.

PRINCIPAL TELEVISION WORK—Specials: Director, *Willie Stark* (opera), PBS, 1981; director, *Sweeney Todd*, Entertainment Channel, 1982; director, "Candide," *Live from Lincoln Center*, PBS, 1986.

RELATED CAREER—Artistic director (with Stephen Porter and Michael Montel), New Phoenix Repertory Company, 1972—; narrator of a revue for the Festival of American Arts and Humanities.

WRITINGS: Contradictions: Notes on Twenty-Six Years in the Theatre (autobiography), Dodd, Mead and Company, 1974.

AWARDS: Antoinette Perry Award, Best Musical, 1955, for *The Pajama Game;* Antoinette Perry Award, Best Musical, 1956, for *Damn Yankees;* Antoinette Perry Award nomination, Best Musical, 1958, for *West Side Story;* Antoinette Perry Award, Best Musical, and New York Drama Critics' Circle Award, Best Musical Production, both 1960, for *Fiorello!;* Antoinette Perry Award, Best Musical, 1963, for *A Funny Thing Happened on the Way to the Forum;* Antoinette Perry Award nominations, Best Musical and Best Director of a Musical, both 1964, for *She Loves Me;* Antoinette Perry Award, Best Musical, and New York Drama Critics' Circle Award, Best Musical Production, both 1965, for *Fiddler on the Roof;* Antoinette Perry Awards, Best Musical and Best Director of a Musical, and New York Drama Critics' Circle Award, Best Musical Production, all 1967, for *Cabaret;* Shubert Foundation Award, 1969; Antoinette Perry Award nominations, Best Musical and Best Director of a Musical, both 1969, for *Zorba; Variety*-New York Drama Critics' Poll Award, Best Director, and New York Drama Critics' Circle Award, Best Musical Production, 1970, and Antoinette Perry Awards, Best Musical and Best Director of a Musical, 1971, all for *Company;* New York Drama Critics' Circle Award, Best Musical Production, 1971, for *Follies;* Antoinette Perry Award, Best Director of a Musical, Antoinette Perry Award nomination, Best Musical, both 1972, for *Follies;* Antoinette Perry Award, Best Musical, Antoinette Perry Award nomination, Best Director of a Musical, and New York Drama Critics' Circle Award, Best Musical Production, all 1973, for *A Little Night Music;* Antoinette Perry Award, Best Director of a Musical, special Antoinette Perry Award citation, Best Musical, New York Drama Critics' Circle Award, Best Musical, and Obie Award from the *Village Voice*, Distinguished Direction, all 1974, for *Candide.*

Antoinette Perry Award nominations, Best Musical and Best Director of a Musical, both 1976, for *Pacific Overtures;* Antoinette Perry Award nomination, Best Musical, 1977, for *Side By Side By Sondheim;* Antoinette Perry Award nomination, Best Director of a Musical, 1978, for *On the Twentieth Century;* Antoinette Perry Award and Drama Desk Award, both Best Director of a Musical, 1979, for *Sweeney Todd, the Demon Barber of Fleet Street;* 1980, Antoinette Perry Award and Drama Desk Award, both Best Director of a Musical, for *Evita;* Commonwealth Award in Dramatic Arts from the Bank of Delaware, 1982; Antoinette Perry Award nominations, Best Musical and Best Director of a Musical, both 1985, for *Grind;* Antoinette Perry Award and Drama Desk Award, both Best Director of a Musical, 1988, for *The Phantom of the Opera.* HONORARY DEGREES—University of Pennsylvania, D.F.A., 1971; Emerson College, Litt.D., 1971.

MEMBER: League of New York Theatres (president, 1963-65), National Council for the Arts, National Institute for Music Theatre

(chairman), Society of Stage Directors and Choreographers, Coffee House Club.

SIDELIGHTS: RECREATIONS—Walking, tennis, and swimming.

ADDRESSES: OFFICE—1270 Avenue of the Americas, New York, NY 10020.*

*   *   *

PSACHAROPOULOS, Nikos   1928-1989

PERSONAL: Born January 18, 1928, in Athens, Greece; immigrated to the United States in 1947; died following surgery for colon cancer, January 12, 1989, in the Virgin Islands; son of Konstantin Nicholas and Helen (Mitsakos) Psacharopoulos. EDUCATION—Oberlin College, B.A., 1951; Yale University, M.F.A., theatre direction, 1954; also trained for the stage at the Actors' Studio.

VOCATION: Director.

CAREER: PRINCIPAL STAGE WORK—Director: *Legend of Lovers,* Yale University School of Drama, New Haven, CT, 1958; *The Play of Daniel,* New York Pro Musica, the Cloisters, New York City, 1958; *Agamemnon,* Yale University School of Drama, 1959; *He Who Must Die* and *The Flowering Peach,* both Yale University School of Drama, 1960; *Man Better Man* and *The Visit,* both Yale University School of Drama, 1963; *Tambourines to Glory,* Little Theatre, New York City, 1963; *The Play of Herod,* New York Pro Musica, the Cloisters, 1963; *Arms and the Man,* Yale University School of Drama, 1965; *Lizzie Borden,* New York City Opera, City Center Theatre, New York City, 1965; *Cavalleria Rusticana* and *Miss Julie,* both State Theatre, New York City, 1965; *Peer Gynt,* Yale University School of Drama, 1966; *Dialogues of the Carmelites,* State Theatre, 1966; *Androcles and the Lion,* American Shakespeare Festival, Stratford, CT, 1968; *The Lion in Winter,* Studio Arena Theatre, Buffalo, NY, 1968; *The Glass Menagerie,* Long Wharf Theatre, New Haven, CT, 1986; *A Streetcar Named Desire,* Circle in the Square, New York City, 1988; *Sweet Bird of Youth,* Royal Alexandra Theatre, Toronto, ON, Canada, 1988. Also director of productions at Rangeley Lakes Summer Theatre, Rangeley, ME, 1954; *Light Up the Sky, The Seagull, Rhinoceros, Once Upon a Mattress, The Visit, Time Remembered, Our Town, The Skin of Our Teeth, Toys in the Attic, The Madwoman of Chaillot, A Streetcar Named Desire, Othello, Becket, Man and Superman, The Cherry Orchard, Pal Joey, A View from the Bridge, A Man for All Seasons, Ondine, Cyrano de Bergerac, Once in a Lifetime, Mary Stuart, Saint Joan, Caesar and Cleopatra, Two for the Seesaw, The Flowering Peach, Heartbreak House, Peer Gynt, Camino Real, Enemies, The Three Sisters, Misalliance,* and *The Legend of Oedipus,* all Williamstown Theatre Festival, Williamstown, MA, 1955-88; and *Arms and the Man,* Pasadena Playhouse, Pasadena, CA.

MAJOR TOURS—Director, *The Play of Daniel,* European cities, 1960.

PRINCIPAL TELEVISION WORK—Episodic: Director, "Night of the Auk," *Play of the Week,* WNTA, 1960. Specials: *The Play of Daniel,* WNET (New York City), 1966; "The Seagull," *Great Performances,* PBS, 1975; also *Agamemnon,* 1960.

RELATED CAREER—Instructor, Amherst College, Amherst, MA,

1954; visiting lecturer, Williams College, Williamstown, MA, 1955; director, New York Pro Musica, New York City, 1955-70; associate professor, Yale University School of Drama, New Haven, CT, 1955-89, also lecturer, 1974-88; founder, executive director, and artistic director, Williamstown Theatre Festival, Williamstown, MA, 1955-89; instructor, Columbia University, New York City, 1961; also board member, American Shakespeare Festival, Stratford, CT; board member, New York City Opera; instructor, New York University, New York City; instructor, Circle in the Square, New York City.

AWARDS: Ford Foundation grant to teach at Amherst College, Amherst, MA, 1954. HONORARY DEGREES—Williams College, L.H.D., 1974; Siena College, D.F.A., 1987.

OBITUARIES AND OTHER SOURCES: New York Times, January 13, 1989, January 29, 1989; *Variety,* January 25-31, 1989.*

*   *   *

PYANT, Paul   1953-

PERSONAL: Surname is pronounced "*Pie*-ant"; born July 22, 1953; son of Leonard Vincent (a business executive) and Jean Phoebe (a medical secretary; maiden name, Frampton). EDUCATION—Attended the Royal Academy of Dramatic Art. POLITICS—Socialist (British Labour Party). RELIGION—Agnostic.

VOCATION: Lighting designer.

CAREER: FIRST STAGE WORK—Stage manager, Kent Opera, Kent, U.K., 1974. FIRST LONDON WORK—Lighting designer, *Oberto,* Bloomsbury Theatre, 1982. FIRST BROADWAY WORK—Lighting designer, *Orpheus Descending,* Neil Simon Theatre, 1989. PRINCIPAL STAGE WORK—All as lighting designer, unless indicated: *The Barber of Seville* and *Le Nozze di Figaro* (operas), both Welsh National Opera, Cardiff, Wales, 1987; *The Devil's Wall,* University College Opera, London, 1987; *This Happy Breed* and *Life's a Dream,* both Drama Centre, London, 1987; *The Merchant of Venice,* Royal Exchange Theatre, Manchester, U.K., 1987; *Masked Ball* (opera), Brighton Festival, Brighton, U.K., 1987; *Lady Macbeth of Mtsensk* (opera), English National Opera, London, 1987; *Macbeth* (opera), Opera North, Leeds, U.K., 1987; *L'ormindo,* Guildhall, London, 1987; *Hansel et Gretel* (opera), Opera House, Geneva, Switzerland, 1987; *A Wholly Healthy Glasgow,* Royal Exchange Theatre, then Edinburgh Festival, Edinburgh, Scotland, both 1987, later Royal Court Theatre, London, 1988; *The Pearl Fishers* (opera) Scottish Opera, Glasgow, Scotland, 1988; *A Place with the Pigs,* National Theatre, London, 1988; *Mother Courage,* Cameri Theatre, Tel Aviv, Israel, 1988; *Factory Girls,* Druid Theatre Company, Galway, Ireland, then Mayfest, Glasgow, later Sense of Ireland Festival, Riverside Studios, London, all 1988; assistant lighting designer, *Winnie,* Royal Exchange Theatre, then Victoria Palace Theatre, London, both 1988; *Xerxes* and *Carmen* (operas), both English National Opera, 1988; *Sinners and Saints,* Croyden Warehouse Theatre, Croyden, U.K., 1988; *Trupets and Raspberrys,* Druid Theatre Company, 1988; *Abduction from the Seraglio* (opera), Opera House, Buxton, U.K., 1988; *La Boheme* and *Abduction from the Seraglio* (operas), both Opera Northern Ireland, Belfast, Ireland, 1988; *Don Giovanni* (opera), *Turandot* (opera), and *The Devil and Kate,* Wexford Festival, Wexford, Ireland, 1988; *Elisa e Claudio,* Wexford Festival, then Queen Elizabeth Hall, London, both 1988; *Le Nozze di Figaro,*

PAUL PYANT

Guildhall, 1988; *Single Spies,* National Theatre, 1988, then Queen's Theatre, London, 1989; *Orpheus Descending,* Peter Hall Company, London, 1988; *L'Italiana in Londra* and *Li Pittor Parigino,* both Buxton Festival, 1989; *Lear, Falstaff,* and *Street Scene* (operas), all English National Opera, 1989; *Who's Afraid of Virginia Woolf?* and *Christmas Carol,* both Birmingham Repertory Theatre, Birmingham, U.K., 1989; *The World According to Me,* Playhouse Theatre, London, 1989; *King Lear* and *The Liar,* both Old Vic Theatre, London, 1989; *The Return of Ulysses,* Kent Opera, Kent, U.K., 1989; *Mlada,* London Symphony Orchestra, Barbican Theatre, London, 1989; *Being Alive* (charity gala), Theatre Royal, London, 1989; *Le Nozze di Figaro* (opera), Glyndebourne Festival Opera, 1989; *Faust* and *Don Giovanni* (operas), both Opera Northern Ireland, 1989; *New Year,* Houston Grand Opera, Houston, TX, 1989; *Pirates of Penzance* and *The Mikado,* both D'Oyly Carte Opera Company, London, 1989; *Two for the Seesaw,* Watford Palace Theatre, Watford, U.K., 1989; *Street Scene,* Scottish Opera, 1989; *Another Time,* Wyndham's Theatre, London, 1989; also *Triple Bill,* Northern Ballet, U.K., 1989.

MAJOR TOURS—Lighting designer: *When Did You Last See Your Trousers?, Twelfth Night,* and *She Stoops to Conquer,* all 1987; *A Tale of Two Cities,* Cambridge Theatre Company, 1988; *Orpheus Descending,* Peter Hall Company, 1988; *Another Time,* 1989; *Death in Venice,* Glyndebourne Touring Opera, 1989.

FIRST TELEVISION WORK—Lighting designer, *King Priam,* Channel Four, 1985. PRINCIPAL TELEVISION WORK—Lighting designer: *Lady Macbeth of Mtsensk* (opera), BBC, 1987; *Xerxes* (opera), Thames, 1988; *The Devil and Kate,* BBC, 1988.

RELATED CAREER—Assistant lighting manager, Glyndebourne

Opera, 1974-87; teacher, Royal Academy of Dramatic Art, 1974—; stage/company manager, Kent Opera, Kent, U.K., 1974-78; lecturer, Croydon College, 1988; associate, Royal Academy of Dramatic Art.

AWARDS: Killick Award from Royal Academy of Dramatic Art, Best Technical Student, 1973.

MEMBER: British Actors' Equity Association, NATKE (BETA), Labour Party, CND, Amnesty International, National Trust.

SIDELIGHTS: RECREATIONS—Classical music, steam locomotives, and walking.

ADDRESSES: AGENT—Jeffrey Cambell Management, 18 Queen Anne Street, London W1M 9LB, England.

Q

QUARTERMASS, Martin
See CARPENTER, John

*   *   *

QUICK, Diana   1946-

PERSONAL: Born November 23, 1946.

VOCATION: Actress.

CAREER: PRINCIPAL STAGE APPEARANCES—Susan, *Lear*, English Stage Company, Royal Court Theatre, London, 1971; Betty, *The Threepenny Opera*, Prince of Wales Theatre, London, 1972; strange lady, *Man of Destiny*, Open Space Theatre, London, 1973; Rose Jones, *The Sea*, Royal Court Theatre, 1973; Liz Benson, *Billy*, Drury Lane Theatre, London, 1974; Lilamani, *Phaedra Britannica*, National Theatre Company, Old Vic Theatre, London, 1975; Prudence Malone, *Plunder*, National Theatre Company, Old Vic Theatre, 1976; Cressida, *Troilus and Cressida*, National Theatre Company, Young Vic Theatre, London, 1976; Olympia, *Tamburlaine the Great, Parts I and II*, National Theatre Company, Olivier Theatre, London, 1976; Pegg and Ann, *The Women Pirates Ann Bonney and Mary Read* and Beatrice-Joanna, *The Changeling*, both Royal Shakespeare Company, Aldwych Theatre, London, 1978.

PRINCIPAL FILM APPEARANCES—Sonya, *Nicholas and Alexandra*, Columbia, 1971; Laura, *The Duellists*, Paramount, 1977; Mona Mars Grant, *The Big Sleep*, United Artists, 1978; Fiona Harris, *The Odd Job*, Columbia, 1978; Gwenda Vaughan, *Ordeal By Innocence*, Metro-Goldwyn-Mayer/United Artists, 1984; Anna, *1919*, British Film Institute/Channel Four, 1984; Camille, *Max mon amour* (also known as *Max My Love*), Allied Artists, 1986; Susan, *Vroom*, Film Four, 1988. Also appeared in *A Private Enterprise*, British Film Institute, 1975; *Wilt*, Rank Film Distributors, 1989.

PRINCIPAL TELEVISION APPEARANCES—Series: Lady Julia Flyte, *Brideshead Revisited*, Granada, 1980-81, then *Great Performances*, PBS, 1982; also *Word for Word*, 1979-80; host, *Friday Night/Saturday Morning*, 1982. Mini-Series: Marian Halcombe, *The Woman in White*, Arts and Entertainment, 1982-83. Episodic: *Smith and Jones*, BBC-1. Movies: Brigida Bianchi, *Phantom of the Opera*, CBS, 1983; also *The Justice Game*, BBC-1, 1989. Specials: Voice of Beryl Markham, *World Without Walls: Beryl Markham's African Memoir* (documentary), PBS, 1986; narrator, *Chanel, Chanel* (documentary), Arts and Entertainment, 1989; also Ophelia, *Hamlet*, 1974. Also appeared in *Christ Recrucified*, 1969; *Hopcraft into Europe*, 1974; *Napoleon in Love*, 1974; *Bedtime Story*, 1974; *The Sleeping Beauty*, 1974; *Mr. Garrick and Mrs. Woffington*, 1975; *Holding On*, 1975; *The Three Hostages*, 1977; *It's My Pleasure, Dorothy Parker*, 1982.

ADDRESSES: AGENT—Duncan Heath Associates Ltd., Paramount House, 162-170 Wardour Street, London W1V 3AT, England.*

*   *   *

QUIGLEY, Linnea
(Linnea)

PERSONAL: Born in Davenport, IA; daughter of W. Heath and Dorothy Quigley. EDUCATION—Attended the John Robert Powers Modeling School.

VOCATION: Actress.

CAREER: PRINCIPAL FILM APPEARANCES—Sleeping Beauty, *Adult Fairy Tales* (also known as *Fairy Tales*), Productions Associates, 1978; Ginger, *Young Warriors*, Cannon, 1983; Milly, *The Black Room*, CI, 1984; Heather, *Savage Streets*, Motion Picture Marketing, 1984; Denise, *Silent Night, Deadly Night*, Tri-Star, 1984; Trash, *The Return of the Living Dead*, Orion, 1985; Bianca, *Creepozoids*, Urban Classics, 1987; Melody, *Nightmare Sisters* (also known as *Sorority Sisters*), Trans World Entertainment/Filmtrust, 1987; Suzanne, *Night of the Demons*, International Film Market, 1988; Spider, *Sorority Babes in the Slimeball Bowl-o-Rama*, Urban Classics, 1988; Samantha Kelso, *Hollywood Chainsaw Hookers*, Camp Motion Pictures/American Independent, 1988; soul from Freddy's chest, *A Nightmare on Elm Street IV: The Dream Master*, New Line Cinema, 1988; Lu DeBelle, *Treasure of the Moon Goddess*, Ascot, 1988; Didi, *Vice Academy*, Rick Sloane Productions, 1989; (as Linnea) Phoebe Love, *Sexbomb*, Phillips and Mora Entertainment, 1989; Bambi, *Assault of the Party Nerds* (also known as *Party Nerds*), Prism Entertainment, 1989; Ginger, *Witchtrap* (also known as *The Haunted*), Magnum Home Entertainment/Imperial Entertainment, 1989; Miss Barbeau, *Robot Ninja*, Cinema Home Video, 1989; Michelle Arno, *Deadly Embrace*, Prism Entertainment/Filmtrust, 1989. Also appeared in *Graduation Day*, Scope III, 1979; *Summer Camp*, Seymour Borde, 1979; *Nightstalker*, 1979; *Stone Cold Dead*, Dimension, 1979; *Still Smokin'* (also known as *Cheech and Chong's Still Smokin'*), Paramount, 1980; *Cheech and Chong's Nice Dreams*, Columbia, 1981; *Don't Go Near the Park*, 1981; *Silent Night, Deadly Night Part II*, Ascot, 1986; *Doctor Alien* (also known as *I Was a Teenage Sex Mutant*), Phantom Video, 1988; *American Rampage*, 1988; *Murder Weapon*, Cinema Home Video, 1989.

PRINCIPAL FILM WORK—Producer (with Fred Kennamer) *Murder Weapon*, Cinema Home Video, 1989.

RELATED CAREER—Professional model.*

*   *   *

QUINE, Richard   1920-1989

PERSONAL: Born November 12, 1920, in Detroit, MI; died of a self-inflicted gunshot wound, June 10, 1989, in Los Angeles, CA; son of Thomas R. Quine (a vaudeville performer); married Susan Peters (an actress; divorced, 1948); married Barbara Bushman (divorced); married Fran Jefferies (a singer; divorced); fourth wife's name, Diana; children: one son (adopted; first marriage); two daughters (second marriage). MILITARY—U.S. Coast Guard.

VOCATION: Director, producer, writer, and actor.

CAREER: Also see *WRITINGS* below. STAGE DEBUT—*Cardinal Richelieu*, Los Angeles. BROADWAY DEBUT—*Very Warm for May*, Alvin Theatre, 1939. PRINCIPAL STAGE APPEARANCES—Frank Lippencott, *My Sister Eileen*, Biltmore Theatre, New York City, 1940; also appeared as Richard, *Counsellor-at-Law*.

FILM DEBUT—*The World Changes*, Warner Brothers/First National, 1933. PRINCIPAL FILM APPEARANCES—Richard, *Counsellor-at-Law*, Universal, 1933; Jackie Shaw, *Dinky*, Warner Brothers, 1935; Pieter, *A Dog of Flanders*, RKO, 1935; John Reed, *Jane Eyre*, First Division, 1935; Ned, *Little Men*, Mascot, 1935; student, *King of the Underworld*, Warner Brothers, 1939; Morton Hammond, *Babes on Broadway*, Metro-Goldwyn-Mayer (MGM), 1941; Doctor Dennis Lindsey, *Dr. Gillespie's New Assistant*, MGM, 1942; Danny Hayden, *For Me and My Gal*, MGM, 1942; Frank Lippencott, *My Sister Eileen*, Columbia, 1942; Ensign Martin, *Stand By for Action* (also known as *Cargo of Innocents*), MGM, 1942; Ted Bowser, *Tish*, MGM, 1942; Brad Craig, *We've Never Been Licked* (also known as *Fighting Command*), Universal, 1943; Howard Bankson, *The Cockeyed Miracle*, MGM, 1946; Major George Rockton, *Command Decision*, MGM, 1948; Ben Feiner, Jr., *Words and Music*, MGM, 1948; Ted Niles, *The Clay Pigeon*, RKO, 1949; Hank Weber, *Flying Missile*, Columbia, 1950; Brownie, *No Sad Songs for Me*, Columbia, 1950; Johnny Truitt, *Rookie Fireman*, Columbia, 1950. Also appeared in *Life Returns*, Scienart, 1939.

FIRST FILM WORK—Producer and director (both with William Asher), *Leather Gloves* (also known as *Loser Take All*), Columbia, 1948. PRINCIPAL FILM WORK—All as director, unless indicated: *Purple Heart Diary* (also known as *No Time for Tears*), Columbia, 1951; *Sunny Side of the Street*, Columbia, 1951; *Rainbow 'round My Shoulder*, Columbia, 1952; *Sound Off*, Columbia, 1952; *All Ashore*, Columbia, 1953; *Cruisin' Down the River*, Columbia, 1953; *Siren of Baghdad*, Columbia, 1953; *Drive a Crooked Road*, Columbia, 1954; *Pushover*, Columbia, 1954; *So This Is Paris*, Universal, 1954; *My Sister Eileen*, Columbia, 1955; *The Solid Gold Cadillac*, Columbia, 1956; *Operation Mad Ball*, Columbia, 1957; *Bell, Book, and Candle*, Columbia, 1958; (also producer) *It Happened to Jane* (also known as *Twinkle and Shine*), Columbia, 1959; (also producer) *Strangers When We Meet*, Columbia, 1960; *The World of Suzie Wong*, Paramount, 1960; *The Notorious Landlady*, Columbia, 1962; producer, *Paris When It Sizzles*, Paramount, 1964; *Sex and the Single Girl*, Warner Brothers, 1964; *How to*

Murder Your Wife, United Artists, 1965; (also producer) *Synanon* (also known as *Get Off My Back*), Columbia, 1965; *Hotel*, Warner Brothers, 1967; (with Alexander Mackendrick) *Oh Dad, Poor Dad, Mama's Hung You in the Closet and I'm Feelin' So Sad*, Paramount, 1967; *The Moonshine War*, Metro-Goldwyn-Mayer, 1970; *W* (also known as *I Want Her Dead*), Cinerama, 1974; *The Prisoner of Zenda*, Universal, 1979.

PRINCIPAL TELEVISION WORK—All as director, unless indicated. Series: *Hey Mulligan* (also known as *The Mickey Rooney Show*), NBC, 1954-55; executive producer (with Richard Kennedy), *The Jean Arthur Show*, CBS, 1966; (with Stan Dragoti) *McCoy*, NBC, 1975-76. Pilots: *Catch-22*, ABC, 1973; *The Specialists*, NBC, 1975. Episodic: *Columbo*, NBC, 1971; *Hec Ramsey*, NBC, 1972; *Project UFO*, NBC, 1978.

PRINCIPAL RADIO APPEARANCES—Title role, *Tom Sawyer*.

RELATED CAREER—Child performer in vaudeville for six years.

WRITINGS: FILM—See production details above, unless indicated: (With Blake Edwards) *Rainbow 'round My Shoulder*, 1952; (with Edwards) *Sound Off*, 1952; (with Edwards) *All Ashore*, 1953; (with Edwards) *Cruisin' Down the River*, 1953; (with Edwards) *Bring Your Smile Along*, Columbia, 1955; (with Edwards) *My Sister Eileen*, 1955; (with Edwards) *He Laughed Last*, Columbia, 1956; composer (with Fred Karger and Stanley Styne), *Juke Box Rhythm*, Columbia, 1959. TELEVISION—Episodic: (With Edwards) *Hey Mulligan*, NBC, 1954-55.

OBITUARIES AND OTHER SOURCES: New York Times, June 14, 1989; *Variety*, 21-27, 1989.*

*   *   *

QUINN, J.C.

VOCATION: Actor.

CAREER: PRINCIPAL STAGE APPEARANCES—Sergeant Morrison, *Short Eyes*, New York Shakespeare Festival, (NYSF), Public Theatre, then Vivian Beaumont Theatre, both New York City, 1974; Jackie, *The Petrified Forest*, St. Clement's Church Theatre, New York City, 1974; Carl, *Fathers and Sons*, NYSF, Public Theatre, 1978; Jerusalem Slim, *Salt Lake City Skyline*, NYSF, Public Theatre, 1980; Skeet, *Heartland*, Century Theatre, New York City, 1981; Walsh, *Legends*, Center Theatre Group, Mark Taper Forum, Los Angeles, 1986.

PRINCIPAL FILM APPEARANCES—Luther, *On the Yard*, Midwest Film, 1978; Dunn, *Fire Power*, Associated Film Distribution, 1979; Simon, *Times Square*, Associated Film Distribution, 1980; man on Riverside Drive, *Gloria*, Columbia, 1980; barber, *Brubaker*, Twentieth Century-Fox, 1980; Shorter, *Eddie Macon's Run*, Universal, 1983; Curtis Schultz, *Silkwood*, Twentieth Century-Fox, 1983; Texas voice, *Places in the Heart*, Tri-Star, 1984; Murphy, *C.H.U.D.*, New World, 1984; Elmo, *Vision Quest*, Warner Brothers, 1985; Boyd, *At Close Range*, Orion, 1986; quartermaster sergeant, *Heartbreak Ridge*, Warner Brothers, 1986; Duncan, *Maximum Overdrive*, Dino De Laurentiis, 1986; Kevin McBane, *Violated*, Cinematronics, 1986; Jim, *Barfly*, Cannon, 1987; Garth Ratliff, *Big Business*, Buena Vista, 1988; Mayotte, *Blanc de Chine* (also known as *Chinese White*), AMLF, 1988;

Sonny Dawson, *The Abyss*, Twentieth Century-Fox, 1989; comedy coach, *Wired*, Taurus Entertainment, 1989; Walter Boyett, *Turner and Hooch*, Buena Vista, 1989; Papa Slovak, *Gross Anatomy*, Buena Vista, 1989. Also appeared in *Love Dream* (also known as *Priceless Beauty*), Titanus Distribuzione/Film Jacques Leitienne, 1988.

PRINCIPAL TELEVISION APPEARANCES—Pilots: Bailiff, *O'Malley*, NBC, 1983. Episodic: Red Griswald, *1st & 10*, HBO, 1985; Slats, "Young Harry Houdini," *Disney Sunday Movie*, ABC, 1987; sheriff, *Stingray*, NBC, 1987; Armstrong, *A Year in the Life*, NBC, 1987; Hartwell, *Crime Story*, NBC, 1988. Movies: Wilbur Purdy, *An Invasion of Privacy*, CBS, 1983; mayor, *North Beach and Rawhide*, CBS, 1985; Schmidler, *Nutcracker: Money, Madness, and Murder*, NBC, 1987; Jack Dorrian, *The Preppie Murder*, ABC, 1989; Ben, *The China Lake Murders*, USA Network, 1990.*

*   *   *

QUINTERO, Jose   1924-

PERSONAL: Full name, Jose Benjamin Quintero; born October 15, 1924, in Panama City, Panama; son of Carlos Rivira (a cattleman and politician) and Consuelo (Palmorala) Quintero. EDUCATION—University of Southern California, B.A., 1948; also attended Los Angeles City College; trained for the stage at the Goodman Theatre School, 1948-49.

VOCATION: Director, producer, and writer.

CAREER: Also see *WRITINGS* below. PRINCIPAL STAGE APPEARANCES—*Valesa, a Nightmare*, Detroit Repertory Theatre, Detroit, MI, 1983.

FIRST STAGE WORK—Director, *The Glass Menagerie* and *Riders to the Sea*, both Woodstock Summer Theatre, Woodstock, NY, 1949. FIRST LONDON WORK—Director, Globe Theatre, 1958. PRINCIPAL STAGE WORK—All as director, unless indicated: *Dark of the Moon*, Circle in the Square, New York City, 1950; *The Bonds of Interest*, *The Enchanted*, *Yerma*, and *Burning Bright*, all Circle in the Square, 1951; *Summer and Smoke*, Circle in the Square, 1952; *The Grass Harp*, Circle in the Square, 1953; *In the Summer House*, Playhouse Theatre, New York City, 1953; *The Girl on the Via Flaminia*, Circle in the Square, 1954; *Portrait of a Lady*, American National Theatre and Academy Theatre, New York City, 1954; (also co-producer) *La Ronde* and *Cradle Song*, both Circle in the Square, 1955; *The Innkeepers*, John Golden Theatre, New York City, 1956; (also producer with Leigh Connell and Theodore Mann) *The Iceman Cometh*, Circle in the Square, 1956; (also producer with Connell and Mann) *Long Day's Journey into Night*, Helen Hayes Theatre, New York City, 1956; *The Quare Fellow* and (also co-producer) *Children of Darkness*, both Circle in the Square, 1958; *A Moon for the Misbegotten*, Festival of the Two Worlds, Spoleto, Italy, 1958; *Lost in the Stars* (opera) and *The Triumph of St. Joan* (opera), both City Center Theatre, New York City, 1958; *Cavalleria Rusticana* and *I Pagliacci* (operas; double-bill), Metropolitan Opera House, New York City, 1958; *Our Town*, Circle in the Square, 1959; *Macbeth*, Cambridge Drama Festival, Cambridge, MA, 1959.

The Balcony, Circle in the Square, 1960; *Camino Real*, St. Mark's Playhouse, New York City, 1960; *Laurette*, Shubert Theatre, New Haven, CT, 1960; (also producer with Mann) *Under Milk Wood*, Circle in the Square, 1961; *Look, We've Come Through*, Hudson Theatre, New York City, 1961; (also co-producer) *Plays for Bleecker Street*, Circle in the Square, 1962; *Great Day in the Morning*, Henry Miller's Theatre, New York City, 1962; producer (with Mann), *Under Milk Wood* and (also producer with Mann) *Pullman Car Hiawatha* (double-bill), Circle in the Square, 1962; (also producer with Mann) *Desire Under the Elms*, Circle in the Square, 1963; *Strange Interlude*, Actors' Studio Company, Theatre, then Martin Beck Theatre, New York City, both 1963; *Marco Millions*, Repertory Company of Lincoln Center, Washington Square Theatre, New York City, 1964; *Hughie*, Royale Theatre, New York City, 1964; *Diamond Orchid*, Henry Miller's Theatre, 1965; *Matty and the Moron and Madonna*, Orpheum Theatre, New York City, 1965; *A Moon for the Misbegotten*, Studio Arena Theatre, Buffalo, NY, 1965; *Pousse-Cafe*, 46th Street Theatre, New York City, 1966; *More Stately Mansions*, Ahmanson Theatre, Los Angeles, then Broadhurst Theatre, New York City, both 1967; *The Seven Descents of Myrtle*, Ethel Barrymore Theatre, New York City, 1968; *Episode in the Life of an Author* and *The Orchestra*, both Studio Arena Theatre, 1969.

Gandhi, Playhouse Theatre, 1970; *Johnny Johnson*, Edison Theatre, New York City, 1971; *A Moon for the Misbegotten*, Morosco Theatre, New York City, 1973, then Center Theatre Group, Ahmanson Theatre, 1974; *Gabrielle*, Studio Arena Theatre, later Ford's Theatre Society, Washington, DC, both 1974; *The Skin of Our Teeth*, Eisenhower Theatre, Kennedy Center for the Performing Arts, Washington, DC, 1975; *Knock Knock*, Biltmore Theatre, New York City, 1976; *Anna Christie*, Imperial Theatre, New York City, 1977; *A Touch of the Poet*, Helen Hayes Theatre, 1977; *Faith Healer*, Longacre Theatre, New York City, 1979; *Clothes for a Summer Hotel*, Cort Theatre, New York, 1980; *Welded*, Horace Mann Theatre, New York City, 1981; *Cat on a Hot Tin Roof*, Center Theatre Group, Mark Taper Forum, Los Angeles, 1983; *Rainsnakes*, Long Wharf Theatre, New Haven, CT, 1984; *The Iceman Cometh*, Lunt-Fontanne Theatre, New York City, 1985; *Long Day's Journey into Night*, Neil Simon Theatre, New York City, 1988. Also director, *The Iceman Cometh*, Amsterdam, Netherlands, 1957; *The Big Coca-Cola Swamp in the Sky*, Westport, CT, 1971; *Hughie*, Lake Forest, IL, 1976; *The Human Voice*, Melbourne, Australia, 1978; and *Ah! Wilderness*, 1980.

MAJOR TOURS—Director, *Long's Day's Journey into Night*, U.S. cities, 1957-58.

PRINCIPAL FILM WORK—Director, *The Roman Spring of Mrs. Stone*, Warner Brothers, 1961; associate producer (with Jose Berrios), *Lola la Loca*, Lola la Loca Associates/Electric, 1987.

PRINCIPAL TELEVISION APPEARANCES—Mini-Series: Don Diego de la Pena, *Fresno*, CBS, 1986.

PRINCIPAL TELEVISION WORK—All as director, unless indicated. Series: (With Leonard Valenta, John Stix, and Jack Garfein) *Windows*, CBS, 1955. Episodic: "Medea," *Play of the Week*, WNTA, 1959; "The Thunder of Ernie Bass" and "A Strange and Distant Place," *The Nurses*, CBS, 1962. Specials: *Our Town*, NBC, 1959; *A Moon for the Misbegotten*, ABC, 1975; "The Human Voice," *Great Performances*, PBS, 1979; also *Hughie*.

RELATED CAREER—Director (With Neal DuBrock, Marvin Gordon, and Warren Enters), Studio Arena Theatre, Buffalo, NY, 1969-70; artistic associate director, Center Theatre Group, Mark Taper Forum, Los Angeles, 1984.

WRITINGS: STAGE—*Gabrielle,* Studio Arena Theatre, Buffalo, NY, 1974. OTHER—*If You Won't Dance, They Beat You.*

AWARDS: Obie Award from the *Village Voice,* Best Director, and Vernon Rice Award, both 1956, for *The Iceman Cometh;* Antoinette Perry Award nomination, Best Director, all 1957, for *Long Day's Journey into Night;* New York Newspaper Guild (Page One) Award, Outstanding Theatre Personality, 1957; Grand Prix du Television from the Monte Carlo Festival, 1959, for *Medea;* Lola d'Annunzio Award, 1960; Antoinette Perry Award, Best Director of a Play, and Drama Desk Award, 1974, both for *A Moon for the Misbegotten;* Distinguished Artist Award, 1985; Unique Contributions to the Theatre Award from the Drama League, 1987, for ''sensitive and brilliant interpretation of Eugene O'Neill's dramatic masterpieces''; Caballero de la Order de Vasco Nunez de Balboa; La Asamblea Nacional de Panama.

MEMBER: Directors Guild of America, Society of Stage Directors and Choreographers.

SIDELIGHTS: RECREATIONS—Reading.

ADDRESSES: OFFICE—c/o Thomas A. Andrews, 7 E. 67th Street, New York, NY 10021. AGENT—The Kohner Agency, 9169 Sunset Boulevard, Los Angeles, CA 90069.*

R

RADEMAKERS, Fons   1920-

PERSONAL: Born September 5, 1920, in Roosendaal, Holland. EDUCATION—Trained at the Academy of Dramatic Art (Amsterdam).

VOCATION: Producer, director, actor, and writer.

CAREER: PRINCIPAL FILM APPEARANCES—Mother, *Le Rouge aux levres* (also known as *Daughters of Darkness*), Gemini, 1971; commissioner, *Mysteries*, Cine-Vog, 1979.

PRINCIPAL FILM WORK—All as director, unless indicated: *Mysteries*, Cine-Vog, 1979; (also producer) *The Assault*, Cannon, 1986; producer (with Henry Lange and Pierre Drouot), *Diary of a Mad Old Man* (also known as *Dagboek Van een oude dwaas*), Cannon, 1987; also *Village on the River* (also known as *Dorp aan de river* and *Doctor in the Village*), 1958; *That Joyous Eve . . .* (also known as *Makkers staaki uw wild geraas*), 1960; *The Knife* (also known as *Het mes*), 1961; *The Spitting Image* (also known as *Like Two Drops of Water* and *Als 2 druppels water*), 1963; *The Dance of Heron* (also known as *De dans van de reiger*), 1966; *Mira*, 1971; *Because of the Cats* (also known as *The Rape* and *Niet voor de posen*), 1973; *Max Havelaar*, 1976; *My Friend* (also known as *The Judge's Friend*), 1979.

RELATED CAREER—Assistant to the film directors Vittorio De Sica, Federico Fellini, Jacques Becker, David Lean, Jean Renoir, and Charles Crichton; also directed for the stage.

WRITINGS: FILM—(With Hugo Claus) *That Joyous Eve . . .* (also known as *Makkers staaki uw wild geraas*), 1960; *The Spitting Image* (also known as *Like Two Drops of Water* and *Als 2 druppels water*), 1963.

AWARDS: International Film Guide Award, Director of the Year, 1979.*

*   *   *

RADNER, Gilda   1946-1989

PERSONAL: Born June 28, 1946, in Detroit, MI; died of cancer, May 20, 1989, in Los Angeles, CA; father, a hotel owner; married G.E. Smith (a musician), April, 1980 (divorced); married Gene Wilder (an actor, director, and writer), September 18, 1984. EDUCATION—Attended the University of Michigan.

VOCATION: Actress, comedienne, and writer.

CAREER: Also see *WRITINGS* below. STAGE DEBUT—With the Second City Improvisational Theatre, Toronto, ON, Canada, 1973-74. BROADWAY DEBUT—*Gilda Radner Live from New York*, Winter Garden Theatre, 1979. PRINCIPAL STAGE APPEARANCES—Ensemble, *The National Lampoon Show* (revue), New Palladium Theatre, New York City, 1975; Carrie, *Lunch Hour*, Ethel Barrymore Theatre, New York City, 1980-81; also appeared in *Godspell*, Global Village Theatre, Toronto, ON, Canada; *Gilda Radner Live from New York*, Boston, MA and Chicago, IL.

PRINCIPAL FILM APPEARANCES—Soshu member, *The Last Detail*, Columbia, 1973; Gloria Link, *First Family*, Warner Brothers, 1980; various roles, *Gilda Live*, Warner Brothers, 1980; Kate Hellman, *Hanky-Panky*, Columbia, 1982; Ms. Milner, *The Woman in Red*, Orion, 1984; Livia Machado, *Movers and Shakers*, United Artists, 1985; Vickie Pearle, *Haunted Honeymoon*, Orion, 1986. Also appeared in *It Came from Hollywood*, Paramount, 1982; *Mr. Mike's Mondo Video*, New Line Cinema, 1979; *Animalympics* (animated), Barber Rose International, 1979.

PRINCIPAL TELEVISION APPEARANCES—Series: Regular, *Saturday Night Live*, NBC, 1975-80. Episodic: As herself, *It's Garry Shandling's Show*, Fox, 1988. Specials: Jill of Hearts, "Jack: A Flash Fantasy," *Opera Theatre*, PBS, 1977; *King Orange Jamboree Parade*, NBC, 1977; passerby, *All You Need Is Cash*, NBC, 1978; *Things We Did Last Summer*, NBC, 1978; *Bob and Ray and Jane, Laraine, and Gilda*, NBC, 1981; *Steve Martin's The Winds of Whoopie*, NBC, 1983.

PRINCIPAL RADIO APPEARANCES—Series: Regular, *The National Lampoon Radio Hour*.

WRITINGS: STAGE—(With Lorne Michaels and Don Novello) *Gilda Radner Live from New York*, Winter Garden Theatre, New York City, 1979. FILM—(With Michaels and Novello) *Gilda Live*, Warner Brothers, 1980. RADIO—*The National Lampoon Radio Hour*. OTHER—*It's Always Something* (autobiography), Simon and Schuster, 1989.

RECORDINGS: ALBUMS—*Gilda Radner Live from New York* (original cast recording).

AWARDS: Emmy Award, Outstanding Performance By an Actress in a Supporting Role in a Variety Series, 1978, for *Saturday Night Live*.

OBITUARIES AND OTHER SOURCES: New York Times, May 21, 1989; *Variety*, May 24-30, 1989.*

RAKOFF, Alvin   1927-

PERSONAL: Born February 6, 1927, in Toronto, ON, Canada; son of Samuel (a shopkeeper) and Pearl (Himmelspring) Rakoff; married Jacqueline Hill (an actress), June 4, 1958; children: Sasha Victoria, John Dmitri. EDUCATION—University of Toronto, B.A., 1948.

VOCATION: Director and writer.

CAREER: Also see *WRITINGS* below. PRINCIPAL FILM WORK—Director: *Room 43* (also known as *Passport to Shame*), Cory, 1959; *Hot Money Girl* (also known as *Long Distance, The Treasure of San Teresa,* and *Rhapsodie in Blei*), United Producers, 1962; *The World in My Pocket* (also known as *On Friday at Eleven*), Metro-Goldwyn-Mayer, 1962; *The Comedy Man*, British Lion, 1964; *Crossplot*, United Artists, 1969; *Hoffman*, Levitt/Pickman, 1970; *Say Hello to Yesterday*, Cinerama, 1971; (also producer) *King Solomon's Treasure*, Canafox Towers, 1978; *City on Fire*, AVCO-Embassy, 1979; *Death Ship*, AVCO-Embassy, 1980; *Dirty Tricks*, AVCO-Embassy, 1981.

PRINCIPAL TELEVISION WORK—All as director, unless indicated. Mini-Series: *Paradise Postponed*, Thames, then *Masterpiece Theatre*, PBS, 1983. Movies: *The Adventures of Don Quixote*, BBC, 1972, then CBS, 1973; *The First Olympics—Athens 1896*, NBC, 1984. Specials: *Mr. Halperin and Mr. Johnson*, HBO, 1983. Also *The Caine Mutiny Court Martial*, BBC, 1958; *Our Town*, BBC, 1957; producer, *Waiting for Gillian*, 1957; *Call Me Daddy*, 1968; *Summer and Smoke*, BBC, 1971; *In Praise of Love*, Anglia Television, 1975; *Romeo and Juliet*, BBC, 1978; *A Voyage 'round My Father*, 1982; *Requiem for a Heavyweight, The Velvet Alley, A Town Was Turned to Dust, Jokers Justice, Call Me Back, Day Before Atlanta, Heart to Heart, The Seekers, Sweet War Man, The Move After Checkmate, The Stars in My Eyes, Shadow of a Gunman, The Impeachment of Andrew Johnson, Cheap in August, Nicest Man in the World, Dame of Sark,* and *The Kitchen*.

RELATED CAREER—Writer, director, and producer, British Broadcasting Corporation (BBC-TV), 1953-57.

NON-RELATED CAREER—Journalist, *Northern Daily News, Windsor Star, Toronto Globe and Mail,* and *Lakeshore Advertiser*, 1949-52.

WRITINGS: FILM—(With Peter King) *Say Hello to Yesterday*, Cinerama, 1971; *City on Fire*, AVCO-Embassy, 1979. TELEVISION—*A Flight of Fancy*, BBC, 1952; (adaptor) *The Troubled Air*, BBC, 1953; *Thunder in the Realms*, BBC, 1955; (adaptor) *Our Town*, BBC, 1957; (adaptor) *The Caine Mutiny Court Martial*, BBC, 1958; (adaptor) *Summer and Smoke*, BBC, 1971; (adaptor) *A Kiss Is Just a Kiss*, Anglia Television, 1971; (adaptor) *A Man About a Dog*, Anglia Television, 1972; (adaptor) *The Adventures of Don Quixote*, BBC, 1972, then CBS, 1973; *Rooms*, Thames Television, 1974; *O Canada*, BBC, 1974; *Mineshaft*, BBC, 1975; (adaptor) *Lulu Street*, CBC, 1975; (adaptor) *In Praise of Love*, Anglia Television, 1975; (adaptor) *Romeo and Juliet*, BBC, 1978.

AWARDS: London Daily Mail National Television Award, 1955, for *Waiting for Gillian;* Emmy Award, 1968, for *Call Me Daddy;* Emmy Award, 1982, for *A Voyage 'round My Father*.

MEMBER: Association of Cinema and Television Technicians, Directors Guild of Canada, Writers Guild of Great Britain.*

RAMIN, Sid   1924-

PERSONAL: Full name, Sidney Norton Ramin; born January 22, 1924, in Boston, MA; son of Ezra (a window trimmer) and Beatrice D. (Salamoff) Ramin; married Gloria Breit (a singer and model), January 9, 1949; children: Ronald. EDUCATION—Attended the New England Conservatory of Music, Boston University, and Columbia University; also studied musical theory with Leonard Bernstein. MILITARY—U.S. Army, sergeant, Infantry, 1940-45.

VOCATION: Orchestrator, musical arranger, and composer.

CAREER: Also see *WRITINGS* below. FIRST STAGE WORK—Orchestrator (with Leonard Bernstein and Irwin Kostal), *West Side Story*, Winter Garden Theatre, New York City, 1957. PRINCIPAL STAGE WORK—All as orchestrator, unless indicated: (With Robert Ginzler) *Gypsy*, Broadway Theatre, New York City, 1959; *The Girls Against the Boys*, Alvin Theatre, New York City, 1959; (with Ginzler; also arranger), *Wildcat*, Alvin Theatre, 1960; (also arranger) *The Conquering Hero*, American National Theatre and Academy Theatre, New York City, 1961; (with Irwin Kostal) *Kwamina*, 54th Street Theatre, New York City, 1961; *I Can Get It for You Wholesale*, Shubert Theatre, New York City, 1962; (with Kostal) *A Funny Thing Happened on the Way to the Forum*, Alvin Theatre, 1962; (with Leonard Bernstein and Kostal) *West Side Story*, Music Theatre of Lincoln Theatre, State Theatre, New York City, 1968; (with Kostal) *A Funny Thing Happened on the Way to the Forum*, Lunt-Fontanne Theatre, New York City, 1972; *Leonard Bernstein's Mass* (chamber-orchestra version), Mark Taper Forum, Los Angeles, CA, 1973; (with Ginzler) *Gypsy*, Winter Garden Theatre, New York City, 1974; *1600 Pennsylvania Avenue*, Mark Hellinger Theatre, New York City, 1976; (with Bernstein and Kostal) *West Side Story*, Minskoff Theatre, New York City, 1980; (with Bill Byers, Dick Hazard, and Torrie Zito) *Smile*, Lunt-Fontanne Theatre, 1986; (with William D. Brohn) *Jerome Robbins' Broadway*, Imperial Theatre, New York City, 1989; *Gypsy*, St. James Theatre, New York City, 1989.

MAJOR TOURS—(With Robert Ginzler) *Gypsy*, U.S. cities, 1961.

FIRST FILM WORK—Orchestrator (with Irwin Kostal, Saul Chaplin, and Johnny Breen), *West Side Story*, United Artists, 1961.

FIRST TELEVISION WORK—Musical arranger, *The Milton Berle Show*, NBC, 1949-56. PRINCIPAL TELEVISION WORK—Series: Musical director, *Candid Camera*, CBS, 1963-66.

RELATED CAREER—Musical arranger for the Boston Pops and Barbra Streisand; composer, musical arranger, and conductor for numerous radio and television commercials.

WRITINGS: All as composer of score, unless indicated. STAGE—Title song, *Agatha Sue, I Love You*, Henry Miller's Theatre, New York City, 1966. FILM—*Too Many Thieves*, United Artists, 1967; *Stiletto*, AVCO-Embassy, 1969. TELEVISION—Series: *The Patty Duke Show*, CBS, 1964-66; *Trials of O'Brien*, CBS, 1966; *Nancy*, NBC, 1970-71; also *All My Children*, ABC. Pilots: *Popi*, CBS, 1975. Specials: *Miracle on 34th Street*, CBS, 1973.

AWARDS: Academy Award (with Irwin Kostal, Saul Chaplin, and Johnny Breen), Best Music (Scoring of a Musical Picture), and Grammy Award, Best Soundtrack Album, both 1961, for *West Side Story;* Emmy Award for *All My Children;* fifteen Clio Awards from the American Television Commercial Festival. MILITARY HONORS—Bronze Star from the U.S. Army.

MEMBER: Academy of Motion Picture Arts and Sciences, American Society of Composers, Authors, and Publishers, National Academy of Television Arts and Sciences, National Academy of Recording Arts and Sciences, Composers and Lyricists Guild of America, Affiliated Federation of Musicians.

ADDRESSES: OFFICE—140 W. 57th Street, New York, NY 10019.

*   *   *

RAMONT, Mark S.   1956-

PERSONAL: Born June 22, 1956, in Loma Linda, CA; son of Raymond Jonathan (a manufacturer) and Gloria Dene (a house cleaner; maiden name, Kronholm) Ramont. EDUCATION—California State University, B.A., theatre arts, 1978; University of Texas, Austin, M.F.A., drama (directing), 1980; also internship in directing, stage management, and literary management, Asolo State Theatre, Sarasota, FL.

VOCATION: Director.

CAREER: FIRST STAGE WORK—Director, *Talley's Folly,* Capital City Playhouse, Austin, TX, 1981. PRINCIPAL STAGE WORK—Stage manager (with John Toia), *The Keeper, The Diary of Anne Frank, Talley's Folly, Daughters,* and *All My Sons,* all Philadelphia Drama Guild, Philadelphia, PA, 1982-83; director, *A Raisin in the Sun,* Capital City Playhouse, Austin, TX, 1983; director, *Agnes of God,* Capital City Playhouse, 1984; assistant director, *Blue Window,* Production Company, Theatre Guinevere, New York City, 1984; artistic associate (with Christian Angermann), *El Salvador, Only You, Cave Life, Borderlines,* and *V and V Only,* all Circle Repertory Theatre, New York City, 1987-88; stage manager, *Living Color,* American Conservatory Theatre, Don't Tell Mama Theatre, New York City, 1986; director, *Dalton's Back,* Circle Repertory Theatre, 1989; director, *Beside Herself,* Circle Repertory Theatre, 1990. Also assistant director, *The Song Is Kern!* and *The Three Musketeers,* both Asolo State Theatre, Sarasota, FL; director, *Perth Road, The Bricklayer's Poet,* and *Joe La Porte,* all Circle Repertory Lab, New York City; director, *Veronica's Room,* Kanawha Players, Charleston, SC; director, *Changes* and *Barefoot Every where,* both Shoestring Theatre, Austin, TX; director, *Who's Afraid of Virginia Woolf,* Bloomsburg Theatre Ensemble, Bloomsburg, PA; director, *Master Harold . . . and the Boys, Educating Rita, Crossing Niagara,* and *Mass Appeal,* all Dorset Theatre Festival, Dorset, VT; director, *The Fantasticks,* Santa Rita Dinner Theatre, Santa Rita, NM; director, *Steel Magnolias* and *'night Mother,* both Cortland Repertory Theatre.

RELATED CAREER—Artistic associate, Circle Repertory Theatre, New York City, 1987-89, then associate artistic director, 1989—.

WRITINGS: Contributor of articles, reviews, and interviews for *Broadway Bill of Fare* magazine.

AWARDS: Austin Circle of Theatres Award nomination, Best Director, 1981, for *Talley's Folly;* Austin Circle of Theatres Award nomination, Best Director, 1983, for *A Raisin in the Sun;* Austin Circle of Theatres Award, Best Director, 1984, for *Agnes of God;* Princess Grace Foundation USA Theatre Fellow, 1988; Princess Grace Foundation USA Statuette Award, 1989, for Outstanding Achievement and Professional Development.

MEMBER: Actors' Equity Association.

ADDRESSES: OFFICE—Circle Repertory Theatre, 161 Avenue of the Americas, New York, NY 10013.

*   *   *

RANDOLPH, John   1915-

PERSONAL: Born Emanuel Hirsch Cohen, June 1, 1915, in Bronx, NY; son of Louis (a hat manufacturer) and Dorothy (an insurance agent; maiden name, Shore) Cohen; name changed to Mortimer Lippman at age 12 by his stepfather, Joseph Lippman; name legally changed to John Randolph in 1940; married Sarah Lucie Cunningham (an actress), January 3, 1942; children: Harrison Henry, Martha Eoline. EDUCATION—Graduated from City College of New York, 1935; also attended Columbia University, 1934 (summer semester); studied acting with Stella Adler and Erwin Piscator at the Dramatic Workshop of the New School for Social Research, 1940-42, with William Hansen at the American Theatre Wing, 1947, and at the Actors' Studio, 1948-54. MILITARY—U.S. Army Air Forces, corporal, 1942-45.

VOCATION: Actor and writer.

CAREER: Also see *WRITINGS* below. STAGE DEBUT—Jacob Engstrand, *Ghosts,* East Houston Street Theatre, New York City, 1935, for eighty-one performances. BROADWAY DEBUT—Tuff, *Revolt of the Beavers,* Federal Theatre Project, Adelphi Theatre,

JOHN RANDOLPH

1937. PRINCIPAL STAGE APPEARANCES—Private, *Private Hicks* and the Old Man, *You Can't Change Human Nature,* both Theatre Collective, Provincetown Playhouse, New York City, 1936; the Weaver, *The Emperor's New Clothes,* Federal Theatre Project, Adelphi Theatre, New York City, 1937; *Times* reporter, *Captain Jinks of the Horse Marines,* Jacob, *No More Peace,* and Roman herald, *Coriolanus,* all Maxine Elliott's Theatre, New York City, 1938; St. Bernard H. Blackwood, *The Great Barrington* and second beau, *Created Equal,* both Federal Theatre Project, Empire Theatre, New York City, 1938; Mac, *Medicine Show,* New Yorker Theatre, New York City, 1940; radio announcer, *Hold On to Your Hats,* Shubert Theatre, New York City, 1940; title role, *Wozzeck* and Rudolf Dvoracek, *Any Day Now,* both Erwin Piscator Dramatic Workshop, New School for Social Research, New York City, 1941; Endicott, *The Front Page,* Civic Theatre, Chicago, IL, 1947; Lieutenant Jake Goldberg, *Command Decision,* Fulton Theatre, New York City, 1947; Dan, *The Sun and I,* New Stages Theatre, New York City, 1949; Fred, *The Respectful Prostitute,* Harris Theatre, Chicago, then East Hartford Theatre, East Hartford, CT, 1949; McCarthy, *The Time of Your Life* and the Milkman, *Come Back, Little Sheba,* both Westport Country Playhouse, Westport, CT, 1949.

Joe Williamson, *The Golden State,* Fulton Theatre, 1950; Aslak, a voice, and Herr Trompetstaale, *Peer Gynt,* American National Theatre and Academy (ANTA) Theatre, New York City, 1951; Mike Mooney, *Paint Your Wagon,* Shubert Theatre, 1951; the Milkman, *Come Back, Little Sheba,* Booth Theatre, New York City, 1952; Lofty, *Seagulls Over Sorrento,* John Golden Theatre, New York City, 1952; the Delivery Man, *The Grey-Eyed People,* Martin Beck Theatre, New York City, 1952; Gordon Miller, *Room Service,* Playhouse Theatre, New York City, 1953; sailor, *Maya,* Theatre de Lys, New York City, 1953; Sir Lawrence Wargrave, *Ten Little Indians,* Cecilwood Theatre, Fishkill, NY, 1953; Mike Mooney, *Paint Your Wagon,* State Fair Music Hall, Dallas, TX, 1953; Officer Mallon, *Madam, Will You Walk?,* Phoenix Theatre, New York City, 1953; Junius Brutus, *Coriolanus,* Phoenix Theatre, 1954; Sergeant Fielding, *Too True to Be Good,* Playhouse-in-the-Park, Philadelphia, PA, 1954; Joe Rugg, *The Farmer's Hotel* and Reverend Davidson, *Rain,* both Cecilwood Theatre, 1954; Harry, *All Summer Long,* Coronet Theatre, New York City, 1954; Gus Kennedy, *Glad Tidings,* Shubert Theatre, Washington, DC, 1954; McCarthy, *The Time of Your Life* and Nathan Detroit, *Guys and Dolls,* both City Center Theatre, New York City, 1955; Captain Jonas, *House of Flowers,* Alvin Theatre, New York City, 1955; Ed Devery, *Born Yesterday,* Playhouse-in-the-Park, 1955; Don Pedro, *Much Ado about Nothing,* Brattle Shakespeare Festival, Cambridge, MA, 1955; Ed Mason, *The Wooden Dish,* Booth Theatre, 1955; Doc Earl, *Fever for Life,* Hyde Park Playhouse, Hyde Park, NY, 1957; Howard, *Miss Isobel,* Royale Theatre, New York City, 1957; Chief of Police Shultz, *The Visit,* Lunt-Fontanne Theatre, New York City, 1958; Mr. Abrams, "Portrait of a Madonna" in *Triple Play,* Playhouse Theatre, 1959; Franz, *The Sound of Music,* Lunt-Fontanne Theatre, 1959.

Recruiting officer, *Mother Courage and Her Children,* Martin Beck Theatre, 1963; Dennis Corcoran, *A Case of Libel,* Longacre Theatre, New York City, 1963; first gravedigger, *Hamlet,* New York Shakespeare Festival, Delacorte Theatre, New York City, 1964; narrator, *An Evening's Frost,* Theatre de Lys, 1965; Mickey, *After the Fall,* Playhouse-in-the-Park, 1966; Treadwell, *My Sweet Charlie,* Longacre Theatre, 1966; Hofrat Behrens, *The Magic Mountain,* Brandeis University, Waltham, MA, 1967; Judge Jerome Stern, *Little Murders,* Wilbur Theatre, Boston, MA, 1967; Art Steinmiller, *The Peddler* and Russ Nowack, *The Dodo Bird*

(double-bill), Martinique Theatre, New York City, 1967; Hofrat Behrens, *The Magic Mountain,* Camden Group Theatre, London, 1968; John Lansdale, *In the Matter of J. Robert Oppenheimer,* Center Theatre Group, Mark Taper Forum, Los Angeles, 1968; Louis, *Dance Next Door,* President of the United States, *God Bless,* and Fleming, *Line,* all Mark Taper Forum, 1969; Editor Webb, *Our Town,* ANTA Theatre, 1969, then Huntington Hartford Theatre, Los Angeles, 1970; Fleming, *Line,* Theatre de Lys, 1971; Andrew Creed, *Motive,* Playhouse-in-the-Park, 1971; Harry Brock, *Born Yesterday,* Walnut Street Theatre, Philadelphia, 1972; Charley, *Death of a Salesman,* Arlington Park Theatre, Arlington Heights, IL, 1972; Dr. Bonfant, *The Waltz of the Toreadors,* Philadelphia Drama Guild, Walnut Street Theatre, then Royal Poinciana Playhouse, Palm Beach, FL, both 1973; Mario, *Baba Goya,* American Place Theatre, New York City, 1973; Mario, *Nourish the Beast,* Cherry Lane Theatre, New York City, 1973; Charley, *Death of a Salesman,* Walnut Street Theatre, 1974; Moe and farmer, *The American Clock,* Harold Clurman Theatre, then as Moe Baum, Biltmore Theatre, both New York City, 1980; Cliff, *Back in the Race: A Family Album,* Circle Repertory Theatre, New York City, 1980; Moe and farmer, *The American Clock,* Center Theatre Group, Mark Taper Forum, 1983; juror, *Twelve Angry Men,* Henry Fonda Theatre, Los Angeles, 1985; Ben, *Broadway Bound,* Broadhurst Theatre, New York City, 1986-87. Also appeared in *My Sister Eileen* and *The Bishop Misbehaves,* both Sayville Playhouse, Sayville, NY, 1946; *Conversation at Midnight,* Billy Rose Theatre, New York City, 1964; as Andrew Creed, *Motive,* Corning, NY, and Kennebunkport, ME, both 1971; in *At the End of Long Island,* Center Theatre Group, Mark Taper Forum Laboratory Productions, 1978; *Eulogy,* Ensemble Studio Theatre, New York City, 1983.

PRINCIPAL STAGE WORK—Director, *Plant in the Sun,* Brattle Theatre, Cambridge, MA, 1938; director, *Transit* and *Plant in the Sun,* both Transit Theatre of Boston, Peabody Playhouse, Boston, MA, 1938; producer, *A Portrait of the Artist As a Young Man,* Martinique Theatre, New York City, 1962.

MAJOR TOURS—Jan Erlone, *Native Son,* U.S. cities, 1941-42; Lieutenant Jake Goldberg, *Command Decision,* U.S. cities, 1948-49; Reverend Jeremiah Brown, *Inherit the Wind,* U.S. cities, 1956-57; title role, *Macbeth,* Connecticut Theatre in Education tour of high schools, 1957; also *Our Town,* U.S. cities.

PRINCIPAL FILM APPEARANCES—Policeman, *The Naked City,* Universal, 1948; fire chief, *Fourteen Hours,* Twentieth Century-Fox, 1951; vice-president in charge of labor, *Partners in Production,* Twentieth Century Fund, 1952; Arthur Hamilton, *Seconds,* Paramount, 1966; narrator, *Like a Beautiful Child,* Local 1199, 1967; Azenauer, *Pretty Poison,* Twentieth Century-Fox, 1968; Father Harvey, *Gaily, Gaily* (also known as *Chicago, Chicago*), United Artists, 1969; Coach Jim Southerd, *Number One* (also known as *The Pro*), United Artists, 1969; Mr. Smith, *Smith,* Buena Vista, 1969; Cyrus McNutt, *There Was a Crooked Man,* Warner Brothers, 1970; chairman, *Escape from the Planet of the Apes,* Twentieth Century-Fox, 1971; Mr. Chamberlain, *Little Murders,* Twentieth Century-Fox, 1971; Mr. Victor, *The Victors,* New York University, 1971; commission chairman, *Conquest of the Planet of the Apes,* Twentieth Century-Fox, 1972; Chief Sidney Green, *Serpico,* Paramount, 1973; Mayor, *Earthquake,* Universal, 1974; as himself, *The Rehearsal* (documentary), Jules Dassin, 1974; Captain Ross, *King Kong,* Paramount, 1976; Samuel Adams, *Independence,* Twentieth Century-Fox, 1976; former team owner, *Heaven Can Wait,* Paramount, 1978; judge, *Frances,* Universal, 1982; Franklin Van Dyke, *Lovely But Deadly,* Juniper Releasing,

1983; Angelo "Pop" Partanna, *Prizzi's Honor*, Twentieth Century-Fox, 1985; Bill Henderson, *Means and Ends*, Progressive Film, 1987; Doc, *The Wizard of Loneliness*, Skouras, 1988; Clark Griswold, Sr., *National Lampoon's Christmas Vacation*, Warner Brothers, 1989. Also appeared as a disk jockey, *Night Song*, 1965; in *Homesick* (short film), 1988.

TELEVISION DEBUT—Chief Guard Jordan, *Captain Video*, Dumont, 1947. PRINCIPAL TELEVISION APPEARANCES—Series: John Hamilton, *Lucas Tanner*, NBC, 1975; Dr. Hoagland, *Lucan*, ABC, 1977-78; Randall Benson, *Angie*, ABC, 1979-80; Mr. Brockelman, *Richie Brockelman, Private Eye*, NBC, 1978; Red McGuire, *Annie McGuire*, CBS, 1988; Jacob Brofman, *Peaceable Kingdom*, CBS, 1989; Harris Weldon, *Grand*, NBC, 1990; also *Another World*, NBC, 1964-66; *As the World Turns*, CBS, 1965-66. Mini-Series: Simon Cameron, *Sandburg's Lincoln*, NBC, 1974-76; Bennett Lowman, *Washington: Behind Closed Doors*, ABC, 1977; John Mitchell, *Blind Ambition*, CBS, 1979; Mr. Johnson, *Backstairs at the White House*, NBC, 1979. Pilots: James Rockmore, *The Judge and Jake Wyler*, NBC, 1972; Judge Charles Leland, *Partners in Crime*, NBC, 1973; General Blankenship, *The New, Original Wonder Woman*, ABC, 1975; Dr. Hoagland, *Lucan*, ABC, 1977; narrator, *Nowhere to Hide*, CBS, 1977; Irv, *Doctors' Private Lives*, ABC, 1978; Lou Cohen, *Nero Wolf*, ABC, 1979; Eldon Radford, *In Security*, CBS, 1982; Mr. Muller, *The Adventures of Pollyanna*, CBS, 1982; Stevenson, *Shooting Stars*, ABC, 1983; Hank Bashaw, *The Sheriff and the Astronaut*, CBS, 1984; Phil Forbes, *Old Friends*, ABC, 1984; also *Topper Returns*, NBC, 1973; *Ann in Blue*, ABC, 1974.

Episodic: Governor, *The Senator*, NBC, 1970; Corneilius "Junior" Harrison, *The Bob Newhart Show*, CBS, 1972-76; General Philip Blankenship, *Wonder Woman*, ABC, 1975; Sy Bookerman, *Executive Suite*, CBS, 1976; Ward Beaumont, *The Facts of Life*, NBC, 1979 and 1983; Jake Keaton, *Family Ties*, NBC, 1982; Admiral John Marquette, *Emerald Point, N.A.S.*, CBS, 1983; Nick McGowan, *Our Family Honor*, ABC, 1985; Art Rutledge, *Fortune Dane*, ABC, 1986; Dr. Francis McDuffy, *Trapper John, M.D.*, CBS, 1986; Frank Vionelli, *Who's the Boss?*, ABC, 1986; Jack Rattigan, *The Equalizer*, CBS, 1987; Sam Gerard, *Matlock*, NBC, 1989; Al Harris, *Roseanne*, ABC, 1989; also *Treasury Men in Action*, NBC, 1947-49; *The Web*, CBS, 1947-49; "Bulletin 120" and "The Floyd Collins Story," *Philco Television Playhouse*, NBC, 1950; *Kraft Television Theatre*, NBC, 1950; "Mrs. McThing," *Omnibus*, CBS, 1958; *East Side/West Side*, CBS, 1963; *The Defenders*, CBS, 1964; *The Ed Sullivan Show*, CBS, 1964; *The Reporter*, CBS, 1964; "Yiddish Stories of Two Worlds," *Camera Three*, CBS, 1965; *For the People*, CBS, 1965; *The Patty Duke Show*, ABC, 1965; *Slattery's People*, CBS, 1965; *N.Y.P.D.*, ABC, 1967; "Unknown Chekhov," *Camera Three*, CBS, 1967; *Mission: Impossible*, CBS, 1967; *The Invaders*, ABC, 1967; *Mannix*, CBS, 1967, 1969, and 1973; *Judd for the Defense*, ABC, 1968; *Bonanza*, NBC, 1968, 1970, and 1972; *Hawaii Five-0*, CBS, 1969; "They're Tearing Down Tim Riley's Bar," *Night Gallery*, NBC, 1970; *Step Out of Line*, CBS, 1970; *Bracken's World*, NBC, 1970; *The Name of the Game*, NBC, 1970; *The Interns*, CBS, 1970; *The Lawyers*, NBC, 1970 and 1971; *O'Hara, U.S. Treasury*, CBS, 1971; *The Rookies*, ABC, 1972; *All in the Family*, CBS, 1972; *The Secret Storm*, CBS, 1973; *Young Dr. Kildare*, ABC, 1973; *Police Story*, NBC, 1974; *Wide World of Entertainment*, ABC, 1974; *Columbo*, NBC, 1974; *M*A*S*H*, CBS, 1979.

Movies: Smith, *The Borgia Stick*, NBC, 1967; Charles Cameron, *A Death of Innocence*, CBS, 1971; Detective John Riddle, *A Step Out of Line*, CBS, 1971; Frederick D. Cooper, *The Cable Car Murder*,

CBS, 1971; Malakas, *The Family Rico*, CBS, 1972; Lou, *Tell Me Where It Hurts*, CBS, 1974; George Collingwood, *The Runaways*, CBS, 1975; John Howe, *Adventures of the Queen*, CBS, 1975; Rupert Wahler, *F. Scott Fitzgerald in Hollywood*, ABC, 1976; Dr. John Hodges, *The Gathering*, ABC, 1977; Ed Warner, *Secrets*, ABC, 1977; General Larkin, *Tail Gunner Joe*, NBC, 1977; Judge Lewis Goodman, *Kill Me If You Can*, NBC, 1977; Alexander Graham Bell, *The Winds of Kitty Hawk*, NBC, 1978; Marian's father, *Nowhere to Run*, NBC, 1978; attorney general, *Killing at Hell's Gate*, CBS, 1981; Joseph Pulitzer, *The Adventures of Nellie Bly*, NBC, 1981; Reverend Palkstater, *Kentucky Woman*, CBS, 1983; judge, *The Execution*, NBC, 1985; Andy Williams, *Vital Signs*, CBS, 1986; Augustus Tompkins, *As Summers Die*, HBO, 1986; Chief Everett Hollander, *The Right of the People*, ABC, 1986. Specials: *My Three Brothers*, World Video, 1945; *Hands of Murder*, WARB, 1949; Reverend Brown, "Inherit the Wind," *Hallmark Hall of Fame*, NBC, 1965; Whit, *Of Mice and Men*, ABC, 1968; *Trail of Tears*, PBS, 1969; Lieutenant General Si McKee, "Pueblo," *ABC Theatre*, ABC, 1973; George Ball, *The Missiles of October*, ABC, 1974; Mario, *Nourish the Beast*, PBS, 1974; James Mayo, "Beyond the Horizon," *Theatre in America*, PBS, 1976; Judge Waites Waring, *With All Deliberate Speed*, CBS, 1976; General David Norman, *My Dissident Mom*, CBS, 1987; Justice Charles Evans Hughes and Chief Justice Earl Warren, *The Blessings of Liberty*, ABC, 1987; *Superman's Fiftieth Anniversary: A Celebration of the Man of Steel*, CBS, 1988.

PRINCIPAL RADIO APPEARANCES—Episodic: *Five Star Final*, WMCA (New York City), 1934; *Americans at Work*, CBS, 1939.

RELATED CAREER—Founder (with Frank Silvera), Transit Theatre of Boston, Boston, MA, 1938; radio announcer, WORL and WHDH, both Boston, 1938, then WHN (New York City), 1939; board of directors, Foundation for the Extension and Development of the American Theatre, 1970-72; artistic consultant, Philadelphia Drama Guild, Philadelphia, PA, 1971-74; board of directors, Theatricum Botanicum, Topanga, CA.

NON-RELATED CAREER—Vice-president, United States Society for Friendship with the German Democratic Republic, 1978-84; chairman, National Council for U.S.-Soviet Friendship, 1987-88; board of directors, Summer Solstice Celebration, Santa Barbara, CA; board of directors, National Committee Against Racist and Political Repression; board of directors, Fund for Open Information and Accountability.

WRITINGS: STAGE—(Adaptor with Phoebe Brand and Frederic Ewen) *A Portrait of the Artist As a Young Man*, Martinique Theatre, New York City, 1962; (adaptor with Brand and Ewen) *The Magic Mountain*, Brandeis University, Waltham, MA, 1967, then Camden Group Theatre, London, 1968; also (with Ewen) *The Nihilist*, unproduced. TELEVISION—(Adaptor with Brand and Ewen) "Yiddish Stories of Two Worlds," *Camera Three*, CBS, 1965; (adaptor with Brand and Ewen) "Unknown Chekhov," *Camera Three*, CBS, 1967.

AWARDS: Richard Watts's Stardust Citation from the *New York Post*, 1951, for *Come Back, Little Sheba; Cinema* magazine Award, Best Supporting Actor, 1966, for *Seconds;* Hospital Workers Union Award, 1969; Friends of a Democratic Spain Award, 1972; Paul Robeson Medal from the German Democratic Republic, 1979; Abraham Lincoln Brigade Award, 1983; Antoinette Perry Award and Drama Desk Award, both Best Featured Actor in a Play, 1987, for *Broadway Bound.*

MEMBER: Academy of Motion Picture Arts and Sciences, Actors' Equity Association (council member, 1966-72, then director), Screen Actors Guild (director, 1972-84), American Federation of Television and Radio Artists (board of directors, 1986-88), National Academy of Television Arts and Sciences, Actors Fund of America (life member), Foundation for the Extension and Development of the American Theatre (board member, 1970-72), American Civil Liberties Union, Abraham Lincoln Brigade, Hospital Workers Union.

SIDELIGHTS: RECREATIONS—Stamp collecting.

ADDRESSES: AGENT—Gores/Fields Agency, 10100 Santa Monica Boulevard, Suite 700, Los Angeles, CA 90067.*

*   *   *

RASULALA, Thalmus 1939-
(Jack Crowder)

PERSONAL: Born Jack Crowder, November 15, 1939, in Miami, FL. EDUCATION—Attended the University of Redlands.

VOCATION: Actor.

CAREER: PRINCIPAL STAGE APPEARANCES—As Jack Crowder: Member of the Lodge, *Fly Blackbird,* Mayfair Theatre, New York City, 1962; Cornelius Hackl, *Hello, Dolly!,* St. James Theatre, New York City, 1964-69; also appeared as the narrator (El Gallo), *The Fantasticks,* Sullivan Street Playhouse, New York City; and in *One Is a Crowd,* Inner City Repertory Theatre, Los Angeles, 1970.

PRINCIPAL FILM APPEARANCES—(As Jack Crowder) Police officer, *The Out of Towners,* Paramount, 1970; Gordon Thomas, *Blacula,* American International, 1972; Sidney Lord Jones, *Cool Breeze,* Metro-Goldwyn-Mayer, 1972; Robert Daniels, *Willie Dynamite,* Universal, 1973; Noah, *Adios Amigo,* Atlas, 1975; Roy, *Bucktown,* American International, 1975; Charlie, *Cornbread, Earl, and Me,* American International, 1975; Blake Tarr, *Friday Foster,* American International, 1975; Frankie Steele, *Mr. Ricco,* United Artists, 1975; George Weed, *The Last Hard Men,* Twentieth Century-Fox, 1976; Mr. Johnson, *Fun with Dick and Jane,* Columbia, 1977; coast guard officer, *The Bermuda Triangle,* Sunn Classic, 1978; the Admiral, *Born American* (also known as *Arctic Heat*), Concorde, 1986; Barney, *The Boss's Wife,* Tri-Star, 1986; Billy Dunbar, *Bulletproof,* CineTel, 1987; Deputy Superintendant Crowder, *Above the Law* (also known as *Nico*), Warner Brothers, 1988; Secret Service commander, *The Package* (also known as *Operation Crepuscle*), Orion, 1989.

PRINCIPAL FILM WORK—Assistant director, *The Slam,* Metro-Goldwyn-Mayer, 1973.

PRINCIPAL TELEVISION APPEARANCES—Series: (As Jack Crowder) Lieutenant Jack Neal, *One Life to Live,* ABC, 1969-70; Bill Thomas, *What's Happening!!,* ABC, 1976-77. Mini-Series: Omoro, *Roots,* ABC, 1977. Pilots: Crossroads, *The Jerk, Too,* NBC, 1984; Clarence, *The Circus,* ABC, 1987. Episodic: (As Jack Crowder) Real estate salesman, *All in the Family,* CBS, 1971; Aaron Kramer, *T.J. Hooker,* ABC, 1985; Lou Casey, *Cagney and Lacey,* CBS, 1985; Arthur Pick, *Simon and Simon,* CBS, 1986; Ben Cooper, *Melba,* CBS, 1986; Eddie Bender, *He's the Mayor,* ABC, 1986; Jake, *Highway to Heaven,* NBC, 1987; Ray Palmer, *Scare-*

crow and Mrs. King, CBS, 1986; Mother, *Stingray,* NBC, 1987; Ben Hargiss, *227,* NBC, 1988; Lance, *Duet,* Fox, 1988; Mason Tribes, *Simon and Simon,* CBS, 1988; Captain Donald Varley, "Contagion," *Star Trek: The Next Generation,* syndicated, 1989. Movies: Eddie Nugent, *The Bait,* ABC, 1973; Ned, *The Autobiography of Miss Jane Pittman,* CBS, 1974; Justice Sullivan, *Last Hours Before Morning,* NBC, 1975; Dr. Alvarez, *Killer on Board,* NBC, 1977; Lieutenant Gordon, *The President's Mistress,* CBS, 1978; Kenneth "Snake" Dobson, *The Sophisticated Gents,* NBC, 1981; Deputy Fred, *The Defiant Ones,* ABC, 1986; Judge Bell, *The Preppie Murder,* ABC, 1989. Specials: "The Trial of the Moke," *Great Performances,* PBS, 1978; Marshall Cook, "My Past Is My Own," *CBS Schoolbreak Special,* CBS, 1989.

RELATED CAREER—Company member, Inner City Repertory Theatre, Los Angeles, 1972-75.

AWARDS: Theatre World Award, 1968, for *Hello, Dolly!.*

ADDRESSES: AGENT—Harry Abrams, Abrams Artists, 9200 Sunset Boulevard, Suite 625, Los Angeles, CA 90069.*

*   *   *

RAY, Aldo 1926-
(Aldo DaRe)

PERSONAL: Born Aldo DaRe, September 25, 1926, in Pen Argyl, PA; son of Silvo M. and Marie T. (De Pizzol) DaRe; married Shirley Green, August, 1951 (marriage ended); married Jean Marie (Jeff) Donnell (an actress), September 30, 1954 (divorced, 1956); married Johanna Bennett (a casting director), 1960 (divorced, March 1967); children: Paul, Eric. EDUCATION—Attended University of California at Berkeley, 1946-50. MILITARY—U.S. Navy, 1944-46. POLITICS—Republican.

VOCATION: Actor.

CAREER: STAGE DEBUT—Sefton, *Stalag 17,* La Jolla Playhouse, La Jolla, CA, 1983.

FILM DEBUT—(As Aldo DaRe) Hausler, *Saturday's Hero* (also known *Idols in the Dust*), Columbia, 1950. PRINCIPAL FILM APPEARANCES—(As Aldo DaRe) Mark Foster, *The Violent Ones,* Columbia, 1951; Chet Keefer, *The Marrying Kind,* Columbia, 1952; Davie Hucko, *Pat and Mike,* Metro-Goldwyn-Mayer (MGM), 1952; Gary Stuart, *Let's Do It Again,* Columbia, 1953; Sergeant Phil O'Hara, *Miss Sadie Thompson,* Columbia, 1953; Andy, *Battle Cry,* Warner Brothers, 1955; Hugh O'Reilly, *Three Stripes in the Sun* (also known as *The Gentle Sergeant*), Columbia, 1955; Albert, *We're No Angels,* Paramount, 1955; James Vanning, *Nightfall,* Columbia, 1956; Montana, *Men in War,* United Artists, 1957; Bill Thompson, *God's Little Acre,* United Artists, 1958; Croft, *The Naked and the Dead,* Warner Brothers, 1958; Norgate, *The Day They Robbed the Bank of England,* MGM, 1960; Matt Kirk, *Four Desperate Men* (also known as *The Siege of Pinchgut*), Continental, 1960; sheriff, *Nightmare in the Sun,* Zodiac, 1964; Johnny, *Johnny Nobody,* Medallion, 1965; Jonas Karoki, *Sylvia,* Paramount, 1965; Eddie Hart, *Dead Heat on a Merry-Go-Round,* Columbia, 1966; Sergeant Rizzo, *What Did You Do in the War, Daddy?,* United Artists, 1966; Vigo, *Kill a Dragon,* United Artists, 1967; Lieutenant Walt Lorimer, *Riot on Sunset Strip,* American International, 1967; man from Bodie, *Welcome to Hard Times* (also known as *Killer on a Horse*), MGM, 1967; Sergeant Muldoon, *The Green Berets*, Warner Brothers, 1968; Bruce, *The Power*, MGM, 1968.

Sheriff, *Angel Unchained*, American International, 1970; Mattone, *La Course du lievre a travers les champs* (also known as *And Hope to Die*), Twentieth Century-Fox, 1972; Lieutenant Stans, *Tom* (also known as *Mothers, Fathers, and Lovers* and *The American Love Thing*), Four Star International, 1973; Ed Walker, *The Centerfold Girls*, General Film, 1974; Sergeant Prior, *Inside Out* (also known as *Hitler's Gold* and *The Golden Heist*), Warner Brothers, 1975; Frank Keefer, *The Man Who Would Not Die*, Centaur/Dandrea, 1975; Anderson, *Psychic Killer*, AVCO-Embassy, 1975; Dr. Dutch, *Seven Alone* (also known as *House without Windows*), Doty/Dayton, 1975; Stubby Stebbins, *Won Ton Ton, the Dog Who Saved Hollywood*, Paramount, 1976; sheriff, *Haunts* (also known as *The Veil*), Intercontinental, 1977; Nemo, *Little Moon and Jud McGraw* (also known as *Gone with the West*), Prism Entertainment, 1978; Sheriff Neal Rydholm, *Bog*, Marshall, 1978.

Prison guard, *The Glove* (also known as *Blood Mad*), Pro International, 1980; Mat Tibbs, *Human Experiments* (also known as *Beyond the Gate*), Crown International, 1980; Lew, *Boxoffice*, Josef Bogdanovich, 1982; voice of Sullivan, *The Secret of Nimh* (animated), Metro-Goldwyn-Mayer/United Artists (MGM/UA), 1982; General Randolph, *Biohazard*, Twenty-First Century, 1983; police commissioner, *The Executioner, Part II*, Twenty-First Century, 1984; Fred, *Evils of the Night*, Shapiro, 1985; Inspector Benedict, *To Kill a Stranger* (also known as *Tiempo de morir*), VCL/Media Home Entertainment, 1985; Don Siano of Bisacquino, *The Sicilian*, Twentieth Century-Fox, 1987; torturer, *Prison Ship* (also known as *Star Slammer*), Worldwide Entertainment, 1987; Fong, *Hollywood Cop*, Peacock, 1988. Also appeared in *My True Story*, Feature, 1967; *The Dynamite Brothers*, Cinemation, 1974; *Stud Brown*, Cinemation, 1975; *Terror in Alcatraz*, Trans World Entertainment, 1975; *The Bad Bunch*, Dimension, 1976; *Haunted* (also known as *The Haunted*), Northgate Communications, 1976; *Kino, the Padre on Horseback* (also known as *Mission to Glory*), Key International, 1977; *The Lucifer Complex*, Four Star Entertainment, 1978; *Death Dimension* (also known as *The Kill Factor*), Movietime, 1978; narrator, *Samuel Fuller and the Big Red One* (documentary), 1980; *Freeze Bomb*, 1980; *Straight Jacket*, Genesis Home Video, 1980; *Don't Go Near the Park*, 1981; *Mongrel*, Rondo/Sutherland/Jenkins, 1982; *The Great Skycopter Rescue*, Star Cinema Group III/MGM/UA Home Video, 1982; *Vultures in Paradise* (also known as *Vultures*), Star World/Prism Entertainment, 1984; *Frankenstein's Great Aunt Tillie*, Myron J. Gold/Video City, 1984; *Flesh and Bullets*, Hollywood International Film Corporation of America, 1985; *Star Slammer, the Escape*, Vidmark Entertainment, 1988; *Blood Red*, Hemdale Releasing, 1989; *Dark Sanity*, Prism Entertainment, 1989; *Swift Justice* (also known as *Pop's Oasis*), Trans World Entertainment, 1989.

PRINCIPAL TELEVISION APPEARANCES—Series: Voice of Muscle Mutt, *The Houndcats* (animated), NBC, 1972-73. Pilots: Louie Mastraeani, "Lollipop Louie," *Alcoa Premiere*, ABC, 1963; Edward Logan, *Deadlock*, NBC, 1969. Episodic: Hotel clerk, *Falcon Crest*, CBS, 1985; also in "K.O. Kitty," *Westinghouse Desilu Playhouse*, CBS, 1958; *The Virginian*, NBC; *Bonanza*, NBC. Movies: Cop, *Promise Him Anything . . .*, ABC, 1975; Frederick Thaler, *Women in White*, NBC, 1979. Specials: Moose, *Have Girls—Will Travel*, NBC, 1964.

NON-RELATED CAREER—Town constable, Crockett, CA, 1950-51.

AWARDS: Star of Tomorrow, 1954.

MEMBER: Screen Actors Guild, American Federation of Television and Radio Artists, American Legion.

ADDRESSES: AGENT—Mark Candiotty, Associated Talent International, 1930 Century Park W., Suite 303, Los Angeles, CA 90067.*

*   *   *

READ, James   1952-

PERSONAL: Born July 31, 1952, in Buffalo, NY.

VOCATION: Actor.

CAREER: PRINCIPAL FILM APPEARANCES—Bridge policeman, *Blue Thunder*, Columbia, 1983; Peter, *The Initiation*, New World, 1984; Lefty Williams, *Eight Men Out*, Orion, 1988; Michael Essex, *Beaches*, Buena Vista, 1988.

PRINCIPAL TELEVISION APPEARANCES—Series: Murphy Michaels, *Remington Steele*, NBC, 1982-83; John Reid, *Shell Game*, CBS, 1987. Mini-Series: Ted Kennedy, *Robert Kennedy and His Times*, CBS, 1985; George Hazard, *North and South*, ABC, 1985; George Hazard, *North and South, Book II*, ABC, 1986; Cary Grant, *Poor Little Rich Girl: The Barbara Hutton Story*, NBC, 1987. Pilots: Josh Landau, *Midas Valley*, ABC, 1985. Episodic: *Cheers*, NBC, 1982. Movies: Daryl Webster, *Lace II*, ABC, 1985; James Marston, *Celebration Family*, ABC, 1987.

RELATED CAREER—Company member, Denver Center Theatre Company, Denver, CO, 1980-81.

ADDRESSES: AGENT—Triad Artists, 10100 Santa Monica Boulevard, 16th Floor, Los Angeles, CA 90067. MANAGER—Phyllis Carlyle Management, Columbia Plaza, Producers Building 8, Room 2-B, Burbank, CA 91505.*

*   *   *

REED, Rex   1938-

PERSONAL: Full name, Rex Taylor Reed; born October 2, 1938 (some sources say 1939), in Fort Worth, TX; son of James M. (an oil company supervisor) and Jewell (Smith) Reed. EDUCATION—Louisiana State University, B.A., journalism, 1960.

VOCATION: Critic, writer, and actor.

CAREER: Also see *WRITINGS* below. PRINCIPAL FILM APPEARANCES—As himself, *Superman*, Warner Brothers, 1978; Longfellow, *Inchon*, Metro-Goldwyn-Mayer/United Artists, 1981; entertainment editor, *Irreconcilable Differences*, Warner Brothers, 1984; also appeared in *Myra Breckinridge*, Twentieth Century-Fox, 1970.

PRINCIPAL TELEVISION APPEARANCES—Series: Panelist, *The Gong Show*, syndicated, 1976-80; host, *Rex Reed's Movie Guide*, syndicated, 1980; correspondent, *Inside America*, ABC, 1982; co-host, *At the Movies,* syndicated, 1986—; also regular, *Tomorrow,* NBC. Pilots: *Hellzapoppin',* ABC, 1972. Specials: *That Was the Year That Was,* NBC, 1976; also *Judy Garland: The Concert Years,* 1985.

RELATED CAREER—Film critic, *Women's Wear Daily,* 1965-69; music critic, *Stereo Review,* 1968-75; film critic, [New York] *Daily News,* 1971-75; also film critic, *Cosmopolitan, Status, Gentleman's Quarterly, Vogue,* and *Holiday* magazines, and the *New York Post;* syndicated columnist, Chicago Tribune-New York Daily News syndicate; contributor to *Esquire, Ladies Home Journal, Harper's Bazaar, New York, Playboy,* and the *New York Times;* jury member, Berlin Film Festival, Venice Film Festival, and the U.S.A. Film Festival; lecturer.

NON-RELATED CAREER—Pancake cook, record salesman, and jazz singer, 1960-65.

WRITINGS: TELEVISION—Series: *Rex Reed's Movie Guide,* syndicated, 1980. OTHER—*Do You Sleep in the Nude?* (nonfiction), New American Library, 1968; *Conversations in the Raw* (nonfiction), World Publishing, 1970; *Big Screen, Little Screen* (nonfiction), Macmillan, 1971; *People Are Crazy Here* (nonfiction), Delacorte, 1974; *Valentines and Vitriol* (nonfiction), Delacorte, 1977; *Travolta to Keaton* (nonfiction), Morrow, 1979; *Personal Effects* (fiction), Arbor House, 1986.

ADDRESSES: OFFICE—c/o *At the Movies,* 435 N. Michigan Avenue, Suite 1829, Chicago, IL 60611. AGENT—International Creative Management, 40 W. 57th Street, New York, NY 10019.*

*   *   *

REES, Angharad   1949-

PERSONAL: Full name, Angharad Mary Rees; born in 1949 in Wales; married Christopher Cazenove (an actor), September 18, 1973; children: Linford, Rhys William.

VOCATION: Actress.

CAREER: PRINCIPAL STAGE APPEARANCES—Sibyl Vane and Duchess of Monmouth, *The Picture of Dorian Gray,* Greenwich Theatre, London, 1975; Patricia Smith, *The Millionairess,* Royal Haymarket Theatre, London, 1978.

PRINCIPAL FILM APPEARANCES—Victoria, *Catch Me a Spy,* Rank, 1971; Anna, *Hands of the Ripper,* Universal, 1971; Gossamer Benyon, *Under Milk Wood,* Altura Films International, 1973; Macha, *La Petite Fille en velours bleu* (also known as *The Little Girl in Blue Velvet*), Columbia-Warner Distributors/Felix, 1978. Also appeared in *Moments,* Pemini Organisation, 1974.

PRINCIPAL TELEVISION APPEARANCES—Series: *Close to Home,* ITV, 1989-90. Mini-Series: Demelza, *Poldark,* BBC, then *Masterpiece Theatre,* PBS, 1977; Demelza Poldark, *Poldark II,* BBC, then *Masterpiece Theatre,* PBS, 1978; Marianne, *Master of the Game,* NBC, 1984. Episodic: Katherine Gault, *Remington Steele,* NBC, 1985. Movies: Louise, *Jane Eyre,* NBC, 1971; Peggy Tracewell, *Baffled!,* NBC, 1973; Lady Evelyn Herbert, *The Curse of King Tut's Tomb,* NBC, 1980. Specials: Stella Mason, *Once the Killing Starts,* ABC, 1974; Celia, *As You Like It,* BBC, then *The*

Shakespeare Plays, PBS, 1979. Also appeared in *Anyone for Tennis?,* BBC-1, 1968.

ADDRESSES: AGENT—Smith-Freedman and Associates, 121 N. San Vicente Boulevard, Beverly Hills, CA 90211.*

*   *   *

REGALBUTO, Joe

PERSONAL: Born August 24, in Brooklyn, NY.

VOCATION: Actor.

CAREER: PRINCIPAL STAGE APPEARANCES—First Gentleman, *Measure for Measure,* New York Shakespeare Festival, Delacorte Theatre, New York City, 1976; Roger, *Division Street,* Center Theatre Group, Mark Taper Forum, Los Angeles, then Ambassador Theatre, New York City, both 1980; also appeared in *Twelfth Night,* Syracuse Stage, Syracuse, NY, 1977; *Bonjour la Bonjour,* Tyrone Guthrie Theatre, Minneapolis, MN, 1978.

PRINCIPAL FILM APPEARANCES—Chuck, *Cheaper to Keep Her,* American Cinema, 1980; Jake Schizoid, *Schizoid* (also known as *Murder By Mail*), Cannon, 1980; Henry Axle, *Honkytonk Man,* Warner Brothers, 1982; Frank Teruggi, *Missing,* Universal, 1982; Bob Crowther, *Six Weeks,* Universal, 1982; Darius, *The Sword and the Sorcerer,* Group I, 1982; Arthur Cooms, *The Star Chamber,* Twentieth Century-Fox, 1983; Breeze, *Lassiter,* Warner Brothers, 1984; Daniel Baxter, *Raw Deal,* De Laurentiis Entertainment Group, 1986; Father Doldana, *The Sicilian,* Twentieth Century-Fox, 1987. Also appeared in *The Goodbye Girl,* Warner Brothers, 1977; *Deadly Weapon,* Trans World Entertainment, 1989.

PRINCIPAL TELEVISION APPEARANCES—Series: Eliot Streeter, *The Associates,* ABC, 1979-80, then Entertainment Channel, 1982; Toomey, *Ace Crawford, Private Eye,* CBS, 1983; Harry Fisher, *Knots Landing,* CBS, 1985; Norman Tuttle, *Street Hawk,* ABC, 1985; Frank Fontana, *Murphy Brown,* CBS, 1988—. Pilots: Dr. Harwood, *Harry's Battles,* ABC, 1981; Joseph Landrum, *You Are the Jury,* NBC, 1984. Episodic: Kalnik, *Mork and Mindy,* ABC, 1982; Dad, "Fuzzbucket," *Disney Sunday Movie,* ABC, 1986; also *Barney Miller,* ABC, 1980 and 1981; *Scene of the Crime,* NBC, 1985. Movies: Barry Henry, *Divorce Wars,* ABC, 1982; Jeff Marisol, *The Other Woman,* CBS, 1983; Tom Peterson, *Invitation to Hell,* ABC, 1984; Dr. Dan, *Love Lives On,* ABC, 1985; Willie Fitz, *That Secret Sunday,* CBS, 1986; William S. Sullivan, *J. Edgar Hoover* (also known as *Hoover*), Showtime, 1987; Charlie Capute, *Fatal Judgment,* CBS, 1988; Grady Dolin, *Cop Killer,* ABC, 1988; Tom Janssen, *Prime Target,* NBC, 1989; Tony Blanchard, *The Love Boat: A Valentine Voyage,* CBS, 1990.

AWARDS: Emmy Award nomination, Outstanding Supporting Actor in a Comedy Series, 1989, for *Murphy Brown.*

ADDRESSES: AGENT—Triad Artists, 10100 Santa Monica Boulevard, 16th Floor, Los Angeles, CA 90067. MANAGER—Bobby Edrick, Edrick and Gotler Management (Artist Circle Entertainment), 8957 Norma Place, Los Angeles, CA 90069.*

REMAR, James 1953-

PERSONAL: Born December 31, 1953, in Boston, MA; wife's name Atsuko; children: Jason Kemji. EDUCATION—Studied acting at the Neighborhood Playhouse.

VOCATION: Actor.

CAREER: BROADWAY DEBUT—Wolf, *Bent,* New Apollo Theatre, 1979. OFF-BROADWAY DEBUT—*Yo-Yo,* 1977. PRINCIPAL STAGE APPEARANCES—Wesley, *Early Dark,* WPA Theatre, New York City, 1978; Pete, *California Dog Fight,* Manhattan Theatre Club, Space at City Center Theatre, New York City, 1985; also appeared in *Grease,* Paper Mill Playhouse, Millburn, NJ, 1977.

PRINCIPAL FILM APPEARANCES—Larson, *On the Yard,* Midwest Films, 1978; Ajax, *The Warriors,* Paramount, 1979; Gregory, *Cruising,* United Artists, 1980; Sam Starr, *The Long Riders,* United Artists, 1980; Windwalker as a young man, *Windwalker,* Pacific International, 1980; Edward K. Peterson, *Partners,* Paramount, 1982; Albert Ganz, *48 Hours,* Paramount, 1982; Dutch Schultz, *The Cotton Club,* Orion, 1984; Nestor, *Band of the Hand,* Tri-Star, 1986; Creb, *The Clan of the Cave Bear,* Warner Brothers, 1986; Joe Dillons, *Quiet Cool,* New Line Cinema, 1986; Dancer, *Rent-a-Cop,* Kings Road Entertainment, 1988; Gianelli, *The Dream Team,* Universal, 1989; Gentry, *Drugstore Cowboy,* Avenue Entertainment/Samuel Goldwyn, 1989; Charley, *Zwei Frauen* (also known as *Silence Like Glass*), Majestic Films International, 1989; Preston, *Tales of the Darkside,* Paramount, 1990.

PRINCIPAL TELEVISION APPEARANCES—Mini-Series: Pesla, *The Mystic Warrior,* ABC, 1984. Episodic: Robbie Can, *Miami Vice,* NBC, 1985; Douglas Tremaine, *The Equalizer,* CBS, 1987. Movies: John Sikes, *Desperado: The Outlaw Wars,* NBC, 1989.

ADDRESSES: AGENTS—Risa Shapiro and Bonnie Owens, William Morris Agency, 151 El Camino Drive, Beverly Hills, CA 90212; Katy Rotmaker, William Morris Agency, 1350 Avenue of the Americas, New York, NY 10019.

*   *   *

REMME, John 1935-

PERSONAL: Born November 21, 1935, in Fargo, ND; son of Amos Engvald and Solveig Alvina (Ingberg) Remme. EDUCATION—Attended the University of Minnesota, 1953-55.

VOCATION: Actor and singer.

CAREER: BROADWAY DEBUT—Patron in chaps, *The Ritz,* Longacre Theatre, 1975. PRINCIPAL STAGE APPEARANCES—Bill Berry, *Young Abe Lincoln,* Town Hall, New York City, 1971; ensemble, *One for the Money, Two for the Show, Three to Make Ready* (revue), Equity Library Theatre, Master Theatre, New York City, 1972; Jo, *The Royal Family,* Helen Hayes Theatre, New York City, 1976; Elmo Roper, *The Counterpart Cure,* New Dramatists Inc., New York City, 1977; waiter, policeman, and guard, *Can-Can,* Minskoff Theatre, New York City, 1981; Moonface, *Anything Goes,* Equity Library Theatre, Master Theatre, New York City, 1981; Mouse, Three of Hearts, and Tweedledee, *Alice in Wonderland,* Virginia Theatre, New York City, 1982; Patch Riley, *A Touch of the Poet,* Yale Repertory Theatre, New Haven, CT, 1983;

JOHN REMME

LeBeau and Hymen, *As You Like It,* Arena Stage, Washington, DC, 1983; Star-Man, *The Tooth of Crime,* Hartford Stage Company, Hartford, CT, 1986; King, *Jubilee,* Town Hall, 1986; Wheeler, *Teddy and Alice,* Minskoff Theatre, 1987; Mr. Goldstone, *Gypsy,* St. James Theatre, New York City, 1989-90. Also appeared as Jim, *Sunny,* Bobby, *Good News,* Rupert, *Sweet Adeline,* Wally, *Lady, Be Good,* Senator Liver P. Loganberry, *Louisiana Purchase,* and numerous other roles, all with the Goodspeed Opera House, East Haddam, CT, 1969-82; with the Pittsburgh Playhouse, Pittsburgh, PA, 1970-71; in *Funny Face,* Studio Arena Theatre, Buffalo, NY, 1973 and 1978; *The Mousetrap,* Studio Arena Theatre, 1979; and productions of *The Firefly in Concert, The Rise of David Levinsky,* and *George White's Scandals in Concert,* all in New York City.

MAJOR TOURS—Budurus, *The Rothschilds,* U.S. cities, 1972.

TELEVISION DEBUT—Jo, "The Royal Family," *Great Performances,* PBS, 1977. PRINCIPAL TELEVISION APPEARANCES—Episodic: Medical examiner, *The Equalizer,* CBS, 1988.

MEMBER: Actors' Equity Association, Screen Actors Guild, Actors Fund of America.

ADDRESSES: AGENT—Bret Adams Ltd., 448 W. 44th Street, New York, NY 10036.

REY, Fernando   1917-

PERSONAL: Born Fernando Casado Arambillet Veiga, September 20, 1917, in La Coruna, Spain; son of Fernando Casada; married Mabel Karr (an actress), 1960; children: Mabel. EDUCATION— Attended the University of Madrid School of Architecture. MILITARY—Fought in the Spanish Civil War, 1936-39.

VOCATION: Actor.

CAREER: PRINCIPAL STAGE APPEARANCES—*Las mocedades del Cid,* Teatro Espanol; also appeared in a production of *Becket,* 1968.

FILM DEBUT—*Nuestra Natacha,* 1936. PRINCIPAL FILM APPEARANCES—Don Felipe, *Locura de amor* (also known as *The Mad Queen*), 1948, released in the United States by Azteca, 1950; inspector, *Tangier Assignment,* New Realm, 1954; high priest, *The Last Days of Pompeii* (also known as *Ultimi giorni di Pompeii* and *Los ultimos dias de Pompeya*), United Artists, 1960; Valerio, *The Revolt of the Slaves* (also known as *La rivolti degli schiavi, La rebelion de los esclavos,* and *Die Sklaven Roms*), United Artists, 1961; Don Hernan, *The Savage Guns* (also known as *Tierra brutal*), Metro-Goldwyn-Mayer (MGM), 1962; Don Jaime, *Viridiana,* Kingsley International, 1962; Dr. Charles Taylor, *La cara del terror* (also known as *Face of Fear* and *Face of Terror*), 1962, released in the United States by Cinema-Video International/ Futuramic Releasing, 1964; King Ramiro II of Leon, *The Castilian* (also known as *Valley of the Swords* and *El valle de las espadas*), Warner Brothers, 1963; Sanchez, *The Ceremony* (also known as *La ceremonia*), United Artists, 1963; Bokan, *Goliath Against the Giants* (also known as *Goliath and the Giants, Goliat contra los gigantes,* and *Goliath contro i giganti*), Medallion, 1963; police official, *The Running Man,* Columbia, 1963.

Don Fortuna, *El hijo del pistolero* (also known as *Son of a Gunfighter*), 1965, released in the United States by MGM, 1966; King Philip II, *El Greco* (also known as *Le Greco*), Twentieth Century-Fox, 1966; priest, *Return of the Seven* (also known as *El regreso de los siete magnificos*), United Artists, 1966; Parson Rattigan, *Un dollaro a testa* (also known as *Navajo Joe* and *Joe, el implacable*), 1966, released in the United States by United Artists, 1967; Worcester, *Chimes at Midnight* (also known as *Falstaff* and *Campanadas a medianoche*), Peppercorn/Wormser/U-M, 1967; Marco Demoigne, *The Viscount* (also known as *Le vicomte regle ses comptes, Les Aventures du vicomte, Atraco al hampa, Las aventuras del vizconde,* and *The Viscount, Furto alla banca mondiale*), Warner Brothers, 1967; Ibram, *The Desperate Ones* (also known as *Beyond the Mountains* and *Mas alla de las montanas*), American International, 1968; Colonel Romero, *Run Like a Thief* (also known as *Robo de diamantes*), Feature, 1968; Colonel Fuentes, *Villa Rides,* Paramount, 1968; merchant, *Une histoire immortelle* (also known as *The Immortal Story*), 1968, released in the United States by Altura, 1969; King Philip II of Spain, *Les Aventures extraordinaires de Cervantes* (also known as *The Young Rebel, Cervantes,* and *Le aventure e gli amori di Miguel Cervantes*), 1968, released in the United States by American International/Commonwealth United, 1969; Quintero, *Guns of the Magnificent Seven,* United Artists, 1969.

Priest, *Land Raiders* (also known as *Day of the Landgrabbers*), Columbia, 1970; Feature, *La colera del viente* (also known as *The Wind's Anger*), Fair Film, 1970; Jaime Xenos, *The Adventurers,* Paramount, 1970; Don Lope, *Tristana,* Maron, 1970; Alain Charnier, *The French Connection,* Twentieth Century-Fox, 1971; Captain

Moriz, *The Light at the Edge of the World* (also known as *La Luz del fin del mundo*), National General, 1971; old blind farmer, *A Town Called Hell* (also known as *A Town Called Bastard*), Scotia International, 1971; Ambassador of Miranda, *Le Charme discret de la bourgeoisie* (also known as *The Discreet Charm of the Bourgeoisie*), Twentieth Century-Fox/Castle Hill, 1972; Don Rodrigo, *La Duda,* Paramount, 1972; Lepidus, *Antony and Cleopatra,* Rank, 1973; Giovanna's father, *Questa specie d'amore* (also known as *This Kind of Love*), Titanus Distribuzione, 1973; Mage, *La Chute d'un corps* (also known as *Fall of a Body*), Albina, 1973; chief physician, *Bianco, rosso, e . . .* (also known as *The Sin, White Sister,* and *White, Red, and . . .*), Columbia/Warner Brothers, 1973; Jacques, *Dites-le avec des fleurs* (also known as *Say It with Flowers*), Gaumont, 1974; Vanini, *Corruzione al Palazzo di Giustizia* (also known as *Corruption in the Halls of Justice*), Istituto Luce Italnoleggio Cinematografio, 1974; Augusto Murri, *Fatti di gente perbene* (also known as *Drama of the Rich, La Grande bourgeoise,* and *Fate genti perbene*), Production Artistique Cinematographique/ Curzon Film Distributors, 1974; Perrot, *La Femme aux bottes rouges* (also known as *The Woman with Red Boots*), Union Generale Cinematographique/Sirius, 1974, released in the United States by Gamma III, 1977.

Alain Charnier, *The French Connection II,* Twentieth Century-Fox, 1975; Minister of Justice, *Cadaveri eccellenti* (also known as *Illustrious Corpses* and *The Context*), Cinegate, 1975, released in the United States by United Artists, 1976; Nathanson, *Le Desert des Tartares* (also known as *The Desert of the Tartars*), Gaumont, 1976; Charles Van Maar, *A Matter of Time* (also known as *Nina*), American International, 1976; Pedro, *Pasqualino settebellezze* (also known as *Seven Beauties* and *Pasqualino: Seven Beauties*), Cinema V, 1976; President Bru of Cuba, *Voyage of the Damned,* AVCO-Embassy, 1976; Augusto Murri, *La Grande Bourgeoise* (also known as *The Murri Affair*), Atlantic/Buckley Brothers, 1977; Bidarra, *Uppdraget* (also known as *The Assignment*), Svenska Filminstitutet, 1977; Mathieu, *Cet obscur objet du desir* (also known as *That Obscure Object of Desire*), First Artists, 1977; Cardinal, *El segundo poder* (also known as *The Second Power*), Oteo Films/CB Films, 1977; father, *Elisa, vida mia* (also known as *Elisa, My Love*), Interama, 1977; Max, *Le Dernier amant romantique* (also known as *The Last Romantic Lover*), World Marketing/ Columbia/Warner Brothers, 1978; Grigor, *Quintet,* Twentieth Century-Fox, 1979.

Teredo, *Caboblanco,* AVCO-Embassy, 1980; Count Stechelberg, *Cera storia della Signora delle Camilie* (also known as *The True Story of Camille*), Gaumont, 1981; Cardinal Santoni, *Monsignor,* Twentieth Century-Fox, 1982; Don Andre, *La Straniera* (also known as *The Stranger*), VO Films, 1982; Antonio, *Bearn* (also known as *La Sala de las Munecas*), Alfredo Matas/Ecran Sud/ Films du Semaphore, 1982; chief inspector, *The Hit,* Island Alive, 1984; Piachi, *Una strana passione/Nicolo ou l'enfant trouve* (also known as *A Strange Passion* and *Nicole ou l'enfant trouve*), World Marketing, 1984; railroad colonel, *Rustler's Rhapsody,* Paramount, 1985; cardinal, *Padre Nuestro* (also known as *Our Father*), International Film Exchange/Heritage Entertainment/Classic, 1985; Fray Lupo, *El caballero del dragon* (also known as *The Knight of the Dragon* and *Star Knight*), CineTel/Manson International, 1986; Cardinal Stefano Biondi, *Saving Grace,* Columbia, 1986; Joseph Goldman, *Hotel du paradis,* Umbrella Films/Global Distribution, 1987; Admiral Comesana, *Mi general* (also known as *My General, Educating the Generals,* and *Yes, General*), Figaro/Television Espanola, 1987; Don Nuno, *Pasodoble* (also known as *Two-Step*), Tesauro, 1988; Allende, *El tunel* (also known as *The Tunnel*), Hemdale Releasing/Interaccess Film Distribution, 1988; father,

Diario de invierno (also known as *A Winter's Diary*), United International/Radiotelevision Espanola, 1988; Alejandro, *Moon Over Parador*, Universal, 1988.

Also appeared in *La gitanilla*, 1940; *Los cuatro Robinsones*, 1940; *Eugenia de Montijo*, 1944; *El rey que rabio*, 1944; *Los ultimos de Filipinas*, 1945; *Mision blanca*, 1945; *Tierra sedienta*, 1945; *La prodiga*, 1946; as Sanson Carrasco, *Don Quixote de la Mancha*, 1947; in *Reina Santa*, 1947; *La Princesa de los Ursinos*, 1947; *Fuentovejuna*, 1947; *Noche de Reyes*, 1947; *Si te hubieses casado con migo*, 1948; *Las aventuras de Juan Lucas*, 1949; *Augustina de Aragon*, 1950; *Mare nostrum*, 1950; *Cielo negro*, 1951; *La Senora de Fatima*, 1951; *Esa pareja feliz*, 1951; *Bienvenido, Mr. Marshall* (also known as *Welcome Mr. Marshall*), 1952; *Comicos*, 1952; *La laguna negra*, 1952; *Rebeldia*, 1953; *El alcalde de Zalamea*, 1953; *Aeropuerto*, 1953; *Cabaret*, 1953; *Marcelino, pan y vino*, 1954; *Un marido de ida y vuelta*, 1955; as Don Juan, *El amor de Don Juan*, 1956; Brother Moderno, *Marcelino*, 1956; Don Inigo, *Pantaloons*, 1956; in *Faustina*, 1956; *Una aventura de Gil Blas*, 1956; as Forastero, *La vanganza*, 1957; in *Les Bijoutiers au clair de lune* (also known as *Heaven Fell That Night*), 1957; *Culpables*, 1958; *Les habitantes de la casa deshabitada*, 1958; *Parque de Madrid*, 1958; as Casares, *Sonatas*, 1959; in *Operacion Relampage*, 1959; *Las dos y media y venuno*, 1959; *Nacido para la musica* (also known as *Ne pour la musique*), 1959.

Fabiola, 1960; *Don Lucio y el harmano pio*, 1960; *A las cinco de la tarde*, 1960; *Teresa de Jesus*, 1960; *Rogelia*, 1962; as painter, *El espontanes*, 1963; in *Dios eligio sus viajeros*, 1963; *Scheherazade* (also known as *La schiava di Baghdad*), 1963, released in the United States by Shawn International, 1965; *Los palomas*, 1964; *El senor de la salle*, 1964; *La nueva cenicienta*, 1964; *Echappement libre* (also known as *Backfire*), 1964, released in the United States by Royal Films International, 1965; *Espana insolita*, 1965; *Mision Lisboa*, 1965; *Zampo y yo*, 1965; *Cartas boca arriba* (also known as *Cards on the Table*), 1965; *The Amazing Dr. G.*, 1965; *Toto de Arabia* (also known as *Toto d'Arabia*), 1965; *Due mafiosi contro Goldginger* (also known as *Dos de la Mafia*), 1965; *Dulcinea del Toboso*, 1966; *Das Vermachtnis des Inka*, 1966; *Los jueces de la Biblia*, 1966; *Don Quixote*, 1966; *Attack of the Robots*, American International, 1967; as Saldiez, *Amor en el aire*, 1967; in *The Price of Power* (also known as *Il prezzo del potere*), Films Montana, 1969; *Fellini Satyricon* (also known as *Satyricon*), United Artists, 1969; *Candidato per un assassino* (also known as *Un sudario a la medida* and *Candidate for a Killing*), 1969.

Companeros (also known as *Vamos a matar, companeros!*), TerraFilmkunst, 1970; *Muerte de un presidente*, 1970; *Histoira de una traicion*, 1970; *Los frios ojos miedo*, 1970; *Coartada en disco rojo* (also known as *I due volti della paura*), 1970; *Chicas de club*, 1972; *One Way* (also known as *Senso unico*), 1973; *Zanna bianca*, 1973; *La polizia incrimina, la legge assolve*, 1973; *Tarot*, 1973; *Pena de muerte*, 1973; *El mejor alcalde, el Rey*, 1973; *Le Fantome de la liberte* (also known as *The Phantom of Liberty*), Twentieth Century-Fox, 1974; *Strip-Tease*, 1976; *Le Grand embouteillage* (also known as *L'ingorgo, Bottleneck*, and *The Traffic Jam*), CineTel/Titanus Distribuzione, 1978; *Cercasi Gesu* (also known as *Jesus Wanted*), Intercontinental, 1982; *El bosque animado* (also known as *The Enchanted Forest, La Foret animee*, and *The Animated Forest*), Radiotelevision Espanola/Colifilms/Classic, 1987; *Les Predateurs de la nuit* (also known as *Faceless, L'Ange de la mort, Angel of Death*, and *Commando Mengele*), New World/World Marketing, 1987; *Esmeralda Bay*, Eurocine, 1988; *El Aire de un crimen* (also known as *The Hint of a Crime*), Isasi Productions Cinematografica/Televisio de Catalunya, 1988; *Hard to Be a God*

(also known as *Es ist nicht leicht ein gott zu sein* and *E' difficile essere un dio*), Union Generale Cinematographique/Titanus Distribuzione/Jugendfilm Verleigh, 1989.

PRINCIPAL TELEVISION APPEARANCES—Mini-Series: Gaspar, *Jesus of Nazareth*, NBC, 1977; Seneca, *A.D.*, NBC, 1985. Movies: Earl of Warwick, *Black Arrow*, Disney Channel, 1985; Sir Edward Hawke, *Captain Cook*, TNT, 1989.

RELATED CAREER—Member, Francisco Melgarae's theatre company; dubbed dialogue of foreign films into Spanish before becoming an actor.

AWARDS: Best Actor Award from the Cannes Film Festival, 1977, for *Elisa, My Love;* Knight of Arts and Letters (France), 1986.

ADDRESSES: OFFICE—Avenida Habana 19, Madrid, Spain. AGENT—The Kohner Agency Inc., 9169 Sunset Boulevard, Los Angeles, CA 90069.*

*   *   *

RHOADES, Barbara 1947-

PERSONAL: Born March 23, 1947, in Poughkeepsie, NY.

VOCATION: Actress.

CAREER: PRINCIPAL STAGE APPEARANCES—Showgirl, *Funny Girl*, Winter Garden Theatre, New York City, 1964.

PRINCIPAL FILM APPEARANCES—Kendall Flanagan, *Don't Just Stand There*, Universal, 1968; Penelope Cushings, *The Shakiest Gun in the West*, Universal, 1968; Miss Jessie Brundidge, *There Was a Crooked Man*, Warner Brothers, 1970; Dr. Boden, *Up the Sandbox*, National General, 1972; Elaine, *Scream Blacula Scream*, American International, 1973; happy hooker, *Harry and Tonto*, Twentieth Century-Fox, 1974; Hadley, *The Choirboys*, Universal, 1977; Donna Douglas, *The Goodbye Girl*, Metro-Goldwyn-Mayer/Warner Brothers, 1977; Vivian, *Serial*, Paramount, 1980. Also appeared in *Out Cold*, Hemdale, 1989.

PRINCIPAL TELEVISION APPEARANCES—Series: Melody Feebeck, *Busting Loose*, CBS, 1977; women's coach, *Celebrity Challenge of the Sexes*, CBS, 1978; Maggie Gallagher, *Hanging In* (also known as *Mr. Dugan*), CBS, 1979 (never broadcast); Maggie Chandler, *Soap*, ABC, 1980-81; Maggie Davis, *You Again?*, NBC, 1986-87; Jessica Gardner, *Generations*, NBC, 1989—. Pilots: Chloe Jones, *The Judge and Jake Wyler*, NBC, 1972; girl, *Hunter*, CBS, 1973; Marnie, *Police Story*, NBC, 1973; Barbara, *Punch and Jody*, NBC, 1974; Helen Horowitz, *Conspiracy of Terror*, NBC, 1975; Carrie Williamson, *The Blue Knight*, CBS, 1975; Angela Swoboda, *Crime Club*, CBS, 1975; Sheila Rainier, *Twin Detectives*, ABC, 1976; Kate Peterson, *The Bureau*, NBC, 1976; Dinah, *Tabitha*, ABC, 1976; DeeDee Fields, *The Day the Women Got Even*, NBC, 1980; Nurse Ruth O'Malley, *Venice Medical*, ABC, 1983; also *Scene of the Crime*, NBC, 1985.

Episodic: Britte Martin, *Stone*, ABC, 1980; Dr. Polly Toledo, *Trapper John, M.D.*, CBS, 1985; Dr. Dorothy Harcroft, *Simon and Simon*, CBS, 1985; Lieutenant Leslie Lynch, *Crazy Like a Fox*, CBS, 1985; Flo Oakes, *Murder, She Wrote*, CBS, 1988; Linda Steadman, *thirtysomething*, ABC, 1988; Barbara Sterling, *Booker*,

Fox, 1990; Daphne Dumont, *Father Dowling Mysteries*, NBC, 1990; also *Ironside*, NBC, 1967; *The Virginian*, NBC, 1968; *It Takes a Thief*, ABC, 1968; *Mannix*, CBS, 1968; *The Partridge Family*, ABC, 1970; *Griff*, ABC, 1973; *Kojak*, CBS, 1973; *McMillan and Wife*, NBC, 1973; *Toma*, ABC, 1973 and 1974; *Happy Days*, ABC, 1974; *Mannix*, CBS, 1974; *Nakia*, ABC, 1974; *Lucas Tanner*, NBC, 1975; *The Six Million Dollar Man*, ABC, 1975; *Joe Forrester*, NBC, 1975; *Ellery Queen*, NBC, 1975; *Harry O*, ABC, 1976; *Switch*, CBS, 1976; *Serpico*, NBC, 1976; *Sanford and Son*, NBC, 1976; *Police Story*, NBC, 1976; *New Love, American Style*, ABC, 1985; *Bewitched*, ABC; "Love and the Unlikely Couple" and "Love and the Amateur Night," both *Love, American Style*, ABC; *The Odd Couple*, ABC; *Rhoda*, CBS; *What's Happening!*, ABC. Movies: Hostess, *The Silent Gun*, ABC, 1969; Marge, *What Are Best Friends For?*, ABC, 1973; Margery Crandon, *The Great Houdini*, ABC, 1976; Paula, *Sex and the Single Parent*, CBS, 1979; Paula Picasso, *Side Show*, NBC, 1981; Denise, *Picking Up the Pieces*, CBS, 1985; Mrs. Bundy, *Double Switch*, ABC, 1987. Specials: *The Paul Lynde Comedy Hour*, ABC, 1975; *National Love, Sex, and Marriage Test*, NBC, 1978.*

*   *   *

RHUE, Madlyn   1934-

PERSONAL: Born Madeline Roche, October 3, 1934, in Washington, DC.

VOCATION: Actress.

CAREER: PRINCIPAL FILM APPEARANCES—Lieutenant Claire Reid, *Operation Petticoat*, Universal, 1959; Alice Black, *A Majority of One*, Warner Brothers, 1961; Laila, *Escape from Zahrain*, Paramount, 1962; police secretary, *It's a Mad, Mad, Mad, Mad World*, United Artists, 1963; Ellie Daniels, *He Rides Tall*, Universal, 1964; Ana Suya, *Kenner* (also known as *Year of the Cricket*), Metro-Goldwyn-Mayer, 1969; Gloria Seagar, *Stand Up and Be Counted*, Columbia, 1972; also appeared in *The Ladies Man*, Paramount, 1961.

PRINCIPAL TELEVISION APPEARANCES—Series: Marjorie Grant, *Bracken's World*, NBC, 1969-70; Hilary Madison, *Executive Suite*, CBS, 1976-77; Daphne DiMera, *Days of Our Lives*, NBC, 1982-84; Annie, *Houston Knights*, CBS, 1987-88; judge, *Trial By Jury*, syndicated, 1989-90. Pilots: Frances Emerson, *Poor Devil*, NBC, 1973; Mrs. Doran, *Medical Story*, NBC, 1975.

Episodic: Lieutenant Marla McGivers, "Space Seed," *Star Trek*, NBC, 1967; Shirley, *Bridges to Cross*, CBS, 1986; Doris West, *Murder, She Wrote*, CBS, 1989; also *Adventures in Paradise*, ABC, 1961; *Hong Kong*, ABC, 1961; *Bus Stop*, ABC, 1961; *Cain's Hundred*, NBC, 1962; *The Third Man*, NBC, 1962; *Route 66*, CBS, 1962; *The Nurses*, CBS, 1963; "The Dark Pool," *Alfred Hitchcock Theatre*, CBS, 1963; *Rawhide*, CBS, 1963; "Man Without a Witness," *Mystery Theatre*, NBC, 1963; *Arrest and Trial*, ABC, 1963; *The Virginian*, NBC, 1963; *The Lieutenant*, NBC, 1963; *Espionage*, NBC, 1964; "The Game with Glass Pieces," *Bob Hope Chrysler Theatre*, NBC, 1964; *The Man from U.N.C.L.E.*, NBC, 1964 and 1967; *Daniel Boone*, NBC, 1965; *The Defenders*, CBS, 1965; *Slattery's People*, CBS, 1965; *I Spy*, NBC, 1965; *Shenandoah*, ABC, 1965; *Laredo*, NBC, 1966; *The Fugitive*, ABC, 1966; *The Iron Horse*, ABC, 1966; *Captain Nice*, NBC, 1967; *Wild, Wild West*, CBS, 1967; *Ironside*, NBC, 1967, 1971,

1973, and 1974; *Cowboy in Africa*, ABC, 1968; *It Takes a Thief*, ABC, 1968; *The Guns of Will Sonnett*, ABC, 1968; *Mannix*, CBS, 1969, 1972, and 1975; *The Land of the Giants*, ABC, 1970; *Hawaii Five-0*, CBS, 1970 and 1973; *Men from Shiloh*, NBC, 1971; *Longstreet*, ABC, 1971; *Banacek*, NBC, 1972; *Mission: Impossible*, CBS, 1972; *Ghost Story*, NBC, 1972; *Barnaby Jones*, CBS, 1973; *Owen Marshall, Counselor at Law*, ABC, 1973; *Cannon*, CBS, 1974 and 1976; *The Night Stalker*, ABC, 1974; *Police Story*, NBC, 1975; *Baretta*, ABC, 1975; *Petrocelli*, NBC, 1975; *Switch*, CBS, 1975; *Starsky and Hutch*, ABC, 1976; *Streets of San Francisco*, ABC, 1976; "Six Characters in Search of an Author," *Hollywood Television Theatre*, PBS, 1976; Lucy, *Dynasty*, ABC; Charlotte Schwartz, *Fame*, NBC.

Movies: Alma Britten, *Stranger on the Run*, NBC, 1967; Joy Hudson, *The Sex Symbol*, ABC, 1974; Teresa Taylor, *The Manhunter*, NBC, 1976; Marsha Miller, *Goldie and the Boxer*, NBC, 1979; Emily Stockwood, *The Best Place to Be*, NBC, 1979; Rebecca, *Fantasies*, ABC, 1982; Elaine Porter, *Games Mother Never Taught You*, CBS, 1982.

NON-RELATED CAREER—Painter.

ADDRESSES: AGENT—Crickett Haskell, J. Carter Gibson Agency, 9000 Sunset Boulevard, Suite 801, Los Angeles, CA 90069.*

*   *   *

RICHMAN, Mark
See RICHMAN, Peter Mark

*   *   *

RICHMAN, Peter Mark   1927-
(Mark Richman)

PERSONAL: Born Marvin Jack Richman, April 16, 1927, in Philadelphia, PA; assumed spiritual first name, Peter, 1971; son of Benjamin (an interior house contractor) and Yetta Dora (Peck) Richman; married Helen Theodora Landess (an actress), May 10, 1953; children: Howard Bennett, Kelly Allyn, Lucas Dion, Orien, Roger Lloyd. EDUCATION—Philadelphia College of Pharmacy and Science, B.S., pharmacy, ,1951; studied acting with Lee Strasberg, 1952-54. MILITARY—U.S. Navy, 1945-46.

VOCATION: Actor.

CAREER: OFF-BROADWAY DEBUT—(As Mark Richman) Larrence Corger, *End As a Man*, Theatre De Lys, 1953. BROADWAY DEBUT—(As Mark Richman) Larrence Corger, *End As a Man*, Vanderbilt Theatre, 1953. PRINCIPAL STAGE APPEARANCES—All as Mark Richman, unless indicated: Billy, *This Happy Breed*, Philadelphia Neighborhood Players, Philadelphia, PA, 1947; title role, *Liliom*, Philadelphia Neighborhood Players, 1949; Jarvis Addams, *The Member of the Wedding*, Alvaro Mangiacavallo, *The Rose Tattoo*, Ben Goodman, *Remains To Be Seen*, Horace William Dodd, *Season in the Sun*, Owen O'Malley, *Twentieth Century*, Clark Wilson, *Twilight Walk*, Matt Burke, *Anna Christie*, Eliot, *Private Lives*, Charles Steward, *Gramercy Ghost*, Sinclair Heybore, *Fancy Meeting You Again*, and Steve, *Pretty Lady*, all Grove Theatre, Nuangola, PA, 1952; Stefanowski, *Mister Roberts* and Joe

PETER MARK RICHMAN

Feinson, *Detective Story,* both Westchester Playhouse, Mt. Kisco, NY, 1953; the Gentleman Caller, *The Glass Menagerie,* Mr. Manningham, *Angel Street,* Harry Binion, *Room Service,* and Charles Grant, *The Family Upstairs,* all Guthsville Playhouse, Guthsville, PA, 1954; Channon, *The Dybbuk,* Fourth Street Theatre, New York City, 1954; Johnny Pope, *A Hatful of Rain,* Lyceum Theatre, New York City, 1956; Sergius, *Arms and the Man,* Drury Lane Theatre, Chicago, IL, 1957; Jimmy Porter, *Look Back in Anger,* Atlantic Beach Playhouse, NJ, 1959; Ralph Glenville, *Masquerade,* John Golden Theatre, New York City, 1959.

Jerry, *The Zoo Story,* Provincetown Playhouse, New York City, 1960-61; David, *Write Me a Murder,* Ogunquit Playhouse, ME, then Cape Playhouse, Dennis, MA, both 1962; Glen Griffin, *The Desperate Hours,* Deertrees Theatre, Harrison, ME, 1962; Senator Joe Cantwell, *The Best Man,* Playhouse-in-the Park, Philadelphia, PA, 1962; Joe Garfield, *Have I Got a Girl for You!,* Biltmore Theatre, Los Angeles, 1963; Shannon, *The Night of the Iguana,* Playhouse-in-the-Park, 1963; the Doctor, *The Deputy,* Theatre Group, University of California, Los Angeles, 1965; Nicky Arnstein, *Funny Girl,* Sacramento Music Circus, Sacramento, CA, 1967; (as Peter Mark Richman) Dysart, *Equus,* Mary Moody Northern Theatre, Austin, TX, 1982; (as Peter Mark Richman) Charles, *Blithe Spirit,* Lobero Theatre, Santa Barbara, CA, 1984; (as Peter Mark Richman) juror, *Twelve Angry Men,* Henry Fonda Theatre, Los Angeles, 1985; (as Peter Mark Richman) Barnaby, *Babes in Toyland,* Pasadena Civic Auditorium, then Orange County Performing Arts Center, Costa Mesa, CA, both 1988. Also appeared in *Lo and Behold* and *Apron Strings,* both Grove Theatre, 1952; (as Peter Mark Richman) *The Owl and the Pussycat,* Atlanta, GA, 1977; (as

Peter Mark Richman) *Hold Me,* Westwood Playhouse, Los Angeles, 1977; *Heartbreak House,* summer theatre production.

PRINCIPAL STAGE WORK—(As Mark Richman) Director, *Apple of His Eye* and *The Glass Menagerie,* both Guthsville Playhouse, Guthsville, PA, 1954.

MAJOR TOURS—All as Mark Richman: Mannion, *Mister Roberts,* U.S. cities, 1954; File, *The Rainmaker,* U.S. cities, 1955; Johnny Pope, *A Hatful of Rain,* U.S. cities, 1956-57; also *Arms and the Man,* U.S. cities, 1957.

FILM DEBUT—(As Mark Richman) Gardner Jordan, *Friendly Persuasion,* Allied Artists, 1956. PRINCIPAL FILM APPEARANCES— All as Mark Richman, unless indicated: Cadet Colonel Corger, *The Strange One* (also known as *End As a Man*), Columbia, 1957; Lieutenant Bill Hanley, *Girls on the Loose,* Universal, 1958; Noble, *Black Orchid,* Paramount, 1959; Robert Vandenburg, *Dark Intruder,* Universal, 1965; Adam Chance, *Agent for H.A.R.M.,* Universal, 1966; Gerald Pryor, *For Singles Only,* Universal, 1968; (as Peter Mark Richman) Colonel Brigg, *Conquest of the Earth,* Universal, 1980; (as Peter Mark Richman) Sam, *Judgment Day,* Rockport, 1989; (as Peter Mark Richman) Charles McCulloch, *Friday the 13th Part VII: Jason Takes Manhattan,* Paramount, 1989; also appeared (as Peter Mark Richman) in *The Third Hand,* Interfilm-Colombia Ltd., 1988.

TELEVISION DEBUT—(As Mark Richman) *Papa Pietro's Place,* WPTZ (Philadelphia, PA), 1950. PRINCIPAL TELEVISION APPEARANCES—As Peter Mark Richman, unless indicated. Series: (As Mark Richman) Nicholas "Nick" Cain, *Cain's Hundred,* NBC, 1961-62; Duke Paige, *Longstreet,* ABC, 1971-72; Pharoah, *Electra Woman and Dyna Girl,* ABC, 1976-77; Andrew Laird, *Dynasty,* ABC, 1981-84; Channing "C.C." Capwell, *Santa Barbara,* NBC, 1984; also voice of God, *Greatest Stories of the Bible,* 1979; voice of the Phantom, *Defenders of the Earth* (animated), 1986. Mini-Series: Robert Mardian, *Blind Ambition,* CBS, 1979. Pilots. (As Mark Richman) Sal Gilman, *The House on Greenapple Road,* ABC, 1970; (as Mark Richman) Chief Peter B. Clifford, *McCloud: Who Killed Miss USA?* (also known as *Portrait of a Dead Girl*), NBC 1970; Major Lucas, *Yuma,* ABC, 1971; John Shields, *Mallory: Circumstantial Evidence,* NBC, 1976; Lieutenant Larkin, *The Islander,* CBS, 1978.

Episodic: (As Mark Richman) Ian Frazer, "The Borderland," *The Outer Limits,* ABC, 1963; (as Mark Richman) Jefferson Rome, "The Probe," *The Outer Limits,* ABC, 1965; Sam, *Vega$,* ABC, 1980; Frank, *The Fall Guy,* ABC, 1982; Dr. Donald Rafelman, *Crazy Like a Fox,* CBS, 1985; Kleist, *Knight Rider,* NBC, 1985; Bennett, *Murder, She Wrote,* CBS, 1986; Ross Paterno, *T.J. Hooker,* CBS, 1986; Roy Barlow, *Hardcastle and McCormick,* ABC, 1986; Dr. Lyman, *Hotel,* ABC, 1988; Smythe, *Supercarrier,* ABC, 1988; Ralph Offenhouse, "Neutral Zone," *Star Trek . . . The Next Generation,* syndicated, 1988; Adam Whitley, *Matlock,* NBC, 1989; also as Mark Richman: "Star in the Night," *Goodyear Playhouse,* NBC, 1954; "Middle of the Night," *Philco Playhouse,* NBC, 1954; "Backfire," *Goodyear Playhouse,* NBC, 1955; "The Bold and the Brave," *Philco Playhouse,* NBC, 1955; "The Center of the Maze," *Playwrights '56,* NBC, 1956; "The Partners," *U.S. Steel Hour,* NBC, 1956; "Sheriff's Man," *Kraft Theatre,* NBC, 1957; "The House," *Goodyear Playhouse,* NBC 1957; "Roadblock Number Seven," *Jane Wyman Theatre,* NBC, 1957; "The Last Man," *Playhouse 90,* CBS, 1958; "Home Again," *Schlitz Playhouse of Stars,* 1958; "Death Wears Many Faces," *Kraft Theatre,* NBC, 1958; "Man with a Problem," *Alfred Hitchcock*

Presents, CBS, 1958; "Mission to Marathon," *Zane Grey Theatre* (also known as *Dick Powell's Zane Grey Theatre*), CBS, 1959; "Ruth and Naomi," *The June Allyson Show*, CBS, 1959; "The Hours Before Dawn" and "Act of Terror," *U.S. Steel Hour*, CBS, 1959; *Hotel de Paree*, CBS, 1959.

As Mark Richman: "The Cure," *Alfred Hitchcock Presents*, CBS, 1960; "Fire By Night," *Moment of Fear*, NBC, 1960; "Emmanuel," *Play of the Week*, PBS, 1960; "Therese Raquin," *Play of the Week*, syndicated, 1961; "Shame of Paula Marsten," *U.S. Steel Hour*, CBS, 1961; "You Can't Escape," *U.S. Steel Hour*, CBS, 1962; *Stoney Burke*, ABC, 1963; "Crack in an Image," *Breaking Point*, ABC, 1963; *The Virginian*, NBC, 1963; *Ben Casey*, ABC, 1963; *Combat*, ABC, 1964; *The Virginian*, NBC, 1964; *The Fugitive*, ABC, 1964; *Profiles in Courage*, NBC, 1965; *The F.B.I.*, ABC, 1965; *The Wild, Wild West*, CBS, 1965; *Twelve O'Clock High*, ABC, 1965; *Combat*, ABC, 1966; *Voyage to the Bottom of the Sea*, ABC, 1966; *Blue Light*, ABC, 1966; *The Fugitive*, ABC, 1966; *T.H.E. Cat*, NBC, 1966; *The Loner*, CBS, 1966; *Jericho*, CBS, 1966; *The Virginian*, NBC, 1967; *The Iron Horse*, ABC, 1967; *Daniel Boone*, NBC, 1967; *Ironside*, NBC, 1967; *The Man from U.N.C.L.E.*, NBC, 1968; *It Takes a Thief*, ABC, 1968; *Gunsmoke*, CBS, 1968; *The Invaders*, ABC, 1968; *The F.B.I.*, ABC, 1968; *The Name of the Game*, NBC, 1968; *Bonanza*, NBC, 1968; *My Friend Tony*, NBC, 1969; *It Takes a Thief*, ABC, 1969; *Insight*, syndicated, 1969; *Hawaii Five-0*, CBS, 1969; *Lancer*, CBS, 1969; *The Name of the Game*, NBC, 1969.

As Peter Mark Richman, unless indicated: (As Mark Richman) *Mannix*, CBS, 1970; (as Mark Richman) *Mission: Impossible*, CBS, 1970; (as Mark Richman) *The F.B.I.*, ABC, 1970; (as Mark Richman) *Silent Force*, ABC, 1970; *Men from Shiloh*, NBC, 1971; *Yuma*, ABC, 1971; *The F.B.I.*, ABC, 1971 and 1972; *Mission: Impossible*, CBS, 1972; *Marcus Welby, M.D.*, ABC, 1973; *Search*, NBC, 1973; *The New Adventures of Perry Mason*, CBS, 1973; *The Streets of San Francisco*, ABC, 1973; *Hawkins*, CBS, 1974; *Police Story*, NBC, 1974; *The F.B.I.*, ABC, 1974; "Nightmare at 43 Hillcrest," *Wide World of Mystery*, ABC, 1974; *Get Christie Love!*, ABC, 1974; *Barnaby Jones*, CBS, 1974; *McCloud*, NBC, 1974; *Ironside*, NBC, 1974; *Caribe*, ABC, 1975; *Petrocelli*, NBC, 1975; *Police Story*, NBC, 1975 and 1976; *Barnaby Jones*, CBS, 1976; *Switch*, CBS, 1976; *Cannon*, CBS, 1976; *Bert D'Angelo, Superstar*, ABC, 1976; *Baretta*, ABC, 1976; *Family*, ABC, 1976; *Dog and Cat*, ABC, 1977; Reverend Luther Snow, *Three's Company*, ABC, 1977; (as Mark Richman) *The Twilight Zone*, CBS; (as Mark Richman) *Suspense*, CBS; (as Mark Richman) *Studio One*, CBS; (as Mark Richman) *Camera Three*, CBS; (as Mark Richman) *Rawhide*, CBS; *Apple's Way*, CBS; *The Young Lawyers*, ABC; *Banacek*, NBC; *Medical Story*, NBC; *Quincy, M.E.*, NBC; *Sword of Justice*, NBC; *Starsky and Hutch*, ABC; *Fantasy Island*, ABC; *The Love Boat*, ABC; *Finder of Lost Loves*, ABC; *Hart to Hart*, ABC; *B.J. and the Bear*, NBC; *Lobo*, NBC; *The Incredible Hulk*, CBS; *240-Robert*, ABC; *The Six Million Dollar Man*, ABC; *Dallas*, CBS; *The Bionic Woman*, ABC; *Seaways*, Canadian television; *Wonder Woman*; *The Ted Knight Show*; *The Lutheran Hour*; and (as Mark Richman) *Armstrong Circle Theatre*.

Movies: Tex Rickard, *Dempsey*, CBS, 1983; Lieutenant Walling, *City Killer*, NBC, 1984; Cele Dunston, *Bonanza . . . The Next Generation*, syndicated, 1988; also *The PSI Factor*, 1980. Specials: (As Mark Richman) David, *David Chapter III*, CBC, 1966. Also appeared (as Mark Richman) in *A Question of Chairs*, CBS, 1961.

NON-RELATED CAREER—Licensed pharmacist in Pennsylvania

and New York; painter, works exhibited in one-man and group shows and in permanent collections in galleries throughout the United States.

WRITINGS: STAGE—*Heavy, Heavy What Hangs Over*.

MEMBER: American Federation of Radio Artists (renamed American Federation of Television and Radio Artists; 1946—), Screen Actors Guild (1953—), Actors' Studio (1954—), Actors' Equity Association, Association of Canadian Radio and Television Artists, Motion Picture and Television Fund (board of trustees), Academy of Motion Picture Arts and Sciences, National Academy of Television Arts and Sciences.

ADDRESSES: AGENT—Barry Freed Company, 9255 Sunset Boulevard, Suite 603, Los Angeles, 90069. MANAGER—Barbara Silver, 3300 Red Rose Drive, Encino, CA 91436.

*   *   *

RICKMAN, Alan

VOCATION: Actor.

CAREER: PRINCIPAL STAGE APPEARANCES—Wittipol, *The Devil Is an Ass* and Friar Peter, *Measure for Measure*, both Birmingham Repertory Theatre Company, Lyttelton Theatre, London, 1977; Farquarson, *Captain Swing*, Royal Shakespeare Company (RSC), Other Place Theatre, Stratford-on-Avon, U.K., 1978; Thidias and Alexa, *Antony and Cleopatra* and Antonio, *The Tempest*, both RSC, Royal Shakespeare Theatre, Stratford-on-Avon, 1978; Boyet, *Love's Labour's Lost*, RSC, Royal Shakespeare Theatre, 1978, then Aldwych Theatre, London, 1979; Jacques, *As You Like It*, RSC, Stratford-on-Avon, then Barbican Theatre, London, both 1985; Hendrik Hofgen, *Mephisto*, RSC, Barbican Theatre, 1986; Le Vicomte de Valmont, *Les Liaisons Dangereuses*, RSC, Music Box Theatre, New York City, 1987. Also appeared as Ferdinand, *The Tempest*, RSC, 1978; Achilles, *Troilus and Cressida*, RSC, 1985; Le Vicomte de Valmont, *Les Liaisons Dangereuses*, RSC; Jacques, *As You Like It*, Crucible Theatre, Sheffield, U.K.

PRINCIPAL STAGE WORK—Director, *Desperately Yours*, Colonnades Theatre, New York City, 1980.

PRINCIPAL FILM APPEARANCES—Hans Gruber, *Die Hard*, Twentieth Century-Fox, 1988; Ed, *The January Man*, Metro-Goldwyn-Mayer/United Artists/United International, 1989.

PRINCIPAL TELEVISION APPEARANCES—Mini-Series: Vidal, *Therese Raquin*, BBC, then *Masterpiece Theatre*, PBS, 1981; Brownlow, *Smiley's People*, BBC, then syndicated, 1982; Obadiah Slope, "Barchester Chronicles," *Masterpiece Theatre*, PBS, 1984. Specials: Tybalt, *Romeo and Juliet*, BBC, then *The Shakespeare Plays*, PBS, 1979.

WRITINGS: "Jaques in *As You Like It*" in *Players of Shakespeare 2*, Cambridge University Press, 1988.

AWARDS: Antoinette Perry Award nomination, Best Actor in a Play, 1987, for *Les Liaisons Dangereuses*.

ADDRESSES: AGENT—Jusy Hofflund, Intertalent Agency, 9200 Sunset Boulevard, Penthouse 25, Los Angeles, CA 90069.*

RIVERA, Chita   1933-

PERSONAL: Born Dolores Concita del Rivero, January 23, 1933, in Washington, DC; daughter of Pedro Julio Figueroa (a musician) and Katherine (a government clerk) del Rivero; married Anthony Mordente (an actor; divorced); children: Lisa. EDUCATION—Trained at the American School of Ballet, 1950-51.

VOCATION: Actress, singer, and dancer.

CAREER: BROADWAY DEBUT—Dancer, *Guys and Dolls,* 46th Street Theatre, 1950. LONDON DEBUT—Anita, *West Side Story,* Her Majesty's Theatre, 1958. PRINCIPAL STAGE APPEARANCES—(As Conchita del Rivero) Dancer, *Call Me Madam,* Imperial Theatre, New York City, 1952; dancer, *Can-Can,* Shubert Theatre, New York City, 1953; ensemble, *Shoestring Revue* (revue), President Theatre, New York City, 1955; Fifi, *Seventh Heaven,* American National Theatre and Academy Theatre, New York City, 1955; Rita Romano, *Mr. Wonderful,* Broadway Theatre, New York City, 1956; Anita, *West Side Story,* Winter Garden Theatre, New York City, 1957; Rosie Grant, *Bye Bye Birdie,* Martin Beck Theatre, New York City, 1960, then Her Majesty's Theatre, London, 1961; Athena Constantine, *Zenda,* Curran Theatre, San Francisco, CA, then Pasadena Civic Auditorium, Pasadena, CA, both 1963; Anyanka, *Bajour,* Shubert Theatre, 1964; Jenny, *The Threepenny Opera,* Mineola Theatre, Mineola, NY, 1966; Billie Dawn, *Born Yesterday,* Walnut Street Theatre, Philadelphia, PA, 1972; *Sondheim: A Musical Tribute* (revue), Shubert Theatre, 1973; Velma Kelly, *Chicago,* 46th Street Theatre, New York City, 1975; *Sing Happy!* (revue), Avery Fisher Hall, New York City, 1978; *V.I.P. Night on Broadway* (revue), Shubert Theatre, 1979; Rose, *Bring Back Birdie,* Martin Beck Theatre, 1981; the Queen, *Merlin,* Mark Hellinger Theatre, New York City, 1983; Anna, *The Rink,* Martin Beck Theatre, 1984; ensemble, *Jerry's Girls* (revue), St. James Theatre, New York City, 1985-86; La Mome Pistache, *Can-Can,* Chicago Theatre, Chicago, IL, 1988. Also appeared in *Shinbone Alley,* Broadway Theatre, 1957; *Flower Drum Song,* Melody Top Theatre, Milwaukee, WI, 1966; *Zorba,* Westbury Music Fair, Westbury NY, 1970; *Milliken Breakfast Show,* Waldorf-Astoria Hotel, New York City, 1972; *Father's Day,* Ivanhoe Theatre, Chicago, 1974; *Hey Look Me Over,* Avery Fisher Hall, 1981.

MAJOR TOURS—(As Conchita del Rivero) Principal dancer, *Call Me Madam,* U.S. cities, 1952; Rosie Grant, *Bye Bye Birdie,* U.S. cities, 1962; title role, *Sweet Charity,* U.S. and Canadian cities, 1967-68; Leader, *Zorba,* U.S. cities, 1969; *Jacques Brel Is Alive and Well and Living in Paris,* U.S. cities, 1972; Lilli Vanessi/Katherine, *Kiss Me Kate,* U.S. cities, 1974; Velma Kelly, *Chicago,* U.S. cities, 1977-78.

PRINCIPAL FILM APPEARANCES—Nickie, *Sweet Charity,* Universal, 1969; also appeared in *Sergeant Pepper's Lonely Hearts Club Band,* Universal, 1978.

PRINCIPAL TELEVISION APPEARANCES—Series: Connie Richardson, *The New Dick Van Dyke Show,* CBS, 1973-74. Episodic: *The Imogene Coca Show,* NBC, 1954; Mrs. Dame, "The Bellero Shield," *The Outer Limits,* ABC, 1964; also *The Garry Moore Show,* CBS; *The Ed Sullivan Show,* CBS; *The Arthur Godfrey Show,* CBS; *The Sid Caesar Show,* NBC; *The Dinah Shore Show,* NBC; *Max Liebman,* NBC; *London Palladium Show,* British television. Movies: Josie Hopper, *The Marcus-Nelson Murders* (also known as *Kojak and the Marcus-Nelson Murders*), CBS, 1973; Risa Dickstein, *The Mayflower Madam,* CBS, 1987.

Specials: *The Maurice Chevalier Show,* NBC, 1956; *The General Motors 50th Anniversary Show,* NBC, 1957; *Tiptoe Through TV,* CBS, 1960; *Variety: The World of Show Biz,* CBS, 1960; *Arthur Godfrey and the Sounds of New York,* CBS, 1963; *The George Burns Special,* CBS, 1976; *The Stars and Stripes Show,* NBC, 1976; gingerbread lady, "Hansel and Gretel," *Once Upon a Brothers Grimm,* CBS, 1977; *Broadway Plays Washington: Kennedy Center Tonight,* PBS, 1982; *Night of 100 Stars II,* NBC, 1982; *Macy's Thanksgiving Day Parade,* NBC, 1985; *Broadway Sings: The Music of Jule Styne,* PBS, 1987; *Celebrating Gershwin,* PBS, 1987; *Sammy Davis, Jr.'s 60th Birthday Celebration,* ABC, 1990.

RELATED CAREER—Performer in nightclubs and cabarets throughout the world, including the Grand Finale, New York City, and Studio One, Los Angeles, both 1975; performer on two tours for the Oldsmobile Industrial Show.

AWARDS: Antoinette Perry Award nomination, Best Supporting or Featured Actress in a Musical, 1961, for *Bye Bye Birdie;* Antoinette Perry Award nomination, Best Actress in a Musical, 1976, for *Chicago;* National Academy of Concert and Cabaret Arts Award, Best Variety Performance, 1980; Antoinette Perry Award nomination, Best Actress in a Musical, 1981, for *Bring Back Birdie;* Antoinette Perry Award nomination, Best Actress in a Musical, 1983, for *Merlin;* Antoinette Perry Award, Best Actress in a Musical, 1984, for *The Rink;* inducted into the Television Academy Hall of Fame, 1985; Antoinette Perry Award nomination, Best Actress in a Musical, 1986, for *Jerry's Girls;* Best Plays citation for *Bajour.*

MEMBER: American Federation of Television and Radio Artists, Actors' Equity Association, Screen Actors Guild.

SIDELIGHTS: RECREATIONS—Cooking, bowling, horseback riding, tennis, and swimming.

ADDRESSES: OFFICE—c/o Armando Rivera, 825 Columbus Avenue, New York, NY 10002.*

*   *   *

ROBBE-GRILLET, Alain   1922-

PERSONAL: Born August 18, 1922, in Brest, France; son of Gaston (an engineer) and Yvonne (Canu) Robbe-Grillet; married Catherine Rstakian, October 23, 1957. EDUCATION—Graduated from the the Institut National Agronomique, 1944.

VOCATION: Screenwriter, director, and novelist.

CAREER: Also see *WRITINGS* below. PRINCIPAL FILM APPEARANCES—Jean (the director), *Trans-Europ-Express,* 1966, released in the United States by Trans American, 1968; also appeared in *Je t'aime, Je t'aime,* New Yorker, 1972.

PRINCIPAL FILM WORK—Director: *L'Immortelle,* 1963, released in the United States by Grove, 1969; *Trans-Europ-Express,* 1966, released in the United States by Trans American, 1968; *L'Homme qui ment* (also known as *The Man Who Lies*), 1968, released in the United States by Grove, 1970; *Glissements progressifs du plaisir* (also known as *Successive Slidings of Pleasure*), Fox-Lira, 1973; *Le Jeu avec le feu* (also known as *Playing with Fire* and *Giocare col fuoco*), Union Generale Cinematographique/CFDC, 1974; *La Belle*

Captive (also known as *The Beautiful Prisoner*), Argos Films, 1983. Also directed *L'Eden et apres,* 1971; *Les Gommes,* 1972; *Piege a fourrure,* 1977.

RELATED CAREER—Literary advisor, Editions de Minuit, Paris, France, 1954—.

NON-RELATED CAREER—Charge de mission, Institut National des Statistiques, Paris, France, 1945-48; agricultural engineer, Institut des Fruits et Agrumes Coloniaux in Morocco, French Guinea, Martinique, and Guadeloupe, 1949-51.

WRITINGS: FILM—See production details above, unless indicated: *L'Annee derniere a Marienbad* (also known as *Last Year at Marienbad*), 1961, released in the United States by Astor, 1962, published by Editions de Minuit, 1961, then in the United States by Grove, 1962; *L'Immortelle,* 1963, published by Editions de Minuit, 1963; *Trans-Europ-Express,* 1966; *L'Homme que ment,* 1968; *L'Eden et apres,* 1971; *Les Gommes,* 1972; *Glissements progressifs du plaisir,* 1972; (co-writer) *Le Jeu avec le feu,* 1974; *Piege a fourrure,* 1977; (with Framl Verpillat) *La Belle Captive,* 1983.

OTHER—*Les Gommes* (novel), Editions de Minuit, 1953, published in the United States as *The Erasers,* Grove, 1964; *Le Voyeur* (novel), Editions de Minuit, 1955, published in the United States as *The Voyeur,* Grove, 1958; *La Jalousie* (novel), Editions de Minuit, 1957, published in the United States as *Jealousy,* Grove, 1959; *Dans le labyrinthe* (novel), Editions de Minuit, 1959, published in the United States as *In the Labyrinth,* Grove, 1960; *Instantanes* (short stories), Editions de Minuit, 1962, published in the United States as *Snapshots,* Grove, 1968; *Pour un nouveau roman* (non-fiction), Editions de Minuit, 1963, published in the United States as *For a New Novel: Essays on Fiction,* Grove, 1966; *La Maison de rendez-vous* (novel), Editions de Minuit, 1965, published in the United States by Grove, 1966; *Projet pour une revolution a New York* (novel), Editions de Minuit, 1970, published in the United States as *Project for a Revolution in New York,* Grove, 1972; (with David Hamilton) *Reves de jeunes filles* (novel), Montel, 1971, published in the United States as *Dreams of a Young Girl,* Morrow, 1971; (with Hamilton) *Les Demoiselles d'Hamilton* (novel), Laffont, 1972; also *Topologie d'une cite fantome* (novel), 1976; *La Belle Captive* (novel), 1977; *Un regicide* (novel), 1978; *Souvenirs du triangle d'or* (novel), 1978; *Djinn* (novel), 1981; *Le Miroir qui revient* (novel), 1984.

AWARDS: Feneon Prize, 1954, for *Les Gommes;* Prix des Critiques, 1955, for *Le Voyeur;* Prix Louis Delluc, 1963, for *L'Immortelle;* also Officer, Order of Merit (France); Chevalier, Legion of Honor (France).

ADDRESSES: OFFICE—7 rue Bernard-Palissy, 75006 Paris, France.*

*   *   *

ROBERTS, Christian   1944-

PERSONAL: Born March 17, 1944, in Berkshire, England; son of Douglas Henry (in the dairy business) and Betty Alison Roberts; married Christine Carswell, September 26, 1973; children: Lucinda Alison, Benjamin Henry. EDUCATION—Studied acting at the Royal Academy of Dramatic Art, 1964-66.

CHRISTIAN ROBERTS

VOCATION: Actor and producer.

CAREER: STAGE DEBUT—Tournel, *A Flea in Her Ear,* Castle Theatre, Farnham, U.K., 1973, for twenty-five performances. LONDON DEBUT—Dr. Prospero, *Return to the Forbidden Planet,* Cambridge Theatre, 1989. PRINCIPAL STAGE APPEARANCES—Reporter, *Free As Air,* Castle Theatre, Farnham, U.K., 1973; Paris, *Romeo and Juliet,* Jack Chesney, *Charley's Aunt,* Cliff Bradshaw, *Cabaret,* Diego, *A Royal Hunt of the Sun,* Sergeant, *The Devil's Disciple,* and Johnny King, *The Lord's Lieutenant,* all Redgrave Theatre, Farnham, 1974; Trofimov, *The Cherry Orchard,* Bob Acres, *The Rivals,* Henry, *Move Over, Mrs. Markham,* Alfieri, *A View from the Bridge,* Philip Lombard, *Ten Little Niggers,* and Mortimer Brewster, *Arsenic and Old Lace,* all Redgrave Theatre, 1975; Philip Harrison, *The Gentle Hook,* Salisbury Playhouse, Salisbury, U.K., 1976; Richard D'Oyly-Carte, *Tarantara Tarantara,* Theatre Royal, York, U.K., 1976; title role, *Foxy,* Watford Palace Theatre, Watford, U.K., then Redgrave Theatre, both 1977; J.M. Barrie, *The Peter Pan Man,* Rodger, *A Slight Accident,* Tegeus, *A Phoenix Too Frequent,* and Charles, *All in the Mind,* all Bellerby Theatre, Guildford, U.K., 1978; Peter, *Time and Time Again* and Fred Castle, *Bed Before Yesterday,* both Redgrave Theatre, 1978; Frankie Basata, *Bird Bath,* Bellerby Theatre, 1981; Sven, *Ball Boys,* Yvonne Arnaud Theatre, Guildford, 1981; Malcolm, *Having a Ball,* Haymarket Theatre, Basingstoke, U.K., 1987; Duke Box, *From a Jack to a King,* Edinburgh Festival, Edinburgh, Scotland, 1988; Lloyd Dallas, *Noises Off,* Redgrave Theatre, 1988. Also appeared as Geoffrey Jackson, *Absurd Person Singular,* 1976; Lennox, *Macbeth,* 1976; in *Cowardly Custard,* 1976; as Jeremy Warrender, *The Spider's Web,* Timothy, *Salad*

Days, John Worthing, *The Importance of Being Earnest*, Tristan Tzara, *Travesties*, and David Ryder, *Murder with Love*, all in 1977.

PRINCIPAL STAGE WORK—Producer, *Return to the Forbidden Planet*, Cambridge Theatre, London, 1989.

FILM DEBUT—Denham, *To Sir, with Love*, Columbia, 1967. PRINCIPAL FILM APPEARANCES—Tom Taggert, *The Anniversary*, Hammer, 1968; Adam Galt, *The Desperados*, Columbia, 1969; Philip Harvey, *Twisted Nerve*, National General, 1969; Robert, *The Adventurers*, Paramount, 1970; Thomas Fleming, *The Mind of Mr. Soames*, Columbia, 1970; Andreas, *The Last Valley*, Cinerama, 1971; also appeared in *The Mountain of Fire*, Paramount, 1972.

PRINCIPAL TELEVISION APPEARANCES—Series: Frank Faith, *Feet First*, Thames, 1979; also *Saturday While Sunday*, Granada, 1967. Mini-Series: *Clochemerle*, BBC, 1972. Episodic: Dr. Renor, *Blake's Seven*, BBC, 1978; Horst, *Secret Army*, BBC, 1978; young lecturer, "Degree of Uncertainty," *Play for Today*, BBC, 1978; also *The Avengers*, ITV, 1968; *The Persuaders*, ITV, 1971; *U.F.O.*, ITV, 1971. Movies: Albert, *The Berlin Affair*, NBC, 1970. Also appeared in *Epic '66*, BBC, 1966; *Haunted*, ABC, 1967.

PRINCIPAL RADIO APPEARANCES—Lieutenant Champion, *When the Gatling Jammed*, BBC, 1978; Edward Digby, *A Gallant Romantic*, BBC, 1978.

RELATED CAREER—Board of directors, Theatre Royal, Windsor, U.K., 1987—; co-founder, Rhythm Method Productions, 1988—.

NON-RELATED CAREER—Director, Job's Dairy Limited, 1981-87.

AWARDS: International Laurel Award from the Motion Picture Exhibitors and named one of Filmdom's Famous Fives by *Film Daily*, both 1967.

MEMBER: Freeman, City of London, 1966; liveryman, Bakers Company, 1983.

SIDELIGHTS: RECREATIONS—Tennis, golf, horseback riding, philately, autograph collecting.

ADDRESSES: AGENT—Denis Selinger, International Creative Management, 388 Oxford Street, London W1N 9HE, England.

*   *   *

ROGERS, Kenny   1938-

PERSONAL: Full name, Kenneth Ray Rogers; born August 21, 1938, in Houston, TX (some sources say Crockett, TX); son of Edward Floyd and Lucille (Hester) Rogers; married fourth wife, Marianne Gordon (an actress), October 2, 1977; children: Carol (first marriage); Kenneth, Jr. (second marriage); Christopher Cody (fourth marriage). EDUCATION—Attended the University of Houston.

VOCATION: Actor and singer.

CAREER: Also see *WRITINGS* below. PRINCIPAL FILM APPEARANCES—Brewster Baker, *Six Pack*, Twentieth Century-Fox, 1982.

KENNY ROGERS

PRINCIPAL TELEVISION APPEARANCES—Series: Host, *Rollin' on the River*, syndicated, 1971-73. Episodic: *American Bandstand*, ABC, 1958; also *Barbara Mandrell and the Mandrell Sisters*, NBC; *The Tonight Show*, NBC. Movies: Earl, *The Dream Makers*, NBC, 1975; Brandy Hawkes, *Kenny Rogers as "The Gambler,"* CBS, 1980; Matthew Spencer, *Coward of the County*, CBS, 1981; Brandy Hawkes, *Kenny Rogers as "The Gambler"—The Adventure Continues*, CBS, 1983; Matt Cooper, *Wild Horses*, CBS, 1985; Brandy Hawkes, *Kenny Rogers as "The Gambler" III*, CBS, 1987.

Specials: Host, *The World's Largest Indoor Country Music Show*, NBC, 1978; *The Captain and Tennille in Hawaii*, ABC, 1978; *American Music Awards*, ABC, 1978; *Country Music Association Awards*, CBS, 1978; *Perry Como's Easter By the Sea*, ABC, 1978; *Variety '77—The Year in Entertainment*, CBS, 1978; host, *The Kenny Rogers Special*, CBS, 1979; *A Christmas Special . . . With Love, Mac Davis*, NBC, 1979; *Lynda Carter's Special*, CBS, 1980; host, *A Special Kenny Rogers*, CBS, 1981; *I Love Liberty*, ABC, 1982; *Roy Acuff—Fifty Years the King of Country Music*, NBC, 1982; host, *Kenny Rogers in Concert*, HBO, 1983; *Sheena Easton, Act 1*, NBC, 1983; *Grandpa, Will You Run with Me?*, NBC, 1983; host, *18th Annual Country Music Association Awards*, CBS, 1984; *Kenny and Dolly: A Christmas to Remember*, CBS, 1984; *Glen Campbell and Friends: The Silver Anniversary*, HBO, 1984; *Salute to Lady Liberty*, CBS, 1984; *Liberty Weekend*, ABC, 1986; *Kenny Rogers: Working America*, CBS, 1987; host, *21st Annual Country Music Awards*, CBS, 1987; *The Smothers Brothers Comedy Special*, CBS, 1988; *The Smothers Brothers Thanksgiving Special*, CBS, 1988; host, *American Music Awards*, CBS, 1989; host, *23rd Annual Country Music Association Awards*, CBS, 1989; *From the*

Heart . . . The First International Very Special Arts Festival, NBC, 1989; *America's All-Star Tribute to Elizabeth Taylor,* ABC, 1989; *Kenny Rogers in Concert: A Holiday Special for Public Television,* PBS, 1989; also *Donald Duck's Fiftieth Birthday,* 1984; *Kenny Rogers and Dolly Parton,* 1985; host, *28th Annual Grammy Awards,* 1986; *The Best of Farm Aid: An American Event,* 1986; *Texas One Hundred and Fifty: A Celebration Special,* 1986; *Kraft Salutes the George Burns 90th Birthday Special,* 1986; *Kenny Rogers Classic Weekend,* 1988; *Hee Haw 20th Anniversary Show,* 1988; *Kenny, Dolly, and Willie: Something Inside So Strong,* 1989; *Mike Tyson—A Portrait of the People's Champion,* 1989; *The Songwriters Hall of Fame 20th Anniversary . . . The Magic of Music,* 1989.

PRINCIPAL TELEVISION WORK—Movies: Executive producer, *A Different Affair,* CBS, 1987. Specials: Executive producer (with Ken Kragen), *Kenny Rogers in Concert,* HBO, 1983.

RELATED CAREER—Bass fiddle player with the jazz group, the Bobby Doyle Trio, 1959-66; member of the pop-folk band, the New Christy Minstrels, 1966-67; singer with the rock group, the First Edition, 1967-73; spokesperson, Dole Foods Company, 1986—; as a concert performer, has appeared throughout the world.

WRITINGS: (With Len Epand) *Making It with Music,* Harper & Row, 1978; *Kenny Rogers' America* (photographs), Little, Brown, 1986; *Your Friends and Mine* (photographs), Little, Brown, 1987.

RECORDINGS: ALBUMS—*Kenny Rogers,* United Artists, 1977; *Daytime Friends,* United Artists, 1977; (with Dottie West) *Every Time Two Fools Collide,* United Artists, 1978; *Love or Something Like It,* United Artists, 1978; *The Gambler,* United Artists, 1979; *Kenny,* United Artists, 1979; *Gideon,* United Artists, 1980; *Love Lifted Me,* United Artists, 1980; *Share Your Love,* Liberty, 1981; (with West) *Classics,* Liberty, 1981; *Christmas,* Liberty, 1981; *Love Will Turn You Around,* Liberty, 1982; *We've Got Tonight,* Liberty, 1983; *Eyes That See in the Dark,* RCA, 1983; *What About Me?,* RCA, 1984; (with Dolly Parton) *Once Upon a Christmas,* RCA, 1984; also *Love Is What We Make It,* Liberty; *Love Lifted Me,* Liberty; *Short Stories,* Liberty; *The Heart of the Matter,* RCA; *I Prefer the Moonlight,* RCA; *They Don't Make Them Like They Used To,* RCA. With the First Edition: *Something's Burning,* Reprise, 1970.

SINGLES—"She Believed in Me," 1970; (with Kim Carnes) "Don't Fall in Love with a Dreamer," 1980; "Lady," 1980; "Love Is What We Make It," 1985; "The Heart of the Matter," 1985; "I Prefer the Moonlight," 1987; "When You Put our Heart in It," 1988; also "They Don't Make Them Like They Used To," "What About Me?," "That Crazy Feeling," "I Don't Need You," "Lucille," "Homemade Love," "The Gambler," "Laura," "While the Feeling's Good," (with West) "Everytime Two Fools Collide." With the First Edition: "Just Dropped in to See What Condition My Condition Was In," "Ruby (Don't Take Your Love to Town)," and "Something's Burnin'."

AWARDS: Grammy Award, Best Male Country Vocalist, and Academy of Country Music Awards, Best Single and Best Song, all 1977, for "Lucille"; Billboard's Cross-Over Artist of the Year, 1977; Academy of Country Music Award, Album of the Year, 1977, for *Kenny Rogers;* Academy of Country Music Awards, Top Male Vocalist, 1977 and 1978; Academy of Country Music Award, Entertainer of the Year, 1978; America's Juke Box Operators Association Award, 1978; Academy of Country Music Awards (with Dottie West), Vocal Duo of the Year, 1978 and 1979;

Grammy Award, Best Male Vocal (Country), 1979; Academy of Country Music Award, Male Vocalist of the Year, 1979; *People* magazine's Top Male Vocalist, 1979 and 1980; *People* magazine's Most Popular Male Singer Awards, 1981, 1982, and 1983; Academy of Country Music Award (with Dolly Parton), Best Vocal Group and/or Duet, 1983; *Rolling Stone* magazine Readers' Poll, Country Artist of the Year, 1984; United Nations Peace Award, 1984; Record Industry Assocation of America Award, Most Awarded Artist, 1984, for eighteen gold and eleven platinum albums; Roy Acuff Award from the Country Music Foundation, 1985; Best Country Vocal Duet Award (with Ronnie Milsap), 1987; Harry Chapin Award for Humanitarianism from the American Society of Composers, Authors, and Publishers, 1988.

SIDELIGHTS: RECREATIONS—Softball and tennis.

ADDRESSES: OFFICE—Kragen and Company, 1112 N. Sherbourne Drive, Los Angeles, CA 90069.*

*   *   *

ROKER, Roxie   1929-

PERSONAL: Born August 28, 1929, in Miami, FL; daughter of Albert and Bessie Roker; married Sy Kravitz (a television network assignment editor); children: Leonard. EDUCATION—Received B.A. in drama from Howard University; studied at the Shakespeare Institute, Stratford-on-Avon, U.K., as a Hattie M. Strong Foundation fellow.

VOCATION: Actress.

CAREER: STAGE DEBUT—Chorus, *Faith of Our Fathers,* Rock Creek Amphitheatre, Washington, DC. PRINCIPAL STAGE APPEARANCES—Irene, "The Dreamy Kid" in *Three By O'Neill,* West End Collegiate Chapel, New York City, 1957; Queen, *The Blacks,* Negro Ensemble Company, St. Mark's Playhouse, New York City, 1961; Dorothea Ellen (Dorry) Sanders, *Rosalee Pritchett* Negro Ensemble Company, St. Mark's Playhouse, 1971; Desiree Vanderkellan, *Behold! Cometh the Vanderkellans,* Theatre De Lys, New York City, 1971; Viola Caine Robinson, *Jamimma,* New Federal Theatre, Henry Street Playhouse, New York City, 1972; Mattie Williams, *The River Niger,* Negro Ensemble Company, St. Mark's Playhouse, 1972, then Brooks Atkinson Theatre, New York City, 1973; also appeared in *Ododo,* Negro Ensemble Company, St. Mark's Playhouse, 1970; *Nevis Mountain Dew,* Los Angeles Actors' Theatre, Los Angeles, 1981-82.

PRINCIPAL FILM APPEARANCES—Mrs. Winston, *Claudine,* Twentieth Century-Fox, 1974; radio operator on "Bohemiar," *The Bermuda Triangle,* Sunn Classic, 1978; female Republican, *Amazon Women on the Moon,* Universal, 1987.

PRINCIPAL TELEVISION APPEARANCES—Series: Co-host, *Inside Bedford Stuyvesant,* WNEW (New York City), 1968; Helen Willis, *The Jeffersons,* CBS, 1975-85. Mini-Series: Melissa, *Roots,* ABC, 1977. Pilots: Eloise Morse, *Change at 125th Street,* CBS, 1974. Episodic: Alverta Edwards, *Cagney and Lacey,* CBS, 1985; Mrs. Gooden, *Trapper John, M.D.,* CBS, 1986; Rhonda Whitney, *The Love Boat,* ABC, 1986; Esther, *The New Mike Hammer,* CBS, 1987; Dr. Thelma Butler, *227,* NBC, 1988. Movies: Mrs. Peoples, *Billy: Portrait of a Street Kid,* CBS, 1977; Madge Davis, *Making of a Male Model,* ABC, 1983. Specials: Aunt Helen, "The Celebrity and the Arcade Kid,'' *ABC Afterschool Specials*, ABC, 1983; Phyllis Brooks, ''The Day My Kid Went Punk,'' *ABC Afterschool Specials*, ABC, 1987.

PRINCIPAL TELEVISION WORK—Series: Associate producer, *Family Living*, NBC, 1962-69.

RELATED CAREER—Featured singer, *Caribbean Fantasy*, the El Morocco nightclub, Montreal, PQ, Canada.

NON-RELATED CAREER—Secretary and administrator, NBC; office clerk; television production assistant.

AWARDS: Antoinette Perry Award nomination, Best Supporting or Featured Actress, and Obie Award from the *Village Voice*, both 1974, for *The River Niger;* Alumni Award from Howard University for distinguished postgraduate achievement in the field of performing arts.

ADDRESSES: AGENT—Twentieth Century Artists, 3800 Barham Boulevard, Suite 303, Los Angeles, CA 90068.*

*   *   *

ROSENBLUM, M. Edgar   1932-

PERSONAL: Full name, Morton Edgar Rosenblum; born January 8, 1932, in Brooklyn, NY; son of Jacob (a physician) and Pauline (a nurse and social worker; maiden name, Feldman) Rosenblum; married Cornelia Hartmann (a graphic designer), May 1, 1960;

M. EDGAR ROSENBLUM

children: Jessica. EDUCATION—Attended Bard College, 1952-55. MILITARY—U.S. Army, private, 1953.

VOCATION: Producer and manager.

CAREER: PRINCIPAL STAGE WORK—Producer (with Arnold Tager) and company manager, *When I Was a Child*, 41st Street Theatre, New York City, 1960; producer and manager, *Barabbas*, Woodstock Playhouse, Woodstock, NY, 1961; also producer, *Let Man Live*, American Scandinavian Foundation, 1958; producer and manager, *Schweik in the Second World War*, Woodstock Playhouse.

As executive director, Long Wharf Theatre, New Haven CT: *Tartuffe, Tango, The Pirate, Country People, Black Comedy, Joe Egg, Spoon River Anthology*, and *A Thousand Clowns*, all 1969-70; *The Skin of Our Teeth, Yegor Bulichov, A Place Without Doors, She Stoops to Conquer, The Blood Knot, Heartbreak House, The Price, Winnie the Pooh, Wind in the Willows, Thirteen Clocks, Go Jump in the Lake, Hansel and Gretel*, and *Solitaire/Double Solitaire* (double-bill), all 1970-71; *You Can't Take It with You, The Contractor, A Streetcar Named Desire, Hamlet, The Way of the World, Troika: An Evening of Russian Comedy, The Iceman Cometh*, and *Patrick's Day*, all 1971-72; *The Lady's Not for Burning, What Price Glory?, Trelawny of the Wells, Juno and the Paycock, Forget-Me-Not-Lane, Dance of Death, Miss Julie*, and *The Changing Room*, all 1972-73; *The Master Builder, Morning's at Seven, The Seagull, The National Health, The Resistable Rise of Arturo Ui, The Widowing of Mrs. Holroyd*, and *A Pagan Place*, all 1973-74; *Circus!, Adventures in the Magic Circle, Gypsies, Doors of Mystery*, and *The Many Faces of Johnny Appleseed*, all Young People's Theatre, 1973-74; *Sizwe Banzi Is Dead* and *The Island* (double-bill), *The Soldier's Tale* and *The Knight of the Burning Pestle* (double-bill), *Ah, Wilderness!, Pygmalion, Afore Night Come, Richard III*, and *You're Too Tall, But Come Back in Two Weeks*, all 1974-75; *Troubadour's Carnival, Frolicks, Creation of Myths, Ticket to Tomorrow*, and *The Hour of Need*, all Young People's Theatre, 1974-75; *Artichoke, The Show-Off, What Every Woman Knows, Streamers, The House of Mirth, Daarlin' Juno*, and *On the Outside* and *On the Inside* (double bill), all 1975-76; *Alphabetical Order, The Autumn Garden, Home, The Shadow Box, Saint Joan, Absent Friends, The Rose Tattoo*, and *The Gin Game*, all 1976-77; *Hobson's Choice, The Lunch Girls, The Recruiting Officer, Spokesong, S.S. Glencairn, The Philadelphia Story, Macbeth, Two Brothers*, and *Starting Here, Starting Now*, all 1977-78; *Journey's End, I Sent a Letter to My Love, Summerfolk, Biography, Romersholm, Hillbilly Women*, and *Privates on Parade*, all 1978-79; *Watch on the Rhine, Jitters, Double Feature, The Beach House, The Caretaker, Mary Barnes, Who's Afraid of Virginia Woolf?*, and *Cyrano de Bergerac*, all 1979-80.

As executive director, Long Wharf Theatre: *American Buffalo, Solomon's Child, Waiting for Godot, The Admirable Crichton, Close Ties, Romeo and Juliet, Bodies, A Life, The Lion in Winter*, and *Private Lives*, all 1980-81; *This Story of Yours, A Day in the Death of Joe Egg, A View from the Bridge, The Workroom, Lakeboat, The Doctor's Dilemma, The Carmone Brothers Italian Food Products Corp's Annual Pasta Pageant, Ethan Frome*, and *The Front Page*, all 1981-82; *Open Admissions, Holiday, Another Country, The Guardsman, Pal Joey, The Cherry Orchard, Two By A.M., Quartermaine's Terms, The Lady and the Clarinet*, and *Free and Clear*, all 1982-83; *The Hostage, Accent on Youth, Requiem for a Heavyweight, The Homesteaders, The Bathers, Under the Ilex, Not Quite Jerusalem*, and *Shivaree*, all 1983-84; *Tobacco Road, Rainsnakes, Oliver Oliver, The Common Pursuit, Blue Window, Cat on a Hot Tin Roof, Albert Herring*, and *Bullie's*

House, all 1984-85; *Paris Bound, Pride and Prejudice, Crystal Clear, The Normal Heart, The Glass Menagerie, Fugue*, and *Lost in the Stars*, all 1985-86; *All My Sons, Camille, Self Defense, Dalliance, The Tender Land, Progress, Painting Churches, Duse Died in Pittsburgh, Men in the Kitchen, The Traveling Squirrel*, and *When It's Over*, all 1986-87; *The Downside, Laughing Stock, Our Town, Scenes from American Life, Fathers and Sons, Fighting Chance*, and *Regina*, all 1987-88.

MAJOR TOURS—Producer (with Arnold Tager) and company manager, *When I Was a Child*, U.S. cities, 1960; stage manager, Robert Joffrey Ballet, U.S. cities, 1961; stage manager, *The Turn of the Screw* (opera), U.S. cities, 1963.

RELATED CAREER—Executive director, Long Wharf Theatre, New Haven, CT, 1970—; consultant to the state arts councils of New York, Rhode Island, Arkansas, Connecticut, and Ohio, 1970—; visiting lecturer, Yale University School of Drama, New Haven, CT, 1985—; producer, manager, and owner, Woodstock Playhouse, Woodstock, NY, for fourteen years; producer, Hyde Park Playhouse, Hyde Park, NY; executive director, Hudson Valley Repertory Theatre, NY.

NON-RELATED CAREER—Secretary to designer Norman Bel Geddes, 1956; copywriter and music manager, National Music League; director, Polari Art Gallery, New York, NY and Woodstock, NY.

MEMBER: League of Resident Theatres (member of the executive, liaison, and negotiating committees, 1970—); National Corporate Theatre Fund (founding president, 1976—); Connecticut Advocates for the Arts (board of directors, 1978—).

ADDRESSES: OFFICE—c/o Long Wharf Theatre, 222 Sargent Drive, New Haven, CT 06511.

*   *   *

ROTUNNO, Giuseppe   1923-

PERSONAL: Born March 19, 1923, in Rome, Italy.

VOCATION: Cinematographer.

CAREER: FIRST FILM WORK—Camera operator, *Senso*, 1954. PRINCIPAL FILM WORK—Cinematographer: *Pane amore e . . .* (also known as *Scandal in Sorrento*), 1955, released in the United States by Distributors Corporation of America, 1957; *The Monte Carlo Story*, United Artists, 1957; *Le notti bianche* (also known as *White Nights* and *Nuits blanches*), 1957, released in the United States by United Motion Picture Organization, 1961; *Anna of Brooklyn*, RKO, 1958, rereleased as *Fast and Sexy*, Columbia, 1960; *La Maja desnuda* (also known as *The Naked Maja*), 1958, released in the United States by United Artists, 1959; *La ragazza del palio* (also known as *The Love Specialist*), Medallion, 1959; (with Daniel Fapp) *On the Beach*, United Artists, 1959; (with Robert Gerardi) *La grande guerra* (also known as *La Grande guerre* and *The Great War*), 1959, released in the United States by Lopert, 1961.

The Angel Wore Red, Metro-Goldwyn-Mayer (MGM), 1960; *Five Branded Women*, Paramount, 1960; *Rocco e i suoi fratelli* (also known as *Rocco et ses freres* and *Rocco and His Brothers*), 1960,

released in the United States by Astor, 1961; *The Best of Enemies*, Columbia, 1962; "The Job" in *Boccaccio '70*, Gray Film, 1962; *Cronaca familiare* (also known as *Family Diary*), 1962, released in the United States by MGM, 1963; *Le guepard* (also known as *Il gattopardo* and *The Leopard*), Twentieth Century-Fox, 1963; *I compagni* (also known as *The Organizer, Les camarades*, and *The Strikers*), 1963, released in the United States by Continental Distributing, 1964; *Ieri, oggi e domani* (also known as *Yesterday, Today, and Tomorrow* and *She Got What She Asked For*), 1963, released in the United States by Embassy, 1964; *The Bible . . . In the Beginning* (also known as *The Bible* and *La Bibbia*), Twentieth Century-Fox, 1966; *Lo straniero* (also known as *L'etranger* and *The Stranger*), Paramount, 1967; *Le streghe* (also known as *The Witches* and *Les Sorcieres*), 1967, released in the United States by Lopert, 1969; *Anzio* (also known as *Lo Sbarco di Anzio* and *The Battle for Anzio*), Columbia, 1968; (with Aldo Graziata and Robert Krasker) *Senso* (also known as *The Wanton Contessa*), Fleetwood, 1968; *Candy* (also known as *Candy e il sul pazzo mondo*), Cinerama, 1968; *Fellini Satyricon* (also known as *Satyricon*), United Artists, 1969; *The Secret of Santa Vittoria*, United Artists, 1969; "Never Bet the Devil Your Head" or "Toby Dammit" *Histoires extraordinaires* (also known as *Spirits of the Dead* and *Tre passi nel delirio*), 1968, released in the United States by American International, 1969; *Sunflower* (also known as *Les Fleurs du soleil* and *Il girasoli*), 1969, released in the United States by AVCO-Embassy, 1970.

Carnal Knowledge, AVCO-Embassy, 1971; *Man of La Mancha*, United Artists, 1972; *Roma* (also known as *Fellini's Roma*), United Artists, 1972; *Film d'amore e d'anarchia* (also known as *Love and Anarchy, Story of Love and Anarchy, Un film d'amore e d'anarchia ovvero stamattina alle 10, in Via dei Fiori nella nota casa di Tolleranza*, and *A Film of Love and Anarchy, or: At 10:00 A.M. in the Well-Known House of Prostitution at Flower Street*), Euro International/Almi/Cinema V, 1973, released in the United States by Peppercorn-Wormsler, 1974; *Amarcord*, Warner Brothers/New World, 1974; *Il bestione* (also known as *The Beast*), Warner Brothers, 1974; *Tutto a posto e niente in ordine* (also known as *All Screwed Up, Everything in Place, Nothing Works*, and *All in Place, Nothing in Order*), Euro International, 1974, released in the United States by New Line Cinema, 1976; *Il Casanova di Federico Fellini* (also known as *Casanova* and *Fellini's Casanova*), Universal, 1976; *Sturmtruppen* (also known as *Stormtroopers*), CIDIF, 1976; *Divina Creatura* (also known as *The Divine Nymph* and *Divine Creature*), Titanus Distribuzione, 1976, released in the United States by Film Releasing Corporation, 1979; *The End of the World in Our Usual Bed in a Night Full of Rain*, Warner Brothers, 1978; *Prova d'orchestra* (also known as *Orchestra Rehearsal*), Gaumont/SACIS/Premier Releasing, 1978; *All That Jazz*, Twentieth Century-Fox, 1979.

La Citta delle donne (also known as *City of Women*), Gaumont, 1980; *Popeye*, Paramount, 1980; (with William Garroni) *Rollover*, Warner Brothers, 1981; *Bello mio bellezza mia* (also known as *My Handsome My Beautiful*), PLM Film Produzione, 1982; *Five Days One Summer*, Warner Brothers, 1982; *E la nave va* (also known as *And the Ship Sails On*), Vides, 1983; *American Dreamer*, Warner Brothers, 1984; *Non ci resta che piangere* (also known as *Nothing Left to Do But Cry*), Columbia, 1984; *Desiderio* (also known as *Desire*), Gaumont, 1984; *The Assisi Underground*, Golan-Globus, 1985; *Red Sonja*, Metro-Goldwyn-Mayer/United Artists, 1985; *Hotel Colonial*, Hemdale Releasing/Orion, 1986; *Julia and Julia*, Cinecom International, 1987; *Rent-a-Cop*, Kings Road Entertainment, 1988; *Haunted Summer*, Pathe Releasing, 1988; *The Adventures of Baron Munchausen*, Columbia, 1989; *Rebus*, Columbia/Tri-Star, 1989. Also cinematographer, *Tosca*, 1956.

PRINCIPAL TELEVISION WORK—Movies: Cinematographer, *The Scarlet and the Black*, CBS, 1983.

RELATED CAREER—Still photographer, camera assistant, camera operator, and lighting cameraman; worked with Federico Fellini, Lina Wertmuller, and Luchino Visconti.*

*   *   *

ROZSA, Miklos   1907-

PERSONAL: Full name, Nicholas Rozsa; born April 18, 1907, in Budapest, Hungary; naturalized U.S. citizen. EDUCATION—Studied violin with Lajos Berkovits; studied music at the Leipzig Conservatory under Hermann Grabner and Theodor Kroyer.

VOCATION: Composer.

CAREER: Also see *WRITINGS* below. PRINCIPAL FILM APPEARANCES—Conductor, "The Jealous Lover" in *The Story of Three Loves*, Metro-Goldwyn-Mayer, 1953. PRINCIPAL FILM WORK—Music director: *That Hamilton Woman* (also known as *Lady Hamilton*), United Artists, 1941; *Dark Waters*, United Artists, 1944; *The Macomber Affair*, United Artists, 1947; *Song of Scheherazade*, Universal, 1947; *The Light Touch*, Metro-Goldwyn-Mayer (MGM), 1951; *The King's Thief*, MGM, 1955; *Lust for Life*, MGM, 1956; *The Power*, MGM, 1968.

RELATED CAREER—Professor of musical composition, University of Southern California, Los Angeles, CA, 1945.

WRITINGS: FILM—All as composer. *Knight Without Armor*, United Artists, 1937; *Thunder in the City*, Columbia, 1937; *Murder on Diamond Row* (also known as *The Squeaker*), United Artists, 1937; (with John Greenwood) *Drums* (also known as *The Drum*), United Artists, 1938; *The Divorce of Lady X*, United Artists, 1938; *The Four Feathers*, United Artists, 1939; *On the Night of the Fire* (also known as *The Fugitive*), Universal, 1939; *U-Boat 29* (also known as *The Spy in Black*), Columbia, 1939.

The Thief of Baghdad, United Artists, 1940; *Four Dark Hours* (also known as *The Green Cockatoo* and *Race Gang*), Devonshire Films, 1940; *Lydia*, United Artists, 1941; *Sundown*, United Artists, 1941; *That Hamilton Woman* (also known as *Lady Hamilton*), United Artists, 1941; *Jungle Book* (also known as *Rudyard Kipling's Jungle Book*), United Artists, 1942; *To Be or Not to Be*, United Artists, 1942; *Five Graves to Cairo*, Paramount, 1943; *Sahara*, Columbia, 1943; *So Proudly We Hail*, Paramount, 1943; *Dark Waters*, United Artists, 1944; *Double Indemnity*, Paramount, 1944; *The Hour Before the Dawn*, Paramount, 1944; *The Man in Half-Moon Street*, Paramount, 1944; *Woman of the Town*, United Artists, 1944; *Blood on the Sun*, United Artists, 1945; *Lady on a Train*, Universal, 1945; *The Lost Weekend*, Paramount, 1945; (with Morris Stoloff) *A Song to Remember*, Columbia, 1945; *Spellbound*, United Artists, 1945; *The Killers*, Universal, 1946; *Because of Him*, Universal, 1946; *The Strange Love of Martha Ivers*, Paramount, 1946; *Brute Force*, Universal, 1947; *Song of Scheherazade*, Universal, 1947; *Desert Fury*, Paramount, 1947; *A Double Life*, Universal, 1947; *The Macomber Affair*, United Artists, 1947; *The Other Love* (also known as *Mankiller*), United Artists, 1947; *The Red House*, United Artists, 1947; (with Mario Casatelnuovo-Tedesco) *Time Out of Mind*, Universal, 1947; *A Woman's Vengeance* (also known as *The Gioconda Smile*), Universal, 1947;

Command Decision, Metro-Goldwyn-Mayer (MGM), 1948; *Kiss the Blood Off My Hands*, (also known as *Blood on My Hands*), Universal, 1948; (with Frank Skinner) *The Naked City* Universal, 1948; *The Secret Beyond the Door*, Universal, 1948; *The Bribe*, MGM, 1949; *Criss Cross*, Universal, 1949; *East Side, West Side*, MGM, 1949; *Adam's Rib*, MGM, 1949; *Madame Bovary*, MGM, 1949; *The Red Danube*, MGM, 1949.

(With Herbert Stothart) *The Miniver Story*, MGM, 1950; *Crisis*, MGM, 1950; *The Asphalt Jungle*, MGM, 1950; *The Light Touch*, MGM, 1951; *Quo Vadis*, MGM, 1951; *Plymouth Adventure*, MGM, 1952; *Ivanhoe*, MGM, 1952; (also song contributor with Paul Francis Webster) *El Cid*, Allied Artists, 1952; *Julius Caesar*, MGM, 1953; *All the Brothers Were Valiant*, MGM, 1953; *Knights of the Round Table*, MGM, 1953; "Mademoiselle" in *The Story of Three Loves*, MGM, 1953; *Young Bess*, MGM, 1953; *Crest of the Wave* (also known as *Seagulls Over Sorrento*), MGM, 1954; *Men of the Fighting Lady* (also known as *Panther Squadron*), MGM, 1954; *Valley of the Kings*, MGM, 1954; *Diane*, MGM, 1955; *The King's Thief*, MGM, 1955; (with Vicente Gomez) *Moonfleet*, MGM, 1955; *Green Fire*, MGM, 1955; *Bhowani Junction*, MGM, 1956; *Lust for Life*, MGM, 1956; *Tribute to a Badman*, MGM, 1956; *Something of Value*, MGM, 1957; *The Seventh Sin*, MGM, 1957; *Tip on a Dead Jockey* (also known as *Time for Action*), MGM, 1957; *A Time to Love and a Time to Die*, Universal, 1958; *Ben Hur*, MGM, 1959; *The World, the Flesh, and the Devil*, MGM, 1959; *King of Kings*, MGM, 1961; *Sodom and Gomorrah* (also known as *The Last Days of Sodom and Gomorah*), Twentieth Century-Fox, 1962; *The V.I.P.'s*, MGM, 1963; *The Green Berets*, Warner Brothers, 1968; *The Power*, MGM, 1968; *The Private Life of Sherlock Holmes*, United Artists, 1970; *The Golden Voyage of Sinbad*, Columbia, 1974; *Providence*, Cinema V, 1977; *Fedora*, United Artists, 1978; *The Private Files of J. Edgar Hoover*, American International, 1978; *The Last Embrace*, United Artists, 1979; *Time After Time*, Warner Brothers/Orion, 1979; *Eye of the Needle*, United Artists, 1981; *Dead Men Don't Wear Plaid*, Universal, 1982. Also *Ten Days in Paris* (also known as *Missing Ten Days* and *Spy in the Pantry*), 1939; *Jacare* (also known as *Jacare—Killer of the Amazon*), 1942.

OTHER—*Double Life* (autobiography), Hippocrene Books, 1982; also composer of music for symphonies and chamber groups.

AWARDS: Academy Award nomination, Best Music (Original Score), 1940, for *The Thief of Baghdad;* Academy Award nominations, both Best Music (Scoring of a Dramatic Picture), 1941, for *Lydia* and *Sundown;* Academy Award nomination, Best Music (Scoring of a Dramatic or Comedy Picture), 1942, for *Jungle Book;* Academy Award nominations, both Best Music (Scoring of a Dramatic or Comedy Picture), 1944, for *Double Indemnity* and *Woman of the Town;* Academy Award, Best Music (Scoring of a Dramatic or Comedy Picture), 1945, for *Spellbound;* Academy Award nominations, both Best Music (Scoring of a Dramatic or Comedy Picture), 1945, for *The Lost Weekend* and (with Morris Stoloff) *A Song to Remember;* Academy Award nomination, Best Music (Scoring of a Dramatic or Comedy Picture), 1946, for *The Killers;* Academy Award, Best Music (Scoring of a Dramatic or Comedy Picture), 1947, for *A Double Life;* Academy Award nomination, Best Music (Scoring of a Dramatic or Comedy Picture), 1951, for *Quo Vadis;* Academy Award nomination, Best Music (Scoring of a Dramatic or Comedy Picture), 1952, for *Ivanhoe;* Academy Award nomination, Best Music (Scoring of a Dramatic or Comedy Picture), 1953, for *Julius Caesar;* Academy Award, Best Music (Scoring of a Dramatic or Comedy Picture), 1959, for *Ben Hur;* Academy Award nomination (with Paul Francis

Webster), Best Music (Song), 1961, for "Love Theme from *El Cid* (The Falcon and the Dove)"; Academy Award nomination, Best Music (Scoring of a Dramatic or Comedy Picture), 1961, for *El Cid;* Cesar Award from the French Academy, 1978, for *Providence.*

MEMBER: Screen Composers Association (president, 1956).*

*   *   *

RYAN, John P.   1938-

PERSONAL: Born July 30, 1938, in New York, NY. EDUCATION—Graduated from the City College of New York.

VOCATION: Actor.

CAREER: BROADWAY DEBUT—Joseph (understudy), *Daphne in Cottage D,* Longacre Theatre, 1967. PRINCIPAL STAGE APPEARANCES—John, *Duet for Three,* Cherry Lane Theatre, New York City, 1966; constable, *Serjeant Musgrave's Dance,* Theatre De Lys, New York City, 1966; villager, *Yerma,* Vivian Beaumont Theatre, New York City, 1966; Jamie O'Hanlin, *Nobody Hears a Broken Drum,* Fortune Theatre, New York City, 1970; Major Cassidy, *The Love Suicide at Schofield Barracks,* American National Theatre and Academy Theatre, New York City, 1972; rich man's son and contestant, *Gypsy,* Unitarian Church of All Souls, New York City, 1972; Mr. Drumm, *The Silent Partner,* Actors' Studio Theatre, New York City, 1972; juror, *Twelve Angry Men,* Queens Playhouse, New York City, 1972; Jason, *Medea,* Circle in the Square/Joseph E. Levine Theatre, New York City, 1973. Also appeared in *The Country Girl,* Stagewest, West Springfield, MA, 1975-76; and with the Arena Stage, Washington, DC, 1976-77.

PRINCIPAL FILM APPEARANCES—Toni's escort, *The Tiger Makes Out,* Columbia, 1967; Harry Samson, *A Lovely Way to Die* (also known as *A Lovely Way to Go*), Universal, 1968; Roger, *What's So Bad About Feeling Good?,* Universal, 1968; Spicer, *Five Easy Pieces,* Columbia, 1970; Surtees, *The King of Marvin Gardens,* Columbia, 1972; Houston, *The Legend of Nigger Charley,* Paramount, 1972; Patsy, *Cops and Robbers,* United Artists, 1973; Charles Mackley, *Dillinger,* American International, 1973; Colonel Hardcore, *Shamus,* Columbia, 1973; Frank Davis, *It's Alive,* Warner Brothers, 1974; Gardner, *Persecution* (also known as *Terror of Sheba* and *Sheba*), Fanfare, 1974; Dr. Schneider, *Futureworld,* American International, 1976; Si, *The Missouri Breaks,* United Artists, 1976; Frank Davis, *It Lives Again* (also known as *It's Alive II*), Warner Brothers, 1978; Coslough, *The Last Flight of Noah's Ark,* Buena Vista, 1980; Kennedy, *The Postman Always Rings Twice,* Paramount, 1981; Vernon, *The Escape Artist,* Orion/Warner Brothers, 1982; Lieutenant Parmentel, *Breathless,* Orion, 1983; head of program, *The Right Stuff,* Warner Brothers, 1983; Joe Flynn, *The Cotton Club,* Orion, 1984; Warden Ranken, *Runaway Train,* Cannon, 1985; Glastebury, *Avenging Force,* Cannon, 1986; Norton White, *Death Wish 4: The Crackdown,* Cannon, 1987; Lieutenant Kellerman, *Fatal Beauty,* Metro-Goldwyn-Mayer/United Artists, 1987; Mr. O'Rourke, *Three O'Clock High,* Universal, 1987; Wieser, *Rent-a-Cop,* Kings Road Entertainment, 1988; Captain Prescott, *Paramedics,* Vestron, 1988; Captain Fireman, *City of Shadows* (also known as *City of Night, Cry of Shadows,* and *Pater Noster*), Shapiro/Glickenhaus Entertainment, 1989. Also appeared in *On the Nickel,* Rose's Park, 1980; *Best of the Best,* Taurus Entertainment Group, 1989.

PRINCIPAL FILM WORK—Producer (with George Mendeluk), *The Kidnapping of the President,* Crown International, 1980; producer (with Mendeluk), *Stone Cold Dead,* Dimension, 1980.

PRINCIPAL TELEVISION APPEARANCES—Series: Lieutenant Barney Brighton, *Archer,* NBC, 1975. Pilots: Ralph Sloan, *Target Risk,* NBC, 1975; Mr. Canady, *Willow B: Women in Prison,* ABC, 1980; Captain McGee, *Shooting Stars,* ABC, 1983. Episodic: Blackie Scanlon, *Hollywood Beat,* ABC, 1985; Jake Manning, *Miami Vice,* NBC, 1989; also *M*A*S*H,* CBS, 1982. Movies: Detective Dave Lambert, *Death Scream,* ABC, 1975; Johnson, *Kill Me If You Can,* NBC, 1977; Flagler, *A Killing Affair,* CBS, 1977; David Burnet, *Houston: The Legend of Texas,* CBS, 1986.*

*   *   *

RYDER, Winona   1971-

PERSONAL: Born Winona Laura Horowitz, October 29, 1971, in Rochester, MN; daughter of Michael (an antiquarian book seller) and Cynthia (a video producer; maiden name, Istas) Horowitz. EDUCATION—Studied acting at the American Conservatory Theatre, San Francisco, CA.

VOCATION: Actress.

CAREER: FILM DEBUT—Rina, *Lucas,* Twentieth Century-Fox, 1986. PRINCIPAL FILM APPEARANCES—Gemma, *Square Dance,* Island, 1987; Lydia, *Beetlejuice,* Warner Brothers, 1988; Beth, *1969,* Atlantic Entertainment Group, 1988; Veronica Sawyer,

WINONA RYDER

Heathers, New World, 1989; Myra Gale Lewis, *Great Balls of Fire!,* Orion, 1989.

AWARDS: Best Actress Award at the Gijon (Spain) Film Festival, 1987, for *Square Dance.*

MEMBER: Screen Actors Guild.

ADDRESSES: AGENT—Andrea Eastman, International Creative Management, 8899 Beverly Boulevard, Los Angeles, CA 90048.

S

SABELLA, Ernie

PERSONAL: Full name, Ernest Sabella; born September 19 in Westchester, NY.

VOCATION: Actor.

CAREER: PRINCIPAL STAGE APPEARANCES—(As Ernest Sabella) Larry, *Broadway*, Equity Library Theatre, New York City, 1973; Lee, *A Nestless Bird*, Tobias, Eames, and Watson, ". . . *Twenty Years of Furniture*," and second friar, *Veil of Infamy*, all New Dramatists Inc., New York City, 1974; Little Harp, *The Robber Bridegroom*, St. Clement's Church Theatre, New York City, 1974, then as Big Harp, Biltmore Theatre, New York City, 1976; Grumio, *The Taming of the Shrew*, Equity Library Theatre, New York City, 1978; Whitney Wilson, *Little Johnny Jones*, Alvin Theatre, New York City, 1982. Also appeared in *The Robber Bridegroom*, Center Theatre Group, Mark Taper Forum, Los Angeles, 1976, then Ford's Theatre Society, Washington, DC, 1978, later Alliance Theatre, Atlanta, GA, 1979; *Richard III*, Repertory Theatre of St. Louis, St. Louis, MO, 1981.

PRINCIPAL FILM APPEARANCES—Ballistics expert, *City Heat*, Warner Brothers, 1984; hotel clerk, *Tough Guys*, Buena Vista, 1986; Dr. Harrison, *Fright Night, Part II*, New Century/Vista, 1988.

PRINCIPAL TELEVISION APPEARANCES—Series: Margaux's father, *Punky Brewster*, NBC, 1984; Lou Donatelli, *It's Your Move*, NBC, 1984-85; Donald "Twinkie" Twinkacetti, *Perfect Strangers*, ABC, 1986-87; Vito Carteri, *Roxie*, CBS, 1987; George Shipman, *A Fine Romance*, ABC, 1989. Pilots: Vlastock Spoltechzep, *13 Thirteenth Avenue*, CBS, 1983; Harry Pike, *100 Centre Street*, ABC, 1984. Episodic: Mr. Pond, *Married with Children*, Fox, 1987; Richard Dinsmore, *She's the Sheriff*, syndicated, 1987; Clyde Whitney, *Hardcastle and McCormick*, ABC, 1985; Ben, *Different Strokes*, ABC, 1985; Bo, *Benson*, ABC, 1986; Talbot, *The Last Precinct*, NBC, 1986; Angelo, *The Law and Harry McGraw*, CBS, 1988; Al Fresco, *Sledge Hammer!*, ABC, 1988; Mr. Palmer, *Mr. Belvedere*, ABC, 1988; also *Cheers*, CBS, 1985. Movies: Sam Gropper, *Copacabana*, CBS, 1985.

ADDRESSES: AGENT—Harris and Goldberg, 2121 Avenue of the Stars, Suite 950, Los Angeles, CA 90067.*

SADDLER, Donald 1918-

PERSONAL: Full name, Donald Edward Saddler; born January 24, 1918, in Van Nuys, CA; son of Elmer Edward (a landscape designer) and Mary Elizabeth (Roberts) Saddler. EDUCATION—Attended Los Angeles City College for two years; studied dance with Carmalita Maracci, Anton Dolin, Anthony Tudor, and Madame Anderson Ivantzova. MILITARY—U.S. Army, sergeant, 1943-45.

VOCATION: Choreographer, director, dancer, and producer.

CAREER: STAGE DEBUT Dancer, *Grand Canyon Suite*, Hollywood Bowl, Hollywood, CA, 1937. BROADWAY DEBUT—Uncle Willie, *High Button Shoes*, Century Theatre, 1947. PRINCIPAL STAGE APPEARANCES—Dancer, *Dance Me a Song*, Royale Theatre, New York City, 1950; dancer, *Bless You All*, Mark Hellinger Theatre, New York City, 1950; dancer, *The Song of Norway*, State Fair Music Hall, Dallas, TX, 1951; Reverend Curtis Brown, *Winesburg, Ohio*, Jacob's Pillow, Lee, MA, 1958; Macbeth, *The Golden Round*, Valerie Bettis Company, Jacob's Pillow, 1960; dancer, *The Castle Period*, Boston Arts Festival, Boston, MA, 1961. Also appeared in the *Fiftieth Anniversary Programme of the Ballet Theatre*, New York City, 1955; *Early Voyagers*, Valerie Bettis Company, Jacob's Pillow, 1960; *Happy Birthday, Mr. Abbott!*, Palace Theatre, New York City, 1987; as Harry Beaton, *Brigadoon*, State Fair Music Hall; and as the title role, *Bluebeard*, Alias, *Billy the Kid*, Benno, *Swan Lake*, the Rose Cavalier, *Aurora's Wedding*, the White Cavalier, *Les Patineurs*, the Hussar, *Lilac Garden*, Italian Ballerina's partner, *Gala Performance*, Paris, *Romeo and Juliet*, and the Head Hunter, *Peter and the Wolf*, all with the Ballet Theatre, New York City.

FIRST STAGE WORK—Choreographer, *Blue Mountain Ballads*, Markova-Dolin Dance Company, 1948. FIRST LONDON WORK—Choreographer, *Wonderful Town*, Prince's Theatre, 1955. PRINCIPAL STAGE WORK—All as choreographer, unless indicated: *Wish You Were Here*, Imperial Theatre, New York City, 1952; *Wonderful Town*, Winter Garden Theatre, New York City, 1953; *John Murray Anderson's Almanac*, Imperial Theatre, 1953; *Tobia la Candida Spia*, Teatro Sistina, Rome, Italy, 1954; (also director) *Wonderful Town*, Greek Theatre, Los Angeles, 1955; *La patrona di raddio di luna*, Teatro Sistina, 1955; *Shangri-La*, Winter Garden Theatre, 1956; *Buona notte Bettina*, Teatro Lirico, Milan, Italy, 1956; *L'adorabile Giulio*, Teatro Sistina, 1957; *Winesburg, Ohio* and *This Property Is Condemned*, both Jacob's Pillow, Lee, MA, 1958; *Un trapezio per Lisistrata*, Teatro Sistina, 1958; *When in Rome*, Adelphi Theatre, London, 1959; *Dreams of Glory*, Joffrey Ballet Company, New York City, 1961; *Milk and Honey*, Martin Beck Theatre, New York City, 1961; *Sophie*, Winter Garden Theatre, 1963; *Morning Sun*, Phoenix Theatre, New York City,

1963; *To Broadway, with Love*, Texas Pavilion, World's Fair, Flushing, NY, 1964.

No, No, Nanette, 46th Street Theatre, New York City, 1971; *Much Ado About Nothing*, New York Shakespeare Festival (NYSF), Delacorte Theatre, New York City, then Winter Garden Theatre, both 1972; director, *Berlin to Broadway with Kurt Weill*, Theatre De Lys, New York City, 1972; *Tricks*, Alvin Theatre, New York City, 1973; *No, No, Nanette*, Drury Lane Theatre, London, 1973; *Fanfare Gala*, City Center Theatre, New York City, 1973; *Good News*, St. James Theatre, New York City, 1973; producer, *The Sol Hurok Birthday Gala*, Metropolitan Opera House, New York City, 1973; *The Merry Wives of Windsor*, NYSF, Delacorte Theatre, 1974; *Miss Moffat*, Shubert Theatre, Philadelphia, PA, 1974; *A Midsummer Night's Dream*, Mitzie E. Newhouse Theatre, New York City, 1975; *A Doll's House*, Vivian Beaumont Theatre, New York City, 1975; *A Gala Tribute to Joshua Logan*, Imperial Theatre, 1975; producer, *The 30th Anniversary of City Center Theatre*, City Center Theatre, 1975; *Rodgers and Hart*, Helen Hayes Theatre, New York City, 1975; *The Robber Bridegroom*, Acting Company, Harkness Theatre, New York City, 1975, then Biltmore Theatre, New York City, 1976; director, *George Abbott . . . A Celebration*, Shubert Theatre, New York City, 1976; *Koshare* and *Vaudeville* (ballets), both Harkness Ballet, New York City, 1976; *Dear Friends and Gentle Hearts* (ballet), Cincinnati Ballet, Cincinnati, OH, 1976; (with others) *Icedancing*, Minskoff Theatre, New York City, 1978; *The Grand Tour*, Palace Theatre, New York City, 1979.

Happy New Year, Morosco Theatre, New York City, 1980; *Hey, Look Me Over!*, Avery Fisher Hall, New York City, 1981; producer (with Martin Feinstein), *The Pre-Inaugural Ballet-Opera Gala*, Kennedy Center for the Performing Arts, Washington, DC, 1981; director, *Life with Father*, Westside YMCA, New York City, 1982; *On Your Toes*, Virginia Theatre, New York City, 1983; director, *I Hear Music . . . of Frank Loesser and Friends*, Ballroom Theatre, New York City, 1984; (also director) *A Celebration for Sir Anton Dolin*, Royal Opera House, London, 1984; *The Loves of Anatol*, Circle in the Square, New York City, 1985; *The Golden Land*, Second Avenue Theatre, New York City, 1985; *Broadway*, Great Lakes Theatre Festival, Cleveland, OH, then Royale Theatre, New York City, both 1987; *The Student Prince*, New York City Opera, State Theatre, New York City, 1987; *Teddy and Alice*, Minskoff Theatre, 1987; (also director) *Kiss Me Kate*, Stratford Shakespeare Festival, Stratford, ON, Canada, 1989. Also director, State Fair Music Hall, Dallas, TX, 1957 and 1959; director, Carousel Theatre, Framingham, MA, 1958; choreographer, *Un manderino per Teo*, in Italy, 1959; producer, *The Dance Collection Gala*, New York City, 1972; producer, *The 35th Anniversary of the American Ballet Theatre*, New York City, 1975; choreographer, *A Long Way to Boston*, 1979; director, Stratford Shakespeare Festival, 1979; choreographer, *Pardon, Monsieur Moliere*, Rome, 1982; director and choreographer of the opening of the Roger L. Stevens Center for the Performing Arts, Dallas, 1983; director and choreographer, *100 Years of Performing Arts at the Metropolitan*, New York City, 1984.

Choreographer, *The Boys from Syracuse*, Great Lakes Theatre Festival; choreographer, *My Fair Lady*, Stratford Shakespeare Festival; director and choreographer, *Bitter Sweet* (opera), Orlando Opera, Orlando, FL; director and choreographer, *Weiner Blut*, *Abduction from the Seraglio* (operas), and *Washinton Opera Follies*, all Washington Opera, Washington, DC; choreographer, *Aida* (opera), Dallas Civic Opera, Dallas; choreographer, *La Perichole* (opera), Metropolitan Opera House; choreographer, *The Merry*

Widow (opera), New York City Opera, State Theatre; director and choreographer, *American Ballet Theatre's Fortieth Anniversary*, Metropolitan Opera House; director and choreographer, *Tribute to Lucille Lortel*, Lucille Lortel Theatre, New York City; director and choreographer, *Tribute to Richard Rodgers*, Imperial Theatre; director and choreographer, *Merman-Martin Gala*, Broadway Theatre, New York City; director and choreographer, *Tribute to Cy Coleman*, Avery Fisher Hall; director and choreographer, *An Evening with Kurt Weill*, Philharmonic Hall, New York City; director and choreographer, *Jo Sullivan in Concert*, Ballroom Theatre, White Barn Theatre, Westport, CT, and Carnegie Hall, New York City; director and choreographer, *Tribute to George Abbott*, Broadway Theatre; director and choreographer, *Tribute to Lerner and Loewe*, Broadway Theatre; producer, *The Cynthia Gregory Gala*, Metropolitan Opera House; director and choreographer, *Stratford Shakespeare Festival Gala*; choreographer, *Tropicana*, Off-Broadway production; director and choreographer, *American Guild of Musical Artists 100th Anniversary Gala*; director and choreographer of the Theatre Hall of Fame ceremonies for seven years; director and choreographer of the first International Ballet Competition, Jackson, MS; and producer of the Lincoln Center Perform-a-Thon, New York City.

MAJOR TOURS—Choreographer: *We Take the Town*, U.S. cities, 1962; *Knickerbocker Holiday*, U.S. cities, 1971; *No, No, Nanette*, U.S. cities, 1971-73; *Good News*, U.S. cities, 1973-74; *Hellzapoppin'*, U.S. cities, 1976-77; (also director) *Oh, Kay!*, U.S. and Canadian cities, 1978; *On Your Toes*, U.S. cities, 1984.

PRINCIPAL FILM WORK—Choreographer: *April in Paris*, Warner Brothers, 1952; *By the Light of the Silvery Moon*, Warner Brothers, 1953; *Young at Heart*, Warner Brothers, 1954; *The Main Attraction*, Metro-Goldwyn-Mayer/Seven Arts, 1963; *The Happy Hooker*, Cannon, 1975; *Radio Days*, Orion, 1987.

PRINCIPAL TELEVISION APPEARANCES—Series: Regular, *Holiday Hotel*, ABC, 1950.

PRINCIPAL TELEVISION WORK—All as choreographer. Series: *Holiday Hotel*, ABC, 1950; *Bell Telephone Hour*, NBC, 1961-64; also *Canozionissima*, Italian television, 1959-60. Episodic: *The Perry Como Show*, CBS, 1950. Specials: *Much Ado About Nothing*, CBS, 1973; *Verna: U.S.O. Girl*, PBS, 1978; also *Alice in Wonderland*, PBS; *In Fashion*, PBS; and the Antoinette Perry Awards broadcasts, 1973, 1975-78, and 1983.

RELATED CAREER—Dancer in nightclubs, New York City, 1939; member, Ballet Theatre, New York City, 1940-43, then 1946-47; assistant director, then artistic director, Harkness Ballet, New York City, 1964-70; executive vice-president, Rebekah Harkness Foundation, New York City, 1967-69; executive board member, International Ballet Corporation, 1979; also producer of the New York Dance Festival, Delacorte Theatre, New York City, for five years; choreographer of industrial shows.

AWARDS: Antoinette Perry Award, Best Choreographer, 1953, for *Wonderful Town;* Maschera d'Argento, 1954, for *Tobia la Candida Spia;* Antoinette Perry Award and Drama Desk Award, both Best Choreographer, 1971, for *No, No, Nanette;* Antoinette Perry Award nomination, Best Choreographer, 1973, for *Much Ado About Nothing;* Antoinette Perry Award nomination, Best Choreographer, 1983, for *On Your Toes; Dance* magazine Award, 1984.

MEMBER: Actors' Equity Association, Society of Stage Directors and Choreographers.

ADDRESSES: AGENT—Coleman-Rosenberg Agency, 210 E. 58th Street, New York, NY 10022.

*   *   *

SAFAN, Craig   1948-

PERSONAL: Born December 17, 1948, in Los Angeles, CA; son of Eugene (in business) and Betty (a concert pianist and piano teacher; maiden name, Torchin) Safan; married Linda McClelland (an artist), July 27, 1977; children: Alec, Kira. EDUCATION—Brandeis University, B.A., 1970.

VOCATION: Composer.

CAREER: Also see *WRITINGS* below. PRINCIPAL STAGE WORK—Assistant musical director, *More Than You Deserve*, New York Shakespeare Festival, Public Theatre, New York City, 1974.

RELATED CAREER—Writer of lead sheets for music publishing companies; arranger and conductor, Reprise Records; lecturer on film composition at the American Film Institute, the University of Southern California Film School, the University of California, Los Angeles Film School, and at Independent Feature Projects West.

WRITINGS: All as composer, unless indicated. STAGE—Music and (with Mark Mueller) book, *Butterfly*, Goodspeed Opera House, East Haddam, CT, 1988.

FILM—*The Great Texas Dynamite Chase* (also known as *Dynamite*

CRAIG SAFAN

Women), New World, 1976; (also lyrics) *The Bad News Bears in Breaking Training,* Paramount, 1977; *Corvette Summer* (also known as *The Hot One*), United Artists, 1978; *Good Guys Wear Black,* Mar Vista, 1978; *The Great Smokey Roadblock* (also known as *The Last of the Cowboys*), Mar Vista, 1978; *Roller Boogie,* United Artists, 1979; *Fade to Black,* American Cinema, 1980; *Die Laughing,* Warner Brothers, 1980; (contributor) *Thief,* United Artists, 1981; *T.A.G.: The Assassination Game,* New World, 1982; *Nightmares,* Universal, 1983; *Angel,* New World, 1984; *The Last Starfighter,* Universal, 1984; *The Legend of Billie Jean,* Tri-Star, 1985; *Remo Williams: The Adventure Begins,* Orion, 1985; *Warning Sign,* Twentieth Century-Fox, 1985; *Lady Beware,* International Video Entertainment, 1987; *The Stranger,* Columbia, 1987; *Stand and Deliver,* Warner Brothers, 1988; *A Nightmare on Elm Street IV: The Dream Master,* New Line Cinema, 1988.

TELEVISION—Series: *Counterattack: Crime in America,* ABC, 1982; *Cheers,* NBC, 1982—; *Detective in the House,* CBS, 1985; *Spies,* CBS, 1987; *Remo Williams,* ABC, 1988; *Supercarrier,* ABC, 1988; *Life Goes On,* ABC, 1989—. Pilots: *Hardcase,* NBC, 1981; *The Best of Times,* CBS, 1983; *Poor Richard,* CBS, 1984; *Help Wanted: Kids,* ABC, 1986; *I-Man,* ABC, 1986. Episodic: *Darkroom,* ABC, 1981-82; *Ripley's Believe It or Not,* ABC, 1982-86; *Call to Glory,* ABC, 1984-85; *Alfred Hitchcock Presents,* NBC, 1985-86; *The Twilight Zone,* CBS, 1985-87; *Amazing Stories,* NBC, 1985-87; "My Town," *Disney Sunday Movie,* ABC, 1986; *Island Son,* CBS, 1989. Movies: *Getting Married,* CBS, 1978; *Survival of Dana,* CBS, 1979; *The Imposter,* ABC, 1984; *Mirrors,* NBC, 1985; *Samaritan: The Mitch Snyder Story,* CBS, 1986; *Courage,* CBS, 1986; *Timestalkers,* CBS, 1987; *Shootdown,* NBC, 1988; *Almost Grown,* CBS, 1988; *The Comeback,* CBS, 1989; *Revenge of Al Capone,* NBC, 1989. Specials: "Secrets of the Titanic," *National Geographic Explorer,* WTBS (Atlanta, GA), 1987; "Elephant," *National Geographic Special,* PBS, 1989; also *The California Reich* (documentary), 1975.

RECORDINGS: ALBUMS—*Warning Sign* (original soundtrack), Southern Cross, 1985; also *The Last Starfighter* (original soundtrack), Southern Cross; *Thief* (original soundtrack), Elektra; *A Nightmare on Elm Street IV: The Dream Master* (original soundtrack); *Stand and Deliver* (original soundtrack); *Lady Beware* (original soundtrack); *The Stranger* (original soundtrack).

AWARDS: Special American Society of Composers, Authors, and Publishers (ASCAP) Award for *Cheers;* Award for Musical Composition and Award for Dramatic Achievement, both from Brandeis University; Watson Foundation fellowship.

MEMBER: Academy of Motion Picture Arts and Sciences (executive music committee member), National Academy of Recording Arts and Sciences, American Society of Composers, Authors, and Publishers.

SIDELIGHTS: RECREATIONS—Collecting art and pre-World War I sheet music.

Craig Safan, with Mark Mueller, developed the original idea for the feature film *Tap* (also known as *Tap Dance*), Tri-Star, 1989.

ADDRESSES: AGENT—Charles Ryan, International Creative Management, 8899 Beverly Boulevard, Los Angeles, CA 90048. PUBLICIST—Flaherty/Winters/Greenberg and Partners, 9884 Santa Monica Boulevard, Beverly Hills, CA 90212.

SAINT JAMES, Susan 1946-

PERSONAL: Born Susan Jane Miller, August 14, 1946, in Los Angeles, CA; daughter of Charles Daniel (in business) and Constance (Geiger) Miller; married Richard Newbert (divorced); married Tom Lucas (divorced); married Dick Ebersol (a television executive); children: Charlie, William James (third marriage); Sunshine, Harmony. EDUCATION—Attended the Connecticut College for Women.

VOCATION: Actress.

CAREER: PRINCIPAL STAGE APPEARANCES—*Ready When You Are, C.B.!*, Marriott's Lincolnshire Theatre, Lincolnshire, IL, 1978.

PRINCIPAL FILM APPEARANCES—Linette Orbison, *P.J.* (also known as *New Face in Hell*), Universal, 1968; Ida, *Jigsaw*, Universal, 1968; Aida, *What's So Bad About Feeling Good?*, Universal, 1968; Rosabelle, *Where Angels Go . . . Trouble Follows*, Columbia, 1968; Tina Waters, *Outlaw Blues*, Warner Brothers, 1977; Cindy Sondheim, *Love at First Bite*, American International, 1979; Jane Mahoney, *How to Beat the High Cost of Living*, American International, 1980; Vivian Whitney, *Carbon Copy*, AVCO-Embassy, 1981; Katherine, *Don't Cry, It's Only Thunder*, Sanrio Communications, 1982.

PRINCIPAL TELEVISION APPEARANCES—Series: Peggy Maxwell, *The Name of the Game*, NBC, 1968-71; Sally McMillan, *McMillan and Wife*, NBC, 1971-76; Kate McArdle, *Kate and Allie*, CBS, 1984-89. Pilots: Peggy Maxwell, *Fame Is the Name of the Game*, NBC, 1966; Miss Porter, *Alias Smith and Jones*, ABC, 1971; Sally McMillan, *Once Upon a Dead Man*, NBC, 1971; Julia Prescott, *Ready and Willing*, CBS, 1974; Holly, *Scott Free*, NBC, 1976; Susan Roberts, *After George*, CBS, 1983. Episodic: *M*A*S*H*, CBS, 1980; *Saturday Night Live*, NBC; *Friday Night Videos*, NBC; *Ironside*, NBC; *It Takes a Thief*, ABC; *McCloud*, NBC; *Love, American Style*, ABC. Movies: Timothea Lamb, *Magic Carpet*, ABC, 1972; Esther Winters, *Desperate Women*, NBC, 1978; Jeannie Haskins, *Night Cries*, ABC, 1978; Rita Massaro, *The Girls in the Office*, ABC, 1979; Sally Bass, *Sex and the Single Parent*, CBS, 1979; Leigh Goodwin, *S.O.S. Titanic*, ABC, 1979; Samantha Kandal, *The Kid from Nowhere*, NBC, 1982; Carol Sherwood, *I Take These Men*, CBS, 1983. Specials: *Celebrity Challenge of the Sexes*, CBS, 1977; *Circus of the Stars*, CBS, 1977; *John Denver in Australia*, ABC, 1978; *Life's Most Embarrassing Moments*, syndicated, 1985; *The Flintstones 25th Anniversary Celebration*, CBS, 1986; *A Very Special Christmas Party* (also known as *Special Olympics Christmas Party*), ABC, 1988.

RELATED CAREER—Professional model in Paris, France; stagehand, Olympia Theatre, Paris, France; assistant to Charles Aznavour.

NON-RELATED CAREER—Vice-president and national chairperson, Connecticut Special Olympics Inc.

AWARDS: Emmy Award, Outstanding Continued Performance By an Actress in a Supporting Role in a Series, 1969, and two additional Emmy Award nominations, all for *The Name of the Game;* also three Emmy Award nominations for *McMillan and Wife;* two Emmy Award nominations for *Kate and Allie;* and received an honorary doctorate for her on-going involvement with Special Olympics.*

PETER SALLIS

SALLIS, Peter 1921-

PERSONAL: Born February 1, 1921, in Twickenham, England; son of Harry (a bank manager) and Dorothy Amea Frances (Barnard) Sallis; married Elaine Usher (an actress), February 9, 1957. EDUCATION—Trained for the stage at the Royal Academy of Dramatic Art. MILITARY—Royal Air Force.

VOCATION: Actor and playwright.

CAREER: Also see *WRITINGS* below. STAGE DEBUT—Soldier and servant, *The Scheming Lieutenant*, Arts Theatre, London, 1946. BROADWAY DEBUT—Dr. Watson, *Baker Street*, Broadway Theatre, 1965. PRINCIPAL STAGE APPEARANCES—Fedotik, *The Three Sisters*, Aldwych Theatre, London, 1951; Roger Doremus, *Summer and Smoke*, Lyric Hammersmith Theatre, London, 1951, then Duchess Theatre, London, 1952; jeweller, *Timon of Athens*, Old Vic Theatre, London, 1952; porter and doctor, *Macbeth* and Hoard, *A Trick to Catch the Old One*, both Mermaid Theatre, London, 1952; Waitwell, *The Way of the World* and Retrosi, *Venice Preserved*, both Lyric Hammersmith Theatre, 1952-53; first soldier, *The Dark Is Light Enough*, Aldwych Theatre, 1954; Joe Scanlon, *The Matchmaker*, Haymarket Theatre, London, 1954; Virgil Penny, *Into Thin Air*, Globe Theatre, London, 1955; the Stage Manager, *Moby Dick*, Duke of York's Theatre, London, 1955; priest, *The Count of Clerembard*, Garrick Theatre, London, 1955; Fag, *The Rivals*, Saville Theatre, London, 1956; J.G., *Who Cares?*, Fortune Theatre, London, 1956; Denny, *Janus*, Aldwych Theatre, 1957; Frank Braddock, *Be My Guest*, Winter Garden Theatre, London, 1957; Simon and Barere, *Danton's Death*, Thrifty, *The Cheats of Scapin*, and doctor and provost, *Brand*, all Lyric

Hammersmith Theatre, 1959; Gigot, then Van Putzeboom, *Look After Lulu,* Royal Court Theatre, London, 1959-60.

Bottard, *Rhinoceros,* Royal Court Theatre, then Strand Theatre, London, 1960; Peter, *The Zoo Story,* Arts Theatre, London, 1960; Phillip Vanderkamp, *Masterpiece,* Royalty Theatre, London, 1961; Mr. Moxer, *Two Stars for Comfort,* Garrick Theatre, 1962; Morestan, *A Shot in the Dark,* Lyric Theatre, London, 1963; Ladislav Sipos, *She Loves Me,* Lyric Theatre, 1964; Hudson, *Inadmissible Evidence,* Belasco Theatre, New York City, 1965, then Shubert Theatre, New York City, 1966; Roat, *Wait Until Dark,* Strand Theatre, 1966; Herr Schultz, *Cabaret,* Palace Theatre, London, 1968; Edwin Palmer, *The Pay-Off,* Comedy Theatre, London, 1972; Dogberry, *Much Ado About Nothing,* Strand Theatre, 1989; also appeared in repertory theatre productions, 1947-50.

PRINCIPAL FILM APPEARANCES—Grischa, *Anastasia,* Twentieth Century-Fox, 1956; secretary of the picture gallery, *The Doctor's Dilemma,* Metro-Goldwyn-Mayer (MGM), 1958; customs official, *The Scapegoat,* MGM, 1959; Don Enrique, *The Curse of the Werewolf,* Universal, 1961; sleazy doctor, *I Thank a Fool,* MGM, 1962; Russian delegate, *The Mouse on the Moon,* United Artists, 1963; doctor, *The V.I.P.s,* MGM, 1963; Lawrence Jacks, *The Third Secret,* Twentieth Century-Fox, 1964; Victor Lush, *Escape By Night* (also known as *Clash By Night*), Allied Artists, 1965; Armand, *Rapture,* Twentieth Century-Fox, 1965; solicitor, *Charlie Bubbles,* Universal, 1968; Hudson, *Inadmissible Evidence,* Paramount, 1968; Sir Sidney Brent, *My Lover, My Son,* MGM, 1970; Schweitz, *Scream and Scream Again,* American International, 1970; Samuel Paxton, *Taste the Blood of Dracula,* Warner Brothers, 1970; Mr. Shielders, *Wuthering Heights,* American International, 1970; Reverend Palafox, *The Night Digger* (also known as *The Road Builder*), MGM, 1971; Keresley, *The Reckoning,* Columbia, 1971; Thierry, *The Incredible Sarah,* Readers Digest Productions, 1976; Geoffrey Branscombe, *Full Circle,* Fester, 1977, rereleased as *The Haunting of Julia,* Discovery, 1981; St. Claire, *Who Is Killing the Great Chefs of Europe?* (also known as *Someone Is Killing the Great Chefs of Europe* and *Too Many Chefs*), Warner Brothers, 1978. Also appeared in *Saturday Night and Sunday Morning,* Continental Distributing, 1961.

PRINCIPAL TELEVISION APPEARANCES—Series: Clegg, *Last of the Summer Wine,* Entertainment Channel, 1983. Mini-Series: Mr. Bonteen, *The Pallisers,* BBC, then PBS, 1977. Movies: Carter, *Witness for the Prosecution,* CBS, 1982. Specials: Sipos, *She Loves Me,* BBC, then PBS, 1979. Also appeared in *The Diary of Samuel Pepys.*

NON-RELATED CAREER—Bank clerk.

WRITINGS: STAGE—*End of Term.* RADIO—Author of three plays broadcast on British radio.

MEMBER: Garrick Club.

SIDELIGHTS: FAVORITE ROLES—Roat in *Wait Until Dark* and Ladislav Sipos in *She Loves Me.* RECREATIONS—Painting and gardening.

ADDRESSES: AGENT—Duncan Heath Associates Ltd., Paramount House, 162-170 Wardour Street, London W1, England.

SANDS, Julian   1958-

PERSONAL: Born in 1958 in Yorkshire, England; wife's name, Sarah (a journalist; divorced); children: Henry. EDUCATION—Studied acting at the Central School of Speech and Drama.

VOCATION: Actor.

CAREER: PRINCIPAL FILM APPEARANCES—Sailor, *Privates on Parade,* Orion Classics, 1982; Jon Swain, *The Killing Fields,* Warner Brothers, 1984; Colin, *Oxford Blues,* Metro-Goldwyn-Mayer/United Artists, 1984; Laurence Huninger, *After Darkness,* Green Man/Philum, 1985; Dr. Murray, *The Doctor and the Devils,* Twentieth Century-Fox, 1985; George Emerson, *A Room with a View,* Cinecom, 1986; Percy Bysshe Shelley, *Gothic,* Virgin, 1987; Kit, *Siesta,* Lorimar, 1987; Dr. Harrison Steele, *Vibes,* Columbia, 1988; Julian, *Wherever You Are* (also known as *Wherever She Is* and *Gdzieskolwiek jest, jeslis jest*), Gerhard Schmidt/Film Polski, 1988; Father Daniel, *Manika* (also known as *Manika: Une vie plus tard, Manika: The Girl Who Lived Twice, Manika Manika,* and *Une Passerelle sur le gange*), Films du Scorpion/Twentieth Century-Fox/Manley, 1988; Wolfgang Leighton, *Tennessee Nights* (also known as *Tennessee Waltz*), Nelson Entertainment, 1989; title role, *Warlock,* J & M Entertainment, 1989.

PRINCIPAL TELEVISION APPEARANCES—Series: Guy Lough, *A Married Man,* Channel Four, 1982, then syndicated, 1984. Movies: Sandy, *Romance on the Orient Express,* NBC, 1985; Forest, *Harem,* ABC, 1986; Todd Sands, *The Room,* ABC, 1987; Major Stefan Kirilenko, *Murder By Moonlight,* CBS, 1989.

RELATED CAREER—Stage manager, writer, and director.

SIDELIGHTS: RECREATIONS—Reading, listening to classical music, and running in marathons.

ADDRESSES: AGENT—Tracy Jacobs, Triad Artists, 10100 Santa Monica Boulevard, 16th Floor, Los Angeles, CA 90067.*

*   *   *

SAVAGE, Fred   1976-

PERSONAL: Born July 9, 1976, in Highland Park, IL; son of Lewis M. (an industrial real estate broker) and Joanne F. (a personal manager) Savage.

VOCATION: Actor.

CAREER: FILM DEBUT—Louis Michaelson, *The Boy Who Could Fly,* Twentieth Century-Fox, 1986. PRINCIPAL FILM APPEARANCES—Grandson, *The Princess Bride,* Twentieth Century-Fox, 1987; Charlie Seymour, *Vice Versa,* Columbia, 1988; Brian Stevenson, *Little Monsters,* Metro-Goldwyn-Mayer/United Artists, 1989; Corey Woods, *The Wizard,* Universal, 1989.

PRINCIPAL TELEVISION APPEARANCES—Series: Alan Bishop, *Morningstar/Eveningstar,* CBS, 1986; Kevin Arnold, *The Wonder Years,* ABC, 1988—. Episodic: *The Twilight Zone,* CBS, 1986; *Saturday Night Live,* NBC, 1990. Movies: Davy Reuben, *Run Till You Fall,* CBS, 1988; Matthew Nickerson, *Convicted: A Mother's Story,* CBS, 1987. Specials: Garf, ''Runaway Ralph,'' *ABC Week-*

FRED SAVAGE

end Specials, ABC, 1987; *Comic Relief III,* HBO, 1989. Also appeared in *What Are Friends For?,* CBS, 1986.

RELATED CAREER—Actor in television commercials.

AWARDS: Emmy Award nomination, Outstanding Lead Actor in a Comedy Series, 1989, for *The Wonder Years.*

ADDRESSES: AGENT—Iris Burton Agency, 1450 Belfast Drive, Los Angeles, CA 90069.

*   *   *

SAYLE, Alexei   1952-

PERSONAL: Born August 7, 1952, in Liverpool, England.

VOCATION: Actor and writer.

CAREER: PRINCIPAL FILM APPEARANCES—Second detective, *Repeater,* British Film Institute, 1982; Golodkin, *Gorky Park,* Rank, 1983; Magar, *The Bride,* Columbia, 1985; Perryman, *The Supergrass,* Hemdale, 1985; as himself in a Hawaiian shirt, *Whoops Apocalypse,* Metro-Goldwyn-Mayer, 1986; cabbie, *Siesta,* Lorimar, 1987; the voices, *The Love Child,* British Film Institute/Frontroom, 1987; Carl and Sterling Moss, *Didn't You Kill My Brother?,* Recorded Releasing, 1987; Paul, *The Strike,* Palace, 1987; Sultan, *Indiana Jones and the Last Crusade,* Paramount, 1989. Also

appeared in *Live a Life,* Other Cinema, 1982; *The Secret Policeman's Other Ball,* United International, 1981.

PRINCIPAL TELEVISION APPEARANCES—Series: Host, *Alexei Sayle's Stuff: Fun with Magnets,* BBC, 1989; also *Comic Strip,* Channel Four, 1987; *The Young Ones* and *Comic Roots.*

WRITINGS: FILM—(With Pauline Melville) *Didn't You Kill My Brother?,* Recorded Releasing, 1987.

ADDRESSES: AGENT—Simon Astaire, International Creative Management, 388-396 Oxford Street, London W1, England.*

*   *   *

SBARGE, Raphael   1964-

PERSONAL: Born February 12, 1964, in New York, NY. EDUCATION—Trained for the stage at the HB Studios.

VOCATION: Actor.

CAREER: OFF-BROADWAY DEBUT—John of Lancaster, *Henry IV, Part One,* New York Shakespeare Festival, Delacorte Theatre, 1981, for thirty-nine performances. PRINCIPAL STAGE APPEARANCES—Martin Thomas Walsh, *The Curse of an Aching Heart,* Little Theatre, New York City, 1982; Reynaldo and Player, *Hamlet,* New York Shakespeare Festival, Public Theatre, New York City, 1982-83; Benjamin, *Short Change,* Samuel Beckett Theatre, New York City, 1985; Bucky, "Sorrows and Sons" and "Spittin' Image," in *Sorrows and Sons,* Vineyard Theatre, New York City, 1986; Richard Miller, *Ah, Wilderness!,* Yale Repertory Theatre, New Haven, CT, 1987, then Neil Simon Theatre, New York City, 1988; also appeared in *The Red Snake,* New York City.

PRINCIPAL FILM APPEARANCES—Thomas Carroll, *Abuse,* Promovision International, 1982; Glenn, *Risky Business,* Warner Brothers, 1983; Sherman, *My Science Project,* Buena Vista, 1985; Schmoozler, *Vision Quest,* Warner Brothers, 1985; Adam Swit, *My Man Adam,* Tri-Star, 1986; narrator, *Dear America* (also known as *Dear America: Letters Home from Vietnam*), HBO Films, 1987; voice of Chip, *Miracle Mile,* Hemdale, 1988; Matt Harman, *Riding the Edge,* Trans World Entertainment, 1989.

PRINCIPAL TELEVISION APPEARANCES—Series: Brian McGuire, *Better Days,* CBS, 1986. Episodic: Ted Nichols, *Werewolf,* Fox, 1987; Mr. Jenkins, *The Cosby Show,* NBC, 1988; Charlie Darrow, *Island Son,* CBS, 1989; Will, *Quantum Leap,* NBC, 1990. Movies: The Collector, *A Streetcar Named Desire,* ABC, 1984; John Parsons, *Prison for Children,* CBS, 1987; Chris McNally, *Cracked Up,* ABC, 1987; Eric Fairmont, *The Billionaire Boys Club,* NBC, 1987; Dr. Nelman, *Baby Girl Scott,* CBS, 1987; Henry Ernst, *So Proudly We Hail* (also known as *Skinheads*), CBS, 1990.

ADDRESSES: MANAGER—Frank Andrews, New York, NY.*

GEORGE SCHAEFER

SCHAEFER, George   1920-

PERSONAL: Full name, George Louis Schaefer; born December 16, 1920, in Wallingford, CT; son of Louis (in sales) and Elsie (Otterbein) Schaefer; married Mildred Trares (an actress), February 5, 1954. EDUCATION—Lafayette College, B.A., 1941; graduate work at the Yale University School of Drama, 1942. MILITARY— U.S. Army, Special Services, sergeant, 1942-45.

VOCATION: Director and producer.

CAREER: FIRST BROADWAY WORK—Director, *Hamlet* (also known as *G.I. Hamlet*), City Center Theatre, 1946. FIRST LONDON WORK—Producer (with Maurice Evans) and director, *Teahouse of the August Moon*, Her Majesty's Theatre, 1954. PRINCIPAL STAGE WORK—All as director, unless indicated: *Leave It to Smith*, Pastime Players, Oak Park, IL, 1937; *Hamlet* (also known as *G.I. Hamlet*), Columbus Circle Theatre, New York City, 1945; (with Maurice Evans) *Man and Superman*, Alvin Theatre, New York City, 1947; *The Linden Tree*, Music Box Theatre, New York City, 1948; (also producer) *Man and Superman* and *She Stoops to Conquer*, both City Center Theatre, 1949; (also producer) *The Corn Is Green, The Heiress, The Devil's Disciple*, and *Captain Brassbound's Conversion*, all City Center Theatre, 1950; (also producer) *The Royal Family, Richard II, The Taming of the Shrew, Dream Girl, Idiot's Delight*, and *The Wild Duck*, all City Center Theatre, 1951; (also producer) *Anna Christie, Come of Age, The Male Animal, Tovarich*, and *First Lady*, all City Center Theatre, 1952; producer (with Evans), *Teahouse of the August Moon*, Martin Beck Theatre, New York City, 1953; *Kiss Me Kate*, City Center Theatre, 1955; *The Southwest Corner*, Holiday Theatre, New York

City, 1955; *The Apple Cart*, Plymouth Theatre, New York City, 1956; *The Body Beautiful*, Broadway Theatre, New York City, 1958; (also producer) *Write Me a Murder*, Belasco Theatre, New York City, 1961, then Lyric Theatre, London, 1962; producer, *To Broadway with Love*, Texas Pavilion, New York World's Fair, Flushing, NY, 1964; *The Great Indoors*, Eugene O'Neill Theatre, New York City, 1966; *The Last of Mrs. Lincoln*, Kennedy Center for the Performing Arts, Opera House, Washington, DC, then American National Theatre and Academy Theatre, New York City, both 1972; *On Golden Pond*, Center Theatre Group, Ahmanson Theatre, Los Angeles, 1980; *Mixed Couples*, Brooks Atkinson Theatre, New York City, 1980; *Another Part of the Forest*, Center Theatre Group, Ahmanson Theatre, 1981; *Lyndon*, Wilmington Playhouse, Wilmington, DE, 1984. Also director of productions at the State Fair Music Hall, Dallas, TX, 1952-56, then 1958; director, *Leave It to Jane*, Los Angeles, 1987.

MAJOR TOURS—Director: *Hamlet*, U.S. cities, 1946-47; *Darling, Darling, Darling*, U.S. cities, 1947; (with Maurice Evans) *Man and Superman*, U.S. cities, 1948-49; *Teahouse of the August Moon*, U.S. cities, 1954, then 1956; *The Apple Cart*, U.S. cities, 1957; *Zenda*, U.S. cities, 1963; *The Student Prince*, U.S. cities, 1973; *Ah! Wilderness*, U.S. cities, 1975; *Lyndon*, U.S. cities, 1984.

PRINCIPAL FILM WORK—Director: *Macbeth*, Prominent, 1963; *Pendulum*, Columbia, 1969; *Generation*, AVCO-Embassy, 1969; *Doctors' Wives*, Columbia, 1971; *Once Upon a Scoundrel*, Carlyle, 1973; (also producer) *An Enemy of the People*, Warner Brothers, 1978.

PRINCIPAL TELEVISION APPEARANCES—Specials: *The Television Makers*, PBS, 1987. PRINCIPAL TELEVISION WORK—All as director, unless indicated. Series: Executive producer, *Love Story*, NBC, 1973-74. Pilots: *Land of Hope*, CBS, 1976. Episodic: "Hour of the Bath," *Alcoa Theatre*, NBC, 1962; "The Hands of Donofrio," *Alcoa Premiere*, ABC, 1962; *Love Story*, NBC, 1973 and 1974 (two episodes). Movies: (Also producer) *A War of Children*, CBS, 1972; *F. Scott Fitzgerald and "The Last of the Belles,"* ABC, 1974; (also producer) *In This House of Brede*, CBS, 1975; *Amelia Earhart*, NBC, 1976; (also producer) *The Girl Called Hatter Fox*, CBS, 1977; *First You Cry*, CBS, 1978; (also producer) *Who'll Save Our Children?*, CBS, 1978; (also producer with Renee Valente) *Blind Ambition*, CBS, 1979; *Mayflower: The Pilgrims' Adventure*, CBS, 1979; (also producer) *People vs. Jean Harris*, NBC, 1981; (also producer with Aida Young) *The Bunker*, CBS, 1981; (also producer) *A Piano for Mrs. Cimino*, CBS, 1982; (also producer) *Right of Way*, HBO, 1983; (also producer with Frank Prendergast and Charles Haid) *Children in the Crossfire*, NBC, 1984; (also producer) *Stone Pillow*, CBS, 1985; (also producer) *Mrs. Delafield Wants to Marry*, CBS, 1986; (also co-producer) *Laura Lansing Slept Here*, NBC, 1988.

Specials: "Hamlet," *Hallmark Hall of Fame*, NBC, 1953; "Richard II" and "Macbeth," *Hallmark Hall of Fame*, NBC, 1954; *One Touch of Venus*, NBC, 1955; "Alice in Wonderland," "Dream Girl," and "The Devil's Disciple," *Hallmark Hall of Fame*, NBC, 1955; "Taming of the Shrew," "The Good Fairy," "The Corn Is Green," (also producer) "Man and Superman," (also producer) "The Little Foxes," (also producer) "The Cradle Song," and producer, "Born Yesterday," *Hallmark Hall of Fame*, NBC, 1956; (also producer) "The Lark," (also producer) "The Green Pastures," (also producer) "On Borrowed Time," (also producer) "Twelfth Night," (also producer) "There Shall Be No Night," and (also producer) "The Yeomen of the Guard," *Hallmark Hall of*

Fame, NBC, 1957; *Harvey*, CBS, 1958; (also producer) "Dial 'M' for Murder," (also producer) "Little Moon of Alban," (also producer) "Kiss Me Kate," (also producer) "Johnny Belinda," and (also producer) "Hans Brinker, or The Silver Skates," *Hallmark Hall of Fame*, NBC, 1958; (also producer) *Gift of the Magi*, CBS, 1958; director, *Meet Me in St. Louis*, CBS, 1959; (also producer) "A Doll's House," (also producer) "Berkeley Square," (also producer) "Ah! Wilderness," and (also producer) "Winterset," *Hallmark Hall of Fame*, NBC, 1959; (also producer) *Hallmark Hall of Fame Christmas Festival*, NBC, 1959.

(Also producer) "Captain Brassbound's Conversion," (also producer) "Macbeth," (also producer) "The Tempest," (also producer) "Shangri-La," and producer, "Golden Child," *Hallmark Hall of Fame*, NBC, 1960; (also producer) "Give Us Barabbas!," (also producer) "The Joke and the Valley," (also producer) "Time Remembered," and (also producer) "Victoria Regina," *Hallmark Hall of Fame*, NBC, 1961; (also producer) "Arsenic and Old Lace," (also producer) "The Invincible Mr. Disraeli," and (also producer) "Cyrano de Bergerac," *Hallmark Hall of Fame*, NBC, 1962; (also producer) *Teahouse of the August Moon*, NBC, 1962; (also producer) "Pygmalion," (also producer) "The Patriots," and (also producer) "A Cry of Angels," *Hallmark Hall of Fame*, NBC, 1963; (also producer) "Abe Lincoln in Illinois," (also producer) "The Fantasticks," and (also producer) "Little Moon of Alban," *Hallmark Hall of Fame*, NBC, 1964; (also producer) "The Magnificent Yankee," (also producer) "Inherit the Wind," (also producer) "The Holy Terror," and (also producer) "Eagle in a Cage," *Hallmark Hall of Fame*, NBC, 1965; (also producer) "Blithe Spirit," (also producer) "Barefoot in Athens," and (also producer) "Lamp at Midnight," *Hallmark Hall of Fame*, NBC, 1966; (also producer) "Anastasia," (also producer) "Soldier in Love," and (also producer) "Saint Joan," *Hallmark Hall of Fame*, NBC, 1967; "Do Not Go Gentle into That Good Night," *CBS Playhouse*, CBS, 1967; (also producer) "The Admirable Crichton," (also producer) "My Father and My Mother," and (also producer) "Elizabeth the Queen," *Hallmark Hall of Fame*, NBC, 1968; (also producer) "The File on Devlin," *Hallmark Hall of Fame*, NBC, 1969.

Producer, "Hamlet," *Hallmark Hall of Fame*, NBC, 1970; (also producer) "Gideon," *Hallmark Hall of Fame*, NBC, 1971; *U.S.A.*, PBS, 1971; (also producer) *Sandburg's Lincoln* (a series of six specials), NBC, 1974-76; "Truman at Potsdam," *Hallmark Hall of Fame*, NBC, 1976; (also producer) *Our Town*, NBC, 1977; *The Second Barry Manilow Special*, ABC, 1978; *Barry Manilow—One Voice*, ABC, 1980; (also producer) *Answers*, NBC, 1982; *Deadly Game*, HBO, 1982; (also producer) *The Best Christmas Pageant Ever*, ABC, 1983; (also producer) *The Booth*, PBS, 1985.

RELATED CAREER—Director of productions for the U.S. Army Special Services, Honolulu, HI, 1942-45; executive producer and artistic director, City Center Theatre, New York City, 1949-52; president, Compass Productions Inc., 1959-86; founder (with Merrill H. Karpf), Schaefer/Karpf Productions, 1982; National Council of the Arts, 1983-88; associate dean, department of theatre, film, and television, University of California, Los Angeles, 1986—.

WRITINGS: TELEVISION—Specials: (With James Prideaux, Israel Horovitz, and Rose Leiman Goldemberg) *The Booth*, PBS, 1985.

AWARDS: Antoinette Perry Award (with Maurice Evans), Best Producer of a Play, 1954, for *Teahouse of the August Moon;* Sylvania Award, Outstanding Dramatic Series, and Peabody Award, Outstanding Television Entertainment, both 1958, for *Hallmark*

Hall of Fame; Look magazine Award and *Radio-Television Daily* Award, both 1957, for "The Green Pastures," *Hallmark Hall of Fame; Radio-Television Daily* Award, Director of the Year, 1957; *Radio-Television Daily* Award, 1959, for "Johnny Belinda," *Hallmark Hall of Fame;* Sylvania Award, Peabody Award, and Emmy Awards, Best Special Dramatic Program and Best Direction of a Single Dramatic Program, all 1959, for "Little Moon of Alban," *Hallmark Hall of Fame;* Outstanding Achievement Award from the Directors Guild of America, 1960, *TV Guide* Award, Best Single Dramatic Program on Television, *Radio-Television Daily* Award, Dramatic Show of the Year, and Emmy Awards, Program of the Year, Outstanding Program Achievement in the Field of Drama, and Outstanding Directorial Achievement in Drama, 1961, all for "Macbeth," *Hallmark Hall of Fame; Radio-Television Daily* Award, Director of the Year, 1961; *Saturday Review* Special Commendation for Notable Production and Emmy Award, Program of the Year, both 1962, for "Victoria Regina," *Hallmark Hall of Fame; Radio-Television Daily* All-American Award, Producer of the Year and Director of the Year, 1963; Outstanding Achievement Award from the Directors Guild of America, Best Television Director, 1963, for "Pygmalion," *Hallmark Hall of Fame; Radio-Television Daily* Award, Director of the Year, 1964; Dineen Award from the National Catholic Theatre Conference, 1964; Emmy Award, Outstanding Program Achievement in Entertainment, 1965, for "The Magnificent Yankee," *Hallmark Hall of Fame; Radio-Television Daily* Award, Director of the Year, 1965; Emmy Award, Outstanding Dramatic Program, 1968, for "Elizabeth the Queen," *Hallmark Hall of Fame;* Outstanding Achievement Award from the Directors Guild of America, Best Television Director, 1967, for "Do Not Go Gentle into That Good Night," *CBS Playhouse;* Outstanding Achievement Award from the Directors Guild of America, Best Television Director, 1968, for "My Father and My Mother," *Hallmark Hall of Fame;* Emmy Award, Outstanding Single Program—Drama or Comedy, 1973, for *A War of Children;* Emmy Award nomination, 1983, for *The Best Christmas Pageant Ever.* HONORARY DEGREES—Lafayette College, Doctor of Literature, 1963; Coker College, L.H.D., 1973.

MEMBER: Directors Guild of America (national board of directors, 1960-75, vice-president, 1961-79, president, 1979-81), Academy of Motion Picture Arts and Sciences, Academy of Television Arts and Sciences, Caucus for Producers, Writers, and Directors, American National Theatre and Academy—West (board of directors), Variety Clubs International, Players Club, Phi Beta Kappa Society.

SIDELIGHTS: RECREATONS—Contract bridge, travel, theatre, and film going.

ADDRESSES: OFFICES—Schaefer/Karpf Productions, 12711 Ventura Boulevard, Suite 307, Studio City, CA 91604; c/o University of California, Los Angeles, Department of Theatre, Film, and Television, 415 Hilgard Macgowan Hall, Room 2310-B, Los Angeles, CA 90024.*

*   *   *

SCHLOENDORFF, Volker   1939-

PERSONAL: Born March 31, 1939, in Wiesbaden, Germany; married Margarethe von Trotta (a film director, screenwriter, and actress), 1969. EDUCATION—Studied political science and economics in Paris; studied film directing at Institut des Hautes Etudes Cinematographiques.

VOCATION: Director, screenwriter, and producer.

CAREER: Also see WRITINGS below. PRINCIPAL STAGE WORK—Director: Katja Kabanova (opera), Frankfurt, Germany, 1974; Wir erreichen den Fluss (opera), Berlin, Germany, 1976.

PRINCIPAL FILM WORK—Director: Der Junge Torless (also known as Les Desarrois de l'eleve Torless, Young Toerless, and Young Torless), 1966, released in the United States by Kanawha, 1968; Mord und Totschlag (also known as A Degree of Murder), 1967, released in the United States by Universal, 1969; Der Plotzliche Reichtum der Armen Leute von Kombach (also known as The Sudden Fortune of the Poor People of Kombach and The Sudden Wealth of the Poor People of Kombach), Hallelujah-Film/Hessischer Rundfunk, 1970; Strohfeuer (also known as A Free Woman, Strawfire, and Summer Lightning), Hallelujah-Film/New Yorker, 1971; Die Moral der Ruth Halbfass (also known as The Moral of Ruth Halbfass), CIC/Paramount/Universal, 1971; (with Margarethe von Trotta) Die Verlorene Ehre der Katharina Blum (also known as The Lost Honor of Katharina Blum), Cinema International, 1975; Der Fangschuss (also known as Coup de grace), Cine-International Filmvertrieb/Almi Cinema V, 1976; (also producer) Nur zum Spass—Nur zum Spiel. Kaleidoskop: Valeska Gert (also known as Just for Fun, Just for Play, Only for Fun—Only for Play, Kaleidoscope: Valeska Gert, Kaleidoskop: Valeska Gert, Nur zum Spass-nur zum Spiel, and Kaleidoscope: Valeska Gert, For Fun—For Play; documentary), Bioskop, 1977; (with others) Deutschland im Herbst (also known as Germany in Autumn), Osiris/Filverlag der Autoren, 1978; The Tin Drum (also known as Die Blechtrommel), New World, 1979.

(With Stefan Aust, Alexander von Eschwege, and Alexander Kluge) Der Kandidat (also known as The Candidate; documentary), Bioskop/Kairos/Pro-ject Filmproduction, 1980; Die Falschung (also known as Circle of Deceit and The Forgery), United International, 1981; (with Aust, Kluge, Heinrich Boll, and Axel Engstfeld) Krieg und Frieden (also known as War and Peace) Filmverlag der Autoren/New Line Cinema, 1983; Un Amour de Swann (also known as Eine Liebe von Swann, Swann's Way, Remembrance of Things Past, and Swann in Love), Artificial Eye/Gaumont International/Orion Classics, 1984; (c-director) Vermischte Nachrichten (also known as Odds and Ends), Filmverlag der Autoren, 1987; The Handmaid's Tale, Cinecom, 1990. Also directed Wen kummert's . . . (also known as Who Cares . . .; short film), 1960; Michael Kohlhaas—Der Rebell (also known as Michael Kohlhaas—The Rebel), 1969; Ein Unheimlicher Moment (also known as An Uneasy Moment; short film), 1970.

PRINCIPAL TELEVISION APPEARANCES—Specials: Private Conversations: On the Set of "Death of a Salesman," PBS, 1986. PRINCIPAL TELEVISION WORK—All as director. Movies: A Gathering of Old Men, CBS, 1987. Specials: Death of a Salesman, CBS, 1985. Also Baal, 1970; Ubernachtung in Tirol (also known as Overnight Stay in the Tyrol, and Overnight in Tirol), 1974; Georginas Grunde (also known as Georgina's Reasons), 1975.

RELATED CAREER—Assistant director to Louis Malle, Jean-Pierre Melville, and Alain Resnais, 1960-64; founder (with Peter Fleischmann), Hallelujah-Film, 1969; founder (with Reinhard Hauff), Bioskop-Film, 1973.

WRITINGS: FILM—See production details above. Der Junge Torless, 1966; (with Gregor von Rezzori, Niklas Franz, and Arne Boyer) Mord und Totschlag, 1967; (with Margarethe Von Trotta) Der Plotzliche Reichtum der Armen Leute von Kombach, 1970; (with Peter Hamm) Die Moral der Ruth Halbfass, 1971; Strohfeuer, 1972; (with Von Trotta) Die verlorene Ehre der Katharina Blum, 1975; Nur zum Spass—Nur zum Spiel. Kaleidoskop: Valeska Gert, 1977; (with Franz Seitz, Jean-Claude Carriere, and Gunter Grass) The Tin Drum, 1979; Der Kandidat, 1980; (with Von Trotta, Kai Hermann, and Carriere) Die Falschung, 1981; (adaptor) L'Amour de Swann, 1984; also (co-writer) Michael Kohlhaas—Der Rebell, 1969. TELEVISION—Baal, 1970; Ubernachtung in Tirol, 1974.

AWARDS: FIPRESCI Prize from the Cannes Film Festival, 1966, for Der Junge Torless; Golden Palm Award from the Cannes Film Festival and Academy Award, Best Foreign Language Film, both 1979, for The Tin Drum; Emmy Award nomination, Best Director, 1985, for Death of a Salesman.

MEMBER: German P.E.N. Centre.*

*　　*　　*

SCOLA, Ettore　1931-

PERSONAL: Born May 10, 1931, in Trevico, Italy; children: Paola. EDUCATION—Studied law at the University of Rome.

VOCATION: Director and screenwriter.

CAREER: Also see WRITINGS below. FIRST FILM WORK—Se permettete, parliamo di donne (also known as Parliamo di donne and Let's Talk About Women), Embassy, 1964. PRINCIPAL FILM WORK—Director: La congiuntura (also known as One Million Dollars), Ceiad/Columbia, 1965; L'arcidiavolo (also known as The Devil in Love and Il diavolo innamorato), 1966, released in the United States by Warner Brothers, 1968; Dramma della gelosia—tutti i particolari in cronaca (also known as The Pizza Triangle, The Motive Was Jealousy, A Drama of Jealousy (and Other Things), and Jealousy Italian Style), Warner Brothers, 1970; Permette? Rocco Papaleo (also known as Rocco Papaleo and Excuse Me, My Name Is Rocco Papaleo), Cineriz, 1971, released in the United States by Rumson, 1974; La piu bella serata della mia vita (also known as The Most Wonderful Evening of My Life), Columbia, 1972; C'eravamo tanto amati (also known as Those Were the Years), Delta, 1974; (with others) Brutti, sporchi e cattivi (also known as Down and Dirty and Ugly, Dirty, and Bad), Gold, 1976; (with others) Signore e signori, buonanotte (also known as Goodnight, Ladies and Gentlemen), 1976, released in the United States by Titanus Distribuzione, 1977; We All Loved Each Other So Much, Almi/Cinema V, 1977; Una giornata particolare (also known as Una giornata speciale, A Special Day, and The Great Day), Cinema V/Gold Film Distributors, 1977; (with Mario Monicelli and Dino Risi) I nuovi mostri (also known as The New Monsters and Viva Italia!), Filmverlag der Autoren/Cinema V, 1978.

La terrazza (also known as The Terrace), United Artists, 1980; Passione d'amore (also known as Passion of Love), Connoisseur, 1981, released in the United States by Putnam Square, 1982; La Nuit de Varennes (also known as Il mondo nuovo, The New World, and La Varennes Nuit), Electric/Contemporary, 1982, released in the United States by Triumph, 1983; Le Bal (also known as The Ball), AMLF, 1982, released in the United States by Almi Classics, 1984; Macaroni (also known as Maccheroni), Paramount, 1985;

(also editor) *La famiglia* (also known as *The Family*), Vestron, 1987; *Splendor* (also known as *The Last Movie*), Warner Brothers, 1989. Also "Il vittimista" in *Thrilling*, 1965; *Il commissario Pepe* (also known as *Inspector Pepe*), 1968; *Riusciranno i nostri eroi a trovare il loro amico misteriosamente scomparso in Africa?* (also known as *Will Your Heroes Find Their Friends Who Disappeared So Mysteriously in Africa?*), 1968; *Trevico-Torino . . . Viaggio nel Fiat Nam*, 1973; *Che si dice a Roma*, 1979.

RELATED CAREER—Journalist, 1947; writer for radio shows, 1950; writer and illustrator for satirical magazines; ghost writer for Italian comedies; documentary filmmaker.

NON-RELATED CAREER—Nominated to the European Parliament, Strasbourg.

WRITINGS: See production details above, unless indicated. FILM— (With Ruggero Maccari) *Un americano a Roma*, 1954; (with Maccari) *Una Parigina a Roma*, 1954; (with Maccari) *Due notti con Cleopatra* (also known as *Two Nights with Cleopatra*), 1954, released in the United States by Ultra, 1963; (with Maccari) *Lo scapolo*, 1956; (with Maccari) *Nata di marzo*, 1958.

(With Maccari, Barratti, and Luciano Salce) *Le Pillole de Ercole* (also known as *Hercules' Pills*), Dino De Laurentiis, 1960; (with Maccari) *Fantasmi a Roma* (also known as *Ghosts of Rome*), 1960; (with Maccari) *La storia di un soldato* (also known as *The Soldier*), 1960; (with Maccari, Sandro Continenza, and Sergio Pugliese) *Il mattatore* (also known as *L'Homme aux cent visages* and *Love and Larceny*), 1960, released in the United States by Major Film Distributing, 1963; (with Maccari, Antonio Pietrangeli, and Tullio Pinelli) *Adua e le compagne* (also known as *Love a la Carte*, *Adua and Her Friends*, and *Adua and Her Companions*), 1960, released in the United States by Promenade, 1965; (with Maccari) *Anni ruggenti* (also known as *Roaring Years*), 1962; (with Maccari and Dino Risi) *Il sorpasso* (also known as *The Easy Life*), 1962, released in the United States by Embassy, 1963; (with Continenza) "The Women" and (with Fabio Carpi, Giuseppe Orlandini, and Nino Manfredi) "The Soldier" in *L'amore difficile* (also known as *Of Wayward Love* and *Erotica*), 1962, released in the United States by Pathe Contemporary, 1964; (with Maccari) *Il successo*, 1963, released in the United States by Embassy, 1965; (with Maccari and Pietrangeli) *La visita*, 1963, released in the United States by Promenade, 1966; (with Maccari, Risi, Furio Scarpelli, Agenore Incrocci ("Age"), and Elio Petri) *I mostri* (also known as *Opiate '67*, *Les Monstres*, and *15 from Rome*), 1963, released in the United States by McAbbe/Janus, 1967; (with Maccari) *Se permettete, parliamo di donne*, 1964; (with Maccari) *Il gaucho* (also known as *The Gaucho*), 1964; (with Maccari, Diego Fabbri, and Stefano Strucchi) *Il magnifico cornuto* (also known as *The Magnificent Cuckold* and *Le Cocu magnifique*), 1964, released in the United States by Continental Distributing, 1965; (with Age, Maccari, and Scarpelli) *Alta infedelta* (also known as *High Infidelity* and *Haute infidelite*), 1964, released in the United States by Magna, 1965.

(With Maccari) *Io la conoscevo bene*, 1965; (with Maccari) *La congiuntura*, 1965; (with Maccari) "Il vittimista" in *Thrilling*, 1965; (with Maccari and Nanni Loy) *Made in Italy* (also known as *A l'Italienne*), 1965, released in the United States by Royal Films International, 1967; (with Maccari) *L'arcidiavolo*, 1966; *Follie d'estate*, 1966; (with Maccari and Strucchi) *Le dolci signore* (also known as *Anyone Can Play*), 1967, released in the United States by Paramount, 1968; (with Maccari) *Il commissario Pepe* (also known as *Inspector Pepe*), 1968; (with Maccari) *Riusciranno i nostri eroi a trovare il loro amico misteriosamente scomparso in Africa?* (also

known as *Will Your Heroes Find Their Friends Who Disappeared So Mysteriously in Africa?*), 1968.

(With Age and Scarpelli) *Dramma della gelosia—tutti i particolari in cronaca*, 1970; (with Maccari) *Permette? Rocco Papaleo*, 1971; *Noi donne siamo fatte cosi* (also known as *Women: So We Are Made*), 1971; (with Sergio Amidei) *La piu bella serata della mia vita*, 1972; *Trevico-Torino . . . Viaggio nel Fiat Nam*, 1973; (with Scarpelli and Age) *C'eravamo tanto amati*, 1974; (with Maccari) *Brutti, sporchi e cattivi*, 1976; (with others) *Signore e signori, buonanotte*, 1976; (with Scarpelli and Age) *We All Loved Each Other So Much*, 1977; (with Maccari and Maurizio Costanzo) *Una giornata particolare*, 1977; *Che si dice a Roma*, 1979; (with Scarpelli and Age) *La terrazza*, 1980; (with Maccari) *Passione d'amore*, 1981; (with Amidei) *La Nuit de Varennes*, 1982; (with Maccari, Scarpelli, and Jean-Claude Penchenat) *Le Bal*, 1983; (with Maccari and Scarpelli) *Macaroni*, 1985; (with Maccari and Scarpelli) *La famiglia*, 1987; *Splendor*, 1989.

AWARDS: Cesar Award, 1975, for *C'eravamo tanto amati*; Best Director Award from the Cannes Film Festival, 1976, for *Brutti, sporchi e cattivi*; Special Jury Prize from the Cannes Film Festival, 1977, for *Una giornata speciale*.

OTHER SOURCES: New York Times, January 17, 1988.*

*   *   *

SCOTT, Walter M.   1906-1989

PERSONAL: Born November 7, 1906, in Cleveland, OH; died of a respiratory ailment, February 2, 1989, in Los Angeles, CA; children: one son, one daughter. EDUCATION—Attended the University of Southern California, 1929; also attended the Chouinard School of Art.

VOCATION: Set designer.

CAREER: PRINCIPAL FILM WORK—All as set designer, unless indicated: (With Thomas Little) *The Moon Is Down* and art director (with Little, James Basevi, and Leland Fuller), *Heaven Can Wait*, both Twentieth Century-Fox, 1943; (both with Little) *The Lodger* and *The Purple Heart*, Twentieth Century-Fox, 1944; (with Little and Joseph C. Wright) *Nob Hill* and (with Little) *Where Do We Go from Here?*, both Twentieth Century-Fox, 1945; (all with Little) *Forever Amber*, *The Homestretch*, and *Daisy Kenyon*, Twentieth Century-Fox, 1947; (all with Little) *Apartment for Peggy*, *Call Northside 777* (also known as *Calling Northside 777*), *A Letter to Three Wives*, *That Lady in Ermine*, and *That Wonderful Urge*, Twentieth Century-Fox, 1948; (all with Little) *House of Strangers*, *I Was a Male War Bride* (also known as *You Can't Sleep Here*), and *Whirlpool*, Twentieth Century-Fox, 1949.

(All with Little) *Under My Skin*, *All About Eve*, and *Where the Sidewalk Ends*, Twentieth Century-Fox, 1950; (with Little) *People Will Talk*, (with Little and Wright) *On the Riviera*, and (with Little) *The Thirteenth Letter*, all Twentieth Century-Fox, 1951; *My Cousin Rachel*, (with Little) *Deadline—U.S.A.* (also known as *Deadline*), (with Little) *Les Miserables*, (with Little) *Monkey Business*, and (with Little) *With a Song in My Heart*, all Twentieth Century-Fox, 1952; *King of the Khyber Rifles* and (with Paul S. Fox) *The Robe*, both Twentieth Century-Fox, 1953; (with Fox) *Desiree*, (with Fox) *The Egyptian*, (with Stuart Reiss) *Hell and*

High Water, (with Reiss) *Broken Lance*, and (with Chester Bayhi) *River of No Return*, all Twentieth Century-Fox, 1954.

(With Fox) *Daddy Long Legs*, (with Fox) *Good Morning, Miss Dove*, (with Frank Wade) *The Left Hand of God*, (with Jack Stubbs) *Love Is a Many-Splendored Thing*, (with Reiss) *House of Bamboo*, (with Fox) *The Rains of Ranchipur*, (with Reiss) *The Seven Year Itch*, (with Reiss) *Soldier of Fortune*, (with Bayhi) *The Tall Men*, (with Bayhi) *Untamed*, and (with Fox) *The View from Pompey's Head* (also known as *Secret Interlude*), all Twentieth Century-Fox, 1955; (with Fox) *The King and I*, (with Reiss) *The Man in the Grey Flannel Suit*, (with Reiss) *Teenage Rebel*, and (with Fay Babcock) *23 Paces to Baker Street*, all Twentieth Century-Fox, 1956; *Forty Guns* (also known as *Woman with a Whip*), (with Fox) *An Affair to Remember*, (with Fox) *Desk Set* (also known as *His Other Woman*), (with Reiss) *Kiss Them for Me*, (with Bayhi) *Kronos*, (with Reiss) *Oh, Men! Oh, Women!*, (with Bertram Granger) *Peyton Place*, (with Fox and Stubbs) *The Sun Also Rises*, (with Eli Benneche) *The Three Faces of Eve*, and (with Reiss) *The True Story of Jesse James* (also known as *The James Brothers*), all Twentieth Century-Fox, 1957; *The Long, Hot Summer*, (with Fox) *A Certain Smile*, (with Granger) *Gang War*, (with Babcock) *In Love and War*, (with Maurice Mulcahy) *Showdown at Boot Hill*, (with Reiss) *The Young Lions*, (with Benneche) *10 North Frederick*, and art director (with Wheeler, Fox, and John DeCuir) *South Pacific*, all Twentieth Century-Fox, 1958; (with Joseph Kish) *Journey to the Center of the Earth*, (with Fox) *The Man Who Understood Women*, *A Private's Affair*, (with Kish) *Return of the Fly*, (with Reiss) *The Diary of Anne Frank*, (with Benneche) *Say One for Me*, (with Gustav W. Bernsten) *The Story on Page One*, (with Reiss) *Warlock*, and (with Reiss) *Woman Obsessed*, all Twentieth Century-Fox, 1959.

(With Fox) *Can-Can*, (with Bernsten) *Flaming Star*, (with Fox) *From the Terrace*, (with Kish and John Sturtevant) *The Lost World*, (with Reiss) *North to Alaska*, (with Reiss) *Seven Thieves*, and (with Kish) *Wild River*, all Twentieth Century-Fox, 1960; (with Robert Priestly) *The Comancheros*, (with Reiss) *The Fiercest Heart*, (with Fernandino Ruffo) *Francis of Assisi*, (with Reiss) *Misty*, (with Lou Hafley) *Pirates of Tortuga*, (with Fred Maclean) *Return to Peyton Place*, (with Maclean) *The Right Approach*, (with Maclean) *Sanctuary*, (with Reiss) *The Second Time Around*, (with Fox) *Snow White and the Three Stooges* (also known as *Snow White and the Three Clowns*), (with Fox) *Tender Is the Night*, (with Sturtevant) *Voyage to the Bottom of the Sea*, and (with Reiss) *Wild in the Country*, all Twentieth Century-Fox, 1961; (with Priestly) *Adventures of a Young Man* (also known as *Hemingway's Adventures of a Young Man*), (with Reiss) *Five Weeks in a Balloon*, (with Sturtevant) *Madison Avenue*, (with Reiss) *Mr. Hobbs Takes a Vacation*, (with Lou Hafley) *State Fair*, and (with Lou Hafley) *Swingin' Along* (also known as *Double Trouble*), all Twentieth Century-Fox, 1962; (with Fox and Ray Moyer) *Cleopatra*, (with Fox) *Move Over, Darling*, (with Reiss and Norman Rockett) *The Stripper* (also known as *Woman of Summer*), and (with Reiss) *Take Her, She's Mine*, all Twentieth Century-Fox, 1963; (with Reiss) *Fate Is the Hunter*, (with Keogh Gleason) *Goodbye Charlie*, (with Reiss) *John Goldfarb, Please Come Home*, (with Reiss) *The Pleasure Seekers*, (with Lou Hafley) *Rio Conchos*, (with Fox) *Shock Treatment*, and (with Reiss) *What a Way to Go*, all Twentieth Century-Fox, 1964.

(With Steven Potter) *Dear Brigette*, (with Jerry Wunderlich) *Do Not Disturb*, (with Wunderlich) *Morituri* (also known as *The Saboteur: Code Name Morituri* and *The Saboteur*), (with Lucien Hafley) *The Reward*, and (with Ruby Levitt) *The Sound of Music*, all Twentieth Century-Fox, 1965; (with Lucien Hafley) *I Deal in Danger*, (with Raphael Bretton) *Our Man Flint*, (with Reiss) *Fantastic Voyage* (also known as *Microscipia* and *Strange Journey*), (with Sturtevant and William Kiernan) *The Sand Pebbles*, (with Reiss) *Stagecoach*, and (with Reiss) *Way . . . Way Out*, all Twentieth Century-Fox, 1966; (with Reiss) *Dr. Dolittle*, (with Sturtevant) *The Flim-Flam Man* (also known as *One Born Every Minute*), (with Bretton) *A Guide for the Married Man*, (with Bretton) *Hombre*, (with James W. Payne) *In Like Flint*, (with Potter) *The St. Valentine's Day Massacre*, (with Warren Welch) *Tony Rome*, and (with Bretton) *Valley of the Dolls*, all Twentieth Century-Fox, 1967; (with Wunderlich) *The Detective*, (with Wunderlich) *Lady in Cement*, (with Rockett) *Planet of the Apes*, (with Bretton) *The Secret Life of an American Wife*, (with Howard Bristol) *Star!* (also known as *Those Were the Happy Times*), (with Reiss) *The Sweet Ride*, and (with Reiss and Bretton) *The Boston Strangler*, all Twentieth Century-Fox, 1968; (with Bayhi) *Butch Cassidy and the Sundance Kid*, (with Reiss) *Che!*, (with Bretton and George James Hopkins) *Hello, Dolly!*, (with Bretton) *Justine*, and (with Bayhi) *The Undefeated*, all Twentieth Century-Fox, 1969.

(With Sven Wickman) *Beneath the Planet of the Apes*, (with Robert De Vestel) *Cover Me Babe*, (with Bretton) *The Great White Hope*, (with Reiss) *M*A*S*H*, (with Kiernan) *Move*, (with Wunderlich) *The Only Game in Town*, (with Rockett and Carl Biddiscombe) *Tora! Tora! Tora!*, and (with Wunderlich) *Tribes*, all Twentieth Century-Fox, 1970; (with Reiss) *Escape from Planet of the Apes*, (with Audrey A. Blasdel) *The Marriage of a Young Stockbroker*, (with Bretton) *The Mephisto Waltz*, and (with Bretton) *The Seven Minutes*, all Twentieth Century-Fox, 1971; *The Culpepper Cattle Company*, Twentieth Century-Fox, 1972; (with Ralph Sylos) *Hex*, Twentieth Century-Fox, 1973.

PRINCIPAL TELEVISION WORK—All as set designer. Pilots: *They Call It Murder*, NBC, 1971. Movies: *Tribes*, ABC, 1970; *The Challenge*, ABC, 1970.

RELATED CAREER—Interior decorator, Fred B. Martin Company, 1929-30; assistant manager, United Studios, 1930-31; supervising set designer, Twentieth Century-Fox, 1952-72; consultant on set design, Twentieth Century-Fox, 1972-1989.

AWARDS: Academy Award nomination, Best Art Direction—Set Decoration (Black and White), 1950, for *All About Eve;* Academy Award nomination, Best Art Direction—Set Decoration (Color), 1951, for *On the Riviera;* Academy Award nomination, Best Art Direction—Set Decoration (Black and White), 1952, for *My Cousin Rachel;* Academy Award, Best Art Direction—Set Decoration (Color), 1953, for *The Robe;* Academy Award nomination, Best Art Direction—Set Decoration (Color), 1954, for *Desiree;* Academy Award nominations, Best Art Direction—Set Decoration (Color), 1955, for *Daddy Long Legs* and *Love Is a Many-Splendored Thing;* Academy Award nomination, Best Art Direction—Set Decoration (Black and White), 1956, for *Teenage Rebel;* Academy Award, Best Art Direction—Set Decoration (Color), 1956, for *The King and I;* Academy Award nomination, Best Art Direction—Set Decoration (Black and White or Color), 1958, for *A Certain Smile;* Academy Award, Best Art Direction—Set Decoration (Black and White), 1959, for *The Diary of Anne Frank;* Academy Award nomination, Best Art Direction—Set Decoration (Color), 1959, for *Journey to the Center of the Earth;* Academy Award, Best Art Direction—Set Decoration (Color), 1963, for *Cleopatra;* Academy Award nomination, Best Art Direction—Set Decoration, 1964, for *What a Way to Go;* Academy Award nomination, Best Art Direction—Set Decoration (Color), 1965, for *The Sound of Music;*

Academy Award, Best Art Direction—Set Decoration (Color), 1966, for *Fantastic Voyage;* Academy Award nomination, Best Art Direction—Set Decoration (Color), 1966, for *The Sand Pebbles;* Academy Award nomination, Best Art Direction—Set Decoration, 1967, for *Dr. Dolittle;* Academy Award nomination, Best Art Direction—Set Decoration, 1968, for *Star!;* Academy Award, Best Art Direction—Set Decoration, 1969, for *Hello, Dolly!;* Academy Award nomination, Best Art Direction—Set Decoration, 1970, for *Tora! Tora! Tora!*

MEMBER: Academy of Motion Picture Arts and Sciences (board of governors, 1968-76, then 1980-85).

OBITUARIES AND OTHER SOURCES: Variety, February 8-14, 1989.*

* * *

SEAMON, Edward 1932-

PERSONAL: Born April 15, 1932, in San Diego, CA; son of Thomas B. (in business) and Ocie B. (a telephone operator; maiden name, Taylor) Seamon; married Mai Hoffer (an artist), August 31, 1989. EDUCATION—Attended San Diego State College; trained for the stage with Herbert Berghof at the HB Studios. MILITARY—U.S. Navy, 1951-53.

VOCATION: Actor.

CAREER: STAGE DEBUT—Owens, *Light Up the Sky,* Hilltop

EDWARD SEAMON

Theatre, Edgartown, MA, 1961. OFF-BROADWAY DEBUT—Edward and manager, *Life and Times of J. Walter Sminthons,* New York Shakespeare Festival, Public Theatre, 1971. PRINCIPAL STAGE APPEARANCES—Stanley, *A Streetcar Named Desire,* Hilltop Theatre, Edgartown, MA, 1961; Frederick, *A Far Country,* Woodstock Playhouse, Woodstock, NY, 1963; Edward, *Underground,* New York Shakespeare Festival (NYSF), Public Theatre, New York City, 1971; Fitzpatrick, *The Contractor,* Chelsea Westside Theatre, New York City, 1973; Ralph Keptner, "49 West 87th" and Harold McCullough, "Cabin Twelve" in *49 West 87th* (double-bill), Schreiber Studio Theatre, New York City, 1974; Reilly, *Fishing,* NYSF, Public Theatre, 1975; Sydney, *The Private Secretary,* Lakewood Theatre, Lakewood, ME, 1975; Will Horvath, *The Trip Back Down,* Longacre Theatre, New York City, 1977; Kelly, *Feedlot,* Circle Repertory Company, Circle Repertory Theatre, New York City, 1977; Old Mahon, *Playboy of the Western World,* Almady, *The Play's the Thing,* Oronte, *The Misanthrope,* and Andrew, *Sleuth,* all State University of New York, Stony Brook, NY, 1977; Harold McCullough, *Cabin Twelve,* Circle Repertory Company, Circle Repertory Theatre, 1978; H.M. Stanley, *The Rear Column,* Manhattan Theatre Club, New York City, 1978; understudy for Dodge, Tilden, Bradley, and Father Dewis, *Buried Child,* Theatre de Lys, New York City, 1978, then as Dodge, Playhouse in the Park, Philadelphia, PA, later Circle Repertory Company, Circle Repertory Theatre, both 1979; Bill Foster and understudy for Lewis, *Devour the Snow,* Hudson Guild Theatre, then John Golden Theatre, both New York City, 1979; Taylor, Tony, and Dugan, *The American Clock,* Biltmore Theatre, New York City, 1979.

Weller Martin, *Gin Game,* Theatre By the Sea, Portsmouth, NH, 1980; Oates, *Terra Nova,* Pittsburgh Public Theatre, Allegheny Theatre, Pittsburgh, PA, 1981; Wilcocks, *Extenuating Circumstances,* Horizon Theatre, Perry Street Theatre, New York City, 1981; Earl, *Confluence,* Circle Repertory Company, Circle Repertory Theatre, 1982; outlaw, *The Holdup,* Little Theatre SPAC, Saratoga, NY 1982; Duke of York, *Richard II* and Jedediah, father, and cop, *The Great Grandson of Jedediah Kohler,* both Circle Repertory Company, Entermedia Theatre, New York City, 1982; sound man, *Marvelous Gray,* Lion Theatre, New York City, 1982; Halvard Solness, *The Master Builder,* Roundabout Theatre, New York City, 1983; Red Pewsy, *Coyote Ugly,* Yale Repertory Theatre, New Haven, CT, 1983; Dr. Jim Bayliss, *All My Sons,* Zellerback Theatre, Philadelphia, PA, 1983; Dr. Dorn, *The Seagull,* Little Theatre SPAC, 1983; Les, *Full Hookup,* Circle Repertory Company, Circle Repertory Theatre, 1983; Hector, *Foxfire,* Guthrie Theatre, Minneapolis, MN, 1984; Bim Miller, *The Harvesting* and Boyet, *Love's Labour's Lost,* both Circle Repertory Company, Circle Repertory Theatre, 1984; Old Man, *Fool for Love,* Douglas Fairbanks Theatre, New York City, 1984; Jimmy Thorne, *A Country for Old Men,* American Stage, Terrace Theatre, New York City, 1984.

Mr. Talley, *A Tale Told,* Little Theatre SPAC, 1985; Mr. Talley, *Talley and Son,* Circle Repertory Company, Circle Repertory Theatre, 1985; Mereia, *Caligula,* August, *The Mound Builders,* and Chris, *Quiet in the Land,* all Circle Repertory Company, Triplex Theatre, New York City, 1986; Candy, *Of Mice and Men,* Roundabout Theatre, New York City, 1987; Ferdinand de'Lesseps, *To Culebra,* Indiana Rerpertory Theatre, Indianapolis, IN, 1987; Antonio, *The Tempest,* Virginia Stage Company, Norfolk, VA, 1987; Old Man, *Fool for Love,* Power Center Theatre, Ann Arbor, MI, 1987; Leroy, *The Bad Seed,* Cape Dennis Playhouse, Cape Dennis, MA, 1988; detective and Louie, *Borderlines* and Vito and Antonio, *V and V Only,* both Circle Repertory Company, Circle

Repertory Theatre, 1988; Engstrand, *Ghosts,* Roundabout Theatre, 1988; Jim, *Tales of the Lost Formicans,* Actors Theatre of Louisville, Louisville, KY, 1989; Candy, *Of Mice and Men,* Levin Theatre, New Brunswick, NJ, 1989; Harry-Bear, *Beside Herself,* Circle Repertory Company, Circle Repertory Theatre, 1989; pawnbroker, *Woyzeck,* Hartford Stage, Hartford, CT, 1990; also appeared in *Marvelous Brown* and *The Private Eye of Hiram Bodoni,* New Dramatists Inc., New York City, 1977; *All My Sons,* Philadelphia Drama Guild, Philadelphia, 1982.

MAJOR TOURS—Various roles, *To Be Young, Gifted, and Black,* U.S. cities, 1972; Mr. Willis, *Moonchildren,* U.S. cities, 1974; Hector, *Foxfire,* with the Tyrone Guthrie Theatre Company, U.S. cities, 1985; Old Man, *Fool for Love,* with the Circle Repertory Company, Japanese cities, 1985.

FILM DEBUT—Father Steele, *The Rosary Murders,* New Line Cinema, 1987.

TELEVISION DEBUT—Malcolm Granger, *The Guiding Light,* CBS, 1976. PRINCIPAL TELEVISION APPEARANCES Episodic: Zeke, *Legwork,* CBS, 1987. Movies: Hawkins, *Rascals and Robbers—The Secret Adventures of Tom Sawyer and Huck Finn,* CBS, 1982; Al, *Stone Pillow,* CBS, 1985; also Mr. O'Brian, *Mystery at Fire Island,* 1981.

RELATED CAREER—Performer, Eugene O'Neill Playwright's Conference, Waterford, CT, 1975; member, Circle Repertory Company.

ADDRESSES: AGENT—Peggy Hadley Enterprises Ltd., 250 W. 57th Street, New York, NY 10107.

*   *   *

SENECA, Joe

VOCATION: Actor.

CAREER: PRINCIPAL STAGE APPEARANCES—Crooks, *Of Mice and Men,* Brooks Atkinson Theatre, New York City, 1974; Peter, *Les Blancs,* AMDA Studio One, New York City, 1980; Cal, *The Little Foxes,* Martin Beck Theatre, New York City, then Center Theatre Group, Ahmanson Theatre, Los Angeles, both 1981; Dodd's father and headwaiter, *Rhinestone,* Richard Allen Center, New York City, 1982; Cutler, *Ma Rainey's Black Bottom,* Yale Repertory Theatre, New Haven, CT, then Cort Theatre, New York City, both 1984. Also appeared in *Sizwe Banzi Is Dead,* Pittsburgh Public Theatre, Pittsburgh, PA, then Studio Arena Theatre, Buffalo, NY, both 1976; and in *Sizwe Banzi Is Dead* and *Statements After an Arrest Under the Immorality Act* (double-bill), George Street Playhouse, New Brunswick, NJ, 1978.

PRINCIPAL FILM APPEARANCES—Partygoer, *Kramer vs. Kramer,* Columbia, 1979; Dr. Thompson, *The Verdict,* Twentieth Century-Fox, 1982; Santiago, *The Evil That Men Do,* Tri-Star, 1984; Ezra, *Silverado,* Columbia, 1985; Nimrod, *Heart of the Garden,* Roland, 1985; Willie Brown, *Crossroads,* Columbia, 1986; Ferryman, *Big Shots,* Twentieth Century-Fox, 1987; Dr. Meddows, *The Blob,* Tri-Star, 1988; President McPherson, *School Daze,* Columbia, 1988.

PRINCIPAL TELEVISION APPEARANCES—Episodic: Joe Adams,

JOE SENECA

Spenser: For Hire, ABC, 1985; Ben Dumfy, "Dorothy and Son," *Amazing Stories,* NBC, 1986; Alvin, *The Golden Girls,* NBC, 1987; Dr. Haynes, *The Cosby Show,* NBC, 1987; Victor, *Mr. President,* Fox, 1987; Wailing Eddie "T" Thompson, *227,* NBC, 1988; Eddie "Cougar" Haynes, *Matlock,* NBC, 1989; Fossil, *The Equalizer,* CBS, 1989; portrait voice, *A Man Called Hawk,* ABC, 1989; also "Solomon Northup's Odyssey," *American Playhouse,* PBS, 1985. Movies: Ed Rudolph, *Wilma,* NBC, 1977; Reverend Keys, *Samaritan: The Mitch Snyder Story,* CBS, 1986; doorman, *The Tenth Month,* CBS, 1979; boxer, *Terrible Joe Moran,* CBS, 1984; Clatoo, *A Gathering of Old Men,* CBS, 1987; Joseph, *Tarzan in Manhattan* (also known as *Tarzan in New York* and *Tarzan of Manhattan*), CBS, 1989. Specials: Levi Pearson, *With All Deliberate Speed,* CBS, 1976; *NAACP Image Awards,* NBC, 1987; *Gordon Parks: Moments Without Proper Names,* PBS, 1988. Also appeared in *The House of Dies Drear.*

RELATED CAREER—Singer with a satirical singing group the Three Riffs, performing at Le Ruban Bleu, New York City, during the 1950s; songwriter during the 1950s and 1960s.

WRITINGS: FILM—Composer (with Ry Cooder), "Willie Brown Blues" (song), *Crossroads,* Columbia, 1986. TELEVISION—Series: *Sesame Street,* PBS, 1970-73.

AWARDS: NAACP Image Award nominations for *Crossroads* and *Amazing Stories.*

ADDRESSES: AGENT—Dulcina Eisen Associates, 154 E. 61st Street, New York, NY 10021.

SERBAN, Andrei   1943-

PERSONAL: Full name, Andrei George Serban; born June 21, 1943, in Bucharest, Romania; son of George and Elpis (Lichardopu) Serban; immigrated to the United States in 1969. EDUCATION—Attended the Theatre Institute of Bucharest, 1963-68; also attended the University of Bucharest.

VOCATION: Director.

CAREER: Also see *WRITINGS* below. FIRST OFF-OFF-BROAD-WAY WORK—Director, *Arden of Faversham,* La Mama Experimental Theatre Club, 1970. FIRST LONDON WORK—Director, *The Umbrellas of Cherbourg,* Phoenix Theatre, 1980. PRINCIPAL STAGE WORK—All as director, unless indicated: *The Trojan Women, Medea,* and *Electra,* all La Mama Experimental Theatre Club (E.T.C.), New York City, 1974-76; *The Good Woman of Setzuan,* La Mama E.T.C., 1975; *As You Like It,* La Mama E.T.C., 1976; *The Cherry Orchard,* New York Shakespeare Festival (NYSF), Vivian Beaumont Theatre, New York City, 1977; *Agamemnon,* NYSF, Vivian Beaumont Theatre, then Delacorte Theatre, New York City, both 1977; *The Ghost Sonata,* Yale Repertory Theatre, New Haven, CT, 1977; *Sganarelle: An Evening of Moliere Farces,* Yale Repertory Theatre, then NYSF, Public Theatre, New York City, both 1978; (also set designer) *The Master and Margarita,* NYSF, Public Theatre, 1978; *The Umbrellas of Cherbourg* and *Happy Days,* both NYSF, Public Theatre, 1979.

The Seagull, NYSF, Public Theatre, 1980; *Sganarelle,* American Repertory Theatre, Cambridge, MA, 1981; *Zastrozzi,* NYSF, Public Theatre, 1982; *The Three Sisters,* American Repertory Theatre, 1982; *Uncle Vanya,* La Mama Annex, New York City, 1983; *Orpheus Descending,* Circle in the Square, New York City, 1984; *The King Stag* and *The Love of Three Oranges,* both American Repertory Theatre, 1984; *The Juniper Tree,* American Repertory Theatre, 1985; *The Marriage of Figaro,* Circle in the Square, 1985; *Sweet Table at the Richelieu* and *The Good Woman of Setzuan,* both American Repertory Theatre, 1986; *Fragments of a Greek Trilogy,* La Mama E.T.C., 1987; *Twelfth Night,* American Repertory Theatre, 1989. Also directed the operas *Eugene Onegin,* Welsh National Opera, Cardiff, Wales, 1980; *Puritani* and *Norma,* both Welsh National Opera, 1981; *The Magic Flute,* Paris Opera; *Turandot,* Royal Opera House, London; *Alcina,* New York City Opera, State Theatre, New York City; and *The Marriage of Figaro,* Tyrone Guthrie Theatre, Minneapolis, MN.

PRINCIPAL FILM WORK—Workshop sequence supervisor, *Jane Austen in Manhattan,* Contemporary/Cinecom International/New Yorker, 1980.

RELATED CAREER—Assistant to Peter Brook, International Theatre Institute, Paris, France, 1970-71; director, La Mama Experimental Theatre Club, New York City, 1970-77; professor of drama, Carnegie Institute of Technology, Pittsburgh, PA, and Sarah Lawrence College, Bronxville, NY, both 1974; professor of drama, Paris Conservatory, Paris, France, 1975; guest professor of drama, Yale University, New Haven, CT, 1977; associate director, Yale Repertory Theatre, New Haven, CT, 1977—; resident director, American Repertory Theatre, Cambridge, MA, 1986-87.

WRITINGS: STAGE—All as adaptor: *The Master and Margarita,* New York Shakespeare Festival (NYSF), Public Theatre, New York City, 1978; (with Elizabeth Swados) *Agamemnon,* NYSF, Vivian Beaumont Theatre, then Delacorte Theatre, New York City,

both 1977; *Fragments of a Greek Trilogy,* La Mama Experimental Theatre Club, New York City, 1987.

AWARDS: European Festival Awards, 1972, 1973, and 1975; Obie Award from the *Village Voice,* 1975, for distinguished direction of Greek tragedy; Outer Critics' Circle Award, 1977, for *The Cherry Orchard;* Drama Desk Award, 1975, for *Medea;* Ford Foundation fellowship, 1969-70; Guggenheim fellowship, 1976-77.

ADDRESSES: OFFICE—35 E. 10th Street, New York, NY 10003.*

*   *   *

SHACKELFORD, Ted   1946-

PERSONAL: Born June 23, 1946, in Oklahoma City, OK; son of Paul Olden (a physician) and Mary Jane (Kennedy) Shackelford; married Janis M. Leverenz, August 6, 1976. EDUCATION—Attended Westminster College, 1964-67; University of Denver, B.A., English and theatre, 1969.

VOCATION: Actor.

CAREER: PRINCIPAL STAGE APPEARANCES—*Murder Among Friends,* Biltmore Theatre, New York City, 1975; also appeared in productions of *Hogan's Goat, The Night of the Iguana, Bus Stop, Sunday in New York, My Three Angels,* and *The Pleasure of His Company,* all in Denver, CO, 1972-74; also *Key Exchange,* Santa Barbara, CA.

PRINCIPAL FILM APPEARANCES—Boone, *Sweet Revenge,* Concorde, 1987.

PRINCIPAL TELEVISION APPEARANCES—Series: Ray Gordon, *Another World,* NBC, 1975-76; Gary Ewing, *Dallas,* CBS, 1979-81; Gary Ewing, *Knots Landing,* CBS, 1979—. Pilots: Brian Klosky, *The Jordan Chance,* CBS, 1978; Barnes, *Ebony, Ivory, and Jade,* CBS, 1979; Helmut Pendl, *Dirty Dozen: The Series,* syndicated, 1988; Preston McMillan, *Paradise,* CBS, 1989. Episodic: Preston McMillan, *Paradise,* CBS, 1989; also *Big Hawaii,* NBC, 1977; *Wonder Woman,* CBS, 1977 and 1979; *The Rockford Files,* NBC; *Soap,* ABC; *Hotel,* ABC. Movies: Blain, *The Defection of Simas Kudirka,* CBS, 1978; Delbert Ramsey, *Terror Among Us,* CBC, 1981; Carlisle, *Summer Fantasy,* NBC, 1984; also *The Love Boat: The Valentine Voyage,* CBS, 1990. Specials: *Battle of the Network Stars,* ABC, 1983; *CBS Cotton Bowl Parade,* CBS, 1984; *CBS All-American Thanksgiving Day Parade,* CBS, 1985 and 1987; host, *Miss America Pageant,* CBS, 1988; also *TV's Bloopers and Practical Jokes,* NBC.

NON-RELATED CAREER—Hotel night manager, New York City.

MEMBER: Actors' Equity Association, Screen Actors Guild, American Federation of Television and Radio Artists.

SIDELIGHTS: RECREATIONS—Hiking, playing cards, swimming, environmental activist.

ADDRESSES: ADDRESSES—Le Mond/Zetter Inc., 8370 Wilshire Boulevard, Suite 310, Beverly Hills, CA 90211-2333.*

MICHAEL SHALLARD

SHALLARD, Michael 1951-

PERSONAL: Born Michael Noakes, August 1, 1951, in London, England; son of Frederick and Dora Jean (Aslett) Noakes. EDUCATION—Trained for the stage at the Royal Academy of Dramatic Art.

VOCATION: Actor.

CAREER: STAGE DEBUT—Silvius, *As You Like It*, New Shakespeare Company, London, 1973. PRINCIPAL STAGE APPEARANCES—Eric Smith, *Funny Peculiar*, Garrick Theatre, London, 1977; Chamberlain, *Dirty Linen*, Arts Theatre, London, 1979; Dalton, *Equus*, Young Vic Theatre, London, 1982; Bud, *Sweet Bird of Youth*, Haymarket Theatre, London, 1985; Seton Cram, *Holiday*, Old Vic Theatre, London, 1987; subeditor, *Exclusive*, Strand Theatre, London, 1989; also appeared in *Harlequinade*, National Theatre Company, Baltimore International Festival, Baltimore, MD, 1981; with the Theatre Royal, York, U.K., 1974; with the Leeds Playhouse, Leeds, U.K., 1975; with the National Theatre, London, 1980-81.

MAJOR TOURS—Silvius, *As You Like It*, with the New Shakespeare Company, U.K. cities, 1973; *Thee and Me, Harlequinade*, and *Caretaker*, with the National Theatre Company, U.K. cities, 1980-81.

TELEVISION DEBUT—Taffy Morgan, *By the Sword Divided*, BBC, 1983, then *Masterpiece Theatre*, PBS. PRINCIPAL TELEVISION APPEARANCES—Episodic: Adrian, *Only Fools and Horses*,

BBC, 1989; also *Dead Head*, BBC, 1984; *Yes, Prime Minister*, BBC, 1987, then PBS.

MEMBER: Actors Centre.

ADDRESSES: AGENT—Kean and Garrick, 6-8 Paved Court, The Green, Richmond, Surrey, England.

*   *   *

SHAPIRO, Debbie 1954-

PERSONAL: Born September 29, 1954, in Los Angeles, CA; married Beau Gravitte (an actor), 1986. EDUCATION—Graduated from Los Angeles Community College.

VOCATION: Actress.

CAREER: BROADWAY DEBUT—Chorus and understudy, *They're Playing Our Song*, Imperial Theatre, 1979. PRINCIPAL STAGE APPEARANCES—Louisa May, *Spotlight*, National Theatre, Washington, DC, 1978; ensemble, *Perfectly Frank* (revue), Helen Hayes Theatre, New York City, 1980; Julie, *The New Moon in Concert*, Town Hall, New York City, 1981; ensemble, *They Say It's Wonderful* (revue), St. Regis-Sheraton/King Cole Room, New York City, 1982; Woman #2, *Blues in the Night*, Rialto Theatre, New York City, 1982; the Woman, *Zorba*, Broadway Theatre, New York City, 1983; Lotta, *Rainbow*, Off Center Theatre, New York City, 1986; overture soloist, Hildy, Rosalia, Mazeppa, "Monotony" singer, and ensemble, *Jerome Robbins' Broadway*, Imperial Theatre, New York City, 1989. Also appeared in *Swing*, Washington, DC; and in *Annie Get Your Gun*.

MAJOR TOURS—The Woman, *Zorba*, U.S. cities, 1983.

PRINCIPAL FILM APPEARANCES—Voice characterizations, *The Little Mermaid* (animated), Buena Vista, 1989.

PRINCIPAL TELEVISION APPEARANCES—Series: Rhonda, *Trial and Error*, CBS, 1988. Specials: *Broadway Plays Washington! Kennedy Center Tonight*, PBS, 1982.

RELATED CAREER—Lounge singer, Ramada Inn, Darien, CT.

AWARDS: Antoinette Perry Award and Drama Desk Award nomination, both Best Actress in a Musical, 1989, for *Jerome Robbins' Broadway*.*

*   *   *

SHAPIRO, Esther 1934-

PERSONAL: Full name, Esther June Shapiro; born June 6, 1934, in Brooklyn, NY; daughter of Jack and Flora (Salmoni) Mayesh; married Richard Shapiro (a producer and screenwriter), December 4, 1960; children: Florie Sonya, Eden Jacqueline. EDUCATION—University of Southern California, B.A., 1952; graduate work, University of California, Los Angeles, 1955-56.

VOCATION: Producer and screenwriter.

CAREER: Also see *WRITINGS* below. PRINCIPAL TELEVISION WORK—Series: Executive story consultant, *Love Story,* NBC, 1973-74; creator (with Richard Shapiro) and executive producer (with Richard Shapiro, Douglas S. Cramer, and Aaron Spelling), *Dynasty,* ABC, 1981-89; creator (with Richard Shapiro) and executive producer (with Richard Shapiro and Michael Filerman), *Emerald Point, N.A.S.,* CBS, 1983-84; creator and executive producer (with Richard Shapiro), *Dynasty II: The Colbys* (also known as *The Colbys*), ABC, 1985-87; executive producer, *HeartBeat,* ABC, 1988. Pilots: Executive producer (with Richard Shapiro), *When We Were Young,* NBC, 1989. Movies: Producer (with Richard Shapiro), *Intimate Strangers,* ABC, 1977; executive producer (with Spelling and Cramer), *The Three Kings,* ABC, 1987; executive producer (with Spelling and Cramer), *Cracked Up,* ABC, 1987.

RELATED CAREER—Executive story consultant, Paramount Pictures, 1973; vice-president in charge of mini-series and novels for television, ABC-TV, 1977-79; founder (with Richard Shapiro), Richard and Esther Shapiro Productions, then Shapiro Entertainment Corporation, 1979—; steering committee, Hollywood Women's Coalition, 1984; board of directors, Los Angeles Actors Theatre, 1984; senior vice-president for creative and corporate affairs, Aaron Spelling Productions, 1986-87.

NON-RELATED CAREER—Board of directors, World Interdependence Fund.

WRITINGS: TELEVISION—Episodic: *Love of Life,* CBS, 1969-70; *Love Story,* NBC, 1973; *Dynasty,* ABC, 1981-89; *Emerald Point, N.A.S.,* CBS, 1983-84; *The Colbys,* ABC, 1985-86; *HeartBeat,* ABC, 1988. Pilots: (With Richard Shapiro) *When We Were Young,* NBC, 1989. Movies: (With Richard Shapiro) *Sarah T.: Portrait of a Teenage Alcoholic,* NBC, 1975; (with Richard Shapiro) *Minstrel Man,* CBS, 1977; (with Richard Shapiro) *Intimate Strangers,* ABC, 1977.

AWARDS: Christopher Award, International Catholic Association for Radio and Television Award, World Association of Christian Communicators Award, 1977, and Prix Italia, 1978, all for *Minstrel Man;* US magazine Awards, 1982 and 1983, Golden Globe, 1983, and *Soap Opera Digest* Award, 1984, all for *Dynasty;* Distinguished Community Service Award from Beverly Hills, CA, 1984; Genii Award from the American Women in Radio and Television (Southern California chapter), 1985; Bullock's Wilshire Portfolio Award for Executive Women, 1985; National Women's Committee of Brandeis University Award, 1985; Leadership Award from the American Women's Economic Development Corporation.

MEMBER: Writers Guild of America—West, Academy of Television Arts and Sciences, Caucus for Producers, Writers, and Directors (trustee), American Film Institute, Regency Club.

ADDRESSES: OFFICE—Shapiro Entertainment Corporation, 335 N. Maple Drive, Beverly Hills, CA 90046.*

*   *   *

SHAPIRO, Richard   1934-

PERSONAL: Full name, Richard Allen Shapiro; born June 27, 1934, in Los Angeles, CA; son of Edward and Florence (Blank) Shapiro; married Esther June Mayesh (a producer and screenwriter),

December 4, 1960; children: Florie Sonya, Eden Jacqueline. EDUCATION—University of California, Los Angeles, B.A., 1956.

VOCATION: Producer and screenwriter.

CAREER: Also see *WRITINGS* below. PRINCIPAL TELEVISION WORK—Series: Creator (with Esther Shapiro) and executive producer (with Esther Shapiro, Douglas S. Cramer, and Aaron Spelling), *Dynasty,* ABC, 1981-89; creator (with Esther Shapiro) and executive producer (with Esther Shapiro and Michael Filerman), *Emerald Point, N.A.S.,* CBS, 1983-84; creator and executive producer (with Esther Shapiro), *Dynasty II: The Colbys* (also known as *The Colbys*), ABC, 1985-87. Pilots: Executive producer (with Esther Shapiro), *When We Were Young,* NBC, 1989. Movies: Producer (with Esther Shapiro), *Intimate Strangers,* ABC, 1977; producer, *The Cracker Factory,* ABC, 1979.

RELATED CAREER—Founder (with Esther Shapiro), Richard and Esther Shapiro Productions, then Shapiro Entertainment Corporation, 1979—.

WRITINGS: FILM—*The Great Scout and Cathouse Thursday* (also known as *Wildcat*), American International, 1976. TELEVISION—Episodic: *Love of Life,* CBS, 1969-70; *Land of the Giants,* ABC, 1969-70; *Dynasty,* ABC, 1981-89; *Emerald Point, N.A.S.,* CBS, 1983-84; *The Colbys,* ABC, 1985-86. Mini-Series: *John Steinbeck's "East of Eden,"* ABC, 1981. Pilots: (With Esther Shapiro) *When We Were Young,* NBC, 1989. Movies: (With Esther Shapiro) *Sarah T.: Portrait of a Teenage Alcoholic,* NBC, 1975; (with Esther Shapiro) *Minstrel Man,* CBS, 1977; (with Esther Shapiro) *Intimate Strangers,* ABC, 1977; *The Cracker Factory,* ABC, 1979.

AWARDS: Christopher Award, International Catholic Association for Radio and Television Award, World Association of Christian Communicators Award, all 1977, and Prix Italia, 1978, all for *Minstrel Man;* Golden Globe, 1981, for *John Steinbeck's "East of Eden";* US magazine Awards, 1982 and 1983, Golden Globe, 1983, and *Soap Opera Digest* Award, 1984, all for *Dynasty;* Distinguished Community Service Award from Beverly Hills, CA, 1984.

MEMBER: Writers Guild of America—West, Academy of Television Arts and Sciences, Caucus for Producers, Writers, and Directors, American Film Institute, Regency Club.

ADDRESSES: OFFICE—Shapiro Entertainment Corporation, 335 N. Maple Drive, Beverly Hills, CA 90046.*

*   *   *

SHAW, Run Run   1907-

PERSONAL: Born October 14, 1907, in Shanghai, China; married Wong Mee Chun, 1932 (deceased); children: Vee Meng, Dorothy, Violet, Harold.

VOCATION: Producer.

CAREER: PRINCIPAL FILM WORK—All as producer, unless indicated: *Madame White Snake* (also known as *Pai-She Chuan*), Frank Lee International, 1963; *The Last Woman of Shang* (also known as *Ta Chi*), Frank Lee International, 1964; *The Love Eterne* (also known as *Liang Shan-Po Yu Chu Ying-T'ai*), Frank Lee Interna-

RUN RUN SHAW

tional, 1964; (with Runme Shaw) *Empress Wu* (also known as *Wu-Hou*), Shaw Brothers, 1965; *The Enchanting Shadow* (also known as *Chin, Nu Yu Hun*), Shaw Brothers, 1965; *The Grand Substitution*, Frank Lee International, 1965; *The Lady General* (also known as *Hua Mu-Lan*), Frank Lee International, 1965; *The Shepherd Girl*, Frank Lee International, 1965; *Lovers' Rock*, Shaw Brothers, 1966; *Sons of Good Earth*, Frank Lee International, 1967; *Vermilion Door*, Shaw Brothers, 1969.

Five Fingers of Death (also known as *Hand of Death*), Warner Brothers, 1973; *Man of Iron*, Bardene International, 1973; production supervisor, *Triple Irons*, National General, 1973; (with Gustave Berne) *Blood Money*, Shaw Brothers/Compagnia Cinematografica Champion/Midega/Harbor, 1974; *The Sacred Knives of Vengeance* (also known as *The Killer*), Warner Brothers, 1974; (with William Tennant) *Cleopatra Jones and the Casino of Gold*, Warner Brothers, 1975; *King Gambler*, Shaw Brothers, 1975; *Big Bad Sis*, Shaw Brothers, 1976; (with Runme Shaw) *Bruce Lee and I* (also known as *Bruce and I*), Shaw Brothers, 1976; *The Brotherhood*, Shaw Brothers, 1976; *The Crooks*, Shaw Brothers, 1976; *Deadly Angels*, Shaw Brothers, 1976; *Girls for Sale*, Shaw Brothers, 1976; *Oily Maniac*, Shaw Brothers, 1976; *Shaolin Avenger*, Shaw Brothers, 1976; *The Dream of the Red Chamber*, Shaw Brothers, 1976; *Dreams of Eroticism*, Shaw Brothers, 1977; *Gang of Four*, Shaw Brothers, 1977; *Innocent Lust*, Shaw Brothers, 1977; *Judgment of an Assassin*, Shaw Brothers, 1977; *Life Gamble*, Shaw Brothers, 1977; *The Mad Monk*, Shaw Brothers, 1977; *The Mad Monk Strikes Again*, Shaw Brothers, 1977; *The Brave Archer*, Shaw Brothers, 1977; executive producer, *The Mad Love Chase*, Shaw Brothers, 1977; executive producer, *The Proud Youth*, Shaw Brothers, 1977;

executive producer, *Pursuit of Vengeance*, Shaw Brothers, 1977; *Delinquent Teenagers*, Shaw Brothers, 1978; *Island of Virgins*, Shaw Brothers, 1978; executive producer, *The Brave Archers, Part II*, Shaw Brothers, 1978; executive producer, *The Psychopath*, Shaw Brothers, 1978; *The Proud Twins*, Shaw Brothers, 1979; *Shaolin Abbot*, Shaw Brothers, 1979; (with Mona Fong) *Shaolin Rescuers*, Shaw Brothers, 1979; *Tragedy of Love*, Shaw Brothers, 1979.

The Convict Killer, Shaw Brothers, 1980; (with Richard Gordon and David Speechly) *Horror Planet* (also known as *Inseminoid*), Almi/Brent Walker/Embassy Home Entertainment, 1980; *Two Champions of Shaolin*, Shaw Brothers, 1980; *Ghosts Galore*, Shaw Brothers, 1982; *Twinkle, Twinkle, Little Star*, Shaw Brothers, 1982; *On the Wrong Track*, Shaw Brothers, 1983; *Behind the Yellow Line*, Shaw Brothers, 1984; executive producer, *Prince Charming*, Shaw Brothers, 1984; *Girl with the Diamond Slipper*, Shaw Brothers, 1985; (with Mona Fong and Wong Kar Hee) *My Name Ain't Suzie*, Shaw Brothers, 1985; *Zuodian Yuanyang* (also known as *Love with the Perfect Stranger*), Shaw Brothers, 1985; *Curry On Doctors and Nurses*, Shaw Brothers, 1985. Also produced *Oriental Playgirls*, 1975.

RELATED CAREER—Chairman, Shaw Brothers Ltd., Hong Kong, 1959—; executive chairman, Television Broadcasts Ltd., 1980—; executive chairman, TVE Holdings Ltd., 1980—.

NON-RELATED CAREER—President, Hong Kong Red Cross Society, 1972—; council member, Chinese University of Hong Kong, 1977—; chairman, board of trustees, Chinese University of Hong Kong, 1983—; founder, Shaw College, Chinese University of Hong Kong, 1986.

AWARDS: Commander of the Order of the British Empire, 1974; knighted, 1977; Queen's Badge from the Red Cross, 1982; Commander in the Order of the Crown of Belgium, 1989. HONORARY DEGREES—University of Hong Kong, LL.D., 1980; Chinese University of Hong Kong, Doctor of Social Sciences, 1981; University of East Asia, Macau, Doctor of Social Sciences, 1985; University of Sussex, Doctor of Letters, 1987; City Polytechnic of Hong Kong, Doctor of Science, 1988; State University of New York, Stony Brook, Doctor of Humane Letters, 1989.

ADDRESSES: OFFICE c/o Shaw Brothers Ltd., Lot 220, Clear Water Bay Road, Kowloon, Hong Kong and Box 95638, Tsim Sha Tsui Post Office, Kowloon, Hong Kong.

*   *   *

SHEARER, Harry   1943-

PERSONAL: Born December 23, 1943, in Los Angeles, CA; son of Mack Shearer and Dora (Kohn) Warren; married Penelope Joyce Nichols, October, 1974 (divorced, 1977). EDUCATION—University of California, Los Angeles, B.A., political science, 1964; graduate studies at Harvard University, 1964-65.

VOCATION: Writer, actor, director, and producer.

CAREER: Also see WRITINGS below. PRINCIPAL STAGE APPEARANCES—*Beyond Therapy*, Los Angeles Public Theatre, Los Angeles, 1983; *Accomplice*, Pasadena Playhouse, Pasadena, CA, 1989.

FILM DEBUT—*Abbott and Costello Go to Mars*, Universal, 1953. PRINCIPAL FILM APPEARANCES—David, *The Robe*, Twentieth Century-Fox, 1953; Pete, *Real Life*, Paramount, 1979; Bernie Wepner, *One-Trick Pony*, Warner Brothers, 1980; recruiter, *The Right Stuff*, Warner Brothers, 1983; Derek Smalls, *This Is Spinal Tap*, Embassy, 1984; voiceover, *Flicks* (also known as *Hollyweird* and *Loose Joints*), United Film Distribution, 1987; Simon Feck, *Plain Clothes*, Paramount, 1988; voice of Carl Sagan, *My Stepmother Is an Alien*, Columbia, 1988. Also appeared in *Cracking Up*, American International, 1977; *The Fish That Saved Pittsburgh*, United Artists, 1979; *Animalympics* (animated), Barber Rose International, 1979; *Loose Shoes* (also known as *Coming Attractions*), Atlantic, 1980; *Serial*, Paramount, 1980.

TELEVISION DEBUT—*The Jack Benny Show*, CBS. PRINCIPAL TELEVISION APPEARANCES—Series: Regular, *Not Necessarily the News*, HBO, 1983; regular, *Saturday Night Live*, NBC, 1984-85. Pilots: Frankie, "It's a Small World," *Studio '57*, syndicated, 1957; Hippy, *Serpico: The Deadly Game*, NBC, 1976. Episodic: Timothy Anderson, *Miami Vice*, NBC, 1988; voice characterizations, *The Simpsons* (animated), Fox, 1990. Movies: Jack Savage, *Million Dollar Infield*, CBS, 1982. Specials: *The TV Show*, ABC, 1979; *David Letterman's Late Night Film Festival*, NBC, 1985; "It's Just TV!," *Cinemax Comedy Experiment*, Cinemax, 1985; voice characterization, *Spitting Image: Down and Out in the White House*, NBC, 1986; voice characterization, *Down and Out with Donald Duck* (animated), NBC, 1987; voice characterization, *Spitting Image: The 1987 Movie Awards*, NBC, 1987; voice characterization, *Spitting Image: The Ronnie and Nancy Show*, NBC, 1987; *Not Necessarily the News: Inside Entertainment*, HBO, 1987; "This Week Indoors," *Cinemax Comedy Experiment*, Cinemax, 1987; "Paul Shaffer: Viva Shaf Vegas," *Cinemax Comedy Experiment*, Cinemax, 1987; *An All-Star Celebration: The '88 Vote*, ABC, 1988; "Merrill Markoe's Guide to Glamorous Living," *Cinemax Comedy Experiment*, Cinemax, 1988; Al Silvers, *Martin Mull in Portrait of a White Marriage* (also known as *Portrait of a White Marriage*, *Martin Mull's Scenes from a White Marriage*, and *Scenes from a White Marriage*), Cinemax, 1988; "Harry Shearer . . . The Magic of Live," *HBO Comedy Hour*, HBO, 1988; voices of Principal Skinner, Mr. Largo, Mr. Burns, and Moe, *Simpsons Roasting on an Open Fire* (animated), Fox, 1989; *ALF Takes Over the Network*, NBC, 1989.

PRINCIPAL TELEVISION WORK—Specials: Creative consultant, *Fernwood 2-Night*, syndicated, 1977; creative consultant, *America 2-Night*, syndicated, 1977-78; producer, *The TV Show*, ABC, 1979; director, "It's Just TV!," *Cinemax Comedy Experiment*, Cinemax, 1985; director, *The History of White People in America*, Cinemax, 1985; executive producer (with Paul Shaffer and Tom Leopold) and director, "Paul Shaffer: Viva Shaf Vegas," *Cinemax Comedy Experiment*, Cinemax, 1987; executive producer (with Merrill Markoe) and director (with Markoe), "This Week Indoors," *Cinemax Comedy Experiment*, Cinemax, 1987; director, *Martin Mull in Portrait of a White Marriage* (also known as *Portrait of a White Marriage*, *Martin Mull's Scenes from a White Marriage*, and *Scenes from a White Marriage*), Cinemax, 1988; executive producer (with Kevin S. Bright), "Harry Shearer . . . The Magic of Live," *HBO Comedy Hour*, HBO, 1988.

PRINCIPAL RADIO APPEARANCES—Series: Host, *Le Show*.

RELATED CAREER—Writer, actor, and producer for the Credibility Gap (a comedy group), Los Angeles, 1968-76; creator of a radio program for National Public Radio, 1983.

NON-RELATED CAREER—Reporter, *Newsweek*, Los Angeles and Boston, MA, 1964-65; legislative intern, California State Assembly, 1965-66; reporter, *Los Angeles Times*; high school English and social studies teacher, Compton Unified School District, Compton, CA, 1966-68.

WRITINGS: FILM—(With others) *Cracking Up*, American International, 1977; (with Albert Brooks and Monica Johnson) *Real Life*, Paramount, 1979; (with Christopher Guest, Michael McKean, and Rob Reiner; also composer, with Guest, McKean, and Reiner) *This Is Spinal Tap*, Embassy, 1984.

TELEVISION—Series: *Saturday Night Live*, NBC, 1979-80 and 1984-85. Specials: "It's Just TV!," *Cinemax Comedy Experiment*, Cinemax, 1985; (with Merrill Markoe; also composer and lyricist) "This Week Indoors," *Cinemax Comedy Experiment*, Cinemax, 1987; (with Paul Shaffer and Tom Leopold) "Paul Shaffer: Viva Shaf Vegas," *Cinemax Comedy Experiment*, Cinemax, 1987; "Harry Shearer . . . The Magic of Live," *HBO Comedy Hour*, HBO, 1988.

OTHER—Contributor of articles to such publications as *New West*, *Los Angeles Magazine* and *Film Comment*.

RECORDINGS: ALBUMS—(With the Credibility Gap) *A Great Gift Idea*, 1974; also (with the Credibility Gap) *The Bronze Age of Radio*.

AWARDS: Emmy Award nominations, 1977 and 1980; ACE Award from the Cable Television Academy, 1988.

ADDRESSES: AGENT—Marty Klein, Agency for the Performing Arts, 9000 Sunset Boulevard, Suite 1200, Los Angeles, CA 90069.*

*   *   *

SHEEHAN, Douglas   1949-

PERSONAL: Born April 27, 1949, in Santa Monica, CA; wife's name, Cate. EDUCATION—Attended San Diego Mesa College. MILITARY—U.S. Army.

VOCATION: Actor.

CAREER: STAGE DEBUT—Summer Repertory Theatre, Santa Rosa, CA. PRINCIPAL STAGE APPEARANCES—Nestor, *Troilus and Cressida*, National Shakespeare Festival, Old Globe Theatre, San Diego, CA, 1976; Bob, *How the Other Half Loves*, National Shakespeare Festival, Old Globe Theatre, 1978; also appeared as Sir Toby Belch, *Twelfth Night*, National Shakespeare Festival, Old Globe Theatre.

PRINCIPAL FILM APPEARANCES—Cop, *10*, Warner Brothers, 1979.

PRINCIPAL TELEVISION APPEARANCES—Series: Joe Kelly, *General Hospital*, ABC, 1979-82; Ben Gibson, *Knots Landing*, CBS, 1983-87; Brian Harper, *Day By Day*, NBC, 1988-89. Pilots: Angel Jerry Davidson, *Heaven on Earth*, NBC, 1981. Episodic: *Cheers*, NBC, 1983; also *Charlie's Angels*, ABC; *Kaz*, CBS. Movies: Roger, *Stranger in My Bed*, NBC, 1987; F.B.I. Commander Gordon McNeill, *In the Line of Duty: The F.B.I. Murders*, NBC, 1988; Specials: *Battle of the Network Stars*, ABC, 1984.

RELATED CAREER—Company member, National Shakespeare Festival, Old Globe Theatre, San Diego, CA, 1976-78; appeared in cologne advertisements as the Aramis man.

AWARDS: Emmy Award nomination, Outstanding Supporting Actor in a Daytime Drama Series, 1982, and two *Soap Opera Digest* Readers' Poll Awards, Outstanding Actor, all for *General Hospital;* Soap Opera Award, Best Newcomer on Prime Time, for *Knots Landing.*

SIDELIGHTS: RECREATIONS—Polo.

ADDRESSES: AGENT—Dick Berman, The Agency, 10351 Santa Monica Boulevard, Suite 211, Los Angeles, CA 90025. PUBLICIST—Monique Moss, Levine Public Relations, 8730 Sunset Boulevard, Sixth Floor, Los Angeles, CA 90069.*

*　　*　　*

SHELDON, Sidney   1917-

PERSONAL: Born February 11, 1917, in Chicago, IL; son of Otto (in sales) and Natalie (Marcus) Sheldon; married Jorja Curtright (an actress), March 28, 1951 (died, 1985); married Alexandra Kosoff, December, 1989; children: Mary (first marriage). EDUCATION—Attended Northwestern University for one year. MILITARY—U.S. Army Air Forces, 1941.

VOCATION: Writer and producer.

CAREER: Also see *WRITINGS* below. PRINCIPAL FILM WORK—Director, *Dream Wife,* Metro-Goldwyn-Mayer, 1953; producer (with Robert Smith) and director, *The Buster Keaton Story,* Paramount, 1957.

PRINCIPAL TELEVISION WORK—Series: Creator (with William Asher), *The Patty Duke Show,* ABC, 1963-66; creator and producer (with Claudio Guzman), *I Dream of Jeannie,* NBC, 1965-70; creator and executive producer, *Nancy,* NBC, 1970-71; creator, *Hart to Hart,* ABC, 1979-84. Mini-Series: Executive producer, *Sidney Sheldon's "Windmills of the Gods,"* CBS, 1988. Movies: Executive producer, *Rage of Angels,* NBC, 1983; executive producer, *Rage of Angels: The Story Continues,* NBC, 1986.

RELATED CAREER—Script reader, Universal and Twentieth Century-Fox studios.

NON-RELATED CAREER—Composer.

WRITINGS: STAGE—(Adaptor with Ben Roberts) *The Merry Widow,* Majestic Theatre, New York City, 1943; *Jackpot,* Alvin Theatre, New York City, 1944; *Dream with Music,* Majestic Theatre, 1944; *Alice in Arms,* National Theatre, New York City, 1945; (with Dorothy and Herbert Fields and David Shaw) *Redhead,* 46th Street Theatre, New York City, 1959; *Roman Candle,* Cort Theatre, New York City, 1960.

FILM—(With Jack Natteford) *Dangerous Lady,* Producers Releasing Corporation, 1941; (with Ben Roberts) *South of Panama,* Producers Releasing Corporation, 1941; *She's in the Army,* Monogram, 1942; *The Bachelor and the Bobby-Soxer* (also known as *Bachelor Knight*), RKO, 1947; (with Roberts) *The Carter Case,* Republic, 1947; (with Frances Goodrich, Albert Hackett, and Guy

Bolton) *Easter Parade,* Metro-Goldwyn-Mayer (MGM), 1948; *Nancy Goes to Rio,* MGM, 1950; *Annie Get Your Gun,* MGM, 1950; *No Questions Asked,* MGM, 1951; (with Dorothy Cooper) *Rich, Young, and Pretty,* MGM, 1951; *Three Guys Named Mike,* MGM, 1951; *Just This Once,* MGM, 1952; (with Herbert Baker and Alfred Lewis Levitt) *Dream Wife,* MGM, 1953; *Remains to Be Seen,* MGM, 1953; *You're Never Too Young,* Paramount, 1955; *Anything Goes,* Paramount, 1956; (with Jerry Davis) *Pardners,* Paramount, 1956; (with Preston Sturges) *The Birds and the Bees,* Paramount, 1956; (with Robert Smith) *The Buster Keaton Story,* Paramount, 1957; (with Edmund Beloin and Maurice Richlin) *All in a Night's Work,* Paramount, 1961; *Jumbo* (also known as *Billy Rose's Jumbo*), MGM, 1962.

TELEVISION—Pilots: *Adventures of a Model,* NBC, 1958; (with Tom Mankiewicz) *Hart to Hart,* ABC, 1979. Episodic: *I Dream of Jeannie,* NBC; *The Patty Duke Show,* ABC; "Need to Know," *The Twilight Zone,* CBS, 1986.

OTHER—Novels: *The Naked Face,* Morrow, 1970; *The Other Side of Midnight,* Morrow, 1974; *A Stranger in the Mirror,* Morrow, 1976; *Bloodline,* Morrow, 1978; *Rage of Angels,* Morrow, 1980; *Master of the Game,* Morrow, 1982; *If Tomorrow Comes,* Morrow, 1985; *Windmills of the Gods,* Morrow, 1987; *The Sands of Time,* Morrow, 1988; *Memories of Midnight,* Morrow, 1990.

AWARDS: Academy Award, Best Screenplay, 1947, for *The Bachelor and the Bobby-Soxer;* Writers Guild of America Award, 1948, for *Easter Parade;* Writers Guild of America Award, 1950, for *Annie Get Your Gun;* Antoinette Perry Award (with Herbert and Dorothy Fields and David Shaw), Best Author of a Musical, 1959, for *Redhead;* also received an Edgar Award from the Mystery Writers of America.

SIDELIGHTS: In addition to the films noted above for which he has written screenplays, Sidney Sheldon's novels have been adapted to such other projects as *The Other Side of Midnight,* Twentieth Century-Fox, 1977; *Bloodline,* Paramount, 1979; *The Naked Face,* Cannon, 1984; and the television mini-series *Master of the Game,* CBS, 1984 and *If Tomorrow Comes,* CBS, 1986.

ADDRESSES: AGENT—Bill Haber, Creative Artists Agency, 9830 Wilshire Boulevard, Beverly Hills, CA 90212. PUBLICIST—Dick Guttman, Guttman and Pam, 8500 Wilshire Boulevard, Suite 801, Beverly Hills, CA 90211.*

*　　*　　*

SHENAR, Paul   1936-1989

PERSONAL: Full name, Albert Paul Shenar; born February 12, 1936, in Milwaukee, WI; died of AIDS, October 11, 1989, in West Hollywood, CA; son of Eugene Joseph and Mary Rosella (Puhek) Shenar. EDUCATION—University of Wisconsin, B.S., 1962. MILITARY—U.S. Air Force, 1954-57.

VOCATION: Actor.

CAREER: OFF-BROADWAY DEBUT—Michael, *Pullman Car Hiawatha,* Circle in the Square, 1962. BROADWAY DEBUT—Brother Julian, *Tiny Alice* and Baron Nikolai Lvovich Tusenbach, *The Three Sisters* (in repertory), both American Conservatory Theatre, American National Theatre and Academy Theatre, 1969.

PRINCIPAL STAGE APPEARANCES—Paul, *Six Characters in Search of an Author,* Martinique Theatre, 1963; Brother Julian, *Tiny Alice,* American Conservatory Theatre, San Francisco, CA, 1966-68; title role, *Oedipus Rex,* American Conservatory Theatre, 1970; Eilert Lovborg, *Hedda Gabler,* Roundabout Theatre, New York City, 1981; Charles, *Blithe Spirit,* McCarter Theatre, Princeton, NJ, 1982; Mikhail Alexandrovich Rakitin, *A Month in the Country* and voice of the King's herald, *Richard III,* both Center Theatre Group, Mark Taper Forum, Los Angeles, 1983; Banquo, *Macbeth,* Mark Hellinger Theatre, New York City, 1988. Also appeared in *Antony and Cleopatra* and *A Midsummer Night's Dream,* both National Shakespeare Festival, San Diego, CA, 1971; *Paradise Lost,* American Conservatory Theatre, 1972; *That Championship Season,* American Conservatory Theatre, 1973; *Shadow Play,* American Conservatory Theatre, 1974; *Ring 'round the Moon,* Center Theatre Group, Ahmanson Theatre, Los Angeles, 1975; *The Heiress,* Westwood Playhouse, Los Angeles; and at the Yale Repertory Theatre, New Haven, CT; Tyrone Guthrie Theatre, Minneapolis, MN; Long Wharf Theatre, New Haven, CT; and with the Lincoln Center Repertory Theatre, New York City.

MAJOR TOURS—Banquo, *Macbeth,* U.S. cities, 1988.

MAJOR FILM APPEARANCES—Ludwig Schon, *Lulu,* Chase, 1978; Arobin, *The End of August,* Quartet, 1982; voice of Jenner, *The Secret of NIMH* (animated), Metro-Goldwyn-Mayer/United Artists, 1982; Joshua Adams, *Deadly Force,* Embassy, 1983; Alejandro Sosa, *Scarface,* Universal, 1983; Ben Gardner, *Dream Lover,* United Artists, 1986; Rocca, *Raw Deal,* De Laurentiis Entertainment Group, 1986; Colin Wentworth, *The Bedroom Window,* De Laurentiis Entertainment Group, 1987; David Madlock, *Best Seller,* Orion, 1987; Ettore Balletto, *Man on Fire,* Tri-Star, 1987; Laurence, *The Big Blue* (also known as *Le Grand Bleu*), Gaumont, 1988.

PRINCIPAL TELEVISION APPEARANCES—Mini-Series: Carrington, *Roots,* ABC, 1977; Roscoe Corlay, *Beaulah Land,* NBC, 1980. Pilots: Charles Edward Royce, *Gemini Man* (also known as *Code Name: Minus One*), NBC, 1976; Joe Silvano, *Three Eyes,* NBC, 1982; J. Elliott Sloan, *Streets of Justice,* NBC, 1985; Philip Drake, *Dark Mansions,* ABC, 1986; Chase, *Time Out for Dad,* NBC, 1987. Episodic: Matthew Lowington, *Spenser: for Hire,* ABC, 1985; also *Paper Dolls,* ABC, 1984; *Dynasty,* ABC, 1985; *Scarecrow and Mrs. King,* CBS. Movies: Crawford, *The Execution of Private Slovik,* NBC, 1974; Orson Welles, *The Night That Panicked America,* ABC, 1975; Rudi Portinari, *The Keegans,* CBS, 1976; James Cardone, *The Hostage Heart,* CBS, 1977; Nick Silcox, *The Courage and the Passion,* NBC, 1978; Jack Graham, *Suddenly, Love,* NBC, 1978; Flo Ziegfeld, *Ziegfeld: The Man and His Women,* NBC, 1978; Schuyler Ross, *Brass,* CBS, 1985; Jerry Worth, *Rage of Angels: The Story Continues,* NBC, 1986. Specials: De Guiche, "Cyrano de Bergerac," *Great Performances,* PBS, 1974. Also appeared in *Richard II.*

RELATED CAREER—Company member and acting teacher, American Conservatory Theatre, San Francisco, CA, 1965-74; voiceover artist for television commercials.

OBITUARIES AND OTHER SOURCES: Variety, October 25-31, 1989.*

SHERMAN, Hiram   1908-1989

PERSONAL: Born February 11, 1908, in Boston, MA; died of a stroke, April 11, 1989, in Springfield, IL; son of Clifford and Gwendolen (Lawrence) Sherman. EDUCATION—Attended the University of Illinois; trained for the stage with the Goodman Theatre Repertory Company. MILITARY—U.S. Navy, 1941-46.

VOCATION: Actor.

CAREER: STAGE DEBUT—Murderer, *Le Tour de Nesle,* Goodman Theatre, Chicago, IL, 1927. BROADWAY DEBUT—Robbin, *Horse Eats Hat,* Federal Theatre Project, Maxine Elliott's Theatre, 1936. LONDON DEBUT—Jeff, *Brigadoon,* His Majesty's Theatre, 1949. PRINCIPAL STAGE APPEARANCES—Reverend Salvation and Junior Mister, *The Cradle Will Rock,* Venice Theatre, New York City, 1937; Casca, *Julius Caesar* and Firk, *The Shoemaker's Holiday,* both Mercury Theatre, New York City, 1937; ensemble, *Sing Out the News* (revue), Music Box Theatre, New York City, 1938; Bottom, *A Midsummer Night's Dream* and Touchstone, *As You Like It,* both Globe Theatre, New York World's Fair, Flushing, NY, 1939; Ogden Quiler, *Very Warm for May,* Alvin Theatre, New York City, 1939; Reverend Ernest Dunwoody, *Boyd's Daughter,* Booth Theatre, New York City, 1940; Copmere, *Mum's the Word,* Belmont Theatre, New York City, 1940; Cy Blodgett, *The Talley Method,* Henry Miller's Theatre, New York City, 1941; Ragueneau, *Cyrano de Bergerac,* Alvin Theatre, 1946; Kastril, *The Alchemist,* City Center Theatre, New York City, 1948; Pete Murray, *Town House,* National Theatre, New York City, 1948; Jeff, *Brigadoon,* Opera House, Manchester, U.K., 1949.

Philip Dupre, *Four Twelves Are 48,* 48th Street Theatre, New York City, 1951; Harry, *I Married an Angel* and Baron Popoff, *The Merry Widow,* both Fair Park Auditorium, Dallas, TX, 1951; David Slater, *The Moon Is Blue,* Harris Theatre, Chicago, IL, 1952; Cowardly Lion, *The Wizard of Oz,* Fair Park Auditorium, 1952; ensemble, *Two's Company* (revue), Alvin Theatre, 1952; Edward, *Dear Charles,* New Parsons Theatre, Hartford, CT, 1953; Charles Belden, *The Frogs of Spring,* Broadhurst Theatre, New York City, 1953; compere, *Three for Tonight* (revue), Plymouth Theatre, New York City, 1955; Harvey Wilson, *Goodbye Again,* Helen Hayes Theatre, New York City, 1956; Pompey, *Measure for Measure* and Hubert de Burgh, *King John,* both American Shakespeare Festival, Stratford, CT, 1956; Jupiter, *Orpheus in the Underworld,* City Center Theatre, 1956; Pompey, *Measure for Measure,* Phoenix Theatre, New York City, 1957; Panisse, *Fanny,* State Fair Music Hall, Dallas, TX, 1957; Baron Popoff, *The Merry Widow,* City Center Theatre, 1957; compere, *International Soiree* (revue), Bijou Theatre, New York City, 1958; Polonius, *Hamlet,* Bottom, *A Midsummer Night's Dream,* and shepherd and third gentleman, *The Winter's Tale,* all American Shakespeare Festival, 1958; Friar Laurence, *Romeo and Juliet,* Ford, *The Merry Wives of Windsor,* and Sergeant, *All's Well That Ends Well,* all American Shakespeare Festival, 1959.

Berenger, *The Killer,* Seven Arts Center, New York City, 1960; ensemble, *The Art of Living* (revue), Criterion Theatre, London, 1960; Touchstone, *As You Like It,* Porter, *Macbeth,* and Pandarus, *Troilus and Cressida,* all American Shakespeare Festival, 1961; Porter, *Macbeth* and Pandarus, *Troilus and Cressida,* both American Shakespeare Festival Performance at the White House, Washington, DC, 1961; narrator, *Die Lustige Witwe,* Carnegie Hall, New York City, 1962; Oscar Nelson, *Mary, Mary,* Helen Hayes Theatre, 1963; Reverend Salvation, *The Cradle Will Rock,* Philharmonic Hall, New York City, 1964; Albert Denison, *Everybody*

Out, the Castle Is Sinking, Colonial Theatre, Boston, MA, 1964; Pinky, *Family Things, Etc.,* Westport, CT, 1965, retitled *Where's Daddy?,* Billy Rose Theatre, New York City, 1966; Wingate, *How Now, Dow Jones,* Lunt-Fontanne Theatre, New York City, 1967; Matthew Cuthbert, *Anne of Green Gables,* New Theatre, London, 1969. Also appeared in a dedicatory program of one-act plays by William Saroyan and Thornton Wilder, Congress Hall, Berlin, Germany, 1957; *War, Women, and Other Trivia,* Shaw Festival, Niagara-on-the-Lake, ON, Canada, 1971; and with the Goodman Theatre, Chicago, IL, 1971-72.

MAJOR TOURS—David Slater, *The Moon Is Blue,* U.S. cities, 1951-52; Charles Belden, *The Frogs of Spring,* U.S. cities, 1953; Philip, *The Little Hut,* U.S. cities, 1954; Baron Popoff, *The Merry Widow,* U.S. cities, 1957; Oscar Nelson, *Mary, Mary,* U.S. cities, 1962-63; Harbour Gage, *Heart's Delight,* U.S. cities, 1964.

FILM DEBUT—Donald Hinchley, *One Third of a Nation,* Paramount, 1939. PRINCIPAL FILM APPEARANCES—English commentary, *Fan-Fan the Tulip* (also known as *Soldier in Love*), Lopert, 1952; Harry Harkness, *The Solid Gold Cadillac,* Columbia, 1956; Oscar Nelson, *Mary, Mary,* Warner Brothers, 1963; Breckenduff, *Oh Dad, Poor Dad, Mama's Hung You in the Closet and I'm Feelin' So Sad,* Paramount, 1967.

PRINCIPAL TELEVISION APPEARANCES—Series: Uncle Simon, *The Tammy Grimes Show,* ABC, 1966. Pilots: Title role, *That's Our Sherman,* NBC, 1948. Episodic: *Alcoa Hour,* NBC; *Studio One,* CBS; also *Prudential Family Playhouse.* Specials: King of Hearts, "Alice in Wonderland," *Hallmark Hall of Fame,* NBC, 1955; R.H. Macy, *Miracle on 34th Street,* NBC, 1959; Henry Stoddard, *The Man in the Dog Suit,* NBC, 1960; Judge Bowling Greene, "Abe Lincoln in Illinois," *Hallmark Hall of Fame,* NBC, 1964.

RELATED CAREER—Master of ceremonies, American Shakespeare Festival Performance at the White House, Washington, DC, 1961; playwright.

AWARDS: Antoinette Perry Award, Best Supporting or Featured Actor in a Musical, 1953, for *Two's Company;* Antoinette Perry Award, Best Supporting or Featured Actor in a Musical, 1968, for *How Now, Dow Jones.*

OBITUARIES AND OTHER SOURCES: *Variety,* April 19-25, 1989.*

*   *   *

SHIGETA, James   1933-

PERSONAL: Born in 1933 in Hawaii.

VOCATION: Actor.

CAREER: PRINCIPAL STAGE APPEARANCES—Prince Eagle, *Chu Chem,* New Locust Theatre, Philadelphia, PA, 1966.

PRINCIPAL FILM APPEARANCES—Detective Joe Kojaku, *The Crimson Kimono,* Columbia, 1959; Cheng Lu, *Walk Like a Dragon,* Paramount, 1960; Hidenari Terasaki, *Bridge to the Sun,* Metro-Goldwyn-Mayer, 1961; Suzuki, *Cry for Happy,* Columbia, 1961; Wang Ta, *Flower Drum Song,* Universal, 1961; Danny Kohana,

Paradise, Hawaiian Style, Paramount, 1966; Toshi O'Hara, *Nobody's Perfect,* Universal, 1968; Brother Tolenn, *Lost Horizon,* Columbia, 1973; Goro, *The Yakuza* (also known as *Brotherhood of the Yakuza*), Warner Brothers/Toei, 1975; Vice-Admiral Chuichi Nagumo, *Midway* (also known as *Battle of Midway*), Universal, 1976; Takagi, *Die Hard,* Twentieth Century-Fox, 1988.

PRINCIPAL TELEVISION APPEARANCES—Mini-Series: Wizard Wong, *Arthur Hailey's "The Moneychangers,"* NBC, 1976; Lin Tsu-Han, *Once an Eagle,* NBC, 1976-77. Pilots: George Ti-Ming, *The Hardy Boys,* NBC, 1967; Chief Resident, *U.M.C.,* CBS, 1969; Dr. Chen, *The Questor Tapes,* NBC, 1974; Thomas McCauley, *Matt Helm,* ABC, 1975; David Lao, *The Killer Who Wouldn't Die,* ABC, 1976; Takeo Chisato, *Samurai,* ABC, 1979; Jimmy Lee, *The Renegades,* ABC, 1982; also *The Young Lawyers,* ABC, 1969. Episodic: Major Jong, "Nightmare," *The Outer Limits,* ABC, 1963; A.I.O. Captain Ngo Newa, "The Inheritors," *The Outer Limits,* ABC, 1964; Dr. Okaua, *Peaceable Kingdom,* CBS, 1989; Kozo Nakasone, *Jake and the Fatman,* CBS, 1989. Movies: Lieutenant Takahashi, *Escape to Mindanao,* NBC, 1968; Field Marshall Abehata, *Enola Gay,* NBC, 1980; Donald Shibura, *Tomorrow's Child,* ABC, 1982. Specials: Doctor, *Carol for Another Christmas,* ABC, 1964.*

*   *   *

SHORES, Del   1957-

PERSONAL: Full name, Delferd Lynn Shores; born December 3, 1957, in Winters, TX; son of William David (a Southern Baptist minister) and Loraine (a real estate broker; maiden name, Fuller) Shores; married Kelley Alexander (a coach), January 7, 1986. EDUCATION—Baylor University, B.A., journalism and Spanish, 1980.

VOCATION: Actor and writer.

CAREER: Also see *WRITINGS* below. STAGE DEBUT—Clarence Hopkins, *Cheatin',* Main Stage Theatre, North Hollywood, CA, 1984. PRINCIPAL STAGE APPEARANCES—Clarence Hopkins, *Cheatin',* Tiffany's Attic Theatre, Kansas City, MO, 1986; Harmony Rhodes and Orville Turnover, *Daddy's Dyin' (Who's Got the Will?),* Theatre-Theater, Hollywood, CA, 1987-88.

PRINCIPAL FILM APPEARANCES—Clarence Hopkins, *Daddy's Dyin',* Propaganda Films, 1989.

TELEVISION DEBUT—Purdy Mantel, *The Quick and the Dead,* HBO, 1987. PRINCIPAL TELEVISION APPEARANCES—Episodic: *Days of Our Lives,* CBS; *Divorce Court,* syndicated.

RELATED CAREER—Actor in and provides voiceovers for television commercials.

WRITINGS: STAGE—*Cheatin',* Main Stage Theatre, North Hollywood, CA, 1984; *Daddy's Dyin' (Who's Got the Will?),* Theater-Theatre, Hollywood, CA, 1986, published by Samuel French Inc., 1988; *Daughters of the Lone Star State,* Casa Manana Theatre, Fort Worth, TX, 1990. FILM—*Daddy's Dyin',* Propaganda Films, 1989. TELEVISION—Pilots: *Mickey and Travis,* CBS, 1989. Episodic: *Family Ties,* NBC; *Eunice,* Disney Channel.

AWARDS: *Drama-Logue* Award, 1985, for his performance in

DEL SHORES

Cheatin'; Los Angeles Times, Los Angeles Reader, Los Angeles Herald Examiner, Los Angeles Daily News, Los Angeles Weekly, Seattle Times, and *Seattle Post* critics' awards, 1987-88, all for *Daddy's Dyin' (Who's Got the Will?); Drama-Logue, Los Angeles Reader, Los Angeles Daily News,* and *Los Angeles Weekly* critics' awards, 1988, all for *Cheatin'.*

ADDRESSES: OFFICE—c/o Warner Brothers Inc., 4000 Warner Boulevard, Production Building 1, Room 17-B, Burbank, CA 91522. MANAGER—Bobbie Edrick, Artists Circle Entertainment, 8957 Norma Place, Los Angeles, CA 90069. PUBLICIST—Virginia Mastroianni, Mastroianni Public Relations, 3166 Arizona Avenue, Suite B, Santa Monica, CA 90404.

*   *   *

SHOWALTER, Max   1917-
(Casey Adams)

PERSONAL: Born June 2, 1917, in Caldwell, KS; son of Ira Edward (a banker, farmer, and worker in the oil industry) and Elma Roxanna (a music teacher; maiden name, Dodson) Showalter. EDUCATION—Trained for the stage at the Pasadena Playhouse for three years. MILITARY—U.S. Army.

VOCATION: Actor, composer, producer, and director.

CAREER: Also see *WRITINGS* below. STAGE DEBUT—Lord Ansel, *Knights of Song,* St. Louis Municipal Opera, St. Louis, MO, 1938, for seven performances. BROADWAY DEBUT—Lord Ansel,

Knights of Song, 51st Street Theatre, 1938, for fourteen performances. PRINCIPAL STAGE APPEARANCES—Lowell Pennyfeather, *Very Warm for May,* Alvin Theatre, New York City, 1939; Frank Lippincott, *My Sister Eileen,* Martin Beck Theatre, New York City, 1941; Jake, *Show Boat,* Ziegfeld Theatre, New York City, 1946; George Beechwood, *John Loves Mary,* Booth Theatre, then Music Box Theatre, both New York City, 1947; ensemble, *Make Mine Manhattan* (revue), Broadhurst Theatre, New York City, 1948; Horace Vandergelder, *Hello, Dolly!,* St. James Theatre, New York City, 1966; Dr. Morris Ritz, *The Grass Harp,* Martin Beck Theatre, 1971; Captain Andy Hawks, *Show Boat,* Jones Beach Theatre, Long Island, NY, 1976; also appeared with the Meadow Brook Theatre, Rochester, MI, 1975-76; in workshop productions of *Farenheit 451* and *A Fine and Private Place,* both Eugene O'Neill Theatre Center, Waterford, CT, 1986-87; as Horace Vandergelder, *Hello, Dolly!,* Starlight Theatre, Kansas City, MO; in *Who Was That Lady?,* summer theatre production, Indianapolis, IN.

PRINCIPAL STAGE WORK—Producer, "My Thirteenth Year," "Bipartisan Blame," and (also director) "The Track of Our Years" in *Three About Love,* Chester Meeting House, Chester, CT, 1989.

MAJOR TOURS—Horace Vandergelder, *Hello, Dolly!,* U.S. cities, 1965-66; Horace Vandergelder, *Hello, Dolly!,* U.S. cities, 1981; also *This Is the Army,* international cities, during World War II; *Lend an Ear,* U.S. cities; *Lunatics and Lovers,* U.S. cities.

FILM DEBUT—Fountain pen salesman, *Always Leave Them Laughing,* Warner Brothers, 1949. PRINCIPAL FILM APPEARANCES—Guild, *With a Song in My Heart,* Twentieth Century-Fox, 1952; (as Casey Adams) Pete Bentham, *My Wife's Best Friend,* Twentieth

MAX SHOWALTER

Century-Fox, 1952; (as Casey Adams) Lieutenant Moore, *What Price Glory?*, Twentieth Century-Fox, 1952; (as Casey Adams) Jim Logan, *Dangerous Crossing*, Twentieth Century-Fox, 1953; (as Casey Adams) Walter Landers, *Destination Gobi*, Twentieth Century-Fox, 1953; (as Casey Adams) Ray Cutler, *Niagara*, Twentieth Century-Fox, 1953; (as Casey Adams) Larry Evans, *Vicki*, Twentieth Century-Fox, 1953; (as Casey Adams) Dave Millson, *Down Three Dark Streets*, United Artists, 1954; (as Casey Adams) Detective Lieutenant Parks, *Naked Alibi*, Universal, 1954; (as Casey Adams) Frederick S. Hobart, *Night People*, Twentieth Century-Fox, 1954; (as Casey Adams) Billy Wilcox, *The Return of Jack Slade* (also known as *Texas Rose*), Allied Artists, 1955; (as Casey Adams) Chasen, *The Indestructible Man*, Allied Artists, 1956; (as Casey Adams) Andy Leonard, *Never Say Goodbye*, Universal, 1956; (as Casey Adams) *Life* reporter, *Bus Stop* (also known as *The Wrong Kind of Girl*), Twentieth Century-Fox, 1956; (as Casey Adams) Phillip Scott, *Dragon Wells Massacre*, Allied Artists, 1957; (as Casey Adams) Tad Johns, *The Monster That Challenged the World* (also known as *The Monster That Challenged New York*), United Artists, 1957; (as Casey Adams) Charlie Grant, *The Female Animal*, Universal, 1958; (as Casey Adams) Don Martin, *Voice in the Mirror*, Universal, 1958; (as Casey Adams) Dalleson, *The Naked and the Dead*, Warner Brothers, 1958; (as Casey Adams) Selwyn Harris, *It Happened to Jane* (also known as *Twinkle and Shine*), Columbia, 1959.

(As Casey Adams) Deaf man, *Elmer Gantry*, United Artists, 1960; (as Casey Adams) Nick Parker, *Return to Peyton Place*, Twentieth Century-Fox, 1961; (as Casey Adams) Roger, *Summer and Smoke*, Paramount, 1961; (as Casey Adams) Tight Suit, *Bon Voyage*, Buena Vista, 1962; desk clerk, *Move Over, Darling*, Twentieth Century-Fox, 1963; B.J. Smith, *My Six Loves*, Paramount, 1963; Crawford, *Fate Is the Hunter*, Twentieth Century-Fox, 1964; Holmes, *Sex and the Single Girl*, Warner Brothers, 1964; Tobey Rawlins, *How to Murder Your Wife*, United Artists, 1965; Howard Greene, *Lord Love a Duck*, United Artists, 1966; Mr. Worthman, *The Moonshine War*, Metro-Goldwyn-Mayer (MGM), 1970; Mr. Bingham, *The Anderson Tapes*, Columbia, 1971; Earnest Shears, *Sergeant Pepper's Lonely Hearts Club Band*, Universal, 1978; minister, *10*, Warner Brothers, 1979; Grandpa Fred, *Sixteen Candles*, Universal, 1984; Mr. Arthur, *Racing with the Moon*, Paramount, 1984; also (as Casey Adams) *Designing Women*, MGM, 1957; (as Casey Adams) *The Music Man*, Warner Brothers, 1962; *Smog*, *A Talent for Loving*, and *Bonnie's Kids*.

TELEVISION DEBUT—*Texaco Star Theatre*, NBC, 1948. PRINCIPAL TELEVISION APPEARANCES—Series: Regular, *Texaco Star Theatre*, NBC, 1948-49; regular, *The Swift Show*, NBC, 1949; Gus Clyde, *The Stockard Channing Show*, CBS, 1980. Pilots: (As Casey Adams) Ward Cleaver, "It's a Small World," *Studio '57*, syndicated, 1957; J.P. Biggey, *How to Succeed in Business Without Really Trying*, ABC, 1975; Dawson, *Valentine's Second Chance*, ABC, 1977; also *It's Always Sunny*, *Boss of the House*, *Last of the Mohicans*, *Petticoat Marshall*, *Private Eyeful*, and *Daphne*.

Episodic: *Young Broadway*, NBC, 1949; (as Casey Adams) *General Electric Summer Originals*, ABC, 1956; (as Casey Adams) *O. Henry Playhouse*, syndicated, 1957; (as Casey Adams) *The David Niven Show*, NBC, 1959; (as Casey Adams) Ralph Mason, *The Andy Griffith Show*, CBS, 1961; *The Bob Newhart Show*, CBS, 1977; *W.E.B.*, NBC, 1978; *The Incredible Hulk*, CBS, 1981; *Foul Play*, ABC, 1981; *The Love Boat*, ABC, 1983; also *Over Easy*, 1982; *Matinee Theatre*, NBC; *The Milton Berle Show*, NBC; *The Jack Sterling Show*, CBS; *Star Stage*, NBC; *My Favorite Husband*, CBS; *The Phil Silvers Show*, CBS; *Private Secretary*, CBS; *Schlitz*

Playhouse of Stars, CBS; *Mr. Adams and Eve*, CBS; *The Loretta Young Show*, NBC; *Crossroads*, ABC; *Studio One*, CBS; *Playhouse 90*, CBS; *General Electric Theatre*, CBS; *The Twilight Zone*, CBS; *Perry Mason*, CBS; *Dr. Kildare*, NBC; *Gunsmoke*, CBS; *The Lucy Show*, CBS; *The Doris Day Show*, CBS; *Bewitched*, ABC; *Police Story*, NBC; *Kojak*, CBS; *Quincy, M.E.*, NBC; *Hazel*; *Ford Theatre*; *Richard Diamond, Private Detective*; *Navy Log*; and *The Real McCoys*. Movies: (As Casey Adams) Raun Kaufman, *Son Rise: A Miracle of Love*, NBC, 1979; Peter Schechter, *Gun in the House*, CBS, 1981. Specials: *Jimmy Durante Meets the Lively Arts*, ABC, 1965; Walter, *The Lucille Ball Comedy Hour*, CBS, 1967; also *Ernie Kovacs on Music*, NBC.

PRINCIPAL TELEVISION WORK—Series: Music director, *Hold It Please*, CBS, 1949.

RELATED CAREER—Board member, Connecticut Governor's Commission for the Arts (motion picture division), 1987-89; also founder, Showalter Music; executive board member, National Theatre of the Deaf, Chester, CT; executive board member, Eugene O'Neill Theatre Center, Waterford, CT; theatre, film, and television instructor, "Project Learn," Eugene O'Neill Theatre Center—Elderhostel, Centerbrook, CT; composer of nightclub material for such artists as Marge and Gower Champion, Celeste Holm, Mary Martin, Lucille Ball, Arthur Godfrey, and Ethel Merman; commercial voiceover artist.

NON-RELATED CAREER   Painter.

WRITINGS: All as composer, unless indicated. STAGE—*Touch of the Child*, St. Paul the Apostle Church, Los Angeles, 1982, then Bel Air, CA; *Harrigan 'n' Hart*, Goodspeed Opera House, Norma Terris Theatre, East Haddam, CT, 1984, then Longacre Theatre, New York City, 1985; also *Little Boy Blue*, El Capitan Theatre, Hollywood, CA; *Joy Ride*, Huntington Hartford Theatre, Hollywood, then Chicago, IL; *Hermione Gingold Revue*, Brattle Theatre, Cambridge, MA; *Live a Little* (revue), first produced in East Hampton, NY; *Go for Your Gun*, produced in England and Scotland.

FILM—(Song contributor with Jack Woodford) *With a Song in My Heart*, Twentieth Century-Fox, 1952; (song contributor with Ken Darby) *Vicki*, Twentieth Century-Fox, 1953; (song adaptor) *Return of Jack Slade* (also known as *Texas Rose*), Allied Artists, 1955.

TELEVISION—Episodic: *The Stockard Channing Show*, CBS, 1980; also *Over Easy*, 1982; *The Chevy Show*, NBC; *The Jeanne Carson Show*, BBC; *The Lucy Show*, CBS. Specials: *Time for Love*, NBC, 1939; *The Ray Bolger Show*, NBC, 1957.

RECORDINGS: ALBUMS—*The Grass Harp* (original cast recording), Painted Smiles, 1971; *10* (original soundtrack), Warner Brothers, 1979; *Do Black Patent Leather Shoes Really Reflect Up?*, Columbia, 1986; *The Secret Garden* (original soundtrack), Columbia, 1987; also *Kenward Elmslie Visited*, Painted Smiles.

MEMBER: American Society of Composers, Authors, and Publishers (1952—), Players Club.

AWARDS: Composers' Award from the American Society of Composers, Authors, and Publishers, 1985, for *Harrigan 'n' Hart*; elected to the Kansas Historical Society Hall of Fame, 1985.

ADDRESSES: AGENT—International Creative Management, 40 W. 57th Street, New York, NY 10019.

SHYER, Charles   1941-

PERSONAL: Full name, Charles Richard Shyer; born October 11, 1941, in Los Angeles, CA; son of Melville Shyer and Lois Jones.

VOCATION: Producer, director, and screenwriter.

CAREER: Also see *WRITINGS* below. PRINCIPAL FILM WORK— Producer (with Goldie Hawn, Nancy Meyers, and Harvey Miller), *Private Benjamin,* Warner Brothers, 1980; director, *Irreconcilable Differences,* Warner Brothers, 1984; producer (with Meyers) and director, *Baby Boom,* Metro-Goldwyn-Mayer/United Artists, 1987.

PRINCIPAL TELEVISION WORK—Pilots: Producer (with Alan Mandel), *Cops,* CBS, 1973; executive producer (with Nancy Meyers) and director, *Baby Boom,* NBC, 1988.

WRITINGS: FILM—(With James Lee Barret and Alan Mandel) *Smokey and the Bandit,* Universal, 1977; (with Mandel, John Herman Shanner, and Al Ramrus) *Goin' South,* Paramount, 1978; (with Mandel, Max Shulman, and Julius J. Epstein) *House Calls,* Universal, 1978; (with Nancy Meyers and Harvey Miller) *Private Benjamin,* Warner Brothers, 1980; (with Meyers) *Irreconcilable Differences,* Warner Brothers, 1984; (with Buck Henry) *Protocol,* Warner Brothers, 1984; (with Meyers) *Baby Boom,* Metro-Goldwyn-Mayer/United Artists, 1987.

TELEVISION—Pilots: (With Mandel and Dean Hargrove) *Lady Luck,* NBC, 1973; (with Meyers) *Baby Boom,* NBC, 1988. Episodic: *The Partridge Family,* ABC.

AWARDS: Academy Award nomination, Best Screenplay Written Directly for the Screen, and Writers Guild of America-West Award, Best Original Screenplay, both 1980, for *Private Benjamin.*

MEMBER: Academy of Motion Picture Arts and Sciences, Writers Guild of America-West, Directors Guild of America, American Society of Composers, Authors, and Publishers.*

*   *   *

SILVA, Henry   1928-

PERSONAL: Born in 1928 in Brooklyn NY. EDUCATION—Trained for the stage with the Group Theatre and the Actors' Studio.

VOCATION: Actor.

CAREER: PRINCIPAL FILM APPEARANCES—Hernandez, *Viva Zapata!,* Twentieth Century-Fox, 1952; Mother, *A Hatful of Rain,* Twentieth Century-Fox, 1957; Chink, *The Tall T,* Columbia, 1957; Lujan, *The Bravados,* Twentieth Century-Fox, 1958; Rennie, *The Law and Jake Wade,* Metro-Goldwyn-Mayer, 1958; Sam Teeler, *Ride a Crooked Trail,* Universal, 1958; Kua-Ko, *Green Mansions,* Metro-Goldwyn-Mayer, 1959; Lordan, *The Jayhawkers,* Paramount, 1959; Maximilian, *Cinderfella,* Paramount, 1960; Roger Corneal, *Ocean's Eleven,* Warner Brothers, 1960; Chunjim, *The Manchurian Candidate,* United Artists, 1962; Mountain Hawk, *Sergeants 3,* United Artists, 1962; Colonel Garcia, *A Gathering of Eagles,* Universal, 1963; Johnny Cool/Giordano, *Johnny Cool,* United Artists, 1963; John Durell, *The Secret Invasion,* United Artists, 1964; Schaft, *Hail Mafia* (also known as *Je vous salue*

Mafia and *Da New York: Mafia uccide*), Goldstone, 1965; title role, *The Return of Mr. Moto,* Twentieth Century-Fox, 1965; Joaquin, *The Reward,* Twentieth Century-Fox, 1965; Crazy Knife, *The Plainsman,* Universal, 1966; Mendez, *The Hills Run Red* (also known as *Un fiume di dollari* and *A River of Dollars*), United Artists, 1967; Hank Norris, *Matchless,* United Artists, 1967; Frank Boley, *Never a Dull Moment,* Buena Vista, 1968.

Chatto, *The Animals,* XYZ, 1971; Caine, *Man and Boy,* Levitt/ Pickman, 1972; Dave, *The Italian Connection* (also known as *La mala ordina* and *Manhunt*), American International, 1973; Everett, *Les Hommes* (also known as *The Men*), Cocinor, 1973; Inspector Walter Grandi, *Milano odia: La polizia non puo' sparare* (also known as *Almost Human*), Joseph Brenner Associates, 1974; Zeke Springer, *Shoot,* AVCO-Embassy, 1976; Kane, *Buck Rogers in the 25th Century,* Universal, 1979; Vittorio Farroni, *Love and Bullets,* Associated Film Distribution, 1979; Dr. Gauss, *Thirst,* New Line Cinema, 1979; Colonel Brock, *Alligator,* Group 1, 1980; Garland, *Virus,* Media, 1980; Henry Chatwill, *Trapped,* Video Film Organization, 1981; Guerera, *Megaforce,* Twentieth Century-Fox, 1982; Billy Score, *Sharky's Machine,* Warner Brothers, 1982; Rafeeq, *Wrong Is Right* (also known as *The Man with the Deadly Lens*), Columbia, 1982; Lester, *Chained Heat,* Jensen Farley, 1983; Slim, *Cannonball Run II,* Warner Brothers, 1984; Luis Comacho, *Code of Silence,* Orion, 1985; Wangler, *Escape from the Bronx,* New Line Cinema, 1985; Bernardo, *Lust in the Dust,* New World, 1985; prison boss, *The Manhunt,* Samuel Goldwyn, 1986; Kirk Cooper, *The Violent Breed,* Metro-Goldwyn-Mayer/United Artists, 1986; Agon, *Allan Quatermain and the Lost City of Gold,* Cannon, 1987; Colonel Kartiff, *Bulletproof,* Cinetel, 1987; Zagon, *Above the Law,* Warner Brothers, 1988. Also appeared in *Crowded Paradise,* Tudor, 1956; *Assassination,* 1967; *The Kidnap of Mary Lou,* 1974; *L'uomo della strada fa giustizia,* 1976; *Eviolenti,* 1976; *Le Marginal* (also known as *The Outsider*), Roissy/Gaumont/Cerito-Rene Chateau, 1983; *Amazon Women on the Moon,* Universal, 1987; *Beverly Hills Brats,* Skouras/Taurus Entertainment, 1989.

PRINCIPAL TELEVISION APPEARANCES—Series: Kane, *Buck Rogers in the 25th Century,* NBC, 1979. Pilots: Matt Elder, *Weapons Man* (broadcast as an episode of *Stoney Burke*), ABC, 1963. Episodic: General Juan Mercurio, "Tourist Attraction," *The Outer Limits,* ABC, 1963; Chino Rivera, "The Mice," *The Outer Limits,* ABC, 1964; also "Dark Legacy," *Thriller,* NBC, 1961; *Voyage to the Bottom of the Sea,* ABC, 1965; "The Doll," *Night Gallery,* NBC, 1971. Movies: Moon, *Black Noon,* CBS, 1971; "Deek" La Costa, *Drive Hard, Drive Fast,* NBC, 1973; Roberto Obregon, *Contract on Cherry Street,* NBC, 1977; Sinclair, *Happy,* CBS, 1983.

NON-RELATED CAREER—Delivery boy and longshoreman.

ADDRESSES: OFFICE—5226 Backford Avenue, Tarzana, CA 91356.*

*   *   *

SILVER, Joe   1922-1989

PERSONAL: Born September 28, 1922, in Chicago, IL; died of a heart attack, February 27, 1989, in New York, NY; son of Morris (in sales) and Sonja (in sales) Silver; married Chevi Colton (an actress), January 8, 1950; children: Christopher, Jennifer. EDUCA-TION—Attended the University of Wisconsin, 1940-42; trained for the stage at the American Theatre Wing, 1946-47. MILITARY—U.S. Army, Signal Corps, high speed code operator, sergeant, 1944-46.

VOCATION: Actor and director.

CAREER: BROADWAY DEBUT—Lov Bensey, *Tobacco Road,* Forrest Theatre, 1942. PRINCIPAL STAGE APPEARANCES—Burton Snead, *Heads or Tails,* Cort Theatre, New York City, 1947; Aldobrandini, *Lamp at Midnight,* New Stages Theatre, New York City, 1947; Dubois, *The Victors,* Gad, *The Sun and I,* and man, *Blood Wedding,* all New Stages Theatre, 1949; waiter, *Nature's Way,* Coronet Theatre, New York City, 1957; Weber, *Gypsy,* Broadway Theatre, New York City, 1959; Squire Hardcastle, *O Marry Me!,* Gate Theatre, New York City, 1961; Phil Barr, *The Heroine,* Lyceum Theatre, New York City, 1963; Harry Grossman, *The Zulu and the Zayda,* Cort Theatre, 1965; Herb Miller, "The Shock of Recognition" in *You Know I Can't Hear You When the Water's Running,* Ambassador Theatre, New York City, 1967; ensemble, *Jacques Brel Is Alive and Well and Living in Paris* (revue), Village Gate Theatre, New York City, 1968.

Julius Katz, *The Shrinking Bride,* Mercury Theatre, New York City, 1971; judge, Sherman Hart, general, vampire priest, plainclothesman, Mr. Wollenstein, and photographer, *Lenny,* Brooks Atkinson Theatre, New York City, 1971; narrator, *Bits and Pieces,* Manhattan Theatre Club, New York City, 1974; Moe, *Cakes with the Wine,* New Dramatists Inc., New York City, 1974; host, *Encore,* National Musical Theatre, St. Malachy's Theatre, New York City, 1979; Garry Allen, *The Roast,* Winter Garden Theatre, New York City, 1980; Mendele, the book seller, and bandit, *The World of Sholom Aleichem,* Rialto Theatre, New York City, 1982; Max, *The Homecoming,* Jewish Repertory Theatre, New York City, 1984; Joseph Parmigian, *Cold Storage,* Jewish Repertory Theatre, 1984-85; Hinson, *Rich Relations,* Second Stage Theatre, New York City, 1986; Fleischer, *Old Business,* New York Shakespeare Festival, Public Theatre, New York City, 1987; Arnold Rothstein, *Legs Diamond,* Mark Hellinger Theatre, New York City, 1988. Also appeared in *See My Lawyer* and *Boy Meets Girl,* both Adams Theatre, Newark, NJ, 1943; *The Goldfish Bowl,* Theatre Showcase, New York City, 1943; *The Octoroon,* Putnam County Playhouse, Lake Mahopac, NY, 1946; *The Terrorists,* Carnegie Hall, New York City, 1948; *Nobody Starts Out to Be a Pirate,* Whole Theatre Company, Montclair, NJ, 1983; *Teahouse of the August Moon* and *I'm Not Rappaport,* both Burt Reynolds' Jupiter Theatre, Jupiter, FL, 1987; *Joseph and His Brethren* and *Family Pieces,* both New York City.

PRINCIPAL STAGE WORK—Director, *Shoe Store,* Equity Library Theatre, New York City, 1971; director, *The Rabinowitz Gambit,* New Dramatists Inc., New York City, 1974.

MAJOR TOURS—The Bellboy, *Doughgirls,* U.S. cities, 1943.

PRINCIPAL FILM APPEARANCES—Charlie Barrett, *Diary of a Bachelor,* American International, 1964; Oscar, *Move,* Twentieth Century-Fox, 1970; Dr. Spangler, *Klute,* Warner Brothers, 1971; Farber, *The Apprenticeship of Duddy Kravitz,* Paramount, 1974; Norman, *Rhinoceros,* American Film Theatre, 1974; Rollo Linsky, *They Came from Within* (also known as *The Parasite Murders, Frissons,* and *Shivers*), American International, 1976; Murray Cypher, *Rabid* (also known as *Rage*), New World, 1976; voice of the Greedy, *Raggedy Ann and Andy* (animated), Twentieth Century-Fox, 1977; Si Robinson, *You Light Up My Life,* Columbia, 1977; Leo, *Boardwalk,* Atlantic Releasing, 1979; Seymour Starger,

Deathtrap, Warner Brothers, 1982; Uncle Stu, *Almost You,* TLC, 1984; Abe Mitgang, *The Gig,* The Gig Company, 1985; voice of Creep, *Creepshow 2,* New World, 1987; Lazer Fish, *Mr. Nice Guy,* Shapiro Entertainment, 1987; pawnbroker, *Magic Sticks,* Wolfgang Odentahl Filmproduktion/Tale Film, 1987; Morosini, *Switching Channels,* Tri-Star, 1988.

TELEVISION DEBUT—Panelist, *What's It Worth?,* CBS, 1947. PRINCIPAL TELEVISION APPEARANCES—Series: Regular, *The 54th Street Revue,* CBS, 1949-50; regular, *Mr. I Magination,* CBS, 1949-52; regular, *Joey Faye's Frolics,* CBS, 1950; regular, *Ad Libbers,* CBS, 1951; regular, *The Red Buttons Show,* CBS, 1952-54, then NBC, 1954-55; voice characterization, *Captain Jet* (animated), CBS, 1954; voice characterization, *Space Funnies* (animated), CBS, 1959-60; Max Spier, *Coronet Blue,* CBS, 1967; Jack Stewart, *Fay,* NBC, 1975-76; also Elliott Silverstein, *Ryan's Hope,* ABC; *Love of Life,* CBS. Pilots: Max, *Starstruck,* CBS, 1979. Episodic: Dzershinsky, *The Equalizer,* CBS, 1985; Guzman, *Spenser: For Hire,* ABC, 1986; also *Studio One,* CBS, 1949; *Winston Telefinds,* CBS, 1949; *Gunsmoke,* CBS, 1972; *Love, American Style,* ABC, 1972; *The Phil Silvers Show,* CBS; *Alice,* CBS. Movies: Alvin Jessop, *Crash,* ABC, 1978; Arnie, *Illusions,* CBS, 1983. Specials: Voice of Teacher and Noah, "It's a Brand New World" (animated), *Special Treat,* NBC, 1977.

RELATED CAREER—As a member of the Wry Guys (a comedy trio), appeared at the Embassy Club, New York City, 1946; commercial spokesman on radio and television, 1950-1989; actor in more than 1,000 television programs.

NON-RELATED CAREER—Shoe salesman and hospital orderly.

AWARDS: Antoinette Perry Award nomination, Best Supporting or Featured Actor in a Play, 1972, for *Lenny.*

OBITUARIES AND OTHER SOURCES: Variety, March 1-7, 1989; *Jersey Journal,* February 28, 1989; *New York Times,* February 28, 1989.*

*　　*　　*

SIMMONS, Gene   1949-

PERSONAL: Born Gene Klein, August 25, 1949, in Haifa, Israel (some sources say Queens, NY); immigrated to the United States in 1958; naturalized U.S. citizen, 1963; children: one son (with Shannon Tweed; an actress). EDUCATION—State University of New York, A.B.A., 1970; City University of New York, B.A., 1972.

VOCATION: Musician, singer, and actor.

CAREER: PRINCIPAL FILM APPEARANCES—Dr. Charles Luther, *Runaway,* Tri-Star, 1984; Velvet Von Ragner and Carruther, *Never Too Young to Die,* Paul Entertainment, 1986; Nuke, *Trick or Treat,* De Laurentiis Entertainment Group, 1986; Malak Al Rahim, *Wanted: Dead or Alive,* New World, 1987; as himself, *The Decline of Western Civilization, Part II: The Metal Years* (documentary), New Line, 1988.

PRINCIPAL TELEVISION APPEARANCES—Movies: *KISS Meets the Phantom of the Park* (also known as *Attack of the Phantoms*), NBC, 1978.

RELATED CAREER—Co-founder, bass guitarist, and vocalist with the rock group, KISS, 1973—.

RECORDINGS: ALBUMS—*Gene Simmons,* Casablanca, 1978. With KISS: *KISS,* Casablanca, 1974; *Hotter Than Hell,* Casablanca, 1974; *Dressed to Kill,* Casablanca, 1975; *Alive,* Casablanca, 1975; *Destroyer,* Casablanca, 1976; *The Originals,* Casablanca, 1976; *Rock and Roll Over,* Casablanca, 1976; *Love Gun,* Casablanca, 1977; *KISS Alive II,* Casablanca, 1977; *Dynasty,* Casablanca, 1979; *Unmasked,* Casablanca, 1980; *The Elder,* Casablanca, 1981; *Creatures of the Night,* Casablanca, 1982; *Lick It Up,* Mercury, 1983; *Animalize,* Mercury, 1984; *Asylum,* Mercury, 1985; *Crazy Nights,* Mercury, 1987.

SINGLES—With KISS: "Rock and Roll All Night," Casablanca, 1975; "Shout It Out Loud," Casablanca, 1976; "Beth," Casablanca, 1976; "Hard Luck Woman," Casablanca, 1977; "Calling Dr. Love," Casablanca, 1977; "Christine Sixteen," Casablanca, 1977; "Rocket Ride," Casablanca, 1978; "I Was Made for Lovin' You," Casablanca, 1979.

AWARDS: With the group KISS, received sixteen Gold Record Albums (indicating sales in excess of 500,000 copies), twelve Platinum Record Albums (indicating sales in excess of one million copies), and two Gold Single Records (indicating sales in excess of one million copies).

MEMBER: American Federation of Musicians, American Federation of Television and Radio Artists, American Society of Composers, Authors, and Publishers.

SIDELIGHTS: Inventor of the Axe bass guitar, 1980.*

*   *   *

SIROLA, Joseph   1929-

PERSONAL: Born October 7, 1929, in New York, NY; son of Anthony (a carpenter) and Ana (Dubrovich) Sirola. EDUCATION—Columbia University, B.A., business, then M.A., 1951. MILITARY—U.S. Army, 1952.

VOCATION: Actor.

CAREER: OFF-BROADWAY DEBUT—Dr. Ordway, *Child of the Morning,* Blackfriar's Theatre, 1954, for one hundred performances. BROADWAY DEBUT—Christmas Morgan, *The Unsinkable Molly Brown,* Winter Garden Theatre, 1960, for four hundred performances. PRINCIPAL STAGE APPEARANCES—Ward Donahue, *Song for a Certain Midnight,* Jan Hus Playhouse, New York City, 1959; Lou Garrity, *Golden Rainbow,* Shubert Theatre, New York City, 1968; also appeared as Ludlow Lowell, *Pal Joey,* New York City; Stanley, *A Streetcar Named Desire,* Maurice Duclos, *Fallen Angels,* Quilary, *Idiot's Delight,* Insigna, *Mr. Roberts,* and in *Phaedra,* all summer theatre productions.

FILM DEBUT—Petracini, *Strange Bedfellows,* Universal, 1965. PRINCIPAL FILM APPEARANCES—Dumah, *The Greatest Story Ever Told,* United Artists, 1965; Baldwin, *Chuka,* Paramount, 1967; Reno, *Hang 'em High,* United Artists, 1968; Sal Dekker, *The Delta Factor,* Continental Distributing, 1970; Reverend Williams, *Hail* (also known as *Hail to the Chief* and *Washington B.C.*), Hail, 1973; Charlie, *Seizure,* American International, 1974; Lieutenant

JOSEPH SIROLA

O'Shaughnessy, *The Super Cops,* Metro-Goldwyn-Mayer/United Artists, 1974.

TELEVISION DEBUT—"Notes from the Underground," *Camera Three,* CBS, 1958. PRINCIPAL TELEVISION APPEARANCES—Series: Peter Nino, *The Brighter Day,* CBS, 1959-60; Dominick, *The Magician,* NBC, 1973-74; Tony Montefusco, *The Montefuscos,* NBC, 1975; Sal Lupo, *Wolf,* CBS, 1989. Mini-Series: Ozymandias, *Washington: Behind Closed Doors,* ABC, 1977. Pilots: Guthrie, *High Risk,* ABC, 1976; George Carriere, *The Rowdies,* NBC, 1986. Episodic: Vincent, *The Untouchables,* ABC, 1961; Thomas Paine, *Meeting of Minds,* PBS, 1977; Judge Locke, *Ohara,* ABC, 1987; also *Love, American Style,* ABC; *Get Smart,* NBC; *Rhoda,* CBS; *Quincy, M.E.,* NBC; *Matt Houston,* ABC; *Mission: Impossible,* CBS; *Hawaii Five-0,* CBS; *The Man from U.N.C.L.E.,* NBC; *The Rockford Files,* NBC; *Charlie's Angels,* ABC; *Riptide,* NBC; *The A-Team,* NBC; *Kojak,* CBS. Movies: George Simpson, *Visions . . .* (also known as *Visions of Death*), CBS, 1972; Detective Sloane, *Cry Rape!,* CBS, 1973; Adolfo, *Swan Song,* ABC, 1980; Capo, *Terrible Joe Moran,* CBS, 1984.

RELATED CAREER—Voiceover commercial spokesman for radio and television including the "I Love New York" campaign; performed in *The 19th Hole* (golf video), Joy and Roses Incorporated.

NON-RELATED CAREER—Executive, Kimberly-Clark Corporation; president, Smylon Corporation; developer (with Bud Westmore) of a dental stain eraser; artist specializing in sketching and oil painting.

AWARDS: Received more than 25 Clio Awards and numerous

Andy Awards for commercial voiceover work. MILITARY HONORS—Bronze Star and Commendation Medal.

SIDELIGHTS: RECREATIONS—Swimming, skiing, horseback riding, golf, tennis, gourmet cooking, cultivating roses, and maintaining his large rooftop garden.

ADDRESSES: AGENT—Mike Eisenstadt, Fred Amsel and Associates, 6310 San Vicente Boulevard, Suite 407, Los Angeles, CA, 90048.

*   *   *

SKELTON, Red   1913-
(Richard Skelton)

PERSONAL: Born Richard Bernard Skelton, July 18, 1913, in Vincennes, IN; son of Joseph (a circus clown) and Ida Mae Skelton; married Edna Marie Stillwell, June 1932 (divorced, 1940); married Georgia Maurine Davis, March, 1945 (divorced, 1973); married Lothian Toland, March, 1973; children: Valentina Maris Alonso and Richard Freeman (deceased; both second marriage). EDUCATION—Attended Northwestern University. MILITARY— U.S. Army, Field Artillery, 1944-45.

VOCATION: Comedian, actor, and writer.

CAREER: Also see WRITINGS below. PRINCIPAL STAGE APPEARANCES—Red Skelton in Concert, Carnegie Hall, New York City, 1977.

FILM DEBUT—(As Richard Skelton) Itchy Faulkner, Having Wonderful Time, RKO, 1938. PRINCIPAL FILM APPEARANCES—Lieutenant Mugger Martin, Flight Command, Metro-Goldwyn-Mayer (MGM), 1940; Vernon Briggs, Dr. Kildare's Wedding Day (also known as Mary Names the Day), MGM, 1941; Joe "Red" Willet, Lady Be Good, MGM, 1941; Vernon Briggs, The People vs. Dr. Kildare (also known as My Life Is Yours), MGM, 1941; Wally Benton, Whistling in the Dark, MGM, 1941; Hap Hixby, Maisie Gets Her Man (also known as She Got Her Man), MGM, 1942; Red, Panama Hattie, MGM, 1942; Merton K. Kibble, Ship Ahoy, MGM, 1942; Wally Benton, Whistling in Dixie, MGM, 1942; Louis Blore and King Louis, DuBarry Was a Lady, MGM, 1943; Joseph Rivington Reynolds, I Dood It (also known as By Hook or By Crook), MGM, 1943; as himself, Thousands Cheer, MGM, 1943; Wally Benton, Whistling in Brooklyn, MGM, 1943; Steve Elliott, Bathing Beauty, MGM, 1945; television announcer, "When Television Comes," Ziegfeld Follies, MGM, 1945; Aubrey Piper, The Show-Off, MGM, 1946; Merton Gill, Merton of the Movies, MGM, 1947; Red Jones, Fuller Brush Man (also known as That Man Mr. Jones), Columbia, 1948; Aubrey Filmore, A Southern Yankee (also known as My Hero!), MGM, 1948; Jack Spratt, Neptune's Daughter, MGM, 1949.

As himself, The Duchess of Idaho, MGM, 1950; Fuller brush man, The Fuller Brush Girl (also known as The Affairs of Sally), Columbia, 1950; Harry Ruby, Three Little Words, MGM, 1950; Rusty Cameron, Pop Cameron, and Grandpop Cameron, Watch the Birdie, MGM, 1950; Augustus "Red" Pirdy, The Yellow Cab Man, MGM, 1950; Joe Belden, Excuse My Dust, MGM, 1951; Cornie Quinell, Texas Carnival, MGM, 1951; Al Marsh, Lovely to Look At, MGM, 1952; Dodo Delwyn, The Clown, MGM, 1953; Ambrose C. Park, Great Diamond Robbery, MGM, 1953; Ben

Dobson, Half a Hero, MGM, 1953; drunk, Around the World in Eighty Days, United Artists, 1956; Rusty Morgan, Public Pigeon Number One, Universal, 1957; client, Ocean's Eleven, Warner Brothers, 1960; Neanderthal man, Those Magnificent Men in Their Flying Machines; or, How I Flew from London to Paris in Twenty-Five Hours and Eleven Minutes (also known as Those Magnificent Men in Their Flying Machines), Twentieth Century-Fox, 1965.

PRINCIPAL TELEVISION APPEARANCES—Series: Host, The Red Skelton Show, NBC, 1951-53, then CBS, 1953-70, later NBC, 1970-71. Episodic: "Public Pigeon Number One," Climax!, CBS, 1955; "The Big Slide," Playhouse 90, CBS, 1956; The Lucille Ball-Desi Arnaz Hour, CBS, 1959; "The Man in the Funny Suit," Desilu Playhouse, CBS, 1960. Specials: Host, The Red Skelton Revue, CBS, 1954; host, The Red Skelton Chevy Special, CBS, 1959; host, The Red Skelton Timex Special, CBS, 1960; host, Clown Alley, CBS, 1966; Jack Benny's 20th Anniversary Television Special, NBC, 1970; voice of Father Time and narrator, Rudolph's Shiny New Year (animated), ABC, 1976; Swing Out, Sweet Land, NBC, 1976; General Electric's All-Star Anniversary, ABC, 1978; Happy Birthday, Bob, NBC, 1978; host, TV: The Fabulous '50s, NBC, 1978; Bob Hope's All-Star Christmas Show, NBC, 1978; Sinatra—The First Forty Years, NBC, 1980; Freddy the Freeloader, Red Skelton's Christmas Dinner, HBO, 1982; host, Red Skelton's Funny Faces, HBO, 1983; host, Red Skelton: A Royal Performance, HBO, 1984; The Television Academy Hall of Fame, Fox, 1987 and 1989; The Third Annual American Comedy Awards, ABC, 1989.

RADIO DEBUT—The Rudy Vallee Show, 1937. PRINCIPAL RADIO APPEARANCES—Series: Host, The Red Skelton Scrapbook of Satire, NBC, 1941-53. Episodic: Avalon Time, 1939; Juvenile Jury.

RELATED CAREER—Vaudeville performer and pantomime artist with the Loew's Montreal Theatre, Montreal, PQ, Canada, 1936; performer with the "Doc" R.E. Lewis traveling medicine show, with the John Lawrence Stock Company, and with the Clarence Stout Minstrels; entertainer in burlesque shows throughout the Midwest; master of ceremonies in walkathons; clown with the Hagenbeck and Wallace Circus; Las Vegas nightclub performer; entertainer in military shows during World War II and the Korean War.

NON-RELATED CAREER—Short story writer; painter; mail-order catologue businessman; founder and president, Red Skelton Needy Children's Fund.

WRITINGS: STAGE—Composer, Red Skelton in Concert, Carnegie Hall, New York City, 1977. TELEVISION—Series: (With others) The Red Skelton Show, NBC, 1951-53, then CBS, 1953-70, later NBC, 1970-71. Episodic: "I Hear America Singing," Ford Star Jubilee, CBS; Shower of Stars, CBS. Specials: (With Sherwood Schwartz, Al Schwartz, and Dave O'Brien) The Red Skelton Chevy Special, CBS, 1959; (with Hal Goldman and Larry Klein) The Red Skelton Timex Special, CBS, 1960; (with O'Brien and Mort Greene) Clown Alley, CBS, 1966; Red Skelton's Christmas Dinner, HBO, 1982; Red Skelton's Funny Faces, HBO, 1983; Red Skelton: A Royal Performance, HBO, 1984. OTHER—(Editor) A Red Skeleton in Your Closet: Ghost Stories Gay and Grim, Grosset, 1965; Red Skelton's Gertrude and Heathcliffe, Desert Publications, 1971, reprinted as Gertrude and Heathcliffe (self-illustrated), Scribner, 1974; also Clown Alley (story coloring book).

AWARDS: Emmy Award, Best Comedian, 1952, for The Red

Skelton Show; Emmy Award, Outstanding Writing Achievement in Comedy, 1961, for *The Red Skelton Show;* Golden Globe, 1978; Cecil B. DeMille Award from the Hollywood Foreign Press Association for Outstanding Contributions to the Entertainment Industry, 1978; Governor's Award from the Academy of Television Arts and Sciences, 1986; Screen Actors Guild Achievement Award, 1987; inducted into the Television Academy Hall of Fame, 1989. HONORARY DEGREES—Ball State University, H.H.D., 1986. MILITARY HONORS—Silver Helmet Americanism Award from the American Veterans of World War II, Korea, and Vietnam, 1969; Freedom Foundation Award, 1970; National Commanders' Award from the American Legion, 1970.

MEMBER: American Federation of Television and Radio Artists, Masons, American Society of Composers, Authors, and Publishers.

SIDELIGHTS: RECREATIONS—Gardening, writing music, and painting.

ADDRESSES: OFFICES—Van Bernard Productions, 37-715 Thompson Road, Rancho Mirage, CA 92270 and P.O. Box 136, Anza, CA 92306.*

*   *   *

SLOYAN, James

PERSONAL: Full name, James J. Sloyan; born February 24, in Indianapolis, IN.

VOCATION: Actor and fight choreographer.

CAREER: PRINCIPAL STAGE APPEARANCES—(As James J. Sloyan) King's master-at-arms, *Henry V,* and one of the madcaps and strolling players, *The Taming of the Shrew,* both New York Shakespeare Festival (NYSF), Delacorte Mobile Theatre, New York City, 1965; (as James J. Sloyan) Guilderstone, *Hamlet,* NYSF, Public Theatre, New York City, 1967; understudy, *Spitting Image,* Theatre De Lys, New York City, 1969; (as James J. Sloyan) Neil Lapides, *Spiro Who?,* Tambellini's Gate Theatre, New York City, 1969; (as James J. Sloyan) Mike, *A Dream Out of Time,* Promenade Theatre, New York City, 1970; (as James J. Sloyan) Dale Harding, *One Flew Over the Cuckoo's Nest,* Mercer-Hansberry Theatre, New York City, 1971. Also appeared in *Gethsemane Springs,* Center Theatre Group, Mark Taper Forum, Los Angeles, 1977.

PRINCIPAL STAGE WORK—Fight choreographer: (As James J. Sloyan) *Troilus and Cressida,* New York Shakespeare Festival (NYSF), Delacorte Theatre, New York City, 1965; (as James J. Sloyan) *King John,* NYSF, Delacorte Theatre, 1967; (as James J. Sloyan) *Romeo and Juliet,* NYSF, Delacorte Theatre, 1968; *Richard III, Henry VI, Part One,* and *Henry VI, Part Two,* all NYSF, Delacorte Theatre, 1970.

PRINCIPAL FILM APPEARANCES—Piquant, *The Traveling Executioner,* Metro-Goldwyn-Mayer (MGM), 1970; Simpson, *Xanadu,* Universal, 1980; also appeared in *The Gang That Couldn't Shoot Straight,* MGM, 1971; *The Sting,* Universal, 1973.

PRINCIPAL TELEVISION APPEARANCES—Series: Dr. Sam Lanagan, *Westside Medical,* ABC, 1977; Mitch Bronsky, *Ryan's Hope,* ABC, 1982; Charlie Wayne, *Oh Madeline,* ABC, 1983-84. Mini-

Series: Spade Larkin, *Centennial,* NBC, 1978-79; Ronald Ziegler, *Blind Ambition,* CBS, 1979. Pilots: Vinnie Kovack, *The Family Kovack,* CBS, 1974; John David Yeager, *Trouble in High Timber Country,* ABC, 1980; candy man, *The Asphalt Cowboy,* NBC, 1980; Stein, *Pros and Cons,* ABC, 1986.

Episodic: Mike Magill, *Tenspeed and Brown Shoe,* ABC, 1980; Harry Wanamaker, *Misfits of Science,* NBC, 1985; Don Shoop, *Simon and Simon,* CBS, 1986; Dr. Bryant, *Highway to Heaven,* NBC, 1986; Jay Taylor, *The Fall Guy,* ABC, 1986; Lieutenant Spoletti, *Murder, She Wrote,* CBS, 1986; Louie Malloy, *Jack and Mike,* ABC, 1986; teacher's husband, *the Love Boat,* ABC, 1986; Lyle Everett, *Who's the Boss?,* ABC, 1987; Max Drummond, *Growing Pains,* ABC, 1987; Butterfield, *Murder, She Wrote,* CBS, 1988; Ed Dryden, *Houston Knights,* CBS, 1987; Elliot Atkins, *Matlock,* NBC, 1988; Frank Marley, *Mission: Impossible,* ABC, 1988; Henry, *HeartBeat,* ABC, 1988; Martin Isaacson, *The Bronx Zoo,* NBC, 1988; Dr. Lucas Forbes, *Matlock,* NBC, 1989; Harv, *Baywatch,* NBC, 1989; Henry Colter, *MacGyver,* ABC, 1989; George Fraley, *MacGyver,* ABC, 1990; Steve Romano, *Jake and the Fatman,* CBS, 1990; Admiral Aladar Jarok, *Star Trek: The Next Generation,* syndicated, 1990.

Movies: Frankie Scamantino, *Panic on the 5:22,* ABC, 1974; Pete Notario, *Honor Thy Father,* CBS, 1973; Lubeck, *The Million Dollar Rip-Off,* NBC, 1976; District Attorney Asa Keyes, *The Disappearance of Aimee,* NBC, 1976; Tony Bonelli, *Act of Violence,* CBS, 1979; Eddie Rodelo, *The Violation of Sarah McDavid,* CBS, 1981; Bubba Wrench, *Callie and Son,* CBS, 1981; John Malloy, *Prime Suspect,* CBS, 1982; Sheriff John Thomas, *Amos,* CBS, 1985; Roger Gaines, *Vital Signs,* CBS, 1986; Fred Wapner, *The Billionaire Boys Club,* NBC, 1987; Dr. Zach Emerson, *Bigfoot,* ABC, 1987; Wardell, *Her Secret Life,* ABC, 1987; Lou McClinton, *Who Gets the Friends?,* CBS, 1988.

ADDRESSES: AGENTS—The Ambrose Company, 1466 Broadway, New York, NY 10036; Gores/Fields Agency, 10100 Santa Monica Boulevard, Suite 700, Los Angeles, CA 90067.*

*   *   *

SMITH, Derek David   1959-

PERSONAL: Born Derek Smith, December 4, 1959, in Seattle, WA; son of David Warren (a sales representative) and Shirley Yvonne (an interior designer; maiden name, Bakken) Smith; children: Savannah Smith-Migliuri. EDUCATION—Attended the University of Washington, 1978-80; Juilliard School, B.F.A., 1984.

VOCATION: Actor.

CAREER: OFF-BROADWAY DEBUT—Rick Hyde, *Cruise Control,* WPA Theatre, 1985. PRINCIPAL STAGE APPEARANCES— Fortune Teller, *The Skin of Our Teeth,* Wellborn, *A New Way to Pay Old Debts,* and Orlando, *As You Like It,* all the Acting Company, Marymount Manhattan Theatre, New York City, 1985; Man, "Talk to Me Like the Rain and Let Me Listen," Doctor, "Portrait of a Madonna," Silva, "The Long Goodbye," and Little Man, "The Strangest Kind of Romance," in *Ten By Tennessee,* the Acting Company, Lucille Lortel Theatre, New York City, 1986; Romeo, *Romeo and Juliet,* Folger Theatre, Washington, DC, 1986; Leslie, *The Hostage,* Coconut Grove Playhouse, Miami, FL, 1987; Frank, *The Witch of Edmonton,* Folger Theatre, 1987; Thomas

Gradgrind, Young Tom, and Stephen Blackpool, *Charles Dickens' Hard Times,* Portland Stage Company, Portland, ME, 1988; Giovanni, *'Tis Pity She's a Whore* and Farruscad, *The Serpent Woman,* both American Repertory Theatre, Cambridge, MA, 1988; Triletsky, *Platonov,* Valere, *The Miser,* and Clarin, *Life Is a Dream,* both American Repertory Theatre, 1989; Reynoldo, *Hyde in Hollywood,* American Place Theatre, New York City, 1989. Also appeared *Traps,* Theatre Upstairs, New York City, 1988; Ben Hubbard, *Another Part of the Forest,* Moon, *Blood Wedding,* Hugo and Frederick, *Ring 'round the Moon,* Theseus and Oberon, *A Midsummer Night's Dream,* Sganarelle, *The Flying Doctor,* Commandant, *To the Ninth Circle,* Stephan Undershaft, *Major Barbara,* title role, *Uncle Vanya,* and Romeo, *Romeo and Juliet,* all Juilliard Theatre Ensemble, New York City; Bernard, *Pieces of Eight,* the Acting Company.

MAJOR TOURS—With the Acting Company, 1984-85.

TELEVISION DEBUT—*Another World,* NBC, 1984. PRINCIPAL TELEVISION APPEARANCES—Series: *Ryan's Hope,* ABC, 1984. Episodic: *The Equalizer,* NBC, 1986; Reynoldo, "Hyde in Hollywood," *American Playhouse,* PBS, 1989. Movies: Marc Gates, *Internal Affairs,* CBS, 1988.

AWARDS: Richard Rodgers Award; Leonard Bernstein's Felicia Montealegre Award; Outstanding Achievement Award from the Juilliard School.

MEMBER: Actors' Equity Association, American Federation of Television and Radio Artists.

*   *   *

SMITH, Kurtwood

PERSONAL: Born July 3, in New Lisbon, WI; married Joan Pirkle (an actress), November 5, 1988.

VOCATION: Actor.

CAREER: PRINCIPAL STAGE APPEARANCES—Ward Henshaw, *Plymouth Rock,* California Actors Theatre, Los Gatos, CA, 1979; also appeared in *The Price,* California Actors Theatre, 1977-78; *Farces By Chekhov,* California Actors Theatre, 1978-79; *Familiar Faces/Mixed Feelings,* Los Angeles Actors Theatre, Los Angeles, 1982-83; *Enemy of the People,* Los Angeles Actors Theatre, 1983-84; *The Debutante Ball,* South Coast Repertory, Costa Mesa, CA, 1984-85.

PRINCIPAL FILM APPEARANCES—Security guard, *Roadie,* United Artists, 1980; Sergeant Smith, *Zoot Suit,* Universal, 1981; Clarence, *Going Berserk,* Universal, 1983; choreographer, *Staying Alive,* Paramount, 1983; Carson, *Flashpoint,* Tri-Star, 1984; Arthur McNeil, *The Delos Adventure,* American Cinema, 1985; Clarence J. Boddicker, *Robocop,* Orion, 1987; Griggs, *Rambo III,* Tri-Star, 1988; District Attorney Robert Reynard, *True Believer,* Columbia, 1989; Mr. Perry, *Dead Poets Society,* Buena Vista, 1989; Professor Flournoy, *Heart of Dixie,* Orion, 1989.

PRINCIPAL TELEVISION APPEARANCES—Series: Captain Frank Scanlon, *The Renegades,* ABC, 1983; Mr. Sue, *The New Adventures of Beans Baxter,* Fox, 1987-88. Mini-Series: Colonel Hiram Berdan, *North and South, Book II,* ABC, 1986. Pilots: Captain

Frank Scanlon, *The Renegades,* ABC, 1982; Major Heckinkamp, *Powers Play,* CBS, 1986. Episodic: Bo Carter, *Stir Crazy,* CBS, 1985; Jonathan, *The Insiders,* ABC, 1985; Al Fiddler, *Stingray,* NBC, 1986; Chet, *Newhart,* CBS, 1986; Phil, *Melba,* CBS, 1986; Spencer Phillips, *21 Jump Street,* Fox, 1987. Movies: Gus Kalb, *Murder in Texas,* NBC, 1981; Edward Sincoff, *Missing Pieces,* CBS, 1983; Warren Jensen, *The Midnight Hour,* ABC, 1985; Gilbert, *International Airport,* ABC, 1985; Lieutenant Burton, *Deadly Messages,* ABC, 1985; Jake Richards, *The Christmas Gift,* CBS, 1986; Dr. Josef Goebbels, *The Nightmare Years,* TNT, 1989.

RELATED CAREER—Company member, California Actors Theatre, Los Gatos, CA, 1975-79.

ADDRESSES: AGENT—Belle Zwerdling, Progressive Artists Agency, 400 S. Beverly Drive, Suite 216, Beverly Hills, CA 90212.*

*   *   *

SMITH, Lois

PERSONAL: Born Lois Arlene Humbert, November 3, in Topeka, KS; daughter of William Oren (a telephone company employee) and Carrie Davis (Gottshalk) Humbert; married Wesley Dale Smith (a teacher), November 5, 1948 (divorced, 1970); children: Moon Elizabeth. EDUCATION—Trained for the stage with Donal Harrington at the University of Washington, 1948-50, and with Lee Strasberg at the Actors' Studio.

LOIS SMITH

VOCATION: Actress and playwright.

CAREER: Also see *WRITINGS* below. STAGE DEBUT—Jeannie, *Time Out for Ginger,* Wilmington Playhouse, Wilmington, DE, 1952. BROADWAY DEBUT—Jeannie, *Time Out for Ginger,* Lyceum Theatre, 1952. LONDON DEBUT—Josephine Perry, *The Young and Beautiful,* Arts Theatre, 1956. PRINCIPAL STAGE APPEARANCES—Cathy, *Mardi Gras,* Locust Theatre, Philadelphia, PA, 1955; Antoinette, *The Wisteria Trees,* City Center Theatre, New York City, 1955; Josephine Perry, *The Young and Beautiful,* Longacre Theatre, New York City, 1955; Laura Wingfield, *The Glass Menagerie,* City Center Theatre, 1956; Carol Cutrere, *Orpheus Descending,* Martin Beck Theatre, New York City, 1957; Mary Devlin, *Edwin Booth,* 46th Street Theatre, New York City, 1958; Alley, *Ding Dong Bell,* Westport Country Playhouse, Westport, CT, 1961; Sheila Knight, *Time of Hope,* Playhouse in the Park, Philadelphia, 1963; Lucha Moreno, *Bicycle Ride to Nevada,* Cort Theatre, New York City, 1963; Jo Britten, *Blues for Mr. Charlie,* American National Theatre and Academy Theatre, New York City, 1964; Virginia, *Galileo,* Andromache, *Tiger at the Gates,* Celimene, *The Misanthrope,* Yelena, *Uncle Vanya,* and Confidante, *The Critic,* all Theatre of the Living Arts, Philadelphia, 1965; title role, *Miss Julie,* Pamela, *The Last Analysis,* and the Preacher Woman, *Bechlch,* all Theatre of the Living Arts, 1966; Mary L., *The Time of Your Life,* Theatre of the Living Arts, 1967; Sonya, *Uncle Vanya,* Center Theatre Group, Mark Taper Forum, Los Angeles, 1969.

Mary, *Sunday Dinner,* American Place Theatre, St. Clement's Church Theatre, New York City, 1970; Louise Harper, "Come Next Tuesday," Judith Kalmus, "'Twas Brillig," the Woman, "So Please Be Kind," and the Mother, "Present Tense," in *Present Tense,* Sheridan Square Playhouse, New York City, 1972; Mission Control voice, *A Break in the Skin,* Actors' Studio Theatre, New York City, 1973; Cora, *The Iceman Cometh,* Circle in the Square/Joseph E. Levine Theatre, New York City, 1973-74; Trina Halvey, *Summer,* Kennedy Center for the Performing Arts, Washington, DC, 1974-75; woman, *Eh, Joe?,* Harvard University, Cambridge, MA, 1975; Gabby, *Harry Outside,* Circle Repertory Theatre, New York City, 1975; various roles, *Touching Bottom,* American Place Theatre, New York City, 1978; Denise, *Hillbilly Women,* Actors' Studio Theatre, then Long Wharf Theatre, New Haven, CT, both 1979; old woman, *Tennessee,* Ensemble Studio Theatre, New York City, 1979.

Emily, *Deer Season,* St. Clement's Church Theatre, 1980; various roles, *After All,* Manhattan Theatre Club, New York City, 1981; Molly Malloy, *The Front Page,* Long Wharf Theatre, 1982; Catherine Senesh, *Hannah,* Harold Clurman Theatre, New York City, 1983; Madam Arkadina, *The Seagull,* Tyrone Guthrie Theatre, Minneapolis, MN, 1983; Madeleine Bejart, *Cabal of Hypocrites,* Actors' Studio Theatre, 1984; Linda, *Special Family Things,* Festival of One-Act Plays, American Place Women's Project, American Place Theatre, New York City, 1984; Reba, *Bite the Hand,* One-Act Play Marathon, Ensemble Studio Theatre, 1984; Rivers, *The Vienna Notes,* Second Stage, New York City, 1985; Blanche, *Brighton Beach Memoirs,* A Contemporary Theatre, Seattle, WA, 1986; Mrs. Dotson and the Bride, *Bodies, Rest, and Motion,* Mitzie E. Newhouse Theatre, New York City, 1986-87; Jessie Bliss, *The Stick Wife,* Hartford Stage Company, Hartford, CT, 1987; Grady, *April Snow,* One-Act Play Marathon, Ensemble Studio Theatre, 1987; Natalie Bauer-Lechner, *Gus and Al* and Dolly, *27 Benedict Street,* both Playwrights Horizons, New York City, 1988; Esther French, *Juliet* and Mrs. Campbell, *The Man Who Climbed the Pecan Trees,* both Ensemble Studio Theatre, 1988; Ma Joad, *The Grapes of Wrath,* Steppenwolf Theatre Com-

pany, Royal George Theatre, Chicago, IL, 1988; Mistress Overdone, *Measure for Measure,* Lincoln Center Theatre, New York City, 1989; Ma Joad, *The Grapes of Wrath,* Steppenwolf Theatre Company, La Jolla Playhouse, La Jolla, CA, then International Theatre Festival, Lyttelton Theatre, London, both 1989; Mary, *Beside Herself,* Circle Repertory Theatre, New York City, 1989; Ma Joad, *The Grapes of Wrath,* Steppenwolf Theatre Company, Cort Theatre, 1990. Also appeared in *A Dream of Love,* Theatre of the Living Arts, 1966; *Stages,* Belasco Theatre, New York City, 1978.

PRINCIPAL STAGE WORK—Director, *Measure for Measure,* Juilliard School, New York City, 1987.

MAJOR TOURS—Trina Halvey, *Summer,* U.S. cities, 1974.

FILM DEBUT—Ann, *East of Eden,* Warner Brothers, 1955. PRINCIPAL FILM APPEARANCES—Spurs O'Brien, *Strange Lady in Town,* Warner Brothers, 1955; Partita Dupea, *Five Easy Pieces,* Columbia, 1970; Jane, *The Way We Live Now,* United Artists, 1970; neighbor, *Brother John,* Columbia, 1971; Elinore, *Up the Sandbox,* National General, 1972; Anita, *Next Stop, Greenwich Village,* Twentieth Century-Fox, 1976; Kathy, *Resurrection,* Universal, 1980; Mrs. Axman, *Foxes,* United Artists, 1980; Mrs. Carnahan, *Four Friends* (also known as *Georgia's Friends*), Filmways, 1981; Mary Spofford, *Reuben, Reuben,* Twentieth Century-Fox, 1983; Mrs. Prescott, *Reckless,* Metro-Goldwyn-Mayer/United Artists, 1984; Sara, *Black Widow,* Twentieth Century-Fox, 1987; Martha, *Fatal Attraction,* Paramount, 1987; Mrs. Nelson, *Midnight Run,* Universal, 1988.

TELEVISION DEBUT—Megan, "The Apple Tree," *Kraft Television Theatre,* NBC, 1953. PRINCIPAL TELEVISION APPEARANCES—Series: Zoe Cannel, *Somerset,* NBC, 1972-73; Eleanor Conrad, *The Doctors,* NBC, 1975-77; also Mrs. Bendarik, *Love of Life,* CBS. Pilots: Doris Adams, *Adams Apple,* CBS, 1986. Episodic: Title role, "Miss Julie," *Play of the Week,* WNTA, 1960; Hilda, "The Master Builder," *Play of the Week,* WNTA, 1961; Maria Gannucci, *The Equalizer,* CBS, 1985; Dorothy Hermes, *The Equalizer,* CBS, 1987; also "Cindy's Fella," *Ford Startime,* NBC, 1959; "Do Not Go Gentle into That Good Night," *CBS Playhouse,* CBS, 1967; "Proxy," *Tales of the Unexpected,* syndicated, 1982; *Spenser: For Hire,* ABC, 1988; *Star Tonight,* ABC; *Robert Montgomery Presents,* NBC; *Studio One,* CBS; *Matinee Theatre,* NBC; *Justice,* NBC; *U.S. Steel Hour,* CBS; *The Loretta Young Show,* NBC; *The Defenders,* CBS; *The Naked City,* ABC; *Dr. Kildare,* NBC; *Route 66,* CBS. Movies: Clara, *Rage of Angels,* NBC, 1983; Sarah, *Doubletake,* CBS, 1985; Mary Neal, *The Execution of Raymond Graham,* ABC, 1985. Specials: Alma, *Victory,* NBC, 1960; *Talk to Me Like the Rain and Let Me Listen,* WNET (New York City), 1970; Margaret, "The Unforgivable Secret," *ABC Afterschool Specials,* ABC, 1981; *Juliet,* Arts and Entertainment, 1989; also *The House of Mirth,* 1980; *Particular Men,* WNET; and *The Jilting of Granny Wetherall.*

RELATED CAREER—Member of the advisory panel on program funding, Public Broadcasting Service, 1981-82; member, Actors' Studio; acting teacher; member, Ensemble Studio Theatre Workshop.

WRITINGS: STAGE—*All There Is,* 1982, first act produced in workshop at the Ensemble Studio Theatre, New York City, 1985.

AWARDS: Film Daily Critics' Poll Award ("Filmdom's Famous Fives"), 1955, for *East of Eden;* National Society of Film Critics' Award, Best Supporting Actress, 1971, for *Five Easy Pieces;*

Clarence Ross fellow at the American Theatre Wing, Eugene O'Neill Theatre Center, Waterbury, CT, 1983; Joseph Jefferson Award nomination, 1989, for *The Grapes of Wrath*.

MEMBER: Actors' Equity Association, Screen Actors Guild, American Federation of Television and Radio Artists, Dramatists Guild, Harold Clurman Theatre Artists Fund Center for the Arts at the State University of New York, Purchase (honorary founder).

SIDELIGHTS: FAVORITE ROLES—Sonya and Yelena in *Uncle Vanya*, Carol Cutrere in *Orpheus Descending*, and Josephine Perry in *The Young and Beautiful*.

ADDRESSES: AGENT—Writers and Artists Agency, 70 W. 36th Street, New York, NY 10018.

*   *   *

SMITHERS, William   1927-

PERSONAL: Born July 10, 1927, in Richmond, VA; son of Marion Wilkinson (a systems engineer) and Marion Albany (Thompson) Smithers; married Claire Heller, July 13, 1955 (divorced, 1960). EDUCATION—Attended Hampden-Sydney College, 1946-48, and Catholic University, 1948-50. MILITARY—U.S. Navy, seaman first class, 1945-46.

VOCATION: Actor.

CAREER: STAGE DEBUT—Thomas Jefferson, *The Common Glo-*

WILLIAM SMITHERS

ry, Williamsburg, VA, 1947. BROADWAY DEBUT—Tybalt, *Romeo and Juliet*, Broadhurst Theatre, 1951. LONDON DEBUT—David Beeston, *Man and Boy*, Queen's Theatre, 1963. PRINCIPAL STAGE APPEARANCES—Hotel waiter, *Legend of Lovers*, Plymouth Theatre, New York City, 1951-52; Treplev, *The Seagull*, Fourth Street Theatre, New York City, 1956; Philip Lovejoy, *The Square Root of Wonderful*, National Theatre, New York City, 1957; Donal Davoren, *The Shadow of a Gunman*, Bijou Theatre, New York City, 1958; Demetrius, *A Midsummer Night's Dream* and Mercutio, *Romeo and Juliet*, both American Shakespeare Festival, Stratford, CT, 1959; Larry Doyle, *Who'll Save the Plowboy?*, Phoenix Theatre, New York City, 1962; David Beeston, *Man and Boy*, Brooks Atkinson Theatre, New York City, 1963. Also appeared in *End As a Man*, Theatre De Lys, New York City, 1954; *The Troublemakers*, President Theatre, New York City, 1954-55.

MAJOR TOURS—Tom, *The Glass Menagerie* and doctor, *The Skin of Our Teeth*, both Theatre Guild American Repertory Company, U.S. cities, 1961.

FILM DEBUT—Lieutenant Harold Woodruff, *Attack!*, United Artists, 1956. PRINCIPAL FILM APPEARANCES—Captain Joe Marks, *Trouble Man*, Twentieth Century-Fox, 1972; Warden Barrot, *Papillon*, Allied Artists, 1973; Mitchell, *Scorpio*, United Artists, 1973; Dr. Karl, *Deathsport*, New World, 1978.

PRINCIPAL TELEVISION APPEARANCES—Series: Committee member, *The Witness*, CBS, 1960-61; David Schuster, *Peyton Place*, ABC, 1965-66; Stanley Norris, *The Guiding Light*, CBS, 1970-71; Anderson Galt, *Executive Suite*, CBS, 1976-77; Dr. Trilling, *Doctors' Private Lives*, ABC, 1979; Jeremy Wendell, *Dallas*, CBS, 1981, then 1984-89. Pilots: Joseph Kane, *Call to Danger*, CBS, 1968; Leo Barnes, *The Monk*, ABC, 1969; Wilson Barrett, *The Return of Frank Cannon*, CBS, 1980. Episodic: Captain R.M. Merik, "Bread and Circuses," *Star Trek*, NBC, 1968; Colonel Poltz, *Sledge Hammer!*, ABC, 1987; also *Espionage*, NBC; *The Lawman*, ABC; *Most Wanted*, ABC; *The Name of the Game*, NBC; *Felony Squad*, ABC; *The Road West*, NBC; *The Invaders*, ABC; *Judd for the Defense*, ABC; *The Mod Squad*, ABC; *Cade's County*, CBS; *Marcus Welby, M.D.*, ABC; *Owen Marshall, Counselor at Law*, ABC; *Ironside*, NBC; *The F.B.I.*, ABC; *Mission: Impossible*, CBS; *Barnaby Jones*, CBS; *Hawkins*, CBS; *Quincy, M.E.*, NBC; *Julie Farr, M.D.* (also known as *Having Babies*), ABC; *Lucan*, ABC; *The Six Million Dollar Man*, ABC; *Scarecrow and Mrs. King*, CBS. Movies: Jerry Fielder, *Brotherhood of the Bell*, CBS, 1970; Dr. Miller, *The Neon Ceiling*, NBC, 1971; Mullen, *Where the Ladies Go*, ABC, 1980. Specials: Laertes, "Hamlet," *Hallmark Hall of Fame*, NBC, 1953; Gourgaud, "Eagle in a Cage," *Hallmark Hall of Fame*, NBC, 1965.

RELATED CAREER—Member, Actors' Studio, 1952—.

AWARDS: Theatre World Award, 1951, for *Romeo and Juliet;* Obie Award from the *Village Voice*, Best Performance By an Actor in an Off-Broadway Play, 1956, for *The Seagull*.

MEMBER: Actors' Equity Association, American Federation of Television and Radio Artists, Screen Actors Guild.

ADDRESSES: AGENT—Beakel and Jennings, 427 N. Canon Drive, Beverly Hills, CA 90210.*

BILL SMITROVICH

SMITROVICH, Bill 1947-

PERSONAL: Surname is pronounced "Smit-tro-vitch;" born William S. Zmitrowicz, May 16, 1947, in Bridgeport, CT; son of Stanley William (a tool and die maker) and Anna (Wojna) Zmitrowicz; married Shaw Purnell, June 8, 1985; children: Alexander John ("A.J."). EDUCATION—Received B.S. in education from the University of Bridgeport; received M.F.A. in dramatic arts from Smith College; studied acting at the Actors' and Directors' Lab and with Morris Carnovsky.

VOCATION: Actor.

CAREER: BROADWAY DEBUT—Rudy, waiter, bicycle thief, piano mover, and Ryan, *The American Clock,* Biltmore Theatre, 1980. PRINCIPAL STAGE APPEARANCES—Moose Corwin, *Never Say Die,* Classic Theatre, New York City, 1982; Johnny Bear, *Requiem for a Heavyweight,* Long Wharf Theatre, New Haven, CT, 1983; Sudden Pisanger, *Food from Trash,* Humana New Play Festival, Actors Theatre of Louisville, Louisville, KY, 1983; Lennie, *Of Mice and Men,* Hong Kong International Arts Festival, 1984; Johnny, *Frankie and Johnny in the Claire de Lune,* Westside Arts Center, New York City, 1988-89. Also appeared in *Zeks,* Theatre for the New City, New York City, 1982; *The Love Suicide at Schofield Barracks,* Fifth Annual New Play Festival, People's Light and Theatre Company, Malvern, PA, 1985.

PRINCIPAL FILM APPEARANCES—Policeman, *Without a Trace,* Twentieth Century-Fox, 1983; Ralph Bauer, *Splash,* Buena Vista, 1984; Lenny, *Key Exchange,* Twentieth Century-Fox, 1985; bartender, *Maria's Lovers,* Cannon, 1985; Andy Fairton, *Stephen*

King's Silver Bullet, Paramount, 1985; Chavez, *Band of the Hand,* Tri-Star, 1986; Lloyd Bowman, *Manhunter,* De Laurentiis Entertainment Group, 1986; Finch, *Renegades,* Universal, 1989; Farrell, *Her Alibi,* Warner Brothers, 1989; Bruce Concannon, *Crazy People,* Paramount, 1990. Also appeared in *A Little Sex,* Universal, 1982; *A Killing Affair* (also known as *Monday, Tuesday, Wednesday*), Hemdale, 1986.

PRINCIPAL TELEVISION APPEARANCES—Series: Detective Danny Krychek, *Crime Story,* NBC, 1986-88; Drew Thacher, *Life Goes On,* ABC, 1989—. Pilots: Steve Enright, *Johnny Garage,* CBS, 1983; Lloyd Bowman, *Manhunter,* 1986. Episodic: Scotty Wheeler, *Miami Vice,* NBC, 1984. Movies: Jake O'Neill, *Born Beautiful,* NBC, 1982; Charlie Hack, *Muggable Mary: Street Cop,* CBS, 1982.

RELATED CAREER—Original company member, NO Theatre Company, Northhampton, MA, 1975-78; acting instructor, University of Massachusetts, Amherst, MA, 1976-78.

ADDRESSES: AGENT—Don Buchwald and Associates, 10 E. 44th Street, New York, NY 10017.

* * *

SOMMARS, Julie

PERSONAL: Born April 15, in Fremont, NE; daughter of Louis Frank (a government grain inspector) and Helen Margaret (a teacher; maiden name, Drummond); married John Harris Karns (an attorney), April 2, 1983; children: Jacey Collyer Erwin. EDUCATION—Studied political science at San Bernardino Valley College; studied acting with Robert O'Neill at the Actors' Workshop.

VOCATION: Actress.

CAREER: PRINCIPAL STAGE APPEARANCES—*Same Time Next Year,* Fiesta Dinner Playhouse, San Antonio, TX, 1983, then Dallas, TX; *The Story of Mary Surratt,* Equity Library Theatre, New York City; *Our Town,* LeGrand Theatre, Los Angeles; *Miss Pell Is Missing,* Civic Theatre, Los Angeles; *I Won't Dance,* Gene Dynarski Theatre, Los Angeles; also appeared with the Redding Summer Theatre, Redding, CA; with the Canal Fulton Summer Theatre, Canal, OH; and with the Hooksett Theatre, Hooksett, NH.

PRINCIPAL FILM APPEARANCES—Caroline Reno, *The Great Sioux Massacre* (also known as *Custer Massacre* and *The Massacre at the Rosebud*), Columbia, 1965; Doreen Marshall, *The Pad . . . (And How to Use It),* Universal, 1966; Diane Darcy, *Herbie Goes to Monte Carlo,* Buena Vista, 1977; also appeared in *Bat 21,* Tri-Star, 1988.

TELEVISION DEBUT—*The Loretta Young Show,* NBC. PRINCIPAL TELEVISION APPEARANCES—Series: Jennifer Jo ("J.J.") Drinkwater, *The Governor and J.J.,* CBS, 1969-70; Tracey, *Rituals,* syndicated, 1984; District Attorney Julie March, *Matlock,* NBC, 1987—. Mini-Series: Alice Grebe, *Centennial,* NBC, 1978-79. Pilots: Alice Shoemaker, *Fools, Females, and Fun: I've Gotta Be Me,* NBC, 1974; Molly, *The Search,* CBS, 1968; Patricia, *Epicac* (broadcast as an episode of *Rex Harrison Presents Short Stories of Love*), NBC, 1974; Suzy Bassett, *My Wife Next Door,* NBC, 1975. Episodic: *Harry O,* ABC, 1974; *The Rockford Files,* NBC, 1974; *Three for the Road,* CBS, 1975; *Switch,* CBS, 1975; *Partners in*

JULIE SOMMARS

Crime, NBC, 1984; *Great Adventure*, CBS; *Gunsmoke*, CBS; *The Man from U.N.C.L.E.*, NBC; *Barnaby Jones*, CBS; *McMillan and Wife*, NBC; *McCloud*, NBC; *Fantasy Island*, ABC; *Magnum, P.I.*, CBS. Movies: Mary Grace, *Five Desperate Women*, ABC, 1971; Jennifer Shagaras, *The Harness*, NBC, 1971; Dorothy, *How to Steal an Airplane* (also known as *Only One Day Left Before Tomorrow*), NBC, 1972; Bonnie McGee, *Sex and the Single Parent*, CBS, 1979; Liz Johnson, *Cave-In!*, NBC, 1983; Nina Cole, *Emergency Room*, syndicated, 1983. Specials: Ann Rogers, *I'm the Girl He Wants to Kill*, ABC, 1974. Also appeared in *Wilderness Trail.*

RELATED CAREER—Apprentice, Michigan Stock Company, Manistee, MI.

AWARDS: Golden Globe, Best Television Actress in a Comedy Series, 1969, and the Television Critics' Award, Best New Star, 1970, both for *The Governor and J.J.*

ADDRESSES: HOME—Hollywood Hills, CA.

*   *   *

SOTHERN, Ann 1909-
(Harriette Lake)

PERSONAL: Born Harriette Lake, January 2, 1909, in Valley City, ND; daughter of Herbert and Annette (an opera singer; maiden name, Yde) Lake; married Roger Pryor (a musician), 1936 (divorced, 1942); married Robert Sterling (an actor), 1943 (divorced,

1949); children: Patricia Ann. EDUCATION—Attended the University of Washington; studied acting with Stella Adler, 1961.

VOCATION: Actress.

CAREER: BROADWAY DEBUT—(As Harriette Lake) *Smiles*, Ziegfeld Theatre, 1930. PRINCIPAL STAGE APPEARANCES—(As Harriette Lake) Geraldine March, *America's Sweetheart*, Broadhurst Theatre, New York City, 1931; (as Harriette Lake) Ann Cathway, *Everybody's Welcome*, Shubert Theatre, New York City, 1931; (as Harriette Lake) Mary Turner, *Of Thee I Sing*, Imperial Theatre, New York City, 1933. Also appeared in productions of *The Glass Menagerie*, *Gypsy*, and *The Solid Gold Cadillac*, all 1966-68; and in *The Duchess of Pasadena*, 1978.

FILM DEBUT—(As Harriette Lake) *Broadway Nights*, First National, 1927. PRINCIPAL FILM APPEARANCES—(As Harriette Lake) As herself, *The Show of Shows*, Warner Brothers, 1929; (as Harriette Lake) dancer, *Broadway thru a Keyhole*, Twentieth Century-Fox, 1933; Kitty Taylor, *Blind Date* (also known as *Her Sacrifice*), Columbia, 1934; Geraldine, *The Hell Cat*, Columbia, 1934; Joan Larrabee, *Kid Millions*, United Artists, 1934; Jean, *Let's Fall in Love*, Columbia, 1934; Jane Blodgett, *Melody in Spring*, Paramount, 1934; Ruth, *The Party's Over*, Columbia, 1934; Marge Walker, *Eight Bells*, Columbia, 1935; Mimi, *Folies Bergere* (also known as *The Man from the Follies Bergere*), Twentieth Century-Fox, 1935; Linda, *The Girl Friend*, Columbia, 1935; Adrienne Martin, *Grand Exit*, Columbia, 1935; Pat, *Hooray for Love*, RKO, 1935; Ann Edwards, *Don't Gamble with Love*, Columbia, 1936; Mary, *Hell-Ship Morgan*, Columbia, 1936; Mary Cantillon, *My American Wife*, Paramount, 1936; Frances Cooke, *Smartest Girl in Town*, RKO, 1936; Kit Bennett, *Walking on Air*, RKO, 1936; Fay Stevens, *You May Be Next* (also known as *Panic on the Air*, *Calling All G-Men*, and *Trapped By Wireless*), Columbia, 1936; Toni Pemberton, *Danger—Love at Work*, Twentieth Century-Fox, 1937; Elinor, *Dangerous Number*, Metro-Goldwyn-Mayer (MGM), 1937; Millicent Kendall, *Fifty Roads to Town*, Twentieth Century-Fox, 1937; Mary Strand, *Super Sleuth*, RKO, 1937; Connie Taylor, *There Goes My Girl*, RKO, 1937; Betty Russell, *There Goes the Groom*, RKO, 1937; Carol Rogers, *She's Got Everything*, RKO, 1938; Jean Livingston, *Trade Winds*, United Artists, 1938; Garda Sloane, *Fast and Furious*, MGM, 1939; Eileen Connelly, *Hotel for Women* (also known as *Elsa Maxwell's Hotel for Women*), Twentieth Century-Fox, 1939; Ethel Turp, *Joe and Ethel Turp Call on the President*, MGM, 1939; Maisie Ravier, *Maisie*, MGM, 1939.

Flo Addams, *Brother Orchid*, Warner Brothers, 1940; Maisie Ravier, *Congo Maisie*, MGM, 1940; Dulcy Ward, *Dulcy*, MGM, 1940; Maisie Ravier, *Gold Rush Maisie*, MGM, 1940; Dixie Donegan, *Lady Be Good*, MGM, 1941; Maisie Ravier, *Maisie Was a Lady*, MGM, 1941; Maisie Ravier, *Ringside Maisie*, MGM, 1941; Maisie Ravier, *Maisie Gets Her Man* (also known as *She Gets Her Man*), MGM, 1942; Hattie Maloney, *Panama Hattie*, MGM, 1942; Pat, *Cry Havoc*, MGM, 1943; Maisie Ravier, *Swing Shift Maisie*, MGM, 1943; as herself, *Thousands Cheer*, MGM, 1943; Julia Seabrook, *Three Hearts for Julia*, MGM, 1943; Maisie Ravier, *Maisie Goes to Reno*, MGM, 1944; Maisie Ravier, *Up Goes Maisie*, MGM, 1946; Maisie Ravier, *Undercover Maisie*, MGM, 1947; Joyce Harmon, *Words and Music*, MGM, 1948; June Tyme, *April Showers*, Warner Brothers, 1948; Rita Phipps, *A Letter to Three Wives*, Twentieth Century-Fox, 1948; Peggy, *The Judge Steps Out* (also known as *Indian Summer*), RKO, 1949; Frances Elliott, *Nancy Goes to Rio*, MGM, 1950; Dell Faring, *Shadow on the Wall* (also known as *Death in the Doll's House*),

MGM, 1950; Crystal Carpenter, *The Blue Gardenia*, Warner Brothers, 1953; Mrs. Gamadge, *The Best Man*, United Artists, 1964; Sade, *Lady in a Cage*, Paramount, 1964; Grace Argona, *Sylvia*, Paramount, 1965; Angela, *Chubasco*, Warner Brothers, 1968; Thelma, *The Killing Kind*, Media Trend, 1973; Finzie, *Golden Needles* (also known as *Chase for the Golden Needles*), American International, 1974; Sheba, *Crazy Mama*, New World, 1975; Mrs. Karmann, *The Manitou*, AVCO-Embassy, 1978; Angel, *The Little Dragons*, Aurora, 1980; Tisha Doughty, *The Whales of August*, Alive, 1987. Also appeared (as Harriette Lake) in *Hearts in Exile*, Warner Brothers, 1929; (as Harriette Lake) *Hold Everything*, Warner Brothers, 1930; (as Harriette Lake) *Whoopie*, United Artists, 1930; (as Harriette Lake) *Doughboys* (also known as *Forward March*), MGM, 1930.

PRINCIPAL TELEVISION APPEARANCES—Series: Susie McNamara, *Private Secretary*, CBS, 1953-57; Katy O'Connor, *The Ann Sothern Show*, CBS, 1958-61; voice of mother, *My Mother the Car*, NBC, 1965-66. Mini-Series: Mrs. Finch, *Captains and the Kings*, NBC, 1976. Pilots: Katy, *Always April*, CBS, 1961; Mrs. Kozzek, *The Outsider*, NBC, 1967. Episodic: *The June Allyson Show*, CBS, 1961; also Blackjack Jenny, *Alias Smith and Jones*, ABC; *Schlitz Playhouse of Stars*, CBS; *Hollywood Opening Night*. Movies: Ethel Gaines, *Congratulations: It's a Boy!*, ABC, 1971; Annie LaCossitt, *A Death of Innocence*, CBS, 1971; Mother Bonaventure, *The Weekend Nun*, ABC, 1972; Aunt Margaret Bancroft, *The Great Man's Whiskers*, NBC, 1973; Ma Finney, *A Letter to Three Wives*, NBC, 1985. Specials: Liza Elliott, *Lady in the Dark*, NBC, 1954; hostess, *Holiday in Las Vegas*, NBC, 1957; the Queen, *Fol-De-Rol*, ABC, 1972.

RELATED CAREER—Performer (as Harriette Lake), Civic Light Opera Company, 1930-31; founder and president, Vincent Productions, 1954; founder, Anso Productions, 1958.

NON-RELATED CAREER—Founder and president, Ann Sothern's Sewing Center, Sun Valley, ID; owner, A Bar S Cattle Company.

AWARDS: Academy Award nomination, Best Supporting Actress, 1988, for *The Whales of August.*

ADDRESSES: AGENT—Tom Korman, Agency for the Performing Arts, 9000 Sunset Boulevard, Suite 1200, Los Angeles, CA 90069.*

*   *   *

SPINELL, Joe   ?-1989

PERSONAL: Born Joseph J. Spagnuolo in New York, NY; died of a heart attack, January 13, 1989, in New York, NY.

VOCATION: Actor.

CAREER: FILM DEBUT—Willie Cicci, *The Godfather*, Paramount, 1972. PRINCIPAL FILM APPEARANCES—Toredano, *The Seven Ups*, Twentieth Century-Fox, 1973; Marty, *Cops and Robbers*, United Artists, 1973; Willie Cicci, *The Godfather, Part II*, Paramount, 1974; Nick, *Farewell, My Lovely*, AVCO-Embassy, 1975; Ollie Slatt, *92 in the Shade*, United Artists, 1975; Mr. Colson, *Rancho Deluxe*, United Artists, 1975; Tom Gazzo, *Rocky*, United Artists, 1976; Jabo, *Stay Hungry*, United Artists, 1976; personnel officer, *Taxi Driver*, Columbia, 1976; Spinell, *Sorcerer* (also known as *Wages of Fear*), Universal/Paramount, 1977;

Angelo, *Nunzio*, Universal, 1978; Burp, *Paradise Alley*, Universal, 1978; Mike, *One Man Jury*, Cal-Am Artists, 1978; psychologist, *Big Wednesday*, Warner Brothers, 1978; Gazzo, *Rocky II*, United Artists, 1979; man in cantina, *Last Embrace*, United Artists, 1979; Count Zarth Arn, *Starcrash*, New World, 1979; Arthur Fletcher, *Winter Kills*, AVCO-Embassy, 1979.

Birdwell, *Brubaker*, Twentieth Century-Fox, 1980; Patrolman DiSimone, *Cruising*, United Artists, 1980; Yancey, *The Little Dragons*, Aurora, 1980; doorman, *The First Deadly Sin*, Filmways, 1980; Frank Zito, *Maniac*, Analysis, 1980; Spinell, *The Ninth Configuration* (also known as *Twinkle, Twinkle, Killer Kane*), Warner Brothers, 1980; Lieutenant Munafo, *Nighthawks*, Universal, 1981; emcee, "Success Wanters" in *National Lampoon Goes to the Movies* (also known as *National Lampoon's Movie Madness*), Metro-Goldwyn-Mayer/United Artists, 1981; bride's father, *Monsignor*, Twentieth Century-Fox, 1982; Joe Spangler, *One Down, Two to Go*, Almi, 1982; Manetti, *Night Shift*, Warner Brothers, 1982; Pete, *Eureka*, United Artists, 1983; Mayfield, *The Big Score*, Almi, 1983; Boss, *The Last Fight*, Best Film and Video, 1983; border patrolman, *Losin' It*, Embassy, 1983; Eisenberg, *Vigilante* (also known as *Street Gang*), Film Ventures, 1983; Vinny Durand, *The Last Horror Film* (also known as *The Fanatic*), Twin Continental, 1984; Max, *Hollywood Harry*, Shapiro, 1985; Brusstar, *Walking the Edge*, Empire, 1985; Guido Antonucci, *The Whoopee Boys*, Paramount, 1986; man with gun, *Deadly Illusion*, Cinetel, 1987; Rico, *The Messenger*, Snizzlefritz, 1987; Eddie, *The Pick-Up Artist*, Twentieth Century-Fox, 1987. Also appeared in *Tilt*, Warner Brothers, 1979; *Melvin and Howard*, Universal, 1980; *Married to the Mob*, Orion, 1988; *The Cop Who Played God*; and *The Undertaker.*

PRINCIPAL FILM WORK—Executive producer (with Judd Hamilton), *Maniac*, Analysis, 1980.

PRINCIPAL TELEVISION APPEARANCES—Pilots: Sol Terranova, *Strike Force*, NBC, 1975; Michael Vincent, *Nightside*, ABC, 1980. Episodic: Joe Latimer, *Night Heat*, CBS, 1986; Ruggiero, *The Equalizer*, CBS, 1986; Carlucci, *Night Heat*, CBS, 1987; Tommy Angel, *Night Heat*, CBS, 1987; Singh, *Diamonds*, CBS, 1987. Movies: Desk captain, *Vampire*, ABC, 1979; Escobar, *Trackdown: Finding the Goodbar Killer*, CBS, 1983; Jim Halsey, *Out of the Darkness*, CBS, 1985; also *The Children of Times Square*, ABC, 1986; *Blood Ties*, Showtime, 1986. Specials: Tony LaRosa, "K.O. Kippers," *Cinemax Comedy Experiment*, Cinemax, 1988.

WRITINGS: FILM—(With C.A. Rosenberg) *Maniac*, Analysis, 1980.

OBITUARIES AND OTHER SOURCES: Variety, February 1-7, 1989.*

*   *   *

STALLONE, Sylvester   1946-   (Q. Moonblood)

PERSONAL: Full name, Sylvester Enzio Stallone (some sources say Michael Sylvester Stallone); born July 6, 1946, in New York, NY; son of Frank (a hairdresser) and Jacquline (Labofish) Stallone;

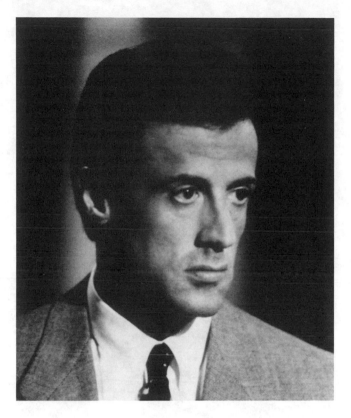

SYLVESTER STALLONE

married Sasha Czack, December 28, 1974 (divorced); married Brigitte Nielsen (an actress), December 15, 1985 (divorced, 1987); children: Sage Moonblood, Seth (first marriage). EDUCATION— Attended the American College of Switzerland, 1965-67; also attended the University of Miami, 1967-69.

VOCATION: Actor, director, producer, and screenwriter.

CAREER: Also see *WRITINGS* below. PRINCIPAL FILM APPEAR-ANCES—Mugger, *Bananas*, United Artists, 1971; Stanley Rosiello, *The Lords of Flatbush*, Columbia, 1974; Frank Nitti, *Capone*, Twentieth Century-Fox, 1975; Machine Gun Joe Viterbo, *Death Race 2000*, New World, 1975; Kelly and Jonnie, *Farewell, My Lovely*, AVCO-Embassy, 1975; Jerry, *No Place to Hide*, American, 1975; youth in park, *The Prisoner of Second Avenue*, Warner Brothers, 1975; Rocky Balboa, *Rocky*, United Artists, 1976; Johnny Kovak, *F.I.S.T.*, United Artists, 1978; Cosmo Carboni, *Paradise Alley*, Universal, 1978; Rocky Balboa, *Rocky II*, United Artists, 1979; Deke DaSilva, *Nighthawks*, Universal, 1981; Robert Hatch, *Victory* (also known as *Escape to Victory*), Paramount, 1981; Rambo, *First Blood*, Orion, 1982; Rocky Balboa, *Rocky III*, Metro-Goldwyn-Mayer/United Artists (MGM/UA), 1982; Nick, *Rhinestone*, Twentieth Century-Fox, 1984; John Rambo, *Rambo: First Blood, Part II*, Tri-Star, 1985; Rocky Balboa, *Rocky IV*, MGM/UA, 1985; Marion "Cobra" Cobretti, *Cobra*, Warner Brothers, 1986; Lincoln Hawk, *Over the Top*, Warner Brothers, 1987; John Rambo, *Rambo III*, Tri-Star, 1988; Frank Leone, *Lock Up*, Tri-Star, 1989. Also appeared in *Cannonball* (also known as *CarQuake*), New World, 1976.

PRINCIPAL FILM WORK—Fight choreographer, *Rocky*, United Artists, 1976; director, *Paradise Alley*, Universal, 1978; director

and fight choreographer, *Rocky II*, United Artists, 1979; director and fight choreographer, *Rocky III*, Metro-Goldwyn-Mayer/ United Artists (MGM/UA), 1982; producer (with Robert Stigwood) and director, *Staying Alive*, Paramount, 1983; director, *Rocky IV*, MGM/UA, 1985.

PRINCIPAL TELEVISION APPEARANCES—Specials: *American Film Institute Salute to Billy Wilder*, NBC, 1986; *The Barbara Walters Special*, ABC, 1988. PRINCIPAL TELEVISION WORK—Executive producer and fight choreographer, *Heart of a Champion: The Ray Mancini Story*, CBS, 1985.

NON-RELATED CAREER—Teacher, American College in Switzerland; also worked as an usher, fish salesman, horse trainer, delicatessen worker, truck driver, bouncer, zoo attendant, bookstore detective, short order cook, pizza demonstrator, and motel superintendant.

WRITINGS: FILM—See production details above. (With Stephen F. Verona, Martin Davidson, and Gayle Glecker) *The Lords of Flatbush*, 1974; *Rocky*, 1976; *Paradise Alley*, 1978; (with Joe Eszterhas) *F.I.S.T.*, 1978; *Rocky II*, 1979; *Rocky III*, 1982; (as Q. Moonblood; with Michael Kozoll and William Sackheim) *First Blood*, 1982; (with Norman Wexler) *Staying Alive*, 1983; (with Phil Alden Robinson) *Rhinestone*, 1984; (with James Cameron) *Rambo: First Blood, Part II*, 1985; *Rocky IV*, 1985; *Cobra*, 1986; (with Stirling Silliphant) *Over the Top*, 1987; (with Sheldon Lettich) *Rambo III*, 1988.

TELEVISION—Episodic: (As Q. Moonblood) "The Monster of Manchester," "Heart to Heart," and "The Ballad of Butcher Bloom," *A Touch of Evil*. OTHER—*Paradise Alley* (novelization), Putnam, 1977; *The Official Rocky Handbook*, 1977; *Rocky II* (novelization), Ballantine, 1982; *Rocky III* (novelization), Ballantine, 1982; *Rocky IV* (novelization), Ballantine, 1985.

AWARDS: Academy Award nominations, Best Actor and Best Original Screenplay, Donatello Award, Best Actor in Europe, National Theatre Owners Award, Christopher Award, and Bell Ringer Award from *Scholastic* magazine, all 1976, for *Rocky;* Star of the Year, 1977; Show West Actor of the Year, 1979.

MEMBER: Screen Actors Guild, Writers Guild, Directors Guild, Stuntman's Association (honorary).

ADDRESSES: AGENT—Ron Meyer, Creative Artists Agency, 9830 Wilshire Boulevard, Beverly Hills, CA 90212.

*   *   *

STANTON, Robert   1963-

PERSONAL: Full name, Robert Lloyd Stanton; born March 8, 1963, in San Antonio, TX; son of Lloyd Winter, Jr. (a government contract negotiator) and Billie Loree (a U.S. Navy budget analyst; maiden name, Baker) Stanton. EDUCATION—Attended George Mason University, 1980-82; New York University Tisch School of the Arts, B.F.A., acting, 1984, M.F.A., acting, 1985.

VOCATION: Actor.

CAREER: OFF-BROADWAY DEBUT—Froth, *Measure for Measure*, New York Shakespeare Festival, Delacorte Theatre, 1985. PRINCIPAL STAGE APPEARANCES—Clarence Day, Jr., *Life with Father*, Pittsburgh Public Theatre, Pittsburgh, PA, 1985; Bob Stanton, waiter, second child, and first soldier, *Rum and Coke*, New York Shakespeare Festival, Public Theatre, New York City, 1986; William Shakespeare, *Cheapside*, Roundabout Theatre, New York City, 1986; Rodger Potter, waiter, man at bus stop, and Eskimo Pie man, *Highest Standard of Living*, Playwrights Horizons, New York City, 1986; Albert Adam, *The Play's the Thing*, Pittsburgh Public Theatre, 1987; the big squirrel, *Afterschool Special*, Marathon '87, Ensemble Studio Theatre, New York City, 1987; Herbert Pocket, *Great Expectations*, Arizona Theatre Company, Tucson and Scottsdale, AZ, 1987; Bill, *Sure Thing* and Patrick, *Best Half-Foot Forward*, both Festival of One-Act Plays, Manhattan Punch Line, New York City, 1988; Hill and various roles, *Emily*, Manhattan Theatre Club, City Center Stage One Theatre, New York City, 1988; Flute, *A Midsummer Night's Dream* Hartford Stage Company, Hartford, CT, 1988; Arkody, *Nothing Sacred*, Hartford Stage Company, 1989; Ubu's conscience, *Ubu*, Mitzie E. Newhouse Theatre, New York City, 1989; Sir Andrew Aguecheek, *Twelfth Night*, American Repertory Theatre, Cambridge, MA, 1989; Charles Lomax, *Major Barbara*, American Repertory Theatre, 1990. Also appeared in *Beau-ootiful Soo-oop*, DearKnows Company, Whole Theatre, Montclair, NJ, 1988, then Whole Theatre and Home for Contemporary Theatre and Art, New York City, 1989.

FILM DEBUT—Dionysus, *The House on Carroll Street*, Orion, 1988. PRINCIPAL FILM APPEARANCES—Dudley, *Love or Money*, Hemdale, 1989.

PRINCIPAL TELEVISION APPEARANCES—Movies: Parker Lloyd-Smith, *Margaret Bourke-White*, TNT, 1989.

RELATED CAREER—Company member, DearKnows (resident company at Home for Contemporary Theatre and Art), New York City, 1989—; founding member, NYU Works (studio for graduate acting and directing alumni of New York University's Tisch School of the Arts), 1989—.

MEMBER: Actors' Equity Association, American Federation of Television and Radio Artists, Screen Actors Guild.

ADDRESSES: AGENT—Michael Braun, Abrams Artists and Associates Ltd., 420 Madison Avenue, New York, NY 10017.

*   *   *

STANWYCK, Barbara   1907-1990

PERSONAL: Born Ruby Stevens, July 16, 1907, in Brooklyn, NY; died of heart failure, January 20, 1990, in Santa Monica, CA; daughter of Byron and Catherine (McGee) Stevens; married Frank Fay (a comedian), August 26, 1928 (divorced, 1935); married Robert Taylor (an actor), May 14, 1939 (divorced, 1951); children: Dion Anthony (first marriage; adopted).

VOCATION: Actress.

CAREER: PRINCIPAL STAGE APPEARANCES—Dancer, *Keep Kool*

BARBARA STANWYCK

(revue), Morosco Theatre, New York City, 1924; dancer, *The Ziegfeld Follies* (revue), New Amsterdam Theatre, New York City, 1925; dancer, *Gay Paree* (revue), Shubert Theatre, New York City, 1925; dancer, *George White's Scandals* (revue), Apollo Theatre, New York City, 1926; Dot, *The Noose*, Hudson Theatre, New York City, 1926; Bonny, *Burlesque*, Plymouth Theatre, New York City, 1927-29; ensemble, *Tattle Tales* (revue), Broadhurst Theatre, New York City, 1933.

MAJOR TOURS—*Ziegfeld Follies of 1923*, U.S. cities, 1923.

FILM DEBUT—Dancer, *Broadway Nights*, First National, 1927. PRINCIPAL FILM APPEARANCES—Ann Carter, *The Locked Door*, United Artists, 1929; title role, *Mexicali Rose* (also known as *Girl from Mexico*), Columbia, 1929; Kay Arnold, *Ladies of Leisure*, Columbia, 1930; Anne Vincent, *Illicit*, Warner Brothers, 1931; Florence Faith Fallon, *The Miracle Woman*, Columbia, 1931; Lora Hart, *Night Nurse*, Warner Brothers, 1931; Barbara O'Neill, *Ten Cents a Dance*, Columbia, 1931; Lulu Smith, *Forbidden*, Columbia, 1932; Joan Gordon, *The Purchase Price*, Warner Brothers, 1932; Kitty Lane, *Shopworn*, Columbia, 1932; Selina Peake Dejong, *So Big*, Warner Brothers, 1932; Lily "Baby Face" Powers, *Baby Face*, Warner Brothers, 1933; Megan Davis, *The Bitter Tea of General Yen*, Columbia, 1933; Mary, *Ever in My Heart*, Warner Brothers, 1933; Nan Taylor, *Ladies They Talk About* (also known as *Women in Prison*), Warner Brothers, 1933; Lady Lee, *Gambling Lady*, Warner Brothers, 1934; Marian Ormsby, *A Lost Lady* (also known as *Courageous*), Warner Brothers, 1934; title role, *Annie Oakley*, RKO, 1935; Drue Van Allen, *Red Salute* (also known as *Arms and the Girl, Runaway Daughter*, and *Her Enlisted Man*), United Artists, 1935; Ruth Vincent, *The Secret Bride* (also known as *Concealment*), Warner Brothers, 1935; Shelby Barrett, *The Woman in Red*, Warner Brothers/First National, 1935; Pearl, *Banjo on My Knee*, Twentieth Century-Fox, 1936; Carolyn Martin, *The Bride Walks Out*, RKO, 1936; Rita Wilson, *His Brother's Wife*, Metro-Goldwyn-Mayer (MGM), 1936; Raphaelita Maderos, *A Message to Garcia*, Twentieth Century-Fox, 1936; Nora Clitheroe, *The Plough and the Stars*, RKO, 1936; Valentine Ransome, *Breakfast for Two*, RKO, 1937; Janet Haley, *Interns Can't Take Money* (also known as *You Can't Take Money*), Paramount, 1937; title role, *Stella Dallas*, United Artists, 1937; Lil Duryea, *This Is My Affair* (also known as *His Affair*), Twentieth Century-Fox, 1937; Margot Weston, *Always Goodbye*, Twentieth Century-Fox, 1938; Melsa Manton, *The Mad Miss Manton*, RKO, 1938; Lorna Moon, *Golden Boy*, Columbia, 1939; Mollie Monaham, *Union Pacific*, Paramount, 1939.

Lee Leander, *Remember the Night*, Paramount, 1940; Sugarpuss O'Shea, *Ball of Fire*, RKO, 1941; Jean Harrington, *The Lady Eve*, Paramount, 1941; Ann Mitchell, *Meet John Doe*, Warner Brothers, 1941; Helen Hunt, *You Belong to Me* (also known as *Good Morning, Doctor*), Columbia, 1941; Fiona Gaylord, *The Gay Sisters*, Warner Brothers/First National, 1942; Hannah Sempler, *The Great Man's Lady*, Paramount, 1942; Joan Stanley, *Flesh and Fantasy*, Universal, 1943; Dixie Daisy, *Lady of Burlesque* (also known as *Strip Tease Lady*), United Artists, 1943; Phyllis Dietrichson, *Double Indemnity*, Paramount, 1944; as herself, *Hollywood Canteen*, Warner Brothers, 1944; Elisabeth Lane, *Christmas in Connecticut* (also known as *Indiscretion*), First National, 1945; Sally Warren, *The Bride Wore Boots*, Paramount, 1946; Lily Bishop, *California*, Paramount, 1946; Jessica Drummond, *My Reputation*, Warner Brothers, 1946; Martha Ivers, *The Strange Love of Martha Ivers*, Paramount, 1946; Sandra Marshall, *Cry Wolf*, Warner Brothers, 1947; Karen Duncan, *The Other Love* (also known as *Man Killer*), United Artists, 1947; Sally Morton, *The Two Mrs. Carrolls*, Warner Brothers, 1947; as herself, *Variety Girl*, Paramount, 1947; Polly Fulton, *B.F.'s Daughter* (also known as *Polly Fulton*), MGM, 1948; Leona Stevenson, *Sorry, Wrong Number*, Paramount, 1948; Jessie Bourne, *East Side, West Side*, MGM, 1949; Joan Boothe, *The Lady Gambles*, Universal, 1949.

Thelma Jordan, *The File on Thelma Jordan* (also known as *Thelma Jordan*), Paramount, 1950; Vance Jeffords, *The Furies*, Paramount, 1950; Helen Ferguson, *No Man of Her Own*, Paramount, 1950; Regina Forbes, *To Please a Lady* (also known as *Red Hot Wheels*), MGM, 1950; Lorna Bounty, *The Man with a Cloak*, MGM, 1951; Mae Doyle, *Clash By Night*, RKO, 1952; Naomi Murdoch, *All I Desire*, Universal, 1953; Marina, *Blowing Wild*, Warner Brothers, 1953; Helen Stilwin, *Jeopardy*, MGM, 1953; Rela, *The Moonlighter*, Warner Brothers, 1953; Julia Sturges, *Titanic*, Twentieth Century-Fox, 1953; Sierra Nevada Jones, *Cattle Queen of Montana*, RKO, 1954; Julia O. Tredway, *Executive Suite*, MGM, 1954; Cheryl Draper, *Witness to Murder*, United Artists, 1954; Gwen Moore, *Escape to Burma*, RKO, 1955; Martha Wilkison, *The Violent Men* (also known as *Rough Company*), Columbia, 1955; Kit Banion, *The Maverick Queen*, Republic, 1956; Norma Miller, *There's Always Tomorrow*, Universal, 1956; Ann Dempster, *These Wilder Years*, MGM, 1956; Kathy, *Crime of Passion*, United Artists, 1957; Jessica Drummond, *Forty Guns* (also known as *Woman with a Whip*), Twentieth Century-Fox, 1957; Cora Stutliff, *Trooper Hook*, United Artists, 1957; Jo Courtney, *Walk on the Wild Side*, Columbia, 1962; Irene Trent, *The Night Walker*, Universal, 1964; Maggie Morgan, *Roustabout*, Paramount, 1964. Also appeared in *Brief Moment*, Columbia, 1933; *The Lie*, 1949.

PRINCIPAL TELEVISION APPEARANCES—Series: Hostess, *The Barbara Stanwyck Show*, NBC, 1960-61; Victoria Barkley, *The Big Valley*, ABC, 1965-69; Constance Colby, *The Colbys*, ABC, 1985-86. Mini-Series: Mary Carson, *The Thorn Birds*, ABC, 1983. Pilots: Irene Frazier, *Sudden Silence* (broadcast as an episode of *Ford Theatre*), ABC, 1956; title role, *Josephine Little: The Miraculous Journey of Tadpole Chan* (broadcast as an episode of *The Barbara Stanwyck Show;* pilot for a proposed series to be called *Josephine Little*), NBC, 1960; Trixie Cochran, *Along the Barbary Coast* (broadcast as an episode of *The Barbara Stanwyck Show*), NBC, 1961; title role, *Josephine Little: Adventures in Happiness* (broadcast as an episode of *The Barbara Stanwyck Show;* second pilot for a proposed series to be called *Josephine Little*), NBC, 1961; title role, *Josephine Little: Dragon By the Tail* (broadcast as an episode of *The Barbara Stanwyck Show;* third pilot for a proposed series to be called *Josephine Little*), NBC, 1961; Lieutenant Agatha Stewart, *Elegy* (broadcast as an episode of *The Untouchables;* pilot for a proposed series to be called *The Seekers*), ABC, 1962; Lieutenant Agatha Stewart, *Search for a Dead Man* (broadcast as an episode of *The Untouchables;* second pilot for a proposed series to be called *The Seekers*), ABC, 1963; Geraldine Parkington, "The Parkington's: Dear Penelope" in *The Letters*, ABC, 1973; Antonia "Toni" Blake, *Toni's Boys* (broadcast as an episode of *Charlie's Angels*), ABC, 1980.

Episodic: Kate Crowley, "The Maud Frazer Story," *Wagon Train*, NBC, 1961; Kate Crowley, "The Caroline Casteel Story," *Wagon Train*, ABC, 1962; Kate Crowley, "The Molly Kincaid Story," *Wagon Train*, ABC, 1963; title role, "The Kate Crowley Story," *Wagon Train*, ABC, 1964; also "My Uncles O'More" and "The Waiting Game," *The Loretta Young Show*, NBC, 1955; "The Freighter" and "Trail to Nowhere," *Zane Grey Theatre* (also known as *Dick Powell's Zane Grey Theatre*), CBS, 1958; "Three Dark Years," *Goodyear Theatre*, NBC, 1958; "Sudden Silence," *Decision*, NBC, 1958; *The Jack Benny Show*, CBS, 1959; "Hang the Heart High" and "Lone Woman," *Zane Grey Theatre* (also known as *Dick Powell's Zane Grey Theatre*), CBS, 1959; *Joey Bishop Show*, NBC, 1961; "The Captain's Wife," *Rawhide*, CBS, 1962; "Special Assignment," *Dick Powell Theatre*, NBC, 1962; *Ford Television Theatre*, ABC; *Alcoa Theatre*, NBC; *The General Electric Theatre*, CBS. Movies: Ruth Bennett, *The House That Would Not Die*, ABC, 1970; Miriam Jannings, *A Taste of Evil*, ABC, 1971. Specials: *The American Film Institute Salute to Henry Fonda*, CBS, 1978; *The American Film Institute Salute to Barbara Stanwyck*, ABC, 1987.

PRINCIPAL RADIO APPEARANCES—Episodic: *Lux Radio Theatre*, NBC (fifteen episodes); *Nobody's Children*, Mutual; *Screen Guild Theatre*, CBS; *The Edgar Bergen and Charlie McCarthy Show*, NBC.

RELATED CAREER—Founder, Barwyck Corporation (a production company), 1956; also appeared in nightclubs as a dancer and chorus girl.

NON-RELATED CAREER—Gift wrapper in a department store, telephone operator, pattern cutter, and file clerk.

AWARDS: Academy Award nomination, Best Actress, 1937, for *Stella Dallas;* Academy Award nomination, Best Actress, 1941, for *Ball of Fire;* Academy Award nomination, Best Actress, 1944, for *Double Indemnity;* Academy Award nomination, Best Actress, 1948, for *Sorry, Wrong Number;* Special Jury Prize (with cast) from the Venice Film Festival for Ensemble Acting, 1954, for *Executive Suite;* Emmy Award, Outstanding Performance By a

Leading Actress in a Series, 1961, for *The Barbara Stanwyck Show;* Golden Apple Star of the Year Award from the Hollywood Women's Press Club, 1961; Emmy Award, Outstanding Continued Performance By an Actress in a Leading Role in a Dramatic Series, 1966, for *The Big Valley;* honored by the Film Society of Lincoln Center, 1981, for career-long excellence; special honorary Academy Award, 1982; Emmy Award, Outstanding Lead Actress in a Limited Series or a Special, 1983, and Golden Globe, Best Performance By an Actress in a Supporting Role (Mini-Series or Motion Picture Made for Television), 1984, both for *The Thorn Birds;* Cecil B. De Mille Award from the Hollywood Foreign Press Association, 1986; Life Achievement Award from the American Film Institute, 1987.

OBITUARIES AND OTHER SOURCES: [New York] *Daily News,* January 22, 1990; *Hollywood Reporter,* January 22, 1990; *New York Times,* January 22, 1990; *Variety,* January 24, 1990.*

*   *   *

STEAFEL, Sheila   1935-

PERSONAL: Surname rhymes with "Steeple"; born May 26, 1935; daughter of Harold (a singer, inventor, engineer, and harp maker) and Eda (a pianist; maiden name, Cohen) Steafel; married Harry H. Corbett, October 10, 1958 (divorced, August, 1964). EDUCATION—Attended the University of Witwatersrand (Johannesburg, South Africa), 1951-52; trained for the stage at the Webber-Douglas Drama School in London, 1955-57.

VOCATION: Actress.

CAREER: STAGE DEBUT—Players Theatre, London. PRINCIPAL STAGE APPEARANCES—Ensemble, *Splits on the Infinitive* (revue), Hampstead Theatre Club, London, 1965; ensemble, *Anyone for England?* (revue), Lyric Hammersmith Theatre, London, 1965; Olga, *The Three Sisters,* Leicester Repertory Theatre, Leicester, U.K., 1970; Magda, *Jump,* Queen's Theatre, London, 1971; Lady Margery Panton, *You'll Never Be Michelangelo,* Hampstead Theatre Club, 1976; Timothy's mother, Heloise, Asphynxia, and Marguerite, *Salad Days,* Windsor Theatre, then Duke of York's Theatre, both London, 1976; Enid Blyton, *Balmoral,* Guildford, U.K., 1978; Harpo Marx, *A Day in Hollywood, A Night in the Ukraine,* New End Theatre, then May Fair Theatre, both London, 1979; *The Late Sheila Steafel* (one-woman show), New End Theatre, then Edinburgh Festival, Scotland, both 1981; *Steafel Solo* (one-woman show), King's Head Theatre, London, 1981-82, then Adelaide Festival, Australia, 1982; *Steafel Revisited* (one-woman show), Edinburgh Festival, 1982; *Steafel Variations* (one-woman show), Apollo Theatre, London, 1982; *Steafel Lately* (one-woman show), Edinburgh Festival, 1983; the Witch, *Hansel and Gretel* (opera), Bloomsbury Theatre, London, 1983; *Steafel Express* (one-woman show), Ambassadors' Theatre, London, 1985; Mistress Quickly, *Merry Wives of Windsor,* Royal Shakespeare Company (RSC), Barbican Theatre, London, 1986 and 1987.

Also appeared in *The Guardsman,* Watford Theatre, 1969; *Billy Liar,* London, 1960; *Headful of Crocodiles* and *Man with the Iron Chest,* both Armchair Theatre, 1965; *How the Other Half Loves,* Leicester Repertory Theatre, 1970; *Who's Who?,* Coventry Repertory Theatre, Coventry, U.K., 1971; *How the Other Half Loves,* Lyric Theatre, London, then Alexandra Theatre, Toronto, ON, Canada, both 1972; *Old Times,* Bristol Old Vic Theatre, Bristol, U.K., 1974; *Old Time Music Hall,* Players Theatre, London, 1974; *Twelfth Night,* and *The Duenna,* both Young Vic Theatre, London, 1983; *Adrian Mole,* Leicester Theatre, 1984; *Starbreakers,* 1984; *Merry Wives of Windsor* and *Candle Bearer,* both RSC, Stratford-on-Avon, U.K., 1985; *Facade* (opera), London Mozart Players, 1986; *Ivanov* and *Much Ado About Nothing,* Strand Theatre, London, 1989; and in repertory in Lincoln, Hunstanton, and Blackpool, U.K., 1956-59.

MAJOR TOURS—*Landscape with Figures,* U.K. cities, 1958; *Milk and Honey,* U.K. cities, 1959; *Jump,* U.K. cities, 1971; *No Room for Sex,* U.K. cities, 1975.

PRINCIPAL FILM APPEARANCES—Isolde, *Just Like a Woman,* Monarch, 1967; journalist, *Five Million Years to Earth* (also known as *Quatermass and the Pit*), Twentieth Century-Fox, 1968; Tessa Pearson, *Baby Love,* AVCO-Embassy, 1969; Tilly, *Goodbye Mr. Chips,* Metro-Goldwyn-Mayer (MGM), 1969; ground stewardess, *Otley,* Columbia, 1969; Tania, *Tropic of Cancer,* Paramount, 1970; Sheila Wilcott, *Some Will, Some Won't,* Williams and Pritchard, 1970; woman in elevator, *Catch Me a Spy,* Rank, 1971; Latimer, *Melody* (also known as *S.W.A.L.K.*), Levitt-Pickman, 1971; Mrs. Gold, *Percy,* MGM, 1971; control operator, *Digby, the Biggest Dog in the World,* Cinerama, 1974; Dr. Pitt, *What's Up Superdoc,* Entertainment Film Distributors, 1978; Sheila Finch, *Bloodbath at the House of Death,* EMI, 1984. Also appeared in *The Waiting Room,* 1976; as voice of Maisie and Marlon, *The Perishers* (animated), 1978; and in *Towers of Babel* (short film), 1981.

SHEILA STEAFEL

TELEVISION DEBUT—*Kipps*, Granada, 1964. PRINCIPAL TELE-VISION APPEARANCES—Series: Miss Pennypacker, *Justin Thyme*, BBC, 1964; White Lady, *Ghosts of Motley Hall*, Granada, 1975-78; Miranda, *You Must Be the Husband*, BBC, 1987; also *It's Dark Outside*, Granada, 1965; *The Frost Report*, 1966; *Illustrated Weekly Hudd*, BBC, 1968; *Horne a Plenty*, ABC (U.K.), 1968; *Beachcomber*, BBC, 1969; *How's Your Father?*, Granada, 1974; Popsy Wopsy, Emmaline, and other roles, *Good Old Days*, 1975-78 and 1981; *Q 7*, 1978 and 1981; *Can We Get On Now Please?*, Granada, 1980; *Bluebirds*, BBC, 1989. Mini-Series: Carrie, *Diary of a Nobody*, BBC-2, 1978.

Episodic: Title role, "The Fabulous Frump," *Wednesday Play*, BBC, 1969; also *Frankie Howerd Show*, BBC, 1968; *The Dickie Henderson Show*, ATV, 1968; *The Beryl Reid Show*, 1978; *The Leslie Crowther Show*, 1978; wicked television director, *Jackanory Playhouse*, 1980; *Rainbow*, 1980; *Give Us a Clue* (game show), 1980; *321*, Yorkshire Television, 1980 and 1981; "Supergran," *Jackanory Playhouse*, 1981; *Live on Two*, Granada, 1981; *Punchlines* (game show for *Weekend*), 1981 and 1983; *The Kenny Everett Show*, 1982; *Call My Bluff*, 1982 and 1983; *Celebrity Squares*, 1983; miserable mum, *Z-Cars*, BBC; *De Maupassant Stories*, Granada. Specials: *Cowboys*, Thames, 1980; also *Good Old Days Jubilee Program*, 1977; *The Frankie Howerd Special*, 1980; *Sheila* (one-woman show), Channel Four, 1982. Also appeared in *The Sebrof Story*, ABC, 1973; *Go for Gold*, BBC, 1973; *Second Time Around*, BBC, 1974; *Let's Make a Musical: History of Mr. Polly*, 1977; *Quiz Kids*, ATV, 1978, *In Loving Memory*, Yorkshire Television, 1979; *Honky Tonk Heroes*, 1979; as Joan, *Time and the Conways*, Granada; *Bicycle*, *The Liars*, Granada; in *The Way of All Flesh*, Granada; *Whoopee Cushion*, BBC; *Troubleshooters*, ATV; *A Fat Woman's Tale*, Granada; and *Close Prisoner*.

PRINCIPAL RADIO APPEARANCES—Series: *Week Ending*, Radio 4, 1977; *Jason Explanation*, Radio 4, 1978 and 1980; also *My Sainted Aunt*, 1978. Specials: *Steafel Plus*, Radio 4, 1982; *Steafel with an S.*, 1984.

AWARDS: Golden Rose of Montreux, 1966.

ADDRESSES: AGENT—Ken McReddie, 91 Regent Street, London, W1.

* * *

STERNHAGEN, Frances   1930-

PERSONAL: Full name, Frances Hussey Sternhagen; born January 13, 1930, in Washington, DC; daughter of John M. (a U.S. tax court judge) and Gertrude S. (Wyckoff) Sternhagen; married Thomas A. Carlin, February 13, 1956; children: six. EDUCATION—Vassar College, B.A., 1951; graduate work, Catholic University, 1952; studied at the Perry-Mansfield School of Theatre and with Sanford Meisner at the Neighborhood Playhouse.

VOCATION: Actress.

CAREER: STAGE DEBUT—Laura, *The Glass Menagerie* and Mrs. Manningham, *Angel Street*, both Bryn Mawr Summer Theatre, Bryn Mawr, PA, 1948. OFF-BROADWAY DEBUT—Eva, *Thieves' Carnival*, Cherry Lane Theatre, 1955. LONDON DEBUT—*The War at Home*, Hempstead Theatre Club, 1985. PRINCIPAL STAGE APPEARANCES—Margery Pinchwife, *The Country Wife*, Mrs.

Webb, *Our Town*, Nancy Stoddard, *The Country Girl*, Phyllis Carmichael, *My Heart's in the Highlands*, Juliette, *Thieves' Carnival*, Doto, *A Phoenix Too Frequent*, and Ma Kirby, *The Happy Journey from Trenton to Camden*, all Arena Stage, Washington, DC, 1953; Muriel, *Ah! Wilderness* and Elvira, *Blithe Spirit*, both Arena Stage, 1954; Lavinia Chamberlayne, *The Cocktail Party*, Ann, *Outward Bound*, Georgie Elgin, *The Country Girl*, and Lady Ariadne Utterwood, *Heartbreak House*, all Olney Theatre, Olney, MD, 1954; Miss T. Muse, *The Skin of Our Teeth*, Theatre Sarah Bernhardt, Paris, France, then American National Theatre and Academy Theatre, New York City, both 1955; Widow Yang, *The Carefree Tree*, Phoenix Theatre, New York City, 1955; Lydia Carew, *The Admirable Bashville*, Cherry Lane Theatre, New York City, 1956; Gretchen, *Faust*, Theatre-on-the-Green, Wellesley, MA, 1956; Margery Pinchwife, *The Country Wife*, Renata Theatre, New York City, 1957; Nymph, *Ulysses in Nighttown*, Rooftop Theatre, New York City, 1958; title role, *The Saintliness of Margery Kempe*, York Theatre, New York City, 1959.

Dee Jones, *Viva Madison Avenue!*, Longacre Theatre, New York City, 1960; Selma Chargesse, *Red Eye of Love*, Provincetown Playhouse, New York City, 1960; Gwendolyn, *The Importance of Being Earnest*, McCarter Theatre, Princeton, NJ, 1960; Hypatia Tarleton, *Misalliance*, Sheridan Square Theatre, New York City, 1961; Alice McAnany, *Great Day in the Morning*, Henry Miller's Theatre, New York City, 1962; Mrs. Levi, *The Matchmaker*, Olney Theatre, 1962; Sabina, *The Skin of Our Teeth*, Brandeis Forum Theatre, Brandeis University, Waltham, MA, 1963; Lois, *A Matter of Like Life and Death*, East End Theatre, New York City, 1963; Jan, *Play*, Cherry Lane Theatre, 1964; Rose, "The Room" and Flora, "A Slight Ache" in *The New Pinter Plays*, Writers Stage Theatre, New York City, 1964; Susan Throssel, *Quality Street*, Bucks County Playhouse, New Hope, PA, 1965; Mrs. Ashton Dilke, *The Right Honourable Gentleman*, Billy Rose Theatre, New York City, 1965; Mrs. Hopewell, *The Displaced Person*, American Place Theatre, St. Clement's Church Theatre, New York City, 1966; Lavinia Chaberlayne, *The Cocktail Party*, APA Phoenix Theatre Company, Lyceum Theatre, New York City, 1968; Jan Loreleen, *Cock-a-Doodly Dandy*, APA Phoenix Theatre Company, Lyceum Theatre, 1969.

Widow Quinn, *Playboy of the Western World*, Vivian Beaumont Theatre, New York City, 1971; Mavis Parodus Bryson, *The Sign in Sidney Brustein's Window*, Longacre Theatre, 1972; Paulina, *Enemies*, Repertory Theatre of Lincoln Center, Vivian Beaumont Theatre, 1972; various roles, *The Good Doctor*, Eugene O'Neill Theatre, New York City, 1973; Dora Strang, *Equus*, Plymouth Theatre, New York City, 1974; Eliza Gant, *Angel*, Minskoff Theatre, New York City, 1978; Ethel Thayer, *On Golden Pond*, New Apollo Century Theatre, New York City, 1979; title role, *The Prevalence of Mrs. Seal*, Manhattan Punchline, New York City, 1980; Laura, *The Father*, Circle in the Square, New York City, 1981; Helen, *Grownups*, Lyceum Theatre, 1981; Xenia, *Summer*, Manhattan Theatre Club, New York City, 1982; Miss Prism, *The Importance of Being Earnest*, John Drew Theatre, East Hampton, NY, 1983; Penny, *You Can't Take It with You*, Royale Theatre, New York City, 1984; Sarah, "Goodbye, Howard," Constance Lindell, "F.M.," and Old Woman, "Tennessee" in *Laughing Stock*, Manhattan Punchline, 1984; Maurine, *Home Front*, Royale Theatre, 1985; Florence, *The Return of Herbert Bracewill*, Chelsea Playhouse, New York City, 1985; Constance Oakshot, *Oliver Oliver*, Manhattan Theatre Club, City Center Theatre, New York City, 1985; Marjorie Newquist, *Little Murders*, Second Stage Theatre, New York City, 1987; title role, *Driving Miss Daisy*, Houseman Theatre, New York City, 1988. Also appeared in *The*

Dining Room, Kennedy Center for the Performing Arts, Washington, DC, 1981.

MAJOR TOURS—Mrs. T. Muse, *The Skin of Our Teeth,* U.S. cities, 1955; Opal, "The Isle of Cipango" and Postmistress, "Pound on Demand" in *Triple Play,* U.S. cities, both 1958; Miss Madrigal, *The Chalk Garden,* U.S. cities, 1960.

FILM DEBUT—Charlotte Wolf, *Up the Down Staircase,* Warner Brothers, 1967. PRINCIPAL FILM APPEARANCES—Lady on bus, *The Tiger Makes Out,* Columbia, 1967; Mrs. Cushing, *The Hospital,* United Artists, 1971; Mrs. McCluskey, *Two People,* Universal, 1973; Miss Balfour, *Fedora,* United Artists, 1978; Marva Potter, *Starting Over,* Paramount, 1979; Dr. Lazarus, *Outland,* Warner Brothers, 1981; Carla Taylor, *Independence Day,* Warner Brothers, 1983; Blanche, *Romantic Comedy,* Metro-Goldwyn-Mayer/United Artists, 1983; as herself, *Sanford Meisner—The Theatre's Best Kept Secret* (documentary), Columbia, 1984; Clara Tillinghast, *Bright Lights, Big City,* United Artists, 1988; Neenie, *See You in the Morning,* Warner Brothers, 1989; Dr. Janet Duffy, *Communion,* Vestron, 1989.

TELEVISION DEBUT—Nellie, "The Great Bank Robbery," *Omnibus,* CBS, 1955. PRINCIPAL TELEVISION APPEARANCES—Series: Toni Prentiss Davis, *Love of Life,* CBS, 1967-68; Phyllis Corrigan, *The Doctors,* NBC, 1970; Jessie Reddin, *The Secret Storm,* CBS, 1973-74; Millie Sprague, *Under One Roof,* NBC, 1985; also Jane Overstreet, *Another World,* NBC. Episodic: Eva, "Thieves' Carnival" and Miss Mabee, "In a Garden," both *Play of the Week,* WNTA, 1961; Wilma Atkins, "The Rimers of Eldritch," *Theatre in America,* PBS, 1972; Paulina, "Enemies," *Theatre in America,* PBS, 1974; Esther Clavin, *Cheers,* NBC, 1986 and 1987; also *Camera Three,* CBS; *Lamp Unto My Feet,* CBS; *The Nurses,* CBS; *The Defenders,* CBS; *Robert Montgomery Presents,* NBC; *Alcoa Hour,* NBC; *Studio One,* CBS; *The House on High Street,* NBC; *Profiles in Courage,* NBC; *For the People,* CBS; *Look Up and Live,* CBS; *Directions,* ABC. Movies: Nellie Henderson, *Who'll Save Our Children?,* CBS, 1978; Mrs. Lloyd, *Mother and Daughter: The Loving War,* ABC, 1980; Dorothy Forrester, *Prototype,* CBS, 1983; Eudora McAlister, *Resting Place,* CBS, 1986; also Berenice Bradshaw, *At Mother's Request,* 1987. Specials: Sue, "Where the Cross Is Made," *Three in One,* NBC, 1960; Harriet Beecher Stowe, *Sojourner,* CBS, 1975; also *How He Lied to Her Husband,* 1965; *T.S. Eliot—The Wasteland,* 1965.

RELATED CAREER—Drama teacher, Milton Academy, Milton MA.

AWARDS: Obie Award from the *Village Voice* and Clarence Derwent Award, both 1956, for *The Admirable Bashville;* Obie Award, 1957, for *The Country Wife;* Obie Award, 1965, for "The Room" and "A Slight Ache" in *The New Pinter Plays;* Antoinette Perry Award, Best Supporting or Featured Actress in a Play, 1974, for *The Good Doctor;* Antionette Perry Award nomination, Best Supporting or Featured Actress in a Play, 1975, for *Equus;* Antoinette Perry Award nomination, Best Actress in a Musical, 1978, for *Angel;* Antoinette Perry Award nomination, Best Actress in a Play, 1979, for *On Golden Pond.*

MEMBER: Actors' Equity Association, Screen Actors Guild, American Federation of Television and Radio Artists.

SIDELIGHTS: FAVORITE ROLES—Margery Pinchwife in *The Country Wife,* Sabina in *The Skin of Our Teeth,* Dora Strang in

Equus, and Ethel Thayer in *On Golden Pond.* RECREATIONS—Singing, painting, swimming, sailing.

ADDRESSES: AGENT—Triad Artists, 888 Seventh Avenue, New York, NY 10019.*

*   *   *

STEVENS, Scooter   1973-

PERSONAL: Born April, 1973, in Los Angeles, CA; son of Nina Cohn. EDUCATION—Studied acting with Randy Stone, Terrance Hines, and Don Frankel.

VOCATION: Actor.

CAREER: PRINCIPAL STAGE APPEARANCES—*Too Short for Prime Time Players,* Roxy Theatre, Los Angeles.

FILM DEBUT—*Private Benjamin,* Warner Brothers, 1980. PRINCIPAL FILM APPEARANCES—Badger Myer, *Better Off Dead,* Warner Brothers, 1985; Bonnie's date, *She's Out of Control,* Columbia, 1989; also appeared in *Something Wicked This Way Comes,* Buena Vista, 1983; *Casual Sex?,* Universal, 1988.

PRINCIPAL TELEVISION APPEARANCES—Series: Regular, *Pryor's Place,* CBS, 1984. Pilots: *Making It,* NBC, 1976; *Scamps,* NBC, 1982. Episodic: "The Last Car," *Tales from the Darkside,* syndi-

SCOOTER STEVENS

cated, 1979; *Blacke's Magic*, NBC, 1986; *Coming of Age*, CBS, 1988; also *Archie Bunker's Place*, CBS; *Gloria*, CBS; *Three's Company*, ABC; *CHiPS*, NBC; *Best of the West*, ABC; *Trapper John, M.D.*, CBS; *My Sister Sam*, CBS; *Sidekicks*, ABC; *Punky Brewster*, NBC; *Small Wonder*, syndicated; *You Can't Take It with You*, syndicated; *Our House*, NBC; *Diff'rent Strokes*, NBC; *Hill Street Blues*, NBC; *St. Elsewhere*, NBC; *Night Court*, NBC. Movies: *A Girl Named Sooner*, NBC, 1975. Specials: David Miller, "Have You Tried Talking to Patty?," *CBS Schoolbreak Special*, CBS, 1986.

RELATED CAREER—Voiceover artist and actor in television commercials.

MEMBER: Screen Actors Guild, American Federation of Television and Radio Artists.

ADDRESSES: AGENT—Twentieth Century Artists, 3800 Barham Boulevard, Suite 303, Los Angeles, CA 90068. MANAGER—Joycelyn Engle, P.O. Box 7703, Beverly Hills, CA 90212.

*   *   *

STEWART, Alexandra   1939-

PERSONAL: Born June 10, 1939, in Montreal, PQ, Canada.

VOCATION: Actress.

CAREER: PRINCIPAL FILM APPEARANCES—Jordana, *Exodus*, United Artists, 1960; Laurie, *Tarzan the Magnificent*, Paramount, 1960; Fifine, *L'eau a la bouche* (also known as *A Game for Six Lovers* and *Games for Six Lovers*), 1960, released in the United States by Falcon, 1962; Belle, *La Mort de Belle* (also known as *The Passion of Slow Fire* and *The End of Belle*), 1961, released in the United States by Trans-Lux Distributing, 1962; Helene, *Les Mauvais coups* (also known as *Naked Autumn*), 1961, released in the United States by United Motion Picture Organization, 1963; Sandra, *La Morte-saison des amours* (also known as *The Season for Love*), 1961, released in the United States by Gaston Hakim, 1963; Solange, *Le Feu follet* (also known as *Fuoco fatuo* and *The Fire Within*), 1963, released in the United States by Governor, 1964; Anna, *Dragees au poivre* (also known as *Confetti al Pepe* and *Sweet and Sour*), 1963, released in the United States by Pathe, 1964; Brigitte, *Das Grosse Liebesspiel* (also known as *And So to Bed*), 1963, released in the United States by Medallion, 1965; Jenny, *Mickey One*, Columbia, 1965; Michele Craig, *Maroc Seven*, Paramount, 1967; Liz, *Only When I Larf*, Paramount, 1968; Miss Becker, *La Mariee etait en noir* (also known as *The Bride Wore Black* and *La sposa in nero*), 1968, released in the United States by Lopert, 1968; Caroline, *Waiting for Caroline*, 1967, released in the United States by Lopert, 1969; Eve, *Bye Bye Barbara*, Paramount, 1969.

Marisa, *Kemek*, GHM, 1970; woman, *Valparaiso, Valparaiso!*, Films de la Commune, 1970; Frances, *The Man Who Had Power Over Women*, AVCO-Embassy, 1970; Stephanie Ross, *Zeppelin*, Warner Brothers, 1971; Alexandra, *Ou est passe Tom?* (also known as *Where Did Tom Go?*), Valoria, 1971; wife, *Far from Dallas*, J.P. Faure, 1972; Feodora, *Niet voor de poesen* (also known as *Because of the Cats*), Cinevog, 1972; Alexandra, *Les Soleils de l'ile de Paques* (also known as *The Suns of Easter Island*), Films 13, 1972; Stacey, *La Nuit Americaine* (also known as *Day for Night*),

Warner Brothers/Columbia, 1973; Rita, *The Destructors* (also known as *The Marseilles Contract*), American International, 1974; sister, *Black Moon*, Twentieth Century-Fox, 1975; Mrs. Blake, *The Uncanny*, Rank, 1977; Delphine, *Julie pot de colle* (also known as *Julie Glue Pot*), Davis/Societe nouvelle prodis, 1977; Paula, *In Praise of Older Women*, AVCO-Embassy, 1978; Theo, *Le Petite fille en velours bleu* (also known as *The Little Girl in Blue Velvet*), Orphee Arts/Columbia-Warner Distributors, 1978; Sandra, *Le Soleil en face* (also known as *Face to the Sun*), Union Generale Cinematographique, 1979.

Dorothee, *Goodbye Emmanuelle*, Miramax, 1980; Sam O'Donnell, *Final Assignment*, Inter-Ocean, 1980; Barbara, *Phobia*, Paramount, 1980; Mimi Oliveri, *Agency*, Farley, 1981; Madame Claude, *Madame Claude 2*, Societe nouvelle de cinema/New Realm Distributors, 1981; Eudora, *The Last Chase*, Crown International, 1981; narrator (English narration), *Sans Soleil* (also known as *Sunless*), The Other Cinema/Argos/New Yorker, 1982; Julie, *Le Bon plaisir*, MK2, 1984; narrator (English narration), *Kusameikyu* (short film), Toei Company, 1984; Mademoiselle Lydie, *Le Matou* (also known as *The Alley Cat*), Viva/Cinevideo, 1985; Helena Werner, *Peau d'ange* (also known as *Angel Skin*), Films de l'Atalante/Zora, 1986; Mrs. Sharon, *Under the Cherry Moon*, Warner Brothers, 1986; Edie, *Frantic*, Warner Brothers, 1988; Mrs. Cornfield, *Welcome to Germany*, Film Four, 1988; Madame Dubois-lacour, *Monsieur*, Bac Films, 1990. Also appeared in *Les Motards*, 1958; *Les Liaisons dangereuses* (also known as *Relazioni Pericolose* and *Dangerous Love Affairs*), 1959, released in the United States by Astor, 1961; *Marcia Nuziale*, 1965; *Chanel Solitaire*, United Film Distribution, 1981; *Charlots Connection*, Films du Scorpion, 1983; *Femmes*, Cine 7, 1983.

PRINCIPAL TELEVISION APPEARANCES—Mini-Series: Mary Jane Kilkullen, *Mistral's Daughter*, CBS, 1984; Countess, *Sins*, CBS, 1986. Episodic: *The Hitchhiker*, HBO, 1983. Movies: Madeleine, *The Blood of Others*, HBO, 1984; also *Champagne Charlie*, syndicated, 1989.*

*   *   *

STEWART, James
See GRANGER, Stewart

*   *   *

STOLER, Shirley   1929-

PERSONAL: Born March 30, 1929, in Brooklyn, NY.

VOCATION: Actress.

CAREER: STAGE DEBUT—*Young Disciple*, New York City, 1955. PRINCIPAL STAGE APPEARANCES—Annunziata, *The Breaking Wall*, St. Mark's Playhouse, New York City, 1960; Miss McCutcheon, "Balls" in *First Evening of New Playwrights*, Cherry Lane Theatre, New York City, 1965; Dvoira, *Sunset*, Brooklyn Academy of Music, Brooklyn, NY, 1972; Charlotte, *Lolita*, Brooks Atkinson Theatre, New York City, 1981; Hannah, *Crossing Delancey*, Jewish Repertory Theatre, New York City, 1985. Also appeared in *No Corner in Heaven* and *Can You See a Prince*, both in New York City.

PRINCIPAL FILM APPEARANCES—Martha Beck, *The Honeymoon Killers* (also known as *The Lonely Hearts Killers*), Cinerama, 1969; Mama Reese, *Klute*, Warner Brothers, 1971; Hilde, *Seven Beauties* (also known as *Pasqualino settebellezze* and *Pasqualino: Seven Beauties*), Cinema V, 1976; L'Epiciere, *Une Vraie juene fille*, Art et Gestion Cinematographiques, 1977; Steven's mother, *The Deer Hunter*, Universal, 1978; Trish, *Below the Belt*, Atlantic, 1980; Corky, *Seed of Innocence* (also known as *Teen Mothers*), Cannon, 1980; Maxy, *Second-Hand Hearts* (also known as *Hamsters of Happiness*), Paramount, 1981; Dean Hunta, *Splitz*, Film Ventures, 1984; jail matron, *Desperately Seeking Susan*, Orion, 1985; Eva, *Three O'Clock High*, Universal, 1987; Irma, *Shakedown*, Universal, 1988; Reeba, *Sticky Fingers*, Spectrafilm, 1988; German housewife, *Sons*, Manley, 1989.

PRINCIPAL TELEVISION APPEARANCES—Series: Dottie Jessup, *Skag*, NBC, 1980. Pilots: Woman in window, *Brass*, CBS, 1985. Episodic: Mrs. Steve, *Pee-Wee's Playhouse*, CBS, 1986; Adah Boone, *In the Heat of the Night*, NBC, 1989. Specials: Mrs. Shortley, "The Displaced Person," *The American Short Story*, PBS, 1977; roller rink cashier, *Snowbound*, NBC, 1978.*

*   *   *

STORARO, Vittorio   1940-

PERSONAL: Born in 1940 in Rome, Italy. EDUCATION—Studied photography at Duca D'Aosta; graduated from Italian Cinemagraphic Training Center; also attended Centro Sperimentale di Cinematografia.

VOCATION: Cinematographer.

CAREER: PRINCIPAL FILM WORK—Cinematographer: *Giovinezza, giovinezza* (also known as *Youthful, Youthful* and *Youth March*), Daniela, 1969; *La strategia del ragno* (also known as *The Spider's Strategem* and *The Spider's Strategy*), RAI-TV Channel 1/Artificial Eye, 1969; *L'ucello dalle piume di cristallo* (also known as *The Bird with the Crystal Plumage*, *The Gallery Murders*, and *The Phantom of Terror*), UM, 1969; *Il conformista* (also known as *The Conformist*), Paramount, 1971; *Orlando furioso*, RAI-TV Channel 1/NOC, 1971; *Corpo d'amore* (also known as *Body of Love*), Julia Cinematografica/Capricorno/RTR, 1971; *Last Tango in Paris*, United Artists, 1972; *Giordano Bruno*, Euro International, 1973; *Addio fratello crudele* (also known as '*Tis a Pity She's a Whore*), Euro International, 1973; *Malizia* (also known as *Malicious* and *Malice*), Paramount, 1974; *Identikit* (also known as *The Driver's Seat*), AVCO-Embassy, 1975; *1900* (also known as *Novecento*), Paramount/United Artists/Twentieth Century-Fox, 1976; *Scandalo* (also known as *Submission*), Joseph Brenner Associates, 1977; *Agatha*, Warner Brothers, 1979; *Apocalypse Now*, United Artists, 1979; *La Luna* (also known as *Luna*) Twentieth Century-Fox, 1979.

Reds, Paramount, 1981; (with Ronald V. Garcia) *One from the Heart*, Columbia, 1982; *Wagner*, Alan Landsberg, 1983; *Ladyhawke*, Warner Brothers/Twentieth Century-Fox, 1985; *Ishtar*, Columbia, 1987; *The Last Emperor*, Columbia, 1987; *Tucker: The Man and His Dream*, Paramount, 1988; "Life without Zoe" in *New York Stories*, Touchstone, 1989. Also *Etruscologia* (short film; also known as *Profanatori di tombe*), 1961; *L'urlo* (short film), 1965; *Sortilegio* (short film), 1966; *Il laborinto* (short film), 1966; *Sirtaki* (short film), 1966; *Rapporto segreto* (short film), 1967; *Sed Lodge* (short film), 1968; *Delitto al circolo del tennis*, 1969; *L'Eneide*,

1970; *Giornata nera per l'ariete*, 1971; *Bleu gang . . .*, 1972; *I grandi naif jugoslavi* (short film), 1973; *Le orme*, 1974.

PRINCIPAL TELEVISION APPEARANCES—Specials: *Omnibus*, ABC, 1988. PRINCIPAL TELEVISION WORK—Mini-Series: Cinematographer, *Peter the Great*, NBC, 1986.

RELATED CAREER—Lighting and photographic consultant, *Captain Eo* (3-D film shown exclusively at Disney World, Orlando, FL, and Disney Land, Anaheim, CA), 1986; photography studio apprentice; assistant to photographers Aldo Scavarda and Marco Scarpelli.

AWARDS: Academy Award, Best Cinematography, 1979, for *Apocalypse Now;* Academy Award, Best Cinematography, 1981, for *Reds;* Academy Award, Best Cinematography, 1988, for *The Last Emperor.**

*   *   *

STRADLING, Harry, Jr.   1925-

PERSONAL: Born January 7, 1925, in New York, NY; son of Harry Stradling (a cinematographer).

VOCATION: Cinematographer.

CAREER: PRINCIPAL FILM WORK—Cinematographer: *Welcome to Hard Times* (also known as *Killer on a Horse*), Metro-Goldwyn-Mayer (MGM), 1967; (with Ellsworth Fredricks) *With Six You Get Eggroll* (also known as *A Man in Mommy's Bed*), National General, 1968; *The Good Guys and the Bad Guys*, Warner Brothers, 1969; *The Mad Room*, Columbia, 1969; *Support Your Local Sheriff*, United Artists, 1969; *Young Billy Young* (also known as *Who Rides with Kane*), United Artists, 1969; *There Was a Crooked Man*, Warner Brothers, 1970; *Dirty Dingus Magee*, MGM, 1970; *Little Big Man*, National General, 1970; *The Late Liz*, Gateway, 1971; *Fools' Parade*, Columbia, 1971; *Something Big*, National General, 1971; *Support Your Local Gunfighter*, United Artists, 1971; *Sky-jacked* (also known as *Sky Terror*), MGM, 1972; *1776*, Columbia, 1972; *Thumb Tripping*, AVCO-Embassy, 1972; *The Way We Were*, Columbia, 1973; *The Man Who Loved Cat Dancing*, MGM, 1973; *Nightmare Honeymoon*, MGM, 1973; *McQ*, Warner Brothers, 1974; *Bank Shot*, United Artists, 1974; *Mitchell*, Allied Artists, 1975; *Bite the Bullet*, Columbia, 1975; *Rooster Cogburn*, Universal, 1975; *The Big Bus*, Paramount, 1976; *Midway* (also known as *The Battle of Midway*), Universal, 1976; *Special Delivery*, American International, 1976; *Damnation Alley*, Twentieth Century-Fox, 1977; *Airport '77*, Universal, 1977; *The Greatest*, Columbia, 1977; *Born Again*, AVCO-Embassy, 1978; *Go Tell the Spartans*, AVCO-Embassy, 1978; *Convoy*, United Artists, 1978; *Prophecy*, Paramount, 1979; *Up the Academy* (also known as *Mad Magazine's Up the Academy* and *The Brave Young Men of Weinberg*), Warner Brothers, 1980; *Carny*, United Artists, 1980; *Buddy Buddy*, United Artists, 1981; *The Pursuit of D.B. Cooper*, Universal, 1981; *S.O.B.*, Paramount, 1981; *O'Hara's Wife*, Davis-Panzer, 1983; *Micki and Maude*, Columbia, 1984; *Blind Date*, New Line Cinema, 1984; *A Fine Mess*, Columbia, 1986; *Caddyshack II*, Warner Brothers, 1988.

PRINCIPAL TELEVISION WORK—Mini-Series: Cinematographer, *George Washington*, CBS, 1984.

RELATED CAREER—Camera assistant.*

*   *   *

STRATHAIRN, David

VOCATION: Actor.

CAREER: PRINCIPAL STAGE APPEARANCES—Bobby, *Einstein and the Polar Bear*, Hartford Stage Company, Hartford, CT, 1981; Ricky Jim, *Blue Plate Special*, Manhattan Theatre Club, New York City, 1983; Emil, "Saxophone Music" in *One-Act Play Marathon '84*, Ensemble Studio Theatre, New York City, 1984; Wilson, Frank, Tewson, and Geoffrey, *Fen*, New York Shakespeare Festival (NYSF), Public Theatre, New York City, 1984; Nehemiah Byron, "My Life in Art" in *The New Directors Project*, Perry Street Theatre, New York City, 1984; Cowboy, *I'm Not Rappaport*, Seattle Repertory Theatre, Seattle, WA, 1984-85; Ben, *Salonika*, NYSF, Public Theatre, 1985; Boris, *The Sea Gull*, Eisenhower Theatre, Kennedy Center for the Performing Arts, Washington, DC, 1986; Jake, *A Lie of the Mind*, Promenade Theatre, New York City, 1985-86; Nils, *A Doll's House*, Hartford Stage Company, 1986; Stanley, *The Birthday Party*, Classic Stage Company, CSC Theatre, New York City, 1988; Gilbert, *The Cezanne Syndrome*, SoHo Repertory Theatre, New York City, 1989; officer, *Mountain Language* and Stanley, *The Birthday Party* (double-bill), Classic Stage Company, CSC Theatre, 1989. Also appeared in *About Spontaneous Combustion*, New Dramatists Inc., New York City, 1981; *Danton's Death*, Center Stage Theatre, Baltimore, MD, 1984; *Temptation*, NYSF, Public Theatre, 1989.

PRINCIPAL FILM APPEARANCES—Ron Desjardins, *Return of the Secaucus Seven*, Libra, 1980; Marvin Zuckerman, *Lovesick*, Warner Brothers, 1983; Wesley, *Silkwood*, Twentieth Century-Fox, 1983; man in black, *The Brother from Another Planet*, Cinecom, 1984; Dr. Singe, *Iceman*, Universal, 1984; Jerry, *Enormous Changes at the Last Minute*, ABC/Ordinary Lives, 1985; Weejun, *When Nature Calls*, Troma, 1985; Tony Pine, *At Close Range*, Orion, 1986; Police Chief Sid Hatfield, *Matewan*, Cinecom, 1987; Eddie Cicotte, *Eight Men Out*, Orion, 1988; Charlie, *Stars and Bars*, Columbia, 1988; Martin Chernak, *Dominick and Eugene*, Orion, 1988; Sam, *Call Me*, Vestron, 1988; the Stranger, *The Feud*, Feud Company, 1989.

PRINCIPAL TELEVISION APPEARANCES—Series: Moss Goodman, *The Days and Nights of Molly Dodd*, NBC, 1988, then Lifetime, 1989—. Episodic: Marty Lang, *Miami Vice*, NBC, 1985; Philip Borchek, *The Equalizer*, CBS, 1988. Movies: J. Robert Oppenheimer, *Day One*, CBS, 1989.*

*   *   *

STREEP, Meryl   1949-

PERSONAL: Born Mary Louise Streep, June 22, 1949, in Summit, NJ; daughter of Harry, Jr. and Mary W. Streep; married Donald J. Gummer (a sculptor), 1978; children: Henry, Mary Willa, Grace

MERYL STREEP

Jane. EDUCATION—Vassar College, B.A., 1971; Yale University, M.F.A., 1975; studied singing with Estelle Liebling.

VOCATION: Actress.

CAREER: BROADWAY DEBUT—Imogen Parrot, *Trelawny of the Wells*, New York Shakespeare Festival, Vivian Beaumont Theatre, 1975. PRINCIPAL STAGE APPEARANCES—Lillian Holliday, *Happy End*, Yale Repertory Theatre, New Haven, CT, 1974; Flora Meighan, *27 Wagons Full of Cotton*, Patricia, *A Memory of Two Mondays*, and Edith Varney, *Secret Service*, all Phoenix Repertory Theatre, Playhouse Theatre, New York City, 1976; Katherine, *Henry V* and Juliet and Isabella, *Measure for Measure*, both New York Shakespeare Festival (NYSF), Delacorte Theatre, New York City, 1976; Dunyasha, *The Cherry Orchard*, NYSF, Vivian Beaumont Theatre, New York City, 1977; Lillian Holliday, *Happy End*, Chelsea Theatre Center, Brooklyn Academy of Music, Brooklyn, NY, then Martin Beck Theatre, New York City, both 1977; Katherine, *The Taming of the Shrew*, NYSF, Delacorte Theatre, 1978; Alice, *Wonderland in Concert*, NYSF, Public Theatre, New York City, 1978; Andrea, *Taken in Marriage*, NYSF, Public Theatre, 1979; Alice, *Alice in Concert*, NYSF, Public Theatre, 1980; Cynthia Peterson, *Isn't It Romantic?*, Playwrights Horizons Theatre, New York City, 1983, then Lucille Lortel Theatre, New York City, 1984. Also appeared with the Green Mountain Guild, Woodstock, VT.

FILM DEBUT—Anne Marie, *Julia*, Twentieth Century-Fox, 1977. PRINCIPAL FILM APPEARANCES—Linda, *The Deer Hunter*, Universal, 1978; Jill, *Manhattan*, United Artists, 1979; Karen Traynor, *The Seduction of Joe Tynan*, Universal, 1979; Joanna Kramer,

Kramer vs. Kramer, Columbia, 1979; Sarah Woodruff and Anna, *The French Lieutenant's Woman,* United Artists, 1981; Brooke Reynolds, *Still of the Night,* Metro-Goldwyn-Mayer/United Artists, 1982; Sophie Zawistowska, *Sophie's Choice,* ITC/Universal, 1982; Karen Silkwood, *Silkwood,* Twentieth Century-Fox, 1983; narrator, *In Our Hands,* Libra/Cinema V, 1983; Molly Gilmore, *Falling in Love,* Paramount, 1984; Susan Traherne, *Plenty,* Twentieth Century-Fox, 1985; Karen Blixen-Finecke, *Out of Africa,* Universal, 1985; Rachel Samstat, *Heartburn,* Paramount, 1986; Helen Archer, *Ironweed,* Tri-Star, 1988; Lindy Chamberlain, *A Cry in the Dark,* Warner Brothers, 1988; Mary Fisher, *She-Devil,* Orion, 1989.

PRINCIPAL TELEVISION APPEARANCES—Mini-Series: Inga Helms Weiss, *Holocaust,* NBC, 1978. Episodic: Narrator, "Harold Clurman: A Life of Theatre," *American Masters,* PBS, 1988. Movies: Sharon Miller, *The Deadliest Season,* CBS, 1977. Specials: Edith, *Secret Service,* PBS, 1977; Leilah, "Uncommon Women and Others," *Great Performances,* PBS, 1978; host and narrator, *Power Struggle,* PBS, 1985; narrator, "Little Ears: The Velveteen Rabbit" (also known as "The Velveteen Rabbit"), *Children's Storybook Classics,* PBS, 1985.

AWARDS: Theatre World Award and Outer Critics' Circle Award, both 1975, and Antoinette Perry Award nomination, Best Featured Actress in a Play, 1976, all for *27 Wagons Full of Cotton; Mademoiselle* Award, 1976; Emmy Award, Best Actress in a Limited Series, 1978, for *Holocaust;* Academy Award nomination and National Society of Film Critics' Award, both Best Supporting Actress, 1978, for *The Deer Hunter;* Woman of the Year Award from B'nai Brith and National Board of Review Best Supporting Actress Award, both 1979; Academy Award and Golden Globe, both Best Supporting Actress, and Los Angeles Film Critics' Award and New York Film Critics' Circle Award, both Best Actress, all 1979, for *Kramer vs. Kramer.*

Harvard University Hasty Pudding Award, Woman of the Year, 1980; Academy Award nomination, Best Actress, Los Angeles Film Critics' Award, Best Actress, British Academy Award, and Golden Globe, all 1981, for *The French Lieutenant's Woman;* Obie Award from the *Village Voice,* 1981, for *Alice in Concert;* Academy Award, Los Angeles Film Critics' Award, and Golden Globe, all Best Actress, 1982, for *Sophie's Choice;* Star of the Year Award from the National Association of Theatre Owners, 1982; Academy Award nomination, Best Actress, 1983, for *Silkwood;* Academy Award nomination and Los Angeles Film Critics' Award, both Best Actress, 1985, for *Out of Africa;* Academy Award nomination, Best Actress, 1988, for *Ironweed;* Academy Award nomination, Best Actress, 1989, for *A Cry in the Dark;* HONORARY DEGREES—Dartmouth College, 1981; Yale University, 1983; Vassar College, 1983.

ADDRESSES: AGENT—International Creative Management, 40 W. 57th Street, New York, NY 10019.*

*   *   *

SUGARMAN, Burt

PERSONAL: Born January 4, in Beverly Hills, CA; married Mary Hart (a television personality), 1989. EDUCATION—Attended the University of Southern California.

VOCATION: Producer.

CAREER: PRINCIPAL FILM APPEARANCES—*The Last Fight,* Best Film and Video, 1983. PRINCIPAL FILM WORK—Producer, *Kiss Me Goodbye,* Island Alive, 1985; producer, *Children of a Lesser God,* Paramount, 1986; producer, *Extremities,* Atlantic, 1986; executive producer, *Crimes of the Heart,* De Laurentiis Entertainment Group, 1986.

PRINCIPAL TELEVISION WORK—Series: Producer (with Pierre Cossette and Dean Whitmore), *Johnny Mann's Stand Up and Cheer,* syndicated, 1971; executive producer, *The Mancini Generation,* syndicated, 1972; executive producer, *The Wizard of Odds,* NBC, 1973-74; executive producer, *The Midnight Special,* NBC, 1973-81; executive producer (with Ralph Andrews), *Celebrity Sweepsteaks,* NBC, 1974-76; executive producer, *The Richard Pryor Show,* NBC, 1977; executive producer, *Take My Advice,* NBC, 1976; producer (with Jay Wolpert), *Whew!,* CBS, 1979-80; executive producer (with Chris Beard), *The Gong Show,* syndicated, 1988—; also producer, *The Joker's Wild.* Pilots: Executive producer (with Cossette), *Stand Up and Cheer,* ABC, 1971. Specials: Executive producer (with Cossette), *The Dionne Warwick Special,* CBS, 1969; executive producer (with Cossette), *Movin',* CBS, 1970; executive producer (with Nick Sevano), *Hi, I'm Glen Campbell,* NBC, 1976; executive producer, *The Richard Pryor Special?,* NBC, 1977; executive producer, *The Billboard #1 Music Awards,* NBC, 1977; executive producer, *The Richard Pryor Special,* NBC, 1982.

RELATED CAREER—Chairman and chief executive officer, Giant Group; head of Barris Industries Inc.

ADDRESSES: AGENT—William Morris Agency, 151 El Camino Drive, Beverly Hills, CA 90212.*

*   *   *

SURTEES, Bruce

PERSONAL: Son of Robert L. (a cinematographer) and Maydell Surtees.

VOCATION: Cinematographer.

CAREER: PRINCIPAL FILM WORK—All as cinematographer, unless indicated: *The Beguiled,* Universal, 1971; *Dirty Harry,* Warner Brothers, 1971; *Play Misty for Me,* Universal, 1971; *Conquest of the Planet of the Apes,* Twentieth Century-Fox, 1972; *The Great Northfield, Minnesota Raid,* Universal, 1972; *Joe Kidd,* Universal, 1972; cameraman, *Lost Horizon,* Columbia, 1973; *Blume in Love,* Samuel Bronston, 1973; *High Plains Drifter,* Universal, 1973; *The Outfit* (also known as *The Good Guys Always Win*), Metro-Goldwyn-Mayer, 1973; *Lenny,* United Artists, 1974; *Night Moves,* Warner Brothers, 1975; *Leadbelly,* Paramount, 1976; *The Outlaw Josey Wales,* Warner Brothers, 1976; *The Shootist,* Paramount, 1976; *Sparkle,* Warner Brothers, 1976; *Three Warriors,* Fantasy, 1977; *Big Wednesday,* Warner Brothers, 1978; "Baxter's Beauties" in *Movie Movie,* Warner Brothers, 1978; *Dreamer,* Twentieth Century-Fox, 1979; *Escape from Alcatraz,* Paramount, 1979; *Inchon,* Metro-Goldwyn-Mayer/United Artists, 1981; *Firefox,* Warner Brothers, 1982; *Honkytonk Man,* Warner Brothers, 1982; *Ladies and Gentlemen, The Fabulous Stains,* Paramount, 1982; *White Dog* (also known as *Trained to*

Kill), Paramount, 1982; (with Donald Thorin) *Bad Boys*, Universal, 1983; *Sudden Impact*, Warner Brothers, 1983; (with Reynaldo Villalobos) *Risky Business*, Warner Brothers, 1983; *Beverly Hills Cop*, Paramount, 1984; *Tightrope*, Warner Brothers, 1984; *Pale Rider*, Warner Brothers, 1985; *Out of Bounds*, Columbia, 1986; *Psycho III*, Universal, 1986; *Ratboy*, Warner Brothers, 1986; *Back to the Beach*, Paramount, 1987; *License to Drive*, Twentieth Century-Fox, 1988; *Men Don't Leave*, Warner Brothers, 1990.

AWARDS: Academy Award nomination, Best Cinematography, 1974, for *Lenny.**

*   *   *

SUSSMAN, Peter   1958-

PERSONAL: Born July 16, 1958, in Toronto, ON, Canada.

VOCATION: Producer.

CAREER: PRINCIPAL FILM WORK—Executive producer, *Cowboys Don't Cry*, Cineplex Odeon/Atlantis Releasing/Cinema Plus, 1987; executive producer (with Michael MacMillan), *Destiny to Order*, Cineplex Odeon/Atlantis Releasing/Studio Entertainment, 1988.

PRINCIPAL TELEVISION WORK—Series: Executive producer, *The Ray Bradbury Theatre*, USA, 1986-89; executive producer, *Magic Hour*, CBC, 1989. Movies: Executive producer (with Michael MacMillan and Tom Radford), *Last Train Home*, Family Channel, 1990. Specials: Supervising producer, *110 Lombard*, CBS and CBC, 1987; supervising producer, *Christmas in America: A Love Story*, NBC, 1989.

MEMBER: Academy of Canadian Cinema and Television (1986—), Canadian Film and Television Association (director, 1987—).

ADDRESSES: OFFICE—c/o Atlantis Films, Cinevillage, 65 Heward Avenue, Toronto, ON, Canada M4M-2T5.

*   *   *

SWAIM, Bob   1943-

PERSONAL: Full name, Robert Frank Swaim, Jr.; born November 2, 1943, in Evanston, IL; son of Robert Frank and Eleanor (Connor) Swaim; married, 1968 (divorced, 1983); children: Benjamin Lee, Christopher Thomas. EDUCATION—California State University, Northridge, B.A., 1965; L'Ecole Nationale de la Cinematographie (Paris), BTS, 1969.

VOCATION: Director and screenwriter.

CAREER: Also see *WRITINGS* below. PRINCIPAL FILM APPEARANCES—Special Forces commander, *Spies Like Us*, Warner Brothers, 1985. PRINCIPAL FILM WORK—Director: *La Nuit de Saint Germain des pres*, Megalo Films, 1977; *La Balance* (also known as *The Nark*), Gala, 1983; *Half Moon Street* (also known as *Escort Girl*), Twentieth Century-Fox, 1986; *Masquerade*, Metro-Goldwyn-Mayer/United Artists, 1988. Also *Le Journal de M. Bonnafous* (short film), 1970; *L'Autoportrait d'un pornographe* (also known

as *Self-Portrait of a Pornographer;* short film), 1971; *Vive les Jacques* (short film), 1972.

WRITINGS: FILM—(With Alain Petit and Robert Rea) *La Nuit de Saint Germain des pres*, Megalo Films, 1977; (with M. Fabiani) *La Balance* (also known as *The Nark*), Gala, 1983; (with Edward Behr) *Half Moon Street* (also known as *Escort Girl*), Twentieth Century-Fox, 1986.

RELATED CAREER—Founder, Bob Swain Productions, Los Angeles.

AWARDS: Jury Prize at Hyeres, 1970, for *Le Journal de M. Bonnafous;* Critics' Prize at Grenoble, 1971, for *L'Autoportrait d'un pornographe;* Cesar Award from the French Academy of Motion Pictures, 1982; Chevalier des Arts et des Lettres from the French government, 1985.

MEMBER: Directors Guild of America, Writers Guild of America, Societe des Realisateurs de Film.

ADDRESSES: OFFICE—Bob Swaim Productions, 9255 Sunset Boulevard, Suite 901, Los Angeles, CA 90069.*

*   *   *

SYLVESTER, Harold

VOCATION: Actor.

CAREER: PRINCIPAL FILM APPEARANCES—Nathan Lee Morgan, *Sounder, Part II*, Gamma III, 1976; doctor, *A Hero Ain't Nothin' But a Sandwich*, New World, 1977; D.C., *Fast Break*, Columbia, 1979; Alvin Martin, *Inside Moves*, Associated, 1980; Perryman, *An Officer and a Gentleman*, Paramount, 1982; Johnson, *Uncommon Valor*, Paramount, 1983; Tanneran, *Vision Quest*, Warner Brothers, 1985; Pete Blanchard, *Innerspace*, Warner Brothers, 1987; Max Bryson, *Space Rage*, Vestron, 1987; Brian Armstrong, *Hit List*, New Line Cinema, 1989.

PRINCIPAL TELEVISION APPEARANCES—Series: Deputy Aaron Fairfax, *Walking Tall*, NBC, 1981; Agent Dwayne Thompson, *Today's F.B.I.*, ABC, 1981-82; Harry Dresden, *Mary*, CBS, 1985-86. Mini-Series: Rollie Knight, *Arthur Hailey's "Wheels"* (also known as *Wheels*), NBC, 1978; Hindsman, *The Atlanta Child Murders*, CBS, 1985. Pilots: Rider, *Richie Brockelman: Missing 24 Hours*, NBC, 1976; sergeant, *Uncommon Valor*, CBS, 1983. Episodic: Mr. Moorepark, *Webster*, ABC, 1986; Blaster Boyle, *Murder, She Wrote*, CBS, 1987; Harold, *Mama's Boy*, NBC, 1987; McCaslin, *Scarecrow and Mrs. King*, CBS, 1987; David Black, *The Tracey Ullman Show*, Fox, 1987; homeless bum, *1st and Ten: The Bulls Mean Business*, HBO, 1988. Movies: Al, *If Tomorrow Comes*, CBS, 1986; Father Christopher, *Sister Margarita and the Saturday Night Ladies*, CBS, 1987; Sam, *Double Your Pleasure*, NBC, 1989. Specials: Neighbor, "Secret Agent Boy," *CBS Afternoon Playhouse*, CBS, 1982.

ADDRESSES: AGENT—Susie Schwartz, Century Artists Ltd., 9744 Wilshire Boulevard, Suite 308, Beverly Hills, CA 90212.*

SZABO, Istvan 1938-

PERSONAL: Born February 18, 1938, in Budapest, Hungary; son of Istvan (a doctor) and Maria (Vita) Szabo; married Vera Gyurey. EDUCATION—Graduated from the Budapest Academy of Theatre and Film Arts, 1961.

VOCATION: Director, actor, and screenwriter.

CAREER: Also see *WRITINGS* below. PRINCIPAL FILM APPEARANCES—Abris Kondor, *Magyarok* (also known as *The Hungarians*), Hungarofilm, 1978; Andras, *Fabian Balint Talalkozasa Istennel* (also known as *Balint Fabian Meets God*), Hungarofilm, 1980; Dr. Kalman, *Tusztortenet* (also known as *Stand Off*), Hungarofilm, 1989.

FIRST FILM WORK—Director, *Koncert* (also known as *Concert;* short film), 1961. PRINCIPAL FILM WORK—Director: *Variaciok egy temara* (also known as *Variations on a Theme;* short film), Bela Balazs Studio, 1961; *Te* (also known as *You . . .;* short film), Bela Balazs Studio, 1963; *Almodozasok kora* (also known as *Age of Illusions* and *The Age of Daydreaming*), 1964, released in the United States by Brandon, 1967; *Apa* (also known as *Father*), Continental Distributing, 1967; *Szerelmesfilm* (also known as *A Film of Love, Love Film,* and *Love Story Film*), Hungarofilm, 1970; *Tuzolto utca 25* (also known as *25 Fireman's Street* and *Vie dei Pompieri 25*), Hungarofilm, 1974; *Bizalom* (also known as *Confidence*), Hungarofilm, 1979, released in the United States by Cinegate, 1980; *Mephisto,* Cinegate/Analysis, 1981; *Redl Ezredes* (also known as *Colonel Redl* and *Oberst Redl*), Orion Classics, 1985; *Hanussen* (also known as *Hanussen, Der Hellseher; Hanussen, the Prophet; Hanussen, the Clairvoyant;* and *The Prophet*), Hungarofilm/Columbia, 1988. Also *Kegyelet* (also known as *Piety;* short documentary film), 1967; *Budapest, amiert szeretem* (also known as *Budapest, Why I Love It;* short film), 1971; *Alom a hazrol* (also known as *Dream About the House;* short film), 1971; *Duna—halak—Madarak* (also known as *The Danube—Fishes—Birds;* short film), 1971; *Egy tukor* (also known as *A Mirror;* short film), 1971; *Leanyportre* (also known as *A Portrait of a Girl;* short film), 1971; *Ter* (also known as *A Square;* short film), 1971; *Hajnal* (also known as *Dawn;* short film), 1971; *Alkony* (also known as *Twilight;* short film), 1971; *Budapesti mesek* (also known as *Budapest Tales*), 1976; *Varosterkep* (also known as *City Map;* short documentary

film), 1977; *Der Grune Vogel* (also known as *The Green Bird*), 1979.

PRINCIPAL TELEVISION WORK—Director, *Osbemutato* (also known as *Premiere*), 1974; director, *Katzenspiel* (also known as *Cat Play*), 1982; director, *Bali,* 1983.

RELATED CAREER—Member, Bela Belazs Studio, Budapest, Hungary; member, Hungarian Film Studios; teacher, College of Theatre and Film Arts, Budapest, and Deutsche Film und Fersehakademie, West Berlin.

WRITINGS: See production details above. FILM—*Koncert,* 1961; *Variaciok egy temara,* 1961; *Te,* 1963; *Almodozasok kora,* 1964; *Apa,* 1966; *Kegyelet,* 1967; *Szerelmesfilm,* 1970; *Budapest, amiert szeretem,* 1971; *Alom a hazrol,* 1971; *Duna—halak—madarak,* 1971; *Egy tukor,* 1971; *Leanyportre,* 1971; *Ter,* 1971; *Hajnal,* 1971; *Alkony,* 1971; *Tuzolto utca 25,* 1974; *Budapesti mesek,* 1976; *Varosterkep,* 1977; *Bizalom,* 1979; *Der Grune Vogel,* 1979; (with Peter Dobai) *Mephisto,* 1981; (with Dobai) *Redl Ezredes,* 1985; (with Dobai, Paul Hengge, and Gottfried Reinhard) *Hanussen,* 1988. TELEVISION—*Osbemutato,* 1974.

AWARDS: Hungarian Film Critics' Award, 1961, for *Koncert;* Hungarian Film Critics' Award, 1962, for *Variaciok egy temara;* Grand Prix de Tours, 1963, for *Te;* Bela Balazs Prize, 1967; Oberhausen Main Prize, 1971, for *Alom a hazrol;* Best Film Award from the Locarno Film Festival, 1974, for *Tuzolto utca 25;* Kossuth Prize, 1975; Oberhausen Grand Prix, 1977, for *Varosterkep;* Academy Award nomination, Best Foreign Film, and Silver Bear Award from the Berlin Film Festival, both 1980, for *Bizalom;* Best Screenplay Award and FIPRESCI Prize from the Cannes Film Festival, 1981, Academy Award, Best Foreign Film, 1981, Hungarian Film Critics' Award, 1982, David di Donatello Prize, Prize of Italian Film Critics, and Prize of U.K. Critics, all for *Mephisto;* Academy Award nomination, Best Foreign Film, 1989, for *Hanussen.*

MEMBER: Academy of Motion Picture Arts and Sciences, Akademie de Kunste (Berlin).

ADDRESSES: OFFICE—Objektiv Film Studio—MAFILM, 1149 Budapest, Lumumba utca 174, Hungary.*

T

TAGGART, Rita

PERSONAL: Born in Salinas, CA; married Haskell Wexler (a cinematographer), 1989. EDUCATION—Majored in special education at San Francisco State College; studied acting with Ray Reinhardt at the American Conservatory Theatre, San Francisco.

VOCATION: Actress.

CAREER: PRINCIPAL STAGE APPEARANCES—Hungry Hearts, Ensemble Studio Theatre, Los Angeles.

FILM DEBUT—Carol Schue, Straight Time, Warner Brothers, 1978. PRINCIPAL FILM APPEARANCES—Johnson, Coming Home, United Artists, 1978; Rita Jacovich, The China Syndrome, Columbia, 1979; reporter, 1941, Universal, 1979; Thelma, Die Laughing, Warner Brothers, 1980; woman in bed, Used Cars, Columbia, 1980; Rita, Torchlight, Film Ventures International, 1984; Lillian

RITA TAGGART

Bingington, Weeds, DeLaurentiis Entertainment Group, 1987; Donna McCarthy, The Horror Show, Metro-Goldwyn-Mayer/United Artists, 1989.

PRINCIPAL TELEVISION APPEARANCES—Series: Blanche, Steambath, Showtime, 1984, Diane, Eye to Eye, ABC, 1985; Joan Foley, Almost Grown, CBS, 1988. Pilots: Geri Ballin, Every Stray Dog and Kid, NBC, 1981; Joan Foley, Almost Grown, CBS, 1988. Episodic: Marie Roscini, Hello, Larry, NBC, 1981; Farkis, "Miss Lonelyhearts," American Playhouse, PBS, 1983; Andrea, Hunter, NBC, 1985; Rosie McDonough, Hill Street Blues, NBC, 1985; Sylvia, Kate and Allie, CBS, 1985; Brenda, The Colbys, ABC, 1986; Sheila Jessup, Hotel, ABC, 1986; Fern Hooten, "Splash, Too," Disney Sunday Movie, ABC, 1988; Mrs. Staplin, "Agenda for Murder," Columbo, ABC, 1990; also Taxi, ABC, 1978; Carla B., Night Court, NBC; Rhoda, CBS; St. Elsewhere, NBC; Cagney and Lacey, CBS. Movies: Amy Morrison, Rape and Marriage: The Rideout Case, CBS, 1980; Nina, Seizure: The Story of Kathy Morris, CBS, 1980; Salt, Inmates: A Love Story, ABC, 1981; Janet Carlson, Born to Be Sold, NBC, 1981; Janice, The Other Victim, CBS, 1981; Sally, Mae West, ABC, 1982; Mrs. Walt Johnson, Wait Till Your Mother Gets Home!, NBC, 1983; Monica, The Cartier Heist, NBC, 1984; Kay Joyner, Terror on Highway 91, CBS, 1989; also James Dean, NBC, 1976.

RELATED CAREER—Actress in regional theatre productions.

NON-RELATED CAREER—Cocktail waitress, school teacher, and masseuse for rock singer Rod Stewart.

ADDRESSES: PUBLICIST—Levine/Schneider Public Relations, 8730 Sunset Boulevard, 6th Floor, Los Angeles, CA 90069.

*   *   *

TALBOT, Nita   1930-

PERSONAL: Born August 8, 1930, in New York, NY. EDUCATION—Studied acting at the Irvine Studio and with Charles Laughton.

VOCATION: Actress.

CAREER: BROADWAY DEBUT—Gloria Sampson, Never Say Never, Booth Theatre, 1951. PRINCIPAL STAGE APPEARANCES—Shelly, The Fifth Season, Cort Theatre, New York City, 1953; Steffi Hartman, Zelda, Ethel Barrymore Theatre, New York City, 1969; also appeared in Uncle Willie, John Golden Theatre, New York City, 1956.

PRINCIPAL FILM APPEARANCES—Model, *It's a Great Feeling,* Warner Brothers, 1949; inmate, *Caged,* Warner Brothers, 1950; woman in bar, *On Dangerous Ground,* RKO, 1951; Mary, *Bundle of Joy,* RKO, 1956; chorus girl, *This Could Be the Night,* Metro-Goldwyn-Mayer (MGM), 1957; Miss Anderson, *I Married a Woman,* RKO/Universal, 1958; Miss Dovey Barnes, *Once Upon a Horse* (also known as *Hot Horse*), Universal, 1958; Saturday Knight, *Who's Got the Action?,* Paramount, 1962; Sunny Daze, *Girl Happy,* MGM, 1965; Mickey, *A Very Special Favor,* Universal, 1965; Dee Dee, *The Cool Ones,* Warner Brothers, 1967; Madame Esther, *Buck and the Preacher,* Columbia, 1972; Joan, *The Day of the Locust,* Paramount, 1975; Jasmine, *The Manchu Eagle Murder Caper Mystery,* United Artists, 1975; Firetop Alice Dewey, *The Sweet Creek County War,* Key International, 1979; Angela, *Serial,* Paramount, 1980; Shelly Meyers, *The Concrete Jungle,* Pentagon, 1982; Vivian, *Night Shift,* Warner Brothers, 1982; Mrs. Rohmer, *Frightmare* (also known as *The Horror Star*), Saturn International, 1983; Kaufman, *Chained Heat,* Jensen Farley, 1983; Mrs. Ferret, *Fraternity Vacation,* New World, 1985; Dorothy, *Movers and Shakers,* Metro-Goldwyn-Mayer/United Artists, 1985; Mrs. Rappaport, *The Check Is in the Mail,* Ascot Entertainment Group, 1985; Betty Griffith, *Take Two,* TBJ, 1988. Also appeared in *Montana,* Warner Brothers, 1950; *This Side of the Law,* Warner Brothers, 1950; *Island Claws* (also known as *The Night of the Claw*), CBS, 1981.

PRINCIPAL TELEVISION APPEARANCES—Series: Mabel Spooner, *Joe and Mabel,* CBS, 1956; Beatrice Dane/Blondie Collins, *The Thin Man,* NBC, 1957-59; Dora Miles, *The Jim Backus Show—Hot Off the Wire,* syndicated, 1960; Maggie Prescott, *Funny Face,* CBS, 1971; Judy Evans, *Here We Go Again,* ABC, 1973; Rose Casey, *Supertrain,* NBC, 1979; Rose, *Starting from Scratch,* syndicated, 1988; also Rose Peabody, *Search for Tomorrow,* CBS; Delfina, *General Hospital,* ABC. Pilots: Thelma, *Under the Yum Yum Tree,* NBC, 1969; Rona Corbin, *They Call It Murder,* NBC, 1971; Mildred Elias, *The Rockford Files,* NBC, 1974; Doris Shaughnessey, *Shaughnessey,* NBC, 1976; Sergeant McCallister, *Turnover Smith,* ABC, 1980; Sara Dabney, *You Are the Jury,* NBC, 1984.

Episodic: Lusti Weathers, *Bourbon Street Beat,* ABC, 1959-60; Doris Stevens, *The Partridge Family,* ABC, 1970; Sheila Fyne, *Soap,* ABC, 1977; Elsa Ravenwood, *Leo and Liz in Beverly Hills,* CBS, 1986; also *Eye Witness,* NBC, 1953; *The Inner Sanctum,* syndicated, 1954; *All in the Family,* CBS, 1977; as Marya, *Hogan's Heroes,* CBS; *Jane Wyman Presents the Fireside Theatre,* NBC; *Studio One,* CBS; "The Werewolf," *Kolchak: The Night Stalker,* ABC. Movies: Lois Warwick, *The Movie Murderer,* NBC, 1970; Evelyn Housner, *What Are Best Friends For?,* ABC, 1973; Heidi Lomax, *Sex and the Married Woman,* NBC, 1977; Grace Binns, *The Other Woman,* CBS, 1983. Specials: Judith Canfield, *Stage Door,* CBS, 1955; Olga, *The Women,* NBC, 1955; also *This Will Be the Year That Will Be,* ABC, 1973.*

*   *   *

TANNER, Alain   1929-

PERSONAL: Born December 6, 1929, in Geneva, Switzerland; father, a writer and painter; mother, an actress. EDUCATION—Studied economics at Calvin College, Geneva.

VOCATION: Director, screenwriter, and producer.

CAREER: Also see *WRITINGS* below. PRINCIPAL FILM APPEARANCES—*Francois Simon—La Presence* (documentary), CSS Geneva, 1986. PRINCIPAL FILM WORK—Producer and director, *La Salamandre* (also known as *The Salamander*), Alga, 1971; producer and director, *La Retour d'Afrique* (also known as *Return from Africa*), Groupe 5 Geneve/Television Suisse/Filmanthrope, 1972; producer and director, *Charles mort ou vif* (also known as *Charles, Dead or Alive*), New Yorker, 1972; director, *Le Milieu du monde* (also known as *The Middle of the World*), Artificial Eye/Action/Citel Film Distribution, 1974; director, *Jonas—Qui aura 25 ans en l'an 2000* (also known as *Jonah—Who Will Be 25 in the Year 2000*), New Yorker, 1976; director, *Messidor,* Gaumont International, 1978; director, *Les Annees lumieres* (also known as *Light Years Away*), Artificial Eye, 1981, released in the United States by New Yorker, 1982; executive producer (with Paulo Branco), producer (with Branco and Antonio Vaz da Silver), and director, *Dans la ville blanche* (also known as *In the White City*), Contemporary Films Ltd., 1982, released in the United States by Grey City, 1983; producer (with Marin Karmitz) and director, *No Man's Land,* MK2/Filmograph/Westdeutscher Rundfunk/Channel Four Film on Four/SSR/Films A2, 1985; executive producer (with Karmitz) and director, *La Vallee fantome* (also known as *The Ghost Valley* and *The Phantom Valley*), MK2, 1987; director, *Une Flamme dans mon coeur* (also known as *A Flame in My Heart*), Bac/Roxie Releasing/Films du Volcan, 1987. Also producer (with Claude Goretta) and co-director, *Nice Times* (short film), 1957; director, *Ramuz, passage d'un poete* (short film), 1959; director, *L'Ecole,* 1962; director, *Les Apprentis* (documentary), 1964; director, *Une Ville a Chandigarh,* 1969.

PRINCIPAL TELEVISION WORK—Series: Assistant producer, *Living with Dangers,* BBC, 1958; producer and director, *Cinq Collones a la Une* (filmed reports), ORTF (French television), 1964-69.

RELATED CAREER—Worked at British Film Institute, 1955; co-founder, Association Suisse des Realisateurs (film society), 1960; co-founder, Group 5 (a film production company).

NON-RELATED CAREER—Shipping clerk for cargo ships.

WRITINGS: FILM—(With John Berger) *Une Ville a Chandigarh,* 1966; *Charles mort ou vif,* New Yorker, 1972; (with Berger) *La Salamandre,* Alga, 1971; *Le Retour d'Afrique,* Groupe 5 Geneve/Television Suisse/Filmanthrope, 1972; (with Berger) *Le Milieu du monde,* Artificial Eye/Action/Citel Film Distribution, 1974; (with Berger) *Jonas—Qui aura 25 ans en l'an 2000,* New Yorker, 1976; *Messidor,* Gaumont International, 1978; *Les Annees lumieres,* Artificial Eye, 1981; *Dans la ville blanche,* Contemporary Films Ltd., 1982; *No Man's Land,* MK2/Filmograph/Westdeutscher Rundfunk/Channel Four Film on Four/SSR/Films A2, 1985; *La Vallee Fantome,* MK2, 1987; (with Myriam Mezieres) *Une Flamme dans mon coeur,* Bac/Roxie Releasing/Films du Volcan, 1987. OTHER—*Jonas qui aura 25 ans en l'an 2000* (novelization), 1978.

AWARDS: Experimental Film Prize from the Venice Film Festival, 1957, for *Nice Time;* First Prize from the Locarno Festival, 1969, for *Charles mort ou vif;* National Society of Film Critics' Award, Best Screenplay (with John Berger), 1976, for *Jonas—Qui aura 25 ans en l'an 2000;* Special Jury Prize from the Cannes Film Festival, 1981, for *Les Annees lumiere.**

TAYLOR, Meshach

PERSONAL: Born April 11, in Boston, MA; father, a sociology professor; mother, a college professor; married second wife, Bianca Fergerson (an actress); children: Tamar (first marriage); Yasmine, Esme Alana (second marriage). EDUCATION—Studied theatre at Florida A & M University.

VOCATION: Actor.

CAREER: PRINCIPAL STAGE APPEARANCES—*Streamers* and *Sizwe Banzi Is Dead,* both Goodman Theatre, Chicago, IL, 1976; *Native Son,* Goodman Theatre, 1978; *The Island,* Goodman Theatre, Annenberg Center, Philadelphia, PA, 1979; also appeared in *Sizwe Banzi Is Dead,* Westwood Playhouse, Los Angeles.

MAJOR TOURS—*Hair,* U.S. cities.

PRINCIPAL FILM APPEARANCES—Dr. Kane, *Damien—Omen II,* Twentieth Century-Fox, 1978; Shantz, *The Howling,* AVCO-Embassy, 1981; deputy, *The Beast Within,* Metro-Goldwyn-Mayer/United Artists, 1982; Gordon Miller, *Explorers,* Paramount, 1985; video technician, *Warning Sign,* Twentieth Century-Fox, 1985; Bill Neal, *One More Saturday Night* (also known as *Datenight*), Columbia, 1986; Philip, *The Allnighter,* Universal, 1987; Mr. Dean, *House of Games,* Orion, 1987; Hollywood Montrose, *Mannequin,* Twentieth Century-Fox, 1987. Also appeared in *The Haircut* (short film), 1982; *From the Hip,* De Laurentiis Entertainment Group, 1987.

PRINCIPAL TELEVISION APPEARANCES—Series: Tony, *Buffalo Bill,* NBC, 1983-84; Anthony Bouvier, *Designing Women,* CBS, 1986—; also host, *Black Life,* WMAQ-TV (Chicago, IL). Pilots: Blue collar man, *I'd Rather Be Calm,* CBS, 1982. Episodic: Cop, *The Golden Girls,* NBC, 1985; Rick, *Melba,* CBS, 1986; also *Barney Miller,* ABC, 1982; *Lou Grant,* CBS; *The White Shadow,* CBS; *M*A*S*H,* CBS. Movies: Crosby, *An Innocent Man,* HBO, 1987. Specials: Virgil, "The Rec Room," *NBC Presents the AFI Comedy Special,* NBC, 1987; also *Huckleberry Finn,* PBS.

RELATED CAREER—Member, Organic Theatre Group.

NON-RELATED CAREER—Political reporter for an Indianapolis, IN radio station; head of privately-funded program for rehabilitating street gang members, Indianapolis; also worked as an accountant and security guard.

AWARDS: Joseph Jefferson Award for *Sizwe Banzi Is Dead;* Chicago Emmy Award for *Huckleberry Finn.*

SIDELIGHTS: RECREATIONS—Travel and studying foreign languages.

ADDRESSES: AGENT—David Shapira and Associates, 15301 Ventura Boulevard, Suite 345, Sherman Oaks, CA 91403.*

*   *   *

TAYLOR, Valerie   1902-1988

PERSONAL: Born November 10, 1902, in Fulham, England; died October 24, 1988, in London, England; daughter of Major Frederick Edward Verney and Florence Julia (Robarts) Taylor; married Hugh Sinclair (an actor; divorced); married Desborough William Saunders. EDUCATION—Trained for the stage at the Royal Academy of Dramatic Art, 1920.

VOCATION: Actress.

CAREER: Also see *WRITINGS* below. STAGE DEBUT—Juliet, *French Leave,* Casino Theatre, Menton, France, 1922. LONDON DEBUT—Title role, *Storm,* Royalty Theatre, 1924. BROADWAY DEBUT—Kate Pettigrew, *Berkeley Square,* Lyceum Theatre, 1929. PRINCIPAL STAGE APPEARANCES—Isabella, *Caroline* and Miss Roberts, *The Mollusc,* both Casino Theatre, Menton, France, 1922; Rosario, *The Romantic Young Lady* and the madonna, *The Marvellous History of Saint Bernard,* both Birmingham Repertory Company, Birmingham, U.K., 1925; lady and Anne Morecombe, *The Show,* St. Martin's Theatre, London, 1925; Judith, *Cobra,* Garrick Theatre, London, 1925; Nina Zaretchny, *The Seagull,* Little Theatre, London, 1925; Feemy Evans, *The Shewing-Up of Blanco Posnet* and Lavinia, *Androcles and the Lion,* both Macdona Players, Regent Theatre, London, 1925; Hermione Gordon, *The Rescue Party,* Repertory Players, Regent Theatre, 1926; the madonna, *The Marvellous History of Saint Bernard,* Kingsway Theatre, London, 1926; Kate Pettigrew, *Berkeley Square,* St. Martin's Theatre, 1926; Helen Hayle, *On Approval,* Fortune Theatre, London, 1927; Betty Harlowe, *The House of the Arrow,* Vaudeville Theatre, London, 1928; Kate Pettigrew, *Berkeley Square,* Lyric Theatre, London, 1929; Nina Zaretchny, *The Seagull,* Fortune Theatre, 1929; Countess of Darnaway, *Petticoat Influence,* Empire Theatre, New York City, 1930; Mrs. Deane, *Peter Ibbetson,* Shubert Theatre, New York City, 1931; Elizabeth Trant, *The Good Companions,* 44th Street Theatre, New York City, 1931; Mary Fanshawe, *Red Planet,* Cort Theatre, New York City, 1932; lady, *The Man with a Load of Mischief,* Westminster Theatre, London, 1933; Irene de Montcel, *La Prisonniere,* Arts Theatre, London, 1934.

Beatrice Gwynne, *Call It a Day,* Globe Theatre, London, 1935; Martha Dobie, *The Children's Hour,* Gate Theatre, London, 1936; Hilda McKenna, *The Orchard Walls,* St. James's Theatre, London, 1937; Vere Malcolm, *Love of Women,* John Golden Theatre, New York City, 1937; Anita Karsten, *Surprise Item,* Ambassadors' Theatre, London, 1938; Cynthia Randolph, *Dear Octopus,* Queen's Theatre, London, 1938; Helen Gordon, *A Lady Reflects,* Q Theatre, London, 1940; Cynthia Randolph, *Dear Octopus,* Adelphi Theatre, London, 1940; Myrtle Valentine, *Skylark,* Duchess Theatre, London, 1942; Marthe de Brancovis, *Watch on the Rhine,* Aldwych Theatre, London, 1942; Natalia, *A Month in the Country,* St. James's Theatre, 1943; Dilys Parry, *The Wind of Heaven,* St. James's Theatre, 1945; Imogen, *Cymbeline,* Lady Macbeth, *Macbeth,* and Princess of France, *Love's Labour's Lost,* all Shakespeare Memorial Company, Shakespeare Memorial Theatre, Stratford-on-Avon, U.K., 1946; Marion, *The Anonymous Lover,* Duke of York's Theatre, London, 1947; Naomi Wright, *Happy with Either,* St. James's Theatre, 1948; Janet Spence, *The Gioconda Smile,* Wyndham's Theatre, London, 1948, then Lyceum Theatre, New York City, 1950; Rosabel Fleming, *Venus Observed,* St. James's Theatre, 1950; Lady Crossley, *The Gift,* Edinburgh Festival, Lyceum Theatre, Edinburgh, Scotland, 1952; Mrs. Dennis, *The Living Room,* Edinburgh Festival, Lyceum Theatre, then Wyndham's Theatre, both 1953; Ruth, *Facts of the Heart,* Under Thirty Group, Criterion Theatre, London, 1953; Jessie, *The Art of Living,* Brighton Theatre Royal, Brighton, U.K., 1955; Comtesse Louise de Clerembard, *The Count of Clerembard,* Garrick Theatre, 1955; Felicia, *Who Cares?,* Fortune Theatre, 1956; Mam'selle, *Father's Match,* Brighton Theatre Royal, then retitled *The Happy Man,* Westminster Theatre, both 1957; Myra Bolton, *Each His Own*

Wilderness, English Stage Company, Royal Court Theatre, London, 1958; Blanche Carrell, *Eighty in the Shade,* Globe Theatre, 1959; Queen Elizabeth, *Mary Stuart,* Old Vic Theatre, London, 1960; Alice Jago, *The Masters,* Savoy Theatre, London, 1963; Aunt Agatha, *The Family Reunion,* Yvonne Arnaud Theatre, Guildford, U.K., 1968; Edith, *Time Present,* Royal Court Theatre, then Duke of York's Theatre, both 1968; Amanda Wingfield, *The Glass Menagerie,* University Theatre, Manchester, U.K., 1970. Also appeared in *The Dancers,* Wyndham's Theatre, 1923; as Lady Trevor, *Behind the Beyond,* 1926; Crystal Weatherley, *The Man in Possession,* Magnolia Theatre, in Massachusetts, 1932.

MAJOR TOURS—Fiona Merril, *I'll See You Again* and *Claudia,* U.K. cities, 1944; Lady Bracknell, *The Importance of Being Earnest,* Old Vic Theatre Company, U.K. cities, 1960, then Moscow and Leningrad, 1961; Anna Seward and Mrs. Pritchard, *From China to Peru* and Lady Hurf, *Thieves' Carnival,* Prospect Productions, U.K. cities, 1966; mother, *The Constant Wife,* U.K. cities, 1967; Violet Deering, *Havoc,* U.K. cities.

PRINCIPAL FILM APPEARANCES—Kate Pettigrew, *Berkeley Square,* Twentieth Century-Fox, 1933; Diana Dent, *Designing Women* (also known as *House of Cards*), Metro-Goldwyn-Mayer (MGM), 1934; Nora Ashton, *48 Hours* (also known as *Went the Day Well*), United Artists, 1944; Miss Hopkins, *Faces in the Dark,* Rank, 1960; Janet Broughton, *What a Carve Up!* (also known as *No Place Like Homicide*), Embassy, 1962; first witch, *Macbeth,* Prominent, 1963; Lily Kendrick, *In the Cool of the Day,* MGM, 1963; Mme. Denise, *Repulsion,* Royal, 1965.

PRINCIPAL TELEVISION APPEARANCES—Movies: Louise Sanford, *Baffled,* NBC, 1973. Specials: First witch, "Macbeth," *Hallmark Hall of Fame,* NBC, 1960.

WRITINGS: FILM—(With Winston Graham and Margaret Kennedy) *Take My Life,* Eagle-Lion/Rank, 1948. RADIO—*Persons Unknown.*

OBITUARIES AND OTHER SOURCES: *Variety,* November 2, 1988.*

*   *   *

TERRY, Nigel   1945-

PERSONAL: Born August 15, 1945, in Bristol, England.

VOCATION: Actor.

CAREER: PRINCIPAL STAGE APPEARANCES—Private Evans, *The Long and the Short and the Tall,* Dolphin Theatre Company, Shaw Theatre, London, 1971; Tybalt, *Romeo and Juliet,* Dolphin Theatre Company, Shaw Theatre, 1972; Knife, *Big Wolf,* Royal Court Theatre, London, 1972; Richard, *Rooted,* Hampstead Theatre Club, London, 1973; Stuart, *Kingdom Coming,* Round House Theatre, London, 1973; Darkie, *The Fool,* Royal Court Theatre, 1975; Duke Magnus de la Gardie, *Queen Christina* and John, *The Sons of Light,* both Royal Shakespeare Company (RSC), Other Place Theatre, Stratford-on-Avon, U.K., 1977; Soranzo, *'Tis Pity She's a Whore,* RSC, Other Place Theatre, 1977, then Warehouse Theatre, London, 1978; Duke of Exeter, *Henry VI, Part Three,* RSC, Royal Shakespeare Theatre, Stratford-on-Avon, 1977, then Aldwych Theatre, London, 1978; George, *Look Out . . . Here*

Comes Trouble, RSC, Warehouse Theatre, 1978; Cleon and knight, *Pericles,* Aristarch Dominikovitch Golaschapov, *The Suicide,* and Ekart, *Baal,* all RSC, Other Place Theatre, 1979; Casca and Pindarus, *Julius Caesar,* RSC, Royal Shakespeare Theatre, 1979; Walter Pursar, *Operation Bad Apple,* Royal Court Theatre, 1982; Milton, *Victory,* Royal Court Theatre, 1983; Bosola, *The Duchess of Malfi,* RSC, Swan Theatre, London, 1989. Also appeared in *The Possessed,* Almeida Theatre, London, 1985.

PRINCIPAL FILM APPEARANCES—Prince John, *The Lion in Winter,* AVCO-Embassy, 1968; King Arthur, *Excalibur,* Warner Brothers, 1981; Gregory Thomas and Michael Richardson, *Deja Vu,* Cannon, 1985; Aden Morris, *Sylvia,* Metro-Goldwyn-Mayer/United Artists Classics, 1985; title role, *Caravaggio,* British Film Institute/Cinevista, 1986; narrator, *The Last of England,* Sales Company/International Film Circuit/Blue Dolphin, 1987; Abraham, *War Requiem,* Anglo International, 1989.

ADDRESSES: MANAGER—Kate Feast Management, 43-A Princess Road, Regents Park, London, NW1 8JS, England.*

*   *   *

THELEN, Jodi   1962-

PERSONAL: Born June 12, 1962, in St. Cloud, MN. EDUCATION—Studied acting at the Children's Theatre Company (Minneapolis, MN) and at the American Theatre Arts Conservatory.

VOCATION: Actress.

CAREER: BROADWAY DEBUT—Nora, *Brighton Beach Memoirs,* Alvin Theatre (renamed the Neil Simon Theatre), 1983. PRINCIPAL STAGE APPEARANCES—Nora, *Brighton Beach Memoirs,* Center Theatre Group, Ahmanson Theatre, Los Angeles, 1982-83; Rosa Spivak, *Before the Dawn,* American Place Theatre, New York City, 1985; Mrs. Smith, *Springtime for Henry,* Roundabout Theatre, New York City, 1986; Needa Heitz, *The Nice and the Nasty,* Playwrights Horizons, New York City, 1986; Marketa, *Largo Desolato,* New York Shakespeare Festival (NYSF), Public Theatre, 1986. Also appeared in *Richard's Cork Leg,* American Theatre Arts, Hollywood, CA, 1980; *Nest of the Wood Grouse,* NYSF, Public Theatre; *The Sorrows of Stephen,* Burt Reynolds' Jupiter Dinner Theatre, Jupiter, FL.

FILM DEBUT—Georgia Miles, *Four Friends* (also known as *Georgia's Friends*), Filmways, 1981. PRINCIPAL FILM APPEARANCES—Tabari, *The Black Stallion Returns,* United Artists, 1983; Lena, *Twilight Time,* United Artists, 1983.

PRINCIPAL TELEVISION APPEARANCES—Series: Jane Kelly, *Duet,* Fox, 1987-89. Pilots: Dr. Edie Farmer, *A Doctor's Story,* NBC, 1984; Skylar Hancock, *Starting Now,* CBS, 1989. Episodic: Penny, "The Rise and Rise of Daniel Rocket," *American Playhouse,* PBS, 1986.

SIDELIGHTS: RECREATIONS—Snow skiing, water skiing, bicycle riding, and reading.

ADDRESSES: AGENT—Bauman, Hiller, and Associates, 5750 Wilshire Boulevard, Suite 512, Los Angeles, CA 90038.*

THIGPEN, Lynne

PERSONAL: Born December 22 in Joliet, IL.

VOCATION: Actress and singer.

CAREER: PRINCIPAL STAGE APPEARANCES—Dina, The Magic Show, Cort Theatre, New York City, 1976; Persona Non Grata, But Never Jam Today, Longacre Theatre, New York City, 1979; various roles, Tintypes, Theatre at St. Peter's Church, New York City, 1980, then John Golden Theatre, New York City, 1980-81; ex-slave, Ida B. Wells, Sister Tessie, Gertrude "Ma" Rainey, Hannah Tutson, Jackie "Moms" Mabley, and Fannie Lou Hamer, And I Ain't Finished Yet, Manhattan Theatre Club, New York City, 1981; More of Loesser (revue), King Cole Room, St. Regis-Sheraton, New York City, 1982; Rita, Educating Rita, Alliance Theatre Company, Atlanta, GA, 1983; Joellen, Full Hookup, Circle Repertory Theatre, New York City, 1983-84; Bonnie, Balm in Gilead, Circle Repertory Theatre, 1984, then Minetta Lane Theatre, New York City, 1984-85; Cora, "D", Manhattan Theatre Club, 1985; Mrs. Baker, A Month of Sundays, Ritz Theatre, New York City, 1987; Mrs. Gamadge, The Best Man, Center Theatre Group, Ahmanson Theatre, Los Angeles, 1987; Rose Maxson, Fences, 46th Street Theatre, New York City, 1988.

PRINCIPAL FILM APPEARANCES—Lynne, Godspell, Columbia, 1973; D.J., The Warriors, Paramount, 1979; Jo, Tootsie, Columbia, 1982; Motor Woman, Streets of Fire, Universal/RKO, 1984; Claire, Sweet Liberty, Universal, 1986; reporter, Hello Again, Buena Vista, 1987; Leona Barrett, Lean on Me, Warner Brothers, 1989.

PRINCIPAL TELEVISION APPEARANCES—Series: Nancy, Love, Sidney, NBC, 1982-83; regular, The News Is the News, NBC, 1983. Pilots: Sue, Pottsville, CBS, 1980. Episodic: The Equalizer, CBS, 1987; also Loretta, Gimme a Break, NBC. Movies: Rica Towne, Rockabye, CBS, 1986.

ADDRESSES: AGENT—Michael Thomas Agency, 305 Madison Avenue, Suite 449, New York, NY 10165.*

*   *   *

THOMERSON, Tim

VOCATION: Actor.

CAREER: PRINCIPAL FILM APPEARANCES—Ken, Car Wash, Universal, 1976; tour guide, Which Way Is Up?, Universal, 1977; Marty, Record City, American International, 1978; Jeff, Remember My Name, Columbia, 1978; Russell Bean, A Wedding, Twentieth Century-Fox, 1978; Doubles, Carny, United Artists, 1980; Dr. Moriarty, Fade to Black, American Cinema, 1980; Ray Binkowski, Take This Job and Shove It, AVCO-Embassy, 1981; highway patrolman, Honkytonk Man, Warner Brothers, 1982; Dr. Lanyon, Jekyll and Hyde . . . Together Again, Paramount, 1982; Cal, Some Kind of Hero, Paramount, 1982; Rhodes, Metal Storm: The Destruction of Jared-Syn, Universal, 1983; motorcycle cop, The Osterman Weekend, Twentieth Century-Fox, 1983; Charts, Uncommon Valor, Paramount, 1983; Barnett Cale, Rhinestone, Twentieth Century-Fox, 1984; Jack Deth and Philip Dethon, Trancers (also known as Future Cop), Empire, 1985; John Reynolds, Volunteers, Tri-Star, 1985; Ted, Iron Eagle, Tri-Star, 1986; Sergeant

Patrick "Sarge" Stone, Zone Troopers, Empire, 1986; Lonny, A Tiger's Tale, Atlantic Releasing, 1987; Loy, Near Dark, De Laurentiis Entertainment Group, 1987; Lester, Cherry 2000, Orion, 1988; Tim, The Wrong Guys, New World, 1988; Vince Barnes, Who's Harry Crumb?, Tri-Star, 1989. Also appeared in St. Helens, Parnell, 1981.

PRINCIPAL TELEVISION APPEARANCES—Series: Regular, Cos, ABC, 1976; regular, The Red Foxx Show, ABC, 1977-78; Gene/Jean, Quark, NBC, 1978; Gianni, Angie, ABC, 1979-80; Johnny Danko, The Associates, ABC, 1979-80; Reggie Cavanaugh, The Two of Us, CBS, 1981-82; Theodore Ogilvie, Gun Shy, CBS, 1983; Jerry Baskin, Down and Out in Beverly Hills, Fox, 1987. Mini-Series: Billy Youngblood, Bare Essence, CBS, 1982; Jack, Glory Years, HBO, 1987. Pilots: Chick, A Shadow in the Streets, NBC, 1975; Barney Tuscom, Benny and Barney: Las Vegas Undercover, NBC, 1977; Lester, Getting There, CBS, 1980; Frank Nightingale, Golden Gate, ABC, 1981; Mr. Damrush, In Trouble, ABC, 1981; Damon Rhoades, Cameo By Night, NBC, 1987. Episodic: Sergeant Traynor, Hunter, NBC, 1986; Brom Bones, "The Legend of Sleepy Hollow," Shelley Duvall's Tall Tales and Legends, Showtime, 1986; Mac Dixon, Private Eye, NBC, 1987; Billy Diamond, "Take My Life . . . Please!" The Twilight Zone, CBS, 1986; Sergeant Aubrey Decker, Tour of Duty, CBS, 1987; Ebenezer Wright, St. Elsewhere, NBC, 1987; Mule Muldowski, Hunter, NBC, 1988; Brock Ash, Moonlighting, ABC, 1989; David Treadway, TV 101, CBS, 1989; Colonel Savage, Young Riders, ABC, 1989; also Starsky and Hutch, ABC, 1978; Nero Wolfe, NBC, 1981; Private Benjamin, CBS, 1982; Hunter, NBC, 1984; Hardcastle and McCormick, ABC, 1985; Improv Tonight, syndicated, 1988; Fantasy Island, ABC. Movies: Steve, Terraces, NBC, 1977; Tom Goodman, His Mistress, NBC, 1984; Major Dan Hackett, The B.R.A.T. Patrol, ABC, 1986; also The Incredible Hulk Returns (also known as The Return of the Incredible Hulk), NBC, 1988. Specials: The Richard Pryor Special?, NBC, 1977.

RELATED CAREER—Comedian, Mitzi Shore's Comedy Store, Dunes Hotel, Las Vegas, NV, 1986.

ADDRESSES: AGENT—Harris and Goldberg, 2121 Avenue of the Americas, Suite 950, Los Angeles, CA 90067.*

*   *   *

THOMSON, Gordon   1951-

PERSONAL: Born March 2, 1951, in Ottawa, ON, Canada. EDUCATION—Received a degree in English from McGill University.

VOCATION: Actor.

CAREER: PRINCIPAL STAGE APPEARANCES—Alexei Belaev, A Month in the Country, Stratford Shakespeare Festival, Stratford, ON, Canada, 1973; Cleante, The Imaginary Invalid, Longaville, Love's Labour's Lost, and Lewis, the Dauphin, The Life and Death of King John, all Stratford Shakespeare Festival, 1974. Also appeared A Bee in Her Bonnet, Manitoba Theatre Center, Winnipeg, MB, Canada, 1979; Loot, Studio Arena Theatre, Buffalo, NY, 1980.

MAJOR TOURS—Godspell, Canadian cities, 1972.

PRINCIPAL FILM APPEARANCES—Alan Evans, Explosion (also

known as *The Blast*), American International, 1969; Tony, "Episode 1: Love from the Marketplace," *Love*, Velvet, 1982. Also appeared in *Leopard in the Snow*, New World, 1979.

PRINCIPAL TELEVISION APPEARANCES—Series: Ari Benedict White, *Ryan's Hope*, ABC, 1975; Adam Carrington, *Dynasty*, ABC, 1981-89. Episodic: Harold, "The Lake," *The Ray Bradbury Theatre*, USA, 1989; Major Daniel McGuire, *Murder, She Wrote*, CBS, 1989; also *Baloney*, CBC, 1989; *Fantasy Island*, ABC; *The Love Boat*, ABC; *Finder of Lost Loves*, ABC. Specials: *Miss Hollywood, 1986*, ABC, 1986; *Soap Opera Digest Awards*, NBC, 1988; *Circus of the Stars*, CBS, 1988.

AWARDS: Golden Globe nomination, Best Performance By an Actor in a Series, Mini-Series, or Motion Picture Made for Television, 1988, for *Dynasty*.

ADDRESSES: AGENT—Alan Iezman, William Morris Agency, 151 El Camino Drive, Beverly Hills, CA 90212. MANAGER—Elaine Rich Management, 2400 Whitman Place, Los Angeles, CA 90068.*

*   *   *

THORNTON, Frank   1921-

PERSONAL: Born Frank Ball, January 15, 1921, in London, England; son of William Ernest and Rosina Mary (Thornton) Ball; married Beryl Jane Margaret Evans. EDUCATION—Trained for the stage at the London School of Dramatic Art. MILITARY—Royal Air Force.

VOCATION: Actor.

CAREER: STAGE DEBUT—Brian Curtis, *French Without Tears*, Confraternity Hall, Thurles, Ireland, 1940. PRINCIPAL STAGE APPEARANCES—Fenton and Bardolph, *The Merry Wives of Windsor*, Donald Wolfit's Company, Strand Theatre, London, 1941; Lysander, *A Midsummer Night's Dream* and Laertes, *Hamlet*, both Strand Theatre, 1941-42; Mosca, *Volpone*, Donald Wolfit's Company, St. James's Theatre, London, 1942; Angus and Scottish lord, *Macbeth*, Piccadilly Theatre, London, 1942; Corporal Jones, *Flare Path*, Apollo Theatre, London, 1942; Gregory Throstle (understudy), *One Wild Oat*, Garrick Theatre, London, 1949; Mouche, *The Empty Chair*, Playhouse Theatre, Oxford, U.K., 1956; Dom Joao de Castro, *The Hidden King*, Edinburgh Festival, Edinburgh, Scotland, 1957; Bishop Zog, *The Golden Touch*, Piccadilly Theatre, 1960; ensemble, *Don't Shoot, We're English* (revue), Cambridge Theatre, London, 1960; Caliph, *Hassan*, Dublin Festival, Dublin, Ireland, 1960; Ludovico Nota, *Naked*, Playhouse Theatre, 1960; Edward, *Meals on Wheels*, Royal Court Theatre, London, 1965; Empton QC, *Alibi for a Judge*, Savoy Theatre, London, 1966; Minnit and Procurio, *The Young Visitors*, Piccadilly Theatre, 1968; Charlie Dyer, *Staircase*, Richmond Theatre, London, 1969.

Councillor Parker, *When We Are Married*, Strand Theatre, 1970; Eeyore, *Winnie the Pooh*, Phoenix Theatre, London, 1971, then 1972; Commander Rogers, *French Without Tears*, Lyceum Theatre, Edinburgh, 1974; Sir Andrew Aguecheek, *Twelfth Night* and Duncan, *Macbeth*, both Royal Shakespeare Company, Stratford-on-Avon, U.K., 1974, then Aldwych Theatre, London, 1975; Sir Patrick Cullen, *The Doctor's Dilemma*, Mermaid Theatre, London, 1975; actor #1, *Play By Play*, King's Head Theatre, London, 1975;

FRANK THORNTON

Captain Peacock, *Are You Being Served?*, Winter Gardens Theatre, Blackpool, U.K., 1976; Sir Justin Holbrook, *Shut Your Eyes and Think of England*, Apollo Theatre, 1977; Ernest, *Bedroom Farce*, Theatre Royal, Windsor, U.K., 1979; George, *Jumpers*, Thorndike Theatre, Leatherhead, U.K., 1979; Dr. Sloper, *The Heiress*, Yvonne Arnaud Theatre, Guildford, U.K., 1981; Malvolio, *Twelfth Night*, Watermill Theatre, Newbury, U.K., 1981; Sir Joseph Porter, *H.M.S. Pinafore*, Queen Elizabeth Hall, London, 1982; Sir John Tremayne, *Me and My Girl*, Haymarket Theatre, Leicester, U.K., 1984, then Adelphi Theatre, London, 1985-86; John of Gaunt, *Richard II*, Ludlow Festival, Ludlow, U.K., 1987; Major General Stanley, *The Pirates of Penzance*, Theatre Royal, Plymouth, U.K., 1987; title role, *The Cabinet Minister*, Royal Exchange Theatre, Manchester, U.K., 1987; the Privy Counsellor, *The Tutor*, Old Vic Theatre, London, 1988; General Charles De Gaulle and various roles, *Winnie*, Opera House, Manchester, then Victoria Palace Theatre, London, both 1988; Captain Hook, *Peter Pan*, Connaught Theatre, Worthing, U.K., 1988; Count Shabyelsky, *Ivanov* and Leonato, *Much Ado About Nothing*, both Strand Theatre, 1989. Also appeared in *Five Players in Four Plays*, Aldeburgh Festival, Aldeburgh, U.K., 1962; Dr. Wicksteed, *Habeas Corpus*, Perth, Australia, 1983; Barney Cashman, *Last of the Red Hot Lovers*, Mill-at-Sonning, 1983.

MAJOR TOURS—Dewhurst, *The Scarlet Pimpernel*, Donald Wolfit's Company, U.K. cities, 1941; Franzel, *The Dancing Years*, U.K. cities, 1947-48; Gregory Throstle, *One Wild Oat*, U.K. cities, 1950; Philip, *The Little Hut*, U.K. cities, 1965; Roger, *Roger's Last Stand*, U.K. cities, 1977; Sir Justin Holbrook, *Shut Your Eyes and Think of England*, U.K. cities, 1977; Dr. Wicksteed, *Habeas*

Corpus, Australian cities, 1980-81; Detective Inspector Hubbard, *Dial "M" for Murder,* U.K. cities, 1982.

PRINCIPAL FILM APPEARANCES—Manservant, *Gambling Lady,* Warner Brothers, 1934; guard, *The Man Who Broke the Bank at Monte Carlo,* Twentieth Century-Fox, 1935; television director, *Ring-a-Ding Rhythm* (also known as *It's Trad, Dad!*), Columbia, 1962; barman, *The Tell-Tale Heart* (also known as *The Hidden Room of 1,000 Murders*), Brigadier-Union, 1962; photographer, *Trial and Error* (also known as *The Dock Brief*), Metro-Goldwyn-Mayer, 1962; doctor, *The Early Bird,* Rank, 1965; Mr. A&R, *Gonks Go Beat,* Anglo-Amalgamated, 1965; Peperel, *The Tomb of Ligeia* (also known as *Tomb of the Cat*), American International, 1965; Mr. Jones, *Carry On Screaming,* Warner Brothers/Pathe, 1966; radio announcer, *The Murder Game,* Twentieth Century-Fox, 1966; manager, *The Wild Affair,* Goldstone, 1966; valuation officer, *Alf 'n' Family* (also known as *Till Death Do Us Part*), Sherpix, 1968; Charles, *A Flea in Her Ear,* Twentieth Century-Fox, 1968; registrar, *30 Is a Dangerous Age, Cynthia,* Columbia, 1968; BBC man, *The Bed Sitting Room,* United Artists, 1969.

Police inspector, *The Magic Christian,* Commonwealth, 1970; porter, *The Private Life of Sherlock Holmes,* United Artists, 1970; Stoddart, *The Rise and Rise of Michael Rimmer,* Warner Brothers, 1970; Mr. Driver, *All the Way Up,* Anglo-Amalgamated, 1970; Cyril, *Sophie's Place* (also known as *Crooks and Coronets*), Warner Brothers/Seven Arts, 1970; estate agent, *Digby, the Biggest Dog in the World,* Cinerama, 1974; King, *Old Dracula* (also known as *Vampira* and *Old Drac*), American International, 1975; Inspector Crumb, *Side By Side,* GTO, 1975; Dr. Johnson, *Spanish Fly,* EMI, 1975; Whitlow, *The Bawdy Adventures of Tom Jones,* Universal, 1976. Also appeared in *Cracked Nuts,* RKO, 1931; *Secret of the Chateau,* Universal, 1935; *Radio Cab Murder,* Eros, 1954; *Stock Car,* Butchers Film Service, 1955; *Johnny, You're Wanted,* Anglo-Amalgamated, 1956; *Operation Conspiracy* (also known as *Cloak Without Dagger*), Republic, 1957; *A Funny Thing Happened on the Way to the Forum,* United Artists, 1966; *The Assassination Bureau,* Paramount, 1969.

PRINCIPAL TELEVISION APPEARANCES—Series: Captain Peacock, *Are You Being Served?,* BBC, 1972-84, then PBS. Mini-Series: Mr. Trabb, *Great Expectations,* HTV, then Disney Channel, 1989. Also appeared in *The Taming of the Shrew* and *It's a Square World.*

RELATED CAREER—Member, Southsea Repertory Company.

NON-RELATED CAREER—Insurance clerk.

MEMBER: Garrick Club, Green Room Club.

ADDRESSES: MANAGER—David Daly Personal Management, 68 Old Brompton Road, London SW7 3LQ, England.

*   *   *

THRONE, Malachi

VOCATION: Actor.

CAREER: PRINCIPAL STAGE APPEARANCES—*L.A. Under Siege,* Center Theatre Group, Los Angeles, 1971.

PRINCIPAL FILM APPEARANCES—Professor Schwartz, *The Young Lovers,* Metro-Goldwyn-Mayer, 1964; Kerjacki, *Beau Geste,* Universal, 1966; Bill Windsor, *Frasier, the Sensuous Lion,* LCS, 1973; Payton Jory, *The Greatest,* Columbia, 1977; Earl, *Stunts* (also known as *Who Is Killing the Stuntmen?*), New Line, 1977; opera announcer, *Eat and Run,* New World, 1986.

PRINCIPAL TELEVISION APPEARANCES—Series: Noah Bain, *It Takes a Thief,* ABC, 1968-69; Ali Baba, "Electra Woman and Dyna Girl," *The Krofft Supershow,* ABC, 1976-77; Ted Adamson, *Search for Tomorrow,* CBS, 1978. Pilots: Hoffman, *Code Name: Heraclitus* (broadcast as an episode of *The Bob Hope Chrysler Theatre*), NBC, 1967; Garrison, *Police Story,* NBC, 1967. Episodic: Dr. Mike, "Cold Hands, Warm Heart," *The Outer Limits,* ABC, 1964; Commodore Jose Mendez, "The Menagerie," *Star Trek,* NBC, 1966; False Face, *Batman,* ABC, 1966; also *Love American Style,* ABC; *What's Happening!,* ABC; *General Electric True* (also known as *True*), CBS. Movies: Bartender, *The Doomsday Flight,* NBC, 1966; Dr. Dykers, *Assualt on the Wayne,* ABC, 1971; voice of Dr. Otto Litsky, *The Sex Symbol,* ABC, 1974; also *Longarm,* ABC, 1988.*

*   *   *

TIGAR, Kenneth   1942-

PERSONAL: Born September 24, 1942, in Chelsea, MA. EDUCATION—Graduated from Havard University.

VOCATION: Actor.

CAREER: OFF-BROADWAY DEBUT—Briggs, *Thunder Rock,* Equity Library Theatre, Master Theatre, 1973. PRINCIPAL STAGE APPEARANCES—Ensemble, *The Proposition* (revue), Bitter End, New York City, 1968; Woodcutter, *Rashomon,* Equity Library Theatre, New York City, 1973; Adolf, *Baba Goya,* American Place Theatre, then retitled *Nourish the Beast,* Cherry Lane Theatre, both New York City, 1973; Ferapont, *The Three Sisters,* AMAS Repertory Theatre, Beaumont Hall, New York City, 1973; Foreman Knuckunder, *Cream Cheese* and man, *Love Scene,* both Festival of Short Plays, American Place Theatre, 1974; Walter, *Gallows Humor,* Equity Library Theatre, Library and Museum of Performing Arts, New York City, 1975. Also appeared in *Mississippi Moonshine,* Playwrights Horizons, New York City, 1975; *The Primary English Class,* Los Angeles Actors Theatre, Los Angeles, 1982; and with the South Coast Repertory Theatre, Costa Mesa, CA, 1979-80.

PRINCIPAL FILM APPEARANCES—Steve, *The Happy Hooker,* Cannon, 1975; Pavlo, *Creator,* Universal, 1985; Mr. Raymaker, *Just One of Guys,* Columbia, 1985; Professor Swivet, *18 Again!,* New World, 1988; Father Meyers, *Phantasm II,* Universal, 1988; bomb squad leader, *Lethal Weapon II,* Warner Brothers, 1989.

PRINCIPAL TELEVISION APPEARANCES—Series: Thomas E. Dewey, *The Gangster Chronicles,* NBC, 1981. Pilots: Jim, *The Rock Rainbow,* ABC, 1978; Schulman, *The Gypsy Warriors,* CBS, 1978; Mel Orlofsky, *Love, Natalie,* NBC, 1980; burglar, *Great Day,* CBS, 1983; Martin Halmos, *Dirty Work,* CBS, 1985; Saul Goldman, *Jake's M.O.,* NBC, 1987. Episodic: Dr. Miller Simon, *The Man from Atlantis,* NBC, 1977; Dr. Lowell Greenspon, *Cheers,* NBC, 1985; Slotkin, *Night Court,* NBC, 1985; John McGill, *Stingray,* NBC, 1986; O'Malley, *L.A. Law,* NBC, 1986;

judge, *Hunter*, NBC, 1986; Richard Morris, *Crazy Like a Fox*, CBS, 1986; the Ripper, *Magnum, P.I.*, CBS, 1986; Scripps, *Hill Street Blues*, NBC, 1986; Bill, *Mr. Belvedere*, ABC, 1987; Dr. Gordon, *Dallas*, CBS, 1987; Dr. Robbins, *Mr. President*, Fox, 1987; Eddy Silver, *Ohara*, ABC, 1987; Gus Melman, *Night Court*, NBC, 1987; Mr. Meyers, *Highway to Heaven*, NBC, 1987; Mr. Terry, *Webster*, ABC, 1987; Sid Sidlevich, *Growing Pains*, ABC, 1987, 1988, and 1989; Detective Dorn, *Sonny Spoon*, NBC, 1988; Dr. Russell, *The Bronx Zoo*, NBC, 1988; Fritz Heath, *Dynasty*, ABC, 1988 and 1989; F.B.I. agent, *ALF*, NBC, 1989; judge, *Amen*, NBC, 1989; Mr. Timmons, *Who's the Boss?*, ABC, 1989; Reuben Pomerantz, *Knots Landing*, CBS, 1990; also *Barney Miller*, ABC, 1975, 1978, 1979, and 1981; *Cheers*, NBC, 1983; "Justin Case," *The Disney Sunday Movie*, ABC, 1988; *Baywatch*, NBC, 1990.

Movies: Father O'Brien, *The Golden Gate Murders* (also known as *Specter on the Bridge*), CBS, 1979; Tom Montgomery, *The Babysitter*, ABC, 1980; Parker, *Pray TV*, ABC, 1982; Bill Richardson, *Thursday's Child*, CBS, 1983; Alan Rosenus, *Missing Pieces*, CBS, 1983; pathologist, *Fatal Vision*, NBC, 1984; Raymond, *A Death in California*, ABC, 1985; Ross, *Second Serve*, CBS, 1986; also *The Big Black Pill*, NBC, 1981; *Special Bulletin*, NBC, 1983; *Roe vs. Wade*, NBC, 1989. Specials: Hessian major, "The World Turned Upside Down," *Ourstory*, PBS, 1975; Sam Rinaldo, "Juvi," *CBS Schoolbreak Special*, CBS, 1987.

ADDRESSES: AGENT—Michael Slessinger, Actors Group Agency, 8285 Sunset Boulevard, Suite 12, Los Angeles, CA 90046.*

*   *   *

TILTON, Charlene   1958-

PERSONAL: Born December 1, 1958, in San Diego, CA; mother's name, Katherine (a secretary); married Johnny Lee (a singer), February 14, 1982 (divorced, 1984); married Dominick Allen (a singer, composer, and actor), April 7, 1985; children: Cherish.

VOCATION: Actress.

CAREER: PRINCIPAL FILM APPEARANCES—Bambi, *Freaky Friday*, Buena Vista, 1976; party girl, *Big Wednesday*, Warner Brothers, 1978; Jennifer Cresswell, *The Fall of the House of Usher*, Sunn Classic, 1980.

PRINCIPAL FILM WORK—Co-producer, *Pale Horse, Pale Rider* (short film).

PRINCIPAL TELEVISION APPEARANCES—Series: Lucy Ewing Cooper, *Dallas*, 1978-85, then 1988—. Episodic: Cindy, *Murder, She Wrote*, CBS, 1987; also *Hotel*, ABC, 1983; *The Love Boat*, ABC, 1985; *Happy Days*, ABC; *Police Woman*, NBC; *Eight Is Enough*, ABC; *Saturday Night Live*, NBC; *The Bionic Woman*. ABC. Movies: Julie Thurston, *Diary of a Hitchhiker*, ABC, 1979. Specials: *Battle of the Network Stars*, ABC, 1976, 1978, 1980, 1981, 1984, and 1988; *Circus of the Stars*, CBS, 1979; *The New and Spectacular Guinness Book of World Records*, ABC, 1980; *Bob Hope's Funny Valentine*, NBC, 1981; *Bob Hope's Women I Love—Beautiful But Funny*, NBC, 1982; *The Academy of Country Music's Twentieth Anniversary Reunion*, NBC, 1986; *America—The Great Mississippi* (also known as *The Serendipity Singers Special*), syndicated, 1987; *Diet America Challenge*, NBC, 1989.

CHARLENE TILTON

RELATED CAREER—Actress in television commercials.

AWARDS: Hollywood Presswomen's Award, Best Juvenile Actress, 1979.

ADDRESSES: AGENT—Eleanor Berger, Irv Schechter Company, 9300 Wilshire Boulevard, Suite 410, Beverly Hills, CA 90212.*

*   *   *

TODD, Beverly   1946-

PERSONAL: Born July 11, 1946, in Chicago, IL; daughter of Virena (Skinner) Todd; children: Malik Smith (deceased).

VOCATION: Actress.

CAREER: PRINCIPAL STAGE APPEARANCES—Myrna Jessup, *Carry Me Back to Morningside Heights*, John Golden Theatre, New York City, 1968; Coretta, "Gettin' It Together" in *Black Visions*, New York Shakespeare Festival, Public Theatre, New York City, 1972.

PRINCIPAL FILM APPEARANCES—Sally, *The Lost Man*, Universal, 1969; Puff, *They Call Me Mister Tibbs!*, United Artists, 1970; Louisa MacGill, *Brother John*, Columbia, 1971; Louise Williams, *Vice Squad*, AVCO-Embassy/Hemdale/Brent Walker, 1982; Georgiane, *The Ladies Club*, New Line Cinema, 1986; Laura, *Happy Hour*, Movie Store, 1987; Ann Bowen, *Baby Boom*, Metro-Goldwyn-Mayer/United Artists, 1987; Dora, *Clara's Heart*,

Warner Brothers, 1988; Monica Pear, *Moving,* Warner Brothers, 1988; Ms. Levias, *Lean on Me,* Warner Brothers, 1989. Also appeared in *Homework,* Jensen Farley, 1982.

PRINCIPAL TELEVISION APPEARANCES—Series: Monica Nelson, *Love of Life,* CBS, 1968-70; Kelly Williams, *Julie Farr, M.D.* (also known as *Having Babies*), ABC, 1978-79; Felicia Clemmons-Hughes, *The Redd Foxx Show,* ABC, 1986. Mini-Series: Fanta, *Roots,* ABC, 1977. Pilots: Melissa, *Deadlock,* NBC, 1969; Kelly Williams, *Having Babies III,* ABC, 1978; Deputy Carmen, *Fraud Squad,* ABC, 1985. Episodic: Donna Clemens, *Magnum, P.I.,* CBS, 1985; Valerie, *Me and Mrs. C.,* NBC, 1987; Denise, *The Robert Guillaume Show,* ABC, 1989; Sara Caldwell, *Snoops,* CBS, 1989; also *Falcon Crest,* CBS; *Quincy, M.E.,* NBC; *Lou Grant,* CBS; *Benson,* ABC; *Hill Street Blues,* NBC; *Family,* ABC. Movies: Dana, *The Ghost of Flight 401,* NBC, 1978; Wylene Stills, *The Jericho Mile,* ABC, 1979; Lahoma Brown Paige, *Don't Look Back,* ABC, 1981; Beatty, *A Touch of Scandal,* CBS, 1984; Maria, *A Different Affair,* CBS, 1987. Specials: Louise Hawley, "Please Don't Hit Me, Mom," *ABC Afterschool Specials,* ABC, 1981; *Sixteenth Annual Black Filmmakers Hall of Fame,* ABC, 1989.

ADDRESSES: AGENT—John Kimble, Triad Artists, 10100 Santa Monica Boulevard, 16th Floor, Los Angeles, CA 90067. MANAGER—Michael Mann Management, 8380 Melrose Avenue, Suite 207, Los Angeles, CA 90069.*

*   *   *

TOLKAN, James   1931-

PERSONAL: Full name, James S. Tolkan; born in 1931 in Calumet, MI; son of Ralph M. Tolkan (a cattle dealer); wife's name, Parmalee (a costume designer). EDUCATION—University of Iowa, B.A., drama, 1956; trained for the stage with Stella Adler. MILITARY—U.S. Navy, 1950-51.

VOCATION: Actor.

CAREER: STAGE DEBUT—Improvised council, *Between Two Thieves,* York Playhouse, New York City, 1960. PRINCIPAL STAGE APPEARANCES—Frank, *The Shoemaker and the Peddler,* East 74th Street Theatre, New York City, 1960; Seth Gale, *Abe Lincoln in Illinois,* Phoenix Theatre Company, Anderson Theatre, New York City, 1963; Herman Glogauer, *Once in a Lifetime,* York Playhouse, New York City, 1964; carnival person, *The Three Sisters,* Morosco Theatre, New York City, 1964; Weiss, *The Cannibals,* American Place Theatre, New York City, 1968; officer of the Queen's guard, *Mary Stuart,* Repertory Theatre of Lincoln Center, Vivian Beaumont Theatre, New York City, 1971; Two Ton Tessie (sergeant), *Pinkville,* St. Clement's Church Theatre, New York City, 1971; Pope, *The Silent Partner,* Actors' Studio, New York City, 1972; jury member, *Twelve Angry Men,* Queens Playhouse, New York City, 1972; Tola, *Narrow Road to the Deep North,* Repertory Theatre of Lincoln Center, Vivian Beaumont Theatre, 1972; Dr. Marrow, *Forty-Two Seconds from Broadway,* Playhouse Theatre, New York City, 1973; Katz, *Full Circle,* American National Theatre and Academy Theatre, New York City, 1973; Gonzalo, *The Tempest* and Rosse, *Macbeth,* both New York Shakespeare Festival, Mitzi E. Newhouse Theatre, New York City, 1974; Charlie Allman, *Dream of a Blacklisted Actor,* Ensemble Studio Theatre, New York City, 1975; Allon, Menachem, and D.P., *Golda,* Morosco Theatre, 1977; Skinny, *Jungle of Cities,*

Colonnades Theatre, New York City, 1979; Billy, *Wings,* Lyceum Theatre, New York City, 1979.

Dave Moss, *Glengarry Glen Ross,* Goodman Theatre, Chicago, IL, then John Golden Theatre, New York City, both 1984; Harvey, *One Tennis Shoe,* Marathon '85, Ensemble Studio Theatre, 1985; Detective Lieutenant Fine, "Clara" in *Danger: Memory!,* Mitzi E. Newhouse Theatre, 1987. Also appeared in *A View from the Bridge,* Sheridan Square Playhouse, New York City, 1965; *Wait Until Dark,* Ethel Barrymore Theatre, New York City, 1966; *Dandelion Wine,* Arena Stage, Washington, DC, 1976; *The Life of Galileo,* Pittsburgh Public Theatre, Pittsburgh, PA, 1981; *The Front Page,* Long Wharf Theatre, New Haven, CT, 1982; with the Charles Playhouse, Boston, MA, 1967-68; Stratford Shakespeare Festival, Stratford, ON, Canada, 1969; Center Stage, Baltimore, MD, 1972-73; Barter Theatre, Abingdon, VA, 1976; and Arena Stage, 1981.

MAJOR TOURS—Dr. Artinian, then bell boy, *The Best Man,* U.S. cities, 1961-62.

PRINCIPAL FILM APPEARANCES—Edwards, *Stiletto,* AVCO-Embassy, 1969; Mr. Brown, *They Might Be Giants,* Universal, 1971; contact man, *The Friends of Eddie Coyle,* Paramount, 1973; Napoleon, *Love and Death,* United Artists, 1975; coroner, *The Amityville Horror,* American International, 1979; District Attorney Polito, *Prince of the City,* Warner Brothers, 1981; Baldy, *Wolfen,* Warner Brothers, 1981; St. Glass, *Author! Author!,* Twentieth Century-Fox, 1982; conferee, *Hanky-Panky,* Columbia, 1982; bishop's voice, "The Bishop of Battle" in *Nightmares,* Universal, 1983; Wigan, *WarGames,* United Artists, 1983; Maynard, *Iceman,* Universal, 1984; Howard Simpson, *The River,* Universal, 1984; Hanley, *Turk 182!,* Twentieth Century-Fox, 1985; Turner, *Flanagan* (also known as *Walls of Glass*), United Film Distribution, 1985; Mr. Strickland, *Back to the Future,* Universal, 1985; Brackman, *Armed and Dangerous,* Columbia, 1986; Stinger, *Top Gun,* Paramount, 1986; Harry, *Off Beat,* Buena Vista, 1986; Detective Lubic, *Masters of the Universe,* Cannon, 1987; Mr. Bjornstead, *Made in Heaven,* Lorimar, 1987; Colonel Tanzer, *Viper,* Fries Distributing, 1988; Benny Pistone, *Split Decisions* (also known as *Kid Gloves*), New Century/Vista, 1988; Joe Hanley, *True Blood* (also known as *Edge of Darkness*), Fries Entertainment, 1989.

PRINCIPAL TELEVISION APPEARANCES—Series: Lester Mintz, *Mary,* CBS, 1985-86. Episodic: Roger Williams, "The Peach Gang," *Ourstory,* PBS, 1975; Billy, "Wings," *American Playhouse,* PBS, 1983; Norman Keyes, *Remington Steele,* NBC, 1985, 1986, and 1987; Mason Mather, *Miami Vice,* NBC, 1987; Ruger, *The Equalizer,* CBS, 1989. Movies: Kennel master, *Little Spies,* ABC, 1986; Dr. Siegel, *Leap of Faith,* CBS, 1988; Major Alex Thompson, *Weekend War,* ABC, 1988; Lieutenant Ed Henderson, *The Case of the Hillside Stranglers* (also known as *Bloodbrothers: The Hillside Stranglers*), NBC, 1989. Specials: Narrator, "Do the Guilty Go Free?," *America Undercover,* HBO, 1988.

SIDELIGHTS: RECREATIONS—Collecting folk art.

ADDRESSES: AGENT—Judith Neff, Gores/Fields Agency, 10100 Santa Monica Boulevard, Suite 700, Los Angeles, CA 90067.*

TOMPKINS, Angel

PERSONAL: Born Angeline Stromberg, December 20, in Albany, CA; daughter of Martin (a real estate broker) and Helen (Robertson) Stromberg; children: Troy. EDUCATION—Attended the University of Texas, El Paso and the University of Illinois, Champaign-Urbana; trained for the stage with Milton Katselas, Ned Manderino, and Adele Khoury.

VOCATION: Actress.

CAREER: PRINCIPAL STAGE APPEARANCES—Tracy, *Mary, Mary,* Sahara Tahoe Hotel, Lake Tahoe, NV; Hanna, *Why Hanna's Skirts Won't Stay Down,* Zephyr Theatre, Los Angeles; the Woman, *Courtship,* Richard Shepard Theatre, Los Angeles; Mother, *The Feeling Hour,* Eagle Theatre, Los Angeles; also appeared as the Major's wife, *Unsold Pilots,* Los Angeles.

PRINCIPAL FILM APPEARANCES—Fran Harper, *Hang Your Hat on the Wind,* Buena Vista, 1969; Helene Donnelly, *I Love My Wife,* Universal, 1970; Clarabelle, *Prime Cut,* National General, 1972; Ruby Dunne, *The Don Is Dead* (also known as *Beautiful But Deadly*), Universal, 1973; Cleo, *Little Cigars,* American International, 1973; Pamela Balsam, *How to Seduce a Woman,* Cinerama, 1974; title role, *The Teacher* (also known as *The Seductress*), Crown International, 1974; Marganne Stilson, *Walking Tall, Part II,* American International, 1975; Betty McCral, *The Farmer,* Columbia, 1977; Sandra Miller, *The Bees,* New World, 1978; Kitty, *One Man Jury,* Cal-Am Artists, 1978; news reporter, *Alligator,* Group 1, 1980; Ms. Waters, *Dangerously Close,* Cannon, 1986; Jan, *Murphy's Law,* Cannon, 1986; Diane Wallace, *The Naked Cage,* Cannon, 1986; First Lady, *Amazon Women on the Moon,* Universal, 1987; LaVonne, *A Tiger's Tale,* Atlantic Releasing, 1988; Carmen, *Relentless,* New Line Cinema, 1989. Also appeared as Mother, *Rockhouse,* 1989.

PRINCIPAL TELEVISION APPEARANCES—Series: Gloria Harding, *Search,* NBC, 1972-73. Pilots: Gloria Harding, *Probe* (also known as *Search*), NBC, 1972; townsperson, *The Buffalo Soldiers,* NBC, 1979; also Miss Dunes, *Cousins,* CBS. Episodic: Grace, *Three's Company,* ABC; Ailene Hardesty, *The New F.B.I.,* ABC; Connie Chasen, *Knight Rider,* NBC; Nora Raeburn, *Knight Rider,* NBC; Debbie, *The Rousters,* NBC; Lita, *The Fall Guy,* ABC; surgeon, *Knots Landing,* CBS; Gloria, *Hardcastle and McCormick,* ABC; Dr. Diane, *General Hospital,* ABC; Bitsy Carmichael, *E/R,* CBS; Bonnie Henderson, *Simon and Simon,* CBS; Sylvia Finnegan, *Simon and Simon,* CBS; Diane, *T.J. Hooker,* ABC; Judge Grassblood, *Amazing Stories,* NBC; Janet, *The Hitchhiker,* HBO. Movies: Jennifer Pierce, *You Lie So Deep, My Love,* ABC, 1975. Also appeared as co-host, *Am Am.*

NON-RELATED CAREER—Investor, licensed building contractor, finished carpenter.

AWARDS: Golden Globe, Most Promising Newcomer, 1972; *Billboard* Award, New Young Player, 1975.

MEMBER: Screen Actors Guild, American Federation of Television and Radio Artists, Actors' Equity Association, Women in Film.

ADDRESSES: AGENT—The Artist Group Ltd., 1930 Century Park W., Suite 403, Los Angeles, CA 90067.

TOWNE, Robert 1936-
(P.H. Vazak, Edward Wain)

PERSONAL: Born in 1936; second wife's name, Luisa; children: one daughter. EDUCATION—Studied philosophy and literature at Pomona State College; studied acting with Jeff Corey. MILITARY—U.S. Army.

VOCATION: Writer, director, producer, and actor.

CAREER: Also see *WRITINGS* below. PRINCIPAL FILM APPEARANCES—(As Edward Wain) Martin, *The Last Woman on Earth,* Filmgroup, 1960; (as Edward Wain) Sparks Moran, *The Creature from the Haunted Sea,* Flimgroup, 1961; Richard, *Drive, He Said,* Columbia, 1971; Stan, *The Pick-Up Artist,* Twentieth Century-Fox, 1987.

PRINCIPAL FILM WORK—Producer and director, *Personal Best,* Warner Brothers, 1982; director, *Tequila Sunrise,* Warner Brothers, 1988; executive producer, *The Bedroom Window,* De Laurentis Entertainment Group, 1987.

NON-RELATED CAREER—Real estate agent and commercial fisherman.

WRITINGS: FILM—(As Edward Wain) *The Last Woman on Earth,* Filmgroup, 1960; *The Tomb of Ligeia* (also known as *Tomb of the Cat*), American International, 1965; (with Sam Peckinpah) *Villa Rides,* Paramount, 1968; *The Last Detail,* Columbia, 1973; *Chinatown,* Paramount, 1974; (with Warren Beatty) *Shampoo,* Columbia, 1975; (with Paul Schrader) *The Yakuza* (also known as *Brotherhood of Yakuza*), Warner Brothers/Toei, 1975; *Personal Best,* Warner Brothers, 1982; (as P.H. Vazak; with Michael Austin) *Greystoke: The Legend of Tarzan, Lord of the Apes,* Warner Brothers, 1984; *Tequila Sunrise,* Warner Brothers, 1988; *The Two Jakes,* Paramount, 1990. TELEVISION—Episodic: *The Lloyd Bridges Show,* CBS, 1962 and 1963 (four episodes); "The Chameleon," *The Outer Limits,* ABC, 1964; "The Dove Affair," *The Man from U.N.C.L.E.,* NBC, 1964; "So Many Pretty Girls, So Little Time," *Breaking Point,* ABC, 1964; *The Richard Boone Show,* NBC, 1964. OTHER—"A Screenwriter on Screenwriting," *Anatomy of the Movies,* Macmillan, 1981.

AWARDS: Academy Award nomination, Best Screenplay Based on Material from Another Medium, 1973, for *The Last Detail;* Academy Award, Best Original Screenplay, 1974, for *Chinatown;* Academy Award nomination (with Warren Beatty), Best Original Screenplay, 1975, for *Shampoo;* Academy Award nomination (with Michael Austin), Best Screenplay Based on Material from Another Medium, 1984, for *Greystoke: The Legend of Tarzan, Lord of the Apes.*

SIDELIGHTS: In addition to the films noted above for which he wrote the screenplays, Robert Towne has also acted as an uncredited script doctor on such films as *The Creature from the Haunted Sea,* Filmgroup, 1961; *A Time for Killing,* Columbia, 1967; (received credit as "special consultant") *Bonnie and Clyde,* Warner Brothers, 1967; *Cisco Pike,* Columbia, 1971; *The Godfather,* Paramount, 1972; *Marathon Man,* Paramount, 1977; *Swing Shift,* Warner Brothers, 1984; *Eight Million Ways to Die,* Tri-Star, 1986; *Frantic,* Warner Brothers, 1988.

OTHER SOURCES: American Film, January/February, 1989; *Dictionary of Literary Biography,* Vol. 44, Gale, 1986.

ADDRESSES: OFFICE—Warner Brothers Inc., 4000 Warner Boulevard, Burbank, CA 91522.*

*   *   *

TROELL, Jan   1931-

PERSONAL: Born July 23, 1931, in Limhamn, Sweden.

VOCATION: Director, cinematographer, film editor, and screenwriter.

CAREER: Also see *WRITINGS* below. PRINCIPAL FILM APPEARANCES—*Sagolandet* (also known as *Fairylands, The Fairy Tale Country,* and *Land of Dreams*), Svenska Filminstitutet, 1986. PRINCIPAL FILM WORK—All as director, cinematographer, and editor, unless indicated: *Har har du ditt liv* (also known as *Here's Your Life* and *Here Is Your Life*), Brandon, 1968; *Utvandrarna* (also known as *The Emigrants*), Warner Brothers, 1972; *Nybyggarna* (also known as *The New Land, The Settlers,* and *Unto a Good Land*) Warner Brothers, 1973; (director only) *Zandy's Bride,* Warner Brothers, 1974; *Bang!,* Svenska Filminstutet, 1977; (director only) *Hurricane* (also known as *Forbidden Paradise*), Paramount, 1979; *Ingenjor Andrees luftfard* (also known as *Flight of the Eagle*), Svenska Filminstitutet, 1982, released in the United States by Summit Feature Distributors, 1983; *Sagolandet* (also known as *Fairylands, The Fairy Tale Country,* and *Land of Dreams*), Svenska Filminstitutet, 1986; also *Ole dole doff* (also known as *Eeny Meeny Miny Moe, Who Saw Him Die?*), 1968.

Also director and cinematographer of the following short films and documentaries: *Stad,* 1960; *Baten* (also known as *The Ship*), 1961; *Sommartag* (also known as *Summer Train*), 1961; *Nyarsafton pa skanska slatten* (also known as *New Year's Eve on the Skane Plains*), 1961; *De kom tillbaka* (also known as *The Return*), 1962; *Pojken och draken* (also known as *The Boy and the Kite*), 1962; (co-director) *Var i Dalby hage* (also known as *Spring in Dalby Pastures*), 1962; (cinematographer only) *Barnvagnen* (also known as *The Pram* and *The Baby Carriage*), 1963; *De gamla kvarnen* (also known as *The Old Mill*), 1964; *Johan Ekberg* 1964; *Trakom* (also known as *Trachoma*), 1964; (also editor) "Uppehall i myrlandet" (also known as "Stopover in the Marshland" and "Interlude in the Marshland") in *4 x 4,* 1965.

RELATED CAREER—Documentary filmmaker for Swedish television.

NON-RELATED CAREER—Elementary school teacher, Malmo, Sweden, during the 1950s.

WRITINGS: FILM—(Co-writer) "Uppehall i myrlandet" in *4 X 4,* 1965; *Ole dole doff,* 1968; (with Bengt Forslund) *Har har du ditt liv,* Brandon, 1968; (with Forslund) *Utvandrarna,* Warner Brothers, 1972; (with Forslund) *Nybyggarna,* Warner Brothers, 1973; (with Sven Christer Swahn) *Bang!,* Svenska Filminstitutet, 1977; (with Georg Oddner, Ian Rakoff, and Klaus Rifbjerg) *Ingenjor Andrees luftfard,* Svenska Filminstitutet, 1982; *Sagolandet,* Svenska Filminstitutet, 1986. OTHER—Contributor to periodicals and journals.

AWARDS: Chicago Film Festival Award, 1967, Berlin Film Festival Award, and Montreal Film Festival Award, all for *Here Is Your Life;* Chicago Film Festival Award, 1969, for *Ole dole doff;* Academy Award nomination, Best Foreign Film, 1982, for *Flight of the Eagle.**

PATRICK TULL

TULL, Patrick   1941-

PERSONAL: Born July 28, 1941, in Bexhill, England; son of Richard Tull (a soldier) and Phillida (an actress; maiden name, Pantlin) Tull; married Pamela Eyton-Jones (divorced, 1974); married Nancy Butler (divorced, 1978); married Suellyn M. Dennis (director of the New York Press Association), December 10, 1979; children: Katharine, Siobhan. EDUCATION—Attended the London Academy of Music and Dramatic Arts. RELIGION—Church of England.

VOCATION: Actor.

CAREER: STAGE DEBUT—Caretaker, *Rhinoceros,* Nottingham Playhouse, Nottingham, U.K., 1961. LONDON DEBUT—Cookson, *Peter Pan,* Scala Theatre, 1962. BROADWAY DEBUT—Sergeant Harris, *The Astrakhan Coat,* Helen Hayes Theatre, 1967. OFF-BROADWAY DEBUT—Blore, *Ten Little Indians,* Equity Library Theatre, 1981. PRINCIPAL STAGE APPEARANCES—Vanhattan, *The Apple Cart,* Mermaid Theatre, London, 1969; priest, *Amadeus,* Broadhurst Theatre, New York City, 1982; Seamus Shields, *The Shadow of a Gunman,* Syracuse Stage, Syracuse, NY, 1983; Reverend Chasuble, *The Importance of Being Earnest,* Clarance Brown Company, Knoxville, TN, 1983; Moroso, *The Tamer Tamed,* Westbeth Theatre Center, New York City, 1984; also appeared in *A Christmas Carol,* Pennsylvania Stage Company, Allentown, PA, 1984; *Brand* and *Frankenstein,* both City Stage Company, New York City, 1985-86; *Saint Joan,* Tyrone Guthrie Theatre, Minneapolis, MN, 1986; as the window washer, *Witness,* King's Head Theatre, London; Andrew Wyke, *Sleuth,* Tennessee Williams Fine Arts Center, Key West, FL; title role, *Goodman*

Clocker, first voice, *Under Milk Wood*, and Baptista, *The Taming of the Shrew*, all St. Mary's Festival, St. Mary's City, MD; Giles Corey, *The Crucible*, Empire State Institute for the Performing Arts, Albany, NY; Montague, *Romeo and Juliet*, 28th Street Playhouse, New York City; Captain Cat, *Under Milk Wood*, Dublin Theatre Festival, Dublin, Ireland; Petey, *The Birthday Party*, YM/YWHA, New York City; in *MacBird!*, *The Provok'd Wife*, and *The Marie Lloyd Story*, all Theatre Royal, Stratford East, U.K.; *A Christmas Carol*, Greeley Street Theatre, Chappaqua, NY; *The Rivals*, Berkeley Repertory Theatre, Berkeley, CA; *She Stoops to Conquer*, Pearl Theatre, New York City; Van Helsing, *Dracula*; and appeared in repertory productions in Harrogate, York, Cromer, Sidmouth, Salisbury, and Canterbury, U.K.

FILM DEBUT—Accountant, *Life at the Top*, Columbia, 1965. PRINCIPAL FILM APPEARANCES—Templeton, *Mosquito Squadron*, United Artists, 1970; bearded student, *Tomorrow*, Rank Film Distributors, 1970; Cecil, *Parting Glances*, Cinecom International, 1986; also appeared in *All Neat in Black Stockings*, National General/Warner Brothers, 1969; and in *The Inn Way Out*.

TELEVISION DEBUT—*Z Cars*, BBC, 1963. PRINCIPAL TELEVISION APPEARANCES—Episodic: Voice of God, *One Life to Live*, ABC; monster voices, *Dr. Who*, BBC. Specials: Terry, *Murder Motel*, ABC, 1975. Also appeared as Charlie Modryb, *Progress to the Park*, BBC; in *Comedy for Rent*, KTCA (St. Paul, MN); as George Thorp, *Jamestown: Beware of the People of the Sunrise*; and in *No Hiding Place*, *Dad's Army*, *Softly Softly*, *Hugh and I*, *Lieutenant Tenant*, *Londoners*, *To the Frontier*, *Thirty Minute Theatre*, and *Sentimental Education*.

RELATED CAREER—Company member, Nottingham Playhouse, Nottingham, U.K., 1961-62, and 1964-65; actor in productions for BBC radio; recorded books-on-tape, including most of the works of George Orwell.

WRITINGS: RADIO—(Adaptor) *Foundation Trilogy*, BBC.

MEMBER: Actors' Equity Association, American Federation of Television and Radio Artists, Screen Actors Guild.

*   *   *

TYNER, Charles   1925-

PERSONAL: Born June 8, 1925, in Danville, VA. EDUCATION—Trained for the stage at the American Theatre Wing and with Stella Adler. MILITARY—U.S. Army, infantry, during World War II.

VOCATION: Actor.

CAREER: BROADWAY DEBUT—*Orpheus Descending*, Martin Beck Theatre, 1957. PRINCIPAL STAGE APPEARANCES—Third drowned man, Organ Morgan, and Evans the Death, *Under Milk Wood*, Henry Miller's Theatre, New York City, 1957; the heckler, *Sweet Bird of Youth*, Martin Beck Theatre, New York City, 1959; John Brown, *The Moon Beseiged*, Lyceum Theatre, New York City, 1962; Sefelt, *One Flew Over the Cuckoo's Nest*, Cort Theatre, New York City, 1963. Also appeared as Howie Newsome, *Our Town*, Equity Library Theatre, New York City; and in *Bedford Forest*, Eugene O'Neill Foundation, CT.

MAJOR TOURS—The heckler, *Sweet Bird of Youth*, U.S. cities, 1960.

FILM DEBUT—Boss Higgins, *Cool Hand Luke*, Warner Brothers, 1967. PRINCIPAL FILM APPEARANCES—Dr. Lazarus, *Gaily, Gaily* (also known as *Chicago, Chicago*), United Artists, 1969; Edmonds, *The Reivers*, National General, 1969; Dace, *The Stalking Moon*, National General, 1969; Charlie Bannister, *The Cheyenne Social Club*, National General, 1970; doctor, *Monte Walsh*, National General, 1970; McClendon, *The Moonshine War*, Metro-Goldwyn-Mayer (MGM), 1970; Virgil, *The Traveling Executioner*, MGM, 1970; Uncle Victor, *Harold and Maude*, Paramount, 1971; minister, *Lawman*, United Artists, 1971; Les Gibbons, *Sometimes a Great Notion* (also known as *Never Give an Inch*), Universal, 1971; farmer, *Bad Company*, Paramount, 1972; Jenkins, *The Cowboys*, Warner Brothers, 1972; Pete, *Fuzz*, United Artists, 1972; Robidoux, *Jeremiah Johnson*, Warner Brothers, 1972; psychiatrist, *The Stone Killer*, Columbia, 1973; Cracker, *Emperor of the North Pole* (also known as *Emperor of the North*), Twentieth Century-Fox, 1973; Unger, *The Longest Yard*, MGM, 1974; Ewing, *The Midnight Man*, Universal, 1974; Wheeler, *The Family Plot*, Universal, 1976; Merle, *Pete's Dragon*, Buena Vista, 1977; Colonel Kinkaid, *Evilspeak*, Moreno, 1982; Lyman Vunk, *Hamburger . . . The Motion Picture*, FM Entertainment, 1986; Gus, *Planes, Trains, and Automobiles*, Paramount, 1987; old man, *Pulse*, Columbia, 1988. Also appeared in *Lilith*, Columbia, 1964.

PRINCIPAL TELEVISION APPEARANCES—Series: Howard Rodman, *Father Murphy*, NBC, 1981-82. Mini-Series: Reverend Hutchins, *The Awakening Land*, NBC, 1978; Dracula, *James A. Michener's "Space"* (also known as *Space*), CBS, 1985. Pilots: Hawley, *Sarge: The Badge or the Cross*, NBC, 1971; Amos Goodloe, *The Greatest Gift*, NBC, 1974; Asa Bluel, *Lassie: The New Beginning*, ABC, 1978. Episodic: Herb Applegate, *Paradise*, CBS, 1988; also *Suspense*, CBS; *Danger*, CBS; *Big Town*; *The Gabby Hayes Show*; *Dupont Show of the Month*. Movies: Charley Eastman, *Winter Kill*, NBC, 1974; Mr. Beaton, *Young Pioneers*, ABC, 1976; Lefty Slade, *Peter Lundy and the Medicine Hat Stallion*, NBC, 1977; Doug Slocumb, *The Incredible Journey of Doctor Meg Laurel*, CBS, 1979; Joy's father, *A Matter of Life and Death*, CBS, 1981; George Clark, *Deadly Messages*, ABC, 1985; Isaiah Cawley, *I'll Be Home for Christmas*, NBC, 1988.

ADDRESSES: AGENT—Irv Schechter Company, 9300 Wilshire Boulevard, Suite 410, Beverly Hills, CA 90212.*

U

USTINOV, Peter 1921-

PERSONAL: Full name, Peter Alexander Ustinov; born April 16, 1921, in London, England; son of Iona (a journalist; professional name, "Klop") and Nadia (a painter and scenic designer; maiden name, Benois) Ustinov; married Isolde Denham, 1940 (divorced, 1950); married Suzanne Cloutier (an actress), 1953 (divorced, 1971); married Helene du Lau d'Allemans, June 17, 1972; children: Tamara (first marriage); Pavla, Igor, Andrea (second marriage). EDUCATION—Studied acting with Michel Saint Denis at the London Theatre Studio, 1937-39. MILITARY—British Army, Royal Sussex Regiment, 1942-46; also served with the Royal Army Ordnance Corps, the Kinematograph Service, and the Directorate of Army Psychiatry.

VOCATION: Actor, writer, director, and producer.

CAREER: Also see *WRITINGS* below. STAGE DEBUT—Waffles, *The Wood Demon*, Barn Theatre, Shere, U.K., 1938. LONDON DEBUT—Title role, *The Bishop of Limpopoland* (sketch), Players' Theatre Club, 1939. BROADWAY DEBUT—The General, *Romanoff and Juliet*, Plymouth Theatre, 1957. PRINCIPAL STAGE APPEARANCES—Reverend Alroy Whittingstall, *First Night*, Richmond Theatre, London, 1940; ensemble, *Swinging the Gate* (revue), Ambassadors' Theatre, London, 1940; M. Lescure, *Fishing for Shadows*, Threshold Theatre, London, 1940; ensemble, *Diversion* (revue), Wyndham's Theatre, London, 1940; ensemble, *Diversion 2* (revue), Wyndham's Theatre, 1941; Petrovitch, *Crime and Punishment*, New Theatre, London, 1946; Caligula, *Frenzy*, St. Martin's Theatre, London, 1948; Sergeant Dohda, *Love in Albania*, Lyric Hammersmith Theatre, then St. James's Theatre, both London, 1949; Carabosse, *The Love of Four Colonels*, Wyndham's Theatre, 1951; the General, *Romanoff and Juliet*, Piccadilly Theatre, London, 1956-57; Old Sam, *Photo Finish*, Saville Theatre, London, 1962, then Brooks Atkinson Theatre, New York City, 1963; the Archbishop, *The Unknown Soldier and His Wife*, Chichester Theatre Festival, Chichester, U.K., 1968, then New London Theatre, London, 1973; Boris Vassilievtch Krivelov, *Who's Who in Hell*, Lunt-Fontanne Theatre, New York City, 1974; title role, *King Lear*, Stratford Shakespeare Festival, Stratford, ON, Canada, 1979, then 1980; the Stage Manager, *The Marriage* (opera), Piccola Scala, Milan, Italy, 1981, then Edinburgh Festival, Edinburgh, Scotland, 1982; Ludwig, *Beethoven's Tenth*, Birmingham, Repertory Theatre, Birmingham, U.K., then Vaudeville Theatre, London, later Center Theatre Group, Ahmanson Theatre, Los Angeles, all 1983, then Nederlander Theatre, New York City, 1984; *An Evening with Peter Ustinov* (one-man show), Royal Haymarket Theatre, London, 1990. Also appeared in *French Without Tears, Pygmalion, White Cargo, Rookery Nook*, and *Laburnum Grove*, all Aylesbury Repertory Theatre, Aylesbury,

PETER USTINOV

U.K., 1939; ensemble, *Hermoine Gingold Revue*, London, 1940; Ludwig, *Beethoven's Tenth*, Paris, France, 1982.

PRINCIPAL STAGE WORK—Director: *Fishing for Shadows*, Threshold Theatre, London, 1940; *Squaring the Circle*, Vaudeville Theatre, London, 1941; *The Man in the Raincoat*, Edinburgh Festival, Edinburgh, Scotland, 1949; *Love in Albania*, Lyric Hammersmith Theatre, then St. James's Theatre, both London, 1949; *The Love of Four Colonels*, Wyndham's Theatre, 1951; *A Fiddle at the Wedding*, Royal Theatre, Brighton, U.K., 1952; *No Sign of the Dove*, Savoy Theatre, London, 1953; (with Nicholas Garland) *Photo Finish*, Saville Theatre, London, 1962, then Brooks Atkinson Theatre, New York City, 1963; *L'Heure Espagnole, Erwartung*, and *Gianni Schicci* (operas), all Royal Opera, Covent Garden Opera House, London, 1962; *Halfway Up the Tree*, Brooks Atkinson Theatre, 1967; *The Magic Flute* (opera), Hamburg Opera, Hamburg, West Germany, 1968; *The Unknown Soldier and His Wife*, Chichester Theatre Festival, Chichester, U.K., 1968, then New

433

London Theatre, London, 1973; (also producer, set designer, and costume designer) *Don Quichotte* (opera), Paris Opera, Paris, France, 1973; (also set designer and costume designer) *Don Giovanni* (opera), Edinburgh Festival, 1973; *Les Brigands* (opera), Berlin Opera, Berlin, West Germany, 1978; *The Marriage* (opera), Piccola Scala, Milan, Italy, 1981, then Edinburgh Festival, 1982; *Mavra* and *The Flood* (operas), Piccola Scala, 1982; *Katja Kabanowa* (opera), Hamburg Opera, 1985; also *The Love of Four Colonels*, Birmingham, U.K., 1951; *No Sign of the Dove*, Leeds, U.K., 1953; (with Nicholas Garland) *Photo Finish*, Dublin, Ireland, then Paris, 1964; *Halfway Up the Tree*, London, 1967; *King Lear*, Stratford Shakespeare Festival, Stratford, ON, Canada.

MAJOR TOURS—The General, *Romanoff and Juliet*, U.S. and Canadian cities, 1958-59; also toured U.S.S.R. in this role.

FILM DEBUT—*Mein Kampf—My Crimes*, Associated British, 1940. PRINCIPAL FILM APPEARANCES—Krauss, *The Goose Steps Out*, United Artists, 1942; priest, *One of Our Aircraft Is Missing*, United Artists, 1942; Rispoli, *The Way Ahead* (also known as *The Immortal Battalion*), Twentieth Century-Fox, 1945; title role, *Private Angelo*, Associated British/Pathe, 1949; Emad, *Hotel Sahara*, United Artists, 1951; Arnaud, *Odette*, United Artists, 1951; Nero, *Quo Vadis*, Metro-Goldwyn-Mayer (MGM), 1951; film distributor, *The Magic Box*, British Lion, 1952; Prince of Wales, *Beau Brummel*, MGM, 1954; Kaptah, *The Egyptian*, Twentieth Century-Fox, 1954; narrator, *House of Pleasure* (also known as *Le Plaisir*), Meyer-Kingsley, 1954; circus master, *Lola Montes* (also known as *The Sins of Lola Montes* and *The Fall of Lola Montes*), Brandon, 1955; Jules, *We're No Angels*, Paramount, 1955; Lentulus Batiatus, *Spartacus*, Universal, 1960; Venneker, *The Sundowners*, Warner Brothers, 1960; Mr. Bossi, *The Man Who Wagged His Tail* (also known as *An Angel Passed Over Brooklyn*, *Un angelo e sceso a Brooklyn*, and *Un angel paso por Brooklyn*), Continental, 1961; the General, *Romanoff and Juliet*, Universal, 1961; Captain Edward Fairfax Vere, *Billy Budd*, United Artists, 1962; King Fawz, *John Goldfarb, Please Come Home*, Twentieth Century-Fox, 1964; Arthur Simpson, *Topkapi*, United Artists, 1964; Prince Otto, *Lady L.*, MGM, 1965; Ambassador Pinada, *The Comedians*, MGM, 1967; Captain Blackbeard, *Blackbeard's Ghost*, Buena Vista, 1968; Marcus Pendleton, *Hot Millions*, MGM, 1968; General Maximilian Rodrigues de Santos, *Viva Max!*, Commonwealth United, 1969.

Doctor, *Hammersmith Is Out*, Cinerama, 1972; voice of Prince John, *Robin Hood* (animated), Buena Vista, 1973; Hnup Wan, *One of Our Dinosaurs Is Missing*, Buena Vista, 1975; Old Man, *Logan's Run*, Metro-Goldwyn-Mayer/United Artists, 1976; Dr. Snodgrass, *Treasure of Matecumbe*, Buena Vista, 1976; Sergeant Markov, *The Last Remake of Beau Geste*, Universal, 1977; voice of Manny, *The Mouse and His Child* (animated), Sanrio, 1977; Taubelman, *The Purple Taxi* (also known as *Un Taxi Mauve*), Quartet, 1977; narrator, *Tarka the Otter*, Rank Film Distributors, 1978; Hercule Poirot, *Death on the Nile*, Paramount, 1978; Harry Hellman, *Double Murders* (also known as *Doppio delitto*), Warner Brothers/Prduzione Internationale Cinematografica, 1978; narrator, *Metamorphosis* (also known as *Winds of Change;* animated), Sanrio, 1978; spectator, *Players*, Paramount, 1979; Suleiman, *Ashanti*, Columbia, 1979; Victor, *We'll Grow Thin Together* (also known as *Nous maigrirons ensemble*), Silenes, 1979; Charlie Chan, *Charlie Chan and the Curse of the Dragon Queen*, American Cinema, 1981; voice of Grendel, *Grendel, Grendel, Grendel* (animated), Victorian Film Corporation, 1981; truck driver, *The Great Muppet Caper*, Universal, 1981; Hercule Poirot, *Evil Under the Sun*, Universal, 1982; Abdi Aga, *Memed My Hawk*, Focus,

1984; Hercule Poirot, *Appointment with Death*, Cannon, 1988; narrator, *Peep and the Big Wide World* (animated short film), National Film Board of Canada, 1988. Also appeared in *Hullo Fame!*, 1941; *Let the People Sing*, Anglo-American, 1942; *The New Lot* (documentary), 1943; *The True Glory* (documentary), 1945; as Don Alfonso, *The Wanderers* (also known as *I girovaghi*), 1956; Michael Kiminsky, *The Spies* (also known as *Les Espions*), 1957; voice, *The Adventures of Mr. Wonderful*, 1959; narrator, *Women of the World* (also known as *La donna del mondo*), 1963; narrator, *The Peaches*, 1964; *Big Truck and Sister Clare*, 1973.

FIRST FILM WORK—Producer (with George H. Brown) and director, *School for Secrets* (also known as *Secret Flight*), General Film Distributors, 1946. PRINCIPAL FILM WORK—Director: (Also producer with George H. Brown) *Vice-Versa*, General Film Distributors, 1948; (with Michael Anderson; also producer) *Private Angelo*, Associated British/Pathe, 1949; (also producer) *Romanoff and Juliet*, Universal, 1961; (also producer) *Billy Budd*, United Artists, 1962; *Lady L.*, MGM, 1965; *Hammersmith Is Out*, Cinerama, 1972; *Memed My Hawk*, Focus, 1984.

PRINCIPAL TELEVISION APPEARANCES—Series: Host, *Omni: The New Frontier*, syndicated, 1981; host, *Peter Ustinov's Russia: A Personal History*, BBC, 1986; also host, *In All Directions*, BBC. Mini-Series: Host, *Nicholas Nickleby*, syndicated, 1983. Episodic: "Moment of Truth," *Omnibus*, NBC, 1958. Movies: Herod the Great, *Jesus of Nazareth*, NBC, 1977; Caliph, *The Thief of Baghdad*, NBC, 1978; Hercule Poirot, *Agatha Christie's "Thirteen at Dinner,"* CBS, 1985; Hercule Poirot, *Agatha Christie's "Murder in Three Acts,"* CBS, 1986; Hercule Poirot, *Agatha Christie's "Dead Man's Folly,"* CBS, 1986; Detective Fix, *Around the World in 80 Days*, NBC, 1989. Specials: "The Life of Samuel Johnson," *Omnibus*, NBC, 1957; *Crescendo*, CBS, 1957; narrator, *The Countdown*, CBS, 1958; Danton, *The Empty Chair*, NBC, 1958; Socrates, "Barefoot in Athens," *Hallmark Hall of Fame*, NBC, 1966; Herman Washington, "Storm in Summer," *Hallmark Hall of Fame*, NBC, 1970; title role, "Gideon," *Hallmark Hall of Fame*, NBC, 1971; *Burt Bacharach—Opus No. 3*, ABC, 1973; Admiral, *Love, Life, Liberty, and Lunch*, ABC, 1976; narrator, *Einstein's Universe*, BBC, then PBS, 1979; voice of title role, *Doctor Snuggles* (animated), syndicated, 1981; host, *The Seven Dials Mystery*, syndicated, 1981; host, *Why Didn't They Ask Evans?*, syndicated, 1981; *The Kennedy Center Honors: A Celebration of the Performing Arts*, CBS, 1986; host, *The Immortal Beethoven with Peter Ustinov*, PBS, 1987; host, *Peter Ustinov in China*, Global TV (Toronto, ON, Canada), 1988; host, *The Secret Identity of Jack the Ripper* (also known as *The Secret of Jack the Ripper*), syndicated, 1988; also *Ustinov ad lib*, 1969; *Conversation with Lord North*, 1971; narrator, *The Mighty Continent*, 1974; *A Quiet War*, 1976; various roles, *Imaginary Friends*, 1982; *The Well Tempered Bach*, 1984; *World Challenge*, 1986; narrator, *History of Europe*, BBC; narrator, *The Hermitage;* in *Peer Gynt*, BBC; narrator, *The Ballerinas*. Also *Ustinov in Orbit*, ATV, 1962.

PRINCIPAL TELEVISION WORK—Series: Producer, *In All Directions*, BBC. Specials: Director, *Love, Life, Liberty, and Lunch*, ABC, 1976.

RELATED CAREER—Joint director, Nottingham Playhouse, Nottingham, U.K., 1963—; worked as a professional impersonator in clubs and traveling revues.

NON-RELATED CAREER—Rector, Dundee University, Dundee, Scotland, 1968-73; goodwill ambassador for UNICEF, 1969—; owner of a vineyard.

WRITINGS: STAGE—*The Bishop of Limpopoland* (sketch), Players' Theatre Club, London, 1939; (contributor) *Swinging the Gate* (revue), Ambassadors' Theatre, London, 1940; (translator and adaptor) *Fishing for Shadows*, Threshold Theatre, London, 1940; (contributor) *Diversion* (revue), Wyndham's Theatre, London, 1940; (contributor) *Diversion 2* (revue), Wyndham's Theatre, 1941; *House of Regrets*, Arts Theatre, London, 1942, published by Jonathan Cape, 1943; *Beyond*, Arts Theatre, 1943, published by English Theatre Guild, 1944, then in *Five Plays*, Little, Brown, 1965; *Blow Your Own Trumpet*, Playhouse Theatre, London, 1943, published in *Plays About People*, Jonathan Cape, 1950; *The Banbury Nose*, Wyndham's Theatre, 1944, published by Jonathan Cape, 1945; *The Tragedy of Good Intentions*, Liverpool Playhouse, Liverpool, U.K., 1945, published in *Plays About People*, 1950; *The Man Behind the Statue*, Opera House, Manchester, U.K., 1946; *The Indifferent Shepherd*, Criterion Theatre, London, 1948, published in *Plays About People*, 1950; (adaptor) *Frenzy*, St. Martin's Theatre, London, 1948; *The Man in the Raincoat*, Edinburgh Festival, Edinburgh, Scotland, 1949; *The Love of Four Colonels*, first produced in Birmingham, U.K., then Wyndham's Theatre, both 1951, later Shubert Theatre, New York City, 1953, published by English Theatre Guild, 1951, then Dramatists Play Service, 1953, later in *Five Plays*, Little, Brown, 1965; *The Moment of Truth*, first produced in Nottingham, U.K., then Adelphi Theatre, London, both 1951, published by English Theatre Guild, 1953, then in *Five Plays*, 1965; *High Balcony*, first produced in London, 1952; *No Sign of the Dove*, first produced in Leeds, U.K., then Savoy Theatre, London, both 1953, published in *Five Plays*, 1965; *The Empty Chair*, Bristol Old Vic Theatre, Bristol, U.K., 1956; *Romanoff and Juliet*, first produced in Manchester, then Piccadilly Theatre, London, both 1956, later Plymouth Theatre, New York City, 1957, published by English Theatre Guild, 1957, then Random House, 1958, later in *Five Plays*, 1965; *Paris Not So Gay*, Oxford Playhouse, Oxford, U.K., 1958.

Photo Finish, first produced in Dublin, Ireland, then Saville Theatre, London, both 1962, later Brooks Atkinson Theatre, New York City, 1963, published by Heinemann, 1962, then Little, Brown, 1963, revised acting edition published by Dramatists Play Service, 1964; *The Life in My Hands*, Nottingham Playhouse, Nottingham, U.K., 1963; *The Unknown Soldier and His Wife*, Vivian Beaumont Theatre, New York City, 1967, then Chichester Theatre Festival, Chichester, U.K., 1968, later New London Theatre, London, 1973, published by Random House, 1967, then Heinemann, 1968; *Halfway Up the Tree*, first produced in West Germany, then Brooks Atkinson Theatre, later Queen's Theatre, London, all 1967, published by Random House, 1968, then English Theatre Guild, 1970; (book for musical) *R Loves J*, Chichester Theatre Festival, 1973; *Who's Who in Hell*, Lunt-Fontanne Theatre, New York City, 1974; *Overheard*, Royal Theatre, Brighton, U.K., then Royal Haymarket Theatre, London, both 1981; (adaptor of libretto) *The Marriage* (opera), Piccola Scala, Milan, Italy, 1981, then Edinburgh Festival, 1982; *Beethoven's Tenth*, first produced in Paris, 1982, then Birmingham Repertory Theatre, Birmingham, U.K., later Vaudeville Theatre, London, and Center Theatre Group, Ahmanson Theatre, Los Angeles, all 1983, then Nederlander Theatre, New York City, 1984; *An Evening with Peter Ustinov* (one-man show), Royal Haymarket Theatre, London, 1990.

FILM—*The New Lot* (documentary), 1943; (co-writer) *The True Glory* (documentary), 1944; (with Eric Ambler) *The Way Ahead* (also known as *The Immortal Battalion*), Twentieth Century-Fox, 1945; (with Eric Maschwitz, Stanley Haynes, and Guy Green) *Carnival*, General Film Distributors, 1946; *School for Secrets* (also known as *Secret Flight*), General Film Distributors, 1946; *Vice-*

Versa, General Film Distributors, 1948; *Private Angelo*, Associated British/Pathe, 1949; (with Hal E. Chester and Patricia Moyes) *School for Scoundrels*, Continental Distributing, 1960; *Romanoff and Juliet*, Universal, 1961; (with Robert Rossen) *Billy Budd*, United Artists, 1962; *Lady L.*, MGM, 1965; (with Ira Wallach) *Hot Millions*, MGM, 1968; *Memed My Hawk*, Focus, 1984.

TELEVISION—Series: *In All Directions*, BBC. Episodic: "Moment of Truth," *Omnibus*, NBC, 1958. Specials: (With Leslie Stevens) *Crescendo*, CBS, 1957; *The Empty Chair*, NBC, 1958; *Ustinov ad lib*, 1969; *Love, Life, Liberty, and Lunch*, ABC, 1976; *Imaginary Friends*, 1982.

OTHER—*Add a Dash of Pity* (short stories), Little, Brown, 1959; *Ustinov's Diplomats* (photographs and commentary), Bernard Geis Associates, 1960; *The Loser* (novel), Little, Brown, 1961; *We Were Only Human* (cartoons), Little, Brown, 1961; (illustrator) *Poodlestan: A Poodle's Eye View of History* by Paul Marc Henry, Reynal, 1965; *The Frontiers of the Sea* (short stories), Little, Brown, 1966; *Krumnagel* (novel), Little, Brown, 1971; *Rectorial Address Delivered in the University, 3rd November, 1972* (lecture), University of Dundee Press, 1972; *Dear Me* (autobiography), Little, Brown, 1977; (introduction) *A Handful of Summers* by Gordon Forbes, Paddington, 1979; *Happiness* (lecture), University of Birmingham, 1980; *My Russia* (nonfiction), Little, Brown, 1983; (introduction) *Niven's Hollywood* by Tom Hutchinson, Salem House, 1984; *Peter Ustinov in Russia* (nonfiction), Summit Books, 1988. Contributor of articles to such periodicals as *Atlantic* and *Listener*.

RECORDINGS: ALBUMS—Narrator, *Baron Munchausen: Eighteen Truly Tall Tales*, Caedmon, 1972; also *Mock Mozart and Phoney Folk Lore*, Parlophone; *The Grand Prix of Gibralter*, Orpheum; narrator: *Peter and the Wolf, The Nutcracker Suite, The Soldier's Tale, Hary Janos, The Little Prince,* and *The Old Man of Lochnagar.*

AWARDS: Academy Award nomination, Best Supporting Actor, 1951, and Golden Globe, Best Supporting Actor, 1952, both for *Quo Vadis;* Donaldson Award, Best First Play, and New York Drama Critics' Circle Award, Best Foreign Play, both 1953, for *The Love of Four Colonels; Evening Standard* Award, Best New Play, 1956, and Antoinette Perry Award nomination, Best Actor in a Play, 1958, both for *Romanoff and Juliet;* Benjamin Franklin Medal from the Royal Society of Arts, 1957; Emmy Award, 1957, for "The Life of Samuel Johnson," *Omnibus;* Academy Award, Best Supporting Actor, 1961, for *Spartacus;* Academy Award, Best Supporting Actor, 1964, for *Topkapi;* First Prize from the Syndicat des journalistes et ecrivains (France), 1964, for *Photo Finish;* Emmy Award, Outstanding Single Performance in a Leading Role, 1966, for "Barefoot in Athens, *Hallmark Hall of Fame;* Academy Award nomination (with Ira Wallach), Best Story and Screenplay Written Directly for the Screen, 1968, and British comedy screenplay award from the Writers Guild, 1969, both for *Hot Millions;* Emmy Award, Outstanding Single Performance in a Leading Role, 1970, for "Storm in Summer," *Hallmark Hall of Fame;* Peabody Award, 1972; special Silver Bear Award from the Berlin Film Festival, 1972, for creative work and for direction of *Hammersmith Is Out;* Order of the Smile (Warsaw, Poland), 1974, for dedication to the idea of international assistance to children; Commander of the British Empire, 1975; Jordanian Independence Medal, 1978; Distinguished Service Award from UNICEF, 1978; Prix de la Butte, 1979; Variety Club of Great Britain Award, Best Actor, 1979; Emmy Award nomination, 1984, for *The Well Tempered Bach;* Commander, Order of Arts and Letters (France), 1985; Grammy Award for *Peter and the Wolf.* HONORARY DEGREES—

Cleveland Institute of Music, D.Mus., 1967; University of Dundee, L.L.D., 1969; La Salle College, D.F.A., 1971; University of Lancaster, Litt.D., 1972; also University of Toronto, 1984.

MEMBER: British Actors' Equity Association, Screen Actors Guild, British Film Academy, Dramatists Guild, British League of Dramatists, British Screenwriters Society, London Society of Authors, Royal Society of Arts (fellow), Societe des Auteurs (France), Arts Theatre, Royal Society of Literature (fellow, 1978), Academy of Fine Arts (Paris, 1988), Garrick Club, Savage Club, Royal Automobile Club, Queen's Club.

SIDELIGHTS: RECREATIONS—Reading, collecting prints and drawings, classical music, cars, lawn tennis, and squash.

ADDRESSES: OFFICE—11 rue de Silly, 92100 Boulogne, France. AGENT—Steve Kenis, William Morris Agency, 31-32 Soho Square, London W1V 5DG, England.*

V

VANCE, Courtney 1960-

PERSONAL: Full name, Courtney Bernard Vance; born March 12, 1960, in Detriot, MI. EDUCATION—Attended Harvard University.

VOCATION: Actor.

CAREER: BROADWAY DEBUT—Cory, *Fences*, 46th Street Theatre, 1987. PRINCIPAL STAGE APPEARANCES—Attendant, *The Comedy of Errors*, Shakespeare and Company, Lenox, MA, 1982; Cory, *Fences*, Goodman Theatre, Chicago, IL, 1986; Mercutio, *Romeo and Juliet*, New York Shakespeare Festival, Public Theatre, New York City, 1988; Thami Mbikwana, *My Children! My Africa!*, New York Theatre Workshop, Perry Street Theatre, New York City, 1989. Also appeared in *A Raisin in the Sun*, Yale Repertory Theatre, New Haven, CT, 1983.

PRINCIPAL FILM APPEARANCES—Doc, *Hamburger Hill*, Paramount, 1987.

PRINCIPAL TELEVISION APPEARANCES—Episodic: Curtis Caldwell, *thirtysomething*, ABC, 1989. Movies: Student, *First Affair*, CBS, 1983.

RELATED CAREER—Company member, Shakespeare and Company, Lenox, MA, 1981.

AWARDS: Theatre World Award and Antoinette Perry Award nomination, Best Featured Actor in a Play, both 1987, for *Fences*.

ADDRESSES: AGENT—Brian Mann, International Creative Management, 8899 Beverly Boulevard, Los Angeles, CA 90048.*

*　　*　　*

VAN CLEEF, Lee 1925-1989

PERSONAL: Born January 9, 1925, in Somerville, NJ; died of a heart attack, December 16, 1989, in Oxnard, CA; son of Clarence LeRoy and Marion Levinia (Van Fleet) Van Cleef; first wife's name, Ruth Ann (divorced); second wife's name, Joan (divorced); married Barbara Hevelone, July 13, 1976; children: Alan, Deborah, David (second marriage). MILITARY—U.S. Navy, 1942-46.

VOCATION: Actor.

CAREER: PRINCIPAL STAGE APPEARANCES—*Mister Roberts*, tour of U.S. cities, 1950.

FILM DEBUT—Jack Colby, *High Noon*, United Artists, 1952. PRINCIPAL FILM APPEARANCES—Dirk Hanley, *The Lawless Breed*, Universal, 1952; Tony Romano, *Kansas City Confidential* (also known as *The Secret Four*), United Artists, 1952; Dave Chittun, *Untamed Frontier*, Universal, 1952; Smitty, *Arena*, Metro-Goldwyn-Mayer (MGM), 1953; Nerva, *The Bandits of Corsica* (also known as *Return of the Corsican Brothers*), United Artists, 1953; Corporal Stone, *The Beast from 20,000 Fathoms*, Warner Brothers, 1953; Toby Mackay, *Jack Slade* (also known as *Slade*), Allied Artists, 1953; Reno, *The Nebraskan*, Columbia, 1953; Karl, *Private Eyes*, Allied Artists, 1953; Marv, *Tumbleweed*, Universal, 1953; Pete Monte, *Vice Squad* (also known as *The Girl in Room One*), United Artists, 1953; Brutus, *White Lightning*, Monogram, 1953; crew boss, *Arrow in the Dust*, Allied Artists, 1954; Earl Ferris, *Dawn at Socorro*, Universal, 1954; Buck and Paul Creyton, *The Desperado*, Allied Artists, 1954; Hank, *Gypsy Colt*, MGM, 1954; Hakar, *Princess of the Nile*, Twentieth Century-Fox, 1954; Ace Winton, *Rails into Laramie*, Universal, 1954; Fireknife, *The Yellow Tomahawk*, United Artists, 1954.

Fante, *The Big Combo*, Allied Artists, 1955; Flash Logan, *I Cover the Underworld*, Republic, 1955; Clantin, *A Man Alone*, Republic, 1955; Pecos Larry, *The Road to Denver*, Republic, 1955; Al Drucker, *Ten Wanted Men*, Columbia, 1955; Emmett, *Treasure of Ruby Hills*, Allied Artists, 1955; Jay Lord, *The Vanishing American*, Republic, 1955; Sergeant Lackey, *Accused of Murder*, Republic, 1956; Chepei, *The Conqueror*, RKO, 1956; Gus, *Pardners*, Paramount, 1956; Tom Anderson, *It Conquered the World*, American International, 1956; Fat Jones, *Tribute to a Badman*, MGM, 1956; Shad Donaphin, *The Badge of Marshall Brennan*, Allied Artists, 1957; Major Cham, *China Gate*, Twentieth Century-Fox, 1957; Kirby, *Gun Battle at Monterey*, Allied Artists, 1957; Ed Bailey, *Gunfight at the O.K. Corral*, Paramount, 1957; Adam Grant, *Joe Dakota*, Universal, 1957; Faro, *The Lonely Man*, Paramount, 1957; Sadler, *The Quiet Gun*, Twentieth Century-Fox, 1957; Ed McGaffey, *The Tin Star*, Paramount, 1957; Alfonso Parral, *The Bravados*, Twentieth Century-Fox, 1958; Jake Hayes, *Day of the Badman*, Universal, 1958; Mike Bennett, *Guns, Girls, and Gangsters*, United Artists, 1958; Miguel, *Machete*, United Artists, 1958; Sergeant Rickett, *The Young Lions*, Twentieth Century-Fox, 1958; Frank, *Ride Lonesome*, Columbia, 1959.

Leo, *Posse from Hell*, Universal, 1961; Marty, *How the West Was Won*, Cinerama, 1962; Reese, *The Man Who Shot Liberty Valance*, Paramount, 1962; Colonel Douglas Mortimer, *Perqualche dollaro in piu* (also known as *For a Few Dollars More*), 1966, released in the United States by United Artists, 1967; Setenza, *Il buono, il brutto, il cattivo* (also known as *The Good, the Bad, and the Ugly*), 1966, released in the United States by United Artists, 1967; bandit turned sheriff, *Beyond the Law*, Roxy, 1967; Ryan, *Da uomo a uomo* (also known as *Death Rides a Horse*), 1967, released in the

United States by United Artists, 1969; Frank Talby, *I giorni dell'ira* (also known as *Day of Anger* and *Der Tod Titt Dienstags*), 1967, released in the United States by National General, 1970; Jonathan Corbett, *The Big Gundown* (also known as *La resa dei conti*), Columbia, 1968; title role, *Sabata* (also known as *Ehi, amico . . . c'e Sabata, hai chiuso*), United Artists, 1969; Travis, *Barquero*, United Artists, 1970; Jaroo, *El Condor*, National General, 1970; title role, *Captain Apache*, Scotia International, 1971; King, *Bad Man's River*, Scotia International, 1972; Chris, *The Magnificent Seven Ride!*, United Artists, 1972; title role, *Return of Sabata* (also known as *E'tornato Sabata* and *Hai chiuso un'altra volta*), United Artists, 1972; Kiefer, *Take a Hard Ride*, Twentieth Century-Fox, 1975.

McCarn, *The Octagon*, American Cinema, 1980; Chris, *The Squeez* (also known as *The Big Ripoff* and *Controrapin*), Maverick, 1980; Bob Hauk, *Escape from New York*, AVCO-Embassy, 1981; Burt Roth, *Armed Response*, CineTel, 1986; Inspector Warren, *Jungle Raiders* (also known as *Captain Yankee* and *La legenda del Rudio Malese*), Cannon, 1986; Maitre Julot, *Killing Machine*, Embassy, 1986. Also appeared in *Man Without a Star*, Universal, 1955; *The Naked Street*, United Artists, 1955; *The Kentuckian*, United Artists, 1955; *Backlash*, Universal, 1956; *Red Sundown*, Universal, 1956; *The Last Stagecoach West*, Republic, 1957; *Raiders of Old California*, Republic, 1957; *The Guns of Zangara*, 1960; *Call to Glory*, 1966; *Commandos*, 1968; *The Man from Far Away* (also known as *L'uomo che viene de lontano*), 1968; *Beyond the Law* (also known as *Al di la della legge*), 1968; *Bite the Dust*, 1969; *Creed of Violence*, 1969; *. . . e continuavano a fregarsi il millione di dollari*, 1971; *The Grand Duel* (also known as *El gran duelo*), 1972; *Gangster Story* (also known as *The Gun, Il suo nome faceva tremare . . . Interpol in allarme!*, and *Dio, sei proprio un padreterno*), 1973; *Blood Money* (also known as *Moneda sangrienta*), Shaw Brothers, 1974; *Crime Boss*, Cinema Shares International, 1976; *Mean Frank and Crazy Tony* (also known as *Johnny le Fligueur*), Aquarius, 1976; *The Stranger and the Gunfighter*, 1976; *Killers* (also known as *Verano sangrieto*), 1977; *God's Gun*, Irwin Yablansy, 1977; *The Perfect Killer*, 1977; *Kid Vengeance*, Golan/Globus/ Irwin Yablans, 1977; *The Hard Way*, 1979; *Trieste File*, 1980; *Code Name: Wild Geese* (also known as *Geheimecode Wild Ganse*), Entertainment, 1985; *The Commander*.

PRINCIPAL TELEVISION APPEARANCES—Series: John Peter McAllister, *The Master*, NBC, 1984. Pilots: Steve Margolis, *Last Stagecoach West*, syndicated, 1954; Ike Scanlon, *Nowhere to Hide*, CBS, 1977. Episodic: *The Lone Ranger*, syndicated, 1952; "Four Things He'd Do," *Schlitz Playhouse of Stars*, CBS, 1954; "Duel at the O.K. Corral," *Cavalcade of America*, ABC, 1954; "The Case of the Desperate Moment," *The Man Behind the Badge*, CBS, 1955; *Brave Eagle*, CBS, 1956; "Deadline," *Studio 57*, syndicated, 1956; *Wire Service*, ABC, 1956; "Sky Pilot of the Cumberlands," *Crossroads*, ABC, 1956; "Alder Gulch," *Tales of Wells Fargo*, NBC, 1957; "The Blue Hotel," *Schlitz Playhouse of Stars*, CBS, 1957; "The Town," *Trackdown*, CBS, 1957; *Wagon Train*, NBC, 1958; *Colt .45*, ABC, 1958; *The Rifleman*, ABC, 1959; *Tombstone Territory*, ABC, 1959; *Yancy Derringer*, CBS, 1959; *The Real McCoys*, ABC, 1959; *Hotel de Paree*, CBS, 1960; *The Untouchables*, ABC, 1960; *Alaskans*, ABC, 1960; *The Deputy*, NBC, 1960; *Gunsmoke*, CBS, 1960; *77 Sunset Strip*, ABC, 1960; *The Lawman*, ABC, 1960; *Laramie*, NBC, 1960; *Bonanza*, NBC, 1960; *Hawaiian Eye*, ABC, 1961; *Maverick*, ABC, 1961; *The Rifleman*, ABC, 1961 and 1962; *The Joey Bishop Show*, NBC, 1962; *Cheyenne*, ABC, 1962; *Have Gun, Will Travel*, CBS, 1962 and 1963; "Colossus," *The Dick Powell Show* (also known as *Hollywood Showcase*), NBC, 1963; *Laramie*, NBC, 1963; *Ripcord*, syndicated, 1963; *The*

Dakotas, ABC, 1963; *Destry*, ABC, 1964; *Rawhide*, CBS, 1964; *Laredo*, NBC, 1966; *Gunsmoke*, CBS, 1966; Skip, *The Andy Griffith Show*, CBS. Specials: Sam Bass, *The Slowest Gun in the West*, CBS, 1963.

NON-RELATED CAREER—Farm worker, assistant manager in a summer camp, factory worker, and accountant.

OBITUARIES AND OTHER SOURCES: New York Times, December 18, 1989.*

*   *   *

VARDA, Agnes 1928-

PERSONAL: Born May 30, 1928, in Brussels, Belgium; daughter of Eugene Jean (an engineer) and Christiane (Pasquet) Varda; married Jacques Demy (a director), January 8, 1962; children: Rosalie and Mathieu. EDUCATION—Studied art history at the Ecole du Louvre, 1944-47, and literature and psychology at the University de Paris a la Sorbonne, 1947.

VOCATION: Director, producer, and screenwriter.

CAREER: Also see *WRITINGS* below. PRINCIPAL FILM APPEARANCES—Nun, *Les Demoiselles de Rochefort* (also known as *The Young Girls of Rochefort*), Warner Brothers/Seven Arts, 1968; also appeared in *Lions Love*, Raab, 1969; *Jane B. par Agnes V.* (also known as *Birkin Double Jeu I, Birkin Diptych I*, and *Jane B. By Agnes V.*), Capital Cinema/Cine Tamaris, 1988.

FIRST FILM WORK—Director and producer, *La Pointe courte*, Cine Tamaris, 1954. PRINCIPAL FILM WORK—Director: *O Saisons, o chateaux* (short documentary film), Films de la Pleiade, 1957; *L'Opera-Mouffe* (short documentary film), Cine Tamaris, 1958; *Du cote de la cote* (short documentary film), Argos, 1958; *Cleo de 5 a 7* (also known as *Cleo from 5 to 7*), Rome-Paris Films, 1961, released in the United States by Zenith International, 1962; *Salut les Cubains* (short documentary film; also known as *Salute to Cuba*), S.N. Pathe Cinema, 1962; *Le Bonheur* (also known as *Happiness*), Parc, 1965, released in the United States by Clover, 1966; *Les Creatures* (also known as *Varelserna*), Parc, 1966, released in the United States by New Yorker, 1969; (co-director) *Loin du Vietnam* (also known as *Far from Vietnam*), Slon/New Yorker, 1967; *Black Panthers* (also known as *Huey;* short documentary film), Cine Tamaris, 1968; *Oncle Janco* (short documentary film), Cine Tamaris, 1968; (also producer) *Lions Love*, Raab, 1969.

(Also producer) *Daguerreotypes* (documentary), Cine Tamaris, 1975, released in the United States by Films Incorporated, 1976; *Reponse de femmes* (short film), Cine Tamaris, 1975, released in the United States, 1977; (also producer) *L'Une chante l'autre pas* (also known as *One Sings, the Other Doesn't*), Cine Tamaris/ Societe Francaise de Production/Institut National de l'Audiovisuel and Contretemps/Paradise/Population, 1976, released in the United States by Cinema V, 1977; (also producer) *Mur Murs* (also known as *Wall Walls* and *Mural Murals;* documentary), Cine Tamaris, 1981; (also producer) *Documenteur* (also known as *Documenteur: An Emotion Picture*), Cine Tamaris, 1981; (also editor) *Sans toit ni loi* (also known as *Vagabond*), Cine Tamaris, 1985, released in the United States by International Film Exchange, 1986; (also producer and editor) *Jane B. par Agnes V.* (also known as *Birkin Double Jeu I, Birkin Diptych I*, and *Jane B. by Agnes V.*),

Capital Cinema/Cine Tamaris, 1988; (also producer) *Kung Fu Master*, Expanded Entertainment, 1989. Also director, unless indicated, of the following short films and documentaries: *Plaisir d'amour en Iran*, 1975; producer, *Lady Oscar*, 1978; *Ulysse*, 1982; *Une Minute pour une image*, 1983; *7P; Cuis, S. de B . . . a saisir*, 1984; *Les Dites cariatides*, 1984; *T'as de beaux escaliers, tu sais . . .*, 1986.

PRINCIPAL TELEVISION APPEARANCES—Specials: *Three Women Filmmakers*, PBS, 1987.

RELATED CAREER—Stage photographer, Theater Festival of Avignon, Avignon, France, 1947; photographer, Theatre National Populaire, Paris, 1951-61; founder, Cine-Tamaris (a film production company), 1977; also magazine photojournalist.

WRITINGS: FILM—See production details above, unless indicated: *La Pointe courte*, 1954; *O Saisons, o chateaux*, 1957; *Du cote de la cote*, 1958; *L'Opera-Mouffe*, 1958; (also composer and lyricist) *Cleo de 5 a 7*, 1961; *Salut les Cubains*, 1962; *Le Bonheur*, 1965; *Les Creatures*, 1966; (co-writer) *Loin du Vietnam*, 1967; *Black Panthers*, 1968; *Oncle Janco*, 1968; *Lions Love*, 1969; (dialogue only with others) *L'Ultimo tango a Parigi* (also known as *Last Tango in Paris*), United Artists, 1971; *Daguerreotypes*, 1975; *Reponse de femmes*, 1975, (also songwriter) *L'Une chante l'autre pas*, 1976; *Mur Murs*, 1981; *Documenteur*, 1981; *Ulysse*, 1982; *Une Minute pour une image*, 1983; *Les Dites cariatides*, 1984; *7P; Cuis, S. de B . . . a saisir*, 1984; *Sans toit ni loi*, 1985; *T'as de beaux escaliers, tu sais . . .*, 1986; *Jane B. par Agnes V.*, 1988; *Kung Fu Master*, 1989. TELEVISION—*Nausicaa*, 1970. OTHER—Contributor to journals and periodicals.

AWARDS: International Federation of Film Clubs Prize from the Brussels Experimental Film Festival, 1958, for *L'Opera-Mouffe;* Prix Melies, 1962, for *Cleo de 5 a 7;* Bronze Lion from the Venice Film Festival, 1964, for *Salut les Cubains;* Silver Bear from the Berlin Film Festival, Prix Louis Delluc, and David O. Selznick Award, all 1965, for *Le Bonheur;* First Prize from the Oberhausen Film Festival, 1969, for *Black Panthers;* Golden Prize from the Italian Film Festival and Grand Prix from the Taormina Film Festival, both 1977, for *L'Une chante l'autre pas;* Firenze Award, 1981, for *Mur Murs;* Cesar Award, 1984, for *Ulysse;* Golden Lion from the Venice Film Festival, Prix Melies, and Los Angeles Film Critics' Association Award, Best Foreign Film, all 1985, for *Sans toit ni loi;* also named to the Legion of Honor (France).

ADDRESSES: OFFICE—c/o Cine Tamaris, 86 Rue Daguerre, 75014 Paris, France.*

*　　*　　*

VAZAK, P.H.
See TOWNE, Robert

*　　*　　*

VEREEN, Ben　1946-

PERSONAL: Full name, Benjamin Augustus Vereen; born October 10, 1946, in Miami, FL; father, a paint factory worker; mother, a maid; married second wife, Nancy Brunner; children: Benjamin

BEN VEREEN

(first marriage); Malakia, Naja, Kabara, Karon (second marriage). EDUCATION—Attended the High School of Performing Arts; attended Pentecostal Theological Seminary for six months.

VOCATION: Actor, singer, and dancer.

CAREER: STAGE DEBUT—*The Prodigal Son*, Greenwich Mews Theatre, New York City, 1965. PRINCIPAL STAGE APPEARANCES—Brother Ben, *Sweet Charity*, Caesar's Palace, Las Vegas, NV, 1966; flight announcer, *Golden Boy*, Auditorium Theatre, Chicago, IL, 1968; Claude, *Hair*, Biltmore Theatre, New York City, 1968; alternated roles of Hud and Berger, *Hair*, Aquarius Theatre, Los Angeles, 1968-70; Judas Iscariot, *Jesus Christ Superstar*, Mark Hellinger Theatre, New York City, 1971; the Leading Player, *Pippin*, Imperial Theatre, New York City, 1972; Leroy, *Grind*, Mark Hellinger Theatre, 1985; also appeared in *Sweet Charity*, San Francisco, CA, 1966.

MAJOR TOURS—Daddy Johann Sebastian Brubeck and policeman, *Sweet Charity*, U.S. and Canadian cities, 1967-68; Hud, *Hair*, U.S. cities, 1968; the Leading Player, *Pippin*, U.S. cities, 1968; Johnny Williams, *No Place to Be Somebody*, National Shakespeare Company, U.S. cities, 1970-71.

PRINCIPAL FILM APPEARANCES—Frug dancer, *Sweet Charity*, Universal, 1969; Carlos, *Gas-s-s-s!* (also known as *Gas-s-s-s, or It Became Necessary to Destroy the World in Order to Save It*), American International, 1970; Bert Robbins, *Funny Lady*, Columbia, 1975; O'Connor Flood, *All That Jazz*, Columbia/Twentieth Century-Fox, 1979; Leatherface, *The Zoo Gang*, New World,

1985; Shaka, *Buy and Cell*, Trans World Entertainment, 1988. Also appeared in *Winners Take All*, New World, 1985.

PRINCIPAL TELEVISION APPEARANCES—Series: *Ben Vereen . . . Comin' At Ya*, NBC, 1975; E.L. "Tenspeed" Turner, *Tenspeed and Brown Shoe*, ABC, 1980; Uncle Phillip Long, *Webster*, ABC, 1984-85; Mayor Ben, *Zoobilee Zoo*, syndicated, 1986; host, *You Write the Songs*, syndicated, 1986-87; E.L. "Tenspeed" Turner, *J.J. Starbuck*, NBC, 1988. Mini-Series: Chicken George, *Roots*, ABC, 1977; Roscoe Haines, *Ellis Island*, CBS, 1984; Ethiopian, *A.D.*, NBC, 1985. Pilots: Nightclub singer, *The Saint* (broadcast as an episode of *CBS Summer Playhouse*), CBS, 1987. Episodic: Ben McQueen, *Booker*, Fox, 1990; also "Puss 'n' Boots," *Faerie Tale Theatre*, Showtime. Movies: Louis Armstrong, *Louis Armstrong—Chicago Style*, ABC, 1976; Herb Douglas, *The Jesse Owens Story*, syndicated, 1984; Paul Williams, *Lost in London*, CBS, 1985; marina manager, *Jenny's Song*, syndicated, 1988.

Specials: Devil, Noah, and man, *Mary's Incredible Dream*, CBS, 1976; *Jubilee*, NBC, 1976; *Ben Vereen—His Roots*, ABC, 1978; *The Stars Salute Israel at 30*, ABC, 1978; *The Cheryl Ladd Special*, ABC, 1979; *Uptown—A Tribute to the Apollo Theatre*, NBC, 1980; *Walt Disney . . . One Man's Dream*, CBS, 1981; *Opryland: Night of Stars and Future Stars*, NBC, 1981; *Christmas in Washington*, NBC, 1982; *Night of 100 Stars*, NBC, 1983; *Lynda Carter: Body and Soul*, CBS, 1984; *Here's Television Entertainment*, 1984; *Salute to Lady Liberty*, CBS, 1984; *Secret World of the Very Young*, CBS, 1984; host, *115th Edition of the Ringling Brothers and Barnum and Bailey Circus*, CBS, 1985; host, *Here's Television Entertainment*, syndicated, 1985; voice of Dragonweed, *The Charmkins* (animated), syndicated, 1985; *52nd Annual King Orange Jamboree Parade*, NBC, 1985; *The ABC All-Star Spectacular*, ABC, 1985; *All Star Party for "Dutch" Reagan*, CBS, 1985; *Kraft Salutes the Magic of David Copperfield . . . In China*, CBS, 1986; host, *Walt Disney World's Very Merry Christmas Parade*, ABC, 1986; *116th Edition of the Ringling Brothers and Barnum and Bailey Circus*, CBS, 1986; *Miss Hollywood, 1986*, ABC, 1986; co-host, *Walt Disney World's Happy Easter*, ABC, 1987; host, *Happy New Year, America*, CBS, 1987; host, *Six Hours for Life*, syndicated, 1987; *Macy's Thanksgiving Day Parade*, NBC, 1987; *A Star-Spangled Celebration*, ABC, 1987; *Circus of the Stars*, CBS, 1989; *Starathon '90*, syndicated, 1990.

RELATED CAREER—Performer in nightclubs and theatres throughout the world.

NON-RELATED CAREER—Chairman, American Lung Association, 1977; established the Naja Vereen Memorial Scholarship Fund, 1988; also chairman, American Heart Association's Dance for Heart campaign.

RECORDINGS: ALBUMS—*Jesus Christ Superstar* (original cast recording), Decca; *Pippin* (original cast recording), Motown; also *High Steppin' Mama*.

AWARDS: Antoinette Perry Award nomination, Best Supporting or Featured Actor in a Musical, *Variety*-New York Drama Critics' Poll winner, Best Supporting Actor, and Theatre World Award, all 1972, for *Jesus Christ Superstar;* Antoinette Perry Award, Best Actor in a Musical, and Drama Desk Award, both 1973, and CLIO Award, 1975, all for *Pippin;* George M. Cohan Award from the American Guild of Variety Artists, 1976; Television Critics' Award, 1977, for *Roots;* Entertainer of the Year, Rising Star, and Song and Dance Star awards, all from the American Guild of Variety Artists, 1978; NAACP Image Awards, 1978 and 1979; Cultural Award

(Israel), 1978; Humanitarian Award (Israel), 1979; Eleanor Roosevelt Humanitarian Award, 1983; Dolores Kohl Education Foundation Award, 1987, for *Zoobilee Zoo*. HONORARY DEGREES—Emerson College, L.H.D., 1977.

MEMBER: Actors' Equity Association, American Guild of Variety Artists, American Federation of Television and Radio Artists, Screen Actors Guild.

ADDRESSES: AGENT—Lee Solomon, William Morris Agency, 1350 Avenue of the Americas, New York, NY 10019. OFFICE—Michelle Marx Inc., 9044 Melrose Avenue, Los Angeles, CA 90069.*

*   *   *

VERHOEVEN, Paul   1940-

PERSONAL: Born in 1940 in the Netherlands. EDUCATION—Received Ph.D. in mathematics and physics from the University of Leiden.

VOCATION: Director and screenwriter.

CAREER: Also see *WRITINGS* below. PRINCIPAL FILM APPEARANCES—*Oh Jonathan, Oh Jonathan*, Constantin Film, 1973. PRINCIPAL FILM WORK—Director: *Wat Zien Ik* (also known as *Memories of a Streetwalker*), Nederland Film, 1971; *Turks Fruit* (also known as *Turkish Delight*), Nederland Film, 1972; *Keetje Tippel*, Tuschinski Film Distribution, 1975; *Soldier of Orange*, International Picture Show, 1979; *Spetters*, Embassy, 1983; *Die Vierde Man* (also known as *The Fourth Man*), International Spectrafilm/New Yorker, 1984; *Flesh and Blood*, Riverside, 1985; *Robocop*, Orion, 1987; also *Unwilling Agent*, 1968.

WRITINGS: FILM—(With Gerard Soeteman and Kees Holierhoek) *Soldier of Orange*, International Picture Show, 1979; (with Soeteman) *Flesh and Blood*, Riverside, 1985.*

*   *   *

VERLAQUE, Robert   1955-

PERSONAL: Born August 7, 1955, in Tunis, Tunisia; son of Jules L. (in business) and Giselle (Wilkes) Verlaque. EDUCATION—Loyola College, B.A., 1977; trained for the stage at the American Academy of Dramatic Arts and with Fred Kareman, Wynn Handman, Caymichael Patten, and Tim Phillips.

VOCATION: Actor and playwright.

CAREER: Also see *WRITINGS* below. STAGE DEBUT—Title role, *Jesus Christ, Superstar*, Priscilla Beach Theatre, Manomet, MA, 1980. OFF-BROADWAY DEBUT—Stagehand, *Isn't It Romantic*, Playwrights Horizons, 1983. PRINCIPAL STAGE APPEARANCES—Stagehand, *Isn't It Romantic*, Lucille Lortel Theatre, New York City, 1984; Jurgen Sallow, *Hollywood Scheherezade*, Primary Stages Company, 45th Street Theatre, New York City, 1989; also appeared as A.D., *Elm Circle*, Playwrights Horizons; Adler, *Roger Casement*, Theatre Off Park, New York City; Sheldon, *So Long Brooklyn*, Arthur, *Waiting for Lillie*, and Barton, *Swimming Out to*

ROBERT VERLAQUE

Sea, all Ensemble Studio Theatre, New York City; David Allen, *The Trip Back Down,* Warren Robertson Theatre Workshop, New York City; Jake, *Lament,* Meat and Potatoes Company, New York City; Harold Pertiner, *Rosaries,* Riverwest Theatre, New York City; Butterworth, *Dracula,* Candlewood Playhouse, New Fairfield, CT; McMurphy, *One Flew Over the Cuckoo's Nest* and James Keller, *The Miracle Worker,* both Priscilla Beach Theatre, Manomet, MA; He, *A Night with Dorothy Parker,* Acorn Theatre Company; Joe Casey, *Them,* Spuyten Duyvil Company, New York City.

PRINCIPAL FILM APPEARANCES—Michael, *Pieces,* Cederquist-Chase Productions; Jonathan, *Judgement,* New York University student film directed by Lee Levitt.

PRINCIPAL TELEVISION APPEARANCES—Episodic: Henri Picard, *All My Children,* ABC, 1989; also host, *Baltimore Is Best,* WBAL (Baltimore, MD).

WRITINGS: STAGE—*Sundown Rockers* (a collection of one-act plays), Primary Stages Company, New York City, 1988; *Bank Shot,* Spuyten Duyvil Company, 1989.

AWARDS: Drama League of New York Award, 1979; Jehlinger Award from the American Academy of Dramatic Arts, 1980.

MEMBER: Actors' Equity Association, Screen Actors Guild, American Federation of Television and Radio Artists.

SIDELIGHTS: RECREATIONS—Sports, music, and fishing.

ADDRESSES: AGENT—Whatley Management, 315 E. 57th Street, Suite 5-B, New York, NY 10022.

*   *   *

VINOVICH, Steve   1945-

PERSONAL: Born January 22, 1945, in Peoria, IL; son of Stephen J. (an insurance salesman) and Jennie J. (a secretary; maiden name, Kuhel) Vinovich; married Carolyn Mignini (an actress), November 27, 1982; children: Nicholas. EDUCATION—University of Illinois, B.A., journalism, 1967; University of California, Los Angeles, M.F.A., acting, 1969; also studied acting at the Strasberg Institute and the Juilliard School of Music, 1972-74.

VOCATION: Actor.

CAREER: BROADWAY DEBUT—Clemment Musgrove, *The Robber Bridegroom,* Biltmore Theatre, 1976. PRINCIPAL STAGE APPEARANCES—Quentin, *After the Fall,* Comedia II Theatre, Los Angeles, 1971; title role, *King John,* New York Shakespeare Festival (NYSF), Public Theatre, New York City, 1974; Clemment Musgrove, *The Robber Bridegroom,* St. Clement's Church Theatre, New York City, 1974; Jourdain, *Would Be Gentleman Present Strauss' Ariadne auf Naxos,* Juilliard School Theatre, New York City, 1974; the Angel, *The Butterfinger's Angel,* Syracuse Stage Theatre, Syracuse, NY, 1974; Norden, *Father Uxbridge Wants to Marry,* Daniel, *Esther,* and Reverend Sykes, *The Last Christians,*

STEVE VINOVICH

all New Dramatists Inc., New York City, 1975; Feldman the Magnificent, *The Magic Show*, Cort Theatre, New York City, 1976; Sam, *Awake and Sing*, McCarter Theatre, Princeton, NJ, 1976; Henry, *Rosa*, St. Clement's Church Theatre, 1978; Sir Andrew Aguecheek, *Twelfth Night*, American Shakespeare Festival, Stratford, CT, 1978; Szabuniewicz, *The Grand Tour*, Palace Theatre, New York City, 1979; Ben, *Loose Ends*, Circle in the Square, New York City, 1979.

Peter Quince, *A Midsummer Night's Dream*, NYSF, Delacorte Theatre, New York City, 1981; Matt, *Talley's Folly*, Royal Palm Theatre, Palm Beach, FL, 1982; Alan, *Double Feature*, Theatre at St. Peter's Church, New York City, 1982; Michael, *A Private View*, NYSF, Public Theatre, 1984; Milt Manville, *Love*, Audrey Wood Theatre, New York City, 1984; Teddy, *The Poker Session*, Theatre-Off-Park, New York City, 1984; Dan, *Paradise!*, Playwrights Horizons, New York City, 1985; Al Capone, *America's Sweetheart*, Hartford Stage Company, Hartford, CT, then Coconut Grove Playhouse, Miami, FL, 1985; Tom, *The Secret Rapture*, Ethel Barrymore Theatre, New York City, 1989. Also appeared in *Tornado*, New Dramatists Inc., 1978; *Hard Sell*, NYSF, Public Theatre, 1980; *Cradlesong*, Musical Theatre Works, New York City, 1984; *Tender Places*, Young Playwrights Festival, NYSF, Public Theatre, 1984.

FILM DEBUT—Dancer, *They Shoot Horses, Don't They?*, ABC/Cinerama, 1969. PRINCIPAL FILM APPEARANCES—Snitch, *Weekend with the Babysitter* (also known as *Weekend Babysitter*), Crown, 1970; Ornstein, *Jennifer on My Mind*, United Artists, 1971; hippie, *The Mechanic* (also known as *Killer of Killers*), United Artists, 1972; B.J. Wert, *Mannequin*, Twentieth Century-Fox, 1987; studio executive, *Wired*, Taurus Entertainment, 1989; also appeared in *Romancing the Stone*, Twentieth Century-Fox, 1984; *Back to Hollywood Boulevard*, New Horizons, 1989; *Awakenings*, 1990.

TELEVISION DEBUT—Randall Feigelbaum, *Call Her Mom*, ABC, 1972. PRINCIPAL TELEVISION APPEARANCES—Series: Bob Hoodenpyle, *Raising Miranda*, CBS, 1988. Pilots: Dwight Purdy III, *Catalina C-Lab*, NBC, 1982. Episodic: Dr. Tobinick, *Hometown*, CBS, 1985; Gallagher, *Stingray*, NBC, 1986; Randy, *The Cavanaughs*, CBS, 1986; Hanhart, *Wiseguy*, CBS, 1987; Bob Keeler, *Roseanne*, ABC, 1988; Joel, *Perfect Strangers*, ABC, 1988; Ken Seaver, *L.A. Law*, NBC, 1988; Tubbs, *Sonny Spoon*, NBC, 1988; Richard, *Valerie's Family*, NBC, 1988, then retitled *The Hogan Family*, NBC, 1989; also *Three's Company*, ABC, 1982; "Seize the Day," *American Playhouse*, PBS, 1984; "The Richest Cat in the World," *Disney Sunday Movie*, ABC, 1985; *Remington Steele*, NBC, 1985; *Hill Street Blues*, NBC, 1987; *Webster*, ABC, 1987 and 1988; *Hooperman*, ABC, 1988.

AWARDS: Best Actor nomination for *Talley's Folly*.

SIDELIGHTS: FAVORITE ROLES—Ben in *Loose Ends*, Clemment Musgrove in *The Robber Bridegroom*, Peter Quince in *A Midsummer Night's Dream*, Matt in *Talley's Folly*, Sir Andrew Aguecheek in *Twelfth Night*, the Angel in *The Butterfinger's Angel*, Jourdain in *Would Be Gentleman Presents Strauss' Ariadne Auf Naxos*, and Quentin in *After the Fall*. RECREATIONS—Reading, golf, racquetball, environmental concerns, traveling, and spending time with his son.

ADDRESSES: AGENT—Harris and Goldberg, 2121 Avenue of the Stars, Los Angeles, CA 90067.

*   *   *

VOLZ, Nedra

VOCATION: Actress.

CAREER: PRINCIPAL FILM APPEARANCES—Free press lady, *Your Three Minutes Are Up*, Cinerama, 1973; Mrs. Kissel, *10*, Warner Brothers, 1979; Mrs. Clancy, *Little Miss Marker*, Universal, 1980; Big Ed, *Lust in the Dust*, New World, 1985; Mrs. Loretta Houk, *Moving Violations*, Twentieth Century-Fox, 1985; Lana, *Earth Girls Are Easy*, Vestron, 1989.

PRINCIPAL TELEVISION APPEARANCES—Series: Grandma Belle Durbin, *A Year at the Top*, CBS, 1977; Pinky Nolan, *Mr. Dugan*, CBS, 1979 (three episodes produced but never broadcast); Pinky Nolan, *Hanging In*, CBS, 1979; Adelaide Brubaker, *Diff'rent Strokes*, NBC, 1980-82; Miz Tisdale, *The Dukes of Hazzard*, CBS, 1981-83; Winona "Mother B" Beck, *Filthy Rich*, CBS, 1982-83; Pearl Sperling, *The Fall Guy*, ABC, 1985-86. Mini-Series: Mrs. Conlaw, *Condominium*, HBO, 1980. Pilots: Elderly woman, *They Only Come Out at Night*, NBC, 1975; Mrs. Hickey, *King of the Road*, CBS, 1978; Emily Baines, *Pals*, NBC, 1981. Episodic: Aunt Iola, *All in the Family*, CBS, 1978; Babbette, *The A-Team*, NBC, 1986; Ethel, *Who's the Boss?*, ABC, 1986; Glynnis Mendelson, *Scarecrow and Mrs. King*, CBS, 1986; cat woman, *Alf*, NBC, 1987; Estelle, *Mr. Belvedere*, ABC, 1988; Momma Steadman, *TV 101*, CBS, 1989. Movies: Mrs. Felcher, *Gridlock* (also known as *The Great American Traffic Jam*), NBC, 1980; Hypatia Flowers, *For Love or Money*, CBS, 1984; Gladys, *Last of the Great Survivors*, CBS, 1984. Specials: *The Screen Actors Guild 50th Anniversary Celebration*, CBS, 1984.

ADDRESSES: AGENT—Dale Garrick International Agency, 8831 Sunset Boulevard, Suite 402, Los Angeles, CA 90069.*

W

WAIN, Edward
See TOWNE, Robert

* * *

WAITE, Ralph 1928-

PERSONAL: Born June 22, 1928, in White Plains, NY; son of Ralph H. (a construction engineer) and Esther (Mitchell) Waite; married first wife, Beverly, 1951 (divorced, 1966); married Kerry Shear, 1972 (divorced, 1980); married Linda East (an interior decorator), December 4, 1982; children: Kathleen, Suzanne, Liam. EDUCATION—Received B.A. from Bucknell University; received B.D. from Yale University; trained for the stage with Lee Strasberg and Mary Tarchi. MILITARY—U.S. Marine Corps, 1946-48.

VOCATION: Actor, director, producer, and writer.

CAREER: STAGE DEBUT—Chief of police, *The Balcony,* Circle in the Square, New York City, 1960. LONDON DEBUT—*Blues for Mister Charlie,* Aldwych Theatre, 1966. PRINCIPAL STAGE APPEARANCES—Minister, *Marathon '33,* American National Theatre and Academy (ANTA) Theatre, New York City, 1963; Ralph and Judge, *Blues for Mister Charlie,* ANTA Theatre, 1964; Matthew Stanton, *Hogan's Goat,* American Place Theatre, New York City, 1965; Henry and Bruno, "The Mutilated" in *Slapstick Tragedy,* Longacre Theatre, New York City, 1966; Azdak, *The Caucasian Chalk Circle,* Theatre Company of Boston, Boston, MA, 1966; Andrew Kragler, *Drums in the Night,* Circle in the Square, New York City, 1967; Defense Counsel Rogers, *The Trial of Lee Harvey Oswald,* ANTA Theatre, 1967; Claudius, *Hamlet,* New York Shakespeare Festival (NYSF), Public Theatre, New York City, 1967, then Mobile Theatre, New York City, 1968; Orsino, *Twelfth Night,* NYSF, Delacorte Theatre, New York City, 1969; the Father, *Watering Place,* Music Box Theatre, New York City, 1969; Ted, *The Killdeer,* NYSF, Public Theatre, 1969; captain, *The Father,* Circle in the Square, 1981; Joe Keller, *All My Sons,* Long Wharf Theatre, New Haven, CT, 1986. Also *Traveller Without Luggage,* ANTA Theatre, 1964; *The Peacemaker,* Theatre Company of Boston, 1969; *Buried Child,* South Coast Repertory Theatre, Costa Mesa, CA, 1985; *Bunker Reveries,* Roundabout Theatre, New York City, 1987; and appeared with the Theatre Company of Boston, 1966-68; and the Long Wharf Theatre, New Haven, CT, 1968-69.

FILM DEBUT—Alibi, *Cool Hand Luke,* Warner Brothers, 1967. PRINCIPAL FILM APPEARANCES—Sean Magruder, *A Lovely Way to Die* (also known as *A Lovely Way to Go*), Universal, 1968; Peter's father, *Last Summer,* Allied Artists, 1969; Carl Fidelio

Dupea, *Five Easy Pieces,* Columbia, 1970; Mace, *The Grissom Gang,* Cinerama, 1971; Jack Dekker, *Lawman,* United Artists, 1971; Detective Cromie, *The Pursuit of Happiness,* Columbia, 1971; Olson, *The Sporting Club,* AVCO-Embassy, 1971; Elias Hooker, *Chato's Land,* United Artists, 1972; Jim MacKay, *The Magnificent Seven Ride,* United Artists, 1972; Pete Cockrell, *Trouble Man,* Twentieth Century-Fox, 1972; Drummer, *Kid Blue,* Twentieth Century-Fox, 1973; Detective Mathews, *The Stone Killer,* Columbia, 1973; C.G., *On the Nickel,* Rose's Park, 1980. Also appeared in *Hot Summer Week,* Fanfare, 1973.

PRINCIPAL FILM WORK—Producer and director, *On the Nickel,* Rose's Park, 1980.

PRINCIPAL TELEVISION APPEARANCES—Series: John Walton, *The Waltons,* CBS, 1972-81; Ben Walker, *The Mississippi* (also known as *On the Mississippi*), CBS, 1983-84. Mini-Series: Third Mate Slater, *Roots,* ABC, 1977. Episodic: Paul Robbins, *Murder, She Wrote,* CBS, 1989; also *Bonanza,* NBC. Movies: The man from Toledo, *The Borgia Stick,* NBC, 1967; title role, *The Secret Life of John Chapman,* CBS, 1976; Henry Stone, *Red Alert,* CBS, 1977; Jared Teeter, *Angel City,* CBS, 1980; Floyd Wing, *Ohms,* CBS, 1980; Father Bernard Pagano, *The Gentleman Bandit,* CBS, 1981; John Walton, *A Wedding on Walton's Mountain,* NBC, 1982; John Walton, *Mother's Day on Walton's Mountain,* NBC, 1982; John Walton, *A Day for Thanks on Walton's Mountain,* NBC, 1982; Tommy O'Bannon, *A Good Sport,* CBS, 1984; Frank Hayward, *Crime of Innocence,* NBC, 1985; Martin Pehrsson, *Red Earth, White Earth,* CBS, 1989. Specials: Lieutenant Colonel Fredericks, *The Desperate Hours,* ABC, 1967; Pozzo, "Waiting for Godot," *Great Performances,* PBS, 1977; *CBS: On the Air,* CBS, 1978.

PRINCIPAL TELEVISION WORK—Series: Supervising producer (with Christopher Morgan), *The Mississippi* (also known as *On the Mississippi*), CBS, 1983-84. Episodic: Director, *The Waltons,* CBS. Movies: Executive producer, *A Good Sport,* CBS, 1984.

RELATED CAREER—Founder and artistic director, Los Angeles Actors Theatre, Los Angeles, 1975—.

NON-RELATED CAREER—Social worker, Westchester County, NY; Presbyterian minister, Garden City, NY; publicity director and assistant editor of religious books, Harper & Row, New York City.

WRITINGS: FILM—*On the Nickel,* Rose's Park, 1980.

SIDELIGHTS: FAVORITE ROLES—Azdak in *The Caucasian Chalk Circle.*

ADDRESSES: AGENTS—Ron Meyer, Creative Artists Agency,

9830 Wilshire Boulevard, Beverly Hills, CA 90212; Smith-Freedman & Associates, 123 San Vicente Boulevard, Beverly Hills, CA 90211.*

*   *   *

WAJDA, Andrzej   1926-

PERSONAL: Born March 6, 1926 (some sources say 1927), in Suwalki, Poland; son of Jakub (a cavalry officer) and Aniela (a school teacher; maiden name, Biaxowas) Wajda; married Beata Tyszkiewicz (an actress), 1967 (divorced); married Krystyna Zachwatowicz (a set and costume designer), 1975; children: one daughter (first marriage). EDUCATION—Attended the Fine Arts Academy (Cracow, Poland), 1945-48, and the Higher School of Cinematography (Lodz, Poland), 1950-52. MILITARY—Served in the A.K. (Polish Home Army Resistance) during World War II.

VOCATION: Director and screenwriter.

CAREER: Also see *WRITINGS* below. FIRST STAGE WORK— Director and scenographer, *A Hatful of Rain*, Gdansk, Poland, 1959. PRINCIPAL STAGE WORK—All as director, unless indicated: *The Possessed,* Yale Repertory Theatre, New Haven, CT, 1974-75; *Crime and Punishment,* Stary Theatre, Cracow, Poland, 1984; *Crime and Punishment,* Pepsico Summerfare International Performing Arts Festival, State University of New York, Purchase, NY, 1986; *The Dybbuk,* Stary Theatre, Cracow, Poland, 1988, then Habima Theatre, Tel Aviv, Israel, later Habima Theatre Company, Moscow, 1990; *The Dybbuk* and *Hamlet IV,* both Pepsico Summerfare International Performing Arts Festival, 1989; also *Hamlet,* 1960; *Two on the Seesaw,* 1960; *Wesele,* 1962; *The Devils,* 1963; *Play Strindberg,* 1969; *Sticks and Bones,* Moscow, 1972; scenographer, *The Devils,* 1972; *Derr Mittmacher,* 1973; (also scenographer) *November Night,* 1974; *The Danton Affair,* 1975; *The Demons,* 1975; *The Idiot,* 1975; *Kiedy rozum spi* (also known as *When Reason Sleeps*), 1976; *Emigranci* (also known as *The Emigrants*), 1976; *Nastasia Philipovna,* 1977; *Conversation with the Executioner,* 1977; *The Danton Affair,* 1978; *Z biegiem lat, z biegiem dni* (also known as *Down the Years, Down the Days*), 1978; *Hamlet,* 1980; *Antigone,* 1984.

PRINCIPAL FILM APPEARANCES—As himself, *Wajda's Danton* (documentary), Cori Films International/Channel Four, 1983. FIRST FILM WORK—Director, *Kiedy ty spisz* (also known as *While You Sleep;* short film), 1950. PRINCIPAL FILM WORK—All as director, unless indicated: *Kanal* (also known as *They Loved Life* and *Sewer*), 1957, released in the United States by MJP/Kingsley International, 1961; *Popiol i diament* (also known as *Ashes and Diamonds*), 1958, released in the United States by Janus, 1961; *Lotna,* Film Polski, 1959, released in the United States by Pol-Ton, 1966; *Samson,* Film Polski, 1961; *Sibirska Ledi Magbet* (also known as *Lady Macbeth of Mtsensk, Fury Is a Woman,* and *Siberian Lady Macbeth*), Avala Films, 1962; "Warszawa" in *L'Amour a vingt ans* (also known as *Love at Twenty, Amore a vent'anni, Milosc Dwudziestolatkow,* and *Liebe Mit Zwanzig*), 1962, released in the United States by Embassy, 1963; *Bramy raju* (also known as *Gates to Paradise, The Gates of Heaven,* and *The Holy Apes*), 1967, released in the United States by Jointex, 1968; *Wszystko na sprzedaz* (also known as *Everything for Sale*), Film Polski, 1968; *Krajobraz po bitwie* (also known as *Krajobraz na much, Landscape After Battle,* and *Landscape After the Battle*), Film Polski, 1970; *Brzezina* (also known as *The Birch-Wood*), Film Polski, 1970;

Wesele (also known as *The Wedding*), Film Polski, 1972; *Ziemia obiecana* (also known as *Promised Land* and *Land of Promise*), Film Polski, 1974, released in the United States by Tinc Production, 1975; *Bez znieczulenia* (also known as *Without Anesthetic* and *Rough Treatment*), Film Polski, 1978; (also producer) *Czlowiek z marmuru* (also known as *Man of Marble*), 1978, released in the United States by Film Polski, 1979; *Panny z Wilka* (also known as *Sziewka z Wilko, The Young Girls of Wilko, Maidens from Wilko, The Girls from Wilko,* and *The Young Ladies of Wilko*), Artificial Eye, 1979; *Dyrygent* (also known as *The Orchestra Conductor* and *The Conductor*), Film Polski/New Yorker, 1979, released in the United States by Cinegate, 1981.

Czlowiek z zelaza (also known as *Man of Iron*), United Artists, 1981; *Danton,* 1982, released in the United States by Triumph, 1983; *Eine Liebe in Deutschland* (also known as *A Love in Germany* and *Un Amour en Allemagne*), Triumph/Artificial Eye/Columbia, 1984; technical advisor, *Visage de chien* (also known as *Dogface*), K Films, 1985; *Kronika wypadkow milosnych* (also known as *A Chronicle of Amorous Accidents*), Zespoly/Film Group Perspektyva, 1986; *Les Possedes* (also known as *The Possessed*), Gaumont International, 1987. Also *Zly chlopiec* (also known as *The Bad Boy;* short film), 1950; *Ceramika Ilzecka* (also known as *The Pottery of Ilzecka;* short documentary), 1951; assistant director, *Piatka z ulicy Barskiej* (also known as *Five Boys from Barska Street*), 1954; *Pokolenie* (also known as *A Generation*), 1954; *Ide ku sloncu* (also known as *Ide do slonca* and *I Walk to the Sun;* short film), 1955; *Niewinni czarodzieje* (also known as *Innocent Sorcerers*), 1960; *Popioly* (also known as *Ashes*), 1965; *Polowanie na muchy* (also known as *Hunting Flies*), 1969; *Smuga cienia* (also known as *The Shadow Line*), 1976; *Zaproszenie do wnetrza* (also known as *Invitation to the Inside;* documentary), 1978.

PRINCIPAL TELEVISION WORK—All as director. Series: *Ziemia obiecana* (also known as *Promised Land* and *The Promised Land*), Polish television, 1974. Also *Przekladaniec* (also known as *Roly-Poly* and *Jigsaw Puzzle*), Polish television, 1968; *Macbeth,* Polish television, 1969; (also art director and costume designer) *Pilatus und andere* (also known as *Pilate and the Others*), West German television, 1972; *Death Class,* Polish television, 1976; and *November Night.*

RELATED CAREER—Assistant stage manager, 1953; stage manager, Stary Theatre, Cracow, Poland, 1973—; founder, Studio X (a film production group; dissolved by the Polish government, 1983); president, Polish Film Association, 1978-84 (resigned under government pressure); president of the jury, Moscow Film Festival, 1989; artistic director, Contemporary Theatre, Warsaw, Poland.

NON-RELATED CAREER—Assisted in the restoration of church paintings, Radom, Poland, 1940-43; senator, Polish government, 1989.

WRITINGS: See production details above. FILM—*Kiedy ty spisz,* 1950; *Zly chlopiec,* 1950; *Ceramika Ilzecka,* 1951; *Ide ku sloncu,* 1955; (with Jerzy Andrzejewski) *Popiol i diament,* 1958, published in *The Wajda Trilogy,* Simon & Schuster, 1973; (with Wojciech Zukrowski) *Lotna,* 1959; *Niewinni czarodzieje,* 1960; (with Kazimierz Brandys) *Samson,* 1961; (with Sveta Lukic) *Sibirska Ledi Magbet,* 1962; (with Jerzy Stefan Stawinski) "Warszawa" in *L'Amour a vingt ans,* 1962; *Popioly,* 1965; (with Andrzejewski) *Bramy raju,* 1967; *Wszystko na sprzedaz,* 1968; *Polowanie na muchy,* 1969; (with Andrzej Brzozowski) *Krajobraz po bitwie,* 1970; (with Jaroslaw Iwaszkiewicz) *Brzezina,* 1970; (with Andrzej Kijowski) *Wesele,* 1972; *Ziemia obiecana,* 1974; (co-writer) *Smuga cienia,* 1976;

(with Agnieszka Holland) *Bez znieczulenia*, 1978; *Zaproszenie do wnetrza*, 1978; (with Holland, Jean-Claude Carriere, Boleslaw Michalek, and Jacek Gasiorowski) *Danton*, 1982; (with Holland and Michalek) *Eine Liebe in Deutschland*, 1984; (with Tadeusz Konwicki) *Kronika wypadkow milosnych*, 1986; (with Holland, Carriere, and Edward Zebrowsky) *Les Possedes*, 1987.

TELEVISION—*Przekladaniec*, 1968; *Pilatus und andere*, 1972. OTHER—*Double Vision* (autobiography), Henry Holt & Company, 1989; also contributor of articles to such periodicals as *Films and Filming*, *Kino*, and *Filmcritica*.

AWARDS: State Prize (Poland), 1954, for *Pokolenie;* Special Jury Prize from the Cannes Film Festival, 1957, for *Kanal;* Fipresci Prize from the Venice Film Festival, 1958, for *Popiol i diament;* Milan Film Festival Award, 1970, and Moscow Film Festival Award, 1971, both for *Brzezina;* Milan Film Festival Award, 1970, and Grand Prize from the Colombo (Sri Lanka) Film Festival, 1973, both for *Krajobraz po bitwie;* Bambi Prize, 1973, for *Pilatus und andere;* Silver Prize from the San Sebastian Film Festival, 1973, for *Wesele;* State Prize (Poland), 1974, Grand Prize from the Moscow Film Festival and Golden Hugo from the Chicago Film Festival, both 1975, Academy Award nomination, Best Foreign Language Film, 1976, Gold Laceno Prize, 1978, and Cartegena Film Festival Award, 1978, all for *Ziemia obiecana;* Order of Banner of Labour (second class), 1975; K. Swinarski Prize, 1976; Valladolid Prize, 1976; Fipresci Prize from the Cannes Film Festival, 1978, for *Czlowiek z marmuru;* Order of Kirill and Methodius (first class; Bulgaria), 1978; Luchino Visconti Prize, 1978, Grand Prize "Gdansk Lions," 1978, and Ecumenical Prize from the Cannes Film Festival, 1979, all for *Bez znieczulenia;* Prize of the Committee for Polish Radio and Television, 1980; Golden Palm Award from the Cannes Film Festival, 1981, for *Czlowiek z zelaza;* Cesar Awards, 1981 and 1982; British Academy Award for Services to Film and British Academy of Film and Television Arts Fellowship, both 1982; Officer, French Legion of Honor, 1982; Louis Delluc Prize, 1982, for *Danton;* Athinai-Onassis Prize for Man and Mankind from the Alexander S. Onassis Public Benefit Foundation, 1983; also Officers' Cross from the Order of Polonia Restituta. HONORARY DEGREES—American University, Dr. H.C., 1981.

MEMBER: Union of Polish Artists and Designers (ZPAP; honorary member).

ADDRESSES: OFFICE—Film Polski, ul. Mazowiecka 6/8, Warsaw, Poland.*

* * *

WALLACE, Marcia   1942-

PERSONAL: Born November 1, 1942, in Creston, IA. EDUCATION—Trained for the stage at the HB Studios.

VOCATION: Actress.

CAREER: OFF-BROADWAY DEBUT—*The Fourth Wall*, Theatre East, 1968. PRINCIPAL STAGE APPEARANCES—Nerissa, *Calling in Crazy*, Fortune Theatre, New York City, 1969; Miss Metcalf, *Dark of the Moon*, Mercer-Shaw Arena Theatre, New York City, 1970.

PRINCIPAL FILM APPEARANCES—Ms. Molloy, *Teen Witch*, Trans

World Entertainment, 1989; also appeared in *My Mom's a Werewolf*, Crown International, 1989.

PRINCIPAL TELEVISION APPEARANCES—Series: Carol Kester, *The Bob Newhart Show*, CBS, 1972-78; regular, *The New Love, American Style*, ABC, 1985. Pilots: Connie Martin, *Flying High*, CBS, 1978; Myra Elliot, *The Castaways on Gilligan's Island*, NBC, 1979; Lelia Flynn, *Characters*, NBC, 1980. Episodic: As herself, *Taxi*, NBC, 1982; Polly Barth, *Murder, She Wrote*, CBS, 1986; Mrs. Lyman, *ALF*, NBC, 1987; Miss Phillips, *Night Court*, NBC, 1988; also Betty, *Bewitched*, ABC. Movies: Boom Boom Shavelson, *Gridlock* (also known as *The Great American Traffic Jam*), NBC, 1980. Specials: *Battle of the Network Stars*, ABC, 1977; *Destined to Live: One Hundred Roads to Recovery*, NBC, 1988.

ADDRESSES: AGENT—Rainford Agency, 7471 Melrose Avenue, Suite 14, Los Angeles, CA 90046. MANAGER—Charter Management, 9000 Sunset Boulevard, Suite 1112, Los Angeles, CA 90210.*

* * *

WALTERS, Ewart James   1950-

PERSONAL: Born November 9, 1950, in Clarendon, Jamaica; son of Glaister James (an engineer) and Isabell Christina (a nurse; maiden name, Clarke) Walters; married Mary Tempest (an actress), April 29, 1978; children: Zara. EDUCATION—Trained for the stage

EWART JAMES WALTERS

at Webber Douglas School of Dramatic Art. RELIGION—Church of England.

VOCATION: Actor.

CAREER: PRINCIPAL STAGE APPEARANCES—Giorgio, *The Gondoliers,* Bristol Old Vic Theatre, Bristol, U.K., 1985; also appeared in *Having a Ball!,* Leeds Playhouse, Leeds, U.K., 1982; *Hamlet,* Young Vic Theatre, London, 1985; *Exclusive,* Strand Theatre, London, 1989; as Oberon, *A Midsummer Night's Dream* and horse, *Equus,* both Leeds Playhouse; Delroy, *Sus,* Yvonne Arnaud Theatre, Guildford, U.K.; John the Baptist and Judas, *Godspell,* Churchill Theatre, Bromley, U.K.; Nelson, *Scenes from Soweto,* Contact Theatre, Manchester, U.K.; narrator, *Joseph and His Amazing Technicolor Dreamcoat,* Ashcroft Theatre, Croyden, U.K.; Abe and Jemmy, *Moll Flanders,* Half Moon Theatre, London; *Jesus Christ Superstar,* Palace Theatre, London; *Measure for Measure* and *The Pied Piper,* both National Theatre, London; *On the Twentieth Century,* Her Majesty's Theatre, London; *The Admirable Bashville,* Regents Park Theatre, London; *Abduction from the Seraglio,* Grand Theatre, Leeds, U.K.; *Carmen Jones,* Crucible Theatre, Sheffield, U.K.; *Moby Dick,* Royal Exchange Theatre, Manchester, U.K.

MAJOR TOURS—Hud, *Hair,* U.K. cities; Blosson, *The Hasty Heart,* U.K. cities; also Harper, *Independence.*

PRINCIPAL FILM APPEARANCES—*AD 72,* AD Productions; *Fox,* Thames Euston; *Born Free,* Screen Gems.

PRINCIPAL TELEVISION APPEARANCES—Episodic: Superintendent Akimbo, *Rumpole of the Bailey,* Thames, then *Mystery!,* PBS; "A Brush with Mr. Porter on the Way to Eldorado," *Play for Today,* BBC. Also appeared as Dion, *The Cleopatras,* BBC; and in *The Bill,* Thames; *Visitors to Anderson,* ATV.

ADDRESSES: AGENT—Rolf Kruger, Morley House, 314-322 Regent Street, London W1, England.

*   *   *

WARD, Jay   1920-1989

PERSONAL: Born September 21, 1920, in San Francisco, CA; died of kidney cancer, October 12, 1989, in Los Angeles, CA; wife's name, Ramona; children: Ron, Carey, Tiffany. EDUCATION—Graduated from the University of California, Berkeley; graduate work in business at Harvard University. MILITARY—U.S. Army Air Corps during World War II.

VOCATION: Producer.

CAREER: PRINCIPAL FILM WORK—Producer, *The Crazy World of Laurel and Hardy* (documentary), 1967; also producer, *Golden Age of Buster Keaton* (documentary).

PRINCIPAL TELEVISION WORK—Series: Creator and producer (with Alexander Anderson), *Crusader Rabbit* (animated), syndicated, 1949-51, then 1957-58; creator and producer (with Bill Scott), *Rocky and His Friends* (also featuring *Fractured Fairy Tales, Aesop's Fables, Peabody's Improbable History, Dudley Do-Right,* and *Bullwinkle's Corner;* animated), ABC, 1959-61; creator (with Scott) and producer (with Scott and Bud Courley), *The Bullwinkle*

Show (also featuring *Dudley Do-Right, Peabody's Improbable History, Aesop's Fables,* and *Fractured Fairy Tales;* animated), NBC, 1961-64; creator and producer, *The Adventures of Hoppity Hopper from Foggy Bogg* (animated), syndicated, 1962, renamed *Hoppity Hopper,* ABC, 1964-65; creator and (with Scott) producer, *Fractured Flickers* (live-action), syndicated, 1963; producer, *George of the Jungle* (also featuring *Super Chicken* and *Tom Slick;* animated), ABC, 1967-70; producer (with Scott), *The Dudley Do-Right Show* (also featuring *The Hunter, The World of Commander McBragg,* and *Tutor the Turtle;* animated), ABC, 1969-70.

RELATED CAREER—Founder, Jay Ward Productions; producer of animated television commercials for the Quaker Oats Company, late 1960s to the mid-1980s.

NON-RELATED CAREER—Owner of a real estate business, Berkeley, CA, 1947-87.

WRITINGS: TELEVISION—Series: (With Alexander Anderson) *Crusader Rabbit,* syndicated, 1949-51, then 1957-58; (with others) *The Bullwinkle Show,* ABC, 1961-64.

SIDELIGHTS: For his work in television animation, Jay Ward has been honored at the U.S. Film Festival in Park City, Utah, and was the subject of tributes in Miami, FL, and Montreal, PQ, Canada in 1989.

OBITUARIES AND OTHER SOURCES: Broadcasting, October 23, 1989; *New York Times,* October 14, 1989; *Variety,* October 18-24, 1989.*

*   *   *

WARDEN, Jack   1920-

PERSONAL: Born Jack Warden Lebzelter, September 18, 1920, in Newark, NJ; son of John W. (an engineer and technician) and Laura (Costello) Lebzelter; married Wanda Dupree, October 11, 1958 (divorced); children: Christopher. EDUCATION—Trained for the stage with Margo Jones. POLITICS—Democrat. MILITARY—U.S. Navy, 1938-41; U.S. Maritime Service, 1941-42; U.S. Army, Paratroopers, 1941-46.

VOCATION: Actor.

CAREER: STAGE DEBUT—Sir Toby Belch, *Twelfth Night,* Margo Jones Theatre, Dallas, TX, 1947. OFF-BROADWAY DEBUT—Mickey, *Golden Boy,* American National Theatre and Academy Theatre, 1952. PRINCIPAL STAGE APPEARANCES—Johnny, *Lullaby,* Lyceum Theatre, New York City, 1954; Mike Hertzog, *Sing Me No Lullaby,* Phoenix Theatre, New York City, 1954; Marco, *A View from the Bridge,* Coronet Theatre, New York City, 1955; Joey, *A Very Special Baby,* Playhouse Theatre, New York City, 1956; Dave, *The Body Beautiful,* Broadway Theatre, New York City, 1958; Arthur Goldman, *The Man in the Glass Booth,* Royale Theatre, New York City, 1969; various roles, *Stages,* Belasco Theatre, New York City, 1978. Also appeared as Algernon Moncrieff, *The Importance of Being Earnest,* Tony Lumpkin, *She Stoops to Conquer,* Trisotin, *The Learned Ladies,* Petruchio, *The Taming of the Shrew,* Yasha, *The Cherry Orchard,* and in *Front Porch* (later retitled *Picnic*), *Summer and Smoke,* and *Leaf and Bough,* all Margo Jones Theatre Company, 1947-51; "Snowangel" and "Epiphany," in *Cages* (double-bill), York Theatre, New York

JACK WARDEN

City, 1963; "A Wen" and "Orange Souffle," in *Under the Weather*, Festival of Two Worlds, Spoleto, Italy, 1966; *Death of a Salesman*, Arlington Park Theatre, Arlington Heights, IL, 1972.

MAJOR TOURS—Pete, *An Old Beat-Up Woman*, U.S. cities, 1950; Eddie Harmon, *Conversations in the Dark*, U.S. cities, 1963-64; also *There Is Always Juliet*, Theatre of the Open Road, U.S. cities.

PRINCIPAL FILM APPEARANCES—Crew member, *The Frogmen*, Twentieth Century-Fox, 1951; Walt Davis, *The Man with My Face*, United Artists, 1951; Morse, *You're in the Navy Now* (also known as *U.S.S. Teakettle*), Twentieth Century-Fox, 1951; Corporal Buckley, *From Here to Eternity*, Columbia, 1953; Eddie, *The Bachelor Party*, United Artists, 1957; Charles Malik, *Edge of the City* (also known as *A Man Is Ten Feet Tall*), Metro-Goldwyn-Mayer (MGM), 1957; juror, *Twelve Angry Men*, United Artists, 1957; Master Sergeant Saul Rosen, *Darby's Rangers* (also known as *Young Invaders*), Warner Brothers, 1958; Mueller, *Run Silent, Run Deep*, United Artists, 1958; Ben Compson, *The Sound and the Fury*, Twentieth Century-Fox, 1959; Kelly, *That Kind of Woman*, Paramount, 1959; Doc Farrington, *Wake Me When It's Over*, Twentieth Century-Fox, 1960; Huston, *Escape from Zahrain*, Paramount, 1962; Dr. Dedham, *Donovan's Reef*, Paramount, 1963; First Sergeant Welsh, *The Thin Red Line*, Allied Artists, 1964; General Pratt, *Blindfold*, Universal, 1966; Barnet Weiner, *Bye, Bye Braverman*, Warner Brothers, 1968.

Earl Olive, *The Sporting Club*, AVCO-Embassy, 1971; Herb McAdams, *Summertree*, Columbia, 1971; General Strapp, *Welcome to the Club*, Columbia, 1971; Dr. Moses, *Who Is Harry Kellerman and Why Is He Saying Those Terrible Things About Me?*, National General, 1971; Gifford, *Billy Two Hats* (also known as *The Lady and the Outlaw*), United Artists, 1973; Dawes, *The Man Who Loved Cat Dancing*, MGM, 1973; Max, *The Apprenticeship of Duddy Kravitz*, Paramount, 1974; Lester Carr, *Shampoo*, Columbia, 1975; Harry Rosenfeld, *All the President's Men*, Warner Brothers, 1976; Charlie Zane, *The White Buffalo* (also known as *Hunt to Kill*), United Artists, 1977; Dr. Bessner, *Death on the Nile*, Paramount, 1978; Max Corkle, *Heaven Can Wait*, Paramount, 1978; Judge Rayford, . . . *And Justice for All*, Columbia, 1979; the President, *Being There*, United Artists, 1979; Harold Meredith, *Beyond The Poseidon Adventure*, Warner Brothers, 1979; Jackie, *The Champ*, Metro-Goldwyn-Mayer/United Artists (MGM/UA), 1979; Harry, *Dreamer*, Twentieth Century-Fox, 1979; Roy L. Fuchs and Luke Fuchs, *Used Cars*, Columbia, 1980; Nelson, *Carbon Copy*, AVCO-Embassy, 1981; Commander, *Chu Chu and the Philly Flash*, Twentieth Century-Fox, 1981; as himself, *The Great Muppet Caper*, Universal, 1981; Jack, *So Fine*, Warner Brothers, 1981; Mickey Morrissey, *The Verdict*, Twentieth Century-Fox, 1982; Garvey, *Crackers*, Universal, 1984; Moravia, *The Aviator*, MGM/UA, 1985; Lloyd, *September*, Orion, 1987; Sergeant Major MacLure, *The Presidio*, Paramount, 1988. Also appeared in *Red Ball Express*, Universal, 1952.

TELEVISION DEBUT—Arthur Clary, "Ann Rutledge," *Philco Television Playhouse*, NBC, 1950. PRINCIPAL TELEVISION APPEARANCES—Series: Coach Frank Whip, *Mr. Peepers*, NBC, 1953-55; Bobo, *Norby*, NBC, 1955; Matthew Gower, *The Asphalt Jungle*, ABC, 1961; Major Simon Butcher, *The Wackiest Ship in the Army*, NBC, 1965-66; Lieutenant Fergus, *Gallagher* and *The Further Adventures of Gallagher* (both broadcast on *Walt Disney's Wonderful World of Color*), NBC, 1965; Lieutenant Fergus, *Gallagher Goes West* (broadcast on *Walt Disney's Wonderful World of Color*), NBC, 1967; Detective Lieutenant Mike Haines, *N.Y.P.D.*, ABC, 1967-69; John "Jigsaw John" St. John, *Jigsaw John*, NBC, 1976; Morris Buttermaker, *The Bad News Bears*, CBS, 1979-80; Harry Fox, *Crazy Like a Fox*, CBS, 1984-86. Mini-Series: Joseph Kennedy, Sr., *Robert Kennedy and His Times*, CBS, 1985; Nerva, *A.D.*, NBC, 1985. Pilots: Joe Cushing, *The Blue Men* (broadcast as an episode of *Playhouse 90*), CBS, 1959; Jack Fleming, *The Watchman* (broadcast as an episode of *Kraft Suspense Theatre*), NBC, 1964; Jake Moniker, *Man on a String*, CBS, 1972; John St. John, *They Only Come Out at Night*, NBC, 1975; Cosmo Topper, *Topper*, ABC, 1979.

Episodic: Gorman, "Retaliation," *Cavalier Theatre*, NBC, 1951; title role, "The Champ," *Manhunt* (also known as *Assignment: Manhunt*), NBC, 1952; Lefty, "Snookie," *Kraft Television Theatre*, NBC, 1953; Teddy Merrill, "Chester Potter of the Pittsburgh Press," *The Big Story*, NBC, 1953; Jerry French, "Comeback," *Gulf Playhouse: First Person*, NBC, 1953; Brick Nelson, "The Promise," *The Campbell Television Soundstage* (also known as *Campbell Playhouse* and *TV Soundstage*), NBC, 1953; Blik, "Train to Trouble," *Goodyear Television Playhouse*, NBC, 1953; taxi driver, "Dream House," *Kraft Television Theatre*, NBC, 1953; Dr. Max, "Native Dancer," *Goodyear Television Playhouse*, NBC, 1954; Pete, "Jean Barrett of the Philadelphia Evening Bulletin," *The Big Story*, NBC, 1954; Sheriff Bass, "Dr. Rainwater Goes A-Courtin'," *Kraft Television Theatre*, NBC, 1954; Stamper, "The Worried Man Blues," *Kraft Television Theatre*, NBC, 1954; Hal, "Class of '58," *Goodyear Television Playhouse*, NBC, 1954.

Lieutenant Earl Floyd, *Justice*, NBC, 1955; title role, "Ted Link of the St. Louis Post Dispatch," *The Big Story*, NBC, 1955; Buzz Calderone, "Shadow of the Champ," *Philco Television Playhouse*,

NBC, 1955; Alex Hamner, *Justice*, NBC, 1955; Boze, "The Petrified Forest," *Producers' Showcase*, NBC, 1955; Harry Pomeroy, "The Mechanical Heart," *Goodyear Television Playhouse*, NBC, 1955; Frank Doran, "Tragedy in a Temporary Town," *Alcoa Hour*, NBC, 1956; Sergeant Debb, "A Real Fine Cutting Edge," *Kaiser Aluminum Hour*, NBC, 1957; newspaperman, "The Flight," *Suspicion*, NBC, 1957; Jack Armstrong, "Abraham Lincoln: The Early Years," *Omnibus*, NBC, 1959; Mike Wilson, *Bonanza*, NBC, 1959; James A. Corey, "The Lonely," *The Twilight Zone*, CBS, 1959; Emmet Fitzgerald, *Five Fingers*, NBC, 1959; Ollie, *The Outlaws*, NBC, 1960; Martin, *Wagon Train*, NBC, 1962; Axton, *Tales of Wells Fargo*, NBC, 1962; Jubal Tatum, *The Virginian*, NBC, 1962; also "Old MacDonald Had a Curve," *Kraft Television Theatre*, NBC, 1953; *The Imogene Coca Show*, NBC, 1954; "Courant," *The Big Story*, NBC, 1954; "A Very Special Baby," *Home Show*, NBC, 1956; *Bewitched*, ABC, 1964; "The Ivy Curtain," *The Invaders*, ABC, 1967; "Meeting at Appalachian," *Westinghouse Desilu Playhouse*, CBS; Bill Foley, *Roger Dove*, syndicated; *The Man Behind the Badge*, CBS; *Danger*, CBS; *The Armstrong Circle Theatre*, NBC; *The Trailmaster*, ABC; *Dr. Kildare*, NBC; *Naked City*, ABC; *Bob Hope Presents*, NBC; *Slattery's People*, CBS; *The Untouchables*, ABC; *Route 66*, CBS; *Ben Casey*, ABC; *The Fugitive*, ABC; *Great Adventure*, CBS; *The Breaking Point*, syndicated; *Bus Stop*, syndicated.

Movies: Coach George Halas, *Brian's Song*, ABC, 1971; Lieutenant George Coye, *The Face of Fear*, CBS, 1971; Lieutenant Joe Burton, *What's a Nice Girl Like You. . .?*, ABC, 1971; Captain Patrick Lonergan, *Lieutenant Schuster's Wife*, ABC, 1972; Sergeant Dobbs, *The Godchild*, ABC, 1974; Joe Hodges, *Remember When*, NBC, 1974; Fred Hartman, *Journey from Darkness*, NBC, 1975; Lieutenant General Mordechai Gur, *Raid on Entebbe*, NBC, 1977; Cornelius Ryan, *A Private Battle*, CBS, 1980; Henry Hobson, *Hobson's Choice*, CBS, 1983; Mark Twain, *Helen Keller—The Miracle Continues*, syndicated, 1984; Owl, *Alice in Wonderland*, CBS, 1985; J. Edgar Hoover, *Hoover vs. the Kennedys: The Second Civil War*, syndicated, 1987; Harry Fox, *Still Crazy Like a Fox*, CBS, 1987; Bad Hair Wimberly, *Dead Solid Perfect*, HBO, 1988. Specials: Robert de Beaudrincourt, "The Lark," *Hallmark Hall of Fame*, NBC, 1957; Ken, *The Three Kings*, ABC, 1987. Also appeared in *Knight and Day*, NBC, 1989; *A Memory of Two Mondays*.

NON-RELATED CAREER—Professional boxer during the 1930s; tugboat deck hand, New York City; lifeguard; dance hall bouncer.

AWARDS: Obie Award from the *Village Voice*, Distinguished Performance, 1964, for "Epiphany" in *Cages;* Emmy Award, Outstanding Performance By an Actor in a Supporting Role in a Drama, 1972, for *Brian's Song;* Academy Award nomination, Best Supporting Actor, 1975, for *Shampoo;* Academy Award nomination, Best Supporting Actor, 1978, for *Heaven Can Wait.*

MEMBER: Actors' Equity Association, Screen Actors Guild, American Federation of Television and Radio Artists, National Maritime Union, Players Club.

SIDELIGHTS: FAVORITE ROLES—Arthur Goldman in *The Man in the Glass Booth*, Marco in *A View from the Bridge*, juror number seven in *Twelve Angry Men*, Judge Rayford in *. . .And Justice for All*, Mickey Morrissey in *The Verdict*, Max Corkle in *Heaven Can Wait*, and Eddie in *The Bachelor Party*. RECREATIONS—Singing, swimming, skiing, sailing, sunset watching, reading, walking, dancing, fishing, caprentry, tennis, and golfing.

ADDRESSES: AGENT—John Gaines, Agency for the Performing Arts, 9000 Sunset Boulevard, Los Angeles, CA 90069.*

*   *   *

WASHBOURNE, Mona   1903-1988

PERSONAL: Born November 27, 1903, in Birmingham, England; died November 15, 1988, in London, England; daughter of Arthur Edmund and Kate (Robinson) Washbourne; married Basil Dignam. EDUCATION—Studied piano at the Birmingham School of Music.

VOCATION: Actress.

CAREER: STAGE DEBUT—Pianist and soubrette, Modern Follies concert party, Yarmouth, U.K., 1924. LONDON DEBUT—Minnie and Mrs. Hills, *Mourning Becomes Electra*, Westminster Theatre, 1937. BROADWAY DEBUT—Cherry-May Waterton, *Nude with Violin*, Belasco Theatre, 1957. PRINCIPAL STAGE APPEARANCES—Madame Arcati and understudy, *Blithe Spirit*, Duchess Theatre, London, 1945; Miss Barnes, *The Winslow Boy*, Lyric Theatre, London, 1946; Helen Poulter, *Cupid and Mars*, Arts Theatre, London, 1947; Dorothy Pilkington, *Honour and Obey*, Saville Theatre, London, 1947; Mrs. Poole, *The Foolish Gentlewoman*, Duchess Theatre, 1948; mother, *Ring Round the Moon*, Globe Theatre, London, 1950; Mrs. Bonamy, *The Mortimer Touch*, Duke of York's Theatre, London, 1952; Mrs. Osbourne, *Hippo Dancing*, Lyric Theatre, 1954; Cora Swanson, *Morning's at Seven*, Comedy Theatre, London, 1955, then Westminster Theatre, London, 1956; Honorine, *Fanny*, Drury Lane Theatre, London, 1956; Alice Fisher, *Billy Liar*, Cambridge Theatre, London, 1960; Hilda Midway, *Semi-Detached*, Saville Theatre, 1962; Mum, *The Anniversary*, Duke of York's Theatre, 1966; Kathleen, *Home*, Royal Court Theatre, London, then Apollo Theatre, London, later Morosco Theatre, New York City, all 1970; Enid Baker, *Getting On*, Queen's Theatre, London, 1971; Veta Louise Simmonds, *Harvey*, Prince of Wales Theatre, London, 1975; the Aunt, *Stevie*, Vaudeville Theatre, London, 1977. Also appeared in *Landscape with Figures;* as Cherry-May Warterton, *Nude with Violin* and Monica, *Present Laughter*, Los Angeles and San Francisco, CA; and in repertory with Harry Hanson's Court Players and Matthew Forsythe's Company, both in the U.K.

MAJOR TOURS—Mrs. Tarleton, *Misalliance*, Prospect Productions and the British Council, Indian, Ceylonese, and Pakistani cities, 1967; toured as a pianist and soubrette with the Fol-de-Rols for three years; and with the Malvern Company during World War II.

PRINCIPAL FILM APPEARANCES—Vicar's wife, *Once Upon a Dream*, General Film Distributors, 1949; Miss Barnes, *The Winslow Boy*, Eagle-Lion, 1950; Lady Leveson, *Maytime in Mayfair*, Real Art, 1952; fussy mother, *Double Confession*, Associated British/Pathe, 1953; Mrs. MacGregor, *Johnny on the Run*, Associated British, 1953; Miss Goslett, *Child's Play*, British Lion, 1954; Mrs. McBain, *Adventure in the Hopfields*, Associated British, 1954; Nurse Appleby, *Cash on Delivery* (also known as *To Dorothy, a Son*), RKO, 1956; Miss Morrow, *It's Great to Be Young*, Associated British/Pathe, 1956; Mrs. Joe, *The Good Companions*, Associated British/Pathe, 1957; Agnes Smith, *Stranger in Town*, Eros, 1957; Monica Bare, *Cast a Dark Shadow*, Eros, 1958; nanny, *Count Your Blessings*, Metro-Goldwyn-Mayer (MGM), 1959; Mrs. Daniels, *A Cry from the Street*, Eros, 1959; Frau Lang, *The*

Brides of Dracula, Universal, 1960; Alice Fisher, *Billy Liar*, Warner Brothers/Pathe, 1963; Aunt Lil, *Ferry Across the Mersey*, United Artists, 1964; Mrs. Pearce, *My Fair Lady*, Warner Brothers, 1964; Mrs. Bramson, *Night Must Fall*, MGM, 1964; Aunt Anne, *The Collector*, Columbia, 1965; Aunt Mildred, *One Way Pendulum*, Lopert, 1965; Catherine Parsons, *The Third Day*, WD, 1965; Mrs. Duckett, *Two a Penny*, Worldwide, 1968; Mrs. Brown, *Mrs. Brown, You've Got a Lovely Daughter*, MGM, 1968; Matron, *If . . .*, Paramount, 1968; mother, *The Bed Sitting Room*, United Artists, 1969.

Mrs. Hayes, *The Games*, Twentieth Century-Fox, 1970; Mrs. Gray, *Fragment of Fear*, Columbia, 1971; Gran, *What Became of Jack and Jill?* (also known as *Romeo and Juliet* and *A Gentle Tale of Sex and Violence, Corruption and Murder*), Twentieth Century-Fox, 1972; Sister Hallett and Usher neighbor, *O Lucky Man!*, Warner Brothers, 1973; Mrs. Fiedke, *The Driver's Seat* (also known as *Identikit*), AVCO-Embassy, 1975; Mrs. Jarley, *Mr. Quilp* (also known as *The Old Curiosity Shop*), AVCO-Embassy, 1975; grandmother, *The Blue Bird*, Twentieth Century-Fox, 1976; Miss Spear—''The Lion Aunt,'' *Stevie*, First Artists, 1978; Aunt Lydia, *The Omega Connection* (also known as *The London Connection*), Buena Vista, 1979. Also appeared in *Dark Interval*, Apex, 1950; *The Gambler and the Lady*, Exclusive, 1952; *Wide Boy*, Anglo-Amalgamated, 1952; *Doctor In the House*, General Film Distributors, 1954; *Star of My Night*, General Film Distributors, 1954; *The Yellow Robe*, Associated British/Pathe, 1954; *Count of Twelve*, Associated British/Pathe, 1955; *John and Julie*, British Lion, 1957; *Son of a Stranger*, United Artists, 1957; *Tears for Simon* (also known as *Lost*), Republic, 1957; *Three Sundays to Live*, United Artists, 1957.

TELEVISION DEBUT—Appeared in a sketch for Baird Television (U.K.), 1929. PRINCIPAL TELEVISION APPEARANCES—Mini-Series: Madame Raquin, *Therese Raquin*, BBC, then *Masterpiece Theatre*, PBS, 1981; Nanny Hawkins, *Brideshead Revisited*, Granada, then *Great Performances*, PBS, 1982. Episodic: *The Lili Palmer Theatre*, syndicated, 1956. Movies: Queen Mother, *Charles and Diana: A Royal Love Story*, ABC, 1982. Specials: Aunt M, *December Flower*, Granada, then *Great Performances*, PBS, 1987. Also appeared in *London Affair*, *A Hundred Years Old*, *Dear Petitioner*, and *Homecoming*.

RELATED CAREER—Sketch writer, Baird Television (U.K.), 1929.

OBITUARIES AND OTHER SOURCES: Variety, November 30, 1988.*

*   *   *

WASSERSTEIN, Wendy   1950-

PERSONAL: Born October 18, 1950, in New York, NY; daughter of Morris W. (a textile manufacturer) and Lola (a dancer; maiden name, Schleifer) Wasserstein. EDUCATION—Mount Holyoke College, B.A., 1971; City College of New York, M.A., 1973; Yale Drama School, M.F.A., 1976.

VOCATION: Playwright.

CAREER: Also see *WRITINGS* below. PRINCIPAL STAGE AP-

PEARANCES—*The Hotel Play*, La Mama Experimental Theatre Club, New York City, 1981.

PRINCIPAL STAGE WORK—Dramaturg, *A New Approach to Human Sacrifice*, Young Playwrights Festival, Circle Repertory Theatre, New York City, 1983.

NON-RELATED CAREER—Teacher, Columbia University, 1985.

WRITINGS: STAGE—*Any Woman Can't*, Playwrights Horizons, Westside YWCA/Clark Center, New York City, 1973; *Happy Birthday, Montpelier Pizz-zazz*, first produced in New Haven, CT, 1974, then Playwrights Horizons, 1976; (with Christopher Durang) *When Dinah Shore Ruled the Earth*, first produced in New Haven, CT, 1975; *Uncommon Women and Others*, first produced in New Haven, CT, 1975, then Phoenix Theatre, New York City, 1977, later Edinburgh Festival, Edinburgh, Scotland, 1985, then Los Angeles Stage Company, Los Angeles, published by Dramatists Play Service, 1978, then Avon, 1979; (contributor of additional material with Mimi Kennedy, Ted Mann, and Herb Sargent), *Hard Sell*, New York Shakespeare Festival, Public Theatre, New York City, 1980; *Isn't It Romantic?*, Phoenix Theatre, Marymount Manhattan Theatre, New York City, 1981, then Playwrights Horizons, 1983, published by Doubleday, 1984, then Dramatists Play Service, 1985; *Tender Offer*, first produced in New York City, 1983; (adaptor) *The Man in a Case*, first produced in Urbana, IL, 1985, then the Acting Company, Lucille Lortel Theatre, New York City, 1986; *Miami*, Playwrights Horizons, 1986; ''Smart Women, Brilliant Choices'' in *Urban Blight*, Manhattan Theatre Club, City Center Theatre, New York City, 1988; *The Heidi Chronicles*, Playwrights Horizons, 1988, then Plymouth Theatre, New York City, 1989. TELEVISION—Episodic: *The Comdey Zone*, CBS, 1984; ''Driving School,'' *The Way We Are*, CBC (Toronto, ON, Canada), then broadcast as an episode of *Trying Times*, PBS, 1987. Specials: (With Terence McNally) Playlets #2 and #3, *Liza Minnelli in Sam Found Out: A Triple Play*, ABC, 1988. Also *Uncommon Women and Others*, 1978; (adaptor) *The Sorrows of Gin*, 1979; *Drive, She Said*, 1987.

AWARDS: Guggenheim fellowship, 1983; New York Drama Critics' Circle Award, Best New Play, Drama Desk Award, Best New Play, Pulitzer Prize for Drama, Susan Smith Blackburn Prize, Dramatists Guild Award, and Outer Critics' Circle Award, Best Broadway Play, all 1989, for *The Heidi Chronicles*; also Obie Award from the *Village Voice*, Joseph Jefferson Award, *Drama-Logue* Award, and Inner Boston Critics' Award, all for *Uncommon Women and Others*; Hale Mathews Foundation Award.

MEMBER: Dramatists Guild, Playwrights Horizons (artistic board), Dramatists Guild for Young Playwrights.

ADDRESSES: AGENT—Luis Sanjurjo, International Creative Management, 40 W. 57th Street, New York, NY 10019.*

*   *   *

WASSON, Craig   1954-

PERSONAL: Born March 15, 1954, in Ontario, OR. EDUCATION—Attended Lane Community College.

VOCATION: Actor, composer, and musician.

CRAIG WASSON

CAREER: BROADWAY DEBUT—Harmonica player and singer, *All God's Chillun Got Wings*, Circle in the Square, 1975. PRINCIPAL STAGE APPEARANCES—Second waiter, *Death of a Salesman*, Circle in the Square, New York City, 1975; Michael Price, *For Sale*, Playhouse 91, New York City, 1985; also appeared in *Five in the Mind House*, Circle Repertory Theatre, New York City.

MAJOR TOURS—*Godspell*, U.S. cities, 1973-74.

PRINCIPAL FILM APPEARANCES—Hippie, *Rollercoaster*, Universal, 1977; Dave Bisbee, *The Boys in Company C*, Columbia, 1978; Corporal Stephen Courcey, *Go Tell the Spartans*, AVCO-Embassy, 1978; Mickey, *Carny*, United Artists, 1980; Michael Flaherty, *The Outsider*, Paramount, 1980; Doug, *Schizoid* (also known as *Murder By Mail*), Cannon, 1980; Max Corley, *Nights at O'Rear's*, American Film Institute, 1980; Danilo Prozer, *Four Friends* (also known as *Georgia's Friends*), Filmways, 1981; Don and David Wanderley, *Ghost Story*, Universal, 1981; Will Thorson, *Second Thoughts*, Universal, 1983; Jack Scully, *Body Double*, Columbia, 1984; Paul, *The Men's Club*, Atlantic Releasing, 1986; Dr. Neil Goldman, *A Nightmare on Elm Street 3: Dream Warriors*, New Line Cinema, 1987; Paul Colson, *Bum Rap*, Fox/Lorber Associates, 1988. Also appeared in *Trackers*, Film Ventures International, 1990.

PRINCIPAL TELEVISION APPEARANCES—Series: Mark Valenti, *Phyllis*, CBS, 1975-77; David Skagska, *Skag*, NBC, 1980. Pilots: Russell Parkinson, *Butterflies*, NBC, 1979; David Skagska, *Skag*, NBC, 1979. Episodic: *The Bob Newhart Show*, CBS, 1977; *M*A*S*H*, CBS, 1983; *For Jenny with Love*, Family Channel, 1989; also *Baa Baa Black Sheep*, NBC; *Serpico*, NBC; "Geezeus

Talks," *Tales of the Darkside*, syndicated. Movies: Hal, *The Silence*, NBC, 1975; Andy Webb, *Mrs. R.'s Daughter*, NBC, 1979; Captain Busher, *Thornwell*, CBS, 1981; Brian Harmon, *Why Me?*, ABC, 1984. Specials: Soldier, *Koscuiszko: An American Portrait*, PBS, 1976; Mark Twain, "The Innocents Abroad," *Great Performances*, PBS, 1983. Also James Madison, *A More Perfect Union*.

RELATED CAREER—Writer and performer of songs for film and for the television series *Skag* and *Phyllis;* musician.

WRITINGS: All as composer. STAGE—(Incidental music) *The Glass Menagerie* and *Death of a Salesman*, both Circle in the Square, New York City, 1975. FILM—*The Boys in Company C*, Columbia, 1978; *Second Thoughts*, Universal, 1983.

AWARDS: Golden Globe nomination, Best New Performer, 1982.

ADDRESSES: AGENT—Russ Lyster, Irv Schechter Company, 9300 Wilshire Boulevard, Beverly Hills, CA 90212.

*   *   *

WATKINS, Peter   1935-

PERSONAL: Born October 29, 1935, in Norbiton, England. EDUCATION—Attended Christ College; studied acting at the Royal Academy of Dramatic Art, 1953. MILITARY—British Army, East Surrey Regiment.

VOCATION: Director, screenwriter, editor, and producer.

CAREER: Also see *WRITINGS* below. PRINCIPAL FILM APPEARANCES—*It Happened Here*, Lopert, 1966; narrator, *Punishment Park*, Sherpix Chartwell/Francoise, 1971.

PRINCIPAL FILM WORK—Director: (Also producer) *The War Game* (documentary), 1966, released in the United States by Pathe, 1967; *Privilege*, Universal, 1967; *Gladiatorerna* (also known as *The Peace Game* and *The Gladiators*), 1969, released in the United States by New Line Cinema, 1970; (also editor) *Punishment Park*, Sherpix Chartwell/Francoise, 1971; (also editor) *Edvard Munch*, 1974, released in the United States by New Yorker, 1976; also *The Web*, 1956; *The Field of Red*, 1958; *Diary of an Unknown Soldier*, 1959; *The Forgotten Faces*, 1961; *70 Talets Manniskor* (also known as *The Seventies People*), 1975; *Fallen* (also known as *The Trap*), 1975; (also editor) *Aftenlandet* (also known as *Evening Land*), 1976; (also editor) *The Journey*, 1986.

PRINCIPAL TELEVISION WORK—Movies: Director, *Culloden*, BBC, 1964.

RELATED CAREER—Assistant producer of short television films and commercials for a London advertising agency, 1950s; assistant editor, producer, and director, BBC, 1961-67; contributor of articles and essays to magazines and journals.

WRITINGS: FILM—See production details above. *The War Game*, 1967; (with Norman Bogner) *Privilege*, 1967; (with Nicholas Gosling) *Gladiatorerna*, 1970; (with Terry Hodel) *Punishment Park*, 1971; *Edvard Munch*, 1975; *Aftenlandet*, 1976; *The Journey*, 1986.

AWARDS: British Academy of Film and Television Arts Award, Television Progam/Series Without Category, 1965; Academy Award, Best Documentary, 1966, for *The War Game.*

ADDRESSES: OFFICE—Swedish Film Institute, Film House, Box 271-26, 102 52 Stockholm, Sweden.*

*   *   *

WATSON, Douglass   1921-1989

PERSONAL: Full name, Larkin Douglass Watson III; born February 24, 1921, in Jackson, GA; died of a heart attack, May 1, 1989, in Arizona; son of Larkin Douglass, Jr. (a teacher) and Caroline (Smith) Watson; married Harriett Eugenia Loaring-Clark, November 28, 1942; children: Larkin, Celia, Randall. EDUCATION—University of North Carolina, A.B., 1942; studied acting with Maria Ouspenskaya, 1942-43. MILITARY—U.S. Army Air Forces.

VOCATION: Actor.

CAREER: Also see *WRITINGS* below. STAGE DEBUT—Rugby, *The Merry Wives of Windsor*, Playhouse Theatre, Wilmington, DE, 1946. BROADWAY DEBUT—Don Parritt, *The Iceman Cometh,* Martin Beck Theatre, 1946. PRINCIPAL STAGE APPEARANCES—Eros, *Antony and Cleopatra*, Martin Beck Theatre, 1947; Captain Jenks, *Command Decision*, Fulton Theatre, New York City, 1947; Eugene, *The Leading Lady*, National Theatre, New York City, 1948; Dorset, *Richard III*, Booth Theatre, New York City, 1949; Richard Johnson, *The Happiest Years*, Lyceum Theatre, New York City, 1949; Bert Warren (understudy), *Leaf and Bough*, Cort Theatre, New York City, 1949; Rodrigo, *That Lady*, Martin Beck Theatre, 1949; Peter Whitfield, *The Wisteria Trees*, Martin Beck Theatre, 1950; Romeo, *Romeo and Juliet*, Broadhurst Theatre, New York City, 1951; messenger, *Medea*, Berlin Festival, Germany, 1951; Eben Cabot, *Desire Under the Elms*, American National Theatre and Academy (ANTA) Theatre, New York City, 1952; Herbert Westman, *The Brass Ring*, Lyceum Theatre, 1952; Mike Decker, *Sunday Breakfast*, Coronet Theatre, New York City, 1952; Lord Ravensbane, *The Scarecrow*, Theatre De Lys, New York City, 1953; Don, *The Time of the Cuckoo*, Central City Festival, Central City, CO, 1953; Christian de Neuvillette, *Cyrano de Bergerac* and Henry, Earl of Richmond, *Richard III*, both New York City Center Theatre, New York City, 1953; Colby Simpkins, *The Confidential Clerk*, Morosco Theatre, New York City, 1954; son, *This Happy Breed*, John Drew Theatre, East Hampton, NY, 1954; Ralph Touchett, *Portrait of a Lady*, ANTA Theatre, 1954.

Valere, *The Miser*, Downtown National Theatre, New York City, 1955; Hippolytos, *The Cretan Woman* and Kilroy, *Camino Real,* both Stanford University, Stanford, CA, 1955; Anthony Harker, *The Young and Beautiful*, Longacre Theatre, New York City, 1955; Armand, Comte de Montfort, *Little Glass Clock*, John Golden Theatre, New York City, 1956; title role, *Henry V*, Cambridge Drama Festival, Harvard University, Sanders Theatre, Cambridge, MA, 1956; Valentine, *You Never Can Tell*, John Drew Theatre, 1956; Gregor Samsa, *Metamorphosis* and Golaud, *Pelleas and Melisande* (double-bill), Kuriakos Theatre, ANTA Matinee Series, Theatre De Lys, 1957; Val Xavier (understudy), *Orpheus Descending,* Martin Beck Theatre, 1957; narrator, *Pale Horse, Pale Rider,* Kuriakos Theatre, White Barn Theatre, Westport, CT, then Jan Hus Theatre, New York City, both 1957; Mr. Harcourt, *The Country*

Wife, Adelphi Theatre, New York City, 1957; Jason Redwine, *Season of Choice*, Barbizon-Plaza Theatre, New York City, 1959.

Leontes, *The Winter's Tale* and Canidius, *Antony and Cleopatra,* both American Shakespeare Festival, Stratford, CT, 1960; Orsino, *Twelfth Night*, American Shakespeare Festival, 1961; title role, *Richard III*, Antonio, *The Merchant of Venice*, and Orsino, *Twelfth Night*, all National Shakespeare Festival, Old Globe Theatre, San Diego, CA, 1961; Reverend T. Lawrence Shannon (understudy), *The Night of the Iguana*, Royale Theatre, New York City, 1961; King Henry VIII, *A Man for All Seasons*, ANTA Theatre, 1962; Bassanio, *The Merchant of Venice*, Gate Theatre, New York City, 1962; Edmund, *King Lear*, Antipholus, *The Comedy of Errors*, and Dauphin, *Henry V*, all American Shakespeare Festival, 1963; Brother Dominic, *Jeanne d'Arc au bucher* (also known as *Joan at the Stake*), New York City Center, 1963; Tarver, *The Chinese Prime Minister*, Royale Theatre, 1964; title role, *Richard III* and Don Pedro, *Much Ado About Nothing*, both American Shakespeare Festival, 1964; Prospero, *The Tempest*, University of Southern Florida, FL, 1964.

Arthur, *The Right Honorable Gentleman*, Billy Rose Theatre, New York City, 1965; Pistol, *Falstaff (Henry IV, Part II)*, Sir Hugh de Morville, *Murder in the Cathedral*, and Brutus, *Julius Caesar*, all American Shakespeare Festival, 1966; Wadsworth, *Come Slowly, Eden (A Portrait of Emily Dickinson)*, ANTA Matinee Series, Theatre De Lys, 1966; herald, *The Persecution and Assassination of Jean-Paul Marat As Performed By the Inmates of the Asylum of Charenton Under the Direction of the Marquis de Sade* (also known as *Marat/Sade*), National Players Company, Majestic Theatre, New York City, 1967; Sir Thomas More, *A Man for All Seasons,* University of Wisconsin, Madison, WI, 1967; title role, *Othello* and Parolles, *All's Well That Ends Well*, both National Shakespeare Festival, Old Globe Theatre, 1967; Mr. Perry, then as Teddy Lloyd, *The Prime of Miss Jean Brodie*, Helen Hayes Theatre, New York City, 1968; Major-General Stanley, *The Pirates of Penzance*, New York City Center, 1968; Vershinin, *The Three Sisters*, Seattle Repertory Theatre, Seattle, WA, 1969; Jack, *L.A. Under Siege,* New Theatre for Now, Mark Taper Forum, Los Angeles, 1970; Buffalo Bill, *Indians*, Seattle Repertory Theatre, 1970; John of Gaunt, *Richard II*, Seattle Repertory Theatre, 1971; Father Phillip Berrigan, *The Trial of the Catonsville Nine*, Center Theatre Group, Mark Taper Forum, 1971; title role, *The Hunter*, New York Shakespeare Festival (NYSF), Public Theatre, New York City, 1972; Don Pedro, *Much Ado About Nothing*, NYSF, Delacorte Theatre, then Winter Garden Theatre, both New York City, 1972; Duke Senior, *As You Like It*, Earl of Kent, *King Lear*, both NYSF, Delacorte Theatre, 1973; Norwin Spokesman, *Over Here!*, Shubert Theatre, New York City, 1974.

Douglas North Wicksteed, *Dancing for the Kaiser*, Circle Repertory Company, Circle Repertory Theatre, New York City, 1975; Wallace Howe, *My Life*, Circle Repertory Company, Circle Repertory Theatre, 1977; Marcus, *The Archbishop's Ceiling*, Eisenhower Theatre, Kennedy Center for the Performing Arts, Washington, DC, 1977; Charles, *The Middle Ages*, Hartman Theatre Company, Stamford, CT, 1978; Frank, *Glorious Morning*, Circle Repertory Company, Circle Repertory Theatre, 1978; Seth Lord, *The Philadelphia Story*, Lincoln Center Theatre Company, Vivian Beaumont Theatre, New York City, 1980; Ben Gerard, *Upside Down on the Handlebars*, Open Space Theatre Experiment, New York City, 1983; Claudius, *Hamlet*, Musical Theatre Works, Classic Stage Company Theatre, New York City, 1987; also appeared in *Murder in the Family*, Berkshire Playhouse, Stockbridge, MA, 1952; *Patience*, New York City Center, 1968.

MAJOR TOURS—Fenton, *The Merry Wives of Windsor*, U.S. and Canadian cities, 1946; Don Parritt, *The Iceman Cometh*, Theatre Guild, U.S. cities, 1946; Andre, *Her Cardboard Lover*, U.S. cities, 1951; Sefton, *Stalag 17*, U.S. cities, 1953; Brian O'Bannion, *Auntie Mame*, U.S. cities, 1958-59; M. Redon-la Mur, *Nina*, U.S. cities, 1959; Leontes, *The Winter's Tale* and Lysander, *A Midsummer Night's Dream*, U.S. cities, 1960-61; Dylan Thomas, *Dylan*, U.S. cities, 1969; Teddy Lloyd, *The Prime of Miss Jean Brodie*, U.S. cities, 1969; Victor Franz, *The Price*, U.S. cities, 1970.

PRINCIPAL FILM APPEARANCES—Octavius Caesar, *Julius Caesar*, Metro-Goldwyn-Mayer, 1953; Colonel Crawford, *Sayonara*, Warner Brothers, 1957; Father Philip Berrigan, *The Trial of the Catonsville Nine*, Melville, 1972; Major Cartwright, *Ulzana's Raid*, Universal, 1972; Walter Felding, Sr., *The Money Pit*, Universal, 1986; also appeared in *Who Says I Can't Ride a Rainbow?*, Transvue, 1971.

PRINCIPAL TELEVISION APPEARANCES—Series: Dr. Robert Wallace *Moment of Truth*, NBC, 1965; Walter Haskins, *Search for Tomorrow*, CBS, 1967-68; Dr. Lloyd Phillips, *Love of Life*, CBS, 1972-73; Mackenzie "Mac" Cory, *Another World*, NBC, 1974-89. Episodic: "Richard III," *Masterpiece Playhouse*, NBC, 1950; "The Sire de Maletroit's Door," *Starlight Theatre*, CBS, 1950; "Brief Candle," *Kraft Television Theatre*, NBC, 1951; "The Young and Beautiful," *Robert Montgomery Presents*, NBC, 1956; *The Doctors and the Nurses* (also known as *The Nurses*), CBS, 1965; Mackenzie "Mac" Cory, *For Richer, for Poorer*, NBC. Specials: Hector Malone, Jr., "Man and Superman," *Hallmark Hall of Fame*, NBC, 1956; Hortensio, "Taming of the Shrew," *Hallmark Hall of Fame*, NBC, 1956; Ninian Edwards, "Abe Lincoln in Illinois," *Hallmark Hall of Fame*, NBC, 1964; narrator, *Continuing Creation*, NBC, 1978. Also *The Dark Side of the Moon*, NBC, 1957; *Lamp Unto My Feet*, CBS; *Much Ado About Nothing*.

RELATED CAREER—Performer with the Martha Graham Dance Company in productions of *Dark Meadow* and *Letter to the World;* also with the company in various Broadway productions and on tour.

WRITINGS: STAGE—(Adaptor) *Metamorphosis* and *Pellas and Melisande* (double-bill), Kuriakos Theatre, American National Theatre and Academy Matinee Series, Theatre De Lys, New York City, 1957; *Haven't a Clue*, Virginia Museum Theatre, Richmond, VA, 1982.

AWARDS: Theatre World Award, 1948, for *Anthony and Cleopatra;* *Variety*-New York Drama Critics' Poll, Most Promising New Actor, 1950, for *The Wisteria Trees;* Clarence Derwent Award, 1950, for *That Lady* and *The Wisteria Trees;* Drama Desk Award, 1973, for *Much Ado About Nothing;* Emmy Award, Outstanding Actor in a Daytime Drama Series, 1980 and 1981, both for *Another World*. MILITARY HONORS—Distinguished Flying Cross and two Purple Hearts from the U.S. Army Air Forces.

OBITUARIES AND OTHER SOURCES: *Variety*, May 10-16, 1989.*

WEAVER, Fritz   1926-

PERSONAL: Full name, Fritz William Weaver; born January 19, 1926, in Pittsburgh, PA; son of John Carson and Elsa W. (Stringaro) Weaver; married Sylvia Short, February 7, 1953; children: Lydia Charlotte, Anthony Ballou. EDUCATION—University of Chicago, B.A., 1952; studied acting at the HB Studios, 1955-56.

VOCATION: Actor.

CAREER: STAGE DEBUT—With the Barter Theatre, Abingdon, VA, 1952. OFF-BROADWAY DEBUT—Fainall, *The Way of the World*, Cherry Lane Theatre, 1954. BROADWAY DEBUT—Maitland, *The Chalk Garden*, Ethel Barrymore Theatre, 1955. PRINCIPAL STAGE APPEARANCES—Petruchio, *The Taming of the Shrew*, Sir Francis Chesney, *Charley's Aunt*, preacher, *Dark of the Moon*, Oberon, *A Midsummer Night's Dream*, Caesar, *Androcles and the Lion*, and Edward II, *Carnival King*, all with the Group 20 Players, Wellesley, MA, 1953; secretary, *The Doctor's Dilemma* and Flamineo, *The White Devil*, both Phoenix Theatre, New York City, 1955; Casca, *Julius Caesar* and Antonio, *The Tempest*, both American Shakespeare Festival, Stratford, CT, 1955; Philip Faulconbridge, *King John* and Gremio, *The Taming of the Shrew*, both American Shakespeare Festival, 1956; Marc Bradley, *Protective Custody*, Ambassador Theatre, New York City, 1956; title role, *Miss Lonelyhearts*, Music Box Theatre, New York City, 1957; title role, *Hamlet*, American Shakespeare Festival, 1958; Harry, Lord Monchensey, *The Family Reunion* and priest, *The Power and the Glory*, both Phoenix Theatre Company, Phoenix Theatre, 1958; Malvolio, *Twelfth Night*, Cambridge Drama Festival, Cambridge, MA, 1959; Dion Anthony, *The Great God Brown*, Phoenix Theatre Company, Coronet Theatre, New York City, 1959.

Title role, *Peer Gynt*, Phoenix Theatre Company, 1960; title role, *Henry IV, Part One* and title role, *Henry IV, Part Two*, both Phoenix Theatre Company, then Cambridge Drama Festival, all 1960; Mark, *Men, Women, and Angels*, Vancouver Festival, Queen Elizabeth Theatre, Vancouver, BC, Canada, 1961; M. Beaurevers, *A Shot in the Dark*, Booth Theatre, New York City, 1961; Henderson, *All American*, Winter Garden Theatre, New York City, 1962; narrator, *The Martyrdom of St. Sebastian*, New York City Philharmonic, Philharmonic Hall, New York City, 1962; Van Miessen, *Lorenzo*, Plymouth Theatre, New York City, 1963; Phileas Fogg, *Around the World in Eighty Days*, Jones Beach Marine Theatre, New York City, 1963; various roles, *The White House*, Henry Miller's Theatre, New York City, 1964; Sherlock Holmes, *Baker Street*, Broadway Theatre, New York City, 1965; Frederick the Great, *The Sorrows of Frederick*, Mark Taper Forum, Los Angeles, 1967; Henry Higgins, *My Fair Lady*, City Center Theatre, New York City, 1968.

Jerome Malley, *Child's Play*, Royale Theatre, New York City, 1970; title role, *Macbeth*, American Shakespeare Festival, 1973; Patrick Power, *Patrick's Day*, Long Wharf Theatre, New Haven, CT, 1973; Ronald, *Absurd Person Singular*, Music Box Theatre, 1975; title role, *Lincoln* (one-man show), Chelsea Theatre Center, Brooklyn Academy of Music, Brooklyn, NY, then Theatre Four, New York City, both 1976; Sidney Kentridge, *The Biko Inquest*, Theatre Four, 1978; Walter Franz, *The Price*, Playhouse Theatre, New York City, 1979; man, *Dialogue for Lovers*, Symphony Space, New York City, 1980; Mr. Talley, *A Tale Told*, Circle Repertory Company, New York City, then Mark Taper Forum, both 1981; Niles Harris, *Angel's Fall*, Circle Repertory Company, 1982, then Longacre Theatre, New York City, 1983; Stephen,

Beethoven's Tenth, Center Theatre Group, Ahmanson Theatre, Los Angeles, 1983; Carleton Fitzgerald, *Light Up the Sky,* Center Theatre Group, Ahmanson Theatre, 1987. Also appeared in *Over My Dead Body,* Hartman Theatre, Stamford, CT, 1984; *L'Histoire du Soldat,* 1954; and in productions of *Time Framed* and *A Christmas Carol.*

MAJOR TOURS—Father Day, *Life with Father,* U.S. cities, 1974; Stephen, *Beethoven's Tenth,* U.S. cities, 1983-84; also appeared with the Barter Theatre Company on a tour of U.S. cities, 1952-54.

FILM DEBUT—Narrator, *The Crimson Curtain,* Rembrandt, 1955. PRINCIPAL FILM APPEARANCES—Colonel Cascio, *Fail Safe,* Columbia, 1964; narrator, *The Guns of August,* Universal, 1965; Vulcan, *To Trap a Spy,* Metro-Goldwyn-Mayer (MGM), 1966; Mr. Ravenswood, *The Maltese Bippy,* MGM, 1969; John Shankalien, *Company of Killers,* Universal, 1970; Roger Meredith, *A Walk in the Spring Rain,* Columbia, 1970; Harold DeMilo, *The Day of the Dolphin,* AVCO-Embassy, 1973; Professor Biesenthal, *Marathon Man,* Paramount, 1976; Corley, *Black Sunday,* Paramount, 1977; Dr. Alex Harris, *Demon Seed,* Metro-Goldwyn-Mayer/United Artists, 1977; Oscar Procari, Sr., *The Big Fix,* Universal, 1978; Father Farrow, *Jaws of Satan* (also known as *King Cobra*), United Artists, 1980; Dexter Stanley, "The Crate" in *Creepshow,* Warner Brothers, 1982, Wallace Furman, *Power,* Twentieth Century-Fox, 1986.

PRINCIPAL TELEVISION APPEARANCES—Mini-Series: Josef Weiss, *Holocaust,* NBC, 1978; Father Peregrine, *The Martian Chronicles,* NBC, 1980; Senator Thomas Hart Benton, *Dream West,* CBS, 1986; Mr. Amberville, *I'll Take Manhattan,* CBS, 1987. Pilots: Anton de Tourolet, *The Snoop Sisters* (also known as *Female Instinct*), NBC, 1972; Vincent Kagel, *Heat of Anger,* CBS, 1972; Daniel Kemper, *Rx for the Defense,* ABC, 1973; Cirrak, *Hunter,* CBS, 1973; Mr. Foster, *Momma the Detective,* NBC, 1981; Stewart Moffitt, *The City,* ABC, 1986; Maxwell Vane, *D.C. Cop,* CBS, 1986. Episodic: William Sturka, "Third from the Sun," *The Twilight Zone,* CBS, 1960; Chancellor, "The Obsolete Man," *The Twilight Zone,* CBS, 1961; Mason, "Jane Eyre," *Family Classics,* CBS, 1961; David, "The People Next Door," *CBS Playhouse,* CBS, 1968; Niklaus, "Lost Treasure," *Suspense Playhouse,* CBS, 1971; Matthew Costigan, "The Star," *The Twilight Zone,* CBS, 1985; Edwin Dupont, *Murder, She Wrote,* CBS, 1987; Inspector Panassie, *Murder, She Wrote,* CBS, 1987; Astaroth, *Friday the 13th,* syndicated, 1989; narrator, "Preston Sturges: The Rise and Fall of an American Dreamer," *American Masters,* PBS, 1990; also *Kraft Television Theatre,* NBC, 1955; "She Stoops to Conquer," *Omnibus,* ABC, 1955; *Lamp Unto My Feet,* CBS, 1955; "We Must Kill Tony," *U.S. Steel Hour,* CBS, 1956; "The Playwright and the Star" and "The Deaf Heart," *Studio One,* CBS, 1957; "Beyond This Place," *Dupont Show of the Month,* CBS, 1957; "The New Class," *Armstrong Circle Theatre,* NBC, 1958; "A Moment of Truth," *Omnibus,* NBC, 1958; "A Tale of Two Cities," *Dupont Show of the Month,* CBS, 1958; "The Little Tin God," *U.S. Steel Hour,* CBS, 1959; "Out of the Dust," *Playhouse 90,* CBS, 1959.

"The Potting Shed," *Play of the Week,* WNTA, 1961; "The Devil Makes Sunday," *U.S. Steel Hour,* CBS, 1961; "The Night of the Storm," *Dupont Show of the Month,* CBS, 1961; *Asphalt Jungle,* ABC, 1961; *The New Breed,* ABC, 1961; *The Defenders,* CBS, 1961, 1962, and 1963; "The Duchess and the Mugs," *U.S. Steel Hour,* CBS, 1962; *Cain's Hundred,* NBC, 1962; *Dr. Kildare,* NBC, 1962 and 1963; *The Nurses,* CBS, 1962 and 1964; *Espionage,* NBC, 1964; *The Man from U.N.C.L.E.,* NBC, 1964; *Great*

Adventures, CBS, 1964; *The Rogues,* NBC, 1964; *Rawhide,* CBS, 1964; *Twelve O'Clock High,* ABC, 1964; *The Fugitive,* ABC, 1966; "The Good Lieutenant," *Showcase,* 1966; *Combat,* ABC, 1966; *Mission: Impossible,* CBS, 1966, 1967, 1969, and 1971; *The F.B.I.,* ABC, 1966, 1968, 1970 and 1971; "The Questions," *Experiment in Television,* NBC, 1967; *The Invaders,* ABC, 1967; *Gunsmoke,* CBS, 1967; *The Big Valley,* ABC, 1967 and 1969; *Gentle Ben,* CBS, 1968; *N.Y.P.D.,* ABC, 1968; *The Outcasts,* ABC, 1968; *The Name of the Game,* NBC, 1968 and 1969; *Mannix,* CBS, 1968 and 1973; *Room 222,* ABC, 1969; *Felony Squad,* ABC, 1969; *Ironside,* NBC, 1970; *Dan August,* ABC, 1971; *Men at Law,* CBS, 1971; *Cannon,* CBS, 1971 and 1973; "A Question of Fear," *Night Gallery,* NBC, 1971; *Owen Marshall, Counselor at Law,* ABC, 1972; *Banyon,* NBC, 1972; *Medical Center,* CBS, 1972; "Columbus," *You Are There,* CBS, 1972; *The Mod Squad,* ABC, 1972; "Antigone," *Playhouse New York,* PBS, 1973; *Kung Fu,* ABC, 1973; *The Delphi Bureau,* ABC, 1973; *Barnaby Jones,* CBS, 1973 and 1974; Corneliu Melody, "A Touch of the Poet," *Theatre in America,* PBS, 1974; *Movin' On,* NBC, 1974; *Petrocelli,* NBC, 1974; *Streets of San Francisco,* ABC, 1975; *Tales from the Darkside,* syndicated.

Movies: Anderson, *The Borgia Stick,* NBC, 1967; Joe Mallicent, *Berlin Affair,* NBC, 1970; Andrew Borden, *The Legend of Lizzie Borden,* ABC, 1975; Harvey Cheyne, Sr., *Captains Courageous,* ABC, 1977; Eli Sorenson, *Children of Divorce,* NBC, 1980; Jonas Angstrom, *Maid in America,* CBS, 1982; Van Niven, *A Death in California,* ABC, 1985; Arthur Beal, *The Hearst and Davies Affair,* ABC, 1985; Bernard Hughes, *Under Siege,* NBC, 1986. Specials: "The Crucible," *Salute to the American Theatre,* CBS, 1959; Brutus, *Julius Caesar,* Canadian Broadcasting Company, 1960; schoolmaster, *The Power and the Glory,* CBS, 1961; *We the People 200: The Constitutional Gala,* CBS, 1987; Dr. Burnham, "My Name Is Bill W.," *Hallmark Hall of Fame,* ABC, 1989; narrator, *The Great Dinosaur Hunt,* PBS, 1989; also *From Sea to Shining Sea,* 1974; *Give Me Liberty,* 1975.

AWARDS: Clarence Derwent Award, 1956, for *The White Devil;* Theatre World Award and Antoinette Perry Award nomination, Best Supporting or Featured Actor in a Play, both 1956, for *The Chalk Garden;* Antoinette Perry Award, Best Actor in a Play, *Variety*-New York Critics' Poll Award, Drama Desk Award, and Outer Critics' Circle Award, all 1971, for *Child's Play.*

MEMBER: Actors' Equity Association, Screen Actors Guild, American Federation of Television and Radio Artists, American Guild of Musical Artists.

ADDRESSES: AGENTS—Lucy Kroll Agency, 390 West End Avenue, New York, NY 10023; Camden Artists, 2121 Avenue of the Stars, Suite 410, Los Angeles, CA 90067.

*   *   *

WEBB, Chloe

PERSONAL: Born in New York, NY. EDUCATION—Attended the Boston Conservatory of Music and Drama.

VOCATION: Actress.

CAREER: PRINCIPAL STAGE APPEARANCES—Angela Lansbury, Mary Martin, and Carol Channing, *Forbidden Broadway* (revue),

Palsson's Theatre, New York City, 1982-83, then the Comedy Store, Los Angeles, 1983; also appeared in *The House of Blue Leaves*, Pasadena Playhouse, Pasadena, CA.

FILM DEBUT—Nancy Spungen, *Sid and Nancy*, Samuel Goldwyn, 1986. PRINCIPAL FILM APPEARANCES—Louisa Kracklite, *The Belly of an Architect*, Hemdale, 1987; Linda Mason, *Twins*, Universal, 1988; Crystal Gerrity, *Heart Condition*, New Line Cinema, 1990.

PRINCIPAL TELEVISION APPEARANCES—Series: Regular, *Thicke of the Night*, syndicated, 1983. Pilots: Laurette Barber, *China Beach*, ABC, 1988. Episodic: Barbara, *Who's the Boss?*, ABC, 1986; Cassie, *Mary*, CBS, 1986; Laurette Barber, *China Beach*, ABC, 1988 (six episodes); also *Remington Steele*, NBC. Movies: *Who Am I This Time?*, PBS.

RELATED CAREER—Appeared with the Boston Shakespeare Company, Boston, MA, the Goodman Theatre Company, Chicago, IL, and at the Mark Taper Forum, Los Angeles, CA.

AWARDS: National Society of Film Critics Award, Best Actress, 1986, for *Sid and Nancy;* Emmy Award nomination, Outstanding Guest Actress in a Drama Series, 1989, for *China Beach.*

ADDRESSES: AGENT—Connie Tavel, International Creative Management, 8899 Beverly Boulevard, Los Angeles, CA 90048.*

*   *   *

WEINTRAUB, Fred   1928-

PERSONAL: Born April 27, 1928, in Bronx, NY; children: Sandra. EDUCATION—Attended the Wharton School of Business, University of Pennsylvania.

VOCATION: Producer and personal manager.

CAREER: Also see WRITINGS below. PRINCIPAL FILM APPEARANCES—*Black Belt Jones*, Warner Brothers, 1974. PRINCIPAL FILM WORK—All as producer, unless indicated: *Woodstock*, Warner Brothers, 1970; (with Francois Reichenbach and Tom Donahue) *Medicine Ball Caravan* (also known as *We Have Come for Your Daughters*), Warner Brothers, 1971; *Rage*, Warner Brothers, 1972; (with Paul Heller) *Enter the Dragon*, Warner Brothers, 1973; (with Heller) *Black Belt Jones*, Warner Brothers, 1974; (with Heller) *Golden Needles* (also known as *Chase for the Golden Needles*), American International, 1974; (with Heller) *Truck Turner*, American International, 1974; (with Heller) *The Ultimate Warrior*, Warner Brothers, 1975; (with Heller) *Dirty Knight's Work* (also known as *Trial By Combat* and *Choice of Arms*), Gamma III, 1976; (with Heller) *Hot Potato*, Warner Brothers, 1976; (with Heller) *The Pack* (also known as *The Long Dark Night*), Warner Brothers, 1977; *Outlaw Blues*, Warner Brothers, 1977; (with Heller) *Checkered Flag or Crash*, Universal, 1978; (with Heller) *The Promise* (also known as *Face of a Stranger*), 1979; (with Terry Morse, Jr.) *The Big Brawl*, Warner Brothers, 1980; *Tom Horn*, Warner Brothers, 1980; *Force: Five*, American Cinema, 1981; *High Road to China*, Warner Brothers, 1983; *Gymkata*, Metro-Goldwyn-Mayer/United Artists, 1985; (with Daniel Grodnik) *Out of Control*, New World, 1985; executive producer, *The Princess Academy*, Empire, 1987; *The Women's Club*, Inter-Ocean Film Sales, 1987.

PRINCIPAL TELEVISION APPEARANCES—Series: Host, *From the Bitter End*, syndicated. PRINCIPAL TELEVISION WORK—Series: Creator, *Hootenanny*, ABC, 1963-64; creator, *The Dukes of Hazard*, CBS, 1979-85. Movies: Producer, *My Father, My Son*, CBS, 1988.

RELATED CAREER—Vice-president of creative services, Warner Brothers Inc., 1969; co-founder, Weintraub-Heller Productions, 1974; also personal manager, Campus Coffee House Entertainment Circuit and for Joan Rivers, Neil Diamond, Bill Cosby, and the Four Seasons; former owner, the Bitter End (nightclub), New York City.

WRITINGS: See production details above. FILM—*Black Belt Jones*, 1974; *Dirty Knight's Work*, 1976; *Hot Potato*, 1976; *The Promise*, 1979; *The Big Brawl*, 1980.

ADDRESSES: OFFICE—Metro-Goldwyn-Mayer/United Artists Entertainment Company, 10000 W. Washington Boulevard, Culver City, CA 90230.*

*   *   *

WENDKOS, Paul   1922-

PERSONAL: Born September 20, 1922, in Philadelphia, PA. EDUCATION—Attended Columbia University.

VOCATION: Director.

CAREER: PRINCIPAL FILM WORK—Director: *The Burglar*, Columbia, 1956; *The Case Against Brooklyn*, Columbia, 1958; *Tarawa Beachhead*, Columbia, 1958; *Battle of the Coral Sea*, Columbia, 1959; *Face of a Fugitive*, Columbia, 1959; *Gidget*, Columbia, 1959; *Because They're Young*, Columbia, 1960; *Angel Baby*, Allied Artists, 1961; *Gidget Goes Hawaiian*, Columbia, 1961; *Gidget Goes to Rome*, Columbia, 1963; *Johnny Tiger*, Universal, 1966; *Attack on the Iron Coast*, United Artists, 1968; *Guns of the Magnificent Seven*, United Artists, 1969; *Cannon for Cordoba* (also known as *Dragon Master*), United Artists, 1970; *Hell Boats*, United Artists, 1970; *The Mephisto Waltz*, Twentieth Century-Fox, 1971; *Special Delivery*, American International, 1976.

PRINCIPAL TELEVISION WORK—All as director. Mini-Series: (Also producer) *Harold Robbins' "79 Park Avenue"* (also known as *79 Park Avenue*), NBC, 1977; *Celebrity*, NBC, 1984. Pilots: *333 Montgomery* (broadcast as an episode of *Alcoa Theatre*), NBC, 1960; *Hawaii Five-0*, CBS, 1968; *Travis Logan, D.A.*, CBS, 1971; *Crisis*, CBS, 1971; *The Delphi Bureau*, NBC, 1972; *The Underground Man*, NBC, 1974; *Mrs. R—Death Among Friends* (also known as *Death Among Friends*), NBC, 1975; *Golden Gate*, ABC, 1981; *Farrell: For the People*, NBC, 1982; *Big John*, NBC, 1983. Episodic: "The Mutation," "The Leeches," "Vikor," "Nightmare," "Doomsday Minus One," "Storm," and "Moonshot," *The Invaders*, ABC, 1967; "The Believers" and "The Life Seekers," *The Invaders*, ABC, 1968; *Hagen*, CBS, 1980; *Boone*, NBC, 1983; *The Alcoa Hour*, NBC; *Ben Casey*, ABC; *The Big Valley*, ABC; *The Dick Powell Show*, NBC; *Honey West*, ABC; *I Spy*, NBC; *Law of the Plainsman*, NBC; *Naked City*, NBC; *The Rifleman*, ABC; *Route 66*, CBS; *Saints and Sinners*, NBC; *The Untouchables*, ABC; *The Wild Wild West*, CBS; *Harry O*, ABC; *Medical Story*, NBC; *Burke's Law*, ABC; *The Detectives* (also known as *Robert Taylor's The Detectives*), ABC; *Mr. Novak*, NBC.

Movies: *Fear No Evil*, NBC, 1969; *Brotherhood of the Bell*, CBS, 1970; *A Death of Innocence*, CBS, 1971; *A Little Game*, ABC, 1971; *A Tattered Web*, CBS, 1971; *The Family Rico*, CBS, 1972; *The Strangers in 7-A*, CBS, 1972; *Footsteps* (also known as *Footsteps: Nice Guys Finish Last*), CBS, 1972; *Haunts of the Very Rich*, ABC, 1972; *Terror on the Beach*, CBS, 1973; *Honor Thy Father*, CBS, 1973; *The Legend of Lizzie Borden*, ABC, 1975; *Good Against Evil*, ABC, 1977; *Secrets*, ABC, 1977; *The Death of Richie*, NBC, 1977; *Betrayal*, NBC, 1978; *A Woman Called Moses*, NBC, 1978; *Act of Violence*, CBS, 1979; *The Ordeal of Patty Hearst*, ABC, 1979; *A Cry for Love*, NBC, 1980; *The Ordeal of Dr. Mudd*, CBS, 1980; *The Five of Me*, CBS, 1981; *The Awakening of Candra*, CBS, 1983; *Intimate Agony*, ABC, 1983; *Cocaine: One Man's Seduction*, NBC, 1983; *Scorned and Swindled*, CBS, 1984; *Picking Up the Pieces*, CBS, 1985; *The Bad Seed*, ABC, 1985; *The Execution*, NBC, 1985; *Rage of Angels: The Story Continues*, NBC, 1986; *Six Against the Rock*, NBC, 1987; *Right to Die*, NBC, 1987; *Blood Vows: The Story of a Mafia Wife*, NBC, 1987; *Sister Margaret and the Saturday Night Ladies*, CBS, 1957; *The Taking of Flight 847: The Uli Derickson Story*, NBC, 1988; *The Great Escape II: The Untold Story*, NBC, 1988; *Cross of Fire*, NBC, 1989; *From the Dead of Night*, NBC, 1989; *Blind Faith*, NBC, 1990.

RELATED CAREER—Documentary filmmaker.

ADDRESSES: AGENT—Fred Specktor, Creative Artists Agency, 9830 Wilshire Boulevard, Beverly Hills, CA 90212.*

*   *   *

WEST, Adam   1928-

PERSONAL: Born William West Anderson, September 19, 1928, in Walla Walla, WA. EDUCATION—Graduated from Whitman College.

VOCATION: Actor.

CAREER: PRINCIPAL STAGE APPEARANCES—*Volpone*, Center Theatre Group, Mark Taper Forum, Los Angeles, 1972.

PRINCIPAL FILM APPEARANCES—William Lawrence, *The Young Philadelphians* (also known as *The City Jungle*), Warner Brothers, 1959; Delahay, *Geronimo*, United Artists, 1962; Captain Blekeley, *Soldier in the Rain*, Allied Artists, 1963; Dr. Eric Hassler, *Tammy and the Doctor*, Universal, 1963; Colonel Daniel McReady, *Robinson Crusoe on Mars*, Paramount, 1964; Kenneth Cabot, *The Outlaws Is Coming* (also known as *The Three Stooges Meet the Gunslinger*), Columbia, 1965; Bruce Wayne/Batman, *Batman*, Twentieth Century-Fox, 1966; Ken Williams, *Mara of the Wilderness* (also known as *Valley of the White Wolves*), Allied Artists, 1966; Johnny Cain, *The Girl Who Knew Too Much*, Commonwealth, 1969; Chester, *The Marriage of a Young Stockbroker*, Twentieth Century-Fox, 1971; Jerry, *The Specialist*, Crown, 1975; Adam, *Hooper*, Warner Brothers, 1978; Allan McKenna, *One Dark Night*, Comworld, 1983; Arthur Bohart, Jr., *Young Lady Chatterley* (also known as *Private Property*), Cine-Circle Distributors, 1985; Dr. Dave Stanley, *Hell Riders*, 21st Century Releasing, 1985; Captain Churchman, *Zombie Nightmare*, Gold-Gems, 1987;

Charles Pinsky, *Doin' Time on Planet Earth*, Cannon, 1988; Edward Harris, *Mad About You*, Pinnacle, 1988. Also appeared in *Curse of the Moon Child*, 1972; *Partisani* (also known as *Hell River*), Yugoslavia Film, 1974; *Blonde Ambition*, Black Cat, 1980; *The Happy Hooker Goes to Hollywood*, Cannon, 1980.

PRINCIPAL TELEVISION APPEARANCES—Series: Sergeant Steve Nelson, *The Detectives* (also known as *Robert Taylor's The Detectives*), ABC, 1961-62; Bruce Wayne/Batman, *Batman*, ABC, 1966-68; voice of Bruce Wayne/Batman, *The New Adventures of Batman* (animated), CBS, 1977-78; voice of Bruce Wayne/Batman, *Batman and the Super Seven* (animated), NBC, 1980-81; voice of Batman, *Super Powers Team: Galactic Guardians* (animated), ABC, 1985-86; Captain Rick Wright, *The Last Precinct*, NBC, 1986. Pilots: David, *All in the Family* (broadcast as an episode of *Goodyear Theatre*), NBC, 1960; Cleander, *Alexander the Great*, ABC, 1968; Jannes Crawford, *Poor Devil*, NBC, 1973; Frank Hartlee, *Nevada Smith*, NBC, 1975; Captain Rick Wright, *The Last Precinct*, NBC, 1986.

Episodic: Bill Crawford, *Guestward Ho!*, ABC, 1961; Major Charles "Lucky" Merritt, "The Invisible Enemy," *The Outer Limits*, ABC, 1964; Wade Talmadge, *Murder, She Wrote*, CBS, 1987; also *Sugarfoot*, ABC, 1959; *Maverick*, ABC, 1959 (three episodes); *Colt .45*, ABC, 1959; *Lawman*, ABC, 1959; *77 Sunset Strip*, ABC, 1959; *Hawaiian Eye*, ABC, 1959; "Murder Is a Private Affair," *Desilu Playhouse*, CBS, 1960; *Tales of Wells Fargo*, NBC, 1961; *Bonanza*, NBC, 1961; *Perry Mason*, CBS, 1962; *The Real McCoys*, CBS, 1963; *Laramie*, NBC, 1963; *Petticoat Junction*, CBS, 1964; *Bewitched*, ABC, 1964; *The Virginian*, NBC, 1965; *Big Valley*, ABC, 1968; *Love, American Style*, ABC, 1970; "With Apologies to Mr. Hyde," *Night Gallery*, NBC, 1971; *This Is the Life*, syndicated, 1972; *Alias Smith and Jones*, ABC, 1972; *Mannix*, CBS, 1972; *Emergency*, NBC, 1974; *Alice*, CBS, 1976. Movies: Dr. Paul Scott, *The Eyes of Charles Sand*, ABC, 1972; Jock Higgins, *For the Love of It*, ABC, 1980; Craig Wyler, *I Take These Men*, CBS, 1983. Specials: *Celebrity Daredevils*, ABC, 1983.

ADDRESSES: AGENT—Lew Sherrell Agency, 7060 Hollywood Boulevard, Suite 610, Hollywood, CA 90028.*

*   *   *

WEST, Caryn

PERSONAL: Born June 23, in Washington, DC; daughter of Fraser Edwards (a rancher and Marine Corps colonel) and Thelma (Charlton) West. EDUCATION—Received B.A. in film and drama from Stanford University; received M.F.A. in acting from Temple University; studied acting with Joel Friedman, Wynn Handman, Robert W. Smith, Alan Langdon; studied advanced commercial technique with Joan See and voiceovers with Gerrianne Raphael.

VOCATION: Actress.

CAREER: STAGE DEBUT—Mina, *Count Dracula*, Paper Mill Playhouse, Millburn, NJ, 1978. BROADWAY DEBUT—Lenny MaGrath, *Crimes of the Heart*, John Golden Theatre, 1982-83. PRINCIPAL STAGE APPEARANCES—Rosalind, *As You Like It*, Riverside Shakespeare Company, New York City, 1978; Desdemona, *Othello*, American Revels Company, Richmond, VA, 1979; Olivia, *Twelfth Night*, Cincinnati Playhouse, Cincinnati, OH, 1979; Hele-

CARYN WEST

na Bulgakova, *Red River,* Goodman Theatre, Chicago, IL, 1982-83; Jess Burke, *Burkie,* Hudson Guild Theatre, New York City, 1984; May, *Fool for Love,* Theatre By the Sea, Portsmouth, NH, 1985, then Missouri Repertory Theatre, Kansas City, MO, 1986; Elizabeth, *The Art of Self Defense,* Festival of Original One-Act Comedies, Manhattan Punch Line, Judith Anderson Theatre, New York City, 1985; Carter, *8 x 10 Glossy,* Octoberfest, Ensemble Studio Theatre, New York City, 1985; Lydie Breeze, *Gardenia,* Pittsburgh Public Theatre, Pittsburgh, PA, 1986; Julia, *Fallen Angels,* Missouri Repertory Theatre, 1986. Also appeared as Beatrice, *Much Ado About Nothing,* New York Actors Unit; Irina, *The Three Sisters,* Central Theatre Company; May, *Fool for Love,* Cleveland Playhouse, Cleveland, OH; and Tansy (understudy), *The Nerd.*

MAJOR TOURS—Lenny MaGrath, *Crimes of the Heart,* U.S. cities, 1983-84.

FILM DEBUT—Jalon, *The Exterminator,* AVCO-Embassy, 1980.

TELEVISION DEBUT—Cora Munro, *Leatherstocking Tales,* PBS, 1979. PRINCIPAL TELEVISION APPEARANCES—Episodic: Mom, *Beauty and the Beast,* CBS, 1988 and 1989; Lauren Casey, *In the Heat of the Night,* NBC, 1989; Valerie Casey, *Jake and the Fatman,* CBS, 1990; also *Our Family Honor,* ABC, 1985; *J.J. Starbuck,* NBC, 1988; *Another World,* NBC; *One Life to Live,* ABC; *All My Children,* ABC; *Ryan's Hope,* ABC; *Tales from the Darkside,* syndicated. Movies: Receptionist, *Doubletake,* NBC, 1985; Margaret Morris, *Good Old Boy,* Disney Channel, 1988; also *Out of the Darkness,* CBS, 1985.

RELATED CAREER—Teacher, Actors in Advertising, 1985—; private acting coach for professional actors.

NON-RELATED CAREER—Member, U.S. National Alpine Ski Team, 1968-72.

MEMBER: Screen Actors Guild, American Federation of Television and Radio Artists, Actors' Equity Association, Performing Artists for Nuclear Disarmament.

SIDELIGHTS: RECREATIONS—Fencing, horsemanship (concentrating in English riding and western/steer team roping), tennis, and stage combat; ran in the New York City Marathon, 1985.

ADDRESSES: AGENTS—Meg Martin/Louis Ambrosio, Ambrosio/Mortimer and Associates Inc., 165 W. 46th Street, Suite 1109, New York, NY 10036 and 9000 Sunset Boulevard, Suite 900, Los Angeles, CA 90069.

*   *   *

WEST, Lockwood   1905-1989

PERSONAL: Full name, Harry Lockwood West; born July 28, 1905, in Birkenhead, England; died of cancer, March 28, 1989, in Brighton, England; son of Henry Cope and Mildred (Hartley) West; married Olive Carleton-Crowe (an actress; died, 1985); children: Timothy, Patricia.

VOCATION: Actor.

CAREER: STAGE DEBUT—Lieutenant Allen, *Alf's Button,* Hippodrome Theatre, Margate, U.K., 1926. LONDON DEBUT—Henry Bevan, *The Barretts of Wimpole Street,* Queen's Theatre, 1931. PRINCIPAL STAGE APPEARANCES—Mr. Toobad, *Nightmare Abbey,* Westminster Theatre, London, 1952; Dr. Macgregor, *The White Carnation,* Globe Theatre, London, 1953; Humphrey Caldwell, *A Day By the Sea,* Haymarket Theatre, London, 1953; the Agent de Police, *Nina,* Wimbledon Theatre, London, then Haymarket Theatre, both 1955; Major Swindon, *The Devil's Disciple,* Winter Garden Theatre, London, 1956; John Callifer, *The Potting Shed,* Globe Theatre, 1958; William Howard, *The Complaisant Lover,* Globe Theatre, 1959; M. Damiens, *The Rehearsal,* Theatre Royal, Bristol, U.K., then Globe Theatre, later Queen's Theatre, London, and Apollo Theatre, London, all 1961-62; Oscar Nelson, *Mary, Mary,* Queen's Theatre, 1963; Ferguson, *Wanted on the Voyage,* Grand Theatre, Leeds, U.K., 1964; Elliott, *He Was Gone When They Got There,* Mermaid Theatre, London, 1966; Emperor, *The Brass Butterfly,* Shaw Festival, Niagara-on-the-Lake, ON, Canada, 1973; Councillor Duxbury, *Billy,* Drury Lane Theatre, London, 1974; Reggie, *The Ordeal of Gilbert Pinfold,* Royal Exchange Theatre, Manchester, U.K., 1976, then Round House Theatre, London, 1979; Jones, *Half-Life,* Cottesloe Theatre, then Duke of York's Theatre, both London, 1978; Geoffrey Thornton, *The Dresser,* Royal Exchange Theatre, then Queen's Theatre, both 1980. Also appeared in *The Masters* and *The Right Honourable Gentleman,* both Theatre Royal, Windsor, U.K., 1969; *While the Sun Shines,* London production, 1987; and in repertory at the Bristol Little Theatre, Bristol, U.K., in Edinburgh, Scotland, and in Coventry, U.K., 1932-39.

MAJOR TOURS—Jones, *Half-Life,* U.K. and Canadian cities, 1978.

FILM DEBUT—*A Song for Tomorrow*, General Film Distributors, 1948. PRINCIPAL FILM APPEARANCES—Dr. Cresswell, *Celia*, Exclusive, 1949; Kennedy, *Hammer the Toff*, Butchers, 1952; Mr. Barraclough, *The Birthday Present*, British Lion, 1957; magistrate, *The Mark of the Hawk* (also known as *Accused*), Universal, 1958; police inspector, *Strong Room*, Union, 1962; Reggie's father, *The Leather Boys*, Allied Artists, 1965; St. Peter, *Bedazzled*, Twentieth Century-Fox, 1967; Quince, *A Dandy in Aspic*, Columbia, 1968; magistrate, *Up the Junction*, Paramount, 1968; Ebert, *One Brief Summer*, Cinevision, 1971; Reverend Wood, *Jane Eyre*, British Lion, 1971; Freeborne, *Count Dracula and His Vampire Bride* (also known as *Satanic Rites of Dracula*), Dynamic Entertainment, 1978; Geoffrey Thornton, *The Dresser*, Columbia, 1983; Rogers, *The Shooting Party*, European Classics, 1985; curio shop owner, *Young Sherlock Holmes*, Paramount, 1985. Also appeared in *Last Holiday*, Stratford, 1950; *No Place for Jennifer*, Associated British/Pathe, 1950; *High Treason*, General Film Distributors/Pacemaker/Mayer/Kingsley, 1951; *The Horse's Mouth* (also known as *The Oracle*), General Film Distributors, 1953; *Sailor of the King* (also known as *Single-Handed* and *Able Seaman Brown*), Twentieth Century-Fox, 1953; *Private's Progress*, British Lion, 1956; *The Man Who Could Cheat Death*, Paramount, 1959; *The Running Man*, Columbia, 1963; *Life at the Top*, Columbia, 1965; *Game for Three Losers*, AVCO-Embassy, 1965.

PRINCIPAL TELEVISION APPEARANCES—Series: Chaplain, *Porterhouse Blue*, 1986. Mini-Series: *Disraeli*, ATV, then *Masterpiece Theatre*, PBS, 1980l Admiral Beaumont, *The Last Place on Earth*, Central Television, then *Masterpiece Theatre*, PBS, 1985. Episodic: King Edward VII, *Upstairs, Downstairs*, London Weekend Television, 1972, then *Masterpiece Theatre*, PBS, 1974; also *The Pallisers*, BBC, 1974, then PBS, 1977. Movies: Reverend Wood, *Jane Eyre*, NBC, 1971; Professor Hardy, *Family Ties Vacation*, NBC, 1985. Also appeared in *The Power Game*, *The Newcomers*, *Brett*, *No Hiding Place*, *Big Brother*, *Raffles*.

RELATED CAREER—Actor in nearly 3,000 radio programs.

NON-RELATED CAREER—Served with the Police War Reserve, Bristol, U.K., 1940-45; worked for a coal mining company.

OBITUARIES AND OTHER SOURCES: Hollywood Reporter, April 6, 1989; *Variety*, April 5-11, 1989.*

*   *   *

WESTON, Jack   1915-

PERSONAL: Born Morris Weinstein, August 21, 1915 (some sources say 1924), in Cleveland, OH; married Marge Redmond (an actress). EDUCATION—Trained for the stage at the Cleveland Playhouse, 1934, and with the American Theatre Wing. MILITARY—U.S. Army.

VOCATION: Actor.

CAREER: BROADWAY DEBUT—Michael Lindsey, *Season in the Sun*, Cort Theatre, 1950. PRINCIPAL STAGE APPEARANCES—Stewpot, *South Pacific*, Majestic Theatre, New York City, 1952; Francis, *Bells Are Ringing*, Shubert Theatre, New York City, 1956; Gaetano Proclo, *The Ritz*, Longacre Theatre, New York City, 1975; Marvin Michaels, "Visitor from Philadelphia" and Mort Hollender, "Visitors from Chicago" in *California Suite*, Eugene O'Neill

Theatre, New York City, 1976; Sam, *Cheaters*, Biltmore Theatre, New York City, 1978; Dietrich Merkenschrift, *Break a Leg*, Palace Theatre, New York City, 1979; Eddie, *One Night Stand*, Nederlander Theatre, New York City, 1980; Jerry Wexler, *The Floating Light Bulb*, Vivian Beaumont Theatre, New York City, 1981; Aimable Castagnet, *The Baker's Wife*, York Theatre Company, Church of the Heavenly Rest, New York City, 1985; Zitorsky, *The Tenth Man*, Vivian Beaumont Theatre, 1989. Also appeared in *The Trouble with People . . . and Other Things*, Coconut Grove Playhouse, Miami Beach, FL, 1974.

MAJOR TOURS—Rudy "Baby" Filbertson, *Crazy October*, U.S. cities, 1958-59; Pfancoo, *The Office*, U.S. cities, 1966; Barney Cashman, *The Last of the Red Hot Lovers*, U.S. cities, 1970-71.

FILM DEBUT—Frank, *Stage Struck*, RKO/Buena Vista, 1958. PRINCIPAL FILM APPEARANCES—Stage manager, *Imitation of Life*, Universal, 1959; Joe Positano, *Please Don't Eat the Daisies*, Metro-Goldwyn-Mayer (MGM), 1960; Lasker, *All in a Night's Work*, Paramount, 1961; Signalman Burford Taylor, *The Honeymoon Machine*, MGM, 1961; Leopold, *It's Only Money*, Paramount, 1962; Coach Campbell, *Palm Springs Weekend*, Warner Brothers, 1963; Lieutenant George Stickle, *The Incredible Mr. Limpet*, Warner Brothers, 1964; Lester, *Mirage*, Universal, 1965; Pig, *The Cincinnati Kid*, MGM, 1965; Carlino, *Wait Until Dark*, Warner Brothers, 1967; Randolph Riker, *The Counterfeit Killer*, Universal, 1968; Erwin Weaver, *The Thomas Crown Affair* (also known as *Thomas Crown and Company* and *The Crown Caper*), United Artists, 1968; Potter Shrader, *The April Fools*, National General, 1969; Harvey Greenfield, *Cactus Flower*, Columbia, 1969; Andrew McPherson, *A New Leaf*, Paramount, 1971; Detective Meyer Meyer, *Fuzz*, United Artists, 1972; Maffio Polo, *Marco*, Cinerama, 1973; Irving Greenfield, *Gator*, United Artists, 1976; Gaetano Proclo, *The Ritz*, Warner Brothers, 1976; Gutman, *Cuba*, United Artists, 1979; Benny Murray, *Can't Stop the Music*, Associated Film Distribution, 1980; Danny Zimmer, *The Four Seasons*, Universal, 1981; Struts, *High Road to China*, Warner Brothers, 1983; Elton, *The Longshot*, Orion, 1986; Duke Best, *Rad*, Tri-Star, 1986; Max Kellerman, *Dirty Dancing*, Vestron, 1987; Marty Freed, *Ishtar*, Columbia, 1987; Oscar Baldwin, *Short Circuit 2*, Tri-Star, 1988. Also appeared in *I Want to Live!*, NCO/United Artists, 1958.

PRINCIPAL TELEVISION APPEARANCES—Series: Ranger Wilbur Wormsey, *Rod Brown of the Rocket Rangers*, CBS, 1953-54; Chick Adams, *My Sister Eileen*, CBS, 1960-61; Walter Hathaway, *The Hathaways*, ABC, 1961-62; Danny Zimmer, *The Four Seasons*, CBS, 1984. Mini-Series: Joker Martin, *Harold Robbins' "79 Park Avenue,"* NBC, 1977; Uncle Willie, *If Tomorrow Comes*, CBS, 1986. Pilots: Kenny, *The Third Commandment*, NBC, 1959; Freddie Pringle, *Band of Gold* (broadcast as an episode of *General Electric Theatre*), CBS, 1961; Ed Broxton, *For the Love of Mike*, CBS, 1962; Fireman Hogan, *Where There's Smokey*, CBS, 1966; Griffin, *Fame Is the Name of the Game*, NBC, 1966; Gerberman, *Code Name: Heraclitus*, NBC, 1967; Job Cheyne, *I Love a Mystery*, NBC, 1973; Mr. Randall, *D.H.O.*, ABC, 1973; Sergeant Herbert Willing, *Ready and Willing*, CBS, 1974; Julius V. Hickey, *Hickey vs. Anybody*, NBC, 1976.

Episodic: Charlie, "The Monsters Are Due on Maple Street," *The Twilight Zone*, CBS, 1960; Julius Moomer, "The Bard," *The Twilight Zone*, CBS, 1963; also "The Cheaters," *Thriller*, NBC, 1961; "Flowers of Evil," *Thriller*, NBC, 1962; *All in the Family*, CBS, 1972; Louis Gruber, *Betwitched*, ABC; *The Carol Burnett Show*, CBS; *Gunsmoke*, CBS; *Philco Television Playhouse*, NBC;

Studio One, CBS; *The Untouchables*, ABC; *Kraft Television Theatre*. Movies: Prince Haroun, *Now You See It, Now You Don't*, NBC, 1968; Al Zabrocki, *Deliver Us from Evil*, ABC, 1973. Specials: Larry Westcott, *Stage Door*, CBS, 1955; Wilson, *Harvey*, CBS, 1958; Cash, *The Lucille Ball Comedy Hour*, CBS, 1967; Ben, "Story 4," *The Trouble with People*, NBC, 1972; *Alan King Looks Back in Anger—A Review of 1972*, ABC, 1973; "You're a Poet and Don't Know It! The Poetry Power Hour," *CBS Festival of Lively Arts for Young People*, CBS, 1976.

AWARDS: Antoinette Perry Award nomination, Best Actor in a Play, 1981, for *The Floating Light Bulb*.

ADDRESSES: AGENT—McCart, Oreck, and Barrett, 10390 Santa Monica Boulevard, Suite 310, Los Angeles, CA 90025.*

*   *   *

WHITAKER, Forest 1961-

PERSONAL: Born July 15, 1961, in Longview, TX; father, an insurance salesman; mother, a teacher. EDUCATION—Studied music at California State Polytechnic University, Pomona; studied drama and opera at the University of Southern California; attended the Drama Studio London (Berkeley, CA).

VOCATION: Actor.

CAREER: FILM DEBUT—Charles Jefferson, *Fast Times at Ridgemont High*, Universal, 1982. PRINCIPAL FILM APPEARANCES—Bulldozer, *Vision Quest*, Warner Brothers, 1985; Amos, *The Color of Money*, Buena Vista, 1986; Big Harold, *Platoon*, Orion, 1986; Edward Montesque Garlick, *Good Morning, Vietnam*, Buena Vista, 1987; Jack Pismo, *Stakeout*, Buena Vista, 1987; Charlie "Bird" Parker, *Bird*, Warner Brothers, 1988; Rawlins, *Bloodsport*, Cannon, 1988; Dr. Steven Resher, *Johnny Handsome*, Tri-Star, 1989; Dennis Curren, *Downtown*, Twentieth Century-Fox, 1990.

PRINCIPAL TELEVISION APPEARANCES—Mini-Series: Cuffey, *North and South*, ABC, 1985; Cuffey, *North and South, Book II*, ABC, 1986. Episodic: Jerry, *Amazing Stories*, NBC, 1986; Harris, *He's the Mayor*, ABC, 1986; also Herman, *Diff'rent Strokes*, NBC. Movies: Sergeant Delaney, *Hands of a Stranger*, CBS, 1987. Specials: *The 21st Annual NAACP Image Awards*, syndicated, 1989.

AWARDS: Best Actor Award from the Cannes Film Festival, 1988, for *Bird*.

OTHER SOURCES: The Hollywood Reporter, January 9, 1989; *Premiere*, November, 1988.

ADDRESSES: AGENT—David Eidenberg, S.T.E. Representation, 9301 Wilshire Boulevard, Suite 312, Beverly Hills, CA 90210. PUBLICIST—Les Cripe, Dennis Davidson Associates, 211 S. Beverly Drive, Suite 200, Beverly Hills, CA 90212.*

WILBY, James 1958-

PERSONAL: Born in 1958 in Rangoon, Burma. EDUCATION—Attended Durham University; studied acting at the Royal Academy of Dramatic Art.

VOCATION: Actor.

CAREER: LONDON DEBUT—*Another Country*. PRINCIPAL STAGE APPEARANCES—*The Common Pursuit*, U.K., 1988.

FILM DEBUT—Jamie, *Privileged*, New Yorker, 1982. PRINCIPAL FILM APPEARANCES—Baker, *Dreamchild*, Universal, 1985; Maurice Hall, *Maurice*, Cinecom, 1987; Tony Last, *A Handful of Dust*, New Line Cinema, 1988; Ashton, *A Summer Story*, Atlantic, 1988; also appeared in *A Room with a View*, Cinecom, 1986.

PRINCIPAL TELEVISION APPEARANCES—Mini-Series: Sidney Carton, *A Tale of Two Cities*, Granada, then *Masterpiece Theatre*, PBS, 1989; also *Mother Love*, BBC-1, 1989. Also appeared in *Sherlock Holmes, The Crooked Man*, and *Dutch Girls*.*

*   *   *

WILCOX, Larry 1947-

PERSONAL: Full name, Larry Dee Wilcox; born August 8, 1947, in San Diego, CA; married Judy Vagner, March 29, 1969 (divorced, 1978); married Johanna Strasser, April 11, 1980 (divorced); married Marlene Rae Harmon, March 22, 1986; children: Derek Scott, Heidi Kirsten (first marriage); Wendy Johanna (second marriage). EDUCATION—Attended the University of Wyoming, 1965, Pierce College, 1970-71, and California State University, Northridge, 1971-74. MILITARY—U.S. Marine Corps, sergeant, 1967-70.

VOCATION: Actor and producer.

CAREER: PRINCIPAL FILM APPEARANCES—Mike Shelby, *The Last Hard Men*, Twentieth Century-Fox, 1976; Web, *Mission Manila*, MCEG/Virgin Home Entertainment, 1987.

PRINCIPAL FILM WORK—Producer (with others), *The Bradbury Trilogy*, Atlantic, 1985.

PRINCIPAL TELEVISION APPEARANCES—Series: Dale Mitchell, *Lassie*, syndicated, 1972-74; Officer Jon Baker, *CHiPs*, NBC, 1977-82. Episodic: *Police Story*, NBC; *Streets of San Francisco*, ABC; *The Wonderful World of Disney*, NBC. Movies: Charlie Saunders, *Mr. and Mrs. Bo Jo Jones*, ABC, 1971; Joe Bunch, *The Great American Beauty Contest*, ABC, 1973; Moose Meyers, *The Girl Most Likely To . . .*, ABC, 1973; Roy Joad, *Death Stalk*, NBC, 1975; Deputy Jim Schiller, *Sky Hei$t*, NBC, 1975; Buck, *Relentless*, CBS, 1977; Em Dalton, *The Last Ride of the Dalton Gang*, NBC, 1979; Detective Russ Kemper, *Deadly Lessons*, ABC, 1983; Tommy Wells, *The Dirty Dozen: The Next Mission*, NBC, 1985; Lieutenant Colonel Kevin Parks, *Perry Mason: The Case of the Avenging Ace*, NBC, 1988; Mark, *Rich Men, Single Women*, ABC, 1990. Specials: Jarvis, *Member of the Wedding*, CBS, 1958; *Battle of the Network Stars*, ABC, 1977-80 (four episodes); *Bob Hope's All-Star Look at TV's Prime Time Wars*, NBC, 1980.

PRINCIPAL TELEVISION WORK—Episodic: Executive producer

(with others), "The Screaming Woman," "Banshee," and "The Town Where No One Got Off," *The Ray Bradbury Theatre*, HBO, 1986; also director, *CHiPs*, NBC; producer, *The Ray Bradbury Theatre*, USA. Movies: Executive producer, *Death of a Centerfold: The Dorothy Stratten Story*, NBC, 1981; also director, *Ride the Whirlwind*, 1979; director, *Tow Truck Lady*, 1980.

NON-RELATED CARRER—Rancher, bartender, laborer, and telegrapher.

WRITINGS: TELEVISION—Movies: (Co-writer) *Harvest of Evil*, CBS.

AWARDS: Four ACE Awards for *The Ray Bradbury Theatre.*

MEMBER: Screen Actors Guild, Writers Guild of America, Directors Guild of America, California Highway Patrol (honorary member, 1979), Professional Rodeo Cowboys Association, Federation Internationale de l'Automobile, Sports Car Club of America, American Legion, SCORE-OFF (road racing organization), American Bicycle Association (national safety chairman), Veterans, No Greater Love (national celebrity chairman), Demolay Club.

ADDRESSES: AGENT—David Shapira and Associates Inc., 15301 Ventura Boulevard, Suite 345, Sherman Oaks, CA 91403.*

*   *   *

WILDE, Cornel   1915-1989

PERSONAL. Full name, Cornelius Louis Wilde; born October 13, 1915 (some sources say 1918), in New York, NY; died of leukemia, October 16, 1989, in Los Angeles, CA; son of Beela Louis (in the cosmetics business) and Renee (Vid) Wilde; married Patricia Knight (an actress), September 3, 1938 (divorced, 1951); married Jean Wallace (an actress), September 4, 1951 (divorced, 1981); children: Wendy (first marriage); Cornel Wallace (second marriage); Pascal, Thomas (stepchildren from second marriage). EDUCATION—Attended Columbia University, 1934-35; City College of New York, B.S., 1937; attended the College of Physicians and Surgeons, Columbia University; studied art in Budapest, Hungary; studied acting with Lee Strasberg, Michael Chekhov, and Leo Bulgakov.

VOCATION: Actor, producer, director, and screenwriter.

CAREER: Also see *WRITINGS* below. BROADWAY DEBUT—*Moon Over Mulberry Street*, Lyceum Theatre, 1935, then 44th Street Theatre, 1936. PRINCIPAL STAGE APPEARANCES—Tybalt, *Romeo and Juliet*, 51st Street Theatre, New York City, 1940; also appeared in *Daughters of Atreus*, 44th Street Theatre, New York City, 1936; *Having Wonderful Time*, Lyceum Theatre, New York City, 1937; and in *Love Is Not So Simple*, New York City. PRINCIPAL STAGE WORK—Fencing instructor, *Romeo and Juliet*, 51st Street Theatre, New York City, 1940.

FILM DEBUT—Mr. Williams, *Lady with Red Hair*, Warner Brothers, 1940. PRINCIPAL FILM APPEARANCES—Louis Mendoza, *High Sierra*, Warner Brothers, 1941; Chet Oakley, *Kisses for Breakfast*, Warner Brothers, 1941; Tom Rossi, *Knockout* (also known as *Right to the Heart*), Warner Brothers/First National, 1941; Mike Lord, *The Perfect Snob*, Twentieth Century-Fox, 1941; Robert, *Life Begins at 8:30* (also known as *The Light of*

Heart), Twentieth Century-Fox, 1942; Jeff Bailey, *Manila Calling*, Twentieth Century-Fox, 1942; Freddy Austin, *Wintertime*, Twentieth Century-Fox, 1943; Frederic Chopin, *A Song to Remember*, Columbia, 1945; Aladdin, *A Thousand and One Nights*, Columbia, 1945; Robert of Nottingham, *The Bandit of Sherwood Forest*, Columbia, 1946; Philippe Lascalles, *Centennial Summer*, Twentieth Century-Fox, 1946; Richard Harland, *Leave Her to Heaven*, Twentieth Century-Fox, 1946; Bruce Carlton, *Forever Amber*, Twentieth Century-Fox, 1947; Jock Wallace, *The Homestretch*, Twentieth Century-Fox, 1947; "George"/Johnny Blaine, *It Had to Be You*, Columbia, 1947; Pete Morgan, *Road House*, Twentieth Century-Fox, 1948; Dave Connors, *Walls of Jericho*, Twentieth Century-Fox, 1948; Griff Marat, *Shockproof*, Columbia, 1949.

Stanley Robin, *Four Days Leave*, Film Classics, 1950; Captain Mark Bradford, *Two Flags West*, Twentieth Century-Fox, 1950; D'Artagnan, *At Sword's Point* (also known as *Sons of the Musketeers*), RKO, 1951; Don Arturo Bordega, *California Conquest*, Columbia, 1952; Sebastian, *The Greatest Show on Earth*, Paramount, 1952; Peter Forrester, *Operation Secret*, Warner Brothers, 1952; Si Lahssen, *Saadia*, Metro-Goldwyn-Mayer (MGM), 1953; Jean-Paul, *Treasure of the Golden Condor*, Twentieth Century-Fox, 1953; as himself, *Main Street to Broadway*, MGM, 1953; Juan Obregon, *Passion*, RKO, 1954; Bill Baxter, *Woman's World*, Twentieth Century-Fox, 1954; Diamond, *The Big Combo*, Allied Artists, 1955; Major John Bolton, *The Scarlet Coat*, MGM, 1955; Stephen Torino, *Hot Blood*, Columbia, 1956; Pierre St. Laurent, *Star of India*, United Artists, 1956; Charlie, *Storm Fear*, United Artists, 1956; Matt Campbell, *Beyond Mombasa*, Columbia 1957; Nick, *The Devil's Hairpin*, Paramount, 1957; title role, *Omar Khayyam*, Paramount, 1957; Vic Scott, *Maracaibo*, Paramount, 1958; Les Martin, *Edge of Eternity*, Columbia, 1959.

Constantine, *Constantine and the Cross* (also known as *Constantine the Great*), Embassy, 1962; Sir Lancelot, *The Sword of Lancelot* (also known as *Lancelot and Guinevere*), Universal, 1963; man, *The Naked Prey*, Paramount, 1966; Captain MacDonald, *Beach Red*, United Artists, 1967; Frank Powers, *The Comic*, Columbia, 1969; narrator, *No Blade of Grass*, MGM, 1970; Jim, *Shark's Treasure*, United Artists, 1975; D'Artagnan, *The Fifth Musketeer* (also known as *Behind the Iron Mask*), Columbia, 1977; Raynar, *The Norseman*, American International, 1978. Also appeared in *Guest in the House*, United Artists, 1944; as Jimmy Banks, *Stairway for a Star*, 1947; and in *Flesh and Bullets*, Hollywood International Film Corporation America, 1985.

PRINCIPAL FILM WORK—Producer, *The Big Combo*, Allied Artists, 1955; producer and director, *Storm Fear*, United Artists, 1956; producer and director, *The Devil's Hairpin*, Paramount, 1957; producer and director, *Maracaibo*, Paramount, 1958; executive producer and director, *The Sword of Lancelot*, Universal, 1963; producer and director, *The Naked Prey*, Paramount, 1966; producer and director, *Beach Red*, United Artists, 1967; producer and director, *No Blade of Grass*, MGM, 1970; producer and director, *Shark's Treasure*, United Artists, 1975.

PRINCIPAL TELEVISION APPEARANCES—Episodic: As himself, *I Love Lucy*, CBS, 1955; George Burnett, *The New Mike Hammer*, CBS, 1986; Duncan Barnett, *Murder, She Wrote*, CBS, 1987; also "The Blond Dog," *General Electric Theatre*, CBS, 1955; "Coast to Coast," *Alcoa Theatre*, NBC, 1958; "Around the World with Nellie Bly," *Chevy Show*, NBC, 1960; *Father Knows Best*, CBS, 1960; "The Great Alberti," *General Electric Theatre*, CBS, 1961; *The Greatest Show on Earth*, ABC, 1964; "Doesn't Anyone Know

Who I Am?,'' *Kraft Suspense Theatre,* NBC, 1964; *Suspense Theatre,* ABC, 1969; ''Deliveries in the Rear,'' *Night Gallery,* NBC, 1972. Movies: Mercer Boley, *Gargoyles,* CBS, 1972. Specials: *Your Choice for the Film Awards,* 1987.

RELATED CAREER—Founder (with Jean Wallace), Theodora Productions, 1955.

NON-RELATED CAREER—Member, U.S. Olympic fencing team, 1936; also toy salesman and commercial artist.

WRITINGS: FILM—See production details above. (With James Edmiston) *The Devil's Hairpin,* Paramount, 1957; *Shark's Treasure,* United Artists, 1975. OTHER—*My Very Wilde Life* (autobiography), 1987.

AWARDS: Academy Award nomination, Best Actor, 1945, for *A Song to Remember;* James K. Hackett Award, 1974; Bijou Film Society Award, 1975.

OBITUARIES AND OTHER SOURCES: New York Times, October 17, 1989; *Variety,* October 18-24, 1989.*

*   *   *

WILLIAMS, Barry   1954-

PERSONAL: Born September 30, 1954, in Santa Monica, CA; son of Frank Millar and Doris May (Moore) Blenkorn.

VOCATION: Actor.

CAREER: BROADWAY DEBUT—Alfred Von Wilmers, ''The Little Comedy'' and Sam, ''Summer Share'' in *Romance/Romance,* Helen Hayes Theatre, 1988. PRINCIPAL STAGE APPEARANCES—*Promises, Promises,* Birmingham, MI, 1988; *I Do, I Do,* Kansas City, MO, 1988; *Funny Girl,* Pittsburgh, PA, 1988.

MAJOR TOURS—Title role, *Pippin,* U.S. cities, 1974-75.

PRINCIPAL TELEVISION APPEARANCES—Series: Greg Brady, *The Brady Bunch,* ABC, 1969-74; voice of Greg Brady, *The Brady Kids* (animated), ABC, 1972-74; Greg Brady, *The Brady Bunch Hour,* ABC, 1977; Greg Brady, *The Bradys,* CBS, 1990. Pilots: Junior Fandango, *The Shameful Secrets of Hastings Corners,* NBC, 1970. Episodic: *General Hospital,* ABC; *The F.B.I.,* ABC; *That Girl,* ABC; *Gomer Pyle, U.S.M.C.,* CBS; *It Takes a Thief,* ABC; *The Mod Squad,* ABC; *Marcus Welby, M.D.,* ABC. Movies: Greg Brady, *The Brady Girls Get Married,* NBC, 1981; Greg Brady, *A Very Brady Christmas,* CBS, 1988.

WRITINGS: SONGS—''Till I Met You.''

MEMBER: Screen Actors Guild, American Federation of Television and Radio Artists, American Guild of Variety Artists.

ADDRESSES: AGENT—Exclusive Artists Agency, 2501 W. Burbank Boulevard, Suite 304, Los Angeles, CA 91505.*

BILLY DEE WILLIAMS

WILLIAMS, Billy Dee   1937-

PERSONAL: Born April 6, 1937, in New York, NY; third wife's name, Teruko; children: Miyaka, Hanako, Corey. EDUCATION—Attended the High School of Music and Art; trained for the stage at the National Academy of Fine Arts and Design and with Paul Mann and Sidney Poitier at the Actors' Workshop.

VOCATION: Actor.

CAREER: BROADWAY DEBUT—Duke Custis, *The Cool World,* Eugene O'Neill Theatre, 1960. PRINCIPAL STAGE APPEARANCES—The Boy, *A Taste of Honey,* Lyceum Theatre, New York City, 1960; Robert, *Blue Boy in Black,* Masque Theatre, New York City, 1963; Junie, *Happy Ending* and John, *Days of Absence* (double-bill), St. Mark's Playhouse, New York City, 1965; Willy Lee Irons, *The Firebugs,* Martinique Theatre, New York City, 1968; Theopolis Parker, *Ceremonies in Dark Old Men,* Pocket Theatre, New York City, 1969; Randall, *Slow Dance on the Killing Ground,* Sheridan Square Playhouse, New York City, 1970; Dr. Martin Luther King, Jr., *I Have a Dream,* Ford's Theatre, Washington, DC, 1975, then Ambassador Theatre, New York City, 1976; Troy Maxon, *Fences,* 46th Street Theatre, New York City, 1988. Also appeared in *Firebrand of Florence,* Alvin Theatre, New York City, 1945; in *Tiger, Tiger Burning Bright,* Booth Theatre, New York City, 1962; and in *Hallelujah, Baby!,* Martin Beck Theatre, New York City, 1967.

FILM DEBUT—Josh Quincy, *The Last Angry Man,* Columbia, 1959. PRINCIPAL FILM APPEARANCES—Lost and found supervisor, *The Out-of-Towners,* Paramount, 1970; Johnny Johnson, *The*

Final Comedown, New World, 1972; Louis McKay, *Lady Sings the Blues*, Paramount, 1972; Nick Allen, *Hit*, Paramount, 1973; Sneed, *The Take*, Columbia, 1974; Brian Walker, *Mahogany*, Paramount, 1975; Bingo Long, *The Bingo Long Traveling All-Stars and Motor Kings*, Universal, 1976; title role, *Scott Joplin*, Universal, 1977; Lando Calrissian, *The Empire Strikes Back*, Twentieth Century-Fox, 1980; Matthew Fox, *Nighthawks*, Universal, 1981; Richard Davis, *Marvin and Tige*, Major, 1983; Lando Calrissian, *Return of the Jedi*, Twentieth Century-Fox, 1983; Al Wheeler, *Fear City*, Chevy Chase Distribution, 1984; Hamberger, *Deadly Illusion*, Cinetel, 1987; Frank Hazeltine, *Number One with a Bullet*, Cannon, 1987; Harvey Dent, *Batman*, Twentieth Century-Fox, 1989. Also appeared in *Blast*, New World, 1976.

PRINCIPAL TELEVISION APPEARANCES—Series: Billy Diamond, *Double Dare*, CBS, 1985; also *The Guiding Light*, CBS. Mini-Series: Tyler Watts, *Chiefs*, CBS, 1983. Pilots: Dan Gardner, *Crisis*, CBS, 1968; David Arnold, *Higher and Higher, Attorneys at Law*, CBS, 1968; Douglas Hawke, *Shooting Stars*, ABC, 1983; Wes Tanner, *Time Bomb*, NBC, 1984. Episodic: As himself, *227*, NBC, 1986 and 1987; Brady Lloyd, *Dynasty*, ABC, 1987; also as himself, *The Jeffersons*, CBS; assistant district attorney, *Another World*, NBC; *The Mod Squad*, ABC; *The Interns*, CBS; *The F.B.I.*, ABC; *Mission: Impossible*, CBS; *Police Woman*, NBC. Movies. Lewis, *Carter's Army*, ABC, 1970; Gale Sayers, *Brian's Song*, ABC, 1971; Lennox Beach, *Truman Capote's "The Glass House,"* CBS, 1972; Homer Smith, *Christmas Lilies of the Field*, NBC, 1979; Walter Williams, *Children of Divorce*, NBC, 1980; Clarence Whitlock, *The Hostage Tower*, CBS, 1980; Matthew Raines, *The Imposter*, ABC, 1984; Bobby Jay, *Courage*, CBS, 1986; Jim McKinley, *Oceans of Fire*, CBS, 1986; Mike Trainor, *The Right of the People*, ABC, 1986; Daniel Lancaster, *The Return of Desperado*, NBC, 1988. Specials: *ABC's Silver Anniversary—25 and Still the One*, ABC, 1978; *The American Film Institute Salute to Henry Fonda*, CBS, 1978; *A Celebration at Ford's Theatre*, CBS, 1978; host, *Classic Creatures: Return of the Jedi*, CBS, 1983; host, *Eubie Blake: A Century of Music*, PBS, 1983; host, *"Cougar!,"* ABC *Weekend Specials*, ABC, 1984; host and narrator, *Brown Sugar: Eighty Years of Black Female Superstars*, PBS, 1986; *Bugs Bunny/Looney Tunes All-Star 50th Anniversary*, CBS, 1986; *Diana Ross . . . Red Hot Rhythm and Blues*, ABC, 1987; *Third Annual Soul Train Music Awards*, syndicated, 1989.

RELATED CAREER—Member, Actors' Workshop, New York City; also commercial spokesman for Colt .45 malt liquor.

AWARDS: Emmy Award nomination, 1972, for *Truman Capote's "The Glass House."*

ADDRESSES: AGENT—Pam Prince, William Morris Agency, 151 El Camino Drive, Beverly Hills, CA 90212. PUBLICIST—Cheryl Kagan, Rogers and Cowan, 10000 Santa Monica Boulevard, Suite 400, Los Angeles, CA 90067.*

*   *   *

WILLIAMS, Samm
   See WILLIAMS, Samm-Art

WILLIAMS, Samm-Art   1946-
(Samm Williams)

PERSONAL: Full name, Samuel Arthur Williams; born January 20, 1946, in Burgaw, NC; son of Samuel and Valdosia (a school teacher) Williams. EDUCATION—Morgan State College, B.A., political science, 1968.

VOCATION: Playwright and actor.

CAREER: Also see *WRITINGS* below. PRINCIPAL STAGE APPEARANCES—(As Samm Williams) Chester Pearce, *Nowhere to Run, Nowhere to Hide*, Season-Within-a-Season, Negro Ensemble Company, St. Mark's Playhouse, New York City, 1974; (as Samm Williams) Boatswain Mate First Class John Wilheart, *Liberty Call* and (as Samm-Art Williams) Argus and klansman, *Waiting for Mongo*, both Season-Within-a-Season, Negro Ensemble Company, St. Mark's Playhouse, 1975; Harper Edwards, *The First Breeze of Summer*, Palace Theatre, New York City, 1975; Eustace, *Eden*, Negro Ensemble Company, St. Mark's Playhouse, 1976; Corporal Clifford Adair, *The Brownsville Raid*, Negro Ensemble Company, Theatre de Lys, New York City, 1976-77; the Window Washer, *Night Shift*, Playhouse Theatre, New York City, 1977; Arthur, *Black Body Blues*, Negro Ensemble Company, St. Mark's Playhouse, 1978; Boise McCanles, *Nevis Mountain Dew*, Negro Ensemble Company, St. Mark's Playhouse, 1978-79, then Arena Stage, Washington, DC, 1979; James, *Old Phantoms*, Negro Ensemble Company, St. Mark's Playhouse, 1979; Cephus Miles, *Home*, Virginia Museum Theatre, Richmond, VA, and Stagewest, West Springfield, MA, both 1982-83. Also appeared in *Black Jesus*, New York City, 1973; *Plays from Africa*, Negro Ensemble Company, St. Mark's Playhouse, 1979; *Night and Day*, Kennedy Center for the Performing Arts, Washington, DC, 1979; *Ajax* and *The Bob Hope War Zone Special* (double-bill), both Terrace Theatre, Kennedy Center for the Performing Arts, 1986.

PRINCIPAL FILM APPEARANCES—Roger, *The Wanderers*, Orion, 1979; cop, *Dressed to Kill*, Filmways, 1980; Maurice, *Blood Simple*, Circle, 1984; Bill Martin, *Hot Resort*, Cannon Releasing, 1985; also appeared in *Night of the Juggler*, Columbia, 1980.

PRINCIPAL TELEVISION APPEARANCES—Episodic: Title role, "Denmark Vesey," *American Playhouse*, PBS, 1985; Jim, "The Adventures of Huckleberry Finn," *American Playhouse*, PBS, 1986; Bubba Crown, *The New Mike Hammer*, CBS, 1986; Jim Manning, *227*, NBC, 1987; Sheriff, *Frank's Place*, CBS, 1987; also "My Man Bovanne," *Ossie and Ruby*, PBS, 1987; *All My Children*, ABC; *Search for Tomorrow*, CBS. Movies: Matthew Henson, *Cook and Peary: The Race to the Pole*, CBS, 1983.

PRINCIPAL TELEVISION WORK—Series: Story editor, *Frank's Place*, CBS, 1987-88.

RELATED CAREER—Company member, Freedom Theatre, Philadelphia, PA, 1968-73; company member, Negro Ensemble Company, New York City, 1973-78; actor in television commercials.

NON-RELATED CAREER—Salesman, gas station attendant, and bartender.

WRITINGS: STAGE—(As Samm Williams) *Welcome to Black River*, Season-Within-a-Season, Negro Ensemble Company, St. Mark's Playhouse, New York City, 1975; *The Coming* and *Do Unto Others*, both Billie Holiday Theatre, Brooklyn, NY, 1976; *A Love Play*, Negro Ensemble Company, St. Mark's Playhouse, 1976; *The*

Last Caravan, 1977; *Brass Birds Don't Sing,* Stage 73, New York City, 1978; *Home,* Negro Ensemble Company, St. Mark's Playhouse, 1979-80, then Cort Theatre, New York City, 1980, published by Dramatists Play Service, 1980; *The Sixteenth Round,* Negro Ensemble Company, Theatre Four, New York City, 1980; (contributor) *Sophisticated Ladies,* Lunt-Fontanne Theatre, New York City, 1981; *Friends,* Billie Holiday Theatre, 1983; (book for musical) *Bojangles,* first produced in New York City, 1985; *Eyes of the American,* Negro Ensemble Company, Theatre Four, New York City, 1985, then Los Angeles Theatre Center, Los Angeles, 1986; "Eve of the Trial" in *Orchards,* the Acting Company, Lucille Lortel Theatre, New York City, 1986; *Cork,* Courtyard Theatre, New York City, 1986. Also *The Frost of Renaissance,* Theatre of Riverside Church, New York City; and *Kamilla, Sometime from Now,* and *Break of Day Arising,* all unproduced.

TELEVISION—Pilots: *Lenny's Neighborhood,* CBS. Episodic: "Kneeslappers," *With Ossie and Ruby,* PBS, 1980; "Solomon Northup's Odyssey" and "Charlotte Forten's Mission: Experiment in Freedom," *American Playhouse,* PBS, 1985; *Cagney and Lacey,* CBS, 1987; *Frank's Place,* CBS, 1987; *The New Mike Hammer,* CBS, 1987; "John Henry," *Shelley Duvall's Tall Tales and Legends,* Showtime, 1987. Specials: *Motown Returns to the Apollo,* NBC, 1986; (with others) *The Debbie Allen Special,* ABC, 1989. Also *Mackron,* 1975.

AWARDS: Audelco Recognition Award, Governor's Award from North Carolina, John Gassner Playwriting Award from the Outer Critics' Circle, Most Provocative New Play By an American, and Antoinette Perry Award nomination, Best Play, all 1980, for *Home;* Guggenheim fellowship for playwriting, 1981-82; National Endowment fellowship for playwriting, 1984.

MEMBER: Screen Actors Guild, Writers Guild of America, Dramatists Guild, Omega Psi Phi (1967—).*

*   *   *

WILLIAMS, Treat   1951-

PERSONAL: Full name, Richard Treat Williams; born December 1, 1951, in Stamford, CT; son of Richard Norman and Marion (Andrew) Williams; married Pamela Van Sant (a dancer and actress), June, 1988. EDUCATION—Franklin and Marshall College, B.A., 1973.

VOCATION: Actor.

CAREER: PRINCIPAL STAGE APPEARANCES—Danny Zuko, *Grease,* Royale Theatre, New York City, 1973; Utah, *Over Here,* Shubert Theatre, New York City, 1974; Bo Decker, *Bus Stop,* Equity Library Theatre, New York City, 1975; Jerry Hyland, *Once in a Lifetime,* Circle in the Square, New York City, 1978; ensemble, *Randy Newman's Maybe I'm Doing It Wrong* (revue), Production Company Theatre, New York City, 1981; Pirate King, *The Pirates of Penzance,* New York Shakespeare Festival, Minskoff Theatre, New York City, 1981; Hudley T. Singleton III, *Some Men Need Help,* 47th Street Theatre, New York City, 1982; Tom Wingfield, *The Glass Menagerie,* Long Wharf Theatre, New Haven, CT, 1986; Andrew Makepeace Ladd III, *Love Letters,* Promenade Theatre, New York City, 1989. Also appeared in *Claptrap,* American Repertory Theatre, Cambridge, MA, 1984; as Zeppo, *Picnic on the Battlefield;* Prince Hal, *Henry IV;* Sam

TREAT WILLIAMS

Jenkins, *Of Thee I Sing;* Lysander, *A Midsummer Night's Dream;* title role, *Captain Jinks of the Horse Marines;* Jack, *Charley's Aunt;* Nicholas and Alan, *Canterbury Tales;* Malvolio, *Twelfth Night;* Dick, *Play It Again, Sam;* and in *Servant of Two Masters.*

FILM DEBUT—Michael Brick, *The Ritz,* Warner Brothers, 1976. PRINCIPAL FILM APPEARANCES—Billings, *Deadly Hero,* AVCO-Embassy, 1976; Captain Harry Clark, *The Eagle Has Landed,* Columbia, 1976; Berger, *Hair,* United Artists, 1979; Sitarski, *1941,* Universal, 1979; Cletus, *Why Would I Lie?,* Metro-Goldwyn-Mayer/United Artists, 1980; Daniel Ciello, *Prince of the City,* Warner Brothers, 1981; Meade, *The Pursuit of D.B. Cooper,* Universal, 1981; Jimmy O'Donnell, *Once Upon a Time in America,* Warner Brothers, 1984; Ernie Wiatt, *Flashpoint,* Tri-Star, 1984; Arnold Friend, *Smooth Talk,* Spectrafilm, 1985; Terry, *The Men's Club,* Atlantic Releasing, 1986; Roger Mortis, *Dead Heat,* New World, 1988; Hoyt Cunningham, *The Heart of Dixie,* Orion/Rank Film Distributors, 1989; Peter, *Sweet Lies,* J&M Entertainment/Alexander Beck Enterprises, 1989. Also appeared in *Stangata napoletana—La trastola* (also known as *Something About the Sting*), RAI-TV Channel 1/Registi Tecnici Associati, 1983; *La notti degli squali* (also known as *Night of the Sharks*), VIP International, 1987; and in *Russicum* and *Napoli.*

PRINCIPAL TELEVISION APPEARANCES—Mini-Series: Drug Enforcement Agent Ray Carson, *Drug Wars: The Camarena Story,* NBC, 1990. Episodic: Prince Andrew, "The Little Mermaid," *Faerie Tale Theatre,* Showtime, 1984; also "Some Men Need Help," *American Playhouse,* PBS, 1985. Movies: Jack Dempsey, *Dempsey,* CBS, 1983; Stanley Kowalski, *A Streetcar Named*

Desire, ABC, 1984; title role, *J. Edgar Hoover*, Showtime, 1987; Deputy Attorney General Rick Guida, *Echoes in the Darkness*, CBS, 1987; Scott Weston, *Third Degree Burn*, HBO, 1989; Max Rosenberg, *Max and Helen*, TNT, 1990. Specials: *Happy Birthday, Hollywood*, ABC, 1987.

MEMBER: Actors' Equity Association, Screen Actors Guild, American Federation of Television and Radio Artists.

SIDELIGHTS: RECREATIONS—Airplane pilot.

ADDRESSES: AGENTS—Steve Starr, William Morris Agency, 1350 Avenue of the Americas, New York, NY 10019; Jay Julien, 1501 Broadway, New York, NY 10036.

*   *   *

WILLIAMSON, Nicol   1938-

PERSONAL: Born September 14, 1938, in Hamilton, Scotland; son of Hugh and Mary (Storrie) Williamson; married Jill Townsend (an actress), July 17, 1973 (divorced, 1977); children: one son. EDUCATION—Studied acting at the Birmingham School of Speech Training and Dramatic Art, 1953-56.

VOCATION: Actor and director.

CAREER: STAGE DEBUT—Dundee Repertory Theatre, Dundee, Scotland, 1960-61. LONDON DEBUT—I-ti, *That's Us*, Royal Court Theatre, 1961. BROADWAY DEBUT—Bill Maitland, *Inadmissible Evidence*, Belasco Theatre, 1965. PRINCIPAL STAGE APPEARANCES—I-ti, *That's Us*, Arts Theatre, Cambridge, U.K., 1961; Flute, *A Midsummer Night's Dream*, Malvolio, *Twelfth Night*, and man at the end, *Spring Awakening*, all Royal Court Theatre, London, 1962; S.A.C. Albert Meakin, *Nil Carborundum*, Satin, *The Lower Depths*, and Leantio, *Women, Beware Women*, all Royal Shakespeare Company (RSC), New Arts Theatre, London, 1962; Kelly, *Kelly's Eye*, Royal Court Theatre, 1963; Sebastian Dangerfield, *The Ginger Man*, Ashcroft Theatre, Croydon, U.K., then Royal Court Theatre, both 1963; Bill Maitland, *Inadmissible Evidence*, Peter Wykeham, *A Cuckoo in the Nest*, and Vladimir, *Waiting for Godot*, all Royal Court Theatre, 1964; Bill Maitland, *Inadmissible Evidence*, Wyndham's Theatre, London, 1965; Joe Johnson, *Miniatures*, Royal Court Theatre, 1965; Sweeney, *Sweeney Agonistes*, Globe Theatre, London, 1965; Alexei Ivanovitch Poprichtchine, *Diary of a Madman*, Duchess Theatre, London, 1967; Sam Nash, "Visitor from Mamaroneck," Jesse Kiplinger, "Visitor from Hollywood," and Roy Hubley, "Visitor from Forest Hills" in *Plaza Suite*, Plymouth Theatre, New York City, 1968; title role, *Hamlet*, Round House Theatre, London, then Lunt-Fontanne Theatre, New York City, both 1969.

Ivan Voinitsky, *Uncle Vanya*, Circle in the Square/Joseph E. Levine Theatre, New York City, 1973; *Nicol Williamson's Late Show* (one-man show), Eastside Playhouse, New York City, 1973; title role, *Coriolanus*, RSC, Aldwych Theatre, London, 1973; *Midwinter Spring* (one-man show), Aldwych Theatre, 1973; Malvolio, *Twelfth Night* and title role, *Macbeth*, both RSC, Stratford-on-Avon, U.K., 1974, then Aldwych Theatre, 1975; Ivan Voinitsky, *Uncle Vanya*, RSC, Other Place Theatre, Stratford-on-Avon, 1975; Henry VIII, *Rex*, Lunt-Fontanne Theatre, 1976; Bill Maitland, *Inadmissible Evidence*, Royal Court Theatre, 1978, then Roundabout Theatre, New York City, 1981; title role, *Macbeth*,

Circle in the Square, 1982; Archie Rice, *The Entertainer*, Roundabout Theatre, 1983; Henry Boot, *The Real Thing*, Plymouth Theatre, 1985.

PRINCIPAL STAGE WORK—Director, *Uncle Vanya*, Royal Shakespeare Company, Other Place Theatre, Stratford-on-Avon, U.K., 1975; director, *Macbeth*, Circle in the Square, 1982. Also director, *The Lark*, Edmonton, AB, Canada, 1983.

MAJOR TOURS—Black Will, *Arden of Faversham*, U.K. cities, 1961; title role, *Hamlet*, U.S. cities, 1969-70.

PRINCIPAL FILM APPEARANCES—O'Rourke, *The Bofors Gun*, Universal, 1968; Bill Maitland, *Inadmissible Evidence*, Paramount, 1968; title role, *Hamlet*, Columbia, 1969; Sir Edward More, *Laughter in the Dark*, Lopert, 1969; Michael Marler, *The Reckoning*, Columbia, 1971; Professor Lang, *The Jerusalem File*, Metro-Goldwyn-Mayer, 1972; Duke, *Le Moine* (also known as *The Monk*), Maya, 1973; Major Horn, *The Wilby Conspiracy*, United Artists, 1975; Little John, *Robin and Marian*, Columbia, 1976; Sherlock Holmes, *The Seven-Per-Cent Solution*, Universal, 1977; Oliver Fry, *The Goodbye Girl*, Warner Brothers, 1977; Colonel Schissel, *The Cheap Detective*, Columbia, 1978; Maurice Castle, *The Human Factor*, Metro-Goldwyn-Mayer/United Artists, 1979; Merlin, *Excalibur*, Warner Brothers, 1981; Derek Bauer, *I'm Dancing As Fast As I Can*, Paramount, 1982; Commander William Bulloch, *Venom*, Paramount, 1982; Dr. Worley and Nome King, *Return to Oz*, Buena Vista, 1985; William Macauley, *Black Widow*, Twentieth Century-Fox, 1987.

PRINCIPAL TELEVISION APPEARANCES—Mini-Series: Maertin de Vroome, *The Word*, CBS, 1978; King Ferdinand, *Christopher Columbus*, CBS, 1985; Louis Mountbatten, "Lord Mountbatten: The Last Viceroy," *Masterpiece Theatre*, PBS, 1986. Movies: Malyarov, *Sakharov*, HBO, 1984; Albert Coskins, *Passion Flower*, CBS, 1986. Specials: Lenny, *Of Mice and Men*, ABC, 1968; *The Tom Jones Special*, ABC, 1971; Richard M. Nixon, *I Know What I Meant*, Granada, 1974; title role, "Macbeth," *The Shakespeare Plays*, PBS, 1982; *Masterpiece Theatre: Fifteen Years*, PBS, 1986. Also appeared in title role, *Arturo Ui*, 1972; as Pierre, *War and Peace;* Warwick, *The Lark;* and in *Terrible Jim Fitch*.

RELATED CAREER—Performed in a one-man show at the White House, Washington, DC, 1970.

RECORDINGS: ALBUMS—*Nicol Williamson*, CBS, 1971.

AWARDS: Evening Standard Award, Best Actor, 1964, for *Inadmissible Evidence; Variety*-New York Drama Critics' Award and Antoinette Perry Award nomination, Best Actor in a Play, both 1966, for *Inadmissible Evidence; Evening Standard* Award, Best Actor, 1969, for *Hamlet;* Antoinette Perry Award nomination, Best Actor in a Play, 1974, for *Uncle Vanya*.

ADDRESSES: AGENTS—International Creative Management, 388 Oxford Street, London W1, England; Camden Artists, 2121 Avenue of the Stars, Suite 410, Los Angeles, CA 90067.*

WILLMAN, Noel   1918-1988

PERSONAL: Full name, Noel Bath Willman; born August 4, 1918, in Londonderry, Northern Ireland; died of a heart attack, December 24, 1988, in New York, NY; son of Romain and Charlotte Ellis (O'Neil) Willman. EDUCATION—Trained for the stage with Michel St. Denis at the London Theatre Studio.

VOCATION: Actor and director.

CAREER: STAGE DEBUT—*Hamlet,* Lyceum Theatre, London, 1939. BROADWAY DEBUT—Monsieur Henri, *Legend of Lovers,* Plymouth Theatre, 1951. PRINCIPAL STAGE APPEARANCES—Player, *The Beggar's Opera,* Haymarket Theatre, London, 1940; ensemble, *Light and Shade* (revue), Ambassadors' Theatre, London, 1942; Grigori Tansmann, *House of Regrets,* Arts Theatre, London, 1942; Lorenzo, *The Merchant of Venice,* New Theatre, London, 1943; Baron Foehn, *The Eagle Has Two Heads,* Lyric Hammersmith Theatre, London, 1946; Robert Falconbridge, *King John,* Antonio, *The Merchant of Venice,* Osric, *Hamlet,* Gremio, *The Taming of the Shrew,* and Pandarus, *Troilus and Cressida,* all Shakespeare Memorial Theatre, Stratford-on-Avon, U.K., 1948; Darius, *Adventure Story,* St. James's Theatre, London, 1949; Sir Joseph Wrathie, *Shall We Join the Ladies?* and Old Tawn, *The Boy with a Cart,* both Lyric Hammersmith Theatre, 1950; the Stylish Young Man and the Prison Chaplain, *The Trial,* Winter Garden Theatre, London, 1950; Daker, *Accolade,* Aldwych Theatre, London, 1950; Colonel Izquierdo, *Montserrat,* Lyric Hammersmith Theatre, 1952; the Interrogator, *The Prisoner,* Globe Theatre, London, 1954; Brack, *Hedda Gabler,* Westminster Theatre, London, 1954; General Burgoyne, *The Devil's Disciple,* Winter Garden Theatre, 1956; the Husband, *Roshomon,* Music Box Theatre, New York City, 1959; Don Pedro, *Much Ado About Nothing* and Claudius, *Hamlet,* both Royal Shakespeare Company, Stratford-on-Avon, U.K., 1961; Eugene Striden, *Isle of Children,* Cort Theatre, New York City, 1962; Peter Cauchon, *Saint Joan,* Oxford Festival, Oxford, U.K., 1974. Also appeared with the Old Vic Company, Playhouse Theatre, Liverpool, U.K., 1943-45; with the Bristol Old Vic Company, Bristol, U.K., 1946.

PRINCIPAL STAGE WORK—Director: *A Doll's House,* Winter Garden Theatre, London, 1946; *A Phoenix Too Frequent, Back to Methuselah,* and *The Turn of the Screw,* all Arts Theatre, London, 1946-47; (with Nigel Green) *Montserrat,* Lyric Hammersmith Theatre, London, 1952; *The White Carnation* and *Someone Waiting,* both Globe Theatre, London, 1953; *All's Well That Ends Well,* Shakespeare Memorial Theatre, Stratford-on-Avon, U.K., 1955; *The Devil's Disciple,* Winter Garden Theatre, 1956; *It's the Geography That Counts,* St. James's Theatre, London, 1957; *A Man for All Seasons,* Globe Theatre, 1960, then American National Theatre and Academy Theatre, New York City, 1961; *The Beauty Part,* Music Box Theatre, New York City, 1962; *Gentle Jack,* Queen's Theatre, London, 1963; *Rich Little Rich Girl,* Walnut Street Theatre, Philadephia, PA, 1964; *The Lion in Winter,* Ambassador Theatre, New York City, 1966; *Othello* and *Beware of the Dog,* both Nottingham Playhouse, Nottingham, U.K., 1967; *Brother and Sister* and *Beware of the Dog,* both St. Martin's Theatre, London, 1967; *Ring 'round the Moon,* Haymarket Theatre, London, 1968; *Darling of the Day,* George Abbott Theatre, New York City, 1968; *The Beheading,* Apollo Theatre, London, 1971; *The Three Arrows,* Actors' Company, New York City, 1972; *A Matter of Gravity,* Broadhurst Theatre, New York City, 1976; *The Apple Cart,* Shaw Festival, Niagara-on-the-Lake, ON, Canada, 1976; *The Inconstant Couple* and *Heartbreak House,* both Chichester Theatre Festival, Chichester, U.K., 1978; *The West Side Waltz,* Ethel

Barrymore Theatre, New York City, 1981. Also with the Old Vic Company, Playhouse Theatre, Liverpool, U.K., 1943-45.

MAJOR TOURS—Director, *Brother and Sister,* U.K. cities, 1967; director, *Lolita My Love,* U.S. cities, 1971; director, *The West Side Waltz,* U.S. cities, 1980-81; as an actor, toured in *The Witch* and *The Merchant of Venice,* Old Vic Company, U.K. cities, 1940; and toured South African cities, 1947.

PRINCIPAL FILM APPEARANCES—Spintho, *Androcles and the Lion,* RKO, 1952; Dr. Dennis Bord, *Project M7* (also known as *The Net*), Universal, 1953; Lord Byron, *Beau Brummell,* Metro-Goldwyn-Mayer (MGM), 1954; DuGueselin, *The Warriors* (also known as *The Dark Avenger*), Allied Artists, 1955; Woburn, *The Man Who Knew Too Much,* Paramount, 1956; Aubrey Clark, *Abandon Ship* (also know as *Seven Waves Away*), Columbia, 1957; Chief of Police, *Across the Bridge,* Rank/IPF, 1957; interrogator, *Carve Her Name with Pride,* Rank, 1958; Inspector Thomas, *Never Let Go,* Continental, 1960; Nigel Pickering, *Trouble in the Sky* (also known as *Cone of Silence*), Universal, 1961; prison governor, *The Concrete Jungle* (also known as *The Criminal*), Amalgamated, 1962; Webster, *The Girl on the Boat,* Knightsbridge, 1962; Dr. Ravna, *Kiss of Evil* (also known as *The Kiss of the Vampire*), Universal, 1963; Inspector Johnson, *Two Living, One Dead* (also known as *Tva le vande och en dod*), Emerson, 1964; Razin, *Doctor Zhivago,* MGM, 1965; Dr. Franklyn, *The Reptile,* Twentieth Century-Fox, 1966; Za-Tor (high priest), *The Vengeance of She* (also known as *The Return of She*), Twentieth Century-Fox, 1968; Franz Bayer, *The Odessa File,* Columbia, 1974; also *The Pickwick Papers,* Mayer Kingsley, 1952.

PRINCIPAL TELEVISION APPEARANCES—Episodic: "The Winslow Boy" and "The Count of Monte Cristo," *Dupont Show of the Month,* CBS, 1958. Movies: Interior Minister Bruno Merk, *Twenty-One Hours at Munich,* ABC, 1976. Specials: Pothinus, "Caesar and Cleopatra," *Hallmark Hall of Fame,* NBC, 1976. Also *The Royal Victorians,* 1974; *The Green Bay Tree, Strange Interlude, The Crucible,* and *Edward VII,* all for British television.

PRINCIPAL TELEVISION WORK—Director, *The Autumn Garden,* British television, 1966.

RELATED CAREER—Artistic director (with Beatrix Lehmann), Arts Theatre, London, 1946-47.

AWARDS: Clarence Derwent Award, 1955, for *The Prisoner;* Antoinette Perry Award, Best Director of a Play, 1962, for *A Man for All Seasons.*

OBITUARIES AND OTHER SOURCES: Variety, December 28, 1988-January 3, 1989.*

*   *   *

WILSON, Elizabeth   1921-

PERSONAL: Full name, Elizabeth Welter Wilson; born April 4, 1921, in Grand Rapids, MI; daughter of Henry Dunning (an insurance agent) and Marie Ethel (Welter) Wilson. EDUCATION—Attended Grand Rapids Junior College; studied for the stage at the Neighborhood Playhouse with Sanford Meisner, Martha Graham, and Harold Clurman.

ELIZABETH WILSON

VOCATION: Actress.

CAREER: STAGE DEBUT—Cape May Playhouse, Cape May, NJ, 1943. BROADWAY DEBUT—Christine Schoenwalder, *Picnic,* Music Box Theatre, 1953. PRINCIPAL STAGE APPEARANCES—Miss Warriner, *Desk Set,* Broadhurst Theatre, New York City, 1955; Mrs. McCracken, *The Tunnel of Love,* Royale Theatre, New York City, 1957; Hilda Rose, *Big Fish, Little Fish,* American National Theatre and Academy Theatre, New York City, 1961; Constance, *Yes Is for a Very Young Man,* Players Theatre, New York City, 1963; Liz Cantriss, *Rich Little Rich Girl,* Walnut Street Theatre, Philadelphia, PA, 1964; Mrs. Murray, *Eh?,* Circle in the Square, New York City, 1967; Marjorie Newquist, *Little Murders,* Circle in the Square, 1969; Martha Wilkins, *Sheep on the Runway,* Helen Hayes Theatre, New York City, 1970; Karen Nash, "Visitor from Mamaroneck," Muriel Tate, "Visitor from Hollywood," and Norma Hubley, "Visitor from Forest Hills" in *Plaza Suite,* Plymouth Theatre, New York City, 1970; Mrs. Shin, *The Good Woman of Setzuan,* Vivian Beaumont Theatre, New York City, 1970; Mrs. Summey, *Dark of the Moon,* Mercer-Shaw Arena Theatre, New York City, 1970; Harriet, *Sticks and Bones,* New York Shakespeare Festival (NYSF), Public Theatre, New York City, 1971, then John Golden Theatre, New York City, 1972; Helen Wild, *The Secret Affairs of Mildred Wild,* Ambassador Theatre, New York City, 1972; Sonya, *Uncle Vanya,* Joseph E. Levine Theatre, New York City, 1973; Mrs. Peachum, *The Threepenny Opera,* Vivian Beaumont Theatre, 1976; Lady Bracknell, *The Importance of Being Earnest,* Circle in the Square, 1977; Countess of Roussillon, *All's Well That Ends Well,* NYSF, Delacorte

Theatre, New York City, 1978; Aunt Helen, *Taken in Marriage,* NYSF, Public Theatre, 1979.

Aaronetta Gibbs, *Morning's at Seven,* Lyceum Theatre, New York City, 1980, then Center Theatre Group, Ahmanson Theatre, Los Angeles, 1981; Penelope "Penny" Sycamore, *You Can't Take It with You,* Paper Mill Playhouse, Millburn, NJ, 1982, then Plymouth Theatre, 1983; Enid, *Salonika,* NYSF, Public Theatre, 1985; Fay, *Anteroom,* Playwrights Horizons, New York City, 1985; Lilly Miller, *Ah, Wilderness!,* Neil Simon Theatre, New York City, 1988. Also appeared in summer theatre productions at the Nantucket Playhouse, Nantucket, MA, 1940; Barter Theatre, Abingdon, VA, 1946; and in *Plaza 9,* New York City.

FILM DEBUT—Christine Schoenwalder, *Picnic,* Columbia, 1956. PRINCIPAL FILM APPEARANCES—Marge Fleming, *Patterns* (also known as *Patterns of Power*), United Artists, 1956; secretary, *The Goddess,* Columbia, 1958; Miss McCracken, *The Tunnel of Love,* Metro-Goldwyn-Mayer (MGM), 1958; Millie, *Happy Anniversary,* United Artists, 1959; Jacky, *Too Hot to Handle* (also known as *Playgirl After Dark*), Topaz, 1961; Miss Fogarty, *A Child Is Waiting,* Warner Brothers, 1963; Mrs. Marsh, *Jenny* (also known as *And Jenny Makes Three*), Cinerama, 1969; Mrs. Braddock, *The Graduate,* Embassy, 1967; receptionist, *The Tiger Makes Out,* Columbia, 1967; mother, *Catch-22,* Paramount/Filmways, 1970; Mrs. Newquist, *Little Murders,* Twentieth Century-Fox, 1971; Mrs. Rome, *The Day of the Dolphin,* AVCO-Embassy, 1973; Dr. Anna Wilson, *Man on a Swing,* Paramount, 1974; Mrs. Gordon, *The Happy Hooker,* Cannon, 1975; Pauline, *The Prisoner of Second Avenue,* Warner Brothers, 1975; Roz, *Nine to Five,* Twentieth Century-Fox, 1980; Dr. Ruth Ruth, *The Incredible Shrinking Woman,* Universal, 1981; Emily Watkins, *The Ultimate Solution of Grace Quigley* (also known as *Grace Quigley*), Metro-Goldwyn-Mayer/United Artists/Cannon, 1984; Dorothy Prentiss, *Where Are the Children?,* Columbia, 1986; Kate Maslow, *The Believers,* Orion, 1987. Also appeared in *The Birds,* Universal, 1963.

PRINCIPAL TELEVISION APPEARANCES—Series: Frieda Hechlinger, *East Side/West Side,* CBS, 1963-64; Annie Bogert, *Doc,* CBS, 1975-76; Kathy Kelly, *Morningstar/Eveningstar,* CBS, 1986. Pilots: Ruth Weston, *Another April,* CBS, 1974; Mrs. Coyle, *The Easter Promise,* CBS, 1975; Mrs. Glidden, *Sanctuary of Fear,* NBC, 1979. Episodic: Marg, "Patterns," *Kraft Television Theatre,* NBC, 1955; Amelia, *All in the Family,* CBS, 1975. Movies: Kate Stanton, *Miles to Go Before I Sleep,* CBS, 1975; Sally Ephron, *Million Dollar Infield,* CBS, 1982; Judge Norma Soloman, *Once Upon a Family,* CBS, 1980; Lillie Wykowski, *Conspiracy of Love,* CBS, 1987; Berenice Bradshaw, *Nutcracker: Money, Madness, and Murder,* NBC, 1987. Specials: Edna, *Happy Endings,* ABC, 1975; also "Morning's at Seven," *Great Performances,* PBS.

AWARDS: Outer Critics' Circle Award (with cast), Best Ensemble Acting, 1961, for *Big Fish, Little Fish;* Antoinette Perry Award, Best Supporting or Featured Actress in a Drama, *Variety*-New York Drama Critics' Poll, Best Supporting Actress, and Obie Award from the *Village Voice,* Distinguished Performance, all 1972, for *Sticks and Bones;* Drama Desk Award, 1976, for *The Threepenny Opera;* Obie Award, 1979, for *Taken in Marriage.*

MEMBER: Actors' Equity Association, Screen Actors Guild, American Federation of Television and Radio Artists, American Guild of Variety Artists.

ADDRESSES: AGENT—STE Representation, 888 Seventh Avenue, New York, NY 10019.*

*   *   *

WILSON, Trey   1948-1989

PERSONAL: Born January 21, 1948, in Houston, TX; died of a cerebral hemorrhage, January 16, 1989, in New York, NY; wife's name, Judy; children: one stepson. EDUCATION—Attended the University of Houston.

VOCATION: Actor.

CAREER: BROADWAY DEBUT—Cecco, *Peter Pan,* Lunt-Fontanne Theatre, 1979. PRINCIPAL STAGE APPEARANCES—Various roles, *Tintypes,* American National Theatre and Academy, Theatre at St. Peter's Church, then John Golden Theatre, both New York City, 1980; Leo Durocher, *The First,* Martin Beck Theatre, New York City, 1981; Prince Carpenter, *Foxfire,* Ethel Barrymore Theatre, New York City, 1982; typesetter and various roles, *Personals,* Minetta Lane Theatre, New York City, 1985; Elmer Moffatt, *The Custom of the Country,* Second Stage Theatre, New York City, 1985; McCue, *The Front Page,* Vivian Beaumont Theatre, New York City, 1986; Hank Turner, *The Debutante Ball,* City Center Theatre Stage II, New York City, 1988.

PRINCIPAL FILM APPEARANCES—Gifford, *Drive-In,* Columbia, 1976; voice characterization, *Lord of the Rings* (also known as *J.R.R. Tolkein's The Lord of the Rings;* animated), United Artists, 1978; Texas voice, *Places in the Heart,* Tri-Star, 1984; Colonel Nivens, *A Soldier's Story,* Columbia, 1984; F.B.I. agent, *Marie,* Metro-Goldwyn-Mayer/United Artists, 1985; truck driver, *The Protector,* Warner Brothers, 1985; Lieutenant Murdoch, *F/X,* Orion, 1986; Nathan Arizona, Sr., *Raising Arizona,* Twentieth Century-Fox, 1987; Maxie Howell, *End of the Line,* Orion Classics, 1987; Skip, *Bull Durham,* Orion, 1988; Regional Director Franklin, *Married to the Mob,* Orion, 1988; Beetroot McKinley, *Twins,* Universal, 1988; Lieutenant Sloan, *The House on Carroll Street,* Orion, 1988; Benjamin Drapper, *Miss Firecracker,* Corsair, 1989; Colonel Barnes, *Welcome Home,* Columbia, 1989; Sam Phillips, *Great Balls of Fire!,* Orion, 1989. Also appeared in *The Vampire Hookers* (also known as *Sensuous Vampires* and *Cemetery Girls*), Capricorn Three, 1979; *The Believers,* Orion, 1987.

PRINCIPAL TELEVISION APPEARANCES—Series: Regular, *The News Is the News,* NBC, 1983; also Murray, *All My Children,* ABC. Mini-Series: Kenneth O'Donnell, *Kennedy,* NBC, 1983; Jimmy Hoffa, *Robert Kennedy and His Times,* CBS, 1985. Episodic: Jack Weller, *Spenser: For Hire,* ABC, 1986; Shumway, *The Equalizer,* CBS, 1986; Terry Vogel, *Spenser: For Hire,* ABC, 1987; Peter Marstand, *The Equalizer,* CBS, 1987; Sheriff Bo Cray, *Crime Story,* NBC, 1988; also *Legwork,* CBS, 1987; *Law and Order.* Movies: Lester, *A Few Days in Weasel Creek,* CBS, 1981; Paul Brown, *Scandal Sheet,* ABC, 1985. Specials: Shorty Rollins, "Daddy, I'm Their Mama Now," *ABC Afterschool Specials,* ABC, 1982.

RELATED CAREER—Appeared in a comedy act with Randy Quaid; actor in regional and summer theatre productions.

OBITUARIES AND OTHER SOURCES: [New York] *Daily News,* January 18, 1989; *Variety,* January 25-31, 1989.*

WINN, Kitty   1944-

PERSONAL: Born February 21, 1944, in Washington, DC. EDUCATION—Graduated from Boston University.

VOCATION: Actress.

CAREER: BROADWAY DEBUT—Irina Sergeyevna Prozorov, *The Three Sisters,* American National Theatre and Academy Theatre, 1969. PRINCIPAL STAGE APPEARANCES—Ophelia, *Hamlet,* New York Shakespeare Festival, Delacorte Theatre, New York City, 1972; Ophelia, *Hamlet,* Long Wharf Theatre, New Haven, CT, 1972; Ophelia, *Hamlet,* Center Theatre Group, Mark Taper Forum, Los Angeles, 1974; Jenny, *Knuckle,* Phoenix Sideshows, Playhouse II, New York City, 1975. Also appeared in *Ring 'round the Moon,* Center Theatre Group, Ahmanson Theatre, Los Angeles, 1975.

PRINCIPAL FILM APPEARANCES—Helen, *Panic in Needle Park,* Twentieth Century-Fox, 1971; Grace, *They Might Be Giants,* Universal, 1971; Sharon, *The Exorcist,* Warner Brothers, 1973; Mianne Prendergast, *Peeper* (also known as *Fat Chance*), Twentieth Century-Fox, 1975; Sharon Spencer, *Exorcist II: The Heretic,* Warner Brothers, 1977; Marianne, *Mirrors* (also known as *Marianne*), First American, 1984.

PRINCIPAL TELEVISION APPEARANCES—Series: Rosamond Lassiter, *Beacon Hill,* CBS, 1975. Episodic: Carla Magid, *Kojak,* CBS. Movies: Sara Dunning, *The House That Would Not Die,* ABC, 1970; Angela Canyon, *Man on a String,* CBS, 1972; Miranda Thatcher, *Message to My Daughter,* ABC, 1973; Maggie Stanton, *Miles to Go Before I Sleep,* CBS, 1975; Sister Beth, *Most Wanted,* ABC, 1976; Maeve Skeffington, *The Last Hurrah,* NBC, 1977.

RELATED CAREER—Company member, American Conservatory Theatre, San Francisco, CA, 1966-70.

AWARDS: Cannes Film Festival Award, Best Actress, 1971, for *Panic in Needle Park.*

ADDRESSES: AGENT—The Artists Agency, 10000 Santa Monica Boulevard, Suite 305, Los Angeles, CA 90067.*

*   *   *

WISEMAN, Fredrick   1930-

PERSONAL: Born January 1, 1930, in Boston, MA; son of Jacob Leo and Gertrude Leah (Kotzen) Wiseman; married Zipporah Batshaw, May 29, 1955; children: David, Eric. EDUCATION—Williams College, B.A., 1951; Yale University School of Law, L.L.B., 1954. MILITARY—U.S. Army, 1955-56.

VOCATION: Producer, director, and film editor.

CAREER: PRINCIPAL STAGE WORK—Producer and director of video sequences, *Tonight We Improvise,* American Repertory Theatre, Cambridge, MA, 1986.

PRINCIPAL FILM WORK—All as producer, director, and editor of documentaries, unless indicated: Producer (with Shirley Clarke), *The Cool World,* Cinema V, 1963; *Welfare,* The Other Cinema/Zipporah, 1975; *Manoeuvre* (also known as *Maneuver*), Zipporah,

1979; (also sound recording mixer) *Model,* Cinegate/Zipporah, 1981; *The Store,* Zipporah, 1983; (also sound) *Missile,* Zipporah, 1987; also *Titicut Follies,* 1967; *High School,* 1968; *Basic Training,* 1971; *Essene,* 1972; *Juvenile Court,* 1973; *Primate,* 1974; *Sinai Field Mission,* 1978; *Seraphita's Diary,* 1982; (also sound) *Racetrack,* 1985.

PRINCIPAL TELEVISION WORK—All as producer, director, and editor of documentaries. Specials: *Meat,* PBS, 1976; *Canal Zone,* PBS, 1977; *Welfare,* PBS, 1978; (also sound) *Blind* (also known as *Blind and Deaf—Part I* and *Deaf and Blind—Part I*), PBS, 1987; (also sound) *Deaf* (also known as *Blind and Deaf—Part II* and *Deaf and Blind—Part II*), PBS, 1988; (also sound) *Adjustment and Work* (also known as *Blind and Deaf—Part III* and *Deaf and Blind—Part III*), PBS, 1988; (also sound) *Multi-Handicapped* (also known as *Blind and Deaf—Part IV* and *Deaf and Blind—Part IV*), PBS, 1988; (also sound) *Near Death,* PBS, 1990; also *Law and Order,* 1969; *Hospital,* 1970.

RELATED CAREER—Founder, Zipporah Films, Cambridge, MA, 1970—.

NON-RELATED CAREER—Lawyer, Paris, France, 1956-58; lecturer in law, Boston University Law School, Boston, MA, 1958-61; research associate in the department of sociology, Brandeis University, Waltham, MA, 1962-66; also visiting lecturer at numerous universities.

AWARDS: Russell Sage Foundation Fellowship from Harvard University, 1961-62; Emmy Award, Outstanding News Documentary Progam, 1969, for *Law and Order;* Emmy Award, Outstanding Achievement in News Documentary Programming, 1970, for *Hospital;* Gabriel Award for Personal Achievement from the Catholic Broadcasters' Association, 1975; Guggenheim Foundation Fellowship, 1980-81; MacArthur Prize, 1982-87. HONORARY DEGREES—University of Cincinnati, L.H.D., 1973; Williams College, L.H.D., 1976.

MEMBER: Massachusetts Bar Association, 1955—; Organization for Social and Technological Innovation (treasurer, 1966-70).

OTHER SOURCES: Contemporary Literary Criticism, Vol. 20, Gale, 1982.

ADDRESSES: OFFICE—1 Richdale Avenue, Unit Four, Cambridge, MA 02140.*

*　　*　　*

WOOLAND, Norman   1905-1989

PERSONAL: Born March 16, 1905, in Dusseldorf, Germany; died April 3, 1989, in Staplehurst, England; married Jane Smith; children: two daughters.

VOCATION: Actor.

CAREER: STAGE DEBUT—Lorenzo, *The Merchant of Venice,* Grand Theatre, Oldham, U.K., 1926. LONDON DEBUT—*Night Club Queen,* Playhouse Theatre, 1937. BROADWAY DEBUT—Gerald, *Time and the Conways,* Ritz Theatre, 1938. PRINCIPAL STAGE APPEARANCES—Mr. Sheltie, *What Say They?,* Malvern Festival, Malvern, U.K., 1939; Robert Murrison, *Cornelius,* West-

minster Theatre, London, 1940; Aubrey Tanqueray, *The Second Mrs. Tanqueray,* Haymarket Theatre, London, 1950; Enobarbus, *Antony and Cleopatra,* St. James's Theatre, London, 1951; Matthew, *Dragon's Mouth,* Winter Garden Theatre, London, 1952; Mr. Fielding, *A Passage to India,* Comedy Theatre, London, 1960; Sergeant Ruff, *Gaslight,* Playhouse Theatre, Oxford, U.K., 1967; Dr. Stockman, *An Enemy of the People,* Playhouse Theatre, Oxford, 1968; Haakon Werle, *The Wild Duck,* Criterion Theatre, London, 1970; the Father, *Six Characters in Search of an Author,* Yvonne Arnaud Theatre, Guildford, U.K., 1972; Max Weiner, *A Touch of Purple,* Globe Theatre, London, 1972; Bob Cherry, *Flowering Cherry,* Yvonne Arnaud Theatre, 1973; the Father, *A Voyage 'round My Father,* Everyman Theatre, Cheltenham, U.K., 1973; Wilson, *The Butcher,* Belgrade Studio Theatre, Coventry, U.K., 1973; George, *Jumpers,* Birmingham Repertory Theatre, Birmingham, U.K., 1975; Captain Shotover, *Heartbreak House,* Harrogate Festival, Harrogate, U.K., 1976. Also appeared in *Hadrian VII,* Haymarket Theatre, 1969; in repertory at the Shakespeare Memorial Theatre, Stratford-on-Avon, U.K., 1933-37; and at the Malvern Festival, 1938.

MAJOR TOURS—Thomas More, *A Man for All Seasons,* U.K. cities, 1971; Colonel Strang, *Conduct Unbecoming,* U.K. cities, 1972; Gilles de Rais, *Abelard and Heloise,* U.K. cities, 1973; Sergeant Rough, *Gaslight,* U.K. cities, 1974; Mr. Bennet, *Pride and Prejudice,* U.K. cities, 1975; Frank Strang, *Equus,* U.K. cities, 1976; Don Jerome, *The Duenna,* U.K. cities, 1977; Sir Cecil, *The Kingfisher,* U.K. cities, 1978; Old Ekdal, *The Wild Duck,* U.K. cities, 1979.

PRINCIPAL FILM APPEARANCES—Lodge keeper, *The Five Pound Man,* Fox British, 1937; Parson, *Escape,* Twentieth Century-Fox, 1948; Horatio, *Hamlet,* General Film Distributors, 1948; Ashley Morehouse, *Look Before You Love,* General Film Distributors, 1948; Nat Hearn, *All Over the Town,* General Film Distributors, 1949; Prince Rudolph, *The Angel with the Trumpet,* British Lion, 1950; William Minnoch, *Madeleine* (also known as *The Strange Case of Madeline*), Universal, 1950; Nerva, *Quo Vadis,* Metro-Goldwyn-Mayer (MGM), 1951; King Richard, *Ivanhoe,* MGM, 1952; Bill Ogden, *Background* (also known as *Edge of Divorce*), Group 3, 1953; Inspector Bliss, *The Ringer,* Regent, 1953; Paris, *Romeo and Juliet,* United Artists, 1954; Colonel Cleaver, *The Master Plan,* Grand National, 1955; Pelton, *Guilty?,* Gibraltar, 1956; Catesby, *Richard III,* Lopert, 1956; Inspector Kingcombe, *The Flesh Is Weak,* Eros, 1957; Inspector Harris, *No Road Back,* RKO, 1957; May Crowley, *The Bandit of Zhobe,* Columbia, 1959; Brutus Smith, *An Honourable Murder,* Warner Brothers/Pathe, 1959; Hugh Manning, *Teenage Bad Girl* (also known as *My Teenage Daughter* and *Bad Girl*), DCA, 1959; Roy Lewis, *Night Train for Inverness,* Paramount, 1960; group captain, *The Guns of Navarone,* Columbia, 1961; David Fraser, *Portrait of a Sinner* (also known as *The Rough and the Smooth*), American International, 1961; Rufio, *Barabbas,* Columbia, 1962; Virgilianus, *The Fall of the Roman Empire,* Paramount, 1964; Sir John Perrott, *The Fighting Prince of Donegal,* Buena Vista, 1966; Crown counsel, *Walk in the Shadow* (also known as *Life for Ruth*), Continental Distributing, 1966; Dr. Blanchard, *The Projected Man,* Universal, 1967; King Saul, *Saul and David,* Rizzoli, 1968; team doctor, *International Velvet,* Metro-Goldwyn-Mayer/United Artists, 1978. Also appeared in *This England* (also known as *Our Heritage*), World, 1941; *The Mirror Crack'd,* Associated Film Distribution, 1980.

PRINCIPAL TELEVISION APPEARANCES—Mini-Series: Simon, *Cover Her Face,* Anglia Television, then *Mystery!,* PBS, 1987.

Also appeared in *All for Love, Diamonds, Life at Stake,* and *The Chief Mourner,* all British television.

RELATED CAREER—Staff announcer and compere, BBC Radio, 1941-46.

OBITUARIES AND OTHER SOURCES: Variety, April 12-18, 1989.*

*　　*　　*

WOOLDRIDGE, Susan

PERSONAL: Born in London, England; daughter of John De Lacy (a composer and conductor) and Margaretta (an actress; maiden name, Scott) Wooldridge. EDUCATION—Studied acting at the Central School of Speech and Drama and attended the Ecole Jacques Lecoq.

VOCATION: Actress.

CAREER: STAGE DEBUT—*Peer Gynt,* Crucible Theatre Company, Sheffield, U.K., 1971. PRINCIPAL STAGE APPEARANCES—Margaret More, *A Man for All Seasons,* Crucible Theatre Company, Sheffield, U.K., then Bankside Globe Theatre, London, both 1972; Alison Porter, *Look Back in Anger,* Young Vic Theatre, London, 1979; Jessie Cates, *'night Mother,* Hampstead Theatre Club, London, 1985; also appeared in productions of *Macbeth, The*

SUSAN WOOLDRIDGE

School for Scandal, The Merchant of Venice, and *The Cherry Orchard.*

PRINCIPAL STAGE WORK—Assistant stage manager, *Peer Gynt,* Crucible Theatre Company, Sheffield, U.K., 1971.

PRINCIPAL FILM APPEARANCES—Harriet, *The Shout,* Films Inc., 1978; Lily Sutton, *Loyalties,* Norstar, 1986; Molly, *Hope and Glory,* Columbia, 1987; Monica, *How to Get Ahead in Advertising,* Warner Brothers, 1988; Lady Wilson, *Bye Bye Blues,* Festival/ Image Organization, 1989. Also appeared in *Butley,* American Film Theatre, 1974.

PRINCIPAL TELEVISION APPEARANCES—Mini-Series: Daphne Manners, *The Jewel in the Crown,* Granada, then *Masterpiece Theatre,* PBS, 1984; Kathleen Scott, *The Last Place on Earth,* Central Television, then *Masterpiece Theatre,* PBS, 1985. Episodic: Ann Biddle, *A Fine Romance,* ABC, 1989; also *Bergerac,* BBC-1, 1990. Movies: Amanda Brewis, *Agatha Christie's "Dead Man's Folly"* (also known as *Dead Man's Folly*), CBS, 1986; also *Changing Step,* 1989; *Pied Piper,* 1989; *Crimestrike,* 1989. Specials: *Masterpiece Theatre: Fifteen Years,* PBS, 1986. Also appeared in *Hay Fever,* 1983; *Time and the Conways,* 1984; *Frankenstein,* 1985; *The Dark Room,* 1987; *The Naked Civil Servant, John McNab, The Racing Game, The Devil's Disciple, Pastoralcare,* and *The Small Assassin.*

AWARDS: British Academy of Film and Television Arts Award nomination, Best Actress, and Alva Award, Best Actress, both 1984, for *The Jewel in the Crown;* British Academy of Film and Television Arts Award, Best Supporting Actress, 1987, for *Hope and Glory.*

ADDRESSES: AGENTS—Markham and Froggatt Ltd., 4 Windmill Street, London W1, England; International Creative Management, 8899 Beverly Boulevard, Los Angeles, CA 90048 and 40 W. 57th Street, New York, NY 10019.

*　　*　　*

WORONOV, Mary   1946-

PERSONAL: Born December 8, 1943, in Brooklyn, NY; daughter of Victor D. (a doctor) and Carol (Eschholz) Woronov; married Ted Gershuny (a bond broker), 1969 (marriage ended); married Ted Whitehead (a race car driver and agent), 1979. EDUCATION—Graduated from Cornell University.

VOCATION: Actress.

CAREER: OFF-BROADWAY DEBUT—*Kitchenette,* 1968. PRINCIPAL STAGE APPEARANCES—Gloria Jean Kojax, *Women Behind Bars,* New York Theatre Ensemble, New York City, 1974; Susan, *Boom Boom Room,* New York Shakespeare Festival, Vivian Beaumont Theatre, New York City, 1974. Also appeared in *Queen of Greece,* La Mama Experimental Theatre Club, New York City, 1969; *Vynil,* Cafe Chino, New York City; *Clearing House* and *Two Noble Kinsmen,* both in New York City.

FILM DEBUT—*The Chelsea Girls,* Filmmakers' Distribution Center, 1967. PRINCIPAL FILM APPEARANCES—Mary, *Kemek,* GHM, 1970; Mikki, *Seizure,* American International, 1974; Diane, *Silent Night, Bloody Night* (also known as *Night of the Dark Full Moon*

MARY WORONOV

APPEARANCES—Episodic: Irene, *Logan's Run*, CBS, 1977; Brady, *Murder, She Wrote*, CBS, 1985; Dr. Von Furst, *Knight Rider*, NBC, 1985; nurse, *Amazing Stories*, NBC, 1986; Bean Sweeney, *Shell Game*, CBS, 1987; Dr. Flynn, *You Again?*, NBC, 1987; Jill Taylor, *Sledge Hammer!*, ABC, 1987; Officer Burdette, *Trial and Error*, CBS, 1988; also *Taxi*, ABC, 1979; *Buck Rogers in the 25th Century*, NBC, 1980. Movies: Bartender, *In the Glitter Palace*, NBC, 1977; Mary Garritee, *Challenge of a Lifetime*, ABC, 1985; Miss Renfro, *A Bunny's Tale*, ABC, 1985. Specials: *Cheech and Chong: Get Out of My Room*, Showtime, 1985; governess, *The Princess Who Had Never Laughed*, Showtime, 1986.

NON-RELATED CAREER—Painter.

AWARDS: Theatre World Award, 1974, for *Boom Boom Room*.

SIDELIGHTS: Mary Woronov told *CTFT*, "As an artist, I considered it interesting to be used as an object. This developed into a life-long love of acting as an expression."

ADDRESSES: AGENT—Progressive Artists Agency, 400 S. Beverly Drive, Suite 216, Beverly Hills, CA 90212.

*   *   *

and *Death House*), Cannon, 1974; Calamity Jane, *Death Race 2000*, New World, 1975; Sandy, *Cannonball* (also known as *Car Quake*), New World, 1976; Mary McQueen, *Hollywood Boulevard*, New World, 1976; Pearl, *Jackson County Jail*, New World, 1976; actress, *Mr. Billion*, Twentieth Century-Fox, 1977; Arlene, *The One and Only*, Paramount, 1978; woman bankrobber, *The Lady in Red* (also known as *Guns, Sin, and Bathtub Gin*), New World, 1979; Evelyn Togar, *Rock 'n' Roll High School*, New World, 1979.

Samantha Vitesse, *The Protectors, Book I* (also known as *Angel of H.E.A.T.*), Studios Pan Imago, 1981; party house owner, *Heartbeeps*, Universal, 1981; secretary, "Success Goes to the Movies" in *National Lampoon Goes to the Movies*, Metro-Goldwyn-Mayer/United Artists, 1981; Mary Bland, *Eating Raoul*, Twentieth Century-Fox, 1982; Violetta, *Get Crazy*, Embassy, 1983; Audrey, *Night of the Comet*, Atlantic, 1984; Dr. Fletcher, *Hellhole*, Arkoff, 1985; Dancing Mary, *Nomads*, PSO, 1985; Mary Bland, *Chopping Mall* (also known as *Killbots* and *R.O.B.O.T.*), Concorde, 1986; Raquel Putterman, *TerrorVision*, Empire, 1986; Shelley, *Black Widow*, Twentieth Century-Fox, 1987; Shelley, *Mortuary Academy*, Skouras, 1988; channeller, *Warlock*, J&M Entertainment, 1989; Quinella, *Let It Ride*, Paramount, 1989; Lisabeth Hepburn-Saravian, *Scenes from the Class Struggle in Beverly Hills*, Rank Film Distributors/Cinecom Entertainment Group, 1989. Also appeared in *Sugar Cookies*, General Film, 1973; *Cover Girl Models*, New World, 1975; *Bad Georgia Road*, Dimension, 1977; *My Man Adam*, Tri-Star, 1985; *Movie House Massacre*, Movie House, 1986.

TELEVISION DEBUT—*Somerset*, NBC. PRINCIPAL TELEVISION

WRAY, Fay   1907-

PERSONAL: Born September 10 (some sources say September 15), 1907, in Alberta, Canada; married John Monk Saunders (a playwright and screenwriter), 1928 (divorced, 1939); married Robert Riskin (a screenwriter), August 23, 1942 (died, September 20, 1955); children: Susan, Robert, Victoria (second marriage).

VOCATION: Actress.

CAREER: FILM DEBUT—*Gasoline Love*, 1923. PRINCIPAL FILM APPEARANCES—Beth Slocum, *The Coast Patrol*, Bud Barsky Corporation, 1925; Lila Rogers, *Lazy Lightning*, Universal, 1926; Pauline Stewart, *The Man in the Saddle*, Universal, 1926; Jessie Hayden, *The Wild Horse Stampede*, Universal, 1926; Molly Vernon, *Loco Luck*, Universal, 1927; Roberts, *A One Man Game*, Universal, 1927; Mildred Orth, *Spurs and Saddles*, Universal, 1927; Mitzi Schrammell, *The Wedding March*, Paramount, 1927; Christine Charteris, *Legion of the Condemned*, Paramount, 1928; Anna Lee, *The First Kiss*, Paramount, 1928; Elizabeth, *The Street of Sin*, Paramount, 1928; Ethne Eustace, *The Four Feathers*, Paramount, 1929; Mary ("Ritzy"), *Thunderbolt*, Paramount, 1929.

Marie, *Behind the Makeup*, Paramount, 1930; Joan Randall, *The Border Legion*, Paramount, 1930; as herself, *Paramount on Parade*, Paramount, 1930; Lora Nixon, *Pointed Heels*, Paramount, 1930; Daisy, *The Sea God*, Paramount, 1930; Consuelo, *The Texan*, Paramount, 1930; Joisie Lockhart, *The Conquering Horde*, Paramount, 1931; Kay Roberts, *The Lawyer's Secret*, Paramount, 1931; Helen, *Dirigible*, Columbia, 1931; Lee Carlton, *Three Rogues* (also known as *Not Exactly Gentlemen*), Twentieth Century-Fox, 1931; Camille de Jonghe, *The Unholy Garden*, United Artists, 1931; Ynez Dominguez, *Captain Thunder*, Warner Brothers, 1931; Marcia Collins, *The Finger Points*, Warner Brothers, 1931; Joan, *Doctor X*, Warner Brothers, 1932; Eve Trowbridge, *The Most Dangerous Game* (also known as *The Hounds of Zaroff*), RKO, 1932; Ann Darrow, *King Kong*, RKO, 1932; Ann Carver, *Ann Carver's Profession*, Columbia, 1933; Diane Templeton, *Below the Sea*, Columbia, 1933; Cynthia Glennon, *The Big Brain* (also known as *Enemies of Society*), RKO, 1933; Virginia Brush, *One Sunday Afternoon*, Warner Brothers, 1933; Lucy Calhoun, *The Bowery*, Twentieth Century-Fox, 1933; Kay Walling, *Master of Men*, Columbia, 1933; Charlotte Duncan, *The Mystery of the Wax Museum*, Warner Brothers, 1933; Wildeth Christie, *Shanghai Madness*, Twentieth Century, 1933; Ruth Bertin, *The Vampire Bat*, Majestic, 1933; Voila Corew, *The Woman I Stole*, Columbia, 1933; Angela, *The Affairs of Cellini*, United Artists, 1934; Gail, *Black Moon*, Columbia, 1934; Nan Brockton, *Cheating Cheaters*, Universal, 1934; Janet, *The Countess of Monte Cristo*, Universal, 1934; Maria, *Madame Spy*, Universal, 1934; Head Nurse Fanshawe, *Once to Every Woman*, Columbia, 1934; Sylvia Vernon, *The Richest Girl in the World*, RKO, 1934; Teresa, *Viva Villa*, Metro-Goldwyn-Mayer (MGM), 1934; Louise Lorimer, *Woman in the Dark*, RKO, 1934.

Ann Manders, *Alias Bull Dog Drummond* (also known as *Bull Dog Jack*), Gaumont, 1935; Rene, *The Clairvoyant* (also known as *Evil Mind*), Twentieth Century-Fox, 1935; Hild, *Come Out of the Pantry*, United Artists, 1935; Jean, *Mills of the God*, Columbia, 1935; Joan Mitchell, *White Lies*, Columbia, 1935; Joyce, *Roaming Lady*, Columbia, 1936; Mary, *They Met in a Taxi*, Columbia, 1936; Lady Rowena, *When Kinghts Were Bold*, Capital Films, 1936, released in the United States by Fine Arts, 1942; Gloria, *It Happened in Hollywood*, Columbia, 1937; Kay Cabot, *Murder in Greenwich Village*, Columbia, 1937; Linda Ware, *The Jury's Secret*, Universal, 1938; Carol, *Navy Secrets*, Monogram, 1939; Eleanor Dunlap, *Smashing the Spy Ring*, Columbia, 1939; Ted Dawson, *Wildcat Bus*, RKO, 1940; Molly, *Adam Had Four Sons*, Columbia, 1941; Mary Stanley, *Melody for Three*, RKO, 1941; Mrs. Gordon Kimbell, *Small Town Girl*, MGM, 1953; Marquise, *Treasure of the Golden Condor*, Twentieth Century-Fox, 1953; Edna Devanal, *The Cobweb*, MGM, 1955; Sue McKinnon, *Queen Bee*, Columbia, 1955; Kay Stanley, *Hell on Frisco Bay* (also known as *The Darkest Hour*), Warner Brothers, 1956; Beth Daley, *Rock, Pretty Baby*, Universal, 1956; Alice Pope, *Crime of Passion*, United Artists, 1957; Mrs. Brent, *Tammy and the Bachelor* (also known as *Tammy*), Universal, 1957; Mrs. Martin, *Dragstrip Riot*, American International, 1958; Beth Daley, *Summer Love*, Universal, 1958. Also appeared in *Stowaway*, Universal, 1932; *The Captain Hates the Sea*, Columbia, 1934; *Once a Hero*, 1937; *Not a Ladies' Man*, 1942; and *Out of Time*.

PRINCIPAL TELEVISION APPEARANCES—Series: Catherine Morrison, *The Pride of the Family*, ABC, 1953-54. Pilots: Mary Parker, *It's Always Sunday* (broadcast as an episode of *Screen Directors Playhouse*), NBC, 1956. Episodic: *The David Niven Theater*, NBC, 1959; also *Damon Runyon Theater*, CBS; *The General Electric Theater*, CBS; *Jane Wyman Presents the Fireside Theater*, NBC; *Playhouse 90*, CBS; *Perry Mason*, CBS; *Alfred Hitchcock Presents*; *Kraft Television Theater*. Movies: Edna Curtis, *Gideon's Trumpet*, CBS, 1980.

WRITINGS: FILM—(With Sinclair Lewis and Wanda Tuchock) *This Is the Life*, Universal, 1944. OTHER—*On the Other Hand: A Life Story* (autobiography), St. Martin's Press, 1989.*

WRIGHT, Max   1943-

PERSONAL: Born August 2, 1943, in Detroit, MI; son of George Herman Wright; wife's name, Linda; children: Ben, Daisy. EDUCATION—Attended Wabash College and Wayne State University; studied drama at the National Theatre School, Montreal, PQ, Canada.

VOCATION: Actor.

CAREER: BROADWAY DEBUT—Mr. Coates, *The Great White Hope*, Alvin Theatre, 1968. PRINCIPAL STAGE APPEARANCES—Murderer, *Public Prosecutor Is Sick of It All*, Arena Stage, Washington, DC, 1972; Parker, *The Basic Training of Pavlo Hummel*, Longacre Theatre, New York City, 1977; Yepikhodor/Semyon Panteleyevich, *The Cherry Orchard*, New York Shakespeare Festival (NYSF), Vivian Beaumont Theatre, New York City, 1977; Lawrence Vail, *Once in a Lifetime*, Circle in the Square, New York City, 1978; second murderer, *Richard III*, Cort Theatre, New York City, 1979; Ivan Alexandrovich Khlestakov, *The Inspector General*, American Repertory Theatre, Cambridge, MA, then Circle in the Square, both 1979; Leo, *Lunch Hour*, Ethel Barrymore Theatre, New York City, 1980; Owen Glendower, *Henry IV, Part One*, NYSF, Delacorte Theatre, New York City, 1981; Man #2, *For No Good Reason*, Samuel Beckett Theatre, then Harold Clurman Theatre, both New York City, 1985. Also appeared in *Tom* and *Inherit the Wind*, both Arena Stage, 1973-74; *Long Day's Journey into Night*, Arena Stage, 1975; *The Recruiting Officer*, Long Wharf Theatre, New Haven, CT, 1977; *The Ghost Sonata* and *Terra Nova*, both Yale Repertory Theatre, New Haven, CT, 1977; *Stages*, Belasco Theatre, New York City, 1978; *A Midsummer Night's Dream* and *Happy End*, both American Repertory Theatre, 1979; *The Front Page*, Long Wharf Theatre, 1981.

PRINCIPAL FILM APPEARANCES—Joshua Benn, *All That Jazz*, Twentieth Century-Fox, 1979; commuter, *Last Embrace*, United Artists, 1979; Hundertwasser, *Simon*, Orion, 1980; Floyd Dell, *Reds*, Paramount, 1981; floor manager, *The Sting II*, Universal, 1983; Lester, *Touch and Go*, Tri-Star, 1986.

PRINCIPAL TELEVISION APPEARANCES—Series: Karl Shub, *Buffalo Bill*, NBC, 1983-84; Richard Stetmeyer, *Misfits of Science*, ABC, 1985-86; Willie Tanner, *ALF*, NBC, 1986—. Mini-Series: Scientist, *James A. Michener's "Space,"* CBS, 1985. Pilots: Mr. Bundle, *Tales from the Dark Side*, syndicated, 1983; Jimbo, *I Gave at the Office*, NBC, 1984; Leon Pakulski, *The Faculty*, ABC, 1986. Episodic: *Taxi*. Movies: Dr. Mengele, *Playing for Time*, CBS, 1980; second director, *For Ladies Only*, NBC, 1981; Dr. Boone, *Dangerous Company*, CBS, 1982; Stan Clark, *Scandal Sheet*, ABC, 1985; Alexandre Gustave Eiffel, *Liberty*, NBC, 1986; Howard Haldan, *Going to the Chapel*, NBC, 1988. Specials: Judge Rhodes, *You Are the Jury*, NBC, 1978.

RELATED CAREER—Company member: Arena Stage, Washington, DC, 1969-70; Actors Theatre of Louisville, Louisville, KY, 1969-70 and 1971-72; and Tyrone Guthrie Theatre, Minneapolis, MN, 1970-72.

AWARDS: Theatre World Award, 1978-79, for *Once in a Lifetime*.

SIDELIGHTS: RECREATIONS—Gardening.*

WYNN, Tracy Keenan   1945-

PERSONAL: Born February 28, 1945, in Hollywood, CA; son of Keenan (an actor) and Eve (Abbott) Wynn; married Kerstin Wassgren, 1976; children: Aidan, Amanda, Brendan. EDUCATION—University of California, Los Angeles, B.A., 1967. RELIGION—Episcopalian. MILITARY—U.S. Air Force Reserve.

VOCATION: Screenwriter and producer.

CAREER: Also see *WRITINGS* below. PRINCIPAL FILM APPEARANCES—Soldier in truck, *Up from the Beach*, Twentieth Century-Fox, 1965.

PRINCIPAL TELEVISION WORK—Movies: Associate producer, *Tribes*, ABC, 1970; director, *Hit Lady*, ABC, 1974; co-producer, *In the Line of Duty: The F.B.I. Murders* (also known as *Bloody Friday* and *The F.B.I. Murders*), NBC, 1988; co-producer, *The Revenge of Al Capone* (also known as *Capone in Jail* and *Al Capone in Jail*), NBC, 1989.

RELATED CAREER—Screenwriting instructor.

WRITINGS: FILM—*The Longest Yard*, Paramount, 1974; (with Lorenzo Semple, Jr. and Walter Hill) *The Drowning Pool*, Warner Brothers, 1975; (with Peter Benchley) *The Deep*, Columbia, 1977. TELEVISION—Pilots: *The Quest*, NBC, 1976. Movies: (With Marvin Schwartz) *Tribes*, ABC, 1970; *Truman Capote's "The Glass House,"* CBS, 1972; *The Autobiography of Miss Jane Pittman*, CBS, 1974; *In the Line of Duty: The F.B.I. Murders* (also known as *Bloody Friday* and *The F.B.I. Murders*), NBC, 1988; *The Revenge of Al Capone* (also known as *Capone in Jail* and *Al Capone in Jail*), NBC, 1989.

AWARDS: Writers Guild Award, 1970, and Emmy Award, Outstanding Writing Achievement in Drama, Original Teleplay (Special), 1971, both for *Tribes;* Emmy Award nomination, 1972, for *Truman Capote's "The Glass House,";* Emmy Award, Best Writing in a Drama Adaptation (Single Program—Comedy or Drama), and Writers Guild Award, both 1974, for *The Autobiography of Miss Jane Pittman.*

MEMBER: Writers Guild of America, Directors Guild of America.

ADDRESSES: AGENT—Bill Haber, Creative Artists Agency, 9830 Wilshire Boulevard, Beverly Hills, CA 90212.*

Y

YABLANS, Frank   1935-

PERSONAL: Born August 27, 1935, in New York, NY; son of Morris and Annette Yablans; married Ruth Edelstein, December 21; children: Robert, Sharon, Edward. EDUCATION—Attended the City College of New York and the University of Wisconsin. MILITARY—U.S. Army, 1954-56.

VOCATION: Producer, screenwriter, and motion picture executive.

CAREER: Also see *WRITINGS* below. PRINCIPAL FILM APPEAR-ANCES—Goon on radio, *The Fury,* Twentieth Century-Fox, 1978. PRINCIPAL FILM WORK—All as producer, unless indicated: Executive producer, *Silver Streak,* Twentieth Century-Fox, 1976; *The Other Side of Midnight,* Twentieth Century-Fox, 1977; *The Fury,* Twentieth Century-Fox, 1978; *North Dallas Forty,* Paramount, 1979; *Mommie Dearest,* Paramount, 1981; (with David Niven, Jr.) *Monsignor,* Twentieth Century-Fox, 1982; *The Star Chamber,* Twentieth Century-Fox, 1983; *Kidco,* Twentieth Century-Fox, 1984; executive producer, *The Caller,* Empire, 1987; *Buy and Cell,* Trans World Entertainment, 1988.

RELATED CAREER—Salesman, Warner Brothers, New York, Boston, Milwaukee, and Chicago, 1957-59; booking manager, Walt Disney Productions, Milwaukee, WI, 1958-66; midwest sales manager, Sigma III, 1966; vice-president, Filmways Productions, 1966-69; vice-president, sales, then vice-president, marketing, later executive vice-president, Paramount Pictures Corporation, New York City, 1969-71, then president, 1971-75; founder and president, Frank Yablans Presentations Inc., 1975—; chief operating officer and board chairman, Metro-Goldwyn-Mayer/United Artists, 1983-1985; founder (with PSO Delphi), Northstar Entertainment Company, 1985; non-exclusive production arrangement with Empire Entertainment, 1986 non-exclusive production arrangement with Columbia Pictures, 1988; board of directors, Directors' Company, Cinema International Corporation; chairman, Variety Club International; director, Motion Picture Association; corporate chairman, entertainment division, Federation of Jewish Philanthropies; trustee, American Film Institute.

NON-RELATED CAREER—Board of directors, Boys' Clubs of America; board of directors, Will Rogers Hospital.

WRITINGS: FILM—(With Ted Kotcheff and Peter Gent) *North Dallas Forty,* Paramount, 1979; (with Frank Perry, Tracy Hotchner, and Robert Getchell) *Mommie Dearest,* Paramount, 1981.

AWARDS: Decorated Commendatore Repubblica Italiana.

MEMBER: Fairview Country Club.*

YABLANS, Irwin   1934-

PERSONAL: Born June 25, 1934, in Brooklyn, NY. MILITARY—U.S. Army, 1954-56.

VOCATION: Producer and motion picture executive.

CAREER: PRINCIPAL FILM WORK—All as executive producer, unless indicated: Associate producer, *Badge 373,* Paramount, 1972; producer, *The Education of Sonny Carson,* Paramount, 1974; *Halloween,* Compass, 1978; *Roller Boogie,* United Artists, 1979; *Fade to Black,* American Cinema, 1979; production representative, *Apocalypse Now,* United Artists, 1979; producer, *Hell Night,* Compass International, 1981; *Halloween II,* Universal, 1981; *Halloween III: The Season of the Witch,* Universal, 1982; producer, *The Seduction,* AVCO-Embassy, 1982; *Parasite,* Embassy, 1982; *Scream for Help,* Lorimar, 1984; producer, *Tank,* Lorimar/Universal, 1984; producer, *Prison,* Empire, 1988.

RELATED CAREER—Sales representative, Warner Brothers, Washington, DC, Albany, NY, Detroit, MI, Milwaukee, WI, and Portland, OR, all 1956; Los Angeles manager, Paramount Productions, 1962, then Western sales manager, 1972; president, Compass International Pictures, 1974; executive vice-president, Lorimar Productions, 1984; chairman, Orion Pictures Distributing Corporation, 1985; chairman and chief executive officer, Epic Pictures Enterprises, 1988—.

ADDRESSES: OFFICE—Epic Pictures Enterprises Inc., 1551 N. LaBrea Avenue, Los Angeles, CA 90028.*

*   *   *

YOUNG, Chris   1971-

PERSONAL: Full name, Christopher Tyler Young; born April 28, 1971, in Chambersburg, PA; son of Dick (in business) and Judy (a librarian and teacher; maiden name, Kreutz) Young. EDUCATION—Attended commercial acting classes at Weist-Barron School.

VOCATION: Actor.

CAREER: STAGE DEBUT—Theo, *Pippin,* Marycrest College, Davenport, IA. PRINCIPAL STAGE APPEARANCES—Billy Ray, *On Golden Pond,* dinner theatre production.

FILM DEBUT—Buck Ripley, *The Great Outdoors,* Universal, 1988.

CHRIS YOUNG

PRINCIPAL TELEVISION APPEARANCES—Series: Bryce Lynch, *Max Headroom,* ABC, 1987; Chris Agretti, *Falcon Crest,* CBS, 1989; Danny Mathews, *Live-In,* CBS, 1989. Pilots: Title role, *Jake's Journey,* CBS, 1988. Movies: Dan Leafcourt, *Dance 'til Dawn* (also known as *Prom Night*), NBC, 1988. Specials: *Square One,* PBS.

RELATED CAREER—Appeared in a calendar featuring young stars for M.A.D.D. (Mothers Against Drunk Driving); actor in television commercials.

SIDELIGHTS: RECREATIONS—Skiing, golfing, swimming, juggling, and biking.

ADDRESSES: PUBLICIST—Brenda Feldman, Julie Nathanson Public Relations, 9229 Sunset Boulevard, Suite 201, Los Angeles, CA 90069.

*   *   *

YOUNG, Karen

PERSONAL: Married Tom Noonan (an actor). EDUCATION—Studied writing and English literature at Douglass College.

VOCATION: Actress.

CAREER: PRINCIPAL STAGE APPEARANCES—Marlies, *Three Acts of Recognition,* New York Shakespeare Festival, Public Theatre, New York City, 1982; Rebecca, *Desperadoes,* Marathon '85,

Ensemble Studio Theatre, New York City, 1985; Megan Feather, *Energumen,* Soho Repertory Theatre, New York City, 1985.

PRINCIPAL FILM APPEARANCES—Kathleen Sullivan, *Deep in the Heart* (also known as *Handgun*), Warner Brothers, 1983; Lisa Willoughby, *Almost You,* Twentieth Century-Fox/TLC, 1984; Hannah Rourke, *Birdy,* Tri-Star, 1984; Rosie, *Maria's Lovers,* Cannon, 1985; Sue, *9 1/2 Weeks,* United Artists, 1986; narrator, *Painted Landscapes of the Times* (also known as *Painted Landscapes of the Times: The Art of Sue Coe;* documentary), Cinema Libre, 1987; Holly, *Heat,* New Century/Vista, 1987; Carla Brody, *Jaws: The Revenge,* Universal, 1987; Dorothea, *Little Sweetheart,* Nelson Entertainment, 1988; Ellen Faulkner, *Criminal Law,* Tri-Star, 1988; Laurel, *Torch Song Trilogy,* New Line Cinema, 1988; Jane, *Wild Things,* BBC Enterprises, 1988; Roxy, *Night Games,* Trans World Entertainment, 1989.

PRINCIPAL TELEVISION APPEARANCES—Episodic: Sandra Stahl, *The Equalizer,* CBS, 1985. Movies: Robin Benedict, *The High Price of Passion,* NBC, 1986. Specials: *This Time It's Personal—Jaws: The Revenge,* syndicated, 1987.

ADDRESSES: AGENT—The Gersh Agency, 222 N. Canon Drive, Suite 202, Beverly Hills, CA 90210.*

*   *   *

YOUNG, Loretta   1913-

PERSONAL: Born Gretchen Michaela Young; January 6, 1913 (some sources say 1914), in Salt Lake City, UT; married Grant Withers (an actor), 1930 (divorced, 1931); married Thomas H.A. Lewis, 1940; children: Judy (first marriage; adopted); Christopher Paul, Peter (second marriage). EDUCATION—Attended Immaculate Heart College.

VOCATION: Actress.

CAREER: PRINCIPAL STAGE APPEARANCES—*An Evening with Loretta Young,* American Museum of Broadcasting Television Festival, New York City, then Los Angeles, County Museum of Art, Leo Bing Theatre, Los Angeles, both 1989.

FILM DEBUT—Child on operating table, *The Only Way,* 1919. PRINCIPAL FILM APPEARANCES—Carol Watts, *The Head Man,* First National, 1928; Simonetta, *Laugh, Clown, Laugh,* Metro-Goldwyn-Mayer (MGM), 1928; Denise Laverne, *The Magnificent Flirt,* Famous Players, 1928; the girl, *The Whip Woman,* First National, 1928; Margaret Barbour, *Scarlet Seas,* First National, 1929; Patricia, *Fast Life,* Warner Brothers/First National, 1929; Patricia Carlyle, *The Forward Pass,* Warner Brothers/First National, 1929; Gladys Cosgrove, *The Girl in the Glass Cage,* Warner Brothers/First National, 1929; Irma, *The Squall,* Warner Brothers/First National, 1929; Muriel, *The Careless Age,* First National, 1929; as herself, *The Show of Shows,* Warner Brothers, 1929.

Dorothy Hope, *The Devil to Pay,* United Artists, 1930; Marsinah, *Kismet,* Warner Brothers/First National, 1930; Ann Harper Berry, *Loose Ankles,* Warner Brothers/First National, 1930; Margery Seaton, *The Man from Blankley's,* Warner Brothers, 1930; Margaret Waring and Mary Brennan, *Road to Paradise,* First National, 1930; Marian Ferguson, *The Second Floor Mystery* (also known as *The Second-Story Murder*), Warner Brothers, 1930; Phyllis Ericson, *The Truth About Youth,* First National, 1930; Isobel Brandon, *Beau Ideal,* RKO, 1931; Claire McIntyre, *Big Business Girl,* First National, 1931; Diane, *I Like Your Nerve,* Warner Brothers/First National, 1931; Gallagher, *Platinum Blonde,* Columbia, 1931; Rosalie Evantural, *The Right of Way,* Warner Brothers/First National, 1931; Noreen McMann, *Three Girls Lost,* Twentieth Century, 1931; Elaine Bumstead, *Too Young to Marry* (also known as *Broken Dishes*), Warner Brothers, 1931; Gloria Bannister, *The Ruling Voice* (also known as *Upper Underworld*), Warner Brothers/First National, 1931; Toya San, *The Hatchet Man* (also known as *The Honorable Mr. Wong*), Warner Brothers, 1932; Grace Sutton, *Life Begins* (also known as *Dream of Life*), Warner Brothers/First National, 1932; Buster, *Play Girl* (also known as *Love on a Budget*), Warner Brothers, 1932; Sue Riley, *Taxi!,* Warner Brothers, 1932; Marion Cullen, *They Call It Sin* (also known as *The Way of Life*), Warner Brothers/First National, 1932; Lola Davis, *Weekend Marriage* (also known as *Weekend Lives* and *Working Wives*), Warner Brothers/First National, 1932; Margot, *The Devil's in Love,* Twentieth Century-Fox, 1933; Madeline, *Employee's Entrance,* Warner Brothers, 1933; Marcia Stanislavsky, *Grand Slam,* Warner Brothers, 1933; Ruth, *Heroes for Sale* (also known as *Breadline*), Warner Brothers/First National, 1933; Peggy, *The Life of Jimmy Dolan* (also known as *The Kid's Last Fight* and *The Sucker*), Warner Brothers, 1933; Trina, *A Man's Castle,* Columbia, 1933; Mary Martin, *Midnight Mary* (also known as *Lady of the Night*), MGM, 1933; Florence Denny, *She Had to Say Yes,* Warner Brothers/First National, 1933; Eve, *Zoo in Budapest,* Twentieth Century-Fox, 1933; Letty Strong, *Born to Be Bad,* United Artists, 1934; Lola Field, *Bulldog Drummond Strikes Back,* United Artists, 1934; Countess Wilma, *Caravan,* Twentieth Century-Fox, 1934; Julie Rothschild, *The House of Rothschild,* Twentieth Century-Fox, 1934; June Arden, *The White Parade,* Twentieth Century-Fox, 1934.

Claire Blake, *Call of the Wild,* Twentieth Century-Fox, 1935; Margaret Maskelyne Clive, *Clive of India,* United Artists, 1935; Berengaria, *The Crusades,* Paramount, 1935; Barbara Howard, *Shanghai,* Paramount, 1935; Susie Schmidt, *Ladies in Love,* Twentieth Century-Fox, 1936; Ellen Neal, *Private Number* (also known as *Secret Interlude*), Twentieth Century-Fox, 1936; title role, *Ramona,* Twentieth Century-Fox, 1936; Lady Helen Dearden, *The Unguarded Hour,* MGM, 1936; Laura Ridgeway, *Cafe Metropole,* Twentieth Century-Fox, 1937; Tony Gateson, *Love Is News,* Twentieth Century-Fox, 1937; Myra Cooper, *Love Under Fire,* Twentieth Century-Fox, 1937; Vicki, *Second Honeymoon,* Twentieth Century-Fox, 1937; Ina, *Wife, Doctor, and Nurse,* Twentieth Century-Fox, 1937; Lynn Cherrington, *Four Men and a Prayer,* Twentiety Century-Fox, 1938; Sally Goodwin, *Kentucky,* Twentieth Century-Fox, 1938; Empress Eugenie, *Suez,* Twentieth Century-Fox, 1938; Pamela Charters, *Three Blind Mice,* Twentieth Century-Fox, 1938; Anita Halstead, *Eternally Yours,* United Artists, 1939; Mrs. Bell, *The Story of Alexander Graham Bell* (also known as *The Modern Miracle*), Twentieth Century-Fox, 1939; Doris Blair Borland, *Wife, Husband, and Friend,* Twentieth Century-Fox, 1939.

June Cameron, *The Doctor Takes a Wife,* Columbia, 1940; Marianne Duval, *He Stayed for Breakfast,* Columbia, 1940; Annie, *Lady from Cheyenne,* Universal, 1941; Lina Varsavina, *The Men in Her Life,* Columbia, 1941; Jane Drake, *Bedtime Story,* Columbia, 1942; Nancy Troy, *A Night to Remember,* Columbia, 1942; Carolyn Grant, *China,* Paramount, 1943; Emily Blair, *And Now Tomorrow,* Paramount, 1944; Roberta Courageous, *Ladies Courageous,* Universal, 1944; Cherry de Longpre, *Along Came Jones,* RKO, 1945; Maggie Williams, *The Perfect Marriage,* Paramount, 1946; Mary Longstreet, *The Stranger,* RKO, 1946; Katrin Holstrom, *The Farmer's Daughter,* RKO, 1947; Julia Brougham, *The Bishop's Wife,* RKO, 1947; Rachel, *Rachel and the Stranger,* RKO, 1948; Wilma Tuttle, *The Accused* (also known as *Strange Deception*), Paramount, 1949; Sister Margaret, *Come to the Stable,* Abigail "Abby" Fortitude Abbott, *Mother Is a Freshman* (also known as *Mother Knows Best*), Twentieth Century-Fox, 1949; Clarissa Standish, *Key to the City,* MGM, 1950; Ellen Jones, *Cause for Alarm,* MGM, 1951; Nora, *Half Angel,* Twentieth Century-Fox, 1951; Christine Carroll, *Because of You,* Universal, 1952; Paula Rogers, *Paula* (also known as *The Silent Voice*), Columbia, 1952; Jane MacAvoy, *It Happens Every Thursday,* Universal, 1953. Also appeared in *Sirens of the Sea,* United Artists, 1921; as Arab child, *The Son of the Sheik,* 1921; in *Naughty But Nice,* First National, 1927; *Her Wild Oats,* First National, 1928.

PRINCIPAL TELEVISION APPEARANCES—Series: Host, *A Letter to Loretta,* NBC, 1953-54; host, *The Loretta Young Theatre,* NBC, 1954-61; Christine Massey, *The Loretta Young Show* (also known as *The New Loretta Young Show*), CBS, 1962-63. Movies: Amanda Kingsley, *Christmas Eve,* NBC, 1986; Grace Guthrie, *Lady in a Corner,* NBC, 1989. Specials: *Happy Birthday Hollywood,* ABC, 1987.

PRINCIPAL RADIO APPEARANCES—Episodic: "Flight from Home," *The Family Theatre,* Mutual, 1947; *Four Star Playhouse,* NBC, 1949; "Liberty's Lady," *Screen Guild Theatre,* CBS; *Theatre of Romance,* CBS; *Lux Radio Theatre,* NBC (fourteen episodes); *One Man's Family,* NBC.

WRITINGS: *The Things I've Learned* (autobiography), 1961.

AWARDS: Academy Award, Best Actress, 1947, for *The Farmer's Daughter;* Academy Award nomination, Best Actress, 1949, for *Come to the Stable;* Golden Apple Star of the Year Award from the Hollywood Women's Press Club, 1950; Emmy Awards, Best Actress Starring in a Regular Series, 1955, Best Continuing Performance By an Actress in a Dramatic Series, 1957, and Best Actress in a Leading Role in a Dramatic Series, 1959, all for *The Loretta Young Show;* Golden Globe, Best Performance By an Actress in a Mini-Series or Motion Picture Made for Television, 1987, for *Christmas Eve.*

SIDELIGHTS: Loretta Young is very active in Catholic charity organizations.

ADDRESSES: PUBLICIST—Joel Brokaw, The Brokaw Company, 9255 Sunset Boulevard, Suite 706, Los Angeles, CA 90069.*

Z

ZABRISKIE, Grace

VOCATION: Actress.

CAREER: PRINCIPAL STAGE APPEARANCES—Marks, *Talking With,* Center Theatre Group, Mark Taper Forum, Taper Too, Los Angeles, 1985; Jessie, *Rose Cottages,* Ensemble Studio Theatre, New York City, 1986; Rosa, *Camaralenta,* Stages Theatre Center, Los Angeles, 1987; Emma, *Cold Sweat,* Playwrights Horizons, New York City, 1988.

PRINCIPAL FILM APPEARANCES—Linette Adum, *Norma Rae,* Twentieth Century-Fox, 1979; Nanny, *The Private Eyes,* New World, 1980; Captain Trantor, *Galaxy of Terror* (also known as *An Infinity of Terror, Planet of Horrors,* and *Mindwarp*), New World, 1981; Esther Pokrifki, *An Officer and a Gentleman,* Paramount, 1982; Chilly's mother, *Body Rock,* New World, 1984; Ellie Wells, *Nickel Mountain,* Ziv International, 1985; Jefferson, *Leonard, Part Six,* Columbia, 1987; Mama McSwain, *The Big Easy,* Columbia, 1987; Sheryl, *The Boost,* Hemdale, 1988; Naomi Reece, *Rampage,* De Laurentiis Entertainment Group, 1988; Bob's mother, *Drugstore Cowboy,* Avenue, 1989. Also appeared in *The Devil's Clone,* 1979.

PRINCIPAL TELEVISION APPEARANCES—Mini-Series: Mrs. Ames, *John Steinbeck's "East of Eden,"* ABC, 1981. Pilots: Alma Kresser, *UNSUB,* NBC, 1989; also Mrs. Clinton, *One Too Many,* 1985. Episodic: Mrs. Komatar, *Shadow Chasers,* ABC, 1985; Terri, *Hill Street Blues,* NBC, 1986; Mabel Burton, *Falcon Crest,* CBS, 1987; Agnes, *Mama's Boy,* NBC, 1987; Rita, *Moonlighting,* ABC, 1989; Eva Barrett, *Empty Nest,* NBC, 1988. Movies: Ruth Lait, *Freedom Road,* NBC, 1979; Peg, *The Concrete Cowboys,* CBS, 1979; Emily, *Blinded By the Light,* CBS, 1980; Kathryne Baker, *The Executioner's Song,* NBC, 1982; Silvie Alice Kohler, *M.A.D.D.: Mothers Against Drunk Driving,* NBC, 1983; Maggie Ryan, *My Mother's Secret Life,* ABC, 1984; Flossie Hughes, *The Burning Bed,* NBC, 1984; hearings officer, *North Beach and Rawhide,* CBS, 1985; Deanie, *Mistress,* CBS, 1987; Mouza Zumwalt, *My Father, My Son,* CBS, 1988; Sister Marie, *Shooter,* NBC, 1988; Cheryl's therapist, *A Deadly Silence,* ABC, 1989; Gloria Hale, *The Ryan White Story,* ABC, 1989.

AWARDS: Los Angeles Drama Critics' Circle Award nomination, Best Featured Performance, 1988, for *Camaralenta.*

ADDRESSES: AGENT—Writers and Artists Agency, 11726 San Vicente Boulevard, Suite 300, Los Angeles, CA 90049.*

ZANUSSI, Krzysztof   1939-

PERSONAL: Born June 17, 1939, in Warsaw, Poland; son of Jerzy and Jadwiga Zanussi. EDUCATION—Studied physics at Warsaw University, 1955-59; postgraduate work in philosophy at the University of Cracow, 1959-62; attended lectures on film at the Institute of Arts of Polish Academy of Science, 1955-58; studied film at Lodz Higher Film School, 1966.

VOCATION: Director, producer, and writer.

CAREER: Also see *WRITINGS* below. PRINCIPAL STAGE WORK—Director, *One Flew Over the Cuckoo's Nest,* 1979; *Der Konig stirbt,* 1980; *Mattatoio,* 1982; *Day and Night,* 1983; *Duo for One,* 1983; *Hiob,* 1985; *Les Joeux des Femmes,* 1985; *Alle Meine Sonne,* 1986.

PRINCIPAL FILM APPEARANCES—As himself, *Amator* (also known as *Camera Buff*), Film Polski/Cinegate, 1979, released in the United States by New Yorker, 1983.

FIRST FILM WORK—Director (with Wincenty Ronisz), *Droga do nieba* (also known as *The Way to the Skies;* short film), 1958. PRINCIPAL FILM WORK—All as director, unless indicated: *Zycie rodzinne* (also known as *Family Life* and *Family Cycle*), Polish Corporation for Film Production, 1970; *Za sciana* (also known as *Behind the Wall*), Tor Film Unit, 1971; *Iluminacja* (also known as *Illumination*), Film Polski, 1973; *The Catamount Killing,* Atlas International, 1974, released in the United States by Hallmark, 1975; *Bilans kwartalny* (also known as *A Woman's Decision*), Tinc Productions, 1975, released in the United States by Almi Cinema V, 1977; *Barwy ochronne* (also known as *Camouflage*), Film Polski, 1976, released in the United States by Comtemporary Films Ltd., 1977; *Spirala* (also known as *Spiral*), Polish Corporation for Film Production, 1978; *Wege in der Nacht* (also known as *Ways in the Night, Paths into the Night,* and *Night Paths*), Westdeutscher Rundfunk, 1979.

Constans (also known as *The Constant Factor*), Polish Corporation for Film Production/New Yorker, 1980; *Kontrakt* (also known as *The Contract*), New Yorker, 1980, Cinegate, 1982; *Die Unerreichbare* (also known as *The Unapproachable*), Regina Ziegler/Zweites Deutsches Fernsehen/Osterreichischer Rundfunk Fernsehen, 1982; *Imperativ* (also known as *Imperative*), Telefilm Saar, 1982, released in the United States by Teleculture, 1985; *Rok Spokonjnego Slonca* (also known as *The Year of the Quiet Sun*), Sandstar Releasing/Blue Dolphin Film Distributors, 1984; *Blaubart* (also known as *Bluebeard*), Westdeutscher Rundfunk/DRS Television, 1984; *Le Pouvoir du mal* (also known as *The Power of Evil*), Films Moliere/Films du Scorpion, 1985; producer (with Rock Demers), *Le Jeune magicien* (also known as *Cudowne dziecko, The Young*

Magician, The Wondrous Child, and *Tales for All [Part 4]*), Les Productions La Fete/Film Tor Unit, 1987; *Gdzieskolwiek jest, jeslis jest* (also known as *Wherever You Are* and *Wherever She Is*), Film Polski/Liberty Film Sales, 1988; executive producer, *And the Violins Stopped Playing,* Film Polski/August Entertainment, 1989; *Stan Posiadania* (also known as *State of Possession* and *Inventory*), TOR Film Unit/Polish Television/Regina Ziegler Filmproduktion, 1989.

Also directed *Smierc prowincjala* (also known as *The Death of a Provincial;* short film), 1966; *Przemysl* (short film), 1966; *Maria Dabrowska* (short film), 1966; *Komputery* (also known as *Computers;* short film), 1967; *Struktura krszatalu* (also known as *The Structure of Crystals*), 1969; *Quarterly Balance,* 1975; *Haus der Frauen* (also known as *House of Women*), 1977; *Penderecki,* 1977; *Lutoslawa,* 1977; *Brigitte Horney,* 1977; *Versuchung,* 1981; *Temptation; Vatican Capitale.*

PRINCIPAL TELEVISION WORK—All as director. Movies: *Portrait of the Composer,* 1967; *Twarza w twarz* (also known as *Face to Face;* short film), 1968; *Credit,* 1968; *Krzysztof Penderecki,* 1968; *Zaliczenie* (also known as *An Examination* and *Pass Mark;* short film), 1969; *Gory o zmierzchu* (also known as *Mountains at Dusk;* short film), 1970; *Rola* (also known as *Die Rolle* and *The Role*), West German television, 1971; *Hipoteza* (also known as *Hypothesis;* short film), 1972; *Milosierdzie platne z gory* (also known as *Nachtdienst* and *Night Duty*), 1975; *Anatomie stunde* (also known as *Lekcja anatomii* and *Anatomy Lesson*), 1977. Specials: *From a Far Country: Pope John Paul II,* NBC, 1981; also *Penderecki Lutoslawski Baird,* 1976; *Mein Krakau* (also known as *My Cracow*), 1979.

RELATED CAREER—Vice-chairman, Polish Film Association, 1971-81; faculty member, Lodz Higher Film School, 1973.

WRITINGS: FILM—See above for production details: (With others) *Struktura krszatalu,* 1969; *Zycie rodzinne,* 1971; (with Edward Zebrowski) *Za Sciana,* 1971; *Iluminacja,* 1973; *Bilans kwartalny,* 1975; *Barwy ochronne,* 1976; *Spirala,* 1978; *Wege in der Nacht,* 1979; *Constans,* 1980; *Kontrakt,* 1980; *Versuchung,* 1981; *Imperativ,* 1982; (with Zebrowski) *Die Unerreichbare,* 1982; *Rok Spolojnego Slonca,* 1984; *Le Pouvoir du mal,* 1985; (with Michael Hirst) *Gdzieskolwiek jest, jeslis jest,* 1988; *Stan Posiadania,* 1989.

TELEVISION—(With others) *Twarza w twarz,* 1968; (with others) *Zaliczenie,* 1969; *Rola,* 1971; *Hipoteza,* 1972.

OTHER—*Nowele Filmowe* (short film scripts), 1976; *Scenariusze Filmowe* (film scripts), 1978; *Un rigorista nella fortezza assediata,* 1982.

AWARDS: Awards in Venice, Mannheim, Valladolid, and Moscow, all 1966, for *Smierc prowincjala;* Prizes in Cracow and Leipzig, both 1967, for *Portrait of the Composer;* Award from Mar del Plata, 1969, and Best Film Award from Polish Film Critics, 1970, both for *Struktura krszatalu;* Awards in Chicago, Valladolid, and Colombo, all 1971, for *Zycie rodzinne;* Grand Prix from the San Remo International Film Festival, 1972, for *Za sciana;* Leopardo d'Oro from the Locarno International Film Festival, Best Film, 1973, for *Illuminacja;* State Award from the Polish Minister of Culture and Arts, 1973; OCIC Prize from the Berlin International Film Festival, 1975, for *Quarterly Balance;* Special Prize from the Teheran International Film Festival and Grand Prix from the Polish Film Festival, both 1977, for *Barwy ochronne;* Prize of Journalists from the Polish Film Festival and OCIC Prize from the Cannes Film

Festival, both 1978, for *Spirala;* Best Director Award and OCIC Prize, both from the Cannes Film Festival, 1980, for *Constans;* Distribution Prize from the Venice Film Festival, 1980, for *Kontrakt;* Donatello Prize (Florence, Italy), 1980, for *Man from a Far Country: Pope John Paul II;* Special Prize from the Polish Film Festival, 1980, Special Jury Prize from the Venice Film Festival, 1982, and State Prize First Class, 1984, all for *Illuminacja;* Golden Lion from the Venice Film Festival, Pasinetti Award, 1984, for *Rok spokonjnego slonca;* Prize from the Venice Film Festival, 1984, for *Blaubart.*

MEMBER: Formerly active in Solidarity labor union.

SIDELIGHTS: RECREATIONS—Travel.

ADDRESSES: OFFICES—Kaniowska 114, 01-529 Warsaw, Poland; 8 Rue Richepance, Paris, France 75001.*

*   *   *

ZMED, Adrian   1954-

PERSONAL: Born March 14, 1954, in Chicago, IL; son of George (a Romanian Orthodox priest) and Sadie (Golub) Zmed; married Barbara Fitzner, July 24, 1976; children: Zachary, Dylan. EDUCATION—Received B.F.A. from the Goodman Theatre School of Drama.

VOCATION: Actor.

ADRIAN ZMED

CAREER: STAGE DEBUT—*Benito Cereno*, Goodman Theatre, Chicago, IL, for forty performances. BROADWAY DEBUT—Danny Zuko, *Grease*, Royale Theatre, 1977, for four hundred fifty performances. PRINCIPAL STAGE APPEARANCES—*Relay*, Main Stage Theatre, North Hollywood, CA, 1988; also appeared in *Romeo and Juliet, She Stoops to Conquer*, and *Merton of the Movies*, all Goodman Theatre, Chicago, IL; *Beginners Luck*, Tiffany's Attic Dinner Theatre; *Little Shop of Horrors*, Loberco Theatre; *Irma La Douce* and *The Fantasticks*, both Forum Theatre; *Godspell*, Muni Opera; *Gangs*.

MAJOR TOURS—Danny Zuko, *Grease*, U.S. cities, 1976-77.

FILM DEBUT—Johnny Nogerilli, *Grease 2*, Paramount, 1982. PRINCIPAL FILM APPEARANCES—Cerone, *The Final Terror* (also known as *Campsite Massacre, Bump in the Night*, and *The Forest Primeval*), Comworld/Watershed/Roth, 1983; Jay O'Neill, *Bachelor Party*, Twentieth Century-Fox, 1983; also appeared in *Eyewitness to Murder*, Saphire Productions.

TELEVISION DEBUT—Socks Palermo, *Flatbush*, CBS, 1979. PRINCIPAL TELEVISION APPEARANCES—Series: Frankie Millardo, *Goodtime Girls*, ABC, 1980; Officer Vince Romano, *T.J. Hooker*, ABC, 1982-85; host, *Dance Fever*, syndicated, 1985-87. Pilots: Jimmy Steinbrenner, *Revenge of the Gray Gang*, NBC, 1981. Episodic: Robert Morton, *Hotel*, ABC, 1986; assassin, *Hotel*, ABC, 1987; Stanley Mannings, *You Are the Jury*, NBC, 1987; Gary, *Empty Nest*, NBC, 1988; Bert Firman, *Murder, She Wrote*, CBS, 1989; also *The Love Boat*, ABC, 1986; *Starsky and Hutch*, ABC; *Angie*, ABC; *Bosom Buddies*, ABC; *I'm a Big Girl Now*, ABC; *Riker*, NBC; *Alfred Hitchcock Presents*. Movies: Fernando Forsalito, *For the Love of It*, ABC, 1980; Fred Feliciano, *Victims for Victims: The Theresa Saldana Story*, NBC, 1984. Specials: *Battle of the Network Stars*, ABC, 1983; *Rickles on the Loose*, Showtime, 1986.

RELATED CAREER—Actor in television commercials; musician in the band Ephrus.

NON-RELATED CAREER—Member of the board of directors and youth spokesman, National Council on Alcoholism and Drug Dependency.

MEMBER: American Federation of Television and Radio Artists, Screen Actors Guild, Actors' Equity Association.

ADDRESSES: AGENT-The Agency, 10351 Santa Monica Boulevard, Suite 211, Los Angeles, CA 90025. MANAGER—Gary George, Lemond-Zetter Management, 8370 Wilshire Boulevard, Suite 310, Beverly Hills, CA 90211. PUBLICIST—Dourie Bolwell, The Group, 723 1/2 N. La Cienega Boulevard, Los Angeles, CA 90069.

*   *   *

ZSIGMOND, Vilmos   1930-
(William Zsigmond)

PERSONAL: Surname is pronounced "Vilmosh Gigmond"; born June 16, 1930, in Czeged, Hungary; immigrated to the United States in 1957; naturalized U.S. citizen, 1962; son of Vilmo (a soccer goalie and coach) and Bozena (an administrator; maiden name, Illichman) Zsigmond; married Elizabeth Fuzes (divorced);

VILMOS ZSIGMOND

children: Julia, Susi. EDUCATION—State Academy of Motion Picture and Theatre Arts (Budapest), M.A., cinematography, 1956.

VOCATION: Cinematographer.

CAREER: PRINCIPAL FILM WORK—Cinematographer: (As William Zsigmond) *Living Between Two Worlds*, Empire, 1963; (as William Zsigmond) *The Sadist* (also known as *The Profile of Terror*), Fairway International, 1963; (as William Zsigmond) *The Nasty Rabbit* (also known as *Spies A Go-Go*), Fairway International, 1964; (as William Zsigmond) *The Time Travelers* (also known as *Time Trap*), American International, 1964; (as William Zsigmond) *What's Up Front* (also known as *The Fall Guy* and *A Fourth for Marriage*), Fairway International, 1964; *Psycho A Go-Go!* (also known as *Blood of Ghastly Horror, The Fiend with the Electric Brain*, and *Man with the Synthetic Brain*), Hemisphere/American General, 1965; (as William Zsigmond) *Deadwood '76*, Fairway International, 1965; (as William Zsigmond) *The Incredibly Strange Creatures Who Stopped Living and Became Crazy Mixed-Up Zombies* (also known as *Teenage Psycho Meets Bloody Mary* and *The Incredibly Strange Creatures*), Hollywood Star, 1965; (as William Zsigmond) *Rat Fink* (also known as *Wild and Willing, My Soul Runs Naked*, and *The Swinging Fink*), Genesis/Cinema, 1965; (as William Zsigmond) *A Hot Summer Game* (also known as *It's All in the Game*), European Producers International, 1965; (as William Zsigmond) *Tales of a Salesman* (also known as *Tales of a Traveling Salesman*), Rossmore, 1965; (as William Zsigmond; additional photography) *Road to Nashville*, Crown International, 1966; (as William Zsigmond; with Leslie Kovaks) *Mondo Mod* (documentary), Timely Motion Pictures, 1967; (as William Zsigmond) *The Name of the Game Is Kill* (also known as *Lovers in Limbo* and *The*

Female Trap), Fanfare, 1968; (as William Zsigmond; with Robert Carl Cohen) *Jennie, Wife/Child*, Emerson Film Enterprises, 1968; (as William Zsigmond) *The Monitors*, Commonwealth United Entertainment, 1969; (as William Zsigmond; with Vilis Lapenieks and Mario Tosi) *Hot Rod Action* (documentary), Cinerama, 1969; *Futz*, Commonwealth United International, 1969; *The Gun Riders* (also known as *Five Bloody Graves, Lonely Man*, and *Five Bloody Days to Tombstone*), Independent International, 1969.

(As William Zsigmond) *The Horror of the Blood Monsters* (also known as *Creatures of the Prehistoric Planet, Horror Creatures of the Red Planet, Flesh Creatures of the Red Planet, The Flesh Creatures, Space Mission of the Lost Planet*, and *Vampire Men of the Lost Planet*), Independent International, 1970; *The Hired Hand*, Universal, 1971; *McCabe and Mrs. Miller*, Warner Brothers, 1971; *Red Sky at Morning*, Universal, 1971; *The Ski Bum*, AVCO-Embassy, 1971; *Deliverance*, Warner Brothers, 1972; *Images*, Columbia, 1972; *Cinderella Liberty*, Twentieth Century-Fox, 1973; *The Long Goodbye*, United Artists, 1973; *Scarecrow*, Warner Brothers, 1973; *The Girl from Petrovka*, Universal, 1974; *The Sugarland Express*, Universal, 1974; *Dandy, the All-American Girl* (also known as *Sweet Revenge*), Metro-Goldwyn-Mayer/United Artists (MGM/UA), 1976; *Death Riders*, Crown International, 1976; *Obsession*, Columbia, 1976; *Close Encounters of the Third Kind*, Columbia, 1977; *The Last Waltz*, United Artists, 1978; *The Deer Hunter*, Universal, 1978; *The Rose*, Twentieth Century-Fox, 1979; *Winter Kills*, AVCO-Embassy, 1979.

Heaven's Gate, United Artists, 1980; *Blow Out*, Filmways, 1981; (with Ric Waite) *The Border*, Universal, 1982; *Jinxed!*, MGM/UA, 1982; *Table for Five*, Warner Brothers, 1983; *No Small Affair*, Columbia, 1984; *The River*, Universal, 1984; *Real Genius*, Tri-Star, 1985; *The Witches of Eastwick*, Warner Brothers, 1987; *Journey to Spirit Island*, World Wide Releasing, 1988; *Fat Man and Little Boy*, Paramount, 1989; also (co-cinematographer) *Hungarn in flammen* (also known as *Revolt in Hungary;* documentary), 1957; *Picasso Summer*, 1970.

PRINCIPAL TELEVISION WORK—Series: Cinematographer, *The Protectors*, NBC, 1969-70. Mini-Series: Cinematographer, *Flesh and Blood*, CBS, 1979.

RELATED CAREER—Founder, Cinematic Directions, 1985; director of television commercials with Cinematic Directions and Filmfair; cinematographer of television documentaries for Wolper Productions; still photographer; laboratory technician; camera assistant.

AWARDS: Academy Award, Best Cinematography, 1977, for *Close Encounters of the Third Kind;* Academy Award nomination, Best Cinematography, 1978, and British Academy of Film and Television Arts Award, Best Cinematography, 1979, both for *The Deer Hunter;* Academy Award nomination, Best Cinematography, 1984, for *The River.*

MEMBER: American Society of Cinematographers, Academy of Motion Picture Arts and Sciences, International Alliance of Theatrical Stage Employees (Local #659), Directors Guild of America.

ADDRESSES: OFFICE—7700 Sunset Boulevard, Suite 200, Hollywood, CA 90046. AGENT—Smith-Gosnell Agency, 3872 Las Flores Canyon Road, Malibu, CA 90265.*

ZSIGMOND, William
See ZSIGMOND, Vilmos

*   *   *

ZUCKER, Jerry   1950-

PERSONAL: Born March 11, 1950, in Milwaukee, WI. EDUCATION—Studied film at the University of Wisconsin.

VOCATION: Producer, director, and screenwriter.

CAREER: Also see *WRITINGS* below. PRINCIPAL FILM APPEARANCES—*Kentucky Fried Movie*, United Films, 1977. PRINCIPAL FILM WORK—Second unit director, *Rock 'n' Roll High School*, New World, 1979; executive producer and director (both with David Zucker and Jim Abrahams), *Airplane!*, Paramount, 1980; director (with Zucker and Abrahams), *Top Secret!*, Paramount, 1984; director (with Zucker and Abrahams), *Ruthless People*, Buena Vista, 1986; executive producer (with Zucker and Abrahams), *The Naked Gun—From the Files of Police Squad!*, Paramount, 1988.

PRINCIPAL TELEVISION WORK—Series: Executive producer (with David Zucker and Jim Abrahams), *Police Squad!*, ABC, 1982. Episodic: Director, *Police Squad!*, ABC, 1982.

RELATED CAREER—Founder (with David Zucker and Jim Abrahams), Kentucky Fried Theatre, Madison, WI, 1979.

WRITINGS: See production details above. FILM—(With Zucker and Abrahams) *Kentucky Fried Movie*, 1977; (with Zucker and Abrahams) *Airplane!*, 1980; (with Zucker, Abrahams, and Martyn Burke) *Top Secret!*, 1984; (with Zucker, Abrahams, and Pat Proft) *The Naked Gun—From the Files of Police Squad!*, 1988. TELEVISION—Episodic: *Police Squad!*, 1982.

ADDRESSES: OFFICE—11777 San Vicente Boulevard, Los Angeles, CA 90049.*

*   *   *

ZUNIGA, Daphne

PERSONAL: Father, a philosophy professor; mother, a Unitarian minister. EDUCATION—Studied theatre arts at the University of California, Los Angeles.

CAREER: PRINCIPAL FILM APPEARANCES—Kelly/Terry, *The Initiation*, New World, 1984; Margie Epstein, *Vision Quest*, Warner Brothers, 1985; Allison Bradbury, *The Sure Thing*, Embassy, 1985; Margo, *Modern Girls*, Atlantic, 1986; Princess Vespa, *Spaceballs*, Metro-Goldwyn-Mayer/United Artists (MGM/UA), 1987; Angela, *Last Rites*, MGM/UA, 1988; Beth Logan, *The Fly II*, Twentieth Century-Fox, 1989; Beverly Young, *Staying Together*, Hemdale, 1989; Laurie Rorbach, *Gross Anatomy*, Buena Vista, 1989. Also appeared in *The Dorm That Dripped Blood*, New Image Releasing, 1971.

PRINCIPAL TELEVISION APPEARANCES—Movies: Kim Maida, *Quarterback Princess*, CBS, 1983; Carrie Lang, *Stone Pillow*,

CBS, 1985. Episodic: Irene Marlowe, "Eye of the Panther," *Nightmare Classics,* Showtime, 1989.

ADDRESSES: AGENT—Intertalent Agency, 9200 Sunset Boulevard, Penthouse 25, Los Angeles, CA 90069. MANAGER—Keith Addis and Associates, 8444 Wilshire Boulevard, Fifth Floor, Beverly Hills, CA 90211.*